COMMITTIES AND COMMISSIONS IN INDIA 1947-73

Details of Published Volumes

COMMITTEES AND COMMISSIONS IN INDIA 1947-80

(In 18 Vols.)

Vol. 1	1947-54	Rs. 1500
Vol. 2	1955-57	Rs. 1500
Vol. 3	1958-59	Rs. 1500
Vol. 4	1960-61	Rs. 1500
Vol. 5	1962-63	Rs. 1500
Vol. 6	1964-65	Rs. 1500
Vol. 7	1966	Rs. 1500
Vol. 8	1967	Rs. 1500
Vol. 9	1968-69	Rs. 1500
Vol. 10	1970	Rs. 1500
Vol. 11	1971-73	Rs. 1500
Vol. 12	1974	Rs. 450
Vol. 13	1975	Rs. 450
Vol. 14	1976	Rs. 450
Vol. 15A	1977	Rs. 450
Vol. 15B	1977	Rs. 450
Vol. 15C	1977	Rs. 450
Vol. 15D	1977	Rs. 450
Vol. 16A	1978	Rs. 450
Vol. 16B	1978	Rs. 450
Vol. 17A	1979	Rs. 450
Vol. 17B	1979	Rs. 450
Vol. 18A	1980	Rs. 450
Vol. 18B	1980	Rs. 450

COMMITTIES AND COMMISSIONS IN INDIA 1947-73

Volume I
1947-54

Virendra Kumar

CONCEPT PUBLISHING COMPANY, NEW DELHI-110059

ISBN 81-7022-196-X (Vol I)

First Published 1976
Reprinted 1988, 2004

Published and Printed by
Ashok Kumar Mittal
Concept Publishing Company
A/15-16, Commercial Block, Mohan Garden
NEW DELHI-110059 (India)

Phones : 25351460, 25351794
Fax : 091-11-25357103
Email : publishing@conceptpub.com

To

The Memory Of My Father

FOREWORD

Shri Virendra Kumar's compilation on 'Committees and Commissions in India' is a singularly valuable research and reference tool and promises to be of immense practical utility to libraries and scholars.

The cynics may often proclaim the wisdom of the facetius epigram that committees and commissions consist of men who can do nothing individually and who decide collectively that nothing can be done. In fact, committees and commissions ideally provide opportunities to men and women of ability and competence to contribute the quintessence of their understanding and experience for the commonweal. The committees and commissions gather relevant information, subject it to a process of sifting and analysis and weigh and appraise diverse considerations on the scale of appropriate norms and criteria. The committees and commissions thus provide a machinery for data processing and policy judgements, epitomising the principle of true and tested facts leading to sober reflections and conclusions. As a brains trust, committees and commissions can fruitfully function as a part of the continuous process of evaluation, innovation and reform.

That is why the rationale of public enquiries is too well established in the modern world to require any elaborate reiteration. Committees and commissions are rightly and universally recognised today as an indispensable arm of government, an invaluable aid to the administration and policy-making processes and an effective instrument of public participation.

Shri Virendra Kumar has pointed out that the universe of commissions and committees is extremely heterogeneous for systematic study as a single category. This compilation will not only assist the researcher interested in a particular committee or commission but will also help in a systematic study of committees and commissions, their contribution to the data gathering and policy making processes, their techniques and their effectiveness.

I take this opportunity to congratulate Shri Virendra Kumar for his painstaking, methodical and imaginative effort and wish this venture the success it deserves.

L. M. Singhvi

CONTENTS

1949

1950

1951

1952

1953

1954

INTRODUCTION

The matrix of commissions is too heterogeneous to lend itself to a systematic study or some type of general categorisation.

The present study attempts to understand and analyse the activities of the various commissions and committees, something which has received only scant attention of even bibliophiles and documentation experts. Whether or not the commissions can be studied under one classification the fact remains that democratic governments all over the world have largely come to rely on them. Such governments make an extensive use of the instrument of public inquiries which ultimately help in lessening managemental tensions as well as quietening allegations of misrule. According to John Stuart Mill, "a man seldom judges right, even in his own concerns, still less in those of the public, when he makes habitual use of no knowlege but his own or that of some single adviser." As such, the 'Committee System' greatly helps in the proper functioning of a democratic set-up.

A 'Commission' is a "governmental agency created to perform a particular function, such as special investigation or governmental regulations of business". It is appointed mainly when it is thought that a matter involves some financial questions. There are other aspects as well for which a Commission is appointed, e.g., in matters pertaining to welfare of the state and its citizens and for improving the efficiency of an administration. The status of a 'Committee' is also the same as that of a Commission. But it does not have as wide powers as enjoyed by a Commission and would have to limit itself in relation to specific work assigned to it under the terms of reference. While arriving at decisions in the form of recommendations a committee or a commission ensures that such decisions are representative of the interest of various types of people and also a safeguard against abuse of power.

In India, the origion of public inquiries is the legacy of the British system. In the United Kingdom, the commissions are known as 'Royal Commissions of Inquiry' and their origin is traced to the Norman times. This method of inquiry had been the instrument of the King since 1066 A.D., and later of the Parliament and the Cabinet. In the olden days the appointment of members of these investigative bodies was the prerogative of the Crown. These members performed their duties permanently or temporarily on behalf of the King. Occasionally, special commissioners were also appointed for inspectional and investigative purposes. For example, there was an extraordinary inquiry into the fiscal rights of the King in 1194 A.D. During the time of Edward I, the inquest for local liberties and franchise of the Barons had led to a further statutory inquiry by the Commissioners throughout the quowarranto proceedings for the jurisdiction held by the local magnates.

Thus, before the establishment of the British Parliament, Royal Commissions of Inquiry were in vogue in the British administration and were appointed under Statutes. During the Tudor Period such agencies of the Government were Privy Council and Royal Commissions and no one ever questioned the powers of the Council to inquire into matters affecting the State and the Government. As early as in 1553 A.D., the Privy Council was divided into five committees, the function of each of which was to pursue official inquiries whenever it was necessary by means of commissions of inquiry.

During the Stuart Period the Council was converted into a typical Parliamentary agency—The Committee—and the use of such committees by both the Houses of Parliament was in existence in the 14th Century. At the end of the 16th Century the procedure of setting up select committees, which had been evolving for a long time, was properly established, and there was also a Committee on Grievances.

The Royal commissions of inquiry were extensively used during the Victorian Age because the guardians of the state were more interested in investigating every sphere of social life with a view to cleansing the existing evils. The original intention of the commissions was to provide relief to industry and labour and to impose restrictions on the capitalist enterprises and the vested interests.

In 1833 the Whig Party revived the Royal commissions of inquiry and in the last decades of the 19th Century many Royal commissions were appointed. The spirit of inquiry which dominated the then Parliament found expression after 1830 and scores of committees and commissions were appointed during each session of Parliament.

According to Professor Redlich: "A Royal commission has many advantages over a Parliamentary committee; it can, while a Parliamentary committee cannot, prolong its work beyond the limits of a session, if necessary even for years; and it is possible to appoint scientific experts as members, so as to secure a complete impartial treatment of the subject; the consequence is that commissions have largely superseded Parliamentary committees when elaborate enquiries have to be made" (*The Procedure of the House of Commons*, II, 1931).

The appointment of Royal commissions was at the peak after 1850 and a number of Royal commissions were appointed. The Royal commissions have thus become a legitimate method of inquiry and are appointed for the purpose of investigating a subject about which there is not much knowledge. They are useful for clarification of difficult subjects which agitate the minds of the people and on which there is no information. They serve, therefore, as a fact finding commission, and the procedure is to hold inquiries.

The appointment of Royal commissions had two main purposes:

(i) Compiling information on some major topics of political dispute, and (ii) reconciliating public opinion.

As a consequence of the East India Company's affairs coming frequently at this time under the notice of Parliament, committees of the House of Commons were appointed to investigate them; and the result of the committees' enquiries is contained in several voluminous reports made available during 1772-73 and again during 1781-82-83. After 1783, no committee was appointed and no inquiry conducted.

There were many commissions of inquiry for India such as the Indian Commission on Education, Statutory Commission, Calcutta University Commission, Royal Commission on Labour, and various committees (for the "improvement of the condition of the Indian people") on various subjects, e.g., agriculture, railways, weights and measures, taxation, finance, industrial development, tariff, riots, decentralization, working of a department, production of salt, welfare of the people and the like.

The appointing authorities of these commissions and committees were:

(i) The crown; (ii) the Secretary of State for India with instructions from the British Parliament; (iii) the Governor-General-in-Council and the Viceroy of India; and (iv) local boards and councils for advising on various special subjects prevailing under the then Indian conditions.

In independent India, we have chosen to have a parliamentary government based on a popular mandate. In a system like this it is necessary for the government for winning over the people to make its policies more and more acceptable to them. This implementation of the policies is largely based on the extent to which the people are convinced that the policies formulated, plans drawn up and surveys undertaken are in general interest of the society.

Whenever an allegation is made against the Government about the failure of its policies, corruption, frequency of communal riots and similar other issues, it may appoint a fact finding inquiry commission and subject to the allegations sustained, the government may accept its recommendations and implement them. The government may even have to resign in the best traditions of a democracy.

Public inquiries are conducted by special tribunals appointed for investigating a dispute between the government and a citizen; between employees and their employers on questions like the quantum of bonus, payment of salaries on time, enhanced allowances due to rise in prices of essential commodities, etc. Such types of disputes are investigated through a Commissioner, Inspector or some such official.

Sometimes, a public inquiry is instituted to evaluate the result of a governmental plan or project implemented with a view to providing a stable and efficient administration. These public inquiries educate the people about the actions taken by the government on the public policies so that good relations may develop between the government and the people.

The Commissions can be classified into two groups: *Ad hoc* and Permanent. *Ad hoc* commissions cease to exist after they complete their inquiry and submit the report to the appointing authority. Permanent commissions have a longer life and are constituted under some Act of Parliament. Examples of the latter group are: Law Commission, University Grants Commission, Planning Commission and Tariff Commission. There are also commissions like the Union Public Service Commission and the state public service commissions which are constituted in terms of the provision of the Constitution of India. The Election Commission of India, charged with the responsibility of conducting elections throughout India is also created in accordance with the provision of Article 324 of the Constitution.

The word 'Committee' has commonly come to be associated with the committees of Parliament, though it is also used in the context of a commission. But when used in the latter context, it implies that a committee generally enjoys less powers than a commission. The role of the committees of Parliament is entirely different and this can best be understood by having a glance at the working of the Indian Parliament.

As the Parliament has to complete a heavy business within a limited time, it entrusts its business to the committees. The permanent committees are called Standing Committees. These are constituted by the Chairman of the Rajya Sabha or the Speaker of the Lok Sabha as the case may be in pursuance of the 'Rules of Procedure' of the House. The important Standing Committees are:

1. **Financial Committees**: Estimates Committee; Public Accounts Committee; and Committee on Public Undertakings, etc.

2. **Advisory Committees**: Business Advisory Committee; Committee on Private Members' Bills and Resolutions; Rules Committee; Committee on Absence of Members from the Sitting of the House.

3. **Committees to Enquire**: Committee of Priviliges; Committee on Petitions.

4. **House-Keeping Committees**: Library Committee; Joint Committee on Salaries and Allowances of Members; Catering Committee.

5. **Committees to Scrutinize and Control**: Committee on Government Assurances; Committee on Subordinate Legislation.

6. **Committees for Welfare**: Committee on Welfare of the Scheduled Castes and Scheduled Tribes.

7. **Committees to Legislate**: At the beginning of each session, the Lok Sabha appoints two large Standing Committees called Committees to Legislate, one dealing with the Bills relating to law, justice, courts and legal procedure and the other with the Bills relating to agriculture, trade, shipping, fisheries etc. This second committee may consider all the topics in the Bill and also propose amendments and these are called Parliamentary Committees.

The Parliamentary Committees are elected or appointed by the House or nominated by the Speaker. They work under the direction of the Speaker and present their report to the House or to the Speaker. The Members of the Committee on Public Accounts, Estimates and Public Undertakings are elected every year by the Members of Lok Sabha. Members of a specified Parliamentary committee may be nominated by the Speaker after consultation with the leader of the House and the leaders of the opposition parties and groups in the House. The Committee on Subordinate Legislation and the Committee on Government Assurances are nominated by the Speaker for a period not exceeding one year.

To make these commissions and committees statutory the Government of India enacted the following Act through Parliament which is called 'The Commissions of Inquiry Act, 1952' (No. IX of 1952).

Definition

In this Act, unless the context otherwise requires:

(a) "appropriate Government" means:

i. the Central Government in relation to a commission appointed by it to make an inquiry into any matter relatable to any of the entries enumerated in List I or List II or List III in the Seventh Schedule of the Constitution; and

ii. the state government in relation to a commission appointed by it to make an inquiry into any matter relatable to any of the entries enumerated in List II or List III in the Seventh Schedule of the Constitution.

(b) "Commission" means a commission of inquiry appointed under Section 3.

(c) "Prescribed" means prescribed by rules made under this Act.

Appointment of Commission

(1) The appropriate government may, if it is of opinion that it is necessary so to do, and shall, if a resolution in this behalf is passed by the House of the People or as the case may be, the Legislative Assembly of the state, by notification in the official Gazette, appoint a commission of inquiry for the purpose of making an inquiry into any definite matter of public importance and performing such functions and within such time as may be specified in the notification and the commission so appointed shall make the inquiry and perform the functions accordingly:

Provided that where any such commission has been appointed to inquire into any matter:

(a) by the Central Government, no state government shall, except with the approval of the Central Government, appoint another commission to inquire into the same matter for so long as the commission appointed by the Central Government is functioning;

(b) by a state government, the Central Government shall not appoint another commission to inquire into the same matter for so long as the commission appointed by the state government is functioning, unless the Central Government is of opinion that the scope of the inquiry should be extended to two or more states.

(2) The Commission may consist of one or more members appointed by the appropriate government, and where the commission consists of more than one members, one of them may be appointed as the Chairman thereof.

Powers of Commission

The commission shall have the powers of a civil court, while trying a suit under the Code of Civil Procedure, 1908 (Act V of 1908), in respect of the following matters, namely:

(a) Summoning and enforcing the attendance of any person and examining him on oath;
(b) requiring the discovery and production of any document;
(c) receiving evidence on affidavits;
(d) requisitioning any public record or copy thereof from any court or office;
(e) issuing commissions for the examination of witnesses or documents;
(f) Any other matter which may be prescribed.

Additional Powers of Commission

(1) Where the appropriate government is of opinion that, having regard to the nature of the inquiry to be made and other circumstances of the case, all or any of the provisions of sub-section (2) or sub-section (3) or sub-section (4) or sub-section (5) should be made applicable to a commission the appropriate government may, by notification in the official gazette, direct that all or such of the said provisions as may be specified in the notification shall apply to that Commission and on the issue of such a notification, the provisions shall apply accordingly.

(2) The commission shall have power to require any person subject to any privilege which may be claimed by that person under any law for the time being in force, to furnish information on such points or matters as in the opinion of the commission, may be useful for, relevant to, the subject matter of the inquiry.

(3) The commission or any officer, not below the rank of a gazetted officer, specially authorised in this behalf by the commission may enter any building or place where the commission has reason to believe that any books of account or other documents relating to the subject matter of the inquiry may be found, and may seize any such books of account or documents or take extracts or copies therefrom, subject to the provisions of Section 102 and Section 103 of the Code of Criminal Procedure, 1898 (Act V of 1898) in so far as they may be applicable.

(4) The commission shall be deemed to be a civil court and when any offence as is described in Section 175, Section 178, Section 179, Section 180 or Section 228 of the Indian Penal Code (Act XLV of 1860) is committed in the view or presence of the commission, the commission may, after recording the facts constituting the offence and the statement of the accused as provided for in the Code of Criminal Procedure, 1898 (Act V of 1898), forward the case to a magistrate having jurisdiction to try the same and the magistrate to whom any such case is forwarded shall proceed to hear the complaint against the accused as if the case had been forwarded to him under Section 482 of the Code of Criminal Procedure, 1898.

(5) Any proceeding before the Commission shall be deemed to be a judicial proceeding within the meaning of Sections 193 and 228 of the Indian Penal Code (Act XLV of 1860).

Statement Made by Persons to the Commission

No statement made by a person in the course of giving evidence before the commission shall subject him to, or be used against him in, any civil or criminal proceeding except a prosecution for giving false evidence by such statement:

Provided that the statement

(a) is made in reply to a question which he is required by the commission to answer, or

(b) is relevant to the subject matter of the inquiry.

Commission to Cease to Exist When so Notified

The appropriate government may, if it is of opinion that the continued existence of a commission is unnecessary, by notification in the official gazette, declare that the commission shall cease to exist from such date as may be specified in this behalf in such notification, and thereupon, the commisson shall cease to exist.

Procedure to be Followed by the Commission

The Commission shall, subject to any rules that may be made in this behalf, have power to regulate its own procedure (including the fixing of places and times of its sitting and deciding whether to sit in public or in private) and may act not withstanding the temporary absence of any member or the existence of a vacancy among its members.

Protection of Action Taken in Good Faith

No suit or other legal proceeding shall lie against the appropriate government, the commission or any member thereof, or any person acting under the direction either of the appropriate government or of the commission in respect of anything which is in good faith done or intended to be done in pursuance of this Act or of any rules or orders made thereunder in respect of the publication by, or under the authority of the appropriate government or the commission, of any report, paper or proceedings.

Members, etc. to be Public Servants

Every member of the commission and every officer appointed or authorised by the Commssion to exercise functions under this Act shall be deemed to be a public servant within the meaning of Section 21 of the Indian Penal Code (Act XLV of 1860).

Act to Apply to Other Inquiring Authorities in Certain Cases

Where any authority (by whatever name called), other than a commission appointed under section 3, has been or is set up under any resolution or order of the appropriate government for the purpose of making an inquiry into any definite matter of public importance and that government is of opinion that all or any of the provisions of this Act should be made applicable to that authority, that government may, subject to the prohibition contained in the provision to sub-section (1) of section 3, by notification in the official gazette, direct that the said provisions of the Act shall apply to that authority, and on the issue of such a notification, that authority shall be deemed to be a commission appointed under section 3 for the purpose of this Act.

Power to Make Rules

(1) The appropriate government may by notification in the official gazette, make rules to carry out the purposes of this Act.

(2) In particular, and without prejudice to the generality of the foregoing power, such rules may provide for all or any of the following matters, namely:

(a) the term of office and the conditions of service of the members of the commission;

(b) the manner in which inquiries may be held under this Act and the procedure to be followed by the commission in respect of the proceedings before it;

(c) the powers of civil court which may be vested in the commission;

(d) any other matter which has to be or may be prescribed.

According to Article 246, Schedule VII, of the Constitution of India the commission or committee may be appointed on the subjects as defined in List I (Union List), List II (State List) and List III (Concurrent List).

List I : Union List

1. Defence of India and every part thereof including preparation for defence and all such acts as may be conducive in times of war to its prosecution and after its termination to effective demobilisation;

2. Naval, military and air forces; any other armed forces of the Union;

[1]3. Delimitation of cantonment areas, local self-government in such areas, the constitution and powers within such areas of cantonment authorities and the regulation of house accommodation (including the control of rents) in such areas;

4. Naval, military and airforce workers;

5. Arms, firearms, ammunition and explosives;

6. Atomic energy and mineral resources necessary for its production;

7. Industries declared by Parliament by law to be necessary for the purpose of defence or for the prosecution of war;

[2]8. Central Bureau of Intelligence and Investigation;

[2]9. Preventive detention for reasons connected with defence, foreign affairs, or the security of India; persons subjected to such detention;

10. Foreign affairs; all matters which bring the Union into relation with any foreign country;

11. Diplomatic, consular and trade representation;

12. United Nations Organization;

13. Participation in international conferences, associations and other bodies and implementing of decisions made thereat;

14. Entering into treaties and agreements with foreign countries and implementing of treaties, agreements and conventions with foreign countries;

15. War and peace;

16. Foreign jurisdiction;

17. Citizenship, naturalisation and aliens;

18. Extradition;

19. Admission into, and emigration and expulsion from, India; passports and visas;

20. Pilgrimages to places outside India;

21. Piracies and crimes committed on the high seas or in the air; offences against the law of nations committed on land or the high seas or in the air;

[1]In its application to the State of Jammu and Kashmir, for entry 3, the following entry shall be substituted, namely :

"3. Administration of cantonments."

[2]Not applicable to the State of Jammu and Kashmir.

22. Railways;

23. Highways declared by or under law made by Parliament to be National Highways;

24. Shipping and navigation on inland waterways, declared by Parliament by law to be national waterways, as regards mechanically propelled vessels; the rule of the road on such waterways;

25. Maritime shipping and navigation, including shipping and navigation on tidal waters; provision of education and training for the mercantile marine and regulation of such education and training provided by states and other agencies;

26. Lighthouses, including lightships, beacons and other provision for the safety of shipping and aircraft;

27. Ports declared by or under law made by Parliament or existing law to be major ports, including their delimitation, and the constitution and powers of port authorities therein;

28. Ports quarantine, including hospitals connected therewith; seamen's and marine hospitals;

29. Airways, aircraft and air navigation; provision of aerodromes; regulation and organization of air traffic and regulation of such education and training provided by states and other agencies;

30. Carriage of passengers and goods by railways, sea or air, or by national waterways in mechanically propelled vessels;

31. Posts and telegraphs; telephones, wireless, broadcasting and other like forms of communication;

32. Property of the Union and the revenue therefrom, but as regards property situated in a state subject to legislation by the state[1]*** subject to legislation by the state save in so far as Parliament by law otherwise provides;

[2]33. *** * * * * * *

[3]34. Courts of wards for the estates of Rulers of Indian States;

35. Public debt of the Union;

36. Currency, coinage and legal tender; foreign exchange;

37. Foreign loans;

38. Reserve Bank of India;

39. Post Office Savings Bank;

40. Lotteries organized by the Government of India or the government of a state;

41. Trade and commerce with foreign countries; import and export across customs frontiers; definition of customs frontiers;

42. Inter-state trade and commerce.

43. Incorporation, regulation and winding up of trading corporations, including banking, insurance and financial corporations but not including cooperative societies.

44. Incorporation, regulation and winding up of corporations, whether trading or not, with objects not confined to one state, but not including universities;

45. Banking;

46. Bills of exchange, cheques, promissory notes and other like instruments;

47. Insurance;

[1]The words and letters "Specified in Part A or Part B of the First Schedule" omitted by the Constitution (Seventh Amendment) Act, 1956, S. 29 and Sch.

[2]Entry 33 omitted by S. 26, *ibid*.

[3]Not applicable to the State of Jammu and Kashmir.

48. Stock exchanges and future markets;

49. Patents, inventions and designs, copyright; trade-marks and merchandise marks;

50. Establishment of standards of weight and measure;

51. Establishment of standards of quality for goods to be exported out of India or transported from one state to another;

52. Industries, the control of which by the Union is declared by Parliament by law to be expedient in the public interest;

53. Regulation and development of oilfields and mineral oil resources; petroleum and petroleum products; other liquids and substances declared by Parliament by law to be dangerously inflammable;

54. Regulation of mines and mineral development to the extent to which such regulation and development under the control of the Union is declared by Parliament by law to be expedient in the Public interest;

55. Regulation of labour and safety in mines and oilfields;

56. Regulation and development of inter-state rivers and river vallleys to the extent to which such regulation and development under control of the Union is declared by Parliament by law to be expedient in the public interest;

57. Fishing and fisheries beyond territorial waters;

58. Manufacture, supply and distribution of salt by Union agencies; regulation and control of manufacture, supply and distribution of salt by other agencies;

59. Cultivation, manufacture and sale for export of opium;

60. Sanctioning of cinematograph films for exhibition;

61. Industrial disputes concerning union employees;

62. The institution known at the commencement of this Constitution as the National Library, the Indian Museum, the Imperial War Museum, the Victoria Memorial and the Indian War Memorial, and any other like institution financed by the Government of India wholly or in part and declared by Parliament by law to be an institution of national importance;

63. The institutions known at the commencement of this Constitution as Banaras Hindu University, the Aligarh Muslim University and the Delhi University and any other institution declared by Parliament by law to be an institution of national importance;

64. Institutions for scientific or technical education financed by the Government of India wholly or in part and declared by Parliament by law to be institutions of national importance;

65. Union agencies and institutions for—(a) professional, vocational or technical training including the training of Police officers; or (b) the promotion of special studies or research; or (c) scientific or technical assistance in the investigation or detection of crime;

66. Coordination and determination of standards in institutions for higher education or research and scientific and technical institutions;

[1]67. Ancient and historical monuments and records, and archaeological sites and remains, [2][declared by or under law made by Parliament] to be of national importance;

68. The Survey of India, the Geological, Botanical, Zoological and Anthropological Surveys of India, Meteorological Organizations;

69. Census;

[1]In its application to the State of Jammu and Kashmir, in entry 67, the words "and records" shall be omitted.

[2]Subs. by the Constitution (Seventh Amendment) Act, 1956, S. 27, for "declared by Parliament by law."

70. Union public services, all-India services, Union Public Service Commission;

71. Union pensions, that is to say, pensions payable by the Government of India or out of the Consolidated Fund of India;

[1]72. Elections of Parliament, to legislatures of States and to the offices of President and Vice-President; the Election Commission;

73. Salaries and allowances of members of Parliament, the Chairman and Deputy Chairman of the Council of States and the Speaker and Deputy Speaker of the House of the People;

74. Powers, privileges and immunities of each House of Parliament and of the members and the committees of each House; enforcement of attendance of persons for giving evidence or producing documents before Committees of Parliament or Commissions appointed by Parliament;

75. Emoluments, allowances, privileges and rights in respect of leave of absence, of the President and Governors; salaries and allowances of the Ministries for the Union; the salaries, allowances, and rights in respect of leave of absence and other conditions of service of the Comptroller and Auditor-General;

76. Audit of the accounts of the Union and of the States;

77. Constitution, organization, jurisdiction and powers of the Supreme Court (including contempt of such court), and the fees taken therein; persons entitled to practise before the Supreme Court;

78. Constitution and Organization [2][including Vacations] of the High Courts except provisions as to officers and servants of High Courts; persons entitled to practise before the High Court;

[3][[4]79. Extension of jurisdiction of a High Court to, and exclusion of the jurisdiction of a High Court from any Union territory];

80. Extension of the powers and the jurisdiction of members of a police force belonging to any State to any area outside that State, but not so as to enable the Police of one State to exercise powers and jurisdiction in any area outside that State without the consent of the Government of the State in which such area is situated; extension of the powers and jurisdiction of members of a police force belonging to any State to railway areas outside the State;

[5]81. Inter-state migration; inter-State quarantine;

82. Taxes on income other than agricultural income;

83. Duties of customs including export duties;

84. Duties of excise on tobacco and other goods manufactured or produced in India except (a) alcoholic liquors for human consumption; (b) opium, Indian hemp and other narcotic drugs and narcotics;

[1]In its application to the State of Jammu and Kashmir, in entry 72, the reference to the States shall be construed,

(a) in relation to appeals to the Supreme Court from any decision or order of the High Court of the State of Jammu and Kashmir made in an election petition whereby an election to either House of the legislature of that State has been called in question, as including a reference to the State of Jammu and Kashmir.

(b) in relation to other matters, as not including a reference to that State.

[2]Ins. by the Constitution (Fifteenth Amendment) Act, 1963, S. 12 (with retrospective effect).

[3]Subs. by the Constitution (Seventh Amendment) Act, 1956, S. 29 and Sch., for entry 79.

[4]Not applicable to the State of Jammu and Kashmir.

[5]In its application to the State of Jammu and Kashmir, in item 81, the words "inter-state migration," shall be omitted.

85. Corporation Tax;

86. Taxes on the capital value of the assets, exclusive of agricultural land, of individuals and companies; taxes on the capital of companies;

87. Estate Duty in respect of property other than agricultural land;

88. Duties in respect of succession to property other than agricultural land;

89. Terminal taxes on goods or passengers, carried by railway, sea or air; taxes on railway fares and freights;

90. Taxes other than stamp duties on transactions in stock exchanges and future markets;

91. Rates of stamp duty in respect of bills of exchange, cheques, promissory notes, bills of lading, letters of credit, policies of insurance, transfer of shares, debentures, proxies and receipts;

92. Taxes on the sale or purchase of newspapers and on advertisements published therein;

[1]92A. Taxes on the sale or purchase of goods other than newspapers, where such sale or purchase takes place in the course of inter-state trade or commerce];

93. Offences against laws with respect to any of the matters in this List;

94. Inquiries, surveys and statistics for the purpose of any of the matters in this List;

95. Jurisdiction and powers of all courts, except the Supreme Court, with respect to any of the matters in this List; admiralty jurisdiction;

96. Fees in respect of any of the matters in this List, but not including fees taken in any Court;

[2]97. Any other matter not enumerated in Lists II or III including any tax not mentioned in either of those Lists.

[3]List II: State List

1. Public Order (but not including the use of naval, military or air forces or any other armed forces of the Union in aid of civil power);

2. Police, including railway and village police;

3. Administration of justice; constitution and organization of all courts, except the Supreme Court and the High Court; officers and servants of the High Court; procedure in rent and revenue courts; fees taken in all courts except the Supreme Court.

4. Prisons, reformatories, Borstal institutions and other institutions of a like nature, and persons detained therein; arrangements with other States for the use of prisons and other institutions;

5. Local government, that is to say, the constitution and powers of municipal corporations, improvement trusts, district boards, mining settlement authorities and other local authorities for the purpose of local self-government or village administration;

[1]Ins. by the Constitution (Sixth Amendment) Act, 1956, S. 2.

[2]In its application to the State of Jammu and Kashmir, for entry 97, the following entry shall be substituted, namely:

"97. Prevention of the activities directed towards disclaiming, questioning or disrupting the sovereignty and territorial integrity of India or bringing about session of a part of the territory of India or secession of a part of the territory of India from the Union or causing insult to the Indian National Flag, the Indian National Anthem and this Constitution; taxes on foreign travel by sea or air, on inland air travel and on postal articles, including moneyorders, phonograms and telegrams."

[3]Not applicable to the State of Jammu and Kashmir.

6. Public health and sanitation; hospitals and dispensaries;

7. Pilgrimages, other than pilgrimages to places outside India;

8. Intoxicating liquors, that is to say, the production, manufacture, possession, transport, purchase and sale of intoxicating liquors;

9. Relief of the disabled and unemployable;

10. Burials and burial grounds; cremations and cremation grounds;

11. Education including universities, subject to the provisions of entries 63, 64, 65 and 66 of List I and entry 25 of List III;

12. Libraries, museums and other similar institutions controlled or financed by the States; ancient and historical monuments and records other than those [1][declared by or under law made by Parliament] to be of national importance;

13. Communications, that is to say, roads, bridges, ferries, and other means of communication not specified in List I; municipal tramways; ropeways; inland waterways and traffic there on subject to the provisions of List I and List III with regard to such waterways; vehicles other than mechanically propelled vehicles;

14. Agriculture, including agricultural education and research, protection against pests and prevention of plant diseases;

15. Preservation, protection and improvement of stock and prevention of animal diseases; veterinary training and practice;

16. Pounds and the prevention of cattle trespass;

17. Water, that is to say, water supplies, irrigation and canals, drainage and embankments, water storage and water power subject to the provisions of entry 56 of List I;

18. Land, that is to say, rights in or over land, land tenures including the relation of landlord and tenant, and the collection of rents; transfer and alienation of agricultural land; land improvement and agricultural loans; colonization;

19. Forests;

20. Proctection of wild animals and birds:

21. Fisheries;

22. Courts of wards subject to the provisions of entry 34 of List I; encumbered and attached estates;

23. Regulation of mines and mineral development subject to the provisions of List I with respect to regulation and development under the control of the Union;

24. Industries subject to the provisions of [2][entries 7 and 52] of List I;

25. Gas and gas-works;

26. Trade and commerce within the state subject to the provisions of entry 33 of List III;

27. Production, supply and distribution of goods subject to the provisions of entry 33 of List III;

28. Markets and fairs;

29. Weights and measures except establishment of standards;

30. Money-lending and money-lenders; relief of agricultural indebtedness;

31. Inns and inn-keepers;

32. Incorporation, regulation and winding up of corporations, other than those specified

[1]Subs. by the Constitution (Seventh Amendment) Act, 1956, S. 27, for "declared by Parliament by law."

[2]Subs. by the Constitution (Seventh Amendment) Act, 1956 S. 28 for "entry 52".

in List I, and universities; unincorporated trading, literary, scientific, religious and other societies and associations; cooperative societies.

33. Theatres and dramatic performances; cinemas subject to the provisions of entry 60 of List I; sports, entertainments and amusements;

34. Betting and gambling;

35. Works, lands and buildings vested in or in the possession of the State;

[1]36. **** * * * * * * *

37. Elections to the legislature of the State subject to the provisions of any law made by Parliament;

38. Salaries and allowances of members of the legislature of the state, of the Speaker and Deputy Speaker of the Legislative Assembly and, if there is a Legislative Council, of the Chairman and Deputy Chairman thereof;

39. Powers, privileges and immunities of the Legislative Assembly and of the members and the committees thereof and, if there is a Legislative Council, of that Council and of the members of the committees thereof; enforcement of attendance of persons for giving evidence or producing documents before committees of the legislature of the State;

40. Salaries and allowances of Ministers for the state;

41. State public services, State Public Service Commission;

42. State pensions, that is to say, pensions payable by the state or out of the Consolidated Fund of the state;

43. Public debt of the State;

44. Treasure trove;

45. Land revenue, including the assessment and collection of revenue, the maintenance of land records, survey for revenue purposes and records of rights, and alienation of revenues;

46. Taxes on agricultural income;

47. Duties in respect of succession to agricultural land;

48. Estate duty in respect of agricultural land;

49. Taxes on lands and buildings;

50. Taxes on mineral rights subject to any limitations imposed by Parliament by law relating to mineral development;

51. Duties of excise on the following goods manufactured or produced in the state and countervailing duties at the same or lower rates on similar goods manufactured or produced elsewhere in India:

(a) alcoholic liquors for human consumption;

(b) opium, Indian hemp and other narcotic drugs and narcotics;

but not including medicinal and toilet preparations containing alcohol or any substance included in sub-paragraph (b) of this entry;

52. Taxes on the entry of goods into a local area for consumption, use or sale therein;

53. Taxes on the consumption or sale of electricity;

[2][54. Taxes on the sale or purchase of goods other than newspapers, subject to the provisions of entry 92A of List I];

55. Taxes on advertisements other than advertisements published in the newspapers;

56. Taxes on goods and passengers carried by road or on inland waterways;

[1]Entry 36 omitted by the Constitution (Seventh Amendment) Act, 1956 S. 26.

[2]Subs. by the Constitution (Sixth Amendment) Act, 1956, S. 2, for the original entry 54.

57. Taxes on vehicles, whether mechanically propelled or not, suitable for use on roads, including tramcars subject to the provisions of entry 35 of List III;

58. Taxes on animals and boats;

59. Tolls;

60. Taxes on professions, trades, callings and employments;

61. Capitation taxes;

62. Taxes on [luxuries, including taxes on entertainments, amusements, betting and gambling;

63. Rates of stamp duty in respect of documents other than those specified in the provisions of List I with regard to rates of stamp duty;

64. Offences against laws with respect to any of the matters in this List;

65. Jurisdiction and powers of all courts, except the Supreme Court, with respect to any of the matters in this List;

66. Fees in respect of any of the matters in this List, but not including fees taken in any court.

List III : Concurrent List

[1]1. Criminal law, including all matters included in the Indian Penal Code at the commencement of this Constitution but excluding offences against laws with respect to any of the matters specified in List I or List II and excluding the use of naval, military or air forces or any other armed forces of the Union in aid of the civil power;

[2]2. Criminal procedure, including all matters included in the Code of Criminal Procedure at the commencement of this Constitution;

[2]3. Preventive detention for reasons connected with the security of a state, the maintenance of public order, or the maintenance of supplies, and services essential to the community; persons subjected to such detention;

4. Removal from one State to another State of prisoners, accused persons and persons subjected to preventive detention for reasons specified in entry 3 of this List;

[2]5. Marriage and divorce; infants and minors; adoption; wills, intestacy and succession; joint family and partition; all matters in respect of which parties in judicial proceedings were immediately before the commencement of this constitution subject to their personal law;

[2]6. Transfer of property other than agricultural land; registration of deeds and documents;

[2]7. Contracts, including partnership, agency, contracts of carriage, and other special forms of contracts, but not including contracts relating to agricultural land;

[2]8. Actionable wrongs;

[2]9. Bankruptcy and insolvency;

[2]10. Trust and trustees;

11. Administrators-general and official trustees;

[1]In its application to the State of Jammu and Kashmir, for entry 1, the following entry shall be substituted, namely:

"1. Criminal law (excluding offences against laws with respect to any of the matters specified in List I and excluding the use of naval, military or air forces or any other armed forces of the Union in aid of the civil power) in so far such criminal law relates to offences against laws with respect to any of the matters specified in this list."

[2]Not applicable to the State of Jammu and Kashmir.

[1]12. Evidence and oaths; recognition of laws, public acts and records, and judicial proceedings;

[1]13. Civil procedure, including all matters included in the Code of Civil Procedure at the commencement of this Constitution, limitation and arbitration;

[1]14. Contempt of court, but not including contempt of the Supreme Court;

[1]15. Vagrancy; nomadic and migratory tribes;

16. Lunacy and mental deficiency, including places for the reception or treatment of lunatics and mental deficients;

[1]17. Prevention of cruelty to animals;

18. Adulteration of foodstuffs and other goods;

19. Drugs and poisons, subject to the provision of entry 59 of List I with respect to opium;

[1]20. Economic and social planning;

[1]21. Commercial and industrial monopolies, combines and trusts;

22. Trade unions; industrial and labour disputes;

23. Social security and social insurance; employment and unemployment;

24. Welfare of labour including conditions of work, provident funds, employers' liability, workmen's compensation, invalidity and old age pensions and maternity benefits;

25. Vocational and technical training of labour;

26. Legal, medical and other professions;

[1]27. Relief and rehabilitation of persons displaced from their original place of residence by reason of the setting up of the Dominions of India and Pakistan;

[1]28. Charities and charitable instituions, charitable and religious endowments and religious institutions;

[1]29. Prevention of the extension from one state to another of infectious or contagious diseases or pests affecting men, animals or plants;

[2]30. Vital statistics including registration of births and deaths;

[1]31. Ports other than those declared by or under law made by Parliament or existing law to be major ports;

[1]32. Shipping and navigation on inland waterways as regards mechanically propelled vessels, and the rule of the road on such waterways, and the carriage of passengers and goods on inland waterways subject to the provisions of List I with respect to national waterways;

[3][33. Trade and commerce in, and the production, supply and distribution of;

(a) the products of any industry where the control of such industry by the Union is declared by Parliament by law to be expedient in the public interest, and imported goods of the same kind as such products;

(b) foodstuffs, including edible oilseeds and oils;

(c) cattle feeder, including oilcakes and other concentrates;

(d) raw cotton, whether ginned or unginned, and cotton seeds; and

(e) raw jute];

[1]Not applicable to the state of Jammu and Kashmir.

[2]In its application to the state of Jammu and Kashmir, for entry 30, the following entry shall be substituted, namely:

"30. Vital statistics in so far as they relate to births and deaths including registration of births and deaths."

[3]Subs. by the Constitution (Third Amendment), Act, 1954, S. 2

34. Price Control;

35. Mechanically propelled vehicles including the principles on which taxes on such vehicles are to be levied;

36. Factories;

[1]37. Boilers;

[1]38. Electricity;

39. Newspapers, books and printing presses;

[1]40. Archaeological sites and remains other than those [2][declared by or under law made by Praliament] to be of national importance;

[1]41. Custody, management and disposal of property (including agricultural land) declared by law to be evacuee property;

[3][[1]42. Acquisition and requisitioning of property];

43. Recovery in a state of claims in respect of taxes and other public demands, including arrears of land-revenue and sums recoverable as such arrears, arising outside that state;

[1]44. Stamp duties other than duties or fees collected by means of judicial stamps, but not including rates of stamp duty;

[4]45. Inquiries and statistics for the purposes of any of the matters specified in List II or List III;

46. Jurisdiction and powers of all courts, except the Supreme Court, with respect to any of the matters in this List;

47. Fees in respect of any of the matters in this List, but not including fees taken in any court.

When a commission or committee is large (like the National Commission on Labour) and its work becomes somewhat unwieldy, it is bifurcated into many study groups or sub-committees. These study groups or sub-committees submit their reports on the specific issues as laid down in their terms of reference. Finally, the main committee or commission takes cognizance of their recommendations and after scrutinizing incorporates them into the main or final recommendations.

The committees which are set up to enquire are also Advisory Committees. They give suggestions to the government and are almost on a par with tribunals which are set up to enquire into a particular accident or disaster, malpractices or maladministration.

The committtees to enquire are also empowered to record evidence in camera if circumstances so require and provide protection, if necessary, to a person or persons giving evidence before these. The recommendations of these committees are in the nature of judgement. Investigation is an important function of such committees; e.g., Punjab Commission, appointed by the Government of India "to enquire into the alleged discrimination and differential treatment of Sikhs" in 1961; the Railway Accidents Committee or the Committee on Prevention of Corruption also known as Santhanam Committee; Commission to enquire into the allegations made against Pratap Singh Kairon; Ayyangar Commission to probe into the charges against Bakshi Ghulam Mohammad; Wanchoo Commission currently looking into the alleged acts of irregularities committed by some Ministers of West Bengal Government.

[1]Not aplicable to the state of Jammu and Kashmir.

[2]Subs. by the Constitution (Seventh Amendment) Act,1956, S. 27, for "declared by Parliament by law."

[3]Subs. by s. 26, *ibid*, for the orginal entry 42.

[4]In its application to the State of Jammu and Kashmir, in entry 45, for the words and figures "List II or List III", the words "this List" shall be substituted.

The committees or commissions to negotiate enquiry into the relations between employees and the employer; they cover a wide field of employment, wages, conditions of service, etc. These committees or study groups and commissions are: Bonus Commission, 1961; Central Wage Board for Cement Industry Committee, 1964; Central Wage Board for Iron and Steel Industry Committee, 1965; Working of Minimum Wages Act Committee, 1965; Commission on the question of adequacy of the dearness allowance admissible to Central Government employees as from December 1, 1965; Calcutta Tramway Workers' Strike Inquiry Committee, 1958; Committee to examine the feasibility of evolving a system of payment by results to certain categories of employees under the Bombay and Madras Port Trust and the Bombay Dock Labour Board, 1960; Dock Workers (Regulation of Employment) Enquiry Committee, 1955; Scavenging Conditions Enquiry Committee, 1957; Third Pay Commission, 1970-73, etc.

The committees or commissions which enquire into administrative deficiencies at the Central, state or local levels are necessary for an efficient and healthy administrative machinery. These are appointed as the case may be by the Parliament, the Prime Minister, Minister of a particulur depertmant or ministry etc., e.g., Education Commission; Administrative Reforms Commission; Public Works Department Committee; Expert Committee on Small Pox and Cholera, 1958; Committee on Broadcasting and Information Media, 1964; Committee on Central National Museum; Reviewing Committee for the three Akademies (Sahitya, Lalit and Sangeet Natak) and the Indian Council for Cultural Relations, 1964; Study Team on Centre-State Relations of the Administrative Reforms Commission; Secretariat Procedure Committee, etc.

Commissions appointed by the President under Article 280 (I), 339, 340 & 344 of the Constitution of India, e.g., the Finance Commission which was first constituted after two years of the commencement of the Indian Constitution, Backward Classes Commission, 1955, Official Languages Commission, 1956 etc.

Whenever there is some subject of national importance and for the welfare of the people and there is the feeling among the Members of Parliament that the government is ignoring such an important issue, the Parliament appoints a committee or commission after discussion in both the Houses under Article 246 of the Constitution of India, e.g., Committee of Members of Parliament on Higher Education, 1963; and Committee of Members of Parliament on Education, 1967.

The committees or commissions appointed by the ministries and departments are mainly for that subject assigned to the department and for the welfare of the people or for their own benefit, that is, for proper and efficient administration. For instance, the Reserve Bank of India appointed a Working Group to have expert advice on the appraisal of applications for Term Loans in 1961; the Ministry of Home Affairs appointed a special Working Group on Cooperation for Backward Classes in 1961; the Ministry of Commerce and Industry appointed a Jute Commission in 1962; the Department of Tourism appointed an Ad-hoc Committee on Tourism in 1963; the Planning Commission appointed a Committee on Transport and Coordination in 1963; the Ministry of Education appointed an Emotional Integration Committee in 1961.

Not only this the various Advisory Boards, Councils and Authorities also appoint committees for the benefit of those they serve or for their own improvement. For instance, the National Cooperative Development and Warehousing Board, New Delhi, appointed a Study Team on Cooperative Marketing in 1961; the Central Advisory Board of Education, a permanent Advisory Board, has appointed from time to time a large number of committees and study teams relating to Education. The Railway Board, also a permanent Advisory Board under the Ministry of Railway has appointed many enquiries, investigation committees, etc., on various subjects relating to Railways.

In 1954 the Central Government made Commission of Inquiry (Assessors) Rules, for assisting and to advise a commission on any matter connected with its inquiry, which is as follows:

Ministry of Home Affairs

New Delhi, the 9th April, 1954

S. R. O. 1218 : In exercise of the powers conferred by Section 12 of the Commission of Inquiry Act, 1952 (LX of 1952), the Central Government hereby makes the following rules, namely:

1. Short Title : These rules may be called the Commission of Inquiry (Assessors) Rules, 1954.

2. Definition : In these Rules, "assessor" means an assessor appointed under these Rules.

3. Appointment of Assessors : The Central Government or with the previous approval of the Central Government a Commission, may, from time to time appoint one or more assessors to assist and advise the Commission on any matter connected with its inquiry.

4. Functions of Assessors : It shall be the duty of the assessors to assist and advise the Commission on any matter on which the Commission may consult them in course of its inquiry:

Provided that advice tendered by the Assessors shall not be binding on the Commission.

5. Manner of Consultation with Assessors : The Commission shall have the power to regulate the manner in which it may consult the assessors. (*No. 16/4/54-Judl.*)

On July 26, 1955 the Government of India made rules for the issue of and service of summons by a commission of inquiry to persons whose attendance is required either to give evidence or to produce documents, which is as follows:

Ministry of Home Affairs

New Delhi, the 26th July, 1955

S.R.O. 1676 : In exercise of the powers conferred by Section 12 of the Commissions of Inquiry Act, 1952 (LX of 1952), the Central Government hereby makes the following rules for the issue and service of summons by a Commission of Inquiry appointed by that Government, namely:

Rules

1. The Commission may issue summons to persons whose attendance is required either to give evidence or to produce documents.

2. Every summons issued by the Commission shall be in duplicate and signed by the Chairman or such person as he empowers in this behalf and sealed with the seal of the Commission;

and it shall specify the time and place at which the person summoned is required to attend and also whether his attendance is required for the purpose of giving evidence or to produce a document, or for both purposes.

3. A person may be summoned to produce a document, without being summoned to give evidence; and any person summoned merely to produce a document shall be deemed to have complied with the summons if he can see such document to be produced instead of attending personally to produce the same.

4. A summons to produce documents may be for the production of certain specified documents or for the production of all documents of a certain description in the possession or power of the person summoned.

5. Every summons shall be served by sending it by post to the person for whom it is intended or in such other manner as the Commission may direct.

6. The provisions of the foregoing rules shall apply, as far as may be, to every other process issued by the Commission. [*No. 16/1/55-Judicial (I)*]

On May 7th 1960 the Government of India made Rules entitled 'The Central Commission of Inquiry (Procedure) Rules' for issuing notices to persons for giving evidence, recording of evidence, etc. to enquire into the conduct of any person and for cross-examination. The Rule is as follows:

Ministry of Home Affairs

New Delhi, the 7th May, 1960

G.S.R. 531 : In exercise of the powers conferred by Section 12 of the Commissions of Inquiry Act, 1952 (60 of 1952), the Central Government hereby makes the following rules, namely:

The Central Commissions of Inquiry (Procedure) Rules, 1960

1. **Short Title and Application** : (i) These rules may be called the Central Commissions of Inquiry (Procedure) Rules, 1960. (ii) They shall apply to Commissions of Inquiry appointed by the Central Government.

2. **Notice to Persons for Giving Evidence** : (i) The Commission shall, as soon as may be after its appointment:

(a) issue a notice to every person, who in its opinion should be given an opportunity of being heard in the inquiry, to furnish to the Commission a statement relating to such matters as may be specified in the notice;

(b) issue a notification to be published in such manner as it may deem fit, inviting all persons acquainted with the subject-matter of the inquiry to furnish to the Commission a statement relating to such matters as may be specified in the notification.

(ii) Every statement furnished under sub-rule (i) shall be accompanied by an affidavit in support of the facts set out in the statement sworn by the person furnishing the statement.

(iii) Every person furnishing a statement under sub-rule (1) shall also furnish to the Commission along with the statement a list of the documents, if any, on which he proposes to rely and forward to the Commission, wherever practicable the originals or true copies of such of the documents as may be in his possession or power and shall state the name and address of the person from whom the remaining documents may be obtained.

3. **Recording of Evidence** : (i) The Commission shall examine all the statements furnished to it under rule 2 and if, after such examination, the Commission considers it necessary to record evidence, it shall first record the evidence, if any, produced by the Central Government and may thereafter record in such order as it may deem fit:

(a) the evidence of any person who has furnished a statement under Rule 2 and whose evidence the Commission, having regard to the statement considers relevant for the purpose of the inquiry;

(b) the evidence of any other person whose evidence, in the opinion of the Commission, is relevant to the inquiry.

(ii) If, after all the the evidence is recorded under sub-rule (1) the Central Government applies to the Commission to recall any witness already examined or to examine any new witness, the Commission shall, if satisfied that it is necessary for the proper determination of any relevant fact so to do, recall such witness or examine such new witness.

4. Persons Likely to be Prejudicially Affected to be Heard : If, at any stage of the inquiry the Commission

(a) considers it necessary to inquire into the conduct of any person ; or

(b) is of the opinion that the reputation of any person is likely to be prejudicially affected by the inquiry, the Commission shall give to that person a reasonable opportunity of being heard in the inquiry and to produce evidence in his defence.

5. Right of Cross-Examination and Representation by Legal Practitioner : The Central Government, every person referred to in rule 4 and with the permission of the Commission, any other person whose evidence is recorded under rule 3;

(a) may cross examine a witness other than a witness produced by it or him;

(b) may address the court; and

(c) may be represented before the Commission by a legal practitioner or, with the consent of the Commission, by any other person.

6. Procedure in Matters Not Provided in the Rules: The Commission shall have the power to regulate its own procedure in respect of any matter for which no provision is made in these rules.

(No. F. 25/8/60-AVD.)

CONCLUSION

To conclude, committees and commissions are always advising the government, offering valuable suggestions and recommendations to run smoothly and efficiently the administration for the welfare of the people.

The staff of committee or commission comprises:

Chairman, Members and Member-Secretary (sometimes there is also an Assistant Secretary). In some cases there are one-man commissions, and the inquiry is entrusted to an Officer-on-Special Duty, e.g., Shri L.S. Mishra was appointed as Officer-on-Special Duty for the Bellary Taluk Commission, 1953; Shri S.R. Das was appointed by the Government of India as Chairman of the one-man Commission on the Question of Adequacy of the Dearness Allowance Admissible to Central Government Employees from December 1, 1965.

The Chairman of a commission is mostly a person well-versed in legal affairs and is often a retired Judge of a High Court or the Supreme Court of India. Occasionally, a Member of Parliament is also appointed Chairman of a Commission.

The Members of a Commission or Committee are specialists in their respective fields and provide valuable guidance to the Commission in making its recommendations.

The Member-Secretary is nominated from among the experienced officials who have the requisite competent knowledge of the subject on which the committee or commission is appointed.

The study of committees and commissions is divided into two main parts:

(i) Pre-Independence: from 1772 to August 1947; and

(ii) Post-Independence: from August 1947 to 1973.

The present volume covers the period from August 1947 to 1954.

I am sure this reference work is of a nature the like of which has not been undertaken before. I have spared no efforts to make it a comprehensive reference tool and the work will be of great use to the research scholars, sociologists, historians, students of political science and all those connected with the study of administration and legal affairs. If there are any omissions or errors I may be forgiven as it is a work of pioneering nature undertaken single handedly. But, I am bound to cover up any lacunae in its future editions.

The work gives information on:

(i) Bibliographical data of the committees and commissions.

(ii) Chairman, Members, etc. of the Committees and Commissions

(iii) Appointment.

(iv) Terms of Reference.

(v) Contents; and

(vi) Recommendations.

In the end, I would be failing in my duty if I do not pay homage to Late Padmashri Dr. S.R. Ranganathan, a great librarian and a world renowned personality in the field of Library Science, who inspired me to undertake this work. I must also express my gratitude to Shri D.R. Kalia, Director, Central Secretariat Library, New Delhi for his valuable guidance without which it would not have been possible for me to bring out this work. I am also indebted to Shri J.C. Shrivastava, Librarian, National Archives of India, New Delhi, who has helped me a lot in the process of compilation of this work. I am thankful to the Ministry of Education and Social Welfare, Department of Culture, Government of India, for giving me permission to publish this reference work. Heartfelt thanks are also due to my friends and colleagues for their constant help and encouragement. I also owe a debt of gratitude to my wife who at sacrifice of much personal comfort provided every facility to finalise this work within a reasonably short time.

NEW DELHI
Deepavali
November 13, 1974.

VIRENDRA KUMAR

1947

COMMITTEE ON MEASUREMENT OF GEOLOGICAL TIME IN INDIA

1947—REPORT

New Delhi, Council of Scientific and Industrial Research, 1954. 23p.

Chairman : Dr. D. N. Wadia.

Members : Prof. C. Mahadevan; Prof. R. S. Krishnan; Dr. O. A. Hoeg; Dr. S. C. D. Sah.

APPOINTMENT

Recognizing the importance of geochronological studies the Council of Scientific and Industrial Research constituted, in 1947, a Committee on Measurement of Geological Time in India.

TERMS OF REFERENCE

To organize, systematize and finance schemes of research on the subject.

CONTENTS

Introduction by Dr. D. N. Wadia; Investigations on the Age of Madras Granites and South Indian Rocks by Prof. C. Mahadevan; Age Determination of Crystal Rocks by Radioactive Methods by Prof. R. S. Krishnan; Palaeobotanical Investigations by Dr. O. A. Hoeg and Dr. S. C. D. Sah.

RECOMMENDATIONS

On the recommendation of the Committee, the Council approved a plan for initiating the following research schemes in four institutions:

(1) Investigations on the uranium, thorium and radium contents of Madras Granites, Gneisses, etc.—Professor C. Mahadevan, Geology Department, Andhra University, Waltair, and Professor R. S. Krishnan, Indian Institute of Science, Bangalore.

(2) Chemical analysis of radioactive minerals from Gaya and Nellore Districts—Professor P. B. Sarkar, University College of Science, Calcutta.

(3) Palaeobotanical research—Birbal Sahni Institute of Palaeobotany, Lucknow.

The work carried out in these institutions is recorded in technical papers and reports.

INSURANCE ADVISORY COMMITTEE, POST-WAR SUB-COMMITTEE 1947—REPORT

New Delhi, Insurance Advisory Committee, 1947. 26p.

Chairman : Shri L. S. Vaidyanathan.
Members : Shri M. A. Aziz Ansari; Shri J. C. Setalvad; Shri S. C. Majumdar; Shri N. V. Nayudu; Shri T. C. Kapur; Shri T. M. Sturgess; Shri Ashutosh Banerjea; Shri K. M. Naik; Shri K. C. Desai.
Secretary : Shri A. Rajagopalan.

APPOINTMENT

The Insurance Advisory Committee, Post-War Sub-Committee, was constituted under the Government of India in 1947.

TERMS OF REFERENCE

To consider "all the problems relating to post-war India", to the comparatively narrow field covered by voluntary insurance as transacted commercially by private companies ; to explore the various other fields of insurance which are usually the responsibility of the State.

CONTENTS

Part I : Introduction; Limitations of Planning; Insurance Publicity; Improved Service to Policyholders; Insurance Education Library and Research; Mortality Investigation; Medico-Actuarial Investigation; Birth and Death Statistics; Limitation of Expenses; Amalgamation and Transfer; Investment Policy; Capital Structure and Voting Rights; Dividends; Taxation; Additional Reserves in the Case of Non-Life Companies; Losses due to War; Re-insurance Facilities for Non-Life Companies; Non-Medical Business; Provident Societies.

Part II : Minutes of Dissent.

RECOMMENDATIONS

We feel that there are directions in which the field of insurance is so far unexplored in this country and these should be explored if the country is to ensure progressive economical improvement to the utmost limit possible. For example, cattle insurance is almost unknown in this country at present. Some years ago there were a number of cattle insurance co-operative societies in the rural districts of the Bombay Presidency and the Punjab, but they all failed, firstly, because of the absence of adequate and reliable statistics on which to base operations, and, secondly, because the management of the societies left much to be desired in the matter of efficiency. We think that a fresh well-planned start should be made in this direction, and we strongly recommend that for this purpose the Imperial Council of Agricultural Research should be requested to collect suitable statistics so that in 5 to 10 years' time adequate statistical material may become available without which the venture might prove a leap in the dark.

Crop insurance is another direction in which this country is very much backward. We strongly recommend that the Imperial Council of Agricultural Research should be requested to collect the relevant statistics for this purpose. Credit insurance and export insurance are two which this country might usefully adopt even now.

One direction in which we feel action can be taken is introduction of compulsory insurance of factory workers.

Concerted measures are necessary to make the public acquainted with the benefits of insurance and to make them more "insurance-minded".

It has been suggested that the publicity work could best be undertaken by a board more or less similar to the Indian Coffee Board and supported by a levy from all insurers. There is no necessity to associate the Government in this matter at least at this stage, and that the publicity could be achieved by voluntary joint effort on the part of all insurers. With a view to bringing in all insurers into the scheme, a board should be set up jointly by all the associations of insurers and this board entrusted with the scheme and its detailed working. Insurers who are not members of any of the associations should also be invited to join the scheme and contribute towards its expenses.

The creation of a joint medical research board to be financed by all insurers which will study diseases and suggest preventive measures. The measures that are suggested will have to take into account the conditions in this country which differ widely from those obtaining in other countries due to climatic and economic differences and should utilize to the utmost the indigenous resources so as to be within the reach of the poor masses of this country.

Satisfactory service to the policy-holders can be rendered only if the insurer has a well-trained staff. The aim should be to bring into being an institute like the Chartered Insurance Institute of the United Kingdom. This Institute should provide an efficient tuition service, both oral and correspondence. It should also be an examining body the diplomas of which should be recognized by insurers as well as by the Government. Insurers should encourage their staff to appear at these examinations and success in these should be rewarded as is done in other advanced countries by increased salaries and improved prospects.

It is also very desirable to have a Central Organization which would keep up-to-date information regarding all matters in the investment field and circulate the information to all insurers who desire to have it and are prepared to pay for it. This matter can also be entrusted to the proposed Institute or its Department which is in charge of the library and research.

A combined mortality table will furnish a better standard with which the individual experience of each company can be usefully compared. It is recommended that the work of compiling such a table should be undertaken by a committee of actuaries under the auspices of all the associations of life insurers.

In addition to a mortality investigation it is highly desirable to have a combined medico-actuarial investigation on the lines of the one made in the United States of America a few years ago.

Necessary steps should be taken by the Government without any delay to ensure the keeping of accurate births and deaths records in the country.

To help the insurers to reduce expenses limitation of commission of licensed agents and chief agents will also be necessary. We also recommend that the intermediaries between the branch office or the chief agent and the insurance agent should be restricted to the barest minimum on the basis of the volume of business and the number of agents, the aim being to have only bona fide intermediaries. Our recommendations accordingly are :

(i) Further limitation of agent's commission.
(ii) Limitation of chief agent's commission.
(iii) Limitation of number of intermediaries.
(iv) Limitation of over-all expenses.

The high expense ratios of many insurance companies in India is that they are too small and therefore are uneconomic units. We recommend that they should combine with strong units.

We recommend that the principle already adopted in the case of the Reserve Bank of India, namely, that no shareholder can have more than a certain number of votes irrespective of his holding, should be followed in the case of insurance companies transacting life insurance business and that the maximum number of votes may be fixed at 10. To prevent some insurers getting round this provision by raising the face value of the share we also recommend that the face value of each share should not be allowed to be changed so as to exceed Rs. 100.

Both life and general insurance companies should be adequately capitalized before they commence underwriting business.

We recommend legislation to the effect that no insurer can utilize more than 10% of the surplus for the benefit of shareholders.

With the present high rates of taxation we feel that the companies will not be able to build up Additional Reserves of an appreciable size within a reasonable period in the future unless transfers to such reserves are exempt from taxation.

If any portion of the Additional Reserves is transferred to the Profit & Loss Account at any time that portion should be subject to tax.

It is well known that Indian insurers who have been carrying on business in enemy-occupied territories have suffered losses due directly or indirectly to the acts of the enemy. It is too early to say whether these insurers will be able to get any compensation for these losses suffered but it is suggested that some arrangement should immediately be made whereby full information can be collected in regard to the details of all such losses so that when the time of signing the peace treaty comes, necessary information might be readily available.

Two points referring to provident societies, however, need specific mention. One is the necessity of raising the limit of the sum assured by the policies which provident societies are entitled to issue. The limit holding at present, viz., Rs. 500, is in our opinion too low to enable provident societies to transact business economically. We recommend that the limit should be raised to Rs. 900 and as a corollary the lower limit for insurers should be raised to Rs. 1,000. This lower limit should also apply to mutual insurance companies. Co-operative life insurance societies may, however, continue to enjoy their present privilege of issuing policies for any amount.

The other point relates to Section 85 of the Act. We recommend that the "Government Securities" referred to in that Section should be replaced by "approved securities" and the latter expression should include the items already recommended for inclusion for the purposes of Section 27.

OVERSEAS SCHOLARSHIPS COMMITTEE, 1947—REPORT

New Delhi, Ministry of Education, 1949. 15p.

(Bureau of Education, India, Pamphlet No. 52)

Chairman : Dr. B. C. Roy.

Members : Dr. M. J. Bhaba; Dr. B. B. Dey; Prof. N. K. Sidhanta.

APPOINTMENT

The Committee was appointed by the Hon'ble Minister for Education to enquire into the progress and scope of the Overseas Scholarships Scheme which was initiated in 1945 and to make recommendations for effective improvements in the year 1947.

TERMS OF REFERENCE

(a) To consider whether, in the light of the experience gained since the scheme was initiated in 1945, the award of Government Scholarships is serving the purpose for which it was established and whether, having reference to the prospects of their being absorbed in suitable employment and of facilities for training becoming available in India, the number of scholars to be sent abroad in 1948 and the subsequent years should be increased or reduced and whether the range of subjects should be enlarged. If so, to what extent ;

(b) To consider further what avenues of study in the different branches are available or may be available in India if the existing institutions in the country are developed with suitable help from the Government;

(c) To consider what modifications, if any, may be desirable in the existing arrangements for inviting applications, selecting candidates, placing them in training institutions abroad, and generally supervising their welfare while overseas;

(d) To consider what arrangements should be made in this country to ensure that scholars who have successfully completed their courses abroad are absorbed without delay in suitable empolyment on their return;

(e) To consider what steps should be taken to coordinate the Overseas Scholarships Scheme with any existing arrangements by other Government Department or by any University for sending persons abroad for advance training.

CONTENTS

Preface; Report of the Overseas Scholarships Committee; Selection of Candidates.

RECOMMENDATIONS—SUMMARY

As hardly any of the scholars sent abroad under the Overseas Scholarships Scheme has returned to India, it is felt that it is still too early to indicate whether or not this Scheme has succeeded in achieving its aim. But it will be seen from observations made above that the operation of the Scheme can be greatly improved if effect is given to our recommendations. In observing this we, however, recognize the fact that the Overseas Scholarships Scheme has so far worked under abnormal conditions due to World War II and that the Ministry of Education have had to surmount enormous difficulties which arose out of the War during the last three years.

The proposals we have made, if followed, would reduce the possibility of any person coming back after training abroad not being absorbed in suitable employment.

It is difficult for us, with the information at our disposal, to give any categorical answer as to the extent to which the requisite facilities for training in India in the subjects for which scholarships have been given (or will be given) will become available in India either in 1948 or in the near future. As we have indicated above, the main objective of the Scheme should be provision of personnel for the upgrading of the existing institutions and the starting of new ones. This will, in time, reduce the total number of scholars to be sent abroad. We would ask the Ministry of Education to make proper enquiries as to the conditions of existing institutions and the possibility of opening now ones. These enquiries should include the facilities now obtaining in the Universities and in technical and teaching institutions in this country.

It is not possible for the Committee, within the short period of time at its disposal, to give definite opinion as to the extent to which study in the different branches may be available in India if the existing institutions in the country were developed with suitable help from the Government. This question can only be answered if the enquiries suggested [in Paragraph (iii) above] have been made and the findings are put before the Committee. In this connection it is understood that information of this type is also being collected by the Scientific Manpower Committee.

We have indicated certain modifications which are desirable in the existing arrangements for inviting applications, selecting candidates, and placing them in training institutions abroad, and generally supervising their welfare.

The Ministry of Education should get in touch with the Universities and other teaching institutions in order to find out to what extent they would co-ordinate and co-operate with the Overseas Scholarships Scheme for sending persons abroad for advanced training so that overlapping of effort and wastage might be avoided. As far as the Departments of the Central and Provincial Governments are concerned, we have already stated that all Overseas Scholarships should be administered by one agency except in the case of the Ministry of Labour's Scheme.

The Government asked us whether we were in a position to indicate the desirability of extending or curtailing the scope of the Overseas Scholarships Scheme.

Bearing in mind the real aim of the Scheme and assuming that the methods of choosing scholars which have been explained fully in paras 7, 8 and 16 are put into effective operation, we are of the opinion that the total number of scholarships may with advantage be reduced progressively, in the course of the next five years, to about half of that awarded now. The money so saved might be utilized for giving opportunities to students in existing Indian institutions to hear and be taught by eminent foreign scholars. Experience during the last two years has shown that while the top men in any country cannot be spared for long periods, most of them are willing and able to come out to India for a few months or even a year. Courses of lectures at Universities and research institutions by eminent foreigners invited by the Ministry of Education on the advice of the institutions concerned would be of inestimable value not only in imparting knowledge on the subjects which may not be very advanced in India but in raising the general level of teaching and education in the country. Indeed, we are of the opinion that it may be desirable to appoint a special committee to devise a machinery for putting this suggestion into operation as a regular feature of our higher educational system, and although such a project would be outside the scope of this Committee and its modifications in the method of operating the Overseas Scholarships Scheme.

We have carefully considered the present system of providing scholarships for overseas training on the basis of the Home Ministry's circular regarding representation of communities in service. In view of the fact, however, that the scholars sponsored by the Government would be persons who on return are to be the leaders of scientific and educational development of the country, we are definitely of the opinion that merit alone should be the basis on which scholarships should be awarded. Instructions may, however, be given to the Selection Boards to give preference to candidates belonging to a community which is educationally backward in cases where two or more candidates are available possessing roughly equal qualifications and ability. If this point of view is accepted by the Government of India and the Ministry of Education, then corresponding instructions should be issued to the Provincial Governments, the Universities and the Industry, to be followed in choosing Scholars sponsored by these bodies.

Finally, we desire to thank all the Ministries of the Government for co-operating with us in arriving at our conclusions, and our special thanks are due to the Ministry of Education for giving us facilities for making the enquiry and placing our findings before the Government.

EXCLUDED AND PARTIALLY EXCLUDED AREAS (OTHER THAN ASSAM) SUB-COMMITTEE, 1947—FINAL REPORT

New Delhi, Constituent Assembly, 1947. 69p.

Chairman : Shri A. V. Thakkar.

Members : Shri Jaipal Singh; Shri Devendra Nath Samanta; Shri Phul Bhanu Shah; The Hon'ble Dr. Proffulla Chandra Ghosh; Shri Raj Krushna Bose.

Co-opted Members : Shri Khetramani Panda—Phulbani Area; Shri Sadasiv Tripathi—Orissa P.E. Areas; Shri Kodanda Ramiah—Madras P.E. Areas; Shri Sneha Kumar Chakma—Chittagong Hill Tracts; Shri Damber Singh Gurung—Darjeeling District.

Secretary : Shri R. K. Ramadhiyani.

APPOINTMENT

The Excluded and Partially Excluded Areas (Other Than Assam) Sub-Committee had been set up by the Advisory Committee on Minorities and Fundamental Rights, etc., in their meeting held on February 27,

1947, in pursuance of paragraphs 19(IV) and 20 of the Cabinet Mission's Statement dated May 16, 1946.

TERMS OF REFERENCE

The terms of reference of the Sub-Committee were in pursuance of paragraphs 19(IV) and 20 of the Cabinet Mission's Statement dated May 16, 1946.

CONTENTS

Introductory; Bihar; United Provinces; East Punjab; A Central Department; Recruitment to Armed Forces; Village And Tribal Headmen; Non-Official Welfare Organizations; Officials to Learn Tribal Languages; Minute of Dissent; Note by Chairman on Minute of Dissent by Shri Jaipal Singh.

RECOMMENDATIONS—SUMMARY

Tribes who live in the non-excluded areas as part of the problem and the tribes as a whole should be treated as a minority. Tribals should have reserved seats in a joint electorate based on adult franchise in proportion to their population. One representative each is recommended for the Laccadive, Amindivi and Minicoy Islands, respectively, in the Madras Legislature and one for the Lahaul and Spiti Waziris in the East Punjab Legislature.

It will be necessary to provide for the exclusion of unsuitable legislation in such matters as land, village management and social customs in certain areas inhabited predominantly or to an appreciable extent by tribals. These areas will be known as Scheduled Areas.

Legislation in such matters as land and social customs should not be applied to Scheduled Areas if the Tribes Advisory Council advises to the contrary.

Simplified procedure should be continued for the disposal of petty criminal and civil cases.

Seats should be reserved in the Federal Legislature on the basis of the tribal population of the Province. A Tribal Advisory Council should be set up with a minimum of 10 and a maximum of 25 members in Madras, Bombay, Bengal, Bihar, C.P. and Orissa.

There should be provision for the Federal Government to institute a special commission to enquire into the progress of plans of development and also into the conditions of the Scheduled Areas and tribals in general.

It will be necessary for the Central Government to come to the assistance of Provincial Governments for the execution of schemes of development by providing the necessary funds. The Central Government should also be in a position to require Provincial Governments to draw up schemes for the Scheduled Areas.

The revenues derived from and the expenses incurred on the Scheduled Areas from the Provincial budget should be shown separately in the annual financial statement of the Province.

It should be the Governor's responsibility to see that schemes of development are drawn up and implemented.

There should be a separate Minister for Tribal Welfare in C.P., Orissa and Bihar, and provision for this should be contained in the statute.

There should be a due proportion of aboriginals recruited into the various Government Services. A separate service is not recommended but non-tribal officials posted to the Scheduled Areas should be selected with care.

Tribal panchayats should be encouraged wherever possible.

Shifting cultivation should be discouraged.

Temperance propaganda should be carried on as part of tribal welfare work.

The alienation of land belonging to tribals to non-tribals should be prohibited. Allotment of new land in Scheduled Areas should not be made to non-aboriginals except in exceptional cases.

There should be provision for control of money-lenders by a system of licensing.

Sambalpur, Angul and Darjeeling and certain areas in Bombay need not be treated as Scheduled Areas. In Bihar the three districts of Ranchi, Singhbhum, and Santhal Parganas only, where the tribes are in a majority, are included in the Schedule provisionally. The U.P. and Punjab areas are not included.

Bihar

We consider it necessary in addition to refer to certain matters connected with the administration of this, the largest compact block of territory comprising any excluded area in India, which came to our notice during our tour. To begin with, the Christian section of the tribals, though small in number, is educationally and economically far in advance of the non-Christian tribals. The demand for education among non-Christians is said to be negligible and this presumably is the result of their economic backwardness which makes it necessary that children should assist their parents in earning their livelihood. There are, however, allegations that the Christian teachers and educational officials encourage only Christian children, and as a good number of the schools are run by Christian Missions, non-Christians lack facilities for education. The Christians again appear to be much better organized and vocal and they are found to take a prominent part in local and political organizations. The other striking feature of this area is the feeling common among educated tribals and shared by non-tribals in considerable measure that Chota Nagpur has little share in the administration commensurate with its area, population and industrial importance and is being neglected by the Government which is made up of elements interested mostly in the rest of Bihar. Certain non-aboriginal witnesses have expressed their views of the neglect of Chota Nagpur in no uncertain terms and suggested that the ameliorative measures claimed by the Government are purely defensive action prompted by the separation movement. Even when the Government is supposed to be resident at Ranchi, it is given as concrete proof of their lack of interest that they are mostly absent on tour in areas other than Chota Nagpur in which they are interested. Dr. Sinha has also stated that the present Government has yet to do something "to capture the imagination of the people" and that under the present practice "the Hon'ble Ministers stay for a very short period at Ranchi—at their own will and convenience—and do not usually visit so much the aboriginal areas as they do those of the other three Divisions of Bihar". We have referred to these statements not because we are in agreement with them or with a view to adjudicating on them but purely as indicative of the local atmosphere. Dr. Sinha has referred to the absence of the aboriginal element in the Ministry and has recommended reconstitution.

The extreme expression of the discontent prevalent in Chota Nagpur is the separation movement which demands the formation of a new province of Jharkhand out of the partially excluded area. This movement is sponsored at present by the Adibasi Mahasabha containing a very large advanced or Christian element but in Singhbhum and in the Santhal Parganas also, a good proportion of non-Christians seems to have been affected by it. To borrow Dr. Sinha's words it is "capturing the imagination" of the tribals. Unmistakably also the movement is gaining sympathy among the non-aboriginals ; and even if it be partly due to mere local ambition, the virtual exclusion of tribal elements from the Cabinet has undoubtedly contributed much to it. We have already held in our interim report that the question of the formation of a separate province is not for us to tackle but we would invite the attention of the Provincial and Central Governments to the separation movement, which seems to be gaining strength, as a symptom of the discontent which is simmering in varying intensity among all sections of the Chota Nagpur population. At the same time we have noticed that the Cabinet of the Bihar Government and such an eminent public man as Dr. S. Sinha oppose the separation movement on grounds very well shown in the brochure of Dr. Sinha. We have also received a number of telegrams from these areas saying that they thoroughly disapprove of the separatist movement.

We are inclined to the view, which seems to be shared by Dr. Sinha also, that there should be adequate association of the people of the partially excluded areas, particularly the tribals, in the different branches of the administration including the Cabinet and that there can be neither satisfaction nor adequate progress until this is done. In short, the problem of administration in this tract must be dealt with not only by economic and educational improvements but also by remedies which recognize its political and psychological aspects ; and we would lay the maximum emphasis on the urgency of action in both these directions.

United Provinces

As regards the partially excluded areas of the United Provinces, viz., the Jaunsar-Bawar Pargana in Dehra Dun District and the area comprising the Dudhi Tahsil and part of the Robertsganj Tahsil of Mirzapur District, we find that both of these comparatively small areas are suffering from serious neglect. Although a Committee was set up as early as 1939 to enquire into the administration of the Jaunsar-Bawar Pargana and a report was submitted by it in 1941, it is a matter for regret that no action has yet been possible although the report was ultimately made only by the official members of the Committee. We understand that another Committee has been appointed recently this year to go into the matter by the Provincial Government and hope that speedy action will be taken on its report. The main matters which require attention in this area are as follows :

(1) The fixation and collection of land revenue and distribution of "right timber" through the agency of the Sayanas as well as the position of the Sayana in the village panchayat which gives rise to a great deal of oppression.

(2) Survey and resettlement of the area and removal of restrictions on the possession of land and reclamation of the waste land by Koltas (local depressed castes of Hindus).

(3) The elimination of social evils like polyandry and venereal disease.

In the partially excluded area of Mirzapur District which is inhabited by a majority of tribals, we find that the administration is of a pretty primitive character. The figures given in the U.P. Government's factual memorandum for the Dudhi Government Estate which are shown below indicate that the revenue from it is not utilized to the extent of even two-fifths of the administration of the area.

Year		Income	Expenditure
1944-45		1,64,430	83,421
1945-46		2,96,002	88,002
1946-47		2,34,797	89,854
	Total	6,95,229	2,61,277 i.e. 33% of the income

We would draw particular attention to the statement of witnesses that a very large percentage of the population of this area is suffering from venereal diseases. In Dudhi Estate the U.P. Government noted that there is a passage of land from the hands of the aboriginals to the non-aboriginals. It would appear that the rules of Dudhi Estate are ineffective in preventing this since land can be surrendered to the Supurdar who re-allots the same to another person, most probably a non-aboriginal. Such a transfer unfortunately does not require the approval of the S.D.O. or the Collector. It does not appear that suitable steps have been taken to put a stop to this. Among other complaints are the working of the monopoly given to Messrs. Gladstone Wyllie & Co., Ltd., for the collection and sale of lac which is terminable in the year 1952. The working of this monopoly under which only about one-seventh, or if the price realized by the Company for the sale of the lac is obtained by the aboriginal cultivator, tends to keep the aboriginal in a miserable condition. It does not appear to us that the Government has any comprehensive or fully considered programme for this area as yet.

The population of this tract is very small ($\frac{1}{3}$%) in comparison with the total population of the United Provinces. We would not on that account recommend for its future administration the proposals which we have recommended for some of the backward tracts of other Provinces, but we are equally definite that special provisions for its development are essential, as without them it is certain that due attention will not be paid to its needs. Similarly although the inhabitants of the Jaunsar-Bawar Area, as pointed out in our interim report, are not tribals by race and we do not recommend inclusion in the schedule of our Interim Report, special provisions are necessary for this area also. We recommend therefore Constitutional provisions for both of these tracts as follows :

(1) There should be an advisory committee consisting of tribals or backward people to the extent of not less than two-thirds of its membership to advise the Government on the development of the area ;

(2) The estimated revenue and expenditure (including development schemes) pertaining to the area should be shown separately in the Provincial budget;

(3) Although general administration of the type in force in other districts may be applied to the tract, the trial of petty civil and criminal cases should be permissible under special regulations ;

(4) There should be provision in the Constitution prohibiting the transfer of land from aboriginals to non-aboriginals except with the sanction of an authorized officer ;

(5) The powers of Supurdars in the Dudhi area of Mirzapur District to allot waste lands and accept surrender of land should be withdrawn and in Jaunsar-Bawar the system of Sayanas should be abolished and the Sayanas replaced by Government employees ;

(6) The U.P. Government should report to the Central Government annually or as may be required by the Central Government regarding the administration of this area and abide by its directive;

(7) There shall be one seat reserved in the Provincial Assembly for a tribal from the area of Mirzapur District which is now partially excluded.

East Punjab

The disturbed conditions in the East Punjab have prevented the appearance of witnesses from Spiti and Lahaul before us and it is equally not possible for us to visit the area. It is unlikely that settled conditions will prevail in the Punjab before the passes are blocked and we do not propose therefore to postpone our recommendations which will now be based on the factual memorandum sent by the Provincial Government.

We consider that Constitutional provisions should be made as follows :

(a) An Advisory Committee of which at least two-thirds shall be local residents shall be set up to advise the Provincial Government regarding the administration of Lahaul and Spiti.

(b) The Provincial Government may declare any law passed by the Federal or Provincial Legislature as not applicable to the tracts or applicable with specified modifications.

(c) The Provincial Government may make special regulations for the administration of criminal and civil laws and the protection of rights of local Tibetan inhabitants in land.

(d) The Provincial Government shall report to the Central Government annually or as may be required by the Central Government regarding the administration of this area and abide by its directive.

(e) We confirm the recommendation made in paragraph 9 of the Interim Report that there should be a representative for Lahaul and Spiti in the Provincial Legislature.

A Central Department

After surveying the position in all the Provinces, we have been forced to the conclusion that unless there is a separate department of the Federal Government prescribed by the statute to supervise and watch the development of the scheduled areas and the tribals in the different Provinces and to furnish such advice and guidance as may be needed, the pace of progress of the tribes will not be sufficiently swift. The Central Government has already recognized the need for a Directorate of Anthropological Survey and we recommend that provision for a Central Department of Tribal Welfare should be made in the Constitution.

Recruitment To Armed Forces

We are also of the view that special attention should be paid to the recruitment of the tribals to the armed forces of India. The tribes people can in our opinion furnish valuable material for this purpose as experience in the last war goes to show.

Village And Tribal Headmen

During the course of our enquiry many complaints of oppression and mishandling of the tribes people by the hereditary chiefs or heads of villages like the Mustadars, Bissois and Paros and Muthadars of South Orissa, the Parganaits and Pradhans of the Santhal Parganas and the Mankis and Mundas of Singhbhum have reached us. We are of the view that a general review of the powers and functions of such village or tribal heads should be undertaken by the Provincial Government with a view to removing the grievances of the tribal villagers, the abolition of powers which are exercised in an oppressive manner and the general reform of these ancient systems.

Non-Official Welfare Organizations

We recommend that the Provincial Governments should utilize the services of approved non-official organizations which are at present doing welfare work in the Provinces for the tribals or which may hereafter come into existence by giving them grants-in-aid with a view to supplementing the volume of development work.

Officials To Learn Tribal Languages

We have found that officials posted to aborigina areas rarely know the local language. This obviously does not conduce to satisfactory administration and we are of the view that it should be made compulsory for officials posted to the aboriginal areas to obtain a working knowledge of the language within a reasonable period. Proficiency in these languages or dialects should be encouraged by the grant of suitable awards.

NORTH-EAST FRONTIER (ASSAM) TRIBAL AND EXCLUDED AREAS SUB-COMMITTEE, 1947—REPORT

Delhi, Manager of Publications, 1950. 2 Vols.

Chairman : The Hon'ble Mr. Gopinath Bardoloi.

Members : The Hon'ble Rev. J. J. M. Nichols-Roy; The Hon'ble Shri Rup Nath Brahma; Shri A. V. Thakkar; Shri Aliba Imti (has not been able to attend the meeting to sign the report).

Co-opted Members :

Shri Khawtinkhuma Shri Saprawng	Co-opted for Lushai Hills Area
Shri Harison W. Momin Shri Mainram Marak	Co-opted for Garo Hills Area
Shri S. S. Engti Shri K. S. Terang	Co-opted for Mikir Hills Area
Shri Kezehol (has since resigned the membership) Shri Khelhoshe	Co-opted for Kohima Area
Shri Swat Daulagopu Shri C.T. Tnanga Biete	Co-opted for Haflong Area
Shri Josing Rynja Shri Larsingh Khyriem	Co-opted for Khasi & Jaintia Hills Area

Secretary : Mr. R. K. Ramadhiyani.

APPOINTMENT

The North-East Frontier (Assam) Tribal and Excluded Areas Sub-Committee was appointed by the Advisory Committee on Minorities' Fundamental Rights, etc., to the Constituent Assembly of India in their meeting held on February 27, 1947, in pursuance of paragraphs 19 (IV) and 20 of the Cabinet Mission's Statement dated May 16, 1946.

TERMS OF REFERENCE

The Sub-Committee was to look into paragraphs 19 (IV) and 20 of the Cabinet Mission's Statement dated May 16, 1946.

CONTENTS

Part I : Introductory; General Description; Development; Hill People's View; Special Features; Political Experience; Provisions of 1935 Act; Future Policy; The Hill People's Land; Forest; Jhuming; Civil and Criminal Courts; Other Local Self-

Governments; Finance; Control of Immigration; Mines and Minerals; Legislation; Regional Councils; Emergency Provisions; The Frontier Tracts; Representation; The Provincial Ministry; The Services; A Commission; Plains Tribals; Boundaries; Non-Tribal Residents; Transitional Provisions; Appendix A; Appendix B.

Part II : The Balipara Frontier Tract; The Sadiya Frontier Tract; The Lakhimpur and Tirap Frontier Tract; Naga Hills District; Lushai Hills District; The North Cachar Hills Sub-Division; Khasi and Jaintia Hills; The Garo Hills; The Mikir Hills; Summary of Recommendations of the Sub-Committee.

RECOMMENDATIONS—SUMMARY

District Councils should be set up in the Hill Districts (see Section B of Appendix A) with powers of legislation over occupation or use of the land other than land comprising reserved forests under the Assam Forest Regulation of 1891 or other law applicable. This is subject to the proviso that no payment would be required for the occupation of vacant land by the Provincial Government for public purposes and private land required for public purposes by the Provincial Government will be acquired for it on payment of compensation.

Reserved forests will be managed by the Provincial Government in question of actual management including the appointment of the forest staff and the granting of contracts and leases, the susceptibilities and the legitimate desires and needs of the Hill people should be taken into account.

On account of its disastrous effects upon the forest rainfall and other climatic features, Jhuming should be discouraged and stopped wherever possible but the initiative for this should come from the tribes themselves and the control of Jhuming should be left to the Local Councils.

All social law and custom is left to be controlled or regulated by the tribes. All criminal offences except those punishable with death, transportation or imprisonment for five years and upward should be left to be dealt with in accordance with local practice and the Code of Criminal Procedure will not apply to such cases. As regards the serious offences punishable with imprisonment of five years or more they should be tried henceforth regularly under the Criminal Procedure Code. To try such cases, powers should be conferred by the Provincial Government wherever suitable upon Tribal Councils or courts set up by the District Councils themselves.

All ordinary civil suits should be disposed of by Tribal Courts and Local Councils may have full powers to deal with them including appeal and revision.

Where non-tribals are involved, civil or criminal cases should be tried under the regular law and the Provincial Government should make suitable arrangements for the expeditious disposal of such cases by employing circuit magistrates or judges.

District Councils should have powers of management over primary schools, dispensaries and other institutions which normally come under the scope of local self-governing institutions in the plains. They should have full control over primary education. As regards secondary school education, there should be some integration with the general system of the Province and it is left open to the Provincial Government to entrust Local Councils with responsibility for secondary schools wherever they find this suitable.

For the Mikir and North Cachar Hills the District or Sub-Divisional Officer, as the case may be, should be ex-officio President of the Local Council with powers, subject to the control of the Government of Assam, to modify or annul resolutions or decisions of the Local Councils and to issue such instructions as may be necessary.

Certain taxes and financial powers should be allocated to the Councils. They should have all the powers which local bodies in a regulation district enjoy and in addition they should have powers to impose house tax or poll tax, land revenue and levies arising out of the powers of management of village forest.

Statutory provision for a fixed proportion of the Provincial Fund to be spent on the Hill districts is not considered practicable. A separate financial statement for each Hill district showing the revenue derived from the district and the expenditure proposed on it is recommended. The framing of a suitable programme of development should be enjoined either by statute or by Instrument of Instructions.

It is quite clear that the urgent requirements of the Hill districts by way of expenditure on development schemes are beyond the resources of the Provincial Government. The development of the Hill districts should be as much the concern of the Federal Government as of the Provincial Government. Financial assistance should be provided by the Federation to meet the deficit in the ordinary administration on the basis of the average deficit during the past three years and the cost of development schemes should also be borne by the Central Exchequer.

The claim of Hill District Councils for assistance from General Provincial Revenues to the extent that they are unable to raise the necessary finances within their own powers is recognized.

If Local Councils decide by a majority of three-fourths of their members to license money-lenders or traders they should have powers to require money-lenders and professional dealers from outside to take out licences.

The management of mineral resources should be centralized in the hands of the Provincial Government but the right of the District Councils to a fair share of the revenues is recognized. No licence or lease shall be given by the Provincial Government except in consultation with the Local Council. If there is no agreement between the Provincial Government and the District Council regarding the share of the revenue, the Governor will decide the matter in his discretion.

Provincial legislation which deals with the subjects in which the Hill Councils have legislative powers will not apply to the Hill districts. Legislation prohibiting consumption of non-distilled liquors like Zu will also not apply; the District Council may, however, apply the legislation.

It is necessary to provide for the creation of Regional Councils for the different tribes inhabiting an autonomous district if they so desire. Regional Councils have powers limited to their customary law and the management of lands and villages and courts. Regional Councils may delegate their powers to District Councils.

The Governor is empowered to set aside any act or resolution of a Council if the safety of the country is prejudiced and to take such action as may be necessary, including dissolution of Local Councils subject to the approval of the Legislature. The Governor is also given powers to dissolve the Council if gross mismanagement is reported by a Commission.

The Central Government should continue to administer the Frontier Tracts and Tribal Area with the Government of Assam as its agent until administration has been satisfactorily established over a sufficiently wide area. Areas over which administration has been satisfactorily established may be taken over by the Provincial Government with the approval of the Federal Government.

The pace of extending administration should be greatly accelerated and separate officers appointed for the Lohit Valley, the Siang Valley and the Naga Tribal Area.

The Lakhimpur Frontier Tract should be attached to the regular administration of the district. The case of the portion of the Lakhimpur Frontier Tract recently included in the Tirap Frontier Tract should be examined by the Provincial Government with a view to a decision whether it could immediately be brought under the Provincial administration. A similar examination of the position in the plains portion of the Sadiya Frontier Tract is recommended. The portion of the Balipara Frontier Tract around Charduar should also be subject to a similar examination.

The excluded areas other than the Frontier Tracts should be enfranchized immediately and restrictions on the franchise in the Garo and Mikir Hills should be removed and adult franchise introduced.

Weightage is not considered necessary but the Hill districts should be represented in the Provincial Legislature in proportion not less than what is due on their population even if this involves a certain weightage in rounding off. The total number of representatives for the Hills thus arrived at should not be taken into account in determining the number of representatives to the Provincial Legislature from the rest of Assam.

The total population of the Hill districts justifies a seat for the Hill tribes in the Federal Legislature on the scale proposed in Section 13 (c) of the Draft Union Constitution.

Joint electorate is recommended but constituencies are confined to the autonomous districts. Reservation of seats, in view of this restriction, is not necessary.

Non-tribals should not be eligible for election from Hill constituencies except in the constituency which includes the Municipality and Cantonment of Shillong.

Representation for the Hills in the Ministry should be guaranteed by a statutory provision, if possible, or at least by a suitable instruction in the Instrument of Instructions or a corresponding provision.

Non-tribal officials should not be barred from serving in the Hills but they should be selected with care if posted to the Hills. The appointment of a due proportion of Hill people in the Services should be particularly kept in mind and provided for in rules or executive instructions of the Provincial Government.

A commission may be appointed at any time or permanently to enable the Government to watch the progress of the development plans or to examine any particular aspects of the administration.

Plains tribals number 1.6 million. Their case for special representation and safeguards should be considered by the Minorities Sub-Committee.

The question of altering boundaries so as to bring the people of the same tribe under a common administration should be considered by the Provincial Government. The Barpathar and Sarupathar Mouzas included in the Mikir Hills should be included in the regularly administered areas henceforth.

Non-tribal residents may be provided with representation in the Local Councils if they are sufficiently numerous. For this purpose non-tribal constituencies may be formed if justified and if the population is not below 8,500.

Provincial Councils should be set up by the Governor of Assam after consulting such local organizations as exist. These Provincial Councils which will be for one year will have powers to frame their own constitution and rules for the future.

PRESS LAWS ENQUIRY COMMITTEE, 1947—REPORT

New Delhi, Ministry of Home Affairs, 1948. 52p.

Chairman : Shri Ganga Nath.

Members : Shri Mohan Lal Saksena; Shri Tushar Kanti Ghosh; Diwan Chaman Lall; Shri Mohd. Ismail Khan; Shri Narayan Mahtha; Shri S. A. Brelvi; Shri Kasturi Srinivasan.

Secretary : Shri G. V. Bedekar.

APPOINTMENT

The Press Laws Enquiry Committee was constituted under the Home Department vide their Resolution No. 33/33/46-Poll (1) dated March 15, 1947, and October 4, 1947.

TERMS OF REFERENCE

(i) To examine and report to the Government on the laws regulating the Press in the principal countries of the world including India;

(ii) To review the Press Laws of India with a view to examine if they are in accord with the Fundamental Rights formulated by the Constituent Assembly of India; and

(iii) To recommend to the Government any measures of reform in the Press Laws considered expedient upon such review.

CONTENTS

Introductory; Review of the Press Laws of India; Fundamental Rights and Press Laws of other Countries; Rights and Responsibilities of the Press; Recommendations; Appendices A to E.

RECOMMENDATIONS

(1) **Press and Registration of Books Act** : Certain amendments are suggested in Section 3, Section 5 (2), Section 5 (3), Section 5 (4) and Section 11.

(2) The Indian States (Protection Against Disaffection) Act, 1922, and the Indian States (Protection) Act, 1934, should be repealed.

(3) The Indian Press (Emergency Powers) Act, 1931, should be repealed but the following provisions of this Act should be incorporated in the ordinary law of the country :

(a) Clauses (a) to (i) of Section 4 (1) which define offences should be incorporated in the Indian Penal Code, or other law.

(b) Sections 15, 16, 17, 18 and 32 should be incorporated in the Press and Registration of Books Act.

(c) Section 19 should be incorporated in the Criminal Procedure Code.

(d) Section 20 should be incorporated in the Sea Customs Act.

(e) Sections 21 and 22 should be incorporated in the Indian Post Offices Act.

(f) Separate provision should be made to vest courts of justice with powers to order the closing down of a Press for a specified period in case of repeated violation of the law by the Press.

(4) The Foreign Relations Act, 1932, should be repealed and more comprehensive legislation should be undertaken to make provision on a reciprocal basis for protection of Heads of Foreign States, Foreign Governments and their diplomatic representatives in India from defamatory attacks, etc.

(5) (a) Section 124 A of the Indian Penal Code should be amended to give effect to the judgment of the Federal Court in the case of N. D. Mazumdar.

(b) An explanation should be added to Section 153 A of I.P.C. to the effect that it does not amount to an offence under that Section to advocate a change in the social or economic order provided such advocacy does not involve violence.

(6) Section 144 of the Criminal Procedure Code should not be applied to the Press; and separate provision should, if necessary, be made by law for dealing with Press in urgent cases of apprehended danger.

(7) Section 5 of the Indian Telegraph Act and Section 26 of the Indian Post Offices Act should be amended to provide that the actions and orders of subordinate officers are reported to and reviewed by responsible Ministers of the Government.

(8) Before taking action against the Press under emergency legislation, the Provincial Government should invariably consult the Press Advisory Committee or a similar body.

SCIENTIFIC MAN-POWER COMMITTEE, 1947—REPORT

Delhi, Manager of Publications, 1949. 99p.

Chairman : Dr. Shanti Swarup Bhatnagar.

Members : Dr. Homi J. Bhabha; Dr. J. C. Ghosh; Shri Ram Rattan Gupta; Dr. K. A. Hamied; Shri Humayun Kabir; Shri A. N. Khosla; Dr. K. S. Krishnan; Mrs. Hansa Mehta; Prof. J. N. Mukherjee; Dr. Baini Prasad; Dr. K. C. K. E. Raja; Dr. Birbal Sahni; W/Cdr. H. Singh (replaced by Dr. R. S. Kothari); Dr R. S. Thakur (replaced by Shri Raghunath Pershad); Dr. D. N. Wadia.

Secretary : Dr. S. R. Sen Gupta.

APPOINTMENT

The Scientific Man-Power Committee was constituted under the Ministry of Education vide their Press Communique dated April 20, 1947.

TERMS OF REFERENCE

(i) To assess the requirements for different grades of scientific and technical man-power taking a comprehensive view over a period of the next 10 years of the needs of the Government (Civil and Defence) of teaching and research and of industry, agriculture, transport, medicine and other fields dependent on the use of scientific and technical man-power;

(ii) To make recommendations regarding the action to be taken during the next five years to meet these requirements, in particular with reference to :

(a) The immediate improvement and expansion of facilities for scientific and technical training in Indian Universities and special institutions;

(b) Training overseas in scientific and technical subjects;

(c) The promotion and development of scientific and technical research;

(d) The utilization of scientific and technical man-power; and

(e) The maintenance of a register of scientific and technical personnel to facilitate their utilization to the best advantage.

CONTENTS

Introduction; Assessment of Requirements for Scientific and Technical Man-Power; Review of Resources of Scientific and Technical Man-Power and Research Development; Development of Scientific and Technical Man-Power Resources—A Five-Year Education Plan; Industrial Training of Engineers and Technologists; Overseers Training; Equal Opportunities, Free Places, Science Talent Search, Shortage of Teachers, etc.; Unemployment, Drift and Leakage of Talent, National Register of Scientific and Technical Personnel; Summary; Annexures I to X.

RECOMMENDATIONS

The first approach to the problem of development of engineering and technological education should be to strengthen the existing facilities in the institutions by equipping and staffing them adequately for the present intake of students and to bring up the standard of training to the desired level.

The existing facilities in respect of staff, equipment, accommodation, etc., should be improved not only for teaching but also for research purposes and there should be close liaison between Industry and Educational Institutions so that the latter might cater to the needs of industry both in the matter of research and in the training of personnel.

The Committee considers that the training of medical personnel up to the degree standard is perhaps the most important aspect of medical education in the context of the requirements for medical personnel.

There are 18 medical schools in the Indian Union which used to account for an annual outturn of about 700 licentiates. But, following the accepted principle of raising the standard of medical education in the country, 11 of these medical schools have already been converted into medical colleges for training up to the degree standard. The Committee hopes that all the other medical schools in the country will, before long, be reorganized into medical colleges.

The Committee observes that both for undergraduate and post-graduate training in dentistry the available facilities in the country offering training up to the degree standard in dentistry.

The Committee estimates that the total number of qualified and practising nurses in India is about 7,000 in the proportion of 1 for every 43,000 of the population, which obviously is very low when compared to corresponding ratios obtaining in other countries.

On the basis of a comparative study of the requirements for scientific and technical man-power for the next 5-year period (1947-52) and the existing resources, the Committee estimates that there are wide gaps between the possible requirements and the anticipated output and that the available resources of man-power are inadequate to meet our requirements, let alone our having a small potential reserve to draw upon in case of an emergency or unforeseen circumstances. The Committee observes that even on stretching the 5-year requirements to the next 10 years the gaps still exist. The gaps are both qualitative and quantitative. In order to make up the gaps the Committee recommends that a 5-year plan for the development of education and research facilities in the country be worked out having the following main features :

(a) Establishment of four Higher Technical Institutions as recommended by the All-India Council for Technical Education for advanced and post-graduate technical training.

(b) Implementation of the various development plans of institutions described in the Survey Report which envisage:

(i) Introduction of specialized or post-graduate courses of study and research in certain branches of science and technology not catered for now;

(ii) Rationalization of the existing courses of study and their diversification;

(iii) Full development of institutions which are in a formative stage at present;

(iv) Expansion of training and research facilities in institutions where these are not of the requisite standard or where there is scope for such expansion;

(v) Reorganization of some of the existing polytechnics or lower technical institutions in order to impart in them higher instruction;

(vi) Increasing the intake of students in various courses in some of the existing institutions.

(c) Creation of facilities for training in production engineering, design engineering, fuel and furnace technology and other special fields at certain selected institutions on a regional basis.

(d) Establishment of a college of marine engineering and naval architecture or creation of facilities for training in the subject at one or two selected institutions.

(e) Establishment of new medical colleges for increasing the outturn of doctors.

(f) Opening of post-graduate science departments in such of the Universities as do not have them at present, and strengthening of the existing ones in order to increase the outturn of scientists of all categories to the desired extent.

(g) Training of supervisory category of technical personnel in conjunction with industry.

The Committee also recommends that the effective outturn of I. Sc.s during the next 10 years should more than double itself; and the outturn of science graduates should be nearly double the present.

Considering the vast number of technically trained personnel that would be trained for various development projects during the next few years, the Committee recommends that urgent and far-reaching measures should be adopted to make available existing facilities for practical training to as many qualified students as possible. Towards this end the Committee recommends that the Government should introduce legislative measures so that it becomes incumbent on every established industrial concern to provide training facilities for qualified candidates in all grades notwithstanding whether the persons thus trained are required by the concern or not. The large number of Government and Government-sponsored departments should provide practical training facilities no less than industrial concerns. As a general measure the Committee also recommends the following :

The technical departments of the Government should organize in their establishments facilities for the industrial training of

(a) Artisan type of personnel;

(b) Supervisory or foreman type of personnel; and

(c) Executive type of personnel;

and the expenses for the organization and careful supervision of training for all the above three types should be borne by them.

All factories or industrial establishments, both private and State-owned, should include schemes of practical training and expenditure on this account should be regarded as legitimate expenditure of the establishment.

In all the above three types of establishments trainees should be paid wages or stipends the value of which, in the case of scientific or technically trained men, should be adequate to meet the expenses on board and lodging.

Industrial and Government Departments should recruit fresh graduates as officer-trainees and put them through any organized training programme with a view to their ultimate employment as executive officers.

The Committee recommends that every effort should be made to mobilize fully all available training facilities now as well as in the years to come and to utilize them in a planned and co-ordinated manner.

In view of the unavailability of facilities for both theoretical and practical training of personnel required for rayon and cellulose industries, special arrangements should be made for such training in certain selected institutions or in the co-operative research laboratory that might be established for this group of industries.

The Indian scientific and technical personnel need be trained abroad with a different emphasis on the scholar's educational and training programme so as to meet the immediate needs of the country for specialists.

Personnel whom it is required to train abroad for industrial developmemt should be selected from among those who have had a certain amount of industrial experience in the particular industry concerned and also have the necessary academic qualifications.

In order to meet the needs of Government Departments, members of the staff of technical departments should get an opportunity to visit corresponding departments or institutions abroad to acquaint themselves with the latest developments in their own fields.

The Committee is of the considered opinion that special efforts should be made to search out scientific talent suited to take to research in the various National Laboratories and other research establishments and recommends that a National Science Talent Search Competition as adopted in the U.S.A. should also be inaugurated in this country for locating and encouraging scientific talent in this country.

In order to overcome the shortage of teachers and to improve the standard of training in educational institutions specially from the practical points of view, the Committee recommends that suitable arrangements be worked out whereby the services of senior officers of engineering departments of Governments and technical executives of industrial concerns might be utilized for the training of students in engineering and technological institutions located close to their headquarters.

INDIAN RAILWAY ENQUIRY COMMITTEE, 1947—REPORT

New Delhi, Ministry of Railways, 1949. 302p.

Owing to the political changes in the country, the Committee's life was divided into two phases, viz., from April 24 to October 15, 1947, and from March 15 to November 6, 1948. The constitution of the Committee in the second period underwent a change owing to the termination of connection of three members from the Committee.

First Phase—April 24 to October 15, 1947

Chairman : Mr. K. C. Neogy.

Members : Sir Mohd. Yamin Khan; Mr. Humayun Kabir; Sir George E. Cuffe; Mr. J. N. Nanda; Mr. K. R. Rama Iyer; Col. N. D. Ballantine (a Railway consultant from the U.S.A.).

Secretary : Mr. M. N. Chakravarti.

The Chairman, Mr. K. C. Neogy, was called upon to serve as a Minister of the Government of India and the Committee were consequently deprived of his mature judgment and wise guidance. The American railway consultant, Col. N. D. Ballantine, also had to leave India on September 12, owing to his ill health. Meanwhile, the political situation of the country deteriorated rapidly, resulting in large-scale disturbances and exchange of populations. This prevented the Committee from progressing with their work satisfactorily and it became evident very soon that many points that emerged from the examination of the material with the Committee could not be finally settled, as most of the railway administrations and the Railway Board were fully occupied with other immediate problems.

The Committee were again granted an interview by the Honourable Minister for Transport and Railways on September 15 and discussed with him the situation arising out of the depletion in the membership of the Committee, and the uncertain political situation in the country. They suggested that the members of the Committee should prepare draft notes to facilitate the preparation of their report and should then disperse temporarily, about the middle of October, leaving behind a reduced staff. When conditions became more favourable the Government could re-assemble the Committee to enable them to complete the unfinished portion of their tour and prepare their report. The Honourable Minister accepted this proposal and the Committee dispersed on October 15, 1947.

The Honourable Minister explained the position in regard to the Committee to the Constituent Assembly (Legislative) on November 20, 1947, in the following terms :

"The Railway Enquiry Committee which has been looking into this (increased economics) question unfortunately has had to be suspended for a period of a few months on account of the disturbances and adjustments following partition, but I hope they will re-assemble within a short period and give us the benefit of their proposals in this matter."

The Secretary to the Committee and a skeleton staff continued to work after October 15, 1947, and carried out the instructions given by the Committee before their dispersal.

Second Phase—Mar. 15 to Nov. 6, 1948

In his speech introducing the Railway Budget for 1948-49 in the Constituent Assembly (Legislative) the Honourable Minister for Transport and Railways made the following statement about the appointment of another Chairman :

"With regard to the Railway Enquiry Committee, as I told the House in answer to a question, the Committee will begin to function in the course of a week or two. Mr. Neogy, who with great ability set the lines on which the enquiry is to proceed, will now be replaced by my honourable friend, Pandit Hirday Nath Kunzru, who, I am sure, will bring to bear on this important work his unique knowledge and experience of public affairs."

The Committee were sorry to lose the services of Mr. Humayun Kabir, who was unable to continue as a member of the Committee on his joining the Ministry of Education. His place on the Committee was taken by Mr. S. Guruswami, General Secretary, All-India Railwaymen's Federation. Col. N. D. Ballantine, who had left India on September 12, 1947, was not recalled owing to his failing health.

The Committee was accordingly reconstituted as follows :

Chairman : Pandit Hirday Nath Kunzru.
Members : Sir Mohd. Yamin Khan; Mr. S. Guruswami; Sir George E. Cuffe; Mr. J. N. Nanda; Mr. K. R. Rama Iyer.
Secretary : Mr. M. N. Chakravarti.

APPOINTMENT

The Government of India notified the appointment of the Committee in their Press Communique dated November 26, 1946, in the following terms :

"In pursuance of the recommendations contained in the Resolution passed by the Railway Standing Finance Committee on June 14, 1946, the Government of India have decided to appoint a high-power Railway Enquiry Committee.

The Committee will consist of :

Mr. K. C. Neogy, M.L.A. (Central)—Chairman.

Mr. I. S. Puri, C.I.E., Additional Financial Commissioner, Railways—Member.

Mr. J. N. Nanda, General Manager, H.E.H. the Nizam's State Railway—Member.

Sir Mohd. Yamin Khan, Deputy President, Central Legislative Assembly—Member.

Mr. Humayun Kabir, Vice-President, All-India Railwaymen's Federation—Member.

There will be two more members, one of whom will probably be a Railway expert from the U.S.A., and the other a high-ranking railway officer on the Indian Railways. Their names will be announced later. Mr. M. N. Chakravarti, an officer of the Transportation (Traffic) and Commercial Departments of North-Western Railway, will act as Secretary.

The Committee, which will be known as "The Indian Railway Enquiry Committee—1947" is expected to assemble early in April, 1947, by which time the Government hope to have received and dealt with the Adjudicator's Award in regard to hours of work, weekly rest, leave reserve and leave rules. In the meantime, Mr. Puri will be engaged in collecting data germane to the enquiry in order to facilitate its deliberations when it starts work.

Mr. Puri, having subsequently been appointed Financial Commissioner of Railways, was replaced on April 14, 1947, by Mr. K. R. Rama Iyer, Financial Adviser and Chief Accounts Officer, Oudh Tirhut Railway, lately on Special Duty as Member, Terminal Facilities Committee, Calcutta. Col. N. D. Ballantine, who possessed considerable experience of railway working in the U.S.A., and Sir George Cuffe, General Manager, Bombay, Baroda and Central India Railway, were appointed as members of the Committee in accordance with the Government of India Press Communique of November 26 referred to above.

TERMS OF REFERENCE

(1) Suggesting ways and means of securing improvement in net earnings by :

(a) Economies in all branches of the Railway Administration; and

(b) Any other means.

(2) Ascertaining the extent of staff surplus to requirements and suggesting practical methods of absorbing them in Railway service.

CONTENTS

Introductory; General Survey of the Indian Government Railways; Civil Engineering; Mechanical Engineering; Operation; Commercial Organization and other Matters; Electrical Organization and Electrification; Railway Stores Organization; Finance; Staff; Research; Central Controlling Authority and Railway Organization; Regrouping of Railways; Railway Grainshops Organization; Miscellaneous Matters; Summary of Conclusions and Recommendations; Acknowledgments; Appendices I to XXXI.

CONCLUSIONS AND RECOMMENDATIONS—SUMMARY

General Survey Of The I.G.R.

We made a broad financial and statistical survey of the Indian Government Railways since 1924. We conclude that the financial results so far cannot be considered bright.

The statistical survey of the major operating and rolling-stock statistics indicates, with minor exceptions, that there has been a substantial fall in the standard of efficiency and performance since 1938-39. During the war years the standard had improved but this was not maintained.

Civil Engineering

Track : We recommend that the urgent relaying programmes should be implemented thus improving the standard of track sufficiently to meet the future demands.

Track standards should not be raised merely to comply with new standards. Greater use of second-hand released materials should be made.

We recommend that investigations should be pushed forward for evolving lighter and modified sections of rails as standards for the Indian Railways.

We recommend that similar investigations should be made to lighten metal sleepers.

We recommend that researches as to the density of sleepers required under different conditions of traffic and types of rails and sleepers should be pursued. This would yield sufficient data to enable impressive economies being made.

The tendency on some railways for increasing the temporary gang strength should be checked. We recommend that an officer should be placed on special duty to make a close study of the methods of track maintenance actually pursued by the Railways, and reach conclusions. He should also ascertain best methods of utilizing gang labour.

Experiments with mechanical appliances for the maintenance of track should be pushed forward as early as possible.

Experiments with mobile gangs should be pursued.

We recommend that the gang length should be gradually increased to four miles which would economise the number of mates and keymen.

The special officer recommended by us for investigating the system of track maintenance should also investigate the question of the economical ballast section for varying formations and conditions of traffic, etc. Mechanical crushers may be used departmentally, if financially justified. Reputable contractors should be encouraged to go in for the use of these crushers.

Experiments with the welding of rails should continue on a sufficiently large scale. The experience of other countries supports the conclusion that economies would be substantial, in addition to making the running smoother and, therefore, more comfortable.

We recommend that vigorous research should be made on the problem of treatment of black cotton and other unstable soil and the best method of drainage of waterlogged banks and cuttings.

Supervision

Normally, a District Engineer's charge should be between 400 and 500 equated track miles and that of an Assistant Engineer between 150 and 200 miles. The average length of the beat of the Permanent-Way Inspector (P.W.I.) and Assistant or Sub-P.W.I. should be about 45 equated track miles.

We recommend that the Railways should obtain records of the condition of track by the use of test cars or Hallade Instrument twice a year and that the annotated records should be in the hands of the Permanent-Way supervising staff expeditiously.

Manufacture Of Equipment

There is a tendency for perpetuating departmental manufacture of materials in Engineering Workshops, which cannot be justified either on the score of economy or availability. We urge periodical reviews.

There is a wide scope for an extensive reconditioning of track materials and tools; rails with battered ends can be re-used by cropping up the ends and welding them; sleepers, fishplates, points and crossings can be reconditioned and re-used. Pooling of information in this respect would be useful.

Structural Maintenance

We recommend that the Railways should carefully scrutinize details of expenditure on maintenance of buildings and the methods of maintenance with a view to effecting economies.

We recommend that research should be undertaken for evolving an economical and suitable design for buildings in the black-cotton soil areas.

The renewal of girders of bridges should be decided on condition basis.

Control Of Expenditure

The possibility of control of expenditure on a unit-cost basis should be investigated as soon as prices stabilize.

Mechanical Engineering

Locomotive Stock : The utilization of locomotives on the Indian Government Railways in 1946-47 was low with the result that a substantial number was employed in excess, which could have been used for carrying additional traffic. On the basis of the performance of 1938-39, and with a reasonable number under or awaiting repairs (say 15% of stock), the percentage of locomotives used in excess would amount to about 10% of the total stock.

Another method for determining the excess is to basc the calculation on the average number of engine miles per engine per day, actually reached in 1941-42. This is certainly capable of achievement and would yield a figure of 17% of the total stock as the measure of the excess.

The performance could have been better, in spite of the deteriorated condition of the locomotives brought about through excessive wear and tear during the war years and the increasing age of locomotives.

Locomotive Repairs in Workshops : All Railways are heavily in arrears. This is alarming, particularly as the output from the workshops is much lower than their capacity and even below the current requirements of the Railways. We realize the difficulties regarding the shortage of spare parts, etc., still the position is considered most unsatisfactory. Excluding the E.P. and Assam Railways, the workshop capacity is adequate.

Coaching Stock : The number of passenger coaches under or awaiting repairs is high.

Coaching Stock Repairs in Workshops and Future Outlook : The shortage of passenger coaches is very acute which is the primary cause of the serious overcrowding. Further, a large proportion of such coaches is normally due to be replaced. We reckon that at a conservative estimate the passenger stock on the B.G. would require to be augmented by 25% and on the M.G. by 50% in the near future.

While we appreciate the Railway Board's action in attempting to tap indigenous sources we wish to emphasize that top priority should be given to the setting up of Central Workshops for the construction of coaching stock.

All-steel coaches are likely to be put in service and we suggest that before reaching final conclusions experiments should be carried out in the hottest part of the country in the months of May and June.

We, however, stress the value of all-steel stock in that it has generally been found that in the event of a serious accident, all-steel stock is less liable to telescoping than is wooden-bodied stock. For the same reason, we recommend the fitting of automatic control couplers to the new 11'—8" stock.

Wagon Stock and Repairs in Workshops : The percentage of wagons immobilized for repairs is very high.

There has been a considerable deterioration in the output of repairs to wagons in workshops, with the result that over 20% of the total stock is overdue periodical overhaul.

Workshop Organization and Layout : On the basis of the work performed in the workshops, measured by the number of standard repair to locomotives and by the number of coaching stock and goods wagons given periodical overhaul, there appears to be a surplus of staff. We recommend a careful job analysis to ascertain the extent of the surplus, taking into consideration the present quantum of work, arrears of maintenance, and other relevant factors.

Though some of the workshops require remodelling or modifications, which should be carried out without delay, in our opinion the present deplorable condition of the workshops is largely attributable to faulty direction and management.

We are impressed with the working of the "Belt System" as it exists in the Kharagpur Workshops of the B. N. Railway, and recommend that this system should be adopted whenever a new workshop is planned or constructed. When any major reconstruction of the existing workshops is undertaken, the principles underlying the "Belt System" should be applied as far as possible.

Effective steps should be taken to control and stabilize prices and making consumer goods available at reasonable rates. It is also imperative to pursue schemes of literacy in order to step up production.

Trade unionism should be encouraged.

Special supervisors should be appointed to guide and supervise the apprentices in their practical work in the workshops.

Statistics on man-hour basis should be introduced for the different operations.

Priority for steel should be given to the Railways and supplies assured to them.

Replacement of locomotives should be made on a 40-year basis, subject, however, to rigid condition tests.

Operation

All officers and staff, both technical and non-technical, dealing with the actual movement of traffic should belong to one operating department or branch.

In the case of major cities where shortage of technical capacity is manifest, early action should be taken to review the present and future requirements and to formulate plans for improving terminal facilities.

A small technical committee of senior officers should be set up in three years' time to examine the gauge question generally and to make recommendations for gauge conversion with the object of reducing the number of transhipment points.

To secure a good general standard of maintenance it is recommended that neutral control-stations should be located at points where large numbers of wagons are dealt with daily, and where adequate repair facilities exist, but not necessarily at interchange junctions.

The provision of steel for carriage underframes and body construction should receive the highest priority even at the expense of wagon construction.

We recommend the preparation of I.R.S. drawings for all double-wire components.

We also recommend the attachment to the Board's office of an experienced signal engineer, capable of examining signal and interlocking schemes, for advising the Board.

We also recommend the deputation of Indian Signal Officers to study signalling and interlocking work on the continent of Europe.

Commercial Organization And Other Matters

We recommend that the arrangements for the training of officers in the Operating and Commercial Departments should be better organized.

There should be a separate Head of Department for commercial work on the B.B. & C.I. Railway.

Railways should devote greater attention to the subject of quick transit of goods in smalls.

Action should be taken to develop gradually a suitable collection and delivery service on a large scale.

Departmental catering should be built up with caution and should be regarded as a long-term development.

The majority of the members of the Central Advisory Council should be chosen by Commercial and Industrial Associations and there should be direct representation of rural interests and of the travelling public.

The strength necessary for the Railway Protection Police should be periodically reviewed.

Electrical Organization And Electrification

The officers of the technical departments should have some electrical qualifications.

Electrical traction work should be entrusted to a sub-department, until it becomes so widespread on a Railway as to require a separate Traction Department.

Railway Stores Organization

A Joint Committee should draw up a further list of items available locally, for which the powers of purchase should be decentralized to the Railways.

Quarterly joint meetings of the Railway Controllers of Stores, representatives of the Industry and Supply Ministry and the Railway Board be held.

Finance

We consider that it is desirable to have in the Finance Branch of the Railway Board a separate unit whose primary duty would be to explore constantly means for improving the earnings.

A collective financial survey should be made annually by the F.A. & C.A.O.s.

The Budget work in the Railway Board's office should be transferred from the control of the Director of Accounts to the Director of Finance.

A beginning should be made to write down the cost of the intangible assets by contributing 1% of the gross earnings every year to an Amortization Fund.

We recommend that an annual contribution to the Fund for the next five years be made at Rs. 22 crores per annum. Thereafter, as and when the prices stabilize, an enquiry should be undertaken to find out how and at what rate contribution should be made. It is tentatively suggested that the contribution should ultimately be related inter alia to gross earnings.

Staff

Organized labour should be requested to embark upon a campaign of propaganda to stimulate greater effort. Similar propaganda might be launched through the leaders of men.

We recommend that subject to the right of appeal, the usual penalties of withholding of increments or promotion, including stoppage at an efficiency bar, the reduction to a lower post or time scale or to a lower stage in the time scale, the recovery from pay of the whole or part of the pecuniary loss caused to the Government, should be capable of imposition by the competent authority; and for this purpose the Payment of Wages Act should be suitably amended.

For recruitment to the lower grades of Class III Services, greater preference should be given to the sons and nephews of the railway employees who have rendered not less than 15 years of efficient and continuous service; 10% of the vacancies should be reserved for them subject to their being suitably qualified.

Area schools for the training of Class III staff should be established on all Railways.

Research

Railway Research Organization is at present inadequate for the essential needs of the Indian Railways and the Railway Board contemplate forming an advisory committee under the chairmanship of the Chief Commissioner. This should be done very early. The Civil and Mechanical Engineering Research Organization already exists under the Central Standards Office, and should be sufficiently strengthened and expanded. It should be watched that research work is not duplicated, full use being made of the National or University Laboratories and Institutions.

Central Controlling Authority And Railway Organization

We recommend the vesting of the control and management of the Union Railways in a Statutory Authority; for important reasons, however, we suggest that the setting up of the Authority should be deferred for about five years from now.

The accounts of the Authority should be in a form prescribed by the Auditor-General of India and that he should audit and certify them.

We recommend the retention of the Railway Rates

Tribunal after the setting up of the Authority. We also recommend that the Central Advisory Council for Railways and the Local Advisory Committees should be retained.

We recommend that a careful examination of the question of "divisional" or "departmental" working should be made before definitely condemning the "divisional" system.

Regrouping Of Railways

We recommend that the E. P. Railway should continue as a separate entity for some years to come and this Railway should be provided, without any avoidable delay, with basic resources necessary for efficient management.

Railway Grainshop Organization

In view of the serious dissatisfaction among the workers and the abuses brought to light by the Grainshop Committee, we recommend that steps should be taken to end the Grainshop Organization as it exists today, the staff being compensated for the loss of the measure of relief in kind now received by them.

Miscellaneous

We recommend that the method of apportionment of earnings between the Indian Government Railways should be simplified and all of them should participate in the Clearing Office Scheme, which should then be retained as a permanent measure.

Each Railway should have a statistical officer who should interpret and review statistics and bring to notice the salient points emerging from the statistics.

We recommend the preparation of a Statistical Manual which would set forth the meaning of the various units and the methods of employing them intelligently.

AD HOC COMMITTEE ON CITIZENSHIP CLAUSE, 1947—REPORT

Delhi, Manager of Publications, 1950.

Chairman : Shri S. Varadachari.

Members : Shri Tek Chand; Shri B. L. Mitter; Shri A. Krishnaswami Ayyar; Shri K. N. Katju; Shri B. R. Ambedkar; Shri K. M. Munshi.

APPOINTMENT

The Ad Hoc Committee on Citizenship Clause was appointed by the Constituent Assembly of India on May 1, 1947.

TERMS OF REFERENCE

"Every person born in the Union and subject to its jurisdiction; every person either of whose parents was at the time of such person's birth a citizen of the Union; and every person naturalized in the Union shall be a citizen of the Union."

"Further provision [regarding the acquisition and termination of Union citizenship may be made by the law of the Union."

CONTENTS

Report; Recommendations.

RECOMMENDATIONS

The inclusion in the Clause of children born in the Union, even of non-citizens, provided they are subject to Union jurisdiction, is a well-marked feature of Anglo-American public law. This principle has been accepted in the Indian Naturalization Act, 1926. There is some authority for the view that the children of visiting foreigners are on the same footing as the children of foreign ambassadors and would as such be regarded as non-citizens even if born in the Union, because of the qualifying phrase "and subject to its jurisdiction". In any event, such cases are likely to be so few and far between that it is necessary in our opinion to make a special exception to exclude them from citizenship. As regards the possibility of double nationality, this is a well-known phenomenon, but it can be provided against by appropriate provisions in the Union Naturalization Law calling upon the persons concerned to choose one or the other. For this purpose, the Clause makes express provision for supplementary legislation terminating citizenship. We recommend that the Clause as redrafted by us be adopted.

Clause 11 (b) does not, in our opinion, include conscription for military service. But the expression "forced labour" being very comprehensive, we think that the Explanation should be retained in order to make an exception in the case of compulsory service for public purposes. We suggest that instead of the word "Explanation", the words "Provided that" be substituted, so that the amended Clause will stand thus:

"Traffic in human beings and 'begar' and other similar forms of forced labour are prohibited, and any contravention of this prohibition shall be an offence.

"Provided that nothing in this Clause shall prevent the State from imposing compulsory service for public purpose without any discrimination on the ground of race, religion, caste or class."

BENGAL BOUNDARY COMMISSION, 1947, OR RADCLIFFE AWARD—REPORT

New Delhi, 1958. 9p.

Chairman : Sir Cyril Radcliffe.
Members : Justice Bijan Kumar Mukherjea; Justice C. C. Biswas; Justice Abu Saleh Mohammed Akram; Justice S. R. Rahman.

APPOINTMENT

The Bengal Boundary Commission was constituted by the announcement of the Governor-General dated June 30, 1947. Reference No. D 50/7/47/R.

TERMS OF REFERENCE

"The Boundary Commission is instructed to demarcate the boundaries of the two parts of Bengal on the basis of ascertaining the contiguous areas of Muslims and non-Muslims. In doing so, it will also take into account other factors."

CONTENTS

Report; The Schedule; Annexure A; Report of the Bengal Boundary Commission (Sylhet District).

RECOMMENDATIONS

Annexure A

A line shall be drawn along the boundary between the Thana of Phansidewa in the district of Darjeeling and Thana Tetulia in the district of Jalpaiguri from the point where that boundary meets the province of Bihar and then along the boundary between the Thanas of Tetulia and Rajganj: the Thanas of Pachagar and Rajganj, and the Thanas of Pachagar and Jalpaiguri, and shall then continue along the northern corner of the Thana Debiganj to the boundary of the State of Cooch-Behar. The district of Jalpaiguri as lies north of this line shall belong to West Bengal, but the Thana of Patgram and any other portion of Jalpaiguri District which lies to the east or south shall belong to East Bengal.

A line shall then be drawn from the point where the boundary between the Thanas of Haripur and Rajganj in the district of 24-Parganas and the Khulna meets the Bay of Bengal. This line shall follow the course indicated in the following paragraphs. So much of the province of Bengal as lies to the west of it shall belong to West Bengal. Subject to what has been provided in paragraph 1 above with regard to the districts of Darjeeling and Jalpaiguri, the remainder of the Province of Bengal shall belong to East Bengal.

The line shall run along the boundary between the following Thanas:

Haripur and Rajganj; Haripur and Hemtabad; Ranisankail and Hemtabad; Pirganj and Hemtabad; Pirganj and Kaliganj; Bochaganj and Kaliganj; Biral and Kaliganj; Biral and Kushmundi; Biral and Gangarampur; Dinajpur and Gangarampur; Dinajpur and Kumarganj; Chirirbandar and Kumarganj; Phulbari and Kumarganj; Phulbari and Balurghat. It shall terminate at the point where the boundary between Phulbari and Balurghat meets the north-south line of the Bengal-Assam Railway in the eastern corner of the Thana of Balurghat. The line shall turn down the western edge of the Railway lands belonging to that Railway and follow that edge until it meets the boundary between the Thanas of Balurghat and Panchbibi.

From that point the line shall run along the boundary between the following Thanas:

Balurghat and Panchbibi; Balurghat and Joypurhat; Balurghat and Dhamairhat; Tapan and Dhamairhat; Tapan and Patnitala; Tapan and Porsha; Bamangola and Porsha; Habibpur and Porsha; Habibpur and Gomastapur; Habibpur and Bholahat; Malda and Bholahat; English Bazar and Bholahat; English Bazar and Shibganj; Kaliachak and Shibganj; to the point where the boundary between the two last mentioned Thanas meets the boundary between the districts of Malda and Murshidabad on river Ganges.

The line shall then turn south-east down river Ganges along the boundary between the districts of Malda and Murshidabad; Rajshahi and Murshidabad; Rajshahi and Nadia; to the point in the north-western corner of the district of Nadia where the channel of river Mathabanga takes off from river Ganges.

The district boundaries, and not the actual course of river Ganges, shall constitute the boundary between East and West Bengal.

From the point on river Ganges where the channel of river Mathabanga takes off, the line shall run along that channel to the northernmost point where it meets the boundary between the Thanas of Daulatpur and Karimpur. The middle line of the main channel shall constitute the actual boundary.

From this point the boundary between East and West Bengal shall run along the boundaries between the Thanas of Daulatpur and Karimpur; Gangani and Karimpur; Meherpur and Karimpur; Meherpur and Tehatta; Meherpur and Chapra; Damurhuda and Chapra; Damurhuda and Krishnaganj; Chuadanga and Krishnaganj; Jibannagar and Krishnaganj; Jibannagar and Hanskhali; Maheshpur and Hanskhali; Maheshpur and Ranaghat; Maheshpur and Bongaon; Jhikargacha and Bongaon; Sarsa and Bongaon; Sarsa and Gaighata; Gaighata and Kalaroa; to the point where the boundary between those Thanas meets the boundary between the districts of Khulna and 24-Parganas.

The line shall then run southwards along the boundary between the districts of Khulna and 24-Parganas to the point where that boundary meets the Bay of Bengal.

In my view the question is limited to the districts of Sylhet and Cachar, since of the other districts of Assam that can be said to adjoin Sylhet neither the Garo Hills nor the Khasi and Jaintia Hills nor the Lushai Hills have anything approaching a Muslim majority of the population in respect of which a claim could be made.

Out of 35 Thanas in Sylhet, eight have non-Muslim majorities; but of these eight, two, Sulla and Anjiriganj (which is in any event divided almost evenly between Muslims and non-Muslims), are entirely surrounded by preponderatingly Muslim areas, and must therefore go with them to East Bengal. The other six Thanas comprising a population of over 5,30,000 people stretch in a continuous line along part of the southern border of Sylhet District. They are divided between two sub-divisions of which one, South Sylhet, comprising a population of over 5,15,000 people has in fact a non-Muslim majority of some 40,000; while the other, Karimganj, with a population of over 5,68,000 people, has a Muslim majority that is a little larger.

With regard to the District of Cachar, one Thana, Hailakandi, has a Muslim majority and is contiguous to the Muslim Thanas of Badarpur and Karimganj in the district of Sylhet. This Thana forms, with Thana of Katlichara, immediately to its south, the sub-division of Hailakandi, and in the sub-division, as a whole, Muslims enjoy a very small majority, being 51% of the total population. I think that the dependence of Katlichara on Hailakandi for normal communications makes it important that the area should be under one jurisdiction, and that the Muslims would have at any rate a strong presumptive claim for the transfer of the sub-division of Hailakandi, comprising a population of 1,66,536 from the Province of Assam to the Province of East Bengal.

But a study of the map shows, in my judgement, that a division on these lines would present problems of administration that might gravely affect the future welfare and happiness of the whole District. Not only would the six non-Muslim Thanas of Sylhet be completely divorced from the rest of Assam if the Muslim claim to Hailakandi were recognized, but they form a strip running east and west whereas the natural division of the land is north and south and they effect an awkward severance of the railway line through Sylhet so that, for instance, the junction for the town of Sylhet itself, the capital of the district, would lie in Assam, not in East Bengal.

In those circumstances I think that some exchange of territories must be effected if a workable division is to result. Some of the non-Muslim Thanas must go to East Bengal and some Muslim territory and Hailakandi must be retained by Assam. Accordingly, I decide and award as follows :

A line shall be drawn from the point where the boundary between the Thanas of Patharkandi and Kulaura meets the frontier of Tripura State and shall run north along the boundary between those Thanas, then along the boundary between the Thanas of Patharkandi and Barlekha, then along the boundary between the Thanas of Karimganj and Barlekha, and then along the boundary between the Thanas of Karimganj and Beani Bazar to the point where that boundary meets river Kusiyara. The line shall then turn to the east taking river Kusiyara as the boundary and run to the point where that river meets the boundary between the districts of Sylhet and Cachar. The centre line of the main stream or channel shall constitute the boundary. So much of the district of Sylhet as lies to the west and north of this line shall be detached from the province of Assam and transferred to the province of East Bengal. No other part of the province of Assam shall be transferred.

PUNJAB BOUNDARY COMMISSION OR RADCLIFFE AWARD 1947—REPORT

New Delhi, 1958.

Chairman : Sir Cyril Radcliffe.
Members : Justice Din Muhammad; Justice Muhammad Munir; Justice Mehr Chand Mahajan; Justice Teja Singh.

APPOINTMENT

The Punjab Boundary Commission was constituted by the announcement of the Governor-General dated June 30, 1947. Reference No. D50/7/47R.

TERMS OF REFERENCE

"The Boundary Commission is instructed to demarcate the boundaries of the two parts of the Punjab on the basis of ascertaining the contiguous majority areas of Muslims and non-Muslims. In doing so, it will also take into account other factors."

CONTENTS

Report; Annexures; Schedule.

RECOMMENDATIONS

The boundary between the East and West Punjab shall commence on the north at the point where the west branch of river Ujh enters the Punjab Province from the State of Kashmir. The boundary shall follow the line of that river down the western boundary of the Pathankot Tahsil to the point where the Pathankot, Shakargarh and Gurdaspur Tahsils meet. The tahsil boundary and not the actual course of river Ujh shall constitute the boundary between the East and West Punjab.

From the point of meeting of the three tahsils mentioned above, the boundary between the East and West Punjab shall follow the line of river Ujh to its junction with river Ravi and thereafter the line of river Ravi along the boundary between the Tahsils of Gurdaspur and Shakargarh, the boundary between the Tahsils of Batala and Shakargarh, the boundary between the tahsils of Bata'a and Narowal, the boundary between the Tahsils of Ajnala and Narowal, and the boundary between the Tahsils of Ajnala and Shahdara, to the point on river Ravi where the district of Amritsar is divided from the district of Lahore. The tahsil boundaries referred to, and not the actual course of river Ujh or river Ravi, shall constitute the boundary between the East and West Punjab.

From the point on river Ravi where the district of Amritsar is divided from the district of Lahore, the boundary between the East and West Punjab shall turn southwards following the boundary between the Tahsils of Ajnala and Lahore and then the Tahsils of Tarn Taran meet. The line will then turn south-westward along the boundary between the Tahsils of Tarn Taran and Lahore, to the point where the Tahsils of Kasur, Lahore and Tarn Taran meet. The line will then turn south-westward along the boundary between the Tahsils of Lahore and Kasur to the point where that boundary meets the north-east corner of village Theh Jharolian. It will then run along the eastern boundary of that village to its junction with village Chathianwala, turn along the northern boundary of that village and then run down its eastern boundary to its junction with village Waigal. It will then run along the eastern boundary of village Waigal to its junction with village Kalia, and then along the southern boundary of village Waigal to its junction with village Panhuwan. The line will then run down the eastern boundary of village Panhuwan to its junction with village Gaddoke. The line will then run down the eastern border of village Gaddoke to its junction with village Nurwala. It will then turn along the southern boundary of village Gaddoke to its junction with village Katluni Kalan. The line will then run down the eastern boundary of village Katluni Kalan to its junction with villages Kals and Mastgarh. It will then run along the southern boundary of village Katluni Kalan to the north-west corner of village Kals. It will then run along the western boundary of village Kals to its junction with village Khem Karan. The line will then run along the western and southern boundaries of village Khem Karan to its junction with village Maewala. It will then run down the western and southern boundaries of village Maewala, proceeding eastward along the boundaries between village Mahaidepur on the north and villages Sheikhupura Kuhna, Kamalpuran, Fatehwala and Mahewala. The line will then turn northward along the western boundary of village Sahjra to its junction with village Mahaidepur and Machhike. It will then turn northeastward along the boundaries between villages Machhike and Sahjra and then proceed along the boundary between villages Rattoke and Sahjra to the junction between villages Rattoke : Sahjra and Mabbuke. The line will then run north-east between villages Rattoke and Mabbuke to the junction of villages Rattoke, Mabbuke and Gajjal. From the point the line will run along the boundary between villages Mabbuke and Gajjal, and then turn south along the eastern boundary of village Mabbuke to its junction with village Nagar Aimanpur. It will then turn along the north-eastern boundary to its junction with village Masteke. From there it will run along the eastern boundary of village Masteke to where it meets the boundary between the tahsils of Kasur and Ferozepore.

For the purpose of identifying the villages referred to in this paragraph, I attach a map of Kasur Tahsil authorized by the then Settlement Officer, Lahore District, which was supplied to the Commission by the Provincial Government.

The line will then run in a south-westerly direction down river Sutlej on the boundary between the districts of Lahore and Ferozepore to the point where the districts of Ferozepore, Lahore and Montgomery meet. It will continue along the boundary between the disrricts of Ferozepore and Montgomery to the point where this boundary meets the border of Bahawalpur State. The district boundaries, and not the actual course of river Sutlej, shall in each case constitute the boundary between the East and West Punjab.

It is my intention that this boundary line should ensure that the canal headworks of Sulemanke will fall within the territorial jurisdiction of the West Punjab. If the existing delimitation of the boundaries of Montgomery District does not ensure this I award to the West Punjab so much of the territory concerned as covers the headworks, and the boundary shall be adjusted accordingly.

So much of the Punjab Province as lies to the west of the line demarcated in the preceding paragraphs shall be the territory of the West Punjab. So much of the territory of the Punjab Province as lies to the east of that line shall be the territory of the East Punjab.

SUB-COMMITTEE OF THE SCIENTIFIC MAN-POWER COMMITTEE, 1947—INTERIM REPORT

New Delhi, Ministry of Education, 1947. 123p.

Chairman : Sir Shanti Swarup Bhatnagar.

Members : Dr. Homi Bhabha; Dr. K. A. Hamed; Mian Afzal Husain; Prof. Humayun Kabir; Rai Bahadur A. N. Khosla; Shri K. S. Krishnan; Shri G. L. Mehta; Mrs. Hansa Mehta; Major B. N. Mitra; Prof. J. N. Mukherji; Dr. M. Qureshi; Dr. K. C. K. E. Raja; Dr. Birbal Sahni; Wing-Comdr. H. Singh; Shri D. N. Wadia.

Secretary : Dr. S. R. Sen Gupta.

APPOINTMENT

The Scientific Man-Power Committee was set up by the Government of India in April, 1947, under the chairmanship of the late Sir Shafaat Ahmed Khan as notified in a Press communique issued on April 19, 1947. Sir Shanti Swarup Bhatnagar has since been appointed Chairman in place of late Sir Shafaat Ahmed Khan with effect from July 23, 1947.

TERMS OF REFERENCE

(1) To assess the requirements for different grades of scientific and technical man-power, taking a comprehensive view over a period of the next 10 years of the needs of the Government (civil and defence), of teaching and research and of industry, agriculture, transport, medicine and other fields dependent on the use of scientific and technical man-power;

(2) To make recommendations regarding action to be taken during the next five years to meet these requirements, in particular with reference to :

(a) The immediate improvement and expansion of facilities for scientific and technical training in Indian Universities and special institutions;

(b) Training overseas in scientific and technical subjects;

(c) The promotion and development of scientific and technical research;

(d) The utilization of scientific and technical man-power; and

(e) The maintenance of a register of scientific and technical personnel to facilitate their utilization to the best advantage.

At its third meeting held on August 22 and 23, 1947, the Scientific Man-Power Committee adopted the report prepared by its Sub-Committee adumbrating measures for the immediate improvement and expansion of facilities for scientific and technical education, research and training.

On July 7, 1947, the acting Chairman was requested by the Government to let them have by

August 5, at the latest, an Interim Report based on available information, however inadequate, recommending measures which should be given the highest priority and initiated within six months in order to meet, to some extent at least, the shortage of scientific and technical personnel—a shortage which is admitted on all hands.

In view of the urgency of the situation Sir Shanti Swarup Bhatnagar agreed to undertake this work. A Sub-Committee consisting mainly of the local members of the Main Committee was constituted at the instance of the Government. The purpose of the Sub-Committee was to formulate certain interim recommendations, prompt action on which on the part of the Government could pave the way to meet partially the scientific and technical man-power shortage. The Sub-Committee consisted of

Chairman : Sir S. S. Bhatnagar

Members : Rai Bahadur A. N. Khosla; Dr. J. N. Mukherji; Rao Bahadur Dr. K. C. K. E. Raja; Dr. J. N. Ray; Wing-Comdr. H. Singh; Shri D. N. Wadia.

Secretary : Dr. S. R. Sen Gupta

and had before it the following Terms of Reference :

To advise the Government of India on measures which should be given the highest priority and initiative within the next six months in respect of :

(a) The immediate improvement and expansion of facilities for scientific and technical training in Indian Universities, and in special institutions; and

(b) The promotion and development of scientific and technical research.

CONTENTS

Personnel and Terms of Reference; Introduction; **Part I:** Interim Report of the Scientific Man-Power Committee; Education; **Section I:** Basic Scientific Education; Double Shift System; Higher Scientific Education; Higher Geological Education; Engineering and Technical Education; Engineering Short-Term Programme; Engineering Long-Term Programme; Education and Training of 'C' Grade Technicians; Practical Training of Engineers; Education of Agricultural Personnel; Education for Health; **Section II:** Training of Personnel for Scientific and Industrial Research; Special Measures to be Initiated within the next six months; **Section III:** Industrial Training; **Section IV:** Technical Training for Defence Services; **Section V:** Shortage of Equipment and other Related Questions; Housing; **Section VI:** Steps to Expedite Government Projects; Summary of Recommendations.

Part II: Notes by Members; Training of Personnel for Scientific and Industrial Research and for Industry by Sir S. S. Bhatnagar; Programme for Provision of Facilities for Education, Training and Research for Engineering Personnel which can be initiated within the next six months by Rai Bahadur A. N. Khosla; Measures which can be implemented during the next six months for speeding up Education, Training and Research in Agriculture and allied subjects by Dr. J. N. Mukherji; Training for Health Personnel by Rao Bahadur Dr. K. C. K. E. Raja; Requirements of Technical and Scientific Personnel for Industrial Development and their Training Programme by Dr. J. N. Ray; R.I.A.F. Training, Research and Development in Collaboration with Civil Institutions by Wing-Comdr. H. Singh; Programme for Provision of Facilities for Education, Training and Research in Geology, Training and Research in Geology and Mining which can be initiated within the next six months by Mr. D. N. Wadia; Programme for the Improvement and Development of Higher Technical Education by Dr. S. R. Sen Gupta.

RECOMMENDATIONS

The Sub-Committee of the Scientific Man-Power Committee makes the following recommendations to the Government of India for immediate implementation.

For an immediate improvement in the outturn of scientific man-power the Government should utilize the existing sources, viz., universities, special institutions and industrial concerns by helping to create in these places adequate facilities for higher education, research and practical training. Such help as is to be given should largely be in the form of grants for (a) the creation of scholarships on a generous scale, (b) the purchase of equipment, (c) the opening of post-graduate research departments in the Universities which do not have any at the moment. In addition to the above, the several educational development plans, which have been prepared by the Departments of Education, etc., should be pushed through immediately.

For the objectives generally set forth above the Sub-Committee makes the following detailed recommendations under various heads.

Education

(a) **Basic Scientific Education :** A substantial increase in the facilities for education in General Science up to the Intermediate Science and B.Sc. standards should be aimed at so that the output from these courses may be adequate to feed the post-graduate institutions.

As an interim measure, to meet the present emergency double shifts should be introduced in such institutions where there is some spare teaching accommodation and equipment but a completely new set of staff should be engaged for the second shift. The Government should, wherever the introduction of double shift is considered feasible, come to the aid of the institution by bearing a share of the expenses on staff salary and contingencies and by assisting the institution in securing a certain amount of equipment and building materials.

The Provincial Governments should be requested to convert without delay some of their existing ordinary High Schools into Technical High Schools.

(b) Higher Scientific Education: The Government of India should come to the aid of all Universities by giving them suitable financial assistance to expand their post-graduate departments so that the output of post-graduate science students may be increased.

The recommendations of the Geological Education Committee should be acted on immediately so that trained geologists in adequate number may be available for the survey and development of India's mineral resources. The Geological Survey of India should increase the number of their present training camps so as to be able to train annually at least 50 geologists in field work.

(c) Engineering and Technological Education: In the matter of education in engineering and technology a short-term and a long-term programme should be initiated within the next six months.

Short-Term Programme: Introduction of an intensive 12-month training programme for M.Sc.'s and Graduates in Chemical Technology to be run on a co-operative basis between (14 different technical institutions and corresponding industries) at a cost of Rs. 34 lakhs in capital and Rs. 13.3 lakhs in recurring.

The Universities should introduce 3-year degree course in engineering as proposed by the All-India Council for Technical Education.

Double-shift system should be introduced in engineering colleges, if conditions justify.

Whatever possible use should be made of the teaching facilities of the Science Departments of general colleges to assist in the education in basic sciences for engineering students.

As an interim measure, engineers in Government service should be encouraged to assist in the instruction in Engineering Colleges.

Long-Term Programme : For ensuring co-ordinated development of technical education and generally to raise its standards, the Regional Committees, recommended by the All-India Council for Technical Education, be established immediately.

For the improvement of the standards of education as well as the expansion of some of the institutions of engineering and technology, so that the present facilities may be fully utilized, the Government of India should immediately make grants to such institutions as are recommended by the All-India Council for Technical Education. The grants required will be about Rs. 2 crores in capital spread over 5 years and Rs. 31 lakhs in recurring.

Building construction, at present contemplated to increase the annual intake of Architecture and Engineering classes of the Delhi Polytechnic, should be expedited. The existing unsatisfactory conditions in the Delhi Polytechnic, especially in the matter of salaries to teachers, accommodation, etc., should be removed and certain departments of the institution be affiliated to Delhi University. The Government should also consider the desirability of setting up a small technical committee to advise the governing body of the Polytechnic.

The Indian Institute of Science should be urged to expedite the opening of the Power Engineering Department so that the outturn of engineers, adequately qualified to handle hydro-electric power development projects, etc., may be available soon.

Within the next six months the Government should complete the purchase of sites and appoint planning staff and, if possible, arrange to hire temporary buildings for starting work on the Eastern and the Western Higher Technical Institutions.

The Government should give immediate effect to the recommendations of the Indian School of Mines Reorganization Committee for the improvement and expansion of facilities for mining and applied geological education.

The scheme of training of 'C' Grade technicians prepared by the Department of Labour should be put into operation as far as possible within the next six months. For this purpose and for training of craftsmen or overseers, the Government should take over some of the private engineering schools and develop them.

For the special needs of leather and footwear industries, leather chemistry should be introduced as one of the subjects in M.Sc. Industrial Chemistry course and the existing training institutions of leather technology should be made more efficient and useful by adding to their equipment and by enabling them to have better-paid staff.

(d) Agricultural Education : For the co-ordinated development of agricultural education, the Government should constitute on an all-India basis an Advisory Council for Agricultural Education.

In order to bring about an improvement in the flow of trained personnel the system of double-shift should be introduced, wherever possible, as an interim measure.

The programme of development of training and research facilities of the Indian Agricultural Research Institute, Central Agricultural College and other Central Research Institutes dealing with different aspects of agricultural forestry and fisheries should be implemented and all facilities given to increase the scope of the training programme so as to be able to train double the present number.

The Indian Universities should be encouraged by financial grants and otherwise to establish and/or develop their facilities of agriculture and diversify the scope of their training.

(e) **Medical Education** : For an immediate increase in the outturn of medical personnel, the double shift system should be tried as an interim experimental measure in the Calcutta Medical College and a grant of Rs. 1.3 lakhs in recurring and Rs. 0.10 lakhs in capital be made for the purpose. The possibility of introducing this system in G.S. Medical College, Bombay, should also be investigated.

As a long-term measure the following grants should be sanctioned for the general improvement and expansion of training facilities in the existing medical colleges and certain other purposes :

Existing Colleges in	India	Pakistan
	(Rs. in lakhs)	
Capital Expenditure	432.0	54.0
Recurring Expenditure	115.5	16.5

Rs. 6 lakhs in capital and Rs. 6.75 lakhs in recurring for starting Departments of Preventive Medicine and Public Health in the medical colleges of Bombay and Calcutta.

Rs. 0.825 lakhs for instituting 50 medical research scholarships at various centres in India.

Rs. 2.8 lakhs in capital and Rs. 2.66 lakhs in recurring for expanding the existing training facilities of the All-India Institute of Public Health and Hygiene.

Rs. 3.38 lakhs in capital and Rs. 2.98 lakhs in recurring for the improvement and expansion of the Calcutta Dental College and the Dental College in Bombay.

A capital grant of Rs. 1 lakh and a recurring grant of Rs. 1.5 lakhs to the Nursing College over and above the presen t expenditure.

A recurring grant of Rs. 71,000 to the Lady Reading Health School, Delhi, for the next three years.

Rs. 2.05 lakhs in recurring and Rs. 11,000 in capital for schemes for training of certain types of non-medical personnel such as midwives, health inspectors, health visitors and vaccinators in the Provinces.

Rs. 0.60 lakhs in recurring for instituting 12 research scholarships in medical and social welfare work at the Tata Institute of Social Sciences, Bombay.

Rs. 446.3 lakhs in capital and Rs. 132.8 lakhs in recurring for a college of pharmacy in Calcutta, a start being made within the next six months.

Scientific Research Training

The rigidity of the system of training obtaining in certain Universities and research institutions should be removed and the system made more flexible and diversified so that a wider field of activity could be covered.

The draft of wastage of scientific talent now going on should be prevented ; and such available talent should be assessed and properly made use of.

For an immediate improvement in the research training facilities in Universities and special institutions following measures should be given effect to :

(a) Institution of 250 scholarships in Indian Universities and non-Government research institutions at an estimated expenditure of Rs. 3 lakhs in recurring.

(b) Creation of 20 professorships, 20 readerships and 40 lectureships in certain Universities.

(c) The Universities of Madras, Nagpur, Delhi, Agra, Patna and Annamalai be asked to start post-graduate research departments in certain important subjects and a total grant of Rs. 30 lakhs in capital and Rs. 7.0 lakhs in recurring, which includes (b) above, be sanctioned.

(d) The Universities of Calcutta, Bombay, Andhra, Benaras, Lucknow, Allahabad, Aligarh, Punjab and Dacca be asked to expand their research training facilities by way of equipment, library, etc., to take in additional workers and that a total grant of Rs. 18 lakhs in capital and Rs. 3 lakhs in recurring be sanctioned.

(e) Indian Institute of Sciences, Bose Research Institute, Tata Institute of Fundamental Research, Nutrition Research Laboratory, Cotton Technological Laboratory, Indian Association for the Cultivation of Science, Lac Research Institute, Jute Research Institute and Laboratories of the Indian Academy of Sciences and the Palaeobotanical Research Institute be asked to expand their research facilities to accommodate more workers and that a grant of Rs. 14 lakhs in capital and Rs. 2.50 lakhs in recurring be sanctioned for the purpose.

(f) The Council of Scientific and Industrial Research be asked to admit at least 20 research workers for training in their present laboratories and that a grant of Rs. 35,000 in recurring be sanctioned for the purpose.

(g) Bengal Tanning Institute, Leather Trades Institute, Madras, Harcourt Butler Technological Institute, Kerala Soap Institute, Imperial Institute of Sugar Technology and the Indian School of Mines be asked to expand their research facilities to take in more men and that a grant of Rs. 0.75 lakhs in recurring be sanctioned for the purpose.

(h) The various scientific departments of the Government, which are about 20 in number, be asked to formulate immediately proposals for training as many men as possible, not less than 200 in any case, for all the departments and the Government take appropriate action on the proposals.

(i) A scheme of Railway Scientific Research for the training of about 200 workers be instituted immediately, and a grant of Rs. 3.42 lakhs in recurring be sanctioned for the purpose.

(j) For the organization and development of Scientific and Industrial Research in the country the Government should implement the recommendations of the Industrial Research Planning Committee especially in regard to the levy of statutory cess on industry for research purposes.

Industrial Training

All the established industrial concerns in the country should be approached to provide facilities for advanced and lower grades of training in their factories for more men. In case response from the concerns is poor the Government should introduce a suitable legislative measure whereby it should become incumbent on industrial concerns to provide technical training for qualified students notwithstanding whether the personnel thus trained would be required by the particular concerns or not.

In all contracts entered into by the Government for the purchase of industrial machinery, plant and equipment from foreign and Indian firms, there should be a provision in terms of purchase for the training of a suitable number of Indians in the workshops of the firms.

The following immediate programme of training of men in industry should be implemented :

(1) Advanced training of 300 men in 24 major industries at an estimated cost of Rs. 3.6 lakhs (recurring).

(2) Foremanship training of 500 men in 24 major industries at an estimated cost of Rs. 4.6 lakhs (recurring).

Technical Training In Institutions

A certain number of 'A' Grade technicians (experts) should be trained in India possibly in accordance with the tentative list of priority subjects drawn up by the Sub-Committee.

A scheme of imparting an immediate intensive short-course training to 'B' Grade technicians as mentioned in II (c) should be implemented forthwith.

A grant of Rs. 5 lakhs be made for instituting a system of scholarships to make it possible for 'C' Grade technicians already engaged in industry to undergo a short refresher and supplementary course in suitable institutions or industrial concerns.

Defence

The Defence Organization of the country should be developed on up-to-date scientific lines partly by organizing defence research on an extensive scale through a strong scientific section dealing with the training and utilization of resources available in the country for forward advance in the manufacture of defence materials. For this purpose the Defence Department should be asked to formulate a scientific project which should include research, design and engineering construction for the several branches of the Defence Forces, viz., Army, Navy and Air Force, and the project examined by a commission of experts.

Since Defence research cannot progress without the co-operation of "Civil" research, effective liaison should be established immediately between the "Civil" and "Defence" Organizations.

Adequate information relating to the requirements of the Defence Organization in respect of scientific and technical man-power being not available at this stage, the necessary details should be collected from the Defence Department immediately and examined.

With reference to the Air Force the following measures should be adopted as far as possible :

(a) The existing scheme of technical training in civil aviation be correlated with that in the R.I.A.F. This measure will not only quicken the pace in the training of mechanics but also enable us to create a common pool of trained personnel between the two organizations.

(b) The Civil Aviation Training Centre at Saharanpur be utilized for the training of Air Force and Civil Aviation personnel.

(c) Ground Engineers in Civil Aviation with A, B, C, D, & X licences should be employed by the Air Force; and the Air Force should be fully represented on the examination boards and the certificates endorsed as "Acceptable to the Defence Services"

General Recommendations

For the successful expansion of research and training facilities in Universities and special institutions, especially in regard to the various programmes recommended above, the Government should immediately adopt the following special measures :

(a) The existing handicaps in the matter of import of scientific equipment and apparatus for educational institutions should be removed and top priority given for such imports. The Government should also endeavour to secure from abroad through the official trade agencies whatever equipment the institutions concerned fail to obtain themselves. The Government should, as far as possible, also allow rebate on the import duty on scientific equipment.

(b) In order to augment the existing equipment resources for scientific institutions the Government should reconsider its present policy of disposal of surplus war materials of scientific value and adopt necessary measures to prevent the passing of such materials into the hands of private dealers and ensure that the materials are made available to educational and research institutions easily and as far as possible free of cost.

(c) In order to facilitate the training of additional workers in institutions and industrial concerns, the Government should immediately evolve a suitable machinery for expediting building construction, especially at various training centres, and also provide necessary funds for the purpose.

The following concrete steps may be favourably considered by the Government :

(i) Construction of additional wings to the existing hostels in Universities, research and technical institutions where the additional men are intended to be trained and the cost of such construction to be entirely borne by the Government.

(ii) Construction of residential buildings in factories where training is to be provided on the basis of 50% of the cost as interest-free loan to be repaid to the Government in instalments and the buildings constructed to become the property of the concerns after a certain period.

In order to overcome the great difficulties experienced by the Government in implementing most of their schemes for the improvement and expansion of research and training facilities, the Government should :

(a) Leave it to the Administrative Department to decide as to how any particular scientific or technical post should be filled. The normal procedure of recruitment through the Federal Public Service Commission can be followed generally but in special cases, at the discretion of the Administrative Department, posts may be filled through negotiations with prospective candidates through the medium of a selection committee with which it may be possible to associate the Federal Public Service Commission.

(b) Create a Scientific Service on a par in status and emoluments with the administrative service, similar to that created in Great Britain.

(c) Improve the salary scales of teachers, especially those engaged in technical education.

(d) Provide funds to enable the institutions to send their experienced staff overseas to visit important centres of scientific and technical education and research.

(e) Institute a large number of scholarships for post-graduate and research training in institutions in India.

(f) Ask the Administrative Department to set up a building committee on which representatives of the C.P.W.D. and the Finance Department may sit together with the departmental representatives and wherever necessary to entrust the department at its discretion to have their building planned and executed through the private agencies.

(g) Delegate a greater amount of power than at present to heads of educational and research institutions.

(h) Place at the disposal of the institutions the funds in the form of block grants to implement programmes approved by the Government. Normally, the head of the institution should have the authority, as a matter of course, once the scheme has been approved and funds allotted, to take the action he considers most appropriate to achieve the desired result without delay.

(i) Decisions on technical matters should be arrived at in fullest consultation with the scientific and technical men at all stages. For any change in the technical proposals, including policy, technical men of the department should be given an opportunity to represent their viewpoint.

COMMITTEE TO RECOMMEND SUITABLE CONSTITUTIONAL CHANGES IN THE ADMINISTRATIVE SYSTEMS OF THE CHIEF COMMISSIONER'S PROVINCES, 1947—REPORT

Delhi, Manager of Publications, 1950.

Chairman : Shri B. Pattabhi Sitaramayya.

Members : Shri N. Gopalaswamy Ayyangar; Shri Deshbandhu Gupta; Shri K. Santhanam; Shri C. M. Poonacha; Shri Mukat Behari Lal Bhargava.

APPOINTMENT

The Committee was appointed by the President, Constituent Assembly of India, in accordance with the motion adopted by the Constituent Assembly on July 30, 1947.

TERMS OF REFERENCE

For the purpose of recommending constitutional changes in the five Centrally administered areas, viz., Panth Piploda, Andaman and Nicobar Islands, Coorg, Ajmer-Merwara and Delhi.

CONTENTS

Report; Annexure.

RECOMMENDATIONS

Delhi, Ajmer-Merwara including Panth Piploda, Coorg and such other Provinces as may be so designated shall be the Lieutenant-Governor's Province.

The Provincial Executive

In each Province there shall be a Lieutenant-Governor who shall be appointed by the Federation.

The provisions of the Constitution Act relating to the term of office, qualifications for appointment, eligibility for re-appointment, conditions of office, declaration before entering office by the Governor shall as far as possible be applicable in the case of a Lieutenant-Governor. He may be removed from office by the President on the grounds upon which a Governor may be impeached.

(i) The Executive Authority of the Province shall be vested in the Lieutenant-Governor and may be exercised by him either directly or through persons acting under his authority.

(ii) The power to suspend, remit or commute the sentence of any person convicted of any offence shall be vested in the Lieutenant-Governor as in the case of major Provinces.

(iii) Nothing in this Section shall prevent the President of the Federation or the Provincial Legislature from delegating functions to subordinate authorities.

Administration Of Provincial Affairs

(i) There shall be a Council of Ministers with the Chief Minister at the head to aid and advise the Lieutenant-Governor in the exercise of his functions except in so far as he is by or under this Constitution required to exercise his functions or any of them in his discretion. The number of Ministers shall not exceed three except with the approval of the President of the Federation.

(ii) In case of difference of opinion between the Lieutenant-Governor and his Ministers on any issue, which he considers important, he may refer the matter to the President of the Federation, whose decision shall be final and binding upon the Province.

The provisions of the Constitution Act relating to the appointment, dismissal and with respect to the determination of the salaries of the Ministers in the Governor's Provinces shall, as far as possible, be applicable in the case of Lieutenant-Governor's Provinces.

Legislature

There shall for each of the Lieutenant-Governor's Province be a Legislature, consisting of a single Chamber to be known as the Legislative Assembly. It shall be composed of members chosen by direct election.

The term of office of the elected members of the Assembly on the basis of franchise and other general provisions shall be on the lines as provided in the Constitution Act for Governor's Provinces except that the representation of the different territorial constituencies in the Assembly shall be on a scale of not more than one representative for every 5,000 persons subject to a minimum of 33 for Coorg; 15,000, subject to a minimum of 40 in the case of Ajmer-Merwara including Panth Piploda; and 20,000, subject to a maximum of 50 in the case of Delhi.

The Provincial Assembly shall not have the power to make laws for Federal subjects, and the subjects included in both the Provincial and Concurrent Lists in the new Constitution will be treated as concurrent in respect of these minor provinces. Laws made by the Federal Legislature for these provinces in respect of any of these subjects shall prevail over laws passed by the Provincial Assembly in so far as the latter are inconsistent with the Federal laws.

Laws passed by the Provincial Assembly shall require the assent of the President of the Federation.

The provisions of the Constitution Act relating to prorogation and dissolution of the Legislature, the right of the Governor to address and send messages, election of members as officers of the Legislature and fixation of their salaries in Governor's Provinces shall apply *mutatis mutandis* in the case of Lieutenant-Governor's Provinces.

The provisions of the Constitution Act relating to the making of declaration by members, vacation of seats, disqualifications of members, their privileges and immunities, salaries and allowances in the Provincial Legislatures shall as far as possible be applicable in Lieutenant-Governor's Provinces.

The provisions of the Constitution Act relating to the langauge to be used in the Provincial Legislature shall as far as possible be applicable in the case of these Provinces.

Administrative Breakdown

If at any time the President of the Federation is satisfied that the Government of the Province cannot be carried on in accordance with these provisions, he should have power to supersede these arrangements, take the administration into his own hands and make such other provision for conducting it as he may consider necessary. The exercise of this power will be subject to the usual provisions relating to report to and control by the Federal Legislature in the case of emergencies in a Governor's Province.

Judiciary

(i) In the case of Coorg, the powers of a High Court shall be exercised by the Madras High Court.

(ii) For Delhi and Ajmer-Merwara there shall be a High Court established in Delhi having original as well as appellate jurisdiction over both the Provinces. The constitution of this High Court, the appointment of judges and their salaries, its jurisdiction and administrative function shall be governed by the provisions of the Constitution Act applicable to High Courts.

Provincial Services

(i) For higher appointments provision shall be made in the recruitment of All India Administrative Services for meeting the requirements of these Provinces.

(ii) Provision shall be made for transfers *inter se* of service personnel recruited in the above manner in these three provinces.

Representation In The Federal Legislature

Notwithstanding anything to the contrary in the Union Constitution regarding the basis of representation for the Houses of Federal Legislature, each of these three minor Provinces should be treated as a unit of the Federation for purposes of representation in the two Houses of the Federal Legislature.

Chief Commissioner's Provinces

(i) Andaman and Nicobar Islands and such other areas as may be so designated shall be the Chief Commissioner's Provinces.

(ii) The Andaman and Nicobar Islands shall continue to be administered as at present with such adjustments in the administrative machinery as may be deemed necessary.

Additional Note by Shri Mukat Behari Lal Bhargava and Shri C. M. Poonacha to the Chief Commissioner's Provinces Constitution Committee Report :

We the members representing Ajmer-Merwara and Coorg having signed the report find it necessary to append this additional note regarding the future of these two Provinces.

The special problem arising out of the smallness of area, geographical position, scantiness of resources attended with what may be called administrative difficulties of many a complex nature may, at no distant future, necessitate the joining of each of these areas with a contiguous unit. Therefore, we feel that a specific provision should be made in this chapter of the Constitution to make possible such a union after ascertaining the wishes of the people of these areas. No doubt our attention was drawn to Clause 3 of the Union Constitution Committee Report which is yet to be adopted by the Constituent Assembly, wherein certain provisions relating to the creation of a Province, altering the boundaries of a Province, etc., are embodied. But after careful examination we feel that the proposed Clause 3 of the Union Constitution Committee Report is of a very restrictive nature and does not in specific terms contemplate the inclusion of an Indian Province or areas with a State or a group of States. Taking into account the situation of Ajmer-Merwara which is surrounded on all sides by Rajputana States such a Clause would perpetually leave Ajmer-Merwara in isolation even though the people of Ajmer-Merwara may at any time decide against it. Accordingly we press upon the Constituent Assembly the urgency of incorporating a suitable provision in this chapter of the Constitution so as to make it possible for each of these areas to join a contiguous unit.

FOODGRAINS POLICY COMMITTEE, 1947—INTERIM REPORT

Delhi, Manager of Publications, 1948. 56p.

Chairman : Sir Purshotamdas Thakurdas.

Members : Seth Ghanshyam Das Birla; Sir Shri Ram; Dr. Ram Manohar Lohia; Thakur Phool Singh; Shri Dip Narain Sinha; Shri Hussain Imam; Shri Lakshmidas Purshotam; Dr. V. K. R. V. Rao; Shri R. L. Gupta; Shri. D. S. Bakhle; Shri S. Y. Krishnaswami; Shri D. R. Sethi; Shri D. N. Mahta.

Secretary : Shri R. A. Gopalaswami.

APPOINTMENT

The Foodgrains Policy Committee was constituted under the Ministry of Food vide their letter No. 432/S— dated September 27, 1947.

TERMS OF REFERENCE

To examine the present position in regard to foodgrains in India and the prospective position in the next five years in the light of considerations of production, procurement, imports, distribution and controls and advise the Government :

(i) On the measures which can be taken to increase domestic production and procurement;

(ii) The extent to which reliance can and should be placed on imports; and

(iii) In the light of the above, the modifications which may be necessary in the foodgrains policy so far pursued.

CONTENTS

Introduction; Rewiew of Foodgrains Controls; Reduction of Central Government Commitments; Reduction of Provincial Government Commitments; Prices; Retention and Removal of Controls; Supplemental Foods; Summary of Conclusions; Statistical Appendix; Minute of Dissent ; Separate Note (No. 1) by Shri Hussain Imam; Separate Note (No. II) by Dr. Ram Manohar Lohia; Supplemental Note by Thakur Phool Singh.

RECOMMENDATIONS

I. Reduction Of Government Commitments

Recommendations to be made to Provincial Governments regarding the Food Control Policy :

(i) Acceptance of policy of reduction of Government commitments under rationing and controlled distribution.

(ii) The beginning to be made with those rationing commitments which were accepted in recent years and reduction to be effected in the reverse order to the original process of extension.

(iii) The basis of reduction to be decided with reference to local conditions with the definite aim of liquidating Government commitments as early as possible.

II. Prices Of Controlled Foodgrains

An increase of procurement prices for controlled foodgrains is necessary. The amount of increase to be allowed in different areas to be settled in accordance with the principles and procedure set out below.

Provincial Governments to propose whether and if so what increase they consider to be necessary; and forward their proposals to the Central Government' with a statement of the circumstances justifying the increase proposed, whether and if so to what extent the increased cost is recoverable from consumers, and the net cost, if any, which is not so recoverable.

Before passing on the cost of increasing the procurement price in whole or in part to the consumer, both the Central Government and the Provincial Government should satisfy themselves that this can be done without raising the consumer price to an unduly high level.

The Central Government to reimburse to the Provincial Government one-half of the net cost of the increased procurement price which is not recoverable from consumers.

III. Imports From Abroad And Basic Plan

The following recommendations to be made to the Central Government regarding Import and Basic Plan Policy :

(i) A ceiling to be fixed for imports from abroad during 1948.

(ii) A decision to be taken and announced that the policy of the Central Government is to terminate its dependence on imports at the earliest possible date.

(iii) Out of the quantities actually imported from abroad, not less than a specified quantity to be retained by the Central Government as an "Emergency Reserve".

(iv) The Central Government to determine, in agreement with the Governments of surplus provinces and States, a "Basic Export Quota" for each. The Provincial (or State) Government concerned to accept responsibility for procuring and making available this "Basic Export Quota" during 1948, and to endeavour to make available as much grain as possible in the form of "Supplementary Export Quotas".

(v) The Central Government to determine, after consultation with the Governments of deficit Provinces and States, the "Ceiling Import Quotas" to be made available to each during 1948. Decision to be taken and announced that the "Ceiling Import Quota" will not be exceeded during 1948. The Government of the deficit Province or State concerned to accept responsibility for management of its food affairs, without making larger demands on the Centre and to endeavour to reduce its requirements from the Centre as much as possible.

IV. Fixation Of Import Ceiling

The ceiling referred to earlier under Item III (i) has been communicated separately and confidentially to the Ministry of Food.

V. Fixation Of Reserve

The reserve referred to earlier under Item III (iii) has been communicated separately and confidentially to the Ministry of Food.

VI. Fixation Of "Basic Export Quotas" And "Ceiling Import Quotas"

Recommended figures for "Basic Export Quotas"

and "Ceiling Import Quotas" referred to earlier under Item III (iv) and (v) to be as follows :

Basic Export Quotas	(Figures in thousand tons)
Coorg	12
Assam	50
Central Provinces	150
Orissa	150
Indian States	120
	482

Ceiling Import Quotas	
Bihar	0
West Bengal	150
Madras	150
Bombay	350
Central Provinces	50
United Provinces	0
Delhi	120
Miscellaneous Areas	100
Defence Services	80
East Punjab	100
Indian States	400
	1,500

VII. Specification Of Controlled Foodgrains

The following foodgrains to continue to be subject to controls, viz. :

(i) Rice (including paddy).

(ii) Wheat (including atta and flour).

(iii) Millets (including jowar, bajra, and any other millet at present procured and distributed in rationed areas).

(iv) Maize.

Whether or not controls should be retained in respect of gram to be considered further later.

All controls to be removed and complete free trade established in respect of all cereals except those mentioned above and all pulses other than gram.

VIII. Nature Of Controls To Be Retained And Removed In Respect Of Controlled Foodgrains

In order to secure supplies necessary for meeting Government commitments, within the Province (reduced in the manner recommended already) and in order to meet the requirements for export from surplus Provinces, freedom should be given to individual Provinces to use the method of compulsory levy or monopoly purchase in selected districts, or a combination of both; details regarding the assessment and collection of the levy as also the operation of monopoly purchase, to be settled by Provincial Governments with reference to these commitments and other relevant local conditions.

All grain traders, and those grain growers who fall within a category to be defined (so as to cover holders of stocks exceeding 50 maunds of controlled foodgrains), to be licensed, and made subject to the following conditions:

(a) Submission of returns of stocks; and

(b) Anti-hoarding restrictions.

The control of movements across Provincial boundaries to remain. Restrictions on the movement of foodgrains within the Province should generally be removed, excepting in so far as they are necessary in the opinion of Provincial Governments concerned to enable them to complete their purchases.

Apart from the liability to deliver either on a monopoly or a compulsory levy basis, at a fixed price, control over prices to be removed.

A sufficiently high priority on the railways, to be allotted for transport of foodgrains on private account; the quantities of which would be increased through complete decontrol of certain grains and the reduction of Government commitments in respect of controlled foodgrains.

IX. Supplemental Foodstuffs

Meat consumption in statutorily rationed urban areas : A suggestion has been made that arrangements should be instituted for ensuring that some part of his cereal ration is surrendered by a consumer who buys meat, in proportion to the quantity of meat purchased by him. The purpose underlying the suggestion is to secure greater equality among consumers, and to save cereals.

The question whether such supplemental foods as groundnuts, bananas, sweet potatoes, carrots and turnips can be made available at reasonable prices, in such a manner as to bring about a reduction of cereal offtakes, to be also suggested for examination.

FOODGRAINS POLICY COMMITTEE, 1947—FINAL REPORT

Delhi, Manager of Publications, 1948. 70p.

Chairman : Sir Purshotamdas Thakurdas.

Members : Seth Ghanshyam Das Birla; Sir Shri Ram; Dr. V. K. R. V. Rao; Dr. Ram Manohar Lohia; Thakur Phool Singh; Shri Dip Narain Sinha; Shri Lakshmidas Purshotam; Shri Hussain Imam; Shri R. L. Gupta; Shri D. S. Bakhle (resigned); Shri S. Y. Krishnaswamy; Shri D. R. Sethi; Shri D. N. Mahta; Shri N. G. Abhyankar; Shri C. Bali Reddi.

Secretary : Shri R. A. Gopalaswami (resigned, replaced by Dr. B. M. Piplani).

APPOINTMENT

The Foodgrains Policy Committee was constituted under the Ministry of Food vide their letter No. 432/S., dated September 27, 1947.

TERMS OF REFERENCE

To examine the present position in regard to foodgrains in India and the prospective position in the next five years in the light of considerations of production, procurement, imports, distribution and controls, and advise the Government on:

(a) the measures which can be taken to increase domestic production;

(b) the extent to which reliance can and should be placed on imports; and

(c) in the light of the above, the modifications which may be necessary in the Foodgrains Policy so far pursued.

CONTENTS

Foreword; Introduction; Review of the "Grow More Food" Campaign from 1943 to 1947; The Problem of Food Shortage and Potentialities of Development; The Outline of the Revised Food Production Policy and Plan; Subsidiary Foods; Food Policy During the Next Five Years; Appendix; Note by Sir Shri Ram; Note by Dr. V. K. R. V. Rao; Note by Thakur Phool Singh; Note by Mr. Hussain Imam; Note by Shri C. Bali Reddi.

RECOMMENDATIONS

Review Of The "Grow More Food" Campaign From 1943 To 1947

The "Grow More Food" efforts between 1943 and 1947 were inadequate and in most areas lacked the necessary vigour and drive, and the Campaign has not produced the results aimed at.

The restriction of area under jute and cotton has not led to corresponding increase in the production of substitute food crops. We recommend that the Central Government should immediately consult the Provinces and States with a view to examining the advisability of continuing the policy of restriction of area under cash crops in favour of food crops.

If definite results are to be achieved, a radical revision in the present food production policy and machinery is called for.

The Problem Of Food Shortage And Potentialities Of Development

The country should set itself the goal of increasing foodgrain production by 10 million tons annually within the shortest possible time.

An all-sided effort must be made with new vigour and new drive to develop the resources through a clear-cut programme of development backed and supported by necessary finances and organization.

The Outline Of The Revised Food Production Policy And Plan

The development of agriculture must remain primarily the responsibility of the Provinces and States. The activities of the Central Government should be limited to:

(i) the co-ordination of individual plans of the Provinces and States into the framework of a common all-India plan;

(ii) the procurement and allocation of essential supplies to Provinces and States required by them for their own plans; and

(iii) the reclamation of cultivable waste lands.

We recommend a target of 10 million tons increased production. All-sided efforts must be made to secure this target within the shortest possible time.

Every effort should be made to complete the multipurpose projects which are now under the consideration of the Government with utmost vigour and despatch.

The Provinces and States should pay the greatest attention to:

(i) minor irrigation projects such as open-surface wells, bandharas, tanks, inundation channels, etc.;

(ii) development of local manurial resources such as compost and green manure; and

(iii) distribution of improved seeds.

The Central Government should set up a committee of experts to examine in all its aspects the possibility of establishing additional units for the production of suitable types of fertilizers. They should also undertake an immediate survey to prospect, prove and develop the known gypsum and phosphate deposits in the country.

The success of the Food Production Drive will depend on the creation of an effective and adequate organization for the purpose. We recommend the immediate creation of an organization on the following lines:

(i) the establishment of a Central Board of Agricultural Planning to co-ordinate food production plans, to determine priorities and allocate supplies and to examine and approve plans for the reclamation of cultivable waste land;

(ii) the setting up of Provincial Boards of Agriculture to advise the Central Board and the Provincial Governments and to assist the Central Land Reclamation Organization; and

(iii) the setting up of an autonomous Central Land Reclamation Organization, with a capital of Rs. 50 crores to be given by the Central Government, with a full-time Board of Directors to undertake the planning and execution of land reclamation projects.

Subsidiary Foods

There is scope for the extension of area and production under high-yielding tuber crops like potatoes and sweet potatoes.

Encouragement should be given to increase the production of potatoes and sweet potatoes on suitable uncultivated lands in all Provinces and States.

We recommend that the exploratory work in regard to the development of deep-sea fishing and a concentrated programme to develop inland fisheries should be given priority in the Central and Provincial food production plans.

Food Policy During The Next Five Years

The dependence of the country on the imports of foodgrains should be terminated as early as possible.

Steps should be taken to terminate all need for imports after a period of not more than five years.

The imports of foodgrains should continue to be a monopoly of the Government during the five-year period.

A minimum reserve of a million tons in wheat and rice should be maintained throughout the five-year period of the first Food Production Plan.

An urgent enquiry should be made into the desirability of setting up an autonomous executive organization to handle the foodgrains imports under Government auspices.

EXPERT COMMITTEE ON THE FINANCIAL PROVISIONS OF UNION CONSTITUTION, 1947—REPORT

Delhi, Manager of Publications, 1950.

Chairman : Shri Nalini Ranjan Sarkar.
Member : Shri V. S. Sundaram.
Member-Secretary : Shri M. V. Rangachari.

APPOINTMENT

The Expert Committee on the Financial Provisions of Union Constitution was appointed on December 5, 1947, by the President of the Constituent Assembly to examine and report on the Financial Provisions of the Constitution Act.

TERMS OF REFERENCE

I. To examine, with the aid of the memoranda on the distribution of revenue between the Centre and the Provinces sent by the Government of India and the Provinces, the existing provisions relating to finance and borrowing powers in the Government of India Act, 1935, and their working during the last 10 years and to make recommendations as to the entries in the lists and sections to be embodied in the new Constitution.

The following points shall, in particular, be kept in view in making the recommendations:

(a) How are taxes to be allocated between the Centre and the Units as regards legislation, levy and collection?

(b) Which are the Federal taxes

(i) whose net proceeds are to be retained entirely by the Centre;

(ii) whose net proceeds are to be entirely made over to Units; and

(iii) whose net proceeds are to be shared between the Centre and the Units?

(c) On what principles the taxes mentioned in (b) (iii) are to be shared between the Centre and the Units?

(d) What is to be the machinery for determining the shares, e.g., whether a Financial Commission should be appointed immediately after the enactment of the Constitution to report on the principle of sharing and their application to be brought into effect when the Constitution comes into force; and whether the same or a similar Commission should review these principles and their concrete application periodically, say, once in five years?

II. What should be the principles on which Federal grants should be made to the Units in future? What should be the machinery for the determination of such grants : Could the same Financial Commission as is referred to in I (d) above act as the machinery for this purpose also, or should it be a different one?

III. How could the Indian States be fitted into this general system as far as possible on the same terms as Provinces? Should a time lag be provided for their being so fitted in?

IV. On the assumption of financial responsibility for Defence, Foreign Affairs and Communications on behalf of the Indian States under arrangements for accession to the Federation, what special financial arrangements, if any, are necessary between the acceding States and the Federation?

V. Should the existing rights of the Indian States as to Federal taxes now levied by them be acquired on payment of compensation?

VI. How far is it feasible, on the centralization of all Customs levied at the Federal frontiers, to permit Indian States affected by such centralization to retain such portion of the Customs so levied at their frontiers as might be attributed to consumption in the States, etc.?

[A review of the existing agreements between the Centre and certain important Indian States as regards maritime Customs, exercises, etc., may be of value in this connection.]

VII. Some Provinces have claimed a large percentage of the income-tax to be made over to them than under the existing system. Does this claim merit consideration; if so, to what extent?

VIII. A suggestion has been made that the Centre should be allocated only the excise on specified commodities; the rest of the field of excise being left to the Provinces to tap according to their needs. Would this be possible without any material detriment to Federal revenues?

IX. On the basis that the residuary powers are vested in the Centre in the new Constitution so far as the Provinces are concerned, and in the States so far as the States are concerned, is it necessary that any additional specific taxes should be entered in the Provincial List, and, if so, what?

X. Is it necessary to make any modifications in the existing provisions as regards procedure in financial matters contained in Sections 33 to 37 and 78 to 83 of the Government of India Act, 1935?

XI. A large number of Indian States at present derive substantial revenues from land Customs levied at the frontiers between their limits and those of neighbouring States or Provinces. One of the fundamental rights already adopted by the Constituent Assembly is to remove all internal barriers in regard to trade between Unit and Unit. Could these land Customs be done away with either immediately or over a period of years, and, if so, should any prejudice caused thereby to the finances of particular States be compensated and in what manner?

[The Committee should kindly indicate clearly which of its recommendations should go into the body of the Constitution and which should be provided for by Federal Law.]

CONTENTS

Report; Terms of Reference; Prefatory Remarks; Brief History of Financial Relations; Present Constitutional Position; Review of Finances of Provinces and the Centre; Claims of Provinces; General Observations; List of Taxes for the Centre and the Units; Shares in Certain Taxes; Taxes on Income; Central Excise Duty; Grants-in-Aid and Subventions; Taxes on Agricultural Income and Property; Division of Proceeds of Revenue Between Provinces; Effect of the Proposals; Finance Commission; Residuary Powers of Taxation; Exemption of Provincial Governments from Taxation; Emergency Provisions; Procedure in Financial Matters; Auditor-General; Borrowing Powers; Problems of Indian States; Summary of Recommendations; Conclusion; Appendix from I to VI.

RECOMMENDATIONS—SUMMARY

No major changes to be made in the list of taxes in the Federal Legislative List as recommended by the Union Powers Committee.

The limit of Rs. 50 to be raised to Rs. 250 for taxes on professions, etc., levied by the local bodies.

Any entry to be made in the Federal Legislative List of a new item "Stock Exchange and Future Markets", etc.

A few minor changes of a drafting nature to be made in the list of taxes in the Provincial Legislative List; and no new items for insertion in the Provincial Legislative List.

The Centre to retain the whole of the net proceeds of the following taxes, viz.

(a) duties of Customs including Export Duties;

(b) tax on capital value of assets, etc.;

(c) taxes on railway fares and freights; and

(d) Central Excise other than on tobacco.

The grant of fixed assignments for a period of years to the jute-growing Provinces to make up for their loss of revenue.

The net proceeds of the following taxes to be shared with the Provincial Governments, viz.

(1) Income-tax, including Corporation Tax;

(2) Central Excise on Tobacco; and

(3) Estate or Succession Duties.

The suggestion that the Centre should be allotted only the excises on specified commodities not accepted.

Federal stamp duties and terminal taxes on goods, etc., to be administered Centrally, but wholly for the benefit of the Provinces.

Larger fixed subventions than now necessary for Assam and Orissa and subventions for limited periods for East Punjab and West Bengal but no precise figures recommended for lack of data.

Grants-in-aid on the Australian model not favoured.

Merging the tax on agricultural income in the Central Income-tax and similarly the Estate and Succession Duties on agricultural property in the similar duties on property in general to be examined in consultation with Provincial Governments and transfers made from the Provincial List of Subjects, if necessary.

Not less than 60% of the net proceeds of Income-tax, including Corporation Tax and the tax on Federal emoluments, to be divided between Provinces in the following manner:

20% on the basis of population, 35% on the basis of collection and 5% as an adjusting factor to mitigate hardship.

Not less than 50% of the net proceeds of the excise on tobacco to be divided between Provinces on the basis of estimated consumption.

Not less than 60% of the net proceeds from Succession and Estate Duties to be divided between the Provinces on the following basis : Duties in respect of real property on the basis of allocation of the property and on the basis of the residence of the deceased and one-fourth on the basis of population.

Net effect of the recommendations, to transfer annually a sum of the order of Rs. 30 crores from the Centre to the Provinces.

A Finance Commission with a High Court judge or an ex-High Court judge as Chairman and four other members to be entrusted with the following functions :

(a) allocation between the Provinces of their shares of Centrally administered taxes assigned to them;

(b) to consider applications for grants-in-aid for Provinces and report thereon; and

(c) to consider and report on other matters referred to it by the President.

The Commission to review the position every five years, or, in special circumstances, earlier.

A tax levied by the Centre under its residuary powers, not to ensure the benefit of a non-acceding State unless it agrees to accede to the Centre in respect of that subject.

Trading operations of Units, as also of Local Bodies, whether carried on within or without their jurisdiction, to be liable to Central Income-tax or a contribution in lieu, but quasi trading operations incidental to the normal functions of the Government not to be taxed.

The President to be empowered in an emergency to suspend or vary the normal financial provisions in the Constitution.

A few minor changes suggested in regard to the procedure in financial matters.

No change to be made in respect of borrowing powers of Units.

Early arrangements to be made for the preparation of regular budgets and the maintenance of appropriate accounts and audit by all acceding States.

States gradually to develop all the taxes in the Provincial Legislative List and correspondingly give up taxes in the Federal List.

Maritime Customs and excises in States to be taken

over by the Centre, the States being compensated therefor, if necessary.

The Indian Income-tax Act to be applied to all the federating States, and 75% of the net proceeds attributable to the States to be divided between them.

A States Commission to be set up with five members with wide knowledge of the financial administration of Provincial, Federal or State Governments.

The States Commission to examine the privileges, immunities, etc., of States and to suggest suitable compensation for the extinction of these rights and liabilities.

States which do not come into the arrangements to pay a contribution to the Centre to be determined by the States Commission.

The interim Constitutional arrangements with the States to be flexible and small States to be grouped together.

Conclusion

Some of our recommendations would need to be embodied in the Constitution while others would be given effect to by the order of the President. We have attempted a draft of the necessary provisions in the Constitution to give effect to the former; and these are set out in Appendix VI.

1948

COMMITTEE ON SECONDARY EDUCATION IN INDIA 1948—REPORT

New Delhi, Ministry of Education, 1948. 11p.
(Bureau of Education, Pamphlet No. 52)

Chairman : Dr. Tara Chand. (In the absence of the Educationals Adviser, Prof. Humayun Kabir, Joint Educational Adviser, was to act as Chairman.)

Members : Shri P. C. Sanyal; Dr. Snehamoy Dutta; Shri Kamta Prasad; Shri D. C. Pavate; Dr. V. S. Jha; Shri D. S. Reddy; Shri S. C. Tripathi; Shri G. C. Chatterji; Rai Bahadur Chuni Lall Sahney; Dr. J. M. Mehta; a representative from Kashmir State; Director of Public Instruction, Mysore; Shri A. Narayanantampi; Shri P. V. R. Rao; Shri K. G. Saiyidain; Mrs. Hannah Sen; Shri K. Zacharia; Principal, St. Mary's Training College for Women, Poona; Shri I. R. Sethi.

Secretary : Dr. (Mrs.) Bina Chatterjee.

APPOINTMENT

The Central Advisory Board of Education at their 14th meeting held in January, 1948, considered the question of Secondary Education in the country. In view of its importance for the educational system as a whole, the Board resolved that (a) a commission may be appointed by the Government of India and (b) make recommendations in regard to the various problems related thereto. The resolution of the Central Advisory Board of Education was endorsed by the All-India Education Conference convened by the Hon'ble Minister for Education in January, 1948. In pursuance of these recommendations the Government of India appointed a committee.

TERMS OF REFERENCE

(1) To examine the aims and objects of Secondary Education as defined in the Report of the Central Advisory Board of Education on Post-War Education.

(2) To determine the period of and gradations in Secondary Education.

(3) To consider the place of the national language and English in Secondary Education.

(4) To consider the different types of Secondary Schools to be established and whether they should be unilateral or multilateral.

(5) To consider the procedure to be adopted for selecting pupils for Secondary Education.

(6) To consider the relation of Secondary Education to Basic Education and University Education.

(7) To consider the nature of the examination to be held at the end of the Secondary Stage and how far it could be utilized for admission to Universities.

(8) To consider the steps to be taken for training an adequate number of teachers with the qualifications necessary and the conditions of their service.

(9) To consider the short and long term measures necessary for giving effect to the proposed system of Secondary Education including methods of instruction, examinations, control and administration and building and equipment.

(10) To consider the special steps to be taken for the growth of leadership both for the Armed Forces and for the civil life.

(11) To consider the financial implications of the proposed system of Secondary Education.

(12) To consider any other matters relevant to the terms of reference.

CONTENTS

Report ; Annexures.

RECOMMENDATIONS

Admission to the degree course should be preceded by a course of Primary and Secondary Education for at least 12 years.

Of the above 12 years, five years should be spent at the Junior Basic Stage, three years at the Senior Basic or pre-Secondary and four years at the Secondary Stage.

The teaching of the Federal language should be started at the end of the Junior Basic Stage and should be compulsory throughout the pre-Secondary Stage, but may be optional thereafter.

English may be an optional subject at the Senior Basic Stage and should be compulsory throughout the pre-Secondary and Secondary Stages, so long as it remains the medium of instruction in the Universities.

The Federal language should become a compulsory subject at the Secondary Stage when English ceases to be the medium of instruction in the Universities.

Secondary Schools should be ordinarily of the multilateral type but where the local circumstances demand, unilateral schools should not be discouraged.

There should be one public examination at the end of the Secondary Stage; the Universities may, for admission purposes, lay down such conditions as they deem fit.

The pay and conditions of service of teachers should be the same as recommended by the C. A. B. of Education. The scales of pay should be revised in the light of the changes that have recently taken place.

Trained Graduates can take charge of the teaching in the first two years of the Secondary Stage but Trained M.A.s should teach in the last two years.

The period of training should not be less than one year and after every five years there should be a refresher course.

Education should be one of the subjects in the University Course of studies.

Provincial Boards should be set up to advise Provincial Educational Authorities on problems connected with Secondary Education.

There should be an All-India Council at the Centre to act as a co-ordinating body for the proposed Provincial Boards.

Youth Movements, Scout Movements, etc., should be encouraged in all schools.

A number of Public Schools may be established to foster the growth of leadership among pupils. Admission to such schools should be governed by merit alone. There should also be provision for scholarships and free places up to 50% of available seats in such schools.

COMMITTEE ON THE WAYS AND MEANS OF FINANCING EDUCATIONAL DEVELOPMENT IN INDIA, 1948—REPORT

Delhi, Manager of Publications, 1950. 78p. (Bureau of Education, Pamphlet No. 64)

Chairman : Shri B. G. Kher.
Members : Dr. B. P. Adarkar; Dr. Tara Chand; Acharya Narendra Deo; Prof. Humayun Kabir; Shri Rustom P. Masani; Shri V. Narahari Rao; Shri N. R. Sarkar; Prof. K. T. Shah.
Secretary : Dr. (Mrs.) Bina Chatterjee.

APPOINTMENT

The outline of educational development of the country has been laid down in the Report of the Central Advisory Board of Education known as "Post-War Educational Development in India" published in January, 1944. This Report has also supplied estimates of the cost of the various programmes and stages of educational development. The practical experience gained since then in the Provinces as well as at the Centre, however, indicates that the recommendations made in the above report require to be modified in certain material respects.

The question of our future programme of education was raised at the 14th meeting of the Central Advisory Board of Education and at the All-India Education Conference held in January, 1948. It was generally agreed that the period of 40 years laid down in the report for including an eight-year course of compulsory education must be curtailed and, if necessary for the purpose, the stage up to which compulsion should be enforced would also be reduced. It was, however, agreed that the period of compulsion would in no case be less than five years, i.e., for the age group 6-11.

The estimates of cost, as calculated in the report, were also out of date. Owing to increased cost of living, basic pay must be higher and dearness and other allowance must also be provided for.

It was decided to appoint a committee to examine the existing financial resources and the programme for educational development for all Provinces and States and to make suggestions to ensure that educational development may not be held up for want of funds.

TERMS OF REFERENCE

(1) To consider in the light of present conditions the finance (recurring and non-recurring) required for the different stages of a comprehensive system of education in India.

(2) To consider the ways and means of raising the necessary finances by means of any or all of the following methods:

- (i) allocation of sources of revenue between the Central and Provincial Governments under the new Constitution; scope and extent of grants from the Central Revenue:
  - (a) to Provincial Governments;
  - (b) for Central All-India Schemes of Development;
  - (c) to Universities and other All-India Institutions;
- (ii) Levy of an Education Cess : Its feasibility and details of its levy, administration and distribution;
- (iii) Educational Loans: Purposes for which educational loans may be raised and the terms on which they should be raised and applied.

(3) To consider any other feasible suggestions for raising the finances for educational development programme.

CONTENTS

Report of the Committee on Ways and Means of Financing Education; Appendix A—Terms of Reference; Appendix B—Extracts from the Memorandum for the Committee on the Ways and Means of Financing Educational Development by N.R. Sarkar, Finance Minister, West Bengal; Appendix II—Note on Educational Finance in the United Kingdom; Appendix III ; Appendix C—Index to Tables: Part I—General; Part II—Compulsory Basic Education; Part III—Post Compulsory and Other Education; Part IV—Technical Education; Part V—Present Cost of Education.

RECOMMENDATIONS

(i) The State must undertake the responsibility of providing at least Junior Basic Education for everybody without, however, detriment to existing facilities for Secondary and Higher Education, Special attention should be given to the provision of such higher studies as will be necessary for increasing the industrial and agricultural potential of the country.

(ii) The Provinces should aim at introducing Universal Compulsory Education for children in the 6-11 age group within a period of 10 years but if financial conditions compel, the programme may be extended over a larger period but in no circumstances should it be given up.

(iii) The basic minimum salary of Trained Basic School teachers should be Rs. 40 per mensem and should on no account be reduced.

(iv) In view of the present emergency, the Committee, with great reluctance, agrees that only for five years, the teacher-pupil ratio may be 1 : 40 instead of 1 : 30, though from the educational point of view, this change would be most undesirable. The ratio of 1 : 30 should be restored earlier if possible, but in any case the position must be reviewed at the end of five years.

(v) In urban areas, where conditions justify, the same school buildings should be used for two shifts provided different teachers are employed in each shift.

(vi) Some increase in the fees in the post-compulsory stage of education, i.e., Senior Basic, Pre-Secondary and above, may be permitted, provided a substantial number of free places are available to meritorious students in straitened circumstances.

(vii) The Government may enact suitable legislation for ensuring that an adequate percentage of the income of all charitable trusts is allocated for expenditure on education provided that the Government may exempt certain specified types of trust, e.g., a medical trust, etc., from the operation of such law.

(viii) Students, after passing their Matriculation or equivalent examination, should, subject to such conditions as may be laid down, be required to serve as teachers for Adult Education for a period of at least six months and the Government may enact necessary legislation for the purpose.

(ix) Voluntary efforts should be encouraged for meeting the capital and recurring cost of education and voluntary organizations should be induced to run educational institutions with such assistance from the Government as may be feasible.

(x) Wherever conditions permit, loans should be raised for meeting the capital cost or such part thereof as may be necessary.

(xi) A fixed percentage of Central and Provincial Revenues—about 10% of the Central and 20% of the Provincial—should be earmarked for education by the respective Governments.

(xii) About 70% of the expenditure on education should be borne by the Local Bodies and Provinces and the remaining 30% by the Centre.

(xiii) All contributions for education approved by the Provincial or Central Government should be exempted from income-tax.

(xiv) The expenditure incurred on education by industrial or business concerns should also, if approved by the Provincial or Central Government, be treated as establishment expenses for purposes of income-tax.

WEST COAST MAJOR PORT DEVELOPMENT COMMITTEE REGARDING THE POSSIBILITY OF SITING A MAJOR PORT ON THE COAST COVERED BY KATHIAWAR AND CUTCH, 1948—REPORT

Delhi, Manager of Publications, 1949. Maps, 14p.

Chairman : Shri Kasturbhai Lalbhai.
Members : Shri N. S. Sen; Shri S. N. Haji; Shri K. Mitter; Shri J. B. Murray; Shri D. Shankar.
Secretary : Shri V. V. Bhide.

APPOINTMENT

The West Coast Major Port Development Committee was constituted under the Ministry of Transport vide their Resolution No. 19-P (53)/47 dated February 17, 1948.

TERMS OF REFERENCE

I. (a) Whether a deep-sea port on the stretch of the coast covering Kathiawar and Cutch for the accommodation of ships of large size and tonnage at all seasons of the year is required;

(b) if so, where it should be sited, having regard to construction and maintenance costs, allied transport developments, possibilities of developing existing ports and the needs of the entire area to be served.

II. (a) Whether a deep-sea port between Murmugao and Cochin for the accommodation of ships of large size and tonnage at all seasons of the year is required;

(b) if so, where it should be sited, having regard to economy of construction and maintenance of the port and allied transport developments required and having regard to the needs of the entire area; also what measures are necessary for establishing it;

(c) What improvements are necessary in communications to the existing ports; also what other measures should be taken for the development or provision of additional facilities in these ports as may be found necessary or desirable.

CONTENTS

First Term of Reference I (a); The Necessity of Having a Major Port (Hinterland; Length of Coast Line; Loss of Karachi; Congestion in Bombay; Relief to Rail Congestion; Traffic Potential); Significant Events; Definition of Major Port; Ship Turn-round; First Term of Reference I (b); Method of Approach; (A) Needs of Entire Area, Estimated Traffic, Railway Connections, Ability to Meet Growth in Traffic, Area Reserved for Development, Land Appreciation; (B) Marine Conditions; (C) Information on Existing Ports; (D) Rail Distances to Hinterland; (E) Visits to Ports; Investigation of Alternative Sites; Ports on the West and South Coasts of Kathiawar; The Gulf of Cambay; Bhavnagar; Port Albert Victor; Cambay; Dholera; The Gulf of Cutch; Navlakhi; Port Bedi; Port Okha; Sika; Salaya; Kandla; Other Possible Sites; Advantages and Disadvantages of Kandla; Future of Minor Ports; Summary of Recommendations; Implementation: (A) Major Ports; (B) Development of Bhavnagar Port; Conclusion; Appendices A to J.

RECOMMENDATIONS

The need for a major port is immediate and imperative.

The major port should be sited at Kandla.

All the existing ports of Kathiawar should be placed under one Port Commission.

A concentrated effort must be made to get better dredging results at Bhavnagar so as to maintain an adequate depth of water at the berths.

After satisfactory dredging results have been obtained, one extra berth should be constructed, so that Bhavnagar can, to some extent, serve the area marked as Zone "B" in Appendix "G".

INCOME-TAX INVESTIGATION COMMISSION, 1948--REPORT

Delhi, Manager of Publications, 1949. 276p. 2 parts.

Chairman : Sir Srinivasa Varadachariar.
Members : Justice G. S. Rajadhyaksha; Rao Bahadur V. D. Mazumdar.
Secretary : Rao Sahib H. S. Ramaswami.

APPOINTMENT

The Income-tax Investigation Commission was constituted under the Government of India on February 28, 1948.

TERMS OF REFERENCE

(a) To investigate and report to the Central Government on all matters relating to taxation on income, with particular reference to the extent to which the existing law relating to, and procedure for, the assessment and collection of such taxation is adequate to prevent evasion thereof; and

(b) To investigate any cases referred to it under Section 5 and report thereon to the Central Government.

CONTENTS

Part I : Terms of Reference; The Background—Recent History of Income-tax Law in India; Recent History of Income-tax Administration; The Scope of the Reference—Some Suggestions Considered; Some Preliminary Steps Taken by the Commission; Recommendations; Substantive Provisions; Procedural Sections; Miscellaneous Recommendations; Administration; Summary of Recommendations.

Part II : Investigation Reports on Individual Cases.

RECOMMENDATIONS

Residents And Non-Residents

A radical change is both necessary and justified in the treatment by the Indian Income-tax Law of persons resident in the Indian States. Arrangements, legal or political, should be made so as to bring into the category of "residents" for the purpose of the Indian Income-tax Law at least such of the residents of the

Indian States as have business connections or sources of income in the Indian Union. So far as it concerns the assessment of persons, who derive taxable income from both the Union Territory and the State Territory, and of Indian residents deriving taxable income from State Territory, it must be arranged that the assessment may be made by the officers of the Indian Income-tax Department, subject to any arrangement between the Union and the State as to the division of the proceeds of the tax. The Assessing Officer should be able to exercise the same powers in the State as he has in the Indian Union for collecting information relevant to the assessment, and enjoy all the other facilities required to make those powers effective. As regards other categories of non-residents, it may be necessary to consider in due course the justification for or propriety of continuing the discrimination made in favour of British subjects and the approximate manner of dealing with residents of French and Portuguese Possessions in India and of Pakistan and Burma and Ceylon, who may have sources of income in India.

The special category of "Not Ordinarily Resident" be omitted.

The abolition of the special provisions relating to persons "not ordinarily resident" may have the effect of imposing a tax liability on some categories of Indians now living abroad in respect of their foreign savings which they may bring with them when they come over to India for good, because some of them may fall within the terms of Section 4 (1) (b) (iii). Appropriate provision should be made to exempt such costs.

Special Officers should be appointed to keep a watch on remittances sent abroad of profits made in India, and they must collect information from Exchange Banks and other Banks as to remittances to foreign countries and scrutinize them to see which of them are remittances in the ordinary course of trade and which are remittances of profits.

The Hindu Undivided Family

Legislation on the lines of Section 10 (4) (b) even in respect of joint family members, except so far as interest on self-acquired or separate funds lent to the family may be concerned.

A mere division in status of a Hindu family governed by the Mitakshara Law will only place such a family in the same position as a Hindu undivided family governed by the Dayabhaga Law. Both can appropriately be assessed as units. A division by *metes and bounds* would be necessary before the family assessment. Perhaps a real demand for division by *metes and bounds*, if not complied with by other members, may create circumstances justifying individual assessment of the sharer who makes such demand.

Section 14 (1)—Effect Of The Decisions

Section 14 (1) may be recast as follows :

"The tax shall not be payable by an assessee in respect of any sum which he receives as a member of a Hindu undivided family out of income in respect of which the family itself has been, or can be, assessed as a unit."

Taxation Of Companies

When 60% of the profits of a non-public limited company has not been distributed as a kind of penal consequence an order has to be made under Section 23-A to the effect that the undistributed portion of the assessable income shall be deemed to have been distributed as dividend, it seems reasonable to provide that such notional distribution shall be subject to the provisions of Section 277-K of the Companies Act. In the case of Banking Companies, some portion of the profit is compulsorily transferable to the Reserve Fund.

Treating Salaries And Loans As Distribution Of Dividends

If it is clear that the Income-tax Officer has power to determine the reasonableness of the amount paid as salary to Directors and other principal persons behind the company in relation to the services rendered, no difficulty arises.

If loans should in certain circumstances be treated as distribution of dividends, they should be taken into account in the application of Section 23-A.

Partnerships

So long as the practice of creating nominal intermediary concerns with a view to show a reduced profit for the principal concern subsists, Income-tax authorities must have power to go behind the document and determine the person or persons into whose pockets the profits of the nominal partnership have gone. It is, therefore, necessary to insist that the production of a deed of partnership should not automatically entitle the person producing it to have it registered by the Income-tax authorities and that registration should not preclude the authorities from going behind the document, if there arises ground for suspicion, and determining who has the real control over the income.

Mutual Associations

The recent decision of the Privy Council in English and Scottish Joint Cooperative Wholesale Society, Ltd., vs. Commissioner of Income-tax, Assam (1948), 2 M.L.J., p. 242, may call for a reconsideration of some of the Indian decisions and the Income-tax Department itself may have to reconsider certain questions in the light of the rationale of the Privy Council judgment.

Life Insurance Companies

The logic of the claim for the full exclusion of the bonus amount, before arriving at the taxable income of a life insurance company on the valuation surplus basis, is not altogether unassailable.

In Rule 2 (d) of the Schedule to the Income-tax Act, the figure 15 be substituted for the figure 12. This will mean that as regards renewal premium the allowance for the expenses will be 15% of such premium instead of 12% as at present. The rest of the rule, viz., that relating to 90% of the first year's premium where the premium-paying period of the policy is 12 years or more and 7½% of the first year's premium multiplied by the number of years for which premiums are payable where the premium-paying period is less than 12 years, will stand.

Mutual Insurance Associations

In view of the decision of the House of Lords in Inland Revenue Commissioners vs. Ayrshire Employers Mutual Insurance Association, Ltd. (1948 I.T.R. Supp. p. 80), it is doubtful whether there can be any "profits" arising out of the business of mutual life insurance associations. The Government must make up its mind whether it is going to treat mutual insurance transactions as transactions yielding profits. If it so decides, it must specifically use charging words to make the surplus arising from such transactions liable to tax, or declare "income" as including, in the case of mutual insurance companies, the surplus arising from transactions with members. This criticism may not apply to taxation of the investment income of the company as interest and not as profits.

Religious And Charitable Trusts

From the observations of Lord Hobhouse in Webb vs. England (1898 A.C. 758) it would seem to follow that the exemption from taxation of income according from property set apart for the benefit of religious and charitable trusts will be available only in cases in which the purpose of the trust substantially relates to anything done within this country. If this view commends itself to the Government, it would be desirable to enact the same clearly by the addition of the necessary words to Section 4, Sub-Section (3), Clause (i).

Collection And Information At Source

The obligation to give verified information on requisition may be imposed on any person who may be assumed or suspected to have made payments of rent, premium, interest, commission, royalty, brokerage, annuity, etc.

Advance Payments And Interest Thereon

If the assessment is not completed before the end of the assessment year, the assessee who has made an advance payment can legitimately claim that he should not be made to suffer for the delay on the part of the Department. In this view it seems to us right to allow interest to the assessee at least at 4% on the deposited amount from the close of the assessment year, except where the completion of the assessment before that date has been prevented by the conduct of the assessee.

Deductions And Allowances

On the question of expenses incurred for business purposes, we recommend that Income-tax Officers may be instructed not to be unduly strict about the amount of expenditure under heads like motor cars maintained and entertainments and amenities provided for the benefit of customers so long as they are satisfied that such amount was actually spent and that no attempt was continuously made to pass off private expenses as business expenses.

Stock Valuation

It may be made compulsory on Auditors to certify the correctness of the stock and not to rely on the certificate of the Manager, and that the Income-tax authorities should be given power to check stock lists at or about the time of their preparation and to enter premises to satisfy themselves that the stock lists are accurate.

Usufructuary Mortgages

We recommend the adoption of the advice given by the Ayers Committee that the income derived by a usufructuary mortgagee of agricultural land be excluded from the definition of "Agricultural Income" in so far as it represents interest payable to him on the mortgage loan.

Premium On Leases

Premia received in connection with leases should be treated as part of the lessor's taxable income.

Unclaimed Balances

We recommend that unclaimed and waived surpluses to the credit of customers, suppliers and employees to the extent they are made up of deductions or allowances previously allowed as admissible expenditure when determining assessable income may be deemed to be profits if they have remained unpaid for over three years. It is not intended to compel the trader or employer to plead limitation.

Superannuation Funds

The provisions of the Indian Act with respect to Superannuation Funds need to be amplified and a general power must be given to the Central Board of Revenue to make rules or regulations as has been given to the Commissioners in the United Kingdom under Section 32 of the Finance Act of 1921. We further suggest that provisions should be made in the Act itself similar to Regulation 8 of Superannuation Funds under the U.K. Act as amended in 1931, as an exception to the proviso to Explanation 2 of the Indian Income-tax Act.

Suitable amendments may be made in the Indian Act restricting the maximum limit to which the contributions by the employee and employer may be made to 25% of the employee's salary.

Super-Tax On Associations

The second proviso to Section 55 should be recast so as to permit an assessee's share in the profits of an unregistered firm or other association being included in his total income even though such profits have suffered super-tax. The assessee should, however, get credit on the analogy of Section 49-B for the super-tax paid by the firm or association in respect of his share of the income of the firm or association.

Avoidance And Evasion

An explanation may be added to Section 16, Sub-Section (3), to the effect that for the purpose of that Sub-Section the word "Child" shall include adopted child, foster child, step-child, illegitimate child and grandchild.

It is desirable to make express provision in respect of shares standing jointly in the name of a person and his wife or his minor child. The appropriate provision will be that where the wife or child became entitled to an interest in the shares without any contribution direct or indirect by or from the estate of the other joint holder (being the husband or ancestor), each of the joint holders must be assessed separately in respect of the dividend in proportion to their beneficial interest in the shares. In other cases, their share of the dividend should also be treated as part of the income of the husband or ancestor, as the case may be.

Bankruptcy And Winding-up

The language of Section 230, Sub-Section (1) of the Indian Companies Act should be amended at least to the extent of allowing preferential payment of one year's assessment if assessed for a period anterior to the winding-up, notwithstanding that the assessment is not made until after the winding-up. Whether the period for which priority could be claimed can reasonably be extended to more than one year is a matter for consideration.

It is desirable also to make express provision for tax leviable in respect of profits (if any) earned after the commencement of the winding-up or bankruptcy.

Submission Of Returns

An Income-tax Officer may require every person to submit a return if his total income in the previous year does not fall short of the maximum amount not chargeable to income-tax by Rs. 500.

Failure to submit a return under Section 22 (1) may be made an offence if the income of the person is found to exceed the maximum amount not chargeable to income-tax by more than Rs. 2,000.

It is desirable to empower the Inspectorate staff to examine the accounts and to take sworn statements from persons whom an Inspector has reasonable grounds to believe to be persons with a taxable income.

Maintenance Of Accounts

Maintenance of accounts should be encouraged by accepting them wherever feasible, unless the defects disclose a desire to conceal profits, or the accounts are so badly kept as to make them useless. The Central Board of Revenue should issue directions in this sense.

Income-tax Officers should have power to :

(1) pay surprise visits to the houses of assessees and their business premises;
(2) search for account books and seize them, if necessary; and
(3) call for succeeding year's account books.

Primary and subsidiary account books should be preserved for a period of at least four years.

Income-tax Officers should have power to call upon Auditors to disclose the names of the businesses whose accounts they have audited.

Best Judgment Assessment

An effort should be made to maintain records of market conditions and of statistical data with regard to the rise of prices and such other matters so that when the time of assessment comes the Income-tax Officer may have some material on which to make as fair an estimate as possible of the profits of the business under assessment.

Penalties

The discretion of the Income-tax authorities to regulate the quantum of penalty should be retained.

With regard to the penalty under Clause (c) of Section 28, the element of *mens rea* should not be done away with altogether. The Clause should be recast on the lines of Sections 329 and 330 of the Codification Committee's draft making a distinction between a person who submits an incorrect return negligently and a person who submits such a return fraudulently. The penalty in the case of the latter may be heavier than in the case of the former.

Imposition of a penalty should not be merely mechanical, and judicial discretion should be exercised in the matter.

Secrecy And Publicity

The principle of secrecy and confidence attaching to the Income-tax proceedings is not to be lightly violated, but it is equally important that these principles should not afford a cloak to the assessee to make reckless statements in order to avoid tax liability with the assurance that such statements will not involve him in any serious consequences.

The proposal of giving wide publicity to persons who are found to have made gross understatements of their income may be dropped.

Cancellation Of Assessments, Revision And Review

Freer use may be made, especially in cases decided under the proviso to Section 13 or under Section 23(4), of the power under Section 27 to cancel assessments, particularly where the Income-tax Officer is satisfied that the true accounts of the assessee are forthcoming at that stage.

Where justice cannot be done by the exercise of the revisional powers under Section 33-A, or by way of rectification under Section 35, a limited power of review may be conferred on the Income-tax authorities similar to that possessed by the Civil Courts on discovery of new material which could not have been produced with due diligence during the original proceedings.

Appeals

There should be a right of appeal, (1) against an order under Section 35 (rectification), and (2) against an order of an Appellate Assistant Commissioner refusing to extend the time for filing an appeal or dismissing an appeal as not filed within time.

There should be a right of appeal against an order appointing a person as an agent of a non-resident.

Stay Of Recovery Proceedings

Specific provision should be made in the Act enabling the Appellate Assistant Commissioner, the Appellate Tribunal, the Commissioner or the High Court to stay the recovery of the tax, penalty or interest pending the disposal of the appeal, application or reference, as the case may be to the extent to which such tax, penalty or interest is in issue before them.

Appellate Procedure

It would be unfair to forbid the production of evidence at the appeal stage, where the assessee had no opportunity to produce the necessary evidence or was not sufficiently informed of the points on which evidence was required to be adduced. But the Appellate Assistant Commissioner should not allow fresh evidence to be brought on record in cases where the relevant material was wilfully withheld by the assessee before the Income-tax Officer. In order to enable the Appellate Assistant Commissioner, or the Appellate Tribunal, to decide whether the evidence was wilfully withheld, the Order Sheet should show what opportunity was given to the assessee to adduce evidence and on what points evidence was required to be produced. Notice under Section 22(4) should indicate with some degree of precision what documents and accounts were required to be produced. All this may be provided for by a statutory rule.

Refunds

It should be possible to expedite the work of refund with some planning and proper supervision. Where the staff is inadequate, its hould be brought to the proper strength required for quick disposal. The Central Board of Revenue might consider if some system on the lines indicated in Para. 125 of the Report of the Departmental Committee on Income-tax in the United Kingdom might not be adopted with profit.

Section 50 may be suitably amended so as to provide that an application for double Income-tax relief in cases falling under Sections 49, 49-A and 49-D may be made within one year from the date of assessment either in India or in a foreign country, whichever is later, in spite of the fact that the period prescribed for making such claims under Section 50 may have expired.

owers Of Income-tax Officers

Income-tax Officers should have powers to gather relevant information, particularly (1) to deal effectively with persons suspected of having black-market dealings; (2) to enter business premises and inspect accounts maintained therein, place identification marks thereon, and make copies therefrom and, if the officer has reason to think that they may not be forthcoming when required, to impound them; (3) to make a search of places where there are reasonable grounds for believing that relevant books and records have been kept; and (4) to call for relevant information from banks and other business houses.

Inspecting Assistant Commissioners

In a large majority of cases, assessments may continue to be made by the Income-tax Officers as at present, but there should be no interference whatsoever by the Inspecting Assistant Commissioner in respect of pending assessments. If a case is of any special difficulty, it would be desirable that the whole assessment should be done by the Inspecting Assistant Commissioner himself by taking advantage of the provisions of Sub-Section (5) of Section 5. Such cases should be investigated by the Income-tax Officer but the assessment should be made by the Inspecting Assistant Commissioner. It should be provided that, from the order of the Inspecting Assistant Commissioner in such cases, appeal shall lie direct to the Appellate Tribunal.

Appellate Assistant Commissioners

The experiment begun in 1938 should be carried forward, and Appellate Assistant Commissioners should be removed from the control of the Commissioners and the Central Board of Revenue, and should be placed under the Appellate Tribunal. Their leave, transfers and postings should be in the hands of the Tribunal.

Appellate Tribunal

Some adequate machinery should be devised, after consultation with the Tribunal, for the reporting of the decisions of the various Branches, and also for the conflict in the decisions being resolved by a Full Bench of the Tribunal.

Whenever a conflict exists between the decisions of two High Courts, it should be within the power of the Tribunal to refer the point of law for the opinion of the Supreme Court, whose decision will be binding on all the High Courts.

The Tribunal should have power to order costs to be paid in any appeal pending before it. It should also have discretion to order that the whole or part of the fees paid by the appellant assessee under Sub-Section (3) of Section 33 be refunded to the appellant, depending upon the degree of success which such appellant has obtained in his appeal.

Miscellaneous

Section 2(11) : It is necessary to link up the option given to an assessee to say when his "previous year" ends under Clause (c) with a similar option under Clause (a) so that the profits of some period of the business may not escape assessment. The option under Clause (c) should be exercisable within 12 months of the setting up of the business.

Section 4(1)(b) : As it has been held that the remittances made during the accounting year cannot be assessed as "profits" of that year, because no "profits" can arise until the accounts are made up at the end of the year, a provision may be added as another explanation after the Explanation (1) to Section 4(1) that where remittances are made to or received in the Indian Union by a person earning income outside the Union, and it is ascertained that the accounts were made up in respect of the year during which the remittance was made, that such person earns a profit in the business carried on by him outside the Union, such remittances made to the extent to which they could have been sent out of the ascertained profits be presumed to have been remitted out of such profits.

In Explanation 2 to Section 4(1), the words "and not being pension payable without India" may be omitted, as there is no longer any need or justification for that exemption.

Section 4-A (b) : It should be safer to insert the expression "in any year" in Sub-Section (v) of Section 4-A, and the Sub-Section may be recast as follows :

> "A Hindu undivided family, firm, or other association of persons is resident in British India in any year in which the control and management of its affairs is not situate wholly without British India."

Section 10(2) (vii) : This Clause should be amended by the inclusion of the words "or furniture" so as to permit allowance being claimed for furniture which has been sold or discarded.

Section 45 : It should be provided either in Section 29 or in Section 45 that the time allowed for payment of tax should be not less than a month.

Administration

Recruitment : Recruitment to the cadre of Income-tax Officers should be made partly directly through the Federal Public Service Commission and partly by promotion from the subordinate ranks.

The proportion of promotions from the subordinate ranks to direct recruitment to the Income-tax Officers' cadre should be one-third to two-thirds and, once a person is promoted to Class I Service by this method, no distinction should be made on account of the method of his recruitment in his future prospects and promotion.

Training Of Officers

The training to be given to Officers directly recruited to the Department should be improved in the direction of giving them greater experience of outdoor work such as Survey and Inquiries and more varied acquaintance with accounts, particularly of important trades and industries.

The training scheme should also include training of non-Gazetted subordinates.

Organization And Distribution Of Work

A change in the duties of the Directorate of Inspection is recommended.

The Directorate might concentrate more on developing and maintaining an Investigation Branch in addition to its present duties. It might also be in charge of special assessment circles.

The designation of the Director might be changed to that of "Chief Commissioner of Income-tax" with a status corresponding to that of the Deputy Chief Inspector of Taxes under the U.K. system.

Jurisdictions of Income-tax Officers should be rearranged so as to provide for multiple Income-tax Officers' jurisdictions in preference to single Income-tax Officers' jurisdiction.

Inspectors And Survey

More importance should be given to Survey than is given at present and the staff of Inspectors may be increased for the purpose, if necessary.

Investigation Branch

The Investigation Branch should be expanded and strengthened.

Equipment

The equipment and furnishings in the Income-tax offices should be improved and better accommodation should be made available for both Income-tax assessees and the offices.

Relations With The Public

The Income-tax Officer must show by his conduct that he is not the tax-grabber he is described to be but a referee standing between the State on the one hand and the tax-payer on the other, with the sole idea and desire that both get a square deal.

Commissioners, Assistant Commissioners, Director of Inspection and the Member of the Board might advertise their tours and arrange them so as to be able to meet Associations and assessees more frequently.

RAILWAY GRAINSHOPS ENQUIRY COMMITTEE, 1948—REPORT

New Delhi, Ministry of Railways, 1948. 48p.

Chairman : Shri Mohan Lal Saksena.
Members : Shri K. Santhanam; Shri Khandubhai Kasanji Desai.
Secretary : Shri K. L. Ghei.

APPOINTMENT

The Railway Grainshops Enquiry Committee was constituted under the Ministry of Railways vide their communique dated February 28, 1948.

TERMS OF REFERENCE

(i) Whether the existing scheme of supplying foodgrains and other commodities to railway employees at concessional rates is fair and equitable as regards categories of staff admitted to the concession, range of commodities, quantities supplied and the rates charged, and whether the organization is efficient and economical as regards procurement, stocking and distribution, and otherwise capable of giving the most satisfactory results;

(ii) Whether the overhead charges are reasonable;

(iii) Whether the existing methods of accounting, inspection and control are adequate;

(iv) Whether the losses that are being incurred are reasonable in the circumstances;

(v) Whether the present system requires to be modified or altered in any respect;

(vi) Whether the present system may be wholly or partially replaced by any other system while retaining all those benefits of the existing scheme to which the workers are reasonably entitled and keeping the cost within the limits which the Railways can afford.

CONTENTS

Introductory (Assembly Debate and Appointment of Committee; Terms of Reference; Tour and Mode of Enquiry; Acknowledgments); Historical Development (Origin and Growth; Review by a Sub-Committee of the Standing Finance Committee for Railways; Further Development and Range of Commodities; Recommendations of the Central Pay Commission; Collective Option by All-India Railwaymen's Federation); Working of Grainshops (Eligibility for Concession—Categories of Staff; The Family; Organization; Procurement; The Retail Shop; Commodities; Corruption); Financial Results (Financial Transaction; Cash Dearness Allowance on Railways; Dearness

Allowance for Other Central Government Employees; Analysis of Loss; Average Loss Per Employee; Overhead Charges); Findings (First Term of Reference; Second Term of Reference; Third Term of Reference; Fourth Term of Reference); Recommendations (Abolition or Limitation; Individual Option; Eligibility for Concession; Future Management; Co-operative Stores; Control by the Railway Board; Conclusion); Appendices I to VI.

RECOMMENDATIONS

There should be no question of retaining the grain-shops as a permanent part of the Railway Administrations, though during the transitional stage the shops may continue to cater only for essential commodities on a uniform basis. Adequate arrangements should be made to ensure regular supplies at all the shops of these articles, the quantity being such as can satisfy any reasonable person.

The new grainshops should supply the essential articles at uniform concessional prices, fixed at a little lower than the average of the present selling prices on Railways, and on scales noted below:

(i) Cereals: Excluding rationed areas workers should be free to take their entire ration in wheat or rice of medium quality. The scale should be increased for the worker himself from 12 oz. (6 chhattacks, to 1 lb. (8 chhattacks) per day with the usual 12 oz. (6 chhattacks) for other adult members of the family including dependants. The distinction between heavy manual workers and others should go. The concessional sale price for wheat and rice should be 2½ annas per seer.

(ii) Pulses: Including gram, not more than three varieties of pulses, common to the area, should be stocked, and each worker should be allowed to take only two. The scale of ration should be rationalized to two seers per unit per month, the employee himself being allowed four seers with a maximum of 12 seers per family. The concessional sale price should be four annas per seer.

(iii) Cooking Oils: Not more than two varieties of cooking oils should be available in any shop and the scale of ration should be two seers per month for the first unit and one seer per additional unit subject to a ceiling of six seers per family. The concessional sale rate should be eight annas per seer.

(iv) Salt: The scale should be one seer per unit with a family limit of five seers per month and the selling rate one anna per seer.

(v) Matches: Six boxes of matches per card per month may be supplied at the rate of six pies per box.

The Purchasing Organization should be improved and simplified. Supplies of wheat and rice should be obtained from the Food Ministry of the Government of India, either out of the imports or out of the purchase made by surplus areas. In the Provinces where this is not feasible, small joint organizations consisting of representatives of the various Railways working in these Provinces should be created for purchasing grains. Pulses, cooking oils and salt should be purchased through open tenders. For this purpose joint Boards of Railways should be created in Bombay, Madras, Calcutta, Lucknow and one or two other places, consisting of Grainshop Officers, Accounts Officers, and two representatives of Labour Unions. Purchase of matches should be arranged for directly by the Railway Board from the factories.

Staff participation in the grainshop management should be secured through a single Grainshop Committee attached to each shop consisting of two nominees of the Railway Administration (to act as Chairman and Secretary) and one elected representative for every 200 (in workshop 500) workers. These Committees should be given powers to decide all matters relating to shops except the appointment of staff, accounts and cash.

A Sub-Committee of the Grainshops Committee should be responsible for checking the quality of articles supplied according to the tender samples.

Non-concessional supplies should not be permitted and in the new grainshop scheme, employees getting a basic pay of Rs. 250 or more should not be entitled to any concessional supplies.

Casual labour, i.e., temporary labour recruited for specific works and specific periods, should be paid at market rates and not given gainshop concession.

No new recruit to the Railway services should be entitled to grainshop concession.

Railway workers should be given individual option to choose either the new grainshops or the dearness allowance admissible to other Central Government employees. If an employee opts for the latter, the option should be taken as final and he should, in no case, be allowed to revert to the gainshop concession. A date should be fixed before which the individual option should be exercised—a period of two months after the acceptance of this scheme by the Government is suggested.

If the exercise of individual options makes the running of a static or a mobile shop in some area impracticable, Railway Administrations should be free to make local arrangements for the supply of prescribed commodities for those who have not opted out or, where this is not feasible, treat them as if they have opted out.

Workers drawing Rs. 50 and less who exercise their option in favour of cash allowance should be given a single lump sum payment, not to be regarded as a permanent addition to the dearness allowance, according to the various areas of dearness allowance as follows:

"X" Area...Rs. 120
"A" Area...Rs. 90
"B" Area...Rs. 60
"C" Area ..Rs. 30

The workers should be entitled to this payment only if the option is exercised within the period stipulated above and if at any future time they have to revert to the cash allowance applicable to other Central Government employees no such payment should be made.

In view of the universal demand of the workers on the Eastern Punjab Railway all grainshops should be immediately closed down and the workers put on the Central Government dearness allowance scales, employees drawing a basic pay of Rs. 50 and less receiving the lump sum payment suggested above.

Earnest efforts should be made to promote autonomous Co-operative Stores confined to particular areas, entirely managed by Railway servants without Railway Administrations having any direct responsibility for them except the provision of premises at nominal rent and a subsidy amounting to not more than half the administration and shop charges for the first three years subject to the Provincial Co-operative Department certifying to their proper working.

M. & S. M. and S. I. Railway Administration should invite the Triplicane Urban Co-operative Stores of Madras to open branches in areas in Madras City now served by the Railway Grainshops.

The Railway Board should keep a close watch and co-ordinate the activities relating to grainshops on railways. Proper disposal of stocks of commodities which are to be discontinued should be ensured so that no avoidable loss occurs.

ADVISORY COMMITTEE FOR HIRAKUD DAM PROJECT 1948—REPORT

New Delhi, Ministry of Works, Mines and Power, 1948. 57p. Charts

Chairman : Shri J. L. Savage.
Members : Shri L. L. MeClellan (not joined); Shri M. Narasimhaiya; Shri S. A. Gadkari.

APPOINTMENT

The Advisory Committee for Hirakud Dam Project was constituted under the Ministry of Works, Mines and Power vide their letter No. D. W. 106 (112) dated March 12, 1948.

TERMS OF REFERENCE

To give advice to the Central Water, Power, Irrigation and Navigation Commission on the Project in general and its technical and other features.

CONTENTS

Letter of Submission; Summary of Recommendations; Part I; Part II; Part III; Enclosures; Figures.

RECOMMENDATIONS

For the design of the reservoir for flood absorption the recommendations of the Consulting Engineer with the Government of India as made in his note dated May 12, 1948 (Enclosure I), be adopted.

The silt observations of 1947 having given higher figures of silt load than assumed in the project report, the silt reserve as now recommended by the Consulting Engineer be adopted and the dead storage level be fixed at 590.0 accordingly.

Taking the flood reserve and silt reserve as under Items 1 and 2 the maximum reservoir level will be R. L. 625.0 (adequate for 100-year flood) and this may be fixed as the reservoir level. The lands coming under submersion will be acquired up to this level.

A free board of 10 ft. be allowed above R.L. 625.0, the top of the dam being R. L. 635.0. A 4-ft-high parapet be provided all along. In the case of 1,000-year flood and 10,000-year flood the free board will be encroached to the extent of 5 ft.

The regulated flood of 780,000 cusecs should be arranged to be disposed of through deep-set sluices adding 10% to 20% extra capacity for gates under repairs, etc.

Two siphons of Ganesa Iyer Volute type be put in as an experimental measure.

The difference of regulated flood between the 10,000-year and 100-year floods, i.e., 830,000 minus 740,000 cusecs, should be provided for through emergency spillway siphons including Ganesa Iyer Volute siphons.

The main dam in the two branches of the river to be of concrete, the right section (which will provide for the necessary penstocks for the power house, locks, fish ladder, etc.) will be 1,570 ft. and the left section (housing the deep-set sluices) will be 2,475 ft.

The main dam on the Kolarikud and Hirakud islands including the deep section in between to be of earth. The remaining length on the left bank will also be of earth. The lengths will be 6,725 ft. and 4,165 ft. respectively.

The sections of the concrete and the earth bund for the main dam as designed be adopted.

The dykes should be of earth as designed; precautions for cut-off and creep walls being taken where the depth of water exceeds 25 ft.

The modified proposals of Mr. Khosla for the power channel be adopted, as they result in economy and efficiency of power operation.

Pending detailed surveys of canals and further investigation, the proposals for irrigation made in the project report be adopted. Under lift irrigation, however, the provision for one-third of the proposed area in the first instance, or, say, 100,000 acres, be made in the estimate. The location and the manner in which this is to be planned to be fully investigated.

The storage in the reservoir earmarked for irrigation will remain unaffected.

The duties proposed for different crops be adopted.

The water rates proposed in the Project Report may be adopted—the position being reviewed at the end of eight years after irrigation commences.

In view of the magnitude of the problem and the period of six years fixed for the completion of work, the question of resettlement and rehabilitation of people that will be dispossessed by submersion of their villages and lands to be taken up at once.

Steps for overhauling the delta irrigation in the Mahanadi Valley to be taken up at once as also the investigation to utilize the continuous supply of 8,000 to 10,000 cusecs in dry weather for extension of rabi crop cultivation and bringing new areas under irrigation.

The proposal of Sir M. Visveswaraya to divert Mahanadi waters to the Chilka Lake with the possible generation of power and irrigation of large tracts in the southern delta should be fully investigated.

To achieve these objects expeditiously a special division under the Central Water, Power, Irrigation and Navigation Commission should be immediately constituted.

Soil surveys in irrigated areas must be carried out soon for purposes of crop planning.

Malaria surveys in the area should be conducted to prepare schemes for preventing increase of malaria incidence.

The present laboratory set up in connection with investigations should be expanded to deal with soil materials, aggregates, cements and concrete.

The questions such as soil conservation, fish culture, industrial survey, agricultural survey should receive attention as a part of the multi-purpose development.

For the development of irrigation in Kharif and Rabi seasons, the Development Committee should pay attention to organize propaganda for better cultivation, research station, agricultural farms, demonstration plots in representative areas.

The question of the levy of water rates and payment of part of additional profits by tenants in lieu of betterment tax should be studied.

Immediate steps should be taken to set up an organization for preparing specifications, details of design, working at schedule of quantities for power house and grid sub-station equipment, etc.

Preparation of papers for calling tenders for power house machinery, switch-gear, transformers, etc., should be taken in hand early.

Design of towers and other structures for extra high tension lines should be undertaken.

Steps to be taken to make arrangements for the manufacture of towers for different voltages in this country.

Installed capacity of six units of 37,500 KW in Power House No. 1 and four units of 24,000 KW in Power House No. 2, giving maximum primary power of 218,000 KW may be catered for, while the secondary power should be generated and the necessary machinery and equipment installed only after the primary power is booked for sale.

Local distribution work should be undertaken by the Government as it is a very profitable concern. Therefore, necessary cost may be provided for in the project.

The navigation question should be taken up at once and investigations of the Dhamra Port pursued with vigour.

The staff engaged on this scheme should be given special concessions in the shape of construction allowance, rent-free quarters, etc., in view of the arduous nature of the work.

The programme of work to complete the work in six years be adopted. Month-by-month programmes for these years should be worked out, before October, 1948, so that a basis may be readily available for the building up of a suitable and adequate organization and collection of equipment.

The project as envisaged should be started at once and pushed through with vigour to completion as it will usher in an area of incalculable benefit to Orissa and open up a vista of great possibilities of industrial expansion and increased food production.

SAILING VESSELS COMMITTEE, 1948—REPORT

New Delhi, Ministry of Commerce, 1949. 62p.

Chairman : Shri C. A. Buch.
Members : Shri M. C. Veerabahu Pillai; Shri B. M. Desai.
Secretary : Shri G. Dattatreya Rao.

APPOINTMENT

The Sailing Vessels Committee was constituted under the Ministry of Commerce vide their letter No. 19 M. IV (2) 48 dated May 24, 1948.

TERMS OF REFERENCE

To examine and report on the steps necessary to ensure the fullest utilization of Country Craft (Sailing Vessels) to sustain and develop the economy of the country and *inter alia*, to prevent wasteful competition between country craft and steamers, due regard being paid to the different needs served by the two classes of transport.

CONTENTS

Prefatory; Procedure of Enquiry; The Set-up of the Trade; Organization of the Industry and Rationalization of Traffic; The Sailing Vessel Defined; Registration of Vessels; Measurement of Vessels and Load Line; New Construction; Seamen; Jettisoning; Auxiliary Power; Port Facilities; Organization of the Industry; Economic Structure; Wages Structure—Seamen; Reservation—Ports—Commodities; General; Conclusion; Recommendations; Appendix A to F.

RECOMMENDATIONS

Legislative

The Control of Shipping Act, 1947, as amended by the Control of Shipping (Amendment) Act, 1948, should be further amended to define "SHIP" 2 (e) "to include sailing ships as are employed in the "Coasting Trade" as defined in this Act 2 (a) as also in adjacent and overseas trade of India". A coasting vessel under sail, so long as the extant smallish vessels are in commission in the Coasting Trade, shall be of 40 tons or over, subject to such vessel being of a type and equipment which, in the opinion of the Government, would render the vessel fit to be regarded as a "Coasting Vessel". This limit ultimately should be raised to 60 tons or over.

A Special Officer under the Director-General of Shipping, not below the existing rank of an Assistant Controller of Shipping, should be appointed and he should be declared a "Shipping Authority" for shipping under sail, as defined under the above Act 2 (f) and be vested with the responsibility and authority of taking all such steps as would assist to ensure a more evenly balanced economy in the traffic under sail.

The Customs and Port Officers at various ports as are frequented by sailing ports as are frequented by sailing ships shall represent the authority of the above Officer within their own jurisdictions as Regional Officers (Sails) and shall have the responsibility and authority to carry out all such directives as may be issued to them by the said Officer. The Regional Officers (Sails) also shall be assisted by Local Advisory Committees representing all direct and allied interests in the industry. These Local Advisory Committees may be invited to send delegates to the Annual or periodical meetings of the Central Advisory Committee.

Suitable amendments should be enacted whereby sailing vessels may come within the operation of the relevant Section of the Indian Merchant Shipping Act of 1923 especially with regard to surveys, safety appliances, etc., or to exempt partly or wholly such sailing vessels which are fitted with auxiliary engines from the overall operation of Sections like Section 3 of that Act.

Trade

No individual or firm should be allowed to do business as a "sailing ship broker" or broker-cum-agent unless he is in possession of a licence. The licence may be made valid for a period not exceeding three years after which it may be renewed on application from the holder.

Such licences shall be valid only for the port or ports or districts specified therein.

Traffic—Jettisoning

All "Protests" involving loss of life or cargo or damage to cargo by jettisoning or otherwise shall be noted and lodged only with the Assistant Controller of Shipping (Sails), or with his corresponding Regional Officers at various ports and not before a Notary Public; and the Master of the vessel or his agent lodging such Protest shall, along with the Note of Protest, lodge the following papers with the authority concerned, namely:

(a) a Bond countersigned if so demanded by the authority concerned by a scheduled bank or by two approved sureties or a personal bond by the owner or his local Agent for an amount equivalent in cash to 25% of the damage assessed on the cargo or to the invoice value of the cargo lost;

(b) the ship's licence;

(c) the Master's licence and, if the ship carries a Mate, the Mate's licence.

The Ship

Every vessel that is classed on the Register as a "Coasting Vessel" which shall include a vessel meant for adjacent or overseas trades shall have to be in possession of a licence issued under the Control of Shipping Act (1947) or any other enactment in that behalf that may come into force hereinafter.

All existing vessels of 40 tons or over and under the Indian Flag may be granted a licence as a "Coasting Vessel" but no vessel, whose keel has been laid after these recommendations become operative, shall be granted such licence unless its tonnage is 60 or over. Such licence shall not be granted to vessels which are specially designed to act as barges or lighters and are not deemed by competent Government authority to be fit to move out of sheltered waters for the time being or permanently.

Every Coasting Vessel, irrespective of its size or type, shall carry such life-saving appliances as are prescribed from time to time by a competent authority. Failure to do so shall be liable to result in suspension or cancellation of a ship's licence as well as the licences held by the Master and the Mate of the vessel and to penalties as may be prescribed by the Government under relevant Sections of the Indian Merchant Shipping Act.

The licences of Master and/or Mate are liable to be cancelled if the vessel under their charge, whether under way or at anchor, whether in port or on the high seas, fails to display the prescribed regulation lights from sunset to sunrise, or such signals as are prescribed during hours of daylight.

A consolidated Register for all sailing vessels registered at any Port of Registry in India shall be maintained in the Directorate-General of Shipping—port by port—and in serially progressive numbers, containing all the particulars referred to in paragraph 36, 38 and 39 above and excerpts from this and regional registers should be made available to the public for a prescribed fee.

The owners and builders of all future coasting vessels shall have the construction of their vessels inspected and supervised by approved shipwrights and surveyors appointed by the Government for the purpose at every such stage of construction as may be prescribed.

Floating Personnel

Every Master of a Coasting Vessel not under 40 tons in existence at present, who has acted as a Master of a Coasting Vessel for at least 12 months precedent to this recommendation being operative, shall be issued, against a prescribed fee, a "Master's Licence", which licence shall be duly endorsed with the following or similar words, namely:

"This licence is by no means any testimony of the ability or competency of the holder to be the Master of a Coasting Vessel under sail but is only to establish his identity. Without this licence he is disqualified to take charge of a vessel as Master. It is liable to be endorsed, suspended or cancelled if the holder thereof is found guilty of any breach of regulations regarding the vessel under his charge, or its navigation and/or of any negligence or misdemeanour whatsoever as Master of the vessel."

The Government should actively encourage the introduction by official or non-official administrations in the country, of pre-sea or post-sea training in nautical subjects especially in scholastic and technical institutions and Fishery Schools, more so in coastal regions by sanctioning Central and/or provisional grants and scholarships to such schools or institutions who undertake to impart theoretical and/or practical instruction in these subjects.

Seamen employed under sail on Coasting Vessels, or on vessels plying in overseas trades should by right be regarded as Merchant Navy Personnel and be included in all welfare schemes like Seamen's Societies, Homes, Clinics, Clubs, Cloth and Ration Shops, etc.

Port Facilities

The Government should direct all such quasi-official and official administrations like Port Fund Committees, Port Administrations as also Governments of Maritime Provinces to make adequate provisions in ports under their jurisdiction for sufficiently deep, lighted and buoyed channels, anchorage, quay space, etc., for sailing vessels, for expeditions and economic working of cargo, docking and repair facilities, etc., and to equip a few minor ports with facilities like loading and unloading berths alongside quay walls with adequate linear footage, cranes, warehouses and/or all-weather sheds (and sidings where Railways exist) and a fair sized drydock or slipway about 100 ft. by 30 ft. to be used by sailing vessels, as also ample sea-room and deep enough anchorage for at least six ships of 100 tons or over. The minimum depths in approach channels, anchorage area and alongside quay walls should be 12 to 15 ft. at all stages of tides.

Orissa may be encouraged to open out at least two good minor ports with port facilities for the use of sailing vessels as described above. Similarly ports may be opened and equipped in the Province of West Bengal as well.

THE ENVIRONMENTAL HYGIENE COMMITTEE, 1948—REPORT

Delhi, Ministry of Health, 1950. 208p.

Chairman : Dr. B. C. Das Gupta.
Members : Shri P. C. Bose; Shri R. S. Mehta; Shri N. V. Modak; Shri A. V. Raman (resigned); Shri K. Subrahmanyan.
Secretary : Shri G. C. Mitroo.

APPOINTMENT

The Environmental Hygiene Committee was constituted under the Ministry of Health vide their letter No. F. 3-22/48—PR, dated June 16, 1948.

TERMS OF REFERENCE

(i) Investigation of the whole field of Environmental Hygiene with special reference to:

(a) town and village planning;
(b) housing, urban and rural;
(c) water supply;
(d) general sanitation, including conservancy and drainage;
(e) prevention of river and beach pollution;
(f) control of insect vectors of diseases; and
(g) regulation of certain trades, industries and occupations dangerous to health and offensive to the community.

(ii) The framing of a programme of development for the consideration of the Government based on an examination of the recommendations of the Health Survey and Development Committee regarding Environmental Hygiene and of the Five-Year Plans of Provinces.

In framing the programme, the Committee should take into consideration the following factors:

(a) the programme will require to be placed on a basis of adequate and comprehensive planning while at the same time taking into account the financial capacity of the Governments to implement the programme. The Committee should, therefore, suggest, wherever possible, ways and means by which the funds necessary for implementing their proposals can be found;

(b) the need for promoting the training of an adequate number of technical personnel of various categories required for a modern programme of environmental improvement and for promoting the production of the necessary equipment. The Committee should make specific recommendations in this regard;

(c) in view of the varying resources of the Provinces, the measures required to assist the less favoured Provinces so that the programme can be implemented on as uniform a basis as possible.

(iii) To investigate the advantages of composting in preference to other methods of disposal of urban refuse and make suitable recommendations.

CONTENTS

Introduction; The Problems Before Us; Housing (New Housing Required; Building Materials; Methods and Costs; Standards of Healthful Housing; Positive Plans for New Housing; Housing of Government and Municipal Employees; Housing of Industrial Labour; Housing Co-operative Societies; Sub-standard Houses); Town and Village Planning (Urban Planning; Planning in Villages; Regional Planning; Improvement Trusts; Legislation and Administration); Water Supply (Survey of Existing Position; Plans Drawn up by Other Committees; A Positive Plan; Standard; Materials Required; Personnel and Organization; Finance); Measures for the Hygienic Collection and Disposal of Community Wastes (Sewerage; Sullage Drains and Open Drains; Sewage Disposal; Public Cleaning; Disposal of Refuse; Collection and Disposal of Excreta in Unsewered Areas; Materials; Personnel and Organization); Food, Drink and Milk (Processing Establishments; Milk and Other Farms; Storage Establishments; Retailing Establishments; Food Sanitation in Pilgrim Centres and Alms Houses); Light and Air (Building Bye-laws about Windows; Smoke and Dust Control; Ventilation); Congregations (Camps, Fairs and Festivals; Schools; Places of Public Resort; Public Transport); Pollution of Streams, Lakes and Beaches; Industrial Environment; Hygiene of the Rural Environment (Water Supply; Excreta Disposal; Housing; Approaches; Planning; Food (Sanitation; Organization); Control of the Environment of Insect and Animal Vectors of Disease (Mosquito Control; Rat Control; Fly Control; Control of Sandflies, Fleas, Ticks, Bugs, Lice, etc.); Design and Construction of Medical and Health Centres; Some Aspects of Environmental Hygiene not Covered in Previous Chapters (Prisons; Disposal of the Dead; Barber Shops and Saloons; Dhobi Ghats; Disinfection Stations; Plumbing); Constructional Materials (Bricks; Coal; Lime; Cement; Iron and Steel;

Doors and Windows; Timber; Tiles and other Roofing Materials; Cast-iron Pipes; Galvanized-iron and Wrought-iron Pipes; Ceramics; Chlorine; Alum; D.D.T.; Other Chemicals; Planning for Production; Transport); Organization and Administration); Training of Personnel (Public Health Engineers; Public Health Engineering Subordinates; Town Planners; Plant Operators; Medical Health Officers; Sanitary Inspectors; Specialists in Public Health Chemistry, Biology, etc.; Industrial Hygienists); Finance (Training; Organization; Materials; Water Supply; Measures for Hygienic Collection and Disposal of Community Wastes; Housing and Town Planning; Congregations; Pollution of Streams, Lakes and Beaches; Industrial Environment; Rural Environment; Control of Insect and Animal Vectors of Disease); Summary; Appendix I to VII.

RECOMMENDATIONS

Housing

It is estimated that 2.84 million dwelling units should be built in five years to meet the housing shortage in urban areas; of these one million will be for displaced persons and 1.84 million for meeting the requirements of normal increase in population. For this purpose, at least a quarter of the steel and cement production, coal, transport, etc., should be allocated for house building in the country and, at the same time, steps should be taken to increase the production of steel, cement, lime, bricks, etc.

It may be natural to think of temporary structures to afford quick relief, but we consider that it is false economy for Governments and public authorities to go in for mud walls, bamboo matting and thatched roofs for houses, even though their initial cost may be one-fourth or one-fifth of the cost of the conventional houses. The cheap house is suitable only under the fond care and maintenance of the rural owner. It is unjustifiable when built out of public funds.

The best way to meet housing shortage is to develop "satellite towns" and "neighbourhood units" to promote self-sufficiency and mixing up of social groups for housing populations of 10,000 to 20,000 instead of adding on the fringe of an existing town.

Provision of water supply and latrines is indispensable in the practical maintenance of standards of decent living; anyone who lets a house to a family for occupation without these facilities should be punished by law.

A house should be built at least as a two-roomed structure apart from the kitchen, the bath, etc., according to specified standards, even if exigencies require that it should be occupied by two families till the shortage is relieved. If a single-room house is absolutely unavoidable, it should have a floor space in the living room of at least 200 sq. ft. and there should be a separate kitchen of at least 50 sq. ft.

Research should be undertaken in institutions of technology and engineering to evolve new designs, materials and methods of construction with a view to promoting better fulfilment of the basic principles of healthful housing at lower costs.

Positive plans for new housing particularly as a "Public Utility" through the agency of Public Housing Corporations are detailed in paras 36-37 of Chapter III. If this is done, the problem of housing the lower-income groups will be largely solved without straining the finances of the State.

In big cities like Calcutta, Bombay, Delhi and Madras, the Government should provide quarters for at least 60% of their employees. The Government should also provide accommodation for their employees in small towns of less than 10,000, where it is extremely difficult to find suitable rented accommodation.

The Government should provide accommodation for all employees in essential services.

In fixing minimum rates of wages for industrial workers under the Minimum Wages Act, 1948, either a house or an allowance equivalent to the economic rent for the minimum standard house should be given.

The Government should adopt a firm attitude with respect to industrial housing and divert the Excess Profits Tax towards solving this problem.

The Central Government should enact a law of compensation to enable Provinces and Improvement Trusts to proceed with slum clearance schemes without being overwhelmed by claims for compensation.

New accommodation for slum dwellers must be found before a slum is cleared. In the present state of housing shortage, all slum clearance schemes should be suspended for five years—till an adequate number of new houses are built.

Often a place becomes a slum on account of substandard arrangements for water supply, drainages, latrines and refuse collection service. For the next five years, instead of going through dilatory procedures for finding the owner of a slum and compelling him to provide these amenities, the Municipality should be enabled to effect these improvements at its expense, one half of the cost being met from Municipal Funds and the other half from a Special Government Grant which may be made for this purpose.

Municipalities should be vested with summary powers to carry out such improvements and recover the cost from the owner as the first charge on the property.

A civic survey should be conducted in respect of

sub-standard houses in each urban area spread over two years.

In villages, the main defects in houses are the absence of latrines and water supply. The latrine should be provided by the house-owner and the water supply by the Government.

Town And Village Planning

Town and village planning should always precede housing.

When the improvement needed is of considerable magnitude, a small executive body like an Improvement Trust is better suited to carry it out.

Those provinces which have no Town Planning Acts should enact them immediately. Existing Acts in some Provinces are inadequate. They should be amended.

The Provincial Town Planner should be on the staff of the Ministry of Health as an Adviser. In the practical execution of large housing projects, an engineer with knowledge of public health engineering, including town planning, will be more suitable than a pure town planner to direct and execute the work.

Provincial Housing Boards may be established as statutory bodies—with the Chief Public Health Engineer as Chairman, a Financial Adviser, and two or three members chosen for their administrative ability and integrity and appointed for a term of years. These Boards may be authorized to float loans at ⅛% above the Government borrowing rates and use them for land acquisition. They may be authorized also to license Public Housing Corporations or to engage in housing activities themselves.

Water Supply

Only 16% of the total number of towns in India have protected water supplies, which serve 6.15% of the total population or 48.5% of the urban population. In the rural areas and smaller urban areas the water supply continues to be as unsatisfactory as it was when the Health Survey and Development Committee reported. There is very little protection in the water supply, as it is drawn from sources open to contamination of all sorts.

Recommendations for a modest five-year plan in respect of water supply, taking into consideration the urgency of other post-war plans and the scarcity of money and materials, are:

(a) To install new water supplies and improve existing water supplies in all towns of over 50,000 to check the rapid deterioration of urban water supplies and the programme already set out for new housing;

(b) To install protected water supplies in all permanent projects for the accommodation of displaced persons;

(c) To provide protected water supplies in all permanent pilgrim centres in India;

(d) To provide protected water supplies to at least 75% of the people in districts where cholera death rate has been 100 or over per 100,000 per annum during the last 10 years;

(e) To provide protected water supplies in areas of greater water scarcity;

(f) To develop and maintain water supplies in areas covered by Health Centres where intensive personal and impersonal health services are being developed.

In addition, we should:

(1) Establish plant control laboratories.

(2) Organize the training of plant operators.

(3) Organize public health engineering services on a strong and sound basis in the Health Ministries and to entrust them with the responsibility for design, construction and maintenance of public health engineering works (Impersonal Health Services).

(4) Plan for gradual extension of protected water supplies to 90% of the population in 40 years.

The greatest handicap to the construction of waterworks today is the lack of materials. Our short-term plans envisage an expenditure of about Rs. 26 crores a year for five years on water supplies. At least Rs. 14 to 18 crores a year will be spent on cast-iron pipes. We cannot and should not import cast-iron pipes from abroad owing to the urgent need for conserving foreign exchange. The Government should therefore take immediate steps to put up cast-iron pipe factories with a capacity of 12,000 to 15,000 tons per month.

The larger waterworks will require steel pipes. Even smaller waterworks may use steel pipes on account of economy and ease of transport.

About 40,000 tons of steel pipes per annum can be consumed for water supplies. Production of steel sheets and manufacture of steel pipes should be promoted by the Government on this basis.

Galvanized-iron and wrought-iron tubes are essential for rural water supplies from wells and tube-wells, and equally so for house connections in urban supplies. They are not manufactured in India. A tube mill with about 15,000 to 20,000 tons capacity per annum should be set up by the Government within two years.

The Government should also facilitate the import of larger sizes of pumps and motors for water supplies.

Present consumption of chlorine for water purification is probably about 300 tons per annum. When our Five-Year Plan is implemented, this consumption will be about 800 tons per annum. Chlorine is an important chemical, used for general public health work, for bleaching in textiles and paper manufacture and for the manutacture of D.D.T. Production of chlorine should therefore be stepped up immediately.

Alum is also used in water purification. Its annual production is about 6,000 to 7,000 tons in India. The demand for this chemical will probably be about 12,000 to 15,000 tons per annum, when our short-term plan for water supplies is implemented. Increased production of alum should be organized by the Government.

Many other chemicals may be required for water supplies. Specifications should be standardized as far as possible for their supply.

The capital cost of water supplies in rural areas should be met entirely by Provincial Governments. The cost and organization for the maintenance of these supplies should also be provided by them through their public health engineering department. If the Local Board engineer is made answerable to the Chief Public Health Engineer, he may be charged with the duty of maintaining rural water supplies.

The capital cost of Municipal water supplies should, in principle, be borne, at least partly, by the Municipality itself. Its share may be fixed at 50%. The cost of maintenance should be borne entirely by Municipalities. Their share of the capital cost may be advanced as a loan by the Government and recovered over a long term of years.

The Chief Public Health Engineer of every Province should have funds placed at his disposal every year for experimentation and research to be conducted in his laboratories or in collaboration with other workers on any water supply problem.

Collection And Disposal Of Community Wastes

The introduction of protected water supplies alone will not be sufficient for achieving healthful living. It is also essential to adopt measures for the hygienic collection and disposal of community wastes.

As a short-term plan, to be achieved in five to 10 years, the following modest programme for sewerage is suggested in the order of priority given below:

(1) Urgent improvements to existing installations and prevailing methods of disposal in sewered cities to cope with overload and wear and tear.

(2) Extension of sewerage to new housing developments and extension of city limits in cities where there is already a sewerage system.

(3) Laying of sewers in all permanent pilgrim centres.

(4) Laying of sewers, following the introduction of satisfactory protected water supply, in all unsewered cities either with a population of over 100,000 or with a high density of population.

(5) Laying of sewers in predominantly industrial areas.

(6) More complete utilization of sewers in sewered areas.

The total outlay required for this programme may be about Rs. 15 crores which can be shared equally between the Municipalities and Provincial Governments except in the case of permanent pilgrim centres.

The Provincial Governments should, on their own initiative, prepare the sewerage schemes and have them carried out. The share of expenditure chargeable to the Municipality may perhaps be financed out of the proceeds of the entertainment tax collected by the Municipality.

The cost of laying sewers in all permanent pilgrim centres should be shared equally between the Central Government and the Provincial Government concerned. The share of the Provincial Government may be met out of the funds of religious endowment boards or other interests that may benefit by improved sanitation.

With regard to the more complete utilization of sewers in existing sewered towns, Provincial Governments should press Municipalities to accelerate progress. If a householder does not connect his premises within a year from the date of service of notice, the Municipality should carry out the work by a system of subvention through its own agency without waiting further and recover the cost along with rates from him. Provincial Governments should advance loans every year to Municipalities for this specific purpose and ensure that at least 90% of the premises are connected within the next 10 years.

We are against the indiscriminate construction of sullage drains. They ought not to be built without ensuring that the houses served by them have sanitary latrines; otherwise these drains are likely to be used as latrines and urinals.

Nothing which is likely to come in contact with sewage and likely to be consumed raw should be grown on a sewage farm.

Sewage farms should be managed under the direction of a competent agricultural expert.

Refuse should be collected and disposed of in a manner free from hazard to public health. The hazards arise from fly and rat breeding. "Wealth from waste" is not to be produced at the expense of health.

The Government should insist that even the smallest local authority or board should carry out refuse collection and disposal satisfactorily.

Every Municipality with a population of over 100,000 should have a well-equipped workshop in which Municipal transport vehicles can be repaired and machinery belonging to waterworks and sewage works can also be repaired. Such workshops should be run on a commercial basis. They should undertake repairs of transport vehicles of smaller Municipalities, Panchayat Boards, etc., if required.

Composting is no doubt a good method of integrated disposal of refuse and human excreta. If carried out under proper supervision, it will help in food production.

We are of the opinion that the value and potentialities of composting of human excreta have been overrated, while the accompanying dangers to public health have been overlooked.

Composting is not advocated for Municipalities with a population of over 100,000. Underground sewers to transport human excreta are safer in every respect than manual removal of night soil from latrines and should be installed in such cities. If large Municipalities are allowed to compost night soil, they will develop a complacency about insanitation and put off sewerage for ever. When cities with a population of over 100,000 are sewered, the nitrogen in the waste can be conserved for agricultural use by sewage farming wherever possible.

In sewered towns, water closets only should be permitted.

As regards smaller Municipalities, we would recommend composting of night soil on a site at least half a mile away from the Municipal limits on the leeward side under good supervision.

Any proposals to encourage composting in private compounds in Municipal areas will be positively dangerous and should be firmly resisted.

In villages and other places where there is no organized refuse or night soil collection, composting cannot be carried out efficiently. Only cattle dung will be available. That can be dumped into a manure pit in each compound and covered with straw and ash. Eventually, it can be used as manure every year or half-year.

We strongly recommend the construction of such manure pits for cattle dung, straw and leaves, but not the composting of human excreta in rural areas.

We have come across a suggestion that villagers should put up public latrines, defecate in them and cover the excreta with refuse before leaving. These are said to be designed to produce compost for village use. Knowing the frailties of ordinary human beings and the difficulty of collecting and bringing refuse to a public latrine in a village, we have to state in all humility that the scheme is utterly impracticable.

In unsewered towns, service latrines are not very satisfactory. We recommend the construction of latrines which require no service and in which the excreta can be disposed of at the site of the latrine in a hygienic manner. The best type is a latrine in which solid and liquid excreta can be washed into a domestic septic tank.

The septic tanks should be provided with means of desludging and should be desludged regularly.

Even if there is not sufficient land for the absorption of effluent from the domestic septic tank, the discharge of effluent into Municipal sullage drains should be permitted if it is already there. The effluent from the tank is not likely to be worse than the raw urine and faeces which the drain actually carries.

For villages where 85% of the population lives but hardly 5% of the houses have any latrines, septic tank latrines, well latrines, "Hazari" (Mysore type) latrines, borehole latrines and pit privies are suitable. They require no sweeper service and are reasonably safe and clean within the limitation of low cost and the imperfections of a rural environment. We require millions of them. They cannot, however, be built and presented to each house by Health Departments of Provincial Governments. Only technical service can be given and inducements offered. A few model latrines of each type should be built in each village for educative purposes.

The villagers can be induced to put up latrines in their houses if there is good leadership, backed by an organization for technical service. Rural Panchayats, social service organizations, schools, health centres, etc., are all means of reaching the villager. Rural Panchayats specially have potentialities for improving the rural hygiene and getting latrines built in rural areas if their activities are regulated and oriented properly.

In rural areas, the aim should be to promote latrines in each house and not public latrines. Expenditure on public latrines should be limited to the barest requirements in rural sanitation programmes. The education of the individual is far more important than the mere provision of a physiological need.

Public latrines should be built at railway stations, bus stands, parks, places of public entertainment, markets, schools and colleges, hostels, dharamsalas, public offices and places of public worship. The number of seats should be on a standardized scale.

The provision and maintenance of water supplies in villages and the introduction of D.D.T. spraying for mosquito control are two services which people readily appreciate and should be used as levers for pushing on latrine construction in villages.

Building of a new house in old or new villages should not be allowed unless a latrine is also built. This power should be vested in the Rural Panchayat Board. The Government should also make available to the people designs, materials and equipment for putting up latrines. Standard concrete squatting plates can be made and supplied to villagers at cost price. Equipment for putting down borehole latrines should be maintained at every Health Centre and every Sanitary Inspector's office in the rural areas.

As in the case of housing and water supplies, the shortage of materials is a deterrent factor in the implementation of plans for the hygienic collection and disposal of community wastes. It should be overcome by increase of production and better allocation of existing production.

There are only three or four large sources and some small sources of supply of stoneware pipes in India and their total production does not exceed 1,200 tons per month. If our modest plans for sewering all cities of over 100,000 are to be implemented, at least three more potteries should be built and the total production of stoneware pipes and drainage fittings stepped up to at least 3,000 tons a month. The production of sanitary fittings, galvanized pipes, etc., should also be ensured.

It will be worth while for the engineers in charge of large sewage undertakings to arrange for the manufacture of cement pipes in their on factories.

Sewage plants need trained personnel for operation. Besides mechanical engineers and electrical engineers for pumping stations, there should be agriculturists for sewage farming and chemists for analysis. Above all, there should be a public health engineer to co-ordinate the work of the people in charge. In the large self-governing Corporations, the Drainage Department should have a public health engineer at the helm. In smaller Municipalities, the Municipal engineers should be provincialized and placed under the Chief Public Health Engineer. As in the case of water supplies, the Chief Public Health Engineer of a Province should be authorized to certify a work as essential and have it carried out at the expense of the Municipality when he finds that the Municipality is not co-operative.

Refuse collection and disposal can be entrusted to the Municipal engineer. The maintenance of transport vehicles and the organization of labour are the preponderant features of the work and an engineer can do it better than the Health Officer, provided he has had sufficient training to keep the public health objectives in the forefront.

The collection and disposal of excreta and the cleansing of drains are actually carried out by bhangis or sweepers. They are doing a great humanitarian service and should be given good housing, water supply, latrines and other amenities. Their physical environment should be improved by the Municipalities immediately. This should receive a high priority among our short-term plans.

Substitution of the human agency by mechanical methods in the collection, removal and disposal of community wastes should be encouraged as far as practicable.

Food, Drink And Milk

The danger of transmission of disease through food, drink and milk is great, especially in urban areas where people have to resort to public food and drink establishments. Food, drink and milk should be produced, stored, transported and served under environmental conditions which are free from the dangers of contamination.

Some of the food processing establishments may be outside the limits of a Municipality and may escape control by the Municipal health authority. The law should be amended so as to ensure better co-ordination between different health authorities in urban and rural areas, so that the wholesale producer can be controlled and not merely the retailer.

Private slaughter-houses should not be allowed in any Municipal town. Municipal slaughter-houses should be built in all towns to type plans approved by the Chief Public Health Engineer of the Province.

The workers in food processing establishments, such as flour mills, bakeries, confectioneries, ice canneries, sweetmeet shops, biscuit factories, ice-cream plants, aerated water and ice factories, papad, vegetable ghee, vanaspati, papadam manufactories and manufacture of scented arecanuts and large public kitchens, should be certified medically fit. The control of large food processing establishments should be tightened up by suitable provisions in a Provincial Public Health Act designed to secure closer co-ordination of the Municipal and Provincial Health Departments. An inspectorate should be established in the Province for regular inspection and quality control in these establishments. Breaches of regulations by these establishments should be liable to deterrent punishment.

The standards for dairies and cattle sheds are detailed in Para. 14 of Chapter VII. Municipalities will not be able to enforce these standards merely by prosecution. They will have to build model dairies and then compel the owners of cattle to keep their cattle there on payment of rent. Provincial Governments may also launch schemes like the one that the Bombay Government is carrying out at Aare outside Bombay City. Co-operative milk farms may also be permitted outside the Municipal limits.

Buildings used for storage of food and foodgrains should be free from dampness and should be rendered rat free. The ventilation, temperature and other conditions of the storage establishment should be such as not to encourage spoilage of the articles stored or to endanger the health of the workers there. No wholesale godowns, warehouses and cold storages in the Province should be opened without consulting the Public Health Engineer and the Health Officer concerned.

Sale of exposed food, cut-fruit, etc., on pavements

and in other places should be stopped. To achieve this, public opinion and police action are necessary. Model markets should be built in every urban area. Wholesale markets should have adequate facilities for storage of perishables. In restaurants, eating houses, etc., provision of adequate supply of safe water, provision of a boiler for hot water for sterilization of utensils, provision of a garbage bin with a lid and provision of washing facilities for customers and staff are essential. The penalty for failing to provide these should be deterrent. Regular spraying of a suitable insecticide should be made a condition for granting a licence for food retailing establishments to operate.

The ordinary standard of sanitation relating to restaurants and eating places cannot be applied to these situations. However, it is necessary at pilgrim and poor feeding centres that kitchens should be well lighted and ventilated; that food should be kept covered and not exposed till it is served; that water and food should be served by ladles and spoons untouched by hand; that washing facilities should be provided for those who eat; and that the leaves and garbage should be cleaned up and disposed of by burial or by feeding them to cows, etc.

Light And Air

Good lighting and good ventilation are conducive to better endeavour, better co-operation and greater and better output in homes, schools, offices, factories, etc.

Windows are used for natural lighting and natural ventilation.

Smoke fumes and dust are irritating. They obscure light and pollute the atmosphere.

Atmospheric pollution can be effectively controlled by zoning and gradual shifting of factories from residential zones to industrial zones by legal compulsion and by offering suitable inducements and facilities to factories to shift. In addition, pollution of the atmosphere can be controlled also by offering feasible technical advice to the factories.

All cinemas and theatres in electrified towns and villages should have artificial ventilation, by means of which the air in the occupied building will be circulated as well as changed.

Operation theatres should be air-conditioned in Provincial and District Headquarters hospitals, where the effective temperature is likely to exceed 95°F.

Third-class carriages in railways should be fitted with fans.

Congregations

Opportunities for transmission of diseases arise and increase wherever people congregate indiscriminately. It is, therefore, necessary to exclude the dangerous people, to immunize the healthy people and to modify the environment so as to reduce its potentiality for transmitting disease. The exclusion of dangerous people and the immunization of the healthy are duties for which the Medical Officer of Health is better qualified. The modification of the environment is a duty for which the Public Health Engineer is better qualified.

In India, more attention is paid to the control of disease in congregations than to other aspects of public health work. It is accorded the highest priority among the various activities of a Health Department, and we recommend that it should continue to be accorded that priority.

The housing of people in places pilgrimage is generally unsatisfactory. As every room in a pilgrim centre is likely to be occupied by a family, the minimum size of rooms in such places and in all dharamsalas should be 200 sq.ft. The rooms should be at least 10 ft. high and have at least 10% of the floor area in the windows.

Places which are prominently pilgrim centres, sanitaria or spas should be run as Government townships. Central legislation should be passed to enable a Provincial Government to take over the sanitation, health and other Municipal functions of such places in the Province.

Schools are places where children from all classes of society congregate and can communicate diseases to one another. The hygiene of the environment in the schools should be of a high standard from the point of view of prevention of disease and, even more so, from that of practical health education.

Cinema houses and theatres are popular places of public resort. Their standard in cities is fairly satisfactory, though in mofussil towns they are not so clean.

The three important means of public transport, which we have considered, are railways, tramways and buses. Overcrowding has become insufferable in all three and the chances of spreading disease by contact have also increased. It is, therefore, recommended that periodical disinfection of public transport vehicles should be carried out with D.D.T. or other insecticides.

Pollution Of Streams, Lakes And Beaches

Rivers, lakes and beaches, which have been revered and sanctified by religious traditions in India, are polluted by the discharge of wastes and excreta by individuals, Municipalities and factories without sufficient consideration for the health of other users of the same water or for conservation of aquatic life or for beauty. The Central and Provincial Water and Drainage Boards recommended by the Health Survey and Development Committee will be useful for the control of river and beach pollution. If these Boards are not established, due emphasis should be given to the supply of drinking water and to the prevention of the pollution of rivers in the activities of the Central Water, Power, Irrigation and Navigation Commission.

Sewage treatment and industrial waste treatment should be carried out to the extent necessary to adjust the pollutional load to the capacity of the receiving body of water for self-purification. Though we are not yet ripe for laying down standards by legislative enactments, we can control pollution by investigation in each case.

The pollutional status of our rivers should be studied, reaeration constants should be computed and standards should be evolved. Research is necessary. The Water and Drainage Boards, if established, can promote this type of research. Otherwise, the All-India Institute of Hygiene and Public Health, Calcutta, may be encouraged to develop research in a few river basins.

Provincial Public Health Acts should contain a provision to the effect that the discharge of sewage or industrial waste into a body of water will be allowed only after the party responsible for the discharge undertakes to carry out the recommendations of the Ministry of Health with regard to the mode of treatment and standard of effluent.

The Ministry of Labour should instruct all Factory Inspectors to refer all questions of treatment and disposal of industrial wastes to the Ministry of Health and get its recommendations implemented.

The disposal of sewage on land by farming during dry months after some preliminary treatment may be a suitable means of reducing river pollution. The discharge of the sewage in wet months into a flooded river may be unobjectionable with sufficiently large dilution.

Pollution of rivers, lakes and beaches by individuals can be controlled to some extent by constructing and maintaining sanitary latrines and urinals at bathing beaches and ghats. The effluent and excreta from these latrines and urinals should be either connected to public sewers or absorbed in the soil.

If problems of river pollution arising between different Provinces or States cannot be solved by negotiation between representatives of their Ministries of Health, the Central Ministry of Health should settle the matter as arbitrator.

Industrial Environment

Industries have been growing in India rapidly. They have been associated with the growth of slums and vice in certain places. The subject is vast and we have confined ourselves to some broad observations. In considering the hygiene of the industrial environment, there is a tendency among many to think only of the worker's environment in the factory and ignore his home environment. This, in our opinion, is incorrect and injurious. Bad housing conditions blight the character and efficiency of the worker and his family and also blight the character and tone of the neighbourhood where the worker lives. Broader perspective and better co-ordination should be brought to bear on the solution of industrial hygiene problems.

The number of factory inspectors should be increased so that factories may be inspected more often, preferably twice a year. Small factories require more frequent inspections than larger ones.

The buildings should be passed as fit for the industry by a competent person before a licence is issued or renewed annually.

Factual data should be collected concerning actual environmental conditions in various industries. Such work is going on now under the auspices of the Indian Research Fund Association; it should be continued and its scope extended.

Training in industrial hygiene should be given to three classes of professional men—doctors, engineers and chemists—with a slight difference in emphasis, so that each can collaborate with the other two in fulfilling his role.

Among other amenities to be provided for the comfort of a worker in a factory, the following should receive special attention:

(a) supply of drinking water,
(b) provision of latrines and urinals,
(c) washing facilities,
(d) canteens, and
(e) creches.

The drinking water should be disinfected, cooled and supplied untouched by hand. It is not expensive to put up an ice-box with a cooling coil and supply the water through the coil and a fountain, if there is a piped water supply.

The scale of latrine accommodation prescribed in Provincial rules under the Factories Act should be revised to conform to that recommended by us for public latrines.

In public latrines in labourers' colonies, the number of latrines should be provided on the basis of users and not of workers only.

Washing facilities provided for labourers in factories are not inadequate but their maintenance is far from clean. This should be improved.

Hygiene Of The Rural Environment

About 85% of the people in India live in villages. Villages are the backbone of our national economy and it is recognized that the rural reconstruction is essential. It has many facets but we have confined ourselves to the reconstruction of the environment from the health point of view.

Water supply in villages is most unsatisfactory. It is the most urgent need. Next in importance to malaria, diarrhoea and dysentery are the causes of sickness. Whatever may be the financial stringency, Provinces should carry out a sustained programme of planned rural water supplies spread over a number of years. The work should be carried out by the Public Health Engineering Department or at least under its direction and funds should not be spent without its control. On an average the capital expenditure may be about Rs. 3 per head of population served and the annual maintenance expenditure can be limited to one to two annas per head per annum.

The means of disposal of excreta in villages is very unsatisfactory. There are few latrines and naturally the soil is polluted.

The houses in villages are generally owned and not rented. These are not generally overcrowded but there are not sufficient windows for lighting and effective cross-ventilation. There is no scope for radical alteration as the villagers are poor. Some improvement can, however, be effected. For example, villagers may be persuaded to construct their cattle sheds away from the house and to dig a manure pit in a corner of the backyard. In addition, the "premises-sanitation" of the house should include spray of D.D.T. at least once in two to six months to control the transmission of mosquito and fly-borne diseases.

Village communications are bad, especially in deltaic areas. This is a great handicap to rural reconstruction and health work. Improvement of village communications is essential.

The wholesale replanning of an existing village is not practicable.

Control Of Insects And Other Causes Of Disease

Malaria ranks highest among the causes of death and sickness in India. Means directed against the mosquito-transmission of malaria are, in the existing state of knowledge, the only methods which give permanent control. Mosquito control is also required in the case of dengue and filaria.

Public Health Engineers should be given training in malaria engineering.

Provincial Governments should extend rural malaria control by indoor residual spraying of D.D.T. in all districts where malaria is endemic.

In malarial areas D.D.T. should be sprayed in every house periodically like white-washing.

Factories for the manufacture of at least 3,000 tons of D.D.T. per annum should be set up in India by the Government or with Government aid and control.

Permanent measures of rat control are necessary for conservation of foodgrains and for the control of plague in the areas where it is endemic.

Fly is the agent for mechanical transmission of many diseases. D.D.T. spray will control sandflies, fleas, ticks, bugs, lice, etc.

Design And Construction Of Medical And Health Centres

Demand for hospital accommodation is increasing.

The design of medical buildings is therefore a matter of great importance in national planning.

Other Aspects Of Environmental Hygiene

These are sanitation in prisons, proper disposal of the dead, hygiene of the barber shops and saloons, dhobi ghats, disinfection stations and plumbing.

Constructional Materials

Acute shortage of materials is now the most serious handicap in the implementation of any scheme. The production in the country is insufficient for our requirements even if conditions had remained as they were before the War. We cannot look for relief to imports from other countries due to limited foreign exchange resources.

The first step that the Government should take for the implementation of our plans is to review the production of constructional materials against our requirements and to adjust industrial policy with a view to increasing production of essential materials for attaining a measure of national self-sufficiency. Existing production should be controlled and allocated more equitably with due recognition of the extreme urgency of some of our plans for housing, water supply, malarial control, etc. At the same time, new factories should be set up to attain the targets of production by private enterprise with or without State aid and by State enterprise within three years. The available foreign exchange resources should be conserved for importing the capital equipment required for setting up these factories and for importing those articles which cannot be produced in India.

Organization And Administration

It is essential that both at the Centre and in the Provinces there should be a strong technical organization which will be constantly at work to make use of every opportunity to improve environmental hygiene and whose special responsibility will be to ensure that recommendations made in this behalf are carried out. Such an organization is not found now in the Central Government and in many of the Provinces.

Plans for environmental hygiene can be implemented only by engineering methods directed towards the public health objective. They are the special field of the Public Health Engineer, who is the right person to take charge of environmental hygiene. The maintenance of health depends on personal health services, which the Medical Health Officer alone is competent to give, and on impersonal health services (or environmental hygiene) which the Public Health Engineer alone is competent to render. Both are essential and both should be organized and co-ordinated in every Province and at the Centre. This co-ordination should be arranged by the heads of the two services as equals.

The Public Health Engineering Department should be attached to the Ministry of Health.

At the Centre, there should be a Consulting Public Health Engineer attached to the Ministry of Health as an Adviser.

In the Provinces, there should be a Chief Public Health Engineer in the Ministry of Health, with headquarters staff for design, investigation, research, etc., and with executive field staff for construction and inspections.

The services of Municipal Engineers and Operators of Water Sewage Works should be provincialized.

A comprehensive Public Health Act should be passed in every Province.

Necessary legislation should also be enacted to ensure that local bodies perform elementary functions of environmental hygiene to standards prescribed by the Ministry of Health.

A revenue of Rs. 13 per capita per annum will be necessary to maintain efficient Municipal services. The actual revenues of many Municipalities are only Rs. 3 to Rs. 5 per capita. The Local Finance Enquiry Committee, set up by the Central Ministry of Health, is investigating ways and means of improving these revenues. The recommendations of that Committee should receive due consideration. Unless the finances of Local Bodies are increased, they cannot improve environmental hygiene.

Training Of Personnel

The Public Health Engineering Service that has been proposed in Chapter XVII can be an effective instrument for rendering service and can produce results if qualified personnel is appointed at least to the senior posts. Hence, the organization of training is of the utmost importance. However, the utilization of trained personnel should not lag behind training. If it does, there will be wastage of talent, frustration and discredit to the courses of training.

The training of personnel for responsible positions in Public Health Engineering should be both academic and practical. What is ingested in the lecture room is digested and assimilated only in the field. The value of experience should not be underrated. If it is combined with academic methods of approach to problems, it is possible to develop leadership in the profession. At least in the earlier stages more opportunities should be given to people with mature experience to undergo training than to immature persons who have not made up their minds about their future career. A definite percentage of foreign scholarships, etc., should be earmarked for Public Health Engineering.

The Central Government should assume responsibility for training personnel required for improving environmental hygiene. Different categories of personnel required for improving environmental hygiene are :

(a) Public Health Engineers.
(b) Public Health Engineering Subordinates.
(c) Town Planners.
(d) Plant Operators.
(e) Medical Health Officers.
(f) Sanitary Inspectors.
(g) Specialists in Public Health Chemistry, Biology, etc.
(h) Industrial Hygienists.

The training of high-grade personnel should be the responsibility of the Central Government for at least 10 years to ensure uniformity of standards.

Public Health Engineers should be basically engineers and not civil engineers only.

The course of training organized at the All-India Institute of Hygiene and Public Health, Calcutta, for the degree of Master of Engineering (Public Health) and the syllabus prescribed therefor are suitable for training men for senior posts.

When the demand for Public Health Engineers increases as a result of the implementation of our recommendations, other centres for training Public Health Engineers should be opened in addition to the one at the All-India Institute of Hygiene and Public Health. If there are three or four engineering colleges in a Province, all of them need not have such a specialized course. We would warn against mass production under poor training facilities.

The specialized training for Public Health Engineering should be given as a post-graduate course and not an under-graduate course.

Finance

The beginnings will not cost much and, during the time required for organizing personnel and materials, the financial position may improve.

LINGUISTIC PROVINCES COMMISSION, 1948—REPORT

New Delhi, Constituent Assembly of India, 1948. 56p.

Chairman : Shri S. K. Dar.
Members : Shri Panna Lall; Shri Jagatnarain Lal.
Secretary : Shri B. C. Banerji.

APPOINTMENT

The Linguistic Provinces Commission was constituted under the Constituent Assembly of India vide their notification dated June 17, 1948, to report on the question of formation of the Provinces of Andhra, Kerala, Karnataka and Maharashtra; the financial, economic, administrative and other consequences thereof; and their approximate boundaries.

TERMS OF REFERENCE

(i) What new provinces, if any, from among those specified above should be created and what broadly should be their boundaries, it being understood that the precise demarcation of the boundaries would be considered later by a Boundary Commission?

(ii) What would be the administrative, economic, financial and other consequences in each Province to be so created?

(iii) What would be the administrative, economic, financial and other consequences in the adjoining territories of India?

CONTENTS

Letter to the Hon'ble President, Constituent Assembly of India, New Delhi; Introduction; The Linguistic Provinces; The Linguistic Areas and their Boundaries; Financial Position of the Proposed Provinces; Financial, Economic, Administrative and other Consequences; Summary and Conclusions; Appendix I to V; Statement I to III.

RECOMMENDATIONS

The existing Provinces of Madras, Bombay and the Central Provinces and Berar hold together within their respective territories large linguistic groups which are unequally matched for the struggle for existence or for the struggle for political power. In the struggle for political power, which the British imperialism and subsequently democracy under British rule introduced in this country, these heterogeneous elements were not completely successful in producing harmonious Governments, with the result that a demand grew up in course of time on the part of the groups, which felt that they had suffered in the struggle for a separate Government of their own.

When a conflict of interest, real or imaginary, arises between linguistic groups differing in numerical strength and in mental and moral equipment, it does not take long for the minority to feel that it has no chance against the majority, and it finds an easy solution of its difficulty in a desire for separation. Whether this demand is due to the aggressiveness of the more successful groups or to some inherent or accidental weakness in the less successful ones or to both it is not easy to determine; nor is it necessary to do so. It is sufficient to note the conditions which bring it into existence and to observe that it originates in a desire for power which, in its lower sense, is a desire for jobs and offices and, in its higher sense, a desire for service to the community and for its material and moral advancement. And it actuates the conduct of both honest and patriotic persons and of self-seekers in the groups in which such a demand has sprung up.

The intensity of the demand and its duration as also its justification vary from province to province, and within linguistic groups of the same province and also within the different sections of the same group. It has a long and persistent history of agitation behind it in Andhra, and exists in its strongest form in the coastal districts thereof. The Rayalaseema districts of Andhra are not affected by the demand to the same extent, and a substantial section is opposed to it. Just as there is a genuine apprehension in the coastal Andhra mind against Tamil domination, so, too, there is an apprehension, though in a somewhat lesser degree, in the Rayalaseema mind against coastal domination. Next to Andhra, the demand is insistent in Karnataka, though there it is moderated by the knowledge that, for the unification of Karnataka, the co-operation of Mysore State is essential and that it may require some time for preparation. In Kerala there is a general recognition that, without the merger of Cochin and Travancore States, a separate province cannot exist; and the demand there is weakest and is rightly conditional upon the formation of any other linguistic province out of Madras, and the people are prepared to wait till a United Kerala comes into existence. Maharashtra is a late-comer in the field of agitation for linguistic provinces, and it is still a divided house comprising three cross-divisions of Konkan, Desh and Mahavidarbha, none of whom has suffered in any way in the struggle for political power.

The main ground put forward for the demand for linguistic provinces is that these are essential for the working of democracy, as also for the working of the

Constitution, and a linguistic province is the best form of a homogeneous province, which the existing circumstances in India permit to be formed. It is said that the working of democracy is impeded in the field of Education, Legislature and Administration by a multiplicity of languages spoken in a province. It is further said that autonomous provinces are embodied in our Federal Constitution and autonomous provinces imply autonomous States. And as the larger linguistic groups now existing in India claim historically to have formed sub-nations, they contend that the appropriate place for these sub-nations is in a linguistic State, just as, for the same reason, the correct principle upon which autonomous provinces should be formed is the linguistic principle.

Linguistic homogeneity in the formation of new provinces is certainly attainable within certain limits but only at the cost of creating a fresh minority problem. More than half the Malayalam and Kannada-speaking people are living in Indian States, and only a little less than half of the Telugu and Marathi-speaking people are living either in Indian States or in Union Provinces from which they cannot be transferred to new linguistic provinces either for want of geographical contiguity or want of their consent to be so transferred. These must remain, at least for many years to come, outside the sphere of a linguistic province. Even in the limited areas of the Union, which can be made homogeneous linguistically, border districts on each side and the capital cities of Bombay and Madras will remain bilingual or multi-lingual. And, as has been explained before, nowhere will it be possible to form a linguistic province of more than 70 to 80% of the people speaking the same language, thus leaving in each province a minority of at least 20% of people speaking other languages. And considering the evidence, which has come before us in regard to the Telugus, who were transferred to Orissa from Madras at the time of the formation of the Orissa Province, and the Tamils, who live in Southern Travancore, it is easy to foresee that similar minority problems on a much more extensive scale will arise all over the linguistic provinces.

As for persons speaking the same language forming a sub-nation, whatever may have been their condition in the past, now for 200 years the sepeople have got separated and scattered over different areas in British-made Provinces or Indian States and have become assimilated with them, so much so that the Rayalaseema districts are not at present eager to throw in their lot with the coastal districts; Cochin and Travancore would not easily coalesce with Malabar; and there are difficulties in the way of Mysore merging in Coorg and Karnataka districts; and Mahavidarbha is not keen on joining Bombay (Maharashtra). Each of these differing elements now has its own special needs and problems, which require individual treatment and which prevent these elements from easily coming together in one homogeneous province contemplated by the Constitution unless special provisions be made for them.

It may, therefore, be safely assumed that linguistic groups as sub-nations do not exist anywhere at present. But if the intention were to bring sub-nations into existence, there could not be a better way of doing it than by putting together these differing elements in a linguistic province. An autonomous linguistic province, in other words, means an autonomous linguistic State and an autonomous linguistic State means, in the words of one of its exponents, that its territories are inviolate. And if in a linguistic province the majority language group comes to regard the territory of the entire province as exclusively its own, the time cannot be far distant when it will come to regard the minority living in that province and people living outside it as not their own. And once that stage is reached it will only be a question of time for that sub-nation to consider itself a full nation.

The strength of the demand for linguistic provinces lies in the fact that there is some advantage in imparting education, in working the Legislature, and in administration if a large majority of the people speak the same language and in the fact that these linguistic groups do not seem to live happily in the existing provinces and are anxious to separate. The demand receives added force from the fact that several of the existing provinces more or less possess linguistic homogeneity. That one part of the country is linguistically homogeneous, including the small Province of Orissa, which has to be maintained by subvention from the Centre, is a source of constant irritation to linguistically heterogeneous provinces. It certainly does not lie in the mouth of those who are living in a linguistically homogeneous province to point out its evils to those living in a heterogeneous province. Moreover the formation of linguistic provinces has been an article of faith in the current political thought of the country during the last 30 years and has received the support of the Congress and the blessings of Mahatma Gandhi.

The weakness of the demand lies in the fact that it involves the recognition of the principle of Government of a province by a linguistic group, which is basically wrong. Further it paves the way for the recognition of other group Governments for which there may exist a tendency in the country, for example, Government by Southerners in the south of India, Government by Sikhs and Jats in the north of India, and even Government by the non-Brahmins in certain areas of this country. It leads to the breaking up or deterioration of vital organisms like capital cities and border districts where, for generations, a bilingual or multi-lingual life has flourished happily. It would further create minority problems and State problems of a kind which did not exist before. And, above all, it would bring into existence provinces with a sub-national bias at a time when nationalism is yet in its infancy and is not in a position to bear any strain. And, lastly, the motive behind the demand is open to serious challenge. It is not the ostensible ground of making democracy run smoother, but the fact that these several communities living in the province cannot get on together, that is behind the proposal to separate and form Governments of their own.

The existing Indian Provinces are administrative units of British imperialism. They came into existence in a somewhat haphazard way, and were not designed to work democratic institutions; they are certainly susceptible of more scientific and rational planning. But they have taken root and are now living vital organisms and have served the useful purpose of bringing together people, who might otherwise have remained separated. And though they may be somewhat disadvantageous in working modern democracy, they are not bad instruments for submerging a sub-national consciousness and moulding a nation.

In any rational and scientific planning that may take place in regard to the provinces of India in the future, homogeneity of language alone cannot be a decisive or even an important factor. Administrative convenience, history, geography, economy, culture, and many other matters will also have to be given due weight. It may be that the provinces thus formed will also show homogeneity of language and, in a way, might resemble linguistic provinces. But, in forming the provinces, the emphasis should be primarily on administrative convenience, and homogeneity of language will enter into consideration only as a matter of administrative convenience and not by its own independent force.

But this is certainly not the time for embarking upon the enterprise of re-drawing the map of the whole of southern India, including the Deccan, Bombay, and the Central Provinces. India is yet to become a nation, and Indian States are yet to be integrated. The problem of regrouping the provinces would become simpler when the future of the remaining States is definitely known. Again, India can ill spare at this moment and for some time to come the money, material, or administrative talent, which will be required for setting up half a dozen new Governments and new capitals. It cannot afford to add to its anxieties the heat, controversy and bitterness, which the demarcation of boundaries and allotment of the capital cities of Bombay and Madras will involve. And lastly by splitting three existing provinces into half a dozen the economy of almost half the country will be so seriously upset that it should not be attempted without a great deal of study, preparation and planning. However urgent the problem of redistribution of provinces may be, it is not more urgent than the Defence problem, the inflation problem, the refugee problem, the food problem, the production problem, and many other problems with which India is burdened today. All these must get priority and the redistribution of provinces must wait till India has become a nation and has been fully integrated. If India lives, all her problems will be solved; if India does not survive, nothing will be gained by solving her linguistic provinces problem alone.

In order to secure this stability and integration, India should have a strong Centre and a national language. Indian nationalism is deeply wedded to its regional languages; Indian patriotism is aggressively attached to its provincial frontiers. If India is to survive, Indian nationalism and patriotism will have to sacrifice some of its cherished sentiments in the larger interests of the country. India has chosen for herself the destiny of a Federal Republic. In the Constitution, which is now being forged for her, a framework may be set up, which would enable her to find her destiny. Provide, if you will, for autonomous provinces and for adult franchise; but also recognize that there will be a period of transition, a period of trial and error, during which India will have to prepare for its destiny and during which the Centre must possess large, overriding powers of control and direction—powers which may be kept in reserve and may be sparingly used and finally abandoned, but which must be available for effective use if and when occasion arises.

Till nationalism has acquired sufficient strength to permit the formation of autonomous provinces, the true nature and function of a province under our Constitution should be that of an administrative unit functioning under delegated authority from the Centre and subject to the Centre's overriding powers in regard to its territory, its existence, and its functions. These powers are required to form new provinces and to mitigate the rigour of Government by linguistic majorities, to prevent a breakdown of the administration on account of disputes amongst linguistic groups, to check fissiparous tendencies and strengthen national feeling, and above all to build up an Indian nation.

An immediate solution has, however, to be found for the desire for separation which exists among the Telugus, Malayalees, Kannadigas, and Maharashtrians. These linguistic groups are entitled to their legitimate share in the administration, Government and development of their provinces. Two of these linguistic groups, namely, Malayalees and Kannadigas, are situated at the tail-end of their provinces and represented by ineffectual minorities in their Legislatures. Two others, namely, the Telugus and the Maharashtrians in C.P. and Berar, are represented by large, virile, and group-conscious minorities; but they are faced with equally group-conscious majorities and the two refuse to coalesce and produce a harmonious Government. The clash and conflict, which exists between them, has brought the administration in Madras to a breaking point, and C.P. and Berar are also showing signs of going the same way. No particular grievance would seem to exist in the case of the Bombay Maharashtra group.

A number of constitutional safeguards were suggested to us to prevent such a breakdown. One commonly-favoured suggestion was that the Governor should always come from another province and should be selected by the Centre for his character and ability and armed with powers to prevent injustice to minorities, and charged with this duty in his Instrument of Instructions. Another suggestion was that Provincial Subjects should be reduced and Joint Subjects enlarged, and the Centre given residuary and overriding powers. The third was that the Government in these provinces should be run by turns by linguistic groups, or be divided into administrative regions, and that the Centre should impose conventions in regard to these matters under which the administration might be carried on. We have not considered in detail these and other similar suggestions made to us as it is not strictly within our province to do so. They all, however, lead to the inference that the Centre must be armed with overriding powers and must assume responsibility to guide democracy till Indian nationalism has been sufficiently strengthened and democracy is able to stand on its own legs.

The only good that we can see in a linguistic province is the possible advantage it has in working the legislature in the regional language. But this is more than counter-balanced by the obstruction the linguistic provinces will inevitably cause to the spread of national language or national feeling in the country. It is claimed—and the view is sincerely held—that the Telugu, Malayalee, Kannadiga, or Maharashtrian will be a better nationalist by being put in a linguistic province than without it. It is said that, by being put in a linguistic province, each linguistic group will be happier and stronger and will be able to develop according to its genius, and a stronger group will be able to serve India better and consequently will be a better nationalist. We are convinced that this is a mistaken view. The emotional response will always be greater than the one received by the national sentiment. The linguistic group, by being put into a linguistic province, may or may not become stronger; but it does not follow that by being stronger it will become more nationalistic in outlook. Nationalism and sub-nationalism are two emotional experiences which grow at the expense of each other. In a linguistic province sub-nationalism will always be the dominant force and will always evoke greater emotional response; and, in a conflict between the two, the nascent nationalism is sure to lose ground and will ultimately be submerged.

No doubt it is a fact that in some of the existing provinces linguistic homogeneity exists, and this is a source of constant irritation to the other linguistic groups who are living in heterogeneous provinces. As soon as India has been physically and emotionally integrated, the Indian State problem solved and the national sentiment strengthened, the scientific planning of the existing provinces of India can be taken in hand as far as practicable and this invidious distinction obliterated; but till then it has to be accepted as an accident of history and all sub-national tendencies in the existing linguistic provinces should be suppressed.

It is true that these linguistic groups, who are clamouring for separate provinces, are not happy in their present surroundings and the friction and differences which subsist between them constitute a serious threat to good Government. This has already become a major administrative problem. But the mere fact that two large communities cannot get on together is no valid reason for breaking up a province even when these communities are numerically large enough, economically strong enough, and geographically contiguous enough to form provinces of their own. The principle underlying this separation would be so dangerous in its application to the rest of India that the strongest advocates of linguistic provinces have been compelled not to base their demand on this ground which is really at the back of their minds, but to make it on other ostensible grounds like benefit to democracy or preservation and development of their language and culture. Not only the groups, whose cases we are considering, but many other linguistic groups in so-called homogeneous provinces, and also many other communal groups, who have as strong an individuality as these linguistic groups possess, are not happy in their present surroundings. And if once this principle is recognized, it will set the ball rolling for the disintegration of the entire country. And we do not think that the case is any further advanced by the fact that these groups are not only discounted groups but also linguistic groups.

It is said that Congress pledges are behind this demand, and that the Congress has formed its provinces on a linguistic basis, that the present political leadership of the country is committed to it, that the desire for these provinces has sunk deep down into the masses, and that, if it is now delayed or denied, it will cause serious discontent. There may be some truth in all this, but we trust that the political leadership in the country will rise to the occasion and guide the country to its duty. The Congress did not form its provinces on a linguistic basis alone, and so far as we are aware has not committed itself to any time limit in regard to the formation of these provinces, unless it be that the time-limit intended by the Congress was the attainment of Swaraj. But freedom has come to us in a way unforeseen and unthought of and has brought in its train problems and dangers never dreamt of. In view of the dangers, which now surround our country, and in the circumstances that now exist, the Congress stands relieved of all past commitments and it is its right as also its duty to come to a fresh decision on the subject in the light of the present circumstances.

The caste system and sectional and group interests stir up some of the deepest emotions in the Indian heart. Those patriotic persons, who fought the battle of freedom under the banner of the Congress and who are now agitating for separate provinces, share the sentiments of their countrymen. They find it difficult to understand how they will become less national-minded and less patriotic by harbouring sentiments, which they had cherished all along and for which a linguistic province is a natural expression, when these very sentiments did not stand in the way of their uniting and making immense sacrifices for the cause of Indian freedom in the struggle against British imperialism. They do not realize that nationalism born under the stress of foreign domination or of the fear of external aggression cannot stand the strain of normal times unless there is some deeper unity to support it when the stresses which have brought it into being disappear. History is replete with examples of great movements born of a sudden surge of feeling meeting with disaster when the moving stimulus was withdrawn. And Indian unity and Indian nationalism, which are yet in their infancy, will not be able to bear the strain of normal ties, unless the mass psychology undergoes a radical change and ceases to think in terms of "mine" and "thine" in so far as the nation and the State are concerned. If India is to live, there simply cannot be an autonomous State anywhere in India for any group, linguistic or otherwise; and no sub-national province can be formed without preparing the way for ultimate disaster.

So clear is the force of logic with which the case of Indian nationalism presents itself to an unprejudiced mind, and at the same time so keen is the desire for linguistic provinces in certain areas that all sensible advocates of such provinces are even prepared to abandon provincial autonomy and accept a unitary Government for India. All the best evidence presented before us is unanimous regarding a strong Centre with overriding powers and a compulsory national and official language to be enforced by statute. If India decides that the existing linguistic provinces should be retained and others formed in the future it must prepare itself for a unitary government at least for the period of transition. And the Constitution should provide for a gradual devolution of power to provinces with full autonomy only when Indian nationalism has been sufficiently strengthened. This is the least margin of safety under which these linguistic provinces can be permitted to function.

This inquiry in some ways has been an eye-opener to us. The work of 60 years of the Indian National Congress was standing before us face to face with centuries-old India of narrow loyalties, petty jealousies, and ignorant prejudices engaged in a mortal conflict, and we were simply horrified to see how thin was the ice upon which we were skating. Some of the ablest men in the country came before us and confidently and emphatically stated that language in this country stood for and represented the culture, tradition, race, history, individuality and, finally, a sub-nation; that the government of a linguistic group could not be safely left in the hands of a multi-lingual group; and that each linguistic group must have a territory of its own and that its territory was inviolate and could not be shared by any other linguistic group. And it is fair to state that these were not individual views, but the views of a great many of our countrymen. The bitter dispute which rages between Tamils and Telugus in regard to the city of Madras and, in a greater degree, between the Marathas and Gujaratis about the city of Bombay reveals a mentality which to our mind will be the death-knell of Indian nationalism.

The basic facts of the Indian situation are well known and well settled, and are not in dispute on either side. India can only live by the strength of its nationalism; Indian nationalism must find its expression in democracy and not in a kind of fascism; that democracy in this country can only function through a Federation as an absolute unitary Government for such a vast country is neither desirable nor practicable; and a Federation requires contented and happy units and some measure of autonomy for these units.

Our masses have been exploited and have long been suffering and their relief is overdue; and they are entitled immediately to the widest possible education and the widest possible franchise; and all these objectives have to be achieved within the framework of a society, which is cast-ridden, group-conscious, and in the grip of reactionary vested interests, religious and secular. So far there is no dispute. The dispute arises in marking out the spheres within which the nationalism of the country and its reactionary tendencies have to find an outlet.

These linguistic provinces make a strong appeal to the imagination of many of our countrymen and there exists a large volume of public support in their favour. Indeed, in the coastal districts of Andhra, the demand has become, in the words of one of its leading advocates, "a passion and has ceased to be a matter of reason"; and the heat and passion and controversy, which gathered round the work of this Commission and which we witnessed during the course of our work, are in themselves a proof of the intensity of feeling which exists on this subject. The non-fulfilment of a demand of this nature may easily lead to a sense of frustration, and there is grave risk in turning it down; and such a risk can only be justified in the interests of national emergency.

In our opinion, however, such an emergency exists at present in this country. The first and last need of India at the present moment is that it should be a nation. The Constitution, which is now being forged for India, as also all the multifarious problems, which clamour for an immediate solution, have got to be considered in relation to this paramount necessity. Everything which helps the growth of nationalism has to go forward, and everything, which throws obstacles in its way, has to be rejected or should stand over. We have applied this test to linguistic provinces also, and judged by this test, in our opinion, they fail and cannot be supported.

It has given us no pleasure to come to a decision, which runs counter to the cherished desires of so many countrymen of ours in Andhra, Kerala, Karnataka and Maharashtra. Throughout this inquiry a strong and able opinion has ranged itself against the formation of these linguistic provinces outside the areas in which the demand was put forward. This opinion proceeded from persons in all walks of life, including some of our ablest administrators and most distinguished countrymen. The case against the formation of linguistic provinces and the arguments by which it was supported have been adverted to in an earlier portion of this Report. If it were possible to decide the question of formation of linguistic provinces with reference to the wishes of the people who want these provinces alone, we should have been prepared to gratify their wishes. We do not think, however, that a question of such national importance can be decided with reference to such wishes without taking into account the repercussions which they would have on the country as a whole. And, judging that way, we have come to the conclusion, reluctantly but definitely, that the case against linguistic provinces is the sounder of the two.

But this finding does not dispose of the administrative problems, which already exist, having regard to the mutual relations of these linguistic groups, nor does it in any way militate against the formation of administrative provinces out of these linguistic areas should such provinces be decided upon in future on purely administrative considerations.

An urgent case, however, exists for adjusting the relations of the various linguistic groups in the Government of the existing provinces. Two of these linguistic groups, Kerala and Karnataka, being situated at the tail-end of their provinces and represented by ineffective minorities, have undoubtedly suffered in their development. There can be no doubt that they would prosper and be able to manage their affairs much better under their own Government nearer home if such a Government were possible. The cases of Andhra, C.P. and Maharashtra are more complicated and have a political colouring. The clash and conflict, which strains the relations between Telugus and Tamils in Madras, is a serious handicap to the efficient administration of that province. And this is also true, though in a much lesser degree, of the relations between Mahavidarbha and Mahakoshal in the province of C.P. and Berar.

The evidence placed before us does not lead to the conclusion that the existing provinces of Madras, Bombay, C.P. and Berar are administratively inconvenient or that their re-formation on administrative grounds is immediately necessary and cannot wait. But it is not unlikely that when Indian States have aligned themselves with Indian provinces and India has been physically and emotionally integrated and has stabilized itself some of the existing Indian provinces may have to be re-framed. In any rational and scientific planning, which may then take place, the natural place of Malabar will be with Cochin and Travancore and of the Union Karnataka with Mysore and their problems will be automatically solved. In such a planning it may not be generally necessary to break up the bilingual border districts and they may be disposed of on their individual economic and historical affinities, and capital cities like Bombay and Madras should receive special treatment, which their interest and the larger interests of the nation may demand. Subject to the above and other relevant considerations, if re-formed provinces present features of linguistic homogeneity also that will be an additional advantage. If the Government of the day should decide to re-form these provinces, an attempt should be made to secure the agreement of the parties concerned, which alone would ensure future harmonious relations.

Our conclusions, therefore, are:

(1) The formation of provinces on exclusively or even mainly linguistic considerations is not in the larger

interests of the Indian nation and should not be taken in hand.

(2) The existing Provinces of Madras, Bombay, C.P. and Berar present serious administrative problems for which an administrative solution is urgently necessary and it is for the Centre to find a satisfactory solution of these problems.

(3) The aforesaid problems do not call for an immediate re-formation of provinces. As soon as Indian States have been integrated and the country has stabilized itself and other conditions are favourable they may be re-formed and convenient administrative provinces set up.

(4) In the formation of new provinces, whenever such a work is taken in hand, oneness of language may be one of the factors to be taken into consideration along with others; but it should not be the decisive or even the main factor. Generally speaking, bilingual districts in border areas, which have developed an economic and organic life of their own, should not be broken up and should be disposed of on considerations of their own special needs. Similarly, the cities of Bombay and Madras should receive special treatment and be disposed of in the best interests of India as a whole and in their own interests. Subject to above and other relevant and paramount considerations, if some new provinces come into being and produce more or less linguistic homogeneity they need not be objected to.

(5) If any powers are necessary for the Centre for a proper solution of the administrative problems in the provinces the Constitution should provide for them.

We find that no new provinces out of those referred to us should be formed for the present; and, in view of this finding, the other questions referred to us do not arise and need no answer.

RUNNING STAFF PAY AND ALLOWANCES COMMITTEE, 1948—REPORT

New Delhi, Railway Board, 1949. 79p.

Chairman : Shri D. P. Mathur.
Members : Shri M. D. Balaraman; Shri N. G. Hoskote.

APPOINTMENT

The Running Staff Pay and Allowances Committee was constituted under the Railway Board vide their letter No. E47-CPC/AL/(1), dated July 1, 1948.

TERMS OF REFERENCE

(i) To examine the prescribed scales of pay recommended for Drivers, Firemen, Guards and other Running Staff on Railways by the Central Pay Commission, and to make recommendations in respect of reasonable basic scales to replace these prescribed scales in the light of actual conditions of work and of the reduction in the hours of work, as recommended in the Adjudicator's Award and also in view of the desirability of obtaining suitable direct recruits for these categories.

(ii) To frame revised Running Allowance Rules for Running Staff on a uniform basis for all Indian Government Railways, keeping in mind the desirability of ensuring that the total emoluments of running staff prior to the introduction of the prescribed scales are, as far as possible, not reduced upon the alteration in the basic scales, and the formulation of the new basis for the payment of running allowances.

(iii) To make recommendations regarding the standards that should be adopted uniformly on Indian Government Railways in designating and classifying Drivers, Firemen, Guards, etc., in the various grades finally fixed for them.

(iv) To make recommendations regarding the recruitment, training and channels of promotion for Drivers, Firemen, Guards, etc.

(v) To make any other recommendations concerning Drivers, Firemen, Guards, etc.

CONTENTS

Part I: Appointment of the Committee and its Terms of Reference; General Considerations and Historical Background; General Review of Systems in force on the various Railways regulating the Emoluments of Running Staff—Section A: Running Allowances; Section B: Scales of Pay in force on Railways and proportion which Running Allowances bear to Basic Pay; Part II: Principles that should govern the future Pay and Allowance Structure of Running Staff—Section A: Distribution of Total Emoluments as between Pay and Running Allowances; Section B: Levels of Total Emoluments; Scales of Pay to be adopted for Running Staff in the future Pay Structure; Principles which should govern allotment of Grades; General Principles which should govern payment of Running Allowances; Draft Rules for payment of Running Allowances and Overtime to Running Staff; Channels of Promotion for Loco and Traffic Running Staff; Miscellaneous Recommendations; Annexures; Appendices.

RECOMMENDATIONS

Protection Of Emoluments Of Individual Staff

The desirability of ensuring that the total emoluments of Running Staff prior to the introduction of the Prescribed Scales are as far as possible not reduced, as a result of the application of the Scales of Pay and Running Allowances, has been borne in mind by the Committee in framing their recommendations. It is, however, impracticable to legislate in a manner that will ensure that every individual's emoluments are preserved. Cases may arise where the emoluments of individual employees may be adversely affected by the revisions proposed. Such a possibility is envisaged particularly in view of the general feeling prevailing that the rules for the fixation of pay in the Prescribed Scales did not help very much to improve the position due to the absence of provisions giving adequate weightage for length of service. Human nature being what it is, the staff might welcome a substantial reduction in the hours of work but they would not reconcile themselves easily to even a small decrease in their emoluments. In the absence of adequate weightage for length of service, the Committee visualize that loss of emoluments may take place as the rise in basic pay on fixation in the proposed scales of pay may, in some cases, bring little gain while the allowances undergo a substantial reduction. Pending the full implementation of the Adjudicator's Award, however, it is anticipated that Running Staff, working up to their present level of hours of duty, would qualify for emoluments generally in excess of the levels of remuneration envisaged in the Report. Enhanced earnings from Running Allowances during the interregnum should be regarded as reasonable remuneration for the excessive hours of work put in by members of the Running Staff on duty. In the fullness of time, when the Adjudicator's Award is fully implemented, the emoluments of the Running Staff will ultimately decline to the level contemplated in the Report. In any case, the necessity for some form of protection to save individuals from loss of emoluments may arise.

In making their recommendations regarding the pay and allowances, the Committee have assumed that they would compulsorily apply to post-1931 staff and optionally to pre-1931 employees who may, if they so choose, elect the Prescribed Scales of Pay and Allowances. It is normally expected that the pre-1931 employees drawing a high level of allowances would not ordinarily elect the revised Running Allowance Rules. It is also evident that Running Allowances drawn by pre-1931 staff will suffer a reduction on implementation of the Award. It was not possible for the Committee to have formulated a scheme of Pay and Allowances which would have covered pre-1931 staff without unduly raising the proposed level of total emoluments.

To ensure uniformity in application of rules regulating Running Allowances, it might be advantageous to offer as inducement pre-1931 staff to elect the new Running Allowance Rules. The requisite inducement would rest on protection being afforded to their present level of Running Allowances. The occasion for offering such inducement would arise when the Adjudicator's Award has been fiually implemented because pre-1931 staff might conceivably ask for compensation for loss of Running Allowances arising from the implementation of the Award. The grant of the compensation could then be made contingent on their adopting the New Running Allowance Rules.

Employment Of Intermediate-Grade Guards To Tranship (Van And S.Q.T.) Services

The E.I. Railway run their Tranship Trains (S.Q.T.s) with intermediate grades of Guards. The Committee consider that employment of higher-grade employees possessing more experience and higher sense of responsibility in dealings with a large number of small packages should make for improvement in the running of these trains. In view of the unsatisfactory running of Tranship and Section Trains generally, it is recommended that the E.I. Railway practice may be adopted with advantage on all Railways.

Appointment Of Brakesmen In Place Of Guards And Clerks

The E.P. and E.I. Railways employ so-called Luggage Guards who are fully qualified Guards to run on trains in addition to the Guard in charge of the train. E. I. Railway have recently started employing Brakesmen. This system of working in which Guards are employed to perform duties analogous to those of Brakesmen would appear to be uneconomic and should, in the opinion of the Committee, be replaced uniformly by employment of Brakesmen. Similarly, the practice of employing Van Clerks on the O.T. Railway in place of Brakesmen needs replacement to secure uniformity of practice on all Railways.

REVIEWING COMMITTEE OF THE INDIAN INSTITUTE OF SCIENCE, BANGALORE, 1948—REPORT

New Delhi, Ministry of Education, 1949. 68p.

Chairman : Sir Alfred Egerton.
Members : Sir Ben Lockspeiser; Dr. J. N. Mukherjee.
Secretary : Shri G. K. Chandiramani.

APPOINTMENT

The Reviewing Committee of the Indian Institute of Bangalore was constituted under the Government of India vide their Resolution No. F. 9-27(94)/46-E. III(A) dated August 5, 1948.

TERMS OF REFERENCE

(1) To review the working and development of the Institute with special reference to the purposes for which it was founded and, if any changes are considered desirable in the organization or activities of the Institute for the better achievement of these purposes, to make recommendations accordingly with due regard to the Institute's actual or reasonably augmentable financial resources, in particular:

(i) to report on the progress made with the execution of the development plans already undertaken.

(ii) to examine the work of each department and the library of the Institute during the last decade with special reference to:

(a) the extent and quality of research work done;

(b) the formation of sections and their grouping within various departments;

(c) the extent of co-operation and co-ordination amongst the various departments; and

(d) the development of team-work in research

and to make recommendations in regard to the possibilities for further effective collaboration amongst departments and sections in their research activities.

(iii) to make recommendations with the object of increasing the quantity and quality of research work in regard to the selection of research staff and workers and to consider whether the guidance of students for M.Sc. degrees of Universities is a proper function of the Institute.

(iv) to examine the extent to which researches in applied sciences have been carried out and utilized by industry; to consider the rules made in this behalf and to make recommendations for an effective liaison between the Institute and Industry for the greater benefit of the country, as contemplated by the donor in his original scheme of Endowment.

(v) to review the work done during the War at the request of the Government of India and to consider how best the Institute can assist the Government in research matters.

(vi) to report on the adequacy or otherwise and the utilization of the existing scientific equipment and apparatus and to make recommendations in regard to the provision that should be made for new equipment over the next three years.

(vii) to consider the plans for expansion of the activities of the Institute, such as establishment of a Central Production Workshop, reorganization of the Aeronautical Engineering Department, etc.

(viii) to consider whether any revision of the pay scales of teaching staff is necessary.

(ix) to review the financial position in the light of the normal revenues of the Institute for the maintenance of the old departments and the ad hoc grant for the new departments; to consider the extent to which the original grant of the Government of India for the recurring expenditure should be enhanced; and to consider the advisability of augmenting the fee income.

(x) to report on the working of the Court, the Council and the Senate of the Institute.

(2) To advise generally on any matter which, in the opinion of the Committee, is of importance to the Institute.

CONTENTS

Letter to H. E. the Governor-General of India; Introduction; Terms of Reference; Structure of the Report; Summary and Main Recommendations; Main Recommendations; General Considerations and Character of the Institute; Organization and Administration; Organization and Work of the Institute; Financial Review.

RECOMMENDATIONS

The Institute should continue its development as a higher technical institute.

The main recommendations on the development of the departments are:

(a) **Mathematics**, establishment of a Department of Applied Mathematics.

(b) **Chemistry,** creation of a chair of Physical Chemistry and appointment of a Superintendent Professor.

(c) **Radio and Radar,** the Department of Electrical Communication should concentrate on teaching radio and radar.

(d) **Aeronautics,** the Aeronautical Engineering Department should widen its scope and co-ordinate teaching in other departments to provide a fuller course.

(e) **Instrumentation,** an Instrument Section should be established in the Department of Mechanical Engineering and Workshop.

(f) **Information Bureau,** the activities should be consolidated and considerably expanded.

The powers, functions and responsibilities of the various authorities should be more clearly defined and procedure regularized. In particular :

(a) **Council** should lay down a broad policy. Its scientific membership should be increased.

(b) **Director** should have full powers for administration and should be an eminent scientist.

Selection Committees should be strengthened.

Salary Scales should be increased.

Scholarships should be increased.

Student amenities should be improved and accommodation increased.

Means for Balancing Budget should include increased financial assistance to the Institute.

THE HOMOEOPATHIC ENQUIRY COMMITTEE, 1948—REPORT

Delhi, Manager of Publications, 1949. 125p.

Chairman : Dr. J. N. Mukherjee.
Members : Col. Amir Chand; Dr. P. N. Chopra; Dr. L. D. Dhawale; Dr. J. N. Hazra; Dr. Diwan Jai Chand; Dr. J. N. Majumdar; Col. K. V. Ramana Rao; Dr. S. C. Sen.

N.B.—Captain H. N. Shivapuri resigned and Col. Amir Chand took his place from January 21, 1949.
Secretary : Dr. Diwan Chand Chopra.

APPOINTMENT

The Homoeopathic Enquiry Committee was constituted under the Ministry of Health vide their letter No. F. 6-5/48-MI dated August 31, 1948.

TERMS OF REFERENCE

(i) To report on the place of homoeopathy in relation to medicine in all its aspects including the treatment, prevention and control of diseases;

(ii) to survey the existing facilities for the teaching of homoeopathy in India, the extent to which this system of treatment is practised in the country, and the manner in which such practice is carried on, i.e., whether by people adequately trained or not; and

(iii) to make recommendations to the Government on,

(a) the measures to be taken to improve facilities for training in homoeopathy and to regulate such training; and

(b) the desirability of State control of the practice of homoeopathy and, if control is desirable, the manner of such control.

CONTENTS

Introduction; Scope of Enquiry; Present State of Medicine as a Science and the Developments which have preceded it; Measures for the Treatment, Prevention and Control of Disease; General Conditions of Medical Aid in India; Functions of the State in the Matter of Medicine and Public Health and the Conditions to be Fulfilled by a System of Medicine; Principles of Homoeopathy and its Distinctive Approach Towards Treatment of Diseased Conditions; Homoeopathy in Other Countries; Place of Homoeopathy in Medicine in all its Aspects; Action Taken or Contemplated by Provincial and State Governments to Regulate the Practice of Homoeopathy; Survey of the Existing Facilities for the Teaching of Homoeopathy in India; Extent to which the Homoeopathic System is Practised in the Country; Conditions of Practice of Homoeopathy; Views of Certain Honourable Ministers of Health of the Provinces on Homoeopathy as Practised in India; Other Views; Recommendations; Central Council of Homoeopathic Medicine; Training in Homoeopathy; Summary; Annexures.

RECOMMENDATIONS

I. Central Council Of Homoeopathic Medicine

In Ch. II we have mentioned the conditions which must, in our opinion, be satisfied by any system of medicine in order to deserve recognition and administrative and financial assistance from the State. We have pointed out that the conditions precedent to such recognition and assistance must be that the particular system of medicine should be able to diagnose a diseased condition, to participate in Public Health measures of the Government for prevention and control of disease and to make available to the State the services of qualified medical men with supplementary training, if need be, in times of emergency, e.g. during war or epidemics. The system must also keep abreast of scientific developments. If the main conditions stated above are held to be satisfied by a particular System of Medicine, it would fully deserve State recognition and support. It seems redundant on our part to emphasize the fact that a State, which does not apply the above criteria before giving its recognition and support to a system of medicine, accepts, unjustifiably to our mind, a risk which is bound to have far-reaching consequences. Again, the first and foremost duty of a State is that it must adopt effective measures to ensure that the life of its citizens is not endangered by persons who have no scientific training and systematic education for medical and surgical practice. It is its bounden duty to take all steps necessary to ensure that its citizens have reasonable facilities to maintain good health. It is the function of a State to provide adequate medical aid as regards both curative and preventive measures. It follows that the State must have proper and adequate control and supervision over the practice of medicine and medical education.

We note that the World Medical Association has recently collected information on the adequacy or otherwise of official or unofficial control of medical practice in different countries. National Medical Associations of 12 countries held the view that the controls were adequate and effective. Three of these 12, namely, Switzerland, Sweden and the U.S.A., had both legislative and unofficial controls while nine others, namely, Bulgaria, Canada, Chili, Denmark, Eire, France, Haiti, Iceland and Norway, had had legislative provisions but no unofficial organizations. In Belgium, Luxemburg and the Philippines, the control was considered to be inadequate and ineffectual. Belgium had both legislative and unofficial machinery for control. China, New Foundland, New Zealand and South Africa reported insufficient or partial control although China had both legislative and unofficial control. Great Britain reported improvement but considered that more control was desirable although it had legislative and unofficial machinery for control. Australia had effective control in three States, ineffective control in two States and information regarding the other States was not available. Australia had legislative control in all but one State and unofficial machinery in all States. India and Pakistan having no control desired to have an effective system of control.

The views expressed by the National Medical Associations in outlining the further steps needed varied widely. They included suggestions regarding:

(1) Strict enforcement of existing regulations with severe penalties for infractions;

(2) Adequate funds, personnel and facilities for purposes of control;

(3) Improved legislative measures;

(4) Support by the medical profession to check illegal advertisements even to the extent of prosecutions by the National Medical Association in cases of illegal advertising;

(5) Maintenance of distinction between Articles of Hygiene and modifications with control over both;

(6) Higher standards for pharmacists;

(7) Control of cult practice and unqualified individuals prescribing medications;

(8) Popular health education programmes; and

(9) Better co-ordination of law governing advertisement and sale of secret remedies and appliances, registration of manufacturers, proprietors and importers who would be required to pay the prescribed fees and furnish lists of medicines and appliances; exact and complete statement of ingredients and their use; maintenance of a sample of each appliance, issue of registration numbers for each remedy permitted to be sold and imprinted on the bottle or label: prohibition by law of invitations to sufferers to correspond with vendors and of the use of fictitious testimony.

In so for as India is concerned, an initial stage towards this direction of control can be traced to the Bombay Medical Act of 1912, the Bengal Medical Act of 1914, the Madras Medical Registration Act of 1914, the Punjab Medical Registration Act of 1916 and the U.P. Medical Act of 1917. These Acts applied mainly to the practitioners of the Western system of medicine for whom certain minimum qualifications were laid down. None of these Acts provided for compulsory registration nor did they make a reference to the innumerable practitioners or other systems of medicine.

The Indian Medical Degrees Act, 1916, regulates the grant of titles implying qualifications in Western Medical Science and prohibits the assumption and use by unqualified persons of such titles. Western Medical Science is defined to mean Western method of Allopathic Medicine, Obstetrics and Surgery but does not include Homoeopathic, Unani or Ayurvedic Systems of Medicine. The right of conferring or issuing degrees, diplomas, licences and certificates is exercised by the Government of India or the Provincial Governments. It prohibits any person other than holders of such titles to use diplomas. The penalty for non-compliance is a fine which may extend to Rs. 1,000. This provision does not apply to people who had been using these degrees prior to 1916. The provisions have been modified by the Madras, Bengal, Bihar and U.P. Governments. The Bombay Indigenous Medical Act, 1949, has included other Systems of Medicine and C.P. and Berar in their Degrees Amendment Bill, 1948, have also included practitioners of other Systems of Medicine. It is understood that the Act is being revised at present in the East Punjab.

It was in 1933 that the Government of India enacted the Government of India Medical Council Act which gave the Indian Medical Council supervisory powers over "certain medical qualifications which are granted by Indian Universities and which are incorporated in the First Schedule of the Indian Medical Council Act". The Act deals with the "Western System of Medical Education" only and makes no reference to education in any of the other Systems of Medicine.

The question of registration and control over the Homoeopathic System of Medicine was, however, taken up subsequently on a Provincial basis by the Governments of Bengal, Bombay, Madras, Bihar, Central Provinces and Berar and the United Provinces and by certain Indian States like Baroda and Travancore. An account of the action taken by Provincial and State Governments has been given in Ch. VI of this Report.

We feel that it is difficult to lay down exhaustively the conditions of State control but we consider that legislation for the control of the practice of and training in Homoeopathy should aim at:

(i) Adequate provision for the supervision and control of Homoeopathic educational institutions and hospitals;

(ii) Registration of practitioners of the Homoeopathic system; and

(iii) Control over Homoeopathic pharmacies, pharmaceutical laboratories and manufacturing concerns.

In Ch. VII we have given facts and figures to show that by far the vast majority of existing Homoeopathic practitioners had received no training in the basic and medical sciences. We have also referred to the extent to which quackery is prevalent and have pointed out that the duty of the State is to ensure that the health of the people is not jeopardized by sueh conditions. We definitely recommend that in future no person who has not undergone a regular course of training in the basic and medical sciences, as discussed earlier in the report, should be allowed to engage himself in the practice of Homoeopathy in future. We also recommend that their names must be entered into a register in a manner to be prescribed by law.

We have indicated that while four of the existing institutions attempted to impart a course of basic scientific training, even though the standard of teaching and equipment falls far short of that obtaining in the least equipped medical schools in India, no other existing Homoeopathic institution can be said to be capable of giving such a training. We have, however, to consider the large number of existing Homoeopathic practitioners who are now earning a livelihood and on whom a section of the population depends for medical relief, whatever this may mean in actual practice. We also feel that we have to take note of the action taken by different Provincial Governments, which has been detailed in Ch. VI. We have given very careful consideration to all aspects of the case and while we feel that for human reasons we have to consider sympathetically the claims of existing unqualified Homoeopathic practitioners, we cannot shirk the duty of making recommendations to ensure that minimum harm is done to the health of the population.

Various suggestions have been made to us as to the manner in which we can bring the existing practitioners on a register or a list. We have given careful thought to these and we think that the following recommendations not only represent the general consensus of opinion expressed before us but also will best achieve which we have in view. We recommend therefore that:

(a) The categories (i) to (iv) below should be placed on a "Register".

(i) Registered Medical Practitioners who have taken to the practice of Homoeopathy;

(ii) Medical Practitioners holding degrees from foreign countries, which entitled them to practise medicine in the countries where such qualifications were obtained;

(iii) Those who have successfully gone through the four-year course of training in any one of the four institutions mentioned in Para. 116;

(iv) Graduates of the Central College of Homoeopathy, Calcutta, the Regular College of Homoeopathy, Calcutta, and the Ashutosh Homoeopathic College, Calcutta, which have ceased to exist but used to have four-year course of training in Basic Sciences and in Homoeopathy, should be put on the Register.

(b) The following category (v) should be placed on a "List":

(v) Those who satisfy the Board we have recommended to be set up that they are bona fide whole-time practitioners of Homoeopathy for not less than 7 years at the time when effect is given to our recommendations.

The following category (vi) may also be placed on the "List" subject to the conditions mentioned below:

(vi) All other categories of existing Homoeopathic practitioners should be included in the List, provided they pass a test in both the Theory and Practice of Medicine of Homoeopathy, as may be laid down by the Board mentioned above. We are definitely of the opinion, however, that the test should conform at least to the existing standard as has been laid down by the General Council of State Faculty of Homoeopathic Medicine, West Bengal. The test will be continued for a period of not more than three years and may be held twice a year. Any existing Homoeopathic practitioners who will not be able to pass the examination within the above period of three years from the date when effect is given to our recommendations should be debarred from practising Homoeopathy.

We unanimously and emphatically recommend that immediate steps should be taken by the Central and Provincial Governments and States to declare illegal the use of bogus degrees, diplomas, or titles, and their colourable imitations not obtained as a result of regular institutional training in an institution recognized by the Government of the Province or State in which the institution is situated and institutions mentioned in Para. 116 which we have recognized for the purpose of registration of Homoeopathic practitioners. We recommend to the Central and Provincial Governments to take appropriate legal action to penalize the use of such bogus degrees, diplomas, titles and their colourable imitations.

Two members of our Committee representing the regular system of medicine were definitely of the opinion that in future nobody without adequate training and qualifications recognized by the Government should be allowed to practise medicine but as a temporary measure and in view of the large number of persons who are now practising and who will be deprived of their livelihood they agreed with the rest of us to the maintenance of a List to absorb some of those people who are practising Homoeopathy at present provided that they had a minimum of experience as may be laid down by law. No further additions should, however, be made to that List after it was once compiled so that the numbers included will diminish and the class will vanish in course of time. They felt that all persons practising Homoeopathy for a period of not less than 10 years, subject to this fact being certified in a prescribed manner and the passing of a satisfactory test, should be put on the List.

We have distinguished between a "Register" and a "List" because we feel such a distinction to be essential. Registration which means the entering of the names of practitioners on a prescribed Register is intended:

(i) to safeguard the public;

(ii) to facilitate control of practice;

(iii) to enable practitioners to get the privileges and rights of bona fide medical practitioners and to protect them against unfair competition by unqualified persons;

(iv) to provide an electorate for the Provincial branches of the Central Board; and

(v) to protect the public from being exploited by quacks.

The "Registered" Homoeopathic Practitioners will be entitled to sign or authenticate a birth or death certificate and a medical or physical fitness certificate and to give evidence at any inquest or in a court of law as an expert under Section 45 of the Indian Evidence Act, 1872. The "Listed" practitioners will not enjoy any of the above privileges although they will be entitled to practise Homoeopathy.

We carefully considered whether control by the State was necessary and, if so, what steps should be taken by the Government in that direction. We examined also what would be the functions of the Centre and of the Provinces and the States, if control was to be introduced. Excepting two members of the Committee whose views have been stated later, we feel that in order to secure uniformity both in standard and conditions of practice and training, there should be a Central Council of Homoeopathic Medicine as also Provincial Boards or Faculties of Homoeopathy. The functions of the Central Council would be co-ordination and advice and control with regard to the maintenance of standards. We further considered that in view of the facts revealed before us and of the almost complete absence of uniformity in the standards of Homoeopathic training and practice and the prevalence of quackery, the Central Council should be constituted immediately in order to enable it to take action for the constitution of the Provincial Boards through the Provincial Governments or State Union Governments.

We recommend, therefore, as follows:

A Council of Homoeopathic Medicine shall be established by law and called the Central Council of Homoeopathic Medicine, India, hereafter referred to as the Council. It shall come into existence on such date as the Central Government may fix by a notification in the Gazette. The members constituting the first Council will hold office for a period of five years; any vacancy during this period will be filled by nomination by the Government of India as provided below. The term of office of elected members shall be for three years after the first period of five years of the life of the Council.

The Council shall consist of the following members:

(i) A President who shall be a whole-time recognized Homoeopathic practitioner, to be elected from amongst the members of the Council subject to the proviso that the Director-General of Health Services, Government of India, shall be the President of the

Council during the first term of five years. Subsequently the President will be elected by the Council from amongst its members and he will hold office for a period of three years, but the Director-General of Health Services, Government of India, will be the ex-officio member of the Council.

(ii) A Vice-President to be elected from amongst the members of the Council for a period of three years. He should be a whole-time recognized Homoeopathic practitioner.

(iii) One member to be elected from each Province and State Union from amongst the recognized Homoeopathic practitioners of the Province or the State Union.

For the first five years, these members will be nominated by the Ministry of Health, Government of India, in consultation with the Provincial or State Union Governments.

(iv) Two members to be elected by the Inter-University Board of India, one of whom shall be a member of the said Board and the other shall be a member of the Faculty of Medicine of an Indian University.

(v) The Director-General of Health Services, Government of India—ex-officio.

(vi) One member each from the two Houses of the Indian Parliament.

(vii) Three members who are "recognized" Homoeopathic practitioners to be elected from amongst the Heads of the Homoeopathic Educational Institutions recognized by the Provincial or State Union Governments, subject to the proviso that not more than one member will be elected from any one Province or State Union. For the first term of five years of the Council, these members will be nominated by the Ministry of Health, Government of India, in consultation with the Provincial or State Union Governments.

(viii) One member from the National Institute of Science from amongst the Fellows of the said Institute.

(ix) Four members who shall be recognized Homoeopathic practitioners to be nominated by the Central Government.

The Government of India will appoint a whole-time paid Secretary who will conduct and administer the affairs of the Council, but will not be a member of the latter.

The word "recognized" shall mean Homoeopathic practitioners who hold a qualification as laid down in Para. 159 entitling them to be put on the Register and have practised Homoeopathy for at least five years previous to the date of nomination.

The functions of the Council shall be mainly of a co-ordinating and advisory nature, but the Council will have powers to control, which will be exercised through the Provincial Boards or Faculties, in the following matters:

(i) Standard, equipment and training of affiliated Homoeopathic institutions;

(ii) Standard of examinations to be held for Homoeopathic students;

(iii) Registration of existing Homoeopathic practitioners; and

(iv) Homoeopathic pharmacies, pharmaceutical laboratories and manufacturing concerns.

The Council will have full powers of inspection in all matters.

Provincial or State Boards or Faculties, as may be set up by Governments of Provincial or State Unions, will be responsible for the maintenance of registers, for the actual conducting of examinations, publication of results and enforcement of disciplinary action, subject to the supervisory authority of the Council.

The Provincial Boards or Faculties shall be constituted with the following as members:

A President: The Surgeon-General or the Inspector-General of Civil Hospitals shall be the President of the Provincial or State Union Boards during the first term of five years, after which the President will be elected by the Board from amongst its members, but the Inspector-General of Civil Hospitals or the Surgeon-General, as the case may be, will continue to be an ex-officio member of the Board.

A Vice-President: To be elected from amongst the members of the Board. He shall be a whole-time recognized Homoeopathic practitioner.

Ten members to be nominated by the Provincial Government for the first term of five years of the Board and to be elected thereafter from amongst the recognized Homoeopathic practitioners, one from each of the 10 areas into which the Province or the State Union will be divided for this purpose. These areas will not include the provincial capitals, which constitute separate electoral areas.

Five recognized Homoeopathic practitioners from the capital of the Province or State Union.

One member who shall not be a medical practitioner to be nominated by the Corporation or the Municipality of the capital town of the Province.

One member, who shall not be a medical practitioner, nominated by the Provincial University or Universities wherever they exist.

One member from the heads of such Homoeopathic educational institutions as are affiliated to the respective Provincial Boards. These members shall be recognized Homoeopathic practitioners.

Two members, who shall not be medical practitioners from the Provincial Legislature.

There shall be a whole-time paid Registrar who will also act as Secretary to the Board.

The word "recognized" has the same meaning as defined in Para. 165(2).

Subject to the provision that in all matters coming within the functions of the Central Council, the Provincial Boards will act under the authority of the former, the functions of the latter shall be :

(1) To maintain a "Register" and a "List" of Homoeopathic Practitioners;

(2) To maintain the standard of teaching and of equipment of Homoeopathic medical institutions, as laid down by the Central Council of Homoeopathic Medicine;

(3) To affiliate Homoeopathic institutions to the Provincial Board;

(4) To hold examinations and to grant licences or diplomas to the successful candidates, according to such rules as may be laid down by the Central Council;

(5) To advise the Provincial Government and general public on all matters relating to advancement of Homoeopathic studies and medical relief;

(6) To control and administer all Homoeopathic charitable organizations aided by the Provincial Government; and

(7) To appoint sub-committees for carrying out the work of the Board.

We visualize that the organizations, the establishment of which has been recommended by us, will among other things ensure that :

(1) Only persons who have been trained in institutions recognized by the State and have passed an examination according to the approved procedure will be allowed to practise medicine in future. They may be awarded suitable degrees, diplomas or certificates;

(2) All other persons will be debarred by law to practise medicine or to assume degrees or titles, and practice of medicine by such persons would be made a cognizable offence;

(3) No medical practitioner would be allowed to advertise the efficacy of his medicine or treatment;

(4) Advertisements of medicines and bringing them to the notice of the public would he suitably controlled by law;

(5) No person including Registered Medical Practitioner would be allowed to do anything to create an impression that he was a "Specialist", except as might be provided by law;

(6) The purchase, sale, award or assumption of title, or advertisement of medicines by persons other than those authorized by law would be made a penal offence;

(7) Provision would be made by legislation for proper and regular inspection in a prescribed manner of establishments manufacturing medicines and other pharmaceutical products, pharmacies, dispensaries and individuals preparing and dispensing medicines; and

(8) Undesirable advertisements claiming the efficacy of patent and proprietary medicines and circulation of objectionable literature, especially about sex matters, would be controlled by legislation.

We recommend for the consideration of the Government the establishment of one Central Model Homoeopathic teaching institution for the training of under-graduates and of post-graduates.

The two members of the Committee representing the regular system of medicine do not subscribe to the view that it is necessary to establish a Central Council of Homoeopathic Medicine and Provincial Boards of Homoeopathy with the constitution and functions as proposed above. They hold that the functions of the Councils and the Boards are traditionally and necessarily of two kinds, first, to prescribe and ensure a minimum standard of medical education and examination and, secondly, to maintain a Register of qualified practitioners and to control the conduct of medical practice by them. Their recommendations are stated below.

"So far as training in Homoeopathy is concerned, no arrangements exist in India and if they do here and there, they are totally inadequate and unsatisfactory. If Homoeopathy is to be taught in India it should, in our opinion, be done as in other countries such as the U.K. and the U.S.A., after the attainment of a basic qualification in scientific medical education recognized by the Medical Council of India or the Provincial Medical Councils, and arrangements should be made for it in the colleges of modern medical science and not in separate institutions and only those parts of Homoeopathy should be taught that have stood the test of science. The reason for this is obvious. Homoeopathy is admitted not to be a medical science by itself but only a system of therapy. The basic, preclinical and clinical sciences are the same in Homoeopathy as in the modern medical science, only the approach to therapy is different. For regulation of training and to prescribe and ensure a minimum standard of Homoeopathic education and examinations all that is rational and necessary is to establish a Faculty of Homoeopathy under the Medical Council of India and the Provincial Medical Councils on the same lines as various faculties under a University. The membership of such faculties should be open to only those who possess a medical qualification recognized by the Medical Council of India or the Provincial Medical Councils and are registered with it and are practitioners in Homoeopathy of not less than five years' standing, preferably with teaching experience in recognized Homoeopathic teaching institutions.

The control of Homoeopathic practice in the case of future entrants all of whom will possess a recognized basic qualification in scientific medicine as suggested by us will be exercised by the Medical Council of India or the Provincial Medical Councils with whom they will be registered and it will neither be advisable nor necessary to constitute separate Councils and Boards. So far as the existing Homoeopathic practitioners are concerned, those who possess a qualification recognized by the Medical Council of India or a Provincial Medical Council should be registered. For the rest, Homoeopathic Councils should be established in the Provinces and these Councils should maintain "Lists" and not "Registers" of such of the existing Homoeopathic practitioners who come under this category and who have practised Homoeopathy as a profession for not less than 10 years and who pass a test to be prescribed by such Councils. This condition may be relaxed in the case of those who possess a qualification recognized by the West Bengal Government or a qualification from a foreign country entitling the holder to practise medicine in that country. Such practitioners should be called "Listed Homoeopathic Practitioners" and not "Registered Homoeopathic Practitioners". Their number will gradually decrease and will not be added to.

The constitution of the Provincial Homoeopathic Council should be as follows:

A President: The Surgeon-General or the Inspector-General of Civil Hospitals, as the case may be, during the first term of five years, after which the President will be elected by the Council from amongst its members, but the Surgeon-General or Inspector-General of Civil Hospitals will continue to be an ex-officio member of the Council.

Vice-President: He shall be elected from amongst the members of the Council and shall be a Registered or a Listed whole-time Homoeopathic practitioner.

Four members to be nominated by the Provincial or State Union Government for the first term of five years from amongst the Homoeopathic practitioners residing in the Province or State Union and thereafter to be elected from amongst the Listed Homoeopathic Practitioners in the Province or the State Union.

One member to be nominated by the Provincial or State Union Government for the first term of five years from amongst the members of the staff of the Homoeopathic medical institutions recognized by the Provincial or State Union Government and thereafter to be elected from amongst themselves by such members of the staff. Such members will not be eligible for election under any other Clause.

Two members to be nominated by the Provincial or State Union Government for the first term of five years and thereafter to be elected from amongst the Homoeopathic practitioners holding qualifications in scientific medicine recognized by the Medical Council of India or the Provincial Medical Council and residing in the Provinces or the State Union.

There will be a Registrar who will be a whole-time paid officer of the Council and who will also act as Secretary to it.

Regarding the type of Homoeopathic training institutions to be set up in future and the control of Homoeopathy in general there has been sharp difference of opinion amongst our colleagues. Several suggestions were placed before us regarding the manner in which Homoeopathic training should be imparted, that is to say, the type of institutions which should undertake this task. We considered in detail the three types of institutions:

(1) Institutions which will be devoted only to the teaching of Homoeopathic medicine along with the basic, pre-clinical and clinical sciences;

(2) Institutions where the basic, pre-clinical and clinical sciences will be common both to students of Homoeopathy and of the regular system of medicine with the difference that students going in for Homoeopathy will not have to take up the courses in Materia Medica and Therapeutics.

In the case of students going in for Homoeopathy the courses in clinical sciences will have an orientation characteristic of Homoeopathy and the Homoeopathic Philosophy, Therapeutics, Materia Medica and Repertory studies will be specially provided for;

(3) Institutions which contemplate only training in Homoeopathy (this training has been described as post-graduate training in Homoeopathy in other parts of the report) for those who have obtained a basic qualification in the regular system of medicine.

The great majority of persons practising Homoeopathy are in favour of institutions which are devoted solely to Homoeopathic medical education. The establishment of post-graduate institutions for training regular medical graduates in Homoeopathy has also been supported by the great majority in addition to the last type of institutions. In other words, the majority of Homoeopathic practitioners have supported the third type in addition to the first type. Medical men belonging to the regular system and a small number of Homoeopathic practitioners have supported the third type of institutions. Three of the five Hon'ble Ministers of Health of the Provinces, who have expressed their views on this subject, consider the third type to be the most preferable. One Hon'ble Minister favoured separate institutions for training in Homoeopathy as an alternative; two were in favour of bifurcation into two channels, one leading to the regular system and the other to the Homoeopathic system of training in the basic and pre-clinical sciences was the same (i.e., the second type institution).

Two Hon'ble Ministers favoured separate institutions if the contents of the training were the same. One Hon'ble Minister expressed no view on the type of institutions but said that the two systems should not be mixed together and they should be kept separate. The medical men representing the regular system of medicine including two members of our Committee think that the post-graduate course is the only rational one. They are, however, not opposed to the provision of training in Homoeopathy in medical colleges but then definitely do not consider purely Homoeopathic teaching institutions to be desirable. The main argument adduced by Homoeopaths including the Homoeopathic members of our Committee in support of purely Homoeopathic medical teaching institutions is the apathy and perhaps active antagonism which the practitioners of the regular system have, according to them, towards Homoeopathy. They think the other most important reason for their demanding separate institutions is the entirely distinctive approach of Homoeopathy in the realm of all therapeutics. They feel that Homoeopathy will not have a chance of developing Homoeopathic training and research unless they get institutions of their own. They, however, agree that in matters of research there should be co-operatioa between the workers of the two systems as also with pure scientists.

The two members of our Committee representing the regular system of medicine do not agree with the Homoeopathic members of the Committee that there should be separate Homoeopathic teaching institutions. Since all witnesses interested in Homoeopathy and all the Homoeopathic members of the Committee admit that training in the basic, pre-clinical and clinical sciences up to the Indian Universities' standard is an essential part of Homoeopathic education and the science of medicine like all other sciences is one and indivisible, in their view there cannot be two anatomies or two physiologies. The same applies tc all the other pre-clinical and clinical sciences. These cannot be different in Homoeopathy which has been admitted to differ from the Modern System of Medicine in its approach to therapeutics only, being in itself only a system of pharmaco-therapeutics. It follows therefore from the above that it is neither scientific nor logical to multiply the institutions without any justification. They ask the question "Why have two institutions for what can be taught in one ?" and emphasize that a poor country like India cannot afford to do that. In their opinion the proposal of having separate institutions would not only cause enormous waste of money, men, material and time, but would be unscientific. For the teaching of those subjects which are a peculiarity of Homoeopathy, all the other subjects being common to both the systems, satisfactory arrangements can be easily and most economically made in the colleges and hospitals of the Modern System of Medicine. The taunt of apathy going on to antagonism of the votaries of the Modern Scientific System of Medicine against Homoeopathy can, in their opinion, be met best by quoting the late Lord Passmore : "If you meet what you call an unprejudiced person that means simply he has the same prejudices as yourself."

The Homoeopathic members of the Committee are of the opinion that for the evolution of Homoeopathy in its proper perspective, there must be separate institutions, preferably for under-graduates and post-graduates but they would under no circumstances recommend association of these institutions with the regular system of medicine in the form of chairs of Homoeopathy or otherwise. We, with the exception of two of our colleagues representing the regular system, however, recommend that the choice of under-graduate or of the post-graduate type of institutions should be left to the Provincial Boards in consultation with the Central Council which we have recommended to be set up.

II. Training In Homoeopathy

We now come to a very important subject, namely, that regarding the nature and extent of training in the science and practice of Homoeopathy. In our earlier remarks we have left no room for doubt as regards the paramount necessity of proper scientific training of all persons who desire to practise Homoeopathy as a profession.

The subject of training has to be considered from various aspects, such as :

(i) Nature of training and courses of study;
(ii) Minimum qualifications for admission;
(iii) Duration of the course;
(iv) Minimum age for admission;
(v) Degrees, diplomas, certificates, etc., to be given to successful candidates;
(vi) Syllabi of courses and programme of studies;
(vii) Nature and extent of the basic training in pre-clinical and clinical sciences and of what is known as "bed-side experience";
(viii) Post-graduate training and research; and
(ix) Establishment, administration and standardization of institutions for training.

Most of the above items will require careful consideration by the Central Council and the Provincial Boards if the recommendations we have made in this report are accepted by the Government. As regards the more important aspects of the training we have indicated below our views and made our recommendations.

We are of the opinion that there should be a single course, namely, a University course and the minimum qualification for admission to the course should be the same as has been laid down by the Indian Universities in respect of the regular system of medicine. That is, a candidate to be eligible for admission to the course should have passed either the Intermediate Science Examination of a recognized University or of a Provincial Board of Intermediate Studies with Chemistry, Physics and Biology as combinations.

The college course should be of the same standard as has been laid down by the Indian Universities. The duration of the course of studies should, in our opinion, be five academic years. As regards age limit we hold the view that the minimum age at the time of admission should not be less than 16 years. The two members of our Committee representing the regular system of medicine think, however, that the age of admission should be not less than either 17 or 18 years.

The following subjects must be included in the syllabus, namely,

(i) Pre-clinical Subjects—Anatomy, Physiology, Biochemistry, Pharmacology, Homoeopathic Materia Medica, Bacteriology and Pathology;

(ii) Clinical Subjects—Medicine in General (which also includes Preventive Medicine and Hygiene), Surgery in general (which also includes eye, ear, nose and throat), Obstetrics, Gynaecology and Medical Jurisprudence;

(iii) Principles and Philosophy of Homoeopathy (Organon and Chronic Diseases), Homoeopathic Therapeutics, Repertory Study.

Regarding anaesthetics and antiseptics we were given to understand that these subjects were being taught in Homoeopathic colleges as part of surgical therapeutics. Toxicology was also being taught by them. They should, of course, be included in the courses of training.

Four Homoeopathic members of the Committee were of the opinion that there should be a Diploma Course in addition to the University Course as an interim measure. For this course also the qualifications for admission should be the same as for the course mentioned in Para. 180. The course will be for four years in all branches of medicine. The training in pre-clinical and clinical subjects would be on a lower level as compared to the course mentioned earlier.

Five Homoeopathic members of our Committee were of the opinion that Homoeopathic subjects should be taught from the very first year, while others thought that it should be taught from the second year. We recommend that the majority view stated above be accepted.

We recommend for the consideration of the Central Council the model syllabus for the Diploma Course given in Annexure IV prepared by one of the Homoeopathic members of the Committee.

Our recommendations regarding research are as follows :

Co-operation of Homoeopathic system of therapeutics with the progress of science, thus providing for the training and research in all relevant subjects, as, for example, biochemistry, physiology, immunology, surgery, etc.;

The biochemical and clinical changes in the human organism, e.g., changes in the blood picture, etc., should be studied in relation to the "provings" of Homoeopathic drugs;

Animal experimentation with slides for teaching Homoeopathic pathology and materia medica;

The research on the action of potentized dilutions of Homoeopathic medicines in the light of modern scientific developments;

"Provings" of new drugs and "Reprovings" of older ones in the light of Modern Medical and Scientific Developments;

Statistical studies of different types of cases treated Homoeopathically;

Confirmatory animal experiments on new drugs;

Experiments from the Homoeopathic point of view on healthy human beings;

Study of the modifying effect of toxins and of substances in the body which modify the action of drugs;

To ascertain the rationale of Homoeopathic cure by drugs when the drug does not produce pathological changes;

Serological and other tests which should be evolved to find the indicated Homoeopathic remedy;

Further study from the statistical point of view of the Law of Similars and correlation with clinical findings under State control by laboratory studies and experiments on physiology, pathology and other relevant sciences; and

More extensive study of drugs isolated from plants or parts of plants, animal tissues, diseased products and the provings of such drugs.

We consider that facilities should be provided in recognized institutions for research on the above lines. The two members representing the regular system opined that facilities for research as outlined above should be provided in institutions meant for modern scientific research and not in separate Homoeopathic institutions.

We desire to reiterate and re-emphasize the necessity of competent statistical studies of patients suffering from specific diseases under the following conditions:

(a) A control group suffering from the same disease but without any medicine being administered, all adjuvant measures being adopted;

(b) A second control group in which medicine is administered in the Homoeopathic way, e.g., the globules or drops will be given but they will be without the Homoeopathic drug;

(c) A third control group in which Homoeopathic drugs will be administered; and

(d) A fourth group in which the patients will be treated on the lines of the scientific medicine known as the regular medical system.

We are definitely of the opinion that it is essential in the interest of the public that a person desiring to practise Homoeopathy as a profession must have what is called actual bed-side experience. In other words he must have an opportunity to acquire practical experience in hospitals under expert supervision. This condition must be satisfied by all those who may be recruited for service under the Government. This matter will have to be examined in detail by the Government in due course.

As regards Homoeopathic training institutions, we have already pointed out that those that exist at present to serve the cause of Homoeopathy are far from satisfactory. Apart from properly equipped schools and colleges for purposes of teaching and training in Homoeopathy there should be an adequate number of Homoeopathic hospitals and dispensaries in the country under the charge of Homoeopathic doctors with the qualifications we have laid down. Pharmacies and organizations concerned with the preparation and manufacture of Homoeopathic drugs in India should also be placed on a proper footing and the Government should assume the authority to intervene in cases of lowering down of standards, adulteration of drugs, bad dispensing, etc. The education, qualifications and training of dispensers to be attached to dispensaries should be laid down.

We feel that when implementing this recommendation the Government should consider the necessity of providing facilities for training in Homoeopathy in order to give it a chance to evolve its own genius.

We consider that it is essential to give effect to all these recommendations we have made, not only for the sake of public health but also because the future of Homoeopathy, in common with that of other systems of medicine, depends to a large extent on public support and faith. Philanthropists and public-spirited men will then come forward to render financial assistance for the purpose of the establishment of hospitals and dispensaries. All persons concerned with or interested in Homoeopathy should, therefore, sincerely endeavour to create the necessary tradition for the all-round improvement of Homoeopathy in India..

PATENTS ENQUIRY COMMITTEE, 1948—REPORT

New Delhi, Ministry of Industry and Supply, 1950. 217,IIp.

Chairman : Dr. Bakshi Tek Chand.
Members : Shri Gurunath Bewoor; Maj.-Gen. S. S. Sokhey; Shri S. M. Basu; Shri N. Barwell; Shri S. P. Sen; Dr. S. D. Mahant.
Secretary : Shri K. Rama Pai.

APPOINTMENT

The Patents Enquiry Committee was constituted under the Ministry of Industry and Supply vide their Resolution No. 223-IRP (6)/48 dated October 1, 1948.

TERMS OF REFERENCE

(i) To survey and report on the working of the Patent System in India;

(ii) To examine the existing Patent Legislation in India and to make recommendations for improving it, particularly with reference to the provisions concerned with the prevention of abuse of Patent Rights;

(iii) To consider whether any special restrictions should be imposed on Patents regarding food and medicine;

(iv) To suggest steps for ensuring effective publicity to the Patent System and to Patent Literature, particularly as regards Patents obtained by Indian inventors;

(v) To consider the necessity and feasibility of setting up a National Patents Trust;

(vi) To consider the desirability or otherwise of regulating the profession of patent agents;

(vii) To examine the working of the Patent Office and the services rendered by it to the public and make suitable recommendations for improvement; and

(viii) To report generally on any improvement that the Committee thinks fit to recommend for enabling the Indian Patent System to be more conducive to national interest, by encouraging invention and the commercial development and use of inventions.

CONTENTS

Forwarding Letter; The Report; The Patent System: Its Origin and Development with particular reference to Patent Legislation in India; Resume of the existing Law of Patents in India; A Survey of the working of the Patent System in India; Defects in existing Law and Procedure; Recommendations for improving the Law of Patents in India; The Patent Office: Its origin, present set-up and recommendations for improving its organization and functions; Additional Recommendations; Summary of Recommendations; Appendix I to V; Annexure A to C.

RECOMMENDATIONS

Legislation

The existing Act (II of 1911) has in many respects become out of date and it is desirable to replace it by a new Act. In framing the new Act the following points be kept in view:

The Act should contain a clear and specific provision as to what is patentable.

"Invention" should be given a wider meaning than in the present Act, so as to include inventions capable of application for industrial uses, even if they are concerned with processes only and do not result in the manufacture of any article.

Substances prepared or produced by chemical processes, or intended for food or medicine, should not be patentable, except when made by the invented processes or their obvious equivalents.

Inventions of which the primary or intended use would be contrary to law or morality should not be patentable.

Novelty should be determined on the basis of prior knowledge or prior uses in India.

The expression "true and first inventor" be defined so as to include not only the actual inventor but also the importer or the communicatee of a new invention from abroad.

Provision be made in the Act that where the "true and first inventor" claims to be the actual inventor of the invention, his name shouldbe mentioned as such on the patent specification as well as the letters patent.

The Act should contain a specific provision requiring the Controller to make a search for "novelty" in respect of every application for patent.

The Act should contain clear provision that:

(a) In the case of a patented invention of any article, the patentee shall have the exclusive right to make, use and/or sell such article or to authorize others to do so:

(b) In the case of a patented invention of a process, the patentee shall have the exclusive right to use such process and to use and/or sell articles made by such process or to authorize others to do so; and

(c) The exclusive right conferred by any patent shall be subject to rights already subsisting in respect of any other patent.

Provision should be made in the Act declaring that the Government would, apart from the special privileges provided in Section 21 of the existing Act, have the same rights and privileges as a private person.

Section 21 should be so modified as to limit its applicability to use or exercise of the patent for Government purpose by the Central Government only.

The Act should contain a provision on the lines of Section 66 of the British Act permitting the institution of a "declaratory suit" by any person who has reasonable cause to doubt whether the use of a process, or the making, using or selling of any article would constitute an infringement of a claim of any particular patent.

The requirement in the present Act that the "year" be marked on a patented article, in addition to the serial number of the patent, be dispensed with.

The Patent Office

The Patent Office requires to be reorganized, and its immediate needs are better and more suitable accommodation and additional supervisory staff.

The office should have five Divisions as under:

(a) Engineering Division, dealing with patent applications for inventions in the field of Mechanical, Electrical, Communication, Civil and Textile Engineering. This Division, will be in charge of a Deputy Controller (Engineering).

(b) Chemistry Division dealing with patent applications for inventions in other fields, including Chemical and Metallurgical industries. This Division will be in charge of a Deputy Controller (Chemistry).

(c) Public Relations Division under a Public Relations Officer in charge of Publications Section, Printing and Sales Section, Publicity Section, Search Section, Documents, Inspection and Copying Section, Enquiries Section and the Library.

(d) Establishment Division having Budget, Accounts and other Sections under an Administrative Officer.

(e) Policy and Special Proceedings Division, directly under the Controller.

Branch Offices should be established at Bombay, Madras and Delhi, and if at any time the Head Office is shifted from Calcutta, there should be a Branch Office at Calcutta also.

The publications of the Patent Office should be improved, both qualitatively and quantitatively. It is necessary that the Patent Office should publish a weekly Official Journal containing its notifications.

"Classified Abridgements" of published specifications are incomplete and out of date. They should be completed without delay and maintained up-to-date in future.

INDIAN STATES FINANCES ENQUIRY COMMITTEE, 1948—REPORT

New Delhi, Ministry of States, 1949. 138p.

Chairman : Shri V. T. Krishnamachari.
Members : Shri S. K. Patil: Shri N. Dandekar.
Secretary : Shri G. Swaminathan.

APPOINTMENT

The Indian States Finances Enquiry Committee was constituted under the Ministry of States vide their Resolution No. F. 60-1B/48 dated October 22, 1948.

TERMS OF REFERENCE

To examine and report upon :

(i) the present structure of Public Finance in Indian States and Unions of States:

(ii) the desirability and feasibility of integrating Federal Finance in Indian States and Unions of States with that of the rest of India, to the end that a uniform system of Federal Finance may be established throughout the Dominion of India:

(iii) whether, and if so, the extent to which the process of so integrating Federal Finance in the Indian States and Unions with that of the rest of India should be gradual and the manner in which it should be brought about; and the machinery required for this purpose, especially as regards the legislative ground work and the administrative organization necessary for the imposition, assessment and collection of Federal Taxes;

(iv) the results of such a policy of integrating Federal Finance upon the finances of Indian States and Unions and the consequential financial adjustments and relations which should subsist between the Governments of the Indian States and Unions on the one hand and the Government of India on the other;

(v) the measures which the Committee may consider necessary and/or desirable for revising, in the light of present-day conditions and standards, and having regard to the requirements of modern administration, the structure of Provincial Finance and, in particular, the levels and sources of Provincial Revenues in Indian States and Unions of States;

(vi) any other consequential and/or cognate matters which the Committee may consider as arising out of the foregoing terms of reference.

CONTENTS

Section I: Preliminary; Section II: Financial Relationship between the Centre and the States—Constitutional and Economic Position; Section III: Financial Integration—General Principles followed by the Committee; Section IV: Summary of Recommendations; Annexure: Section I: Introductory; Section II: Gradual Raising of State Rates of Income-tax; Section III: Technical Matters Relating to Income-tax; Section IV: Other Taxes on Income and Taxes on Capital, etc.; Section V: Summary; Appendix I and II.

RECOMMENDATIONS

The new relationship established between States and the rest of India based on the "Objectives" Resolution demands that the Central Government should have the same range of powers and authority over Provinces and States alike and function in them in the same manner through its own agency and derive the same revenues from them. Federal Financial Integration inevitably follows from this.

Financial integration is necessary and desirable on broad economic considerations as well.

When federal financial integration comes into effect, all "Central" Revenues and all "Federal" Services (including Railways, Posts and Telegraphs, Telephones and Currency and Coinage), together with the administration of the Departments concerned, should be taken over by the Central Government. Accounting and Audit should also be taken over, if possible.

Except in one or two States, internal Customs duties can be totally abolished in all States simultaneously with federal financial integration; the loss of revenue will be covered by the direct and indirect gains resulting from financial integration together with proceeds from Sales Tax. In the excepted cases the abolition of these duties should be gradual. No compensation should be paid in any case.

As regards Armed Forces, financial integration should affect only the regular "Indian States Forces", properly so called; even there, it need not involve any change in the present administrative arrangements concerning them.

The question whether Privy Purses should be a "Federal" or "Provincial" liability is left upon, and financial integration schemes have been worked out on the assumption that the liability will continue with the States; but the modifications required, in the event of this liability being undertaken by the Centre, have been indicated.

Integration of federal finance in States involves also the allocation of assets and liabilities of States between them and the Centre on a "functional" basis.

The integration of federal finances in States need not be gradual; but provision should be made for a degree of gradualness in the full effect of its impact in certain directions.

No compensation should be paid for any "federal" assets (such as Railways) or revenues (such as Customs) which would pass to the Centre, or for any "rights and immunities" which would be extinguished, as a result of federal financial integration; but provision should be made for the prevention of dislocation of finances of States that may be caused by the loss to them of these sources of revenue in the manner indicated; also, public debt and other liabilities should be shared.

Financial integration schemes for individual States have been evolved upon the basis of principles which take account of their varying circumstances, the need to avoid any sudden dislocation of their finances, and the necessity to provide for smooth transition to the full "provincial" pattern in the eleventh year, or the sixteenth year, as may be provided under Article 258 of the (Draft) Constitution of India.

The detailed integration schemes for individual States, except Hyderabad, are in the Committee's two Interim Reports and in Part II of this Report, that for Hyderabad, will follow in a Supplementary Report. These schemes are workable. They are also equitable, both to the States and to the Centre. Their legal basis would be as "agreements" entered into with States under Article 258 of the (Draft) Constitution of India.

A Committee should be appointed to watch the working of these schemes.

Income-tax should be introduced in all States (including those where there is none at present) at rates adjusted to local conditions. Its assessment and collection should be by officers of the Central Government under the Indian Income-tax Act.

The existing distribution to Provinces of the proceeds from Income-tax needs revision; it will need further revision when federal financial integration takes effect in the States. In this respect no distinction should be made between Provinces and States.

Except as regards the "Anchal" post in the Travancore-Cochin Union (for which special arrangements are needed) the regular "Indian States Forces", and some miscellaneous "federal" Service Departments, the administration of all other "federal" subjects in States should be taken over by the Centre simultaneously with the integration of federal finances. Consideration of the problems arising out of this recommendation —staff, training, organization, etc.—should receive immediate attention.

Financial integration should be effective from the April 1, 1950, the necessary "agreements" under Article 258 being executed before that date, after the new Constitution has been enacted.

It should be announced that upon financial integration, States and Provinces will be treated alike in the matter of all grants, "subsidies", and other forms of financial and technical assistance from the Centre.

During a transitional period, the general revenues of the Centre should receive a subvention from the Railway Budget.

Integration of federal finances in States will have most important and far-reaching consequences; there is need, therefore, for caution in proceeding with such matters as prohibition, abolition of Jagirs, etc.

A Deputy Auditor-General for States should be immediately appointed with certain special responsibilities between now and the date of financial integration.

INDIAN STATES FINANCES ENQUIRY COMMITTEE—BARODA, 1948—REPORT—FIRST INTERIM

New Delhi, Ministry of States, 1949. 48p.

Chairman : Shri V. T. Krishnamachari.
Members : Shri S. K. Patil; Shri N. Dandekar.
Secretary : Shri G. Swaminathan.

APPOINTMENT

The Indian States Finances Enquiry Committee—Baroda was constituted under the Ministry of States vide their Resolution No. F-60-IB/48 dated October 22, 1948.

TERMS OF REFERENCE

To examine and report upon:

(i) the present structure of Public Finance in Indian States and Unions of States;

(ii) the desirability and feasibility of integrating Federal Finance in Indian States and Unions of States with that of the rest of India, to the end that a uniform system of Federal Finance may be established throughout the Dominion of India;

(iii) whether, and if so, the extent to which the process of so integrating Federal Finance in the Indian States and Unions with that of the rest of India should be gradual and the manner in which it should be brought about, and the machinery required for this purpose, especially as regards the legislative groundwork and the administrative organization necessary for the imposition, assessment and collection of Federal Taxes;

(iv) the results of such a policy of integrating Federal Finance upon the finances of Indian States and Unions and the consequential financial adjustments and relations which should subsist between the Governments of the Indian States and Unions on the one hand and the Government of India on the other;

(v) the measures which the Committee may consider necessary and/or desirable for revising, in the light of present-day conditions and standards, and having regard to the requirements of modern administration, the structure of Provincial Finance and, in particular, the levels and sources of Provincial Revenues in Indian States and Unions of States;

(vi) any other consequential and/or cognate matters which the Committee may consider as arising out of the foregoing Terms of Reference.

CONTENTS

Introductory; Analysis of the Problem; General Principles; Integration of "Central" Revenues and Expenditure; Allocation of Assets and Liabilities; Summary; Annexures.

RECOMMENDATIONS

Allocation Of Departments, Assets, Liabilities, Etc.

As from the date of the merger the Central Government will take over all "Central" sources of revenue and the administration of all Departments concerned with "Central" functions, together with all connected unproductive capital assets, current liabilities, outstandings, refunds, etc.

Similarly, all specific productive capital assets connected with "Central" functions (e.g., railways and telephones), together with any debt, cash balances, liabilities and outstandings specifically relating to them, should also be taken over by the Government of India.

"Current" liabilities and funded obligations of the State must be allocated between the Central Government and the Bombay Government on a "functional" basis, coupled with the principle of public convenience. The allocation of such liabilities should be accompanied, so far as may be possible, by an equivalent allocation of Current (Liquid) Assets. There will then remain a net surplus of Liquid Assets or of current liabilities, to be apportioned between the two successor Governments.

Financial (Revenue) Adjustments Required Between The Central Government And The Government Of Bombay

We recommend that the net revenue gap in the finances of Baroda (viz., Rs. 126 lakhs per annum), arising from the loss of "Central" revenues and taxes, as reduced by the savings in respect of "Central" expenditure, after Federal Financial Integration, should be made good as follows:

(a) by the Bombay Government assuming responsibility, with effect from 1950-51, for Rs. 50 lakhs per annum, i.e., 40% of Rs. 126 lakhs;

(b) by the Central Government assuming responsibility for, and guaranteeing to pay to the Bombay Government as from the date of the merger, a sum of Rs. 126 lakhs per annum up to March 31, 1950, and thereafter a sum of Rs. 76 lakhs per annum for a period of 10 years, in the shape of:

(i) the share of divisible Income-tax and other divisible federal taxes, if any, which will accrue to the Bombay Government on account of the addition of the Baroda territory to the Provinces; and

(ii) an ad-hoc revenue subsidy to the extent to which (i) should fall short of the guaranteed amount.

In our considered opinion, the Bombay Government should have no difficulty in bearing a share of the net revenue gap as suggested above.

Ruler's Immunities And Privy Purse

Steps should be taken to secure, by necessary executive orders, statutory notifications and/or amendments (as may be appropriate), the continuance of the personal immunities of the Ruler in the matter of taxation, etc.

With regard to the Privy Purse, our proposals have been evolved on the basis that it will not be a "Central" liability. If, however, the Privy Purse should, for any reason, be made payable out of Central Revenues, the net "Central" revenue gap of Baroda will be reduced by that amount; we have suggested consequential changes in the amount thereof to be borne by Bombay and the amount to be guaranteed by the Central Government, respectively.

Assets and Liabilities

"Unproductive" specific capital assets pertaining to "Central" functions will be taken over by the Government of India without valuation; the rest of such assets will go to the Government of Bombay.

"Productive" capital assets of a "Central" nature will similarly be taken over by the Government of India; their book value, less specific debt attached to the assets, amounted to Rs. 624.17 lakhs on July 31, 1948.

"Productive" capital assets of a "Provincial" nature will vest in the Bombay Government; these were valued in the books at Rs. 192.33 lakhs on the same date.

In view of the complexities and importance of the issues arising out of the merger, and the large amount of detail to be attended to purely from the accountancy and financial points of view, it would be desirable, if possible, to invite the Auditor-General of India to appoint an Officer on Special Duty to assist in the implementation of the decisions which may be taken on the various suggestions and recommendations made by us.

INDIAN STATES FINANCES ENQUIRY COMMITTEE—TRAVANCORE AND COCHIN, 1948—REPORT—SECOND INTERIM

New Delhi, Ministry of States, 1949. 61p.

Chairman : Shri V. T. Krishnamachari
Members : Shri N. Dandekar; Shri S. K. Patil.
Secretary : Shri G. Swaminathan.

APPOINTMENT

The Indian States Finances Enquiry Committee—Travancore & Cochin was constituted under the Ministry of States vide their Resolution No. F. 60-IB/48 dated October 22, 1948.

TERMS OF REFERENCE

To examine and report upon:

(i) The desirability and feasibility of integrating Federal Finance in Indian States and Unions of States with that of the rest of India, to the end that a uniform system of Federal Finance may be established throughout the Dominion of India;

(ii) Whether, and if so, the extent to which the process of so integrating Federal Finance in the Indian States and Unions with that of the rest of India should be gradual and the manner in which it should be brought about, and the machinery required for this purpose, especially as regards the legislative groundwork and the administrative organization necessary for the imposition, assessment and collection of Federal Taxes;

(iii) The results of such a policy of integrating Federal Finance upon the finances of Indian States and Unions and the consequential financial adjustments and relations which should subsist between the Governments of the Indian States and Unions on the one hand and the Government of India on the other;

(iv) Any other consequential and/or cognate matters which the Committee may consider as arising out of the foregoing Terms of Reference.

CONTENTS

General Principles; Basic Requirements of Federal Financial Integration; The "Revenue Gap" arising out of Federal Financial Integration; Certain Specific Matters relating to "Central" Revenue and Expenditure Departments; Assets and Liabilities; Summary; Annexures.

RECOMMENDATIONS

General Line Of Approach

In our view no question of paying any "compensation" can arise; but a balanced scheme of financial adjustments over a transitional period will be necessary for avoiding financial dislocation.

Constitutional Requirements

We recommend that:

(i) federal financial integration should be preceded by complete "accession" on all subjects in Lists I and III including Finance and Taxation Matters;

(ii) transitional financial adjustments should terminate after a maximum period of 10 or 15 years as may be provided by Article 258 of the Draft Constitution;

(iii) all Customs duties on internal trade, i.e., on trade with the rest of India should be abolished as soon as the integration of the Federal Finances of these States becomes effective.

Date Of Federal Financial Integration

Ordinarily, Federal Financial Integration should be effective from April 1, 1950, but the State Governments would be willing to make it effective from August 17, 1949, under the present Government of India Act. We recommend accordingly.

Revenue Gap Arising Out Of Federal Financial Integration

We recommend that:

(a) the loss resulting from the immediate abolition of Internal Customs Duties of Travancore must be borne by the State Government;

(b) as regards the residual net "Central" Revenue Gap of the two States taken together (Rs. 230 lakhs), there should be a guaranteed reimbursement by the Central Government to the following extent during a transitional period:

From the date of Federal Financial Integration Rs. 230 lakhs per annum to March 31, 1955.

From April 1, 1955, to March 31, 1960: the residual net Revenue Gap of Travancore in full (i.e., Rs. 127 lakhs) plus a gradually reducing part of the Cochin net Revenue Gap of Rs. 103 lakhs, so as to work it down to 60% thereof in 1959-60.

The amount payable in 1959-60 will continue to be paid as a guaranteed reimbursement for a further period of five years, if the Constituent Assembly should accept an extension of the transitional period to 15 years (under Article 258).

The above guarantee should be implemented by the Central Government by paying to the States:

(a) their share of Income-tax and other divisible Federal taxes, computed on the same basis and principles as are applicable to Provinces; and

(b) an additional grant-in-aid to the extent to which the share of divisible taxes under (a) should fall short of the total guaranteed amount.

If in any year the State Governments' share of divisible Federal taxes should exceed the guaranteed amount, they will be entitled to the larger sum.

The State Governments should be entitled to all forms of financial and other assistance from the Central Government in exactly the same way as Provinces, in addition to the amounts guaranteed as above.

Privy Purse

Our proposals have been evolved on the basis that "Privy Purse" will not be a Central liability. If, however, "Privy Purse" should, for any reason, be made payable out of Central Revenues, our computations of the net Revenue Gap resulting from Federal Financial Integration and of the amounts guaranteed during the transition period will require consequential revision.

Assets And Liabilities

The Central Government should take over unproductive capital assets connected with Central functions or Revenues, by inventory without valuation. The Travancore and Cochin States will retain the rest of the unproductive capital assets.

"Productive" Capital assets connected with "Central" functions should similary be taken over by the Government of India along with the "specific debt" associated with such assets. The net book value of such assets as at the end of 1123 M. E. was Rs. 118 lakhs and Rs. 48 lakhs in the Travancore and Cochin States, respectively.

Productive Capital assets connected with "Provincial" functions along with the specific debt attached thereto should be retained by the State Governments. Their value on the date mentioned was Rs. 609 lakhs and Rs. 144 lakhs in Travancore and Cochin respectively.

INDIAN UNIVERSITY EDUCATION COMMISSION, 1948-49—REPORT

Delhi, Manager of Publications, 1949. 1,356p. Charts. 2 Vols.

Chairman : Dr. S. Radhakrishnan.
Members : Dr. Tara Chand; Dr. Sir James F. Daff; Dr. Zakir Husain; Dr. Arthur E. Morgan; Dr. A. Lakshmanaswami Mudaliar; Dr. Meghnad Saha; Dr. Karm Narayan Bahl; Dr. John J. Tigert.
Secretary : Shri Nirmal Kumar Sidhanta.

APPOINTMENT

The Commission was appointed under a Resolution of the Government of India, Ministry of Education, No. 55-5/47-D/3 dated November 4, 1948, to report on Indian University Education and suggest improvements and extensions that may be desirable to suit present and future requirements of the country.

TERMS OF REFERENCE

To consider and make recommendations in regard to:

(i) The aims and objects of University Education and research in India.

(ii) The changes considered necessary and desirable in the Constitution, Control, Functions and Jurisdiction of Universities in India and their relations with Governments, Central and Provincial.

(iii) The Finance of Universities.

(iv) The maintenance of the highest standards of teaching and examination in the Universities and colleges under their control.

(v) The course of study in the Universities with special reference to the maintenance of a sound balance between the Humanities and Sciences and between Pure Science and Technological Training and the duration of such courses.

(vi) The standards of admission to University courses of study with reference to the desirability of an independent University Entrance Examination and the avoidance of unfair discriminations which militate against Fundamental Right 23(2).

(vii) The medium of instruction in the Universities.

(viii) The provision for advanced study in Indian Culture, History, Literature, Languages, Philosophy and Fine Arts.

(ix) The need for more Universities on a regional or other basis.

(x) The organization of advanced research in all

branches of knowledge in the Universities and institutes of higher research in a well-coordinated fashion avoiding waste of efforts and resources.

(xi) Religious instruction in the Universities.

(xii) The special problems of Banaras Hindu University, Aligarh Muslim University, Delhi University and other institutions of an all-India character.

(xiii) The qualifications, conditions of service, salaries, privileges and functions of teachers and the encouragement of original research by teachers.

(xiv) The discipline of students, hostels and the organization of tutorial work and any other matter which is germane and essential to a complete and comprehensive enquiry into all aspects of University education and advanced research in India.

CONTENTS

Introduction—Appointment and Procedure of the Commission; Historical Retrospect; The Aims of University Education; Teaching Staff: Universities and Colleges; Standard of Teaching; Courses of Study: Arts and Sciences; Post-graduate Training and Research: Arts and Sciences; Professional Education—Introduction; (a) Agriculture, (b) Commerce, (c) Education, (d) Engineering and Technology, (e) Law, (f) Medicine, (g) New Profession; Religious Education; Medium of Instruction; Examinations; Students, their Activities and Welfare; Women's Education; Constitution and Control; Finance; Banaras, Aligarh and Delhi Universities; Other Universities; New Universities; Rural Universities; Conclusion; Appendices from A to R; Graphs.

RECOMMENDATIONS

1. That the ordinary amenities and decencies of life should be provided for women in colleges originally planned for men, but in which women are being admitted in increasing numbers.

2. That there should be no curtailment in educational opportunities for women, but rather a great increase.

3. That there should be intelligent educational guidance, by qualified men and women, to help women to get a clearer view of their real educational interest, to the end that they shall not try to imitate men, but shall desire as good an education as men get. Women's and men's education should have many elements in common, but should not in general be identical in all respects, as is usually the case today.

4. That women students in general should be helped to see their normal places in a normal society, both as citizens and as women and to prepare for it, and college programmes should be so designed that it will be possible for them to do so.

5. That through educational counsel and by example the prevailing prejudice against study of Home Economics and Home Management should be overcome.

6. That standards of courtesy and social responsibility should be emphasized on the part of men in mixed colleges.

7. That where new colleges are established to serve both men and women students, they should be truly co-educational institutions, with as much thought and consideration given to the life needs of women as to those of men. Except as such colleges come into existence there are no valid criteria for comparing segregated education with co-education.

8. That women teachers should be paid the same salaries as men teachers for equal work.

Separate Schools Between The Age Of 13 And 18

The University Education Commission was of the view that there seems to be a definite preponderance of opinion that from the thirteenth or fourteenth year of age until about the eighteenth, separate schools for boys and girls are desirable. The Commission felt that it was not wholly clear whether this opinion was chiefly based on custom or upon experience. The Commission cited the following:

One of India's prominent educators states: "The modern trend is for equality of opportunity for women in all spheres, and it cannot be arrested. There should be no distinctions of any kind of women from men, after the matriculation stage."

On the other hand many, probably a majority of those who commented, favour separate colleges for women when that is feasible though not to the extent of denying women educational opportunity by excluding them from existing colleges organized primarily for men.

Some of the arguments given are that a woman cannot develop her personality in a men's college; that there is no need for women to undergo the nervous strain of examinations; that women's education should be more in keeping with the temperament and needs of women as wives and mothers; and that overcrowding is more serious for women than for men. "A pleasing feature of colleges for women has been the intimate relations of students and teachers." Some of the arguments have greater weight in the absence of truly co-educational colleges where the needs of men and women would be given equal weight in designing the programme.

Co-education At The College Level

As the age of entry to degree colleges would, on our recommendation, be approximately 18, college education may be co-educational as it is at present in many medical colleges. Separate institutions at this level would demand an unjustified increase in expense. To maintain separate institutions for men and women side by side, duplicating equipment, even when it is very inadequate, would be an undue tax upon limited financial resources. Separate women's colleges commonly have poorer buildings, poorer equipment, and less able teachers. So far as possible, co-educational institutions should be encouraged at the degree level.

Scales For University Teachers

The University Education Commission recommended:

1. That the importance of a teacher and his responsibility be recognized.

2. That conditions in universities which are suffering from lack of finances and consequent demoralization be greatly improved.

3. That there be four classes of teachers—Professors, Readers, Lecturers and Instructors.

4. That promotions from one category to another be solely on grounds of merit.

5. That each University should have some Research Fellows.

6. That the scales of salaries for University teachers be:

Professors	Rs. 900-50-1,350
Readers	Rs. 600-30-900
Lecturers	Rs. 300-25-600
Instructors of Fellows	Rs. 250
Research Fellows	Rs. 250-25-500

7. That the scales of salaries for affiliated colleges with no post-graduate classes be :

Lecturers	Rs. 200-15-320-20-400
Senior posts (two in each college)	Rs. 400-25-600
Principals	Rs. 600-45-800

That for colleges which have post-graduate classes, the grades be:

Lecturers	Rs. 200-15-310-20-400-25-500
Senior Posts (two in each college)	Rs. 500-25-800
Principals	Rs. 800-40-1000

8. That care be taken for the selection of proper teachers.

9. That the proportion of junior posts (Lecturers and Instructors) to senior ones (Professors and Readers) be roughly 2.

10. That the age of retirement be ordinarily 60 years but extension be allowed up to 64 in the case of a Professor.

11. That conditions regarding Provident Fund, Leave and Hours of Work be definitely laid down.

Finance

The Commission recommended:

1. That the State should recognize its responsibility for the financing of higher education.

2. That the aid to private colleges should be for buildings and equipment as also for the recurring expenditure, the latter to be on a uniform basis, say, half of the present teachers' salaries and one-third of other approved expenditure.

3 That steps be taken to amend Income-tax laws to encourage donations for educational purposes.

4. That additional grants be made to colleges and Universities in order to enable them to give effect to our recommendations.

5. That the Government should contribute an additional annual amount of about Rs. 10 crores for the development of University education during the next quinquennium.

6. That the University Grants Commission be set up for allocating grants.

1949

COMMITTEE ON THE REORGANIZATION OF THE MACHINERY OF GOVERNMENT, 1949—REPORT

New Delhi, Reorganization Secretariat, 1949. 59p.

One-man Committee : Shri Gopalaswami Ayyangar.

APPOINTMENT

The Reorganization of the Machinery of Government was constituted under the Reorganization Secretariat in 1949.

TERMS OF REFERENCE

(i) To present a basic plan for the approval of the Cabinet; and

(ii) Outline the general principles governing the formulation of a detailed scheme of reorganization.

CONTENTS

Pictorial Chart; Summary of Conclusions and Recommendations; Introductory; Basic Plan; Ministries and Departments; Bureaus and Central Administrative Offices; Council of Ministers and Cabinet Organization; Reorganization Machinery and Procedure; Organization and Methods of Financial Control.

RECOMMENDATIONS

Need for changes in the set-up.

Insufficiency of mere changes in the set-up. Improvement can and should be brought about through the combined effect of (a) Organizational changes in the existing set-up of the machinery of the Government, (b) Improvements in the methods of transaction of governmental business (Administrative and Financial).

There should be distinction between Basic Plan and Detailed Schemes.

The main changes involved in the Basic Plan of Reorganization are divisible under four heads as shown below:

(i) The Central Secretariat should be divided into 37 primary units of organization consisting of 28

Departments, 8 Central Administrative Offices and a Cabinet Secretariat.

(ii) The distinction should be drawn between a Department as an Organizational Unit and a Ministry as an Organizational Unit. 28 Departments should be accommodated within 20 Ministries.

(iii) A new grouping of Ministries responsible for economic and social services should be established under the name of bureaus. There should be a Bureau of National Resources and Agriculture, a Bureau of Industry and Commerce, a Bureau of Transport and Communications and a Bureau of Labour and Social Services.

(iv) The Cabinet Organization should be strengthened by the establishment on a permanent basis of certain Standing Committees of Cabinet, in addition to Ad Hoc Committees set up from time to time.

A Department should be identified with a Secretary's charge and a Ministry with a Minister's charge and this be the basis of distinction between Ministries and Departments.

Each Department should constitute a clearly manageable charge for one Secretary, the responsibility of the Secretary as the Head of the Department should be complete and undivided. Each Department should be manageable and substantially homogeneous in respect of functions entrusted to it.

The best set-up of the organization be as Secretary or Head of a Department; Deputy Secretary or Head of the Division; Under-Secretary or Head of a Branch; Section Officer; Assistant. There should not be any Additional Secretary.

The inter-position of an officer between a Secretary and a Deputy Secretary is not a satisfactory arrangement as this would give rise to serious organizational defects.

With the increase in the number of Departments appointment of Joint Secretaries would become necessary in some Departments. In that case the work assigned to Joint Secretaries should be clearly localized in separate wings within a Department and that there should be maximum measure of independent functioning and responsibility invested in them.

A Secretariat Organization consisting of three Deputy Secretaries each in charge of one Secretariat Division should be regarded as the upper limit of the manageable charge of a single Secretary unassisted by a Joint Secretary. A similar organization with five Deputy Secretaries and five Secretariat Divisions with a "Wing" located in it would be the ordinary upper limit of the manageable charge of one Secretary assisted by a Joint Secretary.

The internal organization of the Secretariat Division should follow the pattern prescribed in the Central Secretariat Service (Reorganization) Scheme. The "Superintendent" and "Assistant Superintendent" in that scheme may preferably be referred to by a common designation, namely, Section Officer.

The proposed reorganization should be effected in such a manner as to involve no increase either in the number of the highest paid posts or their cost.

The Ministries and Departments dealing with economic and social services should be grouped together in four bureaus for purposes of securing co-ordination of policy and planning. The establishment of a Common Financial Advisory Organization and a Common Central Administrative Officer for the efficient performance of common services and administrative co-ordination is recommended.

The four Ministries of Finance, External Affairs, Home Affairs and Defence will continue to be unitary Minister's charges.

There should continue to be three categories of members of the Council of Ministers.

A considerable degree of flexibility is necessary regarding the fixation of numbers of Ministers.

There should be a proper division of labour and effective delegation within the Cabinet. For this purpose Committees of Cabinet are necessary. A clear distinction should be drawn between Standing Committees and Ad Hoc Committees of the Cabinet.

Four Standing Committees of Cabinet be, namely, the Defence Committee of Cabinet, the Economic Committee of Cabinet, the Administrative Organization Committee of Cabinet and the Parliamentary and Legal Affairs Committee of Cabinet. Their functions, etc., have been specified.

Provision should be made for a Cabinet Minister without portfolio and where necessary more than one.

The Cabinet Secretariat to have an Economic Wing.

The Reorganization Secretariat should complete the preparation of schemes of establishment of Ministries, Departments, etc.

The Administrative Organization Committee of Cabinet should be set up forthwith and authority should be conferred on it to give binding decisions on points of disagreement, if any, which may arise.

The process of bringing about necessary changes in organization will not be completed without taking the following steps:

Detailed schemes of organization of services as distinguished from establishment will be necessary.

The preparation of work relating to the revision of Rules of Business should be undertaken.

A manual of Office Procedure should be prepared.

The Civil Service Act should be passed, and a self-contained Code of Civil Service Regulations be promulgated.

The responsibility for securing that all these measures are undertaken be vested with the proposed "Organization and Methods Division" of the Home Department of the Ministry of Home Affairs on the lines similar to agencies in the U.K. and the U.S.A.

Improvement and administrative organization and methods should go hand in hand with improvement of organization and methods of financial control. There should be really effective safeguards against extravagance. Ultimate responsibility for both economy and efficiency must be placed squarely on the shoulders of Administrative Departments.

SPECIAL POLICE ESTABLISHMENT ENQUIRY COMMITTEE, 1949—REPORT

New Delhi, Ministry of Home Affairs, 1952. 28p.

Chairman : Dr. Bakshi Tek Chand.

Members : Shri Mahavir Tyagi; Shri L. Krishnaswami Bharati; Shri S. K. Patil; Pt. Lakshmi Kanta Maitra; Pt. Thakur Das Bhargava. (Shri Mahavir Tyagi has expressed his inability to append his signatures as he felt that by reason of his official position his signatures might be taken to commit the Government.)

APPOINTMENT

The Special Police Establishment Enquiry Committee was constituted under the Ministry of Home Affairs vide their letter No. 38/9/48-S.P.E. dated March 4, 1949.

TERMS OF REFERENCE

(i) To review the working of the Prevention of Corruption Act, 1947, and to make recommendations with regard to any improvement that may be considered necessary in the law as well as in regard to the machinery for enforcing it;

(ii) To assess the amount of success achieved by the Special Police Establishment in combating corruption and to make recommendations regarding the continuance, strengthening, curtailment or abolition of the Special Police Establishment.

CONTENTS

Composition and Terms of Reference; Method of work of the Committee; Special Police Establishment and its method of work; Amendment of Laws; Indian Penal Code, 1860, Criminal Procedure Code, 1898, Delhi Special Police Establishment Act, 1946, Indian Railways Act, 1890, Prevention of Corruption Act, 1947; Administrative Matters; Enforcement Directoraet and the S.P.E., Quick disposal of departmental proceedings in cases investigated by the S.P.E; Continuance of the S.P.E. Organization; Summary of Recommendations; Appendix A to E.

RECOMMENDATIONS

Indian Penal Code, 1860

The offering of illegal gratification should be made a substantive offence since a person who voluntarily offers a bribe to a public servant is, in our opinion, morally as guilty as the public servant who accepts the bribe.

The maximum punishment for an offence under Section 165 I.P.C. (acceptance of a "valuable thing" by a public servant) is now simple imprisonment for 2 years or fine or both. This should be changed and should be the same as the maximum punishment for an offence under Section 161 I.P.C. (acceptance of illegal gratification by a public servant), namely, imprisonment of either description for 3 years or fine or both.

Criminal Procedure Code, 1898

Section 337(1) Cr.P.C. should be so amended as to permit the court to tender pardon to an approver in cases under Sections 161 and 165 I.P.C. and the Section suggested in item 1 above. This amendment should, however, have a limited life of two years in the first instance, and during this time the effect of the amendment may be watched.

Sub-Section (2-A) of Section 337 Cr.P.C. should be amended so as to provide for the trial of cases (where a pardon has been tendered as in item 3 above) by

Special Judges of the status of a Sessions Judge who should be empowered to take cognizance without committal, and an appeal should lie from an order of the Special Judge to the High Court.

Section 164 Cr.P.C. should be applicable to the Presidency Towns of Bombay, Calcutta and Madras so as to enable the recording of statements of witnesses during an investigation by Magistrates in these cities.

Section 422 Cr.P.C.: State Governments should be requested to issue executive instructions to District Magistrates to inform the I.G., Special Police Establishment, of notices of appeals in S.P.E. cases.

The Prevention Of Corruption Act, 1947

The Proviso to Section 3 and Sub-Section (4) of Section 5 should be amended so that officers of the Special Police Establishment down to the rank of Inspector are empowered to take cognizance of and investigate certain offences without the prior order of a Magistrate where there is serious risk of valuable evidence being lost, but the Inspector should make a report to a First Class Magistrate of appropriate jurisdiction as soon as possible after taking action.

The provisions mentioned above refer to Deputy Superintendents of Police. In the three Presidency Towns there are no Police Officers bearing this designation. The Act should be amended so as to confer the requisite powers on officers of corresponding ranks in Bombay, Calcutta and Madras.

Section 5 (2) should be amended so as to make it clear that this Section has not repealed Section 409 I.P.C. by implication (as has been held by a High Court), and that it is open to the prosecution to proceed under either provision or under both.

The appropriate authority for according sanction under Section 6 of the Act should be the authority competent to remove the accused public servant from service at the time when the offence is alleged to have been committed.

Section 1 (3) of the Act should be amended to read "10 years" in place of "5 years". (This will extend the life of the offence of "criminal misconduct in discharge of official duty" up to March 10, 1957.)

The Delhi Special Police Establishment Act, 1946

The Act should be amended so as to confer jurisdiction on the Special Police Establishment to investigate cases arising in the Departments of Chief Commissioners.

The Special Police Establishment should likewise be vested with jurisdiction to investigate cases arising in statutory bodies like the Damodar Valley Corporation] and other undertakings where large amounts of Central Funds are involved.

The Indian Railways Act, 1890

Section 137 of the Act should be amended so that employees of State Railways are treated as "public servants" for all purposes.

Administrative Action

In view of the continuing difficulty in securing the loan of the services of officers belonging to State Police Forces the Special Police Establishment should be permitted to make direct recruitment from the open market.

The S.P.E. should concentrate on really important cases and should not dissipate its energy on cases of minor importance—which should be left to be dealt with by the State Police.

The Government might consider revising the Terms of Service in the Special Police Establishment if they are satisfied that the existing terms are not sufficiently attractive.

It would be justifiable to create a post of Handwriting Expert (attached to the Government Examiner of Questioned Documents) whose primary responsibility will be to deal with documents sent up by the Special Police Establishment.

A general circular should be issued to all Ministries and Departments of the Central Government stressing the importance of close co-operation with the Special Police Establishment. The circular should add that instances of lack of co-operation have been taken note of by the Committee, who desire that the causes should be investigated by appropriate authorities. The attention of Ministries and Heads of Departments should also be drawn to the cases of delay in the issue of sanction to prosecute, and the importance of early issue of sanction should be stressed.

The facility of the Railway Warrant System should be extended to officers of the Special Police Establishment even though they may be above the rank of Sub-Inspector.

The Special Police Establishment should not take over the functions of the Directorate of Enforcement under the Ministry of Commerce and Industry, as this can only lead to a reduction in the efficiency of the S.P.E.

A machinery should be evolved for the speedier disposal of departmental proceedings.

The Special Police Establishment has justified its existence, and should be continued for some time to come; the Government should consider at periodical intervals the question of its further continuance.

LOCAL FINANCE ENQUIRY COMMITTEE, 1949—REPORT

Delhi, Manager of Publications, 1951. 502, VI, CXVp.

Chairman : Shri P. K. Wattal.

Members : Shri R. K. Sidhva; Shri C. D. Barfiwala; Shri Rameshwar Narain Agarwala; Shri T. K. T. Veeraraghavachariar (resigned; replaced by Shri K. A. Nachiappa Gounder); Shri P. B. Gole; Shri R. D. Kapila; Shri L. T. Gholap (resigned; replaced by Shri B. D. Mirchandani); Shri M. B. L. Dar; Shri S. K. Gupta; Shri S. N. Sapru; Shri Raizada Hansraj (not joined; replaced by Shri Yashwant Rai, he also resigned).

Secretary : Shri Labhu Ram Mehra (not joined; replaced by Shri D. P. Gupta, replaced by Shri Dayaldas Sobhraj Parwani).

APPOINTMENT

The Local Finance Enquiry Committee was constituted under the Ministry of Health vide their letter No. 13-7/48-63 LSG, dated April 2, 1949.

TERMS OF REFERENCE

To enquire into the question of the finances of local bodies and to make recommendations for the improvement of local finance and for that purpose:

(1) To examine whether the existing resources are adequate for the performance of the functions assigned to the local bodies and to consider whether, and if so, what further sources of revenue should be provided;

(2) To examine the methods of Government assistance to local bodies;

(3) To examine the existing machinery and methods of (i) assessment, and (ii) collection of taxes.

CONTENTS

Appointment and Terms of Reference of the Committee; History of Local Finance (Lord Mayo's Resolution of 1870; Lord Ripon's Resolution of 1882; Functions of Municipalities in Lord Ripon's time; Financial Resources of Municipalities in Lord Ripon's time; Functions and Financial Resources of Rural Boards in Lord Ripon's time; Government of India Resolution of 1896; Municipal Income; Municipal Expenditure; Government of India Resolution of 1897; Income of Rural Boards (1895-96); Expenditure of Rural Boards (1895-96); The Decentralization Commission (1907-08); Mr. Gokhale's Resolution in the Indian Legislative Council; Government of India Resolution, 1915; Municipal Income and Expenditure (1912-13); Municipal Taxation (1912-13); Municipal Control over Services; Control over Municipal Budgets; Control over Sanction to Works; Control over Municipal Establishment; Finances of District Boards; Income and Expenditure of District Boards; Power to Raise Cesses; Control over District Board Budgets; Control over Sanctions to Works; Control of District Boards over Establishments; Functions and Finances of Village Panchayats; The Declaration of August 20, 1917; The Montagu-Chelmsford Report; Government of India Resolution of May, 1918; The Simon Commission Report; The Government of India Act, 1935, and after; Incidence of Taxation and Total Income (per capita) 1946-47; Incidence of Taxation and Income—City Corporations (1894-95 to 1947-48); Inadequacy of Financial Resources of Local Bodies; Elementary Education; Roads; Water Supply; Sanitation; Medical Relief; Functions and Financial Resources of Local Bodies (Education; Public Health and Sanitation; Medical Relief; Public Works; Rural Boards); Power of Taxation (position before Government of India Act, 1919; Position after Government of India Act, 1919; Position under Government of India Act, 1935; Position under the Present Constitution and Recommendation; Present Position of Power Taxation in Various States; General Observations); Property Tax—General: **Part I**: Position Regarding Levy of Property Tax; Income; Rates; Compulsory Levy of Property Tax; Recommendations Regarding Rates, Maximum and Minimum, and Progressive Scale; Exemptions from Property Tax; Vacancy Remissions; Basis of Assessment and Valuation; Machinery of Assessment, Revision and Appeal; Revision of Assessment; Assessment of Properties belonging to Executive Authorities; Right of Appeal to Local Bodies; Creation of a Central Valuation Organization; **Part II**: Madras; Bombay; West Bengal; Uttar Pradesh; Punjab; Bihar; Orissa; Madhya Pradesh; Assam; Property Tax—Service Taxes (General; Water Rate; Lighting Rate; Drainage Rate; Latrine Rate; Recommendations); Local Fund Cess (Levy of Cess and the Basis of Assessment; Income; Rates of Cess in each State and Recommendations Regarding Abolition of Zamindari and its Effect on Cess); Octroi and Terminal Taxes (History of Octroi up to the Government of India Act, 1919; Position of Octroi and Terminal Taxes under the Government of India Act, 1919; Terminal Taxes under the Government of India Act, 1935; Terminal Taxes under the Constitution);

Recommendation for Retransferring Terminal Taxes to the State List; Recommendations; Present Position Regarding Levy of Octroi in various States; Bombay; Levy of Octroi on Government Trading Enterprises; Levy of Octroi on Articles Received Through Post (Uttar Pradesh; Madhya Pradesh; Punjab); Profession Tax (Constitutional Limitations on the Levy of Profession Tax; Position in each State: Income; Basis of Assessment; Recommendations—Compulsory Levy Basis of Assessment; Agency for Assessment and Collection); Licence Fees (Income; Position in each State; General Observations; Municipal Monopoly of Markets; Licensing to be Self-Supporting; Periodical Review of Fees for Licences; Distinction Between Licence Fee and Tax): Taxation of Railways (Difficulty of Valuing Railways; Railways Act, 1890; Enunciation of Policy, 1901; Declaration of Policy, 1907; Change of Attitude; Government of India Act, 1935, and after; Railways (Local Authorities Taxation) Act, 1941; Present Policy of the Railway Board; Criterion of "Services Rendered"; Position under the Constitution; Railway Board's Memorandum of 1948; Position in Other Countries; Present System of Assessment of Railway Properties; British System of Valuation of Railways; U.K. Local Government Act, 1948; Recommendations); Taxation of Government Property (Position before Government of India Act, 1935; Position under Government of India Act, 1935; Position under the Constitution; Position in Other Countries; Arguments Against Local Taxation of Union Government Property; Arguments in Favour of Local Taxation of Union Government Property; Observations and Recommendations); Betterment Levy of Union Property); Taxation of Port Trust Properties (Madras; Calcutta; Bombay; General); Taxation of Floating Population (Tax on Railway Passengers; Hotel Tax; Tax on Food Ration Cards); Taxation of Mines (Basis of Assessment; Mining Boards; Special Cesses for Mining Boards; Special Laws; General Observations; Quarries); Collection of Taxes (Position State-wise; Need for Improvement in Collections; Levy of Penal Interest; Coercive Processes; Need for Improving the Efficiency of Financial Personnel; Disqualification of Members of Local Bodies in Arrears); Grants-in-Aid and Assignments of Revenue (General; Grants-in-Aid in England; U.K. Local Government Act, 1929; U.K. Local Government Act, 1948; General Exchequer Grants and Transitional Grants; Grants in India; Madras; Bombay; West Bengal; Uttar Pradesh; Punjab; Bihar; Orissa; Madhya Pradesh; Assam; General Observations; Assignment and Sharing of Provincial Taxes; Grants to Supplement Assigned Taxes; Information about Grants-inAid); Education (General; Madras; Bombay; West Bengal; Uttar Pradesh; Punjab; Bihar; Orissa; Madhya Pradesh; Assam); Medical and Public Health [General; Total Expenditure; Per-Capita Expenditure (Urban); Per-Capita Expenditure (Rural); Government Assistance; Madras; Bombay; West Bengal; Uttar Pradesh; Punjab; Bihar; Orissa; Madhya Pradesh; Assam; General Observations]; Communications (General; Road Mileage Statistics; Statewise Positions Regarding Grants for Communications: Madras; Bombay; West Bengal; Uttar Pradesh; Punjab; Bihar; Orissa; Madhya Pradesh; Assam; Need for Prescription of Standards of Road Maintenance; Tax on Bullock Carts; Tax on Road Transport; Tax on Rickshaws; Payment of Compensation from Motor Vehicles Tax; Extraordinary Damage to Local Roads During the War and Partition); Finances of Improvement Trusts/ Development Boards (General; History of Improvement Trusts; Finances; Financial Aid for Housing in Other Countries; Recommendations); Finances of Village Panchayats (General; Constitution; Functions; Finances; General Observations and Recommendations); Finances of City Corporations (Madras; Bombay; Calcutta); Public Utility Undertakings (General; Transport; Cinemas, etc.; Electricity Distribution); Borrowings (General; Local Authorities Loans Act, 1914, and Rules; Ways and Means Advances; Rate af Interest; Repayment; Position of Securities of Local Bodies as "Trustee Securities"; Municipal Banking); Audit (General; Internal Audit; Extension of Scope of Audit; Surcharge); Budget (Power to Sanction Budgets; Allotment of Fixed Proportions of Revenue to Particular Objects; Power of Sanction to Works Expenditure; Investment of Funds; Control over Establishment; General Observations; Minute of Dissent by Shri S. N. Sapru; Minute of Dissent by Shri M. B. L. Dar; Minute of Dissent by Shri Chunilal D. Burfiwala; Minute of Dissent by Shri P. B. Gole; Minute of Dissent by Shri R. K. Sidhva; Minute of Dissent by Shri R.D. Kapila); Summary of Recommendations; Appendices (General); Statistical Appendices.

RECOMMENDATIONS

History Of Local Finance

We are of the opinion that wholesale transfer of functions from local bodies to State Governments is a retrograde step and should be avoided. Whatever be the criterion for demarcations of functions between the State Government and the local bodies, the desperate financial plight of the latter should not be made a ground for reducing them to practical impotence.

It is hoped that in the new set-up local bodies will be used more and more as instruments of national policy and there will be a steady enlargement of their functions.

Power Of Taxation

In order to give to the local bodies definite sources of revenue it is suggested that a convention may be established by which the net proceeds from the following sources of revenue shall be exclusively available for the local authorities.

Union List

(1) Item No. 89: Terminal Taxes on goods or passengers carried by railway, sea or air.

State List

(2) Item No. 49: Taxes on lands and buildings.

(3) Item No. 50: Taxes on mineral rights subject to any limitations imposed by Parliament by law relating to mineral development.

(4) Item No. 52: Taxes on the entry of goods into a local area for consumption, use or sale therein.

(5) Item No. 53: Taxes on the consumption or sale of electricity.

(6) Item No. 56: Taxes on advertisements other than advertisements published in newspapers.

(7) Item No. 56: Taxes on goods and passengers carried by road or on inland waterways.

(8) Item No. 57: Taxes on vehicles, other than those mechanically propelled.

(9) Item No. 58: Taxes on animals and boats.

(10) Item No. 59: Tolls.

(11) Item No. 60: Taxes on professions, trades, callings and employments.

(12) Item No. 61: Capitation taxes.

(13) Item No. 62: Taxes on entertainments including amusements.

We consider that no useful purpose will be served by going into details of cases where rates of taxation have remained unchanged over long periods of time. We would only bring the point to the notice of the State Governments so that they might take appropriate action with the local bodies in question. Local bodies which do not utilize their existing powers of taxation can have no claim on the financial resources of the State.

We think that where local bodies have not got independent powers of taxation, they should be given such powers, subject to maximum limits in each case to be prescribed by the Acts or the rules framed thereunder.

Within these limits, local bodies should have a free hand in determining the rates of taxes. Where a local body is unwilling to impose a tax at an adequate rate, the State Government should have the right, in the first instance, to give friendly advice and if the local body fails to carry it out, the State Government should in the last resort have the power to impose or raise the tax themselves, particularly in emergencies.

Property Tax (General)

There is a difference of opinion as to whether the rates on property are the most appropriate form of taxation for local purposes. We are of the opinion that the existing system should continue, though hardship to owner-occupiers may be alleviated by introducing some flexibility in the method of valuation of properties of different categories.

Property Tax seems to us a tax particularly suitable for exploitation by local bodies and we think it desirable that State Governments should withdraw from this field on the condition that an equivalent local tax is imposed by the municipality.

We are of the opinion that in the place of the present optional provision for the levy of the Property Tax in the various Municipal Acts, there should be an obligatory provision as it is in the Acts constituting the City Corporations of Bombay and Calcutta. Should, however, any Municipality fail to levy the tax in spite of such statutory provision, the State Government should have power to levy the tax at such rates as they deem fit in any Municipal area for the benefit of the Municipality. We would suggest that this power should be exercised by the State Government only when a Municipality has refused the advice tendered to it by the State Government in the first instance.

We recommend that a maximum rate for the Property Tax should be prescribed by statute where it is not done at present. A minimum should likewise be prescribed in the Acts.

We are generally in favour of a progressive scale, adoptable at the discretion of the Municipality concerned.

We are of the opinion that in all cases where exemption is granted at the instance of a Government, an equivalent contribution should be paid by that Government to the Municipal funds.

We are of the view that it is necessary to ensure that an institution claiming exemption on the ground of being a charitable institution is actually being used for purposes of charity. We also think that the list of charitable institutions which at present get exemption from Property Tax should be subjected to periodical review in order to see whether the exemption given in each case is justified or not. This review should be undertaken either by the State Government or the Municipality according as the exemption is under the Act or the rules made thereunder.

Where an actual service like supply of water is rendered there should be no exemption.

It does not appear that a complete list of exemptions granted (together with annual value in each case) is kept by every local body. Such a list should be prepared and should be scrutinized from year to year with a view to seeing that the exemption is fully deserved in every case.

We are of the opinion that there should be no exemption from the property tax merely on the ground of the annual value falling below a particular monetary limit. Such exemptions, wherever they exist, should be done away with.

In view of the fact that the major portion of the services rendered by local bodies such as street repairs, maintenance of main roads, fire brigades, public lighting, drainage, street cleansing, etc., has to be performed, whether the building remains occupied or not, there seems no justification for giving a greater remission than one-half of the tax due in all such cases. Remission should not be granted for a vacancy of less than 90 consecutive days in a year. No rate payers who are in arrears should be entitled to vacancy remission.

We are of the opinion that where the actual rent is lower than the "reasonable" rent, the latter should be adopted as the basis of assessment.

We see no reason why such a machinery as is rateable in England should be excluded in India, and recommend that the Acts of the various States may be amended on the lines of English practice in this matter.

We are not in favour of the inclusion of furniture for valuation.

We are of the opinion that there should be no change from the well-tried basis of rent to the more or less uncertain basis of capital value. Where, however, Municipalities are actually adopting capital value as the basis and there is no complaint that basis may continue.

If alternative bases are to be retained, we think that the choice of basis should not, either directly or indirectly, be left with the owner of the property. There should be only one basis of assessment, namely, the rental basis. Where alternative bases are in existence, the position may be reviewed and remedied.

We recommend that the entire proceeds of the local fund cess within Municipal areas be handed over to Municipalities instead of to District Boards.

Nazul lands should be handed over to Municipalities for management, as in U.P., and the income from leases may be distributed between the Government and the local bodies.

We see no reason for the continuance of the concession in regard to levy of Property Tax in the Municipal Acts of Bengal, Bihar and Orissa in respect of buildings the cost of construction of which exceeds one lakh of rupees.

We are of the opinion that the Calcutta City Municipal Act should be amended so as to provide for a simultaneous revision of valuation in all wards.

We consider the provision in the Madras City Municipal Act and the District Municipalities Act, whereby the annual value of any building or land, the tax for which is payable by the Commissioner (Chief Executive Officer), is to be determined by the Mayor or the Revenue Divisional Officer, as the case may be, a very salutary provision and recommend its adoption.

We think that the Municipal Acts should be amended so as to make it obligatory to record the grounds for each reduction of valuation or assessment.

A local body should have a right of appeal when it feels aggrieved by any decision of a revising authority.

While the power to tax should continue to be vested in the local bodies, the detailed work connected with the preparation of the valuation list of all the properties within the jurisdiction of a local body should be entrusted to a Central Organization (to be created for this purpose) which will consist of trained valuers, as in Western countries. A Valuation Department should be brought into being for all the local bodies in each State.

Property Taxes (Part II)

We are of the view that where an exemption is granted at the instance of the State Government, which has not been proposed by the Municipality, the Municipality should be given compensation to that extent by the Government.

Property Tax—Service Taxes

As regards the question whether or not the services of water supply, drainage, lighting and conservancy should be self-supporting, we are of the opinion that the cost-of-service principle, however equitable it may seem in the abstract, is not capable of practical application.

The present classification of Municipal services into two categories, one to be financed from General Revenues and the other from Special Rates, does not appear to rest on any logical basis.

A Special Service Rate is justified when the areas within Municipal limits are differently developed. When the development is uniform and all the services are evenly spread throughout the area, the case for Special Service Rates disappears.

Local Fund Cess

As the Land Revenue staff which collects the land cess would in any case have to be maintained for the collection of land revenue, and the cost of special staff for the adjustment of accounts between the Land Revenue Department and the District Boards must be insignificant, we think that the Government might well remit this charge.

We consider that the rates of the public works cess and road cess in Bengal should be doubled.

In District Boards in the Punjab where the cess is being levied at 24 pies in the rupee of land revenue, we recommend that the cess should be raised to at least 36 pies.

We are of the opinion that the rate of two annas in the rupee in Bihar District Boards should be ear-marked for general purposes and a separate education cess of one anna levied.

We think that the rate of cess in Orissa should be raised to three annas.

The rate at present levied by Janapadas in Madhya Pradesh is low and should be raised to three annas in the rupee.

We think that the local rate in Assam should be raised to three annas in the rupee.

The present rate of cess in Ajmer-Merwara is low and should be raised to one-and-half annas and by gradual stages to three annas.

The rate of cess in Coorg should be the same as in Madras.

With the abolition of Zamindari, the responsibility for the payment of cess will have to be definitely fixed either on the Government or on the tenant who holds directly from the Government. The interests of District Boards should not be prejudicially affected by the abolition of Zamindari.

Octroi And Terminal Taxes

We recommend the transfer of the entry relating to Terminal Taxes from the Union List to the State List.

If that is not possible we recommend that the Government of India should consider favourably any proposal which may be made to them by State Governments for the levy and collection of Terminal Taxes.

If the above suggestion cannot be adopted there is no alternative to octroi, as it is the most productive single item of Indirect Taxation available.

There should be in each State a model schedule for octroi approved by the State Government and departures from this schedule should not be permitted except with the previous approval of the Government. In framing the model schedule the rates on the necessaries of life should be kept as low as possible.

Octroi should be levied generally on an *ad valorem* basis. There should be no objection to a "maundage" or other basis in the case of articles where the *ad valorem* basis is not suitable.

All public utility and commercial undertakings of the Government should be treated, so far as local taxation is concerned, in the same manner as if they were conducted by private enterprise. If they are to be exempted from local taxation the Government concerned should make a contribution in lieu of such taxation. The provision in Article 285 of the Constitution is unfair to local bodies. We recommend that nesessary legislation may be undertaken to provide for local taxation of State property used in connection with State trading or running of public utility concerns.

To prevent evasion of Octroi duties on postal parcels the post office should render every assistance to Municipalities.

Profession Tax

The Government should advise local bodies to revise their schedules of Profession Tax so as to correspond to the limit permitted by the Constitution.

We consider that the present limit of Rs. 250 in the Constitution is very low and should be raised to Rs. 1,000.

Where the Municipal or Local Board Acts do not contain any provision for the levy of Profession Tax, such provision should be made. We are, however, not in favour of the tax being made compulsory in the case of all local bodies. It may be possible in the case of many local bodies to raise sufficient funds by the levy of Octroi and House Tax. In such cases it may not be necessary to compel the local bodies to levy a Profession Tax. We recommend the compulsory levy of Profession Tax under the orders of the State Government only in cases where only one of the other taxes, namely, House Tax or Octroi or Terminal Tax, is being levied.

The basis of actual income would be the ideal one, but in view of the very great practical difficulties in the way of its adoption, we recommend that local bodies should have the choice to adopt all or any of several bases according to their convenience.

The assessment and collection of Profession Tax should be done by the Municipalities themselves, but they should not have the power to call for accounts.

So far as rural areas other than those covered by Village Panchayats are concerned, we think that in view of the large areas to be covered, the agency for assessment and collection should be the Revenue Department.

In areas where Village Panchayats are constituted, we think that Profession Tax should be levied by the panchayats and should be assessed and collected by them.

Licence Fees

We are of the opinion that markets and slaughter-houses should generally be self-supporting. While endeavour should be to make the markets and slaughter-houses a remunerative enterprise bringing an appreciable net income to the local bodies, in no case should the investment of capital and the recurring expenditure on markets and slaughter-houses be a burden on the local revenues. The State Government should issue instructions to the local bodies to this effect and from time to time see that this is done whenever the account or budget of a local body comes up for review.

The Government of Madras are considering the giving of monopoly of opening markets to Municipalities and prohibiting by legislation the opening of private markets. We recommend that other State Governments should consider whether such a step would be feasible.

The scale of the various licence fees levied by Municipalities should come in for a regular periodical review, at least once in three or five years.

We recommend that the rates of licence fees should be adequate to cover the cost of regulation and supervision of the trade or activity licensed. An attempt should be made to keep proforma accounts in relation to receipts and expenditure of the licensing branch and to ensure that these balance each other. When, however, there is a separate Licence Department the expenditure on that department should not be a net charge on the General Funds of the local body.

A proper scrutiny of various licence fees levied in different States would show that some of the trades, professions, callings or occupations which are subject to licence fees can be more suitably made the objects of Profession Tax. We recommend such a scrutiny and change in the method of this imposition, whatever is suitable.

Taxation Of Railways

We are of the opinion that until the system of local taxation of railways is rationalized and railway undertakings considered as a whole it will not be possible to secure any worthwhile improvement in the existing position. The present lack of uniformity and piecemeal valuation should go. An Act of Parliament should prescribe the principles of valuation, taxation and apportionment. If a Railway Assessment Authority is set up it should be so constituted as to secure adequate representation of local bodies. The right of appeal against the awards of Arbitrators appointed by the Government of India under the Railways Act should be conferred on local bodies and a Special Tribunal constituted under Parliamentary authority for hearing such appeals. The liability of Railways for both General and Service Taxes should be recognized as in the Notification of 1907.

The stress now laid on payment for services rendered as a criterion for local taxation of Railway properties is, in our opinion, not justified.

Taxation Of Government Property

We recommend that State Government properties are not liable to local taxation under the Acts constituting local bodies; the Acts should be amended to provide for such taxation. If the liability is accepted, there should be no objection to an independent machinery for valuation of Government property.

While Union Government properties may continue to enjoy statutory immunity from local taxation, the Union Government should adopt the practice of Governments in other countries and make a contribution to local bodies in lieu of such taxes. That contribution should not be limited by any artificial dateline. In regard to the valuation of these properties, we recommend that the procedure prevailing in England may be adopted, i.e., the valuation may be done by a special machinery constituted by the Central Government.

In regard to official residences, the privileged treatment at present accorded, namely, the annual value being based on the concessional rent paid by Government servants, should be withdrawn and the normal assessment levied.

There is no reason to treat the property of the Central Government differently from other property in respect of levy of betterment charges. Should, however, there be any legal or other objection to the payment of betterment charges in the form of taxes or fees, an equivalent contribution should be made by the Government in lieu thereof.

Taxation Of Port Trust Properties

As the Madras City Corporation and the Port Trust are in favour of the continuance of the existing system of assessment, namely, a percentage of gross earnings, and also in view of its decided advantages we recommend that the existing arrangement be continued.

As the Corporation of Calcutta and the Calcutta Port Commissioners have expressed satisfaction with the recent agreement that they have entered into we suggest that steps may be taken to give legislative effect to its terms.

If in the case of assessment of any Port Trust properties the profit basis is adopted it is necessary that the form of keeping accounts should be determined by an independent authority.

We suggest the constitution of a tribunal to deal with disputes relating to the determination of rateable value of Port Trust properties. Such a tribunal may consist of a qualified accountant and an experienced engineer and be presided over by a High Court judge.

Taxation Of Floating Population

We recommend that the levy of a tax on railway passengers in important centres of trade and industry may be permitted as is done in Calcutta.

We suggested that State Governments should authorize Municipalities to levy a tax on such visitors to important centres of trade and industry as reside in hotels. Such a tax might be levied in the form of a surcharge on the hotel bill, subject to a minimum exemption limit of Rs. 5 per visitor.

Taxation Of Mines

Local taxation of mines on the basis of output appears to us to be appropriate. That basis may be adopted by States which are not doing so at present.

Exemption from the payment of general cess to District Boards at present enjoyed by Railway collieries should cease.

We have suggested that the land cess on agricultural lands in West Bengal should be doubled. If this suggestion is accepted the general cess payable by mines in West Bengal should also be doubled.

The local taxation of quarries should be on the same basis as for mines.

Collection Of Taxes

Each State Government should prescribe for their local bodies a standard percentage of collection to demand and see that it is attained.

The Examiner of Local Fund Accounts should be instructed to give figures in his audit reports of the percentages of collection of taxes to demand for every local body. The figures should be compiled on a uniform basis in all the States, to facilitate comparison.

We are not in favour of any rebates being granted for punctual payment. But we suggest that penal interest at 6¼% per annum should be charged on arrears of taxes.

Where the Acts do not provide for coercive powers for local bodies necessary amendments should be made to incorporate such powers. It should be impressed upon local bodies that a freer use should be made of these powers for collection of taxes.

We are not in favour of issue of distress warrants for recovery of contractual dues, but only for recovery of taxes and fees. In regard to rents of lands vested in or managed by Municipalities, we recommend the adoption of the procedure prescribed in Section 291 of the U.P. Municipalities Act, 1916, i.e., the Municipality may apply to the Collector for the recovery of such rents as arrears of land revenue.

Local bodies should have the power to proceed not only against movable but also against immovable property for the recovery of their taxes and fees.

The head of the financial administration in bigger Municipalities should be a qualified and specially selected person. He should also be in charge of accounts and should examine the position with regard to collection of taxes and submit monthly reports to the chief executive authority, and bring to his notice any failures in collection and suggest suitable remedies. No liabilities of a financial nature should be incurred before he has examined and reported thereon.

With regard to recruitment of the higher financial personnel, we are of the opinion that there should be a Provincial Cadre for such services. Such a cadre should be controlled by a board with statutory powers on which there should be representatives of local bodies.

We recommend that:

(i) No person should be eligible to stand for election to any office in a local body, if on the date of filing nominations he is in arrears of local taxes; and

(ii) If within three months of the notice of demand of any dues to the local body, a member of such a body fails to pay up the arrears, a warning notice, that if he does not pay the arrears before the date of expiry of the original notice of demand, he becomes disqualified under the relevant section of the Act, should be given.

Grant-in-Aid And Assignment Of Revenues

It is felt that if the functions imposed on local bodies under the Constitution (Articles 45, 47, etc.) are to continue to be the responsibility of local bodies as a means of encouraging local initiative, enterprise and co-operation, the State should come to the assistance of local bodies by way of adequate grants-in-aid where they are unable, out of their own resources, to achieve the minimum national standard of efficiency.

The State Governments while investing local bodies with wider responsibilities must place at their disposal adequate funds to discharge those responsibilities.

Grants-in-aid should be so given that, while achieving clearly defined objects of policy and administration, they do not encourage unwillingness on the part of local bodies to develop their own resources.

We prefer assignment of sources of revenue, whereever possible, to grants-in-aid. Where it is not possible to meet the full requirements of a local body from assigned revenues, grants should be given as a last resort. We suggest that the system of grants-in-aid should be utilized to remedy inequalities which are inherent in a system of assigned revenues. Otherwise, generally we would prefer that independent sources of revenue should be placed at the disposal of local bodies.

We recommend that 15% of the net proceeds of land revenue accruing within the area of a District Board (which is not already assigned to a Village Panchayat) should be assigned to District Boards.

We are not in favour of the imposition of a separate vehicle tax on motor cars by local bodies in addition to the State tax. We recommend the sharing of the net proceeds of the Motor Vehicles Tax with the local bodies.

The Sales Tax should remain wholly a State source of revenue and not be shared with the local bodies.

It is desirable that all grants, whether statutory or non-statutory, should be given on some definite and understandable principles, and each State Government should formulate such principles for its guidance.

We suggest that each State Government may, at the time of preparing the budget, include in the Finance Department's explanatory memorandum details of financial assistance rendered to local bodies. Such a statement should also include items which do not appear in the budget, e.g., transfer of land, or any other form the financial assistance for which no vote of the Legislature is required.

Education

In respect of secondary, technical and collegiate education, we consider that there should be no financial responsibility on local bodies and that they should be entirely relieved of this liability.

In regard to Madras we recommend that after the levy of education tax at a proper level, of which the State Government must be the judge, contribution from General Funds of local bodies for educational purposes shall not exceed the proportion that such contribution now bears to the income (excluding Government grants) of such local bodies and the whole of the remaining expenditure should be borne by the State Government.

In regard to Bombay we suggest that the State Government should consider whether an education cess may be levied as in Madras.

We suggest that in every Municipality in West Bengal an education rate as prescribed in the Bengal Primary Education Act, 1919, should be levied. Any increase in expenditure considered necessary to introduce compulsory primary education should not exceed the proportion which the present expenditure of Municipalities on this subject bears to local income.

As regards U.P., we suggest that the Government should consider the desirability of levying an Education Cess at a suitable rate.

As regards Punjab, we suggest that an education cess should be levied in urban and rural areas at rates approved by the Government. The balance of the expenditure should be met from State funds in accordance with the same formula as we have suggested for other States.

If the Education Cess now levied in Bihar is not adequate for any area we suggest that it should be raised to an adequate level. The balance of the expenditure not covered by the Education Cess should be met from Provincial Funds in the same manner as recommended by us in the case of other States.

The financial assistance which local bodies receive from the Government in Orissa is not inadequate and we have therefore no recommendation to make in this regard.

We understand that in Madhya Pradesh the State Government has decided to take over compulsory primary education. We have, therefore, no recommendation to make in this regard.

Under the Assam Primary Education Act, 1947 (which came into force with effect from November 1, 1948), local bodies have been relieved of the responsibility for primary education; therefore, the question of apportionment of local expenditure under this head does not arise.

Medical And Public Health

The distribution of expenditure in regard to Public Health should be as follows:

Local Bodies : (a) Construction, maintenance and cleansing of drains and drainage works and of public latrines, urinals and similar conveniences;

(b) Scavenging and removal and disposal of excrementitious and other filthy matter and of all ashes, refuse and rubbish;

(c) Reclamation of unhealthy localities, removal of noxious vegetation and generally the abatement of all nuisances;

(d) Regulation of places for disposal of the dead and the provision of new places for the said purpose; and

(e) Registration of births and deaths.

State Governments : (f) Public vaccination;

(g) Prevention and suppression of infectious and dangerous diseases; and

(h) Establishing and maintaining public hospitals and dispensaries and carrying out other measures necessary for public medical relief.

We recommend that the division of functions may remain as it is at present.

Communications

Grants for the maintenance of roads should be based on the road mileage which has to be maintained. State Governments should prescribe certain standards of maintenance for metalled and unmetalled roads and make grants on such basis, especially in rural areas, where the need for financial assistance in this matter is very great. We realize that, as a result of such prescription of standards, the financial burden on State Governments will become heavy and they may not be able to give adequate grants-in-aid within the next few years, but it is better to prescribe standards and reach them by slow stages than to allow the present unregulated state of affairs to continue.

We recommend that a tax on bullock carts should be levied in rural areas. It would be very difficult in practice to discriminate between carts used for hire and carts not so used. We, therefore, are not in favour of the exemption of the latter.

The question of the rate at which the tax might be levied we would leave to the discretion of each State Government. Where a tax on bullock carts is already being levied in any Village Panchayat and is at the same level as the tax now proposed for levy by the District Board, there should be no further levy on the individual paying the Panchayat Tax. But should the level of taxation of the Panchayat be lower than that of the District Board, the latter may levy the tax at the difference between the two rates. The net proceeds of such taxation should be exclusively earmarked for purposes of road development in rural areas.

We are in favour of road transport paying a tax which should be levied as a State tax in the first instance. The tax should be in the nature of a surcharge on the fare and range between 3 pies and 12 pies according to distance. Not less than two-thirds of the net proceeds of the tax should go to local bodies and the balance may be retained by the State Government. The basis of allocation of the portion which is intended for local bodies should be either population or road mileage within the jurisdiction of each local body.

We suggest that the power to impose taxation on rickshaws should be conferred on local bodies where it does not already exist.

The basis of the compensation for loss of income due to the abolition of tolls on motor vehicles should be re-opened and fresh amounts fixed in the light of altered facts.

The damage done to the roads of local bodies by extraordinarily heavy traffic can be made good either by the State sharing the proceeds of the motor vehicle tax with them or by the levy of a surcharge on trucks above one ton in weight for the benefit of local bodies concerned.

As regards the damage done by motor trucks during the War, there is a good case for compensation, but the matter is one which should be pursued by the State Governments concerned with the Defence Department.

There is a similar case for compensation to certain local bodies in the Punjab, particularly the Amritsar Municipality, for damage done to roads in consequence of the partition of the Province.

Finances Of Improvement Trusts And Development Boards

The existing resources of the Improvement Trusts are not adequate. The State Government should make these bodies financially self-sufficient so that they may be able to discharge their obligations. We recommend that Improvement Trusts and Development Boards should have the following sources of revenue:

(1) Annual contribution of 2% of the annual rateable value from Municipal funds;

(2) Share of the proceeds of the Entertainment Tax;

(3) Share of the proceeds of the Terminal Tax on persons coming by rail, road or inland waterways;

(4) Betterment Tax; and

(5) Government grants.

In regard to item (2) above, the Madras Corporation at present gets practically the whole of the Entertainment Tax. Similarly, in regard to item (3), the Calcutta Improvement Trust gets the entire income of the terminal tax on passengers coming by rail. We do not suggest that either of these arrangements should be disturbed by the recommendations made above.

Calcutta, Nagpur and some other Trusts are permitted to levy a surcharge on Stamp Duty on transfer of immovable property. Where this is actually being done, we do not recommend any change. But we are not in favour of its extension to other Trusts.

Improvement Trusts and Development Boards should ordinarily borrow from the Government, and the rate of interest charged by the Government should in no case be more than ½% above the rate at which the Government have borrowed themselves.

As regards slums, we recommend the adoption of the provisions of the English Housing Act which requires slums to be cleared at the cost of the owners. We suggest that the law should be so amended that compensation for acquisition of properties for purposes of slum clearance should be limited to the market value of land without any payment being made for the structure and without the addition of 15% solatium on account of compulsory acquisition.

Finances Of Village Panchayats

Every Panchayat should levy the following two taxes compulsorily:

(i) House Tax or *chulla* tax or circumstances and property tax; and

(ii) General sanitary cess.

Other taxes may be levied by Panchayats according to their needs and local conditions.

As regards Labour Tax, there should be no compulsion.

If a person renders such labour willingly, he should be allowed to do so. Alternatively he may be permitted to make a payment in kind in lieu thereof. Should he be unable to work or make any payment in kind on account of poverty, he should not be subjected to any penalty.

We recommend an unconditional allotment to Village Panchayats of 15% of the land revenue raised in the Panchayat areas.

There should be a surcharge on the transfer of immovable property within the Panchayat jurisdiction for the benefit of Village Panchayats.

We recommend that in regard to elementary education Village Panchayats should be dealt with on the same lines as other local bodies.

Village Panchayats should also be assisted in the following ways:

(i) Salaries and allowances of Panchayat officers should be borne by the State Government at least to the extent of three-fourths;

(ii) Wherever Panchayats are compulsorily required to maintain chowkidars and daffadars for watch and ward duties, the State Government should bear the cost on account of their salaries and allowances;

(iii) Panchayats should be allowed the use of State lands within their jurisdiction. When alienation of these lands takes place, it should be subject to the sanction of the State Government.

(iv) Village Panchayats, wherever possible, should be encouraged to collect land revenue and land cess on behalf of the State Government on a commission basis.

Panchayats should also be encouraged to undertake as many remunerative enterprises as possible, namely, markets, slaughter-houses, cart and bus stands and ferries. They may also be encouraged to take up co-operative farming, dairies and like activities under the guidance of the State Government.

Finance Of City Corporations

Madras Corporation: We recommend that the question of raising the rate of Property Tax in respect of properties with annual valuation of Rs. 500 and below from 16½% to 17½% should be revived.

We recommend that the rate of tax on timber be raised to Rs. 20.

Bombay Corporation: In the event of the Bombay Government withdrawing the Urban Immovable Property Tax the Bombay Corporation should consider its replacement by an equivalent addition to the Municipal Tax.

The administrative machinery should be tightened and necessary steps taken to improve collection of taxes.

As regards the distribution of expenditure on primary education we recommend the same formula for the Corporation as we have suggested for other local bodies.

The machinery of valuation and collection should be tightened. This alone will lead to an increase of revenue under the consolidated rate by about 50%.

Public Utility Undertakings

Motor transport can be successfully undertaken only by bigger city Municipalities within their local area but we are not in favour of its being undertaken by smaller Municipalities and rural local bodies.

In rural areas and smaller Municipalities, passenger transport should be managed by the State and the net proceeds shared with local bodies over whose roads the services are run.

Where State Electricity Boards are set up, the financial interests of local bodies should not be disregarded. Local bodies engaged in the business of generation and distribution of electricity should continue to do so and have a free hand in the matter of utilization of the net profits of the undertaking. In regard to new schemes, however, local bodies competent to run electricity undertakings should be given first preference, particularly in regard to retail distribution, subject of course to such restrictions as the Provincial Board may wish to impose.

Borrowings

We suggest that the procedure in regard to loan applicants be simplified so that final orders on a loan application can be issued within four months of its receipt by the Government.

The State Governments are in a position to borrow more cheaply on behalf of local bodies. It is desirable to have a co-ordinated loan policy in which the interests of the Union Government, the State Governments and the local bodies should be considered together.

We support the request made by the Calcutta and Bombay Corporations for the amendment of their respective Acts to allow them to receive ways and means advances repayable within the year from their respective banks with which they keep their accounts on much the same lines and subject to the same conditions on which the State Governments receive such advances from the Reserve Bank.

With regard to other local bodies we recommend that they should also be in a position to receive such advances from the bank in which the Government has permitted them to keep their account, if they keep their funds in the Government Treasury from the Government itself, on the same lines and subject to the same conditions as for City Corporations.

The rate of interest to be charged to local bodies on loans taken from the Government should not be more than one-fourth over the rate of interest paid by the State Government on its own loan for the year in question. The period of repayment in the case of productive schemes may well be extended from 30 to 40 years.

If a local body is able or willing to repay a Government loan earlier than the due date it should be encouraged to do so.

We do not favour the State Government guaranteeing the principal and interest of loans raised by local bodies, but the question whether Section 20 of the Indian Trusts Act may be amended so as to include local bodies in the bigger cities may be considered.

Establishment of Municipal banks by individual Municipalities, except perhaps by big City Corporations, does not appear to us practicable. A Municipal bank for each State would have a better chance of success than banks run by individual Municipalities. The State Government should, however, continue to exercise its powers under the Local Authorities Loans Act in regard to the sanctioning of loans advanced by the bank to local bodies.

Audit

In addition to a qualified accountant, there must in the major Municipalities be an internal audit staff, paid for by the local body, which should be responsible for the initial audit of all transactions of receipts and payments.

With the setting up of an internal audit staff local bodies should be relieved of the liability to contribute to the cost of the audit staff of the Examiner of Local Fund Accounts, where such liability exists.

It is essential that the Examiner of Local Fund Accounts should regard himself not only as an auditor but also as a financial adviser of the local bodies whose accounts he audits. He should be responsible for the checking of all assessment lists and collections against assessment and should bring to notice cases where the collections fall below a prescribed minimum.

The provision for surcharge is a healthy one and should exist in relation to all local bodies.

The surcharge should be both against any person through whose negligence or wrong action such liability has occurred, whether he is an employee of the local body or a member voting for it.

Budget

The power to sanction budgets should vest entirely in local bodies. They should be required to maintain a prescribed closing balance which should not be drawn upon, except temporarily and in an emergency, without the sanction of the State Government or of such officers as may be nominated by the Government in this behalf.

Local bodies should also have full powers of re-appropriation and making supplementary allotments during the currency of a financial year, as long as the prescribed minimum balance is not trenched upon.

The practice prevailing in certain States to require local bodies to allot a percentage of their revenues to particular objects should be discontinued. Where, however, the Government gives a grant for a specific purpose that grant may not be diverted to some other purpose.

Where the Government considers it essential to control a service, it should pay for it and not ask for any contribution from the local body.

The present restrictions on the powers of sanction to works expenditure are very minute and should be relaxed.

The control in respect of non-gazetted and inferior establishments of local bodies by some State Governments is very minute and needs to be relaxed. The Government should prescribe rules in regard to various categories of local bodies in respect of matters such as pay, allowances, leave, travelling allowances, pensions, provident funds, etc. If a local body considers that its circumstances warrant any modification of such rules the variation desired should be with the sanction of the State Government. In other respects, however, local bodies should have a free hand in regard to their establishments.

The restrictions placed on the investment of spare funds by local bodies require revision. A list of banks with which funds may be invested may be drawn up with the approval of the Reserve Bank of India. Subject to the maintenance of the prescribed minimum balance investment of all spare funds with approved institutions should require no outside sanction.

FISCAL COMMISSION, 1949-50—REPORT

Delhi, Manager of Publications, 1950. 4 Vols.

Chairman : Shri V. T. Krishnamachari.
Members : Dr. B. N. Ganguli; Shri B. M. Birla; Shri M. Ananthasayanam Ayyangar; Shri Mukhtar Singh; Shri Khandubhai Desai; Shri Ambalal Sarabhai.
Member-Secretary : Shri D. L. Mazumdar.

APPOINTMENT

The Fiscal Commission was appointed vide Resolution No 34-T(37)/48 dated April 20, 1949, by the Government of India in the Ministry of Commerce. It was inspired by the Industrial Policy Statement by the Government and owes its origin to the statement on Industrial Policy made by the Government of India in 1948. In this statement the Government of India reaffirmed their intention of designing the country's long-term Tariff Policy to suit the needs of Post-War India in the following words:

"the Government of India are fully alive to their direct responsibility for the development of those industries which they have found necessary to reserve exclusively for State enterprise. They are equally ready to extend their assistance to private or co-operative enterprise in the report of the industrial field and, in particular, by removing transport difficulties and by facilitating the import of essential raw materials to the maximum possible extent. The tariff policy of the Government will be designed to prevent unfair competition and to promote the utilization of India's resources without imposing unjustifiable burdens on the consumer."

It was in pursuance of this undertaking that the Fiscal Commission was set up.

In their Resolution No. 34-T(37)/48 dated April 20, 1949, setting up the Fiscal Commission, the Government of India in the Ministry of Commerce referred to the last sentence of the above excerpt from the Government of India's statement of Industrial Policy and added :

"Having regard to the importance of the issues involved and the necessity to synthesize the needs of the divergent interests that are concerned, it has been decided that a Fiscal Commission be appointed to enquire into this matter in detail with the following terms of reference."

TERMS OF REFERENCE

(1) To examine, in consultation with all the interests concerned, the working of the policy of the Government of India with regard to protection of industries since 1922 when the last Fiscal Commission was reported; and

(2) To make recommendations as to:

(a) The future policy which the Government should adopt in regard to protection to and assistance of industries and the treatment and obligations of the industries which may be protected or assisted;

(b) The machinery required to implement such policy; and

(c) Any other matter having a direct bearing on the effective implementation of this policy.

(3) In considering these issues the Commission will be free to distinguish between short-and long-term aspects of the problems and also advise in the light of the country's requirements how far it would be desirable to undertake international obligations of the kind involved in the General Agreement on Tariffs and Trade or Charter of the International Trade Organization.

CONTENTS

Volume I: Book I—Introduction and Approach; Book II—Historical Retrospect; Book III—Patterns of Economic Development; Book IV—Fiscal Policy and Industrial Development; Book V—Other Factors in Industrial Development; Book VI—Organization and Machinery of Administration; Book VII—Fiscal Policy in Relation to International Obligations; Book VIII—Conclusion; Appendices from I to XIII.

Volume II: Evidences.

Volume III: Evidences.

Volume IV: Annexures.

FINDINGS AND RECOMMENDATIONS—SUMMARY

BOOK I

Introduction And Approach

This Chapter is purely introductory. In it we elucidate our general approach to the question referred to us, viz., the place of protection and other forms of assistance in a co-ordinated policy of economic development, and explain the plan of the Report.

We consider it necessary to preface our enquiry with an enunciation of the fundamental objectives of the country's economic policy because it is only against their background that any policy for protection of or assistance to industries can be adequately formulated.

The fundamental objectives of an Economic Policy for India must conform to the "Directive Principles of State Policy" as laid down in the Constitution and the Industrial Policy Statement of 1948 and should be broadly as follows:

(1) avoidance of unemployment, or underemployment through the achievement and maintenance in each country of useful employment opportunities for those able and willing to work and of a large and steadily growing volume of production and effective demand for goods and services;

(2) sound, efficient and fuller utilization of natural resources;

(3) steady and progressive increase in standards of productivity, elimination of sub-standard conditions of labour and the creation of incentives that will stimulate enterprise;

(4) special measures for the development of agriculture, including animal husbandry, on modern scientific lines for the production of food and of essential raw materials for industries (cotton, jute, etc.); for the establishment and development of industries for the processing of domestic primary commodities;

(5) special measures for the development of cottage industries and small-scale industries on co-operative or individual lines;

(6) ensuring that large-scale industrialization occupies a prominent place in any programme of development as capital equipment and modern techniques can make a notable contribution to increases in production, productivity and standards of living—in this field a mixed economy is indicated;

(7) the introduction of a diversified economy which would lead to a better utilization of the diversified talents of the community and its diversified human and natural resources and would enable the population to lead a full and a richer life than would otherwise be attainable.

In implementing these objectives, we recommend that early attention should be given to the following problems:

(a) A close study of the problem of population;

(b) The need for enlisting popular enthusiasm in economic development plans.

As a preliminary to (a), we recommend the constitution of a small expert committee to review the population data available to suggest what additional information should be collected to study the trends in population growth.

BOOK II

A Historical Retrospect

We have examined the changes that have taken place in different sectors of the country's economy—agriculture, industry and foreign trade—as a result of the following factors:

(a) The Great Depression of 1929-33;

(b) The separation of Burma;

(c) World War II; and

(d) The partition of India, 1947.

Our review of the changes that have taken place since 1923 reveals that in spite of the advances made in some lines of manufacture, the deficiency in the different sectors of the country's economy still remains considerable and a great effort will be needed to make up the leeway in the country's agricultural and industrial production.

Our finding is that so far as the pre-War Tariff Policy is concerned, it can be claimed that the policy of discriminating protection within its limited scope has achieved a fairly large measure of success and that on balance the direct and indirect advantages to the community resulting from the protection granted to the major industries which received it have offset the burden on the consumers.

The results of protection granted since 1945 to the new industries are, however, less conclusive. We find that the burden of protection of some of these war-time industries on the consumers has not yet been appreciably reduced. It is, however, too early to express any views on the success of the Policy of Protection in respect of these industries.

BOOK III

Pattern Of Economic Development

We are convinced that in formulating a development policy for India, we should keep in the forefront the basic significance of agriculture in the country's life and economy.

The solution of the problem of underemployment in agriculture has to be sought in the concurrent adoption of a two-fold programme:

First, rationalization of agriculture, i.e., maximization of production in terms of yield per acre by steadily improving agricultural methods and promoting an intensive system of mixed farming, and

Secondly, drawing away the surplus forces from land into industries—an occupation subsidiary to agriculture, cottage and small-scale industries, large-scale industries and tertiary occupations.

The main problem in agricultural development is how to evoke the enthusiasm of the agriculturist for plans for the betterment of his condition.

The greatest need at present in India is an extension service with the object of bridging the gap between research and the practices of producers, similar to those which have been found so valuable in the U.S.A., the U.K., etc.

An important role should be assigned in future plans to industries subsidiary to agriculture and cottage and small-scale industries and a radical change should be effected in their technique and organization by continuous research and in other ways to enable them to meet the increased demand for profitable employment that will be made on them. It should also be laid down that in regard to industries in which certain processes can be suitably "decentralized" these processes should be carried on in small-scale establishments, allowances being made for the private and social costs involved. There should also be a much wider recognition than at present of the opportunity for profitable employment afforded in fairly developed economies by tertiary occupations.

The process of industrialization in this country, seen in its true perspective, is basically a problem of the reorganization of India's occupational pattern. Whether this process should take the form of cottage, small-scale or large-scale industries will depend primarily on:

(a) the nature of the industry;

(b) the technological character of the industry;

(c) the relative proportion of capital and labour needed for the organization of the industry;

(d) the extent to which decentralization in production in small units is economical on the basis not merely of its private cost but also of its social cost; and

(e) the rate at which it is desired to effect a change in the occupational pattern.

The case for cottage and small-scale industries rests fundamentally on the "employment aspect" and that its true place in the economy of the country is determined by the relative importance of their private and social costs in relation to similar costs of large-scale industries. We elucidate this argument in paragraphs 102—104.

The rural industries that can be most economically developed are primarily those that depend on the produce of agriculture (including forests) and the manufacture of utility articles of common consumption that do not call for intensive physical effort or the exercise of a high degree of skill or complicated technical processes. The absence of electrical power in the village will, for many years, compel the rural industries to depend on other forms of motive power, e.g., steam or oil engines.

State initiative and assistance should play an important part in the promotion of cottage and small-scale industries. In our view in each State there might be set up a statutory corporation aided by the State Government to be in charge of the measures which should be adopted for stimulating the growth of cottage and small-scale industries.

In cases where no conflict exists between large-scale cottage and small-scale industries, we recommend that the detailed investigations which were promised in the Industrial Policy Statement should be pressed forward with the utmost expedition and a programme of action should be drawn up as early as possible in consultation with all the interests concerned.

Where, however, large-scale industries compete with cottage and small-scale industries and it is established that the latter deserve support against the competition from the former, we recommend that the Government should take such steps as may be necessary to safeguard the position of the latter after consultation with the interests affected, till such time as they are able to stand on their legs.

On a study of the natural and mutable factors of production we conclude that the pattern of industrialization in India will follow broadly on the lines of development in countries such as East Continental Europe, China and Japan and that within the limits set by these basic factors, the pattern of India's heavy industries will be determined by the natural advantages which its iron and steel industry enjoys.

The broad picture of the development of large-scale industries that emerges from our analysis is briefly as follows:

(i) Defence industries, including not only the industries concerned with the manufacture of arms, ammunition but also a large number of other highly-skilled ancillary industries like aircraft manufacture, wireless communications, cables, etc., which will serve not only defence but also civilian requirements;

(ii) Heavy key industries whose products are of such importance that any interference with the supply such as might arise from a cessation of imports would bring other industries to a standstill, e.g., industries for the manufacture of transportation equipment, rolling stock, wagons, etc.; ship-building to the extent that it provides the nucleus of a merchant marine, etc.;

(iii) Heavy basic industries, which provide the foundations of many other capital goods as well as consumption goods industries, e.g., iron and steel industry, machine tools industry, automobiles, tractors and other heavy machinery;

(iv) Light basic industries, e.g., some important chemical industries, whose products are essential for the manufacturing processes of other industries, e.g., caustic soda, non-ferrous metals, electro-chemical engineering, agricultural implements, prime movers, etc.;

(v) Essential consumption goods industries with a nation-wide market, e.g., cotton and woollen textiles, cement, sugar, paper, etc.

We recognize that it may not be possible for India to achieve the pattern of development envisaged above, and it may be necessary to proceed step by step on the basis of an order of priorities. On the assumption that there will be planned policy we suggest the following order of priorities for the public sector:

(i) Essential defence industries;

(ii) Industries connected with the development of natural resources, e.g., water-power, i.e., the multi-purpose projects and key minerals like coal and petroleum;

(iii) Public utility industries, e.g., railway transportation, electric power generation (where it is State-managed), etc.;

(iv) Heavy key and basic industries which in the absence of private enterprise the State may have to initiate and develop.

In the private sector the following priorities may be observed:

(i) Increase in production in existing undertakings up to the maximum of their installed capacity;

(ii) Expansion of existing industries up to the limits of effective demand in their market with special reference, wherever possible, to export markets;

(iii) Establishment and development of industries which are complementary to existing industries in the public or the private sector, e.g., industries which manufacture components of other industries or which carry the processes of production a stage nearer final consumption;

(iv) Establishment of such industries as are related to existing industries and may increase the external economies resulting from the establishment of a group of connected industries;

(v) Establishment of industries catering for a large market, internal and external, rather than those satisfying a limited or specific demand.

One important problem on the future pattern of large-scale industries requires special consideration, namely, location of industries. The site for many industries is predetermined by the nature of their requirements of raw material, labour supply, water supply, and other services that can be provided elsewhere only at a higher social cost. In the case of other industries which are more mobile, various factors will have to be taken into account before the location can be planned. These will include: (i) security factors, (ii) sources of raw material and power, (iii) labour supply, (iv) communications and transport facilities, (v) distance from the consuming centres, and (vi) the existence of related industries.

We recommend that in planning the location of industries it will be prudent for the Government to rely, in the first instance, on negative measures to prevent the further concentration of industries in areas which are already overcongested. Simultaneously positive steps might be taken to improve the attractiveness of areas where, from the social point of view, it is proposed to encourage migration of existing or new industries. The extent to which the agency of trading estates on the lines of those in the U.K. may be utilized for this purpose merits careful study.

We further recommend that, subject to the criteria laid down, the processes of decentralization of large-scale industries and the establishment of large-scale industries in rural areas should be encouraged.

Having regard to the available capital resources and technical ability we do not think that it is possible to achieve a more intensive pattern of large-scale industrialization than that visualized in this Chapter except through a measure of austerity or regimentation which in the circumstances of this country we consider it extremely difficult to enforce.

The aim of a short-term foreign trade policy should not merely be to achieve equilibrium at an easily attainable level but to create conditions in which current foreign exchange receipts are sufficient to pay for the volume of imports necessary:

(i) To carry out a production plan based on the most efficient use of existing productive resources and plant capacities;

(ii) To achieve a predetermined programme of investment in essential replacements, re-stocking and in essential new lines of manufacture; and

(iii) To maintain a predetermined level and structure of current consumption.

In order to attain these objectives, it is necessary to attack the balance of payments position both on the demand and supply side. These measures will include:

(i) Monetary, budgetary and other economic measures designed to achieve internal economic stability, i.e., what are known as "disinflationary measures".

(ii) Exchange rate adjustments, i.e., devaluation of the currency;

(iii) Bilateral or regional trading arrangements; and

(iv) Adjustments in the structure of production.

The object of the country's long-term foreign trade policy should be:

(i) to direct these short-term developments along channels which will eventually enable the country to consolidate its position in those fields;

(ii) to promote a pattern of import trade by means of which India can obtain the foreign resources necessary for the development of its agriculture and those cottage, small-scale and large-scale industries which it may wish to develop according to the patterns of development foreshadowed in the previous chapters;

(iii) to promote a pattern of export trade (i.e., in volume, composition and direction) that will enable India (a) to pay for its essential imports, (b) to specialize in those exports in which it may have a comparative advantage and (c) to direct its export trade to those markets in which it will have the least difficulty in maintaining its hold against competition from other countries.

To create conditions necessary for bringing about the desired changes in the pattern of export trade, a national shipping policy and the establishment of Indian banking and insurance houses require special mention.

Development of Agriculture—Without the initiative and sustained assistance of the State, there is little likelihood of any substantial improvement in the standards of living of cultivators. This means that for many years to come the resources of the State would have to be devoted in a large measure to these purposes and the Central Government should supplement the efforts of State Governments by assisting them specially in regard to multi-purpose and large-scale irrigation schemes.

Small-Scale Industries—State policy in regard to development of small-scale industries will be concerned with the following:

(i) The types of activities associated with the improvement of their production and marketing methods. These activities will include all forms of assistance to existing cottage industries, whether in urban or rural areas, to such small manufacturing units as operate in rural areas and to all small-scale establishments in urban areas. These different types of cottage and small-scale industries will necessarily require different forms of administrative organization. Appropriate organization would need to be set up not merely for specific purposes, e.g., supply of raw materials, supply of finance, provision of marketing facilities, but also to deal with special problems of different types of cottage and small-scale industries in respect of their requirement of these facilities.

(ii) Another major field of State activity will centre round the establishment and administration of new small industries in rural areas that may be set up in conformity with the pattern of development that we visualize. It will be the responsibility of the State to set up the right type of organizations for this purpose. Organized trade and industry might no doubt help but this will be forthcoming mostly in a consultative or advisory capacity and for specialized ad-hoc services.

(iii) There is a third type of activity that the State will have to undertake in this connection. It will have to regulate the relations between cottage and small-scale industries on the one hand and large-scale industries on the other, and to integrate their production and distribution patterns according to the broad principles that we have suggested. Clearly this function of the State will have to be discharged in consultation with the interests concerned and with the object of maximizing economic welfare.

Large-Scale Industries—In regard to the large-scale industries, State policy will be primarily concerned with:

(i) various forms of assistance that the existing organized industries will require. Here the role of the State will be to arrange for such necessary supplies and services as cannot be obtained without State assistance and to ensure their equitable distribution so that production may be maximized and quality ensured;

(ii) establishment under the control and management of the Government of all such industries in the nationalized sector as it may decide upon;

(iii) encouraging the establishment of such key or basic industries as need to be promoted and fostered in conformity with the desired pattern of industrial development;

(iv) giving facilities necessary for the establishment of other industries in the private sector.

Foreign Trade—As regards foreign trade, the role of the State in the short period will be to exercise control over imports and exports so as to solve the balance of payments problems. In the long period in order to promote the patterns of industrial development outlined in the report, the State may have to regulate the volume and composition of import trade in the interests of India's industrialization policy and also to encourage actively the development of new lines of export. The forms of regulation and assistance will depend on developments in national and international policy. One of the impediments in the way of efficient execution of State policy is the weakness of the present administrative machinery.

In the long run the country should be able to solve the dilemma arising out of the urgency of planned development and the shortcomings in the administrative machinery. In the short period it will be forced by these very limitations to regulate the pace and direction of advance and keep it within the limits set by the capacity of the available administrative machinery. The Government will have to concentrate in the earlier years on the most essential tasks including in this the "creation of an administrative machine that can do work of planning".

BOOK IV

Fiscal Policy And Industrial Development

Tariff protection is primarily a means to an end—one of the instruments of policy which the State must employ to further economic development of a country. The protection of industries should be related to an overall planning of economic development—otherwise there may be unequal distribution of burden and un-coordinated growth of industries. However until such a plan has been approved, protection to industries should continue to be granted on the principles given below:

A. Industries coming under the planned sector immediately may be grouped under the following classes:

(1) Defence and other strategic industries;

(2) Basic and key industries; and

(3) Other industries.

Industries falling under group (1) should be protected, whatever the cost may be, on national considerations. Regarding basic and key industries coming under the plan, the Tariff Authority will decide the form of protection and the quantum thereof and will:

(i) lay down terms and conditions for the grant of protection or assistance; and

(ii) review from time to time the extent to which these conditions have been or are being complied with by the industries.

As regards the third category, we recommend that the criteria to be applied for granting protection should be as follows:

"Having regard to the economic advantages enjoyed by the industry or available to it and its actual or probable cost of production, it is likely, within a reasonable time, to develop sufficiently to be able to carry on successfully without protection or assistance and/or it is an industry to which it is desirable in the national interest to grant protection or assistance and, having regard to the direct and indirect advantages, the probable cost of such protection or assistance to the community is not excessive."

B. As regards industries which are not included in approved plans, the Tariff Authority should examine the claim for protection on the criteria set out above and submit its recommendations to the Government.

C. Where no approved plan exists, the position should be as follows:

(i) Defence and other strategic industries—they should be given protection, whatever the cost may be, on national considerations;

(ii) As regards other industries, the criteria to be applied will be the same as those set out in A above.

Some Specific Issues Of Protectionist Policy:

(a) Availability of Raw Materials—Local availability of raw materials should not be a condition for the grant of protection if the industry possesses other economic advantages, e.g., internal market, availability of labour, etc.

(b) Potential Export Market—It seems to us legitimate to take into account a potential export market in order to determine the comparative advantages of an industry vis-a-vis its rivals.

(c) Ability of an Industry to meet the Domestic Demand—Although ordinarily a protected industry should be eventually able to satisfy the needs of the entire domestic market this should not be laid down as a condition of grant of protection and in the short period it would suffice for the Tariff Authority to consider the potentialities of the industry for expansion so as to cover a sizable portion of the internal market within a reasonable period of time.

(d) Protection to Industry which produces the Raw Materials or Stores of other Industries—Industries using the products of protected industries may require compensatory protection. The type of compensatory protection that may be needed in a particular case will depend on (a) the type of raw materials or stores produced; (b) the nature of the additional burden likely to be imposed; (c) the proportion that the cost of raw materials or stores bears to the total cost of manufacture of the finished product; and (d) the nature of demand for the finished product and other connected considerations.

(e) Protection to New or Embryonic Industries—The need for an assurance of protection prior to the actual establishment of an industry is particularly strong in those industries which require heavy capital outlay or a high degree of specialization in personnel, and plant equipment and are likely to be subjected to intense competition from well-organized and established producers abroad. In such cases we recommend that the Tariff Authority should be asked to examine the facts and estimates relating to the industry and the nature of foreign competition that it is likely to encounter and then advise the Government as to the protection or assistance needed by the industry in the light of the conditions laid down in paragraph 161.

(f) Agricultural Protection—We recommend that, if national interests so require, agricultural products may be protected but in granting such protection it should be stipulated that:

(1) the number of commodities should be kept as small as possible;

(2) the principle of selection should be (a) the importance of the raw materials of industry that they provide; and (b) the volume of employment that they offer;

(3) protection should be on an interim basis limited to short periods—never more than five years at a time;

(4) a programme of agricultural improvement must accompany the scheme of protection and form an integral part of it; and

(5) it should be the special responsibility of the Tariff Authority to report to the Government annually on the progress of technological improvements in the production of these commodities.

(g) **Internal Taxation and Protection:**

(i) **Central Excises**—On broad grounds, the levy of Excises on protected articles is inadvisable and it should be resorted to only where it is needed for budgetary purposes and no alternative sources equally suitable are available;

(ii) **Sales Taxes by States**—Most of the complaints which we heard regarding the imposition of Sales Taxes should be removed under the provisions of Article 286 of the Constitution which regulates the levy of Sales Taxes by the States;

(iii) **Levy of Cesses**—The levy of cesses for promoting research is unobjectionable so long as the rates are moderate and the whole of the tax is actually spent on research and not diverted to other purposes;

(iv) **Fixation of Prices of Raw Materials**—We consider it legitimate that the Central Government should fix the prices of raw materials of protected industries by Central legislation whenever such price fixation becomes necessary. Legislation by individual States for this purpose leads to difficulties.

Tariffs—The form of import duty to be imposed in a particular case will depend on the nature of the commodity and the administrative problems involved in the appraisal of value for Customs purposes.

We suggest that a Development Fund should be created by setting aside every year a portion of the revenue collections from protective tariffs. With such a fund, subsidies, in lieu of or in addition to protective tariffs, can be given more freely than is possible under the budgetary conditions of the present. We also recommend that a strong "after-care" organization to provide facilities necessary for rapid development of protected industries may be set up in the appropriate Ministry.

Quantitative Restrictions—We recommend that for purposes of protection to domestic industries, in normal cases quantitative restrictions should be used sparingly. Temporary quantitative restrictions would, however, be justified against abnormal imports.

Subsidies—As a general rule subsidies would be preferable to tariff protection in the following cases:

(i) where domestic production meets only a small fraction of domestic demand;

(ii) where the commodities are essential raw materials or ingredients of production; and

(iii) where the manufacture of certain quantities or grades of commodities produced in the country needs protection but it is difficult for purposes of levy of import duty to distinguish those grades or qualities from others against which no protection is needed.

Pooling is applicable only to commodities of a highly standardized nature. We recommend that the Tariff Authority should examine cases where pooling arrangements would eventually reduce the burden on the consumer.

Tariff Quota—It is difficult, on *a priori* grounds, to decide on the particular stage of development of an industry at which such a scheme would be suitable. In certain cases where the initial capacity of the industry to supply the requirements is low the tariff quota assures the consumer of the availability of sufficient supplies. It also puts a premium on efficiency and rapid progress thereby guarding against the formation of local monopolies to exploit a situation where imports are rigidly restricted by quantitative restrictions.

Quantum of Protection—In determining the cost of production of a commodity, we consider it necessary for the Tariff Authority to lay down uniform and standardized rules.

We understand that the question of depreciation allowance is under the examination of the Government of India. We would emphasize the importance of an early decision.

We also suggest that a standardized practice might be evolved by the future Tariff Authority in consultation with all interests in the industries concerned regarding the remuneration to be allowed to managing agents for purposes of calculation of costs.

The entire subject of the return on capital in protected industries and the valuation of the capital employed or the block on which such return is to be allowed should be subject to detailed investigation by the Tariff Authority. We need not add that this return on capital should be fair.

We consider that where an element of prejudice is established, the Tariff Authority should add an appropriate margin to the quantum of protection proposed for the industry.

Period of Protection—As a general principle industries should be assured of protection for a reasonably long period so that capital may be attracted and a suitable programme of improvements may be drawn pu and implemented.

Administrative Protection—We consider restrictions, etc., under the Sea Customs Act for purposes of protection unjustifiable not only from the point of view of international relations but also because their use conceals the true character and burden of protection to the community.

Stores Purchase Policy—The stores purchase policy of the Government should be so framed that the indigenous industry receives a reasonable margin of preferenee over foreign articles. For this purpose we lay down the following conditions:

(1) All industries run on sound business lines should be eligible for preference on condition that the products conform to such specifications as may be laid down by the Government on the recommendations of the Indian Standards Institute.

(2) A higher margin of preference should be given to the products of cottage and small-scale industries and conforming to such specifications as may be laid down for them.

The obligations of protected industries should mainly be with regard to price policy, production or output policy, quality of production, adoption of technological improvements, research, training of apprentices and higher grades of labour and anti-social activities.

It is not our view that the obligations regarding these matters should be embodied in the relevant Statutes dealing with protected or assisted industries as this would introduce a needless element of rigidity into the working of the schemes of protection. The plan of implementation that we visualize is broadly as follows:

(i) These obligations should be treated as Directive Principles of Tariff Administration and should be embodied in the Statute dealing with the establishment of the tariff-making authority. These principles will not, however, be "enforceable" in the juridical sense but it should be the duty of the Tariff Authority to bear them in mind when they examine the claims of protection of particular industries.

(ii) Having made up its mind as to the obligations that should be imposed, the Tariff Authority should work out the conditions subject to which the obligations should be imposed. A programme for implementation should also be worked out.

(iii) (a) The Tariff Authority should report to the Government in its periodical reviews the manner in which the obligations are being discharged by the protected industries;

(b) The difficulties that hamper the discharge of these obligations;

(c) The further measures necessary to secure enforcement of the obligations; and

(d) The changes in the terms of obligations, if any, that may be called for.

BOOK V

Other Factors In Industrial Development

The difficulty of securing investable funds for financing industrial undertakings has become acute since the beginning of 1947. The major handicaps to capital formation are stated to be as follows:

(a) Fear of nationalization;

(b) High level of taxation;

(c) Abuses of Managing Agency system;

(d) Speculation leading to gambling at Stock Exchanges; and

(e) The shift in the distribution of national income from urban areas to rural areas.

Remarks are made under each of these heads.

We consider that capital control in its present form should be abolished. As, however, the Planning Commission has now been appointed, a new machinery may be devised for directing capital into approved channels.

On a study of some recent estimates of the rate of savings and investment in India we conclude that India's minimum requirements of capital expenditure will be roughly of the order of Rs. 330 crores a year at the current level of prices. We find that it may be difficult for the country to achieve a higher rate of savings and investment unless coercive measures are adopted and the people are subject to a degree of austerity in current consumption which it may be very difficult in practice to enforce.

The consensus of opinion is that, as a general rule, foreign capital should be invited for

(a) Projects in the public sector of the economy which depend on the import of capital goods, plant, machinery, equipment, stores, etc., from abroad;

(b) Undertakings in the private sector which involve new lines of production and where indigenous capital and management are not likely to be forthcoming.

We are in general agreement with this view but would stipulate that in special cases where the quantity of domestic production is small in relation to the total domestic demand and the indigenous industry is not likely to expand at a sufficiently fast rate, there should be nothing to prevent the Government from inviting foreign capital on such terms and conditions as they may lay down.

Broadly speaking the indirect form of investment is preferable when foreign capital is needed only to pay for foreign machinery and equipment and the type of consultant service that is provided by the manufacturer of such equipment. The direct or equity form of investment is more appropriate in those cases where, besides capital, the technical know-how of the foreigner or his technical knowledge or experience is also needed.

The problems of industrial management have acquired increasing importance since the end of the War. The circumstances of modern industry require the assistance of experts at all stages of industrial management. We find that the deficiencies of private industry in this country—particularly small-scale industry—arise from lack of expert guidance and supervision. We, therefore, recommend that the Government of India in the appropriate Ministry should set up a bureau of consultants whose services can be drawn upon by private industry on such terms and conditions as the Government may lay down.

We also recommend that particular care should be taken by industries to appoint duly qualified technical men and to train suitable men for such positions. The types of expert service that we feel our industries should develop are those connected with plant capacity and production control, stores and organization control, raw material control, quality control and costing.

Industrial Management in the Public Sector—The growing importance of the Public Sector in India's economy and the increasing interest of the State in economic problems calls for the creation of a specialized service. We recommend that early steps be taken to constitute an Economic Service as envisaged in the Industrial Policy Statement of April 6, 1948.

The structure and conditions of working of Government or quasi-Government undertakings should be such as to ensure:

(a) That the community knows the cost of what it is doing;

(b) That the community is satisfied that this cost is equitably distributed; and

(c) That the decisions of the public authority are taken democratically.

Apart from the usual accounting safeguards and the obligation to submit periodical accounts in an approved or prescribed form, we would suggest the following measures to ensure this:

(a) A periodical review of the working of these undertakings by a competent authority with a view to assessing their efficiency;

(b) Constitution of a Consumers' Council to be attached to each Government or quasi-Government undertaking, with well-defined powers and duties which should include the study of cost statistics, price structure and price policy, enquiry into complaints from consumers about unfair practices or discriminatory treatment according to a definite procedure laid down by the Government;

(c) Constitution of a Tribunal on Services and Charges on the lines of the Railway Rates Tribunal with functions more or less similar to those of the latter.

The accounts should be maintained on a commercial basis and audited by a competent staff. These audit notes with reviews thereof should be placed before the Minister concerned so that Parliament may be kept informed of the manner in which these undertakings are working and their cost to the community.

We further recommend that having regard to the increasing importance of the subject, the Government should have special studies made of the problems of management of Government and quasi-Government undertakings in the light of the experiences which countries like the U.K., Australia, Canada and the U.S.A. have acquired.

Industrial Research—Organized industrial research in this country is of comparatively recent growth. There are two aspects of research which deserve special mention:

(1) Establishment of Industrial Research Institutes should be the joint task of the Government and the industries.

(2) Work of the Research Institutes organized by private industries should be integrated with the activities of the Research Institutes established or administered by Government or quasi-Government authorities.

Standardization and Quality Control—We are in general agreement with the principles evolved by the Indian Standards Institute in prescribing standards for various articles. There is a prima facie case for making observance of the approved standards obligatory on the industries concerned—at any rate on those industries which have a large export market or which provide the raw materials of exportable commodities.

There are indications that in recent years there has been an appreciable fall in labour efficiency and this presents a problem that must be tackled in a co-operative spirit by the Government, industry and labour.

The solution of the problem of deterioration in labour efficiency rests in the short period on an effective machinery for collective bargaining and arbitration and sound employer-labour relations and in the long run on training and education and on the far-seeing management of business undertakings.

Training of Labour—One important lacuna in our scheme of technical training is the lack of facilities for training of technicians of the foreman class. To remedy this drawback, Technical Institutes on the model of the one recently started by the Indian Jute Mills' Association should be extended to other industries also.

Transport: (a) **Roads**—While we appreciate the reasons for the importance attached to national highways, we feel that one consequence of recent policy has been to tip the balance against roads of "local" as distinct from "all-India" importance. We attach the greatest importance to the development of village and district roads. We, therefore, recommend that consistent with the needs of the defence and internal security, high priority should be given to the development of district and village roads.

(b) **Railways**—We think that the question may be examined whether it would not be possible for the railway authorities to introduce rates to assist in the local or regional processing of agricultural or mineral produce and in the decentralization of industries. We also recommend that the Railway Board might examine the question of simplifying the present procedure for granting station-to-station rates.

(c) **Shipping**—We consider that the development of Indian shipping is no less important and urgent than that of the basic industries. The Government of India are already committed to a policy of assisting shipping.

(d) **Banking**—The basic limitation of commercial banking in the country arises from the absence of an effective link between the organized money-market and the moneylender-cum-indigenous bankers. Even within this limitation, the credit facilities offered by the commercial banks to trade and industry are inadequate. We recommend that the entire subject to be examined by the Reserve Bank and the Government of India, keeping in view the needs of an expanding economy, and the potential contribution of a sound credit policy to the development of trade and industry.

Another defect of the banking system in this country is the lack of specialized banking institutions, including a sufficient number of Indian exchange banks. We find that small-scale industries are in a particularly difficult situation as regards finance and recommend that the formulation of special measures to meet their requirements should engage the attention.

We further suggest that the Reserve Bank should study the modern practice in respect of Developmental Credit in countries like Australia with a view to drawing such lessons from it as may be applicable to the circumstances of this country.

BOOK VI

Organization And Machinery Of Administration

We examine the relations between Planning and Protection, and refer to certain fundamental issues of policy and techniques which will confront the Planning Commission in a mixed economy like ours.

Measures for securing co-ordination of the activities of the different Ministries concerned with economic matters are under consideration. In this connection we commend a suggestion for the establishment of a Board of Trade and Industry for consideration by the Government.

The Tariff Making Authority should be placed on a permanent and statutory footing and designated as the Tariff Commission.

The Commission should consist of five members including the Chairman but power should be taken in the proposed Statute to increase the number to seven if necessary. There should also be power to co-opt assessors or advisers for particular purposes. We are definitely opposed to the representation of interests or regions on the Commission and would emphasize that members should be selected primarily on the basis of their competence for the functions which they will have to perform, coupled with their standing in their profession, business or service in which they are engaged, or in public life.

We recommend that two important conditions of membership should be:

(a) That members on appointment must disclose the nature of their interest in private companies, if any, and

(b) The members on relinquishment of their office should be debarred from holding any position of trust and responsibility in any private industrial undertaking for a period of three years except with the prior approval of the Government of India.

The following functions should be entrusted to the Commission:

(a) Enquiries connected with Protective and Revenue Tariffs. This will include:

(1) Tariff enquiries proper, i.e., enquiries into applications for protection;

(2) Enquiries into cases of alleged dumping;

(3) Enquiry into variation of protective and revenue duties; and

(4) Enquiry into Tariff concessions under trade agreements.

Enquiries under (1) and (4) should normally be initiated at the instance of the Government of India.

(b) Enquiries connected with prices and the general effects of protection on the economy of the country.

(c) Review of protected industries.

Apart from ad-hoc investigations the Commission should submit to the Government a periodical review, preferably triennial, on the working of protected industries.

In order that the Tariff Commission can perform its function efficiently, it will require special powers for the summoning of witnesses and compelling the production of evidence which it considers essential.

We consider that the Commission's enquiries into the various matters enumerated in paragraph 269 should normally be held in public.

As soon as an enquiry is completed, the Tariff Commission should submit its report to the Government of India in the appropriate Ministry and the Government should be in a position to arrive at a decision on the recommendations of the Commission ordinarily within a period of two months.

We recommend that the authorities concerned with the grant of non-fiscal assistance should give special attention to it and furnish to the Tariff Commission an annual statement on the measures of the assistance given.

The Commission should be given powers to frame its own rules regarding the internal management of its business including the appointment of personnel up to a certain level, rules of business relating to enquiries, review of the effects of protection and other matters.

BOOK VII

Fiscal Policy In Relation To International Obligations

We analyse the provisions of the Havana Charter with particular reference to the sections dealing with Commercial Policy, Restrictive Business Practice, and Economic Development and Reconstruction in underdeveloped areas.

We examined the pros and cons of the Charter and find that in the short period (i.e., as long as the present Balance of Payment difficulties continue) the provisions of the Charter will, in practice, hardly impose any serious limitation on India's freedom to mould its commercial policy in the interests of its domestic economy. In the long run, however, the obligations which the Charter imposes on the members may detract from their right to initiate and pursue commercial policies solely in the national interest. The decisive consideration for the country is, therefore, whether or not it should submit to this limitation on its sovereign rights for such advantages may accrue to it by reason of its membership of the International Trade Organization.

On a consideration of all the relevant factors and consistent attitude which India has hitherto adopted towards measures of international economic co-operation, all of us, except our colleague, Shri B. M. Birla, recommend that India should ratify the Charter provided:

(1) That the other countries of major economic importance including the U.S.A. and the U.K. have by then ratified it; and

(2) The economic conditions in the country at that time justify this course.

In making this recommendation to the Government we reiterate our hope that the provisions of the Charter concerning the economic development of the underdeveloped countries of the world will be interpreted liberally by the leading industrially advanced countries of the world.

We analyse the tariff concessions granted and received by India under the General Agreement on Tariffs and Trade and find that no definite conclusions as to the effect of these concessions on India's import and export trade can be drawn from the relevant trade figures.

On general grounds, however, and having regard to our attitude towards the Havana Charter, we consider that it will not be to India's benefit to keep out of the General Agreement on Tariffs and Trade till the future of the International Trade Organization is definitely known. The existing principles for negotiating tariff reduction appears to be sound and we suggest that in all future negotiations the following principles should also be borne in mind:

First, in regard to the tariff concessions to be received from other countries, India should concentrate on:

(a) Commodities which meet with competition from similar commodities from other countries in the world market;

(b) Commodities which meet with competition from possible substitutes from other countries in the world market;

(c) Manufactured commodities rather than raw materials.

Secondly, in the matter of granting tariff concessions, India should concentrate on :

(a) Capital goods;

(b) Other machinery and equipment;

(c) Essential raw materials.

We also make three further suggestions:

(1) The special export requirements of the unorganized cottage and small-scale industries, which depend on the foreign market to a large extent, should be borne in mind when India enters into trade negotiations with foreign countries. It should be the particular aim of India's representatives to secure for them the maximum of tariff concessions in the foreign market and to safeguard their position against competitive imports from abroad.

(2) A close watch should be kept on the course of trade in GATT items, and half-yearly trade returns should be published within six weeks of every half-yearly period.

(3) Before any fresh negotiations are started, the representatives of trade, industry and other interests concerned should be consulted as regards the nature of the concessions that India may claim from other countries and of the reciprocal concessions that the other countries, in their turn, may demand of it.

We find it difficult to assess the effects of the Indo-British Trade Agreement of 1939 on the trade between India and the U.K. because (a) the relevant trade returns are available only for a period of six months after the execution of the Agreement till the War broke out and (b) during the War and post-War years the effects of the Preferences granted and received by India were masked by the restrictions on imports and exports imposed during the War and continued in some form or other ever since.

We consider that our attitude towards this question should depend on the policy that the Government of India have already laid down in regard to Preferences and that in the light of this policy the Government should initiate negotiations with the U.K. and Colonies for a review of the Tariff Preferences now granted to them or received by us. The continuance or otherwise of Preferences should be decided exclusively on economic considerations and on a basis of mutual interest.

BOOK VIII

Conclusion

In this Chapter we set out the objectives and priorities of a short-term economic policy as a basis for the formulation of a plan of action in the short period.

The objectives of a short-term economic policy are enumerated in paragraphs 327-328.

Defence and basic and key industries stand in a special position. Excluding these the priority should be as follows :

(1) Schemes for agricultural improvement especially irrigation and multi-purpose project including minor irrigation works.

(2) Industries necessary for the implementation of the agricultural programme and the construction and maintenance of irrigation and multi-purpose projects.

(3) Schemes for increased production in industries producing basic raw material and consumption goods.

(4) Manufacture and repair of the machinery and equipment needed by the industries in (3).

(5) Establishment of industries complementary to the industries in (3) and (4) and those that will increase external economies of these industries.

(6) *Pari Passu* with the developments mentioned in (1) to (5).

(a) Encouragement of tertiary industries; and

(b) Promotion of exports.

RAILWAY JOINT ADVISORY COMMITTEE, 1949—REPORT

New Delhi, Ministry of Railways (Railway Board). n.d. 39p.

Chairman : Shri F. Jeejeebhoy.

Members : Shri S. Guruswami; Shri Hariharnath Shastri; Shri R. A. Khedgikar; Shri P. K. Chatterji (As regards Railway Representatives, there were changes from time to time and Shri R. Ramaswami Ayyar; Shri K. P. Mushram; Shri P. N. Saxena; Shri S. S. Gore; Shri M. E. Bartely; Shri K. S. Bhandari; Shri Y. P. Kulkarni; Shri V. T. Narayanan served on the Committee for varying periods).

Secretary : Shri Y. P. Kulkarni (replaced by Shri V. T. Narayanan).

APPOINTMENT

The Railway Joint Advisory Committee was constituted under the Ministry of Railways in May, 1949.

TERMS OF REFERENCE

The acceptance of the Central Pay Commission's recommendations by the Government not only liberalized the wage structure of the Indian Railways but also introduced considerable standardization in the large number of grades, denominations and rules which had been evolved in nearly 100 years over the various Railway systems. Inevitably, in this process a number of anomalies arose and were brought to the notice of the Railway Administrations by representatives of organized labour.

CONTENTS

Introduction; A Review of the Committee's Work; Recommendations Affecting Large Bodies of Staff; Recommendations Affecting Smaller Bodies or Numbers; Appendix.

RECOMMENDATIONS

Recommendations Affecting Large Bodies Of Staff

The number of posts of clerks in the lowest grade Rs. 55—130 should not exceed 72½% to 75% of the total number of posts of clerks, the existing position on the B.B.&C.I. and the G.I.P. Railways being left undisturbed.

Graduates who were appointed to posts requiring graduation, before the C.P.C. scales, should be placed in the scale of Rs. 80—220.

Stores Clerks, Ledger Clerks, Travelling Store Keepers, Stores Distributors, Store Van Clerks And Store Delivery Clerks

The Principal Stores Clerks in major running sheds should be allocated to grades not lower than Rs. 80—160.

Ledger Clerks should be regarded as Office Clerks and the recommendation regarding Office Clerks that 25% of the posts should be in higher grades should apply to them.

The scale of pay Rs. 55—130 should be abolished in the case of Travelling Store Keepers, Stores Distributors, Store Van Clerks and Store Deilvery Clerks.

Typists And Stenographers

The number of posts of Typists in the intermediate grade of Rs. 80—160 should be 16% to 20% of the posts in the lowest grade of Rs. 55—130.

The number of posts of Stenographers in the intermediate grade of Rs. 200—300 should be 16% to 20% of the posts in the lowest grade Rs. 80—220.

Accounts Clerks Class I

The scale of Rs. 80—220 should be allotted to this category of staff.

The number of posts of Accounts Clerks Class I should not be less than one-third of the number of clerks in the scale of Rs. 55—130.

Station Masters and Asstt. Station Masters

The number of Station Masters and Asstt. Station Masters in the grade Rs.100—185 shall be between 20% and 25% of the Asstt. Station Masters and Station Masters in the grade Rs. 64—170.

Running Staff

The scale of pay of Drivers—Grade C should be revised from Rs. 80-5-130-EB-8-170 to 80-5-130-EB-10-185.

The scales of pay Rs. 60—150, 75—105 and 60—80 as recommended by the C.P.C. should be allotted to Shunters, instead of Rs. 75—105 and 60—85 at present.

The grades as recommended by the C.P.C., i.e., Rs. 75—105, 60—80 and 40—60 should be adopted for Firemen instead of Rs. 60—80, 50—60 and 40—50.

The scale of pay for Guards—Grade C should be revised from Rs. 60—170 to 80—170.

The scales of Rs. 60-5/2-80 and 40-1-50-2-60 for Brakesmen should be revised to Rs. 60-3-72-4-80 and 40-2-60.

The rate of Running Allowance for Drivers—Grade A should be increased from Rs. 4 to Rs. 4.6 an. per 100 miles.

The rate of Running Allowance for Drivers—Grade B should be increased from Rs. 3.12 an. to Rs. 4 per 100 miles.

The rate of Running Allowance for Drivers—Grade C should be increased from Rs. 3.4 an. to Rs. 3.6 an. per 100 miles.

The rate of Running Allowance for Guards—Grade A should be increased from Rs. 2 to Rs. 2.6 an. per 100 miles.

The rate of Running Allowance for Guards—Grade B should be increased from Re. 1.12 an. to Rs. 2 per 100 miles.

Running Staff

The classification of Drivers and Guards in Ghat Sections and their allowances should be dealt with individually by the administrations concerned.

Guards of Ballast Trains when personally supervising the working and loading and unloading of trains shall be paid in addition to substantive pay and Running Allowance, an Engineering Allowance per day for days on which work is done. The rate of Rs. 2.8 an. on the E. I. Railway, and the past rate on the other Railways should continue.

Guards of Main-line S.Q.T. trains of the type working on the E.I. Railway should be given 'B' Grade.

25% of the total number of posts of Brakesmen shall be in Grade 'A'.

The rate for payment for shunting performed by the train engines at terminals covered by shunting orders should be increased from 8 to 10 miles an hour.

Running Allowance for staff learning the road should be increased from 1/2 to 3/4th of the actual mileage.

Conductor Guards should be placed in Grade 'A'.

The scale of Rs. 150—225 should be allotted to Motormen, instead of Rs. 80—170.

Assistant Guards, O.T. Rly., who are recruited with Matriculation as minimum qualification should be placed in the scale Rs.60—80 as personal to themselves.

Drivers And Guards

The Drivers of the following trains should be given Grade 'B'.

Passenger trains on the main line other than mail and express and excluding shuttle services.

Trains carrying passengers on main (important) branch lines but excluding shuttle services.

The classification of Guards should follow the classification of Drivers.

Gangmates And Keymen In The Engg. Deptt.

Gangmates in the Engineering Department should be fixed in the scale Rs. 40—60 instead of 35—50.

The prescribed scale of pay for Keymen should be raised to Rs. 35—50.

Commercial Clerks And Chief Booking Clerks And Head Booking Clerks

In the matter of allocation of posts of Commercial Clerks to the various grades, the recommendation regarding Clerks should apply. A fairer allocation of posts to the grade of Rs. 150—225 should be made.

The allocation of posts to the grade of Rs. 200—300 should be reviewed with a view to securing a fairer allocation to the grade.

Travelling Ticket Examiners, Head Ticket Collectors And Ticket Collectors

In respect of the allocation to the grades of TTEs, the percentage in the lowest category should be between 65 and 67½; in the intermediate category between 25 and 27½; and in the highest category approximately 7½. Those already in higher grades beyond these percentages will not be reduced but as wastage occurs, necessary adjustments will be made.

Head Ticket Collectors should be placed in the scale Rs. 100—185 with a few posts in the Selection Grade of Rs. 200—300.

All those on Rs. 80—160 should be in the scale Rs. 100—185.

The total number of Selection Posts of Ticket Collecting staff on all Railways in the grade Rs. 200—300 should be 75.

The number of Ticket Collectors in the lowest grade should not exceed 80% of the total number of stationary Ticket Collectors.

Traffic Technical Staff

Coupling and Shunting Porters employed in marshalling yards and big stations should be allotted Rs. 40—60, all other Coupling and Shunting Porters Rs. 35—50.

All persons performing the duties of Shunting Jemadars on all Railways should be allotted Rs. 60—75.

The word "Porter" should be replaced by some other term.

Trains Clerks

The number of posts in the scale of Rs. 80—160 should not be less than 12½% and 15% of the number in the lowest grade.

The allocation of the posts of Trains Clerks to the several grades should be reviewed with a view to securing, wherever it was justified, a more equitable allotment to the scales higher than the scale Rs. 80—160.

Chargemen

The scale of Rs. 100—185 should not be allotted to Chargemen.

If the duties and responsibilities of workmen who have been allotted Rs. 100—185 scale are found to be equivalent to those of workmen classified as 'C' on the E.I. Railway, the former shall be placed in the scale of Rs. 150—225.

Staff In The Cash And Pay Department

The scale of pay for Pay Clerks should be Rs. 80—160 instead of Rs. 60—150.

The scale of pay of Rs. 150—225 for Senior Pay Clerks should be replaced by Rs. 160—220.

The scale of Rs. 200—300 allotted to Sub-Cashiers should be changed to Rs. 200—350.

The scale of Rs. 200—300 for Asstt. Cashiers and Asstt. Treasurers should be changed to the scale Rs. 250—400.

The scale of pay of Rs. 200—300 for Asstt. Pay Masters should be changed to the scale of Rs. 200—350.

Gazetted status should be given to Chief Cashiers of such of the Railways as have Cl. III Chief Cashiers at present.

Any Pay Clerks not being in the grade applicable to Asstt. Pay Masters who supervise more than six disbursing Pay Clerks should not be in a scale lower than Rs. 160—220.

There should be single scale of Rs. 55—130 for Shroffs.

Staff In The Watch And Ward Department

Special Watch employees should be placed in the scale Rs. 40—60.

Chief Watch and Ward Overseers, B.B.&C.I. Railway; Chief Head Watchmen, B.N. Railway; and Subedars, G.I.P., M.&S.M. and S.I. Railways, who are in the scale Rs. 60—75, should be given the scale Rs. 60—120.

Sub-Inspectors, Watch and Ward, in the scale Rs. 60—150 should be given the scale Rs. 80—160 provided that persons whose duties are analogous to those of Chief Head Watchmen do not come within the enhanced scale.

Asstt. Sub-Inspectors, Assam Rly. and ex-B.A. Rly. portion of the E.I. Rly., should be given the scale Rs. 60—120 with protection to any higher scale which may have been given to any individual.

Efforts should be made to conform as nearly as possible to the general average of 65% and 35% respectively in the case of Sub and Assistant Inspectors.

The G.I.P. Rly. should review the allocation of posts to the different scales of Inspectors with a view to a fair distribution of posts to the various scales.

Armed Supervisors of Armed Guards should be placed on equal scales of pay on all Railways, viz., Rs. 40—60.

Highly Skilled Workers And Master Craftsmen

There should be two grades for highly skilled workers, viz., Rs. 125—185 and Rs. 80—160. Master Craftsmen should be in the former grade.

Switchmen, E.I. Railway

The scale of pay Rs. 61-3-85 should be allotted to this category of staff.

Section Controllers

The allocation of posts of Section Controllers in the scale Rs. 260—350 and Rs. 200—300 should be revised.

Head Signallers

They should be granted the scales Rs. 100—185 and Rs. 150—225.

Semi-Skilled Workers

There should be an additional scale of Rs. 60-3/2—75.

Apprentice Mechanics

The Apprentice Mechanics on first appointment to a working post should be given Rs. 100—185. For purpose of promotion to the grade of Chargemen, the claims of persons promoted from skilled ranks should be taken into account.

Stores Issuers

The staff should be placed on Rs. 55—85.

Sanitary And Asstt. Sanitary Inspectors

The scale of Rs. 55—130 for Assistant Sanitary Inspectors is not applicable and is not operative.

Labour Welfare Advisers And Inspectors

There should be 3 scales, e.g., Rs. 260—350, 200—300 and 150—225 and should be allocated according to the duties and responsibilities.

All Non-Gazetted Staff

The formula suggested by the representatives of labour for giving weightage for service in the matter of fixation of initial pay in the prescribed scale was forwarded to the Government for consideration.

All Class IV Staff

The rate of daily allowance should be raised from 11 annas to 13 annas.

Travelling Ticket Examiners

The rates of daily allowance should be increased as follows:

Rs. 55—130	Re. 1.14 an.
Rs. 100—200	Rs. 2.14 an.
Rs. 200—300	Rs. 4.4 an.

All Categories Of Staff

Dearness Allowance should be reviewed in accordance with the C.P.C recommendations.

Cases where substantive and officiating posts have overlapping scales and employees were fixed on the same or lower rate in the higher scale should be reviewed to see whether there was any hardship involved.

The cases of all employees of temporary departments who were appointed prior to 15-9-1945 should be examined with the object of their absorption in the regular departments. On thus being filled in any department, they shall become permanent therein even though they may continue in the temporary department for the time being.

Recommendation Affecting Smaller Bodies Or Numbers

Asstt. Yard Foreman, E.I. Rly., should be given the scale Rs. 64—170 in place of the scale Rs. 60—150.

The proportion of posts of Asstt. Surgeons—Gr. I is inadequate on the E.I. and M.&S.M. Rlys. and should be increased.

The scale of pay for Midwives should be Rs. 60—105.

Writers (Hd. Watchmen) and Watchmen Writers, G.I.P. Rly., should be given the scales Rs. 40—60 and Rs. 35—50 so long as they hold these posts.

Crane Inspectors, S.I., should be given the scale Rs. 150—225 if their duties and responsibilities approximate to those of Chargemen on E.I. Rly. in the scale Rs. 150—225.

Gunners on the Assam and E.I. Rlys. should be given the scale Rs. 75—105 so long as the category of Gunners exists, those at present in receipt of salary above Rs. 105 being protected for their pay.

Waterworks Superintendent, S.I. Rly., should be given the scale Rs. 150—225.

The Journalist, S.I. Rly., should be given the scale of Rs. 160—220 if he is a graduate and has had two years' experience in journalism.

The category of Drivers and Cleaners wherever it exists should be given the scale Rs. 35—40.

Refreshment Room Managers should be placed in the scale Rs. 80—160.

Servers in the Railway Catering Department should be given the scale Rs. 35-1-40 in place of the present scale Rs. 30-½-35.

Pier Lascars, S.I. Rly., who are in the scale Rs. 30-½-35 should be given the scale Rs. 35—50.

The Chief Court Clerk and the Court Clerks, M.& S.M. Rly., who are in the scale Rs. 200—300 and Rs. 160—220 should be redesignated as Chief Court Inspector and Court Inspectors and given the scale Rs. 260—350 and Rs. 200—300, if they were recruited with the qualification of having been practising lawyers.

The Junior Instructors in the Sealdah Training School should be given the scale Rs. 100—185 in the place of Rs. 80—160.

Accounts Clerks of the Engineering Department, B.B.&C.I. Rly., should be given the same prescribed scale whether they work on the Broad Gauge or Metre Gauge.

A selection grade of Rs. 250—400 should be given to Teachers in Railway Schools.

Lead Burners who perform the work of Cell or Battery Fitters should be given the scale Rs. 55—130.

The Lamp Tindals and Head Lampmen on the E.I. Rly. should be placed in the scale Rs. 35—50.

In the case of the staff drafted from the signallers' group to perform the work of Telegraph Check Office Clerks, the same scale of pay should be given as applicable to Signallers, namely, Rs. 60—150.

Belt Makers and/or Mochis on B.B.&C.I. Rly. should be correctly designated and fitted in a proper scale if they were doing the work of Trimmers.

The allocation of posts of Inspectors in the Food Department, O.T. Rly., should be as follows:

3 posts (including one post of Purchase Inspector)	Rs. 200—300
6 posts	Rs. 150—225
10 posts	Rs. 100—185

The incumbents of the posts of Head Cash Witness, O.T. Rly., and Asstt. Cash Witnesses, B.B.&C.I. Rly., should have proper avenues of promotion and should not be frozen to their jobs.

The Flagmen in workshops, E.I. Rly., should be allotted the scale Rs. 35—50 or Rs. 40—60 by applying the same yardstick as was applied to Shunting Porters.

Sanitary Peons, M.&S.M. Rly., should be designated and graded accordingly if they were doing the work of Sweeper Jemadars.

Air-conditioned Coach Attendants, E.I. Rly., should be given the scale of pay Rs. 75-3-105-5-120 in place of the present scale Rs. 75-3-105.

Such non-technical Progressmen, M.&S.M. Rly., as perform semi-clerical duties such as preparation of indents, stores returns, foils return of surplus materials and issue of routine work orders on repeat-items jobs, should be placed on the minimum scale of Rs. 55—85.

One of the posts of Circle Inspectors (Ticket Branch) on Assam Railway should be placed in the scale Rs. 260—350 and re-designated as Chief Ticket Inspector.

If Dressers on the M.&S.M. Rly. have been wrongly designated as Dispensary Peons, the mistake should by rectified.

Wiremen and Linemen Fitters, E.I. Railway, should get the scale of Rs. 80—160 if they were actually supervising any skilled workmen.

The scale of pay Rs. 120—220 applicable to the Asstt. Head Reader, E.I. Rly. Press, should be replaced by the scale Rs. 160—220.

Litho Draftsmen of the Printing Press, E.I. Rly., should be placed in the scale Rs. 100—185 if they were Draftsmen in the Engineering Department and had been brought from that department to the Press.

Two posts of Foremen in the Printing Press, M. &S.M. Rly., should be allotted the scale of Rs. 150—225 in place of the scale of pay Rs. 125—185.

Workshop Firemen (Mechanical Department), G.I.P. Rly., should get the pay and allowances applicable to Running Staff if they belong to the cadre of Running Staff.

In the case of those Telephone Operators on the S. I. Rly. who had been fixed in the prescribed scale from January 1, 1948, instead of January 1, 1947, any misapplication of rules should be rectified.

The case of the G.I.P. Rly. employee who was a Booking Clerk on January 1, 1947, and was transferred as a Ticket Collector on April 1, 1947, but did not get protection of the pay fixed as Booking Clerk on January 1, 1947, after his transfer as Ticket Collector, should be examined for any rectification of the position called for. He might also be permitted to go back as Booking Clerk if he desired unless he had already been confirmed as Ticket Collector.

The Inspector of Vegetable Gardens, G.I.P. Rly., Bombay, should be given House Rent and Compensatory Allowances under the appropriate rules if he has been properly fixed in a prescribed scale and is no longer on a contract basis.

Junior Inspectors (called Assistant Inspectors) of the Indian Refreshment Rooms, M.&S.M. Rly., should be given the scale Rs. 80—160 in place of the present scale Rs. 60—150.

The representations submitted by Messrs. Lakshmi Narain Misra and others of the B.B.&C.I., Nilmani Bannerji and Satish Chandra Gupta and others of the E.I. Rly., Mohd. Yusuf of the G.I.P. Rly., S. Dakshinamurti of S.I. Rly., and K. V. Venkata Rao of the B.N. Railway should be considered in accordance with the recommendation of the Committee relating to the distribution of the posts of Head Clerks.

The case of such categories of Railway Press Workers as have not been classified by the Railway Workers Classification Tribunal or by the Trade Test Panel, or categories claiming to be classified as Master Craftsmen or Highly Skilled, should be referred to Trade Test Panels constituted under the Award. The cases of the categories of staff shown in the Appendix should also be dealt with in accordance with this recommendation.

Wherever the work of a Cabin A.S.M. justified it, the post should carry a higher scale.

The original relative seniority of the Asstt. Carriage

Cleaner Chargemen on the S.I. Railway who had opted to become Rolling Stock Fitters when the latter were given a higher scale should not be adversely affected.

The scale of pay of Delivery Munshis in the Grainshops on O.T. Railway should be raised from Rs. 40—60 to Rs. 60—75.

If any persons in the categories of Drillers, Blasters and Furnacemen in the B.E. Shops, Manmad, G.I.P. Rly., now declared as semi-skilled, were previously getting higher pay, their scale should be protected.

If the duties of the Chargemen in the Bridge Engineering Workshops at Manmad, G.I.P. Rly., and in the Engineering Deptt. of the M.&S.M. Rly. correspond to those of 'C' Grade Chargemen on the E.I. Rly., they should be given the same scale, viz., 'C' Grade.

Muccadams in the Mechanical Deptt. of the G.I.P. Rly. should be given higher scales if they were not merely supervisors of unskilled workmen.

The Tool Issuer (Car Shed), S.I. Rly., should be allotted the scale of Rs. 55—85 if he performed, as in the past, the clerical duties which were since decided by the Railway Administration to be taken away from him.

First Grade Compositors 'and Ticket Printers in the Byculla Printing Press, G.I.P. Rly., should be fixed in the scale of Rs. 80—160, if they supervise the work of compositors and printers, respectively.

Senior Ticket Printer of the Accounts Press, the Section Head and the Printing Press Machine Mistry should be fixed in the scale of Rs. 80—160 if they supervise the work of Ticket Printers, Binders and Skilled Workmen, respectively.

Compositor, O.T. Rly. Press, working as Binding Supervisor, Press, should be fixed in the scale of Rs. 80—160 if he is supervising the work of skilled workmen.

The Printing Press Store-Keeper and Asstt. Store-keeper, M.&S.M. Rly., should be treated as Ward Keeper and Asstt. Ward Keeper, respectively.

The minimum scale of Engine Examiners, M.& S.M. Rly., should be Rs. 150—225 if they are doing the same type of work as is done by Engine Examiners of the B.N. and G.I.P. Railways.

Any Record Lascar on the M.&S.M. Rly., who is doing the work of a Daftry, should be designated and paid accordingly.

Tindals of Grainshops, Assam Rly., should be given the scale of Rs. 35—50 if they were supervisors of unskilled labour.

The Maintainer, Central Training School, S.I. Rly., should be given the option to revert to his previous category if he was promoted from a category now classified as Skilled and if his present post is classified as Unskilled on a reference to the Trade Test Panel.

The period during which the Steno-typists on the B.B.&C.I. Rly. worked as regular Stenographers should be taken into consideration on the fixation of their pay in the prescribed scales.

If the post of the Portuguese Customs Clerk, Marmugao Harbour, M.&S.M. Rly., was filled with the minimum qualification of being a graduate, the incumbent should be given the scale recommended by the Committee for graduate clerks, viz., Rs. 80—220.

The scale of pay of Senior Clerk, Marmugao Harbour, should be determined in accordance with the recommendation of the Committee on the distribution of the posts of Head Clerks.

The scale of pay of the Shed Manager and his Asstt. Trains & Claim Clerk, M.&S.M. Rly., should be reviewed in accordance with the Committee's recommendation on the distribution of posts of Commercial Clerks.

The case of the Asstt. Workshop Instructor, Alambagh, E.I. Rly., should be examined with a view to fixing his pay in the prescribed scale of Rs. 200—300, if he was on the post-1931 scale of Rs. 200, fixed.

One of the three posts of Fire Inspectors on the Assam Railway should be re-designated as Chief Fire Inspector and given the scale of Rs. 260—350.

The representations submitted by Mr. Bhagat Ram and others, Sub-Inspectors, Watch & World, E.P. Rly., and Mr. S. M. Khan and others, Inspectors, Watch & Ward, G.I.P. Rly., should be considered in accordance with the Committee's recommendations on the scale of pay and the allocation of the posts of Sub-Inspectors and Inspectors, Watch & Ward, respectively.

The scale of pay of Head Stenographer, B.B.& C.I. Rly., should be dealt with in accordance with the Committee's decision of the distribution of posts of Stenographers.

The work and responsibilities of the Head Calculators and Calculators, Assam Rly., should be compared with those of the Chief Computer and Computers, E.I. Rly., with a view to curing any disparity which might exist in the allotment of their respective scales.

Enquiry or Enquiry plus Reservation Clerks should be placed in the minimum grade of Rs. 100—185 and Clerks doing purely reservation work should not be put on a scale lower than Rs. 60—150.

Road Van Porters should be placed in the scale Rs. 35—40 in place of the scale Rs. 30—35 at present applicable.

The scale of pay of Rs. 100—185 should be one of the scales applicable to Ward Keepers.

The allocation of posts to the several grades in the case of Ward Keepers and Assistant Ward Keepers should be reviewed with a view to securing a fair allocation.

Apprentics should be granted House Rent and Compensatory Allowances as for Railway servants.

The principles stated in paragraph 88 of the Report of the Central Pay Commission should be observed in the matter of grant of Island, Ghat and Hill Allowances.

The question of grant of House Rent and City Allowances to staff at Delhi should be reviewed with a view to suitable increase in these allowances.

The principle applied in the case of the Running Shed staff of the E.P. Railway should be applied in the case of Running Shed staff on other Railways, i.e., the conversion of daily rate into monthly, should be on the basis of 30 5/12 days instead of 26 1/12 days.

The question of the grant of Madras City Compensatory Allowance to staff at St. Thomas Mount Station should be sympathetically considered as an exception to the general rules.

For purposes of promotion of Train Examiners in the grade of Rs. 80—160, the claims of Train Examiners who have been promoted from Skilled Artisans should be taken into account.

Water Softening Mistry and Head Block Fitters on E.I. Rly. should be given the prescribed scale of Rs. 80—160 if they supervise the work of skilled workmen.

The case of Tele-Communication Mechanic and M.I.C.s, Senior and Junior, should be referred to the Trade Test Panel and their scales fixed according to their classification by the Panel.

The prescribed scale of Gangmates on the Kalka-Simla Section of the E.P. Rly. should be higher than the scale of Keymen whose work they supervise.

The case of Fitters-in-Charge (Electrical) on B.B.&C.I. who claim higher scales of pay should be referred to the Trade Test Panel for classification.

The case of Ledger Keeper, T. and P. Depot, Golden Rock, S.I. Rly., who demands the scale of Rs. 80—160 should be dealt with in accordance with the Committee's decision regarding distribution of the posts of Clerks in the various grades.

The case of Print Order Reader, Printing Branch, E.P. Rly., for a higher scale should be dealt with in accordance with the Committee's decision regarding distribution of the posts of Clerks on the various grades.

The case of Cabin Staff at Howrah, E.I. Rly., who claim higher scales of pay, should be dealt with in accordance with the Committee's decision on the distribution of posts of S.M.s and A.S.M.s.

The case of Mr. S. K. Ghosh, Rationing Assistant, E.I. Rly., who claims a higher scale of pay, should be reviewed. If it was a case of promotion on transfer, he should be allowed to opt back to his previous post of Inspector; if a case of wrong fixation of pay, it should be referred to the Railway Administration for investigation and disposal.

The case of Shunting Masters on B.N. Rly., who claim higher scales of pay, should be dealt with in accordance with the Committee's decision relating to Gunners of the E.I. Rly.

The Inspector of Casting, Kanchrapara Shops, E.I. Rly., should be given the scale of Rs. 80—160 if he supervises the work of skilled staff.

Teleprinter Operators on the M.&S.M. Rly. should be given the scale of Rs. 60—150 if they were required to be qualified Signallers.

The case of T.T.I., S.I. Railway, for a higher scale should be dealt with in accordance with the Committee's recommendation regarding the distribution of the posts of T.T.E.s.

The case of Tally Board Supervisor on the M. & S.M. Rly. for a higher scale should be dealt with in accordance with the Committee's recommendation regarding the distribution of the posts of Head Clerks.

The Asstt. Cash Witness, Ajmer, B.B.&C.I. Rly., should have an avenue of promotion and should not be frozen to his job.

The case of Senior Cabinmen, E.P. Rly., should be dealt with in accordance with the Committee's decision on the scales of pay for Traffic Technical Staff.

The case of Chief Clerk, C.M.E.'s Office, S.I. Rly., should be dealt with in accordance with the Committee's decision on the distribution of the posts of Head Clerks.

The case of Mr. Narendranath Ghosh, Clerk-in-Charge, E.I. Rly., should be dealt with in accordance with the Committee's decision regarding Commercial Clerks.

The cases of the following individuals or categories of staff should be dealt with in accordance with the Committee's recommendation relating to Commercial Clerks.

(i) Radha Krishna, Shed Clerk, G.I.P. Rly.
(ii) Chugrai Mulrai, C.G.C., Moradabad, E.I. Rly.
(iii) General Assistants working as Parcel Clerks and Booking Clerks on the E.I. Rly.
(iv) Ticket Stock Clerks, E.I. Rly.
(v) Goods & Coaching Clerks, B.B.&C.I. Rly.
(vi) Head Book-Keeper, Wadi Bunder, G.I.P. Rly.
(vii) Commercial Staff of Wadi Bunder Depot, G.I.P. Rly.

The case of Storemen of Tool Stores, Kharagpur Workshop, B.N. Rly., should be dealt with in accordance with the Committee's recommendation relating to Stores Issuers.

The case of Travelling Ticket Examiners of the Assam Railway who are in the old A.B. Rly. scale of Rs. 75—10—200 should be dealt with in accordance

Both the Association of Producers and the Association of Artistes should arrive at a working arrangement by which no artiste is permitted to take part in more than two pictures at a time and that, in turn, the productions themselves must be completed within a reasonable time, say, six months, so that the artistes can feature in a maximum of four pictures in each year. Similarly the Association of Technicians should enter into arrangements with the Association of Producers regarding the rules for the training of apprentices and for the interchange of technicians between this country and others.

We would recommend that the Government should set up the Production Code Administration as soon as possible.

The functions of the P.C.A. should be the same as those of the P.C.A. in America. It should have four regional branches in Delhi, Calcutta, Bombay and Madras, and a Central Office the location of which could be decided later. Each Regional Committee should have five members and a Chairman (to be nominated by the Government)—the members to represent as far as possible the regional languages.

Only a nominal fee should be charged by the P.C.A. to be set up, and that its budget should be met from the Film Council Fund. For the period the P.C.A. is operated by the Government, a monetary limit may be fixed, as in the case of the Boards of Censors, to the contribution from the Film Council Fund towards its operation of expenses.

The Production Code Administration should be entrusted with the work of approving films for purposes of export outside India.

That legislative action should be taken immediately to declare the control of production of films by the Union expedient in the public interest and thereby to entrust full responsibility for the production side of the industry to the Central Government.

The regulation of cinemas would also prove more satisfactory if, as originally, the rule-making powers were retained at the Centre. A comprehensive code of regulations should, in our opinion, be drawn up by the Centre and made uniformly applicable to all places of public resort in all States of the Union. In addition, the Centre should also draw up a brief code covering cinemas in particular with special reference to the layout and safety devices in the projection booths as well as to the question of visibility of the screen from all the seats in the auditorium. The regulations in regard to projection booths should, however, be reduced to the minimum in the case of cinemas which show exclusively safety film.

In any show there should not be a display of pictures on the screen for a duration in excess of 120 minutes without interruption. Shows of longer durations should be split up so that each part does not exceed the duration mentioned above and is separated by at least 10 minutes from the next part of the show.

Establishment of a Film Finance Corporation is urgent and essential.

The fee charged from producers for the issue of a certificate should be nominal.

Cinema films should be exempted from the Octroi and Terminal Taxes.

In the case of artistes, we recommend that their earnings should be treated as professional income and that they should be permitted to pay income-tax after deducting all expenditure for professional reasons.

The licences granted to touring cinemas should enable them not merely to visit all parts of a district but also to move from one district to another within the same State.

We would recommend to the Film Industry the production of pictures with an eye on the different export markets. We consider that even in Western countries the exhibitors might be able to find a market for Indian films since people there demand a certain amount of variety in their daily fare, and Indian producers should consider the possibility of producing English versions of features which, they feel, would have universal appeal or special appeal o Western audiences; versions of pictures for export to the West could also be made by using sub-titles and captions.

Films in Indian languages imported from abroad should not be permitted to circulate in this country unless in each case the Production Code Administration are convinced that the film possesses special merit by way of being a classic or of great educational, historical or artistic value.

The practice of sending students abroad for basic training in cinematography which had been in force in the immediate post-War years need not be revived. The academic training they received in educational institutions, mainly in the United States, could easily be provided in this country, and we recommend the starting of an Institute of Film Technique for training all categories of technicians including directors.

The Institute should be located in Bombay and that both for purposes of basic training and for field training the resources of the Films Division should be made available to the students of the Institute.

In field-training, it is necessary that aspiring young men should have opportunities to work under people with originality and imagination, in circumstances where these two qualities can be exercised. In India the production of short films is carried on at present mainly under Government auspices. Their organization can, therefore, be used for providing field training to technicians who have had basic training.

No control over raw film would be effective unless there is control over distribution.

In all States visual education, whether in the classroom or in the rural areas, should be developed hand in hand.

In the field of adult education through the film, we feel that the ground covered by the use of mobile vans cannot be extensive and we therefore recommend the establishment of open-air theatres in rural areas. These should be put up by local authorities to suit the climatic conditions of the place and should be made available for free cinema shows where instructional and informative short films are screened for the benefit of the public. The same theatres could be used for the encouragement of local talents in music, dancing or acting.

The Film Council should bring out a journal containing sound criticism of current productions, and we would further recommend that in their selection of reviewers they should pay special attention to the essentials that we have mentioned above and by granting awards to the best piece of criticism or to the best work on film craft they should encourage qualified critics.

CRIMINAL TRIBES ACT ENQUIRY COMMITTEE, 1949—REPORT
Delhi, Manager of Publications, 1951. 177p.

Chairman : Shri Ananthasayanam Ayyangar.
Members : Shri A. V. Thakkar; Shri K. Chaliha; Shri V. N. Tivary; Sardar Gurbachan Singh; Shri J. K. Biswas.
Secretary : Shri P. C. Dave.

APPOINTMENT

The Criminal Tribes Act Enquiry Committee was constituted under the Ministry of Home Affairs vide their Resolution No. 22/1/49-Police-I dated September 28, 1949.

TERMS OF REFERENCE

(i) To enquire into the working of the Criminal Tribes Act, 1924, in the Provinces; and

(ii) To make recommendations for its modification or repeal.

CONTENTS

Introductory; Historical; Criminal Tribes; Working of the Criminal Tribes Act in the States; General Observations and Recommendations; Summary of Conclusions; Appendices.

RECOMMENDATIONS

General

Given proper opportunities and systematic help, it is neither impossible nor even difficult to reclaim the so-called Criminal Tribes. The problem requires to be tackled from three sides—economic, educational and social.

Working Of The Criminal Tribes Act

This would have been useful if a definite period, after which registration of a Criminal Tribe member should be cancelled, was fixed in the rules issued under the Criminal Tribes Act by the States.

The tented accommodation provided in the Reformatory Settlement at Amritsar, Punjab State, requires to be replaced by suitable buildings, and there is scope for improving the wages of the settlers in that settlement.

In Fazalpur Settlement (Uttar Pradesh), it was observed that undue strictness was shown in registering persons and more attention was required for satisfactory employment of all the able-bodied people in the settlement and for other welfare work.

The institutional life in the Reformatory School, Amritsar, requires to be made more attractive by introduction of more games and by giving more personal liberty to the boys. The system of releasing boys on probation also requires to be introduced early.

The Rajasthan Government should intensify the reclamation work among the Criminal Tribes by opening schools in every colony and by providing the Criminal Tribe members more facilities for agriculture.

Recommendation For The Repeal Of The Criminal Tribes Act And Reasons For The Repeal

A provision in Section 3 of the Criminal Tribes Act, 1924, is against the spirit of our Constitution. The Act indirectly sanctions begar or forced labour which is an offence under the Indian Penal Code and is opposed to the International Labour Convention and also Article 23 of the Constitution of India.

The Criminal Tribes Act, 1924, should be replaced by a Central legislation applicable to all habitual offenders without any distinction based on caste, creed or birth and the newly formed States included in Parts B and C of the First Schedule to the Constitution, which have local laws for the surveillance of the Criminal Tribes, should be advised to replace their laws in this respect by the Central legislation for habitual offenders, when passed.

The ordinary criminal and police laws are not adequate for the surveillance and control of the habitual offenders and it is necessary to have a Central legislation providing for the adequate surveillance and control of the habitual offenders.

There is no necessity to provide for the restrictions of ordinary wandering gangs.

The State Governments may be advised to use Section 401 of the Criminal Procedure Code more frequently in case of habitual offenders on condition that they live in specified Settlements for the unexpired portion of their sentence.

Provisions Recommended For Inclusion In The Proposed Restriction Of Habitual Offenders Act

Section 562 of the Criminal Procedure Code should be so amended that in necessary cases the courts could pass orders of restriction or detention in a Settlement for training in craft or industry even on a first offender.

A person who has two convictions for any non-bailable offences under Ch. XII, XVI and XVII of the Indian Penal Code, including an order under Section 118 of the Criminal Procedure Code within five years just before the date of issue of the Notification, may be notified as a habitual offender and on such Notification he should be liable to report his residence, change or intended change of, or absence or intended absence from his residence and also to allow his finger impressions to be recorded.

Section 565 of the Criminal Procedure Code should be suitably amended so as to empower the courts to order restriction of or confinement in Settlements of persons convicted by them under the penal law in lieu of part or whole of the sentence of imprisonment passed against such persons.

The courts should be empowered to order restriction of movements to a certain area or detention in a Settlement in lieu of an order to furnish security under Section 118 of the Criminal Procedure Code. A court acting under Sub-Section 3 of Section 123 of the Criminal Procedure Code or an Appellate Court, acting under Section 406 of the Criminal Procedure Code, may also be authorized to pass an order of restriction or detention in a Settlement in lieu of an order requiring a person to give security under Section 110 of the Criminal Procedure Code.

Habitual offenders who have not less than 3 convictions for non-bailable offences under Ch. XII, XVI and XVII of the Indian Penal Code spread over a period of five years immediately before the date on which the new Act comes into force and who are at present in the Settlements may be ordered to be detained in the Settlements for three years by executive orders.

A habitual offender, who is ordered to be detained in a Settlement, should be allowed to bring his wife and other dependants to the Settlement but he should be responsible to see that his dependants obey the Settlement rules.

When an order of detention in a Settlement is passed against a habitual offender, the detention should be ordered for a minimum period of two years.

Settlements should be directly managed by the Government through their Welfare or Labour Departments. In no case should management of Settlements be entrusted to the Police Department.

There should be a general provision for separation of children of habitual offenders from their parents and placing them in residential schools and children falling under particular categories should invariably be removed from their parents and placed in such schools.

Where special laws for the treatment of children are in force, action against the children of habitual offenders should be taken under such laws as far as possible.

Children should be committed to schools for a sufficiently long time.

No provisions similar to Sections 23, 24, 26 and 27 of the Criminal Tribes Act, 1924, are necessary in the new Act.

Incidental provisions that may be considered necessary and provisions for making rules for the proper administration of the Act may be made but, unless the breach of rules is for the purpose of committing offences, the punishment should be light.

Action Suggested To Be Taken Pending The Repeal Of The Act

The system of automatic registration of members of the Criminal Tribes, on their attaining a particular age, is neither necessary nor desirable and pending the repeal of the Act, the existing powers of exempting persons from registration should be liberally used in the case of all persons other than those who have been proved guilty of offences or reasonably suspected of such offences. It is suggested that registration of members of the Criminal Tribes, who are not convicted of any offences or are not reasonably suspected of any offences during the last three years, may be cancelled.

Pending the repeal of the Act, the preliminary enquiry under a proviso to Section 16 of the Criminal Tribes Act should be carried out by a judicial officer giving adequate opportunity to the Criminal Tribe members, likely to be affected, to urge their reasons against the proposed internment order.

Pending repeal of the Act, the administration of the Criminal Tribes Act, 1924, should be liberalized and no new tribe should be notified as a Criminal Tribe.

Suggestion For The Amelioration Of The Criminal Tribes After The Repeal Of The Act

Suitable steps for the amelioration of the Criminal Tribes should be taken after the repeal of the Act.

The Central Government should make a liberal contribution not exceeding 50% to the State Governments for the initiation and execution of the schemes for a period of 10 years in the first instance.

COMMITTEE ON STATE TRADING, 1949—REPORT

New Delhi, Ministry of Commerce, 1950. 119p.

Chairman : Dr. Panjabrao Shamrao Deshmukh.
Members : Shri Prabhudayal Himatsingka; Shri H. V. Kamath; Shri B. P. Jhunjhunwala; Shri S. V. Krishnamoorthy Rao; Shri R. N. Goenka; Shri N. Dandekar (resigned).
Secretaries : Shri V. L. Goswami; Shri B. N. Adarkar.

APPOINTMENT

The Committee on State Trading was constituted under the Ministry of Commerce vide their Resolution No. 11-TP(P) (1)/49 dated October 8, 1949.

TERMS OF REFERENCE

(i) Whether, having regard to present-day conditions and future trends of India's international trade, it would be of advantage to set up a State-owned or State-sponsored organization for handling any sector of the foreign trade of the country;

(ii) If so, what the structure of the organization should be and what the field and scope of the activities of the organization should be.

CONTENTS

Introductory; Main Features of the Foreign Trade Situation; State Trading in Imports; State Trading in Exports; General Considerations Affecting State Trading; Organization of the State Trading Corporation; Summary of Conclusions and Recommendations; Appendix I to IV.

RECOMMENDATIONS

The question of stores purchase and disposals be taken up for separate examination.

Barter agreements should be resorted to only in exceptional circumstances, and in all other cases the normal type of agreement should be the one in which the two parties commit themselves only to license specified quantities of goods for export or import.

Violent fluctuations in imports could be prevented by effecting certain procedural improvements in the existing system. A rationalization of the Import Control Policy and Procedure is one of the most urgent problems which deserve the Government's attention.

A State Trading Corporation can, however, sponsor negotiations on behalf of private importers and exporters with considerable advantage to them and to the country as a whole. In view of the growing trend towards the establishment of monopolies in other countries, traders in this country should be encouraged to resort to collective bargaining.

It is only when the commodity in question is suitable for State trading that the possibility of raising revenues for the State should be considered as an additional justification for resorting to State trading.

Imports of foodgrains on Government account should, in future, be handled by the State Trading Corporation.

State trading in fertilizers should be continued in order to eliminate middlemen's profits and to ensure that fertilizers are made available to State Governments at reasonable prices so as to enable them to carry out the "Grow More Food" Campaign effectively.

Malpractices like underinvoicing of exports of jute manufactures should be dealt with through a stricter enforcement of exchange control.

It should be one of the functions of the State Trading Corporation to advise the Government on the desirability of adopting State trading for the purpose of price discrimination in individual cases on a consideration of the merits of each case.

The question of utilizing national banking, shipping and insurance services to the fullest possible extent in connection with all Government transactions should be given urgent consideration.

The State Trading Corporation should be developed as a model enterprise, adopting modern methods of business administration, publicity, market research, etc., and thus setting an example to other business enterprises.

A State Trading Corporation to be called "The Indian Commercial Corporation" should be established by statute. The amount of authorized capital and the initial issue may be settled after a detailed examination by the Government. Not less than 51% of the capital should be held by the Central Government, and the balance offered to State Governments and private investors.

No statutory limit need be placed on the borrowing capacity of the Corporation.

Early steps should be taken towards the organization of a well-trained economic and commercial service on a permanent basis.

RURAL BANKING ENQUIRY COMMITTEE, 1949—REPORT

Delhi, Manager of Publications, 1953. 214p.

Chairman : Shri Purshottamdas Thakurdas.
Vice-Chairman : Shri C. H. Bhabha.
Members : Shri B. Venkatappiah; Shri Ram Gopal; Shri V. R. Sonalker; Shri J. C. Ryan.
Secretary : Shri N. D. Nangia.

APPOINTMENT

The Rural Banking Enquiry Committee was constituted under the Ministry of Finance vide their Resolution No. F. 4(196) FI/49 dated November 8, 1949.

TERMS OF REFERENCE

(i) To consider the measures that can be immediately adopted for the extension of banking facilities in rural areas;

(ii) To review in this connection the present arrangements for the management of the cash work at Government Treasuries and Sub-Treasuries including those where the work is at present managed by the Imperial Bank of India;

(iii) To consider to what extent the extension of banking facilities will be facilitated by entrusting the cash work at Government Treasuries and Sub-Treasuries at places where the work is not at present being managed by the Imperial Bank of India to commercial banks and co-operative banks, and in this connection to consider:

(a) The future management of such work in the Provinces of India as well as in the States and Unions whose financial integration with the Indian Union will take effect from April 1, 1950; and

(b) To what extent the management of the cash work in Government Treasuries and Sub-Treasuries could be entrusted to either a new State-sponsored bank or to one or more of the existing commercial banks or co-operative banks; and the conditions to be fulfilled by and the assistance to be given to such banks;

(iv) To make recommendations in regard to the banks which may now be handling the Treasury work in the States and the Unions; and

(v) To make any other recommendations.

CONTENTS

Part I: Preliminary—Introductory; Scope and Objects of the Enquiry; Part II: Extension of Banking Facilities—Present Position of Banking Facilities; Mobilization of Rural Savings; Machinery for Rural Credits; Proposals for the Extension of Banking Facilities; Part III: Treasury Arrangements in the Provinces—Treasuries and the Extension of Banking Facilities; Desirability and Feasibility of a Multi-agency System; Future Role of the Imperial Bank in the Banking and Treasury Set-up; Part IV: Treasury Arrangements in the States—Necessity for Separate Treatment; Proposals Regarding Individual States; Part V: Formation of a New State-Sponsored Bank; Part VI: Summary of Conclusions and Recommendations; Appendices.

RECOMMENDATIONS

Present Position Of Banking Facilities

Post Office Savings Banks are the most widespread governmental agency; they enjoy the confidence of the people, and can be developed to collect the savings of the rural people to an increasing extent.

The diversity of banking institutions is inherent in the variety of conditions and circumstances obtaining in different regions of this country, and is the natural consequence of historical circumstances. The differing requirements of people cannot all be provided by one set of institutions and all the various types of institutions have their place in the banking system. What is necessary is to ensure co-ordination in their activities and the maintenance of a minimum standard of soundness, efficiency and service to the people.

Mobilization Of Rural Savings

Under existing conditions it would be advisable to concentrate on the consolidation of the progress already achieved, and to plan further expansion on sound and cautious lines rather than undertake any costly and hasty schemes of expansion of the banking system on the basis of overoptimistic expectations. Such expansion would have to be conceived largely from the point of view of bringing within the framework of the banking system the savings already accumulated and being currently made by the relatively well-to-do rural classes, particularly in the more prosperous regions. To this end, encouragement should be offered to sound commercial banks to open offices as near the rural areas as possible.

For the smaller people in rural areas, emphasis will largely have to be placed on the expansion and more effective utilization of machinery like Post Office Savings Banks and co-operative societies. Attempts will also have to be made to promote Thrift and Small Savings by means of propaganda, and group effort utilized to the maximum possible extent.

Apart from inculcating the habit of thrift, necessary at all times to promote self-help and self-reliance, it is essential, in the changed political conditions, that all sections of the community should contribute to the general uplift of the country.

Machinery For Rural Credit

Attention should more properly be concentrated on building up the institutional machinery for rural credit.

The establishment of a single financial agency to cover the entire field of rural credit would not be feasible in existing conditions, and in each region a varied and adequate machinery should be developed in conformity with local conditions.

In any scheme for a sound and efficient system of agricultural finance, sufficient emphasis must be laid on the building up of a sound structure of primary institutions—whether co-operative credit societies or multipurpose societies.

While the establishment of new organizations, e.g., Agricultural Credit Corporation or Agricultural Banks may be necessary in some regions such as the former Indian States, full use should be made of the existing institutions.

Separate institutions would be necessary to provide long-term credit, and land mortgage banks are the most appropriate agencies for this purpose.

A satisfactory machinery to deal with the credit needs of "disadvantaged" farmers will have to be developed gradually and the task will, in the first instance, have to be undertaken on an experimental basis.

Proposals For The Extension Of Banking Facilities

There is some scope for extending facilities for the receipt of deposits by an expansion in the number of branches of sound banks in semi-urban and rural areas, and of Post Office Savings Banks. The need of the rural areas for advances is considerable, and is capable of continued increase. Co-operative institutions are the most important agencies for providing credit and should, therefore, receive special attention and assistance.

The Imperial Bank and other commercial banks should be allowed and encouraged to expand up to taluka (or tehsil) towns, mandis or market towns, or other towns of some commercial or industrial importance. An expansion in the number of offices of the Imperial Bank is desirable in the interest of the rural areas as well as of the banking system as a whole. Co-operative banks can be established in the larger as well as smaller towns, and can go deeper into rural areas than commercial banks. Small villages can only be served by co-operative societies and rural Post Office Savings Banks.

Existing legislation concerning money-lending, debt relief and allied matters should be reviewed and amended so as to place commercial banks on the same footing as the co-operative institutions.

Liberalization of remittance facilities would encourage banks to open branches in the countryside and would lead to other beneficial results.

The Reserve Bank should see that adequate facilities are made available throughout the country for the conversion and exchange of notes and coins. The Imperial Bank should examine the feasibility of adopting at its branches the system of accepting tenders, where they are unduly large, on a guarantee basis.

Co-operative banks and societies would need special assistance and some subsidies in addition to the concessions and privileges they are already enjoying.

The procedure and working of the Post Office Savings Bank should be examined in detail by an officer with banking experience.

Treasuries And The Extension Of Banking Facilities

Steps should be taken to convert non-bank treasuries into bank treasuries at as many centres as possible.

The question of opening offices by the Imperial Bank at places where the treasury turnover may not be large but where the potentialities of general banking business are good should also be examined.

To encourage the Imperial Bank to expand further on the proposed scale, the rate of commission on turnover at its new branches and treasury pay offices should, at any rate for a period of five years, be fixed separately.

Urgent steps should be taken towards the reorganization of treasuries for improving their efficiency and for enabling them to provide certain basic facilities essential for the extension of banks to the less developed areas.

The present practice of making payments by means of pay orders on the original bills should be replaced by the system of payment by cheques to as large an extent as possible.

Desirability And Feasibility Of A Multi-Agency System

It would not be in the interest of the country to do anything which will weaken or impair the organizational and financial strength of the Imperial Bank towards the building of which much of the nation's efforts and resources have been spent. The present unsatisfactory features of the working of the Imperial Bank can be remedied by legislative and other measures.

The cash work at treasuries and sub-treasuries in the provinces at centres where the Reserve Bank is not established should, therefore, continue to be handled either by the Imperial Bank as agent of the Reserve Bank, or by the Government themselves.

Future Role Of The Imperial Bank In The Banking And Treasury Set-up

The role of the Imperial Bank in the future banking and treasury set-up of the country should primarily be that of an auxiliary to the Reserve Bank.

The Imperial Bank should continue its commercial activities, and the existing restrictions on its business are considered sufficient.

Necessity For Separate Treatment

Every State should appoint the Reserve Bank as its banker and entrust it with all its monies and balances, free of interest. The Reserve Bank must also be entrusted with all the remittance, exchange investment and other banking transactions as well as with the management of the public debt of each State. Any other bank can handle the cash work of any State but only as the agent of the Reserve Bank.

Proposals Regarding Individual States

Hyderabad : The Reserve Bank should be appointed as bankers to the State, and the various central banking functions of the Hyderabad State Bank should be transferred to that bank.

The Hyderabad State Bank should be appointed as agent of the Reserve Bank in the State for five years, and be permitted to manage cash work at treasuries and sub-treasuries at centres where it was managing the work on April 1, 1950.

Madhya Bharat: The present arrangements for the conduct of cash work should be continued except at Indore where the Imperial Bank should undertake State Government business in addition to that of the Central Government which it is managing at present as agent of the Reserve Bank.

Mysore: At Bangalore, the cash work may continue to be handled by the Imperial Bank, but this should be done under its general agreement with the Reserve Bank. As soon as possible, the Reserve Bank should establish an office, and take over Government business and the custody of the chest from the Imperial Bank at Bangalore.

PEPSU: With the appointment of the Reserve Bank as bankers to the State it will be unnecessary for the State Government to maintain balances with any other bank, and the accounts maintained by the State Government with the various banks inside and outside the State should be closed.

The monopoly of general banking business and other extraordinary concessions enjoyed by the Imperial Bank should be terminated.

Rajasthan: The Imperial Bank should be appointed agent of the Reserve Bank at Sambhar, Jodhpur and Alwar and entrusted with the cash work of the Central and State Governments at those centres. As soon as the agreement with the Bank of Jaipur expires, the Imperial Bank should also be appointed agent of the Reserve Bank to manage Government business at Jaipur.

Saurashtra: The Imperial Bank may continue to be entrusted with treasury work at Rajkot, but this should be under its general agreement with the Reserve Bank and not under a separate agreement with the State Government.

At the remaining centres, the State Government should arrange for the cash work at treasuries and sub-treasuries to be carried on departmentally.

Travancore and Cochin: The Imperial Bank which is at present managing the Central Government treasury work at Trivandrum should also be entrusted with the business of the State at that centre under its general agreement with the Reserve Bank.

The Central Bank may continue to handle the State Government cash work at Ernakulam and at the sub-treasury at Trichur on the existing basis until the expiry of its present agreement on February 1, 1951. Thereafter, the Government must make their own arrangements for the management of the work.

At the remaining centres, the State Government should continue to carry on the work through their own staff.

Formation Of A New State-Sponsored Bank

The present organization of the Reserve Bank is inadequate to meet the requirements of the country, and energetic steps should be taken to secure the establishment of a branch of the Bank at the headquarters of each of the major Provinces and States, special attention being paid to the requirements of States where the Reserve Bank has no office at present.

1950

DELHI IMPROVEMENT TRUST ENQUIRY COMMITTEE, 1950—REPORT

New Delhi, Ministry of Health, 1951. 2 Vols.

Chairman : Shri G. D. Birla.
Members : Dr. Bakhshi Tek Chand; Shri Deshbandhu Gupta; Shri B. Shiva Rao; Dr. Yudhvir Singh; Shri Amar Nath Nanda (died).
Secretary : Shri K. K. Sharma.

APPOINTMENT

The Delhi Improvement Trust Enquiry Committee was constituted under the Ministry of Health in 1950.

TERMS OF REFERENCE

(i) To review the working of the Trust and in particular to examine and report on the difficulties, if any, experienced by the Trust in fulfilling the targets originally fixed.

(ii) To advise, keeping in view the rapid growth of population and prevailing high land values in Delhi, what should be the Trust's policy as regards housing, especially poor class housing.

(iii) To fix new targets (immediate and long-term) for the Trust and make suggestions for giving it adequate financial and other resources for their attainment.

(iv) To examine whether any, and if so, what changes should be made in the Constitution of the Trust.

CONTENTS

Volume I: Introductory; A Review of the Working of the Delhi Improvement Trust; The Problem; The Solution; The Authority; Targets; Summary of Major Conclusions and Recommendations; Volume II: Appendices.

RECOMMENDATIONS

There should be a single Planning and Controlling Authority for the whole of the urban area of Delhi. It should be an independent Authority with a non-official majority.

The Authority should be given extensive planning

powers. In matters of actual development, the Authority should provide collective services (i.e., highways, water mains, sewerage and lighting); the internal development of developable areas should be left to private parties. The Authority should have powers to recover the cost of collective services from private parties.

As regards areas with a bad layout, the Authority should have the power to pool compulsorily all the plots owned by different persons and re-divide the land among the former owners, after reserving a portion of the area for public amenities.

Facilities should be provided for the provision of land and building materials at reasonable rates to local bodies, co-operative societies, business societies, associations, private parties, etc., together with cheap credit facilities.

The first option to clear and rebuild a slum area should be given to its owner. Should he fail to co-operate the slum should be cleared by the Authority at his expense, acquired, developed and disposed of.

The Authority should have the power to enforce the carrying out of repairs or minor works in the case of sub-standard buildings situated in a slum area.

The following sources of income should be placed at the disposal of the Authority:

(i) Two per cent of the gross annual income of each Municipal or Notified Area Committee.

(ii) Proceeds from a surcharge of 2% on stamp duty on transfer of property.

(iii) Proceeds from a terminal tax of half-an-anna on passengers coming by rail to Delhi.

(iv) The entire net proceeds from the Entertainment Tax.

(v) Proceeds of tax on the presentation of building applications within the scheme areas of the Authority.

The Authority should be a financially autonomous organization.

The Authority should be allowed to raise loans in the open market.

FOODGRAINS PROCUREMENT COMMITTEE, 1950—REPORT
Delhi, Manager of Publications, 1950. 186p.

Chairman : Shri M. Tirumala Rao.
Members : Shri C. P. K. Menon; Shri E N Mangat Rai; Shri R. P. Noronha.
Secretary : Shri C. Banerji.

APPOINTMENT

The Foodgrains Procurement Committee was constituted under the Ministry of Food vide their Resolution No. Py. I-619/117/50 dated February 8, 1950.

TERMS OF REFERENCE

(i) To enquire into the systems of procurement and distribution adopted in the States;

(ii) Recommend such changes as may be necessary in the existing system of procurement and distribution to minimize imports in the case of a deficit State and to maximize exports in the case of a surplus State, and to reduce the difference between the prices in the market and the prescribed control prices;

(iii) Recommend such modifications as may be necessary in the food organization of the State to ensure efficient procurement and distribution;

(iv) Recommend the extent to which uniformity in the systems of procurement and distribution in the country as a whole is desirable and practicable with reference to the circumstances prevailing in the different areas;

(v) Recommend any changes necessary in the Central Government's organization to supervise and co-ordinate procurement and distribution in the States.

CONTENTS

Introduction; Food Policy and Organization, Uniformity of Systems and Miscellaneous Considerations; The Monopoly Procurement System; The Punjab; The Patiala and East Punjab States Union; Uttar Pradesh; Rajasthan; Madhya Bharat; Saurashtra; Bombay; Hyderabad; Madhya Pradesh; Bihar; West Bengal; Assam; Orissa; Mysore; United States of Travancore-Cochin; Madras; Other States; Appendices I and II.

RECOMMENDATIONS

Food Policy And Organization, Uniformity Of Systems And Miscellaneons Considerations

The Regional Food Commissioners' Organization: We believe that this organization could prove most useful for the purpose. It is decentralized, and can, therefore, achieve the degree of detailed knowledge required to be constructive, rather than the theoretical and irritating. If, however, the Regional Food Commissioner is to really assist State Governments, he must be an officer of adequate experience and knowledge to be able to advise States usefully; and, conversely, to effectively bring their special peculiarities and problems to the notice of the Centre; he must have sufficient status and personality to be able to take up problems, at the highest level, with both States and the Centre; and he must have adequate vision not to take either a merely technical and rigid or a vague view of his responsibilities and duties. These are no small qualifications, and men for these most important posts should be carefully selected.

The Regional Food Commissioner's primary and main duty should be, as a representative of the Centre, to perform the functions of the co-ordinating, supervisory authority, in the Region, for which purpose he must maintain intimate contact, both with State Governments and the Centre, regarding both policy and administrative matters.

It follows from this that the Regional Food Commissioner must be a carefully selected officer, with adequate experience of practical administration, knowledge of the people and personality; and that the post must be adequately paid to ensure this. We consider that the minimum qualification for this post should be administrative experience, of at least five years, of the post of Collector (or Deputy Commissioner), or its equivalent, and a first-class record of work. Actual experience of food work should, wherever available, be considered an additional qualification.

Deputy Regional Food Commissioner

The appointments of Deputy Regional Food Commissioners, posted in individual States within a Region, are in our opinion quite ineffective and unnecessary, and should be abolished.

At The Food Ministry

We have been impressed with the need for two whole-time officers at the Ministry to co-ordinate and supervise procurement and distribution operations.

THE PUNJAB

Special Recommendations To Assist Procurement

This State is a close neighbour of Uttar Pradesh, Delhi, Rajasthan and PEPSU. It is most important that parity control prices should be introduced, and enforced, in this whole area; otherwise the strain on the administrative machinery in a State where prices are controlled may well become intolerable.

The State Government is at present financing foodgrain operations. In the circumstances of the State, owing largely to money being shy in the immediate neighbourhood of Pakistan, finance by the Trade is not practical. Since the Rabi crop, which represents the main production in the State, arrives in markets in a concentrated period of two or three months, the funds involved are very considerable and it is possible that the State Government may find it difficult to provide these in full.

The system of monopoly purchase, which assumes normal marketing by the producer, depends very much for its success on confidence and belief on the part of the consumer, the trader and the producer that the Government is able to meet food requirements. For such confidence, the maintenance of an adequate reserve is essential and the State Government should be encouraged to maintain such a reserve.

THE PATIALA & EAST PUNJAB STATES UNION

Monopoly Procurement

We recommend that the monopoly procurement system should be established in PEPSU for wheat, barley and rice.

A modified form of the monopoly procurement system should be introduced for wheat and barley for 1950.

The full monopoly should be introduced for rice during the coming Kharif 1950.

As soon as possible and in any event from Rabi 1951, the full monopoly should be made effective for wheat and barley.

Interim Period—Modified Monopoly For Wheat And Barley

In surplus districts the whole system should be introduced and a complete monopoly set up at the market, along with restrictions on movement, a limitation on transactions in villages, etc.

It is not possible to achieve Government financing of wholesale transactions in PEPSU immediately. This State should function, therefore, through Grain Dealers' Associations, acting as Government agents not only for purchase but for the financing, storing and maintaining of grain.

In deficit districts a complete monopoly should not be introduced and operations should be left to the trade. It is, however, necessary that the Government should ensure a guaranteed price to the grower throughout the State.

Distribution

In surplus areas distribution should be arranged by releases from local arrivals to authorized retailers and in deficit areas partly from local arrivals, which will be left to the trade, and partly by transfers from surplus areas. Wherever the Government distributes this should be on the basis of family cards and earmarking of particular retailers for specified card-holders. The

PEPSU Government should endeavour progressively to introduce a systematic distribution scheme so that this is established and is in working order by early winter when shortages may begin to appear.

In border and heavily deficit areas, it may be necessary for the Government to go further, from the very beginning, in introducing the complete monopoly system to prevent smuggling or difficulties in the availability of supplies.

Non-Monopoly Grains

The non-monopoly grains will be gram, maize and bajra. These grains should be purchased in the same way as in the neighbouring State of the Punjab.

Administration

In view of the comparatively small urban areas in PEPSU, it will not be necessary to have more than one whole-time District Officer in charge of both food and civil supplies work, who may be designated the District Food and Civil Supplies Controller.

Finance

The position regarding funds must be watched carefully, particularly during the period of peak arrivals, to ensure that the monopoly functions fully and that there is no discouragement of the producer in bringing grain to the market.

Advance Allocations

The Centre should allocate grain in advance of actual arrivals and the PEPSU Government and the Centre should ensure that all preliminary arrangements, such as finance from recipients, despatch instructions, arrangements for inspection, etc., are made in good time so that despatches can take place as soon as the grain arrives.

Reserves

It is essential that reserves should be built up and maintained to stabilize the system of purchase recommended here and the Government will have to take the necessary action in acquiring godown accommodation for this purpose and staff to maintain these reserves.

Prices

It is necessary that prices of foodgrains in PEPSU should be fixed and enforced in parity with those in the Punjab, U.P., Delhi and Rajasthan.

Transport

As financing of the monopoly is to be done largely by the trade, it is essential to ensure that their turnover is speedy so that they maintain sufficient fluid funds to meet the needs of procurement.

Supervision By The Centre

It is recommended that the Centre should review progress continually and remain in constant touch with the State Government, providing the necessary advice and pressure to ensure results.

UTTAR PRADESH

Recommendations Limited By Actual Developments

The two biggest needs in Uttar Pradesh seem to be:

(a) To get market prices down to the procurement level; and

(b) To establish a settled, well-defined policy and an adequate standard of efficiency in enforcing it.

The cultivator should not be compelled to surrender grain which he has not produced.

He should not be given the choice to substitute one Rabi grain for another, but must supply the specific grain produced, according to the quantity produced, and the levy demand served upon him.

Movement bans should be constant throughout the year irrespective of the procurement season, and should be imposed on smaller and more compact areas than at present.

Rationing should be extended to all urban areas so that the demand on the remainder of the cultivators' surplus will be reduced and open-market prices brought down. As soon as the prices come down the Government should proceed to purchase also the balance of the surpluses offered by the cultivator, so as to meet its additional commitments.

Monopoly Procurement

The monopoly should apply to wheat, barley, rice, millets and maize; to gram also if the Uttar Pradesh Government considers necessary. For Rabi foodgrains, it has already been introduced but care must be taken to ensure that all its provisions, without exception, are enforced. In the case of Kharif foodgrains, it should be introduced from the harvest of 1950.

The monopoly should be enforced in all areas, both surplus and deficit for wheat, rice and barley. Maize and millets are probably local in production and consumption, and it may be possible for the Government to work the monopoly for them, by applying it only to producing areas.

The Government must ensure that the number of purchasing centres opened are adequate.

Special attention is required, in view of high prices, to the distribution side of the scheme, which means:

(a) That rationing and distribution should be undertaken to the fullest extent laid down by us in the Monopoly Scheme; and

(b) These arrangements should be as efficient as possible.

No free market, and this includes rural markets, should be allowed.

Additional Imports

The Uttar Pradesh problem is essentially that of prices. A steady price level can only be established by rationing and distribution, which will cut off competitive demand on supplies. It is imperative that rationing and distribution arrangements should be established and should not be withdrawn under any circumstances. It was in this background that a recommendation for additional imports, during the current year, was made in the Interim Report. In principle, this position remains unchanged. In fact, initial procurement has been satisfactory and, therefore, there may be no immediate need for such imports. It would, however, be a mistake to consider that these should be abandoned finally.

Prices

A suitable maximum price to start the monopoly scheme which would be Rs. 15 per maund for the best quality and proportionately less for other varieties.

Administration

In respect of all areas, other than statutorily rationed areas, we suggest that distribution should be in the hands of the Principal Procurement Officer in the district, so that he may be in a position to relieve shortages as and when they develop. The Collector should be the head of the food organization in the district.

RAJASTHAN

Levy Scheme

The quantity left with the Jagirdars should be substantially reduced and only sufficient should be allowed for his *bona fide* requirements.

As Rajasthan is heavily deficit, we feel that there is no justification for permitting the cultivator to sell any part of his surplus except to the Government over and above the levy.

Rationing schemes will have to be tightened up and extended to all urban areas as well as deficit rural pockets as laid down for the monopoly.

The State Government should prepare a rough and ready list of holdings in the Jagirdari area so that some check may be exercised on the Jagirdars' own statement of rent paid in kind. In view of the deficit in Rajasthan the monopoly should be applied to all foodgrains and in all areas.

Distribution

There is no justification for allowing free sales to continue in statutorily rationed areas like Jaipur city, because, as we have already pointed out, such sales act as a standing inducement to the cultivator to evade procurement because the price offered is much more than the procurement rate. Open sales in Jaipur city should be prohibited forthwith and the scale of ration should be made the same as is allowed in Jodhpur and Bikaner.

As regards the other 59 towns where distribution is against ration cards, the more important amongst them should be statutorily rationed and free imports and open sales should be banned.

In Jodhpur and Udaipur Divisions scarcity conditions are likely to get worse and it is, therefore, necessary that all rural areas should be informally rationed against family ration cards, at a slightly lower scale than in the towns.

General

We find that efficiency in the implementation of food schemes in this State could be considerably improved if the present confusion regarding pay scales of staff was removed.

A proper plan of control and co-ordination between the Revenue and the Food Staff should be worked out.

MADHYA BHARAT

Monopoly Procurement

The levy should be abolished and a Monopoly Procurement System should be introduced.

The monopoly should be introduced for Kharif grains from the harvest of 1950 and for Rabi grains from that of 1951.

An adequate number of purchasing centres should be opened so that the monopoly draws grain from the producer.

Even in the intervening period before the monopoly is introduced, the open market should be closed immediately in rationed towns and in areas where a system of distribution, substantially amounting to rationing, is in existence.

In heavily deficit rural areas distribution should be systematized straightaway and should be against family ration cards.

A major difficulty in Madhya Bharat is lack of finance, which holds up and even stops procurement, at particular times of the year. Since the State is surplus it is in the general interest to remove this defect, and we recommend that the Central and State Governments should take it up immediately and evolve means to ensure adequate finance. If necessary, the Centre should finance procurement operations at a nominal rate of interest, and permit this interest to be passed on to the consumer or the recipient administration.

SAURASHTRA

Levy Plus Monopoly

The existing levy should continue in full.

In addition, the monopoly procurement system, with its concomitants in distribution, should be established for the Government to obtain the balance of surpluses available with producers.

In regard to existing rationed towns, rationing should be strictly enforced, and the present concession allowing consumers to bring in supplies against the cancellation of ration cards should be withdrawn immediately. The proposed concessions for gradual derationing should be abandoned.

Rationing should be extended to all important urban areas which, in the case of Saurashtra, we would describe as all towns where the present population is above 25,000. This will mean, in addition to the existing three towns, the Government introducing rationing in another 10.

The monopoly should be introduced with the arrival of the new Kharif crop.

BOMBAY

Universal Procurement And Universal Distribution

Bombay should now proceed to universal procurement and universal distribution, so that its net dependence on the Central Government resources may be reduced.

This recommendation, on the procurement side, would mean assessing each individual producer's total actual production, leaving with him his actual requirements and taking away the whole of the surplus. Such a system of procurement, considered in the background of the present arrangements in Bombay, implies:

(a) The calculation of the levy on the actual areas sown with food crops;

(b) Where rent is paid in kind, the assessment of the levy separately on the landlord and the tenant;

(c) Working out figures of production by assuming separate yields for each kind of crop in each area and calculating production on the full yield for soils above average and for irrigated areas;

(d) The levy to be paid in terms of the actual grain or grains sown and the abolition of interchangeability; and

(e) The preparation of levy bills, separately for Kharif and Rabi, and their modification according to what the producer receives, if anything, from the smaller of the two crops harvested by him.

Extension Of Levy To Non-Levy Areas

The Committee recommended that the Bombay Government should consider the extension of the levy to the excluded homogeneous rice areas.

HYDERABAD

Possibility Of Reverting To Previous System Of Procurement

In the circumstances of Hyderabad a levy continues to be necessary and a monopoly alone will not meet the situation.

Rationing And Distribution

We recommend:

(a) The rationing of all towns, with a population above 50,000, before the arrival of the new crop;

(b) An extension of rationing to towns, with a population above 25,000, as soon as possible after the new crop arrives; and

(c) The abolition of the 10 seers exemption in the monopoly; this should be reduced to 3 lb. The Government should substantially undertake the feeding of non-producers and underproducers who require grain in deficit rural areas.

The Alternative Temporary Abolition Of The Monopoly

Movement bans, as between districts, should be maintained in full and, even within each district, as far as possible, movement should only be permitted within a group of villages, or from a group of villages to an unrationed town, which requires to be fed.

Administration

The present duplicate system of administration, partly by direct Government agency and partly through the H.C.C.C., should be replaced by a unified administration.

The Civil Administrator or Collector should be in charge of food work in each district, both on the procurement and distribution sides.

He should be assisted, in each district, by a District Food Officer of the rank of Deputy Collector or similar status.

MADHYA PRADESH

Monopoly Procurement

We recommend that the Monopoly Procurement System should be introduced in Madhya Pradesh.

In the case of jowar and rice, which are Kharif grains, it should be introduced with the arrival of the 1950 Kharif crop. In the case of wheat its introduction will have to await the Rabi 1950 crop.

The prices fixed for the monopoly should be somewhat higher than present procurement rates, and thereafter should be fixed in parity with prices in the region.

Non-Monopoly Grains

The non-monopoly grains will be, in order of importance, gram, barley and maize. The production of the last two is negligible. The Government should continue to buy gram to the extent, and in such a manner, as it considers necessary. The price of these foodgrains should, however, be controlled in parity with monopoly foodgrains.

Premium For Good Quality

In the case of superior rice the procurement price is fixed in terms of specifications which prescribe tolerance limits. No premium is allowed for rice, where the tolerance limit has been improved upon, with the result that the Government tends not to get any really first-class rice. It is recommended that the specifications should be amended so as to allow a premium for better quality than tolerance, or alternatively that a premium should be paid for this quality. The measure will have the effect of getting into Government hands some of the best rice produced.

BIHAR

In North Bihar, there should be no procurement or price control. Movement should not be allowed from the North to the Centre and South of the State, and strictly banned from the Centre and South to the North. The latter must be isolated and any movements which take place will be on Government account only. This is quite practicable as the river forms an excellent barrier.

The Government should strictly ration all towns in the North, with a population of 25,000 and above.

The monopoly should apply to paddy, rice, wheat, gram, maize and barley.

It should be enforced from the arrival of the new harvest, in each case, that means for Kharif grains in 1950 and Rabi grains in 1951.

Nepal Paddy

Fairly liberal quantities of the rice should be moved into North Bihar for rationed towns from the current procurement so as to depress the price level there at the beginning of the season.

The West Bengal tea estates should be prohibited from purchasing Nepal paddy. Purchases of such paddy should only be on Government account and at a fixed rate. If this rate is the same as the procurement rate for West Bengal, it is almost certain that the major part of the Nepal paddy will be rediverted to Bihar.

WEST BENGAL

Monopoly Procurement

Our recommendation for West Bengal is the Monopoly Procurement System.

The whole system should be introduced, on both the procurement and distribution sides, with the arrival of the new crop. The Administration, particularly in districts, should be trained and informed of its duties well in advance of this.

In West Bengal, the Government will have to provide for the collection of grain, not only at the purchasing centre but also in the village. This implies, at the executive level, more careful and detailed check against abuse.

The monopoly implies a fixed guaranteed price. Steps will have to be taken to ensure that while the producer receives this, he does not get a higher price. This means the elimination of competition between agents.

The Government must appoint as agents, if it continues to use these, the best people available and merit must be the sole criterion for determining appointment.

The monopoly should be established in all areas, surplus and deficit.

Illicit Movement

The rationed area of Calcutta might itself be divided into belts, movement from one belt to another being prohibited. More careful cordoning should be done in regard to such movements from the deficit districts of Hooghly and Howrah into the rationed area of Calcutta.

Requisitioning

Before harvesting an exhaustive list of all producers with an estimate of their production should be made.

Actual disposal of the surplus by each producer should be watched.

Administration

Food and Civil Supplies controls should be administered by the same department, under the same Minister.

In districts procurement and distribution should be under the same officer, who should be assisted suitably by staff to make it possible for him to perform these functions.

The district should be the unit of organization and the Collector should be in charge and responsible for procurement and distribution work.

The Food Administration should endeavour to retain personnel with experience of food work and not surrender trained employees to other branches of the Government. Recruitment of personnel for new posts should be done strictly on merit.

ASSAM

Monopoly Procurement With Defined Exemptions

The Monopoly Procurement System should be established in Assam.

With the start of the 1951 crop, full monopoly, on both the purchase and distribution sides, should be introduced.

Procurement; Movement Control

A complete ban should be imposed on movements from surplus areas to places outside them.

Movement from surplus to deficit areas or between surplus areas or between deficit areas should be banned absolutely, and the many exemptions, at present a feature of the Assam Administration, should be eliminated.

Procurement Centres

The setting up of an adequate number of procurement centres is, in our opinion, a fundamental pre-condition to any scheme of procurement in Assam. The general rule should be that there are enough procurement centres to ensure that a villager does not have to travel, however remote his village, a distance of more than 10 miles to bring his grain to the Government. In heavily surplus areas, or areas where there is danger of smuggling or of movement to a deficit district, the number should be larger.

Government Monopoly

Transactions of five maunds and below may be permitted between producers and consumers direct. It should also be permitted, for a licensee under the Foodgrains Control Order, to buy up to five maunds in a single transaction and thereafter sell in retail to consumers, provided the total quantity he stores at any one time does not exceed a prescribed limit, of, say, 25 maunds.

All other transactions should be under Government monopoly.

Finance

The scheme must provide, and this should be rigidly enforced, that payments are made to the miller or the procurement agent within three days of the offer of grain by him, even if the grain has not been despatched.

Inspection for quality should be done at the spot though there may be a system of superinspection, in order to keep a check on abuse.

The Government must have the finance to be able to pay immediately for all grain offered to it.

Requisitioning

Produce hoarding is one of the main problems in Assam. In order to combat this, requisitioning from producers must be accepted as part of normal policy.

Checks

A proper system of checks on millers and procurement agents buying for the Government should be introduced and enforced.

Distribution

Open markets in rationed towns should be closed immediately so as to derive the maximum benefit, in procurement operations, from the fact of rationing.

In hill areas, where the Government has to provide regularly help in food, distribution should be put on a systematic basis.

Immediate arrangements should be made to put distribution to tea estate labour on a satisfactory basis.

Administration

The district should be the unit of administration and the Deputy Commissioner should be in charge of operations, both on the procurement and distribution sides.

He should be assisted, in each district, by a District Food and Civil Supplies Officer.

Help From The Centre—Finance

The provision of adequate funds to make immediate payment for procurement is basic to the whole scheme and we recommend that the Central Government should recognize that it must provide funds to the Assam Government.

ORISSA

The procurement zones should be clearly demarcated and only one agent, or at the most two, should be appointed for each zone.

The number of centres for the procurement should be increased, so that purchasing depots are brought within five or six miles of every cultivator.

District bans on movement should be imposed so that procurement may not be evaded by transfer and concealment of stocks.

MYSORE

No change is required in the principles of the Mysore system, nor in the organization. In the circumstances of the State the use of a levy is necessary.

Procurement should be more strictly enforced, in all its details, particularly of millets.

In statutorily rationed towns, the scale of rations should immediately be raised to 12 oz. per adult per day, with the incidental increases involved for children and heavy manual workers.

The exemption limit, permitting two seers into rationed towns, for personal consumption, should be stopped simultaneously with action at (2) and measures to prevent illicit imports into rationed areas should be tightened up.

In informally rationed areas, the actual ration given should, on no account, be less than 8 oz. An attempt should be made to improve on this figure as procurement becomes effective.

The present system of subsidizing internal procurement is suicidal, in the long run, and cannot be justified except on grounds of sheer inertia.

UNITED STATES OF TRAVANCORE-COCHIN

The deficit of the area as a whole is so large, even if we take as its basis the average imports prior to 1941, that no system other than one of intensive procurement can possibly solve the twin problem of prices and supplies.

In regard to Cochin, the existing system is satisfactory and no changes are necessary.

In regard to Travancore, the registers maintained in Cochin should be introduced for the purpose of checking and cross-checking the production, surpluses, demands and purchases.

Two prices should be fixed, one for local grain and the other for imported grain, local production being reserved as far as possible for the areas in which it is procured.

Wholesalers should be abolished and all food work should be done by the Government, with Government finance, as in the case of Cochin. The question of retailers should also be examined and their number, which is excessive, may be reduced if possible.

MADRAS

The intensive procurement system together with universal rationing should be reimposed in all areas of the State. This recommendation involves introduction of statutory rationing in the surplus Northern districts and the giving up of the levy system in Coimbatore.

In the case of millets the exemption granted to holders of five acres or less should be removed and precisely the same system introduced as that in force for rice.

The Intensive Procurement System would be quantitatively more successful if village-to-village bans were imposed.

The Monopoly System cannot be introduced in the heavily deficit Malabar District, where Intensive Procurement and informal rationing must continue in full.

THE WORKING PARTY FOR THE COTTON TEXTILE INDUSTRY, 1950—REPORT

Delhi, Manager of Publications, 1953. 613p.

Chairman : Shri A. Ramaswami Mudaliar.
Members : Shri T. Sivasankar; Shri Radha Kamal Mukherji; Shri Raja Kulkarni; Shri D. P. Joshi; Shri S. R. Vasavada; Shri Gautam Sarabhai; Shri P. H. Bhutta.
Secretary : Shri M. S. Ramnath.

APPOINTMENT

The Working Party for the Cotton Textile Industry was constituted under the Ministry of Industry and Supply vide their Notification No. 1 (4)/WOP (1), dated March 31, 1950.

TERMS OF REFERENCE

To examine and make recommendations on:

(a) Measures necessary to achieve increase of production in the industry;

(b) Measures for reducing cost of production;

(c) Measures for improving quality of production;

(d) Measures to improve the efficiency of labour management and organization of the industry as a whole;

(e) Measures to achieve rationalization of the industry; and

(f) Measures for better marketing of the products of the industry at home and abroad.

CONTENTS

Introduction; Historical Development; Recent Developments in the Industry; Measures Necessary for Increased Production; Reduction of Costs; Indigenous Textile Machinery; Rationalization of the Industry; Rehabilitation of the Industry; Supervision and Efficiency of Technical Labour; Industrial Relations; Target for Production; Marketing Methods; The Technical Sub-Committee and Its Report; Postscript; Summary of Conclusions and Recommendations; Conclusions; Annexure A to D; Explananatory Notes.

RECOMMENDATIONS

The fact has to be emphasized that while protection to the Indian Textile Industry was largely based on the ground that raw material was available in abundance within the country and that the Industry was helping the agriculturists to find a market for such raw material, the situation is tending to take a reverse turn and requires careful watching.

Our examination of the present state of the Industry has unfortunately revealed a new factor and a new development which has an important bearing on the healthy growth of the Industry and on its productivity. The fact cannot be denied that owing to the change of management in some cases to inexperienced hands, both production and quality have suffered.

While we are in sympathy with the general opinion expressed by the Textile Industry that it may be left free to cater to the needs of the consumer without the irksome intervention of the present control measures, we are equally clear that, unless the Industry as a whole is in a position to put its house in order and adopt measures which will expose erring members and mete out suitable punishment to such if necessary by claiming powers from the Government for such reform measures, it will be difficult to get out of the era of controls which many of them desire.

The Committee find it impossible to accept the suggestion that cotton cultivation should be encouraged even at the expense of foodstuffs—however well based on economic grounds—as the essential which will keep body and soul together, namely, foodstuffs, should be first made available from local sources, and dependence on imports of foodstuffs may lead to catastrophic results especially when owing to war or world crisis import is made impossible.

The real factor which militated against the larger growth of cotton is the fact that the cultivator could have better returns by growing cash crops other than cotton which, owing to their being exportable, commanded a higher international price, and therefore a higher internal price than cotton.

While giving credit to certain State Governments which have consistently and conscientiously encouraged the growth of more and better cotton it has to be stated that many of the State Governments have allowed the agriculturists to divert lands from both food production and cotton production to the growth of other cash crops like oilseeds and sugarcane in the belief that in their particular jurisdiction the peasants will be more prosperous.

We are constrained to state that some State Governments have taken a somewhat narrow and parochial view of the comparative prosperity thereby ensured to their own agriculturists without realizing the particular bearing which such an attitude has on the economy of the country as a whole and ultimately on the economy of the State itself and the population whose prosperity it wants to ensure.

We would, therefore, strongly recommend that a more consistent policy should be followed by State Governments without exception and that without interfering with the "Grow More Food" Campaign, priority should be given, at least with respect to areas where cotton was being grown a decade ago, to the growth of such cotton.

The suggestion that compulsory reduction of cash crops other than cotton should be resorted to in certain areas by State Governments does not appear to us to be so violently antagonistic to agriculturists' interests as to be discarded.

The Committee is convinced that the problem of purification of the varieties of cotton is as important as the growing of more cotton. It suggests that local Governments can and should, by enforcing more strictly the Cotton Ginning and Pressing Factories Act, by sealing off areas of particular varieties of cotton, and by distributing the necessary pure seeds to the cotton cultivator, gradually attain the position in their respective areas which a decade before they maintained, whereby the purity of the varieties will be unquestionable.

It is clear that strenuous efforts must be made to enlarge the area of cultivation where staple and long staple cotton can be grown and to give every facility to States where such areas existed to grow such varieties. These States, however, would need an assurance from the Centre that their requirements of food would be adequately met if it is found necessary by them to divert certain areas of low food production to the comparatively high yielding cotton production of the requisite staple and long staple kinds.

Now that artificial fertilizers of the requisite kind are being produced in the country, specifically at the Sindri factory, State Governments may, through their Agricultural Departments, induce cultivators, by granting subsidies at the initial stages to utilize such fertilizers and thereby enable them to produce more cotton from the same area.

The utilization of low-staple cotton (Bengal Desi) by spinning yarns of low counts which could be used mainly for durries should, in the opinion of the Committee, be encouraged as this will release the better varieties of cotton which are now used for the same purpose, for cloth production.

We feel that a watch should be kept over the export of comber waste and justification should be adduced by any mill which is unable to utilize it and desires to have it exported.

We see no objection to mills being permitted to use larger quantities of staple fibre and to import such fibre as a means of relieving the shortage in cotton supply, provided it is made perfectly evident to the consumer that the cloth produced is of staple fibre.

The evidence and report of the Technical Sub-Committee reveals that, in quite a number of mills, there is constant change over from one pattern of production to another at somewhat short intervals.

A large number of mills producing a large variety of cloth and constantly changing the types of production has certainly been a source of diminishing the quantity, and in fact putting on the market types of cloth which are often unwanted.

The present system of distribution involving the nominees of the Government taking the cloth wanted and unwanted together and trying to recoup their loss on the unwanted by larger margins on the wanted has made it easy for some mills to go in for this variegated system of production.

Some of the mills at least have gone in for types of cloth which they know may not be easily consumed partly because they have no responsibility for its distribution and ultimate sale and partly because the margin of profit thereon was better than on other qualities.

We feel in the light of what we have seen regarding the production programme of various mills and the complaints about the nature and quality of cloth produced by mills that the recommendations made by the Textile Production (Control) Committee, 1948, regarding the regulation of mill production may now be implemented by the Governments, particularly as they have had the full support of the industry's representatives on the Committee.

We feel that the lead and whatever measure of control is necessary regarding the regulation of mill output may preferably come from the Industry itself; that millowners' organizations are best calculated to check the tendency to produce unwanted cloth or cloth of inferior quality by some of the mills; and that provided millowners' organizations can exercise the power to take punitive measures on erring mills, the disease may, to a certain extent, be checked.

While we recognize that, normally speaking, third-shift work may not be quite desirable, we feel that a certain fluidity should prevail in the discretion which both the management and labour have in regard to the application of the third shift.

We are unable to commend the suggestion that mills which produced quantities of yarn or cloth above a prescribed target by special inducements to workers or by improved efficient methods may be permitted to export 50% of such surplus production. We feel that there are a number of mills in the country which do not require such a temptation for expanding their production and we believe that we shall be guilty of giving the wrong kind of encouragement for increased production by adopting the method that has been suggested.

It has to be conceded that in many cases it is not the agriculturists so much as the middlemen into whose hands the production of cotton passes at a very early stage, who may be hit by the system of bulk purchase. Where, however, Co-operative Marketing Societies exist, the agriculturist may be in a better position to obtain fair prices. Even so, unless these Societies are organized on a much wider scale, the agriculturist may not get a fair deal.

It is clear that, on the basis of bulk purchase, either all mills should contribute the finance according to their requirements for a period, or a central fund should be created which will allow individual mills to take their stocks as and when necessary and pay for them according to consumption.

The finance involved in bulk purchase of locally produced cotton is so large that it is not always possible to depend upon banks for key loan advances; nor is the present position of the banks, having regard to the instructions received by them from time to time from the Reserve Bank, calculated to facilitate such a course.

Having regard to these conflicting views, the Committee has come to the conclusion that it cannot recommend the system of bulk purchase by an individual on behalf of the entire body of mills, or by a Committee of the millowners at the present stage, but it nevertheless feels that there are obvious advantages in such a system of bulk purchase of foreign cotton and would commend the idea to the mills in the hope that, if not for the entire body of mills which require foreign cotton, at least for a group of mills in common, an agency can be voluntarily designed and a common purchase on behalf of these mills can be effected.

No exception has been taken to the system of bulk purchase of foreign cotton where the transaction was between Government and Government and the Committee recommends that such a system should continue.

Having given due consideration to all factors, the Committee feels that if the mills can take the responsibility for the bulk purchase of mill stores through an organization of their own associations, facility should be given to them to do so; the present state of controls over imports necessarily means that licences for import of these mill stores should be granted to the organization which mills may establish for the purpose, and we recommend both to the Government and to the Industry that these steps may be adopted.

The Committee agrees with the need for encouraging these industries (Mill Stores) and helping them to be firmly established and feels that the one method by which it can be done is to make it obligatory on the mills to purchase their requirements in the non-excepted categories from local producers.

The quality of the production of local Mill Stores has to be kept at a high level and in fact continuously improved upon if the indigenous manufacturer desires to retain his market and expects governmental assistance in this behalf.

There is too often a tendency, particularly in recent years, for quality to deteriorate and for manufacturers to produce articles which are cheap, especially when an embargo is placed on the import of such articles, and the consumer is obliged to buy locally produced materials.

While we strongly recommend that protection should be afforded to these industries (Mill Stores) by virtual compulsory purchases from local manufacturers, we feel that there is a clear need for a constant inspection of the goods so produced and for the quality being approved by some agency set up either by the Government or by the Mill Industry itself.

We feel that the problem of co-operative fire and other miscellaneous insurance may not prove so intractable of solution now as before, and we recommend that the millowners regionally may take up the question of co-operative insurance against fire and other risks and so bring about a reduction in the cost of their overheads.

The Committee is bound to record that the Industry as a whole has shown great uneasinses in regard to the compulsory utilization of either the ring frames or the looms which are of indigenous manufacture.

We would emphasize that, in the manufacture of capital goods, a higher degree of technical efficiency has to be guaranteed and that the Industry should not be averse to utilizing the experience of foreign experts in the initial stages of production.

We also feel that, apart from the level of protection that may be granted, it should be obligatory to have a proper system of inspection of the machinery produced locally, particularly when the Government has decided that every purchaser should purchase a certain ratio of his requirements from the local producer.

We recommend, especially as the Textile Machinery Manufacturing Industry is willing to accept the proposal, that in consultation with the Textile Industry and the Textile Machinery Manufacturing Industry, a competent and adequate system of inspectorate should be organized by the Government and that such an Inspectorate should be authorized to certify the quality of the products of the Industry.

Our reaction to the recent Notification issued by the Government announcing their policy for import of textile machinery in the period January-June, 1952, after a study of the psychology of the millowners, is that it may lead to further postponement of the process of rehabilitation and renovation by mills generally which we have emphasized is the crying need of the Industry at present.

We hope that by the constant guidance of the Tariff Commission, the capital goods industry, which we wish to see encouraged and strengthened, will play its proper part in furnishing to the country the right type of capital goods which can bear comparison in quality with any of the imported goods.

The disparity in workloads obtaining in mills with similar working conditions led the Committee to the view that it was essential that some sort of scientific workload should be ascertained and that it would promote healthier relations between workers and management if such scientific workloads were accepted by both managements and labour unions.

We suggest that the highest priority should be given to the question of the scientific assessment of workload for the Industry as a whole and its application with proper modifications according to the circumstances existing in each individual mill.

We recommend that a panel of names of experts approved both by management and labour unions should be set up for the purpose of assessing the workload in the Industry region-wise. In the first place, a small body of men amongst them—not more than five—should be commissioned to undertake the work of determining normal workloads in a region, having regard to the conditions prevailing in a sample of mills (which may form a cross-section of the industrial units in the region, ranging from the best organized to those that are sub-normal in their set-up) and to the provision for healthy conditions of work.

This normal workload will, we hope, be accepted by both millowners and labour unions except in the case of any individual unit where either the management or the labour union considers that the normal workload is not fair and that it should be modified in the light of the existing conditions.

In this event, an Ad Hoc Committee of experts, membership of which will be drawn from the agreed panel, will examine the specific conditions in the mill concerned and lay down what modifications should be made to the general recommendations of the Expert Committee which has suggested the normal workloads for the region.

In the opinion of the Committee, this is the essence of the whole problem of establishing and improving the efficiency of labour and management and of organizing the Industry as a whole on a more satisfactory basis.

It is obvious that rationalization of the Industry in itself will be facilitated if the preliminary question of establishing normal workloads and of individual workloads in the case of certain mills were resolved satisfactorily.

The problem of rationalization has to be looked at not merely from the point of view of whether a slight reduction in costs will be possible on such rationalization, but also from a much wider angle.

The fact that the Textile Industry which a decade back had sought protection against foreign competition is now in a position to meet such foreign competition in outside countries, and in fact to compete so effectively as to capture markets which were hitherto held by foreign competitors, is significant and is a healthy development which must be safeguarded.

The Committee wishes to point out that, in the distribution of the gains of rationalization, some more definite and precise method should be adopted than that suggested, of giving first preference to the raising of the standard of wages to a living wage. On the whole, it seems to the Committee that a fair allocation would be to divide equally between the management and the worker the gains so realized from rationalization.

It is well known that during the War years, particularly from 1943 onwards, the Industry had earned profits very much in excess of those that were earned in the previous decade.

Few managements have had any doubt that the cost of replacement of such machinery would be very much higher than the original cost at which depreciation had been allowed, and while it is true that the Government did not relieve from the incidence of Income-tax any larger amounts set aside for depreciation, it was nevertheless open for a prudent management to reserve greater amounts even after incurring the incidence of Income-tax as depreciation or reserves.

It is beyond the capacity of the Industry taken as a whole to replace or rehabilitate the existing machinery even over a period of 10 or 15 years without some sort of financial assistance.

In spite of the Government's warnings, it is regrettable to note that in many of the units of the Textile Industry, profits have not been conserved for the future benefit of the Industry, and large dividends have been declared during these years of abnormal profits.

The Committee generally feels that, while it entirely agrees that proper funds should be allotted for depreciation and reserve and while it deprecates the frittering away of unexpected profits by the distribution of large dividends, a statutory provision for limitation of dividends in any industry will have an unhealthy and detrimental effect not merely on the industry concerned but on the flow of capital to industries generally.

Some of the members of the Committee feel inclined to accept the proposition as fair that the capital employed in the Industry should be calculated as "paid-up" capital plus 50% of reserves, and that dividends should be calculated on this basis.

Where the resources have been transferred into bonus shares for the original shareholders, we feel that the bonus shares should rank equally with the original paid-up capital for the purpose of calculating the capital employed in the Industry.

The Managing Agents should have no direct financial interest in the sale of the products or purchase of articles for the mills, and other agencies unconnected with the Managing Agencies should be set up if it is necessary to have such an organization for this purpose.

The Committee recommends that a company should, out of the profits, first set apart the depreciation fund according to Income-tax regulations; next give 10% or 12½% commission out of the balance to the Managing Agents; then an amount which will give 6% dividend on the "paid-up" capital as interpreted in Para. 91 to the shareholders; and out of the balance remaining, allocate equal amounts for distribution to workers, for reserves, for rehabilitation, and for additional dividends to shareholders.

The Committee is of the opinion that the money to be found for replacement and renovation of the machinery employed in the Industry can only be found by a loan being granted by the Government and not by any outright grant either through a surcharge or otherwise. The Committee strongly recommends that such a loan for purposes of rehabilitation should carry a low rate of interest not exceeding 4%.

The Committee emphasizes the need for rehabilitation of the Industry over a period of 10 to 15 years and for making available such amount as is required for this purpose by the Industry by way of loan.

The problem of re-building old mill structures presents a greater difficulty, but the Committee is quite certain that this difficulty ought to be faced, and that the State Governments concerned should require the units which are badly housed to make suitable alterations and modifications to their structures.

The Supervisory Staff has devolved on it now a special responsibility—a responsibility not merely of checking the work of the workers and seeing that they discharge their duties properly, but even more, or trying to make new relationship with the workers which will take into account the human factor connected with the conditions of work both in the mill and even more outside the mill.

A management which treats its labour properly and establishes human contacts with individual workers as far as possible commands from these workers a loyalty to the unit at least as great as the loyalty to the trade union concerned. It must therefore be the attempt of every enlightened management to secure this loyalty which is not incompatible with and certainly does not militate against the loyalty of the worker to his trade union.

The need of securing supervisors of the right type, able to understand the human element in the treatment of the workers, technically well qualified, capable of leadership both on the technical and on the personnel side, is so obvious that it is regrettable that many managements have not appreciated this fact.

We are inclined to believe that of one the main serious drawbacks in the Industry which militates against the interests of the workers and the management, which jeopardizes production in the mill, and which sometimes leads to serious consequences of strikes and lockouts, is the management's treatment of the supervisory staff.

We recommend that it being of the utmost importance to the Industry both from the point of view of production and from the point of view of labour relationship which assists such production that a properly trained and well-qualified supervisory staff should be employed by each industrial unit and that their tenure of service should be secured; that their emoluments should be at a reasonably high level; and that managements should not take advantage of the fact that at the present time trained technicians are available in sufficient numbers.

If the morale of the worker has to be maintained by the technician or supervisor, the morale of the technical or supervisory staff in turn has to be maintained, and only the management can secure such morale on the part of the supervisory staff.

While we do not express any opinion on the desirability or otherwise of trade union rights and of the privileges that follow from membership of trade unions being granted to technical and supervisory staff, we are convinced that the treatment of technicians and supervisory staff in many of the textile units deserves to be placed on a better basis not merely because of the importance of the supervisory staff in the Industry, but even more because such conditions go to the very root of healthy industrial relations and result in proper productivity in the unit concerned.

We recommend the suggestion that in those textile colleges where technicians are trained, the subject of a proper human relationship to the worker, the social side of the activities of the technicians may also be studied, and a course of studies prescribed so composed as to give an opportunity to the student to acquire at least a primary and preliminary knowledge of these matters and of how these relations can be properly adjusted.

The examination of these problems and the issues connected with them lead us to conclude that there should be a chain of proper understanding between the management, the supervisory staff and the worker. To the extent that the hands of the supervisor are strengthened by the management; to the extent that there is perfect understanding between the management and the supervisor; and to the extent that there is devolution of responsibility on the supervisor for certain aspects of work and of the prospects of the worker, to that extent will an integrated scheme of human relationship be successful.

In fact the supervisor should be taken into the confidence of the management to a very large extent if the administrative machinery is to work smoothly from top to bottom and the loyalty of the worker and the supervisor is to be supreme to the unit concerned.

Both State Governments and Managements of mills should seriously consider the setting up of institutions where the apprentice-workers can be properly trained. It is a process that is not elaborate, what is required essentially being machinery which will enable them to get such training, and we commend the suggestion that such training centres should be established at least in the big centres of the Textile Industry.

Apart from the preparatory training which a worker should get before he is introduced into a mill, there is also the need for continual post-employment training of workers in the Industry.

Post-employment training of workers is, in any event, and not merely in connection with novel machinery, a desirable thing, and we trust that both Governments and Managements will bestow their proper attention on this problem and afford facilities for such training.

We recognize that a strict legal code cannot be established for resolving all the disputes that are often referred to Industrial Tribunals, and that to a certain extent these Industrial Tribunals are not completely judicial bodies having a law to administer and having the main responsibility of establishing facts. Nevertheless owing to the far-reaching effects of these decisions, including those of Appellate Tribunals, we feel that some sort of governing principles or directives may be laid down which will enable both Industrial Tribunals and Appellate Tribunals to give decisions with less risk of dissatisfaction to either of the parties concerned.

We recommend that any tripartite or other agreements arrived at between labour and management should be circulated to Industrial Tribunals and Appellate Tribunals, and that these Tribunals may take note of these agreements in giving their decisions. If such agreements were to be multiplied and if they could be referred as guiding principles to Industrial

Tribunals, the chances of minimizing references to such Tribunals will be better and in any case decisions will be more acceptable to the parties concerned.

Apart from this, it may be possible for the Central Government to lay down certain directive principles with reference to some at least of the numerous matters that come up for disposal before the Industrial Tribunals, which do not necessarily involve a study of the question of wages or a claim for bonus or anything incidental thereto.

It seems to us that the Planning Commission's estimated figure of production in 1955-56 is to some extent an underestimate, and that it can confidently be expected that with better conditions of availability of cotton, more regular working of mills and such improvements in the plant and machinery as may be effected—apart from the new installations which are coming into production—this estimate may be revised to at least 5,000 million yards of cloth.

The question of what the per-capita consumption within the next five years should be must be viewed not merely from the angle of the rate of production possible with improved machinery and better relations of labour and more enlightened management. The question is also associated with the standard of living of the people and the purchasing power of the consumer.

We believe that the expansion of the Industry will take place without special encouragement if capital is available and if entrepreneurs are not afraid of investing such capital in new ventures.

The reform measures suggested by the Technical Sub-Committee of mills producing fewer varieties, over continuous periods, of good-quality cloth suited to the needs of the consumers may bring down the price of cloth and may incidentally increase the production and determine more effectively the per-capita consumption of cloth by the year 1955-56.

If co-operative societies run on proper lines with adequate financial resources and with enthusiastic directors can take up the distribution of cloth, it would no doubt be a healthy check on the abuses by others more indisciplined.

At a time when no controls are necessary it seems to us that the distributory system will resume its normal state and the only precaution that the State has to take in the interest of the ultimate consumer is to check the possibility of too many intermediate agencies intervening between the mill and the last retailer.

The Committee trusts that more mills will copy the example followed by some who have organized a system of inspectorate and ensure that the prices quoted by the mill for the retail shop are adhered to by the retail seller on pain of termination of the agency, and that the distributory system will be so arranged as to guarantee that the ultimate consumer is not exploited.

It is essential for the good name of the country and for maintaining continuously the export markets abroad that some measures have to be adopted either by the Government or by the Industry to control the quality of goods exported.

In the case of textiles, it is suggested that the necessary inspectorate should be set up by the Textiles Fund Committee: in case any exporter is found seriously to deviate from the sample in accordance with which he has contracted to supply goods and defaults in a considerable measure not on one occasion but on more than one occasion, the recommendation of the inspecting authority should be that the Government should deprive him of the licence to export cloth.

We recommend that this agency for inspecting export cloth should be started as soon as possible, and hope that the Industry will co-operate with the Government in carrying out this very necessary reform if the already shrinking export market for Indian goods is to be maintained.

While the recommendation made by the Technical Sub-Committee that there should be roughly a dozen textile centres distributed evenly over the whole continent may be theoretically a most desirable thing, we feel that it is not a practical measure capable of adoption.

In accepting the recommendation of the Technical Sub-Committee regarding the desirability of replacing the existing wage schedules by a scientific wage structure "where the wage will be a function of the workload, skill and hazard, where the duties will be clearly defined and where the provisions for incentives by the operative will lead them to put forth greater efforts, leading to higher efficiencies and higher production", we interpret it to mean:

(a) The existing average work load should be linked to the existing standardized wage in each centre; and

(b) If after scientific study, it is determined that the standard workload for a normal worker under specified working conditions can be higher than the average existing workload referred to in (a) above, the workload may be increased, provided there is no unemployment and provided the gains of rationalization are shared with the worker and his earnings are progressively raised towards a living wage: the wage structure to be evolved after the introduction of rationalization, linking the higher workloads with higher earnings, should be based on principles enunciated in para. 5, page 29 of the Sub-Committee's report, which has been quoted above.

We are unable to agree with the Technical Sub-

Committee that all female workers should be retired and that only male workers should be employed in the mills.

In the opinion of the Committee, the Indian Cotton Textile Industry must come into line with the Industry in other countries in regard to the quality of cloth and the price at which it should be sold, and this can only be done by a prompt re-adjustment in which the Committee hope both labour and enlightened management will co-operate fully.

CACHAR PLANTATION ENQUIRY COMMITTEE, 1950—REPORT

Delhi, Manager of Publications. 1952. 164p.

Chairman : Shri S. K. Sinha.

Members Representing Employers : Shri A. H. Galloway; Shri Baidyanath Mukherjee (resigned, replaced by Shri P. C. Chatterjee).

Members Representing Workers : Shri Paresh Chandra Chaudhury; Shri Suresh Chandra Deb.

Representing the Govt. of Assam : Shri H. P. Duara

Tea Expert: Shri P. M. Glover.

Secretary : Shri R. R. Bhatnagar.

APPOINTMENT

The Cachar Plantation Enquiry Committee was constituted under the Ministry of Labour on April 4, 1950.

TERMS OF REFERENCE

(i) To enquire into the cost structure and financial conditions of the tea gardens in the Cachar District of Assam;

(ii) To enquire into the causes of the present uneconomic working of certain gardens;

(iii) To make recommendations regarding the measures required to place uneconomic gardens on a sound basis;

(iv) To report in particular (a) whether the concessional supply of foodgrains to labour should be discontinued in any estate; and, if so, in what circumstances and to what extent, and (b) what arrangements should be made for the supply of foodgrains to workers on these estates.

CONTENTS

Introductory; Technical Problems and Their Remedies; The Financial Condition of the Cachar Gardens, Reasons for Uneconomic Working and Recommendations for Improvement; List of Appendices; Summary of Recommendations.

RECOMMENDATIONS

A study of the cost structure discloses that in an industry like Tea Plantation, which is more of the nature of agriculture than industry, the present cost in labour is not high; in fact the wages are too low and require early revision to enable the workers to get a "fair wage".

An inspectorate should be set up immediately to report on how far and how effectively the Tea Estates in Cachar are carrying out the policy outlined in the recommendations of the expert, if the industry in Cachar is to be saved. No reliance can be placed on Visiting Agents as the system which has been in force for many years has failed to serve any useful purpose.

Finance is the most baffling question. We recommend creation of a fund from Excise and Export Duties, collected from the manufacture and export of tea, and issue of long-term loans to the derelict Estates, especially to the Indian-owned Estates, subject to expert assessment of properties and control and guidance of the Inspectorate.

Managing Agency System should be abolished and till this is done the expenditure should be curtailed to the minimum.

Recruitment to the managerial cadres should be under a definite policy of selecting better educated Managers who should not only be able to do this job of better planting but should be able to deal with the human material under them with better understanding. A progressive policy of Indianization is strongly advocated.

In clerical and supervisory cadres, recruitment should be through an Employment Board set up by the Industry and if the Industry does not agree, the Government of India should take up the matter and regulate through the Employment Exchange. The scope for promotion to managerial cadres should be there to create an incentive for better work.

Pay-scales of Sirdars and Jamadars should be revised and a policy of recruiting in these posts qualified, intelligent persons with drive, experience and integrity should be adopted, with scope for promotion.

To create interest in the workers they must be paid a fair wage. Side by side with the appeal to produce more and produce quality, there should be a clear-cut employment policy, suitable provision for old age, suitable guarantee against sickness and loss of earning therefrom, suitable scope for the education of children, suitable living conditions, paid leave and introduction of the system of sharing in profits. Labourers now know what will happen to them if adversity overtakes the Industry but are debarred from sharing in its prosperity.

A scheme for training workers, especially the Sirdars, Tilla Babus and Factory Babus, should be introduced. They should have the rudiments of the science of Tea Planting and Manufacture to be a bulwark against apathy and incompetence of planters. For this purpose opening of a Training Centre in Cachar along with a Branch of Tocklai Institute is recommended.

We visualize a shrinkage in the employment of labour. To arrest increase in unemployment and stop wastage of man-power, a policy of giving the adolescent opportunity of picking up different trades and professions by working in the factory workshop should be introduced so that there may be an incentive for surplus population to migrate elsewhere from the Estates for livelihood. Surplus labour may also be profitably employed for growing food in garden waste land.

Workers should be made to retire on attainment of certain age by giving pension as there is no Provident Fund now. Provident Fund Benefit should be introduced without further delay.

We are on principle in favour of Cash Conversion of the concessional foodstuff. The amount of payment in lieu of ration should be determined by the Provincial Wage Committee and introduction of the Cash Conversion should synchronize with the enforcement of payment of minimum wage.

Co-operatives should be started in every garden with a Central Trading Society to import goods from outside the State. Till this is done, the Industry should continue the present arrangement of procurement and sale of commodities.

MOTOR VEHICLE TAXATION ENQUIRY COMMITTEE, 1950—REPORT

New Delhi, Ministry of Transport, 1950. 244p., xp.

Chairman : Shri M. N. Dalal.
Members : Shri G. M. McKelvie; Shri N. C. Ghosh; Shri T. S. Krishna; Shri K. R. P. Aiyangar; Shri A. A. Brown.
Secretaries: Shri C. S. Anantapadmanabhan; Shri C. S. Nair.

APPOINTMENT

The Motor Vehicle Taxation Enquiry Committee was constituted under the Ministry of Transport vide their Resolution No. 30-T(14)/49 dated April 20, 1950.

TERMS OF REFERENCE

(i) Survey the existing systems of taxation of motor vehicle users in India; and

(ii) Recommend:

(a) The basis of a scientific system of taxation of the motor vehicle users to ensure the provision and development of cheap, rapid, and efficient transport for different categories of users by the means best suited for the kind of traffic involved and with a view to obtaining proper co-ordination between the different forms of inland transport;

(b) The method of securing reciprocity in taxation between the various taxing authorities; and

(c) The principles nn which any part of the proceeds of the taxation of motor vehicle users by the Union and State Governments and Local Authorities should be made available for road maintenance and development.

CONTENTS

Introductory; A Survey of the Existing Taxes Paid by the Motor Vehicle User in India; Inland Transport Co-ordination and Regulation; Other Cognate Matters; The Present Position In Respect to Road Maintenance and Development In India; Taxation of Motor Transport In Foreign Countries; Recommendations: Inland Transport Policy; Recommendations: Motor Vehicle

Taxation; Summary of the Committee's Conclusions and Recommendations; Appendices I to XX.

RECOMMENDATIONS

A scientific system of taxation of the motor vehicle user cannot be evolved unless the Union and State Governments accept a common transport policy. The transport policy recommended for acceptance is generally that recommended by the United Nations.

The motor vehicle user as a general tax-payer should contribute to General Revenues only to the same extent as does the railway user; and

The taxation policies of the Union and States should be so adjusted that the motor vehicle user as such is not called upon to pay the expense of implementing any extraneous Union or State policy (Defence, Welfare, Prohibition, etc.), nor to pay for the establishment of a motor vehicle manufacturing industry in India.

The balance of the proceeds of taxes on the motor vehicle user after deducting the contributions to General Revenues should be earmarked for expenditure on roads; and

These proceeds should be paid into non-lapsing road funds.

The aim should be to have complete reciprocity between States in the matter of permission to operate motor vehicles.

More liberal issue of permits for inter-regional traffic is desirable and also closer liaison between the Transport Authorities of adjoining States.

Any review of the acts and orders of Transport Authorities with respect to their legality, regularity, or propriety should be carried out by a judicial authority and the State Government should not issue any orders with respect thereto without the concurrence of the judicial authority.

State Governments should give increased attention to the development of motor transport in the interior of their States by giving tax concessions to operators and priority to bridge construction, etc., on selected routes.

Minimum fares and freights for transport services need not be fixed at present.

Scope should be allowed deliberately and as a matter of policy to private enterprise to develop new routes.

The discretion of Transport Authorities in the matter of giving permits to commercial vehicles should not be interfered with by State Governments. This applies particularly to the question of giving licences to single-vehicle owners as the Transport Authorities are under a statutory obligation to associate remunerative and unremunerative bus services.

State Governments should study the procedure adopted in the United Kingdom and arrange for a more expeditious method of collecting taxes from the motor vehicle user. The Central Government should assist by permitting selected post offices to collect these taxes (as in the United Kingdom) or the State Governments should permit their taxing authorities to accept "crossed" Postal Orders.

The States should, where necessary, increase the number and quantity of their motor vehicles inspecting staff and raise the fees charged for this purpose where necessary.

The question of maintenance of transport statistics and submission of returns should be studied by the Transport Advisory Council.

The restrictions on the carriage of goods by road imposed by the Code of Principles and Practice should not be enforced during the next three years.

Transport Authorities should grant private carrier permits freely as provided by Section 53 of the Motor Vehicles Act of 1939.

A Tribunal should be established with all-India jurisdiction to deal with complaints against State Undertakings.

The Motor Vehicles Act should be amended in respect of Sections 47 and 55 to provide when granting permits for consideration of the adequacy of other transport services of whatever kind operating or likely to operate in the near future.

The tariff policy of the Central Government should take into account the effect very high duties on transport have on agricultural and industrial development.

Motor vehicles used for commercial purposes should not be regarded as luxuries for purposes of taxation. The tariffs should be brought down at least to the pre-1950 level.

Subsidies should be given to assist in the development of the motor vehicle manufacturing industry in India. These are better than Protective Tariffs.

Fuel for diesel-engined motor vehicles should continue to receive preferential treatment.

Cultivators' carts should not be separately taxed but a "road cess" of one anna in the rupee on land revenue should be imposed for road-use and available.

Carts plying for hire and reward in and near towns should be reasonably taxed.

The use of rubber tyred carts plying in and near towns should be encouraged.

Local bodies should not be permitted to tax motor vehicles.

The losses incurred on any form of transport-communications maintained for purposes of Defence or National Welfare should not throw any additional charge on transport users as such but should be borne by the general tax-payer.

Co-ordination of inland transport under present

conditions in India should be achieved by methods other than the giving of artificial support to alternative forms of transport. The controlled elimination of obsolete and obsolescent forms of transport would be in keeping with a dynamic policy as opposed to a static policy that would aim merely at maintaining the *status quo* in spite of modern technical developments.

The road engineers of the Centre and States should discuss in conference the question of limitation of vehicle weights.

The principles advocated in the "Nagpur Plan" as applicable to Road Maintenance and Development should be accepted and applied by the Union and State Governments.

The Union and State Governments should consider raising loans to fund their Road Development Programmes.

Legislation should be enacted in India on the broad lines of the American Federal Aid Road Acts or similar Acts in Australia embodying the principles listed in Para 72.

An "Associated Council" of the Transport Advisory Council should be created to make known the views of the users of motor vehicle transport.

The Railways should not add to their route mileage by constructing uneconomic lines (except for purposes of Defence) or restoring such lines dismantled during the last war. Many short-distance feeder and link railway lines that are not paying their way should be dismantled.

The statutory obligations imposed on the Railways with respect to the carriage of goods should be "eased" to permit them to refuse to carry "short-distance smalls" in certain cases.

No new State Transport Undertakings should be set up nor should the existing undertakings be further developed until the State concerned is satisfied that it is in a position to provide better road transport services than those provided by private operators. The proof that theservice is "better" to be ascertained by comparing with competitive private services operatting on the same routes or on comparable routes in the neighbourhood.

The States should not attempt any large-scale development of the road-haulage business until State passenger transport undertakings have established their efficiency.

Until road communications in India are better developed than at present no change should be made in the present duties of Customs and Excise on motor spirit.

An amount representing 4½ annas of these duties should be credited to the States Road Funds to "make" on a three-quarters basis the proceeds of the States' fuel tax credited to those funds.

The duties of Customs and Excise on motor vehicles, tyres, parts, and accessories should remain at the level they stood before March 1, 1950, but should higher duties have to be imposed for any reason, the differences between these higher duties and the duties at the 1950 rates should be credited to the Central Road Fund.

The Centre besides matching the States' fuel tax should support liberally plans for road development.

The Centre should also levy a "transport cess" of 1½ annas a gallon on motor spirit in addition to the existing duties of Customs and Excise on this commodity. The proceeds of this cess should be used to pay the cost of distributing motor spirit by rail so that its selling price will be sensibly the same throughout India.

The duties on diesel oil and other fuels should remain as at present but a countervailing tax should be imposed on diesel-engined motor vehicles.

Only two taxes on the motor vehicle user should be levied by the States, the States' Fuel Tax and the States' Motor Vehicle Tax. All other taxes on transport including Sales Tax on transport including Sales Tax on fuel and taxes on the carriage of passengers or goods by road should be abolished as also all "Entrance Fees", Octrois, and all local taxes on motor transport or on passengers or goods in transit.

The proposed taxes are NOT to be regarded as additional taxes but as substitutes for existing taxes. The tax recommendations made by the Committee follow logically from the acceptance of the Transport Policy outlined in Paras 112 to 121 and no tax that is not in accordance with this policy should be levied.

The States' Fuel Tax should be fixed at present at six annas a gallon on motor spirit.

This tax should be collected by the Centre as a surcharge on the Central duty on motor spirit and credited ultimately to the various States' Road Funds (to be created). In the agreement that authorizes the Centre to collect this surcharge, it is to be made quite clear the monies collected are State monies.

The Sales Tax on motor vehicles and accessories to remain but the rate should be the same as for other non-luxury goods.

The only tolls that should remain are those levied at ferries (ferry charges), the rates being so adjusted that the ferries yield no net profit, and tolls levied at new bridges when the toll proceeds are used to redeem loans taken for constructing the bridges, the tolls being abolished as soon as the loans are paid off.

Assistance is to be given to local bodies when this is justified.

Fees should be so adjusted as to cover the cost of services rendered; fees should not be allowed to grow into taxes.

The States' Motor Vehicle Tax should ultimately

be the same in all States and should conform for the present to the Schedule laid down in Table 22. The proceeds should be paid into the States' Road Funds (to be created).

The Central and State Governments should regard themselves as partners in all Road Transport Undertakings as they supply the roads, the main capital asset of these undertakings. It is in the interests of these Governments to supply good roads and, for this reason, the main yield of the taxes on the motor vehicle user should be regarded as a road rent.

The general tax-payer must also contribute to the upkeep of roads paying for the "community use" of roads.

There should be no "double taxation" on motor vehicles, even if the taxes in all States are not the same, but uniform taxes are recommended.

Taxation measures should not deny the country the benefits of technical progress.

The proceeds of the modified taxes recommended by the Committee should all be credited into non-lapsing road funds as should also the States' contribution from General Revenues for "community use" of roads. Capital grants should also be non-lapsing.

The taxation principles recommended for adoption by the Committee should be embodied in the All-India Motor Vehicles Taxation Act parallel to the Motor Vehicles Act of 1939 vide item 35 of List III (the Concurrent List) of the Seventh Schedule of the Constitution of India.

COMMITTEE TO EXAMINE THE SYSTEM OF LAND TENURE IN PEPSU, 1950 – REPORT ON AGRARIAN REFORMS IN PEPSU

New Delhi, Ministry of States, 1952. 86p.

Chairman : Shri C. S. Venkatachar.
Members : Shri J. M. Shrinagesh; Sardar Tarlok Singh.
Secretary : Sardar Rajbir Singh Kang.

APPOINTMENT

The Committee to Examine the System of Land Tenure in PEPSU was constituted under the Ministry of States vide their Resolution No. F. 53 (39)—P/49 dated May 11, 1950.

TERMS OF REFERENCE

(i) To examine the existing tenancy relationships (other than the rights of occupancy) in land in the Patiala and East Punjab States Union and to propose such changes in them as may be necessary;

(ii) To examine the existing system of land tenure in the Patiala and East Punjab States Union; and

(iii) To propose such changes in it as may be necessary keeping in view the requirements of the agricultural economy and the welfare of different sections of the rural population.

CONTENTS

Introduction; Tenancy Problems in PEPSU; Occupancy Tenants; Special Tenures; Rights of Superior Landlords; Tenants-at-will; Reorganization of the Rural Economy; Summary of Recommendations and Conclusion; Acknowledgments; Appendices.

RECOMMENDATIONS

Evacuee Lands

In respect of tenancy reforms evacuee lands should continue to be treated as a category apart from other lands until allottees obtain full ownership. There are, however, certain exceptions to this rule.

Occupancy Tenants

The present legislation regarding occupancy tenants should be reviewed. The abolition of landlord rights in those cases in which the status of occupancy tenants is accepted should be made easier. On the other hand, occupancy tenants who claim to be proprietors of their holdings should be afforded one more opportunity of establishing their rights. While it is important to provide a reasonable solution for the problem of occupancy tenants in the former Patiala State, it is also extremely important to enforce and implement the decisions in a sustained and effective manner without further room for doubt and questioning and without fear or favour. To this end, it is recommended that:

(i) The benefits of the Biswedari abolition legislation should be extended to those occupancy tenants who held these rights on March 11, 1940, and were dispossessed for non-payment of amounts decreed against them;

(ii) Instead of the option to acquire proprietary rights being left to occupancy tenants and the possibility of physical partition of a holding, the legislation should provide for the vesting of proprietary rights in occupancy tenants and extinction of the rights of landlords holding no occupancy tenants without a suitable procedure for the payment of compensation;

(iii) The amount of compensation due to a landlord should not include arrears of rent due to him. As regards buildings, Kacha farm houses should not be considered for compensation. Compensation to the landlord for Banjar and Ghair Mumkin land should be reduced from the present level of 50 times and 25 times respectively of the land revenue assessable on the lowest Barani class in the estate on the landlord's share to 25 and 5 times.

(iv) Compensation to the landlord should be payable in four six-monthly instalments spread over a period of two years, but the Collector may allow the occupancy tenant to pay the compensation in six-monthly instalments over a period which may extend to six years; and

(v) A Special Tribunal presided over by a Judge of the High Court and consisting of two other members, one of whom may be a Judicial Officer and the other a senior Revenue Officer, should be set up. The Tribunal should be authorized to receive and decide finally upon applications for the recognition of the status of proprietary rights from occupancy tenants whose cases have been in dispute in any Civil or Revenue Court since March 11, 1940. The Tribunal should, however, have the power, if it deems fit, to entertain an application in a case which has not been the subject in dispute during the prescribed period.

Special Tenures

(i) Proprietary rights should be conferred by the Government of the Patiala and East Punjab States Union, without payment of compensation, upon the special tenants of the former Faridkot State who held land in which the ruler of Faridkot State was shown as both superior and inferior landlord. This measure may be taken with effect from July 1, 1952;

(ii) Rights of occupancy conferred by the Government of the Patiala and East Punjab States Union by Notification No. 8-B of April 28, 1951, on special tenants of the former Faridkot State should also devolve on holders of special tenancies in land in which the ruler of Faridkot held the rights of an inferior landlord and which had been granted to him as the personal property by the Government of India.

Rights Of Superior Landlords

The rights of superior owners should be abolished on payment of compensation amounting to eight times the amount of rent or other dues, if any, payable to the superior owner.

Tenants-at-Will

(i) 100 acres should be fixed as the limit of the area which an individual may reserve for personal cultivation. Detailed suggestions on the administration of the proposal are made;

(ii) The period of tenancy for all tenants-at-will should be five years. This will be subject to the right of a land-owner to resume the land, after giving due notice, for personal cultivation. In the case of those owners who hold more than 100 acres of land, only 100 acres could be resumed for personal cultivation. This recommendation should apply to evacuee lands;

(iii) Tenants-at-will who have continued to hold land in an estate under the same landlord from a date prior to May 1, 1940, should be declared as "Protected Tenants". Protected Tenants should have the right, within a period of three years, to purchase land cultivated by them in the preceding agricultural year. They should be given financial assistance to purchase their tenancies. Where the purchase price is fixed by a Revenue Court, the latter may allow payments up to a maximum of 12 six-monthly instalments extending over a period of six years. The Protected Tenants' option to purchase his holding will be subject to the right of the land-owner to reserve or secure the permissible area for personal cultivation;

(iv) Legislation should provide for the grant of adequate compensation for improvements effected by tenants. One-third of the produce of land held in a tenancy of the value thereof should be regarded as the maximum rent which may be recovered from the tenant. This maximum limit of rent should apply uniformly to all tenancies, whether below or in excess of the limit prescribed for personal cultivation. This recommendation will also apply to evacuee lands.

Reorganization Of The Rural Economy

(i) The alienation of agricultural land for agricultural purposes in favour of non-cultivation should be restricted by legislation;

(ii) The Committee favours, in principle, the imposition of a ceiling on existing agricultural holdings, but recommends that such a ceiling should be a part of a comprehensive programme of reorganization of the rural economy. The Committee proposes that steps should be taken to reorganize the agricultural economy on the basis of a system of co-operative village management over a period of five to 10 years. With the institution of co-operative village management ownership in excess of the prescribed limit is to be extinguished and only such ownership is recognized for purposes of the grant of ownership dividend as falls within the limit. The Committee suggests a limit of 100 acres or 50 "standard" acres, and proposes that if the majority of owners and permanent tenants holding more than one-half of the land of the village (subject in each case to the ceiling) are in favour of co-operative management of the land of a village, the Government should take steps to provide the necessary measures of assistance to establish the new system;

(iii) A limit of 100 acres is also proposed as the ceiling for future acquisition of land;

(iv) To provide for certain well-developed farms of substantial size belonging to individual owners which need to be kept intact in the general interest of agricultural development, it is proposed that such farms should be maintained by their owners on special conditions to be prescribed by the Government and later they may be acquired and turned into State farms.

THE AGRARIAN REFORMS COMMISSION, SAURASHTRA, 1950—REPORT

New Delhi, Ministry of States, 1950. 121p.

Chairman : Shri J. A. Madan.
Members : Shri D. V. Rege; Shri R. S. Mane Patil.
Secretary : Shri R. K. Joshi.

APPOINTMENT

The Agrarian Reforms Commission, Saurashtra, was constituted under the Ministry of States vide their Resolution No. F.1 (28)-P/50, dated May 13, 1950.

TERMS OF REFERENCE

To examine and report on:

(i) The history and the present position of the relations between landholders and their tenants in non-Khalsa areas (Note: the word landholder would include, *inter alia*, a Zamindar, Jagirdar, Garasdar, Talukdar, Bhayat, Bhagdar, Peta Bhagdar, Mulgirasia, Barkhalidar, Inamdar and Jiwaidar);

(ii) The state of land revenue administration including survey, settlement and maintenance of village records in the non-Khalsa areas of Saurashtra;

(iii) The existing tenancy legislation regulating the relations between landholders and tenants, the mode of realization of rent, the status of the tenant and the security of the tenure and quantum of Gharkhed, if any, to be given to the landholder;

(iv) The need and the desirability of determining in the light of present-day conditions and the requirements of modern administration and, in particular, the need for improving agrarian conditions, the respective shares of the State, the landholders and the cultivators in the produce and the assets of the holding;

(v) The desirability of extinguishing differences between the Khalsa and non-Khalsa areas so that a uniform land revenue and land tenure system is established throughout Saurashtra, the manner in which this should be brought about and the administrative organization and legislation necessary therefor;

(vi) The steps to be taken to improve the economic condition of the smaller landholders and tenants, having regard to the effects of Tenancy and Agrarian Reforms on them; and

(vii) Any other constituent and/or cognate matters which the Commission may consider as arising out of the foregoing Terms of Reference.

CONTENTS

Introduction; Historical Background; Origin of States and Estates; Garasdars and other Grantees; Land Tenure and Revenue Administration; Agricultural Lands and Tenancy Legislation; Agrarian Reforms; Small Landholders and Tenants; Summary of Recommendations; Appendices I to VIII.

RECOMMENDATIONS

Garasdari and Barkhali systems should be immediately abolished.

For the purpose of compensation for their agricultural land, Garasdars should be divided into three classes:

(a) Those having one or more villages or more than 800 acres;

(b) Those having between 80 and 800 acres;

(c) Those having up to and including 80 acres.

Class (a) should be paid six times cash assessment in lump sum or two annual instalments by their present tenants plus cash assessment annually for 12 years by the Government.

Class (b) should be paid six times cash assessment as in the case of Class (a) plus cash assessment annually for 15 years by the Government.

Class (c) should be paid six times cash assessment as in the case of Classes (a) and (b) plus cash assessment annually for 18 years by the Government.

The amount of compensation should not be liable

to deduction of 12½% as assessment to the Government. The Government should guarantee payment of compensation by the tenants as the non-Gharkhed lands will immediately vest in it as soon as the necessary legislation is passed and it will recover the amount from the tenants who will become occupants of the Government without being required to pay any price for occupancy rights. The Government should also bear interest at 3% on the deferred instalments of compensation payable by it.

Compensation amount should be proportionately reduced in the case of those holdings in the produce or assets of which Garasdars have limited rights.

Compensation for non-agricultural lands, assets and dues should be paid to Garasdars.

All cesses, haks, taxes, etc., payable to Garasdars should be abolished forthwith without any compensation.

All Garasdars will retain as Gharkhed whatever land they have in their actual cultivation at present. They should have a right to resume land from their tenants who have been continuously on land for less than six years ending on January 1, 1951, except those who have acquired Chau or Buta Haks. Garasdars of Classes (a) and (b) should be allowed to resume excess land over an economic holding from their protected tenants up to three times the size of an economic holding including their Gharkhed, if any, and the land resumed from their unprotected tenants.

Garasdars of Class (c) should be allowed to resume land from their protected tenants which, together with their own Gharkhed, if any, and the land resumed from non-protected tenants, will give them an economic holding. Garasdars of this class who own less than an economic holding should not be allowed to resume land from any of their tenants. The total number of evictions would be about 4,800, which gives an average of less than three evictions per alienated village.

Evictions of tenants by Garasdars between August 15, 1947, and the passing of the Saurashtra Protection of Tenants Ordinance No. XXII of 1948 should be ignored in computing the six-year period.

If there is any cultivable waste land in the village, Garasdars of Class (c) should have first preference to it for making their holdings economic.

If land which is resumed from tenants for Gharkhed is not cultivated personally within one year of resumption by the Garasdar, it should revert to the tenants concerned. No evictions should take place without reasonable notice and while making evictions, if there is a choice between two or more tenants, those who are on the land for a lesser period should be displaced first.

Until precise economic holdings are determined under the Prevention of Fragmentation and Consolidation of Holdings legislation which the Government has under contemplation, the acreages given in Para 130 of economic holdings in various parts of Saurashtra should be taken as a guide.

Garasdars will continue to pay four annas as assessment per acre of Gharkhed during the period of compensation at the end of which they will have to pay full assessment. If the land is sold to a non-Garasdar in the meantime, it will lose the character of Gharkhed.

Talukdars, who have not entered into agreements for privy purse, may still be given an option, to be exercised within a month from the date of intimation, either to convert the Zamindari agreement into a cash hereditary allowance payable by the Government of Saurashtra or to abide by the decision that may eventually be reached on allotment of Gharkhed, compensation and ancillary matters. The cash hereditary allowance should be fixed on the average income of the last 15 years.

Quasi-Mulgarasias and Maiyas should be treated for reservation and allottment of Gharkhed in the same manner as the Garasdars. As the Maiyas have commuted the assessment payable by them by relinquishing a part of their land, they should not be required to pay any assessment on their lands in future unless they wish to become occupancy tenants.

Barkhalidars have no proprietary rights in the lands granted to them and their grants were always resumable. Their grants must, therefore, revert to the State without compensation; but to enable these grantees to adjust themselves to the changed circumstances, we recommend payment of a rehabilitation grant.

Inamdars and Jiwaidars who hold one or more villages should get the rehabilitation grant in the shape of assessment from the Government annually for nine years, while the remaining Inamdars and Jiwaidars should get it for 12 years.

In the case of Hathgarna Jiwai grants, the daughters should get the assessment for their life-time. If a male Jiwaidar dies within the above period, the assessment would be payable to his widow if she is left in indigent circumstances.

Inamdars and Jiwaidars who already possess Gharkhed should be allowed to retain it on payment of assessment at four annas per acre during the period they receive rehabilitation grant, after which they will pay full assessment. If, in the meantime, the land is transferred, it will be fully assessed.

Many of the institutions receiving Dharmada grants have small incomes and are situated in villages. Their management should be handed over to the Gram Panchayat, if any, or to the Village Panch to which the Government should pay an amount equal to the income derived at present from their grants.

For institutions having a large income or situated in towns, a statutory Religious and Charitable Endowments Board should be set up. The lands held by these institutions will vest in the Government and the tenants will become occupants of the Government.

In the case of Dharmada grants to individuals, if they are cultivating land personally, they should become occupants of their holdings without payment of occupancy price. If these lands are in the possession of tenants they will become occupants and the Government will pay the grantees assessment for six years annually as a rehabilitation grant.

Service tenure holders may be allowed to retain the land, if cultivated by them, free of assessment as long as their services are required. If they are not cultivating the land, they should be paid in cash and their tenants treated as occupants of the Government.

Crop share system should be abolished once for all.

The present method of computing cash assessment in non-Khalsa areas by taking the average of the assessments in the adjoining Khalsa villages, though not quite scientific, appears to us to be fair.

A Settlement Commissioner and Director of Land Records should be appointed to be in general charge of assessing compensation and rehabilitation grants. Actual assessment work will be done by Special Officers of the grade of Mamlatdars who should be appointed for one or more talukas as may be necessary. Appeals against their orders will lie to the Deputy Collectors of the sub-divisions. Revision against the appellate orders will lie to the Settlement Commissioner whose decision will be final. Preparation of land records will have to be done simultaneously with the assessment of compensation and rehabilitation grants by the Special Officers with the assistance of the local officials of the Revenue Department.

There should be a Settlement Officer of the Collector's grade under the Settlement Commissioner for survey and settlement work. The settlement of the whole State should be completed as soon as possible, but as the necessary personnel will not be easily available, we think that this will take about 10 years. Compensation and rehabilitation grants will be paid according to the present rates of assessment until the revised rates come into force.

The Gharkhed Ordinance (XLI of 1949) should be repealed when the new legislation incorporating the final decisions on our various proposals comes into force. A new tenancy legislation, largely based on the Bombay model, would also be necessary. The Act should provide for sub-letting only in the cases of disability, viz., minors, widows and other disabled persons. Transfer of land should be absolutely banned if this reduces the area left with the transferring tenant below an economic holding, unless he wants to sell his entire land.

While assuming management of landholder's estate during the interim period, it should be seen that the requirements of Section 35 of the Gharkhed Ordinance are fully satisfied.

The Government should, out of its General Revenues, meet the development charges of such alienated villages as go in for Village Panchayat until the entire revenues of these villages become available.

In the allotment of cultivable waste land to small landholders and tenants, no assessment should be charged for the first three years. Fragment holders should be encouraged to form co-operative joint farming societies.

Small fragment-holders should be settled on lands which are being reclaimed.

It is essential to provide against fragmentation of holdings, which is one of the principal banes of agriculture in this country.

Effective steps should be taken to prevent soil deterioration resulting from erosion.

Forest areas should not be allowed to be denuded for temporary gains. Pasture lands should not be allowed to be indiscriminately turned into farm lands.

Debt conciliation and regulation of money-lenders on the lines recommended by the Gadgil Committee and supported by the Congress Agrarian Reforms Committee should be adopted in Saurashtra.

Early steps should be taken to organize financing agencies like banking unions, district banks or an apex bank to finance co-operative credit societies.

There should be a network of co-operative credit societies, and non-credit activities should also be organized on a co-operative basis. For training staff as well as members of societies and for doing propaganda work, the Government help would be necessary in the initial stages.

A Land Mortgage Bank should be established for supplying long-term credit not only for repayment of debts but also for the purchase and improvement of lands and betterment of cultivation.

Cottage and small-scale industries should be established in villages so as to give the smaller landholders and tenants alternative or supplementary employment.

There should be a non-official organization to help the Committee and the Industries Department for starting such industries.

As Garasdars have generally an aptitude for service in the Police Department or in the Defence Forces, they may be given preference for recruitment in these services.

SUGAR ENQUIRY COMMITTEE ON THE SUGAR CRISIS OF JULY-AUGUST, 1949, 1950—REPORT

Delhi, Manager of Publications, 1951. 88p., iiip.

One-Man Committee : Shri Ganga Nath.

APPOINTMENT

The Sugar Enquiry Committee on the Sugar Crisis of July-August, 1949, was constituted under the Ministry of Food & Agriculture vide their Resolution No. SV-101 (4-15)/50 dated June 12, 1950.

TERMS OF REFERENCE

The Government of India in their Resolution No. 33 (1)-T.B./50, dated March 6, 1950, issued by the Ministry of Commerce on the report of the Tariff Board on the Sugar Industry had stated *inter alia* that the question whether any further enquiry into the Sugar Crisis of July-August, 1949, was necessary and if so what its scope should be was engaging their attention and a decision thereon would be taken shortly. The Government have now completed their examination of the Tariff Board Report and having regard to the assurance given to Parliament that an enquiry will be made about such aspects of the Sugar Crisis as were not fully covered by the Tariff Board, they have decided that the enquiry should be held into the following matters of which Items 1 and 2 were recommended by the Tariff Board themselves for further investigation:

(i) The suggestion that the wagon supply to sugar factories for movement of sugar during the season 1948-49 was excessive.

(ii) The allegation that sugar intended for consumption in India was in fact moved into Pakistan on an appreciable scale during 1949.

(iii) The allegation that several factories despatched sugar in breach of the Freezing Order of the U.P. Government on August 26, 1949, and of the Central Government on September 2, 1949.

(iv) The allegation that many factories or their sales agents charged heavy premia over the fixed price during July-August, 1949.

(v) The circumstances under which the proposal for export of the 50,000 tons of sugar was made in May-June, 1949, by spokesmen of the Industry and the circumstances under which the proposal was dropped.

(vi) The allegation that substantial stocks of sugar were moved out by the factories to their own godowns before the crisis, that large stocks were moved by the factories and trade from the Bihar Factories during the interval between the U.P. and the Central Government's Freezing Orders and that in July-August, 1949, considerable movement of sugar by factories and trade took place in various directions to facilitate the sale at exorbitant prices of sugar purchased at high premia.

(vii) Any other matter which may be germane to or incidental to any one or more of the afore-stated matters or to any finding of the Tariff Board on the Sugar Crisis.

CONTENTS

Introductory; The suggestion that wagon supply to the sugar factories for movement of sugar during 1948-49 was excessive; The allegation that sugar intended for consumption in India was in fact moved to Pakistan on an appreciable scale; The allegation that several factories despatched sugar in breach of the Freezing Order of the U.P. Government on August 26, 1949, and of the Central Government on September 2, 1949; The allegation that many factories or their sales agents charged heavy premia over the fixed price during July-August, 1949; The circumstances under which the proposal for export of 50,000 tons of sugar was made in May-June, 1949, by spokesmen of the Industry and the circumstances under which the proposal was dropped; The allegation that substantial stocks of sugar were moved out by the factories to their own godowns before the crisis, that large stocks were moved by the factories and trade from the Bihar factories during the interval between the U.P. and the Central Government's Freezing Orders and that in July-August, 1949, considerable movement of sugar by factories and trade took place in various directions to facilitate the sale at exorbitant prices of sugar purchased at high premia (The allegation that substantial stocks of sugar were moved out by the factories to their own godowns before the crisis; Movement of sugar by factories and trade from Bihar factories during the interval of the Freezing Orders of the U.P. Government and the Central Government); Any other matter which may be germane to or incidental to any one or more of the afore-stated matters or any finding of the Tariff Board on the Sugar Crisis; and Tables.

RECOMMENDATIONS

The main causes of the Sugar Crisis of 1949 in the opinion of the Committee as also of the Tariff Board were the uncontrolled and accelerated releases from the factories by the Indian Sugar Syndicate and the decision taken towards the end of June, 1949, to facilitate the export of a substantial quantity of sugar. Both these factors had a marked bullish effect on the sugar markets. The situation was fully exploited by the Industry and the trade to their advantage. Consequently, a feeling of scarcity was created in the latter half of 1949 leading to high prices of sugar. Unless releases from factories are regulated and properly controlled, or, alternatively, sufficient stocks are at the disposal of the State, there will inevitably be a tendency towards hoarding and profiteering in a commodity like sugar in the later part of the season.

IMPORT CONTROL ENQUIRY COMMITTEE, 1950—REPORT

Delhi, Manager of Publications, 1950. 130p. Charts.

Chairman : Shri G. L. Mehta.
Member : Shri Tulsidas Kilachand.
Secretary : Shri D. L. Mazumdar.

APPOINTMENT

The Import Control Enquiry Committee was constituted under the Ministry of Commerce vide their Resolution No. 1 (26)-I.T.C./50 dated July 3, 1950.

TERMS OF REFERENCE

(i) To enquire into the working of Import Control with reference to:

(a) The procedure followed in the fixation of import quotas for individual commodities;

(b) The procedure and methods followed in dealing with applications for import licences;

(c) The organization of the existing machinery for Import Control;

(d) Any other matter incidental to the working of the Import Control Organization; and

(ii) To make recommendations on the above subjects with a view to improving the efficiency of the Import Control Organization in such a way that applications for licences may be promptly dealt with and disposed of and the complaints against its present working may be removed.

CONTENTS

Introductory; Import Trade Control Policy in India —A Historical Review (Section A: Genesis of Import Trade Control; Section B: Growth and Development of Import Policy); Import Control Policy (Section A: Objectives and Principles; Section B: The Foreign Exchange Budget); Problems of Import Licensing (Section A: Priorities in Import Control; Section B: Licensing Policy); Problems of Organization and Administration (Section A: Organization of Licensing Work; Section B: Administrative Procedure—Handling and Disposal of Applications); Miscellaneous Recommendations; Conclusion; Summary of Findings and Recommendations; Appendix A to E.

RECOMMENDATIONS

The basic objectives of the Import Control Policy in this country should be:

(a) To limit the aggregate imports, on Government or Commercial account, to the total available foreign exchange earnings from different sources, including sterling releases;

(b) To distribute the available foreign exchange resources in the most equitable manner among the commodities required for:

(i) The planned development of agriculture and industry; and

(ii) The essential requirements of consumers;

(c) Consistently with the above, to moderate the fluctuations in the prices of particular commodities, where they may have abruptly risen much above the parity of the general level of prices on account of shortages resulting from deficiencies in supply or other causes.

Our Trade Commissioners and Consular Agents should be trained and equipped to make an intelligent forecast of the trends in the principal Indian exports to foreign countries concerned.

The Reserve Bank of India should undertake a systematic study of the modern technique of foreign trade forecasting and adapt it to the requirements of this country.

The Government must do all that they can to increase our invisible earnings of foreign exchange by encouraging the use of the services of:

(a) Indian shipping in our import and export trade;

(b) Indian banking for the transport and financing of our trade; and

(c) Indian insurance in underwriting the risks of our foreign trade.

While a case for protection is pending examination with the Tariff Board, there should not be any sudden change in the Import Policy concerning that commodity without consultation with the Tariff Board.

The working of the current O.G.L.'s should be reviewed immediately in consultation with the trade interests concerned, the Import Trade Controllers and the Collectors of Customs at the three main ports before our recommendation about their indefinite continuance is given effect to.

In future licensing should be only in respect of the two currency blocs, viz., hard and soft currency countries; while the conversion of the latter into the former will be permissible only according to the general licensing policy in regard to hard currency areas that may be adopted as a result of recent Commonwealth Ministers' Conference. In special cases applications for the conversion of soft currency licences into hard currency ones may be considered on merits.

We recommend a liberal extension of the facilities regarding the issue of bulk licences. In the case of those organized industries which are under the control and supervision of well-established and effective Associations, licences should be issued to the Associations in preference to individual firms.

A Standing Inter-Ministry Committee for Capital Goods and Heavy Electrical Plant licensing should be constituted for a period of one year at a time. The scope of the Capital Goods and Heavy Electrical Plant schemes should be limited to new projects.

In addition to the transfer of the bulk of licensing work to the Ports, we recommend that the procedure for the issue of licences to established importers should be simplified so as to render it as automatic as possible.

The revalidation of Capital Goods and Heavy Electrical Plant licences already issued should be granted within a week and that the Import Trade Controllers should be authorized to grant revalidation.

There should be provision in the licensing procedure for the issue of Emergency Licences.

The Import Trade Controllers at the Ports should be authorized to issue such licences up to Rs. 50,000 under any one serial of the ITC Schedule. Applications for Emergency Licences for higher amounts should be submitted to the Chief Controller of Imports.

The present procedure for the grant of Customs Clearance Permits for the import of personal baggage should be revised on the lines indicated by us in the Report.

The Indian Trade Commissioners in foreign countries should be kept regularly informed of the changes in licensing instructions or procedure so that they may be in a position to advise foreign suppliers in good time.

COMMITTEE OF INQUIRY (RELATING TO CIVILIAN EMPLOYEES UNDER THE MINISTRY OF DEFENCE), 1950—REPORT

Delhi, Manager of Publications, 1952. 331p.+vp.

Chairman : Shri F. N. Kalyanvala (died).
Members : Shri B. B. Ghosh; Shri K. N. Subramanian.
Secretary : Shri B. Vasudeva Rao.

APPOINTMENT

The Committee of Inquiry (Relating to Civilian Employees under the Ministry of Defence) was constituted under the Ministry of Defence vide their Resolution No. 19-E dated September 15, 1950.

TERMS OF REFERENCE

(i) To examine whether the report, generally known as the Shahaney Report, on the basis of which the present pay scales in the Ordnance Factories have been fixed provides a satisfactory basis for the implementation of the Pay Commission's recommendations regarding pay scales, having regard to the nature of the work to be performed in the Ordnance Factories.

(ii) To examine and make suggestions regarding the rectification of any anomalies in pay scales existing in the present orders applying the revised scales of pay to Defence installations.

(iii) In the light of the Pay Commission's recommendations on the subject, to examine whether conditions in any Defence installation are so special as to justify the grant of a Conveyance Allowance to any class of personnel employed therein.

(iv) To examine whether service conditions regarding permanency of industrial and non-industrial employees in Defence installations need any alteration.

In their letter No. 15 (56) 50/12446/D-11, dated October 30, 1950, addressed to the General Secretary, All India Ordnance Employees' Federation, Calcutta, the Ministry of Defence stated that overtime pay and gratuity and/or pension could be additional subjects for examination by the Committee.

In another letter No. 15 (56) 50/12848/D-11, dated December 6, 1950, the Ministry of Defence stated that the question of piece-work rates might also be examined by the Committee.

Further, in their letter No. 15 (51) 50/1571/D-11, dated February 8, 1951, the following items were added to the Terms of Reference of the Committee of Inquiry:

(a) To examine and make recommendations regarding the leave rules of industrial employees serving in the Defence Establishments, including all kinds of leave.

(b) To examine and make recommendations regarding the scale of contribution by the Government to the Provident Fund of the employees serving in Defence Establishments, where a Provident Fund Scheme exists.

As the exact scope of the examination of the subjects of overtime pay, gratuity and/or pension was not clear, the Ministry of Defence elucidated the position in their letter No. 759/D-11, dated January 19, 1951, as follows:

Overtime Pay

The Committee may examine the eligibility of personnel, who are not at present allowed overtime pay, to such payment, if any representation is made to it. As the Committee is not expected to deal with the question of working hours, the intention was that while examining any question of overtime pay the Committee should start with the basic point that certain working hours are already prescribed.

Gratuity And/Or Pension

The point for consideration was how the period of extra temporary service of non-industrial employees (i. e., service prior to August 1, 1949) should be counted for purposes of gratuity for such personnel. Under the existing orders that service does not count at all. The Committee would examine this and make necessary recommendations. On the question of pension there was no special dispute but if the Committee should recommend permanency for industrial employees it would be within their scope of examination to consider whether the normal pension rules should be applied to such employees in lieu of the Contributory Provident Fund benefits which are, at present, admissible to them.

As regards the piece-work rates the Ministry of Defence in their letter No. 136-JS (P)/51, dated August 18, 1951, desired the Committee to advise on the following points:

(a) Whether the present methods of calculations of piece-work earnings of high-paid and low-paid piece-workers should be continued;

(b) Whether all piece-work rates for new jobs in future should be correlated to the new monthly scales in consonance with the principle that a piece-worker of average ability, working at standard speed, should earn 25% profit over time rates; if so, what should be the reference point in the monthly scales to which the piece-work should be correlated;

(c) Whether any revision of piece-work rates is necessary/desirable and, if so, in what manner should such piece-work rate revision be done; and

(d) Should there be a guarantee of the minimum wage to all piece-workers, even when there is no limitation against the ceiling earnings?

CONTENTS

Introductory; Term of Reference I (Pay Scales of Industrial Workers in Ordnance Factories; Mr. Ghosh's Recommendations; Mr. Subramanian's Recommendations); Term of Reference II (Anomalies in Pay Scales); Section I: Clerical and Allied Establishments (Head Clerks—Ordnance Factories; Head Clerks —M.G.O.'s Establishments; Charge Allowance—Supervisory Clerks; Mr. Ghosh's Recommendations; Mr. Subramanian's Recommendations); Senior Temporary Clerks—Ordnance Factories; Cashiers—Ordnance Factories; Cashiers—Ordnance Depots; Cashiers— Technical Development Establishments; Stenographers; Typists; Checkers—Ordnance Factories (Mr. Ghosh's Recommendations; Mr. Subramanian's Recommendations); Unified Scales—Cut in pay on account of supervisory element (Mr. Ghosh's Recommendations; Mr. Subramanian's Recommendations); Unified Scales—Application to Ordnance Factories (Mr. Ghosh's Recommendations; Mr. Subramanian's Recommendations); Unified Scales—Grading of 'B' grade clerks in the revised scale; Unified Scales—Fixation of Pay of 'C' grade clerks in the revised scale; Unified Scales—Fresh option to clerks of the regular establishment (Mr. Ghosh's Recommendations; Mr. Subramanian's Recommendations); Unified Scales—Extra element of pay sanctioned at Calcutta and Bombay; Unified Scales—Application of—to Timekeepers in Kirkee Ordnance Depot; Lower Division Clerks—Fixation of pay taking into account previous service rendered as daily rated Clerks, Godown Keepers, etc., in the Ordnance Factories; Lower Division Clerks—Fixation of pay taking into account previous service rendered as Leading Hands, etc., in the T.D.E. (Stores), Kanpur; Section II: Storekeeping Establishment—Godown Keepers, Leading Hand (Stores) and Supervisors (Stores)—Ordnance Factories and Depots (Mr. Ghosh's Recommendations; Mr Subramanian's Recommendations); Packers—M.G.O.'s

Establishments (Mr. Ghosh's Recommendations; Mr. Subramanian's Recommendations); Packers—Protection to demoted Packers in A.I.G.S., Bengal Area (Mr. Ghosh's Recommendations; Mr. Subramanian's Recommendations); Storekeeping Establishment—M.E.S. (Mr. Ghosh's Recommendations; Mr. Subramanian's Recommendations); Packers—Engineer Store Depot, Avadi; Storekeepers (E.T.E.)—E.M.E. Workshops (Mr. Ghosh's Recommendations; Mr. Subramanian's Recommendations); Loaders and Unloaders—Ordnance Depots; Supervisors (Non-technical)—Fixation of grade of—in Ordnance Depots; Section III: Supervisory Establishment (Technical)—Supervisors—Ordnance Factories (Mr. Ghosh's Recommendations; Mr. Subramanian's Recommendations); Supervisors— A.I.G.S., Bengal Area, and other T.D.E.s; Creation of Higher Grades of Supervisory Posts—E.M.E. Workshops; Supervisors (Grade III)—Abolition of Installations under M.G.O. (Mr. Ghosh's Recommendations; Mr. Subramanian's Recommendations); Supervisors—Retrospective effect of promotion to 'B' Grade in the case of Supervisors in Factories and T.D.E.s; Motor Transport Supervisors—Downgradation as Supervisors (Non-technical) in Depots; Supervisor (Chemists)—Ordnance Factories (Mr. Ghosh's Recommendations; Mr. Subramanian's Recommendations); Junior Scientific Assistants—T.D.E.s; Laboratory Attendants—T.D.E.s; Leading Hands (Technical)—M.G.O.'s Establishments (Mr. Ghosh's Recommendations; Mr. Subramanian's Recommendations); Inspectors—Creation of this category in E.M.E. Workshops (Mr. Ghosh's Recommendations; Mr. Subramanian's Recommendations); Superintendents B/R & E/M (Grade II)—Charge Allowance; Section IV: Draughtsmen and Tracers (Draughtsmen, Estimators, Rate-fixers and Planners—Ordnance Factories; Draughtsmen—T.D.E.s; Draughtsmen—M.E.S.; Tracers—Defence Establishments); Section V: Viewers—Viewers—T.D.E.s (Mr. Ghosh's Recommendations; Mr. Subramanian's Recommendations); Viewers—Fixation of pay in the revised scales on the basis of 26 times the daily rates instead of 24 times; Section VI: Other Non-Industrial Categories (Teachers—Schools attached to Ordnance Factories; Civilian Medical Officers—Non-Practising Allowance; Compounders—Defence Establishments; Nurses—Ordnance Factory Hospitals; Ayahs—Ordnance Factory Hospitals; Dhobis/Washermen—Defence Establishments; Sweepers—Retrospective effect of the revised scale from January 1, 1947; Motor Drivers—Defence Establishments; Armoured Fighting Vehicle Drivers—Ordnance Depots; Fire Patrolmen—Recategorization in Ordnance Depots; Fire Brigade Staff—Ordnance Factories; Photographers—T.D.E.s; Telephone Operators—Defence Establishments; Gatekeepers—Ordnance Factories; Subedar Durwans and Jamadar Durwans—Ordnance Factories); Section VII: Industrial Establishments—Engravers—T.D.E.s; Lappers—T.D.E.s (Mr. Ghosh's Recommendations; Mr. Subramanian's Recommendations); Shooters—T.D.E.s; Proof Firers—T.D.E.s; Book-binders, Compositors and Printers—Ordnance Depot Presses; Fitters—Reclassification as Fitter Mates in T.D.E.s; Fitter Mates—Defence Establishments; Instrument Mechanics & Tele-communication Mechanics—T.D.E.s; Turners and Grinders employed in Gauge Rooms—T.D.E.s; Tradesmen—Wage Structure in M.E.S.; Semi-skilled Tradesmen—M.E.S.; Tradesmen—Naval Dockyard, Bombay; Tradesmen—Naval Armament Depot, Waltair, Visakhapatnam; Tradesmen—Wage structure in D.O.S., D.M.E., D.T.D. and M.E.S. (Mr. Ghosh's Recommendations; Mr. Subramanian's Recommendations); Labourers engaged in lifting heavy loads—Defence Establishments (other than Ordnance Factories) (Mr. Ghosh's Recommendations; Mr. Subramanian's Recommendations); Beldars—M.E.S.; Section VIII: General Points—Loss of pay on promotion; Protection of pay last drawn in a post on re-promotion to the post in the case of Industrial Employees; All India Service Liability Allowance (Mr. Ghosh's Recommendations; Mr. Subramanian's Recommendations); Arrears under the revised pay rules to persons discharged in the year 1947 (Mr. Subramanian's Recommendations; Mr. Ghosh's Recommendations); Pay of Displaced Personnel (Mr. Subramanian's Recommendations; Mr. Ghosh's Recommendations); Continuity of Service on Transfer from E.T.E. to Regular Establishment; Classification of Employees as Industrial and Non-Industrial (Mr. Ghosh's Recommendations; Mr. Subramanian's Recommendations); Fixation of Pay in the Revised Scales on the basis of pay in the lower grades to which personnel were reverted subsequent to January 1, 1947; Method of converting daily rate of pay into monthly rate; Term of Reference III: Conveyance Allowance (Mr. Ghosh's Recommendations; Mr. Subramanian's Recommendations); Term of Reference IV: Permanency; Term of Reference V: Piece-work Rates (Mr. Ghosh's Recommendations; Mr. Subramanian's Recommendations); Term of Reference VI: Leave; Term of Reference VII: Government's Contribution to Provident Fund; Term of Reference VIII: Overtime Pay (Mr. Ghosh's Recommendations; Mr. Subramanian's Recommendations); Term of Reference IX: Gratuity (Mr. Ghosh's Recommendations; Mr. Subramanian's Recommendations); Acknowledgments; Appendices A to G.

RECOMMENDATIONS

Pay Of Industrial Workers In Ordnance Factories

Mr. Ghosh's Recommendations: There is no doubt whatsoever that for industrial workers the Pay Commission advocated short-time scales and a number of scales within one trade.

The Pay Commission did not consider it either necessary or desirable to classify or to re-classify trades into Skilled, Semi-Skilled, etc., with a view to applying the scales of pay recommended by them. Recognizing that one category merges into the other the Pay Commission recommended certain common scales for Skilled and Semi-Skilled Categories.

The classification of certain trades as "Skilled" without consideration of the different degrees of skill, etc., within one trade and the adoption of one long-time scale for all such trades would be not only not in accordance with the recommendations of the Pay Commission, but would be wholly unsuited to the Ordnance Factories.

For a production organization like the Ordnance Factories, men of varying degrees of skill, experience, etc., in the same trade are required and the payment of the same scale of pay to all would be unjustified and would take away all incentive for improving one's skill.

An additional reason for not adopting a long-time scale for any category in the Ordnance Factories is the incompatibility of a long-time scale with the system of piece-work.

The variations made by Mr. Shahaney from the scales suggested by the Pay Commission are on the whole beneficial to the workers.

Not only has Mr. Shahaney adopted a system of pay scales which is in accordance with the Pay Commission's Recommendations and suited to the requirements of the Ordnance Factories, he has framed his detailed proposals for the different trades with due care and keeping in view all the essential elements. Although he has tried to bring about uniformity out of diversity in the various factories, he has given due weight to past practice, to the extent necessary. He has taken every care to ensure that his gradation is correct and that it is such as should be acceptable to all concerned including the workers and the management. The gradation has received the general approval of the Superintendents of all the factories, and the labour representatives have not been able to establish and defect in this grading.

Mr. Shahaney does not claim to have followed an ideal or a prefect method of job evaluation based entirly on independent data and covering all trades and grades. Since this was neither necessary nor practicable, he adopted a simplified method designed to achieve the limited objective of bringing about uniformity between the different factories with the minimum of disturbance.

In the method of job evaluation followed by Mr. Shahaney, the maximum number of marks were allotted to the degree of skill and while therefore the final grading is very largely based on the degree o skill, it does not ignore other important factors. It must, therefore, be considered an improvement on a system of classification with reference to skill only.

The so-called downgradation of workers does not disclose any defect in the Shahaney Report. Such seeming downgradations are an inevitable consequence of a Rationalization Scheme. The perpetuation of the old classification which was not based on any scientific or uniform standard would have only perpetuated the old diversity and defeated the object of rationalization. The interests of workers have been sufficiently safeguarded by appropriate instructions that trade tests should be conducted on practical lines and that promotion to the old grade should be permitted irrespective of vacancy. The workers have also been assured of their old daily scale of pay.

From the views summarized above, it follows that in my opinion "the Shahaney Report, on the basis of which the present scales in the Ordnance Factories have been laid down, provides a satisfactory basis for the implementation of the Pay Commission's Recommendations regarding pay scales, having regard to the nature of the work to be performed in the Ordnance Factories".

While holding that the Shahaney Report as a whole is sound, I have suggested that the two scales of Rs. 35—45 and Rs. 36—50 for Semi-Skilled workers should be combined into one scale of Rs. 35—50. I have suggested this mainly for the sake of simplicity and for removing a grievance which can be removed without upsetting the pay scheme.

I consider that the other pay scales should remain as they are. In my view, they are better in some respects than the scales recommended by the Pay Commission. The existing pay scales fall into a pattern and I do not think it is possible to make any significant alteration to any of the scales without destroying the pattern.

I do not agree with the suggestion that all learners and mates should be given the scale of Rs. 40—60 and that the scale of Rs. 36—50 should apply mainly to those who are slightly above the Unskilled category. In my view, the normal scale for Learners and Semi-Skilled workers should be Rs. 35—50. The scale of Rs. 40—60 should apply to those who possess higher skill though not of the same degree as would enable them to pass the trade test prescribed for Fully Skilled tradesmen.

I suggest that those workers who, before the introduction of the new scales, were classified in a higher grade should be promoted to the corresponding higher grade with retrospective effect from the date of election of the new scales, if they pass the necessary trade test in one attempt within a period of six months. It follows that those (similarly downgraded men) who have already passed in the first attempt should be given retrospective effect to their promotion to the higher grade.

I do not recommend that interim relief should be considered as basic pay for the purpose of fixation of pay in the new scales under the Revision of Pay Rules. I consider that a special dispensation in this matter for Defence employees only is not feasible.

I recommend that the pay should be fixed in the final scales sanctioned on the basis of the Shahaney Report, in terms of the second option, under the Revision of Pay Rules and, for this purpose, the pre-prescribed pay should be taken as the daily rate appropriate to the date from which the new scales are elected and not the pay on the provisional monthly scales.

Mr. Subramanian's Recommendations: The Recommendations made by the Pay Commission in respect of the industrial staff in Ordnance Factories cannot be deemed to be anything more than a broad indication of the principles and of the level of salaries that must be taken into account in framing a wage structure.

The wage structure in ordnance factories under the daily-rated system was very defective.

The evolution of a new scale each for the Unskilled, Semi-Skilled and Skilled categories and the making of minor changes in the rates of increments in certain scales constituted the main difference between the Provisional Scales and the Shahaney Scales.

The main defects of the job evaluation done by Mr. Shahaney are :

(a) Secrecy of the Report;

(b) Absence of mention of job evaluation in the Report;

(c) Non-consultation with workers;

(d) Omission to carry out job analysis and description;

(e) Failure to take into account working conditions and hazards for purposes of job evaluation; and

(f) Assumption rather than ascertainment of differentials.

A system of short scales is preferable to a single long scale in ordnance factories.

The scale of Rs. 40-2-60 recommended by the Pay Commission as one of the scales for the Skilled Category is not for the full-fledged or truly Skilled Category but is for a category which is less than truly Skilled.

The lowest of the short scales prescribed for truly Skilled Tradesmen should start at a minimum of Rs. 60.

Three scales are recommended for the Skilled category, viz., Rs. 60-3-75, 75-3-90-5-105, and 105-5-130.

Trade tests should be prescribed both for entry into the Skilled category at the Rs. 60 level and for promotion to the higher scales.

A scale of Rs. 40-2-60 is recommended for Learners and Mates in trades classified as Skilled.

The scale of Rs. 35—45 for the Semi-Skilled category should be abolished.

Two scales, viz., Rs. 36-1-40-2-50 and Rs. 40-2-60, are recommended for the Semi-Skilled category.

Downgraded workers would be well advised to take tests as early as possible.

It is suggested that all downgraded persons who pass Trade Tests in the first attempt should be restored to the grades for which they have been tested from January 1, 1947, or other date of option.

"Interim Relief" should be treated as part and parcel of basic pay for the purpose of fixation of pay on the revised scales.

There are advantages in ensuring that for comparable trades and grades within each trade in factories and workshops under the more important Departments the same standard of trade test specifications is observed.

The multiple for the conversion of daily rates into monthly rates should be 26 and not 30.

The method of giving effect to the second option has been explained.

A Classification Tribunal should be set up, first for classifying all trades into the Highly Skilled, Skilled, Semi-Skilled and Unskilled categories, and then, if need be, for sub-dividing particular trades into Skilled I, Skilled II and Skilled III or Semi-Skilled I and Semi-Skilled II, according to requirements.

Recommendations regarding the classification of trades and the appropriate pay scales are given.

The Classification Tribunal should consist of three technical persons, of whom one should be nominated by the Federations acting jointly, another by the Director-General of Ordnance Factories and the third by the Defence Ministry. The last mentioned who should be appointed as Chairman should be an officer not under the control of the Defence Ministry.

Special arrangements should be made for the prompt trade testing of workers for their initial fixation in the appropriate grades in all cases in which fresh testing is considered necessary.

Clerical And Allied Establishments

Pay of Head Clerks In Ordnance Factories

We recommend that the normal scale of pay for Head Clerks in the Ordnance Factories should be Rs. 200-10-300, but for the very big factories where the strength of the clerical staff is appreciably higher than the average, the scale should be Rs. 260-15-350. Below the Head Clerk the Upper Division Clerks in actual charge of sections of groups or men should be entitled to the usual Charge Allowance as sanctioned in other Defence Establishments.

Pay Of Head Clerks In Ordnance Depots, Technical Development Establishments And E.M.E. Workshops

This matter, in so far as it affects Ordnance Factories, has already been dealt with, and we have recommended the adoption of the following two scales of pay for Head Clerks:

(i) Rs. 200-10-300;
(ii) Rs. 260-15-350.

We recommend the adoption of the same scales for the appointment of Head Clerks sanctioned in the other Establishments mentioned. It has been pointed out that there are a number of very small Establishments which employ 15 to 30 clerks. In such cases, it may not be necessary, unless the special nature of work justifies it, to sanction a post of Head Clerk on either of these scales. Either only a post of Assistant-in-Charge with the usual Charge Allowance should be sanctioned or, where it is necessary to create an appointment of Head Clerk, he should be on the existing scale of Rs. 160-10-250.

Charge Allowance To Clerks-in-Charge In Ordnance Depots

Mr. Ghosh's Recommendations: The number of posts carrying Charge Allowance will naturally depend on the organization of each office because obviously the question of payment of Charge Allowance arises only if someone is made to supervise the work of other clerks. The Committee has been given to understand, however, that there is always uncertainty about anyone drawing Charge Allowance for any length of time, because it happens quite often that a J.C.O. is posted to a Depot and since a J.C.O. is intended to be employed as a Supervisor, a civilian clerk already drawing Charge Allowance has to drop the allowance. While there is nothing wrong in this system, it is felt that it would be an advantage and it would lead to greater satisfaction if administrative arrangements can be made in such a manner that large-scale reversions of this nature do not take place. That could be achieved by allocating a minimum number of supervisory appointments to the civilian clerical cadre.

Mr. Subramanian's Recommendations: While I agree with Mr. Ghosh's report as far as it goes, I would point out that A.I. 845 of 1945 which regulates payment of Charge Allowances has been differently interpreted by different authorities and that according to a recent report from the Adjutant-General's Branch even a clarification issued by the Ministry of Defence after due consultation with the Financial Adviser has been held to be inconsistent with A.I. 845/45 by the C.D.D.A. It is, therefore, necessary that further instructions should be issued on the subject. In particular it should be made clear whether the number of Charge Allowances of both Rs. 40 and Rs. 20 should be based on the total clerical strength of a Depot or other establishment or whether they would be admissible only if the clerical establishment lent itself to grouping into "independent" sections—whether compact or scattered. I feel that it is not a satisfactory arrangement to assign the supervision of the first 25 clerks to one called a "Head Clerk" on an allowance of Rs. 40, who will also be expected to have "general supervision" over all Assistant Head Clerks in the establishment. I would suggest that there should be at least one Head Clerk in each establishment on a scale of pay comparable to the new scales of pay recommended by the Committee for Head Clerks in Ordnance Factories, who will be in charge of the overall supervision of the entire clerical cadre in the establishment. The clerical establishment should then be divided into sections. In such sections an Assistant Head Clerk drawing a uniform rate of allowance should be placed in direct charge of a prescribed number of clerks. Where in a section there are two or more Assistant Head Clerks, the seniormost among them should be given a higher rate of allowance and asked to exercise general supervision over the charges of the other Assistant Head Clerks besides supervising the work of the clerks placed directly under his charge. This pattern of organization would need to be departed from only in the case of small establishments with a clerical strength of, say, less than 25. In such a case all that would be required is to have one Head Clerk on a scale of pay of Rs. 160-10-250.

The Position Of Senior Temporary Clerks In The Ordnance Factories

Any straightforward protection of pay of Head Clerks and Senior Temporary Clerks, Grade I, or for that matter of that of anyone holding a non-permanent post would amount to a clear departure from the general orders of the Government. In other words, if the matter is to be considered at all, it has to be considered as a general proposition. A suggestion was made that a protection should be given to non-gazetted employees. It is not strictly a matter within the province of the Committee and it is for the Government to consider the suggestion.

Cashiers And Assistant Cashiers In The Ordnance Factories

We do not consider that any revision of the scale of pay of Cashiers and Assistant Cashiers is called for.

Cashiers In Ordnance Depots

As long as the Clerks are not responsible for the disbursement and custody of cash they cannot be regarded as Cashiers.

Cashiers And Assistant Cashiers In Certain Technical Development Establishments

We recommend that Cashiers and Assistant Cashiers in the T.D.E.s who are pre-1931 entrants should be allowed to retain their prescribed scales of Rs. 200-10-300 and Rs. 100-10-150. The Assistant Cashiers who may elect to move on to the revised scale, namely, Rs. 80-5-120-EB-8-200-10/2-220 should be allowed to have their starting pay fixed in the revised scale on the basis of their existing pay in the scale of Rs. 100-10-150 because this being a pre-1931 scale applicable to the corresponding post in the factories cannot be regarded as inflated.

Stenographers

This is not a proposition which can be considered under the Terms of Reference of this Committee, because it is not an anomaly which requires to be rectified, but it is an entirely new demand which goes beyond the recommendation of the Pay Commission.

Typists

We do not consider that any modification of the existing pay scale of Typists in the Defence establishments is called for.

Checkers In Ordnance Factories

Mr. Ghosh's Recommendations: The category of Checkers is peculiar to the Ordnance Factories. It is not unnatural that in an industrial establishment there will be a variety of work of a very routine nature not requiring any special educational qualification or experience. There is nothing inappropriate, therefore, in laying down a special rate of pay lower than the scale prescribed for the Lower Division Clerks for such a category where Matriculation is not required to be the minimum educational qualification.

I am of the opinion that the category of Checkers should be retained as a separate category, but such of the appointments as, on a proper assessment, can be considered as clerical appointments should be merged into the clerical cadre. The mere fact that the holders of such appointments were in the past on daily rates of pay is no justification for keeping them in a separate category. From the information supplied by the Director-General, it seems that a considerable number of these Checkers are in actual practice employed on clerical duties. (It is seen that a very large number of Checkers are Matriculates.) If these appointments are converted into Lower Division Clerks' appointments, it is possible that the majority of the Matriculates amongst them will be absorbed as Lower Division Clerks. On the whole I think that would meet the situation.

If those who are employed on clerical duties are merged in the clerks cadre, as I have suggested previously, for the rest there is no need or justification for laying down Matriculation as the minimum qualification.

If the clerical appointments in Grade I of Checkers are merged with the clerical cadre, I doubt whether for the remaining appointments two distinct grades would be justified or necessary. I consider that the best course would then be to have one scale of Rs. 45-2-55-3-85. This incidentally is the scale applicable to non-Matriculate Leading Hands in the Ordnance Depots.

Mr. Subramanian's Recommendations: I feel that even the 885 Checkers who are supposed to be doing semi-clerical duties according to the Director-General are, in fact, doing work comparable to that of Lower Division Clerks in the Government offices and that the posts of Checkers should be abolished and replaced by those of Lower Division Clerks.

As the duties performed by Checkers are comparable to those of Lower Division Clerks, I feel that for future recruits the Matriculation should be fixed as the requisite educational qualification. As for the existing non-Matriculates, special exemption from the minimum educational qualification will be necessary on the lines of A.I. No. 16/S/49 for non-Matriculate clerks.

Fixation Of Pay Of Extra Temporary Establishment—Clerks

Mr. Ghosh's Recommendations: It cannot be said that the E.T.E. clerks on daily rates of pay have done at all badly. I, therefore, do not consider that a case exists for reviewing the orders relating to the fixation of pay in the unified scales of pay.

It was stated that in certain Ordnance Depots, clerks who were employed on monthly scales of pay (pre-unified) and were in receipt of a maximum pay of Rs. 80 per month were not graded 'B' but were moved on to Grade 'C' only, contrary to the orders issued by the Government. If this is a fact, it was a mistake and it is for the administration to rectify it.

Mr. Subramanian's Recommendations: I am convinced that the so-called clerical supervisors were only Senior Clerks and that their rates of pay even up to Rs. 7 per day were not excessive even if unauthorized. That being so, deduction of the supervisory element is, in my opinion, not proper. I suggest cancellation of the orders relating to the deduction of the supervisory element.

In view of the new situations created by the considerable delay that took place in the implementation of the unified scales of pay and as there was every possibility of the numerous orders issued from time to time not being fully understood by the affected persons,

I suggest that the request of the Federations may be acceded to.

Application Of The Unified Scales Of Pay To The Clerical Establishment Of Ordnance Factories

Mr. Ghosh's Recommendations: The Director-General has explained to the Committee why the unified scales were not introduced in the Ordnance Factories and has further pointed out the difficulties of introducing them now, after so many years, with retrospective effect, mainly because of promotions and demotions during this long period. I think it is necessary at this stage to examine whether it was right for the factories not to introduce the unified scales of pay because apart from anything else it is not a matter before this Committee. The only question is whether, even though the unified scales were not in actual fact applied, there is justification for recalculating the pre-prescribed pay of clerks as if they had been brought on to the unified scales of pay with effect from September 1, 1944, for the purpose of fixation of pay in the revised scales under the Revision of Pay Rules. I consider that it is administratively impossible to re-open things which happened seven or eight years ago and to set right past irregularities, even assuming there was an unjustified irregularity in this case.

When unified scales were introduced in other establishments, the existing employees were given an option to retain their old scales or to come on to the unified scales.

I can find no justification for suggesting that the pay of Ordnance Factory clerks should be recalculated as if unified scales were introduced in the Ordnance Factories with effect from September 1, 1944.

Mr. Subramanian's Recommendations: I wish that the orders already passed by the Government in respect of clerks in all establishments under the Defence Ministry had been implemented.

The salaries of clerks in Ordnance Factories brought on to the revised scales be recalculated on the assumption that the unified scales of pay had been applied to them with effect from September 1, 1944, or June 1, 1946, as may be found more advantageous to the individual concerned.

The Grading Of Clerks Who Were In 'B' Grade Of Unified Scale As Lower Division Clerks

The case of the Upper Division Clerks of the Defence Accounts Department, who were graded 'B' under the unified scales of pay scheme, is not comparable to the case of Grade 'B' clerks of the other Defence Establishments. The Grade 'B' clerks of the other Defence Establishments were all L.D.C.s, and the U.D.C.s were all in Grade 'A'. We do not find any substance in the grievance of the Clerical Association.

Anomaly In The Fixation Of Pay Of L.D.C.s Who Were Previously In Grade 'C' Of The Unified Scales Of Pay

The demand of the Clerical Employees is that the starting pay of Rs. 60 which they were allowed initially should be treated as basic pay without any deductions. The Association quoted the instance of Storemen who were similarly started on Rs. 60 in the scale of Rs. 45-3-75-EB-80-5/2-105 on similar considerations and in their case the Government had allowed the starting pay to be fixed in the revised scales on the basis of the higher pay of Rs. 60.

We do not find the claim of the Association justified. Their pay at no time was reduced below Rs. 60 and had not the unified scales of pay been introduced they would have had to stay on at the stage of Rs. 60 till their advance increments were absorbed. Though it is true that the All India and Field Service Liability Allowances as separate entities have not been provided for in the revised scales of Pay Scheme, it is to be noted that under the orders previously in force also the element of a higher start on account of these liabilities would have been reduced and after a time they would not have been entitled to any extra element of pay for these liabilities.

We do not also regard the case of Storemen quite analogous in view of the fact that the Storemen were not admitted to the unified scales of pay and did not draw any All India and Field Service Liability Allowances separately as did the clerks.

We therefore do not consider that there is any anomaly.

Fresh Option To Elect The Unified Scales In The Case Of Those Employees Who Did Not Elect To Be Governed By Those Scales

Mr. Ghosh's Recommendations: It is not administratively feasible now to recalculate a man's pay from September 1, 1944, and refix it from January 1, 1947, or January 1, 1948, and then to adjust subsequent payments. So far as this particular demand from clerks, who were given the option to elect unified scales but exercised the option in a manner which has turned out to their disadvantage for the future, is concerned, it is undoubtedly unfortunate; but it is in my view difficult for the Government to give fresh options to employees in such cases whenever it turns out later that the new circumstances have made the original option disadvantageous.

Mr. Subramanian's Recommendations: If employees had known that the unified scales were a stepping stone to the eventual permanent scale, it stands to reason that they would have elected it. As all the facts necessary in such cases for making up one's mind were not before the clerks, I feel that this is a fit case for giving a fresh opportunity to the affected persons to be brought over to the revised scales through the unified scales.

Treatment Of The Extra Element Of Pay Sanctioned For Clerks On Unified Scales Of Pay Stationed At Bombay And Calcutta As Part Of Basic Pay For Fixation Of Pay In The Revised Scales

We do not find any justification in this grievance since the personnel have been allowed compensation for high cost of living separately.

Application Of Unified Scales Of Pay To Time-keepers Employed In The Kirkee Ordnance Depot

We consider that the Time-keepers of the Kirkee Ordnance Depot cannot be treated differently from those in other Depots, and that the former too should be moved on to the revised scales through the unified scales. If any overpayment has been made, no recovery need be effected.

Counting Of Service Rendered By Temporary Clerks Of Ordnance Factories, As Daily Rated Clerks, Godown Keepers, Supervisors Grade 'C' And Miscellaneous Appointments Having Identical Scales Of Pay Of Temporary Clerks Grade 'B', For The Purpose Of Fixing The Starting Pay In The Revised Scale Of Lower Division Clerks.

We recommend that prior service of temporary clerks rendered on daily rates, when substantially clerical, should be allowed to count for increments, while fixing the starting pay in the revised scale.

We recommend that service as Junior Godown Keepers should also be treated as service in corresponding scale for the purpose of fixing the starting pay of temporary clerks in the revised scale of L.D.C.s.

Loss In Pay Due To Classification Of Clerks As Leading Hands And Later Again As Clerks In The Technical Development Establishments (Stores), Kanpur

As it is apparent that the duties of the individuals affected had not undergone any change during the period they were classified as Leading Hands and re-classified as Clerks and as the scales of pay are also practically the same (except that the scale applicable to Leading Hands stops at Rs. 125 and the scale applicable to Clerks goes up to Rs. 130) we recommend that the pay of the individuals should be re-fixed from the beginning as though they have continued as clerks.

As regards the Leading Hands (Stores), who have continued in the T.D.E. (Stores), the D.T.D. has stated that there is a proposal to abolish the category of Leading Hands (Stores) and to absorb the existing incumbents as Storemen. The representatives of the Kanpur Federation have suggested that when this is done, the existing incumbents should move on the same rate of pay which they are drawing at present. The D.T.D. is also of the same view.

We recommend that this should be done, since here too there is no difference in the duties of Leading Hands (Stores) or Storemen and if any Government orders are necessary they should be issued.

Store-keeping Establishment

Store-keeping Establishment In Ordnance Factories And Ordnance Depots

Mr. Ghosh's Recommendations: Since the E.T.E. has been abolished and as the duties are more or less the same, I consider that there is no longer any justification for maintaining two categories like Leading Hands (Stores) and Storemen. It is suggested that there should be only one category of Storemen on the scale of Rs. 55—130 and the Leading Hands should be re-designated as Storemen. Supervisors are in two grades, Grade II being on Rs. 80—120 and Grade I being on Rs. 100—180. It is suggested that Supervisors, Grade II, may be re-designated as Storemen on the scale of Rs. 55—130 (unless any particular individual wishes to retain his existing scale of pay, in which case it may be protected to him or unless anyone is fit to be made a Store-keeper straightaway) and Supervisors Grade I may be re-designated as Store-keepers, Grade IV, on the scale of Rs. 100—185.

In determining the scale of pay of an appointment it is necessary to consider not only the duties and responsibilities but also the type of man required to hold such an appointment. I consider that in a case of this nature, where the assessment of duties and responsibilities is difficult, it is more desirable to consider what qualifications are required of an individual, to determine an appropriate pay for him or his class because, apart from anything else, qualifications are an indication of what an individual is capable of doing. Godown-Keepers are not Tradesmen and the D.G.O.F. has stated that no minimum educational qualification has been laid down for Godown-Keepers. In other words, neither are they skilled nor have they any prescribed educational qualifications. Whatever may be the organizational difference, the lowest level of store-keeping personnel is a Godown-Keeper in Ordnance Factories and a Storeman in Ordnance Depots. It may be that the former, because of a somewhat different organization, is required to undertake a little higher responsibility but one cannot go on weighing responsibilities in a scale in this manner. I find that the number of higher appointments open to

Godown-Keepers in the Ordnance Factories is proportionately very much higher than the number of appointments open to Storemen and equivalent category of Leading Hands (Stores). Roughly the proportion works out as 1 to 1 in the Ordnance Factories and about 1 to 5 or 6 in the Ordnance Depots. In the clerical cadre, the proportion between the Upper Division and Lower Division varies from 1 to 4 and 1 to 6. Therefore, on the whole, the Godown-Keepers in the Ordnance Factories have better prospects and there can be no justifiable grievance if their pay is similar to that of Storemen. To give them the pay of Supervisors would be wholly unjustified.

At present, there are two scales of Godown-Keepers. Both the grades start with the same minimum of 55, but while the Junior Grade stops at 105, the Senior Grade goes up to 130. I see no particular merit in this system. I suggest that the two grades be abolished and all be placed on the scale of Rs. 55—130, a scale which is common to Lower Division Clerks and Storemen.

Mr. Subramanian's Recommendations: I agree that Leading Hands (Stores) should be re-designated as Storemen and brought on to the scale of Rs. 55-3-85-4-125-130.

Supervisors, Grade I and Grade II, be re-designated as Store-keepers, Grade III and Grade IV, on the scales of Rs. 150—225 and Rs. 100—185. In view of the responsibilities shouldered by Supervisors, Grade II, I do not think that it is proper to re-designate them as Storemen on Rs. 55—130.

Godown-Keepers should be equated at least to Store-keepers, Grade IV, i.e., Supervisors, Grade B, Ordnance Factories, on the scale of Rs. 100—185. I recommend that the categories of Godown-Keepers, junior and senior, be abolished and merged in Supervisor, Grade B, on Rs. 100—185.

Scale Of Pay Of Packers

Mr. Ghosh's Recommendations: I suggest that the D.O.S. and the Director-General, Ordnance Factories, should jointly consider whether the scale of Packers calls for any improvement and, if so, what improvement is justified comparing their duties and responsibilities with those of other tradesmen.

Mr. Subramanian's Recommendations: I suggest the scale of Rs. 40-2-60-EB-3/2-75 for Packers (Ordinary). This would necessitate upgradation of the scale of pay of Packers (Special). For them I would suggest the scale of Rs. 55-3-85, which is the first part of the scale prescribed for Leading Hands.

Demotion Of Packers—A.I.G.s, Bengal Area

Mr. Ghosh's Recommendations: The issue involved is one of principle. Should the Government accept the proposition that once a man has been fixed on a scale of pay, he must necessarily be continued on that scale even if the number of appointments in that scale is reduced? Though the number of cases involved here is small and one could perhaps make a departure just to satisfy the men, it is necessary to consider this matter in the light of day-to-day events in administration and particularly in the Defence Services. In the Defence Organization the numbers of posts in the aggregate as well as in the different grades are liable to wide fluctuations due to variation in the load of work and if posts have to be reduced as a result of a fall in the workload, it may involve not only retrenchment but also demotion. In such cases also, the men may point out that they have drawn the higher scales for years and ask for protection. Such a demand has never been accepted and cannot, I suggest, be accepted. I cannot see any essential difference between such cases and the case of Packers we are dealing with (except that the case of Packers is even weaker in that it may be held that their fixation in the higher scale was never intended). I suggest that the only practicable way of satisfying these few men is to consider the possibility of transferring them elsewhere where appointments in the higher scale may exist.

Mr. Subramanian's Recommendations: When the same set of percentages are allocated to the various grades of a particular trade or job in all the establishments under a directorate, it is a reasonable presumption that the percentages are not based on the actual requirements of each establishment and that they have been laid down after taking into account an average sample of work found in the establishments. If then a particular establishment had, in the past, been employing comparatively higher-grade staff and such staff were drawing pay, at the time of transition to the new scales, at a level which would take them to a higher grade, there is *prima facie* a presumption that that establishment requires still higher-grade posts. Even if further examination justifies more lower-grade posts I should say that existing incumbents, placed where they are for no fault of theirs, should be allowed the higher scales warranted by their previous daily rates, at least as a personal concession. The practice adopted in Ordnance Factories at the time of the initial fixation of workers on the revised scales of pay was based on this principle. Many trades in Ordnance Factories have a number of grades and percentages have been laid down for those grades. Nevertheless all workers were initially placed in the grades in which 26-times their daily wages fell. There was even a further concession. When workers found themselves demoted by the 26-times-the-daily-wages formula, they had only to pass a trade test to be restored to their old grades, irrespective of percentages or vacancies. In the present case the placing of four out of five

Packers in the scale of Rs. 40—75 by the application of the 26-times-the-daily-wages formula was in accordance with the practice in Ordnance Factories and hence, in my opinion, correct. The strict application of a fixed ratio as between the various grades, on the initial constitution of a proper cadre, is bound to cause hardship to existing workers even though such a ratio might be appropriate for eventual attainments. I feel, therefore, that the three demoted Packers should be restored to the scale of Rs. 40—75 and that their posts should be converted into the lower category ones only when they next fall vacant.

Pay Of Store-keeping Organization In The M.E.S.

Mr. Ghosh's Recommendations: I do not consider that the prospects of the store-keeping establishment in the M.E.S. are on the whole worse than either in the Central P.W.D. or in the Ordnance Services. The Pay Commission had recommended that the M.E.S. and the Central P.W.D. scales should be similar and I do not see any justification for departing from this principle. However, as in the case of the C.P.W.D. (and also the Ordnance Depots), the scale of pay for Matriculate Store-keepers, Grade II, in the M.E.S. should be Rs. 55-3-85-4-125-130 and suggest that they should be redesignated as Storemen to indicate that they are a lower category than Store-keepers in other Defence establishments and similar to Storeman/Godown-keeper. If this is done, the position of the lowest grade of Store-keeping staff will be the same in the M.E.S. and C.P.W.D. While the highest grade in the Central P.W.D. is Rs. 80—220, in the M.E.S. this is, in a way, split up into two grades of Rs. 80—160 and Rs. 100—200, but there is provision for a still higher grade of Rs. 200—410. There are further opportunities for promotion to gazetted rank. In my view it would on the whole be better to leave the pay scales as they are, except in the case of the Storemen where the scale may be improved to Rs. 55—130 in which case future recruitment should be restricted to Matriculates.

Mr. Subramanian's Recommendations: The scales of Rs. 80-5-120-EB-8-160 for Store-keepers, Grade I, and Rs. 100-8-140-10-200 for Supervisor, Grade II, should be changed to the corresponding conventional scales, viz., Rs. 100-5-125-6-185 and Rs. 150-7-185-8-225. The scale of Supervisor, Grade I, namely, Rs. 200—410 will then correspond to the two higher grades of Rs. 200—300 and Rs. 260—350. If Store-keepers, Grade II, are independently responsible for receipt, custody and issue of stores, they should be promoted to the next higher category for which I have suggested a scale of Rs. 100—185 above. If, however, they are not in independent charge and are more in the nature of Assistants, they should be re-classified as Storemen on Rs. 55—130 and the present Storemen on Rs. 35—50 designated differently.

Pay Of Packers In The M.E.S.

There are two grades of Packers in the M.E.S., Grade I, in the scale of Rs. 40-2-60-3/2-75 and Grade II in the scale of Rs. 35-1-50. One of the Unions brought out that although there are two grades of Packers, the higher grade has not been sanctioned for the Engineer Store Depot, Avadi.

This is a matter which the Engineer-in-Chief may look into and if there is work for the higher grade, he will no doubt get the necessary post sanctioned as soon as possible. Unless higher grade work exists, there is no justification for granting automatically the higher grade, particularly, as in the Central P.W.D. the Packers are all in the lower scale of Rs. 35-1-50.

Fixing A Scale Of Pay For Store-keepers In The E.M.E Who Were On E.T.E. On Daily Rates From Rs. 3 To Rs. 5

Mr. Ghosh's Recommendations: I find that Store-keepers have not all been automatically fixed in the grade of Store-keeper on the introduction of the revised scales. For example, Store-keepers M.T.L.D. on the pre-prescribed scale of Rs. 45—100 have been brought on to the scale of Rs. 55—130. Therefore, I cannot see any great force in the argument that simply because these men were designated Store-keepers in the past, they must automatically be brought on to the grade of Store-keepers now. E.T.E. Clerks also were on varying rates of pay and even though those drawing between Rs. 3 and Rs. 5 were called Clerical Supervisors, they have been brought on to the Lower Division scale of Rs. 55—130. The men concerned in the E.M.E. Workshops have been protected against any actual loss in pay. I think that sufficiently meets the case. To put them straightaway on to the scale of Rs. 100—185 would either deprive an equivalent number of regular Storemen of promotion or would necessitate the creation of the same number of supernumerary appointments for them. I cannot see adequate justification for either.

Mr. Subramanian's Recommendations: I feel that E.T.E. Store-keepers who were on Rs. 3 to Rs. 5 were really Store-keepers and not Storemen. If that is the case, there should be no question of their having to compete with Storemen of the regular establishment for getting on to the grade of Store-keepers. They should have been brought over to the regular Store-keeper's grade on the scale of Rs. 100—185 by the application of 26-times-the-daily-wages formula. I suggest that this be done. In order to accommodate the claims of Storemen of the regular establishment for promotion to the grade of Store-keeper, it may be necessary temporarily to increase the number of Store-keepers, but that seems inevitable in view of the liability already incurred by the department by the creation of Store-keepers in E.T.E.

Scale Of Pay Applicable To Loaders And Unloaders In The Ordnance Depots

The scale of Rs. 55—125, which is intended for posts requiring Matriculation qualification, is, therefore, not recommended for the Loaders and Unloaders though under the existing orders a section of this category has already been allowed this scale. It is noticed in this connection that for the Leading Hands who are not Matriculates and who may be recruited after February, 1950, a scale of Rs. 45-2-55-3-85 has been sanctioned by the Government. We consider that this scale of pay may be prescribed for all Loaders and Unloaders but those already categorized as Leading Hands in the scale of Rs. 55—125 should be left as they are.

Allotment Of Grades To Supervisors (Non-Technical) In The Ordnance Depots

There are two grades of Supervisors (non-Technical) viz., Rs. 80-5-120 and Rs. 100-8-140-10-180. We are given to understand that since then orders have been issued in A.H.Q. letter No. 48699/AG/Org.4 (a), dated April 25-26, 1952, that the Grade I posts should be allotted on the basis of the daily rates of pay.

Supervisory Establishment (Technical) Pay Of Supervisors In Ordnance Factories

Mr. Ghosh's Recommendations: While arguing for a higher scale of pay for the ex-Apprentice Supervisors, it has been agreed that the scale of pay for promoted workmen can continue to be Rs. 100—185 as on the Railways. It seems that in the Ordnance Factories, by and large, these promoted workmen and the raw ex-Apprentice Supervisors perform more or less the same functions. Therefore, in my view, to increase the pay of the ex-Apprentice Supervisor while retaining the existing scale for the promoted workmen would be hardly justified. While for the ordinary workmen, the scale of Supervisor, Grade 'B', may be the highest which he can ordinarily hope to reach, for the apprentices it is the stepping stone to higher grades. I see nothing wrong, therefore, in apprentices getting the same scale of pay as promoted workmen for a period of time.

As the Director-General has explained, the Ordnance Factory apprentices are in no way worse off compared to the apprentices in the Railways, so far as their prospects, etc., are concerned. Therefore, neither on equity nor on technical grounds can I see any justification for altering the existing scales of pay.

Mr. Subramanian's Recommendations: As there are already two grades of Chargemen on Rs. 260—350 and Rs. 200—300 in factories, there is scope only for one more category of the Supervisory Staff corresponding to the grade of Chargemen C on the Railways on Rs. 150-225. I suggest that if the Department wishes to retain the designation of Supervisor, there should be only one category of Supervisor on the scale of Rs. 150—225. There will have to be a lower grade of Rs. 100—185 but that, as on the Railways, should be confined to:

(a) Mistries promoted in a suitable proportion from skilled workmen who are not technically and educationally qualified for promotion as Supervisors on Rs. 150—225; and

(b) Journeymen appointed from qualified apprentices who have successfully completed their period of apprenticeship, if it considered that such apprentices are not fit straightaway to be appointed as full-fledged Supervisors.

Scale Of Pay Of Supervisors (Technical) Of The Inspectorate-General Stores And In Other Technical Development Establishments

We are informed that the pre-prescribed scale of the Examiners in the Indian Stores Department was Rs. 150-10-300-EB-20-400 (though the scale of Rs. 150-10-240 was applicable only for posts created during the War), and the prescribed scale is, therefore, definitely lower rather than higher, as argued by the Federation. We are also informed that the duties of Examiners in the Stores Department and the Supervisors in the T.D.E. are not strictly comparable. The scales prescribed for Supervisors under D.G.O.F., D.M.E. and D.T.D. are the same at present and it would be advisable to increase the pay of the Supervisors in the A.I.G.S., Calcutta, simply on the analogy of the scale applicable to Examiners in the Stores Department, even if this analogy were correct. The scale of Chargemen, the next higher post, is Rs. 200-10-300 and any increase in the Supervisor's scale will call for a similar increase in the Chargemen's scale and the still higher scales. We, therefore, consider that no change is called for in the existing pay structure.

The other claim made by the Uttar and Madhya Pradesh Ordnance Employees Federation, Kanpur, is that a new grade of Supervisors in Grade I (Rs. 260-15-350) should be created in the T.D.E. (Weapons). From the statement of the Organization it is seen that there are already posts of Chargemen above the Supervisors, Grade II, in the scales of Rs. 200-10-300 and Rs. 260-10-350. There is, therefore, no need to create another category of Supervisors in the scale of Rs. 260-15-350.

Scale Of Pay Of Civilian Workshop Supervisors In The E.M.E. Workshops And Creation Of Higher Grades Such As Foremen And Assistant Foremen

It has been represented that the posts of Civilian Workshop Supervisors created during the War due to the shortage of B.O.R.s and J.C.O.s carried the scales of pay of Rs. 280-10-500 and 180-7½-240, and as these Workshop Supervisors are still doing the same type of duties, their scales should not have been reduced. It has been suggested, therefore, that higher posts of the pre-prescribed pay range should be created for these men with the designations of Foremen and Assistant Foreman.

Restriction Of The Scale Of Supervisor, Grade III, viz., Rs. 100—185 To Mistries And Promoted Tradesmen In The Establishments Under The M.G.O. (D.T.D., D.O.S., D.M.E.)

Mr. Ghosh's Recommendations: Supervisors, Grade II, in the Ordnance Depots and E.M.G. Workshops and Supervisors, Grade II—I can see no justification whatsoever for abolishing this scale or for raising it further.

Technical Development Establishments—I see no case for altering the existing pay structure.

Mr. Subramanian's Recommendations: I suggest that the category of Supervisor, Grade III, on Rs. 100—185 should be abolished. Mistries who are not qualified for promotion to Grade II may be allowed to continue on the scale of Rs. 100—185, but there need not be any further recruitment to that category as I am suggesting that that scale might be prescribed as one of the scales for Leading Hands (Technical). As the category of Leading Hands is an intermediate stage between Tradesmen and Supervisors, there should be no objection to competent Tradesmen, who may not have the requisite technical and educational qualification for becoming Supervisors, being put in the category of Leading Hands. In other words, the higher grade of Leading Hands (Technical) should in Directorates other than that of factories take the place of Mistries in factories.

Promotion Of Supervisors Grade 'C' To Supervisors Grade 'B' In Ordnance Factories And Technical Development Establishments

We recommend that the promotion of Grade 'C' Supervisors who were promoted with effect from April 1, 1948, in the Ordnance Factories or from October 1, 1948, in the Inspectorates should be effective from January 1, 1947.

Downgradation Of Motor Transport Supervisors Of The Ordnance Depots As Non-Technical Supervisors

In some of the Ordnance Depots, Motor Transport Supervisors were appointed during War time in the scale of Rs. 180-7½-240. They were thereafter reverted as Supervisors on daily rates of Rs. 5 and on the introduction of the revised scales were classified as Non-Technical Supervisors in the scale of Rs. 80—120 or Rs. 100—180 according to the availability of posts. The contention of the Federation is that these Supervisors are technical persons and should be classified as Technical Supervisors in the scale of Rs. 100—185 or 150—225. We suggest that efforts may be made to absorb, if possible, such personnel as Technical Supervisors subject to their passing the necessary qualifying test.

Graduate Chemists In Factories Employed As Supervisors, Grades 'A' And 'B'

Mr. Ghosh's Recommendations: I do not recommend any change in the existing pay scales.

Mr. Subramanian's Recommendations: In another section I have recommended that there should be only one grade of Supervisor in Ordnance Factories on Rs. 150—225. I would repeat that recommendation in the present case also and suggest that the first regular appointment of a graduate chemist fully trained in his work should be on the scale of Rs. 150—225. This would not, however, debar payment to recruits during the first year or two of their probation of the lower scale of Rs. 100—185 as in the case of Journeymen in the regular establishment.

Abolition Of The Scale Of Rs. 100-5-120-8-200 Applicable To Junior Scientific Assistants Grade II In The T.D.E.s.

We do not regard that there is any anomaly in retaining the scale of Rs. 100—200 for Junior Scientific Assistants, Grade II, who in the past used to be called Laboratory Assistants. The scale of Rs. 100—200 for raw science graduates cannot be considered inadequate when the normal pay of Graduate Clerks is Rs. 80—220.

Improvement Of The Pay Scales Of Laboratory Attendants In The T.D.E.s

The scale of Laboratory Attendants is Rs. 35-1-40-2-60. The Uttar and Madhya Pradesh Ordnance Employees Federation argued that Laboratory Attendants after experience acquired skill and were capable of assisting the Scientific Assistants in their less important tasks and, therefore, their scale should be improved.

We do not consider that there is any anomaly in the existing orders since the Laboratory Attendants in other Laboratories are also in the same pay range and in some cases they are on even lower scales, e.g., Rs. 35-1-50.

Pay Of Leading Hands (Technical)

Mr. Ghosh's Recommendations: I cannot see any justification for either raising the scale of the Leading Hands or for creating a new grade of Leading Hands higher than the scale laid down for the Group 'A' tradesmen.

I would suggest, however, a slight modification of the existing scale of Leading Hands. The present scale is identical with the Lower Division Clerks' scale except that the maximum is less by Rs. 5 only. I see no point in having this slight difference. I sugget that the scale of pay for Leading Hands (Technical) and Matriculate Leading Hands (non-Technical) be revised to Rs. 55—130, the scale which applies to Lower Division Clerks.

Mr. Subramanian's Recommendations: I suggest that a scale of Rs. 100—185 may be prescribed for Leading Hands (Technical) in addition to the present scale of Rs. 55—125. As usual, these could be marked as Grades I and II. This will be in accord with the view I have held elswhere that the lowest scale of a full-fledged Technical Supervisor should be Rs. 150—225 and that the lower grade of Rs. 100—185 should apply only to Journeymen, Mistries and—now I add —one engaged in an intermediate stage of supervision. I also feel that it should be recognized that Tradesmen belonging to Group A who are technically and educationally qualified should be eligible for promotion to the category of Supervisor, Grade II, on Rs. 150—225.

Creation Of A Category Of Inspectors In The E.M.E.

Mr. Ghosh's Recommendations: I cannot see any justification for creating a new category of Tradesmen with the designation of Inspectors simply in order to give them a higher scale of pay.

Mr. Subramanian's Recommendations: That there is need for a category of Inspectors now appears clear from the fact that D.M.E. is thinking of constituting a Central Inspectorate. The new scheme may take time. Meanwhile I feel that those who are actually doing the work of inspection must be paid suitably. I should say that an Inspector drawn from Group B (Rs. 60—105) should, like Mistries and the higher grade of Leading Hands, be placed on the scale of Rs. 100—185. Those drawn from lower groups (Rs. 50—75 and below) might be placed appropriately on the present scale for Leading Hands, viz., Rs. 55—125. As my recommendation elsewhere is that full-fledged Supervisors (Technical) should have a minimum scale of Rs. 150—225, the recommendations made above will maintain the necessary differential between Inspectors and Supervisors.

Special Pay For Superintendents B/R & E/M When In Charge Of A Station

At present Suprintendents B/R and Suprintendents E/M Grade I in the scale of Rs. 250—400 get a special pay of Rs. 50 when they are in charge of Sub-divisions. The M.E.S. Unions suggested that there should be a Charge Allowance for Superintendents, Grade II, when they are in charge of stations.

This is a demand for increase of pay of Superintendents, Grade II, in certain conditions. There is no anomaly in this case which brings it within the Terms of Reference of the Committee. The Engineer-in-Chief has stated that the Superintendents, Grade II, are comparable to Overseers of the Central P.W.D. who are on the same scale of Rs. 100—300. The latter are not entitled to any special pay unless they are placed in charge of sub-divisions. The Overseers are also employed in various capacities just as Superintendents, Grade II, are. The Engineer-in-Chief does not consider that the duties and responsibilities of Superintendent, Grade II, in charge of a station justify the grant of a special pay. We do not find any reason to differ from this view.

Draughtsmen And Tracers

Scales Of Pay Of Draughtsmen, Estimators, Rate-Fixers And Planners In The Ordnance Factories

We recommend that it would be appropriate to lay down for Senior Draughtsmen, Jigs and Tools, a higher scale of Rs. 200-10-300.

Draughtsmen In The Technical Development Establishments

The Labour Federations have asked for two intermediary scales for Draughtsmen—Rs. 200-10-300 and Rs. 260-15-350—in between existing Grades I and II, namely, Rs. 300-20-500 and Rs. 150-7-185-8-225 for the Technical Development Establishment. The scales of pay of Draughtsmen vary rather widely in different departments as the qualities of Draughtsmen required also vary. The mere fact that a scale exists in one department does not indicate that a similar scale is necessarily required in another department. However, it has been brought to our notice that the Government have recently issued orders creating another grade of Draughtsmen in the scale of Rs. 260-15-350. We consider that the case has been adequately met.

Pay Of Draughtsmen In The M.E.S.

The M.E.S. Unions suggested that there should be a selection grade of Draughtsmen in the scale of Rs. 260-15-350 as in the Central P.W.D. and that further a new category of Architectural Draughtsmen on the scale of Rs. 150-10-300 should he sanctioned since there was such a category on this scale of pay in the past. The Engineer-in-Chief has stated that the Architectural Draughtsmen are doing the same type of work as other Draughtsmen in Grade I and, therefore, he does not see any reason for creating a new category with this designation. He has, however, stated that there should be a Selection Grade of Rs. 260-15-350 as in the Central P.W.D. We recommend the introduction of this Selection Grade.

Scale Of Pay Of Tracers

We consider that the scale of Rs. 55-3-85 is low for the Tracers and they should be at least allowed the minimum scale applicable to Matriculates, viz., Rs. 55—130. As, however, the scale of Rs. 60—150 has already been sanctioned for this category in most departments, we recommned that this scale may be admitted to all the Tracers in the Defence Establishments. We understand that a minimum qualification of Matriculation has been prescribed for recruitment to this post in the T.D.E.s., the M.E.S., the Railways, and the C.P.W.D. This qualification may also be insisted upon for future recruits in offices where such a minimum qualification has not been prescribed.

Viewers

Scale Of Pay Of Viewers In The Technical Development Establishments

Mr. Ghosh's Recommendations: The Director of Technical Development seems to be of the view that the solution to all the difficulties is to give him discretion to fix the establishments, i.e., the number of higher grade Viewers required in each establishment from time to time. He is, however, prepared to ensure that taking all the Viewers throughout India together the percentages of Viewers in the higher grades do dot exceed the percentages indicated below:

Grade 'A'...10
Grade 'B'...30
Grade 'C'...30
Grade 'D'...30

It does not appear that the present proportion laid down for the calculation of the number of appointments of Viewers in the various grades was based on any scientific assessment of requirements. It seems to have been an ad hoc decision. It looks as if it is too rigid for an organization of this nature and in any case there is no doubt that the adoption of the same proportions in every establishment is not correct. The question is whether the proportions should be laid down at all or the appointments should be sanctioned by number for each establishment. The latter would certainly be the most satisfactory method. If, however, that is found to be administratively too inconvenient, then of course the only alternative is to have a system as recommended by the Director of Technical Development, which is that he should be given powers to fix the number of Viewers in the higher grades in each establishment subject to an overall limit for the whole of India.

Mr. Subramanian's Recommendations: Percentages can be worked out on an all-India basis only if the cadre is also an all-India one. In other words, if workers are liable to be transferred from place to place, a set of percentages on an all-India basis will not cause hardship as those entitled to promotion will get it wherever they might be stationed. But if the staff is not to be made transferable and the actual numbers are fixed for each establishment, then over-all percentages have little significance as far as the employees are concerned.

In principle, I would not object to the requirements of each establishment being fixed separately. In so doing, however, the authorities concerned should not overlook the fact that reasonable prospects of promotion are necessary in each establishment if the staff is not to be made transferable. I do not consider that it is a practical proposition to devise all-India cadres and to insist on transfer from one establishment to another. That being so, the distribution between the four grades in some establishments may have to be somewhat different from what strict requirements may dictate so that workers of the lower grades may have reasonable prospects of promotion. I also feel that if the fixation of numbers establishmentwise based on requirements leads to demotion of workers already placed on higher scales, there will be serious discontent and that such a course should be avoided. If the system of fixing grades establishmentwise cannot be worked out at least to the satisfaction of the existing workers, the only alternative is to stick to the percentages already prescribed even though that might not be wholly satisfactory.

The Case Of Viewers In Certain T.D.E.s Who Were On Daily Rates Of Pay And Were Moved On To Monthly Scales In 1942

The Federations suggest that in the case of the Viewers, who were brought on to the monthly scales on the basis of 24 times their daily rates in 1942, their monthly rate of pay on the date of election of the prescribed scales should first be converted into a daily rate at one-twentyfourth of the monthly rate, thereafter the pay in the prescribed scale should be fixed on the basis of 26 times of such daily rate. We understand that such a procedure was adopted in an identical case of the workmen of the Cordite Factory, Arvankadu. It is, therefore, recommended that the same procedure may be adopted in the case of the Viewers referred to.

Other Non-Industrial Categories

Scales Of Pay Of Teachers In The Schools Attached To Ordnance Factories

1. Headmasters and Headmistresses, High Schools: (i) Rs. 200-10-300; (ii) 300-20-400; (iii) 400-20-500.

2. Headmasters and Headmistresses, Vernacular and Anglo-Vernacular Schools: (i) Rs. 100-8-140-10-200 (up to six classes); (ii) 140-10-200-E.B.-10-300 (for more than six classes).

3. Headmasters and Headmistresses of Primary Schools: (i) Grade Pay+S.P. Rs. 10 for schools with one or two class sections; (ii) Grade Pay+S.P. Rs. 20 for schools with three, four or five class sections; (iii) 100-5-125-6-155-E.B.-6-185 for schools with more than five sections.

4. Graduates in High Schools: Rs. 80-5-120-E.B.-8-200-10/2-220 (with a Selection Grade of Rs. 150-15-300) or 80-5-120-8-200-10-300, with an initial start at Rs. 120 per month for B.T.s and L.T.s.

5. Graduate Teachers in other schools (Middle School Standard): Rs. 80-5-120-E.B.-8-200-10/2-220.

6. Trained Teachers in Primary Schools: Rs. 50-2-60-3-90 for (non-Matriculates); 68-4-120-5-170 (for Matriculates).

7. Untrained Teachers in Primary School: Rs. 35-1-40-2-60.

8. Inter (Honours in Oriental Classical Languages): Rs. 80-5-120-E.B.-8-200-10-220.

9. Inter (Honours in Vernacular Languages): Rs. 68-4-120-5-170.

10. Oriental Teachers (Shastris, etc.) non-Matriculates, but teaching in High and Middle Classes: Rs. 68-4-120-5-170.

11. Junior Oriental Teachers (Vernacular non-Matric Teachers): Rs. 50-2-60-3-90.

12. Junior Vernacular Teachers: (a) Matriculates: Rs. 60-4-120-5-170; (b) Non-Matriculates: 50-2-60-3-90.

We recommend that the scales for the Teachers in the Ordnance Factories should be prescribed on the basis of the above standards.

Civilian Medical Officers

We consider that it would be reasonable to grant a Non-Practising Allowance at the rates usually applicable to Medical Officers in other Ministries, where private practice is in fact not possible. In such places it would be in order to prohibit practice and to grant the allowance.

Scales Of Pay Of Compounders

We do not recommend any further increase.

Scales Of Pay Of Nurses In The Hospitals Of The Ordnance Factories

The hospitals of Ordnance Factories are comparable, from the point of view of bed strength, with Railway hospitals. We suggest, therefore, that a higher grade of fully qualified Nurse be sanctioned on a scale of pay of Rs. 150—225 and that the scale of pay of the 'Matron and Sister-in-Charge' category be raised from Rs. 150—225 to Rs. 200—300. These are the scales recommended by the Pay Commission.

Scale Of Pay Of Ayahs

The Ayahs are in the scale of Rs. 30-½-35. The Labour Federations have suggested that this scale should be upgraded to Rs. 35-1-50. The scale applicable to Ayahs generally in other departments is Rs. 30-½-35. We, therefore, do not consider any improvement in the existing scale of pay called for.

Pay Of Dhobis/Washermen

The scale sanctioned for Dhobis/Washermen is not uniform in the different establishments. In some they are on the same grade as other unskilled labour, i.e., Rs. 30—35 while in others the semi-skilled scale of Rs. 35—50 has been sanctioned. Dhobis/Washermen ought to be at least treated as semi-skilled workers. We, therefore. recommend that the scale of Rs. 35—50. may be adopted uniformly in all the establishments.

Giving Effect To The Revised Scale Of Pay In The Case Of Sweepers Paid From Contingencies From January 1, 1947

The claim of the Labour Federations is that the Sweepers of the Ordnance Factories should be allowed arrears from January 1, 1947, the date from which the revised scales had effect in the case of employees not paid from contingencies. As all the Sweepers paid from contingencies in other Defence Establishments and in establishments under other Ministries of the Government of India have been allowed this scale only with effect from June 1, 1949, we are unable to recommend treating the Sweepers of the Ordnance Factories still more favourably by allowing the arrears from January 1, 1947.

Scale Of Pay Of Motor Drivers

We feel that there is no need to change the existing scale of pay applicable to Motor Drivers.

Scale Of Pay Of Armoured Fighting Vehicle Drivers

We recommend that the scale applicable to Tractor Drivers in the Military Farms may be made applicable to Drivers of Armoured Fighting Vehicles.

Recategorization Of Fire Patrolmen

It has been brought to our notice that orders have

been issued by the Ministry of Defence reclassifying the Fire Patrolmen as Supervisors (Non-technical).

Scales Of Pay Of Leaders Of Fire-Brigade Staff And Firemen In Ordnance Factories

In view of the fact that Leading Hands (Fire) generally start on Rs. 50 or Rs. 55 and go up to Rs. 75, 85, or even 125, we suggest a scale of Rs. 55-3-85 for Leading Hands (Fire) in Ordnance Factories as also in the M.E.S.

In the case of Firemen the scale of Rs. 35-1-50 seems to be reasonable for beginners, but a higher grade may be created on the scale of Rs. 40-1-50-260 as in Ordnance Depots, in establishments under the Naval Headquarters, and in the Delhi State Fire Service.

Scale Of Pay Of Photographers

The D.T.D. has recommended two grades, namely, Rs. 160-10-330 Grade I and Rs. 80-5-120-EB-8-160 Grade II, taking into consideration the different degrees of responsibilities and skill required. We recommend this suggestion for the consideration of the Government.

Scales Of Pay Of Telephone Operators

In the case of the clerical grade, it may be said that a Matriculate is likely to give better service than a non-Matriculate, but in the case of a Telephone Operator, there is no reason why a non-Matriculate may not prove as efficient as a result of practice and experience as a Matriculate because the work is essentially of a manual nature. Since the value of the post is recognized as Rs. 60—170, there is little justification for denying the full scale to those who are retained on the ground of their usefulness. This does not, however, necessarily mean that the Government would not be justified in insisting on Matriculation qualification for future recruitment.

Scale Of Pay Of Gatekeepers In Ordnance Factories

We feel that a comparison of the duties and responsibilities of the Inspectors in the Railways with those of Gatekeepers in the Ordnance Factories is not appropriate and do not consider that any anomaly exists in the present orders.

Scales Of Pay Of Subedar Durwans And Jamadar Durwans In The Ordnance Factories

The scales prescribed for the categories mentioned are Rs. 35-1-50 and Rs. 40-1-50-2-60, respectively. The Labour Federations have suggested that these categories should be in the scale of Rs. 40-2-90. We do not see any justification for the suggestion.

Industrial Establishment

Pay Of Engravers In The Technical Development Establishments

It is understood that in the Ordnance Factories Machine Engravers may be on 'C' and 'D' Grades only while Hand Engravers may be on any of the four grades. It is obvious that if any alteration is to be made on the basis of the scales obtaining in the Factories, it would be appropriate to introduce lower scales as it would be appropriate to introduce scales which are higher. However, if the existing pay structure in the Technical Development Establishments is not to be altered, we can see the justification for prescribing the Groop 'B' scale, viz., Rs. 60—105, for Hand Engravers doing fine work. Whether all Hand Engravers are in fact doing fine work or whether some of them are doing only rough work, such as would merit no more than the existing scale, are, of conrse, questions of fact which should be settled by the Director. Those who are in fact employed on high grade work and pass the necessary trade test should be promoted to this category.

Pay Of Lappers In The Technical Development Establishment

Mr. Ghosh's Recommendations: If the existing system is to continue in the T.D.E., I consider that the category of Lapper (Precision) may be raised from Grade 'D' to Grade 'C', i.e., its scale may be Rs. 50-2-60-3/2-75. I can not see any *prima facie* justification for jumping one group and raising it from Group 'D' to Group 'B' straightaway. So far as Lappers (Ordinary) are concerned, the existing scale, the maximum of which is higher than the manimum of the lowest grade of Lappers in the Ordnance Factories, seems adequate.

Mr. Subramanian's Recommendations: The scale prescribed for D.T.D. and other establishments starting from Rs. 60 is Rs. 60-5/2-75-EB-3-105. I suggest that this scale should be prescribed for Lappers (Precision). As for Lappers (Ordinary) I feel that the existing scale of Rs. 35-1-50-2-60 is adequate as it is not very different from the scale suggested by D.T.D.

Scale Of Pay Of Shooters (in T.D.E.s)

The D.T.D. is also of the view that the existing scale of pay of shooters is inadequate and has recommended two grades of Pay for Shooters in the scale of Rs. 50-2-60-EB-3/2-75 and Rs. 40-2-60-EB-3/2-75. In view of the fact that Grade I as proposed is the same as Grade II except that Grade I starts higher up, the Committee considers that there is no advantage in creating a higher grade. If Shooters of some experience and skill are required, it would necessarily mean that they must have undergone about five years of service at least in Grade II after which period they would, in any case, be drawing Rs. 50. Considering the duties of the Shooters, we feel that an improvement in their scale is called for and recommend that the scale of Shooters be revised to Rs. 40-2-60-EB-3/2-75.

Scale Of Pay For Proof Firers

The D.T.D. is of the view that the present scale is inadequate and has recommended an improvement in the existing scale but has suggested that there may be two grades of Proof Firers, the first grade in the scale of Rs. 40-2-60-EB-3/2-75 and the second grade in the scale of Rs. 35-1-50-EB-2-60.

We recommend that the proposal of the D.T.D. may be accepted. But here again adequate trade test justifying the higher scale should be laid down.

Scales Of Pay Of Book-Binders, Compositors And Printers Of The C.A.F.V. Depot, Kirkee Press

Book-Binders: We recommend that the scale may be improved to Rs. 35-1-50-2-60 applicable to Group 'E' Tradesmen under the D.O.S.

Printers: Taking into consideration that the Ordnance Depot Press is not as large as a Central Government Press, we regard that the existing scale of pay is adequate.

Compositors: We consider that the existing scale for Compositors in the Ordnance Depot Press compares fairly with the scale for Compositors in the lower grade at the Central Government Presses and no further improvement is necessary.

Re-classification Of Fitters As Fitter Mates In Technical Development Establishments

We agree that it would be not correct to admit the scale of Rs. 60—105, which is intended for full-fledged Fitters, to the lower category of Fitters in the old set-up who were in fact nothing but Fitter Mates although not designated as such. We however recommend that all such Fitters who have been reclassified as Fitter Mates should be allowed a chance to appear for a trade test to prove their fitness to be classified as Fitters.

Scale Of Pay For Fitter Mates In the T.D.E.s

We regard that the scale for Fitter Mates should be Rs. 35-1-50 applicable to the semi-skilled trade and other tradesmen's mates.

Higher Starting Pay For Instrument Mechanics And Tele-Communication Mechanics In The Scale Of Rs. 90-185 After Passing A Trade Test

The Uttar and Madhya Pradesh Ordnance Employers Federation drew attention to a Government order according to which recruitment to the posts of tradesmen could be made at the stage above the efficiency bar if tradesmen with higher skill and experience were required. They had to pass a special trade test. The existing men also were permitted to take their chance along with direct recruits and could be promoted above the efficiency bar on passing the trade test. The complaint is that in the T.D.E.s. Instrument Mechanics and Tele-Communication Mechanics are started only on the minimum of the scale of Rs. 90—185 without being given an opportunity to pass a special trade test.

Since Government orders, referred to by the Federation, were issued mainly to enable the Heads of Establishments to recruit persons with previous experience and higher skill who were not prepared to start on the minimum of the time scale, we consider that where men are available on the minimum or where more experienced men are not actually required, there could be no justification for invoking these orders and promoting men to higher stages in the time scale. We do not feel that there has been any anomaly.

Reclassification Of Turners And Grinders In Gauge Rooms In The T.D.E.s Who Are Employed As Tool-Makers

We agree that specialization in individual trades does not necessarily qualify tradesmen to become Tool-Makers. Where, however, a full-fledged Tool-Maker is required and the tradesman possesses the necessary qualifications, he should be appointed as a Tool-Maker.

Pay Of Tradesmen In The M.E.S.

Since the nature of the work is essentially the same in the two organizations, it seems *prima facie* likely that if there is need for different degrees of skill in the Central P.W.D., there should be a similar need in the M.E.S. though there may be some variation in the actual degree of skill required or the proportion of men required with different degrees of skill. The correct course would be to re-examine the requirements of the M.E.S. and to compare them with the requirements of the Central P.W.D. for tradesmen of varying degrees of skill and then to lay down for the M.E.S. comparable short-time scales for different degrees of skill within one trade, wherever necessary.

Pay Of Semi-Skilled Categories In The M.E.S.

The M.E.S. Unions suggested that certain categories which are now classed as semi-skilled and for whom the scales of Rs. 35-1-50 or Rs. 35-1-50-2-60 have been sanctioned should be categorized as skilled and given the scale of Rs. 40-2-60-3/2-75.

It is for the technical experts to compare the skill required in these grades with the skill required of the tradesmen who have been given the minimum scale of

Rs. 40—75. There would be a case for an equalization of the pay scales if the degrees of skill and other qualifications required are similar. Of the abovementioned categories the Meter Reader and Storeman probably require to be considered separately. The scale of pay for a Meter Reader in the Central P.W.D. appears to be Rs. 35-1-50 while it is understood that recently the scale of the Meter Reader in the M.E.S. has been raised to the scale of Rs. 50-2-60-3/2-75-3-105. It is not quite clear whether this disparity in the scale of pay is justified. The matter should be examined with reference to the qualifications required. The category of Storeman does not exist in the Central P.W.D. The Engineer-in-Chief has stated that this category is mostly employed in Engineer Store Depots. The existing scale of Rs. 35-1-50 seems to be too low for this category and the Engineer-in-Chief himself has recommended the scale of Rs. 40-1-50-2-60. The proposal of the Engineer-in-Chief is supported.

Pay Of Tradesmen In The M.E.S.

Mr. Subramanian's Recommendations: While agreeing with the view mentioned in the note above, I would suggest that an attempt should be made to evolve a uniform wage structure in all establishments under the Defence Ministry. I have recommended in a separate note dealing with Ordrance Factories that all jobs should first be divided into the categories of Highly-skilled, Skilled, Semi-skilled and Unskilled and then, if necessary, be divided further into grades within each category. I have also suggested the pay-scales which I consider suitable for each category and grade. If those recommendations are accepted, I suggest that an effort be made to introduce the same structure in the M.E.S.

Pay Of Tradesmen In The Naval Dockyard

As explained previously in connection with Industrial workers in the M.G.O.'s establishments and in the M.E.S., the Committee is of the opinion that the basis of the Pay Commission's recommendations in regard to industrial workers generally is that there are varying degrees of skill even within one trade. They accordingly recommended short time scales for varying degrees of skill. It appears that in so far as the Naval Dockyard is concerned, a compromise arrangement has been made. To a limited extent varying degrees of skill have been recognized by creating two grades in the same trade in a number of cases. The scales of pay, though modelled somewhat on the scales sanctioned for the M.G.O. establishments, have generally higher maxima. If the scales were framed in accordance with the Pay Commission's recommendations, they would have been, generally speaking, lower, and it cannot, therefore, be held that the Pay Commission's recommendations justify further improvements in the existing scales.

There is no justification in the proposals that the system of trade tests should be abolished or that promotion should have no relation to vacancies. Recruitment and promotion in the case of tradesmen must be based on trade tests. As a man's pay should be related to the job on which he is employed, it is obvious also that promotion should be against vacancies.

Pay Of Workmen In Naval Armament Depot, Waltair

It is true that in the case of the workers of the Naval Armament Depot the Pay Commission's recommendations have not been strictly followed but the departure has been to the advantage of the workers rather than to their disadvantage. In the circumstances, it is considered that no case has been made out for a further improvement in the pay scales.

1. **Pay Of Tradesmen In The Naval Dockyard, Bombay**
2. **Pay Of Workmen In The Naval Armament Depot, Waltair**

Mr. Subramanian's Recommendations: I suggest that the wage structure obtaining in these establishments be brought in line with the wage structure obtaining in Ordnance Factories. In the case of the latter, I have recommended that all trades should, in the first instance, be divided into the major categories of Highly-skilled, Skilled, Semi-skilled and Unskilled and, if need be, into further grades within each category. I have also suggested the pay scales which I consider appropriate. I feel that an attempt should be made to evolve a uniform wage structure for all establishments under the Defence Ministry.

Wage Structure Of Tradesmen Under The D.O.S., D.M.E., D.T.D. And E-in-C.

Mr. Ghosh's Recommendations: If the Technical Directors, after a joint discussion, find that there requirements can be met, consistent with the interest of the workers, within the present framework, but with relatively minor variations, there is no reason why the entire pay structure should be upset and recast on the lines recommended by the Pay Commission. As I see it, the strict application of the Pay Commission's recommendations or the adoption of the pattern followed in the Ordnance Factories may not be in the general interest of the workers in the M.G.O. establishments, etc.

Mr. Subramainan's Recommendations: In my report on pay scales in Ordnance Factories, I have recommended a scheme based on the division of trades, first into the Highly-skilled, Skilled, Semi-skilled, and

Unskilled Categories and then, if necessary, into grades within each category depending on the degree of skill required. I would suggest the adoption of the same system in these establishments also and the application of the same scales. There will, no doubt, be some differences, depending on the degree of skill required, regarding the particular grades of a trade that may be found necessary or suitable, but subject to such variations, I feel, that the basic system and structure should be the same for all establishments under the Defence Ministry.

Pay Of Labourers Engaged In Lifting Heavy Loads

Mr. Ghosh's Recommendations: I consider that if the present anomaly is to be removed, it should be removed by abolishing the higher scale for the labourers employed on lifting heavy loads in the Ordnance Factories and not by extending the higher scale to all other Defence installations.

Mr. Subramanian's Recommendations: I suggest that the anomaly be removed by extending the scale of Rs. 32-½-35-1-40 to all Defence installations and prescribing it in sections or departments where heavy loads have habitually to be lifted.

A slightly higher scale for persons who have constantly to handle particularly heavy loads is, in my opinion, fully justified. Whether the lifting of heavy loads occurs as a regular feature of work in a particular section or department is, of course, a question of fact which has to be decided by men on the spot.

Pay Of Beldars In The M.E.S.

We do not consider that a case has been made out for the introduction of a higher scale for Beldars. In the C.P.W.D. also they are paid on the same scale of Rs. 30-½-35, the scale applicable to Unskilled labourers in general. Besides, the Pay Commission recommended a uniform scale of Rs. 30-½-35 for all Unskilled labourers on the living wage principle although previously different types of Unskilled workers might have got different rates of pay.

General Points

Loss Of Pay On Promotion To A Higher Post

Since this matter was represented to the Committee, orders have been issued that the fixation of pay in such cases should be regulated in accordance with the following principles:

(i) In cases of officiating promotion in the direct line of appointment—If the pay drawn by a Government servant (whether permanent or temporary) in a post held temporarily or in an officiating capacity exceeds the minimum of the scale of the higher post to which he is promoted, he may be given the next higher stage in the scale of the higher post subject to the fulfilment of the following conditions:

(a) That the Government servant is qualified to be confirmed in the lower post or cadre and that he has acquired stability of tenure therein by working for more than three years at the time of promotion;

(b) The lower post or cadre continues to exist on a long-term basis; and

(c) The Government servant would have continued to work in the lower post or cadre but for his promotion to the higher post.

(ii) In case of officiating promotions not in the direct line of appointment—No protection will generally be afforded in such cases.

As fixation of pay in accordance with these principles is a relaxation of the existing rules, it has been laid down that Government orders will be necessary in each case. When dealing with a large number of employees as in the Defence establishments, it is inevitable that if each case has to be referred to the Government, there will be considerable delay in the issue of orders. We realize that this matter does not fall within the Terms of Reference, but since it affects a large number of employees in the Defence Organization, in particular, we feel that it might be advisable to bring to the the notice of the Government the suggestion that powers to fix the pay in accordance with the principles laid down should be delegated to lower authorities.

Anomaly In The Matter Of Fixation Of Pay Resulting From The Classification Of Posts Into Industrial And Non-Industrial Sections

It is recommended that the Government may issue suitable instructions stating that in the matter of fixation of pay, the rules applicable to the non-industrial employees should generally apply to the industrial employees also, now that the latter have been brought on to monthly scales of pay.

All-India Service Liability Allowance

Mr. Ghosh's Recommendations: The Commission has made certain observations in different places in its report indicating that the employees should not ordinarily be transferred from one area to another unless absolutely essential and that such transfers should generally be limited to higher-grade officers. The question whether any particular category should be transferred or not from one area to another is for the administration to decide in the light of the requirements. I find no support in the Pay Commission's recommendations, however (except in the case of the Divisional Accounts of the office of the A.G.C.R. and the P.&T. Department) that the pay should be enhanced on the ground of liability to all-India service. However, if any category is, in fact, transferable anywhere in India in the same manner as the staff in the Defence Accounts and Defence Audit Departments, it is difficult to hold that an allowance is justified in the case of the latter but not in the case of the former. I consider that this anomaly should be rectified as early as possible.

Mr. Subramanian's Recommendations: So long as it is considered proper to grant an allowance to the staff in the Defence Accounts and Defence Audit Departments, a similar allowance should, I feel, be given to all other staff in Defence establisements who are subject to the same liability. The question of an allowance would arise only if the liability were imposed. In this connection I would invite attention to the Pay Commission's recommendation, at page 340 of their Report, "that liability to serve in all parts of the country should ordinarily be limited to the higher-grade appointments only". Again at page 24 they have stated that "it has been rightly insisted on that public employees in the lower levels of pay should, as far as possible, not be transferred out of their Provinces". Observance of this principle, if found feasible, would eliminate the bulk of the lower categories from the list liable to all-India service. I suggest that an attempt be made to put this principle into practice.

1. **Time-Barred Arrears On Account Of Revised Scales Of Pay Payable To Persons Retrenched During The Year 1947**

2. **Payment Of Arrears To Those Retrenched And Re-employed On Or Before January 1, 1948**

Mr. Subramanian's Recommendations: The Civilians in Defence Services (Revision of Pay) Rules, promulgated on December 31, 1947, contain a provision that employees may elect the revised scales of pay with effect from either January 1, 1947, or January 1, 1948. The question arose whether the benefit of the retrospective application of the revised scales from January 1, 1947, should be extended to those who were discharged from service in the course of the year 1947. The Government finally passed orders in their O.M. No. 4083/331/D-11, dated May 4, 1948, allowing payment of arrears of pay and dearness allowance based on the revised scales of pay to those whose services were terminated between January 1, 1947, and January 1, 1948, on account of retirement, death or discharge on termination of sanctioned posts, subject to two conditions, viz.,

(i) That payment of arrears would be permissible only if the person concerned (or in the case of a claim pertaining to a person who has died, his legal heir) applied for it in writing within six months from the date of issue of the orders; and

(ii) That persons who were in service on January 1, 1948, would not be allowed the concession in respect of any broken period of service prior to that date.

The Federations have represented that the orders passed were not publicized, that they were not communicated to the persons who were entitled to claim arrears, and that a number of discharged persons, having gone to distant places and lost touch with their old establishments, were unable, for no fault of theirs, to prefer claims. They, therefore, request that a fresh opportunity should be given to all such persons to put in their claims and that on this occasion no time limit should be fixed. The complaint of the Federations that the orders did not receive adequate publicity and that they were not communicated to the individuals concerned seems to be correct. Some time necessarily elapses between the passing of orders by the Government and the notification of those orders in the individual establishments. The remainder of the six-month period is, in my opinion, not sufficient to enable a discharged employee who has probably left the place and gone far away in search of a job to make a claim unless, of course, he is informed of it through a notice. As this was not done, I feel that discharged workers did not get a reasonable opportunity of preferring claims. I would, therefore, suggest that a fresh opportunity should be given to all such persons to put in claims and that on this occasion adequate publicity might be given to the orders. As the offer cannot be kept open indefinitely, a time limit of one year may be fixed from the date of communication of the orders to the Federations.

The rights of the persons who, by virtue of their seniority, were allowed re-employment before January 1, 1948, should not in any way be less than those of persons who were discharged without any subsequent re-employment; nor should persons appointed before January 1, 1948, be treated less generously than their juniors who were re-appointed after January 1, 1948. In view of these circumstances, I feel that discharged employees who were re-employed before January 1, 1948, should also be allowed the benefit of the concession.

Mr. Ghosh's Views: I feel that the question of payment of arrears is outside the Terms of Reference and therefore it is inappropriate for the Committee to express any views on it. Similar cases may have occurred in other Departments also.

Pay of Displaced Personnel

Mr. Subramanian's Recommendations: The Federations have made two demands, viz.:

(1) That all displaced E.T.E. personnel appointed in Defence Establishments should be given the right

of election of the prescribed scales from January 1, 1947; and

(2) That increments should be allowed on being brought over to the revised scales to all displaced personnel whether they joined establishments in India before or after January 1, 1948.

The request for being allowed the right of election of the prescribed scales from January 1, 1947, cannot be supported.

Displaced persons who managed to secure employment in India before January 1, 1948, being in position on the relevant date, were allowed the right of election of the revised scales from January 1, 1948, or the actual date of employment in India. The consequence of this was that they got at least the benefit of Clause (c) of Rule 8 (1) of the Revision of Pay Rules and were placed on the prescribed scale at the stage next above their present pay. Thus invariably they got at least one increment by the operation of this rule. No such benefit accrued to persons who joined the establishments in India after January 1, 1948, as, in their case, the question of electing the revised scales of pay from January 1, 1948, did not arise. They were brought on to the new scales under the normal rules, i.e., without the benefit of the next higher stage. The request is that persons who, through the exigencies of the times, happened to secure employment after January 1, 1948, should not be placed in a worse position than their colleagues who, through good fortune, happened to secure employment before that date.

I feel that though this is strictly not a case of anomaly in the implementation of the pay scales, the circumstances are such as would warrant redress. In 1947 the times were exceptional; many persons were unable to get out of Pakistan in time and those who managed to come away to India did not know where to go or what to do. In view of all these circumstances, it is through no merit or fault of displaced personnel that some secured employment before January 1, 1948, and others after that date. It would be a slight mitigation of the hardship caused to such persons if all were treated alike and those who joined after January 1, 1948, given the benefit which would have accrued to them had they joined before that date.

Mr. Ghosh's Views: Whether, in view of the circumstances obtaining at the time of partition and thereafter, displaced persons, who were either late in coming out of Pakistan or even if they came to India before January 1, 1948, were actually absorbed after that date, should be treated in the same manner as those who were luckier and came to India and were absorbed earlier is a general question of policy which it is not for this Committee to consider. The representation should be examined by the Ministry of Defence.

Continuity of Service On Transfer From E.T.E. To Regular Establishment

It has been represented that in the past persons have been transferred from E.T.E. to temporary establishment, and vice versa and that in such cases the service should be regarded as continuous. We are informed that Government orders have been issued recognizing continuity of service in such cases for the purpose of fixation of pay.

Classification Of Employees As Industrial And Non-Industrial

Mr. Ghosh's Recommendations: Of the categories now classified as Industrial the Federations want that Switch-board Attendants, Laboratory Attendants and Viewers should be classified as Non-industrial.

I do not think that Switch-board Attendants should be classified as Non-industrial. They are tradesmen and classified as Industrial everywhere. As regards Laboratory Attendants they should, if possible, be treated alike in the Inspectorates and Factories. I suggest that the D.T.D. and D.G.O.F. should jointly examine this matter.

The problem of Viewers is a special one. Although this category exists both in the Inspectorates under the D.T.D. and also in the Factories, the matter was not evidently considered jointly by the two Directors with the result that an anomaly was created by T.D.E. Viewers being declared as Non-industrial, while Viewers in Factories continued to be treated as Industrial. If the matter is considered objectively with reference to the nature of work of Viewers, one must classify all of them as Industrial.

Mr. Subramanian's Recommendations: I agree with the suggestion to classify Laboratory Attendants as 'Non-industrial' and Switch-board Attendants as 'Industrial'.

The present attempt to transfer the bulk of 'A' Grade Viewers into examiners is liable to be misconstrued by the lower-grade Viewers.

Above all there must be consistency in classification. The top men cannot be classified as Non-industrial while the rest are classified as Industrial. Similarly, the same category should not be classified as Industrial in one establishment and as Non-industrial in another. So long as these are observed, I would leave the classification to be done jointly by the Directors of the two establishments, namely, Factories and Technical Development.

Fixation Of Pay In The Prescribed Scales Based On Pay In Lower Grades To Which Personnel Were Reverted Subsequent To January 1, 1947

We do not regard that the pays of the persons have been incorrectly fixed.

Method Of Converting The Daily Rate Of Pay Into Monthly Rate Of Pay For The Purpose Of Fixing The Starting Pay In The Revised Scales

The grievance of the Federation is that though they were paid on daily rates of pay they were also often called upon to work on holidays and receive pay and, therefore, their monthly pay should have been calculated at 30 times their daily rate instead of 26 times as has been done.

We do not appreciate the argument since even now if the employees are called upon to work on Sundays and holidays then get overtime pay or compensatory holiday in lieu and, therefore, the pay the daily-rated persons got for holidays should not be taken into consideration. We understand that the principle adopted in determining the monthly pay of daily-rated workers in other Ministries is also similar to that followed in the case of personnel of Defence Establishments, and, therefore, no anomaly has been established.

Conveyance Allowance—Term of Reference III

Mr. Ghosh's Recommendations: In my view, the demand for the general grant of a conveyance allowance to all Defence employees is not reasonable.

Only where men have to travel long distances by train or other public conveyance and the fare is considerably more could there be a case for assistance.

Mr. Subramanian's Recommendations: I find myself unable to agree with the view that the uniqueness of the case of the Defence installations alone will qualify for a conveyance allowance.

In my opinion there are the following special circumstances which would necessitate payment of a conveyance allowance to the employees of a large number of Defernce Establishments, viz.:

(i) That many Defence installations are situated at considerable distances from large towns or other large centres of residence;

(ii) That even where installations are situated in or near towns the concentration of thousands of workers at one place creates problems which force workers to go far in search of housing;

(iii) That large numbers of workers have to spend appreciable sums on transport;

(iv) That such expenditure is a permanent feature of their entire working life and is not such as can eventually be avoided by securing a transfer or the allotment of Government quarters as in the case of the majority of the employees of other Departments; and

(v) That physical tiredness in a manual worker is detrimental to the employer himself.

As regards the amount of the allowance, I feel that while it should not become a source of profit to the recipient, it should be sufficient to meet the extra expenditure on transport.

I suggest a scale as follows:

1. Not more than five miles—nil.
2. More than five miles but not more than 10 miles —Rs. 5 p.m.
3. More than 10 miles but not more than 15 miles —Rs. 10 p.m.
4. More than 15 milles—Rs. 12 p.m. or the actual cost of a ticket if it exceeds Rs. 12 p.m. but subjeet to a maximum of Rs. 15 p.m.

Permanency—Term of Reference IV

Industrial Employees : It has been brought to our notice that while by and large industrial employees under the Government may be on a temporary basis, it is not an absolutely uniform rule. There are certain establishments where permanent posts have been created for industrial employees, e.g., the C.P.W.D., the Mints at Bombay and Calcutta, the Security Printing Press, Nasik, and, as far as information is available, also the Railway Workshops.

After considering all the aspects of the question we have come to the conclusion that such of the appointments, held by industrial employees, as are certain to be continued indefinitely should be declared as permanent. Obviously, no uniform method of determining the number of such appointments can be laid down. For example, while in the Technical Development Establishment, it may be possible for the Government to declare a large number of appointments as permanent, on the ground that there is unlikely to be a contraction in this establishment, in the Ordnance Depots which are likely to contract the number must proportionately be very much less. In other words, each establishment must be considered on its own merits. We recommend, however, that the Government should take a decision in this matter in respect of each of the establishments at an early date. In some establishments, the Government may have to proceed stage by stage, i.e., to start with a small number may be declared as permanent and it may be increased gradually as the future of the organization becomes clearer.

A demand was put forward by the labour Federations that all industrial employees who have put in a certain number of years, say, three years or so, should all be made permanent straightaway. We consider that it is not a proposition which can be accepted. Persons can be confirmed only if there are permanent appointments and appointments can be declared as permanent only if they are likely to continue on a permanent basis. In some offices or departments it may be possible to adopt length of service as a criterion for confirmation, where the number of permanent appointments is in no case likely to be less than the number of men to be confirmed on this basis but even in this case, permanent strength is determined with reference to the permanent requirement of staff. But in an organization like the Defence Services, this is obviously not possible. It is well known that during an emergency the Defence Services have to expand and that the emergency may sometimes continue for a number of years, but obviously the Government cannot agree to confirm automatically all employees who were recruited originally for the emergency and who may have continued for a number of years. On behalf of the Defence Ministry, it has been mentioned that the Defence Organization in India has not yet come to its normal peace-time conditions. Therefore, confirmation cannot be made purely with reference to the length of service of an individual and a prerequisite of confirmation must be the creation of permanent appointments.

Non-Industrial Employees: On behalf of the Non-industrial employees, it was brought to our notice that even though the Government had directed as early as in 1949 that a permanent nucleus should be created, the direction has not yet been given effect to. It is suggested that steps may be taken to implement the decision already arrived at.

Piece-Work Rates—Term of Reference V

Mr. Ghosh's Recommendations: There are various systems of payment by results the object of all of which is to achieve greater output by providing an incentive the workers to produce more than they would otherwise do. But whatever the system or the extent of incentive may be, it is of the utmost importance that the rate should be correctly fixed. Otherwise, the disadvantages may sametimes outweigh the advantages of the system.

Ignoring for the time being the existence of unduly high profits in some cases, it is obvious that unless the piece-work rates are related to the current rates, the principle that a piece-worker of average ability working at a standard speed should earn 25% of profit over time-rates may itself be vitiated. The old daily rates are no longer in force and it is not correct to cling to the piece-work rates based on them only in order to avoid an increase in the rates which are unduly high. The problem of unduly high rates should be faced squarely by reviewing them, taking into consideration the persent methods and instruments of production; but, in any case, the piece-rates should be related to the new scales.

Mr. Subramanian's Recommendations: The present methods of calculation of piece-work earnings are unsuitable and should be replaced by a system in which the piece-rates will be directly related to, and evolved from, the revised monthly scales of pay.

I feel that the minimum of a scale has no special significance in relation to the skill of the worker or the value of the worker to the employer and should, therefore, not be taken as the appropriate reference point for correlating time-rates with piece-rates.

I suggest that the actual monthly rates, not the minimum of the scale as at present, should be guaranteed to all piece-workers, high or low. I do not think that it is sufficient to guarantee the minimum of the scale. What the workers are asking for is their actual wages, i.e., their time-rates, and the minimum does not represent the time-rate in the case of all workers other than new recruits.

Leave—Term of Reference VI

We consider that the provisions of the Factories Act must be regarded as satisfying the need for requisite rest and therefore, purely from the point of view of need, it would be difficult to establish that an improvement in the leave terms of the industrial employees is justified. As the existing rules may, by and large, be considered to be no less favourable than the rules contained in the Factories Act, any improvement of the former would naturally widen the difference between the leave rules applicable to the industrial employees in the Government industrial undertakings and those in the private industries which, according to the Pay Commission, would be desirable to avoid. Even so, we have come to the conclusion that the considerations urged by the representatives of labour are sufficiently important to justify a reconsideration of this attitude.

The Industrial employees at present get 14 paid holidays while the Non-industrial employees generally get 20 to 21 paid holidays. There is a great deal of criticism already about the excessive leave given to Government employees. Apart from this, the need of the present time is to increase production. We are, therefore, opposed to any increase in the number of holidays to industrial workers. Uniformity can, therefore, be achieved only by reduction of the number of holidays for Non-industrial employees, but if this is not possible, there is no reason why the holidays of the Industrial workers should be increased.

We do not recommend the introduction of a system of casual leave to Industrial workers. That would lead to a lot of administrative difficulties and would affect production. The equalization of the basic leave rules will confer a substantial benefit on the Industrial workers and no further additional benefit is, in our opinion, justified.

Government's Contribution To Provident Fund—Term Of Reference VII

We recommend that the Pay Commission's recommendation should be implemented. In other words the Government's contribution should be equal to employees' compulsory contribution, which is 8⅓% of the emoluments (as defined in the Provident Fund Rules).

Overtime Pay—Term Of Reference VIII

Mr. Ghosh's Recommendations: I am given to understand that the legal view is that apart from the workers employed in shops, only those employed in estimating, planning and drawing offices directly connected with production would come under the definition of workers under the Factories Act. Storekeepers, gate-keepers, durwans, lorry drivers, nurses, fire brigade staff, etc., do not come under the definition of workers under the Factories Act. My view, therefore, is that there can be no case for the grant of overtime pay to such employees under the Factories Act. As regards the application of the departmental rules which provide for overtime pay for systematic overtime work in the case of Non-industrial workers, I think there should rarely be any occasion for these categories to work systematic overtime. Such staff like gate-keepers, durwans, fire brigade staff, etc., generally work on shift system and any increase in the work of the production section would not affect their hours of work.

The only category which requires further consideration is the category of clerks. It has been represented that the clerks in administrative offices who have now to work to the same working hours as shop clerks and Industrial workers should be eligible for overtime payment. It is understood that clerks in administrative offices (except those who work in estimating, drawing and planning offices directly connected with production) do not fall under the definition of "workers" under the Factories Act. We see no objection to this category being treated on a par with industrial staff in the matter of overtime.

Mr. Subramanian's Recommendations: In view of the fact that clerks in ordinary civil offices work only for 36 hours and that clerks in factories have to keep pace with Industrial workers, there would be every justification for treating them on a par with Industrial workers even in respect of the quantum of overtime and paying them at twice the rate on those occasions on which they are required to work beyond 48 hours. These recommendations would apply equally to Checkers.

As regards other categories of Non-industrial staff in factories such as gate-keepers, durwans, lorry drivers, orderlies, nurses, fire-brigade staff and telephone operators, it is understood that while some of them may be working on a three-shift basis, others have to work the same working hours including overtime as Industrial workers. Those working on a three-shift basis are not normally liable to be subjected to systematic overtime. If at any time they are called upon to work systematic overtime and are so certified to be working, they should be given both departmental overtime and overtime over 48 hours on the same terms as the rest of the Non-industrial staff who are presumed to be working systematic overtime.

As regards the complaint that Supervisors in Ordnance Factories are not being paid overtime pay on account of their exemption under Section 64 (1) of the Factories Act, I feel that the question whether exemption should be sought in respect of the lowest category of employees in the chain of supervision should be re-examined. If there are no great advantages in seeking exemption, it would be as well to leave them within the scope of the Factories Act so that they might be entitled to overtime at double the rate for work beyond 48 hours. If, on the other hand, there are any compelling reasons why exemption should be sought in respect of them, I agree that they should at least be equated to chargemen and similar categories who are entitled to a higher rate of departmental overtime.

Gratuity—Term Of Reference IX

Mr. Ghosh's Recommendations: Taking everything into account, I suggest the following:

(i) In the case of ex-E.T.D. personnel who are eventually confirmed, E.T.E. service should count as equivalent to temporary service.

(ii) In the case of ex-E.T.E. personnel who retire without being confirmed, gratuity should be sanctioned for E.T.E. service on the same scale as applicable to the Industrial employees.

Mr. Subramanian's Recommendations: As the claim of the Federations that extra-temporary service should count for pension has not been referred to the Committee, the main question for the decision of the Committee is whether gratuity should be allowed to Non-industrial employees in respect of their extra-temporary service prior to August 1, 1949, on the same terms as the concession shown to Industrial employees. The answer seems to be clear: they should be given a gratuity on the same terms. The two sets of employees classified as Industrial and Non-industrial in pursuance of the Government's orders of August 19, 1949, were all, prior to August 1, 1949, members of one and the same category, known as Extra Temporary, with the same service conditions, rights and liabilities. No doubt a division of the cadre was affected on August 1, 1949, one group being sent over to the benefits of the Provident Fund and the other to the benefits of quasi-permanency and eventual permanency and pension. It is true that as from August 1, 1949, the two categories could not look forward to treatment identical in all respects because of the inherent differences in the features of the two systems of retirement benefits, but there is no reason why all of them should not be treated alike in the matter of retirement benefits for the period prior to August 1, 1949, when they were all indistinguishably part and parcel of one and the same service. If then the group classified as Industrial Employees was allowed gratuity, I feel that the group classified as Non-industrial should also have been allowed gratuity on the same terms.

I feel that Non-industrial employees who were members of the former extra-temporary service should be allowed a gratuity on the same terms as Industrial employees. In the case of some who are not too old and may eventually become permanent, it may be more advantageous to treat half the extra-temporary service as qualifying for pension in the same way as the regular temporary service. I suggest that this concession may be extended to those who claim it in preference to gratuity.

The Federations have made the following demands in respect of the gratuity admissible to Industrial employees, namely:

(1) That the condition of five years' continuous service prior to August 1, 1949, should not be enforced;

(2) That gratuity should be paid at the rate of one month's pay for every completed year of service instead of half a month's pay; and

(3) That the amount of the gratuity should not be restricted to a maximum of 9 months' pay.

I am not inclined to consider demands (2) and (3) as it cannot be said that the existing provisions are unreasonable. As regards demand (1), viz., the condition of five years' service prior to August 1, 1949, I realize that this condition obtains in other departments also, but feel that it requires reconsideration.

In my opinion, the War Bonus paid should not be deducted from the gratuity sanctioned to Industrial employees under the Government's orders of August 19, 1949, in respect of their extra-temporary service prior to August 1, 1949.

COMMITTEE OF EXPERTS FOR BUILDING WORKS, 1950—REPORT

New Delhi, Ministry of Works, Production and Supply, 1952. 59p.

Convener : Shri B. S. Puri.
Members : Shri F. C. Badhwar; Maj-Gen. H. Williams.
Secretary : Shri C. B. Patel.

APPOINTMENT

The Committee of Experts for Building Works was constituted under the Ministry of Works, Production and Supply vide their Resolution No. AG 88(123), dated September 21, 1950.

TERMS OF REFERENCE

(i) To collect plans, specifications and construction costs of all types of cheap but durable buildings;

(ii) To continuously review building costs on both the civil and the military sides of Government activity with a view to advising the Ministries of the Government of India, and, if desirable, the public, on how to obtain the best value for money; and

(iii) To draw up an annual consolidation programme of construction of buildings, office, residential, etc., by the Government of India and estimate of the materials necessary for the purpose;

(iv) Any other matter on which the advice of the Committee is sought for by the Government.

CONTENTS

Letter to the Government of India; Summary of Report and Conclusions; Background; Planning of Works; Materials and Labour; Standards of Accommodation; Architectural Design; Structural Design; Ceiling Costs; Administrative and Executive Procedures; Appendices A to C.

RECOMMENDATIONS

Building Costs

Building costs are correlated to the cost of living. However, same degree of economy can be effected by.

(a) Expert architectural planning and structural designing; and

(b) Adopting utility scales of accommodation.

Notification Of Allotments Of Funds Two Years In Advance

Considerable time is required to progress a project through the different stages of planning. To ensure good economical planning, the practice followed in advanced countries of notifying the allotment of funds for capital projects two years in advance must be adopted. No major project should be included in a budget unless it has been administratively approved and technically examined in detail in the previous year.

National Building Organization

There is a need for the establishment of an expert organization to collect, collate and disseminate technical information available both at home and from abroad. This body should be essentially advisory in nature, and should have administrative, technical and co-ordinating functions.

Standardization Of The Quality Of Materials And Better Outturn From Labour

The standards laid down for various locally produced materials by the I.S.I. should be enforced in order to enable the designer to allow the maximum permissible stresses.

Similarly imported materials should be subjected to strict inspections and rigid compliance to specifications.

Time-honoured practice of paying labour on the basis of units of work done instead of daily or monthly basis should continue for higher production.

Standards Of Accommodation

Seven types of residential accommodation with the appropriate pay range of the occupants shown against each have been drawn up for housing Government employees. A 10% variation in plinth area is allowed for local conditions. In special circumstances exceptions will, however, have to be made to the application of these standards. Accommodation in the houses of upper class can be appreciably reduced.

Economy Through Architectural Design

Plans should be developed so as to utilize all available space to the fullest advantage.

The various components of the structure should be balanced in quality, quantity and cost and so arranged as to give a pleasing appearance.

Cost Reduction Through Structural Design

Traditional materials and building methods are generally most economical in India, but traditional specifications should not be followed blindly. The functional requirement of each component of a structure should be considered and materials and methods selected to ensure a sound permanent building with minimum cost. A departure from the usual specification in many instances will result in a saving in cost. Buildings erected from public funds should be durable as temporary buildings are more expensive due to heavy maintenance and depreciation costs.

Ceiling Costs

The Committee were of the opinion that some indication of reasonable ceiling costs of various types of buildings would be a useful guide to engineers and architects. It would also encourage them to explore methods to bring down the costs of buildings without sacrificing essentials.

Ceiling costs for Delhi in 1950 have been calculated and coefficients for variations in building costs indices have been worked out for a number of other localities to determine the permissible ceiling costs for the latter.

Economy In Construction Through Administrative And Executive Procedures

The tendency to design oversafe and therefore uneconomical structure must be discouraged. Engineers must be made more cost-minded. Quality control of works must be instituted, and laboratories set up both in the centre and in the field to test strength of materials and structures.

Contractors should be paid promptly but not later than 90 days after satisfactory completion of works. Delay in payment means higher tender costs.

ENQUIRY COMMITTEE ON GOVERNMENT HOUSING FACTORY, 1950—REPORT

New Delhi, Ministry of Health, 1951. 76p.

Chairman : Shri S. Moolgaokar.
Member : Shri Kanwar Sain.
Secretary : Shri S. V. Ayyar

APPOINTMENT

The Enquiry Committee on Government Housing Factory was constituted under the Ministry of Health vide their letter No. 4304-LSG/50 dated November 2, 1950.

TERMS OF REFERENCE

(i) To examine the organization of the factory that has been set up for the manufacture of Alcrete House-Building Material, and to make recommendations regarding its adequacy, or otherwise, for the purpose in view;

(ii) To examine the house-building material produced in the Alcrete factory and the design of the house, and to pronounce on their suitability from a structural and qualitative point of view;

(iii) To examine the operation of the Alcrete factory from the commercial (including financial) point of view, and to advise on the fixation of the sale price of the house in the initial period.

CONTENTS

Introductory; History of the Housing Project; Capital Expenditure of the Project; Proposed Design of the Low Cost House, Suitable for mass prefabrication; Comparison of original specifications of wall panels and specifications of wall panels as now produced; House-Building Material produced in the Factory and its suitability from a structural and qualitative point of view; Factory Production Capacity; **Section 1**: Estimated Cost of Production of MZ-2 Type houses; **Section 2**: Estimated Cost of Production of FR-1 Type houses; Comparative Study of Costs; Traditional type versus Prefabricated House MZ-2 and FR-1; Organization of the Factory; Fixation of the Selling Price for FR-1 Type house during the initial period; Summary of Conclusions and Recommendations; Acknowledgments; Appendices I to IV.

RECOMMENDATIONS

For the maintenance of production, a fairly satisfactory organization has been built up, but the factory has been staffed on a very generous scale. It is recommended that the economies suggested in Chapter X be carried out.

The house-building material produced in the factory at the moment comprises Foam Concrete Wall Panels which bear no relation whatsoever to the type of patented Wall Panels previously specified by the Consultants. The present type of plain Foam Concrete Load Bearing Panels bears all traces of a complex product, the commercial production of which does not appear to be a straightforward job. Production of a uniform product with the desired properties would appear to require considerable experience and close control of the manufacturing process. The Consultants' lack of experience in the production, on a commercial scale, of this complex product has been abundantly revealed. The performance of the factory product in actual practice has so far turned out to be unsatisfactory. Even with large-scale production, the cost per unit volume of Foam Concrete will not be comparable with that of ordinary dense concrete.

The original design known as MZ-2 Type with an aluminium roof and other expensive aluminium alloy parts may have been suitable from the point of view of quick production and erection, and also from the point of view of quick production and erection, and also from the point of view of the Consultants whose function it is to promote the use of aluminium products, but from the point of even reasonably low cost, the design has failed badly. Its production can no longer be considered in view of its high cost.

As far as the general design of the flat roof house is concerned there can be no complaints. The design would appear to be generally to the taste of the buying public.

The choice of Foam Concrete Wall Panels as a principal ingredient of a Low Cost House is not justified, because it is definitely more expensive than the traditional type of construction.

The Committee recommends that the Government should obtain from the Consultants a definite indication of the time required by them to complete the tuning up of the factory, which has been laid out at such heavy cost, strictly in accordance with the Consultants' designs and specifications.

The Committee recommends that future production at the factory should not be confined to the manufacture of the complex Foam Concrete Load Bearing Panels but should be extended so as to cover the vastly greater field of ordinary concrete products, such as hollow building blocks and various other types of precast products, which are in great demand for all types of building activities. It is felt that the future bread aud butter line for this factory should be the production of Hollow Concrete Building Blocks, used in place of ordinary bricks.

A precasting section should be set up for manufacturing concrete products of various types, so largely used by the C.P.W.D. and other house-builders.

1951

COMMITTEE ON PROPOSED LEGISLATION FOR THE REGULATION OF STOCK EXCHANGES AND CONTRACTS IN SECURITIES, 1951—REPORT

New Delhi, Ministry of Finance, Economic Affairs Department, 1951. 75p.

Chairman : Shri A. D. Gorwala.
Members : Shri K. R. P. Shroff; Shri B. N. Chaturvedi; Shri V. S. Krishnaswamy; Shri Pranlal Devkaran Nanjee; Shri L. S. Vaidyanathan; Shri P. D. Himatsinghka; Shri Jagmohandas J. Kapadia; Shri G. P. Kapadia.
Secretary : Shri P. S. Nadkarni.

APPOINTMENT

The Committee on Proposed Legislation for the Regulation of Stock Exchanges and Contracts in Securities was constituted under the Ministry of Finance, Economic Affairs Department, vide their Resolution No. 7 (85)-F.1/51 dated June 23, 1951.

TERMS OF REFERENCE

(i) To consider and report on the draft proposals of the Government;

(ii) To submit a revised draft Bill with a memorandum explaining in brief the reasons for each clause of the Bill; and

(iii) To make any other recommendations on the subject.

CONTENTS

Report; Draft Bill; Notes on Clauses; Notes on Blank Transfers.

RECOMMENDATIONS

The blank transfer system is an integral part of the Stock Exchange mechanism, directly affects the banking world and the capital market and enters into the daily trade, commerce and industry of that country.

The case for abolition or limitation of blank transfers must be established by reasoned arguments and not by dogmatic associations or appeals to opinions, however distinguished, as seems to have been attempted.

The assertions in favour of abolition or limitation of blank transfers fall into two categories:

(a) Those germane to Stock Exchanges (Section II) and therefore relevant for purposes of Stock Exchange legislation; and

(b) Those extraneous to Stock Exchanges (Section II) and therefore not strictly relevant.

The blank transfer system is alleged to stimulate unhealthy speculation. But in effect it does not even touch or influence short-term speculation which is 80 to 90% of the total speculation--speculation of a type which in certain circumstances is more apt to develop on unhealthy lines. The system is solely concerned with long-term speculation which amounts to only 10 to 20% of the total speculation and which in the main is *bona fide* healthy speculation. It follows that abolition or limitation of blank transfers can in no way curb unhealthy speculation.

The abolition or limitation of blank transfers will be not only unhelpful but will directly lead to serious and most harmful consequences, namely,

(a) Periodic artificial squeezes and emergencies in the market necessitating undesirable outside interference;

(b) Stimulation of unhealthy speculation and gambling for differences and sharp price fluctuations;

(c) Encouragement to monopoly practices complicating the problem of control; and

(d) Destruction of ready marketability and negotiability of shares with adverse repercussions on borrowing, lending and banking credit and on the finance of joint stock enterprises.

The system of blank transfers exists all over the world, particularly in America where it has reached a high stage of perfection and on the continent of Europe where bearer securities predominate. The system has been necessary for promoting progress and development. India is no exception and hence the necessity and widespread use of the blank transfer system whose usefulness must be recognized and appreciated rather than unthinkingly condemned.

It is not correct that blank transfers are bad delivery on the London Stock Exchange. The London rule merely discourages blank transfers by denying protection to holders on blank. Similar rules exist, for example, on the Bombay and Madras Stock Exchanges and are strictly observed. It is the unique differentiation between brokers and jobbers on the London Stock Exchange, the provision of special privileges to jobbers in the form of nominal stamp duties and the facilities for quick registration of shares by specialized corporations acting within the few square miles of the City of London on behalf of Companies spread over different parts of the country which together have produced conditions in which in the natural course of things it is more advantageous to register them to take the risk of carrying shares on blank. These conditions are non-existent in other parts of the world. For instance, in India brokers are not distinguished from jobbers, the stamp duties are extortionate without suitable exemptions, and the distances and delays involved in registration of shares are notorious. It follows that, contrary to London, for other parts of the world and particularly India the blank transfer system is not only desirable but also indispensable.

Government Securities are in the form of promissory notes and bearer bonds which are transferable on delivery and which therefore are a more perfect instrument than shares on blank transfers. If compulsory registration of Government Securities even without stamp duty is deemed destructive of free negotiability, what is the warrant for abolishing or limiting blank transfers for shares? If there are possibilities of abuse, the scope is much larger in regard to Government Securities whose total outstanding amount of about Rs. 1,600 crores exceeds by two or three times the market value of quoted shares computed at about Rs. 600 crores, particularly if it is remembered that shares generally do go up for registration at least at dividend time. If promissory notes and bearer bonds are necessary for financing Government borrowing, blank transfers are even more necessary for financing industry and providing credit for the trade and commerce of the country.

The whole trend of evolution has been to depersonalize ownership imparting to it mobility and liquidity. To advocate abolition or limitation of blank transfers to compel the owner to hold and "freeze" the share in his own name is to go back to the bullock-cart days and attempt to undo an evolutionary process not peculiar to India but common everywhere, more particularly in advanced and progressive countries.

It is not only that abolition or limitation of blank transfers is unnecessary, undesirable and potentially dangerous. The proposal as embodied in the scheme put forward is *prima facie* not feasible at all, evasion will be easy and widespread, and to the extent the scheme operates it will work to the disadvantage of *bona fide* market interests.

The scheme by which the proposal is intended to be enforced contemplates that all securities must pass through a Clearing House which all recognized Stock Exchanges must maintain and such a Clearing House must date the transfers. But it is forgotten that spot delivery contracts in the area to which the Act applies and all contracts—spot delivery or otherwise—in all parts of India other than the notified area will not pass through a Clearing House and in such cases the procedure for stamping transfers will not operate at all. Further the organization, maintenance and working of a Clearing House involve questions of expense, risk and administration. These practical problems are of formidable dimensions and therefore breakdowns of the Clearing House and therefore of the scheme are not only possible but more than probable. The proposition that all securities must pass through the Clearing House is far from feasible and as the only argument in favour of such a proposal is that the Act applies to all securities and not to listed securities only it would be by far the better thing to limit the scope of the Bill to listed securities only.

Apart from the Clearing House, the scheme for effectuating abolition or limitation of blank transfer also envisages that Companies should not register transfers if presented six months after they have passed through the Clearing House unless heavy penalties are paid. But companies cannot discriminate between one transfer and another and the method cannot work since in regard to spot delivery contracts and contracts in non-notified areas no question of transfers passing through a Clearing House can at all arise.

The scheme for abolition or limitation of blank transfers is open to evasion at almost every point and to the extent it operates it will penalize *bona fide* market delivery business and deliberately encourage monopolistic practices. On the London Exchange jobbers are distinct from brokers and they receive special exemptions in the matter of registration and stamp duties. No such exemptions will be available here as it is not feasible to differentiate between jobbers and brokers. As a result *bona fide* market interests will be heavily penalized and monopoly elements will gain at their expense.

Abolition or limitation of blank transfers has also been suggested on grounds not strictly germane to Stock Exchanges but even otherwise they have no inherent validity or compelling justification.

It has been contended that the holder on blank benefits at the expense of the Government. This belief is erroneous. The taxing statute gives the holder a choice between paying the stamp duty and thereby perfecting his title or not paying the stamp duty and risking the consequences, and there is nothing inequitable in such a position.

It has been urged that the abolition or limitation of blank transfers will bring the Government a large revenue. Consideration of revenue is no doubt important but it cannot be the determining factor when deciding questions of economic policy. If the stamp duties are made uniform and drastically reduced, as it has been recommended they must be if blank transfers are abolished or limited, the ultimate gain in revenue may not be as popularly imagined.

It has been objected that blank transfers make Company records incomplete, inaccurate and misleading. In this connection it is not generally appreciated that all shares do not circulate on blank indefinitely. Shares generally do go up for registration every six months or year at dividend time as can be confirmed by making inquiries. As an encouragement to this normal practice it has been suggested, and the Report has accepted the suggestion, that an option may be given in law to the registered holder not to pay to the beneficial holder the dividend collected unless the shares are transferred out of his name. This will ensure that shares are lodged for transfer when the annual list of shareholders is prepared. But so long as a floating stock exists—and it must exist in the nature of things—and shares are held by nominees, the share registers will remain in any event incomplete and inaccurate, no matter what is done and no matter whether blank transfers are abolished or limited or not.

It is observed, and rightly, that blank transfers often saddle the registered holders of partly-paid shares with an indefinite capital liability even after the shares are sold. Registration at dividend time as suggested above offers a partial solution. But the seller desiring complete protection has the remedy in his own hands. He must make an appropriate stipulation when he sells the partly-paid shares and for that the Stock Exchanges provide special facilities.

It has been asserted that blank transfers help evasion of income-tax. The Income-tax Investigation Commission has also complained to this effect. But there seems to be some misunderstanding. The blank transfer system occupies a completely neutral position in this matter. No doubt evaded moneys are held in the form of Government Securities, bullion, precious stones, etc., none of which carry identity labels and the scope here is much greater. To argue that blank transfers should be abolished or limited because evaded moneys are held in this form is tantamount to arguing that Government Securities, bullion, precious stones, etc., which are also employed as a medium for the same purpose, should also be similarly done away with. The proposition can hardly be sustained.

The last contention is that blank transfers should be either abolished or limited because they directly contribute to establishment of monopoly control over joint stock companies. The argument seems to be misconceived. The monopolist acquires control the moment he purchases the shares, no matter whether the shares are retained on blank or subsequently lodged for transfer in his own name, or in the name of his bankers, or in the name of the companies under his control, or in the names of his nominees. In fact, in such cases, shares are more often lodged for registration than held on blank so as to avoid difficulties of mobilizing voting control. It is the concentration of money power which enables the monopolist to purchase shares from *bona fide* investors and others at fabulous prices and it is this concentration of money power and not the prevalence of the blank transfer system which is responsible for the developments that have attracted so much attention. The abolition or limitation of blank transfers will not influence the position one way or the other as here again it functions as a purely neutral agent.

Economic, Political And Psychological Considerations

The issues summarized in the last para dispose of many prejudices and clarify many misconceptions. It is easy to be led away by slogans but the question demands dispassionate thinking. The critical argument that has been developed in this Note is vaguely present in many minds. But it is only when the argument is systematically set out and defined in terms that its true import is grasped. It is then apparent that every attempt at abolishing or limiting blank transfers will only succeed in touching off a chain of adverse reactions in every direction and that will make the last state worse than the first. The inherent dangers seem to have been subconsciously realized. The very admission that blank transfers should be limited to six months or to a year as later suggested as a compromise; that the transfer stamp duty should be substantially reduced; that all possible arrangements should be made so that shares do not "freeze" in the process of registration: all these admissions are in themselves the clearest proof that everything should be done to preserve liquidity and negotiability of shares and maintain banking and other credit facilities and that nothing should be done to disturb the economy of the country or interrupt the smooth flow of the business in the capital market. The question of questions then is— why impose artificial restrictions interfering with an old established and universal practice and then make elaborate suggestions and provisions of doubtful utility for surmounting the very obstacles thus artificially imposed? In between the imposition and the relief, all sorts of awkward, undesirable and harmful consequences intervene. The dangers of any hasty or immature legislation are well known. As pointed out by Mr. L. S. Vaidyanathan, Chairman of the Insurance Companies' Association, in the course of discussions on the Bill, the recent insurance legislation is found in practice to be impossible of full compliance in many respects and those charged with the management of insurance companies are constantly struggling with problems artificially created by a legislation some of the provisions of which were enacted without consultation with or in opposition to the views of those who are vitally concerned in their day-to-day administration. It seems to be the better part of commonsense not to inflict unnatural restraints rather than to impose them and then discover means of relief and remedy. The Fabian fallacies of the era inaugurated by the Liaquat Ali Khan Budget are a standing reminder of how ruinous are the consequences of blind ideological pursuits no matter how honest and laudable the underlying intentions. The world of trade, commerce and industry and the Stock Exchanges particularly have scarcely recovered their poise and while yet they are at this delicate stage, is it necessary to repeat the costly errors of the past which cannot but dislocate the economy, affect banking practices and have serious repercussions on the capital market shaking it to its very foundations? The proposal of abolishing or limiting blank transfers has these widespread ramifications and the question must be carefully weighed again and again because nothing should be done which destroys the free circulation of shares or retards the free circulation of shares or retards the free flow of capital that is so desirable in the public interest and on which the growth and development of trade, commerce and industry of the country depend.

SPICES ENQUIRY COMMITTEE, 1951—REPORT

New Delhi, Indian Council of Agricultural Research, 1954. 199p.

Chairman : Shri K. R. Damle.
Members : Shri A. K. Menon; Shri N. Alexander; Dr. B. N. Uppal; Dr. M. B. Ghatge; Dr. T. G. Shirname; Shri C. M. John.
Secretary : Shri J. V. A. Nehemiah.

APPOINTMENT

The Spices Enquiry Committee was constituted under the Indian Council of Agricultural Research vide their letter No. F.63(4)/51-A dated October 23, 1951.

TERMS OF REFERENCE

(i) To examine the whole position regarding the production and marketing of six agricultural commodities, viz., pepper, cardamom, ginger, turmeric, cashewnut and lemon-grass oil and make recommendations as to how the production and marketing of these commodities could be improved;

(ii) The Committee was also asked to see whether centralized direction was necessary and feasible and, if so, in what form to bring about the desired improvements.

CONTENTS

Introduction; Pepper (Kali Mirich) (General Outlook; Position of the Industry in India; Research, Technology and Development; Summary of Conclusions and Recommendations); Cardamom (Elaichi) (General Outlook; Position of the Industry in India; Research, Technology and Development; Summary of Conclusions and Recommendations); Ginger (Adrak) (General Outlook; Position of the Industry in India; Research, Technology and Development; Summary of Conclusions and Recommendations); Turmeric (Haldi) (General Outlook; Position of the Industry in India; Research, Technology and Development; Summary of Conclusions and Recommendations); Cashewnut (Kaju) (General Outlook; Position of the Industry in India; Research, Technology and Development; Summary of Conclusions and Recommendations); Lemon-Grass Oil (Pul Thylam) (General Outlook; Position of the Industry in India; Research, Technology and Development; Summary of Conclusions and Recommendations); Appendices I to XXXVI; List of Illustrations.

RECOMMENDATIONS

Pepper (Kali Mirich):
General Outlook

The Indian pepper industry should utilize the present opportunity and take early steps to reduce the cost of production and distribution so as to enable it to offer more competitive prices in the foreign markets.

Need For Agricultural Research

There is urgent need for research for reducing the cultivation expenses and production costs by adopting scientific methods of farming. Two regional research stations should be started in the two important producing areas of Travancore-Cochin and Malabar and two regional sub-stations at Sirsi in North Kanara and some suitable hill areas of Assam. Investigations should be carried out for popularizing pepper cultivation in various parts of Assam.

In order to minimize the expenditure on staff and equipment, it is suggested that these regional research stations and sub-stations for pepper should be utilized for conducting research on other spices and allied crops as well, as far as possible.

Increasing Internal Production

For reducing the gap between the present world demand and supply, it is necessary to step up internal production of black pepper. In order to increase internal production of this spice, we recommend that steps should be taken to encourage:

(i) Intensive methods of cultivation in all the existing pepper gardens;

(ii) Replacement of old and uneconomic vines in all the existing plantations; and

(iii) Cultivation of pepper in new areas wherever there are possibilities of extending the crop.

Better Basis For Crop Estimation

Pilot sample surveys should be undertaken to determine the normal yield of the pepper crop in the different producing areas. Such surveys should also examine the possibility of enumerating the total number of old and new vines in different plantations so as to determine more accurately their yielding capacities.

Special Agency For Export Promotion

The Central Government should set up a special Export-Promotion Agency in New York and another in London with the sole object of expanding India's trade in pepper and other spices by co-operating with similar agencies already functioning at present. The Export-Promotion Agency which had its headquarters in New York should be entrusted with the work in the U.S.A., Canada and other American markets while its counterpart in London should be asked to take over the publicity and sales promotion work in the U.K. and other European Markets.

Documentary Films

Exhibition of documentary films will be an effective aid to greater publicity and sales promotion. The Government of India should prepare documentary films showing the various stages of the pepper industry and of other spices and arrange for their exhibition in all important markets, both present and potential.

Exploring New Markets

The Government of India Trade Representatives in foreign countries should survey the potentialities of developing these new markets.

Uniformity In Grade Standards

In order to maintain the reputation of Indian black pepper and to give satisfaction to the foreign consumers, it is necessary to frame suitable grades and grade specifications for this commodity under the Agricultural Produce (Grading and Marking) Act, and encourage the shippers to conduct export trade on the basis of these grades and grade specifications. These standards of quality should then be included in the trade contract terms also.

Standardizing Trade Contract Terms

The present contracts for foreign exports of pepper and other spices are made largely according to the terms prescribed by the American Spice Trade Association of New York or the General Produce Brokers' Association of London. None of these associations provides for mutual allowances of quality or for arbitration facilities in India in the case of disputes. The Indian industry should frame standard contract terms of their own providing for these facilities and utilize the present opportunity in order to persuade the foreign buyers to accept the same.

Uniform Weights In West Coast Markets

The Governments of Madras and Travancore-Cochin should agree to take early steps to adopt uniform weights in all the West Coast markets.

Regulation Of Markets

Improper deduction and market practices should be eliminated by bringing all important assembling centres in the West Coast within the scope of the Regulated Markets Act as soon as possible.

Co-operative Marketing

There is urgent need for organizing Producers' Co-operative Societies for the sale of pepper in all the primary markets. These societies should be gradually combined into District Unions and brought under a State or Regional Federation. The Central and State Governments should encourage the formation of such co-operatives and give all facilities to these federations for undertaking the export trade. Such facilities may also include loans or subsidies for construction of warehouses, etc., and liberalization of rules governing the issue of co-operative loans. Wherever there is no scope for organizing co-operative societies, the possibilities of establishing licensed warehouses should be considered.

Improving Road Communications

Most of the pepper-producing areas are concentrated in the hilly tracts at the foothills of the Western Ghats. The opening up of these areas by means of proper road communications would make these areas more accessible and facilitate marketing of the produce.

'Market News' Service

In order to determine his selling price, the seller in the primary and secondary market should possess an up-to-date information regarding arrivals, stocks, despatches and prevailing prices at various centres. Arrangements should be made for supplying such information regularly to the sellers in the primary and assembling markets by organizing a 'Market News' service in the important producing States, including daily broadcasts of these particulars from the regional stations of All India Radio.

Central Plan For Development

The Government of India should create a Pepper Development Fund and earmark from the export duty a sum of not less than one crore of rupees for organizing and subsidizing all the development measures such as supply of standards, raising of special nurseries, supply of rooted cuttings, replacement of uneconomic vines, extension of cultivation, control of pests and diseases, provision of better storage facilities, framing of grade standards, promotion of orderly marketing and dissemination of agricultural information regarding production, marketing, etc.

As a first step, the Central Government should consult the State Governments concerned and prepare an integrated ten-year plan for the development of the Indian pepper industry. This plan should also be executed expeditiously.

Organization And Control

A small Central Advisory Committee for the development of spices should be constituted by the Government of India. This Committee should be assisted by three Regional Advisory Committees, one for Travancore-Cochin, second for Malabar and South Kanara and the third for Mysore including Coorg and North Kanara. While the Central Committee will be responsible for planning and co-ordination as well as allocation of funds for various developmental measures, the responsibility for the successful working of the ten-year plan and for proper utilization of the funds provided therein will rest with the three Regional Advisory Committees.

Cardamom (Elaichi): General Outlook

Instead of trying to expand the foreign trade, steps should be taken to retain the position already gained in the overseas markets by maintaining the quality of the cardamoms exported from India.

Alternative Uses For Cardamom And Cardamom Oil

Since cardamom and cardamom oil have only limited uses, research should be conducted to find out alternative uses for these products. The National

Chemical Laboratory at Poona and the Council of Scientific and Industrial Research should investigate the possibilities and also subsidize suitable schemes in this connection.

Need For New Research Stations

Agronomic and botanical research on the cardamom crop has been inadequate in all the producing areas. Considering the need for scientific aid in these problems, we recommend that two additional Cardamom Research Stations should be opened, one in the Saklaspur region of Mysore State and another in the Cardamom Hills of Travancore-Cochin. The regional research station at Mysore should study the problems of Coorg also.

Scarcity Of Planting Material

In many plantations, great difficulty is experienced in obtaining reliable planting material. Early arrangements should, therefore, be made to select suitable sites in the main producing areas and propagate seedlings and disease-free rhizomes so as to meet the requirements of all the planters. A Five-Year Nursery Scheme should be prepared and worked in this connection.

Control Of Pests And Diseases

Experiments conducted at Madras (Singampatti) and Bombay (Sirsi) have found out suitable remedies for controlling thrips and mosaic which take a heavy toll of the cardamom crop in India. The State Department of Agriculture should give wide publicity to these remedial measures and include these as important items of their extension work.

Publish All-India Crop Forecasts

The Central Government should, therefore, conduct pilot sample surveys to find out the normal yield in all the important producing areas and arrange to publish regular forecasts of areas and yield of this crop on an all-India basis.

Increase Consumption In Upper India

In order to enable the producers to sell at cheaper rates and to reduce the cost of distribution, it is recommended that specially reduced station-to-station rates should be charged by the Railways for transporting cardamom from the producing areas of South India to the distribution centres of Upper India.

Publicity In Foreign Markets

The important foreign markets for Indian Cardamom are the countries of the Middle East and Europe, particularly Saudi Arabia and Sweden. The India Government Trade Representatives concerned and the Special Export Promotion Agency we have proposed in the case of pepper should give wider publicity to the better aroma and greater oil-content of the Indian cardamoms and take all possible steps to help sales promotion in these markets.

Uniformity In Grade Standards

In order to make price quotations comparable, it is necessary to frame standard grades and grade specifications on an all-India basis. Early steps in this direction should be taken under the Agricultural Produce (Grading and Marking) Act. These standards of quality should then be included in the trade contract terms.

Premium For The Producers

In view of the higher premium obtained for the better qualities of cardamom, it would be more remunerative for the producers if they could themselves undertake to grade the produce before taking it to the auction floors.

Organizing Co-operative Marketing Societies

The co-operative societies engaged in the marketing of cardamom, particularly those at Saklaspur and Mysore, were found to do useful work. For want of better storage and credit facilities the volume of business handled by these societies was comparatively small. The State Governments concerned and the Central Government should provide these facilities and thus encourage the formation of more co-operatives. The facilities may be in the form of loans and subsidies for the construction of warehouses and liberalization of the rules governing the issue of loans by the societies.

Regulation Of Markets

By standardizing the weights and various market practices and charges, under the provisions of the Regulated Markets Act, it should be possible to increase the margin of profit of the producers. Early steps in this direction should be taken by the State Governments concerned.

Organize Market News Service

There is need for organizing a market news service at least in all the important assembling centres with a view to enabling the producers to determine their selling price and derive the maximum benefit.

Organization For Development

The Central and Regional Committees proposed for the development of the pepper industry should also deal with the various measures which we have recommended above for developing the cardamom industry in India.

Ginger (Adrak):

General Outlook

Further expansion of India's foreign trade in this spice depends largely upon the improvement in the intrinsic quality and costs of Indian ginger.

Need For Starting New Research Stations

Regional research stations should be opened in typical ginger-producing areas for evolving a better type of ginger having less fibre-content and finding out other improved agronomic practices.

Credit Facilities During Cultivation Season

The Governments of the States concerned and the Central Government should assist in removing all credit restrictions in the working of co-operative societies and make available adequate production credit. There is considerable scope for expanding production if such seasonal credit facilities are provided.

Crop Estimates

The forecasts of area and yield of the ginger crop do not include the figures for States like Uttar Pradesh where nearly 14,800 tons of green ginger equivalent to 2,960 tons of dry ginger are produced in nearly 4,000 acres. These and other producing States should be brought under the reporting regions and the forecasts made more comprehensive. It should, however, be stated in the forecast that the bulk of the local production is consumed as green ginger in most of the producing areas, and the conversion of green ginger into the dry form for export purposes is concentrated in the West Coast regions of Travancore-Cochin and Malabar.

Uniformity In Grade Standards

To obtain price quotations on a comparable basis and create better confidence in the foreign buyers, it is necessary to frame suitable grade standards for this product on an all-India basis. Early steps in this direction should be taken under the Agricultural Produce (Grading and Marking) Act. These standards of quality should then be included in the trade contract terms which should also provide facilities for arbitration in India in case of disputes between the parties.

Trend Of Foreign Exports

Although the post-war exports showed an increase over the pre-war period, recent exports have shown a decline particularly to the U.S.A., the U.K., Aden and dependencies and Iran. The causes of this decline and the scope for export promotion in these countries should be investigated by the Government of India Trade Representatives abroad.

Co-operative Marketing

The co operative agency plays a very insignificant part in the marketing of dry ginger. The main difficulty that stood in the way of the development of some of these societies did not provide for adequate storage facilities. Necessary financial assistance should be given by the Central and State Governments to these co-operatives for the construction of warehouses in all the important marketing centres.

Regulation Of Markets

The producers' share of the prevailing prices could be increased by extending the operation of the Regulated Markets Act to this article also in all important markets in the West Coast.

Fumigation At The Ports

In order to reduce insect infestation in the products exported from India, arrangements should be made for their proper storage and fumigation at the ports of shipment.

Market News Service

It is necessary to organize a Market News Service and disseminate up-to-date information regularly by means of radio broadcasts, bulletins, etc.

Organization For Development

The Central and Regional Committees proposed for the development of pepper should deal also with the various measures which we have recommended above for developing the ginger industry in India.

Turmeric (Haldi):

General

A detailed marketing survey should be conducted by the Central Government in order to assess all the problems concerning this industry.

Need For All-India Crop Estimates

The Central Government should arrange to publish regularly all-India forecasts of area and yield of turmeric.

More Research Stations

Except in Orissa, no systematic attempt has been made to develop the industry on scientific lines. There is an urgent need for improving the local varieties under cultivation and for finding out suitable remedies for seed diseases which are carried from season to season. Arrangements should therefore be made to start Turmeric Research Stations in all other typical producing areas. These stations should tackle all the problems of botanical and agronomic improvements concerning this crop including problems of storage and control of stored products pests.

Credit Facilities

Greater production credit should be made available to the cultivators through the co-operative agencies.

Transport

In common with all other agricultural commodities, the marketing of this crop also suffers because of lack of suitable communications, particularly in the agency tracts of Orissa. Improvements in this direction are, therefore, necessary to open up the producing areas.

Better Equipment For Curing And Polishing

The improved type of furnace evolved at Orissa has been found to be more efficient and economical in fuel consumption than the local type. The cured product when also polished by the equipment evolved in this State has fetched a premium of 20%. Greater use of these and similar equipment should be encouraged by the Agriculture Departments of the States concerned.

Foreign Publicity

In all trade exhibitions organized by the Government of India in foreign countries, greater publicity should be given to this product in order to increase the offtake.

Uniformity In Grade Standards

Turmeric has well-defined quality factors which are also recognized by the trade. These factors should be taken advantage of for framing uniform grades and grade standards under the Agricultural Produce (Grading and Marking) Act.

A sizable proportion of the turmeric trade takes place in the form of powder. As there are serious complaints regarding its quality, grades and grade specifications for this product also should be framed and an effort should be made to induce the trade to adopt these standards for internal distribution.

Cashewnut (Kaju):
Main Problem

The immediate problem of the cashewnut processing industry is to reduce India's dependence on foreign imports by taking early steps to increase the supplies of raw cashewnuts within the country.

Increase Internal Supply Of Raw Cashewnuts

There are extensive lands available for cashew cultivation in the East Coast region of Madras, the coastal districts of Ratnagiri and North Kanara in the Bombay State and parts of Coorg and Mysore. In all these regions, extensive cultivation of the crop on a plantation basis should be encouraged. The Forest Departments in the producing States should also encourage its spread and growth in all the reserve areas and arrange to collect the nuts along with other minor forest produce. Wherever possible, the Public Works Departments should also undertake to extend the cultivation of this crop in suitable lands under their jurisdiction. A Co-ordinated Ten-Year Plan (Cashewnut Plantation Scheme) should be prepared in this connection in consultation with the State Governments and put through expeditiously.

Greater Central Aid For Agricultural Research

Although sanction has been accorded by the Indian Council of Agricultural Research for the starting of three Regional Research Stations for cashewnut at Madras (Mangalore), Bombay (Ratnagiri) and Travancore-Cochin (Kottarakara), actual research work has not commenced in any of these regions, mainly due to lack of funds. Adequate funds should be made available by the Central Government, so as to enable the respective States to overcome the financial difficulties and start systematic scientific studies at these three research stations without any further delay.

All-India Crop Estimates

Except for what is given out by some of the leading business firms in the West Coast region, no attempt has been made by the Governments at the Centre or in the States to publish regular forecasts of the local production of cashewnuts, cashew kernels and cashew-shell liquid. Considering the size and value of the crop and the importance of the products as dollar-earners, it is necessary to maintain these statistics on an all-India basis.

Quicker Transport To The Factories

The movement of raw cashewnuts from the assembling centres or the ports to the factories has to be done quickly. The railway authorities should give greater facilities for the quick transport of raw nuts to the processing factories.

Government Assistance For Procurement Of Raw Nuts

The Government should give all assistance to the factory owners in regard to the procurement of raw nuts from foreign countries.

Standardizing Local Methods Of Marketing

As formation of Producers' Co-operative Societies is difficult in the case of cashewnuts, we suggest that the buyers in the primary and assembling markets should be licensed by the State Governments and the issue of such licences should be subject to the condition that the licensee should buy only ripe and mature nuts and use standard weights in the transactions.

Adopting Better Methods Of Processing

Out of the various methods of processing employed in the extraction of cashew kernels from raw nuts, the oil-bath method is more efficient. The cost of the equipment and installation charges are, however, heavy. Small owners of cashewnut factories should, therefore, combine themselves into recognized associations and necessary financial assistance should be given by the Governments to such associations in the form of loans for the setting up of such improved processing plants.

The Council of Scientific and Industrial Research should also take up for investigation the possibilities of evolving cheaper processing plants.

Uniformity In Grade Standards

It will be helpful to the manufacturers and consumers if all-India standards of quality are framed for this product under the Agricultural Produce (Grading and Marking) Act and all price quotations are made on the basis of such standard qualities. These standards of quality should then be included in the trade contract terms also.

Regulation Of Quality

In order to prevent development of worms in the cases shipped from India, factory owners should:

(1) Pay greater attention to the environmental hygiene of the factory premises;

(2) Use new tin containers for packing kernels; and

(3) Adopt airtight packing.

Cashewnut Development Fund

The Central Government should create a separate fund and earmark a lump sum of Rs. 25 lakhs for undertaking the various developmental measures stated above. The administration and control of this fund should also vest in the Central Committee which we have already proposed for developing the spice industry in India.

Indigenous Utilization Of Cashew-Shell Liquid

Its distillation products can be used in various industries such as the manufacture of insulating varnishes, typewriter rolls, oil and acid-proof cold-setting cements, industrial flooring tiles and automobile break-linings. Wider publicity should be given to these uses in order to encourage greater utilization of this by-product by the indigenous industries.

Standardizing Quality Of Cashew-Shell Liquid

All industrial uses of cashew-shell liquid presuppose a uniform quality of the commercial product. The Indian Standards Institution has drafted some tentative specifications for this oil, which should be adopted by the manufacturers to put a uniform product on the market. By such standardization of quality, the exports of this oil to foreign countries are also likely to increase.

Publicity And Sales Promotion

The special export-promotion agencies we have proposed in the case of pepper should undertake publicity work in respect of this product also in their respective areas.

Internally also, publicity is necessary to increase the demand for cashew kernels.

Amenities For Factory Workers

Quite a large number of persons are employed by the Indian cashewnut industry. Although certain amenities such as fans, light, drinking water, nursery, etc., have been provided under the Factories Act, these were not found to be uniform or quite satisfactory in all the factories. Considering the difficult conditions and the nature of the work involved in processing, it is imperative that the standard of amenities provided in all these factories should be uniformly high.

Lemon-Grass Oil (Pull Thylam):

General Outlook

Although India is the largest supplier of lemon-grass oil in the world markets, the total demand for this Indian product has declined since last year. This is attributed partly to larger supplies received from Guatemala and partly to the curtailment of demand from the manufacturers in America and other foreign countries. Unless steps are taken to find alternative uses for this oil in India, the prospects of this Indian industry are not bright.

Commercial Manufacture of Ionones

A pilot plant should be set up in Travancore-Cochin State and early arrangements made for the commercial manufacture of ionones and other products. The Central Government should subsidize this project and encourage the use of these manufactured products in the Indian industries.

Adequate Supply Of Red-Stemmed Grass Seeds

The cultivation of lemon-grass is simple and presents no difficulty but in most of the fields the cultivated variety of red-stemmed grass is often found mixed with a white-stemmed variety which yields an inferior quality of oil. In order to prevent such admixtures, adequate arrangements should be made for the supply of sufficient quantities of seeds of the red-stemmed grass. The Lemon-Grass Research Station at Odakkali, Travancore-Cochin, which has facilities for the cultivation of this grass, could be entrusted with arrangements in this connection.

Need For Improved Type Of Country Still

The present type of country stills used in India for the distillation of oil is crude in design and construction and involves considerable wastage. It has been found that by adopting steam distillation both the total recovery and the quality of the oil could be increased by about 20%. In order to reduce the costs of extraction and to improve the quality, there is need for evolving an improved type of equipment in the producing areas for the distillation of oil from lemon-grass. The Governments of Travancore-Cochin and Madras and the Central Government should take early steps in this direction and arrange to supply improved type of stills to the producers on a subsidized basis.

Mutual Allowances For Quality Of Oil

Although Indian lemon-grass oil contains up to 85% citral, the shippers are asked to guarantee only a minimum of 75% citral-content in their consignments under the present shipping contract terms. This provision encourages adulteration and also unnecessarily brings down the reputation of the Indian product. The producers are also not able to realize the premium for the better quality of their products. The trade contract terms should, therefore, be amended so as to guarantee a minimum citral-content of 75% and provide for payment of premium for any higher citral-content above 75%. The Indian Standards Institution has prescribed minimum standards of quality for Indian lemon-grass oil. These standards should be suitably amended under the Agricultural Produce (Grading and Marking) Act so as to provide mutual allowances for quality as stated above on the basis of citral-content.

Preventing Export Of Sub-standard Qualities

Necessary arrangements should also be made to prevent the export of sub-standard qualities for India under the provisions of the Central Sea Customs Act.

Co-operative Marketing

The extraction and marketing of the oil is all done by a small number of producers. Greater economies could be effected in installation charges and manufacturing costs if they could combine themselves into co-operative marketing societies.

Such societies should own laboratories for the regular testing of the oil and its correct determination of citral-content and other quality factors. Necessary facilities should be given by the Governments at the Centre and in the States in organizing such co-operatives.

Uniform Weights And Measures

Arrangements should be made to adopt uniform weights and measures and also to regulate the marketing of this product under the Regulated Markets Act.

Maintenance Of Statistics

Reliable statistics of acreage under lemon-grass or of the supply of oil are not available in the different producing States. The Governments of Travancore-Cochin and Madras which are the most important producers of this oil should arrange to collect this information and regularly publish it in their Season and Crop Report.

Market News Service

Very little reliable information regarding supply, stocks, demand and prices of this oil filters down from the exporters to the producers in the village markets. The need for such commercial intelligence exists greatly in Travancore-Cochin and Malabar. The Governments of the respective States should arrange to disseminate such news regularly in the rural markets through bulletins and broadcasts from the regional stations of All India Radio.

Organization For Development

The Central and Regional Committees for spices proposed in the case of pepper should function also for carrying out the various measures which we have recommended for developing the lemon-grass oil industry in India.

RAILWAY FUEL ECONOMY ENQUIRY COMMITTEE, 1951—REPORT

New Delhi, Railway Board, 1953. 2 Vols.

Chairman : Shri Darab Cursetji Driver.
Members : Shri R. A. Massey; Dr. J. W. Whitekar; Shri A. B. Guha; Shri L. S. Corbett.
Co-opted Members : Shri P. L. Verma; Shri I. S. Malik.
Secretary : Shri M. V. Kamlani.

APPOINTMENT

The Railway Fuel Economy Enquiry Committee was constituted under the Ministry of Railways vide their letter No. E 51C01/11/3 dated October 27, 1951.

TERMS OF REFERENCE

(i) To examine the supply, consumption and reserve stocks of coal on Railways; and

(ii) To make recommendations for economy in expenditure on coal used as fuel.

CONTENTS

Volume I : Part I—The Railway Fuel Problem and the Committee's Recommendations; The Railway Fuel Problem; Summary of Recommendations; **Part II**—Coal Resources of the Country—Coal Reserves, Production and Demand; Grading and Pricing of Coal; Preparation of Coal; Lignite or Brown Coal; **Part III**—Supply and Transport—Loco Coal Requirements and a Rational Basis of Assessment; Existing Conditions of Supply and Distribution of Loco Coal; Proposed Plan for Supply and Distribution of Coal; Plan for Supply of Coal to the South; Transport Deficiencies; **Part IV**—Fuel Economy Measures—Economy in Consumption and Prevention of Losses; Fuel Accounts and Statistics; Different Types of Railway Traction; Power and Fuel Research; Fuel Control Organizations and Training Centres. **Volume II**: Appendices.

RECOMMENDATIONS

Production Of Coal

Immediate steps should be taken to develop the outlying fields, particularly in Vindhya Pradesh, Madhya Pradesh and Hyderabad State, in order to meet as far as practicable the requirements of Western and Southern India and a part of Rajasthan. Northern India and the rest of Rajasthan may draw upon the coalfields of Bengal and Bihar.

The lignite resources in South Arcot, Madras, should be developed without delay.

Coal production in the Assam and Orissa States should be such as will meet the requirements of these States; special qualities of coal, however, may be obtained from outside sources.

Production of high-grade non-caking coal should be increased in the Raniganj and Karanpura coalfields in order to release caking coals for (a) metallurgical purpose and (b) feeding the export market.

Government collieries at Kurasia, Deulbera and Talchar should be developed and extended by acquiring new areas without delay, wherever possible.

Properties should be immediately acquired and Government Mines opened up in the Karanpura and Korba Coalfields.

Grading And Pricing Of Coal

An official Committee under the Coal Board should be appointed immediately to examine in detail new proposals for coal grading and pricing. The Fuel Research Institute and the Ministry of Railways should be represented in this Committee.

Prompt steps should be taken to grade the coals of the outlying fields.

Arrangements should be made to ensure continuous testing at pitheads (by Collieries) of the quality of coal loaded.

Preparation Of Coal

Different types of Pilot Washing Plant should be installed at the Fuel Research Institute without delay to obtain evidence on the most suitable and economical types of coals of different washability characteristics.

The Government should take steps to explore the possibilities of coal washing and to set up Washing Plants at selected sites.

Lignite Or Brown Coal

High priority should be given by the Government to the mining and exploitation of the South Arcot lignite and to the establishment of thermal generating plant and industries in the vicinity of mines.

Steps should be taken to draw upon the experience and knowledge of Brown Coal mining in Germany, where the problems of water infiltration and handling have been solved.

Selected Mining Engineers from India should be sent to gain experience of the methods employed in working the Brown Coals of Germany and Australia.

Research should be undertaken into:

(a) The best method of using the lignite in locomotives (including Gas Turbine type) and in industrial plants; and

(b) Problems of Briquetting, Gasification, Carbonization and Hydrogenation.

Loco Coal Requirements

Loco coal requirements should be estimated on the basis of the suitability of each grade of caking or non-caking coal for different categories of locomotives, adjustments being made for accepting inferior coals from nearer sources.

Efforts should be made to exclude from the future Loco Coal Programmes, as far as transport permits, coals whose calorific value is below 11,500 HTU/LB.

The use of low-grade coals (calorific value below 11,500 HTU/LB) on shunting locomotives should be gradually discontinued; districts or zones which receive supplies of coal over long leads should receive prior attention.

Existing Supply Conditions:
Quality

Efficient control is exercised on the quality of coal so that supplies made to Railways are in accordance with the specifications.

Supply And Grouping

Districts or zones of a Railway receive coals from fixed sources, a source being either a group of collieries or a single colliery. The collieries selected to form a group should be on the same "Pilot". They should be chosen so that the mixing of their coals may be done without causing combustion trouble. The quantities drawn from each group towards Railway supplies should be guaranteed in advance.

Distribution And Grouping

As far as practicable, coal for any consuming point on a Railway should be obtained from the nearest group source. The group and the connected base station are such as will permit the movement of coal to districts or zones without entailing much marshalling at base stations (and en route) and without involving cross movements.

Future Loco Coal Supplies

The Railways should in future select their own coals by inviting offers from collieries and by arranging for supplies on contract basis.

A Standing Loco Coal Committee should be set up to undertake all work connected with the framing of Loco Coal Programmes, inviting offers from collieries, for scrutiny and acceptance, allocation of their approved offers according to the supplies and transport available. The Committee should consist of representatives of Railways, the Ministry of Railways and the Coal Commissioner. The Chairman of the Railway Board or his nominee may act as Chairman and the Chief Mining Engineer, Railway Board, as Member Secretary of the Standing Loco Coal Committee.

In order to simplify and rationalize transport and to ensure regular and reliable supplies of coal to Railways, steps should be taken to introduce the system of grouping collieries, with distributing centres to serve as primary receiving points in respect of supplies to Railway Zones.

Supply Of Coal To The South

Wagons should be loaded to the maximum permissible degree.

To meet the fuel requirements of the South, the Government should give priority to the development of Talcher, Singareni and CP/CIC coalfields.

The Ministry of Railways should immediately undertake the development of the junction yards and line capacities along the rail routes from the abovementioned outlying fields to the South.

Transport Deficiencies

A "Standing Coal Transport Planning Committee" should be set up, consisting of the representatives of the Ministries of Railways and Production and of the Planning Commission, to undertake necessary planning in respect of coal transport, and to ensure that due importance is given to coal (and other goods) transport in the economic development of the country.

Wagon turn-round and carrying capacity should be improved by:

(a) Allocating coal orders colliery-wise and pilot-wise in order to form block loads. The colliery and consuming areas should be in zones and rationally linked up to afford movement of block loads along specified directions.

(b) Ensuring that wagons are fully loaded to the carrying capacity and that full use is made of the two-ton overload allowance. For the purpose the Measuring Gauge, shown in Appendix 20, or a similar device should be adopted.

(c) Removing transport "bottlenecks" and improving line capacities as recommended in the short-term and long-term plans.

The existing practice of allocating coal orders and wagons should be modified to give effect to regional distribution of coal as far as possible, and to incorporate the following features:

(a) Allocation of coal orders on the basis of wagon availability.

(b) Linking of supplies with specified supply sources and colliery base stations.

(c) Advance programming of public supplies on a quarterly or half-yearly basis.

(d) Provision of a "cushion" of 200 wagons daily

for the Bengal and Bihar coalfields and 50 wagons daily for other coalfields to meet emergency demands, the allotment of this number being left to the discretion of the Coal Commissioner.

A Railway Officer of senior administrative rank (director) should be immediately appointed and housed in the office of the Coal Commissioner. He should function as Liaison Transport Officer and make day-to-day allotment of wagons in collaboration with the Coal Commissioner.

Control Over Consumption And Losses Of Railway Coal

More attention should be given to provide proper stacking facilities and stacking ground and to the adequate stacking of all supplies as a check on consumption and pilferage.

Immediate steps should be taken to set up a machinery for giving effect to the proposed economy measures, which can be broadly divided into:

(a) Control over consumption; and

(b) Power and fuel research.

The control measures should be the function of the fuel control organization, and power and fuel research should be the concern of the Railway Testing and Research Centre, working in collaboration with the Fuel Research Institute.

Fuel Accounts And Statistics

Examine the report of the Chartered Accountants in the light of the Committee's remarks with a view to evolving a simple and effective system of fuel accounts for adoption on all the Indian Railways.

Enlarge the scope of railway fuel statistics so that the effects of various direct and indirect factors affecting coal consumption are adequately brought out by the statistical figures.

Different Types Of Traction And Power And Fuel Research

Electrification of the undermentioned sections should be given consideration:

Railway	Section to be electrified	Route Miles
Eastern	Suburban Services	
	Howrah Division	151
	Sealdah Division	138
	Main Line	
	Burdwan-Gaya	242
	Gaya-Moghalsarai	126
Central	Igatpuri-Bhusaval	192
	(Extension of the present Electrified Section—Bombay-Igatpuri)	
Southern	Quilon-Ernakulam	96
	Madras-Trichinopoly	358
	Madras-Bangalore	222
	Madras-Bezwada	268
Western	Virar-Ahmedabad	271
	(Extension of the present Electrified Section—Bombay Central-Virar	
Northern	Delhi-Ambala	123
		2,187

Steps should be taken to introduce:

(a) Diesel traction on the Saurashtra Section (Gondal Division) of the Western Railway;

(b) Diesel light railcar services on suitable Sections; and

(c) Diesel power for shunting services.

Power and fuel research should be enlarged and intensified to:

(a) Establish the reliability, in operation and maintenance, of design improvements in order to expedite their incorporation in future Steam Locomotives;

(b) Develop other types of locomotive power to meet the growing traffic requirements of the country most efficiently;

(c) Develop designs of gas producers, using coal or coke, for ratings up to 400/500 H.P. in order to give impetus to dieselization of railcar and shunting services;

(d) Investigate the possibilities of using lignite in steam locomotives and in gas turbines;

(e) Develop designs of combustor and heat-exchanger suitable for Indian coals, to facilitate the adoption of external combustion gas-turbine locomotives; and

(f) Determine the performance and advantages of the high-tension 50 cycle A.C. system for electric traction.

Early action should be taken to set up a "Standing Railway Power and Electrification Planning Committee", consisting of representatives of the Ministry of Railways, the Planning Commission, and the Central Water and Power Commission, for:

(a) Ensuring co-ordination among the authorities responsible for industrial, power, transport, fuel and other national developments;

(b) Initiating, scrutinizing, and recommending the execution of railway electrification and dieselization schemes in a specified order of priority; and

(c) Examine the possibilities of indigenous manufacture of machinery and components to meet the maintenance requirements of electric, diesel and other types of traction.

Fuel Control Organizations And Training Centres

Immediate setting up of:

(a) Six regional fuel control departments,

(b) A central fuel directorate,

(c) Six regional training schools, and

(d) A central training school.

1952

GROW MORE FOOD ENQUIRY COMMITTEE, 1952—REPORT

New Delhi, Ministry of Food and Agriculture, 1952. 128p.

Chairman : Shri V. T. Krishnamachari.

Members : Shri R. K. Patil; Hon'ble Shri M. P. Patil; Hon'ble Shri Dip Narain Sinha; Pandit Thakurdas Bhargava; Shri Tribhuwan Narain Singh; Dr. Mono Mohon Das; Dr. V. K. R. V. Rao; Dr. B. Venkataratnam; Sardar Datar Singh.

Secretary : Shri S. T. Raja.

APPOINTMENT

The Grow More Food Enquiry Committee was constituted under the Ministry of Food and Agriculture vide their Resolution No. F.1-2/52-GS(P) dated February 8, 1952.

TERMS OF REFERENCE

(i) To examine the categories of G. M. F. schemes for which funds have been sanctioned and the extent to which the utilization of the funds has been in conformity with the intended purposes;

(ii) To assess the relative efficiency of the different categories of schemes for increasing food production in the context of the available means and the prevalent agricultural practices, particularly with respect to the use of fertilizers, compost and improved seeds, and taking into account the lag between the grant of money and the actual production of the crop;

(iii) To enquire whether the follow-up arrangements for demonstrating and teaching the cultivators have been properly organized in the areas in which G. M. F. funds have been spent;

(iv) To examine whether the results achieved by the G. M. F. campaign since April 1, 1949, in terms of units of work, acreage benefited and increased food production over a specified base figure have been commensurate with the scale of expenditure involved;

(v) To suggest measures for ensuring the optimum utilization of the available production requisites by the cultivators and for checking up on the actual expenditure of money and the results achieved; and

(vi) To examine and report on any other matter germane or incidental to the above.

CONTENTS

Introductory; The Food Problem; Progress of G. M. F. Campaign (1943-44 to 1950-51); G. M. F. Campaign (1951-52 and 1952-53); Results of the Campaign; Terms of Reference; Our Proposals Regarding Future Policy; Summary of Conclusions and Recommendations; Appendices I to XI.

RECOMMENDATIONS

The present G.M.F. Campaign should be enlarged so as to cover a wider plan for development of village life in all its aspects. This is a permanent problem.

The administrative machinery of the Governments should be reorganized and equipped for the efficient discharge of the duties imposed on it, under the new conception of India as a Welfare State.

The best non-official leadership available should be mobilized for guiding the rural families in their efforts to improve their own condition.

An extension organization should be set up for rural work which would reach every farmer and assist in the co-ordinated development of all aspects of rural life.

The Taluq or "Tahsil" consisting of 100 to 120 villages will be the development block and the unit best suited for extension service. Below it there would be a group of villages, five to 10 in number, and then the village itself.

The extension work in the Taluq will be in the charge of the Development Officer or "Extension Officer" who will be the Revenue Officer. This officer will be relieved of his other duties by a special assistant appointed for the purpose. The "Extension Officer" will be assisted by four technical officers for agriculture, animal husbandry, co-operation and engineering. This organization will function as a team.

The "Extension" organization should be spread all over the country within the shortest practicable time, not exceeding 10 years.

For associating the non-official leadership with the schemes of village development, any of the existing village organizations, e.g., panchayat, multi-purpose co-operative society, or the village production council, may be utilized. When such organizations do not exist necessary steps should be taken to set them up.

The development activities in the district should be unified under the Collector as "Extension Officer" assisted by the specialist officers.

At the State level there should be a Cabinet committee, and a non-official Board for formulation of co-ordinated policies and for facilitating joint action.

At the Centre, there should be an Advisory Council for village development which should include representatives of the Central Ministries concerned, of some of the State Governments and of Parliament and also selected non-officials with special experience or qualifications.

Financial assistance from the Centre will be necessary to enable the States to set up the "Extension" service.

Loans advanced to cultivators should as far as possible be made through approved co-operative societies.

As large a portion as possible of the available funds should be earmarked for permanent works of utility. Subsidies should be reduced and eventually abolished.

The role of the Government of India should be confined to:

(a) Formulation of overall policies and co-ordination of programmes of village development including targets of additional production;

(b) Giving of financial and technical assistance;

(c) Making arrangements for supplies and movement of essential materials; and

(d) Assessment of results of the programme.

A Special Division in the Central Ministry of Food and Agriculture should deal with these functions with regard to the entire programme.

Surveys should be undertaken in all States of areas suitable for minor irrigation, tanks, wells, tubewells, etc., and details of programmes should be formulated in the order of priority.

As between the different permanent schemes, prominence should be given to schemes of minor irrigation.

Before undertaking the land reclamation programme on a large scale, systematic surveys of areas suitable for the purpose should be undertaken.

Adequate steps should be taken to ensure that follow-up cultivation is undertaken on lands reclaimed by the Central Tractor Organization.

The land reclamation and mechanical cultivation schemes of the State Governments should be worked on a self-financing basis.

Facilities for repairs, spare parts and servicing in respect of tractors should be made available to the cultivators close at hand to ensure the success of mechanical cultivation.

Adequate numbers of seed farms should be established for providing nucleus seeds.

It is important to ensure that seeds are made available in time and are of good quality.

There is much scope for increasing the use of green manures, especially in irrigated paddy areas, and more efforts should be made to popularize them.

There should be continuous efforts made to develop local manurial resources to the maximum extent.

State Governments should undertake responsibility for dealing with widespread pests and diseases promptly. As regards stray cattle the main difficulty is regarding useless cattle which are not claimed by their owners. The only remedy for this appears to be the starting of Gosadans.

Crop competition schemes are very important and should be continued and extended.

More attention should be paid to problems of dry farming in areas of inadequate rainfall.

The Government of India should make a declaration accepting the principle of guarantee of minimum prices as this will provide an incentive to agricultural production.

COMMITTEE ON TRAINING OF CIVIL AIR PILOTS, 1952—REPORT

Delhi, Manager of Publications, 1952. 312p.

Chairman : Shri M. A. Master.
Members : Shri T. P. Bhalla; Group Capt. H. N. Chatterjee; Rai Bajrang Bahadur Singh; Shri K. K. Roy; W/Cdr. W. H. Burbury; Capt. S. Bujakowski; Prof. C. N. Vakil.
Secretary : Shri G. S. Subramaniam.

APPOINTMENT

The Committee on Training of Civil Air Pilots was constituted under the Ministry of Communications vide their Order No. 14-A/25-52, dated April 15, 1952.

TERMS OF REFERENCE

To examine the existing system of civil air pilots' training in all its aspects and recommend measures for its improvement consistent with economy, with particular reference to the following:

I. Training Of Commercial Pilots

(a) Qualifications, number and method of selection of trainees;

(b) Organization of institutions for training of commercial pilots—study of the working of the Civil Aviation Training Centre and proposals for its improvement;

(c) Legislation pertaining to commercial flying;

(d) Curricula for the training of commercial pilots, of various grades, namely, Junior airline pilots, Command pilots and Co-pilots for single-engined, twin-engined and multi-engined aircraft;

(e) Training for special types of aircraft and special types of work, e.g., helicopters, aerial survey and spraying of chemicals;

(f) Standardization of training aircraft and equipment;

(g) Scheme for financial assistance for training of commercial pilots—incidence of costs on pilots, airlines and the Government;

(h) Ensuring operational efficiency of pilots—system of periodical checks and refresher courses, laying down of conditions for avoidance of fatigue of air crew;

(i) Qualifications for check pilots and instructors for conversion courses and their periodical checks;

(j) Standardization of scales of pay of different grades of pilots, check pilots and conversion course instructors;

(k) Liability of airline pilots to serve under the State, if required.

II. Training Of Private Pilots

(a) Qualifications, number and method of selection of trainees;

(b) Evaluation of flying clubs and other agencies for the training of private and commercial pilots and recommendations for organization of Model Institutions, giving details of organization and equipment;

(c) Legislation pertaining to private flying;

(d) Curriculum for the training of private pilots;

(e) Standardization of training aircraft and equipment;

(f) Scheme for financial assistance for training private pilots, including concessions in Customs duty on light aircraft, aircraft parts, light aircraft radio, landing and housing fees and duty on aviation petrol;

(g) Qualifications of Flight Instructors and other staff engaged in flying training institutions;

(h) Scales of pay for Flight Instructors and other staff employed in the training institutions;

(i) Encouragement of private flying generally, and in particular by students of colleges and technical institutions.

III. Gliding And Other Media For Encouraging Air-mindedness Among The Young.

CONTENTS

Part I: Introductory; Flying Club Movement in India; Civil Aviation Training Centre, Allahabad; Legislation pertaining to the licensing of Private and

Commercial Pilots; Operational Efficiency; Policy of Recruitment and Training; Cost of Training and Responsibility of the State; Future role of the Flying School at the Civil Aviation Training Centre; Flying Activities of the Air Wing of the National Cadet Corps; The Future of the Flying Clubs; Problem of Unemployment; Civil Air Board; Miscellaneous Matters; Development of Gliding in India; Development of Air-mindedness; Financial Implications of the Recommendations; Summary of Recommendations; Acknowledgments.

Part II: Appendices A to G; Statistics.

Part III: Observations of Shri T. P. Bhalla on the Terms of Reference of the Committee on Training of Civil Air Pilots.

RECOMMENDATIONS

The pilots in charge flying and co-pilot flying engaged in scheduled air transport services should undergo two to four hours' refresher flying training respectively every six months. These hours should include the flying tests prescribed for the renewal of the instrument rating. These flying tests will be carried out by the Check Pilots appointed by the company for that purpose.

The Government should persuade the airline operators in the country to voluntarily restrict the maximum number of hours up to which they should allow their pilots to fly to 100 hours per month and 1,000 hours per year.

Training for Private or Sport flying should be continued to be given at flying clubs in the future as in the past. No restriction should be put on those who wish to undergo training for obtaining a Commercial Pilot Licence at their own cost, and we recommend that they may be given such training at flying clubs.

The maximum number of pilots who should be trained as Commercial Pilots per year for absorption in the air transport industry should not be more than 30.

With a view to developing Sport flying and to spread air-mindedness in the country, a person under 28 years of age, irrespective of his nationality, undergoing flying training at flying clubs, should not be charged more than Rs. 10 per hour for every hour flown to enable him to obtain his Private Pilot Licence and for five hours' flying experience which he will require to keep his licence current,

The conversion training on aircraft other than Dakota should be continued to be given in the future by the airline companies or by the merged Corporation, as the case may be, as in the past, but the cost incurred for such training should be met by a subsidy from the Central Government.

Flying clubs are a great storehouse of enthusiasm and inspiration for drawing out the potential air sense of the people of the country. We, therefore, strongly recommend that all possible steps should be taken to keep flying clubs alive and in full vigour in the country in the future, as in the past.

The Central Government and the States should continue in the future their policy of subsidizing flying clubs in India.

The trainees should not be given the right to vote as long as they are trainees.

The Flying Instructors should undergo a course of regular training for the purpose of ensuring a uniformity of standard at the Flying Instructors' School of the Air Force at Ambala, and it should be a condition of their employment that they should undergo periodically a refresher course and a categorization test at that school.

Pupils undergoing training for Private Pilot's Licence or for Commercial Pilot's Licence should neither be under an obligation to sign agreements nor be subjected to restrictions and penalty as are imposed on them at present.

Anyone who is medically fit and shows an aptitude for flying should be admitted to flying clubs by their managements. The number of cadets to be admitted for training to the clubs should be such as would not increase the flying work of the clubs beyond 4,500 hours per annum.

The Light Aircraft not exceeding a gross weight of 5,000 lbs., aircraft parts and light aircraft radio imported for the purpose of training in India should be exempt from Customs duty.

As a matter of principle privately owned aircraft as well as flying club aircraft not exceeding a gross weight of 5,000 lbs. should be exempt from the payment of the Landing and Housing Fees at all airports when they are engaged in Sport or Pleasure flight.

The Flying School at the Civil Aviation Training Centre should not be continued on an experimental basis, year after year. The Flying School should be made a permanent institution for giving training to pilots who intend to follow a professional career in the air transport industry in India.

The Flying School at the Civil Aviation Training Centre should be equipped and developed in such a manner as may enable it to give training on the best modern lines. We recommend that a Civil Air Board should be constituted as a statutory body. The Board shall consist of the following members:

(1) A non-official Chairman of standing in public life and preferably with knowledge and experience of educational activities in the country;

(2) A representative of the Air Headquarters;

(3) The Director-General of Civil Aviation or his representative;

(4) Two representatives of the Air Transport Association or two representatives of the new Air Corporation when it is formed, one of whom shall be a man possessing knowledge and experience of technical subjects;

(5) A pilot of outstanding ability and experience;

(6) A representative of flying clubs;

(7) A Member of Parliament.

We recommend that the free grant of land and the financial assistance which the Aero Club has asked for to enable it to have its own office with qualified and adequate staff, an ante-room, a reference library, and residential accommodation for five to 10 visiting members should be given to it to enable it to achieve its object.

As gliding will promote air-mindedness amongst the youth of the country, both the Central and the State Governments should develop gliding activities in India.

Gliding clubs should be started under the auspices of all the Universities in the country and the students of Colleges should be given training in gliding free of cost.

DEARNESS ALLOWANCE COMMITTEE, 1952—REPORT

Delhi, Manager of Publications, 1953. 56p.

Chairman : Shri N. V. Gadgil.
Members : Shri S. Guruswami; Shri Khandubhai K. Desai; Shri J. Dayal; Shri P. N. Saxena.
Secretary : Shri S. K. Majumdar.

APPOINTMENT

The Dearness Allowance Committee was constituted under the Ministry of Finance vide their Resolution No. F.6(2)-E-II/52 dated July 15, 1952.

TERMS OF REFERENCE

Taking into consideration the rates of dearness allowance that have been sanctioned to date for Central Government servants, and the level at which the cost-of-living index is likely to stabilize in the foreseeable future, to recommend the percentage of the dearness allowance now given to Central Government servants which should be allowed to be treated as pay for all purposes in future, provided that by doing so the present total of pay and dearness allowance is not enhanced.

CONTENTS

Introductory; Cost-of-Living Index; Pay and Dearness Allowance of Central Government Servants; Consideration of the Question of Stabilization in the Cost of Living; Recommendation as regards portion of Dearness Allowance to be treated as pay; Other Recommendations; Minute of Dissent; Appendices.

RECOMMENDATIONS

Recommendation As Regards Portion Of Dearness Allowance To Be Treated As Pay

We find that for the index figure of 265, the Central Pay Commission's formula allows Government employees in the lowest pay group a dearness allowance of Rs. 20 and this amount remains unchanged until the cost-of-living index goes above the index of the rent slab, i.e., 285. We, therefore, consider that for employees in this pay group, a sum of Rs. 20 which represents 50% of the present dearness allowance of Rs. 40 p.m. should be treated as pay.

As regards the higher pay groups, we have considered the percentage of the dearness allowance that should be treated as pay and also the highest pay range up to which this should be applied.

Our recommendation should apply to those in receipt of a pay not exceeding Rs. 750 p.m.

As regards the quantum of dearness allowance to be treated as pay, the largest measure of benefit should be given to those in the lowest pay group. We find, however, that the dearness allowance given at present to the higher pay groups already bears a diminishing percentage to the pay. We also observe that although the employees in the lowest pay groups were given an increase in dearness allowance in the past, those in the higher pay groups either received no increases at all or, up to certain pay limits, only a proportionately small measure of increase. Taking these factors into account, we recommend that the same percentage, as applied in the lowest pay group, should also be applied to employees in the higher groups up to a pay of Rs. 750 p.m., namely, that 50% of the dearness allowance drawn at present might be treated as pay.

We have observed that the Government accepted the grant of dearness allowance at the rates suggested by the Central Pay Commission for the index figure of 285. In accordance with the Pay Commission's formula, these rates would continue to hold good until the index figure reached 305. When the cost-of-living index crosses this figure and prices started rising, the Government found itself enable to grant dearness allowance in accordance with the Central Pay Commission's formula. To alleviate the hardship caused to its employees, it gave two *ad hoc* increases in the dearness allowance to those in receipt of pay not exceeding Rs. 300. The representatives of various unions who gave evidence before us stressed that these *ad hoc* increases were both inadequate (according to the Pay Commission's formula) and belated. They also argued that the *ad hoc* increases should not be reduced. In the event of a fall in the cost of living, a reduction in the dearness allowance seems unavoidable. However, we feel that a reduction should come about only when the fall in the cost of living is fairly substantial and is not purely of a temporary nature. This would afford a certain degree of stability even in the fluctuating element of their emoluments and would give them a reasonable sense of security. Having regard to the circumstances in which the *ad hoc* increases were given, we would recommend that these *ad hoc* increases should not be reduced until the All-India Cost of Living Index reaches the figure of 305.

Other Recommendations

The purposes for which the approved percentage of the dearness allowance should be treated as pay are indicated below:

(a) Retirement benefits:

(i) Subscription to the Contributory Provident Fund, the Government's contribution thereof and the Special Contribution.

(ii) Pension and gratuities.

It has been urged before us by the Central Government employees who are on the verge of retirement that the full pensionary benefit arising from our recommendations should be made available to them. We have been told that as the pension is calculated on "Average Emoluments" (as defined in the Pension Rules) relating to the period of three years before retirement, the full benefit of treating a portion of dearness allowance as pay will be felt in pension only after a period of three years from the date from which this measure is given effect to. We recommend that the "Average Emoluments" should first be calculated under the normal pension rules (excluding for the purpose of such calculation the element of dearness allowance that is treated as pay), and the following should be added:

"After determining the dearness allowance in respect of an amount of pay equal to the 'Average Emolument', and taking 50% thereof as representing the portion to be treated as pay,

(i) Half of such portion should be taken for addition to the Average Emoluments for those retiring within one year from the date from which the recommendations are given effect to, and

(ii) The whole of such portion should be taken for addition to the Average Emoluments for those retiring in the second or third year after the date from which the recommendations are given effect to."

(b) Travelling Allowance.

(c) Compensatory Allowance.

(d) House Rent Allowance.

It has been brought to our notice, however, that Government servants in Group "C" towns who are not provided with Government quarters and who are in receipt of pay not exceeding Rs. 100 p.m. and who are entitled to a house rent allowance of Rs. 7 p.m. would stand to lose in cases where their pay together with the portion of dearness allowance to be treated as pay exceeds Rs. 100 p.m. We have considered this matter and feel that while it would be correct to determine the house rent allowance on pay plus the portion of dearness allowance to be treated as pay, we would recommend that in the case of an employee who is in receipt of house rent allowance on the date on which our recommendation is given effect to, any immediate drop in emoluments caused by the inclusion of the appropriate portion of the dearness allowance as pay should be protected by the grant of a personal allowance which will be absorbed in increases in emoluments consequent on the drawal of increments, promotions, etc.

(e) Recovery of house rent from Government employees in occupation of Government quarters.

In order to prevent a sudden drop in the net emoluments of an individual who is occupying Government quarters on the date on which our recommendations are given effect to, we could recommend that the additional amount of house rent to be charged on such portion of the dearness allowance as is treated as pay should be limited to 5% instead of the usual 10%. This personal concession will cease either on promotion or on an individual becoming entitled to Government quarters of a different class.

(f) Computation of leave salary: We recommend that for purposes of computing the leave salary, the average pay, half average pay, etc., should be calculated as at present on the basic pay (i.e., excluding the element of dearness allowance to be treated as pay) and the dearness allowance should then be determined on the amount of average pay, half average pay, etc., so arrived at.

There are a few service conditions which are peculiar to the employees of certain departments and they require special mention:

(a) Piece Workers in Ordnance Factories.

(b) Railway employees who are in receipt of grainshop concession: They should be eligible to all the concessions as if they were in receipt of full dearness allowance in cash.

(c) Railway employees who are in receipt of Educational Assistance: In the case of an employee who is in receipt of educational assistance on the date from which the recommendations are given effect to, the amount of educational assistance admissible shall, as a personal concession, be based on his basic pay (i.e., excluding the portion of dearness allowance treated as pay) till such time as his basic pay exceeds the upper limit of the slab in which he is on the relevant date. When the limit referred to is exceeded, the portion of dearness allowance treated as pay shall be taken into account with the basic pay for regulating the grant of educational assistance.

(d) Running allowances to traffic and loco running staff on Railways: We recommend that the portion of dearness allowance which is to be treated as pay should not affect the determination of the rates of running allowance under the old Running Allowance Rules.

DAMODAR VALLEY CORPORATION ENQUIRY COMMITTEE, 1952—REPORT

New Delhi, Ministry of Irrigation and Power, 1953. 152p., Map.

Chairman : Shri P. S. Rau.
Members : Shri V. D. Dantyagi; Shri S. B. Capoor (replaced by Shri B. N. Lokur); Shri G. R. Garg.
Secretary : Shri B. D. Nanda.

APPOINTMENT

The Damodar Valley Corporation Enquiry Committee was constituted under the Ministry of Irrigation and Power vide their Resolution No. DW.10 dated September 20, 1952.

TERMS OF REFERENCE

To examine and make recommendations on:

(i) Land reclamation and rehabilitation works undertaken by the Damodar Valley Corporation;

(ii) The changes in the design and construction features of the Konar and Tilaiya Dams; the award of contracts and the rates for various items of works;

(iii) The planning and purchase of stores and equipment for works on the Damodar Valley Corporation and the procedure therefor;

(iv) The appointment of a Chief Engineer for the Damodar Valley Corporation;

(v) The adequacy of the Damodar Valley Corporation Act, 1948, and the organizational set-up of the Corporation.

CONTENTS

Introductory; Historical; Land Reclamation and Rehabilitation Works Undertaken by the Damodar Valley Corporation; The Changes in the Design and Construction Features of the Tilaiya Dam; The Planning and Purchase of Stores and Equipment for Works on Damodar Valley Corporation and the Procedure Therefor; The Appointment of a Chief Engineer for the Damodar Valley Corporation; The Adequacy of the Damodar Valley Corporation Act, 1948; Organizational Set-up of the Damodar Valley Corporation; Conclusion and Acknowledgments; Summary of Conclusions and Recommendations; Appendices I to X.

RECOMMENDATIONS

Land Reclamation And Rehabilitation Works Undertaken By The DVC

The work of rehabilitation should remain with the Corporation.

Payment of compensation in cash in all cases is neither fair in itself nor in consonance with the declared policy of the Government and must be rejected.

The proposal that land for land may be given 60 to 100 miles away where it can be reclaimed at a lower cost is bound to lead to a justified agitation by displaced persons and cause difficulties and will involve a change in policy which will lead to charges of a breach of faith.

Land of equal productivity must be given to the displaced persons; any other course would be unfair.

The proposal that the Corporation should acquire culturable waste and hand over to displaced persons an equivalent number of acres and give suitable plots for houses in a new *abadi*, though cheaper, would not provide real rehabilitation.

The method may be tried of entrusting the construction of houses to an approved village co-operative society under the guidance of the Corporation's engineers.

The Changes In The Design And Construction Features Of Tilaiya Dam

Though the advice of the Board of Consultants for a change of design from masonry to concrete was not unanimous, no formal decision was taken by the Corporation, but Shri Venkatachari's advice was tacitly accepted. It is surprising that no record exists of so important a decision with such technical and financial implications.

The numerous changes in design were due to the absence of a Chief Engineer who could have given the Corporation authoritative advice.

The possibility of linking the Tilaiya Power Station with Bokaro may be investigated. As soon as that is done, the thermal power plant at Tilaiya may either be disposed of or used elsewhere.

It may be considered whether the waters of both Tilaiya and Konar cannot be put to immediate use.

The Planning And Purchase Of Stores And Equipment

It would not be proper to compel the Corporation to make all its purchases through the D.G.S.&D. At the same time, it should be advantageous to the Corporation to enforce more strictly the procedure laid down to ensure that requirements are foreseen by indenting officers as far as possible. If this is done, it should be possible for the Corporation to utilize the agency of the D.G.S.&D. to a greater extent.

The possibility of entering into rate contracts with regard to spare parts of the machinery in common use may be explored by the Government.

The possibility of standardizing equipment to be used in the river valley projects needs consideration by the Government.

The Appointment Of A Chief Engineer

The efforts made by the Corporation to secure the services of an Indian Chief Engineer were genuine and serious.

The results of the absence of a Chief Engineer for two and a half years are writ large on the work of the Corporation—in expert advice and frequent changes of design, increase in costs, waste of public funds.

For the vacillation and indecision in appointing the Chief Engineer the Corporation is, as a whole, technically responsible but the personal responsibility of the Chairman in the matter is by no means negligible.

The Adequacy Of The Damodar Valley Corporation Act, 1948

A Corporation should be created only when a project has been investigated in sufficient detail, and a fairly firm estimate has been sanctioned by the Government.

Within the sanctioned project estimate, the Corporation should have full powers to execute the project, without any outside interference. The Corporation should not have any power to modify the scope of the project. That power should rest only in the Government.

After completion of the project, the Corporation should have full powers to run its commercial or quasi-commercial activities, like irrigation, navigation, power and flood control.

In regard to non-commercial activities like soil conservation, afforestation, etc., schemes should be submitted by the Corporation to the Government for approval, before they are taken up. Such schemes should be implemented only to the extent approved by the Government.

A "policy-making corporation" is in every way better than a "functional" one.

The provisions of Sections 30 and 31 are being worked in the right spirit, but their full implications may be clarified when the amendment of the Act is undertaken.

The Central Government should authorize the Corporation under Section 29 (2) of the Act to open accounts with any of the more important Indian banks wherever necessary.

The Advisory Committee Rules may also be rescinded.

Functions listed in Sub-Section 12 (f) of the Act should be undertaken only after the scheme has been specifically sanctioned by the Central Government unless the State Government concerned desire to entrust any similar work to the Corporation after making provision in the State budget.

Afforestation and soil conservation as provided under Section 12 (e) of the Act should be subject to the prior approval of the Central Government.

The Government should lay down priorities between the various functions with regard to each project, if necessary by directions under Section 48.

The procedure for initiating and making plans laid down by the Planning Commission in the Five Year Plan is recommended.

When large projects are sanctioned self-sufficient organizations for designing are necessary.

The DVC Act and the Land Acquisition Act should be amended in its application to the Corporation.

The Organizational Set-up Of The DVC

There is too much centralization in the Corporation's methods of administration. While the Corporation should concern itself with policy matters and broad features of general administration, supervision and control, there should be generous delegation of powers at all levels indicating both well-defined responsibility and adequate powers.

The Soil Conservation Department should be placed under a first-rate specialist.

A high-ranking social worker with some knowledge of economics should assist the Corporation in the development of the Valley.

The Chief Electrical Engineer's headquarters could be more conveniently located in the Valley.

The absence of a Law Division in the Corporation office is a serious omission and should be supplied without delay.

All the three members of the Corporation should sit on the Selection Board when appointments carrying pay of Rs. 1,000 p.m. and above are under consideration.

A system of "merit awards" based on objective tests should be introduced as an incentive to good work.

The headquarters of the Corporation should be located at Maithon as early as circumstances permit.

The Corporation should engage the services of a reputed firm of efficiency experts to go into the question of the staff and their efficiency.

SECONDARY EDUCATION COMMISSION, 1952-53—REPORT

New Delhi, Ministry of Education, 1953. 309p. Charts

Chairman : Dr. A. Lakshmanaswami Mudaliar.
Members : Principal John Christie; Dr. Kenneth Rast Williams; Mrs. Hansa Mehta; Shri J. A. Taraporevala; Dr. K. L. Shrimali; Shri M. T. Vyas; Shri K. G. Saiyidain.
Member-Secretary : Shri A. N. Basu.
Assistant Secretary : Dr. S. M. S. Chari.

APPOINTMENT

The Secondary Education Commission was appointed by the Government of India in terms of their Resolution No. F. 9-5/52-B-I dated September 23, 1952.

The Government of India, in their Communique quoted above, referred to the recommendations of the Central Advisory Board of Education made at its 14th meeting held in January, 1948, that a Commission be appointed to examine the prevailing system of Secondary Education in the country and suggest measures for its reorganization and improvement. The Board reiterated its recommendation in January, 1951. The Government of India had also other considerations in mind when appointing this Commission, such as the desirability of changing over from the prevailing system of Secondary Education which is unilateral and predominantly academic in nature to one which will cater at the secondary stage for different aptitudes and interests.

TERMS OF REFERENCE

Under the Terms of Reference, the Government was asked:

(a) To enquire into and report on the present position of Secondary Education in India in all its aspects; and

(b) To suggest measures for its reorganization and improvement with particular reference to:

(i) The aims, organization and content of Secondary Education;

(ii) Its relationship to Primary, Basic and Higher Education;

(iii) The inter-relation of Secondary schools of different types; and

(iv) Other allied problems

so that a sound and reasonable uniform system of Secondary Education suited to our needs and resources may be provided for the whole country.

CONTENTS

Introductory; Appraisal of the Existing Situation; Reorientation of Aims and Objectives; New Organizational Pattern of Secondary Education; Study of Languages; Curriculam in Secondary Schools; Dynamic Methods of Teaching; The Education of Character; Guidance and Counselling in Secondary Schools; The Physical Welfare of Students; A New Approach to Examination and Evaluation; Improvement of the Teaching Personnel; Problems of Administration; Finance; The Secondary School as we visualize it; Conclusions; Summary of Recommendations; Appendices from I to X; Administrative Set-up of the State Department of Education; Educational Ladder—Proposed Organizational Pattern.

RECOMMENDATIONS—SUMMARY

I. Aims And Objectives Of Secondary Education

The Commission have said in their report: "As political, social and economic conditions change and new problems arise, it becomes necessary to re-examine carefully and study clearly the objectives which education at each stage should keep in view. Moreover, this statement must take into account not only the facts of the existing situation but also the direction of its development and the nature and type of the social order that we envisage for the future to which education has to be geared."

In the Commission's opinion, the most outstanding and educationally relevant facts in the Indian situation were:

(1) The adoption of the goals of democracy and socialism necessitating the development among the people of a broad, national and secular outlook;

(2) The extreme poverty of the country and urgency for promoting its economic growth; and

(3) The absence of educational facilities needed for developing all aspects of the human personality and the neglect of cultural pursuits and activities.

On the basis of this analysis, the Commission recommended that Secondary Education should be re-oriented to the following aims and objects:

(a) Development of Qualities Essential for Creative Citizenship : This includes the development in the students of Secondary Schools of those habits, attitudes and qualities of character which are essential for creative citizenship in a democratic society. Among these qualities, which are to be fostered through curricular and co-curricular activities in Secondary Schools, are:

(i) The capacity for clear thinking (allied to which is the capacity for clearness in speech and writing);

(ii) The scientific attitude of mind;

(iii) A receptivity to new ideas;

(iv) A respect for the dignity and worth of every individual;

(v) The ability to live harmoniously with one's fellow-men through the cultivation of discipline, co-operation, social sensitiveness and tolerance; and

(vi) A sense of true patriotism.

(b) The Promotion of Vocational Efficiency: This involves not only the creation of a new attitude to work and an appreciation of the dignity of manual labour but also the development of the students' technical skill and efficiency through greater emphasis on craft and productive work and the diversification of courses at the Secondary stage.

(c) Development of Personality: This implies cultivation of the students' literary, artistic and cultural interests for a fuller development of their personalities. This means the provision of subjects like art, craft, music, dancing and hobbies in the Secondary School curricula.

(d) The Training for Leadership: The training of persons who, on completion of the Secondary stage, would be able to assume the responsibilities of leadership at the Intermediate level.

II. Proposed Pattern Of School Education

Under the new organized structure, education should commence after a four or five-year period of Primary or Junior Basic Education and should include:

(a) Middle or Senior Basic or Junior Secondary stage of three years; and

(b) The Higher Secondary stage of four years.

Transition State: During the transitional stage, the existing High Schools and the Higher Secondary Schools should function on the lines laid down.

Replacement of Intermediate Stage: The present Intermediate stage should be replaced by the Higher Secondary stage which should be of four years' duration, one year of the present Intermediate being included in it.

First Degree Course: As a consequence of the preceding recommendations, the first degree course in the university should be of three years' duration.

Pre-University Course for those who pass out of the High School: For those who pass out of High School there should be provision for a pre-university course of one year, during which period the scheme of students' studies should be planned with due regard to the needs of the degree or the professional course to be taken by the students, and special emphasis should be placed on the quickening of intellectual interests, training in methods of study at college and the study of English so long as it continues to be the medium of instruction at the university.

Admission to Professional Colleges: Admission to professional colleges should be open to those who have completed the Higher Secondary course, or have taken the one year's pre-university course.

Pre-Professional Course: In the professional colleges, a pre-professional course of one year should be provided for the students, preferably in the professional colleges themselves, but, as a transitory measure, they may be given in the degree colleges where facilities exist, till professional colleges are able to provide for such courses.

Place of Public Schools: Public schools should continue to exist for the present and the pattern of education given in them should be brought into reasonable conformity with the general pattern of national education. Such schools should gradually become self-supporting, but during the transitional period of the next five years, State or Central assistance should be given to them on a gradually diminishing scale.

Additional Residential Schools: A number of residential schools should be established, more particularly in certain rural areas, to provide proper opportunities for the education of children and particularly to meet the needs of children whose education suffers at present owing to the exigencies of service of their parents.

Residential Day Schools: "Residential Day Schools" should be established in suitable centres to provide greater opportunities for teacher-pupil contact and for developing recreational and extra-curricular activities.

Co-operation between Centre and States: In matters connected with reorganization and improvement of Secondary Education, there should be close co-operation between the Centre and the States.

Centre's Responsibility for Reorganization of Secondary Education: The Centre should assume a certain amount of direct responsibility for the contemplated reorganization of Secondary Education and give financial aid for the purpose.

III. School Hours And Admissions Latitude In School Hours To Suit Community Activities

Considerable latitude should be given to schools to arrange their school hours in such a way as not to interfere with the activities of the community and the general climatic and occupational conditions prevailing in the locality.

School Day—School Week: As a rule, the total number of working days in a school should not be less than two hundred, the working hours per week should be at least 35 periods of about 45 minutes each; the school should work regularly for six days in the week, one of the days being a half-day when the teachers and students might meet informally and work together on various extra-curricular and social projects.

Holidays and Vacations: School holidays need not be identical with public holidays as declared by the Government, and normally during the year there should be a summer vacation of two months and two breaks of 10 to 15 days at suitable periods during the year.

IV. Language And Medium Of Instruction

Languages at the Middle School Stage: During the Mi dle School stage, every child should be taught at least two languages. English and Hindi should be introduced at the end of the Junior Basic stage, subject to the principle that no two languages should be introduced in the same year.

Languages at the High and Higher Secondary Stage: At the High and Higher Secondary stage, at least two languages should be studied, one of which being the mother-tongue or the regional language.

Medium of Instruction should be the Mother-Tongue or the Regional Language: The mother-tongue or the regional language should generally be the medium of instruction throughout the Secondary School stage, subject to the provision that for linguistic minorities special facilities should be made available on the lines suggested by the Central Advisory Board of Education.

V. Methods Of Teaching

Inculcation of Values, Attitudes and Work Habits: The methods of teaching in schools should aim not merely at the imparting of knowledge in an efficient manner, but also at inculcating desirable values and proper attitudes and habits of work in the students.

They should, in particular, endeavour to create in the students a genuine attachment to work and a desire to do it as efficiently, honestly and thoroughly as possible.

Activity and Project Methods: The emphasis in teaching should shift from verbalism and memorization to learning through purposeful, concrete and realistic situations and, for this purpose, the principles of "Activity Method" and "Project Method" should be assimilated in school practice.

Teaching methods should provide opportunities for students to learn actively and to apply practically the knowledge that they have acquired in the class-room. "Expression Work" of different kinds must, therefore, form part of the programme in every school subject.

Emphasis on Clear Thinking and Expression: In the teaching of all subjects special stress should be placed on clear thinking and clear expression both in speech and writing.

Training Pupils in Techniques of Study: Teaching methods should aim less at imparting the maximum quantum of knowledge possible, and more on training students in the techniques of study and methods of acquiring knowledge through personal effort and initiative.

Instruction to Suit Different Student Abilities: A well-thought-out attempt should be made to adopt methods of instruction to the needs of individual students as much as possible so that dull, average and bright students may all have a chance to progress at their own pace.

Group Projects and Activities: Students should be given an adequate opportunity to work in groups and to carry out group projects and activities so as to develop in them the qualities necessary for group life and co-operative work.

VI. Moral And Religious Instruction

Religious Instruction: Religious instruction may be given in schools only on a voluntary basis and outside the regular school hours, such instruction being confined to the children of the particular faith concerned and given with the consent of the parents and the managements.

VII. Text Books

High-Power Text Book Committee for Quality Text Books: With a view to improving the quality of text books prescribed, a high-power Text Book Committee should be constituted which should consist of a high dignitary of the judiciary of the State, preferably a Judge of the High Court, a member of the Public Service Commission of the region concerned, a Vice-Chancellor of the region, a headmaster or headmistress in the State, two distinguished educationists, and the Director of Education. The Committee should function as an independent body.

Sale Proceeds for Award of Scholarships: A fund should be maintained from the amount realized from the sale of publications which may be utilized for awarding scholarships and providing books and certain other amenities for schoolchildren.

Criteria for Text Books: The Text Book Committee should lay down clear criteria for the type of paper, illustration, printing and format of the book.

Libraries of Blocks of Illustrations: The Central and State Governments should maintain libraries of blocks of good illustrations which could be loaned to Text Book Committees and publishers in order to improve the standard of book illustration.

A Range of Books should be Recommended: Single text books should not be prescribed for every subject of study, but a reasonable number of books which satisfy the standards laid down should be recommended leaving the choice to the schools concerned.

Language Text Books should be Prescribed: In the case of languages, however, definite text books should be prescribed for each class to ensure proper gradation.

Text Books should not Offend or Indoctrinate: No book prescribed as a text book or as a book for general study should contain any passage or statement which might offend the religious or social susceptibilities of any section of the community or might indoctrinate the minds of the young students with particular political or religious ideologies.

Discouraging Frequent Change of Text Books: Frequent changes in text books and books prescribed for study should be discouraged.

VIII. Examinations And Evaluation

Reviewing the defects of examinations at the Secondary stage, the Secondary Education Commission said:

"The examinations today dictate the curriculum instead of following it, prevent any experimentation, hamper the proper treatment of subjects and sound methods of teaching, foster a dull uniformity rather than originality, encourage the average pupil to concentrate too rigidly upon too narrow a field and thus help him to develop wrong values in education. Pupils assess education in terms of success in examinations. Teachers, recognizing the importance of the external examination to the individual pupils, are constrained to relate their teaching to an examination which can test only a narrow field of the pupil's interests and capacities and so inevitably neglect the qualities which are more important though less tangible."

(a) **External Examinations—Introduction of Objective Type Tests:** The number of external examinations should be reduced and the element of subjectivity in the essay-type tests should be minimized by introducing objective tests and also by changing the type of questions.

(b) **School Records for Assessment of All-round Progress:** In order to find out the pupil's all-round progress and to determine his future, a proper system of school records should be maintained for every pupil indicating the work done by him from time to time and his attainments in the different spheres.

(c) **In the Final Assessment** of the pupils due credit should be given to the internal tests and the school records of the pupils.

(d) **Symbolic Marking to Replace Numerical Marking:** The system of symbolic rather than numerical marking should be adopted for evaluating and grading the work of the pupils in external and internal examinations and in maintaining the school records.

(e) **One Public Examination—Final Comprehensive Certificate:** There should be only one public examination at the completion of the Secondary School course.

(f) **The Certificate awarded** should contain, besides the results of the public examination in different subjects, the results of the school tests in subjects not included in the public examination as well as the gist of the school records.

(g) **The System of** compartmental examinations should be introduced at the final public examination.

(h) **Board of Secondary Education to be Set Up:** There should be a Board of Secondary Education consisting of not more than 25 members with the Director of Education as its chairman to deal with all matters of education at the Secondary stage and to lay down general policies.

A sub-committee of the Board should deal with the conduct of examinations.

IX. Buildings And Equipment

School Buildings—Space per Pupil: Normally, in designing buildings for schools, care should be taken to see that an area of not less than 10 sq. ft. is provided per student in the classroom.

Optimum Strength of Class and School: The optimum number of boys to be admitted to any class should be 30 and the maximum should not in any case exceed 40; the optimum number in the whole school should be 500 while the maximum should not exceed 750.

Research Required on School Buildings, Furniture and Equipment: In the type design of schools as well as the furniture, etc., research should be carried on to improve functional efficiency and to adjust them to Indian conditions.

An Expert Committee should be appointed to lay down carefully the amount and the kind of equipment required for various types of diversified courses and workshops.

Land for Educational Purposes: The State Governments and the Centre should, wherever possible, assign lands to schools for playgrounds, buildings or agricultural farms and other necessary purposes without any charge.

Exemption from Customs Duty for Equipment and Books: The educational institutions which have to obtain necessary scientific apparatus, workshop appliances and books for school library should be exempted from Customs duty.

X. Experimentation In Schools

Schools to be Encouraged to Experiment on New Methods: In order to popularize progressive teaching methods and facilitate their introduction, "Experimental" and "Demonstration" schools should be established and given special encouragement where they exist, so that they may try out new methods freely without being fettered by too many departmental restrictions.

XI. Educational Finance

Contributions to Secondary Education to be Exempted from Income-Tax: Contributions for the development of secondary education should be exempted from the operation of the Income-tax Act.

Surplus Endowment Funds for Education: Surplus funds from the religious and charitable endowments should be diverted to educational purposes.

Amount Bequeathed for Educational Purposes to be Exempted from Duty: The amount bequeathed to public institutions for general educational purposes in the will of a deceased person should not be subject to any duty by the Centre and the whole of it should be appropriated to the educational purpose.

Educational Institutions should be Exempted from Property Tax: All educational institutions and the grounds attached thereto should be exempted from the levy of Property Taxes.

XII. Fees And Freeships

Free Studentships: The States or the Centre should provide for certain free studentships in them (public schools) to be given on the basis of merit to select students.

No Fees to be Levied—Stipends to Student-Teachers No fees should be charged in training colleges, while during the period of training all the student-teachers should be given suitable stipends by the State; the teachers who are already in service should be given the same salary which they were getting.

Rates of Fees: The scales of fees fixed by the Management of a school should be subject to approval by the Department of Education.

A Committee should be appointed when necessary by the Department of Education to go into the question of levying a uniform scale of tuition and other fees and all accounts of the school should be subject to audit by the Department.

XIII. Girls' Education

Facilities for Home Science in Girls' Schools: While no distinction need be made between education imparted to boys and girls, special facilities for the study of Home Science should be made available in all girls' schools and co-educational or mixed schools.

Separate Schools for Girls: Effort should be made by State Governments to open separate schools for girls wherever there is demand for them.

Facilities to be Provided in Co-educational Schools: Definite conditions should be laid down in regard to co-educational or mixed schools to satisfy the special needs of girl students and women members of the teaching staff.

XIV. Guidance And Counselling

Importance of Educational Guidance: Educational guidance should receive much greater attention on the part of the educational authorities.

Films on Occupations and Industries: In order to broaden the pupils' understanding of the scope, nature and significance of various occupations and industries, films should be prepared to show the nature of the work in various industries and this should be supplemented by actual visits.

Guidance Officers and Career Masters Training: The services of trained Guidance Officers and Career Masters should be made available gradually and in an increasing measure to all educational institutions.

The Centre should take up the responsibility of opening in different regions centres of training for Guidance Officers and Career Masters to which each State may send a member of teachers or other suitable persons for training.

XV. Health And Physical Education

School Medical Services—Follow-up Treatment: A

properly organized School Medical Service should be built up in all States.

A thorough medical examination of all pupils, and necessary follow-up treatment where necessary, should be carried out in all schools.

Teachers to be Trained in First Aid and Health Principles: Some of the teachers should be trained in first aid and general principles of health so that they may co-operate intelligently with the medical staff.

Nutritional Standards in Residential Schools: Proper nutritional standards should be maintained in hostels and residential schools.

School and Sanitation of Community: The school should assist, where possible, in the maintenance of sanitation of the area, and the schoolchildren should thus be trained to appreciate the dignity of manual labour.

Physical Activities—Adapted to Individual Capacity: Physical activities should be made to suit the individual and his capacity for physical endurance.

Teachers should Participate in Physical Activities: All teachers below the age of 40 should actively participate in many of the physical activities of students and thus make them a lively part of the school programme.

Records of Physical Activities: Full records of physical activities of students must be maintained.

Physical Education to be Comprehensive: The training in physical education should be comprehensive enough to include all aspects of health education.

Physical Education Teachers to Teach Physiology and Hygiene: Teachers of Physical Education should be associated with the teaching of subjects like physiology and hygiene and given the same status as other teachers with similar qualifications.

Training of Physical Education Teachers: The existing facilities for training of teachers of Physical Education should be expanded by increasing the seats in the existing colleges, by opening new colleges, where necessary, and by reorganizing some of the institutions as All-India Training Centres to which aid may be given both by the Centre and the States.

XVI. School Libraries And Reading Habits

Importance of School Libraries: As the proper use of a well-equipped school library is absolutely essential for the efficient working of every educational institution and for encouraging literacy and cultural interests in students, every Secondary School should have such a library; class libraries and subject libraries should also be utilized for this purpose.

Training in Library Work: Trained Librarians, who have love for books and an understanding of students' interests, should be provided in all Secondary Schools and all teachers should be given some training in the basic principles of library work, in the training colleges as well as through refresher courses.

School Libraries vis-a-vis Public Libraries: Where there are no separate public libraries, the school libraries should, as far as possible, make their facilities available to the local public and all public libraries should have a special section for children and adolescents.

Production of General Reading Books: In order to improve general standards of work in schools, necessary steps should be taken to produce text books as well as books of general reading which are distinctly superior in quality to the books at present available.

XVII. School Management And Recognition

Recognition of Schools: Recognition to schools should be given only on clearly defined conditions which will ensure their proper running and the maintenance of proper standards.

Managing Boards of Schools—Rules of Service: The managing boards of all schools should be registered and should consist of a limited number of persons with the Headmaster as an ex-officio member.

No member of the Managing Board should directly or indirectly interfere with the internal administration of the school.

Every management should be required to draw up definite rules of service wherein the conditions pertaining to salary, leave, etc., should be definitely laid down.

Endowment of Schools: For proper running of a school, every management should be required to provide an endowment and the income accruing from this should be shown in the receipts of the year.

Requirements of Staff: Accommodation and Equipment for Recognition: The managements should satisfy the Department that qualified staff is available and will be appointed in accordance with the rules laid down by the Department of Affiliation.

The management should satisfy the Department that adequate accommodation and equipment, etc., have been provided for the efficient running of the school.

Sections in Each Class: The number of sections in each class should be limited and before any increase in the numbers of sections is made, the prior approval of the Department should be obtained.

Opening of New Schools: Rules to Prevent Unhealthy Competition: In the interest of the general efficiency of schools, rules should be framed preventing undue competition amongst neighbouring schools.

Minimum Conditions to be Fulfilled: Managements should obtain prior approval of the Director of Education before opening schools and the approval should not be given unless the minimum conditions prescribed have been scrupulously fulfilled.

XVIII. Teachers

Guide Material for Teachers: Suitable literature for the guidance and inspiration of teachers should be produced by the Education Departments of all States and either the Office of the Director of Education or one of the training colleges should be adequately equipped for the purpose.

Selection and Appointment: A reasonable uniform procedure should be devised for the selection and appointment of teachers for all types of schools.

Selection Committee for Private Schools: In all privately managed institutions and in schools maintained by local boards there should be a small Selection Committee entrusted with the responsibility of recruiting the staff, with the Headmaster as an ex-officio member.

The normal period of probation for a Trained Teacher should be one year.

Qualification of Teachers: Teachers working in High Schools should be Graduates with a Degree in Education; those who teach technical subjects should be Graduates in the subjects concerned with the necessary training for teaching it; teachers in Higher Secondary Schools should possess higher qualifications somewhat similar to those prescribed in some universities for teachers of the Intermediate Colleges.

Qualifications; Type of Work; Grades of Pay: The teachers possessing the same qualifications and performing the same type of work should be treated on a par in the matter of grades of salary irrespective of the type of institution in which they are working.

Special Committee to Review the Scales of Pay: A Special Committee should be set up to review the scales of pay of teachers of all grades and recommend such scales of pay that will meet in a fair and just manner the varying cost of living.

Triple Benefit Scheme for Teachers: In order to relieve teachers from anxieties about their own and their dependants' future which will affect the efficiency of their work, the system of Triple Benefit Scheme, pension-cum-provident fund-cum-insurance, should be introduced in all States.

Arbitration Boards to Look into Teachers' Appeals: Arbitration Boards or Committees should be established to look into the appeals and grievances of teachers and to consider matters relating to suspension, dismissal, etc.

Age of Retirement: The age of retirement in the case of a physically fit and competent teacher may be extended to 60 with the approval of the Director of Education.

Free Education to Teachers' Children: The children of teachers should be given free education throughout the school stage.

Co-operative Housing Scheme for Teachers: Through a system of co-operative house-building societies, teachers should be provided with quarters so as to enable them to live near the school and devote more time to the many-sided activities of the school.

Travel Concessions and Leave Facilities; Medical Facilities: Teachers wishing to go to health resorts or holiday camps or to attend educational conferences, seminars, etc., should be given travel concessions and leave facilities.

They should be given free medical attention and treatment in hospitals and dispensaries.

Uniform Leave Rules: Opportunities to Visit Institutions in India and Abroad: The leave rules should, as far as possible, be uniform for all educational institutions.

Opportunities should be provided on a generous scale for teachers to visit different institutions within the country and in special cases to go abroad on study leave for higher studies.

Private Tuitions: Teachers' Social and Professional Status: The practice of private tuitions by teachers should be abolished.

Persons in high public position should give special recognition to the teachers' social status and the dignity of their profession.

Recruitment of Headmasters: In order to attract persons of the right type to the responsible position of the headmaster, the emoluments of the post should be made sufficiently attractive.

Teacher Training—Two Types: There should be only two types of institutions for teacher training:

(i) For those who have taken the School Leaving Certificate or Higher Secondary School Leaving Certificate, for whom the period of training should be two years; and

(ii) For graduates for whom the training may, for the present, be of one academic year, but extended as a long-term programme to two academic years.

Graduate teacher-training institutions should be recognized by and affiliated to the universities which should grant the degrees, while the Secondary Grade training institutions should be under the control of a separate Board appointed for the purpose.

The teacher-trainees should receive training in one or more of the various extra-curricular activities.

Training Colleges and In-service Responsibilities: The training colleges should, as a normal part of their work, arrange refresher courses, short intensive courses in special subjects, practical training in workshops and professional conferences.

Teacher's Training: Board for Maintaining Standard of Teacher Training: There should be a Teachers' Training Board for supervising and laying down the conditions necessary for the proper training of undergraduates and for suggesting, for the consideration of the universities, improvements that may be needed in the training of graduates.

Recruitment of Teachers: The teaching staff should not be limited to any particular caste or community but should, as far as possible, be recruited on a wide basis.

Quarters For Teachers: So far as possible, quarters should be provided for teachers in rural areas as well as urban areas to attract suitable persons to the profession and to facilitate development of a corporate community life in the schools.

XIX. Recommendations Of The Secondary Education Commission On School Buildings And Equipment

1. Secondary schools should be established in rural areas in central places with sufficient population which are easily accessible to the surrounding villages.

2. Schools in urban areas should, as far as possible, be so located that they are free from the noise and congestion of the city and necessary transport facilities should be made available for students.

3. The open spaces available in cities must be conserved to be utilized as playgrounds by groups of schools and the State and Central Governments should prevent, through legislation, encroachment on them for industrial or commercial purposes or by housing societies.

4. Normally, in designing buildings for schools, care should be taken to see that an area of not less than 10 sq. ft. is provided per student in the class-rooms.

5. The optimum number of boys to be admitted to any class should be 30 and the maximum should not exceed 40 in any case. The optimum number in the whole school should be 500, while the maximum should not exceed 750.

6. The schools constructed in future should provide facilities for the introduction of diversified courses.

7. In the type design of schools as well as the furniture, etc., research should be carried on to improve functional efficiency and to adjust them to Indian conditions.

8. Expert Committees should be appointed to lay down carefully the amount and the kind of equipment required for various types of diversified courses and workshops.

9. Co-operative stores should be established in all schools where books, stationery and other materials required by students are made available to them at cost price.

10. So far as possible, quarters should be provided for teachers in rural areas as well as urban areas to attract suitable persons to the profession and to facilitate development of a corporate community life in the schools.

XX. Supervision And Inspection Of Schools

Existing Defects: The present system of inspection of schools was subjected to criticism by several witnesses. It was pointed out that inspections were perfunctory, that the time spent by the Inspector at any particular place was insufficient, that the greater part of this time was taken up with routine work like checking accounts and looking into the administrative aspects of the school. There was not enough time devoted to the academic side, and contacts between the Inspectors and teachers were casual. It was also stated that the number of schools entrusted to the care of an Inspector was too large and the range too wide for him to be able to acquaint himself with their work and appreciate their problems; nor was he in a position to advise and guide the teaching staff in improving the work of the school. It occasionally happened that the Inspector instead of being "the friend, philosopher and guide" of the school behaved in such a critical and unsympathetic way that his visit was looked upon with some degree of apprehension, if not of resentment. In our view the true role of an Inspector—for whom we would prefer the term Educational Adviser—is to study the problems of each school, to take a comprehensive view of all its functions and to help the teachers to carry out his advice and recommendations. We also recommend that for special subjects like Physical Education, Domestic Science, Art, Music, etc., there should be attached to the Director's Office certain experts in these subjects who will inspect the different schools periodically and help in improving the standards of teaching.

Selection of Inspectorate: At present the Inspectorate is made up in diverse ways by different States. In some cases Inspectors are recruited directly to inspectional posts and while certain academic qualifications are prescribed, experience and other relevant qualifications are not duly emphasized. Once a person has been chosen for the Inspectorate he often continues in that line till the age of retirement. We are of the view that a person, to be chosen as an Inspector, should possess high academic qualifications (an Honours or Master's degree) and should have had teaching experience in schools for at least 10 years, or should have been a Headmaster of a High School for a minimum period of three years. In addition to direct recruitment the Inspectors should also be drawn from:

(i) Teachers of 10 years' experience;
(ii) Experienced Headmasters of High Schools; and
(iii) Qualified staff of Training Colleges.

We recommend further that suitable persons from any of these categories may be appointed as Inspectors for a period of three to five years after which they may revert to their original posts. In the initial stages, we suggest that 50% of such posts may be reserved for recruitment on this basis. It is necessary that Professors of Training Colleges should be conversant with the work done in the schools; and that Headmasters should likewise have a chance to serve as Inspecting Officers for short periods. This will enable them to appreciate the position of the Inspectors and to approach the problems of the schools with greater appreciation of the realities from their own experience.

Duties of Inspectors: The duties of an Inspector are divisible into administrative and academic. The administrative duties relate to the annual inspection of records, accounts, office routine, etc. For this purpose he must have the assistance of a competent staff. With the increase in the number and types of schools, this duty will require a considerable amount of his time if he is to discharge these functions properly and efficiently. The time needed for the purpose has necessarily restricted the scope of his activities on the academic side. Moreover, the multiplicity of the subjects taught in the school by specially qualified staff now makes it very difficult for any single officer, however qualified, to inspect them thoroughly and to advise on all their problems. We, therefore, recommend that the academic work of the school should be thoroughly inspected by a panel of experts with the Inspector as Chairman and this should be done once in three years. We recommend that three persons may be chosen from senior teachers or headmasters to visit schools in the company of the Inspector and to spend two or three days with the staff, discussing with them all aspects of school life—the library and laboratory facilities, the curriculum, the organization of extra-curricular activities, the use of the holidays and all other problems connected with school activities. Through these full and frank discussions, the inspectors will be in a far better position to help in the improvement of the schools. What is suggested is nothing new—colleges affiliated to Universities are visited by commissions of experts who inspect their working, discuss their problems and report to the University.

PRESS COMMISSION, 1952—REPORT

Delhi, Manager of Publications, 1954. 3 Parts.

Chairman : Shri Justice G. S. Rajadhyaksha.

Members : Dr. C. P. Ramaswami Aiyar; Acharya Narendra Deva; Dr. Zakir Husain; Dr. V. K. R. V. Rao; Shri P. H. Patwardhan; Shri T. N. Singh; Shri Jaipal Singh; Shri J. Natarajan; Shri A. R. Bhat; Shri M. Chalapathi Rao.

Secretary : Shri M. L. Chowla (died on 19.2.1953 and Shri S. Gopalan took over as Secretary).

APPOINTMENT

The Press Commission was constituted under the Ministry of Information and Broadcasting vide their Notification No. 10/1/52-IP dated October 3, 1952.

TERMS OF REFERENCE

The Press Commission shall enquire into the state of the Press in India, its present and future lines of development and shall in particular examine:

(i) The control, management and ownership and financial structure of newspapers, large and small, the periodical Press and news agencies and feature syndicates;

(ii) The working of monopolies and chains and their effect on the presentation of accurate news and fair views;

(iii) The effect of holding companies, the distribution of advertisements and such other forms of external influence as may have a bearing on the development of healthy journalism;

(iv) The method of recruitment, training, scales of remuneration, benefits and other conditions of employment of working journalists, settlement of disputes affecting them and factors which influence the establishment and maintenance of high professional standards;

(v) The adequacy of newsprint supplies and their distribution among all classes of newspapers and the possibilities of promoting indigenous manufacture of (i) newsprint and (ii) printing and composing machinery;

(vi) Machinery for (a) ensuring high standards of journalism and (b) liaison between the Government and the Press; the functioning of Press Advisory Committees and organizations of editors and working journalists, etc.;

(vii) Freedom of the Press and repeal or amendment of laws not in consonance with it; and to make recommendations thereon.

CONTENTS

Course of Enquiry; Newspapers and Periodicals; Capital Investment and Turnover; Economics of Newspapers; Advertisements; Supplies; Communications and Transport; News Agencies; Feature Syndicates; Liaison with Government; Employment; Working Journalists; Associations of Newspapermen; Newspaper Content; Ownership and Control; Competition and Monopolies; Bias and External Pressure; Editorial Control; Standards and Performance; Press Legislation; Conclusions and Recommendations; Annexures.

RECOMMENDATIONS

Statistics Of Newspapers And Periodicals

At the outset we found that the statistics of newspapers and periodicals were grossly inaccurate.

Daily Newspapers

There are about 330 daily newspapers currently being published (including editions published from different centres) and their total circulation is just over 25 lakhs. The figures have to be approximate in the circumstances, but it may be added that if there are a few more newspapers that have not been included they would be essentially those with small circulations.

Newspapers Predominantly Urban

While the growth of circulation of daily newspapers has been satisfactory in comparison with what existed a decade or so ago, the development of journalism has not been adequate in terms of the total population. The penetration of daily newspapers into the rural areas, which house the bulk of India's population, has been very slight.

Scope For Expansion Of Newspapers

On the basis of the number of literate households covered by our sample survey who have expressed interest in newspapers, there exists an immediate potential for a very large increase in readership, much greater in the rural areas than in the urban areas. The results of the survey indicate that the reasons at present preventing interested households from going in for newspapers are primarily the cost and the lack of distribution facilities.

Number Of Papers Should Increase

If we take into account such factors as distance and poor communications, we need a large increase in the number of newspapers.

One way that can be suggested to minimize the losses in the early stages, particularly where no daily paper exists already, would be to start the paper initially as a weekly, and when circulation has been built up to some extent, to convert it into a daily. We would also suggest that where adequate printing facilities exist, such papers should not install their own printing equipment, even if they can find the necessary capital for it. It might be preferable to entrust the printing to a press that has already established itself locally.

Local sale of most nationally advertised products is generally small. We feel that local advertising can be built up by educating the people about the advantages of advertising.

Statutory Collection Of Statistics

We consider it essential that there should be some statutory authority responsible for the collection of reliable statistics regarding the Press in the country and periodical publication. The authority responsible for the collection of statistics would, therefore, be a central authority. There should be Press Registrars for each State who will be responsible for the primary collection and compilation of the statistics. All newspapers should be called upon to file periodic returns regarding employees, consumption of raw material, changes in ownership and control, and changes in management so that the public can get, from one source, authentic statistics about the industry. It should also be made incumbent on the newspapers to file periodic statements regarding the circulation of the paper as well as to send one copy of each edition to the National Library of India.

Periodical Publications

A very large proportion of the periodical publications, particularly of those appearing monthly or oftener, are published on newsprint. This not merely adds to the demand for newsprint but gives a poorer appearance to the periodicals and a number of potential purchasers may be put off by the poor production quality. If, however, their standards of production can be raised, it is possible that advertisement revenues can be built up to such an extent that they would more than offset the increased cost.

Publishers should realize the large market that exists for periodicals in this country and the possibilities of a large-scale expansion of this profitable field of public service.

An important aspect in which the Indian periodical Press is today found deficient is in the publication of technical and specialist periodicals. When science, technology and medicine are advancing rapidly, the interchange of the latest information on research and application is achieved not so much by books as through periodicals.

We must mention with regret that a great deal of the objectionable writings—scurrilous, obscene, indecent and personal—does exist in the Indian Press, though it is confined to the periodical Press, and the daily newspapers have been comparatively free from these evils. While it is necessary for the Press to develop so as to meet the needs of the country, it is also essential that effective checks should exist against publications of this character.

Under-capitalization And Indebtedness

We found that unsecured loans had been obtained mostly from the same sources as the original capital. Whether the additional funds are brought in as regular capital or as loan would not be very significant so long as the interest on the loans does not cripple the resources of the newspaper and the fact of indebtedness does not lay the paper open to external influences.

Sources Of Capital

Provision for regular ploughing back of a substantial part of the profits into the industry is essential in the interest of normal and healthy development of the Press.

Costs Of Production

Some managements have followed certain practices that have added to the costs and thus reduced the profit for distribution as bonus. We have examined specific cases which were cited to us and in some of them we have noticed one or more of such practices. The methods adopted were mainly to employ a number of relations on higher salaries, creation of supernumerary posts for them and payment of excessive commission to concerns in which the main shareholders or directors are interested. These work to the detriment of the development of the industry and creation of goodwill among the employees.

Main Sources Of Revenue

The circulation revenue alone does not cover the cost of production and a newspaper has to rely on advertisement revenue for making both ends meet. To the extent that a paper can get more advertisement revenue it can afford to reduce its price or improve its news and features.

Auxiliary Sources Of Revenue

Crosswords and similar competitions did form an important source of revenue in the past, but now they appear to serve the dailies more as a means of promoting circulation than as a source of revenue and are conducted for this purpose even if they are not returning direct profits.

Advertisement Revenue

If newspaper readership expands faster than commercial and industrial activity, as is very likely with the rapid spread of education, we expect a fall in the advertisement revenue per copy. Therefore any step that may help newspapers to be less dependent on advertisement revenue would be welcome. A price-page schedule would be one such measure.

The Fight For Circulation

The range of commission that should be paid to news agents should be narrowed down, say, between 25 and 33½%. Any payment of commission above this rate as well as offer of other inducements to news-agents or allowing them to sell the papers at reduced prices should be considered unfair practices and should be stopped.

A healthy method of competition is to give better, more varied and specialized coverage. Merely offering a large number of pages does not increase the standard of service, but on the other hand gives an unfair advantage in competition to those papers which have higher financial resources.

The publication of entry forms for prize competitions in newspapers and periodicals is an unjournalistic activity and we recommend the insertion of a provision in the Act regulating the printing of any form of entry to competition or prize schemes.

Where delivery charges exceed 15% of the nett value, the excess should be recovered from the agent or as a surcharge from the subscribers. Any violation of these price restrictions should be considered an unfair practice and should be checked.

Circulation Statistics

We are suggesting the appointment of a Press Registrar with whom publishers of newspapers have to file certain factual statements periodically. State Governments and the Central Government should be guided by these statements when placing advertisements.

Restrictive Practices

There are other practices connected with large-scale operation which we consider unfair and undesirable. One is the insistence by the management that any advertiser in the most important paper of a group or chain should book space at the same time in their other papers also. Another is to insist that news-agents handling one of the papers of the group should also take a specified number or proportion of the other papers published by the group, or to insist that news-agents handling one paper of a group, say, in English, shall not handle any Indian language paper from any other publisher. Some provision should be made in the contemplated legislation governing newspapers and periodicals to put a stop to such restrictive practices.

Economics Of Groups And Chains

Common ownership of more than one daily newspaper takes the form of combines, chains, multiple units and group. Certain economies are possible in group operation but the extent to which these economies are realized varies from one paper to another.

Separation Of Accounts

We would like, if it were possible, that every paper

should be constituted as a separate unit so that its profits and losses are definitely ascertainable and both the proprietor and the employees know where they stand. In the case of multiple editions, each unit should be separated from the other in the matter of accounts. Where a chain consists of a number of groups, each group should be separated from the other. Inside the group itself, it may be difficult to make a division of capital investment and of certain categories of expenditure. The revenue account should be maintained separately and cost accounts should be kept in respect of production of each of the papers. This system of book-keeping should invariably be adopted wherever the managements find it inconvenient to divide the group into its component units.

We envisage the expansion of some of our metropolitan papers to provide a national or continental coverage, or the establishment of papers by national or political parties to cover the whole country, but in all these cases, the principles we have enunciated above should always be kept in mind. If, however, the parent papers have made adequate provisions for replacement costs and other necessary reserves and are paying their staff reasonable salaries and wages, then there could be no objection to their using the funds obtained from the profits of the parent papers for starting multiple editions in other parts of the country.

Competition Should Be More Even

Newspapers serve as media for the free exchange of information and of ideas. The proper functioning of democracy requires that every individual should have equal opportunity, in so far as this can be achieved to put forward his opinions. Measures should therefore be adopted to reduce the differences due to economic advantages or other causes and to enable newcomers to start with a fair chance of achieving success. To fix a minimum price at which papers of a particular size can be sold would be the most effective measure to bring about this end.

Price-Page Schedule

If the price is fixed too high, it would have a doubly unwelcome effect on the fortunes of the Press. Circulation would fall directly and as a consequence of such fall, advertisement revenues would also shrink. This would force papers to reduce the quality of their services and the cumulative effect may well be disastrous.

The Price-Page Schedule should prescribe not only the maximum number of pages that could be sold at a particular price, but also the minimum number that must be offered. The quantum of advertisement in a week's issue of a newspaper should not exceed 40% of the total area. On the present costs of production a schedule based on a price of 3 pies per page of standard size may prove adequate to meet all costs of production in the case of the average Indian language and English papers after allowing for the normal expectation of advertisement revenue in each case.

Volume And Sources Of Advertisements

Legislation Recommended—Summary

A. The newspaper a d periodical industry should be brought within the list of industries under the control of the Union Government.

B. An Act should be passed to regulate the industry and should *inter alia* provide for the following matters:

(1) The appointment of Press Registrars both at the Centre and in the States, whose duties and functions would be prescribed in the Act on the lines indicated in our recommendations; (2) The collection of statistics of the newspaper industry; (3) The fixing, by the Government, from time to time, of a Price-Page Schedule on the lines we have recomme ıded; (4) The definition and punishment of practices which are unfair or restrictive; (5) Laying down the manner in which accounts of different enterprises shall be maintained by a proprietor controlling more than one newspaper or publishing them from more than one centre; (6) Making the issue and publication of fraudulent advertisements punishable; (7) Making the new Industrial Relations legislation applicable to newspaper employees; (8) Prescribing the method of assessment and distribution of profits from the industry, including the payment of bonus to the employees; (9) Prescribing the terms of employment, including the notice period, minimum wage, leave, provident fund, gratuity, etc.; (10) Making it compulsory for newspapers to publish periodically a statement of ownership and control in the form prescribed; (11) Making provisions of the Provident Fund Act applicable to the employees.

C. There will have to be new enactments for:

(1) Establishing a Press Council; (2) Bringing into existence of a State Trading Corporation for dealing in newsprint and for furnishing finances for the operation of the Press Council; (3) Establishing a Public Corporation to take over the Press Trust of India; (4) Defining the powers, privileges and immunities of legislatures.

D. Amending legislation would also be necessary, on the lines suggested by us, in the case of:

(1) The Press and Registration of Books Act; (2) The Drugs and Magic Remedies (Objectionable Advertisements) Act; (3) The Post Offices Act; (4) The Indian Penal Code (repeal of Section 124A, addition of a new Section 121B, amendments of Sections 153A, 295A and 499); (5) The Criminal Procedure Code (amendment of Sections 99A, 198 and 202); (6) The Sea Customs Act; and (7) The Indian Telegraph Act.

COMMODITY CONTROLS COMMITTEE, 1952—REPORT

Delhi, Manager of Publications, 1953. 133p.

Chairman : Shri S. V. Krishnamoorthy Rao.
Members : Shri M. P. Pai; Shri P. A. Gopalakrishnan (replaced by Dr. S. R. Sen); Shri L. K. Jha; Shri B. N. Lokur; Shri P. M. Nabar.
Secretary : Shri M. A. Mulky.

APPOINTMENT

The Commodity Controls Committee was constituted under the Ministry of Commerce and Industry vide their Memorandum No. 24(31)-PC/52 dated October 24, 1952.

TERMS OF REFERENCE

(a) To examine and review the working of:

(i) The Essential Supplies (Temporary Powers) Act, 1946;

(ii) The Supply and Prices of Goods Act, 1950;

(iii) The Drugs (Control) Act, 1950, and the Orders and Notifications issued thereunder;

(b) To make recommendations for the revision or repeal of any of the said laws with a view to improving the existing systems of controls; and

(c) To streamline the Control Orders and Notifications.

CONTENTS

Introductory; Origin and Present Position of Commodity Controls; Effects of Commodity Controls on the Economy of the Country; Continuance of Commodity Controls; Enforcement of Control Laws; Improvement of the Control System; Fixation of Prices; The Essential Supplies (Temporary Powers) Act, 1946; Food Stuffs and Fodder; The Essential Supplies (Temporary Powers) Act, 1946; Raw Cotton and Textile (Cloth and Yarn); The Essential Supplies (Temporary Powers) Act, 1946: Coal and Salt; The Essential Supplies (Temporary Powers) Act, 1946; Iron and Steel; The Supply and Prices of Goods Act, 1950; The Drugs (Control) Act, 1950; Summary of Recommendations; Appendices I to V.

RECOMMENDATIONS

There are times when controls are necessary and equally at times controls are harmful. Controls can, however, be used for a positive purpose. For planned progress in the economic field, the Government must, in the last analysis, retain the powers of overall guidance and control.

The controls of all essential commodities should be regulated on an all-India basis.

The maximum imprisonment for any offence against control laws need not be more than three years.

The trial of control offences should be concluded within the minimum possible time.

A sound system of numbering the Orders and Notifications and amendments thereto should be evolved so that everyone concerned can easily check the up-to-date position of the control laws.

Each officer in charge of the administration of controls should maintain master copies, brought up to date, of the Control Orders and Notifications with which they may be concerned, and a complete list of all amendments to such Orders and Notifications.

Whenever it is necessary to control prices by law, every effort should be made to make a thorough examination of all the factors involved, to assess the long-term effects of the policy no less than its immediate effects and to ensure that the policies followed in allied economic fields are not such as to undermine the effectiveness of the control measures.

To avoid liability from adulteration the manufacturers of vegetable oil products should devise a method of sealing the tins with their seals and warning the consumers not to buy tins which show signs of having been tampered.

The Central Government should keep a watch on the restrictions imposed on oilcakes and ensure that they are not abused or kept in force beyond the barest minimum period which the emergency may require.

A definite announcement should be made each year regarding floor and ceiling prices of cotton, even if it is intended that there should be no change in the prices. This announcement should be made before the end of June at the latest.

Special efforts should be made to create coal dumps in the South in central places like Madras and Bangalore to assure regular supplies of coal to industries.

Some control over quality of re-rolled steel is desirable, especially when it is used for constructional purposes, where there may be danger to human life if the material is below standard.

The suggestion that dealers and producers of drugs and medicines should mark prices on the drugs and medicines sold by them is commended to them.

CALENDAR REFORM COMMITTEE, 1952—REPORT

New Delhi, Council of Scientific and Industrial Research, 1955. 280p, xiip.

Chairman : Prof. M. N. Saha.
Members : Prof. A. C. Banerji; Dr. K. L. Daftari; Shri J. S. Karandikar; Dr. Gorakh Prasad; Prof. R. V. Vaidya.
Secretary : Shri N. C. Lahiri.

APPOINTMENT

The Calendar Reform Committee was constituted under the Council of Scientific and Industrial Research in November, 1952.

TERMS OF REFERENCE

(i) To examine all the existing calendars which are being followed in the country at present after a scientific study of the subject.

(ii) To submit proposals far an accurate and uniform calendar for the whole of India.

CONTENTS

Message from the Prime Minister; Members of the Calendar Reform Committee; Translation; Preface; **Part A** : Introductory; Appointment of the Committee; Final Recommendations of the Committee; Annexure I to VIII; **Part B** : Explanation; Reformed Calendar of India for each month of the five years 1876 to 1880 Saka; General Rules for Religious Festivals; Lunar Festivals; Solar Festivals; Criteria of Some Festivals for South India; Certain Special Tithis and Combinations; Certain Special Yogas; Tithis, Naksatras, Muhurtas and their Lords; Yogas and Karanas; Alphabetical List of Festivals; Sunrise and Sunset for certain Important Places; List of Holidays; **Part C** : History of the Calendar in Different Countries through the Ages; General Principles of Calendar Making; The Solar Calendar; The Luni-Solar and Lunar Calendars; Calendaric Astronomy; Indian Calendar; Corrigenda and Addenda; Bibliography; Index.

RECOMMENDATIONS

The Committee recommends that the unified National Calendar should be used uniformly in all States of India for civil purposes wherever necessary, in place of local calendars.

Civil Calendar

The Saka era should be used in the Unified National Calendar. The year 1954-55 A.D. corresponds to 1876 Saka, in other words the year 1954 A.D. corresponds to 1875-76 Saka.

The year should start from the day following the vernal equinox day.

A normal year would consist of 365 days while a leap year would have 366 days. After adding 78 to the Saka era, if the sum is divisible by 4, then it is a leap year. But when the sum becomes a multiple of 100, it would be a leap year only when it is divisible by 400, otherwise it would be a common year.

Caitra (pronounced as Chaitra) should be the first month of the year, and the lengths of the different months would be fixed as follows:

Caitra	(31 days in a leap year)	30 days
Vaisakha		31 days
Jyaistha		31 days
Asadha		31 days
Sravana		31 days
Bhadra		31 days
Asvina		30 days
Kartika		30 days
Agrahayana (Margasirsa)		30 days
Pausa		30 days
Magha		30 days
Phalguna		30 days

The dates of the reformed Indian Calendar would thus have a permanent correspondence with the dates of the present Gregorian Calendar.

The corresponding dates are as follows:

Caitra	1	March 22 in a common year and March 21 in a leap year
Vaisakha	1	April 21
Jyaistha	1	May 22
Asadha	1	June 22
Sravana	1	July 23
Bhadra	1	August 23
Asvina	1	September 23
Kartika	1	October 23
Agrahayana	1	November 22
Pausa	1	December 22
Magha	1	January 21
Phalguna	1	February 20

The Indian seasons would thus be permanently fixed with respect to the reformed calendar as follows:

Seasons	Calendar Months
Grisma (Summer)	Vaisakha and Jyaistha
Varsa (Rains)	Asadha and Sravana
Sarat (Autumn)	Bhadra and Asvina
Hemanta (Late Autumn)	Kartika and Agrahayana
Sisira (Winter)	Pausa and Magha
Vasanta (Spring)	Phalguna and Caitra.

Religious Calendar

The calculation of Solar (Saura) months necessary for determining the lunar months of the same name will start 23°15′ ahead of the vernal equinoctial point. This tallies with the present practice of most almanac-makers.

As usual the lunar months for religious purposes would commence from the moment of New Moon and would be named after the Saura Masa in which the New Moon falls. If there be two New Moons during the period of a Saura Masa, the lunar month beginning from the first New Moon is the Adhika or Mala and the Lunar Month beginning from the moment of the second New Moon is the Suddha or Nija, as usual.

The moments of the moon's exit from a Naksatra division of 13°20′ each or the sun's entry into it would be calculated with a valuable Ayanamsa, i.e, on the supposition that they are fixed with respect to the stars. The value of this Ayanamsa would amount to 23°15′ 0″ on March 21, 1956. Thereafter it would gradually increase with the usual annual rate, the mean value of which is about 50″.27.

The day should be reckoned from midnight to midnight of the central station (82½° E. Long. and 23°11′ N. Lat.) for civil purposes, but for religious purposes the local sunrise system may be followed.

For the purpose of all calculations, the longitudes of the sun and the moon should be obtained by applying the most up-to-date and complete equations of their motions, so that they may tally with their observed values.

Steps should be taken to compile an "Indian Ephemeris and Nautical Almanac" by the Government of India, showing in advance the positions of the sun, the moon, planets and other heavenly bodies. The Indian Calendar—both civil and religious—prepared according to the above recommendations should be included in that publication every year.

A permanent Standing Committee to be called the Indian Ephemeris and National Almanac Committee may be constituted for this purpose and attached to a scientific department of the Government of India.

Steps should be taken to establish a National Astronomical Observatory at a suitable place, provided with modern equipment, apparatus and time-service.

TRAINING AND EMPLOYMENT SERVICES ORGANIZATION COMMITTEE, 1952—REPORT

New Delhi, Ministry of Labour, 1954. 252p.

Chairman : Shri B. Shiva Rao.

Members : Shri Hariraj Swarup; Shri Ratan Lal Malviya; Shri V. K. R. Menon; Shri C. S. Menon; Shri G. K. Chandiramani; Shri P. M. Sundaram (replaced by Shri R. K. Rangan).

Secretary : Shri F. M. Nathaniel.

APPOINTMENT

The Training and Employment Services Organization Committee was constituted under the Ministry of Labour vide their Notification No. RCO-320(2) dated November 10, 1952.

TERMS OF REFERENCE

To assess the need for the continuance of the Resettlement and Employment Organization in the context of the country's economic and social development and to suggest with reference to such need what its future shape should be. In particular:

(a) To enquire into the whole question of the future of the Resettlement and Employment Organization and examine whether part of the Organization should be transferred to the State Governments or not; in the latter event, what degree of superintendence and control should be retained by the Central Government;

(b) To assess the results obtained by the Employment Exchanges and Training Schemes, including the Scheme for the Training of Instructors and Supervisors at the Central Institute, Koni-Bilaspur;

(c) To consider on what basis the Training Schemes should be continued and whether the present system of granting stipends should be abolished or modified;

(d) To examine whether there should be further

expansion of Employment Exchanges and Training Programmes consonant with the increased requirements of the country;

(e) To consider whether legislation should be introduced making it obligatory for industry to recruit personnel, at least in the larger industrial centres, through Employment Exchanges; and

(f) To consider whether the Government should make a small levy from employers and/or employment seekers in order to finance part of the cost of the Organization.

CONTENTS

Introduction; **Part I**: Employment Service in India —A Historical Survey; General Administrative Organization; Review of Work Performed by the Employment Exchanges; Shortcomings and Defects in the Existing Organization; Need for an Employment Service; Administration and Financing of the Employment Service Organization; Scope of the Employment Exchanges; Functions, Programme and Procedure; Utilization of Employment Exchange Facilities; Proposed Plan of Organization of the Employment Service under a Central-State System; **Part II**:—Training Schemes for Craftsmen sponsored by Central Government—A Historical Survey; Present Training Schemes of the D.G.R.&E.; General Administrative Organization; Training of Craftsmen and Instructors—A Plan for the Future; Future Administrative Organization; A Note by Shri Hariraj Swarup; Summary of Recommendations; Appendices.

RECOMMENDATIONS

Need For An Employment Service

The Employment Exchange Organization should be placed on a permanent footing without further delay.

Additional Employment Exchanges should be set up only when the need for such is fully established.

Administration And Financing Of The Employment Service Organization

With the object that the Employment Exchange Organization might continue to function as a nationwide system and at the same time be integrated with the plans and programmes of the States, day-to-day administration of the Exchanges should be handed over to the States, the Central Government being responsible for laying down policy and standards and for co-ordination and supervision of the work of the Employment Exchanges.

The Central Government should continue to bear the entire cost of the Central Headquarters, while State Governments should provide, at their cost, the necessary accommodation for the Employment Exchanges.

The expenditure of the Central Government on the Employment Exchange Organization should not on the whole be reduced from the present level.

Scope Of The Employment Exchanges

Employment Exchanges should render assistance to all employment seekers who seek their assistance. They should stay away from traditional assembly points, work sites or other places where workers assemble on their own and where they (Employment Exchanges) can make no positive contribution towards the employment process.

Employment Exchanges should not register applicants for jobs for which they do not possess the prescribed qualifications or satisfy conditions laid down by the respective State Governments from time to time.

In cases where the wages or salary offered is so unreasonably low that the time of the Exchange is likely to be wasted in trying to get the men required, the Exchange should explain the position to the employer and not accept such vacancies. In regard to employment in respect of which minimum wages have been fixed under the Minimum Wages Act, 1948, the Exchanges should not accept vacancies which violate the provisions of the Act.

Functions, Programme And Procedure

Employment Exchanges should make adequate seating arrangements for callers and for the prompt handling of their requests.

Verification of character and antecedents of applicants should be the responsibility in the main of the employers themselves. Employment Exchanges should not let their selection of applicants be influenced mainly by the opinion regarding their character expressed by their previous employers.

Even in the case of employed persons, the basic referral policy, viz., that the best qualified applicant should be submitted, should apply.

The present practice by which Government employers request nomination of particular individuals is likely to lead to abuse and should be stopped.

Completion of Index Cards is not necessary in the case of unskilled workers. Vacancies for unskilled workers should not be formally registered, nor should any formal submission be made against them.

State Governments may, however, consider it necessary that Employment Exchanges should participate more actively in some special cases of large-scale recruitment of unskilled workers so as to eliminate exploitation of such workers by intermediary agencies.

More comprehensive information should be furnished to the Exchanges regarding the terms and conditions attached to the vacancies to be circulated.

The work at present handled by the Regional

Employment Co-ordination Offices located at the Regional Employment Exchanges should be transferred to the State Headquarters.

The Employment Service should develop standardized aptitude tests and trade tests to assess wherever necessary the aptitude and/or proficiency of applicants desiring training or employment in skilled trades.

Suitable tests should be developed in respect of the general clerical categories denoted by the Trade Index Numbers N. II. 14 and N. II. 15, specifically in regard to fresh entrants to the employment market.

The Central Headquarters of the Service should undertake responsibility for the development and standardization of tests and for imparting training to Employment Officers in the administration of the tests.

Side by side with the development of trade tests, the Service should undertake, in collaboration with technical experts and representatives of workers, industry and the Government, the task of standardizing definitions of skills and functions of the different types of tradesmen.

If the Exchanges are to achieve the overall objective of the Service, a counselling programme is essential. Advice in the choice of a career or an occupation should be made available to all who need such advice.

Employment Exchanges should maintain a close liaison and develop co-operative arrangements with schools and colleges and other agencies engaged or interested in vocational guidance.

Mobile Sections as a normal feature of Employment Exchange work should be discontinued.

Employment Exchanges should collect comprehensive information on a continuing basis regarding the supply as well as the current and anticipated demand for labour in all its aspects.

Effective steps should be taken to ensure that each Employment Exchange carries out a programme of visits to employers in the Exchange area on a pre-planned and continuous basis. Special staff should be provided for the purpose wherever necessary.

Central Headquarters should also establish and maintain regular and systematic contacts with national organizations of workers so that all policies regarding Employment Exchange operations might be framed with due regard to their viewpoint also.

The Central Headquarters should arrange to issue a periodical bulletin dealing with all topics of interest relating to the Service.

Before deciding on the continuance or abolition of the existing schemes, the whole matter should be reviewed by the State Governments concerned.

Training of staff should continue to form an important part of the overall programme of the Employment Service.

Utilization Of Employment Exchange Facilities

In so far as the Central Government Departments are concerned, the existing arrangements should continue and the Employment Exchange Organization should as hitherto perform the role as the main agency for recruitment to Central Government employment, reflecting Central Government policy in the matter of priority for those categories for whom the Central Government has assumed moral responsibility to provide employment.

Recruitment to State Government vacancies and vacancies under Local Bodies should be made through the Employment Exchanges. The scope of this compulsory measure should be the same as in the case of Central Government vacancies. The obligation to recruit through the Employment Exchanges should apply equally to all State-owned enterprises and to all quasi-Government and Statutory Bodies.

No fee should be levied on employers or employment seekers who seek the assistance of the Employment Exchanges.

Proposed Plan Of Organization Of Employment Service Under A Central-State System

The Employment Exchange Organization, with the Central Headquarters, State Administrative Offices and Employment Exchanges, should constitute a unit by itself and be renamed as the "National Employment Service"

The Directorate of Employment Exchanges, which should perform the role of the Central Headquarters of the National Employment Service, should be redesignated as the Department of National Employment Service. The Department should function as an Attached Office, headed by a Director of National Employment Service, under the Ministry of Labour.

The services of an experienced officer should be obtained through the I.L.O. or the Colombo Plan or other similar agencies to assist the Director in organizing programmes of counselling and testing and occupational analysis and research.

For administrative purposes, the Employment Service in the States should be placed under the Department of Labour or, where a separate Department of Labour does not exist, under the State Government authority responsible for the administration of labour laws.

State Governments should establish, under their Departments of Labour, State Directorates of Employment Service placed under the charge of State Directors.

The present location of Employment Exchanges should be reviewed in the light of the principles enunciated in the Report and necessary changes brought about.

The Department of National Employment Service should, on the basis of objective studies, develop standards to help State Governments to assess the staff strength of individual offices in relation to the actual work performed.

Training Of Craftsmen And Instructors—A Plan For The Future

The training facilities now provided in the centres run by the D.G.R.&E. should be integrated with similar facilities provided by State Governments, the administrative responsibility for the D.G.R.&E. Scheme being also transferred to State Governments.

Neither the Central nor the State Governments should decrease their respective current level of expenditure on technical training as a whole.

The Ministry of Labour should assume the overall responsibility and continue to lay down policy for the craftsmen's training of labour. Within the Ministry of Labour itself, responsibility for the organization of training should be entrusted to a Department of Training with a Director at the head.

Selections for admission to the training centres should be based on the result of suitable tests and industry should be closely associated with the selections.

The Central Training Institute for Instructors should be placed on a permanent footing and should continue to remain the direct responsibility of the Government of India.

Early steps should be taken to provide the Institute with more up-to-date equipment.

Future Administrative Organization

The Directorate of Training should be transformed into a separate Department under the Ministry of Labour, with the status of an Attached Office. The Department, which may be designated as the Department of Training, should be headed by a Director of Training, who should be responsible to the Secretary in the Ministry of Labour and through him to the Minister of Labour.

The staff of the Department of Training should, in addition to the Director, comprise one Deputy Director, five Assistant Directors and one Section Officer with a complement of Class III and Class IV staff as indicated in the body of the Report.

TEXTILE ENQUIRY COMMITTEE, 1952—REPORT

Delhi, Manager of Publications, 1954. 3 Vols.

Chairman : Shri Nityananda Kanungo.
Members : Shri H. C. Dasappa; Shri V. N. Tivary; Shri A. R. Bhat; Prof. S. K. Muranjan; Prof. R. Balakrishna; Prof. S. K. Basu; Shri S. P. Chopra; Shri T. Swaminathan; Shri S. Subramanian.
Secretary Shri M. S. Ramnath.

APPOINTMENT

The Textile Enquiry Committee was constituted under the Ministry of Commerce and Industry vide their Resolution No. CT (A)/52 dated November 25, 1952.

TERMS OF REFERENCE

(i) An examination of the structure and organization of the various sectors of the cotton textile industry;

(ii) A study of the nature and volume of the demand for cotton textiles internally as well as in the export market;

(iii) An assessment, if possible, of the extent to which each of the three sectors may be utilized for the production of cotton textiles, having in view the following factors:

(a) Providing supplies of cotton textiles at reasonable prices for internal consumption;

(b) Ensuring maximum earning of foreign exchange;

(c) Utilization of our resources both in men and material in the direction that is socially most desirable;

(d) The size, organization, and the lines of development of each sector including reservation, if necessary, of particular fields of production to one or more sectors; and

(iv) An inquiry into all other matters incidental and ancillary; and make suitable recommendations to the Government.

CONTENTS

Vol. I: Introductory; Structure and Organization of the Textile Industry of India; The Demand for Cloth Internally and in the Export Market; Pattern for the Future; Summary of Conclusions and Recommendations; Acknowledgments; **Vol. II**: Tables I to III; Annexure A to G; **Vol. III**: Annexure G to S.

RECOMMENDATIONS

Much of the equipment of the industry, however, is old and somewhat out of date and needs replacement.

It is very desirable that the handloom weaver through the length and breadth of the country should be organized into a sound co-operative fabrics in such a way that the society keeps the weaver employed at a reasonable wage steadily in good times and in bad and the weaver for his part is pledged to purchase his raw materials, dyes, etc., from the society and market, as much of his products through the society as it can handle.

It is of great importance both for reasons of earning foreign exchange and for reasons of maintaining employment in the mill and, even more so, in the handloom industry that every effort should be made to promote exports up to a figure of 1,000 million yards a year.

As the manufacturing charges are a considerably larger fraction of the final cost in superfine and fine goods as contrasted with coarse and medium goods (where raw material costs are the larger element in costs), it is obvious that we would earn a great deal more by exporting fine and superfine varieties (after allowing for payments for imports of cotton).

Again in all categories, we would earn a good deal more by exporting dyed, printed, and finished goods rather than grey goods.

In a country such as India, where the requirements of resources for the development of the basic projects are large and the progress of capital formation is slow owing to the low levels of income and of the margin available for saving, the husbanding of capital resources for such projects appears essential.

The maintenance over the short term of a relatively less efficient means of production in use in order to sustain the levels of employment while alternative employment is being generated by the fruition of the larger and basic projects also appears inevitable. In the process a slightly higher price of such consumer goods is inescapable.

As a rough guide, it may be taken that 60,000 powerlooms and 1.5 lakh improved (semi-automatic) handlooms should replace the 3 lakh ordinary handlooms over the six-year period.

An annual conversion of 20,000 handlooms into 10,000 powerlooms and of roughly 38,000 handlooms into 25,000 improved (semi-automatic) looms has to be planned.

As far as possible, preference should be given to co-operative institutions and their members for bringing about this conversion.

If conversion through the co-operative organization does not take place at a fast pace, then there should be a larger resort to private enterprise in the form of, say, joint stock companies.

The Committee states emphatically that it is of the opinion that the ownership of the loom must, except in the case of existing karkhanas (factories), vest under all circumstances in the weaver, whether the form of organization adopted is the co-operative or the joint stock company.

In the case of the existing karkhanas, the conversion may be on the basis of the average number of looms working daily on 250 days in a year at the rate of two handlooms to one powerloom or three handlooms to two improved (semi-automatic) handlooms.

The karkhana is to be the last in priority for the purpose of conversion, preference being given to co-operative organizations and joint stock companies wherein the weavers have a share in the profits.

In order to secure the necessary speed of conversion, the Committee is of the opinion that private enterprise should also be harnessed.

The Committee recommends the continuance of the existing arrangements of bulk purchase by the Central Co-operative or other organizations reinforced by the setting up of at least a few co-operatively owned spinning mills on the pattern of the mill recently started at Guntakal and the mill being projected for Tinnelvelli in Madras State.

The Committee endorses very strongly the view of the All-India Handloom Board that as much as possible of the handloom industry must be brought within the co-operative fold at as rapid a pace as possible.

The principle of assisted sales with some feasibility should continue wherever the small sector is in genuine need of such assistance.

At least for the export market the manufacture of coarse and medium plain clothes like sheetings ought to be allowed on automatic looms in order to ensure both higher quality that is possible on these looms and a reduction in costs, in order to enable Indian mills to compete the better with countries which produce plain cloths on automatic looms.

Matters of design, weavers, etc., are evidently such as have to be the subject of research on a regional basis. Technical and technological questions such as fibre and yarn strengths, techniques, dyeing and finishing, etc., are subjects which may appropriately be dealt with on a basis other than strictly local or regional.

Statistics will become immediately essential in order that the scheme of conversion of handlooms into improved handlooms and powerlooms may be properly executed without undue hardship to any particular area or undue preference to any others.

The Committee would recommend that a scheme of quality marking similar to that run by the U.P. Government for handloom fabrics should be adopted widely on a voluntary basis for the handloom industry (or the improved handloom or domestic powerloom industry) so that some standardization of quality may become possible.

The All-India Handloom Board must be expanded and greatly strengthened in order to provide the necessary knowledge, executive ability, energy and drive.

On the All-India Handloom Board, it is essential tc have, in particular, people with extensive practical experience of organizing the handloom industry in the co-operative fold.

INQUIRY INTO FINANCIAL AND OTHER IMPLICATIONS RELATING TO THE CREATION OF THE NEW ANDHRA STATE, 1952—REPORT

New Delhi, Ministry of Home Affairs, 1953. 66p.

Official On Special Duty : Mr. Justice K. N. Wanchoo (one-man enquiry).

APPOINTMENT

The Government of India have decided to establish an Andhra State and the Prime Minister made the following statement on December 19, 1952, in the House of the People in that connection:

"In furtherance of the statement I made in the Council of States on the 9th December, 1952, and in terms of that statement, the Government of India have decided to establish an Andhra State consisting of the Telugu-speaking areas of the present Madras State, but not including the City of Madras and intend to take early steps to this end in accordance with Article 3 of the Constitution. The Government are appointing Mr. Justice K. N. Wanchoo, Chief Justice of the Rajasthan High Court, to consider and report on the financial and other implications of this decision and the questions to be considered in implementing it. Mr. Justice Wanchoo will report by the end of January, 1953. On receipt of this report, the Government will take other necessary steps. They are anxious to avoid all possible delay in establishing the new State. They hope that the establishment of this State will be brought about with the friendly co-operation of all the people concerned."

TERMS OF REFERENCE

The Terms of Reference were as follows which were intimated on January 5, 1953:

"Chief Justice Wanchoo will set out, consider and report on the financial and other implications of this division and the various questions which will arise in the course of implementing the decision of the Government of India more particularly by reason of the non-inclusion of the City of Madras in the Andhra State. For the consideration of the whole problem he will receive representations from such individuals, groups, organizations and parties as he may think fit and hear their representatives, if they desire to be heard. He may, if he so chooses, tour the different parts of the Telugu-speaking districts if he considers that it will facilitate the execution of the task entrusted to him. He will submit his report by the 31st of January, 1953."

CONTENTS

Introductory; Report; Annexures I to VII.

RECOMMENDATIONS

Boundaries Of The New State

The new State has to be carved out of the following 12 districts of the present Madras State, namely, (1) Srikakulam, (2) Visakhapatnam, (3) East Godavari, (4) West Godavari, (5) Krishna, (6) Guntur, (7) Nellore, (8) Kurnool, (9) Anantapur, (10) Cuddapah, (11) Chittoor, and (12) Bellary.

Appointment Of A Boundary Commission

If the Government of India so desire, a Boundary Commission may be appointed for the purpose. I feel, however, that it would be better to wait for some time till the new State has stabilized so that the emotional upheaval, which is visible at present, settles down. If a Boundary Commission were to be appointed at once before the new State has settled down, the excitement will continue and the process of organization of the new State will be retarded. Further if it is decided to have the temporary capital of the new State in Madras City for some time (a matter with which I shall deal later in this report), it would be advisable not to appoint the Boundary Commission till the temporary capital remains in Madras. Further, areas which will go from one side to the other are not very large and if the Government of India do not desire to correct these boundaries, it may not be necessary to appoint a Boundary Commission. The correction will be a small matter in itself but it will raise a good deal of emotion and it may, therefore, not be worth while to appoint a Boundary Commission at all. The matter could be easily settled by taking the population firka-wise. A "firka" is a sub-division of a Taluk and a Taluk is an equivalent of a Tehsil. It is not necessary that there should be a village-wise correction of boundaries, and firka-wise correction can be easily made without the appointment of a Boundary Commission if the Census figures of 1951 are accepted as correct. I may mention, however, that interested parties against whom these figures go have already started challenging the correctness of these figures, and would like to have a plebiscite in these matters.

Capital Of The New State

There is no one place where the temporary capital can be shifted at once (with perhaps the possible exception of Waltair-Visakhapatnam with which I shall deal later). The best solution would be to allow the temporary capital of the new State to be located in the City of Madras for a period of three to five years at the outset. It should be clearly understood that the jurisdiction over the City of Madras will in all matters rest in the residuary State and the Government of the new State will merely be in the nature of guests or tenants in Madras City. In any case if the temporary capital of the new State is located in Madras City, it will be for the Government of India to make it clear that the location is only temporary, for a fixed period, and to see that the Andhra Government gets out after the period is over. This solution is, in my opinion, the best and if it can be enforced, it will minimize many of the difficulties inherent in the birth of a new State. If, however, for any reason it is not possible to locate the Andhra capital even temporarily in Madras City for a limited period, an alternative solution has to be looked for.

That alternative solution is to shift certain essential parts of the Government from Madras City at once. These essential parts are the Governor, the Legislature, the Ministers, and the Secretariat and certain other essential Heads of Departments like the Inspector-General of Police. The one place in Andhra Desa to which all these officers can be shifted (though even there difficulties will be great) is Waltair-Visakhapatnam. There are a number of large vacant buildings available there. Some of these are not in very good condition but they can be made to serve the purpose with small expenditure on repairs. The Headquarters of the District will have to be shifted from there to Vizyanagram where, I understand, there is sufficient space for their location, though here again difficulties will be felt. It should, however, be clearly understood that this shift to Waltair-Visakhapatnam is merely for the temporary location of the capital. This place is at one end of the new State and would, from the geographical point of view, be inconvenient as a permanent capital. Waltair-Visakhapatnam has already got a harbour and the university and is a city which will grow whether the capital is placed there or not. It will be best to have all the important organs of the Government at one place. The task of organization and settlement will require day-to-day consultations and these will be facilitated if all the important organs of the executive Government are, as far as possible, in one place. That is why I have suggested a place which is in one corner of the new State for the temporary location of the capital for a period of, say, five years till the new State builds a permanent capital at a more suitable place. This alternative solution should only be thought of if it is not possible to locate the temporary capital of the new State in Madras City even for the short period mentioned by me above.

High Court

So far as the permanent location of the High Court is concerned, the main question, however, is about the temporary location of the High Court of the new State and whether there should be a separate High Court for the new State from the very beginning. In one sense, the High Court is a smaller institution than the executive Government because the number of judges, officers and clerks employed in the High Court is smaller than the number of Ministers and officers and clerks in the Secretariat. It is, therefore, even more necessary that the High Court should remain in Madras for some time to come and the period at which I would put it would be longer than the period I have recommended for the executive Government. It will, therefore, be conducive to efficiency and will lead to least disturbance if with the creation of the new State the jurisdiction of the Madras High Court is extended to it under Article 230 of the Constitution.

But as the High Court will be looking after two States, certain conventions may have to be observed in order that there may not be friction in the day-to-day working. The Andhra Wing may consist of six judges and the Non-Andhra wing of the remaining nine judges. It may be left to the Chief Justice and the judges to separate these two Wings. The Chief Justice will preside over both the Wings. I understand that it would be possible for the High Court to work this convention satisfactorily till a separate High Court can be conveniently created for the new State after five to 10 years.

As for the expenses of the High Court, I understand that the income from Court fees, stamps, etc., in the High Court is sufficient to meet the expenses. All this income should go to the residuary State and the residuary State should meet all the expenses of the High Court. The Madras High Court having extended jurisdiction for a period of five to 10 years over Andhra State to begin with will be most conducive to efficiency and cause least disturbance to the litigant public and the lawyers and others. It is true that a separate High Court will have to come one day but the public will have notice of it well in advance as soon as the new State starts constructing a building for the High Court. The shifting will be so sudden after this period of five to 10 years is over that everybody would be expecting it to take place.

Finally, if, for some reason, the High Court has also to be separated and moved out of Madras City at once (though I would strongly recommend against this course), it may be located in Guntur till such time as proper buildings can be constructed for it in the place which is eventually decided upon as its permanent seat.

Governor

It would be advantageous to have a separate Governor for the new State from the very beginning, whether the temporary capital is at Madras City or not. The new State will have a large number of problems and a whole-time Governor would be desirable so that his advice and guidance may be available all the time. It is also possible that there may be problems in which the interests of the new State and the residuary State might conflict. In such circumstances the position of a common Governor would be embarrassing. If the temporary capital of the new State remains in Madras City, its Governor can also stay there. There should be no difficulty in the matter of precedence as the Governor of the new State will be outside his State and will therefore rank below the Governor of the residuary State at all times. So long as the temporary capital is in Madras City, his permanent residence should be there. It would perhaps be difficult to find a suitable residence for the Governor just now in any town of the new State with the possible exception of Waltair-Visakhapatnam. If the new Governor likes, a suitable place can be arranged for him at Waltair in one of the palaces of Rajahs which are lying vacant there. But if the temporary capital remains in Madras City, he will have to live there for most of the time and it should not be difficult to find a suitable residence for him there.

PUBLIC SERVICE COMMISSION

It would be better if a separate Public Service Commission is established for the new State from the very beginning consisting of a Chairman and two members. The office of the Public Service Commission is a small one and should be shifted at once to a central place in the new State. I suggest that it may be shifted to Guntur where it will be possible to find accommodation for it.

Facilities For Andhras In Institutions In The Residuary State

As Madras City has been excluded from the new State, the question of providing facilities in Government hospitals and educational institutions has to be explored. When this matter was considered by the Partition Committee presided over by Shri P. S. Kumaraswamy Raja in 1950, the following provision was made at paragraph 16 of the Annexure (1) of that Committee's report:

"(1) The provisions of this paragraph shall be in force for 25 years commencing on the appointed day and shall have effect with respect to such Government hospitals and educational institutions in Madras City as before the appointed day served the areas included in both the provinces.

(2) There shall be reserved for the Andhra Province either,

(a) The specific number of places reserved for residents in the Andhra Province immediately before the appointed day, or

(b) If a specific number of places was not so reserved, a number of places as near as may be equal to the average number of places filled by residents in the Andhra Province during the three years immediately preceding the appointed day.

(3) The charge for admittance to the aforesaid institutions shall be the same for persons of both the provinces provided the excess of recurring expenditure in any year over the receipts during that year in respect of each such institution shall be divided between the two provinces in proportion to the number of persons admitted from each province.

(4) If for any five consecutive years after the appointed day the Andhra Province fails to fill any of the places so reserved, the right of that province to that place shall lapse."

The educational facilities should be available for Andhras in the residuary State for some time till they can make arrangements of their own. These facilities should be available only in Government institutions; so far as private institutions in the two States are concerned, they may be left to regulate their admissions as they consider best.

For this purpose the educational and training institutions should be divided into two categories. The first category consists of institutions which only exist in the residuary State, e.g., the Veterinary College in Madras City and the King Institute at Guindy and others of this kind. In the case of these institutions 36% of the seats should be reserved for students from the new State. For this purpose the students from the new State would be those who are residents of the area comprising the new State, whatever may be the language that they speak. If any seat so reserved is not filled in any year, it may be filled by admitting students from the residuary State; but the right to the seat should only lapse if for five consecutive years the new State fails to fill up the seat, as provided in Clause 4 of the paragraph from the Partition Committee's Report quoted above. It may be added that if there are institutions in the new State for which there are no counterparts in the residuary State, the same principle would apply and students from the residuary State to the extent of 64% should be admitted to those institutions. The expenses should be shared as provided in Clause 3 of the paragraph quoted above.

The second category is of institutions in the residuary State which have their counterparts in Andhra Desa also, e.g., Engineering, Law, Medical and Agricultural colleges, etc. In such cases the new State should use the entire seats available for its own students and if there is any deficiency compared to the total number of seats available to Andhra students on the date of separation, that deficiency should be made up by reserving statutorily seats in institutions in Madras City to the extent required. Complete figures are not available to me on account of the shortness of time; but I understand there will be deficiencies in professional colleges of this kind and to that extent facilities will have to be provided for Andhra students (i.e., students resident in the areas of the new State whatever their language) for some years.

Another point which may be made clear is about Government hospitals. The paragraph quoted above reserves a number of places for the Andhra Province in Government hospitals in Madras City. So far as these places are required for training of students, there is no objection to reservation on the principles which I have already set out; but if the intention was that beds for patients should also be reserved in a certain proportion, I must say that is not right. So far as patients are concerned, the principle must be first come first served. No non-Andhra should be refused admission to a Government hospital on the ground that the bed available is earmarked for an Andhra. Similarly, no Andhra should be refused admission on the ground that the bed is earmarked for a non-Andhra. Admission of patients should be left to the discretion of the doctors entirely.

At present colleges in the five Rayalaseema districts are affiliated to Madras University. It may be that with the creation of the new State the affiliation of these colleges may be changed and they may be affiliated to Andhra University. If that happens, provision should be made for at least one year, and, if necessary, three years, that boys reading in the institutions in Rayalaseema should continue to appear at the examinations of Madras University. Such provision is common whenever a change of this kind takes place and there should be no difficulty about providing for it.

Another question raised is about the selection of students for the seats reserved for Andhras in institutions in the residuary State. It seems to me that the correct thing is that the selection should be made by the new State and the names of students supplied to the institutions concerned for admission. I should like to make it clear that for purposes of admissions to Government educational institutions and hospitals an Andhra should be one who is resident in the area under the new State whatever the language he speaks and a non-Andhra is one who is resident in the residuary State whether he speaks Tamil, Telugu, Kanarese, Malayalam or any other language.

Lastly, some provision would also have to be made for students of Rayalaseema who appear within the period of adjustment allowed in the examinations of Madras University and fail. Such students should be allowed to appear at the examinations of Madras University.

Sri Baug Pact

The Pact was approved by the Andhra Pradesh Congress Committee and its terms are:

University: This Committee is of the opinion that two University centres are to be developed under Andhra University, one at Waltair and the other at Anantapur, so as to distribute the centres of culture over the Andhra Desa and create opportunities for social and cultural intercourse amongst the Andhras and locate colleges in areas favourable to the subjects dealt with.

Irrigation: That, to ensure the rapid development of the agricultural and economic interests of Rayalaseema and Nellore on to the level of those in the coastal districts, schemes of irrigation should, for a period of 10 years or such longer period as conditions may necessitate, be given a preferential claim specially in respect of the utilization of the waters of the Tungabhadra, Krishna and Pennar, giving for 10 years exclusive attention in respect of major projects beneficial to these areas.

That whenever the question of the sharing of waters arises, the needs of the aforesaid areas be first met and that this policy be implemented as from today in the administration of the province.

Legislature: That, in the matter of general seats in the Legislature, the distribution shall be generally on an equal district basis.

It is agreed that the location of the University, the Headquarters and the High Court may advantageously be in different places, so as not to concentrate all civic importance at the same centre.

Accordingly, it is agreed that, while the University may continue to be where it is, the High Court and the Metropolis be located in suitable places in the coastal districts and the Rayalaseema, the choice being given to the Rayalaseema.

It shall, however, be open to vary these terms by common consent.

Division Of Services

(1) Non-gazetted staff in the districts.

(2) Non-gazetted staff in the Secretariat, in Regional offices and offices of Heads of Departments.

(3) State Services, i.e., officers of gazetted rank.

(4) All-India Services.

Those Government servants who are in temporary service (whatever may be the period for which they may have served) will not be considered for division. If such temporary staff become surplus, their services will be dispensed with.

The second main principle which must be kept in view is that the two States should, on division, have a balanced cadre in each Service as far as possible. In order to get this balanced cadre, the division may be made taking the officers and the staff in groups of, say, three to five years, whichever may be convenient.

Another principle which should be applied in the same connection is this:

There is likelihood of an increase in the cadre to a certain extent on account of the creation of the new State. Wherever there is such an increase in the cadre, the benefit of that increase should be given to the new State and the residuary State should take its full complement of the staff from the existing personnel. The matter may be briefly illustrated by taking the instance of the Public Service Commission. At present, the strength of the staff of the Public Service Commission is 49 from the Secretary downwards. When the division takes place, the Chairman calculates that the staff required for the Andhra Public Service Commission would be 22 while the staff required for the Public Service Commission of the residuary State would be 33, the total being 55, an increase of six over the present total. When the staff is divided, the residuary State should take its full complement of 33. This will leave only 16 members of the staff for the new State and there will be a deficiency of six in the new State. This deficiency should be left for the new State to fill so that it may have the full benefit of the increase in staff due to the division. Further, it will also have a chance of deciding whether this deficiency should be made up or not. This may give it some scope for economy considering that it might be difficult for it to balance its budget. The principle, therefore, should be that the benefit of the increase in staff due to partition should go to the new State. This will also enable it to correct to a certain extent the proportion of Andhras in its Services immediately. The increase, it may be mentioned, is coming about mainly because of the creation of the new State and this is also a reason, apart from the other reasons, that the benefit should go to the new State.

Then I come to the question of selection of personnel for the new State and how that should be done. The difficulty, as I pointed out, arises from the fact that there is a deficiency of Andhra personnel in many Departments. The order of allotment should be as follows:

(1) Persons whose families continue to have their domicile in the Andhra area, i.e., in any of the districts constituting the new State. It is immaterial what language such persons speak as their mother tongue.

(2) Persons not falling under class (1) above who opt for service in the new State.

(3) Persons whose mother tongue is Telugu and whose families had their domicile in the Andhra area within the last 25 years.

(4) The balance may be made up from other persons who may be required to serve the new State. In this category, those persons whose mother tongue is Telugu but who do not come under (3) above or who know Telugu and have served in the Andhra area should be first considered for transfer to the new State in preference to others.

Those persons, who fall in classes (1) and (2) above, must go to the new State except in those cases where there are no posts in the new State to which they can be transferred, or the two State Governments agree that for special reasons a deviation from this principle is necessary. These persons will get the usual protection provided under the law and the Special Protection Rules which I am proposing will only apply to persons falling in classes (3) and (4).

For the purpose of ensuring smooth working of the Special Protection Rules which will be found as Annexure I to this Report, the following arrangements shall be adopted:

(1) During the period of 2½ years reckoning from the date of separation, no confirmation should be ordered in permanent posts in either State. A margin of six months is necessary for making the necessary

adjustment to provide for persons who have elected to revert.

(2) During the further period during which persons have been compelled to stay on in the State which they have elected to leave, they should be protected by the device of provisionally substantive arrangements.

(3) Except by agreement between the two State Governments or by the operation of the Special Protection Rules, there should be no disturbance in either State of the set-up agreed to at the time of the separation during the 2½ years specified above in respect of any Services.

All India Services

These Services may be divided into two groups, namely,

(1) The former Secretary of State Services which are now coming to an end, including the Indian Civil Service, the Indian Police, the Indian Service Engineers and the Indian Forest Service; and

(2) The new All India Services, viz., the Indian Administrative Service and the Indian Police Service. The officers serving in the All India Services desire that their cadres for the two States should remain joint. So far as the former Secretary of State Services is concerned, this desire of the officers may be taken into account; but it would perhaps be difficult to work with a joint cadre even for the initial period of five years, as desired by these officers. If the Government of India decides to keep the cadres joint, a provision will have to be made that 36% of the officers should serve in the new State and the remaining in the residuary State. If, on the other hand, it is decided to separate the cadres of the former Secretary of State Services also, the division may be made on the basis of population, keeping in mind that the Services should contain a balanced cadre of senior and junior officers so that prospects of promotion may be even in both States as far as possible. It may perhaps be advantageous to apply the three-to-five-year Service Group principle in the case of these Services also.

Each State would, of course, have its own Advocate-General, Public Prosecutor and Government Pleader even though the High Court of Madras may be provided with extended jurisdiction over the new State. The law creating the new State must necessarily contain a provision for continuance of existing laws until the enactments are modified by a competent authority.

No special rules are required for Class IV staff. It will be divided according to the needs of each State and the personnel allocated accordingly.

Budget

I now turn to the financial implications of the partition and will begin with the budget for the new State. The Finance Department has supplied me statements indicating the receipts and expenditure in the Andhra districts and the other districts in Madras State during the year 1951-52. The figures are based on the actuals of the year 1951-52 and allocations have been made, as far as possible, with reference to the area to which each transaction relates and in other cases on the basis of population, i.e., 36% for the new State and 64% for the residuary State. The details will be found in Annexure III of this Report. I may add that the Finance Department has worked out the figures on the basis of three Taluks of Bellary District in the new State and the remaining Taluks in the residuary State. I have suggested that the whole of Bellary District should be included in the new State. That would, however, not make any appreciable difference to the picture which briefly may be summarized as follows:

Revenue For The New State

Note: All figures are in rupees lakhs

Direct Receipts	1,408.70
Share of Allocable Items	361.19
Grand Total	1,769.89

The total revenue thus works out to Rs. 1,769.89 lakhs. As against this, the expenditure is as follows:

Direct Expenditure	1,698.82
Share of Allocable Expenditure	573.89
Total Expenditure	2,272.71

This leaves a deficit of Rs. 502.82 lakhs. If the whole of Bellary District is included in the new State, the deficit will be slightly larger.

The main question, therefore, which has to be considered is how to bridge this gap of over five crores of rupees.

So far as the residuary State is concerned, the problem is not so acute. The budget of the residuary State shows a slight surplus as will be clear from the following figures:

Revenue

Note: All figures are in rupees lakhs

Direct Receipts	3,168.64
Share of Allocable Receipts	1,004.62
Total Receipts	4,173.26

The expenditure of the residuary State is given below:

(Figures in rupees lakhs)

Direct Expenditure including Payments of Local Nature in Madras City	3,037.21
Share of Allocable Expenditure	1,133.92
Total Expenditure	4,171.13

This leaves a small surplus of Rs. 2.13 lakhs. It may be pointed out that the main cause why the residuary State is surplus is that Madras City has been included in it. The city gives an income of Rs. 709.47 lakhs to the residuary State while the expenditure on the city for local payments is only Rs. 337.28 lakhs, leaving a surplus of about Rs. 3.75 crores. It is this item of revenue which enabled the residuary State to balance its part of the budget in 1951-52 and will enable it in future also to avoid a deficit.

To sum up, therefore, there appears a possibility of an increase of revenue by Rs. 2 crores and a decrease in expenditure by Rs. 50 lakhs (I include in this Rs. 33 lakhs for the Rationing Department and the remainder for the abolition of the Legislative Council and for correction of the concentration of the Armed Police in Andhra districts). This will reduce the deficit from Rs. 5 crores to Rs. 2.5 crores.

Thus, I find that the deficit which has been reduced to Rs. 2.5 crores will still remain. The only other method which I can think of for reducing this deficit immediately is by scrapping Prohibition in the new State. The only way which I can see for balancing the budget immediately is by getting this Excise income. I would, therefore, recommend for the serious consideration of the leaders of the new State the necessity of giving up Prohibition if their State is to avoid bankruptcy from the very beginning.

Tungabhadra Irrigation Project, Machkund Hydro-Electric Scheme And The Five Year Plan

I propose to examine the Tungabhadra Project and the Machkund Scheme as they will be affected by the creation of the new State.

The Kanarese-speaking people apprehend that if the management of the Project is to vest in the new State, water in their area may be stopped. However, as I have recommended that the whole of Bellary District should form, for the present, part of the new State, I do not think that the new State will discriminate against the Kanarese-speaking area of Bellary District.

Division Of Assets And Liabilities And Adjustments Consequent Thereon

The first principle, so far as the division of assets is concerned, is that all assets attached to land shall pass to the State in which they are situate. Thus, all lands, works, forests and buildings shall remain the property of or, as the case may be, pass to the State in which they are situate. There can be no dispute about this basic principle.

It would, in my opinion, be an impossible task if every kind of asset attached to land was to be valued and then adjustment made accordingly. It seems, therefore, that all those assets attached to land, which are the usual concomitants of a State, should be ignored in making adjustments, if any. Thus, all roads, Administration buildings, hospitals, schools, colleges and so on, which exist all over the State, should be left out of account except Government buildings in Madras City which stand on a footing of their own. In effect, therefore, the only assets, which have to be taken into account in case adjustments have to be made, are assets arising out of capital expenditure on irrigation, navigation, electricity schemes, industrial schemes and State Transport Services. These assets, generally speaking, yield some income, even though in some cases the income may not be sufficient to cover the expenses of management and the interest charges.

Let me now turn to the division of debts. Here again I refer to the position as it was on March 31, 1952, and necessary adjustments will have to be made up to the date on which the separation actually takes place. The total debt on March 31, 1952, was Rs. 4,342.02 lakhs. Of this, Rs. 2,178.11 lakhs was recoverable from Local Bodies, etc. The balance was thus only Rs. 2,163.91 lakhs. As I have found that the capital outlay is roughly in proportion to the population figure, namely, 36:64, the debt should also be divided in the same ratio. The figures given in Annexure IV, which are based on a different ratio, will have to be revised so far as this item of Rs. 2,163.91 lakhs is concerned. The same principle of division, namely, 36:64, would apply to the position which may be found on the actual date of partition.

Then there are certain items of liabilities which have to be divided between the two States. These items are mentioned in Annexure IV as:

(1) Special irredeemable loans.

(2) State Provident Funds.

(3) Deposit Accounts.

(4) Portion of debt equal to the recoverable advances to Local Bodies, agriculturists, etc.

These liabilities have been shown in Annexure IV as divided according to the area to which they relate or where the officers are posted or where the advances have been made. This method is correct and it may be applied to the situation as it exists on the date of separation.

That deficit will have to be shared by the two States and may perhaps wipe out the credit of Rs. 230.4 lakhs which the new State may be entitled to on account of Madras City being excluded from it.

I now turn to certain special provisions for special matters arising in connection with the division of assets and liabilities. These recommendations are based on the Report of the Partition Committee of 1950 with such modifications as I consider necessary. Provision will have to be made on these lines and to complete the division of finances between the two States. These recommendations are in addition to those which have already been made by me in the foregoing paragraphs.

(1) Any substantial quantities of unissued stores of any class shall be divided between the two States in proportion to the indents for stores of that class made in the three years immediately preceding April 1, 1953, for the areas comprised in the two States respectively.

(2) The new State's share of the printing machinery in the Government Press, Madras, shall be 36%. This share shall, as far as may be possible, be given to the new State in the shape of physically separable printing machinery which can be utilized by the new State and to the extent to which this is not found practical, an adjustment shall be made in cash or otherwise.

(3) Arrears of taxes shall belong to the State in which the taxed property is situate or the tax transaction took place.

(4) Each sinking fund shall be apportioned in the same proportion as loans in respect of which it has been created (this will now be theoretical for the most part).

(5) The assets and liabilities relating to commercial undertakings of the undivided State shall pass to the State in which they are situate.

(6) Civil and Local Fund Deposits shall pass to the State in which the deposits have been made and the liability to pay shall fall on that State.

(7) (i) The shares held by the undivided State for the Fertilizers, Chemicals Travancore, Ltd., Radio and Electrical, Ltd., Madras, and the Madras Industrial Investment Corporation shall be divided between the two States in the proportion of 36:64 and the necessary adjustment made when assets and liabilities are finally worked out as on the date of separation.

(ii) All interest in the Madras Bus Service shall pass to the residuary State and necessary adjustment shall be made as above.

(8) Revenue Reserve Fund, Village Reconstruction Fund, Harijan Uplift, Funds for the Rural Water Supply and Famine Relief Fund.—There are no assets in these Funds now. They may be notionally divided in the proportion of 36:64.

(9) Cash Balances, if any, Ways and Means Advances and Treasury Bills.—These assets and liabilities shall be divided in the proportion of 36:64.

(10) Provincial Road Fund.—The aggregate undisbursed amount payable to the Local Bodies situate in each State shall pass to that State.

(11) Provident Fund.—Each Government shall take over the Provident Fund Accounts of the Government servants allotted to it.

(12) Pensions.—(i) Subject to the adjustment mentioned in sub-paragraph 2, each State shall, in respect of pensions granted before the appointed day, pay the pensions from its Treasury and sub-Treasury;

(ii) These will be computed in respect of each financial year after the appointment day a total payment made in each State in respect of such pensions and the new State shall pay to or receive from the residuary State the amount by which the total payments in the residuary State for that year exceeds, or, as the case may be, falls short of, 64% of the total payment made in both States for that year; and

(iii) The liability in respect of pension granted on or after the appointed day shall be the liability of the State granting the pension. In respect of officers whose service after the appointed day was partly in one State and partly in the other, the amounts of their pensions shall be allocated between the two States in proportion to their total service qualifying for pension in the respective States whether such service was before, on or after the appointed day. For the purpose of this allocation, the period of qualifying service in the Secretariat or in the office of any Head of Department in Madras City before the appointed day shall be divided between the new State and the residuary State in the proportion of 36:64.

(13) If and in so far as any item in suspense is ultimately found to affect any matter referred to in the financial part of this Report, it shall be dealt with in accordance with the relevant provision of the Report.

(14) The benefit or burden of any assets or liabilities not dealt with in the financial provisions of this Report shall be divided between the new State and the residuary State in the proportion of 36:64 provided that any such asset or liability may be apportioned in any other manner if the Governments of the two States so agree.

(15) The new State shall be responsible for the execution of further works in connection with the Tungabhadra Project and shall also be responsible for meeting the expenditure.

(16) Unless otherwise stated or required by the context the assets and liabilities shall be determined as at the close of business on the day immediately preceding the appointed day.

Lastly, I address myself to the question of the date on which the new State should be created. There was a general desire on the part of Andhras that the new State should be created on the Telugu New Year Day, viz., March 16, 1953. That is, however, impossible as there will be innumerable difficulties of accounting if a date in the middle of the month is chosen, particularly when that date is so near the end of the financial year. The Accountant-General points out that the creation of a new State with effect from a date other than April 1 would cause a good deal of confusion and inconvenience. He urges that it would be more convenient from the point of view of accounting if the new State were to be formed from the beginning of the financial year as that will eliminate many complications and reduce labour in the Audit office as well as in the Administrative offices. It would, therefore, be advisable to form the new State from April 1, 1953, if possible. But I realize that it may be impossible within the short period of two months to carry through all the measures necessary for bringing the new State into existence. If, therefore, the new State cannot be brought into existence by April 1, 1953, the Accountant-General would prefer that it should come into existence on April 1, 1954. I may, however, point out that this delay of one year would cause profound disappointment and, therefore, if the new State cannot be brought into existence on April 1, 1953, it should be created as early thereafter as possible. It would, however, be preferable if it comes into existence on any day at the end of a quarter as that would reduce accounting troubles to some extent. Thus, July 1 or October 1 or January 1, are the other likely dates if the new State cannot come into existence from April 1, 1953. I would, therefore, recommend any of these three dates—the earlier the better.

1953

BACKWARD CLASSES COMMISSION, 1953—REPORT

New Delhi, Ministry of Home Affairs, 1955. Various pages.

Chairman : Shri Kakasaheb Kalelkar.

Members : Shri Narayan Sadoba Kajrolkar; Shri Bheeksha Bhai; Shri Shivdayal Singh Chaurasia; Shri Rajeshwar Patel; Shri Abdul Qaiyum Ansari; Shri T. Mariappa; Lala Jagannath (resigned, replaced by Shri P. G. Shah); Shri Atma Singh Namdhari (died, Dr. Anup Singh was appointed in his place); Shri N. R. M. Swamy.

Secretary : Shri Arunangshu De.

APPOINTMENT

The Backward Classes Commission was appointed by the President in pursuance of Article 340 vide the Ministry of Home Affairs Notification No. 70/53-Public dated January 29, 1953.

TERMS OF REFERENCE

The Backward Classes Commission shall:

(a) Determine the criteria to be adopted in considering whether any sections of the people in the territory of India (in addition to the Scheduled Castes and Scheduled Tribes specified by Notifications issued under Articles 341 and 342 of the Constitution) should be treated as socially and educationally backward classes; and, in accordance with such criteria, prepare a list of such classes setting out also their approximate numbers and their territorial distribution;

(b) Investigate the conditions of all such socially and educationally backward classes and the difficulties under which they labour, and make recommendations:

(i) as to the steps that should be taken by the Union or any State to remove such difficulties or to improve their condition; and

(ii) as to the grants that should be made for the purpose by the Union or any State and the conditions subject to which such grants should be made;

(c) Investigate such other matters as the President may hereafter refer to them; and

(d) Present to the President a Report setting out the facts as found by them and making such recommendations as they think proper.

The Commission may:

(a) Obtain such information as they may consider necessary or relevant for their purpose in such form and such manner as they may think appropriate from the Central Government, the State Governments and such other authorities, organizations or individuals as may, in the opinion of the Commission, be of assistance to them;

(b) Hold their sittings or the sittings of such sub-committees as they may appoint from amongst their own members at such times and such places as may be determined by, or under the authority of, the Chairman; and

(c) Visit or depute a sub-committee of theirs to visit such parts of the territory of India as they consider necessary or convenient.

CONTENTS

Forwarding Letter of the Chairman; General; Census and Castes; Caste and Society; Problems of Special Groups—Muslims; Christians; Anglo-Indians; Eurasians in Travancore-Cochin; Sikhs; Gurkhas; Bhangis (Sweepers and Scavengers); Women; Unfortunate Women; Delinquent Children; Denotified Communities; Backwardness; Conditions of Backwardness and Measures for their Removal; Ministry for the Advancement of Backward Classes; Grants; Revision of Lists of Scheduled Castes and Scheduled Tribes; Summary of Recommendations; Acknowledgment; Appendices.

RECOMMENDATIONS

Census And Caste

Before the disease of caste is destroyed all facts about it have to be noted and classified in a scientific manner as in a clinical record. To this end we suggest that the 1961 census be remodelled and reorganized so as to secure the required information on the following lines:

The census operation should be conducted as a well-equipped continuous organization competent to supply information on various topics of sociological importance.

The Census Offices must have permanent ethnologists and sociologists in addition to the economists attached to them.

Special Groups

It would not be correct or just to list all Muslims as socially and educationally backward.

Christianity has consistently refused to recognize caste. And yet, in practice, it was found that segregation of converts from the Scheduled Castes was not successfully overcome in certain parts of South India. We have included such communities, especially in the South, in the list of Other Backward Classes. We added if Scheduled Caste converts to Christianity in other parts of the country also suffer from any recognizable degree of segregation and social disability their case should be considered for being included in the list of Other Backward Classes.

A small community in the extreme South which is really Emasian in character is now being called Anglo-Indian in the list published by the Education Ministry, Government of India. The nomenclature is a mistake. It may be renamed Eurasian for the purpose of relief and included in the list of Other Backward Classes of Travancore-Cochin.

We recommend that the communities or groups who are treated as untouchables among the Sikhs should be included in the list of Scheduled Castes.

Such of the communities among the Gurkhas found in Uttar Pradesh, Bihar and West Bengal, who are educationally and socially backward, are included in the list of Other Backward Classes.

The Bhangis should not be condemned to live in segregated localities. They should be distributed and given quarters among other groups.

Women in India have lived under great social hardships and as a class must be regarded as backward.

The following measures are recommended for the advancement of women in general:

(1) Free education at all stages to all girls whose parents' income is less than Rs. 3,000 per annum.

(2) Scholarships for girls belonging to the Backward Classes.

(3) Residential hostels for girl students, with priority for girls of the Backward Classes.

(4) Samata Ashrams for girls of all communities to be run by trained staffs of women and men.

(5) Creation of special facilities for girls to study Medicine, Home Sciences, and other subjects specially suited for women.

(6) More facilities for training women in the Fine Arts, and in Social Service.

The administration of the "Suppression of Immoral Traffic Act" is found to be more punitive than reformative. There is great scope for starting rescue homes and the Government should be able to help such efforts with finance and legislation. Rescue homes should not be mere asylums for such women. Such homes must be controlled by committees consisting of social workers under Government supervision. Women social workers from well-to-do sections of society should accept an increasingly larger role in tackling this problem.

The provisions for the rehabilitation of delinquent children are totally inadequate. The State must help persons who take up the work of amelioration of these delinquent children.

The ex-Criminal Tribes should hereafter be called denotified communities—Vimochit Jatian.

These communities have been classed as Scheduled Castes, Scheduled Tribes or Other Backward Classes according to the criteria applicable to them for the purpose of relief.

The nomadic groups should be given facilities for leading a settled life.

The children of these groups should be trained in Basic Education. They must also be trained in cottage industries, handicrafts and agriculture.

Group criminality should be treated differently from the acquired criminality of the individuals.

Backward areas in Himachal Pradesh, Uttar Pradesh, Udaipur and in Rajasthan, Bastar in Madhya Pradesh, Amarakantak in Vindhya Pradesh should be developed by allocating more Community Projects, National Extension Service Blocs, Social Welfare Extension Projects and other developmental schemes.

Criteria Of Backwardness

After consideration of the social conditions in Indian society and the causes for backwardness of a large section of the people, the following criteria are adopted for general guidance:

(1) Low social position, in the traditional caste hierarchy of Hindu Society.

(2) Lack of general educational advancement among the major section of a caste or community.

(3) Inadequate or no representation in Government service.

(4) Inadequate representation in the field of trade, commerce and industry.

Classification Of Communities

The economic backwardness had also to be kept in view in order to find out the ability of the community to take advantage of the available opportunities as also the recent trends in its advancement.

Conditions Of Backwardness And Measures For Their Removal

Political parties in the country should take note of the unhealthy symptoms in the body politic and draw people together under a well-defined economic and social programme.

Any plan for economic reconstruction of the country must necessarily include measures designed for the speedy uplift of the Backward Classes. Conditions must be recreated in which the development of these classes takes a natural growth. Removal of economic and social causes that are operating to their detriment should receive first priority.

Land Policy

For the uplift of the Backward Classes, it is vital to have a proper land policy. It is necessary that all kinds of intermediary tenures should be abolished to help in the formulation and implementation of a national land policy.

Large Landowners And Ceilings On Holdings

Fixing a ceiling on land holdings is necessary as a social principle to remove the existing inequality of the cultivator's holdings in the countryside. But it should be followed almost immediately by placing limits on incomes from other fields of national economy. Only then would it be possible to create a psychological satisfaction among those who are required to surrender their property for the common good. The ceilings should be different for different types of land and conditions of rainfall, types of crops grown, pressure of population, etc., should be taken into consideration in determining the ceilings.

Distribution Of Land

The available Government land should firstly be distributed among the landless and then among the owners of uneconomic holdings. To this end land revenue rules should be suitably amended. Any infringement of this rule should be severely dealt with by the State authorities.

Small And Middle Owners

These groups include almost all backward communities. Their holdings are uneconomic and seriously fragmented. The general aim should be to bring about consolidation of holdings.

Fragmentation beyond a certain limit should be prohibited by law.

Regulation Of Tenancy Rights

It is necessary to protect the tenants under large holders from arbitrary eviction and from the levy of unreasonable rent.

Record Of Rights

Peasant proprietorship, however small the holding, will for some years be the pattern in most rural areas. The rights of all interests in land should be correctly recorded and maintained.

Agricultural Class Structure

The economic conditions of communities engaged in agriculture are far from satisfactory and a large majority of them have necessarily to live below subsistence level. Their position has become such that they are inevitably the helpless victims of exploitation. They need State help in abundant measure, not only to improve agriculture which is their mainstay but to bring about general improvement in their living conditions. It is equally necessary to remove all forms of exploitation from rural life, and establish co-operatives on a planned basis—both functional and regional—manned by proper type of persons who would work devotedly for the betterment of the rural people.

Rural Indebtedness

Agricultural communities habitually run into debts and more so when adverse seasonal conditions prevail. It is necessary that provision should be made either through land marketing societies or through the proposed State Bank for long-term credits to redeem them from the clutches of unconscionable money-lenders. Relief from usurious rates of interests is also needed. Scaling down of the debts of impecunious cultivators is equally desirable.

Marketing Facilities

It is necessary to establish co-operative marketing societies, regulated markets at suitable centres with warehouse and banking facilities.

Price Support

Minimum fair prices should be guaranteed to the cultivators both from the point of view of keeping up agricultural production and of the prosperity of the agricultural communities.

Irrigation

Greater attention should be paid to the execution of small and medium irrigation works and to provide irrigation from wells and rivers wherever it is not possible to have tanks and anicuts.

Land Tax Policy

The system of land taxation in its relation to the capacity of the cultivator should be thoroughly examined and an equitable system of taxation evolved.

Rural Savings

There is need for organizing rural savings schemes at village level.

Communities Engaged In The Cultivation Of Vegetables And Flowers

Enough land should be made available for growing vegetables and fruits.

The exorbitant rents in all cases of tenancies should be scaled down as in the case of other tenancies.

Instruction should be given to the young men of these communities on improved methods of fruit and vegetable cultivation.

Scholarships should be established for the purpose of training qualified students among them in general horticulture.

Communities Engaged In Growing Betel Vine

The following measures are recommended for their amelioration:

(1) Grant of sufficient and suitable land for raising betel vine to members of this community and reduction of oppressive rents.

(2) Establishment of co-operatives to grant medium-term loans for the purchase of agricultural implements and manure and for marketing the betel leaves.

(3) Exploration of foreign markets by States for betel leaves.

(4) Research work for the eradication of pests and diseases and for improving the quality of the vines, and in the nutritional and medicinal value of Pan.

Reorganization Of Village Economy

The basic causes hindering the development of the co-operative spirit must be removed before agriculture could be reorganized on the co-operative principle.

Bhoodan Movement

We recommend both to the Government and to the nation that they should take up the work of Bhoodan Movement and spread it to every nook and corner of the country.

Development Of Livestock

The cattle wealth of the country should be improved.

Cattle-breeding stations to improve the breed of cattle as also to improve the milk-yielding qualities of cows should be established.

Steps should be taken to conserve the existing pasture land in the interest of village cattle.

More veterinary institutions should be established.

Dairying

Efforts should be made to organize small producers into co-operative Milk Unions and to give them monetary help and other assistance needed for developing dairying.

Cattle Insurance

Cattle in India are subject to periodical epidemics, and loss of cattle during such epidemics renders agriculturists helpless. It is necessary to safeguard their interest by sponsoring schemes of cattle insurance.

Sheep And Wool

Besides establishing regional centres for improving the quality of wool by selective breeding and cross-breeding, it is necessary to make available sufficient breeding areas to the sheep-breeders in several States. Steps should be taken to protect the flocks of sheep from disease and epidemics.

Poultry And Bee-Keeping

Improved breeds like white leghorn, Rhode-Island, etc., should be introduced in the rural areas. The rural population should also be instructed in the art of bee-keeping, and State help extended to popularize it.

Piggery

State Governments should give more facilities to communities engaged in this occupation and they must be induced to lead a more settled life.

Fisheries

Fisheries have to be developed to supply adequate food to the nation. Fishermen should be organized and helped to form multi-purpose co-operative societies.

The Khalasi community could be encouraged to join the Indian Navy.

Agricultural Labour

Agricultural labour forms the most vulnerable section of the population, and the question of rehabilitation of communities in this group should receive the earnest consideration of the Governments—Central and State. The redistribution of land among the landless would further improve the economic conditions of these classes.

Minimum Wages

In the case of agricultural labour, we feel that, barring a few exceptional cases, fixation of the minimum wage is desirable. All the facilities granted to industrial labour should also be extended to the agricultural labour.

Development Of Industries

The conflict between heavy industries on the one hand and cottage and rural industries on the other be removed. Steps should be taken to disperse industries all over the country according to a definite plan.

Rural And Cottage Industries

The policy of giving subsidies to sustain these industries is at best only a palliative. The only feasible course would be to remove all factors hindering natural development of these industries and recreate favourable conditions in which these industries could flourish spontaneously.

Khadi Industry

Improved Charkhas and improved looms should be introduced to cut down cost and to step up production.

Handloom Industry

Clear demarcation of spheres of production exclusively for the handloom should be made with immediate effect. Since the weavers are accustomed to produce varieties of fabrics like saris, dhotis and lungis, all these varieties should be exclusively reserved for the handloom industry.

Regular and adequate supply of yarn of required counts and colours at reasonable prices should be ensured to the handloom weavers.

After full protection and patronage to Khadi, only handloom products should be purchased by Governments—Central and State—for their requirements.

Special Features Of Cotton And Silk Weaving In Assam And Manipur

The entry of mill-cloth should be prohibited and the State Governments should give special help to hand-spinning and weaving and also set up a yarn mill with required spindleage. Cotton cultivation in some parts of Assam should also be encouraged.

Silk Handloom Industry

The All-India Handloom Board should draw programmes for improving the conditions of weavers and in marketing their cloth.

Sericulture

There is great scope both for expansion and for improvement in the method of production of silk. This industry needs stabilization and it is only then it can develop sufficiently rapidly.

Wool Spinning And Weaving Industry

Proper organizations should be set up preferably on co-operative lines in suitable places for the purchase and supply of wool to the spinners and weavers. Marketing facilities for the sale of woollen blankets should be provided so that weavers may get proper price for their products.

Village Oil Industry

Immediate steps should be taken to stop the use of machinery for crushing edible oil. It is also necessary to stop further licensing of new oil mills and gradually stop the crushing of edible oils in the existing mills.

Village Potter

The potters should be encouraged to improve their methods of production by giving them training and better implements.

Bamboo And Cane Workers

Steps should be taken to encourage these communities by arranging supply of raw materials at reasonable prices and proper marketing facilities. Proper housing and educational facilities should be provided for improving the conditions of the people.

Paddy Husking

It is desirable to eliminate rice mills altogether from the rural areas.

Minor Industries

Special measures should be taken for their uplift and rehabilitation.

Village Handicrafts

The Governments should purchase these articles of art to adorn Parliament, Legislatures and Embassies. The Government of India should assist in building up foreign markets for such articles.

Beedi Industry

Steps are necessary not only to prevent exploitation but also to organize beedi workers on a co-operative basis.

Mill And Factory Competition

Protection of cottage and rural industries from unrestricted competition of the mills and factories and decentralization of industries will greatly contribute towards rehabilitation of Backward Classes.

Communities Whose Traditional Occupation Is Personal Service

They are the washermen, the barber, the Kahar or the water-carrier and other classes of domestic servants. They need special help for ameliorating their conditions.

Measures To Prevent Exploitation Of The Backward Classes

Proper institutions must be set up for the distribution of wealth produced. A chain of suitable co-operative institutions or Government stores is badly needed for this purpose. Steps should be taken to train these communities in running institutions set up for their benefit.

Unless all kinds of communications are developed it will not be possible to remove either the backwardness of areas cut off from urban centres or of people inhabiting these areas.

It is absolutely essential that the rural public should be educated in the necessity of maintaining sanitary conditions.

Rural water supply should be improved a great deal.

A planned programme of rural housing should be drawn up to provide housing for the poorer sections in proper village layouts.

The measures that the Governments—Central and State—should undertake for the eradication of social evils:

A Clear enunciation and effective implementation of this policy of social solidarity and national progress.

Necessary legislation on marriage and inheritance laws.

Prohibition by law of social disabilities.

Liberal use of the Press, Films, Platform and Radio for the removal of social evils.

Full assistance to promote education as speedily as possible among the Backward Classes.

Non-communal hostels should be established and the cost of board and lodging for the poorer sections of the Backward Classes should be borne by the Government.

Special type of Ashram Schools (Samata Ashrams) where teachers with their families live with the students should be established.

University Education

The present-day Universities should confine themselves to technical education and research, certain percentage of seats being reserved for qualified students of the Backward Classes and liberal scholarships being granted to poorer amongst them.

Adequate provision should be made both by the State and Central Governments for training students of all Backward Classes in post-graduate courses and in research centres both in India and abroad.

Reading-rooms and libraries in rural areas should be established and a judicious selection of books made for stocking rural libraries.

In all science, engineering, medicine, agriculture, veterinary and other technical and technological institutions, a reservation of 70% of seats should be made for qualified students of Backward Classes till such time as accommodation is provided for all the students eligible for admission.

Ministry For The Advancement Of Backward Classes

A new Ministry should be created both at the Centre and in the States similar to the Ministry of Rehabilitation to handle in an effective manner the problems for the advancement of Backward Classes and also to prevent anti-social elements from fostering disruptive tendencies among the Backward Classes by exploiting discontentment among them.

Members of Scheduled Castes and Scheduled Tribes when they go from one State to another should receive the amount of their help that is given to other Backward Classes in the State where they have gone to reside.

PHARMACEUTICAL ENQUIRY COMMITTEE, 1953—REPORT

Delhi, Manager of Publications, 1954. 402p. viip.

Chairman : Major-General S. L. Bhatia.
Members : Dr. K. Vasudeva Rao; Dr. B. B. Yodh; Dr. J. C. Ghosh; Dr. A. K. Sen (died, replaced by Dr. T. N. Banerji); Dr. R. C. Shah; Dr. T. R. Seshadri; Dr. H. R. Nanji; Shri K. R. Chandran; Shri P. M. Nabar; Dr. A. Nagaraja Rao.
Secretary : Dr. B. Shah.

APPOINTMENT

The Pharmaceutical Enquiry Committee was constituted under the Ministry of Commerce & Industry vide their Resolution No. CI-1(12)/52 dated February 14, 1953.

TERMS OF REFERENCE

(i) To study the working of the existing pharmaceutical manufacturing concerns in India with particular reference to:

(a) The demand for the drugs produced and their essentiality;

(b) The quality of the drugs;

(c) The cost of production;

(d) The efficiency of the process employed; and

(e) Whether the product is made from imported intermediates and penultimate products or from basic raw materials and chemicals;

(ii) To study the operations of foreign and/or Indian concerns, who import drugs and pack them in the country. The extent of the tie-up between the wholly or partly owned Indian concerns with foreign companies;

(iii) To recommend steps for encouraging the manufacture of important drugs, which are imported into the country;

(iv) To enquire into the scheme of distribution of pharmaceutical products, whether imported or manufactured or packed in the country, the profit margins to Trade or Industry and the part played in this by purely Indian as well as other concerns;

(v) All ancillary matters connected with the above.

CONTENTS

Introduction; Pharmaceutical Industry, Its Scope and Development; Basic Raw Materials and Packing Materials of the Industry; Demand and Production; Standardization, Control of Quality and Administration; Research Work; Distribution and Advertisement; Medical Profession and the Pharmaceutical Industry; Technical Training for the Profession of Pharmacy; Summary of Recommendations; Conclusions and Acknowledgments; Appendices; Bibliography; List of Tables.

RECOMMENDATIONS

Pharmaceutical Industry—Its Scope And Development

Scope Of The Industry

Each manufacturing concern should endeavour to produce as many fine chemicals and drugs starting from basic chemicals and/or intermediates as close to the basic chemicals as practicable for the time being, in quantities sufficient to meet not only its own requirements but also of other firms which process them. By such co-operation between different units and the pooling of their resources, the Pharmaceutical Industry will undergo rapid development.

Government Medical Stores

The manufacturing activities of the Government Medical Stores should be reorganized and their method of management changed to conform to commercial practices.

Opium Factory

Experimental plantations should be set up (i) for investigating methods for improving the yield of opium; (ii) to render technical advice; (iii) to supply better grades of seeds; and (iv) to demonstrate improved methods of cultivation to the opium cultivators.

All unit operations such as mixing and bricketting which are, at present, carried out manually should be mechanized.

Commercial methods of marketing the different products of the factory should be adopted.

Penicillin Factory—(Hindustan Antibiotics Ltd.)

A well-equipped research laboratory and a pilot plant should be set up for carrying out investigations side by side with manufacture to keep pace with the rapid developments in the field of antibiotics.

As the manufacture of penicillin needs certain chemicals, whose production will have to be undertaken at Pimpri, it will be economical to extend the activities of the penicillin factory to include the production of synthetic antimalarials, sulpha drugs, other chemotherapeutic products and vitamins.

D.D.T. Factory—(Hindustan Insecticides Ltd.)

A research unit and a pilot plant should be provided in this factory to carry out investigations on the production of new type of insecticides and conduct experiments on their production.

Madras Cinchona Plantations And Quinine Factories

The programme of replacing the existing plants with those whose bark yields a higher quinine content should be accelerated.

Sufficient attention has not been paid by the Madras Government for providing elementary amenities, like electricity for lighting the quarters, to the staff of the Cinchona Department stationed in the plantations. Every amenity should be afforded to the staff especially as they are living in isolation without any social contacts.

Bengal Cinchona Plantations And Quinine Factory

Some of the operations now carried out manually like the transport of the mixture of bark powder and lime for lixiviating with caustic soda solution in tanks should be mechanized.

The programme of replacing the existing cinchona plants with those whose bark yields a higher percentage of quinine should be accelerated.

Assam Cinchona Plantations

As the special Cinchona Committee have advised against any expansion of the existing plantations in the country, in view of the uncertain position of quinine, the Assam Government should not spend their finances and energies in expanding these plantations specially when the State is endowed with all the natural advantages for cultivating other medicinal plants for which a great shortage exists in the country.

Assistance To Quinine Factories

Commercial methods of marketing quinine should be adopted by the Governments concerned. Dumping of foreign quinine into the country should be prevented. Customs duty should be imposed on synthetic antimalarials and foreign quinine.

Shark Liver Oil Factories

The two State Governments (Bombay and Madras) are competing with each other in the sale of their products and trying to obtain the raw materials at as cheap a price as possible from the local fishermen to whom has been entrusted the work of catching sharks. By unregulated fishing, a very valuable source of Vitamin "A" may be lost to the country. The Central Government should, therefore, look into this matter urgently and see that necessary steps are taken for conserving this important source and bring about a better co-ordination in its exploitation by the two State Governments.

The manufacturing and marketing activities of the two State Government factories at Bombay and Kozhikode should be co-ordinated. A uniformity in quality and packing and a common brand name instead of calling them differently as "Madras Government Shark Liver Oil" and "Bombay Government Shark Liver Oil" should be adopted by the two factories.

They should endeavour to adopt (a) a uniform selling price for the different grades, (b) scale of discount to traders, and (c) a common publicity for the products made. If necessary, the territories, where their products should be marketed, can be defined by the two Governments.

Other Government Institutions

The production of hyperimmune rabies serum in institutes like the Haffkine Institute, Bombay, where facilities for its production exist should be taken up in adequate quantities to meet the needs of the country. All schemes for its production should be actively assisted both by the Central and State Governments. For eradicating the danger of rabies in the country, the production of Avianized Rabies Vaccine at the Haffkine Institute should be increased and the vaccine made more easily available.

Steps should be taken to increase the output of diphtheria and tetanus vaccines. An attempt should be made to manufacture the triple vaccine required for the simultaneous prophylaxis of vulnerable groups of population against these diseases.

It is necessary to keep facilities for the production of influenza vaccine ready at hand to meet emergencies.

The Government should afford the necessary facilities to the Haffkine Institute, Bombay, to expand the snake farm and increase its output, and other institutions should be encouraged to start snake farms and produce the antivenin serum.

At present the vaccines and sera made by the Government institutions are only available at Government hospitals. The practice should be revised and the products made available to the general public through the retail trade by adopting commercial methods of marketing.

Large Scale Private Enterprise Under Foreign Control And/Or Foreign Collaboration

The firms should progressively extend their manufacturing activities to include the production of bulk pharmaceuticals, starting from basic chemicals and/or intermediates as near to the basic chemicals as possible.

While planning the production of bulk pharmaceuticals the production capacity should not be confined merely to the requirements of the particular factory, but should be large enough to be able to supply, as far as possible, the requirements in the country.

No new foreign concerns should be allowed to set up factories unless they undertake to manufacture products which have not been manufactured in adequate quantities by other factories starting from basic chemicals and/or intermediates as near to the basic chemicals as possible, within a reasonable time.

Arrangements made by certain manufacturers, whether Indian or foreign, forbidding the selling of bulk chemicals to other processors based on agreements entered into with foreign firms should be discouraged.

The Patent Laws of the country should be amended to secure effective utilization of all developments in the field of science and medicine, wherever necessary, in the interest of the country.

Firms with 100% foreign capital—the so-called "India Ltd."—and branches of foreign firms should not be permitted to be established except under special circumstances for the manufacture of basic chemicals and drugs, which the Indian-managed factories are not able to take up.

Payment of rates of royalty for "pure know-how" as agreed to by some firms is excessive and this should be reduced to a reasonable figure when current agreements come up for revision.

In all agreements, suitable provision should be made for the training of Indian personnel.

Large-Scale Private Enterprise Under Indian Management

New firms should not be allowed to start the manufacture of galenicals for which there is already a surplus capacity.

Once a development programme of a particular firm has been approved, a constant watch on the progress made by it should be kept. The progress being satisfactory, all facilities should be given for its furtherance.

A large number of firms should not be allowed to carry out almost identical type of work without due regard to the requirements of the country or the existing capacity as this will defeat the very object of the Industries (Development and Regulation) Act and retard the development of the industry.

Small-Scale Private Enterprise

The Government should take early steps to cancel licences and close down all pharmaceutical establishments which do not possess the minimum requirements of premises, equipment and staff that the Committee have specified. New factories should not be licensed unless they fulfil these requirements.

To prevent hardships that may result from it to small-scale manufacturers they should be induced to get together and, by pooling their resources, put up properly equipped co-operative units.

A group of firms may be encouraged to join together and put up well-equipped testing laboratories for keeping control on their raw materials and finished products.

Basic Raw Materials And Packing Materials Of The Industry

Medicinal Plants

The Government should take immediate steps to organize the cultivation of medicinal plants in a scientific manner and sponsor agencies for their proper collection, storage and marketing.

For carrying out experimental work on the cultivation of medicinal plants, adequate grants should be made available by both the Central and State Governments.

Ethyl Alcohol

The restrictions imposed by certain State Governments, in the interests of Prohibition, on the supply of alcohol to the industry such as (i) making rectified spirit a monopoly of the Government and insisting that all manufacturers should buy their requirements from Government distilleries only, at high prices; (ii) restricting production of alcohol of pharmaceutical firms, which have their own distilleries, to their actual requirements; (iii) controlling the supply of molasses to such distilleries; and (iv) charging heavy vend fee on the alcohol of their own manufacture used in their factory hampers the development of the industry and should be removed.

To prevent the misuse of tinctures, especially in the States where Prohibition exists, the following steps are recommended:

(i) The production of tinctures which are in the older editions of pharmacopoeia and for which a genuine demand exists should be allowed to be produced on the basis of production and consumption before the introduction of Prohibition; and

(ii) On those tinctures which appear in the latest edition of the pharmacopoeia and are liable to misuse, the duty should be raised to the same level as on pure ethyl alcohol.

Methyl Alcohol

The policy adopted, at present, should be revised and the existing restrictions removed as they come in the way of the development of the synthetic drug industry and research and testing work in scientific laboratories, where methyl alcohol forms an important item. The existing requirements are small and should be allowed to come in without any restriction.

Coal-tar Products

To improve the production of coal-tar products, the recovery of benzol in the coke ovens operated in the country should be made compulsory unless the units are too small for its economical recovery.

The existing practice of burning coal-tar by the steel companies in their open-hearth furnaces leads to a waste of an important national resource and should be stopped till such time as enough coal-tar is available for purposes of distillation.

The Government themselves should take up the manufacture of essential coal-tar products if sufficient response from the private sector is not forthcoming.

Animal Glands And Organs

Modern slaughter-houses with facilities for proper collection and storage of glands and organs should be established, to start with, in cities such as Bombay, Madras, Calcutta and Delhi.

The collection and preservation of these glands and organs should be supervised by qualified personnel and not left to the butchers as at present.

Glass Bottles

The pharmaceutical concerns and pharmacies, while indenting their requirements of glass containers from glass manufacturers, should insist on standard specifications and decline to purchase cheap goods that do not conform to them.

Ampoules, Vials, Etc.

To enable the pharmaceutical manufacturers to adopt more automatic filling and sealing, the production of machine-made tubing and ampoules should be expanded. The production of neutral glass tubing and its use in ampoule-making should be encouraged.

Standardization

Standards for the quality of the glass and/or alternative containers required for different purposes should be drawn up with the help of the Central Glass and Ceramic Institute and the Indian Standards Institution.

The Weights and Measures Act should be enforced strictly in all States and the practice of dispensing in bottles of lower capacity than that stated should be penalized.

Cork

Several species of Quercus are found at different levels of the Himalayas. Investigations should be carried out to see if these could serve as substitutes for cork. Simultaneously, cork-oak cultivation should be undertaken in suitable climates after investigations in the selected areas.

Demand And Production

Essentiality Of Drugs

A tentative list of essential drugs, whose production should be encouraged in the country, has been given in Appendix 10.

Estimates And Demand And Production

In future, a detailed tariff classification indicating the imports and exports of all essential drugs should be included in the Imports and Customs Schedules published by the Government of India. Basic chemicals and intermediates required by the pharmaceutical industry should also be classified in detail in the above Schedules.

Steps Necessary To Increase Production

The import duty on industrial machinery and scientific equipment, not made in the country and yet required by the pharmaceutical industry for manufacturing and testing purposes, should be brought to the same level as that levied on capital equipment for other industries.

Assistance should be given in the form of reduction, remission or rebate of import duties on the raw materials and intermediates required by the Industry. The rebate or reduction should be so adjusted as to amount to a total incidence which would be less than the duty levied on the finished products.

Cost Of Production And Efficiency Of Process Employed

A detailed examination of books of different firms for estimating both the cost of individual drugs and the cost of processing different formulations should be undertaken.

To enable manufacturers to assess the cost of production of pharmaceuticals and drugs from imported basic chemicals and the economics of their production, the rates of Customs duty levied on the various raw materials and finished products should be indicated in the Customs Tariffs.

Standardization, Control Of Quality And Administration

Administration Of The Drugs Act

Administration of the Drugs Act requires specialized knowledge. Training should, therefore, be provided under one of the Foreign Fellowship Schemes. At least two persons should be sent out for such training every year till an adequate number of persons is available.

Need For Centralizing The Administration

In order to overcome the defects in the operation of the drug control existing at present, and to bring about a uniformity in the standard of products manufactured, administration of the Drugs Control should be centralized by bringing control on manufacture, sale and distribution, which is at present exercised by the State Drugs Controllers under the Drugs Controller (India).

Central Government Laboratories

For primary testing, additional testing laboratories should be set up at the ports of entry of drugs. To ensure that importers have adequate facilities for the storage of the drugs imported by them, additional staff to inspect their premises and take samples more frequently from their godowns should be appointed.

State Government Laboratories

In every State or a group of small States a well-equipped independent laboratory should be set up which should not form an appendage to any of the existing Public Health, Food or Chemical Laboratories.

Manufacturers' Laboratories

In addition to a scrutiny of the testing facilities maintained by manufacturing concerns, a frequent check of the records and test reports maintained by them in these laboratories should be made to see that their products are being regularly and properly tested.

The medical profession and pharmaceutical industry should join together in setting up testing laboratories for the purpose of certifying the products made by the Industry and thus create confidence among the public in the products manufactured by them.

Public Analytical Laboratories

The Drugs Control authorities should keep a constant check on their activities and also verify the adequacy of equipment, staff and their technical competency.

Industries (Development And Regulation) Act

The definition of a factory in the Industries Act as applied to the pharmaceutical industry should be amended to that given under the Factories Act, 1948, so as to bring smaller units under the purview of the Act and thus facilitate their development.

Co-ordination With Drugs Act

There should be a perfect co-ordination between licensing under the Drugs Act and licensing under the Industries Act. Licences should be issued under the respective Acts only after consultation between the two concerned Departments of the Government.

New Grouping

Firms should be licensed to manufacture drugs under the Industries (Development and Regulation) Act, according to any of the two groupings given in the classification in Lists A & B of Table No. 35.

Development Council For Pharmaceuticals And Drugs

To ensure future development of the pharmaceutical industry on the lines of our recommendations, immediate steps should be taken by the Government to constitute a Development Council for Pharmaceuticals and Drugs.

Amendments To The Drugs Act And The Rules Thereunder

At present, there is provision for the marketing of proprietaries with secret formulae after registration in the Central Drugs Laboratory. This provision should be withdrawn and no patent or proprietary preparation with secret formulae should be allowed to be marketed. Any product to be marketed must have its composition and method of usage published on its label.

Offences under the Drugs Act for trading in spurious and sub-standard drugs should be made cognizable. Deterrent punishment with an adequate fine and a compulsory period of rigorous imprisonment should be given.

Giving of adequate publicity to an offender's name and address should be made compulsory.

Revision Of Licence Fees

The Rules under the Drugs Act prescribing licence fees for the importing, stocking, exhibiting, selling and manufacturing of drugs and medicines should be revised and the fees increased in order to prevent unhealthy competition in the trade which has been flooded with unqualified people.

Licensing Of Crude Drug Dealers

For the proper development of the pharmaceutical industry, it is necessary to see that the quality of the crude drugs used as raw materials is ensured.

It should be made compulsory that every licensed dealer in such drugs should give a warranty about their active constituents.

Manufacturers who obtain their crude drugs requirements directly should be licensed as dealers in crude drugs.

Chemical Name Vis-a-Vis Proprietary Name

Rule 109 (1) (a), which reads as follows, is at present applicable to Schedule "C" drugs. This Rule should be made applicable to all drugs and rigidly enforced. It should apply, in addition to the labels on the containers, to advertisements in medical, scientific and trade journals and the literature distributed to the medical profession and chemists and druggists.

Rule 109 (1) (a): Labelling: (1) Every phial ampoule

or other container of a substance specified in Schedule "C" shall bear a label on which is printed or written in indelible ink the following particulars, if any, as are specified in Schedule "F".

(a) The proper name of the substance in letters not less conspicuous than those in which the proprietary name, if any, is printed or written and following immediately after or under such proprietary name.

In the case of combinations the names of the main ingredients should be displayed in letters of readable size on the labels of the containers and in the advertisements and in the medical literature.

Staff For Inspection And Testing

A sufficient number of well-qualified and properly paid inspectors should be appointed so that the premises of drug manufacturers, distributors and traders may be more frequently inspected and samples drawn and tested.

Problem Of Reuse Of Old Containers

The problem of reuse of old containers has assumed serious proportions. Wide publicity to this is required and the co-operation of the public, the medical profession and chemists and druggists should be sought for the prompt destruction of such containers and thus prevent them from falling into the hands of unsocial elements. Documentary films, cinema slides and posters should be used for giving wide publicity to check this malpractice.

Research Work

Evaluation of drugs requires team-work by several groups of scientists. It should be actively encouraged as and when facilities for such team-work become available with the setting up of more Research Laboratories.

In order to provide the required number of research workers, it is necessary to train a large number of chemists and biologists in pharmacology in addition to medical men.

Distribution And Advertisement

Distribution

Drugs and medicines should not be allowed to be sold in grocers' shops, restaurants and by general merchants in cities and large towns.

Goods should be sold only at the prices so fixed and any deviation should entail cancellation of licence.

High priority should be given to the transport of pharmaceutical products. Consignments of medicines should be provided with special "rush labels" so that even small packages could be moved at a faster rate.

Advertisement

Newspapers and especially publishers of journals in Indian languages in this country should themselves evolve a code of advertising and, if necessary, the State should step in to put an end to suggestive advertisements which exploit the credulous public.

Medical Profession And The Pharmaceutical Industry

The Expert body proposed for determining the essentiality of drugs should prepare a list of standard combinations which are considered essential and which should be allowed to be manufactured or imported.

Technical Training For The Profession Of Pharmacy

Status Of The Profession

The profession of pharmacy should be given a recognized place in society.

Training In Pharmacy

To enable students to migrate from one university to another at an appropriate stage, there should be a uniform minimum standard of education in the different universities. There should be provision for postgraduate training in different branches of pharmacy in the various universities.

Pharmacy Act

The Pharmacy Act should be made operative uniformly throughout the country by extending it to all the States of the Indian Union.

The Pharmacy Council should be empowered to draw up a code of ethics for the profession of pharmacists which should be enforced rigorously.

Dispensing of Drugs

The question of requirements for a general practitioner in maintaining his dispensary in a proper way should be examined by the State and Central Medical Councils. It should be considered necessary for them to maintain minimum equipment and requisite storage arrangements and adequate maintenance of proper records on the lines of those provided under the Drug Rules.

Employment Of Pharmacists

The scales of pay that are applicable to pharmacists in the Centre and States should be upgraded wherever they are low.

Chief Pharmacists for all large hospitals should be graduates in Pharmacy.

STORES PURCHASE COMMITTEE, 1953—REPORT
Delhi, Manager of Publications, 1955. 239p.

Chairman : Shri S. N. Buragohain (Shri G. B. Kotak became the Chairman of the Committee after the death of Shri S. N. Buragohain).

Members : Shri T. Sivasankar; Shri M. P. Pai (resigned); Shri N. M. Buch (died); Shri N. N. Wanchoo; Shri K. R. P. Aiyangar (replaced by Shri S. Ratnam); Shri K. L. Ghei; Shri G. S. Rao; Shri N. V. Rajan.

Secretary : Shri D. P. Karnik.

APPOINTMENT

The Stores Purchase Committee was constituted under the Government of India, Ministry of Works, Housing and Supply, vide their Resolution No. P-3(201) dated March 11, 1953.

TERMS OF REFERENCE

(i) To examine the scope and functions of the Central Purchasing Organization in India and the extent of delegation of powers necessary for the Indenting Departments for direct purchases with particular reference to specialized stores and special or emergent demands; and to consider the advisability of utilizing the Central Purchasing Organization for purchases by State-owned industrial enterprises and important River Valley and other Projects.

(ii) To examine the organization of the Central Purchasing Agency and to consider reorganization that may be necessary, including the extent of powers, provision of adequate and suitable personnel to man the organization, scales of pay, service conditions, technical qualifications of the staff, etc., with a view to securing greater efficiency.

(iii) To consider the manner of determination of Government demands and the authorities at appropriate levels competent for approving such demands, rationalized planning, provisioning and indenting of stores and screening and processing of such demands and the procedure for the communication of sanctions and contracts to Audit.

(iv) To examine the procedure and methods of purchase, progressing of deliveries and payment of bills with special reference to avoidance of delays and achieving better results in respect of quality and economy.

(v) To examine the procedure of inspection of stores by various agencies and to suggest general improvements, including simplification and rationalization of procedure.

(vi) To examine the working of the stores purchasing system in relation to assistance to articles of Indian manufacture and encouragement to small-scale and cottage industries.

(vii) To examine whether any modifications are required in the general conditions of contract, in particular whether the Arbitration Procedure now in force in the Supply Contracts is suitable.

(viii) To examine the policy, procedure and method of disposals of surplus stores with particular reference to their utilization against Government requirements.

(ix) To examine any other matters considered to be relevant to this enquiry.

CONTENTS

Introductory; Central Purchase Organization—History and Review of Current Working; Retrospect; Working of the Directorate-General of Supplies and Disposals; Scope and Functions of the Central Purchase Organization; Purchase and Development Board and Non-Official Advisory Councils; Purchase and Development Board; Non-Official Purchase Advisory Councils; Purchase Corporation; Assistance to Industry; Screening of Indents for Imported Stores; Indents for Development Items; Price Preference; Relaxation in Quality; Definition of Cottage and Small-Scale Industries; Protection to Industry—Unfair Competition; Permanent Exhibitions; Directory of Government Requirements; Liaison Between "Purchase" and the "Development" Wing; Purchase of Imported Stores; Imported Stores—Purchase in India; Indents under "Foreign Aid"; Cross Mandate (Transfer) of Indents to Purchase Missions Abroad; Assistance to Indian Shipping; Purchase Missions Abroad; Determination and Planning of Demands; Assessment of Requirements; Programme for Indents; Special Indents; Indents for Proprietary Makes and Brands; Incomplete Indents; Changes in Specifications; Uniform Specifications; Indent Estimates—Prices and Deliveries; Budget Provision for Supplies of Stores; Purchase Procedure—**Part I** : General; Indent Forms; Registration of Suppliers; Tenders; Negotiated Purchases; Special Contracts; Sales Tax; Reckoning of Inland Freight; Purchase of Stores from State-owned Industries; Preference to Tried Firms, Makes and Brands; Issue of Import Licences; Purchase of Spare Parts; Purchase Procedure: **Part II** : Central Purchase Organization; Bulking of Indents; Rate/Running Contracts and Price Agreements; Repeat Orders; Ignoring of Lower Tenders;

Referring Tenders to Indenting Departments; Discretion to Exceed Prices Indicated by Indentors; Small Shortages and Excesses in Supply; Speedy Communication of Purchase Orders and Amendments to Paying Authority; "Control Data"; Financial Data; Financial Advice; Audit; Fees Charged by the Central Purchase Organization; "Write-Off" of Losses; Manuals of Instructions; Stores Purchase Rules; Delays in Supplies; Delays in Pre-contract Stage; Delays in Post-contract Stage; Progressing of Supplies; Payment Terms and Other Conditions of Contract; Uniform Terms of Payment and Conditions of Contract; Payment Authority; Delays in Payment; Refund of Security Deposits; Power of Attorney; Financial Accommodation; Consignee's Right of Rejection; Arbitration; "Liquidated Damages" for Delays in Supply; Other Conditions of Contract; Inspection of Stores; Inspection Agencies; Facilities for Routine Tests with Inspectors; State Inspection; Percentage Inspection; Delays in Inspection; Test Houses; Disposal of Surplus Stores; Disposals Organization; Determination of Surplus; General Policy and Procedure; Utilization of Surpluses Against Government Demands; Pricing Policy; Disposal "As Is, Where Is"; Disposal of Scrap; Non-official Disposals Advisory Councils; Directorate-General of Supplies and Disposals: Organizational Set-up, Personnel, Powers, etc.; Organizational Set-up of the Directorate-General of Supplies and Disposals; Strength of Personnel; Scales of Pay; Need for Permanency; Recruitment and Calibre of Personnel; Administration, Co-ordination and Statistics Personnel; Powers of Purchase and Disposal; Regional Purchase Offices; Commercial Intelligence; Complaints; Indentors' Liaison Officers; Office Accommodation; Conclusion and Summary of Recommendations; Appendix 1 to 46.

RECOMMENDATIONS

The existing Central Purchase Organization (C.P.O.), i.e., the Directorate-General of Supplies, should continue. For the present, the *status quo* should generally be maintained between centralized purchases and direct purchases by Indenting Departments. Purchases of specialized stores should be progressively transferred to the C.P.O., as it becomes effectively equipped to handle larger purchases.

Purchases for industrial and other undertakings owned by the Central Government should be made through the C.P.O. subject to exceptions to be agreed upon.

State Governments, Port Trusts and larger Municipal Corporations should be persuaded to make their purchases of imported stores through the C.P.O.

The Railways, the Posts and Telegraphs and the Defence Departments should be authorized to make direct purchases up to the enhanced value of Rs. 10,000 in each case.

Indenting Departments should have the authority to make direct purchases in emergencies.

Direct purchases may be made by the Indenting Departments in the case of arms and ammunition, or where intervention/assistance of, or negotiation with, a foreign Government is necessary.

In respect of imported stores proposed to be manufactured indigenously with the technical assistance of foreign manufacturers or consultants, Departments may make direct purchases.

During the construction period, Industrial and River Valley Projects may make direct purchases subject to certain conditions; for other major projects, direct purchases may be authorized in suitable cases.

A high-power Purchase and Development Board should be established to control and co-ordinate the Government's purchase activities with particular reference to development of industries.

A non-official Purchase Advisory Council should be established to advise the Government on procurement policy and procedure; non-official Purchase Advisory Committees should also be established to advise the regional offices of the C.P.O.

The Purchase and Development Board should be kept informed of the direct purchases of imported stores made by the Defence, Railways and other Departments, Industrial and River Valley Projects, Corporate Bodies and State Governments.

Certain classes of stores should be reserved for purchase only from cottage and small-scale industries.

Permanent exhibitions should be opened in large cities to display samples, drawings, models, etc., of the stores required by the various Government Departments, which are at present being imported.

The "Purchase" and "Development" Organizations of the Government of India should be placed under a common Ministry.

Indents should be classified under five categories: "Programme" or "Normal", "Ad Hoc", "Urgent", "Operational", and "Development" indents; specific coloured forms should be used for each type.

Indenting Departments should reduce the number of special indents, i.e., "Ad Hoc", "Urgent", "Operational"; purchase procedure should be so devised as to meet such requirements with minimum delay.

The present policy in regard to purchases from Ordnance Factories may continue. The spare capacity in the Ordnance Factories should be first utilized to meet Government requirements of stores normally imported or where indigenous capacity is insufficient to meet the country's demands.

The Progress Wing of the C.P.O. should maintain "Progress Cards" for watching deliveries.

A time-schedule should be fixed in the C.P.O. for completion of action at each stage on the indents received till conclusion of contracts. A period of 90 days from the receipt of an indent should be prescribed for placing orders for stores of common type and 150 days for stores of complicated nature. "Emergent" and "Operational" indents should be dealt with personally by senior officers not below the rank of Director.

The Government should discourage payment of advances against contracts and encourage a wider application of the system of "progress" payments. Suppliers in India should not receive less favourable financing terms than those allowed when purchases are made abroad.

All available information regarding the condition of the stores should be notified to the public while inviting tenders for disposal of surplus.

Arrangements should be made to fill all the permanent posts in the C.P.O. on a permanent basis.

Two Central Services, one for "Supply" and the other for "Inspection", should be constituted for the C.P.O.

The "Central" and "Regional" lists of stores should be revised; the "Central" list should be kept to the minimum.

The C.P.O. should have its own bi-weekly "Commercial Bulletin" for prompt publication of information of commercial interest to give advance intimation of probable demands. Copies of the Bulletin should be mailed free to the registered cottage and small-scale industrial units.

To ensure that complaints from indentors and suppliers are dealt with expeditiously, a special officer should be appointed in the Progress Wing. This arrangement should be notified to indentors and suppliers.

BELLARY TALUQ ENQUIRY COMMISSION, 1953—REPORT

Delhi, Manager of Publications, 1953. 55p.

One-Man Commission : Mr. Justice L. S. Misra.

APPOINTMENT

The Bellary Taluq Enquiry Commission was constituted under the Ministry of Home Affairs vide their Memorandum No. 110/53-P.S.S. dated April 28, 1953.

TERMS OF REFERENCE

To enquire into the various factors regarding the future of Bellary Taluq, and to report thereon.

CONTENTS

Introductory; Reference; Enquiry; Topography; The Kannadiga Case; The Andhra Case; Linguistic Composition: Administrative Convenience; Financial Implications; Economic Well-being; Cultural Affinity; Historical Background; Appendices; Tables.

RECOMMENDATIONS

Bellary Taluq should go as a whole to the State of Mysore subject to the transitional arrangements which I shall now proceed to set out. These transitional arrangements are designed to provide facilities to Andhra State and its people in order to enable it to function with facility and ease for a reasonable period. From the talk that I had with the Government of Mysore I gathered that in the matter of transitional arrangements there would be no difficulty in arriving at a sympathetic settlement. Of course, the Government of India can arbitrate where necessary.

Subject to the above observations, I would indicate below the principal matters about which arrangements between the two States may be necessary and the lines on which they may be settled.

1. Regional Offices

There are a number of Regional Government Offices located at Bellary. Andhra State may find it difficult to secure immediate accommodation in its territory for most of them. I would, therefore, recommend that it should be allowed five years' time to shift these offices. An exception will have to be made in the case of the office of the D.I.G., Police, which should be shifted immediately after the formation of the new State.

2. Jails

Besides the District Jail, there are three other jails in Bellary town of a regional nature. They are:

Name of Jail	Present Population
1. Central Jail	1,076
2. Allipuram Borstal School	158
3. Junior Certified School	443

The bulk of the inmates of these institutions belong to districts other than Bellary. It would take time for Andhra State to provide alternative accommodation and I would recommend that, while the administration of these institutions must be transferred to Mysore State, there should be adequate reservation for a period of 10 years of accommodation for Andhra State on payment of the expenses involved.

3. The Rayalaseema Polytechnic

The Polytechnic has at present 208 students on its rolls of which 108 belong to Bellary District and 100 to other districts of the would-be Andhra State (including 72 from Rayalaseema District alone). There are only two other polytechnics in Andhra State—at Vuyyuru (Krishna District) and Kakinada. Obviously, these two cannot be expected to cater to the needs of the whole State. The Rayalaseema Polytechnic at Bellary has recently shifted to new buildings which have been put up at a cost of Rs. 3.65 lakhs and it has equipment costing Rs. 4.27 lakhs. It will take considerable time for the new Andhra State to be able to provide a new polytechnic for the Rayalaseema area. I would, therefore, recommend that about half the seats in the Bellary Polytechnic should be reserved for Andhra State students on payment of the necessary cost for a period of 10 years.

Government Wellesley T.B. Sanatorium, Bellary

Bellary is noted for its excellent climate and has been chosen as the site of the T.B. Sanatorium for this reason. The present number of patients in the Sanatorium is 265. The bulk of them belong to districts other than Bellary. I would recommend that a proportion of beds should be reserved for Andhras by mutual arrangements between the two States and on payment of the necessary expenses. The proportion and the time during which the arrangements are to subsist should also be settled by negotiation between the two States.

PART B STATES (SPECIAL ASSISTANCE) ENQUIRY COMMITTEE, 1953—REPORT

Delhi, Manager of Publications, 1953. 61p.

Chairman : Shri N. V. Gadgil.
Members : Shri Bimal Comar Ghose; Shri S. V. Ramamurty.
Secretary : Shri C. Ganesan.

APPOINTMENT

The Part B States (Special Assistance) Enquiry Committee was constituted under the Ministry of States vide their Resolution No. 66-SF/53 dated April 28, 1953.

TERMS OF REFERENCE

(a) To review the results of the progress made in the internal integration of the administration and services in these States and the problems, financial and technical, if any, created for them by such integration;

(b) To enquire into the developmental needs of these States; and

(c) To make recommendations regarding any financial and technical assistance still required by these States to enable them to attain a reasonable standard of development, taking into account:

(i) the efforts made by the State Governments to increase their available resources by additional taxation;

(ii) the assistance envisaged in the Five Year Plan to these States and the extent to which their special circumstances have been taken into account in fixing the quantum of such assistance; and

(iii) the additional resources made available to them under the recommendations of the Finance Commission.

CONTENTS

Preliminary; Background of the Enquiry; Federal Financial Integration; Analysis of the Memoranda Presented by the States; Internal Integration of Administration and Services; Development; Taxation Efforts of the States; Recommendations; Appendices.

RECOMMENDATIONS

The brief analysis which we have attempted of the position in regard to the various matters in the Part B States will, we think, establish fairly conclusively that so far as the developmental requirements are concerned these have been considered in the framing of the Five Year Plan by the Planning Commission. There are some long-term projects to which the States naturally attach particular importance. Prominent among these are the proposals for contour bunding which the Saurashtra Government have included as part of their Agricultural Programme and the Afforestation Programme as laid down by the Government of Saurashtra in respect of which they feel that the provision under the Five Year Plan does not enable them to progress fast enough. Similar programmes of other States will also require consideration but we feel, as we have pointed out above, that the most appropriate method of preparing phased programmes for implementing these requirements will be in consultation between the State Governments and the Planning Commission. While there may be shortcomings in certain directions, it seems that taking an overall picture, the general backwardness of these States in regard to development has been adequately taken into account by the Planning Commission.

Nevertheless we feel that having regard to the background of the problems which the State Governments had and to their peculiar difficulties, a certain amount of initial financial help is still necessary and that this should be given to them by the Centre. In this respect these four States must be considered in a somewhat different position from the other States which have had comparatively simpler tasks to face.

In fixing the Central assistance for these States the Planning Commission has taken into account the question of the Special Assistance which they require. In the case of Saurashtra, we understand that, on account of certain special circumstances, a sum of Rs. 2 crores is to be treated as grant.

In view of the special circumstances of these States and their need for financial assistance in the initial stages we recommend that out of the Central assistance which has been envisaged in the Five Year Plans of these States an amount of Rs. 4 crores (in addition to whatever amounts the Government of India have so far decided to allot in the shape of grants) should be treated as outright grant.

There is one more direction in which we think the States deserve some assistance. They have represented that they are short of administrative buildings inclusive of police buildings and some of the States have brought forcefully to our notice that they lack in certain essential directions, namely, link roads, public health services in rural areas, etc. We recommend, therefore, that a sum of Rs. 4 crores should be given to these States as an *ad hoc* grant during the next two years.

This amount is to be in addition to the assistance which the States have so far received from the Government of India in various directions and is to be spent on plans approved by the Centre but formulated by the States themselves having regard to their individual requirements. We also recommend that, if any balance of this amount remains unspent at the end of the two-year period, it should not be allowed to lapse but should be made available in the subsequent period, also on the same conditions as before.

We also wish to make the following recommendations with a view to strengthening the administrative machinery of the State Governments:

(i) Each of the States may be provided with two senior officers, one specially competent to deal with general administration and the other with development, so that their services may be utilized as Chief Secretary and Development Commissioner respectively.

(ii) In the initial stages of planning and development, in each of these States a Planning and Development Board may be entrusted with planning and implementation of the Plan, the relation of the Board to the State Government being analogous to that of the National Planning Commission to the Central Government and one member of the Board being nominated in consultation with the National Planning Commission.

PORT AND SHIPPING STATISTICS COMMITTEE, 1953—REPORT

Delhi, Ministry of Transport, 1955. 322p.+viip.

Chairman : Shri M. A. Master.

Members : Shri S. N. Haji; Shri C. R. B. Menon; Shri P. R. Subramaniam; Dr. B. Ramamurti; Shri A. Mudie (retired from service and replaced by Shri L. H. Cornish); Shri B. B. Gujral.

Secretary : Shri D. K. Guha.

APPOINTMENT

The Port and Shipping Statistics Committee was constituted under the Ministry of Transport on May 7, 1953.

TERMS OF REFERENCE

(i) The type of port and shipping statistics that

are already being collected and maintained in major and minor ports;

(ii) The extent to which such statistics are being published either by Government Departments or Port Authorities and whether there is any duplication of effort;

(iii) Having regard to the needs of the Government, the trade and international agencies, what further statistics should be collected in regard to ports and coastal and ocean-going shipping; the agencies for collection and compilation; the material that should be published and the manner of publication.

AMENDED AND AMPLIFIED TERMS OF REFERENCE

As a result of the correspondence passed between the Chairman of the Committee, the Ministry of Transport and the Directorate-General of Shipping, it was felt by the Ministry of Transport that the Terms of Reference of the Committee should be amplified and it was decided by the Ministry that the question whether the Terms of Reference of the Committee required to be amended or not might be left over to be discussed by the Committee itself at its first meeting in the first instance. Accordingly, at the first meeting of the Committee held on August 17, 18, 19, 1953, the matter was fully discussed and sanction of the Government sought for the proposed Amended Terms of Reference.

The final Terms of Reference, as approved by the Government, are as under:

I. To examine and report:

(a) On port and shipping statistics that are already being collected and maintained in major and minor ports;

(b) The extent to which such statistics are being published either by the Central or the State Government, or port authorities, and whether there is any duplication of effort;

(c) On shipping statistics that are collected, maintained and published by the Government of India and State Governments.

II. The Committee shall examine the existing system of collection, maintenance and publication of port and shipping statistics, in all its aspects, and make recommendations:

(a) As to what measures should be taken for collecting information regarding the cargo carried by all shipping companies in the coastal and overseas trades and the amount of freight payable thereon;

(b) As to what measures should be taken for collecting information in regard to the nature and quantity of cargo to be imported into India or to be exported from India, which may be under the ownership and/or control of the Central or the State Government, or the local authority, and the amount of freight that may be paid thereon;

(c) As to what measures should be taken for collecting further statistics in regard to ports and coastal and ocean-going shipping, with particular reference to the needs of the Government, the trade and international agencies and the shipping industry;

(d) In regard to the agencies that should collect and compile the statistics mentioned in (a), (b) and (c) above;

(e) In regard to the publication of the material referred to in (a), (b) and (c) above, and the manner of its publication;

(f) As to what further statutory powers will be necessary for giving effect to their recommendations.

In making their recommendations, the Committee may take into consideration the nature and extent of the collection, maintenance and publication of port and shipping statistics in such leading maritime countries as the United Kingdom, the United States of America, Japan, Germany, Norway, Italy, Holland, Belgium and France.

CONTENTS

Introductory (Appointment of the Committee and the Original Terms of Reference; Amended and Amplified Terms of Reference; Other points discussed in the first meeting; Issue of Questionnaire; Appointment of a Sub-Committee—study of all questions on the spot by Personal Interviews; Information regarding Port and Shipping Statistics in Leading Maritime Countries; Cargo carried under the ownership and/or control of the Central or State Governments; Total Deadweight Tons of Imports into and Exports from India and the freight paid or payable thereon; Cargo coming to India under the T.C.A. Aid; Second Meeting; Passenger Traffic Statistics; Further Interviews with the Director-General of Shipping; Additional Interviews at Bombay; Concluding Meeting and Signing of the Report); Statistics Collected and Maintained by Major Ports (Control and Administration of Major Ports; Share of Major Ports in the Total Tonnages Imported and Exported; Maintenance of Statistics under different groups; Subjects and Fields which Statistics should cover; Tonnages of Principal Commodities Exported and Imported; Number of Commodities for which Statistics Maintained—their conversion into Deadweight Tons; Tonnage of Principal Commodities—Coastal and Foreign; Statistics for Transhipment Cargo; Region-wise Tonnages of Imports and Exports of Principal Commodities; Madras Cautions Against the Correctness of Region-wise Statistics; Flag-wise Tonnages of Imports and Exports; Imports and Exports according to Shipping Lines and Agencies; Statistics of Cargo and Passengers carried by and of the Shipping Tonnage of the Sailing Vessels; Passenger Statistics; Number and Tonnage of the Ships that arrived or departed and entered and cleared; Import and Export by Dry Cargo Vessels and Tankers; Turn-round of Vessels at Ports; Statistical expression not used in the same sense at all ports; Different Basis of Classifying Ships at Different Ports; No uniform basis of allocating cargo to coastal and foreign trade; Different Systems followed at Different Ports for entering or clearing ships in Foreign Trade; How the Customs Authorities enter and clear vessels into Foreign Trade: How the U.K. defines "Foreign" and "Coastal" Trade: How vessels are entered and cleared into Foreign Trade in the U.K.; Port-wise Statement of Commodities at Madras Defective: All Statistical Expressions must have the same meaning at all the ports: Circulation and Supply of Statistics; Statistics supplied to the Ministry of Transport by the Major and Minor Port Authorities; Statistics supplied to the Director-General of Shipping, Bombay, by the Major and Minor Port Authorities; Comparative Statements of Statistics of the Major and Minor Ports); Statistics Collected and Maintained at Minor Ports (Number of Minor Ports and the Authority controlling them; Who Administers the Affairs of Minor Ports: Who Collects the Statistics at Minor Ports: Basic Documents from which Statistics are Collected: the Nature of Statistics Collected—General Observations: Tonnages of Commodities—separate figures for Coastal and Foreign Trades: Line-wise and Agent-wise particulars of Imports and Exports: Flag-wise Statistics of Imports and Exports; Separate Statistics for Dry Cargo Vessels and Tankers: Particulars of Transhipment Cargo: Passenger Statistics: Shipping Statistics—number and tonnage of vessels that arrive and depart or enter and clear the ports; Tonnages of Commodities Imported and Exported and Passengers carried by sailing vessels: Circulation and Supply of Statistics): Basic Documents for Statistics Collected by Ports (Basic Documents for Cargo Statistics: Columns in the Basic Documents and how they are filled in: Basic Documents for Customs Trade Statistics: Number of Bills of Entry and Shipping Bills filed and their distribution at the different ports; Procedure in respect of delivery of imports and shipment of exports differ from port to port: How the particulars about weight are obtained in Import and Export Applications: The Forms of the Basic Documents: Names of the Basic Documents should be same at different ports: Gross weight to be shown in every Import and Export Application; Uniform Nomenclature for charges of similar nature; Uniform Procedure as regards Delivery of Imports and Shipment of Exports; Basic Documents for Cargo Statistics at the ports which have no Documents of their own; Basic Documents for Vessels and Passengers: Forms of the Arrival and Departure Reports; Basic Documents for Sailing Vessel Statistics); Commodities for which Statistics are collected by Ports (Names of Principal Commodities; Number of Principal Commodities); Publication of Statistics of Ports (Who publishes Statistics of Major Ports; Who publishes Statistics of Minor Ports; Nature and Extent of Statistics published; Total Tonnages of Imports and Exports; Tonnages of Principal Commodities; Transhipment Cargo; Flag-wise Statement; Line-wise Statement; Agency-wise Statement; Region-wise Statement; Separate Figures for Dry Cargo Vessels and Tankers; Tonnage of Principal Commodities Imported and Exported by Sailing Vessels; Passengers; Entry and Clearance of vessels with cargo and in ballast broken up into Foreign and Coastal Trades; Entry and Clearance of Vessels; Entry alone of Vessels broken up into Coastal and Foreign; Entry and Clearance of Sailing Vessels; Turn-round of Ships; Important Statistics Collected and Maintained but not Published; Who publishes the Annual Administration Reports and the Traffic Reviews; Does the Central Government publish Statistics: Availability of the Administrative Report and the Traffic Reviews); Shipment Statistics Published by the Government of India and State Governments (Coasting Trade; Foreign Trade; Shipping Statistics published by the D.G.C.I.S.; Special features of the Shipping Statistics in the Annual Statement; Field which Shipping Statistics should cover); Statistics Maintained by the Directorate-General of Shipping (Cargo Statistics—Statistics received from Indian Shipping Companies; Statements received from the different Major Ports and Minor Ports Authorities; Shipping Statistics in respect of Indian Vessels; Register of Indian Ships—particulars of ships on the Indian Register; Register of Sailing Vessels—particulars of Vessels of the Indian Register: Passenger Statistics: Statistics in respect of Indian Crew and Statistics in respect of Indian and non-Indian Officers on Indian Vessels; Statistics in respect of Freight on Imports and Exports; Sailing Vessels Statistics; General Information about the Indian Shipping Companies): International Obligations for Supplying Statistics (Agencies to which Statistics are to be supplied; Standardization of Transport Statistics: Statistics to be supplied to the United Nations; Statistics required by E.C.A.F.E.; Statistics to be Published and Supplied under the Convention of 1928; Collection of Additional Statistics; Statistics to be Supplied to the International Monetary Fund): Statistics which Government Trade and Shipping Industry require (Commodity Data for shaping Government Policy; Region-wise Statistics Essential for Regulating Exchange Control Policy; Region-wise Data useful for Trade Agreements: Region-wise Data helps determining of Tariff Policy; Country-wise Commodities Data necessary for developing Import-Export Business;

Region-wise Statistics and Economic Operations on Ships; Development of Sailing Vessel Industry requires Separate Statistics; Flag-wise Statistics and Development of Indian Shipping; Study of Flag-wise Data for opening new Shipping Services; Purposes for which the Government require Passenger Statistics; Statistics for the Implementation of the Emigration Policy; Statistics of the Entry and Exit of Foreigners; Statistics for the Development of the Tourist Traffic; Statistics regarding the Entry of Foreign Tourists; Passenger List furnished to the Police and the Port Health Officers; Passenger Statistics to be collected under the Indian Merchant Shipping Act; Data of Passenger Traffic—Routes and Internal Arrangements of Passenger Ships; Details essential for future Passenger Statistics; Movement of Passengers in the Coastal Trade of India; National Shipping Policy and Security and Flags that carry India's Trades; Turn-round of Ships and Port and Shipping Economy; Records kept by the Directorate-General of Shipping); Study of Port and Shipping Statistics in Leading Maritime Countries (Difficulties in the way of Study; Detailed Data not received from all countries; Port Statistical Systems vary; Statistical Work carried on by several Organizations; Responsibility of different Government Departments for Statistics in the U.S.A.; Fairly good field covered by Cargo Statistics at Indian Ports; Necessity to maintain Region-wise and Flag-wise Commodities Statistics; Combination of Region and Flag in Commodities Statistics; Considerable scope in improvement of our Passenger Statistics; Statutory Obligations for supplying Passenger Statistics in the U.K.; System of maintaining Shipping Statistics in India compared with that of the U.K.; Freight Statistics; How Freight Statistics are collected in Foreign Countries; Vessel Utilization and Performance Report; Labour Statistics; Statistics and Special Studies Office in the U.S.A); Additional Port and Shipping Statistics—Agency for Collection (Uniform Commodity Schedule; Additional Cargo Statistics—Commodity—Flag-wise; Number of Flags; Commodity—Region-wise; Number of Regions; Statistics available from Commodity—Flag-wise and Commodity—Region-wise Statements; Statistics of Coastal Cargo carried by Foreign Flags; Tonnages of Commodities carried by steamers and sailing vessels; Line-wise and Agency-wise Particulars of Imports and Exports; Flag-wise Statement and the Tonnages of Total Imports and Exports; Same Bottom cargo and Transhipment cargo; Maintenance of Separate Statistics for Tonnages Imported and Exported by Dry Cargo Vessels and Tankers; How International Obligations regarding Statistics for Cargo will be met; Basic Documents for Additional Cargo Statistics; How International Obligations regarding Shipping Statistics will be fulfilled; Shipping Statistics; Passenger Statistics; Supply of Statistics of Different Types of Vessels under International Obligations; Statistics of Sea Personnel; Turn-round of Vessels; Statistics regarding Port Facilities, Navigational Aids and Port Flotilla, etc.; Statistics regarding Officers who handle ships at Ports; Labour Statistics at all Ports; Construction of Ships; Laid-up Tonnage; Institutions for the Training of Sea Personnel; Feasibility of drawing up, in future, a form based on the U.S. and Japanese Forms; Proposed Uniform Commodity Schedule); Agency for Collection, Compilation and Publication of Statistics (Collecting Agencies recommended by us; Primary Collecting Agency for Cargo Statistics; Central Agency; Statistics that should be published—Agency for Publication; Formation of Groups of Ports for Submitting Statistics; Publication of Shipping Statistics; Publication of Passenger Statistics; Publication of Statistics maintained by D.G. of Shipping; New Staff for Additional Statistics at Ports; Proposed Statistical Branch in the D.G. Shipping's Office; Mechanization of Statistics); What further Statutory Powers are necessary for Collecting Additional Statistics (Present Statutory Powers of the Ports, Customs and D.G., Shipping; Existing Statutory Powers for collecting Cargo Statistics; Rule 2 of the Landing and Shipping Fees; No fresh Statutory Power necessary for collecting Additional Cargo Statistics; Additional Shipping Statistics; Additional Passenger Statistics; Additional Statistics of Other Nature); Summary of Conclusions and Recommendations (Conclusions; Recommendations); Acknowledgments; Appendices I to XXVIII.

RECOMMENDATIONS

Primary Collecting Agency For Cargo Statistics

Statistics regarding the deadweight tonnage of cargo imported or exported, classified according to different cross-sections, should be compiled by the ports and sent to the Central Agency for compiling statistics on an all-India basis.

Central Agency For All-India Compilation And Publication Of Statistics

The Directorate-General of Shipping should be the appropriate Central Agency for all-India compilation and publication of the various types of statistics recommended by the Committee.

Thirty-Two Port And Port Groups To Send Statements To The Directorate-General Of Shipping

All the statements mentioned in Chapter XII which are to be forwarded by the ports to the Directorate-General of Shipping should be sent by 32 Ports and Groups mentioned in the Schedule given in Appendix XXVIII.

Cargo Statistics

Commodity-wise Cargo Statistics

All the Major and Minor Ports should, in future, maintain all their commodity-wise cargo statistics according to a uniform standard commodity schedule given at the end of Chapter XII.

Basic Documents For Cargo Statistics For All Ports

The basic documents for collection of cargo statistics at all the ports, including the 111 Minor Ports, where there are at present no port documents, should be the Port Revenue Documents.

Same Name For Basic Documents

The names of these basic documents should, in future, be the same at all ports, viz., Import and Export Applications.

Basic Documents For Statistics Of Cargo Carried By Sailing Vessels

The basic documents for statistics of cargo carried by sailing vessels should be also the Import and Export Applications.

Essential Items To Appear On Import And Export Applications

The Import and Export Applications should have, amongst other items which the port might find necessary to have for other purposes, the following columns:

Import Application	Export Application
(1) Vessel's Name.	(1) Vessel's Name.
(2) Name of the Line.	(2) Name of the Line.
(3) Name of the Agent or Charterer.	(3) Name of the Agent or Charterer.
(4) Nationality of the Flag.	(4) Nationality of the Flag.
(5) The Port and Country of Shipment.	(5) Port and Country of Destination.
(6) Name of the Commodity.	(6) Name of the Commodity.
(7) Country of Origin.	(7) Country to which Consigned.
(8) Marks and Numbers of the Consignment.	(8) Marks and Numbers of the Consignment.
(9) Gross Weight of the Consignment.	(9) Gross Weight of the Consignment.

Gross Weight Particulars And Uniform Standard Conversion Table

The gross weight of the consignment must always be recorded in the Import or Export Applications. In the cases where gross weight particulars are not necessary for the port to realize its charges and the particulars are shown in gallonage, measurement, units, etc., the gross weight of the consignment should be arrived at by applying a Standard Conversion Table, which has been given in Appendix XV.

Every Port To Have Copies Of Bills Of Entry And Shipping Bills

A definite procedure should be laid down for supplying port authorities with a copy of the Bill of Entry or Shipping Bill for each consignment at every Major and Minor Port in India.

Uniform Nomenclature For Charges

A proper study should be made for ensuring uniform nomenclature at all the ports, as far as possible, for the port charges for same types of operations, services rendered, etc.

Uniform Procedure

All possible steps should be taken to ensure uniformity of procedure, as far as possible, at all ports for making them responsible for the delivery and shipment of cargo that passes through their jurisdiction.

Tonnages Of Imports And Exports

The ports should send monthly statements to the Directorate-General of Shipping (Central Agency) showing total tonnages of imports and exports, broken up into coastal and foreign, and the Directorate-General should compile them on an all-India basis and publish the figures in its monthly Bulletin.

Commodity Flag-wise Statements

Every port should maintain a monthly flag-wise statement giving particulars of the tonnages of commodities mentioned in the Schedule of Commodities, imported into or exported from that port, according to the nationality of the flag of the ship which brought or carried them. This monthly flag-wise statement should be forwarded by the ports to the Directorate-General of Shipping (Central Agency) and the Directorate-General should compile and publish the figures in its monthly Bulletin.

The Flags For Commodity Flag-wise Statement

The commodity flag-wise statement should be maintained under the following flags:

1. Indian, 2. British, 3. Dutch, 4. Danish, 5. Greek, 6. Italian, 7. Japanese, 8. Norwegian, 9. Panamanian, 10. Pakistani, 11. Swedish, 12. U.S., 13. Canadian, 14. German, 15. French, 16. Liberian, 17. Belgian, 18. Chinese, 19. Russian, 20. Burmese, 21. Ceylonese, 22. All other flags.

Commodity Region-wise Statements

Every port should maintain a monthly region-wise commodity statement giving separate figures for the total tonnage of each commodity mentioned in the Schedule of Commodities, imported from or exported to these regions. The ports should forward every month this monthly region-wise commodity statement to the Directorate-General of Shipping (Central Agency), which should compile and publish the figures in its monthly Bulletin on an all-India basis.

The Regions For Commodity Region-wise Statement

The region-wise commodity statement should be maintained, both for imports and exports, for the following regions:

Coastal Trade

1. West Bengal, 2. Orissa, 3. Madras, 4. Andhra, 5. Travancore-Cochin, 6. Cochin Port, 7. Bombay, 8. Saurashtra, Okha and Cutch, 9. French Indian Possessions, 10. Indian Portuguese Possessions.

Adjacent Trades

11. Pakistan, 12. Ceylon, 13. Burma.

Overseas Trades

14. Malaya and Straights, 15. Other South East Asian Countries, 16. Japan, 17. China, 18. Persian Gulf Ports, 19. Saudi Arabia and Red Sea Ports, 20. Other Asian Countries, 21. Egypt, 22. East Africa, 23. South Africa, 24. Other African Countries, 25. Australia and New Zealand, 26. United Kingdom, 27. France, 28. Belgium, 29. Netherlands, 30. Germany, 31. Scandinavian Countries, 32. Union of Soviet Socialist Republics, 33. Other European Countries, 34. Canada, 35. United States of America, 36. Central America, 37. South America, 38. All other countries.

Commodities Carried In Coastal Trade By Non-Indian Ships

The Directorate-General of Shipping should maintain tonnages of the commodities which are carried in the coastal trade by ships of non-Indian flags. These figures should be shown separately in the monthly Bulletin, which should be published by the Directorate in its monthly Bulletin.

Tonnages Of Commodities Imported And Exported

The ports should send a monthly statement giving separate figures of the tonnages of commodities, imported and exported, broken up into "by steamer" and "by sailing vessel", in coastal and foreign trade to the Directorate-General of Shipping (Central Agency) and the Directorate-General should compile and publish the figures on an all-India basis in its monthly Bulletin.

Line-wise And Agent-wise Statements

The ports should send separately monthly statements of the tonnages, of imports and xeports, brought or carried by different shipping companies as well as by the shipping companies under different agencies to the Directorate-General of Shipping (Central Agency) and the Directorate-General should compile and publish the figures on an all-India basis in its monthly Bulletin.

Flag-wise Statements

The ports should send monthly flag-wise statements, showing the total number of vessels, total tonnages of imports and exports brought or carried by each flag, broken up into coastal and foreign, to the Directorate-General of Shipping (Central Agency) and the Directorate-General should compile and publish the same on an all-India basis in its monthly Bulletin.

Same Bottom Cargo Not Discharged In India And Transhipment Cargo

The port should send monthly statements showing particulars of total tonnage of transhipment cargo at every port and the particulars of the same bottom cargo not to be discharged at any port in India only at the first port of call of the vessel, to the Directorate-General of Shipping (Central Agency) and the Directorate-General shall compile and publish the same on an all-India basis in its monthly Bulletin.

Dry Cargo Vessels And Tankers

The ports, where tankers call, should furnish a monthly statement showing the number of dry cargo vessels and tankers and total tonnages of imports and exports carried by them to the Directorate-General of Shipping and that the Directorate should compile and publish the same on an all-India basis in its monthly Bulletin.

Shipping Statistics

Standard Definitions For Certain Statistical Terms

The following statistical terms should be defined as under:

(1) Coastal Ports: All ports lying on the coast of Indian Union, together with the ports within the French and Portuguese territories in India.

(2) Foreign Ports: Ports other than the Coastal Ports, as defined above.

(3) Coastal Cargo: Any cargo imported into a port of India from any other Indian coastal port or any cargo exported from a port in India to another Indian coastal port.

(4) Foreign Cargo: Any cargo imported into a port of India from a port other than an Indian coastal port of any cargo exported from a port of India to a port other than a coastal port of India.

(5) Coastal Trade: Import or export trade at an Indian port with a port other than an Indian coastal port.

(6) Foreign Trade: Import or export trade at an Indian port with a port other than an Indian coastal port.

(7) Arrivals and Departures: Every port will show the number and net registered tonnages of vessels arrived and departed—irrespective of the fact whether it was running in the Coastal or Foreign Trade.

(8) Entries and Clearances in Foreign Trade: A vessel will be treated as entered in foreign trade when it arrives from a foreign port at the first port in India. Similarly, a vessel will be treated as cleared in foreign trade when it leaves for a foreign port at the last port in India. If, however, the vessel carries no cargo, it will be shown as entered in foreign trade in ballast at the first port in India and cleared in foreign trade in ballast at the last port in India.

(9) Arrivals and Departures in Coasting Trade: Vessels engaged in exclusively coastal trade will be recorded as Arrivals and Departures in Coasting Trade. There will be no such items as entries and clearances in Coasting Trade.

Shipping Statistics To Be Maintained By Ports

The ports should maintain figures showing the number and N.R.T. of all vessels, steamers and sailing vessels separately, with cargo and in ballast, arrived and departed for their own use.

Essential Items In Arrival And Departure Reports

Every vessel should submit an "Arrival Report" when it arrives at a port and "Departure Report" when it leaves a port to the Port Authorities at all the ports, Major and Minor. While it will be competent for each port to have its own Arrival and Departure Report forms, each of such forms must contain the following essential items for the collection of shipping and passenger statistics by the ports themselves.

Arrival Report

(1) Name of the Vessel.
(2) Name of the Master.
(3) Name of the Agents or Charterers.
(4) Name of the Line.
(5) Nationality of the Flag.
(6) Gross Registered Tonnage.
(7) Net Registered Tonnage.
(8) Name of the First Port the Vessel left on voyage.
(9) Names of the Intermediate Ports and the Last Port the vessel left.
(10) Whether the vessel is carrying any cargo or arrived in ballast.
(11) If carrying cargo, Approximate Deadweight Tonnage of cargo carried for discharge at the port.

From ... Tons ...
From ... Tons ...
From ... Tons ...
From ... Tons ...

(12) Approximate Deadweight Tonnage of the cargo which the vessel is carrying but will not discharge at any Indian port.

From ... to ... Tons.

(13) If carrying passengers, number of passengers:

Saloon
Total
Unberthed
Embarked from

Departure Report

(14) If carrying mails, number of packages and Deadweight Tonnage.

(1) Name of the Vessel.
(2) Name of the Master.
(3) Name of the Agents or Charterers.
(4) Name of the Line.
(5) Nationality of the Flag.
(6) Net and Gross Registered Tonnage.
(7) Whether leaving with Cargo or in Ballast.
(8) If leaving with Cargo, Deadweight Tonnage of Cargo and the Name of the Port of Destination.

Tonnage ... Port ...
Tonnage ... Port ...
Tonnage ... Port ...
Tonnage ... Port ...

(9) Next Port of Call.
(10) Final Port of Call.
(11) Intermediate Ports of Call.
(12) If carrying passengers embarked from the port (separately for each port of disembarkation), number of passengers:

Saloon
Unberthed
Total
Port of Disembarkation

(13) If carrying passengers not embarked at the port, number of passengers:

Saloon
Deck
Total
Port of Disembarkation

(14) If carrying mails, number of packages and approximate tonnage.

Basic Documents For Shipping Statistics In Case Of Sailing Vessels

The basic documents for ports for collecting Shipping Statistics in respect of sailing vessels should be the Arrival and Departure Reports which the sailing vessels must submit to the ports.

Shipping Statistics To Be Maintained By Customs And Sent To D.G. Shipping

The Customs Authorities should maintain the following shipping statistics:

(i) Figures showing number and N.R.T. of vessels, steamers and sailing vessels separately with cargo and in ballast entered and cleared in foreign trade. The figures should be maintained both region-wise and flag-wise as at present.

(ii) Figures showing number and N.R.T. of vessels, steamers and sailing vessels separately with cargo and in ballast arrived and departed in coasting trade.

(iii) Figures showing number and N.R.T. of all vessels, steamers and sailing vessels separately with cargo and in ballast, arrived at or departed from a port.

The Customs Authorities should send these figures monthly and annually to the Directorate-General of Shipping (Central Agency) and the Directorate-General should compile and publish the figures on an all-India basis in its Bulletin. The Director-General of Shipping in consultation with the Customs Authorities should examine the existing forms and registers kept by the Customs for recording shipping statistics and make suitable modifications and introduce such new forms as may be found necessary.

Classification Of Ships According To Flags

The present system of classification of ships as "Indian", "British" and "Foreign", for the purposes of maintenance of shipping statistics by the Customs Authorities, has been examined. In future there should be two broad classifications, viz., "Indian" and "Non-Indian". The non-Indian ships will be again broken up into different flags.

Passenger Statistics

Passenger Statistics To Be Maintained By Ports

Every port should maintain figures showing the total number of passengers, according to regions of travel broken up into Saloon and Deck, but the ports which are maintaining more detailed statistics at present should continue to do so.

Basic Documents For Passenger Statistics To Be Maintained By Ports

Every vessel should submit an Arrival Report when it arrives at a port and a Departure Report when it leaves a port to the Port Authorities at all ports, Major and Minor. While it will be competent for each port to have its own Arrival and Departure Report Forms, each of such forms must contain certain essential items already mentioned in Para 618 for the collection of shipping and passenger statistics.

Basic Documents For Statistics Of Passengers By Sailings Vessels

The basic documents for the ports to collect statistics of passengers arriving or departing by sailing vessels should be the Arrival and Departure Reports.

How Passenger Statistics In Foreign Trade To Be Maintained

As more detailed information about passengers than what is maintained by ports is necessary, the statistics of passengers leaving India or arriving in India from abroad should contain information about the class of travel, sex, age, nationality, region, profession or calling and the object and duration of visit of the passengers.

How Passenger Statistics In Coastal Trade To Be Maintained

In case of passengers in the coastal traffic, only the total number of passengers, broken up into Saloon and Deck, from one port to another should be maintained.

Shipping Companies To Furnish Statements For Passengers

Information in regard to passengers entering or leaving India should be collected from the shipping companies.

Returns To Be Submitted By Ships In Case Of Passengers In Foreign Trade

Every ship arriving from abroad at an Indian port with passengers, or leaving for foreign ports with passengers from an Indian port, should furnish to the Directorate-General of Shipping (Central Agency), through the Port Authorities, immediately after arrival of the ship and before the departure of the ship, lists of passengers, one for passengers disembarking and the other for passengers embarking, in accordance with the forms given in Appendix XXV and Appendix XXVI respectively. The Directorate-General should compile and publish the figures, on an all-India basis, in its monthly Bulletin.

Returns To Be Submitted By Shipping Companies In Case Of Passengers In Coastal Trade

Every shipping company, licensed to carry passengers in the coastal traffic, should send, for each of its Lines, a monthly statement in the form shown in Appendix XXVII to the Directorate-General of Shipping and the Directorate-General should compile and publish the figures, on an all-India basis, in its monthly Bulletin.

Other Statistics To Be Maintained By Ports And Published By The Directorate-General Of Shipping

Turn-Round Of Ships

The reports of the turn-round of ships should be furnished once in every three months by the ports to the Directorate-General of Shipping (Central Agency) and the Directorate-General should publish the reports once in every three months in its Bulletin.

Port Facilities, Etc.

Every port should send an annual statement to the Directorate-General of Shipping (Central Agency) giving full particulars of the facilities available at that port, such as berths, jetties, docks, cranes, transit sheds, warehouses, facilities for supply of water, bunkering, flotilla, dry docks, etc. The Directorate-General should compile the same, on an all-India basis, and publish it once in every three years in its Bulletin.

Officers Handling Ships At Ports

Every port should send an annual statement to the Directorate-General of Shipping (Central Agency) giving the strength of the different categories of officers at the ports who handle ships. The Directorate-General should compile these figures on an all-India basis and publish the same once a year in its Bulletin.

Labour Statistics

Every port should submit an annual report to the Directorate-General giving a broad picture of the output of labour in handling cargo and the cost which the port incurs in doing so. The report should also give particulars of the average number of the port labour employed under the different services which the port renders to trade and shipping. The Directorate-General should publish the reports on an all-India basis once a year.

Statistics Maintained Are To Be Maintained By The Directorate-General Of Shipping

Register Of Indian Ships

The Register of Indian Ships, at present maintained by the Directorate-General of Shipping, should be amplified so that further details might be kept. The particulars shown in this Register should be published annually in the Directorate-General's Bulletin.

Register Of Sailing Vessels

A separate Register should be maintained by the Directorate-General of Shipping for sailing ves sels. The particulars given in this Register should be published annually in the Directorate-General's Bulletin.

Casualty Register

The "Casualty Register" at present maintained by the Directorate-General of Shipping should be amplified as shown in Para 327.

Register Of Sea Personnel

The Directorate-General of Shipping should maintain a Monthly Register showing the position of the Executive and Engineering Officers and the crew employed by Indian Shipping Companies in a certain form as shown in Para 362. The particulars shown in this Register should be published annually in the Directorate-General's Bulletin.

Losses And Gains Of Sea Personnel

The figures in respect of gains and losses of the Officers and Ratings of the Indian Merchant Navy should be collected and maintained, in accordance with the form shown in Appendix XVII, and such statistics should be published in the Directorate-General of Shipping's monthly Bulletin.

Register Of Indian Shipping Companies

The Directorate-General of Shipping should maintain a register showing information about the Indian Shipping Companies under certain heads.

Construction And Launching Of Ships

The Directorate-General of Shipping should collect information of ships constructed, launched and under construction in India, every quarter, and should publish the same on an all-India basis once in every three months in its Bulletin.

Vessels Laid Up Or Under Repairs

The Directorate-General of Shipping should collect particulars about Indian ships laid up or under repairs and should compile and publish, on an all-India basis, these figures every month in its Bulletin.

Training Institution For Sea Personnel

The Directorate-General of Shipping should collect information in regard to the training institutions for training sea personnel that exist in India and those that may come into existence in future and should also compile information on an all-India basis in regard to the cadets, officers and seamen, trained by such institutions. The particulars should be published on an all-India basis by the Directorate-General once a year in its Bulletin.

Further Statutory Powers Necessary For The Following: For Passenger Statistics In The Foreign Trade

As regards the statistics in respect of passengers arriving from or leaving for foreign countries, which would have to be collected by the Directorate-General of Shipping from the returns shown in Appendices XXV and XXVI, to be submitted by all Shipping Companies, the Government should obtain the opinion of the Ministry of Law whether the Collection of Statistics Act, 1953, provides for the necessary statutory powers. If the reply is in the negative, the Government should enact necessary legislation as early as possible. The Government should also provide for the required statutory powers when the Indian Merchant Shipping Act is revised.

General

Inception Of An Office Similar To The Statistics And Special Studies Office In The U.S.A.

Both the Government and the Directorate-General of Shipping should carefully examine whether Statistics and Special Studies Office similar to that in the U.S.A. would not be useful in the study of the problems connected with our Maritime Industries.

New Staff At The Ports For Additional Statistics

The collection of the statistics, which the ports have been recommended to maintain, is in the interest of the ports themselves and as such the Port Authorities and the respective State Governments should provide for the necessary staff. Whatever the additional expenditure might be, it should be incurred.

Setting Up And Manning Of The Statistical Branch In The Directorate-General Of Shipping

The Statistical Branch to be set up in the Directorate-General of Shipping for collecting, compiling and publishing all the statistics recommended by the Committee should be manned by an adequate, properly trained and competent staff and should be headed by a competent Senior Statistician.

Employment Of System For Mechanization Of Statistics

Considering the range, volume and variety of the statistical work that the Committee's proposals entail, the mechanized system should be introduced in the statistical branch to be set up in the office of the Directorate-General of Shipping.

Statement Showing The Manner Of Collection And Publication Of Statistics On An All-India Basis

A statement showing the Nature of the Statistics, the names of the Collecting Agency, Furnishing Agency, the manner in which such statistics are to be furnished, the names of Agency for Compilation and Publication, and the manner of publication of such statistics, as recommended by the Committee, has been given in a tabular form at the end of Chapter XIII.

COURT OF ENQUIRY ON THE ACCIDENT TO AIR-INDIA DAKOTA VT-AUD ON MAY 9, 1953, NEAR DELHI (PALAM), 1953—REPORT

Delhi, Ministry of Communications, 1953. 44p.

Court : Shri Sankar Saran.
Assessors : Shri V. B. Gandhi; Shri D. Chakraverti.
Secretary : Shri B. S. Gidwani.

APPOINTMENT

The Court of Enquiry on the Accident to Air-India Dakota VT-AUD on May 9, 1953, Near Delhi (Palam) was constituted under the Ministry of Communications' Order of May 12, 1953, in exercise of the powers conferred under Rule 75 of the Indian Aircraft Rules, 1937.

TERMS OF REFERENCE

To make a formal investigation of the accident, which occurred on May 9, 1953, near Delhi to a Dakota aircraft of Air-India Ltd., VT-AUD, while engaged in a scheduled flight from Delhi to Bombay, resulting in the death of all the crew and the passengers on board.

CONTENTS

Introductory; Circumstances of the Accident (Location of Accident; Date and Time Notification issued; Date and Time site of accident first visited; Action taken after crash); Particulars of the Aircraft (Aircraft, Engines, Propellers); Crew (Captain Bhalchandra Yeshwant Mohone; Co-pilot Vishwa Mitter Bali; Supernumerary Pilot R. N. Postvala; Radio Officer W. J. Wadke; Air-hostess Miss G. Lee); Passengers; Maintenance, Inspection and Loading of the Aircraft (Maintenance and Inspection; Loading of the Aircraft);

Briefing of Crew (General; Meteorological; Communication and Navigation Briefing; Air Traffic Control Briefing); The Weather; Site of the Wreckage and Topography of the Surrounding Area; Special Flying Tests; Observations at Site and Description and Distribution of the Wreckage; The Main Wreckage; Flight Control System Wreckage; Discussion of Various Factors as Possible Causes (Operational Safety of Dakota Aircraft; Structural Failure; Engine Failure; Damage During Storm; Caged Artificial Horizon; Cockpit Light Failure; Auto-Pilot in "on" position; Faulty Loading; Fire; Lightning; Hitting an Object in the Air; Shortage of Fuel; Drunkenness of the Members of the Crew; Sabotage; Locked Ailerons; Crew Fatigue; Sensory Illusion; Pilot's Error of Judgment); Findings; Conclusion; Recommendations.

RECOMMENDATIONS

With a view to the preservation of life and the avoidance of accidents in future, the Court makes the following recommendations:

The existing rule that unlicensed personnel should not fly the aircraft should be strictly enforced and anyone acting in contravention or in abetment thereof should be severely dealt with.

Although we are satisfied in this case that the crew took no alcoholic drink, we recommend that a provision should be made in the Indian Aircraft Rules that none of the operating crew of an aircraft should have any alcoholic or intoxicating drink, sedative, narcotic or stimulant drug or preparation within 12 hours of the commencement of the flight or during the flight.

The existing regulations that the Captain of the aircraft (or the Flight Despatcher where a company employs such an officer) should personally obtain briefing should be strictly enforced.

The briefing should be given to the members of the crew personally by the officers competent to do so.

A senior officer of the operator should be present at the time of departure of a scheduled service from a terminal station to ensure that both the engineering and operational staff of the operator carry out their respective duties in accordance with the regulations and procedures laid down.

The Proficiency or Instrument and Route Checks of Pilots should be carried out frequently by Government Check Pilots. The number of Government Check Pilots should be increased to enable them to cope with the thorough and frequent checks of Pilots.

Co-pilots should receive an Instrument or Proficiency Check once a year. The new Captains, that is, those with less than one year's service as Commanders, should be given a Proficiency or Instrument Check at frequent intervals, roughly every quarter. In the case of Captains with over one year's service as Pilots-in-Command, their Proficiency and Instrument Checks may be less frequent, say, once in every six months. The procedure of checking to be followed for these checks can be laid down by the Civil Aviation administration.

The Check Pilots appointed by the Government should be qualified, experienced and competent to fly the type of aircraft on which the check is to be carried out. They should themselves be subjected to checks at least once a year by independent and competent Check Pilots.

It should be ensured that proper use is made by the Pilots of the Cockpit Check Lists. A pilot should not be permitted to rely on his memory in preference to the Cockpit Check Lists. These Lists should be as detailed and thorough as possible and should include all critical items and emergency procedures. Disciplinary action should be taken against Pilots not making proper use of Cockpit Check Lists.

Adequate link training equipment and sufficient number of Instructors should be made available in India for airline pilot training. The cost of training during the course of an actual flight has at times proved to be a deterring factor and considering the reduced cost in link training, their provision will encourage airlines to devote greater attention to increasing of Pilot Proficiency.

Uniform standards and procedures of training should be maintained throughout the country in respect of civil aviation personnel. Therefore, the Directorate of Training of the Civil Aviation Department should be strengthened along the latest trends that obtain in other parts of the world.

Standards and recommended practices of the International Civil Aviation Organization relating to Personnel Licensing, as laid down in Annex. I to the Convention on International Civil Aviation, should be implemented by India.

Every opportunity should be utilized to send officers abroad for training and familiarization of the techniques, procedures and standards which prevail in other countries. Opportunities for training in the International Civil Aviation Organization and such other organizations should also be explored.

The Accident Investigation Branch of the Civil Aviation Department should be strengthened to enable them to initiate a thorough study and detailed analysis of the causes of accidents which occur in India and other parts of the world.

A provision should be made to ensure that the Certificate of Safety for Flight issued by an Aircraft Maintenance Engineer of the operators should be handed over to the Pilot personally by the former.

JUTE ENQUIRY COMMISSION, 1953—REPORT

New Delhi, Ministry of Commerce and Industry, 1954. 274, viiip. 3 parts.

Chairman : Shri K. R. P. Aiyangar.
Members : Dr. B. V. Narayanaswamy Naidu; Shri P. S. Gupta; Shri D. Sandilya.
Secretary : Shri T. S. Seshukutty.

APPOINTMENT

The Jute Enquiry Commission was constituted under the Ministry of Commerce and Industry vide their Notification No. 2 (4)-Jute/53 dated August 8, 1953.

TERMS OF REFERENCE

(i) To examine and inquire into the operations of the tiers in the jute industry and trade from the grower of raw jute to the seller of jute goods;

(ii) To examine and inquire into the factors which determine the return to the grower of raw jute for his product and the part played in it by the cost and the adequacy or otherwise of transport, the lack of contact between the grower of raw jute and its consumer, the absence of market information to the growers of raw jute and all matters relating thereto;

(iii) To examine and inquire into the nature and content of speculations both in raw jute trade and the jute goods trade, the extent to which market prices are affected by the operation of millowners, jute dealers and the speculative operators in the market and to consider in relation to the circumstances which rendered the closing of the Fatka market in Calcutta in December, 1952, the malpractices indulged in by the various units that operated in the Fatka market resulting in undue depression of prices of raw jute as well as jute goods;

(iv) And after such examination, inquiry and consideration, to make recommendations to the Central Government on the measures necessary:

(a) To secure for the grower as well as the industry a fair price for raw jute and jute goods;

(b) To put down the malpractices indulged in by certain sectors of the jute industry in order to rig up or depress prices for their own ends; and

(c) To ensure that the jute export trade is not affected by frequent manipulation of the market by interested persons.

The Ministry of Commerce and Industry further desired that the working time agreement of the mills be gone into by the Commission. They also sought the Commission's views on the Assam Government's proposal for the starting of a jute mill in the State.

CONTENTS

Part I: Introductory; Jute—A Historical Retrospect; Supply of Raw Jute—Area and Production; Cultivator's Costs; Marketing of Jute—General; Marketing of Jute—Transport; Marketing of Jute—Indebtedness—Other Handicaps; Marketing of Jute—Classification and Grading; Marketing of Jute—Regulated Markets Co-operatives; Raw Jute—Ancillary Recommendations; The Problem of Prices; **Part II**: Organization and Growth of the Industry; Jute Baling Industry; Mill Purchases; Mill Production and Factors Influencing It; The Export Markets; Costing and Prices of Jute Goods; Basis for Fair Prices of Jute Goods; Interaction of Raw Jute and Jute Goods Prices; Working Time Agreement of Mills; **Part III**: Marketing—Miscellaneous; Jute Statistics; Speculation in Jute Markets; Future Markets; The Need for a Futures Market; Future of Jute Industry; Summary of Conclusions and Recommendations; List of Annexures: Annexure I to XXVI; Appendix I to XIV.

RECOMMENDATIONS

In the long-term interests of jute-growing in India and of the jute industry, the import of jute from Pakistan should be restricted to grades which are not yet available in the required quantity in India.

Railway authorities should examine freight rates and consider the possibility of reduction in rates in view of the export importance of the industry and the incidence to the grower. River transport companies should also evolve a more equitable freight.

The specification of the Indian Standards Institution regarding grades of raw jute should be adopted and applied by the trade and industry.

We recommend the establishment of regulated markets at important centres in the jute-growing areas of each State. Warehouses should also be set up at such markets.

For bettering the conditions of the cultivator the organization of multi-purpose co-operatives is essential and State Governments should give all possible help for this purpose. The scheme should be tried out as an experimental one at important centres.

As jute is the raw material of an important industry, we consider State Governments should not levy Sales Tax or similar taxes on raw jute.

The demand for the establishment of more research-demonstration farms should be given sympathetic consideration.

Use of manures and improved seed should be encouraged with a view to obtaining the Planning Commission's target yield (54 lakh bales) from the minimum acreage.

To assist and stabilize the industry the appointment of a Jute Commissioner, the establishment of a Jute Board and setting up of a Development Council for the industry are recommended.

Indication of fair prices for raw jute in relation to jute goods prices should be an important function of the Board. Notification of such parity of prices is of particular significance to the grower before the sowing season. The prescription of such a price would improve the morale of the grower and support him in his unequal struggle with the middle-men in the trade.

In its struggle for building up and retaining its market in the future, the jute industry must continue vigorous market research and make a more positive endeavour to diversify its pattern of production.

As far as raw jute is concerned, a Fair Price can be determined with reference only to the terminal market, Calcutta.

The Jute Board should examine the appropriateness of the present contract forms in use for markets overseas and make suitable changes in the forms used in India.

The normal arbitration practice should be followed and an award should be precise and complete and not leave the door open for any option to be exercised by either party later. The Indian Chamber of Commerce should also be included in the arbitration panel.

The Pucca Delivery Order has so far been regarded as a document of title to goods on the basis of which discounting facilities have been given freely by banks.

A system of verifying goods against uncashed P.O.S.s is desirable.

We recommend the establishment of a futures market for jute and jute goods. A single well-knit and regulated organization like the East India Cotton Association, Bombay, should be set up.

We recommend that problems connected with modernization of plant and industry in the jute mill industry should receive the highest consideration of the Government.

RAILWAY CORRUPTION ENQUIRY COMMITTEE, 1953—REPORT

New Delhi, Ministry of Railways. 1955. 180, ivp.

Chairman : Shri Hriday Nath Kunzru (resigned, replaced by Acharya J. B. Kripalani).

Members : Shri Sahnawaz Khan; Dr. W. S. Barlingay; Shri K. S. Hedge; Shri K. L. More; Dr. A. Krishnaswami; Shri K. Raghuramiah; Shri P. S. Rajagopal Naidu; Shri Ramsubhag Singh; Shri S. C. Samanta; Shri Sarangadhar Das; Shri M. D. Upadhyay.

Secretary : Shri H. N. Trivedi.

APPOINTMENT

The Railway Corruption Enquiry Committee was constituted under the Ministry of Railways vide their Press Communique dated September 9, 1953.

TERMS OF REFERENCE

To enquire into and report on:

(i) Extent of corruption prevalent among various categories of Railway employees in their dealings with the public.

(ii) Methods adopted by the staff concerned.

(iii) The causes of corruption.

(iv) Responsibility of the using public.

(v) Defects, if any, in the Rules and Regulations which leave loopholes for corruption.

(vi) Remedial measures, both administrative and legal, to eradicate this evil in all its aspects.

CONTENTS

Introductory; Problem of Corruption in its Setting (Approach to the Problem); Booking of Goods and Parcels Traffic (Modes of Corruption; The Amount of Gratification and Categories of Staff Involved; Causes of Corruption; Responsibility of the Using Public; Defects in Rules and Regulations which leave loopholes for corruption); Booking of Passengers and Luggage; Catering and Vending (Policy followed; Subletting; Departmental Catering); Engineering; Compensation Claims on Indian Railways (Causes of high incidence of claims and remedial measures; Crime on Railways; Settlement of Claims; Assessment of Damage to Goods;

Responsibility of the Railways as Carriers; Linking up the Freight Structure with Transit Time); Public Complaints and General Efficiency (Analysis of the Complaints received and dealt with by the Railways; Complaints Organizations on Railways; General Efficiency); Internal Working of the Railways (Modes of corruption among staff *inter se*); Working of the Special Police Establishment (Genesis and Work; Comparative data of the work done; Difficulties experienced by the Special Police Establishment); Working of the Anti-Corruption Organization on the Railways; Administrative Measures (Preventive Measures; Punitive Measures); Legal Measures; Miscellaneous Matters (Pilferage of coal; Thefts of Railway Property excluding coal; Cinder and Ash Contracts; Licensed Porters; Railway Grainshops; Railway Service Commissions Light Railways; Stores Departments on Railways); Conclusion; Summary of Recommendations; Appendix I to XIII.

RECOMMENDATIONS

A concentrated drive should be made and sustained for a long period for removal of corruption.

When there is suspicion about an officer's integrity, his actions, his financial position and the financial position of such of his relatives and close friends as seem to be enjoying a luxurious life should be investigated. He should not in any case be kept in any position of responsibility or influence.

There should be a steady drive for improving wagon position.

Procedure for the booking of goods should be made more uniform on all Railways. A chapter should be added in the Goods Tariff laying down a clear procedure for indent, allotment and supply of wagons.

Information about the quotas in force, the current restrictions and the day-to-day allotment orders should be exhibited on the notice boards and should also be supplied to local Chambers of Commerce or other mercantile associations. Where no such association exists, the higher officials should try to help the merchants to organize it.

Railway Receipts should be issued on the day the consignments are accepted for booking.

There should be advance planning and adequate arrangements for clearance of seasonal perishable traffic.

The bottlenecks at the transhipment points should be eliminated by increasing the transhipment capacity.

Brokers who transact business at stations be licensed by the Railways.

Entry into marshalling yards and goods sheds should be suitably regulated by issue of identity cards or otherwise to eliminate unauthorized entry.

Monthly suburban tickets should have a photograph and signature of the owner of the ticket to facilitate check and avoid misuse.

A reasonable limit should be fixed to the luggage allowed with the passengers in the compartment and the balance should be put in the brake-van.

The members of the National Railway Users' Consultative Council, authorized to conduct surprise checks through the Ticket Checking Staff, should make one surprise check each at least every three months and submit brief reports to the Council for scrutinizing and suggesting further measures.

Ticket-checking on trains must be enforced as a regular measure so that no traveller normally goes unchecked, the minimum checks being (i) at the entraining station; (ii) at the detraining station; and (iii) en route, on long journeys at every junction.

Surprise checks should be kept strictly secret and the plans therefore should be made and supervised at high levels. The out-of-course stoppage of a through train for a concentrated check would be useful.

There should be a certain number of Ticket Checking Staff in plain clothes with proper letters of authority to make surprise checks to catch ticketless passengers.

Booking facilities at stations should be reviewed from time to time and increased where necessary.

All station entrances and exits should be controlled properly and proper fencing provided.

The strength of Ticket Collectors should be increased at rush periods.

The stoppage of passenger trains outside signals should be avoided as far as possible.

Cases of ticketless travelling by responsible officials and students should be reported to the higher authorities who should take prompt and drastic action.

Ticket Checking Staff who, at personal risk, face intimidation and help in checking organized ticketless travel should be rewarded. Police protection should also be afforded to such Ticket Checking Staff where trouble is apprehended.

No leniency should be shown in proved cases of harassment of poor and illiterate villagers by the Railway Staff. Removal from service is the only suitable punishment in such cases.

Higher authorities should pay special attention to cases of molestation by the Railway Staff to lady passengers.

The system of giving refreshment and vending contracts to big contractors should be abolished.

The practice of station staff having free supplies of tea and refreshments from the vending and catering contractors should be put a stop to by proper supervision and by taking disciplinary action against staff guilty of it.

The licence fees from the vending contractors should

be taken in advance and outstanding arrears due from them cleared up without delay.

Refreshments and meals on trains should be provided at popular prices by the Department.

Constant vigilance will be necessary to check corrupt practices in Departmental Catering.

Drastic action should be taken against staff involved in theft of Railway property.

Recruitment of casual labour and temporary staff should be kept to the minimum.

A post of Claims Prevention Officer in the Senior Scale should be created on each Railway.

Complaint Books should be provided at all stations, in the Refreshment Rooms, Dining Cars and important Goods Sheds. Complainants should have easy access to them without asking for them from a Railway employee.

Complaint Books at Stations, in Refreshment Rooms and in Goods Sheds should be scrutinized daily by the Station Master who should send a copy of the complaint to the higher authorities with his remarks within 24 hours.

Complaints should be dealt with at a level not lower than that of a District or Divisional Officer.

Recruitment of Class IV staff should be done only through Recruitment Boards with some officers belonging to Departments other than those for which recruitment is made.

Chairmen of the Railway Service Commissions should not, as far as possible, be retired Government officials.

The question of honesty and integrity of the candidates should be given greater emphasis while considering them for promotion from Class III to Class II.

Removal of Railway material from the Railway workshops for private use by the employees should be viewed seriously. Greater supervision, proper accountal and stock verification will minimize such irregularities.

Complaints regarding misuse of Railway labour by officers and staff should be properly investigated.

Names of Informers and Railway Servants who help the Special Police Establishment in investigation should be kept confidential to avoid possibility of victimization. Complaints of victimization should be promptly looked into by an Officer of not less than Administrative Rank.

Requests from the Special Police Establishment for transfer of accused Railway servants should be promptly agreed to.

In proved cases of bribery and corruption, punishment must be swift and deterrent. Appropriate fines should invariably form part of the punishment.

Anti-Corruption Organizations on Railways should be separated from Security Organizations of Railways and placed under an officer of Senior Administrative Rank on each Railway, loaned from a Government Department other than the Railway and designated as Chief Investigating Officer. He should be assisted by an Anti-Corruption Officer in senior scale. He should maintain close co-ordination with the Chief Security Officer and the General Manager. He should be responsible for the work of this Organization to the Railway Board directly.

The Anti-Corruption Organization should not depend merely on complaints but should on its own initiate probes into the working of the various Departments and unearth cases involving bribery, corruption and frauds. For this purpose, there should be a Detective Force under this Organization.

Wider publicity should be given to the existence of the Anti-Corruption Organizations on the Railways by suitable notices to be inserted in the public time-tables and Railway Gazettes and by posters. Names and designations of the Railway staff punished in corruption cases should be published in the Railway Gazettes, giving the nature of offence committed and the punishment inflicted.

The Efficiency Bureau of the Railway Board's Office should analyse the quantum of work performed by Gazetted Officers in various Departments and suggest measures for reduction of desk work, increase in supervision work, and also suggest if any increase in the strength of Class I and II staff is necessary.

Rules of Conduct of Railway employees in relation to the public should be made known to the public. They may be given in a summarized form in Railway time-tables.

Exceptional and outstanding work should receive special recognition by grant of honoraria, letters of appreciation and medals, honoraria being confined to non-Gazetted employees only. Successful efforts of an officer to root out corruption should be a qualification for accelerated promotion.

Disparity in the emoluments of the lowest-paid and highest-paid Government employees should be narrowed down.

Suitable publicity should be given to the various facilities available to the employees, particularly those in lower categories. There should be constant propaganda through posters, pamphlets and films both among the public and the Railway staff bringing home the evils of corruption. The public should also be warned, through posters at all the Railway stations and through microphones and loudspeakers at certain selected larger stations, against offering illegal gratification and should be informed that thereby they make themselves liable to criminal prosecution.

Passengers' Associations and Chambers of Commerce should make it a rule that an individual or a firm found to have indulged in offering illegal gratification will be debarred from membership of these bodies. They should come forward with information and evidence if they have knowledge when a charge of corruption is made against a Railway employee.

Surprise re-weighments of the wagons loaded with coal should be conducted and drastic action taken against staff responsible for over-weighments.

Provision of expanded metal cover, fencing of stacking areas and proper lighting, better watch and ward arrangements and strict supervision would minimize pilferage of coal.

There should be stricter physical verification of stock both at the time of purchase as well as at suitable intervals.

There should be independent spot checks on all transactions of the Stores Department by the Audit.

COMMITTEE ON FINANCE FOR THE PRIVATE SECTOR, 1953—REPORT

Bombay, Reserve Bank of India, 1954. 162p.

Chairman : Shri A. D. Shroff.

Members : Shri J. V. Joshi; Shri S. Anantharamakrishnan; Shri C. W. Middleton; Shri B. T. Thakur; Shri V. R. Sonalker; Shri B. K. Dutt.

Joint Secretaries : Shri M. S. Nadkarni; Dr. K. S. Krishnaswamy.

APPOINTMENT

The Committee on Finance for the Private Sector was constituted under the Reserve Bank of India vide their Press Communique dated October 5, 1953.

TERMS OF REFERENCE

(i) To examine why investment in the private sector has not reached the level envisaged in the First Five Year Plan and in this connection to consider the factors, other than taxation, which influence investment in this sector;

(ii) To examine how increased finance could be made available to the private sector through sources other than those which are under the consideration of the Taxation Enquiry Commission; and

(iii) In particular, to examine the possibility of providing on a larger scale bank finance for development in the private sector.

CONTENTS

Introductory; Role of the Private Sector in the Five Year Plan; Factors Inhibiting Investment in the Private Sector; Existing Agencies for Industrial Finance in India; Credit Expansion and Development; Commercial Banks and Industrial Finance; Indigenous Bankers and Money-lenders; Long-term Financial Requirements of Industries; Small-Scale Industries; Special Institutions for Providing Finance to Industries; Summary of Recommendations; Appendices.

RECOMMENDATIONS

The Committee feels that in the past few years several changes have occurred in the socio-economic climate of this country which tend to discourage and discredit private enterprise. The Committee is of the opinion that unless these inhibiting factors are remedied, mere multiplication or strengthening of agencies supplying finance will not add much to industrial development.

In respect of large investments in scheduled industries which take time to fructify, it should be possible for the Government to give some assurance of immunity from nationalization, at least for a reasonable period.

The Committee considers it essential that the work of the several authorities from which licences or sanctions have to be obtained should be co-ordinated and the procedure for obtaining such licences or sanctions should be simplified and rationalized.

The Committee considers it desirable that the technical organization in Government Ministries should be adequately strengthened so as to provide in course of time the specialized services of these agencies to private parties also in drawing up plans for expansion. The attitude of such Departments should be to assist applicants in completing the necessary technical details.

Early steps should be taken to remove the confusions and uncertainties in regard to labour legislations and Awards and to ensure that a rise in the rewards of labour does not run ahead of the increase in the productivity of labour.

Organized bodies of business men and industrialists should make all possible effort to enforce proper codes of conduct and to raise the standards of business management and morality.

The Reserve Bank should take up with the Government the question of obtaining promptly and systematizing the data relating to joint stock companies.

Banks should endeavour to increase their investments in the shares and debentures of first-class industrial concerns, to make larger advances to approved parties against such shares and debentures and subscribe to a greater extent to the shares and bonds of specialized institutions like the Industrial Finance Corporation of India and the State Financial Corporations.

The Reserve Bank should treat shares and bonds of the Industrial Finance Corporation of India and State Financial Corporations on a par with Government securities for advances under Section 17(4)(a) of the Reserve Bank of India Act, on such terms regarding margin, etc., as the Reserve Bank may deem appropriate. In order to ensure the marketability of these shares, the statutory restrictions on the holdings of such shares should be removed.

In view of the steep rise in the operating costs of banks in recent years as a result of the Awards given by various Industrial Tribunals, the Committee recommends that the Government of India should immediately appoint an Expert Committee to examine, among other things, ways and means of rationalizing the wage and salary structure in the banking sector and to explore possible avenues of reducing the burden of operating costs to banks.

Having regard to the peculiar difficulties of the smaller banks, the Committee suggests for the consideration of the Reserve Bank of India whether any of the directives or criteria laid down by the Bank could be suitably relaxed, without prejudice to sound banking principles, in view of the special characteristics of the smaller banks such as their deposit structure, and other local conditions.

Facilities under the Bill Market Scheme should be made available to all scheduled banks with deposits of Rs. 1 crore or over. Further, the individual minimum amount for bills should be reduced from Rs. 1 lakh to Rs. 50,000 and for parcels of bills from Rs. 25 lakhs to Rs. 10 lakhs.

The Committee recommends that the Reserve Bank of India should, in consultation with the Government of India, work out a detailed scheme of financial assistance to licensed scheduled banks opening branches in accordance with an expansion programme submitted by the banks and approved by the Reserve Bank. The assistance may for instance take the form of a lump-sum to cover part of the initial expenses of the branch and a commission in respect of deposits collected over a prescribed minimum. The Reserve Bank may also consider the desirability of not allowing more than one banking office to be opened in an undeveloped area for a limited period, say, up to five years.

Mobile banks have useful potentialities in developing the banking habit and should therefore be encouraged and supported.

An All-India Association of Banks should be brought into being at the earliest possible moment for protecting the interests of bankers and reaching agreements on matters of common interest.

The question of linking indigenous Bankers and Shroffs directly with the Reserve Bank should be actively pursued by the Bank in consultation with the Shroffs.

The Government should examine, in consultation with insurance interests, the various anomalies in the Insurance Act, with a view to removing them.

The Industrial Finance Corporation of India and the State Financial Corporations should give banks an opportunity to participate in the loans sanctioned by them. The Corporations should also examine the question of guaranteeing long-term loans advanced by Scheduled Banks or Insurance Companies.

The limit of Rs. 1 crore prescribed in Section 24 of the Industrial Finance Corporation Act for advances to any single concern should be relaxed in the case of key industries.

The Central and State Governments should explore the possibility of opening Letters of Credit in favour of suppliers stipulating for payments on the presentation of Inspection Notes by a duly authorized officer of the Indenting Department.

The Government of India should take steps to amend the State Financial Corporations Act, 1951, in a manner that will permit joint working of a financial corporation by two or more adjoining States.

In order to augment the finance available to small industries, a Special Development Corporation for small industries should be constituted immediately.

The proposed Special Development Corporation for small industries should, through a separate and specialized department, take a lead in organizing the small industries and rendering assistance in the matter of co-operative or joint purchase of raw materials, standardization of products, organized marketing, distribution and publicity.

A Central organization for the provision of technical and managerial assistance to industries should be set up jointly by the Government, special financial institutions like the Industrial Finance Corporation of India, the privately-owned Industrial Development and Finance Corporation, etc., and private industries.

MODEL PUBLIC HEALTH ACT COMMITTEE, 1953—REPORT

New Delhi, Ministry of Health, 1955. 203, 29p.

Chairman : Dr. B. C. Das Gupta.
Members : Dr. K. S. Viswanathan; Dr. W. Mathur; Shri P. C. Bose.
Secretary : Dr. K. C. Patnaik.

APPOINTMENT

The Model Public Health Act Committee was constituted under the Ministry of Health vide letter No. F-1411/53-PH II dated October 6, 1953.

TERMS OF REFERENCE

(i) To draw up a model comprehensive Public Health Act, which the various States in India may enact with such modifications as may be necessary to suit local conditions. Such an Act will aim at serving the following purposes:

(a) To bring together existing legal provisions relating to health, which are scattered over various enactments;

(b) To modify those sections of the law which require change in the light of recent advances in knowledge with a view to promoting efficient administration;

(c) To incorporate the new provisions which will be necessary for the development of future health programmes of the States; and

(d) To embrace, on the basis of the recommendations of the Environmental Hygiene Committee, all phases of Environmental Hygiene, such as Housing, Provision and Maintenance of Safe Water Supply, General Sanitation, including Conservancy and Drainage, Prevention of River and Beach Pollution, Control of Insect Vectors of Diseases, Regulation of Certain Trades, Industries and Occupations dangerous to health and offensive to community; and

(ii) To recommend, after surveying the existing position, suitable bye-laws for the fixation of standards of pipe-water supply, sewage systems, sullage drains, sanitary latrines, public cleaning, refuse collection and sewage disposal, septic tanks, pollution of streams and beaches, slaughter-houses, healthful housing, town and village planning, industrial environments and disposal of trade wastes and various other items connected with environmental sanitation.

CONTENTS

Part I: Administration—Boards, Councils and Committees; Organization of the State Health Services; State Health Services; State Public Health Engineering Services; Model Relief and Public Health Services of the Local Authorities; Health Officers and Health Engineers of Local Authorities. **Part II**: Medical Relief and Public Health Measures—Hospitals, Dispensaries and Clinics; Prevention and Control of Infectious Diseases; Vaccination; School Health Services; Maternity and Child Welfare Services; Control and Prevention of Leprosy; Control and Prevention of Tuberculosis; Venereal Diseases and Prostitution; Aftercare Homes and Houses for Invalids; Nursing Homes; Ophthalmic Services; Treatment of Rabies; Blood Bank; Mental Health Services; Social Welfare Services; Vagrants; Nutrition; Laboratory Services; Ambulance Services. **Part III**: Sanitation—Water Supply; Collection and Disposal of Community Wastes; Town and Village Planning; Housing; Improvement of Slum and Bustee Areas; Improvement Trust; Control of Malaria and other mosquito-borne diseases; Places of Pilgrimage; Health Resorts; Holiday Camps; Park, Playground and Open Spaces; Miscellaneous Institutions; Fairs and Festivals; Burial and Burning Ground; Lodging Houses; Eating Houses; Markets; Control of Foodstuffs; Milk Supply; Drug Control; Cosmetics; Slaughter-Houses; Factories; Offensive Trades; Registration of Births and Deaths; Nuisances; Disinfection; Plumbers. **Part IV**: General Provisions—Financial Provisions; Miscellaneous; Penalties; Definitions; Schedules I to IV; Appendices I to XIII.

RECOMMENDATIONS

The recommendations of the Committee defining the standards and other particulars in connection with various items of environmental sanitation, which might be found suitable for incorporation in the rules or bye-laws to be framed by the State Governments or the Local Authorities, as the case may be, under the Model Public Health Act, are given in the Appendix.

Town And Village Planning

Basic Requirements Of Site Selection

Regard may be had to the following conditions for heathful development and maintenance in the selection of a site:

(a) Sub-soil condition should afford suitable bearing capacity for economical construction of buildings of the types contemplated. Bearing capacity will be adversely affected if the site contains muck, peat, poorly compacted fill, shifting sand or quicksand.

(b) Essential factors in site selection include a water table low enough to protect against flooding and interference with sewerage, the absence of swamps or marshes and sufficient slope to permit surface drainage of normal rainfall and free flow of sanitary sewers. Periodic flooding due to high ground water table should disqualify a site unless preventive measures can be applied. High ground water may cause dampness beneath the buildings. Flooding due to ground water may occur not only through conditions on the site itself, but also from present or future drainage onto the site from adjacent areas.

(c) The development area should be free from danger of surface flooding by streams, lakes or tidal waters.

(d) Land should not be too steep for satisfactory grading in relation to dwelling construction.

(e) The development area should be free from topographic conditions which might be a serious cause of accidents. Hazards of this type include landslides, earth settlement above disused mine workings and earthquake slippage along known geological fault lines.

Availability Of Sanitary And Protective Services

(a) A healthful town or village can only be developed on a site with water supply that is adequate and certain as to amount, that will not be a means of conveying disease and that is reasonably free from chemical and physical impurities. Equally important is the collection and ultimate disposal of human excreta without sanitary hazard.

(b) It is of utmost importance that before a site is selected, the water and sewerage systems must be visualized as long-term sanitary services. Preference should be given to a site having access to a public system. Where a public water supply is unavailable, it is necessary to be certain that a local supply can be developed at a reasonable cost.

(c) Removal of wastes from the site by a public sewerage system that is properly designed and operated affords the greatest safety, if every residence can be connected to a public sewerage system of sufficient capacity. In the absence of a public sewerage system, an on-site community system is generally safer than septic tanks or other individual installations, provided adequate maintenance is assured.

(d) It is essential that a projected site shall have facilities for the effective removal of domestic wastes —notably garbage—or that ultimate disposal on the site can be provided without sanitary hazard.

Freedom From Local Hazards And Nuisances

(a) The site should be entirely free from grave hazards to life or health, and as free as possible from minor hazards and nuisances.

(b) Residents of the site should not be unduly exposed to sources of animal or insect carriers of disease on or adjoining the site, or to polluted water courses, lakes or ponds. If control or elimination of the sources is not practicable, housing areas should be located outside the range of any substantial breeding places for rodents and insects and of any sizable deposits of refuse which might contribute to the spread of fly-borne or rodent-borne disease.

Water Supply

(a) An adequate supply of safe and potable water, delivered under pressure within the dwellings, is a *sine qua non* of healthful housing.

(b) Where connections to a public supply is not possible, provision must be made for the development of an on-site community supply or for the installation of individual wells.

(c) Whatever the system used, the location, construction operation of the water supply must meet requirements of Public Health authorities having jurisdiction. The Chief Public Health Engineer should be consulted whenever a public supply is not available.

Sewage Disposal

(a) It is essential to plan for the collection of sewage from all dwellings and non-residential structures on the site and for its disposal by one of the following means:

(i) Discharge to an existing public sewerage system;

(ii) Treatment in a community disposal plant;

(iii) Treatment in individual septic tanks with disposal by absorption field or percolation;

(b) Where a public sewerage system is not available, the location and design of on-site community disposal plants and the installation of individual septic tanks or soakage pits should meet the requirements of the Public Health Department of the State Government.

Density And Floor-Space Index

(a) Gross density should be not more than 10 houses to the acre—the maximum allowable should be 20 to the acre. In one or two-storey development in ordinary suburban housing, the floor-space index should be kept below 0.5. Vertical development is optional where land is scarce as in the present congested towns. In places where vertical development is planned, the floor-space index should be limited to 1.5. Where the floor-space index exceeds 1.25, buildings should be planned in open plan forms, staggered so as to offer the least obstruction to light and air.

(b) In new satellite towns and suburban planning, the gross density of population should be about 60 per acre but not more than 120 per acre. To reduce congestion in existing towns, the aim should be to reduce the density to at least 250 per acre.

Roads Classified With Regard To Traffic

In town planning, the roads should be designed to ensure swift movement of traffic consistent with safety. In the places where fast and slow traffic are both likely to use the road, the width should be sufficient for segregation of traffic in lanes. The surface should be suitable for the kind of traffic using it. Through roads should avoid passing through residential areas. They should afford a clear vision avoiding sharp curves and obstructions. Level crossing should be replaced by separation of grades if the volume of traffic is heavy. The width of roads should be fixed in relation to their function and traffic load.

Civic Amenities

In every town and village planning scheme there should be provision for shopping centres, educational institutions, clubs, parks and playgrounds, health centres, hospital, post office and other public offices, places of worship and places for disposal of the dead.

Zoning Of Residential And Industrial Areas

The planning should provide for zoning to segregate industrial areas, big transport centres and godowns, dangerous and offensive trades, and dairies from residential areas and business areas. There should be a thinning out of the population from the centre to the fringes and, if possible, a green belt all round. The planning of the residential areas should ensure a fair mix-up of all social groups and avoid too much segregation.

Population Limits

In planning of new towns, the population should be limited to 100,000.

Planning In Villages

(a) Population to be limited to 5,000.

(b) Gross density should be restricted to 10 houses per acre.

(c) Water supply in the form of wells or tubewells should be provided at one source for every 250 persons.

(d) Houses should be served by proper streets; they should be detached or semi-detached and should have definite space for cowshed and manure pits.

(e) There should be open space for public resort and public utility halls.

Planning of towns and villages to be integrated with the Master Plan of the region.

Healthful Housing

The following points may be given due consideration in the manner of construction of healthful housing accommodation:

(1) The site should have an independent access to a street of adequate width and should be in pleasing surroundings free from hazards of flooding, landslides, fly breeding, mosquito breeding nuisances, dust, smoke, smells and excessive noise. The soil should be dry and safe for founding the structure.

(2) The set-back of the house from the road and the surrounding houses should be such as to make lighting and ventilation through windows effective without obstruction of light and air. The proportion of built-up area to site may not exceed 1:3 in the smaller municipalities and fringes of big cities where the density thins out, but may be 2:3 in the areas of high land values.

(3) A house designed for family life should have independent access with sufficient privacy.

(4) Floor should be impervious. Height of plinth 2′×6″ from centre of public road with adequate damp-proof course.

(5) The walls should have low heat capacity. They should be smooth, easy to keep clean, weather resistant, unsuitable for harbourage of rats or vermin, not easily damaged and reasonably strong against impact.

(6) The roof of the house should be heat-resistant and the height of the rooms should be such as to give an air space of at least 500 cubic feet per capita, preferably 1,000 cubic feet.

(7) The floor area of a living room should be at least 120 square feet for occupancy by more than one person and at least 100 square feet for occupancy by a single person. The floor area available in living rooms per person should be not less than 50 square feet; 100 square feet is recommended as the optimum.

(8) A domestic house should be provided with at least two rooms and one of them should open directly or through an unobstructed verandah on to open space. The windows should be placed at a height not exceeding three feet above ground.

(9) For living rooms, total window openings to be at least 1/15th the floor space and window and door openings combined not to be less than 1/7th floor space.

(10) The house is to have a kitchen of minimum size 8′×6′, adequately lighted by windows (1/5th of floor area) and to have arrangements for storing food, fuel and provisions.

(11) The house is to have an independent source of safe and adequate water supply.

(12) Every house to have a latrine of minimum size 3′0″×2′6″ non-service sanitary type, with floor and seat made of impervious material, and readily accessible.

(13) An enclosed courtyard, open space or terrace of sufficient area should be provided in each house.

(14) In the rural areas, the "approved" standards

may be lower than in towns. The minimum should be a two-roomed house on a dry site with separate access, giving sufficient security. It should be provided with a separate kitchen, a platform for washing utensils, a properly sloped "pucca" drain, and a sanitary latrine; effective windows equal in area to at least 10% of the floor space; a well, tubewell or tap for water supply within the house and in any case within a quarter of a mile from the house; open space in front, within or behind not less than twice the built-up area; separate and adequate accommodation for the animals and implements associated with rural occupations; a manure pit, and arrangements for safe disposal of waste water.

Piped Water Supply

Sources Of Intake And Treatment

(a) Upland water (b) Rain water over a catchment area.	impounding— coagulation— sedimentation — filtration— chlorination — to supply mains.
(c) River or stream water	—intake at suitable place and depth—preliminary settlement — coagulation — sedimentation — filtration— chlorination — to supply mains.
(d) Lake water	—intake at suitable place and depth — coagulation — sedimentation— filtration –chlorination—to supply mains.
(e) Spring water	—impounding—chlorination— to supply mains.
(f) Underground water below impervious strata (drawn by mechanical pumps from tubewells of diam. 4″ or more)	—softening, if necessary— chlorination — to supply mains.

Filtration

(a) Slow sand filter, at the rate of 4″ per square foot per hour

or

(b) Rapid filter, at the rate of 3″ to 4″ per square foot per minute

or

(c) A combination of (a) and (b) as may be advised by the Chief Public Health Engineer of the State.

Chlorination

Chlorination should be done by any of the approved methods or appliances to ensure a residual chlorine at the rate of 0.2 ppm for the water to be supplied irrespective of its source of intake.

Supply Mains

(a) Terminal mains shall have internal diameters not less than 3

(b) Where in any street both water and sewer mains are laid, the water mains shall be at least 3′ vertically above and at a distance of 6′ from the sewer.

Terminal Pressure: Recommended 35′, must not be less than 25′.

Quantity: To be supplied per capita per diem, will vary with the population and the requirements for various purposes, and taking into consideration possible wastage from leaks, defective fittings and careless handling to the extent of nearly 10% of the total supply.

Quality

(a) **General:** Water for drinking and other domestic purposes shall be clear, odourless, palatable, of neutral taste, of reasonable temperature, neither corrosive nor scale-forming.

(b) **Physical Standards:** (i) turbidity—not exceeding 10 ppm on silica scale;

(ii) colour—not exceeding 20 ppm on cobalt scale;

(iii) total solids—500 ppm for good water; maximum permissible 1000 ppm.

(c) **Chemical Standards:** (i) Total Hardness—150 to 200 ppm as Calcium Carbonate is the maximum permissible hardness where the source is other than spring or underground. This may, however, be relaxed up to 250 to 300 ppm under exceptional circumstances.

(ii) Alkalinity: (a) for treated waters Phenolphthalein alkalinity as Calcium Carbonate not to exceed 15 ppm plus 0.4 x total alkalinity at pH 10.6 and 25°C;

(b) normal Carbonate alkalinity not to exceed 120 ppm;

(c) total alkalinity shall not exceed hardness by 35 ppm.

(iii) Chemical Standards: (a) Rigid limits—

Lead...less than 0.1 ppm.

Arsenic...less than 0.05 ppm.

Selenium... ,, ,, 0.05 ppm.

Fluoride ... { not less than 1.00 ppm. / not more than 1.30 ppm.

(b) Limits not so rigid—(limited variation admissible after investigation of local conditions):

Copper ... less than 3 ppm.

Iron & Manganese together less than 0.4 ppm.

Magnesium	...	125 ppm.
Zinc	...	15 ppm.
Chloride	...	500 ppm.
Sulphate	...	250 ppm.
Phenolic Compounds	...	0.001 ppm. in terms of phenol.

Bacteriological Standards

(a) Excellent...no coliform bacilli in 100 c.c.

(b) Satisfactory...1 to 2 coliform bacilli in 100 c.c.

(c) Suspicious...3 to 10 coliform in 100 c.c.

(d) Unsatisfactory or bad...over 10 coliform in 100 c.c.

If in (c) all coliform bacilli are aerogenons and no faecal coli—recommend chlorination.

If 1 to 2 coli type—insist on chlorination.

Hours of Supply: Preferably continuous, but in no case less than eight hours per day.

Dispersed Sources Of Water Supply

Sources: Generally from tubewells, masonry wells, reinforced concrete ring wells or reserved surface tanks.

(i) Tubewells

(a) internal diameter of pipes—1½″ to 2″;

(b) depth—below at least one impervious stratum;

(c) strainers—2 x 6′ each of same diameter as the pipes;

(d) pumps—suitable type to draw 300 to 500 gallons per hour according to size of pipes and strainers;

(e) platform and overflow drain—usually 4′x4′ to 6′x6′ with drain along the sides of the platform to lead to soakpit or suitable point of discharge.

(ii) Masonry Or C.C. Wells

(a) recommended internal diameter—4′;

(b) depth—according to geological condition;

(c) platform and overflow drain—width 3′x4′ sloped outward. The parapet should be sharply sloped on top and not flat;

(d) fittings—the well should be covered and fitted with pump and pipes or provided with a water lifting device or a common rope-and-bucket arrangement over pulley.

Drainage And Sewerage

A. Sewers

(1) To be introduced in areas where adequate water supply is available for the purpose—minimum 5 gallons per capita per diem (exclusive of water required for other purposes).

(2) Minimum diameter of a public sewer to be 6". Minimum diameter of a domestic sewer should be 4".

(3) Velocity of sewage flow to be between 2.5 and 3 ft. per second.

(4) Sewers to be well ventilated—ventilation pipe at the summit and fresh air entry at the lowest point to be provided.

(5) Industrial waste not to be allowed into town sewer without treatment as may be prescribed by the Chief Public Health Engineer.

(6) Flushing chambers to be provided at top end of the sewers.

(7) Manholes to be located at every junction and at intervals of 200 ft. (maximum) on straight lengths. Every manhole to have easy access and working space inside for maintenance and provided with sturdy water-tight cover.

B. Sewage Disposal

(1) Before sewage is discharged into the river, stream or channel or on land, the same to be treated by one or combination of the methods as under and according to the directions of the Chief Public Health Engineer:

(a) Screening and land irrigation after dilution—provided no food crops which are eaten raw are grown in the fields;

(b) screening, primary settlement and discharge after chlorination;

(c) screening, primary settlement followed by biological treatment and chlorination;

(d) screening, primary settlement followed by biological treatment and chlorination with sludge digestion in lagoons, tanks with or without provision for gas collection.

The treatment plant to work continuously throughout day and night and septicity of sewage is to be prevented.

Standards Of Treatment

(a) Land irrigation—Raw sewage after sedimentation:

(i) on grassy soil—25,000 g a d

(ii) on sandy soil—50,000 g a d

(b) Intermittent sand filters:

(i) Raw sewage—80,000 g a d

(ii) Settled sewage—120,000 g a d.

(c) Contact beds:

Range—125,000—150,000 gals. acre ft/day.

(d) Standard Filter:

(i) Low rate—1—3 m g a d

(ii) High rate—16—30 m g a d

(e) Activated Sludge Process:

Tank capacity—0.35—0.39 cft/gal. of sewage.

N.B.:—ppm—parts per million

g a d—gallons per acre per day

BOD—biochemical oxygen demand

Standards Of Effluent

(a) When the dilution is over 500 volumes, raw sewage to be discharged after removing floating matters only.

(b) When the dilution range is between 300 and 150, sedimentation is essential and suspended solids in the effluent to be kept at 60 ppm.

(c) When the dilution range is between 500 and 300, sedimentation to be adopted and suspended solids in the effluent may be as high as 150 ppm.

(d) Generally, treated effluent not to contain more than 30 ppm. of suspended solids and not to take up dissolved oxygen more than 20 ppm in a 5-day BOD test at 65°F.

C. Sullage Drains

(1) Sullage drains to carry only rain water from roofs and yards, wastes from kitchen and bathroom. They are not to be allowed to receive the wastes from latrines and urinals.

(2) The whole system of open drains should be well-planned, with the best available gradients, an outfall and a method of disposal. The authorities concerned should arrange for daily flushing and cleansing of open drains.

(3) A minimum self-cleansing velocity of 2 ft. per second to be maintained.

(4) These drains to be provided with such a capacity that during rains flooding is avoided.

(5) Where the water supply is less than 15 gallons per capita per day, or the flushing is defective, kitchen and bath water shall be led into properly constructed soakage wells.

Sanitary Latrines, Septic Tanks And Disposal Of Nightsoil

A. Sanitary Latrines

(1) Every house to have at least one latrine and this is to be non-service type sanitary latrine—either dug well, bore-hole or septic tank.

(2) seat—to be of impervious material: of the type suitable for local habits and of age groups, with water seal of minimum ½ inch.

B. Septic Tanks

(1) Septic tanks—for temperate climates, capacity provided to be 2.5 cft/user while for cold climates this to be increased to 3.5 cft./user.

(2) Minimum water depth 4′, 6″, with an additional air space of 1′ to 1½′ shall be maintained. But the capacity shall be guided by temperature condition of the place.

(3) Adequate ventilation to be provided for: size of ventilator pipe 3″ or more.

(4) Effluent from domestic septic tanks should be used, if possible, in the soil for kitchen gardens, by subsoil percolation or surface irrigation if the subsoil water is not too high and land at the rate of 70 sq. ft. per user is available. If there is not sufficient land, the effluent may be discharged into a sullage drain after chlorination.

(5) Septic tanks should be provided with means of desludging and should be desludged regularly.

(6) Septic tank latrines with flushing arrangements, and not bore-hole or dug-well latrines, may be used for public latrines in unsewered areas provided sufficient water is available for the purpose.

C. Disposal Of Nightsoil

(1) Service privy is the least satisfactory type of latrine and should be prohibited. It may be allowed only if no other method of disposal of nightsoil is possible.

(2) For house-to-house collection, pails made of G.I. sheets provided with handles and cover shall be used and carried to pail depots or nightsoil carts, or poured down into a public sewer inside a well-protected enclosure.

(3) Nightsoil Carts—Commercial size 100-gallon capacity—and able to turn 180, for emptying.

Pail Depots

(i) shall be located in a place away from inhabited locality;

(ii) shall have brick walls all round—minimum height 10 ft;

(iii) must have an impervious floor;

(iv) shall have a hydrant for flushing—minimum size 3″ with a minimum discharge of 400 gallons per minute.

Trenching And Composting

(a) Mechanical transport is preferred.

(b) Trenches—trapezoidal in section with top 2′ 6″ wide and not more then 3' deep and 40—100 ft long; longitudinal slope 1 in 100. A layer of 6″—9″ of nightsoil shall be spread and covered with excavated earth with the top in the form of a mound and left in that state for a minimum period of 6 months before the trench can be used again. Minimum space between the trenches to be at least 3′

(c) The trenching ground shall be selected at a site at least ½ mile away from human habitation and shall be connected with a good road for mechanized transport.

(d) Washing arrangement at the trenching ground shall be provided.

(e) For composting, a similar trench is recommended; the trench shall be started with a layer of refuse and finished with the same, the alternate layers being 6″ refuse and 2″ nightsoil, and finally covered with earth.

(f) In composting, the trench should be allowed to rest for 4 to 5 months and subsequently the compost may be taken out and allowed to cool for one month before it can be pulverized and utilized as manure.

Refuse Collection And Disposal

(1) Refuse to be collected from house to house in covered house-service bins and public bin system may, if possible, be eliminated.

(2) These house-service bins shall be made of impervious materials and have a capacity to hold refuse for at least 2 days. They should be placed on impervious platforms.

(3) Number of collections shall be not less than 3 times a week for household purposes in less congested areas, whereas in congested parts, collection to be made at least once a day. In market places minimum service to be given should be twice a day.

(4) Refuse must not be mixed with nightsoil: nightsoil to be collected separately and "dalao" system abolished.

(5) Refuse to be disposed of by either of the following methods as directed by the Chief Public Health Engineer:

(a) dumping at sea;

(b) dumping in other waterways (not meant for human use);

(c) dumping in low-lying areas—controlled dumping;

(d) ploughing in lands (only for villages);

(e) dumping in small pits (only for villages),

(f) incineration;

(g) composting (for a population below one lakh);

(h) trenching.

Treatment And Disposal Of Industrial Wastes

The wastes from industries shall be treated prior to its discharge into a public sewer, river, stream, channel or inland water collection or on land, by adopting one of the methods or combination of methods such as sedimentation, screening, coagulation, chemical precipitation, septic tank treatment, activated sludge process, biofiltration method followed by chlorination, superchlorination or any other chemical treatment to prevent pollution of water-sources and of the soil and to avoid abnoxious odour, fly and other nuisances.

Wastes From Milk Products Industry

The wastes from processing of milk products consisting of washing, spillage, spoiled products and by-products and almost entirely composed of organic material in solution or colloidal suspension, larger suspended organic solids, sand and other foreign particles shall be disposed of in the manner indicated below:

(1) By-products and spoiled products shall not be discharged into the drains, sewers, streams or land but shall be utilized for animal feeding and other purposes.

(2) (a) Land irrigation of wastes from plants in sparsely populated areas provided the land is light and sandy and is kept under constant cultivation to prevent pooling and that the production of odour, if any, is controlled by application of chlorine at the rate of 20 parts per million.

(b) Screening with ½″ inch wire mesh into a girt chamber of such size as to reduce the velocity to about 1 foot per second, the deposits being disposed of by burial. Subsequent treatment of the waste may be carried out by either biological filtration or activated sludge to produce an effluent that can be satisfactorily disposed of in drain, sewer, stream or land. The BOD of the final effluent after treatment should not exceed 50 ppm.

Wastes From Vegetable Canning, Freezing And Dehydration Industry

The wastes from vegetable canning, freezing and dehydration industry consisting largely of carbohydrates in suspension and foreign matters from spillage and washing and not containing organic substances inimical to normal biological treatment shall be disposed of in the manner indicated below:

(1) Solid wastes to be handled separately by composting and converting into manure or by burial.

(2) Liquid wastes may be disposed of by :

(a) land irrigation with or without any treatment, provided sufficient land with suitable porosity is available and there is no underground seepage which might contaminate streams, wells or tanks and there is no possibility of surface run off from flooding;

(b) (i) before discharge into a stream, lake of large collection of water or into public sewers, screening through 40 mesh screens is necessary;

(ii) chemical precipitation with lime or with coagulants may be used to bring about 50% reduction in BOD; the sludge may be dried on open beds or let out for field irrigation;

(iii) biological treatment in trickling filters for BOD removal to about 80 to 90%.

Caution : Stack liquor heavily laden with soluble organic matter and having an obnoxious odour of butyric acid and other decomposition products should not be discharged as it is or mixed with other wastes into sewage treatment plants. They may be segregated in tanks and disposed of separately on land or streams.

Wastes From Slaughter-House

The wastes from slaughter-houses and meat-packing processes containing large amount of suspended solids are highly putriscible, quickly becoming septic with a disagreeable odour and high oxygen demand and having pollutional effects such as oxygen depletion, discolouration, sludge deposits, scum formation and insect nuisance; these shall be disposed of in the manner indicated below:

(a) Sedimentation, with or without coagulants, followed by septic tank treatment, roughing filters, superchlorination or activated sludge and low rate sand filtration to give BOD reduction varying from 40% to 90%.

(b) After settling, aeration and passage through trickling filters, the effluent may be discharged into sewers for further treatment.

Wastes From Fermentation Industries

The wastes from fermentation industries after recovery of useful products vary with the nature of fermenting processes and raw materials and may be disposed of after suitable treatment into large volumes of water on or land.

Wastes From Grain Starch Industry

The wastes from grain starch industry from wet-milling and bottled up processes consisting of condensates from stripping towers, entertainment from evaporators and washing waters polluted with organic solubles from the kernals are amenable to treatment when mixed with domestic sewage and may be disposed of in the sewers after screening and primary sedimentation.

Wastes From Tanning, Fat-Processing And Laundry Soap Industries

The composite wastes from tannery which vary widely in strength carrying large amounts of suspended matter, including various constituents such as hair, particles of flesh and suspended practices of lime and calcium carbonate, are inherently putritive and eventually become highly offensive. Wastes from vegetable canneries are highly coloured from spent tan liquors and the colour persists for long periods in the stream receiving tannery wastes. In wastes from chrome tanneries colour is absent. But Anthrax may be transmitted, though very rarely, and arsenic, which is sometimes used for hair removal, may be present and may check biological action.

Tannery wastes may be disposed of in the manner indicated below:

(1) Tannery wastes not exceeding 10% of total flow of the sewage from any city present no difficulty in sewage treatment process. Mixtures of tannery wastes and domestic sewage can be adequately treated in properly designed plants.

(2) Tannery wastes may form lime mortar inside receiving sewer, and this requires treatment with flue gas prior to discharge.

(3) Treatment of tannery wastes for disposal into watercourses involves one or a combination of the following processes: collocation and sedimentation with or without coagulants, biological treatment in sand filters or trickling filters and adequate means for disposal.

Wastes From Edible Oil Refining And Soap Manufacture

The wastes usually consisting of wash water from the washes immediately following a caustic treatment and floors may interfere with sewage plants because of their high grease contents and excessive acidity acting on concrete sewers unless neutralized with lime before discharge and may be finally disposed of after screening, sedimentation and anaerobic digestion.

Wastes From Textile Dyeing And Finishing Works

(1) Wools-scouring liquors should be treated at their sources and the treated effluents after centrifuging, chlorination, coagulation and secondary treatment may by discharged to the sewage system or to neighbouring stream.

(2) The final effluent from the wastes from dyeing and finishing processes contributed by the spent liquors and subsequent washing after singeing, bleaching, dyeing and finishing, after treatment by usual methods of chemical precipitation followed by sedimentation and filtration or other suitable treatment, may be discharged into a watercourse.

Wastes From Pulp, Paper And Paperboard And Strawboard Industries

The wastes produced by the industry are of the group classed or organic wastes, both suspended and dissolved. The main objections to the discharge of mill effluents in respect to the condition of receiving stream, when dilution is low, are oxygen depletion, floating materials, deposits of suspended matter, toxicity to fish, colour, and odour. The final effluent may be disposed of after treatment methods such as screening, sedimentation, precipitation, coagulation, activated sludge, trickling filter, evaporation and burning or other suitable treatment, to avoid stream pollution difficulties.

Acid Wastes

Acid wastes which may be a solution of one or a mixture of several acids with or without suspended matters or highly dissolved salt concentration may be disposed of after adoption of remedial measures for volume reduction, strength reduction, equalization and interaction with other wastes. Equalization may be necessary even where the total amount of acid waste is insufficient to damage stream life, sewers or sewage treatment processes.

(a) Equalization of acid chemical wastes detained in large water collections with or without mixing devices and baffles is essential. The quality of the industrial wastes discharged into sewers shall have a pH between 4.2 and 8.4 indicating that the wastes have a low mineral acidity or caustic alkalinity.

(b) Neutralization with lime and other substances is necessary for wastes with high acid concentration which when discharged into streams may interfere with natural self purification, rise the hardness and cause a decrease of fish population.

Caution: The high nitrate concentration wastes from explosive factories even after neutralization may cause excessive growth of algae and may impart colour, taste and odour to the water of the stream. Disposal by mixing with sewage may be tolerated to a certain extent without affecting the BOD reduction in the activated sludge process.

Wastes From Steel Pickling Industry

Wastes from steel factory consisting of 1—9% of sulphuric acid and ferrous sulphate or in the disposal of sewage where ferrous sulphate acts as a coagulant and brings about improved clarification in the primary settling tanks. Neutralization of the free acid is usually done by the soda ash because it is easy to apply and avoids sludge deposits in sewers

Planting Wastes

The wastes usually consist of low concentrations of metals as ions or as cyanide complexes in solution and may be either acid or alkaline depending on the type of baths used. Electroplating wastes are toxic to fish and fish food, corrosive to metal and concrete structures of the sewers and affect sewage because of the toxic reaction of the waste chemicals on the biological organisms which cause purification.

(a) It is highly advisable to isolate the wastes containing cyanides and treat these separately from other wastes.

(b) Because of the toxicity of the cyanide wastes great care must be taken for location, design and operation of such plants.

(c) After treatment by approved methods in sealed tanks and use of blowers for diffusion of poisonous gas the effluents which may contain about 1 ppm of cyanide may be disposed of in such manner as would provide sufficient dilution for the complete safety of the effluent after discharge into a stream or a sewage system.

Wastes From Coal Industry

Treatment of acid water and reduction of the acid content in mine drainage should be done before discharge into streams.

Wastes From Oil Refining Industry

Oilfield brine may be disposed of after removal of suspended matters and necessary chemical treatment and aeration into sea or into subterranean formations. Other wastes may be dealt with by appropriate treatment methods.

Laundry Wastes

Large volume of soap wastes with high oxygen demand from power laundries may require treatment by sedimentation chemicals, trickling filters, and activated sludge before discharge.

Sugar Wastes

Disposal of wastes is frequently done either on land or into streams, and pollutional characteristics may widely vary both in BOD and suspended solids. All waste products should be re-used, as far as possible, as a source of fuel, fertilizers and irrigation water.

Wastes From Rubber Industry

Wastes to be treated by neutralization, settling tanks and save all to remove suspended matter including rubber particles and the effluent to be treated suitably for disposal on land or water.

Prevention Of Pollution Of Water

In the disposal of sewage and other oxidizable organic wastes into surface waters, regard shall be had to the effects of pollution on such waters and the subsequent use or uses of such waters for different purposes.

Note On Biological Zones In A Polluted Stream

The over-all physical, chemical and biological changes brought about as a result of discharge of sewage and other oxidizable organic wastes have been divided into different zones on the basis of various criteria. A system of zoning on the basis of biological characteristics has been suggested as under:

Zone I: Zone Of Active Bacterial Decomposition

This zone is immediately below the source of pollution and is characterized by a low dissolved oxygen content (between 3 and 0 ppm), a high BOD, a high bacterial count, the presence of bacteria-eating protozoa such as Paramecium, Colpidium, Vorticella and Carechesium, and a few Flagellata. The total volume of plankton is low. In the bottom deposits are found Tubifex and Liminodrilus worms. Gas evolution often brings sludge to the surface. Sewage fungus is present. Only a few coarse fish such as carp and buffalo are found at the mouth of the sewer.

Zone II: Zone Of Intermediate Bacterial Decomposition

The rate of biochemical activity is decreased and as a result the dissolved oxygen increases to 3 to 5 ppm. The plankton volume is higher but the plankton is still made up of pollutional forms requiring a rich medium or feeding on bacteria and solid particles. There is an increase in green and blue-green organisms. In addition to carp and buffalo, shiners, minnows, suckers and sunfish are found.

Zone III: Fertile Zone

This zone has a dissolved oxygen content above 5 ppm and is characterized by a large variety and volume of green algae and a decrease of pollutional protozoa. The fertilizing effect of the decomposed sewage and wastage has resulted in an increase in biological productivity. Forage and market fish increase in numbers.

Zone IV: Game Fish Zone

In this section the plankton volume diminishes sharply and only the clean water forms remain. The dissolved oxygen level remains near the saturation point. Bass, perch, wall-eyed pike and other game and forage fish predominate.

Zone V: Biological Poor Zone

Plankton volume is even lower in this zone and consists entirely of clean water forms. Fish are scarce in comparison with the previous zone and are mainly forage and game fish. The reduction of fish is associated with the low plankton population resulting from the exhaustion of available food.

Waste Disposal By Dilution

Disposal of sewage by dilution shall include sufficient diluting water high in dissolved oxygen to prevent putrefaction and to maintain fish life; adequate current to prevent sedimentation and to carry sewage away; absence of back current or quiet pools favourable to sedimentation in the body of water in which disposal is taking place. Conditions to be prevented are: offensive odours, sludge banks, rise of septic gases, deposit on shores, excessive oxygen depletion, unsightly discolouration, pollution of shell fish and killing of other fish life and unsightly floating or suspended matter.

Permissible Pollution

Permissible limits of pollution for particular body of water depends on subsequent use, which are:

(1) natural state;
(2) drinking water standard;
(3) preservation of fish;
(4) safety for agricultural use;
(5) industries;
(6) recreational standard;
(7) freedom from nuisance;
(8) commercial use, such as navigation.

No uniform standard of quality is possible because of different conditions in various regions. The principal consideration shall be, in promulgation of standard:

(1) health;
(2) aesthetic; and
(3) economics.

In all waters dissolved oxygen shall be above 3 ppm and carbon dioxide not more than 40 ppm. For bathing purposes, coli-aerogenes index to be preferably below 100 in 100 c.c. and maximum limit 1000 in 100 c.c.

Sewage Outfalls

Before discharging sewage hydrological survey of the body of receiving water to be made, to satisfy the conditions referred to in 3 and 4 above, as well as for direction of flow and intake points for water supply on the downstream side.

Treatment

In all cases of disposal of sewage by dilution, screening, sedimentation of heavy grits and removal of grease and oil prior to discharge are to be carried out.

(see Table on p. 296).

Slaughter-House—Location

Preferably away from residential areas; may be located in a market if suitable accommodation is available. Sheds to be kept out of public eyes by high walls all round.

Structure

Floor and walls up to 3′ should be impervious and easy to clean.

Disposal Of Wastes

Blood, offal, etc., should not be discharged in public sewer and should be collected separately. Intestines, hoofs and horns to be disposed of separately.

Water Supply

Independent, adequate and continuous.

Examination Of Animals

Ante-mortem and post-mortem examination to be

Stream Conditions And Its Relative Fitness For Various Uses

Characteristics	Stream uses	Range of characteristics	Remarks
Dissolved oxyzen (DO) (minimum monthly average DO in ppm)	Fish life; General sanitary condition. Reaction	0.3.0	Heavy pollution and probable nuisance at times; little fish life.
		3.0—5.0	Moderate to heavy pollution; no nuisance; fish life restricted to coarse species.
		Above 5.0	Slight to moderate pollution; fish life varied, abundant and healthy; game fish at higher minimum levels.
Biochemical Oxygen Demands (BOD) (maximum monthly average BOD in ppm)	General sanitary condition; Reaction	0—3.0	Slight to moderate pollution.
		3.0—5.0	Moderate to moderately heavy pollution.
		Over 5.	Heavy pollution.
pH (average daily pH value)	Water Supply; Fish life reaction; Navigation; Industry	6.5—8.6	Normal for unpolluted stream; favourable to fish life; suitable for water supplies.
		5.5—6.5	Moderate acid pollution; tolerable to fish life; suitable for water supply prior to treatment.
		4.0—5.5	Moderate acid pollution; detrimental to fish life; fairly suitable for water supplies prior to treatment.
		Less than 4.0	Heavy acid pollution; lethal to fish life; unfavourable to water supplies prior to treatment.
Coliform (bacterial) organism (limiting monthly average coliform per c.c.)	Water Supply: Water Sports & Bathing	0—0.5	Suitable for purification by simple chlorination.
		Not over 1.0	Bathing; sports
		0.5—50.0	Suitable for purification by filtration and other methods of treatment.
		Over 200	Unsuitable for treatment.

arranged. Animals or meat found unfit for human consumption should be destroyed or denatured.

Miscellaneous

Animals other than those to be slaughtered shall not be allowed inside the shed.

Storage Of Meat

If fly-proof and rat-proof rooms under sanitary conditions; for overnight storage the temperature of the room shall be maintained at 35°F.

Transportation Of Meat

Meat shall be transported in fly-proof covered vans during slack period of traffic.

Camps, Fairs And Festivals

Lodging Houses And Dharamsalas

(a) Every room in lodging houses and dharamsalas shall not be less than 200 sq. ft. with a minimum height of 10 ft., and 10% of the floor area as window opening.

(b) Every such place shall have a separate kitchen and cooking inside the living room shall be strictly prohibited.

(c) All floors shall be of impervious materials and easy to clean and wash.

Temporary Sheds

Each shed shall not be more than 100 ft. in length and 20 ft. in width, with separate working place.

Water Supply

(a) In permanent pilgrimage places for periodical gathering of 50,000 or more persons, permanent water supply arrangement at the rate calculated at 6 gallons per capita per diem shall be provided from public taps at the rate of one for every 150 persons, and the supply should preferably be chlorinated and continuous.

(b) In case of temporary gatherings, disinfected water to be supplied by trucks and trailers at convenient points. Where the gathering is to last for more than two days, temporary spot tubewells or temporary pipe water supply is to be arranged.

(c) Mass disinfection of neighbouring water sources —both private and public—like masonry wells, ring wells, tubewells, etc., to be started a week prior to congregation and to continue for a week after the congregation is over.

Latrines

(a) Shallow or deep trench latrines, maximum length not exceeding 100 ft., to be constructed. Number of seats to be calculated @ one for 20 persons. There should be an adequate number of sweepers and mehtars.

(b) Ablution water to be made available near latrines.

(c) Separate enclosure to be provided for women and sadhus.

(d) Sites for all latrines to be at least 50′ away from drinking water sources and foodstuffs.

Refuse Collection

Public bins to be provided at convenient places for collection and particularly in front of eating shops, and should be disposed of once or twice daily as may be required.

Restaurants And Eating Shops

Shall be located away from any collection of filth, latrines or sources of nuisance. To be kept clean and free from flies.

Use Of Disinfectants

(a) Bleaching powder and other disinfectants shall be liberally used.

(b) DDT residual spraying method shall be adopted for keeping down flies and mosquitos.

Restaurants And Eating Houses

Location

Shall not be near any accumulation of filth or open drain, stable, manure-pit and other sources of nuisance.

Floors

To be higher than the adjoining land, made with impervious material and easy to keep clean.

Rooms

(a) Rooms where meals are served shall not be less than 100 sq. ft. and shall provide accommodation for maximum 10 persons.

(b) Walls up to 3′ height; should be smooth, corners to be rounded; should be impervious and easily washable.

(c) Lighting and Ventilation.—Ample natural lighting facilities aided by artificial lighting with good circulation of air are necessary.

Kitchen

(a) Floor space minimum 60 sq. ft.

(b) Window opening to be 25% of floor area.

(c) Floor to be impervious, smooth, easy to keep clean but non-slippery.

(d) Doors and windows to be rat-proof and fly-proof —of self-closing type.

(e) Ventilators 2% of floor area, in addition to smoke pipes.

Storage Of Cooked Food

Separate room to be provided. For long storage, control of temperature is necessary.

Storage For Un-Cooked Foodstuff

Perishable and non-perishable articles to be kept separately, in rat-proof and vermin-proof space; for storage of perishable articles temperature control should be adopted.

Furniture

Should be reasonably strong and easy to keep clean and dry.

Disposal Of Refuse

To be collected in covered, impervious bins and disposed of twice a day.

Water Supply

To be independent source, adequate, continuous and safe.

Washing Facilities

To be provided. Cleansing of utensils and crockeries to be done in hot water and followed by disinfection.

Schools

Site

(a) The site should be on suitable high land, not subject to inundation or dampness and can be properly drained, not far from inhabited localities and with good approach.

(b) Area of the land, including playground, shall be between 60 and 100 sq.ft. per student; minimum in congested areas 30 sq. ft. per student; in such congested areas, the nearest public park or playground should be made available to the students.

Structure

(a) Nursery and Secondary schools should, as far as possible, be single-storied.

(b) Exterior walls shall have a minimum thickness of 10″ masonry and should be heat resisting.

Classrooms

(a) Verandahs should be attached to classrooms.

(b) Classrooms shall not be less than 100 sq. ft.

(c) Length of the room maximum 30 ft., width maximum 20 ft., with a minimum height of 10 ft.

(d) No classroom to accommodate more than 40 students.

(e) Per capita space for students in a classroom shall not be less than 10 sq. ft.

Furniture

(a) To suit the age-group of students.

(b) Chairs and desks or high benches to be provided with proper back-rests, with facilities for desk work.

Doors And Windows

(a) Broad windows with bottom sill at a height of 2′ 6″ from the floor level.

(b) Combined door and window area shall be at least 25% of the floor space.

(c) Windows to be placed on different walls for cross ventilation.

(d) If ventilators are provided, the area of the ventilator shall not be less than 2% of the floor area.

Colour

Inside colour of the classroom to be white and should be periodically white-washed.

Lighting

Classrooms to have sufficient natural light, preferably from the left, and shall not be from the front.

Water Supply

There should be an independent source of safe and potable water supply, which should be continuous. Distribution should be from taps.

Eating Facilities

(a) Vendors other than approved by the school authorities are not to be allowed inside school premises.

(b) School authorities to arrange for mid-day tiffin or meals of such standard as may be approved by the Director of Health Services.

(c) There should be a separate room provided for mid-day tiffins.

Lavatory

Privies and urinals should be provided on the basis of one seat for 25 students. Arrangements should be separately provided for boys and girls.

COMMITTEE APPOINTED TO EXAMINE ALL ASPECTS OF CATERING ARRANGEMENTS AND SERVICE ON RAILWAYS, 1953—REPORT

New Delhi, Railway Board, 1954. 81p.

Chairman : Shri O. V. Alagesan.
Members : Shri Shahnawaz Khan; Shri P. C. Bhattacharyya; Shri K. B. Mathur.
Secretary : Shri S. K. Guha.

APPOINTMENT

The Committee was appointed by the Ministry of Railways on November 3, 1953.

TERMS OF REFERENCE

To put up proposals for re-organizing the present catering system on Railways, including:

(a) The consideration of the feasibility of the extension of Departmental Catering, steps required to minimize the loss at present experienced in such catering, prices being suitably raised, if necessary, having regard, however, to the fact that these were not such as were to be beyond the reach of the middle-class persons.

(b) As an immediate aim, to minimize and check the evils inherent in the Contract System of Catering where it has to continue, by

(i) Devising methods to prevent the tendency for some caterers to become monopolists and widening the field with a view to awarding contracts to smaller concerns as well. This should include consideration whether sub-contractors could not be awarded contracts to eliminate the bigger contractors who were more or less middle-men;

(ii) Devising deterrent penalties against contractors who sublet their contracts or fail to supply food of the requisite quality;

(iii) Feasibility of bringing down the prices at which the contractors are allowed to sell foodstuffs;

(iv) Practicability of having two standard "thalis" priced, say, at Rs. 2 and Re. 1 each so as to satisfy people of moderate means;

(v) Perfecting the arrangement for inspection of the quality of foodstuff and checking the prices charged by vending contractors; and

(vi) Steps necessary to effect improvements in dining cars meant for lower-class passengers.

CONTENTS

Introductory; Contract Catering; Different Types of Catering; Departmental Catering; Improvements in Contract Catering; Restaurant/Dining Cars; Vending Contracts; Prices of Meals; Licence Fees; Relief to Catering Contractors; Other Miscellaneous Matters brought up before the Committee; Summary of Conclusions and Recommendations; Appendices.

RECOMMENDATIONS

Contract Catering

On a review of the present position of catering on the Railways, the Committee found that Contract Catering was in force over a very wide field. The Committee noted that about 84% of catering establishments were, in fact, in the hands of contractors; the other 16% or so only being departmentally run. So far as vending was concerned, this was almost entirely in the hands of contractors.

The Committee also noted that although Contract Catering had the advantage of lower costs and was, therefore, in a better position to give satisfactory service, there was a large volume of complaints against such catering. They also noticed that some catering contractors who have large holdings are not in a position to exercise adequate personal supervision over their staff or services rendered in their establishments spread over a wide area or to pay due attention to public complaints and to take adequate remedial measures.

After having carefully examined the present state of affairs in Contract Catering establishments and the numerous complaints received in respect of the services rendered, the Committee came to the conclusion that the following steps were necessary to achieve the desired improvement:

(i) Railways with no Departmental Catering should start with an experiment with an Economic Departmental Catering Organization so as to set the standard and service as a model;

(ii) The holdings of contractors should be compact and of a manageable size and the existing large holdings which have resulted in unsatisfactory service should be reduced;

(iii) Railway Administrations should ensure more effective supervision and take prompt and vigorous action against unsatisfactory service.

Different Types Of Catering

The Committee after examining the different types of catering establishments now run on the Indian Railways came to the conclusion that, with the changed conditions in the country, the Western-style catering at wayside stations had no future as a separate entity. They consider that restaurants now catering exclusively in the Western style may be closed down, except in places where contractors find that they have adequate custom. Likewise, restaurants run departmentally may also be closed down if they are uneconomic. Isolated demands for this type of catering at wayside stations could be met by the Non-Vegetarian Refreshment Rooms where they exist and are considered suitable for taking up this kind of catering in addition.

While the Committee consider that Western-style catering in restaurants will largely disappear, they feel that it will be necessary to maintain this style of catering in the restaurant cars running on important long-distance trains for catering to meet the special requirements of overseas tourists and other higher-class passengers for some time to come.

Departmental Catering

The Committee have noted the opinions expressed in favour of Departmental Catering and agree that satisfactory catering is one of the needs of the travelling public. They also agree that Departmental Catering could be an inducement to catering contractors to improve their service as well. They have, therefore, already recommended that Railways with no Departmental Catering should start with an experiment with an Economic Departmental Catering Organization.

While recommending organization of Departmental Catering to a limited extent on each Railway, the Committee have noted the possible difficulties in the way of implementing the recommendation both from the points of view of administrative responsibility and its financial implications and have suggested ways and means of meeting them. They have come to the conclusion that Departmental Catering should be capable of running on a "no-profit-no-loss" basis if certain measures were adopted to reduce expenditure, including combining different types of catering to form an economic unit for departmental working.

The Committee have stated that it was not their intention to recommend elimination of Contract Catering on the Railways. They would like to see an efficient Contract Catering running side by side with Departmental Catering, each profiting from the experience of the other, and fulfilling a complementary role.

Improvements In Contract Catering

The Committee have noted *inter alia* the desirability to reduce the existing large holdings to reasonable and manageable proportions. The holdings must necessarily be compact and capable of working economically, but at the same time should not be too large as such holdings have resulted in practice in unsatisfactory service. The Committee realize that it is difficult to lay down any rigid limitation of holdings either by defining an area, number of contracts or monthly sales. Taking all factors into consideration, they agree that some discretion must be left with General Managers so that the local factors and satisfactory services of contractors may be taken into account in determining the reasonable size of a holding in each individual case. They have, however, set out, as a broad indication of policy, the following directive principles:

(i) In the case of Restaurant/Dining Cars, a contract may, if necessary, extend over the whole Railway and the contiguous Railways;

(ii) In the case of Restaurants and Refreshment Rooms, holdings may extend to about 10 to 12 contracts within a compact area on the Indian Railways;

(iii) In the case of Vending Contracts, holdings may extend to about five to seven contracts within a compact area on the Indian Railways. Local interests should, however, be encouraged in this case;

(iv) A combination of Vending, Catering and Dining Car Contracts in any individual case is permissible wherever deemed expedient to form an economic unit. Where such a combination is permitted, the total number of holdings may extend to about 15 to 20 contracts;

(v) Care should be taken to see that the same contractor does not operate under different names on the Indian Railways;

(vi) Before giving a contract, a declaration in writing should be obtained to show:

(a) That the contractor does not operate under a different name anywhere else on the Indian Railways;

(b) The number of Catering or Vending Contracts, if any, the Contractor holds on the Indian Railways.

If, in any particular case, circumstances warrant the extension of the holdings beyond the limits specified, the General Manager should obtain the approval of the Railway Board.

The Committee recommend that each Railway should review all its Catering and Vending Contracts with a view to implementing the directive principles set out in Paragraph 27 of the Report.

The Committee feel that although comprehensive instructions already exist regarding inspection of catering arrangements on Railways, in actual practice there has been some slackness in their implementation, and that supervision by those who are required to carry out these duties has been deficient. They recommend that more effective supervision must be enforced. Surprise inspections should also be encouraged.

The Committee also feel that a specific provision should be made for the imposition of fines on Catering and Vending Contractors for unsatisfactory service.

These should be sufficiently deterrent and may extend up to Rs. 100 in any particular case.

The Committee recommend that in the event of a wholesale termination of contracts of a contractor for grave reasons on one Railway, he should not be reappointed anywhere else on any other Indian Railway. If employees of a contractor are likewise dismissed for good and sufficient reasons, they should be debarred from appointment by any other contractor on any Indian Railway.

The Committee consider that instructions regarding maintenance of Complaint Books should also be strictly observed and cases of complaints such as non-production of Complaint Books viewed seriously, and adequate action taken against the contractors concerned by the appropriate Railway officer.

The Committee consider elimination of subletting of contracts essential for improvement in the existing state of affairs particularly in the context of Vending Contracts.

The Committee noted the present multifarious affairs for the different types of meals as confusing to the unwary passengers who were often defrauded and made to pay exorbitant rates not authorized by the Railway Administrations. The Committee have, therefore, evolved certain standard means at standard prices for Indian-style meals served in Refreshment Rooms.

The Committee consider that in awarding contracts, the appointment of suitable local men with requisite experience of catering should be encouraged. The Committee also consider that to ensure that subletting is not resorted to, Railway Administrations should carefully examine the *bona fides* of displaced persons before giving special preference to them in the matter of award of contracts.

The Committee recommend that the tenure of all catering contracts to be entered in the future should be of three years only, terminable on a month's notice from either party, subject, however, to the present proviso that contracts are liable to be summarily terminated in the event of a breach of the conditions of the contract, including unsatisfactory service, subletting or any other improper act. The Chief Commercial Superintendent should be treated as the authority who would take a decision whether a particular contract should be terminated in terms of the proviso referred to above.

The Committee consider that a reasonable security deposit related to the business turnover for a specified period should be charged at the discretion of the General Manager. The basis should, however, be uniform on each Railway applicable to all types of contracts.

Restaurant/Dining Cars

Having inspected the different types of Indian-style dining and buffet cars now running on the Indian Railways, the Committee felt that the present arrangements were generally unsatisfactory and that, in future, there should be provision for only two types of dining cars —one designated "Restaurant Car" and the other "Dining Car". Restaurant Cars should be full dining cars catering mainly in the Western style as at present running on all important long-distance mail and express trains having fairly heavy upper-class passenger traffic and tourist traffic in particular. Dining Cars catering mainly in the Indian style should also have a larger seating accommodation. The Committee have in this context suggested that the future Dining Cars should be designed on the basis of their recommendations contained in Paragraph 42 of the Report.

The Committee also recommend that in future both Restaurant and Dining Cars should be open to all classes of passengers during meal times. This recommendation has already been implemented by the Railway Board.

The Committee also recommend that the construction of Dining Cars of the proposed design should be accelerated and a definite programme laid down by the Railway Board for early replacement of the existing buffet cars and catering compartments used for Indian-style catering.

The Committee have also evolved a standard design of containers in the "thali" service as indicated in Appendix "G" for general use in all dining cars for serving Indian-style food.

Vending Contracts

The Committee have noted that of all the different types of catering establishments on Railways, those for vending are usually the most profitable, and that, as the scope for profit is large, there has been a tendency on the part of middle-men having the necessary capital and influence of entering the business by securing contracts and then subletting them to vendors or salesmen at exorbitant rates. This has in turn led to the vendors and salesmen giving bad service and unsatisfactory food. Extortionate charging by such vendors has also been noticeable in the cases where Vending Contracts have been sublet. The Committee have also examined the various data made available to them in connection with the complaints for subletting and come to the conclusion that subletting was frequently and freely being resorted to by some contractors.

The Committee feel that the recommendation that they have already made earlier for reducing the size of holdings of contractors in terms of the directive principles will help in the elimination of subletting to a large extent. They further recommend that the number of salesmen per vendor or per platform should also be carefully fixed and strictly enforced to prevent any scope for subletting of contracts. At large stations, separate Vending Contracts should be given for separate commodities. The Railway Administration must also be vigilant and watchful and take prompt action both in letter and spirit of Paragraphs 7 and 8 of the Railway Board's directive at Appendix "C"

Prices Of Meals

The Committee have in consultation with the representatives of the Catering Contractors evolved certain standard menu and standard price for Indian-style meals and these have already been notified, at their request. They have in fact come into force from September 1, 1954. The particulars of the standard menu and standard price are given at Appendix "I".

In regard to Indian-style meals served in Indian-style dining or buffet cars and Western-style meals where they continue to be served on the Indian Railways, the Committee, after making certain suggestions, recommend that Railways should examine them with a view to introducing a standard menu and standard prices applying, as far as possible, to all Indian Railways. In regard to prices of tea and coffee also, suitable standardization should similarly be considered by the Railway Board.

The Committee feel that so far as prices of foodstuffs, including sweetmeat and other edibles, sold at vending stalls or hawked by vendors are concerned, there is some scope for reduction, and that Railways should pursue the matter further.

Licence Fees

The Committee recommend that Railways should examine the scope for a further enhancement in the licence fees generally for the various types of catering establishments. So far as the actual revision of licence fees is concerned, the Committee consider that this should be left to the General Managers of Railways subject to the principle that the licence fees are not to be treated as a source of revenue but, at the same time, a reasonable fee should be charged having regard to the turnover with a view to meeting the Railways' expenses in connection with the provision of facilities for running the service and supervision and inspection of the establishments. A reasonable rent should also be charged for providing accommodation and this must normally be related to the floor area placed at the disposal of the contractor and the type of accommodation provided. After the first review, the licence fees and rents should continue to be reviewed every three years. To what extent the turnover figures are reliable should be left for examination by the Chief Commercial Superintendent in consultation with the Financial Adviser and the Chief Accounts Officer. Certain suggestions in regard to the basis of fixation of the licence fees made by the Southern Railway were commended for examination by all the Railways. In the light of the result of the examination, the Railway Board should lay down certain standards for adoption on different Railways.

Relief To Catering Contractors

The Committee recommend certain reliefs to Catering Contractors, such as avoidance of unnecessary duplication of contracts at stations and unauthorized vending at stations or on trains; protection against dual control of Central and local Acts, bye-laws, rules and regulations in the matter of medical and sanitary inspections of catering establishments and extortion by Railway staff.

The Committee also recommend the setting up of an Advisory Committee consisting of representatives of caterers nominated by General Managers on each Railway.

Other Miscellaneous Matters Brought Up Before The Committee

The Committee recommend the continuance of Railway employees' concession now allowed by Catering Contractors in the matter of meal tariffs but desire it to be rationalized and placed on a uniform basis, the extent of concession not exceeding 25% in any case. No concession need be given so far as Departmental Catering is concerned.

The Committee considered the question of giving preference in the matter of award of contracts to co-operative societies of vendors but did not favour the idea for reasons set out in Paragraph 65.

The Committee recommend experiments being carried out by departmental establishments on Railways to see if cooking generally cannot be improved by the adoption of what may be called "Army School Cookery" method. Certain standard tinned meat dishes might also be evolved by experiments in these establishments.

The Committee feel that the Railways can, with advantage, issue from time to time suitably worded appeals to their Catering and Vending Contractors to improve their service in all respects and also arrange "Courtesy to Customers Week" once or twice a year.

COLLECTION OF AGRICULTURAL PRICES IN INDIA ENQUIRY COMMITTEE, 1953—REPORT

Delhi, Manager of Publications, 1954. 114p.

Chairman : Shri P. N. Thapar.
Members : Dr. S. R. Sen; Dr. B. Ramamurti.
Secretary : Shri J. S. Sarma.

APPOINTMENT

The Collection of Agricultural Prices in India Enquiry Committee was constituted under the Ministry of Food and Agriculture vide their Resolution No. F.7-5/53-P.C. III, dated November 11, 1953.

TERMS OF REFERENCE

(i) To examine the existing machinery for the reporting of prices of agricultural commodities, including cash crops and foodgrains; and

(ii) To suggest improvements necessary in the existing machinery.

CONTENTS

Introductory; Present Position Regarding the Availability of Price Data; Some Technical Problems Connected With Price Reporting; Suggestions for Improvement; Economic Adviser's Index Numbers of Wholesale Prices; Summary of Conclusions and Recommendations; Appendices I to XIV.

RECOMMENDATIONS

Technical Aspects Of Price Reporting

The system of wholesale prices reported should cover representative prices at all stages of commercial transactions in goods, i.e., in primary, secondary and terminal markets. In selecting primary markets, while the importance of the market from the point of view of transactions should be the guidi g factor, the availability of continuous price data should also be a criterion.

At each market, the quotation reported should relate to the actual price at which the transaction takes place irrespective of the Terms of Contract and without excluding the different incidentals such as charges for weighment, wholesaler's commission, etc.

The variety and quality of the commodity to which the prices should relate should be specified for each market. If only a single variety is commonly transacted and its arrivals are continuous throughout the year, this variety should be selected for that centre. If this is not possible, two or three additional varieties which are most common and which are sufficiently close to the original variety should be fixed in advance, and one of them should be quoted if the original variety ceases to arrive in the market. The prices should be reported for the fair average quality.

Whenever there is a change in variety, the price of the new variety during the previous one or two weeks should also be given to enable comparison. This will also facilitate splicing if Index Numbers are to be compiled from the data.

When both the old and new crops are marketed simultaneously, the prices of both should be quoted, for about four to six weeks.

For each market, the quotations should relate to the model price, i.e., the price at which most of the transactions take place, during the peak period of marketing.

The wholesale prices should be collected as on Friday every week, where markets are held every day. Where markets are held on specified days of the week, the prices reported should relate to the nearest market day, preceding Friday.

The prices collected should relate to actual transactions, nominal quotations being avoided as far as possible.

During the period when statutory rationing is in force, the wholesale issue rates to ration shops should be quoted. Where Fair Price Shop prices and Open Market quotations are simultaneously available due to partial control, both should be quoted. A rough estimate of the relative proportion of the respective transactions at Fair Price Shops and in the Open Market might be formed and submitted once in two months or so.

The Primary Reporter should collect the prices in terms of local measures and should convert them into standard measures. The prices reported and published should relate to all-India standard measures, e.g., maund of $82\frac{2}{7}$ lbs. for grain, bale of 392 lbs. for cotton.

The proforma and instructions prescribed in Appendices IX and X should be adopted for the primary collection of data.

Machinery For Collection Of Wholesale Prices

Any agency which is associated with the market in the normal course of its duties and is intimately acquainted with the market conditions is the most suitable agency for purposes of price reporting at the

Primary Level. It is an added advantage if the agency is located at or near the markets.

In States where the Agricultural Produce Markets Act has been enacted and regulated markets have been established under the Act, the staff of the Market Committees is the best agency for reporting prices.

The States which have not passed an Agricultural Produce Markets Act should undertake the necessary legislation expeditiously and establish regulated markets at the more important marketing centres as early as possible. Then alone can a permanent and reliable agency be created for the recording and reporting of wholesale prices. The other advantages of the regulated markets are given in Paragraph 4.4.

In applying the Agricultural Produce Markets Act, the State Governments should give priority to the centres selected for reporting of prices to the Ministry of Food and Agriculture given in Appendix XI. In States where the coverage of the commodities in the regulated market is limited, the Act should be extended to all commodities which are commonly sold in the market.

The States which have not yet enacted an Agricultural Produce Markets Act are advised to study the Hyderabad legislation and to follow the same with such modifications as may be necessary in the light of local conditions. The other States which are at present following a different system might also examine the working of the Hyderabad model with a view to seeing what suitable improvements can be made in the existing arrangements.

Till such regulated markets are brought into existence, other marketing agencies which already exist could, as an interim measure, be entrusted with the work of price collection provided they have adequate field staff in the districts, sub-divisions or tehsils.

Next in importance comes the Economic Intelligence Staff belonging to the Departments of Economics and Statistics. This can be entrusted with price reporting, as an interim measure, at places where regulated markets or other suitable marketing staff does not exist.

The revenue agency may continue to be entrusted with price collection work, as an interim measure, at such centres where regulated markets or other marketing or economic intelligence staff does not exist, subject however to certain improvements designed to enhance the reliability of the prices reported by it. The first is the provision of adequate and effective supervision over its work. The second is that the responsibility for price collection should be definitely fixed on a single specified person. Thirdly, the Primary Reporter should be trained properly in the procedures for the collection of prices.

As and when the regulated markets are established, the staff of the market committees should take over the work of primary collection of price data from the interim agencies. Then, even for the requirements of revenue administration, the District Collectors should utilize the data collected through marketing agencies rather than collect their own price data independently.

The staff of the Civil Supplies Department is not suitable as a permanent agency because it is mostly a temporary organization and is not likely to continue after the relaxation of controls.

For purposes of comparison, each State may attempt to collect prices for a few selected centres through non-official agencies also, e.g., Imperial Bank of India, Chambers of Commerce, etc.

In the regulated markets where the price data are reported by the marketing staff, inspection should be done by the officers of the Marketing Department.

Where the Revenue or other agency reports the price data, whole-time Prices Current Inspectors should be appointed, as an interim measure. The number of Inspectors that will be needed has been suggested for each State.

As regards permanent arrangements for the supervision of price data, in each district there should be a District Statistical Officer who should be entrusted with the task of supervision of all statistics including agricultural statistics and agricultural prices. This officer should belong to the Cadre of Statisticians and have the proper technical qualifications and the necessary training in statistics. He should be located at the headquarters of the district under the general supervision of the District Collector subject to technical guidance and co-ordination of a Statistical Organization at the State level.

The District Statistical Officer should not normally be required to do any routine collection of statistics. His main function should be to supervise the work of the various Primary Collecting Agencies and give them necessary technical guidance and training and also to co-ordinate their work.

Before the Primary Reporters begin reporting of prices, they should be adequately trained in the procedures of collection.

The duplication in the matter of price collection at present in existence should be avoided as far as practicable. At the State level, only one agency should be designated as the Price Collecting Authority.

The requirements of price data at the different levels, viz., the District, the State Headquarters and the Government of India, should be carefully assessed. Four Lists of Market Centres should be prepared for reporting prices to the District Officer, State Government, Central Ministry of Food and Agriculture and Office of the Economic Adviser, in the Ministry of Commerce and Industry. The first List should be inclusive of the second, and so on. The nature of the markets, e.g., Primary, Secondary or Terminal, should be specified in each case. The authorities at each level should know exactly the names and types of centres selected at the other levels so that whenever the need for such data arises, they can get the information by telegram or otherwise from the appropriate authorities. In respect of common centres, the Primary Reporter should prepare the requisite number of copies and post them simultaneously.

In order to enable an assessment of the relative importance of different markets, data on arrivals of the various agricultural commodities into each market should be collected and maintained. In the absence of this information, statistics of movement by rail of these commodities to and from the railway station or stations near the market should be collected through the railway authorities.

The Ministry of Food and Agriculture are receiving price data from a large number of centres in respect of cereals and gram and a small number in respect of other crops. There is scope for reduction in the number of quotations for cereals. The list of centres for which the Ministry should obtain prices is given in Appendix XI.

With regard to agricultural commodities other than cereals and gram, the existing number of quotations is inadequate and should be enlarged. An illustrative list of centres for which the Ministry should obtain prices is given in Appendix XI.

Processing And Publication

The time-lag in the publication of the data should be reduced by the State Governments. A weekly Price Bulletin should be published by every State within seven days of the date to which the data relate. Ordinarily this should be printed, if it could be brought out in time. Where this is not possible, the Price Bulletins should be cyclostyled. In the latter case, we recommend that the weekly price data should be published in a separate monthly Bulletin, to serve as a permanent record.

The Ministry of Food and Agriculture might consider the question of preparing Regional Index Numbers of Wholesale Prices of cereals and other agricultural commodities based on a larger number of centres than those covered by the Economic Adviser's Index. These Regional Indices might be ultimately combined into an All-India Index Number of Agricultural Prices.

All the major States should consider the desirability of compiling Index Numbers of wholesale prices in order to give a clear indication of the trends in prices.

Collection Of Retail And Other Prices

The collection of Retail Prices should be organized on the same lines as those suggested for Wholesale Prices. Adequate arrangements for supervision and improvements in the quality of data and the techniques of price collection should be made.

Where the data are required for the Cost of Living and Retail Price Index Numbers and are compiled by the Departments of Labour or Economics and Statistics, the data should continue to be collected through the existing agencies. The scope of the price data collected might be expanded to cover commonly used articles entering the consumption of other important urban classes, e.g., Middle Classes.

In other centres, wherever it is possible, the agency which is collecting Wholesale Prices should also collect Retail Prices.

As in the case of Wholesale Prices, the existing duplication of work relating to collection of Retail Prices should be avoided as far as possible and the lists of centres should be prepared in the manner described in Paragraph 4.30.

The procedure suggested by the Ministry of Food and Agriculture for the compilation of Farm Prices appears to be satisfactory. The States which have not so far adopted this method should start collecting the data on this basis immediately.

The States might also compile Index Numbers of Parity between the prices received and prices paid by the farmer. These State Indices might be ultimately combined into an All-India Index of Parity.

In States where "Futures" Markets are important, the respective State Governments should organize the collection of "Futures" Prices also. The Central Government might also collect data on "Futures" Prices in respect of important crops.

The list of 50 centres proposed for inclusion in the Cereals Sub-Group of the All-India Index Number of Wholesale Prices issued by the Economic Adviser to the Ministry of Commerce and Industry should be enlarged as suggested by us in Paragraph 5.5.

STUDY GROUP (TRANSPORT PLANNING), 1953—REPORT

New Delhi, Ministry of Transport, 1955. 222p.

Chairman : Shri N. M. Ayyar.
Members : Shri H. P. Mathrani; Shri J. N. Nanda; Shri A. Nanu; Shri B. B. Saksena; Shri M. D. Sethna; Shri S. C. Chaudhri; Shri M. V. Bhavnani; Shri H. Davenport; Shri C. Parthasarathi.
Secretary : Shri D. D. Suri.

APPOINTMENT

Complaints were received during the year 1953 from various quarters about the difficulties experienced by industry and trade in securing adequate railway transport for the carriage of raw materials and finished goods. Suggestions were also made that road transport should be expanded so as to fill the gap between the demand for transport on the one hand and the availability of railway wagons on the other. The Planning Commission took note of these criticism and invited the comments of the State Governments as to the extent to which their plans had been affected by the shortage of transport. On receipt of replies from the State Governments an inter-departmental meeting was convened by the Planning Commission on August 19, 1953, to review the position. It was then decided to set up a Small Study Group consisting of the representatives of the Planning Commission and the Ministries of Transport, Railways, Commerce and Industry and Food and Agriculture to examine and make recommendations on the planning of transport industry so as to meet the increasing demands.

The Study Group (Transport Planning) was set up in December, 1953.

TERMS OF REFERENCE

(i) Study the data regarding targets of additional production and demand on regional basis and work out the additional transport capacity required to be created for facilitating the movement of traffic arising therefrom.

(ii) Examine more thoroughly the suggestion to demarcate 50-mile zones in the congested areas round Calcutta, Madras, Bombay, Ahmedabad, Kanpur, etc., for road traffic (it being understood that the Railways would not accept transport of certain categories of goods within the zones) with special reference to:

(a) The economics of the proposal;

(b) Relief to railway traffic (wagon capacity to be released);

(c) Problems, if any, arising out of an increase in road traffic like capacity of roads and their conditions, suitability of bridges for coping with additional traffic;

(d) Additional employment likely to be created and other related aspects.

(iii) Go into all aspects of the problem of rail-road transport co-ordination and make recommendations to the Government.

(iv) Study the problems of Light Railways like the Martin and Burn Railways, who, it is understood, are finding it difficult to face the competition from road traffic.

CONTENTS

Introductory; Need for a National Transportation Policy; General Review of the extent to which Transport Requirements have been met by Railways; Comments of the Railways on the complaints and criticism by State Governments and others regarding inadequacy of Rail Transport Capacity; Coal Transport; Measures taken by the Railways to increase the Line Capacity and Rolling Stock to remove existing bottlenecks; General assessment of transport requirements arising out of the implementation of the Five Year Plan and the role to be played by the different forms of transport; Road Transport—a General Survey; Roads; Road Transport—an analysis of the factors affecting cost of operation; Taxation of Motor Vehicles; Regulation of Motor Transport; Nationalization of Road Transport; Further measures for encouraging road transport; Inland Water Transport; Coastal Shipping; Co-ordination of Inland Transport; Summary of Conclusions and Recommendations; Appendix.

RECOMMENDATIONS

In India Railways have overshadowed other means of transport like Road, Inland Waterways and Coastal Shipping. It is necessary in the national interest to have a co-ordinated development of all forms of transport. As a first step it is essential to formulate a National Transportation Policy which will give due recognition to the part to be played by each of the different forms of transport and embody it in a statute.

A more realistic objective would be, first, to enable replacement of overaged trucks; secondly, to obtain full employment for the existing trucks; thirdly, to provide sufficient road transport capacity to carry the "small" traffic which the Railways are not now able to carry; and, fourthly, provision of additional road transport in rural areas gradually. In the light of the current manufacturing programme, an addition to the total road transport fleet for goods by 10,000 to 12,000 vehicles per year during the next two years may be aimed at in addition to the replacement of overaged trucks. A fleet strength of about 160,000 trucks by the end of the Second Plan period would be a reasonable target to aim at. In addition, there will have to be expansion of passenger transport.

There is still a tendency to construct roads parallel and adjacent to the railways leading to duplication of transport services. It is desirable that State Road Plans should give priority to Feeder Roads connecting the interior with rail-heads. It is also desirable that whenever the construction of a major road, whether it is a National Highway or a State Highway, is decided upon the project should have the approval of the Central Board of Transport or the State Road Board, if one exists, as the case may be. The Railways should have representation on such Road Boards.

Road Transport Policies should generally be directed towards the control of the industry in a manner which would help in increasing the load factor and vehicle utilization, in the improvement of roads, in the encouragement of diesel-operated vehicles, and in the development of the type of vehicles most suited to conditions of operation in India.

The work of the Regional and State Transport Authorities should be reviewed carefully in the light of the remarks made by Appellate Authorities and Courts in the country and the set-up should be reorganized.

The Central Government should take power by legislation to regulate the inter-State movement of road transport vehicles as the present method of regulation by the State Governments is unsatisfactory and highly restrictive.

The automobile industry in India should take a long-range view of their own interests and of the country and try to offer their products at a reasonable price range. The marketing and distribution technique adopted by them will also require a revolutionary change if the products are to be sold in substantial numbers. In regard to passenger cars there is no doubt that the basic factor discouraging demand is the price of the vehicle.

A careful watch should be kept over the performance in India of the vehicles included in the manufacturing programme so that in due course the evolution of types of vehicles most suited for this country may be facilitated.

It is desirable to adopt the following order of priority in the development of road transport in the country:

(1) Passenger and Goods Traffic in areas not served by Railways.

(2) Passenger and Goods Traffic in rural areas.

(3) Passenger and Goods Traffic on Feeder Roads to rail-heads.

(4) Passenger Transport over distances not exceeding 150 miles in areas served by Railways.

(5) Carriage of goods over distances ordinarily not exceeding 150 miles in areas served by Railways.

State Governments may draw up special schemes for encouraging the use of lorries in selected rural areas by partly subsidizing co-operative societies or a group of Panchayats if they take the initiative by purchasing a suitable motor truck. Provision may have to be made for small workshops in and around the centres and for mobile vans for carrying out repairs.

Intermediaries, such as Goods Booking and Forwarding Agencies, should be subjected to statutory regulation.

Inland Water Transport should obtain better consideration in the Second Five Year Plan.

There should be definite understanding between Railways and shipping regarding the traffic that should be left to be carried by the sea route.

It is desirable that the Government should set up a High Level Committee to go into all aspects of sea-rail co-ordination.

Several complex problems of co-ordination have to be tackled in India. These include co-ordination between Road and Rail, Rail and Coastal Shipping, Rail and Inland Waterways, among Road Transport Operators themselves, and between Nationalized Operated Services and Private Services.

An expansion of the system of road operation by Road Transport Corporations in which the Railways and State Governments should take part is desirable.

It is desirable to examine the feasibility of operating integrated services over the railways and inland waterways. An extension of through booking facilities is also desirable. The Government also may have to adopt special measures to stimulate traffic by Inland Waterways.

The constitution and working of the Transport Advisory Council should be changed so as to make it a less unwieldy body which could take quick decisions. Efforts should also be directed towards making the decisions of the Council binding on the State Governments.

The Central Board of Transport should meet more regularly and it should consider not only the major decisions affecting the transport position proposed to be taken by the various Ministries but also review the progress made in the implementation of the various projects and the transport problems generally.

STATES REORGANIZATION COMMISSION, 1953—REPORT

Delhi, Manager of Publications, 1953. 267p.

Chairman : Shri S. Fazl Ali.
Members : Shri H. N. Kunzru; Shri K. M. Panikkar.
Secretary : Shri P. C. Chaudhuri.

APPOINTMENT

The States Reorganization Commission was constituted under the Ministry of Home Affairs vide their Resolution No. 53/69/53-Public dated December 29, 1953.

TERMS OF REFERENCE

The Commission will investigate the conditions of the problem, the historical background, the existing situation and the bearing of all important and relevant factors thereon.

CONTENTS

Introductory; **Part I:** The Conditions of the Problem: State of the Indian Union; Rationale of Reorganization; Time for Reorganization; **Part II:** Factors Bearing on Reorganization: Cost of Change; Unity and Security of India; Language and Culture; Financial Viability; Requirements of National Development Plans; Regional Planning and a Balanced Economy; Smaller vs. Larger States; Some Other Factors; **Part III:** Proposals for Reorganization: Basic Pattern of the Component Units; Madras; Kerala; Karnataka; Hyderabad; Andhra; Bombay; Vidarbha; Madhya Pradesh; Rajasthan; The Punjab; Delhi; Uttar Pradesh; Bihar; West Bengal; Assam; Manipur; Orissa; The Reorganized Units; **Part IV:** Administrative and Allied Matters: Safeguards for Linguistic Groups; The Integration of Services; Financial and other Administrative Measures; The Unity of India; Notes and Summary; Note on Himachal Pradesh; Note on Uttar Pradesh; Summary of Conclusions and Recommendations; Appendices I and II.

RECOMMENDATIONS

The problem of the reorganization of States is urgent as with large-scale planning the country has to think in terms of enduring political units. The integration of States has removed the main hurdle in the way of rationalization of the existing units. Further deferment of a general reorganization will cause dissatisfaction and disappointment.

In proposing any changes in the existing structure, due consideration should be given to the unsettling consequences of reorganization. The changes proposed should be such as would compensate, in terms of the welfare of the people, for the administrative dislocation and the heavy burden on the administrative and financial resources of the country which they entail.

In the interests of the national unity, it is necessary that the administrative and political structure of the country should be based on the primacy of the nation.

The administrative set-up in strategic areas should be determined primarily by considerations of national security. Where border areas are not under the direct control of the Centre, it would be safer to have relatively large and resourceful States.

It is neither possible nor desirable to reorganize States on the basis of a single test of either language or culture; a balanced approach, which takes all relevant factors into account, is necessary.

Financial viability has an important bearing on reorganization proposals, but it has to be considered along with other relevant factors.

Some degree of dislocation in the working of the next plan is likely to be caused by any scheme of reorganization; this dislocation, however, should be considered along with the possible advantages of reorganization. Steps should also be taken to minimize the unsettling effects of reorganization.

The States cannot be so reorganized as to conform to economic regions. Nor can the principle of economic self-sufficiency within an administrative unit be regarded as a clear criterion. Consistently with these principles it would be desirable to avoid as far as possible wide disparities in resources between the various States.

The wishes of the people should be regarded as an important factor bearing on reorganization but they have to be considered along with other relevant factors.

The facts of the existing situation are more important than the previous historical associations of different areas. Undue importance cannot be attached, therefore, to historical arguments.

Geographical contiguity of the units is important from the point of view of administrative convenience. Other geographical factors have to be regarded as secondary.

The existing constitutional disparity between the different constituent units of the Indian Union should disappear as a necessary consequence of reorganization.

In respect of three of the Part C States, namely, Himachal Pradesh, Kutch and Tripura, the Central Government should retain supervisory powers for a specified period to maintain their present pace of development.

Such of the existing Part C States as cannot be merged in the adjoining areas for security and other imperative considerations should be administered by the Centre as "territories".

The component units of the Indian Union should thus consist of two categories:

(a) "States" forming primary federating units of the Indian Union; and

(b) "Territories" which are Centrally-administered.

Madras

This State should include the existing territories subject to the following adjustments, namely:

(i) The five taluks of Agastheeswaram, Thovala, Kalkulam, Vilavancode and Shencotta, now forming part of Travancore-Cochin, should be transferred to the State of Madras; and

(ii) The districts of Malabar and South Kanara and Kollegal Taluk of Coimbatore District should be detached from Madras.

Kerala

The State of Kerala should be formed, which should consist of the following areas:

(a) The State of Travancore-Cochin minus the five taluks proposed to be transferred to Madras;

(b) Malabar District (including Fort Cochin and the Laccadive Islands), Kasaragod Taluk of South Kanara District and the Amindive Islands.

Karnataka

The State of Karnataka should be created consisting of the following areas:

(a) The present State of Mysore, excluding Siruguppa Taluk, Bellary Taluk, Hospet Taluk and a small portion of Mallapuram Sub-Taluk of Bellary District;

(b) The four Kannada-speaking districts of Bombay, namely, Dharwar, Bijapur, North Kanara and Belgaum (except Chandgad Taluk of Belgaum District);

(c) The districts of Raichur and Gulbarga from Hyderabad;

(d) South Kanara District of Madras minus Kasaragod Taluk;

(e) Kollegal Taluk of Coimbatore District of Madras; and

(f) Coorg.

Hyderabad

Apart from the districts of Raichur and Gulbarga, the Marathwada districts should also be detached from Hyderabad State. The residuary State which should continue to be known as Hyderabad should consist of the Telugu-speaking districts of the present State of Hyderabad, namely, Mahbubnagar, Nalgonda, Warangal (including Khammam), Karimnagar, Adilabad, Nizamabad, Hyderabad and Medak, along with Bidar District, and Munagala Enclave in Nalgonda District belonging to Krishna District of Andhra.

The residuary State of Hyderabad might unite with Andhra after the General Elections likely to be held in or about 1961, if by a two-thirds majority the Legislature of Hyderabad State expresses itself in favour of such unification.

The future of the remaining areas of Hyderabad, consisting of the districts known as Marathwada, is dealt with later on under Bombay.

Andhra

Andhra State should for the time being continue as it is, subject to certain minor adjustments which are mentioned below.

The taluks of Siruguppa, Bellary and Hospet and a portion of Mallapuram Sub-Taluk of Bellary District should be transferred to Andhra.

Munagala Enclave of Krishna District, as has already been stated, should be transferred to Hyderabad.

There should be no change in the present position regarding Madras City and its future should be regarded as finally settled.

Bombay

The State of Bombay should be reconstituted so as to include the existing Bombay State minus Abu Road Taluk of Banaskantha District and the Kannada-speaking districts of Dharwar, Bijapur, North Kanara and Belgaum (excluding Chandgad Taluk), plus the following areas:

(a) The Marathi-speaking districts of Hyderabad, namely, Osmanabad, Bhir, Aurangabad, Parbhani and Nanded;

(b) Saurashtra; and

(c) Kutch.

Vidarbha

A new State to be known as Vidarbha should be created, consisting of the following Marathi-speaking districts of Madhya Pradesh, namely, Buldana, Akola, Amravati, Yeotmal, Wardha, Nagpur, Bhandara and Chanda.

Madhya Pradesh

After the separation of Vidarbha, a new State, which may be known as Madhya Pradesh, should be created consisting of:

(i) The 14 districts of the residuary Madhya Pradesh;

(ii) The whole of Bhopal and the whole of Vindhya Pradesh;

(iii) Madhya Bharat except Sunel Enclave of Mandsaur District; and

(iv) Sironj Sub-Division of Kotah District of Rajasthan.

Rajasthan

After the proposed merger of Sironj in the new Madhya Pradesh State, Rajasthan should continue in its present form subject to the addition of territories mentioned below:

(i) Ajmer; and

(ii) Abu Road Taluk of Banaskantha District of Bombay, Sunel Enclave of Mandsaur District of Madhya Bharat and Loharu Sub-Tehsil of Hissar District of the Punjab.

The Punjab

There is no case for dividing the present Punjab State. PEPSU and Himachal Pradesh should, however, be merged in the Punjab.

Loharu Sub-Tehsil of Hissar District, as already stated, should be transferred to Rajasthan.

Apart from the safeguards referred to in Paragraph 24 of this Summary, Himachal Pradesh should be represented in the Punjab Cabinet by at least one member.

Uttar Pradesh

There is no case for dividing Uttar Pradesh, and this State should continue in its existing form.

Bihar

It does not seem to be either necessary or desirable to create a Jharkhand State in South Bihar; the special needs of this area should, however, be recognized.

Seraikella and Kharsawan should continue to be part of Bihar.

Some adjustments in the two eastern districts belonging to Bihar are indicated under West Bengal.

West Bengal

A portion of Purnea District east of the river Mahananda and Purulia Sub-District of Manbhum District minus the Chas Thana should be transferred from Bihar to West Bengal.

Subject to the recommendations summarized in the immediately preceding paragraph, no boundary adjustments seem to be called for in order to satisfy claims and counter-claims in respect of the border areas of Bihar, West Bengal, Assam and Orissa.

Assam

Assam should continue as it is subject to the changes mentioned below:

The demand for the creation of a Hill State in Assam is impracticable and there is also no reason, having regard to the peculiar features and circumstances of Assam, why a separate Hill State should be created; Special attention should, however, be paid to the development of the hill districts and an enquiry into the working of the autonomous bodies created under the Sixth Schedule to the Constitution should be undertaken.

Tripura should be merged in Assam.

The present arrangements with regard to the North-East Frontier Agency should continue.

Orissa

No changes are called for in the boundaries of Orissa which were fixed in 1936 after a prolonged and detailed examination.

Jammu And Kashmir

No recommendations are made in regard to Jammu and Kashmir.

The units or areas which have not been dealt with so far will be directly administered by the Centre and will be known as territories.

Delhi

Delhi should be constituted into such a Centrally-administered territory; the question of creating a Municipal Corporation with substantial powers should be considered.

Manipur

Manipur should be a Centrally-administered territory for the time being. The ultimate merger of this State in Assam should be kept in view.

Andaman And Nicobar Islands

The *status quo* in the Andaman and Nicobar Islands should continue.

The arrangements in regard to areas which have been or may be brought under Central administration in future, either before or after becoming *de jure* part of the territory of India, must be flexible, until the position is finally clarified.

Constitutional recognition should be given to the right of linguistic minorities to have instruction in their mother tongues at the primary school stage subject to a sufficient number of students being available. The Central Government should acquire powers to enforce this right on the lines of the provisions contained in Article 347 of the Constitution.

The Government of India should adopt, in consultation with the State Governments, a clear code to govern the use of different languages at different levels of State administrations and take steps, under Article 347, to ensure that this code is followed.

The domicile tests in force in certain States operate to the disadvantage of minority groups. The Government of India should, therefore, undertake legislation under Article 16 (3) of the Constitution in order to simplify and liberalize the requirements as to residence.

In examinations regulating entry into the Public Service of the States, a candidate should have the option to elect as the medium, apart from the main language of the State, the Union language, namely, English or Hindi, or the language of a minority constituting about 15% to 20% or more of the population of the State.

As far as possible, Public Service Commissions should be constituted to serve more than one State.

Appointments to Public Service Commissions serving even single States should be made by the President as in the case of appointments to joint Public Service Commissions.

The reconstitution of the sanctioned State Cadres and the integration of Services should be accorded very high priority, and must be decided on the basis of certain general principles, due regard being paid to the options of the employees, the need for a mixed element in the services, *inter se* seniority in the State of origin, etc., and also the needs of the new States.

The body constituted to integrate the service personnel of different States should be one that inspires confidence, and only one appeal against decisions regarding integration should be permitted.

After the scheme of reorganization has been given effect to, it may be necessary for some of the new administrations to review the number and territorial extent of the existing districts as well as Commissioners' charges and the rationalization of the administrative structure.

Decisions on the reorganization proposals should, if possible, be taken before the next Finance Commission commences its enquiries.

If may be necessary to grant ways and means advances to newly-constituted units in order to help them to tide over temporary difficulties.

Pending a comprehensive review, grants-in-aid on Revenue or Capital account as well as long-term loans should be made available to the new units as nearly as possible on the existing basis. The Government of India should fix the existing statutory and development grants and long-term loans with reference to the principles on which such grants or loans have been sanctioned.

Payments under Article 278 of the Constitution may be continued and apportioned population-wise among new units until such time as the position is reviewed by the Finance Commission.

Pending the amendment of Article 264 (b) of the Constitution, appropriate portions of the divisible pools pertaining to Part C States, which are now retained by the Centre, may be distributed among the new units, where necessary, in proportion to their population.

Assets and liabilities should be divided on the basis of principles which should, as far as practicable, be of general application.

Financial settlements in the case of Part C States need not be elaborate, but may be based on a review of the position as it exists today and the needs of these areas.

The question of setting up some special machinery to expedite the final settlements regarding assets and liabilities should be considered.

It will be necessary to adapt current inter-State agreements regarding water rights, etc., with due regard to the broad basis on which they may have been drawn up, and this question should be taken up as soon as possible after decisions regarding reorganization have been reached.

The creation of Special Development Boards for certain areas which are underdeveloped should be considered.

A permanent body, in which members of the Planning Commission may be included, should be set up in order to examine the grievances, if any, on the score of the alleged neglect of certain areas.

The Government of India should consider the question of formulating an Industrial Location Policy for the whole of India, in order to ensure an equitable distribution of development expenditure.

As a general rule, 50% of the new entrants in the All-India Services should be from outside the State concerned, this computation being made after deducting the number of posts in any State which are to be filled by promotion.

Certain All-India Services, namely, the Indian Service of Engineers, the Indian Forest Service and the Indian Medical and Health Service, should be constituted.

Regular transfers to and from the Centre and the States in respect of personnel belonging to the All-India Services should, as far as possible, be arranged.

The curriculum of studies for the new entrants to the All-India and Central Services should include such basic and essential subjects as Indian history, geography, religions, customs and manners.

In formulating a policy regarding the recognition of Hindi in Competitive Examinations for the All-India and other services, the need for encouraging the study of other Indian languages, and particularly of the South Indian languages, should be kept in view.

At least one-third of the number of Judges in the High Court of a State should consist of persons who are recruited from outside that State.

For some time to come, English should continue to occupy an important place in our universities and institutions of higher learning even after the adoption of Hindi and the regional languages for official and educational purposes.

Osmania University should be placed under the Central Government and the medium of instruction in this University should be Hindi. One more Central University should be established further South and arrangements should be made for the study of South Indian languages in the North.

Reorganization has a legitimate place in this country, but its limitations must be recognized. If the supremacy of the Union not merely in the political but also in the economic thinking of the country is fully realized, the issues arising out of the reorganization of States should not assume the proportions of major political controversies.

1954

RATES AND COSTS COMMITTEE, 1954—REPORT

New Delhi, Ministry of Irrigation and Power, 1956. 2 Parts.

Chairman : Shri P. C. Agrawal.
Members : Shri Raunaq Lal (left); Shri N. S. Sandhu (left); Shri M. R. Varadarajan; Shri S. Ramier.
Secretary Shri G. G. Dhanak (replaced by Shri B. D. Nanda).

APPOINTMENT

The Rates and Costs Committee was constituted under the Ministry of Irrigation and Power vide their letter No. DW-III-7(I) dated February 16, 1954.

TERMS OF REFERENCE

The Committee was required to make recommendations on the following terms:

(i) A Comprehensive Standard Schedule of rates for manual as well as machinery work, which can be used as a basic schedule for all projects with such modifications as may be necessary for zonal consideration;

(ii) Standard analysis of rates for the main items of River Valley Projects estimates which would enable rates being worked out for any project with the help of the basic schedule, after allowing for differences in cost of carriage and other local factors involved;

(iii) The causes which have led to the difference in rates at present prevalent on the various major projects (dams and canal works); and

(iv) To examine the present P.W.D. forms with a view to suggesting modifications which would serve the purpose of better cost accounting on all River Valley Projects.

These Terms of Reference were further amplified by the Government of India with the concurrence of the Comptroller and Auditor-General in their letter No. DW-III-22(108) dated June 4, 1954, stating that "the Committee will also visit a typical Railway Workshop (Central Railway Workshop, Parel), and after studying the system of maintenance and accounting of stores in force on the Projects, the Railway, and the Electricity Department of the Government of Madras and the procedure on Stock Control as laid down in B.S.S.

1100—Part 5 by the British Standard Institution, and make recommendation on:

(i) Stock account rules to be adopted for both quantity and value of accounts of stores for River Valley Projects;

(ii) Suitable forms for the maintenance of accounts of special tools and plants and machinery and the forms pertaining thereto;

(iii) Procedure for the maintenance of accounts of special tools and plants and machinery and the forms pertaining thereto; and

(iv) Rules for placing orders for stores, taking delivery from railway (or other carriages), carriage to godowns, safe custody (including construction of godowns, bins and yards), employment of guards, physical verification, issues, etc., with form such as challans, gate-passes, etc., for upkeep and custody of stores (including all tools and plants) to guard against thefts, shortages, etc., and ensure fixing of responsibility thereof.

In so far as the Terms of Reference of the Committee relating to matters falling within Article 160 of the Constitution are concerned, the Committee was deemed to function for and under the Comptroller and Auditor-General of India, vide the Government of India, Ministry of Irrigation and Power, letter No. DW-III-22 (108) dated June 4, 1954. Briefly these terms were:

(i) To make suggestions for the introduction of such subsidiary rules or accounts as would ensure a more effective control over the cost of certain items of works; and

(ii) To suggest improvements *inter alia* in the system of store accounting as far as possible.

CONTENTS

Part I: Introductory; Construction Cost; Economics of Construction Equipment; Stores; Cost Control; Excavation, Loading, Hauling and Compaction Units; Earthwork by Manual Labour; Transport; Drilling and Quarrying; Tunnelling; Brick Work and Lining of Canals; Steelworks and Gates; Store Masonry; Concrete and Formwork; Analyses and Schedules of Rates; Observations; Annexures; Appendices; **Part II**: Introductory; Existing Conditions and Remedies; Central Workshops; Stores; Cost Control; Forms; Summary of Recommendations; Appendices from I to VI.

RECOMMENDATIONS — SUMMARY

That the existing Muster Roll System be replaced by Time-Keeping System on large River Valley Projects.

That Costing should be done in a separate section.

That Stores Accounts be kept on the lines detailed in Chapter 4.

That inspection and issue of inspection notes and payments for supplies should be prompt.

That a system of payment for supplies on indemnity bonds be introduced.

That advance payments should be permissible in the case of local deliveries also.

That it should be permissible to raise debits for the supply of stores falling under Transfer between P.W. Office on the basis of issues from godowns supplemented by the receipts of the indentor or his Clearing Agents.

That it should be permissible to make payment for supplies made within the country against Running Rate Contracts made by the Director-General, Supplies and Disposals, direct to the supplier instead of through the Director-General, Supplies and Disposals.

That it should be permissible to make payment of freight to the Railways by cheque or in cash.

That it should be necessary to clear the Workshop Suspense either by cash recovery or by adjustment made periodically in case of completed jobs.

That an annual requirement of stores on a project should be budgeted carefully and a revenue limit laid down.

That disposal of surplus and unserviceable stores should be prompt.

That non-standard and obsolete equipment should not be purchased.

That proper discretion for purchase of spares should be exercised and a comprehensive list of interchangeable spares also prepared for use.

That physical check of stores should be carried out continuously.

That the use of present form of register of works (C.P.W.A. Forms 40 & 41) and work abstract (C.P.W.A. Forms 33 & 34) may continue on smaller projects.

That simplified forms of work abstract (Form N-34) should be used on larger projects.

That the register of works in a simplified form (N-35) be used on larger projects.

That maintenance of material at site accounts be dispensed with and all stores passed through Stock Accounts.

That only quantity account of stores received and issued on works for material at site be kept in a Maukawar register and physical verification carried out periodically.

That classification and coding of stores items be done on a decimal system as described in Chapter 4.

That adequate and trained stores personnel be posted in a Stores Section in advance.

That measurement book (C.P.W.A. Form 23) so far as supplies are concerned should be replaced by a new form (N-8) of stores received book.

That a standard issue rate should be fixed for each item of store for duration of the project.

That some of C.P.W.A. forms be amended and some replaced.

That proper stores yards and bins be constructed for keeping stores and watch and ward staff employed for security.

That a ledger for all equipment in Form N-28 be maintained.

That figures of Cost Section and Financial Accounts Section should be agreed and differences reconciled.

That field report for labour, equipment material issued should be introduced.

That a system of designating physical quantities and details of accounts by units be introduced to facilitate classification of expenditure.

That decimal system of classification be adopted for classification of accounts.

That service conditions for accounts personnel be made more attractive and competitive examinations introduced.

That a qualifying examination in accounts be prescribed for all officers.

That routine clerks should compulsorily pass an accounts examination before becoming entitled to promotion above certain grade.

That in heavy divisions S.A.S. accountants should be kept to perform the duties of accountants.

That the Accounts Branch on large River Valley Projects should be split into a number of sections, each headed by a senior accountant.

That recruitment of workcharged and other establishments be made through the Employment Section of the Project.

That a Time-Keeping System be adopted in workshops as described in Appendix V.

That each shop should be under a Chargeman and Time-Officer under a Time-Keeper.

That Foreman or Sub-Divisional Officer should be in charge of two or more shops.

That hours of work be fixed according to the Factory Act and that sanction for overtime be obtained in Form W-5.

That wages for half-hour should be disallowed for late attendance of five to 15 minutes and one hour's wages for late attendance exceeding 15 minutes but not exceeding 30 minutes.

That a worker leaving work before the expiry of day's shift should be allowed only proportionate wages for the period he actually worked.

That leave should be granted and holidays observed according to Factory Rules.

That annual proforma accounts of each workshop should be prepared in forms and details prescribed by the Government in consultation with the Accountant-General.

That there should be a requisition in Form W-1, sanctioned estimate for each job and also a deposit in case of private jobs.

That access to the Token Board should be provided for only five minutes before commencement of shifts.

That late-comers should be given their tickets at the window of the Time Office.

That the Time-Keeper should report daily the total number of each category of labour present to the Officer I/C of the workshop.

That the Chargeman should keep a record of each worker of jobs on which each worked on a shop board.

That the Chargeman should complete the Time Card in Form No. 21

That Gate Passes in Form TK-7 should be used for all articles going out of gate.

That Gate Passes should be signed by an Officer not below the rank of Foreman.

That a Gate Pass should be checked at the gate by the Time Office and Watch and Ward Staff who should sign it in token of check of passing materials, etc., as entered in it.

That the counterfoils of Gate Passes should be frequently verified by the Accountant by a tally with the original copies.

That Gate Passes should also be used in the case of staff going out on duty.

That no Gate Pass should be necessary in case of accident, and that the person concerned should be marked present for the whole morning or afternoon term in which the accident occurred.

That payment of wages to staff other than that employed on monthly basis be made weekly or so notifying the same two days before.

That the Time-Keeper should prepare a Form W-7 of Wages Allocation Sheet and send it to the Divisional Office.

That the Foreman should maintain a register in Form W-8 of the time for which each worker is employed each day.

That each shop having machines with tools, etc., should be provided with a lock-up cupboard with a list of the tools fixed on the inner side of the door.

That each workman taking charge of the machine should check tools, etc., with the list.

That special tools, jigs, etc., should be obtained under the Foreman's signatures who will be responsible till their return to Stores or transfer elsewhere.

That the Foreman should obtain foundry materials from Stores in quantities sufficient roughly for a month.

That the cost of stores drawn for the foundry should remain charged to the Suspense Work Order till its eventual transfer to jobs concerned or Stores.

That there may be created a Sub-Stores in a workshop and that stores drawn should be charged to the Stores Suspense Work Order.

That the balance under the Stores Suspense Work

Order should be cleared by transfer to jobs concerned or Stores.

That the stores from the Workshop Store should be issued on Form N-13 and the Store-Keeper send the receipted indent daily to H.O. with a covering list in Form W-6.

That the Store-Keeper should complete Bin Card Form No. 10 and prepare in duplicate Form W-6 as transactions occur and send the indents to the Head Office.

That the Divisional Officer should maintain a Store Ledger in Form N-18 and prepare material analysis in Form W-10 by Jobs.

That over-head charges should be levied on all jobs to fix their total cost.

That no work should be undertaken in a workshop without an order in Form W-2.

That there should be a Work Order in Form W-2, Job Card in duplicate in Form W-3, and an entry made in the Job Register in Form W-4.

That the entries in the Job Card in respect of labour should be filled in by the Foreman and those for stores from the Store-Keeper report in Form W-6.

That the total of Pay Roll should be agreed by the Divisional Accountant with that of sheet in Form W-7.

That the register of Work Order and Job Cards should be completed on the completion of a job and an entry in a ledger in Form W-11 made.

That at the end of every month over-heads should be levied on all completed jobs and adjustment made to clear workshop suspense.

That a monthly schedule of workshop suspense be prepared in a manuscript form on the lines of Form CPWA 67.

That a monthly consolidated account of workshop suspense by jobs should be kept in CPWA Form 67.

That there should be no balance under General Charges Suspense at the commencement of a fresh year—the balance, if any, being adjusted by credit to R. R. on capital account or by write-off under an order of a competent authority.

That a bill in Form W-12 should be issued for acceptance or payment.

That a proforma account should be prepared at the end of the year to show the financial aspect of the shops, the existing centage charges for over-head reviewed and new ones determined for the ensuing year.

That a Decimal System of Classification should be adopted for Stores.

That the maximum limit should not exceed the minimum limit by more than the requirement for one year.

That the minimum limit for stock should not exceed 6-8 weeks' requirements in the case of local supplies. A higher limit may be fixed in the case of imported articles.

That bulking of orders for purchases should be limited to three months' requirements.

That mechanical equipment should be standardized, and the supply of spare parts during life-time of a machine should be made a condition of the purchase.

That the prices of spares should also be controlled.

That there should be constituted a Stores Purchase Committee with full powers to make purchases direct and a senior officer of the Ministry of I. & P. or a Stores Purchase Officer made a member.

That the Project Manager should normally be the Chairman of the Stores Purchase Committee, Stores Purchase Officer of D.G. of Supplies and Disposals, Chief Mechanical Engineer, Financial Adviser, and Chief Accounts Officers as Members and the Central Stores Officers as Member Secretaries.

That there should be an annual budget for purchase of stores approved by the Committee before placing orders.

That the Chief Stores Officer should be placed directly under the Project Manager.

That demands for an urgent and immediate purchase of stores should be kept to the minimum.

That the powers of officers to make emergency purchases should be clearly defined.

That shortages in consignments should be immediately notified to the supplier.

That payment for shortage should be made and charged to Misc. Advances in case the Railways have accepted it and granted "Short Certificate".

That payment for railway freight should be made by cheque and cash.

That the bills for supplies should be entered in a register in Form N-12.

That the bills for supplies should invariably contain references to Purchase Orders and Railway Receipts.

That the Stores Received Book should be completed in respect of rate, amount, etc., as soon as the bill is received.

That a supplementary Stores Received Book should be prepared if necessary in respect of incidental charges, etc., so that the two Stores Received Books will tie up the accounts between the value of the stores received and the actual expenditure through the Cash Book.

That the officer receiving the stores should check the bill with entries made in the relative Stores Received Book and Purchase Order and record a Certificate of Verification.

That all purchases of stores should be passed through Stock Accounts.

That all purchases of stores should pass through

Purchase Account in the first instance and clearance effected as bills are paid.

That the Purchase Register should contain a reference to the Stores Received Book No. and Date, R/R No. and Date, Purchase Order and names of a few prominent items.

That a monthly Abstract of Stores Received Books should be prepared sub-divided by stock sub-heads in Form N-11.

That one copy of the Stores Received Book should be used for posting the Store Ledger.

That monthly reconciliation of the value of Abstract of Receipts should be carried out with figures in the Purchase Register and the total in the Ledger under each stock sub-heads.

That pressure gauges should be used for checking the quantity of gases, etc.

That the Stores Receiving Officer should notify the receipt of stores to the indentors promptly.

That the first purchase price should be adopted as standard price for that store for the duration of the project except for violent fluctuations.

That issue rates for an article of store should be worked out again when violent fluctuations are noticed.

That the original Stores Received Book with stores should be sent by the Officer receiving the stores to the store holder who after completing the Stores Received Book in respect of the Bin Card No., etc., should return it to that officer for the completion of the other two copies and pass on the original to the Divisional Office for further processing.

That the Bin Card should be posted immediately on receipt of articles in the Stores.

That a new Bin Card should be issued only under the signature of the officer holding the Store.

That there should be separate Stores for combustible materials.

That the issue rate should be mentioned on the Bin Cards.

That the indents for stores in Form N-13 should be prepared in triplicate in indelible ink or with copying pencil.

That two copies of the indents in Form N-13 should be presented at the Stores out of which one copy should accompany the stores supplied.

That the two copies of the indents presented at the Stores should be completed after issue of the stores and registered in the Stores Issue Book Form N-14.

That the person collecting the stores should sign the Stores copy and the Store-Keeper the copy intended to accompany the stores in token of having received the stores and issued the stores respectively.

That three copies of the Stores Issue Book Form N-14 should be prepared.

That an abstract of Stores Issue Books grouped by sub-heads of stock and each group classified by works and its sub-heads should be prepared in Form N-16.

That each Sectional Store Holder should prepare separate Stores Issue Books for the different sub-heads of stock daily for the issues, total being carried forward from page to page for an accounting month.

That Sectional Store Holders should prepare also an abstract of the indents supplied for each work and its sub-heads and post it under the proper sub-head of stock in Form N-15.

That Form N-15 should be posted daily from the Stores Issue Book and an abstract in Form N-16 prepared at the close of a month.

That at the close of a month each Sectional Store Holder should submit a set of Stores Issue Books and a copy of the monthly abstract of issues to the Officer who compiles the account of the stock.

That the officer should consolidate all the abstracts in a Monthly Abstract Form for his entire charge to give the values of the stores issued by stock sub-heads, by work and its sub-heads and by the fundamental heads of account.

That one card for tools in Form N-24 should be prepared for each item of plant (Plant Card) and one card for each employee (Personnel Card).

That one corner of the Plant Card should be cut off to distinguish it from the "Personnel Card"

That the Store-Keeper while issuing tools should note down the employees' No. on the Plant Card and the Plant No. on the Personnel Card.

That the Store Price Ledger should be maintained for the reconciliation of receipts, issues and balance of stock.

That the Ledger should be posted from the Stores Received Book and the Stores Issue Book.

That each Ledger should have a few pages at the end reserved for abstracting transactions.

That a copy of the Ledger abstract should be given to the Accounts Branch for financial reconciliation.

That financial reconciliation of Stock Account should be gradually and regularly carried out by one or two sub-heads each month.

That the discrepancy between the Financial Account and the Ledger Account should be adjusted on a pro-rata basis.

That the adjustment of profit and loss should be carried out annually.

That the physical verification of the ground balances and reconciliation of value account of the same sub-heads should be simultaneously carried out in the same month, and that a Perpetual Inventory of Stores be made.

That a detached Store sub-division should be maintained at the site of work, if necessary, subordinate to the main Store.

That the main Store should issue materials to Detached Stores as transfer of stock.

That the Sub-Stores should send a monthly abstract of their own ledgers to the H.O. for reconciliation.

That the Sub-Stores should be kept posted with the revised issue rates for materials.

That there should be a Special Officer set apart for stock-taking.

That stores verification should be carried out according to a programme.

That the Stock Verifier should report also the condition of stores.

That the subordinate incharge of Stores should render all possible help to the Stock Verifier in his work.

That Bin Cards should be brought up-to-date before a section is subjected to a physical check.

That the Stock Verifier should prepare a report of verification in Form N-19.

That the store of an allied nature should be verified at the same time.

That stock-taking should be carried out in the presence of a representative of the Store Holder.

That articles like coal, coke, etc., should be checked by weighing or counting on average sample.

That the verification report should be prepared in quadruplicate.

That the Stock Verifier should initial and date the Bin Cards of the articles checked by him.

That the discrepancies noticed in stock-taking should be carefully inquired into to know the cause.

That the discrepancies should be written off, recovered or adjusted under a proper authority.

That prompt action should be taken to correct the account without delay.

That "Changed Stores" should be indicated as such.

That articles pertaining to the "Returned Stores" should be returned on Form N-17.

That the scraps, empties, etc., should be returned on Form N-17.

That the Central Store Organization should also handle articles of tools and plant.

That the Stores should be located at sites involving minimum carriage, etc.

That lack of space should be avoided by having gangways of the size as necessary only.

That heavier goods should be stored in lower bins.

That there should be at least a four-foot clearance from the roof.

That the articles should be judiciously stored in bins.

That the steel racks should be used with bigger bins at the bottom and smaller at the top.

That adequate arrangements should be made to provide good light in the Stores.

That arrangements to keep off dust should be made.

That the Stores should be protected with wrappers, anti-rust paint, etc.

That the bins should be lettered and numbered at eye-level in letters and figures at least 3 inches high. The numbers should run from left to right.

That colour should be used for identification of materials, if necessary.

That fire-extinguishers and fire-buckets should be placed at convenient intervals in the Stores.

That fire-fighting squads be formed from among the staff and fire-fighting drills held.

That notice boards prohibiting smoking should be hung at the entrance of the Stores.

That adequate security measures should be adopted by frequent checking and providing overalls, etc., and Store yards well lighted.

That the personnel for the Stores should be given training in the job.

That accounting machines should be introduced in large Stores.

That units for bidding, measurement and payments should conform to a Standard Estimating Practice.

That a Manual should be got out on the Standard Methods of Measurement.

That Estimates should be prepared in detail to enable distribution of cost into elements of work.

That the Estimates should show physical quantities of work also.

That a Unit Price Contract is preferable to all other types.

That the composition of specification of work should be systematic and logical.

That the language of the Contract Document should be free from ambiguities.

That there should be a clause in the agreement invalidating all commitments in relation to the contract from any but legally authorized sources.

That a pre-selection of contractors be based on qualifications.

That the lowest tenders should be accepted from among the pre-selected contractors.

The Project Organization should have the following cells:

1. Cost Engineer.
2. Construction Officer.
3. Construction Engineer.
4. Field Engineer.
5. Chief Store Officer.
6. Administrator.
7. Development Officer.
8. Financial Adviser.

That Flow Diagrams should be used for planning works.

That equipment should be properly planned.

That labour requirements should be planned.

That a Costing Section is necessary to control costs.

That the Cost System should be flexible.

That the costing organization should be conversant with the technical aspects of work.

That punctuality in the submission of data should be ensured.

That when exact figures are not available best approximation may be made.

That the Costing Section should be under a competent Cost Engineer.

That each official should keep a diary to record all essentials regarding work under him.

That Daily Reports should be submitted for works, materials, labourers, field repairs and outputs.

That the units of measurement should be the same as the units in the estimates.

That a monthly reconciliation of figures for quantities of work and expenditure be made between the Costing and Accounts Sections.

That Monthly Progress Reports should be prepared in the prescribed forms, giving quantities of work done, unit rates obtained and variations in cost.

That the C.P.W.A. Forms 1 to 6, 13 to 19, 23 to 28, 31 to 32, 39, 42 to 46, 48 to 86 and 88 to 98 should be retained intact.

That the original C.P.W.A. Forms 7 to 12, 21, 22, 29, 35 to 38 may be deleted.

That the C.P.W.A. Forms, 33, 34, 40, 41 should be amended.

That new Forms N-1 to N-39 should be introduced.

That the original C.P.W.A. Form 7—Indents for Stores—should be replaced by a new Form N-13.

That the old Form C.P.W.A. 8—Register of Stock Receipts/Issues—should be replaced by a Bin Card in Form N-10.

That the old Form C.P.W.A. 9 of Abstract of Stock Receipts should be replaced by Form N-11.

That the old Form C.P.W.A. 10 of Abstract of Stock Issues should be replaced by Form N-16.

That the old Forms C.P.W.A. 11 and 12 should be replaced by Forms N-10 and N-18.

That the old Form C.P.W.A. 21 of Muster Roll should be abolished and a system of time-keeping described in Appendix V adopted.

That old Form 23 of Measurement Book should be replaced by Form N-8 of the Stores Received Book in the case of supplies only.

That the old Form 29 of Pay Bill of work-charged establishments should be replaced by a new Form N-23 of Pay Roll.

That the old C.P.W.A. Forms 33 and 34 of Work Abstract should be replaced by a new Form N-34.

That the old Forms of M.A.S. accounts Nos. 35 to 38 be abolished and only a register in Form N-36 maintained with a supplementary register of daily transactions.

That the old Forms 40 and 41 of Register of Work be replaced by the new Form N-35.

That Field Engineers should send their requirements of stores in Form N-1 in duplicate to Construction Engineer.

That the enquiries from supplier be standardized regarding stores and issued on Form N-2.

That the order for supply of stores be issued in the new Form N-3 prepared in as many copies as necessary, at least 6.

That a copy of Purchase Orders issued in Form N-3 should each be supplied to the supplier, officer receiving the store, officer holding the store, ultimate user, Accounts Branch and the sixth used as office copy.

That a consolidated record of all the Purchase Orders should be maintained in a register in Form N-4 by the Procurement Officer.

That a Register of Railway Receipts be maintained in Form N-5.

That prompt action for the disposal of rejected stores should be taken. A Form N-6 Rejection Memo has been proposed.

That a consolidated record of all rejections should be maintained in a register in Form N-7.

That new Form N-8 of the Stores Received Book should be used to record entries of receipts of all stores and that it should be prepared in triplicate by sub-heads of stock in an indelible ink or copying pencil in accordance with the instructions.

That one copy of the Stores Received Book with a necessary Certificate of Verification should be sent to the disbursing officer for making payment and posting of the Stores Price Ledgers.

That the third copy of Form N-8 should be utilized to prepare a monthly Abstract of Stores Received.

That Stores Received Books should be given the same attention and importance as is given at present to Measurement Books.

That a register of Bin Cards issued should be maintained in Form N-9 as a permanent record.

That there should be a Bin Card in Form N-10 for each item of the Stores.

That the new Form N-11 of Abstract of Stores Received be prepared by stock sub-heads.

That the disposal of bills for supplies should be watched through a register in Form N-12.

That stores should be drawn in the new Form N-13.

That the new Form N-14 of Stores Issue Book should replace the old Form 10 and should be prepared by the sub-heads of stock classified by works and their sub-heads.

That each Sectional Store Holder should prepare separate Stores Issue Books for different sub-heads of stock daily.

That each Store Holder should prepare an abstract of Issue Indents in Form N-15 for each work and its sub-heads day to day.

That a monthly Abstract of Issues in Form N-16 should be prepared by the sub-heads of stock from Stores Issue Books.

That for all goods previously issued and required to be returned to the Stores Form N-17 of the Return Note should be urged.

That a Store Price Ledger in Form N-18 should be maintained.

That results of all physical verifications of stores should be reported in Form N-19.

That a programme of physical verification of stores should be maintained in a register in Form N-20.

That a Time Card in Form N-21 should be maintained for each worker.

That a Time Check Sheet in Form N-22 should be maintained by the Time-Keeper.

That payment to workmen should be made on the new Form N-23 of Pay Roll.

That a record of movements of tools should be kept in a Tool Card Form N-24.

That a ledger in Form N-25 should be maintained for each equipment.

That the time for which a machine has worked should be summarized in Form N-26 for the distribution of the cost of jobs.

That a report of daily issue of stores for machines should be reported in Form N-27.

That a daily report of the use of automobiles should be prepared in Form N-28.

That the daily output of machines should be reported in Form N-29.

That the daily output by the manual labour should be reported in Form N-30.

That a statement of the monthly production by machines be prepared in Form N-31.

That a cost report of mass concrete should be submitted in Form N-32.

That estimates should be framed in a new Form N-33.

That the work abstract be prepared in Form N-34.

That a new Form N-35 should be used for Register of Works.

That the Sub-Store Register for stores issued for Materials at Site should be maintained.

That field repairs should be reported daily in Form N-37.

That a daily report of accidents and breakdowns be sent in Form N-38.

That a daily mass concrete report should be sent in Form N-39.

PLANTATION INQUIRY COMMISSION, 1954—REPORT

Delhi, Manager of Publications, 1956. 994p.

Chairman : Shri P. Madhava Menon.
Members : Shri K. G. Sivaswamy; Prof. M. V. Mathur.
Secretary : Shri T. S. Seshukutty.

APPOINTMENT

The Plantation Inquiry Commission was constituted under the Ministry of Commerce and Industry vide their Notification No. S.R.O. 1261 dated April 17, 1954.

TERMS OF REFERENCE

To make a comprehensive enquiry and in particular to:

(a) Ascertain separately the amount of capital, Indian and non-Indian, invested respectively in Tea, Coffee and Rubber Plantations;

(b) Examine the methods of production and the costs of production of Tea, Coffee and Rubber in the different important growing areas in India;

(c) Examine the present methods of financing Tea, Coffee and Rubber Plantations;

(d) Examine the present methods of marketing Tea, Coffee and Rubber including all the factors which affect the price paid by the consumer;

(e) Examine the possibilities of further expansion and development of the Tea, Coffee and Rubber Plantation industries.

On the conclusion of the Enquiry the Commission were required to make recommendations to the Government on the measures necessary:

(a) To secure for the producer a Fair Price for his product and to the consumer a Fair Price for the article he buys;

(b) To enable the provision of necessary finance for the plantation industries;

(c) To ensure suitable marketing arrangements; and

(d) To develop and expand the Tea, Coffee and Rubber Plantation industries.

CONTENTS

Introductory; General; Geographical Location of the Tea Growing Areas in India; The Structure of the Tea Industry in India; Capital Structure; Maintenance and Up-keep of Tea Bushes; Methods of Production—A Description; Cost of Production of Tea; Higher Productivity and Labour (**Section A**: External Facilities; **Section B**: Regulation of Temporary Labour; **Section C**: Reduction of Labour Turnover and Absenteeism; **Section D**: Surplus Labour and Employment; **Section E**: Wage Structure; **Section F**: Industrial Relations); Transport Supplies and Services; Finance; Marketing of Tea—Primary Sales; Marketing of Tea—Retail Distribution of Tea in India; Consumption and Export; Profits and Their Allocation; Taxation; Plantation Labour Act and Labour Welfare; The Small Producer; Research Training and Advisory Services; Regulation of the Working of Companies; Sales of Tea Estates; Expansion and Development; Summary of Conclusions and Recommendations; Acknowledgments.

RECOMMENDATIONS

The Structure Of The Tea Industry In India

In order to provide for a continuous growth of the industry, it is necessary that finance should be made available in sufficient quantities and that the agencies providing the finance should operate with greater flexibility.

We feel that the response of the capital market to debenture issues by tea companies should be favourable. We recommend that tea companies adopt this source of finance for future capital to an increasing extent.

Maintenance And Up-keep Of Tea Bushes

The tea gardens should be required to lay aside every year a certain sum of money for the purpose of financing programmes of replanting.

The contributions to the fund made by the tea gardens should be allowed as an admissible charge for the purpose of computing income-tax.

In many estates rehabilitation is necessary not only as regards tea bushes but also as regards plant and machinery and other fixed equipment. Some of the gardens are working with old and worn out machinery which affects the quality of the tea manufactured by them. These old and worn out machinery would require replacement.

We recommend that the Tea Board in consultation with the producers concerned should draw up a programme of phased replanting as well as replacement and renewal of plant and machinery. After such a phased programme has been drawn up, the Government should take steps to ensure that the necessary financial provision for it is made by various gardens before they declare dividends or repatriate profits.

When tea gardens of 100 acres or more are sold, the approval of the Tea Board should be obtained.

Cost Of Production Of Tea

A well-planned and regular study of Cost Data is necessary for keeping the industry informed about its economic efficiency and competitive position. The Tea Board should, therefore, undertake this function as part of its regular work. A "Cost of Production" Section should be set up in the Tea Board for this purpose. This section of the Tea Board should collect relevant data regarding costs of production from all estates. In order to maintain uniformity and secure better comparability, the forms for cost of production returns should be standardized by the Tea Board with the help of experienced Tea Planters and Chartered Accountants.

Higher Productivity And Labour

The success of Productivity Schemes primarily hinges on the Inspector at the bottom, his training and his capacity to promote labour-management relations.

An improvement in the working conditions would certainly increase labour productivity.

Rationalization of operations is necessary to increase productivity.

A major part of the success of the industry depends on plucking.

Supplies of tools and implements should be reviewed from the point of view of reducing physical efforts and increasing productivity.

Training of recruited labour should be given priority in every estate.

A Special Committee should devise a uniform set of registers and records.

The Government should enforce a slightly higher wage than the minimum in the case of casual labour so as to include the cost of amenities which resident labour got from the estates.

The possibility of using Employment Exchanges should be explored by the State Governments and employers' organizations.

We recommend that the State Governments in collaboration with the Tea Board and the Tea Industry should have detailed surveys made of the land resources other than land under tea at present held by the tea plantations and the use to which they are put.

Provision should be made for giving advice on Family Planning to the workers and their families.

Minimum wages should be the same in all States unless they varied on account of differences in cost of living.

A progressively higher rate for overtime hours of work will be an incentive to labour productivity.

Transport, Supplies And Services

There is need for keeping the line connecting Dhubri with the Central Dooars secure from breaching as this will keep the alternative river route to Calcutta open even when the rail route is disrupted. This deserves consideration by the Railway authorities.

The requests from the industry that at stations where there are bookings of tea, suitable covered accommodation should be provided to hold the tea awaiting despatch and that only leak-proof wagons should be provided for the transport of tea are reasonable and we recommend that these facilities should be provided.

We recommend that the Excise authorities should consider the possibilities of allowing gardens the facility of having duty-paid godowns where teas can be stored after payment of Excise duty and from which teas can be moved quickly to the rail-head on receipt of information regarding the placement of wagons.

Tea estates in the Darjeeling region may be granted permits for plying their vehicles on the Darjeeling-Siliguri Road for transport of tea and their stores.

The main difficulty regarding transport experienced by the South Indian Tea Industry is with regard to shortage of wagons, especially in the monsoon months. The Railway authorities should consider the request and do what is possible in the matter.

The Tea Board should promote establishment of co-operative organizations for supplying stores.

Finance

The Industrial Finance Corporation and State Finance Corporations of the States in which the gardens are situated should meet the need for long-term finance. In the case of Tripura, we recommend that the facilities of the State Finance Corporation of a neighbouring State, either Assam or West Bengal, should be extended to Tripura by necessary amendment of the relevant Act and Rules.

Marketing Of Tea—Primary Sales

We recommend that the Tea Board should assume the function of regulating the sale of tea in the Cochin and Calcutta auctions. The rules governing the auction sales and other matters pertinent to the primary marketing of tea should be made by the Tea Board. To help the Board in performing its functions regarding the regulation of sales it should appoint a Standing Committee.

The Tea Board should look into the question of warehousing and brokerage charges about which complaints have been made.

If in the future the need arises for a centralized warehousing system in Cochin, the Tea Board through the relevant Committee should be responsible for its administration also.

The Quota System should be abolished.

Future regulation of tea exports can be done under the Import and Export Control Act as for other commodities, which are subject to quantitative restrictions for exports.

Marketing Of Tea—Retail Distribution Of Tea In India

The differential rates of Excise duties on packaged and loose tea should be abolished and the old uniform rate of duty of three annas per lb. on all teas restored.

We recommend that the Central Board of Revenue should evolve a system by which companies and proprietors having less than 500 acres will be permitted to move their teas from factories on pre-payment of only half the amount of Excise duty provided they undertake payment of the balance within 90 days. The scheme evolved should be a flexible one.

Consumption And Export

In order that market expansion may be guided properly and effectively there should be Marketing and Tea Promotion Directorate in the Tea Board which will make studies of various marketing problems in India and abroad.

Profits And Their Allocation

Any scheme that may be evolved should incorporate the following essential requirements:

(i) The depreciation allowance by the Income Tax authorities should be separately funded and drawn upon only for meeting expenditure on replacement and renewal of fixed assets.

(ii) The Tea Replanting Fund should be set apart as already recommended.

(iii) After providing for taxation, each company should build out of its profits a Statutory Reserve for meeting development expenditure and unforeseen charges; this Reserve should be kept in a fairly liquid form.

(iv) From what is left over, a certain minimum dividend should be provided for as a percentage on share capital.

(v) The remainder should be divided between the shareholders and labour and staff according to a suitable formula.

Taxation

We recommend that the rates and conditions regarding levy of Agricultural Income Tax on tea plantation in the several States be made uniform. Also the mode of collection will be simplified and duplicate collecting agencies avoided if the Central Income Tax authorities collect both the taxes themselves and pass on the agricultural portion of the collection to the States.

Levy should be abolished.

Plantation Labour Act And Labour Welfare

Government loans should be made available to the plantation industry at rates of interest and terms of repayment as available to other industries under the Industrial Housing Scheme.

The local authorities should not levy any rates or taxes on plantations in respect of conservancy and lighting, etc., unless they are in a position to provide these services in a satisfactory manner.

Wherever the employers have to provide for the maintenance of civic services such as conservancy, water supply, etc., it would be desirable to manage these through committees on which workers are adequately represented. The maintenance of canteens may also be delegated to the same committees with advantage.

A Plantation Labour Welfare Organization may be instituted. This organization should be established and controlled by the Government of India.

In the event of an estate being brought to sale before the phased programme of implementation is completed, we recommend that the State Government should assess the undischarged liability of the seller in regard to his obligations under the Plantation Labour Act and recover such amounts as may be necessary for this purpose from the seller before registering the sale.

Small Producer

When the small holders form co-operative societies, they should be granted assistance somewhat on the lines on which the Government of Ceylon grants loans to the tea growers' co-operative societies.

Voluntary amalgamation of small gardens into larger ones where there is a desire for it would of course be given every encouragement.

Research Training And Advisory Services

The Tea Board should organize in a suitable manner Regional Advisory Committees of representative and influential planters whose help will be available to the Advisory Officer to facilitate his work by securing necessary local co-operation.

The Tea Experimental Farm at Palampur should be transferred to the Tea Board to be developed into a suitable Demonstration Farm to meet the needs of Kangra District. The State Government should transfer the farm to the Tea Board free of charge.

The Tea Board should make necessary arrangements for specialized training of their Advisory Officers in tea culture in collaboration with existing tea experimental stations and agricultural colleges.

Regulation Of The Working Of Companies

Remuneration to staff should take the form of a fixed salary.

An increasing number of Indians be appointed in the Managerial Cadre of tea companies.

It is essential that a system of local audit of the garden expenditure and other branch office expenditure should be insisted upon by the Government in the case of all companies.

Sale Of Tea Estates

If the seller or a prospective buyer so desired, the Tea Board should send its expert evaluators to assess the price of a tea estate. Such evaluations should also be done for the benefit of the Department of Company Law Administration and the Reserve Bank of India, as and when necessary.

Expansion And Development

It would be desirable to continue the machinery provided by the International Tea Agreement so that all problems of the industry concerning production and absorption may be kept under constant and close study by the International Committee and regulations initiated if and when the situation demands it.

It will be necessary for the Government and the Tea Board to have necessary reserve powers to regulate the orderly development of tea cultivation and exports.

RAILWAY CONVENTION COMMITTEE, 1954—REPORT

New Delhi, Lok Sabha Secretariat, 1954. 21, IIp.

Chairman : Shri M. Ananthasayanam Ayyangar.

Members : Shri C. D. Deshmukh; Shri Lal Bahadur Shastri; Shri R. Venkataraman; Shri Basanta Kumar Das; Shri Satyendra Narayan Sinha; Shri Nageshwar Prasad Sinha; Shri Narendra P. Nathwani; Shri Ram Saran; Shri B. Ramachandra Reddi; Sardar Lal Singh; Shri Tulsidas Kilachand; Shri K. Ananda Nambiar; Shri R. M. Deshmukh; Shri B. C. Ghose; Babu Gopinath Singh; Shri T.V. Kamalaswamy; Shri V. M. Obaidullah Sahib.

Joint Secretary : Shri S. L Shakdher.

Deputy Secretary : Shri V. Subramanian.

APPOINTMENT

The Convention Resolution of 1949, which was passed by the Constituent Assembly of India (Legislative) on December 21, 1949, *inter alia* laid down that a Committee of the House should review the rate of dividend towards the end of the aforesaid period and suggest for the years following it any adjustment considered necessary, having regard to the revenue returns of the Undertaking, the average borrowing rate of the Government and any other relevant factors. A Committee of both Houses of Parliament was accordingly constituted in pursuance of the following Resolution adopted by the Lok Sabha on May 12, 1954, and concurred in by the Rajya Sabha on May 14, 1954.

"That this House resolved that—

(i) A Parliamentary Committee consisting of 12 members of this House to be nominated by the Speaker be appointed to review the rate of dividend which is at present payable by the Railway Undertaking to the General Revenues as well as other ancillary matters in connection with the separation of Railway Finance from General Finance, and make recommendations thereon by November 30, 1954; and

(ii) That this House recommends to the Council of States to agree to associate six members from the Council with the Committee and to communicate the names of the members so appointed to this House."

TERMS OF REFERENCE

The first sitting of the Committee was held on October 1, 1954. At this sitting the Committee drew up the undermentioned list of subjects which they liked to take up for a detailed investigation with reference to the above Resolution and asked the Railway Board to furnish detailed memoranda:

(i) The future financial prospects of the Railway Undertaking on the basis of the present rates and fares;

(ii) The average borrowing rate of the Government in the recent past;

(iii) Whether it will be desirable to have an Amortization Fund, and, if so, what should be the contribution to the Fund having regard to the actual contribution to General Revenues?

(iv) The rate at which contributions to the Depreciation Reserve Fund should be made to ensure that adequate funds are available for renewals and replacements of Railway assets;

(v) The needs of the Development Fund to meet the demands for amenities to users of the Railways, for Welfare Schemes for Railway staff, for unremunerative developmental work, etc.;

(vi) The rate of growth of the Railway Capital-at-Charge and ways and means of financing such expenditure; and

(vii) The appropriate size of the Revenue Reserve Fund and the demands that may be made upon it.

(viii) New Lines: Should any special concession in regard to payment of dividend be given to Capital invested on new lines so as to encourage the undertaking of the construction of such lines for development purposes?

(ix) Whether the test of remunerativeness of a Project requires revision in the light of the result of the review of the dividend payable.

(x) Whether any alterations in the Rules of Allocation of Railway expenditure introduced in 1950 as between Capital, Revenue and Development Fund are considered necessary in the light of the actual working during the last four years.

(xi) Whether the rate of dividend of 4% on the Capital-at-Charge payable to General Revenues requires to be revised, and if so, what should be the revised rate and how it should be met by the Railways?

(xii) In the event of any difficulty in fixing a new rate of dividend, whether alternative methods of contribution to General Revenues, e.g.,

(a) A small fixed percentage on the Capital-at-Charge, plus sharing of profits after payment of interest, or

(b) Interest on Capital, plus a levy of Income Tax

as on other Government Undertakings together with or without any contribution for investment, fixed or varying, may not be resorted to.

(xiii) Whether the element of over-capitalization in the Loan Capital should be eliminated in keeping with sound commercial practice and, if so, to what extent, and how?

(xiv) Whether any alternative method of financing unremunerative development work is feasible if adequate resources are not available in the Development Fund.

CONTENTS

Composition of the Railway Convention Committee, 1954; Introduction; Report; Appendix; Summary of the Principal Recommendations of the Committee.

RECOMMENDATIONS

It would be advantageous from all points of view to express the rate of dividend in terms of a percentage on the Capital-at-Charge and the amount paid annually through a fixed rate of dividend inclusive of the element of interest.

The present rate of dividend should remain unaltered for another period of five years. However, the Committee feel that in the matter of calculation of the Capital-at-Charge and arriving at the total of the dividend payable, some minor adjustments are called for.

The element of over-capitalization should be precisely assessed by the Railway Board and on that portion of the loan capital the Railways shall pay the dividend at the rate equivalent to the average borrowing rate charged by the Government of India to Commercial Departments from year to year.

The dividend on the Capital-at-Charge of new lines should be computed at a lesser rate, viz., the average borrowing rate charged to Commercial Departments and a moratorium should be granted in respect of the dividend payable on the Capital invested on the new lines during the period of construction and up to the end of the fifth year of their opening for traffic, the deferred amount being repaid from the sixth year onwards in addition to the current dividend out of the net income of the new lines.

The annual contribution to the Depreciation Reserve Fund which had been maintained at a level of Rs. 30 crores during the five-year period ending March 31, 1955, should be raised to Rs. 35 crores during the next quinquennium.

The Committee recognize that the appropriation to the Development Fund and the solvency of the Fund are dependent on the availability and the size of the surplus, while the provision for depreciation should be based on the life of the assets, and their replacement on the actual conditions which cannot be deferred, if their earning potential is to be maintained. They, therefore, feel that the replacement of these assets should bear no relationship to the ultimate loss or gain of the Undertaking but should be met out of the Depreciation Reserve Fund.

The Committee are in favour of extending the scope of the Development Fund so as to include amenities for all "users of Railway transport", such as improvement to goods sheds, loading and unloading platforms, waiting sheds for the trading public, etc., which they consider as absolutely essential and recommend the continuance of the present practice of earmarking a minimum of Rs. 3 crores per annum on this account.

The Railway Board should look into the matter of assessment of rent realized for Railway quarters and ensure that a return of rent more commensurate with the capital cost is obtained on all residential buildings built for Class III staff.

The Committee are anxious that the primary amenity which the Railways must provide is that of safety of travel. They, therefore, desire that the expenditure on Safety Works should be given due priority in any allocations of funds from the Development Fund over the next few years.

The Committee agree with the Railway Board that the distinction of splitting up of expenditure on works between the Development Fund and Revenue for the purpose of allocation is unnecessary. The allocation should be determined as in the case of other works according to the total outlay expected on each work. The expenditure on unremunerative operating improvement works costing more than Rs. 3 lakhs each should be charged entirely to the Development Fund.

The cost of construction of all new lines when decided to be constructed might be debited to Capital from the very beginning.

In the event of the Development Fund not being in a position to meet the programme of expenditure chargeable to that Fund from its own resources, money should be advanced from General Revenues to the Railways for utilization on those projects or Works which are of a developmental nature. Such advances should be treated as Temporary Loans to the Railways and will not be added to the Capital-at-Charge on which 4% dividend is payable annually. The Railways will pay interest on this loan to General Revenues at the average borrowing rate chargeable to Commercial Departments. It shall, however, be open to the Railways to repay this loan in instalments, if necessary, from accretions to the Development Fund in more prosperous years and thus liquidate the debt and the interest liability thereon.

In view of the fact that the annual loss on the working of strategic lines is insignificant, the Committee consider that the suggestion made by the Railway

Board whether the operating loss on strategic lines should not be deducted from the contribution calculated for payment to General Revenues on non-strategic lines should not be pressed for a decision now, but brought up before the next Convention Committee, if the loss on this account is sizable.

The criterion for classifying a project as remunerative should be 5%.

While the Committee agree that amortization would eventually be of benefit to the Railways and the users of Railway transport alike, they agree with the Railway Board that the time is not yet ripe for amortization; they would, however, suggest that this question may be taken up at the time of next revision of the Convention.

The Committee consider that in the present financial prospects, it will be idle either to prescribe any minimum limit for the balance in the Revenue Reserve Fund or to extend its scope so as to include amortization of Capital and this should wait till better days come.

A Parliamentary Committee should review the rate of dividend towards the end of the next quinquennium and suggest for the years following it any adjustment considered necessary, in the light of the situation obtaining then.

It would be enough if the Ministry of Railways submitted a review on the general working of the Railways during these five years to the next Convention Committee for their consideration.

EXPERT COMMITTEE ON THE PREVENTION OF SLAUGHTER OF CATTLE IN INDIA, 1954—REPORT

Delhi, Manager of Publications, 1955. 84, IIIp.

Chairman : Shri P. N. Nanda.
Members : Dr. K. C. Sen; Shri D. N. Khurody; Shri L. C. Sikka; Shri B. N. Handa; Shri V. R. Rajagopalan; Sardar Santokh Singh.
Secretary : Shri K. P. R. Kartha.

APPOINTMENT

The Expert Committee on the Prevention of Slaughter of Cattle in India was constituted under the Ministry of Food and Agriculture vide their Resolution No. F. 24-I/54-L. S. dated June 10, 1954.

TERMS OF REFERENCE

To suggest measures which should be taken:

(i) To prevent the killing of milch cows, particularly in the cities of Calcutta and Bombay even when they had gone temporarily dry;

(ii) To make the present law under the subject more effective so as to put an end to such an evil practice as "Phooka";

(iii) To explore the possibility of making milk powder in suitable centres; and

(iv) To impose some effective control on the inter-State movement of cattle.

CONTENTS

Preface; Slaughter of Milch Animals in Cities; Past Efforts to Control Slaughter—Historical Retrospects; Position in Greater Bombay; The Problem in Calcutta City; Position in Madras City; Problem in other Cities; Consideration of Item I in Terms of Reference; Consideration of Item II in Terms of Reference; Consideration of Item III in Terms of Reference; Consideration of Item IV in Terms of Reference; General Problem of Cattle Slaughter in India; Summary of Recommendations; Appendices.

RECOMMENDATIONS

Item 1

The wholesale removal of milch cattle from cities and the replacement of city-produced milk by milk produced by animals kept in their natural surroundings in rural areas is the only permanent method of solving the problem of prevention of slaughter of milch animals.

A comprehensive organization should be set up immediately in each State for efficiently handling the numerous aspects of the complicated matter of developing milk production in rural areas to its maximum capacity and for its collection, processing and transport to and distribution in urban areas.

The milk plan should be worked in the best interests of both the producer in the villages and the consumer in the urban areas so that it may result in a large-scale development of cattle and dairy industries of the country.

The establishment of farms for the salvage of dry

cows and buffaloes and for the rearing of calves, at suitable places, should be part of the colony scheme.

The colony part of the scheme should be financially self-supporting except in regard to the capital outlay, but in regard to salvage of dry animals and the rearing of calves, subsidies should be given by the Government.

Legislation, where necessary, should be enacted to enforce compulsory pasteurization of all milk distributed in cities so that the work of quality control may be effectively enforced.

Item 2

To prevent "Phooka", milch cows should be maintained under conditions where their calves can be reared.

The relevant provision in the Prevention of Cruelty to Animals Act should be more effectively enforced.

The rewards offered to the informants, provided in the Act, should be enhanced and made more attractive.

The punishment prescribed under the existing law should also include cancellation of the licence of the offenders for the keeping of milch animals.

Item 3

The replacement of export of milch animals from breeding areas by the export of milk powder manufactured there is not considered feasible.

Surveys should be carried out in areas considered to be actual or potential milk pockets in parts of the country like Gujarat, Saurashtra, Nilgiris, Karnal, Jullundur, Sangrur, Aligarh, Darjeeling and Guntur to examine their suitability for the establishment of milk condensing or drying plants, in order to fully utilize seasonal surpluses and to make the country independent of foreign supplies.

Researches should be undertaken on both cow and buffalo milk, produced under village conditions, for investigating the technological and organizational problems connected with drying and condensing.

Item 4

As high-quality milch animals have already become scarce in the breeding tracts, the following steps should be taken for their resuscitation to prevent further depletion:

(a) A remunerative market for the sale of milk produced in the breeding areas should be developed.

(b) Export from the breeding areas should be restricted to such cows and she-buffaloes as have dropped at least two calves in the breeding tracts.

(c) The rearing and breeding of high-class animals in the breeding tracts should be encouraged. To a large extent this will automatically follow the full implementation of Recommendation Nos. 1 and 2.

(d) In the selection of breeding stock in the Haryana tract, more emphasis should be laid on milk rather than on draught alone.

(e) Cattle and buffaloes in the breeding tracts should be registered and the retention of selected high-class stock should be subsidized.

An organization to purchase dry cows and buffaloes from cities and to sell them to the breeders in the breeding tract should be set up by the State Governments in the exporting areas.

General Recommendations

Legislation for the prevention of slaughter of useful cattle should be uniform in all States.

A complete ban on the slaughter of cattle would not be in the best interest of the country as it is merely a negative and not a positive approach to the problem.

A full-fledged statistical section should be set up in the Animal Husbandry Department in each State for the regular collection, collation and dissemination of statistical data and other information relating to all aspects of animal husbandry.

In view of the undeveloped state of the potentially large cattle and dairy industries of India, the Central Government should pay much greater attention and take more initiative in the development of these industries than they have done hitherto. It is, therefore, essential that there should be a whole-time member in the Planning Commission to devote his entire attention to the development of cattle and dairy industries in the country.

Interim Measures

Until such time as the milk supply of cities can be reorganized in accordance with the foregoing recommendations, the following interim measures should be adopted to arrest further depletion of high-class milch animals:

(a) Stables and cattle in cities must be licensed and movement of cattle allowed only under a permit.

(b) To prevent further growth of city milch cattle population, import of animals should be allowed only on the basis of animals which die or are salvaged or are disposed of under a certificate.

(c) Adequate breeding facilities should be made available free of cost in the cities.

(d) Self-contained salvage and calf-rearing farms should be set up by State Governments.

(e) Maintenance of dry cattle and calves in these farms should be subsidized, and salvage of dry cows and buffaloes should be restricted to high-yielding animals which are in calf.

(f) Selected Goshalas and Pinjrapoles should be helped with additional facilities and funds, where necessary, to enable them to undertake salvage of dry animals and rearing of calves.

(g) The existing method of assessment for levying income-tax should be revised to enable the owners to retain their dry stock without inflating their assets.

(h) Concession in railway freight for return of dry animals and their calves from cities to rural areas should be further liberalized to 25% of the normal freight and should be applicable to all cities instead of to Bombay, Calcutta and Madras only as at present.

(i) Salvage farms should also be set up in the breeding tracts by the State Governments concerned.

(j) An export fee of Rs. 20 per animal exported by rail from a breeding tract should be levied and constituted into a Cattle Improvement and Salvage Fund for defraying the cost of salvage, as well as for subsidizing the retention of basic stock.

(k) The State Governments concerned should set up an organization for purchasing dry cows and buffaloes from cities, transporting them to the breeding tracts and disposing of them there.

(l) The legislation against the slaughter of useful cattle should be made fully effective by making it applicable to the entire State and not only to a part of it, and by the provision of adequate veterinary and police staff.

(m) The provision against sale of contraband beef should be rigorously enforced and fresh legislation enacted where necessary.

(n) Male calves of buffaloes should be excluded from the categories of animals whose slaughter is prohibited.

RIVER VALLEY PROJECTS TECHNICAL PERSONNEL COMMITTEE, 1954—REPORT

New Delhi, Ministry of Irrigation and Power, 1957. 117p.

Chairman : Shri W. X. Mascarenhas.

Members : Shri B. N. Datar; Shri G. K. Chandiramani; Shri A. K. Char.

Co-opted Members : Shri N. S. Gupchup; Lt.-Col. J. V. P. Braganza; Shri R. S. Basrur.

Secretary : Shri Ripudaman Singh.

APPOINTMENT

The River Valley Projects Technical Personnel Committee was constituted under the Ministry of Irrigation and Power vide their Resolution No. 24(14)/54-Adm. dated July 10, 1954.

TERMS OF REFERENCE

The Committee was asked to visit the River Valley Projects under construction in the country and, after studying the various factors affecting the requirements of technical personnel, to make recommendations on the following:

(i) The strength of the technical and accounts personnel of various categories required for the planning and execution of River Valley Projects and Flood Control Schemes, proposed to be undertaken in the country during the next 15 years, including those already under execution, and of the operational personnel required after their completion.

(ii) The steps that must be taken in order that the theoretical and practical talent necessary to meet the requirements under (i) above is forthcoming in this country and specially that the higher planning staff, capable in due course of assuming positions of the highest trust and responsibility, is progressively trained for the purpose.

(iii) The means of securing the co-operation of universities and professional institutions and service organizations, e.g., the Corps of Army Engineers, in the training of personnel for the Projects.

(iv) The extent to which the assistance of foreign experts and technicians will be necessary and the agencies through whom such assistance should be secured.

(v) The procedure to be followed in securing liaison and co-ordination between the various States *inter se* and between the States and the Central Government in the employment of available personnel in the best interests of the country.

(vi) Ways and means of improving efficiency and raising the morale of the engineering services of the Central and State Governments, with special reference to the Irrigation and Power Cadres.

The Committee was requested subsequently to include within the scope of its inquiry the question of facilities already existing for the training of personnel for handling various types of machinery and plant on the River Valley Projects.

CONTENTS

Introductory; Retrospect and Prospect; Assessment of Demand; Officer Personnel and Their Recruitment; Post-Recruitment Training; Departmental Organization and Efficiency; Foreign Experts; Miscellaneous; Summary of Conclusions and Recommendations; Appendix I to VIII.

RECOMMENDATIONS

In the vast majority of cases, the country's demands could be more conveniently and economically met by a large number of medium-sized projects than a small number of gigantic size.

Mobility of the various categories of personnel required for River Valley Projects excepting graduate engineers is, generally speaking, limited.

To meet partially the large demand for overseers short-term functional training should be organized for "Technical Assistants"

It will be necessary to turn out about 2,200 Technical Assistants (Civil) and 550 Technical Assistants (Electrical and Mechanical) per year for the two years 1957-58 and 1958-59.

The new category of Technical Assistants may be continued on a permanent basis in partial replacement of Diploma-holders if the experience justifies it.

Technical Assistants should be trained at the rate of 400 Civil and 250 Mechanical and Electrical per year during the years 1959-60 and 1960-61. During the Third Five Year Plan period (1961-66), 400 Civils and 250 Mechanicals and Electricals per year would require to be trained.

Training facilities for Mechanical and Electrical Assistants must be very widespread. Training centres should be set up at the project headquarters or near the sites of works.

A uniform duration of four years for courses leading to an engineering degree recommended by the Joint Committee of the All-India Council for Technical Education and the Inter-University Board should be adopted.

For post-graduate degrees, the courses should aim at depth rather than breadth.

To raise the standard of technical education, the Government should loan the services of experienced officers to serve as teachers in engineering colleges, particularly in the fields of irrigation and power engineering, where experience is almost exclusively restricted to Government engineers.

More time and attention should be devoted to the study of Social Sciences, Industrial Psychology, Labour Relations, etc., in the undergraduate engineering courses.

The two Cadres for Irrigation and Roads and Buildings should be separated and there must be specialization and research within the Cadres.

An All-India Service of Irrigation and Power Engineers should be created.

Officers should be encouraged to take post-graduate courses and to specialize in particular fields.

All engineers should be required to take refresher courses at periodical intervals, say, every five or seven years and these courses should be organized either in the individual States or on an inter-State basis or even by the Central Government.

Seminars and conferences should be held once in two years and attended by only selected persons, the subjects discussed being strictly limited.

A Staff College should be established for the study of socio-economic, administrative and practical aspects of planning and execution of big projects.

Every State should have a Research Station of its own.

The Hydro-Dynamical Research Station at Khadakvasla should be constituted into a National Laboratory on a par with the other National Laboratories in the country; it should confine itself to purely hydro-dynamical problems. Other work should be carried out only in an ancillary capacity.

The friction between Engineers and Administrators, especially Officers of the Revenue Department, at District and Divisional levels, must be eliminated by a clear recognition by the administrators that co-ordination does not mean subordination.

Our first need is to build up a planning and construction organization for River Valley Projects on a comprehensive and rational basis.

Zonal Development Organizations each covering one or more complete river basins as far as possible are the best solution in the existing circumstances.

A Central Organization to co-ordinate the work of the Zonal Authorities would be necessary and the Central Water and Power Commission could fill this role.

As the idea of Zonal Development Authorities develops the Central Water and Power Commission should progressively restrict its activity to that of a "Brain Trust" for the country.

The Central Board of Irrigation should act as a high-power consultative body which could review not only irrigation development in the country but also discuss the irrigation and power policies of the Government.

For so long as we do not produce heavy electrical and mechanical plant and equipment in this country and such equipment is imported, the advice of foreign consultants in regard to its use may be necessary.

There should be no need in future to recruit foreign executives or technicians for actual employment in this country.

Retired engineers of proven ability should be invited to join panels which could be consulted whenever problems of which they have had personal experience arise.

Every State Government should establish a proper Statistical Section for collecting and analysing statistical data relating to Irrigation and Power Projects.

Released Army personnel may be employed as Instructors in Training Centres in the use and maintenance of heavy earth-moving machinery.

A Cadre of Surveyors of Works may be created with a view to enabling engineering officers to concentrate as far as possible exclusively on technical matters.

The Government should boldly announce a new charter for engineers under which they should be appointed to Secretariat posts in Government administration, including that of Secretary to Government, managerial posts in public corporations, chairmanship of Port Trusts, Improvement Trusts, etc., in short, all those posts which can, with advantage, be held by persons with a technical background. In other words, engineers should be free to aspire to fill the highest posts in the country's service and not be restricted, as at present, to their own strictly professional field for preferment in office.

COMFORT SURVEY COMMITTEE ON LOW COST HOUSES, 1954—REPORT

New Delhi, Ministry of Works, Housing and Supply (National Buildings Organization), 1957. 146p.

Chairman : Lt.-Gen. H. Williams.
Members : Shri H. D. Awasty; Shri J. M. Rijhwani; Shri C. B. Patel; Shri H. C. Vijh; Sardar Sarup Singh; Shri K. L. Aggarwal.
Secretary : Shri K. Rama Varman.

APPOINTMENT

The Comfort Survey Committee on Low Cost Housing was constituted under the Ministry of Works, Housing and Supply (National Buildings Organization), in August, 1954.

TERMS OF REFERENCE

To study the different methods in the designs adopted by the International Low Cost Housing Exhibition, 1954.

CONTENTS

Part A: Introduction; Size of Plots; Orientation of Buildings; Architectural Treatment; Standards of Accommodation and Planning of Space; Foundation; Damp Proof Course; Termite-Proofing; Superstructure; Ceiling Heights; Roofs; Doors and Windows; Plastering; General Remarks; Appendices I to V; **Part B**: Introduction; Design Requirements; Work Done Abroad; Thermal Investigations; Thermal Properties of Surfaces; Ventilation; Day Light Illumination; Dampness Penetration; Minimum Ceiling Heights; Tentative Recommendations; References; Tables and Figures.

RECOMMENDATIONS

In orienting a building two factors are of consideration—isolation and ventilation—and at times these give conflicting indications. For climates as in Delhi the mean wind direction in the afternoon during the monsoon should guide the orientation, a thermally sound roof taking care of the isolation.

The heating effect of the sun on a building with faulty orientation can be remedied by attention to the roof and by an intelligent use of *chhajjas* and shady trees.

Closeable ventilators should be provided at ceiling level; permanent ventilators should, as far as possible, be avoided.

Heat capacity plays an important role in deciding the thermal performance of a building.

Where no artificial cooling aids are used, thermal diffusivity plays an important part; thermal conductivity alone is not so important.

As far as thermal comfort is concerned, the roof is the most important component of a building and it should on this account receive special attention.

The ceiling temperature can be brought down considerably by whitewashing the exposed surface of the roof.

A roof of built-up thickness of 6½ in. or more consisting of R. C. C. or reinforced brick work with or without mud-phuska, lime, concrete, etc., gave satisfactory results (due to moisture penetration, roofs of reinforced brick work have deteriorated after a time and their use is not generally recommended). R.C.C. roofs up to a thickness of 4½ in. and store roofs should not be used without some insulation. A.C. sheets, G.I. sheets or Mangalore tile roofing should not be used without a false ceiling.

Nine-inch brick walls in cement, lime or mud mortar with ½ in. plaster on both sides afford adequate thermal protection. Eight-inch hollow blocks of concrete or gypsum are not thermally adequate.

White, cream, biscuit and similar light-coloured washes are thermally desirable for exterior surfaces.

Cement wash, red and similar deep-colour washes should be avoided.

Where mud is used as an insulating material a waterproof rendering should be used on the roof.

When using precast roofs, special care is necessary to avoid dampness penetration at the joints.

Corrugated A.C. and G.I. sheets, if properly laid, may be relied upon as roofing materials.

Cavity walls and hollow-block walls can be safely depended upon.

Four-and-a-half-inch-thick brick walls, even of first class bricks and with rendering on both sides, have leaked and cannot be trusted.

Nine-inch brick walls with plaster on both sides have given satisfactory results in the Delhi climate, but may not be adequate in very exposed locations.

It is not sufficient to prescribe only the window area as a percentage of floor area. The distribution is also important and should be indicated.

When deciding the location of windows the mean monsoon wind direction during the afternoons should be the guiding factor. The effect of faulty orientation may be remedied to some extent by suitably locating the windows.

From the point of view of ventilation the width of a window is more important than its height.

The openings required for adequate ventilation generally produce adequate illumination conditions indoors.

From the illumination point of view the height of the window is more important than its width.

Little difference was noticed in the indoor temperature of four identical rooms of 12 ft. by 10 ft. and with ceiling heights varying between 8 ft. and 11 ft. and in four other identical rooms of 11 ft. 6 in. by 9 ft. 6 in. and with ceiling heights varying between 7½ ft. and 12 ft.

COMMITTEE FOR THE PREVENTION OF CRUELTY TO ANIMALS, 1954—REPORT

New Delhi, Ministry of Food and Agriculture (Department of Agriculture), 1957. 383p.

Chairman : Shri V. K. Krishna Menon (resigned, replaced by Shri V. B. Gandhi).

Vice-Chairman : Shrimati Rukmini Devi Arundale.

Members : Dr. M. D. D. Gilder; Shri Kakasaheb Kalelkar; Prof. N. R. Malkani; Shrimati Lakshmi N. Menon; Shri Dewan Chand Sharma; Dr. Syed Mahmud (resigned, Pt. Munishwar Dutt Upadhyaya was replaced and he also resigned and Shri Krishna Chandra was appointed in his place); Shri G. Srinivasa Murty; Dr. K. Mitra; Dr. P. Subbarayan; Shri G. R. Rajagopal; Shri Ahmed Mohiuddin; Shri R. L. Kaura.

Secretary : Shri R. L. Mehta.

APPOINTMENT

The Committee for the Prevention of Cruelty to Animals was constituted under the Ministry of Food and Agriculture (Department of Agriculture) vide their Resolution No. F. 2-136/53-PC. II dated August 16, 1954.

CONTENTS

Introductory; Cruelty to Animals Generally and Growth of Legislation for the Prevention of Cruelty to Animals in India; Experimentation of Animals; Slaughter of Animals; Animal Sacrifices; Animal Sport; Performing Animals; The Keeping or Confining of Animals; Transport of Animals; Export and Import of Animals; Animal Welfare in General; Summary of Conclusions and Recommendations; Note Received from Shrimati Rukmini Devi Arundale; Appendices.

RECOMMENDATIONS

Experimentation On Animals

The legislation to be undertaken may envisage the constitution of a Committee of 15 persons. The Central Government will nominate: (i) two representatives of each of the three Councils, viz., the Indian Council of Medical Research, the Indian Council of Agricultural Research and the Council of Scientific and Industrial Research; (ii) two persons to represent Universities in India; and (iii) five non-officials actively interested in animal welfare work. The remaining two persons will be members of Parliament of India. The Committee shall lay down rules, which shall be binding on all persons and institutions carrying on experiments on animals, so as to ensure that:

(a) Experiments are performed in any institution on the responsibility of the person in charge of the institution, and if they are performed outside an institution, the individuals performing them are fully qualified and assume full responsibility therefor;

(b) As far as possible, experiments involving operations are performed under the influence of some anaesthetic of sufficient power to prevent the animal feeling pain;

(c) No experiments are conducted:

(i) as an illustration of lectures, except when it is absolutely necessary, and

(ii) merely for attaining manual skill;

(d) Experiments on larger animals are avoided when it is possible to achieve the same results by experimenting upon small laboratory animals like guinea-pigs, rabbits, rats, etc.;

(e) Animals are properly looked after both before and after experiments; and

(f) Suitable records are maintained about the experiments performed.

The Committee shall have powers to inspect any institution engaged in animal experimentation to satisfy itself that its rules are being properly observed. Any violation of the rules shall render punishable the person in charge of the institution in which the breach has occurred or any other person (if the breach has occurred outside an institution), the punishment being a fine extending to Rs. 200.

Procurement, Housing, Breeding And Care Of Experimental Animal

The housing as well as breeding of experimental animals should be done, as far as possible, under natural conditions. Proper care should be observed in the disposal of animals after experimentation.

Alternatives To Animal Experimentation

Special efforts should be made to develop suitable alternatives to animal experimentation. To the extent that the systems of medicine other than the modern system need not rely on animal experimentation they deserve encouragement.

Slaughter Of Animals

Animals should be provided with food, water and rest at regular intervals during transit to slaughter-houses.

Pens or lairs should be large enough to accommodate comfortably the animals brought for slaughter; they should be well-paved, well-drained, properly ventilated and lighted. There should be adequate arrangements for the supply of food and water.

For proper ante-mortem inspection whole-time Veterinary Surgeons and other trained staff should be employed and slaughter-houses should be constructed on scientific lines. Uniform procedures should be laid down by Municipalities for the guidance of Meat Inspectors in their inspection work. Special legislation may have to be enacted, making it obligatory on Municipalities to effect these improvements.

Conservation Of Modern Slaughter-Houses

As the establishment of a sufficient number of modern slaughter-houses in the country will take a considerable time, a beginning may be made in this direction by setting up model slaughter-houses in big cities. Central and State Governments should consider providing suitable financial and technical aid to Municipalities for this purpose.

Humane Methods Of Slaughter

A law may be passed providing for the adoption of humane methods of slaughter in general terms, i.e., for the adoption of mechanical, electrical, chemical or other means which are found to be rapid, effective and humane.

Municipalization Of Slaughter-Houses

For the proper enforcement of municipal regulations and to enable improvements to be made in slaughter-houses, it is recommended that municipalities should assume complete control over all operations relating to the slaughter of animals from the pre-slaughter stage to slaughter, flaying or skinning of carcasses, etc. Further, the income derived from slaughter-houses should be spent on effecting improvements in slaughter-houses instead of being treated as part of the General Revenues of Municipalities.

Model Rules For Regulation Of Slaughter-Houses

Municipalities in India should adopt the Model Rules for the regulation of slaughter-houses to the maximum possible extent, depending on local conditions, and enforce them strictly.

Women and children should not be allowed under any circumstances to enter slaughter-houses nor should they be employed in any operation connected with a slaughter-house.

"Visitors" including public men should be nominated by Municipalities to visit slaughter-houses to ensure that Municipal regulations are fully observed.

Animal Sacrifices

The sacrifice of animals, including birds, to propitiate a deity should be banned by legislation. To achieve this, widespread educative propaganda is essential.

Animal Sport

The existing game laws should be strictly enforced and to that end the requisite administrative machinery should be set up.

Game licences should be issued with utmost caution. They should be granted only to those who produce certificates of proficiency in handling guns, rifles, etc., and in shooting at moving targets. Every licence should be accompanied by a pamphlet which should highlight the important provisions of game-laws, give information on the proper use of weapons and regarding the choice of arms and ammunition for shooting different classes of wild animals and birds and other necessary details.

As the use of traps and snares almost invariably causes suffering to the captured animal, it is necessary that only such traps are allowed to be used the design of which has been approved by a competent authority.

Capture And Training Of Elephant

The stockade method for capturing elephants is the least objectionable and should gradually replace the pit method. All precautions should be taken to avoid suffering involved in the capturing of elephants.

Crop Protection Licences

The question of abuse of such licences may be considered. One suggestion is that instead of issuing such licences to individual agriculturists, some kind of a Crop Protection Corps may be created for killing animals in the areas where they have become a menace to crops.

Game Sanctuaries

Game Sanctuaries and National Parks should be set up all over the country.

Publicity And Propaganda

For this purpose, increasing use should be made of documentary films, radio broadcasts, Press and other means of publicity and propaganda.

Performing Animals

Circuses of performing animals may continue subject to regulations.

Street Performances

Street performances should be licensed and adequate supervision and control exercised on the proper health and maintenance of animals by subjecting them to periodical inspections, so that any cruelties involved may be prevented.

Animal And Bird Fights

Such fights should be prohibited by law.

Keeping Or Confining Animals In Municipal Market

Confinement of animals in Municipal markets should be regulated by comprehensive rules to be prescribed and enforced by Municipalities.

Khatals

Highest priority should be given to the implementation of Cattle Colonization Schemes so as to cover all the big and densely populated cities of India. Meanwhile, urgent steps should be taken to improve the existing conditions in Khatals. They should be licensed and controlled by Municipalities.

Keeping Of Pets

The selling and keeping of pets should be licensed by Municipalities. It should be made obligatory on the sellers of pets to supply booklets to the buyers containing all necessary information about the habits and the way of life of the pets sold.

Zoos

The zoos in India should be reorganized on scientific lines keeping in view the need to provide natural habitat to animals.

Transport Of Animals By Rail

Animals should be transported in wagons specially constructed for the purpose. There should be adequate arrangements for the provision of food and water during transit. Loose-shunting of wagons containing animals should be strictly prohibited. Animals should not be allowed to be transported during hot months.

Transport By Road

Animals should be transported only in vehicles suitably designed for this purpose and there should be no overcrowding. Wells or small tanks should be constructed at suitable distances on roads so that animals can get water when thirsty. The carrying of animals and birds in unnatural positions should be prohibited.

Export Of Monkeys

The Government should exercise stricter control at the various stages of export trade. There should be a comprehensive system of licensing of the trapper, animal dealer, exporter and carrier and the licence should specify all conditions to ensure humane treatment. Inspectors should be appointed for enforcing the licensing provisions and deterrent penalties imposed for breaches.

Export Of Wild And Other Animals And Birds

The Government should undertake legislation more or less on the lines of the U.K. Animals (Sea Transport) Order of 1930 to regulate the loading and unloading of animals and their transport by our ships.

The Problem Of Stray Animals

The conditions prevailing in the cattle pounds should be improved with regard to housing, feeding, watering, protection from exposure to weather and veterinary treatment.

Gaushalas And Pinjrapoles

Gosadans should also accept other old and useless animals besides cattle; failing this, institutions may be established where under Government or private auspices useless and decrepit animals other than cattle can be housed. Every encouragement should be given to pinjrapoles which admit all kinds of animals in addition to cattle.

Castration Of Animals

The use of Burdizzo Castrator should be popularized.

Specific Measures To Ameliorate The Condition Of Beasts Of Burden

Municipalities and S.P.C.A.s should construct sheds and water troughs at suitable distances.

All States should maintain an adequate number of mobile vans which may go into villages, treat sick and wounded animals on the spot and carry on educative propaganda among villagers.

Municipalities should introduce a system of hire-purchase so that even the poor cart-driver may be enabled to purchase pneumatic tyres for his cart.

Reorganization Of S.P.C.A.s In India

The S.P.C.A.s should be manned by sincere and honest persons. Their constitution should be so amended that at least the Secretary and half of the Members of the Managing and Executive Committees are nominated by the Government. The Secretary should be an official of the Animal Husbandry Department.

Need For Humane Education

An "Animal Welfare Week" should be observed throughout the country. During this week all available means of publicity and propaganda should be made use of to arouse public consciousness.

There is no limit to the imparting of humane education but the actual textual education for the purpose may be continued at least up to the Matriculation standard. Lessons on kindness to animals stressing the advantages of treating them humanely may be included in the text-books prescribed for children. Interesting stories on the subject may also be included.

Animal Welfare Board

An Animal Welfare Board should be set up at the Centre, with its counterparts in States, for giving an over-all advice to the Government as well as humanitarian organizations on problems of animal welfare.

AD HOC COMMITTEE FOR EXTERNAL MARKETING, 1954—REPORT

Ernakulam, Coir Board, 1955. 47, XXIXp.

Chairman & Convener : Shri K. Narayana Menon.

Members : Shri R. Krishna Aiyar; Shri T. M. Antony; Shri C. T. Jacob; Shri N. Kunjuraman; Shri H. Smith; Shri Revi Karunakaran; Shri J. Murukandi; Shri K. Raman; Shri J. L. White; Shri K. Kesavan Nair; Shri B. Bueler; Shri T. V. Thomas; Shri T. K. Divakaran; Shri B. V. Abdulla Koya.

APPOINTMENT

The Ad Hoc Committee for External Marketing was constituted under the Coir Board on August 20, 1954.

TERMS OF REFERENCE

The Committee was directed to enquire into and advise the Coir Board on the policy to be adopted and the steps to be taken in furtherance of that policy by the Board in carrying out the functions assigned to it under Sections 10, 12 and 13 of the Coir Industry Act. These functions, in relation to external marketing, particularly, are:

(i) Promoting exports of coir yarn and coir products, and carrying on propaganda for that purpose—Section 10(2) (a);

(ii) Licensing exporters of coir, coir yarn and coir products—Section 10(2) (b) and Section 12;

(iii) Improving the marketing of coir fibre, coir yarn and coir products in foreign countries and preventing unfair competition—Section 10(2) (f);

(iv) Licensing of warehouses and otherwise regulating the stocking and sale of coir fibre, coir yarn and coir products for exports—Section 10(2) (i);

(v) Control of export of coir fibre, coir yarn and coir products—Section 12;

(vi) Imposition of a duty of Customs on export of coir fibre, coir yarn and coir products—Section 13.

CONTENTS

Introductory (Preliminary; Terms of Reference; Questionnaire; Scope of the Report); Coir Fibre; Coir Yarn (India's Export Trade; Coir Yarn Exports; Need for Market Survey; Price Movements; Coir Yarn and other Industrial Fibres; Diversification of Exports; Licensing; Warehousing; Standardization of Qualities); Coir Mats and Mattings (History of the Trade; General Review of Exports; Present Condition of the Trade—Price Cutting and Wage Reduction; Effects of Uneconomic Competition; Licensing System; Difficulties of Export Trade—Tariffs and Import Restriction; Competition from other Manufacturing Countries; Measures for Development of Foreign Markets; Co-operative Marketing); Summary of Recommendations; Appendices (Questionnaire); List of those who sent answers to the Questionnaire; Shipment of Coir Fibre from Alleppey, Cochin, Calicut and other Malabar Coast Ports; Shipments of Coir Yarn from Alleppey, Cochin, Calicut and other Malabar Coast Ports; Price of Coir Yarn (Superior Anjengo) at Alleppey Ex-Warehouse per ton, Bailed Weight Basis; World Production of Hard Fibres; Shippers of Coir Yarn Bales from Alleppey and Cochin; Shippers who have been Shipping Coir Yarn Regularly before and after the War (in Bales); Shipments of Mats, Mattings, Rugs and Carpets from Alleppey, Cochin, Calicut and other Malabar Coast Ports; Comparative Statement of New Shippers and number of Shippers dropping out between 1929-38 and 1949-54; Distribution of Shipments amongst Shippers of Coir Mats, Mattings and Rugs from Alleppey and Cochin; Scheme for Licensing of Exporters and Exports of Coir Products (Excluding Ropes); List of Import Duties in Foreign Countries; Decisions of the Coir Board on the Recommendations of the Committee for External Marketing.

RECOMMENDATIONS

The Committee recommends that the position of export of coir fibre and the end uses of fibre should be carefully watched by the Coir Board and periodically examined. With a view to enabling the Board to watch the situation carefully and exercise control, if it becomes necessary, all exporters of coir fibre should be licensed by the Board and no export should be permitted except under a licence issued by the Board.

It is said that coir fibre does not easily lend itself to be spun into yarn by a mechanical process. It must be one of the duties of the Research Department of the Coir Board to examine this position.

No exhaustive study has been made by India as a producing country in the end uses of coir yarn and the Committee recommends that an early marketing survey in the consuming countries be made.

There is no precise information as to how much of coir yarn in importing countries is used for industrial purposes such as manufacture of floor coverings and ropes. The Committee recommends that a market survey should be undertaken immediately. A delegation of the Board visiting those countries would be most useful. An endeavour may first be made through existing trade organizations of the Government of India to collect the necessary data.

It is understood that the United Kingdom and the Continental countries obtain East African sisal as fibre and spin it into yarn, and the spinners, by agreement, seem to be fixing the price of East African sisal yarn both in the United Kingdom and Continental countries and such agreement seems to have enabled spinners to secure reasonable profits. The Committee recommends an investigation being made into this matter so that the results of the investigation may be utilized in the coir trade for introducing any measure of voluntary price agreement.

Ceylon can develop into a potential rival to the coir industry in India.

A diversification of the export trade is calculated to make for stability in that sector and for this purpose more and more people capable of doing a fair amount of business should be given facilities to enter the trade. The Committee recommends that the Coir Board should vigilantly watch the trend of exports of coir yarn, and if this trend does not indicate a tendency towards progressive diversification, the Board should take immediate steps to regulate the exports in whatever manner it thinks fit.

The development of Central Co-operative Marketing Societies can exert a very wholesome influence upon the quality of yarn and also on the price stability as the Central Marketing Societies would form the apex of a system of several co-operative societies for the production and marketing of yarn. The Committee strongly recommends to State Governments interested that they should render every financial aid both for the capital outlay and for working capital, if existing funds are found to be insufficient.

Exporters and exports of coir yarn should be licensed in the same manner as is contemplated in the scheme recommended in the case of coir products, subject to necessary modifications regarding ownership of a factory by shippers. The fees for licensing should be the same as in the case of export of coir products.

The Committee is in general agreement with the recommendation of the Ad Hoc Committee on Coir Yarn regarding establishment of licensed warehouses. The Committee however thinks that fundamental changes have to be made in the method of production, in grading, etc., before it would be possible to introduce a compulsory licensed warehousing system. Otherwise compulsion might result in confusion in the trade with no advantage either to the primary producer or the final exporter.

Exporters of coir yarn may have their own trade marks; but they must have relation to the standardized qualities. If a scheme for this purpose is evolved, along with standardization of coir yarn, the marketing of coir yarn in foreign countries is bound to be facilitated and beneficial to the industry. The Committee recommends a closer examination of this subject.

Since opinion is unanimous that proper organization of the export trade is necessary, the Committee has gone into the methods by which this can be best secured, and has prepared an elastic scheme of licensing of exporters and exports of coir products (excluding ropes). Adoption of the scheme by the Board and immediate action thereon are recommended.

In view of the existing condition of backwardness of areas like Malabar in the matter of manufacture of coir mats and mattings, the Committee considers that exemption may be granted to such areas from provisions in the scheme relating to registration of new exporters and renewal of licences.

Most importing countries have imposed high tariffs against entry of coir mats and mattings. Coir yarn, however, is allowed import free of duty or at nominal duty. The Board should collect full information regarding the scale of duties or restrictions imposed on import of coir and coir products in various countries from time to time.

The Continental countries have been importing large quantities of yarn and almost all yarn imported is used for the manufacture of mats and mattings. The Committee recommends that the Government of India should immediately take the strongest possible line when negotiating Trade Agreements with such countries as Holland, Germany, France and Belgium with a view to ensuring that these countries would permit import of at least 25% on a weight basis of coir mats and mattings in proportion to the coir yarn which these countries import. If, however, these countries refuse to co-operate with India, action should then be taken to regulate the exports of coir yarn to those destinations by suitable steps.

Coir mats and mattings have not lost ground because of quality. It must, however, be stated that there is ample room for improvement of quality and Indian coir products should be brought up to the standards reached in the U. K., Germany and Holland.

No organized attempt has hitherto been made by the industry as such in foreign markets for advertisement and propaganda. With effective advertisement and propaganda India's markets in foreign countries could be developed very considerably. A study of the foreign markets and a close market survey are an essential preliminary to any organized scheme of advertisement and propaganda. The manner of advertisement and propaganda would vary with the requirements of each market. No hard and fast rule could be laid down as to the lines which advertisement and propaganda should follow. It is recommended that advertisement and propaganda in foreign countries must be handled by experts in the line and that the Coir Board should take urgent and suitable action in this regard.

When the Coir Board has organized itself fully and made arrangements for advertisement and propaganda, it should issue an attractive bulletin which would contain all necessary features about the coir industry in the same way as bulletins appear in foreign countries in respect of other floor coverings.

The Committee is in full agreement with the recommendations regarding standardization of quality and on designs and planning contained in the report of the Ad Hoc Committee for Coir Products.

Manufacturers of coir mats and mattings in India are at a disadvantage as compared with the manufacturers of mats and mattings in those countries which import coir yarn and manufacture it into mats and mattings because of the rates of freight levied on coir mats and mattings as compared to those on coir yarn.

Apart from the question of the difference between the freight on coir mats and mattings and the raw material, the Committee finds that the present rate of freight is itself very high.

Coir yarn and coir mats and mattings are in no way at a disadvantage in relation to freight rates on jute goods.

The organization of a Central Marketing Society could be of immense benefit not only to the exporters but also in bringing about a solution for the unhealthy competition amongst the manufacturers and shippers. The possibilities of organizing a Central Co-operative Marketing Board for coir mats and mattings should be carefully studied, which is strongly recommended by the Committee.

AD HOC COMMITTEE FOR HUSK AND FIBRE, 1954—REPORT

Ernakulam, Coir Board, 1955. 15p.

Chairman : Shri K. Narayana Menon.
Vice-Chairman and Convener : Shri N. Kunjuraman.
Members : Shri K. V. Nanu; Shri V. K. Kumaran; Shri R. Janardhanan Pillai; Shri S. C. Roy; Shri P. K. Dewer; Shri N. Narayana Kurup; Shri B. M. Peter; Shri A. P. Raman; Shri Kochu Pillai; Shri V. K. Purushothaman.

APPOINTMENT

The Ad Hoc Committee for Husk and Fibre was constituted under the Coir Board on August 20, 1954.

TERMS OF REFERENCE

To enquire into and advise the Coir Board on the policy to be adopted and the measures necessary for carrying out the policy in respect of the following functions assigned to the Board under Section 10 of the Coir Industry Act:

(i) Regulating under the supervision of the Central Government the production of husk and coir fibre.

(ii) Fixing grade standards and arranging when necessary for inspection of coir fibre.

(iii) Promoting co-operative organization among producers of husks and coir fibre.

(iv) Ensuring remunerative returns to producers of husks and coir fibre.

(v) Licensing of the retting places.

At the meeting held on August 21, 1954, the scope of enquiry for the Committee was discussed and it was decided that it should include:

(a) Collection of statistical data regarding total production of coconut husk in India and the percentage of husk used for retting and extraction of fibre; the various uses to which husk is put in different States; investigation of the different methods of retting in different places, etc.

(b) Formulating proposals for improved methods of retting and artificial methods of retting where natural facilities are not available.

(c) Consideration of licensing of retting places.

(d) Investigation of the different kinds of fibre produced, grading such fibres, and to define minimum standards for them.

(e) Examination of the scope and advantage of co-operative organization among husk retters and producers of fibre, and appraisal of the results so far achieved by the Coir Co-operative Scheme working in Travancore-Cochin State.

(f) Formulating proposals for remunerative return to husk retters and producers of fibre and examination of the desirability of introducing minimum wages in the industry.

CONTENTS

Introductory; Scope of Enquiry; Availability of Husks; Retting Facilities; Extraction of Fibre; By-Products; Co-operative Organization among Producers of Husk and Fibre; Coir Minimum Wages and Its Reactions; Price Control of Husk; Relationship Between the Prices of Husk, Fibre and Yarn; Competition from Other Fibres; Export of Fibre; Standardization and Grading of Fibre; Collection of Statistical Data; Summary of Conclusions and Recommendations; Appendices.

RECOMMENDATIONS

Reliable information regarding the extent of husk used for extracting fibre in India and other uses to which husk is put is not available. For considering measures for developing the coir industry, it is essential to have such statistics relating to the above. The Statistical Section of the Coir Board should take up this matter.

The effect of different methods of retting husk on fibre and the devising of artificial method of retting, where there are no natural retting facilities, may form the subject matter of study and research by the Coir Board (Research Section).

The Committee does not recommend at this stage the introduction of machinery for the extraction of fibre as this would tend to make more acute the unemployment position of labour engaged in the industry. But it would recommend the use of machinery in places where extraction of fibre is done from raw husk and artificial retting devices would be employed.

The Committee would recommend the issue of licences for retting on a sliding scale. It is recommended further that the various Governments should be approached by the Board to let out for retting Government *poromboke* lands suitable for the purpose, at nominal rates.

The pith and outer cover of the husk can be used for making cardboards and insulators. It can also be used for making building construction materials. Investigation may be made into the various uses to which the pith and the outer cover can be put. This may be done by the Research Section.

Co-operative organization among producers of husk and fibre must be started and encouraged in all States. In the opinion of the Committee, the working of the existing Coir Co-operatives of Travancore-Cochin State must be enquired into and strengthened and quickened with necessary modifications.

Minimum Wages in the Coir Industry must be enforced to ensure a fair deal to the labour employed therein. Minimum Wages have come to stay in Travancore-Cochin State and it is producing salutary effects in that it tends to stabilize the price of husk and link it on a more stable and reasonable basis with the price of fibre and yarn. Minimum Wages should be introduced in the other States.

The Committee is of the view that price control—let alone its legal difficulties—does not seem to be feasible at this stage. The co-operative machinery and minimum wages would help to establish a reasonable relationship between the prices of yarn, fibre and husk.

Experience does not warrant any serious threat to the industry from other fibres; and does, as Ceylon competition in the field of coir fibre offers an immediate threat.

Export of fibre is negligible and practically the entire fibre produced in India is utilized internally. The Committee does not at this stage consider it necessary to recommend any measure to restrict export of fibre.

Fixing of grade standards of fibre may be left to the Indian Standards Institution.

The Committee feels it necessary that this report should be supplemented and made fuller by further recommendations on the basis of facts ascertained as a result of on-the-spot enquiries in the coconut-producing areas in States like Mysore, Bengal, Bombay, Andhra and Orissa.

COMMITTEE ON OFFICES OF PROFIT, 1954—REPORT

New Delhi, Lok Sabha Secretariat, 1955. 2 Vols.

Chairman : Pandit Thakurdas Bhargava.

Members : Shri V. B. Gandhi; Shri S. V. Ramaswamy; Shri K. Raghuramaiah; Shri Vishwambhar Dayal Tripathi; Shri R. V. Dhulekar; Shri Anirudha Sinha; Shri S. S. More; Shri Kamal Kumar Basu; Shri N. Ramaseshaiah; Shri M. Govinda Reddy; Shri Kazi Karimuddin; Shri Amolakh Chand; Prof. G. Ranga; Shri Rajendra Pratap Sinha.

Secretary : Shri M. N. Kaul.

APPOINTMENT

The Committee on Offices of Profit was constituted under the Lok Sabha Secretariat on August 21, 1954.

TERMS OF REFERENCE

(i) To study various matters connected with the disqualification of members and to make recommendations in order to enable the Government to consider the lines along which a comprehensive legislation should be brought before the House; and

(ii) To collect facts, data and to make suggestions as to how the matter should be dealt with.

CONTENTS

Members of the Committee on Offices of Profit; Report; Annexures.

RECOMMENDATIONS

In view of the immensity of the task involved in collecting material and in studying relevant matter extension of the life of Act I of 1954 for one year was recommended.

The word "Office" used in Article 102(1) (a) would include membership of a Committee, Commission, etc., appointed for a particular or temporary purpose.

The word "Profit" should be interpreted in a broad sense.

The word "under" used in Article 102(1) (a) should include offices held directly or indirectly under the control of the Central or State Governments.

Holders of ministerial offices (Ministers of State, Deputy Ministers, Parliamentary Secretaries and Parliamentary Under Secretaries) should be exempted from disqualification.

Holders of the offices of Chief and Deputy Chief Whips in Parliament should be exempted from disqualification.

Members of Parliament sent on delegation to foreign countries should be exempted from disqualification.

Holders of offices of Vice-Chancellors of Universities should not be exempted from disqualification. The disqualification clause should not apply to Chancellors and Pro-Chancellors of Universities.

Members of Parliament nominated/elected as members of Senate, Syndicate, Executive Council/ Committees of various Universities should be exempted from disqualification.

Holders of offices of Honorary Magistrates, Revenue Officers, Munsiffs, Judges, Coroners, Members appointed on Tribunals and other Judicial Officers should not be exempted from disqualification.

Holders of offices of Sheriff should be exempted from disqualification.

Village officials mentioned in Section 123 (8) of the Representation of the People Act, 1951 (Act 43 of 1951), should not be exempted from disqualification.

Lambardars in States where they have been declared as exempted under Section 123 (8) of the Representation of the People Act, 1951, should not be disqualified.

Persons belonging to the National Cadet Corps, Territorial Army, Members of the Home Guards in various States raised under special enactments should be exempted from disqualification.

Pension holders drawing pensions for services rendered should be exempted from disqualification. Pension holders who receive other pensions, like political pensions, during the pleasure of the granting authority should not be exempted from disqualification.

A person receiving an allowance from the Government on the condition of rendering some service, though of an occasional character, should be deemed to be a person who holds an office of profit under the Government. The disqualification should not, however, apply to erstwhile rulers.

Employees of local bodies should be treated on a par with other Government employees and should not be exempted from disqualification. The disqualification should not apply to Presidents, Chairmen, or Members of Municipalities, District Boards, Corporations or like bodies.

A Technical Adviser to advise the Government on a particular matter and drawing only the travelling allowance permissible under rules and fee subject to the ceiling of Rs. 21 per day should not incur disqualification.

Members of Parliament invited to broadcast from All India Radio should not incur disqualification provided that they are not paid anything except travelling allowance permissible under the rules and fee subject to the ceiling of Rs. 21 per day.

Members of Parliament appointed for setting question papers or examining answer-books and receiving remuneration thereby should not incur disqualification.

Members of Parliament appointed as part-time Professors, Lecturers, Instructors, Inspectors or Teachers in Government educational institutions, medical practitioners rendering part-time service in Government institutions, etc., should not be exempted from disqualification.

Members of Parliament should be encouraged to go on Committees which are of an advisory character. Members of Parliament should not be permitted to go on Committees which jeopardize their independence or place them in a position of power or influence or in a position where they receive some patronage from the Government or are themselves in a position to distribute patronage.

Members of Parliament appointed to Committees formed for the purpose of advising the Government for making an enquiry into or collecting statistics should not incur disqualification.

Members of Parliament appointed to Committees on election by Parliament should not incur disqualification.

Membership of Commodity Committees and Development Councils should be exempted from disqualification. Chairmanship, Vice-Chairmanship or Secretaryship of Commodity Committees or of their Standing Committees or Sub-Committees should not be exempted from disqualification. There should be no distinction between office holders nominated by the Government and those elected by the Committees for the purpose of disqualification.

Members of Parliament nominated by the Speaker of the Lok Sabha or the Chairman of the Rajya Sabha should be exempted from disqualification.

Members of Parliament appointed to Committees of a non-advisory character should be exempted from disqualification. A practice should be developed by which members of such Committees may either be elected by Parliament or nominated by the Speaker of the Lok Sabha or the Chairman of the Rajya Sabha.

Membership of Committees entrusted with executive, judicial or like powers should incur disqualification.

No member of Parliament should be appointed on any Committee, especially those entailing disqualifications, without his consent in writing.

Members of Parliament nominated or elected by sectional or other interests, such as employers, employees, consumers, etc., should not incur disqualification.

Provision should be made in the Statute constituting a corporation in which the Government has any share or financial interest for specifically disqualifying a director as provided for in Section 8(e) of the Representation of the People Act, 1951. The words, "financial interest" used in Section 7(e) of the Act should be clearly defined in the proposed legislation.

The exemption from disqualification recommended in the case of advisory committees and non-advisory committees membership of which is non-objectionable should be subject to the overriding condition that Members of Parliament appointed to such committees are not given an allowance or fee of more than Rs. 21 per day.

A Standing Parliamentary Committee composed of Members of both the Houses should be constituted to undertake the work of continuous scrutiny in respect of offices of profit which have escaped the notice of the Committee or offices of profit which may come into existence in future.

All proposed appointments of Members of Parliament to any office or any committee, commission, etc., should be communicated to the Standing Parliamentary Committee. Any future legislation undertaken affecting such offices or committees should be placed before this Committee and its views should be duly considered before a Bill is brought before Parliament.

The legislation recommended may be introduced as soon as possible.

REVIEWING COMMITTEE (REVIEW OF THE REPORT OF THE RAILWAY ACCIDENTS ENQUIRY COMMITTEE), 1954—REPORT

New Delhi, Railway Board, 1957. 57,10p.

Chairman : Shri Shah Nawaz Khan.
Members : Shri L. P. Mishra; Shri T. S. Pattabhiraman; Shri F. C. Badhwar.
Secretary : Shri Ranjit Singh.

APPOINTMENT

The Reviewing Committee (Review of the Report of the Railway Accidents Enquiry Committee) was constituted under the Ministry of Railways (Railway Board) vide their Memorandum No. 4894-TT/II dated August 25-26, 1954.

TERMS OF REFERENCE

To review the various conclusions and recommendations of the Accidents Enquiry Committee in the light of the latest information received from Railways.

CONTENTS

Main Reports: General; Permanent Way and Level Crossings; Vacuum Brakes; Fires on Trains; Minor Accidents; Train Examination; Shortages, Delays and Uncertainties in the supply of Materials through Agencies outside the control of Railways; Traffic Working Rules; The Safety Authority for Railways; The Effective Promotion of Safety through Internal Checks and Supervision vis-a-vis External Inspections; Staff and Accident Prevention; Penalties for Negligence as Deterrent for Offences Against Safety; Accident Prevention Aspects of External Inspections by G. I. R.s ; Accident Preventive Aspects of Servicing, Repairs and Overhauls in Workshops, Sheds, Sick Lines, etc.; Effectiveness of Internal Checks and Supervision on Quality of Work; Adequate and Timely Supplies of Stores Essential for Safety and Good Performance; Surprise [Checks by Experts; Judicial Enquiries into Major Railway Accidents; Reversion to Pre-War Practice for External Inspection; Encouragement of Maximum Availability and Intensive Utilization of Rolling Stock Consistent with Safety Standards; Inspection and Patrolling of Permanent Way; Concluding Paragraph; Appendices.

RECOMMENDATIONS

Vacuum Brakes

We agree that vacuum brakes should be fitted on all trains on the broad and metre gauges as early as possible, priority being given to the stock that is required to operate on Ghat and other sections where gradients are steep or speeds high. As regards the narrow gauge, however, we feel that some latitude should be allowed for local conditions, comparatively low speeds, and for current schemes for their conversion into the gauge of the surrounding railway systems within a reasonable period.

Fires On Trains

We have been informed that fire extinguishers are now standard fittings on all passenger trains and also that electrical wiring is carefully examined at regular intervals. The Accident Enquiry Committee's recommendation for adding to the scale of fire extinguishers on each train will not improve matters until vestibulated trains are generally adopted or an extinguisher of a type which any passenger can easily operate is fitted in each compartment. This is hardly practicable at present. Spark arrestors are already standard fittings on all locomotives.

Train Examination

Facilities for train examinations should also be modernized, wherever necessary, and well-trained staff, keen supervisors and adequate stocks of materials and spares provided. We consider that, at present, train examination in its various aspects is the weakest link in the "safety chain" on Railways, and we recommend that every Railway should carry out a thorough and early probe into the working of each Train Examining Depot.

Shortages, Delays And Uncertainties In The Supply Of Materials Through Agencies Outside The Control Of Railways

On this matter we fully endorse the views of the Accident Enquiry Committee and, in fact, would like to go further and point out that no appreciable improvements in safety promotion, or the maintenance and operation on Railways, are possible unless timely and adequate supplies of all essential stores can be ensured.

Traffic Working Rules

We are in complete agreement with the Accident Enquiry Committee that all the Traffic Working Rules for all stations, as well as any special procedures necessitated by local conditions, should be available to the staff concerned in a clear and simple language, which they can read and digest.

The Safety Authority For Railways

The technical wings of the Railway Board must always remain the safety-controlling authority for Indian Railways.

The Effective Promotion Of Safety Through Internal Checks And Supervision Vis-a-Vis External Inspections

While paying a tribute to the excellent work performed by the Government Inspectors of Railways over a period of many years under varying conditions, which were not always favourable, we feel that the time has come to recognize the many changes, having wide repercussions, which have taken place in the country since the War and to remodel and adjust the present Inspectorate to these changed conditions.

The increased office work is taking up too large a proportion of the time of certain supervisory categories and we would like to draw the attention of the Railway Ministry to this development and to stress that they should redistribute, or otherwise adjust, the office work in a suitable manner to permit technical staff to concentrate on their essential duties in accordance with the actual work-load.

Staff And Accident Prevention

Outstanding individual performance deserves special consideration, and if this cannot be given in the shape of special or extra emoluments, then some form of accelerated advancement should be approved. Careful selection and training of all staff, especially Class IV, are as important as choosing good machines and equipment, and both pay high dividends.

Temporary arrangements for providing special instruction outside working hours in suitable centres for technical and train passing staff might be examined, as the provision of modern and well-equipped training schools in adequate numbers over the widespread Indian Railway System may take some years to fructify.

The delays in filling working vacancies on the Railways are regrettable and early improvements in the system of recruitment and training are necessary in this connection. We do not consider it fair to a Railway to have to depend for its recruits on an organization, which it can neither hurry up nor guide in the matter of quality. We, therefore, recommend strongly that each Railway should have its own separate Service Commission or other recruiting agency for Class III staff and the sooner this can be arranged the better as this has a bearing on safety.

Penalties For Negligence As Deterrents For Offences Against Safety

The proposals to amend the Payment of Wages Act or to alter the existing Code rules may perhaps present practical difficulties, but the Railway Ministry should make a special effort to distinguish between staff offences which endanger the public safety, or public property, and other offences and to take speedier and more severe deterrent action to deal with the former. We feel that a special set of regulations, based on summary procedures, should be introduced for all offences likely to endanger public safety, or public property and that punishments in such cases should be prompt and effective, in the deterrent sense.

Accident Prevention Aspects Of External Inspections By G. I. R.s

The composition of the Inspectorate would also have to be altered to meet the present-day conditions by including an element of mechanical, electrical, signalling and, perhaps, operating experts.

Expert enquiries into major Railway accidents could be considered as suitably by an organization under the Railway Ministry as by an organization under any other Ministry. The time has come to take a wider view and deal with all matters affecting public safety, and public property, under the common law of the land. If judicial or magisterial enquiries into major

Railway accidents are accepted, then we suggest that the appropriate Ministry to "father" such enquiries would be the Ministry of Home Affairs, which could also ensure that prompt action is taken to commence an enquiry as soon as an accident occurs.

Accident Preventive Aspects Of Servicing, Repairs And Overhauls In Workshops, Sheds, Sick Lines, Etc.

All Railways are endeavouring to attain self-sufficiency by using Indian materials to the greatest extent and it is not at present always possible to obtain these in quality quite comparable with the best imported materials, which the former British regime used to insist upon. A higher degree of checking and testing has been recommended for draw-bars, springs, etc., and it will undoubtedly pay the Railways to arrange this as part of the internal supervision and quality control for each workshop, and C. & W. Depot.

High standards of maintenance and operation and quality generally have to be built into a product by competent workmen using good materials under helpful and intensive supervision. Internal tests, checks and other quality-control measures on Railways should, therefore, be overhauled and strengthened where necessary to ensure uniformly high standards that will stand up to robust and intensive usage with safety.

Departmental, or ministerial, considerations at the Centre, based on the theoretical advantages of centralization, should be relaxed as far as the provisioning of Railways is concerned, as this factor, more than any other, is handicapping them in their efforts to provide additional carrying capacity, with safe operation. The present practice in the D. G. & S. D. of insisting on indents two years, or more, before the material is expected to be used, and the artificialities of the Stores Accounting System are all additional major handicaps which require immediate remedy.

Safety Promotion can best be achieved through increased efficiency in all aspects of servicing, repairs, overhauls, maintenance and operation, and we have no doubt that the most effective contribution can be made through internal measures like competence of workmanship and checks by supervisors who have to share the responsibility for defective work.

Early steps be taken for enquiries into major railway accidents to be conducted by judicial officers, who should be provided with such expert assessors as they may require, in replacement of the present Government Railway Inspectors.

The Government Railway Inspectorate should revert to its pre-War (1941) location, from which it is reported to have functioned quite well in inspection matters.

In respect of technical matters, however, facilities should be provided by the Railway Board for the Government Inspectorate to maintain close and constant liaison with the various experts sections that comprise the Central Standards Office, the Railway Testing and Research Directorate and the various other technical Directorates of the Board's office.

Adequate and timely supplies of materials, provision of competent workmen in sufficient numbers, intensive and expert supervision, the additional capacity and equipment required in servicing depots and workshops, and the requisite funds to sustain these special efforts should be made readily available to the Railways to enable them to operate with reasonable safety, the large proportion of over-age rolling stock, well past its economic life, which the country cannot afford these days to withdraw from regular service.

We feel that each gang length, or every second gang length, should be provided with a trolley-cycle for use in emergencies as is the practice in some Western countries. This should enable a keyman, or a two-man patrol, to cover a gang length in one-third or one-fourth of the time that would be taken if they had to walk. We feel that the evolution of a suitable slow speed (20 m.p.h.) design, which three men can comfortably lift, should be within the scope of the Railway Research Centre. Replacement of the old, slow and heavy four-man push trolleys by these motor rail-tricycles should facilitate more frequent inspections of track and bridges as supervisors can get round faster and more frequently.

BANK AWARD COMMISSION, 1954—REPORT

New Delhi, Ministry of Labour, 2 Vols.

Chairman : Justice Shri Rajadhyaksha (died, replaced by Shri P. B. Gajendragadkar).
Secretary : Shri W. T. Korke.

APPOINTMENT

The Bank Award Commission was constituted under the Ministry of Labour vide their Resolution No. LR-100(56)/54 dated September 17, 1954.

TERMS OF REFERENCE

To enquire into and ascertain the effects on the

emoluments which the employees were in receipt of prior to August, 1954.

(a) Of the Appellate Tribunal Decision without modification, and

(b) Of the Appellate Tribunal Decision as modified by the Government's Order No. S. R. O. 2732, dated August 24, 1954.

To ascertain:

(a) The additional burden on individual banks that would have been caused by the Appellate Tribunal Decision over the expenses under the frozen Sen Award:

(b) The extent and amount of relief obtained by them as a result of the modifications made by the Government:

(c) The additional expenditure now to be borne by banks under the modified decision over the expenditure incurred under the frozen Sen Award that would have been incurred under the Sastry Award.

To scrutinize the information already collected and to collect further information relevant to the consideration of these issues.

To recommend, having regard to the facts ascertained and to the need for ensuring an equitable treatment to bank employees consistent with the capacity to pay of the various classes of banking companies or individual units:

(a) Whether the Appellate Tribunal Decision, as modified, should be continued;

(b) Whether the Appellate Tribunal Decision should be restored and, if so, whether fully or in part:

(c) Whether the Appellate Tribunal Decision should be enforced with any other modifications considered necessary.

In considering this, due regard should also be paid to the desirability of avoiding widespread closures of banking companies or their branches, to the necessity to promote development of banking in the country generally and in the rural areas in particular and to any possibilities of effecting economies in the expenses of banking companies.

To consider and recommend what special modifications, if any, are necessary in the Decision in order to encourage the spread of banking facilities in the Class IV Areas of Part "B" States and Part "C" States other than Delhi, Ajmer and Coorg.

CONTENTS

Foreword: The Commission at Work—A Brief Account of the Proceedings: Background of the Dispute: The Task Before the Commission: The Approach to the Problem—General Considerations: Preliminary Questions in Regard to the Implementation of the Labour Appellate Tribunal Decision; Expansion of Banking and the Problem of Area 4: Capacity to Pay of Classes of Banks and Individual Units; Government-Modified Decision—The Approach Underlying the Decision Considered and Commented on; Problems Connected with Some Special Class; Recommendations; Appendices; Statements.

RECOMMENDATIONS

Labour Appellate Tribunal Decision With Modifications To Be Restored In Case Of A And B Classes And Specified Banks In C Class

1. The Labour Appellate Tribunal Decision should be restored in the case of the following banks subject to the modifications mentioned below in Clauses 1(a) to 1(f). In view of the Government's assurance in Parliament, this recommendation should have retrospective effect as from April 1, 1954.

A Class : All banks—Indian and Foreign.

B Class : All banks except the Bank of Bikaner and the United Bank of India.

C Class : (i) Bank of Behar
(ii) Bank of Indore
(iii) Bank of Jaipur
(iv) Bank of Maharashtra
(v) Canara Banking Corporation
(vi) Canara Industrial and Banking Syndicate
(vii) Hind Bank
(viii) Travancore Bank.

Medical Relief

(a) The provision for accumulation of Medical Relief in the Labour Appellate Tribunal Decision should be dropped; the provisions in the Sastry Award in regard to Medical Relief should be confirmed.

Subject And Reference To Relevant Paragraph In The Report

Area 4

(b) The provision for the creation of an additional Area 4 as per Clause 3(a) of the Government-modified decision dated August 24, 1954, together with the wage structure and dearness allowance prescribed for this Area should be confirmed.

Area 5

(i) The creation of a further Sub-Area under Area 4 described as Area 5 in this Report, which under the Government-modified decision dated August 24, 1954, now enjoys complete exemption from any award should, however, be set aside except in the case of banks incorporated in Travancore-Cochin State excluding the Travancore Bank.

Banks Incorporated In Travancore-Cochin State

(ii) Banks incorporated in Travancore-Cochin State except the Travancore Bank should be allowed complete exemption from the operation of any award in respect of their business within the limits of the Sub-Area as defined above for a maximum period of two years from the date of announcement of the Government's final decision on the Commission's report or until the recommendations of the Special Commission referred to below are implemented, whichever event happens earlier. In case, however, such a Commission is not appointed or after appointment is unable to make its recommendations within two years or in case its recommendations are received but not implemented within two years, the exemption granted to the branches of these banks in the Sub-Area referred to above should be withdrawn.

Cuts To Be Phased With Adjustment Of Increments

(c) Clause 3(g) in the Government-modified decision should be confirmed and applied to the Government-modified or Labour Appellate Tribunal Decision, as the case may be, save that in making deductions in three instalments as contemplated by the said provision banks should be entitled to adjust the increments due to employees against the temporary adjustment difference payable to them. This clause should have retrospective effect from April 1, 1954, the first cut falling due on April 1, 1955. However, in giving effect to this changed provision, employees should not be required to refund any amount already received by them as a result of Clause 3(g) of the Government-modified decision dated August 24, 1954.

Payment Of Arrears For 1954-55 To Be Spread Over Three Accounting Years

(d) With a view to affording some relief to banks from the initial impact of the retrospective implementation of the Labour Appellate Tribunal Decision, the implementation of the aforesaid first impact should be phased over three accounting years in such a manner that 40% of the additional emoluments due to employees in 1954-55 (April to March) will be payable by December 31, 1955, 30% by June 30, 1956, and the balance 30% by January 31, 1957. This will, however, be subject to the condition that in case during this period the services of any of the employees concerned are terminated by way of dismissal or discharge or in other ways, or in case an employee retires or leaves his employment for any reason whatever or dies, the total dues that would have become payable to him at the time the final decision of the Government on my recommendations came into force inclusive of all benefits should be paid to him or his assignee forthwith.

Adjustment Of Dearness Allowance

(e) The following formulae should be adopted for adjustment of the dearness allowance for variations in the Cost of Living Index for clerical and subordinate staff respectively in lieu of the provision in the Labour Appellate Tribunal Decision:

Clerical Staff

If the average All-India Cost of Living Index for the half-year ending June or December of any year should rise or fall by more than 10 points as compared to 144 (1944=100), the dearness allowance for the succeeding half-year will be raised or lowered by one-seventh of the dearness allowance admissible at the Index level of 144 for each variation of 10 points.

Subordinate Staff

If the average All-India Cost of Living Index for the half-year ending June or December of any year should rise or fall by more than 10 points as compared to 144 (1944=100), the dearness allowance for the succeeding half-year will be raised or lowered by one-tenth of the dearness allowance admissible at the Index level of 144 for each variation of 10 points.

Adjustment Of Employees In The New Wage Structure

(f) The provision made in the Labour Appellate Tribunal Decision in regard to fitting employees in the new wage structure should be confirmed only in the case of A Class banks. In the case of B, C and D Classes of banks, the corresponding provision in the Sastry Award which has been upheld in the Government-modified decision dated August 24, 1954, should be applied.

Government-Modified Decision Dated August 24, 1954, To Continue In Case Of Banks Specified

2. As regards C Class banks other than those mentioned in Clauses 1, 6 and 7, and D Class banks other than those in Clause 7, the Government-modified decision dated August 24, 1954, should operate subject to the modifications mentioned in Clauses 1 (a), 1(b), 1(c), and 1(e). Displaced banks and banks incorporated in Travancore-Cochin State excluding the Travancore Bank should likewise implement the Government-modified decision subject to the aforesaid modifications.

Position Of D Class Banks Including Displaced Banks To Be Reviewed In 1959

(i) In the case D Class banks, including displaced banks but excluding D Class banks incorporated in Travancore-Cochin State the provision made in the Labour Appellate Tribunal Decision that as from April 1, 1959, they should automatically step into C Class should be set aside and in its place a provision added that the position of these banks as at the end of March, 1959, will be examined afresh in order to arrive at a decision as to their promotion or otherwise to C Class.

Provision As To D Class Banks In Travancore-Cochin State

(ii) In case a Commission is not appointed for banks incorporated in Travancore-Cochin State as recommended, the recommendation made in Clause 2(i) in respect of D Class banks will apply to D Class banks in Travancore-Cochin State also.

Time For Exercising Right Of Option To Be Refixed

3. Employees should be entitled to the right of option to the existing terms of service as confirmed by the Labour Appellate Tribunal decision but the period for such option mentioned in that Decision should, as a consequence of my recommendations, be refixed and extended to three months from the date of pronouncement of the Government's final decision on my report. Where employees of any bank have already exercised their option on the assumption that the Government-modified decision has come to stay, such option should be allowed to be revised and another opportunity given to employees to opt either for the final decision of the Government on my report or for the terms offered by the individual banks.

Dues For The Current Year To Be Settled On Or Before December 31, 1955

4. Payment of emoluments to bank employees for the current year according to the Government's final decision on my recommendations should be settled by December 31, 1955.

Promotion Of The Indian Bank To A Class

5. The agreement entered into between the Indian Bank and its employees' representatives in regard to its promotion from B Class to A Class as from January 1, 1956, should be approved and enforced.

Agreements Before The Commission

6. In respect of the following banks which entered into agreements with employees' representatives before this Commission, the decision should be in terms of the agreements forwarded to the Government.

(a) Bank of Bikaner.

(b) Jodhpur Commercial Bank.

Other Agreements

7. The following banks have independently entered into agreements with their employees as to the pay scales and other conditions of service applicable to them:

(i) Salem Bank.

(ii) Vysya Bank.

(iii) Bharatha Lakshmi Bank.

(iv) Pandyan Bank.

The agreements of the first two banks have been recorded by the Labour Appellate Tribunal. The last two banks have sent to this Commission authenticated copies of agreements signed by them and their employees. These agreements should also be approved and enforced.

The United Bank Of India

8. The United Bank of India should implement the Sastry Award applicable to banks in B Class with effect from August 1, 1955, subject to the following conditions:

(i) The initial additional burden arising from the implementation of the said Award should be spread over a period of three years, one-third of the increase in each of the components of the monthly emoluments being paid to the employees year by year during this period:

(ii) The employees whose monthly emoluments would be reduced should have their emoluments adjusted downward during a similar period of three years, the reduction every year being one-third of the difference in their emoluments for the month of July, 1955, and the emoluments they would be entitled to under the above provisions as from August 1, 1955;

(iii) The employees should be entitled to regular increments in the Award scales during the above period and where salaries would be reduced such increments should be adjusted towards the reduction in the temporary adjustment difference which would become payable to the employees as a result of implementation of the above recommendation;

(iv) The Tribunal to which the question of retrenchment of staff has been referred should be requested to decide the said question as early as possible and the recommendations of the Tribunal when received should be implemented without delay; and

(v) At the end of three years or after the recommendations of the Tribunal appointed to deal with the question of retrenchment of staff are received and implemented, whichever event happens earlier, the financial position of the bank should be considered afresh by a Tribunal appointed in that behalf and the wage structure and allowances should be fixed in the light of the decision of the said Tribunal.

Banks Incorporated In Travancore-Cochin State—Commission To Be Appointed

9. In view of the special problem of banking in Travancore-Cochin State, the Government should, as soon as may be expedient, appoint a Commission with wide powers to examine the financial position of banks incorporated in that State in relation to its economy, suggest measures for their integration and make recommendations in regard to the terms and conditions of service of their employees.

COMMITTEE ON HIGHER EDUCATION FOR RURAL AREAS : RURAL INSTITUTES, 1954—REPORT

New Delhi, Ministry of Education, 1955. 77p. Charts.

Convener : Shri K. L. Shrimali.
Members : Shri L. K. Elmhirst; Shri L. H. Foster; Shri J. C. Mathur.
Secretary : Shri I. R. Khan.

APPOINTMENT

The Committee on Higher Education for Rural Areas: Rural Institutes was appointed by the Ministry of Education, Government of India, in October, 1954.

TERMS OF REFERENCE

(a) To undertake a comprehensive survey and appraisal of promising ideas, institutions and experiments in the field of Higher Education in rural areas;

(b) To determine what specific projects and institutions should be encouraged to carry on experimental work in this field;

(c) To recommend a possible pattern for rural universities with particular reference to:

(i) The aims, organization and content of Higher Education in rural areas;

(ii) Its relationship to Basic and Secondary Education;

(iii) Other allied problems;

(d) To suggest ways and means of making education in the existing universities more useful and more closely related to rural needs and problems,

so that a sound and reasonably uniform system of Rural Higher Education suited to our needs and resources may be evolved for the whole country.

CONTENTS

Foreword; Preface; Appointment and Terms of Reference; Aims and Objectives; Research Courses and Services to the Community; Admission and Examinations; Organization and Administration; Finance; Implementation; Summary of Main Recommendations; Appendices from 1 to 4.

SUMMARY OF MAIN RECOMMENDATIONS

The aims and objectives of Higher Education in rural areas are not fundamentally different from those of Higher Education in urban areas.

Rural Institutes will help in breaking down economic and geographic barriers between the rural and the urban population. They will also help in bridging the gulf which exists in our country between culture and work, between the humanities and technology and between the practical and the ideal.

Rural Institutes which aim at serving the entire community will have a variety of functions:

(i) They will admit students who after completing their Post-Basic or Higher Secondary education wish to proceed for higher studies.

(ii) They will make provision for certificate courses in subjects such as Rural Hygiene, Agriculture and Rural Engineering and also for shorter courses to meet the requirements of those persons—men or women—who wish to increase their knowledge and skill without having to go through a regular course.

(iii) By providing a comprehensive teaching-cum-research-cum-extension programme, Rural Institutes will strive to meet the educational needs of every one in the area they set out to serve.

The Rural Institute will, in short, need to function as a cultural and training centre and as a centre for development planning for the entire community.

Students at the Rural Institutes should devote sufficient time to studies of the fundamentals of science and technology.

The requirements for recruitment to Government services will need adjustment to afford the products of Rural Institutes their rightful place in the administrative services.

In recommending the establishment of Rural Institutes, it is not intended to create a permanent or ultimate separation of rural and urban institutions. The programme of national education must develop as an organic whole.

Rural Institutes

Part I

The five main aspects of any region in India today are:

(i) The Economic aspect; (ii) The Health and Hygiene aspect; (iii) The Educational aspect; (iv) The Sociological aspect; and (v) The Cultural aspect.

Each of these aspects will be reflected in the courses and research at the institute and in extension work in the field.

The site of the Rural Institute should be carefully chosen keeping in view not only practical considerations but also the natural beauty of the surroundings.

The Institute will be residential for students of both

sexes and for staff, with adequate amenities for living rooms, classrooms, workshops, farms, etc.

Close and constant contact between the Rural Institute and other agencies working in the field of rural reconstruction such as the Community Projects Administration and National Extension Service is highly desirable and likely to be of no little mutual benefit.

Rural Institutes will take every aspect of the regional or village problem as their field of research, and with a view to action.

Some fields of research in the various aspects of rural life are suggested.

The following courses should be provided at the Rural Institute with minor adjustments in their duration and content to suit different regions:

(i) A three-year Diploma Course in Rural Services;

(ii) A one-year course for a Teaching Diploma;

(iii) A one-year course for a Teaching Certificate;

(iv) A two-year Certificate Course for Rural Health Workers (Women).

(v) A two-year Certificate Course for Overseers; and

(vi) A two-year Certificate Course in Agricultural Sciences.

All students will undertake some "useful work" on the Campus. Paid jobs will also be available for needy students and will, where possible, be related to the nature of their courses of study.

The language requirements will be the regional languages, Hindi and English.

Students at the Rural Institute will be given facilities and scope to develop their own activities and societies in their own leisure time.

The extension service of the Rural Institute represents the chief means of contact between the Institute and the people of its region whether for promoting Higher Education or for enlivening the process of research.

As part of the extension programme, we recommend short courses of study at the Vidyapeeths that would combine cultural orientation with the learning of new agricultural and craft techniques. Such courses would improve the cultural and economic level of the region.

The short residential courses here proposed will make the Institute a home for a much wider public than just their own regular student body.

We visualize the eventual establishment of a *Lok Vidyapeeth* in every district of India.

The ultimate end of such community programmes must be a vital cultural growth which releases new energies, reveals suppressed emotions and finds new forms of expression through the Arts and develops new qualities of trust in human relations.

Part II

The three-year Diploma Course as well as the two- and one-year Certificate Courses should be open to candidates who have completed the Higher Secondary or Post-Basic course.

Candidates who have passed the High School Examination should not be admitted unless they have put in an extra year of practical work.

The Teaching Diploma Course should be of two kinds. One for graduates and the other for those who have done Higher Secondary or the Post-Basic course, and also for those who have completed the one or two years' Certificate Course.

No educational qualification need be prescribed for short courses in special techniques.

Lok Vidyapeeths may admit trainees irrespective of their academic background.

The Director and the Faculties should try different methods for the selection of those candidates who are most likely to benefit from the Institute.

Women will be encouraged to take advantage of all the facilities offered by the Institute.

Standards of admission and of selection should remain flexible.

A final test on completion of the three-year Diploma Course will be given.

The Diplomas will be awarded by the National Council of Higher Education for Rural Areas and will be called the National Diploma in Rural Services.

For Certificate Courses of one or two years' duration, the award of certificate will be the responsibility of the State Councils. The emphasis in assessment should be on the practical side of the students' work.

No formal tests need be held in the case of shorter courses of less than a year's duration.

A definite shift in emphasis away from the stereotyped written examinations and towards depending for assessment on cumulative records of practical and social activities of the student will be essential for the success of the Rural Institutes.

Organization And Administration

In the early stages of development of Higher Education for rural areas, privately sponsored Rural Institutes should be particularly encouraged.

At the Centre, Government efforts to develop Higher Education for rural areas should concentrate on nation-wide co-ordination, financial support, development and maintenance of standards and encouragement for programmes of demonstrated value.

A National Council of Higher Education for Rural Areas should be established as Advisory Body to the Central Ministry of Education.

At the Central Ministry of Education, a Division of Higher Education for Rural Areas should be established to encourage the development of Higher Education in rural areas.

At the State level, there should be established a State Council of Higher Education for Rural Areas in the Department of Education along the same lines as suggested for the Centre.

Each Rural Institute should have a governing body to determine major policy to facilitate the general understanding and support of its programme, and to ensure academic and financial integrity in all phases of the Institute's work.

The internal organization of the Rural Institute should establish authority and responsibility clearly, in order to achieve the Institute's comprehensive goal of teaching, research and extension.

There should be provision for:

(a) A Director to be the Chief Executive Officer who will administer the total programme, being responsible only to the Governing Board.

(b) Separate Departments for the Library and for the six major fields of study (Agriculture, Engineering, Hygiene, Rural Services, Teacher-Training and General Studies), each under the direction of a Department Head responsible to the Director of the Institute.

(c) An Extension Service Department, directed by a Head responsible to the Director, to co-ordinate the field work of the educational departments and to promote the total extension service programme of the Institute.

(d) A Student Guidance Counsellor, responsible to the Director, to stimulate and co-ordinate programme concerned with out-of-class life of students.

(e) A Finance Department, headed by a Bursar responsible to the Director, to manage all business affairs.

(f) Standing Committees to advise the Director on general administration, educational programme, extension service, and other major matters; and temporary Committees as required for special studies and to expedite the Institute's work.

The Rural Institute should make every effort to build a good working relationship with existing universities, with the State schools, and with administrative and other agencies engaged in work related to that of the Institute.

Finance

Simplicity of style and manner should guide all planning at the Rural Institute in order that operating costs may be kept low; but high quality should always be maintained.

Students at the Rural Institute should work to help pay the costs of their education. Student work experiences should be integrated into the student's total educational programme.

The Rural Institute should undertake productive activities to improve the economy of the community and to provide some income for the Institute.

The possible sources of Revenue for a Rural Institute include the Central and State Governments, the students, the local people, the alumni of the Institute and philanthropy.

The recurring budget of Rs. 5,50,000 and capital investment of Rs. 65,00,000 are conservative estimates of costs which should be provided for each Rural Institute.

Implementation

We recommend that the Government select for immediate development into Rural Institutes five or six existing which are already doing pioneering work in this field.

If the Heads of these Institutions are willing to accept help and suggestion from the Government, they should be invited to draw up plans immediately for submission to the Government. Once agreement is reached funds should be made available by the Government.

We recommend the immediate establishment of a National and State Councils of Higher Education for Rural Areas to guide and maintain the standards of these Institutes and to explore the possibility of setting up new Institutes, or of developing other existing ones.

We also urge the establishment of a new Division in the Central Ministry of Education to take immediate steps to promote the development of Rural Institutes.

Each State will need to set up a Section in the Department of Education to deal with these matters at the State level.

As soon as possible, the National Council of Higher Education for Rural Areas should set up an expert committee to draw up suggestions for courses, suggestions for suitable buildings, sample budgets for the proposed institutes and appropriate qualifications for personnel.

RICE MILLING COMMITTEE, 1954—REPORT

Delhi, Manager of Publications, 1958. 180p.

Chairman : Shri C. P. Karunakara Menon.
Members : Shri G. Parameswaran Pillai; Shri I. U. Lakhia; Shri Jhaverbhai Patel; Shri Raojibhai N. Patel; Mrs. P. Johri; Dr. D. V. Karmarkar.
Secretary : Shri N. M. Bardhan.

APPOINTMENT

The Rice Milling Committee was constituted under the Ministry of Food and Agriculture vide their Resolution No. P4-I-608(5)/54 dated October 8, 1954.

TERMS OF REFERENCE

(i) To examine the working of the different types of rice milling now in vogue in the country from all relevant aspects such as Technical, Nutritional, Consumer Preference, Economic and Employment; and

(ii) To make recommendations as to the future policy that should be adopted and to indicate the Administrative, Financial and Legislative measures which may be needed on the part of the Central and State Governments to give effect to them.

CONTENTS

Introductory; Implements of Hand-Pounding; Rice Milling by Power-driven Machine; Adverse effects of Government Control and other factors on the Hand-Pounding Industry; Rice Milling after Decontrol; Rural Unemployment and Employment Potential of the Hand-Pounding Industry; Impediments in the way of Organizing and Developing Hand-Pounding Industry; Encouragement of Hand-Pounding Industry; Co-operative Hand-Pounding Centres; Nutrition; Summary of Recommendations for Rice Milling; Pulse-Milling and Recommendations; Note by Dr. D. V. Karmarkar; Appendices I to XII.

RECOMMENDATIONS

Licensing of all types of power-driven rice mills, and recognized hand-pounding centres organized as co-operative societies or by recognized institutions and social workers or by trade engaged in producing hand-pounded rice working on factory scale should be immediately introduced in all States under the Essential Commodities Act, 1955, where this has not already been done under a State Act.

A census should be taken by the State Governments of all existing rice mills.

No licences for new rice mills or rice milling in combined mills should be granted. If, however, a new mill is considered by the Local Government to be absolutely essential in the public interest in special circumstances, for example, in emergencies, the licence should be given to the required number of the smallest unit managed either by the Government or by Co-operative Societies as the Government may decide. The decision in this matter should be taken in each case at State Government level.

No additional capacity to any of the existing rice mills should be allowed.

No rice mill should be permitted to work for more than six hours a day, the object being that the existing over-all production of the rice mills should not only not be increased, but should be decreased.

Immediate action should be taken to eliminate small huller machines operated with one or two hullers; similarly rice hullers working in combination such as pumping out or lifting water for agricultural or other purposes should be prohibited. In no case should the licence of any such small huller machine be renewed to work after December 31, 1956, and the Government should take suitable steps, where necessary, for example, in the case of displaced persons, for rehabilitating owners of husking machines in some alternative employment.

A cess at annas six per maund of paddy milled should be imposed on all rice mills and the proceeds of the cess should be utilized for organizing the hand-pounding industry, for research to improve hand-pounding implements and for a subsidy to hand-pounded rice. Necessary legislation should be made for the imposition of a cess on rice mills.

The existing average subsidy of annas six per maund of paddy hand-pounded should be increased to annas eight per maund of paddy. The subsidy should be granted through recognized hand-pounding centres organized as Co-operative Societies or by recognized institutions and social workers (wherever the price of the hand-pounded rice is higher than [that of] milled rice). The subsidy should be for a specified period of, say, five years, after which the position should be reviewed by the Government.

Individuals engaged in producing hand-pounded rice and certified by the All-India Khadi and Village Industries Commission may be allowed concessions in the form of easy credit and implements at subsidized rates.

The hand-pounded rice produced at hand-pounding centres certified by the All-India Khadi and Village

Industries Commission should be exempted from sales tax in States where rice is subjected to sales tax. The existing rules should be amended accordingly.

State Governments should purchase only hand-pounded rice, preferably from Government-subsidized hand-pounding centres where they exist, for their requirements for jails, hospitals, Government hostels, the Railways, the Army, the police, etc. The Government should issue a directive to all Government-aided and controlled concerns, institutions and canteens (such as Railway Canteens) to purchase only hand-pounded rice, preferably from Government-subsidized hand-pounding centres where they exist.

Each State Government should immediately formulate a programme for the speedy organization of hand-pounding for home consumption and at centres for sale, so as to cover within the shortest possible time the milling capacity released by the proposed closure of small huller machines, in order that the supply position of rice is ensured.

Hand-pounding industry should be further organized in other areas also for improving the employment position and for producing the supplies required in those areas so as to replace production by the rice mills. Each State Government should draw a five-year phased programme on the lines indicated in this Report for the speedy organization and development of the hand-pounding industry, with a view to the employment of the maximum number possible of the unemployed or under-employed rural labour, and for the elimination of rice mills in the States within that period, regard being had to the maintenance of normal supplies of rice to the community. Each State Government should review this five-year plan every year and revise it with reference to the progress achieved in the previous years and the target to be achieved.

The programme of State Governments for a speedy organization of the hand-pounding industry should proceed on a co-operative basis and should follow the recommendations made by the Reserve Bank of India in their Rural Credit Survey Report regarding co-operative processing and marketing of village produce. At the end of three years there should be a review by the Government of India of the progress made by each State in the implementation of these recommendations, so far as hand-pounding of rice is concerned.

All State Governments, by issuing orders in exercise of powers conferred on them by the Essential Commodities Act, 1955, should restrict the milling of rice by rice mills to 5% with a minimum milling of 3%.

Exemption from the restriction under Item (12) should be granted for rice produced for the export market in which case the milling should be adjusted to the requirements of the purchasing country. Such production should be with the special permission of the Government of India and under their close supervision.

In the case of any import of rice, the rice of the same standard of milling as stated above should be imported as far as possible.

Any rice mill which may be retained to meet the essential needs for production, for export, or for any other reason should be only of the sheller type or of the combined sheller-huller type.

The Essential Commodities Act, 1955, and, if necessary, the Constitution should be suitably amended to enable State Governments:

(i) To issue orders under Items (2) to (6) with the object of creating work for the rural unemployed;

(ii) To restrict milling by rice mills (Item 12) with the object of retaining the nutritive value of milled rice; and

(iii) To convert any huller mills into sheller mills or combined sheller-huller mills.

Publicity and propaganda should be made through Schools, Colleges, the Community Development and National Extension Blocks, Women's Organizations, the Red Cross, the Cinema, the Radio, the Stage and Literature:

(i) To emphasize the nutritive value of under-milled rice and hand-pounded rice and induce consumers to eat hand-pounded rice;

(ii) To emphasize the greater potentiality of the hand-pounding industry to provide employment;

(iii) To discourage the present practice of washing and cooking rice by which its nutritive value is lost and to propagate the correct method for retaining it in cooked rice.

Research should be conducted for evolving simpler and better hand-pounding implements with a view to increasing their output and at the same time making them easier to handle.

Each State Government should have a special agency under its Co-operative Department to organize Co-operative Societies as suggested in these Recommendations.

The Central Government should appoint a Special Agency to act as liaison between them and the State Government with a view to enforcing the Government of India's policy in those matters.

FERTILIZER PRODUCTION COMMITTEE, 1954—REPORT

New Delhi, Ministry of Production, 1955. 2 Vols.

Chairman Shri B. C. Mukharji.
Members : Dr. A. Nagaraja Rao; Dr. M. D. Parekh; Shri K. C. Sharma.
Secretary : Shri P. M. Nayak.

APPOINTMENT

The Fertilizer Production Committee was constituted under the Ministry of Production vide their Resolution No.Fy.I-17(1)/54 dated October 29, 1954.

TERMS OF REFERENCE

(i) To suggest possible locations for the new fertilizer factories for the production of ammonium sulphate, ammonium sulphate-nitrate and urea having regard to all relevant considerations including adequacy of transport and the proximity of consumer points;

(ii) To indicate the quantities of one or more of these fertilizers that could be produced at each location on an economic basis, the processes to be adopted and the probable cost of production;

(iii) To estimate roughly the capital and working cost of the plants recommended at different locations;

(iv) To make recommendations regarding the requirements and the provision of technical personnel for staffing the new plants; and

(v) To suggest the best method of further processing the Committee's Recommendations.

CONTENTS

Introductory; Production Targets; Raw Materials; Review of State Governments' Proposals; Production Units—Number and Location; Technical, Financial and Administrative Consequences; Mode of Implementation of Recommendations; Miscellaneous; Annexures.

RECOMMENDATIONS

For any new factory, however large it may be, it is necessary at the present juncture to appoint a firm of constructors as the Government's general agents charged with the task of arranging for contractors and supervising and co-ordinating their work. We have come to the conclusion that while it will be necessary, even on the present occasion, to depend largely on imported technique and know-how for designing the new plants, on imported plant, equipment and machinery for their construction at site and, to some extent, on imported technicians for supervising their assembly and commissioning, our contractual arrangements with the selected foreign firms should be so devised as to secure full association of Indian Technical Personnel at every stage of the work and also full utilization, as well as maximum development, of whatever construction and fabrication facilities exist in the country today.

The technique of making heavy water is new and uncommon and its knowledge is, we understand, confined to only a handful of firms in the world. We consider in the circumstances that it would be expedient to engage, on the best possible terms, the services of one of them for technical guidance in the designing, construction and commissioning of the heavy water plant from start to finish.

We advocate, as the first step in the process of implementation of our Recommendations, the setting up of a common Fertilizer Board to administer and control all State-owned fertilizer production units including Sindri.

While the common Board must have a body of common Directors, whole-time and part-time, it may, we recognize, be necessary to devise a system of appointing Associate Directors for individual projects. In the case of the Nangal Plant, for example, it may be considered expedient to have on the Board a representative of the Atomic Energy Commission and/or a representative of the Bhakra Control Board; these representatives cannot for obvious reasons be accepted as common Directors for all projects and should therefore be given a distinctive designation so that they may exercise their powers and fulfil their responsibilities only in relation to the particular project for which they may be specifically named. There should, we suggest, be a paid whole-time Executive Chairman for the common Board and not a Chairman for only presiding at meetings as currently provided by the Articles of Association of Sindri and other State-owned industrial concerns. The Board should have, alternatively, a paid whole-time Managing Director as its Chief Executive. With a whole-time Executive Chairman, there should be as many Managing Directors as there are production units. With a single whole-time Managing Director each factory should have a General Manager, all the General Managers being also Directors of the common Board.

To the Management Committee for each factory fairly wide powers should be delegated by the Board; in addition, restricted delegations should be made to the General Manager or the Managing Director himself with powers to sub-delegate his authority to any of his principal lieutenants individually.

As the very first step we would recommend immediate recruitment of the following four senior officials for each approved factory including Nangal Plant:

(i) The Administrative head, i.e., the General Manager/Managing Director;

(ii) A fully qualified Chief Engineer; there should be no hesitation in recruiting a foreigner to this post if no qualified and experienced Indian national is available for the office;

(iii) A qualified and experienced Production Manager of proved merit and having the requisite operational and administrative experience; we expect that there are at least some technicians in the country, at Sindri or elsewhere, who would come up to the expectations; for the rest, recruitment from abroad may have to be resorted to; and

(iv) A Chief Accounts Officer.

Simultaneously two foreign experts should be engaged on short-term contracts (not more than three years) to fill the position of consultants and technical advisers without any executive authority. These experts should be direct employees of the Central Fertilizer Board and not attached to any particular factory. The type of men we have in mind can be recruited only in one way, namely, by a direct approach to foreign Governments who are interested in, and are genuinely anxious to help, the industrialization of India coupled simultaneously with an approach to friendly firms with whom we have already developed business contacts.

A Standing Technical Committee should be set up consisting of:

(i) The three foreign experts or consultants;

(ii) The Chief Engineers of the new production units;

(iii) Their Production Managers; and

(iv) Two or three technicians of experience drawn from Sindri or elsewhere including firms in the private sector.

This Standing Committee should to a large extent fulfil the functions of Consulting Engineers for the new production units and their jurisdiction should also cover Nangal to a limited extent.

The first task of the Standing Technical Committee should be to prepare a layout design of the new plants with necessary drawings for the approval of the Central Fertilizer Board; and thereafter to prepare specifications for each plant on the basis of the approved designs. In the case of the Nangal Plant the plant designs will have to be made and specifications prepared by the Consulting Engineers in consultation with the Standing Technical Committee and under their general instructions.

For Nangal a firm of consulting engineers having special experience in designing and building heavy water plants should be engaged and required to function in close collaboration with, and under the supervisory control of, the Standing Technical Committee.

On the basis of the specifications prepared by the Standing Technical Committee (in the case of Nangal by the consulting engineers under the supervision of the Standing Technical Committee) tenders should be invited for each section of each plant. After the tenders received are scrutinized by the Standing Technical Committee (in the case of Nangal by the Consulting Engineers under the supervision of the Standing Technical Committee) contracts should be awarded for individual plants or groups of plants, not on the basis of turn-key jobs, but on the basis of either supply of plant and equipment alone or their supply and erection or, in exceptional cases, their supply, erection and commissioning.

Adequate local organizations for individual production units as well as a Headquarters Central Organization for the Central Fertilizer Board should be built up as early as possible.

As an interim measure the processing of the programme visualized above should be entrusted to either a small Ad Hoc Committee or preferably a Special Officer invested with the necessary status and powers and assisted by competent lieutenants of appropriate rank.

COKE-OVEN PROJECTS ENQUIRY COMMITTEE, 1954—REPORT

New Delhi, Planning Commission, 1955. 80p.

Chairman : Shri Darab C. Driver.
Members : Shri R. K. Ramadhyani; Dr. A. Nagaraja Rao; Shri C. S. N. Raju; Shri S. V. Aiyer; Shri S. N. Ray.
Secretary : Shri K. Vyasulu.

APPOINTMENT

The Coke-Oven Projects Enquiry Committee was constituted under the Planning Commission vide their Resolution dated November 27, 1954.

TERMS OF REFERENCE

(i) To make an assessment of the demand for coke as at present and over the next Five Year Plan period;

(ii) To examine the replacement and expansion programme of existing producers of coke in the country and assess the additional production likely to be available from existing and projected cokeries;

(iii) In case the need for additional coke production is established, to advise on the exact quantum of development and the size of the plant or plants that will have to be established, and on their appropriate locations and in this connection to make an appraisal of the economics of the West Bengal Government Scheme referred to in Para 1 taking into account the scope for utilization of by-products dealt with in (iv), (v) and (vi) below;

(iv) To examine the prospects of by-product recovery and coal-tar distillation plants, against the demand, current and expected, during the Second Five Year Plan, for the primary organic chemicals obtained as by-products directly from coke-oven gas or from distillation of coal-tar;

(v) To examine the scope for and economics of a thermal power plant as an adjunct to a coke-oven plant, if established at Durgapur taking into consideration the power generation programme of the Damodar Valley Corporation and the anticipated growth of load for electric power in the Bengal-Bihar areas;

(vi) To examine other possibilities of utilizing coke-oven gas in the vicinity of a coke-oven plant if established at Durgapur for improving the economics of operation of the coke-oven plant;

(vii) To advise on the best method of organization and management of any independent coke-oven plant or plants and ancillary industries that might be recommended to be established in the public sector.

CONTENTS

Introduction dealing with history of the Durgapur Project and the Appointment of the Committee; Assessment of Demand for Coke; Replacement and expansion programme of existing producers and additional production from these and any other projected cokeries; Appraisement of different locations for creating additional capacity for coke; Demand for primary organic chemicals and other by-products, coal-tar distillation products, price levels for these products by 1960; Establishment of a Thermal Power Plant as an adjunct to the Durgapur Coke-Oven Plant for improving its economics of operation; Economics of the Durgapur Coke-Oven Project; Organization and Management of Coke-Oven Plant; Summary of Conclusions and Recommendations; Explanatory Notes by Shri S. V. Aiyer, Shri S. N. Ray and Shri R. K. Ramadhyani; Appendices.

RECOMMENDATIONS

The demand within the country for hard coke in 1953 was estimated at 462,478 tons. The estimated demand for hard coke by 1960, exclusive of the requirements of the steel works and their subsidiaries and the Sindri Fertilizer Factory, would be about 875,000 tons of which 831,000 tons would be for sized coke. The increase in requirements is expected to arise mainly from foundries, Mysore Iron & Steel Works, soda ash, sugar, calcium carbide and ferro-manganese industries.

Of the total demand by 1960, about 100,000 to 110,000 tons of hard sized coke would have to be of a grade required in ferro manganese and ferro alloys production, i.e., with phosphorus not exceeding 0.05 per cent and ash below 20 per cent. A very special grade of another 15,000 to 20,000 tons of coke with phosphorus not exceeding 0.03 per cent and ash below 12 per cent would be needed for the production of calcium carbide, sodium sulphide and special castings.

No supplies of sized coke for the market could be envisaged from the steel works and the Sindri Fertilizer Factory with the exception of the Indian Iron & Steel Company, who have indicated a possible supply of sized coke during the period of the Second Five Year Plan varying between 66,000 tons in 1955 and 44,000 tons in 1960, the supply in 1959 being nil.

On the assumption that the renovation programmes furnished by the four private merchant cokeries in existence would be completed, their capacity by 1960 would be 307,000 tons per annum; a production of 269,500 tons of sized coke is expected from them in 1960. The supplies of sized coke from the Giridih Coke Ovens have been placed at 27,600 tons in 1960. The total availability of by-product sized coke from the existing sources indicated above (i.e., private merchant cokeries, Giridih Plant and IISCO) is expected to be 341,100 tons in 1960. Including supplies of sized bee-hive coke estimated at 105,000 tons in 1960, the total domestic supplies of sized coke would come to 446,100 tons.

The deficit in supplies of sized coke to be covered by the erection of additional coke capacity would amount to 384,900 tons. The tonnage of normal grade of sized coke would correspond to 250,000 to 270,000 tons of the total deficit, the balance being of special grades.

The deficit in supplies of sized coke to be covered by the erection of additional coke capacity would amount to 384,900 tons. The tonnage of normal grade of sized coke would correspond to 250,000 to 270,000 tons of the total deficit, the balance being of special grades.

To investigate the question of appropriate locations for coke-oven plants, the Committee would have had to study several aspects of the different coal fields and their coal, select several possible areas and make a comparative study of the merits and demerits of each location before the most suitable location/locations could be indicated. The volume of work and the investigation that would be involved would take a considerably longer period for the Committee to complete such a study, if required. If the Planning Commission consider that such an investigation is required and it would be advantageous for them to have ready data on the subject for their further guidance, the Committee would like to suggest that separate arrangements for undertaking such an exhaustive enquiry should be made.

In the light of the position explained above, even while considering the question of location of the plant proposed by the West Bengal Government, the Committee were not able to discuss any location other than Durgapur. An examination of the several aspects relating to Durgapur reveals that facilities of quick transport towards Calcutta side from a four-track railway system soon to be electrified, cheaper railway freight for coke compared to freight from Jharia, etc., future availability of water transport through Durgapur Canal towards Calcutta and places in between, cheap land, water supplies and a developed colony obtain at Durgapur which is also favourably situated in respect of availability of coal and power and the market of Greater Calcutta. The Committee are, therefore , of the opinion that taking the deficit into account, the Durgapur site is suitable for the location of the plant proposed by the West Bengal Government with a capacity of 292,950 tons of sized coke over 1" per annum.

The sections of the Durgapur Scheme, whose economics have been worked out by the Committee, comprise the following:

(a) Coke-Oven Plant with a daily throughput of 1,300 tons of coal and coke breeze (1,235 tons of coal and 65 tons of coke breeze).

(b) Auxiliary Plants for the recovery of by-products from coke-oven gas (Ammonia, Sulphuric Acid, Coal-tar, Crude Benzol and its rectified products).

(c) Coal-tar Distillation Plant with a daily input of 50 tons of coal-tar.

The fixed capital investment on the sections covered in the economic appraisal is estimated at Rs. 525 lakhs. The requirements of working capital have been estimated at Rs. 35 lakhs.

In calculating the credits, the Committee are of the opinion that counting the potentialities for industrial development in the Bengal-Bihar area, there would be a market for 500,000 gallons of benzene and corresponding quantities of other by-products of benzol rectification. The balance of crude benzol would have to be processed and sold as motor benzol. The surplus coke-oven gas amounting to 8.18 million c.ft. of 450-460 BTU per c.ft. per day will be utilized in the beginning for firing the boilers of the Thermal Power Plant of 30,000 KW capacity. The total credits from the sale of different products are estimated at Rs. 193.61 lakhs as against manufacturing charges and provisions for depreciation and interest on working capital totalling Rs. 157.9 lakhs.

The operating results show a return of 6.8% over the capital investment of Rs. 525 lakhs, the two items of preliminary expenses, i.e., expenditure on the project report and interest during the period of construction on any loan capital that might be secured, estimated at an extra Rs. 30 lakhs, being written off from the profits gradually year by year, according to existing commercial practice. These items have not been provided for in computing the 6.8% referred to. The above return is visualized after providing depreciation and interest on working capital, without providing for interest on fixed capital.

Having regard to the agreement entered into by the West Bengal Government and the Damodar Valley Corporation in January, 1955, on the installation of a 30,000-KW Thermal Power Plant by the latter, it is not considered necessary to assess the growth of load in the Bengal-Bihar area as required under the Terms of Reference. The installation of this power station provides an outlet for the by-product coke-oven gas and thus improves the economics of the Scheme.

Having regard to certain industrial demands in prospect near Durgapur, which have been intimated to the Committee by the West Bengal Government, it is not clear at this stage whether there would be enough gas for being transported to Chittaranjan area or to Calcutta. On re-examination of the Terms of Reference since the submission of the Interim Report, the Committee are of the opinion that since they were only called upon to examine the possibilities of utilizing coke-oven gas in the vicinity of a coke-oven plant if established at Durgapur, it is not necessary for them to report on the proposals relating to the gas grid intimated by the West Bengal Government as part of the First Phase of their Durgapur Scheme.

The State Government, who have sponsored the Durgapur Project, would naturally be the authority to decide on the form of organization and management for the Project. According to the Committee, the operation of the Project should be based on strict commercial principles.

ADVISORY COMMITTEE ON AFTER-CARE PROGRAMMES, 1954—REPORT

New Delhi, Central Social Welfare Board, 1955. 2 Vols.

Chairman : Shri M. S. Gore.
Members : Smt. Mary Clubwala Jadhav; Smt. Premvati Thapar; Shri P. R. Bhatt; Shri K. K. Balbir.

APPOINTMENT

The Advisory Committee on After-Care Programmes was constituted under the Central Social Welfare Board in December, 1954.

TERMS OF REFERENCE

(i) To study the nature and size of the problem of those adults and juveniles who have been discharged from correctional institutions and institutions for the physically and socially handicapped.

(ii) To determine the scope of After-Care Programmes for these individuals.

(iii) To assess the extent to which the existing After-Care Services meet the needs of the situation and specify the manner in which they need to be developed and modified.

(iv) To suggest ways and means for the establishing of these additional services by statutory and voluntary agencies with the aid of the Central Social Welfare Board.

(v) To indicate the manner in which the pre-discharge policies and practices of institutions may have to be modified if the suggested after-care programmes are to be effective.

CONTENTS

Vol. I: Preface; **Part I**: Introduction; Orphanages; **Part II** : Homes for Women; Homes for the Destitute; Institutions for the Blind, the Deaf and the Leprosy Patients; Institutions for Juvenile Offenders; The Jails in India; Discharged Prisoners' Aid Societies and After-Care Associations; **Part III**: Recommendations; **Vol. II**: Appendices.

RECOMMENDATIONS

The total programme of rehabilitation consists of two phases: Institutional Care and Post-Institutional or After-Care. After-Care has itself two aspects: Vocational Rehabilitation and Social Rehabilitation. The two sets of services are mutually supportive.

For Vocational Rehabilitation the Committee recommend the following services:

(i) The issuing of Letters of Recommendation after proper investigation;

(ii) The organizing of Job Placement Service;

(iii) The Removal of Restrictions on the employment of ex-convicts;

(iv) The Reservation of a Certain Percentage of Jobs for the physically handicapped;

(v) The Issuing of Small Loans for self-employment;

(vi) The organization of Producers' Co-operatives;

(vii) The organization of Small-Scale Industrial Units;

(viii) The provision of Sheltered Workshops and Home Workers' Schemes for the Physically Handicapped.

For Social Rehabilitation of the dischargees from institutions the Committee recommended:

(i) The organizing of After-Care Hostels;

(ii) The providing of Guidance, Counselling and Follow-up Services;

(iii) The providing of Legal Aid and Protection Services.

The best machinery for providing the above-mentioned services would be a nation wide organization of Voluntary After-Care Agencies.

The initiation of after-care work by the Central Social Welfare Board which would be advised in this field by (i) a Central Advisory Committee and (ii) State Advisory Committees.

The Central Advisory Committee would help the CSWB to develop a co-ordinated policy and programme for the development of After-Care Services. This Committee would also assist and guide the work of the State Advisory Committees.

The State Advisory Committees, which will function as specialized bodies of the State Welfare Advisory Boards, will be responsible for preparing detailed programmes of development for their particular States. Their recommendations, routed through the State Boards, would have to receive the approval of the Central Social Welfare Board.

The State Advisory Committees in their own turn will implement the programmes through the instrumentality of Project Implementing Committees.

Targets For The Next Plan Period

The Committee have also suggested specific targets of work for the next five-year period. These targets have been visualized in two types of After-Care Units —Type A and Type B.

(i) Type A would provide basic pre-discharge and After-Care Services. This unit will also provide temporary shelter to the dischargees. It will employ at least one After-Care Officer, one typist-clerk and one peon involving a salary bill of Rs. 6,000 annually. Office expenditure and provision of shelter services will involve about Rs. 5,500 annually. The Committee recommend that each unit should have about Rs. 5,000 at its disposal from which Occupational Loans could be granted to its clients. Thus the total outlay for each such unit will be about Rs.17,000.

(ii) Type B would provide all the above services and also have a regular hostel for about 30 inmates and a fully organized Production Centre. The additional recurring expenditure of this unit will be about Rs. 10,000 not chargeable to the workshops and also involving about Rs. 1,00,000 for a hostel building providing accommodation for 30 people.

Ultimately each one of the 330 districts will have one After-Care Unit of either of the above two types.

In view of the limited organizational resources, however, the Committee have recommended that 150 District Units be established all over the country—120 Type A units and 30 Type B units during the next five years.

Sources Of Financial Support

In the opinion of the Committee the following governmental agencies may have to work together to find the necessary finances for implementing the recommendations:

(i) The Central Social Welfare Board.

(ii) The Ministry of Home Affairs and its corresponding State Departments.

(iii) The Ministry of Education and the State Departments of Education.

(iv) The Ministry of Commerce and Industry and its State counterparts.

PROHIBITION ENQUIRY COMMITTEE, 1954—REPORT

Delhi, Manager of Publications, 1955. 183, IVp.

Chairman : Shri Shriman Narayan.

Members : Shrimati Sucheta Kripalani; Shri S. R. Vasavada; Shri Jaglal Choudhry; Shri G. Ramachandran; Dr. Bhasker Patel; Shri V. D. Dantyagi (died, replaced by Shri R. N. Samarth); Dr. P. J. Thomas.

Co-opted Members : Shri P. Kodanda Rao; Prof. D. S. Nag.

Secretary : Shri N. S. Varadachari.

APPOINTMENT

The Prohibition Enquiry Committee was constituted under the Planning Commission vide their Resolution No. PC/Proh/1/54 dated December 16, 1954.

TERMS OF REFERENCE

(i) To examine the experience gained regarding measures adopted by State Governments to promote prohibition with a view to assessing the extent to which these have been successful and analysing the practical difficulties—administrative, economic, social and others—which have come in the way of implementation of the Programme of Prohibition;

(ii) To make recommendations for a Programme of Prohibition on a national basis;

(iii) To indicate the manner and the stages in which, and the machinery through which, this programme should be carried out; and

(iv) To make such other recommendations on the subject as the Committee may consider necessary.

CONTENTS

Introductory; Historical Background and Factual Position; National Programme; Enforcement; Financial Aspect; Conclusions; Summary of Recommendations; Appendices; Dissenting Minute.

RECOMMENDATIONS

National Programme

Prohibition should be regarded as an integral part of the Second Five Year Plan.

The target date for completing Nationwide Prohibition should be April 1, 1958.

Before the end of the current year the State Governments may declare their acceptance of Prohibition Policy and the target date and prepare the public to fully co-operate in the fulfilment of the Prohibition Programme.

A clear-cut statement may be issued by the Union Government to the effect that Prohibition has become the national policy of the Government and that through the gradual process of education, tightening of restrictions and enforcement, the use of intoxicating drinks and of drugs injurious to health, except for medicinal purposes, is to be completely stopped and before April 1, 1958, Prohibition will become national law through the State Legislatures.

In States which have yet made no beginning towards Prohibition and in the wet areas of Partial Prohibition States, from April 1, 1956, there should be stoppage of drinking in hotels, bars, restaurants, messes, clubs, cinemas and in parties and functions—social, religious and otherwise.

During the transition period, in the case of hotels catering to foreign visitors and tourists, a separate room may be provided for service of liquor to them. Such hotels should be specified by State Governments and rules made in regard to the serving of liquor on temporary permits for foreign visitors and tourists.

During the transition period, in regard to the messes of Defence Services, liquor should not be served at the table when outsiders are invited.

From April 1, 1956, advertisements and all other public inducements relating to drink should be prohibited.

Provision may be made for the following:

(a) Foreign tourists and visitors and foreigners resident in this country may be allowed to have liquor privately in their homes on the basis of special permits. They should in no case indulge in drinking in public after the target date.

(b) For sacramental purposes, liquor may be allowed on permits to Christian, Jewish and Parsee places of worship.

(c) Small quantities of liquor and opium and its derivatives may be permitted for medical treatment of cases under proper safeguards.

Enforcement

It is of the utmost importance that the public conscience should be roused to combat the growing evil of drink and drugs.

Enforcement should proceed on two definite lines:

(a) Educative and Preventive; and

(b) Legal and Administrative.

To achieve co-ordination between the two wings of the enforcement machinery, an Administrator of Prohibition should be appointed in every State with effect from April 1, 1956. The Administrator should work directly under the Minister for Prohibition.

There should be a Prohibition Board at the State level consisting of representatives of both the wings of the enforcement machinery as well as some representatives of public opinion. The Minister in charge of Prohibition will be the President of the Board and the Administrator its Chairman.

It would also be necessary to establish Prohibition Committees in each district and even up to the village and mohalla level.

There should be a Prohibition Act in every State. In the States where no such Act is in force, steps should be taken as early as possible to frame the necessary legislation. The Acts of Bombay and Madras which are already in force may serve as models.

Prohibition offences should be treated on a par with other offences and the police should be made responsible for the legal enforcement of prohibition. All powers in connection with investigation, prevention, detection, prosecution, etc., will vest with the Police Department.

Within the Police Department, there should be a special enforcement branch for Prohibition work, consisting of trained personnel.

Mobile squads of police be organized especially for attacking sources of illicit supplies of liquor and drugs. For this purpose, the State Governments should provide adequate transport and other facilities.

The following changes in law and procedure are suggested:

(1) All offences connected with illicit distillation, import and export of liquor and drugs, bottling of illicit liquor for sale, rendering denatured spirit potable, cultivation of hemp plant, etc., should be made non-bailable.

(2) Punishments in connection with non-bailable offences should be made deterrent. The law should prescribe a minimum punishment for the first offence which may be imprisonment for six months and a heavy fine, and for the second offence, a minimum of one year and a heavier fine.

(3) There should be summary trials for Prohibition offences other than non-bailable offences mentioned above. A time-limit of two months for each case may be set for ensuring an expeditious disposal. The intention is to simplify procedure without taking away the right of the citizen to defend himself properly before a court of law.

(4) State Governments should devise ways and means of protecting witnesses who furnish important information relating to non-bailable offences.

(5) Where a person continues to defy the law and is engaged in illicit manufacture or illicit traffic in drinks and drugs, the possibility of the use of Security Sections of the Criminal Procedure Code may be examined for the prevention of such offences.

Concerted measures are necessary to strike at the roots of illicit distillation and trade.

Great care should be taken in the matter of selecting personnel for the enforcement of Prohibition.

Machinery for education and propaganda should be immediately organized by State Governments.

The Education Department has a special function to perform in the matter of educating students and younger people in regard to the harmful effects of alcohol and drugs.

The Press should be fully utilized to rally public opinion around Prohibition.

The immediate steps to be taken in Prohibition Areas and non-Prohibition Areas will take distinct forms; in the former attention should be focussed on the enlarging of entertainment and recreation facilities and the application of persuasion to addicts to give up drinking. In non-Prohibition States immediate attention should be given to preparing the ground for the introduction of Prohibition and creating the nucleus of the enforcement machinery.

Special efforts should be made to persuade ex-toddy tappers to take up suitable cottage industries. Liquor contractors and vendors should be weaned off from their present occupations and encouraged to take up more productive lines of work.

A Central Research Institute should be set up for the study of mental and physical disorders and psychological problems connected with alcoholism.

It would be useful to conduct research on the industrial utilization of such base materials as molasses and palm juice which are used for illicit distillation.

Financial Aspects

The Excise duties on narcotics and intoxicants collected in the States are highly iniquitous, regressive and anti-social. This kind of levy has no justification to exist in a progressive tax system and should be wiped out at the earliest.

The Union Government would give adequate assistance to those States which depend on Excise for a considerable part of their revenue to introduce Prohibition in their areas and to push through other social welfare schemes.

ADVISORY COMMITTEE ON SOCIAL AND MORAL HYGIENE, 1954—REPORT

New Delhi, Central Social Welfare Board, 1956. 175p.

Chairman : Smt. Dhanwanthi Rama Rau.

Members : Smt. Shanti Kabir; Smt. Vimala Deshmukh; Smt. Maitreyee Bose; Smt. P. Parijatham Naidu; Shri V. V. Sastri.

APPOINTMENT

The Advisory Committee on Social and Moral Hygiene was constituted under the Central Social Welfare Board on December 24, 1954.

TERMS OF REFERENCE

(i) A study of the extent of the problem of immoral traffic in women and children throughout the whole of India be made;

(ii) The background information that was conducive to the victimization of women and children for immoral purposes be collected;

(iii) The laws concerning the problem of Immoral Traffic, Brothels and Prostitution be examined from State to State and an investigation made with regard to prosecutions that may have taken place under any of the laws relating to the subject—Central, State, Municipal Bye-laws, etc;

(iv) More effective remedial measures be suggested that may apply in a uniform manner to all the States of India;

(v) Existing institutions for destitute women and girls, rescue homes and orphanages be visited and programmes of education and training in these institutions examined;

(vi) Methods of work for the rescue of women and girls who are led into an immoral life be suggested;

(vii) Suggestions be made for the creation of new institutions for rescued women, where more comprehensive work may be undertaken on sound scientific lines for their education, training and rehabilitation to wean them away from a life of vice and degradation;

(viii) After-care programmes be suggested for the permanent mental and economic regeneration of those who have been rescued and rehabilitated.

CONTENTS

Introductory; General Information; Prostitution; Institutions; Legislation; Reclamation, Rehabilitation, and After-Care (Part I); Scheme of Reclamation, Rehabilitation and After-Care (Part II); Concluding Remarks; Appendix I to V.

RECOMMENDATIONS

Governmental

Sex Education: It is necessary that in every Educational Institution at all stages Sex Education of a progressive nature should be given to children and adults. It is the opinion of the Committee that many of the lapses from an honest way of life can be avoided if in adolescence children are made aware of their awakening emotions and are helped and guided by those they can trust. This specialized education is desirable also in their homes, but judging by the conditions at present it will be a long time before they can expect such guidance from their parents unless courses on this subject are introduced also in Programmes for Social Education. A carefully worked out syllabus must be evolved to suit the child, at each stage of its development and educational career. It is only with this knowledge that boys and girls could be guided into decent ways of living, respect each other and learn the necessity of keeping their bodies clean and healthy for the assumption of natural family life.

Child Guidance Clinics: (These) should be opened in every area with suitable qualified personnel in charge. This service has developed in Western countries with undisputed success and we may well take advantage of the experience gained abroad. It is not always that a child has a happy home, which may be due to various causes. Sometimes it is difficult for parents themselves to understand the factors that need examination or they do not find it easy to resolve the tensions unaided. The advice of trained and experienced men and women could be of invaluable help. Some children grow perverse and ungovernable, and the parents themselves wonder why one child should be different from the other in the same family. Wrong treatment, punishment, enforced discipline may have very injurious effects, unless experts can help parents diagnose the trouble and apply the correct remedies. Such children when wrongly handled can become delinquents and sex delinquency is often attributed to such causes. Help of the right type at the right time can bring about a re-adjustment to a normality of behaviour.

The Committee recommends that the Child Guidance Clinics be staffed with clinicians, who have a specialized knowledge of Child Psychology and Child Care.

Marriage Guidance And Counselling: Child Guidance Clinics cannot produce results unless an attempt is made for the solving of the problems of the home in which the child lives. A problem child is created by the atmosphere and environment of its home and this atmosphere is often due to the fact of marital discord and disharmony. Besides young wives and husbands could be helped over hurdles that are often responsible for the break-up of marital relations creating situations that prove dangerous. This integration of the home with those that live in it, the parents, the children, all other relations, could remove the conflicts which often are the cause of mal-adjustment and produce a most harmful effect on children who subconsciously reject the strain. Such conflicts are also often responsible for resentments between married couples that may open the door to immorality on the part of the husband or the wife. Such clinics therefore would have a far-reaching effect in improving the conditions of our homes.

Parent-Teacher Associations: It would be necessary to encourage in all educational institutions Parent-Teacher Associations. A child spends a good part of its day at school. It would greatly help the parents as well as the teachers, if they could get together periodically, and discuss the problems concerning the child. Such organizations would create a medium for a better understanding of the personality of the child by those who share the privilege of helping to develop the character and special aptitudes of the child. The parents would realize that they must assume the responsibility, which is not recognized today, of co-operating with the school authorities, so that they may apply the correctives that are suggested by the school authorities with understanding and sympathy at home.

Venereal Disease: The question of venereal disease is closely associated with prostitution, promiscuity and lapses in moral conduct. This Committee, throughout its tours, interviewed doctors on the subject and arrived at the conclusion that although a universal anxiety was expressed at the endemic nature of the many types of this disease there was hardly any uniform governmental machinery to detect and help eradicate it in spite of its dire consequences. A comprehensive picture could not be placed before the Committee, for the figures and statistics obtainable were limited. In some parts of the country, intensive work is being done, whereas in other parts no heed is being paid and no special clinics have been established.

Factual information, however, can be obtained from a report of the investigations carried out by Sir John Megaw, in 1933, into Village Health Conditions, which states that approximately 13 million people were suffering from venereal diseases. He states, "It would probably be well within the mark to assume that 10 to 15% of the inhabitants suffer from syphillis, at some time or the other during their lifetime". It is also estimated that among the States, Madras and Bengal lead the rest in having the highest incidence of venereal disease. Expert work in this field is being done in Madras, under Dr. Rajan, a specialist with an international reputation, and Dr. Murti, in Visakhapatnam. In the latter town the Committee visited a large and efficiently run hospital where a praiseworthy effort is being made, not only to give treatment to sufferers in the Special Department for Venereal Disease and Skin Diseases, but a careful follow-up work by paid medical social workers, both men and women, is also undertaken.

We were told in Srinagar that a World Health Organization team had been responsible for excellent work in villages in the Jammu area, where the population was being wiped out by this scourge.

The Bombay Municipality has a special Venereal Disease Control Department. The Committee was only able to collect fragmentary information on this important topic. The full implication of the evil was realized when we visited the hospital in Visakhapatnam where we were shown the horror of the ravages of this disease on innocent victims, women and children, who were in-patients in the wards. We were told that those suffering from the disease discontinue the treatment as soon as the first symptoms disappear, not realizing that until the treatment is complete they still carried the infection. The doctor explained that unless an adequate staff of doctors and medical social workers could be appointed to do intensive work, not only in curing sufferers but to discover the contacts that were responsible for the infection in the original case, and the contacts made by the infected men or women after the infection, the work in this field would be incomplete. We consider this subject so important that we recommend to the Government that :

(1) An educational programme be devised for the layman and woman on the subject of venereal disease on the lines of programmes of other epidemics.

(2) An all-India plan for detection and curing of venereal diseases be undertaken.

(3) Compulsion be used for complete treatment, wherever sufferers are detected.

The Committee has received a comprehensive report made on the subject from the Social and Moral Hygiene Association of India, which makes interesting reading.

Family Planning : The Committee considers that the subject of Family Planning is closely related to the subject of Social and Moral Hygiene and would recommend that the Government strengthen Family Planning Programmes throughout the country. It stands to reason that when large families of eight or nine comprising parents and children of all ages are crowded in single-room tenements, sex knowledge is acquired with neither understanding nor restraint.

Conditions produced by unplanned families tend to the weakening of moral codes and social values. We have already commented on the importance of improving economic conditions and housing facilities, and on the raising of living standards to help with the problem of prostitution and promiscuity. No progress in these measures can be effected unless men and women are taught that they should raise only as many children as their economic condition can support, recognizing the requirements of parental care, clothing, health and education to which the child is entitled. Programmes for Family Planning therefore should be emphasized.

Voluntary Welfare Societies

The Committee recommends that all voluntary welfare societies should undertake countrywide programmes to :

(a) Advocate suitable changes in social life and community practices and customs to meet the requirements of modern times without breaking down traditions which may be healthy.

(b) Propagate the eradication of the double moral standard so common in Indian homes. Society is usually prepared to reject the woman who may have made a mistake, but there is no rejection of the man who is known to be immoral. The stigma that attaches to the prostitute has no counterpart for the prostitute's paramour. Laws that penalize the prostitute take no cognizance of the client who has made the prostitution possible. In our opinion he is more worthy of blame, for while the woman may be driven to prostitution through necessity, financial or otherwise, he may be a married man with a comfortable home and growing children, economically well placed, but driven to seek an outlet for casual lusts.

(c) Study and devote some time to the propagation of spiritual and moral codes to replace the narrow religious precepts blindly followed in most Indian homes today. It is necessary to discriminate between true and false values and change socio-religious laws that lay down restrictions that today have no place in life. It should be the function of respected social workers to propagate ideals and convince those they work for that inner strength of character has to be developed and discrimination between right and wrong has to be engendered in the individual so that men and women should automatically choose the right path without social compulsions. This no doubt would be a long-term programme and different too, because of the complicated social pattern of the thousands of communities of our people and the varying degrees of changes that are affecting them with changing conditions today.

Basic Requirements And Institutions for Reclamation, Rehabilitation And After-Care

No official measures in any of these departments should be organized without the active co-operation of suitable voluntary agencies and individual workers.

Sympathy and understanding are often unobtainable from those who follow strict official procedures and we believe that the class of women for whom such work is initiated are specially in need of a sympathetic approach to their problems. A happy relationship between officials and non-officials should be established for co-operation and material advice and consultation.

No institution organized for work in connection with rescued women should have any but women in charge of the internal management of the Institution and intimate dealings with the inmates. Men should be strictly excluded, though they may be employed for dealing with the police and the courts of law, general protection, accounts departments and external management.

No institution should be allowed to exist unless its management undertakes to provide decent healthy surroundings, general education and vocational training for the inmates with the purpose of making them independent in a fixed period (three to five years). No marriage be allowed to take place unless the woman has been trained in Elementary Domestic Science and Child-Care to fit her for marriage. No home be allowed to exist that is not registered, licensed and open to inspection from time to time—by official authorities.

The Committee realizes the inadequacies of the enquiry it has attempted to carry out. Except for getting a general picture of the position, with regard to brothels and prostitution and the other immoral traffickers who support them, we have not been able to carry out any research study into the many aspects of this important subject. The time was too short for detailed work and the equipment of the Members was insufficient to approach the problems from the scientific angle. It is, however, our recommendation that Trained Social Scientists be appointed by the Central Social Welfare Board to study the subject from the research angle. The following is a list of subjects that may well be taken up for a deeper study so that a background could be obtained, for a more effective work in the future.

Subjects such as the following would be suitable for research work and other topics could be added from time to time:

(1) Case-study of the inmates of a Vigilance Home with special reference to the problem of rehabilitation.

(2) Analytical study of the family background of the brothel-keepers.

(3) Socio-economic study of the pimps and procurers.

(4) Study of the attitudes of the young women towards their stay in a Vigilance Home.

(5) Home conditions inducing prostitution among women and girls in poor families.

(6) Attitudes of women prostitutes towards the profession of prostitution.

(7) Prostitution and correctional administration (i.e., critical survey of the police, judicial, probation service and institutional administration, with a view to improving their methods which would be helpful for rehabilitation of women and children convicted and rescued under the Suppression of Immoral Traffic Act).

(8) A comparative study of the economic, professional and human values, as achieved or realized by the two groups of prostitutes, viz., prostitutes from hereditary homes and street prostitutes.

(9) Study of the attitudes of some of the inmates of a Rescue Home or jail in regard to their future rehabilitation.

(10) Case-study of some of the women who have been rehabilitated from a Rescue Home.

(11) Study of the attitudes of men who marry women from Rescue Homes.

(12) Case-study of the habitual offenders, i.e., prostitutes who go back to the profession.

(13) Study of spheres of co-operation between paid officials in charge and voluntary and public workers.

(14) Producer Co-operatives and their value in rehabilitation work with study of the demand and supply of the varied products of Women's Institutions.

(15) Research into the motivations of married men with homes and families who are habitual frequenters of brothel areas.

(16) Research into the hormones determining the sex life and sex behaviour of an individual, e.g., the action and interaction of the hormones produced by the Anterior Pituitary, Adrenal, Cortex and Ovary.

(17) Study of the taboos and moral codes of different ethnic groups including tribals.

CHAIRMAN—INDEX

INDEX

COMMITTEES AND COMMISSIONS IN INDIA

Details of Published Volumes

COMMITTEES AND COMMISSIONS IN INDIA 1947-80
(In 18 Vols.)

Vol. 1	1947-54	Rs. 1500
Vol. 2	1955-57	Rs. 1500
Vol. 3	1958-59	Rs. 1500
Vol. 4	1960-61	Rs. 1500
Vol. 5	1962-63	Rs. 1500
Vol. 6	1964-65	Rs. 1500
Vol. 7	1966	Rs. 1500
Vol. 8	1967	Rs. 1500
Vol. 9	1968-69	Rs. 1500
Vol. 10	1970	Rs. 1500
Vol. 11	1971-73	Rs. 1500
Vol. 12	1974	Rs. 750
Vol. 13	1975	Rs. 750
Vol. 14	1976	Rs. 750
Vol. 15A	1977	Rs. 750
Vol. 15B	1977	Rs. 750
Vol. 15C	1977	Rs. 750
Vol. 15D	1977	Rs. 750
Vol. 16A	1978	Rs. 750
Vol. 16B	1978	Rs. 750
Vol. 17A	1979	Rs. 750
Vol. 17B	1979	Rs. 750
Vol. 18A	1980	Rs. 750
Vol. 18B	1980	Rs. 750

COMMITTEES AND COMMISSIONS IN INDIA 1947-1973

Volume II : 1955-57

Virendra Kumar

CONCEPT PUBLISHING COMPANY, PVT. LTD. NEW DELHI-110059

ISBN : 81-7022-211-7 (Vol. II)

First Published 1976
Reprinted 1988, 2011

Virendra Kumar *(b. 1933-)*

Published and Printed by
Ashok Kumar Mittal
Concept Publishing Company Pvt. Ltd.
A/15-16, Commercial Block, Mohan Garden
NEW DELHI-110059 (India)

Phones : 25351460, 25351794
Fax : 091-11-25357109
Email : publishing@conceptpub.com
Website : www.conceptpub.com

DEDICATED

TO

my mother
who inspired me
to rise in life

PREFACE

This second volume attempts to understand and analyse the activities of the various Committees and Commissions during the period 1955-1957, which has received, as far as the previous volume is concerned only scant attention—of even bibliophiles and documentation experts. It is known that the governments all over the world largely rely on Committees and Commissions or their decisions on particular subjects. Governments make an extensive use of the instruments of the Public Inquiries which ultimately help in lessening managerial tensions as well as quietening allegations of misrule. According to John Stuart Mill, "A man seldom judges right, even in his own concerns, still less in those of the public, when he makes habitual use of knowledge but his own or that of some single adviser." As such the "committee system" greatly helps the proper functioning of a democratic set-up.

A "Commission" is a 'Governmental agency created to perform a particular function such as special investigations or on governmental regulations of business'. It is appointed mainly when it is thought that a matter involves some financial questions. There are other reasons for which a Commission is appointed, e.g., in matters pertaining to welfare of the State and its citizens and for improving the efficiency in an administration. The status of a "Committee" is also the same as that of a Commission. but it does not possess as wide powers as are enjoyed by a Commission and has to limit itself in relation to specific work assigned to it under its terms of reference. While arriving at decisions in the form of recommendations, a Committee or a Commission ensures that such decisions are representative of interests of various types of people and also a safeguard against abuse of power.

The "Committees and Commissions" always advise a Government; offering valuable suggestions and recommendations for smooth operation and efficiency in administration for the welfare of the people.

A Committee or a Commission comprises a Chairman, the Members and Member-Secretary (sometimes there is also an Assistant Secretary). In some cases there are even One-man Commissions and the enquiry in such Commission is entrusted to an Officer-on-Special Duty.

The Chairman of a Commission is a person well-versed mostly in legal affairs and is often a retired Judge of a High Court or the Supreme Court of India. Occasionally, a member of Parliament is also appointed as the Chairman of a Commission: Regarding Committees, the Chairman is mostly a specialist in the subject of the Committee. He can be a Leader or a Convenor also, if he heads a Panel, a Study Group, or a Delegation, etc.

The Members of a Commission, Committee, Panel, Study Group, etc., are specialists in their respective Fields and provide valuable guidance to the Commission in making recommendations.

The Member-Secretary or Secretary is nominated from among the experienced officials who have the requisite competent knowledge of the subject on which the Commission or the Committee is appointed.

This Study of Committees and Commissions is divided into two main parts :—

(I) PRE-INDEPENDENCE : From 1772 to August, 1947 ; and

(II) POST-INDEPENDENCE : From August, 1947 to 1973.

The first volume covers the period from August, 1947 to 1954. The present bool Volume II in the series covers the period from 1955 to 1957.

The work provides information on subjects like : Bibliographical Data of the Con mittees and Commissions; Chairman, Leader, Convenor, etc., of the Committees or Commi: sions; Appointments; Terms of Reference; Contents; and Recommendations.

ARRANGEMENTS: The Arrangement of the "Committees and Commissions" is firstl chronological and within it items are arranged according to their Dates of Appointment an not according to their Dates of Publication.

I am sure that this Reference Work will continue into a number of Volumes. For, is unique in nature. I have spared no efforts to make it a comprehensive reference work an it will be of great use to the research scholars, sociologists, historians, economists, students (political science and all those connected with the study of administration and legal affairs. have tried my level best, to rectify all omissions or errors that I noticed in the previou Volume. It will be my effort to go on improving these volumes. The introductory part i the Volume I deals in detail about the Why, What and How of the Committees and Commissions.

In the end, I must express my gratitude to Shri D.R. Kalia, Director, Central Secre tariat Library, New Delhi, for his valuable guidance without which it would not hav been possible for me to bring out this work. I am also indebted to Shri J.C Srivastava, Lib rarian, National Archives of India, New Delhi, Shri S.P. Kulsreshtha, Librarian, Admini: trative Reforms Department and other friends who have helped me a lot in the process c compilation of this Volume. I must also express my gratitude to the Press that reviewe and appreciated the first Volume in the series.

I am immensely grateful to Dr. L.M. Singhvi, Advocate-General of Rajasthan an Executive Chairman of Institute of Constitutional and Parliamentary Studies, New Delhi, fo writing a Foreword.

I am also thankful to my wife and children who have sacrificed their personal com forts by providing me every facility to finalise this Volume within a reasonably short time.

NEW DELHI
Dusshera
October 2, 1976

VIRENDRA KUMAR

CONTENTS

1956

1957

1955

DOCK WORKERS (REGULATION OF EMPLOYMENT) ENQUIRY COMMITTEE, 1955—REPORT

Delhi, Manager of Publications, 1955. 371p.

Chairman : Shri S. S. Vasist.

Members : Shri A. Ramaswami Mudaliar; Shri S. C. Sheth; Shri A. N. Chowdhury; Shri Biswanath Dubey; Shri G. S. Dhara Singh; Shri Adhir Banerjee; Shri Vincent Vaz; Shri K. Mitter; Shri V. A. Jaywant.

Co-opted Members : Shri R. Gupta; Shri Makhan Chatterjee; Dr. (Mrs.) Maitreyee Bose; Shri Naresh Nath Mookerjee; Shri G. Venkateshwara Ayyar; Shri S. C. C. Anthoni Pillai; Shri C. Govindarajloo; Shri P. Lakshmipathi Naidu; Shri L. T. Gholap; Shri P. D. Mello; Shri H. N. Trivedi.

Secretary : Shri D. K. Guha.

APPOINTMENT

The Dock Workers (Regulation of Employment) Enquiry Committee was constituted under the Ministry of Labour vide their Resolution No.Fac.80(6)/55, dated January 14, 1955.

TERMS OF REFERENCE

(i) To enquire into the working of the Dock Workers (Regulation of Employment) Schemes in Bombay, Calcutta and Madras, to examine all difficulties encountered by the parties interested in the working of the Schemes, and to recommend what modifications, if any, in the Schemes are necessary;

(ii) To enquire into the necessity and feasibility of decasualising other categories of labour covered by the Dock Workers (Regulation of Employment) Act, 1948 (IX of 1948), at the three Ports—whether by inclusion in the existing Schemes or by the framing of special Schemes; and

(iii) To prepare amendments to existing Schemes or to frame new Schemes for the further categories of labour, if any, recommended for decasualisation.

CONTENTS

Part I—Findings and Recommendations: Introductory; A Survey of the Implementation of the Schemes; Effects of the Schemes; Turnround of Ships; Productivity and Cost of Handling Cargo; Shore Labour and

Facilities; Constitution and Functions of the Dock Labour Board; Regulation of Employment; the Obligations, Labour Relations and Discipline; Wages and Allowances; other Important Aspects (Shifts, Overtime, Weekly Off, Holidays and Holiday Work, Cost of Operation of the Scheme and Levy, Workers' Welfare Fund, Exemption from Taxation, Illegal Gratification, Objects of the Scheme, Institution of Stevedores, Productivity and Turnround Statistics, Central Coordination); Decasualisation of other Categories of Dock Workers and Regulation of Employment of Unregistered Dock Workers; Training, Welfare, Health and Safety Measures; Conclusions; Note of Dissent Submitted by Shri G. S. Dhara Singh; Note of Dissent Submitted by Shri B. N. Dubey and Shri A. C. Banerjee; Comments on the Joint Note of Dissent of Shri B. N. Dubey and Shri A. C. Banerjee; Summary of Conclusions and Recommendations. **Part II**—Draft Amendment Schemes and Draft Rules: Amended Bombay Dock Workers (Regulation of Employment) Scheme; Amended Calcutta Dock Workers (Regulation of Employment) Scheme; Amended Madras Dock Workers (Regulation of Employment) Scheme; Proposed Rules for the Regulation of the Employment of Unregistered Dock Workers. **Part III**—Appendices I to X.

CONCLUSIONS AND RECOMMENDATIONS—SUMMARY

According to Clause 7(1)(a) of the Schemes it is one of the functions of the Dock Labour Boards to secure economic turnround of vessels and speedy transit of goods through the Port; it would appear that this item has not received their due attention.

There has been a progressive deterioration in the turnround of ships at Bombay and Calcutta up to 1954 which was the worst year in this respect. This deterioration was due to a decline in the effective output of labour, for whatever reasons. In Madras, there has been a deterioration in the overall cargo handling period in respect of imports in the post-decasualisation period, partly due to a slight increase in the proportion of difficult-handling cargo and partly for loss in effective productivity. There has been a slight improvement in respect of exports in which the proportion of easy-handling cargo has also increased.

There has almost been a progressive deterioration in the output of dock labour at Bombay and 1954 was the worst year in this respect. The overall decline in the output during that year was of the order of 30 per cent as compared with that of 1951, the year just preceding the introduction of the Scheme. The deterioration in the turnround of vessels at Bombay, which was also worst in 1954, is entirely explained by the deterioration in the labour output.

The extent of the decline in the effective output of labour in the post-decasualisation period would account for the deterioration in the turnround of ships in the Calcutta Port.

At Madras, in the post-decasualisation period while there has been a decline in productivity in case of general cargo and sugar by 34 per cent and 23 per cent respectively, there has been an improvement in the case of bag cargo by 11.7 per cent. In the case of ore, the level of output before and after the introduction of the Scheme has been the same.

The output of both pool and monthly stevedore workers at Calcutta was the lowest in the three Ports and there is a considerable difference between the productivity of the workers at Calcutta and that of the workers at Bombay and Madras.

Workers arrive late for duty and leave early. The Deputy Chairman, the Executive Officer and other Officers of the Dock Labour Board should make frequent checks to ensure that workers start work punctually and do not leave before time.

The stevedoring expenses form a small part of the total of other expenses. The actual labour cost will be even less. A slight increase in the direct stevedore labour cost, if necessitated by the provisions of the Scheme, should not, therefore, normally make a considerable difference in the overall transport expenses.

It cannot be accepted that there has been a deterioration in the shore facilities provided at these Ports. There has, however, been little or no modernisation or improvement in respect of the lifting appliances at Calcutta and Madras. The attention of the Port Authorities may be invited to the desirability of providing modern and more efficient appliances, not only while making replacements of existing assets, but also as additions, if necessary.

At all the three Ports casual labour is employed by the Port Authorities in varying magnitudes. The proportion of casual employment to the total employment is considerable. In order to create a proper healthy atmosphere amongst the shore and stevedore labour, who have to work side by side and on whose joint and coordinated efforts the rate of handling and the turnround of vessels depend, the question of decasualisation of the shore casual labour should be taken up. The Government may review the situation and suggest to the Port Authorities that a suitable decasualisation scheme in respect of casual shore labour may be framed by them.

The question of eliminating contractors' labour from work, which has come to be recognised as shore work to be done by the labour employed directly by the Port Authorities, should also be taken up when the framing of a Scheme for the decasualisation of shore labour is taken in hand.

The inability of the Dock Labour Boards to discharge their responsibilities has largely been due to the following reasons:

(a) The Scheme has certain loopholes and does not enable the Dock Labour Board to take adequate and effective steps to remove the causes of some failures complained of:

(b) No one in the Dock Labour Board has been vested, under the Scheme, with adequate executive authority to enforce the decisions of the Board;

(c) Certain functionaries under the Dock Labour Board, viz. the Administrative Officer, the Special Officer and the Inspectors, have failed to discharge efficiently the responsibilities that have been vested in them;

(d) The time of the Dock Labour Board has mostly been taken up by matters mainly concerning wages, allowances and service conditions of workers; little attention would appear to have been given to other important matters.

The Dock Labour Board should continue to be a tripartite body as at present.

The Chairman of the Port Authority, ex-officio, should continue to be the Chairman of the Dock Labour Board and the Scheme should specifically provide for that.

The Scheme should contain a provision which should authorise the Chairman, Dock Labour Board, to recommend to the Central Government the withdrawal of the representation of any organisation from the Board on the ground that the organisation has collectively failed to implement a unanimous or a majority decision of the Board; this provision however should not apply if the decision concerned is the basis of an industrial dispute under the law.

The Chairman of the Dock Labour Boards in all the Ports should be vested with powers like the Chairman, Dock Labour Board, Calcutta, for dealing with "go-slow" and "emergency" under present Clauses 36-A and 40-A of the Calcutta Scheme.

The Board should primarily devote its full attention to important matters of policy and the responsibility to implement decisions should rest on the Chairman who should be the Chief Executive of the Board. It is considered expedient that the powers and duties of the Chairman, Dock Labour Board, should be specifically defined in the Scheme and that the powers which can be exercised by the Board only should also be clearly stated.

All matters of policy, and in particular the matters itemised in Para. 711 of the Report, will be dealt with by the Dock Labour Board in the meeting.

The Chairman of the Dock Labour Board should have full powers to deal with all matters relating to the day-to-day administration of the Scheme with particular reference to the matters itemised in Para. 712 of the Report.

There should be a whole-time Deputy Chairman each at Calcutta and Bombay and an Executive Officer at Madras to assist the Chairman. The status of the Deputy Chairman should be comparable with that of the Head of a Department under the Port Authority and he should be appointed by the Central Government. The Executive Officer should be of the status of the Assistant Traffic Manager, Madras Port Trust, and may be appointed by the Dock Labour Board. The Chairman may delegate, in writing, his duties, excepting those specifically mentioned in Para. 713 of the Report, to the Deputy Chairman or the Executive Officer, as the case may be.

The Government representatives on the Dock Labour Board should be effective and give to the Board the benefit of their experience by taking an active part in its deliberations.

The Port Traffic Managers at Calcutta and Madras and the Docks Manager at Bombay may also be nominated by the Government as ex-officio Members of the Board apart from the Chairman of the Port Authority.

At Bombay and Calcutta, the Deputy Chairman will also be one of the Government representatives on the Board.

It will be expedient if the Regional Labour Commissioner (Central) is not nominated on the Dock Labour Board; if at all it is necessary to nominate on the Government side someone concerned with the employment of labour, the Regional Director of Resettlement and Employment will be a suitable choice.

The continuity of the presence of the same member, as far as possible, was very necessary when the original Schemes were implemented and it will be more so when the amended Schemes are brought into force. This may be pointed out to the organisations which are asked in future to nominate their representatives on the Board.

The Administrative Bodies at Bombay and Madras have satisfactorily discharged the responsibilities and functions vested in them under the Schemes. The Administrative Bodies at Bombay and Madras should continue as at present.

The Administrative Officer at Calcutta has not been able to discharge effectively and satisfactorily the responsibilities and functions entrusted to him under the Scheme.

Should the stevedores at Calcutta be now able to make up their differences and come to the Government with a proposal, agreed to by both the Associations, for the constitution of the Administrative Body, the request should be favourably considered. Failing that an Administrative Superintendent of the status comparable with that of the Superintendent of Labour, Calcutta Port Commissioners, should be appointed by the Board. This Officer, though in immediate charge of the duties and responsibilities vested in the Administrative Body, should work under the direction and control of the Deputy Chairman and refer all important matters to him for decision.

The institution of Special Officers should be abolished altogether and the responsibility to enforce discipline should be vested in the Chairman, the Deputy Chairman and the Executive Officer, as the case may be, and to a limited extent in the employers. The Chairman, the Deputy Chairman and the Executive Officer may be assisted by Personnel Officers appointed mainly for this purpose. The status of the Personnel Officers may be determined by each Dock Labour Board having regard to local conditions.

At Bombay, notwithstanding the abolition of the post of the Special Officer, the Inspectors may continue at the discretion of the Bombay Dock Labour Board, but as there is a possibility of confusion with the Inspectors appointed under Clause 6 of the Act, the designation of the Inspectors should be changed by the Bombay Dock Labour Board to Dock Overseers. At Calcutta, the Inspectors have not at all been useful and should be withdrawn. It may be left to the Dock Labour Board to devise, if necessary, a suitable machinery to achieve the object for which these Inspectors were appointed.

The Calcutta Dock Labour Board should have its own Secretary.

At Bombay, the supply of registered workers has, more or less, throughout the working of the Scheme, been inadequate. This factor could not but have adverse effects on the efficiency of the dock work there. After the recent recruitment in May, 1955, of 70 additional gangs and other workers, the labour supply has improved.

The registration at Calcutta had no relation to actual demands. The excess registration caused almost a financial crisis for the Dock Labour Board.

At Calcutta, the position at present is that there is definitely an excess in respect of Sirdars and Mates and a shortage in the category of Winchmen; the number of Rolias and Kamalias on register may not entail the payment of guaranteed minimum wages to them in any large proportions even when the labour output is at a reasonable level and the demands are normal, but there is a considerable scope for an increase in their average employment per month. It is not necessary, at present, for the Dock Labour Board to take any special steps other than offering voluntary retirement on existing terms to reduce the number of registered workers in these categories.

The incomplete gangs at Calcutta should be immediately completed with workers now available on the Register. Should the resultant reduction in the number of gangs result in some Sirdars and Mates becoming surplus, they may be kept unattached and utilised for relieving duties.

The Dock Labour Board, Madras, should review the Register and the position in regard to anticipated demands and take suitable steps early to avoid employment of casual labour. Should it be found necessary to make fresh recruitment, preference should be given to those workers who can prove to have worked in the Docks for long periods but failed to obtain registration after application because they had not worked during the prescribed qualifying period for registration.

The Dock Labour Boards should make periodical assessment of their labour requirements and determine the anticipated demands based on long-term trade prospects affecting exports and imports as well as short-term fluctuations in trade and normal seasonal variations. The demands resulting from short-term and seasonal fluctuations should be separated from the long-term requirements and adjustments in the Register, whether implying increase or decrease, should be based on long-term variations only.

In order to meet the demands resulting from short-term or seasonal fluctuations, the Dock Labour Boards should have the authority to permit temporary registrations. They should specify the number of workers and the period of their temporary registration, which should be communicated to the "workers registered temporarily" who for brevity may be called WRT's. The WRT's should be entitled to attendance wages under the same conditions as permanent registered workers and their other service conditions may be prescribed by the Dock Labour Boards. They must comply with all the conditions of the Scheme and have the same obligations as permanent registered workers.

All registrations of new categories in future should be very carefully planned and carried out so that the problems which resulted from the registration already made do not come up again. The principles detailed in Para. 811 of the Report should apply in respect of all categories which have not yet been registered but may be registered hereafter.

Having regard to the local conditions, the Dock Labour Boards may prescribe maximum age limits for recruitment of fresh labour, whether permanent or temporary, and preference should generally be given to younger applicants.

In case any fresh recruitment is necessary, whether on a temporary or permanent basis, in any category already registered, the recruitment should be done from amongst workers registered with the local Employment Exchange. If, however, the requirement exceeds the number of suitable men available on the Register of the Employment Exchange on the day of the requisition, direct recruitment, after absorbing suitable men from the Employment Exchange Register, may be resorted to.

Each individual registered worker should have a proper photo identity card and an attendance and wage card. A proper Service Record for each registered worker should also be maintained which should be a complete record of all disciplinary actions taken against him as well as of promotions and commendations for good work.

It would be in the furtherance of greater regularity

of employment and the efficient performance of dock work if the monthly registers are not only retained but progressively expanded. The rate of expansion of the monthly register can be considerably quickened if the employment of workers on a monthly basis is allowed not only by individual "employers" but also by "groups of employers". The "employers" or "group of employers" should be allowed to select workers for monthly employment. Necessary provisions should be made in the Schemes accordingly and the limitation placed by the Delhi Settlement of May, 1954, on the number of monthly gangs to be retained by stevedores at Calcutta should be removed.

Monthly workers should have a reasonable security of retention on the monthly register. No transfer of a monthly worker to the pool should take place without the prior approval of the Chairman or the Deputy Chairman and that the employer or the worker asking for such a transfer should submit an application in writing explaining fully the reason for the transfer. The request will be complied with only if the reason is good and valid. No transfer should take place in anticipation of the Chairman's or the Deputy Chairman's approval.

The Calcutta Port Authority should be asked to take the responsibility of licensing stevedores, as is the case at Bombay and Madras, and Clause 10(1) of the Calcutta Scheme may be amended to be in line with the corresponding clauses in the Bombay and Madras Schemes. The registration fee for employers in future should be uniform for all the three Ports and the fee at Madras should be raised from Rs. 400 to Rs. 500.

At Bombay, the junior stevedore workers in the sub-pool maintained for relieving pursoses may be called LRW's (Leave Reserve Workers). The practice of having such a sub-pool is considered sound.

At Calcutta, the procedure of booking of stevedore workers should be overhauled with a view to reducing the period, for which a worker has to wait to prove attendance, to not more than an hour normally.

The Calcutta Dock Labour Board also should have a sub-pool of LRW's (Leave Reserve Workers) from amongst the existing workers to fill casual vacancies in pool as well as monthly gangs.

All the members of the gang should present cards individually for booking. The head of the gang should notify to the booking office, at the time of booking, the number of vacancies in his gang. The booking office will then fill these vacancies from amongst the LRW's on attendance.

The Dock Labour Board, Madras, also should have a sub-pool of LRW's for filling casual vacancies. This will be particularly necessary if workers are formed in gangs.

The transfer of a worker from the Reserve Pool Register to the Monthly Register will not be considered as a promotion and will not be subject to rules applicable to promotions. Such a transfer will be by selection by the employer or the group of employers who undertake to employ him as a monthly worker.

The Madras Dock Labour Board should pursue the question of forming regular gangs. The demands for half gangs, in addition to a full gang, which appear to be a frequent and unavoidable feature at Madras, may be met from amongst the sub-pool of LRW's.

The designations of senior and junior stevedore workers at Bombay and Kamalias and Rolias at Calcutta should be abolished and all these workers may be classified as "Stevedore Workers" or "Mazdoors". In view of the fact that there has been a difference in the wages of some of these workers, the stevedore workers under the new designation may be put on incremental scales of pay which may be fixed having regard to the fact that some of them enjoyed the benefit of officiating on a higher wage in the same or the higher group. The present wages of any worker should not be adversely affected by this change.

The three categories of Foremen Grade I, Foremen Grade II and Foremen Grade III, mentioned in Clause 11 of the Bombay Scheme, should also be abolished and in their place there should be one category named "Foremen" and a suitable incremental scale of pay should be fixed for this category so that they do not incur any financial disadvantage due to the abolition of the three grades.

The Sirdar of a gang in Calcutta has no well-defined duties apart from taking booking for the gang. There is no need for having two Supervisors in a gang of nine workers and the Dock Labour Board should re-allocate the duties between the Sirdar and the Mate of a gang in such a way that the Sirdar alone supervises the work of the gang and the Mate does the signalling work thus relieving a Rolia for normal cargo handling work.

The designation of Hatch Foreman at Bombay may be abolished and the present Hatch Foremen should be merged in the existing gangs as stevedore workers, but they may continue to carry on the signalling work. This change in designation, however, should be made without affecting the wages of the existing workers in this category and also without reducing the number of men in the gang who handle cargo at present. When this change is carried out, the number of workers in a gang will be nine instead of eight.

The extent and intensity of indiscipline, particularly at Bombay and Calcutta, are of an order that cannot but cause concern to those interested in port working as well as to the Government. Employer-employee relations at Calcutta have been particularly strained and those at Bombay have also not been happy.

The Dock Labour Board should endeavour to settle disputes about which a request for arbitration has been made to the Central Government by the parties concerned and report to the Government the results of its endeavours. The Government should give due weight to the views of the Board which is a tripartite body and to a decision which may have been taken by the board unanimously or by a majority vote.

The Committee is of the opinion that the words "the rules of the port or place where he is working" in Sub-Clause (5) of Clause 29 of the Scheme are necessary as the rules of the port or the place of working must, in all cases, be enforced. Suitable amendment of the Clause, however, is necessary so that authorised representatives and supervisors of the employers are deemed to have proper authority to give directions hereunder. If the workers consider that the direction of the employer in any particular matter is not in order, they should seek correction by a reference to the appropriate authority and not stop the work. The Dock Labour Boards should get the employers' and employees' representatives together and persuade them to enter into joint agreements so that stoppages of work or lock-outs pending settlement of disputes are not resorted to.

It would be most expedient, without in any way infringing the rights of workers or a sound disciplinary practice, if the Chairman of the Dock Labour Board is made the highest administrative authority in disciplinary matters and disciplinary powers are delegated to the Deputy Chairman, the Executive Officer, the Personnel Officer, and the Employers to the extent appropriate in each case.

The object of giving certain disciplinary powers to the employers can be secured, to a large extent, if the Administrative Body which consists of employers only is vested with such powers.

The Administrative Body should have a Labour Officer or Labour Officers appointed by that Body with the approval of the Dock Labour Board. It will be the duty and responsibility of the Administrative Body, on receipt of a complaint from an employer in regard to an act of indiscipline or misdemeanour committed by a reserve pool worker while he was allocated to that employer, to apply through the Labour Officer the disciplinary procedure and, if necessary, to impose a suitable penalty within its powers against the pool worker. If on enquiry the offence calls for a penalty beyond its powers, it will report the case to the Deputy Chairman at Calcutta and Bombay or the Executive Officer at Madras for suitable action. Where there is no Administrative Body consisting of employers, the disciplinary procedure will be applied by the Personnel Officer on receipt of a complaint in writing from an employer.

A Record Sheet should be maintained in respect of every employer and the warnings in writing given to him under Clause 36(1)(a) should be recorded in that sheet. If any employer is found guilty of an offence for which the penalty under Clause 36(1)(a) would be inadequate and that under Clause 36(1)(b) too heavy, the Chairman or the Deputy Chairman may record a censure in the Record Sheet advising the employer in writing that in the event of his being found guilty of a repetition of the offence for which he is being censured, the imposition of the next higher penalty, viz. "removal of his name from the Employers' Register" for a period to be determined by the Board, will have to be considered. A provision for a censure in this manner may be made in the Scheme. Further, the Scheme should also provide for the permanent removal of the name of a registered employer from the Employers' Register in grave cases.

Sub-Clause 2(d) of Clause 36 should, as an alternative to "termination of service", provide for "the removal of the name of the worker from the Workers' Register for a period not exceeding three months".

The Schemes for Calcutta and Bombay contain a provision for suspension pending enquiry. This provision should be incorporated in the Scheme for Madras also. The payment of subsistence allowance to the workers under suspension pending enquiry should not be limited to the "attendance wages" only and it should be one-fourth of the total daily time-scale wage inclusive of dearness allowance, or the attendance allowance, whichever is more. The Chairman may have the discretion in exceptional cases to grant a higher subsistence allowance not exceeding half the total daily wage inclusive of dearness allowance for the suspension period in excess of over a month. Further, if the suspended worker is honourably acquitted he should be entitled to the time-rate wages inclusive of dearness allowance that he would have earned had he not been under suspension.

A provision may be made in the Scheme to the effect that penalties leviable for acts of indiscipline or misdemeanour should also apply to cases of inefficiency.

The Scheme should specifically vest in the registered employers full disciplinary powers in respect of monthly workers and it should be entirely their responsibility to take disciplinary action against monthly workers employed under them without prejudice to the powers of the Chairman under Clauses 36-A and 40-A of the Scheme.

The maximum penalties which can be imposed by different authorities should be as follows:

1. **Chairman**: All disciplinary powers against registered employers and registered reserve pool workers and the special powers under Clauses 36-A and 40-A against all registered workers.

2. **Deputy Chairman or Executive Officer**: All disciplinary powers against registered employers and registered reserve pool workers excepting powers under Clauses 36-A and 40-A.

3. **Personnel Officer**: (i) Disciplinary powers against pool workers prescribed under Sub-Clauses 36(2)(a), (b) and (c), viz.

(a) to determine that, for such period as he thinks proper, the worker shall not be entitled to any payment under Clause 34;

(b) to give him a warning in writing;

(c) to suspend him without pay for a period not exceeding three days; and

(d) to suspend a worker pending enquiry.

(ii) Powers against registered employers should be limited only to warning in writing.

4. **Administrative Body**: Powers will be restricted to those permitted to the Personnel Officer and Clause 3(i) above.

Powers to deal with cases of inefficiency will vest in the Chairman and the Deputy Chairman only.

Appeals by workers against the decisions of the Administrative Body and the Personnel Officer shall lie with the Deputy Chairman at Bombay and Calcutta and the Executive Officer at Madras. Appeals against the decision of the Deputy Chairman or the Executive Officer, whether in original or on appeal, shall lie with the Appeal Tribunal. The decision of the Appeal Tribunal shall be final and there shall be no further appeal against its decision.

Appeals by registered employers against the decision of the Personnel Officer shall lie with the Deputy Chairman at Bombay and Calcutta, and the Executive Officer at Madras. Appeals against the decision of the Deputy Chairman or the Executive Officer, whether in original or on appeal, shall lie with the Chairman who shall forthwith refer the matter to the Central Government. The Central Government shall pass such orders on the appeal as it thinks fit.

The present system of time-rate wages, even though linked with an incentive bonus in one Port, has been totally ineffective in securing reasonable productivity from workers.

In order to ensure a reasonable output from workers and minimise the possibilities of the turnround of ships in Indian Ports not being maintained at an acceptable level of efficiency in future, wages paid to workers employed in connection with loading and unloading of cargo must be linked with productivity and a system of "payment by results" should replace the present system of time-rate wages. It will also be desirable to provide for an "Incentive Bonus" in the system.

(a) Norms for productivity in respect of cargoes of different kinds and/or Lines and/or Zones should be determined by a Special Committee to be appointed by the Dock Labour Board consisting of representatives of employers, shipping companies, workers, Port authorities and a nominee of the Central Government. These norms should be fixed after giving due consideration to all relevant factors and local conditions including past performances in normal periods free from disputes between workers and employers. The norms should be reasonably less than the maximum working potential of the workers. If any recognised norms are already in existence they may be adopted. Should the Committee be not able to prescribe agreed norms within a period of two months of having been asked to do so, the Chairman of the Dock Labour Board may determine such norms and submit them to the Central Government for their approval. The norms may be called the "Standard Output". To be entitled to the normal time-rate wages, a gang of stevedore workers should produce the standard output during a standard shift. If the durations of the shifts vary, the standard output for different shifts may vary proportionately.

(b) Workers producing more than the standard output should be entitled to an "Incentive Bonus" on a scale to be determined by the Dock Labour Board. In order that labour may not "sweat", the Dock Labour Board may prescribe the maximum tonnage beyond which no incentive bonus payment will be due.

(c) The Dock Labour Board may also allow a special "Target Bonus" to be paid at the end of each month to workers who consistently have produced the standard output but have not been able to earn Incentive Bonus.

(d) Workers who fail to produce a standard output in more than 50 per cent of the shifts worked by them should be liable to disciplinary action for inefficiency.

(e) Each Dock Labour Board should devise a suitable scheme which, inter alia, should relate the quantum of wages earned to the actual output of workers when they do not produce the standard output subject to the conditions:

(i) that a worker will be entitled to the normal daily time-rate wage only if he produces the standard output;

(ii) that the daily wage earned by a worker should in no case be less than a guaranteed minimum wage which shall be equivalent to three-fifths of his normal time-rate wage.

(f) The Scheme for payment by results prepared in accordance with (e) above should provide that a worker should be entitled to the normal time-rate wage for any period or periods for which loading or unloading may be held up for reasons beyond the worker's control, such as inclement weather or non-availability of cargo in case of export, or completion of work before the expiry of the full shift period.

(g) The scheme should be submitted to the Central Government for approval before it is implemented. Should the Dock Labour Board fail to submit a Scheme to the Central Government within three months of the direction from the Central Government to do so, the Government may prepare a Scheme and direct the Dock Labour Board concerned to implement that.

(h) All the foregoing provisions will apply to the monthly workers for determining their wages on the days they work, and for the balance of the days for which they are entitled to payment, they will draw wages on a calculated daily time-rate.

(i) If any direction, action or failure of an employer or his representatives is likely to result in the output being adversely affected, it will be the duty of the head of the stevedoring gang to bring that to the notice of the Foreman immediately. On receipt of such a report, the Foreman must immediately advise the official of the Dock Labour Board appointed to deal with such reports. The head of the gang may also report to this official after having reported to the Foreman.

A method of determining the wages of a worker when his production is less than the standard output as required under Para. 1014(e) together with two examples have been given in Para. 1015.

It is extremely desirable that shore workers employed for loading and unloading of cargoes must also be brought under a piece-rate system of wages where this is not so at present and that this must be done immediately in respect of the Cranemen, in particular.

The Committee is unable to accept that the minimum wages which a dock worker must get, irrespective of any other consideration, should not be less than Rs. 100 p.m. Dock workers cannot be singled out to be entitled to any ideal minimum wages without any regard to other relevant and vital considerations.

Dock workers' earnings should be stabilised progressively at higher levels until a guarantee of 21 days in a month is reached. The progressive increase, however, should definitely be related to the quantum of total employment available in the docks and the wages which, on the basis of average employment, workers in the pool may expect.

The minimum number of days guaranteed for wages every month should be assessed annually on the basis of the average employment during the immediately preceding 12 months according to procedure laid down in Paras. 1020 and 1021.

If the average number of days in any year works out to be less than the minimum number of days for which wages have already been guaranteed, the latter number will not be reduced. In other words, the minimum number of days in a month for which wages are guaranteed will progressively increase but will never be decreased.

While deciding the question of additional recruitment under any category for meeting additional demands of work, the Dock Labour Boards must always bear in mind the repercussions which such additional recruitment may have on the average employment of workers which, as already stated, should be progressively improved.

It is neither necessary nor desirable to increase the quantum of attendance wage which should remain at Re. 1 as at present. The Dock Labour Boards, particularly the Dock Labour Board, Calcutta, should take steps to improve the organisation in regard to booking so that a worker is normally required to attend the Call Stand only once a day and has not to wait for more than an hour to get his attendance marked. So long as a registered daily worker fulfils his obligations under Clause 29 there need be no ban on his seeking occasional employment elsewhere while he is not allocated for work to a registered employer.

The Calcutta and Madras Dock Labour Boards should also provide for payment of gratuity to registered workers as has already been done at Bombay.

The Madras Dock Labour Board should also have a Provident Fund Scheme as has already been done at Bombay and recently at Calcutta.

At each of the three Ports there should be three shifts round the clock with no interval between them; of these, two should be compulsory and the third optional for the employers subject to the approval of the Port Authorities.

Normally a worker should not be called upon to work even in two consecutive shifts. There should, however, be a mandatory ban on the employment of a worker in three consecutive shifts.

Pool workers should not be allowed to work more than nine shifts in a week or 33 shifts in a month. Further, when pool workers who have not reached this maximum limit of employment are not available, monthly workers may also be employed up to nine shifts in a week or 33 shifts in a month. Should these arrangements necessitate a monthly or a pool worker having to work in two consecutive shifts, he should be treated as having worked in two separate normal shifts and not deemed as having performed overtime work.

The Chairman, Dock Labour Board, may, however, in emergent circumstances allow a general relaxation in the ceiling mentioned above but such a condition should not be allowed to continue for any length of time and steps must be taken immediately so that the employment is brought within the maximum time limit permissible. If any permanent or temporary registration is necessary it should be so adjusted that the chances for employment of the existing workers during a month may not go below 26 shifts.

The Chairman, Dock Labour Board, in special circumstances may also authorise individual exceptions to the ceiling rule.

Normally overtime work should be permitted in respect of finishing ships only and it should not exceed two hours at a time. In exceptional circumstances, the Chairman, Dock Labour Board, may allow exceptions both in regard to the time and the reasons for working overtime.

Every worker should be given a weekly off on the

seventh day if he has worked for six consecutive days and the off-day should be staggered for daily as well as monthly workers so that the dock work goes on normally on all days including Sundays. The question of making the "off-day" a paid day should be examined by each Dock Labour Board after a reasonable period and if it is found then that the desired improvement in the output of labour has been achieved and sustained, it may be favourably considered by the Board.

While each Port may have certain closed holidays as may be decided by the Dock Labour Board, the number of 12 closed days at Bombay is excessive. The number of closed days in any Port should not be more than six in a year which may include the three national holidays, i.e. Independence Day, Republic Day and Gandhiji's Birthday. The Dock Labour Board, Bombay, should take steps to reduce the number of closed days within this limit.

Out of the days recognised as holidays by the Dock Labour Boards, eight days in a year may be treated as paid holidays for workers, i.e. workers enjoying these holidays should receive a normal day's wage for each day. The paid holidays should include all the closed days for the Port to be decided by the Dock Labour Board. The workers may choose any other recognised holidays to make up the total number of eight paid holidays in a year, but it should be ensured that the Port does not remain closed for more than six days in a year.

Workers required to work on recognised holidays, which are not treated as paid holidays, should be paid according to the existing practice in each Port and the payment made for the paid holidays or for working on any of the recognised holidays should not count towards the guaranteed minimum wages under Clause 23 of the Scheme.

The administrative cost per hundred registered workers is the highest at Calcutta. The Dock Labour Board, Calcutta, may examine the position with a view to seeing what economies are possible.

The levy should not be fixed at a high percentage merely for building progressively a large reserve, but each Dock Labour Board should have a reasonable financial reserve to provide against any unfavourable position which may arise from a sudden or sharp slump in the business of the Port and consequent depression in the stevedoring industry.

The Calcutta and Madras Dock Labour Boards should also take some steps, as has been done at Bombay, so that losses on account of non-payment of wages and levy by defaulting employers are avoided.

There should be a separate fund for providing amenities and welfare measures for workers. This fund may be called "Workers Welfare Fund" contribution to which should be made by all dock employers. This fund should be maintained and administered by the Dock Labour Board who should frame suitable rules for this purpose. To start with, part of the levy at present available at each Port should be credited to this fund.

The Government should take suitable action so that the income, property and operations of the Boards are not subject to income tax.

The payment of "Speed Money" by the stevedores and its acceptance by the crane-drivers is, strictly speaking, illegal.

The payment of "Speed Money" should hereafter be stopped, but a suitable increase in the present ordinary daily time-rate wages of the crane men may be made by the Port Authorities simultaneously with bringing them on a piece-rate system of wages.

Payments in any form or manner which are not authorised by the Dock Labour Board or the Port Authorities are nothing less than illegal gratifications. These are immoral and must be stopped with a strong hand. There need however be no objection to entertainment of workers by employers on recognised festive or other occasions approved by the Dock Labour Boards as they foster better employer-employee relations and should, therefore, be encouraged.

The Preamble of the Dock Workers (Regulation of Employment) Act, 1948, is not comprehensive enough inasmuch as it makes no reference to the "efficient performance of dock work". The Preamble of the Act may be amended so as fully to cover the objects of the Scheme.

Irrespective of the feasibility, desirability or otherwise, of doing away with the institution of stevedores, time is not yet opportune to contemplate such a major change in the system of dock working because the working under the present Schemes has not yet completely settled down and it may take some time before it does and is extended fully to cover other dock workers whose nature of employment is still casual. It will not be desirable at this stage to face the Dock Labour Boards with such problems having far-reaching repercussions.

In order that the Dock Labour Boards should be able to exercise proper vigilance and take timely action to maintain productivity of labour and turnround of ships at satisfactory levels, they should collect necessary data and compile statistics for each month separately under imports and exports pertaining to productivity and turnround as mentioned in Para. 1137 of the Report.

The Dock Workers Advisory Committee has not yet functioned as regularly and effectively as was expected of it. In order to make the Advisory Committee really effective the Government representatives on the Committee should be of sufficiently high status and the Chairman of the Committee should be a high Government Officer; besides it should include among others the Chairmen of the Dock Labour Boards. Representation may also be given to Export and Import and Shipping interests. The Advisory Committee should meet as often as necessary, but not less than twice a year.

Whilst the establishment of a National Dock Labour Board here is not yet warranted, the need for the whole-time and effective superintendence from the centre of the working of the Schemes at different Ports and the co-ordination of important measures under the Schemes, so that all the Ports may benefit by the experience of one another, must be fully realised. Unless immediate steps are taken to provide a suitable organisation at the centre, the required superintendence, direction and co-ordination cannot be secured. The need for central co-ordination will be all the more increased when the Port Authorities also take up the question of further decasualisation of the labour employed under them as recommended. The Government of India should depute a high-level officer at the centre to carry out these functions and such other duties in the furtherance of the Schemes as may be found necessary from time to time. This officer should also be the Chairman of the Advisory Committee referred to in Para. 1139.

The term "vessel" for the purpose of the Dock Workers (Regulation of Employment) Act of 1948 and the Schemes thereunder should apply to "all ocean-going vessels of 350 gross registered tons and over".

The Scheme is only a means to an end which is to eliminate casualness of employment and to secure efficient performance of dock work, and there is no point in bringing under the Scheme workers who are already permanently employed on a monthly salary basis.

The present Schemes cover only the employment of dock workers who are employed by stevedores. For others separate Schemes modelled on these Schemes will be necessary.

Foremen and Chargemen working in Bombay Port, who were in the permanent employment of stevedores on June 30, 1955, should not be brought under the Scheme. Of the remainder, those who are hereafter offered permanent employment and are so employed should also not be brought under the Scheme. If all the existing Foremen and Chargemen are so absorbed, no registration should be necessary, but the designations "Foremen" and "Chargemen" may continue to remain in the Schedule. No recruitment in these categories, however, should be permitted so long as stevedores meet their requirements by their permanent employees, irrespective of when they are so appointed. If, however, any Foremen or Chargemen from the existing force remain unemployed permanently, or any of the Foremen or Chargemen, employed permanently by stevedores on or after July 1, 1955, wish to come under the Dock Labour Board with their prior sanction, such Foremen or Chargemen may be recognised by the Dock Labour Board.

The Apprentice Hatch-Foremen or Gunners at Calcutta and Apprentice Foremen at Bombay may be dealt with by the respective Dock Labour Boards in the light of the following suggestions :

(a) The Dock Labour Board should keep a panel of the names of bona fide apprentices who may have been trained, or are under training of any registered employer on or before August 1, 1955.

(b) If any additions to the registers in the categories of Hatch-Foremen or Gunners at Calcutta and Foremen at Bombay are considered necessary, first preference for registration should be given to the apprentices on the panel mentioned under (a) above.

(c) Since the Registration Committee at Calcutta already has under scrutiny some applications for registrations as Hatch-Foremen or Gunners, applicants who had applied before August 1, 1955, and are selected for registration should have preference over the apprentices on the panel.

Shipping Companies should be allowed to employ their permanent staff for tallying and sorting work on their ships. They however cannot employ casual workers. Should they require at any time the services of clerks, other than their own permanent staff, they should ask the stevedores working on their ships to provide them.

At Calcutta, the stevedores should not be allowed to employ for tallying and sorting work any casual worker or any of their permanent staff appointed after March 16, 1955. To meet their and the Shipping Companies' additional requirements they must employ clerks registered with the Dock Labour Board.

In order to meet additional requirements of stevedores, the Dock Labour Board, Calcutta, should register "clerks". The number of clerks to be registered should be determined on the basis of estimated requirements and those clerks who have been working in that capacity in the docks prior to January 1, 1965, will only be eligible for registration. If the number of eligible clerks are more than the number actually required, a selection should be made on the basis of length of service and age, younger men with similar length of service getting preference.

Clerks including Tally and Sorting Clerks should also be included in the Schedules of the Schemes for Bombay and Madras and registered under the Act, but the Shipping Companies should be free to utilise their permanent staff for this work. The stevedores also should be allowed to employ their permanent staff for this work provided they were appointed on or before June 30, 1955.

"Derrick Fitters" and "Riggers" should be included in the Schedule of the Calcutta Scheme and registered by the Dock Labour Board, Calcutta. The employment of "Derrick Fitters" and "Riggers" will be through stevedores from the Dock Labour Board Registers. No other agency will be permitted to employ "Derrick Fitters" and "Riggers".

The Dock Workers (Regulation of Employment) Act, Clause 3, provides for the regulation of employment of dock workers "whether registered or not". The first step should be to prescribe simple Rules under the Act aiming at some "Regulation of Employment" of all dock workers. These Rules may provide for the measures itemised in Para. 1220.

Further regulation of employment of certain categories of dock workers to be decided by the Dock Labour Board from time to time should be secured by adopting a procedure of "listing" the workers in those categories as well as the employers of those workers. Rules may be framed under the Act to regulate the employment of listed workers and they may provide for the measures itemised in Para. 1221.

"Listing" under the Rules mentioned in Para. 1221 may be taken in hand at all the three Ports in respect of the following categories:

(a) Chipping and Painting Workers,
(b) Stitchers and Baggers,
(c) Sale Workers,
(d) Coal Workers.

Listing in accordance with the procedure detailed in Para. 1221 must hereafter always precede registration under the Act in the case of all new categories which are not included in the existing Schedules or have not already been recommended for registration by the Committee. The Dock Labour Board should obtain the sanction of the Central Government before a new category is included in the Schedule and registered under the Act.

Facilities should be provided by each Dock Labour Board for training existing registered workers in the duties of Winchmen, Signallers, Derrick Fitters or Khalasis, so that trained workers are readily available when permanent vacancies occur or temporary demands arise for these categories.

As an incentive to acquire proficiency in their day-to-day work for all categories of workers the Dock Labour Boards may periodically hold competitions amongst workers and award prizes.

It is the responsibility of the Port Authorities to provide necessary facilities for workers within the Dock area. They should, therefore, incur the capital expenditure in connection with their provision. In regard to the canteens provided and maintained by the Port Authorities, necessary financial arrangements in regard to their maintenance and running, if necessary, may be entered into between the Port Authorities and the Dock Labour Boards.

The Dock Labour Board should take the responsibility for providing the necessary facilities and amenities outside the Dock area. Amenities to be provided by the Dock Labour Board should be planned in advance for a number of years and financial resources under the "Workers Welfare Fund' should be accordingly secured. The Dock Labour Board may have a special Sub-Committee to work out a detailed programme and to see that it is implemented according to schedule, after it has been approved by the Board. The Sub-Committee may include, if necessary, representatives of listed employers and workers.

The provision of bathing, washing and sanitary facilities should be liberal and need not be limited to what is required under certain statutory obligations.

Canteens should be located at convenient places so that workers do not have to spend much time to go there from their place of work. They should be commodious and sufficient in number so that all the dock workers can be comfortably catered for. They should provide wholesome refreshments and meals at cheap rates.

Drinking water should be available at convenient places on shore and near the call stands. Special arrangements should be made to supply drinking water to the stevedore workers on ships; it would be desirable that the Dock Labour Boards should take the responsibility for these arrangements, which may be made in consultation with the Shipping Companies.

The call stands should be spacious, airy and well lit and should provide sufficient covering and adequate protection against rain and sun. There should be no obstruction of any kind in the circulating area inside the call stand, but benches, drinking water and refreshment arrangements may be provided along the sides. Steps should be taken to see that the call stands do not become places of shelter for outsiders, beggars, vagrants, etc.

The purpose of providing lockers can be substantially served, if necessary, by making arrangements for the custody of the clothes and closed space specially provided for this purpose. Numbered tokens or other means may be used to facilitate identification of the deposited belongings and their owners at the time of their return.

The provision of adequate and suitable housing for workers is necessary, both from the workers' welfare and efficiency points of view and recommends that the Government should consider favourably the requests of the Dock Labour Boards for financial assistance and grant suitable subsidies for housing to this industry also. The repayment of loans may be spread over 15 to 20 years, so that the present employers only do not have to bear the entire burden for a long-term facility.

Well-equipped dispensaries with just a few beds for emergency cases would meet the requirements better than large hospitals. Each Dock Labour Board should provide one or more, as may be necessary, well-equipped dispensaries located near the Docks. They should be adequately staffed with doctors, nurses and other attendants and have a few beds for emergency cases. In addition, First-Aid equipment should also be provided at convenient and readily accessible places and the Dock

Labour Boards in conjunction with the Port Authorities should arrange for holding First-Aid classes to train workers and the supervisory staff in First-Aid. The names of those who pass the First-Aid test should be prominently exhibited so that they may be called upon for aid whenever necessary.

Every new worker selected for registration should undergo, free of charge, a medical examination for physical fitness before he is registered and employed.

The Dock Labour Boards should take steps to ensure that employers as well as workers conform to the requirements of the Dock Labourers Regulations, 1948, and that protective equipment suggested and approved by the Dock Safety Inspectors is provided and used.

The Dock Labour Boards should take steps to provide facilities for sports, games, cultural activities and other healthy entertainments which should make for close contacts between the employers and the employees.

At Calcutta, liquor shops should not be allowed within a prescribed distance from the Docks and the Central Government may request the Government of West Bengal to give this matter their attention and take suitable action in consultation with the Port Authorities.

The Act should be suitably amended so that Rules can be framed under this Act for the regulation of employment of dock workers who are not registered under any Scheme, or for any other purpose.

The Dock Labour Boards and the Government must ensure that failures to carry out the obligations under the Scheme are not allowed to occur with impunity but are immediately and effectively dealt with. Any individual or group found to be persistently responsible for breaches of the condition of the Scheme and disrupting the working in the Port cannot but be regarded as deliberately working against the objectives of the Scheme and not interested in the welfare of the industry.

PULSE MILLING COMMITTEE, 1955—REPORT

Delhi, Manager of Publications, 1958. 46-48p. (Bound with Rice Milling Committee)

Chairman : Shri C. P. Karunakara Menon.

Members : Shri G. Parameswaran Pillai; Shri I. U. Lakhia; Shri Jhaverbhai Patel; Shri Raojibhai N. Patel; Mrs. P. Johri; Dr. D. V. Karmarkar.

Secretary : Shri N. M. Bardhan.

APPOINTMENT

The Pulse Milling Committee was constituted under the Ministry of Food and Agriculture vide their Resolution No. Py.I-608(5)54, dated January 8, 1955.

TERMS OF REFERENCE

(i) To examine the working of the different types of pulse milling now in vogue in the country from all relevant aspects such as technical, nutritional, consumer preference, economic and employment; and

(ii) To make recommendations as to the future policy that should be adopted and to indicate the administrative, financial and legislative measures which may be needed on the part of the Central and State Governments to give effect to them.

CONTENTS

Introduction; Appointment; Terms of Reference; Pulse Milling; Summary of Recommendations.

RECOMMENDATIONS

Licensing of power-driven *dal* mills should be immediately introduced in all States.

No licences for new dal mills should be granted.

No additional capacity should be allowed to existing dal mills.

No dal mills should be permitted to work for more than six hours a day, the object being that the existing over-all production of the dal mills should not only not be increased but should be decreased.

A cess at the rate of 6 annas per maund of whole pulses (not dal) milled should be imposed on all dal mills and the proceeds of the cess should be utilised for organising pulse milling by hand chakkis, for research to improve the hand chakkis, and for a subsidy to dal producers by hand chakkis. Necessary legislation should be made for imposition of a cess on dal mills.

A subsidy of 8 annas per maund of whole pulse milled by hand chakkis should be given through recognised hand chakkis centres organised as Cooperative Societies or by recognised institutions and social workers certified by the All-India Khadi and Village Industries Commission, wherever the price of hand-chakki dal is higher than dal milled by dal mills. The subsidy should be for a specified period of three years, at the end of which the position should be reviewed by the Government. Individuals engaged in producing hand-chakki dal and certified by the State Khadi and Village Industries Commission may be allowed concessions in the form of easy credit and implements at subsidised rates.

Dal milled by hand chakkis should be exempted from sales tax in States where dal is subject to sales tax. The existing rules should be amended accordingly.

The State Governments should purchase dal produced only by hand chakkis preferably from Government subsidised hand-chakki centres, where they exist, for their requirements for Jails, Hospitals, Government Hostels, the Railways, the Army, the Police, etc. The State Governments should issue a directive to all Government aided and controlled concerns, institutions and canteens (such as railway canteens) to purchase dal produced only by hand chakkis.

Each State Government should draw up a three-year programme for speedy organisation of production of dal by hand chakkis and replacement of all dal mills within that period. For that purpose each State Government should each year formulate a programme for developing the hand-chakki industry and correspondingly reducing the production by dal mills.

The programme of the State Governments for speedy organisation of pulse milling with hand chakkis should proceed on a co-operative basis.

Research should be undertaken with financial assistance from the Government evolving simple and better type hand chakkis with a view to increasing their output and at the same time making it easier to handle.

EDUCATION COMMITTEE FOR THE ANDAMAN AND NICOBAR ISLANDS 1955—REPORT

New Delhi, Ministry of Education, 1956. 107p.

Chairman : Shri A. N. Basu.
Members : Dr. K. D. Ghosh; Shri D. S. Achtani; Shri A. C. Erickson.
Member-Secretary : Pandit Sham Narayan.

APPOINTMENT

The Government of India, Ministry of Education, vide their Order No. F. 2-16/54-H.3, dated February 22, 1955, appointed an Education Committee for the Andaman and Nicobar Islands.

TERMS OF REFERENCE

The terms of reference of the Committee were as follows:

(a) To study the existing educational set-up in these islands; and

(b) To recommend plans for the improvement and reorganisation of the education system.

In view of the special conditions prevailing in these Islands, it was decided that the scope for investigation of the Committee might be, if necessary, widened.

CONTENTS

Introductory; Background of the Problems of Education; Geography and History of the Islands; Primary Education; A general Picture; Middle School Education; Recommendations for opening new schools; Compulsory Primary Education; Senior Basic Schools; High School Education; Vocational Education; Administration; Teachers, their Recruitment and Training; Proposals for better Service Conditions; Training School; Its Working and Staffing; Medium of Instruction, Primary Stage, High School Stage, the Lingua Franca of the Islands, Script, the place of Hindi, the Nicobar, Background, the Present Set-up, the Middle School, Hostels for High School Students, Language; Social Education, its Importance under the Present Conditions, a Scheme for Social Education; Finance; Conclusions; Summary of Recommendations; Appendices from I to IX.

RECOMMENDATIONS—SUMMARY

I Primary Education

At least 19 Basic Trained Teachers (14+5) should be immediately appointed, one for each of the Primary Schools (Grade Rs. 68-4-120-5-170).

These teachers should be able to teach Hindi as well as other subjects.

Four sets of peripatetic teachers (12 teachers) should be appointed for Drawing, Music and Physical Education for the three Zones, South Andamans, Middle and North Andamans and Nicobar Islands (Grade Rs. 68-4-120-5-170).

Co-operation of local women should be sought in teaching, sewing and knitting to girls in schools, if need be, on small honoraria.

The peripatetic teachers are to be under the Education Officer and should work in collaboration with the two Supervisors in these areas.

Each school should have at least three rooms.

As an immediate measure, bamboo partitions should be set up in big rooms for purposes of effective teaching.

To remove the dearth of textbooks, etc., the Co-operative Book Depot at the High School should be the agency for ordering textbooks and educational appliances for Primary and Basic Schools.

Slates should be replaced by wooden takhtis which can be made inexpensively in these areas.

Hand-made mats (made by children) and flat wooden writing desks, according to specifications given, should replace high benches and desks.

The blackboards should get a yearly coat of paint, preferably made in the school itself according to the formula given.

There should be a morning assembly in each school for non-denominational prayers, community singing, reading from sacred books and talks by the Headmaster and other teachers.

There should be systematic training in singing the National Anthem (which the pupils must understand) correctly, as also a number of selected songs including school songs.

The school walls should be decorated with pictures and children's drawings.

There should be a school museum, housing children's collection of shells, pebbles, butterflies and other objects of interest.

Every child should have the following subjects:

Mother tongue, Hindi, Social Studies (History, Geography and Civics), Arithmetic, Music, Drawing, Craft, Health and Physical Education and Gardening.

A detailed syllabus in each subject should be provided by the Education Department.

To enable parents to have children's help and to give some relief to teachers, hours of school work should be from 11 a.m. to 4.30 p.m., the younger children being let off at 3 p.m.

The Paddy Vacation may be extended by a fortnight.

Every school be given an initial capital grant of at least Rs. 200 to start the nucleus of a library.

The Education Department should receive a capital grant of Rs. 2,000 to start a Central Library at Port Blair for circulating books to different schools.

There being no newspapers in these Islands, the Education Department should publish a Hindi bi-weekly edition of the *Daily Press Telegrams,* brought out by the Administration and send it regularly to the schools.

There should be a School Medical Service, started with the help of the Public Health Authorities. Arrangements should also be made for cheap but nourishing midday tiffin.

All new appointments should be of Matriculate Trained Teachers. The existing teachers should be required to add to their educational qualifications and get themselves trained within a period of five years.

Schools should be started in schoolless areas as indicated and the Primary Department of the High School be split into four or five schools to serve Port Blair itself.

All the 19 Primary Schools should be converted into proper Basic Schools by 1957-58, according to the time schedule given in the Report.

One of the following Crafts is to be introduced in the school with at least two hours' practice: Cane and Bamboo work, Gardening, Carpentry and Spinning.

Free compulsory Primary Education should be introduced but before it is actually enforced, the schools should be strengthened by provision of school places and appointment of Trained Teachers.

Three new Senior Basic Schools (Middle Schools) should be started at Chouldari, Tusonabad and Rangat.

Cheap hostels should be attached to the Senior Basic (Middle) schools, children being allowed to bring their own rations.

In the Senior Basic (Middle) schools, crafts suggested for the Junior Basic schools should be continued, spinning being followed by weaving and carpentry being given a forest bias.

Stress should be laid in the Senior Basic (Middle) schools on group games, mass drill and Scouting, Guiding and Bratachari.

Each of the Senior Basic (Middle) schools must have at least two additional teachers, the Headmaster being a trained graduate.

Each Senior Basic (Middle) school must have at least five rooms.

There should be two Supervisors, for the present, under the Education Officer for purposes of inspection and guidance.

The Education Department should organise from time to time inter-school activities of various types such as Sports, Debates, Music and Craft Work competitions.

Teachers should be brought together from time to time for short week-end courses and for discussing problems connected with their work.

Educational exhibitions and excursions should be regularly organised by the Education Department.

II High School Education

The present mixed High School may be converted into a Higher Secondary Multipurpose School for boys and a Senior Basic School for girls may be opened at a separate place.

Besides M.A.B.T.'s required for the Multipurpose School, the following additional staff should be appointed: (1) Two trained and qualified teachers, (2) One Sanskrit teacher, (3) Two Drawing teachers, (4) One Domestic Science teacher for girls school and (5) Two

Physical Instructors for both the schools—one for each, one for boys and one for girls, in the grade of Rs. 120-300.

Unqualified and underqualified teachers be replaced by qualified staff.

Furniture should be replaced by desks and chairs, black boards may be renovated; maps, charts, models, strip projector for the teaching of geography be provided: library should be completely overhauled—Rs. 5,000 be given as grant.

Suitable periodicals, magazines, journals be submitted for the use of teachers and students.

Science laboratory should be properly equipped and be used for both boys and girls. A substantial amount of Rs. 5,000 be spent in the first instance and Rs. 1,000 be allowed annually.

Schools should have their own playgrounds. Trained Physical Instructors in the grade of Rs. 120-300 be appointed for physical instruction.

Excursions and tours should be organised.

Students be encouraged to grow their school garden.

Medical inspection be done twice a year and Rs. 2,000 a year be earmarked for remuneration to the doctors.

The question of affiliation be decided once for all.

III Vocational Education

A trade school may be opened either near the Marine Dockyard or at the Chatham Saw Mills. Chatham Saw Mills have the advantage of Staff Training School, while the Marine Dockyard have got much of other facilities. The age limit for admission should be 14 plus.

Selection of the candidates, if possible, be made by competition.

No fee may be charged from the students except a nominal admission fee of Rs. 2 and caution money of Rs. 15.

The students will receive instruction in Elementary Mathematics, Technical Drawing, Elementary English, General Knowledge and also Workshop Practice. Total periods will be 45 per week of 40 minutes' duration each.

During the first year, all training will have Basic all-round training in General Workshop Practice and Theory and in the second year they will specialise in either Mechanics or Carpentry.

There will be an examination at the end of the first year and another examination at the end of the second year. The successful candidates may be employed as apprentices in the Government Departments, particularly in Forest Department and Marine Dockyard with a stipend of Rs. 30 or Rs. 40.

The students of the Trade School may be housed in the Government hostel.

The following posts may be created.

(a) A Headmaster in the grade of Rs. 250-10-300-20-400-E.B.-25-500.

(b) One Assistant Teacher in the grade of Rs. 120-8-200-E.B.-10-300.

This Institute will produce the following technicians: Carpenters, Fitters, Smiths, Mechanics, Welders, Moulders, etc.

IV Administration

The present system of administration of education is centralised in the hands of the Chief Commissioner, assisted by an Advisory Committee for Education and a High School Managing Committee. The Secretary of these bodies, consisting of non-official and official members, is generally an officer of some Department other than Education. The Committee recommend the creation of the following posts:

(1) Education Officer, Grade Rs. 400-25-500-30-800, equivalent to the rank of a District Inspector of Schools in Delhi.

(2) Two Supervisors, one for Maya Bander and Middle Islands, the other for Port Blair and Nicobar group of Islands, Grade Rs. 180-10-320-E.B.-350, equivalent to the grade of an A.D.I. in Delhi.

(3) One steno-typist, one U.D.C., three Lower Grade clerks and three peons, for the office establishment of the Education Officer and the Supervisors.

The functions of these officers will be as follows:

(a) **Education Officer**

(i) To work as the Head of the Department of Education under the Chief Commissioner.

(ii) Conversion of the existing High School for boys into a Multipurpose School, and the starting of a new Higher Secondary Multipurpose School for girls.

(iii) To look after Social Education.

(iv) To convert the existing Primary Schools into Basic Schools.

(v) To direct, supervise and reorganise the existing schools.

(vi) To manage, direct and supervise Technical Schools in the Islands.

(vii) To arrange for the training of teachers, and the recruitment of suitable teachers.

(b) **Supervisors**

(i) To assist the Education Officer in the direction, supervision and organisation of Basic Schools. One of them will be for the Andamans and the other for Nicobar Islands.

V Medium Of Instruction

At the Primary stage, mother tongue of the child should be the medium of instruction. Hindi should be begun from Class III in the Andamans and Class II in the Nicobars schools, where the mother tongue is not Hindi.

In the Secondary stage, Hindi should be the medium of instruction. Urdu may for some time continue side by side.

Hindi is the regional language in the Andamans; but there are linguistic minorities.

Devanagari script may be given to dialects in Nancowry group and also to Car Nicobar dialect.

Improvement in the teaching of Hindi, or other subjects through Hindi may be made by the appointment of qualified teachers.

VI Teachers

At the moment, all the schools are staffed generally by untrained and unqualified teachers, but it is necessary to make arrangements for their training.

Untrained teachers in the High Schools should be sent to Training Colleges in India for their training. They should be considered on duty during the period of training and should also be given passage money and a small allowance in addition to their salaries on the lines of Tripura and Manipur States.

A school for the training of Primary School teachers may be opened in Andamans and the following posts be created:

1. Headmaster: Trained Graduate in the grade of Rs. 250-10-300-20-400-E.B.-25-500.

2. One Instructor: Matric-Basic Trained with five years' teaching experience, grade Rs. 60-4-120-E.B.-5-170.

3. One qualified Craft Instructor, grade Rs. 60-4-120-5-170.

4. One Peon.

The Principal and some of the teachers on the staff of the Higher Secondary School may also assist in the teaching work.

The Director of Education should direct, guide and assist in the training at the institution. This training institution will be an evening institution and housed in the building of the Higher Secondary School for boys.

In the first year, six untrained teachers from the schools and six fresh Matriculates may be admitted. Next year, the Trained Teachers may be posted in schools and another similar batch will be trained. In four years, all the untrained teachers in the Andamans will have received training and would provide sufficient number of trained teachers for schools. This School, then, should be transferred to Nicobar Islands. This school is expected to finish its job in five years. Only those teachers should be admitted to the school who have passed the Middle School Examination. Others should pass the Middle School Examination before being admitted to the School. All these Middle Passed Teachers should after training be required to pass the Matriculation Examination in a reasonable time. Graduate Trained Teachers should be obtained on deputation from the mainland through the good offices of the Ministry of Education.

To attract teachers the following action should be taken:

(a) Existing grades should be revised and brought in line with those prevailing in Delhi. They should continue to receive the usual Andaman allowance.

(b) The existing service conditions may be revised and teachers may be allowed to visit their homes during long vacations with free passage to and from their homes. If a teacher is detained on duty during vacation this should be confirmed, as early as possible.

VII Social Education

In view of the large number of illiterate mazdoors, apart from the general adult illiterate population, the employees of the Forest Department and the Saw Mills need an urgent scheme for Social Education in the Islands. This work should be taken in hand immediately.

A Department of Social Education with the following staff may be created under the supervision of the Social Education Officer (Grade Rs. 250-10-300-20-400-E.B.-25-500). He should be a person trained from centres like Sewa Gram or Shanti Niketan.

1. Six Social Workers in the grade of Rs. 68-4-120-E.B.-5-170. They should be at least Matric trained. Two of them should be good singers and actors, capable of organising and training music and dramatic parties, etc. Two Social Workers should be able to train pupil-workers, selected from amongst the mazdoors themselves in the art of imparting instruction in three R's to adults. The remaining two should be adept in Audio-visual Aids and should be able to work a moving library. These Social Workers should preferably be selected from the persons trained in a Janta College.

2. One Senior Operator in the grade of Rs. 80-5-120-E.B.-210/220.

3. Night schools may be organised for labourers in the Forest Labour Camps. The building for the purpose which should serve as a Community Centre may be provided by the Forest Department. At several places the school buildings may be utilised for this purpose.

4. One Social Worker may be selected from amongst the labourers from each of the Camps and may be given a sum of Rs. 30 per mensem as remuneration or honorarium.

After training local people in the Andamans the Social Education Officer may shift to Car Nicobar for a year with four of his Social Workers to organise evening classes or Community Centres in those Islands.

This work of training local people and organising Community Centres, etc., should be completed in three years' time. Co-operation of the Village Panchayats and the Headmen in the Nicobar villages may be obtained.

A 16 mm. projector may also be supplied, if it is not already available.

All literature, books and charts for the purpose should be supplied by the Education Ministry to the Social Education Officer.

VIII Nicobar

The existing Middle School at Mus may be shifted to Big Lapati.

In 1956, Class VIII may be added to this. There is no need for further extension or opening of new schools in the near future in the Car Nicobar.

At other places also the existing schools may be developed wherever number justifies. The subject of fine arts should be introduced in the Government schools. People here are very good musicians and should be given benefits of learning Guitar, Banjo and Violin.

The Craft suitable for the schools, as mat-making or coir-making, etc., should be introduced.

The Staff is highly unqualified, and arrangements for the training of the unqualified staff may be made as mentioned in the chapter on Teachers. Hindi should be the medium of instruction at the High School stage. In the Primary classes Hindi should be introduced in Class II, after which the medium of instruction should be Hindi.

The children sit on the bare floor. Arrangements should be made for mats to seat them. These mats, if possible, should be woven by womenfolk in homes for their children. The Government should supply small wooden tables of reasonable size to serve as writing desks.

A hostel may be started for the students of distant villages to get education in the Middle School, proposed to be shifted to Big Lapati. For High School education the students may be sent back to the Andamans and a separate hostel may be opened for the Nicobarese students in view of their tastes and habits of food and way of life. Bishop Richardson's proposal for a hostel may be encouraged.

LOWER DAMODAR INVESTIGATION COMMITTEE, 1955—REPORT

Calcutta, Domodar Valley Corporation, 1957. 2 vols.

Chairman : Shri G. R. Garg.
Members : Dr. N. K. Bose; Shri G. B. Mondal; Shri S. P. Sarathy; Shri D. Mookerjea; Shri A. L. Dias.
Secretary : Shri H. J. Ajwani (replaced by Shri N. S. Iyengar).

APPOINTMENT

The Damodar Valley Corporation vide Memorandum No.WI-G/21-1880, dated February 24, 1955, set up a Committee to examine the possible effects of the D.V.C. dams on the lower reaches of the Damodar River and the Rupnarain.

TERMS OF REFERENCE

(a) To examine in detail the available data and suggest what further information will be required with respect to the regime of the Lower Damodar and the Rupnarain;

(b) To assess the possible effects of the DVC dams on the lower reaches of the Damodar river and the Rupnarain;

(c) To suggest what steps, if any, should be taken for preventing deterioration of the Lower Damodar and the Rupnarain; and

(d) To make such other recommendations pertinent to the subject which they may consider necessary.

CONTENTS

Volume I—Introduction; Examination of the available data and suggestions regarding further information to be collected; Existing (pre-dam) condition of the Lower Reaches of the Damodar and the Rupnarain; Possible effects of the D.V.C. Dams on the Lower Reaches of the Damodar and the Rupnarain; Suggestions regarding the steps to be taken for preventing deterioration of the Lower Damodar and the Rupnarain; Plates I and II. **Volume II**—Appendices.

RECOMMENDATIONS

Suggestions regarding the steps to be taken for preventing deterioration of the Lower Damodar and the Rupnarain:

(1) Encroachment on the river by private interests must be prevented by suitable legislative and other measures.

(2) The growth of vegetation in the bed of the river and also along the banks should be carefully watched and suitable action taken so as to cause minimum obstruction to the flood flow, frequency of which would be

definitely less than what it is now. Controlled cultivation above normal high flood level and in *chars* will be helpful in restricting jungle growth.

(3) Concentrated flushing doses should be occasionally released down the river in the interest of the conservancy of the river channels. Proper studies should be made while releasing the flushing doses as to the effect of such operation on the regime of the river as well as on the various interests on the banks. Such studies would be of valuable guidance for future operation of the reservoirs.

(4) In fixing the priority of water uses the conservancy of the river channel itself must not be ignored and should be given due consideration along with other uses of water, viz. irrigation and generation of power. The operation of the reservoirs should be flexible enough in the initial stages, so that a proper and careful study can be made and suitable adjustments in the plan of operation are introduced for the benefit of all concerned.

(5) Some suitable method of supply of irrigation water for the trans-Damodar area may be investigated.

(6) The problem of drainage of local area in the Lower Valley should be separately studied and investigated and suitable action for drainage of these areas should be taken up by the appropriate authorities.

(7) Detailed investigations should be carried out to effect improvement over the present condition of the Amta channel. Care should, however, be taken to ensure that it does not affect the river Rupnarain adversely.

(8) Immediate and suitable steps should be taken for carrying out systematic hydrological investigations and observation in this area.

(9) It is well-known that several problems arise in the Lower Reaches of the river after construction of the dams. In the present case the problems are further complicated by the tides in the Lower Reaches. It is, therefore, difficult to forecast the actual problems that would crop up in this area after the completion of the Damodar Valley Project. It would, therefore, be necessary to have a proper control so as to co-ordinate the activities of the different authorities concerned.

We suggest that a Board to be called the "Lower Damodar Conservancy Board" be set up with the representatives of the Government of West Bengal, Calcutta Port Commissioners and the Damodar Valley Corporation. The functions of this Board will be:

(a) to formulate the necessary hydrological and engineering investigations that will have to be carried out to study the effect of operation of dams especially the releases during the floods;

(b) to suggest alternative plans of operation if any; and

(c) to formulate schemes for improvement of channels and any local area in the Lower Valley.

It is necessary to have a proper unified development of the entire Lower Valley as a whole instead of solution of individual problems for local and short-term benefits.

AD HOC COMMITTEE FOR COIR ROPE, 1955—REPORT

Ernakulam, The Coir Board, 1956. 11p.+ixp.

Convener : C. T. Jacob.
Members : Shri P. K. Dewer; Shri B. V. Abdulla Koya; Shri S. C. Roy; Shri B. M. Peter; Shri A. M. Barbhaya; Shri C. E. Menon.

APPOINTMENT

The Ad Hoc Committee for Coir Rope is an offshoot and part of the Ad Hoc Committee for Coir Products. Paragraph 37 of the Report of the Ad Hoc Committee for Coir Products reads as follows:

"This Committee should have examined the question of manufacture of coir rope also as this forms one of the 'coir products'. But because manufacturers of rope were not adequately represented on the Ad Hoc Committee when it was originally constituted, the questionnaire did not contain any questions relating to the production of coir rope. Since then, Shri B. M. Peter and Shri C. E. Menon were added to the Ad Hoc Committee, but it was unfortunately too late to include questions relating to coir rope. In view of this and with a view not to delay the report of this Committee, we recommend to the Coir Board that a smaller Ad Hoc Committee be appointed to consider the production of coir rope and when that Committee submits its Report, it may be added on to this Report to form one complete Report on Coir Products."

In accordance with the above recommendation which was accepted by the Coir Board at its meeting held on March 25, 1955, this Ad Hoc Committee was constituted.

TERMS OF REFERENCE

To consider the production of coir rope.

CONTENTS

Introduction; Production; Demand for Coir Rope; Prospects for Development; Factors; Standardisation; General Recommendations; Conclusions and Recommendations; Appendices I to V.

RECOMMENDATIONS

(1) Although accurate statistics are not available, it can be estimated that the total production of coir rope in India amounts to about 14,100 tons. Of this, internal consumption may be estimated at 10,650 tons and exports to foreign countries at 3,450 tons.

(2) The principal buyers of coir cordage and rope are the Middle East countries, Turkey and Malaya, and a tendency is visible of declining exports to other countries. During the War, there was an acute shortage of other hard fibres which were traditionally used in the manufacture of cordage and rope, e.g. Manila, Hemp and Sisal. Since the War, Sisal production has increased in Africa, and likewise more Manila and Hemp have been released for civil consumption in Indonesia and the Far East. It is therefore reasonable to assume that the off-take by these countries, particularly of coir cordage and rope, has declined because of displacement by other fibres.

(3) It is important to ensure supplies of yarn of a uniform quality to the manufacturers. The Committee is in entire agreement with the recommendations made by the Ad Hoc Committee for Coir Yarn on this subject.

(4) Competition for coir rope is mainly from Aloe, Manila and Hemp ropes. The Committee recommends that a technical study should be made by the Technological Department of the Coir Board of the tensile strength and other properties of the coir fibre as compared with other industrial fibres used for rope manufacture and of the possibilities of improving the quality of coir rope so as to increase its usefulness and enlarge its market.

(5) Coir yarn prices in India are controlled by many factors and it is by no means possible to make the raw material available to producers of coir cordage and rope at lower prices unless production methods are improved, especially in Malabar, thereby increasing production and reducing production costs.

(6) A reduction in production costs can also be achieved by improving the efficiency of the rather crude equipments now used by roperies in the Malabar Coast, not by mechanisation, but by technological improvements to the equipment for which the necessary technical advice should be rendered by the Coir Board's technical staff.

(7) There are no factors in the rope manufacturing industry, but there are merchants who play a useful role in the industry as at present organised.

(8) The Committee feels that it is desirable to have specifications laid down for coir cordage and rope, which will eventually be helpful to the progress of the industry. TDC:14 of the Indian Standards Institution is now engaged in this work. For the present these specifications need not be enforced, but they should be given adequate publicity.

(9) With a view to enabling the Coir Board to maintain fuller statistical information regarding production and marketing of coir rope, the Committee recommends:

(a) that no exports of coir rope shall be made except under a licence issued by the Coir Board; the licence may however be issued freely;

(b) that coir rope be given a separate heading in the accounts of the sea-borne trade of India—both foreign and coastwise;

(c) that statistics of rail-borne trade in coir rope be collected by the Coir Board;

(d) that in the event of the Coir Board sending a delegation to foreign countries, that delegation be asked to collect full information regarding the extent of production of coir rope in foreign countries and the methods of manufacture adopted.

(10) The Committee also recommends that any delegation sent out by the Coir Board inquire into the reasons why our exports to certain countries have declined and also into the possibilities of our reviving such exports.

OILSEEDS CRUSHING INDUSTRY INQUIRY COMMITTEE, 1955—REPORT

New Delhi, Ministry of Food and Agriculture, 1956. 111p.

Chairman : Shri P. A. Gopalkrishnan (resigned, replaced by Shri T. C. Puri).

Members : Shri R. L. Mehta; Shri Ratilal M. Gandhi; Shri Jhaverbhai Patel; Shri Satish Chandra Das Gupta; Mrs. Prema Johari; Dr. K. S. Murti.

Secretary : Shri F. C. Gera.

APPOINTMENT

The Oilseeds Crushing Industry Inquiry Committee was constituted under the Ministry of Food and Agriculture vide their Resolution No. F. 5-54/ 54-Com. I, dated April 1, 1955.

TERMS OF REFERENCE

To carry out a rapid survey of the state of Oilseeds Crushing Industry (crushing both by mills and by village ghanis) in the country and to recommend the lines on which this industry should be developed in future, in particular, to examine and report:

(a) whether it is necessary to increase or to reduce the existing oilseeds crushing capacity of mills in the country;

(b) whether it would be desirable to reserve any particular oilseeds for crushing by the village ghani only having regard to the effect of such reservation on the efficiency of production of oil and its nutritional value and having regard further to its effect on employment, supply of oil to consuming industries and exports; and

(c) whether it is necessary to give any assistance to the village oil-crushing industry and, if so, in what form.

CONTENTS

Introduction; Efficiency of Mills and Ghanis; Nutritional Value of Oils and Oilcakes produced by Mills and Ghanis; Industries dependent upon vegetable oils; Employment possibilities of the Oilseeds Crushing Industry; Reservation of Edible Oilseeds for Ghani Industry; Exports of Oils and Oilseeds; Cess on Oils and Oilseeds; Assistance to the Village Oilseeds Crushing Industry; Organisation for control of Oilseeds Crushing Industry; Minor Oilseeds; Development of Cottonseed Crushing Industry; Acknowledgements; Summary of Conclusions and Recommendations; Appendices.

CONCLUSIONS AND RECOMMENDATIONS—SUMMARY

There is a marked preference in the country for the ghani oil over the mill oil so far as domestic consumption is concerned. Ghani oil is more palatable than mill oil and according to popular opinion, it is slightly more nutritious than mill oil.

There is every justification for ensuring that ghani oil unadulterated with mill oil is made available to the consumers for domestic consumption in the quantities required by them.

Filtration of ghani oil should be encouraged on a large scale.

In the conditions prevailing in India where malnutrition of animals is the rule and their balanced feeding an exception, it is important that they are fed on oilcakes containing a higher percentage of oil.

One result of crushing of oilseeds by ghani is that the cake remains in the village and is fed to the cattle.

Ghani-pressed cake undergoes quicker spoilage but ghani cakes produced in small quantities by village oilmen are easily sold and there is little danger of the ghani cake being spoiled by long storage for the reason that this will not be stored for a long time.

Vanaspati industry, the paints and varnishes industry and the soap factories may continue to draw their requirements of vegetable oil from the existing sources, namely, vegetable oil mills.

If the pharmaceutical industry needs any quantity of vegetable oils from the mill sector, there is no objection to that sector continuing to meet the requirements of that industry.

Ghani has superior employment possibilities compared to the mills and there is a case for giving every possible encouragement to it even if it means a slight loss of the total vegetable oil resources of the country.

The existing number of ghanis will not be able to cope with the crushing of all the edible oilseeds produced in the country. The suggestion to reserve all edible oilseeds for crushing by ghanis is, therefore, impracticable.

While encouragement should be given to the ghanis, oil milling industry is also entitled to a place in India's economy.

Installed crushing capacity of the milling industry may be allowed to operate in respect of all oilseeds except sesamum.

Regarding sesamum, the mill sector may continue to supply sesamum oil for the requirements of the vanaspati and other industries and for exports. All requirements of sesamum oil for domestic consumption should be met by the ghanis.

No more power-driven mills should be set up in the country.

It is not desirable to ban the export of oils and oilseeds. If it is necessary to export small quantities of oils and oilseeds to maintain prices in the country, these should be allowed.

It is not desirable to permit export of large quantities of oilcakes, but there is no objection to small quantities of de-oiled cakes produced by mills being allowed to be exported after allowing for the needs of the country.

There should only be an excise duty on mill oil and this excise should enter the General Revenues.

It would not be desirable to levy a cess on the oil mills for utilising the proceeds for the benefit of the ghani. Any money required for the benefit of the village industry should come from the General Revenues and this need not be equal to the amount of income from the excise duty. The expenditure on the village industry should be according to its requirements.

At least 10,000 improved ghanis should be supplied annually on a subsidized basis to the village oilmen to replace the old-type ghanis.

Supply of improved-type ghanis should continue to be subsidized at Rs. 150 per ghani.

Research should be arranged at a few selected centres for effecting improvements in the Wardha Ghani.

It is desirable to have a network of oilmen's co-operative societies whose chief duty should be to ensure a continuous supply of raw material to the oilmen and to buy all the oils and oilcakes produced by them, as only a rapid sale of the oils and oilcakes could keep the ghanis going. If the co-operative societies do not have sufficient finances to discharge this responsibility, it would be desirable to consider the possibility of setting up marketing organisations in each State for doing this work.

The Government should remove the difficulties experienced by the oilmen and Co-operative Societies in arranging finances. Mainly due to the oilseeds' prices being subject to fluctuations, credit is not easy to arrange and the State should therefore guarantee the losses to enable the oilmen to hold out at the time of fall in prices. Whatever payment the Government may have to make on this account should be treated as a loan to the Co-operative Societies. In the usual course, the loss of one season could be made up by the profits of the next. In exceptional cases, the loan may be written off.

The production subsidy of Rs. 2, 8 an. per maund of oil produced by the ghanis should be reduced to Re. 1, 14 an. per maund.

The Government's requirements of vegetable oils for use in hospitals, jails, police establishments, messes, hostels, etc., should be met by the purchase of ghani oil only.

Purchases of oilcakes required for immediate consumption in Government institutions should be confined to ghani cakes only. The keeping quality of ghani cakes is inferior to the keeping quality of mill cakes and it would not, therefore, be proper to make the use of ghani cakes compulsory where the cakes have to be stored for long periods.

The Railways should sanction a concessional rate of freight for the movement of ghanis and allied equipment.

There is need for technical advice being given to the mill sector regarding the type of machinery to be used, the manner of maintaining it, the treatment of seed before crushing, the storage of oilseeds, etc. The duty of giving this advice could be entrusted to the Indian Central Oilseeds Committee.

There is need for Governmental measures to ensure healthful conditions of work for the workmen employed in the mills.

Village-level workers in the National Extension Service Blocks and the Community Project Areas should be told to popularise the collection of minor oilseeds where they grow in natural state so that their exploitation may be a source of income to the rural population and may incidentally add to the oil resources of this country.

The Indian Central Oilseeds Committee is engaged in a survey of minor oilseeds in the country. After this survey is completed, the possibility of making arrangements for regular collection and publication of statistics of production of minor oilseeds may be examined.

The country should go slow in the matter of development of cottonseed crushing by mills. During the Second Five Year Plan the quantity of cottonseed crushed in the country should not exceed 20% of the total production of cottonseed.

There is no reason why any special concession should be given to the cottonseed industry. There is a real danger that if direct or indirect subsidies are given to this industry, the consequential large-scale diversion of cottonseed from Indian villages to the urban areas for crushing by mills might have a dangerous effect on the health of the Indian cattle. However, licences for import of machinery for crushing cottonseed might be given freely up to the limit of crushing capacity indicated above.

Hand presses used for the crushing of certain oilseeds involve a considerable amount of cruelty to the workmen and these presses may be replaced by power-driven mills with the crushing capacity equal to that of the presses. If any financial assistance in the shape of loans and grants to the owners of these presses is necessary, this should be given by the Government.

There is need for separate Central legislation to carry out the recommendations of the Oilseeds Crushing Industry Inquiry Committee. This legislation should provide for the creation of a statutory office of a Controller of the Vegetable Oilseeds Crushing Industry who should be entrusted with the duty of seeing that no new mills are set up for crushing oilseeds, that the existing installed capacity of the mills is not exceeded and that the crushing of sesamum by the mills is not undertaken except for requirements of exports and industries using vegetable oils as a raw material. There may be Regional Officers working under the Controller of the Vegetable Oilseeds Crushing Industry in the various States who can be delegated suitable powers.

PUBLIC SERVICES (QUALIFICATIONS FOR RECRUITMENT) COMMITTEE, 1955—REPORT

Delhi, Manager of Publications, 1956. 34p.

Chairman : Dr. A. Ramaswami Mudaliar.

Members : Dr. C. P. Ramaswamy Aiyar; Dr. Amar Nath Jha (died); Dr. J. C. Ghosh; Dr. Sushila Nayar; Shri N. K. Sidhanta; Prof. Humayun Kabir; Shri K. P. Mushran; Shri A. K. Roy.

Secretary : Shri R. C. Dutt.

APPOINTMENT

The Public Services (Qualifications for Recruitment) Committee was constituted under the Ministry of Education vide their Resolution No. F. 23-49/54. A. 1, dated April 16, 1955, to examine the need for a university degree as a prerequisite qualification for the public services.

TERMS OF REFERENCE

(i) To examine the question as to how far and at what levels the possession of a university degree is necessary for recruitment to public services.

(ii) To consider the type of tests which should be instituted to assess the relative merits of candidates in an objective manner in the absence of a university degree.

(iii) To consider measures to ensure that the number of candidates competing for posts and services under the Government is not wastefully large.

CONTENTS

Introduction; the Problem; the Problem Analysed; Recommendations; General Recommendations; Minute of Dissent; Appendices I to IV.

RECOMMENDATIONS

In the course of the evidence adduced before us and in the discussions which we have had with representatives of the various authorities and organisations, three points of view have broadly emerged. Of these, two may be regarded as belonging to two extremes. The first point of view is that the standard of university education having deteriorated in recent years, a university degree does not represent that standard of academic attainment that was associated with it earlier. This being so, it is argued, a university degree is not really a very high standard to set for even the middle levels of Government service. A person who does not acquire a university degree even in the present circumstances when such degrees are comparatively easy to acquire is obviously of a lower standard still in educational and cultural attainment. It would be in the interests of efficiency to recruit such persons to the public services. It is argued by the protagonists of this view that in practical administration the Government must be realistic enough to recognise the standards that obtain at present at various levels of education. To ignore such standards and to recruit non-graduates to various levels of Government service merely because non-graduates are recruited to corresponding levels in other countries would be highly unrealistic.

The other extreme view on the contrary maintains that competence and even academic attainment cannot be measured by certificates and degrees given by universities. No such qualification should be prescribed at all. Recruitment to the public services should be on the basis of competitive examinations. The standard of such examinations may be as high as is considered necessary for the level to which recruitment is made. Success in such examinations would by itself carry sufficient assurance of the intellectual qualities of the candidate, and would render unnecessary such artificial standards as School Final Certificate or a university degree. It is argued by the supporters of this view that it is quite possible for a person to attain a high intellectual standard without going anywhere near a university. In fact, lack of economic resources and other reasons might prevent bright young persons from studying at a university, and yet they may have by private study attained the same intellectual standard as, if not even higher than, those who have obtained their B.A. or M.A. degrees. There is no reason why such persons should be kept out of the public services.

Between these two extreme views, a large number of witnesses who appeared before us expressed the view that while a university degree should continue to be the minimum qualification for the higher levels of Government service, it need not be insisted upon for levels which are not so high. While agreeing on this broad generalisation, there were naturally differences of opinion even among such witnesses as to the level at which the line should be drawn. Some witnesses felt that the present requirements were by and large fair, and that only slight modifications need be made. Others however were of the opinion that the level of public services at which non-graduates could be admitted could be raised considerably above what it is today.

We have given careful consideration to the three

points of view. We are unable to agree with the first view because it not only holds out no solution of the problem which has arisen but, in fact, perpetuates the vicious circle to which we have already referred. The result of the indiscriminate insistence on university degrees has been to create a rush for university education even among people who can neither afford such education economically, nor are likely to profit by it intellectually. There are numerous instances where families have been hard put to finance the university education of their children only to discover after a number of years that either

(a) the persons in question have not the aptitude to pass the course successfully; or

(b) even if they do pass and ultimately obtain the long-cherished degree, it does not help them to find the type of employment they desire.

Naturally there is disillusionment which is all the more bitter as it follows a comparatively long period of economic hardship and misery. In these circumstances, it would be a counsel of despair to suggest that the vicious circle cannot be broken at any stage. The circle must be broken and can be done either

(a) by refusing admission to universities to persons who do not attain a certain standard in the Secondary Schools; or

(b) by removing the inducements which make persons go in for university education even when they have no special taste for it.

It can certainly be argued by the protagonists of the view under discussion that the first alternative is the only right course. The universities, it may be contended, should strictly limit admission on the basis of candidates' performance in schools. While undoubtedly there is some scope for action in this respect, it would be highly unrealistic to suppose that in the face of a strong public desire to obtain admission to universities it would be possible for the latter to refuse admission to any considerable proportion of the intending entrants. By refusing such admission universities would not only lay themselves open to the charge of denying higher education to a proportion of the population but also of practically denying them decent employment thereafter, as no such employment would be available except to university graduates. In any case, the second alternative should be immediately pursued. University education must be placed in its proper perspective in relation to employment opportunities, and the desire to obtain some sort of a degree only to get employment thereafter discouraged.

It has been urged that there is no positive evidence to support the view that the rush for university education arises out of a desire for employment, or, to put it in a different form, that the elimination of the degree requirement for public services would to any appreciable extent reduce this rush. In a matter like this it is extremely difficult, if not impossible, to collect evidence which would establish casual relationship between the two phenomena, namely, the rush for university education, on the one hand, and the desire for employment on the other. In fact, it would be simplifying matters unduly if the desire for employment were regarded as the only reason for the congestion at universities. There are certainly other reasons, not the least of which is the absence of employment opportunities at the pre-university stage. The fact that there is unemployment on a large scale among the middle classes is certainly one of the reasons why in the absence of any better occupation, both parents and students find the continuance of education the only useful occupation. From our experience, and this was corroborated by those of the witnesses who appeared before us, it is not different to conclude that many students enter universities merely because at this stage they have nothing better to do. Nevertheless, there is no doubt that the hope of improving their prospects of getting employment is an important factor which induces many students to enter universities. Recruitment is also effected on an *ad hoc* basis, direct by the Commissions or other Government agencies.

The desire for employment is at least an important consideration which induces students to take up university education. If such employment, or at least a proportion of it, could be made available to persons without university education, there will at least be one factor less contributing to overcrowding at universities. Besides, if a proportion of students could be drawn into the services at the end of their school careers, the number of persons who would continue with university education in the absence of better occupation would also be correspondingly reduced.

The second view referred to above, namely, that competence and academic attainment cannot be measured by university degrees, in the opinion of the Committee, goes to the other extreme. To dispense with academic qualifications altogether and to rely on competitive recruitment examinations in order to ensure maintenance of intellectual standards in public services would, in our opinion, be unwise. It is, of course, possible to point to stray cases in which persons have obtained high intellectual and cultural standards completely outside the universities. Instances can be cited of literary geniuses like Shakespeare and Rabindranath Tagore who have never had any university education. Genius has no law, but to base a scheme on such exceptions would be dangerous. The fact, on the other hand, remains that university education, apart from the intellectual standard that goes with it, does carry certain cultural values and a maturity of outlook. These values cannot be assessed by examinations, however thorough. There is no system of examination so far conceived that can completely and correctly assess the total personality of an individual. Personality is a complex phenomenon and is built up through a variety of experiences, of which experience in a university is an important one. However poor the university standard may be, its contribution to the development of personality cannot be altogether ignored. Nor should university education be condemned because the present standard of such education in our country is not uniformly high. If the standard of university education is not as high in India as it should be, our efforts should be directed towards improving the standard. To condemn university education or to ignore it because we fail to improve the standard is at best a counsel of despair. We must presume, therefore, that the very fact that a person has passed through a university and done the usual course carries with it some assurance that he has developed a certain degree of personality. There is no means of judging with complete assurance to what extent this personality has been developed by those who have not had this experience.

A view has been put forward by some of our colleagues that university education should be dissociated from employment prospects. It has been argued that as long as these two are connected, university atmosphere will continue to be vitiated by the influx into the universities of persons whose main, if not only, objective is to obtain some advantage in the matter of employment. We appreciate the high idealism which inspires this view and which seeks to maintain the purity of academic education. We do not agree, however, that elimination of the degree qualification from public service requirements will lead to the objective which the advocates of this view have in mind. There is no doubt that at the highest levels of public services there is need for persons who have attained high intellectual and cultural standards. Organised opportunities for attainment of such standards exist, at present, only in the universities. The public services, therefore, have a definite need for persons trained in these universities. Employment in these spheres cannot, as a consequence, be divorced entirely from university education, nor would it be in the larger public interest to do so. Our colleagues who advocate this view under discussion would rely on a sufficiently searching recruitment examination for entry into the public services and would eliminate degree requirements. It is admitted by them however that as long as a high standard of recruitment examination is maintained, very few persons without university training are likely to succeed in such competitive examinations. Those ambitious to enter at these levels would therefore continue to avail themselves of the training which university education has to offer, for they would realise that it is only by doing so that they would have any reasonable chance of fulfilling their ambitions. As long as this is so, a complete divorce between university education and employment prospects is not possible, and there is no way of ensuring that persons who go in for university education do so solely because of their love for such education.

On these grounds, we are of the opinion that university degrees cannot and should not be dispensed with entirely. There is no doubt however that there has been exaggerated emphasis on such degrees in our country for reasons which have already been stated. A re-examination of the requirements in relation to the different levels of Government services is, therefore, what is required. For this purpose we have broadly divided public services into three categories:

(a) Senior Officers—Executive and Administrative.

(b) Junior Officers—Executive and Administrative.

(c) Clerical Services.

The first category, namely, that of senior executive and administrative services, would include the All India Services as well as the Central and State Class I Services where persons would be required to take important decisions and have intimate acquaintance with the policy-making activities of the Government. As an illustration, it may be stated that the services to which recruitment is now made on the results of the Combined Competitive Examinations held by the Union Public Service Commission for recruiting to the I.A.S., I.F.S., etc., and the services which are described as Class I Executive Services in the State Governments would fall under this category. The third category would comprise the clerical or ministerial services where duties are of a routine nature. All the rest will come under the second category.

In classifying the services in these three categories we have excluded those of a technical and professional nature for which special considerations would apply. By technical services we mean those that require not merely specialised experience but qualifications or training of a technical nature. There is a tendency today for all services to be more and more specialised. This, however, only means that those services have to be manned by persons who have acquired some specialised experience of these branches of activity. They are not, strictly speaking, technical services. On the other hand, there are services like engineering which require special training and qualifications. These are the services that can rightly be regarded as technical services. There are, besides, what may be termed professional services, such as services relating to law, medicine and teaching. These technical and professional services we have excluded from our purview.

In our opinion, a university degree should definitely not be insisted upon for the clerical services. We would in fact go a step further, and while we would not disqualify graduates from entering the clerical services, we would discourage them from doing so. This, we feel, can best be done by fixing the age limits at suitable levels which would preclude graduates from entering this service. Against the background of the reorganised system of education to which we have referred, we would suggest that for clerical services the age limit should be 17-19. When the new system of education comes into force, it would not be possible for anyone to obtain a degree before the age of 20. To fix the maximum age limit at 19 would therefore preclude graduates from competing for such services.

This, we feel, will have a distinct advantage. Persons who are interested in services of this type would know as soon as they complete the Secondary school stage that they would have to compete for these services without going in for a university course. In fact, those who do go in for university course will do so with the realisation that the clerical services would be closed to them. There will thus be no question of any disillusionment at the end of university career arising out of a graduate not being able to get even a clerical post.

It has, however, been pointed out to us that for certain types of employment it would not be appropriate to insist rigidly on the age limit 17-19 recommended by us. There are posts in certain departments which are grouped with the clerical services mainly because they carry the clerical rates of pay. They are lower executive in nature and in some cases carry a marked degree of responsibility, though not perhaps much of discretion. Such posts to which our attention has in particular been drawn are posts in the lower formations of the Revenue, Railway and Communication Departments. Normally, even in such cases it should be possible to recruit at the age level suggested by us and to give the recruits adequate training for a sufficiently long period to enable them to discharge their duties satisfactorily. This, however, naturally presumes that recruitment will be made in due anticipation of the requirements by the Departments concerned. In an expanding economy where the State has, without sufficient notice, to undertake new activities, such planned anticipation is not always possible. A new taxation introduced in a new financial year may well require a large number of tax collectors for whom there is no time to be trained. In such emergent situations it would hardly be possible to entrust the responsibilities to persons of the age level contemplated by us. A higher level of maturity is obviously called for. We agree that in such circumstances there would be a good ground for deviating from the general recommendation we have made.

We suggest that each such case should be considered on its merits, and slightly higher age levels introduced as and where found necessary.

For the middle category we are of the opinion that a university degree should not be made the minimum qualification, but that graduates should be given an opportunity to compete, if they so desire. We, therefore, suggest that the age limit for this group of services should be 19-21. This would render services of this nature open to non-graduates as well as to graduates.

Finally, for the top-most grades we are definitely of the opinion that entry into these services should be restricted to graduates. This view is based on our opinion that for the highest Executive and Administrative Services a maturity of outlook and cultural standard is required which, by and large, can naturally be expected of graduates. For these services, therefore, we recommend the age level of 21 to 23.

It will be noted that for all levels of Government service we have recommended a span of two years as against the usual span of three years between the minimum and the maximum age limits. This recommendation has been made deliberately because we are of the opinion that the mental qualities as also the personality can best be tested in one or, at the most, two examinations. A person who fails to come up to "the standard" in the first two examinations may, on the basis of his experience of the examinations and having acquired the technique thereof, be successful in the third. Such success, however, does not necessarily reflect the innate qualities of the candidate. We have also noted that under the present system of three examinations, the first examination is often taken by the candidates without that degree of seriousness that should normally go with such an effort. It is often taken only in order to acquire some experience of the technique of examinations. This leads to the number of candidates being unnecessarily multiplied, thus adding to the administrative problem of holding examinations. Two chances would obviate this disadvantage and, to that extent, would be of benefit.

We have made no mention so far about the Scheduled Castes and other Backward Classes. We would like to point out that our recommendations are made on the basis that the concessions enjoyed by the Scheduled Castes, Scheduled Tribes and other Backward Classes are not in any way affected.

We would like to mention at this stage that our recommendation throwing open clerical as well as the middle level of Government services to non-graduates is based on the assumption that recruitment to these levels is on the basis of open competitive examinations. We are of the opinion that for these levels it is not necessary to insist on a high level of intellectual and cultural attainment. The standard expected of persons who have passed the School Final under the reorganised system is sufficient for these levels, but it is necessary to ensure that this standard is tested in an examination. Where such recruitment examinations are not held, it would be necessary to fall back, as at present, on university degrees which, in the absence of any other objective test, would guarantee at least a minimum standard of the qualities required for the posts. We recommend that as far as possible individual posts should be grouped together in organised services and competitive examinations held for recruitment to such services, and that the age levels and the educational qualifications should be as suggested by us. Where however, such examinations are not possible a higher standard of qualification should be maintained.

Interim Arrangements: Our recommendations, as already stated, have been conceived against the background of the proposed educational reorganisation. The period which lapses before the reorganised system is adopted should, we feel, be utilised in giving notice to the future recruits about the proposed changes for admission to the recruitment examinations. We recognise that a reasonable period of notice before the introduction of the new scheme is essential to avoid hardship. Persons who have embarked on a course of university education and have perhaps faced difficulties, financial and otherwise, in the hope of obtaining employment under the Government should not certainly find employment prospects disappear on account of a change in the recruitment policy. An interim period of notice is therefore essential for a transition to the new system and we recommend accordingly.

General Recommendations

Recruitment Examinations: We have suggested that the degree qualification should be abolished for the lower and middle levels of public services. We have however recommended that it should continue for the top levels. For all levels of Government service however we are of the opinion that recruitment examinations of adequate standard should be held for the selection of candidates. We would like to make the following observations regarding the nature of such examinations.

The examination should be of a comprehensive nature and should test the mental qualities rather than merely the memory or the fund of information of the candidates. Every paper in the examination for the higher services should be of the Honours standard and every candidate for such services should be required to take at least two subjects. The questions set at the examination should be so framed as to test the capacity of the candidates for rational thinking as well as their sense of values. The questions should deal with the significant phases of the subject and emphasise evaluation and rational thinking. They should compel the candidates to integrate their ideas and draw upon the entire background of their knowledge and also test the candidates' reaction to different circumstances. The questions should also test the mental alertness of the candidates and offer scope for originality of thought and expression.

In addition to these tests, there should also be some test for judging the personality, attitude of candidates. Their past career may offer some insight into these and, in addition, the first three months of the probationary period should be used for forming a correct idea about their personality. Obviously, unsuitable candidates may during these three months be weeded out by a properly constituted Board in consultation with the Public Service Commission. One way of ensuring that the candidates derive full benefit from their period of probation may be to evaluate their achievements during this period and add it to the competitive examination marks for determining their final ranking in the services.

Method of Promotion: A point of view has been expressed before us that lowering the academic standard for certain levels of Government service may be unobjectionable so far as work at those levels is concerned, but that it would have the disadvantage of not qualifying such persons for promotion to higher posts. It has been argued, for instance, that a non-graduate who is appointed as an Executive Officer under a State Government or to a Class II post at the Centre may function satisfactorily enough on these posts. In making such appointments however it would be wrong to confine our view to the particular posts or services to which such persons are appointed. It should be open to every individual in the public services to rise to the highest post available on the basis of his merit. Unless such prospects are available, frustration is bound to creep in, and this will reduce the value and efficiency of the service. A non-graduate, on the other hand, however good he may be for the post to which he is appointed is not likely, it is argued, to have the mental calibre necessary for rising to the highest post in the superior services. To that extent, their promotion will be limited and a feeling of frustration created.

We have considered this problem and we appreciate the validity of the point raised. We have, on the other hand, had evidence to show that a graduate is not always superior in merit to a non-graduate. Several State Governments informed us that there have been numerous instances in which in written examinations non-graduates have successfully beaten graduates who have competed with them. This is specially true where the written examination is conducted not on a purely academic basis but is limited to the work of the department in which it is held. Nevertheless, it cannot be denied that absence of higher education may, to some extent, render persons unfit for promotion to higher posts. We have recommended that university education need not be insisted upon except for the higher levels of Government services. We appreciate that an influx of non-graduates at the lower levels which this recommendation envisages may render a review of promotion prospects necessary. We recommend that such reviews should be undertaken on the basis of actual experience. At the same time it is necessary to ensure that promotions are not denied to non-graduates merely because of certain prejudices against such persons. It is necessary that their merit should be decided in a purely objective manner. We therefore recommend that as far as possible promotion from grade to grade should be made on the basis of departmental examinations. We appreciate that for all levels of Government services and on all occasions this may not be possible. We do feel however that the system of departmental examinations should be utilised to a larger extent than it is at present, especially in established cadres. We therefore recommend that the Government should not only review promotion quotas at present fixed but also undertake re-examination of the methods of promotion, and, to the extent possible, institute departmental examinations particularly in respect of organised services.

Training: We have given careful attention to the question of training of recruits to the various levels of public services. The problem of training is an important one, and there are reasons to believe that one of the reasons for thedifficulty in maintaining a high standard of efficiency in the public services lies in the fact that it has been difficult for the training course of recruits to keep pace with the very much increased rate of recruitment to the expanded services. The administrative problem of training which the expansion of services has created is not only highly important but a very complicated one. We appreciate however that it is beyond the Terms of Reference of this Committee to examine this general problem. Nevertheless, we have a special responsibility in this matter. We have recommended that persons should be recruited to the lowest and the middle levels at ages which are much below those prevailing at present. Our recommendations also envisage that at the lowest levels the recruits would all be non-graduates, and at the middle level a proportion of them would have no university education. The comparative immaturity which goes with lower age levels and the lack of university education in a large proportion of Government servants intensify the need for adequate training before such persons are called upon to discharge the duties for which they are recruited. We therefore consider it an essential part of our recommendations that a proper scheme of training for all levels of Government service should be accepted and implemented by the Governments both at the Centre and in the States. In this Report we can give only an outline of the training which we envisage as the basic minimum. Further details will obviously have to be worked out by the Governments themselves.

For the lower levels of Government service, particularly at the clerical level, training will obviously have to be decentralised. We contemplate training at this level to be given in the districts, preferably at one centre for a group of districts. The period of training should be at least one year and should consist not only of professional items such as typing, maintenance of files, noting, drafting, etc., but also instruction in general subjects aimed at giving the recruits a general education to render them not only good clerks but useful citizens. For the higher levels of Government services a similar scheme should be adopted. In this connection a point of view which has been expressed before us is that at least for the highest level, like the All-India Services, it would be useful to entrust the training to some selected universities. It has been argued that by doing so we shall help to break the barrier which exists at present between Government servants and the general public. While there is undoubtedly considerable force in this suggestion, we feel that the balance of advantage would lie in the Governments themselves organising courses of training with such help as may be necessary from the universities instead of seconding the probationers to a course of study at one of the universities. At the highest level we do envisage a university degree as the minimum qualification. All the recruits to these services, therefore, would have spent a number of years at a university and no useful purpose would therefore be served by sending them back to a university for a further period. On the other hand, there would certainly be considerable advantage in using the facilities which universities have to offer in order to impart instruction in subjects which are important for the training of the higher civil servants. Social subjects, particularly Economics, are of the highest importance in the present context in administration. To a lesser extent a knowledge of Law is essential for the Administrative Services. Instruction in these subjects may well be arranged in co-operation with the universities. We therefore recommend that the courses of training should be arranged in consultation with and with the cooperation of the universities but under the auspices of the appropriate Government department.

We are also of the opinion that for the highest executive and administrative services a period of training abroad after they have seen different parts of India would be highly useful. This will not only help to broaden the outlook of the recruits generally but also help to develop in them an All-India outlook by enabling them to view our own country from outside and give them a more correct perspective of her needs and aspirations.

Limitation of Numbers: The Terms of Reference of this Committee have drawn our attention to the problem of numbers that would inevitably arise from any lowering of academic standards. There is no doubt that if non-graduates are allowed to compete for the various services, larger numbers would apply for these services than would have applied if applicants were limited to graduates. This increase in numbers may well create a serious administrative problem. Apart from the problem of arranging for the examination of large numbers of candidates, the question would arise of maintaining a uniform standard with respect to all those who appear at such an examination. It is well known that uniformity in the assessment of examination is conducted by a number of examiners who do not necessarily follow the same standard of assessment. The problem arises as soon as the number of examiners is more than one. But it can be kept under control so long as the number is reasonably small. With the increase in the number of examinees the number of examiners has to be increased proportionately and the problem of maintaining uniformity among a very large number of examiners throws up a problem of considerable complexity. To meet this problem of numbers, a suggestion has been made that a system of deposits should be insisted on from all examinees. These deposits should be refundable to candidates who secure the prescribed minimum percentage of marks but should be forfeited in the case of those who do not even attain this standard. The fear of forfeiture, it is hoped, will deter frivolous candidates who have no reasonable chance of successfully competing at the examination and will thus help to reduce the number of examinees. The suggestion is an attractive one but it has been opposed on behalf of several institutions and organisations on the ground that it would penalise the poor candidates more than the rich. The system of deposits would be no deterrent to the rich and the well-to-do even if they chose to be frivolous, but would impose a real hardship on those who are hard put to collect the money for deposit. We agree with this criticism and are unable to recommend a system which is obviously open to the criticism of being particularly hard on poorer candidates. As an alternative, we would suggest that where the number of examinees is very large, a system of weeding out by preliminary examination may be adopted. The preliminary examination should be restricted to one or two simple written papers which would test the general alertness and mental calibre of the candidates concerned. As a result of this preliminary test a number of candidates equal to a given multiple of the number to be finally recruited should be selected for the final examination. It is true that the preliminary examination would be subject to the same defect of lack of uniformity as for any examination where large numbers appear. For a preliminary examination however lack of uniformity is not necessarily a serious disadvantage, provided deviations from the norm are not very great As a result of this examination a much larger number would be selected for the final examination than there are vacancies. So long as a liberal margin is allowed, it would not make any serious difference whether a few persons at the margin are or are not allowed to compete for the final examination, because the marginal candidates would not have a serious chance of being finally recruited.

A point which has been brought to our notice often in the course of our discussions is the lack of uniformity in the standards of the various universities all over the country. The same degree or diploma given by two different universities often involves two entirely different standards. A B.A. or a Ph.D. of one university is not necessarily of the same standard as a B.A. or a Ph.D. of another. This is a problem which we are informed has engaged the attention of the education authorities but has defied solution so far on the ground that there is no objective standard on the basis of which the degrees awarded by different universities could be measured. The problem is, however, important from the point of view of the recruitment policy of the Government. We have recommended that a degree should be made a prerequisite qualification for the highest levels of Government service. This recommendation would be without significance if the degree did not at least approximately measure up to a certain standard of academic and cultural attainment. We appreciate, however, that the problem is complicated and a solution must be left to the authorities in charge of higher education in this country. We do feel however that recruiting authorities like Public Service Commissions may help considerably in devising an objective standard for assessing the value of education given by the different universities and thus help the authorities concerned to introduce some uniformity in this respect. We recommend that Public Service Commissions should publish annually tabulated results of the examinations held by them, analysing the marks obtained by candidates from different universities in different subjects. The results thus tabulated would speak for themselves and the long-term trends would clearly indicate the quality of the products of different universities in different subjects in which they are trained. Such materials would provide an objective basis on which the quality of the training imparted by different universities can be assessed.

COMMITTEE TO STUDY THE QUESTION OF FORMULATING UNIFORM STANDARDS IN RESPECT OF EDUCATION AND REGULATION OF PRACTICE OF VAIDYAS, HAKIMS AND HOMOEOPATHS, 1955—FINAL REPORT

New Delhi, Ministry of Health, 1956. 129p.

Chairman : Shri Dayashankar Trikamji Dave.
Members : Shri A. A. Rahim (resigned); Shri Shanti Lal H. Shah; Shri Mehdi Nawaz Jung; Shri A. D. Mukherji.
Adviser : Shri Vasudevbhai M. Dwivedi.
Secretary : Dr. H. B. N. Swift.
Joint Secretaries : Dr. P. M. Mehta; Dr. C L. Malhotra.

APPOINTMENT

In pursuance of the Resolution passed by the Central Council of Health at Trivandrum at their third meeting held on January 23 to 25, 1955, the Government of India appointed vide their letter No. F. 8-11/55M, dated April 27, 1955, a Committee to study and report on the question of establishing uniform standards in respect of education and regulation of practice of Vaidyas, Hakims, and Homoeopaths.

TERMS OF REFERENCE

1. To survey the existing facilities for teaching in Ayurvedic, Unani and Homoeopathic systems of medicine;

2. To recommend specific measures to be taken to improve facilities for training and to establish uniform standards of education in these systems;

3. To make suggestions for the regulation of practice in these systems of medicine including the desirability of State control.

If the opinion of the Committee be in favour of State control, the Committee should examine the Draft Legislation prepared by this Ministry and recommend what modifications, if any, are necessary and submit a Model Draft Legislation. The Committee may also recommend whether the Model Draft Legislation submitted by it should be enacted by the Union Government or by the respective State Governments.

CONTENTS

Introduction; Courses of Instruction for Ayurvedic and Unani Systems of Medicine; Course of Instruction for Homoeopathy; Councils and Directorate; Post-Graduate Instruction and Research; Summary of Recommendations; Conclusion; Appendices I to VI.

RECOMMENDATIONS

1. There must be uniform standard of training.

2. (i) Two Councils should be created similar to the Indian Medical Council which will have control over the maintenance of uniform teaching standards in all the institutions: one Council shall be for Ayurvedic and Unani Systems of Medicine and the other for Homoeopathy. The Councils may be called:

(1) The Central Council of Ayurvedic and Unani Systems of Medicine, and

(2) The Central Council for Homoeopathic System of Medicine.

(ii) The composition of the Council may be as follows:

(1) One member from each State to be nominated by the State Government;

(2) One member from each Indian University, which possesses a Faculty of Ayurvedic, Unani and/or Homoeopathy, to be nominated by the Vice-Chancellor;

(3) Four members to be nominated by the Central Government.

(iii) The first Council will be nominated with a nominated President.

3. The existing institutions should be upgraded so that they can efficiently impart education in these systems.

4. (i) A five-and-a-half year course of study including one year for Internship is recommended with at least three months' training in the rural areas.

(ii) Admission—Intermediate Science examination with Physics, Chemistry and Biology or Higher Secondary examination. Good knowledge of Sanskrit and Arabic or Persian is essential for Ayurveda and Unani respectively.

(iii) Minimum age of the candidates should be 17 years.

5. Next textbooks subjectwise should be written; and those already existing should be revised. The State Governments and Universities should encourage this.

6. The training and syllabus prescribed should be taken up by separate Faculties for Ayurvedic and Unani Systems of Medicine. It is desirable that these Faculties be affiliated to the Universities, if possible.

7. The Pharmacopoeia and Dictionary of Ayurvedic and Unani Systems of Medicine should be compiled.

8. A five-and-a-half-year degree course should be introduced for Homoeopathy four-and-a-half-year course with one year's internship. The course for Homoeopathy would be more or less in the lines suggested by the Homoeopathy Inquiry Committee (1949).

9. All the teaching institutions should have indoor hospital beds and the ratio of students to beds should be 1 : 5.

10. The degrees to be given to the graduates should be:

(1) "G.A.M.S."—Graduate of Ayurvedic Medicine and Surgery;

(2) "G.U.M.S."—Graduate of Unani Medicine and Surgery; and

(3) "G.H.M.S."—Graduate of Homoeopathic Medicine and Surgery.

11. Separate Directorates for (a) Ayurvedic and Unani and (b) Homoeopathic Systems of Medicine should be created in the Central Ministry of Health, Government of India, and also in the States as far as possible.

12. Post-Graduate training and research facilities should be given to all the three systems at suitable places and also to Graduates of Modern Medicine. The duration of the Post-Graduate Course shall be of two years.

13. Refresher courses in Ayurveda, Unani and Homoeopathy should be organised in teaching institutions

COMMITTEE TO STUDY THE QUESTION OF FORMULATING UNIFORM STANDARDS IN RESPECT OF EDUCATION AND REGULATION OF PRACTICE OF VAIDYAS, HAKIMS AND HOMOEOPATHS, 1955—INTERIM REPORT

Delhi, Manager of Publications, 1956. 144p.

Chairman : Shri Dayashankar Trikamji Dave.
Members : Shri A. A. Rahim; Shri Shanti Lal H. Shah; Shri Mehdi Nawaz Jung; Shri A. D. Mukherji.
Adviser : Shri Vasudevbhai M. Dwivedi.
Secretary : Dr. H. B. N. Swift.
Joint Secretaries : Dr. P. M. Mehta; Dr. C. L. Malhotra.

APPOINTMENT

In pursuance of the Resolution passed by the Central Council of Health at Trivandrum at their third meeting held on January 23 to 25, 1955, the Government of India appointed vide their letter No. F. 8-11/55M, dated April 27, 1955, a committee to study and report on the question of establishing uniform standards in respect of Education and Regulation of Practice of Vaidyas, Hakims, and Homoeopaths.

TERMS OF REFERENCE

1. To survey the existing facilities for teaching in Ayurvedic, Unani and Homoeopathic systems of medicine;

2. To recommend specific measures to be taken to improve facilities for training and to establish uniform standards of education in these systems;

3. To make suggestions for the regulation of practice in these systems of medicine including the desirability of State control.

If the opinion of the Committee be in favour of State control, the Committee should examine the Draft legislation prepared by this Ministry and recommend what modifications, if any, are necessary and submit a model draft legislation. The Committee may also recommend whether the model draft legislation submitted by it should be enacted by the Union Government or by the respective State Governments.

CONTENTS

Introduction; Appointment of the Committee; Terms of Reference; Recommendations of the Committee; Appendices from I to VIII.

RECOMMENDATIONS

1. There should be separate registers for Ayurveda, Unani and Homoeopathy.

2. Persons who are of 15 years' standing prior to the appointed day will be on the register along with the institutionally qualified persons and that the rest who have two years' practice on the appointed day should be on a list.

3. Fees should be levied for registration. The amount may however be left to the discretion of each State. Whether only initial registration fee should be charged

or a renewal fee also should be charged may also be left to the discretion of each State.

4. Initially there should be a nominated body to control the practitioners for three years and subsequent bodies may be partly elected and partly nominated.

5. Not more than one-third of the members in the board should be nominated and that the Director, Indigenous Systems of Medicine, if any, or the Officer incharge of the Indigenous Systems of Medicine or a Government nominee should be ex-officio member of the Council. The composition of the Board should be such as the State may think expedient.

6. There should be separate registers for practitioners in Ayurvedic and Unani and Homoeopathic systems. If the number of practitioners exceeded 100 a separate board should be constituted otherwise a joint register and board are favoured in so far as the Ayurvedic and Unani are concerned. Homoeopathy should have a separate register and a separate board.

7. The privileges should be given only to Registered Practitioners and not to Enlisted Practitioners.

8. Registered Medical Practitioners of Ayurvedic, Unani and Homoeopathic systems of medicine should be treated with regard to the privileges mentioned earlier at par with the practitioners in modern medicine.

9. Unregistered or Unenlisted Practitioners can practise in rural areas as defined by the State which have no Registered Practitioners.

10. The term of office of the Board should ordinarily be five years. The first Board (a nominated one) shall be for three years.

11. So far as professional conduct and practice are concerned there should be separate registration by each State bearing in mind the above principles laid down for the sake of uniformity and there should be reciprocity of registration.

12. For regulating academic teaching and standards the control should vest with the Central Body so constituted.

13. The State legislation should be passed within two years and should not await Central legislation.

14. The legislation about Homoeopathy should also be on similar lines. Central legislation embracing regulation of practice, professional ethics and teaching would not be feasible. Since the subject medical qualification is a concurrent subject the Central Body may be a coordinating body exercising control over academic standards and teaching.

15. The Medical Degrees Act should be amended so that the use of a bogus degree in Ayurveda, Unani and Homoeopathy can be prohibited.

16. In case of States which have existing legislation the question of registration and enlistment need not be reopened, but the amendments may be made to bring the legislation in line with our recommendations.

AD HOC COMMITTEE ON SLAUGHTER-HOUSES AND MEAT INSPECTION PRACTICES, 1955—REPORT

New Delhi, Ministry of Food and Agriculture, 1957. 166p.

Chairman : Dr. S. Datta.
Members : Shri S. R. Chadha; Shri H. S. Bawa; Shri V. A. Mehta; Dr. K. Mitra (replaced by Dr. Y. K. Subrahmanyam).
Secretary : Shri R. N. Mohan.

APPOINTMENT

The Ad Hoc Committee on Slaughter-Houses and Meat Inspection Practices was constituted under the Ministry of Food and Agriculture vide their Resolution No. F. 25-2/54-LS, dated May 11, 1955.

TERMS OF REFERENCE

(i) (a) To examine the existing slaughter-houses and meat inspection practices; and

(b) To make suitable recommendations for the purpose of ensuring arrangements in such States as possess or could provide the necessary facilities for ante- and post-mortem examination carried out by veterinarians so as to conform to the regulations of the U.K., the U.S.A., etc.

(ii) (a) To examine the report of the Pharmaceutical Enquiry Committee in regard to improving the supply of animal glands and organs for the manufacture of hormones and glandular products;

(b) To examine the proposal for the establishment of an experimental *abattoir* with facilities for collection and storage of glands to serve as a model for other slaughter-houses; and

(c) To make suitable recommendations in this regard.

Subsequently, problems relating to export of meat, especially piggery products, were also referred to the Committee by the Government of India.

CONTENTS

Introduction; Programme of Work; Slaughter-House; Production and Inspection of Meat; Slaughter-House By-products; Export Trade in Casings; Utilization of Animal Glands and Organs; Export Trade in Meat; Control and Improvement of Meat Inspection; Summary and Recommendations; Appendices I to XII.

RECOMMENDATIONS

Slaughter-Houses

All urban slaughter-houses as well as the butchers and flayers working there should be licensed, and entry to slaughter-houses strictly regulated.

Greater proportion of the income derived from slaughter-houses should be spent on their upkeep, efficient running and improvement.

Slaughtering fees, where these are low, should be suitably enhanced as far as possible.

For accommodating animals awaiting slaughter, every slaughter-house should have a properly constructed lairage, and this should afford protection against sun and rain, allow ample supply of drinking water and provide sufficient accommodation as well as satisfactory arrangements for securing and handling animals for facilitating a quick but careful ante-mortem examination of individual animals.

The general construction and orientation of the lairage, slaughter hall, etc., should be such that the animals awaiting slaughter are not able to see the slaughtering and other operations.

All such urban slaughter-houses as have now fallen within or very close to inhabited areas should be closed down and new slaughter-houses, designed on modern lines and well provided with requisite arrangements and facilities for efficiently conducting the slaughtering, flaying, dressing and all other operations, should be set up well away from inhabited areas. In selecting the new sites, future expansion of the towns should be taken into consideration, and adequate space should be provided for future development of the slaughter-house and for locating around it the various ancillary trades.

In the meantime, all necessary structural alterations and other improvements should be made in the existing slaughter-houses to facilitate slaughter and the various operations before and after slaughter.

In slaughter-houses handling much larger numbers than they were designed for arrangements should be made for slaughter in suitably regulated shifts to relieve congestion and to facilitate operations and inspection.

Production And Inspection Of Meat

Better arrangements for the carriage of animals to slaughter-houses should be provided, and the railway wagons meant for animal transport should be so constructed that they do not become excessively hot during summer or unbearably cold during winter.

Livestock markets should be located as close to the slaughter-houses as possible.

All animals before slaughter should be rested for at least 12 hours in the lairage.

It should be made incumbent on all Municipalities and Local Boards to engage adequate number of Veterinary Officers and to provide the requisite facilities for carrying out proper ante-mortem examination in all slaughter-houses; proper maintenance of records of all animals rejected on ante-mortem examination should be insisted upon.

Gimbals and hooks for hoisting carcases must be provided in sufficient numbers in all slaughter-houses to facilitate flaying and dressing as well as post-mortem examination.

Post-mortem inspection by qualified Veterinary Officers should be made compulsory at all slaughter-houses and should be rigidly enforced by the State Governments, and for this purpose the Municipalities and Local Boards must employ adequate veterinary staff to be determined by the number of animals slaughtered each day and provide all necessary facilities for conducting the examination.

Incinerators or rendering-down plants should be provided in all large slaughter-houses.

Maintenance of proper records of all condemned organs, etc., should be insisted upon.

Municipalities should provide suitable cold-storage at slaughter-houses for storing dressed carcases and glands and organs wherever required.

They should also ensure proper sanitary conditions for the transport and sale of meat and, at least in big cities, provide fly-proof motor transport and cold-storage facilities in the main meat markets or encourage private enterprise to do so.

Slaughter-House Byproducts

Systematic collection, efficient preservation and processing, and full utilization of all slaughter-house by-products and wastes should be properly organised in all towns.

Gut-washing tanks and other facilities for timely washing and clearing of the intestines should be provided in all slaughter-houses.

All slaughter-houses should provide and maintain in workable condition adequate hoisting arrangements to facilitate proper flaying and dressing, and the use of modern tools by flayers should be insisted upon. Curing salt and modern flaying tools should be made available for sale on slaughter-house premises. Flayers should also be fully trained and licensed, and rules for the examination of flayers, conditions of licence, etc., should be framed on an all-India basis. Sale of hides and skins should be on the basis of their quality—for which a reliable system of grading should be introduced—and sale by forward contract should be forbidden. Hide-curing yards should be provided at or close to slaughter-houses.

Special bleeding rails and channels for collecting blood free from admixture with ingesta, etc., should be provided in all urban slaughter-houses. It should be made obligatory on the authorities in charge of urban slaughter-houses to ensure proper collection of blood and its processing for use as animal feed, manure, etc., and in big cities also for pharmaceutical purposes.

Export Trade In Casings

Until conditions in respect of production and inspection of meat can be improved throughout the country, big slaughter-houses where large numbers of animals are slaughtered should be modernised and provided with efficient ante- and post-mortem examination services and suitable facilities for collection, cleaning and handling of the intestines.

The Government of India should then arrange for the required certification and take up with the U.K., the U.S.A. and other countries the question of casings produced at these slaughter-houses being accepted by them. For this purpose, the recommendations made for "Export Trade in Meat" should be implemented.

The Government should also arrange for licensing and regular inspection of all casings manufacturing concerns to ensure observance of necessary sanitary precautions in the handling, processing and packing of this material meant for human consumption.

The Government of India should provide the technical know-how and other facilities, such as machinery required for complete processing, sterilisation and grading of surgical cat-gut in India.

Utilisation Of Animal Glands And Organs

Steps should be taken to make India self-sufficient in its requirements of glandular preparations as quickly as possible and thereby save much valuable foreign exchange which is at present being expended on importing large quantities of such products.

All slaughter-houses in large cities, especially Bombay, Calcutta, Madras and Delhi, should be modernised or rebuilt and equipped with arrangements for expeditious collection of glands and organs and for storing them in cold-storage.

Centralisation of all slaughter in big cities would no doubt greatly facilitate collection and utilisation of glands and organs, but the responsibility of constructing and maintaining model slaughter-houses need not be taken over directly by the Government.

The responsibility of collecting glands and organs and supplying them to pharmaceutical concerns should be taken over by the municipalities and they should suitably compensate the butchers for the extra labour involved in expeditious removal of the glands.

It should be obligatory on the butchers to part with any of the carcase that may be required by the Municipality on payment of a reasonable price.

Butchers should be provided with suitable containers surrounded by crushed ice for chilling glands immediately on collection, and they should be duly compensated for the extra labour involved in expeditious removal of the glands.

The prices of glands and organs should be fixed from time to time by special boards consisting of a representative of the State Government, a representative of the Municipality, and a representative of the pharmaceutical industry. These boards should also settle other problems relating to collection and utilisation of animal glands and organs.

Pharmaceutical concerns should be allowed to purchase glands, organs, etc., required by them only from slaughter-houses certified for the purpose.

The Government of India should arrange for regular inspection of all pharmaceutical concerns engaged in the manufacture of glandular preparations.

Some veterinarians should be deputed to selected foreign countries for training in collection and preservation of glands and organs and their utilisation to best advantage by the pharmaceutical industry.

Well-coordinated programmes of research on the preparation and utilisation of glands and organs for preparing glandular and other pharmaceutical products should be planned and at least one well-equipped research unit for the purpose should be established. Research on this subject should also be undertaken at Research Institutes, such as the Haffkine Institute, Bombay, Indian Institute of Science, Bangalore, Indian Veterinary Research Institute, Izatnagar, and the Central Drugs Research Institute, Lucknow.

Export Trade In Meat

The Government of India should take all necessary steps to promote the export of meat and meat products and thereby earn valuable foreign exchange, and for this purpose they should arrange for proper veterinary certification, inspection of the premises concerned, and such other facilities, etc., as may be required from time to time. It is further recommended that the Government of India should appoint immediately a veterinarian of high status and adequate experience of certifying meats, with adequate staff to assist him, to

(i) make expeditiously interim arrangements for

export of meat, especially piggery products and buffalo flesh,

(ii) inspect and certify slaughter-houses and meat-packing factories for export of meat and meat products,

(iii) organise throughout the country inspection of all meat and slaughter - house products meant for export,

(iv) organise inspection of meat, etc. imported into India, and

(v) keep in touch with the import regulations and requirements of veterinary certification prescribed by the importing countries from time to time.

Control And Improvement Of Meat Inspection

There should be a comprehensive legislation governing the location, construction and management of slaughter-houses, meat inspection practices. and all other allied matters.

Ante-mortem and post-mortem examination of all food animals, as also inspection of all human food derived from animals, should be entrusted only to fully qualified veterinarians. As veterinarians have already started becoming available in larger numbers, the implementation of this recommendation should not be delayed, and municipalities should offer sufficiently remunerative salaries commensurate with the training and experience required and the duties entrusted.

At the same time, the Sanitary Inspectors at present engaged in this work in slaughter-houses should be suitably trained further in the technique of meat inspection. The State Governments may consider starting short-term training courses for this purpose.

A separate Meat Inspection Service should be created for ensuring efficient working of slaughter-houses and proper meat inspection, by integrating the veterinarians and the sanitary inspectors engaged in meat inspection work. This Meat Inspection Service should form part of an over-all Veterinary Public Health Organisation. The veterinary inspectors engaged in meat inspection work should be designated as 'Meat Inspectors' and absorbed in this service.

The Government of India should set up a permanent Central Committee for the Development of Meat Industry and should entrust to it such necessary functions of technical advice co-ordination. supervision and control as may be required from time to time. No substantial progress would be achieved unless such a Committee is established.

The Government of India and the State Governments should provide suitable financial assistance to the municipalities for meeting the capital expenditure required for constructing new slaughter-houses and for substantially improving those not considered necessary to be shifted to new sites.

The Government of India should send a small team to study the organisation and working of slaughter-houses and allied industries in the U.S.A. and the more advanced European countries. This team should also study the organisation and functioning of the Veterinary Public Health Services in those countries where such services exist.

The services of one or more experts in different aspects of the meat industry should be obtained under the Foreign Aid Programme.

Selected officers should be deputed abroad for specialised training in slaughter-house management and meat inspection practices.

Seminars on Veterinary Public Health should be arranged periodically for ensuring co-ordinated development and progress throughout the country.

GENERAL EDUCATION STUDY TEAM, 1955—REPORT

New Delhi, Ministry of Education, 1957. 97p.

Convener : Dr. S. Bhagavantam.

Members : Dr. P. Maheshwari; Dr. S. M. Sethna (Natural Sciences). Dr. K. S. Murty; Prof. G. D. Parikh; Dr. Baljit Singh (Social Sciences). Prof. Umashankar Joshi; Mrs. Mahmud Hosain (Humanities).

APPOINTMENT

The Government of India in the Ministry of Education arranged at Srinagar in June, 1955, a conference of a few Vice-Chancellors to consider a scheme of a General Course of Education for students which would cut across some of the current divisions among the different subjects. At this conference, a Consultative Committee was formed which discussed the desirability of introducing General Education Courses in Indian Universities. A note on the "Indo-American Curricular Project in General Education" prepared by Dr. Ward of the Ford Foundation was also considered by the Committee. In July, 1955, a circular letter was sent out from the Ministry of Education to the Vice-Chancellors of all Universities in India along with the proceedings of the Consultative Committee that met in Srinagar and with a note on the objectives and scope of the General Education courses as envisaged by the Committee. They were requested to communicate the views of their respective universities on the suggestions made in the Proceedings of the Consultative Committee. They were also requested to make a beginning, if possible, with General Education courses that very year, if possible, and the Ministry agreed to give financial assistance where necessary. So the Government appointed the present General Education Study Team.

TERMS OF REFERENCE

(1) The Team should study critically the working of General Education Courses in the various institutions of the U.S.A. and the U.K. in order to find out what approaches to the problem have proved most effective.

(2) In the light of the conditions prevailing in the Indian Universities, they should suggest suitable approaches, which may be tried out in our country.

(3) They should formulate illustrative syllabuses and courses of lectures which may be introduced in our Universities with due regard to the present curricular load and make practicable suggestions about the manner in which they might be produced. In doing this care should be taken to see that these courses are not overloaded with mere informational items, as the object is not to provide a great deal of factual information but to develop broad interests and appreciation and healthy attitudes and to quicken the capacity for clear thinking. The method of work is, therefore, at least as important in this connection as the contents of the courses. Their proposals should include suggestions about the organisational set-up, as well as any additional personnel that may be required for the purpose.

(4) They should work out the approximate financial implications of their proposals with due regard to the limitations of financial resources under which the scheme will have to be implemented.

(5) They should suggest suitable methods for preparing reading materials for use in these courses and, for this purpose, collect, from the U.S.A. as well as the U.K., actual syllabi, books, mimeographed materials and other teaching aids which have been successfully used in these institutions.

CONTENTS

Introduction; the Scope and purpose of General Education; Some Features of Higher Education in U.S.A.; Some Patterns of General Education in Indian Universities; Organisation and Financial Implications; Summary of Recommendations; Appendix I; Appendix II.

RECOMMENDATIONS

We recommend that courses in General Education be introduced in all Indian Universities.

We have drawn up two schemes of General Education—a main Scheme that we ardently hope will be adopted sooner or later in all Universities and an alternative Scheme with which a beginning may be made almost immediately.

In the main Scheme, we recommend that General Education covering basic studies in the fields of (a) Natural Sciences, (b) Social Sciences, and (c) Humanities, together with training in communication skills, be made compulsory for all undergraduates preparing for a degree in a non-professional faculty. Out of the total time available for all studies in the three years, one-third should be devoted to General Education courses. While the bulk of this programme should come in the first year, the rest may be distributed in the second and third years or may all come in the second year.

In the alternative Scheme, we recommend that six periods per week in the first year and six periods per week in the second year of the degree course be devoted to General Education courses.

Illustrative syllabuses are furnished in each of these areas. A certain quantum of General Education, with suitable modifications where necessary, should be given to all students preparing for their first professional degrees also. Passing an examination in the prescribed General Education courses should be made a required condition in the case of all students, before graduation.

Instruction in General Education courses should be so organised that for every two lectures delivered, at least one discussion in small groups should be arranged.

Suitable reading material should be prepared by drawing freely upon source writings and the classics. Such projects should be adequately financed by the University Grants Commission and the Government.

Steps should be taken by which interest amongst a large number of teachers in the General Education programmes is promoted as a result of which participation therein will be widely encouraged.

Expansion of libraries, laboratories and other teaching aids needed for the implementation of the programmes outlined should be provided for on a generous scale.

We envisage that in addition to the present expenditure, an approximate annual average recurring expenditure of Rs. 70 per student per year will be required for putting the Scheme of General Education into operation and we recommend that financial aid on this scale be given to as many colleges and universities as are willing to adopt the measures suggested in our report.

COMMITTEE ON PROBLEMS OF RE-ORGANISATION, 1955—REPORT

Delhi, Planning Commission, 1959. 171-226p. (Bounded with the Committee on Tenancy Reforms, and the Committee on Size of Holdings under the title of The Reports of the Committees of Panel on Land Reforms.) Total 226p.+xp.

Convener : Prof. D. R. Gadgil.

Members : Prof. D. G. Karve; Shri H. D. Malaviya; Shri Jugat Ram Dave; Shri Lal Singh; Shri Loke Nath Mishra; Shri Narsingha Rao; Dr. Pramatha Nath Bannerji; Dr. Radha Kumud Mookerji.

APPOINTMENT

The Committee on Problems of Re-organisation was constituted under the Planning Commission by the Panel on Land Reforms on June 4, 1955.

TERMS OF REFERENCE

To make recommendations on:

(i) Co-operative farming;

(ii) Co-operative village management;

(iii) Consolidation of holdings; and

(iv) Land management legislation.

CONTENTS

Introduction; Co-operative Farming; Co-operative Village Management; Land Management Legislation; Administrative Machinery for Land Reforms; Annexures I and II.

RECOMMENDATIONS

Co-operative Farming

The first recommendation we have to make is that on lands such as surplus lands which become available on the imposition of ceilings, Government waste lands, considered suitable for cultivation, land reclaimed through public effort and land periodically let out by the Government, wherever they are available in sizable areas, co-operative farms should be organised. As a rule, these lands should be settled with co-operatives and individual rights should not be created in them. The tribal areas where the notions of communal ownership still persist in some degree also offer a good field for co-operative experiments.

The lands already under cultivation consist of :

(i) Holdings below the floor limit;

(ii) Holdings between the floor limit and the ceiling; and

(iii) Holdings above the ceiling.

Ordinarily, holdings below the floor limit cannot be cultivated profitably. The object we have in view is that steadily increasing proposition of holdings below the floor limit should be brought into the co-operative pool. As a first step we suggest that the surplus land obtained on imposition of ceiling and other lands available in a village with the Government should be regrouped into a compact unit or units. These lands should constitute the nucleus for co-operative farming. The displaced tenants, the cultivators below the floor limit and the landless agricultural workers. who may be selected for settlement on these lands, will be admitted as members of the co-operative farm. The cultivators below the floor limit will be admitted as members provided they agree to put their lands into the pool. It is not necessary that the whole of this area should constitute a single co-operative farm. Depending upon the size of the optimum or minimum area that may be necessary for co-operative farming, the pooled area could be divided so as to constitute more than one co-operative farm.

The farms below the floor limit, which stay out of a co-operative farm at the commencement, should be located contiguously to the pooled area as part of the operations of consolidation of holdings to enable them to join the co-operative farm at a later date. A deliberate effort should be made to develop intensive co-operative activity on these farms. In the early stages it may take the form of co-operation in ancillary activities, such as credit, marketing, supplies, etc., leading on to joint cultivation at a somewhat later stage.

The terms and conditions on which lands may be pooled and the mode of co-operative management have a considerable bearing on the progress of co-operative farming. As regards the method of pooling of land, the following different forms were considered by the Committee:

(1) The ownership of land may be retained by individuals but the land may be managed as one unit, the owners being compensated through some form of ownership dividend;

(2) The land may be leased to the co-operative society for a period, the owners being paid agreed rents or rents prescribed by law; or

(3) Ownership may be transferred to the co-operative

society but shares representing the value of land may be given to individuals.

As the surplus and other governmental lands will be settled with co-operative groups and not with individuals, no difficulty regarding pooling of land would arise in their case. With regard to lands pooled by individuals, on the basis of experience available so far, it is not possible to recommend any particular method and we suggest that at this stage no rigid conditions need be prescribed and the various alternative forms mentioned above may be tried out.

The adoption of any particular mode of management will depend on the technique of farming that may be applied and the degree of co-operation which has developed among the members. Each co-operative farm will adopt the mode of management which suits it best according to its own circumstances. We suggest that at this stage all the various methods may be tried, till suitable techniques of co-operative management are fully established by experience. Where lands are allotted to individual families for all agricultural operations or merely for subsidiary operations, it should be ensured that vested interests are not created and attachment to any particular plot of land does not develop. Provision should, therefore, be made for the redistribution of plots among the members from time to time.

We recommend that immediate steps should be taken to organise, on a large scale, planned experiments in co-operative farming in various crop regions of the country. These experiments may be located in areas of colonisation and in community project areas and national extension areas. It will also be an advantage, if some of the experiments are located around existing non-official institutions for social welfare work where the participation and guidance of trained social workers could be more easily obtained.

Each State may set up a small Committee at the State headquarters with the Minister of Co-operation as its Chairman. Its members may consist of persons with a faith in the philosophy of co-operation and experience in the methods of co-operation. It should be assisted by an officer whose special charge should be to organise co-operative farming in the State. The planned experiments should be worked under the direct supervision of this Committee. For creating necessary psychological atmosphere and mobilising public opinion, the co-operation of non-official organisations working in the social and political fields is indispensable. In the selected areas seminars should be organised at which intensive discussions may be held on the advantages of and problems presented by co-operative farming.

Each co-operative farm will need the assistance of a properly trained manager. Wherever possible, these managers should be selected from amongst experienced cultivators who possess a broad social outlook. The managers will need training in the management of large farms, maintenance of accounts and above all securing people's co-operation and participation. We suggest that an adequate number of training centres should immediately be set up and steps taken for the selection of suitable hands taking into consideration the needs over the next five years.

At this stage of development we would hesitate to recommend any firm targets for the country as a whole. We suggest that each State Government should formulate its programme in the light of its own circumstances. These programmes should be so framed that over the next 10 years a substantial portion of the area can be brought under co-operative farming.

We suggest that the following facilities should be offered by the State to co-operative farms:

(i) Credit from the Government or from co-operative agencies and preference generally in financial assistance from the government for approved agricultural programmes;

(ii) Preference against the available stock in the supply of improved seed, fertilisers and materials for local construction;

(iii) Facilities for consolidation of lands comprised in a co-operative farm;

(iv) Preference in grant of leases of lands reclaimed by the Government, culturable waste lands, lands whose management is assured by the Government and lands under the management of the Village Panchayats;

(v) Provision that after a co-operative farming society is formed and so long as it continues and is managed in accordance with the conditions prescribed under the law, no new rights adverse to the interest of its members will accrue. Where land is held by the tenants with permanent rights, it is for them to elect to become members of a co-operative farming society. Owners of these lands cannot elect to pool their lands in a co-operative farm. In respect of lands under the cultivation of a tenant who does not possess permanent rights, an owner may join a co-operative farming society if the tenant is also agreeable to becoming a member of the co-operative farm;

(vi) Reduction of land revenue for a period;

(vii) Reduction of or exemption from agricultural income tax, if any;

(viii) Technical assistance of expert personnel employed by the Government in farm operations, marketing, preparation of production programmes, etc.;

(ix) Technical or financial assistance in developing non-agricultural employment for members of the co-operative farming society and others associated with them, such as in cottage industries, dairying and horticulture, etc.; and

(x) Subsidy for managerial expenses.

It has been observed that sometimes fraudulent

societies are formed by large and middle owners with a view to getting certain advantages or to evading the provisions of land reform laws. We suggest that provision should be made to prevent such evasions by providing that a co-operative farm will be registered only if the Registrar is satisfied that the bulk of the labour for the farm will be provided by its members.

Co-operative Village Management

The aim should be to enlarge the co-operative sector till the entire farm land in the village is comprised in co-operative farming societies.

The main instruments for realising co-operative village management are:

(a) The Village Panchayat and the functions assigned to it as a development agency at the village level;

(b) Measures taken to develop co-operative credit, marketing, warehousing, processing, etc.;

(c) Programmes for the development of village industries specially for meeting local needs and offering work opportunities to all persons in the villages;

(d) Programmes for promoting and assisting voluntary co-operative farming societies; and

(e) Development of a "community sector", within the village economy, that is, of land belonging to the village community as a whole (such as common lands, gifted lands, sites, etc.) and activities organised for the village as a whole.

These various activities supplement one another, but their total effect is to emphasise the responsibility of the village community as such for the development of its resources, including land, in the interest of all those who belong to it, without regard to whether they are or are not owners of land.

Consolidation Of Holdings

We recommend that all State Governments should be asked to draw up phased programmes for taking up consolidation work on a large scale during the Second Five Year Plan. We would, however, like to draw attention to one obstacle which may hamper the programme. In some parts of the country, considerable areas are held by tenants-at-will. In such areas consolidation of holdings would be largely a waste of effort and it would be desirable to undertake tenancy legislation before consolidation is taken up. Consolidation facilitates cultivation. The land in which permanent rights are conferred on the tenants should, therefore, be included in their holdings and excluded from owners' holdings.

Land Management Legislation

We regard land management legislation as an instrument of a policy for the progressive improvement of agricultural standards. We agree with the observations of the Sub-Committee that each cultivator should be under a social obligation to maintain a reasonable standard of efficient production and the object of land management legislation is to provide the necessary incentives and sanctions for the performance of this duty. The measure cannot however be regarded (merely as a means of coercion) in isolation from (other) factors which are essential for the maintenance of efficient production. The prescription of standard should necessarily be linked with the fulfilment of certain prerequisite conditions, such as suitability of tenure, consolidation of holdings, progressive development of co-operation in various spheres of agricultural activity and increasing State assistance in the provision of financial resources and technical guidance and supplies.

As recommended by the Sub-Committee, provision should also be made for sanctions in the following cases:

(i) Cultivable waste lands held by large and medium holders, which are not brought under cultivation within a reasonable period, should be taken over under State management and arrangements made for reclamation and cultivation. Where cultivable waste lands held by small holders are not reclaimed with a reasonable period, the State should make arrangements for reclamation and recover the cost from them in suitable instalments.

(ii) With regard to measures relating to levelling, bunding and fencing, where necessary, provision of irrigation facilities and maintenance of irrigation channels, control of insects and diseases and eradication of weeds and terracing of fields, it is suggested that in case the cultivator fails to fulfil the necessary obligations, the State may carry out the work and recover the cost from the cultivator concerned along with a surcharge which may be up to 25 per cent of the cost.

(iii) Where a cultivator cannot be persuaded, after all needed assistance and instructions have been provided, to use improved seeds, or make compost of farm refuse, provision for a small fine may be made.

We recommend that land management legislation should apply to all farms. Till sufficient experience has however been gained and adequate administrative machinery has been built up, we would suggest the enforcement of standards, in the first instance, in selected National Extension and Community Project areas in each State.

Administrative Machinery For Land Reforms

We recommend that in areas where they have not already been set up the establishment of Village Panchayats should be expedited.

Financial Resources

One of the most serious handicaps from which the existing Village Panchayats suffer is lack of adequate financial resources. We would suggest that provision for financial resources for the Village Panchayats should include:

(i) A basic grant which should not be less than 20 per cent of the land revenue with an additional grant up to 15 per cent subject to the condition that the Village Panchayat finds matching resources;

(ii) The imposition of an additional local rent or cess for meeting the recurring costs of institutions such as schools and other development schemes;

(iii) Income from common lands;

(iv) Income from allotment of house sites or lands for the purposes of cultivation;

(v) Income from public markets and ferries;

(vi) A commission for collection of land revenue or other Government dues where this is entrusted to them;

(vii) A tax on trade, professions and callings;

(viii) Free labour for works of improvement;

(ix) Income from land set apart as a result of consolidation of holdings for cultivation through the village community; and

(x) Income from business activities undertaken on a co-operative basis by the Village Panchayat.

Staff

We recommend that the Government should set up training centres for the education and training of the staff required for the Village Panchayat and appointments should be made from among the qualified candidates where they are available. Regarding the strength of the staff of Village Panchayats or their terms and conditions no general conditions can be laid down. Arrangements will have to be made according to local needs and resources. The panchayats may appoint part-time or whole-time secretaries according to local conditions and availability of funds.

Composition Of Village Panchayats

As a general principle there should be a village panchayat for each village.

Where multi-village organisations have been set up already, they may at this stage continue to be treated as the primary organisational units.

It has been suggested in this connection that provision should be made for nominations of suitable persons as members of the Village Panchayats. This proposal, however, is likely to lead to serious difficulties. The Collector of a district or a Sub-Divisional Officer does not possess the necessary knowledge about the inhabitants of the hundreds of villages under his charge. Nomination will, therefore, have to be left, in substance, if not in name, to lower officials with the likely result that unsuitable persons may be nominated in a number of cases. Besides a combination of elected and nominated members will not make for smooth working and it may tend to weaken the sense of democratic responsibility among the elected representatives.

Efforts should be made to ensure that elections to the Village Panchayat are made as far as possible by the general consent of the people and the bitterness and hostility created by election campaigns is avoided.

Gradation Of Village Panchayat

The Congress Village Panchayat Committee which has made a detailed and comprehensive study of the subject suggested that the Panchayats should be classified into three grades, namely, A, B and C. The Tenancy Committee has supported the suggestion. In classifying the Panchayats their experience and ability would naturally be taken into account. Where the Panchayat has been elected on a unanimous basis by genuine and spontaneous agreement, this may also be considered as a significant factor for purposes of gradation. Panchayats which are placed in Grade "A" may be given all the duties listed below. The other Panchayats may be classed in Grade "B" or "C" according to their experience and ability and given less wide powers in the first instance. Effort should be made by providing the necessary training and financial support to enable the Panchayats of lower grades to qualify for higher powers.

Judicial Panchayats

We agree with the recommendation of the Congress Village Panchayat Committee that each village community should elect a panel of five members to work on the Judicial Panchayats, which would thus have about 30 members elected from a few villages. Cases should be heard in the village itself in an atmosphere of informality by a Bench of five (drawn from different villages) by a system of rotation. The Judicial Panchayats should also be graded as suggested with regard to the Village Panchayats. Judicial Panchayats of Grade A may be entrusted with the judicial functions contained in the following list while others may be given less wide powers in the first instance.

The judicial functions may be classified as below:

(1) Decision of disputes regarding land;

(2) Effecting transfers of land;

(3) Administration of civil and criminal justice; and

(4) Enforcement of minimum wages for agricultural labourers.

With regard to item (1), the Tenancy Committee has drawn up a list of disputes regarding land which should be dealt with by Judicial Panchayats. We are in agreement with the recommendations of the Tenancy Committee.

With regard to item 2, the Tenancy Committee has recommended that transfers should not be made by private contract between individuals. They should be made through Village Panchayats at regulated prices and according to an order of preference which should be prescribed by law or rules. In agreement with the Tenancy Committee we would recommend that the price of lands which are to be transferred should be determined by the Judicial Panchayat, while the actual transfer be effected through the Village Panchayat.

With regard to items 3 and 4, the Land Reform Panel is not concerned directly. We have, however, included them in the list to make it comprehensive. With regard to the administration of civil and criminal justice we would suggest that a list may be drawn up indicating the nature of cases which can be made over to the Judicial Panchayat.

Functions

The functions which may be entrusted to the village organisation may be classified as below:

Administrative Functions

Management Of Land

(1) Association with the work of maintenance of land records;

(2) Making leases of land in all cases where the owner is unable to cultivate the land himself and desires that it may be let out for cultivation;

(3) Regulation of the use of common lands such as waste lands, forests, *abadi* sites, tanks, etc.;

(4) Allotment of *abadi* sites; housing condition of Harijans and others, the layout of village sites;

(5) Allotment of cultivable lands for agricultural purposes;

(6) Allotment of land for non-agricultural use;

(7) Adaptation of the standards of good management and cultivation to local conditions;

(8) Inspection and judgment whether the standards of good management and cultivation have been fulfilled and whether the classification of farms has been done according to their efficiency;

(9) Enforcement of standards;

(10) Collection of land revenue.

Development

(11) Development of common lands, such as waste lands, forests, *abadi* sites, tanks, etc., including measures against soil erosion.

(12) Organisation of mutual aid and joint effort;

(13) Promotion of co-operative societies, such as rural credit, marketing, etc.;

(14) Promotion of co-operative farming societies;

(15) Framing programmes of development for the village;

(16) Framing budget of requirements for supply and finance for carrying out programmes;

(17) Acting as the channel through which increasing Government assistance (other than the assistance given through agencies like co-operatives) reaches the village;

(18) Organising voluntary labour for community works;

(19) Improvement of livestock;

(20) Construction, repair and maintenance of public wells, tanks and ponds;

(21) Development of village industries.

Civil And Administrative Functions

(22) Education, culture and sports;

(23) Medical relief, sanitation and hygiene, and maternity and child welfare and relief to the poor;

(24) Registration of births, deaths and marriages;

(25) Construction, repair and maintenance, cleaning and lighting of public streets; removal of encroachments from public streets, construction or maintenance of culverts and bridges;

(26) Regulation of Melas and fairs;

(27) Rendering assistance in extinguishing fires and protecting life and property when fires occur;

(28) Maintenance of records of cattle census, population census and other statistics;

(29) Watch and Ward.

Land Reform Functions

(30) Determination of land to be allotted to the owner in exercise of his right of resumption and the land to be left with the tenant;

(31) Association with the determination of surplus land (arising from legislation for ceilings);

(32) Association with the redistribution of surplus land (arising from legislation for ceilings); and

(33) Association with the work of consolidation of holdings.

Item 1: The correct maintenance of land records is absolutely essential for the effective implementation of land reform measures. The Tenancy Committee has recommended that all Village Panchayats, of whatever grade, should be associated with the preparation and maintenance of land records and has made suggestions in detail in this respect, with which we agree.

Item 2: The Tenancy Committee has recommended that in order to prevent rackrenting of tenants or sub-tenants and to provide for a degree of flexibility in the land system (so that it may be possible for land-owners who wish to seek alternative occupation in the urban areas to lease their lands temporarily and on return to the village to get back their lands for cultivation and further to ensure that tenants are not rendered landless), leases of land should be made by the Village Panchayat. General principles for the guidance of the executive of the village, i.e. the Village Panchayat, should be laid down by the assembly of the village people as a whole within the framework of the law and the rules on the subject.

Items 3—6: The Sub-Committee is of the view that the management of common lands and *abadi* sites, etc., and allotment of *abadi* sites for house building and of plots of land to individuals for cultivation or non-agricultural use should be entrusted to the Village Panchayats so that the common lands may be utilised and developed for the benefit of the village community as a whole. It is understood that in the discharge of these functions as well as others, the Village Panchayat will be required to act in accordance with the State plans or directions and the provisions of the law and rules on the subject.

Items 8—10: The question relating to land management legislation, the fixing of standards of efficient cultivation and management, the procedure and methods for their enforcement and the sanctions to be applied have been examined in detail by the Sub-Committee on Land Management. This committee is concerned with the question of the agency to be employed for the enforcement of these standards. The Reorganisation Committee has decided that the village body should be the pivot of land management legislation, responsible for the adaptation of the standards to the conditions in the village, the classification of various grades, drawing up of phased programmes for development giving directions and supplying the necessary assistance and financial resources. In certain cases provision has been made for punitive action, i.e. assumption or management by the State increases where a substantial or medium holder fails to reclaim cultivable waste, the State undertaking certain items of work on the failure of the cultivator to perform them and the imposition of fines in a few cases. In such cases the cultivator concerned should have a right of appeal to a higher authority. The establishment of such higher authorities is dealt with in the sequel.

Item 11: Wherever the Village Panchayats possess the necessary ability, the responsibility for collecting land revenue may be made over to them on payment of suitable remuneration in the form of a percentage of the revenue collected.

Items 12—22: These should necessarily be dealt with by the Village Panchayats.

Items 23—30: The Land Reform Panel is not concerned with these items which have been included in the list to make it comprehensive. The list is based upon duties which have already been entrusted to Village Panchayats in a number of States.

Item 31: The Sub-Committee is of the view that the Village Panchayats should be entrusted with the determination of land to be allotted to the owner in exercise of his right of resumption and the land to be left with the tenant. The work would necessarily have to be done in accordance with the provisions of the law and rules, but some degree of flexibility may be provided so that the Village Panchayat may be able to make necessary adjustments between the interests of the owners and the tenants.

Item 32: In order to ensure that owners of land above the ceiling do not escape the provisions of the law, the Village Panchayat should be entrusted with the duty of checking up such cases and reporting contravention of the law to the revenue courts.

Item 33: The Village Panchayats should be associated with the redistribution of surplus lands, but their recommendations should be subject to confirmation by the official agency.

Item 34: The Sub-Committee is of the view that the Village Panchayat should be associated with the work of consolidation of holdings so that it may be carried out smoothly and complaints and grievances of the cultivators may be minimised. Where the Consolidation Officer disagrees with the suggestions of the Village Panchayat a reference may be made to a higher consolidation authority.

Sub-Committees

We have referred earlier to the appointment of sub-committees in cases where Village Panchayats have a circle extending over more than one village. The functions to be entrusted to these committees would include Items 1 to 7 and 31 to 34.

Higher Units Of Administration

We suggest as an immediate measure the formation of representative bodies at the District level and Tehsil/Taluka or Development Block level.

It is proposed that every district should have a District Development Council composed as follows:

(1) Representatives of the district in the State Legislature and in Parliament;

(2) Representatives of Municipal Committees and rural local bodies, (say, 10 in number);

(3) Representatives of the co-operative movement (say, 4 in number);

(4) Representatives of Village Panchayats (say, 10 in number);

(5) Co-opted members from leading social service agencies, constructive social workers and educational institutions (say, 6 in number);

(6) The Collector and district officials in charge of various development departments.

It may be convenient at this stage for the Collector to be the Chairman of the District Development Council.

At the Tehsil/Taluka Development Block, there should be Development Committees which may be composed as follows:

(1) Representatives of the area in the State Legislature and in Parliament;

(2) Representatives of all urban local bodies and the Taluka Board or members of the District Board from the area (say, 8 in number);

(3) Representatives of the co-operative movement (say, 15 in number);

(4) Representatives of the Village Panchayats (say, 15 in number);

(5) Co-opted members from leading social service agencies, constructive social workers and educational institutions (say, 6 in number);

(6) Officials-in-charge of development departments.

A fairly senior officer below the rank of Collector, such as a Sub-Divisional Officer, may, to begin with, be the Chairman of the Development Committee.

The representatives of various institutions would be elected by them in the manner prescribed by the State Governments in the light of local conditions.

It is desirable that the Tehsil/Taluka/Block Development Committee should be a statutory body with clearly defined authority and functions. Where, however, the circumstances in a State or region render this difficult, advisory functions may be given in the first instance.

The functions of District Development Councils would, in the earlier stages, be advisory.

More specifically, within their areas the functions of District Development Councils and Tehsil/Taluka/Block Development Committees may be set out as follows:

(1) To advise on the formation of each year's plan of development within the general framework of the Five-Year Plan;

(2) To review progress in the implementation of approved programmes of development;

(3) To recommend measures for the effective and speedy fulfilment, with the maximum support from the people, of schemes of economic and social development and, more especially, of national extension and community projects, agricultural production programmes, local development works, social services, village and small industries;

(4) General supervision over the work of land reforms, land management and development by Village Panchayats;

(5) To promote public participation and co-operation in development programmes and to expand local community effort both in rural and in urban areas;

(6) To promote the Small Savings movement;

(7) To assist the development of co-operatives and Village Panchayats;

(8) To enlist the active association and co-operation of teachers and students in the study and development of local resources; and

(9) To provide opportunities for the education and training of members and Sarpanches of Village Panchayats.

COMMITTEE ON SIZE OF HOLDINGS, 1955—REPORT

New Delhi, Planning Commission, 1959. 95-170p.
(Bound with the Committee on Tenancy Reforms and Committee on Problems of Re-organisations under the Title "Committees of the Panel on Land Reforms".) Total 226p.+xp.

Convener : Prof. M. L. Dantwala.
Members : Shri H. D. Malaviya; Shri Lal Singh; Shri Narsingha Rao; Shri N. Prasada Rao; Dr. Radha Kumud Mookerji; Shri G. Sankaran Nair.

APPOINTMENT

The Committee on the Size of Holdings was constituted under the Planning Commission by the Panel on Land Reforms on June 4, 1955.

TERMS OF REFERENCE

(i) Reviewing the progress in the implementation of land policy proposed in the First Five-Year Plan; and

(ii) Studying further steps in connection with the Second Five-Year Plan.

CONTENTS

General; Appendix A; Minute of Dissent by Sardar Lal Singh, M.P.; A note by Dr. Radha Kumud Mookerji, M.P.; Minute of Dissent by Shri N. Prasada Rao, M.P.

RECOMMENDATIONS

General

The Committee unanimously accepted the principle that there should be an absolute limit to the amount of land which any individual may hold.

The policy of imposition of ceiling would be able to

make a contribution towards fulfilling the following objectives:

(i) Meeting the widespread desire to possess land;

(ii) Reducing glaring inequalities in ownership and use of land;

(iii) Reducing inequalities in agricultural incomes; and

(iv) Enlarging the sphere of self-employment.

The Committee wished to emphasise that the principle of ceiling should be applied to other sectors of economy also with due regard to the conditions prevailing in those sectors. Though the principle of applying it specially to agriculture could be justified on several grounds, it was felt that if the State would announce its policy of application of ceilings to other sectors of the economy as well, imposition of ceiling on agricultural lands would meet with less opposition and there would be greater chances of its proving successful.

Area Of Application Of Ceiling

On the assumption that in respect of leased lands, positive steps will be taken to enable the tenants to become owners within a reasonable period, the Committee recommend that the ceiling should apply to owned land under personal cultivation. In determining the area under personal cultivation, all uncultivated but cultivable lands not leased to tenants should be taken into account. Land taken on lease but not liable to resumption and land given on lease but liable to resumption should be taken in account for the purposes of ceiling.

Level Of Ceiling

We have examined the question whether in applying ceiling, the aggregate area held by all the members of a family should be taken into account or whether the land held by an individual member of a family should be regarded as constituting a separate holding for purposes of ceilings. We are of the view that family is the real operative unit in land ownership as in land management. We therefore recommend that in the fixing of the ceiling, the aggregate area held by all the members of a family should be taken into account. For this purpose, a family should be deemed to consist of husband, wife and dependent sons and daughters and grand-children. Land held by married daughters and earning sons should be excluded. Where the property has already devolved on two or more heirs after the death of the parents but the property has been held in common by them, undivided, the share of each heir should be regarded as a separate holding.

Mala Fide Transfers

It has been brought to our notice that anticipating imposition of ceilings, substantial owners are making benami transactions in favour of near relations and friends to bring their holdings within assumed limits. If such transfers are allowed, they will defeat the very object of imposition of ceilings. We would therefore recommend that any transfer or lease made after a given date should be disregarded in determining the surplus area.

The date could be fixed by each State Government in the light of its own circumstances.

Acquisition Of The Surplus; And Compensation And Method Of Financing

The next question was to decide

(1) Whether the surplus land should be acquired by the State and distributed to the claimants according to some prescribed priority;

(2) Whether it should be requisitioned and tenants settled on it; or

(3) Whether the land owners should be asked to lease out the surplus to tenants of their own choice.

The adoption of the third course, namely, permitting the land owners to lease out the surplus lands may result in malpractices, benami transactions and even extortion of money by the land owners from the tenants to be settled by them. It may also raise same constitutional difficulties. We do not therefore favour this course. If the surplus is acquired, the question of compensation and the mode of payment will arise. If however the surplus is merely requisitioned, the tenants could continue to pay the rent either directly to the land owners or to the State. The following alternative methods, some of which are already in existence, were mentioned:

(1) In a number of States, legislative provisions exist empowering the State Government to arrange for the cultivation of lands which have been allowed to remain uncultivated without a reasonable cause for a period of over two or three years. In such cases, the State Government has the power to admit a tenant to the land. Generally the tenant has the same right as if he has been admitted by the landlord.

If this alternative was adopted, the State Government would settle the surplus land with a tenant, who would have permanent and heritable rights and would be liable to pay rent.

(2) The land could be settled with a tenant who would have permanent and heritable rights and also the right...voluntarily to purchase the land at a reasonable price. The State could make the necessary provision for financial assistance to the tenant to facilitate purchase of land.

In both the alternatives, mentioned above, the State Government would not acquire ownership of the surplus land immediately. In alternative (1), the land owner would remain the owner indefinitely. In alternative (2) the landlord would remain the owner until the tenant purchases his right. In alternative (3), the State acquires ownership of the surplus land immediately and becomes responsible for the payment of compensation. The compensation could be paid in one of the two ways:

(i) The person who is admitted as tenant pays rent to the State Government and the State Government finances the compensation out of its increased revenue;

(ii) The person who is admitted to the land pays annual land revenue to the State and, in addition, he pays instalments of the compensation over a number of years.

There were distinct differences in views on this issue. The Committee however favours the adoption of the following methods:

(i) The surplus land should be acquired. When the surplus is distributed, the recipients should become direct tenants. They should pay fair rent to the State as long as it may be necessary to enable the State to pay the compensation money to the land owner.

(ii) The amount of compensation should in no case be more than 25 per cent of the market value and should not exceed (inclusive of interest charges) the aggregate of the increase in land revenues for 20 years. The increase in land revenue will be due to the fact that the State will be receiving fair rent from the new settlers on the surplus land which will be more than the land revenue paid by the ex-owner.

(iii) The compensation may be paid in bonds redeemable in about 20 years.

(iv) After, say, 20 years' payment of fair rent, the recipient should be declared to be a full-fledged owner, after which he will be liable to pay no more than the prevailing land revenue.

Exemptions

Following categories, which could possibly qualify for exemption, were listed:

(1) Plantations—Tea, coffee, rubber;

(2) Sugarcane farms owned by sugar factories;

(3) Orchards;

(4) Special farms such as cattle-breading, dairy farms, sheep-breeding farms, etc.;

(5) Farms in a compact block;

(6) Efficient farms;

(7) Mechanised farms and farms with heavy investment.

Plantations

It was agreed that the ceiling was not an appropriate measure of reform for plantation. Other measures suggested were—strict enforcement of minimum wages, steep agricultural income tax, State acquisition and subsequent co-operative management was favoured by many. Attention was drawn to large areas within plantations which were leased out to tenants for growing seasonal crops. It was agreed that the question of tenancy rights and ceiling in respect of such lands should be considered in the light of the recommendations of the Plantation Enquiry Commission.

Sugarcane Farms

The unanimous view was that these do not qualify for exemption. How these farms should be operated after the ceiling is enforced needs to be considered; in particular, the question of running them as integrated co-operative farms should be investigated.

Orchards

The Committee are of the view that existing orchards should not be broken up if situated within a reasonably compact area, but the area under them should be taken into consideration for calculating the permissible area under the ceiling. If, as a result, no other land was left for the owner, a basic holding may be permitted in addition to the orchards.

Where orchards are taken over, it should be ensured that they are not cut down and are maintained as orchards.

Cattle-Breeding, Dairy, Wool-Raising Farms

We favour exemption for bona fide farms of the above type, as certified by the Government. Exemption is intended for existing farms of the type and not for contemplated future use.

Compact, Well-Managed Mechanised Farms

All these categories were considered together. Except one member who advocated State acquisition, others favoured exemption of the highly efficiently managed farms which consist of compact blocks, and on which heavy investment for permanent structural improvements has been made. Subsequent to exemption, they will be subject to special responsibilities and obligations, such as conforming to the highest possible standard of efficiency, use of improved practices, payment of minimum wages to labourers, right of State to use them as experimental or demonstration farms, acquisition of crops (produce) by State at reasonable prices.

Distribution Of Surplus

The question of re-distribution is however linked with the question of re-organisation of agriculture. We are informed that the Committee on Problems of Re-organisation has taken the view that the surplus should be settled on co-operative basis. We would therefore defer making any recommendation on this matter.

Floors

While the policy of imposition of ceilings has reference to the problem of distributive justice, imposition of a floor limit is the outcome of the need for national layout of land surface and efficient productive organisation. Land is a scarce resource and the nation cannot afford its wasteful use. None of the problems of inadequate or disproportionate equipment, of backward technique and inefficiency, of underemployment and wasted labour, of poverty and exploitation can be solved as long as the bulk of farming units are small. The concept of floor, thus, derives its imperativeness from the supreme need of operational efficiency rather than from the need to secure minimum income. It therefore implies that no production unit should be smaller than the minimum necessary for good agriculture. If even this unit is too large for the country to be able to provide to every individual cultivator, rather than partitioning the unit and distributing parcels to individual cultivators, the cultivators should be persuaded to come together and practise group or co-operative farming.

The Committee could not achieve unanimity in approaching this problem. Though several members favoured imposition of a floor, say, at one-third of the economic holding as in the Hyderabad legislation, others felt that blanket injunction against individual cultivation of the below-floor farms would unduly restrict the already limited opportunities for owning land and will keep out a large number of the landless from becoming owners. In the distribution of the surplus also, if a minimum floor limit is imposed, the number benefiting from the distribution would be restricted. These members, therefore, opposed any rigid adherence to the concept of the floor.

Imposition of floor has a meaning only if all farms below the floor are grouped in a compact block of what may be called a co-operative sector. Varying degrees of co-operative working may be introduced—from credit and marketing to joint cultivation according to the preparedness of the participants. To make participation in this sector attractive the surplus from the imposition of ceilings may be transferred to it. Of course, the displaced tenants, attached workers and the landless (if so decided) will have to be provided on it. It is evident that this sort of reorganisation and re-alignment is possible only if a scheme of consolidation of holdings for re-designing of the lay out is introduced as a part of ceiling-floor policy.

Regarding the level of floor (those who were in favour of imposing such a limit) some recommended one-third, others one-half, while two members held the view that the floor and the economic level should be the same. However, if the imposition of floor is to result in some sort of re-organisation as suggested above, the effective limit will be organisational, i.e. the Government's capacity to organise the co-operative sectors.

COMMITTEE ON TENANCY REFORMS, 1955—REPORT

New Delhi, Planning Commission, 1959. 1-94p.
(Bound with the Committee on Size of Holdings and Committee on Problems of Re-organisation under the Title of Reports of the Committees of the Panel on Land Reforms.) Total 226p.+xp.

Convener : Shri R. K. Patil.
Members : Shri G. Sankaran Nair; Shri Loke Nath Mishra; Shri N. Prasada Rao; Shri Shriman Narain; Shri H. D. Malaviya; Dr. P. N. Banerjee.

APPOINTMENT

The Committee on Tenancy Reforms was constituted under the Planning Commission by the Panel on Land Reforms on June 4, 1955.

TERMS OF REFERENCE

(i) Reviewing the progress made in the implementation of the policy proposed in the First Five-Year Plan; and

(ii) Recommending further steps in connection with the Second Five-Year Plan.

CONTENTS

Preface; **Part I**—Progress (Introduction; Land Policy in the First Five-Year Plan; Abolition of Intermediaries; Progress of Tenancy Reforms; A Critical Review); **Part II**—Recommendations (some Fundamental Considerations; Abolition of Intermediaries; Rights of Owners of Land; Tenancy Reforms; Administrative Agency); Annexures I to VI.

RECOMMENDATIONS

Some Fundamental Considerations

As it is our object to transform rural society by

peaceful and democratic means, a certain amount of gradualness is necessary and desirable. It is necessary to obtain wide acceptance and common consent for each step that is taken, which in its turn acts as a process of social education for the next. A period of transition is, however, exposed to some dangers. Progressive change may cause a feeling of insecurity and may give an opportunity to the more powerful sections to anticipate further change and make its implementation difficult. These difficulties have to be taken into account in any proposals for land reforms and the pace and direction of social change carefully adjusted to avoid them. It is, for instance, apparent that large land-holders have come to realise that they cannot for long continue to enjoy the rights that they now possess.

And what is more, we do not consider it easy, by any steps which the Government might take, to restore the feeling that the landlords had in the past that their property rights were not liable to be affected by any sudden or immediate change. The circumstances and the atmosphere are against it. Even if the Government were to make a declaration of the inviolability of such holdings, such a declaration cannot bind future Governments, and the prevailing atmosphere indicates that a future Government is bound to impose a ceiling even if the present Government does not do so.

A complementary aspect of the same question is the expectation raised in the minds of the landless population of obtaining a higher social status, greater security and means of employment and the hope of receiving land through some manner of redistribution. The Bhoodan Movement has strengthened the demand for land. Our ideas of social justice are being progressively enlarged and they are bound to become increasingly larger with the passage of time. Unless, therefore, there appears to be a reasonable possibility of providing employment for a large number of the landless population in other non-farm occupations in any reasonable period of time, this demand for land is likely to increase in volume and intensity and assume the form of a mass movement in a short time.

Increase in personal cultivation as distinguished from cultivation through hired labourers must be an important objective of land reform. It goes without saying that other things being equal, a personally cultivated holding is likely to yield more than the one cultivated through hired labour. The advantages to the State of a hard-working, contented and prosperous peasantry working on the land are considerable. It is their purchasing power which will influence increased production of industrial goods, and thus help industrialisation. The ownership of land, besides conferring security and social status on its possession, also provides an opportunity for self-employment and it should be an objective of land policy to increase this sector up to the limit where holdings become so small that these advantages begin to be counter-balanced by other disadvantages.

All proposals for land reforms should aim at establishing such a new pattern of landownership and cultivation that it will have in it the germs of future development. And the next step in land should be such as clearly lays bare the final pattern of landholding involved in the significant expression "land to the tiller". The element of uncertainty should be reduced and the landowning classes including both the small and the large holders should know precisely where they stand. The position of tenants should be established and rendered secure. It is of importance that all proposals for land reforms must carry conviction to all concerned with the holding of land that they are final and unlikely to be disturbed for any reasonable length of time. It is this atmosphere that induces development and it must be our concern to restore it.

One of our most urgent problems is the provision of additional opportunities for employment to those who are engaged on land today whether as landowners, tenants or agricultural labourers. The fundamental cause of our poverty is our inability to utilise fully the labour potential of the bulk of the people who are today engaged on land. In so far as agriculture is a seasonal occupation, even a large holding is ineffective in increasing the period of employment. More employment outside the agricultural season must, therefore, be found by (1) development works and (2) development of village industries. There is also considerable scope for a good deal of development work on the land itself. Soil erosion is our chief technological problem today, and if soil is to be conserved, land will have to be terraced, bunded and afforested. Irrigation sources will have to be developed and where there is no scope for collecting rain-water, wells will have to be dug. A proper system of soil conservation includes all these items and a great deal of labour could be absorbed in all these operations. They would increase production, provide more employment on land and open the way for adoption of modern scientific agricultural practices. It is estimated that it requires about Rs. 90 worth of labour to conserve properly one acre of cotton land. This would give an idea of the scope for absorption of labour in soil conservation operations. The land is there, the surplus labour is there, the nation can afford the capital necessary to start this process of land development, and yet in spite of all these favourable factors, there are considerable difficulties in co-ordinating them and providing more employment on land.

The reason for this difficulty is quite obvious. Land today is divided in a series of fragments, each owned by a separate individual. Individually he has neither the resources nor the inclination to develop the land. Wage-paid employment to develop individual fragments is out of the question. The other alternative is some sort of a co-operative effort by the landowners for this purpose. This is considerably handicapped by the various differences in the landownership pattern of the village community. Some have more land, some have less land and others have no land at all. It is clear that an effort at land development in the existing pattern of land-holding is bound to give differential returns to the various owners owning land in proportion to their ownership. The large holders will benefit more, the smaller holders less, and the landless not at all, except in an indirect way. It is this difficulty which prevents a large-scale effort at land development on the part of the village community.

But if land were owned by the whole village with an equal right to participate in its fruits, on the part of all those who are willing to labour on it, the case would be different. Everybody would have the same interest in developing the land and this should pave the way for a land army in each village working for the maximum produce from the land. Land resources and human resources would be fully co-ordinated without the interposition of any ownership rights or other differences separating them from one another.

The idea of the imposition of ceiling at three times the family holding has already been accepted in the First Five-Year Plan and we recommend that it should be brought into operation in all the States in India during the course of the Second Five-Year Plan. Thus, we would be creating a large body of small peasant proprietors and the pattern can be stabilised. (Future changes will then result only from the development of co-operative activities.)

Where the landless people belong to the Harijan caste this is an essential preliminary for the removal of untouchability itself. Existing disparities in ownership of land and agricultural incomes will, to a certain extent, be reduced. This will facilitate co-operation and rural progress and the State will have laid the fundamental basis for the establishment of a socialistic pattern of society.

Two objections have to be considered before such a course can be recommended for adoption all over the country. The first is economic and the second social. The economic objection can be stated thus: The giving of land in small holdings to a large number of landless persons would increase the number of diminutive holdings and, to that extent, reduce production in agriculture. Further, these small holdings being unable to attract capital, the land will progressively deteriorate and this would amount to living on our capital.

The imposition of a ceiling on land is in the national interest and, therefore, this step has to be followed.

The settling of the landless people on the land and providing them with some security in life is a human problem the solution of which cannot now be delayed. This is the first step which must be taken so that a more homogeneous village community is produced which can come together for various objects of rural development. Co-operation in the village today is handicapped because of the various social and economic differences which beset village life. These come in the way of all co-operative activities. It is necessary to remove them and establish a more homogeneous and broad-based pattern capable of sustaining the rapid strides of national development which are taking place today.

Abolition Of Intermediaries

Abolition of intermediaries has been carried out in the bulk of the country and further legislative measures have to be taken only in some small areas which we have indicated. Abolition of intermediaries does not raise any controversial issues and its main features are well known. We recommend that the process should be completed as early as possible. In some States, it is possible that there may be some feeling that further land reform measures may be taken up when the question of reorganisation of States has been settled and there may perhaps be some reluctance to take up any controversial measure on account of the fact that the areas affected may be transferred to other States. We would, however, urge that this should not be regarded as an obstacle to the completion of the work because abolition of intermediaries has a well-known and common pattern and necessary action can and should be taken even before the re-organisation is complete.

We have mentioned that in a number of States, some of the main tasks consequent on the abolition of intermediaries have yet to be completed. While we are aware that the State Governments concerned are taking necessary action, we would urge that effort should be made to complete the various items of work as early as possible, referred to in Chapter III of Part I of this report particularly:

(a) Cadastral survey and preparation of records wherever necessary;

(b) Strengthening the agency for the maintenance of land records up-to-date;

(c) Setting up of a suitable agency for collection of land revenue; and

(d) Setting up of an agency for management of common lands acquired by the Government.

We consider that it is desirable to pay compensation as quickly as possible in cases where it has not been paid already. Where there are likely to be some delays in the determination of payment of compensation, interim compensation should be paid. Steps should be taken, in particular, to make the payments to small intermediaries and to the intermediaries who are widows or minors. A suggestion has been made to us that there should be a ceiling on the amount of compensation payable to any intermediary. We suggest that this should be carefully considered and implemented if there are no constitutional or legal difficulties.

We recommend that action for the abolition of *inams* should be completed as early as possible on the basis of the general pattern for abolition of intermediaries.

Further, in an area where an owner of land in a village performs an important function like the maintenance of land records, the administration may be biased against the interests of other classes such as tenants. An owner who collects land revenue is likely to be a very powerful person and may, to that extent, tend to weaken the authority of the Village Panchayat. It is conceivable that functions relating to the revenue administration may be performed by Government servants on prescribed scales of pay or by a duly elected representative of the village community as a whole. But a system in which a landlord performs these functions, is inconsistent with our objectives. We, therefore, recommend that the organisation of services to the Government should be based on the normal footing as speedily as possible.

Rights Of Owners Of Land

With the abolition of intermediaries, the existing tenures may be broadly clarified into the following categories:

(1) **Owners,** i.e. the principal tenure holders such as occupant or raiyat or tenants-in-chief (in the former intermediary areas) who hold land directly under the State;

(2) **Tenants,** i.e. sub-tenants or tenants of an occupant or raiyat holding land from an owner either directly or through an intermediate tenure holder.

In any consideration of a comprehensive scheme of land reforms we have to take into account not only the quantum of rights which should be conferred upon the peasants in cultivating possession of land and the degree and nature of social control over these rights, but also the ultimate pattern of our social and economic institutions.

Steps have to be taken to rationalise our land system and to introduce a more or less uniform pattern throughout the country, allowing only for such variations as are justified by economic considerations rather than considerations of historical development. Denial of necessary rights or the conferment of excessive rights can both cause damage to the rural economy. A comprehensive view of this question should be taken so that the quantum of rights of owners is related to their economic functions and the interest of the community as a whole. They should have the rights which will give them the necessary psychological incentive and opportunities for increased agricultural production and should have the obligations which would facilitate the maximum utilisation of land resources in the interest of the community.

(1) **Inheritance:** Inheritance is generally governed by personal law, but in some cases as, for instance, sirdars in U.P., a restricted table of devolution has been prescribed in order to prevent fragmentation of holdings. We consider that there is no need to make a distinction between inheritance of land and inheritance of other forms of property. The measures necessary to prevent excessive fragmentation will be examined in the sequel.

(2) **Right of Transfer:** The Committee recommend that transfers should be made through Village Panchayats at regulated prices (which should give adequate recompense to the transferor, and be also economic for the transferee) and according to an order of preference which should be prescribed by law. The aggregate of the land which the transferee may own (including the area already owned) should not exceed the area which a family can cultivate with their own labour and occasional hired labour to the extent customary. In cases where there are more applicants than one belonging to the same order or preference, who are willing to purchase the land at a regulated price, lots may be drawn.

(3) **Right of Improvement:** The Committee are of the view that an unrestricted right of improvement should be given.

(4) **Right of Simple Mortgage:** The Committee are of the view that all owners should have the right to make a simple mortgage to facilitate rural credit.

(5) **Right of Mortgage with Possession:** The Committee are of the view that the cultivators should not have the right of mortgage with possession, as it can be used to defeat the provisions for regulation of transfers and leases.

(6) **Right of Letting:** It would not be administratively possible to enforce a complete prohibition of letting. Besides, it would make the land system too rigid and would prevent the rural classes from taking up employment in urban areas.

(7) **Right of Use:** The cultivator should have the right to use land for agricultural purposes subject to the observance of standards of efficient cultivation. Use for non-agricultural purposes may also be permitted subject to the approval of the community.

(8) **Right of Exchange:** The right of exchange already exists in order that cultivators may exchange lands among themselves according to their needs. There is no objection to this right being allowed to owners where it does not obtain now.

(9) **Right of Partition:** We suggest that partition of land where it results in the creation of a fragment or in the breaking up of a holding which is already a fragment should be prohibited. The Village Panchayats should

in addition to the revenue agency be required to report cases of contravention and where the Village Panchayat is unable to persuade the co-tenure holders to cultivate their land on a co-operative basis, the land should be sold at a regulated price among the co-tenure holders. The co-tenure holders who do not purchase the land should be paid their share of the compensation.

(10) **Recovery of Rent or Revenue:** We consider that the provision for ejectment should be omitted and arrears of rent or revenue may be recovered by sale of the holding. Such sales should be subject to the same conditions as have been suggested above for voluntary transfers. Land of value equivalent to the rent or revenue should be sold but not in such a way as to create a fragment.

(11) **Processes for Recovery of Arrears of Rent or Revenue:** The processes for recovery of rent or revenue are generally similar in the various States and include (1) issue of writ of a demand, (2) sale of movable property, (3) sale of crops, (4) sale of the holding, (5) sale of other immovable property, and (6) arrest and detention of the defaulter.

The Committee is of the view that arrest or detention of the defaulter should be omitted from the processes of recovery. The other processes are quite adequate for the purpose.

(12) **Rent in Kind:** Under the intermediary system, there were some classes of tenants who paid rent in kind. On abolition, the State Governments have taken steps to commute such a rent into a fixed money rent as it is obviously inconvenient for the State to collect rent in kind.

(13) **Principles Governing the Allotment of Waste Lands for Agricultural Purposes in (a) Rural Areas, and (b) Urban Areas:** The procedure for allotment of such lands (for instance, by auction, to the highest bidder or by allotment either on an ad hoc basis or in accordance with a prescribed order of priority), the terms and conditions of the lease and the level of rents show considerable variations from State to State. The Committee are of the view that the procedure for such allotments and the rights and obligations of the allottees should be rationalised in the light of the objectives which have been mentioned earlier.

Tenancy Reforms

We recommend that pending the enactment of comprehensive legislation for tenancy reforms, the following steps should be taken in this direction with immediate effect :

(i) Ejectment of tenants or sub-tenants should be stayed. Ejectment on grounds of non-payment of rent or misuse of land may be permitted through the due processes of law.

(ii) Tenants who have been dispossessed of their lands in recent years should be restored except where ejectments were made through the courts for non-payment of rent or misuse of land. "Voluntary surrenders" result mainly from the landlords' influence and the tenants' low bargaining power. All such surrenders should be treated as cases of ejectments and restoration provided for.

(iii) All tenants should come into direct relation with the State which should undertake the obligation to recover fair rents from the tenants and pay it to the landlord after deducting the cost of collection.

Security of Tenure: We do not favour the idea that security of tenure should be conferred only where long possession is established and we recommend that:

(1) A tenant who has already held any land continuously for a period of 12 years or is in possession of land which has not been cultivated by the land owner personally at any time during a period of 12 years should have permanent and heritable rights in the land and should not be liable to ejectment on any grounds whatsoever, not even on the ground that the landlord requires the land for personal cultivation.

(2) All other tenants should have security of tenure subject to the landlord's right to resume land bona fide for personal cultivation on terms and conditions described in the succeeding paragraphs.

Landlord's Right of Resumption: We recommend as follows :

(a) Every tenant should have a prior right to retain a family holding for personal cultivation. The family holding has been defined by the Size of Holdings Committee. In determining this area any land owned by him or held under permanent rights should be taken into consideration.

(b) The land held by a tenant in excess of a family holding may be resumed by the landlord for personal cultivation subject to the limit of a family holding.

(c) Any land held by a tenant which he is not entitled to retain and which the landlord is not entitled to resume should be declared surplus to provide land for redistribution.

(d) Provided that where a tenant's family comprises more than one adult worker, the tenant shall, in addition to a family holding, be entitled to retain half a family holding for each additional adult worker.

The family may, for this purpose, be deemed to consist of all persons who are working with the tenant on land and who, if they survived the tenant without nearer heirs would be entitled to inherit his right.

Exemptions to the above rules may be made in the following cases:

(i) **Small Owners:** Social considerations demand a more careful balancing of the rights of the small owners and their tenants. A small owner may be defined as a person who owns less than a family holding. He should be permitted to resume (including the area already held under personal cultivation) half the area owned by him but not less than the floor which will be one-third of the family holding. Where this would reduce the tenant's holding to less than the floor the Government should, before permitting resumption, allot to the tenant, out of the surplus land, an area which will make up his holding up to the floor.

(ii) **Persons Suffering from a Disability:** Where a person was obligated to lease the land, he should have the prior right to land for personal cultivation to the extent he can cultivate with his own labour together with the labour of his family members and occasional assistance of hired labourers. For this purpose, the person may be presumed to be suffering from a disability if he belongs to any one of the following categories:

(a) Unmarried women;

(b) Widows;

(c) Minors;

(d) Persons suffering from mental or physical disability; and

(e) Persons serving in the Armed Forces.

If in the family of such a person there is an adult worker capable of engaging in cultivation, he should not be presumed to be suffering from a disability.

Where as a result of resumption by a person suffering from a disability, the tenant is left with less than the minimum area, he should have the first preference to allotment of land out of the surplus area to the extent it may be necessary to make up his holding up to the minimum area.

In order to remove uncertainty and to stabilise the position of tenants, the areas which the landlord is entitled to resume and the areas to be retained by the tenants should be demarcated in as short a period as possible. A period of, say, six months should be prescribed during which the owner shall be required to apply for reservation of land which is to be resumed.

In demarcating the resumable and the non-resumable area, the tenant in possession should have the right to select the area which he is entitled to retain. The tenant should select the area in the following order of priorities:

(a) Land owned by him, if any, and which he is entitled to retain;

(b) Land held by him from substantial holders;

(c) Land held by him from medium holders; and

(d) Land held by him from small holders.

The landowner will then select the land for resumption out of the remaining area up to the limit mentioned above. The excess land, if any, will then be declared surplus.

Condition for Resumption: The right of resumption will, in all cases, be subject to the condition that the income from the land to be resumed will be the main source of the owner's income.

Period of Resumption: The substantial owner shall exercise the right to actually resume the land by ejectment of the tenant within three years, and in cases where the owner suffers from a disability within three years of the termination of the disability, failing which the right of resumption will lapse. In the case of small owners, the right can be exercised within three years, but if it is not thus exercised, the lease shall be deemed to be renewed for five years, for successive period of the right of resumption being available at the end of each five-year period.

Rights of Tenants in the Non-resumable Area: In respect of the non-resumable area, the tenants should have the right of permanent and heritable possession. They should also have all the other rights and obligations recommended in an earlier section for the owners.

Rights in the Resumable Area: With regard to the resumable area, pending its resumption by the landlord, the tenant may have heritable but not permanent rights together with a right to make improvements. He should be entitled to compensation if it is undertaken with the Government's consent. He should not, however, have a right of transfer, mortgage or exchange.

Definitions of "Personal Cultivation" and "Tenant": The expressions "personal cultivation" and "tenant" need to be defined more precisely than is generally done.

The principal constituents of "personal cultivation" are:

(a) **Risk of Cultivation:** The cultivator should meet the entire risk of cultivation. Where he shares the risk with another person, who receives a share of the produce as his remuneration, the latter has an apparent motive for cultivating the land to the best of his capacity. It is common practice for the landowner to leave the entire management of land to him and become an absentee. As in the definition adopted in Bombay and some other States, the owner should, therefore, bear the entire risk of cultivation.

(b) **Personal Supervision:** By the owner or a member of his family cannot be effectively exercised without residence in the village or in a contiguous village during the major part of the agricultural season.

(c) **Labour:** A bona fide cultivator is one who engages himself in the principal agricultural operations, such as ploughing, sowing and harvesting. Performance of minimum labour should, therefore, be included in the definition of personal cultivation.

When a person resumes land for personal cultivation by ejecting a tenant, he should be required to fulfil the conditions of personal cultivation outlined above. If he fails to satisfy any one of these conditions, the land should revert to the tenant or the State, as the case may be.

It would, however, be difficult to apply these conditions to all existing arrangements in areas where the definition of personal cultivation is less complete and a worker who receives the bulk of his remuneration in the form of a share of the produce is not regarded as a tenant. In such cases, the arrangement should not be considered a lease if the owner also engages in the work of cultivation and performs minimum labour. If he does not do so, it is a lease and tenancy rights should accrue.

Where an owner meets the entire risk of cultivation but does not reside in the village and exercises personal supervision effectively, he should have an opportunity to take up residence in the village. With regard to future arrangements, while the three conditions described above represent the goal which should gradually be achieved, it is not necessary at this stage to insist upon the performance of minimum labour provided the owner meets the entire risk of cultivation, resides in the village and personally supervises agricultural operations.

Fair Rents: Rents should be brought down to the level of one-sixth of the produce or value thereof by the end of the Second Five-Year Plan period. As the State will undertake the responsibility to collect rents, it will be necessary for administrative convenience to commute produce rents into fixed money rents as speedily as possible. In the determination of rents, increase in produce resulting from an improvement made by the tenant at his own expense should not be taken into account.

Ownership for Tenants: In the foregoing paragraphs, we have suggested that all tenants should be brought into direct relationship with the State with immediate effect. As soon as it may be feasible and keeping in view the level of rent and the financial obligations involved, the State Governments may but out the landlord's interest on payment of compensation. In determining the rate of compensation, the aggregate net increase in revenues accruing to the State (i.e. fair rent minus land revenue minus collection charges) over a period not exceeding 20 years may be taken into consideration. Graded rates of compensation might also be considered. The compensation may be paid in the form of bonds redeemable over a period of 20 years. The tenant's liability to pay fair rent should continue so long as it may be necessary for enabling the State Government to meet the liability for payment of compensation. At the end of the period the State Government may review the position, and, if necessary, require the tenants to pay land revenue only. Since acquisition of ownership rights would by this method take about 20 years or so tenants should so have the right voluntarily to purchase ownership at a reasonable price to be prescribed by law.

Administrative Agency

Problems relating to administrative organisation should receive immediate attention.

With regard to difficulties arising from the fact that Village Panchayats are divided by factions or do not truly represent the various interests in the villages, we would suggest that the difficulties can be met by:

(i) the provision that the Village Panchayats may co-opt additional members to find adequate representation to various classes of interests involved, such as tenants, agricultural labourers, etc.; and

(ii) by gradation of Panchayats into Grades A, B and C as recommended by the Congress Panchayat Committee.

The Village Panchayats which have been elected on a unanimous basis and thus command confidence of the whole community and such other Panchayats as possess the necessary competence would be placed in Grade 'A'. These Panchayats would undertake all the functions with regard to the implementation of land reform measures, namely:

(i) association with the work of maintenance of land records;

(ii) making leases of land in all cases where the owner is unable to cultivate the land himself and desires that it may be let out for cultivation;

(iii) association with the determination of surplus lands;

(iv) association with the re-distribution of surplus lands;

(v) allotment of waste lands; and

(vi) where land is being transferred by an owner by sale, the selection of the transferee to whom the land may be transferred.

The other Panchayats can be graded into Class 'B' or 'C' according to their experience and competence and could be given lesser powers to begin with. It would, however, be desirable to associate these Village Panchayats also with the preparation and maintenance of records. A sustained effort should, however, be made to give these Panchayats the necessary training and support so that they become competent to discharge wider responsibilities. We consider it necessary that there should be representative bodies at higher levels to give necessary support to the Village Panchayats and to exercise general supervision over their work. It is not, however, necessary to enter into details as the whole question of village organisation is being considered by the Committee on Problems of Re-organisation.

Judicial functions relating to the enforcement of land reform measures comprise:

(i) disputes regarding tenancies;
(ii) disputes regarding possession of land;
(iii) disputes regarding commutation;
(iv) appeals arising out of correction of records;
(v) cases regarding arrears of rent;
(vi) ejectment of tenants;
(vii) ejectment of trespassers;
(viii) restoration of possession to tenants; and

(ix) fixation of the price of lands where lands are transferred.

The ultimate objective is that these cases should be dealt with in the village itself by Nyaya Panchayats. For this purpose Nyaya Panchayats should be established, where they do not already exist, as speedily as possible. Where the decision of a particular category of cases cannot be entrusted to Panchayats, they should be encouraged to consider and determine facts, and their findings on facts should be subject to confirmation by the revenue or civil courts. It is essential that up-to-date land records should be prepared as a measure of topmost priority and they should contain full particulars about the mode of cultivation of land, the terms and conditions of tenancies, and the names of the actual tillers of land. The progress of work in this connection should be carefully watched and facilities given to State Governments where necessary to complete the preparation or revision of records as soon as possible. Besides, the records frequently contain errors which lead to much litigation. The preparation or revision of such records is the first step in the enforcement of any measure of land reforms. Unfortunately during the preparation or revision of records false claims are often made by different parties. It has been our experience that in such cases the best evidence of the actual fact of possession can be obtained only in the village. It is easy for a few villagers to suppress facts before a Revenue Officer who is far away from the village but it is extremely difficult for them to behave in the same manner in the presence of the whole body of villagers. To ensure correctness of records in future we recommend the adoption of the procedure which has recently been initiated in U.P., namely, that a copy of the record showing the possession of land should be maintained with the Village Panchayat and all subsequent changes with regard to possession of land should be communicated to the panchayats as well as to the affected parties.

As soon as the interim law for the stay of ejectments has been enacted, ejectments under the law would stop. As we stated earlier, dispossession of tenants takes place mainly as a result of "voluntary surrenders". Unless effective steps are taken to prevent these surrenders, it is feared the whole law may become ineffective. It is true that a provision for restoration of tenants which will apply to cases of surrenders also will, to some extent, discourage surrenders. It will not, however, wholly prevent them as is borne out by the present experience. It will, therefore, be necessary to provide in the law that no one shall surrender land and no landlord shall accept surrender from a tenant pending the enactment of the comprehensive law. If any tenant for certain economic reasons is meanwhile unable to cultivate the land, he may surrender it to the Government which should have the authority to settle a new tenant on it.

Restoration of tenants will present a much more difficult task. The law should provide for restoration on application as well as suo moto by the revenue authority. If restoration is to be made only on the application of a tenant, it is feared that due to the influence of the landlord many tenants may not come forward with applications. Suo moto action is, therefore, necessary. To enable the revenue administration to take suo moto action, we suggest that while the record-of-rights is being prepared, information should also be collected regarding the tenants who had been dispossessed of lands. As the Village Panchayats will be associated with the preparation of records, it should be comparatively easier to collect this information. A further difficulty may be experienced where a landlord after ejecting a tenant has admitted another tenant. We suggest that in such cases restoration of tenants may not be insisted upon provided the new tenant has been admitted bona fide and is not merely a relation or a dependent admitted with a view to avoiding the provisions of the law. If, however, the new tenant has, thus, acquired an area exceeding, say, a family holding, the ejected tenant could be admitted to the land held by the new tenant, in excess of the family holding.

Pari passu with the preparation of the record-of-rights, the State Governments will also take action for the enactment of a comprehensive law so that by the time the record-of-rights has been prepared, the comprehensive law is also brought on the anvil. The tenants should then be brought into direct relationship with the State which should collect fair rent from them and pay it to the landlord after deducting a collection charge. The stage will then be reached for the demarcation of the resumable and non-resumable areas. The demarcation of these areas, and all other disputes relating to tenancy rights, will, as stated earlier, be the responsibility of the Judicial Panchayats.

We have mentioned earlier that the ignorance of the people of the provisions of the land reform law constitutes a major factor contributing to the ineffectiveness of the law. It is necessary, therefore, that deliberate efforts should be made to inform the people about the contents of law. The revenue staff and the Village Panchayats are the principal agencies which could be utilised for this purpose. The provisions of the land reform law should be rendered in a simple language which the subordinate staff and the "panches" could understand. Small pamphlets containing the provisions of the law should be widely distributed. Seminars in rural areas may also be organised where these provisions be freely discussed. The local vernacular Press should be encouraged to give wide publicity to the provisions. Where necessary, special agencies should be created for this purpose.

OFFICIAL LANGUAGE COMMISSION, 1955—REPORT

New Delhi, Ministry of Home Affairs, 1957. 495p.

Chairman : Shri B. G. Kher.

Members : Dr. Birinchi Kumar Barua; Dr. S. K. Chatterji; Shri Maganbhai Desai; Shri D. C. Pavate; Prof. P. N. Pushp; Shri M. K. Raja; Dr. P. Subbarayan; Shri G. P. Nene; Dr. P. K. Parija; Sardar Teja Singh; Shri M. Satyanarayana; Dr. Babu Ram Saksena; Dr. Abid Hussain; Dr. Amar Nath Jha (died, replaced by Prof. Ramdhari Sinha); Dr. R.P. Tripathi; Shri Balkrishna Sharma; Shri Mauli Chander Sharma; Dr. Hazari Prasad Dwivedi; Shri Jai Narain Vyas; Shri M. Ananthasayanam Ayyangar.

Secretary : Shri S. G. Barve.

APPOINTMENT

In pursuance of the provisions contained in Article 344 of the Constitution, the Official Language Commission was constituted by the President of India vide the Notification of the Ministry of Home Affairs No. 43/9/55-Public I, dated June 7, 1955.

TERMS OF REFERENCE

To make recommendations to:

(a) The progressive use of the Hindi language for the official purposes of the Union;

(b) Restrictions on the use of the English language for all or any of the official purposes of the Union;

(c) The language to be used for all or any of the purposes mentioned in Article 348 of the Constitution;

(d) The form of numerals to be used for any one or more specified purposes of the Union;

(e) The preparation of a time schedule according to which and the manner in which Hindi may gradually replace English as the official language of the Union and as a language for communication between the Union and State Governments and between one State Government and another.

In making their recommendations, the Commission shall have due regard to the industrial, cultural and scientific advancement of India and the just claims and interests of persons belonging to the non-Hindi speaking areas in regard to the public services.

The Commission may:

(a) obtain such information as they may consider useful for or relevant to any matter under their consideration whether by asking for written memoranda or by examining witnesses, or in such form and in such manner as they may consider appropriate, from the Central Government, the State Governments, the Supreme Court, the High Courts, the Legislatures and such other authorities, organisations or individuals as may, in the opinion of the Commission, be of assistance to them;

(b) regulate their own procedure, including the fixing of places and time of their sittings and deciding whether to sit in public or in private;

(c) appoint such and so many sub-committees from amongst their members to exercise such powers and perform such duties as may be delegated to them by the Commission;

(d) visit or depute any of their sub-committees to visit such parts of the territory of India as they consider necessary or expedient;

(e) act, notwithstanding the temporary absence of any member or the existence of any vacancy among the members.

CONTENTS

Introductory; Language in the Modern World; The Indian Linguistic Scene; The Indian Language Problem and the Lineaments of a Solution; Terminology; The Union Language and the Educational System; Language in Public Administration—I; Language in Public Administration—II; Language of Law and Law Courts—I; Language of Law and Law Courts—II; Language of Law and Law Courts—III; The Union Language and Public Services Examinations; Propagation and Development of Hindi and the Regional Languages; Agencies, etc., for Implementation of the National Language Programme; Concluding Remarks; Appendices I to XV.

RECOMMENDATIONS

Language In The Modern World

Language, in its spoken and written form, is an indispensable tool of all forms of social organisation and basic to the advancement of knowledge and human progress. In modern communities mass literacy is an indispensable means for technological progress and improvement of living standards.

Language is generally an important element in the consciousness of nationality: since modern Governments have to concern themselves intimately with numerous aspects of life in a community, the question of linguistic medium for "official purposes" becomes an important matter for deliberate choice.

In certain countries of the world like Switzerland, Canada, Belgium, the problem of languages, since it arises in respect of no more than three or four languages, is solved, generally speaking, by adoption of a wide-spread multi-lingualism; in the U.S.S.R., the outstanding position of the Russian language from all points of view in the linguistic map of the country simplifies the language problem in that country compared to the Indian situation.

In Japan and in Turkey deliberate programmes of language reform were undertaken and carried through as a measure of national policy; the outstanding issue of language reform in China is the alphabetisation of the script.

While the complexity of the Indian language problem exceeds that of other multi-lingual countries, a solution sought on pragmatic lines and in a spirit of tolerance, understanding and respect for diverse cultural expressions —which have been painfully learnt in certain countries of the world as amelioratives for linguistic difficulties—ought to be available.

In many countries, for keeping abreast of scientific advances in the world, an advanced foreign language is systematically taught as a second language within the educational system: the English language is the foremost amongst such second languages in many parts of the world.

The Indian Linguistic Scene

As the vast sub-continent of India has been the meeting ground throughout the history for the people of diverse racial and demographic origin it is hardly to be wondered at that there should be a great multiplicity and variety in the forms of speech in this country.

Although the number of languages and dialects registered as such in linguistic surveys in India is very large, the cultivated current languages are only a few; besides, there are close affinities and common elements amongst all these languages. The languages that require to be considered in relation to the "language problem" in the country are only the important 13 regional languages (omitting Sanskrit) enlisted in the Eighth Schedule to the Constitution.

The system of public education introduced after the establishment of British rule in the country has had a profound influence on the Indian linguistic scene. Following the famous resolution passed by the Government of India in 1835 for imparting to Indians a knowledge of English literature and science, the policies laid down in Wood's Despatch of 1854 governed the educational system of the country for several decades thereafter. Although this Despatch embodied a clear recognition of the importance of the indigenous languages of the country in the educational system and envisaged literature in such languages as a necessary link in the "percolation" theory of education, in practice, these languages did not feature to any significant extent in the educational system as media of instruction until very recently. Apart from any official neglect of these languages in these early years the demand from the politically conscious Indian opinion was insistently for greater opportunities for learning English which it deemed as a "key" not only to scientific and other advance of the country but also as an instrument of political advance, and withal as a great liberalising social force.

Growingly, over the last 150 years, the English language came to supervene and finally eclipsed entirely the Indian languages in all important fields of public administration, higher education, the professions and public life. As a result of such supersession, these languages continued undeveloped and they are now not in a position to displace English in their appropriate fields until these deficiencies have been made up.

Notwithstanding all this, Indian literature still recorded a very impressive development during these decades. The period of the 19th century represents a great renaissance in the Indian languages brought about by the advent of the printing press, the opening out of new vistas of literary forms and features through acquaintance of English literature and the impact of Western civilisation on Indian conditions. Thanks to this efflorescence in the indigenous languages, we are now in a position to think in terms of switching over to Indian language media in all fields of activity, including those from which they have hitherto been excluded.

It is suggested for the consideration of Census authorities that a question indicative of linguistic ability in the Hindi language on the part of speakers of non-Hindi mother tongues all over the country may be instituted at the next and subsequent censuses.

The Indian Language Problem And The Lineaments Of A Solution

The enfranchisement of the regional languages in their appropriate fields and the forging of a common medium of expression for all relevant purposes, official and non-official, with reference to all aspects of pan-Indian intercourse, constitute the language problem of India.

In the light of the fully democratic basis of the Indian polity as established under the Constitution, it is not possible to envisage English as the common all-India mass medium. About 1 per cent of the population has presently anything like an adequate linguistic ability in English. The programme of compulsory elementary education, enjoined in the Constitution, can be conceived of only in terms of Indian languages.

This conclusion has been reached not on grounds of prejudice against a foreign language, or in disregard of the wealth of literature and scientific knowledge available in it, or merely on grounds of patriotic sentiment; it is also recognised that for the maintenance of high academic standards, particularly in respect of scientific knowledge and research, for maintaining a live communion with the progress of science and thought in the rest of the world, and for other specific purposes like international contacts, as language of diplomacy, etc., a knowledge of the English language will have to be cultivated by appropriate categories of persons. However, there is a vital distinction between the use of a foreign language for specific purposes or as "a second language", and its use as the *principal or general medium* of education, administration, public life and the day-to-day business of the country. It is this aspect which is sought to be rectified.

The obvious linguistic medium for pan-Indian purposes is the Hindi language. Hindi has been adopted as the Union language and the language for inter-State communication in the Indian Constitution having regard to the relative numbers of the population who speak and understand this language, compared to the other regional languages; and not because in point of development, or in point of literary wealth, other regional languages in India are in any way inferior to Hindi.

It is not practicable to adopt two Union languages, one from the Indo-Aryan and the other from the Dravidian families; nor is it possible to think in terms of Sanskrit as such an all-India medium.

In view of all this, the provisions made in the Constitution for adoption of Hindi for the purposes of the Union, Union-State and inter-State communication represent the only practicable course.

On the displacement of the English language as a general medium in these various spheres of national life the "succession" would accrue not wholly to the Union language but to the Union and regional languages in their appropriate spheres.

The Hindi language will replace the English language only to a limited extent in one sense as it would not wholly "step into the shoes" of the English language, the regional languages having been yielded their appropriate places; in another sense, however, having regard to the vast programmes of compulsory education and literacy ahead, the extent of coverage that would accrue to the Union language would be enormously in excess of the population served by the English language at present or of what could possibly be served by any such foreign linguistic medium.

While the Constitution properly limits itself to the question of replacing English by Indian linguistic media in the official business of the country, there are other fields of activity, within, so to say, the "private sector of national life", wherein the question of a single linguistic medium for all pan-Indian levels of intercourse is of the highest significance. In these fields there is little or no scope for legislating with reference to any specific language policy; and the linguistic pattern must be allowed freedom to develop as it may by the voluntary choices of the people and in response to the needs and opportunities of the situation. After initiating necessary steps for the development of the Union language as well as of the regional languages, this sector may be left free for all the different linguistic media to attain their appropriate coverage with reference to the needs and opportunities in different fields, evolving in due course a general linguistic equilibrium.

The constitutional provisions limit themselves to laying down the minimum requirements with reference to the sectors of activity relatable to official business; for our part also we have limited ourselves to this and the necessary consequential measures for sustaining the linguistic provisions for the official sector.

Apart from these strict and minimum requirements of the situation, what the constitutional provisions envisage, and we whole-heartedly endorse, is a "republic of letters" in which each language, including English, will find the place that properly belongs to it in the country's national life.

The language provisions of the Constitution are wise and comprehending; while clearly enunciating the objectives, they make due provision for the need for developing the Union language, the special case of language for law courts and legislation, and the difficulties of the transitional period. They are viable and elastic, and it should be possible to accommodate the situation as it develops without amendment of the constitutional framework.

Practically all responsible opinion accepts the constitutional settlement, although some persons have doubts as to the preparatory period of 15 years being ultimately found adequate; others are of the view that the period will be found adequate for a *general* change-over of the linguistic medium provided sufficiently energetic steps are taken in the meantime. However, this is not an issue on which it is necessary or possible for this Commission to pronounce.

We have no opinion to express regarding the legitimacy of the demands for the inclusion of the Sindhi and the English languages in the Eighth Schedule to the Constitution. The reason is that the question of inclusion of any more languages in that Schedule is not included within, and does not appear to be necessarily relatable to, our Terms of Reference; nor have we taken evidence with reference to these demands which were made to us only towards the end of our labours.

Apart from the constitutional provisions regarding language of the Union and of the States, the Indian Constitution enacts certain general safeguards relating to languages and scripts as a part of the cultural and educational rights of minorities. These provisions are an extension of the same spirit of liberalism and catholicity which characterises the provisions of the Constitution relating to official languages and recognise and allow for the variety and multiform character of the Indian cultural inheritance. In different regions certain local problems arise relating to languages. While these fall outside our purview, we are convinced that all these local problems are capable of being resolved satisfactorily, if they are approached in the same spirit of tolerance and broadmindedness which informs the cultural and linguistic guarantees and other language provisions of the Constitution.

Terminology

The principal ground-work for the development of the Union language and the regional languages is the furnishing to them of an adequate technical terminology wherever it is deficient at present.

In adopting terminology, clarity, precision and simplicity should be primarily aimed at. Doctrinaire insistence on "language purism" is deprecated.

Promising sources for adopting new terminology should be available in the indigenous terms current in the past, and the terms currently used in actual life amongst various categories of craftsmen, artisans, etc. These should be explored. In suitable cases, international terminology may be adopted or adapted to the genius of the Indian languages.

The maximum possible identity in evolving new terminology for all Indian languages should be aimed at.

Suitable arrangements should be made for evolving terminology and for co-ordinating such work as between different authorities with reference to the Union language as well as the other regional languages.

On a review of the work done so far in the Ministry of Education of the Government of India, there would seem to be room for greater acceleration in the work and need for achieving more effective co-ordination as between different terminological efforts.

Before the terminology evolved can be thoroughly assimilated into the corpus of the "host" languages, two stages must be envisaged: (i) to start using the new terminology and (ii) to undertake its periodical re-standardisation.

The Union Language And The Educational System

The problem of language instruction and of language medium in the educational system is considered in this Report only in so far as it is relatable to the language question of the country.

In view of Article 45 of the Directive Principles of State Policy in the Indian Constitution, under which "the State shall endeavour to provide for free and compulsory education for all children until they complete the age of 14 years", the educational system must be re-oriented to achieve the imparting of sufficient literacy in the Hindi language by the age-limit of 14 years, so that every citizen, if so inclined, may be in a position to comprehend and keep in touch with trends and movements in public life at pan-Indian levels including the activities of the Union Government.

The children undergoing compulsory education up to the age of 14 years in terms of Article 45 of the Constitution would receive about eight years of school education, during the whole of which they would have studied the regional language both as a subject and as the medium of instruction for other subjects. It is essential to provide for a minimum of three or four years of instruction in Hindi during the later part of this period.

Even when English ceases to be the medium of instruction in our Universities, it would be necessary, for a long time to come, to provide that the graduates emerging from our Universities, especially in the scientific subjects and professions, are equipped with a sufficient command of English (or other suitable advanced foreign language) to enable them to comprehend and follow further advances in their particular departments of study through journals and new publications available in such a language.

In view of the different purposes that English would now serve in the educational system of the country, it is necessary to review the present teaching methods and the content and character of instruction in English imparted presently. English should be taught hereafter principally as a "language of comprehension" and not as a literary language, excepting when it is taken as a voluntary subject for special study.

It will be for the appropriate authorities, after a study of pedagogic considerations, to formulate the exact curricula for imparting to students. during the secondary school stage and after, the degree of knowledge in the English language that we consider necessary for Undergraduates and Graduates to possess. Tentatively it would seem appropriate if instruction in the English language commenced in the Secondary school at a stage about five years pre-S.L.C.

There may be a suitable "streaming off" of boys destined to follow further academic education from those who would leave off education at the end of the 14-year age-limit of compulsory education, the instruction in English suggested above being imparted, as a rule, only to the former.

The quantum of instruction in the Hindi language which we consider indispensable for students in secondary schools could be imparted to them if instruction in the Hindi language commenced roughly at the close of the Primary stage and continued up to the S.L.C. stage.

In our view instruction in Hindi should be compulsory at the Secondary school stage all over the country and the arguments for such a course of action are strong and decisive. However, reasons of expediency might also have relevance within particular regions and the decision as to when compulsion should be introduced must be left to be made by the State Government concerned in whose jurisdiction the decision anyhow lies.

The suggestion that there should be "compensatory compulsion" to the students in the Hindi-speaking areas in Secondary schools to learn another Indian language (a South Indian language) is examined and negatived.

However, the educational authorities in the Hindi-speaking areas should be encouraged to provide facilities for the learning of other Indian languages to the maximum possible extent and, where necessary, special assistance should be made available from governmental sources for this purpose.

For various reasons the English language must eventually be replaced by an Indian language or languages as a general medium of higher education. The waste of energy that the foreign medium involves, the burden that it imposes on the intellectual development of our youth, the general blighting effect that the whole situation has on an independent and original thinking, and the resultant alienation of the educated classes from the rest of the community, make it imperative that the medium of instruction should be changed. Provided such a change-over is properly phased and made after complete and satisfactory preparations, it would not itself cause any fall in the academic standards, and should indeed eventually open the way for their considerable improvement.

If English is to be displaced as a general medium of university education, the question arises whether it should be replaced by one single common medium, i.e. Hindi in all Universities, or by respective regional languages in the Universities in the different regions. There are certain advantages in a country-wide single medium of university education; at the same time there are strong and comprehensible reasons which urge people to seek to replace the English medium by the regional language.

It is not necessary that the change-over of medium should be simultaneous or uniform or monolithic. It may be that some courses of study, say, the humanities can be more appropriately taught in the regional languages; it may be that for other courses of study the advantages of a common medium in all Universities operate much more powerfully; in yet other faculties it may be preferable, particularly at higher levels, even to continue the English medium; it may also be that in some courses of study, the regional language medium may be adopted for lower levels and a common medium, i.e. the English or Hindi language, adopted for post-graduate studies. Among other things, the decisions of Universities in this regard would depend upon availability of teachers, text-books and other supporting literature in various branches of study.

The whole situation is still fluid and we would advocate that it may be left, in the first instance, to the Universities to judge it after mutual consultation through their customary channels and to decide for themselves what medium or media they would adopt for different courses of study and stages therein.

Certain minimum arrangements from the point of view of the language problem of the country, however, seem to us quite necessary. These may be as under:

All universities in any event be required to arrange to *examine* students offering themselves for any university examination with Hindi as the medium of instruction.

All affiliating universities should also be under obligation to offer affiliation on equal terms to any college or institution teaching through Hindi any of their courses in the territorial jurisdiction of the University.

The establishing, in addition, of Central Universities in the non-Hindi-speaking areas, with Hindi as the medium of instruction and allowing Hindi-medium institutions situate within the jurisdiction of other universities and to affiliate to them, would not be necessary if the above-mentioned arrangements are found sufficient to provide affiliation facilities to institutions adopting the medium of Hindi.

In the case of scientific and technical educational institutions, where students drawn from different linguistic regions avail themselves of the instruction imparted, the common medium of the Hindi language will have to be adopted; where students are drawn exclusively or almost wholly from a single linguistic group, the medium will have to be the regional language concerned. All such cases must be decided pragmatically on the specific merits of each.

So far as the question of the linguistic medium of instruction is concerned, the principle of "autonomy of universities" can, in the final analysis, have only a qualified hearing and the national language policy must ultimately prevail.

The supply of text-books for various university courses in Hindi and the regional languages would of course tend to respond to the greater demand for them; nevertheless, it is necessary to provide for effective and co-ordinated action in this field. As for the production of "reference literature" in these languages, special promotional efforts may be necessary and will have to be organised.

Language in Public Administration—I

Official Language of the Union

The programme chalked out by the Government of India for changing over the medium of business in the affairs of the Union is reviewed. The pre-requisites of a change-over in the language for administration are:

(1) Preparation and standardisation of the necessary special terminology used in the administrative field.

(2) Translation into Hindi of official publications

embodying rules, regulations, manuals, handbooks and other procedural literature relating to the working of the administrative machinery.

(3) Training of administrative personnel of different categories in appropriate standards of linguistic competence for the purpose of using the new linguistic medium with the requisite efficiency and facility of expression.

(4) Development and furnishing in the new linguistic medium of the mechanical and service aids necessary for speeding up and facilitating office work, such as typewriters and typists, stenography and stenographers, printing and duplicating machines, teleprinters and other communication services adapted to the use of the new medium, etc.

Regarding (2) above, it is necessary to ensure that a measure of uniformity is observed in the language used in the translations of all this procedural literature, and for that purpose it may be advisable to invest in a single agency of the Central Government the general responsibility for direction and superintendence over all such work.

As regards (3) above, (training of personnel) the present arrangements made by the Government of India for training their employees on a voluntary basis in the Hindi language are reviewed.

If experience shows that adequate results are not forthcoming under such optional arrangements, it would be legitimate and necessary for the Government to impose, in pursuance of their language policy, obligatory requirements on Government servants to qualify themselves in Hindi within a reasonable period to the extent requisite for the discharge of their duties.

As regards (4) above, schemes should be adopted whereunder stenographers and typists are granted special leave and accorded special facilities to enable them to undertake training in stenography and typing in the new linguistic medium and to acquire knowledge of the Union language.

The standard of linguistic ability in the English language normally associated with the academic education prescribed as a qualification for purposes of recruitment to various categories of posts and services would furnish a guide as to the standard of linguistic ability in Hindi to be aimed at for the different categories of Government personnel. During earlier stages perhaps a slightly lower standard might suffice.

Generally speaking, penalties would seem to be appropriate with reference to failure to attain the prescribed standard by the due date; incentives and rewards would seem to be appropriate with reference to performance above the minimum standard laid down.

In certain segments of the administrative machinery of the Union Government, technical English terms might continue to be used for an indefinite time in the future at levels at which it is not considered necessary to evolve Indian terminology; similarly correspondence may be carried on in the English language where the work involves constant contact with foreign countries through that medium.

Apart from the Ministries or Departments of the Government of India, the linguistic medium will have to change over in the administrative agencies and organisations, such as the Railways, the Posts and Telegraphs, the Excise, Customs, Income-Tax Departments, and so on. Some of these organisations have units and branches located in different parts of the country and the language problem presents a special aspect in regard to them. It is necessary that these administrative organisations should evolve a measure of permanent bilingualism; that is to say, they will use the Hindi language for purposes of internal working and the respective regional languages in their public dealings in the respective regions.

It is necessary that the staff structures of these administrative agencies and departments of the Government of India with a countrywide coverage should be reviewed and decentralised to conform to the requirements of such bilingualism. The recruitment methods and qualifications for recruitment may have also to be revised suitably.

As employers, these all-India departments and organisations have certainly the right to prescribe the standards of Hindi qualification (as of qualification, where necessary, in the respective regional languages) necessary for purposes of recruitment to the different categories of their establishment. It may be that for zonal and regional requirements, the standard of Hindi qualification could be somewhat lower than what would be necessary for the headquarters organisation of these offices as the work in the latter, as distinguished from the former, would be carried on wholly in Hindi.

In order that employment opportunities in the different regions are not curtailed during the transitional period, the requirements of Hindi knowledge may at the start be pitched somewhat lower having due regard to the progress of Hindi in the local educational system, and deficiency being made good by in-service training (after recruitment). The standard may be progressively raised as facilities for instruction in the Hindi language improve in particular regions.

The language policy of the all-India administrative agencies of the Central Government, like the Railways and the Posts and Telegraphs, in their dealings with the public should be framed principally with a view to be convenient to the public whom they are designed to serve: the instrumentality of these Departments should not be used as a "lever" to force the pace of Hindi propagation at the cost of convenience to the public. Where Hindi terms and expressions are used on signboards, forms, etc., for the purpose of familiarising the public with them, the text should also be given in the regional language (or English where relevant) having regard to public convenience.

It is necessary to examine all new Hindi terms and expressions, especially those used by these all-India administrative agencies which come into intimate contact with the public, so as to ensure that the terms and expressions are not discordant with local forms of speech and associations; where certain Sanskrit words have come to acquire in different languages different specialised meanings the employment of inept or unsuitable expressions in disregard or ignorance of these is apt to bring the attempt at "Indianization" of the medium itself into disparagement and ridicule.

It would not be correct, to adopt, instead of training personnel in the new medium, the device of separate translation units or bureaux being maintained at an additional cost to the public funds for translating the work done originally in the English language. While translation services would have their place in the administrative organisation both permanently and as an aid during the transitional stage, these cannot be a substitute for training the personnel to do its work originally in Hindi. In our view, the continuance of the original work in English and its translation at public expense at different stages into Hindi was not the sense in which the changeover in the linguistic medium for the business of the Union was enacted (*sic*) in the Constitution.

The Union Government would be justified in prescribing a reasonable measure of knowledge of the Hindi language as a qualification for entry into their services by new entrants, provided a sufficiently long notice is given and the measure of linguistic ability prescribed is moderate, any deficit being made good by subsequent in-service training.

In the case of officials of the age of 45 and above, the requirement to be prescribed should be for a "comprehending knowledge" of Hindi rather than high levels of linguistic ability for purposes of expression corresponding to the levels of their ability in English. If necessary, separate tests may be devised for the purpose.

The statutory publications of the Government of India would necessarily be in the official language of the Union. It would seem advisable that as many of these as possible, particularly those intended for information of the public, should be published in the Hindi language from now on; translations of such publications should be published in other regional languages depending upon the public to whom they are addressed.

We do not recommend that any restrictions should be imposed for the present on the use of the English language for any of the purposes of the Union.

It has not been possible for us to furnish a regular time-table by dates and stages as to how Hindi should be introduced into the business of the Union so as to accomplish the general changeover within the period fixed by the Constitution. Since the Ministries of the Government of India are components of a single organic unity, the phasing of the progressive use of Hindi must, in general, be lateral and coherent in the different Ministries and Departments. We have not had the benefit of a provisional "plan of action" by the Government of India covering all its Ministries and Departments and comprehending their special difficulties, if any, estimates of workloads of basic preparatory work involved, the present linguistic capacity of all the Government staff and approximate dates by which they could be trained in the new linguistic medium, etc. While we have, therefore, indicated the prerequisites, the general sequence of the phasing and the principles covering various related issues, the actual drawing up of a plan of action and the setting up of a time schedule therewithin must be left to the Government of India themselves to do after a study of the relevant factors.

The special case of the Indian Audit and Accounts Department under the Comptroller and Auditor-General of India is examined. After a State has adopted its regional language as the official language, it will be necessary to arrange that the staff of the Indian Audit and Accounts Department dealing with the affairs of the State is versed in that language sufficiently for the purpose of carrying out its duties of compiling accounts and the exercise of audit. This implies that the Accountant-General's Comptroller's office in a State should be capable of compiling accounts from returns submitted in the regional language and conducting audit with reference to noting and administrative decisions recorded in the regional language.

"Provincialisation of audit" was mentioned as a possible way of resolving this difficulty; it is, however, not necessary to consider such an alternative which would involve a major change in the constitutional arrangements currently in force. We feel that it ought to be possible to devise a solution within the framework of the existing constitutional arrangement whereby, on the one hand, the establishment of the Accountant-General's Comptroller's office in each State would be able to carry out their duties in respect of transactions recorded in the State language, and, on the other, the present system, wherein the accounts and audit responsibility in respect of the Union as well as of the States is centred in the Comptroller and Auditor-General working through a single Indian Audit and Accounts Department, is maintained. The organisation and methods of staffing of the Indian Audit and Accounts Department may have to be revised on lines somewhat similar, to the ones envisaged in respect of the Central Departments comprising activities spread over the whole country.

Language In Public Administration—II

Progress Made In The Use Of Hindi In State Administrations

In general, the progress in the adoption of the Indian language medium, in replacement of the English medium, has been more rapid in the States in the Hindi region than in the rest of the country; however, after the reorganisation of States on a more or less unilingual basis, we would expect the trend, for displacement of the English language by the respective regional languages for the official purposes within such States, to intensify in the non-Hindi-speaking areas as well.

The States concerned will have to consider for themselves at what level administrative occasions would arise for their officers to enter into communication, oral or written, with officers of other States or of the Union. The State Governments must determine for themselves what staff would be affected and what precise steps should be taken for training their personnel at the appropriate levels for dealing with Hindi communications.

As in the case of the Union Government, the State Governments would be justified in imposing obligatory requirements for the acquisition of qualifications in the Hindi language with reference to the staff embraced by the requirements of the new linguistic medium in the field of inter-State and State-Union communications. It would seem that acquisition of a knowledge of the Hindi language beyond these requirements should be on the basis of rewards and incentives rather than compulsion and penalties; however, this is an issue which must be decided by each State for itself.

Arrangements may be made for outgoing communications from the Union Government to a Hindi-speaking State being accompanied by a Hindi translation of the English text, whenever such a State makes a request to this effect. The employment of Hindi in actual work of administration before 1965 in this manner will help in establishing forms of address, expressions, etc., in that language.

The Form Of Numerals

The international form of numerals is itself of Indian origin and as such is nothing but yet another mutation of the ancient Indian numerals, analogous to the several forms of numerals developed, together with their separate scripts, by the modern Indian languages.

It is to be noted that in the South the international form of numerals is in current use in the four great Dravidian languages, sometimes and to a varying extent, alongside the numerals of their respective scripts.

In certain States in the Hindi-speaking region the Devanagari form of numerals is used either exclusively or in addition to the international form of numerals for the internal purposes of the State administration.

It is for the respective State Governments to decide whether this should be so. So far as the Union Government is concerned, there should be a uniform basic policy depending on the public intended to be addressed as to the use of Devanagari numerals in addition to the international form of numerals in the publications of the different Ministries.

We have no recommendation to make for the issue of directions by the President for the use of the Devanagari form of numerals in addition to the international form of Indian numerals for any purposes of the Union between now and the time when the issue will be re-examined by the next Commission to be appointed in 1960.

Language Of Law And Law Courts—I

Language Of Legislation

A distinction must be made between the language to be adopted for the proceedings and deliberations of legislative bodies and the language of the enactments which they legislate. For the deliberative functions of legislatures, the requirements as to a language medium are facility of expression by the concerned speakers and convenience to the general assembly. For the linguistic medium of legislation, the governing considerations are different, namely, that the language must be precise, concise and unambiguous and capable of standing up to the interpretations that will be sought to be put on it in the numerous law courts of the country.

The practice as regards answering interpellations appears to vary. In some cases, provision is made, for furnishing, for the information of the other Members, written translations of the questions and answers in the prescribed language(s) of the legislative body concerned when these have been rendered in another language. Such a practice might be generalised with advantage.

It may happen that for a period of time after (i.e., January 25th, 1965, in the case of the Parliament) English has been replaced by Hindi in Parliament and by the respective official languages of the States in the State Legislatures, cases would arise in which a member may not be able to express himself adequately in Hindi/the State language concerned or in his own mother-tongue; and it would seem advisable that provision should be made to empower the presiding authorities in such cases to permit the members to address the House in English.

We are of the view that the constitutional provisions in regard to the language, relative to proceedings and deliberations of Parliament and legislative bodies of the States, are sufficient for the requirements of the situation.

Apart from the authoritative enactment which, in our opinion, ought to be eventually in Hindi, both in respect of parliamentary legislation and State legislation, there may be need, for the sake of public convenience, to publish translations of the enactments in different regional languages. In respect of State legislation, this would be normally necessary in the regional language(s) prevalent in the State, whereas in respect of parliamentary legislation it may be necessary in all the important regional languages current in the country.

We consider that it is essential, when the time comes for this change-over, that the entire Statute Book of the country should be in one language which cannot of course be other than Hindi. Therefore the language of legislation of the States as well as of Parliament and also, of course, consequently of all statutory orders, rules, etc., issued under any law should be Hindi.

Language Of Law And Law Courts—II

Language Of Law Courts

In some States, like Madhya Bharat, Rajasthan, Hyderabad, etc., the use of Hindi/regional language has been authorised for proceedings, other than judgments, decrees or orders, of the High Courts.

The country's judicial system used to function, ere the last few decades, in languages other than English. The change-over to Indian language media from English may appear novel to the present generation which sees before it the English language proliferated over the entire judicial system. However it is only natural that justice should be administered in a country in its indigenous languages and, provided the change is brought about systematically, the prospect should not provoke alarm or cause apprehension about its basic practicability.

So far as the language of the Supreme Court is concerned, eventually there can be only one language, i.e. Hindi, in respect of the entire court proceedings and records, including, of course, the judgments and orders. When the time comes for the change-over, the Supreme Court will have to function only in the Hindi language. The authoritative texts of reported judgments of the Supreme Court will also be published in the same language.

Processes issued in Hindi by the Supreme Court, when addressed to a non-Hindi region or against a person whose mother-tongue is not Hindi, should be accompanied by a translation for the convenience of the concerned party.

Provision should also be made for reliable translations of Supreme Court decisions being available in the State languages in separate regional language series.

When the time comes for the change-over in the lower levels of the judiciary, that is to say, courts of panchayats, civil and criminal courts at the tehsil level, etc., the language of the courts must be the language best understood by the people, which would be the regional language(s) of the different States. The same considerations might prevail in respect of civil and criminal courts at the district level. Even at present, in varying degrees, in the hierarchy of the judicial structure in the various States the regional languages are current at these levels.

With the Supreme Court functioning in Hindi and the subordinate judiciaries of different States functioning in their respective regional languages, there has to be some stage where the multiple linguistic pattern has to be broken and integrated. The multiple linguistic circuit falls to be broken at the High Court level and it is at this stage that there has to be a 'facing of both ways' viz., Hindi as far as the Supreme Court is concerned and the respective regional language(s) so far as the concerned subordinate judiciary is concerned.

The pros and cons of the regional and the Hindi languages are carefully examined so far as the linguistic medium of the High Court is concerned. There are several strong and, in our opinion, conclusive reasons in favour of deciding that when the time for the change-over arrives, the language of the judgments, decrees and orders of the High Courts must be a common linguistic medium for the whole country and, therefore, these should be in the Hindi language in all regions.

Since subordinate courts are guided by the determination of law given in the High Court judgments, there will have to be translations into the respective regional languages of all reportable High Court judgments. It would be necessary, in our opinion, to ensure that these translations are sufficiently reliable and we would suggest, for consideration by the concerned authorities, at the material time, that a "translation unit" may be established in each High Court for such translation of judgments.

So far as the processes, decrees and orders of High Courts are concerned, we would suggest that, wherever necessary, it may be provided that they would issue in regional languages in their "authorised translations", in addition to their original issue in Hindi.

As in all other such cases, so in regard to the language of the law courts, we consider it important to concentrate on bringing about the general change-over in the linguistic medium for the system as a whole. Wherever it is necessary to make individual exceptions for a good reason, e.g. in order that we may continue to enjoy or to secure afresh the services of suitable personnel for the posts of judges in the Supreme Court and the several High Courts, dispensation as to the language should be readily granted. It may be that for a long time after such a general change-over in the language of the judiciary has taken place, there would still be individual judges, who would prefer to deliver their judgments in English. Such individuals must be accommodated.

Having regard to the recommendations made by the States Reorganisation Commission regarding transfer of High Court judges and the proposals about a single judicial service, it might be worth considering whether certain minimum language tests in appropriate regional languages and Hindi should not be adopted in the case of High Court judges.

Apart from the option of delivering judgments in English, there may be an option to High Court judges to deliver judgments in their regional languages provided English or Hindi translations of such judgments are authenticated by them.

Provision may be made for granting leave by presiding judges to counsel, in suitable cases, to argue in English in the Supreme Court and in English or the regional languages in the several High Courts even after the general change-over in the linguistic medium has taken place.

We would recommend, for consideration by the States concerned, at the appropriate time, the making of a provision (at any rate) at the district levels, whereunder it would be open to parties or counsel to resort to the Hindi language at their option. We expect that this would be particularly necessary in larger towns; but if it is found necessary at lower levels as well, the principle ought to be extended.

So far as the language of special tribunals is concerned, wherever their decisions or orders have a bearing not confined to a single region, it should be prescribed that their judgments and orders shall be delivered originally in Hindi. A translation in another language may be made available to the parties where necessary. As in the case of High Courts, we would envisage the English language being allowed to be used as the language of the judgment or order by individual judges of such special tribunals for a considerable transitional period.

The Universities should provide facilities for examination of law graduates both in the Hindi and the regional languages at the option of the candidates. So far as facilities for imparting instruction in the Universities or Colleges in Hindi/the regional language are concerned, the situation may be left to adjust itself in response to the demand for such instruction in Hindi or the regional language concerned.

Language Of Law And Law Courts—III

The Dynamics Of The Change-Over

In the field of law and administration of justice, a general change-over should not be made until the groundwork has been fully prepared.

In accordance with our policy, with reference to similar other matters, of not indulging in prognostication as to the date by which any particular change-over would become practicable, we have not attempted to frame any estimates of the time-periods that would be required for completion of any of the preliminaries of the various phases through which the transition must pass. We have, however, indicated the particulars of such preliminaries and noticed the more important points in connection therewith that occurred to us; and also indicated the sequence in which the various phases must be articulated.

We have carefully considered the arguments advanced by some people for English continuing for an indefinite period as the language of legislation and of superior tribunals in the judicial hierarchy. We have come to the conclusion that the change-over in the linguistic medium will have to come in the field of legislation and the law courts also (although possibly at a different date, since it is to come by virtue of a special parliamentary legislation for the purpose, in the terms of Article 343 of the Constitution) in consonance with a similar change in the field of public administration and corresponding changes in the educational system.

The following preliminaries appear to us to be prerequisite to the accomplishment of a change-over of the linguistic medium in the field of legislation and administration of justice:

(i) The preparation of a standard legal lexicon;

(ii) Re-enactment of the Statute Book in Hindi in respect of both the Central and State legislation.

For the maintenance of the juridical and judicial unity of the country it is essential that legal terms and expressions should be used in the same significance in all parts of the country.

So far as evolving of legal terminology is concerned, it seems to us necessary to adopt the following plan of action and to carry it out as rapidly as possible:

(1) The present pace of evolving the necessary terminology for the Indian languages in the field of law must be greatly accelerated.

(2) Steps must be taken for the publication, from time to time as they get ready, of glossaries of such terminology, as standard and recognised expressions under the "imprimatur" of a suitable authority.

(3) A rendering of the Statute Book, both Central and State, into Hindi must be projected under the auspices of the Centre. It should be decided as to whether such Hindi versions of the law should not be enacted afresh by the appropriate legislative authority; precise arrangements in this behalf and a programme of action in respect of the Central as well as the State laws should be settled and pursued.

In order that original drafting may commence being attempted in Hindi by persons competent to do so and drafting practices gradually develop in that linguistic medium, it seems to us necessary to allow those States, who may want to do so, to undertake authoritative enactment originally in Hindi itself.

We envisage a transitional period of time during which the Statute Book as well as the case law would be partially in Hindi and partially in English, the Hindi language progressively assuming a larger proportion of the whole. During such a transitional period, resort may be had to the device of texts being made available in both Hindi and English, one of them being the original text for purposes of the law and the other an authorised translation.

The Union Language And Public Services Examinations

For obvious reasons the linguistic media of the competitive examinations should be generally in keeping with the media of instruction in the educational system.

A distinction may be made between the competitive examinations intended for admission to further courses of training, such as the Indian Navy Entrance Cadets Examination or the National Defence Academy Admission Examination, etc., and competitive examinations held for purposes of recruitment on the results of the competition.

It seems there has not yet been an overhaul of the linguistic media of instruction in some of the training establishments; and probably most of such training continues to be in English, although it may be susceptible to replacement, to more or less extent, by the Hindi medium. Such a review should be made, and steps taken for the language media for the appropriate entrance examinations, being related, on the one hand, to the medium of instruction in the different training institutions, and conforming, on the other, to the changes in the system of Secondary education taking place in the country.

If in view of this, English has to be displaced partly or wholly as the medium for these examinations, it might be necessary to introduce regional language media in place of English, as the Secondary education in most parts of the country has now switched over from the English language medium to the medium of the regional language. This might entail a region-wise decentralisation of the entrance examination and, consequentially, a quota system. There are, however, very important distinctions between the adoption of the quota system for admission to training establishments and the adoption of such a system for purposes of actual recruitment to the all-India Services at the highest level of the administrative cadres, where the issue arises.

Having regard to the linguistic abilities that would be needed by members of the all-India and Central Services in future, it would be legitimate in our view to introduce a compulsory paper in Hindi after due notice. In order that non-Hindi students may not be unduly handicapped in the transitional period, the paper may, to start with, be of a fairly low standard and treated as only a "qualifying paper" and later, after due notice, again it may be raised to the status of other compulsory papers as a "marking" and fully competitive paper. Further, candidates having one of the South Indian languages as mother-tongue may be exempted from answering one or two stiffer questions in the Hindi paper which the candidates whose mother-tongues are closer to Hindi may be required to answer.

To equate Hindi candidates with non-Hindi candidates the former should be required to offer a paper, to be answered in their linguistic medium of the general examination, out of a variety of options including subjects of cultural interest bearing on South India and languages of the Eighth Schedule other than Hindi.

We do not see sufficient justification for the suggestion that the "compensatory provision" for Hindi candidates should be that they must offer a paper in a regional language (or a South Indian language) other than Hindi.

Provision may be made for testing candidates for the all-India services examinations in English through specific papers even after the medium of examination is changed to a different language or languages.

As regards the language medium for the combined competitive examination through which candidates are recruited for the all-India and higher Central Services, the principal difficulty arises out of the fact that for obvious reasons it will be prima facie extremely difficult to attain satisfactory standards of "moderation" if the competition is held in linguistic medium anything as numerous as the thirteen regional languages. If the number of linguistic media for the examination exceed the limits of manageability with reference to satisfactory standards of moderation, quota system may become inevitable unless the character of the examination itself is changed.

A quota system would break up the character of the existing all-India Services and would lead to fragmentation of the all-India competition and to deterioration in the quality of recruits to the all-India as well as higher Central Services. Considering the present-day calls on the administrative personnel, we would strongly discountenance proposals leading to any such deterioration in the quality of the recruits to these Services. In the case of the personnel of the all-India Services, the chief consideration even from the point of view of each region exclusively regarding its own interest should be "quality" and not proportionate share in the volume of employment. For like reasons quality is more important in the case of the higher Central Services as well than a proportionate regionwise distribution of the employment available.

On the subject of the linguistic medium of the competitive examination for these Services we, therefore, conclude as under:

(a) So far as the all-India and Central Services are concerned (and this would apply, unless otherwise provided, also to other all-India Services created hereafter), the alternative of the Hindi medium in addition to the existing English medium may be introduced after due notice. As and when other regional languages become a medium of instruction in the universities up to the graduation stage as Hindi has done, the admission of other linguistic media will have to be considered.

Suitable standards will have to be laid down as to what degree of progress as a medium should have been made in university education in respect of any language before its eligibility as a linguistic medium for the competitive examination for recruitment to these Services may be considered.

The medium of the English language may be continued as an alternative for as long as may be necessary: if, eventually, a position should arise when this alternative could be dispensed with, such dispensation should of course be made after a sufficiently long notice.

(b) While "moderation" might still be practicable so long as the number of linguistic media is manageable, having regard to the availability of examiners with suitable bilingual or multi-lingual qualifications, a stage might arrive when the admission of further linguistic media would be found impracticable.

Before such a stage is reached the Union and State Governments must take mutual counsel and decide whether (1) they would accept a change in the scheme of recruitment to the all-India Services or, in the alternative, (2) agree upon a limitation in the number of the linguistic media, or (3) make other appropriate changes in the system of the examination.

(c) We hope and trust that before the contingencies contemplated in (b) above eventuate, the progress of Hindi amongst non-Hindi-speaking university graduates generally would have advanced sufficiently to admit of their competing on equal terms with Hindi-speaking candidates at these examinations through the medium of the Hindi language.

And until then, the availability of the English medium would give to such of the non-Hindi-speaking candidates as may need it an alternative sufficient to safeguard their legitimate interests.

Some of us entertain the hope that it would not, in the upshot, be necessary for the Union and State Governments to make the difficult choice presented by the alternatives in the last sub-paragraph of item (b) above.

As a measure of general encouragement to linguistic studies so badly needed in the special circumstances of this country, the concerned authorities should revise the list of optional subjects tenderable at the various Public Service Commission examinations and consider whether greater scope should not be allowed for the subjects of languages and literatures in the different Indian languages.

In order that candidates preparing themselves for the U.P.S.C. competitive examinations with the Hindi medium may not be handicapped, the State Public Service Commissions might consider allowing the option of the Hindi medium also for their corresponding examinations. In that case the latter examinations would be held in the regional language medium as well as in the Hindi medium besides, until the transition is completed, the English medium.

Propagation And Development Of Hindi And Regional Languages

It is partly due to the patriotic and highly creditable work done by voluntary agencies in the field of Hindi propagation in the non-Hindi areas over the last 35 years that it was at all possible for the Constituent Assembly to think in terms of the adoption of an Indian language for the official purposes of the Union in the place of English.

Since the adoption of the Constitution, this work has assumed a different aspect and it is now necessary that this responsibility is "sponsored" officially.

From what we have seen of the working of voluntary agencies in this field it appears to us that steps ought to be taken in the following directions for the more systematic organisation and expansion of the work of propagation of Hindi:

(1) Co-ordination of work among the various agencies, and where necessary demarcation of their activities.

(2) Survey of their requirements for the purpose of adequate expansion in their allocated fields of activity.

(3) The introduction of some measure of uniformity and comparability in the standards of their examinations; and ensuring that proper methods are adopted and appropriate academic standards maintained in the conduct of the examinations.

(4) Provision of aids for improvement of teaching methods and greater facilities for teachers' training.

(5) Securing an appropriate and graded supply of suitable text-books for the different regions of the country and for different categories of persons receiving Hindi instruction; supply of supporting reading matter and literature for the benefit of neo-literates and special classes of pupils, like children, women, etc.

(6) Ancillary to the propagation of the Hindi language the provision of reading-room and literary facilities for those recently made literate in Hindi.

We recommend that the Central Government should make liberal financial assistance available to the voluntary agencies for enlarging and improving their activities in the various ways referred to above.

Organisationally the Government of India are assisted in discharging their responsibility to propagate Hindi in the non-Hindi areas by the Hindi Shiksha Samiti which comprises one representative from each of the non-Hindi-speaking States and two representatives in all from the Hindi States.

The work done under the auspices of the Union and State Governments in the field of development and enrichment of Hindi (apart from terminological work) is reviewed.

A greater and growing approachment amongst the various Indian languages and a wider understanding and comprehension of the varied cultural inheritance of India would be promoted by the encouragement of studies in the field of linguistics and philology; and such studies and research deserve every encouragement at the hands of the Union and State Governments.

There are tremendous opportunities to linguists working in the field of Indological research to help in promoting a greater integration of the country.

Standardisation Of Indian Scripts

Almost all the Indian scripts have been derived from the Brahmi script. Practically all the Indian scripts, except for Tamil, have almost the same alphabet; in Tamil, the principal difference is the absence of aspirates.

The Devanagari script accounts for an even larger proportion amongst the different scripts in India than the Hindi language accounts for amongst the speakers of the different languages in the Indian population. If, therefore, there is to be one script for the purpose of writing in all Indian languages, the best claimant amongst the Indian scripts would certainly be the Devanagari script.

For a long time, thoughtful persons have been reflecting how powerfully it would make for the integration and unity of the country if a uniform script could be adopted for all the Indian languages, vastly facilitating the study of other languages and literatures in each region. Several eminent persons, including Lokmanya Tilak, Mahatma Gandhi and Pandit Jawaharlal Nehru, have advocated this view.

The adoption of the Roman script as the common script for all Indian languages is advocated by some persons. The pros and cons of the Roman and Devanagari scripts as the common script for Indian languages are examined, and we conclude that, on a balance of considerations, there are no particular advantages to be gained by adopting the Roman script, and that the case for Devanagari as the comman script is conclusively stronger.

Having regard to all these considerations, we would advocate the adoption of the Devanagari script optionally for the writing of other Indian languages besides the Union language.

A script is only a convenience as distinguished from tne language, which in some way, is a cultural embodiment; for the standardisation or reform of script, therefore, there is less room for objections comprehensible in the case of the language.

Reform Of The Devanagari Script

In the field of the Devanagari script reform vastly more useful than the "perfect solution" to be evolved at an indefinite time in the future is a "serviceable solution" presently commending itself to the longest number of interested parties. The Lucknow Conference represents such a laudable attempt to bring some of the issues to a conclusion in the matter of script reform and thus registers an advance.

It is urgently necessary to finalise the typewriter keyboard and authoritatively adopt reforms to be made in the Devanagari script which can only be done on the leadership and under the auspices of the Centre.

As in the case of Hindi, so in the case of the regional languages to a more or less similar extent, we do not expect that there would be any insuperable difficulties in the way of adaptation of the script to the requirements of modern mechanical and multiplying aids. Also intrinsically there is no reason why there should be any difficulty about developing stenography in Hindi or any of the regional languages.

Which Hindi?

The terms of Article 351 of the Constitution would be best fulfilled by carrying out programmes of development of the Hindi language along with similar programmes for other languages.

While everybody agrees that the Hindi language to be developed should be as simple and intelligible as possible, there is a real difficulty in this regard in that what is regarded as "simple" in certain areas is found genuinely difficult in other areas and vice versa; where such a difficulty arises both words, deemed simple and familiar in the different parts, should be adopted in the vocabulary and to that extent variant styles developed in the Union language.

Unless Hindi grammar is found susceptible of being, and is in practice actually, simplified for all persons including those whose mother-tongue is Hindi, any considerable amelioration of the difficulties of non-Hindi-speaking persons in learning Hindi by virtue of such simplification of grammar, etc., could hardly by hoped for.

The Press and The Indian Languages

We recommend that the possibility may be explored of providing news services in Hindi and such other regional languages as it may be remunerative to do—this might be more practicable if the Devanagari script is used for transmissions in regional languages also—for the convenience of Indian language newspapers. Besides being a facility and an impetus to Indian language journalism, such a service might be of use for purposes of standardising terms and expressions in Hindi and the regional languages.

Agencies, Etc., For Implementation Of The National Language Programme

So far as the change-over in the Union administration

is concerned, we would emphasise the need for locating the responsibility specifically in a single administrative unit of the Government to initiate, direct, superintend and co-ordinate the operations involved in all departments and agencies of the Union. Provided the unit is enabled to work with sufficient authority, whether it should be a Ministry or a Department within a Ministry or merely a wing or a division of a Ministry would be for the Government themselves to determine.

It would be of advantage, in our opinion, organisationally, to set up at the Centre an Advisory Board, with representatives of States to co-ordinate the activities of the Union and State administrations so far as they impinge upon each other in the implementation of language policies in the fields of law and administration.

We feel that it would be best if a new single agency, which may be called the National Academy of Indian languages, is set up for carrying out the work relating to the development of the Union as well as the regional languages and for other appropriate and connected purposes including the production of text-books and books of reference. On the governing body of the Academy, representation should be accorded to the Union Government, the State Governments, the Universities and perhaps also recognised professional and literary associations drawn from all parts of the country and working in the different regional languages.

While academic and literary opinion should be allowed to have a full say in the evolution of new terminology and the schemes of development of the Union and regional languages of the country, etc., it would be necessary for the Central Government to possess reserve powers for giving directives to the National Academy on matters of policy.

As regards the location of the Academy, we would suggest for consideration the city of Hyderabad.

A Central Library of literatures of all Indian languages and a National Institute for training of language teachers require to be established; it may be considered whether these institutions should be sited alongside the National Academy of Indian Languages.

We recommend that the Central Government should institute a practice of rendering to Parliament annually a report of the progress made during the previous year in regard to the implementation of the language provisions laid down in the Constitution and connected matters, so far as they appertain to the central field of authority.

It is necessary to give wide publicity to the national policy about languages to inculcate a proper perspective in this matter amongst the people at large and to remove unfounded misconceptions.

Concluding Remarks

In spite of apparent diversities of Indian linguistic and cultural patterns, all the important Indian languages have close and strong affinities. These affinities are a reflection of a basic unity and a common "Indian way of life".

Indian unity is not merely the recent result of "pax Britannica". The idea of an all-India political unity has always inspired Indian political thought; this urge for unification is only the political expression of the cultural identity of Indian life.

The problem of a common pan-Indian linguistic medium is not unprecedented in Indian history. In the past the Sanskrit and Persian languages and in recent decades the English language have served as such a medium.

If energetic steps are taken for promoting a "rapproachment" amongst the various regional languages of the country, within a period of a very few years the "distances" between the different Indian languages would be considerably reduced.

As citizens of a polyglot country, it is essential for us to encourage widespread multilingualism among members of all linguistic regions and to this end to make appropriate provisions in the Secondary and University systems of education.

The language problem is principally one of the contemporary generation. Any reasonable policy steadily and determinedly pursued would furnish an adequate solution as a new generation is brought up on it. Therefore, for a language policy what is important is not so much the *a priori* perfection of a solution but the general acceptance of it by all.

In the solution of the language problem many agencies are concerned besides the Union and State Governments and it is necessary to engage the ready co-operation of all of them. Apart from such agencies—official and non-official—ultimately it is the ordinary citizen who is the arbiter in the matter of new terminologies and new phrases and expressions evolved as a measure of "development" of a language.

It is essential to make a beginning with the use of the new linguistic medium in actual life even as various developments and evolutions are taking place; there must be an interplay of working use and coinage of vocabularies.

Language in its official aspect is only a means for the convenient carrying on of the intercourse between the States and the Union; we have therefore considered the various issues arising in the subject-matter of our inquiry within the framework of the country's constitutional structure.

In language policies it is necessary to be flexible as regards details and time-periods; firm as regards objectives; specific as regards proximate programmes.

The complex linguistic revolution envisaged in the language policy of the country cannot be brought about unless the objective is clearly comprehended, kept in view and steadily pursued under the general stewardship of a single authority.

We were greatly impressed by the general concern for the unity of the country and the anxiety to consolidate it which characterised the greater part of the evidence in all regions; by and large, the issues were approached by all concerned with objectivity, realism and in a spirit of tolerance.

Language is only an instrumentality and there need be no heat or passion on the issue of language. While the complexities of the Indian language problem are unparalleled, we feel that, properly approached, reasonable solutions are available; and we feel confident that the problem will be successfully tackled and solved.

VILLAGE AND SMALL-SCALE INDUSTRIES (SECOND FIVE-YEAR PLAN) COMMITTEE, 1955—REPORT

Delhi, Manager of Publications, 1955. 89p.

Chairman : Prof. D. G. Karve.
Members : Prof. D. R. Gadgil; Shri V. L. Mehta; Shri P. Govindan Nair; Shri V. Nanjappa (Alternate Member).
Secretary : Dr. D. K. Malhotra.

APPOINTMENT

The National Development Council at its meeting held on May 6, 1955, recommended that the measures needed for the organisation of village and small-scale industries on an adequate scale in connection with the Second Five-Year Plan should be taken in hand immediately. In pursuance of this recommendation, a Committee was constituted under the Planning Commission vide their Resolution No. Fy II/CDI/23/55, dated June, 28, 1955, to prepare, in the light of the provision made in the Draft Plan frame for village and small-scale industries and in the light of the recommendations made in the memorandum submitted by the Panel of Economists, a scheme industry-wise, and wherever possible State-wise, for the utilisation of the resources to be earmarked for the purpose of development of these industries as an integral part of the Second Five-Year Plan.

TERMS OF REFERENCE

The Committee should frame its scheme with special reference to the following objects:

(1) That the bulk of the increased production during the Plan period of consumer goods in common demand has to be provided by the village and small-scale industries;

(2) That employment provided by these industries should progressively increase; and

(3) That production and marketing in these industries is organised, in the main, on co-operative lines.

CONTENTS

Introductory; Village and Small-Scale Industries in the First Five-Year Plan: Basic Approach; Principles and Policies; Framework of Suggested Measures; Outlines of Development Programmes; Scheme of Allocation of Resources and Employment; Pattern of Organisation; Acknowledgements; Appendices I & II.

RECOMMENDATIONS

Village And Small-Scale Industries In The First Five-Year Plan

In the First Five-Year Plan, utmost importance should be attached to arrangements for research and training in village industries, handicrafts and small industries, handicrafts and small-scale industries. Among the problems requiring necessary action were mentioned improvements of tools and implements as well as evolving of machines worked by power and suitable for small-scale operation. Proposals for the establishment of an institute of village technology, of research institutions for handicrafts production, of a Central Institute for the study and preparation of designs and of special research sections for small industries in research institutes associated with individual large-scale industries were emphasised in the Plan as requiring special consideration. Further, it was recommended that technical training programmes should be so designed as to fit in with the over-all plan for the development of cottage and small industries in the country and that the training should be directed towards those trades in which prospects of stable employment were reasonably clear.

Basic Approach

When new capital investment has to be made, it should be made as far as possible only in improved equipment or where existing equipment is itself capable of being improved by addition or adaptation. In the adoption of improvements a long-period view must necessarily be taken, so that the improvements now effected are capable of being utilised at higher techniques without being rendered obsolete at an early stage in the process of development. The needs of the future programme emphasise a discriminating attitude in both protecting existing techniques and providing fuller employment, and indicate that additional capital investment and employment or training of new persons has to be oriented towards an improvement in existing techniques.

Principles And Policies

A normal principle of economic planning that whatever the villagers can undertake by way of improved industry in their own village should be organised on a village basis. This would, of course, be subject to physical factors such as location of minerals, availability of transport facilities, etc.

Large schemes of hydro-electric and thermal generation of electricity have been included in the First and Second Five-Year Plans.

Powers to license plants for processing and other industries such as rice milling which affect the working of the programmes of development in the sector of village and small-scale industries should be conferred on the State Governments. Licensing Committees at the Centre and in the States should give adequate representation to the interests of village and small-scale industries.

The essential purposes of the Plan are that the decentralised sector should produce the requisite quantity and quality of goods and that these should actually to made available to the consumers. The various sections of producers will be in need of assured supplies of raw materials, implements and other accessories. To the largest possible extent these supplies should be organised through general purchase and sales co-operatives serving more than one section of producers. On the sales side the products ought to be taken over from the producers as near the place of production as possible. The primary purchase and sale societies which perform these services will form part of a co-operative system which will provide for the needs of all the constituent elements in the sector of village and small-scale industries and which will be closely linked with the agricultural marketing and the general co-operative credit systems. A well-designed buying and selling organisation with branches in all parts of the country is a *sine qua non* of a scheme of planned transformation of the small and village industries.

A far-reaching programme of co-operative marketing and rural warehousing designed to serve the needs of the agricultural sector has been planned. When legislation is enacted for the creation of a Co-operative Development and Warehousing Corporation, provision should be made to include within its scope the marketing of the products of village and small-scale industries.

The agency of State Finance Corporations should be used for the purpose of providing long-term credits to village and small-scale industries. A special cottage industries section should be set up as an essential part of the structure of each Corporation.

To ensure proper co-ordination, a concerted financial policy should, we recommend, be chalked out at as early a stage as possible by the Reserve Bank, the State Bank of India, State Finance Corporations and the Central co-operative banking institutions.

Framework Of Suggested Measures

The effect of reservation, in general though not in specific terms, can be obtained by overall limitations on production or expansion and through control over the licensing of new establishments.

To the extent that the rehabilitation or improvement of techniques of particular industry requires certain common plants, services, etc., these have been included in the plan of that industry. However, the more general provisions are much more important for small decentralised industry than the specific ones. The provision of efficient systems of transport, money and credit, water and power supply, technical training and advice, throughout the country would alone make possible the evolution of an efficient network of decentralised industry.

Outlines Of Development Programmes

A phased production programme for the handloom industry should be drawn up for the five-year period and should be periodically reviewed. If at any stage there are adequate reasons to think that the programme cannot be worked to schedule, the position should be reviewed and alternative arrangements for obtaining the requisite production of cloth examined.

We consider that hand-pounding of rice should be treated as an integral part of village economy for the purpose of meeting domestic and local demand. Factors which operate to dislodge it from this position should be resisted and counter-acted. At the same time we think that for particular purposes, processing of paddy in the mills will be necessary as long as a possible alternative is not available. We, therefore, recommend that new sheller or combined sheller-huller mills or huller mills or single hullers should not be allowed to be set up and no increase in production above the present level should be permitted during the Plan period, except when hand-pounding cannot be organised: for example, when production in an area where labour is scarce has to be augmented quickly or supply to a new industrial area has to be arranged. In such cases, the mills allowed to be set up should be owned wherever possible by co-operative societies or by the Government.

The Government should examine whether cotton seeds which are not being used at present for oil crushing can be utilised for augmenting the supply of vegetable oils in the country.

Scheme Of Allocation Of Resources And Employment

The question of flow of resources from the Centre to the States for meeting expenditure on different types of schemes and the principles and conditions governing such a flow should be treated separately from the allocations themselves.

RAILWAY FREIGHT STRUCTURE ENQUIRY COMMITTEE, 1955—REPORT

New Delhi, Ministry of Railways, 1957. 2 Vols.

Chairman : Dr. A. Ramaswami Mudaliar.
Members : Shri T. N. Singh; Shri D. K. Borooah; Shri I. S. Puri; Shri V. P. Bhandarkar; Shri L. K. Jha; Shri A. K. Basu.

APPOINTMENT

The Railway Freight Structure Enquiry Committee was constituted under the Ministry of Railways vide their Resolution No. 6899-TC, dated June 29, 1955, to review the existing freight structure for transport by goods trains in all its aspects in the light of the present developmental economy and to give ample opportunity to the interests concerned to explain their point of view.

TERMS OF REFERENCE

(i) To review the present railway freight rate structure in all its aspects and to suggest what modifications should be made, bearing in mind the needs of a developing economy and the necessity for maintaining the financial stability of the Railways;

(ii) To examine whether the statutory provisions dealing with the responsibility of Railways as carriers need any, and if so what, modification; and in the light of modification proposed whether any adjustment in freight rates is warranted;

(iii) To examine what changes, if any, are needed in the existing constitution, jurisdiction and rules of procedure of the Railway Rates Tribunal, so that the Tribunal might be a more effective and expeditious instrument for adjudication of railway freight matters at a reasonable cost to the litigant; and

(iv) To make recommendations.

CONTENTS

Introduction; A Brief Survey of the History of Rail Freight Rates in India; The General Pattern of the Revised Rates Structure and its Impact on Public Opinion; Basis for a New Freight Rate Structure; The Scale of Rates, the Impact of the Second Five-Year Plan on its Evolution—The need to keep the Financial Stability of Railways in view whilst Evolving the same; Goods Classification; Industrialisation and Railway Policy; Miscellaneous; Statistical Information; Efficiency; The Liability of Railways for Goods Tendered for Despatch; Railway Rates Tribunal; Committee's Comments on the Minority Note; A Joint Note by Shri I. S. Puri and Shri V. P. Bhandarkar; Summary of Conclusions and Recommendations; Annexures I to XVII.

RECOMMENDATIONS

A Brief Survey Of The History Of Rail Freight Rates In India

In this chapter we have briefly surveyed railway development and industrial growth since the early beginning of railways and the evolution of the Railway Freight Structure vis-a-vis its development. We have referred to the early events which culminated in the historic resolution of 1887, when, for the first time, the Government enunciated the principles to regulate the fixing of rates. We have dealt, in somewhat greater detail, with the changes in the freight structure introduced in 1922, the further refinements effected in 1936 and the major steps towards ultimate standardisation and rationalisation effected by the Revised Freight Structure which was introduced in 1948.

We have recounted the recommendation made on railway rates matters, in reports of various committees, from time to time, and have briefly indicated the impact of the freight structure on the growth of industry and agriculture during the last 100 years.

The General Pattern Of The Revised Rates Structure And Its Impact On Public Opinion

In this chapter we have dealt with the circumstances that led to the introduction of the telescopic freight structure in 1948. We have also given an indication of the principal features of the freight structure and have pin-pointed the criticisms that have been advanced against some of them, particularly those concerning the structure of the Class Rates and Wagonload Scales, the legs of the telescope, ancillary charges like terminal, short-distance and transhipment charges and the rigidity in the railway freight policy that has been associated with the new freight structure.

Basis For A New Freight Rate Structure

We consider a radical revision of the pattern of the legs of the freight structure necessary. We state why a different pattern need be adopted. We recommend adoption of following pattern of legs for traffic both in "smalls" and in wagonloads:

1	—	25 miles
26	—	75 miles
76	—	150 miles
151	—	300 miles
301	—	500 miles
501	—	800 miles
801	—	1,200 miles
1,201 miles and beyond.		

We recommend a regular and progressive increase through a percentage system of rates from the lowest class to the highest class to form an integrated scale of rates covering both class rates and wagonload scales. For this purpose, we recommend a norm or a standard rate, to be called the Class 100 Rate. We have taken the present Class 9 as the most convenient norm and all other classes above and below Class 9 and also the wagonload scales have been expressed as percentages of the new Class 100. We have shown what percentage each class will represent.

We recommend that, for all commodities, there should be a wagonload Classification and a "Smalls" classification.

We also recommend for a few commodities, for which separate "smalls" and wagonload rates will have no special significance, that the rate will apply on an "AQ" (any quantity) basis.

We recommend that there should be a relativity between the rates for wagonloads and "smalls" and we have allowed an increase in the rates for "smalls" as compared with wagonloads to the extent of some 15 to 36 per cent and on this basis we have shown the pattern of the classification for wagonloads and "smalls".

We recommend that the revised classification may be fixed for individual commodities for which at present there is no wagonload classification in the following manner. Where the commodity is reported to move largely in wagonloads, the percentage class rate corresponding to the existing rate will apply for movement in "smalls" and a lower percentage class rate for wagonloads corresponding to the percentage class rate for "smalls".

We have referred to the number of classes that exist at present and we recommend what should be the revised number.

We have dealt with the subject of minimum weight conditions. We are of the opinion that the existing wagonload conditions are on the low side and we recommend that the wagonload conditions should be examined afresh. We have forwarded two recommendations on this subject; one from Shri A. K. Basu with a schedule of minimum weight conditions for wagonloads for all commodities, and the other from Shri Puri and Shri Bhandarkar for commodities for which, in their opinion, an upward revision is necessary.

Shri Puri and Shri Bhandarkar also recommend that for certain articles, for which the classification is subject to a minimum weight per consignment unrelated to the carrying capacity of the wagon, the minimum weights should be raised; also, for explosives, the rule that the minimum charge per consignment is for 54 maunds should be revised and the minimum charge should be for 62 maunds.

To meet the criticism made by some Chambers that the wagonload conditions may prove to be too high for certain commodities for wagonload movements to and from small centres, some of us recommend the policy of adopting intermediate wagonload weights with corresponding higher rates.

We recommend that loading and unloading in respect of wagonloads should be done by consignors and consignees.

We recommend that the wagonload conditions of the forwarding Railway should apply through to the destination, irrespective of break-of-gauge, both in the case of general merchandise and livestock.

We recommend that the terminal charges as such should be abolished, but that this fact should be taken into consideration in evolving the Revised Freight Structure.

We recommend that the additional short-distance charge is not justified and that it may be abolished.

We recommend discontinuance of a separate levy of transhipment charges and of *ghat* charges.

We recommend that the minimum distance for charge should be raised to 25 miles and should apply only once (in bookings) whether the movement is over one or more Railways.

We recommend that the minimum weight for acceptance per package by goods trains should be 20 seers and the charge should be based on 20 seers.

We recommend that the overall minimum charge of Re. 1, 12 annas per ton for wagonload consignments should be abolished.

Shri Puri and Shri Bhandarkar recommend that the minimum charge of Re. 1 per consignment should be discontinued.

We consider that neither maxima nor minima rates should be prescribed in the New Freight Structure.

The Scale Of Rates, The Impact Of The Second Five-Year Plan On Its Evolution—The Need To Keep The Financial Stability Of Railways In View Whilst Evolving The Same

We consider that a Uniform Surcharge on freight rates is not a satisfactory method of raising revenue and we recommend that, if additional revenue is required, it should be acquired by a suitable revision of the scale and taper of telescopic rates.

We have examined the financial position of the Railways during the Second Plan period. We have considered the public views on the financial aspect of railway working.

We have examined the Railways' earnings and expenditure during the Plan period and have reviewed particularly the appropriation to the Depreciation Fund, and we recommend an increase in the appropriation.

We have taken into consideration the adjustments in the expenditure due to an increase in the coal price and due to a rise in costs on account of the inflationary trends, and from these several considerations, we conclude that the gap between revenue and expenditure during the Plan period will be over Rs. 300 crores.

Hence, we recommend that, if the twin objectives, viz. that the Railways play the part they are expected to during the Second Plan period by carrying additional traffic that will be forthcoming, and, secondly, that the financial stability of the Railways is ensured, have to be achieved, it is essential that the existing scale of rates be revised in an upward direction.

We have mentioned the several factors on which a Revised Scale of Rates may be constructed and we recommend the following scale which we consider would be an equitable one and, to a large extent, would meet our requirements:

1— 25 miles	3.60	pies per maund	per mile.
+ 26— 75 ,,	1.40	,,	,,
+ 76— 150 ,,	1.20	,,	,,
+151— 300 ,,	1.05	,,	,,
+301— 500 ,,	0.85	,,	,,
+501— 800 ,,	0.70	,,	,,
+801—1,200 ,,	0.60	,,	,,
+ distances beyond	0.50	,,	,,

We recommend that the rates should be introduced on a Block Mileage Basis with blocks of 5 miles up to 500 miles and 10 miles beyond.

Goods Classification

We have briefly dealt with the principle governing the classification of goods and the relationship in the classification of "smalls" and wagonloads.

We have indicated the consideration that influenced our recommendation to adopt 13 to 27 per cent reduction in rates for wagonloads as compared to "smalls".

We recommend that practically for all commodities, rates should be quoted only at railway risk. Whilst this is our general recommendation, we recognise that there are a few commodities which may continue to be carried at owner's risk, but in regard to which Railway Risk Rates may also be quoted. We recommended that the owner's risk rates for these commodities should be at a level one class below the corresponding percentage class rate and we have listed these commodities.

We have dealt with the anomalies in the classification, which have been complained of by the public.

We have referred to our Interim Recommendation for the setting up of a Classification Anomalies Committee to deal with those anomalies which we have not been able to examine or any fresh anomalies that might arise as a result of our recommendation and we have stated the Government's decision thereon.

We recommend revised classification for some commodities with a view to removing the anomalies.

We recommend revised lower classification for those commodities for which we consider that special consideration should be shown in the interests of industry or more generally in public interest and for certain commodities from cost-of-living consideration.

We recommend that certain groupings in the existing classification may be specially examined by the Anomalies Committee and also any new anomalies that may have arisen in the course of our proposal for reclassification.

In regard to the permanent machinery to deal with the question of classification, we suggest that the Commercial Committee for Interchange, while more or less working to the existing procedure should formally consult and discuss their tentative ideas with representatives of the Federation of Indian Chambers of Commerce and Industry and Associated Chambers of Commerce, across the table before making their final recommendation to the Government. Where necessary, the matter may be referred by their party for the advisory opinion of the Railway Rates Tribunal before a decision is taken.

We recommend that Urea which is used in the plastic industry and which also moves for bona-fide agricultural purposes, should retain its higher classification, but should be given station-to-station rates when moving on the latter account.

Similarly Gypsum moving in limited quantities to specific points for fertilising "Usar" land may be given station-to-station rates.

We recommend different rates for Jute according to as it is unpressed, half-pressed or full-pressed, so as to encourage fibres being offered for transport fully pressed, and we have prescribed qualifying conditions for Full-Pressed and Half-Pressed Jute.

In regard to classification of Oils—Division "D" we forward two recommendations to the Government: (i) 75 per cent rate for wagonloads, and (ii) 65 per cent.

We have dealt with the classification of Coal, Coke and Patent Fuel. Whilst we are unanimously of the opinion that the coal scale needs revision with a view to making it more realistic, we have made two suggestions in regard to the manner of implementing it and we forward both the suggestions to the Government. One suggestion is to assimilate into the freight structure and prescribe 25 per cent rate for Coal, Coke and Patent Fuel when moving in wagonloads with a ceiling, if necessary, at 800 miles or so; the other suggestion is to have a separate scale for coal as follows:

(*In pies per maund per mile*)

First 25 miles	+ For the next 50 miles	+ For the next 75 miles	+ For the next 150 miles	+ For the next 200 miles	+ For the next 300 miles	+ For the next 400 miles	+ For distances beyond
(1—25) 1.10	(26—75) .36	(76—150) .32	(151—300) .24	(301—500) .15	(501—800) .10	(801—1,200) .07	(1,201 and over) .05

With a view to removing the disparity between freight costs for long-distance movement of coal by railway and by coastal steamers, we recommend that the freight rates on the railway portion of the rail-cum-sea route should be on the basis of the combined distance from the collieries to the port and from the port to the destination point, and we also recommend that if the gap needs to be further reduced, any subsidy that might be considered by the Government should be met from General Revenues and not from Railway Revenues.

Industrialisation And Railway Policy

We have dealt with the complaints made about the rates structure introduced in 1948 and the difficulty in obtaining station-to-station rates. In view of the standardisation of the rates structure the scope for quoting station-to-station rates became limited.

With the universal application of wagonload scales recommended by us the occasion for quoting station-to-station rates will continue to be limited.

We have referred to the recommendation made by us when our advice was sought by the Government that all concessional rates for the carriage of raw materials and finished products for established iron and steel industries may be cancelled.

We have examined the suggestion of the Estimates Committee to have a separate Directorate in the Railway Board's office for quoting station-to-station rates. We consider that this may not be necessary and we recommend that individual Railway Administrations should have power to quote station-to-station rates and grant concessions at a percentage below the standard rate. This percentage should be laid down by the Railway Board. Concessions below this limit may be granted by the Railway Board after obtaining the advisory opinion of the Railway Rates Tribunal except in urgent cases where they may grant the concession and make a reference subsequently to the Railway Rates Tribunal.

We are unable to accept the suggestion of the Indian National Steam Ship Owners' Association in the matter of quoting reduced rates for traffic moving to and from ports when carried by ships on the Indian Register. We recommend, however, that the Railways should assist generally in the export drive. This recommendation does not bear directly on the Indian shipping, but embraces all shipping in the interest of enabling export of Indian products abroad. As Railways will only be one of the departments, which will be called upon to make such a concession, we recommend that there should be some authority who will be in a position to assess the situation and we recommend the formation of a high-level committee with representatives of the Commerce and Industry Ministry, Finance Ministry, Railway Ministry and such other Ministries as may be concerned in promoting the export trade of the country. The committee will function with a small secretariat specially constituted for the purpose.

We recommend that the Committee may also examine the provision of priority transport for export needs.

We suggest for consideration of the Tariff Commission that in arriving at the protection or the quantum thereof, they may assume the existing level of rates and leave it to the parties to make representations to the Railway Board for concession in rates, if necessary.

We have dealt with the question of concession to underdeveloped areas. We have drawn the attention of the Government of India to the practice of the Canadian Government which grants low concessional rates for wheat moving from some territories, the value of the concession being reimbursed to the railways by the Federal Government of Canada. We recommend that this practice may be adopted for assisting the backward areas in India.

In regard to Assam, we recommend the proposal of

treating the distance to and from Assam the same as what it was before Partition or that a variant of this treatment which meets the situation may be devised for a period during which the industrial development of Assam may be expedited.

In this connection the present practice of levying ferry charges for traffic passing over Sakrigali-Manihari-ghat in the shape of a lumpsum mileage charge as for 33 miles, calculated separately on the first leg of the telescope, violates the principle of charging on continuous mileage. We recommend that the ferry mileage should be added to the total mileage for charge and not be separately calculated.

In regard to products of cottage and hand industries, we recommend that, to start with, a concession of 25 per cent of the normal freight rates be granted when these products are booked by recognised co-operative societies on the authority of a certificate issued by the All-India Khadi and Village Industry Board, the All-India Handicrafts Board, Director of Industries of State Governments and other bodies, which might be recognised by the Union Government for this purpose.

Though, at first sight, the proposal of a Freight Pool appears attractive, on further examination of the question, we consider that this method of encouraging certain areas where industrial development is backward is not justified.

Miscellaneous

We recommend that the present relativity between goods and parcel rates will have to be maintained if diversion to parcel service is to be avoided. We have not gone into the structure of parcel rates, and these should be reviewed in the light of the freight structure that we have recommended.

We are opposed to making any change in the statutory obligations of Railways, according to which, at present, they have to carry all the traffic offered to them and we are, therefore, unable to accept the suggestion that the Railways should decline to carry traffic for short distances.

We recommend telescopic rate structure to be generally adopted on Indian railways for livestock and other animals; the rates should apply at railway risk and no separate terminal charges are to be levied. In through booking between different gauges, the rate applicable at the forwarding station would apply through to the destination.

We consider it feasible to introduce the procedure, at least at large goods sheds, of obtaining advance information of the probable date of the arrival of the consignment and communicating it to the consignee where his address is known, so that he may make preliminary arrangements for unloading wagons.

We recommend that salt in bulk may be moved when booked to private and assisted sidings under suitable precautions to prevent corrosive action on the steel plates of the wagons.

We recommend to the Government the examination of a proposal that suitable trucks may be constructed for the movement of motor-cars, so that more than one car may be loaded either horizontally or vertically, and the incidence of cost both to the users and to the Railways under the existing rates may be minimised.

We recommend the examination of special type of steel or other covers for open wagons and flats for protection against theft and rain as are used in some countries and as are also used in modern shipbuilding in what are called Mcgregor type of covers used over Mcgregor holds.

We strongly urge that steps may be taken in the matter of providing special types of vans like tank wagons, refrigerator vans, etc.

We consider that standard rules should be provided and standard charges be levied for supply of cranes, for all Railways.

We consider that the Railways should take timely action to develop the existing capacity of inward and outward goods sheds with a view to meeting the complaint that at several stations, there is no outward wharf and goods brought for booking are exposed to the wind and weather in open space.

We suggest that an educative campaign may be undertaken amongst the workers themselves in certain big stations at least, in the matter of handling goods, and a suitable inspectorate may be provided to inspect the loading and unloading of these goods and thereby to educate the workers on the methods to be adopted in such matters.

We consider that the ferry charge for coal traffic should not be levied separately as a lump-sum charge and recommend that coal traffic be charged on the through distance, inclusive of the ferry mileage, as in the case of other traffic.

Statistical Information

We have referred to the sample survey that we conducted for obtaining figures of zonal movement in certain important commodities and we recommend that these figures may be given as a permanent annual feature in the statistics published by the Railways and that the results may be derived from a full compilation and not barely from a sample analysis. We consider that during the high tempo of development economy when heavier and heavier loads will fall on the Railways, these figures will be of great practical assistance not only to the Commercial and Rates Officers, but also to Operating Officers.

We have referred to the sampling survey conducted particularly by the Inter-State Commerce Commission through continuous sampling of way-bills and we recommend to the Government that the method of compiling statistics on the basis of sample surveys may usefully be encouraged on the Indian Railways for the purpose of investigating particular problems from time to time.

We have referred to cost studies in other countries and to the cost figures that we have on the Indian Railways. We have drawn the attention of the Government specially to the cost figures dealing with coaching traffic and have pointed out that if passenger traffic does not pay adequately, additional burden on goods traffic becomes inevitable.

We consider that there is scope for more detailed statistics to enable costs of large-scale and regular movement of important commodities being ascertained.

Efficiency

We have examined the efficiency of the Railways in the light of the criticism that increased efficiency will secure sufficient funds for the Railways. We find that the Railways are making a sustained effort for improvement. We, however, consider that, nevertheless, we must face the fact that the Railways should have additional revenue by an increase in the freight rates to meet their expanding needs.

In connection with the question of operating efficiency, we consider that smaller zones of 3,000 miles or so will conduce to better control and operating efficiency and we consider that a bold attempt be made to review the position and rectify it at an early date.

The Liability Of Railways For Goods Tendered For Despatch

In this chapter, we have dealt with the statutory provisions governing the responsibility of the Railways as carriers. We have described how the Railways' liability, which is ordinarily that of a bailee, may be limited, under certain conditions. In this connection, we have dealt particularly with what is called owner's-risk liability and the developments in this regard from time to time, culminating in the amendments to the Indian Railways Act 1949. We find that there is, at present, virtually no difference between the Railway Risk and the Owner's Risk Liability except in regard to the burden of proof.

We recommend that the general policy of the Railways should be to quote rates at railway risk and with the exception of a few commodities, the classified rates in the revised rates structure should be applicable at railway risk only. With reference to livestock also, we recommend that railway risk rates only should apply.

We have referred to the claims position on the Railways, and the several useful reports that have been made from time to time in the matter of claims. We have also referred to the evidence that we have received on this subject and the large volume of suggestions from the public to prevent the heavy incidence of claims.

We consider that the question of prevention of the causes leading to claims boils down largely to one of prevention of crime in the shape of thefts and pilferages whether inside the Railway premises or outside, in which both Railways and State Governments must play their part if this crime is to be successfully scotched.

We recommend that the Railways should assume common carrier liability and the change-over should be effected within one year from the coming into force of the revised freight rate structure. Some of us are doubtful whether the administrative and organisational reforms can be brought about within a period of one year.

We consider that packing conditions may be reviewed generally and the list of commodities for which compulsory packing conditions are imposed may also be enlarged, and the revised packing conditions may be brought into effect simultaneously with the assumption by the Railways of the liability of the common carriers.

We recommend that in regard to "non-delivery" the position may be clarified and suitable amendments may be made in the Act to provide for specific inclusion of the term "non-delivery".

We recommend for sympathetic examination the question whether Railways cease to be bailees once the free time for wharfage is over.

We recommend that suitable amendments may be made in the Railways Act to provide for certified copies of Forwarding Notes and other documents being admitted as evidence without the originals being produced. This will help in the speedier disposal of claims and avoid hold-up of railway records in most cases.

We recommend that the list of "Excepted Articles" be reviewed and certain commodities like electric bulbs, silk apparel and musical and scientific instruments should no longer find a place in this list.

We recommend that the notice of claims served on the Chief Commercial Superintendent of a Railway should be valid in law and necessary amendments to the Act should be carried out to provide for this.

Railway Rates Tribunal

We have dealt with the developments in the matter of Government control over Railway Freight Rates. We have referred to the provision in the Indian Railways Act, IX of 1890, of a Commission to deal with questions of undue preference. This Commission, however, was never set up. We have referred to subsequent attempts by the public and the recommendation of the Acworth Committee for the constitution of a Railway Rates Tribunal. We have also referred to the appointment of the Railway Rates Advisory Committee and its main features and functions and the subsequent setting up of the Railway Rates Tribunal.

We have dealt with the constitution of the Railway Rates Tribunal and referred to the public opinion in this matter.

We recommend that the constitution should be amended and the Tribunal should consist of an experienced High Court Judge as president with two other members chosen for their knowledge or experience of commercial, industrial and economic conditions in the country, or of the commercial working of railways. We further recommend that the President and members of the Tribunal may be appointed for a period of five years and may, in suitable cases, be eligible for reappointment. The appointments, we recommend, should be made by the President of India on the recommendation of the Law Minister, the Minister for Industry and Commerce and the Minister for Railways.

We have considered the present jurisdiction of the Tribunal and public opinion in this regard.

We recommend that the jurisdiction of the Tribunal be divided into mandatory and advisory functions—mandatory functions where the judgment of the Railway Rates Tribunal is binding on the Government in matters relating to undue preference, unreasonableness of rates and unreasonableness of other charges; advisory functions relating to classification and to references by the Central Government in matters falling within Section 45 of the Act and in cases where the Railway Board decide to grant station-to-station rates involving reductions beyond the limits prescribed by the Board for individual administrations.

In the matter of station-to-station rates, where such reduction is granted by the Railway Board on the recommendation of the high-level committee of representatives of various Ministries of the Union Government, including the Railways, to assist the export drive, we recommend that such decisions may be given effect to by the Railways without obtaining the advisory opinion of the Railway Rates Tribunal.

We recommend that necessary provision be made in the Indian Railways Act, so that the Railway Rates Tribunal may adopt an "informal procedure" in dealing with cases where a formal hearing is unnecessary and may be dispensed with.

We recommend that the question of permitting the Railway Rates Tribunal to award refund of overcharges for a particular period may be considered in greater detail by the Government.

RAIL-SEA CO-ORDINATION COMMITTEE, 1955—REPORT

New Delhi, Ministry of Transport, 1958. 121p.+viip.

Chairman : Justice Shri N. S. Lokur.
Members : Shri B. Das; Shri M. Govinda Reddy; Shri S. R. Kalyanaraman; Shri B. R. Patel (replaced by Shri P. R. Subramanian).
Secretary : Shri D. Mahadevan.

APPOINTMENT

The Rail-Sea Co-ordination Committee was constituted under the Ministry of Transport in June, 1955.

TERMS OF REFERENCE

(1) (a) To examine the reasonableness of freight charged by coastal shipping with reference to its costs of operation;

(b) To examine the existing pattern of trade movements within the country of commodities which could suitably move by sea and suggest measures to ensure effective co-ordination between the Railways and Coastal Shipping with a view to promoting movement of such goods by sea and with particular regard to:

(i) the need for promoting development of coastal shipping on sound lines;

(ii) the need for avoiding overlapping between the two forms of transport;

(iii) the need for developing adequate coastal shipping in the larger and long-term interests of the country;

(iv) the possibility of extending through booking arrangements between Railways and Shipping for movement by combined rail-sea route, wherever possible.

(2) To advise whether any standing machinery should be set up for considering all problems concerning rail-shipping coordination or allocation of traffic between the two forms of transport.

CONTENTS

Introductory; Historical Review of the Coastal and Adjacent Tonnage and Trades; Conference Arrangements Regarding Freight Adjustments; Commodity-wise Analysis of the Volume of Sea and Rail Borne Traffic along the Coast and between Defined Coastal Areas; Comparison made of Relative Levels of Freight Rates and Service Characteristics by Rail and Sea Routes; Main Problems of Coastal Shipping Industry; Problem of Co-ordination in other Countries; Development Plans for Coastal Shipping Tonnage and Additional Cargo Requirements for the Economic and Full Employment of the Target Tonnage visualised for the Second Plan Period; Proposals for Co-ordination and Diversion of Traffic in the Short-Term—The Long-Term Solution; Rates of Freight by the Sea Routes in relation to the Costs of Operation; Through Booking Arrangements by Rail and by Sea; Standing Machinery for Co-ordination; Some General Suggestions for Making the Sea Route more Popular and Attractive; Summary of Recommendations; Annexures Containing Statements.

RECOMMENDATIONS

Re: Item 1(a) Of The Terms Of Reference

We recommend that a general enhancement of 15 per cent in the rates of coastal freight as were in force prior to October 15, 1955, be made without any distinction as between rates for the West Coast trade and the Wider Coast trade and that in regard to the freight rates for coal traffic, an appropriate enhancement be granted with retrospective effect as from April 1, 1956, in view of the undertaking given in this regard by the Government.

We also recommend that the freight rates for salt should generally be brought up to the level of the freight rates for coal in the reverse direction. As, however, such a revision is likely to bring about a sudden and steep enhancement in the freight rates for salt they can be revised in the first instance from Saurashtra port to Calcutta and from Tuticorin to Calcutta as follows:

Commodity	*Stations* from	to	*Rate Per Ton* Rs.	An.	P.
Salt	Saurashtra Ports	Calcutta	37	12	0
,,	Tuticorin	,,	28	8	0

The enhancements recommended are on the basis of the operating costs for the year 1954-55 with due allowance for increases in fuel and other costs that have taken place since then and up to now. In the absence of any special disturbing feature, the revised rates are to remain in force for a period of two years, i.e. up to March 31, 1959. The matter will be reviewed, thereafter, in the light of such additions to the fleet as may have been made, and such increases in operating expenses and improvements in the turn-round of ships at ports as may have been brought about.

Re: Item 1(b) Of The Terms Of Reference

We recommend that in the context of the general policy of development of shipping and the overall transport shortage anticipated during the second half of the present Plan period the Government should take urgent steps to ensure attainment of the target of 4.12 lakh GRT for the coastal and adjacent trades as indicated in the Second Five-Year Plan.

Further, we consider it imperative that, whatever be the method adopted, as much of this tonnage should be reached by the end of the year 1959 as possible as thereafter we anticipate a sharp and substantial increase in the demand for additional transportation facilities.

With this total tonnage of 4.12 lakhs of shipping, we expect that it will be possible to carry about 50 lakh tons of cargo and that if necessary steps are taken cargo pertaining to adjacent trades carried in our ships may increase to about 8 to 10 lakh tons, leaving a total requirement of about 40 lakh tons of cargo in the purely Indian coastal trade. Against this the existing movements by coastal shipping may be expected to increase by about 10 per cent in the Second Plan period over the figures of 1954. The main cargo availability would, therefore, be 31.6 lakh tons leaving a balance of 8.4 lakh tons to be found by promotional means. This may be split up into 6 lakh tons in the loaded direction from East to West on the Wider Coast and the balance in the opposite direction, also on the Wider Coast.

On an analysis of the present pattern of movements, the total volume of general cargo available for diversion from the Rail to Sea route is only of the order of 2 to 3 lakh tons.

It is possible to find additional cargo of 6 lakh tons in the Wider Coast in the East to West direction almost entirely from Coal.

There is also scope for finding some cargo from other items like foodgrains, fertilisers and iron and steel.

In the reverse direction, the main hope of securing additional cargoes is a slight increase in salt shipments and some movements of cement. There may also be increasing volumes of trade in bitumen and packed petroleum products from the Bombay refineries to other coastal ports.

We recommend that in respect of these items of traffic a positive policy of diversion to the sea or rail-cum-sea route be adopted to the extent necessary for adequate utilisation of coastal shipping and in such a manner as to afford maximum relief to the Railways notwithstanding a slightly higher incidence of freight charges which may result.

We do not, however, recommend any enforced diversion to the sea route of any traffic of the private parties except in the case of coal.

So far as coal is concerned, we consider it imperative for the scheme of diversion of traffic to the sea route that some arrangement is made to ensure that the price to consumers in the coastal areas to which coal is diverted is not much higher than if their requirements had moved by rail.

We understand that the question of evolving a scheme of selling coal at a uniform price throughout the country or, alternatively, in several zones into which the country is to be divided is under consideration. If such a scheme is evolved, our recommendation will merely involve pooling of freight for all movements including those by the sea route.

In case such a scheme does not materialise, other specific freight equalisation arrangements will have to be introduced and we leave it to the Government to decide as to how this is to be done.

As a long-term solution for restoring the inherent advantages and the competitive position of coastal shipping, we recommend that, as in other countries, every effort be made to reduce terminal costs for transportation by sea through the provision of improved port facilities for avoiding or minimising delays to coastal shipping, and wherever possible, if necessary even by charging preferential port charges for coastal shipping.

In this context, we feel that we cannot too strongly emphasise the need to improve the working conditions at the ports in every way, so that the enormous national loss that results from undue delays to ships may be avoided.

We suggest also that the assessment made by the Ministry of Transport in regard to the provision for increased capacity of ports during the Second Plan period be reviewed in the light of our remarks made in this connection.

We recommend that the facility of through booking by the rail-cum-sea route as at present in force be continued and extended wherever possible.

Re: Item 2 Of Terms Of Reference

We recommend that the allocation of different descriptions of traffic as between the rail and sea routes be dealt with by a sub-committee of the Central Board of Transport of which senior representatives of the various Ministries are members. This sub-committee should review the tonnage and cargo availability position from time to time and decide on the nature and volume of cargo which should move by the sea or rail-cum-sea route, so as to ensure adequate employment of available shipping tonnage on the one hand and give maximum relief to the Railways on the other.

Apart from this sub-committee at the Centre to deal with the general over-all position, we recommend that local committees be set up at each of the major ports to implement decisions of the Government based on the recommendations of the sub-committee and also to examine all questions concerning local matters of detail.

We do not at this stage recommend the setting up of any standing machinery for purposes of freight fixation. We consider that future variations should, as far as possible, be confined to general increases or decreases and as the volume of work involved would be very limited, a standing machinery as such will not be required. Whenever there are any special circumstances justifying a detailed enquiry, the Government could exercise their powers under the Control of Shipping Act to set up an ad-hoc board for the purpose.

Additional Recommendations

The recommendations we have made for freight increases include an allowance of Rs. 37.14 lakhs per annum towards rehabilitation and the building up of reserves. We recommend that the Government should take suitable steps to ensure that the funds are so utilised.

Although as between the West Coast trade and the Wider Coast trade we have recommended that the same rate of increase be allowed now, we suggest that the Government may arrange for an examination of the question whether the freight tariff of the West Coast should not be entirely detached from that of the Wider Coast at a convenient opportunity so that rates in respect of each of these services and variations therein, made from time to time, may appropriately reflect the economies of the particular service.

We consider that there is scope and need for the rationalisation of the present tariff on as scientific a basis as it is possible without disturbing the total financial return and without causing too violent a variation in the relativity of rates at any one time.

The Coastal Conference has agreed to consider this subject at an early opportunity after the Government has taken its decision on our report.

We recommend that this be further followed up.

We recommend that in order to enable future proposals for variations in the coastal rates to be dealt with satisfactorily and expeditiously suitable arrangements be made to develop on organisation which will collect and maintain necessary statistics in appropriate forms to be prescribed in advance so that they could be used readily for purposes of cost estimation. In our opinion this organisation is now best developed in the Directorate-General of Shipping and that it should work in close collaboration with the Coastal Conference.

Subject to the rationalisation of the freight structure, we are of the opinion that, in future, freight revisions should, as far as possible, be confined to general increases or decreases and that such variations should be made only when any important change involving substantial financial implications takes place in the coastal trade or, alternatively, when over a period of time a number of changes have occurred the cumulative financial implications of which are substantial.

We recommend that consideration be given to the possibility of granting concessional terms for loans advanced for purchase of ships for coastal operations.

We recommend that preferential berthing facilities at ports for general cargo ships on the coast be granted.

We further suggest that consideration be given for the levy, wherever possible, of port dues, wharfage and other charges on coastal shipping on a concessional basis.

We recommend that the Coastal Conference should evolve rationalised sailing schedules with a view to ensuring regular sailings and calls at as many ports as possible, as the prevailing shortage of general cargo is, in a substantial measure, due to the irregular clearing opportunities offered.

We suggested to the Coastal Conference consideration of the possibility of their opening common City Booking Offices and Warehouses in the larger cities where all cargoes could be received for despatch by the first available vessel. The Conference did not receive the suggestion favourably. We consider, however, that the matter should be reviewed by them, as it appears to us that they have not appreciated the full advantages of opening of joint booking offices at the principal ports.

We recommend that detailed examination be made of the economies of topping up coal cargo vessels at Visakhapatnam, coming short-loaded from Calcutta, due to the draft limitations in river Hooghly.

We consider that, in future, control should be exercised by the Director-General of Shipping over coastal shipping in such a way that the entire pool of coastal tonnage is used to the best advantage of the country and as an effective limb in the co-ordinated transport arrangements.

RAILWAY METRIC COMMITTEE, 1955—REPORT

New Delhi, Railway Board, 1957. 82p.+xxxvp.

Chairman : Shri S. L. Kumar.

Members : Shri B. S. Sindhu (replaced by Shri C. S. Lal); Shri V. Venkataramayya (replaced by Shri K. C. Sood); Shri L. C. Mohindra; Shri B. R. Kinra; Shri K. V. Kasturi Rangan (replaced by Shri H. Ramamoorthy); Shri R. E. de Sa (replaced by Shri B. C. Ganguli); Shri L. T. Madnani (replaced by Shri N. N. Tandon); Shri G. D. Khandelwal (replaced by Shri P. C. Mathew); Shri D. R. Suri; Shri D. S. Mehta (replaced by Shri I. C. Bhatt); Dr. B. Lall; Shri P. N. Murti.

Secretary : Shri J. P. Gupta.

APPOINTMENT

The Ministry of Railways (Railway Board) in pursuance of the standing Metric Committee's recommendation set up an ad-hoc Railway Metric Committee in terms of the Board's letter No. E55 CO1/39/3, dated August 20, 1955.

TERMS OF REFERENCE

(a) How the change-over from the present system to the metric system should be effected.

(b) Phasing of the change-over.

(c) Financial implications.

CONTENTS

Introductory; General Preparatory Steps; Administrative and Organisational Measures; Central Standards Office; Civil Engineering Branch: Mechanical Engineering Branch; Production Units; Signal and Tele-Communication Engineering Branch; Electrical Engineering Branch; Stores Branch; Traffic and Commercial Branch; Medical Branch; Accounts Branch; Conclusion; Summary of Financial Implications; Summary of Recommendations; Appendices I to VII.

RECOMMENDATIONS

Recommendations For Immediate Action

A Metric Cell should be set up immediately under the Additional Member (Mechanical) of the Railway Board to plan and direct the change-over to the metric system on the Railways. The Cell should consist of one Joint Director from the Mechanical Engineering branch and one Deputy Director each from the Civil Engineering, Stores and Traffic (Transportation and Commercial) branches.

The Railways should initiate early action in the matter of recalibration of weighing machines and weighbridges to show in addition the metric units of weights.

The Central Standards Office should immediately select suitable metric scales for use in Engineering Drawing Offices and issue a directive to all Railways on this subject.

The Civil Engineering Departments of the Railways should work out the station-to-station distances in kilometres from the longitudinal sections, in advance of the actual fixation of kilometre posts, and supply these particulars to the Commercial Departments, not later than the end of 1957, to enable timely revision of fare and rate tables.

The Railways should be advised immediately to commence marking of tare weight, carrying capacity, floor area on the existing and the metric units on all goods stock during periodical overhaul.

Other Recommendations

The Railway Board Metric Cell should arrange for the immediate revision of the Railway Board's codes and publications, particularly the Schedule of Dimensions, I.R.S. Limits and Fits, Way and Works Manual and State Railway Engineering Code.

Metric Cells should be set up in each branch at the Headquarter Office of each Railway for planning and effecting the change-over.

The expeditious implementation of the change-over will depend on the availability of an adequate number of experienced draftsmen. In order to attract and retain suitable men, the number of additional posts in the higher grades in major Drawing Offices should be considerably increased during the period of the change-over and the outstanding among them should be promoted to fill additional gazetted posts to supervise this work.

All recruiting agencies for the Railways should include an elementary test of the knowledge of the metric system in their syllabi.

In order to adopt the metric system, mere endorsement of the exact equivalents of inch dimensions on the drawings of standard engineering equipment will ordinarily be of little practical utility. Redesigning of the normally replaceable assemblies in our standard equipment including rolling stock would, in most cases, be inescapable. There should be simultaneous development of designs for new standard equipment based entirely on the metric system.

It would be futile to undertake any revision of designs and drawings of non-standard equipment, including non-standard rolling stock, which will not remain in service after 1970. Re-examination should, therefore, be confined mainly to the existing standard designs and drawings of equipment likely to remain in use beyond 1970. Such re-examination for the adoption of the new standards should be so carried out as to reduce the element of redesigning to a minimum and the leading dimensions of standard engineering equipment should, as far as possible, remain unaltered.

Development of new designs of equipment should aim not only at the complete adoption of the newly developed metric standards but also result in such leading dimensions as would be convenient to trade and industry from the point of view of facility of manufacture and of its subsequent maintenance.

The Central Standards Office should take immediate action in the matter of revision of standard designs and drawings, particularly those of standard locomotives to be manufactured in the immediate future. Early availability of new designs for the existing standard equipment would reduce the transitional difficulties in respect of new equipment and may also reduce the period of complete change-over.

In order to eliminate duplication of tracing work at various centres, adequate arrangements for additional printing-room equipment should be made by the Central Standards Office for the preparation and distribution to the Railways of sets of mechanical tracings and *ferros* of revised drawings.

Necessary additional office accommodation for the Central Standard Office should be arranged on a priority basis.

Provision of roving Instructors of the rank of Inspectors or Assistant Inspectors would be necessary on all Zonal Railways for training the Class IV and artisan staff distributed all over the line.

Engineering works, which are likely to commence after 1960-61, should be planned entirely on the metric system. Designs of works in hand at present should show the leading dimensions also in the metric system.

Establishment of Planning Cells in the major Mechanical Workshops and Production Units would be necessary for assisting the local management.

Chittaranjan Locomotive Works should consider commencement of production of each metric assembly as and when its modified drawings are received from the Central Standards Office.

Production of integral design coaches to the metric standards at the Integral Coach Factory, Perambur, should commence with the 10th and 11th batches, sometime in 1961-62.

All Production Units such as the Furnishing Unit at Perambur, Metric Gauge Integral Coach Factory, Duplicates Factory, etc., to be set up in future, should be planned on the metric basis and manufacture from the commencement of production should be based on the metric system only.

Electrification projects likely to be taken in hand after 1960 should be planned on the metric basis.

Two Junior Scale Officers would be necessary for a period of 3 to 5 years, primarily for the revision of nomenclature lists in the Stores Branch of each Zonal Railway.

Existing organizations for the preparation of nomenclature lists should be suitably strengthened immediately so as to expedite the revision of these lists.

The revision of bases for rates and fares and other charges in the Commercial Branches of the Railways may be carried out simultaneously for both decimal coinage and metric weights and measures and brought into effect on and from April 1, 1960.

AIR TRANSPORT COUNCIL, INDIAN AIRLINES CORPORATION'S FARES AND FREIGHT RATES, 1955—REPORT

New Delhi, Ministry of Communications, 1957. 231p.+xivp.

Chairman : Shri S. Lall.

Members : Shri J. R. D. Tata; Shri Chandulal P. Parikh; Shri B. Malik; Shri K. Srinivasan; Shri A. K. Roy; Shri K. B. Mathur; Shri Shankar Prasad; Shri L. C. Jain; Shri J. K. Chaudhuri.

Secretary : Shri G. P. Shahani.

APPOINTMENT

During the debate on the annual report of the Indian Airlines Corporation in the Rajya Sabha on September 9, 1955, Shri Jagjivan Ram, then Minister for Communications, announced the Government's intention to have the Corporation's fare and freight rate structure examined by the Council. On September 19, 1955, the Council received a request "to study the general problem of fares and freight rates to be charged on the air services operated by the Indian Airlines Corporation and to draw up for the consideration of the Government a set of principles on the basis of which such fares and freight rates should be determined".

TERMS OF REFERENCE

(i) To study the general problem of fares and freight rates to be charged on the air services operated by the Indian Airlines Corporation; and

(ii) To draw up for the consideration of the Government a set of principles on the basis of which such fares and freight rates should be determined.

CONTENTS

Introduction; Definitions; **Part I**—Basic Economic Aspects; A Brief Review of Air Transport Results; Possibilities of Promoting, Developing and Expanding Air Traffic; The Corporation's Problems, Working Results and Future Outlook; A Brief History of Regulation of Air Fares and Freight Rates; International Fares and Freight Rates and Domestic Fares and Freight Rates of Foreign Countries; **Part II**—The Objectives; Reasonable Passenger Fares; Reasonable Freight Rates; Corporation's Deficit Operation; **Part III**—Summary of Conclusions and Recommendations; Acknowledgments; Minute of Dissent; **Part IV**—Appendices I to XVII.

RECOMMENDATIONS

Safety Record

Due publicity should be given to the ascertained causes of each serious accident whether investigated by a court or not. Comparative statistics relating to accidents according to a well-accepted pattern should be published annually in fuller detail.

Travel By Air By Government Officers On Duty

The level of entitlement, which has since been reduced to a monthly salary of Rs. 1,600, should be further reduced to Rs. 1,100.

Passenger Insurance

We suggest that the Government consider the possibility of introducing a suitable, cheap Accident Insurance Scheme for air passengers.

Two-Class Air Travel

The Corporation should explore the possibility of introducing a two-class service either in the same aircraft or by different aircraft.

Tourism

We suggest that, in consultation with the Corporation, the Ministries concerned consider what action should be taken.

The Objectives

In an important public utility operated by the State, "business principles" should definitely be subject to overriding considerations of a national or public character.

The objectives of rate-making should be:

(i) To stimulate the maximum economic volume of traffic;

(ii) To generate surplus revenues on high-density traffic routes which would offset to the largest extent possible the gap between costs and revenues on weak traffic routes; and

(iii) To sustain and promote air traffic by creating a preference for it on account of its inherent advantages.

Reasonable Passenger Fares

On no scientific basis is it possible to establish any definite relationship between air fares and air-conditioned-class rail fares. The latter cannot be regarded as a reliable criterion for judging the reasonableness of the former.

If there is any significant diversion from air to rail travel adversely affecting the load factor of air services, the lowering of air fares within the permissible limit hereinafter proposed or introduction of a cheaper, austerity class service would provide the appropriate solution.

The fare structure should be constructed on the basis of single tapering design.

The scale prescribed by such a design cannot be rigidly applied. The Corporation ought to have reasonable scope for experimenting with lower fares in order to promote, sustain or develop traffic. The scope for variation in the exercise of this discretion should be a range of 15 per cent below the prescribed scale. This may be called the range of reasonableness. Any fare proposed by the Corporation within this range may be approved by the Government as a matter of course. Fares may be fixed above or below the range, if the Government is satisfied that sufficient justification exists.

The Corporation, when negotiating foreign fares and rates under bilateral agreements, should, generally bear in mind the objectives and principles of rate-making stated by us.

The fares of foreign sectors of the Bombay-Madras-Tiruchirapalli-Colombo service should be raised at least to the level of domestic fares recommended for the corresponding sectors.

The Council recommends the following fare design:

(For all existing types of aircraft)

(i)	1 — 30 miles	... 0.6.6	per each pax. mile
(ii)	31 — 100 miles	... 0.5.0	,,
(iii)	101 — 200 miles	... 0.4.9	,,
(iv)	201 — 500 miles	... 0.4.6	,,
(v)	501 — 900 miles	... 0.4.3	,,
(vi)	901 and above	... 0.4.0	,,

Raising of the 10 per cent discount of the one-way fare for the round-trip journeys would not be in the best interests of the public as well as the Corporation.

It should be left to the discretion of the Corporation to introduce appropriate Concessional Fare Schemes for special purposes, e.g. to arrest traffic decline, to meet seasonal fluctuations, to give relief in distress, to provide for student concession, family travel, etc.

Whenever feasible, the Corporation should establish appropriate fare differentials between faster and slower services, and where there is appreciable difference between the standard of passenger comfort of the two services.

As there is a long halt at Nagpur on the Night Airmail Services during an inconvenient hour which breaks the passenger's sleep, the current practice of 10 per cent differential between the Day Services and Night Airmail Services should continue.

Also, where the cost of operation is significantly higher on account of the difficult nature of operations, an upward adjustment of the maximum fare rate is justified.

Fare should be computed on the basis of point-to-point mileage except when there is a regular, available service between the two points by a shorter route, in which case the fare should be related to the shorter route distance.

Frequent or marked fluctuations should be avoided as far as possible. Due publicity and adequate notice should be given to any proposed changes in fares.

Reasonable Freight Rates

The Corporation should continue to watch the practices of Freight Agents from time to time and successfully regulate them in its best interests and those of the public through appropriate agreements.

On the one hand it is proposed to increase the Corporation's revenues by raising passenger fares, it would not be consistent, on the other, to recommend that the rebate of 25 per cent of basic cargo rate enjoyed by newspapers should be enhanced.

In view of the great social utility of vaccines and drugs, the freight rate for these commodities, as demanded by the B.C.G. Laboratory, Madras, a regular customer of the Corporation, should be slightly lower.

As the demand for transport of accompanying excess baggage is produced by passenger traffic, its rate should be equated to the passenger fare rate.

The Council, by majority, is of the view that, as the demand for promotional treatment of air cargo is being adequately met to the extent required, the current practice of equating the basic cargo rate to the passenger fare rate or the excess baggage rate should continue, though theoretically it costs less to transport air cargo than air passengers.

A start should be made towards standardisation of class rates, specific commodity rates, bulk rates and back-haul rates.

Taking excess baggage rate as 100, the rates to be fixed for high-grade commodities or cargo requiring special care in transit or in ground handling should, in accordance with current practice, be selected from the range 150 per cent, 200 per cent, 250 per cent, 300 per cent, 350 per cent and 400 per cent. If the basic cargo rate is equated to the excess baggage rate, the other rates should be selected from the following range, viz. 95 per cent, 90 per cent, 85 per cent, 80 per cent, 75 per cent, 70 per cent, 65 per cent, 60 per cent, 55 per cent, 50 per cent, 45 per cent, 40 per cent, 35 per cent, 30 per cent, 25 per cent, 20 per cent, 15 per cent, 10 per cent, according to what the traffic can bear in specified, small or bulk shipments on out-haul or on back-haul.

The last four rates will be for back-haul in the Calcutta-North Bengal, Assam, Tripura, Manipur region.

Admittedly, such rate-fixing is not an easy art and will require some period of trial and error to mature and give fair results.

The break-points or the minimum weights for entitlement to lower bulk rates for out-haul or back-haul should, as far as possible, be standardised.

To meet possible competition from non-scheduled operators, the Corporation should be permitted to offer special rebates for bulk shipments completed within specified periods, which would ensure customers' loyalty.

Greater emphasis should be laid by the Corporation on market survey.

ENGINEERING PERSONNEL COMMITTEE, 1955—REPORT

New Delhi, Planning Commission, 1956. 85p.

Chairman : Shri Y. N. Sukthankar.

Members : Shri Vishnu Sahay; Shri Kanwar Sain; Prof. M. S. Thacker; Shri S. B. Bapat; Shri S. Ranganathan; Shri K. N. Subramanian; Shri K. P. Mushran; Shri H. P. Mathrani; Shri G. K. Chandiramani; Dr. B. D. Kalelkar; Shri N. Govindarajan; Shri H. Davenport.

Secretary : Shri B. N. Datar.

APPOINTMENT

A number of attempts at assessing the requirements of engineering personnel in isolated sectors have recently been made in the Ministries at the Centre and in the States. For instance, the Ministries of Irrigation and Power, Communications, Production, Railways and Iron and Steel have independently assessed their requirements for implementing the development programmes under the Second Plan. A few State Governments which anticipated acute shortages have also assessed their demand for engineering skills. To undertake an overall assessment of demand and supply in this respect, therefore, the Planning Commission set up the Engineering Personnel Committee under its Resolution No. PC (VI) L (E) II-15/55, dated September 26, 1955.

TERMS OF REFERENCE

(i) To make a general assessment of shortages of supervisory and higher grades of engineering personnel anticipated at the end of the First Five-Year Plan;

(ii) To estimate the probable requirements of engineering personnel of supervisory and higher grades for implementing the Second Five-Year Plan in the principal fields of national development such as building and road construction, railways, industrial development in the public and private sectors, mining and irrigation and power etc.;

(iii) To review the programme of the Central and State Governments under the Second Five-Year Plan for the expansion and development of facilities for technical education for engineering personnel of supervisory and higher grades and to recommend such additional or modified programmes as may be considered necessary;

(iv) To review existing facilities for practical training in industrial establishments, including apprenticeships, and to recommend measures for their expansion in co-operation with industry; and

(v) To make such other recommendations as may be essential for ensuring the adequate supply of engineering personnel for the next 15 years with particular reference to the immediate requirements of the Second Five-Year Plan.

CONTENTS

RECOMMENDATIONS

There has been a considerable expansion in engineering education in the country in recent years. Even so, the demand for engineering personnel has outstripped supply.

A high-level of demand is likely to be sustained in view of the future emphasis on development of heavy industries.

Advance assessment of needs is necessary not only for supervisory and higher grades of engineering personnel, but also for skilled workers, who constitute a vital component of technical manpower resources.

There is a certain amount of immobility among technical personnel, especially at lower levels. In spite of incentives that may be thought of for promoting mobility, resistances are likely to persist. The regional aspect of demand and supply has, therefore, to be kept in mind.

In assessing the future demand for technical personnel, the following assumptions have been made:

(a) No major technological change as would seriously affect the requirements of engineering personnel will take place in the next five years;

(b) The present pattern of distribution of work between departments and contractors and as between small and big contractors will continue in the Second Plan also;

(c) An increasing proportion of graduate engineers will be employed in the private sector; and

(d) A substantial number of qualified engineers will be required to staff the additional capacity to be created for institutional training. The cadres will be strengthened to allow for a reserve for refresher training and deputation within and outside the country.

Central Ministries and State Governments had indicated comparatively heavy demands in the initial years of the Second Plan. Since these demands cannot be met all at once, they have been re-distributed between different sectors of development and between the five years of the Second Plan to correspond to a more realistic pattern of demand. This should not be considered as actual allocation of personnel to different regions or Ministries.

It is necessary to create a suitable deployment machinery to co-ordinate the release of personnel from one project and their absorption in another.

Foreign training for our engineers should be made more purposeful by advance mapping of fields in which such training is urgently required and earmarking trainees for suitable positions in the country on successful completion of training. A larger proportion of foreign scholarships should be made available to teachers in engineering institutions.

Post-graduate training facilities in engineering subjects should be provided on a wider scale within the country.

Engineers who have qualified in specialisations for which demand is likely to develop should be afforded facilities for pursuing advanced work in their chosen fields in (a) Design and Development wings attached to State enterprises and (b) Engineering and Technological institutions.

Since demand for specialists has not developed to any considerable extent, it will be more advantageous to continue the present arrangements under which training is more broad-based.

While standards in respect of top students in the engineering institutions have been maintained, there is reason to believe that a certain lowering of average standards has taken place.

Reasons for the deterioration in quality are:

(a) Dearth of teachers of the right calibre,

(b) Inadequate facilities for practical training,

(c) Ineffective methods of examination and enforcement of standards, and

(d) Possibly also, insufficiency of equipment in some institutions.

Standards in engineering institutions should be improved by:

(a) Bringing service conditions for teaching staff on a par with those obtaining in executive positions under the Government,

(b) Sparing competent and experienced men from Government cadres for teaching in colleges,

(c) Arranging field experience in industrial enterprises and engineering projects for teachers to help them keep in touch with the progress taking place in current engineering practices,

(d) Promoting advanced work and research in universities,

(e) Making promotions within the teaching line largely on the basis of research work carried out by staff,

(f) Allowing serving engineers who display a special aptitude and potentiality for research to enter such work on adequate remuneration, and

(g) Encouraging consulting work by University staff.

Standards of examination should be improved by effecting a partial change in favour of a system which will give evidence of the professional attainments of a student rather than his power to memorise.

As an incentive for better performance, employment should be guaranteed to students who top the lists in the examinations.

There is not sufficient justification for the belief that engineering personnel are surplus to the country's requirements.

Lack of experience is the main cause for unemployment among engineers. An engineer may also remain unemployed as a result of temporary imbalance between the supply and demand in certain regions.

Employing authorities should provide opportunities for experience to persons who have potentialities of being "built up".

The practice of advance recruitment of technical personnel and their training prior to posting should be adopted on a wider scale.

It is anticipated that in 1960-61, engineering personnel will be in short supply to the extent of about 1800 graduates and 8,000 diploma holders in different branches.

To meet the shortages, capacity in the existing established institutions should be expanded fully. It may be possible to secure in this manner an average increase of 20 per cent in the outturn of graduates and 25 per cent in the case of diploma holders.

In addition, 18 colleges and 62 diploma institutions will have to be opened. The total cost of setting up these training facilities (establishment of new institutions and expansion of capacity in existing institutions) will be in the neighbourhood of Rs. 16 crores.

It will take three to four years for these additional

facilities to yield results. In the interim period, shortages will have to be met by :

(a) promotion from lower ranks,

(b) more balanced utilisation of available talent,

(c) retention of persons for suitable periods beyond the age of superannuation,

(d) temporary overloading, to some extent, where this is not already being practised, and

(e) the organisation of functional training at the supervisory level.

Functional training for supervisory personnel will have to be continued as a permanent measure, even beyond the interim period, since the additional facilities planned will need only 60 per cent of the prospective demand.

In addition to physical shortages, rigidity in recruitment and financial procedures create difficulties. These should be suitably resolved.

Institutional training for skilled workers, present and future, should be geared to the requirements of employing authorities.

Despite the insufficiency of information on skilled workers, it is possible to state that given the right atmosphere, engineering activities will not suffer for want of craftsmen.

Industrial establishments should train personnel in advance to meet not only their individual needs, but also the expanding requirements of the country.

If anticipated steel production is to find its uses, special efforts will be needed to place apprentices in the existing engineering establishments.

The Government's orders for machinery should be properly phased both in the interest of stepping up internal production and for widening the scope of apprenticeship in engineering trades.

Training opportunities afforded by foreign consultants and suppliers of machinery should be fully utilised.

Voluntary efforts, supported by the Government, should be sufficient to meet the needs of apprenticeship training.

If sufficient progress is not in evidence, legislation or levy of a cess may have to be considered.

There is evidence to show that in the engineering field there is considerable "flight" of personnel from job to job resulting in dislocation of work, unsatisfactory performance and increased expenditure on staff.

"Flight" of personnel is an organisational problem and is tied up with differences in salary scales, security of tenure and regional preferences.

States should agree to a common line of action for the evolution of uniform conditions of service for personnel engaged on development schemes.

The long-term interests of temporary engineers engaged on development projects should be protected.

A suitable authority should be set up by agreement between the States and the Centre for (a) regulation of salary scales and security of tenure and (b) allocation, inter-State movement and welfare of personnel engaged on development projects outside the regular cadres.

Flexibility and speed have to to be secured in recruitment through the Public Service Commissions in the context of the personnel needs of the development programmes.

Recruitment should be speeded up through (a) suitably strengthening the Public Service Commissions, (b) bifurcating their work relating to senior and junior posts, and (c) devising simpler and quicker methods of consultation.

Recruitment to services at the college campus should be tried because of (a) the advantage of speeding up recruitment and (b) the beneficial effect which a Service Commission going round the universities will have on students.

There should be one or two bulk selections every year for technical men of a particular category.

Priority should be given to the creation and maintenance of a Register of Technical Manpower.

Indian nationals receiving technical training abroad should be kept informed of employment opportunities advertised in India.

Future recruitment policy should be guided by the need to keep in balance the age composition of serving engineers.

The successful implementation of a manpower policy implies (a) an effective and continuous collection of the necessary information, (b) framing of policy on the basis of information so collected, and (c) execution of such policy. Each of these functions requires a suitable organisation.

With improved co-ordination among existing agencies, collection and interpretation of the necessary data on a continuing basis would not be difficult.

A Technical Manpower Committee of the Cabinet should be set up, with a corresponding Committee of Secretaries, to evolve policies regarding technical personnel. A Technical Manpower Division should be created in the Planning Commission to serve the Cabinet Committee. Similar Committees will have to be set up at the State level.

The Central Government should explore the possibilities of instituting a suitable All-India Service of Engineers by common consent of the participating States.

Technical and scientific personnel should be introduced at suitable levels in the general administrative machinery, especially to hold posts where their experience is of value.

STUDY GROUP ON EDUCATED UNEMPLOYED, 1955—REPORT

New Delhi, Planning Commission, 1956. Mimographed. 55p.

Chairman : Shri V. K. R. Menon.
Members : Shri G. K. Chandiramani; Shri Jang Bir Singh; Shri G. P. Kane; Shri K. N. Subramanian; Shri B. N. Datar; Shri P. C. Suri; Shri S. A. Qadir.
Secretary : Shri A. N. K. Nair.

APPOINTMENT

The Study Group on Educated Unemployed was set up in the last week of September, 1955, by the Planning Commission for the purpose of assessing the extent of the problem of unemployment among educated persons in the country and for working out schemes which would help tackle the problem.

TERMS OF REFERENCE

(i) To assess generally the extent of unemployment of the educated classes in the country and with special reference to conditions prevailing in areas where the problem is acute;

(ii) To indicate the scope for special programmes for increasing employment opportunities for educated persons in the schemes that are being formulated by the State Governments and Central Ministries and in the private sector;

(iii) To recommend special measures and programmes of training, re-orientation and employment which may facilitate absorption of educated unemployed persons into the economy of the country;

(iv) In particular, to work out detailed programmes to be implemented during 1956-57 and especially pilot programmes in selected areas; and

(v) To recommend a scheme of work and transit camps particularly in areas badly affected by unemployment with the following objectives in view:

(a) to assist the unemployed during the waiting period,

(b) to assist the unemployed to secure suitable employment, and

(c) to enable the unemployed to lead a disciplined life rendering manual work or other services and acquiring secondary skills through vocational training.

CONTENTS

Introduction; Approach to the Problem; Extent of Unemployment; Special Programmes to Reduce Unemployment; Proposals of State Governments; Some Measures to Mitigate Frustration; Long-Term Remedies; Conclusions.

RECOMMENDATIONS

The sum total of our recommendations in regard to items involving fresh capital outlay can be summarised briefly thus:

	Gross cost over 5-year period	*Recoveries*	*Net cost*
	(Rupees in crores)		
(i) Work and Orientation Camps	7.1	nil	7.1
(ii) Small-Scale Industries	84.0	58.3	25.7
(iii) Co-operative Goods Transport	20.0	18.0	2.0
(iv) Other Schemes of State Governments	19.0	not known	not known

Recoveries in the case of schemes under (iv) can be known only after it is decided as to which of the schemes from among the many recommended by State Governments are to be finally selected. If, for the purpose of calculation, we treat half the sum as recoverable, the result will be that, on a gross provision of Rs. 130 crores, the net cost will be about Rs. 44 crores. The additional employment generated is estimated at 235,000 for the educated classes, leaving aside consequential employment created for others. If the co-operative sector is expanded in accordance with our recommendations—which we have omitted here as no financial provision is being separately recommended for it—approximately another 20,000 could be absorbed.

According to the assumptions we have made in Chapter 3, the position in respect of educated unemployed is likely to be about the same at the end of the Second Five-Year Plan period as it is at present if no special measures are undertaken on their behalf. While this is based on the best available data, certain caution is nevertheless desirable. Further, the goal of total elimination of unemployment can be attained only if substantial progressive reduction is achieved during the Second Five-Year Plan period. Broadly, our recommendations will reduce the quantum of unemployment among the educated group to about half the present number at the end of the period. We feel this is not too ambitious a target to work on, remembering that in view of the many administrative and other questions involved, the chances are rather of the target not being reached than of it being exceeded.

As already mentioned, no considered recommendations can be made regarding regional distribution until an indication is available whether the schemes recommended are approved as also whether overall finances to the extent we have recommended will be available. Further, we have still to get detailed recommendations from those States in some of which the problem is generally known to be acute or chronic. Some indication has, however, been given of the degree to which the problem exists in different regions. With this information coupled with further details which are expected from the State Governments concerned, it will be relatively easy to make specific recommendations as to how these amounts could be allocated to the different States. It is, of course, recognised that regional distribution cannot, in the case of every scheme, be based merely on the quantum of unemployment prevalent in a particular State. For instance, in regard to co-operative services for goods transport, distribution will have to be related to actual needs for such services. Nevertheless, it should be possible to make allocations between different States in such a manner that the overall allocations and employment potential can be reasonably related to the size of the problem in the particular States.

In regard to the gross expenditure on the schemes recommended, the major share is for the *one* item, "Small-Scale Industries", and we have made this recommendation after careful consideration and with an awareness of possible criticism. Our justification is first that the bulk of the expenditure is returnable investment. Even of the net cost of Rs. 25.7 crores, Rs. 4 crores represent non-recurring expenditure on buildings and equipment, the use of which will continue well beyond the five years. If account is taken of these factors, the ultimate net expenditure is by no means out of proportion to the importance the Government has been attaching to the development of small-scale industries. There is general admission, though for good reasons, that development in this sector has been poor during the First Five-Year Plan period. That alone is a justification for a larger outlay during the Second Five-Year Plan. Though the Group is primarily concerned with the limited problem of educated unemployed, it is felt that between two types of schemes suited to this class, the one which is more important from the point of view of general economic development should have preference. Finally, the Group is convinced that this is one of the most potential fields which can absorb the educated youth as a permanent measure—not as a mere temporary palliative. Indeed one criticism, often expressed, against any change in the current pattern of education, is that this could be done only after ensuring that adequate facilities for vocational training and subsequent avenues for employment are both readily available. In a way, schemes of the type we have recommended afford one answer to such criticism.

Though the Group is confident that the targets can be effectively worked to—provided early decisions are reached and *adequate* administrative machinery is set up—we suggest that in the unlikely event of practical difficulties arising, the provision under one head could be reduced by a corresponding increase under another. To make such changes quickly a certain number of additional schemes should be held in reserve under each head. In the particular case of small-scale industries, we are clear in our mind that an adequate financial provision should be immediately sanctioned for getting complete schemes prepared.

We have referred to the steady increase in the number of educated men whose career at school or college has not given them a bias towards any particular vocation or specially fitted them for any type of employment. This trend is more pronounced in some regions than in others, and we urge once again the urgent need for the remedial measures recommended. One particular matter to stress here is the need for effective co-ordination between the educational authorities and those responsible for the employment services and vocational training, at all levels. This responsibility should be specifically located, as a continuous function, both at the Centre and in the States in their respective planning organisations.

ADVISORY COMMITTEE FOR LIBRARIES, 1955—REPORT

Delhi, Manager of Publications, 1959. 141p.

Chairman : Shri K. P. Sinha.

Members : Shri N. Bhadriah; Shri J. C. Mathur; Shri B. S. Kesavan; Shri S. S. Saith; Shri T. D. Waknis; Shri D. R. Kalia; Mrs. Achamma John Mathai.

Secretary : Shri Sohan Singh.

APPOINTMENT

In September-October 1955, a Seminar on the "Role of Libraries in Social Education" was organised by the Indian Adult Education Association at Chirag Delhi. One of the recommendations of the Seminar was to set up a Library Commission to investigate the state of libraries in India. The Ministry of Education accepted the recommendation and set up an Advisory Committee for Libraries instead of a Commission.

TERMS OF REFERENCE

(i) To enquire into the present reading needs of the people, how they are met and what part the existing library set-up plays in meeting the needs.

(ii) To enquire into the reading tastes of various sections of the people, what agencies are there to provide suitable literature and how the reading tastes and hence the literature can be improved.

(iii) To recommend the future library structure in India.

(iv) To recommend the forms of co-operation between the library and social education set-up.

(v) To go into the question of the training of librarians and the conditions of their service.

(vi) To make recommendations on the administrative and financial measures necessary to support the future library set-up in India.

CONTENTS

Historical; The Present Position of Library Service in India; Place of Public Libraries; The Structure of Libraries; The Auxiliary Services and Library Co-operation; The Library Personnel; Training Librarianship; Libraries and Social Education; Library Finance and Administration; Appendices I to V.

RECOMMENDATIONS

The Structure Of Libraries

Library service should be free to every citizen of India.

The library pattern in the country should consist of National Library, State Central Libraries, District Libraries, Block Libraries and Panchayat Libraries.

It should be desirable to have an independent Directorate of Social Education and Libraries in every State. Wherever, on account of any special local circumstances, this is not possible, the State Government should have at least one whole-time Senior Class I Officer of the rank of Deputy Director of Education.

The important functions of the State Library Department should, among others, be as follows:

(a) Prepare annual and five-year plans for libraries in the State;

(b) Collect descriptive and statistical reports on the working of all libraries in the State;

(c) Fix minimum standards of Library Service by various libraries under the State Library Department;

(d) Conduct constant evaluation of Library Service in the State;

(e) Ensure training of various types of library workers in adequate numbers and quality;

(f) Assist auxiliary bodies in maintaining their efficient and useful working;

(g) Sponsor library legislation, where necessary;

(h) Maintain an efficient Inspection and Advisory Service for District and Block Libraries in the State;

(i) Supervise and administer the system of grants-in-aid to Subscription Libraries.

The State Central Librarian should be the Chief Technical Adviser of the Library Department.

Every State should have a State Library consisting of two wings—the State Central Library and the State Lending Library. The important functions of the State Central Library should, among others, be as follows:

(a) Build up an exhaustive collection of all publications, official and non-official, in the State;

(b) Undertake bibliographical work, including special bibliographies, for the use of scholars and research workers;

(c) Maintain a union catalogue of the important libraries in the State;

(d) Maintain a strong reference collection and service;

(e) Act as a clearing house of information on the Five-Year Plans of the country, etc.;

(f) Organise book exhibitions and professional conferences;

(g) Be the centre of inter-library loan within and without the State;

(h) Promote library work with children.

The State Lending Library should:

(a) Mainly serve as home-lending library for the city in which it is situated and as the library supplying the stocks of District Libraries;

(b) Provide for lending of films, film strips and recordings.

The State Lending Library should honour the tickets of all service points in the State.

Libraries in big cities as well as District Libraries should have children's wings attached to them.

The State Library should exercise the following functions in the field of Children's Library Service:

(a) Plan the book stocks of libraries having children's wings;

(b) Exchange of children's books between libraries;

(c) Award prizes for those who publish good reading material for children;

(d) Hold conferences of school teachers for discussing children's literature;

(e) Hold travelling children's books exhibitions;

(f) Compile annotated catalogues of children's books;

(g) Prepare posters and artistic book-notices;

(h) Sponsor projects for studying children's reading tastes.

The State Library should have a Council which should be composed as follows:

(a) The Minister of Education, as Chairman;

(b) The Officer-in-Charge of Libraries in the State as Secretary of the Council;

(c) Secretary, Education Department;

(d) Representatives of all District Libraries in the State;

(e) A representative of the State Library Association;

(f) Vice-Chancellors of all Universities in the State;

(g) A representative of the Development Department;

(h) Two members of the Legislature;

(i) Two persons co-opted for their special knowledge of libraries.

The Executive Committee of the Council should consist of not more than seven members, comprising the Chairman, the Secretary, the Secretary of Education Department, and four persons nominated by the Chairman from among the members of the Council.

In a district, Library Service should be a system based on urban centres having responsibility for their surrounding rural areas.

A District Headquarters Library should have two wings, one running a Reference Service and Lending Service as the Central Library of the town in which it is located, and the other running the Circulation Service to the branches in the city and Block Libraries.

A District Library Committee should consist of 15-19 members. Two-thirds of these members should represent Municipal and Block Library Committees and one-third nominated by the Executive Committee of the State Library Council. Of the members who represent the Municipal and Block Libraries, two-thirds will represent Block Library Committees and one-third Municipal Committees.

The important functions of a District Library Committee, among others, should be as follows:

(i) Supervise the work of Municipal and Block Libraries;

(ii) Lay down policy and procedure regarding purchase of books for the District Library;

(iii) Opening of new branches, etc., or purchase of furniture, equipment and mobile vans;

(iv) Issue reports on the working of Municipal and Block Libraries in the district as well as the District Library;

(v) Administer library funds, including grants-in-aid, to Subscription Libraries.

The District Library Committee should be represented on the District Development Board by its Chairman.

A City or Town Library Committee should be composed of 10 persons. Of these, two-thirds should be elected by the Municipal Committee of the city or town and one-third nominated by the Chairman of the District Library Committee. The City or Town Librarian should be the Secretary of the Committee.

The State Government should encourage annual conferences of Chairmen and interested members o District Committees. Expenditure on such conferences should be met from the State Government Library Funds.

Block Libraries should be manned by whole-time staff.

Information Centres in the blocks should form the nuclei of Block Libraries.

A Block Library Committee should consist of 9-12 persons. Of these, one-third should be nominated by the Block Development Committee, one-third should be elected by the members of the Block Development Committee from amongst themselves, and the remaining one-third should be nominated by the Chairman of the District Library Committee.

Every Panchayat should have a library.

The management of Panchayat Libraries should rest in the Panchayat or Village Committees.

At the all-India level, there should be a National Central Library and three National Book Deposit Centres. The National Book Deposit Centres should be run by the Government of India under the National Central Library.

There should be an All-India Library Advisory Council composed as follows:

(a) Union Minister of Education, as Chairman;

(b) Secretary, Ministry of Education;

(c) The Office-in-Charge of Libraries in the Ministry of Education as Secretary of the Council;

(d) Chairmen of all State Library Boards;

(e) A representative each of the Ministry of Community Development and the Planning Commission;

(f) Two Vice-Chancellors of Universities;

(g) Two Members of Parliament;

(h) Two persons co-opted for their expert knowledge of libraries.

The important functions of the Council should be as follows:

(a) Review and assess the work done by the State Library Departments;

(b) Collect and publish descriptive and statistical reports of working of libraries in the States:

(c) Lay down minimum standards of Library Education in the country;

(d) Lay down minimum standards of Library Service for various sectors;

(e) Organise experimental or pilot projects for administering new and better modes of Library Service;

(f) Promote research in library problems;

(g) Organise library conferences, seminars and workshops on national scale;

(h) Collaborate with national or international library associations.

There should be an Executive Committee of the All-India Library Advisory Council consisting of seven persons nominated by the Minister of Education from among the members of the Council, including the Chairman, the Secretary to the Ministry of Education and the Secretary of the Council who will be ex-officio members of the Board.

The Executive Committee will have all the necessary executive powers, and will be supported by a Division of Libraries with a Divisional Head in the Ministry of Education.

The Auxiliary Services And Library Co-operation

State Governments should encourage the setting up of book bureaux in all State capitals in the first instance, to be extended later to district and other towns. All libraries run or assisted by the Government shall buy their books from the bureaux.

Library Associations are essential to the development of library movement and State Governments and the Government of India should encourage development of strong library associations.

The Government should give financial assistance to Library Associations for the following purposes:

(a) Rent for premises of headquarters office;

(b) Remuneration of one whole-time or part-time Secretary or office clerk;

(c) Projects of general usefulness to library movement which the Government may like to sponsor.

The Library Associations should strive to prepare the tax-payers' mind for accepting library legislation and persuade State Governments to enact legislation and set up State Libraries.

Libraries should encourage the formation of *Mitra Mandals* wherever possible.

Every State or region should have a centre where books weeded out from the Public Libraries are sent.

Public Libraries in the country should co-operate with one another as well as with subscription libraries, school libraries, college libraries, departmental and research libraries, university libraries, etc.

In places, where it may not be possible to run independent Public Libraries, school libraries may serve the public after school hours.

In places where Public Libraries are not strong, an inter-lending arrangement with the college libraries should be made.

Pending establishment of efficient reference sections in Public Libraries, Government departmental and research libraries should assist them in compiling annotated book lists on their special subjects and in answering reference enquiries from the public, etc.

The University Library should co-operate with the public library system by:

(a) Issuing book lists on subjects of interest to certain groups in the public;

(b) Admitting as regular members the more serious minded readers among the public; and

(c) Perform reference functions of the State Central Library, where these libraries are not yet established.

The Government of India should sponsor the preparation of four Union Catalogues as follows:

(a) A Union Catalogue of all publications in the various university libraries in the country. This can be undertaken by the University Grants Commission.

(b) A Union Catalogue of all publications in the departmental and research libraries under the Government of India. The Union Ministry of Education should take up this work.

(c) A Union Catalogue of all copyright holdings in the State Central Libraries. The National Library will probably be best fitted to take up this work.

(d) A Union Catalogue of all scientific and learned periodicals in the university and research libraries in the country. This should be entrusted to the Scientific Research wing of the Ministry of Scientific Research and Cultural Affairs.

The Library Personnel

State Governments should accept the responsibility of Public Library Service in their areas. The librarians of these libraries should be State Government employees.

The various positions in the library structure in a State should be equated with those of teachers and educational administrators in the Education Departments.

State Governments should put out vocational pamphlets giving in detail the opportunities available in the public Library Service in the State.

Library Departments in the State should make clear-cut separation between professional and semi-professional work and entrust professional work to trained staff only.

After recruitment, the semi-professional staff should be given elementary library training during their probation period.

For a professional worker the minimum qualification should be Graduation with diploma in librarianship.

As far as possible, librarians should not be transferred too frequently.

Every State Library should have qualified specialists in Children's work and Adult work besides specialists in technical processes.

State Governments should freely grant study leave to librarians going in for ordinary or higher training in the profession.

It should be the responsibility of the State Librarian to see that librarians in the Public Library system keep up with the professional literature after leaving their library schools. The District Librarians and large City Librarians should take up similar responsibility for the staff under them.

State Education Departments and the Ministry of Education should have a programme of library seminars or workshops every year as follows:

(a) The Central Ministry of Education should organise every year at least one all-India seminar or a workshop of librarians and liberally subsidise atleast two regional seminars.

(b) Every State Government should give at least one opportunity in a year to State and District Librarians to come together for one to four days' camp.

(c) District Librarians should similarly organise at least one annual meeting of Block Librarians and three or four conferences or camps where they, along with their Block Librarians, can meet Village Librarians for a day or two.

(d) Every Block Librarian should convene a meeting of Village Librarians three or four times a year.

(e) Apart from general seminars, there should also be special subject seminars and courses for the professional growth of librarians.

Suitable budget provision should be made for such seminars by the Government concerned.

In technical matters a librarian should be required to take orders only from a professionally trained librarian.

Library Departments should prepare manuals defining clearly the duties of all library workers in the State from the State Librarian down to the Village Librarian.

The Director of Libraries should have the following powers:

(a) Plan, organise and administer the Library Service in the State;

(b) Administer a system of State financial grant to Subscription Libraries so long as they exist and determine conditions of their absorption in the State Library System;

(c) A large measure of financial powers to enable him to run the Library Service smoothly. He should be closely associated with the preparation or revision of the State Library budget. His duties and powers vis-a-vis the State Library Committee should be clearly defined.

The State Librarians should have, among others, the following powers:

(a) Incur expenditure from the sanctioned budget for the State Central Library and to re-appropriate from one head in his budget to another with the advice of the Library Committee;

(b) Grant all types of leave to his staff, except study leave and leave for more than two months which will be sanctioned by the Director of Libraries;

(c) Make officiating arrangements in case of a leave of more than a month;

(d) Depute staff members to library seminars and workshops inside and outside the State and sanction their travelling and other expenses;

(e) Appoint certain class of staff which an officer of equivalent status in the Education Department is competent to appoint;

(f) Plan and publish technical works, including tools needed for proper performance of various technical processes;

(g) Organise elementary training programmes.

The District Librarian will have the powers necessary for supervising and co-ordinating the activities of Branch Libraries in the State.

The State Governments should frame rules for defining the powers of the District Librarian regarding grant of leave, appointments, purchases, etc.

In the cities and towns, library appointments should be made by Municipalities or Corporations in accordance with the rules framed by State Governments.

Chief Librarians at all levels should be associated with the selection of staff at their level.

State, District and Block Librarians should have seats on the Development Councils of their States, districts and blocks, respectively.

State Governments may institute certificates of merit to be awarded to persons and groups whose achievements in the field of Library Service may have been outstanding in a particular year.

No State Government should require a librarian to furnish security or to pay for the loss of books, unless gross negligence or dishonesty is proved against him.

Training For Librarianship

A National Scheme of studies for training in librarianship should comprehend (i) the training of semi-professional staff needed by all types of libraries, which requires training only in methods and routines, (ii) the training of the professional staff needed by most of the public libraries, which involves a sound training in general librarianship, and, finally, (iii) advanced or specialised training in Library Science for the leaders in the profession, as also for those who would occupy responsible positions in different types of libraries.

The training of semi-professional staff should be conducted at two levels:

(a) Training for Village Library work;

(b) Training library clerks for performing routine duties.

Block Librarians should give prospective Village Librarians in their jurisdiction a short course of two to four weeks' duration, which should prepare them for Village Library work, instruct them in the aims and scope of Library Service and the relation of Village Library Centre to other Social Agencies working in the field.

No university should run semi-professional courses. They should be run by Library Associations or, where no such association is willing or able to take up the responsibility, the State Government through the State Library.

The Government should lay down the standards with regard to the syllabus and duration of the Elementary Course, the selection of teachers and the conduct of examinations.

The duration of the elementary course should be three to four months, at the end of which the trainees should be required to take an examination comprising three to four papers of one or two hours' duration.

Courses for training professional librarians should be organised by the Universities, State Governments or the National Central Library.

The basic professional training should consist of a full year's course leading to a Diploma. The admission to this basic course should be confined only to First and Second Class Graduates.

The Government of India should set up an expert committee consisting of professional librarians for suggesting complete reorganisation of the syllabus of Library Diploma Course.

The expert committee should also go into the following subjects:

(a) Teaching methods, and

(b) Conduct of examination.

The University Grants Commission should strengthen the existing Diploma Courses in the first instance in order to enable the universities running classes in Library Science to create separate departments of library education and give adequate financial assistance to the Universities for this purpose.

In a University library, teachers should be appointed by the same agency which selects persons for other academic courses. The Library Teachers' status should also be determined according to the standards governing the status of other University teachers.

Teachers for Library classes should be selected on the strength of their research and publications.

Universities should offer to Library teachers salaries equivalent to those received by teachers of other departments.

All universities teaching Library Science should appoint Boards of Studies and Boards of Examiners in Library Science.

Some of the universities should also provide advanced courses in librarianship, leading to M.A. degree in librarianship.

The Central Government and the University Grants Commission should give financial assistance to the universities for this purpose.

The entrance qualifications for the advanced course should be at least a Second Class Graduate and Diploma in Librarianship. The admission may also be open to fresh Diploma holders who have first class or distinction in their first professional examination and for special librarians on the basis of their contributions to the profession.

Universities should also encourage research in librarianship. Special funds should be provided for this purpose.

Libraries And Social Education

In some States demonstration projects should be tried at one or two promising centres where librarians, who are also trained in the teaching of reading, may take some regular classes for improving reading skills and methods of study of the people willing to take such lessons.

In order to be helpful to one another, Librarians and Social Education workers at the Block and District levels should have knowledge of one another's field of work.

Both the Social Education workers and Librarians should try to discover the reading tastes and reading needs of the people and pass on this knowledge to the book production agencies in their State.

Library and Social Education staff should meet regularly to evolve methods of fruitful co-operation.

Library Finance And Administration

The Government of India and State Governments should have a 25-year Library Plan to raise the library structure from its present embryonic dimensions to a size which will do justice to the cultural and educational needs of the people.

The Government should levy a cess of 6 naye paise in a rupee of property tax in all places with permission of the local bodies to raise the cess.

The Government of India should contribute to the Library Funds of a State an amount equal to the cess collected in the State.

To begin with, State Governments should give grants equal to the cess collected and gradually in the course of the next 25 years raise their contribution to three times the cess collected.

Suitable existing Subscription Libraries should continue to receive aid from State Governments subject inter alia to the condition that at least 25 per cent of the membership of an aided library should be free and mainly meant for persons of low economic status. The existing Subscription Libraries should be encouraged to join the proposed free public Library Service in every State.

Subscription Libraries set up after the publication of this Report should not be given grants-in-aid.

There should be a periodical review, after every five years, of the Subscription Libraries in receipt of Government aid and after every such review the freeships of such libraries should be raised by at least 25 per cent. Thus at the beginning of the Sixth Five-Year Plan the entire public library system will have become free.

In each State, the library system should function as follows:

(a) The cess collected in an urban area by a Municipality or a Corporation will constitute the Library Fund of the Municipality or Corporation.

(b) The cess collected in the area within a block will constitute the Block Library Fund.

(c) To each Block or Municipal or Corporation Library Fund the State Government will add an amount equal to the cess collected either in cash or in the form of provision of staff or both.

(d) The Central Library at a District Headquarters will serve as the Central Library for the entire district for purposes of supplementing the book stocks of Block and Municipal Libraries and for strengthening the administration. To enable it to do so, the whole of the State Government's contribution to Municipal and Block Funds in the district will go into a District Library Fund. If necessary, the funds may be reinforced by a percentage of Library Funds of the Blocks and the Municipalities in the District. In addition, subject to a degree of autonomy of large cities with population of over one lakh, the District Library will exercise a certain degree of autonomy over other libraries, especially in the deployment and use of their book stocks, and the areas which they should serve.

State Governments should enact a comprehensive State Library Law which will provide for the following:

(a) Free Public Library Service with the following objectives:

(i) To house materials giving reliable information and wholesome recreation,

(ii) To organise them as to promote their use,

(iii) To stimulate non-readers to be readers and readers to be purposive students,

(b) A library rate of 6 naye paise in a rupee of property tax to be levied by local bodies and Panchayats.

(c) The State Government will aid the local bodies by a matching formula. The law may be brought into operation gradually within a period of 20 years.

(d) There will be Block Library Funds and the Municipal Library Funds, but the district would be regarded as a Unit of Library Service.

(e) The various units of Library Service will have their own Library Committees.

(f) The State will organise a Department of Libraries.

(g) The State Government will recognise Library Associations and provide for adequate assistance to them.

(h) Books will form the bulk of library stocks, which must also include newer media of mass communication like audio-visual materials, etc.

Similarly, the Government of India should enact a Library Law incorporating:

(a) Right of every citizen to have free access to libraries as his Fundamental Right;

(b) Collating the various deposit sections under the Copyright Act, the Delivery of Books Act, and the Press and Registration of Books Act and making them subserve the needs of a National Library Service; and

(c) Providing for financial assistance to State Governments.

ALCOHOL COMMITTEE, 1955—REPORT

Delhi, Manager of Publications, 1956. 137p.

Chairman : Dr. A. Nagaraja Rao.
Alternate Chairman : Dr. G. P. Kane.
Members : Shri M. P. Alexander; Shri Jasjit Singh, Shri Shripat.
Secretary : Shri S. L. Venkateswaran.

APPOINTMENT

The present production of alcohol in the country is being largely utilised as power alcohol which in admixture with petrol is used as an automobile fuel. Quite apart from the fact that the scope for using alcohol in this fashion is for various reasons very limited, it is desirable that the many industrial uses of alcohol should be developed so that many products for which the country is dependent on imports today and the demand for which is going up could be produced in India. With the expansion which is taking place and is expected to take place in the production of sugar, the potentiality for producing alcohol is on the increase. Taking all these circumstances into account, the Alcohol Committee was constituted under the Ministry of Commerce and Industry, vide their Resolution No. Ch. Ind. 33(11)/52, dated October 11, 1955.

TERMS OF REFERENCE

(i) To assess the scope for increasing the production of alcohol in the country having regard to the present materials and to suggest suitable locations for any new units for producing alcohol that may need to be set up.

(ii) To examine the manner in which the total

alcohol production in the country can be fully utilised either as power alcohol or more particularly for industrial purposes and to recommend the industries which can be expanded or established having regard to the increase in the availability of alcohol for industrial purposes in the country.

(iii) To study the system of controls exercised by different States over the production, distribution and transport of alcohol and to make suitable recommendations for their simplification, where necessary, in order to ensure that while the objectives of the controls are adequately safeguarded, the industrial concerns which need alcohol as a raw material have the minimum of difficulty in meeting their requirements.

(iv) To make any other recommendations that the Committee may deem appropriate having regard to the objectives of increasing the production and utilisation of alcohol for industrial purposes.

CONTENTS

Introduction and Scope of the Committee's Work; Brief History of the Growth of Alcohol Industry in India; Present Position of the Alcohol Industry; Prospects for Development of the Alcohol Industry and the setting up of Additional Capacity; The Price of Alcohol; Tax on Alcohol; Regulations governing Price Distribution, Possession, Transport and Use of Industrial Alcohol; Arrangements for Use of Power Alcohol; Miscellaneous Considerations; Summary of the Major Recommendations; Tables I to XII; Appendices 1 to 10.

RECOMMENDATIONS

1. Consumption of alcohol for industrial purposes amounts only to 3 to 4 million gallons per year at the present time. The scope for increased use of alcohol for such purposes has been analysed and major projects based on alcohol as a raw material that should be encouraged on a priority basis have been indicated. If all these projects materialise, their requirements of alcohol would amount to over 31 million gallons per year.

2. The present annual consumption of alcohol as power alcohol is of the order of 10 million gallons. Even when alcohol-based industries develop, it will be necessary to continue to use power alcohol in admixture with petrol so as to provide a flexible demand to cover any imbalance between anticipated production and gradual development of industrial demand for alcohol. For several years to come, it will be necessary to arrange for the utilisation of about 12 million gallons per year as power alcohol.

3. The principal raw material for the production of alcohol will have to continue to be molasses from sugar factories. The availability of molasses estimated on the basis of the programme envisaged for expansion of the Sugar Industry during the Second Five-Year Plan is of the order of 1 million tons per year. After meeting the requirements of other users, it is expected that over 900,000 tons of molasses will become available for the manufacture of alcohol from 1959-60 onwards.

4. The total production of alcohol even from all the available molasses as shown in (3) above together with about 1 million gallons produced from Mahua flowers would be of the order of 46.8 million gallons per year (100% by volume). Installed distillery capacity recommended for achieving this production is of the order of 52 million gallons per year.

5. The minimum capacity for a distillery of economic size, under the present circumstances in India is 1 million gallons per year. The Committee recognises, however, that under special circumstances, the economies of production in units of smaller capacities may not be too disadvantageous.

6. The power alcohol industry has been developed to its present stature on the basis of an ex-distillery price of 14 annas per gallon. It is essential that the basic price for alcohol should not be higher than this figure if its use as a raw material for industries is to be developed. The Committee considers this an essential prerequisite for stimulating industrial development based on alcohol and also in view of the absence of many other organic raw materials for development of these important industries within the country.

The Committee recognises that while the basic price for alcohol may be fixed so as to provide a fair return to the producer, the incidence of price to the consumer may be governed by a system of graded taxation depending upon the use to which the alcohol is to be put.

7. As molasses has been and will continue to be the principal raw material for production of alcohol, control over its price and distribution is essential if the price of 4 annas per maund, for molasses containing not less than 50 per cent total sugars, is recommended. For molasses of a lower sugar content, correspondingly lower prices on the lines prescribed in U.P. may be charged.

In spite of the many representations demanding an increase in the price of molasses, the Committee is unable to recommend any such increase because, while it will not contribute significantly to reducing the price of sugar to the consumer, such an increase would be detrimental to the development of alcohol and alcohol-based industries.

8. In order to ensure uniformity in the control over price and distribution of molasses, it seems preferable that such control should be exercised by the Union Government under powers conferred by the Industries (Development and Regulation) Act.

9. A ceiling price for alcohol has been calculated after taking into account the cost of production in a unit of economic size as well as the actual average

transport charges on molasses from sugar factories to the distilleries. It is recommended that a uniform ceiling price for alcohol ex-distillery should be:

> Rs. 0.12.9 for alcohol of strength 99.5% by volume, Rs. 0.12.5 for alcohol of strength 96% by volume, plus an amount corresponding to an additional charge upto a maximum of Rs. 0.6.0 per gallon towards the actual average transport charges incurred on molasses.

The above price would be applicable to alcohol corresponding to the specifications of power alcohol and rectified spirit (industrial grade) respectively.

10. In the interest of developing alcohol-based industries, it is essential that alcohol of all grades, including power alcohol, should be charged the same freight rates on Railways. It is recommended that one uniform rate should be charged under Class 10 for Railway Risk and under Class 8 for Owner Risk for all grades of alcohol.

11. There is no unanimity of opinion between the Union and State Governments regarding their respective rights to tax alcohol. The Committee feels, however, that if efforts for promotion of a substantial increase in the consumption of alcohol for industrial purposes are to succeed, it is essential that a uniform taxation policy and procedure should be devised by agreement between the Union and State Governments, as has been done already for power alcohol. Such taxation can be enforced more satisfactorily by the Union Government.

The two members of the Committee belonging to the State Governments feel, however, strongly that since excise duties on alcohol represent a major flexible source of revenue to State Governments, even if it decided that the Union Government alone has the power to levy a duty on industrial alcohol, the collection of such duties should be left to the State agencies and the amounts realised retained by the concerned States.

12. It is recognised that for certain categories of uses a higher price of alcohol would not constitute a deterrent to its consumption, and, therefore, any margin between the ceiling price specified earlier and the higher price which such a user could afford to pay may provide a source of revenue to the Government. Variation in excise duties on alcohol used for different purposes has been recommended in the light of this observation.

13. It is recommended that the incidence of Permit or Licence Fees, Vend Fees and Gallonage Charge, etc., may be levied, if at all, at a token figure and that such charges should not be levied as a compensation to cover the costs incurred in the administration of Excise and Prohibition Laws.

14. It is recommended that Excise Laws governing distilleries engaged in the production of alcohol be revised in consonance with the needs of modern design and practice. The lines on which existing State Regulations may be revised have been indicated in broad detail.

15. Control over distribution of industrial alcohol should be exercised under Section 18 (G) of the Industries (Development and Regulation) Act so as to ensure proper correlation between its production and distribution and to guarantee adequate supplies of alcohol at reasonable prices to industries whose development is deserving of encouragement.

16. It is recognised that prevention of misuse of alcohol for potable purposes is the responsibility of State Governments; it is necessary, however, that jurisdiction of State Governments in this respect should be integrated with the need for encouraging industrial developments based on alcohol. The following suggestions have been made to achieve the objective:

(i) Conditions of licences and permits granted by State Governments to producers or users of alcohol should not conflict with any of the objectives of the Industries (Development and Regulation) Act.

(ii) Wide scope should be permitted in the use of special denaturants for alcohol depending upon the specific needs of different industrial processes.

(iii) While denaturants must be tested and certified as conforming to approved specifications before use, it is not necessary to insist on further tests of the denatured spirit before issue from distilleries.

(iv) A permit for each individual consignment drawn by the licensee need not be insisted upon, so long as supplies are made within an annual quota previously fixed and licensed for use by an industrial user and the consignment is moved each time only against passes from the Excise Inspector stationed at the distillery.

17. The general public may be allowed to buy and keep up to a maximum limit of half a gallon of completely denatured spirit without permit or licence for domestic and other miscellaneous uses.

18. The varying pattern which may have to be developed with respect to mixing depots for supplying petrol mixed with power alcohol in different parts of the country during the next few years has been indicated.

To ensure the offtake of power alcohol in different areas from year to year it is considered necessary to adopt a flexible system for the sale of power alcohol, under which the Oil Companies should take over directly from the distilleries the stipulated amount of alcohol allotted to them each year and take charge of arrangements for the purchase, handling, transport and sale of all power alcohol. An outline of the arrangements that should be made for this purpose has heen indicated.

19. The need is felt to have a clear definition of the terms "alcohol" and "spirit" so as to devise methods for extending facilities and assistance exclusively to producers and users of power and industrial alcohol. It is

suggested, therefore, that the term "alcohol" be used for denoting only ethyl alcohol of 66" over proof and above, and the term "spirit" be limited exclusively for alcohol of lower grades.

20. Recently, the Ministry of Finance have issued a Notification exempting methyl alcohol from the purview of the definition of the term "spirit", for purposes of levy of Customs Duty. The Committee recommends that a similar Notification exempting higher alcohols such as isopropyl, amyl, butyl, etc., which are neither potable nor intoxicants be issued immediately and that the scope of control and taxation of all alcohol or spirit be confined scrupulously to ethyl alcohol only.

A similar exemption from control applicable to ethyl alcohol should be granted also to users of fusel oil containing less than 12 proof gallons of ethyl alcohol.

21. The cost of excise supervision should not be realised from distilleries, as it constitutes an appreciable addition to the cost of production of alcohol.

22. Sometimes difficulties arise because of dual control over alcohol producers exercised by the Union and State Government Departments. It is recommended that a system may be devised under which one single officer, either of the Union or the State Government concerned, will be in sole charge of a distillery or a factory.

23. The anticipated movements of molasses and alcohol for the Second Five-Year Plan period have been worked out for the guidance of the Railway Authorities. The Committee wishes to stress that provision of tank wagons in adequate numbers for both is essential to ensure success of the programme of development of alcohol based industries and, therefore, expenditure on tank wagons should be regarded as a developmental item and arrangements made to procure them in adequate numbers in anticipation of the need.

24. It may be possible to build up an export market for over a few million gallons of alcohol per year if the price of alcohol is pegged at the level recommended in this report. Suitable assistance should be given with regard to excise procedure and availability of tank wagons and storage facilities at ports to prospective exporters.

25. A Development Council for Fermentation Industries including alcohol and products obtained therefrom should be constituted as early as possible.

26. Since State Governments issue permits or licences to all consumers of alcohol, they should maintain detailed statistics relating to industrywise consumption of alcohol, because such data would be valuable for estimating the requirements of industries in future.

SETHUSAMUDRAM PROJECT COMMITTEE, 1955—REPORT

New Delhi, Ministry of Transport, 1957. 41p., Charts.

Chairman : Dr. A. Ramaswami Mudaliar.
Members : Shri S. K. Mukerji; Shri B. N. Chatterjee; Captain J. R. Davies.
Secretary : Shri R. A. Gopalaswami.

APPOINTMENT

The Sethusamudram Project Committee was constituted under the Government of India vide their Resolution No. 9-PII(23)/55, dated November 1, 1955, to examine and report on the feasibility and desirability of connecting the Gulf of Mannar and the Palk Bay by cutting a channel at the approaches to the Adam's Bridge for enabling deep-sea ships to navigate in safety from the West to the East Coast of India. It has been suggested that the construction of such a passage would increase the potentiality of the port of Tuticorin if it is to be developed into a deep-sea port.

TERMS OF REFERENCE

(a) What is the extent to which shipping in general is likely to benefit by, and in practice to take advantage of the shortened sea route via the proposed Sethusamudram Passage?

(b) Would the advantages, likely to be secured, be commensurate with the expenditure involved?

(c) What are the traffic prospects of the Tuticorin Port during the next decade—

(i) if the Sethusamudram Passage is provided; and

(ii) if the Sethusamudram Passage is not provided?

(d) In the light of the traffic assessment, should the Tuticorin Development Project be proceeded with? If so, what should be the timing :

(i) immediately by itself and independently by the Sethusamudram Project;

(ii) simultaneously with the Sethusamudram Scheme; or

(iii) at a later stage and, if so, when?

CONTENTS

Introductory; Integrated Project—Proposed Design

and Estimate of Cost; Estimates of Traffic and Revenue; Direct Financial Return; Answers to Terms of Reference; Sethusamudram Project and Rail Traffic; Concluding Remarks; Annexures I & II.

RECOMMENDATIONS

Sethusamudram Legislation

If the project is executed, it will be necessary to make provision by special legislation for the permanent maintenance of the navigational works and facilities brought into being thereby. The canal, the various approach channels, the lock and the bridge will have to be maintained and conserved. The statutory authority will have to be established; its jurisdiction will have to be defined; (this may possibly entail reference to the Sethusamudram Medial Line) and it should be given legal authority to levy dues on ships using the route and to regulate their movements on the route and safeguard their navigational safety and conveniences

Sethusamudram Authority

Since the creation of a Sethusamudram Authority would be essential at a later stage, it would be an advantage, in advance of legislation, to set it up under executive orders immediately upon sanction of the Project. This would enable the execution of the Project to be supervised closely and carried out efficiently and expeditiously. The necessary financial and administrative powers can be delegated so as to secure this result.

It will be necessary to give careful consideration to the composition of this Authority. We think it is essential that it should be composed of representatives of the Government of India, the Government of Madras, the Indian Shipping Companies, the Southern Railway and the Tuticorin Port Trust.

Sethusamudram Shipyard

Before concluding this Report, we desire to invite the attention of the Government of India to the special features of the site which we have selected and recommended for the location of the Sethusamudram Canal. It is situated in the vicinity of a natural harbour with a shore-frontage of about seven miles. There is a railway and a National Highway lying immediately behind this frontage. Land is available in plenty and can be acquired at low cost. Electric power is available. The sea in this area (as in the South generally) has a very low range of tides.

We understand that the coexistence in one place of all these advantages renders the area in the vicinity of Sethusamudram Canal exceptionally well suited for the location of ship building and allied industries. At present, India has got only one shipyard at Visakhapatnam. As our work was nearing conclusion, the newspapers carried the report that the Government of India had taken the decision that a second shipyard should be established somewhere in the country and that they were on the look out for a suitable site.

We have, therefore, considered it appropriate that we should bring these facts to the notice of the Government of India. We suggest that the possibility of establishing the second shipyard required by the country in the vicinity of the Sethusamudram Canal may be investigated.

THE COMMITTEE ON AMALGAMATION OF COLLIERIES, 1955—REPORT

New Delhi, Ministry of Production, 1956. 148p.+ivp.+Map.

Chairman : Shri Balvantray Gopaljee Mehta.
Members : Shri N. P. Nathwani; Shri R. R. Morarka; Shri Ahmed Mohiuddin; Shri M.L. Shome; Shri S. S. Grewal; Shri R. Maulik; Shri J. N. Mukherjee; Shri B.L. Agarwalla; Shri Baidya Nath Banerjee; Shri Chapalendu Bhattacharjee; Shri Kanti Mehta.
Secretary : Shri S. Mayuranathan.

APPOINTMENT

The Committee on Amalgamation of Collieries was constituted under the Ministry of Production vide their Memorandum No. C 2-23 (10)/52, dated November 10, 1955.

TERMS OF REFERENCE

(i) To examine the position of the Collieries in Raniganj and Jharia coalfields and to make proposals for their amalgamation into single economic units taking into account the areas of holdings, the current output and capacity of the collieries, geological and geographical and other relevant features, the need for efficient and economical production, conservation and preparation of coal by such processes as washing, etc.;

(ii) To consider the objective in relation to existing State legislation and to suggest whether Central Legislation will be necessary for carrying out amalgamation, and, if so, to recommend the content of such legislation.

CONTENTS

Introduction (Appointment and Terms of Reference; Amendment of the Terms of Reference; An Interpretation; The Committee's Procedure; Our Approach to the Problem; The Questionnaires of the Committee; Witnesses; Acknowledgments); The Bengal and Bihar Coalfields (Progress and Development of Mining in India; The Present Position; Leases, Intermediaries and Royalties; Production and Methods of Production; Labour; Transport and its Effect on Production; Summary); The Background to the Problem of Amalgamation and the Appointment of the Committee (The 1919 Report and the 1920 Committee; The Views of the Coal Mining Committee, 1937; The Indian Coalfields Committee; The Working Party of the Coal Industry 1951; Discussions with the Industry 1952 to 1955; Summary); Experience in Foreign Countries (General; Great Britain; Germany; France; Netherlands; Belgium; U.S.A.; Australia; Summary); The Laws Affecting the Coal Industry (The Mines Act and the Indian Coal Mines Regulations); The Coal Mines (Conservation and Safety) Act and the Coal Board; The Colliery Control Order 1945 and the Coal Controller; The Welfare, Rescue and Provident Fund Organisations; The Mines and Minerals (Development and Regulation) Act 1948; The Bihar Land Reforms Act 1950; The West Bengal Estates Acquisition Act 1953); The Small Collieries and their Problems (History; Performance; The Colliery Control Order and its Effect; Labour Amenities and other Factors; The Capacity of the Small Collieries; Technical Management; Their Place in the Industrial Structure; Summary and Conclusions); Irregular Boundaries (Present Position; Problems created by Irregular Boundaries etc.; Relation between Geological and Surface Features and Mine Boundaries; Causes of Unsuitability of Barriers; Previous Consideration of the Question; Main Difficulties in Adopting Remedial Measures; Remedial Measures Suggested and Conclusions; Recommendations); Coal Conservation (The Reserves of Coal; Safety and Conservation; Stowing; Coal Washing; Blending; Rotation of Workings; Waste in not working thin seams; Selective Mining; Recommendations); Modernisation and Mechanisation (Planning; Mechanisation; Improving O.M.S. in existing Mines; Mechanisation in Relation to Amalgamation; Recommendations); Proper size of a Colliery and the Collieries to be Amalgamated (Present Classification of Collieries; Classification According to Area, Labour Strength, etc.; The Relation of Output to Various Factors and the Economics of Mining; Various Views Regarding size of a Colliery; Our Conclusions; Summary; Recommendations); The Objectives and Scope of Amalgamation of Collieries (Survey; The General Scope of Amalgamation; Seam-wise Fragmentation of Collieries; Non-Contiguous Collieries; Amalgamation of Working Seams; The Exploitation of Virgin Seams; Discontinued Collieries; Summary; Recommendations); Methods and Procedure of Amalgamation and Adjustment of Irregular Boundaries (Methods of Amalgamation and Adjustment of Boundaries; The Machinery to draw up Schemes; Voluntary Amalgamation before the Appointment of the Commission; The Procedure and the Time-Table; Recommendations); Central Legislation Required (The Position Regarding Mineral Rights; The Recommendation of the Indian Coal Fields Committee; The Bengal and Bihar Acts; Royalties and Intermediaries; Mines and Minerals (Development and Regulation) Act; Other Central Acts; Legislation Required; Summary; Recommendations); Valuation of Collieries, Finance and the Organisation to run the Amalgamation Units (Experience in the U.K. and France; Methods of Valuation; Suggestions Regarding Valuation; General Practice in India; Details of Assets; Procedure for Valuation; The Valuation of Reserves; Exceptional Cases; Compensation to the Participating Owners; Finance for the Amalgamated Units; The Organisation to Run the Amalgamated Units; Recommendations); Effect on Employment of Labour (Views regarding possible Retrenchment of Labour; Mechanisation after Amalgamation; Our Examination of the Problem; O.M.S. in Production Groups; Adjustment Required; Absorption of Workers who may be Rendered Surplus; Conclusions and Recommendations); Conclusions and Recommendations; Notes; Appendices.

RECOMMENDATIONS

The Bengal And Bihar Coalfields

A large number of small collieries is a noticeable feature of the Bengal and Bihar coalfields which produce the bulk of India's coal production. The number of collieries has fluctuated in the past; the number is progressively getting reduced since 1950. The mineral rights in the permanently settled areas belonged to the landlords who gave leases and by a process of subleasing of various lessees' interest a class of intermediaries who collect a royalty from the producer of coal has been created. Labour position has been stabilised since the award of the Conciliation Board in 1947. The Industrial Tribunal for Coal has now given a fresh award. But the conditions under which colliery labour lives and works require further improvement. The need for adequate transport for coal is of paramount importance.

The Background to the Problem of Amalgamation

The existence of small and irregular collieries and the fact that in such areas scientific and planned mining may not be possible and that there is wastage of coal have been observed since 1919. Recommendations have been made by various Committees since 1919 that small collieries should be amalgamated. This Committee has been appointed in 1955 to work out more definite proposals.

Experience in Foreign Countries

In most of the foreign countries, the collieries are large units. In the U.K. the problem of amalgamation of colliery undertakings was tackled in various ways and by making statutory provisions; though some amalgamation took place, the objective aimed at could not be achieved. In Germany unification of mines has taken place voluntarily for the formation of units with large production.

The Laws Affecting The Coal Industry

The existing enactments and statutory orders affecting the Coal Industry which have a bearing on the problem of small collieries and their amalgamation are:

(i) The Mines Act and the Indian Coal Mines Regulations, which deal with safety, labour, etc.

(ii) The Coal Mines (Conservation and Safety) Act which deals with Conservation of Coal and Safety in Coal Mines. It is administered by a Coal Board which grants assistance for measures of conservation and safety and also controls the opening of mines.

(iii) The Colliery Control Order, under which the price of coal is controlled. There is control over the distribution of coal to various classes of consumers by allotment of wagons.

(iv) The Coal Mines Welfare Commissioner is in charge of general welfare and amenities for labour, including Housing, Health, Water Supply, Education and Recreation.

The Coal Mines Rescue Committee trains rescue workers.

The Coal Mines Provident Fund Act is administered by the Coal Mines Provident Fund Commissioner and the Bonus Scheme Act by the Regional Labour Commissioner.

(v) The Mines & Minerals (Development and Regulation) Act controls the leases for minerals including coal. The rules regarding mining leases are administered by the State Governments under the overall control of the Central Government.

(vi) The Bihar Land Reforms Act and the West Bengal Estates Acquisition Act are intended to vest in the State Governments the rights of royalty holders and intermediaries.

The Small Collieries And Their Problems

The small collieries are large in number, but their overall output is small. They are small ventures with no equipment. They have no technical staff. They have no possibility of expansion. They cannot follow scientific and planned methods of exploitation of coal. They cannot tackle fires. They do not provide housing and other amenities to labour. Labour in these mines is not organised and collective bargaining is not generally possible. Labour is not paid wages according to the standards laid down, and Provident Fund and other facilities are denied. There is wastage in production.

The country is going to need more coal and in the next decade or so, the requirements of coal for industrial purposes may increase to more than 200 million tons. New standards to improve the living and working conditions of labour, are being laid down. If the industry is to play its part in the immediate future, it should be reorganised. Such reorganisation is hardly possible if so many small units of production, with all the disadvantages mentioned, are to be allowed to continue. They should, therefore, be amalgamated, brought under unified control, reorganised and modernised so that the existing resources will be exploited in the best possible manner and in the best interest of the nation.

Irregular Boundaries

The existence of irregular boundaries between collieries, of faults and other geological disturbances in seams in different coal mines and the surface features like jores, rivers, railway lines and roads over coal mines cause avoidable waste of coal and difficulties in extraction.

In order to minimise the locking of coal underground due to the existence of railway lines, roads, rivers, etc., the boundaries should be redrawn and readjusted, so that such features form the boundaries wherever necessary.

In cases of geological disturbances like faults, dykes, etc., in coal seams the boundaries should as far as possible be readjusted so that the boundaries overlie such disturbances.

Registration of such transactions as may be necessary for adjustment of boundaries should be exempted from Stamp Duty or nominal Stamp Duties should be charged.

The Government of India may suggest to the State Governments concerned to take measures to ensure that the difficulties in the way of adjustment of boundaries, arising from different lease terms, should be removed.

Coal Conservation

The proper re-estimation of the reserves of coal in India is necessary. We understand that a Committee is being appointed to draw up a procedure for estimation of reserves and to re-estimate the reserves of coal.

Measures should be taken to ensure the maximum extraction of coal and for the best use of coal; at the same time the maximum possible extent of safety in coal production should be ensured.

The Coal Board should make arrangements for the supply of sand and water in the case of collieries where stowing is urgent for safety and conservation of coal. Small collieries cannot carry out stowing even if sand were to be supplied. Stowing can be expanded by the amalgamation of collieries. Studies should also be carried out in regard to methods of pneumatic stowing and mechanical stowing and various methods of large-scale transport of stowing materials.

Amalgamation of collieries will enable the Central Washeries to draw coal of fairly uniform washability characteristics from large units.

We understand that arrangements for coal blending are receiving attention.

Waste of coal in thin seams, and selective mining may be avoided by extensive stowing and washing.

Modernisation and Mechanisation

Mechanisation of the hard operations of mining is essential to cut out the drudgery of human toil and to improve the output per man-shift.

In the working seams of collieries there is no large scope for mechanisation. But virgin seams should be properly laid out and planned.

Intensive mechanisation will be necessary when the coal requirements of the country cannot be met by the present extent of mechanisation. But it is imperative that steps be taken to manufacture machinery and for training operators before such mechanisation can be effected.

Proper Size Of A Colliery And The Collieries To Be Amalgamated

Of the 734 collieries in West Bengal and Bihar, 666 produce less than 10,000 tons a month. Of the 491 collieries which replied to our questionnaire 205 have an area less than 100 acres. Considering the large number of small collieries which did not reply, the percentage of such collieries to the total may also be large. Judged by the criteria of production and area, the bulk of the collieries are small.

Output: In view of the fact that a colliery is expected to work coal without avoidable waste, follow scientific and efficient methods of mining and exploitation of coal, adhere to and implement all labour legislations, by giving adequate facilities and amenities to labour, avoid unnecessary wastage of coal in boundaries and in the support of surface features, the Committee considers that the output of any colliery should not be less than 10,000 tons a month.

Area: The area of a colliery should be such as to be able to produce 10,000 tons a month for a period of 50 years, but the area should not, in any case, be less than 100 acres.

Amalgamation: Any colliery which at the time of the implementation of the scheme of amalgamation is not producing in the region of 10,000 tons per month or has an area of less than 100 acres should be amalgamated with one or more collieries or part or parts thereof.

Amalgamated Unit: The amalgamated units shall consist of such number of collieries or part or parts of collieries as to fulfil the criterion regarding minimum production of 10,000 tons a month.

In forming such units due regard should be paid to the existence of fires, flooded areas, important surface features, such as railways, roads, rivers, etc., and the natural disturbance encountered in or about the area so as to ensure maximum recovery of coal.

Discretionary Power: (a) Notwithstanding anything contained in the preceding paragraphs the Commission may exclude any colliery from the amalgamation scheme, if it is satisfied that due to special circumstances its amalgamation is not advisable, or expedient, or in the public interest.

(b) It may also exclude from the scheme of amalgamation, collieries producing more than 6000 tons of coal per month but less than 10,000 tons, if it is satisfied that such collieries are capable of producing 10,000 tons per month within the period of a year, if demand and transport were available for their output.

The Objectives And Scope Of Amalgamation Of Collieries

We do not anticipate, generally, any technical difficulties arising out of the different collieries having the seams in different stages of development. In the case of non-contiguous collieries and particularly those existing in Karanpura, Ramgarh and Bokaro and other areas of Bihar, amalgamation is not possible now, but they may be amalgamated with any contiguous collieries which may be opened in future. The cases of horizontal fragmentation where separate undertakings work different seams in the same property should be investigated by the Commission. The system of appointment of Managing Contractors for different seams may also be worthy of study by the Commission.

Seam-wise fragmentation of collieries should be permitted only in special cases in the interests of the country. Cases of such fragmentation, wherever occurring should be examined by the ommission and if they are against the interests of Safety and Conservation they should be rectified.

Methods And Procedure Of Amalgamation And Adjustment Of Boundaries

The Central Government shall, in consultation with

the Governments of West Bengal and Bihar, appoint a Statutory Body, called the Collieries Amalgamation Commission, consisting of a Chairman of the rank of a High Court judge and two other members, one being a Senior Mining Engineer and the other a Senior Accounts Expert. This Commission will draw up a scheme of amalgamation of collieries and adjustment of boundaries, hear objections and give decisions regarding the same.

If the Government consider it necessary they may, in order to expedite the work, appoint two or more Commissions. They may also decide upon a common Chairman if considered necessary to ensure uniformity.

The Commission will be authorised to hold enquiries for the discharge of their function and as such will have the powers of a Tribunal under the Investigations Act, 1952.

All schemes of voluntary amalgamation and adjustment of boundaries will be notified to the Commission by the parties concerned.

The Commission will take all necessary steps for the purpose of implementation of the scheme of amalgamation of collieries and adjustment of boundaries including valuation of collieries.

The Time-Table

Submission of the Report	... 31.10.1956
Legislation	... 31.3.1957
Appointment of the Commission and Staff	... 30.4.1957
Collection of material for the Commission completed by	... 30.9.1957
Receipt by the Commission of notices of Voluntary Amalgamation and Adjustment of Boundaries to be effected by collieries	... 30.9.1957
Approval by the Commission of such Voluntary Amalgamation	... 28.2.1958
Completion by the Commission of Schemes of Amalgamation and Adjustment of Boundaries	... 28.2.1958
Expiry of Notices to Collieries to submit Objections to the Schemes (clear two months' notice)	... 30.4.1958
Award of the Commission on the Objections	... 31.7.1958
Date of implementation of Amalgamation and Adjustment of Boundaries	... 31.1.1959

The Central Government should appoint a Committee of three of its Technical Officers with powers to examine all proposals for voluntary amalgamation emanating from the collieries till the appointment of the proposed Collieries Amalgamation Commission.

The Committee will examine and modify, when necessary, and give its decision on any proposal submitted to it within one month from the date of receipt of the scheme.

An amalgamated unit formed voluntarily should have a minimum area of 100 acres, a production of 10,000 tons a month, sufficient reserves and a proper shape; but a unit may be formed to give an output of 6,000 tons a month, if it can be increased when necessary to 10,000 tons within one year.

Central Legislation Required

We have taken note of the fact that suitable steps will be taken by the Governments of West Bengal and Bihar to take over the rights of all intermediaries and we hope that by this step the difficulties in the way of amalgamation and adjustment of boundaries on this account will be removed.

We are informed that there is a proposal to make royalty rates uniform and that necessary steps are being taken.

Powers of amalgamation of mining leases will have to be taken by an amendment of Sections 5 and 7 of the Mines and Minerals (Development and Regulation) Act and the Mineral Concession Rules will also require amendment. Composite legislation is required to effect amalgamation of collieries and adjustment of boundaries and for the appointment of the Collieries Amalgamation Commission.

Valuation Of Collieries, Finance And The Organisation To Run The Amalgamated Units

When one or more collieries are amalgamated the share of each colliery in the amalgamated unit may be decided:

(a) By mutual agreement between the parties;

(b) According to the value of each colliery determined by the Commission on the following basis:

(i) Assets of the colliery consisting of mining rights, initial capital expenditure, shafts and inclines, machinery, plants and buildings, stores, stocks of coal;

(ii) Liabilities consisting of loans or encumbrances charged on the property should be deducted;

(iii) A surcharge equal to four times the net annual average profit, according to the Income Tax returns over a period of 10 years from 1945 should be added. The Commission may also consider whether in addition to these any surcharge should be added in respect of coal reserves in working seams.

In case a colliery owner is not willing to join the amalgamated group, the colliery will be absorbed in the group and the owner will be paid by the amalgamated concern a compensation to be determined in the manner mentioned above. The compensation shall be payable in five equal annual instalments.

In order that the amalgamated units may function efficiently, financial assistance may be required and this will have to be provided through the three Government-sponsored organisations which advance funds for industrial undertakings. If this is not found possible a new Corporation should be started. This may be financed by a cess on despatches of coal.

The form of organisation to run the amalgamated units may be decided by the parties concerned, but when they fail to agree the Commission may decide the form of the organisation. In our opinion, Public Limited Companies would be the best.

Effect On Employment Of Labour

There is no likelihood of any appreciable change in the overall employment of labour due to amalgamation.

Only in the category of clerical and some other staff some workers may be rendered surplus.

Certain adjustments in the employment pattern will be necessary. We endorse the proposal which is separately under consideration for the creation of a pool for surplus colliery workers.

The process of rationalisation and mechanisation after amalgamation should be gradual and only after arrangements for the absorption of surplus hands are made.

If the surplus hands are not absorbed, they should be maintained till natural elimination or absorption elsewhere takes place; such maintenance will be on such terms and conditions as are provided in the Industrial Disputes Act.

Adjustments should be made in consultation with representatives of labour and without adversely affecting the emoluments of the workers or increasing their workloads.

SUBURBAN TRAIN (BOMBAY, CALCUTTA AND MADRAS) OVERCROWDING ENQUIRY COMMITTEE, 1955—REPORT

New Delhi, Ministry of Railways (Railway Board), 1956. 98p., Maps, Diagrams.

Chairman : Shri B. B. Varma.
Members : Shri A. C. Chatterjee; Shri K. M. Rau.
Secretary : Shri K. Sambamurti.

APPOINTMENT

The Suburban Train (Bombay, Calcutta and Madras) Overcrowding Enquiry Committee was constituted under the Ministry of Railways (Railway Board) vide their Resolution No. E55Col/73/3, dated November 10, 1955.

TERMS OF REFERENCE

(i) To investigate into the problem of excessive overcrowding during peak hours in the Suburban Services at Bombay, Calcutta and Madras; and

(ii) To suggest remedial measures.

CONTENTS

Introductory; Bombay Suburban Railway System (Western Railway—Central Railway); Madras Suburban Railway System (Metre Gauge—Broad Gauge); Calcutta Suburban Railway System (Suburban System South of Sealdah—Suburban System North of Sealdah—Suburban System North of Howrah—South-Eastern Railway Suburban System); Overcrowding in Suburban Trains and Staggering of Working Hours and Establishments as a Remedial Measure; Increase in Train Carrying Capacity as a Remedial Measure; Increase in Number of Trains as a Remedial Measure; Other General and Specific Remedial Measures; Conclusion; Appendices I to X; Annexures.

RECOMMENDATIONS

We should like to conclude this report with a brief reiteration of the more important of our Recommendations, Railway by Railway. But before we do so, we would refer to the old adage, "knowledge is power", as apt here as elsewhere. Diagnosis precedes remedies, but a knowledge of the facts of the situation must go before either, which, in the present instance, can best be acquired by setting up an organisation to collect data of the travel needs of the suburban resident, the extent, the range and the time of the day of his journeys. From these details the nature of the train service and its timings follow easily. Hence our emphasis on the census of passengers, train by train, station by station, and space-time-speed studies as the only reliable basis for the fairest distribution of the available resources and their optimum deployment.

One lesson that has to be learnt is that when large passenger concentrations take place, the number travelling from any point is great, and if a Fast Service from the different points can be run by turns, it saves time for the traveller and ensures the maximum utilisation of the stock. To deal with the surges of traffic, therefore, fast trains with a limited number of stops is the ideal solution and there is abundant evidence of it in the data we have collected. People by hundreds collect at each halt to catch the Fast Train even when it is overful and this, in our opinion, gives the key to the solution of the problem. The provision of really Fast Trains from different points in the morning and to different points in the evening is the need which requires to be satisfied.

In the case of Bombay, the Western Railway could do a lot more, in this direction, by replacing Stopping Trains by Fast ones, thereby putting in many more. They could serve their outer suburbs by stock other than EMU, and if during the rush hours, they concentrated their EMU stock on stations short of Borivli, there would be a far larger number of trains and a vastly improved service. This does not mean that the Railway does not require extra stock, but since EMU stock is neither standardised by the Indian Railways nor manufactured in India, the best course is to take early steps in this direction and phase their supply on a regular programme to enable the manufacturing industry to be assured of orders for a term of years.

In the meanwhile, fast long-distance trains should be run with stock indigenously manufactured but adopted for suburban travel and hauled by locomotives, be they electric, diesel or steam, as can be made available. This is not only more economical but just as fast and efficient for the special purpose of clearing large numbers of passengers during the rush hours for distant destinations. Terminals will require to be equipped to deal with engine-hauled trains and the reversal of engines, but there are no insurmountable difficulties in that direction. Even Churchgate could deal with such trains when the proposed yard extensions are completed, but, if this system is adopted extensively, a few more stabling lines would need to be added to that Yard.

The problems of the Central Railway are not very different from the above, and it is gratifying to note that this Railway does run a larger number of Fast Trains, but their operation is severely hit by the endeavour to provide direct train services to each destination, without requiring the passengers to change trains. These direct services to Thana, Bandra and Andheri via the Harbour Branch involve criss-cross movements, reduce the speed of travel and make operation unnecessarily complicated. In doing so, they upset punctuality, regularity and flexibility not only of their own trains but also of the Western Railway, on which they run between Mahim and Andheri. If suitable transfer facilities are developed at stations of interchange the Railways' resources can be conserved by terminating the services from Victoria Terminus at Mahim and cutting out trains from Victoria Terminus to Thana via the Harbour Branch. Harbour Branch trains may run from Vadala Road to Chembur or Mankhurd but not to Thana. Straight services running forwards and backwards are calculated to simplify operation, and divert passengers to the faster runs.

The Central Railway possesses the advantage of having Main and Suburban Lines running right through its Suburban Section, and is in a better position to run engine-hauled Fast Trains to clear the rush-period traffic and to save on EMU stock, which is particularly useful for short runs.

Both the Railways could, with advantage, run their new rakes at greater speeds and fully utilise the large power units installed in them by working them on separate links providing more intensive and faster services. The slow runs, not popular during periods of rush, could be made with single units, thereby releasing more stock for fast trains.

On the electrified section of the Southern Railway, too, the problem is much the same—paucity of stock, and its uneven distribution has led to excessive overcrowding. For lack of terminal facilities, full use during the rush hours is not made of electric-engine hauled trains. Space is available for the development of facilities at the terminus to reverse engines from one end of the train to the other without much expense or trouble. If, during the rush hours, all trains on the Guindy-Beach Section are run with double units, reinforced with a third-class coach in between, and single units are employed on the Guindy-Tambaram Section, the utilisation of stock will fit in with the demands of traffic, overcrowding will diminish, and passengers will be more evenly distributed. If, in addition, each of the three electric locomotives that they have run out one train each during the period of rush, the service will be adequate to the needs of the present traffic.

The EMU stock has very little standing accommodation and is literally filled with seats some of which can, with advantage, be removed to create standing accommodation for short-distance passengers. This aspect can be exploited to a still greater extent on the third-class coaches that augment the loads of these EMU rakes by providing only standing accommodation on them.

On the Broad Gauge Section of the Southern Railway, there is very little overcrowding, and such that there is, can be easily eliminated by the provision of standing room inside the coach, and by running trains with the full number of carriages. The latter step will need the shifting of the motor loading work from the Central station to other stations in Madras, which move is effected easily.

The problem on the Calcutta Railways, where steam traction is being replaced by electric traction, is of an entirely different nature as the vast possibilities of improved service with steam traction have been eclipsed by the general belief that nothing short of electrification will solve the problem of overcrowding. It is true that electric traction means improved speeds and this means enlargement of the area of the suburbs, but where overcrowding is concerned, it is more a matter of the type of the coach and accommodation in it than the mode of traction. Most of the stock of steam trains in Calcutta and elsewhere is of the obsolete pattern, very often unfit for Main Line use, with seating arrangement unsuited to the requirements of Suburban Service. Large crowds literally invade trains as they approach the city terminus. Whereas this area is wide in the case of electrified traction with fast speeds, it is nonetheless there in the case of steam trains, even though it is limited to 10 or 12 miles. It is, therefore, incumbent on the Railways to so alter the seating arrangement that these invading crowds get standing room and take shelter on the train instead of travelling on the footboards. The Railways' programme to spend crores on electrification offers a strange contrast to their parsimony in grudging *sic* an expenditure of even a few lakhs to build suburban coaching stock of adequate width and capacity. This position has perhaps arisen less out of a disregard for the comforts of passengers than out of an imbalance in planning. Passengers in their eagerness, however, make the best of the cheap travel facilities offered on a Season Ticket, brave discomfort, and cram the trains that somehow will take them to work and back at the time that is most convenient to them.

We are firmly of the opinion that much-needed relief to passengers can be given by re-arranging the seats, by providing standing room on the existing stock, by the use of wider and more suitable stock, and by arranging to have those trains, which do not return immediately, hauled by tender engines of greater capacity, which in turn will allow the addition of more coaches. For Sections on which the capacity of terminal yards for the reception of trains, and the facilities for the disposal of engines and rakes have reached the limit, we suggest trials with engines at both ends, so that the trains can be worked backwards and forwards in much the same way as EMU rakes do.

For these observations we should not be regarded as having failed to appreciate the magnificent performance of the Railways in the handling of large volume of traffic with the very meagre equipment at their disposal. They are going all out and keeping the entire suburban stock in service, with the unavoidable consequence that there is no reserve left for emergencies. No wonder that in consequence proper standards of punctuality and regularity are not being maintained. We feel that the standards at present are below the levels, which the Railways desire to set before themselves. or which the public expect of a nationalised undertaking.

1956

ASSESSMENT COMMITTEE ON BASIC EDUCATION, 1956—REPORT

New Delhi, Ministry of Education, 1956. 87p.

Convener : Shri G. Ramachandran.
Members : Shri R.S. Upadhyaya; Dr. Saeed Ansari; Dr. M.D. Paul.

APPOINTMENT

The Committee was appointed by the Ministry of Education in 1956.

TERMS OF REFERENCE

Following are the terms of reference :

(i) To survey the existing situation regarding basic education in the various States, and

(ii) To think out ways and means of bringing about effective improvements.

CONTENTS

Foreword; Introduction; Introductory Remarks; Places and Institutions visited; What we tried to assess and how; the General Factual Picture; Inadequacy of Compact Area Method; Need to turn all schools towards the Basic Education; Too many Interpretations of Basic Education; Training of Administrative and Inspecting Officers; Training of Teachers; Basic Teachers Training at the Graduate Level; Research in Basic Education; Preparation of Literature; Some essential principles that should operate in every Basic Training Institution; Concluding observations on the training of Teachers; Conditions in Basic Schools; Teaching of English in Basic Schools; The type of Craft Teachers needed in Basic Schools; Certain necessary observations on Basic Schools in general; Pulse of public on Basic Education; Administration and Contents of Basic Education; The administrative set-up and Basic Education; Productivity of in Basic Education; Comparison of attainments in Basic and non-Basic Schools; Dovetailing of Basic Education with Higher Education; Linking Basic Institutions with various agencies engaged in Community and Rural Development Work; Conclusion; Summary of Recommendations; Appendices.

RECOMMENDATIONS

Our recommendations are brought together under seven headings as follows :

1. The Government of India.

2. The Government of the States.
3. The Universities.
4. The Administration.
5. Basic Teachers' Training.
6. Basic Schools.
7. The Public.

1. The Government of India

The Government of India should take appropriate steps to make it clear to all those concerned that the elucidation of Basic Education given by the Basic Education Standing Committee of the Central Advisory Board of Education has their concurrence. As a first step, the Central Advisory Board of Education itself should give its early approval formally after which the Union Ministry of Education may adopt it. In this connection, we have specially in mind the place assigned to productive work in Basic Education.

In view of the national significance and urgency of the situation, it has become necessary for the Union Ministry of Education to convene a conference of the Education Ministers as also of the Education Secretaries of the various States to make clear the Standing Committee's concept of Basic Education so that the development of Basic Education in the whole country may take place on generally approved lines and to be completed within specific time limits suited to the conditions of the different States.

The above Conference may well be followed by a declaration of policy by the Central and State Governments reiterating the place of Basic Education in educational reconstruction under the Second Five-Year Plan.

In the wake of the above conference, it will be necessary to hold a Basic Education seminar to be attended by the Directors of Public Instruction from all the States, so that the Heads of Education Departments in the States may be enabled to make their contribution to the development of Basic Education. The officers in overall charge of Basic Education in the Education Departments, whom we have suggested might be designated Joint or Additional Directors of Public Instruction, should also be invited to the seminar. The minimum duration of the seminar should be three weeks. The seminar, to be really effective, should be held in some places where Basic Education has already become a reality.

All-India and regional conferences on Basic Education should be arranged periodically in order that the workers in the field can come together, discuss difficulties, problems and experience and evolve, as far as possible, common solutions.

The Union Ministry of Education should undertake to educate public opinion in regard to the issues concerning Basic Education, through all methods of publicity open to the Government, utilising films, the radio, the press, publications, exhibitions, etc., for the purpose. What is now being done is totally inadequate.

A Central Research Institute of Basic Education should be established under proper direction to initiate schemes of research, with scholarships available for research workers. Unless this Research Institute functions at the highest and broadest level, Education Departments in the States and others working for Basic Education will not look up to it for guidance.

A small special committee of educational experts in close touch with the numerous problems of Basic Education should be set up to lay down the criteria to evaluate the achievements and progress of pupils in Basic institutions and then to carry out assessments from time to time in terms of the criteria so formulated. This should be a high-level and permanent body.

A committee of specialists in the field should be set up to collect, edit and publish the large mass of manuscript literature even now available with innumerable Basic Training schools and Basic schools for the benefit of teachers and pupils. The publications will have to be in the main languages of India. Handbooks for educational administrators and others are urgently called for, as also reading books for children and guide and reference books for teachers and trainees. An authentic all-India magazine in the form of a 'Quarterly' may be published to guide all those engaged in the development of Basic Education. If such a quarterly is issued by the Union Ministry of Education, its value would be greatly enhanced.

A special brochure on the subject of the progressive conversion of all Elementary schools into Basic schools should be issued without delay by the Union Ministry of Education. This publication should show clearly how vital aspects and characteristics of Basic Education can be introduced simultaneously in all Elementary schools in quick stages even during the period of waiting for fully trained Basic teachers to come in with the correlated technique of teaching. The Ministry should also actually help the State Governments to implement this programme of preliminary conversion.

The various official and non-official agencies engaged in village reconstruction have to be brought together, so that these and the Education Departments can cooperate in the development of Basic Education. We have in mind the Community Projects Administration, the All-India Khadi and Village Industries Board, the Sarva Seva Sangh, the Hindustani Talimi Sangh, the Kasturba Gandhi National Memorial Trust, the Social Welfare Board, Rural Welfare Departments in different States, etc. Basic education and village reconstruction are often one and the same to a considerable extent in our country.

The whole question of Basic schools and Training schools being allowed to be conducted in simpler and cheaper buildings suited to the village environment must be taken up seriously and a committee of engineers and administrators of Basic Education should be set up immediately to draw up plans and estimates in this connection.

The establishment of full-fledged postgraduate Basic Training Colleges can no longer be delayed. The Union Government in consultation with State Government should formulate their proposals and initiate negotiations with the universities to obtain their cooperation in this matter. The Inter-University Board and the University Grants Commission may be approached to secure their help.

The Union Government in consultation with State Governments should ensure that post-Basic Education gets due recognition and place in the present schemes for the reorganisation of Secondary education and that an adequate number of post-Basic schools will be provided for in the Second Five-Year Plan alongside of multipurpose high schools. Just as the Union Government has adopted a positive attitude towards Basic Education, it has become necessary equally to adopt a similar attitude towards post-Basic Education. Otherwise, educational reconstruction along lines of Basic Education will stand cut off in the middle.

The Union Government should insist that any financial aid given by it directly or indirectly to improve or spread Elementary Education is strictly earmarked by the States for Basic Education, i.e., Basic schools and Basic training schools.

When, after a few years, there is a greater development of Basic education, an assessment committee may be appointed to assess, scientifically and in a detailed manner, Basic Education in the country.

2. The Governments Of The States

State Governments should no longer delay to make a clear and unambiguous declaration of policy that all Elementary schools will be converted into Basic schools and that all teacher training at this level will become Basic teacher training within reasonable time limits.

State Governments should take immediate steps to establish statutory Basic Education Boards with adequate powers to guide Education Departments and to secure public cooperation. Such Boards should consist of officials and non-officials as in Bihar and Assam.

The compact area method of developing Basic Education should yield place to the whole of Elementary Education becoming Basic by the introduction, simultaneously and in quick stages, of important aspects of Basic Education in all elementary schools, as clearly pointed out in the body of the Report.

To make the above programme a success, Education Officers at all levels should be given short and effective courses of training in seminars on Basic Education arranged by the State Governments.

Even more important is the need for the appointment of a Joint or Additional Director of Public Instruction in each State, to take full responsibility for converting all Elementary schools into Basic schools within a stipulated period. This will necessitate that such an officer should have all the necessary powers to do his job as explained in the Report.

Basic Education conferences should be arranged periodically on intra-district, district and regional levels.

State Governments should also take a clear stand on the economies of productivity in Basic institutions, and therefore take effective steps for the supply of raw materials, equipment, for repairs and for marketing of surplus produce.

A working formula for apportioning a part of the net income for direct benefit to school children and the other part for remittance to the Treasury should be prepared and put into effect.

Preparations of literature, assessment and research should be arranged at the State level, in addition to the work done at the level of the Government of India.

The establishment of full-fledged postgraduate Basic Teachers' Training Colleges should also be taken up at the State level along the same lines as indicated for the Union Government.

State Governments should also make up their minds to give post-Basic schools a full chance in their schemes for the reorganisation of secondary education.

Steps should be taken to effect economy in Basic Education by laying down appropriate rules so that cost of craft equipment is met by the pupils themselves. Those who can afford to pay the full cost should do so at the outset. Poorer children may pay in easy instalments. Craft equipment must essentially belong to the children. Whatever is produced should, as far as possible, be consumed by the teachers and pupils at reasonable rates and only the surplus need be taken over by the State for marketing.

Land gifts for Basic schools and Basic Training schools should be organised with the full moral support of the State Government.

States should arrange for the retraining of ordinary graduate trained teachers. The period of such training should not be less than five months.

States should take sufficient care that truncated Basic schools are not allowed to upset the development of Basic Education. The integrated course of eight years should be continually kept in view and what are called Junior Basic schools should be allowed only as feeder schools to senior Basic schools.

States should guarantee that all teachers' training at the matriculate level becomes Basic within a strict time limit. No new teachers' training at this level, other than Basic, should be allowed from now on.

States should plan to provide every senior Basic school of eight grades with a graduate or equally Basic-trained headmaster.

3. The Universities

At a time when the Union and State Governments intend to go ahead with Basic Education, it would not do for our universities to stand aloof. So far the universities have not taken kindly to Basic Education. But to the four important points of assessment, teachers' training, dovetailing of Basic Education with higher education, and research, the universities can make a valuable contribution. Central and State Governments must, therefore, take up the matter with the universities to help at these points and particularly in regard to the establishment and recognition of post-graduate Basic Teacher's Training Colleges.

It will presently become necessary for universities to recognise post-Basic Education for purposes of admitting pupils passing out of post-Basic schools into colleges.

Provision will have to be made for the affiliation of postgraduate Basic Training Colleges to Universities.

4. Administration

Departmental officers, realising the value and inevitability of Basic Education, should give earnest, detailed and devoted attention to improving Basic schools and Basic Training schools. All the material conditions which alone can make Basic schools and Basic Training schools efficient and fruitful should be furnished in time and without reservation.

Inspecting staff at different levels connected with Basic Education should be fully trained in Basic Education. As Basic Education will remain for many years a revolutionary change in educational concepts and practices, the inspecting officers should cease to be fault-finders and become instead guides, collaborators and inspirers to the teachers in Basic schools.

Decentralisation of administration within the Education Departments is the *sine qua non* for the development of Basic Education. It is the key to efficiency and quick attention to innumerable details at this level. It is also the best way to secure local cooperation.

Examinations in Basic training schools and Basic schools should be mainly a continuous assessment of work and progress of pupils and this should be considered more important than written examinations. But to secure sufficiently high institutional standards there will be need to set up appropriate assessment boards.

It will be necessary to relax rules and regulations governing construction of school buildings to permit Basic schools to be conducted in cheaper buildings which will fit in with the village environment. Grant-in-aid rules will therefore, need to be modified. At the same time, plans should be drawn up for the progressive improvement of school accommodation, consistent with finances available. The introduction of Basic Education should, however, not be made to wait for improved buildings.

Whereas in Travancore-Cochin and some other places, the shift system is firmly established and where it may be proved to be necessary in other places, Basic Education and shift system may be reconciled temporarily. In such cases the shift should be confined only to the earlier grades and subject to the strict condition that proper assignments of work would be given to children in the out-of-school hours and that the assignments will be completed and brought to the school systematically for review and correlation.

After careful study of productivity in Basic schools and Basic training schools in various States, each State Department of Education should lay down fairly elastic targets of production for such Basic institutions. Once such targets are laid down, no efforts should be spared to achieve them. Productive work should in no case become the excuse for lowering standards of learning. On the other hand, learning should become more real and richer through productive work.

English should be offered as an optional subject from the sixth grade onwards, wherever knowledge of English is considered necessary for entrance into high schools and other similar institutions. Where Hindi is not the regional language, it should be compulsory in the senior Basic grades. But where Hindi is the regional language, another suitable Indian language should be made compulsory from the sixth year onwards.

It is of the utmost importance to guarantee proper dovetailing of Basic Education with Secondary Education in such a manner that equal years of study in different types of institutions will be considered as of equal value for purposes of admission into institutions of higher education.

5. Basic Teachers' Training

Though we have stated that the training of teachers for Basic Education is, on the whole, conducted fairly well, we think it urgently necessary to make Teachers' Training more efficient and real. Improvement is called for in craft training in handling the technique of correlated teaching and in a new and dynamic approach to the study of psychology. Truncation of craft has played havoc with craft training and this must not be tolerated. Any craft for Basic Education must be a whole craft and not split into pieces, nor learnt in isolated parts. The technique of correlated teaching has largely remained incomplete because correlation has been mostly with productive work and very little with the natural and social environments. We have dealt with this matter in detail in the Report. The new approach to the study of psychology will consist in giving every pupil-teacher the intellectual certainty that education through productive activities in life situations furnishes the best way of learning. Since any weakening of productivity in training will further weaken productivity in Basic schools, adequate stress must always be given to mastering the various processes of whatever productive work is chosen in Basic teachers' training. Even if Basic teachers' training is for a period of two years, which in our opinion, is certainly the correct period, pupil-teachers should not be given more than one major craft and one or two subsidiary crafts for each of the pupil-teachers has to be even more emphasised when the training period is only for one year, as in some States. Requiring every pupil-teacher to learn too many crafts is a complete mistake and must be strictly avoided.

Every obstacle in the way of appointing traditional craftsmen with highly developed skills as craft instructors in Basic training schools, even if they have no academic qualification, should be removed without delay or hesitation. Every time such a craftsman is appointed, a trained Basic teacher should be closely associated with him in the teaching of the craft.

Whatever crafts are selected for Basic teachers' training should be such as the teachers can later introduce them into the Basic schools as the medium of learning. If this is fully understood, there will be less loose talk of every kind of craft being introduced into Basic training schools.

Basic training schools in close touch with Basic schools and with practice teaching for pupil-teachers in some of them, can become excellent laboratories of research in Basic education. Therefore, one member at least of the teaching staff of such a training school should be made familiar with the technique of educational research and entrusted with research work in Basic education in the area.

Many Basic Teachers' Training Schools have already a growing mass of literature on various aspects of Basic Education. The continued and improved production of such literature should be encouraged. The literature thus produced should be studied and shifted and made available to the State level committee preparing Basic Education literature.

The staff of Basic training schools and the pupil-teachers under training should prepare manuscripts of reading books for Basic school children and these manuscripts should also go to the above State level committees.

Every Basic training school should plan and execute appropriate extension programmes to bring the staff and the trainees into close touch with the surrounding community. An important item of such extension work should be the education of the local public concerning Basic Education. Such extension work will also give training to pupil-teachers in the technique of organising local cooperation.

Basic training schools should be residential for the purpose, among other things, of giving day-to-day training in actual living and practising of the principles of a cooperative democratic community work and learning together and producing much of what is necessary for daily life.

Sanitation, common kitchen and cultural and recreational activities based on community self-government will be the vital centres of such cooperative community and, therefore, of Basic Education.

Retraining of teachers already in service should be for a minimum period of five months and attached to Basic T achers' Training School.

The essential principles indicated in the Report must operate in Basic Teachers' Training Schools.

Every Basic training school should take direct responsibility for the in-service training of all teachers in Basic schools in and around the locality in which the training school is located, and such in-service training should be carried out in collaboration with the local Basic trained inspecting officer.

6. Basic Schools

The grave error of either putting fully trained Basic teachers in Basic schools, lacking adequate facilities of raw materials, equipment, land, etc., and the equal error of sending untrained or inadequately trained teachers into Basic schools with all the necessary facilities, should both be strictly avoided, for both will be bad economy and waste from every point of view. So long as these two errors continue, there will be no efficient or vigorous development of Basic Education.

No school may be considered a Basic school or assessed as such, unless the following requisites at least are fulfilled:

(i) It provides for an integrated course of eight years of Basic Education and where there are only what are called the junior five grades, such a school should necessarily be the feeder for a senior Basic school.

(ii) Adequate quantities of needed raw materials are supplied in time.

(iii) Adequate craft equipment and repair material are provided.

(iv) There is minimum land available, according to local conditions with water facilities and in no case no less than three acres for a senior Basic school of eight grades.

(v) The majority of teachers at least are Basic trained. The untrained teachers get training under them all the time, but only till all teachers are trained or retrained.

(vi) There is community living and work based on democratic student self-government under the guidance of teachers.

(vii) Craft work is systematic and not truncated, ensuring minimum targets of production which may be settled in this regard by the Education Departments.

(viii) There is the correlated method of teaching, with correlation not restricted to productive work only, but also extending to the natural environment and the social environment.

(ix) There is commensurate extension work linking the school with the community and vice versa.

(x) Congregational prayers are organised.

(xi) A library with suitable books is available.

(xii) Cultural and recreational activities are organised.

Examinations in Basic schools will be wholly internal and based on assessment of continuous progress of students and cumulative records.

Emphasis should be laid more on character and personality development and on the cultivation of healthy attitudes and habits than on mere academic attainments. But this would never mean neglect of academic attainments.

As in the case of Basic training schools, we must emphasise the value of traditional craftsmen, possessing high skills, being associated with teaching in suitable manner in Basic schools and ultimately qualifying as Basic school teachers.

The method of assessment of Basic schools should be clearly laid down as per our detailed suggestions in the Report, before assessment is attempted. We stress that the method of assessment should be appropriate to the objectives and processes inherent in Basic Education.

Basic Education should apply equally to urban and rural areas. During the interim period a common syllabus should be introduced in Basic schools and in other Elementary schools.

7. The Public

The public naturally constitute a very vital factor in the problem in a democratic State. The Union and State Governments must, therefore, consider ways and means of convincing the public about Basic Education and securing their co-operation for its rapid development. Our suggestions to the Union and State Governments in this regard may be adopted in this connection. Ultimately, however, it will be the efficient and successful working of Basic schools themselves which will bring public support and cooperation. The peaceful and constructive evolution of a socialistic pattern of society depends so largely on the development of Basic Education, that the education of the public in regard to all the relevant issues in and for Basic Education should be undertaken in all seriousness without delay.

COMMITTEE ON BUILDING FOUNDATIONS IN SHRINKABLE SOILS (BLACK COTTON SOILS), 1956—FIRST REPORT

New Delhi, Ministry of Works, Housing and Supply, 1958. 56p., Charts.

Convener : Sardar Sarup Singh (replaced by Shri C.P. Malik).

Members : Shri U.G.K. Rao; Dr. H.L. Uppal; Shri Dinesh Mohan; Shri J.S. Narasimham; Shri M.S. Bhatia.

Secretary : Shri K. Rama Varman (replaced by Shri Shri Krishna).

APPOINTMENT

The Building Foundations in Shrinkable Soils (Black Cotton Soils) was constituted under the National Buildings Organisation in 1956.

TERMS OF REFERENCE

(i) To enunciate the problem;

(ii) To assess the present status of research;

(iii) To collect the information available;

(iv) To formulate recommendations; and

(v) To initiate further research, if any required.

CONTENTS

Background and Composition of the Committee; The Report; Appendix.

RECOMMENDATIONS

Where the depth of the black cotton soil is shallow it might be necessary to carry foundations to the inert soil below the black cotton soil stratum. While judging the inert nature of soil for founding the structure, mere colour should not be taken for guidance as it is found that even yellow soils met at that depth below black cotton soil layers exhibit swelling and shrinking properties. The footing may be either continuous footings or of pier or pillar and beam or arch construction.

Where the black cotton soil is deep the footing depth should, wherever practicable, be below the zone of seasonal moisture change (which may extend upto about 12 ft. in some parts of the country) especially for buildings that cannot tolerate any movements. It is cautioned that even this depth may not be sufficient since clays are sometimes desiccated by average climatic conditions to depths far greater than those reached by seasonal variations. In such cases a structure which changes moisture equilibrium over a large area or sometimes even a small building with a large paved area adjacent to it, may cause slow swelling of deep layers with consequent having of footings.

In many cases it is impractical or uneconomical to take footings down to soil that will not expand. Under such circumstances the footings may be placed at a higher level, say five feet below ground level, but the footing pressures may be kept high enough to impede expansion. While it is impractical to design the footing to counteract entirely the expansion pressure, the latter is very much reduced if slight expansion is permitted. Thus, if the building superstructure is of a relatively flexible nature and if small movements can be tolerated, a smaller depth than 12 ft. can be considered. Traditional practices of providing rubber filling under foundations and floors and of constructing super-structure in coursed rubble in mud or lime mortar provides a certain measure of flexibility. The pressure at the foundation level from the dead load should not be less than the swelling pressure of the soil when saturated which is to be determined experimentally. Simultaneously there should be an adequate factor of safety against plastic failure.

The interior footings can be put at shallower depths than the exterior, or can have lighter unit loads if at the same depth. If construction is done when the soils are dry, interior depth and loading conditions should be the same as for the exterior.

It is not practicable always to transmit high pressures by means of continuous strips. The load from the building is then transmitted through masonry pillars or through bored piles which may be under-reamed where necessary. Such piles or pillars may be insulated from the surrounding soil by surrounding them with granular non-cohesive material.

Where the load is transmitted through columns or piers, the super-structure is carried on grade beams resting on these columns. The beam is necessarily placed close to the surface of the ground. It is a good practice to avoid contact of these grade beams with the soil to prevent action of swelling soil on the beam. It is best to leave the space between the grade beams and the ground surface empty with a dwarf wall protection on the two faces to prevent entry of materials. This is sometimes done by providing a sand cushion or a cushion of granular material below the beam. This is only a pallative and does not always prevent development of stresses in beams due to swelling of the soil. The beams are designed taking the composite action of the masonry wall coming over it. Design of these beams will be indicated in a subsequent report.

When continuous strip foundation is used, it is sometimes usual to provide reinforced cement concrete bands at plinth level and at lintel level. Design of these bands is empirical and at best then serve only as crack control measures. These beams may be reinforced both at top and bottom. Empirically, the total reinforcement may be kept at one-and-a-half per cent of the area of the section for both the layers together. Raft foundations require careful calculation and have proved successful.

Considering the high cost of foundation of buildings in black cotton soil, it is uneconomical to construct single-storeyed buildings in such areas. Double-storeyed buildings not only distribute the cost of foundation over twice the floor area, but also assist in increasing the foundation pressure to counteract the swelling pressure. It was observed that in several areas with identical designs of foundations, the single storeyed buildings suffered greater damage than the double-storeyed structures.

The excavations for footings of foundations should not be allowed to become excessively dry, or wet, so as to lose its sheer strength. On the other hand, undertaking construction during the dry season and completing it before the outset of monsoon has proved successful.

The effects of moisture changes in active soils below the floors can be vertical movements of the order of several inches and such movements are also non-uniform over a large floor area. Design and construction measures to eliminate or minimise such effects should include—

(a) removal of as much active soil as practicable;

(b) replacement of fill of inactive soil properly compacted.

(c) completion of fill to floor level with properly compacted inactive soil;

(d) separation of floor slabs from contact with walls, footings, etc.;

(e) support of floor slabs on flexible base such as rubber or boulder filling which provide relief against upward expansion pressures; and

(f) floors suspended from the grade beams in the pile or pier and beam construction are the ideal methods of construction.

Sometimes ponding the area under the floor to an optimum condition before or after the foundations have been constructed is practised. In such cases the soil is allowed to get wet and to swell before the fill is placed. A good judgment is however, necessary to see that the soil does not swell excessively and soften to such an extent that reconsolidation will lead to its settlement under the weight of the floor and the fill.

A commonly used specification to interrupt the capillary rise into the fill is by making the bottom one or two feet of fill of clean granular material, continuing upward with cheaper local material and finally topping off with a course of sand at least eight inches in thickness just below the floor. In such cases the local soil should be compacted to atleast 90 per cent of the optimum density and at two or three per cent higher than the optimum moisture content. While compacting these fills special precaution must be taken to avoid failure of external walls which might act as retaining walls for this purpose.

The desiccating action of fast growing trees in the vicinity of buildings should be taken into account while planting of tree is done near a newly constructed or existing building on active soils. Similary, removal of trees from the vicinity of buildings and covering up large areas near the building with pavements or starting extensive gardening operations near the building, should be done after careful consideration of their effects on the moisture movement towards and from the building area.

In the case of boiler rooms, hot process units, etc., measures should be taken to prevent the heat from furnaces, etc., desiccating adjacent or underlying soils. Such measures include use of insulating materials, provision of air space with forced or natural ventilation, use of cooling water and even carefully regulated irrigation of the surface clay to prevent its drying out.

The cracking consequent upon the movement of soil can sometimes be very wide and there is often a tendency to insist on immediate repairs which involve filling the cracks with mortar. This is often a mistake. Cracks of this nature are seasonal and they tend to close in the wet season. The immediate filling of cracks with a dense mortar will, therefore, result in building up of high compressive stresses when the reverse movements take place. It is therefore essential that in such cases before any repairs are attempted the matter should be investigated by a soil engineer. Repair measures may include under pinning and removal of contact between soils and grade beams in the case of pillar and beam construction, correction of drainage conditions, location and repair of water leaks, establishment of evaporation barriers, alteration of thermal gradients by increasing the paved area round the building or decreasing it as necessary, and a variety of other operations followed finally by structural repairs.

INDIAN DELEGATION TO CHINA ON AGRICULTURAL PLANNING AND TECHNIQUES, 1956—REPORT

Delhi, Manager of Publications, 1956. 199p.

Leader : Shri M. V. Krishnappa.

Members : Shri P. N. Thapar; Shri Tarlok Singh; Dr. R. J. Kalamkar. (Shri L. C. Sayal, a staff member of the Ministry of Food & Agriculture also accompanied the delegation.)

APPOINTMENT

The Indian Delegation to China on Agricultural Planning and Techniques was constituted under the Ministry of Food and Agriculture in 1956.

TERMS OF REFERENCE

(i) General planning and inter-relationship between the Planning Commission, the Ministries and the other Governmental Organisations in China.

(ii) Agricultural planning including problems of techniques, fixation of targets, etc.

(iii) Methods of (a) implementation of agricultural plan, (b) agricultural extension, and (c) intensive cultivation.

(iv) Incentives given to farmers (a) through price support and/or parity between industrial and agricultural products, (b) subsidies and/or tax relief, and (c) others.

(v) Agricultural research, education and training.

(vi) Methods of collecting statistics of area and yield of important crops and data regarding area and yield of these crops for the seven years.

(vii) Progress Reports and Assessment of results of agricultural programmes included in the Plan.

CONTENTS

Introduction; The Tour; General Background; Administration and Planning; Techniques of Agricultural Planning; Stat'stical Assessment and Control; Measures for Implementation—Agrarian Reorganisation; Measures for Implementation—Economic and Financial Measures; Measures for Implementation—Technical Reforms; Research, Education and Training; Conclusions and Recommendations.

RECOMMENDATIONS

Organisational Measures

On the whole, in India progress in land reform in recent years has been relatively slow, especially in some States. We consider that the land reform programme set out in our Second Five-Year Plan should be carried out speedily so as to create the conditions necessary for the rapid development of the agriculture.

The early implementation of proposals relating to cooperation in the Second Five-Year Plan is essential. The building up of strong multipurpose cooperatives is an important condition for the successful implementation of the agricultural production programme. In the National Extension and Community Development programmes, cooperation should be given the central place. A major test of progress in the N.E.S. and Community Development Blocks should be achievements in the development of genuine cooperatives through the voluntary participation by peasants. A bold programme of experiments in cooperative farming of different types should be organised, the details being worked out after the report of the Indian Cooperative Delegation to China has been received.

It would be useful to workers engaged in developing cooperative farming in India if accounts of individual agricultural producers' cooperatives in China which have been studied by members of the Agricultural and Cooperative Delegations are brought together as case studies in a single volume and made generally available.

It is important that, within the general National Extension Service pattern, technical staffs should have specific responsibilities and should be assisted in discharging them fully.

In addition to the technical extension service at the block level, there should be agricultural, animal husbandry and cooperative personnel also for each group of, say, 15 to 25 villages.

The agricultural extension staff at the block level should be strengthened by the addition of an engineer who will assist village cooperatives in working out schemes for minor irrigation, drainage and water and soil conservation which can be carried out with local participation and labour. There should also be a plant protection assistant.

For each group of 15 to 25 villages, there should be agricultural, animal husbandry and cooperative personnel.

The jurisdiction of the multi-purpose village level worker, which is now about 10 villages, should be reduced, possibly to about one-half and the training programme for village level workers should be stepped up accordingly.

In-service training and short-term courses should be organised as a matter of normal practice for existing personnel as well.

It is essential that minimum standards of cultivation should be prescribed and enforced especially at the village level. The measures necessary for this purpose should be taken.

In addition to setting targets of additional production potential for the country as a whole and for individual States as is being done at present, targets of yield per acre should be fixed by the local authorities concerned for individual districts, National Extension Blocks and villages. The local people and representative farmers should be closely associated with this work.

Awards and citations to farmers and to villages which do well in the agricultural production programme should be given. The exchange of visits by leading farmers, especially small peasants, exhibitions, discussion groups, conferences, etc. should be organised as a regular feature in different localities.

Conditions should be created in which the bulk of farmers in India will work hard in the manner that only a small proportion do at present.

Economic And Financial Measures

The targets for agricultural credit proposed tentatively in the Second Five-Year Plan need to be revised upward in substantial measures and early steps should be taken to ensure an adequate provision of credit through cooperative channels whenever possible and through government agencies elsewhere. The administrative procedures relating to the grant of credit by cooperatives as well as by government agencies should be re-examined so that farmers can receive financial assistance within a week or at the most two weeks and without having to depend upon the favour of petty officials.

In the interest of agricultural production, it is essential that there should be guaranteed minimum prices for the principal agricultural crops such as foodgrains, cotton, jute, etc., with an assurance that the government would be prepared to purchase quantities offered at these prices. Minimum prices for different agricultural products should be fixed in relation to one another and in such a manner that production is encouraged in accordance with the planned targets.

For the marketing of agricultural produce, cooperative institutions by themselves may not be sufficient. It may be necessary, however, for the State to play a larger role in the organisation of rural supply and marketing than has been contemplated so far.

Technical Measures

With increase in the area under irrigation, there should be targets in every State, district, etc. for area to be put under two or three crops during the year.

The multiplication and distribution of improved seeds should be given the highest priority so that during the period of the Second Plan, the areas under rice and wheat and as far as possible under millets, maize and other crops are brought under improved strains.

Research work on crops for which improved strains have not yet been evolved should be intensified in each State and for this purpose funds should be made available.

An all-out effort should be made to develop local manurial resources such as farm yard manure, night soil, composting and green manuring as well as the utilisation of chemical fertilisers on a much larger scale than at present.

Manurial schedules should be worked out for all types of soils and crops. Experiments to study the effect of different types of fertilisers on the cultivators' fields should be undertaken.

Research on the usefulness of bacterial fertilisers under Indian conditions should be organised and the use of nodule bacteria for inoculating seeds of leguminous crops should be practised.

Advice to cultivators for the use of proper rotations on the basis of soil types and their economic needs should be provided.

Much greater attention than hitherto should be given to dry farming methods which have been found successful.

Planting of high yield crops, such as, maize, potatoes, sweet potatoes and high yielding varieties of paddy should be encouraged. Investigations into the possibilities of developing the Japanese method of cultivation for potatoes should be carried out. Research in the economies of 'close planting' vis-a-vis the 'Japanese method' should be undertaken with reference to different crops and in different areas.

The engineering sections of the agricultural departments of State Governments should be strengthened. Arrangements for the sale of improved implements and supply of spare parts and repair services have to be improved.

Village level workers should be provided with light plant protection, soil testing and soil temperature equipment.

Vigorous measures should be organised in each area for the destruction of pests and animals which destroy crops.

State Governments should strengthen their research organisations and increase their research staffs to meet the demand for improved agricultural techniques which has arisen and is likely to develop further in all areas.

Arrangements for liaison between research and extension workers should be strengthened.

Improved seeds and plant material should be imported from China for trial and breeding in India especially in regard to cotton, rice, groundnut and green manure seeds.

IRRIGATION AND POWER TEAM ON LAKKAVALLI PROJECT (MYSORE STATE), 1956—REPORT

New Delhi, Committee on Plan Projects, 1957. 37p., Maps.

Leader : Shri N. V. Gadgil.
Members : Shri Lal Singh; Shri M. Narasimhaiya; Shri C. L. Handa; Shri G. N. Pandit.
Secretary : Shri D. S. Borker.

APPOINTMENT

The Irrigation and Power Team on Lakkavalli Project (Mysore State) was constituted under the Committee on Plan Projects in 1956.

TERMS OF REFERENCE

To make a study of various aspects of the two Projects with special reference—

To study all aspects of the Project having a bearing on economy and efficiency with special reference to:

(a) Utilisation of trained personnel and materials;

(b) Utilisation of machinery and equipment;

(c) Construction—Plant lay-out;

(d) Adequacy of original estimates and designs as evidenced from actual construction of the Project;

(e) Phasing of construction with a view to studying whether—

(i) timely utilisation of benefits accruing from the Project has been ensured;

(ii) it is possible to accelerate accrual of benefits;

(iii) benefits could be increased by rephasing the Project at this stage;

(f) Sufficiency of investigations conducted at the planning stage with a view to the formulation of Project Estimates;

(g) The effect of the above study on the financial results of the Project, if any.

Generally to assess the progress made in construction, the reasons for shortfall, if any, and to suggest measures for improvements in the future.

To examine the possibility of decreasing dependence upon imported materials and equipment required for the Project.

To examine whether adequate steps have been taken by the authorities concerned for fixing and realising the contemplated water rates, betterment fees and/or any other rates, cesses or taxes.

Any other recommendation that the Team may like to make in order to ensure economy and efficiency in the construction of the Project.

CONTENTS

Introductory; Scope of the Project; Administration; Phasing of Construction Programme; Features of Design and Construction; Canal Works Needing Urgent Attention; Development and Management of Irrigation; Power Generation; Construction Costs; Summary of Report; Appendices.

RECOMMENDATIONS

The Project is designed to impound 90,000 million cubic feet of water on the River Bhadra, irrigating 2,34,000 acres of land in Mysore State, and generating 25,000 kw firm power, installed capacity being 40,400 kw.

The Project was initially started in 1947 and at the time of writing this report i.e., by June 1957, an expenditure of roughly nine crores was incurred out of Rs. 24 crores, the estimated cost of the Project. The dam is raised to nearly half the total height and irrigation was started on the left bank canal during the last year (1956-57). The excavation of the main canal is nearly complete in the first 50 miles, beyond which it has to cross a hill range through a tunnel, approximately two and three-quarters miles in length. This tunnel is yet to be started, to facilitate which special machinery worth about Rs. 30 to 40 lakhs would be necessary and the Team has recommended to Government of India to release the necessary foreign exchange required to purchase such of the machinery as might not be available from the surplus on other Projects in the country. The Government of Mysore have been aware of the urgency of this work and are now busy in taking all the necessary steps to expedite the execution, since the Project is scheduled to deliver irrigation water up to the tail end by June 1961. Also, the report has suggested an alternative list of machinery which would save about Rs. 10 lakhs.

The Irrigation and Power Team noted that there was another factor holding up the execution of the Canal beyond the tunnel portion viz. the problem of by-passing the Shantisagar Reservoir, within a few miles after the tail of the tunnel. This problem could be solved by recourse to any one of a number of alternatives which were being discussed by the Mysore Engineers. The Team of Engineers and the Members of the Consultative Committee after discussing the matter with the State Engineers, proposed one of the alternatives, which happens to be the easiest and cheapest bringing a saving of Rs. 20 to 50 lakhs over the other possible alternatives.

The team has found the construction staff as generally sufficient and efficient. However, they have made recommendations to strengthen the organisations incharge of the designs and quality control over construction materials and techniques. The report reveals that the establishment charges on this project are only four per cent of the outlay, as against 10 to 12 per cent as considered normal by the Engineers' Seminar. The reasons for this are reported to be mainly due to the very low scales of salaries prevailing in the State and partly due to the under-staffing as mentioned before.

The report suggests the creation of another Circle under a Superintending Engineer to take up the construction of the Hiremalali Tunnel and the works beyond, so as to enable finishing of the work before the scheduled date.

The Report appreciates the Mysore practice of appointing a Standing Technical Advisory Board, consisting of the Chief Engineers of the State and retired Chief Engineers of the State and presided over by the Minister for P.W.D. The engineers work almost honorarily and provide an excellent consultation at all the stages of planning, designing and execution of Projects. This practice is recommended for emulation by other States engaged in construction of development projects.

The Report notes with appreciation the excellent manner in which the problem of Development of Irrigation has been tackled by the Mysore Government; who appointed a Committee known as Bhadra Reservoir Development Committee consisting of a Revenue Commissioner as a Chairman, with Chief Engineer, Director of Agriculture, Director of Public Health and the Superintending Engineer of the Project, as members. This Committee prepared the Irrigation Development Report, which not only surveyed all the irrigable area from irrigation point of view, but also from agricultural and health point of view, and prepared zone maps for irrigation with the proposed crop patterns for each village.

To implement the recommendations of the above Committee, another Committee was appointed, so as to expedite actual development of irrigation on the pattern set and enable the State and Society to realise the benefits of the Scheme without loss of time as soon as the irrigation facilities become available.

The State has also seen to it to decide the Betterment Levy etc. However, the report reveals a scope for and recommends recourse to upward revision of water rates, as they are lower than those obtained in the Bombay State. In order that the irrigation management and administration should not be slack and haphazard, the Report recommends the adoption of the Block-system and the Canal Rules and the system of irrigation management, as practised in the Bombay State, as far as possible.

As Bhadra is in the Inter-State River Basin of Tungabhadra Valley, which covers the erstwhile States of Mysore, Hyderabad and Madras the utilisation of the waters by the different States is subject to an agreement reached between these three States. With the recent reorganisation of the States, the position has changed and it is only Mysore and Andhra Pradesh that have rights over these waters. Hence the report points out the need for revising this agreement. Also, it is recommended that the earlier restrictions in regard to carrying over the waters in the Bhadra Reservoir from year to year should be removed; as such a carry-over would increase the firm electrical energy output annually, without affecting the interests of the State lower down.

The Report appreciates the fact that this Project is mostly carried out by utilising only the local labour and material, without adopting much mechanisation, and avoiding rare and costly building materials like cement which are very sparingly used, as the bulk of the masonry is all in lime mortar.

In conclusion the Report recommends expeditious sanction of adequate funds for the Project to enable its completion within the target date.

TEAM FOR THE STUDY OF COMMUNITY PROJECTS AND NATIONAL EXTENSION SERVICE, 1956—REPORT

New Delhi, Committee on Plan Projects, 1957. 175p.

Leader : Shri Balvantray G. Mehta.
Members : Shri Shankar Dayal Sharma; Shri B. G. Rao; Shri Phool Singh; Shri G. Ramachandran.
Secretary : Shri D. P. Singh.

APPOINTMENT

The Team for the Study of Community Projects and National Extension Service was constituted under the Committee on Plan Projects in 1956.

TERMS OF REFERENCE

To study and report on the Community Projects and National Extension Service with a view to economy and efficiency with specific reference to the following aspects:

(i) The content of the programme and the priorities assigned to different fields of activity within it.

(ii) The arrangements for the execution of the programme with special reference to:

(a) Intensification of activities in the sphere of agricultural production;

(b) Coordination between

(1) the different Ministries/Departments at the Centre;

(2) the Centre and the States; and

(3) the different agencies within the Community Projects Administration and other State Government Organisations and Departments;

(c) The organisational structure and methods of work with a view to securing a greater speed in the despatch of business.

(iii) The assessment of the requirements of personnel for Community Projects and National Extension Service and examination of existing training facilities in order to meet the growing requirements of personnel for extending the coverage of the programme.

(iv) The assessment of the extent to which the movement has succeeded in utilising local initiative and in creating institutions to ensure continuity in the process of improving economic and social conditions in rural areas.

(v) The methods adopted for reporting upon the results attained by the Community Projects and National Extension Service.

(vi) Any other recommendation that the Team may like to make in order to ensure economy and efficiency in the working of the Community Projects and the National Extension Service.

CONTENTS

Introduction; **Part I**—Concept and Approach; Democratic Decentralisation; Methods of Work; Programme Planning; Coordination at the Centre and between the Centre and the States; Administrative Pattern—Coordination within the State; **People's** Participation in Community Works; Work Among

Women and Children; Work in Tribal Areas; Surveys, Evaluation and Methods of Reporting; Training of Personnel; Farming; Cooperation; Rural Industries; Health; Primary Education; Social Education; Some Special Programmes (Sarvodaya, Saghan Kshetra and Gramdan etc.); Measures for Economy, Efficiency and Speed; Minute of Dissent by Shri B.G. Rao; **Part II**—Summary of Recommendations; Note on Financial Implications; Subjects for Special Study or Further Examination.

RECOMMENDATIONS

Introduction

In addition to evaluation by Programme Evaluation Organisation another body should make a review, after every few years, of the progress made and problems encountered, and advise on future lines of action in connection with the community development programme.

Concept Of Approach

The emphasis should shift without delay to the move demanding aspects of economic development and the priorities as between the different activities should be supply of drinking water, improvement of agriculture and animal husbandry, co-operative activities, rural industries and health, followed by all others.

Democratic Decentralisation

The government should divert itself completely of certain duties and responsibilities and devolve them to a body which will have the entire charge of all development work within its jurisdiction, reserving to itself only the functions of guidance, supervision and higher planning.

At the block level, an elected self-governing institution should be set up with its jurisdiction co-existensive with a development block.

The panchayat samiti should be constituted by indirect elections from the village panchayats.

Each of the municipalities lying as enclaves within the jurisdiction of a block should elect from amongst its own members one person as a member of the panchayat samiti. Secondly, State Governments may convert predominantly rural municipalities into panchayats.

The functions of the panchayat samiti should cover the development of agriculture in all its aspects, improvement of cattle, promotion of local industries, public health, welfare work, administration of primary schools and collection and maintenance of statistics. It should also act as an agent of State Government in executing special schemes of development entrusted to it.

The annual budget of the samiti should be approved by the Zila Parishad.

Main resources of income of the panchayat will be property or house tax, tax on markets and vehicles, octroi or terminal tax, conservancy tax, water and lighting rate, income [illegible]m cattle ponds, grants from the panchayat samiti and fees charged from the registration of animals sold, etc.

The compulsory duties of the village panchayats should include among others provision of water supply, sanitation, maintenance of roads, land management, collection and maintenance of records and other statistics and the welfare of backward classes.

The judicial panchayat may have much larger jurisdiction than even a Gram Sewak's circle, and out of the panel suggested by village panchayats the sub-divisional or district magistrate may select persons to form judicial panchayats.

Methods Of Work: Programme Planning

The broad distribution of the budget provision should be prescribed by the Centre. Within this pattern each State should evolve its own schematic budget, in consultation with Central Ministries.

All schemes sponsored by different departments in addition to those under the block budget, and financed out of State funds, including loans, and/or people's contributions, should be integrated with the block budget schemes at all levels and an integrated plan for the entire State should be evolved.

The present system of dividing the community development programme into three phases of N.E.S., I.D. and P.I.D. leads to two-fold waste and frustration on account of the non-availability of resources during the N.E.S. and P.I.D. stages. This distinction should be replaced by a continuing programme of six years, the unspent funds of each year being carried forward to the following year within certain limits.

The original budget ceiling of Rs. 15 lakhs should be restored.

Coordination At The Centre And Between The Centre And The States

Where the Central Government desires to introduce any new scheme on a country-wide basis, it would be correct to advise the States only on the broad lines of the scheme and allow them to work it out with necessary modifications.

Research schemes should not merely be appropriately coordinated but mainly worked out by the States, leaving to the Central Ministries the role of helpful adviser.

The Planning Commission and the Central Ministries, dealing with rural development, should evolve a procedure whereby once a scheme is included in the Plan, it should not need further detailed examination in a Central Ministry unless fresh and unforeseeable circumstances have developed.

It is essential to allow State Governments a large measure of discretion in details like fixation of pay-scales of personnel, designs of buildings, etc.

Cooperation and rural self-governing institutions which are not receiving adequate attention in the Ministries concerned and which are closely connected with the programme of Community Development should be brought under the Ministry which deals with the coordination of rural development activities all over the country, namely the Ministry of Community Development.

Administrative Pattern—Coordination Within The State

The area of operation of the Gram Sewak should be reduced and the number of Gram Sewaks increased to about 20 per block.

With the limited funds and scanty trained personnel available, pooling is the only effective answer to the requirements of community development programme. With increasing resources in due course, specialised service agencies may be provided.

A Gram Sewak should not be placed in charge of an area with a population exceeding 800 families or 4000 persons.

A closer link should be established between the Gram Sewak and the village panchayat immediately.

The block should not have more than 20 circles, each circle not exceeding 4000 population.

The most useful arrangement for associating the S.D.O. with development work would be to give him supervisory control over the block development officers under him and to delegate to him some of the powers now vested exclusively in the collector.

People's Participation In Community Works

Public participation in community works should be organised through statutory representative bodies which should also take over the maintenance of these works.

Work Among Women And Children

The work of women welfare should be directed from one point alone and one general policy adopted and followed.

Suitable smokeless chulhas need to be designed for different areas instead of one type all over the country.

Training centres of Gram Sewikas should stress less on theory of sanitation than on its actual practices, personal and environmental cleanliness being drilled in their daily lives at the centres.

The care of the cow, the kitchen garden and poultry keeping which constitute the most effective welfare work for the rural women should receive the primary attention of women workers in the villages.

Knitting, embroidery and tailoring have little economic value excepting in villages near large cities. Training in elementary use of thread and needle is necessary so that women can mend clothes for the family.

In villages which surround large towns and cities, cookery classes can be started with profit.

Work In Tribal Areas

A thorough survey and study should be carried out before a detailed budget of a block is drawn up.

Right type of personnel with sympathy and understanding for the tribal people should be selected, preferably local people.

Efforts should be made to induce the people in tribal areas to take up settled cultivation wherever possible.

A careful attempt should be made to introduce new crops especially cash crops.

Training centres for rural arts and crafts should be started with necessary modifications to suit local conditions, indigenous talent and raw materials available in the area.

The system of education should be of the basic type, so that the gulf between the educated and uneducated may be as narrow as possible.

Surveys, Evaluation And Methods Of Reporting

For a coordinated approach in reporting, the revenue set up, the planning set-up and the statistical department should, as far as possible, work as a unified agency. For certain information, the local school master's services can be utilised on a small additional remuneration.

The Gram Sewak, block level extension officers, as well as the Block Development Officer, should maintain a handbook-cum-diary to enable the district level officers to watch the progress of work.

A progress assistant should be provided at the block level, wherever this has not been done already, for coordinating statistical work of all branches and looking after crop-cutting surveys and special studies.

At the district level, a district statistical officer should function under the technical control of the Director of Economics and Statistics and the administrative control of the Collector.

At the State headquarters a statistical unit should be set up if not already in existence.

A seasonal review of the different activities at the close of each season should be made by each worker in respect of various items of a seasonal nature.

The States can profitably organise evaluation either of the programme as a whole or certain aspects of the programme; *ad hoc* bodies may be set up for the purpose.

Training of Personnel

Age limits for direct recruits as Gram Sewak should be 18 to 30 years. The departmental candidates should be taken purely on the basis of merit and the age limit relaxed upto 40 years.

The criteria for 'rural background' of a candidate should be that his parents or guardians live in non-urban areas and he himself spends his vacations at home.

Various tests, viz., physical fitness, general knowledge, aptitude for development work, leadership and initiative etc. should be the basis of selection and should spread over a number of days.

The training programme of Gram Sewak should also include the use of simple medicine chest, elementary survey training and measures for soil conservation, etc.

Inspection of various institutions imparting training to Gram Sewaks should be done occasionally.

The concept of job training should be strengthened by (i) attaching a block to every centre, and (ii) approach to rural problems followed by work in the blocks.

The integrated course for Gram Sewak should be for full two years with a brief break in the middle.

Training centres should be located in genuine rural areas.

Agriculture research institutions and the training centres should function in close association.

A scheme of apprenticeship as part of the training programme should be drawn up for every Gram Sewak by attaching a small batch of Gram Sewaks under an efficient B.D.O. for a period of at least one month which should not be included in the two years of training.

The training syllabus for Gram Sewikas should include methods of approach to village women and some knowledge of two village industries.

Each training centre should have some land for a flower and kitchen garden and also maintain a small dairy, poultry farm and an apiary.

Farming

The targets for additional production should be broken down upto block and Gram Sewak's circle.

Greater attention should be given for evolving and distributing improved varieties of coarser grains as also of other grains suitable for unirrigated areas.

Distribution of improved seeds on the basis of *sawai* or smaller additional percentage in kind will ensure timely and adequate supply.

Central Government should explore all possibilities of increasing local production of chemical fertilizers.

Village panchayats should buy wheel-barrows for supply to farmers on hire.

The State Governments should examine both types of soil conservation schemes, viz. (i) Bombay type by departmental agency, and (ii) U.P. type worked on self help basis. A judicious combination of good points of both types might produce better results.

Current methods of fruit preservation have to be simplified and made cheaper.

Greater attention needs to be given to starting nurseries in each block.

Rates for the supply of electricity for irrigation works should not exceed the rates for industrial purposes.

Water rates for the second crop should be reduced to encourage double cropping.

More concerted efforts should be made to encourage farmers to raise green fodder crops and for popularisation of silage-making.

Milk cooperative societies have to be organised on proper lines in the vicinity of towns and cities.

Poultry keeping has to be intensified through youth clubs, financial assistance to Harijans, backward classes etc., replacement of indigenous by exotic cocks and giving proper technical guidance.

Greater technical guidance is needed for improving the breed of pigs.

Fisheries should receive larger financial allotments and greater administrative attention especially in Community Development Blocks.

Cooperation

A multi-purpose cooperative society for a village or a group of villages working in close association with local panchayat or panchayats, as against societies for different lines of activity, remains the only correct course to be followed.

The criteria and qualifying conditions for obtaining funds from the Reserve Bank of India should be laid down in precise terms so that the co-operative societies in the blocks can take maximum advantage of the loan facility of Rs. 3 lakhs provided in N.E.S. budget.

The entire training programme should be oriented to the elimination of official control from the field of co-operation.

Students' co-operative societies for the supply of stationery and text books should be organised in high schools.

Rural Industries

Planned coordination in the working of cottage, village and small-scale industries is needed so that they do not cut at and pull down each other.

A number of peripatetic training centres should be opened in rural areas.

Health

The Medical and Public Health Departments should be combined under a single head at the State, regional and district levels in those States where such integration has not yet taken place.

The State Governments should examine the possibilities to train the staff employed in Health Centres for specialised services relating to malaria, filaria, tuberculosis, leprosy and venereal diseases.

Certain tried and proved indigenous remedies for common ailments handed down by way of family tradition should be collected, examined and their knowledge made widely known.

Improvement of the existing houses in rural areas by increasing ventilation and by making them more liberal should be effected.

Primary Education

Provision for primary education in C.D./N.E.S. schemes should be used to supplement allotments of the States to strengthen existing schools except in educationally backward areas.

At least blocks should be provided with necessary funds and trained personnel to achieve the immediate goal of introducing free and compulsory primary education.

Social Education

The aim of social education should be (a) to acquaint people of the meaning of citizenship and the way democracy functions; (b) to induce citizens to learn how to read and write; (c) to impart proper training for refinement of emotions; and (d) to instil a spirit of toleration among citizens.

Vikas Melas, Shibirs or training camps for villagers' campaigns or drives for different activities may be utilised as supplementary activities requiring day-to-day participation by the villages.

Cultural teachers and reformers may be utilised in educating the masses.

Circulating libraries of suitable films should be maintained by the States. Subsidised radio sets should be provided to the villagers.

Village leaders should be asked to broadcast talks; discussions during rural camps etc., recorded and broadcast.

Some Special Programmes—Sarvodaya, Saghan Kshetra and Gramdan

The Sarvodaya Area Committee should not be merely advisory but have fuller powers so that the Sanchalak becomes only the constitutional Chairman.

Area of operation of existing Sarvodaya Block should be extended to cover the whole N.E.S. Block.

The workers of Kshetra Samiti may be utilised to create necessary atmosphere as well as machinery required for intensive development of cottage and village industries, prepare one block and then move to contiguous blocks.

The community development work should be closely interlinked with Gramdan movement, Gramdan village areas being preferred in the selection of new blocks.

Measures For Economy, Efficiency And Speed

The provision for personnel at the block level should not be spent outside the block i.e., on the staff at State headquarters.

No project located outside the block should be financed out of the block funds and no scheme involving a large expenditure undertaken excepting when a scheme is essential and unavoidable.

The grants-in-aid should be non-lapsable at all levels.

All jeeps should be withdrawn from the blocks, only exception can be a jeep for the Mukhya Sewika.

The State and Central Governments should take remedial action to avoid the holding of meetings and seminars with considerable pomp.

Too frequent meetings and too frequent visits by outsiders absorb a very considerable part of the working hours of the block and the village staff.

The publication of too many similar publications printed on expensive paper with unnecessary pictures and a number of articles irrelevant to the purpose needs careful re-examination by the Ministries concerned.

EXPORT CREDIT GUARANTEE COMMITTEE, 1956—REPORT

Delhi, Manager of Publications, 1957. 304p.

Chairman : Shri T. C. Kapur.
Members : Shri W. A. Foges; Shri E. P. W. DaCosta; Shri S. Gupta; Shri S. C. Roy.
Secretary : Shri T. S. Ramaswami.

APPOINTMENT

The Export Credit Guarantee Committee was constituted under the Ministry of Commerce and Industry vide their Resolution No. EP/56, dated January 7, 1956.

TERMS OF REFERENCE

(1) To examine the suggestions made in this behalf and to consider the scope of the Export Credit Guarantee Scheme;

(2) To make recommendations in regard to :

(a) the nature of risks to be covered;

(b) the basis on which premia should be fixed;

(c) the structure of the organisation that will be required for the implementation of the scheme; and

(d) any other matter necessary for the successful operation of the scheme.

CONTENTS

Introductory; Case for Export Credit Insurance; Exporters' Risks; Periods for which Risks can be Covered; Percentages of Cover; Buyers' Risks; Export Finance; Split of Risks; Spread of Risks; How and when Claims should become Payable; Basis of Premium Rates; Structure of the Indian Insurance Organisation; Miscellaneous; Summary of Conclusions and Recommendations; Acknowledgements; Appendices from I to X.

SUMMARY OF CONCLUSIONS AND RECOMMENDATIONS

Case For Export Credit Insurance

An export credit insurance scheme is an important export promotion measure, and this scheme should be started in India without delay, for the following reasons :

(a) Demand for credit terms is being made for all exports and is likely to increase even for traditional exports of jute fabrics, tea, minerals, cotton textiles.

(b) More small and medium-sized firms are coming into the exports business and this class of firms has a great need for insurance.

(c) Export credit insurance makes export finance facilities more readily available.

(d) The insurance helps the exporter to develop new markets.

(e) Competition from exporters from other countries having insurance facilities can be met if, other things being the same. Indian exporters are placed in a similar position as their competitors in regard to credit insurance.

(f) There is a pressing need to earn foreign exchange.

Exporters' Risks

The types and extent of risks covered by export credit guarantee organisations differ from country to country. Nevertheless, the practice of all the countries conforms to two basic principles, viz.,

(a) Except in the case of some pre-shipment risks, only those risks are covered which arise out of events occurring outside the exporter's country.

(b) Only those risks are covered which are outside the control of the exporter and, generally, of the buyer. Any risk which can be avoided by the exporter and/or the buyer should be excluded.

All risks which contravene the above principles or for which cover is available from other insurers are generally excluded.

The Indian Export Credit Insurance Organisation should cover the following risks.

Post-Shipment Risks

(a) **Diversion Risks:** Due to interruption or diversion of voyage outside the exporting country, the exporter may have to incur in respect of goods shipped from his country, additional handling, transport or insurance charges which it is impracticable to recover from the buyer.

(b) **Import Control Risks:** The buyer's import or exchange licence may be cancelled or may have expired and it cannot be renewed; or new restrictions may be imposed on the import or payment. The risk should not be covered where

(i) Import or exchange licence is necessary but is not held by the buyer when the order is placed and he is unable to obtain it when goods arrive; and

(ii) Import or exchange licence is cancelled for buyer's fault.

(c) **Repudiation Risk:** A buyer may repudiate his contract, refuse to open a letter of credit or to accept goods. This risk is to be covered only in the following cases:

(i) When the buyer is a public body which either cancels the contract unilaterally or refuses to accept goods not due to any fault of the exporter;

(ii) When the buyer repudiates the contract and is adjudged insolvent;

(iii) Where a buyer repudiates the contract and the exporter takes legal steps, obtains a final judgement against the buyer and even by executing the decree he cannot receive the full price of the goods because the buyer has no assets from which recoveries can be made.

(d) **Insolvency Risk:** The buyer may become insolvent.

(e) **Default Risk:** The buyer may accept the goods on credit terms and on the due date refuse to make payment or may temporarily be unable to pay.

[Both (d) and (e) together are called Commercial or Del Credere Risks.]

(f) **War and Civil War Risks:** There may occur war between the buyer's country and the exporter's country; or war, hostilities, civil war, rebellion, revolution, insurrection or other disturbance may occur in the buyer's country or other countries through which the goods must pass. In all these contingencies, the exporter may suffer losses.

(g) **Transfer Risk:** The operation of a law or an order, decree or regulation having the force of law, which, in circumstances outside the control of the exporter and of the buyer, may prevent, restrict or control the transfer of payments from the buyer's country to the exporter's country.

(h) **Omnibus Risk:** Any other cause not being within the control of the exporter or of the buyer which arises from events occurring outside the exporter's country. Omnibus risk includes risks of port, strikes overseas, dock clearance delays and natural catastrophes (floods, earthquakes and hurricanes) in the buyer's country. This also includes the risk involved in the change in the standards of food and other products after goods have been shipped, provided the goods at the time of shipment were of the standard then in force.

[Risks (a), (b), (c)(i), (f), (g) and (h) are called Political Risks.]

Pre-Shipment Risks

Risks (a) to (b) of 3 as also the Export Control Risk (i.e., non-renewal or cancellation of the export licence or the imposition of fresh restrictions on the export of goods) should be covered during the pre-shipment period. The Export Control Risk should, however, be not covered in the following cases:

(i) Where export licence is necessary but is not held by the exporter when the order is placed and he is unable to obtain a licence at a later date, and

(ii) Where the export licence is cancelled on account of the fault of the exporter.

Risks Of Special Transactions

The following risks of special transactions should be covered:

(i) C.I.F. Risks, i.e., increase in insurance and freight rates after a sale has been concluded on a "cost, insurance and freight basis".

(ii) Risks of exports on consignment basis.

(iii) Risks [similar to those in (ii) above] of goods sent for display in a foreign fair.

(iv) Risks pertaining to non-receipt of money for services rendered to a principal in a foreign country.

(v) Expenses incurred on market surveys, publicity, stock-holdings and other promotional measures, for the development of a particular market, if such expenses are not fully recouped by sales made in that country.

Risks Not To Be Covered

The following risks should not be covered:

1. Repudiation Risk, except in the cases mentioned in 3(c).

2. Exchange Fluctuation and Devaluation Risks.

3. During the pre-shipment period

(a) Ban or restrictions on the import of raw material or semi-manufactured goods which may be necessary to manufacture the goods to be exported;

(b) Increase in export duty or the imposition of a new export duty which, under the terms of the contract, cannot be recovered from the foreign buyer;

(c) Non-availability of railway transport, shipping space or of berthing space for steamers;

(d) Strikes;

(e) Increase in manufacturing costs.

The Indian Export Credit Insurance Organisation should, when covering commercial risks, set limits on the amount of business which can be covered at any one time for an exporter on any of his buyers. The limits should be of the following types:

(a) **The Credit Limit**, which limits the insurer's liability in respect of the value of shipments which have been delivered to the buyer on credit terms or placed at his disposal on cash against documents or equivalent terms.

(b) **The Contract (or Trading) Limit**, which limits the insurer's maximum liability in respect of all the goods in course of (manufacture and) shipment to the buyer at any one time.

2. The amount of the Credit Limit should be agreed by the insurer for each buyer on application by the exporter, or a discretionary limit can be agreed, within which the exporter, on the basis of his own knowledge and experience of the buyer, can ship without reference to the insurer. Normally the maximum amount of this discretionary limit should be Rs. 4,000 in the case of credit transactions or Rs. 8,000 in the case of transactions on cash against documents or equivalent terms.

The Contract Limit set in the case of shipment policies relating to goods in course of shipment should be equal to twice the amount of the Credit Limit and in the case of pre-shipment policies relating to course of manufacture and shipment should be equal to four times the amount of the Credit Limit.

Periods For Which Risks Can Be Covered

The periods for which the risks of the Indian exporters should be covered are specified below:

(a) **Pre-Shipment Risks:** For a period of four months preceding the date of shipment.

(b) **Post-Shipment Risks:**

(i) **For Exports of Raw Materials:** Upto three months and, exceptionally, four months from the date of shipment.

(ii) **For Exports of Consumer Goods:** Upto six months from the date of shipment.

(iii) **For Exports of Light Capital Goods:** A spread of payments upto two years from the date of shipment.

(iv) **For Exports of Capital Goods:** A spread of payments upto three years from the date of shipment.

These periods may be extended in exceptional cases.

The risks for a credit period of more than six months should be covered only where

(i) Foreign competition warrants such a course;

(ii) The type of goods and the nature of the order justify extended credit;

(iii) A substantial payment has been received before or on shipment;

(iv) The work content is high;

(v) Any necessary authority from the Reserve Bank of India has been obtained.

Percentages Of Cover

An accepted principle of credit insurance is that the

insured should carry a part of every risk. The Indian organisation should in the initial stages give cover for:

(a) commerical risks—upto 80 per cent;

(b) political risks—upto 85 per cent;

(c) promotional policies—equal to 50 per cent of the unrecouped expenses.

These percentages, except in the case of (c), are of the value of an invoice.

Export Finance

Credit Insurance policies are accepted by banks as a satisfactory form of security and therefore export finance becomes more readily available. The Indian export credit insurance organisation should provide by its regulations for the registration of assignments the benefits under their policies made by exporter to their banks.

In the case of contracts of national importance, the Indian Export Credit Insurance Organisation should have the authority—

(a) to provide, in the case of approved parties, financial guarantees to banks and others with no risk to them but with recourse to the exporter where necessary in connection with the export of goods, to the extent of 80 percent of the bills provided a policy to cover both the commercial and political risks has been taken out and assigned to the organisation;

(b) to provide, where necessary, as agents of the Government, financial help for the purchase of Indian exports on extended payment terms.

The Indian organisation should not normally discount or rediscount insured bills so long as such facilities are available from other organisations, unless the Government specially instructs it to do so.

Split Of Risks

The ideal policy for an exporter is that which covers both the commercial and political risks together because every insurable risk which can cause loss will be provided for; but a demand by certain trade interests for a split of commercial and political risks can be accepted.

Having examined the demand regarding split of risks in the light of the practices of foreign Export Credit Insurance Organisations, it is recommended that a limited split of risks should be allowed and separate policies made available for exports to private buyers in respect of:

(a) Commercial and political risks together; and

(b) The following political risks together, viz.

(i) Import Control Risk.

(ii) Diversion risk, if under the sale agreement the charges for diversion have to be borne by the exporter.

(iii) Non-payment due to moratorium or freezing of commercial debts by an order, decree, or law of the Government of the buyer's country.

(iv) Non-transfer provided that the payment has been made within 30 days of the due date. In case devaluation takes place before a claim is paid, the amount to be paid in Indian currency by the insurer to the insured should be based on the devalued rate. After a claim is paid the recoveries should be shared by the insured and the insurer. This will be applicable also in case of any change in the value of the currency.

(v) C.I.F. risk.

(vi) Risk of change in standards imposed in the buyer's country on the import of food and other products after goods have been shipped.

(vii) War between the buyer's country and the exporter's country before expiry of 30 days of due date.

For exports to public buyers, either of the proposed policies described in (a) and (b) of clause (2) should cover all political risks, including default and repudiation of the contracts.

Spread of Risks

It is necessary that an expert credit insurance organisation should have as wide a spread of risks by countries, by trades, by buyers, and over time, as possible. To achieve this object, the Indian organisation should require every exporter to insure all his exports of the trade in a period of twelve months (normally excluding sales on confirmed irrevocable letters of credit). In special cases, however, an exporter may be permitted to exclude his exports to any one or more countries, or to any one or more buyers provided; in the opinion of the organisation, what is left after this exclusion is a proper spread of risks and provided also the exporter agrees to pay an additional premium.

Exporters dealing with goods in more than one trade should be allowed, in appropriate cases, to insure only a substantial group of exports which might come under a single reasonable category. Premium rates should be assessed from the outset at the level, which it is expected will prove economic on the basis of business anticipated at the end of five years. Patience will, therefore, be needed in the first few years which will be spent in building a stable organisation, and some losses may be experienced.

Evidence on the desirability of any element of compulsion for selected commodities has been far from uniform. Broadly, it is thought that the business community does not welcome compulsion in any form, and as the advantages of a limited compulsory scheme are considered to be illusory, it would be inexpedient to depart from the general principle of voluntary credit insurance. However, if after the facilities of the organisation have been available for a reasonable period, a request is made by the great majority of any particular trade that all exports in the trade, not on a letter of credit basis should be covered by the scheme; their request should be examined; if it is agreed, a rebate in premium rates of between 15 and 25 per cent should be possible. Similar arrangements might be made, should the Government be satisfied that the use of credit insurance by all exporters of a particular commodity is in the interest of the export trade as a whole and of the individual trade concerned.

How And When Claims Should Become Payable

(1) Claims, in respect of goods invoiced in foreign currencies, should, like the premiums, be payable in Indian currency at the rate of exchange effective on the date of commencement of risks.

(2) The Indian Export Credit Insurance Organisation should pay claims as under:

(a) For claims under insolvency risk—as soon as the buyer is adjudged insolvent;

(b) For claims under default risk—six months after the due date;

(c) For claims under C.I.F. and diversion risks—as soon as the proof of loss to the satisfaction of the organisation is furnished;

(d) For claims under promotional policies issued in connection with the development of particular markets —60 days after the final audited accounts for the period covered by the policy are furnished to the organisation;

(e) For claims under Transfer Risks—six months after the due date;

(f) For claims under all other risks—six months after the date of the event which is the cause of loss.

(3) Recoveries made after payment of claims should be divided between the insurer, and the insured in the same proportion in which they carry the risks.

Basis Of Premium Rates

As the nature and intensity of political risks depend upon the economic and political conditions of the countries to which the goods are exported, different rates of premiums are necessary for exports to different countries. Premium rates cannot be published and must be kept confidential.

The Indian Export Credit Insurance Organisation, like organisations in other countries should work on a 'no profit, no loss' basis. The premiums therefore should be assessed to cover only the net claims and the expenses of management.

The following factors should be taken into consideration in fixing the premium rates:

(a) The types of risks and their causes;

(b) The markets to which the goods are exported;

(c) The type of goods;

(d) The period for which the risks are covered;

(e) The past experience of the exporter and the spread of risks offered by him for insurance; and

(f) The expenses of management.

For fixing premium rates, countries may be grouped as shown below, according to the nature and intensity of the risk involved:

(a) Countries which are important traditional buyers of Indian goods, where the administration of economic affairs is particularly efficient, and where the foreseeable risks of loss from transfer or other causes are very small;

(b) Countries whose economies are soundly based and well administered and where transfer losses are unlikely to occur;

(c) Countries which are relatively stable, but where minor risks of losses can be foreseen;

(d) Countries whose economies are not broadly based where fluctuations may occur with possible risks of loss;

(e) Countries which are relatively unstable or whose economies are deteriorating and where there is persistent risk of transfer and/or other losses;

(f) Countries whose economies are chronically unstable, where transfer and/or other losses have recently occurred or are in prospect.

Risks also differ according to the nature and/or type of the commodities. To fix premium rates for each commodity separately will not be practicable. The goods exported may, therefore, be grouped as under:

(a) Raw materials;

(b) Manufactured goods which are easily saleable in more than one market; and

(c) All other goods not included in (a) and (b) such as expensive manufactured articles and goods whose resale possibilities are limited that are subject to changing fashions, that deteriorate rapidly; or those goods falling under (a) and (b) of which the insurance organisation has unsatisfactory experience.

The rate of premium will also vary with the period for which credit is allowed by the exporter. It would be advisable to fix basic rates of premium applicable to the cases where cash is to be received against documents in the buyer's country and where credit upto 30 days after delivery is given. Where payment terms provide for credit longer than 30 days an extra premium dependent on the period in excess of 30 days should be charged at a rate fixed for every additional month. These considerations apply to post-shipment risks.

Where pre-shipment risks are also covered, the premium will have to be charged for a longer period than in the case of cover for post-shipment risks only. It is desirable to place the buyers' countries for pre-shipment risks into the following three groups:

(i) Where pre-shipment risks are very slight;

(ii) Where additional risks exist in the pre-shipment period but are not considerable;

(iii) Where the additional risks in the pre-shipment period are very real.

The premium rating schedule for transactions involving payment terms of more than six months' credit from the date of shipment is based on a forward projection of the normal premium schedule, and takes into account the following additional factors:

(a) The length of the manufacturing period;

(b) The spread of shipments and payments;

(c) The class of buyer (whether public or private); and

(d) The degree of specialisation of the goods.

Where an exporter offers for cover under a single policy a large volume of exports, he should be allowed a small rebate in the premium charged, depending on the spread of risk and the saving in administrative work. Conversely, an exporter who wishes to exclude from his policy shipments to one or more markets must expect, if his proposal is accepted, to be charged somewhat higher rates of premium than if he had insured all his good and bad markets together.

An estimate of the expenses of the insurance organisation should be prepared as also of the premiums likely to be collected in the first five years of the working, and on that basis expense leading to the risk premium can be arrived at.

Structure Of The Indian Export Credit Insurance Organisation

A study of the structure of credit insurance organisations in other countries shows that the organisation can be

(a) a government department; or

(b) a corporation owned by the State; or

(c) a private company acting for and on behalf of the State.

There is no private company in India transacting credit insurance business even for home trade. So far as the Indian organisation is concerned, the choice lies between a Government Department and a State-owned Corporation.

The widespread view of the trade should be accepted that the work of the Indian organisation should be entrusted to a Corporation wholly owned by the State.

The Corporation should be named Export Risks Insurance Corporation.

The Corporation should be set up with the following objects:

(a) For the purpose of encouraging, facilitating and developing trade with other countries, it may make arrangements for giving guarantees to or for the benefit of persons carrying on business in India, being guarantees in connection with the export, manufacture, treatment, or distribution of goods, the rendering of services or any other matter which is conducive to the said purpose;

(b) For the purpose referred to in (a), it may make arrangements for giving guarantees to or for the benefit of persons residing in, or belonging to a foreign country, being guarantees in connection with goods exported or services rendered from India;

(c) It may give facilities for financing exports;

(d) It may act as agent of the Government to

(i) give guarantees beyond its scope which are considered by the Government as necessary in national interest;

(ii) acquire any securities (which expression includes bonds, stocks, shares, bills and promissory notes) which the Corporation has guaranteed, hold any such security for such period as may be directed by the Government, collect any sum falling due whether by way of principal or interest in respect thereof, and dispose of any such security at such time and in such a manner as directed by the Government;

(e) it may do all such things as may be incidental to or consequential upon the carrying out of its object mentioned in clauses (a) to (b) above.

The authorised and subscribed capital of the Indian Corporation should be Rs. 5 crores of which 10% should be paid up. This will enable the Corporation to carry at any time, a risk upto 50 crores which is considered to be the maximum that can be achieved by the end of the first 5 years.

To infuse confidence in the mind of the exporters, it is necessary that every policy issued by the Corporation should carry Government guarantee.

The management of the affairs of the Corporation should vest in a Board of Directors consisting of seven members including either a whole-time Chairman or a whole-time Managing Director. The Directors may delegate powers for day-to-day administration to the principal officer whether he be the Chairman or the Managing Director.

There should be an Advisory Council consisting of not more than 21 members representing the export trade, banks engaged in financing exports, various Export Promotion Councils and Commodity Boards. The Council will advise the Corporation regarding the insurance needs of the export trade, the changes taking place in the export trade and the steps to be taken to provide for new conditions. The Advisory Council may elect two members to be appointed as Directors of the Corporation.

The registered and main office of the Corporation should be at New Delhi. The Corporation may open branch offices and, where necessary, set up Local Advisory Boards to help and advise the Branch Offices appoint brokers to introduce business and appoint agents elsewhere than in India for enforcing any right that, as a result of contract of an insurance, may have vested in the Corporation.

The Corporation may borrow monies, raise loans, and for that purpose, if necessary, may issue and sell bonds and debentures bearing such rates of interest and subject to such terms and conditions as the Board of Directors may approve.

Miscellaneous

Export credit insurance would appear to fall under the definition of "miscellaneous insurance business" given in section 2(13B) of the Insurance Act, 1938 (IV of 1938). The Indian export credit insurance organisation would be a Corporation wholly owned by the State and as such would appear to be exempted under section 118 of the Insurance Act. In case business done by the Government through a corporation owned by it is held to be not any insurance business carried on by the Central Government a change in the Insurance Act will be necessary.

Since premium rates are to be kept confidential, if any rule or regulation requires an exporter to show the premium paid separately in any return or statement, suitable amendment should be made to such rule or regulation.

Every policy issued by the Corporation should have clauses to the following effect:

(a) The Proposal and Declaration thereto shall be incorporated with this policy as the basis thereof and if any of the statements contained in the Proposal or Declaration be untrue or incorrect in any respect, this policy shall be void, but the Corporation may retain any premium that has been paid;

(b) Due performance and observance of each and every stipulation contained herein and in the Proposal and Declaration thereto shall be a condition precedent to any liability of the Corporation hereunder.

The export credit insurance organisation being a non-profit making concern, reserves built up should not be treated as profit in the commercial sense and should not be made liable to income-tax. For this purpose necessary legislative or administrative action should be taken.

The premiums paid by an exporter to the Export Risks Insurance Corporation should be an allowable deduction for the purposes of income tax.

The Indian Export Risks Insurance Corporation should become a member of the *Union D'Assureurs Pour Le Controle Des Credits Internationaux* (Union of Insurers for the Supervision of International Credits).

The attention of the Committee has been drawn to various difficulties which appear to be retarding the development of the export trade. These are outside the terms of reference of the Committee. Nevertheless, they have been included in the summaries of the written and oral evidence in Appendices VI and VII, with a view to effective steps being taken by Government to resolve them.

MACHINE TOOL COMMITTEE, 1956—REPORT

Delhi, Manager of Publications, 1956. 30p.

Chairman : Prof. M.S. Thacker.
Members : Shri M.K. Mathulla; Shri S.J. Shahaney; Shri L.T. Madnani; Shri K.S. Raghupati; Shri P.N. Batra; Shri N. Krishnaswamy; Shri S.L. Kirloskar; Shri D.S. Mulla; Shri G.R. Damodaran.
Secretary : Shri R.K. Gejji.

APPOINTMENT

The Machine Tool Committee was constituted under the Ministry of Commerce & Industry vide their Resolution No. E.I. 23(19)/55, dated January 14, 1956.

TERMS OF REFERENCE

(i) To review the existing capacity to manufacture machine tools in the private and public sectors and study their plans for further expansion.

(ii) To assess the country's requirements of machine tools in the different categories and determine the gap between requirements and present manufacturing capacity.

(iii) To investigate causes responsible for impeding faster development of the industry and suggest how they can be eliminated.

(iv) To suggest ways and means of utilising the existing capacity fully and developing it further to meet the requirements of the country for machine tools, as assessed by the Committee and to report whether, after ensuring such full utilization, there is any necessity to set up new units—and if so to indicate the size and scope of such units.

(v) To review the existing capacity to design machine tools, to survey the facilities available for training machine tool designers and to suggest ways and means of helping the industry in securing training facilities at home and abroad for such staff.

(vi) To study the range of general purpose machine tools required by the various Departments of Government with a view to standardising to the most widely popular requirements, and to examine the feasibility of other Government Departments using similar machines and adopting them as their standards. In carrying out this examination, the Committee will take particular note of the standardisation work already completed by the Railways.

(vii) To suggest the machinery for laying down the standards of performance and the specifications for inspection of the final product in order to ensure that the product measures up to the required quality, and to recommend the most suitable organisation for testing, and certifying the products as conforming to the prescribed quality specifications.

(viii) To investigate and report on such other matters as the Committee may think fit regarding the development of the Machine Tool Industry in India.

CONTENTS

Introduction; Working of the Committee; Preliminary Remarks; Recommendations; Demand Forecast; Programme of Manufacturing; Acknowledgements; Appendix.

RECOMMENDATIONS

Terms Of Reference No. (1)

"To review the existing capacity to manufacture machine tools in the private and public sectors and study their plans for further expansion."

The existing capacity to manufacture machine tools has been investigated by Sub-Committee No. 4.

Questionnaires were circulated to ascertain the installed capacity of the various units producing machine tools. The information received was carefully analysed and the capacity of each unit was arrived at on the following basis:

(i) Installed machine-hour capacity.

(ii) An improvement factor was anticipated due to technical help and collaboration reaching proportions of 48% rise in efficiency by 1961.

(iii) The actual time required at present for the production of the different types of machine tools was projected utilising the efficiency factor as per (ii) above in order to determine the proposed manufacturing capacity in 1961.

Another questionnaire was issued to ascertain the plans for expansion of units. The plan of manufacture recommended in Table II at page 11 (of the report) takes into account such programmes for expansion as were considered by the Committee to be reasonable.

Terms Of Reference No. (2)

"To assess the country's requirements of machine tools in different categories and determine the gap between requirements and present manufacturing capacity."

Demand Forecast: The assessment of the requirements of machine tools, especially in an expanding economy is very difficult. Normally forecasts are based on past experience but when rapid industrialisation is taking place, it is difficult to rely on past statistics. In these cirumstances, the Committee feels that any estimate of demand can at best be an intelligent guess.

The following documents were made available to the Committee to enable them to form their assessment:

(i) Report of Railway Equipment Committee regarding the machine tools required by Railways.

(ii) Analysis of the licences issued by the Development Officer (Tools) and the Chief Controller of Imports for machine tools during the year 1955.

(iii) Census of machine tools, which has been referred to in paragraph 3.3.

In this connection, it has been pointed out that the licences issued during the year do not always represent the actual number of machine tools imported during that period. An alternative source, viz., figures of actual imports compiled by the Director-General of Commercial Intelligence & Statistics, and published in the "Accounts relating to the Sea, Air, Land Trade and Navigation of India" was considered but as these are not categorised in sufficient detail, it was felt that the licences issued over a period of one year would be more representative of the approximate demand.

With the information available and based on the experience of the members of the Committee, a reasonable factor has been applied to arrive at the expected increase in the demand. The demand thus estimated is given in Table I. This covers only such categories of machine tools as are expected to be manufactured during the Second Plan Period. The demand for other types is comparatively less and diversified. The manufacture of these may, therefore, be taken up later:

Table I
Demand Forecast

Sl. No.	*Code No.*	*Description*		*Estimated Annual Demand (1960-61) Nos.*
1.	040101 to 040115	Drilling machine	Bench & Floor	2,050
2.	040120 to 040144	Drilling machine	Pillar	1,135
3.	040201 to 040203	Drilling machine	Radial	425

Table I (*Contd.*)

Sl. No.	*Code No.*	*Description*		*Estimated Annual Demand (1960-61) Nos.*
4.	060101 to 060161, 060601 to 060609 and 060701 to 060713	Grinding machine	O.D., Universal & I.D.	180
5.	060801 to 060892	Grinder	Surface	200
6.	060901 to 060999	Grinder	Tool & Cutter	205
7.	090101 to 090103	Capstans	Upto 1"	72
8.	090104 to 090108	Capstans	Above 1"	195
9.	090201 to 090202	Turrets		210
10.	110201 to 110203, 110301 to 110303 and 110401 to 110403	Milling machine	Plain, Vertical & Universal No. 1	105
11.	110204 to 110205, 110304 to 110305 and 110404 to 110405	Milling machine	Plain, Vertical & Universal Nos. 2 & 3	360
12.	120101 to 120103	Planers 3" wide upto 8' stroke		20
13.	120104 to 120132	Planers higher upto 16' stroke		35
14.	100120 to 100123	Lathes 12" to 16" Swing		120
15.	100124 to 100129	Lathes 16" to 20" Swing Heavy		128
		Lathes 16" to 20" Swing Light		205
16.	100130 to 100133	Lathes 20" to 24" Swing Heavy		55
17.	100201 to 100209	Surfacing and boring lathes		12
18.	040204 to 040205	Radial Drilling machine 3" capacity and above		18
19.	110206 to 110208, 110306 to 110308 and 110406 to 110408	Milling machines similar to Cincinnati No. 4 and heavier		18
20.	090203 to 090220	Turrets bigger than Ward 7		42
21.	180104 to 180105	Slotting machines 16" stroke & above		10
22.	020201 to 020228	Vertical boring machines		32
23.	020101 to 020137	Horizontal boring machines		17
24.	101100	Wheel lathes		10
25.	101201 to 101203	Axle lathes		8
26.	101400	Roll turning machines		4
27.	060400	Roll grinding machines		4
28.	120133 to 120173	Planers 20' & above		2
29.	221501 to 221550	Hammers, Power		10
30.	222501 to 222509, 130101 to 130804 and 160101 to 169900	Sheet metal machinery		Rs. 1.5 crores (in value)
31.	400101 to 549900	Wood working machine tools		Rs. 1 crore (in value)

Terms Of Reference No. (3)

"To investigate causes responsible for impeding faster development of the industry and suggest how they can be eliminated."

Lack of Guidance: Although the importance of this industry to the nation has been accepted in principle, effective steps do not appear to have been taken so far to ensure a planned and rapid development. Of necessity, private enterprise has worked to meet the requirements of a fluctuating economic cycle and not as part of a national programme. This has resulted in the manufacture of machine tools most easy to sell. Absence of statistical data regarding the demand from time to time has prevented development of new designs.

Government has taken some steps to protect this industry by banning import of such of those items as are produced indigenously to graded standards. Facilities of free inspection by a third party viz., the Government are provided to ensure quality by granting a certificate of standard by an impartial agency. The Committee, however, feels that much more will have to be done to develop this industry as a national asset. It is essential that topmost priority should be accorded to its requirements.

Technical Know-how: Another important lacuna has

been the lack of technical know-how. The skill developed for the manufacture of machine tools in the industrially advanced countries is the result of long experience. It is possible to close that technological gap in far less time through the willingness of many industrialised countries to share their factories in the public sector collaborated with a foreign firm. It is desirable that Government encourage foreign collaboration on satisfactory terms, for further expansion of the industry.

The Committee has noted that the technical know-how imparted through foreign technical assistance has benefited certain industries. If such foreign technical assistance in the field of machine tool manufacture could be secured, the development of the industry would be accelerated. Experts who might be obtained under these technical assistance schemes should stay with the manufacturing units sufficiently long to demonstrate the results of their suggestions. It is expected that about 5 to 10 experts covering various fields of technology such as foundry, machining, tooling, designing, methods, planning, heat treatment and assembly would be required by each unit. The Committee, therefore, recommends that Government secure a team of technicians and make them available to the indigenous manufacturers at a price they can afford. The services of the experts in the various fields may be phased out as required. As this programme requires very highly specialised engineers, special attention will have to be given to their selection. The Committee is of the opinion that the manufacturers should be represented on any recruiting team which should be composed of personnel with experience of the industry.

Raw Material: The main raw materials required for the manufacture of machine tools are pig iron and steel, carbon and alloys. Due to the sudden spurt of demand, there has been a general shortage of these items. Manufacturers of machine tools have found it difficult to obtain their requirements. Very often applications have to be followed up in person to expedite results. It has been brought to the notice of the Committee that similar conditions exist in the procurement of import licences for some of the essential components. It will be realised that if the senior personnel of the factories are to spend their time and energy in following up, it will be difficult for them to concentrate on their real work of manufacturing and developing machine tools. It is, therefore, requested that necessary action be taken to see that these handicaps do not stand in the way of development of industry.

Financial Assistance: With increased tempo of expansion programmes, individual firms in the private sector are bound to feel the necessity of installing additional plant and equipment to balance production. As some of them may require financial help, the Committee recommends that Government consider such requests liberally.

Terms of Reference No. (4)

"To suggest ways and means of utilising the existing capacity fully and developing it further to meet the requirements of the country for machine tools as assessed by the Committee and to report whether after ensuring such full utilisation, there is any necessity to set up new units and if so, to indicate the size and scope of such units."

Present Production: The present manufacturing activity of the firms either in the private sector or in the public sector is confined to the production of only a few types of machine tools such as lathes, drilling machines and shapers. Though some attempts have been made to manufacture machine tools like hydraulic shapers, capstans and surface grinders, so far only prototypes have been produced. Organized manufacture of large milling machines, grinding machines, turrets and similar other machine tools has not been established. It is essential that the manufacture of all types of machine tools should be developed in the country as early as possible.

Development and Expansion: From the point of view of maximum utilisation of the existing capacity, the Committee has taken into account not only the capacity as represented by the capital equipment installed, but what is of greater importance, the technique and skill developed by the various units. As the Committee's main concern is the development of as many types of machine tools as possible within a short period, it recommends a broad base for the development of this industry. Different types of machine tools can be developed by different units simultaneously to produce within two or three years such items as are required in large numbers. These include milling machines, radial drills, grinding machines, turrets, planers and lathes of modern design. The Committee feels that this broad-based development will require modernisation of plant in some factories. Balancing machinery may also have to be installed which will increase individual capacity by about 30% and help to develop the industry on sound lines.

Programme of Manufacture: Sub-Committee No. 6 has considered a detailed plan and recommends a programme of manufacture for the various units to utilise the existing capacity in the machine tool industry. The Committee has accepted this programme, shown at Table II. It may be pointed out that an analysis of the capacity to produce machine tools is a difficult task. The number which can be produced by a given unit vary with the design and type of the product taken up for manufacture. A rational programme on a broad basis has, therefore, been recommended. Where surplus capacity exists, the Committee recommends the development of additional categories of machine tools. Existing activities of the firms consistent with the programme recommended will be the first priority. Machine tools to be manufactured thereafter should be in the order of priority proposed. It is expected that development of the different items can go on simultaneously depending upon the engineering resources of the individual concern, but production will follow the priority laid down. Particular attention is invited to the fact that Investas who are at present making lathes will give up their manufacture gradually. Similarly, Hindustan Machine Tools have been recommended the manufacture of a production lathe of the same dimensions as their present H.22, as it is felt that the present lathe is over-engineered for general requirements. The programme of manufacture by Pragas will (it is recommended) be confined to lines which are at present well established by them. At Kirloskars, the consumers' preference for modern design will cause the phasing out of cone-pulley lathes. This will also be the case with Coopers.

Table II

Programme of Manufacture

Firm	*Item of Manufacture*	*Code Range*	*Priority*
Messrs. Cooper Engg. Ltd.	Geared shapers upto and including 32″ stroke. (Gradual changeover from cone-pulley to geared head.)	150101 to 150106	I
	Planers, upto and including 6′×6′×16′ table.	120101	II
	Slotters, upto and including 21″ stroke.	180101	III
Messrs. Hindustan Machine Tools (Pvt.) Ltd.	*Lathes 17″ Swing, present and allied models.	100124 to 100129	I
	Milling machines (No. 2 and No. 3) Plain, Vertical, Universal and Manufacturing (Heavy type).	110204, 110205, 110304, 110305, 110404, 110405, & 110504	II
	Grinding machines O.D., Universal and I.D.	060101, 060106, 060601, 060609, 060701 & 060713	III
	**Radial drilling machines 2″ and above	040203, 040205	IV
	*Lathes, 20″ to 28″ Swing	100130, 100139	V
	Production jig borers	0204	VI
	*Lathes (other types)—Capstans and turrets	(Group 10 and 09)	VII
Messrs. Investa Machine Tools & Engineering Co. Ltd.	Drilling machines, Pillar 1¼″ to 2″	040122 & 040123	I
	Drilling machines, Column upto 3″	040124	II
	Drilling machines, Radial below 2″	040201 & 040202	
Machine Tool Prototype Factory	Lathes, Geared head 10″ Swing	100111 & 100112	I
	Lathes, Capstan ½″	090101	II
	Grinders, Surface 18″ and 24″	060801	III
	Grinders—Tool & Cutter	060901 to 060921	IV
	Lathes—Capstan 1¼″	090104	V
Messrs. Mysore Kirloskar Ltd.	*Lathes—12″ to 28″ Swing	100121 to 100139	I
	Lathes—Capstan 1½″	090105	II
	Lathes—Capstan 2½″	090107	III
	Lathes—Turret 3½″	090203	IV
Messrs. Praga Tools Corporation	Drilling Machines Pillar 1″ and 1½″	040122	II
	Milling Machines No. 1	110201, 110203, 110301, 110303 & 110401, 110403	III
	Lathes, Bench	100110	IV

*Shri M.K. Mathulla considered that overlapping in the programme of manufacture of lathes is not desirable.
**Shri D.S. Mulla considered that this item be developed by Investas also.

Implementation: With the programme recommended above, the existing units when modernised and equipped with balancing plant would be booked to capacity during the Second Five-Year Plan period. Detailed phased programmes should be obtained from each manufacturer and approved by Government. It is essential that the individual firms should adhere to the programme once it is approved by Government. Stringent measures should be adopted to see that the programme is implemented. Where a firm fails to take up an item on the programme, another firm doing allied work should be permitted to take it up if their capacity permits.

Additional Capacity: (i) *Heavy Machine Tools.* Existing units in the country are not in a position to manufacture heavy machine tools. It is recommended Government take steps to create capacity for this purpose.

(ii) *Special Machine Tools.* The technological advancement of the country is characterised in general by a gradual changeover from the repair shop technique to manufacturing methods. With increased industrial activity during the Secon Plan Period, it is expected that there will be a transformation from batch production to continuous flow production methods. This will mean the introduction of special purpose machine tools. The present stage is not considered advanced enough in the evolution of the industry for the introduction of such units. With the stress on increased production, the Committee expects greater utilisation of special purpose machine tools towards the end of the Second Plan Period. It is, therefore, recommended that Government encourage the creation of capacity for the manufacture of such units. Special purpose machine tools required will have to be designed to suit Indian conditions. As this would involve evolution of new designs and not merely copying existing ones, it may warrant foreign collaboration.

(iii) *Sheet Metal Machinery.* The Committee is of the opinion that the capacity and specialised skill for the manufacture of presses and sheet metal machinery in the country is limited. The existing units in the field are too small and the committee thinks that even after expansion under the development programme, they will not be able to meet the requirements for these machines during the Second Plan period. The Committee, recommends the establishment of an additional unit for the manufacture of presses and other sheet metal machinery.

(iv) *Wood Working Machinery.* The production of wood working machines has not been attempted in the country to any large extent. As the demand for this is reasonably large and is likely to increase during the Second Plan period, it is recommended that adequate capacity be created for this purpose.

Other Small Units: Apart from the main manufacturers, there are in the country a few units, who are classed among steel processing industries, but they are not large enough to contribute anything substantial at present. If scope of these units is enlarged, they could make a valuable contribution to the development of this industry. They should either concentrate on the manufacture of machine tools or give it up altogether. They are now dividing their energies in different fields with the result that their output is small and uncertain. These units do make graded machine tools, but their equipment has to be modernised and staff trained for the production of modern machine tools.

Small Scale Industries: There are also a number of units in the small scale sector especially in places such as Batala, Ludhiana, Calcutta and Coimbatore. These shops, which are generally one-man shows, make ungraded machines and in the present context of shortage of machine tools sell them profitably. It will be in the interest of the country to develop the skill of these people and persuade them to make graded machine tools by giving them technical know-how and financial assistance.

Terms Of Reference No. (5)

"To review the existing capacity to design machine tools, to survey the facilities available for training machine tool designers and suggest ways and means of helping the industry in securing training facilities at home and abroad for such staff."

Design Facilities: The greatest lacuna in the development of the machine tool industry is the absence of original design technique. The existing talent for machine tool design in the country is negligible. A beginning has been made at Machine Tool Prototype Factory, Ambarnath, to develop a section for the designing of machine tools. The Hydraulic Surface Grinder now in the prototype stage and a few other machines they propose to manufacture have been designed by them. The other unit in the public sector has now formulated plans to develop gradually its own designs. In the private sector, each factory has a design office, but the development of designs is generally not original. Many firms have tried to copy the designs of foreign manufacturers. But even this takes time. By the time the copied product is ready for the market, the original design itself becomes obsolete. Messrs. Investas have evolved an original design for a radial drill. The staff available for such design work is generally not very experienced and consequently the designs developed are none too modern. It may also be mentioned that apart from designers of machine tools, the designers of jigs, fixtures and tools are few. Many of the jigs and tools are fabricated by various shops without any formal design, and could be better designed by specialists trained for the purpose.

What has been stated regarding the facilities available for machine tool design, applies equally to training facilities for design work.

Suggested Design Training: It has been found that

the selection of designers and their training is a difficult process. It is not always that a candidate with high academic record or otherwise brilliant makes a good designer. The present practice is to select a large number of men and retain such of those found suitable for design engineering, transferring the others to wherever they are better suited. These trial and error methods have many disadvantages and should be replaced by modern scientific methods of selection. Even during the initial selection of a candidate, his aptitude for design must be tested. In the opinion of the Committee the requisite tests conducted in some of the more industrialised countries could be tried with advantage.

The training of designers must include practical experience within the shop. Any attempt at centralising this training would lead to the development of a theoretical designer, requiring additional practical 'indoctrination'. If the designer is attached to the shop, he would know the shortcomings of the plant and his designs would take into account the practical difficulties in production. As Indian talent in this particular line is at present meagre, it will be necessary to have well-trained foreign designers in each manufacturing unit to impart training.

Particular attention should be given to engage the services of only first class designers from abroad. Able Indian understudies with adequate practical experience should be attached to these men, so that they could take over eventually. At the same time, carefully selected young engineers should be sent to factories abroad for necessary design training. The 'design aspect' appears to have been missed in many schemes that are now in operation. It is suggested that Government should examine schemes with particular reference to training facilities for design.

Apart from training designers as stated above, designers of a higher calibre would be required to ensure proper growth of the Machine Tool Industry as well as the general Engineering Industry. Such a strata of capable designers can grow only in a healthy atmosphere of mutual exchange of ideas at their level and exchange of information with their counterparts in other industrialised countries. A Post-Graduate Institution where regular courses of a higher standard and short term courses for specialised designers addressed by eminent international authorities on the subject are available from time to time has to be created in the country. This could be tied up with a research programme for the Machine Tool Industry. In this connection, it is understood that proposals for the establishment of a Research Institution for Mechanical Engineering, are already under consideration of the Council of Scientific and Industrial Research. The combined programme for advanced machine tool design training at post-graduate level and machine tool research referred to above could be incorporated in such an institute. A liberal exchange of students and faculty should be established with the highly industrialised countries. The machine tool manufacturers should associate themselves with the institution and help by exchange of information regarding standards etc.

Terms Of Reference No. (6)

"To study the range of general purpose machine tools required by the various Departments of Government with a view to standardising to the most widely popular requirements, and to examine the feasibility of other Government Departments using similar machines and adopting them as their standards. In carrying out this examination, the Committee will take particular note of the standardisation work already completed by the Railways."

The Committee considered the fact that there existed today a demand for a large number of different sizes in almost each type of machine tool and in many cases these sizes did not differ very much from each other.

It also noted the fact that whilst the overall number of machine tools of each of the types required was relatively high, if manufacture had to be undertaken of each of the sizes now demanded, the quantities in each size would be too small to manufacture economically.

It was therefore felt that if the number of sizes in each type of machine tool was limited it would be possible to increase the batches to quantities where economic manufacture could be undertaken.

In consequence the Committee decided to appoint a Sub-Committee No. 2 to prepare such a rationalised list of machine tools by type and sizes using for their guidance the list of Standard Machine Tools prepared by the Railway Equipment Committee.

The Committee endorses the report of Sub-Committee No. 2 standardising the sizes and the types of machine tools to be manufactured in the country in the Second Plan period and since the country is switching on to the metric system the standardised sizes are given in both the British and metric systems. It is understood that the Railways will also fall in line with the metric system.

The Committee would like to point out that the list of standardised machine tools is only indicative in a general way of the sizes and number of different sizes in each type of machine tool and does not take into account overall design consideration.

It agrees with the Sub-Committee's view that the preparation of detailed specifications covering all essential dimensions would involve considerable research work and it is only after such investigation for each type and size of machine. This work, it was felt, should be undertaken as early as possible by such an authority as is being recommended to be created in the Machine Tool Board.

Table III

1. **Drilling Machines:**

(a) Bench type

	Capacity Inch	M.M.
(i) Sensitive	1/4	6
	3/8	9
	1/2	12
(ii) Production	1/2	12
	3/4	20
(b) Pillar type Production	1-1/4	32
	1-3/4	45
(c) Column type		
(i) Sensitive	1	25
(ii) Production	1-1/4	32
	1-3/4	45
	2-1/2	60/63
	3	75

(d) Radials

			Arm Length Inch	M.M.
(i) Sensitive	1	25	42,60	1000,1500
(ii) Production	1-1/4	32	42,60	1000,1500
	1-3/4	45	54,66	1300,1600
	2-1/2	60/63	60,72,84	1500, 1800,2000
	3	75	72,96	1800,2500

2. **Grinding Machines (Single headed or double headed, with or without Twist Drill Grinding attachment):**

(a) Bench type

Wheel diameter Inch	M.M.
6	150
8	200

(b) Floor type

Inch	M.M.
14	350
24	630
32	800

(c) Cylindrical, Plain/Universal

Swing Inch	M.M.	Admits between centres Inch	M.M.
6	150	18,36	450,900
12	300	18,36,48	450,900, 1200
14	350	36,48,72	900,1200, 1800
20	500	72,96,120	1800,2400, 3000

(d) Surface

Table Sizes Inch	M.M.
18×6	450×150
24×8	600×200

(e) Tool & Cutter

Swing Inch	M.M.	Admits between centres Inch	M.M.
10	250	24	600
12	300	24	600

3. **Hack Saw Machines**

Capacity Inch	M.M.
6×6	150×150
9×9	225×225
12×12	300×300

4. **Lathes**

(a) (i) Capstans & Turrets

	By capacity Inch	M.M.	
	1/2	12	
	1	25	
	1-1/4	32	
	1-1/2	38	
	2	50	
(ii) Turrets	2-1/2	52	Combination turrets similar to Herbet No. 7 Senior or Ward No. 6
	3-1/2	68	

(b) Lathes : Centre (Sliding, Surfacing & Screw Cutting; Standardization is done on the basis of Swing)

Swing Inch	M.M.	Admits between centres Inch	M.M.	Inch	M.M.	Inch	M.M.
10	250	22	560	32	800	45	1250
12	300	28	710	40	1000	56	1400
16	300	36	900	50	1250	71	1800
20	500	45	1250	63	1600	90	2240
28	620	56	1400	80	2000	112	2800

5. **Milling Machines**

It is recommended that the standardisation should be effected in terms of traverses, weight and H.P. of the machine (Metric equivalents are given in brackets).

(a) Plain Milling Machines:

	No. 1	No. 2	No. 3
Weight in lbs.	3,000	6,000	8,000
H.P.	3	7-1/2	10
Longitudinal traverse	20″(500)	28″(700)	34″(850)
Cross traverse	6″(15)	10″(250)	12″(300)
Vertical traverse	14″(350)	16″(400)	18″(450)

(b) Universal Milling Machines:

	No. 1	No. 2	No. 3
Weight in lbs.	3,100	6,200	8,200
H.P.	3	7-1/2	10
Longitudinal traverse	20″(500)	28″(700)	34″(850)
Cross traverse	6″(150)	10″(250)	12″(300)
Vertical traverse	14″(350)	16″(400)	18″(450)

(c) Vertical Milling Machines:

	No. 1	No. 2	No. 3
Weight in lbs.	...	6,500	8,500
H.P.	...	7-1/2	10

Longitudinal traverse	...	28″(700)	34″(850)
Cross traverse	...	12″(300)	14″(350)
Vertical traverse	...	14″(350)	16″(400)

6. Planing Machines (Double column/open sides):

Table travel		Width		Height	
Feet	M.M.	Inch	M.M.	Inch	M.M.
6	1800	30	750	30	750
8	2400	36	900	32	800
10	3000	36	900	32	800
12	3500	48	1200	40	1100
16	4500	60	1500	50	1250
		72	1800	72	1800

	Stroke	
	Inch	M.M.
7. Shaping Machines:	12	300
	18	450
	24	600
	32	800
8. Slotting Machines:	8	200
	12	300
	16	400
	20	500

Terms Of Reference No. (7)

"To suggest the machinery for laying down the standards of performance and the specifications for inspection of the final product in order to ensure that the product measures upto the required quality, and to recommend the most suitable organisation for testing and certifying the products as conforming to the prescribed quality specifications."

Sub-Committee No. 5 investigated this question and their recommendations are fully endorsed by this Committee. These recommendations are:

(a) The Indian Standards Institution is the appropriate authority for laying down standards of performance and specifications for inspection of the final product in order to ensure that the product measures upto the required quality.

(b) In cases where the Indian Standards Institution's specifications and standards of performance are not available Schlesinger's standards should be accepted.

(c) The Committee strongly emphasises the necessity of continuing the D.G.S. & D. inspection to ensure that the machine tool industry maintains the quality of its product. It is imperative that all machine tools manufactured by graded manufacturers should be inspected by a third party (at present D.G.S. & D. Inspection Wing), unless the customer specifically states that he does not require this. Government purchases will continue to be inspected by the Inspection Wing of D.G.S. & D.

The Committee commends the action of Government in offering this free inspection and strongly emphasises the necessity for its continuance. It further recommends that Government make available inspection facilities on a larger scale than hitherto in view of the expected increase of activity in this industry.

(d) The Committee recommends that the Indian Standards Institution should extend their quality marking scheme to machine tools as early as possible. The Committee suggests that all machine tools produced for export may have either a quality certification mark from the Indian Standards Institution or the D.G.S.&D. Inspection Certificate.

(e) The Committee recommends the creation of a Central Registry for the maintenance of inspection records of machine tools and periodical inspection of some of the machine tools installed at works for a period of three years, at six-monthly intervals. This, the Committee envisages, will enable an analysis of performance data under different workshop conditions and show up the deficiencies of design, material and other factors further enabling corrective measures to be taken in future designs.

(f) In order to ensure uniformity of inspection all over the country refresher courses should be arranged for the inspection staff at appropriate places.

Terms Of Reference No. (8)

"To investigate and report on such other matters as the Committee may think fit regarding the development of the machine tool industry in India."

Machine Tool Board: The Committee has recommended a broad-based programme so that existing manufacturers could produce the machine tools in general demand in a short period. When Government accept these recommendations; the individual manufacturers may be asked to submit their phased programme for approval. For the adequate supervision of such plans and the consideration of technical details, it is recommended that Government create a Machine Tool Board. The Board which should include representatives of the manufacturers and users of machine tools has to be a small one to be effective. It should have as its chairman an engineer of high standing and eminence who is conversant with the Machine Tool Industry. This Board should amongst other things scrutinise schemes submitted, examine designs, recommended fair prices for indigenously manufactured machine tools, watch the performance of manufacturing units vis-a-vis the phased programme and recommend to Govt. action to be taken on these and allied matters. The machine tool industry suffers in general from many shortcomings including shortage of essential raw materials, technical aid, proper financing, etc. The necessity for giving top priority to this industry has already been stressed. The Committee would like to reiterate this.

Competition: The programme recommended gives a

monopolistic position to some firms which can lead to certain abuses. These can be overcome by exercising stricter control on the industry. One of the means of exercising such control would be through the Machine Tool Board.

The Committee accepts in principle that an element of competition in this industry is desirable for its healthy growth. However, as the total demand envisaged for 1960-61 for different types of machine tools is not large, a limited competition in certain machine tools like shapers, milling machines, radial drilling machines might be possible at that stage. Until then in view of the restricted demand for machine tools in different types and sizes, it is considered necessary that the manufacture for each product is allotted to only one unit—lathes being the exception. As regards lathes, where the demand is relatively large, greater competition is possible.

Banned Machines: The (late) Tariff Board which had enquired into the machine tool industry had come to certain conclusions regarding the methods by which indigenous industry could be protected. One of these was to increase the rate of import duty on the type of machine tools manufactured in the country and to restrict the import of machine tools to the extent necessary to meet the demand after taking into account indigenous production. Since a general increase in the tariff is likely to hamper the industrial growth of the country, Government thought it advisable not to raise the import duty. It was accepted that import of such types of machine tools as are manufactured in the country should be totally banned. This policy has been adhered to ever since. During the Second Five-Year Plan, it is envisaged that it will be possible to manufacture many more types of machine tools. It may be pointed out that it will not be possible for indigenous manufacturers to compete with their foreign counterparts in the initial stages mainly due to "consumer preference". It will, therefore, be necessary to afford protection to indigenous manufacturers against competition from abroad. The argument advanced earlier by the Government against general raising of import duty on machine tools continues to apply. The only course open to protect the indigenous products from similar imported products is by exercising import control. However, to safeguard the interests of consumers of machine tools, fair selling prices should be based on prices they would have to pay for a technically equivalent imported product. If necessary, certain weightage to cover development charges may be allowed. Where import of any banned category of machines has to be permitted for special reasons, a deterrent in the form of a high duty for these may be considered.

With the total ban on the import of the types of machines produced in the country, Government purchases will also be restricted to the machine tools manufactured indigenously. In this connection the Stores Purchase Committee has already recommended a price preference upto 25%. It is recommended that this proposal be accepted in so far as it relates to machine tools.

Government Ordering Procedure: It has been brought to the notice of the Committee that generally funds are made available to Government indentors only from year to year and these funds lapse in case they are not utilised within the financial year for which they are sanctioned. This results in a rush of orders with the indigenous manufacturers, for the machine tools produced by them, at the end of the financial year. In order to enable the manufacturers to plan their production programme suitably, it is suggested that such of those identors as cannot carry funds to the subsequent years be advised to plan their purchase programme for machine tools well in advance, instead of all approaching the manufacturers almost at the end of the financial year. It is also recommended that as the manufacture of machine tools has been allocated to specified units, there should be an approved rate contract system for these machine tools.

Standard Code: The Engineering Capacity Survey Committee had recommended that with a view to obtain statistics of the different types of machine tools required, these machine tools be classified according to a standard code. The Development Wing has already published a code of this nature and it is essential that all statistics compiled for this trade be kept in terms of that code. The licences issued by the Development Officer (Tools) already bear the code numbers of the various items imported. However, licences issued under the capital goods scheme are not classified in this manner. The Committee recommends such classification be insisted upon or in the alternative the licensing of machine tools be centralised so that satisfactory statistical data could be maintained. The Machine Tool Panel of the Engineering Capacity Survey Committee had recommended a comprehensive procedure for collecting data on machine tools imported. It is recommended that the procedure suggested be adopted without delay.

Blanket Licences: It is also noted that certain industries have been given 'blanket' licences for import of machine tools. In such cases returns as regards the exact types and specifications of machine tools are not available. It is, therefore, recommended that it be insisted at the time of the issue of such "blanket" licences that a return showing the full details of the machine tools be filed with the competent authority before they are cleared by the Customs authorities.

Steel: The Committee has investigated through Sub-Committee No. I the standardisation of the types and sizes of alloy steel required in the machine tool industry. Preliminary talks with the representative of Ministry of Defence have indicated that it will be possible to manufacture these indigenously if the requirements of the machine tool industry are pooled and made known to them. The sizes and types as rationalised by the Sub-Committee and adopted by this Committee are given in Table IV.

Table IV
List of Standardised Steels

Selected Steels	*Nearest Equivalent EN*	*Type of Steel*	*To be used instead of* MPF	HMT	Kirloskar	Investa	Cooper	Praga	*Special Conditions*	*Remarks*
MSF III/1	EN8/EN9	Medium Carbon	In use	C.I.	EN8	EN8	.4/.5C	EN8	.	
MSF XII/6	EN24	1.5% Ni Cr	—	C35*	EN24	EN24	50/60	—	C 0.4 to 0.45	*May use instead of
MSF XII/3	EN36	3% Ni Cr	In use	C 2	—	—	Ni Cr	EN36	C 0.12 to 0.18	
MSF XIV/12	EN30	4.5 Ni Cr	XII/1*	C.3	—	—	—	—	C 0.3-0.4	*Also instead of
Limiting Conditions										
MSF III/I										
Upto 4″ diameter & in special cases 6″			In rolled condition			Minimum economic quantities 10 tons.			Allowance 1/8″ on finished size.	
Over 4″ diameter		...	In forged condition						Allowance ¼″ on diameter.	
MSF XIV/6XII/3-XIV/12										
Upto 6″ diameter		...	In rolled condition			Minimum economic quantities 10 tons.			Allowance upto 2″, 1/8″ on finished diameter size. Over 2″, ¼″ on finished diameter size (in case extra clean surface is required otherwise 1/8″ will do).	
Over 6″ diameter			In forged condition			Minimum economic quantities 10 tons.			Allowance ¼″ on finished size.	

Sizes of rolled stock : Strips of 1/8″ on diameter could be rolled, but where the quantities after bulking of orders are less than the minimum economic quantities then the nearest higher size should be ordered.

Forgings : In case of forging—Forging drawing showing finished size and allowance required should be submitted.

Drop Stamp Forgings: 7 to 8 lbs. stampings on 15 cwt. drop hammer. Minimum wt. of stamping 1 lb. on 7 cwt. drop stamp.

TOBACCO EXPERT COMMITTEE, 1956—REPORT

Delhi, Manager of Publications, 1957. 183p.

Chairman : Shri K. Raghu Ramaiah.

Members : Shri M. Nageswara Rao; Shri R.A. Patil; Shri Mohammad Ayub; Shri Fulabhai D. Patel; Dr. M.S. Patel; Dr. M.B. Ghatge; Dr. T.G. Shirname; Shri M. Abu Backer.

Secretary : Shri R.N. Misra.

APPOINTMENT

The structure of the Central Excise Tariff on Tobacco was examined by the Taxation Enquiry Commission set up by the Government of India in the year 1953. That Commission recommended that the present differential tariff on unmanufactured tobacco other than flue-cured should continue but an exhaustive review of the procedure adopted in the working of the criterion for assessment should be made by an expert committee who should examine and recommend the improvements required in the present procedure. The Government of India have accepted this recommendation and have accordingly decided to appoint an Expert Committee for this purpose. The Tobacco Expert Committee was constituted under the Ministry of Finance (Department of Revenue) vide their Resolution No. 20/8/55-CX, dated January 17, 1956.

TERMS OF REFERENCE

(1) To review generally the departmental procedures now in force for giving effect to the criterion of capability of use for the manufacture of biris laid down in items 91(5) and 91(6) of the Central Excise Tariff on Tobacco other than flue-cured, and in particular to ascertain and report:

(i) Whether the executive concessions in the application of this tariff, granted by the Government of India vide letter No. 9/16-CX(I)/51, dated July 12, 1951, addressed by the Central Board of Revenue to Collectors of Central Excise, read with the Government of India, Ministry of Finance (Revenue Division) Notification No. 23-Central Excises, dated July 14, 1951 have been fully effective in providing the relief which they were intended to give, or whether their scope has, in actual practice, been curtailed by undue regidity in operation:

(ii) Whether these concessions have been satisfactorily operated or not in different regions of the country, with special reference to—

(a) the classifications of tobacco under the various categories laid down in the said letter;

(b) "denaturation" (that is to say, treatment of tobacco with foreign ingredients to make it unfit for the manufacture of biris) as a condition precedent to the application of concessional rates of duty;

(c) the extent to which normal movements from one market to another have been affected by the administration of the concessions.

(2) In the light of the observations of the Taxation Enquiry Commission (1953-54) on the subject, to recommend modifications, if any, which are considered necessary in the existing concessions, and in the instructions contained in the letter of the Central Board of Revenue referred to in paragraph 2(I)(i) above, having regard to the legitimate interests of tobacco trade, the security of the revenue, and smooth administration of the concessions.

(3) To consider generally the methods adopted for estimating the produce of tobacco growers for purposes of accounting and assessment, and to recommend measures for remedying the defects, if any, in the existing methods.

(4) To make any other recommendations germane to the objective of the investigation.

CONTENTS

Introductory; Main Features of Tobacco Excise; Assessment of Tobacco; Issue of Questionnaire; Working of the Capability Tariff; Suggestions; Recommendations; Estimation and Accounting of Tobacco Crop; Losses in Storage, Transit etc.; Adjudications, Appeals and Settlement of Disputes; Miscellaneous; Summary of Conclusions and Recommendations; Minute of Dissent; Appendices; Tables 1 to 12.

CONCLUSIONS AND RECOMMENDATIONS

The manner in which lists of varieties have been classified for purposes of assessment under the present scheme, is neither uniform nor scientific, and is not easy to follow. The existence of a large number of varieties, and the several physical forms in which each is consumed, the same variety being often known by different names in different areas, renders a comprehensive listing extremely difficult, and gives rise to considerable confusion and consequent assessment disputes.

The present procedure does not permit movement of lower rated tobacco, moving from one lower rated area to another, through an intervening area where the same variety is liable to assessment at the higher rate, except on payment of the differential duty. Difficulties in movement of lower rated tobacco from one Collectorate to another, where it is similarly classified, still exist in some areas.

Classification of varieties for assessment at different rates in different areas has contributed to the flow of trade in tobacco in certain varieties from higher rated to lower rated areas, has given unfair advantage to operators in certain areas over similar operators in other areas, and has been discriminatory against tobacco grown in certain areas resulting in accumulation of stocks and causing considerable dissatisfaction in contiguous areas where the same variety is classified differently. The size of the area prescribed in the Central Board of Revenue's letter No. 19/16-CXI/51 of the July 12, 1951, is arbitrary and has, in practice, not been uniformly adhered to. Malpractices and evasion have occurred by smuggling of lower rated tobacco to areas where the same variety is assessed at the higher rate.

No uniform or rational method has been followed for ascertaining the extent of actual use of multipurpose varieties consumed in biri-making, nor is any such method practicable. Most varieties are capable of use in biri-making. Disputes under the existing scheme are not capable of being objectively solved.

Alterations and additions to notified varieties have been made too frequently creating a degree of uncertainty in the tobacco trade.

There is no satisfactory method of denaturing tobacco so as to make it unusable for biris without at the same time affecting its quality, saleability, etc. The scheme of denaturation, therefore, has not been quite effective in checking leakage of revenue. It has also caused hardship to the trade. As a result it has been availed only by a very small section of the trade.

The relief contemplated in the scheme of July, 1951, has not been fully implemented.

Chapter V

Various suggestions were considered.

A flat rate of duty for all tobacco, or a tariff based on the actual use of tobacco, is not practicable.

Neither a qualified nor a straightforward *ad valorem* tariff for unmanufactured tobacco is practicable under the existing conditions.

No scheme to relate the rate applicable to the extent to which tobacco has been processed is workable.

There is no valid reason for abandoning the principle of a higher rate of duty for biri and a lower rate for hooka, chewing, snuff etc. tobacco.

Chapter VI

No method of classification is feasible under existing conditions which will be completely objective and fair as there is no absolutely or readily recognisable standard for capability or otherwise of any specified variety for biri-making.

It would be incorrect to classify all forms of the botanical type Nicotiana Rustica as incapable of use in biri-making.

Mere storage does not render tobacco incapable of use in biri-making.

No generalisation is possible as to which varieties are wholly 'chewing types'.

The only workable classification under the existing tariff is that based on the physical form of tobacco which is readily verifiable.

(a) All forms of tobacco dust, Rawa which passes through a seive of 1/16 in. mesh or finer, uncrushed stems, and all whole leaf varieties in the form of bundles, Judis, hanks, twists, Rassa or rope and indee, in any form, whether stripped or not, but in which the whole-leaf is intact, and broken bits of whole leaf tobacco incidental to its handling and packing, should be treated as incapable of use in biri-making and assessed at the lower rate if presented for assessment in these forms.

There is hardly any risk of biri types of tobacco being cured and presented for assessment in whole leaf form to claim assessment at the lower rate. Revenue risk by processing, after payment of duty, whole leaf types for biri-making is negligible.

(b) All broken leaf grades, and crushed stems to tobacco of size 1/16 in. to 1/4 in., should be classified as capable of use in biri-making and therefore, assessable at the higher rate.

(c) As certain inferior varieties of broken leaf forms of tobacco may be adversely affected by this method of classification for assessment, relief should be provided by permitting any type of tobacco to be converted into Rawa or dust for claiming assessment at the lower rate.

(d) Ratoon of tobacco should be classified for assessment on par with the main crop of the same tobacco in the same physical form.

Classification based on physical form is acceptable to majority interests as an improvement over the present methods and is administratively advantageous.

The proposed schemes of classification based on physical form will have a healthy effect on the tobacco industry and yield substantially higher revenue. There is, therefore, a case, on adoption of this basis of classification, for reduction of the gap between the two rates of duty, which would not only give relief to the broken leaf grades, but would further render unprofitable processing of lower rated whole leaf varieties for use in biris.

Chapter VII

Incidence of leakage of revenue is higher in sparse growing areas than in heavy growing tracts. While no accurate estimate can be made, the leakage is substantial. It is not serious in V.F.C. tobacco.

The special scheme operating in certain areas of U.P. and Rajasthan for licensing of growers by village revenue officials has proved a failure.

Reduction in non-productive workload of officers can be achieved if growers who grow tobacco only for their personal and domestic consumption are exempted from registration. The maximum size of holdings to be so exempted should depend on the average yield in the exempted area.

In other areas an improvement in control can be achieved by

(i) timely registration of growers;

(ii) saving avoidable labour by reduction in the scale of compulsory verification of departmental records with local revenue records;

(iii) accurate crop survey, using measuring tapes where necessary;

(iv) carrying out crop surveys on an increased scale;

(v) a proper appreciation of extent of damage due to natural occurrences;

(vi) noting crop condition on a substantially increased scale and in a uniform and fuller way; and

(vii) devising ways of keeping the producer informed of the official estimates of crop expectations.

The tendency of curers to under-declare their cured tobacco is on the increase. Present methods of control are not fully effective in checking leakage specially in areas where jurisdictions are unmanageable. Control over curers can be improved by—

(i) provision of portable weighing scales to the staff;

(ii) weighment of curer's produce on an increased scale and with due regard to the size of individual's produce, the record of weighment being also witnessed;

(iii) speedy collection of annual returns by rationalising staff with reference to workload; and

(iv) adoption of firm methods for penalising curers who under-declare their produce.

The allowance of duty free tobacco for personal consumption of growers should be given on a uniform scale over as large an area as possible. In very sparse growing areas a more liberal scale of allowance would lead to saving in non-productive administrative costs.

No amendment of Rules 15, 16, 36 and 37 of the Central Excise Rules is necessary. The steadily worsening position of duty assessed remaining in arrear calls for determined efforts.

Unwieldy jurisdiction and insufficient preventive activity are partly responsible for inadequate control over growing and curing and should be remedied.

Transport should be provided to supervising officers in areas of high revenue potential and to primary workers with large or difficult jurisdictions for improving control and imparting confidence to the trade.

The time limit under Rule 27 should be enhanced to December 31, and provision made ro authorise local officers to allow extensions in individual cases on the lines of the procedure for warehoused tobacco.

Chapter VIII

Administrative action is necessary to minimise delays in adjudication of technical cases.

Adjudication of losses in storage of varieties normally tied in bundles, judies etc. can be done more satisfactorily if account is maintained showing both the number of judies, bundles, etc. and weight.

Unless it is established that loss is due to pilferage, variations in weight of pressed bales of V.F.C. tobacco should be ignored. Duty, if any, on losses due to pilferage should be charged at the lowest of the several rates applicable, unless it can be established that the tobacco pilfered was used in cigarette manufacture.

Fixing uniform maximum scales for condonation of losses is impracticable in absence of common standards of quality, moisture, etc.

The suggestion of not allowing any abatement for losses in tobacco warehoused has met with widespread opposition. The present practice of condoning losses should continue but efforts should be made to improve the methods of ascertaining normal losses.

Experimental data on which adjudication of loss cases is at present done is not adequate and there is need for revision of the technique of experiments. Experimental observations should be conducted and analysed in a scientific and uniform manner in all major tobacco warehousing centres to provide more reliable guidance. Adjudication of loss cases should be done after full proper appreciation in each case of all factors that affect losses. In a minute of dissent, three Members have advocated trial of the proposed scheme under which no abatement is to be allowed except for duty on refuse etc. destroyed.

In adjudication of transit losses, the extent of moisture added at the despatching should be taken into account, and steps should be taken to ensure that this data is available to the adjudicating officer.

Adjudication of losses in processing under bond should be based on the results of experimental observations.

Annual stock-taking results calculated on prorata weighment are not sufficiently accurate to warrant imposition of penalties for losses not condoned. While the present technique of annual stock-taking may continue, the result of stock-taking should be noted to provide data for decision after final clearance of each lot.

Chapter IX

It is unnecessary to set up separate machinery for initial decisions in technical cases.

Requiring deposit of amounts adjudged payable before consideration of an appeal is an important revenue safeguard and should remain, but the alternative of furnishing acceptable security or surety in lieu of cash deposit should be allowed.

Taxation Enquiry Commission's recommendation for setting up a Tribunal to decide revision petitions against the Collector's and the Central Board of Revenue's appellate orders should be implemented.

Advisory Committees of Collectors of Central Excise should be formed without avoidable delay. Formation of similar committees for Assistant Collectors and Superintendents may be considered after experience of working of Collector's committees.

Subordinate supervisory officers should have informal discussions of the industry's difficulties and specially invite grower's/curer's representatives at such discussions.

The Handbook of Tobacco Excise should be made available in Hindi and important regional languages.

Chapter X

There is genuine hardship arising from the State Sales (including Purchase) Tax Laws and the varying methods and practices in their administrations. Repercussions of some are likely to be unfavourable to Indian tobacco in export markets also. A solution along the lines recommended by the National Development Council will remove most of the present difficulties.

Agricultural Export Cess should be waived on samples of tobacco exported out of India.

Varying interpretations are current regarding processing operations permissible in warehouses. To remove certain obvious hardships in this matter, instructions to secure uniformity are necessary.

Where an applicant for a warehouse licence furnishes security or acceptable surety for his bond, verification of his own solvency is an avoidable and unnecessary formality and should not be necessary.

Requests for clearances for destruction of tobacco should be speedily attended to.

The date of first warehousing of tobacco should continue to be shown on covering excise documents.

Weighment Registers showing a record of all weighments done should be maintained.

Revenue payments by cash or cheque are accepted directly at some offices of the State Bank of India. There should be similar facility at other Centres.

Stock challenges should be so done that tobacco is not damaged.

Delays in attending warehouses to take account of receipts and to supervise removals should be eliminated.

Operations permissible to curers to prepare their produce for marketing should be uniformly allowed.

Arrangements should be made urgently to ensure supply of Government stationery to Central Excise Officers.

EXPERT COMMITTEE ON THE FOREST RESEARCH INSTITUTE AND COLLEGES, DEHRADUN, 1956—REPORT

New Delhi, Ministry of Agriculture, Department of Agriculture, 1956.

Chairman : Prof. H. G. Champion.
Members : Prof. M.S. Thacker; Shri M.D. Chaturvedi; Dr. B.P. Pal; Shri C.R. Ranganathan.
Secretary : Dy. Secretary in the Ministry dealing with 'Forests'.

APPOINTMENT

The Estimates Committee of Parliament, in its Sixth report 1953-54 relating to the Forest Research Institute and Colleges, recommended inter alia that in order to assess the actual achievements of the Institute from time to time, steps should be taken to appoint a Board of eminent scientists and representatives of the Industry to conduct periodically an "Achievement Audit" say after every 3 or 5 years. The recommendation was considered by the Central Advisory Board on Forest utilisation at its meeting held in January 1954 and although it was felt that this Board was already performing the functions referred to by the Estimates Committee, the recommendation was brought to the notice of the Executive Committee of the Board for the specific attention. The Committee supported the suggestion of the Estimates Committee and recommended that an ad-hoc Committee be set up to assess the research work done at the Forest Research Institute and Colleges periodically say after every three to five years. The Government of India accepted the recommendation and in their Resolution No. F. 19-29/54, dated January 31, 1956, appointed an Expert Committee.

TERMS OF REFERENCE

The terms of reference of the Committee were as follows:

(i) To review the progress of research done during the past five years;

(ii) To study the organisation of the Forest Research Institute and suggest improvement;

(iii) To study proposals for improving the quality and progress of research;

(iv) To advise on steps to be taken for ensuring efficiency in the context of investigations;

(v) To advise on steps to be taken for establishing liaison with other research institutions so as to derive advantage from their work and avoid duplication of research; and

(vi) To advise on steps to be taken to secure publicity and quick application of the result of research.

CONTENTS

Introduction; Historical Background; Origin of Research Programmes; Review of the Work of the Research Branches; Central Services; Suggestions received from other Organisations; General Comments on the Research Work of the Institute; Organisation: (i) Existing set-up, (ii) Comments and Proposals, (iii) Liaison with State Forest Departments, Industry and Research Institutes; Staff; Accommodation and Equipment; Linkage with Education; Acknowledgements, Summary of Recommendations.

RECOMMENDATIONS

The chief recommendations of the Committee are as follows:

Replacement of the post of Director of Education by a post of Deputy President of Forest Research and Education.

Replacement of the post of Personal Assistant to the President (at present also holding charge of a Branch) by a post of Deputy President for Forest Products.

Creating of a new Section for Timber Extraction in the Forest Engineering Branch.

Organisation of a strong Section for Forest Genetics to be initiated by a well-known specialist from abroad who should train an Indian officer to succeed him.

Creation of a new Section for Forest Influences in the Silviculture Branch maintaining close liaison with soil conservation and desert research.

Creation of Wood Working Section under the Composite Wood Branch.

Re-organisation of the activities now allotted to the Minor Forest Products Branch, linking up more closely with the Biological Branches and limiting the chemical work to analysis on standard techniques.

Revision of the present allocation of duties to the Publicity and Liaison Officer and appointment of a Public Relations Officer in his place. Besides assisting in the translation of research into production, this officer should be responsible for educational and promotional work with a view to bring home to industry the importance and usefulness of the results obtained. He will also be incharge of some of the general services of the Institute like photography and printing and publication.

As a beginning, it is recommended that the Research Centre at Bangalore under the Government of Mysore should be taken over and developed as a Regional Station for utilisation in the South together with the study of spike disease, working in close liaison with the Indian Institute of Sciences and the Central Virus Research Laboratory at Poona. Similarly the Forest College at Coimbatore should be developed as a base for regional research in the biological and silvicultural fields. On the basis of the experience gained with these Centres, similar regional stations could be developed latter in other regions such as north India, the Himalaya and the Dry West India regions.

Abolition of the cadre of Junior Research Officers of the Class II and the constitution of an integrated Class I service with a proper structure on the lines of the established Central Services with provision for officers passing from the Junior to the Senior scale automatically after a certain period of service subject to work and conduct being satisfactory. A flat rate of special pay should be attached to those holding administrative charge of full-fledged Branches.

Liberalisation of the deputation terms for Forest Officers appointed at the Institute by granting a special pay of not less than Rs. 250/- in addition to their pay in their respective State cadres and the institution of about a dozen Research Studentships of the value of Rs. 200/- per month for post-M.Sc. students and Rs. 400/- for post-D. Phil. students.

The provision of a new centrally located and properly designed building for housing the Central Library and records.

More adequate arrangements for collaboration with National Laboratories and other institutions engaged in similar scientific research, closer liaison with industries using forest products and closer co-ordination with the State Departments.

AMBAR-CHARKHA ENQUIRY COMMITTEE, 1956—REPORT

New Delhi, Ministry of Production, 1956. 489p.

Chairman : Production Secretary.

Members : Shri S.V. Aiyer; Shri H.B. Bhar; Shri Krishandas Gandhi; Shri Gyanchand; Shri A.S.E. Iyer; Shri Purushottam Kanji; Shri S.S. Khera; Shri C.J. Soneji; Shri Morarji Vaidya; Shri S.R. Vasavada.

Secretary : Shrimati P. Johari.

APPOINTMENT

The Ambar-Charkha Enquiry Committee was constituted under the Ministry of Production, Govt. of India vide their Resolution No. 12-Cot. Ind. (1)(3)/55, dated March 5, 1956.

TERMS OF REFERENCE

(a) Whether the different tools or machines comprising the Ambar Charkha set are capable of being worked with hand;

(b) Whether a normal adult can work them for eight hours, with reasonable intervals of rest, say 15 minutes after every two hours and a recess of one or two hours after four hours, without any particular feeling of fatigue;

(c) Whether the Charkha can give a production of about eight hanks of yarn, starting from the carding of cotton; or a production of about 16 hanks if the rovings are separately prepared and supplied for eight hours' effective work, by a person who has received training for six weeks and has regularly practised on the Charkha for a further period of six weeks;

(d) Whether the tools or machines are capable of producing yarn of coarse, medium and fine counts with necessary adjustments, the range being six to 18, 18 to 32 and 32 to 48;

(e) Whether the yarn is fairly even for the purpose of weaving on handlooms i.e., it does not result in too many breakages while passing through the roads, because of variations in the counts;

(f) Whether the yarn is fairly strong for the purpose of weaving on handlooms, i.e. it does not give any particular difficulty in sizing and weaving; whether it is capable of being woven more or less as easily as the average reeled yarn available to handloom weavers and with more or less as much speed;

(g) The availability of different varieties of cotton for producing different counts of yarn and to indicate which varieties of cotton are suitable for spinning different counts with the Ambar Charkha set;

(h) What counts of cloth of specified reeds and picks could be woven on the handloom from Ambar Charkha yarn and which from mill yarn;

(i) The percentage of waste at different stages in spinning and weaving compared with similar wastage in producing mill yarn of identical counts from the same variety of cotton.

CONTENTS

Introductory (Genesis; Appointment and Terms of Reference of the Committee; Assumptions; Procedure of Enquiry); Conclusions and Recommendations (Conclusions; Recommendations); Technological Aspects (Laboratory Tests; Field Tests; Miscellaneous Tests; Data Available; The Ambar Charkha Set; Quantitative Production of Yarn; Count Range in Ambar Yarn; Quality of Yarn and its Weavability; Texture of Ambar Cloth; Availability of Cotton and Varieties of Cotton Suitable for Ambar Yarn; Wastage in Spinning and Weaving; Tables I-V); Economic Aspects (Subsidy for the Production and Distribution of Ambar Charkha; Working Capital Required for the Manufacture of Ambar Charkhas; Wages of Spinners Operating the Ambar Charkhas; Cost of Production of Yarn; Difference in the Cost of Supplying Yarn to Handloom Weavers as between Yarn Manufactured by the Ambar Charkha and Yarn Reeled by the Mills; Subsidy; Working Capital Requirements for the Production of Ambar Cloth: Cost of the Programme); The Proposal: Programme and Organisation (Acknowledgements); Appendices: Summary of the Ambar Charkha Programme of the All India Khadi and Village Industries Board Based on the Board's Pamphlet on the Subject; Questionnaire Issued by the Committee on the Technical Aspects of the Ambar Charkha; Questionnaire Issued by the Committee on the Economic Aspects of the Ambar Charkha; Replies to the Questionnaire on Technical Aspects; Ahmedabad Textile Industry; Research Association; The Director, Technological Laboratory, Central Cotton Committee, Matunga; The Principal, Central Textile Institute, Kanpur: Replies to Questionnaire on Economic Aspects: Director of Industries, West Bengal; Director of Industries, Punjab; Director of Industries, Madras; Director of Industries, Vindhya Pradesh; The All India Khadi and Village Industries Board; Ahmedabad Textile Industry's Research Association; Dr. D.R. Gadgil; Director, School of Economics, Bombay; Reports of the Laboratories on the Tests Carried Out on the Ambar Charkha, Ambar Yarn and Ambar Khadi; Interim Report of A.T.I.R.A. dated March 2, 1956; Supplement to above; Interim Summary Report of A.T.I.R.A.; Final Report of A.T.I.R.A.; Report of the Matunga Laboratory; Report of the Principal, Govt. Central Textile Institute, Kanpur; Report of the All India Khadi and Village Industries Board on the field tests carried out on the Ambar Charkha under the "Ambar Charkha Pilot Project Scheme"; Notes on Inspections made by the Committee: Results of Weaving Tests on Yarn Produced in the Parishramalaya under the Board; Pilot Project Scheme: Report of Shri S.R. Vasavada, Member of the Committee; Report of the Principal, Govt. Textile Institute, Madras; Report of the Director of Industries, PEPSU; Report of the Joint Director of Industries, Kanpur; Report of the Matunga Laboratory; Statistical Data collected by the Committee's Secretariat in respect of the Performance of 84 Parishramalayas under the Board's Pilot Project Scheme; Report on Sampling of Performance data in the Parishramalaya at Meerut; Miscellaneous Letter No. A.C.C. dated May 10, 1956 addressed to the Khadi Board, seeking clarification on certain points arising out of the Ambar Programme; Letter No. E.C.R./A.C./56, dated May 17, 1956 from the Khadi Board in reply to above; Report from the Ahmedabad Textile Industry's Research Association on the Charkha produced by M/s Sunder Das Saw Mills, Bombay; Correspondence between the All India Khadi and Village Industries Board and the Office of the Textile Commissioner on the scope of the experiments conducted at A.T.I.R.A. and the Technological Laboratory of the Central Cotton Committee at Matunga; A Note on Khadi Prepared by the Secretariat of the Committee.

RECOMMENDATIONS

The experimental steps of the scheme should continue for some time longer; experiments should be on an increasing scale, in keeping with our other recommendations.

Both intensive and extensive efforts should be made for improvements in the design of the Ambar Charkha, both in the spinning unit and in the Belni. A design competition for the spinning unit, to conform *inter alia* with Gandhiji's specifications should be organised by Government.

Much more experiment and testing should be done on productivity of yarn on the Ambar Charkha, to see if it can be more than six hanks a day, after three months of training and practice.

Charkhas should be adequately tested for quality and performance, before being used for production.

Government should immediately set up a Textile Research Centre adequately equipped and staffed, mainly devoted to decentralised spinning and weaving; with regional centres to be set up in due course.

There should be an annual review of the progress and further prospect of the scheme, with special attention to technical improvements, quality of the product, productivity, worker's earnings, subsidy element and the extent of its further needs, prices, organisation and disposal of yarn.

Growing of cotton staples suitable for the Ambar Charkha, 3/4" to 7/8", should be encouraged in all villages as part of a drive for self-sufficiency in the C.P.A. and agricultural programmes.

Experiments should be conducted to reduce wastage in spinning to the minimum and possibilities of re-using or otherwise utilising the wastage should be explored.

The Ambar Charkha should be manufactured on a fully decentralised basis, village carpenters from the Ambar areas should be trained and supplied only with the essential precision parts from a central agency; it should not be manufactured in any central factories or even in a number of manufacturing centres.

The distribution of Ambar Charkha sets should be subsidised to some extent. In the first instance, the Ambar Charkha set should be charged at full cost to the spinner to whom it is supplied, the cost being payable in easy instalments over five years, free of interest.

Working capital should be provided, free of interest, for the manufacture and supply of Ambar Charkhas, at the rate approximately of 50 per cent of the cost of the Charkha sets to be made and supplied in any one year; that is, an amount equal to six months' production.

The daily wages earned at spinning should be kept under constant watch and studied by Government.

The concept of "certification" by the Khadi Board should gradually give place to the concept of a normally decentralised village industry.

Special effort should be directed at every point; towards a target, in the first instance of bringing down the need for subsidy to a total of two annas in the rupee for Ambar cloth.

Working capital should be provided, free of interest, at 60 per cent of the annual production of Ambar cloth; i.e. Rs. 500 per Ambar Charkha set, with a six-monthly assessment of the requirements.

The Ambar programme should be integrated with the Community Project Areas and National Extension Service and run by the C.P.A. wherever a C.P.A. or N.E.S. project is sufficiently established.

Special attention should be given to training of both spinners and instructors. Training should be regularly systematic and sufficient.

At the end of the three months' training, every spinner should have an Ambar Charkha set in his home for immediate use, without break.

Training should culminate in a test and certificate of proficiency.

The full cost of training should be met by the Government.

The existing Khadi looms should also go over to Amber yarn, as part of the first phase of the programme and the traditional charkha should be progressively replaced by the Ambar Charkha.

Subject to organisational problems being solved in a practical manner, members of weavers' families should be trained and supplied with Ambar Charkhas in preference to others; at least 75 per cent of the spinners (other than the present spinners of traditional Khadi yarn) should be from weavers' families, until nearly all such families have been provided with at least one, preferably two, Ambar Charkha Sets.

The Scheme should be progressively decentralised. The Central agency (Government or the Khadi and Village Industries Board) should limit its functions to

(a) allotment of grants, subsidies, loans;

(b) advice and directions on technical and organisational matters;

(c) research and testing;

(d) a Directorate to watch and assess the progress for two years;

(e) coordination between the decentralised agencies;

(f) export;

(g) certification to the extent necessary.

Government should set up a special section or a Directorate strongly staffed by persons qualified and experienced in the technical aspects, economics, statistics and administration of large scale organisation of village industries, including community project and cooperatives, to continuously and closely watch the progress of the scheme for the first two years.

The Ambar programme should be organised through cooperatives.

Government should to the maximum extent possible, obtain its requirements of cloth from Ambar cloth; Government requirements should be linked to the production project directly through the headquarters procurement organisation on the one hand and headquarters production organisation on the other.

Sample rooms may be opened under the marketing organisation in important cities and samples of items along with information about rates and ready stocks at different production centres may be kept in the sample rooms in order to secure orders and do wholesale business.

Finishing and stocking centres for Ambar cloth will be needed as production increases. These centres should be planned now; and the possibility of degrees of specialisation examined.

There should be adequate arrangements for quality control of yarn spun in bulk.

THE COMMITTEE ON CONSTRUCTION OF HIGH DAMS IN SEISMIC ZONES, 1956—REPORT

New Delhi, Central Water & Power Commission, 1962. viii, 189p., Maps & Charts

Chairman : Shri Balwant Singh Nag.

Members : Shri George Oomen; Shri P.C. Hazra; Shri A.N. Tandon; Shri O.P. Mittal; Shri D.P. Chatterjee.

Member-Secretary : Shri Kehar Singh.

Reconstituted the Committee as follows:

Chairman : Shri C.L. Handa, Member (D&R), C.W. & P. Commission.

Members : The Chief Engineer, Assam; The Special Engineer, Flood and Flood Control, West Bengal; Representative of Geological Survey of India; Dr. A.N. Tandon.

Coopted Members : The Chief Engineer, Irrigation Department, North Bihar; The Chief Engineer, Kosi Project, Government of Bihar; Dr. Jai Krishna; Shri Y.K. Murthy; Shri I.P. Kapila.

Member-Secretary : The Superintending Engineer, Assam Investigation Circle, C.W. & P. Commission, Gauhati.

APPOINTMENT

The Committee on Construction of High Dams in Seismic Zones was constituted under the Ministry of Irrigation & Power (Central Water & Power Commission) at the fourth meeting of the Brahmaputra River Commission held on March 7, 1956.

TERMS OF REFERENCE

To examine the advisability of constructing high dams in seismic zones.

(It was also decided that the committee should examine only those dam sites which were under investigations in Assam and West Bengal.)

CONTENTS

Foreword; Preface for the Second Edition; Background Note; Meetings and Decisions; Implementation of the Decisions; Appendices A to S.

RECOMMENDATIONS

Seismically, it may be stated that the worst areas are the Shillong plateau and the north-eastern corner of the State where the Himalayan range and the Arakan Yomas meet. The seismic conditions, however, improve progressively from east to west along the Himalayas in this region.

The Committee has given consideration to individual dam sites in Assam and West Bengal in the light of the data and other informations available.

In the Kopili Basin, the Kopili dam site is considered feasible, unless some unfavourable features are revealed during the detailed investigations to render the site unsuitable. The result of the detailed investigations conducted so far seems to reveal no favourable feature at this site. The Diyung dam site in the basin has been found to be geologically unsatisfactory. The Barapani and the Killing dam sites in this basin are considered feasible provided, geologically, satisfactory foundations are available.

No dam site has been found on the Barak which can be considered suitable geologically, but seismologically the construction of a dam in this region is considered feasible.

Construction of dams in the Dihing Basin at the tentative dam site on the Noa-Dihing, the Tirap, the Namphuk and the Namchik is considered feasible, provided suitable rock foundations are available at those sites.

If foundation rocks are satisfactory on detailed explorations, the Subansiri dam site would be feasible for constructing a high dam of the height contemplated provided due allowance is made for the high intensity of earthquake shock experienced in this region. It may, however, be pointed out that the Subansiri catchment area is liable to heavy landslide during earthquakes which may lead to rapid siltation of the reservoir.

The Jia-Bhareli dam site, for the height of the dam contemplated, has not been found suitable geologically, apart from its being in highly seismic area.

The Dihang, the Dibang and the Luhit dam sites lie in an area which was the worst affected during the 1950 earthquakes. Here, the intensity of shock had reached X of M.M. scale. There were very heavy and extensive landslides in this region during the 1950 earthquake, and the area is yielding an adnormal silt load in the rivers. Dams on these three tributaries of the Brahmaputra should be built only if these be considered imperative and if geological conditions at all permit.

The Manas dam site is situated in an area which seismologically is as active as any other along the Himalayan boundary fault region. The site has not yet been investigated geologically and the area has not even been geologically mapped. Before any large-scale investigations are undertaken at this site, a careful geological reconnaissance should be carried out first and if suitable rock foundation is available at the dam site, the construction of a dam would be feasible seismically.

The Kulsi dam site lies in an area which, seismically is the worst affected in this region. In the great Assam earthquake of 1897 the destructive intensity of XI on M.M. scale was reached here and small objects were thrown up in the air. This site which has been found otherwise uneconomic, is considered not feasible on seismic considerations.

The area in West Bengal in which the Tista, the Rangit, the Lish, the Gish, the Chel and the Jaldhaka on which dams have been proposed is seismologically not as bad as the area in the eastern part of Assam, provided suitable rock foundation is available at these dam sites. Construction of dam of the height contemplated is considered feasible.

In Assam and in upper parts of Burma severe earthquakes are fairly frequent and violent. Apart from the consideration of safety to dam structures, the life of reservoir has an important bearing in taking decisions regarding the advisability of construction of dams in these regions. Landslides are common and extensive, particularly in the outer Himalayas, where soft rocks of younger formations predominate, and as a result colossal quantities of detritous and silt flow into the rivers, contributed mostly by these landslides and therefore the life of the reservoirs created in such hilly tracts would be comparatively shorter.

NETAJI INQUIRY COMMITTEE, 1956—REPORT

New Delhi, Ministry of Information and Broadcasting, 1956. 70p., Photographs.

Chairman : Shri Shah Nawaz Khan.
Members : Shri Suresh Chandra Bose; Shri S. N. Maitra.

APPOINTMENTS

The Netaji Inquiry Committee was constituted under the Government of India vide Notification No. F. 30 (26) FEA/55, dated April 5, 1956.

TERMS OF REFERENCE

To enquire into and to report to the Government of India

(i) on the circumstances concerning the departure of Netaji Subhas Chandra Bose from Bangkok about August 16, 1945;

(ii) his alleged death as a result of an aircraft accident; and

(iii) subsequent developments connected therewith.

CONTENTS

Introduction; Last Plans of Netaji Subhas Chandra Bose; Air Crash at Taihoku (Formosa); Death of Netaiji Subhas Chandra Bose; Cremation of Netaji's Body; Netaji's Ashes; Treasure; Recommendation; Annexure: Copies of Relevant Papers; Photographs.

CONCLUSIONS

The Committee has come to the conclusion that Netaji Subhas Chandra Bose met his death in an air crash, and that the ashes now at Renkoji Temple, Tokyo, are his ashes. Rev. Mochizuki and the trustees of the Renkoji Temple have already kept the ashes for a number of years. Their services deserve to be recognised. If the ashes are taken to be genuine, Renkoji Temple cannot obviously be their final resting place. Netaji Subhas Chandra Bose died ten years ago. It is time that his ashes were brought to India with due honour, and a memorial erected over them at a suitable place. This we recommend for the serious consideration of the Government of India. It may be mentioned in this connection that influential circles in Japan are considering putting up a memorial to Netaji in that country. If Netaji's mortal remains are honoured, and his ideals kept alive, then one could truly ask "Where is death's sting, where, grave thy victory?"

COMMITTEE TO ENQUIRE INTO THE POSITION OF SAND SUPPLIES FOR PURPOSES OF STOWING IN THE JHARIA/ RANIGANJ COALFIELDS AFTER COMPLETION OF DAMS BY THE DAMODAR VALLEY CORPORATION, 1956—REPORT

New Delhi, Ministry of Production, 1956. 70p., Maps

Chairman : Shri M. L. Shome.

Members : Shri D. V. Joglekar; Shri P. C. Hazra; Shri H. J. Ajwani; Shri S. G. Krishnan; Shri G. S. Marwaha; Shri R. P. Rosser (left India, replaced by Shri A. D. C. Burbidge; Shri Burbidge also left India and replaced by Shri Ll. D. Hughes); Shri S. C. Ghosh; Shri P.H. Pandya.

Member-Secretary : Shri U. N. Jha.

APPOINTMENT

The Committee to Enquire into the Position of Sand Supplies for purposes of Stowing in the Jharia/Raniganj Coalfields after Completion of Dams by the Damodar Valley Corporation was constituted under the Ministry of Production vide their Memorandum No. 25—CI (38)/55, dated March 6, 1956 supplemented by Memorandum No. 25-CI (38)/55, dated May 8, 1956.

TERMS OF REFERENCE

(i) To examine the position of replacement of sand reserves in the Damodar, Ajoy and Barakar rivers in the areas near the Jharia and the Raniganj Coalfields, and to study the effect of the construction of the dams in the Damodar river on the replacement of sand and to report how far the present availability of sand for stowing in the Jharia and Raniganj Coalfields is likely to be affected.

(ii) To examine the extent of sand deposits which may occur at the top-end of the Panchet Hill Dam and to suggest how this sand can be utilised for stowing in the collieries in Jharia.

(iii) To report on the extent to which silt deposit will occur in the areas in the river below the Maithon and Panchet Hill Dams and whether it is likely to affect arrangements for sand getting in the Barakar areas.

(iv) To indicate the possible extent of and the problems connected with the dredging, transportation and distribution of sand to different collieries in the Jharia and Raniganj Coalfields from the top-ends of the Maithon and Panchet Dams.

CONTENTS

Introduction; Discussion of the Report of the Technical Sub-Committee; The Damodar Valley; The Damodar Valley Project; Production of Coal and Requirements of Sand for Stowing in the Jharia and Raniganj Coalfields; Reserves and Replacements of Sand in the Damodar, Barakar and Ajoy Rivers; Position of the Dams and their probable Effects on the Replacement of Sand in the Rivers; Possibility of Occurrence of Silt Deposit on Sand Beds after Constructions of Dams; Consideration of the Problems of Sand Supplies in the Jharia and Raniganj Coalfields after Construction of D.V.C. Dams; Dredging, Transportation and Distribution of Sand from the Deltas at the Heads of the Reservoirs; Recommendations; Remarks by Shri H. J. Ajwani, Representative of the D.V.C.; Appendices from I to VII; two Maps.

RECOMMENDATIONS

Arrangements should be made for the excavation and transportation of about one million tons of sand annually from each of the deltas that would form at the heads of the Maithon and Panchet reservoirs for distribution to the collieries in the Dishergarh Section of the Raniganj Coalfield. We make this recommendation with a view to augment the life of the so-called "fixed' sand deposits in the Barakar and Damodar rivers downstream of the Maithon and Panchet Dams, and to feed supplies to the collieries which may be affected as a result of scour of the sand beds of the rivers downstream of these dams. These arrangements will also provide supplies of sand to the collieries which do not possess a lease of sand beds in the adjoining areas of these rivers.

To supplement the supplies of sand in the Ondal Section of the Raniganj Coalfield from the adjoining areas of the Damodar and Ajoy rivers, arrangements should be made for collection and transportation of sand for distribution to the collieries in this section from the eight mile stretch of the Damodar river downstream of the Dishergarh Section and lying two miles upstream and six miles downstream of the railway bridge on the Adra-Asansol line. As there are no important mines situated in this reach of the Damodar, its sand reserves may be utilised for supplies to the Ondal Section. The proposal for the collection and transport of sand from the upper reach of the Durgapur Pond for supply to this section of the Raniganj Coalfield should be further examined. It may be feasible and perhaps also desirable to transport sand to collieries by a ropeway which may carry coal on its return journey for onward conveyance in barges to the consumers along the Hoogly River.

Arrangements should be made for excavation and transportation of sand from the delta that will form at the head of the Panchet Reservoir for distribution to the collieries in the Jharia Coalfields. Such arrangements will enable supplies of sand to be made to those collieries of this Coalfield which need stowing urgently for conservation but are unable to arrange for supplies of sand for want of space in the adjoining areas of the Damodar River.

For dregding sand from the deltas, sand dredging pumps, mounted on pontoons, of 300 to 350 tons per hour capacity should be installed at each of the deltas above the Maithon and Panchet Dams for the annual supply of one million tons of sand from each of them.

Experts should be appointed to make detailed surveys and investigations:

To study the merits of the two methods of transportation of sand suggested by us so as to enable final selection of one of them;

To find suitable sites on the shore of the reservoirs for the installation of receiving and loading plant and machinery;

To chalk out economical and practical lay-out of the ropeways (i) from the shore of the reservoirs to the Dishergarh group of collieries, (ii) from the unoccupied eight mile stretch of the Damodar to the groups of collieries in the Ondal Section and (iii) from the delta above the Panchet Dam (perhaps from near Sudamadih bridge) to the Jharia Coalfield;

To select suitable sites for central dumps in the Dishergarh Section, Ondal Section and Jharia Coalfield for later distribution to individual collieries; and

To examine the proposal for transporting sand from the upper reach of the Durgapur Pond to the Ondal Section of the Raniganj Coalfield by an aerial ropeway which, on its return journey to Durgapur, may carry coal for onward conveyance in barges to the consumers along the Hoogly River.

In order to reduce the effect of retrogression, at least for the next few years until arrangements for the supply of sand from the deltas are complete, the Damodar Valley Corporation may consider the possibility of increasing flood reserve and thereby decreasing storages in the reservoirs so as to minimise heavy flood releases.

To ensure the continued supply of sand in the Jharia Coalfield, where stowing on a very large scale has to be adopted for conservation of coking coal in the national interest, further construction of large dams in the Damodar Valley should be delayed till the stowing problem is solved. We are, however, not opposed to the construction of small dams for minor irrigation projects and soil conservation in the upper reaches.

To assess the effect of the dams on the river regime, the Damodar Valley Corporation should arrange to institute observations on the effect of retrogression downstream of the dams and collect silt samples from the bed of the rivers to check on any changes that may occur due to the dams. The observations of delta formation and also of the river upstream of the Panchet reservoir where accretion will continue for a long time, should also be done. Sand samples from the bed of the delta should be collected for classification of silt deposits.

The annual rate of replacement in the Ajoy River is not known. As this river will assume importance for the supply of sand to the Raniganj Coalfield, arrangements should be made for recording yearly replacement and increment of sand in this river.

STUDY GROUP ON EFFICIENCY AND ECONOMY IN THE IRRIGATION AND POWER SECTOR, 1956—REPORT

New Delhi, Central Water and Power Commission, 1957. 204p., II.

Chairman : Dr. K.L. Rao.
Members : Shri L.P. Bhargava; Shri S.S. Kumar; Shri S. Venkataraman; Shri E. Kolet; Shri Hari Singh.
Convener : Shri P.C. Suri.

APPOINTMENT

The Study Group on Efficiency and Economy in the Irrigation and Power Sector was constituted under the Ministry of Irrigation and Power on May 18, 1956.

TERMS OF REFERENCE

(i) To make a study of the problems relating to efficiency and economy in the field of Irrigation and Power; and

(ii) To consolidate and crystallise the thinking available for securing these aims and make recommendations.

CONTENTS

Part I: Report—Approach; Investigation, Designs and Estimates upto Pre-construction Stage; Letter from Chief Natural Resources Division, Planning Commission; Construction; Development of Irrigation and Power Benefits; Coordination of Knowledge and Experience and Improving the Instruments of Control and Planning; Organisation, Personnel and Attitudes; **Part II:** Enclosures; **Part III:** Conclusions and Recommendations.

CHAPTER ONE

RECOMMENDATIONS AND CONCLUSIONS

Pre-construction Stage

In Irrigation and Power field, maximum economies are dependent on long-term planning, building up of accurate realistic schedules of rates, standards, forms, etc. to service the planning authorities for the preparation of the estimates and for evaluating and promoting efficiency.

The arrangements in regard to this stage are distinctly inadequate.

Decision in regard to construction plant lay-out and purchase of machinery will also determine the best use of capital resources.

Experience in regard to drafting of tenders and agreements with the contractors should be studied by the CWPC or in the alternative by the Irrigation Departments in the States, whose experience can be coordinated by the Central Water and Power Commission. Other subjects for study may be:

(a) the relative economies in the use of small vs large contractors; and

(b) profits made by the contractors.

Each State should forthwith establish the Water Resources Investigation Unit under the charge of an Officer not lower than the rank of a Superintending Engineer with a proper compliment of the junior staff and an experienced and competent Agricultural Officer fully conversant with the soils, training conditions and agricultural practices in different areas of the State.

The detailed project reports and estimates for the Third Five-Year Plan must be completed not later than the middle of 1960.

The basin-wise water resources report and fixation of priorities for detailed investigations of projects would, therefore, be completed not later than the end of 1957.

It is for consideration if it will not be advantageous to make available to the Central Water and Power Commission the talent of retired reputed construction and design engineers for either working on individual problems or for making basic scrutiny of project reports. They would be able to give adequate time to the job. It will be, however, necessary for the reputed construction design engineers who have retired to keep themselves up-to-date. Measures to secure this end may be adopted.

Construction Stage

The assessment in regard to the present arrangements is summed up in para 8.1.

The factors responsible for economy and efficiency in the construction stage are summed up in para 8.2.

Attitudes

Basically the problem of efficiency and economy is a problem of attitudes.

The attitude of research enunciated by Mr. Curtis, President of General Motors, in para 12, is commended to all the individuals in the irrigation and power field.

The Fundamental Factors

Integration and co-operation between talents; an attitude of persistent search after efficiency and savings in costs, the development of personnel and their integrity are fundamental factors for securing efficiency and economy.

Recommendations made in this report should be continuously and persistently, followed up by concerned authorities and individuals.

CHAPTER TWO

Investigation, Designs and Estimations Upto The Pre-construction Stage

Decisions which may result in maximum economy have to be taken in the pre-construction stage and depend upon the adequacy of investigations, suitable designs and estimates based on up-to-date analysis of the rates/costs thrown up in actual practice.

The examination of projects included in the Second Plan, shows that 40% of the total allocation of Irrigation Projects in the Second Plan is for projects which are not likely to give the prescribed return.

Where a project, not likely to give the prescribed return, may be justified on the ground of regional development, the investigations should ensure that the project selected is the most economical in that region.

Arrangements For Investigations Etc.

It is of the utmost importance that the two processes, that is (i) overall planning of the river system; and (ii) survey to locate areas which need and can take irrigation economically should be attended to.

These two inter-related aims could be secured by the following arrangements:

(a) By undertaking investigations and planning of development of river systems and investigations (including minor irrigation works) through the Irrigation and Power Ministry/Central Water and Power Commission/ State Irrigation Departments; necessary high level arrangement should be added in the CWPC.

(b) Survey in regard to (ii) (including scope for dry farming) to be done with the cooperation of Agriculture Ministry/Agriculture/Revenue Department of the State Governments.

(c) Development Boards in the States (as suggested in Chapter Four) for coordinating (i) and (ii), the corresponding coordination at the Centre to be secured through Planning Commission.

The pace at which investigations have to be done, will demand immediate establishment of the organisation for investigation and the State Boards for development or irrigation in the States.

The results of the preliminary hydro-electric survey have to be confirmed and supported by reconnaissance field work.

The specialised Directorates of the Central Water and Power Commission (Power Wing) should be utilised by the State Governments in regard to system designs, Hydro and Thermal Plant installations and transmission and inter-connection studies. The scope for consultation with the CWPC may be extended to cover

(i) scrutiny of power station specifications of capacities of 10,000 KW and above, and specifications for transmission lines and sub-stations of 56KW and above;

(ii) consultation before awarding contracts for materials and equipments included in item (i) above; and

(iii) consultation in respect of major alterations, in the designs covering item (i) above.

The survey of India must complete the 50′ contour maps for the portion not covered so far by such surveys.

The estimation of irrigation potential of the country should be completed by 1958 for the whole country and the office work followed by field reconnaissance to be organised in collaboration with State Engineers and agricultural experts.

Investigation Of Schemes For The Second And The Third Plans

The investigations for schemes to be undertaken for the Third Plan and balance of schemes included in the Second Plan should be urgently completed.

There is generally a lack of uniformity and inadequacy of investigations before project reports are prepared.

Manuals For Investigations, Preparations Of Estimates And Project Reports

The services of a suitable retired Chief Engineer should be immediately obtained for getting these Manuals prepared on a high priority basis.

These Manuals will serve three aims:

(a) Preparation of project reports with a view to achieve optimum utilization of water resources commensurate with cost;

(b) Preparation of realistic estimates which are correct within a margin of 10 per cent; and

(c) Permit evaluation of experience and working in terms of rates and costs at the construction stage and for the preparation of up-to-date rates and costs schedules for further planning. To secure this aim, as recommended by the Rates and Costs Committee, a uniform list of ingredients should be adopted in estimates.

The following recommendations should be immediately implemented:

(a) The Manuals in draft form may be issued to the State Governments for compliance specially in view of the fact that Irrigation and Power Seminar has already approved the general lines on which these have to be drafted.

(b) Each State Government should send their schedule for investigation of Schemes for the Second Plan etc. to the Central Water and Power Commission. The investigations for the Schemes in the Second Plan must be completed by 1958.

(c) A basin-wise water resources report and fixation of priorities for detailed investigations and projects should be completed not later than the end of 1957, and the detailed project reports and estimates for the Third Five-Year Plan must be completed not later than the middle of 1960.

(d) Necessary vigorous follow-up may be organised at the level of the Joint Secretary/concerned Member in the Central Water and Power Commission and reports submitted to Secretary/Chairman, Central Water and Power Commission.

Planning And Designing Organisation In The States

The State Governments which do not have Planning and Designing Organisations should set them up immediately and the States which have them, should strengthen them to the extent necessary. The Planning and Designing Organisations should be manned by right type of men and enough incentives should be provided.

Realistic Long-term Schedules

In case of Thermal Power, major economies can be secured in designing and silting of Plant.

Long-term realistic schedules should be worked out to secure the best use of capital as has been done by the Central Authority for Electricity in U.K.

Arrangement For Designing Of Dams

Design of dams requires specialised knowledge. The State Governments may not be in a position to maintain full-fledged design offices with all the requisite experts. A Central Organisation like the Central Water and Power Commission should be enabled to obtain the services of personnel who acquire experience in specialised design work in the country in order to make such specialisation available to all the States, when they need.

After the States have prepared their first designs they may be discussed with the Central Organisation for securing the benefit of their coordinated knowledge and experience at the stage of planning and designs.

A book of specifications and designs should be brought out. Deviations from this should preferably be made in consultation with the Central Organisation.

All the major projects in the country costing more than Rs. 5 crores should finalise the broad designs (specification) before any work is started. Specifications of the works must be prepared along with the designs.

Specifications and designs prepared by the State Engineers, may be scrutinised by the Central Water and Power Commission.

While the CWPC should charge the State Governments for specific services like the preparation of designs, the CWPC should be in a position to give a second opinion and advice in regard to minor matters to State Governments without making any charge. The Chairman, CWPC has a certain discretion in this matter. The CWPC should analyse and classify instances of advice sought and given and frame adequate recommendations for permitting flexibility in this matter, to the Ministry of I & P.

The Central Water and Power Commission in consultation with the State Chief Engineers, should prepare the Manuals giving standardised methods of designs and typical drawings of structures such as regulators and falls etc.

Typical designs on dams and power systems should be printed in a form of Manual for reference.

It is of utmost importance that the preparation of Manuals suggested in this Report is expedited. A programme of work should be immediately finalised for this purpose.

(a) The primary role of the CWPC is consultative and advisory to the Ministry of I & P, the Planning Commission and to the States. Chief Engineer in States should feel free to call upon the CWPC for technical advice. Secondly, the CWPC should, on request, be in a position to prepare workable alternatives in regard to detailed designs and take responsibility for such designs. The design wing of the CWPC may be strengthened, if necessary. A scheme should be framed to secure these aims.

(b) The CWPC should be in a position to adequately attend to the task of designing of dams and big structures which require specialised knowledge.

(c) The design experts, of adequate status, should attend to the task of designing without being involved too much in administrative work. Secondly, the design staff should be drawn from or kept in touch with the construction work.

Estimates

The following suggestions should be implemented:

(a) The State Design should collect the latest rate data of projects completed recently or under execution, so that complete break up of important rates involved in the estimates is readily available for application to the estimates of future projects.

(b) The Rates Section in the Central Water and Power Commission should be strengthened to carry further the work done by the Rates and Costs Committee. These units should be equipped to function with adequate speed.

(c) Data in regard to experience of making lump sum allocations and those items of estimate wherein generally, excesses have occurred in the past, should be regularly analysed for making realistic estimates.

(d) Provision in regard to some items such as maintenance, miscellaneous, preliminaries, establishment, T&P etc. have generally exceeded the estimated provision. The estimates for these items should be supported by experience of similar projects rather than on the individual judgement of officers preparing the estimates. This matter has been dealt with in detail in the Report of the Rates and Costs Committee.

(e) It is essential that the basis for the estimates is given in each case to the maximum extent possible.

CHAPTER THREE

Construction

Productivity, employment of minimum real resources and quality are the three main aims to be secured at the construction stage.

The Chart opposite to page 21 is an attempt to indicate the relationship between planning organisation/ personnel and methods with productivity, employment of minimum real resources and quality for construction programme both in the case of departmental construction as well as construction through contractors.

Setting Up Of The Planning Organisation

After a project estimate has been sanctioned, it is imperative that a Planning Organisation should be set up two to three years in advance of the start of execution of works in full swing.

A major cause of the difficulties and infructuous expenditure in the case of River Valley Projects could have been averted, if time had been available for allowing this build up. The schedules to be prescribed for inclusion of such projects in the Plan should take this factor into account. To ensure this build up in regard to projects in the Second Five-Year Plan, is going to be a difficult proposition.

An adequate Chief Engineer is the major factor in the efficient execution of River Valley Projects. He should stay on the construction job till it is completed.

The award of a contract should be preceded by a good deal of planning by the Initial Planning Organisation (see functions in Group A in the Chart to be performed by the Initial Planning Organisation).

In obtaining tenders the plans and specifications should be definite and should give the exact requirements of item of work.

The award of a contract should be scheduled to enable the contractor to make preliminary arrangement of labour and materials so that he can start the work from the commencement of the working season.

The specifications should require the contractors to provide reasonable amenities for the labour, particularly in regard to living accommodation, pure drinking water, enough water for bathing and washing, sewage disposal, lighting arrangements in their colonies and around and medical aid.

In this connection, alternative schedules, are suggested, for the consideration of the Irrigation and Power Seminar.

	Alternative I	Alternative II
1. Works put to tender	Beginning of April	June
2. Receipt of tenders	End of May	July
3. Decision on tenders	July	August
4. Start of season	Beginning of October	

After the work has been awarded the main role of the Administration would be cooperation and vigilance i.e. (a) inspection in regard to progress of work and for quality control; (b) prompt payments to contractors; (c) ensuring adequate provisions of amenities to labour; and (d) combating corruption.

Construction Plant Layout

Before the construction of a project is started it is essential to have a Master Plan showing the plant layout of the project.

This plant layout has necessarily to be prepared by competent men, who have had considerable experience in the construction of similar projects. The Chief Engineer of the project must have a predominant voice in the choice of the plant as he is ultimately responsible for the successful execution of the project. In the preparation of this general plant layout, it is considered desirable that the Chief Engineer associate himself with two other engineers who have got real experience of the type of equipment that is to be used for construction.

It is also suggested that the CWPC should keep records of all those officers who have got special experience in heavy construction and the lines in which they can give useful advice.

The Engineers (not more than three) should be selected out of this panel.

The Plant Designs Section or the Project Designs Organisation should prepare detailed specifications and detailed working drawings for the plant layout. This section should be placed under the charge of a good structural engineer conversant with the equipment for which designs have to be prepared.

This Organisation should have a field unit also attached to it. Specialised specifications can be drawn up with the assistance of firms who deal with such equipment. It would sometimes be found useful and economical to engage specialists from firms on pay rolls for working out detailed designs and specifications; as such firms would have more specialised knowledge on the particular subject than the designs organisation.

The Central Water and Power Commission should publish the construction plant layouts adopted at various projects in the country.

The construction plant layout must be made with the idea of best utilisation of the available machines from other projects. A list of available machines must be made up-to-date by the CWPC by strengthening the P and M Directorate, if found necessary.

The machines should be transferred only in working condition and, therefore, steps should be taken to overhaul the machines and keep them in working order.

Stores

The Stores constitute the major expenditure in River Valley Projects.

In case of Major River Valley Projects, the stores management should be centralised in a separate organisation in the project itself. The arrangements for transport should also form a part of this Organisation.

In regard to stores, like iron, steel and cement which are controlled by the Government of India or which are scarce, the Purchase Organisation should plan ahead in consultation with the various works engineers in order to secure such stores in time.

Estimates in regard to the requirements of spares for each category of equipment should be made on a proper analysis of the record of spare parts consumed by the machines in use on the project. This can be done by analysing the log books and more preferably the service records of machines in the projects, maintained in the workshop and field servicing units. This analysis may enable more accurate assessment of the requirements of different types of spare parts needed during various periods of life of the machine. The Sections operating and maintaining the plant and who are responsible for making appraisal of the requirements of the spare parts should attend to this. This analysis may be pooled together by the CWPC for indicating standards to be observed in making purchase in regard to spares.

Arrangements For Making Purchases For The T & P Sector

During the construction period, a river valley project may be authorised to purchase its requirements directly, provided it has a properly organised purchase unit which should normally be strengthened by one or more experienced purchase officers deputed by the Directorate General of Supplies and Disposals. Such direct purchases should exclude items covered by the Rate/Running Contracts of the Directorate General (S & D). The Project authorities should, at the same time, establish close collaboration with the Directorate General (S & D), so that items which may be required by more than one project and can, therefore, be purchased more economically by the Directorate General (S & D) by bulking, or any other items which they consider can with advantage be dealt with by the Directorate General (S & D) should be purchased through the Central Purchase Organisation.

Scarce Materials

Regarding Cement: In view of the need to expedite small and medium projects for increasing agricultural production, the same priority as has been given to major products, should be accorded to the medium and small projects.

Regarding Iron & Steel: The arrangements in regard to iron and steel for irrigation and power projects should be based on a basis of two years, i.e., for the emergency period. It will, therefore, be necessary to take the following steps:

(1) Devise measures for securing accurate information of the needs for two years.

(2) Analyse the demand in order to see to what extent the demand e.g. in regard to buildings, can be met by changing the specifications.

(3) Secure adequate allocation of foreign exchange for importing iron and steel.

(4) Determine and set up, in time, the arrangements for purchasing iron and steel.

The reason for non-availability of allocated quota and specific steps required to deal with the problems should be worked out. This matter should be dealt with immediately.

The arrangements made in one project with one or two Oil Companies on a long-term basis may be adopted in other projects.

The recommendations of the Rates and Costs Committee in regard to the following may be implemented:

1. Classification and codification of stores.
2. Procurements of stores, formation of a S.P.C. for projects.
3. Accounting of receipts and issues.
4. Standardisation of price of stores.
5. Stores Management.

Construction Plant & Machinery Committee

The recommendations of the Construction Plant and Machinery Committee as indicated in para 11.1 and regarding standardisation in para 11.2 should be implemented.

Accounts

A high-powered committee should be appointed in consultation with the Comptroller and Auditor General of India to re-examine the CPWD and CPWA codes in order to make them suitable for the present conditions.

The Irrigation and Power Ministry, in consultation with the Comptroller and Auditor General, should examine the extent to which the accounts procedure could be safely relaxed in order to give relief to the field engineers from office work.

The Accounting Departments in the projects are not adequately staffed or trained. These weaknesses have to be removed on a high priority basis.

Prompt Payment

The arrangements for payments should be prompt. A systematic analysis of work load involved should be made for proper distribution of load of work and for preparing a time-table to be followed for making payments. Watch should be kept on the actual working of the arrangements through fortnightly reports which should go upto the Chief Engineer. The selection of pre-audit or post-concurrent audit method should take into account the need for prompt payments.

Cost Control/Work Studies/Cost Accounting

The construction jobs are a mixture of the systems of unique-product production and mass production. Under the unique-product production, the basic principle is organisation into homogeneous stages. This organisation is different from craft organisation. The unique-product production does not go by craft skill, but by stage skills, for which integrated teams are required. The basic principles for securing efficiency for such a system of production are:

(a) division of work into homogeneous stages;

(b) the systematic organisation of the work-groups for specific requirements of each stage; and

(c) the systematic training of large number of people to do all the work required within one stage.

The system of cost control for the job, which is a mixture of unique-product and mass product production, would involve work studies and training for the unique-product part of the job and standard costing involved after work studies in relation to mass production part of the job.

The following arrangements are suggested:

Phasing: (a) In the first stage, the supervisors have to train themselves and their workers in relation to specific jobs from time to time and build up skills.

To secure the best results, the primary need, thus, will be to train the supervisory personnel in work studies (method studies, time and motion studies) and T.W.I. techniques for training workmen.

(b) Simultaneously, the accounting section should work out arrangements for relating costs to estimates. This will include preparation of a code as a part of the classification system of accounts.

(c) After the supervisory and work skills, as well as cost accounting, have been routinised, may come the stage for cost control, with a view to further improving efficiency.

The cost control unit may start as a work study-cum-cost accounting unit and develop as a cost control unit.

The skills to be required for this unit will be an experienced construction engineer with accounting statistical bent, an accountant trained in cost accounting and control; an expert in work studies in the initial stages and computors. This unit should service the top-construction executive direct and its forms and reporting system should be approved by the Chief Engineer. Its work has to be coordinated with the accounting.

At the Centre the Cost Control Cell should be able to:

(a) Advise on the organisation of cost units.

(b) Advise on work-studies.

(c) Analyse and build up set or sets of standards on the basis of actual field experience, for control and planning.

(d) Present an assessment of:

(i) comparison between actual costs and estimated costs;

(ii) increase in efficiency or productivity of men and materials in the projects from time to time.

(e) Publish studies.

The experiments mentioned in para 14.1(4) may be initiated on the basis of the advice of selected engineers/ cost experts, immediately by the Central Water and Power Commission.

O & M Unit

A small O & M Unit should be set up to perform the functions.

Inspection And Control

A separate organisation for inspection and quality control should be set up under the Chief Engineer to perform the functions.

Land Acquisition

It is for consideration whether the use of Section (4) of the Land Acquisition Act of 1894 and the cooperation of the Collector do not in practice secure possession of land even without setting the price and the claims.

In case of large projects, the services of a senior Revenue Officer should be obtained for land acquisition work.

Labour Relations

The basic approach and the recommendations in para 18 may be considered.

Public Cooperation

Irrigation and Flood Control programme provides a good opportunity for seeking the cooperation of the people and in this vital field of national development there is vast scope for voluntary effort. Works on which unskilled labour is entirely employed (like the canal systems), should as a rule be done by villagers themselves and not through contractors and that in each village or group of villages, the villagers should be organised into cooperatives taking up the work in their own area.

Education Of Corruption

An analysis of the opportunities for corruption in irrigation and power projects is given in para 21.1.

There is reason to believe that corruption gets well-organised.

Unlike some other spheres, corruption in this sector is almost entirely at the expense of the public exchequer.

An examination of some preliminary data has disclosed that in emergent situations, delegation of powers, without adequate inspection arrangements or spot supervision may lead to misuse of delegated authority and perhaps even lowering of quality. Straightforward attitude for meeting the emergent situations may not be developed in the staff. Instead, misuse of discretion, misreporting of facts may be indulged in the name of speed and thus provide free scope to the corrupt. There is also prima facie reason to believe that accounting arrangements are not adequate to the speed of execution thereby providing greater freedom to the corrupt but lesser scope for supervision and control.

In a large scale construction work, an inspecting organisation should be promptly fed with indicators for scrutiny (e.g. see item 19 in the Enclosure I) by the account and cost control organisation, etc.

Inspection to be effective should be serviced by well-organised intelligence.

In making arrangements for checks and control the aim should be to stop misuse of discretion, preserve initiative and straightforward relaxation of wasteful rule for lowering of real costs by an adequate authority promptly.

There is a good case for regular training in cost-mindedness to all the engineers engaged in construction.

A most useful instrument for controlling corruption is the sound detailed estimates prepared after adequate investigations. Arrangements should be made for securing prompt reporting of variances in regard to specifications, quantities, etc. from the estimates. These should be followed up immediately by field inspections.

Various suggestions for dealing with scope and opportunities for corruption (as analysed in para 21.1) are given for consideration in paras 21.7, 21.9 to 21.13.

To ensure that these measures operate, it is necessary that there should be: (a) will to combat; (b) will to expose; and (c) facilities and time for combating. Secondly, the strategy and organisational arrangements employed for combating corruption by prevention or by punishment. should function in a coordinated manner and with speed.

Para 21.11 and 21.12 indicate the measures for securing the will to combat corruption, the will to expose corruption and for promoting morale.

Honest men, sandwitched between dishonest superiors and dishonest subordinates are very much handicapped and may even suffer for not falling in line with the superiors. It is, therefore, necessary that measures should be devised for retaining the initiative of such honest men for combating corruption. For instance, steps should be taken to ensure that the records of honest persons are not spoiled and that promotions are ordered in a fair and just manner.

A major instigating factor in regard to corruption is the disparities in income and standards of living between public and private sectors.

A study into the failure of contracts in order to improve drafting of contracts may be made by a team consisting of an Engineer and a Finance man. The Ministry of Irrigation and Power may sponsor the study.

CHAPTER FOUR

Development Of Irrigation And Power Benefits

Suggestions for eliminating the time lag between the availability of supplies and their utilisation are given below:

(a) Simultaneously with the establishment of arrangement for overall planning of the river system, a survey in regard to areas which need and can take irrigation should be organised by the Revenue Agricultural Departments of the State Governments.

(b) Development of land should be planned in advance and form an integral part of the Project Report. The report should include an assessment of the steps to be taken for timely development of the steps e.g., setting up of N.E. Organisation and demonstration centres ahead of availability of water, financial assistance, agricultural implements, fertilisers, livestock and seeds. This should be a condition precedent to the acceptance of the project by the Planning Commission. It is recommended that the proposed Manual on "Preparation of Project Reports" should contain a Chapter dealing with this aspect.

(c) Phasing of construction should promote maximum use of water even during construction.

For purpose of (a) and (b) i.e. for ensuring timely utilisation, a Development Board consisting of representatives of Irrigation, Revenue and Agricultural Departments may be set up in each State.

(d) It may be advisable to offer suitable inducements for one or two seasons to educate the peasant for changing over from dry to wet cultivation.

Suggestions for securing maximum irrigation out of water supplied are given in paras 2 and 3.

Development Of Power Benefits

The various causes leading to delays in utilisation of power supplies are given in para 5.

Suggestions for ensuring efficient and economical generation and utilization of power are given in para 6 and include:

Suggestions for obtaining adequate information of requirements, vide para 6(a);

Timely information in regard to availability, vide para 6(c);

Facilities or utilization, vide para 6(b) and (d);

Standardization, vide paras 6(e); and

Coordinated programming in regard to generation and receipt of power, vide para 6(f).

Coordinated Development Power

In order to secure coordinated development between the States in each zone, it is recommended that a Co-ordination Committee consisting of the Chief Engineers for Power, a representative of the Power Wing of the Central Water and Power Commission and Adviser (Programme Administration concerned with the particular zone), should be set up, to: (i) get studies made in regard to coordinated development of power within the zone; (ii) suggest legislative or administrative measures required for bringing about coordinated development; and (iii) advise and other questions which usually arise when power is obtained by one State from another.

A start might be made for constituting a grid in the south where the conditions are favourable. The constitution of State Electricity Boards would facilitate the constitution of such grids which might ultimately be integrated into a national grid.

Maintenance Of Efficiency

The Central Electricity Authority has been requested to make arrangements for assessing the efficiency of electricity supply undertakings owned by the public sector from time to time.

CHAPTER FIVE

Coordination Of Knowledge And Experience And Improving The Instruments Of Control And Planning

The research work done in regard to irrigation should be analysed and reviewed. The Member (Research) CWPC should send a Report on the subject.

The research work on problems of general applicability is not being tackled due to lack of adequate funds and personnel.

There seems to be some duplication of work in different research stations.

Central Water And Power Commission

The primary function of the Central Water and Power Commission is to coordinate knowledge, experience and reseach in regard to irrigation and power in the country and the rest of the world for securing technical efficiency. It has to function as a sort of staff organisation concerned primarily with setting up of standards in regard to investigation, designing, estimation, preparation of project reports, rates and costs and various matters connected with machinery, equipment, etc. and keep these standards in continuous review on the basis of actual experience in the field.

The adequate discharge of these functions would depend on (a) cooperation of Project Authorities/State Governments etc., (b) prompt arrangement for analysis, extension and application of new ideas.

There should be regular arrangement in the Central Water and Power Commission to keep the work of these Committees (Construction Plant & Machinery Committee and Rates & Costs Committee) up-to-date as well as fill up the gaps which can only be filled up by a proper system of reporting and special studies.

The material for the preparation of completion reports (which should highlight new methods of design and construction resulting in increased technical efficiency and economy), should be prepared side by side, as the construction proceeds.

The completion reports should be ready soon after the completion of projects.

One way to secure this object is to introduce in the progress report a section where special development (including the advice given by Consultants/Experts) and experience are reported, say, every quarter or six months.

All the Project Authorities should report to the Central Water and Power Commission for information any new features in design which may have been developed during process of designing particular structures.

The Central Water and Power Commission should also coordinate experience in regard to organisation and methods relating to stores and workshops.

Evaluation Of Progress And Efficiency

The Control Boards should arrange to develop arrangements in regard to preparation of detailed realistic schedules, cost accounting, cost control and standards as instruments of control without day-to-day interference and for securing increased efficiency and economy, if necessary with the assistance of the Central Water and Power Commission.

These arrangements should function as an integrated mechanism which services all the executive levels down to the foreman, as well as, the management levels, i.e. upto the policy makers.

Progress Report

The following additional information should be given in the progress reports:

(i) Availability of construction material.

(ii) Value of stores in hand, whether it is more than the requirements of the projects, and steps taken.

(iii) Whether sanction to estimates is being received in time or whether any work is held up for want of sanction.

(iv) Whether timely payments are made to the contractors (details about the prescribed schedules may be given).

(v) The number of machines working, number at site as stand-by and number in the stores (to give an indication as to whether large number of machinery is being kept in store or idle).

(vi) Results of cost control studies, detailed comparison of the estimates with the actuals and the advice given by consultants/experts (at suitable intervals).

We feel that the Progress Report should further reflect conscious drive for efficiency and economy (i.e., new methods under application or proved methods for securing efficiency and economy).

CHAPTER SIX

Task For The Third Five-Year Plan

As a result of the discussions on this Chapter, Planning Commission has issued a letter (Enclosure 1) to the State Governments, indicating that the size of the Irrigation and Power Sector in the Third Plan may exceed Rs. 1,500 crores.

Targets For Investigation

The arrangements for investigations for projects should ensure availability of fully investigated schemes for irrigation and power worth Rs. 2,000 crores by the fourth year of the Second Plan in order to permit adequate preparation of the Third Plan and for obtaining the best value for capital resources. This implies preliminary investigations of schemes worth Rs. 3,000 crores at least.

According to the Technical Committee on Irrigation and Power, the present condition in most States is that the existing organisation is fully utilised on the execution of various sanctioned schemes with the result that the essential work of investigations and survey is being neglected.

Some of the States are reluctant to invest on investigation of schemes not to be taken up immediately. Unless this attitude is changed and immediate action taken, it will be physically impossible to carry out this basic task, on which primarily depends the best use of our capital.

Even now, perhaps we may be behind time by three to four years.

Recommendations

(a) The CWPC should examine the implications of the task in regard to investigations in terms of organisation, personnel and finances and report in three months.

(b) State Governments should be requested to send their programme and make arrangements for investigation of schemes to be implemented in the Second Plan urgently. Funds, as loans, required for investigation of schemes have been provided for in the Second Five-Year Plan.

(c) A preliminary discussion in regard to organisation for investigation of schemes for the Third Five-Year Plan should be held on the basis of a paper to be prepared by the CWPC at the Symposium of C.B.I. Annual meeting at Bombay.

The Symposium should specifically examine the suggestion made by the Planning Commission that special arrangements for planning, investigation and preparation of project reports may be immediately made.

Organisation For The I & P Sector

Arrangements at various levels for planning and execution in the Irrigation and Power Sector are given in para 3.

List of issues in regard to organisation are listed in para 4.

Delegation Of Powers

The system of delegation of powers combined with the emergency procedure, vide Enclosure 2, adopted by the Bhakra Control Board to the Chief Engineer may be adequate for the scale and the speed of operations, provided limit is placed on the time to be consumed by the emergency procedure.

Suitable Form Of Organisation For Inter-State Projects

In balance, the Control Board (subject to observations in Chapter Six) is a better arrangement than Corporation in regard to an Organisation for construction, maintenance and utilization of benefits of Inter-State River Valley Projects.

On the other hand, we appreciate need for a statutory organisation for maintenance of the dam etc., and for regulating the distribution of benefits in the case of inter-State projects under one man, with adequate staff. The person incharge could be placed under the control of a Committee representing the State Governments and may be the Centre also.

A representative of the CWPC at the member-level should be a member of each Control Board. It is also necessary that a representative of the Irrigation and Power Ministry should be on the Control Board.

In the case of multi-purpose projects the Chief Engineer for power, who has often to secure decisions of Control Board and also to contribute to the decision-making process in the Control Boards, should be a member of the Control Boards alongwith the Chief Engineer for Irrigation.

Relationship Between The Administrator And The Chief Engineer

The relationship in regard to the operation level should be determined on the following basis:

"Where the decision-making process and the staff are mainly or predominantly technical, the head of the organisation should be a technical person, experienced in organisation.

"He should be assisted with administrative personnel for performing administrative functions. Where, however, the administrative functions e.g., rehabilitation of displaced persons etc. are of a size and complexity demanding a high level Administrator, the Chief Engineer and the Administrator should function as colleagues serving a common aim."

The responsibilities of delegation of power to the

General Manager, Bhakra, should be regarded as a model to be adjusted to suit local conditions.

The Secretary of the Control Board should preferably be a whole-time person and may be appointed in consultation with the Board.

Control Boards

Structurally the Control Boards being high-powered and high level bodies of part-time busy members may function as an okeying body. Its membership leaves little scope for supervision of its work. Some of the Boards have dealt with the question of delays by prescribing emergency procedures. They have been able to provide initiative occasionally in addition to coordination, on the strength of their experience gained by them in other Control Boards.

On the other hand, we feel that the problem of the scrutiny of estimates, construction plant layout and phasing placed before the Control Boards for sanction has to be further considered.

There is also need for personal contact with the work in the field.

Recommendations

Scrutiny Of Estimates Submitted To The Control Boards

The scrutiny of the estimates should be concerned with (a) designs; (b) rates; and (c) inclusion of inappropriate items. It was suggested that if the CWPC could be consulted in regard to specification and design, scrutiny in regard to designs at a later stage would not involve delay.

It will be useful to have a Standing Committee of the Control Board which could examine in detail the estimates submitted to them and report in time for the next meeting of the Control Board.

Being high level, Control Boards should equip themselves for self criticism in regard to their own working.

It is suggested that the Ministry of I & P may organise a study of (a) the manner in which the Control Boards have performed their functions; (b) exercise their powers; and (c) the manner in which they have dealt at their level with specific problems and factors (sanction of estimates, corruption, quality control, evaluation of work, arrangements for scrutiny of estimates, speed of functioning, prompt payments to contractors, building up of personnel, team spirit and so on) essential for securing efficiency and economy. Another practical question for consideration is: How many Control Boards should be serviced by a single officer? In the first instance, this study may be only fact-finding and analytical in its scope.

Committee On Plan Projects

The examination of construction project may be concerned with (a) planning; (b) organisation and personnel; (c) bottlenecks and delays; (d) organised attention to productivity; and (e) quality control. Detailed examination through specialists could also be organised in regard to working of the individual departments or aspects of the project administration. It will be, therefore, essential for the teams to be assisted by specialised personnel. Panels of such experts should be maintained.

In the first instance, we recommend, study and not inspection of three types of projects: (1) projects in a preliminary stage, e.g. Nagarjunasagar, Koyna and Rihand; (2) projects in somewhat anvanced stage of construction, e.g. Chambal and Bhakra Dam; and (3) projects nearing completion like Hirakud and Maithon. The aim of this study should be to work out a paper in consultation with the Chief Engineers in regard to what to inspect and how to inspect. The team should, in particular, study the methods and organisational arrangements evolved by the Chief Engineers for assessment, reporting as well as continuous improvement in the working of organisation and methods. The study should concentrate on positive aspects and may not deal with the past, in the first instance, except to draw conclusion for improving organisation and methods in the future.

After this preliminary study is done, many inspection teams may be organised.

Such teams may be set up by the Control Board. The terms of reference and the membership of the teams may be put up to the Committee on Plan Projects for approval.

Inspections should not be made for, say, more than once in two years.

Quality Control

A separate set of officers, solely employed on inspections and quality control, should be appointed. These arrangements (strength, qualifications of personnel, equipment and the manner of functioning, procedures for record and follow-up action) should be prescribed by a Quality Control Manual to be prepared by the CWPC. This unit should function under the Chief Engineer of the project.

A Quality Control Unit at the Centre should be set up to collect information from different projects, analyse and bring important observations to the notice of the Chief Engineers concerned.

It is also for consideration if a Quality Control Squad should be set up in the CWPC to supplement the quality control efforts and the State Organisations in regard to medium projects at the request of the State Governments.

Coordinatian Board Of Ministers

The Coordination Board of Ministers should meet more frequently and the Board should authorise the CWPC to follow-up the recommendations on its behalf.

Irrigation And Power Seminar

A suitable drill in regard to the actual functioning of the Seminars should be worked out for making adequate use of time and the talent brought together.

Committee On Plan Projects

In regard to Irrigation and Power Sector, the implementation of the term of Reference No. 1 (of the Committee on Plan Projects) should be done through the Ministry of Irrigation and Power/Control Boards.

In regard to Function Nos. 2 and 3 the Committee on Plan Projects may ensure that the arrangements are installed where they are lacking and where necessary, provide support and sanction any improvement to existing arrangements.

The CWPC/The Ministry of I&P/Planning Commission

The issues listed in paras 4(d) & 4(e) are being dealt with separately.

Personnel: Forward Man-Power Planning

The Ministry of Irrigation and Power through the CWPC should attend to forward man-power planning as recommended in paras 16.1 to 16.4.

Provision of Experienced/Quality Engineering Personnel

Cooperative arrangements suggested for obtaining or building up personnel with Governments which have established cadres by adding supernumetary posts at the necessary levels at the cost of the needy party are given in para 17.3.

Information in regard to Superintending Engineers and the work they are engaged on, from year to year may be maintained in order to deploy them in the interest of the country as a whole under the auspices of the Coordination Board of Ministers.

The problem of provision of experienced personnel for training and research institutions deserves to be attended to immediately.

The need for regular and persistent build up of personnel, if they have to succeed as teachers seem to be established. For efficient teaching, the ideal combination may be a theorist with adequate field experience and specialisation in one branch of that field.

There should be a joint cadre for the executive side and the teachers etc., who are not required to stay for continuity or specialisation.

In order to attract right quality of personnel for research, the pay scale at the lowest level should be made higher than the scale provided for executive work through further promotions should be made on selection basis after the recruit has been given an opportunity to show himself up as a fellow after some years' work.

Attitudes

An illustrative sample of generally felt attitude is given in para 18.1.

These attitudes are, in part, a heritage of attitudes of static regulatory administration, in part of defensive inhibitions of a specialist who may not always appreciate the new complexities which he has to manage and the need to keep himself under constant reorientation. A Chief Engineer is not a specialist merely, he is an organiser of a complex production assignment. The same is the case with the finance man.

The finance man has to function with a production cost outlook rather than audit outlook.

The engineer has to be trained to be cost-minded and should learn modern methods of management.

The administrator has got to appreciate his role as an integrator of talents.

Practically all have to learn the problems of handling personnel and labour.

That each public servant must spend Government funds as prudently as he would his own, is a fundamental principle for constant application and guidance.

Integration of and cooperation between talents, an attitude of persistent search after efficiency and savings in cost and the development of personnel, are fundamental factors for securing efficiency and economy.

Recommendations

Engineers at all levels must be given courses in cost control, industrial engineering and the senior amongst the profession should reorientate themselves in the methods of management, through seminars, personal visits, contacts and selected reading.

Training in industrial management should be a part of the syllabus of graduate courses.

Experienced middle level finance men with administrative experience be sent to large-scale projects in the country and even to large-scale industrial-cum-commercial organisations abroad to see in actual practice the approach and methods functioning on large-scale enterprises with speed. No successful enterprise, whether in the public or private sector, can afford to ignore the arrangement for financial control. Yet, in large-scale enterprise outside the country, the management have worked out a balance between delegation and supervision and control which permits over 90% of decision making at the operational level.

The Ministry of Irrigation and Power has been equipped with internal yet independent financial advice as a first step towards the adoption of U.K. arrangements (which include a device for obtaining assessment of finance-mindedness of the Administrative Secretary before the Prime Minister). We feel that the arrangement as in U.K. should be fully adopted as soon as practicable.

A Chief Accounts Officer, responsible to the Chief Engineer, should be provided for maintenance of accounts and for giving internal financial advice to the Chief Engineer.

The Finance-Secretary of the State and the representative of the Ministry of Finance on the Control Board should serve as financial advisers to the Control Boards. In order to secure adequate attention, the number of Joint Secretaries in the Ministry of Finance concerned with River Valley Projects may be increased. It may also be necessary to strengthen the State Finance Departments.

FINANCE COMMISSION, 1956—REPORT

New Delhi, Ministry of Finance, 1958. 215p.

Chairman : Shri K. Santhanam.
Members : Shri Ujjal Singh; Shri L.S. Misra; Shri M.V. Rangachari; Dr. B.N. Ganguli.
Secretary : Shri H.B. Bhar.

APPOINTMENT

The Finance Commission was set up under article 280 of the constitution by an Order of the President Vide No. SRO 1285, dated June 1, 1956.

TERMS OF REFERENCE

The Commission shall, in addition to making recommendations as to the matters specified in sub-clauses (a) to (c) of clause (3) of article 280, make recommendations as to the following matters, namely:

(a) The sums which may be prescribed under article 273 as grants-in-aid of the revenues of the States of Assam, Bihar, Orissa and West Bengal, in lieu of assignment of any share of the net proceeds in each year of export duty on jute and jute products to those States;

(b) The States which are in need of assistance by way of grants-in-aid of the revenues of those States under article 275, and the sums to be paid to those States, having regard, among other considerations, to

(i) the requirements of the Second Five-Year Plan, and

(ii) the efforts made by those States to raise additional revenue from the sources available to them;

(c) The principles which should govern the distribution under article 269 of the net proceeds in any financial year of estate duty in respect of property other than agricultural land, levied by the Government of India in the States within which such duty is leviable; and

(d) The modifications, if any, in the rates of interest and the terms of repayment of the loans made to the various States by the Government of India between August 15, 1947 and March 31, 1956.

Additional References

The Government of India, in consultation with the State Governments, have decided that an additional duty of excise should be levied on mill-made textiles, sugar and tobacco, including manufactured tobacco, in replacement of the sales taxes now levied by the State Governments, the net proceeds being distributed among the States, subject to the present income derived by each of the States being assured to it. Necessary legislation will be promoted shortly for the levy, by the Centre, of this additional duty. In this connection the President has been pleased to decide that the Finance Commission should be requested to make recommendations to him as to the principles which should govern the distribution of the net proceeds of this additional duty among the States and the amounts which should be assured to the States as the income now derived by them from the levy of sales taxes on these commodities.

The President has also been pleased to decide that the Commission should be requested to make recommendations to him as to the principles which should govern the distribution, under article 269 of the Constitution, of the net proceeds in any financial year of the tax on railway fares proposed to be levied by the Railway Passenger Fares Bill, 1957, introduced in the Lok Sabha on May, 15, 1957.

CONTENTS

Introductory; First and Second Commissions; Planning and Finance Commissions; Constitutional Aspects; Recent Trends in Federal Finance; Principles of Grants-in-aid; Review of State Finances; Assessment of Needs of States; Distribution of Income-Tax; Division of Union Excises; Grants-in-aid in lieu of Jute Export Duty; Grants-in-aid of Revenues; Distribution of Estate Duty; Union Loans to States; Distribution of Additional Duties of Excise; Distribution of Tax on Railway Fares;

Miscellaneous: Recommendations; Conclusion; Acknowledgements; Appendices from I to XIII.

RECOMMENDATIONS

Our recommendations to the President are set out below:

Under article 270 of the Constitution—

(a) The percentage of the net proceeds in any financial year of taxes on income other than agricultural income, except in so far as those proceeds represent proceeds attributable to Union Territories or to taxes payable in respect of Union emoluments to be assigned to the States be 60 (sixty);

(b) The percentage of the net proceeds of taxes on income which shall be deemed to represent proceeds attributable to Union Territories be 1 (one); and

(c) The percentage of the net proceeds assigned to the States be distributed among those States as follows:

State	Percentage
Andhra Pradesh	8·12
Assam	2·44
Bihar	9·94
Bombay	15·97
Kerala	3·64
Madhya Pradesh	6·72
Madras	8·40
Mysore	5·14
Orissa	3·73
Punjab	4·24
Rajasthan	4·09
Uttar Pradesh	16·36
West Bengal	10·08
Jammu and Kashmir	1·13

Under article 272 of the Constitution, a sum equal to 25 (twenty-five) per cent of the net proceeds of the Union duties of excise on sugar, matches, tobacco (including manufactured tobacco), vegetable products, coffee, tea, paper and vegetable non-essential oils, be paid out of the Consolidated Fund of India to the States and distributed among them as follows:

State	Percentage
Andhra Pradesh	9·38
Assam	3·46
Bihar	10·57
Bombay	12·17
Kerala	3·84
Madhya Pradesh	7·46
Madras	7·56
Mysore	6·52
Orissa	4·46
Punjab	4·59
Rajasthan	4·71
Uttar Pradesh	15·94
West Bengal	7·59
Jammu and Kashmir	1·75

Under article 273 of the Constitution, the following sums be prescribed as grants-in-aid of the revenues of the States of Assam, Bihar, Orissa and West Bengal, in lieu of assignment of any share of the net proceeds of the export duty on jute and jute products, in each of the three financial years beginning on April 1, 1957:

	(Rupees in lakhs)
Assam	75·00
Bihar	72·31
Orissa	15·00
West Bengal	152·69

Under the substantive portion of article 275(1) of the Constitution, in each of the five financial years beginning on April 1, 1957, the sums shown in the table below be charged on the Consolidated Fund of India as grants-in-aid of the revenues of the States mentioned against them:

State	1957-58	1958-59	1959-60	1960-61	1961-62
			(Rupees in crores)		
Andhra Pradesh	4·00	4·00	4·00	4·00	4·00
Assam	3·75	3·75	3·75	4·50	4·50
Bihar	3·50	3·50	3·50	4·25	4·25
Kerala	1·75	1·75	1·75	1·75	1·75
Madhya Pradesh	3·00	3·00	3·00	3·00	3·00
Mysore	6·00	6·00	6·00	6·00	6·00
Orissa	3·25	3·25	3·25	3·50	3·50
Punjab	2·25	2·25	2·25	2·25	2·25
Rajasthan	2·50	2·50	2·50	2·50	2·50
West Bengal	3·25	3·25	3·25	4·75	4·75
Jammu and Kashmir	3·00	3·00	3·00	3·00	3·00
Total	36·25	36·25	36·25	39·50	39·50

With effect from April 1, 1957:

(1) Out of the net proceeds in each financial year of estate duty in respect of property other than agricultural land, a sum equal to 1 (one) per cent be retained by the Union as proceeds attributable to Union territories:

(2) The balance of the net proceeds be apportioned between immovable property and other property in the ratio of the gross value of all such properties brought into assessment in that year;

(3) The sum thus apportioned to immovable property be distributed among the States in proportion to the gross value of the immovable property located in each State; and

(4) The sum apportioned to property other than immovable property be distributed among the States as follows:

State	Percentage
Andhra Pradesh	8·76
Assam	2·53

Bihar	10·86
Bombay	13·52
Kerala	3·79
Madhya Pradesh	7·30
Madras	8·40
Mysore	5·43
Orissa	4·10
Punjab	4·52
Rajasthan	4·47
Uttar Pradesh	17·71
West Bengal	7·37
Jammu and Kashmir	1·24

In respect of the period prior to April 1, 1957, the distribution already made be legally ratified.

In regard to the loans made by the Government of India to the States between August 15, 1947 and March 31, 1956:

(a) With effect from April 1, 1957, in respect of loans made to the States for the rehabilitation of displaced persons and re-lent by them, the States be allowed to pay to the Union only the amounts of principal and interest collected, including arrears, if any;

(b) No modification be made in the rate of interest or terms of repayment of interest-free loans; and

(c) Of the remaining loans—

(i) The balances on March 31, 1957 of all loans carrying interest at three per cent or more per annum and repayable on or after April 1, 1977, be considered into one single loan at 3(three) per cent per annum repayable on March 31, 1987;

(ii) The balances on March 31, 1957 of all loans carrying interest at 3 (three) per cent or more per annum and repayable on or before March 31, 1977 be consolidated into one single loan at 3 (three) per cent per annum repayable on March 31, 1972;

(iii) The balances on March 31, 1957 of all loans carrying interest at less than three per cent per annum and repayable on or after April 1, 1977 be consolidated into one single loan at 2½ (two-and-a-half) per cent per annum repayable on March 31, 1987; and

(iv) The balances on March 31, 1957 of all loans carrying interest at less than 3 (three) per cent per annum repayable on or before March 31, 1977 be consolidated into one single loan at 2½ (two-and-a-half) per cent per annum repayable on March 31, 1972.

Out of the net proceeds of the additional duties of excise levied in replacement of sales taxes on mill-made textiles, sugar and tobacco (including manufactured tobacco)—

If each of the additional duties is to be distributed separately—

(1) A sum equal to 1(one) per cent of the net proceeds of each additional duty be retained by the Union in respect of Union Territories;

(2) A sum equal to 1¼ (one-and-one-quarter) per cent of the net proceeds of each additional duty be paid to the State of Jammu and Kashmir; and

(3) A sum equal to the balance of the net proceeds of each additional duty, i.e., after deduction of the sums mentioned in sub-paragraphs (1) and (2) above, be distributed as follows:

(a) The sums mentioned below representing the present income of the States on account of sales taxes, by whatever name called, on the three commodities be first paid to them.

State	Mill-made textiles	Sugar	Tobacco
			(Rupees in lakhs)
Andhra Pradesh	120	40	75
Assam	40	15	30
Bihar	80	30	20
Bombay	600	245	115
Kerala	38	20	37
Madhya Pradesh	83	40	32
Madras	168	60	57
Mysore	48	25	27
Orissa	50	20	15
Punjab	95	50	30
Rajasthan	50	25	15
Uttar Pradesh	400	112	63
West Bengal	240	36	40
Total	1976	718	556

(b) The remaining sum, if any, be distributed as follows:

State	Percentages		
	Mill-made textiles	Sugar	Tobacco
Andhra Pradesh	7·38	6·65	1·47
Assam	2·72	2·55	2·98
Bihar	11·19	8·20	8·90
Bombay	16·46	20·17	17·41
Kerala	3·10	3·03	3·43
Madhya Pradesh	6·97	7·67	7·10
Madras	7·26	7·43	9·53
Mysore	4·98	5·13	5·58
Orissa	3·32	2·87	3·21
Punjab	5·56	7·21	4·36
Rajasthan	4·36	4·81	3·59
Uttar Pradesh	18·19	15·63	16·13
West Bengal	8·51	8·65	7·31

(4) If the total net proceeds of the three additional duties taken together are to be distributed:

(i) A sum equal to 1(one) per cent of the net proceeds be retained by the Union in respect of Union Territories;

(ii) A sum equal to 1¼ (one-and-one-quarter) per cent of the net proceeds be paid to the State of Jammu and Kashmir; and

(iii) A sum equal to the balance of the net proceeds, i.e., after deduction of the sums mentioned in sub-paragraphs (i) and (ii) above, be distributed as follows:

(a) The sums mentioned below, representing the present income of the States on account of sales taxes, by whatever name called, on the three commodities be first paid to them:

State	Rupees in lakhs
Andhra Pradesh	235
Assam	85
Bihar	130
Bombay	960
Kerala	95
Madhya Pradesh	155
Madras	285
Mysore	100
Orissa	85
Punjab	175
Rajasthan	90
Uttar Pradesh	575
West Bengal	280
Total	3250

(b) The remainder, if any, of the net proceeds be distributed as follows:

State	Percentage
Andhra Pradesh	7·81
Assam	2·73
Bihar	10·04
Bombay	17·52
Kerala	3·15
Madhya Pradesh	7·16
Madras	7·74
Mysore	5·13
Orissa	3·20
Punjab	5·71
Rajasthan	4·32
Uttar Pradesh	17·18
West Bengal	8·31

(5) (a) Out of the net proceeds in each financial year of the tax on railway fares a sum equal to ¼ (one-quarter) per cent be retained by the Union as proceeds attributable to Union Territories; and

(b) the balance of the net proceeds of the tax on railway fares be distributed among the States as follows:

State	Percentage
Andhra Pradesh	8·86
Assam	2·71
Bihar	9·39
Bombay	16·28
Kerala	1·81
Madhya Pradesh	8·31
Madras	6·46
Mysore	4·45
Orissa	1·78
Punjab	8·11
Rajasthan	6·77
Uttar Pradesh	18·76
West Bengal	6·31

Conclusion

The scheme of devolution recommended by us is an integrated scheme. It takes into account the needs of the States with due regard to the ability of the Union, with its immense responsibilities particularly for defence and national development, to transfer resources to the States. It maintains a balance between devolution by transfer of shares of taxes and devolution by fixed grants-in-aid. We would like to emphasize that any modification of individual recommendations will upset this balance.

We recommend that the decisions taken by the Government of India on this report be given effect to from April 1, 1957, and all payments made on the basis of the interim report submitted by us be readjusted against the final payments. This will be without prejudice to the settlement of past arrears, if any.

Our scheme provides for a devolution of about Rs. 140 crores a year against an average sum of Rs. 93 crores received by the States under the last Commission's recommendations in the five years ending March 31, 1957. The table below summarises what each State may expect to receive under our recommendations taken together in each of the five years beginning on April 1, 1957. The figures shown against shares of taxes are only estimates and indicate the order of the sums to be received; the actuals will vary from year to year.

State	Shares of taxes	Grant under article 273*	Grant under substantive portion of article 275 (1)	Total
	(Rupees in crores)			
Andhra Pradesh	8·50		4·00	12·50
Assam	2·75	0·45	4·05	7·25
Bihar	10·00	0·43	3·80	14·23
Bombay	14·75			14·75
Kerala	3·75		1·75	5·50
Madhya Pradesh	7·00		3·00	10·00
Madras	8·25			8·25
Mysore	5·50		6·50	11·50
Orissa	4·00	0·09	3·35	7·44
Punjab	4·25		2·25	6·50

Rajasthan	4·25		2·50	6·75
Uttar Pradesh	16·25			16·25
West Bengal	9·50	0·91	3·85	14·26
Jammu and Kashmir	1·25		3·00	4·25
Total	100·00	1·88*	37·55	139·43

*This is an average for five years of payments which will actually be made to the State in the three years ending March 31, 1960. Grants-in-aid under article 273 cease on the expiry of ten years from the commencement of the Constitution.

Note 1: Assam will receive in addition, a grant-in-aid of Rs. 40 lakhs under clause (a) of the second proviso to article 275 (1).

Note 2: Under Section 74 of the State Reorganisation Act, the States of Bombay, Kerala, Madras and Mysore are entitled to receive during the three years ending March 31, 1960 the sums by which a prescribed percentage of their share of divisible Central taxes may fall short of average of the revenue gap grants guaranteed to the former Part B States of Saurastra, Travancore-Cochin and Mysore, now merged in them. On the estimate of divisible Central taxes adopted by us, the sums due to Kerala and Madras will be marginal while Bombay and Mysore may receive sums of the order of Rs. 3½ crores and Rs. one crore respectively for all the three years.

The increased devolution just mentioned is not the only source of additional income for the States. During this period the States will receive their share of the new Centrally levied tax under article 269, namely, the tax on railway fares. These receipts, which do not form part of the revenue devolved by us, are likely to be of the order of Rs. 15 crores in full year; a State-wise detailed analysis, on the basis of the distribution recommended by us, is given in the table below:

State	Share of tax on railway fares (Rupees in lakhs)
Andhra Pradesh	131
Assam	40
Bihar	139
Bombay	241
Kerala	27
Madhya Pradesh	123
Madras	96
Mysore	66
Orissa	26
Punjab	120
Rajasthan	100
Uttar Pradesh	278
West Bengal	94
Total	1481

We cannot over-emphasise the paramount importance of States balancing their revenue budgets. We have framed out scheme of devolution so as to enable them to do so. With a massive development plan under implementation, there is a grave risk of the budgetary deficits of the States endangering the country's economy by adding to the inflationary potential. Now that all expenditure creating permanent assets are being treated as capital outlay, deficits on current account covered by borrowing results in unfair shifting by the present generation of its burden to future generations. Development expenditure should, therefore, be adjusted to the available resources and States should not run into a revenue deficit even for meeting such expenditure. We earnestly trust that they will bear this in mind in shaping their financial policies.

COMMITTEE ON CO-OPERATIVE LAW, 1956—REPORT

Delhi, Manager of Publications, 1957. 2 parts.

Chairman : Shri S.T. Raja.

Members : Shri S.K. Hiranandani; Shri J.C. Ryan; Shri K. Subramanyam Nayudu; Shri S.S. Puri; Shri A. Palaniappa Mudaliar; Shri M.D. Vidwans.

Secretary : Shri M.P. Bhargava.

APPOINTMENT

The Committee on Cooperative Law was constituted under the Ministry of Food & Agriculture vide their Resolution No. 5-8/56-Coop. 1, dated June 6, 1956.

TERMS OF REFERENCE

(a) To review the existing cooperative legislation and to make recommendations for a simple legislative measure generally suited to the whole country to facilitate coordinated progress of the movement.

(b) To examine, in the light of recommendations of the Rural Credit Survey Report, the modifications necessary in the Cooperative Societies Act and rules for giving effect to the concept of State partnership in share capital and State participation in management of cooperative societies.

(c) To examine the existing provisions relating to various types of cooperative societies listed below and to suggest if any modifications are required in the Act, Rules as well as bye-laws so that these societies may be able to play an increasingly important role in the economic development of the country.

(i) Credit;
(ii) Marketing;
(iii) Processing;
(iv) Irrigation;
(v) Dairying;
(vi) Farming;
(vii) Small Scale and Village and other Industries;
(viii) Consumers;
(ix) Labour Contract, Construction and Housing;
(x) Transport, etc.

(d) To prepare standard sets of bye-laws which would facilitate the proper and smooth working of the new types of societies which are sought to be encouraged under the changed economic and social policy.

(e) To consider other related matters.

CONTENTS

Introductory; Review of Cooperative Legislation in India; Model Cooperative Societies Bill; Model Rules; Model Bye-Laws; Administration of Cooperative Law; Summary of the Provisions in the Model Cooperative Societies Bill and the Model Rules; Appendices I to VII.

RECOMMENDATIONS

I Model Co-operative Societies Bill

The following are the important provisions in the Model Co-operative Societies Bill.

The State Government may appoint a person to be the Registrar of co-operative societies for the State and may appoint other persons to assist him and confer on such persons all or any of the powers of the Registrar. The persons appointed to assist the Registrar shall exercise the powers conferred on them subject to the general superintendence and control of the Registrar.

A co-operative credit society consisting mainly of agriculturists shall be registered with unlimited liability, unless otherwise directed by the State Government.

For registration as a co-operative society, the objects of the society must not only comply with the provisions of the Act and the rules, but should also be consistent with co-operative principles and with the principles of social justice. The society must also satisfy the requirements of sound business and have a reasonable chance of success.

A society may, by an amendment of its bye-laws, change the form or extent of its liability, provided that the members and creditors of the society are given an opportunity to withdraw their shares or deposits in the society.

In registering an amendment to the bye-laws of a co-operative society, the Registrar is to be satisfied that the proposed amendment is not contrary to the provisions of the Act and the rules and is not inconsistent with the principles of social justice.

A society may transfer its assets and liabilities, in whole or in part, to any other co-operative society or divide itself into two or more co-operative societies. Such amalgamation or division, however, can be effected after giving the members and creditors of the societies concerned an opportunity to withdraw their shares or deposits in them.

A co-operative society shall admit as members only individuals who are competent to contract, any other co-operative society and the State Government. A society may also admit an individual as 'nominal' or 'associate' member. A nominal member shall not be entitled to any share in the assets or profits of the society.

Every member of a co-operative society shall have one vote in the affairs of the society. But where the Government is a member of the society, each person nominated by the State Government or the Committee of the society shall have one vote. Voting by proxy will not be allowed.

An individual member may hold shares in a co-operative society not exceeding rupees five thousand. The State Government may, by notification in the Official Gazette, fix a higher maximum in special cases.

A minor, or a person of an unsound mind, may acquire, by inheritance or otherwise, the shares of a deceased member in a co-operative society.

The liability of the past member or the estate of a deceased member for the debts of a society shall continue for a period of two years from the date of his ceasing to be a member.

A society shall convene at least once a year an annual general meeting for the approval of the programme of its activities for the coming year, for the election of the members of the Committee, for the amendment of bye-laws etc.

The State Government shall have the right to nominate not more than three members or one-third of the total number of members of the Committee of a co-operative society, whichever is less, where the Government has subscribed to its share capital directly or indirectly or has guaranteed debentures issued by it or has guaranteed the repayment of loans advanced to it.

The Registrar may supersede the Committee of a co-operative society, if he is satisfied that it is persistently negligent in the performance of the duties imposed on it by the Act and the bye-laws. Before removing the Committee, the Registrar will give an opportunity to it of being heard. In place of the Committee removed, the Registrar may appoint a new Committee consisting of one or more members of the soeiety or appoint an Administrator who may not be a member of the society.

The new Committee of a co-operative society, an Administrator or a Liquidator may apply to a magistrate for securing records and property of the society which may have been withheld by the outgoing Committee.

Any debt owing to a co-operative society by a member shall be a first charge upon the crops and other agricultural produce, cattle, fodder for cattle, agricultural or industrial implements, raw materials for manufacture and finished products belonging to a member. A member shall not transfer any property which is subject to a first charge of the society, except with its permission in writing. Any transfer of property made in contravention of these provisions will be void. The first charge shall be available as against a claim of the Government arising from any loans granted to a member under the Land Improvement Loans Act, 1883 or the Agriculturists Loans Act, 1884, after the grant of loans to him by the Society.

A member of a co-operative society may execute an agreement in favour of a society authorising his employer to deduct from his salary such amount as may be specified in the agreement and pay the amount so deducted towards the repayment of the loan taken by him from the society.

In addition to exemption from the income-tax, registration and other fees which the co-operative societies at present enjoy, the State Government may exempt any class of co-operative societies from taxes on agricultural income, on sale or purchase of goods and on professions, trades, callings and employments.

It shall be the duty of the State Government to encourage and promote the Co-operative Movement in the State. The State Government may subscribe directly to the share capital of a cooperative society. It shall, however, not be entitled to a dividend at a rate higher than that at which such dividend is payable to any other shareholder of the society.

The State Government may contribute indirectly to the share capital of a co-operative society. For this purpose, it may provide moneys to an apex society which shall credit them to a fund to be called the 'Principal State Partnership Fund'. The Fund is to be utilised by the apex society for directly purchasing shares in its own name in central co-operative societies affiliated to it or in providing moneys to a central co-operative society to enable the latter to purchase shares in primary co-operative societies. The moneys received by the central society out of the 'Principal State Partnership Fund' will be credited by it to a 'Subsidiary State Partnership Fund'.

Every purchase of shares out of the moneys in the 'Principal State Partnership Fund' or a 'Subsidiary State Partnership Fund' shall be made only with the previous approval in writing of the State Government. The liability in respect of shares purchased out of the Funds mentioned above will be limited to the amount paid in respect of such shares. If a central co-operative society in which shares are purchased from the 'Principal State Partnership Fund' or a primary co-operative society in which shares are purchased from a 'Subsidiary State Partnership Fund' is liquidated, the State Government shall not have any claim against the apex society in respect of any loss arising from such purchases. All moneys to the credit of the 'Principal or Subsidiary State Partnership Fund' shall not form part of the assets of the apex or central societies. The State Government may enter into an agreement with an apex society setting out the terms and conditions on which it shall provide moneys to the apex society for the purchase of shares in central societies or for the purposes of providing moneys by it to central societies to enable them to purchase shares in primary societies.

The State Government may assist co-operative societies by giving them loans and advances, by guaranteeing debentures issued by a society, by guaranteeing loans advanced to a co-operative society, or by giving subsidies.

Out of the net profits in a year, a co-operative society shall transfer an amount which is not less than twenty-five per cent of the profits to the reserve fund. It shall also contribute to the Cooperative Education Fund at a rate prescribed in the rules. The balance of the net profits may be utilised by it in payment of dividend, in payment of bonus to members in proposition to the amount or volume of business done by them with the society, in payment of bonus to employees, in creation of funds etc.

A co-operative society may create a provident fund for the benefit of its employees. The provident fund shall not form part of the assets of the society.

The Registrar may inspect the books of a co-operative society on his own motion.

In the course of an audit, inquiry or inspection, if it is found that a person who was entrusted with the management of a society, has made any payment contrary to the Act, the rules and the bye-laws, or has caused any loss to the society by breach of trust or by gross negligence, the Registrar may, after an enquiry into the conduct of the person, order him to restore the money or the property.

A dispute touching the constitution, management or the business of a co-operative society shall be referred to the Registrar and no court will have jurisdiction to enter any suit or other proceedings in respect of such disputes. The disputes may be decided by the Registrar himself or may be transferred to another person who has been invested by the State Government with powers in that behalf, or to an arbitrator.

Before canceiling the registration of a co-operative society, the Registrar may order the society to be wound up and appoint a liquidator for the purpose. On his appointment, a liquidator will take into his custody all the property belonging to the society. The liquidator shall continue to have the custody or control of the property of the society during the period of appeal, and even when an appeal is preferred, until it is decided. If the appeal is rejected the liquidator will proceed with the liquidation proceedings.

The State Government may appoint the Registrar or any other person to act as trustee for the purpose of facilitating the working of co-operative land mortgage banks.

The debentures issued by a State Co-operative Land Mortgage Bank shall carry the guarantee of the State Government as to the repayment of principal and payment of interest.

The State Government may guarantee for any specified period, the repayment of a loan granted by a land mortgage bank in excess of the amount to which a borrower is entitled on the basis of the value of the land determined in accordance with the standards of valuation in force, provided the loan is for the development and improvement of land.

A mortgage in favour of a land mortgage bank will have priority over any claim of the Government arising from loans under the Land Improvement Loans Act, 1883 or the Agriculturists Loans Act, 1884.

A mortgage executed in favour of a primary land mortgage bank will stand automatically vested in the State Co-operative Land Mortgage Bank.

If an instalment payable in respect of a loan made by a land mortgage bank remains unpaid, the Registrar, may, on the application of the land mortgage bank, direct the recovery of the amount due by distraint and sale of the produce of the mortgaged property. Similarly, the Registrar shall have the power to bring the mortgaged property for sale without the intervention of the court, in satisfaction of the debts due by the member to a land mortgage bank.

The Registrar, or any person subordinate to him empowered by the Registrar in this behalf may, on the application of a co-operative society, make an order directing the payment of any debt due to the society by selling the property subject to a first charge.

The orders of the Registrar for the recovery of moneys, the awards of arbitrators and orders of the Tribunal shall be executed by the civil court, by the Collector, or by the Registrar or any person authorised by him.

The Registrar may direct the attachment of the property of a person before judgment, if he is satisfied that the person, with the intention of delaying the enforcement of an order or an award, is likely to remove the property from the jurisdiction of the Registrar.

The State Government shall constitute a Tribunal consisting of not more than three members. Any person aggrieved by the decision of the Registrar, or an award of an arbitrator, given in the settlement of a dispute, may appeal to the Tribunal.

An appeal against the orders of the Registrar in certain cases shall lie to the State Government and against orders passed by any person other than the Registrar, to the Registrar.

No civil or revenue court will have jurisdiction in respect of matters connected with the registration of a co-operative society or its bye-laws the removal of the Committee, the winding up of a society or any dispute required to be referred to the Registrar.

II Model Rules

The following are the important provisions made in the Model Rules.

The bye-laws of a co-operative society shall provide for certain matters essential for its organisation and management, such as the objects of the society, the nature and extent of the liability of the members, the extent to which the society may borrow funds, the purposes for which the funds may be applied for, etc. In addition to these, the bye-laws may also make provision in regard to matters which are incidental to the organisation of the society and the management of its business such as, for instance, the method of recruitment and the conditions of service of the salaried employees etc.

An amendment of the bye-laws of a co-operative society shall be made by a resolution passed by a two-thirds majority of the members present and voting.

A person shall not become a member of two primary credit societies.

The chairman of a meeting of a cooperative society shall have a second or casting vote.

A defaulting member shall not be appointed to represent a society in another co-operative society.

For the purpose of election of members of its Committee, a co-operative society may divide its membership into different groups on a territorial or any other basis. The bye-laws may also specify the number of proportion of the members of the Committee who may be elected to represent each such group on the Committee and may specify further that, the representatives may be elected by all the members of the society or by only that particular group of members to which such representatives belong.

A co-operative society shall not appoint any person as its paid officer or employee in any category of service, unless he possesses such qualifications and furnishes such security as may be specified by the Registrar.

Every co-operative society shall contribute an amount, not exceeding five per cent of its net profits in an year, to the Co-operative Education Fund which will be administered by the State Co-operative Union and if there is no such Union, by a committee appointed by the Registr.r.

The reserve fund of a co-operative society shall be indivisible and no member shall have a claim to any share in it. It shall not be withdrawn without the permission of the Registrar previously obtained in writing. Unless otherwise permitted by the Registrar, the reserve fund shall not be invested by the society in its business.

A co-operative society shall not receive deposits and loans from members or non-members exceeding the limit fixed by the Registrar for that society. However, a co-operative society which accepts deposits from members only and has no other outside liability may accept such deposits in excess of the limit fixed by the Registrar, provided, however, that the excess amount is invested outside the business of the society.

A co-operative society accepting deposits and granting cash credits shall maintain fluid resources in such form and according to such standards as may be fixed by the Registrar.

Every co-operative society shall pay to the State Government a fee for the audit of its accounts in accordance with the scale fixed by the Registrar with the previous approval of the State Government.

No person shall be qualified to be a member of the Tribunal, unless he is a district judge or has exercised the powers of a district judge or is an advocate of at least ten years standing, or is a law-graduate having considerable experience of the Co-operative Movement.

The Registrar may direct a co-operative society to get its accounts written up to any date in such form and within such time as he may direct. In case of failure by the society to do so, the Registrar may get the accounts written up by a person deputed by him for the purpose and may recover the cost thereof from the society.

Every co-operative society shall furnish to the Registrar every year a receipt and disbursement statement, a profit and loss account, a balance sheet and any other returns specified by him. In case the society fails to do so, the Registrar may depute a person to get the returns and recover the cost thereof from the society.

EXPERT COMMITTEE ON ECONOMY IN THE USE OF CEMENT IN BUILDING CONSTRUCTION, 1956—REPORT

Delhi, Manager of Publications, 1957. 15p.

Chairman : Sardar Sarup Singh.

Members : Shri J.M. Rijhwani; Shri H.R. Hay; Shri S.K. Joglekar; Shri C.B. Patel.

Coopted Members : Shri L.P. Bhargava; Shri B.C. Ganguli; Col. H.C. Vij; Shri M.S. Bhatia; Shri K. Rama Varman; Shri G.L. Bhandari.

APPOINTMENT

The Experts Committee on Economy in the use of Cement in Building Construction was constituted under the Ministry of Works, Housing and Supply in July 1956.

TERMS OF REFERENCE

(i) Regarding substitution of cement by lime in mortars;

(ii) Adoption of alternate specifications for buildings to reduce the consumption of cement.

CONTENTS

Introduction; Material for Building Mortars; Properties Required of Building Mortars; Characteristics of Cement and Lime Mortars; Mortars for Different Uses; Use of Cement in Terraces of Flat-roofs; Use of Cement in Floors; Use of Cement in Roofs; Use of Cement in Other Structures; Appendices I and II.

RECOMMENDATIONS

The following recommendations for reduction factors for different slenderness ratios for masonry walls have been taken from the British Standard Code of Practice C.P. 111 (1948). These factors and the associated definitions may be adopted till such time as the Indian Standard Code of Practice for load bearing walls is accepted and published.

Slenderness Ratio	Reduction Factors
1	1·0
2	0·96
4	0·88
6	0·80
8	0·70
10	0·60
12	0·50 (Limit for Lime Mortars)

14	0·40
16	0·35
18	0·30 (Limit for Cement Mortars)

The slenderness ratio is obtained by dividing the effective height of the wall or column by its thickness. The effective height is determined as follows:

(i) For columns provided with complete support at bottom and lateral support parallel to the line of one of the horizontal surface dimensions at the top; the effective height relative to the directions of the top support shall be the height between the support.

The effective height at right angles to this shall be twice the height of the column above the lower support.

In the absence of top support the effective height relative to both directions shall be twice its height from the lower support.

(ii) For walls where laterally support at top and bottom, the effective height shall be ¾th of the height between such lateral support.

In the absence of top lateral support, the effective height shall be 1½ times the height of the walling above bottom lateral support.

The height between lateral support is termed storey height in many building regulations.

COMMITTEE ON ELECTRIC FURNACES, STEEL FOUNDRIES AND STEEL RE-ROLLING MILLS, 1956—REPORT

New Delhi, Ministry of Commerce and Industry, 1957. 84p.

Chairman : Shri B.B. Saksena.
Members : Shri S. Sambasivan; Shri R.M. Agrawal; Shri D.P. Dada; Shri K.S. Raghupathi.
Member-Secretary : Shri S. Banerjee.

APPOINTMENT

The Committee on Electric Furnaces, Steel Foundries and Steel Re-rolling Mills was constituted under the Ministry of Commerce and Industry vide their Resolution No. I.&S.(B)-55(7)/56, dated July 24, 1956.

TERMS OF REFERENCE

The Committee will—

(a) study the raw material requirements of the existing electric furnaces, foundries and re-rolling mills in the country and assess the kind of expansion that is possible having regard to the availability of the raw materials in the future;

(b) suggest ways and means of improving the efficiency of these units and recommend steps that should be taken to make them economic and independent of any form of subsidy in regard to the prices at which they obtain their raw materials;

(c) assess the additional capacity that it may be desirable to set up in the light of the developments which are taking place in other sectors of the economy and the considerations set out in (a) and (b) above;

(d) indicate suitable locations for the new units that may be set up having regard to the importance of promoting regional development and other relevant considerations such as transport facilities and raw materials supplies; and

(e) formulating principles which should govern the examination of the applications for setting up re-rolling mills which have been received in response to the Press Note of April 11, 1956.

CONTENTS

Introduction; The Industry in General; Part I: Steel Re-rolling Industry in India; Steel Re-rolling Industry; Raw Material Requirements of the Existing Re-rolling Mills in India; Possibilities of Expansion of the Industry and the Availability of Raw Materials; Ways and Means of Improving the Efficiency of Re-rolling Units and Steps to be taken to Make them Economical and Independent of any form of Subsidy in Regard to Prices of Raw Materials; Principles to be followed in Establishing Additional Re-rolling Capacity in the Deficient Areas; Matters not Directly Covered by the Terms of Reference; Summary of Conclusions and Recommendations; Part II: Electric Furnaces and Steel Foundries in India: General Observations; Scope of Enquiry and State of Development of Electric Furnaces and Steel Foundries; Raw Material Requirements of Electric Furnaces and Steel Foundries: Possibilities of Expansion of the Industry and the Availability of Raw Materials; Ways and Means of Improving the Efficiency of Steel Foundries and Electric Furnaces; Principles to be followed in Locating new Sites for Proposed Electric Furnaces and Possibilities of Additional Steel Casting Units; Matters not Directly Covered by the Terms of Reference; Summary of Conclusions and Recommendations; General Remarks by the Committee; Appendices from I to XI.

RECOMMENDATIONS

Part I: Steel Re-rolling Industry

The existing capacity of the Re-rolling Mills of various categories including Secondary, Producers as on November 1, 1956 is about 700,000 tons per annum on one shift basis. As certain returns need re-checking, the figure should be regarded as provisional.

Recommendation No. 1

All the existing capacity is not covered by valid sanctions. In some cases, the plant and machinery which was mainly for the purpose of replacement has been put up along with plant already in position. Strictly speaking, the capacity created without proper sanction should not be recognised. It would not, however, be in the national interest to ignore the existence of such plant and machinery.

Recommendation No. 2

In addition, some plant and machinery has been licensed by the Iron and Steel Controller to be obtained from abroad or indigenously, mainly for replacement. There is reason to believe that most of the plant and machinery now to be arranged will have the effect of increasing the capacity of the re-rolling units. Such additional capacity has been assessed at 104,760 tons per annum and may be taken as the projected additional capacity.

Recommendation No. 3

While the major part of the existing capacity is based on the use of billets, quite a few units, particularly smaller units, depend on re-rollable scrap for their operation. Re-rollable scrap is not proper material for the manufacture of quality product, but its use will be continued in mills below 8" sizes. These can operate economically on re-rollable scrap. The capacity of such units which can suitably run on re-rollable scrap is 26,200 tons per annum. The remaining capacity should be taken as based on billets. It comes to 1,325,746 tons on double shift.

No difficulty is anticipated in the mills below 8" in size getting their future requirements of re-rollable scrap as hitherto.

As regards the units based on billets, a number of such units have had to restrict their operations to single shift or even less. It is generally accepted practice for such units to work double shift to ensure economic production. Allowing for wastage at 10 per cent, their total requirements of billets on double shift, work out to 1,458,024 tons per annum.

The indigenous supplies of billets and imports under liberal policy have not proved sufficient to meet the requirements of the re-rolling industry according to the general practice in the line.

The total anticipated availability of billets and electric furnace ingots for re-rolling purposes by 1960-61 is 890,000 tons a year. This quantity in terms of billets comes to 876,250 tons.

Recommendation No. 4

Nothing can be said about the quantum of billets that would be available in the near future. Anyway, it is clear that it would not be possible to cater to the entire industry as it exists today on two shift basis which represents the general practice in industry to achieve economic production. It would, therefore, be necessary to regulate billet supplies in the manner which more or less maintains the present pattern of distribution.

Recommendation Nos. 5 and 6

In spite of the Government of India's liberal import policy in regard to billets, it was found necessary to obtain from abroad substantial supplies of certain sections for which capacity existed in the country. This points to the conclusion that it is difficult to get billets from foreign countries. Government should, therefore, make a special effort to get from steel producing countries, through trade agreements or otherwise, as much billet supply as possible to supplement the indigenous production to enable the re-rollers to work on an economic basis. At least, it should be ensured that the industry as a whole does not get less than what they were given in 1956.

Recommendation Nos. 7 and 8

It would take some time to increase the billet production by utilising the scrap available in the country. Meanwhile it would be in the national interest if the mills of 8" and above are also advised to make use of as much scrap as possible to secure the maximum output. Till such time as the raw material position for the Re-rolling Industry continues to be tight, the Main Producers may be asked to make available to the Re-rolling units scrap at least to the same extent as during the years 1955-56.

Recommendation No. 9

Having regard to the trend of demand for re-rolled sections, we reckon that the demand by 1960-61 will far exceed the estimates given in the Second Five-Year Plan, with reference to the supply position of billets. The advisability of making better provision for billets in the Third Plan period may, therefore, be considered.

Recommendation No. 10

If adequate supplies of billets cannot be arranged, the available supplies may have to be rationed among the re-rollers pro-rata on the capacity as recently assessed by the Iron and Steel Controller. In such allocations of billets (i) the units which were given the option recently to change over to billets but preferred to continue to operate on scrap and (ii) the unauthorised capacity will have to be ignored.

Unless supplies for one shift at least are assured to the industry, there would be a danger of larger units having to suspend their operations.

Recommendation No. 11

The re-rolling industry is amenable to regional development. New capacity should be established so as to fill the gap locally as far as possible.

The following States are deficient in re-rolling capacity:

1. Andhra.
2. Assam (including Manipur, Tripura and N.E.F.A.).
3. Bihar.
4. Himachal Pradesh.
5. Jammu and Kashmir.
6. Madras (including Pondicherry).
7. Madhya Pradesh.
8. Mysore.
9. Kerala.
10. Orissa.

The other States have surplus re-rolling capacity.

Recommendation No. 12

Minimum economic unit in the re-rolling industry defined.

Recommendation No. 13

Additional re-rolling capacity in deficient areas should be created by resorting to the following steps in the order mentioned:

(1) The parties which have been allowed to import or otherwise obtain new rolling mills plants may be advised to establish their plants in a State other than the State where there is already over-concentration of capacity.

(2) Mills in the surplus (congested) areas may be permitted to transfer their existing plant and machinery to the deficient State.

(3) The existing mills in the State may be permitted to expand their plant suitably.

(4) If the gap cannot be filled up in any one or more of the above ways, permission to obtain new plant and machinery for establishing new units should be given.

Recommendation No. 14

If, for a particular State, there be schemes involving the manufacture of (i) Special Sections exclusively (ii) Special Sections in conjunction with Common Sections and (iii) Common Sections alone, they should be considered in that order of preference.

Recommendation No. 15

No re-rolling mills should be allowed to be established in the future on the basis of supplies of ingots or billets from Electric Furnaces which are mainly for Steel Foundries.

Recommendation No. 16

For all billets allocation production orders should be planned by the Iron and Steel Controller in the same way as on the Main and Secondary Producers.

Recommendation No. 17

Future planning of orders should aim at utilising the capacity of the larger mills for meeting the demands for Common Sections which are suitable for mass production and that of the smaller mills for the production of other Sections as far as possible. As large capacity for producing bars and rods, certain sections such as 1/2" and 5/8" diameter rounds and squares flats and light structurals, is available with the Re-rolling Industry, it would be possible to restrict their production by the major steel plants in the country and to utilise their capacity for bigger sections for which the demand is not fully met.

Recommendation No. 18

While mills below 8" may continue to base their operations on scrap as at present, they should be ultimately replaced by modern mills operating on billets.

Recommendation No. 19

In a number of mills equipment is obsolescent and ill-balanced. Ultimately, improved efficiency should be aimed at. It can be secured, among other things, by

(a) improved lay-out obtained by re-vamping;

(b) modernisation and balancing of equipment, for example, furnace capacity to the mill and proper cutting and handling facilities;

(c) providing up-to-date technical know-how and supervision; and

(d) ensuring regular and adequate supplies of raw materials of uniform quality.

Recommendation No. 20

As a long range policy, balanced and modernised plants with effective quality control should be preferred.

Recommendation No. 21

Quality control in the Re-rolling Industry needs to be developed.

Recommendation No. 22

There is a congestion of small re-rolling mills in certain areas. This is primarily due to the availability of the requisite type of skill locally. It would be of greater advantage if two or more of them could be induced to pool their resources and work as a single unit.

Recommendation No. 23

There are some re-rolling mills where the working conditions are not quite satisfactory. Such units should be shifted to better sites, preferably to the Industrial Estates wherever they are being developed.

Recommendation No. 24

Larger mechanised re-rolling units, if given adequate supplies of billets, can pay their way without any 'subsidy'. All such units may be treated as Secondary Producers. Further there will be no need to give any subsidy to the smaller units provided they get regular supply of billets to work double shift. The entire question of subsidy is now before the Tariff Commission.

Recommendation No. 25

It would improve the lot of re-rolling units if they enlarge their scope of activities by providing for processing or fabricating suitable consumer goods or parts for the manufacture of machinery, equipments, etc.

Recommendation No. 26

Existing classification of re-rollers should be revised and in future there should be only two categories on the basis of type of raw material used, billets or scrap.

Recommendation No. 27

The advisability of including rolling mill engineering as a subject in the technical colleges and institutes may be considered.

Recommendation No. 28

It would be conducive to economic production, facilitate distribution of finished products and relieve pressure on the transport system, if mills which are concentrated in certain areas in surplus States could be dispersed over wider areas within such States.

Part II: Electric Furnances And Steel Foundries

The estimated total liquid metal capacity of steel furnaces, existing and projected will be 250,000 tons by 1960-61, and this should be utilised both for casting and for the production of ingots or billets. The melting scrap expected to be available by 1960-61 would be 260,000 tons per year. This would hardly be sufficient to meet the needs of the existing and projected Steel Furnaces, as their actual requirements of scrap would be about 285,000 tons a year.

Recommendation No. 1

The capacity of the existing steel foundries is 21,000 tons per annum. They expect to increase their capacity to 36,000 tons per annum by 1960-61. These Foundries should be encouraged to expand and to utilise all their liquid metal for casting purposes only.

Recommendation No. 2

The estimated demand for steel casting by 1960-61 is 72,000 tons per annum and the steel foundry capacity is expected to be 80,000 tons by that time. This will take care of the entire demand for steel castings. Therefore, there is no need to create any additional casting capacity before 1960-61. The position should be reviewed thereafter.

The estimated availability of melting scrap (other than re-rollable industrial scrap) now is 200,000 tons per annum. This together with about 200,000 tons now being exported makes up a total of 400,000 tons, and with the ingot production of 6 million tons per annum after 1960-61, the expected availability of scrap by 1961-62/1965-66 is expected to be 1,000,000 tons i.e. 600,000 tons over and above the 400,000 tons.

Recommendation No. 3

There is definitely a need in the country for additional steel furnace for the manufacture of steel ingots or billets for meeting the needs of steel rolling industry. By 1960-61, 250,000 tons of Grades 2 and 3 scrap now being allowed to be exported, will be available. 20 per cent of this scrap is comprised of very light varieties, which arise in all parts of the country. Besides, other types of light scrap can be had throughout country. Efforts should be made to use such scrap in the regions where it arises.

In all, about 80,000 tons of this type of scrap would be available per year. Mains frequency induction furnace with monthly capacity of 150/300 tons should be set up to convert this scrap into billets for rolling mills at least one in each State and more than one if an assessment of scrap availability warrants such addition. Balance 80 per cent of the scrap should be pressed into compact bales in power hydraulic presses and should be converted into steel in big mechanically charged electric furnaces and converted into billets by adopting the method of continuous castings.

Recommendation No. 4

Such large furnaces can be installed in Bombay and Calcutta to begin with.

Recommendation No. 5

If individual private parties or co-operatives find it difficult to put up such large electric furnace plants, Government should assist the parties in overcoming the financial difficulties.

If the scrap of the types exported at present is utilised in electric furnaces, 150,000 tons of billets can be made available to the re rolling mills per annum.

The additional scrap estimated as available in the period 1960-61/1965-66 is 600,000 tons and if all of this additional scrap can be utilised in electric furnaces for producing billets an additional 500,000 tons of billets will be available per year.

Recommendation No. 6

Any future plans for the development of the steel industry should provide for the continuance of electric furnace plants that might be put up in present conditions for billet-making.

Recommendation No. 7

It is suggested that the Mysore Iron and Steel Works may expand their electric furnace capacity to 50,000 tons instead of 30,000 tons a year and supply 15,000 tons of billets to the re-rolling mills in the South.

Recommendation No. 8

Until the furnaces are erected to utilise the scrap exported at present, permits may be given for export, subject to review every six months and the exporters making a certain percentage available to electric furnaces. Eventually the export should be stopped.

Recommendation No. 9

Scrap should be de-controlled, so that it may find a price level through normal trade channels.

Recommendation No. 10

Steel foundries should modernise to achieve large scale production utilising their full melting capacity for foundry purposes only.

Recommendation No. 11

The classification of scrap followed at present under the control needs considerable modifications. Fairly identifiable items of scrap should be classified under the category of industrial or re-rolling scrap; the balance as melting scrap only.

Recommendation No. 12

Boring and turnings should be canalised to the steel foundries by establishing a working arrangement between the major producers or borings and turnings and steel foundries or by pressing or compacting this at source to avoid deterioration of the material.

Recommendation No. 13

An organised trade should be developed for supply of high grade silica sands of low iron and alkali contents.

Recommendation No. 14

The possibilities of the setting up of a plant for manufacture of graphite electrodes should be explored with the technical assistance of a leading foreign country in the field.

Recommendation No. 15

Intensive research on the suitability of silica sands, bentonite and other binders should be undertaken.

Recommendation No. 16

Transport facilities and freight rates for steel scrap and silica sand should receive special consideration.

COMMITTEE ON ECONOMY OF IRON AND STEEL BUILDING CONSTRUCTION, 1956—REPORT

Delhi, Manager of Publications, 1958. 59p.

Chairman : Sardar Sarup Singh.

Members : Col. H.C. Vijh; Shri M.S. Bhatia; Shri C.P. Malik; Director Civil Engineering, Railway Board or his representative; Housing Adviser, Ministry of Works, Housing & Supply; Shri T.V. Joseph (alternate Shri C.S. Chandrasekhara); Shri N. Padmanabha Iyer; Shri R.N. Dutt; Shri C.J. Shah.

APPOINTMENT

The Committee on Economy of Iron and Steel in Building Construction was constituted after realising the imperative and urgent need for exploring all possible avenues leading to economy in the use of steel in building construction by the Ministry of Works, Housing and Supply under the National Buildings Organisation in September 1956.

TERMS OF REFERENCE

To examine and report on this matter.

CONTENTS

Background and composition of the Committee; Observations and Recommendations of the Committee; Statement; Appendices; Annexures; Charts.

RECOMMENDATIONS

The Committee realised that economy in the use of steel in buildings can be effected in several ways and concerted and co-ordinated drive is necessary on all possible fronts to obtain conspicuous results. Thus the saving may be through rationalisation of bye-laws and codes of practices, rationalisation of design methods, improvements in constructional practices and substitution by other suitable materials. Some of these measures, specially those of the last category, may be for a short duration i.e., for the period of emergency; some others are for all times and can be brought into operation almost at once while others require a period of preparation, training and re-adjustment in thinking and in operations.

The Committee noted that the Indian Standards Institution have progressed substantially in rationalising bye-laws and codes of practices. Their past work and programme are well set out in their memorandum presented to the Government of India and Planning Commission in February, 1957 (Appendix I). The codes and standards so far finalised on this subject could be brought into use almost immediately, by all institutions and organisations. A specific recommendation to this end has been made in this report (vide Recommendations 10 and 13).

With the aid of these bye-laws and codes of practices the design methods will improve and will be rationalised. For design of steel structures, especially, the Indian Standards Institution have in hand preparation of handbooks covering the design and fabrication of almost all types of structures.

In many places use of structural steel can be avoided by the use of M.S. bars or pre-stressing steel in concrete. Specific recommendations in this direction are given in Recommendations 4 and 5 on page 5 of this report.

Design practices that result in economy in the use of structural steel include adoption of plastic design in place of elastic design currently adopted. Similarly it has been known that definite economies are associated with certain preferred shapes for sections and components.

To obtain the effective practical implementation of various aspects of efficiency in the use of steel in buildings there is a pressing need for a team of structural engineers. This need may be met either in the shape of a special cadre in Government Departments or in the shape of consultants in Government or private practice.

Foremost in the efforts to save steel through improvements of construction practices should come the use of superior constructions material and erection practices which bring in its wake the need for quality control. With this is connected a comparatively greater freedom for the administration to select efficient contractors especially for structures where large savings in steel (and cement) are possible through quality control.

The substitute materials, the Committee has in mind, are pre-stressed concrete, timber and non-ferrous metals like aluminium. The role of these materials in effecting economy in steel by their substitution has been taken into consideration while making Recommendation 3 and the Statement 1 appended therewith. Partial prefabrication and mechanisation that are needed for large scale use of pre-stressed concrete have to be taken as the national evolution in building construction techniques. These methods are even now in use though to a relatively smaller extent, for erection of structural steel.

With these thoughts in the background the Committee desires to place before the Government for their consideration the following recommendations.

Recommendation No. 1

The measures required to ameliorate the existing shortages in iron and steel materials, in so far as the building industry is concerned are partly technical and partly administrative and these should go hand in hand to produce useful results.

Further, such measures are either long term or immediate, permanent or temporary for the duration of this shortage (which as far as can be envisaged is likely to last for a considerable time). The immediate measures include adoption of higher stress, more rational use and design of steel structures and use of substitute materials. The long-term measures include imparting training, encouraging better design practices and use of new techniques and materials.

Recommendation No. 2

The use of structural steel in building construction should be reduced to a minimum by its substitution by reinforced concrete and pre-stressed concrete and where possible and economical, by timber and aluminium where such substitute materials are available. Further reinforced or pre-stressed concrete materials should be efficiently designed to release maximum quantities of M.S. bars and rods and pre-stressing steel for use as substitute for structural steel.

Recommendation No. 3

Statement 1 (Page 11) indicates in broad terms the types of buildings and situations where steel of either category viz. structural or reinforcing, may be used. These have to be adapted to circumstances obtaining in each region. The important point is that a competent technical authority should consider all these alternatives and adopt the one which is economical and suitable for the particular situation. The measures can be termed mostly administrative and partly technical.

Recommendation No. 4

Since M.S. rods and bars are the categories to be preferred to structurals from the foregoing considerations, the Ministry of Steel, Fuel and Mines and the Iron and Steel Controller should investigate the possibilities of turning out more M.S. rods and bars than at present, sacrificing, if necessary, equivalent quantities in the category of structurals.

Recommendation No. 5

(i) The need for substituting structural steel and ordinary reinforced concrete by pre-stressed concrete is vital in the present context of shortages of both cement and steel.

(ii) As a positive step towards this end it is necessary to ensure that adequate quantities of pre-stressing steel should be available in the country from which the intending consumers can draw without going through the time consuming procedure of importing their requirements for each individual use as is being done at present.

(iii) For this purpose it is considered necessary to stock some quantities of this material against anticipated demands.

(iv) The Government may constitute a Committee for the purpose of determining the quantity and specifications of the material, to be so stocked. This Committee may include the Consulting Engineer (Roads), the Engineer-in-Chief, Army Headquarters, the Chief Engineer, Central P.W.D., the Ministry of Railways, Railway Board and representatives from State Governments who ordinarily use this material.

(v) The purchase, stocking and distribution of this material may be handled by the State Trading Corporation, a portion of the foreign exchange at present spent on the purchase of steel from abroad being diverted for this purpose.

(vi) The Committee referred to in para (iv) above will recommend the procedure to be adopted for allocation and distribution of this material to users against approved demands.

(vii) The present practice of permitting import of this material against ad-hoc indents should also continue and may even be liberalised to the maximum possible extent.

Recommendation No. 6

Timber is another substitute material proposed. Roofs of many buildings can be changed to timber construction. There is, however, an acute shortage of structural timber like teak; secondary timber can be used for structural purposes provided they are seasoned and adequately treated. Facilities for such treatment are at present inadequate with the result that this changeover is rendered difficult. Steps should be taken to make available in the market adequate quantities of treated timber of secondary species for structural use. For this purpose a careful study, regionally, of the availability of timber (other than teak) should be made in collaboration with forest departments. If careful planning is done, the Committee feels, the changeover of roofing specifications to timber can be effected in a few years. These measures are technical and administrative.

Recommendation No. 7

To reduce dead weight in structures and consumption of steel, light weight construction is essential for multi-storeyed buildings. Hollow clay tiles and hollow concrete blocks with light-weight aggregates are suitable for this purpose. The Committee considers that the Government should set up plants immediately for producing these materials in principal areas where multi-storeyed construction is coming into practice.*

Recommendation No. 8

Use of Deformed Reinforcing Bars in concrete effect considerable economy in M.S. reinforcement. A note "Use of Deformed Reinforcing Bars in Concrete" prepared by N.B.O. will be found in Appendix II.

The Committee is informed that the Tata Iron and Steel Company is in a position to place these bars on the market at a nominal extra cost above the price of M.S. rods and bars. The Committee recommends that this may be done immediately and that these rods may be made available preferentially to M.S. rods and bars. The Government may inform concerned departments and State Government that this material should be used wherever possible taking advantage of the increased bond. These measures are partly technical but mostly administrative.

Recommendation No. 9

The Committee considers that there is room for economy in steel by its more rational use. This is amplified in the recommendations that follow.

Recommendation No. 10

The Committee has reason to suppose that live loads assumed for buildings of similar occupancies vary in the case of different departments. A fair measure of agreement has been reached in respect of loadings on structures in the draft Code IS: 875. The Government may advise all departments and State Governments to follow these standards as far as possible. This measure is technical.

* The Chief Engineer, Central P.W.D. was of the view that the suitability of hollow clay tiles and concrete blocks with light weight aggregate should be examined further before setting up factories for their manufacture.

Recommendation No. 11

At present design of steel structures is generally being done on the basis of out-moded codes. The Indian Standards Institution's Code (IS:800—1956) is an improvement on this code in several respects. The Government may request and make it mandatory on all departments to follow this code with immediate effect. This measure though technical needs administrative backing.

Recommendation No. 12

It will be seen from the Statement 1 (page 11) that where use of structural steel is unavoidable welding is preferred to rivetting from considerations of steel economy.

The Committee recommends that the Government may direct all departments that where structural steel is used, welded construction by competent welders should be accepted as an alternative and in preference to (if cost is the same for both) rivetted constructions.

For this purpose designs on recognised principles of plastic theory should also be accepted. The measure is technical but requires administrative backing.

Recommendation No. 13

The Committee considers that in order to inculcate in the authorities concerned a direct sense of responsibility in the matter of rational use of steel, it will be advisable if the officer approving the design, records in each major design, certificate to the effect (i) that the use of structural steel has been avoided wherever possible and limited to the minimum in other cases and (ii) that the load stresses and design practices adopted are in conformity with IS: 800—1956.

It is further considered that similar certificates from a Chartered Engineer may be insisted upon in respect of all designs in private sector in which substantial quantities of structural steel is released either by the Provincial Iron and Steel Controller or by the Ministry of Commerce and Industry.

Recommendation No. 14

The Committee considered a proposal that in the present context of acute steel shortage, the permissible stresses in M.S. reinforcements in R.C.C. work may be increased; the Committee recommends that this question may be referred to the concerned Committee of the Indian Standards Institution for their very early consideration and decision.

Recommendation No. 15

About one-third of the quantity of M.S. rods and bars are at present marketed as untested. Permissible stress adopted for this category of steel by some departments is only 16,000 lbs. per square inch. Most of these rods are rolled from billets slightly falling short of the standard specifications. The Committee feels that the Iron and Steel Controller may arrange to market this steel as 'tested' but certified to a lower class, say Class II, with guaranteed physical properties. The permissible stress for reinforcing rods of this class shall be considered and laid down by the relevant Committee of the Indian Standards Institution.

Recommendation No. 16

The Committee observes that considerable economies in cost and in steel will arise out of rational design of foundations and structure. For this purpose the Committee recommends (1) that persons be specially trained as design engineers for structures and foundations and that (2) a specialist individual or body be created for consultations in matters arising out of design of steel and R.C.C. structures and foundations. The Committee further recommends that the National Buildings Organisation will be the appropriate body to contain these specialists. This measure is administrative in character.

Recommendation No. 17

The Committee has seen the preliminary study by the National Buildings Organisation regarding the consumption of cement and steel in 10 multi-storeyed buildings in Delhi and has noticed the wide variations in the use of materials. The Committee feels that most design authorities could keep target figures for use of steel for various types of buildings from analysis of buildings already designed, and the designers should see that these target figures are bettered every time. Periodical publication of such figures by a body like the National Buildings Organisation will be helpful in the sharing of such knowledge.

Recommendation No. 18

The Committee feels that the information on use of twisted steel made available to them was insufficient to arrive at firm conclusions and that more comprehensive information supported by test results may be collected before large scale use of this could be advocated. The National Buildings Organisation and the Central Building Research Institute will collaborate on this project.

APPENDIX I

Indian Standards Institution Report On The Steel Economy Programme (Up To December 31, 1956) Presented By The Structural Steel Plant Committee

1. Preliminary Planning

In 1950, the Planning Commission recommended to the Government of India that the Indian Standards Institution should undertake a programme for increasing efficiency in the use of structural steel, by the formulation and implementation of standards relating to its production and use. Accepting this recommendation, the Government of India requested the ISI to take up a Steel Economy Programme to include:

(a) Formulation of Standards for Hot-rolled sections;

(b) Formulation of Standards for Cold-formed Light-gauge sections;

(c) Formulation of Codes of Practice for the Use of Steel in Structures;

(d) Preparation of Typical Designs and Drawings for and other aids to the implementation of the higher efficiency standards;

(e) Preparation of Standard specifications, Codes of Practice and other publications for popularising welding as a medium of fabrication of steel; and

(f) Sponsoring experimental and other investigations necessary for the formulation and revision of higher efficiency standards, relating to production and use of structural steel.

In the ISI, this work was entrusted to the Structural Steel Sectional Committee, BDC 7, under the Chairmanship of Sir Jehangir Ghandy. The composition of Sectional Committee BDC 7, is given as Annexure I.

The detailed work on steel economy could be initiated in the Directorate only from December 1953 since it took some time to arrange for the services of a suitable senior engineer to take charge of the Steel Economy Section. At the end of November 1953, Shri T.V. Joseph joined the ISI as the Officer on Special Duty. His services had been made available by the Ministry of Railways.

Shortly afterwards, the United States Technical Co-operation Mission in India finalised an agreement for technical assistance to the ISI for the Steel Economy Programme.

2. Inauguration Of Work

The work of the Structural Steel Sectional Committee BDC 7, was inaugurated by Shri T.T. Krishnamachari at Calcutta, on February 13, 1954. Shri T.T. Krishnamachari referred to the importance which the Government of India attached to the tasks allotted to the ISI under the Steel Economy Programme. He mentioned that the experts who had studied the problem of conservation of steel had estimated that more than 25 per cent of steel now used in structural engineering might be considered as wasted because of the use of uneconomic sections and the adoption of uneconomic and outmoded design practices. He pointed out that even with the restricted availability and use of steel in 1954, this wastage amounted to over 1,50,000 tons annually, costing the country 8 to 9 crores of rupees, on the basis of the value of imported steel. Stressing the urgency of the work initiated, he said that the Iron and Steel Control Organisation of the Government of India would be helpful at a later stage in implementing the standards and other findings of the Committee and that, if necessary, the enforcing of these recommendations could be arranged through Government regulations.

3. First Meeting Of The Steel Economy Committee Of The ISI

The first meeting of the Committee was held on February 13, 1954 under the Chairmanship of Sir Jehangir Ghandy.

The Structural Steel Sectional Committee, BDC 7, at its first meeting, distributed the steel economy work to four sub-committees, namely:

(i) Steel Sections Sub-committee (BDC 7:1);

(ii) Structural Codes and Design Sub-committee (BDC 7:2);

(iii) Welding Sub-committee (BDC 7:3); and

(iv) Structural Steel Research Sub-committee (BDC 7:4);

The four sub-committees in turn, had to set up a number of panels, to cover effectively the wide variety and extent of the subjects allotted to them. The names of the conveners of the four sub-committees and of the various panels set up by them are given in Annexure II.

The Steel Sections Sub-committee (BDC 7:1) is responsible for the formulation of standards for and the preparation of a handbook of structural sections. The structural codes and Design Sub-committee (BDC 7:2) is responsible for the formulation of codes of practice for the use of steel in structures and for the preparation of handbooks, typical designs, etc., for structural engineers. The Welding Sub-committee (BDC 7:3) is responsible for the formulation of specifications and codes of practice relating to welding and for the preparation of handbooks, brochures, etc., for the use of welding engineers, inspectors, supervisors, and welders. The Structural Steel Research Sub-committee (BDC 7:4) is responsible for co-ordinating and sponsoring experimental research and also for the formulation of specifications relating to corrosion protection of light-gauge structural steel work.

4. Second Meeting of the Structural Steel Sectional Committee (BDC 7)

The second meeting of the Sectional Committee BDC 7 was held on May 5, 1955 at Calcutta under the Chairmanship of Sir Jehangir Ghandy.

In this meeting the Sectional Committee approved the detailed programmes of work prepared by the Sub-committees and also the issue for wide circulation and comments, of the Draft Indian Standards on

(a) Code of Practice for Use of Steel in General Building Construction;

(b) Schemes of Symbols for Welding;

(c) Code of Practice for Use of Metal Arc Welding for General Construction in Mild Steel;

(d) Glossary of Terms Relating to Welding and Cutting of Metals;

(e) Specification for Covered Electrodes for Metal Arc Welding of Mild Steel;

(f) Classification of Covered Electrodes for Metal Arc Welding of Mild Steel and of Low Alloy High Tensile Steels of Welding Quality; and

(g) Code of Practice for Training and Testing Metal Arc Welders.

These seven draft Indian standards were later on finalised by the Committee through correspondence.

The Committee also considered the subject of 'tested' and 'untested' steels and decided that 'untested' steel should more appropriately be designated as 'commercial quality steel' and recommended to the Basic Ferrous Metal Sectional Committee (EDC 3) of Engineering Division Council (EDC) of the ISI the formulation of one or more additional specifications to cover these steels, in addition to IS:226—1955 specification for structural steel.

5. Third Meeting Of The Structural Steel Sectional Committee (BDC 7)

This meeting was held at Delhi on December 13, 1956, under the Chairmanship of Sir Jehangir Ghandy.

In this meeting, the Sectional Committee finalised for publication, the Indian standards mentioned below:

(a) Specification for Rolled Steel Sections-Beams;

(b) Specification for Rolled Steel Sections-Channels;

(c) Specification for Rolled Steel Sections-Angles;

(d) Code of Practice for Safety and Health Requirements in Electric and Gas Welding and Cutting Operations; and

(e) Code of Practice for Resistance Spot Welding for Light Assemblies in Mild Steel.

The Committee also approved of the issue for wide circulation and comments, the Draft Indian Standard Specifications for

(a) Rolled Steel Sections-Tee Bars; and

(b) Rolled Steel Sections-Bulb Angles.

6. Formulation Of Standard Specifications And Codes Of Practice

Details of the specifications and codes of practice on which work was undertaken as a part of the Steel Economy Programme are given below:

Standards For Structural Sections

(a) Rolled Steel Beams;

(b) Rolled Steel Channels;

(c) Rolled Steel Angles;

(d) Rolled Steel-Tee Bars;

(e) Rolled Steel-Bulb Angles;

(f) Tubular Sections;

(g) Cold Formed Light Gauge Steel Sections;

(h) Special Steel Sections for Structural Use; and

(i) Rolled Steel Piling Sections.

Design Codes

(a) Code of Practice for Use of Structural Steel in General Building Construction;

(b) Code of Practice for Use of Cold Formed Light Gauge Sections in Structures;

(c) Rules for the Design, Construction, Erection, Testing, Operation, Maintenance and Inspection of Cranes and Hoists;

(d) Code of Practice for Pressed Steel Tanks;

(e) Code of Practice for Design, Fabrication and Erection of Mild Steel Tanks for Storage of Oil;

(f) Code of Practice for Design, Fabrication and Erection of Steel Tanks; Standpipes, Reservoirs and Elevated Tanks for Water Storage;

(g) Code of Practice for Gas Storage Tanks;

(h) Code of Practice for Use of Steel Tubes in General Building Construction;

(j) Code of Practice for High Strength Bolting in Structures;

(k) Code of Practice for Light Weight Open Web Steel Joint Construction;

(m) Code of Practice for Use of Steel in Overhead Transmission Line Towers;

(n) Code of Practice for Use of Steel in Radio Masts; and

(p) Code of Practice for Use of Steel in Temporary Construction.

Welding Codes And Standards

(a) Glossary of Terms Relating to Welding and Cutting of Metals;

(b) Scheme of Symbols for Welding;

(c) Specification for Covered Electrodes for Metal Arc Welding of Mild Steel;

(d) Classification and Coding of Covered Electrodes for Metal Arc Welding of Mild Steel and of Low Alloy High Tensile Steels;

(e) Code of Practice for Use of Metal Arc Welding for General Construction in Mild Steel;

(f) Code of Practice for Training and Testing of Metal Arc Welders;

(g) Code of Practice for Safety and Health Requirements in Electric and Gas Welding and Cutting Operations;

(h) Code of Practice for Resistance Spot Welding for Light Assemblies in Mild Steel;

(j) Code of Practice for use of Welding in Weldments (built-up sections for use in place of steel castings);

(k) Code of Practice for Use of Welding in Boilers;

(m) Code of Practice for Use of Gas Welding in Structural Work;

(n) Code of Practice for Use of Welding in Structures Subject to Dynamic Loading—Bridges;

(p) Procedure Code for Electric Arc Welding;

(q) Code of Practice for Inspection of Welds;

(r) Code of Practice for Use of Welding in Pipelines;

(s) Code of Practice for Resistance Steam Welding for Light Gauge Sections; and

(t) Code of Practice for Use of Welding in Tubular Construction.

Standards For Corrosion Protection

(a) Specification for Corrosion Protection of Light Gauge Construction; and

(b) Specification for Performance Tests for Protective Scheme Use in Corrosion Protection of Light Gauge Steel.

The position as on December 31, 1956 regarding the progress of these standards is given in Annexure III.

7. Handbooks And Other Aids For The Implementation Of Standards

Preparation of handbooks and other publications mentioned below form an important part of the ISI's work on Steel Economy:

(a) Handbook of Properties of Structural Steel Sections;

(i) Properties and Dimensions of Structural Shapes for Designing and Detailing;

(ii) Rolling Mill Practices;

(iii) Miscellaneous Data for Estimating and Designing;

(iv) Estimating and Detailing Information;

(v) Allowable Loads on Rivets, Bolts and Constructions; and

(vi) Miscellaneous Data and Mathematical Tables.

(b) Handbook for Structural Engineers (including Typical Designs and Drawings).

(i) Functions of Good Design in Steel Economy;

(ii) Economy of Steel through Choice of Fabrication Methods;

(iii) Choice of Materials and Steel Economy Programme;

(iv) Steel Beams and Plate Girders;

(v) Steel Columns and Struts;

(vi) Roof Trusses in Steel;

(vii) Design of Welded Connections;

(viii) Single Storey Industrial and Mill Type Buildings in Steel;

(ix) Multi-storeyed Steel Framed Structures for Offices and Residences;

(x) Steel Transmission Towers;

(xi) Steel Work in Cranes and Hoists;

(xii) Large Span-Shed Type Buildings in Steel;

(xiii) Design of Storage Tanks;

(xiv) Design of Bunkers;

(xv) Use of Tubes as a Structural Material;

(xvi) Structural Use of Light Gauge Sections;

(xvii) High Strength Bolting in Steel Structures;

(xviii) Light Weight Open Web Steel Joint Construction;

(xix) Design of Rigid Frame Structures in Steel;

(xx) Application of Plastic Theory in Design of Steel Structures; and

(xxi) Commentary on the Code of Practice for Use of Structural Steel in General Building Construction.

(c) Handbook for Welders.

(d) Handbook for Welding Inspectors and Supervisors.

(e) Handbook for Welding Engineers Typical Designs and Drawings.

Progress of this work as on December 31, 1956, is indicated in Annexure III (Page 42).

8. Experimental Investigations

(i) During the course of their work on various standards specifications and codes of practice, the committees entrusted with the steel economy work came across a number of problems on which data are not available or are incomplete. Such items, after scrutiny by the Subcommittee (BDC 7:4) and the Sectional Committee (BDC 7), were submitted to the Council of Scientific and Industrial Research with the request that financial and other assistance, as was required for arranging these investigations, may be made available. Various institutions in India were approached in connection with the investigations, and the items as included in Annexure IV (page 45) have so far been allotted to the Institutions mentioned against them.

(ii) At a meeting held on September 22, 1956, the Board of Engineering Research of the Council of Scientific and Industrial Research, accepted and allotted to the National Physical Laboratory, an extensive programme of investigations relating to the production and use of cold-formed light-gauge structural sections.

(iii) In consultation with the Government Test House, the Directorate of Research of the Ministry of Railways, and the Technical Development Establishment Laboratories, Kanpur, details of an extensive programme relating to corrosion protection of steel structures with particular reference to light-gauge steel are being worked out. This programme includes investigations required in connection with the classification of areas in India on the basis of corrosiveness.

9. Certain Important Aspects Of The Steel Economy Programme

Hot Rolled Steel Sections: Early in 1954, when the work on the re-design and standardisation of hot rolled steel structural sections was initiated, production of structural sections in India was mainly through two organisations, namely, the Tata Iron and Steel Co. Ltd. (TISCO) and the Indian Iron and Steel Co. Ltd. (IISCO). The programme at that time was, therefore, confined to the redesign of the limited variety of sections producable with the existing equipment at these two factories. The decision of Government to set up the Hindustan Steel Ltd., at Rourkela, did not necessitate any change in this programme since the production of that company was to be confined to flat products. In early 1955, however, it came to the notice of the committees that plans for the installation of two new factories, one at Bhillai and the other at Durgapur, were also being considered and it was possible to arrange for the production of a wider range of structural sections through them. TISCO and IISCO had also decided on large expansion programmes, including additional mills and improvements to existing ones. Shortly afterwards, came the decision of the Government about the changeover to the metric system. These developments necessitated a complete reorientation of the work on standardisation of hot-rolled sections. It also became possible for the Indian Standards to cover more effectively the wide field of requirements of steel sections through the provision of a number of types of beams and channels of both lighter and heavier proportions.

Higher Efficiency Sections: In the case of beams and channels, the new sections being standardised give increased efficiency of 5 to 15 per cent when compared to the sections rolled hitherto in India. The new Indian standard sections compare favourably with those of other countries and, in most cases, are an improvement on them. In the case of Angles, Tees, etc., the new standards have achieved rationalisation without affecting economy in use. All the structural sections are standardised in the metric system.

Co-ordination With The Commission Mixte Des Aciers (CMA) and the European Coal & Steel Community (CECA): Early in 1 55, it came to the notice of the ISI that on the initiative of the Commission Mixte des Aciers (CMA) of Bilguime Luxembourg, the countries of the European Coal and Steel Community (CECA), had launched a scheme of re-design and standardisation of hot-rolled structural sections. Since the aim of this scheme was the same as that of the ISI, as regards redesign of structural sections, exchange of information between the ISI and the CMA and CECA, has been maintained. It is gratifying to note that the steps along which the work of the CMA and CECA has developed, closely follow the steps taken by the ISI committees.

Basic Design Code: The basic code for the use of steel in general building construction is now under print. In this code, the committees have tried to prescribe for India, standards in line with present day developments and practices generally accepted in other countries. The increased efficiency in use of steel available through the adoption of this code varies from organisation to organisation depending on the practices are largely modern in approach, the advantages would be small. But, in the large number of cases where outdated and unduly conservative design practices have so far prevailed, the adoption of the Indian Standard Code could yield considerable savings in steel.

Welding: Before the use of weldings can be increased, it is vital that the quality and dependability of welded designs and welding should be improved. Specifications and design codes alone were considered as insufficient to improve these aspects and to create greater confidence in welding. The handbooks for welders, inspectors, supervisors, etc., however, are expected to be of great help in this connection.

Interest in Other Countries of the Commonwealth: At the 1951 meeting of representatives of the National Standards Bodies of the Commonwealth Countries, considerable interest was shown in the Steel Economy Programme which the ISI was proposing to launch. The Commonwealth countries have, therefore, been kept informed of the developments of this programme. At the Commonwealth Standards Conference, to be held in Delhi in January-February 1957, a technical session is to be devoted to the discussion of various aspects of the Steel Economy Programme.

Interest in Latin American Countries: The Steel Economy Programme of the ISI has been of particular interest to the countries of Latin America whose industrial developments and problems are in many respects, similar to ours. At the request of the Economic Commission for Latin America (ECLA), the ISI presented, at the meeting of the Experts on the Steel Making and Transforming Industries held at Sao Paulo, Brazil, from October 15 to 28, 1956, a detailed paper on ISI's work on standardisation in the production and use of rolled steel sections in India. The ISI paper was presented during the integration discussions on October 25. Since conditions in most Latin American countries are parallel to those which exist in India (viz., a relatively small steel industry, large excess demand, limited foreign exchange, active economic development efforts, etc.), the paper was of immediate and direct interest to them. Furthermore, it provided an indication of what might be done as a partial answer to the existing and anticipated future steel shortage. There was considerable discussion following its presentation. At the end of the discussion, the meeting passed a resolution to establish steel economy programmes within the various Latin American countries under a joint committee to be set up by ECLA.

Implementation

General: As mentioned earlier in this report, the Steel Economy Programme of the ISI includes the preparation of not only standard specifications and codes of practice but also of handbooks and other publications as aids to implementation. The effectiveness of the Steel Economy Programme, in terms of actual savings in material and money would depend on the extent to which the particular aspects of the implementation could be followed up. The following paragraphs bring out certain of these aspects.

A co-ordinated plan for the works-cum-field implementation of the Steel Economy Programme has to be formulated and worked. The Government of India and the Planning Commission may consider the setting up of a suitable Body with powers to co-ordinate and effect this implementation. The Structural & Metals Division Council (SMDC) and the committees of the ISI responsible for the formulation of the standards, procedures etc., which are to be implemented, should be closely associated with this Body.

Hot-rolled Sections: The implementation of the Indian Standards for Hot-rolled Sections, does not present any serious difficulties. TISCO in their new mill and the steel mills at Bhillai and Durgapur, are expected to start production with the Indian standard sections. In the preparation of the standards for sections, the capabilities and limitations of these mills have been particularly kept in view. As regards the existing mills of TISCO, IISCO and Mysore, the changeover to new sections would be on a programme phased over a period of time.

Cold-formed Light-gauge Sections: For production of cold formed light-gauge sections, strip steel of properties and widths covering the full requirements would become available in India only after production starts at Rourkela in 1958. Hot rolled strip up to 12½" in width will be available from the Tata Iron and Steel Co., Ltd., if sufficient orders for structural quality material are placed. The immediate implementation of the standards for cold-formed sections, therefore, depends on the imported strip being made available and subsidised to the same extent as mild steel of other categories. It should be possible to give an impetus to the setting up of production units for the manufacture of cold-formed sections through encouragement by Government by way of loans etc., and also through consuming departments of the Central and State Governments accepting tenders for structures made from cold-formed sections, on a competitive basis, as compared to structures made from hot-rolled sections. The savings in steel through use of cold-formed light-gauge sections in certain structures will be as large as 40 per cent. By using strip steel from indigenous production or imported strip subsidised to the same extent as imported mild steel, there will be appreciable savings in overall cost also.

Steel Tubes: It is understood that the indigenous capacity for steel tubes up to 3 in. diameter leaves a surplus which could be diverted for structural use and further that the indigenous production of tubes upto 6 in. diameter is expected to start shortly. With the same type of encouragement as mentioned in para 10.3 above, it should be possible to popularise the use of steel tubes as a structural material.

Efficient Designs: The wide scale adoption in India of IS:800—1956 Code of Practice for use of steel in general building construction, would lead to considerable savings in steel. Since the Central and State Governments have to set the pace in this connection, their co-operation is essential. With this co-operation, there is no doubt that the private agencies would also accept this for their design offices.

The extent to which a code of practice could lead to a satisfactory design, greatly depends on the care and effort applied in the preparation of designs using the code. It is a matter of general opinion that there is considerable scope for improving the standard of design procedures in most organisations. A possible method by which this may be achieved is through a technical check on demands for steel to see that they are based on efficient and economic designs. This check may be enforced at the organisational level and, in some cases, also by the Iron and Steel Controller.

Untested Steel: An appreciable tonnage of steel meant for structural purposes goes, at present, under the category of 'untested steel'. Since the strength property of this steel is not guaranteed or definitely known, it is not possible to use this steel efficiently by allowing stresses and loads to the maximum safe limits. The Structural Steel Sectional Committee (BDC 7), has recommended that a separate standard should be drawn up for 'Commercial' quality steels which, even though not up to the requirements of the normal 'tested' quality steels, are usable, provided their physical and chemical properties are known and guaranteed.

Apart from this, consideration deserves to be given as to how far it is possible to reduce the tonnage of steel which has to be classified as not coming up to the present standards for structural steel.

Welding: There is already in India, a growing appreciation of the advantages which welding could afford in many cases of structural steel fabrication. But the natural reluctance of established fabricators to change over from riveted to welded fabrication procedures is even now acting as a retarding factor on this progress. An increased insistence by Government Organisations for welded fabrication could improve the situation. Apart from this, new fabricating organisations springing up in the private and public sectors, should be encouraged to set apart an appreciable proportion of their capacity for welded fabrication.

In order to implement the standards for welding and for popularising welding in India, it is also necessary that

(a) The Government should help in making available more freely suitable wire for the manufacture of electrodes in this country;

(b) As transformers suitable for welding sets are not produced in India at present, the import of such transformer welding sets should be permitted freely and the import duty on such transformer sets should be reduced in order to make them available more cheaply;

(c) The import of oxygen cutting equipment should also be permitted freely and the import duty on such equipment should be reduced in order to make available in the country equipments of satisfactory quality at reasonable prices;

(d) Technical institutions and universities in India should expand the facilities for the training of welding engineers, who would have a sound knowledge of both practical and theoretical aspects of welding; and

(e) Basic trade schools and other facilities for training welders should be established in various parts of the country. The procedure and syllabus for training and testing welders should be in accordance with the Indian Standard on the subject. The certification of welders should be arranged through a centrally-controlled organisation.

Research: Inspite of the fact that the CSIR had extended its full support to the whole programme of research drawn up by the Structural Steel Research Sub-Committee (BDC 7:4), the progress achieved so far is not quite satisfactory. It has been possible to get accepted for research only 10 out of 21 of the items considered as requiring immediate attention for research. Of the various institutions in India approached with a request that they may take up these investigations, only 8 have found it possible to take up any item. Since the large scale development of research in steel structural engineering is an essential requirement for placing the steel industry in India on a sound footing, thought should be given as to how far the present position can be improved. This need is all the greater, since a very large expansion in steel production and consumption is planned during the Second Five-Year Plan and thereafter.

The steel structural engineering and the welding sections of the research laboratories in India require to be strengthened in order to enable to meet the country's immediate demand for expansion of experimental research in these fields.

11. Structure And Metal Division Council (SMDC)

The considerable amount of work done under the Steel Economy Programme of the ISI, has highlighted the need and advantage of co-ordinating the production and use aspects in the standardisation of metals. This has led to the setting up of the Structural and Metal Division Council (SMDC) of the ISI. This new Division Council which was inaugurated on October 26, 1956, with Sir Jehangir Ghandy as Chairman will hereafter deal with the metallurgical, structural and other use aspects of metals and connected subjects.

12. Technical Assistance

The services of Messrs. Ramseyer and Miller, Inc., Iron and Steel Industry Consultants, New York, were made available by the United States Technical Co-operation Mission in India, to assist the steel economy work of the ISI from early 1954. This first agreement with these consultants, was for a period of two years from February 4, 1954. Arrangements were completed to continue their services for an additional period of one year upto February, 1957, with provision for further extension of one year up to February, 1958. In addition to the consultative service, made available from the New York Office of the Consulting Engineers and selected specialists in the United States, a resident engineer of the Consultants has been posted at Delhi and is co-operating in the day-to-day work of the ISI Directorate on the Steel Economy Programme.

TECHNICAL TRAINING COMMITTEE, 1956—REPORT

New Delhi, Development Commissioner (Small Scale Industries), Ministry of Commerce and Industries, 1957. 91p.

Chairman : Shri P.B. Advani.

Members : Dr. E. Staley; Development Commissioner for Small Scale Industries to the Government of India; Shri R.V. Ramiah.

Member-Secretary : Shri L.N. Renu.

APPOINTMENT

Small Scale Industries, for the development of which a sum of Rs. 61 crores has been earmarked in the Second Five-Year Plan, would, it is estimated, provide employment to additional 1·6 lakh workers. The break up of this figure into skilled, semi-skilled and unskilled categories is not available, nor is there any information on the supply position of the first two categories. The Small Scale Industries Board has been concerned about shortage of technical personnel which may seriously handicap the achievement of targets of employment and production laid down in the plan, and, after discussing this problem at more meetings than one decided on a detailed study of short and long-term measures for devising a planned programme of training technical personnel. Accordingly, at its 7th meeting held on September 17 and 18, 1956, it appointed a Committee.

TERMS OF REFERENCE

The Committee was directed to "examine and report on short term and long term measures which should be taken for the training of skilled workers and supervisors for small industries". For this purpose the Committee was desired inter alia to

(i) assess the demand for such workers based on normal wastage and expansion of industrial development during the Second Five-Year Plan;

(ii) suggest the types and numbers of special institutions to be extended or newly established;

(iii) suggest the classes and types of factories suitable for admission of boys and apprentices for training as skilled workers, conditions under which such training should be taken to ensure the requisite number of boys as apprentices to the factories in question;

(iv) make proposals for organisation of evening classes for apprentices;

(v) make an approximate estimate of cost of proposals; and

(vi) take into consideration all other incidental and connected matters.

CONTENTS

Introductory; Assessment of Demand for Skilled and Semi-skilled Workers; Technical Training Institutions; Apprenticeship and In-plant Training in Factories; Expansion Training Programme; Immediate Training Programme for Small Industries Sector; Conclusions; Appendices from I to VIII.

RECOMMENDATION

Demand Of Small Sector

The demand for skilled and semi-skilled workers for the small industrial sector for expansion, replacement and normal wastage, during the Second Plan period, is estimated at 1·74 lakhs.

Because the existing programme for training falls far short of the total demand of industries, the small industrial sector runs the risk of losing its skilled and semi-skilled workers to the large sector unless adequate arrangements are made for the latter also.

Demand Of Large, Medium And Small Sectors

Arrangements should be made for training 6·35 lakh persons for skilled and semi-skilled jobs to meet the total expansion and replacement demands of the large, medium and small scale industries sectors after allowing for wastage during training.

Institutional Training

Arrangements have been made for training two lakh persons in technical training institutions under the existing and proposed programmes. Half of these may be expected to secure direct employment in factories and the other half may be available for further training as apprentices.

No Spare Capacity In Existing Institutions

No spare capacity would be available for running additional second shifts or evening classes at the existing technical training institutions after meeting the requirements of expansion programmes of the Ministries of Education; and Labour and Employment.

Expansion Of Institutional Training

Following the example of industrially advanced countries, 20 per cent of the total number of apprentices may be recruited from technical schools. As the present institutional training programme will fall short of meeting this demand, the National Council for Training in Vocational Trades should examine the possibility of expansion of institutional training programme to provide an additional 20,000 seats, preferably under the D.G.R.&E. programme for training certificate holders. Of these, arrangements should be made to provide 4,000 seats during 1958-59, an additional 6,000 seats during 1959-60 and the remaining 10,000 seats during 1960-61.

Present Apprenticeship Programme

About 67,000 apprentices would be accepted for training under regular apprenticeship schemes during the Plan period under the existing and proposed programmes.

Programme Falls Short Of Demand

Assuming that one lakh out of the persons going through technical training institutions could be absorbed directly by the factories, the balance left for coverage by apprenticeship training would be 5·35 lakhs. The present apprenticeship programme, therefore, falls far short of the requirements.

Unorganised Training by Factories

Industry is meeting the remaining demand by unorganised training arrangements. This will lead to lowering of standards of workers available for expansion and replacement.

Replace Unorganised Arrangements By Organised Courses

A planned and properly organised training programme should, therefore, replace the unorganised training arrangements and necessary facilities provided to factories for this purpose.

Classes And Types Of Industries

The classes and types of industries and trades which will be suitable for admission of apprentices for training as skilled workers may be seen in tables 2(a) and 2(b).

Up To Five Per Cent Of The Labour Force First

Programmes for apprenticeship training should be expanded to the extent of five per cent of the labour force in large, medium and small factories and apprenticeship capacity of 93,000 seats developed in the first instance under the guidance of the National Council for Training in Vocational Trades. Of this, arrangements for 45,000 seats should be completed by the end of the current year (1957-58), another 18,000 seats developed during 1958-59, and 30,000 additional seats during 1959-60.

Up To 11·5 Per Cent Of The Labour Force Ultimately

An additional 1·21 lakh seats should be developed during 1960-61 bringing the total number of seats for training of apprentices to 2·14 lakhs, which is 11·5 per cent of the labour force.

Average Period Of Training

The average period of training may be brought down from 2½ years to two years to meet the present exigency.

Conditions Under Which Training Should Be Provided

Factories should be assisted to set up separate sections for training with additional equipment and suitably qualified staff attached to the production workshops to enable them to accept apprentices up to 11·5 per cent of their labour force.

Phasing Of Establishment Of Training Sections

Arrangements should be initiated to establish training sections with 30,000 seats during 1958-59, an additional 40,000 seats during 1959-60, and the remaining 51,000 seats during 1960-61.

Measure To Ensure Admission Of Requisite Number Of Apprentices

It will be necessary to introduce a compulsory training scheme under an Act of Parliament, whereby factories will be required compulsorily to admit a prescribed percentage of their total labour force for apprenticeship training. Compulsion may be introduced by stages, industry by industry and the engineering industry should be in the first set to which compulsion should apply.

Training Of Instructors

There is a great shortage of instructors for both institutional schemes as well as apprentice schemes. The National Council for Training in Vocational Trades should prepare a phased programme for training of instructors which should receive a high priority and arrangements should be made for training of instructors which should receive a high priority and arrangements should be made for training at least 3,000 instructors during 1958-59, 6,000 instructors during 1959-60, and 7,400 instructors during 1960-61.

Day Or Evening Classes

Day or evening classes would be necessary for apprentices to acquire knowledge of theory of their crafts. Preference should be given to day-time classes which the apprentices attend one day a week. An additional number of 14,000 seats would be required for running day-time classes for apprentices. Of these arrangements for 1,500 seats should be made during 1958-59, 2,500 additional seats during 1959-60 and the remaining 10,000 seats during 1960-61.

Total Cost Of Expansion Proposals

The total non-recurring cost of the expansion proposals, excluding the cost of the administrative set-up at the Centre and the cost of training instructors, would be about Rs. 58 crores and the annual recurring cost about Rs. 28·5 crores.

Immediate Programme

An immediate programme of apprenticeship training can be started at the Common Facility and Pilot Workshops attached to the Small Industries Service Organisation of the Ministry of Commerce and Industry for training (i) 1850 skilled and semi-skilled workers, (ii) 200 instructors, and (iii) 170 persons who can fit in managerial jobs or as entrepreneurs.

Arrangements should also be made for training an additional number of 250 Degree and Diploma holders per year by placing them in small factories where they could learn all aspects of manufacture of particular items to qualify them to become supervisors of entrepreneurs.

Additional equipment and staff should be provided in these centres to allow them to increase the number of trainees in art skilled and semi-skilled jobs to 5850.

Cost Of Immediate Programme

The non-recurring cost of this programme would be about Rs. 240 lakhs and the recurring cost about Rs. 86 lakhs.

Training Programme Essential For Fulfilment Of Second Plan Targets

We are strongly of the view that unless effect is given

to these proposals and a large number of technically trained men is made available, the targets of employment and production laid down for the small scale industries under the Second Plan are not likely to be met.

It will be an appreciable time before trained men become available under the apprenticeship and institutional training schemes proposed by us. Such of these men who do not complete training in time for the Second Plan period will be available for the Third Plan period.

Assess Requirements Of Third Plan

To train men is a time-consuming process. We accordingly strongly recommend that the National Council for Training in Vocational Trades should, in consultation with the Planning Commission take in hand as soon as possible the work of assessing the probable requirements of skilled and semi-skilled men in the different trades for the Third Plan period and make timely arrangements for their training.

COMMISSION FOR THE ESTABLISHMENT OF A HOTEL TRAINING CENTRE IN INDIA, 1956—REPORT

New Delhi, Ministry of Transport, 1956. 379p., XIII p. (Memeographed)

One-Man Commission : Shri John Fuller.

APPOINTMENT

The Establishment of a Hotel Training Centre in India was constituted under the Ministry of Transport in October 1956.

TERMS OF REFERENCE

(a) To ascertain whether a genuine need exists for a hotel training centre;

(b) Ascertaining the opinions in the hotel industry itself regarding staff training;

(c) Observing the working conditions generally in hotels in India and thus the type of training required; and

(d) To consider possible locations for a hotel training centre.

CONTENTS

Summary of Recommendations; **Part 1:** Introduction (Scope of Tour; Purposes of the Tour); **Part 2:** Tour Report (General Impression of Indian Hotel Industry; Luxury and Tourist Hotels; Other Hotels and Restaurants; Circuit House, Dak Bungalows, etc.; Outside Catering; Railway Catering; Meetings with Hoteliers and Hotel Associations; Conditions of Work and Career Prospects; Existing Facilities for Training in Catering; General Conclusions following Tour); **Part 3:** Training Report (Type of Training Required; Location of Training Centre; Adaptation of Hotel as Training Centre; Standard of Equipment etc.; Scope of Training and Type of Student; Supervised Hotel Training Following the Course; Subjects of the Course; Languages; Syllabus of Training; Staffing the School; Potential Teaching Staff; Recruitment of Students; Qualifications of Students; Women Students; Non-Teaching Staff; Possible Cost of Establishing Hotel Training Centre; Miscellaneous Costs); **Part 4:** Conclusion; **Part 5**: Appendices.

RECOMMENDATIONS

Decor and furnishing of hotels should draw more widely on Indian themes, styles and materials.

It should be the aim eventually to abolish the multiplicity of different types of staff for room cleaning and maintenance on hotel floors.

Training in waiting and cookery should be coupled with an attempt to recruit bearers of better background and higher personal standards.

There should be greater attention devoted to the planning and equipment of hotel kitchens.

Effort should be encouragement (if not specific legal requirement) of the wearing by cooks, bearers and other food handlers of adequate protective clothing maintained in a clean condition.

The compilation should be encouraged of an authoritative repertory of Indian dishes, standardising spellings and recipes in order to help evolve a "classic" Indian cuisine.

Adequate accommodation should be available for tourists in State Circuit Houses and Guest Houses when once a State has agreed to provide these facilities.

The activities of outside caterers should be regulated (particularly those coming in contact with the tourist trade) especially from the point of view of hygiene.

Training should be directed towards railway and other travel catering generally and not only towards hotels and restaurants.

The hotel industry itself should aid recruitment of

better staff by offering reasonable minimum wages to trainees and fair opportunities for advancement.

The industry, once training has been established, should reorganise by additional pay proper qualifications in both craft and administrative fields work.

There should be propaganda directed to the general public by both industry and possibly the Government emphasising the good status of hotel careers.

A Hotel Training Centre should be established without delay.

Such a hotel training centre should be residential and should concentrate on training in the hotel and directly associated with tourist and commercial fields, i.e. should not be linked with "welfare" catering training.

Training should primarily be directed towards full-time courses for potential managers.

The facilities of the school should additionally be used to aid in craft training, for example, of cooks and bearers and for refresher courses for other categories of staff. Priority should be given to short courses for the staff of State hotels, Guest Houses and Circuit Houses.

Part-time craft training in local centres should be a long-term objective of the hotel industry in collaboration with Government and educational authorities.

Consideration should be given to the ultimate establishment of apprenticeship schemes for craft workers in the industry.

The most desirable location for a hotel training centre would be in the centre of a progressive area of hotel activity such as Bombay.

Owing to the pressure of accommodation in large cities and the urgent need for a hotel training centre, it is suggested that as an immediate first step, an existing hotel, e.g. the Hotel Cecil at Agra, should be adapted as a training centre.

The training centre should be a residential establishment.

The centre should be equipped to the highest hotel standards in every department.

The principal course should be a full-time two-year course in hotel management combined with a period of two years supervised continuation training in the industry.

The course itself and the subsequent continuation training should have a strong content of practical craft work particularly in kitchen and restaurant.

Students recruited for this full-time training in hotel management should be either graduates of a University or have passed the University's intermediate examination.

Students gaining post-centre training in hotel management should be paid appropriate wages by employers who should have normal disciplinary control over them as employees.

Consideration should be given to students entering for recognised professional and other examinations of examining bodies of known prestige in the United Kingdom.

The Principal appointed should be an experienced hotelman, desirably with teaching experience and should be appointed at least six months before the opening of the training centre.

The Principal should have freedom to evolve his own detailed syllabus but subjects should be covered broadly as outlined in Appendix E.

There should be a strong emphasis throughout the training of the need for graduates of the centre to augment their period of supervised practical training by further years of experience in hotel departments before aspiring to management.

Initially teaching staff from the Principal downwards should be recruited from experienced hotelmen with teaching experience from outside India and the maximum period of contract should be offered to all teachers except in the case of those, if any, who are lent from their own teaching appointment abroad.

Salaries for staff recruited from overseas should compete favourably with rates obtaining in similar appointments in Europe.

The training centre should collaborate with neighbouring educational establishments in covering certain subjects such as Science and French.

Eventually the staffing of the school should be Indian.

There should still be encouragement given to students with exceptional aptitudes to gain experience in Europe, particularly as such persons may obviously be considered as potential teaching staff for an Indian hotel training centre.

Initial recruitment to the centre should be not less than 16 students and not more than 32 students per annum and that preferably the rate of recruitment should be 32 per annum for the first few.

Entry requirements for students as regards specific subjects should not be too rigid and the yardstick should be good general education, ability to profit by the course and personal aptitudes for a hotel career.

Candidates for hotel training should be required to attend for personal interview by the Principal before acceptance.

Encouragement should be given to the participation of women in the operation of hotels and in their training as students and, possibly, teachers.

The school should be maintained and conducted as a residential hotel (students and staff being "guests") and the work should be carried out by students themselves. It is strongly recommended that all duties including cooking, service and cleaning in all departments should be undertaken by the students themselves.

The sum of Rs. 3,00,000 should be earmarked as a possible cost for equipping the restaurant, kitchens and ancillary kitchen sections of the hotel training centre in addition to the capital cost of the building itself and in addition to the cost of decorating and furnishing.

Rs. 3,69,000 should be earmarked as a possible recurring cost for conducting the school in the first few years.

The cost of training should be off-set by levying reasonable tuition fees and charges for residence but government should be prepared to subsidise training in order that the fees charged should be sufficiently low to attract recruitment.

Recovery of cost by the sale of food in the restaurant to the general public should also be encouraged.

The hotel industry should be encouraged to contribute towards the cost of operating the school.

Hotel proprietors and companies should be encouraged to sponsor training of individual students acceptable to the school, such students being linked by a formal agreement to the hotel concerned.

The hotel industry should be closely associated with the management of the school through the formation of an advisory committee or board of governors.

The work of the school should be directed at improving staffing throughout the industry and not merely of top class hotels.

The Hotel Federation should be given the opportunity of studying this report with a view to inviting their comments.

The Government should regard the hotel industry as an industry and as one capable of development as part of a valuable foreign currency earning tourist industry.

SANSKRIT COMMISSION, 1956—REPORT

Delhi, Manager of Publications, 1958. 439p.

Chairman : Dr. Suniti Kumar Chatterji.
Members : Shri J.H. Dave; Prof. S.K. De; Shri T.R.V. Murti; Dr. V. Raghavan; Asthana Vidwan Panditaraja V.S. Ramachandra Sastry; Shri Vishva Bandhu Shastri.
Secretary : Dr. R.N. Dandekar.

APPOINTMENT

The Sanskrit Commission was constituted under the Ministry of Education vide their Resolution No. F. 34-1/56-A-1, dated October 1, 1956.

TERMS OF REFERENCE

(i) To undertake a survey of the existing facilities for Sanskrit Education in Universities and non-University institutions and to make proposals for promoting the study of Sanskrit, including research; and

(ii) To examine the traditional system of Sanskrit Education in order to find out what features from it could be incorporated into the modern system.

CONTENTS

Introduction; Historical Retrospect; Present Situation; Sanskrit and the Aspirations of Independent India; Sanskrit Education; Teaching of Sanskrit; Sanskrit Research; Manuscripts; Sanskrit University; Other Questions Concerning Sanskrit; Administration and Organisation of Sanskrit Education and Research; Conspectus and Recommendations; Epilogue; Appendices I to IX.

RECOMMENDATIONS

Sanskrit Education

1. Sanskrit In Secondary Schools

In view of the importance of Sanskrit for an adequate understanding of the culture of India; in view of its intimate relation with the modern Indian languages; in view of the desirability of every Indian student having an opportunity to study it; in view of the fact that the Secondary School Education has not only to be complete in itself and well-rounded (as many students would be discontinuing their formal for the further study of Sanskrit in Colleges and Universities); and in view of the various other points made out in Chapter IV; this Commission recommends that such provision should be made in language studies in the Secondary School curriculum as would guarantee for Sanskrit a secure place therein as a language which all students would be able to take up, and that, for this purpose, the necessary modifications should be made in the Three Language Formula which has been already announced by the Central Government and which is being implemented by the States.

The Commission urges upon the Government the need for making an adequate provision for the study of Sanskrit in the scheme of general education, in Schools and Colleges, as otherwise the liberalisation of Sanskrit Education which has taken place in modern times will receive an undesirable set-back (III.49)*.

* The Roman figure indicates the number of the Chapter and the Arabic figure that of the paragraph.

The Commission recommends that this provision should be such that, in some way or other, the young Indian pupils, with such exceptions as may be necessary (V.15), would automatically study Sanskrit;

That, for this purpose, compulsory provision for the teaching of Sanskrit, unaffected by arguments of economy or number of students taking Sanskrit, should be made in all the Schools in the country (V.32); and

That arrangements of groups of subjects should be so designed as not to debar such students as want to study Sanskrit from doing so (V.33).

The Language-Formula

The Commission recommends that, in Secondary Schools, all Indian students should be taught three languages, namely, (1) the mother-tongue (or the regional language), (2) English, and (3) Sanskrit (or, in some special cases, some other classical language as equivalent to Sanskrit, e.g. Arabic, Persian, Old Tamil, Latin or Greek) (V.25, 15);

That Hindi should be taught at the College stage to such students as desire to enter all-India services (V.25); or, if it is to be taught in the School, the three-language scheme recommended by us above should be so modified that Hindi, or, for Hindi-speaking students, some other modern Indian language, preferably South Indian, is allowed as an alternative to English (V.25).

In any scheme of adjustment with Hindi, the Commission is against providing Hindi as an alternative to Sanskrit.

The Commission recommends the following pattern for the study of languages in Schools: (i) Classes 1-5: only the mother-tongue with voluntary extra-curricular lessons in Sanskrit Subhasitas, etc.; (ii) Class 6: the mother-tongue and English, the extra-curricular lessons in Sanskrit Subhasitas etc., being continued; and (iii) Classes 7-11: the mother-tongue (reduced), English and Sanskrit (V.27). In this connection, the Commission thinks that it is not advisable to add the burden of Hindi as the fourth language at the School stage. The best results, in the opinion of the Commission, will be achieved if Hindi is made a subject of study at the College stage, on the basis of a knowledge of the mother-tongue and Sanskrit (V.25).

If the Three-Language Formula, namely, the mother-tongue, English and Sanskrit (or the alternative formula, namely, the mother-tongue, Hindi or some other Modern Indian Language, and Sanskrit), as recommended by the Commission as its first choice, is not feasible in certain parts of the country, then, as a second preference the Commission recommends a Four-Language Formula, namely, the mother-tongue, English, and Hindi (or any other Modern Indian Language for Hindi Speaking students), plus Sanskrit [V.25 (2)].

As a third preference, the Commission favours a course of four languages, namely, the mother-tongue, English and Hindi, plus Sanskrit in a composite course with the mother-tongue or Hindi or both, under certain specific conditions, namely, (i) that, at some stage, such a composite course must be made compulsory in lieu of the mother-tongue, (ii) that the duration of this course must not be less than 5 years, (iii) that the course must begin with an equal emphasis on the two languages, and emphasis on Sanskrit must increase in the higher classes, and (iv) that separate passing in each constituent language of the composite course must be made obligatory [V.25 (4), 28].

The Commission is of the opinion that it is quite practicable to adjust the study of the four languages (the mother-tongue, Sanskrit, English, and Hindi or any other Modern Indian Language for Hindi-speaking students) without there being any trace of burden, if the extraordinarily long course in the mother-tongue is pruned to some extent, if the simultaneous commencement of the learning of two languages is avoided by phasing their introduction, and if English and Hindi are treated as skill subjects and not as content subjects, as indeed they are meant to be treated (V.20, 21, 28, 29).

The preferences of the Commission in the matter of its recommendations are in the order as stated above.

The Commission is definitely against the suggestions made in some quarters that Sanskrit should be provided for out of school hours or as a non-examination subject [V.25 (3)].

The Commission is of the view that a course in Sanskrit in Secondary Schools of less than five years' duration will not be at all adequate as the necessary foundation for the further study of it at the College stage (V.27).

The Commission is against Pali and Prakrits being allowed as alternatives to Sanskrit at the School stage; at the same time, the Commission recommends that the study of the Prakrits should be made an obligatory part of the courses in special Sanskrit in the Universities and the Pathasalas. Provision should also be made for the Prakrits and Pali being taken as special subjects at the Graduate and Post-Graduate stages (V.31).

The Commission further recommends that, in addition to the provision for Sanskrit in the scheme of language studies, some account of the thought, culture and literary productions in Sanskrit should be included in the subject of Social Studies in the Secondary School Curricula.

2. The Traditional System Of Sanskrit Education And Learning

The Commission, agreeing with the view expressed by an overwhelming majority of witnesses, recommends that the traditional Pathasala system of Sanskrit education and higher studies should be continued and preserved and recognised as an accepted form of education, like any type of school and college education.

The Commission recommends—

That the Pathasala system should be revitalised by reorganising the Pathasala courses with the introduction in them of some modern subjects like the mother-tongue, English, General Science including Mathematics, and Social Studies including Ancient Indian History and Culture (V.60-62), adequate care being taken to see that this introduction of the modern subjects does not result in lowering the standard of Pandit scholarships;

That these reorganised Sanskrit High Schools or remodelled Pathasalas, with their students studying mainly Sanskrit (for not less than 16 periods a week) and also some modern subjects as indicated above, should be on par with other High Schools, and their products be treated like S.S.L.C. students for purposes of employment or admission to further courses of study;

That the reorganised Pathasalas should be properly inspected by an adequate Inspectorate, which should see particularly whether proper provision is made in the Pathasalas for the teaching of the modern subjects;

That, where feasible, these reorganised Pathasala courses should be opened as Sanskrit Wings of existing general High Schools;

That these Sanskrit High Schools or remodelled Pathasalas should lead to Sanskrit Colleges; the former (Sanskrit High Schools or the two stages of Prathama and Madhyama of three years' duration each, corresponding respectively to Lower and Higher Secondary; and the latter (Sanskrit Colleges) comprising the Graduate and the Post-Graduate stages of Sastri (of three years) and Acharya (of two years) corresponding respectively to B.A. and M.A.;

That the products of the Sanskrit Colleges should enjoy the same prestige and status as those of the Colleges of Arts, Science, etc.;

That as the apex of the Pathasala system, Sanskrit Universities should be established as indicated in V.75-76 and IX.15;

That, apart from encouraging in every way all proper proposals for Sanskrit Universities from States and Private Foundations or Societies, the Central Government itself should give a lead by founding a Sanskrit University;

That, in respect of the traditional Sanskrit education in the Pathasalas, there should be a uniform system for all India, with the same standards, duration of courses, examinations and nomenclature of Sanskrit degrees and/or diplomas;

That, in the interim period, there should be established an equivalence in respect of the different Sanskrit diplomas current in the different parts of the country, as also an equivalence between the various stages in the traditional Sanskrit education on the one hand and the stages in the University education on the other;

That this parity should comprehend also the scales and grades of pay, as between Pandit-Teachers and Graduate Teachers in the various cadres in Schools, Colleges and Universities; and

That Pandit-Teachers be given the same status as Graduate Teachers in respect of representation on the various University Bodies.

Other recommendations of the Commission relating to Pandits, Pandit-learning and Pathasalas are given subsequently.

College and University

The Commission recommends—

That, in the College course leading up to the Graduate and Post-Graduate Degrees, there should be provision for the study of Sanskrit under general as well as special and optional subjects;

That such of the Universities, as have not so far provided for the study of Sanskrit as a special or an optional subject for B.A. (Hons.) and M.A. Degrees, should make such provision available in their College or Colleges;

That no University in India should be without a Department of Sanskrit or a Chair in Sanskrit for the organisation and teaching of Sanskrit as a special subject for B A. (Hons.) and M.A.; and

That, for facilitating the proper pursuit of such advanced study of Sanskrit under the special branch, the teaching of Sanskrit in the lower collegiate classes should be sufficiently strengthened.

Other recommendations of the Commission in respect of the collegiate study of Sanskrit are given subsequently.

4. Integration Of The Two Systems

The Commission is of the considered view that it is premature and not wise to make any forced attempt at an integration of the Pathasala and the University systems of Sanskrit Education into a single system.

The Commission, however, recommends a greater measure of cooperation between the two systems, helping the two to approximate each other steadily and gradually, so that a healthy and lasting integration of the two might naturally emerge at some future date.

The Commission recommends—

That, for this purpose, Pathasala Pandits should be employed in modern Colleges, Universities and Research Institutes to bring into these modern institutions the traditional method of intensive and line by line study and mastery of the texts, and, correspondingly, Sanskrit M.A.'s should be employed in higher grade Sanskrit Pathasalas to familiarise the Pandits and the students there with modern historical, critical and comparative methods.

That the various other ways set forth in the Chapters on Sanskrit Education, Teaching of Sanskrit, and Sanskrit Research for familiarising the Pandits with modern methods and the results of modern researches should be adopted;

That care should be taken to see that there is no hybridisation by bringing the two systems together in a superficial manner; and

That the integration of the two systems should be tried at higher levels by arranging for some Sanskrit Graduates of the Universities undergoing Pandit-training, and for Pandits. after the completion of their Sastraic study, undergoing training in modern methods.

5. Sanskrit And Other Indian Languages And Allied Subjects

The Commission recommends—

That, in view of the intimate relation of Sanskrit with the several Indian languages and the influence exerted on the latter by Sanskrit, the special study of all the Indian languages at the B.A. (Hons.) and M.A. stages should include a study of Sanskrit; and that, for this purpose, there should be prescribed at least one full paper in Sanskrit in all Degree and Post-Graduate courses in Indian languages;

That particularly in the case of Hindi, which, according to the Constitution, is to draw primarily from Sanskrit, a larger quantum of Sanskrit study, especially from a grammatical point of view, should be prescribed from the school stage onwards upto the M.A. stage;

That, in the syllabus of studies in the Degree and Post-Graduate courses in Indian Philosophy, Ancient Indian History and Archaeology, Indian Music, Indian Architecture, etc., provision should be made for a fair knowledge of Sanskrit and for the study of Sanskrit texts on Philosophy, of Sanskrit inscriptions, of Sanskrit treatises on Music, Architecture, etc.;

That, in the special courses of English literature also, provision should be made for the study of the principles of Sanskrit literary and dramatic criticism, Alankara and Natya-Sastra and for a comparative study of the Sanskrit epic, drama, etc., at least in translations;

That, in the special courses of scientific subjects, like Mathematics and Astronomy, Medicine, etc., the syllabi should include a study, from the historical and comparative points of view, of the contributions of India in those branches as found in old Sanskrit texts; and

That, to enable all graduates of Indian Universities to have some knowledge of the cultural heritage of the country, there should be a general provision for all students in schools and colleges for a graded course in the culture enshrined in Sanskrit, giving an introduction to Sanskrit literature, Indian thought, philosophy and religion, and art and architecture.

Teaching Of Sanskrit

The Commission recommends—

That, in view of the unique character of the Sanskrit language, which can be compared neither with the spoken mother-tongue nor with a dead archaic language, and which is immanent in the thought, vocabulary and form of most of the spoken tongues of India, special steps should be taken to investigate into the methods of teaching it to different categories of students, Indian and foreign;

That Sanskrit Pedagogy should be recognised as a special subject; and

That courses should be organised in Teachers' Colleges for imparting training to Sanskrit Teachers of both the Graduate and the Pandit types in methods of teaching Sanskrit.

1. Schools: The Commission recommends—

That, owing to the peculiar nature of Sanskrit, which a young student does not normally hear spoken around him, a certain amount of memorising, particularly of declensional and conjugational forms, should be made a legitimate part of Sanskrit instruction;

That, in teaching Sanskrit, the teacher should not only use all the modern methods and aids, such as direct method, visual aids, conversation, recitation, dramatic production, etc., but he should also press into service the traditional Khandanvaya and Akanksa methods (V 1.8), so that all these methods would ensure an active participation of the student in the process of teaching and add to his interest and zest in learning the language;

That, at the earlier stages, grammatical forms should be taught as full-fledged parts of speech, rather than as stems, roots and terminations, and that, for this purpose, grammar should be taught as a complement to or as arising out of the speech or the literary material used; and

That, at the School stage, the mother-tongue or the regional language, which is closely related to Sanskrit, should be generally employed as the medium for teaching Sanskrit and that occasionally Sanskrit also should be employed when the direct and conversational method is resorted to.

2. Colleges: The Commission recommends—

That, in the courses of special Sanskrit at the collegiate stage, an adequate amount of Sastraic study should be provided for, and that, for the proper teaching of the Sastras, qualified Pandit-Teachers should be employed in the Degree and Post-Graduate Departments of Sanskrit in Colleges and Universities;

That, as the prescription of a large number of texts prevents adequate justice being done to each text, in some respects, the number of texts prescribed should be reduced so that these texts could be studied with greater intensity;

That the highest University course in Sanskrit should provide for the attainment by students of ability to write and speak Sanskrit freely and to read further Sanskrit texts by themselves;

That, wherever possible, contact and collaboration should be established between the Sanskrit M.A. classes and the teaching of the corresponding texts in the Pathasalas in the same centre; and

That, the curricula of Sanskrit studies should be so designed as to avoid the serious gap that now exists between the Intermediate or the Pre-University standard on the one hand and that required for the B.A. (Hons.) and M.A. courses on the other.

3. **Pathasalas:** The Commission recommends—

That the course of studies in the Pathasalas should be more broadbased, and that too narrow and too premature specialisation in a single Sastra should be avoided;

That a Sastri or equivalent title-holder should not only acquire good grounding in general literature and the basic Sastras, but should master, besides a special Sastra, other related Sastras also;

That, in the syllabus of studies, adequate provision should be made for the study of the Pracina texts in each Sastra and also of hitherto neglected subjects and Sastras, such as Veda (with Bhasya), Bauddha and Jaina Darsanas, Pratyabhijna, Tantra, etc.;

That, as fair grounding in Navya Nyaya should be given to all students who have to study higher texts belonging to the later dialectical phase of each Sastra;

That, in the final stages, students of the different Sastras should be given a knowledge of the corresponding developments in Western thought;

That, in the teaching of Sastraic texts, improvements in the pedagogic methods suggested in VI.35 should be adopted, so that greater interest would be created among the students and there would be a more active participation on their part in the classes;

That, except in the lower classes where the mother-tongue may be used, if necessary, the medium of instruction in the Pathasalas should be Sanskrit;

That, the Pathasalas should develop extra-curricular activities as indicated in VI.37 to create and sustain interest and enthusiasm among the students;

That, in addition to the line-by-line study of the texts, provision should be made in the Pathasala classes for the students acquiring a grasp of the general outlines and a comprehensive view of the contributions of the specific Sastras and texts, through general lectures and essay-writing;

That, with a view to remedying the drawback, namely, that the present Pathasala-system does not produce scholars equal to the Pandits of the old type, the examination system for the Pathasala education should be drastically revised and oral examination of the traditional Sastrartha or Vakyartha type should be introduced as a substantial part of the examination (say, with 50 per cent marks for the written test and 50 per cent for the oral Sastrartha test), and that the new Sastri and Acharya title-holders should be required to appear for a test in open assemblies (Sabhas) presided over the panels of Senior Pandits. The Commission desires to emphasise this as the most effective way to restore to the Sastraic learning its old depth and intensity.

Sanskrit Research

1. **Research:** This Commission thinks that the spirit of research is not something foreign, but is part and parcel of the tradition of Indian scholarship; that Research has an intimate bearing on the deepening and vitalising of Sanskrit study; and that, in this Research, which would consolidate and develop Sanskrit studies today, both the modern Sanskrit scholar and the Pandit have to take their share.

This Commission also thinks that, as the subjects of Research in the field of Sanskrit and Indology are still part of a living tradition and culture in India, Indian Indology is bound to have its own unique nation; and that, today, independent India affords free and ample scope for fresh investigation and interpretation in the field of her culture.

This Commission envisages an ideal Sanskrit scholar who can play a distinct and valuable role today as one who combines in himself the best features of modern methods and traditional equipment (VII.8) and thinks that adequate care ought to be taken to see that a spurious and superficial combination of the two systems does not dilute the standard of scholarly work in the field of Research (VII.11).

2. **Pathasalas And Pandits:** This Commission recommends—

That, in all Universities, facilities for Research should be afforded to the products of the Pathasalas as much as to those of the Universities and Colleges;

That, where the higher Pathasalas or Sanskrit Colleges as affiliated to the Universities, facilities for Research by the staff and students of these Sanskrit Colleges should be provided for;

That Post-Graduate Research Titles or Degrees should be instituted for the Sastris, Siromanis, Tirthas, Vidvans, etc.;

That high grade Sanskrit Colleges, with reputed Pandits on their staffs and well-equipped libraries and collections of manuscripts, should be recognised by the Universities and the University Grants Commissions as centres for Research;

That Pandits should be encouraged and given adequate scope to edit critically difficult Sastraic texts and to bring out expositions of the recondite technique and terminology of Sastraic writing;

That Research Journals in Sanskrit should be started in which research work done through the medium of Sanskrit might be published and Sanskrit abstracts might be given of research work published elsewhere in English and other languages; and

That the Sanskrit University or Universities, recommended by this Commission, should have Research Departments devoted to the different Sastras, where Pandits might be able to make their original contributions.

3. **Universities:** This Commission recommends—

That, in order that higher Research work in Sanskrit might be carried on in the Universities and that adequate guidance might be available there to young research scholars, every Indian University should have a separate Sanskrit Chair and Department of one or more members.

That the University Sanskrit Departments should be so strong as not to allow the quantum of research work to suffer on account of an overload of Degree-class Teaching, and that the Departments should concern themselves mainly with Post-Graduate Teaching and guiding of Research Students and Scholars;

That these Departments should be under the charge of scholars who have a distinguished record of Research work to their credit, who are continuously engaged in Research work and who are capable of giving guidance to Research Students;

That the University Sanskrit Professors should try to inculcate in the Research Students correct ideals and standards in methods of Research as indicated in VII.14-16, and that they should make available to young scholars, who have registered themselves under them for Research Degrees, active guidance and effective supervision of their work;

That the University Departments of Sanskrit should be well equipped with adequate library facilities, including bibliographical and reference material, periodicals, etc., required for Research work;

That all Universities should make awards of Research Studentships of at least Rs. 100 p.m. to such of the brighter graduates, as desire to prosecute Research work, and that at least one or two of such Research Studentships should be made available regularly to the Sanskrit Department every year;

That, as it is desirable and necessary to give further encouragement to those who have qualified themselves in Research, a certain number of scholarships or fellowships should be awarded annually also to those who have taken their first Research Degree; and desire to undertake further Research;

That the Research Scholarships awarded by the University Grants Commission, which are of a higher value, should be treated as continuation scholarships of this type for the further encouragement of those who have taken their first Research Degree;

That the Humanities Scholarships awarded by the Union Ministry of Education, which are still higher in value, should be granted to adult Research Scholars, or to Teachers in affiliated colleges who can take research leave, or to retired Professors who have chalked out a programme of Research work, have materials for such work and require financial assistance to complete that piece of research work;

That, for the first Research Degree, Sanskrit Research Students, who are to be introduced to textual criticism, should take up the work of critically editing an important unpublished text with a critical introduction and study. and that the more interpretative type of work, which requires greater maturity, should be taken up for the higher Research Degree;

That Indian Universities, which now have diverse practices, conventions and standards in the matter of the adjudgement of Research theses submitted to them, should establish some uniformity regarding the type of Research Degrees, the method of appointment of Referees and the valuation of theses;

That there should be an initial Research Degree, called M. Litt., and only one higher Research Degree, called D.Litt.; that, for both these, there should be viva voce test besides the thesis, and that the viva voce for D Litt. should be of the nature of a regular public test;

That, as regards the appointment of Foreign Referees, Indian Universities should follow a uniform policy; that, where Indian experts are available, they should be generally preferred, particularly when the thesis relates to pure Sanskrit studies; that, if Foreign Referees are to be appointed, there should be only one such in a Board of three Referees; and that the practice of appointing the Professor, who has guided the candidate, as an Internal Referee should be discontinued;

That the University Grants Commission and the Universities should revise their policy in respect of Foreign Degrees, especially in a field like that of pure Sanskrit studies (as indicated in VII.22);

That, while young Indian Graduates might be encouraged to go to Foreign Universities to study subjects like Comparative Philology, which are not adequately cultivated in this country, the University Grants Commission, the Universities and the Government should revise their policy in respect of sending Indian Graduate to foreign countries for a higher study of subjects like pure Sanskrit; and

That, on the other hand, since, even in the field of subjects like Sanskrit, sending abroad of more mature scholars of established reputation would have great significance and value (as shown in VII.23), and deputation of such scholars to foreign countries for lecture-tours and in schemes of exchange of Professorships should be more actively pursued.

The Commission recommends—

That greater discrement should be shown in the choice of subjects taken up for Research by young students and scholars, and that, in this connection, attention should be paid more particularly to the many neglected fields demanding investigation by Research scholars (as indicated in VII.24-28);

That adequate facilities should be made available in this country for the proper pursuit of researches in the subject of the spread of Indian culture, Sanskrit language and literature, and Indian art and philosophy in countries outside India; that, for this purpose, a School of Asian Languages should be established in India and facilities should also be afforded in Indian Universities for the study of these languages, so that a tradition of research in these Extra-Indian Studies might be built up in this country; and that the All-India Oriental Conference should be helped to open a new section devoted to the subject of Indian Cultural Contacts outside India.

4. Lectures, Seminars, etc.: The Commission recommends that University Lectures, through Departmental arrangement or by invitation under specific Endowments, Seminars and Inter-disciplinary Studies should be provided for and developed in the Universities with a view to stepping up the quantity and quality of Research work being done under their aegis.

5. Publication: The Commission recommends—

That greater facilities should be made available for the publication of the results of Research done in the different Universities and for making the Research publications of the Universities better known and more easily accessible in other centres of Research both in India and abroad;

That greater interest should be taken by Indian publishers in the publication of Sanskrit and allied Indological works and in improving the standard of the printing of such Research works (as indicated in VII.34-35);

That the Central and the State Governments should give greater encouragement to authors and publishers of Sanskrit and Indological books by making the libraries both in cities and mofussil centres, which receive grant-in-aid from them or which are under the charge of District Boards and other local bodies, purchase such books regularly (VII.36);

That, instead of reprinting old works on ancient Indian literature and culture, written by Western Orientalists at a time when materials were not yet adequately available, publishers in India should arrange with Indian scholars for the writing of new books relating to ancient Indian culture and literature, so that, the latest researches and their significance for the present age might be well reflected in these works; that, at the same time, arrangements should be made for the reprinting of some of the old publications of fundamental value in the field of Sanskrit and Indological research, containing bibliographical material, original records, basic texts, and translations, etc., as also for the re-issue in Devanagari editions of a number of texts (e.g. in the field of Veda, etc.), which are available only in Roman script;

The several agencies, official and non-official, public and private, which are bringing out Series of Sanskrit Texts, should show greater discretion in the matter of the selection of texts to be included in such Series; and that they should ensure the proper critical editing of these texts, which requires careful examination and collation of the available manuscript material and the preparation of the critical apparatus and the introduction;

The facilities should be made available to Manuscript Libraries, University Sanskrit Departments, Institute of Sanskrit Research and other agencies to bring to light larger number of valuable texts still lying in manuscripts in the different libraries; that, for the purpose of ensuring the speedy publication of a larger number of really valuable texts, an inventory (in order of priority) should be drawn up, by scholars conversant with the manuscripts-material, of works of value lying in the different manuscript libraries, which deserve to be printed; and that such an inventory should be made available to all the agencies, public and private, which are engaged in the work of bringing out editions of texts.

6. Periodicals: The Commission recommends—

That periodicals publishing articles relating to Sanskrit and other allied research should make every effort to raise their standard by such means as the proper screening of the papers submitted to them, so that they could play a more effective role in the matter of improving the quality of Research work done in the country; and

That, as the number of Indological Journals and the output of Research published in them is large, plans for preparing and publishing Research Digests, Annual Bibliographies, etc., should be seriously taken in hand.

7. Projects: The Commission recommends—

That, in view of the limited resources in respect of funds and personnel at present available, Research Institutes or University Departments should not, as far as possible, embark on any new big scale Research Projects;

That, in the interest of the entire Sanskrit Research in the country, the Central Government, the University Grants Commission, the State Governments and other authorities should concentrate, for the time being, on helping expeditious execution and completion of the important large-scale subjects, which have already been undertaken at the different centres, such as, the Critical Edition of the Mahabharata (Bhandarkar Oriental Research Institute, Poona), the New Catalogus Catalogorum (Madras University), the Vedic Word Concordance and Vedic Dictionary (Vishveshvaranand Vedic Research Institute, Hoshiarpur), the Sanskrit Dictionary on Historical Principles (Deccan College Research Institute, Poona), the Critical Edition of the Ramayana (M.S. University, Baroda), etc. mentioned in VII.43 and discussed in (VII.43-47); and

That, in the present conditions, it is more desirable to encourage the undertaking of smaller unit of work, rather than big projects, and thereby to step up the production of individual research (VII.48).

8. Non-Official Institutes: The Commission notes that there is a net-work of privately organised Research Institutes, which have been sustaining the work of Research in Sanskrit and allied fields in the different parts of the country; that these Institutes have either been pioneers in the field or are complementing the work of official agencies in their areas (VII.49); and that these private Institutes are severely handicapped on account of extremely limited resources in respect of staff, equipment, accommodation, etc. (VII.50).

The Commission recommends that all these non-official Sanskrit and Indological Institutes in the country should be brought under a comprehensive scheme of co-ordination and should be given by the Central and the State Governments generous grants, both recurring and non-recurring, for, in the opinion of the Commission, these private institutes form a necessary and integral part of the Research activity in the field of Sanskrit and Indology in this country (VII.51).

The Commission recommends that the methods of assessing and assisting Indological work in this country, adopted by the present ad hoc Indology Committee set up by the Ministry of Education, should be revised and rationalised (VII.54).

9. Central Institute of Indology: The Commission recommends that the Government should establish a Central Institute of Indology, which among other things, would supplement the work being done by the existing Research Institutes and would have, as its main objective, Research work which is being neglected at present or which can be carried out only with the special facilities such as the Government alone can provide for (VII.55).

The Commission further recommends—

That the core of this Institute should be the section devoted to Sanskrit, its other sections being devoted to such fields as Munda, Dravidian and Sino-Tibetan Languages and their relation to Sanskrit; History and Antiquities of Egypt and the Near East (Hittite and Iranian); and studies relating to Central Asia, Nepal, Tibet, China, and South-East Asian countries (VII 55);

That this Institute should work in collaboration with or comprehend the Central Manuscripts Survey recommended elsewhere (VII.55); and

That the work of the Central Institute should also include the preparation of annual bibliographies of Indology, publication of Sanskrit texts and Research monographs, and functioning as a Central Clearing House for Research Scholars (VII.56).

10. Co-ordination: The Commission recommends—

That the work of Research being carried on at different centres in this country, in Universities, Research Institutes, etc., should be properly co-ordinated and that duplication of work should be avoided (VII.58):

That, for this and other related purposes, year-to-year inventories of subjects of Research undertaken at different centres should be issued (VII.58); and

That steps (as indicated in VII.58) should be taken to promote a healthy and cooperative atmosphere in the field of Sanskrit Research in the country.

11. Conferences: The Commission recommends—

That the All-India Oriental Conference, which is the premier forum of Orientalists in this country, should be placed on a permanent basis, with adequate financial resources (VII.59);

That the Conference should be helped, in every possible manner, to expand the scope of its work by starting new Sections devoted to hitherto neglected fields such as Indian Cultural Contracts Abroad (VII.60); and

That the Conference should be given adequate aid to enable it to invite, for every Session, delegates from other Asian Countries particularly interested in the study of Indian Cultural Contacts with their own respective regions (VII.59.60).

The Commission feels that, apart from the academic gain accruing from it, this last-mentioned line of work of the Conference will have a lasting benefit on the larger front of promoting Asian Solidarity (VII.61).

12. Prizes, Foundations, Etc.: The Commission recommends that Prizes for Sanskrit and Indological work, on the model of those awarded by the Sahitya Akademi, should be instituted to promote high class Research work (VII.62);

The Commission hopes that the Philanthropists of the country will bring into being big Endowments and Foundations, such as the ones functioning in America, for awards of scholarships and grants of financial aid to Research Scholars and Projects (VII.63).

The Commission thinks that it is the imperative duty of the Government of India to ensure the continuation and expansion of higher Sanskrit Studies in this country, so that several fields, in which Western Indology had hitherto been taking the initiative, might now be properly investigated into by Indian scholars; and that, however much it might be necessary to devote special attention to Scientific and Technological Studies in modern times, the Government should not ignore the need for promoting Humanistic Studies, particularly Sanskrit, Indian Philosophy, Archaeology and Art, which constitute the most precious cultural heritage of India (VII.64-66).

Manuscripts

The Commission recommends that the Government should pay due attention to the question of Manuscripts, as the content, value and standard of the Research work in the field of Sanskrit primarily depend on the discovery of outstanding Sanskrit works among the Manuscripts lying scattered all over the country, and as the reconstruction of Indian History, Thought and Culture is dependent on Manuscript sources as on Archaeological and other materials (VIII.4.12-16.20.26).

The Commission recommends—

That, in order to tackle adequately the problem of the vast collections of Sanskrit Manuscripts lying in the different parts of the country, the Central Government should establish a Central Manuscripts Survey, which would be an independent Central Organisation or would form an important Section of the proposed Central Institute of Indology, or would work under the aegis of the Central Sanskrit Board recommended elsewhere (VIII.24);

That the Central Manuscripts Survey should have regional branches and should work in collaboration with State Governments and locally functioning non-official bodies (VIII.25);

That the work of the Central Manuscripts Survey should consist of Search, Survey, Collection, Cataloguing and Publication of Manuscripts of Sanskrit and allied works, and that, for this purpose it should have in its Central and Regional Branches qualified personnel experienced in Manuscript and editorial work and conversant with the local scripts and conditions (VIII.24);

That the Central Munuscripts Survey should publish a periodical Bulletin or Report giving details about the Manuscripts surveyed, transcribed, loaned or collected from time to time (VIII.27); and

That this Central Manuscripts Survey should function also as a Clearing House in respect of Manuscripts from foreign libraries, which are to be procured for the use of Indian scholars (VIII.27).

The Commission recommends—

That adequate steps should be taken to safeguard the Manuscripts, particularly in private possession, against decay;

That public consciousness should be aroused in respect of the value of Manuscript treasures lying in the nooks and corners of the country; and

That, wherever possible, such Manuscripts should be acquired from their owners or the owners should be helped to preserve them properly (VIII.19.24).

The Commission recommends—

That the Government should, if necessary, enact a suitable legislation to prevent the flow of manuscripts to foreign countries by sale or other means (VIII.17.25); and

That active steps should be taken to build up, in the proposed Central Manuscripts Survey, a library of microfilm copies of Sanskrit and allied Manuscripts from collections in Western countries (VIII.25.27).

The Commission recommends—

That each State Government should start its own Manuscript Library, wherever such Library does not already exist, in order to safeguard the Manuscripts in that region (VIII.10-19.29);

That these States or other local Manuscript Libraries should be under the charge of persons who are specially qualified in Manuscript and editorial work and who have some standing in the field of Research (VIII.31);

That wherever such Libraries, particularly belonging to the State Governments, have stopped the work of Peripatetic Search for Manuscripts, they should resume that work (VIII.22-29);

That, these Libraries should make adequate arrangements for the thorough examination and early cataloguing of the Collections of Manuscripts made by them (VIII.22-29);

That the Manuscript Libraries should have an adequate staff who can examine the Manuscripts, catalogue them, and also edit the rare works discovered among them (VIII.22-29);

That, while preparing Catalogues of Manuscripts, due attention should be paid to the correctness of identification and other information, and that, as far as possible, such Catalogues should follow uniform or standard methods of describing the Manuscripts (VII.23);

That the Government should give necessary financial assistance to the Libraries possessing big collections, the nature and value of the contents of which are not known to scholars, with a view to enabling them to expedite the publication of their descriptive catalogues (VIII. 11-30);

That the Manuscript Libraries should have adequate accommodation and furniture for stocking Manuscripts, and should, as far as possible, possess micro-filming and photostat equipment, micro-film reading apparatus and similar other facilities (VIII.28-29);

That the Manuscript Libraries should afford facilities to bona fide scholars and institutions to consult or borrow Manuscripts from them (VIII.28);

That, wherever the Manuscript Libraries are publishing critical editions of works, they should seek the advice and cooperation of scholars conversant with Manuscript and editorial work, with a view to ensuring that their work is being done on proper lines; and

That the Manuscript Libraries should take due care of the Manuscripts and seek the advice of experts on the methods of their preservation (VIII.31).

The Commission recommends that the Government should take immediate steps to throw open to the public the Manuscript Libraries of the former Native States which are now inaccessible to scholars (VIII.11).

Sanskrit Universities

The Commission recommends—

That, with a view to upgrading and toning up the

traditional system of Sanskrit Education, Sanskrit Universities should be established in different areas (IX.18);

That the Sanskrit Universities should not interfere in any manner with the existing Universities and their Sanskrit Departments and the courses of Studies in Sanskrit on modern lines (IX.12);

That the Sanskrit Universities should constitute the apex of the reorganised Pathasala system of Sanskrit Education (IX.15);

That the function of the Sanskrit Universities should be to co-ordinate Pathasalas and Sanskrit Colleges, regulate their courses of studies, inspect their working, and conduct their examinations (IX.15);

That, besides being co-ordinating, affiliating and examining bodies, the Sanskrit Universities should also function as Centres of Higher Studies and Research in Sanskrit (IX.15);

That the Sanskrit Universities should be brought into being and function under the aegis of the Statutory Body called the Central Sanskrit Board, recommended elsewhere (IX.16.17);

That the Sanskrit Universities should adopt, at all stages, Sanskrit as the medium of teaching, administration, production of books, etc. (IX.13);

That while the Sanskrit Universities should concentrate on pure Sanskrit Studies at the highest level, they should also comprehend the necessary complement of modern knowledge and should provide to the scholars working there facilities to study contemporary developments in the different branches of knowledge; and

That the Sanskrit Universities should have, in their programme of work, the production of Sanskrit works embodying modern knowledge, so that Sanskrit Studies fostered in their set-up do not suffer from segregation (IX.15).

The Commission recommends that the Central Government should make it a point to encourage all proper proposals for Sanskrit Universities coming from the States (e.g., the one relating to the Varanasi Sanskrit University of Uttar Pradesh) (IX.3.16).

The Commission recommends that the Central Government should give a lead in the matter of the Sanskrit Universities by founding a centrally administered Sanskrit University somewhere in the South (IX.17).

The Commission suggests that private bodies and associations, which desire to organise and set up Sanskrit Universities, should bestow due thought on the various problems involved in that connection, should assure themselves of the required resources in respect of men and money, and should obtain the prior approval of the authority or authorities under whose aegis such Universities are to come into being and function (IX.16).

General

The Commission recommends—

That, in view of the cultural importance and pan-Indian character of Sanskrit, and with a view to arresting the growth of fissiparous tendencies and linguistic parochialism, which are at present threatening the unity of India (through the agency of Sanskrit which has, through the ages, played the role of a great unifying force in the country), Sanskrit, which is already one of the languages recognised by the Constitution, should be declared as an Additional Official Language (by the side of Hindi and English, for the time being) to be used for public purposes as may be feasible;

That, in particular, Sanskrit should be officially used on all such ceremonial occasions as the taking of oath, the wearing-in ceremony, the opening and the conclusion of the Sessions of Legislature and of officially sponsored National and International Conferences and Deliberative Bodies, the presentation of credentials, the award of National decorations and honours, and the University Convocations, as also for such purposes as Passports and Mottos of different departments of the Government. In this connection, the Commission desires to emphasise that the use of Sanskrit which commands unique prestige and respect all over India, would add to the dignity and solemnity of such occasions (X.1.21.29).

The Commission recommends that the infinite resources of Sanskrit literature, particularly of its pithy sayings and didactic stanzas (Subhasitas) should be utilised in Schools and Colleges for such moral and non-denominational religious instruction as might be imparted in these Educational Institutions. The Commission further recommends that the Sanskrit Subhasitas which have a knack of sticking to memory and which constitute the popular wisdom of the nation, should be taught to the children from the earliest stages of their school education (X.2.3).

The Commission recommends that, as far as possible, efforts should be made to teach a Uniform Standard Pronunciation of Sanskrit in all parts of the country; that, for this purpose, qualified readers and teachers of Sanskrit from areas, where the standard pronunciation is better, should be employed in areas where pronunciation of Sanskrit is defective, and that, for the same purpose, tape-records and gramophone records, as also the services of the All India Radio, should be utilised (X.4-7).

The Commission recommends that, for pan-Indian purposes, Devanagari should be accepted as the Uniform Script for Sanskrit and should be taught to all students of Sanskrit; at the same time, the practice of using Local Scripts for Sanskrit should be continued as one of the chief ways of maintaining the necessary intimate contact of Sanskrit with the regional languages and promoting the advance of Sanskrit within the various regions; and that the Roman Script, which is used in a number of

Sanskrit texts published in the West, should also be cultivated by Pandits so that they would be able to use the material printed in that script (X.8-15).

The Commission recommends the full exploitation of Sanskrit and the technical and scientific literature available in it for the building up of an All-India Scientific and Technical Terminology. The Commission further recommends that the principle which has been laid down in the Constitution and which has been supported by the Official Language Commission, namely, that the Official Language, Hindi, shall draw primarily from Sanskrit, should be given full effect to, particularly for the purpose of evolving a Scientific and Technical Terminology for all-India use. The Commission recommends, for this purpose, the formation of associations of scientists and specialists in different disciplines who should collect from different branches of Sanskrit literature all such precise technical terms as can be used today, and also recommends the compilation of a comprehensive English-Sanskrit Dictionary of Scientific and Technical Terms (X.16-20).

The Commission recommends that, in view of the importance of Sanskrit for the understanding of the culture and the national genius of India, the personnel recruited for the Indian Administrative and Foreign Services should be given opportunities, through special courses of lectures, to acquire adequate knowledge of Sanskrit Thought and Indian Culture. The Commission further recommends that the Government should take early steps to appoint, in Indian Embassies abroad, Cultural Attaches possessing special competence in Sanskrit Language, Literature and Culture, so that centres of Indic studies in the different countries as well as the public in general interested in Indian culture might derive the necessary help from them. The Commission further recommends that Indian Embassies abroad should put up, now and then exhibitions of Indian literature and other cultural material and maintain a fairly representative library of Indological literature. The Commission desires to point out that the appointment of such Cultural Officers would go a long way in creating among the considerable number of Indians, now living or domiciled in various foreign countries, the necessary awareness for the culture of their motherland (X.30-36).

The Commission recommends that, with a view to enhancing the prestige of Sanskrit and by way of recognition of scholars of real eminence, the Government should revive the award of the Title of Mahamahopadhyaya with an attendant life-honorarium of Rs. 200 p.m. that the Central Government should, in cooperation with the State Governments, also provide for a scheme of life-pensions for the Pandits, who are in indigent circumstances but who are respected for their learning and character in the different parts of the country; that some of the eminent Pandits, who take interest in current affairs and are distinguished writers, should be nominated to Legislative Bodies, at the Centre and in the States; and that the President of India and the Governors of various States should hold Annual Sabhas for honouring eminent Pandits (X.37-42).

The Commission recommends that, in view of the fundamental importance of the Vedas from the point of view of the later development of Sanskrit Literature and Indian Thought and Philosophy, special attention should be paid to the preservation of the Oral Tradition of the different Vedas and their recensions as current in different parts of India, this Oral Tradition being useful even from the point of view of linguistic and literary research; that provision should be made available in temples and religious institutions for the recitation of the Vedas, and that where such provision already exists, it should be continued; that the surplus of temple funds which might be available, should be utilised for the maintenance of schools for the teaching of the Kantha-Patha of the Vedas; that, in those parts of India where the Oral Tradition of the Vedas has died out, authorities of educational and religious Institutions should take steps to revive it; that the Research Institutes working in the field of the Veda should, wherever possible, utilise the services of the Pandits who have preserved the Oral Tradition of the Vedas; that special attention should be paid to the tradition of the Samaveda, which is important from the point of view of Indian Music also, as well as to the tradition of the Atharvaveda, which has become almost extinct (at present being current only in a few families of Nagar Brahmanas in Gujarat); and that the Vedic Endowments, such as those in the Deccan and South India, which are facing difficulties in one way or another, should be helped by the Government to rehabilitate themselves in the matter of realising their annual incomes and utilising them (X.46-51.53).

The Commission further recommends that, apart from helping the preservation of the Oral Tradition of the Vedas in the manner indicated above, the Government should take early steps to prepare complete Tape-recordings of the Vedas, through the All India Radio or through some other official or non-official agency, and thus build up a Library of Vedic Recordings (X.52).

In view of the great role as the popular educator of the Indian masses, which the Epics and the Puranas have efficiently played in the past, and in view of the present efforts of the Government in connection with the spread of education and moral ideals among the masses, the Commission recommends that steps should be taken to train the required personnel for the exposition of Itihasa-Purana, and that the Pathasalas should introduce Itihasa-Purana and other exposition among their regular courses.

The Commission recommends that gifted exponents of the Ramayana, the Mahabharata, the Gita, the

Puranas, etc., should be employed in Community Projects and National Extension Service Schemes for the inculcation among the masses of the proper ideals of conduct and Departments, functioning in some States, should also employ such exponents of the Epics and the Puranas for regular as well as occasional expositions (X.54-55).

The Commission recommends that, wherever possible and necessary, courses in Paurohitya and Karmakanda should be introduced in the Pathasalas. The Commission, however, thinks that it would be desirable if the Vaidikas and the Purohitas were given a better academic grounding in Sanskrit, Veda and allied disciplines (X.56).

The Commission recommends that, in the different scientific and technical subjects in the University courses, students should be given an adequate knowledge of the ancient Indian contribution to those sciences as embodied in old Sanskrit texts, and that research should be carried on in the field of the Indian contribution to sciences, so that ancient Indian scientific knowledge might be properly apprised (X.57).

The Commission recommends that, in respect of Ayurveda, while the necessary quantum of modern knowledge and equipment needs to be introduced in its study, such large-scale integration with modern medicine, as would destroy the essential character of the Ayurvedic studies, should be discountenanced; that Ayurvedic Title Courses should be converted into Degree Courses; that the Universities should set up Departments of Research in Ayurveda; that text-books for the Ayurvedic students should be prepared in Sanskrit so that they might be used all over India; and that knowledge of Sanskrit should be considered a prerequisite for all students going in for Ayurveda (X.58-60).

The Commission thinks that the attitude of the Centre and the States towards Ayurveda needs to be revised, that greater utilisation of the service of Ayurveda should be encouraged among the people, and that steps should be taken to train larger Ayurvedic personnel. The Commission further thinks that it would be desirable to set up an All-India Council of Indigenous Medical Systems including Indigenous Veterinary Science (X.61).

In connection with Indian Astronomy, Mathematics, etc., the Commission thinks that there is much scope for research in these branches; it, accordingly, recommends that students of Mathematics and Astronomy in the Universities should be given an adequate idea of the work on Jyotisa, etc., embodied in Sanskrit, so that these students might feel inclined to take to research in the field of Sanskrit contribution to these subjects (X.62).

The Commission recommends that, in Schools of Art and Architecture and in modern courses in these subjects organised in the Universities, Sanskrit texts on Silpa-Sastra should also be taught, and that adequate steps should be taken to revitalise the practice and tradition of the ancient Indian Silpa-Sastra (X.63.64).

The Commission favours a simple form of Sanskrit, but not a simplified or Basic Sanskrit, which takes liberties with the grammar of the language. It, therefore, suggests that graded forms of simple Sanskrit should be employed in the initial stages of the teaching of Sanskrit to children and adults (X.65-67).

The Commission recommends that the authorities and the public should support Sanskrit Journals, which form an effective medium for developing Sanskrit as a vehicle of modern thought and current affairs (X.70-72).

The Commission recommends that the following measures should be adopted for the popularisation of Sanskrit:

(1) Organisation of private classes; (2) Study groups; (3) Private examinations; (4) Popular Sanskrit booklets and selections with translations; (5) Establishment of Sanskrit Associations, Clubs, Sabhas, etc.; (6) Celebration of Days in commemoration of important Sanskrit Writers and Works; (7) Popular publications; (8) Simplification of methods of teaching Sanskrit; (9) Sanskrit Literary Conference; (10) Promotion of original writings in Sanskrit; (11) Sanskrit Debates; (12) Competitions in short stories, plays, etc., in Sanskrit; (13) Musical Recitals of Sanskrit classics; (14) Putting on boards of Sanskrit Dramas; and such other measures as have been set forth in Section 14 of Chapter X.

The Commission recommends that, in order that the aesthetic and auditory qualities of Sanskrit might be fully exploited for the growth of popular interest in Sanskrit, the Government should give special encouragement to Sanskrit drama, opera and dance, musical recitals etc., by such means as sponsoring an annual Kalidasa Drama Festival.

The Commission recommends that, as far as feasible, the authorities should extend their help and patronage to the more important and active private academies and bodies, which are working for the popularisation of Sanskrit in their respective regions.

The Commission recommends that the All India Radio and the Film Division of the Ministry of Information and Broadcasting should take all possible steps in the matter of the popularisation of Sanskrit (as indicated in X.78-80).

The Commission recommends that the Indian Press should afford all possible facilities for popularising Sanskrit through their columns (in the manner indicated in X.84).

The Commission recommends that the Union Government and the Sahitya Akademi and the State Governments and the Regional Branches of the Akademi should actively help the publication, in cheap and uniform series, of Sanskrit Classics with translations in Modern Indian Languages and English, as also of works relating to Indian Thought and Culture.

The Commission further recommends that Sanskrit Texts, which are no longer available, should be brought in new editions by the Sahitya Akademi and other bodies; that works like a Dictionary of Sanskrit words current in Regional Languages, handy editions of Poems and Plays of great Sanskrit Authors, a Men of Letters Series of Sanskrit and Prakrit Writers, Studies on Indian Philosophers and Philosophical Schools, and attractive story-books in Sanskrit, should be taken up for publication, and that the National Book Trust of India and the Sahitya Akademi should sponsor the efforts in this direction; and that new and undeveloped types of literary expression should be encouraged in Sanskrit, and that prizes should be offered for the same by the Sahitya Akademi and the State Governments (X.85-91).

Administration And Organisation

Trusts And Endowments: The Commission desires to bring to the notice of the Government that there are in the country a large number of Endowments specifically earmarked for Sanskrit (including the Vedas), as also considerable surplus funds available with Religious Trusts, Temples and other similar Foundations, which, if properly tackled, can be legitimately used towards the implementation of the proposals made in this Report for the reorganisation, promotion and improvement of Sanskrit studies.

As many of such Endowments are either moribund or frozen or mismanaged or diverted for purposes not consistent with their original object and as the surpluses of Religious Trusts referred to above are either unutilised or diverted for secular purposes, this Commission urges upon the Government to take steps to institute, through the Central Sanskrit Board or some other competent agency, a full inquiry into such Endowments, set right their administration, make them operative, help them to realise the proceeds, and redirect the diverted funds of Temples, etc., towards the proper cultivation of the Veda, Itihasa-Purana, Agama, Dharma and other branches of Sanskrit study related to the original objective of the Endowments.

The Commission recommends that the Central Government should pass a suitable Legislation prohibiting the diversion of funds earmarked for Sanskrit studies to other charitable purposes, even with the concurrence of the Trustees and after the orders of the Courts. This Legislation should further prohibit the diversion of the surplus funds of religious institutions like Maths and Temples to secular charitable purposes and should insist upon the utilisation of these for promoting Sanskrit studies, which are broadly speaking regarded as religious objects.

The Commission recommends that where, as a result of the abolition of Estates and Zamindaris and the merger of former Native States and Principalities, the maintenance of Sanskrit studies provided for in the previous set-up has been adversely affected, the Central and the State Governments should take special care to ensure the continuance of the support which Sanskrit used to receive from its former patrons, and that the Government should also honour in full the commitments of former Princes and Zamindars, in respect of the promotion of Sanskrit, Vedic studies etc. (XI.2-16).

Numerous Sanskrit Institutions are dependent on Land-endowments; and the Agrarian Policy which has been recently adopted by some States adversely affected these Institutions. The Commission, therefore, wants to press this matter upon the Governments for their earnest consideration (XI.5).

In view of the facts that Sanskrit possesses an All-India importance, that its interest cannot be wholly taken care of by the States which have to develop the regional languages, and that a uniform policy for the whole of India in respect of Sanskrit is desirable, this Commission recommends that Sanskrit should be specially taken care of by the Centre by placing it in the list of Concurrent Subjects in the Constitution (XI.19); that, while the States should normally look after Sanskrit in their educational set-up, the Centre should, whenever necessary, financially assist the States to fulfil their obligations in respect of Sanskrit; and that the Central Government should promote such activities in the field of Sanskrit as do not receive adequate attention from the State Governments.

Central Sanskrit Board: In view of the fact that several proposals made by this Commission for the cultivation and promotion of Sanskrit presuppose constant attention, co-ordination and direction from the Centre, the Commission recommends—

That the Central Government should take early steps to set up a Central Sanskrit Board;

That this Central Sanskrit Board should not be only a co-ordinating and advisory body like the Central Boards of Secondary Education, Archaeology, etc., but that it should be constituted on the lines of the University Grants Commission, with statutory authority and financial provisions for helping Sanskrit Studies and Research in the country;

That this Board should consist of members representing all aspects of Sanskrit Education and Higher Studies—modern and traditional, academic as well as administrative—and all parts of the country, as also those representing private agencies and Research Institutes functioning in the field of Sanskrit;

That, while the Central Sanskrit Board might function in an advisory capacity in respect of the University Sanskrit Departments, it should have no statutory jurisdiction over them;

That, this Central Sanskrit Board should concern itself mainly with two fields of Sanskrit activity: (i) the

Pathasala education, and (ii) the privately organised Research Institutes in the country;

That the Central Board should be charged with, among other things, the formation of the patterns of Sanskrit Education at different levels; the co-ordination of courses, teaching, publication and similar other activities; the standardisation of syllabuses, examinations and degrees; and the definiting of the qualifications of different types of Sanskrit Teachers and Research Guides;

That the Central Board should function as the agency through which the Central Government might grant subventions to the State Governments for purposes such as the maintaining of Sanskrit teachers in Secondary Schools;

That the Central Board should also function as the agency through which the Central Government might grant subventions to reorganised Sanskrit Schools and Colleges in order to enable them to pay to their teachers in various grades emoluments equal to those paid to teachers in corresponding grades working in general High Schools, Colleges and Universities;

That the Central Board should help the Pathasalas in the matter of accommodation, libraries and other equipment;

That the Central Board should concern itself with the question of adding Research Departments to higher Pathasalas and awarding Research Scholarships and Stipends to the products of the Pathasalas;

That the Central Board should advise the Government in the matter of the State Honours and Awards for Pandits recommended elsewhere;

That the Central Board should be vested with the authority to sanction the starting of Sanskrit Universities, to recognise them as statutory bodies, to make them suitable grants, and generally to control and direct their working;

That the Central Board should co-ordinate and financially help the activities of the privately organised Research Institutes and Manuscript Libraries in the country; and

That the Central Board should generally function in co-operation with the Central Institute of Indology and the Central Manuscripts Survey (XI.17-25).

The Commission recommends—

That in view of the great expansion of educational activities at the present time and the inadequacy of a single Directorate looking after all the different branches, the present Directorates of Public Instruction in the States should be split up, and separate Directors should hold charge of special branches, e.g. University Education, Technical Education, etc. and that, in such a reorganisation, Sanskrit should be placed under a special Director (XI.27); and

That, a sufficient number of Sanskrit Inspectors should be appointed in the States and they be charged with the duty of regularly inspecting the Sanskrit Schools and Colleges in the respective States, particularly with reference to the fulfilment of the provisions of reorganisation (XI.26).

The Commission recommends—

That there should be quality in the matter of status, privileges, and emoluments between the Professors and the Pandits employed in the Universities; and

That the distinction between the Title-courses and the Degree courses should be abolished (XI.28).

The Commission thinks that it would not be advisable to make any sudden drastic changes in the matter of the various facilities, such as free tuition, free lodging and free boarding, which are at present available in many Pathasalas (XI.30-31).

In view of the fact that the significance and standard of Sanskrit studies suffer on account of the indifferent quality of the personnel recruitment for the various posts in the field of Sanskrit, the Commission recommends that only such persons, as possess appropriate qualifications for these posts (as set forth in XI.32-39) should be appointed to these posts.

The Commission recommends that, with a view to securing the unification of all cultural matters now scattered over more than one Ministry, the avoidance of duplication of work, the adoption of a single consistent policy, and the concentration of efforts in the matter of the cultural development of the country, the Central Government should constitute a separate Ministry of Culture and place all cultural affairs under that Ministry. The Commission believes that the setting up of such a Ministry will go a long way in promoting various activities in the field of Sanskrit (XI.44).

The Commission recommends that, as in the case of Scientific Studies and Research, so also in the case of Humanistic Studies and Research, particularly relating to Sanskrit and Indology, the Centre should show special concern. The Commission, indeed, feels that, in view of its peculiar position and significance, Sanskrit should receive a preferential treatment from the Central and the State Governments (IV.57-59).

The Commission recommends that, in the National Plans adopted by the Government, a substantial amount should be set apart for the development of Sanskrit on the lines set forth in the various Chapters of this Report.

The Commission recommends that, besides the major matters on which recommendations have been set forth above, several other matters which are referred to in the various Chapters of this Report and which are intended to further one aspect or another of Sanskrit Studies, should also be attended to by the Central and the State Governments.

THREE-YEAR DEGREE COURSE ESTIMATES COMMITTEE, 1956—REPORT

New Delhi, Ministry of Education, 1958. 23p.

Chairman : Shri C.D. Deshmukh.
Members : Shri K.G. Saiyidain; Shri G.F. Lakani; Shri K.L. Joshi; Shri C.S. Menon (Shri C.S. Menon was transferred and Shri A.C. Bose attended the first meeting; on his transfer, Shri A. Bakshi became the member); Dr. G.S. Mahajani; Dr. A.L. Mudaliar; Shri Vinod Chandra Sharma; Shri K.P. Sinha; Shri S. Govindarajulu; Dr. D.M. Sen.
Secretary : Dr. H.C. Gupta.

APPOINTMENT

The Education Ministers' Conference held on September 2-3, 1956, gave further implements to the reform by recommending the appointment of a Committee to work out the estimates of expenditure to be incurred on introducting this reform, making it impossible for all universities to changeover to the new pattern. In accordance with the above recommendation a Three-Year Degree Course Estimates Committee was set up on October 1, 1956.

TERMS OF REFERENCE

The terms of reference of the Committee were as follows:

(1) To make recommendations regarding the best manner in which Three-Year Degree Course could be introduced in the affiliated Colleges and Universities in the country and the arrangements which would be made during the interim period for admission of students to the reorganised Arts and Science Colleges and the professional colleges as constituted at present till the new pattern is fully introduced;

(2) To frame the estimates of expenditure involved in the reorganisation of collegiate education implicit in the introduction of Three-Year Degree Course in Universities and affiliated Colleges;

(3) To suggest the proportions in which the expenditure may be shared between the Central Government and the State Governments for introducing the Three-Year Degree Course;

(4) To recommend the best manner in which interim grants from Central Government may be made to the State Governments for the year 1956-57 in case formulation of schemes by the State Government is delayed;

(5) To consider and examine the future of the Intermediate Colleges and such other problems as may be ancillary to the main question of introducing Three-Year Degree Course;

(6) To consider any other issues which may be relevant to the question of introducing Three-Year Degree Course in the Universities and the affiliated Colleges.

CONTENTS

Introduction; Nature of the Problem; Financial Implications; Administrative Implications; Summary of Recommendations; Appendices—Terms of Reference; Report of the Sub-Committee of the Estimates Committee.

RECOMMENDATIONS

The Three-Year Degree Course should be introduced in as many universities as possible during the Second Five-Year Plan period.

The unit of reorganisation should be a university and not a college, so that no university will give two types of degrees for the same courses.

During the transitional period, students passing the Intermediate Examination should be admitted to the second year of the Three-Year Degree Course.

The total amount which would be required to introduce the reform including recurring expenditure for four years, will be about Rs. 25 crores.

The expenditure involved in introducing the reform should be shared between the Central and State Governments in equal proportion.

During the Second Five-Year Plan period, the Central Government should give Rs. seven-and-a-half crores, including Rs. two-and-a-half crores to be made available by the University Grants Commission. A similar amount should be found by the State Governments including contributions from Private Managements. The total amount available will thus be Rs. 15 crores which will be sufficient for upgrading 180 Intermediate Colleges and reorganising 300 Degree Colleges which should be taken as the targets for the Second Five-Year Plan.

There should be a public examination at the end of the pre-University Class.

Professional colleges should either conduct their own admission tests or select candidates for pre-professional courses on the basis of Higher Secondary/Pre-University Examination.

The number of students should be restricted to 800-1000 per college.

While the Three-Year Degree Course is introduced, steps should be taken to improve the quality of collegiate education in general. For this purpose from the grants available, it is necessary to revise syllabuses, introduce General Education Courses, reduce over-crowding in colleges, improve the teacher-pupil ratio, strengthen laboratories, replenish libraries and, wherever, possible, institute tutorial system.

The State of U.P. will present a special problem because of the entirely different system operating in that State.

SUB-COMMITTEE OF THE CENTRAL FRUIT PRODUCTS ADVISORY COMMITTEE ON CHUTNEY INDUSTRY IN INDIA, 1956—REPORT

Delhi, Manager of Publications, 1958. 35p.+vip.

Chairman : Dr. Girdhari Lal.
Members : Shri N.S. Pochkhanawala; Shri H.C. Bhatnagar.
Secretary : Shri P.H. Bhatt.

APPOINTMENT

The Central Fruit Products Advisory Committee set up under the Fruit Products Order, 1955, constituted a Sub-Committee on October 31, 1956 to enquire into the Chutney Industry in India.

TERMS OF REFERENCE

To survey the present status of Chutney Industry in India and to study problems faced by the industry particularly in augmenting the export trade and to suggest Plans for its development.

CONTENTS

Preface; Adoption of Resolution; Introduction, History of the Industry; Production; Method of Manufacture; Raw Material Requirements; The Investment Pattern of the Industry; Conditions of Factories; Quality; Research; Demand and Prospects; Summary and Recommendations; Appendices A & B.

RECOMMENDATIONS

The average production for five years for chutney is estimated at 734 tons valued at Rs. 13·6 lakhs.

The manufacture of mango chutney can be divided into two parts—(i) the pickling of green mango slices and (ii) preparation of mango chutney.

The manufacture of chutney is done according to the specifications of the Fruit Products Order, 1955.

The major raw materials required for manufacture of chutney are green mangoes, sugar, salt, vinegar or acetic acid, barrels, bottles, labels, fuel, spices and other packing materials.

The Sub-Committee feels that while pickling of green mangoes, due attention is not given to the quality of the raw material as the manufacturers are inclined to an opinion that this does not reflect on the final product.

The Sub-Committee is of the opinion that in the interest of the chutney industry there is a need for reorganising the pickling industry and putting it on a footing which would not only give a product produced under hygienic and sanitary conditions and of a standard quality but also would safeguard the interest of the primary processors. A small cooperative processing unit can be operated if the Government assistance was available partially in the form of grant and partially in the form of loan.

The Sub-Committee also favours the proposal of expanding the scope of the primary processing societies which can undertake the manufacture of mango chutney.

The Sub-Committee recommends that immediate steps should be taken for establishment of fruit preservation unit at Malda in West Bengal.

Detailed specifications of pickled mango should be worked out and prescribed under the Fruit Products Order.

The Sub-Committee was given to understand that the revised procedure for rebate on excise duty of sugar used in chutney is likely to be announced shortly. This would give an impetus to the chutney industry.

The chutney industry would do well in utilising the better quality salt in pickling.

The chutney industry while making contract for purchases of bottles should give detailed specifications including alkalinity factor and get the various lots examined prior to final purchase.

The Sub-Committee is of the view that good quality corks at a reasonable price should be made available to the chutney industry.

There seemed to be an orthodox approach to various problems and considerations due to conventions and past practices seemed to weigh heavily in the matters of modernisation and even in expansion of activities. Both at Bombay and Calcutta the Director of Industries gave the Sub-Committee to understand that the chutney industry had not approached for assistance in any form.

In spite of availability of accommodation in the factories it was observed that an unorganised manner of handling affected the working of the units.

In the factories the water line should be realigned so that the water can be made available to almost all the centres of processing departments.

More stainless steel equipment should be introduced by chutney industry.

The chutney industry would do well to employ steam cooking which would give better results and would avoid the smoke in the factory. This would also improve the quality of the finished products.

The Sub-Committee is of the view that most of the chutney manufacturers are in a position to instal adequate equipment and machinery. Facilities now being given by the Government to small scale industries should be fully utilised by the industry.

The performance of the chutney manufacturers in conforming to the quality standards prescribed under the Fruit Products Order has been creditable. A pilot scheme for continuous check sampling of all chutney manufactured at Bombay, Calcutta and Madras has yielded useful results.

The Sub-Committee recommends that arrangements should be made for analysis of fruit products samples at the port towns and a system of certification of quality standards according to the minimum requirements under the Fruit Products Order should be started as early as possible. Such a measure would help considerably in export promotion.

It would be advantageous if, most of the manufacturers agreed with the view that a procedure is worked out in consultation with the traders according to the grade and the specifications to be provided under the Agricultural Produce (Grading and Marking) Act, 1937.

The Sub-Committee recommends that a Senior Research Officer should be entrusted a project on chutney at Central Food Technological Research Institute, Mysore. There has not been much work done in preparation and processing of chutney.

Nearly 82 to 83 per cent of the production of chutney was exported.

As there are many resources for developing the chutney industry in India the Sub-Committee recommends that the intensive area scheme for village industries of the Khadi and Village Industry Board as well as some of the Community Development Block should include processing of green mango pickling.

For developing demand within the country the industry should participate in more exhibitions, produce leaflets and pamphlets as well as for developing new recipes to suit the indigenous tastes. There is also need for introducing more varieties of chutneys made of different fruits and vegetables. The prospective demand within the country is estimated to be 500 tons per year by 1960-61.

The Sub-Committee recommends a ban for next five years from 1958 on export of pickled mango which is a raw material for chutney industry.

Although chutney exports are as much as 50 per cent of the total exports of fruit products, the export of chutney has been more or less stationary. This situation, the Sub-Committee feels is due to the lack of incentive amongst the manufacturers.

There is likelihood of serious competition in the chutney trade in the world market. Even to maintain the existing exports the chutney industry should concentrate more on quality, on selling under their own brand and on intensive propaganda and publicity.

The excise duty rebate on sugar used in exported chutney should be collected as a fund to start an export promotion organisation. The Government should make a contribution to this fund on the basis of what is being done for other export promotion councils.

A proposal for forming an export promotion council for all fruit products may be studied and its feasibility examined by the Ministry of Food and Agriculture.

The chutney manufacturers should collectively take up advertising of the Indian mango chutney in foreign markets. Attractive pamphlets and brochures depicting the qualities of chutney should be prepared.

Some European countries are importing mango chutney through established importers in U.K. The expansion of our trade in this country is most likely if our trade representatives bring these parties in contact with our manufacturers.

A reported ban on imports of fruit products from India in certain European countries should be investigated and an attempt be made to remove the same.

Although in trade agreements with some countries export of fruit products has been included, no useful results have been achieved. Our trade representatives may be requested to explore possibilities for promotion of export of chutney as well as other fruit products.

COMMITTEE OF ENQUIRY INTO DEMANDS OF LABOUR OF PORT AND DOCK WORKERS, 1956—REPORT

New Delhi, Ministry of Transport and Communications, 1958. 353p.+xivp.

One-Man Committee : Shri P.C. Chaudhuri.

APPOINTMENT

The Committee on Port and Dock Workers, Enquiry into Demands of Labour was constituted under the Ministry of Transport and Communications on November 27, 1956.

TERMS OF REFERENCE

(i) To enquire into the disparities and anomalies in the pay scales and allowances of Class III and Class IV employees of the Major Ports and to submit proposals for their rationalisation.

(ii) To consider the question of reducing to a minimum the number of casual shore workers and the drawing up of departmental schemes for decasualisation, and to examine the disparities between the wages of permanent, temporary and casual workers and between those of shore labour and stevedore labour on time rate.

The enquiry was also intended to cover posts, corresponding to Class III and Class IV posts in the Major Ports, under the Dock Labour Boards, subject to the proviso that the final decision would rest with the respective Boards.

The terms of Reference further included a number of items relating to the conditions of service of Port and Dock Workers such as working hours, night work, weekly off, provident fund, retiring gratuity, overtime payment, holidays and leave.

CONTENTS

Introduction; Part I—Major Ports; Factors Bearing on Rationalisation; Rationalisation of Pay Scales; Part II—Decasualisation of Shore Workers; Turnround of Shipping and other connected Matters; Part III—Retirement Benefits; Working Hours, Night Shift and Weekly Off; Overtime Work and Rate of Payment; Leave, Holidays and Other Privileges; Tables I to LXXIII.

RECOMMENDATIONS

Factors Bearing On Rationalisation Of Pay Scales And Allowances

Considering the limitations of the various methods and the time and expense involved, it is hardly worthwhile adopting the highly specialised techniques of the Factor-Comparison and point methods for the evaluation of any sets of posts in the Major Ports. An appreciable number of posts, as will be explained later, can easily be identified and their function and responsibilities determined with a fair amount of accuracy from the material already available. For certain posts peculiar to ports, particularly in the Marine/Port, Deputy Conservator and Engineering Departments, additional information would have been helpful, but even in these cases it does not seem difficult to evaluate and grade them for the purposes of working out pay scales most appropriate to them, by bearing in mind the principles of Ranking and Classification. In formulating my proposals for rationalisation, therefore, it has not been necessary to go beyond the first two qualitative methods.

Rationalisation Of Pay Scales

The basic minimum scale for Class IV should be revised to Rs. 30-1-35 in all the Ports. Similarly, the basic minimum scale for Class III staff employed in Clerical duties and for whom Matriculation or equivalent qualification is prescribed as the minimum, should be Rs. 60-3-81-4-125-5-130. Apart from this any other alteration in the present wage structure not based on the recommendations of the Central Pay Commission is not considered to be within the Terms of Reference of this enquiry.

It has not been possible to embark on a detailed job evaluation partly because of the limitations of time and partly because of certain practical difficulties which stand in the way of the application of Factor Comparison or Point Rating methods. The method adopted has, therefore, been to choose certain categories in each Department and endeavour to fix the appropriate pay scales in the light of the recommendations of the Central Pay Commission for comparable posts under the Central Government. There is, however, a clear necessity for work studies to be undertaken by Port Administrations if problems of this type are to be solved in absolute terms.

As regards other posts, fixation of pay scales will have to be done by the Port Administrations having regard to the inter-departmental and intra-departmental relativities and differentials. While due weight has to be given to the last two factors, the Port Administrations should seek to 'broadband' categories of staff;

weightage should nermally be given to the above factors only if these would result in a material alteration of the pay scales or a translation into another standard scale prescribed by the Central Pay Commission.

The possibility of introducing any system of payment of results in the Technical Departments, particularly in regard to categories like Tally Clerks, Crane Driver, etc., should be considered further by the Ports.

In many Administrative Departments, the proportion of Upper Division clerical cadre to the Lower Division and the proportion of the Supervisory staff to the clerical strength is quite low in most of the Ports; higher proportions will be more in consonance with work requirements also.

In the Accounts Department, the Port Administrations of Calcutta and Bombay should examine the possibility of prescribing Departmental Tests to regulate eligibility for appointment to supervisory posts in their Accounts Departments. It is also suggested that the present designations in those Ports should be changed to Junior and Senior Accountants.

The Port Administrations should make a beginning towards the introduction of the Messenger system.

There seem to be weighty reasons for the transfer of control of certain Special Departments like the Port Railways, Lighthouses and Fire Services to the Railway Board, the Central Lighthouse Department and the Fire Services Organisation of the State Governments concerned. This, however, is only a suggestion.

Medical facilities should be pooled between the Port Administrations and the Dock Labour Boards.

While it is premature to suggest any radical changes in view of the fact that the Dock Labour Boards have commenced functioning only recently, there is a possibility of effecting uniformity among the Dock Labour Boards even now by adopting the standard pay scales for Lower and Upper Division Clerks and higher posts. It will be a good principle to follow if both the Port Administrations and the Dock Labour Boards keep one another informed of material revisions in the pay scales and other conditions of service.

The fixation of pays of staff who have elected to come on to the new pay scales should be done on the basis of one increment for every three years of services as was done by the Central Government when implementing the recommendations of the Central Pay Commission. It may be possible to avoid anomalies by readjusting the dates of their increments in respect of periods falling short of multiples of three years.

While the existing staff will naturally have the option to retain their old pay scales if they are more advantageous, it will not be equitable to freeze at a higher level such of the posts whose pay scales at present happen to be higher than those justifiable in the light of the recommendations of the Central Pay Commission.

In the absence of further information in regard to the practice in other State Governments and in view of the fact that the pattern of pay scales of Central Government on which the above proposals are made is different from the pattern of the pay scales of State Governments, it has not been found possible to recommend payment of 'unclean allowance' which is now being paid in Bombay Port to sweepers in other Ports also.

The desirability of providing suitable avenues of promotion requires special emphasis.

Decasualisation Of Shore Workers

The Ports should make every endeavour to keep contract labour below 25 per cent of the total strength of shore labour.

Steps should be taken to approximate the wages paid to contractors' labour on the same basis and at the same rates as those paid to Port labour.

In assessing the required strength of shore labour the following should be regarded as relevant factors:

(a) Volume of trade and its variations;
(b) Types of cargo to be handled;
(c) Availability of mechanical aids;
(d) The rate of output of labour; and
(e) General working conditions.

The minimum labour strength shall be calculated by taking the average daily attendance figures of permanent as well as of casual workers in the last five years; the average daily figures shall be increased by 20 per cent to provide for absenteeism and leave reserves; 75 per cent of the gross total thus obtained shall be the number of workers to be included in the Permanent Register; the remaining 25 per cent shall be the number of workers to be included in the Temporary Register.

Peak requirements will be met by the employment of non-registered labour on the recommendations of Registration Committee provided that the period of their engagement shall not exceed 10 per cent of the strength of the Temporary Register.

Port administrations may examine whether action should not be initiated through the Registration Committee or special agencies of the collection of statistics for further investigation with a view to facilitate the proper allocation of heavy and light work among the workers.

The registered labour shall consist only of two categories, Permanent and Temporary.

Two registers shall be maintained one each for the Permanent and Temporary categories; within each category the names of the workers shall be entered in the strict order of seniority. The register should contain information regarding the name of the worker, his address, date of entry into service, the scale of pay and all such information which may be necessary for the retention, promotion or when called for removal of the name of the worker from the register.

Workers in the Temporary Register should serve as a reservoir to fill up vacancies in the Permanent Register.

Both categories of workers shall be entitled to the payment of attendance money, the benefits of Workmen's Compensation Act, medical assistance, housing facilities, weekly days of rest, etc.

Workers on the Permanent Register will be entitled for the benefit of Provident Fund, special contribution, leave, holidays, etc., under the rules and regulations applicable to the permanent staff of the Ports.

The worker will be liable to undertake any kind of work included in the expression 'shore work'.

A Registration Committee should be formed of three members, one representative each of shore labour and of shipowners with the Chairman of the Port Trust or the Administrator of the Port as Chairman, the Committee shall have power to co-opt the Regional Labour Commissioner or the Traffic Manager for expert advice and assistance.

The Registration Committee shall screen all entrants and classify them according to the registers, go into the question of labour rendered surplus after decasualisation and be responsible for periodic revisions and adjustments of the register.

Where there is sufficient work for both categories the work on the third shift should be shared between them on a strict principle of rotation.

Attendance money for temporary workers should be the same as that for permanent workers and preferably at annas 12 a day.

The constitution of a gang shall be in accordance with the existing practice in the Port; there should be a differential in the payment made to the head of the gang who directs work and the labour who works under his direction.

Seniority, merit and fitness as well as past services should be the basis for promotion as leader of the gang.

The central call stand should be so located as to enable workers to reach the place of work before the shift is due to begin.

Where there are more than one call stand, there should be telephonic communication between stands and transport arrangements to carry labour from one stand to another.

The conditions of the call stands for shore workers require considerable improvement and should conform to the standard laid down for stevedore workers by the Dock Workers (Regulation of Employment) Enquiry Committee Report, 1955.

The normal age of retirement should be 55 years with the option to the Ports to retain workers who are physically fit upto the age of 60 years.

The Ports shall examine the possibility of reducing the number of attendances at call stands particularly by permanent workers.

The minimum wages of decasualised and casual shore workers in Ports should be equalised.

No incremental scale for casual shore workers appear necessary, the better course of action will be to keep the proportion continuously under review to bring the casual workers on to the Permanent Register to the extent possible.

In the present conditions a higher rate for stevedore work seems to be inevitable; but without seeking to anticipate the conclusions of the Tripartite Committee, which is going into the question of introduction of piece work rates, it can be reasonably assumed that the differentials between the wages of stevedore and shore labour will be further narrowed down.

A Model Scheme for direct employment of shore labour has been framed for adoption by the Ports.

The Major Ports should consider the possibility of working out suitable schemes of transfer agreements with the Minor Ports on a selective basis.

Casual labour rendered surplus must be given preference over fresh labour for enrolment in the Temporary Register.

Turn-Round Of Shipping And Other Connected Matters

If a Port is to function properly and continuously, it must have a margin of capacity to enable it to meet sudden or seasonal increase in traffic without congestion.

What is specially important is to regulate the flow of cargo in and out of the docks. This cannot, however, be achieved by unilateral action by the Port administrations and calls for the cooperation of all interests concerned. This may also require a certain conformity to discipline which may be regarded as irksome, though difficulties of individual consignees should receive special considerations.

It would not be proper to minimise in any way the extra cost and wastefulness of congestion in a Port. It is probable that some of the congestion is unavoidable in certain circumstances; this is particularly true of the aftermath of strikes or 'go slow' practices which inevitably lead to a subsequent rush of traffic to clear. Congestion may also result from other circumstances as when foreign shippers, anticipating import restrictions, send out in a hurry as many consignments as possible in the hope that the goods might be cleared at the receiving end, on the plea that these had been ordered long before the restrictions were announced.

Unless proper arrangements on a coordinated basis are made in advance, difficulties will continue. It has been estimated by a representative of shipping interests that in the next few years, 80 per cent of the inward cargo will be Government imports; it has, therefore, been suggested that steps should be taken at the highest level to arrange for the routing of such shipments not only as between the Major Ports but also to Minor Ports where they can be cleared overside into lighters. For this, however, it has been stressed, there must be forward planning at all levels and continuous supervision of its implementation.

The need for detailed planning over a definite period in an under-developed country has been stressed in the First Five-Year Plan. It has been emphasised that "while there is need for concentrating effort on the more immediate problems, planning implies the readiness on the part of the community to view the social process as one whole and to take action designed to shape this process along desired lines for a definite period. Planning as an approach to a rational solution of problems has been accepted. Difficulties may of course arise when policies change or targets are not reached in time. In the matter of foodgrains, the Ports, following the announcement in June, 1949 of complete self-sufficiency by 1951, could hardly envisage and be prepared to deal with foodgrain imports of the present dimensions. With regard to exports, planning can bear excellent results and eliminate congestion at Ports if there is full coordination between all concerned. The routing of traffic should be possible provided there is forward planning based on precise data.

As a substantial portion of the imports particularly of bulk cargo are on Government account, and orders are invariably placed in advance, it should not be difficult to arrange for the routing of ships to different Ports according to a phased programme. The State Trading Corporation have already given much thought to the routing of their exports of mineral ores and other commodities through all available Ports nearest to the sources of supply. A similar approach in regard to the imports of large quantities of foodgrains, iron and steel, machinery, etc., by landing such goods at Ports nearest to the destinations will be an important method of solving the problem of congestion. For this however it is essential to have adequate information about end-use and destination, as also about the facilities available at the Ports for the handling, storage and onward despatch of such cargo. It was the practice, in the earlier days of import control to mark import licences with the name of port of destination; this was done with a view to conserve shipping space and make the best possible use of rail or road transport services. If a similar procedure is now followed, it should not only relieve the burden of some of our Ports and the Railways, but also ensure quicker distribution to the end-use area.

It is essential for the success of any routing of traffic to Ports that there should be complete coordination of sea transport with all other forms of transport.

Considering the successful way in which lighters have been used in the Port of Calcutta for one side handling of cargo and the importance attached to lighterage in other important Ports, there is no adequate reason why this means of expediting the turn-round of ships in the harbour should not be utilised to a greater extent in other Major Ports, particularly in Bombay and Madras.

A point which may have to be considered is the effect of clearance by lighters on the Ports' finances. In Madras Port, no separate charge is made for the use of lighters, which are freely lent on requisition for export work; any extra cost involved is already covered by the Port dues. It is possible that the increased use of lighters may lead to some reduction in Port dues, but in the paramount interest of a quick turnround of shipping, this should not stand in the way of more lighterage facilities. In London, there is in fact a Free Water Clause in the Charter of the Port Authority. A similar provision may well be made at our Ports.

If an adequate and well-equipped fleet of lighters is maintained by the Port authority and is made available on a reasonable charge, it will encourage the best possible use of this mode of transport.

In the Port working of lighter traffic, it is essential to ensure continuous cooperation between all concerned so that the right craft come alongside the ship at the right time, having due regard to the stowage of the ship and the availability of particular cargo; if this is lacking, congestion and delays will remain unsolved.

From the point of view of quicker turnround of shipping, new forms of transport, particularly road haulage and river and canal navigation, are also required to be encouraged. Road transport, if properly regulated, need not adversely compete with the Railways, but rather act as a feeder to them and take off them some of the burden which they are at present unable to carry. Shipping and Ports—the links between the sea and inland transport—must grow in importance if India is to attain economic prosperity.

In some ways, particularly over moderate distances, road haulage has an advantage over carriage of goods by rail. Though the Railways have made considerable progress, it cannot be said that there has really been substantial improvement in the locomotive speed of goods trains, except on the more expensive Parcel Expresses, during the last forty years. Cross-country journeys by rail are often slow and usually involve changes, with long waits at Junctions; a direct route taken by a motor bus can be much quicker and even cheaper. If this be true of passenger traffic, such advantages can also apply to the carriage of goods by motor trucks where direct routes are available.

The Docks at most of the Ports, particularly the Major Ports, were originally built mainly for Railway feeder services and road connections as such were not thought of except for purposes of local transit. If advantage is to be taken of road haulage, steps will have to be taken to construct proper roadways to give access to the quays. There will also have to be careful coordination between rail and road traffic so that one means of transport does not get into the way of the other; an example of the present difficulties is a roadway in one of the Ports, which traverses three sets of railway lines in less than two hundred yards.

If the removal of cargo from the transit sheds and warehouses of the Major Ports is to be expedited by road haulage, it is obvious that there will have to be a substantial improvement in the supply of trucks. Apart from this, considerable improvement will have to be undertaken in the Ports themselves by the provision of road terminals, better road approaches, spaces for parking and turnround; proper loading and unloading bays, suitable handling equipment, etc. It has been observed that "Ports which have not modernised their truck facilities are finding the problem of traffic congestion and turnround delay an increasingly costly one." It is recommended that early steps be taken to make a thorough assessment of the immediate and long term possibilities of road haulage; this is all the more important for our Major Ports in view of continuing inability of the Railways or for that matter of other means of transport such as inland waterways to meet all the requirements of the Ports. In examining the problem with reference to our Ports, it should be considered what steps can be taken to remove any complication arising out of the traditional use of bullock carts.

In the interests of developing inter-State traffic, it was considered desirable that an agency controlled by the Central Government should be set up to regulate the operation of transport vehicles on inter-State routes.

The use of coastal shipping to any appreciable degree to relieve the congestion in the Major Ports will depend on the availability of a sufficient fleet of sailing vessels. As the Sailing Vessels Committee had pointed out, the lack of organisation among owners of sailing vessels is a serious impediment and will have to be removed as an initial measure before the industry can be developed.

It has been suggested that in order to enable the coastal vessels to obtain cargo for their return journeys, encouragement should be given to industries to develop in the regions of the Minor Ports also.

A number of Minor Ports may not be able to function effectively to take over excess cargo from the Major Ports; this will be mainly due to the lack of rail facilities. Coordination between rail and sea transport is thus necessary in the interests of the working of the Ports in general and the progress of our coast-wise trade.

It must be recommended that the transit sheds are designed on the assumption that there will be a reasonably steady flow of goods, through them, from wagons, trucks or carts, to the ship or from the ship, through them again, to wagons, trucks or carts. If circumstances prevent cargo from being moved continuously, the sheds inevitably become congested thereby adversely affecting the unloading of export cargo from wagons etc., and retarding the onward movement of imported goods. The problem could be eased if the sheds were larger, but apart from the additional overhead cost, the location of the transit sheds may be such that it may be physically impossible to enlarge the sheds. This may well be illustrated by the position in Madras, where it is difficult to find any space for expansion within the harbour. Nevertheless, in the general interest of removing congestion and making it easier for the Port and Dock workers to carry out their duties unhampered—an aspect which has been stressed by the representatives of labour—it is desirable that, within the limitations indicated above, steps should be taken to improve shed accommodation at all the principal Major Ports of Bombay, Calcutta and Madras. There should be the maximum freedom of movement about the shed, unimpeded by physical obstructions and aided by an ordered sequence of operations. The sheds should also be well equipped with suitable devices so that there is a minimum risk of bottlenecks. It may be mentioned that since the War, in foreign Ports, improvement has been effected by joining existing sheds on the quays to provide sufficiently large unloading bays to enable more vehicles, in one case a maximum of 17 vehicles, to unload simultaneously under the covered section of the main dock.

Attention will also have to be paid to warehouse facilities at the above three Ports.

Goods are not merely stored in warehouses but have to be dealt with in numerous different ways. A common aspect of this branch of Port activity is in the case of bulk importation, storage at the Port over a period, and gradual sub-division and forwarding in hundreds of small consignments. This is an important commercial function performed at Major Ports which are situated in large distributing centres. Here is an opportunity to introduce a number of modern techniques. Some of the new methods of cargo handling, such as the unit load operation, can lead to a doubling or even trebling of the capacity of a warehouse.

The handling of general cargo, raises many problems on account of the varying sizes and shapes of packages. The more important mechanical appliances that have been developed recently in the handling of general cargo are electrical mobile trucks, mobile diesel cranes and, by far the most important and useful, the fork lifts. While fork lifts are used in Bombay and certain mobile cranes are available in all the Major Ports, there is a similar need for the introduction and greater use of fork lifts in all the Ports. The fork lift is useful for the quick handling of any type of general cargo not only on the quay but in the sheds and should obviously be utilised in larger numbers.

There is scope for the elimination of wasted time and effort both by improvement in the organisation of the work and by the introduction of mechanical aids. Disproportionate efforts now incurred by moving cargo solely by manual labour could be effectively reduced, and labour employed more productively, by moving traffic from point to point at the dock and in transit shed and warehouse by mechanical means. It should be borne in mind that most of the ships calling at our Ports are foreign-owned and many of them are equipped with the latest machinery for the handling of cargoes, to enable our shore labour to keep pace with the work on the hatches of such ships, it is necessary to provide our workers with correspondingly efficient mechanical aids. Cargo handling in our Major Ports can be greatly improved by the more frequent use of fork lifts, mobile cranes and similar appliances.

Work study in selected departments, as in the engineering department and those relating to cargo handling, will be helpful in finding out the anomalies and defects of the existing system and in suggesting ways of improvement so that equal effort can be equally rewarded. Such studies cannot, however, be successfully conducted without the cooperation of the workers themselves; it is therefore desirable that the arrangements for the studies should be made after due consultation with the representatives of Port and Dock workers. As it is, one of the complaints of Labour is that the existing rates of payment were on the basis of past records, some of which were not sufficiently detailed to be reliable, rather than on any kind of work measurement. In such circumstances, it would be all the more necessary to introduce the use of work study.

In the course of the present enquiry, it became increasingly evident that there was no uniformity in the collection of basic data and this rendered a comparative study of the precise duties and functions of various categories of employees at the different Ports difficult. As the objective of uniformity and the principle of equal pay for equal work have been emphasised, as in the Terms of Reference for this enquiry, it would be advisable to initiate a uniform system of collection and maintenance of statistical material by the Ports. The details of some of the requirements of statistical data were suggested by the Port and Shipping Statistics Committee in their Report in July, 1954. For purposes of ready reference and comparison, it would be helpful if the Administration Reports of all the Major Ports are prepared in accordance with definite and uniform proformas; in this matter, the Bombay Administration Report with certain additions, would be a suitable model.

In employment like those in the Major Ports it is clearly to the advantage of both the administration and the employees to have proper schemes of training. Such training becomes all the more necessary if tests of fairly high standards are prescribed to regulate promotions and confirmations after completing a period of probation.

In the Railways, there are as many as 24 Training Schools for the Railway staff, some of which are technical schools attached to the Railway Workshops to train apprentices for eventual appointment as skilled artisans or as supervisors or skilled workers. Refresher and promotion courses have also been arranged. Training on similar lines can be fruitfully undertaken by the Port administrations also. It might be useful to arrange for the training facilities on a joint basis with the Dock Labour Boards if maximum results are to be achieved with the minimum of outlay.

Apart from technical training, a properly planned programme of adult education, encouraging and understanding of the problems of the transport industry and of the means to solve them, is sure to make a vital contribution to the efficient working of the Port. There is also a need for a literacy drive among the class IV staff.

Retirement Benefits

In regard to all categories of staff to whom the Provident Fund Rules apply the rules should be uniform throughout. Any rule in which a particular class of employees has been accorded a lower scale of benefits should be amended to remove the discrimination.

In respect of Port employees governed by Provident Fund Rules the rate of subscription and contribution should be at eight-one-by-three per cent of basic wages and dearness allowance in full. Local compensatory, house rent and overtime allowances should be excluded.

For workers remunerated on a piece work basis, no specific recommendation is made in view of the fact that revised piece-rate scheme for some of the Ports is under consideration.

Eligibility to subscribe to Provident Fund should be determined with reference to the fact whether the employee has been taken on a permanent or temporary basis. In the latter case the subscription should commence only after one year's service has been completed.

No liberalisation in the present rules relating to sanction of advances from Provident Fund is called for. As accumulations in the Provident Fund are also regarded as being held in trust for the benefit of the family of the employees, there is scope for even tightening the present rules.

Without conceding that retirement benefits are in the form of deferred wages, there is ample justification for amending the Provident Fund Rules to provide for payment of the Port's contribution as well as Special Contribution in the event of any kind of discharge other than that caused by misconduct involving loss of the Port's funds.

For the purpose of the application of the Provident Fund Rules, the pay limit up to which an employee can be considered as Class III should be placed at Rs. 500 and for Special Contribution in Bombay and Madras

Ports according as the employee draws a pay of more than Rs. 320 or Rs. 300 or not should be amended accordingly.

There should be a separate Board of Trustees for the management of Provident Funds, in which Labour should be represented, the Board will be responsible to the Port authority.

Special contributions should be regulated on the basis of one month's emoluments for each completed year of service up to a maximum of twenty-five years. Only basic wages and dearness allowance in full should be treated as emoluments for this purpose.

As has been suggested in the case of Provident Fund, the rules relating to Special Contribution should be made uniform for all staff drawing pay up to Rs. 500.

The remarks offered earlier in regard to withholding of the Port's contribution in the Contributory Provident Fund apply also to the Special Contribution.

The increase in Provident Fund accumulations and Special Contributions should be converted into annuities of the joint and survivor type. It may also be necessary to amend the relevant sections of the Port's Acts in order to provide, in the Provident Fund Rules, for annuities on a compulsory basis.

Working Hours, Night Shift And Weekly Off

In the result I am clearly of opinion that the existing 48-hour week should be retained except in the case of office staff who have been dealt with separately and certain intermittent workers for whom a 75-hour week is recommended. This will not place any undue strain on the workers but will on the other hand ensure greater productivity. The crux of the problem of working hours is to decide the length of the working time best suited to a particular stage of social and industrial development. It is my considered opinion that a 48-hour week should achieve the required balance between the workers' right to improved working conditions and the imperative needs of the Second Five-Year Plan. In conclusion, my specific recommendations are as follows:

(i) While a progressive reduction of working hours is a desirable objective, there is no special reason to place the Port Transport Industry on a separate footing; the number of working hours should remain at 48-hours a week;

(ii) Certain categories of staff in the Marine, Lighthouse and other Departments, whose duties are essentially intermittent in character, should observe a 75-hour week; their classification should be undertaken by the Port Administrations; running allowances should be paid to such workers;

(iii) There is no justification for a further reduction in the working hours of the clerical staff by an increase of the lunch interval;

(iv) The working hours of the clerical staff posted to work along with technical staff on outdoor work should be on the same basis as for the latter category;

(v) The working hours of certain Class IV staff attached to offices of the Bombay Port Trust should be on a par with those of other staff subject to slight modifications;

(vi) The port authority should consider the desirability of arranging transport facilities for the workers; where for administrative or other reasons they are unable to do so, evening and night workers should be reimbursed the equivalent of the bus or tram fares when the journeys occur between 11 p.m. and 5 a.m.; and

(vii) Time spent in transit to and from the place of work within the Port during working hours should in all cases be counted as on duty.

Shifts should be as continuous as possible, with comparatively short intervals in between, as at present in Bombay Port.

There should be a uniform night shift of six hours.

The hourly rate for workers on night shift of six hours should be at the rate of one-sixth of the normal wages.

As far as possible, recess periods should be in the middle of the shift.

Recess periods during shifts should be regarded as effective breaks and subject to the exigencies of work, the workers should be permitted to be away from the place of duty.

A few minutes off for smoking should be granted if so desired by a worker.

All Port and Dock workers, except workers in whose case it is not feasible to give a weekly day of rest, should be given a weekly off with full wages after six days' consecutive work.

It will not be obligatory on the Port Authorities to fix Sunday or any other fixed day as the weekly day of rest for all workers but they should try to make suitable arrangements to the extent possible.

The principle laid down in the Award of the Labour Appellate Tribunal, Bombay, in regard to payment for work on weekly day of rest should be followed in the case of all workers with the exception noted above.

Class IV Conservancy Staff should work in rotation on Saturday afternoons and holidays and such workers should be paid overtime at double rates for the period.

Overtime Work And Rate Of Payment

Any additional hours of work in excess of nine hours a day or 48 hours a week, whether or not the worker concerned comes within the purview of the Minimum Wages Act, should be paid for at double the rates.

In principle, the payment of overtime to the clerical staff working short of the general limit of working hours prescribed for other workers does not seem to be justified.

Except in the case of Marine Staff, overtime at double the normal rate should be paid to essentially intermittent staff for work in excess of 75 hours a week and a compensatory allowance should be evolved to replace the present *ad hoc* overtime.

For such Marine Staff whose work is essentially intermittent in character, a scheme of allowance similar to running allowances paid to Railway staff should be evolved; these allowances should count for leave salary, provident fund etc., to the same extent as in the Railways.

A worker should not be called upon to undertake a second consecutive shift except in emergencies when he should be compensated by being paid at overtime rates.

For daily rated workers whose daily wages are determined by dividing the monthly wages by 26, the hourly overtime rate should bear a proportion of 1/208 of the monthly wages instead of 1/240.

Overtime should be calculated on the basis of the entire emoluments drawn by a worker while on regular duty. Emoluments for the calculation of overtime should include house rent allowance also.

Leave, Holidays And Other Privileges

The Leave Rules should be uniform for all categories of staff as well as for decasualised shore labour. In particular, the Rules for the Class IV staff should be brought on par with those for Class III. Similarly, the difference in the Rules applicable to the scheduled and non-scheduled permanent staff, as regards the limit of accumulation of earned leave and eligibility to special disability leave, should be removed.

The present ceilings for the accumulations of earned leave or commuted leave need not be disturbed.

Payment of leave salary in lieu of leave not taken by a worker because of his discharge will not be justified.

The demands that no limit should be placed on special disability and sick leave on full pay, commuted leave, and extraordinary leave are not recommended for acceptance.

Casual leave should be made uniform, at fifteen days in a year, for all categories of staff other than casual labour. This is intended to compensate for the situation that may arise out of the suggestion that there should be no closed holidays in the Ports.

A weekly off-day or holiday should be allowed to be prefixed or suffixed to a period of leave.

It is difficult to fix a definite percentage for leave reserves; depending on the necessity for providing immediate relief, the percentages may vary from 10 per cent to 20 per cent.

The possibility of simplifying the Leave Rules by introducing a system of lump credits on the first day of each year and the payment of a fixed sum as leave salary in the case of decasualised shore labour deserves further examination.

It is necessary that loading and unloading operations in Ports should continue without interruption; there should be no closed holidays for workers employed in handling of cargo and others engaged in work considered essential in that connection; the persons concerned should work on a roster.

The number of holidays for other staff should be fixed at 16 as observed in the Posts and Telegraphs Department; payment for work on holidays should be in accordance with the principle enunciated in the Award of the Labour Appellate Tribunal.

There is no justification for the grant of overtime allowance to the Office staff who work occasionally on holidays; they may have, when possible a compensatory day off within a stipulated period.

The general demand of labour is that the concession should be restored and also extended to cover journeys performed by steamer or road. In opposition to this, it has been urged by certain employers that it is nowhere the practice for any organisation other than the one which is actually engaged in transport services to give such concession to its employees, and that unlike the Central Government employees, the Port and Dock workers are not subject to transfer. As against this point of view, it has to be borne in mind that the principle of according certain privileges has already been considered and recognised. A concession of this type enables a worker to proceed home on short spells of leave; such an opportunity for rest and recuperation in the surroundings of one's own home can only add to the efficiency of the worker returning to duty with renewed health. The restoration of the concession in the form in which it has been applied to the Government servants is, therefore, recommended.

At present no concessions are given for journeys performed by water or road. It was pointed out, in the course of discussion, that a large number of Port workers in Bombay come from districts which are not conveniently connected by rail. The concession in the present form will, therefore, not be of much use to them. In any case, it does not seem very logical to distinguish between the modes of travel for a concession of this nature. It is, therefore, recommended that a similar concession should also be given for journeys by sea, river or road transport to and from places not connected by rail; the concession should be based on the same principles as have been laid down for the P.T.O. concession, that is, the minimum distance should be excluded and the concession should be admissible only once in two years.

JUDICIAL INQUIRY INTO THE CAUSES OF THE ACCIDENT TO TRAIN NO. 603 TUTICORIN EXPRESS BETWEEN ARIYALUR AND KALLAGAM STATIONS ON THE SOUTHERN RAILWAY ON NOVEMBER 23, 1956, 1956—REPORT

New Delhi, Railway Board, 1957. 53p.

One-man Commission : Shri Himansu Kumar Bose.

APPOINTMENT

By a notification of the Government of India, Ministry of Railways (Railway Board) bearing No. E (AO) 56 AP 1-7, November 30, 1956, and published in Part II, Section 3 of the Government of India Gazette of December 1, 1956, the Central Government notified as follows:

"Whereas the Central Government is of opinion that it is necessary to appoint a Commission of Inquiry for the purpose of making an inquiry into the causes of the accident to Train No. 603 Tuticorin Express at Mile 170/14-12 between Ariyalur and Kallagam on the Villupuram—Trichinopoly (Chord) line of the Southern Railway at 5.30 hours on November 23, 1956;

Now therefore, in exercise of the powers conferred by Section 3 of the Commission of Inquiry Act, 1952 (60 of 1952), the Central Government hereby appoints a Commission of Inquiry consisting of Shri Himansu Kumar Bose, a judge of the High Court at Calcutta, as its sole member."

TERMS OF REFERENCE

(i) Make an inquiry into the causes of the said accident and for that purpose take such evidence as may be necessary;

(ii) State its findings as to causes of the said accident and as to the person or persons if any, responsible therefor; and

(iii) Suggest safeguards against similar accidents in future.

CONTENTS

Report; Annexure A.

RECOMMENDATIONS

Unprecedented and unforeseen flood in the river Marudayar and in the areas around the embankments of the river, caused erosion or scour under and around the southern abutment of the bridge No. 252 and its approach, and when the Express Train No. 603 reached the spot of the accident, seventy feet of the approach to the bridge beyond the southern abutment, collapsed or had already collapsed, due to this scour or erosion, and this resulted in the accident.

Some points have been made that the accident was due to defective design and construction of the bridge and its abutments or was due to the bridge being constructed at a site which was not suitable, but it appears to me on the evidence as placed before the Commission that there is no substance in these points. These aspects of the matter, therefore, need not be considered any further.

The following safeguards are suggested for prevention of similar accidents in future:

(a) The foundations of abutments of bridges resting on screw piles should be strengthened and construction of rivetments or pitching of the river banks or margins on either side of the abutments to a sufficient length, should at once be undertaken.

(b) The rules in Chapter X, XI, XIV and XVII of the Indian Railway Way & Works Manual should be rigidly observed and mere nominal compliance should be avoided. Engineers and Inspectors should be instructed to explain the rules to the staff before and during the monsoon each year.

(c) On sections where Railway quarters are not provided to patrolmen, at least two patrollers should be appointed for each beat from experienced gangmen specially trained for the purpose.

(d) The length of beat of patrollers should not exceed three miles.

(e) Night patrolmen should have as part of their equipment a strong electric torch to enable them to observe the level of water and the strength of current flowing through the bridges or along the abutments.

(f) Patrollers should be trained to take soundings, probings near abutments and piers to determine the depth of scour in order to decide whether trains should be slowed down or stopped and piloted over the danger point, and the selection of men for this work should be from people who can usefully function in this manner.

(g) Stationary watchmen should be posted at the bridge during floods or heavy rainfall whether there is imminent danger to the bridge or not, until the flood water subsides and the water reaches the normal level.

(h) In case of doubt the patrolman should not allow trains to pass over bridges when the river is flowing at high velocity.

(i) Signboards should be put up at either end of the bridges at adequate distance from the bridge.

(j) The speed limit of the train should be restricted

to five to 10 miles per hour over bridges whenever there is rise in the level or increase in the flow of water during monsoon.

(k) Good glass should be fitted to the YP Engines to make it possible for the drivers to see through the glass at a distance especially during rains.

(l) Daily water reading should be taken at all important bridges during the monsoon and the Register should be available for perusal by the Supeior Engineering staff, at any time. The staff should be properly trained for the purpose.

(m) The rules in Chapters X and XI of the Way & Works Manual should be amplified to include an appendix on river training and control of big and small rivers and indications to be looked for future trouble clearly described and explained. The Railway Assistant Engineers and District Engineers should undergo a short course on this and also visit river model research stations to acquaint themselves with the behaviour of rivers and their response to training works.

(n) The high flood level mark should be prominently marked on every bridge and a danger level mark below high flood level should be fixed by the Engineering authority and marked in *red*. When the level is exceeded, the patrolman should be prepared to stop trains and pilot them if necessary.

(o) Passenger trains should carry portable telephone instruments so that they can communicate with the nearest Railway Station in the event of trains being halted between stations by patrolmen.

THE COMMISSION OF INQUIRY TO ASCERTAIN THE CAUSES OF THE ACCIDENT TO 565 DOWN PASSENGER TRAIN BETWEEN JADCHERLA AND MAHBUBNAGAR ON THE CENTRAL RAILWAY, ON THE NIGHT OF SEPTEMBER 1/2, 1956, 1956—REPORT

Delhi, Railway Board, 1957. 134p.

One-Member
Commission : Shri Sunderlal Trikamlal Desai.
Assessors : Shri N.K. Mitra; Dr. K.L. Rao.

APPOINTMENT

The Commission of Inquiry to Ascertain the Causes of the Accident to 565 Down Passenger Train between Jadcherla and Mahbubnagar on the Central Railway, on the night of September 1/2, 1956 was constituted under the Ministry of Railways (Railway Board) vide their Notification, dated December 10, 1956, in pursuance of Section 3 of the Commission of Inquiry Act 1952 (LX of 1952).

TERMS OF REFERENCE

(i) To consider the Report of the Government Inspector of Railways on the said accident, and take such additional evidence as may be necessary; and

(ii) State its findings as to the causes of the said accident and the person or persons, if any, responsible therefor.

CONTENTS

Accident; Commission of Inquiry; Report of the Government Inspector of Railways; Inquiry at Hyderabad; Alignment; Pochani Nalla; Bridge No. 229; Breaches at Bridge 229 on August 1, 1956; Restoration work done after breaches of August 1, 1956; Version on Shri Bheemadu, the night watchman on duty on September 1, 1956; Breaches of the embankment of bridge 229 on the night of September 1, 1956; Damage to bridge caused by the Crash; Ventway of Bridge 229; The Jangaon Accident of September 27, 1954; Directives issued by Railway Board in December 1954; Circulars issued by Chief Engineer; Patrolling on the Section and watch at Night; Evidence; Questions for determination; Case for the Railway; What was the Intensity of Rainfall; Was there any defect in the Restoration Work after breaches on August 1, 1956?; Bridge was structurally sound; Removal of speed restriction on August 21, 1956; Ventway was inadequate; Plea of act of God; Plea of inevitable accident; Grouping of bridges 229 and 233; Bheemadu not responsible for the accident; Argument for the Railway; Precautionary measures after Jangaon accident; Watch at tank affected bridges; Modification of instructions; Decision to group bridges; Practice followed by Deputy Chief Engineer; Some considerations overlooked; Principal cause of accident: inadequate ventway; Another cause of accident: inadequate watch; Railway responsible for the accident; Persons responsible for the accident; Opinion of Shri Mitra; Opinion of Dr. Rao; Suggested safeguards against similar accidents in future; Opinion of Shri N.K. Mitra, Assessor; Opinion of Dr. K.L. Rao, Assessor; Table; Enclosure; Appendix.

RECOMMENDATIONS

There was two to two-and-a-half inches of rainfall (according to the Railway about three inches) in the catchment area of the Pochari Nalla during one hour after 11 o'clock on the night of September 1. It appears that the level of the flood water at the bridge rose suddenly after Shri Bheemadu had left the bridge for the second time. It has not been possible to ascertain the exact level to which the flood water rose but I agree with the submission made on behalf of the Railway that water over-topped the railway line by about six inches to one foot and this caused serious breaches to the embankments on both the sides of the bridge.

There was considerable damage done to the Permanent-Way and the Bridge by the crashing of the engine and the two coaches when the accident occurred. Jadcherla-end abutment and the wing walls of the bridge were demolished up to about two feet from the bed level. Mahbubnagar-end was destroyed up to about five feet from the bed level. The structure of the bridge before the accident has been ascertained to be sound and the masonry in the undemolished portion of the abutments has on examination also been ascertained to be sound. As to how exactly the engine and the first two coaches went down must remain a matter of theorising; but so much is clear that the left-hand girder of the bridge was found lying across the track with its leading-end 28 feet, six inches ahead of the engine. The right-hand girder suffered more extensive damage and was badly buckled. It was found 56 feet away from the track on the downstream side. The approach banks were damaged to the extent of 25 feet in length and 15 ft. in depth on the Jadcherla side and 35 ft. in length and 16 ft. in depth on the Mahbubnagar side. The track over the damaged portion was completely smashed.

One factor which features prominently in this inquiry and gives rise to a crucial consideration is that the waterway of Bridge 229 near Mahbubnagar was designed to accommodate a discharge of only 2,400 cusecs at a velocity of about 10 feet per second, the height of the flood section corresponding to this flow being 12 feet including the afflux. Hydrological calculations based on carefully selected data were made by Dr. K.L. Rao, one of the learned Assessors, and he expressed the opinion that the estimated maximum discharge in the Pochani Nalla on the night of September 1, was in the order of 400 cusecs. This was far in excess of the capacity of the bridge and its approach banks to withstand the impact of the flood water. The fact that the approaches to the bridge had been restored on August 2, does not make any difference here because, as I shall have the occasion to point out later on, the breaches to the approaches would have occurred even if they were in their old fully consolidated condition. It is also the case of the Railway that the impact of flood water on the night of September 1, was so great that it over-topped the railway line and even the 40-year old consolidated embankments would not have withstood that impact. It has been admitted before me by two Senior Officers of the Central Railway, the Chief Engineer and the Divisional Engineer, that the ventway of a 20-feet bridge like No. 229 would not be able to resist the flow of water resulting from two inches of rainfall in one hour in a catchment area like that of the Pochani Nalla.

Upon the whole, I have reached the conclusion that the principal cause of the accident was that the ventway of bridge 229 was inadequate to accommodate discharge of flood water resulting from two to two-and-a-half inches of rain which fell in the catchment area within one hour or a little over one hour on the night of September 1/2, 1956.

I have also reached the conclusion that another cause of the accident and one which has also required serious consideration was that the watch kept at bridge 229 on the night of September 1, was not adequate because it was not safe or prudent to group bridges 229 and 233 for being looked after by a single watchman. This grouping, of necessity, meant divided attention by the night watchman of two vulnerable spots at a distance of about two-thirds of a mile from each other. I have already examined this question of bracketting of bridges at some length and expressed the view that the watch kept at the bridge was inadequate and that the reason for this must be found in the arrangement of grouping bridges lying within a distance of about one mile and not in the absence of the watchman from bridge 229 in the emergent situation that suddenly arose. It was not safe or prudent to group bridges 229 and 233. That in my opinion was a serious mistake. The paramount and indispensable consideration of safety made it obligatory that in every case where a bridge or its approaches required attention and that too in a terrain of the nature to be found in this Section of the Railway where there was the possibility of flood water suddenly rising, close and continuous watch should have been insisted upon as the ultimate safeguard. That principle of safety was trenched upon when vulnerable bridges which required close watch were grouped for being looked after by a single watchman. The inadequate ventway notwithstanding the accident could certainly have been avoided if the ultimate safeguard of close and continuous watch had been enforced.

It is for these reasons, which I have sketched, that the Central Railway must be said to be responsible for the accident. Omission by the engineering department of the Railway to maintain an adequate ventway for the bridge and omission to enforce full-time watch at the bridge during monsoon before remedial measures could be taken, renders the Railway responsible on the ground of negligence. The rainfall proved to have occurred at the period of the accident was no doubt heavy, but it cannot be regarded as of unique character or an unpredictable convulsion of nature. It was such as ought to have been foreseen as possible. Having regard to the hilly terrain, the meteorological data available for Mahbubnagar and its vicinity and the other relevant facts which I have already discussed, it is not possible for me to take the view that two inches to two-and-a-half inches of rain in one hour or a little more than an hour in the catchment area of the Nalla was an act of God. Nor is it possible for me to accede to the suggestion that this was a case of inevitable accident. An adequate waterway was of vital importance and till remedial measures were taken it was equally vital to see that close and continuous watch was maintained at the bridge. Grouping for the purposes of watch of two vulnerable bridges lying at a distance of about two-thirds of a mile was a serious error. There are mitigative factors but they are apart and do not disturb the finding of negligence, though in fairness to those responsible for the accident it must be added that those factors would have considerable bearing on other matters.

It remains to consider the question of the person or persons responsible for the accident. In view of the conclusion reached by me that there was an omission to take proper remedial measures in respect of bridge 229, the first thing to be examined is: Whose duty was it to see that the Railway maintained an adequate ventway for the bridges? Now primarily it was for the Chief Engineer and the Deputy Chief Engineer to apply their mind to the question of stability of all bridges on the old Nizam's State Railway after it was merged in the Central Railway. It was for them to direct investigation into the question and especially so after the experience at Jangaon.

Primarily, it was the duty of the Chief Engineer and the Deputy Chief Engineer to see that the ventway of bridge 229 maintained by the Railway was adequate. Investigation of the nature indicated by me should have been started immediately after the Jangaon accident. The fact remains that no attempt was made by them at any time during a period of nearly two years to secure even some prima facie data about the catchment area of the bridge and the possible intensity of rainfall. For all the reasons discussed by me in the preceding paragraphs, both the Chief Engineer and the Deputy Chief Engineer must be held to be responsible for the failure to provide an adequate ventway for the bridge.

Responsibility under this head must also fall on the Divisional Engineer. A copy of the Railway Board's letter of December 2, 1954 had been sent to him. Even if the Chief Engineer and the Deputy Chief Engineer confined their instructions to investigation only of bridges which carried past history, he should have, if not before the washaway of August 1, in any event thereafter, seriously applied his mind to the capacity of the bridge and the possible intensity of rainfall.

I have no doubt that the Divisional Engineer did not apply his mind at any time till after the accident on September 1, to the question of the capacity of the bridge or its catchment area or the possible intensity of rainfall.

After giving most anxious consideration to this head of omission to provide an adequate ventway for the bridge and take any remedial measures in that behalf, I have, for reasons already discussed, reached the conclusion that the responsibility for the same must rest on the Chief Engineer, the Deputy Chief Engineer and the Divisional Engineer. A number of reasons given by them in their evidence before me in support of their conduct would give rise to valid considerations as mitigating circumstances but they are not such as can exonerate any of them from their responsibility.

I have reached the conclusion that no responsibility for grouping bridges 229 and 233 can rest on the Deputy Chief Engineer.

On a consideration of the whole position, I have reached the conclusion that the Divisional Engineer also was responsible for the omission to enforce adequate watch at bridge 229.

Suggested Safeguards Against Similar Accidents In Future

The hydrology of all streams affecting the Sector should be studied with all available data and requisite surveys should be carried out. The importance of hydrographic surveys does not require to be emphasised. Hydrographs where feasible are constructed for analysing surface run-off. The advantage of this is that it brings into the frame the element of time which must be a vital factor in the computation of storm flow. It furnishes what is described as the "time of concentration". It was observed in a Paper laid before the Indian Roads Congress by the Bridge Sub-Committee:

"The basic principle underlying the Hydrograph method is that a continuous rain of constant intensity produces hydrograph of a characteristic shape for any catchment area, and that this shape and the time of concentration are functions of the shape and size of the catchment area. The shape of the hydrograph is also affected if the duration of the storm either exceeds or is less than the time of concentration."

In case of extensive watersheds, detailed information requisite for hydrographs would often be difficult to obtain and correlate but in case of smaller areas the hydrograph furnishes the best available guidance. But systematic hydrographic surveys can only be a long term plan.

In a vast country like India with its varying weather and climatic conditions the possibility of having a uniform code of Rules for calculating maximum discharge of rivers and streams may readily be questioned. Various empirical formulae for estimating the discharge from a catchment have been presented from time to time. These run-off formulae from their very nature are of limited usefulness and the generally accepted principle is to devise rational formulae ground on basic concepts.

The immediate practical course to be adopted in these circumstances would be to direct investigations into the hydrology of all streams in the sector with such data as may be readily available. To start with, catchment areas over one square mile can fairly accurately be determined from topographical maps of the Survey of India. The Public Works Department of Andhra Pradesh, Hyderabad, maintains records of all tanks with irrigation of more than 10 acres. That would also be of use. I would suggest that all culverts should be checked for the maximum flood conditions. For catchments like that of Pochani Nalla the flood discharge should be computed on the basis of the maximum anticipated intensity of rainfall with allowance for a reasonable percentage as run-off. The maximum intensity may be gauged from meteorological records. Results of analysis of severe storms that may have occurred during the past several decades would also have to be considered on the assumption that the storms centre over the catchments. In obtaining this data the Director (Hydrology and Statistics) of the Central Water and Power Commission, Poona, may be requested to furnish relevant data from which the expected intensity of rainfall and storm-depths for any catchment could be estimated.

Any action required for strengthening, widening or rebuilding including resisting of bridges should be taken as expeditiously as reasonably possible. Before action by way of remedial measures can be taken the ultimate safeguard of exclusive and close watch would be strictly enforced during the monsoon.

Grouping of vulnerable mileages is not a salutary principle. Where close and special watch is necessary, bracketting of bridges is most undesirable. In any event in hilly terrains where there is always a distinct possibility of flood-water rising suddenly, full-time watch by day and by night should be maintained during the monsoon.

COMMISSION OF INQUIRY—INQUIRY ON THE ADMINISTRATION OF DALMIA-JAIN COMPANIES, 1956—REPORT

Delhi, Manager of Publications, 1963. 815p.

Chairman : Shri Justice S.R. Tendolkar (resigned, replaced by Shri V.R. Sen).
Members : Shri N.R. Mody; Shri S.C. Chaudhuri.
Secretary : Shri S.N. Lahiri (resigned; replaced by Shri P.S. Nadkarni).

APPOINTMENT

The Commission of Inquiry—Inquiry on the Administration of Dalmia-Jain Companies was constituted under the Ministry of Commerce and Industry vide Notification S.R.O. No. 2993 of the Ministry of Finance (Department of Economic Affairs) dated December 11, 1956 under the Commission of Inquiry Act (No. LX) of 1952.

TERMS OF REFERENCE

To inquire into and report on the administration of nine Companies, the nature and extent of the control, direct and indirect, exercised over such companies and firms or any of them by Ramkrishna Dalmia, Jaidayal Dalmia, Shanti Prasad Jain, Shriyans Prasad Jain, their relatives, employees and persons concerned with them and other matters mentioned in Clause 1 of the notification.

The names of the nine Companies are as follows:

1. Dalmia Jain Airways Ltd.
2. Dalmia Jain Aviation Ltd. (now known as Asia Udyog Ltd.).
3. Lahore Electric Supply Company Ltd. (now known as South Asia Industries Ltd.).
4. Shapurji Broacha Mills Ltd.
5. Madhowji Dharamji Manufacturing Company Ltd.
6. Allenberry & Co. Ltd.
7. Bharat Union Agencies Ltd.
8. Dalmia Cement and Paper Marketing Co. Ltd. (now known as Delhi Glass Works Ltd.).
9. Vastra Vyavasaya Ltd.

CONTENTS

Vol. I—General—Introductory; The Format of the Report; Procedure; Impeded Progress—and Reasons

Therefor; Legal Objections; The D.J. Group; Abuse of Control; Nature and Extent of the Personal Gains; Subscription Obtained from the Investing Public; Responsibility; Finale; Appendix; Vol. II—Dissolution—Introductory; Composition and Functioning of the Group; Effective Date of Dissolution; Documents: Ex.1216; Documents (continued) Ex.S.75; The Lauriya Farm; Account Books of J. Dalmia and Shanti Prasad Jain; Chronological Sequence of Entries; Were the Interpolations Innocent?; Implementation of Ex.1216; Oral Evidence: "Outside Witnesses"; Oral Evidence: Senior Executives and Employees; Broad Criticisms; Selling Agencies; Managing Agencies; Directorships; Senior Executives; Other Documents; Summary of Conclusions; The Dalmia Jain Group; Conclusions; Appendices; **Volume III—Part 1**—Allenberry and D.J. Airways—Pre-Joint Venture Period—Introductory; Allenberry: Acquisition and Control; D.J. Airways: Formation; D.J. Airways: Promotion and Floatation; D.J. Airways: Control through Directors; D.J. Airways: Control through Shareholdings; D.J. Airways: Initial Subscribers: 114 Fictitious Persons; D.J. Airways: Underwriting Commission; D.J. Airways: Managing Agency; **Part 2**—Joint Venture Period: Joint Venture Agreement, Ex.36; The R-3 A Plant; The 2323 Vehicles; Manipulations; Statutory Auditor, P.S. Sodhbans and the Ante-Dating of the Audited Accounts of D.J. Airways; Termination of the Joint Venture; **Vol. IV—Part 1**—Dalmia Jain Aviation—Post-Joint Venture: Allenberry Liquidation of D.J. Airways—D.J. Aviation; **Part 2**—Manipulations and Ante-Dating: Motor Vehicles Section—Under-statement of Sales for half year ended December 31, 1948; Inflation of Selling and Depot Expenses of Disposal Business for the Half Year ending December 31, 1948; Fraudulent Manipulation of Indirect Expenses for 1949, 1950 and 1951; Suppression of Profit on Disposal Business in the half year ending December 31, 1948, year ending December 31, 1949 and year ending December 31, 1950; Ante-Dating of the Accounts of Allenberry for the year ended December 31, 1948; Ante-Dating of the Accounts of Allenberry for the year ended December 31, 1951; **Part 3**—Manipulations and Ante-Dating: Drum and Pipeline Section— Transfer of Rs. 52 lakhs to D.C.P.M.; Under-statement of Sales of Steel Sheets; **Part 4**—Inter-Company Investment and Transfers —Introductory; D.J. Aviation; Investment of Rs. 75,25,000 in D.J. Aviation Shares; Investments in Shares; No Good Faith; **Part 5**—Liquidation—Introductory; Ante-Dating Ex.5; Events leading upto the Liquidation; Voluntary Liquidation of D.J. Airways; C.P. Lal: Voluntary Liquidator; Scheme of Amalgamation; Destruction of Account Books; Defence of C.P. Lal; **Vol. V**—Dalmia Cement and Paper Marketing Co. Ltd.—Introductory; Control; Borrowings, Loans and Advances; Borrowings from Banks (Bharat Bank; Punjab National Bank); Borrowings from Companies (L.E.S. Co.; D.J. Airways: D.J. Aviation; S.S.B. and M.D.M.; Bharat Insurance Co.; Jaipur Traders; Dadri Marketing & Co. Ltd.); Loans and Advances (R. Dalmia; J. Dalmia; Rashtriya Financial Corporation; Bennett Coleman & Co. Ltd.; Ashoka Marketing Co. Ltd.; Ashoka Agencies Ltd.; Vyapari Ltd.; Dalmia Investment Co. Ltd.; Allenberry & Co. Ltd.; Rashtriya Investors Ltd.; Inter-Company Investments; Government Securities; Unauthorised Use and Retention of Sale Proceeds; Nahur Land: Payment of Rs. seven lakhs Compensation to Shriyans Prasad Jain; Personal Expenses Charged to Company's Revenue Accounts; Illegalities; Loss on Share Transactions; The 2323 Vehicles and Transfer of Rs. 52 lakhs; Liquidation, Transfer of Assets and Destruction of Books and Records; Responsibilities: **Vol. VI—Part 1**—Sir Shapurji Broacha Mills Ltd. and Madhowji Dharamji Manufacturing Co. Ltd.—Introductory; Acquisition of Control; Abuse of Control; Selling Agency Agreements; Managing Agency Agreements; Haines Road Property; Loans to D.C.P.M.; Bennett Coleman Shares; Liquidation, Transfer of Assets and Destruction of Books; Responsibility; **Part 2**—Bharat Union Agencies Ltd. and Vastra Vyavasaya Ltd.—Introductory; Acquisition of Control; **Vol. VII—Part 1**—Lahore Electric Supply Company Limited now known as South Asia Industries Limited—Introductory; Misuse of Funds; Loans to D.C.P.M.; Loans to Asia Udyog; Loans to Patiala Biscuits; Deceptive Presentation of the Loans in the Balance Sheets; Buying and Selling of Shares; Amalgamation of S.S.B. Mills and M.D.M.Co. (in Liquidation) under Section 280-C of the Indian Companies Act, 1913; Taking Over of Disputed Claim of Allenberry; Breaches of Trust; **Part 2**—Dalmia Dadri Cement Ltd.—Introductory; Promotion and Control; Fraud-Loan of Rs. 18 lakhs to Allenberry; Loans of Rs. 12 lakhs to Jaipur Udyog and Rs. 25 lakhs to Rajasthan Udyog; Rupees Six lakhs Compensation paid to Dalmia Jain (Jind State) Limited; Breach of Trust; Acquisition of Shares by R. Dalmia; Acquisition of Shares by Swadesh Nirman; Gains by R. Dalmia; Investment in Shares; Inter-Company Investments; Inter-Company Transfers; Inquiry and Recommendations.

RECOMMENDATIONS

Objects Clause Of The Memorandum Of Association

The Act should be suitably amended to provide that every Company shall clearly state its purposes and objects under two separate categories, viz.,

(a) The principal and ancillary objects which the company intends at the time of its incorporation to pursue; and

(b) All other objects which are separate from the principal and ancillary ones mentioned in item (a) above.

A provision should be made in the Act to the effect that a Company shall not engage itself in any activities coming within the scope of Clause (b) unless such activities are sanctioned by a special resolution of the Company in general meeting.

Underwriting Commission

The Commission shall not be paid to any persons on such shares or debentures as are actually subscribed for at the time of the filing of the Company's Prospectus or Statement in lieu of Prospectus.

A copy of the contract or agreement for the payment of the Commission shall be delivered to the Registrar simultaneously with the filing of the Prospectus or the Statement in lieu of Prospectus.

Issue And Allotment Of Shares In The Names Of Fictitious Or Non-existing Persons

A provision should be made in the Companies Act, whereby any person who, either makes an application to the company or otherwise induces the company to allot or transfer its shares in the names of fictitious or, non-existent persons, shall be punishable with imprisonment which may extend to five years.

The penal provision suggested above shall be inserted at a prominent place—

(a) in every prospectus issued by a Company; and

(b) in every form of application for shares that is issued to any person.

Holding Of Shares On "Blank Transfers" And Nominee Holdings

A new provision should be made in the Companies Act, 1956 to adapt Section 308 read with Section 307 so as to—

(a) Require beneficial owners of five per cent or more of the equity capital of a company or shares having the right to vote at general meetings, to notify to the company the extent of their holdings of all such shares; and

(b) Require such persons, so long as they remain beneficial owners of five per cent or more such shares, to notify to the company details of all transactions by them or on their behalf in such shares, within 15 days of such transactions coming to their knowledge.

The beneficial interests to be taken into account for the purposes of disclosure under the aforesaid new provisions should be confined to those shares which are held by a person or in trust for him, or of which he has any right to become the holder, whether on payment or not.

The provision should not require a director who has disclosed his holdings under Section 308 to make any further disclosure in relation to that holding.

Provision for fine or imprisonment should be made [on the same line as in Section 308(3) of the Companies Act, 1956] for wilful failure of a person to notify his beneficial interests in shares to the company as envisaged by the new provision suggested in item (i) above.

The identity of the shareholders notifying the beneficial interest, the extent of their individual holdings of, and the transactions in, the types of shares referred to in item (i) above and the description and amount of such shares should be recorded by the company in a new register within seven working days of notification to it.

The Company should be required to—

(a) keep open the new register for inspection by the same persons and on the same terms as its register of members; and

(b) to make available to the public copies of the new register on the same terms as copies of the register of members.

A return of all such disclosure of beneficial interests in holdings of and transactions in the shares, as recorded by the company, should be filed with the Registrar of Companies along with its Annual Return under Section 159 of the Companies Act, 1956.

Provision for penalty should also be made in respect of the Company's default in complying with any of the requirements of the provisions suggested above on the lines of Section 307(8).

The above requirements should not apply to holdings in a private company as defined in the Companies Act or should they affect the operation of Section 153.

Section 247 of the Companies Act, 1956, should be extended to empower the Central Government to appoint an Inspector to investigate the ownership of the shares of a company when there are circumstances suggesting to the Central Government that there may have been deliberate disregard of provisions for disclosure of ownership as suggested above.

Section 137 of the Income-tax Act, 1961, should be suitably amended to permit disclosure of such information as may be required by—

(a) the concerned officer or Department of the Central Government for the purpose of investigation into the ownership of shares of a Company under Sections 247 and 248 of the Companies' Act, 1956; or

(b) by a Court in connection with the prosecution of any person arising out of any proceeding instituted under Section 621 of the Companies Act, 1956, read with the above proposed provision for fine or imprisonment for deliberate non-compliance of disclosure of ownership as suggested above.

Restrictions should be imposed relating to the period of currency of the blank transfers by making suitable statutory provisions with a view to permit shares being held on blank transfers only for a limited period. In this connection, we make the following broad recommendation, namely—

(i) To prescribe a form for execution of the instrument of transfer to be delivered to the company for having the transfer of shares registered.

(ii) The transfer forms should be in a standardised

form as now obtaining in the case of listed securities in some of the Stock Exchanges in the country.

(iii) The application for registration of a transfer should be made to a company by either the transferor or the transferee within a period of six months from the date of issue of the transfer form as stamped on it in the case of listed securities and two months in the case of non-listed securities.

(iv) The aforesaid restrictions relating to the period of currency of the blank transfers, as mentioned above, should not apply in cases where the shares are held by a company within the ambit of Section 49 or where they are held in a fiduciary capacity or as security by a financial institution, provided that in the last case the shares should be in the name of the borrower with a blank transfer executed in favour of the institution as security for the advance.

(v) We strongly recommend reduction in the rate of stamp duty chargeable on the transfer of shares which in our opinon, would operate as an incentive against keeping the transfers blank. We feel that the loss in revenue on this account may be more than made up by the volume of transfers as well as by the possibility of reducing evasion in the matter of direct taxes.

Dummy Directors

The definition of "officer" contained in Section 2(30) should be expanded by the adding of a Sub-clause (d) to include (as an officer) a person in accordance with those directions or instructions the directors of a Company or any of them are accustomed to act.

Loans To Companies Under The Same Management Or To Other Bodies Corporate

Section 370 should impose a limit on the amount of loans the lending company can give and for this purpose, we would suggest the limit of 20 per cent of the subscribed capital and free reserves of lending company in respect of loans to companies within the same group but with the sanction of a resolution of the shareholders.

The section should be further enlarged to include also loans made to companies not in the same group so that the aggregate of all the loans made by the lending company should not exceed 30 per cent of its paid-up capital and free reserves. Such loans also should be the subject of a resolution of the shareholders.

Loans in excess of the limits prescribed above should be sanctioned by a special resolution of the shareholders followed by the approval of the Central Government.

The same exceptions should apply as at present mentioned in Section 370(2).

Appointment And Termination Of Sole Selling Agents

The Companies' Act should be amended to the effect that—

(i) A Company shall not pay or be liable to pay its sole selling agents any amount by way of compensation for the loss of his office in the following cases:

(a) where the appointment of a sole selling agent ceases to be valid under Section 294(2A);

(b) where the sole selling agent resigns his office in view of the reconstruction of the company or of its amalgamation with any other body corporate or bodies corporate, and is appointed as sole selling agent of the reconstructed company or the body corporate resulting from the amalgamation;

(c) where the sole selling agent resigns his office, otherwise than on the reconstruction of the company or its amalgamation as aforesaid;

(d) where the sole selling agent has been guilty of fraud or breach of trust in relation to, or of gross negligence in the conduct of his duty as the sole selling agent; and

(e) where the sole selling agent has, whether directly or indirectly, himself initiated, or has taken part in bringing about, the termination of the sole selling agency.

(ii) The compensation which may be paid by a Company to the sole selling agent for loss of office shall not exceed the remuneration which he would have earned if he had been in office for the unexpired residue of his term, or for three years, whichever is shorter, actually earned by him during a period of three years immediately. This shall be calculated on the basis of the average remuneration preceding the date of cessation or termination of the office, or when he held the office for a lesser period, during such period.

Power And Obligation To Acquire Shares Of Dissenting Shareholders Under A Scheme Or Contract Approved By The Majority

Suitable provisions should be made, in the Companies' Act to the following effect for governing the procedure to be followed and the information to be disclosed in a take over offer and circular:

(a) The Central Government should have power to frame rules prescribing the information to be disclosed in every offer of a scheme or contract by a transferee company under Section 395 and in every circular containing such an offer, or recommendation to the members of the transferor company by its Directors to accept such an offer;

(b) Every offer of a scheme or contract under Section 395 offering cash for the shares to be acquired, should contain a statement, binding on the transferee company, saying that what steps it has taken to ensure that the necessary cash will be available;

(c) The circulars containing, or recommending acceptance of, the offer of a contract or scheme should be required, before their circulation to be sent for registration to the Registrar of Companies;

(d) The Registrar should be empowered (subject to appeal to the Court) to refuse to register any such circular which does not set out the information required to be given by the statutory rules suggested in (a) above or does so in a manner likely to create a false impression;

(e) The issue of such a circular, which has not been accepted for registration, should be made an offence;

(f) Circulars by directors or the members of the transferor company recommending rejection of the offer of a contract or scheme should not be required to be registered or subject to statutory rules suggested in (a) above.

Sub-section (3) of Section 395 should be suitably amended to provide that the transferor company shall within a month from the date of registration of the transferee company as holder of the shares of the dissenting shareholders intimate to them the fact of such registration and the receipt of the amount or other consideration representing the price payable to them by the transferee company and shall forthwith proceed thereafter to pay the money to the dissenting shareholders.

Liquidation

Section 400 of the Companies' Act should be suitably amended to provide for issue of notice to, and consideration of the representations, if any, submitted by the Central Government, by the Court before it passes the final orders on an application made to it under Sections 391 to 394.

Recovery Of Taxes On Income From Companies In Liquidation

In addition to the existing provisions of Section 530 of the Companies' Act, this section should be modified to the extent of allowing preferential payment of tax in respect of the last complete accounting year preceding the liquidation, notwithstanding that the assessment is actually made subsequent to the commencement of liquidation.

Provision should be made in the Income-tax Act to authorise the issue of a fresh demand notice on a transferee company which takes over all the liabilities of the transferor company including its income-tax liability, under a scheme of arrangement under Section 394 read with Section 391 or under Section 396 of the Companies' Act.

Section 220 of the Income-tax Act, 1961, which lays down the circumstances in which an assessee is 'deemed to be in default' should be modified to include a transferee company which takes over the income-tax liabilities of the transferor company in pursuance of any scheme of arrangement.

Destruction Of Books Of Account

Where a company has been amalgamated with another without liquidation, the provisions of Section 550 shall, notwithstanding there being no liquidation, apply to the books of the transferor company and it shall be made incumbent on the transferee company to retain the books in good order for the period for which it has been directed so to do.

Prohibition Of Allotment Until Receipt Of Minimum Subscription

The words "until the certificate to commence business obtained under Section 149" be deleted from Section 69(4); instead the following words be added, namely, "till the amount stated in the Prospectus as the 'minimum subscription' is raised".

1957

COMMISSION ON CERTAIN ASPECTS OF COOPERATIVE MOVEMENT IN INDIA, 1957—REPORT

Delhi, Manager of Publications, 1957. 53p.

One-Man Commission : Sir Malcolm Darling.

APPOINTMENT

The Certain Aspects of Cooperative Movement in India conducted by Sir Malcolm Darling was due to a request by the Government of India (Planning Commission) under the Technical Cooperation Scheme of the Colombo Plan in 1957.

TERMS OF REFERENCE

(i) To review recent developments in the field of co-operation with reference to programmes in the Second Five-Year Plan; and

(ii) To make recommendations for strengthening the organisation of Cooperative Departments in the States, the training programmes for cooperative personnel, and the organisation of the cooperative movement at and below the district level.

CONTENTS

Prefatory Note; Introduction; **Part I**—General Policy in regard to the Agricultural Thrift and Credit Society; **Part II**—The Agricultural Thrift and Credit Society—Supervision, Audit and Investment of Reserve Funds; **Part III**—Some New Types of Societies; **Part IV**—Recruitment and Training; **Part V**—The Training System and the Teaching of Members of Societies; **Part VI**—The National Extension Service; Summary of Recommendations; Appendix; Itinerary of Tour.

RECOMMENDATIONS

Agricultural Credit Societies

The need for caution in making further credit available is especially necessary in States with less developed movements.

The pace for development set by the Second Five-Year Plan should be slowed down, and in the case of the weakest States 10 instead of five years should be allowed for achieving the targets.

An Officer of standing and experience should be attached to the Ministry of Food and Agriculture to act as Liaison Officer between the Ministry and the State Governments.

Large societies should be of three types and operate under certain conditions.

In due course they should be reviewed in relation to certain points specified in paragraph 34.

A special effort should be made to render the small societies more viable.

Societies with no Secretary of their own should be helped to get one of their members trained to act as Secretary.

Where this is impossible, Unions should be formed experimentally for the employment of peripatetic Secretaries.

The name 'Thrift and Credit Society' should be restored.

A systematic attempt should be made to increase deposits in Thrift and Credit Societies.

A special effort should be made to attract deposits from both young and old, including school children.

Ordinarily a representative of the State Bank of India should not be nominated by Government to the Board of a cooperative bank.

In no circumstances should nomination be governed or influenced by political considerations.

Wherever the general supervision of the Thrift and Credit Society is not the responsibility of the Central Cooperative Bank and the system works satisfactorily, no change should be made.

In Andhra and Madras societies classed A or B should be allowed to apply direct to a Central Bank for loans.

Thrift and Credit Societies with unlimited liability should be allowed to invest their reserve funds in their own business where this has been the practice in the past.

When they are lodged with a Central Bank, they should be kept in some liquid form, the total amount to be in addition to the fluid resource required to cover ordinary deposits; and there should be the same rule for the reserve funds of Central Banks deposited with an Apex Bank.

Audit should remain the responsibility of the Registrar, and in the Punjab and Uttar Pradesh, where this is no longer the case, his responsibility should be restored.

Societies should not be formed without proper preparation, and in each State, where this has not been done already, the Registrar should fix the number of visits by a member of his staff required to secure this.

Societies whose dealings would mainly be with non-members should not be registered under a Cooperative Societies Act.

More attention should be paid to cooperative farming on an individual as opposed to a collective basis.

The name 'Multi-purpose Society' should not be used of societies with only a single activity.

Where the supply and marketing side of the movement is sufficiently well organised, cooperative societies should be used exclusively for the distribution of fertilisers.

Credit and crops should be closely linked.

Recruitment And Training

No one should be appointed Registrar without at least a year's training.

Every Registrar should have on his staff someone competent to succeed him and sufficiently trained and experienced to be able to do so.

Registrars should not be transferred under at least three years, and generally not for five years or more.

Ordinarily, no one from the Indian Administrative Service should be appointed Registrar under twelve years' service.

All appointed Joint or Deputy Registrars direct should attend a Senior Officers' course at Poona and get six months' training in addition.

Technicians employed in connection with any kind of industrial society should have three to four months' training, to include a short course in the theory, history and practice of Cooperation.

Advisers to the Registrar on Banking and Finance, if appointed within the department, should receive a year's training in banking, six months of which should be spent in a commercial bank or in the State Bank of India. If appointed from outside the department, they should get six months' training in cooperative banking and other cooperative financial activities.

A model training scheme for Assistant Registrars is recommended.

For Inspectors, attendance at an Intermediate Level Course should be supplemented by at least six months' field training.

The desirability of a rural background for all in constant contact with the villager should be given full effect to in recruitment.

More persons should be recruited than needed for employment to allow for weeding out the unfit during training.

Special staff will be needed to enable the large areas cooperatively undeveloped to keep pace with the Plan; the Registrars should advise their Governments accordingly.

A statistician should be added to the staff of the Registrar, Andhra Pradesh, Madras and Bombay.

The training courses should be revised to secure a better balance between the practical and the theoretical.

The syllabii of the courses should be revised and shortened.

There should not be more than four lectures a day in any training course.

The seminar system should be more freely used.

More time should be allowed in the courses for reading.

The libraries of the training centres should be better stocked.

There should not be more than one intermediate and one final examination.

Excessive 'home-work' should be discouraged.

Batches of students taken on tour should be limited to ten of large societies.

Societies much used for the practical purposes of training should be given some special staff for the necessary explanations and guidance.

Societies within easy reach of a training centre should be used for practical training.

No one should be allowed to take a course without first receiving the three to six months' field training.

After training no one should be given independent charge of a post without working for a certain period under the personal supervision of an officer of a superior grade.

Men with over five years' service should not be trained with men of less than one year's service.

At both the intermediate and the higher level there should be two courses, one for new entrants, the other for those who require a course to prepare them for new responsibilities.

The course for Senior Officers directly appointed should include 'Rural Economics and Elements of Agriculture' as a compulsory subject; and the shorter course at the same level might well include 'Business Management' as an optional subject.

No one whose post involves attending a course and passing an examination should be confirmed in the post until he has passed it.

Short refresher course should be held regularly in all States.

Experiments should be made with the Study Session as used in France.

The correspondence course as a method of teaching should be borne in mind with a view to its introduction at a later stage.

There should be a short special course in cooperation for entrants into the Indian Administrative and Agricultural Services, and also, if necessary, for key personnel in the Agricultural Credit Department of the Reserve Bank.

Teaching Of Members Of Societies

Regional training centres are needed for training those conerned with teaching members of cooperative societies; and the training should be given in the language of the region.

It might be better to train presidents of societies with other members of Committee rather than with Secretaries.

Special attention should be paid to the education of members of large societies.

The use of the drama in the teaching of members of societies should not be overlooked and might usefully be taken up by the National Extension Service, in collaboration with the Cooperative Departments and the All-India Cooperative Union.

The National Extension Service

No one should be appointed Cooperative Extension Officer without at least a year's field experience.

All Block Development Officers appointed direct should be trained as recommended in paragraph 118.

Coordination with the technical departments concerned can be best secured by the system described in paragraph 120.

If Block Development Officers are given administrative control over Cooperative Extension Officers they should be properly trained in the theory and practice of Cooperation, and Cooperative Extension Officers should be given at least two years' field experience before being posted to a Block.

Block Development Officers should not be liable to frequent transfers.

The posts of Cooperative and Panchayat Extension Officer should not be combined.

The National Extension Service through its cooperative staff should try to persuade groups of villagers of the same tribe or caste to reduce their expenditure on social ceremonies, where it seems out of proportion to their resources.

HEAVY ENGINEERING COMMITTEE, 1957—REPORT

New Delhi, Ministry of Heavy Industries, 1957. 26p. (Memographed)

Chairman : Sir Jehangir Ghandy.

Members : Shri S. Moolgaokar; Shri S.K. Nanavati; Shri P. Mueller; Shri F.C. Bhadwar; Shri P. Bhattacharji; Dr. M.D. Parekh; Shri P.R. Ramakrishna.

APPOINTMENT

The Heavy Engineering Committee was constituted under the Ministry of Heavy Industries in 1957 to examine the two reports submitted by the Soviet Team of Heavy Machinery and the United Kingdom Heavy Engineering Mission and to advise Government on the most suitable plan on the establishment of Heavy Engineering Industry in India.

TERMS OF REFERENCE

(i) To examine the two reports (submitted by the Soviet Team and the U.K. Mission in regard to the establishment of Heavy Engineering Industry in India); and

(ii) To advise Government on the most suitable plan on the establishment of Heavy Engineering Industry in India.

CONTENTS

Introductory; Consideration of Technical data regarding Approximate Capital Cost, Annual Output and Number of Employees, from the Reports Submitted by the Soviet Team of Heavy Machinery Experts and the U.K. Heavy Engineering Mission; Deliberations of the Heavy Engineering Committee (assisted by Government Officers) and Recommendations; Procedure for the Implementation of the Heavy Engineering Industry Projects; Acknowledgement; Enclosures I and II; Appendices A and B.

RECOMMENDATIONS

After considering the British and the Russian reports, the Heavy Engineering Committee was of the unanimous opinion that, for reasons stated below, the proposals contained in the report of the U.K. Heavy Engineering Mission were preferable to those submitted by the Soviet Team of Heavy Machinery Experts. These reasons are:

(i) Whilst the Russian report recommends establishment of an integrated Heavy Machine Building Plant as a homogeneous unit, the British report recommends the establishment of different shops on unit basis. The U.K. report has, however, correctly pointed out that the Heavy Machine Shop should be located in close proximity to the Forge/Foundry Project. With the exception of the Medium Heavy Machine Tool Plant, which could be located near the same site, the other units, namely, the Plate and Vessel Works, the Heavy Structural Works and the Mining Machinery Factory could be located at independent sites.

(ii) The recommendations made by the U.K. Heavy Engineering Mission will permit a greater scope for ultimate development of the Heavy Engineering Industry than units of a composite plant sited at one location.

(iii) The British report covers a wider scope for, in addition to equipment for the iron and steel works, they have envisaged production for other industries, such as chemical and fertilizer industries in a plate and vessel works. The British report also recommends the production of medium/heavy machine tools and of mining machinery in separate factories. These aspects have not been covered by the Russian Report, who, however, submitted a later report on mining machinery production.

(iv) The establishment of the Heavy Engineering Industry on unit basis will enable return on investment to be earned earlier, as it would be possible to obtain production from separate units earlier than in the case of an integrated plant at one site.

(v) Dispersal of some of the units is advisable for strategic considerations and also for reasons of transport facilities.

(vi) Concentration of Heavy Engineering Industry at one site as recommended in the Russian Report may make it difficult to obtain highly skilled layout which is essential for this project. Dispersal of units, on the other hand, as recommended in the U.K. report, will enable generations of skilled labour to be developed more effectively.

2. In regard to the project for Heavy Machine Shop, the Soviet Team in its Aide Memoir dated February 20, 1957, has indicated an approximate range of output of machinery and equipment as shown below:—

S. No.	Name of Machinery and Equipment	Weight (Tons)
1.	Coke Ovens Bye-Product equipment	5,000
2.	Blast Furnace equipment	4,000
3.	Steel Making equipment	5,000
4.	Crushing and Grinding equipment	2,000
5.	Cranes	4,000
6.	Assemblies of Rolling Mill equipment and spare parts	2,000
		22,000

3. On the other hand, the U.K. Heavy Engineering Mission report has not indicated the tonnages or the expected range of output of machinery and equipment. Further, as indicated on page 55 of their report, if two Heavy Machine Shops are to be located the investment involved is Rs. six crores and seventy lakhs. The Soviet Team of Heavy Machinery Experts have indicated to Government that a Heavy Machine Building Plant in the range indicated above would cost approximately Rs. seven crores. Therefore, as the capital investment indicated is approximately the same and, as we were given to understand, the Russians would offer satisfactory credit terms, the Committee is of the opinion that the Russian project for Heavy Machine Shop may be accepted.

4. In regards to the Mining Machinery Works, the U.K. report has provided for capital investment of Rs. two crores and ninety-six lakhs. This estimate is exclusive of Forge/Foundry Shop as they had assumed that the requirements of forgings and castings for this unit would

be supplied from the Forge/Foundry Project to be established under the auspices of the N.I.D.C. However, this Committee considers that, within the financial limit of Rs. 20 crores provided for the Forge/Foundry Project, it will not be possible to provide for additional capacity to supply components to the Mining Machinery Works, in addition to the requirements of the Heavy Machine Shop and the Medium/Heavy Machine Tool Works. Therefore, a small Forge and Grey Iron Foundry will have to be integrated with the Mining Machinery Works to make it a composite unit. With this in view, the capital investment has been increased to approximately Rs. four and a half crores.

5. The Heavy Engineering Committee has been advised that the Soviet Team of Heavy Machinery Experts has recently submitted a more elaborate scheme for the manufacture of mining machinery in a separate works, estimated to produce approximately 30,000 tons of machinery a year, involving a capital investment of approximately Rs. 13 crores. It is, therefore, suggested that the Soviet Team of Heavy Machinery Experts as well as the U.K. Heavy Engineering Mission should be asked by Government to re-examine and submit a revised project for the production of approximately eight to 10 thousand tons of mining machinery requiring a capital investment not exceeding Rs. four-and-a-half crores including its Forge/Foundry Shop. The requirements of mining machinery and other equipment to the tune of eight to 10 thousand tons a year should be worked out in detail by Government in consultation with the Coal Mining Industry, before requesting the Soviet Team and the U.K. Mission to re-examine this project.

6. The Committee recommends that the following shops and the number of units be accepted in the establishment of Heavy Engineering Industry in India, as a beginning.

Works	No. of Units	Approximate Capital investment (Rs. in crores)
Forge/Foundry Shop	1	20.00
Heavy Machine Shop	1	7.00
Heavy Structural Works	1	1.09
Heavy Plate & Vessel Works	1	5.16
Medium/Heavy Machine Tool Works	1	4.70
Mining Machinery Works	1	4.50
Total		42.45
At 15% for contingency		6.37
Total including contingency		48.82 say 49 crores

7. The Committee considers it essential to make a minimum provision of 15% on the estimated investment cost for contingencies. With prices of machinery and equipment on the increase, it is very likely that the actual expenditure to be incurred during the next four years of the Second Five-Year Plan will be higher than the estimates. The above estimates have been taken from the U.K. Mission report, except for the Heavy Machine Shop which has been recommended by the Committee on the pattern offered by the Russians at an estimated cost of approximately Rs. seven crores.

8. The Committee wishes to point out that the capital investment has been indicated on broad outlines. When detail project reports are received, it is very likely that the capital investment may exceed the estimate indicated.

9. It will be observed that the total estimated investment including 15% for contingencies is approximately Rs. 49 crores and therefore, the financial limit of Rs. 40 crores as indicated by Government will not be sufficient.

10. The Committee recommends that if it becomes essential to eliminate some of the projects, then the following should be the order of priority.

(i) The first unit to be set up should be a composite unit comprising of Forge/Foundry Shop and a Heavy Machine Shop.

(ii) One unit of Plate and Vessel Works.

(iii) One unit of Heavy Structural Works.

(iv) One unit for the production of Mining Machinery and Equipment.

(v) One unit for the production of Medium/Heavy Machine Tools (to which should be attached the heavy grey iron section of the N.I.D.C. Forge/Foundry project).

11. One member of the Committee, Mr. P. Bhattacharji, suggested a combination of units to be established for the Heavy Engineering Industry, different to what has been indicated in paragraph six. It will be observed, according to his proposals, that the estimate for capital investment, including 15 per cent for contingencies, works out to approximately Rs. 51 crores.

12. It was the considered opinion of the other members of the Heavy Engineering Committee as well as of the Government officers who were present that early establishment of a Machine Tool Works is essential for providing a broad enough base for the development of Heavy Engineering Industry. In addition, the Committee also felt that Mr. Bhattacharji's proposals would result in a larger number of men to be employed which will further increase the total capital investment to provide for housing and other municipal services for the additional number.

Forge/Foundry Project—N.I.D.C.

13. As stated previously, Government have appointed

a Special Committee to examine the different proposals received for the establishment of a separate Forge/Foundry project under the auspices of the N.I.D.C. At the meeting on March 5, 1957, the Heavy Engineering Committee have indicated the requirements of forgings and castings for the Heavy Machine Shop and for the Medium/Heavy Machine Tool Works.

14. The following is a summary of the requirements:

(a) Steel Castings	
Finish-machined requirement	13,500 tons per annum
Fettled and cleaned casting required for above	18,000 ,, ,, ,,
Liquid metal required for above	26,000 ,, ,, ,,
(b) Forging	
Finish-machined forgings required	10,000 ,, ,, ,,
Ingots required for above	20,000 ,, ,, ,,
Liquid metal required for above	24,000 ,, ,, ,,
(c) Total liquid metal capacity required for steel	50,000 ,, ,, ,,
(d) Grey Iron Casting	
Finish-machined casting required	6,000 ,, ,, ,,
Liquid metal capacity required for above	10,000 ,, ,, ,,

The above tonnages are exclusive of the requirements of rolls for the steel plants.

15. The Heavy Engineering Committee also recommends, finance permitting, that a section for manufacture of non-ferrous components be included in the Forge/Foundry Project with a capacity of approximately 1500 to 2000 tons per annum of finished non-ferrous components.

16. The total requirement of Heavy Machine Shop has been broadly divided into 40 per cent forgings and 60 per cent steel castings. Likewise, for the Medium/Heavy Machine Tool Works, it has been estimated that the requirement of forgings will be 33 per cent and that of grey iron castings will be 67 per cent.

17. This is suggested as the Heavy Machine Shop as offered by the Russians and the Medium/Heavy Machine Tool Works as offered by U.K. Mission, have been recommended by the Committee for acceptance. If any adjustments are necessary in the quantities of castings and forgings, then the revised figures should be indicated by Government to the Forge/Foundry Special Committee for their consideration.

18. To avoid any duplication of machine tools in the Forge/Foundry Project and in the Heavy Machine Building and Medium/Heavy Machine Tool Works, the details of machine tools should be carefully checked by the Special Committee, preferably in consultation with the Soviet Team and U.K. Mission.

19. In the event of the Medium/Heavy Machine Tool Works being established at a site other than for Forge/Foundry Project and Heavy Machine Shop, the Committee recommends that the Grey Iron Foundry should be isolated from the Forge/Foundry Project and should be integrated with the Machine Tool Works, as the requirements of grey iron castings are mainly for this shop.

HOTEL STANDARDS AND RATE STRUCTURE COMMITTEE, 1957—REPORT

New Delhi, Ministry of Transport and Communications (Tourist Department), 1958. 107p.

Chairman : Diwan Chaman Lall.

Members : Shri R.R. Morarka; Shri M.S. Oberoi; Shri K. Heuer; Shri C. Green; Shri Ram Nath Kapur; Shri E.F. Gerald Jr.; Shri N.J. Katgara; Shri N.P. Dube; Shri Nettur P. Damodaran (resigned; replaced by Shri K.T. Achuthan).

Secretary : Shri G.R. Kadapa.

APPOINTMENT

The Hotel Standards and Rate Structure Committee was constituted under the Ministry of Transport and Communications (Tourist Department) in 1957.

TERMS OF REFERENCE

(i) To frame criteria for the classification of hotels keeping in view the criteria laid down by existing International Organisations dealing with the hotel industry.

(ii) To recommend the number and type of classifications that should be applicable e.g. whether to introduce the Star System as is prevalent in some countries or any other suitable system of classification.

(iii) Taking into account the price level obtaining in India, the cost of hotel-keeping and other relevant factors, to recommend a rational rate structure for each category of hotels and other establishments.

(iv) For the purpose of promoting tourist traffic, to consider any other aspect of the hotel industry including the desirability or otherwise of legislation and/or of assistance.

CONTENTS

Introduction; The New Era of Air Travel and Its Impact on the Hotel Trade; Classification and Criteria; Rate Structure; Assistance to the Hotel Industry; Legislation; Service Charge and Tipping; Conciliation; Provision of Common Fund; Prohibition; Training of Hotel Personnel; Public Sector and Private Sector in the Hotel Industry; Foreign Interests; Rest Houses. Dak Bungalows, Circuit Houses and the Like; Indian Style Hotels; Hygiene, Cleanliness and Food; Tourist Publicity; Kashmir; Places of Tourist Interest and Their Development; Acknowledgments; Appendices I to VII.

RECOMMENDATIONS

It is axiomatic that the average traveller in this new age will not require pomp but essential comfort, convenience and good food. The hotel industry has to build a reputation for itself just as any other good business. Therefore, the benefit that would accrue through this increased traffic will necessarily be taken advantage of in a large measure by traditional hoteliers whose reputation is good.

We are convinced that the time has come for the rapid expansion of the hotel industry. We have suggested that this should be done under a proper and planned scheme of development. We had our First Five-Year Plan. The hotel industry was not in that Plan. We are proceeding with our Second Five-Year Plan. Again the hotel industry does not form any part in this Plan. We would urge the Planning Commission and all the interests involved, including the Ministry of Transport that no time should be lost for the purpose of planning the development of the hotel industry on a rapid but rational and scientific basis keeping in view the requirements of the country in this behalf for the next fifteen years or so.

Classification And Criteria

From a study of the prevalent system of classification, the Committee came to the conclusion that the existing modes of classification are divergent and that the number of categories varies from three to six excluding subdivisions and that the classifications are symbolised sometimes by stars, by Roman or Arabic figures or by alphabetical symbols. Considering that the star system is the most popular and the most easily understood method, the Committee feels that it would be worth trying in this country. The Committee, therefore, recommends that this system should be adopted in India and all hotels in any particular class should be listed in an alphabetical order which, indeed, is the prevailing rule in most countries where classification exists. In the case of seasonal hotels it would be necessary to declare the months during the year that such hotel establishments remain open.

In the matter of Dak Bungalows, Rest Houses and other residential establishments used by tourists, the Committee recommends that these should be classified as A, B and C. The Committee further considers that such establishments which provide good service and food, modern sanitation, a high standard of cleanliness, decent and comfortable furniture inclusive of good bed and bath, linen, proper modern kitchen arrangements and electricity may be eligible for 'A' category and those with modern sanitation, good service and food, a high standard of cleanliness, modern sanitation, decent and comfortable furniture but no proper modern kitchen arrangements should be eligible for 'B' category and the rest should be classified as 'C' category.

The Committee also recommends that no establishment which does not primarily offer residential accommodation and is not so used should be permitted to use the word 'hotel'.

Due to the urgent necessity for the classification of hotel establishments in India, we recommend that this task should be undertaken by a small but effective Standing Hotel Committee under the Tourist Department on which there should be adequate representation of the hoteliers. This Committee should, in our opinion, consist of four members; viz. two representing the hotel industry, one representing the consumers—preferably a Member of Parliament and the fourth, who will be the Chairman, representing the Tourist Department of the Government of India. The Committee should have the power to co-opt on a regional basis a representative each of the hotel industry and the Tourist Department in that particular region. We are further of the view that the Committee should not be an unwieldy one but a business-like body. It should meet as and when necessary and should be capable of taking prompt decisions particularly in the matter of re-grading hotels which matter can obviously brook no delay.

The Committee gave a great deal of thought to the method of classifying hotels in India and has came to the conclusion that a scientific basis should be adopted for the purposes of classifying hotel establishments, in order that there should be no doubt whatsoever that justice is being done in the matter of classification. The Committee has, therefore, worked out a suitable system of assigning marks in respect of classification—one class of marks would be 'Esssential' and the other 'Desirable'. It will be necessary for an establishment which is to be categorised to qualify for that category by obtaining a minimum of 50 per cent marks in each 'Essential' item and 65 per cent on the aggregate. And as far as the 'Desirable' items are concerned, a totality of 70 per cent of the aggregate marks is to be considered as the minimum requirement. As already stated the Committee also is aware of the necessity of keeping in view the climatic conditions prevailing in India and, therefore, suggests that hotel establishments should be distinguished namely those maintained in the hills, those maintained on the plains and those at the sea-side resorts. Therefore, the criteria for such types of hotels will have to be slightly different while at the same time not deviating in material respects from the expected stardards. The Committee, therefore considers that the following broad criteria should be applicable to all hotels catering for tourist traffic:—

(*****) Five Star Or De Luxe Category

	Marks Essential	Marks Desirable
1. An artistically designed and substantially constructed building, in a good locality. (For new hotels the building should have been constructed on modern hotel lines.)	10	
2. Public rooms such as lounge, dining rooms, bars, banquet halls etc. and residential rooms should be air-conditioned wherever necessary except in hill stations.	15	
3. A Swimming Pool and/or Tennis Courts.		10
4. Billiard Rooms, Radio in each room.		5
5. There should be adequate public room facilities such as a Lounge, Banqueting Halls, Writing Room, Dining Rooms for private parties, Conference Rooms for meetings, Bars, Restaurants and Grill Rooms, safe deposits, foreign exchange, postal and shopping facilities as well as Airlines and Travel Agencies offices, a Taxi Stand, adequate facilities for garages or parking space. 10% of the total floor area should be earmarked for public rooms.	30	
6. Complete and adequate laundry facilities.	5	
7. Elegant furnishing and appointments in the rooms.	10	
8. 24 Hours' Service.	5	
9. All rooms must have attached bath rooms which should have long baths and showers, toilets and wash basins. The sanitary fittings should be of the highest quality.	15	
10. Provision of running hot and cold water all the time.	5	
11. Provision of proper lighting including bed-lights and bath room lights.	5	
12. Provision of electric points for plugging in electric razors in the rooms.	5	
13. Provision of clean and adequate bed linen, blankets and bath room linen of the highest quality.	10	
14. Provision of toilet soap and paper for each guest.	2	
15. Provision of 'Left Luggage Rooms' and 'Check Rooms'.		5
16. Each room must have a telephone for service. In Metropolitan cities it should have an external telephone service as well.	10	
17. Provision of call bell system in each room.		5
18. Provision of lifts wherever necessary for guests commensurate with the bed capacity and number of floors in the hotel.	10	
19. Provision of orchestras, floor shows and ball room facilities in metropolitan cities only.	10	
20. Provision of highest quality of indigenous crockery, cutlery, glassware, silverware and tableware. (Imported crokery etc. not barred.)	10	
21. Provision of a modern kitchen, pantries and cold storage.	15	
22. Provision of modern equipment in kitchen such as Dishwashing Machines, etc.	10	
23. Provision of Indian and Continental cuisine, vegetarian and/or non-vegetarian.	10	
24. The highest standard of cuisine, catering and service.	25	
25. Smart, efficient, experienced staff in adequate number from the General Manager down to the bell-boy.	10 Senior staff	10 Junior staff
26. Suitable livery of a very high standard for the relevant staff.	10	
27. Senior staff and Service staff should know English and possibly one more European or Asian language.	10	

	Marks Essential	Marks Desirable
28. Provision of public stenographic service.		
29. It is necessary and highly essential that hotel establishments in this category should be guided by business ethics of the highest order and should have an atmosphere of elegance and luxury and provide service, food and appointments appropriate to a luxury hotel.	35	

(****) Four Star

	Marks Essential	Marks Desirable
1. A well constructed building. (For new hotels the buildings should have been constructed on modern hotel lines.)	10	
2. Dining Room and 50% of the bed rooms should be airconditioned wherever necessary.	15	
3. Swimming Pool and/or Tennis Court.		10
4. Indoor recreational facilities such as radios in each room and public Billiard room.		5
5. Adequate well furnished public room facilities such as lounge, licensed bars (in non-prohibition areas), ball room or banquet room (in major cities only) and dining room. At least 7½% of the total floor area of the hotel should be earmarked for public rooms.	30	
6. Provision of facilities such as bookstalls, travel agency, airline offices, banking and postal facilities, garage or parking space.	10	
7. Laundry facilities.	5	
8. Well furnished and well appointed bed rooms and suites.	10	
9. 24 Hours' Service.	5	
10. All rooms must have attached bathrooms which should have long bath and/or showers, toilets and wash basin. The sanitary fittings should be of high quality.	15	
11. Provision of running hot and cold water all the time.	5	
12. Provision of proper lighting including bed lights and bathroom lights.	5	
13. Provision of electric points for plugging in electric razors in the rooms.		5
14. Provision of clean and adequate bed linen, blankets and bathroom linen of a high quality.	10	
15. Provision of toilet soap for each guest.	5	
16. Provision of a 'Left Luggage Room'.		5
17. Each room must have a telephone service. In metropolitan cities it should have an external telephone service as well.	5	
18. Provision of call-bell system in each room.		5
19. Provision of lifts wherever necessary for guests, commensurate with the bed capacity and number of floors in the hotel.	10	
20. Provision of Orchestra and Ball room facilities (in metropolitan cities only).	10	
21. Provision of high quality of indigenous crockey, cutlery, glassware, silverware and tableware. (Imported crockery etc. not barred.)	10	
22. Provision of a modern kitchen, pantries and cold storage.	15	
23. Provision of modern equipment in kitchen such as dish washing machine etc.	10	
24. Provision of Indian and Continental cuisine, vegetarian and/or non-vegetarian.	10	
25. A high standard of cuisine, catering and service.	25	
26. Smart, efficient and experienced staff in adequate number from the Manager down to the bell-boy.	10 Senior staff	10 Junior staff
27. Suitable livery of a high standard for the relevant staff.	10	
28. Senior staff and service staff should know English and possibly one more foreign language.	10	
29. Business ethics of the highest order. The hotel should have an atmosphere of elegance and comfort and provide service, food and appointments appropriate to this category of hotels.	35	

(***) Three Star

	Marks Essential	Marks Desirable
1. A well constructed building. (For new hotels the buildings should have been constructed on modern lines.)	10	
2. 25% of the bedrooms should be air-conditioned wherever necessary except in hill stations.	15	
3. Indoor recreational facilities such as		

	Marks Essential	Marks Desirable
a radio in the lounge, card tables, etc.	5	
4. Provision of adequate and well furnished dining room and lounge. At least 5% of the total floor area of the hotel should be earmarked for public rooms.	30	
5. Provision of facilities such as book-stall and parking space for cars.	10	
6. Laundry facilities.	5	
7. Reasonably well furnished and well appointed bedrooms.	10	
8. Service till 11 P.M.	5	
9. All rooms must have attached bath rooms which should have long baths and/or showers, toilets and wash basins. The sanitary fittings should be modern and of good quality.	15	
10. Provision of running cold water all the time and running hot water mornings and evenings.	5	
11. Provision of proper lighting including bed lights and bedroom lights.	5	
12. Provision of clean and adequate bed linen, blankets and bath room linen of good quality.	10	
13. Provision of toilet soap for each guest.	5	
14. Provision of 'Left Luggage' facilities.	5	
15. Call bell and/or internal telephone system in each room and in metropolitan cities external telephone on each floor.	5	
16. Provision of Lift wherever necessary.	10	
17. Provision of music and dance-floor facilities (in metropolitan cities only).	10	
18. Provision of good quality of indigenous crockery, cutlery, glassware, silverware and tableware. (Imported crockery etc. not barred.)	10	
19. Provision of a modern kitchen, pantries and cold storage.	15	
20. Provision of modern equipment in the kitchen.	10	
21. Provision of Indian and Continental cuisine, vegetarian and/or non-vegetarian.	10	
22. A high standard of cuisine, catering and service.	25	
23. Smart efficient and experienced staff.	10 Senior staff	10 Junior staff

(**) Two Star

	Marks Essential	Marks Desirable
1. The building should be in a good locality and should be suitable for a hotel.	10	
2. All the rooms should have fans wherever necessary and good ventilation.	15	
3. Provision of adequate and reasonably furnished dining room and lounge.	15	
4. Provision of a separate Reception-cum-Enquiry office within the proximity of the main entrance of the building.	10	
5. Provision of laundry facilities.	5	
6. Reasonably well furnished and well appointed bed rooms.	10	
7. Service till 11 p.m.	5	
8. Atleast 50% of the rooms must have attached bath-rooms (public bath rooms to be in the ratio of one for every fcur of the remaining bed rooms) which should have modern sanitation.	20	
9. Provision of running cold water all the time and provision of running hot water mornings and evenings.	10	
10. Provision of proper lighting including table lamps.	5	
11. Provision of adequate and clean blankets and linen including bath room linen.	10	
12. Provision of toilet soap on request.	5	
13. Provision of one or more public telephones on the premises.	5	
14. Provision of good quality indigenous crockery, cutlery and glassware. (Imported crockery etc. not barred.)	10	
15. Provision of a clean, hygienic and well maintained kitchen with smoke exhausts and proper stores and running hot and cold water.	20	
16. Provision of reasonably good standard of cuisine. Indian as well as continental food (vegetarian and/or non-vegetarian) and good service.	25	
17. Efficient and experienced staff.	10	
18. Suitable and clean livery for the relevant staff.	10	

	Marks Essen-tial	Desir-able
19. The senior staff and service staff should possess knowledge of English.	10	
20. Business ethics of the highest order. The hotel must be clean, comfortable and homely and must provide food and service of a good order.	25	
(*) One Star		
1. Building should be suitable for a hotel and should have at least to letting rooms.	10	
2. All the rooms should be clean and properly ventilated with electric feans wherever possible.	10	
3. Rooms must be properly furnished with comfortable spring beds and cotton mattresses etc. etc.	10	
4. Provision of a moderately well equipped dining room which should be clean, properly ventilated and protected from flies and insects. Provision of at least one public room. Fans and/or ceiling punkhas are essential.	10	
5. At least 25% of the rooms must have attached bathrooms and there should be a bath room for every four of the remaining bed rooms.	15	
6. Adequate supply of hot and cold water in bath rooms.	10	
7. Provision of clean bed linen, blankets and towels.	10	
8. Provision of toilet soap on request.	5	
9. Provision of at least one public telephone wherever telephones do exist.	10	
10. Provision of good quality crockery, cutlery and glassware.	10	
11. Provision of a clean, hygienic and well maintained kitchen with smoke-exhaust and proper ventilation with fly proof doors, etc.	20	
12. Provision of clean and wholesome meals.	25	
13. The staff should be experienced and properly dressed, especially those coming into contact with the customers.	10	
14. The relevant staff coming into contact with guest should possess knowledge of English.	15	
15. Business ethics of the highest order. The establishment must be clean, comfortable and homely and must provide good service, food, etc.	25	

Rate Structure

The Committee recommends:

The adoption of modified Hubbart Formula in the matter of fixation of the rate structure applicable to hotel establishments in this country.

The withdrawal of rate control as at present exercised in Bombay or wherever it exists.

The entrusting of the work of looking into the application of the Rate Structure to the Standing Hotel Committee.

Assistance To The Hotel Industry

In keeping with the declared policy of the Government, the Hotel Industry should, by and large, be left to private enterprise, but where the private sector is unable or unwilling to fill the gap, Government should step in.

The Hotel Industry being of national importance, the Government of India and particularly the Planning Commission, should give this industry its due by formally recognising it as an industry.

For the rapid growth of the Hotel Industry, which is essential for quick development of tourist traffic, adequate financial assistance in the shape of loans, grants, subsidies etc., should be made available to the Hotel Industry.

A fund of Rs. 10 crores should be created for the purpose of advancing loans at low interest and easy terms of repayment to deserving hoteliers, since financial assistance is of the utmost importance if more hotels are to be constructed and maintained in this country.

Other sources of loans, such as the Finance Corporation, Insurance Companies, Banks (Indian and International) should be persuaded to offer loans to the Hotel Industry on suitable terms.

The feasibility of giving exemptions from certain types of taxes to new hotels for a certain period of years should be considered.

Lowering of custom duties on certain imported stores and equipment and refund of sales tax in respect of dollar earnings of hotels should be considered with a view to assisting the Hotel Industry.

The refund system on income tax on the basis of percentage of profits earned in foreign exchange should be made applicable to the Hotel Industry.

Depreciation on furniture should be increased from nine per cent to 15 per cent, and the highest rate of depreciation should be allowed on electric motors, air conditioning plants etc., used in hotels.

All anomalies in the matter of sales tax should be eliminated.

The Hotel Industry should be given direct Import Licences in respect of essential equipment and provisions to be imported from abroad for maintaining proper standards of hotel keeping.

With a view to attracting more and more tourists

during the summer season and to spread out tourist arrivals throughout the year and with a view to persuading overseas tourists to lengthen their stay in India, hotels should be encouraged to aircondition both private rooms as well as public rooms and all assistance and facilities should be afforded to them to import the necessary equipment from abroad.

Those willing to start Rest Houses and Dak Bungalows where the existing facilities are inadequate should be assisted by the Government.

Immediate steps should be taken to augment the existing hotel facilities or for providing new ones at all important tourist centres. In Calcutta, particularly where the hotel accommodation is very short, the Committee recommends the erection of a first rate hotel there, and a functional but first rate (with a minimum bed capacity of 200) at the Dum Dum airport and a couple of moderately priced first rate and modern hotels in the city. Hotel accommodation should also be increased on an urgent basis in places like Bombay, Agra, Cochin and Madras, and functional hotels of the type of Tourist Hotels in Italy, should be provided at important tourist centres where at present there are no proper and adequate facilities.

Legislation

Built-In-Conciliation Machinery

A conciliation board should be set up in case of disputes regarding wages and working conditions or of any other kind between the employees and the hotel managements. We recommend as an essential feature a system of built-in Boards of Conciliation at the Unit level, the City level and the Hotel Federation level—the Board to consist of equal numbers of representatives of managements and workers with an independent Chairman at the Unit level, the City level and the Hotel Federation level. All disputes and grievances will thus be dealt with from day-to-day and any unresolved matter will go to the next level and finally, if necessary, to the Hotel Federation level whose verdict must be final and binding on all concerned. This must take the place of the provisions of the Industrial Disputes Act as applicable to hotel establishments.

Regulation of the relationship between the hotelier and the employees, namely, stipulation of hoteliers' obligations towards the workers' emoluments, food, accommodation, clothing and medical aid, the total number of working hours to be put in during a specified spread-over time, overtime wages, recovery against loss or damage to hotel property, service charge, payment of gratuities, bonus, minimum wages, pensions, provident funds etc. Provision for warning, punishment or dismissal of hotel employees on being found slack, negligent, indisciplined, disobedient or found harassing guests for tips or other similar objectionable acts. In fact it is necessary to draw up a code of conduct by agreement between employer and employee.

Workers' obligation towards the hoteliers, namely, good behaviour, efficient service, cleanliness and regular attendance, compliance with the management's special instructions in special circumstances.

Protection for the hotelier from unscrupulous lodgers i.e. those who do not pay their bills in time or who overstay their booked time or those who make a nuisance of themselves vis-a-vis the hotel management and other guests staying in the hotel.

Provision for references to the local Tourist Advisory Committees in case of any complaints by lodgers who feel that they have been subjected to any malpractice such as overcharging and illegal ejectment from the hotel or short supply of materials and amenities and all such matters.

Relationship between the hotel industry and the Government such as:

(i) Protection of the hotelier against undue or excessive claims by lodgers for damage to person or property, theft, food poisoning, missing of train and plane connections.

(ii) Adherence by the hotel industry to a code of ethics.

(iii) Display in the rooms of the room price stating what other additional charges such as sales-tax, service charge, charge for supply of coal, air conditioning etc. are leviable.

(iv) Definition of the terms "American Plan" (Room with Full Board) "European Plan" (Room only) or "Commonwealth Plan" (Room and Breakfast).

(v) Definition of the terms 'bed tea', 'breakfast', 'lunch', 'afternoon tea' and 'dinner'.

(vi) Stipulation for the display of menus and prices outside the dining rooms and inside the lifts.

(vii) Stipulation of a uniform, percentage of service charge and the mode of its collection and distribution.

(viii) Provision of adequate fresh linen each day.

Provision to ensure cleanliness and modern sanitary conditions and proper cleansing arrangements in the kitchen.

Extension of the Employees Health Insurance Legislation to all hotel employees of the requisite category.

Enactment of comprehensive Housing Legislation concerning hotels, restaurants, eating houses and dealing with overcrowding, kitchens, safety, sanitation, airconditioning, ventilation, building construction, plumbing, fixtures, bath rooms, lavatories and all allied matters.

Legislation for the creation and the setting up of catering and training establishments specially designed for the training of staff from the craft level to the management level.

In view of the fact that the enactment of comprehensive legislation recommended by us is, in the nature of things, likely to take some time, it is urged that the Tourist Department should immediately take up with the State Governments concerned the question of relaxation of such of the existing laws as operate adversely against the satisfactory and efficient working of the Hotel Industry and consequently militate against the best interests of tourism.

Service Charge And Tipping

In view of the harassment caused to the tourist, both Indian and foreign, in the matter of the demands made by the staff for what is euphemistically called 'Bakhshish' having assumed serious proportions, there should be strict prohibition under the law against this practice.

The hoteliers organisation should ensure that strict disciplinary action will be taken in order to eliminate the evil of soliciting for tips in the hotels owned by them.

There should be levied a uniform service charge of 10% which should be set apart for distribution on the Continental system. Care should however be taken that this in no way upsets the pay structure i.e. the payment of fair wages to the staff.

Conciliation

It will be apparent that in well organised countries it is not the law which has brought about better conditions of service but the strength of the trade union of the employees operating in a reasonable manner for the purpose of achieving the best standards of work and pay that they can. We, therefore, recommend that the first attempt should be the strengthening of the existing unions and making them representative of the entire staff employed by a hotel establishment. Preferably the unions should be unions of all employees engaged in the hotel industry in a town and if necessary a federation in a State so that any agreements that are arrived at are universal and are binding. This is the ideal method but where this cannot be achieved or until it is achieved our recommendation is that Standing Conciliation Machinery should be established for the Hotel Industry town by town, and, State by State with equal representation of the management and of the staff with an independent Chairman, who, as in the case of the city of San Francisco, should be named and should operate for a certain period but named only after agreement between the two parties namely the employees and the employers. The remuneration of the Chairman should be a charge on the resources of the State, the union and/or the hotel administration. There should be no matter left out of consideration of the Conciliation Board whether it relates to wages, hours of work, meals, conditions of service or disputes of any kind that might arise between employees and the employers. By means of this internal machinery for settlement of these disputes, grievances and bitterness that we have found existing in the hotel industry will be avoided and the employees and the employers are bound to come together instead of living apart and working up anger in their hearts against each other.

Provision Of Common Fund

We suggest that the Statistical Section already in existence in the Ministry of Transport, should be properly strengthened and legislation should provide for obtaining correct information from the hotels and other sources so that not only are the statistics compiled but compiled expeditiously. The objective should be to obtain and issue a weekly report of the progress being made in regard to tourism, followed by monthly, six-monthly or yearly reports without which a planned development will be well nigh impossible.

From 1948-55, the Common Fund administered by the European Travel Commission alone spent 2 million dollars for the purpose of promoting European tourism in the United States and Europe. Thus, it will be seen that Government Agencies and various sections of the industry dealing with hotels have both joined hands to make possible the achievement of this phenomenal increase in tourist towards Europe.

Some such thing has to be done if we are to reap the rich harvest of this increase in some measure. But it can only be done if all agencies combined are ready to spend large sums towards this end both in the provisions of amenities and comforts through the hotel industry and in the matter of publicity throughout the world and in particular in Europe and the United States of America.

What we have to think about today is how to find ways and means of increasing the total number of foreign visitors from 86,000 to at least half a million a year. For this purpose we have to find over 400 thousand new visitors under a planned scheme and wherever assistance is necessary to provide the assistance in order to achieve this end. We have at the same time to ensure for these prospective tourists suitable conditions of stay in our country. In order to achieve this objective the lowering of the cost of travel is one of the essential things. Secondly, it is essential to promote big publicity campaigns boosting the advantages of travel to India. Thirdly, a provision of a fund on the same basis as the Common Fund of the European Travel Commission to which State Governments and Central Government, the hotel industry, travel agencies, shipping firms and Air Companies should contribute in an adequate manner. We recommend towards this end that the Fund should be known as the Common Fund and that it should be augmented by a levy of a two per cent surcharge on all accommodation, supply and service on bills prepared by hotels, restaurants or other catering establishment bills. With this end in view it is necessary therefore, to examine the question of the existing facilities for stay and the manner in which these facilities can be improved at the focal points in the important cities and at places of tourist interest. We have at the same time to realise that the inadequacy of internal air travel, the difficulty of finding connections, the impossibility of being certain of reservations booked in advance, have to be tackled immediately. Such difficulties must be avoided at all cost and any tourists booked on a certain passage from or certain town on a certain date must be guaranteed that accommodation, come what may.

Prohibition

Bombay: Availability of permits to foreign tourists should be made as simple as possible.

Liquor should be allowed to be served to tourists in their rooms at all times and also with their meals.

Each hotel should be allowed to have a permit room where tourists can entertain their guests and the hours should be till such time as the hotel licence permits them to keep open the dining room and the restaurant.

On special occasions permits should be given for late night closing of the dining room and the restaurant.

Permit rooms should be kept open on Sundays and holidays.

There should be no dry days.

The tourists coming to India should be given the necessary permits not only to consume alcoholic drinks in their own rooms, bar room or in public rooms but also along with their meals. These permits should be handed over to them along with their visas for the duration of their stay or, in the alternative, immediately on landing at the Customs Check Post.

For the next 10 years the above method should be adopted which in the opinion of the Committee is not likely to lead to abuse.

Madras: Besides the above facilities which should also apply to Madras, facilities should be given for drinks to be served by the hotel to permit holders both foreign and Indian in their rooms and in the dining rooms with their meals.

Delhi: In the hotels catering for foreign tourists, residents and their guests should be allowed to be served drinks not merely in their own bed rooms, but in the dining room, the lounge and the bar room and with their meals.

There should be no dry days.

The Committee also recommends that the hotel establishments should be given necessary users' licences to import their yearly requirements direct from abroad eliminating the middleman and thus reducing the cost to the consumer. We consider that within the Prohibition policy and the framework of the law the procedure adopted by certain States, including Delhi, should be liberalised.

Training Of Hotel Personnel

With properly trained staff, the cost will go down, the guests will get better service and the staff will receive higher wages.

It is most essential that in the planned development of the hotel industry important steps should be taken towards the establishment of training centres of the highest standard properly housed with adequate modern equipment for training purposes, and a competent staff.

Training

In reference to Training Institutes, we recommend that the courses should be divided into two—full time and part time. Large numbers of staff already in service with some experience and background would be benefited greatly by part time training courses.

The curriculum such as is provided in Institutes abroad should be adopted by the Universities everywhere in India for the conferment of Diplomas and Degrees.

Universities should open courses which should be recognised for the purpose of conferment of Diplomas and Degrees in hotel management and in various crafts concerned with the hotel industry.

In addition, catering establishments should be established in places indicated by us and suitably housed and supported financially by the State, the Centre and the hotel industry. These should incorporate managerial training equivalent to the standard of the Associate Membership Examination of the Hotel Catering Institute of Great Britain.

The number of students in these institutes should be in conformity with the plans for development of the hotel industry envisaged for the next few years, thus ensuring full employment.

The services of experienced foreigners in the country should be utilised and their vast experience made available for this purpose for as long a period as it is necessary.

Licences for the purchase of equipment from abroad should be made available for the purposes of the training institutes. If necessary, assistance may be taken out of the Fund suggested by the Committee for this purpose apart from the assistance given by the States and the Centre, should such a contingency arise.

Apart from the training institute recommended by us, incentive should be provided, as suggested by the Federation of Hotel and Restaurant Associations of India, to private enterprise in order to encourage it to build and operate hotel training schools. The best method for this purpose is the allotment of land free of charge, subsidies and grants for the purpose of meeting operational expenses.

The Committee recommends that training institute of the type suggested should be opened up in as many places as necessary for the requirements of the industry.

We further recommend that until such time that the training institutes as recommended by the Committee are in a position to turn out trained personnel both on the managerial and the credit side, the present scheme of giving scholarships to selected trainees to attend courses abroad should be continued and further the Committee is definitely of the opinion that until such time as managerial or craft personnel can be properly trained in the institutes indicated and capable of taking charge of the top positions in the hotel industry in their respective spheres, foreign expert personnel both managerial and craft, should be allowed to continue or allowed to be engaged from abroad. This, in our opinion, is of vital importance in the development of this industry in view of the fact that trained expert personnel of highest kind is not to be found in India at present.

It will be necessary to adopt a National Apprenticeship Scheme for all classes not only for cooks but also for all employees who are to be trained for this purpose. We recommend the creation of a National Joint Apprenticeship Council of the hotel and catering industry. It should have four representatives of the hotel Federation, four representatives of trade unions serving the hotel and catering industry, two representatives of the Tourist Department, two representatives of the Ministry of Education on the technical side, one representing the Ministry of Labour, four members of Parliament representing the public and the consumer interests. The purpose of this scheme should be to provide for the recruitment and systematic training of men and women workers. The period of apprenticeship should be not less than three years and not more than five years terminable at the maximum age of 23. Apprenticeship should start from the normal school-leaving age but older apprenticeship may also be accepted. Employers will have the right to register not more than two apprentices each but the applications must in all cases be approved by the Council.

Public Sector And Private Sector Industry

The Committee have been informed that provision exists in the Second Five-Year Plan relating to the Ministry of Transport for the establishment of 25 Rest Houses catering for the low income groups and that the Ministry of W.H. & S. has already built Rest Houses in places like Sanchi, Budh Gaya and Kushinagar. A rest house, we learn costing Rs. two-and-a-half lakhs is going to be built at Pathankot and that other steps are in hand in the U.P. and elsewhere for similar developments.

The question has arisen of the control of these new Rest Houses as well as of the existing Dak Bungalows and Rest Houses, Circuit Houses etc. throughout India. We recommend that the Central Committee suggested by us should be in the closest touch with State Governments in respect of the functioning of these Rest Houses and the provision of new ones. The question of functioning includes furnishings, service and other amenities as well as fixation of rates for board and lodging and the provision of linen, bed linen and other amenities. We recommend some uniformity being brought in not only in the construction of these establishments, Dak Bungalows, Rest Houses etc., but also in their functioning, their rate structure, the amenities that they provide and the control to be exercised over them. Obviously India is a country which, for the purposes of tourism, needs literally thousands of Rest Houses of this kind and our experience shows that buildings already in existence could easily be converted to a proper use for the benefit of the tourist—whether Indian or foreign.

We are of the opinion that the organised system of Rest Houses in Ceylon is the method that we should follow in the management of Rest Houses in India and we are firmly of the opinion that this cannot be done if ten different authorities in different parts of India deal with these establishments instead of a central coordinating authority which could delegate its functioning to local organisations either of its own or of the State Governments keeping overall control in its hands.

We suggest, initially an expenditure of two crores on the building and furnishing of one hundred such Rest Houses in different parts of India needing such accommodation for the benefit of tourists, and extra adequate expenditure on renovating and refurnishing and improving existing ones. We also suggest that the extra accommodation, save a room or two, should be made available to tourists in order to avoid the existing complaint that such accommodation is seldom available when needed.

Finally, we suggest that not the Deputy Commissioners or Collectors etc., but Tourist Councils should be the bodies authorised to issue permits for the use of all such Rest Houses etc., in order to eliminate unnecessary harassment of tourists wanting to use such accommodation.

The Committee has been impressed by the necessity of establishing through a widespread system, properly suited to Indian conditions, small roadside Motels for tourists where Dak Bungalows and Rest Houses are not available or are inadequate for this purpose.

Taking the distance to be covered for the purpose of these institutions at about 100,000 miles, we suggest that at least 100 such Motels should be provided for the use of travellers.

The main purpose would be defeated if such accommodation recommended by us for the low income groups is not properly subsidised both in regard to travel charges and in regard to food and accommodation. So far as the youth movement is concerned, the matter should be dealt with in consultation with the Central Ministry of Education (which indeed at present is dealing with it). We understand that the Ministry has agreed in principle to the establishment of Youth Hostels, although the question of the financial details of control and provision are not yet finalised. Obviously all the Ministries concerned will have to cooperate with the Central Tourist Organisation and not only cooperate but assist this organisation financially and otherwise in order that the objectives we aim at are achieved.

Indian Style Hotels

The question of internal tourism is also of the greatest importance and deserves consideration on a top priority basis. The Committee is firmly of the opinion that the possibilities and potentialities of the development of internal tourism are unlimited.

After visiting a cross section of such establishments throughout the country the Committee came to the conclusion that all such establishments should be classified according to the system of A.B.C. keeping in view the amenities, comforts, situation, service and such like factors available in these establishments.

We consider it most important that the working of these establishments should be carefully examined by a separate Committee with a view to the elimination of those establishments which are a danger to the health and well-being of the community and with a view to the standardisation of those that remain, keeping in view the basic necessities of hygiene, comforts, cleanliness and the amenities offered to the Indian traveller. The Committee recommends that it is most essential to encourage private concerns in the first instance to establish low-priced establishments everywhere, failing which it must be the duty of the State, if necessary, to construct and operate such establishments. This is a very vast undertaking and we recommend that, if it is to be undertaken by State Governments or by the Centre an autonomous Corporation should be set up for this purpose utilising all available talent and experience gained by people in the hotel industry.

Hygiene, Cleanliness And Food

In India we have found that some control is exercised in regard to the health of the staff operating in hotel establishments through the appointment of either a Resident Doctor or a Visiting Doctor. But in most cases this control is not adequate. It is not sufficient for instance that an employee should be examined once and then let go. There should be some arrangement for regular checks in regard to health matters. The first essential in the matter of legislation is to provide for adequate and constant health protection methods as far as the employees are concerned and at the same time to see that the standards laid down in the legislation that we have referred to regarding health and cleanliness are adhered to. It is necessary that the Health Departments of Corporations and Municipalities as well as the staff specially deputed for this purpose attached to the Tourist Department should at all times have the right to enter the hotel premises for inspection purposes. It is obvious that there should be no duplication. For instance, where the Corporation or Municipality services are adequate for this purpose, it is not necessary for the Tourist Department to duplicate these services. All owners of restaurants and hotel establishments should be asked to post at prominent places provisions of relevant laws, rules or regulations relating to hygiene and cleanliness in the regional language as well as English. It is the kitchen where the utmost attention has to be paid to the proper lay-out, equipping and cleanliness in all hotels and restaurants. It is necessary that the law should prohibit the use of any utensils which are not in a perfectly clean condition. All multiuse dishes and utensils should be kept free of breaks, corrosion, open seams, cracks and chipped places. It is necessary to provide adequate washing arrangements with proper sinks and drain boards with an adequate supply of running hot and cold water. Wherever possible dish-washing machines should be installed.

The Committee's attention was drawn to the existing state of numerous catering establishments that have sprung up everywhere in recent years, to the rules and regulations applicable to these establishments and to the lack of control being exercised at present in the matter of sanitation resulting in the possibility of infection. Some States have taken measures to examine this situation particularly in the metropolitan cities and we recommend to the attention of the Government the steps taken by the Madras Government and the report prepared by its Committee known as the Hotel Sanitation Committee.

Tourist Publicity

In the opinion of the Committee it is most essential that publicity should be looked at from the double angle, internal and external, and the production and the dissemination of the two types of publicity material should be organised on a separate basis, foreign publicity material being entirely under the supervision and control, in regard to production and dissemination, of the Tourist Department of the Ministry of Transport. From this point of view, the Committee feels that it is necessary to undertake an examination of the present situation, so that the above objectives are achieved as quickly as possible.

The Committee was struck by the fact that a very fine organisation has been set up by the Tourist Department of the Ministry of Transport for the distribution of publicity literature abroad and that that organisation is functioning in a most highly efficient and scientific manner. At the same time the Committee feels that not enough has been spent in the matter of publicity abroad by the private sector, namely, the hoteliers and the Travel Agents. In this connection, the Committee has been informed that in a country like Switzerland, a sum of eight million Swiss Francs is spent annually by the Hotel Industry in publicising their institutions abroad. The Committee suggests that both the Hotel Federation and the Travel Agents Association in India should get together for the purpose of assisting the authorities in the matter of publicising the Hotel Industry in foreign countries on similar lines. It is understood by the Committee that in spite of the difficult foreign exchange position, the Government of India, at the request of the Tourist Department of the Ministry of Transport, has allocated a sum of Rs. two lakhs during the current year for the purpose of enabling the hoteliers and the travel agents to make their contacts abroad, either through travel or through publicity. The Committee feels that on the one hand the Hotel Industry as well as the Travel Agents combined should make a much bigger effort for the purposes of foreign publicity and on the other hand appreciating such an effort the Government of India should make available larger sums in foreign exchange for the purposes of foreign publicity.

Kashmir

The Committee was struck, by the fact that new wooden chateaus or tourist huts were being constructed by the State comfortably furnished with modern sanitation which could be rented at a very moderate price by the season in places like Pahalgaum. It is necessary in our opinion to give wide publicity to this fact and to provide a greater number of such tourist huts for the travelling public visiting Kashmir for a longer stay.

The Committee was greatly impressed by the reduction of the rail-cum-air fares to Kashmir and the step taken by the railways in providing a return ticket at one-and-a-half times the price of the single journey ticket available for a certain period of stay. The Committee recommends that this matter should be constantly kept in mind and reviewed with the objective of a further reduction in rates, if such reduction will help in furthering the visits of tourists to Kashmir.

It is necessary in the opinion of the Committee that youth hostels and accommodation for pilgrims should be available in a large way at various centres in the State and there is no reason, in view of the cheapness of wood and the addiction of the citizens of Kashmir to the use of wood as a principal building material, why the tourist hut system should not be introduced for the purpose of youth hostels and pilgrim accommodation centres throughout the State.

The industrial and mineral possibilities of the State are enormous and we anticipate a very large influx year by year of both tourists and business people into the valley of Kashmir. It is not necessary to provide any further deluxe accommodation in the valley except to the extent of modernising a large number of houseboats in Srinagar.

But it is necessary that the small boarding houses, often run with great efficiency and success, should be encouraged and necessary subsidies and financial assistance given so that they are able to keep up their standards and provide necessary improvements and additions from year to year. The charges levied by these establishments are reasonable and the food and surroundings and the furnishings of the rooms are attractive on the whole. But a strict watch should be kept on the state of cleanliness and the authorities incharge should not hesitate to take prompt penal action, should there be found any deterioration from normal standards laid down in this respect. The Committee recommends that all Travel Agencies and Tourist Organisations should be brought into action for the purpose of publicising the joys of a visit to Kashmir.

In order that tourists visiting northern parts of India or Delhi are induced or are enabled to spend at least a short holiday in Kashmir during their sojourn in northern India, it is necessary that the existing rigid formalities for visits of foreign or Indian tourists to Kashmir should be minimised and permits made available even on holidays and at all reasonable hours of the day.

There are vast areas in Kashmir of great interest from the point of view of *shikar* which are yet to be explored or opened up. The Committee recommends that this aspect should be examined carefully by a Local Committee set up for this purpose whose recommendations should be implemented with expedition, whether they relate to the opening up of new roads, new transport facilities, new Rest Houses, Dak Bungalows or Tourist huts or any other facilities that may be necessary for the purpose of opening up these new avenues of travel.

The Committee was greatly impressed with the officers incharge of the Tourist Organisation in Kashmir which is functioning in a satisfactory manner up to the limit of the experience so far gained. The newly constructed Reception Centre has a lounge, a restaurant attached to it and it is very necessary that cleanliness should be ensured and the charges kept down to the minimum without affecting the quality of the food and drinks available.

For the foreign tourists, it is important to emphasise the fact that there are no restrictions regarding prohibition in the entire valley of Kashmir and in the opinion of the Committee this state of affairs should continue if foreign tourists are to be attracted on a large scale.

The Committee recommends that the Shikar Bungalow at Dachigam should be made available for *Shikar* parties and for parties of tourists wanting complete rest and that similar bungalows should be built elsewhere for this purpose as we are convinced that they can always be madè self-supporting and will constitute an extra attraction for visitors both Indian and foreign.

The Committee recommends that there should be no limit in a reasonable way to the amount of financial assistance that should be made available to the State of Jammu & Kashmir for the purpose of the development of tourism, if out of its own resources the State is unable to meet the expenditure. For this purpose the Committee recommends that the Ministry of Transport in the Tourist Department should confer with the Tourist Organisation in Kashmir and draw up a planned and phased basis for the purpose of providing greater and better amenities for the travelling public in Kashmir. One of the essential things in this respect is the provision of cheap road transport in the valley. A holiday in Kashmir is often marred by the expenditure people have to incur for such transport which often is not available. This is a matter which should be the concern of the Tourist Organisation in Kashmir and we suggest the import of cheap priced diesel vehicles of the Volks-Wagon type or any other suitable type should be permitted to the extent required.

We are finally concerned that proper publicity should be conducted abroad and in India so that the attractions of Kashmir are presented as of primary importance in the tour itineraries arranged by Travel Agencies and other organisations for prospective tourists.

Places Of Tourist Interest And Their Development

Grouping of tourist centres for the purpose of arranging systematic tours, we are told, has been done by some tourist agencies and booklets have been prepared on the subject of 'Tours in India'. The Committee is of the opinion that in the drawing up of a schedule giving a general idea of the centres of tourist interest both youth hostel aspect as well as the aspect of pilgrim accommodation should be kept in view. From the transport point of view, it is necessary to see that adequate rail, air or road connections are available in the existing centres of tourist attraction and for the others that are to be developed. An accelerated drive should be made to develop other centres of tourist attraction, the first essential is the provision of transport. Even at the sacrifice of revenue, it is necessary that places of tourist interest should be connected by air and the road approach improved and modernised. For instance, there is no regular air service to Khajuraho at the present moment. The approach to the Sun Temple at Konarak is only by road and suitable arrangement should be taken in hand for the purpose of building small aerodromes, like the one at Bhuvaneshwar, with centres like Konarak and centres of rest and pleasure like Goalpur-on-sea.

The Committee received some valuable information regarding the Tel Valley Civilization and its rich archaeological remains in Orissa. These sites remain neglected and almost in a forgotten state. Our attention was drawn to the temples and statues of Khichin in Mayurbhanj which date back to the ninth century A.D. It appears that in addition to the sites at Bhuvaneshwar, Puri and Konarak, there is also 'Dev Kund' which is a spot of great natural beauty. The coins and images that have been found in this area date back to the Kushan period. This area attracts thousands of pilgrims every year. It is sacred to the Goddess Ambika. The jungles around are said to contain prehistoric animals like giant flying squirrels. If this site is developed into a tourist centre, it is bound to attract thousands of visitors from abroad as well as from India. This area, Dev Kund and Ambika Mahapith, are already being developed by the Government as a national park because of the extraordinary beauty of their natural surroundings and their association with our cultural past dating back to the first or second century A.D. and its rich heritage of wild life and beautiful flora suggest that immediate attention should be paid to this area with a view to its development and utilisation in the national interest.

We also draw the attention of the Government to the urgent necessity of developing the Kulu and Kangra Valleys for the purposes of tourist traffic. We consider that the following matters should be given priority both by the State Government and the Central Government:

(i) The opening up of a large sized aerodrome in the Bahl Valley which is most suitable for this purpose and is likely to cost a much smaller sum than any other site available in this area. The natural advantages of the utilisation of the site are obvious.

(ii) Small hotels of the Italian tourist type should be established in the valley.

(iii) The State or the Central Government should establish a sanatorium at the site of the Hotel Sulphur Springs and be charged with their maintenance in proper condition with the service of medical assistance available on the spot with accommodation to begin with to at least a 100 beds. Timber from the valley can be utilised for this purpose thus cheapening the cost. Even log huts of the type that are available in places like Lake Louise, Canada, accommodating a family, will be suitable to begin with and later could form the basis for extra accommodation when needed.

(iv) The road from Bhakra to Mandi should be developed. It is only a few miles and the development of this road would be the easiest and quickest means of approach to the Kulu Valley. The economic possibility of opening up this valley by road, rail and aeroplane traffic deserve the immediate attention of the authorities. The economic possibilities include the development of the Pashmina industry, the lifting of high grade fruit, the canning of fruit and vegetables, the manufacture of cider and the development of mineral resources including iron ore, antimony and rock salt and the development on a large scale of cottage industries and handicrafts.

(v) The development of the seed of Spiti peonies which were famous once upon a time and seem to be dying out.

(vi) The road that goes up the valley is on the left side at present. It is very close to the main Beas river. But when there are heavy floods and the river slightly changes its course it knocks against the pillar of the bridge, and the road and the bridge are both liable to destruction. There is no road on the right side of the bank going up and it is necessary to build a road which is now only a pony track and avoid all the dangers of erosion which have caused tremendous financial losses in the past.

We draw the special attention of the authorities to the valuable suggestions made by the representatives of the Himachal Pradesh Government and the need stressed by them of opening a Spa at Tattapani and the development of roads and transport on the Tibet road as well as the necessity of all-the-year-round ice skating rink as well as adequate provision for winter sports in Simla.

We have been greatly impressed by the importance attached to social tourism in the concept of the developing economy of our country. The object of social tourism is not only to provide holidays to people of the lower income groups who normally are unable to afford them but to fit the scheme into the newly developing ideas of paid holidays for workers, assistance to the youth travel movement as well as to the movement of pilgrims throughout our land. Our objective is the welfare State. The welfare State depends for its existence upon the willing cooperation of the working classes and the peasantry who form 98 per cent of the population of our country. The welfare State has to function for their benefit and would have no meaning if it did not. One of the objectives of the welfare State must necessarily be the provision of paid holidays to workers and subsidised travel for the youth of our country. It is one of the essential items and is a kind of education for the younger people to be able to see their country, meet the people of cultural interest as well as of industrial importance. It is only thus, that the lack of understanding of each other's needs of the different people that live in this country can be put an end to. Further, such social tourism would create deep interest and enthusiasm for the great industrial revolution we are witnessing. Planned economy has to be brought home visually to large masses of our people by affording them an opportunity of seeing our industrial plans in action. So visits to Nangal-Bhakra, to the Steel Plants, to Sindri, Chittaranjan, Bangalore and other centres must necessarily be arranged on a concessional basis for those wanting to see the sites and acquaint themselves with the spirit of the great industrial-revolution.

We recommend that the system of paid holidays for workers should be introduced in every hotel establishment and extended elsewhere. This must be a compulsory provision. We recommend further that subsidised tours on a very large basis should be organised by the Railways for the student community and young people generally. We also recommend that similar subsidised tours should be organised on a large scale for pilgrims wanting to travel from their homes to the places of pilgrimage throughout India.

The Committee while drawing the attention of the Government to places of tourist interest worthy of development wants to make it clear that the places mentioned by it are by no means exclusive but that large areas of tourist importance need to be brought to the notice of the public throughout the country, and many beauty spots in the States of Mysore, Kerala, Orissa and elsewhere need special attention from the point of view of tourist interest. In fact there is so much of interest for the tourist in almost every part of India that it is necessary only to draw general attention to the problem, except in the places which we have specified as almost everywhere in India, there is need for special attention being paid to places of tourist importance.

IRRIGATION AND POWER TEAM ON CHAMBAL PROJECT (MADHYA PRADESH AND RAJASTHAN), 1957—REPORT

New Delhi, Committee on Plan Projects, 1958. 119p.+iiip.+Charts.

Leader : Shri N.V. Gadgil.
Members : Shri Lal Singh; Shri M. Narasimhaiya; Shri C.L. Handa; Shri G.N. Pandit.
Secretary : Shri D.S. Borker.

APPOINTMENT

The Irrigation and Power Team on Chambal Project (Madhya Pradesh and Rajasthan) was constituted under the Committee on Plan Projects in 1957 by the National Development Council.

TERMS OF REFERENCE

(1) To study all aspects of the Project having a bearing on economy and efficiency with special reference to:

(a) Utilisation of trained personnel and materials;

(b) Utilisation of machinery and equipment;

(c) Construction—Plant lay-out;

(d) Adequacy of original estimates and designs as evidenced from actual construction of the Project;

(e) Phasing of construction with a view to studying whether:

(i) timely utilisation of benefits accruing from the Project has been ensured;

(ii) it is possible to accelerate accrual of benefits;

(iii) benefits could be increased by rephasing the Project at this stage;

(f) Sufficiency of investigations conducted at the planning stage with a view to the formulation of Project Estimates;

(g) The effect of the above study on the financial results of the Project, if any.

(2) Generally to assess the progress made in construction, the reasons for shortfall, if any, and to suggest measures for improvements in the future.

(3) To examine the possibility of decreasing dependence upon imported materials and equipment required for the Project.

(4) To examine whether adequate steps have been taken by the authorities concerned for fixing and realising the contemplated water rates, betterment fees and/or any other rates, cesses or taxes.

(5) Any other recommendation that the Team may like to make in order to ensure economy and efficiency in the construction of the Project.

CONTENTS

Preface; Introductory; Administration; Features of Design and Construction; Phasing of Project; Management of Irrigation and Utilization of Water; Power Generation; Works Needing Urgent Attention; Costs of Project; Summary of the Report; Appendices I to XXI-B.

RECOMMENDATIONS

History And Salient Features Of Project

The Chambal Project originally estimated to cost Rs. 77 crores would consist of three storage reservoirs with power houses and a barrage with attendant canal works. On completion, it would irrigate 14 lakhs of acres and generate 210,000 kw of electricity. By the end of Second Plan it is planned to achieve almost full irrigation benefits and to generate a maximum of 92,000 kw of power.

The Project has undergone several changes before it was officially sanctioned in 1954 though the work was started in 1953. These changes were inevitable in view of the then existing princely States which were merged in different stages subsequently while active consideration was being given to the preparation of the Project. No precise schedules of materials, technical personnel, machinery and equipment could be drawn at the commencement of the Project.

Administration

The dominant impressions gathered regarding the administration of the Project are as under:

(a) One of the main functions of the Control Board in agricultural planning and phasing of field channels for the proper utilisation of water. The former requires two to three years' experimentation ahead of the target date and the latter involves complex scheduling in advance. In both these cases nothing tangible has been done so far.

(b) Preparation of detailed estimates and schedule of rates is lagging badly.

(c) Inordinate delays are noticed in the States' implementing decision taken by the Board.

To remedy this serious situation, the report recommends:

(i) State Finance Secretaries should be *ex-officio* Members of the Board;

(ii) Technical designs should be regularly subjected to check by an independent technical agency;

(iii) An agricultural expert should be made a Member of the Board or at least consulted regularly;

(iv) The Board should set up machinery for carrying out the main functions assigned to it;

(v) Specified Executive Engineer in each Project and an A.F.A. should be made jointly responsible for preparing estimates and schedule of rates within three to six months;

(vi) Pending completion of work at (v), Chief Engineers may be given larger financial and administrative powers in respect of acceptance of tenders and sanctioning of estimates without obtaining prior concurrence of Financial Adviser; and

(vii) The above proposals would mean a much greater burden on the Chairman of the Board than hitherto rendering his job virtually a whole time function.

Personnel

Staffing position on the Project is difficult particularly in Madhya Pradesh area. To remedy the situation the report suggests:

(a) The State cadres may be expanded to include the post-projects requirements so that some of the temporary incumbents could be absorbed taking into account lengths of their previous services;

(b) The ultimate solution lies in pooling of the existing resources to the best advantage of all the projects in the country by creating an All India Reserve of officers who could be utilised to strengthen the projects as and when necessary since each State cannot appreciate the overall situation;

(c) As it takes a long time to recruit personnel by

each Public Service Commission, a Committee consisting of a Member from each of the Commissions, each acting as Chairman alternately and two eminent engineers as other Members should be empowered to recruit the necessary personnel; and

(d) The Project authorities should organise courses so as to fit the existing personnel to some of the routine tasks connected with the construction of the Dam, the Canals and the electrical equipment for power houses and transmission lines.

Agencies Of Construction

Some works are done departmentally, some by contracts and some in a composite way. M/s Gammons are entrusted with the complicated work of the Kunu Syphon. In addition, the National Projects Construction Corporation has been given a large number of works costing about Rs. two-and-a-half crores. The potentialities of this organisation are considerable especially when contracting resources all over the country are overstressed due to the increasing demands of the Second Five-Year Plan.

Features Of Design And Construction

Design of Kotah Barrage: The design of the earthen dam which forms a part of the barrage has undergone a continuous evolution involving six designs in all. After discussing the fifth design with the C.W.&P.C., the Consultative Committee stressed the necessity of devising other methods of protecting the foundations as neither the clay grouting nor the sheet piles could be considered fully effective in serving their purpose. The Consultative Committee considers that the design number six subject to modifications agreed upon on January 15, 1958, is the most satisfactory and stresses the need to programme the work into its minutest detail including strengthening of personnel. The report suggests that the retired Chief Engineers of the country should be given a proper retainer and distributed over various projects costing more than 15 crores for consultations. Each such project should have a Consultative Committee with the necessary specialised personnel. This device is specially relevant in our country so as to have an independent and objective check over the the designs on Irrigation and Power Projects prepared by the State authorities or the C.W.& P.C., in view of the fact that there are no consultants available in the private sector in this field unlike in the western countries.

Canal Lining: The Team proposes to provide lime surkhi concrete bedding in the canal reaches passing through rocky terrain, instead of cement concrete. This alternative would result in conservation of scarce materials like cement as well as a saving of about 15 to 20 lakhs of rupees.

Designs Organisation: Chief Engineer, Madhya Pradesh gets all the designs from C.W.&P.C. It is the view of the Team that some of these designs which are not of a major character could with advantage and convenience be prepared by the Chief Engineer himself. For this purpose a special design cell with suitable staffing needs to be created under the control of the Chief Engineer. Design Officers both in Rajasthan and Madhya Pradesh may be drawn from the establishment of the C.W.&P.C. who should work under the direction of the Chief Engineers, affording an opportunity to the Project Authorities of knowing the mind of C.W.&P.C. Also the Officers thus drawn from C.W.&P.C. would gain experience of changes in designs in actual construction.

Quality Control: The report recommends the practices followed on the Bhakra Project, that is to appoint a special inspection and control organisation under the Chief Engineers, so as to have an objective analysis of factors influencing quality of work.

Agency for Constructing Field Channels: Customary practice of constructing field channels is to leave the works to the villagers themselves. But the main drawback is that it is not possible to enthuse them to the extent necessary having regard to the existing standards of people in these areas. Therefore, it is most desirable that the Project authorities themselves should construct the channels recovering the cost from the villagers. If this is not done, it may take a long time to realise the irrigation benefits from the Project. In order to euthuse the cultivators village committees working under the guidance of an overall committee in every administrative division under the chairmanship of the commissioner concerned and with Superintending Engineer or Local Executive Engineer as Members to undertake detailed planning, should be instituted.

Phasing Of Construction Programme

Gandhi Sagar Dam and Kotah Barrage: There has been a delay in obtaining penstock gates which resulted in setting back the progress on the Gandhi Sagar Dam, which is now expected to be completed by 1959, instead of 1958 as originally planned. The Kotah Barrage is also now expected to be completed in 1959.

Canals and distributaries are expected to be completed by 1962-63. However, the Team feels that the period of completion of the canals could be advanced provided funds are made available. Looking to the rising tempo of work and the capacity of the machinery, it is considered that this acceleration could be achieved.

Acceleration of Construction of Rana Pratap Sagar Dam: The integrated development of Chambal River Valley envisages construction of Rana Pratap Sagar Dam 20 miles below Gandhi Sagar Dam. Therefore the original intention was to start the construction of the dam in the winter of 1957. Although preliminary Project report has been submitted by the Chief Engineer,

Rajasthan, certain important investigations relating to power house remain to be done. The Team considers it necessary to expedite work on the remaining investigations and dovetail the construction of the Rana Pratap Sagar Dam with that of Gandhi Sagar Dam which would

(a) facilitate installation of power plants at a short notice, when necessary;

(b) incidentally result in a saving of Rs. 54 lakhs by utilising some of the machinery and buildings at Gandhi Sagar Dam.

Agricultural Aspects

The Team worked in close cooperation with the State authorities, both at technical level and administrative (Ministers) level, so that the recommendations are the outcome of joint discussion of the Team and State authorities.

For a Project of the size and nature of Chambal, it was necessary to have a Master Schedule before initiation of the enterprise. This shortcoming could be attributed to (a) two States concerned lacked the necessary institutional arrangement and not having Development Committee consisting of Engineering, Agricultural, Administrative and Revenue Experts to work out the details of utilisation as done by Mysore State, and (b) the Control Board, while consisting of experienced persons in Irrigation, had no agricultural expert on it for giving serious thought to agricultural aspect. It is highly desirable to associate an agricultural expert in all the Control Boards.

The Team considers that the period of 10 years for realising the benefit of irrigation, can be reduced to half, *provided* the recommendations relating to agricultural aspect are immediately implemented. The State Agriculture Department fully agrees with this view. Economic benefit both to the agriculturists and the country, by hastening the utilisation programme, cannot be underestimated.

Presumptions of Project authorities, both in regard to *increased yield* of foodgrains and the *financial return* on the Project, are not likely to be realised. Kharif foodgrain crops would require little irrigation on account of ample rainfall and financial return will depend upon the extent to which the cultivators find irrigation a remunerative practice. On the other hand, anticipated financial returns can be easily realised and even be exceeded, if agricultural aspect of the Project is given due attention with least delay.

The agricultural problems are discussed under three headings:

(a) Changes in agriculture pattern.

(b) Serious problems already existing.

(c) Urgent steps to be taken for deriving maximum benefits from canal irrigation.

The present pattern of agriculture is distressing, people generallyl azy, crop yields poor, elementary principles of dry farming not observed, farmyard manure largely wasted, composting and green manuring almost unknown, even big cities like Kotah (Rajasthan) utilising thousands of tons of town refuse and animal dung just for filling depressions, milk yield of milch-animals disgustingly low on account of poor feeding and poor breeding, and area under cash crops almost insignificant. All this is likely to undergo revolutionary change with the advent of canal irrigation. Future cropping pattern would largely depend upon the extent to which the State Agriculture Department is able to solve the problems of agriculturists under altered conditions.

Water allowance per thousand acres on this canal seems liberal in view of much heavier rainfall and much higher ground water level in the former. Secondly, G.C.A. and C.C.A. require to be confirmed for various reasons.

High salt contents of water and high water table in the percolation wells in several areas of both Rajasthan and Madhya Pradesh—particularly in Digod Tehsil in Rajasthan and Gohad and Mehgaon Tehsils in Madhya Pradesh, point to serious dangers of water-logging and salinity of land which must be safeguarded against, if canal irrigation is not to prove ultimately injurious.

Measures to prevent waterlogging, salinity and bad drainage such as lining canals, distributaries, minors, providing satisfactory drainage system, installation of tubewells, encouraging use of pumping sets, avoiding accumulation of salts by proper culturable practices, study of subsoil etc., are discussed, with which, the State authorities generally agree. The cost of drainage system in Gohad and Mehgaon Tehsils is expected to be 10 lakhs of rupees.

Levelling of land, in many places, in order to ensure maximum advantage from irrigation and to prevent the evils of uneven irrigation, seems indispensable. The total area in each of the State requiring levelling is estimated at 15 to 20 per cent or about lakh or lakh-and-a-half acres in each State—the total provision made being Rs. 30 lakhs for Rajasthan and Rs. 46 lakhs for Madhya Pradesh during three years recoverable from cultivators in five yearly instalmenls. Four alternative methods of attending to this work have been discussed.

Wild *ber* bush infesting the land in most area coming under Chambal Valley Project in both States is a serious pest. Its removal can easily increase the yield by 2 to 3 mds. of foodgrain per acre on an average for the State. Various methods of attending to this evil are discussed.

Kankar layers appearing at depths of two feet to four feet below surface soil, and also hard pan appearing in many places, require immediate experimentation.

Other matters requiring urgent attention are determination of varieties of crops, best suited under irrigation cultural practices, time of sowing, seed-rate etc. under altered conditions, manurial requirements under canal system, irrigation requirements of various crops and such other problems. Upon the proper solution of these questions will depend not only the yield of crops but also financial returns to the Government on this Project. In fact, this work should have been started several years ago. Lack of preparedness can be attributed to the manner in which the States came into existence, as a result of merger of small Princely States which could hardly be expected to do any great deal of research work for want of funds. The States will have to stage double march in order to catch up with other States, not only because these two States are the biggest in India, next to Bombay, but also because there are numerous problems to be tackled, and that also, in the shortest possible time. No doubt, the new research stations are being established, staff being appointed and laboratories being fitted but unfortunately the specialists in various branches are being scattered all over the State in order to satisfy the political claims of capitals of erstwhile Princely States. This is not in the lasting interest of the State agriculture.

Horticulture Industry has immense potentialities and can bring about revolutionary change in the agricultural economy of the two States. Although the area under fruits in both the States, at present, is very small, yet the presence of good number of fruit trees of many kinds—mangoes, citrus and papayas etc.—flourishing in many places and bearing bumper crop of good quality, indicates vast possibilities. For the development of horticulture, the gardens of erstwhile Rulers, containing trees of high quality, can play great part by supplying budwood to the Agriculture Department for mass scale production of nursery plants of pedigree stock for supply to public at 'no profit no loss basis'. The scheme in this connection has also been prepared for both the States.

Sugar Industry: Area under sugarcane in both the States, at present, is very small but fertile soil, good climate free from frost, plentiful supply of canal water, point to immense scope for sugar industry. Most desirable course will be to create "Sugarcane Belts" to concentrate cane cultivation in suitable areas. This will not only lead to high yield of cane but also high recovery of sugar as two factors responsible for low recovery of sugar are (a) the time lag between the time of cutting of cane and its crushing in the factory, and (b) proper degree of maturity of cane at crushing time, and both these factors can be fully controlled if cane cultivation is concentrated in certain areas. In size, Rajasthan and Madhya Pradesh are even bigger than U.P. which has nearly 30 lakhs of acres under sugarcane and 68 sugar mills. Even a quarter of this area and 15 mills can contribute immensely to the prosperity of the two States and their agriculturists.

Storing farm-yard manure in pits, composting of town refuse and green manuring fields to maintain the fertility of soil, will have to be encouraged by necessary propaganda or legislation. Green manuring practices would receive impetus if green manure crops are exempted from irrigation rates as done in the Punjab. The State authorities agree to take necessary steps in this direction. In the interest of dairy industry, irrigation rates on green fodder crops like berseem could be reduced.

Consolidation of holdings would help in the better and more profitable utilisation of canal water and in fixation of *warabandi*. The State authorities agree to give priority to Chambal area for this work.

Village tanks, formerly used for storage of irrigation water, and to prevent erosion, are now going out of use and their utility in future to serve as fish tanks or for production of crops like Saugara or as an insurance against periodic closure of canal for short periods, requires consideration.

In canal-irrigated areas residential houses of farmers have got to be, as near the fields as possible, otherwise canal irrigation has little meaning. Accordingly new villages with new houses are bound to spring up. The West Punjab (now Pakistan) had a happy experience of preparing village sites and house plans for cultivators, simultaneously with the construction of canals. Likewise new sites for mandis (markets) were also thought out. Several old towns like Sheopur (Madhya Pradesh) are growing rapidly but in a most haphazard manner. This evil can be prevented right now and proper plans prepared with warehousing facilities etc.

With the onset of Monsoon, most of the roads in the proposed canal area, both in Rajasthan and Madhya Pradesh, get out of order, and villages remain completely cut off during Monsoon for months at a time. Here again, the happy experience of the Punjab in constructing pucca roads, almost simultaneously with canal construction, could be cited which immensely helped in opening up and developing the new area leading to the prosperity of the people.

The unfortunate practice, already prevalent in several places in Madhya Pradesh like Harsi Dam Canal area, is for the cultivator to take any amount of water at any time and for any length of period with the result that lands at the head of the minor get excess water resulting in water logging and those at the tail-end, die for want of water, besides embittering relations between the farmers. This evil must be checked from the very start in Chambal area by following *warabandi* system as prevalent in the Punjab and even in Bikaner area of Rajasthan. The Chief Engineer, Madhya Pradesh, has sent his Superintending Engineer to the Punjab to study *warabandi* system there.

Construction and maintenance of the main field channels are now the responsibility of the village but it would be better for the Department to undertake this responsibility (construction only) or at any rate, provide technical guidance.

Malaria Problem: It is likely to become more serious as spleen percentage is already said to be very high.

In order to utilise the services of retired persons for the development of fruit industry and enable them to lead a useful and productive life in the rural area, it will be desirable to start cooperative garden colony scheme on the lines adopted in the Punjab.

There is said to be a considerable area of culturable waste land in both the States, which requires to be reclaimed. The States may lease out these areas to progressive enterprising agriculturists for sufficiently long period or (b) start cooperative farm on these areas to see to what extent, even under favourable conditions, cooperative farming can be a success.

Soil Erosion: This is a most serious problem in both the States. In Rajasthan no less than 30 per cent of the total culturable area has already been devastated by soil erosion—gullies, ravines, rills and even sheet erosion. Since the problem of soil erosion is not directly concerned with Chambal Valley Project, the subject is proposed to be separately discussed, except that sheet erosion (although imperceptible to an untrained eye) goes on continuously washing away fertile soil from land that appear almost level or only slightly sloping; and this evil is likely to be accentuated with the advent of canal system. It will be the duty of Irrigation and Agriculture Departments to popularise agricultural practices like contour cultivation, strip cropping, terracing, levelling, proper crop rotation, bunding, etc.

Estimates of expenditure for three years both recurring and non-recurring on various schemes proposed, aggregates to Rs. 59.3 lakhs for Rajasthan and Rs. 57 lakhs for Madhya Pradesh including the amounts recoverable from cultivators.

Incentive for Development: Some of the land to be brought under irrigation needs considerable improvement by way of clearance of ber bushes and levelling of steep slopes and ravines, requiring time and capital. In the interest of expediting development of irrigation, it is recommended that relative bigger holdings may be entrusted to private enterprise and ceiling of ownership of land may not be applied for a period of say 25 years. With persistent effort on all hands the period of development may be reduced to five years instead of 10 provided in the Project report.

Betterment Levy: In view of the increasing value of lands consequent upon availability of irrigation facilities the necessity of betterment levy is beyond any doubt. The main principle to be followed should be that the betterment levy may be half of the estimated increase in the value of land as a result of the benefits of irrigation. It is learnt that necessary legislation in this regard is under consideration of Madhya Pradesh and Rajasthan Government.

Power Generation

Owing to the present financial difficulties in the country, the load growth in the Chambal region will not be as rapid (increasing five-fold in five years) as it was forecast earlier. Hence it is suggested that foreign exchange expenditure on Rana Pratap Sagar Power Plant may be postponed but the civil works should be started in the Second Plan period. The works could be accelerated if any unforeseen development of new loads does come about earlier than now considered probable.

The proposed transmission system lay-out may be modified slightly so as to inter-connect with the Chambal grid the recently installed thermal power plants and those under erection presently, contributing an effective capacity of 34,000 kw.

At the Gandhi Sagar Power Station, the fifth generating unit for which the penstock pipe has already been provided in the dam, may be installed. With this installation and in conjunction with the thermal plants, it is possible to meet a system demand upto 1,20,000 kw. The addition of the fifth unit not only serves to meet the load demand in the interim period till additional hydro-capacity is commissioned in the region, but also provides spare generating capacity for all the three hydro-stations, namely, Gandhi Sagar, Rana Pratap Sagar and Kotah in the ultimate stage.

By the integrated operation of the Gandhi Sagar Station with the new thermal plants, more thermal generation than now may be necessary but it is possible to minimise it. To begin with, irrigation would not have fully developed. Also, in the early stages of load development, the system load factor will be lower than 60 per cent and it may be possible to meet the entire load demand by operating five units at Gandhi Sagar Power Station only. As the system load grows and load factor improves, thermal support could be brought in gradually. Prior to full irrigation development, keeping the reservoir full (R.L. 1312) at the end of the Monsoon on October 1, and by drawing down the reservoir to as low a level as possible by the end of June and building it up during the Monsoon, it is possible to generate maximum hydro energy. In a good year, there will be no need for thermal generation at all except for about an hour or so per day to meet the peak demand. In years of average or low rainfall it would be necessary to supplement the hydro energy by thermal generation. It is expected that the average coal consumption per annum may not exceed what it would be, say in 1958.

Another advantage of the integrated operation would be the improvement in the performance of the unusually extensive (about 1,000 miles) trasmission net-work associated with this Project which has an ultimate hydro potential of about 2,00,000 kw in the three hydro stations. Normally in a well-developed region this quantum of power would be absorbed in a distance of about 200 miles. It is suggested that the performance of the proposed transmission system may be studied on the Network Analyser at the Indian Institute of Science, Bangalore. Based on the results of this study, the design and the lay-out of the transmission system may be suitably modified.

With a view to economise in the use of steel, the possibility of utilising wood-poles or concrete poles for transmission lines of 66 kw and below may be examined.

The major handicap for the speedy execution of the electrical works appears to be the shortage of technical personnel. It is sugested that the C.W.&P.C. may consider sparing for this Project some officers who, being familiar with the designs, could be of help to accelerate executions in the field.

For deriving early and maximum benefits from the sale of power that will be developed by the Chambal Project in successive stages of its construction, it is essential that the State Electricity Boards of Madhya Pradesh and Rajasthan should cooperate very closely and plan on the full utilisation of the hydro power as it becomes available, based on short term power sales understandings between the two Electricity Boards. Power should be utilised fully by whichever administration ready to do so and the programme should not be impeded by a literal interpretation of the Agreement that the power available should be shared equally between Madhya Pradesh and Rajasthan. Power may be made available for all consumers who can make effective use of it irrespective of where they are whether in Madhya Pradesh or in Rajasthan. Such a load-building programme will keep the total power generating facilities fully loaded all the time and will facilitate early and profitable construction of the Rana Pratap Sagar Power Station and other Power Stations down below.

Works Needing Urgent Attention

The progress on transmission lines both in Madhya Pradesh and Rajasthan is almost negligible. Special attention is necessary both as regards procurement of materials and erection so as to obtain the benefits of power soon after the power plant is ready for operation in 1959.

The Kotah Barrage including erection of gates has to be completed by 1959. Up till now progress on earthen dam portion of the barrage is practically nil. In order to complete the same by June 1959, very special efforts and care are necessary in providing the filters, clay grouting of foundation, and placing of bleeder wells. A very careful schedule is considered imperative in view of the necessity to complete all the foundation works before the commencement of coming Monsoon, and the entire earth work, during the next working season before the Monsoon of 1959.

The radial gates on the spillway are required to be fabricated and erected in position before the irrigation season of 1959 commences. Already some delay has taken place due to non-availability of steel in time. The Control Board should arrange for necessary agency to watch the progress of all the works at various stages and schedules attained.

Progress on all the cross drainage works on canals have to be specifically watched so that they are completed before the irrigation commences in their respective zones. The numerous railway crossings need specially attended to as they are to be constructed by railway authorities.

Field channels and water-courses need to be completed before the irrigation starts in respective zones.

Cost of Project

Total development of the scheme with all three dams, power houses and transmission lines, Kotah Barrage and canals system was originally estimated to cost Rs. 77 crores. Out of this, the Gandhi Sagar Dam and its power houses, transmission lines, Kotah Barrage and the canal system intended to be completed up to the end of Second Five-Year Plan originally estimated to cost Rs. 48.03 crores are now revised to Rs. 63.59 crores, in view of rising costs and increase in quantities etc.

The expenditure upto date is Rs. 14.62 crores.

The Team has proposed economies amounting to a crore of rupees, by way of (a) dovetailing construction of Rana Pratap Sagar Dam with that of Gandhi Sagar Dam, (b) accelerating canal construction, and (c) lining canals with lime concrete instead of cement concrete etc.

LIBRARY COMMITTEE TO ADVISE THE U.G.C. ABOUT DEVELOPMENT OF LIBRARIES AND THEIR ORGANISATION, 1957—REPORT

(Report on University and College Libraries and the Proceedings of the Seminar on "From Publisher to Reader" held on March 4-7, 1959) New Delhi, University Grants Commission, 1965. 228p.

Chairman : Dr. S.R. Ranganathan.
Members : Shri S. Bashir-uddin; Shri K.S. Hingwe; Shri B.S. Kesavan; Shri S. Parthasarathy.
Member-Secretary : Dr. P.J. Philip.

APPOINTMENT

The Chairman, University Grants Commission, appointed this Committee in 1957 to advise the Commission on matters relating to the proper functioning and management of libraries.

TERMS OF REFERENCE

(i) To advise the Commission on matters relating to the proper functioning and management of libraries;

(ii) To advise on various problems connected with provision of grant to libraries, book purchase, development of reading habit and help to students in the use of libraries, documentation work and service to research workers, departmental libraries, library personnel and their functions, classification, status, salary scale and strength; and

(iii) To advise on standards for the design of library buildings and fittings and furniture.

CONTENTS

Foreword by Dr. D. S. Kothari; Introduction; **Report of the Library Committee:** Utilisation of UGC Grant; Library Finance; Book Selection and Book Purchase; Promotion of Reading Habit; Weeding out, Wear and Tear and Loss; Documentation; Departmental Collection; Library Personnel; Strength of Library Staff; Training of Library Personnel; Library Building, Fittings and Furniture; Standard for Library Building; Standard for Fittings and Furniture; Summary of Chief Recommendations; Proceedings of the Seminar; **"From Publisher to Reader":** Address of Welcome by Samuel Mathai; Inaugural Address by C.D. Deshmukh; Presidential Address by S.R. Ranganathan; Address of Thanks by P.J. Philip; Working Paper for the Seminar by S.R. Ranganathan; Findings of the Seminar: Address by K.D. Metcalf; Concluding Address by S.R. Ranganathan; Remarks by P.J. Philip; Index.

RECOMMENDATIONS

UGC Grant

A period of 17 months should be allowed for the proper utilisation of the UGC grant for reading and kindred materials, to facilitate book-selection and book-purchase along useful and economic lines without disturbing the weekly rhythm of the administration work of the library and the normal reference and circulation service to readers.

A library may be allowed to spend upto one-fifth of the Commission's grant for reading and kindred materials on the staff required to select and complete the purchase of the materials and to complete the technical work and the processing necessary to bring them into active use.

Commission's grant to a university library should be determined according to an agreed per capita formula.

Subject to local variation, the capacity of the university to spend, and the amount at the disposal of the Commission, for grant for reading and kindred materials, Rs. 15 per capita on the basis of students registered in the university and Rs. 200 per teacher may be given as grant to a university library for the time being. These figures should be revised periodically in the light of the changes in the cost of books and periodicals.

In the case of an affiliating university the number of students and teachers to be counted should be determined in the light of local conditions.

In the case of a newly started university, which is not more than five years old, an additional grant upto a sum of Rs. 300,000 may be given to build up the initial stock of reading materials, such as periodical publications, reference books, and advanced treatises.

These universities may be given permission to spend this amount within a period of three years.

Whenever schemes for the development of Postgraduate Departments are accepted by the Commission some assistance should be given for the purchase of reading and kindred materials and bringing them into active use.

The entire library finance of a university or a college library should be provided by the Commission and the State Government.

The Commission and the State Government should decide from time to time the proportion in which their respective grants to a university or a college library should be determined.

The Commission and the State Government should have an agreed understanding between them that each will actually pay its own share of the library grant.

The Commission should not ordinarily withdraw or lower its grant to a university or a college library because the State Government fails to provide the corresponding matching grant.

The library grant in any year should be based on the statistical data of the preceding year.

Library Fund

The library fund of a university or a college should be maintained and operated as a separate library account.

To make the spending of book-fund useful and to avoid its being dissipated on the rush-purchase of any materials readily available in the nearby market, the unappropriated amount of the budget should not be lost to the library, but should be carried forward to the credit of the library and be available for inclusion in the budget of the next year, as an addition to the normal allotment. Our chief book market is now thousands of miles away. Scholarly treatises, research materials, and particularly back volumes of learned periodicals take a long time in searching and procuring. Therefore, this provision for the revival of unspent balance in the next year's budget is quite essential.

Each library should—

Spread the utilisation of the grant received from the Commission for reading and kindred materials as uniformly as possible over the entire period of 17 months allowed for purchase;

Avoid hastening to spend the grant somehow on the purchase of whatever is available for immediate delivery without fully satisfying itself about the actual or anticipated demand of the reading materials purchased;

Complete all the administrative and technical work on the reading materials and release them for use by readers as expeditiously as possible, say, within less than one month of their receipt in the library;

Allocate the total book fund equitably over all the disciplines pursued by the parent body, subject to the availability of worthwhile reading and kindred materials in the different disciplines and the special extraordinary needs, if any, of particular disciplines;

Avoid duplication of learned periodicals and reference books;

Minimise duplication of advanced treatises;

Purchase a reasonable number of copies of books of the text book standard; and

Distribute the share of the total book-fund of each discipline, equitably on current learned periodicals, their back-volumes, reference books, advanced treatises, and text-books.

It is desirable and economical for the selection of current learned periodicals and their back volumes to be coordinated among the libraries of a locality or a region, so as to minimise duplication and maximise the number of distinct periodicals available in the region, in order that the book-fund of each institution may go the longest way.

Without prejudice to the recurring local needs of students and research workers in different subjects, the libraries of a locality or a region should by mutual agreement specialise in stated subjects and make their collection in them as complete as possible for the requirements of research and invoke the aid of inter-library loan for books in frequent demand in subjects in which they do not specialise.

To prevent any prejudice to the reader's requirements being caused by the co-ordination of selection and purchase mentioned in Sec. 24 and 25, the libraries should co-operate with one another in inter-library loan and, whenever warranted, in exchange of reading materials so that they are housed where they are in greatest demand.

The Commission may frame a set of Rules for Inter-Library Loan and commend them to the University Libraries.

To facilitate inter-library loan and co-ordination of selection, the UGC should promote the production and maintenance of a union catalogue of the learned periodicals and the books in foreign languages other than English and rare books necessary for research in the humanities and the social sciences along the lines in which the Insdoc is doing for the natural sciences.

Book Selection And Book Purchase

The acquisition of reading materials for the libraries should be regulated as follows:

The authority concerned may lay down the policy according to which book-selection should be regulated.

The authority concerned may make the allocation of the amount for the purchase of reading materials as indicated in Sec. 23, items four and eight.

The proportion implied in the allocation should normally be continued for at least three years without undue disturbance unless there are unexpected special factors coming into play. The proportion may be reviewed and re-established periodically, say once in three years.

The authority concerned should provide a panel of experts in different subjects to help the librarian in making the final selection of reading and kindred materials.

It should be regarded as improper to call for tenders or competitive quotations for each order.

Standing vendors may be appointed with stipulated

terms including discount and exchange rate for a year or a longer period with a clause in the agreement that if orders are not filled within a prescribed period the librarian will be free to place orders with others. In this, special weight should be given to advanced books and treatises.

Within the limits of the policy laid down, and in conformity to the advice of the experts concerned, and without exceeding the sanctioned budget and allocation, the librarian should be entrusted with the responsibility of book-selection and the question of reading and kindred materials.

The authority concerned may exercise the power of review to satisfy itself that the acquisition of reading and kindred materials was being done without infringement of the policy and the limitations of the budget and the allocation, and for watching for factors needing amendment in the policy and in the allocation of the fund.

To minimise the harmful effect of the practices in vogue in the choice of ad hoc or standing vendors for the supply of books, such as

1. Leading to failure of prompt supply of nascent books;

2. By-passing of the supply of advanced books and treatises in limited demand, of difficult-to-get-at kinds and without an attractive trade discount; and

3. Resulting in the ultimate lapse of budget allotment for books or for its diversion at the last minute to less important books because of their being available on the spot.

It is necessary to rationalise the vendor-library relation as it is now only in a formative stage.

To facilitate this and reach an agreed standard, such as netbook agreement, which will not either stifle the development of a healthy book trade or vitiate the proper utilisation of the book-fund of the libraries, it would be desirable for the Commission to bring about a conference consisting of a few representatives of publishers, booksellers, the library profession, the top-management of universities, and if feasible, representatives of Statutory Library Authorities in areas in which a Library Act is in force.

In view of the increasing cost of foreign books, it is desirable for the Commission to promote publication of cheap Indian editions of foreign books in wide demand in the universities and colleges or their import in sheets and being bound in India.

To minimise the effect of the

1. Present exchange difficulties;

2. Import licence difficulties; and

3. Frustrating delay caused by these two factors in the procurement of foreign reading materials.

It is desirable for the Commission—

Either

1. To arrange through a suitable agency for pooling together the orders of the different libraries for foreign reference books and advanced treatises of too limited a demand to warrant cheap Indian edition or Indian binding;

2. Their purchase in bulk; and

3. Their distribution to the libraries and debiting of their cost against the grant due to the respective libraries.

Or

To give part of the grant in the form of foreign exchange licence or coupons.

If the first alternative is followed, to minimise the danger of cooperative or centralised purchase resulting in the curtailment of the freedom of libraries in book-selection, the Commission may adopt special methods such as the following:

1. Appoint an Expert Committee for each subject to make a book selection list of reference books and advanced treatises, likely to be needed by many universities and colleges;

2. Circulate these lists to the libraries of the universities and bigger colleges for their respective selection; and

3. Consolidate the returns on these lists for bulk purchase.

Such lists in the different subjects may go out at different times. They may also be promoted by the libraries corresponding among themselves. This device may be given up as soon as the current difficult situation in respect of foreign exchange and import licence disappears.

Promotion Of Reading Habit

The most potent method of developing in the students a book-sense and the desire to own, enjoy, and read worthwhile books is the adoption of a teaching technique which minimises telling facts or giving ready-made opinion but rouses curiosity in the students by posing the pros and cons of a problem, and encouraging the students to seek from books and periodicals the information and the knowledge necessary to satisfy the curiosity and generally inspire the students to seek enjoyment in reading good books.

Safeguarded open access and provision of ample reference service should be provided by each university and college library.

Suitable arrangements may be made by the Commission to prepare and distribute periodically anticipatory reading lists of current and best books in diverse subjects of general interest to the students. Each library should also prepare its own reading lists from time to time on topics of local demand.

Reading circles may be formed on various topics from time to time and they may be given facilities to meet in the library.

Reference librarians should be appointed in sufficient number to help the students with sympathy and understanding in the selection of reading materials.

Each university or college, as the case may be, should encourage the formation of book-shops within its campus through co-operative effort or in any other manner.

Weeding Out And Loss Of Books

The following principles should be adopted by a library for weeding out books:

1. Generally speaking, pedestrian books (for example, text-books and other books without permanent value) may be weeded out once in five years.

2. Books worn out by use beyond repair may be weeded out once in a year.

3. Reference books, which are quite out-of-date and whose later editions are available in the market, may be weeded out once in five years or 10 years according to their nature.

4. A list of the books to be weeded out may be sent to the State Central Library, or its equivalent which should be given the choice to take over such copies as are found necessary to have within the State at least one tolerably sound representative copy.

While rare, costly, and small-size reading materials should be kept safely without direct access to readers and issued out only on formal application, in the case of the other books housed in the open access regions of the library, loss of two volumes for every one thousand volumes issued out is a risk worth taking for getting the books widely used before they go outmoded in thought-content or perish physically; and such a loss should be normally written off by library authorities, unless there is evidence of malpractice on the part of the staff.

Documentation

To save the time of the research workers, the library should—

Make documentation lists on demand as well as in anticipation to supplement the Insdoc list;

Make, on demand from research workers, abstracts of articles in current issues of periodicals not covered by the issues of abstracting serials received in the library;

Procure documents not in the library by inter-library loan;

Procure photostat or microfilm copies of other reprograph of documents on demand from research workers;

Arrange, on demand, translations of articles in foreign languages through the Insdoc or other agencies; and

Employ documentalists in adequate number.

The following policy may, for the time being, be adopted by the Commission in respect of the reprograph of documents and the reading apparatus needed for them.

In view of the fact that facilities for micro-filming, photostating, and duplicating exist in Delhi, Bombay and Bangalore, the following universities, situated in the regions noted against them and having rich collections of periodicals and manuscripts, may be provided with microfilming, photostating, and duplicating equipment:

Eastern India	Calcutta
Western India	Poona
Southern India	Madras
Central India	Hyderabad
Northern India	Lucknow or Banaras

It is desirable to consult the Insdoc, which has experience in this field, for suggesting suitable equipment.

To begin with, one reading apparatus may be useful in each university library.

The demand for a second apparatus should be properly established by statistics and frequency of use, before an application for its supply can be entertained.

Departmental Collection

A post-graduate department of a university may be allowed a permanent loan of up to a maximum of 2,000 volumes that are expected to be frequently needed for the research in progress in the department.

This does not apply to the books whose duplication has been made especially for the use of the Department.

The volumes on permanent loan may be kept in the department for an indefinite period. As and when the needs of the department change, the volumes no longer required in the permanent loan collection may be returned to the Central Library and new volumes taken in their place.

The volumes in the permanent loan collection are subject to recall by the librarian at his discretion in case they are wanted for other readers or for technical purposes.

Besides the permanent loan, each department may be given a temporary loan of upto 100 volumes, returnable only in the last week of the term or the year as may be prescribed.

Copies of text-books, if any, supplied to teachers for teaching purposes should be independent of loan of every kind and should be treated on a par with the material equipments furnished to a teacher.

Current issues of periodicals should be kept on display in the periodicals room of the Central Library for one or two weeks to give a chance for everybody to use them and be released for loan to research workers only after that period.

It is not economical to build independent departmental libraries, unless a department is far away from the campus. It will unnecessarily add to the load of responsibility of the head of the department. Even in the case of a department having its own library for reasons of distance or other reasons, all impersonal work such as book-purchase, classification, cataloguing, and binding of books should be left to the care of the Central Library.

Library Staff

The professional staff of a university library should be distributed into four grades with designations, qualifications, and scales of salary corresponding to those of professors, readers, lecturers, and assistant lecturers as follows:

Designation, Qualification, Salary Scale

The following structure of the library staff, their functional designation, their professional status, their qualifications, their grades in a university library, and the corresponding scales of salary for each grade, are recommended. The salary scale should be changed to coincide with that of the teaching staff, wherever the latter is changed.

Sl. No.	Designation	Professional Status	Qualifications: Minimum	Qualifications: Desirable	Grade	Scale of Pay
1	Librarian	Professional senior	M. Lib. Sc. II class or M.Sc. II class and Dip. Lib. Sc. or B. Lib. Sc. I class; A prescribed minimum experience in a research or a university library	Doctorate in Library Science or any other subject	1	800-50-1250 (Professor's)
2	Document	-do-	-do-	-do-	2	500-25-800 (Reader's)
3	Deputy or Assistant Librarian	-do-	-do-	-do-	-do-	-do-
4	Reference Librarian	-do-	-do-	-do-	-do-	-do-
5	Chief Classifier	-do-	-do-	-do-	-do-	-do-
6	Chief Cataloguer	-do-	-do-	-do-	-do-	-do-
7	Maintenance Librarian	Professional Junior	Dip. Lib. Sc. or B. Lib. Sc. I class and B.A. or B.Sc. or B.Com. II class		3	250-20-500 (Lecturer's)
8	Assistant Classifier	-do-	-do-		-do-	-do-
9	Assistant Cataloguer	-do-	-do-		-do-	-do-
10	Accession Librarian	-do-	-do-		-do-	-do-
11	Periodicals Librarian	-do-	-do-		-do-	-do-
12	Circulation Librarian	-do-	-do-		-do-	-do-
13	Senior Library Assistant in any Section but not the Reference Sec.	Professional Assistant	-do-		4	150-10-250 (Assistant Lecturer's)
14	Junior Library Assistant in any Section but not the Reference Sec.	Semi-Professional	Cer. Lib. Sc. and good Higher Secondary Certificate		5	80-5-150-10-220

There should also be semi-professionals to do the repetitive routine connected with technical work, besides the usual ministerial staff.

The professional staff of a college should have the qualifications and the salary scale given above.

The system of appointing a non-professional person, such as a professor, as honorary librarian as the head of a library should be abolished.

The strength of the staff of a library should be determined on the basis of the load of work in accordance with the staff-formula whose substance is given below:

The strength of the staff for the different sections is to be determined roughly on the following basis.

1. Book Section: One person for every 6,000 volumes added in a year.
2. Periodical Publications Sections: One person for every 500 current periodicals taken.
3. Documentation Section: One person for every 1,000 entries prepared in a year.
4. Technical Section: One person for every 2,000 volumes added in a year.
5. Reference Section: One person for every 50 readers (other than the users of the text-book collection) in a day.
6. Circulation Section: One person for every 1,500 hours for which one wicket gate of the library has to be kept open in a year.
7. Maintenance Section: One person for every 6,000 volumes added in a year, one person for every 500 volumes to be replaced in a day, and one person for every 100,000 volumes in the library.
8. Administrative Section: Minimum of one library accountant, one steno-typist and one correspondence clerk.
9. Supervisory Section: One librarian and one Assistant or Deputy Librarian.
10. Unskilled staff: One cleaner for every 30,000 volumes in the library, one attendant each for every 6,000 volumes added in a year, for every 500 current periodicals taken, and for each of the shifts in the Circulation Section. besides unskilled and the semi-skilled workers normal to any institution.

The salary fund of the university and college libraries should be subsidised by the Commission so as to promote the implementation of the recommendations contained in the beginning of this chapter.

Department Of Library Science

A first grade Department of Library Science may conduct courses for B. Lib. Sc. and M. Lib. Sc. and a second grade one only for B. Lib. Sc. ordinarily. A university Department of Library Science should not conduct certificate courses for semi-professionals. This should be left to the care of the Departments of Libraries and the Library Associations in the Constituent States.

A first grade Department of Library Science should have one professor, one reader, two lecturers, and two demonstrators, and a second grade one should have one reader, one lecturer, and one demonstrator.

For the time being the Commission may help the maintenance of full-time teachers in not more than six Second Grade Departments of Library Science distributed on a regional basis and not more than two First Grade Departments.

During the next ten years, the Commission's help may have to be gradually extended so as to secure one Second Grade Department of Library Science in each constituent State.

The librarian and his staff should devote their full time to the work of the library and should rot be burdened with part-time teaching work; nor should the teachers in the Department of Library Science be burdened with the work of the library.

Course Of Studies In Library Science

Only a graduate should be admitted to the B. Lib. Sc. course.

A person should be allowed to join the B. Lib. Sc. course only after the satisfactory completion of an apprentice course of six months in a library approved for the purpose.

A Committee of Experts should be appointed by the Commission to examine the question of improving and coordinating the standard of teaching and research in the Departments of Library Science of the universities and to give advice on the course of studies, standards, and teaching.

Library Buildings, Fittings, And Furniture

The standards for the Library Buildings, Fittings and Furniture, established by the Indian Standards Institution and extracted in chapters N and O, should be followed by all the university and college libraries.

Any proposal, for a new library buildings, fittings, and furniture, or for the adaptation of an existing building, or for its extension for library purposes, should be examined and approved by a Library Expert appointed by the Commission.

SELECTED BUILDINGS PROJECTS TEAM ON MULTISTOREYED BUILDINGS, 1957—REPORT

New Delhi, Committee on Plan Projects, 1958. 88p., Plates.

Leader : Shri S.K. Patil.
Members : Sardar Sarup Singh; Dr. A. Carbone; Shri C.P. Malik.
Secretary : Shri T.S. Vedagiri.

APPOINTMENT

The Selected Buildings Projects Team on Multistoreyed Buildings was constituted under Planning Commission in 1957.

TERMS OF REFERENCE

To help in the efficient and economic implementation of the Projects included in the Plan.

CONTENTS

Introduction; Space Utilisation and General Planning; Structure and Materials; Programming and Planning of Site Operations; Administrative and Contract Problems; Summary of Recommendations; Remarks by the Selected Buildings Projects Team; Appendices I to VII; Plates.

RECOMMENDATIONS

Space Utilisation

It is desirable to orientate a building so as to avoid exposure of the occupied rooms to Eastern and Western Sun.

The lettable office space or carpet area should be of the order of 65 to 75 per cent of the total built up area.

Clients' requirements should be ascertained in detail before undertaking planning of the building.

Storage space must be properly planned.

An area of 500 sq. ft. is considered adequate for Committee Room required to serve an office with carpet area of one lakh sq. ft.

The requirements of canteen should be assessed in each case separately and suitable provision made for the same.

Scales for sanitary units fixed by ISI should be enforced.

Space requirements of specialised services should be determined at the planning stage.

Eight feet width for corridor is adequate to meet all normal office requirements.

It is economical to construct independent light structures for garages and cycle sheds provided sufficient land is available.

A height of 11 feet from floor to floor is considered adequate.

In view of the scarcity of teak wood and its rising prices, it should be advantageous to specify flush doors for office buildings where superior finish is required.

Light installation should be capable of transporting the whole population to the second and higher floors within 20 to 45 minutes.

It is essential to decide the question of airconditioning at the planning stage as subsequent alterations are costly and cause inconvenience.

A scientific study of the effect of shading window openings with louvers of various shapes and materials should be undertaken by the CBRI.

Structure And Materials

A cavity wall appears to be the best proposition for external cladding.

The type of frame with a central corridor of eight feet and rooms 14 to 16 feet deep on one side and 25 to 30 feet deep on the other side and with a spacing of 12 feet is considered economical.

There is need for setting up permanent centres at important places in the country for exhibiting building materials and advanced techniques of construction.

Tested and untested variety of steel must be stocked separately and tested steel should be used for important projects like multi-storeyed buildings.

It is advantageous to use richer mix for members which are predominantly in compression. Normal mix of 1:2:4 can be adopted for members subject to flextural stresses.

The adoption of limited tendering is recommended to obtain quality concrete.

Where foundation problems are complicated, expert on foundation engineering should be consulted and alternative foundation designs worked out.

All construction agencies should supply data of the break-up of cost to the N.B.O. for consolidation and publication.

Programming and Planning Of Site Operations

All working drawings to eighth scale should be made available with all information necessary for the completion of the building, right at the commencement of construction.

A few building sites should be selected at random and the operations as they exist should be carefully studied from the inception of work to its completion in order to evaluate the wastage in materials, manpower and money due to lack of planning and organisation.

Administrative And Contract Problems

Building work should not be started without finalising all the architectural and service details, on the basis of firm requirements of the user department and making arrangement for materials. It should also be ensured structural details are made available to the contractor, well in advance.

The adoption of three to five year approved programme with priorities is recommended.

The method of letting out a work complete with all services to a general contractor may be tried in a few cases and the results watched for future guidance.

CUSTOMS REORGANISATION COMMITTEE, 1957-58—REPORT

New Delhi, Manager of Publications, 1959. 374p.+iiip.

Chairman : Shri F.C. Badhwar.
Members : Shri S.M. Shah; Shri E.J. Benjamin; Shri W. Saldanha.
Secretary : Shri V.S. Ramaswamy.

APPOINTMENT

The Customs Reorganisation Committee was appointed by the Government of India, in the Ministry of Finance, by Resolution No. 4/10/55-Cus. III, dated January 23, 1957, the terms of which are as follows:

The procedures, for the clearance of goods and passengers, baggage at present followed by the Custom Houses in India have grown into their present form over many years during which rapid changes have taken place in the practices adopted in international trade and commerce. Although these procedures have been under constant review by the Collectors of Customs as well as by the Central Board of Revenue, basically they are still the same as those followed over three-quarters of a century ago. Both the Government of India as well as the commercial public have, therefore, felt the need, particularly in recent years, for a detailed investigation of the content and operation of these procedures so as to achieve the requisite degree of modernisation, especially in respect of speed and efficiency. An examination would simultaneously be necessary of the connected questions of adequacy and level of efficiency of the organisation and staff of the Custom Houses. The Government of India have accordingly decided to appoint a Committee to conduct a comprehensive enquiry into customs procedures and organisation and to make recommendations for their improvement.

TERMS OF REFERENCE

(1) To examine in detail the procedure:

(a) for the clearance of goods and passengers' baggage through the customs at the sea ports, airports and land customs stations;

(b) for the administration of Import, Export and Exchange Control Regulations;

(c) for ensuring uniformity of classification of goods and methods of valuation;

(d) for the grant of Customs refunds and drawbacks; and

(e) other matters of Customs procedure generally;

(2) To examine the liaison between the Customs on the one hand and the trade, the Port Trust/Commissioners, the Import and Export Trade Control authorities, and the Posts and Telegraph Department, on the other;

(3) In the light of examination made under items (1) and (2) above, and having regard to the safety of Government revenue, the adequate enforcement of prohibitions and restrictions, and the legitimate interest of the trade and of passengers, to recommend the modifications required in the various procedures for making them more effective, simple and speedier;

(4) To examine the administration of the existing Customs Department as a whole with reference to the adequacy and disposition of staff provided at various levels, their working conditions, the exercise and delegation of responsibility and methods of recruitment and training;

(5) In the light of the examination referred to in item (4) above, to recommend necessary improvements; and

(6) To make any other recommendations germane to the objective of the investigation.

CONTENTS

Part I: Introductory; Brief Historical Survey; The Committee's Approach; Tariff Structure; Implementation of Import Trade Control; Valuation for Assessment to Import Duties; Assessment of Mixed Goods; Processing of Bills of Entry; Examination of Cargo; Analytical Tests; Detention of Goods; Bonds and Guarantees; Bonded Warehousing; Foreign Post Parcels; Government Stores; Exports; Drawback; Entrepot Trade;

Changes in Import and Export Duties; Short and Excess Levies of Customs Duties; Tourists and other Passengers; Penal Proceedings; Steamer Agents; Air Traffic: Problems of Airlines; Custom House Agents; Customs Advisory Bodies; Public Relations and Information Services; Other Important Problems; Organisation; Summary of Main Recommendations; **Part II:** Introductory; Processing of Bills of Entry; Examination of Cargo; Bonded Warehousing; Foreign Post Parcels; Exports; Transhipment; Precious, Semi-Precious and Synthetic Stones; Jewellery; Imports and Exports; Tourists and other Passengers; Steamer Agents; Problems of the Airlines; Air Freight; Short-Landing; Receipts and Payments; Certain Problems at Minor Ports; Other Problems; Customs Advisory Committees at Ports and Central Customs Advisory Council; **Part III:** Work done by Customs for other Departments of the Government of India and the State Governments; List of Advance Recommendations sent to the Government of India; Copies of the Advance Recommendations sent to the Government of India; Memorandum dated March 4, 1957 issued to Chambers of Commerce and Trade Associations in India; List of Chambers of Commerce and Trade Associations in India to whom the Memorandum dated March 4, 1957 was Issued; List of Chambers of Commerce, Trade Associations, Firms and Individuals who replied to the Memorandum, dated March 4, 1957; Questionnaire dated May 31, 1957 issued to the Public; List of Chambers of Commerce, Trade Associations, Firms and Individuals to whom the Public Questionnaire was issued; List of Chambers of Commerce and Trade Associations who replied to the Public Questionnaire; List of Firms and Individuals who replied to the Public Questionnaire; List of Officers, Individuals, Chambers of Commerce, Trade Associations, etc. interviewed by the Committee; Departmental Questionnaire sent to the Collectors of Customs; Memorandum, dated March 11, 1957 issued to Ministries of the Government of India and State Governments; List of the Ministries and Departments of the Government of India to whom the Memorandum, dated March 11, 1957 was Issued; List of the Ministries and Departments of the Government of India who replied to the Memorandum dated March 11, 1957; List of the State Governments to whom the Memorandum, dated March 11, 1957 was issued; List of the State Government Departments who replied to the Memorandum, dated March 11, 1957; List of the Ministries and Departments of the Government of India who replied to the Public Questionnaire; List of the State Government Departments who replied to the Public Questionnaire; Memorandum, dated March 11, 1957 issued to Diplomatic Missions and U.N. Agencies in India through the Ministry of External Affairs; List of Diplomatic Missions and U.N. Agencies who replied to the Memorandum, dated March 11, 1957; List of Subjects on which facts were obtained from Central Board of Revenue, Collectors of Customs or Central Excise or the Chief Controller of Imports.

RECOMMENDATIONS

Tariff Structure

As a first practical step towards the revision of the Tariff Schedule, footnotes to it, which are of a reasonably permanent character, should be incorporated in the schedule, and anomalies in rates of duty for similar categories of goods should be removed.

The Customs Tariff should be thoroughly revised by aligning it closely with the Import Trade Control Licensing Schedule and such alignment should be continuously maintained.

The "Indian Customs Tariff Guide" should be amplified, brought up-to-date, and published at intervals of not more than six months.

"The Indian Customs Tariff Guide" should be replaced as soon as possible by an amplified edition of the "Alphabetical Index to the Standard Indian Trade Classification", showing against each item the corresponding tariff item. Explanatory notes should be appended in respect of items of doubtful classification. The amplified "Index" should be issued with the approval of the Central Board of Revenue. The correlations in the Index should be kept under constant review.

Cross-references to the Tariff should be inserted in the Import Trade Control Licensing Schedule, to assist in classification for import trade control purposes.

Implementation Of Import Trade Control

The Trade Control authorities should post an officer, preferably of the rank of Deputy Chief Controller, in each major Custom House to help resolve quickly any differences in interpretation of licences, and generally to act as a liaison between the Trade, the Customs and the Joint Chief Controller of Imports.

A list of cases of disputed licences should be sent daily to the Joint Chief Controller of Imports who should convey his advice to the Customs by the following day. Joint meetings of the Customs and Import Trade Control authorities should be convened, if necessary, at a fixed hour and venue, to discuss such cases, and the importer should have the right to ask for a reference to, and personal hearing at, such meetings.

The description on the Licence should be as specific as possible. In the case of items falling under general descriptions, the major items intended to be imported should be specified on the licence, together, where necessary, with a residuary description. Publicity should be given to the availability of the facility of amendment of licence descriptions by the licensing authorities for inclusion of specific articles.

C.I.F. values only should be debited in all cases of

enhanced valuation. Values as enhanced for assessment to duty should be debited only in cases of deliberate under-valuations, or where special relationships exist between supplier and importer.

Valuation For Assessment To Import Duties

Section 30 of the Sea Customs Act should be amended to make the C.I.F. value the sole basis of *ad valorem* assessments.

Detailed and clear instructions should be published regarding the method of valuation under section 30(b), in cases of special relationship between seller and buyer; the possibility of fixing tariff values for raw materials and semi-manufactured goods in such cases should be examined.

Tariff values should be fixed for as large a range of commodities as possible; constant surveys and reviews of imported commodities should be undertaken for this purpose.

Assessment Of Mixed Goods

Each item in a composite set should be assessed separately. Where the value of a single component is over 75 per cent, the entire set should be assessed at the rate applicable to that component.

Processing Of Bills Of Entry

Some positive action should be taken on each bill of entry in the appraising department within two to three hours of its first presentation, and it should receive prompt attention at each stage thereafter.

"Second appraisement" should be the rule and the Principal Appraiser's approval be obtained before resorting to "First appraisement".

Appraisers should sort out bills of entry at least twice a day to fix their priority for attention.

The specific documents that must be initially attached to bills of entry should be widely publicised. Any other documents, if required, should be called for at one time. No second demand for such papers should be permitted without the Principal Appraiser's approval.

Even if a bill of entry contains items pertaining to different groups, it should be disposed of in the group responsible for the article carrying the highest value.

All pre-clearance processes, except pre-audit and registration of licences, should be completed in the dealing group itself, its ministerial strength being suitably increased for the purpose, if required.

As a temporary relief measure, part of the work in an over-loaded group should be farmed out to suitable appraisers working outside it.

Appraisers should be available to the public throughout the hours fixed for interviews. In the event of an extended discussion over a certain case, the Principal Appraiser should make special arrangements for the disposal, without delay, of other bills of entry in his group.

Any fee or fine leviable for the amendment of a bill of entry should be collected simultaneously with the customs duty.

The instructions that all Appraisers should be up-to-date in the maintenance of their references and records should be continually enforced by periodical checks by supervisory officers.

The cent per cent "double check" of Customs documents should be reduced to 10 to 20 per cent both in respect of the Principal Appraiser's and the Docks Supervising Appraiser's checks. The limit of Rs. 100, in duty, in respect of an Appraiser's powers to pass a bill of entry without the Principal Appraiser's verification, should be raised to Rs. 500.

To speed up work, the Principal Appraiser should be delegated the authority to finalise many of the routine cases which only Assistant Collectors are empowered to decide at present.

To ensure efficient operation, Assistant Collectors should pay frequent visits to Appraising groups.

Where the Import General Manifest cannot be submitted in advance of a vessel's arrival, which happens frequently when the port of origin of a vessel's run is close to India, bills of entry should be accepted by the Appraising department, under orders of the Collector, for scrutiny and completion, leaving "noting" by the Import department to a later stage.

Examination Of Cargo

An examination centre, with a supervising Appraiser should be provided at each of the large and normally busy sheds. Otherwise, where sheds are close together, one examination centre, fully staffed, should cover two or three sheds; isolated sheds should each have one centre, supervised by a mobile appraiser.

Supervising officers should ensure that the busier centres are reinforced quickly by reserves of staff from less busy centres.

Day-time working hours and lunch intervals at the examination centres should be the same for Port Trust and Customs staff at each port. Where uniformity is not practicable, Customs working hours should be 8 A.M. to 6 P.M. at these centres.

All examination centres should be self-sufficient in equipment required for examination and weighments and should be provided with furniture, fans and such other amenities for both the public and the Customs staff.

Where a specified package is not readily available for examination, the discretion already vested in the examining staff should be liberally exercised, to examine an alternate package, or to allow part clearance.

The Port Trust authorities should ensure that

cargo is methodically stacked to avoid delays in Customs examination and clearance.

Goods of standard quality, and imported regularly, should be enabled to be cleared quickly by adopting a reduced scale of examination, weighment or other checks.

Analytical Tests

Existing arrangements for Customs sampling and testing should be brought up, without delay, to international standards.

Where there are inadequate facilities with Customs for the testing of certain articles, analysis reports of recognised Indian or foreign agencies should be accepted.

Test procedures should be framed with due regard to trade interests, and urgent steps should be taken to remove existing deficiencies in Customs of qualified staff and equipment for sampling and testing of ores and other bulk commodities.

Private or public bonded warehouses should be provided for storing export cargo before sampling and testing.

Modern systems, like the card-index, should be introduced in each appraising group for maintenance of, and quick references to, test records. The Custom House laboratories should also maintain their own card-index references, so that any unnecessary requisition for test can be rejected.

Detailed analytical data recorded by the Customs laboratory should be made available to parties, and test results of established brands of goods should be treated as valid for a longer period than at present. The period of validity of goods of reputable makers should be at least twelve months, and clearance/shipment allowed on production of a certified copy of a previous and valid test.

When adopting test standards, the utmost consideration should be given to a free and uninterrupted flow of legitimate trade.

When disputes arise on test results, chemists representing each party should be afforded an opportunity to discuss the technical points involved. Samples should, at the option of, and on payment of a fee by the party be permitted to be re-tested by a recognised independent agency whose findings should be accepted. The bill of entry or shipping biil should be endorsed to the effect that a re-test would be admissible.

In dealing with appeals against Customs tests, the existing procedure of consultations with recognised expert agencies other than the Chief Chemist, Central Revenues, should be more liberally adopted on request by the appellant.

Detention Of Goods

In all cases of dispute, subject only to a few exceptions, as for example, where a deliberate fraud has been committed, only such portions of a consignment as are essential to safeguard the interests of the revenue or any regulatory provisions as may be involved, should be detained.

When delays in Customs clearance are due to factors outside the control of the owner, the Port Trust should remit demurrage charges in all cases on production of Customs detention certificates. Only an Assistant Collector should issue detention certificates in cases other than those in which the Port Trust accept such certificates at present.

As an alternative, the Customs should provide a departmental "detained goods warehouse" at each port for the safe storage of goods detained by them. Since it may not be possible for the Customs at major ports to undertake the custody of goods, such warehouse should be maintained for Customs by the Port Trust or some other responsible public body.

There should be the maximum possible uniformity in the calculating of the "free days" and rates for demurrage at the different ports.

Bonds And Guarantees

Bonds should generally be accepted without insisting on the surety from only a bank. When a bank's surety is indispensable, the amount of the guarantee should not exceed 20 per cent of the amount of the bond. Witnessing of signatures of executants, by clearing agents, or under a bank's seal, should be accepted.

Bankers' guarantees should be cancelled within 30 days of the fulfilment of the terms of the bond.

Personal appearance before customs officers for the signing of bonds and guarantees should not be insisted upon.

Continuing bonds should be accepted from established concerns to cover recurring types of import and export transactions.

Forms for bonds intended to cover recurring types of cases, should be prescribed by the Central Board of Revenue, and published in the "Indian Sea Customs Manual".

The financial liability to be covered by the bond should be calculated as precisely as possible and the amount shown in the text of the bond; an amount equal to the value of the goods should not be fixed as a matter of routine.

The period of validity of a bond or a guarantee should be fixed at between six and twelve months in most routine cases.

Bonded Warehousing

Private bonded warehouses should be licensed within the municipal limits of a major port, as for example, to regular importers of industrial raw materials or other bulk commodities.

Bonded warehousing facilities should be provided at Land Customs Stations.

Provision should be made in airport development plans for Customs bonded warehousing accommodation, and meanwhile the possibility of providing such accommodation in hangers or sheds should be explored.

A public bonded warehouse is preferable to a number of small private ones, at each major airport; special provision should also be made for bonding cold storage and hazardous goods at such airports.

Bonded warehouse facilities with trained Customs staff in attendance, should be extended, wherever justified, to inland trade centres for goods sent in bond from Indian customs ports or stations.

Bonded goods should be permitted to be dealt with under the "second appraisement" system.

Relaxations already allowed by executive orders in connection with Section 94 of the Sea Customs Act, for amending declarations on bond bills of entry, after warehousing has been completed, should be freely extended in deserving cases, and these relaxations should be embodied in the Act itself.

Continuing bonds should be accepted from established and regular importers for their warehousing operations.

Foreign Post Parcels

On parcels imported by post, no duty should be levied (i) where the duty does not amount to more than Rs. 10/-, whatever the value of the parcel, or (ii) where the value does not exceed Rs. 25/-(exclusively of postal charges), whatever the duty. The officer-in-charge should also have discretionary powers to waive duty charges and licence requirements in the case of certain used or other articles imported on bona fide personal account in excess of the prescribed exemption limits.

Additional Foreign Post Offices should be established at places where the headquarters of Collectors of Central Excise are situated.

Rules and regulations concerning Foreign Post Offices should be widely publicised in newspapers, and through appropriate brochures issued by the Postal Department.

Government Stores

The regulation regarding submission to Customs, of shipping and other documents, at the time of importation, which is rigidly applied in the case of the private sector, should apply with equal force to Government organisations.

If the existing "Note and Pass" facility of submission of documents after clearance is to continue, it should be confined to stores imported for the sole use of Government's non-commercial departments; there is no justification for its extension to Government's industrial and commercial undertakings or public corporations.

Where the "Note and Pass" system is permitted, a provisional debit for duty should be raised on the basis of available particulars. If the required documents are not furnished by the importing department within three months, the provisional debit should be confirmed. No relaxation of the time-limits under Sections 39 and 40 of Sea Customs Act for recovery of short-levies or refund of excess levies, should be permitted.

Much time and effort would be saved if the stores imported only for consumption in Government's non-commercial departments are exempted from payment of Custom duty.

Exports

An Export Trade Control Unit, to deal with shipping bills for controlled goods, should be housed in each Custom House.

Shipping bills should be passed by the ministerial section or by the appraising unit, according to nature and/or value of goods, as is done at Bombay Customs House.

The existing facilities available on holidays for urgent Customs clearance of goods for export should be extended to Sundays and "closed" holidays also. Wide publicity should be given to these facilities, which should be made available at the minor ports also. Skeleton staff should be provided in all sections where it may be necessary.

Preventive Officers supervising ships which are loading should be called upon to assist in examining export cargo. Preventive Officers should be trained for this work.

The scale of examination, and other checks, of export cargo, should be reviewed periodically to ensure that they are not excessive and burdensome.

Formalities in connection with boat notes should be minimised, and handled only by experienced Customs staff.

The price at which export goods have been sold to purchasers abroad may differ from the value as established under Section 30 of Sea Customs Act. Clear instructions should be issued on this aspect of export valuation. Specific duties or tariff valuations should replace *ad valorem* export duties, wherever possible. Wherever *ad valorem* duty is unavoidable, the F.O.B. price, as contracted under open market conditions, should be accepted.

The abolition of export duties, with a view to earning more foreign exchange, would remove many procedural problems and delays.

Drawback; Entrepot Trade

Drawback of the full Customs duty recovered on import should be allowed in cases of re-export of commercial goods and personal articles in original condition.

Free replacements, under a warranty, of defective

articles, which have been re-exported without drawback, should be exempted from duty.

An extension of the existing time-limit of three years, for re-export of imported goods under drawback, is not necessary.

Admissibility of drawback should be determined much in advance of actual export, if desired by an intending shipper. The Assistant Collector's routine approval in each case of shipment under a drawback claim, should not be necessary. The drawback shipping bill itself should be treated as a claim, and claims should be audited only after payment.

Drawback claims should be settled within three months.

The possibility should be explored, of reducing the period of six months now fixed for determining the rate of drawback on aviation spirit supplied to aircraft. Provision should also be made for these supplies to be made from bonded stock, maintained at the airports. Where this is not possible the drawback procedure should be simplified.

Drawback or bond facilities should be extended to goods imported by sea or air and re-exported by land, and vice-versa.

Creation of "free zones" at port premises, for manufacture of goods for re-export should be considered.

Changes In Import And Export Duties

The existing practice of applying changes in rates of duty, or tariff values, on and from the date of announcement, should continue.

The rate of duty applicable to warehoused goods should be the rate in force on the day the duty on the goods has actually been paid.

Short And Excess Levies Of Customs Duties

Notices of demand for payment of short-levies should be as clear and precise as possible regarding the amounts to be paid and the basis of calculation. When the assessment is qualified as provisional, the reasons for not accepting the declared value should be given.

When demands are issued pending investigation, the Assistant Collector in charge of the Special Investigation Branch should satisfy himself regarding the justification for questioning import invoices and take various measures to ensure that no delay or inconvenience occur in finalising disposal of such cases. Special branches for this purpose should be set-up in Custom Houses, where they do not exist and are justified.

A time limit of six months should be fixed for the final disposal of such cases. On the expiry of this period, the Collector should give his decision on the material available on the file.

In all other types of cases of short-levy demands, the final demand should issue within a period of six months.

The Bombay pattern of the Appraising groups dealing with "current" refund claims, and a special and separate unit dealing with "arrears" should be adopted at the Custom Houses. Care should be taken to ensure that no new refund claims remain undecided beyond a limit of six months, and add to the "arrears". The groups dealing with "current" refund claims should also attend to relevant correspondence.

Tourists And Other Passengers

The Customs procedures governing articles of high value, carried by tourists, should be simplified in consultation with the Tourist Promotion authorities.

Where free allowances are specified by value, the limits should be replaced, subject to certain specified exceptions, by numbers or measures or weights. A list of articles ordinarily carried as personal effects by passengers should be drawn up for this purpose, and all other articles in the bona fide use of passengers, and brought in reasonable numbers, should also be exempted from duty.

The Customs staff required to work at airports should either be housed near their duty posts or transport should be supplied for them to meet all calls of duty. The supervising officers on baggage duty should be sufficiently experienced and adequately empowered to take decisions on the spot. When necessary, appraising staff should also be detailed for the clearance of baggage.

Suitable physical arrangements should be made for both passengers and Customs staff at the baggage examination centres.

The intensity and scales of examination of deck passengers' baggage, should be the same as those of saloon passengers.

Unaccompanied baggage should be cleared under Baggage Declaration Forms with the assistance, when necessary, of appraising staff.

If offending articles are found in a package in a passenger's baggage, these articles only should be detained, and not the entire package, unless the passenger is held to have attempted a deliberate act of smuggling.

The routine body search of passengers wherever it is still carried out, should be discontinued forthwith. When a body search is deemed necessary, it should be entrusted to a responsible and considerate officer.

Customs staff detailed for duty at points of entry and exit of passengers, should be selected with care and be well-trained. The existing system of paying rewards to staff for the detections of irregularities in the course of routine searches, should be abolished.

Penal Proceedings

Penal action should not be taken in the case of bona fide mistakes, or where identical goods have been cleared previously without objection, or where goods have been shipped contrary to importer's instructions.

The Principal Appraiser and, in cases of baggage, the Chief Inspector or Senior Preventive Officer, should have authority to issue "show cause" memos, without the previous approval of the Assistant Collector. Where the "accused" is willing to forego the "show cause" procedure, summary adjudication should be arranged.

Several measures are necessary to speed up the adjudication of penal proceedings; the main among them being the delegation of penal powers to the Principal Appraiser to adjudicate routine cases.

Orders imposing penalties, whether original or appellate, should state clearly the grounds on which decisions are based.

The right of "accused" parties to be heard and represented by legal or other expert advisers should be statutorily recognised. In urgent cases, personal hearings should be arranged on holidays.

There should be a separate Appeal Section, in each Custom House, to handle all appeals; no reference to the original adjudicating officer should be permitted.

The tribunal suggested by the Taxation Enquiry Commission for hearing revision petitions should be set up with the addition of a suitable representative of the trade as a third member.

There are serious delays in the passing of appellate and revisionary orders, which, it is understood, Government are taking steps to remedy.

Personal penalties imposed by "original" decisions, should not be enforced during the pendency of appeals.

Recourse to seizures of trade goods should be made (under Section 178-A of the Sea Customs Act) only when an Assistant Collector is fully satisfied of the grounds for suspicion. A time limit of three months should be fixed for the Collector to dispose of the cases of such seizures, and a similar time limit should also be observed by the Central Board of Revenue in deciding appeals in these cases.

Steamer Agents

Staff and launch facilities should be sufficient at the major ports for officers to board vessels within an hour of arrival. A special officer or officers should make a daily round of vessels in the harbour for the issue of stores for use on board.

An adequate number of launches should be provided for Customs staff, at the larger of the minor ports, to carry out boarding duties of vessels in stream at least twice a day.

The practice of recovering "overtime" fees from steamer agents for Customs supervision provided for the working of ships on Sundays and public holidays, should be abolished.

Steamer agents should be compelled by law to submit Import General Manifests in advance of arrival of ships except where ports of origin are situated not beyond the Middle East and the East Coast of Africa on one side, and the Malayan Peninsula on the other. A scale of time limits for this purpose for foreign ports or geographical regions, depending upon distances from Indian ports, and the availability of airmail services, should be introduced.

The present practice of extending the time limit of 24 hours for coastal shipping to submit import manifests should be given statutory sanction.

There should be uniformity at all ports, based on the Bombay and Cochin practices, in the levy of fees for supplementary manifests.

The maximum penalty of Rs. 500/- authorised under Section 167(17) of the Sea Customs Act, should not be imposed as a matter of routine when manifested goods are not properly accounted for by steamer agents; normally, unless the bona fides of the agents of the steamer company are in doubt, the penalty should not exceed the actual duty involved.

The time limit of five days for filing the Export General Manifest, prescribed in Section 66 of the Sea Customs Act, should be raised to seven days.

Duty should not be recovered on the entire stores of a vessel when it undertakes a temporary coastal run; it should be limited, by the adoption of the necessary procedure, to the quantity necessary, and issued, for such run.

Air Traffic: Problems Of Airlines

It is not necessary, nor would it be useful, in the wider interests of the trade, to have self-contained Customs Units at the international airports in India, at the present stage of development of these airports.

Bonded facilities at the airports should be extended and since airline spares and stores are imported and kept in bond purely as a temporary measure, and are not intended for internal consumption, detailed assessment of them is unnecessary and should not be insisted upon.

Airline spares or stores should not be removed to the Custom House, but should be attended to at the airport itself by the airport Preventive Staff, or, where necessary, by Appraisers. If the volume of work justifies it, Appraisers should be posted permanently at the airport. Airlines should also be allowed to pay duty, or other charges, at the airport at their option.

All Customs formalities in connection with the arrival or departure of an aircraft should be completed at the airport itself, and no overtime fees should be charged except for service provided during transit stops of aircraft.

In the case of aircrafts stopping in transit, Customs documentation should be reduced to a simple application from the Airlines, who should be bound by suitable guarantees for the observance of the indispensable Customs documentary formalities, after departure of the aircraft. Customs supervision should not be made a condition for permitting supplies of engine parts, or essential operating equipment, to waiting aircraft.

Custom House Agents

No major modifications appear necessary in the terms governing the examination for Custom House Agents or their employees as specified in the Rules made under Section 202 of the Sea Customs Act.

The problem of "Muccadams" at Bombay could be met by their merging with "Dalals" to form partnership concerns, and by limiting the examination in their case to actual clearance or shipment processes, which are directly handled by them. Modifying the Rules to provide for a special "Muccadam's licence", valid only for the Customs operations which he is now conducting, should also be considered.

In implementing the Rule requiring a knowledge of Hindi, the case of areas where Hindi is not generally spoken should be taken care of.

Unless his complicity, or positive negligence, is proved, a Custom House Agent should not be held liable for any short, or non-levied, or erroneously refunded duty, after the goods have been cleared from Customs.

The condition prescribed in the Rules for the production of letters of employment by six parties, should not apply except at the time of renewal of an existing licence. At the time of renewal, not merely the numbers but also the volume of the business of clients should be the test of the full employment of an Agent.

Generally, the arrangement proposed in the Rules is designed to secure the requisite, and uniform, standard for Custom House Agents, and adequately provides for both large and small concerns to be employed in this capacity.

Customs Advisory Bodies

A Customs Advisory Council should be set up at the Centre; the existing Customs Advisory Committees at the major ports should be reorganised.

The membership of the local Committees and the Central Council should be limited to about a dozen and two dozen respectively. The ratio of non-officials to officials in each should not be less than 2:1, and special weightage should be given to those who come into close and constant contact with Customs operations. Secretaries of Ministries concerned with Trade Control and Port Trust operations should try to attend the meetings of the Council. The Directorate of Inspection, Customs and Central Excises, should be associated with the meetings of the Committees as well as the Council.

The functions assigned to the Committees and the Council should serve to provide a cross-section of objective public opinion on Customs operations.

The agenda of the local Committee meetings should be framed by inviting suggestions, and including matters on which the Collector thinks the Committee's advice would be useful. The proceedings of the meetings of the bodies should be followed up in a systematic manner both locally and by the Central Board of Revenue. Similar action is necessary in connection with the meetings of the Council.

The Committee should meet normally each month, and the Council once in six moths, alternately at Delhi and at a major Port.

Advisory Committees should also be set up for the minor ports and the important Land Customs Stations.

Public Relations And Information Services

Whenever tariff changes take place, the Customs should issue a circular, within 24 hours, containing the old and the new rates of duty in respect of each item affected, for easy reference by the public.

The "Indian Sea Customs Manual" should be published every two years as statutorily prescribed, and consolidated correction lists to it issued at half-yearly intervals.

Many of the rulings and instructions which now appear in the "departmental" manuals, and which are of concern to the public should be made available in the published manuals.

Local Custom House standing orders should also be made available to the public in the form of quarterly publications.

There should be a separate section at the headquarters of the Central Board of Revenue, as well as at each Custom House, for issuing up-to-date and comprehensive manuals and correction slips at stated intervals. At a major Custom House this section should be attached to the Public Relations Office.

Any instructions from the Government or the Central Board of Revenue, which affect the trade, should be published in notice form within 24 hours. More larger and neater notice-boards, placed at suitable points, should inter alia indicate the sources from which copies of such orders would be available.

A section should be maintained at each Custom House for promptly issuing copies of notices and circulars to registered subscribers.

A reference library should be established at each Public Relations Office where publications, notices and circulars would be available for reference, and also on sale, to the public. A quarterly assessment of the public demand for these should be made so that adequate stocks are available throughout the year.

Information sections should be maintained at minor Custom Houses also, and signboards should indicate the location of such sections.

At major ports, the Public Relations Officer should

be an Assistant Collector promoted from the Principal Appraiser's rank. He may be used as a secretary to the local advisory committee, but this should not interfere with the normal duties he must perform as a Public Relations Officer. He should have atleast one senior Appraiser and sufficient clerical staff. His office should be suitably equipped with an up-to-date library of reference books and furnished on modern lines. An importer should be entitled to clearance of a first importation, without penalties, where full information has been supplied by him, to and recorded with the Public Relations Officer, and declarations have been made on the relative bill of entry in accordance with the advice given by that officer.

The Public Relations Officer should answer enquiries promptly, clearly and helpfully.

Advice on Trade Control matters leading to the issue of licences should be sought from the Trade Control organisation; necessary consultation between Customs and the Trade Control authorities should be completed, and an answer given, as quickly as possible.

In planning improvements in the Public Relations sections, expert publicity orgnisations should be consulted and the views expressed at Advisory Committee meetings considered.

The Public Relations Officer should act in such a manner as to remove the popular impression that Customs practices are slow and the formalities tedious, and are looked upon as indispensable.

Other Important Problems

A. Tariff And Trade Control Classifications

Classification of goods according to the tariff is not the importer's responsibility; where it has been indicated on the bill of entry by the importer in good faith, but is not accepted by the Customs, no penal action should be taken.

A clear directive should be given to the Customs and the Trade Control authorities to adhere to the normal criteria of composition and ordinary use, in classifying articles for assessment and trade control purposes.

The existing orders of Government that changes in established tariff and trade control classifications should not be made without Government's prior approval, should be rigidly enforced. A reasonable notice should be given to the trade when any such changes are authorised.

A Classification Committee of expert officers should be set up at the headquarters of the Central Board of Revenue with the Director of Inspection as Convener, for reaching quick and satisfactory decisions in cases of doubtful or disputed classifications.

There should be no rigidity of attitude in the classification of articles of "special design".

The Central Board of Revenue and the Chief Controller of Imports should issue a directive to ensure that separate classification is not made, of machine parts and accessories which have no special design, and are imported in reasonable quantities along with the equipment for which they are intended.

B. Valuation

The condition that a sole agent for any particular imported article must make 90 per cent of imports of such article on his own account, in order to secure the benefit of duty exemption in respect of his commission from the suppliers should be withdrawn.

The provisions in Sections 33, 34 and 34-A of the Sea Customs Act should be modified so as to allow consideration of claims on account of damage or deterioration without reference to the point of time at which the damage or deterioration took place.

C. Provisional Assessment

When a provisional assessment is made, and a deposit is taken as security, no bond should be necessary; similarly, when a bond is furnished, no deposit should be demanded. Care should be taken to see that the amount of the bond or the deposit demanded is not more than what is reasonable in any particular case. There should be a speedier and simpler procedure for cancellation of bonds and adjustment of deposits.

D. Temporary Imports

Additional facilities are necessary for the clearance and reshipment of equipment and apparatus, which are imported temporarily by organisations of standing.

Goods which are temporarily imported for display at Exhibitions, should not be subjected even to detailed assessment.

E. Reimported Goods

The law should be amended to sanction the existing executive practice of allowing refund of export duty or cess, when reimportation takes place.

The condition in Section 25 of the Sea Customs Act that there should be no change in the ownership of Indian goods, to enable them to duty-free reimportation should be withdrawn. Provision should also be made for the three-year time limit laid down in that section for such reimportation, to be extended by the Central Government in appropriate cases.

The existing concession which entitles scientific instruments and machinery of foreign manufacture, reimported after repairs, to be charged to duty only on the repair costs, should be extended to all types of industrial goods of foreign manufacture.

F. Payments Of Duties And Other Charges

Cheques drawn on scheduled banks and endorsed as

"good for payment" on the day of payment, should be accepted. If considered necessary, a portion of the goods may be detained pending encashment of the cheque.

Debits to deposit accounts should not be made, when a demand for short-levied duty is served, without the prior consent of the account-holder.

The facility of paying minor charges through a system of Customs Revenue Stamps should be introduced in order to reduce the delay in making cash payments.

G. Liaison With Port Commissioners

In order that the necessary degree of liaison between the Customs and the Port Trust authorities may be fully secured, meetings between them should be held regularly at agreed intervals.

H. Goods Consigned To Diplomatic and U.N. Missions

In order to eliminate delays which occur in the delivery of freight and post parcels addressed to U.N. and Foreign Missions and their officers, certain measures are necessary.

U.N. specialised agencies and other recognised bodies importing goods entitled to exemption from duty under schemes approved by the Government of India, should be given the same facilities for clearance as are extended to non-commercial "Government Stores" at any particular time.

I. Air Freight

Special and entirely separate arrangements should be made for disposal of air freight bills of entry in the Cash and Accounts Department.

Six clear "free days" should be allowed for the clearance of air freight from the Customs godown, counting from the date of despatch to the consignee, of the intimation of arrival, by the Airline agents.

J. Miscellaneous

Customs facilities such as bonded warehousing and transhipment of goods, provided at the minor ports should keep in step with the needs of developing ports.

At each Custom House, panel of expert official and non-official advisers should be formed to advise on classification or valuation of specialised types of engineering or scientific goods.

In the case of refunds of duty relating to short-landed packages, six months should be allowed for the lodging of claims from the date of issue of short-landing certificates by the Port Trust.

Any tendency that exists to avoid reopening of assessments, where this has been permitted by Government, should be checked.

In the case of goods which are shipped by mistake, or have not been cleared by importers, and have, therefore, to be reshipped by banks or steamer agents, penalties should not be imposed except after examination of the merits in each case.

Where emergency supplies are imported by a responsible organisation, clearance should be immediately given at the airport itself under orders of the nearest gazetted officer against an undertaking to observe all customs formalities later.

Organisation

Careful forward planning of the Customs set-up should be arranged and necessary facilities provided to cater for speedy clearance of increasing goods and passenger traffic on the scales visualised in approved development plans.

Some additional expenditure on expansions providing better service to the public and improving the working condition of the staff should be undertaken early. A part of this should be met by debiting the cost of agency services to the other Government departments on behalf of whom they are undertaken.

There should be adequate reserves, specially in the Appraising and Preventive departments to meet foreseeable emergencies.

Preventive officers should be trained and employed for examination of export cargo.

Officers with specialised knowledge of scientific and engineering equipment should be periodically recruited in adequate numbers. Such officers should also receive practical training in industrial establishments to enable them to keep up-to-date.

There should be a larger number of "all-rounders" among the Preventive, Examining and Appraising staff to deal with varying situations, specially at the smaller stations.

Training centres should be established for Examining, Appraising and Preventive staff and all new entrants should receive training here. Refresher courses should also be a feature of such centres. A senior officers' course should also be provided for.

Staff meetings with the collector and other supervising officers should be encouraged to improve performance.

Much larger staff, fully-trained in Customs work is necessary for inland Customs stations and the minor ports.

Reorganisations within the Appraiser's cadres and consequential adjustments are suggested to improve overall efficiency.

More facilities and conveniences, particularly in respect of residential accommodation and transport, should be provided.

Clerical work, connected with the Sea Customs or allied Acts, or technical noting and drafting, should be assigned to Upper Division Clerks. Office supervision should be increased to ensure better output and quality.

Modern systems for maintenance of records should

be introduced. Experts should be consulted to get the best results.

The usefulness of the Directorate of Inspection should be developed.

Major aspects of Customs operations should be reviewed at 10-year intervals.

EXPORT RROMOTION COMMITTEE, 1957—REPORT

New Delhi, Ministry of Commerce and Industry, 1957. 200p.

Chairman : Shri V. L. D'Souza.
Members : Shri T. C. Kapur; Shri Karam Chand Thapar; Shri G. B. Kotak; Shri R. M. Gandhi; Shri Nazir Hussain; Shri P. Chentsal Rao.
Secretary : Shri R. Venkateswaran.

APPOINTMENT

The Government of India have had under examination for some time the measures to be taken for bridging the gap between the foreign exchange resources which now appear likely to be available and the resources actually required for the successful implementation of the Second Five-Year Plan. The Government are convinced that an effective contribution in this regard can be made by increasing exports. Accordingly they have been taking all possible measures for stimulating trade; but *ad hoc* export promotion measures are not adequate to secure the required increase in trade. The Government of India have, therefore, decided to set up a Committee vide Resolution No. 38-EP(1)/57, dated February 18, 1957, of the Ministry of Commerce and Consumer Industries to make a comprehensive study of all aspects of trade promotion.

TERMS OF REFERENCE

To make a comprehensive study of the question of promoting Indian Exports and to make recommendations to Government with particular reference to the following:

(1) The nature of fiscal or other concessions that could reasonably be granted for stimulating exports, and the procedure for giving this assistance;

(2) The nature and content of credit facilities for export trade and the manner in which these facilities should be provided;

(3) The lines on which special agencies such as Export Promotion Councils, Commodity Boards etc., should be developed to become effective instruments for export promotion;

(4) The assistance required for expeditious movement for export both by rail and sea;

(5) Simplification of commercial transactions by provision of facilities for:

(i) the settlement of trade disputes;

(ii) conduct of pre-shipment survey;

(iii) quality control for the maintenance of quality standards in export goods.

(6) Nature of propaganda to be conducted in foreign markets and the need for development of marketing agencies abroad;

(7) The adequacy of the service rendered at present by agencies like the Director-General of Commercial Intelligence and Statistics, the Trade Commissioners' Organisations etc., for promoting trade; and

(8) Any other matters relevant to the main object of export promotion.

CONTENTS

Letter of Transmittal; Introductory; India's Trade in the International Setting; Foreign Trade of India; Policy and Programme; India's Foreign Exchange Resources and Balance of Payments; Export Promotion: Aids and Incentives; Export Finance; Trade Agreements; Government and Export Promotion; Publicity and Commercial Information; Invisible Exports; Standardisation and Quality Control; Trade Disputes and Arbitration; Export Services Department; Commodities: A Survey; Summary of Recommendations; Statistics; Appendices A to C.

RECOMMENDATIONS

A detailed analysis of long-term trends in our export commodities should be undertaken.

The likely effects on our exports consequent on the formation of the European Common Market and the proposed European Free Trade Area should be discussed in the GATT with a view to obtaining such concessions and safeguards as will ensure that India's export trade is not materially affected.

We should diversify our exports as well as export markets.

Greater attention should be paid to develop services such as shipping, banking and insurance.

Our traders, manufacturers and industrialists should develop a measure of export consciousness and be prepared to organise themselves to launch a concerted drive for the promotion of exports.

The aim should be to step up exports to Rs. 700 to 750 crores a year from now on.

In the present circumstances devaluation of the rupee will not help export promotion.

The aim should be to increase agricultural output as much as possible. Further, increased production of vegetable oilseeds, especially groundnuts, should receive the most urgent attention of Government.

To help exports, the most modern methods of production should be allowed even on our present lines.

While fixing targets for industrial production, especially in the engineering field, provision should invariably be made for exports.

Over-heads such as administrative, managerial and organisational costs should be reduced to the barest minimum.

When raw-material availabilities are insufficient to work existing industrial units at two or three shifts, production should be concentrated on the more efficient ones and the uneconomic units closed down by mutual agreement among parties concerned.

Wages should be related to production and much greater attention should be devoted to increasing productivity.

The Railways should accord first priority of movement to export freight.

The grant of concessional railway freights to export commodities should be examined in detail on an urgent basis.

Existing restrictions on inter-State road transport should be removed and commercial vehicles licensing and taxation policies in the States should be modified.

Barring exceptional circumstances, the aim should be to keep the level of export duties fairly stable over given periods of time.

The Export Risks Insurance Corporation should be authorised to provide insurance cover to exporters in respect of changes in export duty.

A flat rate of refund of excise duty should be applicable to all manufacturers exported using duty-paid raw materials, semi-processed goods and packing material.

Traders and stockists who buy goods in the open market and export should also benefit from refund of excise duty.

Refunds should be given on the Central Sales Tax as also in cases where the sales tax is levied as a surcharge on excise duty.

Exporters should be given a measure of relief from income-tax, such relief being related to their total business turnover, the total income-tax they have to pay and the increase they have been able to effect in the export of non-quota items.

Relief from income-tax on a different basis should be granted to exporters of commodities which have not so far figured in our export list as also to new exporters.

Earnings by new foreign branches of Indian business houses should be exempted from income-tax during their period of consolidation, say three to five years.

Sections 42 and 43 of the Indian Income Tax Act should be liberally interpreted so that only in cases beyond doubt the exporter is made liable to pay income-tax on the assumed profits of foreign buyers.

Drawback of customs duty should be admissible not merely to goods manufactured in India out of imported materials, but also to imported goods processed, blended, sorted or packed in India.

The drawback system should be effectively simplified by granting refund of customs duties on a flat rate basis.

Five per cent of the increase in exports (by value) of a non-quota item effected by an exporter over his average performance during 1954-57 may be allocated to him for effecting such imports as he likes but allowed under the Import Trade Control policy in force from time to time.

Small quota-holders should be permitted to pool their quotas on mutually agreed terms with better-placed exporters of the same commodity.

It may be examined whether quota-holders cannot be allowed to pool their quotas in order to enable them to obtain higher prices abroad and to ensure that the overall quota set apart for export is actually shipped.

Against exports of better-priced Indian commodities for which there is a good demand abroad, imports of cheaper substitutes may be made.

Government should agree to make available the facilities of the Market Development Plan of the Export Risks Insurance Corporation to exporters on as wide a scale as possible.

Canalising of exports through a single agency, though a useful device, should be considered as an exceptional measure to be taken only in special circumstances.

Government should examine the feasibility of encouraging entrepot trade in India on a limited scale.

Government should actively assist the development of manufacture in bond for export purposes.

Government should encourage our traders to carry on external trading operations with such safeguards as may be necessary.

Trust receipts i.e. documents which exporters execute to obtain credit from banks should be capable of registration with the Registrar of Assurances and on violation of the provisions of such trust receipts, banks should be able rapidly to bring criminal charges against defaulters. The requisite legislation should be passed.

Commercial banks should be enabled increasingly to

rediscount bills through increased credits made available to them by the Reserve Bank. Such re-discounting should be at a rate materially below the bank rate and the benefit of the low rate should be passed on to exporters.

Small producers and exporters should form co-operatives for undertaking exports.

The State Bank of India should increasingly participate in the foreign trade of India.

There is no urgent necessity for the establishment of an Export-Import Bank in India.

Existing trade agreements should be renewed and new ones entered into as occasion demands.

Special payments arrangements of the type agreed to with Egypt may be concluded with countries with which India has a heavy deficit in trade.

Special arrangements within the broad framework of the general policy of non-discrimination and multilateralism should be entered into for promoting exports.

Under-developed countries should be allowed to give aids and incentives to their exports of manufactures.

Government should set up Export Promotion Councils for commodities not already covered.

It will be advantageous for the State Trading Corporation to associate private business with its activities. The Corporation should carry on its business like any other private firm and, consequently, should not, save in exceptional circumstances, receive any privileges or facilities not available to the private sector.

Our Foreign Service officers should, at some stage of their career, be given a period of training of at least six months in an export house or manufacturing establishment.

Procedures and administrative formalities of all kinds in respect of export transactions should be simplified to the extent possible.

Government should explain to the public the urgency and importance of export promotion through suitable publicity in the newspapers etc.

The export trade in India should devote particular attention to packaging.

Exporters should try to pool their export advertising and channel it through a single agency.

Export Promotion Councils, Commodity Boards, trade delegations, travelling salesmen and our overseas commercial establishments should undertake market surveys for Indian products abroad.

The Federation of Indian Chambers of Commerce and Industry should hold exhibitions similar to the Indian Industries Fair held in 1955-56 from time to time.

There is need for a comprehensive directory of importers and exporters in India. The compilation of such a document may be entrusted to a non-official organisation like the F.I.C.C.I. and the venture given every co-operation from Government.

An agency for furnishing status reports on Indian firms should be established in India in due course.

Government should bring out a weekly "Indian Journal of Foreign Commerce".

The Directorate of Commercial Intelligence and Statistics may be so reorganised that its commercial intelligence and related functions are transferred to the proposed Export Services Department in the Ministry of Commerce and Industry.

Foreign exchange should be allowed on a more liberal basis to exporters going abroad to conclude sales or for exploring export possibilities.

We should aim at carrying 50 per cent of our total overseas trade in our own ships within the next 10 years.

Government should encourage shipping corporations, both public and private, to acquire ships on a deferred payment basis.

A third ship-building yard should be planned immediately.

In addition to providing loans for acquisition of ships at low rates of interest, Government should consider the question of selective tax exemptions to shipping companies on amounts spent by them in the acquisition of additional tonnage.

In respect of transport of government imports and exports, Government should use their good offices in persuading conference lines to enable and assist Indian shipping companies to participate increasingly on fair and equal terms on all routes and also to make selective as well as general reductions in the freight rates on Indian commodities.

The possibility of negotiating a measure of relief from high freight rates on certain commodities with the foreign shipping lines concerned may be examined.

The handling capacity and operational efficiency of ports should be improved. The facilities available in ports such as warehouses, storage space for fluids, fumigation facilities etc. should be improved.

The proposal to develop a port at Geonkhali as a satellite to Calcutta should be actively pursued.

Indian firms should increasingly patronise Indian banks for export transactions and the latter should offer attractive terms and satisfactory service to Indian exporters.

The Reserve Bank of India should examine the question of granting loans and advances at low interest rates to banks desiring to open new branches in foreign countries.

Indian importers should increasingly entrust insurance cover for their imports with Indian insurance companies.

Accommodation facilities should be greatly increased in centres of tourist interest.

The Indian Airlines Corporation give facilities to tourists in regard to reservations and cancellation charges.

The Indian Railways should consider the question of giving concessions to tourists on the same scale as foreign railways.

Road transport facilities to tourists should be provided through well-appointed coaches, conducted bus tours etc.

Frontier formalities, police registration, income-tax clearance etc. should be simplified.

Publicity abroad to attract tourist traffic into India should be strengthened.

Grading certificates in respect of commodities already covered should be issued without delay and grading inspectors should have proper training and receive adequate emoluments.

Further grading schemes should be started first on a voluntary basis.

There should be a system of compulsory registration of all exporters.

Government should confer with the principal business associations with a view to investigating the possibility of setting up an all-India agency for pre-shipment inspection and surveys.

The question of forming an Indian Arbitration Association should be studied by the Chambers and Associations presently providing arbitration facilities.

An Export Services Department should be set up in the Ministry of Commerce and Industry.

The head of this Department should be a person of high standing preferably one with wide business and administrative experience. If an officer already in Government is appointed to head it, he should be of the rank of Joint Secretary and also have experience of commercial matters and should not be subject to frequent transfers.

A Standing Committee of representatives of trade and industry should be set up to advise the Export Services Department on export promotion matters. The head of the Export Services Department should be its Chairman.

The Export Services Department should have field officers under Deputy Directors in Bombay, Calcutta and Madras to begin with.

INLAND WATER TRANSPORT COMMITTEE, 1957—REPORT

New Delhi, Ministry of Transport and Communications, 1959. 139p.

Chairman : Shri B.K. Gokhale.
Members : Shri H.P. Mathrani; Shri U.N. Mahida; Shri D.V. Joglekar; Shri D. Mehta (replaced by Dr. K.L. Rao; Dr. Rao left the Committee in 1958 and replaced by Shri Yadava Mohan); Shri S.K. Mukerji; Shri J.B. Craig; Shri B.L. Jalan; Shri K.C. Chatterjee.
Secretary : Shri S.P. Sarathy.

APPOINTMENT

The Government of India have been considering ways and means of restoring Inland Water Transport to its rightful place since independence, and the Ministry of Transport convened an Inter-State Conference of the States in North East India shortly thereafter. The object of this conference was to devise and consider suitable measures to establish Inland Water Transport on a firm and economic footing in the region. In 1949 they collected from the State Governments information on various points connected with development of inland waterborne traffic, construction of craft, training of marine personnel, registered Companies operating inland water transport, and so on.

A Conference of the States of North-East India was again convened in April 1951, which resulted in the formation of the Ganga Brahmaputra Water Transport Board in 1952. Nevertheless, a real start was not made on an All India basis until the Study Group on Transport Planning set up in 1953, recommended that Inland Water Transport should be recognised and allotted its proper place in the Second Five-Year Plan, and in all future Plans. This recommendation was accepted, and an allocation of Rs. three crores was made in the Second Five-Year Plan for the development of Inland Water Transport.

Further in 1956, the Central Board of Transport recommended that the policy to be adopted in future should allow for the integration of Inland Water Transport in the national transport system of the country, and suggested that an enquiry on an "All India" basis should be undertaken with a view to examining the part played by Inland Water Transport, and to make recommendations for its future development. Accordingly, this Committee was set up under the Ministry of Transport (Transport Wing) Resolution No. 3-IWT (44)/56, dated February 18, 1957. The appointment of the Committee was warmly welcomed by the Estimates Committee of the Lok Sabha in their Sixty-first Report of March 1957 on Inland Water Transport.

TERMS OF REFERENCE

(i) To review the part played by Inland Water Transport in the transport system of the country;

(ii) To advise on measures for the increased utilisation of Inland Water Transport including movement of bulk commodities to ports for purposes of export and movement of bulk commodities from the ports to the interior account being taken of what is already contemplated under the Second Five-Year Plan for the development of Inland Water Transport, and to give an estimate of

(a) the time needed for the execution of the schemes recommended, and

(b) their cost;

(iii) To examine the prospects of increasing and extending the river and canal services, including a direct service on the East Coast as well as from some point in the North to the South and to suggest steps to be taken to achieve effective coordination between the railways and inland waterways including financial participation, appropriate allocation of traffic as between the two modes of transport and arrangements for through booking;

(iv) To consider the organisation of an efficient country boat service on a co-operative basis with an appreciable increase in the present number with a view to facilitating the carriage of more goods and the question of mechanising at least some of the boats, with particular reference to cost, time and other implications.

(v) To suggest whether any special organisation is necessary to execute the schemes and how they should be financed.

(vi) To make recommendations regarding important waterways to be declared as "National Waterways" as envisaged in the Constitution.

CONTENTS

Appointment of the Committee—Terms of Reference—Visits and Discussions; Interim Recommendations; Inland Water Transport in Retrospect; Waterways of North-East India—Their Problems and Suggestions for Improvements; Waterways of the Rest of India—Their Problems and Suggestions for Improvements; Outline of Master Plan—Multipurpose Projects and Future Developments, Classification of Waterways; Country Boats and Ferries; Construction of I.W.T. Craft, Engines and Auxiliaries and Training of Personnel; Government Organisation for Development of Inland Water Transport; Replies to Terms of Reference; Conclusions and Acknowledgements; Appendices I to V.

RECOMMENDATIONS

In the past the river valleys were cradles of civilisations and waterways were the main means of communications.

The history of decline of inland water transport is not peculiar to India alone.

Inland water transport has now developed into a flourishing and vital mode of transport in Europe and America because of adequate measures for improvement of waterways adopted by the Governments of those countries and location of industries in close proximity thereto.

Inland water transport nas an important role to play. It can supplement other modes of transport and is particularly suited for commodities in bulk.

The capital and maintenance cost compare very favourably with other modes of transport and it is possible to move a greater quantity of traffic between any two points within a specified time than by any other mode of transport provided the waterways are in good condition.

93 per cent of Assam's tea and 90% of her jute are transported by waterways. Assam is dependent on water transport to a large extent.

Aerial and hydrographic surveys of the main shoals of the Brahmaputra should be carried out.

The conservancy of waterways must no longer be the responsibility of any private operators but should be carried out by Government.

Draft restrictions, taking into consideration available depth over shoals should be enforced on the Brahmaputra to obviate any disruption of water borne traffic.

Terminal facilities in Assam are inadequate. Construction of an inland Port at Pandu should be proceeded with. Terminal facilities at Dhurbi on the Brahmaputra, and on the Kushiyara should be taken in hand in the next Plan. The foreshore at Gauhati should be raised and pitched and parking space for lorries should be provided. At Neamati and a number of Ghats light portable prefabricated aluminium transit sheds should be provided.

Afforestation measures in the catchment areas of the rivers of the Brahmaputra and Surma Valleys are essential.

Ship repair and docking facilities are necessary in Assam.

Hydrographic surveys of feeder rivers in Assam should be undertaken for developing feeder services.

Construction of a lock for craft from Longayi river to enter Kushiyara river through Natiyal Khal should be investigated.

Liaison with I.W.T. Authority in East Pakistan should be established.

Early implementation of the Ganga Barrage Project is essential.

Hydrographic surveys of Sunderbans between Channel creek and Thakuran river should be carried out for planning dredging operations to improve the steamer route.

The Damodar Valley Corporation Canal should be made toll free for a specific period to attract boating interests. This canal serves a highly industrial area where a transport bottleneck exists. Steps should, therefore, be taken to develop water transport on this canal.

The Hijli Tidal Canal should be better maintained in view of lack of other communications.

A suitable launch should be acquired for Customs and Police use at Beharikhal in Sunderbans to obviate undue detentions to I.W.T. craft. Similar facilities are necessary at Dhurbi on the Brahmaputra.

Improvements of terminal facilities on the Hooghly, provision of a non-tidal berth in the Docks and release of number three berth in the King George Dock for tea traffic, are essential in the Port of Calcutta. Possibility of development of a boat basin in Chitpur Canal, improvement of canal lock and lift bridge should be investigated.

There has been considerable decline in the activities of country boats on the Ganga due to altered trade conditions following partition and the levy of ghat charges by ferry contractors.

The responsibility for maintaining transport services on the Ganga and Ghagra lies with the State Governments. A country boat service with tugs to provide the haulage should be started so as to run rail-cum-river services between Calcutta and Upper India *via* Sakrigali Ghat or Rajmahal. Governments should divert adequate traffic for this service.

Industrialists should be encouraged to locate industries on the banks of the Ganga in suitable areas. Conservancy and river training measures should aim at improving the navigability of the Ganga and the Ghagra.

In the deltaic region of Orissa, inland water transport is the most important mode of transport. It is necessary to plan coordinated development of these waterways. The development of the Port of Paradip should also be planned simultaneously.

The High Level Canal Range I and the Kendrapara and the Taldanda Canals should be improved, and the Taldanda canal should be extended to Paradip Port. New locks should be constructed on the canals as the traffic develops on the bridges should have a head clearance of 16 ft. above high water level. Lining of the sides of the canal from three ft. above water level to three ft. below water level is necessary for powered craft to operate. The Mahanadi river from Dholepur to Cuttack should be improved on the basis of hydrographic surveys. There are excellent opportunities for location of industries in this area with adequate raw materials and power from Hirakud available.

The tolls at present charged over Orissa canals are excessive and should be reduced.

The Buckingham Canal suffers from limitations such as inadequate maintenance, lack of head room under the two Railway bridges in the Madras City area, lack of terminal facilities, inadequate road connection with important rail heads and towns, absence of regular tow-paths and difficulties in obtaining fresh water supplies. The cargo transported by this canal does not form part of the trade passing through the Port of Madras. It is not practicable to connect the canal to the Port. The canal should, however, be maintained for existing craft to operate fully loaded (three ft. draft) and facilities including warehouses with compound walls at important wharves, to avoid detentions to craft, should be provided.

The Vedaranyam Canal should be maintained for existing traffic. Beyond that there is no justification for major improvements or extension of this canal.

The Delta Canals of the Krishna and Godavari rivers play an important role in transporting iron ore to the minor ports of Masulipatnam and Kakinada. With the completion of the Krishna Barrage, additional water will be available in Masulipatnam and Ellore Canals. The requirement of water transport should be given adequate weightage in planning additional irrigation facilities. Lining of these two canals for powered craft should be taken up as traffic develops. Suitable locks should be constructed on Pulleru Canal to meet transport requirements.

Improvement of navigability of the Krishna and Godavari rivers should be planned after detailed investigations to facilitate transport of lime kankar to cement factories in Vijayawada and iron ore to Kakinada.

In Kerala, there are a number of industries situated close to the waterways, which use this mode of transport. The most important stretch of the West Coast Canal system is between Cochin and Quilon where the deepening and widening of the channel to a minimum bed-width of 50 ft., and a depth of six ft., at low water, improvement to terminal facilities, and navigational aids are necessary.

In the stretch north of Cochin, two locks should be constructed between Punani and Chetwayi to replace earth dams. New locks should be designed to replace the existing locks which are too small. Road bridges should have a minimum head room of 16 ft. This stretch of the canal should be maintained to a minimum bed width of 30 ft. except in rocky portion where the width may be reduced to 20 ft. The extension of the West Coast Canal, north of Badagara upto Mahe is recommended. The stretch between Trivandrum and Quilon is in a poor state and should be improved. Provision of two new tunnels to replace the existing ones at Verkalla can be considered if there is traffic potential.

The rigid restriction of licensing of tank boats with wooden hulls under Petroleum Rules is affecting the bulk transport of oil by Kerala waterways. As these rules were introduced on the analogy of Rules prevailing in the Port of London, we suggest consideration of the possibility of amending these Rules to suit local conditions.

The coastal strip of Mysore State, north of Mangalore is devoid of through lines of communications. A canal linking Mangalore and Coondapur connecting numerous backwaters is likely to prove a useful waterway. There are a number of factories in this region which are likely to use this canal for transport requirements.

Along the coast of Bombay State, the coastal and inland navigation are closely inter-connected. The following improvements to waterways of Bombay are necessary: (a) hydrographic surveys of the rivers and the creeks; (b) dredging to improve depths; (c) navigational aids for marking shoals, rocks etc.; (d) tugs to assist country boats in tidal stretches to improve their turn round; (e) extensive afforestation measures on the foot hills in the catchment area; (f) improvement of terminal facilities. The problems of siltation of Rewas Jetty in the Dharamtar Creek should be studied in the models at Poona Research Station.

With the likely increase in the population of Greater Bombay, the transport bottleneck will become more acute in future. Development of water transport on the Thana, Bassein Creeks and the Ulhas river is necessary. Immediate investigations such as hydrographic surveys, extent of rock cutting necessary and possibilities of increasing head room under bridges should be undertaken on the basis of which plans could be prepared by experts for development of water transport.

The area commanded by the Rajasthan Canal is void of communications. The proposed canal with a gentle slope is suitable for development of water transport. We suggest there should be coordinated planning of the transport requirements of this region. The works on the canal should be so designed as to readily facilitate development of water transport in this area.

The waterway development in all countries like the U.S.S.R. and the U.S.A., has been mostly multi-purpose in character. In India the navigation aspect has not been given due consideration and should be kept in view while planning the development of river valleys and finalising the design of individual projects. The Central Technical Organisation should examine the provision of facilities such as locks etc., on the multi-purpose projects now being undertaken. It is essential that trees and other obstacles should be removed from the beds of reservoirs before water is stored to enable water transport to be developed.

With regard to the provision of navigation on the proposed Nagarjunasagar Canal, the details available are not adequate for us to give a definite opinion. We suggest that full details such as traffic potential be examined by the Central Organisation.

Investigations are necessary to ascertain to what extent a number of rivers in the country are navigable from their mouth upwards into the hinterland. It is only on basis of this and other data like traffic surveys, that it would be possible to assess the cost and feasibility of extending navigation up these rivers and the possibility of connecting them.

The Central Organisation should classify the navigable rivers and canals of the country following the practice in western countries but keeping in mind our own peculiar conditions. It should be the ultimate aim to develop a unified network of waterways which can accommodate the most economical type of vessels with maximum draft throughout the year. The following classification is suggested for rivers and canals respectively.

Rivers

Class	Navigable minimum depth at		Width of channel
	H.W. Season	L.W. Season	
I	8 ft.	6 ft.	400 ft.
II	6 ft.	4 ft.	300 ft.
III	4 ft.	3 ft.	150 ft.

Canals

Class	Navigable depth	Minimum bed width
I	Over 6 ft.	50 ft.
II	6 ft. to 4 ft.	30 ft.
III	4 ft. to 3 ft.	20 ft.

The country craft play an important role in the transport system of the country. There has been a decline in the activities of country boats all over the country. The State Governments should organise them on cooperative basis and provide facilities, such as tugs, adequate cargo and ancillary occupations. Immediate steps should be taken to see that neither restriction of their operation by ferry contractors nor excessive tolls impede their operation. Mechanisation of country craft is not recommended.

The employment potential of country craft and ferries is considerable. Expenditure on country boats would be fully justified even on this account.

Operation of ferries in the country, with the exception of those operated by the Railways and organised inland water transport operators and one or two States, is inefficient and inadequate. Numerous country boat ferries have capsised with loss of life due to inadequate safety measures and over-crowding. People have a right to expect the Government to run ferry services on all important rivers until they are bridged and ferry services become unnecessary. The system of auctioning ferries is pernicious and must be given up. The North India Ferries Act and other similar Acts should be repealed. Ports like Calcutta, Cochin and Bombay should organise ferry and harbour excursion services and if necessary, existing laws should be amended for this purpose. Ferry services should also be organised on a number of multi-purpose reservoirs all over the country. They assist in making people water minded.

We recommend that the Railway administration should run more ferry services wherever possible as a gesture of their interest in the development of inland water transport.

Manufacture of craft, standard designs of propelling machinery and auxiliaries including marine diesel engines should be encouraged in the country. Manufacture of dredgers in collaboration with foreign firms specialised in this field is necessary.

There is acute shortage of Indian Nationals to man I.W.T. craft especially among qualified personnel like Masters or Serangs and Drivers. Existing training facilities are inadequate and should be improved. Engine room personnel be trained at existing workshops while Serangs, Dredging Masters and officers in-charge of conservancy could be trained at marine organisations at various ports and by I.W.T. organisations. Facilities at the I.L.O. Centre at Rangoon where diesel mechanics are trained, should be better utilised.

The road and Inland Water Transport Advisory Committee, set up by the Government of India should be split up into two separate committees, one for roads and the other for inland water transport, both under the Chairmanship of the Minister of State for Transport & Communications.

An inland water transport organisation in the Ministry of Transport & Communications should be created under an expert technical officer designated Director General of Inland Water Transport who should have the status of a Joint Secretary. The skeleton organisation now available in the Waterways, Irrigation and Navigation Directorate should be expanded and placed in charge of a Chief Engineer. The State Governments should also set up their own technical organisations to prepare schemes for development of waterways and maintenance of existing ones under the guidance of the Central Organisation. Thereafter it will be no longer necessary for regional boards like the Ganga Brahmaputra Water Transport Board to exist.

It is essential to employ technical men with experience of inland water transport at the Centre and State Government levels.

Lack of an organisation to look after the waterways has led to virtual extinction of inland water transport at a number of places and is threatening the continued operation at others where it is still carrying on a precarious existence. It is only through setting up of a strong Central Organisation that the Ministry of Transport and Communications will be able to implement the undertaking given to the Estimates Committee of Parliament to accept responsibility of coordinating and developing inland water transport in India.

In the present neglected state of the waterways, development of water transport in certain areas, where conditions are favourable, should be taken up in the first instance before turning to other and more difficult areas.

There are possibilities of greater utilisation of inland water transport at Calcutta, Bombay, Cochin, Paradip and a number of minor ports. Details of schemes should be worked out. Utilisation of water transport for movement of ores to ports for export or to industrial centres for processing should be examined.

There does not appear to be sufficient justification for a direct service on the East Coast from Calcutta to Cape Comorin connecting the Orissa Coast Canal with the Buckingham and Vedaranyam Canals or to extend the East Coast Canal system to join the West Coast canals *via* Cape Comorin.

The question of linking various rivers can be examined after implementation of various multi-purpose projects during the next 30 years which will make the rivers navigable to a greater extent than at present.

Through-booking facilities with the Railways should be extended to established and organised inland water transport operators in all regions.

Machinery on regional basis should be set up to make proper allocation of traffic from time to time bearing in mind the relative suitability of inland water and other modes of transport. In the present under-developed state of inland water transport, we do not envisage financial participation by the Railways.

We do not recommend any of the waterways in India to be declared as a "National Waterways" at the present stage. We, however, strongly urge that the Government of India should assume responsibility for improving and maintaining all important waterways specified by us in this report. The expenditure involved in maintaining and improving the waterways should be examined by the Central Technical Organisation on the basis of hydrographic surveys and other data.

The provision of funds for development of water transport in the Second Five-Year Plan is inadequate. A provision of at least Rs. 50 crores should be made in the Third Five-Year Plan to ensure some appreciable advance. We do not recommend apportionment of this amount among different States but suggest that the money should be available for all properly worked up schemes from any State Government. The total expenditure for development of inland water transport envisaged in our report will be several times the figure of Rs. 50 crores but we recommend a provision cf only Rs. 50 crores in the Third Five-Year Plan because of the difficulty of usefully spending anything more than this amount.

A concerted drive is necessary to make people water-minded. Government should encourage water sports, ragattas, yacht clubs and organise boat races among a number of villages on similar lines to the traditional boat race in Kerala.

A great deal of propaganda and publicity is necessary.

COMMITTEE ON MILK POWDER INDUSTRY, 1957—REPORT

Delhi, Manager of Publications, 1960. 41p.+iip.

Chairman : Shri Krishan Chand.

Members : Dr. L.C. Sikka; Shri T.R. Sathe (Resigned).

Secretary : Shri V.A. Mehta.

APPOINTMENT

The Government of India appointed a Committee to review the development of milk powder industry in India vide Commerce & Industry Ministry No. 19(3)/57-C-D.(A)(MCI), dated February 19, 1957.

TERMS OF REFERENCE

(i) To review the steps so far taken to develop the milk powder industry in India in the private and public sectors and also under the auspices of the UNICEF.

(ii) To assess the scope for further development of the production of milk powder in India having regard to the present and potential availability of fluid milk and to suggest suitable locations for this purpose.

(iii) To assess (a) present import; (b) indigenous production and (c) consumption of milk powder in India for different purposes.

(iv) To make recommendations regarding the nature of plant and machinery required for the manufacture of milk powder keeping in view the present foreign exchange position and to examine the scope for the fabrication of roller and spray milk drying plants in India in the near future.

(v) To make such other recommendations that the Committee may deem appropriate having regard to the objective of developing the production of milk powder in India.

(vi) The Committee may also make an enquiry on the above lines in regard to condensed milk.

CONTENTS

RECOMMENDATIONS

Demand For Condensed And Dried Milks Is Due To Poor Supply Of Fresh Milk

Milk is in demand by almost every one all over India. But the supply, which varies greatly from one part to another, is generally unsatisfactory from the standpoint of quantity, quality and price, particularly in large consuming centres. This has given rise to the use of condensed and evaporated milks, milk powder, both whole and skim, and proprietory milk foods for infants and invalids. The demand for these products varies in different parts of the country and is, in fact, an index of the supply of fresh milk locally available. There is, undoubtedly, a strong preference for fresh milk. But where that is not available in sufficient quantity, or its quality is considered doubtful, as is the case in most towns, particularly those lying in the eastern and southern States, manufactured products have, per force, to be consumed. The position in this respect will remain unchanged until the existing milk supply arrangements can be improved.

Demand Bound To Continue

According to the 1950 Census, there were 74 cities, the population of each of which exceeded a lakh and another 91, the population of which was between 50,000 and a lakh. With industrialisation and consequent urbanisation, and the growth of population, the number in each category has considerably increased. New townships have also come up, such as at Rourkela, Bhilai and Durgapur and it would be safe to assume that the number of cities with population exceeding 50,000 would be in the neighbourhood of 250. The milk supply of few of these cities is satisfactory at present. Under the Second Five-Year Plan, no doubt, 52 cities are to be equipped with modern milk treatment plants, each, with some expansion in future, capable of ultimately supplying the entire requirements of the city concerned. But it will take these plants some years to be able to meet the full requirements of the entire population and, meanwhile, many people will have to keep on depending upon the manufactured milk products, as they are doing at present. There is also a more or less permanent demand from the defence forces stationed in forward positions. The demand for such products is, therefore, bound to continue for some considerable time inspite of the urban milk supply schemes included in the Second Five-Year Plan or which may be taken up during the future Plan periods.

Demand Met From Imports

As explained in Chapter I, the country has had to depend upon imported products to meet this demand, the value of such products being of the order of Rs. six crores annually. It is only in recent years that a spray-drying milk powder factory was set up within the country, to which has lately been added a section for the manufacture of condensed and evaporated milks. The total production of this factory, however, has been relatively very small to-date.

Great Need For Developing Milk Condensing And Drying Industry

Due to the current balance of payments difficulties, the imports of milk products have had to be curtailed rather heavily so much so that even the quota for baby foods has had to be reduced to about a quarter of the normal imports. The need for the establishment of a well-organised milk condensing and drying industry is, therefore, great and urgent in the interest of consumers.

It is equally necessary to set up milk condensaries and drying plants to provide a remunerative market to primary producers belonging to "milk pockets", which are remote from large consuming centres. In the absence of such plants, milk produced in these areas is disposed of as ghee, which does not give an attractive return to the producers. The Committee are satisfied that by using high fat buffalo milk, which is abundantly produced in many of these milk pockets, condensed and evaporated milk and full-cream milk powder can be produced at prices, which will compare favourably with the imported products and this, if done, will ensure a much higher return to the primary producer than he gets at present. The latter will also be the case where buffalo milk is disposed of as butter or ghee and skim milk powder, although without a material reduction in the cost of production of milk, it will, it is thought, not be possible to produce skim milk powder at as low a price as in some other countries, which have a well-developed dairy industry.

This, however, is hardly of much consequence in the context of the current balance of payments difficulties, due to which, as stated earlier, imports have had to be curtailed thus giving virtually protected market to the indigenous product.

The Committee, therefore, recommend that a well-organised indigenous milk condensing and drying industry should be established as speedily as possible not only to meet the requirements of condensed, evaporated and dried milk, which the country is unable to import at present, but also to provide a remunerative outlet for surplus milk available in certain areas, which is not being marketed very profitably at present. This, they feel, will give a great fillip to the production of more milk in rural areas, as has happened around Anand.

Plants Coming Up

The Committee note with satisfaction the developments in this regard, which are taking place both in the public and private sectors. These developments comprise establishment of two spray-drying milk powder factories at Rajkot and Amritsar in the public sector and three plants are for the manufacture of malted milk at Nabha, second for the production of condensed milk at Moga and the third, a roller drying set up, for the manufacture of a well-known brand of baby food at Aligarh—in the private sector. The Rajkot plant, although located in one of the most prolific cow milk pockets in the country, the Committee understand, has been designed to manufacture butter, ghee, and skim milk powder. They think that the proper use of this plant will be to manufacture baby food instead of skim milk powder and for this purpose the formula developed by the Central Food Technological Research Institute, Mysore, may be tried. Likewise, the Amritsar plant, too, should be used for the manufacture of baby food to the extent cow milk is available for this purpose and preference should be given to the manufacture of full-cream milk powder from buffalo milk rather than using it for producing butter, ghee and skim milk powder. This, if done, the Committee hope, will make the country more or less self-sufficient with respect to condensed, evaporated and dried milks, including baby foods, but excluding skim milk powder, on the basis of her imports of these products in the past. Additional plants will be required to meet the requirements of skim milk powder.

Improvement Of Hygienic Quality Of Milk

Due to the lack of care exercised in the production of milk under average Indian conditions, it gets heavily contaminated with bacteria, which not only reduces its keeping quality and may cause difficulties in condensing and drying, but also leads to the production of a milk powder which contains large number of dead bacteria. In order to avoid such contamination milk should be produced hygienically and extension work should be undertaken by competent technical staff in the milk shed of each plant.

Extension Service

Extension service is also necessary to increase and intensify milk production in the selected areas, so that the quantity required by each plant can be produced from as small an area as possible. The latter will lead to economy in the cost of collection as well as ensure supply of fresh milk to the plant. The extension work should consist of organisation of producers' cooperatives to market milk and to arrange supply of feed, fodder, fertilisers and improved seeds, grant of loans to enable producers to purchase better milching stock, supply of well-bred bulls and/or institution of an efficient artificial insemination service, provision of a good veterinary service and purposeful propaganda to improve the existing feeding and management practices, including care in the production and handling of milk. Special staff necessary for this purpose should be employed by the State Governments concerned.

All Weather Roads

It will also be necessary to provide a net work of all-weather roads in the milk sheds of the plants, where such roads do not exist at present, to speed up transport of milk, as has been done to facilitate transport of sugarcane from cultivators fields to sugar factories. Because of the perishable nature of milk, the need is even greater in case of milk plants. The States concerned should, therefore, give a high priority to this requirement in their overall road building programmes.

Foreign Exchange Required For Remaining Plants Included In The Second Plan

The Second Five-Year Plan also provides for the establishment of six other spray-drying milk powder factories in the public sector two each in Andhra Pradesh and U.P. and one each in Bihar and Punjab. The Plan also includes nine rural creameries each cf which can be equipped with a roller-dryer. It has not so far been possible to execute these projects basically due to non-release of foreign exchange required for the imported equipment. The completion of these projects will give the country installed capacity equalling 47.7 per cent of her past commercial imports of skim milk powder and will necessitate foreign exchange expenditure of the order of Rs. one crore on the assumption that equipment required for these plants cannot be manufactured indigenously, partially or fully, within the current Plan period. The Committee recommend that, as suggested in a subsequent paragraph, the question of indigenous manufacture of the required equipment should be examined speedily by the Ministry of Commerce and Industry in collaboration with the Ministry of Food and Agriculture, and foreign exchange necessary for what cannot be thus obtained should be released so that the projected plants can come up expeditiously.

Scope For Additional Plants

The Committee think that there are many other areas lying in Andhra Pradesh, Bihar, Bombay, Madras, Mysore, Madhya Pradesh, U.P. and Punjab, which can feed a milk condensery and/or milk powder factory. While they have a fairly good idea of the approximate locations of nearly a dozen plants for this purpose, they feel that these should be confirmed by carrying out detailed milk surveys. They recommend, therefore, that a precise plan should be prepared as early as possible for the establishment of these plants in different parts of the country during the next five to seven years. The plan should indicate which particular area will be best suited for the location of a milk condensery, a roller-drying plant or a spray-drying plant.

Milk Surveys

To prepare a realistic plan, it will be necessary to carry out milk surveys in the better known "milk pockets" all over the country. The Committee recommend that such surveys should be undertaken as early as possible. The results of these surveys will be helpfu not only to the State Governments in planning the plants which may come up in the public sector, but also to private parties who may be considering putting up such plants. There is a general impression in other countries that India does not offer much scope for a milk drying industry. This erroneous idea can only be dispelled by factual data regarding availability of milk which the milk surveys would provide. In deciding the locations of plants of different kinds and capacities, the requirements of fresh milk, both present and future, of urban consuming centres lying in the vicinity of the proposed locations should be carefully assessed. Plants should be considered for only such places as can supply milk in excess of the quantity required for liquid consumption. Subject to this overriding condition, it will be an advantage to include equipment for the manufacture of products in an urban milk treatment plant.

Need For Central Staff To Carry Out Milk Surveys

As few States possess experienced staff for carrying out milk surveys, and to ensure uniformity of technique, it will be desirable to entrust this work to a Central staff employed in the Ministry of Food and Agriculture.

Relative Suitability Of Roller-Drying And Spray-Drying Plants

With regard to the relative suitability of roller-drying and spray-drying plants under Indian conditions, the Committee think that plants of both the kinds have their place, the choice depending upon the availability of milk and finances and the usage of milk powder in view. Roller-drying should be adopted where the quantity of milk available is less than 300 mds. per day or where skim milk, butter milk or whey are to be dried for use as animal food or for manufacturing purposes. Baby foods can also be manufactured by that process. But spray-drying must be adopted where dried milk is to be reconstituted for use on table.

Need For Research

Little research work has so far been carried out in the condensing and drying of milk, produced by Indian cows and buffaloes at different times of the year. Many problems in this field have therefore, remained unsolved. These must be tackled if the country is to have an industry which is organised on sound lines. The Committee, therefore, recommend that the National Dairy Research Institute, Karnal, should pay special attention to a study of these problems and should undertake manufacture of evaporated, condensed, malted and dried milks on pilot plant scale, using cow and buffalo milk produced at different times of the year. The plant required for this purpose, the Committee note, is already in possession of the Institute.

Need For Indigenous Manufacture Of Dairy Equipment

The equipment required for a modern milk condensery or drying plant is both varied and complicated. But little of that is manufactured within the country at present. The Committee recommend that the requirements of such equipment (as also equipment for milk treatment plants) over the next five to seven years should be assessed and steps taken to organise its manufacture by private trade or in a plant which may come up in the public sector. They feel that the private trade is likely to show interest if assured of a good demand over a period and suggest that negotiations should be undertaken for this purpose first with the four Indian firms of dairy engineers, who represent some reputed overseas manufacturers. If these prove of no avail, indigenous manufacturers of allied equipment should be induced to take up manufacture under licence from overseas manufacturers, who are not represented in India. But if even that fails, a factory should be put up in the public sector. The Committee wish to emphasise that in the context of the country's current foreign exchange difficulties, which may continue for some years. indigenous manufacture of the required plant and machinery is an essential prerequisite to the development of an organised dairy industry, be it for supply market milk or for condensed and dried milks. They, therefore, hope that the matter will be given the prompt attention it deserves in the interest of national health and well being.

BUILDINGS PROJECTS TEAM OF PUBLIC WORKS ADMINISTRATION, 1957—REPORT

New Delhi, Committee on Plan Projects, 1963. 126p.+ivp.

Leader : Shri S.K. Patil.
Members : Shri Sarup Singh; Shri N.G. Dewan; Maj. Gen. Harkirat Singh; Dr. Eng. A. Carbone (expired; Shri N.V. Modak was appointed in his place); Shri C.P. Malik (transferred; replaced by Shri C.B. Patel).
Secretary : Shri T.S. Vedagiri.

APPOINTMENT

The Buildings Projects Team on Public Works Administration was constituted under the Committee on Plan Projects in March 1957 in order to carry out evaluation of selected building projects and lay down norms and standards with a view to achieving economy in building construction costs on rational lines.

TERMS OF REFERENCE

For evaluation:

(i) Multi-storeyed office accommodation such as on King Edward and Queen Victoria Roads and some of the office buildings constructed by the C.P.W.D. outside Delhi.

(ii) Slum Clearance schemes of a few States.

(iii) Comparable building projects of four to five different States to be selected by the Leader of the Team in consultation with the Chairman, Committee on Plan Projects.

As a result of the evaluation of the above projects, the Team was to make suggestions on the following general questions:

(i) Standardisation of technical requirements of similar types of buildings with a view to achieving the maximum economy in costs and scarce materials consistent with the utility and optimum life of the building.

(ii) Comparative study of rate structure and profit margins.

(iii) Organisational questions, especially the workload on each category of staff, and the principles on which it is computed.

(iv) Organisation of "technical audit" for the work of the Public Works Department, its functions and location i.e. within the P.W.D. or outside it.

(v) Methods of work relating to designing, planning and execution of Projects, including any factors, that impede work and remedies for them.

CONTENTS

Introduction; Planning of Works; Construction Agencies; Execution of Works; Technical Examination; Stores; Accounts and Audit; Organisation and Administration; Summary of Important Recommendations; Appendices I to XIX.

RECOMMENDATIONS

Adequate time should be allowed to engineering departments to plan the works properly with a view to obtaining the most economical results.

The outline of a Five-Year Plan should be finalised at least one year before the commencement of the Plan period to make planning effective.

Budget provision should be made only for those works which have been administratively approved and demands for funds should only be made after consultation with the Chief Engineer.

With a view to an even distribution of construction activity throughout the year, we would suggest that the budget year commences from first of July.

Budgeting for materials is as important as budgeting for works. We recommend the setting up of material budgeting cells in the State and Central Engineering Organisations. The work of these cells should be coordinated by a Central Cell in the Planning Commission which should be in a position to correlate overall requirements and availability of construction materials and equipment.

In the case of proposals involving acquisition of land or materials with long lead times, the budget allotment itself should be given in two parts, the first part to cover the cost of such materials and/or land and the other given subsequently, as for works in progress, to cover the actual cost of execution.

Requirements of projects should be studied by a composite Panel in which all the technological disciplines connected with the particular undertaking including work study are represented.

When once requirements have been arrived at in a logical way, the users should normally refrain from making changes at a later stage.

Check-lists for different types of project should be prepared indicating the norms and standards. The engineering departments may use check-lists prepared by the Committee on Plan Projects for multi-storeyed buildings, residential buildings, industrial estates, hostels etc. In other cases, they can prepare check-lists in consultation with the authorities concerned. If schemes are accompanied by check-lists indicating the figures sought to be realised in comparison with the norms laid down, it would facilitate checking and avoid to a great extent queries and resultant delays.

More public construction undertakings, such as the National Projects Construction Corporation and National Buildings Construction Corporation, should be set up.

Social organisations, such as the Bharat Sewak Samaj, should be given greater encouragement. They may be given exemptions from payment of earnest money and security deposit. Public Works Departments may also hire out initially their tools and equipments to the Samaj.

The earnest money to be paid at the time of tendering should be reduced to one per cent of the cost of works subject to a maximum of Rs. 20,000.

The security deposit should be released in three stages; 50 per cent on completion of work, 25 per cent on payment of final bill and 25 per cent on the completion of defects liability period. This will considerably avoid complaints regarding undue locking-up of contractor's money.

We have taken up the preparation of standard Schedules of Rates by various zones in the country. It is recommended that a permanent cell be formed in each zone for the purpose of keeping this schedule up-to-date. For the purpose of coordination, a cell should be set up in the Planning Commission.

The adoption of lump sum contract would lead to speedier completion of works and reduction in contractual problems.

Some existing conditions of contract are oppressive on one side. Suitable recommendations have been made to modify these conditions with a view to making them equitable.

The necessity of prompt payment to contractors does not require special emphasis. The undisputed portion of the bill should be paid within four months of the completion of the work.

Scrutiny of contractor's claims by departments prior to submitting them for arbitration should be discontinued.

The present system of apointing a sole arbitrator by Government is satisfactory.

Once an award has been given, it should be implemented quickly. For this purpose, a lump sum should be placed at the disposal of the Chief Engineer at the beginning of the financial year.

Engineering authorities should be empowered to accept, where necessary tenders which are not the lowest subject to an intimation to the next higher engineering authority.

If the plan projects are to have an impact on the public, it is essential to see that the flow of benefits is commensurate with the expenditure incurred. This can be achieved by adopting the "Line of Balance Technique" outlined by the Committee on Plan Projects for programming and progressing of works.

The present system of technical examination of works by an outside agency has done more harm than good. While it has disclosed some over payments and lapses in the line of management, it has also had the effect of killing initiative among officers obliging them to play safe and of acting as a strong deterrent to the development of leadership. The Technical Examiners' Organisation as such should be abolished and replaced by measures for strengthening of public works organisations from within such as rationalisation of workloads, preparation of realistic schedules and specifications, increase in powers and institution of work study wings.

Existing procedure for stores accounting is cumbersome. A completely revised scheme has been given which would make stores management simpler and more purposeful.

It is advisable to separate the accounting and audit functions and keep the former (accounting and primary audit) with the Chief Engineer.

An S.A.S. Accountant should replace the existing Divisional Accountant in each Public Works Division.

The procedure for public works accounting is involved. There is a great scope for simplification. Detailed recommendations including the following have been made for streamlining the procedure with reference to payment of bills to suppliers, inter-departmental transactions, accounting for materials, etc.

(1) Payment of bills of supplies could be made direct to the suppliers or to the Accounts Officer of the Supply Deparment.

(2) Payments for railway freight could be made through cheques instead of credit notes.

(3) Inter-departmental adjustments should also be settled by cheques.

(4) Preparation of Capital and Revenue Accounts should be dispensed with.

There should be for each State one unified service of Engineers for all branches of engineering in that State.

The posts of the Secretaries of the engineering departments should be held by the highest technical personnel i.e., Chief Engineers of the State. This would lead to both economy of time and manpower and efficiency in execution of projects.

The offices of the Secretary and the Chief Engineer should be combined thereby avoiding duplication of personnel and work which obtains at present in several States and Central Departments.

A high-power board of technical experts, namely, the Board of Engineers should be set up in each State charged with specific responsibility for coordinating engineering activities and tendering expert advice from day-to-day on important matters affecting the development of the State.

In the context of the vast developmental activity that the country has undertaken, planning assumes great importance. A Central Design and Architectural Branch should be set up in all Public Works Departments.

Engineering organisations in the country should become more alive to work study and the role it can play in improving efficiency and economy all round and especially in the scheme of cost reduction which has assumed importance today. A Work Study Wing should be set up in each department for evaluation of works and works procedures with a view to economy and efficiency.

Powers of engineering officers vary widely and are inadequate to meet the increasing tempo of works. Suggestions for radically altering the powers have been made. Notable among them are mentioned below:

(a) Superintending Engineer should have powers of technical sanction up to Rs. five lakhs and the Executive Engineer upto Rs. one lakh.

(b) The Superintending Engineer should have powers to accept tenders upto Rs. 10 lakhs and Executive Engineer upto Rs. one lakh.

(c) The Superintending Engineer and Executive Engineer should have full powers to sanction extra or substituted items for their own contracts.

(d) The Superintending Engineer should have full powers to grant extension of time.

Workloads of divisions on value basis have been prescribed taking into account the difference in the nature and type of work.

Original works (Bldgs. & Roads) concentrated	... Rs. 40 to 50 lakhs
Original works (Bldgs. & Roads) scattered	... Rs. 25 to 40 lakhs
Minor and Maintenance works (Bldgs. & Roads) Concentrated	... Rs. 16 to 20 lakhs
Minor and Maintenance works (Bldgs. & Roads) scattered	... Rs. 10 to 16 lakhs
Original Works (Electrical)	... Rs. 20 to 30 lakhs
Maintenance works (Electrical)	... Rs. 7 to 10 lakhs.

Staffing norms also have been prescribed. With the norms so prescribed, the Chief Engineer should be empowered to create extra divisions or sub-divisions as the volume of work warrants and to staff them.

COMMITTEE OF ENGINEERS, 1957—REPORT

New Delhi, Ministry of Railways (Railway Board), 1959. 56p., Charts.

Chairman : Dr. A.N. Khosla.

Members : Maj. Genl. R.E. Aserappa; Shri N.K. Roy (replaced by Shri D.R. Kohli); Shri H.P. Sinha; Shri D.R. Mehta (replaced by Shri R.D. Dhir).

Co-opted Members : Shri S.L. Bazaz; Shri P.R. Ahuja; Shri B.B. Varma; Shri P.C. Khanna; Shri M.R. Venkataram; Shri S.D. Bamjee; Shri H.K.L. Sethi; Shri N.K. Roy; Shri S. Basu.

Secretary : Shri B.C. Ganguli (was transferred and Shri D.N. Chopra was appointed in his place; Shri Chopra was also transferred and Shri N.K. Mehra was appointed as Secretary).

APPOINTMENT

A large number of bridges including their protection works were designed and constructed in this country in the latter half of the last century on the basis of technical knowledge and with the data then available. Hydraulic science and technical knowledge in this sphere have since advanced considerably and further data have become available. It was, therefore, considered profitable to review the methods of designs of bridges in the light of the latest knowledge and experience gained and to indicate the standards which should generally guide the design of new bridges in future. With this object in view, the Government of India in the Ministry of Railways decided to set up a committee of engineers to investigate and review the methods of estimating the maximum flood discharge from catchment areas in order to determine the waterway and other connected factors required in connection with the design of bridges. Accordingly, the Ministry of Railways, in Resolution No. E57COI/3 (RB1) dated March 4, 1957, set up this Committee.

TERMS OF REFERENCE

(i) To indicate for different regions the method of determining the maximum discharge to design the waterway for bridges. In places where empirical formulae are recommended to be used, the value of constants to be prescribed for guidance;

(ii) To indicate the general principles for determining the extent of bed scour for the design of foundations and the design of training works, the extent of afflux to be permitted at bridge openings for the peak discharge, the minimum free-board for various types and sizes of bridges and waterways to be provided; and

(iii) To indicate measures to ensure safety of railway bridges against failure of various 'Railway affecting' works like tanks, canals, etc.

CONTENTS

Composition of the Committee; Terms of Reference and Particulars of Meetings; Determination of Maximum Discharge for the Design of Waterways of Bridges; Determination of Bed Scour for the Design of Foundations and Training Works, the Extent of Afflux and the Minimum Free Board for Bridges and Determination of Waterway Required; Organisation for implementing the Short-term and the Long-term Plans and its Functions; Measures to Ensure Safety of Railway Bridges against Failure of various 'Railway Affecting' works; Conclusions and Summary of Recommendations; Appendices A to E; Charts.

RECOMMENDATIONS

Determination Of Maximum Discharge For the Design Of Waterways Of Bridges

The waterway of bridges should be designed to cater for the maximum recorded flood when the data available extends over a period of not less than 50 years, or for a 50-year flood when data available are for a lesser period.

Foundations and protection works should, however, be designed for a larger flood, named as 'foundation design flood'.

For better results, collection of requisite data should be started immediately in accordance with a systematic plan to cover the entire country. As such, the evolution of the revised approach will have to be considered as a long-term measure, but a short-term plan based on available data or data that can be readily collected is proposed with a view to improving the present approach, as soon as possible. In the meantime, however, the established practices as obtaining in different regions have to continue.

The Committee have suggested two plans as under:

I. Short-Term Plan

(a) It is recommended that only one simple formula applicable, if possible, to the whole India should be evolved, with the range in the value of the coefficient reduced to the minimum possible.

(b) India should be divided into various regions and sub-regions of similar hydro-meteorological conditions and the value of coefficient worked out for different slopes and sizes of the catchments for these regions.

(c) A practical approach for the determination of the value of coefficient would be to observe actual flood discharges at a large number of representative bridges covering the whole country and then to correlate these discharges with the size, slope and nature of catchments, rainfall pattern etc.

(d) The Bridge Reviewing Cells already set up on each Railway should continue.

(e) A central cell should be established under an eminent Bridge Engineer in the Railway Board for:

(i) The collection and analysis of a large volume of hydrological, meteorological and topographical data which already exists;

(ii) The preparation and execution of a comprehensive plan for the collection and analysis of further data for at least two monsoon periods;

(iii) The observation of actual discharges at a large number of representative bridges;

(iv) The fixation of value of coefficient in an empirical formula or formulae to be evolved for the determination of the design-flood or the preparation of graphs and charts showing the correlation between discharge, catchment area and the rainfall pattern; and

(v) The study of design practices of other advanced countries.

The results of these studies will be required for application, pending development of better and improved methods under the long-term plan.

II. Long-Term Plan

The long-term plan will include:

(a) The preparation of intensity-frequency charts of rainfall;

(b) The analysis of all past and present storms;

(c) The establishment of unit hydrographs for representative catchments of different regions;

(d) The study of the behaviour of the existing bridges (including other hydraulic structures) and the assessment of the adequacy of current theory and practice; and

(e) The task of bringing up-to-date the information and knowledge continued in the classics on this subject.

The programme of these studies would naturally be adjusted in the light of the subsequent knowledge on the subject.

One of the fundamental requisites for the purpose would be the rapid installation of a network of self-recording rain-gauges and stream-gauges, essential requirements being completed within three years. Necessary foreign exchange required in this connection should be allotted immediately.

The proposal for additional self-recording rain-gauges and stream-gauges should be drawn up by a Committee.

An organisation adequate to deal with the voluminous work required should be set up on a permanent basis, with wings in the Railway Board, Central Water & Power Commission, Indian Meteorological Department and the Roads Wing of the Ministry of Transport.

There should also be a Coordinating and Planning Committee for planning and allocating the work and later reviewing and approving for publication the studies of the various wings.

The observed data where available should be the main basis for the determination of discharge. Empirical formulae should be used only as a guide.

Determination Of Bed Scour For The Design Of Foundations And Training Works, The Extent Of Afflux And The Minimum Free-Board For Bridges And Determination Of Waterway Required

There appears to be need for further investigations and research on river regimes, guide banks and protective works, in order to be able to assess the adequacy of existing theory and current practice and to suggest modifications where called for.

The design practice in respect of hydraulic structures varies considerably in different engineering organisations and even in similar organisations in different States, mainly because of a lack of coordination in respect of interpretation of different hydraulic theories and the assessment of the behaviour of existing structures in the various regions. The Committee has attempted to interpret these theories on the basis of sound practice which has stood the test of time, to focus attention on fundamentals and to evolve uniformity of practice. The correct application of these in actual practice will, however, largely depend on the judgement of the engineer responsible for the design on the basis of his mature experience.

Design Of Waterway

The design of waterway of a bridge is a problem which has two main considerations, namely, hydraulic and economic. A correct balance between these two opposing considerations has to be struck, which will largely be a matter of judgement based on experience. However, some broad principles for determining the correct balance have been laid down.

Depth Of Scour

The pier foundations should be taken to twice the depth of normal scour plus a further depth for grip. It is recommended that the foundations be taken to a depth not less than 1.33D′ (D′ is twice the normal depth of scour) below the 'foundation design-flood' level for all bridges and further research carried out.

Records of depth of scour which exist for a large number of bridges and barrages on the major rivers should be centrally collected and analysed.

Investigations should also be undertaken to establish

relationship between scour depth and flood discharge in gravel and boulder beds and in coherent materials.

Afflux

No hard and fast rules on the permissible limit of afflux can be laid down beyond the general statement that harmful afflux should be avoided.

Clearance

A higher clearance has been recommended in case of smaller bridges than what has been normally allowed in the past.

Free-Board

The free-board for railway embankments should not be less than three feet above the 'foundation design-flood' level plus afflux.

Training Works

For rivers flowing in alluvium, the training works should continue to be designed on the basic principles enunciated by Spring, modified, if necessary, in the light of model experiments which may be carried out for important bridge works where river training presents problems.

For rivers in montane and sub-montane stages

(a) A guide bund of the type adopted in alluvium may not serve effectively;

(b) The length of the downstream portion of the guide bund should be somewhat longer than that considered suitable for a guide bund in alluvial bed;

(c) The thickness of pitching on the slopes of guide bunds and the thickness of the apron protection should also be heavier than that recommended by Spring for guide bunds in alluvial beds; and

(d) The apron should not consist of loose boulders, but should be built of large cement concrete blocks chained together or of wire-crated boulders or a combination of the two. The practice of laying wire-crates along the toe of the slopes which has been generally followed in the past, should be carefully reviewed, as it may be preferable to lay wire-crates perpendicularly to the guide bunds.

Protection Works

No great modifications have been suggested in the existing practice relating to the design of spurs, groynes, and protective pitchings for approach embankments, except that in the case of approach banks which are, or are likely to be, subject to the parallel flow of water, the question of providing an apron at the toe of the pitching or some other alternative protective measure should be seriously considered.

Small bridges should normally be provided with flooring and splayed wing walls. The downstream curtain wall should be protected by an apron designed for the maximum scour.

If a standing wave or hydraulic jump is expected, the apron should have under it a blanket of inverted filter to prevent the bed sand being sucked out by the pressure differentials.

General

The course of the stream sbould be periodically surveyed and, if necessary, measures taken to ensure normal and smooth flow, as far as possible.

If an existing bridge does not satisfy one or more of the standards recommended in the report it need not necessarily be enlarged or reconstructed. A careful study of such bridges should be made and ways and means devised to ensure the safety of these bridges by providing suitable bed protection in cases where foundations are inadequate in depth and in other cases by suitable protection works.

Measures To Ensure Safety Of Railway Bridges Against Failure Of Various 'Railway Affecting' Works

There have been a number of instances where failure of 'Railway affecting' works has led to breaches in railway embankments and in some cases to train accidents. The whole question of responsibility for and maintenance of such works has to be reviewed and a unified procedure evolved.

It is recommended that:

(a) The State Committee of Engineers should prepare a list of and notify all 'Railway affecting' works; and arrange for submission of annual reports of inspection, system of watch and the issue of warnings of apprehended and actual breaches of tanks.

(b) The State Governments should be entrusted with the responsibility for checking up and ensuring the maintenance of all 'Railway affecting' works, their watch and issue of warnings.

(c) The State Irrigation Departments should have the authority to take action against unauthorised excavation of channels from beds of active rivers.

(d) It should be obligatory for the party constructing a work which is likely to become 'Railway affecting' to obtain prior approval of the Railway concerned.

(e) In order that the directions in respect of maintenance and construction of 'Railway affecting' works be comprehensive and unified for all States, a Manual of Instructions should be prepared on an all India basis and the essential requirements of safety, as set forth in this Manual, incorporated in a Central statute either as an amendment to the Indian Railway Act or as a separate Act.

JUTE ENQUIRY COMMITTEE, 1957—REPORT

Delhi, Manager of Publications, 1958. 128p.+vp.

Chairman : Dr. S.R. Sen.
Members : Shri S.A. Teckchandani; Shri A.P. Mathur; Shri K.N. Agha; Shri K.C. Basak.
Secretary : Shri J.S. Sarma (replaced by Dr. S.B.L. Nigam).

APPOINTMENT

The Conference on Promotion of Jute Production, held in the Ministry of Agriculture on January 12, 1957, recommended that a Committee be appointed to consider, *inter alia*, the question of requirements of jute and mesta by the Indian jute mills. Accordingly, the Jute Enquiry Committee was constituted under the Ministry of Agriculture vide their Memorandum No. 5-16/57-Com.II, dated March 7, 1957.

TERMS OF REFERENCE

(i) To consider the requirements of the jute mills in respect of the various qualities of jute and mesta;

(ii) To assess the extent of availability of various qualities of jute and mesta in India including the stocks with mills;

(iii) To determine the quantum of raw jute to be imported from Pakistan and to examine the possibilities of stopping or staggering imports from Pakistan of those varieties of raw jute of which there is enough production in India;

(iv) To consider as to what extent the Indian jute mills should be allowed stock piling and have carry-over stocks; and

(v) To work out and recommend the proportions in which mesta and jute should be grown, particularly whether and how far the growth of mesta should be encouraged in any specified parts of the country.

CONTENTS

Introduction; Requirements of Raw Jute and Mesta; Availability of Raw Jute and Mesta; Imports of Raw Jute; Mesta; Price of Raw Jute; Mills' Stocks of Raw Jute; Improvement of Quality and Marketing of Raw Jute and Mesta; Summary of Conclusions and Recommendations; Minute of Dissent by Sarvashri S.A. Teckchandani and A.P. Mathur; Appendices; Conversion Table.

RECOMMENDATIONS

The total requirements of jute and mesta during the First Plan period 1951-52 to 1955-56 varied widely but on the whole the consumption requirements of raw jute and mesta increased by about 40 per cent during the First Plan period. The total requirements of raw jute and mesta in 1955-56 amounted to 70.9 lakh bales.

The word export demand for jute goods during the Second Plan period is expected to go up by about 15 to 20 per cent over that of 1955-56. India has kept pace with the rate of increase in the world trade since 1950-51. Though the world markets have become increasingly competitive and Pakistan is coming up as India's keen competitor, our share in the world trade during the Second Plan period may not decrease. We, therefore, think that our exports of jute goods in 1960-61 would increase at least by about 15 per cent over those in 1955-56.

In view of the increase in population and rise in the standard of living which is expected to take place during the Second Plan period, the total consumption requirement of raw jute and mesta at the end of 1960-61 may be of the order of 80 lakh bales. Allowing for the likely increase in stocks of raw jute and jute goods during the Second Plan period, the total requirements of raw jute may be assumed at 82 lakh bales.

On the basis of the data available at present it is not possible to work out variety-wise requirements of raw jute and mesta during the Second Plan period. Roughly, however, the break-up of the future requirements of different varieties of the fibre may be taken as 50 per cent white jute, 25 per cent mesta, 15 per cent tossa jute and 10 per cent cuttings.

Requirements of the various grades of the fibre during the Second Plan period may be taken as 34 per cent middles, 54 per cent bottoms and 12 per cent X-bottoms.

For manufacturing Bright Hessian for U.S.A. markets about 50,000 to one lakh bales of superior Jat variety of jute are required. This variety of Jute is not being produced in the country at present in any appreciable quantity.

The target of jute production has been fixed at 55.4 lakh bales in the Second Five-Year Plan. No target of mesta production has, however, been fixed. Judging from the rate at which mesta production has been increasing in recent years, we think that the total production of mesta by the end of 1960-61 would at least be about 20 lakh bales. The total internal supply of jute and mesta would thus be about 75.4 lakh bales at the end of the Second Plan period.

Though no regular data are collected at present about the variety-wise production of raw jute, the information received from the State Governments shows that the total production of jute (excluding mesta) roughly about 70 per cent is white jute and 30 per cent is tossa jute.

The tentative consumption demand and supply position of raw jute during the Second Plan period shows that the country would be short of about 4.4 lakh bales of raw jute at the end of 1960-61. Of this the shortage of white jute would be about 1.2 lakh bales while that of tossa jute and cuttings would be about 3.2 lakh bales. Allowing for the increase in the stocks of raw jute and jute-goods (in terms of raw jute) with the mills which is likely to take place during the coming years, the over-all deficiency of the fibre at the end of 1960-61 may be estimated at about 6.4 lakh bales.

The deficiency of raw jute and mesta according to various grades may be broadly indicated by the imports from Pakistan. Of the white jute imported from Pakistan about 25 per cent is of middle grade, 60 per cent is of bottom grade and 15 per cent is of X-bottom grade. About 80 per cent of the cuttings imported from Pakistan are of white jute while the remaining 20 per cent are of tossa jute. Our basic deficiency is thus of better grades of white jute viz., tops and middles.

There is no doubt about the fact that the country can produce almost all the good quality jute required for maintaining our competitive position in world markets, except perhaps the Jat variety of white jute, a small quantity of which—about 50 thousand to one lakh bales—is required for manufacturing Bright Hessian for U.S. markets.

For meeting the deficiency in the supply of the fibre it does not seem advisable to continue to rely on imports from Pakistan to any large extent.

To be self-sufficient in the supply of the fibre it is necessary to increase the internal production during the Second Five-Year Plan period. There may be little scope for increasing further the target of production of jute which has already been raised from 50 lakh bales to 55.4 lakh bales. We have, therefore, to look mainly to the increase in the production of the substitute for jute i.e., mesta for meeting the deficiency.

Every effort should be made to achieve the plan target of raw jute and to ensure that as large a proportion as possible of this is quality jute specially white jute of superior grades. There are certain areas which are already growing good quality jute and it is in these areas that efforts should be concentrated in future for increasing the production.

In areas where natural supply of slow-flowing good retting water is available the State Government should try to supply better seeds, fertilizers and encourage adoption of improved techniques such as line-sowing, wheel-hoeing, better retting techniques etc. Such areas may to some extent be available also in the neighbourhood of canals in Damodar Valley and Mayurakshi Projects areas in West Bengal. If timely irrigation is made available, it is possible to increase the acreage under jute from the existing one lakh acres to about two lakh acres in the D.V.C. zone. In the Mayurakshi Project areas, if adequate amount of irrigation water is made available from April to July, the jute acreage can be increased considerably in Murshidabad, Burdwan and Birbhum districts.

In those areas where the fibre grown is good and strong but retting water facilities are not adequate the primary work should be to renovate the existing retting tanks as well as to dig more tanks.

We feel that the Indian Central Jute Committee should investigate the complaint that water in the retting tanks gets spoilt after some jute has been steeped into it and subsequent steepings affect the colour and quality of the fibre. Research should be conducted in the matter and some chemical, biological or other process for improving the quality of the water in tanks, may be found out.

Since our efforts in the coming years would have to be confined to increasing the yield per acre in areas where good quality jute is already being grown, it is desirable, in our view, for the State Governments to undertake a detailed survey of the jute growing areas in their States. The Soil Survey recommended by the Expert Committee on the quality of jute should be completed as early as possible.

There are some possibilities in Assam, Orissa and U.P. for bringing in more area under jute without affecting the production of paddy. We suggest these possibilities may be explored by the State Governments.

The imports of raw jute in recent years has been of the order of about 14 to 15 lakh bales, these are mainly of those varieties which are already produced in India. Of the total imports from Pakistan about 60 per cent are cuttings, 30 per cent long jute and 10 per cent Habijabis.

Of the expected deficiency of the fibre during the Second Plan period, we feel that the basic shortage may be only in respect of Jat variety of white jute which at the most may be estimated at about two lakh bales. The balance of the deficiency, which should vary from year to year, may be met by imports of cuttings, preferably of superior grades of jutes. Barring these varieties, namely, Jat variety of white jute and cuttings, no other variety of jute should in our view, be allowed to be imported. Inferior varieties of jute, in particular, should not be allowed to be imported.

We feel that staggering of imports is necessary for protecting the interests of the cultivators. In our view, the issue of import licences should be regulated in such a manner that the requisite quantity of long white jute viz., two lakh bales is imported largely during the months of July, August and September. During the same period a small quota of cuttings, say two lakh bales, may also be allowed. The balance of the import requirements of cuttings in a year may be allowed to be imported only after December.

We suggest that, in future, import policy of raw jute should be decided every season by the Ministry of Commerce and Industry in consultation with the Ministry of Food and Agriculture once in July for the interim quota and again in September/October for the final quota in the light of supply position.

In order to enable the Government to make a proper assessment of the demand and supply position every year we consider it very necessary that variety-wise and, if possible, grade-wise production figures of jute and mesta should be collected on a regular basis. Similarly, the Jute Controller should maintain details of the variety-wise and grade-wise imports of jute and cuttings from Pakistan. It is also desirable to ask the mills to classify their stocks of jute into different grades.

While there is every reason to be watchful about India's competitive position in world markets particularly because of Pakistan's emergence as a formidable competitor in jute goods, we feel that there is no special reason at present to get alarmed at the admixture of mesta in the production of jute manufactures. We are inclined to agree with the view of the trade that the mill industry will be able to take care of the requirements of the foreign markets and the question of admixture of mesta with jute and the extent to which it should be done, should better be left to it.

The sacking manufactured by certain Indian mills suffer from some drawbacks and are sold at a small discount in world markets. These defects are not due to the admixture of mesta but are primarily due to a number of manufacturing defects viz., lack of uniform weaving, bad seeming and under-weight. We feel that the Government should watch the situation and if the voluntary efforts of the Indian Jute Mills Association do not succeed, steps should be taken to ensure the quality of our sackings.

We feel that it is not necessary to regulate the production of mesta in general. On the other hand, it appears desirable and necessary to give more attention to the production of mesta than has been done hitherto especially in areas other than West Bengal. It is also desirable to fix a separate target of mesta production.

The problem of replacement of jute by mesta, however, deserves, consideration. This problem at present can be said to have assumed some significance in West Bengal. We are already short of jute and any encroachment of mesta on jute land should not ordinarily be encouraged.

The State Governments should encourage the production of mesta in those areas where the question of replacement of either paddy or jute does not arise. An illustrative list of such areas has been given by us but a complete list will have to be prepared by each State Government separately.

If the quality of Bimli grown in Andhra Pradesh can be improved by better retting techniques, control of plant diseases etc., its production, in our view, may be further encouraged in the State of Andhra, particularly in Visakhapatnam, Srikakulam and Guntur areas.

As the transport cost to Calcutta from Mysore and Madras is high it will serve little purpose in increasing further the production of Bimlipatam jute in these States unless the mill industry expands there.

The production of mesta in Madhya Pradesh and Bombay can be increased only in those areas from where the fibre can be conveniently and economically transported to Calcutta. Any large scale production of mesta in these States does not seem to us to be economically feasible or desirable.

Adequate plant protection measures must be taken to protect *Hibiscus Cannabinus*, a variety of mesta, which is more susceptible to plant diseases. The Indian Central Jute Committee should intensify their plant protection measures for protecting the *Hibiscus Cannabinus* variety of Mesta from plant diseases and side by side improve the quality and strength of *Hibiscus Sabdariffa*.

We feel that the problem of jute prices is fundamental to the question of increasing the production and improving the quality of raw jute produced in the country.

For the fixation of minimum price of jute all the three criteria, *viz.*, the cost of production of jute, the parity between prices of jute and paddy and the relationship between the prices of raw jute and jute goods need to be considered.

As far as the cost of production factor is concerned we think that the minimum price should cover the cost of production of jute in West Bengal as the bulk of jute is grown in this State and it is also proximate to the main consuming centre, Calcutta.

The reasonable parity between the prices of jute and paddy would, according to our calculations, be 2.7 to one or in other words 1.8 to one between jute and rice.

The fair price indicated by the Jute Enquiry Commission on the basis of relationship between raw jute and jute goods prices was, in our view, an under-estimate to the extent of Rs. 4 to Rs. 6. The industry has in fact, been paying a higher price of raw jute, than indicated by the Jute Enquiry Commission's formula, and has been able to export more jute goods in recent years.

Besides the three main factors to be taken into account of determining the minimum price of jute to be guaranteed to the growers, the cost of transport from the up-country centres in a State to the main consuming centre Calcutta will also have to be considered and adjustments made accordingly.

In our view the mere announcement of the minimum prices should tone up the market and keep prices well above the minimum. In practice, therefore, the possibility of the Government being required to enter into the market for supporting the price is not likely to arise in the present circumstances.

The most effective method of supporting prices is through 'Buffer Stock Operations'. In case, it becomes necessary for the Government to support prices and a buffer stock is built up, we think that not more than two per cent of the raw jute and mesta will have to be bought by the Government at any time. This will require a working capital of about Rs. two crores.

There is very little possibility of incurring a loss in 'Buffer Stock Operations'. Even if some loss is incurred by way of storage charges, administrative expenses, wastage etc., the amount involved is unlikely to be more than Rs. four lakhs. This is not a large amount and can be treated as subsidy by the Government to the grower of jute.

The work relating to buffer stock operations can also be entrusted to a Cooperative Marketing Board or a Marketing Organisation of Trade or of Mills. The State can exercise supervision over such a body and if need arises may make good the loss it may suffer in the process.

An indirect method of ensuring minimum price is to lay down a Buying Programme for the Mills. In our view voluntary efforts of the Indian Jute Mills Association would serve this purpose and it may not be necessary for the Government to prescribe a buying programme statutorily.

If for various reasons it is not found feasible by the Government to fix statutorily minimum prices of jute, it is necessary, in our view, to calculate the minimum price every season and keep it in view so that if market prices fall below the minimum the Government may take one or more of the measures suggested by us.

We feel that if minimum price for rice is fixed in pursuance of the Government's announcement dated June 14, 1957, the fixation of minimum price for jute at a corresponding parity may become necessary.

The tendency of the mills to keep away from the market in India during the beginning of the season and to play between Indian and Pakistani markets in their own interest is borne out, to some extent, by the figures of purchases of raw jute by mills and stocks of raw jute with them.

The reasonable level of stocks of raw jute to be maintained by mills should, in our view, be about three months' requirements i.e., roughly about 15 lakh bales while the maximum stocks to be held at any particular time might be about four to five months' requirements.

In our view the tendency of the mills to keep away from the market at a time which is crucial to the cultivator is undesirable. We feel that about two to three months' stocks, i.e., roughly 10 to 15 lakh bales, ought to be built up by mills, particularly during the first five months of the season i.e., from July to November when most of the produce is marketed by our cultivators.

The long-term and more permanent solution of the problem of price support would be provided only by setting up a Government organisation or Cooperative Marketing Organisation which would buy jute from the cultivators at a reasonable rate at the harvest season and sell to the mills later at a competitive price.

We feel that it will be useful to popularise the use of Tamarind-water treatment of raw jute for improving the colour of shyamla jute grown in some parts of the country. This should, however, be done only when it is proved by research that the strength of the fibre is not weakened by the tamarind-water treatment. To begin with, this process may be tried in a few areas which grow shyamla jute. It will be useful if a pamphlet is prepared by the Indian Central Jute Committee giving the details of the Tamarind process and its advantages which may be distributed widely amongst cultivators growing shyamla or dark colour jute.

In our view the Ministry of Commerce and Industry should take up with the U.S. authorities the question of charging a higher import duty by U.S. on Hessian prepared out of bleached jute. It seems to involve unfair discrimination. In any case the tamarind water process should not be regarded as chemical treatment of the fabric and the goods prepared out of such jute should not be subjected to a higher customs duty.

Intensive cultivation of jute should be achieved by better manuring, improved seeds, improved cultural practices, control of pests and diseases. The efforts in this direction should be accelerated as much as possible.

Top-dressing of jute, which offers the best potentialities for the increase in production, should be taken up in right earnest by the State Governments.

The State Governments may utilise the help offered by the Indian Jute Mills Association and other jute interests for distributing pamphlets and popularising the use of fertilizers amongst cultivators.

Attempts should be made to procure adequate number of seed drills and wheel-hoes and distribute them to the cultivators as widely as possible.

In our view there is urgent need for intensifying plant protection measures for saving the huge loss which is caused by plant pests and diseases.

We suggest that the possibilities of setting up cooperative jute pressing and baling machines in producing centres should be explored so that the cultivator is able to get a better price of his produce.

We can hardly over-emphasise the urgent need for proper grading and standardisation of raw jute and mesta in order to protect the cultivators from exploitation by traders and middlemen.

The displaced persons from East Pakistan have long experience of growing better quality jute and they know better retting techniques. We feel that if the displaced skilled persons are rehabilitated in important jute growing areas the quality of our jute will improve considerably.

The apathy on the part of the cultivators to improve the quality of the fibre is partly due to the fact that the premium paid for better grades of the fibre is not commensurate with the time and labour involved. This state of affairs needs to be remedied.

We would suggest the establishment of Cooperative Marketing Societies which should go a long way in securing to the growers a fair price for their produce.

The importance of abundant supply of retting water for improving the quality of fibre is supreme. Every attempt should be made to renovate the existing retting tanks as well as to provide more retting tanks in important jute growing areas.

TECHNICAL COMMITTEE ON CEMENT, 1957—REPORT

Delhi, Manager of Publications, 1959. 58p.

Chairman : Shri K.C. Sood.
Members : Shri V.N. Pai; Shri S.L. Soni; Shri N.C. Roy; Shri Dwarka Prasad; Shri V.M. Rao; Sardar Sarup Singh; Shri M.S. Bhatia; Shri P.C. Hazra; Prof. G.S. Ramaswamy; Shri George Oommen; Shri C.B. Patel; Dr. R.R. Hattiangadi.
Secretary : Dr. S.P. Varma.

APPOINTMENT

The Government of India, taking cognizance of the acute shortage of cement in the country and the fact that the domestic demand was far in excess of indigenous production—necessitating, therefore, economy, in the use of cement and increasing its availability by all possible manners—appointed a Committee vide Resolution No. Cem-18(174)/56, dated March 23, 1957.

TERMS OF REFERENCE

(i) Investigate and report the availability of materials of pozzolanic nature in various parts of the country, particularly the ones found, close to either the cement-producing centres or where cement is to be consumed in bulk, i.e., dams, etc.;

(ii) Examine the feasibility of admixing such pozzolanic materials available in the country as do not adversely affect the properties of the ultimate mix vis-a-vis Portland Cement for specified jobs; the percentage of the pozzolanic mix as well as the stage at which the mixing should be effected;

(iii) Suggest suitable specifications of the pozzolan cement and suitable marking on the pozzolan cement bags;

(iv) Investigate the nature of blast furnace slags that would be available from the existing steel factories as well as the newly-projected plants with reference to their suitability for manufacturing Blast Furnace Slag Portland Cement in accordance with the Indian Standards Specification No. IS. 455-1953;

(v) Examine the feasibility of using lower grade gypsum (80 per cent—85 per cent) as a retarder and use of other retarders to conserve gypsum;

(vi) Examine the prospects of manufacturing high alumina cement by fusing together limestone and bauxite; and

(vii) Investigate and report on such other matters as the Committee may think fit regarding the economy in the use of cement.

CONTENTS

Introductory; Acknowledgement; Present Position of the Cement Industry, Its Programme of Development, Actual Production and Estimated Demand; Pozzolans and Pozzolanic Cements; Blast Furnace Slag Cement; High Alumina Cements, Masonry Cements, Utilisation of Low Grade Gypsum; Adoption of Metric System, etc.; Summary; Government Resolution on the findings of the Committee; Appendices I to IV.

RECOMMENDATIONS

The Committee observed at the outset that although the position in regard to availability of cement had changed considerably from that of acute shortage to that of easy supply, this is only a temporary phase and that with the general rise in the tempo of developmental activities, demand for cement is certain to revive. The per capita consumption of cement is very low in this country as compared to its consumption in other countries. There is, therefore, scope for further expansion of portland cement industry and for the development of pozzolanic and blast furnace slag cement.

Pozzolanic Cement

(i) There is a wide range of both natural and artificial pozzolanic materials available in the country, but their activity and suitability as pozzolanas needs to be investigated.

(ii) Before the pozzolanic materials are admixed with Portland Cement, it would be necessary to fix Indian Standard Specifications for such materials.

(iii) Pozzolanic cement is not a general purpose cement, but its use in mass masonry construction of dams, marine works etc. has been well established both in India and abroad. In addition, it can be beneficially used for certain specific jobs like Tunnel Lining and Foundations, piers and abutments of bridges etc.

(iv) Use of pozzolanas in the construction of dams should be made on a more extensive scale. The possibility of such use should invariably be examined before any new project is sanctioned.

(v) Mixing of pozzolanas may be done either at the site of the dam or at cement factories located close to the site, as well as in areas which are deficient in the production of portland cement but are close to the source of pozzolanas.

(vi) Unless the use of pozzolanic cement can be extended to the field of general construction, it would not be advisable to establish any regular capacity for its manufacture. Also in view of the present easy availability of cement, some caution would be necessary before any decision is taken to establish capacity for its manufacture. But the industry should be in a position to take up such manufacture, should a contingency arise, and investigations and steps necessary for this end, should not be postponed.

Blast Furnace Slag Cement

(i) Suitability of blast furnace slag for manufacture of portland cement seems to have been established in the case of slag available from the Mysore Iron and Steel Works and Tata Iron and Steel Companies. The schemes which are at present under implementation for utilisation of this slag in the manufacture of cement may be speedily executed.

(ii) The possibility of the use of slag for manufacture of cement has also been kept in view while planning the lay-out of the three steel plants in the public sector. A granulation plant has already been designed in the case of Bhilai Steel Project.

(iii) The new cement factories, specially those near Iron and Steel Plants should provide for 50 per cent additional milling capacity, so as to take to manufacture of blended portland slag cement, whenever necessary.

(iv) Not all the available slag can be utilised for manufacture of cement and its use in the manufacture of slag wool, insulation products, construction of roads etc., should be investigated and encouraged.

Alumina Cement

Alumina cement disintegrates at a temperature of 25°C or 80°F and considering the climatic conditions in the country, it is not advisable to use it as a masonry cement.

Masonry Cement

The Central Building Research Institute should explore the possibilities of experimental production of masonry cement based on low grade limestone and rejects in the country.

Gypsum Used In The Manufacture Of Cement

In view of the overall short supply of good quality gypsum, the Central Building Research Institute should investigate the possibilities of using other materials as retarders in place of gypsum used in the manufacture of cement.

Other Recommendations

No practical difficulty is envisaged in the adoption of metric system by the cement industry.

To overcome the initial reluctance of the consumers to buy portland pozzolana or portland slag cement, it would be necessary to fix concessional price for these types of cement.

To ensure equitable distribution, it would be necessary to bring pozzolana cement under the purview of the Cement Control Order.

SELECTED BUILDINGS PROJECTS TEAM ON GRAIN STORAGE STRUCTURES, 1957—REPORT

New Delhi, Committee on Plan Projects, 1957. 7p., Maps & Charts.

Leader : Shri S.K. Patil.
Members : Sardar Sarup Singh; Dr. A. Carbone; Shri C.P. Malik.
Secretary : Shri T.S. Vedagiri.

APPOINTMENT

The Selected Buildings Projects Team on Grain Storage Structures was constituted under the Committee on Plan Projects at its meeting on March 29, 1957.

TERMS OF REFERENCE

For carrying out a study of the existing designs and specifications for the building of the grain godowns, with a view to evolving improved designs, which, while fulfilling the functions of efficient storage, would be more economical in cost and consumption of scarce materials, viz., steel and cement.

CONTENTS

Background; Existing Design; Observations and Recommendations; Cost and Material Analysis; Administrative and Other Arrangements for Implementation; Appendices I to III; Plates I to VI.

RECOMMENDATIONS

The grain godowns constructed by other agencies also follow the same design with slight modifications in the span of trusses and spacing of columns. Some States have constructed godowns of small capacity with masonry walls and vaulted roofing. Timber trusses have also been adopted for godowns of small width. Only in Punjab bulk storage of grain has been resorted to in a restricted way. Batteries of bunkers of the hexagonal pattern have been constructed at Sonepat, Ambala and a few other places.

Alternative Proposals

The Panel considered silos as one of the alternate means of efficient storage. But as the question of bulk storage was not acceptable to the Ministry of Food, the panel did not consider this in detail. However, some technical information on the problems of overhead and underground storage in silos has been obtained from our Ambassador in Argentina and more information is awaited. The Panel will be considering these in detail and make recommendations in due course regarding their adaptability in this country.

There are many other alternatives to the existing type design for grain godowns but taking a practical view of the question the following three appear to be the feasible solutions:

(a) Specialised forms of timber trusses using secondary grades of timber.

(b) Prestressed concrete girders and rafters.

(c) Shell type of roofing.

The question of utilising timber trusses for the roofing of grain godowns was discussed by the Panel in detail with the officers of the Forest Research Institute at Dehra Dun. The design envisages the use of small Scantlings of secondary grades of timber as members of the truss with nailed joints. The timber used is properly seasoned and treated. Special connectors have been adopted for main joints in some cases. Trusses of spans upto 70 feet have been designed and a few have been erected at the Institute. The efficacy and life of the nailed joints when subject to varying weather conditions are some of the important factors on which further experimental research is necessary. This apart, the Panel understands that the shortage of timber for structural purposes is almost as great, if not greater, than that of steel.

Considering all these and the immediate necessity of putting up a large number of godowns for grain storage, the Panel is not inclined to recommend the adoption of timber trusses for grain godowns at this juncture. It must, however, be added that the development of different varieties of structural timber is an utmost necessity as it can be one of the major substitutes for steel in building construction.

The next alternative was the adoption of prestressed concrete girders, R.C.C. rafters and asbestos cement sheets for roofing. From the functional point of view it is desirable to space the columns as far apart as possible consistent with structural requirements.

The elimination of the central row of columns was also suggested in this connection to improve the manoeuvreability inside the godown. This gives rise to the problem of roofing over large spans with a meagre superimposed load.

Prestressed construction in this context was not found to be economical as the proportion of self weight of the structure to the super load will be too high for an economical design. Apart from this, there is the difficulty of getting the high tensile steel which will be required in large quantities for this purpose. Considering these factors the Panel ruled out the idea of prestressed constructions in this case.

The third alternative was the adoption of shell roofing. The development of shell structure is one of the outstanding achievements of the day resulting in wider and more economical use of reinforced concrete in large span construction. Its structural soundness is already well established. The amazing reduction of self weight achieved by the use of thin shells two to three inches in thickness assists also in reducing structural dimensions throughout the building resulting in all round saving of both space and material. Experience has shown that shell structures have great resistance to damage by bombs or fire owing to their monolithic construction. Exgineering studies made after the recent earthquake at Mexico City have also revealed the resistance of thin membrane roofs to seismic forces. In Europe and other advanced countries this type of construction has gained great currency since the close of the Second World War. Shell roofing is not new to India. Many industrial and factory buildings with shell roof have been constructed recently. The performance of such roofs is also found to be very satisfactory.

Shell Type Design

After having decided that shell construction would be the suitable solution for the problems on hand, the Panel tried several types of shell and came to the conclusion that the barrel shell was the best.

The present plan envisages a unit of godown of 90 feet width and 70 feet length. One row of godown may consist of 4 or 5 such units. The shell roof for the godown is a continuous one with a double span of 35 feet each and a chord of 90 feet. The platform roofs are cantilevered from the main shell itself. This arrangement has a number of advantages:

(a) **Greater Flexibility:** The unrestricted floor space gives ample scope for easy arranging and rearranging of the stacks.

(b) **Better Lighting:** Better standard of lighting inside the godown can be obtained with lesser area of glazing in the roof.

(c) **Possibility of Reducing the Godown Space Required Per Ton of Storage:** The absence of any horizontal obstruction and the greater rise of the shell roof make more space available for stacking inside the godown. It may be possible to rearrange the stacks in such a way as to reduce the area of valuable godown space required per ton of storage.

(d) **Saving in Structural Steel:** The shell structure requires no structural steel. This is a significant advantage particularly with the present acute shortage of structural steel.

The Panel also suggests that further saving in steel can be obtained if the end frames of 90 feet span are prestressed. Modified designs for this are under way and it may be possible to utilise this refinement also, if high tensile wire is available.

Design Features

The cylindrical shell has chord width of 90 feet and is supported by traverses at 35 feet intervals. In addition there are two cantilever slabs on either side, 10 feet and eight feet which are integrally connected to the shell.

The analysis of the cylindrical shell can conveniently be divided into two stages. The first part consists in treating the structure as statically determine and calculating what are known as "Membrane Stresses". From the membrane analysis edge stresses in the nature of normal stresses, shear stresses and bending moments will be found to occur along the edges. But the stresses occurring along the edges found from the membrane analysis will not satisfy the actual boundary conditions that are known to exist along the edges. This means that a subsidiary system of stresses usually known as "Line Loads" will have to be applied along the edges so that the actual boundary conditions may be satisfied.

In accordance with usual practices secondary stresses of an insignificant character have been discarded in the analysis. The next step consists in superimposing the stresses by line loads on the membrane stresses.

The present design does not make any provision for the earthquake factor, but there is no difficulty in designing shell type roofs for safety in seismic areas.

Other Items Of Work

Important items of work involved in the construction of grain godowns were considered in detail and the conclusions arrived at in respect of each are detailed below:

(i) **Foundation:** The existing design shows that the foundations of the filler walls have been carried down to the same depth as the foundations of columns. This is difficult to justify. It appears that the foundation designs are not determined by detailed investigations of the site conditions and the applications of the latest principles of soil mechanics. Perhaps, the rule of thumb has been applied. It is very desirable that in future site investigations are carried out in advance and the designs drawn up accordingly. It will not only result in economy but there will also be greater confidence in the soundness of the structure.

(ii) **Plinth Height:** The present practice is to build the plinth upto the floor level of the wagons. With a formation depth of 1.5 feet this involves earth-filling to the extent of 5 feet. The earth has, in the majority of the cases, to be imported. The design therefore ordinarily proves expensive.

Examination has shown that it is unnecessary to keep the platform level at the floor level of the wagons. The platform height should therefore be kept as low as possible subject to a minimum of one-and-a-half feet above the proposed formation level with a view to secure damp proofness of the floor. Each case must, however, be decided in relation to the site conditions.

To secure the maximum economy the user department should devise suitable portable sloping gangways for the loading and unloading of the bags by manual workers. It is considered that this should not present any unsurmountable difficulty.

(iii) **Height of Walls:** The shell type of roofing being free from any obstruction, the height of the external walls can be profitably lowered. A minimum clearance of 17.5 feet is required by the user. This, however, need not be provided at the extreme end of the godown and it should suffice if it is available at a distance of 2.5 feet from the inner face of the wall. This is agreed to by the Ministry of Food.

(iv) **Thickness of Walls:** The present practice is to keep the walls a brick-and-a-half thick, or 13½ inches in the case of standard nine inches bricks. In the case of shell roof construction the walls have two functions to perform:

(a) To provide rigidity against wind pressure and rolling grain bags, and

(b) Protection against weather conditions. The question of reduction of the thickness has been considered, but in spite of the reduction in the height of the wall, as mentioned in (iii) above a thickness of nine inches would not be safe against wind load, and therefore, the present practice of keeping the wall 13½ inches thick would have to be continued. Wherever, it can prove cheaper, the walls may be built in stone masonry 1.25 feet thick.

(v) **Concrete Mix for Shell:** The concrete for the shell structure is of nominal mix 1:2:4 but the present practice is to specify concrete by strength and not by mix. For work of this type of shell the ultimate cube strength of 3500 lbs. per sq. inch at 28 days is required. By proper grading of aggregates both fine and coarse and careful design of mix, it is possible to attain this strength with less cement. Adoption of discontinuous grading is suggested. It is also emphasised that the mix must be designed on the basis of aggregate size available and the nature of sand.

(vi) **Flooring:** The floor has to perform three functions:

(a) damp proofness,
(b) rigidity, and
(c) durability.

It is considered that nine inches thick layer of pure sand, free from all deleterious materials, especially clay, or cinder, whichever is cheaper should be provided under the rigid part of the floors. Prior to sand or cinder filling, the earth filling under the floor must be properly stabilised in accordance with the modern practice; otherwise, there would be danger of settlement and cracks.

The top layer of the floor may consist of four inches lime or lean cement concrete 1:5:10 with two inches wearing surface of rich concrete 1:2:4 mixed with ironite or rockite.

This type of construction, it is considered, will meet the requirements of Fork Lift trucks of half-ton capacity – the usual size.

Where the sub-soil water level is within five feet of the prevailing ground level or conditions otherwise demand, a membrane of tar-felt or alkathene sheets, may be introduced between the sand and the top layer.

If it is difficult or expensive to obtain clean sand, two-coat treatment of bitumen at 50 lbs. per 100 sq. ft. should be given above the lean concrete course. In such cases, the thickness of the sand layer can be reduced to six inches.

(vii) **Finish of Walls:** For cleanliness it was considered necessary that the inside of the walls may be plastered and white-washed. The outside need only be pointed. Plastering is not necessary as the walls are fully protected by Chhajjas which form part of the shell roof.

(viii) **Ventilation:** Entry of fresh air is needed to keep grain in good condition, but during the monsoon period, it is necessary to shut out moisture, and therefore ventilators must be provided with shutters. The top ventilators should have wire gauze protection on the external side, and top hung shutters. The lower ventilators should have expanded metal protection outside and sliding shutters and wire gauze, on the inside.

(ix) **Lighting:** The proposed plan is considered satisfactory from the point of view of obtaining the required day light. It is estimated that the intensity of lighting at three feet above the floor level within the godown will be 20 lumens per sq. ft. which is very nearly the same as obtained in the conventional type godown. The internal covering should consist of reinforced glass.

(x) **Platform Protection:** To prevent damage to the platform by the backing of the transport vehicles, it should be provided with wooden fenders throughout backed by hard rubber packing at intervals.

SELECTED BUILDINGS PROJECTS TEAM ON SLUM CLEARANCE, 1957—REPORT

New Delhi, Committee on Plan Projects, Planning Commission, 1958. 79p.+Plates.

Leader : Shri S.K. Patil.
Members : Shri Sarup Singh; Dr. A. Carbone; Shri C.P. Malik.
Secretary : Shri T.S. Vedagiri.

APPOINTMENT

The Selected Buildings Projects Team on Slum Clearance was constituted under the Committee on Plan Projects, Planning Commission on March 31, 1957.

TERMS OF REFERENCE

To study the slum clearance schemes of Madras, Bombay, Mysore, U.P., and West Bengal with a view

(1) To find out the existing bottlenecks in the way of pushing forward the schemes with speed, economy and efficiency, and

(2) To recommend measures for the removal of such bottlenecks so as to expedite the execution of schemes already in hand and to smoothen the progress of similar schemes to be undertaken in subsequent years.

CONTENTS

Introduction; Basic Issues; Definition of Slum and Magnitude of Slum Clearance Problem; Slum Prevention; Rehabilitation of Sub-standard Buildings; Slum Improvement and Slum Service; Slum Clearance Schemes; Reducing Cost of Construction; Summary of Recommendations; Appendices I to IV; Plates I to III.

RECOMMENDATIONS

Basic Issues

A Statutory Corporation should be created in every State for implementing the slum clearance programmes included in the Plan.

A Housing Corporation should be created at the Centre and all the State Corporations should be subsidiaries to the same.

The financial assistance by the Central Government should be given at the time of the commencement of the land acquisition proceedings or the local bodies must be exempted from paying the compensation in advance.

Minor matters of detail should be settled by discussion at personal level instead of through repeated correspondence.

Definition Of Slum And Magnitude Of Slum Clearance Problem

A comprehensive definition of a "slum" should be framed by the Government of India.

Slum Prevention

No licences to start new industries or for expansion of the existing industries should be granted by the Central Government unless a "no objection" certificate is produced from the local body.

Studies and research in "product design" should be encouraged with a view to evolve gadgets of common use which can be prepared from the locally available materials without the aid of any big machinery.

A Master Plan should be prepared for each city as a positive measure for slum prevention.

The Municipalities should be given assistance financial as well as technical by the State Government for the preparation of the Master Plan.

The Central Government should make available a "Model Town Planning Legislation" on the basis of which the States can enact their own Town Planning Legislation.

The rent control Acts of different States should be examined with a view to exempt from their application buildings which have finished their useful life, old buildings which are in a bad state of repairs and buildings which are substandard but which can be improved for rehabilitation at a reasonable cost.

Rehabilitation Of Sub-standard Buildings

Permanent allotments may be made in the yearly budgets of the municipalities for slum servicing and improvement of sub-standard housing and that a regular Five-Year Plan may be drawn up by each municipality to deal with this problem.

The municipalities should adopt a Housing Code which would go a long way towards prevention of blight as its enforcement would help in maintaining the existing buildings in good state of repairs.

Slum Improvement And Slum Service

In case the owner fails to carry out improvements where this is feasible, the local authority should be empowered by suitable legislation to carry out these improvements and recover the money spent on improvements.

Slum Clearance

A critical study of the various Slum Clearance Acts should be made by a Special Committee which can then formulate a "Model Slum Clearance Legislature" for the guidance of all States.

The acquisition and development of land on a large scale for housing purposes by the proposed Housing Corporation would ensure the speedy execution of slum clearance schemes.

Encouragement should be given to building societies and cooperative housing societies to step up the progress of new housing.

A proper budgeting for materials is of prime importance for the drawing up of housing schemes on a realistic basis.

The manufacture of clay tiles must be studied at different places in India where good clay is available.

The technique of pre-fabrication of cement concrete units should be further explored in this country.

All possible steps should be taken to utilise secondary species of timber for structural purposes in order to ensure thereby saving of steel and cement.

The municipalities, who have not revised their building bye-laws for a long-time, should revise them now on the lines of the model bye-laws evolved by the Indian Standards Institution.

"Dormitory accommodation" for displaced slum dwellers (who live in the city without their families) should be constructed.

HIGH LEVEL COMMITTEE ON FLOODS, 1957—REPORT

New Delhi, Ministry of Irrigation and Power, 1957. 189p., Charts.

Chairman : Shri A.C. Mitra.
Members : Shri B.S. Nag; Shri C.R. Ranganathan (not joined); Shri N.P. Mohan (resigned); Shri M.P. Mathrani; One or two Foreign Experts (Shri H.E. Hedger).
Secretary : Shri R.D. Dhir (replaced by Shri B.S. Nag).

APPOINTMENT

In order to have an adequate assessment of the flood problem in the country and also an authoritative advice on the measures that should be taken to tackle it, the Government of India decided *vide* Ministry of Irrigation and Power Resolution No. DW.V. 530(1)/56, dated April 12, 1957, to set up a Committee to go into the entire question on the basis of the available data.

TERMS OF REFERENCE

(a) To analyse the factors responsible for a succession of heavy floods in the Ganga and the Brahmaputra basins in the recent years and to indicate, in a general way, after an examination of the hydrological and other relevant data available, the lines on which the flood problems in the various areas should be tackled.

(b) To review the measures undertaken in the last two years to combat floods and to indicate the lines on which work should be proceeded in future both in regard to the construction of flood protection works and in regard to the collection of data for the formulation of long-term flood measures.

(c) To lay down principles for the fixation of priorities in the construction of flood protection works.

(d) To examine specific flood problems of an acute character from States like Andhra, Orissa and the Punjab and to indicate the lines on which they should be tackled.

(e) To report on the circumstances in which embankments can be considered as a suitable method of flood protection.

(f) Any other recommendations bearing on the control of and mitigation of damage by floods.

CONTENTS

Letter of Transmittal; The Nature of Flood Problem in India; A Brief Resume of Past Efforts in Flood Control; Flood Damage in India; The Place of Flood Control in Five-Year Plans; Embankments as a Method of Flood Protection; Other Methods of Controlling Floods or Reducing Flood Losses; Soil Conservation; Principles for the Fixation of Priorities of Flood Control Measures; An Analysis of Factors Responsible for a Succession of Heavy Floods in the Ganga and Brahmaputra Basins in Recent Years; Organisational Aspects; Summary; Recommendations; Statement of Mr. H.E. Hedger, Chief Engineer, Los Angeles County Flood Control District, Flood Control Consultant, Technical Cooperation Mission to India; Appendices A to K; Tables 1 to 16; Figures 1 to 12.

RECOMMENDATIONS

Absolute or permanent immunity from flood damage

is not physically attainable by known methods of flood control. Flood plain zoning, flood forecasting and warning, and like measures should therefore be given due importance, particularly as these do not require large capital investment.

There is lack of precision in flood damage data. The techniques of assessment and reporting flood damage should be improved to make the estimates of damage realistic.

For purposes of economic justification of flood control schemes, it is not necessary to collect daily and weekly information about flood damage, and this might be discontinued. The annual flood damage data under various heads should, however, continue to be collected and reported.

Damage to engineering works pertaining to irrigation, power, and flood control should be reported by Flood Control Organisations of the States to the Union Ministry of Irrigation and Power, and the data collected by other State Departments to the concerned Union Ministry. Copy of all this information should be furnished by the various State Departments to the Flood Control Department of the State. At the Centre all the flood damage information should be made available to the Central Water and Power Commission, by the various Ministries.

The Ministry of Home Affairs, in consultation with other concerned Ministries, may prescribe standards for assessing damage and lay down proformas for collection and reporting of relevant data.

Flood control schemes should fit in with plans for other water resource developments such as irrigation, power, domestic water supply, etc. to the extent feasible.

In multi-purpose projects, care should be taken to ensure that the flood control aspect is not allowed to lose its due importance in the operational stage.

In considering future plans, the flood control aspect of a multi-purpose project should be considered simultaneously with other aspects and financial allocations made for all the aspects at the same time.

Where a delta is extending rapidly, the lower reaches of the river should not be embanked as otherwise the rising flood levels would perpetuate the problems of drainage and waterlogging in the adjoining areas. Similarly, premature embanking of freshly formed lands at the deltas must be avoided.

The flood-moderating effect of the various reservoirs recently constructed or under construction on the tributaries of the Ganga would, more or less, offset any increase in flood peaks caused by the embankments already constructed or planned to be constructed in the current Five-Year Plan.

The extent of rise in the flood heights as a result of embankments on the Brahmaputra already constructed or planned to be constructed during the current Five-Year Plan would be small because of the great width of the river and the small valley storage as compared with large channel storage.

Embankments as proposed on the Ganga and the Brahmaputra river systems for construction during the current Plan period may, therefore, be completed without apprehension of adverse effects.

Proposals for constructing flood embankments which State Governments may have in view for inclusion in the third and subsequent five-year plans, should be studied in detail to determine their effect on the river basin before these schemes are accepted for inclusion in the plan.

In general, embankments are satisfactory means of flood protection when properly designed, satisfactorily executed and adequately maintained in localities where the construction of embankments is technically indicated but a suitable combination of this method with other methods such as storage dams, detention basins, etc., is usually more efficient and should be adopted as resources permit.

When it is not economically possible to preclude floods in certain areas, raising of habitations or other important places may be resorted to in order to prevent damage to property and inconvenience to inhabitants.

Priorities for soil conservation work relative to flood control should be as under:

(i) Catchment areas of the multi-purpose dams;
(ii) Himalayas with their foot hills;
(iii) Indo-Gangetic plain; and
(iv) Deccan plateau.

In order to increase the tempo of soil conservation work relating to flood control, watersheds should be arranged in order of priorities and detailed schemes should be prepared for such works which require immediate treatment. Work commenced in a catchment should not be left incomplete to take up work in other catchments.

Soil Conservation Organisation in the States should be strengthened. There should be a unified authority and responsibility for soil conservation work. Also the State Governments should arm themselves with the necessary legal authority for evolution and execution of soil conservation schemes.

Priorities amongst flood control schemes must be decided by taking an integrated view of the various considerations involved, the human and social aspect receiving its due emphasis. The following order of priorities in general is recommended:

(i) Emergent Schemes;
(ii) Continuing Schemes;
(iii) Schemes for the protection of important urban and industrial communities;
(iv) Schemes which would help in augmenting food production in the country;

(v) Schemes which combine other beneficial utilisation of waters.

In the matter of investigations necessary for the preparation of master plans, the same pattern of priorities should be adopted as for the execution of the schemes.

The priorities for schemes proposed for execution during the current Plan, as also those in the master plans already prepared, should be reviewed and appropriate priorities reallocated.

Priorities should be reviewed from time to time as the factors which go to determine priorities change with time.

Several of the functions allotted to the State Technical Advisory Committees, State Flood Control Boards, River Commissions and the Central Flood Control Board are overlapping. Some of these cannot appropriately be performed by the Organisation to which they are entrusted at present. Modifications in these functions have been suggested in the Report and may be adopted.

In each State, having serious flood problems, requiring extensive flood control measures, there should be a separate Planning Unit, headed preferably by a Senior Superintending Engineer to formulate the various schemes and to prepare an integrated Outline Plan.

All soil conservation schemes requiring Central loan assistance should normally be submitted by the States to the Central Soil Conservation Board for vetting and approval. That Board should obtain the concurrence of other Central Departments if the cost of the schemes is to be shared with them.

COAL PRICE REVISION COMMITTEE ON THE BENGAL-BIHAR COALFIELDS AND THE OUTLYING COALFIELDS (OTHER THAN ASSAM AND ANDHRA PRADESH), 1957—REPORT

Delhi, Manager of Publications, 1959. 56p.

Chairman : Shri S. Bhoothalingam.

Members : Shri P.M. Menon; Shri S.R. Kaiwar (ceased his membership); Shri V. Narayanan; Shri S.R. Kalyanaraman; Shri P.M. Nayak; Shri N.S. Mani.

Secretary : Shri Chhedi Lal.

APPOINTMENT

The Coal Price Revision Committee was constituted under the Ministry of Steel, Mines and Fuel vide their Memorandum No. 12/9/57-CI, dated May 3, 1957.

TERMS OF REFERENCE

(i) To examine and report upon the cost of production of coal/coke in the country taking into account, *inter alia*, the awards and other relevant factors that have a bearing on the coal production programme envisaged in the Second Five-Year Plan;

(ii) On the basis of such investigation to recommend whether, and if so, what changes are necessary in the price structure of coal and coke; and

(iii) To consider and to report on the impact of the price changes recommended by the Committee on the economy of the country and on industry generally.

CONTENTS

Preliminary; History of Coal Prices in India; Our Broad Lines of Investigation; Analysis of Cost Data and Our Conclusions for the Bengal-Bihar Coalfields; "Fixed" Prices versus "Ceiling" Prices for Coal; Outlying Fields other than Assam and Andhra Pradesh; Conclusion; Appendices I and II.

RECOMMENDATIONS

Analysis Of Cost Data And Our Conclusions For The Bengal-Bihar Coalfields

We have carefully considered the reports submitted by the Cost Accounts Officers. We think that for a general appreciation of the cost structure, the report for Bengal-Bihar fields should be treated as providing the basic data, as these fields produce about 80 per cent of the total output of coal in India. While several basic factors in the structure would be equally applicable to the outlying fields of Madhya Pradesh, Bombay and Orissa, these latter fields would require separate treatment because the coals there are not yet graded and the Committee was called upon to examine the question of introducing grading and to recommend prices accordingly. These fields have, therefore, been dealt with in a separate chapter.

The collieries in Assam are, again, a class apart, and we propose dealing with them in a supplementary report. The collieries in Andhra Pradesh also appear to stand in a class by themselves, although not necessarily for the same reasons.

A preliminary examination of the data furnished by the Cost Accounts Officers revealed wide variations in the same elements of cost even among collieries in the same field. In many cases an explanation for these variations was not apparent. It is no doubt true that in any industry there would be variations which are not clearly attributable to obvious reasons. But, in a general way, it should normally be possible to indicate, even if only broadly, the kind of variations which are due to factors beyond the control of the management and the kind of variations which have resulted from differences in methods of management and from varying degrees of efficiency achieved. We also found considerable variations in the output-per-manshift (OMS) even among collieries having more or less similar conditions of working. The cases where these variations could be explained were relatively few. We felt, therefore, that the easy course of striking averages would not be appropriate, even though the representatives of the industry had themselves told us that the collieries selected for cost examination were on the whole representative of the Bengal-Bihar coalfields. If averages are thus to be eschewed, we asked ourselves how the cost data available could be better utilised to yield a more appropriate method. For this purpose we thought that a technical examination, designed to show why actual costs varied so widely, would be useful. We, therefore, requested Shri A.B. Guha, Coal Mining Adviser to the Department of Mines and Fuel (Ministry of Steel, Mines and Fuel), and Shri S.G. Krishnan, Chief Mining Adviser to the Railways, to undertake the technical examination. They were also given the assistance of a Cost Accounts Officer. This team visited the following collieries in June 1958:

(a) New Jinagara (b) Busserya (c) Loyabad (d) Katras	Jharia Coalfield
(e) Bhanora (f) Girimint (g) Dhemo Main	Ranigunj coalfield

These collieries were chosen as typical of those which showed wide variations in such elements as labour costs, incidence of sand stowing, internal consumption of coal and overall working costs in relation to size and output. In particular, the Katras colliery was chosen because one of the seams had been leased to another company and we thought a study of two units working under almost similar conditions would be worthwhile. In order to get a clearer idea of the efforts of mechanisation in deep working conditions, the technical team was also requested to study the Girimint colliery, although it had not been initially chosen for costing.

The technical team gave us their report in the third week of June 1958. The report covered such factors as nature and depth of seams, geological conditions, presence of water and gas underneath, condition of roof, need for timbering and the extent of mechanisation.

After a re-examination of the cost data in the light of the report of the technical team, we were reinforced in our preliminary conclusion that the computation of costs by the method of averaging would definitely be inappropriate. We felt that it would be more appropriate to attempt an assessment of what might be regarded as "normal" for each main item of cost; in other words, that a mere examination of costs actually incurred by various collieries would not be enough and the objective should rather be to determine, by a study and comparison of actual costs, the cost of production, as it should be, in a colliery managed with reasonable efficiency and economy and facing no problems of special difficulty. In making such an assessment, we considered that along with the conditions which actually prevailed during the period of costing, it would be equally necessary to take note of later trends of production and development and the conditions necessary to achieve the target of production set for the Second Five-Year Plan. Expressed in a different way, the concept of "normal" should relate to a colliery working with reasonable efficiency and economy not only to maintain production but also to expand production at the rate envisaged under the Plan.

In the light of the considerations set out in the preceding paragraph we now proceed to assess the "normal" costs under the following heads:—

(1) Wages.

(2) Provision of labour amenities and implementation of the Coal Mines Regulations.

(3) Salaries and expenses on administration.

(4) Cost of stores.

(5) Cost of power, royalties, cesses, collieries' own consumption of coal and other "miscellaneous items".

(6) Depreciation.

(7) Brokerage and Commission.

Wages

Wages constitute the largest single element in the cost of raising coal. As stated earlier, our cost examination related to the period immediately after the Majumdar Award but before the Appellate Award was implemented.

Of the 27 collieries costed on our behalf, the wage element in one major unit could not be ascertained as coal raising was entrusted to contractors on a lump sum, including all charges except depreciation and expenses on administration. The cost data furnished by the other 26 collieries revealed a wage cost per ton ranging from Rs. 6.70 to Rs. 13.99. Among these collieries, the O.M.S. ranged from 0.23 to 0.58. These wide variations naturally called for some explanation. We have carefully examined the variations but are unable to isolate the specific reasons for the variations. We notice, for example, that the level of production in the colliery which showed the highest wage cost is not very different from the level of production in the colliery which showed the lowest: there are also no obvious differences in working conditions which might account for the large difference in wage cost. On the other hand, 14 out of the 26 collieries, which account for 50 per cent of the total production of the 26 collieries, show a wage cost which is less than Rs. 10 per ton and two-thirds of these, again, show a figure of less than Rs. nine per ton. Eighteen out of the 26 collieries constitute a broad cross-section showing a relatively narrow range of variation in the wage cost per ton. We consider that this cross secton affords, under the circumstances, the most reasonable guide for determining the "normal" wage cost. In this group of 18, the figure of Rs. 9.50 per ton appears to be the most representative. Actually, seven out of the 18 show a figure of less than Rs. 9.50 per ton. Another five collieries, not in the central group of 18, also show a wage cost of less than Rs. 9.50. It is true that eight out of the 26 collieries fall in that category in which the cost is higher than in the central group. Two of the collieries in this group have been studied by the technical team. In one case the higher cost has been attributed to higher lead and lift in one of the inclines. But this incline is nearly exhausted and the cost in the remaining portion of the colliery falls within the central range. In the second case, the higher cost is attributed to fall in production from the principal seam which is nearing exhaustion, the opening of a new seam and the gassy nature of the mine. Because of these difficulties, it is not possible, in the opinion of the technical team, to increase the output-per-man shift or to reduce wage costs in this mine. Yet, the quality of the coal is high and one could well regard the continuance of production as essential. These two illustrations will show that without an individual examination of the special problem of each mine it is not possible to say to what extent the higher costs are inevitable and to what extent they are capable of reduction by better management. We consider, therefore, that to the extent there are inherent difficulties, some special treatment will have to be provided for in the case of mines from which continuance of production is necessary in the national interest. We do not think it appropriate to take these special factors into account in assessing the "normal" cost structure. Later in this chapter, we are making our recommendations how these special or exceptional cases may be treated. If these recommendations are accepted, we consider that Rs. 9.50 per ton, suitably adjusted as indicated in the succeeding paragraph, should be regarded as the "normal" wage cost.

As we have stated earlier, the cost examination of collieries related to the period July 1956 to March 1957—a period during which the Majumdar Award was in force but the Appellate Award had not been implemented. The assessment of wage cost, as made in the previous paragraph, will, therefore, have to be increased to provide for the incidence of the Appellate Award. At first sight, it would appear that the simplest way of ascertaining this incidence would be by a further examination of the cost during a period in which the Appellate Award was in force. Such further examination would have caused delay. This delay would have been worthwhile, were one certain that a further examination would make possible a precise and accurate assessment. But the observations which we have made regarding variations in the wage cost as a whole would equally apply to changes in the wage cost caused in different collieries by the implementation of the Appellate Award. In our opinion, therefore, a theoretical calculation of the effect of the Appellate Award on the basis that Rs. 9.50 per ton represents the wage cost of a normal composite labour force, would give results as satisfying as by any other method. We have adopted this method; and, in our judgment, the incidence of the Appellate Award may be assessed at Rs. 1.10 per ton for purposes of price fixation.

The wage cost of coal is directly linked with the output-per-man-shift. Other things remaining equal, any increase in the O.M.S. must involve a proportionate decrease in the cost per ton. But what determines the O.M.S. is not merely the physical effort of the individual worker; the ways in which work is facilitated by mechanisation, provision of adequate arrangements for the conveyance of coal etc., too, have a great bearing on the output-per-man-shift. There is no doubt whatever that over the years, the O.M.S. in the coalfields of India has been gradually increasing. The average O.M.S. in the 26 collieries of the Bengal-Bihar coalfields which have been costed, comes to 0.36 ton. A comparison with the average O.M.S. of all collieries in Bengal-Bihar and all collieries in India is interesting. The figures for 1956 and 1957 for the three main coalfields in Bengal-Bihar are as follows:

	1956	1957
Jharia	0.39	0.40
Ranigunj	0.39	0.42
Karanpura	0.37	0.41

The all-India average for 1956 and 1957 was 0.39 and 0.41 respectively. The trend is, therefore, unmistakable. From later paragraphs dealing with other items of cost, it would be seen that we are making adequate provision for elements which would directly or indirectly help to increase the O.M.S. If, as we expect, the price structure recommended by us would have to be maintained for a period of years, subject only to provisions for certain escalations on known variations, note has to be taken of the increasing trend of the O.M.S. while determining the present wage cost. In the circumstances we regard an O.M.S. of 0.40 ton as fair and reasonable. It would be observed that several collieries among those costed had achieved this output even during the costing period. We consider that other collieries, too, in conditions of reasonable efficiency of working, should be able to attain this rate of output, if not more. On the basis of an O.M.S. of 0.40 ton, the "normal" wage cost (Rs. 9.50 plus Rs. 1.10) would stand adjusted at Rs. 9.55 per ton.

Provision Of Labour Amenities And Implementation Of The Coal Mines Regulation

We consider it necessary to assess separately the element required to enable collieries to fulfil adequately their obligations in regard to labour amenities and the implementation of the various Coal Mines Regulations. The amenities provided to labour by collieries have varied widely from region to region and even among collieries within the same region. Some of these amenities were provided voluntarily and others under various statutory requirements. The Mines Rules of 1955 not only codified these obligations but enlarged them. The Temporary Mines Regulations of 1955, which have now been replaced by the Coal Mines Regulations, 1957, have imposed further obligations on the employers. It has been claimed that the cost of providing these facilities would be considerable. The industry's estimate of the cost ranges from Rs. 1.09 to Rs. 3.23 per ton. Because of the importance of ensuring speedy and adequate implementation of these measures, we consider that there should be no excuse for any one to urge that the cost structure does not make it possible for him to do so. This is the main reason why, as stated earlier, we regard it necessary to isolate this element. Unfortunately, the cost data provide very little guidance in this matter. The accounts maintained by the collieries do not specifically exhibit these items of expenditure separately. The Cost Accounts Officers have, therefore, found it very difficult to isolate what has actually been spent, although we know that expenditure is being incurred by most collieries and a few of them are actually doing even more than what is statutorily required. Further, the implementation of the new regulations of 1957 is far from complete. We have, therefore, to rely mainly on observation, discussion and judgement in assessing the cost of this element. In this connection, we have consulted the Chief Inspector of Mines, who is primarily responsible for enforcing these regulations. Taking all factors into account, we consider that the cost structure should include an element of Rs. 1.10 on this account.

Salaries And Expenses On Administration

The head 'salaries and administration' includes the cost of clerical and supervisory staff and other expenses of administration both in the colliery offices and the head offices in Calcutta or other big towns. One would expect that these expenses would bear some recognisable relationship to total output or the number of employees. But the figures compiled by the Cost Accounts Officers do not reveal any clear relationship. Thus, there are large units in the Bengal-Bihar area (producing from 16,000 to 18,000 tons per month) which show a cost ranging from Rs. 1.38 to Rs. 1.60 per ton. But there are other comparatively smaller units which show a cost ranging from Rs. 2.17 to Rs. 3.24. There are again others which show a cost of less than Re. one per ton. These variations, to some extent, may be attributable to the differences in methods of accounting pattern and procedure. In our judgement an element of Rs. 1.70 per ton would be adequate and reasonable.

Stores

Both in written memoranda submitted by them and in discussions with us, the representatives of the industry have laid great stress on the increases that had taken place in the cost of plant, machinery, spares and other stores. We have pointed out earlier that revisions of coal prices during the last ten years were mainly on account of increase in labour costs. It is an undoubted fact that the cost of machinery, spares and other stores have increased considerably since 1947. The industry's estimate is that as compared to 1947, there has been an average increase of 75 per cent in the cost of stores resulting in an increase in the stores cost, ranging from Annas 14 to Rs. 1-4-0 per ton. One would infer from this that in view of the industry the stores cost in 1947 would have been of the order of Rs. 1-8-0 per ton and the actual cost today would be in the range of Rs. 2-8-0 per ton. We agree that the prices of the various stores used by the industry, e.g., kerosene, timber, explosives, iron and steel, cement, etc., have increased considerably since 1947. But we feel that there is no purpose in trying to evaluate what the stores cost was in 1947. The cost examination (relating to the period July 1956 to March 1957) reveals a stores cost ranging from Rs. 0.59 to Rs. 2.76 per ton. We would, however, observe in this connection that the accounts of the collieries costed have not been kept in a way which makes it easy to isolate this element. This might account partly for the variations. It is difficult to be anything like dogmatic on this matter as the nature and amount of stores necessary would vary according to the conditions prevailing in each colliery. Having regard to all factors, and taking note in particular of the tendency for increased mechanisation, which we consider desirable in the interests of production, and allowing for the increase in prices since the period of costing, we consider that this element could be reasonably assessed at Rs. 1.75 per ton.

Cost On Power, Collieries' Own Consumption Of Coal, Royalty, Cess And Miscellaneous Items

In these elements variations are very wide. Royalty varies according to the terms of the leases. Pre 1949 leases are not governed by the uniform rate prescribed under the Mineral Concession Rules, 1949. The element of royalty ranges from Rs. 0.01 to Rs. 1.18 per ton. Similarly, cesses which are local levies, vary from State to State and even from district to district. The cost per ton under this head, therefore, varies from Rs. 0.03 to Rs. 0.26 per ton. Under the head 'miscellaneous', the variations range from Rs. 0.13 to Rs. 1.00. This element comprises expenditure on such items as stationery, printing, postage, insurance, legal charges and travelling allowances. The few instances below would show that expenditure on these items is perhaps unduly high in relation to raisings:

Colliery	Raisings per month	Cost per ton on "Misc." items	Total Cost per month
		Rs.	Rs.
Colliery A	5,000 tons	1.00	5,000
Colliery B	18,000 ,,	0.94	16,920
Colliery C	2,200 ,,	0.80	1,760
Colliery D	10,000 ,,	0.74	7,400

The most widely spread variations are, however, found in the cost of power and collieries' own consumption of coal. To a certain extent, these elements are related. Many collieries use their own coal to generate power. Certain quantities of coal are also issued to workers, the quantity differing according to local practices. Hardly any colliery maintains a correct account of the quantity of coal consumed in boilers or issued to workers. In many cases, only rejects are issued to the workers.

The only practical way of dealing with these widely varying figures is to lay down an amount which should broadly be sufficient for an average colliery. We assess this amount at Rs. 1.85 per ton.

Depreciation

In their memoranda, and during discussions with us, the representatives of the industry have made a strong plea for an adequate element in the price of coal to provide for depreciation and rehabilitation of plant and machinery. They say that investments in the coal industry were made at a time when prices were much lower than they are today and the cost of replacing the assets would be much higher under present conditions. It has also been urged that, as in the case of some other industries, the price should specifically include an element which would enable the industry to have some internal resources which could be utilised for further development. We think there is force in this argument. In our opinion the price structure should be such as would enable the industry not only to keep the plant and equipment in efficient functioning, but also to permit of further development. In this context, the amount that is admissible for income-tax purposes—which is based generally on the written down value of the plant and other fixed assets from time to time—is not really relevant. We think that the factors which do have a bearing on this question are the capital employed in the industry, the requirements for maintaining existing assets in efficient condition and the likely cost of further development. We find that at the beginning of the Second Plan period the capital employed in the private sector of the coal industry was approximately Rs. 14 per ton of production. At that time, production in the private sector was running at a level of about 35 million tons per annum. According to the target prescribed under the Second Plan, the production in the private sector should go up to about 45 million tons in 1961. For achieving this increase in production, the establishment of new collieries in entirely new areas is not contemplated under the policy laid down by Government. The development envisaged in the private sector will thus be by increase of production in the existing collieries and by opening of areas immediately contiguous to the existing mines. The capital required for expansion of production through existing units and development of immediately contiguous areas will naturally be less than what would be required for opening up entirely new areas. We have carefully considered the matter in the light of such information as we have regarding the cost of expansion under varying conditions and we estimate that on the average the additional capital required for expanding production in the manner envisaged for the private sector would be about Rs. 20 per ton. On this basis, the total capital employed (including new investment for additional production) by the industry after attaining the target of output of 45 million tons would be Rs. 690 million (i.e. $35 \times 14 + 10 \times 20$). The average capital employed per ton of coal would, therefore, be about Rs. 16 which we think should be taken as the basis for determining a suitable depreciation allowance. We consider that in determining this allowance some special provision should be made for development. In our opinion, the best way to do so would be to relate it to the development for which provision exists in the present tax structure. In one sense, the development rebate of 25 per cent available in the present tax structure really means that over a period corresponding to the useful life of the assets concerned, the industry would be enabled to recoup 125 per cent of the initial value of the assets. Following the same principle, we consider that the allowance for depreciation and development should be equal to the average capital employed (about Rs. 16 per ton) plus 25 per cent of that capital divided by the average useful life of the complex of assets of different kinds constituting an average colliery. Buildings, water supply arrangements and such like assets have a relatively longer period of useful life. On the other hand, there are many types of machinery and equipment which have a shorter period of life. Items like earth-moving machinery and haulage equipment have a period of life even shorter. Taking all factors into account, we consider that on an average the capital investment in a coal mine might be taken to have a useful life of 12 years. On this basis, we regard that the depreciation and development allowance should be Rs. 1.70 per ton.

Brokerage And Commission

Under the Colliery Control Order, a brokerage not exceeding 37 naye paise per ton may be paid by the colliery owner to the broker. Collieries also incur some expenses on their sales organisation. The cost examination has revealed that, barring a few exceptions, hardly any colliery pays the maximum brokerage and commission. Of the 27 collieries costed, in 19 the overall expenditure under this head ranged from nil to 27 naye paise per ton. It is also significant that no brokerage or commission is permissible in direct sales to Railways which take about a-third of the total production in the country. We therefore consider that for purposes of the cost structure, an allowance of 25 naye paise would be adequate.

Recoveries

In assessing the ultimate cost, a deduction of Rs. 0.14 was made by the Cost Accounts Officers on account of the average recoveries which the collieries generally make. These pertain to receipts from sale of miscellaneous items such as slack and rejected coal, payments received from contractors, house rent recovery etc. The data in respect of the 26 costed collieries in Bengal and Bihar, however, show that this is a very variable item, which depends on certain factors peculiar to individual units. There are numerous units which do not make any "recovery" at all. We would prefer to ignore this element altogether.

To sum up, the cost structure on the basis of an O.M.S. of 0.40 would be as follows:

Items	Cost per ton Rs.
Wages	9.55
Labour amenities and Coal Mines Regulations	1.10
Salaries and administration	1.70
Stores	1.75
Power, Royalty, Cess, Collieries' own consumption of coal and other 'miscellaneous' items	1.85
Depreciation	1.70
Brokerage and Commission	0.25
	17.90

(It will be observed that no allowance has been made for stowing.)

Profit

We shall now consider what would be the fair margin of profit for an average colliery. Obviously, the price fixed should enable an average colliery working under conditions of reasonable efficiency to earn profits sufficient to permit payment of a reasonable dividend after payment of taxes. A rough and ready method which has proved generally fair and satisfactory, and which is also the simplest, is to relate profits to the capital employed or to the cost of production. Taking both these factors into account, we consider that a profit of Rs. 1.75 per ton would be reasonable. This would represent approximately 11 per cent of the capital employed (Rs. 16 per ton) and nearly 10 per cent of the cost of production. At first sight this might appear only just adequate and not sufficiently attractive for new investments in the industry. We would, however, point out that, in computing the normal cost of production, we have already included under the head 'Depreciation and Development' an element for the creation of internal resources, for development.

Revision Of Prices

It would thus be seen that the object of revision of prices should be to ensure an average sales realisation of Rs. 19.65 per ton (normal cost of Rs. 17.90 plus a profit of Rs. 1.75). It is, therefore, necessary to consider what the average sales realisation is at current prices. For this purpose, we propose to follow the pattern of production in 1957 in the Bengal-Bihar area, ignoring the production of Grade III coal for the reasons given later in the report. In 1957, production grade-wise (excluding Grade III) was as follows:

Selected A	...	24 per cent
Selected B	...	33 ,,
Grade I	...	26 ,,
Grade II	...	17 ,,

Each grade has again two different prices according to the size of coal. Run-of-mine and slack coal are in one group, while steam and rubble form another group. Between these two groups, the proportion is approximately 40 per cent and 60 per cent respectively.

The average price for each grade on this basis works out as follows:

Selected A	...	Rs. 20.46
Selected B	...	Rs. 19.46
Grade I	...	Rs. 18.58
Grade II	...	Rs. 17.45

(The price is exclusive of the increase of Rs. 0.75 given in May, 1958.)

Taking the weighted average of raisings of various grades as quoted above, the gross sales realisation comes to approximately Rs. 19.18 per ton.

The difference between the average sales realisation at existing prices and Rs. 19.65 comes to Rs. 0.47. We, therefore, recommend that the prices of all grades of coal, except Grade III, be increased uniformly by Rs. 0.50 per ton.

Prices Of Grade III Coal

We consider that Grade III coals should be treated somewhat differently from the higher grades. The production of this grade of coal (comprising Grades IIIA and IIIB) accounts for only six the per cent of total production in the Bengal-Bihar coalfields. Unlike the higher grades of coal, Grade III coal is, as a rule produced in comparatively small collieries which do not yield any higher grades. Mining is generally open cast or by shallow inclines. The cost of production is, therefore, less than for the higher grades. Capital investment is generally lower. While labour costs may not be different, expenditure on stores and other overheads is also lower. As most of the collieries are small, statutory obligations in regard to amenities are more limited in scope. For these reasons, and from our general observations, we are satisfied that there is no case for an increase in the present prices. On the other hand, we feel that it will not be possible to assess with any degree of reliability to what extent prices might be reduced. We understand from the Coal Controller that collieries producing Grade III coals do not as a rule maintain accounts of the type that would lend themselves to cost examination. We do not think, however, that on this account alone, prices which appear to us to be capable of some reduction should be left undisturbed. We feel that a better and more practical way of dealing with the situation would be to notify the present prices as ceiling prices, thereby permitting some competition which should result in some reduction. There are very good reasons why the prices of higher grade coals, particularly metallurgical coal, should be fixed prices and not ceilings. These we shall state in a subsequent chapter. We accordingly recommend that the present prices of Grade III coal in the Bengal-Bihar area should be notified as ceiling prices.

Period Of Price Fixation

It is implicit in our approach to the problem that the prices we are recommending should remain stable over a reasonable period. We would recommend a period of five years. This we regard as the minimum. Major variations requiring radical changes in the price structure are unlikely to occur. We think, however, that provision should be made for appropriate changes in the prices to the extent increases in the cost of raising coal are caused by changes in the level of wages. Under the awards now in force, the wage level is related to the All-India average consumer price index. The level of dearness allowance is regulated in accordance with this index, the basic dearness allowance being related to an index of 102. For every increase of 10 points in the index in a half year, the dearness allowance is to be increased by Rs. 4/14/- in the ensuing half year. Further, we cannot state with certainty that the present award will remain operative throughout the five-year period. For making appropriate changes in the prices of coal as a result of changes in the wage level, we consider that our assessment of the wage element in the cost of coal would provide the necessary basis.

Stowing

We have stated earlier that the cost of stowing has been excluded in our previous calculations. Provision should, however, be made for meeting this cost where it has to be incurred. Stowing is not practised in all collieries, nor it is necessary to do so. It is mainly required in thick seams, both for maximum extraction of the reserves and for avoiding dangers of collapses and consequent risks of fire. On both these considerations, the encouragement of stowing, where necessary, is regarded very important. The Coal Board, therefore, subsidises stowing to the extent of 75 per cent or 85 per cent of the stowing costs actually incurred, subject to certain maximum limits. It would not be difficult to calculate the balance of the cost which collieries have to incur themselves. Even these, however, would vary. We have, therefore, thought that it would be inappropriate to include an element for stowing in the general price of coal. At the same time, it is not only necessary to provide for the stowing cost to be met, but to do it in such a way that there will be no disinclination to adopt stowing. We, therefore, recommend that stowing costs should be met in full. Maximum limits should, of course, be prescribed to ensure economy of expenditure on stowing. The additional funds needed for this purpose will have to be found by a suitable enhancement of the stowing cess. In our view, this enhancement may be of the order of Rs. 0.25 per ton.

Special Cases

We have explained earlier that the prices we have recommended are appropriate to an 'average' colliery. The price structure is sufficiently flexible to absorb minor variations in working conditions. But, there are quite a few collieries which are handicapped by one kind or other of several adverse factors which inevitably tend to raise the cost of production. In a purely competitive economy, they might not be regarded as worth exploiting except under conditions of scarcity when prices as a whole are high. Many of these collieries, however, produce superior grades of coal which are very much in demand. In such cases, it is necessary to keep them in production. In a controlled economy it is neither necessary nor desirable to raise all prices to a level sufficient to maintain such units in production. We, therefore, consider that in such cases special assistance should be given in the form of a subsidy to enable them to sell at the prescribed controlled prices. Obviously, the subsidy cannot be determined on a general basis. It should be related to the requirements of each case and should be revised from time to time. Further, no such subsidy should be automatically granted. It must first be established that the continuance of the production from a particular colliery is necessary in the national interest. It should also be established that the working conditions are really exceptional and higher costs have to be necessarily incurred. In our opinion, the exceptional conditions which would qualify for special treatment would fall under the following heads:

(1) Gassy nature of the mine: This would involve both additional capital and revenue expenditure for ventilation arrangements, safety lamps, flame proof equipment, and the use of permitted explosives.

(2) Depth of workings: This will affect winding and pumping charges.

(3) Geological conditions like the existence of dykes and faults which necessitate extensive 'drifting' and increase the depth of underground haulage.

(4) Higher pumping charges resulting from excessive accumulation of water in the mine.

(5) Nature of seams: Their hardness, thickness, inclination, condition of roof, etc.

(6) High transportation costs from the pit-head to the rail-head.

For a consideration of such special cases, we recommend the following procedure.

The colliery concerned should apply for assistance to the Coal Board explaining in detail the special factors and their incidence. After initial examination, the Coal Board will advise the Government whether *prima facie* a case exists for special consideration. Should the Government consider that, in the circumstances prevalent at the time, the continuance of production in the colliery is necessary in the national interest, the Coal Board should be asked to conduct a detailed examination and to grant such quantum of subsidy for such period as it may deem necessary. A fund will have to be established from which the subsidy can be paid. In order to build up the fund, a cess will have to be imposed. We consider that for the present a cess of Rs. 0.25 per ton, which at the current level of production will bring in about Rs. one crore per year would be sufficient to meet the expenditure. Legislation will be necessary to implement these measures. This can be done either by a new Act or by appropriate amendments to the existing law bearing on the subject. In our view the most convenient way appears to be to amend the Coal Mines (Conservation & Safety) Act 1952, to provide for the necessary increase in the existing cess and to expand the purposes for which the cess may be used. There should also be provision to enable Government to give general or specific directions to the Coal Board from time to time.

Impact Of The Proposed Price Increase On The Economy Of The Country

If our recommendations are accepted, the increase in the price of coal to the consumer will be as follows:

(i) General increase	....	Re. 0.50
(ii) Additional cess to meet the full cost of stowing (estimated)	....	Re. 0.25
(iii) Additional cess for subsidy in special cases	....	Re. 0.25
		Re. 1.00

The most important uses of coal are the Railways, Steel Plants and Thermal Power Stations. Almost all industries use some coal. There is also a widespread public demand for coal for brick burning. Any increase in the price of coal will, therefore, have a widespread impact on the economy. We feel, however, that the increase in price to the consumer, resulting from our recommendation, will have only a negligible effect on the users. It must be remembered that except for consumers in the vicinity of the collieries, the transport cost of coal is an element nearly as important as the price of coal itself. Even in the case of industries using large amounts of coal, like steel, cement and some chemical industries, the percentage of increase in the cost of production will be less than one. Because of this we have not thought it necessary to attempt to work out such percentages in detail. It is to be remembered in this context that assurance of supplies and right conditions for the expansion of production of coal are even more important to the consumer than the price of coal itself.

"Fixed" Prices Versus "Ceiling" Prices For Coal

We shall examine in this chapter whether the present system of "fixed" prices under the Colliery Control Order should continue or whether it would be desirable to replace it by a system of "ceiling" prices.

The cycles of fall in production, which were as many

as four between 1920 and 1944, have not recurred since price control was introduced and production has steadily increased from 26 million tons in 1944 to 43.5 million tons in 1957. In an unregulated economy, the coal industry was subject to violent fluctuations and there was a cycle of over-production, cut-throat competition and uneconomic prices followed by scarcity and high prices. Control on prices, coupled with regulation of production (of coking coal) and control over distribution, has eliminated these uncertainties and brought about reasonably stable conditions.

The prices originally fixed for the lower grades undoubtedly contained an excessive margin of profit and very soon it became apparent that these grades were being under-quoted. Some important consumers then proposed that, since collieries were willing to sell coal of lower grades at prices below the statutory price, controlled prices should be converted into "ceiling" prices. The argument was based on the following grounds and related primarily to the lower grades of coal:

(i) The Colliery Control Order was introduced mainly in the interest of the consumer, and, if the industry is able to sell below the statutory price, there should be no objection to permit them to do so;

(ii) So far as lower grade coals are concerned, there is a large pithead stock and it would benefit the industry to be able to dispose of this stock;

(iii) The prices fixed for Grades IIIA and IIIB coal were much too high having regard to the ash content and calorific value and consumers should be allowed to negotiate for their purchase without being fettered by statutory prices below which no prices can be demanded or offered; and

(iv) If coal prices are made competitive, it will help towards disinflation.

After due examination of the proposal, the Government decided that the stability which the industry had achieved through "fixed" prices should not be disturbed by converting them into "ceiling" prices.

The Indian Coalfields Committee, 1946, also gave thought to this question. They were of the view that prices should be "fixed" and not allowed to sag; but they equally emphasised the function of control to ensure that consumers are not charged prices higher than the "fixed" prices. The Committee observed as follows:

"We turn now to the question of control over coal prices. We have shown in earlier chapters how unfavourably the low prices for coal which prevailed some 10 years ago, reflected on mining practice, and we feel that it is essential that the price of coal should not again be allowed to fall to uneconomic levels. This opinion is supported by the fact that we are advocating in this report that every effort should be made to increase the production of coal in order that increased industrialisation of the country, which is now planned, may become possible."

The Working Party for the coal industry endorsed this view in 1951. They observed as follows:

"We have also had the experience of the years 1943 to 1946, when there was serious shortage in coal production caused, in our opinion, by negligence of the coal industry and the failure on the part of the industry to maintain their machinery and plant in order, to develop the mines adequately and maintain a settled and contented labour force in the coalfields. In a free economy the above conditions are likely to repeat themselves and in the interest of continuing production in the country at reasonable prices and of proper exploitation of the mining resources, we feel that steps should be taken to stabilise the coal prices and adopt measures by which not only coal is made available to the consumers at an economic price, but also the producers can obtain an economic price for their produce.

The result of decontrol of price is likely to be an immediate fall in price that may render a large number of marginal mines to be uneconomical and compel them to close down. Such marginal mines should not be called inefficient units as the increased cost of production is due to the conditions prevailing underground caused by secondary mining operations or other factors beyond the control of the management. But such marginal mines cannot in the larger interest of the nation be allowed to be closed down, drowned and lost for ever because many of these mines may be impossible to be recovered except at abnormal expenditure. This is another reason why there should be a state of control on prices with a view to making it possible for the marginal mines to carry on."

In 1953 the Commodity Controls Committee which had an opportunity of examining this matter expressed the opinion that due to the rigidity of the cost structure and the fact that the industry was called upon to bear certain burdens, for example, supply of food at concessional rates, the system of "fixed" prices should continue. They observed as follows:

"We do not support the suggestion that fixed prices should be treated as ceiling prices. For, if the collieries are allowed to sell below the ceiling price, the only result would be that there would be unhealthy competition and the weaker and the marginal mines would go out of production."

We are in general agreement with the above views. We would add that the case for fixed prices rests on another factor as well viz., control over distribution. Transport is inadequate as compared to both demand and availability of coal. The entire distribution system has, therefore, been rationalised so as to economise transport to the maximum and to ensure that the better grades of coal are distributed to industries which need them rather than be wasted by industries which can use lower grades. Certain restrictions are imposed on movement from different coalfields with a view to eliminating avoidable haulage and increasing the turn-round of wagons. In other words, a kind of zonalisation of the sources of supply has been made in respect of various points of consumption to that the supply of coal of a required quality is from the nearest possible colliery. It is an essential part of this rationalisation that the consumers will have to restrict their orders to the collieries in a specified zone. While such rationalisation may be necessitated by Railway operational requirements, it would be difficult to justify it except in a context of "fixed" prices. If a consumer can secure the same quality of coal at a lower price from any zone other than the one allotted to him, rationalisation will not permit him to get that coal, and the freedom given to him under a system of "ceiling" prices would be largely illusory. It was in view of this that the Railway Board observed as far back as 1952 that decontrol of the prices of coal would be inopportune when rationalisation of coal movements is sought to be achieved to the largest possible extent.

Wages and profits also are inextricably linked with prices and all these three elements taken together are the determinants of stability in the industry. It would be unrealistic to dissociate the price element from these and to take a decision in regard to this separately. The extent to which wages have become closely inter-linked with prices will be seen from the fact that a price increase of Rs. 3 was given in 1947 to enable the industry to implement the Conciliation Board Award. Another increase of Rs. 3 was given in July, 1956 in connection with the Industrial Tribunal Award and then again a further increase of Rs. 1/8/- per ton in July, 1957, in connection with the Appellate Tribunal Award. A further increase of As. 12 per ton has been given only very recently on May 17, 1958, to enable the industry to pay enhanced dearness allowance to workers. Thus an element of as much as Rs. 8/4/- in the price structure is connected with wages to labour, and, if price control is removed, there is the danger of attempts being made to lower the level of wages which are statutorily fixed. The result may be straining of the employer-employee relations with its repercussions on production.

The case for ceiling prices rests on general considerations. The main argument is that the consumer should have a choice, as only so he can be certain of getting the right quality of coal he requires. If for any reason the quality offered is lower than what he needs, he should have the choice of paying a lower price or getting better coal. It is argued that there is no better guarantee against the supply of inferior quality than competition. All this would indicate that unless there are other valid reasons, controlled prices should be the ceilings. It would, however, be seen that in the case of the coal industry, such special conditions do exist. All the committees which have gone into this question previously have unanimously come to the conclusion that the maintenance of a system of fixed prices is necessary. After carefully considering the matter, we agree that essentially this policy should be continued. In our opinion a system of ceiling prices can be operated only in conditions where the consumer has a choice of the source of supply. The crucial question, therefore, is whether in the coal industry all consumers can be given this freedom of choice. The answer is clearly in the negative. We would emphasise in particular the necessity to confine the distribution of metallurgical coal to those who cannot do without it. It is the objective of Government's policy to achieve this state of affairs as soon as possible. For this purpose, it is not enough to prescribe that metallurgical coal shall be supplied only to the steel industry and a few others who need it. It is equally necessary to allocate the sources to individual units, taking into account not only the convenience of transport but also a fair distribution of the various qualities available. The establishment of coal washeries increase this necessity. These considerations apply, though perhaps with slightly lesser force, to other high grade coals as well. For these reasons we consider that, by and large, the system of fixed prices should continue.

We find, however, that in the case of Grade III coals, it might be practicable to give a certain freedom of choice to the consumer. In relation to demand, supplies are generally adequate. In fact, there is some over-production of lower grades and the greater part of pit-head stocks in collieries consists of these grades. We have already pointed out that the prices of Grade III coals might be able to bear some reduction. This can best be brought about by a limited competition. The only limits we have in mind will be those set by rationalisation of movement. Subject to this, the consumer will have a free choice of the sources of supply. With such a choice, he will be in a better position to obtain the right quality of coal and negotiate prices. For these reasons, we have recommended earlier that, as an experimental measure, the prices of Grade III coals in the Bengal-Bihar area be notified as the ceiling prices. After experience is gained of the practice of this method, the question of extension of this system to other areas producing low grade coals can be considered.

Outlying Fields Other Than Assam And Andhra Pradesh

In the outlying fields falling in Madhya Pradesh (inclusive of the former Vindhya Pradesh), Bombay and Orissa, 17 collieries were costed. These collieries comprised about 25 per cent of the total number of units in this region and accounted for about 47 per cent of the overall output. The collieries selected represented various levels of production, with the monthly output ranging from 2,716 tons to 40,479 tons. Some of these collieries are mechanised or partly mechanised.

Coals in the outlying fields are not yet graded, and for the purpose of price fixation under the Colliery Control Order, they have been classed under certain groups. These groups, according to the price notification No. S.R.O. 2253, dated July 8, 1957, are as follows:

	Price	
	R.O.M. and slack	Steam and rubble
First Group—16 collieries in Madhya Pradesh	19.75	20.75
Second Group—6 collieries in Hirdagarh area	21.69	22.69
Third Group—9 collieries in former Korea State	18.87	19.87
Fourth Group—11 collieries in the former Vindhya Pradesh area	17.25	18.25
Fifth Group—Korba colliery (subsequently added)	18.87	19.87
Sixth Group—18 "other collieries" in Madhya Pradesh	19.19	20.19
Seventh Group—5 collieries in Talcher (Orissa)	21.06	22.06
Eighth Group—3 "other collieries" in Orissa	20.06	21.06
Ninth Group—7 collieries in Bombay	19.75	20.75
Tenth Group—2 "other collieries" in Bombay	19.19	20.19

It will be seen that prices for the ninth group are the same as for the first, and similarly, those for the tenth and the sixth groups coincide. Before the re-organisation of States in 1956, the areas in which collieries in the ninth and tenth groups are situated formed part of the old Madhya Pradesh State.

Unlike in Bengal-Bihar, the prices thus vary from region to region. The variations arise principally from varying costs of production, these again being dependent on varying standards of workers' wages and amenities and factors of a local character. Thus, the former Korea and Rewa States had their own sanctioned scales of wages, and the higher prices for the second group are related to the higher transportation costs of the collieries in the area, these having to run tramlines of their own to carry coal from the pit-head to the rail-head. Now that wages and amenities have been statutorily standardised on an all-India scale, we consider that the time has come to apply uniformity to the prices of the collieries in all these fields.

As in the case of the Bengal-Bihar coalfields, we have considered the data collected by the Cost Accounts Officers in the light of our discussions with the representatives of the industry. We also visited some of the collieries in this area. We first considered whether we should, following the pattern adopted in the Bengal-Bihar coalfields, try to ascertain norms for each of the ten groups. We come to the conclusion that the groups had come into being more as a result of historical factors than as a result of deliberate decisions based on an assessment of economic and working conditions. Our general conclusion is that, on the whole, there is no special reason or necessity for continuing these groups as they are. Most of the considerations which apply to the Bengal-Bihar coalfields apply equally to these coalfields also. In particular, wage rates are now governed by awards which are uniformly applicable to all coalfields throughout the country, except Assam. Similarly, the coal mines rules and regulations have to be applied uniformly. Statutory requirements regarding the provision of amenities to labour are also the same throughout the country. We have, therefore, considered that, except in regard to two factors which are discussed in the following paragraphs, the principles and standards we have recommended for application in the Bengal-Bihar area should be applied to the outlying collieries as well.

These two factors generally add to the costs in this region and have to be compensated by an allowance over and above what has been provided in the cost structure worked out for Bengal-Bihar. One is the higher cost of stores. These collieries are far away from the two principal ports of the country and the indigenous centres of manufacture of colliery stores. The result is that they have to incur higher freights on all stores, whether imported from abroad or obtained internally. Secondly, the strata being particularly hard are not susceptible to pick mining, and the expenditure on explosives is, therefore, higher. We feel that these factors would justify a provision under "stores" of Rs. 0.75 per ton higher than in Bengal-Bihar.

The other element which calls for recognition is the incidence of royalty. The average rate of royalty in this field is higher. In the Bengal-Bihar fields, leases in the permanently settled areas were obtained at rates of royalty much lower than the 5 per cent of the F. O. R. price prescribed under the Mineral Concession Rules, 1949. In Bengal, the average rate is Re. 0.28 per ton, and in Bihar, Re. 0.22 per ton. In the outlying fields, however, the prescribed rate is five per cent on the sale value of coal and in a few cases it is even higher. It is thus correct to say that for every increase of Re. one in coal prices, five nP. are taken away in the form of royalty. Taking all these factors into consideration, we would provide for Re. 0·70 per ton under this head, in addition to the figure adopted for Bengal-Bihar.

Even after making adjustments as indicated above,

there may still be a few exceptional cases, as in Bengal-Bihar, which would require special treatment. These may arise out of factors like difficult geological conditions or unfavourably long distances from rail-heads. For example, in some of the units in Madhya Pradesh, the seams are traversed by the frequent faults, folds and dykes which reduce the coal-bearing areas and increase the raising costs. We recommend that such units should be dealt with in the manner stated earlier.

The normal cost structure for this area would thus be

Cost structure for Bengal-Bihar	Rs. 17.90
Extra under "Stores"	Re. 0.75
Extra under "power, royalty, cess etc."	Re. 0.70
Total	Rs. 19.35

Adding the same element of profit, viz., Rs. 1.75 per ton, the revised price structure for this area should yield an average sales realisation of Rs. 21.10 per ton.

Grading

We have to consider in this context the question of grading these coals, which has been specially referred to us by the Government. While coals of Bengal-Bihar were graded in 1944, following the introduction of price control, coals of the outlying fields still remain ungraded. There has been a persistent demand from consumers served by these fields that the coals should be graded. The case for grading is generally based on several considerations. For example, it bas been urged that it is obviously illogical that coals of varying qualities and fuel values (although produced in the same coalfield) should bear the same price. Again, consumers should be assured of some consistency in the supplies they receive. The Railways have complained that the coals supplied to them from the Korea and Rewa fields and the Pench Valley field show very wide variations in ash content from day-to-day. This impairs the efficiency of their locomtoives. Grading is also a means of giving an incentive and fillip for improving the quality of production and despatches. It is necessary to improve the quality of coal despatched in order to encourage consumers to draw their requirements from the outlying fields, and thereby reduce the present excessive dependence on supplies from Bengal-Bihar. There will be not only a saving in the actual haulage effort and expenditure, but consumers will be assured of a more regular supply of coal. Thus, a system of grading will serve two purposes: it will improve the quality of despatches and will save transport. In the result, both coal distribution and consumers will be benefited.

We consider that, for the reasons stated, an attempt should be made to introduce grading in this area. Two Sub-Committees of the Coal Advisory Committee have studied this question and drawn up a scheme of grading for these coals. We have studied the reports of the two Sub-Committees and the recommendation thereon by the Coal Controller.

The following basis for grading has been suggested :

		Ash plus moisture content
Selected Grade	...	Not exceeding 19 per cent
Grade I	...	Exceeding 19 per cent but not exceeding 24 per cent
Grade II	...	Exceeding 24 per cent but not exceeding 28 per cent
Grade III	...	Exceeding 28 per cent but not exceeding 35 per cent

Barring only a few exceptions, these coals are all high volatile non-coking coals and the grading indicated above accords with the present grading of high volatile non-coking coals in Bengal-Bihar. The only difference is that only one Selected Grade has been suggested in place of two in Bengal-Bihar) and Grade III is a new grade which is distinct from Grades III-A and III-B of Bengal-Bihar. We consider this to be a suitable and satisfactory basis for grading and recommend that it may be adopted. Taking the production figures for 1957, we find that the production is likely to be shared between these four grades approximately in the following proportion :

Selected Grade	...	4 per cent
Grade I	...	28 ,,
Grade II	...	49 ,,
Grade III	...	19 ,,

In suggesting suitable prices for these different grades, we have tried to keep the price differential between one grade and another sufficiently wide to make grading worthwhile and workable in practice. After careful consideration, we recommend the following grade-wise prices; these will apply to all the collieries in these fields, replacing the groupwise prices mentioned above:

	R.O.M. and Stack	Steam and Rubble	Average
	Rs.	Rs.	Rs.
Selected Grade	21.85	22.85	22.45
Grade I	21.13	22.10	21.70
Grade II	20.35	21.35	20.95
Grade III	19.75	20.75	20.35

On the basis of the *inter se* proportion of the various grades, these prices will result in an average sales realisation of Rs. 21.11 per ton. These prices could be exclusive of the temporary increase recently. Sanctioned in compensation for the higher dearness allowance prescribed in the Award of the Appellate Tribunal. For the reasons already explained earlier, the prices we are recommending should operate as "fixed" prices and not as ceilings.

CLASS IV STAFF PROMOTION COMMITTEE, 1957—REPORT

New Delhi, Ministry of Railways, 1958. 68p.

Chairman : Shri G.D. Tapase.
Members : Shri B.B. Mathur; Shri C.V. Cunningham; Shri A.P. Sharma; Miss Maniben Kara; Shri S.S. Jagota; Shri J.N. Roy; Shri B.N. Datar.
Secretary : Shri P.M. Narasimhan.

APPOINTMENT

While presenting the Statement of Revenue and Expenditure in March, 1957, the Railway Minister stated in the Lok Sabha that in the matter of promotion of Class IV employees to higher grades, the present rules were rather restrictive and in certain categories there were no chances of promotion at all. He expressed his desire to appoint a Committee to examine this and allied issues and the Class IV Staff Promotion Committee was constituted under the Ministry of Railways vide their Press Note, dated May 4, 1957.

TERMS OF REFERENCE

(i) To examine the existing channels of promotion for class IV staff and to determine new channels of promotion preferably for uniform application over all Indian Railways.

(ii) To determine the conditions of eligibility of staff for promotion.

(iii) To prescribe the manner in which employees should be selected for promotion.

(iv) To prescribe the training, if any, that should be given to selected employees before being promoted and the additional training facilities over and above those existing at present that should be provided.

CONTENTS

Introduction; Classification of and Recruitment to Railway Services, The Problem—General Recommendations; Miscellaneous Recommendations; Promotion to Higher Grades; Minimum Qualifications for Recruitment Engineering Department; Mechanical Engineering & Transportation (Power) Department; Transportation (Traffic) and Commercial Department; Medical Department; Stores Department; Signal and Telecommunication Department; Electrical Department; Training; Miscellaneous; Summary of Recommendations; Supplementary Note by Miss Kara and Shri Datar; Appendices A to F.

RECOMMENDATIONS

The cadres in the various departments should be fixed in such a manner that each employee can reasonably expect to get the first promotion and that too even before he has put in 12 to 13 years of service. To achieve this objective, we recommend (i) opening up new channels of promotion where they do not exist; (ii) grouping of posts to avoid dead-ends; (iii) stopping direct recruitment in higher grades of Class IV and to a certain extent in Class III; and (iv) upgrading of posts to make up the balance.

For the categories of staff whom officiating allowance is admissible without regard to the minimum time limit, leave reserve should be provided in the same grade.

The designation and duties of Class IV staff should be standardised as far as possible to ensure uniformity on all railways.

No direct recruitment should be made to higher grades in Class IV except,

(a) In certain categories where the men do not offer from Class IV, and

(b) When they cannot be trained in time in cases of expansion and/or embarking on new projects.

The quota for promotion from Class IV to Class III should be raised from 10 per cent to 25 per cent for categories for which no regular avenue of promotion exists.

There should be a still higher ratio of 50 per cent for train clerks, transhipment clerks and ticket collectors.

The Promotions to Class III in the ministerial and outdoor cadres should be made on the basis of a departmental competitive examination to be held annually railway-wise which will be open to Class IV railway employees who have put in five years' aggregate service.

Class IV staff who appear and pass in the matriculation examination after entry in service should be eligible for promotion to Class III service provided they have put in five years' service or are permanent.

There should be a quota of 10 per cent for promotion from Cabinmen to the lowest grade of Cabin Assistant Station Masters.

The existing orders regarding literacy for purpose of recruitment to Class IV should continue. For the recruits belonging to scheduled castes and scheduled tribes, this condition should be relaxed where mere literacy is required.

In the case of those illiterate railway employees already in service or those who may have to be recruited in future, the administration should make arrangements to impart literacy with the cooperation of the trade unions and social/voluntary agencies.

Engineering Department—Permanent Way Side

Posts of permanent way mistries, gangmates and keymen should be filled only by promotion.

25 per cent of posts of assistant permanent way inspectors should be filled by promotion from the cadre of mistries.

The gang beats should be so adjusted that there are not more than 12 to 14 gangmen in any gang; where the gang strength is less, no change should be made.

The cadre strength of permanent way mistries should be increased.

Trollymen, gatemen and chowkidars should be merged with gangmen and serve as gangmen by rotation subject to the condition that they are medically fit.

10 per cent of the annual intake of gangmen should be encouraged to be transferred to the Mechanical Engineering and Transportation (Power) and Commercial Departments as well as the works side of the Engineering Department.

About 31 per cent to 32 per cent of posts of gangmen should be upgraded; likewise, about five per cent of the unskilled posts of the works side should be upgraded.

Mechanical Engineering And Transportation (Power) Department

30 per cent posts of chargeman 'C' grade and 50 per cent of posts of skilled artisans should be filled by promotion.

The cadre of skilled and semi-skilled posts should be decided on the basis of actual requirements. The posts of basic tradesmen should not count against skilled posts.

In the case of semi-skilled categories for which there are no allied skilled categories, the semi-skilled workmen should be transferred as basic tradesmen to provide an avenue of promotion.

Jamadars should be permitted to go as semi-skilled.

The chances of promotion for Khalasis should be equalised.

Unskilled staff other than in the workshops, should uniformly be designated as Khalasis, the functionary qualification being only incidental; they should seek promotion either in Loco Maintenance or Carriage and Wagon Maintenance sides.

Running Staff

Promotion to the grade of fireman 'A' grade should be made to the extent of 25 per cent of vacancies from the grade of fireman 'B'.

Air-conditioned coach attendants should be placed in the scale of Rs. 40-60.

Transportation And Commercial Department

It is recommended that the staff in grade Rs. 30-35 in the Transportation and Commercial Departments should be combined together for the purposes of promotion.

Categories like box porters, call boys, running room bearers, etc., should also be eligible for promotion as pointsmen, coupling porters, etc.

The balance of posts required should be upgraded.

66-2/3 per cent of posts of guards, grade 'C' should be filled by promotion.

Medical Department—Hospital Staff

All hospital staff should be pooled and be eligible for promotion as dressers and laboratory attendants.

Hospital staff in the lowest grade of Rs.30-35 should be upgraded so that there are in all 50 per cent of posts in the higher grade.

Conservancy Staff

In departments like Carriage and Wagon, Transportation etc., where the sweepers cadre is comparatively small, they should be pooled with khalasis, porters, etc., in the unskilled grade and allowed the same avenues of promotion. The resultant vacancies of sweepers in these departments should be filled by drawing from the conservancy cadre of the Medical/Engineering Department.

A uniform yardstick should be laid down for determining the number of jamadars on a liberal basis.

The balance of posts required to make up 50 per cent of the number of posts of sweepers should be upgraded to higher grade in accordance with the general principle.

Stores Department

Posts in the scale Rs. 55-85 as well as posts in the higher grades in class IV and semi-skilled posts should be filled only by promotion.

After taking into account these posts, the balance required to make up 50 per cent of posts in the scale Rs. 30-35 should be upgraded.

Signal And Telecommunication Department

Recruitment to the lowest grade in this Department should be made from persons with at least middle school standard.

Electrical Department

Recruitment to the lowest grade in this Department should be made from persons with at least fifth standard.

Training

Training should be imparted for various categories to equip them for promotion.

The Railway Board should take all steps to secure expeditious implementation of the accepted recommendations.

COMPANIES ACT AMENDMENT COMMITTEE, 1957—REPORT

New Delhi, Department of Company Law Administration, 1957. 222p.+iip.

Chairman : Shri A.V. Visvanatha Sastri.
Members : Shri C.C. Shah; Shri G. Basu; Shri J.D.K. Brown; Shri K.R.P. Aiyangar.
Secretary : Shri F.N. Sanyal.

APPOINTMENT

The Companies Act Amendment Committee was constituted under the Ministry of Finance (Department of Company Law Administration) vide their Order, dated May 15, 1957.

TERMS OF REFERENCE

Having regard to the aims and objects of the Companies Act, 1956, and in the light of its working—

(i) To consider what amendments in the Act are necessary:

(a) To overcome such practical difficulties in its working as may have been encountered since it came into force;

(b) To remove such drafting defects and obscurities as may have interfered with the working of the Act;

(c) To ensure the better fulfilment of the purposes underlying the Act;

(ii) To consider what changes in the form or structure of the Act, if any, are necessary or desirable to simplify it.

CONTENTS

Introductory; Amendments recommended by the Committee; Nidhis and Benefit Societies; Acknowledgement Annexure (Accounts); Appendices I and II.

RECOMMENDATIONS

Sections of the Companies Act, 1956, Affected	Suggestion made by the Committee
(1)	(2)
2	Amendment of Sub-Sec. (3)(c)(i).
2	Amendment of Sub-Secs. (3)(c)(ii) and (4)(b)(ii).
2	Amendment of Sub-Sec. (7).
2 & 8	Amendment of Sub-Sec. (9) of Sec. 2 and of Sec. 8.
2 & 10	Amendment of Sub-Sec.(ii) of Sec. 2 and of Sec. 10.
2	Amendment of Sub-Sec. (17).
2	Insertion of a new Sub-Sec. as Sub-Sec. (18A).
2	Amendment of Sub-Sec. (26).
2	Amendment of definition in Sub-Sec. (45) so as to accord with policy.
2	Amendment of Sub-Sec. (33) r/w Ss.549 and 643.
2	Amendment of Sub-Sec. (36).
3	Insertion of a proviso to Sub-Sec. (1) (iv).
4	Suggestion for amendment of Section in line with policy.
4	Amendment of Sub-Secs. (1)(b) and (2) (c).
6	Redraft of Section.
7 & 538	Amendment of Sec. 7 and Sub-Sec. (3) of Sec. 538.
13	Amendment of Sub-Sec. (1)(c).
17	Amendment of Sub-Sec. (4).
18	Amendment of Sub-Secs. (1) and (4).
19	Amendment of Sub-Sec. (2).
23	Insertion of a new Sub-Sec. as Sub-Sec. (4).
25	Amendment of Sub-Secs. (6) and (8).
28 & 29	Substitution of a new Sec. for the Sections.
31	Addition of a proviso to Sub-Sec. (1).
31	Insertion of new Sub-Sec. (3) and renumbering of the existing Sub-Sec. (3) as Sub-Sec. (4).
38	Addition of a few words at the end of the proviso to Section.
39	Amendment of Sub-Sec. (1).
41	Amendment of Sub-Sec. (2).
49	Amendment of Sub-Secs. (1), (2), (5) (a) and (6).
60	Amendment of Sub-Sec. (3).
73	Amendment of Sub-Sec. (1)
76	Amendment of Sub-Sec. (2).
80	Amendment of Section.
81	Amendment of Sub-Sec. (1).
84	Addition of a Sub-Section.
88	Amendment of Section.
89	Amendment of Sub-Sec. (1).

(1)	(2)
89	Amendment of Section to provide for Company or Shareholder to apply to Court.
106	Amendment of Section.
108	Provision to be made for allowing transfers on execution of indemnity bond.
111	Amendment of Sub-Secs. (2), (4) and (5).
111	Insertion of two new Sub-Secs. as Sub-Secs. (6) and (10) and renumbering of existing Sub-Secs. (6) to (8) as (7) to (9) in the Section.
111	Further amendment of the Section.
113	Amendment of Sub-Sec. (1).
125	Amendment of Sub-Sec. (1) empowering Registrars to condone delays in applying for registration of a charge.
138 & 139	Substitution of a new Section for the Sections.
142	Deletion of Sub-Sec. (1) (b).
145	Amendment of Section.
147	Amendment of Sub-Sec. (1)(c). Further amendment of Sub-Sec. (1)(c).
149	Omission of Sub-Sec. (8).
154	Amendment of Section.
155	Amendment of Sub-Secs. (1) and (3) and the addition of a new Sub-Section as Sub-Section (5).
156	Amendment of Section.
159	Amendment of Sub-Secs. (1) and (2).
159	Further amendment of Sub-Sec. (1).
161	Amendment of Sub-Sec. (2)(c).
163	Addition of a proviso to Sub-Sec. (1). Amendment of Sub-Secs. (3)(b) and (4).
165	Amendment of Sub-Sec. (4).
166	Amendment of Sub-Sec. (1) and addition of two provisos to Sub-Sec. (2) *inter-alia* empowering the Central Government to grant relaxations of the requirements of Sub-Sec. (2).
169	Amendment of Sub-Sec. (4).
170	Amendment of Sub-Sec. (1).
171 & 190	Amendment of Sec. 171(1) and Sec. 190.
172	Amendment of Sub-Sec. (2)(i) by the addition of a proviso thereto.
176	Amendment of Sub-Sec. (3).
187	Amendment of Sub-Sec. (2).
190	Amendment of Sub-Sec. (1).
192	Amendment of Sub-Secs. (1), (2) and (4)(g).
193	Amendment of Sub-Sec. (1).
194	Redraft of the Section.
196	Amendment of Sub-Sec. (2).
197	Amendment of Sub-Sec. (1).
198	Amendment of Heading of Section.
198	Amendment of Sub-Sec. (1).
198	Deletion of Sub-Sec. (3) (b).
198	Addition of a proviso to Sub-Sec. (1).
198	Insertion of an Explanation in Sub-Sec. (1).
198	Amendment of Sub-Sec. (2).
198	Redraft of Sub-Sec. (3)(a).
198	Amendment of Sub-Sec. (4).
309	Redrafts of Sub-Secs. (2) and (3).
309	Insertion of a new Sub-Sec. as Sub-Sec. (5A).
309	Amendment of Sub-Sec. (8).
310	Amendment of the Section.
204	Power for Govt. to relax provisions of Sub-Sec. (4).
204	Amendment of Sub-Secs. (1) and (5).
205	Redraft of Section.
207	Insertion of a new Sub-Sec. as Sub-Sec. (1) in the Section.
207	Amendment of Sub-Sec. (2).
209	Amendment of Sub-Sec. (1) and the addition of a proviso thereto.
209	Insertion of a new Sub-Sec. as Sub-Sec. (3A).
209	Amendment of proviso to Sub-Sec. (5).
209	Amendment of Sub-Sec. (6).
210	Amendment of Sub-Sec. (4) and of the proviso to Sub-Sec. (5).
211	Amendment of Sub-Sec. (5)(iii).
211	Amendment of the provisos to Sub-Secs. (1), (2) and (7).
212	Amendment of Sub-Sec. (2)(a).
212	Amendment of proviso to Sub-Sec. (9).
217	Amendment of Sub-Sec. (1)(b).
217	Addition of two clauses of clauses (d) and (e) to Sub-Sec. (1).
219	Amendment of Sub-Sec. (1).
220	Amendment of Sub-Sec. (1)(a).
220	Deletion of Sub-Sec. (1)(b).
220	Amendment of Sub-Sec. (2).
224	Amendment of Sub-Secs. (1) and (2).
226	Amendment of Sub-Sec. (2).
227	Redraft of Sub-Sec. (5) recommended.
228	Amendment to Sub-Secs. (1) and (2).
238	Insertion of a new Sub-Sec. as Sub-Sec. (3).

(1)	(2)
234	Amendment of Sub-Secs. (1), (2), (3) and (4).
239	Amendment of Sub-Secs. (1)(c) and (2).
240	Amendment of Sub-Secs. (1) and (3).
240	Penalty to be imposed for disobedience of Court's Order.
245	Amendment of Sub-Secs. (2) and (3).
250	Amendment of Section.
252	Amendment of Section.
255	Amendment of Sub-Sec. (1).
256 & 257	Amendment of Sections.
257	Further amendment of Sec. 257(1).
261	Amendment of Sub-Sec. (5).
263A	Insertion of a new Section as Sec. 263A.
264	Redraft of Section.
269	Redraft of Section.
271	Amendment of Section.
267 & 274	Amendment of Sec. 267(c) and Sec. 274(1)(d).
283	Amendment of Sub-Sec. (1), Sub-Sec. (1)(e) and (1)(h).
283	Insertion of new Clause as Clause (1) in Sub-Sec. (1).
285	Addition of a proviso to Section.
287	Amendment of proviso to Sub-Sec. (2).
292	Amendment of the existing proviso to Sub-Sec. (1).
292	Insertion of a further proviso to Sub-Sec. (1).
292	Insertion of Explanations in Sub-Sec. (1).
292	Amendment of Sub-Sec. (2).
293	Amendment of Sub-Sec. (1)(c).
293	Amendment of Sub-Sec. (1)(b).
293	Insertion of a further Explanation to Sub-Sec. (1).
293	Insertion of a further proviso to Sub-Sec. (1) defining "temporary loans".
293	Redraft of Sub-Sec. (5).
293	Insertion of a new Sub-Sec. as Sub-Sec. (6) in the Section.
293	Amendment of Sub-Sec. (1)(e).
294	Insertion of new provisions in the Section.
294	Amendment of Sub-Secs. (1) and (2).
296	Redraft of Section.
297	Insertion of a proviso to Sub-Sec. (1).
297	Amendment of Sub-Sec. (2).
297	Further amendment of Sub-Sec. (2).
300	Amendment of Sub-Sec. (2)(d).
301	Redraft of Sub-Secs. (1) to (3).
302	Amendment of Sub-Sec. (7).
303	Amendment of Form No. 32 prescribed under the General Rules.
303	Addition of a proviso to Sub-Sec. (2).
305	Suggestions for Amendments of Section. Other amendments to the Section.
307	Addition of a new Sub-Section to Section.
310 & 311	Substitution of a new Section in the place of the two sections.
313	Amendment of Sub-Sec. (2).
314	Redraft of Sub-Sec. (1) with the addition of an 'Explanation'.
314	Insertion of a new Sub-Section as Sub-Section (2).
314	Existing Sub-Sec. (2) with amendments to be renumbered Sub-Sec. (3).
314	Existing Sub-Sec. (3) with amendments to be renumbered Sub-Sec. (5).
314	Insertion of a new Sub-Section as Sub-Sec. (4).
329	Amendment of the Section.
332	Amendment of Sub-Sec. (4)(b).
340	Amendment of Sub-Sec. (1).
342	Amendment of Sub-Sec. (2) and redrafts of Sub-Secs. (3) to (5).
343	Redraft of the Section.
346	Amendment of Sub-Sec. (1).
348	Addition of a new Sub-Sec. to the Section as Sub-Sec. (2), the existing Section being numbered Sub-Sec. (1) with some amendments.
349	Amendment of Sub-Sec. (4)(1). Insertion of a new clause as Clause (o) to Sub-Sec.(4).
349	Amendment of Sub-Sec. (4) (j).
350	Redraft of the Substantive part of Section.
354	Amendment of the Section.
356	Amendment of Sub-Sec. (2).
358	Amendment of Sub-Sec. (2).
360	Amendment of Sub-Sec. (1). Amendment of Sub-Sec. (4). Insertion of an explanation in the Section.
361	Redraft of the Section.
362A	Insertion of a new Section as Section 362A.
363	Amendment of the Section,
369	Amendment of Sub-Sec. (1)(a). Insertion of an explanation in Sub-Sec. (2).
370	Amendment of Sub-Sec. (2)(b). Amend-

(1)	(2)
	ment of Sub-Sec. (3). Insertion of a new Clause as Clause (iii) to Explanation to Sub-Sec. (1). Amendment of Clause (ii) to Explanation to Sub-Section (1). Insertion of a further new Clause as Clause (iv) to Explanation to Sub-Sec. (1). Addition of a Sub-Clause to Sub-Sec. (2). Insertion of a new Section as Section 370A.
372	Amendment of Sub-Section (9).
377	Amendment of Sub-Section (1).
384 & 386	Amendment of Sec. 384 and Sub-Sec. (5) of Section 386.
388A	Insertion of a new Sec. as Sec. 388A.
390	Amendment of Clause (a).
391	Amendment of Sub-Sec. (2).
408	Amendment of Sub-Secs. (1) and (2). Insertion of a new Sub-Sec. as Sub-Sec. (4).
416	Amendment of Sub-Sec. (3)(a).
417	Amendment of Sub-Sec. (1).
418	Amendment of Sub-Sec. (1) and deletion of the proviso thereto. Amendment of Sub-Sec. (4).
426	Amendment of Sub-Sec. (1)(g).
439	Amendment of Sub-Sec. (5).
440 r/w 521	Deletion of Section 521.
446	Amendment of the Section.
449	Amendment of the Section so as to confer power on the Court to appoint person other than the Official Liquidator.
454	Amendment of the Section to vest power in the Court to punish defaults under the Section.
455	Amendment of the Section so as to confer power on the Court to extend time for submission of report by Official Liquidator.
456	Insertion of a new Sub-Sec. in the Section.
457	Amendment of the Section.
463	Amendment of Sub-Sec. (1).
465	Amendment of the Section requiring Courts to give directions as to constitution of Committee of Inspection.
468	Insertion of a provision in the Section similar to Sec. 36 of the Presidency Towns Insolvency Act.

(1)	(2)
468	Further amendment of the Section.
469	Amendment of Sub-Sec. (1).
477	Provisions to be made in the Section on the lines of Sec. 36(4) and (5) of the Presidency Towns Insolvency Act.
481	Amendment of Sub-Sec. (1).
490 r/w, 515	Amendment of Sections 490(1)(b) and 515.
502	Amendment of Sub-Sec. (2) with a view to empower the Court to fix remuneration of Liquidator appointed by it in a voluntary winding up.
512	Amendment of Sub-Sec. (1)(a).
513	Amendment of Sub-Sec. (1).
515	Amendment of Sub-Sec. (3).
522 & 524	Amendment of the Sections.
524	Amendment of the Section.
529	Addition of a Sub-Section to the Section.
531A	Insertion of a new Section as Section 531A.
535	Amendment of Sub-Sec. (4).
537	Amendment of Sub-Sec. (2).
549 r/w, Sec. 2(33) and 643	Amendment of Sub-Sec. (1) of Sec. 549.
555	Amendment of Sub-Sec. (9).
582	Amendment of Clause (b).
595	Amendment of Clause (c).
610	Amendment of Sub-Sections (1)(b) and (4).
611	Insertion of a further proviso to the Section.
614	Insertion of a new Sub-Section as Sub-Sec. (3) of the Section, the existing Sub-Section (3) being renumbered as Sub-Sec. (4).
616	Amendment of Clause (c).
617	Amendment of the Section.
624A	Insertion of a new Section as Section 624A.
626	Redraft of the Section.
629A	Insertion of a new Section as Section 629A to provide generally for penalties for defaults.
643	Amendments of Sub-Secs. (1)(a), (1)(b) and (1)(b)(iv).
645, 647(2), 648, 656 & 658	Suggestion for the deletion of these sections.
647	Further amendment of the Section.

FOODGRAINS ENQUIRY COMMITTEE, 1957—REPORT

New Delhi, Ministry of Food and Agriculture (Department of Food), 1957. 191p. Charts & Maps.

Chairman : Shri Asoka Mehta.

Members : Shri M. Thirumala Rao; Shri S.F.B. Tyabji; Raja Surendra Singh of Nalagarh; Shri Venkatesh Narayan Tivary; Shri B.K. Madan.

Member Secretary : Dr. S.R. Sen.

APPOINTMENT

In the course of a statement made in the Lok Sabha on May, 14, 1957, on the food situation the Minister for Food and Agriculture announced: "The Government have come to the conclusion that the whole question requires thorough investigation and have decided to set up a high-powered Committee to investigate fully into the causes of rise in prices despite higher production and to suggest immediately and from time to time remedial measures which would prevent speculative hoarding and arrest undue rise in prices." It was in accordance with this announcement that the present Committee was constituted under the Government of India Resolution No. 158 (1)/57-PY.1, dated June 24, 1957.

TERMS OF REFERENCE

(i) To review the present food situation and to examine the causes of the rising trend of food prices since about the middle of 1955.

(ii) To assess the likely trend in demand and availability of foodgrains over the next few years, taking into account—

(a) The steps taken and those proposed to be taken under the Second Five-Year Plan by the Central and the State Governments to increase food production;

(b) The impact of growing development expenditure, increase in population and urbanisation, on the demand for marketable surpluses;

(c) Availability of foodgrains from abroad in relation to requirements and in the light of the foreign exchange position; and

(iii) To make recommendations to ensure a level of prices which would provide the necessary incentive to the producer with due regard to the interest of the consumer and the maintenance of a reasonable cost structure in the economy.

Subsequently on September 19, 1957, the Minister requested the Committee also to examine the problem of the areas where the food problem had been one of recurring nature and pay more attention to the food problem of the Eastern U.P.

CONTENTS

Introductory; Review of Food Situation: Trends in Prices since 1950-51; Review of Food Policy in Recent Years; Analysis of Factors in Rise in Prices; Prospects of the Future; Price Stabilisation; Foodgrains Stabilisation Organisation; Short Period Measures; Production and Marketed Surplus; Problem of Scarcity Areas; Conclusion; Appendices from I to VI; Charts from I to X; Map of Uttar Pradesh.

RECOMMENDATIONS

Rise In Prices

The embargo on exports of foodgrains was lifted for the first time after a decade. Government also undertook limited price support operations early in 1955. All these helped to create a general feeling that the bottom was perhaps reached and prices could not fall further.

The rise in prices in India was not an isolated phenomenon. During 1956, there was a rise in price roughly of the order of seven to nine per cent in most of the Asian countries, five to six per cent in U.S.A. and four to five per cent, in European countries. However, the greater rise of prices in India than in world prices during 1956 followed a phase of substantial price decline in 1954 and the first part of 1955 when world prices experienced a small rise. The rise in Indian prices during 1956, therefore, could be regarded as partly compensating the earlier fall in prices.

We have noted the divergence in movements of prices among a large number of important centres during the downward phase of prices in 1954-55. Similar disparities in movement of prices from one centre to another may be observed during the upward phase of prices in the last two years.

These data illustrate clearly the heterogeneous character of and lack of mobility in the Indian economy and also underline the pitfalls of coming to a general conclusion on the basis of average alone. For instance, although all-India averages do not show an appreciable rise in cereals' prices as compared to the base year 1952-53, they do not register the difficulties, say, of the people of Ujjain who have to pay 180 per cent more than in 1955 and 27.3 per cent more than in 1953 for

Mid-Year Prices

	June 1953	June 1955	June 1957	Percentage increase (+) or decrease(—) in 1957 over 1953	1955
	(a) Rice				
1. All-India Index No. (Base : 1952-53=100)	109	77	106	— 2.8	+ 37.6
2. Patna (Bihar)	Rs. 24.00	13.00	23.00	— 4.2	+ 76.9
3. Nowgarh (U.P.)	Rs. 28.00	14.62	21.75	— 22.4	+ 48.7
4. Nandgarh (Mysore)	Rs. 20.39	11.50	20.00	— 2.0	+ 73.9
5. Balurghat (West Bengal)	Rs. 21.50	14.75	22.50	+ 4.6	+ 52.5
6. Kozhikode (Kerala)	Rs. 33.00	13.50	20.55	— 37.8	+ 52.2
7. Imphal (Manipur)	Rs. 14.75	5.00	7.25	— 50.9	+ 45.0
8. Kakinada (Andhra Pradesh)	Rs. 25.25	13.50	20.00	— 20.8	+ 48.1
9. Kalyan (Bombay)	Rs. 26.08	14.00	21.00	— 19.5	+ 50.0
10. Cuttack (Orissa)	Rs. 12.00	17.87	16.75	+ 39.6	— 6.3
11. Calcutta City	Rs. 16.75	17.50	22.50	+ 34.3	+ 28.5
12. Madras City	Rs. 21.37	13.37	19.20	— 10.2	+ 43.6
	(b) Wheat				
1. All India Index No.	95	62	88	— 7.4	+ 41.6
2. Jabalpur (M.P.)	Rs. 20.62	12.50	17.75	— 13.9	+ 42.0
3. Kanpur (U.P.)	Rs. 17.75	9.50	12.81	+ 27.8	+ 34.8
4. Kotah (Rajasthan)	Rs. 14.44	9.00	14.62	+ 1.2	+ 62.4
5. Abohar (Punjab)	Rs. 13.62	11.12	13.50	— 1.9	+ 21.4
6. Dhanduka (Bombay)	Rs. 19.42	11.00	18.50	— 4.8	+ 68.2
7. Rewa (M.P.)	Rs. 20.00	10.00	15.31	— 23.5	+ 53.1
8. Delhi City	Rs. 15.62	10.00	15.00	— 4.0	+ 50.0
9. Bombay City	Rs. 19.42	12.87	19.25	— 0.9	+ 49.5
	(c) Jowar				
1. All India Index No.	109	57	127	+ 16.5	+122.8
2. Amravati (Bombay)	Rs. 11.50	6.00	13.25	+ 15.2	+120.8
3. Ujjain (M.P.)	Rs. 11.00	5.00	14.00*	+ 15.2	+180.0
4. Nandyal (Andhra Pradesh)	Rs. 13.50	5.75	16.00	+ 18.5	+178.2
5. Jhansi (U.P.)	Rs. 13.25	5.31	13.56	+ 2.3	+155.4

* Relates to July 5, 1957.

their Jowar, or of Calcutta who have to pay 28.5 per cent more than in 1955 and 34.3 per cent more than in 1953 for their rice or of Rewa where wheat prices first fell by 50 per cent and then again rose by 50 per cent all within four years. All India average prices do not record the considerable regional disparities in prices, such as are indicated by the fact that in June, 1957, price of rice at Patna was Rs. 23.00 per maund as against Rs. 16.75 at cuttack and Rs. 7.25 at Imphal or of wheat was Rs. 19.25 in Bombay as against Rs. 12.81 in Kanpur. In fact, it was such sharp variations in prices over space as well as the changes over time during the last quinquennium which created many of the stresses and strains in the economy.

We recognise that under our terms of reference we are concerned primarily with the problem of prices in the country as a whole. Regional disparities indicate the development of scarcity pockets caused by vicissitudes of weather or difficulties of transport in a vast country like ours. In an inflationary situation, however, price rise in any area tends to be sticky and the rise in prices in pockets of scarcity tends to spread and thus contributes to a general rise in prices.

Food Distribution

Government's food policy in recent years may be reviewed broadly in relation to its own two main aspects: (i) Short-term and (ii) Long-term. The former consisted chiefly of programmes of food distribution and the latter of food production. They are the regulatory and developmental aspects of policy respectively. However, the regulatory parts of policy are not necessarily all short-term nor are the developmental aspects wholly long-term. Price and selective credit policies are ancillary to both aspects and have recently assumed some importance, the latter having been operated by the Reserve Bank primarily as a restrictive instrument.

Between 1951 and 1957, Government's policy regarding food distribution has undergone a change successively from complete control to complete decontrol and back to partial control.

The existing system of control was held to be adversely affecting production and, even more, the volume of marketed surplus.

Rise in Prices

The causes of the rise in prices in the last two-and-a-half years may be broadly classified as (a) general factors and (b) specific factors. Under general factors may be considered the broad forces—monetary and non-monetary—operating on the price level as a whole including prices of food as well as non-food articles. The specific factors would relate to foodgrains or cereals in particular and may be further classified as (i) factors on the demand side, and (ii) factors on the supply side.

There is no index of velocity of circulation available in respect of the bulk of money-supply which takes the form of currency circulation. But in regard to bank money a reliable indicator of the rate of monetary turnover is to be found in the figures of total bank debits in relation to demand deposits which are now published by the Reserve Bank. These is no basis for assuming that the velocity of currency circulation corresponds to the turnover of bank money.

To some extent, an increased volume of money supply is also required to sustain the same level of prices owing to the steadily expanding boundaries of the money economy or the gradual extension of what is termed the monetised sector of the economy and the resulting increase in the demand for money. This has been placed at about one per cent per annum, but may well be significantly larger owing to the large expansion, e.g., in the sector of bank financed transactions. This is, at any rate, likely to be a somewhat variable or discontinuous factor.

On the whole, a large part of the rise in the general level of prices may be ascribed to a general increase in demand resulting from the increase in investment expenditure on public and private account accompanied by deficit-financing and credit expansion, however, have also been associated with a certain increase in production activity. The increase in production has intended to moderate and absorb the inflationary impact of investment expenditure to a considerable extent, and the rise in prices would have been greater but for the increase in production.

Inflationary trends in India during this period, therefore, were by no means an isolated phenomenon. The effect of the general inflationary forces, however, will be different on different commodities, depending upon their relative demand and supply situations and effectiveness of any controls in operation. It is to a consideration of the specific factors on the demand and supply sides respectively for foodgrains that we now turn.

The system of rationing had converted many who formerly used to live on coarse grains to eating rice and wheat. When rationing was abolished a certain increase in the consumption of rice and wheat probably tended to retain, though there was some shift back to coarse grains. For instance, we were told by the representative of the Tea Association in Assam that the tea garden labourers no longer accept the coarse rice which they used to eat in the old days. Similarly, we were told in Orissa that the mining labour now-a-days insists on having better quality rice. In other areas, we understood that people who used to live an roots like tapioca or sweet potatoes are now transferring their demand to millets or coarse rice and people who used to take millets formerly are now gradually shifting over to rice or wheat. Such analysis of statistical evidence as we have been able to make does not, however, indicate that changes in food habits are of substantial magnitude over the short period.

The per adult availability of food in India amounts only to 2,200 calories as against an estimated 3,000 calories that are required by minimum nutritional standards. Even this average is misleading because there are large sections of the population who hardly get 1,200 to 1,500 calories per adult per diem. With even a small increase in income the first demand of the under-fed people is naturally for more foodgrains. An increase in consumption by half the population by one oz. more of cereals per capita per day would put up the totol requirement by over two million tons.

The supply factor has to be considered in relation not merely to over-all production and net imports of all foodgrains taken together but also to marketed surplus of different types and varieties of foodgrains in different periods of the marketing season and in different areas. It is, therefore, necessary to examine carefully factors affecting production, marketed surplus as also imports.

That the actual increase in production during the First Plan period, i.e., in 1955-56 over 1949-50 was of the order of 13.7 per cent or roughly 7.3 million tons of foodgrains as indicated by production indices and not 20.8 per cent as indicated by the unadjusted figures of production. The increase of 7.3 million tons during the First Plan period does not appear to compare unfavourably with the target of 7.6 million tons. It should, however, be recalled that the latter was essentially a target of additional production-potential and not of actual additional production. In practice, the additional production-potential created during the First Plan period amounted to 5.16 million tons only.

As regards rice, prices at first showed a declining trend in 1956-57 as crop prospects were good but tended to firm up in the earlier months of 1957 as it became clear that the market arrivals were slower than usual and that stocks with the Government were also low.

That if the production increases and prices fall marketed surplus will increase more than proportionately, owing to the tendency to de-hoarding initiated thereby. Similarly, if the production falls and prices rise, marketed surplus will decrease more than proportionately, owing to the stimulus to greater hoarding imparted thereby. But a situation may arise, with prices and production moving in the same direction, when marketed surplus may behave quite erratically.

In an inflationary situation, however, the role of expectations increases and the price tends to settle at a level higher than what would be warranted by purely technical demand and supply factors.

To the extent that corrective action is taken in time, scare and panicky rise in prices can be prevented. On the other hand, to the extent that there is delay in taking action in these areas even a small shortage may lead to a disproportionate rise in prices and consequent hoarding and fall in market supplies especially when general conditions are inflationary.

In a developing economy like ours there is always the risk that disparities of various types will tend to get aggravated unless special care is taken to even them out. Prices may rise faster at times due to a temporary imbalance of supply and demand. With a quickening pace of development, these disparities are likely to become greater. It should, therefore, be an object of Government policy to keep a careful watch over likely development of such disparities and take timely action to minimise their harmful effects.

In retrospect, the total dismantling of controls appears to have been a hasty step, particularly inasmuch as Government failed to take the opportunity to build up buffer stocks as prices fell.

A basic weakness was the absence of a well defined and coordinated policy of price stabilisation and of a machinery to implement it. Nor was there within the administration a unit charged with the specific responsibility of studying the variations of prices in their ramifications and considering by regions and sectors of the economy measures for their comparative stabilisation. The general complacency about the food situation made it difficult to realise that the bumper crop of 1953-54 came at the crest of a periodical cycle of production, and that output might not be sustained at that level. If the excess production could have been husbanded for lean years to come, the cultivators would have been assured that while under economic planning they should not expect very high prices, they would at the same time be insured against unduly low prices. An opportunity to fill the buffers with indigenous stock and thereby to ensure a measure of stability with growth under planning was, however, missed.

The necessary liaison between the Food Ministry and the Reserve Bank, particularly on credit facilities to the traders, developed slowly. Better understanding between the Food Ministry and the Port Authorities could have enabled proper phasing of imports of foodgrains and reduced loss of foreign exchange in demurrage.

We have also found that through most of the period that rice was being sold, price of rice was rising and not falling as alleged. That the stock of rice needed to be sold cannot be gain-said. The question was asked by certain sections of the trade why fresh purchases were not made to replenish the stocks. This is explained by the fact that the reserve stocks with Government were higher than 1.5 million tons of foodgrains and by the decision against engaging in buffer-stocks operations. A somewhat inconsistent statement has been made by the witnesses who have criticised Government's disposal of rice by simultaneously charging the Government with initiating and accentuating rise in food prices with their open market purchases of relatively small quantities of rice for Kashmir and the Defence Forces. The contention that for these purchases prices higher than the ten ruling market prices were paid is difficult to sustain because the rice purchased was of better quality and the price differential covered quality differences.

Many of the shortcomings of policy or execution were, in our view, due to the strong popular preference for total decontrol of foodgrains, a preference that was not unshared in the highest levels of the administration. There appears, however, to have been a misconception about the policy of Shri Kidwai. It was during his regime that the Ministry of Food and Agriculture issued the Foodgrains (Licensing and Procurement) Order in 1952 and prepared the scheme of buffer-stock operations in 1954. Shri Kidwai was obviously not thinking in terms of having complete decontrol and leaving a vacuum behind. He had an alternative method of regulation which may perhaps be described as "regulated decontrol". Shri Kidwai's policy was, we believe, a natural development of the policy of "strategic controls" that his predecessor, Shri K.M. Munshi, had enunciated on the eve of his retirement. And it was the same policy that Shri Kidwai's successor has sought to continue.

Insufficiency of knowledge regarding marketed surplus, which has not yet been remedied, added to the difficulties of evolving an effective food policy. In a developing economy it is not the production of food alone but marketed surplus that is of real importance.

Prospects For The Future

While assessing the effect of population growth on the demand for foodgrains, it is necessary to consider the growth in the rural and the urban populations separately.

We may expect the urban demand for foodgrains to increase by 26.3 per cent and the rural demand by 6.8 per cent which will mean about 10 per cent increase in the total demand for foodgrains. This is the extent of increase in the demand for foodgrains that we may expect only as a result of the increase in population that may take place during the Second Plan period.

We propose to consider the effect of increase in per capita income in the two areas separately. A break up of the total national product into rural and urban sectors is not available. However, the Second Plan gives a break up by main industrial sectors. In order to obtain a break up of the total product into the rural and urban sectors, we propose to treat the entire product in the sectors (i) agriculture and allied pursuits and (ii) small enterprises plus one-fourth of the product in the sectors (a) commerce, transport and communications and (b) professions and services as belonging to the rural sector.

During the Second Plan period we estimate an increase of 1.2 per cent in the per capita expenditure on cereals in the urban areas and an increase of 5.5 per cent in the per capita expenditure on cereals in the rural areas on account of an increase in the per capita total consumer expenditure. When these are combined, they give an estimated increase of 4.7 per cent in the per capita total consumer expenditure on cereals during the Second Plan period on account of an estimated increase in the per capita total consumer expenditure.

However, in the absence of relevant data, it seems reasonable to assume that similar increase in the expenditure on pulses may be expected. We shall, therefore, assume that the estimated increase of 4.7 per cent refers to the per capita expenditure not only on cereals but on all foodgrains.

In the absence of the relevant data we have no basis to judge to what extent the estimated increases in the per capita consumer expenditure on foodgrains due to increases in the per capita consumer expenditure on foodgrains due to increases in the per capita total consumer expenditure may be on account of a possible shift from inferior to superior grains. In order to indicate the magnitude of a possible shift of this nature, we shall proceed on the assumption that rice, wheat and pulses are superior grains while all other cereals are inferior grains. On this basis, the inferior grains form about 30 per cent of the existing supplies of all foodgrains. We shall further assume that the average price of the superior grains is about 50 per cent higher than the average price of the inferior grains. On this assumption, a 4.7 per cent increase in the consumer expenditure on foodgrains may cause an increase between five and six per cent in the per capita consumption of superior grains and anything up to four per cent in that of inferior grains. The increase in the per capita consumption of all foodgrains will be between four and 4.5 per cent.

During the Second Plan period, we expect the consumer demand for foodgrains to increase by about 10 per cent on account of an estimated increase in the total population. This when combined with an increase from four to 4.5 per cent in the per capita consumption of foodgrains on account of an expected increase in the per capita total consumer expenditure gives us an expected increase between 14.4 and 15.0 per cent in the consumer demand for foodgrains during the Second Plan period.

We may say that our estimates of expected increase in the consumer demand for foodgrains may be extended to the total demand for foodgrains. As such, we may expect that during the Second Plan period, the total demand for foodgrains may increase by 14.4 to 15.0 per cent.

The gross availability of foodgrains in 1955-56 was a little over 67 million tons. On this basis the total demand for 1960-61 may be roughly estimated to be 77 million tons excluding demand for variations in stocks. If it is felt that in the absence of data on stocks with farmers and traders it will not be proper to take the figure for only one year and that it will be more realistic to take the average for three years, then the average gross availability during the base period will work out to a little over 69 million tons and the estimate of demand in 1960-61 will approximate 79 million tons.

We have assumed above that the population will increase at a higher rate, namely, two per cent per annum in future. But we could also assume that it will continue to increase at the rate of one-and-a-half per cent computed by the Registrar General. We have assumed that the distribution of income will be according to a particular pattern but the future pattern of distribution could be also assumed to be somewhat different. Similarly, we have got different sets of figures regarding income elasticity of demand for different trends of prices. We do not propose to go into these details in this report. We should like, however, to mention that most of these estimates of demand range between 75 and 80 million tons. We may also note that if money incomes and prices tend to go up sharply during this period, the propensity to consume and propensity to stock will also tend to go up. In that event the demand for foodgrains may conceivably exceed even the upper limit of 80 million tons mentioned above. For our present purpose, however, we shall assume as a working basis that the demand for foodgrains in 1960-61 will be of the order of 79 million tons (which is also obtained even on the basis of one-and-a-half per cent rate of population growth with certain alternative assumptions regarding income, etc.) if prices continue at the present levels. If there is any deflationary trend, demand may be somewhat lower. While if there is any inflationary trend it may be somewhat higher. The breakdown of 79 million tons between rural and urban areas works out roughly to 66 and 13 million tons respectively and between superior grains, namely, rice, wheat and pulses and inferior grains, namely, millets, works out to 56 and 23 million tons respectively.

Supply of foodgrains has two aspects, one of overall supply and the other of supply in the market. Supply at both these levels is affected by the same set of factors, namely, production, imports and exports and changes in stocks or inventories. The first two of these factors are the most important not only in the short run but also in the long run. The third factor may be relatively not so important for an analysis extending over a number of years although its importance over seasons within a year is undoubtedly great. Analysis of the prospect of supply of foodgrains over the next few years will, therefore, be attempted in terms of supply both at the overall level as well as at the market level and in relation mainly to the expected behaviour of production and imports and exports.

We feel that the revised targets of additional foodgrains production are no longer realistic, and future supply has to be estimated in terms of an achievement in the neighbourhood of 60 per cent of the targets laid down. This means that as against a target of additional production-potential of 15.5 million tons of foodgrains by 1961, the actual achievement is likely to be of the order of 10 million tons. On this basis, the level of output of foodgrains in 1960-61 is expected to be in the neighbourhood of 75 million tons.

If the behaviour of production in the last few years is to be taken as a guide, 74 per cent of the revised target is expected to be achieved. This estimate of the overall production needs, however, further examination in respect of its acreage and yield components.

It seems that the rate of growth of wheat and millets production taken together will in future be perhaps lower than has been the case in the past. The same is not, however, true for rice, because the growth of production in the past has been brought about very largely through increases in the yield of expansion of acreage through double dropping on irrigated lands.

Three significant conclusions emerge. First, intensification of cultivation has been proceeding and is likely to proceed at a much higher pace (about double) in the case of rice than in the case of either wheat or other cereals. Secondly, if the present trend is to continue, the phenomenal increase in wheat output observed during the last eight years is likely to slow down considerably unless a drive for more intensive cultivation of wheat is launched. Thirdly, the case of other cereals is somewhat anomalous, though, as a whole, the picture here is a little better than in the case of wheat. In spite of decrease in acreage since 1953-54, increase in yield per acre is keeping up production proportionately higher.

Besides, for any country to make its food economy dependent heavily on the fluctuations of the world trade in other agricultural commodities is a policy fraught with grave dangers. It would, therefore, be wise to continue the present policy of emphasising increase in production of both foodgrains and cash crops.

The world availability of foodgrains has been such that we have come to depend more on wheat than on rice, and this position seems to have come to stay, more or less. Incidentally, this is crucial from the point of view of future food policy.

On present estimate, the import requirements for 1958 would appear to exceed 30 lakh tons. Once, however, a comfortable 'buffer stock' has been built up, the import requirements might be stabilised at a somewhat lower level. The need for imports would still remain. What is, therefore, needed is to ensure adequate supplies from the major exporting countries on a long-term basis.

Price Stabilisation

We think that full control should be resorted to only in cases of emergency like war or famine or extreme inflationary pressures. We do not visualise it as a permanent feature of our developing economy.

The type of controls that we envisage would be largely of a flexible and indirect character, designed to be adapted to changing situations and such as would not require an army of officials exercising restrictive powers for their implementation.

In a period of inflation even a small seasonal rise tends to stick and to accentuate the general tendency for prices to rise. Purchase of stocks in the harvest season and selling the same in the market at a reasonable price in the lean season is an effective way of preventing undue seasonal rise in prices. In a country like India where there is considerable transport difficulty and markets are imperfect it is only natural that there should be regional differences in price. To the extent that these regional variations are caused by transport difficulties they cannot be eliminated until the basic difficulty is overcome. But if semi-monopolistic elements in the trade exploit the regional variations taking advantage of the imperfections of the market, there is strong case for the State to intervene with a view to keeping the prices within reasonable limits. If in a period of inflation or deflation prices in particular regions are allowed to go up or down sharply they generate similar movements in other regions. Hence, the prevention of regional variations becoming abnormally large is important in times of inflation or deflation. The long-term remedy for such disparities is no doubt the improvement of transport facilities and general economic development. But, in the short period considerable relief to the situation can be afforded by the State buying the surplus in surplus areas and meeting the deficit in areas where shortages exist. Finally, there may be an abnormally sharp rise or fall in prices of some commodities compared to that of others with the result that the cost of production of the commodities and the cost of living of the cultivators are affected very differently from what happens in the other sectors. Such distortions of the price structure also create considerable strains and stresses in the economy and if allowed to persist tend to change the consumption and production pattern in such a manner as may adversely affect the whole economy and also upset the allocation of resources envisaged in the Plan. It is important to prevent such sectoral imbalances also as far as practicable.

The main characteristic of a rational system of price stabilisation which seeks to avoid both complete laissez and rigid control should be on the one hand to allow the trade to function on a competitive basis within certain broad limits and on the other to regulate it by suitable countervailing action, over-all as well as selective, by public authority.

In fact according as the circumstances change the nature of the action to be taken as well as the types and combinations of measures must also change correspondingly. There may be some measures which require to be taken on a long-term basis while others may be of a relatively short-term character, being liable to be altered according to the situation as prices show an abnormal rise or fall.

Indeed, monetary and credit policy has to a considerable extent to be adapted to the economic climate created by the general state of fiscal policy or the budgetary operations of Government. If these operations themselves give rise to considerable inflationary tendencies, while the ability of monetary and credit policy by itself to restrain such tendencies is limited, its general tone is indicated by the extent of such tendencies. In this context, while a general cheap or dear money policy may produce a certain effect on over-all price trends, it can be usefully supplemented by a policy of selective credit control for preventing abnormal fluctuations in prices of particular essential commodities like foodgrains, as has been shown by recent experience. Selective credit control has, therefore, to be continued to be used as a flexible instrument of some proved efficacy to curb any undue speculative tendencies. Export and import quotas and duties can also be manipulated with a view to regulating the prices of important commodities having a bearing on food prices which are exported or imported on a significant scale. Excise taxes and subsidies are other fiscal tools available to influence the consumption and production pattern of various commodities in the desired direction.

While the general climate would thus be set by appropriate fiscal, monetary and credit policies, it is obvious that in the general economic and monetary situation that is likely to prevail for some time these have to be supplemented by certain specific action directed to controlling foodgrains and also in respect of related commodities if comparative stabilisation of their prices is desired. These measures are, however, to be used judiciously and in different combinations under different circumstances.

In our view, the formal announcement and effective enforcement of minimum prices throughout the country should be necessary in conditions when there may be a possibility of prices falling sharply. The cultivator does require the assurance that prices will not be allowed to fall below economic levels to maintain his incentive to invest in the improvement of his farm and, thereby, sustain the basis of progressive agriculture. This assurance will, in our view, be available if the general framework of our recommendations is accepted and it is decided to set up an organisation charged with the function of operating in the market and equipped with resources to do so and to counteract through its operations the amplitude of fluctuations which tend to occur. Over and above this, we believe that assurance of the kind that Government recently extended through its Press Note on June 14, 1957, could have a limited use in reinforcing the confidence in Government's policy in this sphere. If, however, certain areas are cordoned off for facilitating certain operations, the announcement of a minimum price would become essential.

We consider that to ensure a level of prices which would provide the necessary incentive to the producer with due regard to the interest of the consumer and the maintenance of reasonable cost structure in the country, as stated in our terms of reference, it is essential to set up such an organisation and machinery for coordinated formulation of measures to be taken from time to time to this end, and implementation of the action proposed by way of market operations within the range of prices and subject to the conditions determined.

We recommend, therefore, firstly, the setting up of a high-powered authority for the formulation of the policy for price stabilisation in general and determining the programme for enforcing it from time to time and, secondly, the establishment of a suitable organisation to execute that part of the policy and programme framed by this authority as may relate specifically to purchase and sale operations in the field of foodgrains. The policy-making body may be called the "Price Stabilisation Board" composed of representatives of the Ministries of Food & Agriculture, Finance, Commerce and Industry and Railways, Planning Commission and the Reserve Bank of India, with a Chairman of the status of Secretary to the Government of India. Food, no doubt, forms the core of our price structure, but prices of competing crops like cotton or oilseeds and of industrial products like cloth, fertilisers, iron and steel etc., are all very important from the point of view of an effective price policy for the country and have to bear a reasonable relationship to food prices. It is only a high-level authority as proposed above, which is properly integrated into the machinery of decisions within Government on economic questions, that will be able to deal effectively with the problem of price stabilisation. The Board should examine not only the food prices as such, but also the prices of all related consumer and producer goods, e.g., cloth, oilcake, fertilisers, iron and steel, etc., study the various margins charged at different stages before sale to the cultivator and make appropriate suggestions. It should be possible for a vigilant Price Stabilisation Board to help in maintaining a reasonably stable price structure by ensuring better coordination of the various measures bearing on prices of foodgrains and other related commodities. As regards the executive organisation for dealing specifically with foodgrains, we think that it would be desirable to set up under the Ministry of Food and Agriculture a separate body called the "Foodgrains Stabilisation Organisation".

It will also be desirable to set up a body of non-officials called Central Food Advisory Council to assist the Food Ministry and the Price Stabilisation Board. The Council should be composed of representatives of agriculture, trade, industry, workers, consumers, banks, cooperatives, leading political parties and economists. It will meet as often as necessary but at least twice a year in connection with the kharif and rabi seasons. It will consider the various aspects of the food problem, long-term as well as short-term. Its views will be placed before Government and before the Price Stabilisation Board to help the latter in the formulation of price policies and programmes.

We have notified that at present considerable misunderstanding is being caused in the public mind by the concentration of attention on the wholesale price index alone. The Division should be able in due course to supply a corrective to this situation by presenting a much wider series of indices relating to prices, incomes and employment in a coordinated and easily intelligible form to the general public from time to time.

Foodgrains Stabilisation Organisation

We consider, however, that for the specific functions of open market purchase and sale, procurement of foodgrains and maintenance of stocks, it will be desirable to have a separate organisation called Foodgrains Stabilisation Organisation under the Ministry.

This Organisation will not only take a part of the work that the Directorate General of Food is handling now but will also operate as a trader in the foodgrains market, with branches or agencies of its own in all important mandis, particularly in surplus areas and centres of distributive trade. This Organisation may either be a department of the Ministry or a statutory corporation or a limited company. Each of these alternatives has its advantages and disadvantages. Considerable experience of all these three forms of organisation is available to Government who will be in the best position to consider what the right organisation for such a purpose should be. We have not been able to estimate how much working capital will be required by this Organisation. It should, not, however, be more than what was required by the Food Administration during the days of control. We feel that in the beginning this Organisation should be able to manage with a capital of about Rs. 100 crores, which may subsequently be increased as its business expands.

In our view, buffer stock operations can be a most effective instrument for the stabilisation of the prices of foodgrains. The main idea of such operations is simple. Whenever prices tend to fall, even if such a fall is not general but is confined to a particular locality, this Organisation should step in and start purchasing at reasonable prices. Similarly, when prices tend to rise, this Organisation should sell at reasonable prices. The Organisation will, from time to time, have to fix limits of prices at which it would buy or sell, within the range of prices for its operations which will be fixed by Government on the advice of the proposed Price Stabilisation Board.

It should also be able to purchase fairly large quantities from depressed pockets where competition from the trade is usually weak. The Organisation will normally be buying in the harvest season and in the depressed pockets and selling in the lean season either of the same year in which it buys or in a subsequent year when there is a short crop. Therefore, ordinarily, there should be no risk of loss for such an organisation, especially over a long period of, say, five years. Even if there is some loss, it would be a worthwhile premium to pay for insurance against instability.

We feel that step by step conditions should be created so that in course of the next three or four years the Foodgrains Stabilisation Organisation may be in a position to control a substantial proportion of the wholesale trade in the country.

We would like to emphasise here that until there is social control over the wholesale trade we shall not be in a position to bring about stabilisation of foodgrains prices. Our policy should, therefore, be that of progressive and planned socialisation of the wholesale trade in foodgrains.

Our proposal that the Foodgrains Stabilisation Organisation should have a dominant share in the foodgrains trade in the country should not be regarded as something which is extraordinary.

Although we believe that the Foodgrains Stabilisation Organisation will be able to control a large part of the marketable surplus during normal years, in the immediate future so long as inflationary trends continue and food shortage persists, open market purchases may push up prices so that the Organisation may find it necessary to stop its operations. Therefore, it will be necessary to undertake some form of compulsory procurement for replenishing the reserve stocks and maintaining supplies to vulnerable sections of the population at reasonable prices.

It will be necessary to resort to some form of compulsory procurement to ensure that at least six to seven lakh tons of rice is procured from the surplus areas in the country.

There are several ways in which compulsory procurement may be enforced. The simplest way would perhaps be to cordon off certain areas and make the Foodgrains Stabilisation Organisation the sole buyer in these areas for the purpose of export. States of Orissa and Punjab should remain cordoned off and the export of surplus rice from these States should be controlled by the Foodgrains Stabilisation Organisation. Although Orissa is a surplus State, the pressure from Calcutta, Jamshedpur and other industrial areas of West Bengal and Bihar with high purchasing power often denudes it of its stocks, raises prices abnormally and creates distress for the local population. Cordoning off of Orissa is, therefore, a necessity. So far as Punjab is concerned, rice is being produced mainly as a cash crop for export and the production has gone up considerably in recent years. Hence, cordoning off of the whole of that State for the purpose of procuring rice should not create any special difficulty. We believe that in a normal year, it should be possible for the Organisation to procure about three to four lakh tons of rice in Orissa and Punjab. The delta districts of Andhra Pradesh and the Chhatisgarh area of Madhya Pradesh are also generally surplus in rice. It should also be possible to export to States not included in the present rice zones—the continuance of which we recommend later—three to four lakh tons from these two areas without upsetting the local price structure. On the other hand, if these States are cordoned off as a whole or an attempt is made to take away from these areas larger quantities, the present zonal balance may be upset causing considerable difficulties. One way, therefore, may be that every year only two to three districts in these areas which are likely to yield the requisite surplus may be cordoned off, and the entire surplus mopped up. Alternatively, the whole area may be cordoned off and out of the surplus procured certain quantities, say, two lakh tons from each area may be taken away from the State and the balance sold back in other areas of the State itself. We are in favour of this alternative. Under this alternative the districts of Tanjore and Tinnevely in Madras would also be cordoned off for procurement of rice, which should then be released to the deficit areas within the southern rice zone itself. If it is decided to impose any restriction for the purpose of procurement in a few districts of a State, it would be essential not only to ensure that the prices ruling in the cordoned districts are reasonable and are not substantially lower than those obtaining at least in the harvest time in neighbouring districts but also to provide special Grow More Food assistance to the farmers of the cordoned districts to obviate any sense of grievance that the rest of the country is exploiting them unduly.

If it is felt that in any area cordoning is not practicable for some reason, one or more of the following systems of procurement may be tried according to local conditions and the relative proportion of the quantity to be procured to the quantity produced. One alternative may be a levy on all rice and flour mills as also on all private traders making purchases in major primary mandis. This method will work only if the quantity to be procured is relatively small compared to the total production and the levy price approximates to the market price at the harvest time. Another alternative is a fixed levy of foodgrains for every acre of land which a farmer possesses above a fixed limit, say 10 standard acres. Another method may be to collect the price of fertilizers and repayment of loans given by Government in the form of grains, the prices at which grains have to be evaluated being fixed previously. This method, we are afraid, may not be feasible until State-owned or cooperative warehouses are set up in sufficient numbers in the areas concerned. Credit given by cooperative societies may be also linked with the marketing of grains and all grains collected by cooperative societies purchased by the Foodgrains Stabilisation Organisation at an agreed price. This method also, we feel, may not be feasible in the areas concerned until the cooperative movement has made very considerable headway. It has been suggested to us by many witnesses that land revenue and irrigation charges should be collected in grain. This proposal has some merits as well as several demerits and on a balance of considerations we do not recommend it. The main attraction of this proposal is that it will enable fairly large quantities to be procured without creating undue resentment. On the other hand, since most of the payments will be small, the cost of collection will ordinarily be very large. The total cropped area in the country is over 360 million acres and the incidence of land revenue per acre of cropped area is only Rs. 2.24 on the average. Also the dangers of corrupt practices by petty officials will be large.

It has been suggested to us by a number of witnesses that maximum prices should be announced every season when price trends are inflationary and Government should take powers to requisition stocks whenever prices go beyond these levels. At the same time, for allaying fears of the farmers that prices may be depressed as a result of zonal cordons and other Government action, minimum prices should also be fixed at which Government should be prepared to buy whatever quantity is offered. These prices should be varied from season to season in the light of various factors, e.g., trends of costs, incomes, price parities. We agree that various relevant factors, e.g., cost of production of the concerned foodgrains and competing crops, cost of living of the agriculturist and industrial labour relative movements in prices of food crops and cash crops, and in incomes of agricultural and non-agricultural workers, may be examined. In the light of all this information and in consultation with the Central Food Advisory Council the range of prices within which the Foodgrains Stabilisation Organisation may carry on its operations may be determined every year and from time to time by the Price Stabilisation Board. It is however, important that no single formula should be announced or relied upon. While a number of formulae may be taken into account, we recognise that the final decision would have to be taken by the Board on a somewhat adhoc basis, particularly owing to the importance of prospective price trends in any assessment of the reasonable prices which might guide operations of the Organisation, for no formula can satisfactorily reflect the prospective position. It has, indeed, been the experience of most countries that no formula can fully cover all contingencies. On the other hand, adoption of a particular formula makes the price policies so rigid that it becomes very difficult to introduce any flexibility even when broader considerations require it. Besides, the prices at which the Foodgrains Stabilisation Organisation should be prepared to buy whatever is offered to it and which it should announce at suitable times the administration should have powers to fix the prices at which the State should be prepared to requisition stocks boonded by traders or big producers. At present, there is a provision that the Government can requisition any stock by paying the average price for the previous three months. We understand that this provision is creating considerable difficulties in practice. We consider that powers should be obtained to give statutory recognition for the purpose of requisitioning at the prices that may be fixed by the Price Stabilisation Board as suggested above. For the current year we feel that prices for coarse paddy may be fixed at between Rs. 9.25 per maund and Rs. 11 per maund and of rice between Rs. 15 and Rs. 17 per maund for fair average quality which will be considered generally reasonable all over the country. Similarly, prices for wheat between Rs. 13 per maund and Rs. 15 per maund for fair average quality would be considered such as would give a reasonable incentive to the producer and be fair to the consumer and would also pay due regard to the cost-structure in the country.

We would like to reiterate that the prices at which the Foodgrains Stabilisation Organisation would be prepared to buy should be economic prices and should be kept reasonably stable to give confidence to the producers.

One of the key measures that will be necessary for making the system proposed above really successful will be the licensing of all dealers in foodgrains. We feel that an order on the lines of the Foodgrains (Procurement and Licensing) Order, 1952, should be issued and strictly enforced. All the traders and big producers in the country who may deal in and stock more than 100 maunds of foodgrains should be required to take a licence. One of the terms of the licence should be that traders will submit fortnightly returns of their stocks, sales and purchases to the prescribed authorities. A further clause may also be added to the licence to the effect that the traders will stop purchase or sale in the district concerned whenever Government may order them to do so and that they will also confine the sales or despatches to particular areas if Government so direct them. We feel that these powers may not have to be exercised ordinarily but it will nevertheless be useful to have these powers.

One of the most important tasks of the Foodgrains Stabilisation Organisation would be to build up and maintain adequate reserve stocks as distinct from any buffer stocks that it may build up from operational considerations. It was the experience in 1955 that even a stock of 1.5 million tons was not sufficient when a real crisis began. Stocks were depleted rapidly as soon as prices started rising but it was not found practicable to replenish them. We are aware that the Government have taken a decision sometime back to build up a reserve stock of two million tons, half of wheat and half of rice, but we are nevertheless emphasising the point in view of the fact that even now the stocks are less than 50 per cent of the target. It is very important that the Government should not only maintain a reserve stock of at least two million tons as decided by them but should arrange for adequate replenishments as soon as they tend to fall below that figure. One advantage of these reserve stocks being maintained by the Foodgrains Stabilisation Organisation would be not only to facilitate storage but also to ensure timely turn-over. Reserve stocks as distinct from buffer stocks should be maintained at certain special points. In our view, these points in order of preference should be (a) ports and metropolitan areas, (b) chronically deficit areas, (c) areas generally affected by floods and drought and (d) important centres from the point of view of transport, e.g., Mokameh, Manmad, Nagpur, Kanpur. Adequate arrangements should also be made for revolving this stock and this turn-over operation should be undertaken in a manner such that it may not unduly upset the market. Turn-over operations of the reserve stocks will also be facilitated by the maintenance of a large number of fair price and modified ration shops that have already been set up in the country.

All the imported grain comes into the hands of the authorities and the entire amount is available for distribution. On the other hand, procurement can only be a fraction of the production. Although during inflation procurement becomes unavoidable, it gives a spurt to the price level which does not get fully corrected when the procured quantity is released.

We should, therefore, be prepared for importing a substantial amount of foodgrains during the next few years. It is important that we should make every effort to enter into a long-term arrangement with Burma. India's share in the total exports of rice from Burma stood at 41 per cent in 1954; this share declined to 17 per cent in 1955 and to 15 per cent in 1956 but increased to 25 per cent in 1957. As rice is the main source of foreign exchange for Burma, the Government of Burma appointed a Special Committee in June, 1956 to make recommendations for planned development of rice acreage during the four years 1956-57 to 1959-60. The Government of Burma have planned for an increase in the acreage under paddy by 12 lakh acres in this four-year period. They are also planning an increase of exports of rice by two lakh tons per year for the next few years. Already, the exports of Burma have gone up from 14.6 lakh tons in 1954 to 20 lakh tons in 1957, an increase of 5.4 lakh tons in four years or an average of 1.3 lakh tons a year. With the prospect of Burmese exports being stepped up by two lakh tons per year in the next few years, it should be possible for Burma to export upto eight lakh tons of rice per year to India. At any rate, it is possible to obtain from Burma large quantities of rice than are provided for in the existing five-year agreement. The question as to what form any long-term agreement with Burma should take may be examined by Government.

We feel that it would be to our advantage to take fairly large quantities of wheat and some quantities of rice from the U.S.A. under P.L. 480. For imports under such concessional terms not only relieve us of our immediate foreign exchange commitments but also help us to build up a rupee fund which can be utilised for development purposes. One of the conditions of P.L. 480 is that we should continue to import our normal requirements at ordinary commercial terms. This means that we shall have to continue to import about 5.5 lakh tons of wheat from Australia, Canada, U.S.A. and other countries under normal commercial terms. We feel that all this import of rice and wheat supplemented by some quantities of coarse grains will continue to be necessary if our development outlay is maintained at the level proposed in the Second Plan.

With long-term agreements concluded with U.S.A. and Burma, India would be able to assure herself of certain quantities of foodgrains from abroad in the years to come. That assured supply of foodgrains from abroad would enable the formulation of a stable and long-term food policy needs no emphasis. In fact, assurance of continued imports of certain quantities of foodgrains will constitute the very basis of a successful food policy for some years to come.

Short Period Measures

We propose now to refer to some short-term measures relating to control of distribution and trading in foodgrains as well as certain miscellaneous matters including food administration.

An important method for distribution of Government supplies which provides for a measure of relief to consumers through assuring them the benefit of Government procurement operations at reasonable rates is by selling foodgrains through fair-price shops or modified ration shops or through institutions like cooperative societies or employers' organisations. Consumers' groups should be encouraged to form cooperative shops and large employers of labour should also be persuaded to run their own fair price shops. Where such shops cannot be set up, Government should set up their own shops. In some areas it may be more convenient to entrust these shops to the trade. But in such cases there should be a strict system of supervision to check corruption and a system of identity cards should invariably be introduced.

Sales from fair-price shops, etc., should be normally made on a "no profit no loss" basis so far as Government is concerned. This in itself should prove to be of benefit to a large group of people. In view of its relatively easy supply position, wheat may be issued freely upto a full quota of 12 oz. per adult per day from these shops, since every one will be free to supplement from the open market. The issue of rice, which is in short supply, may ordinarily be not more than eight oz. per adult per day in South India, six oz. per adult per day in East India and four oz. per adult per day in other areas. Moreover, this amount should be issued only if the purchaser agrees to take the balance of 12 oz. in the shape of wheat. This will not only help in economising rice but also in popularising wheat. In allocating supplies to different areas care should be taken to keep in view local preference e.g., parboiled rice should be supplied to Calcutta, Punjab wheat should be supplied to Delhi and so on as far as practicable as otherwise the pressure on the market for the supply of the preferred variety increases unduly and thus gives rise to a price spiral. Besides, superior and inferior qualities of grain need not all be sold at the same price. There should be no objection, for this purpose, to charging higher prices for the more preferred varieties even compared to the "no profit no loss" price utilising the proceeds for reducing the pool price on the less preferred variety. It has been represented to us that if the same price is charged for more preferred and less preferred varieties then the pressure on the fair-price shops tends to be very elastic. It goes up suddenly when the more preferred variety is issued and goes down suddenly when the less preferred variety is supplied. Similarly, there seems to be a good case for making a small difference in price between the harvest season and the lean season. The grain becomes more dry in the lean season when the consumers are also used to paying a higher price. If the sale price from the fair-price shops is raised to a small extent in the lean season that would only follow the normal seasonal pattern and would have a healthy effect on demand. Besides the "no profit no loss" basis may be applied in terms of even a longer period than what is taken as the basis of the present calculations. On the whole, some of the above suggestions amount to making the sale operations of the fair price shops less rigid and more responsive to market considerations than they are at present. As such they are calculated to reduce the malpractices and corruption observed in their working, to which we refer presently.

We feel that a practicable solution may be to give to each fair-price or modified ration shop a limited number of what may be called "relief quota cards". The issue of these cards may be limited to special categories of persons e.g., expectant and nursing mothers, sick and convalescents, teen age children of families below a certain per capita income limit. The distribution of these cards may be looked after by a responsible Government officer in consultation with a small representative committee of citizens of the locality. A rule should be made that in no case should subsidised grain be sold except on the basis of "relief quota cards". At present whatever subsidy Government is able to provide seems to get dissipated over a large number of recipients each of whom get only a small relief. In the system proposed by us while a larger number of people will get moderate relief from the normal sale of unsubsidised grains through fair-price shops, a smaller number of really distressed people will get much more substantial relief from the sale of subsidised grain on the basis of relief quota cards.

Now that we are recommending the system of fair-price shops or modified ration shops to be maintained as a regular measure for providing relief to vulnerable groups of the population, it is necessary that these shops should be organised on a basis of properly supervised distribution. For each fair price or modified ration shop there should be a small local Committee of officials and non-officials which should meet at least once a month in the early stages of working of the shops. This Committee should supervise the work of the shop as also the preparation of lists of vulnerable families, distribution of identity cards and "relief quota" cards. The non-officials should be nominated after consulting all the important local interests concerned. Apart from these local committees there should be a strict inspecting organisation for supervising and exercising vigilance over the work of all these shops.

As we have noticed earlier, some of these cities tend to have a de-stabilising influence on the prices of food-grains in neighbouring rural areas. The cordoning off of these cities will go some way to relieve distress in these latter areas.

The possibility of obtaining modification of the system of zoning also encourages political pressure. Prior arrangements for adequate supplies for deficit areas outside the zones should invariably be made before any scheme for zoning is implemented. Once a zone is formed it should be maintained on a relatively long-term basis so that the trade patterns are not frequently disturbed.

At present there are three zones in the country. There is a southern rice zone comprising the four States of Andhra Pradesh, Mysore, Madras and Kerala. There are two wheat zones—one comprising Punjab, Delhi and Himachal Pradesh and the second Rajasthan, Madhya Pradesh and Bombay State. In addition to these, Orissa has been cordoned off for rice and U.P. for wheat. When these zones were first formed they created some dislocation for an initial period and caused distress amongst the vulnerable groups of the population outside the zones. But now that the trade has adjusted itself to these new zones and they are working without difficulty, we do not propose to change these zones at this stage. After the Foodgrains Stabilisation Organisation has started purchasing and procurement of rice is made as suggested, e.g., in the surplus areas of the southern zone and the Organisation itself transfers the surplus to deficit areas the utility of the zone may be somewhat reduced. On the other hand, in the initial stages of working of the Organisation the existence of the zone may be definitely helpful to its operations. The time for removal of the zone will, therefore, be only after some experience of working of the Foodgrains Stabilisation Organisation has demonstrated that the zone is no longer necessary; till then the zone may remain.

We understand, however, that if the supply of wagons for foodgrains is to be controlled in this manner it may be necessary to amend the Railway Act suitably. Transport policy will play an increasingly important role in implementing economic policy and requires to be closely integrated with policy regarding distribution and prices of foodgrains. That is why we have recommended earlier that the Ministry of Railways should be represented on the Price Stabilisation Board and it will defeat that recommendation if the Railway Ministry is not given necessary powers for implementing any policy that the Price Stabilisation Board may recommend.

In view of the large regional disparities of price movements and importance of local price rises, we recommend that a special cell or section should be set up within the State Governments with particularly heavy incidence of scarcity and also at the Centre within the Food Ministry for the purpose of anticipating difficulties arising out of possible floods and drought, locating scarcity pockets and initiating prompt measures to deal with them. Such organisations are important for preventing scarcity developing into a scare and causing speculative rise in prices in other areas.

We would recommend that the Development Commissioner in each State should be made specially responsible for schemes of development of these areas. The problems of these areas should also receive special attention at the hands of State and Union Governments in such adaptation of the development programmes and projects as might be considered from time to time.

It is also necessary to promote arrangements to conserve more grain in the rural areas for the lean season. We suggest that for the purpose village panchayats and cooperatives should be encouraged, through advances where necessary, to set up grain golas on the lines of those set up in Orissa in recent years where sufficient quantities of grain should be stored for the lean months. Grain golas may provide at least partial assistance in meeting seasonal scarcities in some of the vulnerable areas. It would also be desirable to liberalise the famine code which was originally drafted to take care of a different type of food shortage to provide now for this new type of seasonal shortage also. We would recommend that provision of more funds for test relief works in these areas should be considered. Besides, the distribution of "relief quota cards" should be more liberal in these areas. We recognise that all these will be at best only temporary palliatives. The more effective and permanent remedy will be setting up of rural industries and improvement of local agriculture by undertaking appropriate development measures.

We believe that the Central Food Advisory Council on which all interests, political, commercial, agricultural etc., will be represented will regularly bring to the notice of Government the views of the informed public. It will be desirable to set up similar advisory bodies also at the State level.

We would recommend that the Food Administration should be put on a permanent footing and all consequential action should be initiated to improve its efficiency.

We would recommend that a special division should be set up in the Ministries of Food and Agriculture in the Centre as well as the States to promote the production and consumption of subsidiary foods.

Production And Marketed Surplus

We believe that if full use is made of all our resources, it may still be possible to reach closer to the Plan target than the above estimate. The prospect of a shortfall from the Plan target has, however, to be faced, unpalatable though its implications may be.

While we do not advocate any diminution in the allocation to major irrigation, we recommend that a careful examination should be made of all major irrigation schemes, and, if there is likely to be a shortfall for any reason, from the target of expenditure on them, the funds that may remain unspent should be reallocated to minor irrigation, which promises quicker results. The procedure for such reallocation may be examined and if possible simplified and made more expeditious.

We recognise that an even phasing of the targets during the five years may not be entirely feasible and that some bunching of the targets in the last year or two of the Plan is unavoidable. However, the less the crowding in the later years of the Plan, the greater will be the chances of fulfilment of the entire targets. We believe that there is scope for more even distribution of the targets so that the earlier years of the Plan receive their due share.

We give below what in our view are fair estimates of the achievements that are likely to take place in the Second Plan period.

Schemes	Production targets (million tons)	Achievements as of percentage of production targets	Additional increase in production
Minor Irrigation	1.89	95	1.80
Fertilisers and Manures	3.77	80	3.02
Improved Seeds	3.42	60	2.05
Land Reclamation and Development	0.94	75	0.71
Improved Agricultural Practices	2.47	50	1.24
Major Irrigation	3.02	50	1.51
Total	15.51	66.6	10.33

In making these estimates, we have first borne in mind that the phasing of the Second Plan targets is similar to that of the First Plan targets and the achievements are, therefore, likely to follow the same pattern. Thus the ratios for all the schemes except fertilizers and manures have been estimated at a level only slightly higher than what was realised in the First Plan. The likely achievement ratio for fertilizers and manures has, however, been estimated much higher than in the First Plan because the evidence shows that the demand for fertilisers has already outstripped the supplies provided for in the first two years of the Second Plan. In fact the achievement ratio could have been taken at even more than the 80 per cent if there had not been the fear that difficulties of foreign exchange might interfere with the fulfilment of the target. There is scope for stepping up effort in respect of the seed schemes. The possibility of obtaining large increases in foodgrains production during the next three years thus seems greatest from the schemes for fertilizers and manures, improved seeds and minor irrigation.

We believe, that there are certain inherent problems in major irrigation, that have not been solved and are largely responsible for this state of affairs.

We are of the opinion that in areas where full use of irrigation facilities needs to be encouraged, cultivators, should be supplied irrigation water at concessional rates during the first few years. The C.D. and N.E.S. blocks in such areas should include as a part of their programme an intensive campaign to teach the cultivators the use and benefits of irrigation.

In a number of areas where rainfall is usually sufficient, irrigation facilities are in the nature of a security measure to be used only when rainfall is untimely or inadequate. In such cases, the full extent of irrigation available is not utilised. It has been suggested that in these areas a more intensive use of land should be made through the production of two or more crops. For example, unless double cropping is introduced there is little prospect of additional production from the Mayurakshi project and the irrigation system of the D.V.C. in West Bengal. Such changes can be brought about only if sufficient inducement by way of concession or exemption from water charges for the second crop is given to the cultivators during the first few years.

We recommend that the responsibility for the construction of the subsidiary channels should generally be on the Irrigation Department.

The lay out and the construction of the distributory system should, therefore, be done after proper consultation with the local people and after taking into account the special needs of each locality.

We suggest that the cultivator may be helped with credit and other facilities.

It is important that ways and means are devised to ensure that irrigation from tube-wells is properly utilised. Our recommendation regarding water rates for major irrigation also hold good for medium irrigation.

It has been represented to us in certain States that electricity for irrigational purposes was being supplied at rates higher than were charged for industrial purposes in the same areas. This raises a policy issue regarding the relative importance and needs of power for irrigation vis-a-vis industrial use. We suggest that the question be examined.

In some States, it was stated that small irrigation works which had formerly been kept in repair by the zamindars are not now being maintained in proper condition after the abolition of zamindaris. This is a matter which requires immediate attention by the State Governments.

It is essential that in the remaining years of the Second Plan the allocation for minor irrigation be separated out into two accounts, one for repair and maintenance and the other for new projects. The repair of the existing works should be given as high a priority as construction of new works.

In Assam large low lying areas in the valley regions offer considerable scope for growing a variety of spring paddy locally known as *boro* paddy, provided irrigation pumps are supplied to the cultivators on reasonable terms. This suggestion should be examined by the State Government.

In Rajasthan, it was represented to us, that artesian well irrigation had produced good results. Cultivators were given 50 per cent of the cost of well as loan. Many farmers, however, could not, avail themselves of this because they could not raise the remaining 50 per cent. It was suggested that the amount of Government loan in such cases should be raised to 75 per cent of the cost. The suggestion should be considered.

The question of providing technical staff to the States for undertaking surveys of water resources should be taken up by the Government of India.

The Grow More Food Enquiry Committee (1952) recommended the setting up of cooperatives of growers for this purpose. We are in agreement with this recommendation.

We stress the urgency for greater progress in this direction particularly since seed schemes require hardly any more funds for a given level of achievement than the other G.M.F. Schemes.

All States should ensure that the procedure for acquiring land for seed farms is simplified so that delay is avoided.

In view of the large potential of improved seeds to increase food production, the number of seed stores in each block should be increased to at least four per block so that improved seeds are brought to the door of the cultivator.

Complaints of delay and adulteration of seed are widespread. State Governments should take administrative action to ensure timely supplies of pure seeds.

We recommend the setting up of more factories for producing chemical fertilizers in India. One way to meet the foreign exchange requirement that would arise in this connection would be either to invite foreign firms to participate with Government or with private enterprise in setting up these factories or even to give them scope to set up factories on their own. In view of its importance as a producer of rice and consumer of fertilizers, Andhra Pradesh would be suitable for location of one such plant.

As regards manures, we emphasise the urgent need to develop local manurial resources, e.g., night soil, farm yard manure, compost, green manure.

The National Forest Policy Resolution of 1952 proposed that the area under forests should be raised steadily to 33 per cent of the total area, the proportion to be aimed at being 60 per cent in the hilly region and 20 per cent in the plains. Very little has been done to implement this resolution. The low percentage of forests in the plains has many harmful effects on agricultural production as has been repeatedly stressed. We recommend that the National Forest Policy Resolution of 1952 should be accepted as early as possible, particularly as regards its provision that the wooded area in the plains should be raised to 20 per cent.

In fact, there is reason to think that some of the land now classified and used as agricultural land could be more profitably turned into forest. This is where the land is of poorer quality, which hardly repays the cost of cultivation but which would become an economic asset if turned into a wooded area. A careful examination of land utilisation from this point of view is, therefore, an urgent necessity.

It seems that if the present pace of reclamation and development work is not stepped up, much less than 75 per cent of the Plan target would be achieved. In Rajasthan, it seems, that a substantial increase in production can be brought about through conservation of rain water by permitting it to percolate in the soil by building with sand. This method, we understand, has large potentialities.

Since one of the difficulties in this direction is the lack of trained personnel, we would recommend to the Government of India to increase the facilities for training in soil conservation methods.

Some other points that were brought to our notice related to (a) difficulties experienced by mechanised farms in obtaining adequate and reasonably-priced spare parts; (b) indiscriminate imports of tractors of unknown makes and without adequate facilities for training and servicing; and (c) lack of follow-up cultivation of reclaimed land. Solution of the first two difficulties has to be sought through restricting the licensing of imports of tractors and mechanical equipment only to such firms as would guarantee training and servicing facilities. Such a decision has already been taken by the Government of India and we recommend that it be enforced strictly. Regarding (c) we suggest that necessary administrative steps may be taken by the State Governments for transfer of reclaimed lands to cultivators immediately after reclamation so that no delay takes place in follow-up cultivation. The question of reducing the cost of diesel and lubricating oils also deserves to be looked into.

However, we have no doubt that as the extension service gets more firmly rooted and production-oriented, substantial increase in production can be brought about by better trained and organised staff. In the opinion of many witnesses it was being too optimistic to expect an increase of 50 per cent in the food production in irrigated areas and 30 per cent in dry areas until production orientation has attained the desired level. We are inclined to agree with this view.

We learn that the Ministry of Community Development has recently re-oriented its programme and policy so that food production received a high priority. We emphasise that these decisions be implemented effectively and quickly. The most far-reaching suggestion extended to us all over the country was that the control and guidance of agricultural programmes in N.E.S. and C.D. areas should be transferred from the non-technical hands of the N.E.S. staff to the technical hands of the State Agricultural Departments. The unduly large jurisdiction of the village level worker was also pointed out to us as a drawback. We do not consider it necessary to go into the subject of C.D. and N.E.S. areas in any great detail. A pointed reference to the administrative difficulties of these areas has been made by the C.D. and N.E.S. Areas Team under the leadership of Shri Balwant Raj Mehta. We understand that recommendations of this Team for the decentralisation of administration at the block level through the formation of statutory block boards on a democratic basis are receiving careful consideration.

We recommend that the aim should be that every Tehsil should have at least one agricultural high school, and that as far as possible all ordinary secondary schools in rural areas should adopt the syllabus for agricultural bias prepared by the All India Council for Secondary Education.

The state of higher education in agriculture is no better. There were in the entire country only 18 Agricultural Colleges in 1954-55. These colleges had 4,827 pupils to meet the growing demand for trained personnel. The number of agricultural colleges requires to be greatly increased.

In our opinion, the State Governments should proceed expeditiously with enacting the necessary legislation for land reforms and, what is more important, following it up with effective implementation. This should indeed contribute to the growth of agricultural production in the country.

What is needed is a stronger decentralised administrative effort in the rural areas, with adequate non-official cooperation to follow up the land reforms legislation with proper enforcement.

Consolidation operations should, therefore, always be carried out with as much speed as possible.

The importance of devoting greater attention to the improvement in design and manufacture of indigenous farm implements, irrigation and transport devices, was also brought to our notice. It was claimed that simple, cheap and easy to repair, hand and bullock-driven devices fall more readily into the pattern of our country's rural economy than imported machinery. At this stage of the country's development we agree with this point of view.

We feel that the seriousness of this menace should be recognised by the Government and steps taken by them for effectively decreasing the number of such cattle.

There is urgent need for modification in the present administrative and financial procedures of the Union and State Governments. What is needed is synchronising the procedure for executive approval and financial sanction of schemes to suit the developmental needs.

In most States, there are large arrears of G.M.F. loans which have not yet been recovered by the State Governments. This tendency of permitting arrears to pile up puts a heavy strain on the resources of the nation and should, therefore, be checked.

We found that in most States large sections of the subordinate staff of the Agriculture and other Development departments are comparatively low paid and kept temporary for a long time. This state of affairs cannot but lead to low efficiency. We suggest that the State Governments may examine these questions.

We suggest the setting up of grain golas in the rural areas as is being done in Orissa. The grain golas are being set up in that State on cooperative basis. The emphasis in the formation of cooperative grain gola societies is on local grain collections by way of share and deposit; Government also deposits paddy with these societies. Paddy comes into the golas in three ways: firstly, in repayment of the paddy loans; secondly, in the discharge of fertiliser loans; and, thirdly, in pursuance of the marketing operations of members through the grain gola society. Grain golas thus help the collection of marketable surplus in the rural areas and, by providing local storages to meet the local needs, facilitate marketing of the surplus to other areas.

We also recommend that in the Community Project areas special efforts may be made to make the farmer market-conscious, encourage him to sell more of his produce in exchange for industrial goods and thereby ensure that increased production in these areas is reflected in the marketable surplus.

We would recommend the setting up of regulated markets in all parts of the country, preferably on the model of the markets of the erstwhile Hyderabad State, and would urge the State Governments to take necessary steps in the matter.

Regular studies of the pace and volume of marketable surplus in relation to fluctuations in production and prices are essential for the formulation and review of policies relating to price stabilisation. For this purpose, arrangements should be made for the collection of all relevant data including the information on market sentiment and expectations which affect the course of prices considerably. In fact, it is on the basis of a regular study of the market behaviour that the Intelligence Division, the setting up of which we have recommended, will provide the necessary guidance to the Price Stabilisation Board and Government.

The need for technical, economic, and social research can hardly be over-emphasised. In fact a number of the recommendations in this report have been for eliciting more facts and figures in areas where the available knowledge is rather inadequate. It has cropped up in our studies of demand, supply, production responses, marketings, marketed surplus and farm management, to list only a few. While a lot of work is being done at present by the Government departments, Universities and other Research Centres, we feel that a lot still remains to be done and Government should allot more funds for research to the various bodies concerned. The role of research in the development of the country cannot be over-emphasised.

Problem Of Scarcity Areas

The remedial measures for each of these areas would depend on the nature and intensity of its problem. We hope that detailed and intensive studies would be undertaken in these areas before long.

From the viewpoint of food scarcity, the districts to be included have to be such as are chronically deficit and form a compact block of territory. The two easternmost and highly deficit Divisions of Varanasi and Gorakhpur have essentially to be a part of the eastern districts, with the exception of Mirzapur District which consists of a thinly populated plateau. Contiguous with these two Divisions are the six districts of Faizabad Division including Pratapgarh, Sultanpur, Faizabad, Barabanki, Gonda and Bahraich. These districts are also subject to the same type of difficulties as are the areas cavered by Varanasi and Gorakhpur Divisions. The three Divisions form an unbroken stretch of territory with common characteristics bearing on food situation. The U.P. Census Report, 1951, also includes four out of six districts of Faizabad Division in the scarcity area of eastern U.P. Volume II, Part I-A, of that Report says, "the whole of Gorakhpur Division, Banaras Division except Mirzapur, Faizabad Division except Gonda and Bahraich and Lucknow and Rai Bareili districts of Lucknow Division are danger spots from the point of view of rural food situation." Gonda and Bahraich which were left out, have been in a relatively better position partly because they have been receiving considerable quantities of rice and paddy from Nepal. With the imposition of a ban on exports from Nepal, these two districts may now have to face scarcity in times of floods which are quite frequent there. Considering all this, we are of the opinion that the scarcity area in the eastern districts of U.P. should include the three Divisions of Gorakhpur, Varanasi (except Mirzapur District) and Faizabad comprising the following districts :

Gorakhpur Division	...	Gorakhpur, Deoria, Basti, Azamgarh.
Varanasi Division	...	Varanasi, Jaunpur, Ghazipur, Ballia.
Faizabad Division	...	Pratapgarh, Sultanpur, Faizabad, Gonda, Bahraich, Barabanki.

In the discussion that follows, it is the 14 districts of these three Divisions that are compendiously described as eastern districts or the eastern region.

In the eastern districts holdings below two acres account for 20 per cent of the area under all holdings; the corresponding figure for the rest of U.P. is only 11 per cent. Similarly, the proportion of area covered by holdings exceeding two acres but not exceeding five acres to the area under all holdings is about 29 per cent in 14 districts and only three per cent in the rest of U.P. On the other hand, the proportion of area covered by holdings exceeding five acres is much greater in the rest of U.P. than in the 14 districts. It is about 86 per cent in the rest of U.P. and in the 14 districts about 50 per cent. All this shows that there is greater concentration of small holdings in eastern districts. What is required is a drive for promotion of cooperative servicing and better farming societies, so as to overcome the difficulties of tiny holdings.

The decline in the number of wells seems to be partly due to their replacement by camels and tube-wells and partly to lack of repair. Wells have a part to play even in the areas receiving canal water, because the grower can draw upon well water at any moment he likes. In other areas, adequate stress on the construction of masonry wells and repair of old ones seems to be necessary to bring a larger area under irrigation. The water level in these districts being high, masonry wells provide cheap and ready means of irrigation.

The State Government constituted a Flood Control Board in 1954 for coordinating all measures relating to control of floods. Under the First Plan, schemes estimated to cost Rs. 9.68 crores were started. Out of this amount, a sum of Rs. 5.41 crores was spent up to the end of 1956-57. Under the Second Plan schemes estimated to cost Rs. 8,29. crores were started, out of which only Rs. 48 lakhs have been spent by the end of 1956-57. This pace is obviously poor and needs to be stepped up.

We were told that the State Government is considering a proposal to give subsidy on the distribution of chemical fertilizers to these districts. That showed help in raising the yield. But because of prevailing difficulties about chemical fertilizers, provision of organic manures and green manuring are urgently called for.

In order to increase the production of foodgrains in these districts, the State Government is exploring the possibility of introducing short-term crops which can mature between the harvest of the rabi crop and the biginning of the rains.

Considering the extent of food deficit in these districts, it is clear that after everything possible has been done to augment food production, the problem of deficit will continue to remain unless steps are simultaneously taken to check the growth of population.

When U.P. as a whole is on the margin or is deficit, it does not seem safe to depend on private trade to meet the needs of the eastern districts, without incurring the risk of an undue rise in prices. In such a situation, the deficit of the eastern districts is likely to put a disproportionately large pressure on the price position in the whole State. Until, therefore, the State as a whole has as comfortable surplus, Government will have to undertake responsibility for the supply of foodgrains to this area. When, however, crops in these districts are affected by floods or drought, Government will have to undertake distribution, irrespective of whether the rest of the State is in a deficit or surplus position. At least for some years to come, the State as a whole is not likely to have a comfortable surplus while these deficit districts will continue to be exposed to floods and drought. Therefore, arrangements for Government supplies to this area on a continuing basis will be necessary.

Despite its having deficit, the region is a substantial exporter of certain foodgrains. There exports enlarge its deficit which is met by imports from the rest of U.P. or from outside U.P.

It is necessary that exports on private account from these districts should be banned.

As already stated, agriculture being the main source of income of the people, any severe damage to crops, in addition to enlarging the deficit creates the problem of low purchasing power. The problem often is not lack of flow of supplies from other areas but lack of means to buy. Opening of test relief works is only a palliative. The solution lies in correcting the unbalanced character of the economy by increasing and diversifying employment opportunities through promotion of village and small-scale industries besides position of better irrigation facilities for agriculture and protecting the economy against flood hazards.

Conclusion

The assessment that we have made of the likely supply and of the demand for foodgrains shows that food position will continue to be difficult. It is for that reason that we have emphasised the need for price stabilisation, control over trade of foodgrains and its progressive socialisation. Our recommendations when implemented, will materially reduce the fluctuations in prices and attendant hardships caused both to the producers and the consumers.

For an effective solution of the food problem, not only determined and all out efforts to step up production have to be made but the high rate of increase of population has to be checked. We, therefore, urge that a nation-wide campaign for family planning enlisting the efforts and energies of social workers particularly women, medical men, scientists, sociologists, economists, administrators and political leaders be launched.

The gravity of the food situation demands national efforts transcending regional and party considerations. Given a sympathetic policy and helpful administration we have no doubt that our cultivators are capable of greatly accelerating production. If India can become the pace-setter in constructing major irrigation projects in the world, there is no reason to believe that her agriculturists cannot match the strides of her engineers. What is needed is a sense of urgency and mobilisation of popular energies on a national scale.

Success of food policy, in the conditions prevailing, demands understanding and cooperation from the people. Adequate and effective contact with the people and flow of information both ways are, therefore, the *sine qua non* of success. In the great experiment of economic development through political democracy that our country is engaged in, the crucial position is occupied by food policv

BANARAS HINDU UNIVERSITY ENQUIRY COMMITTEE, 1957—REPORT

Delhi, Manager of Publications, 1958. 44p.

Chairman : Dr. A.L. Mudaliar.
Members : Shri M.C. Mahajan ; Dr. P. Subbarayan ; Smt. Sucheta Kripalani ; Shri Navroji J. Wadia.

APPOINTMENT

In exercise of the powers conferred by Sub-Section (2) of Section 5 of the Banaras Hindu University Act, 1915 (Act XVI of 1915), the President, in his capacity as Visitor of the University, has directed that an enquiry be made and that a Committee of Enquiry be appointed to enquire into and report on the said matters relating to the University in July 1957.

TERMS OF REFERENCE

(1) To examine the general state of discipline in the university, keeping in view the recent disturbances in some of the Institutions ;

(2) To enquire into the adequacy and effectiveness of the existing rules and procedure for ensuring proper conduct and discipline amongst the employees of the University ;

(3) To examine the working of the Act, the Statutes and the Ordinances of the University in general and with particular reference to :

(a) The Composition of the Authorities of the University ;

(b) The Institution of the Principals and their *ex-officio* appointment as Chief Wardens ; and

(c) The powers of the Vice-Chancellor vis-a-vis the administrative and the teaching personnel of the University ;

(4) To suggest such remedies and measures as are necessary in respect of matters specified in items (1) to (3) above ; and

(5) To suggest such other measures of reform as are necessary for the betterment of the academic life and efficient functioning of the University.

CONTENTS

Report of the Banaras Hindu University Enquiry Committee ; Memoranda ; Constitution of Selection Committees and Appointment of Teachers ; Examinations and Examinerships ; Strike in the College of Technology ; Teacher-Politicians and Group Formations ; Student Welfare Problems ; Law and Order ;

Demand for Increased Admissions ; Procedure to be Adopted for Consideration ; Admission of Students ; Women's College ; College of Music ; Constitution of the University Bodies ; the Visitor ; the Court ; the Chancellor and Pro-Chancellor ; Rector of the University ; Appointment of Vice-Chancellor ; the Pro-Vice-Chancellor ; Treasurer ; the Court ; Representatives of Ex-Students ; Representatives of Parliament ; Nominated Members ; the Executive Council ; the Academic Council ; Standing Committee of the Academic Council; Finance Committee ; Selection of Teaching Personnel ; Library ; Office Reorganisation; Audit and Stock-taking; Construction of Buildings ; Ministerial Staff ; Other Representations ; Other Complaints and Grievances ; Conclusion ; Epilogue; Appendices 1 to 6.

RECOMMENDATIONS

Memoranda

The memoranda received by the Committee dealt with the following aspects :

(1) Reports of occurrences in the University, particularly with reference to certain incidents that took place in recent years.

(2) Complaints regarding the manner in which the University was being administered.

(3) Complaints regarding certain Principals and Professors of the University.

(4) Complaints regarding the method of recruitment of the teaching staff and appointment of examiners and the method of advertisement for such posts.

(5) Complaints regarding elections to University bodies with particular reference to the dominant role played by certain groups in the University in these matters.

(6) Complaints regarding the attitude of certain teachers in student indiscipline and the manner in which the student-body was generally utilised for purposes not conducive to the discipline and the healthy atmosphere in University life.

(7) Complaints about the lack of proper facilities or amenities to the large body of students seeking admission.

(8) Complaints about certain injustices done to individual members of the staff.

In considering all these points, the Committee was naturally led to a study of the history of events in the Banaras Hindu University over a period of years and such study revealed the fact that for some years, the position has been steadily deteriorating in regard to all aspects of University life and administration. This University was founded by the late Pandit Mahamana Madan Mohan Malaviya of revered memory with ideals which appealed to a very large number of persons and which drew large benefactions and donations from various categories of persons. It is understood that during the life-time of the Founder, there were a few occasions when slight disturbances took place; but, on the whole, his personality and his long connection with the University helped to curb the disturbing elements and keep them in their places. Pandit Madan Mohan Malaviya was succeeded as Vice-Chancellor by Dr. S. Radhakrishnan under whose stewardship many improvements were made in the University administration and life. Yet it is disconcerting to note that he had eventually to break his connection with the University owing to certain factors that developed leading to what has been termed as the assertion of group politics in the University. The next Vice-Chancellor to be appointed was the late Dr. Amarnath Jha, who had been Vice-Chancellor of the Allahabad University and held other positions of great responsibility. It is regrettable to note that Dr. Amarnath Jha did not find it possible to continue even for a full year as Vice-Chancellor. When Dr. Amarnath Jha left the University, Pandit Govind Malaviya was appointed as Vice-Chancellor. Even Pandit Govind Malaviya, who at one time was able to satisfy the group, ultimately had to leave as the Rector had to set aside the election on complaint from his very supporters. It was at this time that the Banaras Hindu University Act was revised and the Act of 1951 came into force whereby the power of appointing the Vice-Chancellor out of a panel of names submitted by the Executive Council was vested in the Visitor. The person chosen was a well-known and much respected leader, Acharya Narendra Deva, who had been previously the Vice-Chancellor of the Lucknow University. It has been reported that, during the time of Acharya Narendra Deva, things were not running smoothly and the dominant role played by certain groups of teachers became more accentuated. The absence of the late Acharya Narendra Deva for long periods from the University owing to his other activities and to his poor health is also reported to have been a factor leading to the development of certain unfortunate trends. The conflicts increased and certain incidents are reported to have taken place then. Acharya Narendra Deva left the University before his term expired and probably one of the reasons might have been that his health did not permit him to continue. When Acharya Narendra Deva retired, the following four persons were nominated for selection by the Visitor for the post of Vice-Chancellor:

(1) Shri R.N. Banerji,

(2) Shri K.C. Sen,

(3) Sir C.P. Ramaswami Aiyar,

(4) Shri D.G. Karve.

The Visitor chose Sir C.P. Ramaswami Aiyar who assumed office on July 1, 1954. From all accounts, Sir Ramaswami Aiyar was anxious to do his very best for the University and it is well known that the cause of the University was championed by him both with the

Government of India and with the University Grants Commission of which he was for sometime a member. In spite of all his efforts to improve the conditions of the University, which owing to several factors could not possibly be rectified earlier, Sir C.P. Ramaswami Aiyar met with a very hostile reception both from the students and from certain members of the staff. An incident has been reported when certain members of the staff advised him that, after the inauguration of the Students' Union, it was not customary to give a holiday but the very persons who appeared to have advised the Vice-Chancellor, withdrew their support with the consequence that a very hostile demonstration was staged against him. It is reported that actually some of the teachers, far from controlling the situation, actually encouraged the students to continue the demonstration. The position consequent upon the squabbles and the recriminations so widely prevalent between members of the teaching staff and groups, sometimes based on political ideologies and sometimes on personal loyalties, was such that Sir C.P. Ramaswami Aiyar had to report to the Visitor his inability to continue as Vice-Chancellor. It is no doubt true that Sir C.P. Ramaswami Aiyar also stated that he had some literary work to do for which he wanted peace and quiet, and this is one of the reasons which led to his severing the connection; it must be stated however that had his influence been normal as in some other Universities, notably the Annamalai University whose Vice-Chancellorship he resigned, he would not have felt the necessity to break his connection with the Banaras Hindu University. The resignation by Sir C.P. Ramaswami Aiyar, who had taken such great interest in the work of the University, was a shock to many of the prominent citizens of Banaras and, in particular, some of them wrote expressing their anguish at the situation that had developed and asking for strong and speedy measures to be taken.

When the resignation of Sir C.P. Ramaswami Aiyar was accepted and the Vice-Chancellorship once again became vacant, according to the newly revised Act, the Executive Council suggested four names:—

(1) Shri M.C. Bijawat,
(2) Shri R.S. Tripathi,
(3) Shri Gurumukh Nihal Singh,
(4) Dr. V.S. Jha.

It is significant that one of the names proposed was that of a Principal of a College who, no doubt, had been in service for about 25 years but who, it is reported, was strongly backed by a particular group, commonly termed the "Eastern U.P. Group" by several of the witnesses who appeared before us. The appointment of Dr. V.S. Jha evidently created considerable resentment in this particular group and we were given to understand that they have not reconciled themselves to the position of "an outsider" being appointed as Vice-Chancellor of the University.

The events which have occurred since the appointment of Dr. V.S. Jha, will be enumerated later. At this stage, it would be pertinent to refer to the position of the Banaras Hindu University in Uttar Pradesh and to the relationship that exists between the University and the State Government. The Banaras Hindu University is a Central University and was based on an Act of the Central Legislature. It is expected to function as an all-India University serving the interests of students coming from all over the country and it is on this basis that the Central Government in the Ministry of Education and later the University Grants Commission have taken the full responsibility of meeting all the needs of the University. The point requires some emphasis and witnesses have, in their oral evidence, emphasised the fact that at present, the Banaras Hindu University has lost much of its all-India character. From the statements that have been furnished to us, it would appear that a recurring block grant of Rs. 55 lakhs is being paid to the University besides contributions for other specific objects and towards the building of hostels in the University. The State Government's contribution, which was Rs. two lakhs when the Centre's contribution was Rs. five lakhs at the starting of the University, is at present a recurring grant of Rs. one lakh.

The fundamentals in the constitution of the Banaras Hindu University were (1) its all-India character, and (2) its residential nature. These facts have been emphasised in one of the memoranda submitted to us in the following terms:

"Two important objects which must be vigilantly kept in mind as far as the Banaras Hindu University is concerned are the preservation of its much valued all-India character and its residential nature... It must guard against the danger of in-breeding in its selections of teachers and continue to attract students and teachers from all over India."

The other aspect that it should be a residential University has also been stressed in this memorandum:

"There are few residential Universities and Banaras Hindu University is one of them. In recent years a large number of students in the Faculty of Arts secure their degrees without in any way benefitting from the corporate life of a residential University. So far as the majority of students in the Faculty of Arts is concerned, they are neither fish nor fowl nor good red herring. A large number of them are private candidates or students from the various affiliated colleges. A time has come when the question of permitting private candidates to appear at the examinations of a residential University should be re-examined. Getting degrees by merely passing examinations is not genuine education, no doubt this enables the University to produce a large number of Arts graduates who have never known the incalculable advantage of the contact between mind and mind, between fellow students and students and teachers; that is the most valued factor of proper University education and not merely passing examinations. Let other Universities care for more numbers, let Banaras Hindu University cater for quality."

This aspect of the question will be referred to later. It is no doubt true that in certain of the Technological Departments, this aim has been kept in view. It cannot be said that in several of the Departments, it is functioning as an all-India University. Of greater significance is the fact that this University has come to be looked upon by the student community of Uttar Pradesh in particular and parts of Bihar as a University to which admission should be guaranteed for all students who wish to join the University. The result has been that at the time of admission, a great deal of pressure is exercised on the University authorities to increase the number of admissions, to admit candidates who may not come up to the standards prescribed, and in other words to utilise the occasion for a demonstration of a more or less serious nature, which has contributed not a little to the deterioration of student discipline and academic standards throughout the year. Evidence has been forthcoming that in this attempt to force the authorities to yield to the pressure tactics of certain groups, considerable sympathy, if not support, has been given by some of the Principals and Professors of the University. We are given to understand that on the last occasion, at the beginning of the academic year 1957-58, when things reached a climax and a particular person took to what is a common form of demonstration even to-day, a hunger strike, wild demonstrations took place in the University campus and groups of students went about crying 'Principal-Zindabad' 'Vice-Chancellor—University Officers—Murdabad'. The incident has been graphically described in a memorandum submitted to us in the following words:

"In the last week of July 1957, a very senior student of the Banaras Hindu University commenced a hunger strike in order to obtain concession for admission in some faculties of the University for those students who could not be selected on their merits and fell short of the minimum qualifications prescribed by the Standing Committee of the Academic Council. In the beginning of the strike period, the general body of the students who got admitted to the various faculties on their merit showed very little sympathy for the hunger striker. The heat in the movement came when a few agitators from outside, once students of this University, were imported and who shouted many indecent slogans."

The incident took place on the night of August 1, 1957, and

"If one were to analyse, he will find that apart from Ayurvedic College students, generally the students from 'Arts College', 'Law College' and the 'College of Indology' take prominent part in such movements."

In fact, a representative of the Students' Association and the person who undertook the fast told the Committee that there should be no restriction as to the number of students to be admitted, that there should be no qualifications prescribed for admissions, and that whether a student had a third-class qualification or had qualified at more than one attempt, admissions should be guaranteed.

Standards Of Admission

In one respect, this impression is due to the University itself having prescribed certain lower standards which cannot altogether be justified and which fortunately do not prevail in many other Universities. Special exemption is given to students who are prominent in the field of sports. This, it would appear to the Committee might be a justifiable position to take. But another kind of exemption is that given to the children of the teaching staff and other employees of the University to whom a lower standard is applicable for admission into the University. We can find no justification whatsoever for such exemptions being given, and if the Principals themselves or the Professors want their children to be admitted on a lower qualification, obviously they cannot be parties to maintaining any standards in regard to admission of students.

Another trend in which the responsibilities of the University have increased is the affiliation of a number of Colleges situated outside the residential area of the University on the ground that the Act provides that the "University may found and maintain other Colleges than the Central Hindu College and institutions including High Schools whithin a radius of 15 miles from the main temple of the University for the purpose of carrying out instruction and research." This has resulted in a number of Colleges being admitted to the privileges of the Banaras Hindu University but with little or no possibility of effective supervision of such Colleges in view of their distance from the Centre. Moreover, it has been pointed out by the representatives of these Colleges: "We are often sandwiched between two arguments. The State Government sometimes tells us that we are governed by the Central University and should look to the Centre for aid, but the Central Government says that we are a State responsibility."

There is another aspect of the development of the Banaras Hindu University which has to be taken into consideration. Limited as the numbers were at one stage, most of the students were resident within the campus of the University. But as numbers increased, the present number being somewhere near 10,000, students had necessarily to seek accommodation anywhere in the city of Banaras, although a few lodgings are supposed to have been accepted by the University as approved lodges. The result has, therefore, been that there has been a great deal of pressure for admission into the hostels of the University. The hostels have been overcrowded, the conditions of residence have been far from satisfactory and the bulk of the students have had to face considerable difficulty in securing admission outside the University. Being a Central University, it would almost appear as if the State Government or the Local Board authority constituted by the State Government have not felt it their responsibility to do anything to alleviate the state of affairs existing at present in the University campus. It has been pointed out that even the Local Board which is responsible for the area where the University is situated has done little or nothing for any kind of amenity that is required for the residents within the University, while such taxes as are levied on the residential quarters and hostels are being collected by this local authority. The University campus presents a unique instance of a place where the commonest amenities are not available—water supply, drainage, electric supply in some parts, proper roads, etc. Within the last two years on representations made by the University authorities, steps are being taken by the University Grants Commission to provide funds for improvements for these various purposes.

It would, however, be necessary to consider whether the Banaras Hindu University should be utilised to admit students at the undergraduate level to the extent to which they are being admitted at present, thus relieving the State Government of its responsibility to provide undergraduate instruction to its own students. The information before us goes to prove that the bulk of these undergraduate students for the first degree are students from what are known as the eastern districts of Uttar Pradesh. A few would appear to come from Bihar also. While we sympathise with the needs of the students in these regions for higher education, we do feel that other methods must be explored for giving them the proper type of education that is needed, whether it be within the city of Banaras or in the districts from which they come. It is understood that many students from the eastern Uttar Pradesh districts are not in a position to maintain themselves in Banaras and this adds to the seriousness of the situation created when such students are not in a position to pay their fees or their boarding charges. The result has been a great deal of pressure on the University to raise funds for helping students, and not infrequently such students are used as tools for creating situations embarrassing to the University and sufficiently serious to cause grave indiscipline. We shall refer to some of these aspects later and suggest some methods by which alleviation may be brought about. We do sympathise with the students and feel that to bring students to a large city like Banaras is neither safe nor desirable. In fact, some of the members who appeared before us went so far as to say that it was unfortunate that the Banaras Hindu University itself should have its campus so near a great city like Banaras with its ever changing population consequent on the large number of pilgrims and others visiting the city. Certain incidental factors lend themselves easily to produce disharmony in the atmosphere of an institution devoted solely to learning.

In referring to the increased admission of students, more particularly in recent years, our attention has been drawn to the fact that certain Principals feel that they need not observe any restrictions, even though such restrictions might have been suggested in the admission of students. In the case of one Principal, it was stated that while the number of students to be admitted was limited, he had actually admitted almost double the number of students in the college and once such admissions had been made, it was represented to us by some of the students' organisations that what had been done in one year should be continued in subsequent years. The bulk of evidence placed before us would appear to indicate that the main cause of trouble among students is due to several factors. Firstly, there are a number of students in the University who have been students for many, many years. In fact, the student-leader who went on a hunger strike in July last year has been a student for over 15 years, and at present is stated to be a student of the LL.M. class. These so-called students, who are of the mature age of 35 and over, dominate the whole atmosphere and get a group of indisciplined students to coerce other young students or subjugate them to their wishes. We have been informed that the bulk of the students are not inclined to be so indisciplined and we welcome and accept this statement; but the ring leaders create a situation where they are easily trapped to commit acts of indiscipline. It is unfortunate that the Presidents of Students' Organisations should be persons who are so mature in their age that they can hardly be identified as students of a University.

In the field of sports, it is generally laid down that a student cannot represent his University for more than five years and this has had a wholesome effect upon encouraging sports among the student population. Likewise, it is a matter for serious consideration whether anyone who continues as a student for a long period should be given the opportunity of holding positions of a dominant influence in University Unions for more than a certain period of years. This is a suggestion which may well be considered not only for this University but for other Universities as well.

Secondly, we have had very clear indication that indiscipline prevails among students because of indiscipline among teachers as well. There can be no doubt whatsoever that several of the acts of indiscipline among students have been due directly or indirectly to the manner in which certain teachers have played the role in regard to activities of the student population. We have some names mentioned of such teachers holding very responsible positions and we note with a great deal of regret that the present state of indiscipline in the University is due as much to some of the teachers in the University as to the students thereof.

Thirdly, it has been represented to us that the concentration of power in an increasing measure in recent years among certain members of the staff of the University, notably among certain of the Principals, has led to a position where they hold on the student population and on the teaching staff of their Colleges has increased with possibilities of using that power in a manner not always in the interests of the University. It is unfortunate that within the last three or four years, Principals of Colleges have also been made the Chief Wardens by an executive order of the Vice-Chancellor, and for the increased responsibility of Chief Wardenship, they have been given rent-free quarters with exemption from water-tax and electricity consumption to a certain limit. It has been calculated by some that these may amount to a sum of about Rs. 200 per month. Many of the witnesses took strong exception to this extra burden being placed on Principals of Colleges and stated that it was hardly likely that they would be in a position to deliver the goods as Chief Wardens in view of their other commitments, their administrative duties and their load of teaching. It has been freely commented that this has resulted in making the Principals all powerful, leading to excessive concentration of power and neglect of proper duties. We shall refer to this aspect and to the position of Principals later, but we should at this stage point out that it should not be left to the executive action of the Vice-Chancellor to make such appointments involving also financial liability without the proper approval of the University authorities.

Constitution Of Selection Committees And Appointment Of Teachers

From several of the memoranda presented to us and in the oral evidence tendered by several persons of standing, attention was drawn to the manner in which posts in the departments of teaching are filled. It was stated that the advertisements were generally prepared by the Principals of Colleges who were expected to consult the heads of the departments concerned. In some cases at any rate, such advertisements were very defective or were so framed as to suit particular types of persons only. Even in regard to the appointment to the Selection Committee of experts, the system is far from satisfactory and has led to many errors in the proper selection of the teaching personnel. We were given to understand that not infrequently, in the Executive Council, names were suggested and passed by a majority although some people expressed strong opinions about the suitability of such experts. We would have been inclined to think that this might have been due to an honest difference of opinion; but, in the light of the instances placed at our disposal, we regret we have to come to the conclusion that the selection of teachers is not made on merit and in the best interests of the University but that efforts are made to force the choice and to have a better hold over the teachers so recruited. In one of the memoranda presented to us, it is stated that certain groups have a dominating voice in the appointment of Selection Committees or in other ways, and thereby they influence the whole system of recruitment of the teaching staff. A statement has been furnished containing a list of members who are on the Executive Council or on the staff or other employees, all drawn from one area, and it has been asserted that many of them are related. A statement of the list of members of the staff who are so related and who form a very important group in University politics is given below.

List Of Members Of The Staff Who Are Stated To Be Inter-related

1. Pt. Ram Vyas Pande, Banaras and Balia: Editor, Panchang 1927, unpaid Lecturer and Editor, Panchang 1930, salaried Lecturer 1933, Head of Dept. of Jyotishi 1947, Member, Univ. Council 1946-47, Member of the Senate since 1948.

2. Pt. Ramshanker Pande, Banaras and Balia: Elder son of No. 1, Member, Univ. Court from Regd. Graduates Constituency since 1951, Member, Executive Council from Court after the introduction of new Act.

3. Pt. Umashanker Pande, Banaras and Balia: Second son of No. 1, teacher in C. H. School, under B. H. U.

4. Pt. Ambika Pd. Upadhya, Banaras and Balia: Retired Head of the Department of Vyakaran, Member of University Court, Faculty and father-in-law of son of No. 1.

5. Pt. Daya Sanker Pande, Banaras and Balia: Nephew of No. 1 and son-in-law of Pt. K. D. Tewari, No. 7 and House Surgeon, S. S. Hospital, B. H. U.

6. Pt. Sabhapati Upadhya, Banaras and Balia: Uncle of No. 4, member of the University Court, Board of Examiners and Faculty.

7. Dr. K. D. Tewari: Related to No. 1 through No. 5, Member, Univ. Court and Executive Council for the last many years.

8. Dr. R. S. Ojha, Banaras and Arrah: Son-in-law of No. 7, Reader in English, B. H. U.

9. Dr. R. Misra, Banaras and Jaunpur: Mrs. Misra and wife of No. 7, real sisters, Head of the Department of Botany, B. H. U.; and Member, Univ. Executive Council and Court before he joined University Service.

10. Shri K. C. Misra: Lecturer in Botany, B. H. U. and younger brother of No. 9.

11. Dr. C. S. Misra: Civil Surgeon, Kanpur, elder brother of No. 9, Member, Univ. Court.

12. Shri B. D. Tewari, Banaras and Balia: Lecturer, Dept. of Geology, Son-in-law of No. 4.

13. Shri B. K. Tewari, Banaras and, Balia: Lecturer, Dept. of Physics, son-in-law of No. 4.

14. Pt. Dhaneshwar Pande, Banaras and Balia: Head of Dept. of Hindi, B. H. U. and near relation of Nos. 1 and 4.

15. Dr. Hajari Pd. Dwivedi, Banaras and Balia: Head of the Department of Hindi, B. H. U. and near relation of Nos. 1 and 4.

16. Justice Balram Upadhyaya, Banaras and Allahabad: Judge, Allahabad High Court, Member, Univ. Court.

17. Pt. S. R. Tripathi: Lecturer, College of Indology, daughter married to son of No. 16.

18. Shri Chandra Pande: Near relation of Nos. 1 and 4.

19. Pt. Satya Narayan Pande: Part time in Jyotishi, B. H. U.

20. Pt. Raj Narayan Pande, Banaras: Father-in-law of daughter of No. 11.

We were not inclined to take this statement seriously but, on further examination and from other independent sources, as well as from some of those whose names have been mentioned, we came to the conclusion that there was no reason for us to doubt the veracity of the facts contained therein.

Another significant fact, and a factor which has disturbed us very much, is that looking into the record of several of the teachers, we find that somehow or other, they are generally those who have risen from the lowest positions in the University. They have been selected as demonstrators or tutors and gradually have worked their way up. We would not have thought that this was necessarily a matter for some anxiety but for the fact that, in the actual selection of such persons, there seems to have been an attempt to exclude people who might have been equally competent or more competent from either appearing for interview or from succeeding after appearance. This has produced an unfortunate tendency for in-breeding which in a University of an all-India character would be rather detrimental to its best interests. More particularly in recent years, we have been given to understand that an atmosphere has been created in which only particular types of persons from certain geographical areas have any chance to be appointed as teachers when vacancies occur. In this connection, it has been brought to our notice that in one case, a member of the Selection Committee was himself selected to the post though he was not an applicant. In another case, a post was created and, without any advertisement, the person was appointed the next day. We are very much concerned with these trends and feel that this is an important aspect of the question that should be rectified as early as possible. We shall refer to what we feel should be significant changes in regard to the method of appointing Selection Committees later.

Examinations And Examinerships

In a residential University, there is no doubt a possibility that the bulk of the examiners are from the staff of that University; but, unfortunately, in the particular circumstances under which the students have to study, it has become necessary for us to examine the system of appointment of examiners more closely. Whether it be in the examinations at the higher level which involve the conferment of doctorates or in the other examinations, it has been represented to us that it is not so much the performance of the student as the part he plays in propitiating some of the powerful members of the groups that ensures his success and not infrequently his rank in the University. In the choice of examiners also, it would appear again that group politics play their part, and often examiners are appointed who would be more inclined to support the internal examiner than to express their own independent opinion. It has also been represented to us that in the all-India conferences held on various subjects, where teachers are sent as delegates, much of lobbying takes place in regard to examinerships and suitable names are thereafter suggested from the Universities concerned so that on a mutual benefit process, examiners may be appointed by the different Universities. We realise that examiners are not averse to make complaints in any University but from certain other incidental factors, we are inclined to believe that the evil exists to a large extent in this University. We have been told and we have no reason to disbelieve this information that in certain of the professional examinations, the students are practically at the mercy of their teachers so far as success in the examination is concerned. It is also extraordinary that Professors should wish that their relations should work under them for research qualifications. Under ideal circumstances, this should not lead to much comment but under the circumstances obtaining in the University when things are manipulated, it obviously leads to criticism and comment when a close relation of a Professor, such as son or daughter, is taken as a research student and he or she is guided through research. An instance has been brought to our notice where a thesis was presented in three volumes on a subject which required a great deal of study and experimentation. The examiners themselves were bewildered and one of them is reported to have said that it was a marvel that such a thesis could be presented by a student working for a degree and within a short period. In this case, it has been suggested that this student, who is related to a Principal, submitted a thesis the bulk of which was done by members of the department. One of the Professors has made a serious charge that his daughter was not allowed to work under him for a research degree. The Academic Council would appear to have suggested that she might work under some other Professor. We would ordinarily have thought that instead of taking it as a criticism, the Professor himself would have voluntarily suggested that the daughter might work with another Professor on a subject mutually to be agreed upon. To resent this and to make an attack on the authorities for their decision shows how little the Professor realises his responsibility in the matter.

Strike In The College Of Technology

Early in 1957, there was a strike in the College of Technology which led to some confusion. The following students of the College were detained for shortage of attendance, viz., N.C. Sachiti, M. Venket Ratna, B.K. Lal and A. Setu Ramya. On account of their detention, the students of the third year class of the College boycotted the examinations on March 23, 1957. They accused the authorities for not taking regular attendance and also for improper maintenance of registers, etc. We enquired into this question carefully. The students were afraid of victimisation because, at the time of the examination, the persons responsible held a dominant position in assessing their results. When the Principal was interviewed, he was specifically asked how he came to the conclusion that the attendance register was not maintained; he admitted that the attendance was not taken for some months, probably four months, but stated that as the number of students was limited, say 30, he counted the heads and noted those students who were absent. No register was shown to us containing these details; and we cannot but express our surprise that the Principal should have dealt with students in this manner and refused to certify he had not taken the attendance.

A curious and somewhat comical incident in regard to this taking of attendance happened which was a revelation to the Committee. The students who had been detained represented to the Committee their fears of victimisation. Another batch of students appeared before the Committee. They stated that they were students of the same College of Technology and volunteered the information that the attendance was regularly taken, that the Principal insisted upon attendance and that at no time was it a fact that the attendance register did not indicate who was present and who was absent. When confronted with the statement of the Principal himself as transcribed from the short-hand record of his evidence admitting that attendance was not taken for four months, the students were confused beyond measure, a significant fact which reveals how evidence should have been manipulated.

We have noted that the students of the University have some genuine grievances which we feel ought to be remedied. It is not necessary for us to go into further details to bring home the real cause underlying the indiscipline among students. In fact, the enquiry has revealed in no uncertain terms that the greatest menace to the proper functioning of the University is not the student population but the teacher-politicians and the groups, particularly the dominant section of what is known as the Eastern U.P. group.

Teacher-Politicians And Group Formations

We have had irrefutable evidence from diverse sources, including many members of the academic staff, that the real menace to the satisfactory working of the University lies in the teacher-politicians and the formation of groups which dominate in all affairs of the University. This allegation has been fiercely contested by some who have themselves been styled as leaders of such groups. Recently, the Chairman of the University Grants Commission visited the University and after a thorough study of the present conditions prevalent there referred to the part played by teacher-politicians to the ruin of the University. The Teachers' Association sent a letter to him asking to withdraw these remarks. Incidentally, it may be mentioned that the so-called Teachers' Association itself seems to be dominated by a group and several teachers stated that they had not joined such an association and questioned the very methods adopted to form such an association. We may also here refer to the memorandum presented by this Association, wherein the President's decision to appoint the Enquiry Committee is questioned and criticised. Reference is made to this group in several of the memoranda submitted and even more unequivocally by the witnesses who tendered evidence before us, which we feel we cannot afford to ignore either as regards the existence or the role played by this group. It has been stated that "the voice of the Eastern U.P. group dominates the University Court and affairs" and that "the crux of the problem lies in the fact that people belonging to the Eastern U.P. districts try to capture all positions of vantage in the University, both academic and administrative." In another memorandum submitted by a senior Professor, it has been stated that "peoples of East U.P. and Bihar were responsible for the strike. The fact is that a group of local people from among the staff of the Banaras Hindu University from the eastern Districts of Balia, Gorakhpur, Jaunpur, Deoria, etc. and local citizens have joined together to wrest power and the reigns of the University ever since the time of the founder Vice-Chancellor Pandit Madan Mohan Malaviya, in ousting Dr. Radhakrishnan and Dr. Amarnath Jha in quick succession and again it is they who fought against

Pandit Govind Malaviya, Acharya Narendra Deva, Sir C.P. Ramaswami Aiyar and now against the present Vice-Chancellor. They dominate the University politics, the B.H.U. Teachers' Association, the University Old Boys' Association, the Banaras Hindu University Union and the University Court which in turn sends four or five members to the Executive Council and who gather round them some of the Principals of Colleges and thus acquire a very dominant voice in the Executive Council, making it impossible for the Vice-Chancellor to effect any changes or reforms and forcing the Vice-Chancellor to play to their tune. This brings us to the question of discipline among the staff and employees which is of much greater importance than discipline among students on account of their general influence on the general behaviour and party alignments of the students. Students are floating population but staff is permanent, and it is the staff that seems advantageous often using the students as their tools." We have quoted rather extensively from this memorandum because our enquiries and our close investigations lend support to these observations. Lastly, let us quote from the memorandum presented by the Commissioner of the Banaras Division. "It must, however, be admitted," states the memorandum, "that these agitations are not only those which emanate from the students themselves. The seeds of these agitations are to some considerable extent sown by certain teachers of the University who seem to have been acting for the last six to seven years with the clear intention of bringing the University into disrepute by creating situations and circumstances so as to belittle and embarrass the University authorities, particularly the authority of the Vice-Chancellor. As such, whenever it is felt by this group of teachers that there is a certain amount of unrest amongst the students, they act as agent-provocateurs."

Student Welfare Problems

So far as the welfare problem of the students is concerned, the Committee has been impressed by the fact that conditions in the University, owing to the large and increasing numbers admitted year after year, have deteriorated. Whe have been told and we have verified for ourselves the fact, that there is not enough accommodation for all the students in the class-rooms. Nor is there sufficient space in the laboratories for the increased numbers admitted. The hostels are overcrowded and unfortunately students, who are not hostel-mates, are also accommodated there either openly or in other ways. This overcrowding has become so chronic that the teachers are unable to control the classes. A large number of students are forced to live outside the campus of the University in surroundings that are appalling. Reference will be made to this serious problem when we discuss the question of law and order in the University. It is understood that no attention has been paid to such extra-curricular activities as have a great bearing upon student-welfare. As one of our Commissioners has reported, although the campus is so big and there are large pieces of ground for various games to be played, the playgrounds presented a deserted appearance. Obviously the students have never felt the urge to play. It is unfortunate that even a physical director is not available and no one is interested in promoting sporting activities and games among the students. The canteen arrangements for the students are far from satisfactory. When the bulk of the students are coming from outside and the city is far off, it should be the responsibility of the University to make suitable arrangements for day scholars to have at a convenient place a canteen where proper and nutritious food will be available at minimum cost. The students have also complained that facilities for library study are remote. We shall refer to the Library at a later stage but we must confess that the idea of a centralised library, without proper facilities for Colleges to have a library of their own for undergraduates, lends much support to the criticism of students that books are not available and that poor students have not the opportunity to have recourse to the library.

The state of sanitation is deplorable. No attempt has been made to provide the necessary sanitary conveniences of modern nature even in the hostels whether it be for men students or women students; and, in the Colleges themselves, the arrangements are to say the least very primitive indeed.

It has been reported already that the electrification programme has been considerably delayed owing to lack of power supply. There are many places where electricity has not been made available. The provision of a few fans in the class-rooms when the work is to be conducted in the hottest part of the year might be looked into as one of the necessary amenities.

In a residential University of this nature, many activities could have been fostered. Many competitive forms of physical activities and games, and competitions in the literary field could have been organised by dividing the resident population into what is known as Houses, as is done in such residential places. We regret to say that the supervision of the students is extremely inadequate and the whole system of wardens, and particularly Chief Wardens, has been a fiasco. We consider that the legitimate grievances of the students in this respect should be attended to immediately, that more residential accommodation should be available and that the University should be, as its name implies, a residential University taking such numbers as can be accommodated in a residential University. The limitation of numbers is for the particular purpose of giving to everybody who joins, the benefit of a residential system and thus fostering the growth of healthy citizens who will be a credit to the country. At present, this ideal is far from being reached.

Law And Order

The position with regard to law and order in the University seems to be chaotic. University students are allowed to live in various places outside the campus under surroundings that can only be described as most unfortunate. As the Commissioner of the Banaras Division has stated in his memorandum, in such a campus it would appear as if nobody can control students. It is a healthy convention in most Universities that the University campus itself should be free from any visits by officers responsible for the maintenance of law and order in the District or Town, and it is for this reason that a system of Chief Proctors and Proctors has been devised, who should be in a position to control the students and save them from falling into unfortunate ways. The Commission states: "The students have always been rude whenever a police officer has visited the University in connection with the investigation of crimes or any allied matter. On account of this, the authority of the police in regard to maintenance of law and order in the University campus has dwindled day by day and a sort of tradition has grown up that the police is responsible for the law and order duties only upto the University gates. The Chief Proctor who happens to be invested with Magisterial powers of second class does not perform any function of a Second Class Magistrate to deal with the problem of law and order in the University. This fact coupled with the fact that lawlessness and indiscipline in the University is actively guided by political parties and certain teachers of the University, has, so to say, made University campus out of bounds for the process of law. It may be added, however, that the tendency of the University authorities has so far unfortunately been to solve matters by acceding to a great extent to the demands of the students. Although in the circumstances, it cannot be said that any other solution could have been better, yet it can be said that action has never been taken to eradicate indiscipline from among the students owing to adoption of the temporary expediency of avoiding a showdown. The students have quite often sent bogus telegrams to high personalities and have also been found congregating before girls' schools in the city and brow-beating traffic constables or ridiculing a police officer."

We do hold that the University which is a temple of learning should be in a position to manage its own affairs, to control any acts of indiscipline among students by invoking healthy traditions among students themselves and by creating public opinion among the student population, which is the best preventive for acts of indiscipline. But such state of affairs cannot possibly be prevented if active cooperation from the teaching element is not available. From the statements quoted elsewhere, it would be obvious that if certain of the teacher-politicians themselves are agent-provocateurs as mentioned by the Commissioner of the Division and are inclined to take every opportunity to create more of indiscipline, a stage is often reached when such indiscipline becomes a matter of grave concern to the University authorities.

One aspect of life in the University which has been revealed by the Divisional Commissioner is far more surprising than any of the acts of indiscipline. He has referred in his memorandum to students visiting houses and lodges of disrepute and to certain students being associated with these. He has also mentioned about certain teachers committing offences involving moral turpitude. It was painful reading for the Committee to go through these unvarnished facts and the members do not see any reason to discount the statement made, for, in the evidence tendered by more than one person, charges and imputations of immorality in the University have been made and a case of unnatural offence involving a Professor is stated to be before a court of law.

Mention of the court of law brings to our notice the manner in which the University has been often dragged into a court in matters which should hardly have been taken to a court of law. We feel that in matters academic, it would certainly be embarrassing for a University to be dragged into a court of law on every conceivable occasion by teachers, students and politicians. We give below a list of various disputes pending or which have been recently disposed of in Courts of Justice wherein the University had to be a party.

List Of Disputes Pending Or Disposed Of In Courts Of Justice With University As A Party

1. Dr. Akshaibar Lal, Reader, College of Agriculture.
2. Dr. Raj Bali Pandey, Principal, College of Indology.
3. Dr. S.S. Joshi, Principal, College of Science and Dr. P.N. Bhargava, Reader in Organic Chemistry.
4. Indian Wheat Loan Educational Exchange Programme—Scheme in the Botany Department.
5. Sale of old newspapers and magazines in the B.H.U. Library.
6. Dr. Virendranath, Lecturer in Pharmacology, College of Ayurveda, B.H.U.
7. College of Mining and Metallurgy—Appointment of Readers.
8. Indiscipline in the College of Technology.
9. Re. two posts of Lecturers in Hindi.
10. Re. Pt. Ram Vyas Pandeya, Jyotishi, Sanskrit College, B.H.U.
11. Re. Dr. R.S. Ojha, Reader in English, Central Hindu College.

12. Re. Shri Ganesh Prasad Singh, Lecturer, Teachers' Training College, B.H.U.

13. Re. Pt. Dhaneshwar Pande, Compounder, S.S. Hospital, B.H.U.

14. Re. Dr. B.L. Atreya, Head of the Department of Philosophy.

15. Re. Shri D.S. Pande, Temporary Medical Officer, S.S. Hospital, B.H.U.

16. Re. Shri Uma Shanker Pandeya, Art Teacher, Central Hindu School, Banaras.

17. Re. Pt. K.D. Tewari, Member, B.H.U. Court, Executive Council and Finance Committee.

18. Re. Pt. Kedar Dutt Joshi, Adhyapak in Jyotish, Sanskrit College.

19. Re. Dr. Gopal Tripathi, Principal, College of Technology, B.H.U.

20. Re. Dr. Ramlochan Singh, Head of the Department of Geography, B.H.U.

21. Re. Pt. Ambika Prasad Upadhyaya, Adhyapak in Vyakarna, Sanskrit College, B.H.U.

22. Re. Dr. S.S. Joshi, Principal, College of Science, B.H.U.

23. Re. Appointment of Treasurer.

It has been brought to our notice that in the case of the strike in the College of Technology, the conduct of the Principal was subject to review in the Executive Council, and a retired Chief Justice, was appointed to look into this case on a resolution passed by the Executive Council by a majority vote. From evidence tendered before us by very responsible people, it would appear that one Principal and another, a Registrar of another University who is a member of the Executive Council, who participated in the discussion and did not agree with the suggestion of the Vice-Chancellor, used threatening terms to very respectable members of the Executive Council and who participated in the discussion and voted with the majority, should have appeared for the Principal of the College in the judicial appeal that was preferred by the Principal against the University. We realise that it is open for any Advocate to plead in a court of law in a case on behalf of his client irrespective of his own attitude in the matter, but it does seem incomprehensible that a person holding the position of the Advocate-General and a member of the Executive Council should have gone out of the way to support a case professionally against the University.

We have carefully considered the several memoranda submitted to us by persons who are in the service of the University in one capacity or another, by those connected with one or other of the University authorities, by ex-Vice-Chancellors, by members of the public who have taken a keen interest in the affairs of the University and by the Association of Teachers, students and class IV employees of the University. Several of them have suggested a number of remedies so that the University may function as an all-India University and maintain a proper academic atmosphere and standard of conduct and rectitude. We have also interviewed several of these persons and others and had a free and frank talk with them to elucidate their views about the present state of the University, the reasons for deterioration, if any, in the standards academic, administrative or otherwise, and we have taken note of the remedies suggested by several of them. While a few maintain that there was nothing wrong with the University, that the state of affairs was not different from what prevailed in other Universities in the neighbourhood, the majority of those who could speak with a certain sense of responsibility were, however, of the view that matters had come to such a pitch that radical measures should be immediately undertaken.

It has been brought to our notice that one of the Professors utilised the students' concession fare on railway to take a marriage party and when this was brought to the notice of the authorities, the Professor was let off with a warning. Later, we understand this Professor was the recipient of a Presidential award. Such an incident cannot but be demoralising to the University. This incident found a place in the report of the Railway Inquiry Committee.

The irresistible conclusion that has been forced on us from the evidence placed before us is that the University is in an unfortunately bad predicament. It is not functioning as it should or as it was intended by its eminent founder. It has lost its all-India character and is not at present a residential University by any stretch of imagination. We regret to have to state that from all the material placed at our disposal, we cannot help feeling that it has become a hot-bed of intrigue, nepotism, corruption and even of crimes of various description. It would appear that the ordinary law of the land is not in force within the campus, nor are the authorities of the University, who are entrusted with the maintenance of law and order within the campus, in a position to enforce these under well-known conventions.

It is a sad reflection that the University campus which has been well laid out with extensive playfields has not been put to any proper use at all, and no healthy physical activities are undertaken by the students in the evenings. In fact, the campus gives an appearance of Goldsmith's "deserted village", and no students can be found in the playfields in the evening or taking to healthy recreation in the University premises. Many of the common amenities required for students do not exist. There are no common-rooms or assembly halls. The University does not possess, after so many years of its existence, a trained Physical Director for organising sports and games. Little attention seems to have been paid to provide proper amenities for students to keep them busy and away from unhealthy surroundings in and around the campus. It would appear that little or no attempt has been made to harness young men's activities outside the lecture-rooms into healthy channels and to prevent them from falling into the hands of demagogue politicians of all shades.

The University is supposed to have wardens in charge of the students residing in the different hostels, but we have had on the authority of the Provost that the majority of these wardens have not been able to discharge their duties conscientiously and that probably half a dozen or so are trying to do their best under the difficult circumstances existing in the University. The innovation of having the Principals of Colleges as Chief Wardens has made the situation worse. There has been a feeling of resentment that the Principals should have been entrusted with the duties of Chief Wardens in addition to the multifarious duties that they have to perform in the Colleges as Principals and members of various University authorities and in attending many meetings, conferences and functions. The result is that the hostels are used by a few persons who have no right to be there and some of them have been living for several years, refusing to leave the hostels. It is even more surprising that one of the Professors on retirement refused to vacate the quarter occupied by him and continued to live there at his leisure paying only half the amount of rent that he was paying when in office. Eventually he carried this matter even to a law court. This lack of any control has given room for a number of persons entering the premises of the University, and various leaders of political parties have not hesitated to maintain their offices within the campus. We are informed that their activities are carried on through the agencies in the different hostels and with the cooperation of some of the members of the teaching staff. We have been told by a responsible officer of the Government of India that some offences are committed within and outside the campus involving moral turpitude.

The institution of 'Principals of Colleges' has been subjected to severe criticism at the hands of many of the witnesses. It has been stated that the Principals act in a very autocratic manner with few exceptions and that the other members of the staff and the students have to toe their line if they are to have a peaceful existence. Too much power is concentrated in their hands, much to the detriment of sound academic efficiency, and it has been reported that the Principals have their way of distributing patronage among the staff and act in a most undemocratic manner. We must confess that it has been due to the weak policy followed by some of the Vice-Chancellors who, to propitiate certain dominant persons, have given them more and more power with less and less justification. The head of the Department is not given the status that he ought to have. Moreover, when advertisements have to be inserted in the press or selection of proper personnel is to be made, it is the Principal who has got the chief voice in the matter. There are no staff committees which are expected to meet occasionally and discuss academic and administrative problems of the department. And so far as students are concerned, they are made to feel that their future is entirely in the hands of some of these Principals. Reference has been made to the state of affairs in the College of Technology where the Principal, without taking attendance for four months, exercised his authority in withholding certificates for four students to appear for the examination. Although eventually this order was annulled, it is still a matter which is under investigation. But the main point of emphasis here is that the students naturally feel that they will not get fair play with some persons or group of persons who will be responsible for the conduct of the examination. This has introduced an amount of demoralisation among students which it is unnecessary to describe at length.

Demand For Increased Admissions

We must express our surprise that the situation does not seem to have been as well appreciated by the State Government as one would have expected. Where demands are made for increased admissions in the different States, it is the responsibility of the State Government to see that such demands are satisfied. We gather that in the eastern U.P. districts, there are a few colleges to cater to the needs of the large number of students seeking admission and the idea, that the Banaras Hindu University being a Central University should be open to all, is a very erroneous idea, and is not justified either according to the terms under which the University was constituted or from the point of view of the ideals with which it was founded. We are also of opinion that the time has come when the Banaras Hindu University should be purely a residential University limiting its numbers to the extent to which it is possible so that all students may be resident and that the colleges affiliated to the University should be hereafter affiliated to the Gorakhpur University except for the Kamachcha College which was the old Hindu College and should therefore continue as a Constituent College of the Banaras Hindu University. We shall refer to the financial aspect of this question later.

It has been represented to us that the indiscipline in the University is not a little due to the traditions that were established in the freedom struggle and that those traditions have created an atmosphere which naturally tends to give an impetus to act in this manner. We are unable to appreciate this argument which has been put forward even by some of the members of the teaching staff. The pesent generation of students cannot be said to have done anything to claim their participation in the freedom struggle of 1942. Moreover, it is not only the Banaras Hindu University students but the alumni of all Indian Universities who naturally on account of their youthful enthusiasm and selfless conduct, contributed to the struggle. To put forward this as an argument for the state of thorough indiscipline in the University is to fail to understand the essentials of proper conduct and rectitude.

We have been told that, while in the earlier days of the University even undergraduate and Intermediate classes were given the benefit of the lectures from professors, today the position is that most of those who occupy posts of Professors do not think it worthwhile or consider it even infra dig to teach such classes. We have also been impressed with the fact that the hours of work for different grades in the teaching category are disproportionate. It has been stated that a Professor lectures four or five times a week, each time for a period of 45 minutes. The lecturers have 18 periods a week, whatever may be the amount of research work that is supposed to be carried on. We do not appreciate the manner in which responsible academic duties are being discharged by some of the Professors in the University. We are driven to the conclusion on the materials placed before us that even if some of the members of the teaching staff in the employment of the University possess post-graduate qualifications and may be good teachers, their contribution in the academic development of the University is far from satisfactory, as they have developed the mentality of exploitation and power. It is true that every University, for the matter of that, every organisation, depends upon proper personnel being available; unfortunately, in this University it would appear that merit is not appreciated as it ought to be with the result that the University is controlled by undesirable elements.

Procedure To Be Adopted For Consideration

Reference has been made to the fact that under Section 5(2) the Visitor has been pleased to appoint us as a Committee to inspect and report upon the present state of the Banaras Hindu University under certain terms of reference that have been given to us. Under Section 5(3), the Visitor has given notice to the University of his intention to have an inspection or enquiry to be made and the University has, under powers vested in this Section, appointed a representative, who in this case is the Vice-Chancellor, to be present at such inspection or enquiry. We have given every facility to the representative of the University to be present on all occasions when the enquiry was made. We have also furnished him with the various memoranda but, in view of the request made by some of the members that the fact that they have submitted memoranda should be treated as confidential, we have furnished such memoranda without giving information as to who it was that had forwarded the memoranda. We come to Section 5(4) which is of significance and we wish to invite attention to the language used in this sub-section. It is stated that the Visitor may address the Vice-Chancellor with reference to the result of such inspection or enquiry and the Vice-Chancellor shall communicate to the Executive Council the views of the Visitor with such advice as the Visitor may offer upon the action to be taken."

From a perusal of the report that we have submitted, it will be obvious that in material respects, the report does imply that some of those who are now members of the Executive Council are themselves in some measure or other involved in some of the incidents which have been referred to. To a large extent, the present personnel of the Executive Council has, in our opinion, been responsible for the state of affairs in this University. We have no objection to our report being perused by anybody or being subjected to any fair or just criticism. In our opinion, a discussion in the present Executive Council will lead to considerable trouble and disharmony in the University. It is only from this point of view that we feel, in as much as it is not incumbent upon the Visitor to address the Vice-Chancellor with reference to the result of such inspection and enquiry, the Visitor may consider the desirability or otherwise of taking measures which we feel are necessary in the present condition of the University and in light of the evidence furnished. After very careful consideration we have come to the conclusion that the advice given by very many influential and impartial witnesses that for sometime the Banaras Hindu University Act should be kept in abeyance is a sound one. In fact, if this is not done, it will be difficult to consider dispassionately the steps that should be taken to reform the University and to get a proper atmosphere in the various University bodies which may have to be thoroughly reconstituted. Any other step would only foster agitation being sponsored or aggravated.

The question may be asked how the University is to function under such circumstances. We may give the instances of some Universities where, for a transitional period when the University Act had to be revised, the old University Act was suspended and a Committee was appointed to help the Vice-Chancellor in carrying on the day-to-day functions of the University and for preparing the necessary Statutes, Regulations and Ordinances according to the revised Act. In one University, such an *ad hoc* Committee to help the Vice-Chancellor was constituted for a period of two years, not because of any gross maladministration in the University but because the new Act would take sometime for the various provisions to be ultimately studied and brought before the authorities concerned and the authorities themselves had to be reconstituted in a manner which would involve a time lag before they are finally constituted. The question then arises as to the method of constitution of this advisory body. We feel that this body should consist of not more than nine persons with the Vice-Chancellor as its Chairman. such representatives being chosen from persons with academic and administrative experience and one representative being a nominee of the Rector. We feel that this body may, as occasion needs, coopt upto three members, in particular of the teaching staff, the Provost or Chief Proctor, on the advice of the Vice-Chancellor for particular meetings when special subjects are to be considered. We are anxious that this body should meet frequently and consider the various problems connected with University. In the meantime, we feel that certain essential changes are required in the Act itself in the light of its working for the last seven years. We realise that whatever may be the nature of the Act and whatever its Statutes, the successful working of the University depends upon the personnel more than the rules and regulations and it is our hope that if some of our suggestions are carried out, there will be an improvement in the general atmosphere and in the tone of the people appointed to the teaching staff of the University. We are convinced that student indiscipline is a by-product of the activities of some of the teachers and it would serve no useful purpose to disguise the fact that the main emphasis to root out such indiscipline should be on the methods adopted for changing the attitude of some of the teachers and improving their sense of loyalty, discipline and the ideals which they should entertain towards the University.

All the members of the Enquiry Committee have been connected with Universities in one capacity or other and are staunch supporters of the view point that the Universities should be autonomous bodies but this very phrase 'University autonomy' implies other obligations which are sometimes forgotten. In the very interests of University autonomy therefore, it would be necessary to remove the canker wherever it exists in the body politic of the University, to purify the administration and so to say bring about a revolution which will never allow the destructive forces to creep in again. It is therefore with a strong sense of our responsibility and with a great desire to see that the University, which was launched with great hopes and which is known all over the world, does not slip back into unfortunate trends as it has in recent years, that most of our recommendations have been made. We may state that we have no intention of trying to make out that there are not very many good elements in the University who have been, under depressing and unfavourable circumstances, trying to carry on the good work as befits good academicians. To those members of the teaching staff who have stood loyally by their academic standards, we wish to pay our meed of praise but, even as a few unruly and perverse elements could ruin the whole tone of the University, it is necessary to apply remedies which will root out such group politics.

Admission Of Students

We have already referred to the theory propounded by students' organisations and unfortunately by some teachers that there should be no restriction on the number of students admitted to the University, that the first claim should be of those students who come from the neighbouring areas who are poor and who think that, though they may not satisfy the rigid standards laid down, they have still a claim because of their eligibility for such admission. We have referred to the fact that in a residential University of this nature, only those who can be properly accommodated within the campus should be given these facilities and that restriction of numbers is an absolute necessity in every University. The increased numbers seeking admission to the Banaras Hindu University would appear to be due to the following causes: (1) Facilities not being available in particular parts of the State of Uttar Pradesh, particularly in the eastern Districts thereof; (2) The existence of a large number of students who are encouraged into the belief that the Banaras Hindu University being a Central University, they have a right to gain admission, and also the idea prevalent that the Banaras Hindu University should be treated as a poor man's University and therefore such persons should be admitted without any restriction of numbers and irrespective of standards; (3) The most important cause seems to be the feeling and the active encouragement of the same by Principals and teachers themselves that there should be no restriction on admission of students and that everybody who applies ought to be admitted to the University; and lastly (4), till now it would appear that the State Government has not taken sufficient steps to provide educational institutions for the large numbers who pass out of schools. We give below the strength of University from year to year for the last 34 years.

Total Number Of Students In The University

Year	Total No.
1924-25	1,952
1925-26	2,047
1926-27	1,936
1927-28	2,192
1928-29	2,359
1929-30	2,533
1930-31	3,055
1931-32	3,019
1932-33	3,506
1933-34	3,492
1934-35	3,711
1935-36	3,417
1936-37	3,428
1937-38	3,411
1938-39	3,477
1939-40	3,674
1940-41	3,945

1941-42	4,209
1942-43	3,894
1943-44	3,815
1944-45	4,128
1945-46	4,536
1946-47	4,872
1947-48	5,233
1948-49	5,531
1949-50	5,806
1950-51	6,533
1951-52	7,630
1952-53	7,846
1953-54	8,614
1954-55	8,621
1955-56	8,490
1956-57	8,766
1957-58	8,586

In this connection, we would refer to the report of the Allahabad University Enquiry Committee of 1953, where the question of the number of students to be admitted into the University has been discussed. The report states: "We urge that the number of students to be admitted each year should not depend upon the ability of the Vice-Chancellor and heads of departments to resist the pressure which is put on them to increase the number of admissions, but that the maximum figure be resolutely fixed and rigidly adhered to without any hindrance whatever until such time as circumstances justify a reconsideration of that figure. In determining the maximum figure, there are in our opinion four considerations to be borne in mind:

(1) Limitation of space, equipment and financial resources;

(2) The burden in a unitary University on the administrative machinery and on the Vice-Chancellor if the number is very large;

(3) The danger of less of personal contact between teacher and students; and

(4) In regard to those departments where education of a professional nature is imparted, the problem of unemployment.

The report continues: "The opinion of the witnesses who appeared before us was that the maximum should be between 3,000 and 4,500, and in any case, not greater than 5,000. We hold clearly to the view that if the academic standards of the University are to be maintained, a limit should be placed on the number of students who join the University. The number of students is just over 6,000 and it appears to be impracticable to effect a reduction to the numbers proposed by the witnesses. We recommend that the numbers ought to be fixed at 5,000 exclusive of those taking the Diploma or other courses. It is our view that whatever be the maximum as fixed, under no circumstances, the figure should be exceeded, whatever strong pressure may be and from whatever quarter pressure may emanate." These observations hold good *mutatis mutandis* to the Banaras Hindu University and we entirely agree with the Chairman of the University Grants Commission that the maximum should be fixed and there should be a progressive reduction in the numbers till the number is fixed in such a manner that all the four essentials enumerated in the above report are complied with.

It must not, however, be supposed that we are trying to handicap the students in their natural desire for higher education. At the undergraduate stage, it is the State's responsibility to provide those facilities. We are therefore of opinion that the State Government should be requested immediately to take steps to open colleges if necessary, particularly in the eastern districts of Uttar Pradesh, and to affiliate them to the Gorakhpur University which has been recently started. This would not only enable a more appropriate distribution of student-strength in the different colleges but would also enable the poor students to study nearer their homes at considerably less cost than is possible for them in a city like Banaras and in the University campus. We have already stated that all the colleges outside the campus of the Banaras Hindu University with the exception of the Kamachcha College should likewise be disaffiliated from the Banaras Hindu University and should be affiliated to the Gorakhpur University. We feel that this step is absolutely necessary if we are to ensure the essential nature of the University and the purpose for which the Banaras Hindu University was organised and brought into existence.

There is one peculiar feature of a college in the Banaras Hindu University which has given considerable anxiety—the Ayurvedic College. It would appear at one stage that the founder wanted to encourage pure Ayurveda and started this college with the hope that in association with Sanskrit studies, there would be a renaissance in the branch of Ayurveda and the proper study of this subject. Since then, many changes have been introduced and today, the College is supposed to cater to Ayurvedic studies and to studies in Modern Medicine. It is not our purpose to enter into any discussion on this question nor do we feel competent to do so and it does not come within our terms of reference. The problem with this Ayurvedic College has been that there has been a sense of frustration among the students which, to a very large extent, is due to the manner in which the studies are being organised and the teaching element is recruited. It has been freely stated that the cause of the strikes which were going on for some time was due to the fact that the students were not able to get a Principal whom they wanted, a person who is qualified in Ayurvedic Medicine and in Modern Medicine and with high standards of qualification either foreign or indigenous, ranking with the qualification of

M.D., or M.S., F.R.C.S., M.R.C.P., etc. The best efforts of the Vice-Chancellor have not resulted in securing the services of such a person and the last the Commission heard was that a gentleman in Himachal Pradesh, who was formerly a student of this college and who had gone abroad and obtained a higher qualification, was expected to join as Principal and after much correspondence, it seems very doubtful whether he will be willing to relinquish his present post. The students also insisted that such a person should have been a student of the Ayurvedic College to ensure his sympathetic consideration of the requirements of the students and of their demands. In fact, the qualification has been changed from Ayurvedacharya to A.B.M.S. This problem may be deemed to be an all-India problem and it ought to be decided on an all-India level how the indigenous systems of medicine should be taught and to what extent modern medicine should also be associated with the teaching. We refer to one particular memorandum wherein it has been stated that the best way of securing this result would be to require persons to take a qualification in modern medicine and then to take to Ayurvedic studies or vice-versa so that the person would be equally qualified is both systems. Such a person can be given a higher qualification like M.D. Coming as it does from one of the products of the Ayurvedic College, it seems to us that the suggestion should not be altogether ignored. The position in Western Countries is that a person may practise any system of Medicine—Homoeopathy, Naturopathy, Allopathy, Hydropathy or any other system—but he must possess the basic qualification in Modern Medicine and be registered before he claims to qualify himself to practise any other system. This is the rule in the United Kingdom. We are not expressing any view on this particular system but a point which is worth consideration more seriously is : Can a University afford to maintain a hospital which is to cater to the general public and would it be possible to expand that hospital in the manner in which it has to be expanded without unlimited resources being placed at the disposal of such an institution ? We feel that the maintenance of the Hospital for Ayurveda or modern system of medicine or for both should be the responsibility of the State Government and we do feel that the authorities should consider the desirability of the State taking over the hospital, and if the University is to grant degrees, the teachers in the College and the equipment for the College may be provided out of contributions by the Central Government. The difficulties that have been experienced by a University having to maintain a Medical College and Hospital should convince both the Central and State Governments of the view that a hospital which caters to the patient of the locality is primarily the responsibility of the State. We are also of the opinion that another suggestion thrown out may have to be considered. Recently, the Sanskrit University has been started in Banaras. Ayurveda being so closely associated with Sanskritic studies, the question whether the Sanskrit University started in the heart of the city could not have close liaison with the Aurvedic College and Hospital may be considered. We consider that the Ayurvedic Hospital should function in the Banaras Hindu University but for study of modern medicine, the State should have a properly equipped general hospital in the city which will be open for the students. The amenities for the students at present are meagre and a hostel is an urgent necessity.

Women's College

There is only one Women's College in the Banaras Hindu University but representations have been made to us that unfortunately the College has not had the same amount of attention that other institutions in the University have had. For some reason or other, it has not been possible to start science courses in this College. It has also been brought to our notice that the scales of pay of all women teachers have not been improved. At the time when the Founder was responsible, a Vice-Principal was appointed with no such post having been created and with qualifications which will not pass muster in a University College. The question of appointing a Principal is hanging fire for some time and we regret that a considerable amount of frustration seems to be prevalent among the teaching staff of this College, some of them with very high qualifications and a great deal of teaching experience with their claims not attended to. We think this is a matter which ought to receive attention and a person with proper qualifications should be appointed as Principal.

College Of Music

This College has been under the direction of a distinguished musician of North India. By virtue of the age limit he has retired. It was, however, represented to us that the whole scheme of Music studies was drawn up by him and it was necessary that his guidance should be available if the scheme is to be successfully implemented to the highest stage. We are under the impression that when a scheme has been organised, it should be capable of being implemented by suitably qualified persons. A proper Principal conforming to the academic requirements and as per Regulations should be appointed to carry on the work and the College of Music should be thoroughly reorganised with Music as a branch of the humanities.

Constitution Of The University Bodies

We shall now take up some of the major changes which may be required in the Constitution of the

University and in the working of the several departments. We have already suggested that as an interim measure, the various bodies constituted under the Act should be suspended and their place taken by an ad hoc Committee with the Vice-Chancellor as Chairman to perform the functions under the Act. We have also stated that we do not feel that the procedure contemplated under Section 5(4) should in this particular case be utilised. After careful consideration and with due regard to the provisions of the Act, we feel that the state of affairs in the University is such that emergency action is required. In the interests of the University, and not because we wish that our report should not be spotlighted by persons who can express opinion, we have expressed the view that it would serve no useful purpose if the report is placed before the authorities as contemplated under Section 5(4). On the other hand, even at present, we have received supplementary memoranda which clearly indicate that certain of the groups realise that a good deal of evidence has been placed before us which is not to their credit or in their interest and therefore certain persons or organisations are trying to make it appear that there is nothing wrong with the University, that the only flow is that the Vice-Chancellor and the official bloc do not allow democracy to prevail. In the light of what we have been able to gather through the memoranda and through evidence tendered by very responsible persons, we feel that such a statement is absolutely unwarranted and if the University, before it reopens, is at all to function in a proper atmosphere, urgent and energetic steps should be taken; and, in the meantime, the Constitution will have to be revised carefully taking into consideration the manner in which it has been worked within the last seven years. Before going into the question of the provisions of the Constitution, we feel that it is necessary that a small Committee consisting of a High Court Judge, a Vice-Chancellor and a public man of eminence should be appointed who, with experts co-opted, may act as a screening body to examine the cases of teaching and administrative staff and to what extent the unruly elements have come to play a part in the affairs of the University to its detriment.

We realise that the amended Act was passed in 1951; but the experience of the last seven years shows that unless certain radical changes are introduced and certain categories of personnel are deprived of any part in some of the University authorities, it is idle to expect the University to function as it ought to. We are aware of the fact that whatever may be the amendment of the Act, the success of any University depends not upon the Act, Statutes, Regulations and Ordinances but on the personnel and the sense of responsibility and discipline that they bring to bear in the discharge of their high and onerous duties as academicians. Even so, in the light of the present working of the University, we have had the advantage of several eminent persons coming forward and suggesting certain radical changes. We shall take up some of these changes. We would recommend that an expert Committee consisting of academicians and persons noted for their administrative talent and public spirit should finally advise Government as to the shape of the University Act to be implemented.

The Visitor

The President of India is the Visitor of the University. But we feel taking into account some of the most disorderly scenes enacted in the University that it is very desirable that he should be given the power to suspend the operation of the University Act under conditions where gross indiscipline, organised strikes or chaotic conditions prevailed. The President has such power in the political field in regard to suspension of the administration in the States. It is no doubt true that this will be considered an infringement upon academic life and University autonomy but those who bring in those changes must themselves realise that they are largely responsible for the unfortunate recommendations that have been made by eminent persons of integrity.

The Court

We think that the statement that "the Court shall be the supreme governing body of the University" is inappropriate. In several cases, this has been considered as an indication that the Court can veto or amend any proposals, academic, administrative or otherwise that is put forward by duly constituted authority. It is no doubt true that there is a qualifying clause "save when these authorities have acted in accordance with powers conferred upon them under this Act, the Statutes or the Ordinances," whereby the Court cannot interfere but even so, the tendency for acrimonious discussion and for party politics to creep in consequent upon the misunderstood expression "the supreme governing body of the University" has been made obvious to us by several of the witnesses. Even when the Court is given power to review acts of certain of the University authorities, we feel it is necessary to impose the condition that any such act cannot be overruled unless by two-thirds majority as obtains in the provisions of certain of the Universities and only when the relevant Statutes, Regulations or Ordinances are brought up for consideration or when there is a definite official item on the agenda pertaining to the decision arrived at by such bodies.

We feel that the composition of several authorities of the University requires considerable revision in the light of the experience gained even within these seven years, not to speak of the experience of earlier decades. One of the fundamental considerations which has been forced on us is that the system of elections to various academic bodies and University authorities should, to a certain extent, give place to a system of automatic preferences. In other cases, the system of election should be controlled by adopting the system of proportional representation with the single transferable vote wherever this is possible. A third point which has been advocated is that inasmuch as this is a Central University and practically all the funds are given through the University Grants Commission by the Central Government, the spirit of a Central University should be maintained and the composition of the various bodies should reflect the characteristics of a Central University. It may be necessary wherever possible that due representation is given to the component parts of the Indian Union and no monopoly should be allowed for any particular area wherever the Central University may be situated.

The Chancellor And Pro-Chancellor

We note that the Chancellor and the Pro-Chancellor are to be elected by the Court. This has resulted in a great deal of canvassing and naturally persons who ought to be thought of for these posts are most disinclined to accept such an honour. An instance has been brought to our notice where in the time of the previous Vice-Chancellor, two eminent persons were suggested for these high offices but the Court turned it down on grounds that could not well be understood and this was largely due to the predominance of group politics within the Court. We feel that such exalted offices as those of the Chancellor and Pro-Chancellor should not be filled by election by the Court. We feel that it would add to the prestige of the University if the Vice-President of India and the Chief Justice of the Supreme Court be *ex-officio* Chancellor and Pro-Chancellor respectively.

Rector Of The University

The Act provides that the Visitor may, on his own motion or on the recommendation of the Court, appoint such person as he thinks fit to be the Rector of the University. We feel that under existing conditions and in conformity with the practice in most of the State Universities, it would perhaps be feasible to appoint the Governor of the State as Rector for the time being.

Appointment Of Vice-Chancellor

The appointment of Vice-Chancellor has led to a great deal of comment at all times. This office is to be filled by a person selected from among a panel of at least three persons recommended by the Executive Council. Unless the Executive Council is so composed that it can avoid group politics and come to right decisions, this at once puts the Vice-Chancellor into a very unfortunate position. If the name has been included by a majority vote as is likely to be the case, or if one of those persons whom even the minority,—a vociferous minority, has been backing is not appointed as Vice-Chancellor, the person who assumes office is at once heavily handicapped with the result that attempts are made to suggest that there are rival parties, the Vice-Chancellor's party and the party opposed to the Vice-Chancellor. This has been the bane of the Banaras Hindu University for several years. It would therefore be well for the Vice-Chancellor to be selected by the Visitor.

We do not feel that it is necessary to invest the Vice-Chancellor with more powers than he has. There is one direction however where the Vice-Chancellor's powers should not be curtailed and that it is in the matter of discipline of the students. The present position is that the Standing Committee is expected to deal with all matters of discipline, the result being that this Committee has been a great handicap rather than a help in enforcing discipline among students. The Vice-Chancellor should deal with matters of discipline subject to consideration by the Executive Council in special cases.

The Pro-Vice-Chancellor

It has been suggested that the post of Pro-Vice-Chancellor is not necessary in the University. On the other hand, several persons have stated that it is very necessary in view of the large amount of details of administrative work that is to be carried on in the University. It is laid down that the Pro-Vice-Chancellor shall be appointed by the Executive Council on the recommendation of the Vice-Chancellor and on such terms as may be laid down in the Ordinances and, where the recommendation of the Vice-Chancellor is not accepted, the matter shall be referred to the Visitor. The post of a Pro-Vice-Chancellor seems to us to be unnecessary. It is preferable to have instead an officer in the administrative cadre to relieve the Vice-Chancellor of routine duties.

Treasurer

This office has no doubt been in vogue for many decades but we think the time has come when the whole provision of the Treasurer should be reviewed. When the University Act was first passed in the year 1916, the state of the University was such that the Treasurer might be elected by the Court and he might continue in office for a period of five years. Those were days when the finances of the University were very limited and when it would be possible for a person in an honorary capacity to perform all the duties of a Treasurer. Today, the annual budget of the University exceeds one crore of rupees and we have been told that with *ad hoc* grants that have been given by the University Grants Commission, the amount in some cases is nearer Rs. one-and-a-half crores. While we should state that the distinguished persons who have held the office of Treasurer have done their best for the University and they have discharged their duties in a most conscientious manner, it is time that such heavy responsibility was not laid on a person who is elected by the Court from a panel of three names nominated by the Executive Council. On the last occasion, the very election of Treasurer gave room to considerable disharmony and it is not likely that, if this provision is allowed to continue, persons of the requisite calibre would be forthcoming to act as Treasurers. But even more important than this consideration is that we can no longer expect a person to discharge in an honorary capacity the duties in view of the large administrative and financial responsibilities now devolving upon the University. We therefore suggest that there should be a Finance Committee with a Chairman who will be responsible for the financial administration of the University. Such a Finance Committee has been in existence in other Universities and we think it is time that in a Central University like this, with large funds which are to be spent, such a Committee should be appointed. The Finance Committee which we have in view is a small Committee of five to seven persons with the Vice-Chancellor as Chairman.

The Court

The composition of the Court has been subject to several criticisms from many persons. We have already referred to the manner in which the powers of the Court should be restricted. In the light of our later observations, the composition of the Court will have to be altered.

Representatives Of Ex-Students

It is laid down that 15 representatives should be elected by the alumni (old students) association or old boys' association established in accordance with Statute 29-A. The bulk of the evidence before us goes to show that this constituency has become the monopoly of a particular group and that the elections are manipulated to get the maximum number of members into the Court by methods who do not bring out the intentions of the Act. Two suggestions are placed for consideration. In the first place, these representatives should be elected under a system of proportional representation by the single transferable vote, as exists in many of the Southern Universities. Secondly, a suggestion has been made that in view of the all-India nature, there is little or no chance of the alumni residing in different parts of the Indian Union to gain representation under present conditions; and although it is true that proportional representation would, to a certain extent, cure this state of affairs leading to concentration of power in a small group, we feel that it is worth considering whether representation should not be on a more distributive basis. We would commend the system by which the votes can be exercised in polling booths and where it is very necessary, postal vote may be permitted. The postal ballot has been misused and evidence goes to show that ballot papers are collected in numbers from the Registrar's office or from the Post Offices by interested persons.

We feel that the whole question of donor-representatives should be reviewed. This provision was probably necessary at the time when the funds of the University were limited under a foreign-dominated Government and had to be increased but, under present conditions, it would appear that as practically the whole of the revenue comes from the Central Government, this may be further simplified and limited.

The third category of persons to be represented on the Court are persons representing the learned professions, industry and commerce. Under the Act, 10 persons are to represent the learned professions to be elected by the Court; five persons to represent Industry and Commerce. We are afraid that the elections by the Court have not resulted in the intentions of the Act being duly observed. We do not wish to cast any reflections upon the persons who might have been elected under this category. From the evidence tendered before us, we are convinced that this method of representation has been utilised by the power bloc to import into the Court persons who would at all stages be inclined to support them on the basis of *quid pro quo* for their assistance at the election. Time has come when this representation should be totally removed from the purview of the Court and the Visitor given the power to nominate a certain number representing these interests or the right may be given to the Chambers of Commerce.

Representatives Of Parliament

The representation of Parliament need not be disturbed.

It is laid down in the Act that representatives of Hindu, Buddhist, Sikh and Jain culture and learning should be elected by the Court, five presons representing the Hindu culture, three persons, one each to represent the Buddhist, Sikh and Jain culture and learning. We are constrained to state that there has been a considerable amount of dissatisfaction that these persons may not always command the confidence of the particular interests concerned. In fact, the Sikh community has strongly felt that it was not properly represented and the Hindus have likewise made their comment that these have been used by the power blocs, who by virtue of their election are bound to support them in several of their activities. We feel that if such representatives are to be in the Court, they must be through well defined organisations or should be nominated by the Visitor. It is a matter for consideration whether under the Constitution in a secular State, such representation would be valid or is at any rate desirable.

Nominated Members

This is very necessary but at the same time, we feel that the persons so nominated must be in a position to attend the meetings of the Court, which we understand are generally held only once a year. When important measures are to be discussed, the power groups are dominant, the teaching element which has been given such excessive representation in the Court has not failed to support these groups, and the Vice-Chancellor and members of the Executive Council who propose any mesure find themselves helpless against a virile and not always fair criticism of some of these dominant groups. In fact, meetings of the Court have come to be regarded with some amount of dread by persons in authority and from the proceedings, we feel that it is the Professors and Teachers who have contributed not a little to a great deal of disharmony which prevailed at Court meetings. It seems to us therefore that in making such nominations, particular care should be taken to see that persons nominated are in a position to attend these meetings.

The Executive Council

This is the most important authority of the University which has got to deal with the day-to-day administration of the University in several respects. Theoretically, in a University which is run on academic lines, there may be every reason to suggest that the teaching element should be fairly represented. In actual practice, however, this has again led to a state of affairs where group politics dominated. More than one Vice-Chancellor has had to comment on the fact that some of the Principals and Professors have dominated and even coerced others into submission. We think that this Executive Council should consist of a limited number, not more than 15 with the Vice-Chancellor as Chairman. The Registrar should be the Secretary of all University bodies without any right of participating in the discussion or voting.

Here we may refer to the institution of Principals. Several of the witnesses, both those connected with the teaching posts and others, have stated that the institution of Principals in a residential University has brought about more cleavage and more of bitter estrangement between members of the teaching staff than any other institution. The Principal once appointed continues for life and, with his power and position as such, he dominates, being *ex officio* on all bodies. It has been reported that the Principals are a law unto themselves; they do not allow heads of departments to express their views or at least they ignore their views; they do not give adequate consideration for the needs of the different departments and they play up divided loyalties so that it has been reported in almost every college that there are two blocs, one, the Principal's bloc, the other consisting of those estranged and therefore frustrated. The recent appointment of Principals of Colleges as Chief Wardens has considerably enhanced their hold without increasing their responsibilities. It has been stated by more than one representative that, in their discharge of academic duties, the Principals do not feel that they have any responsibility and some do not take even 15 lectures in an academic year while others have to undertake greater amount of work. We are not prepared to discard altogether the criticism that favourtism and nepotism prevail to a very large extent in some Colleges due to the activities of the Principals. We have also been told that in the Selection Committees, the Principals play an important role and that the selections are by no means in the interests of the University. The very composition of the Selection Committees requires to be changed. We shall refer to this at a later stage. The demand has been made by very responsible persons that the posts of Principals should be abolished and that in their place, there should be Deans of Faculties. We are inclined to view this suggestion with sympathy. We do not see why in a residential University there should be Principals who would be like the fifth wheel in a coach. We are of opinion that the Deans should be elected by virtue of their seniority and that the Deanship should rotate, the maximum period being three years. The only exception would be the Principal of the Women's College who has particular responsibility and should therefore be on the Executive Council. We would call her the Dean of Women's Education and she should be responsible for all aspects of women's education and more primarily for the welfare of women students wherever they may be studying. She can have an assistant to help her who may be a Professor in the Women's College.

We suggest that the departments be grouped as follows:

I. **Arts Including Commerce**

Department of Politics,
Department of Geography,
Department of History,
Department of Philosophy,
Department of Economics,
Department of Commerce,
Department of Ancient Indian History and Culture,
Department of Indo-Sumerian Studies.

II. **Science**

Mathematics,
Botany,
Chemistry,
Geology,
Physics,
Zoology.

III. **Oriental Learning**

Sanskrit and Pali,

Ayurveda,
Mimamsa and Dharma Sastra,
Vyakarna,
Jyotish,
Sahitya,
Darshan,
Theology,
Religious Instruction,
Hindi, Arabic, Persian and Urdu.

IV. **Engineering and Technology**

Metallurgy,
Mining,
Ceramics,
Glass,
Pharmaceutics,
Industrial Chemistry,
Electrical Engineering,
Civil and Mechanical Engineering.

V. **Fine Arts and Other Professional Subjects**

Agriculture,
Surgery,
Arts and Architecture,
Law,
Music and Fine Arts,
Education.

The manner of the composition of the Executive Council should be left to the Expert Committee suggested. The members of the Executive Council may, unless otherwise specified, hold office for a term of three years except the *ex officio* members. The Registrar will be the *ex officio* Secretary.

The Academic Council

The Academic Council may consist as at present of the members mentioned, except that in view of the abolition of the posts of Principals of Colleges suggested, they will not be represented.

Standing Committee Of The Academic Council

The Standing Committee of the Academic Council as composed at present is an unwieldy body. We feel that its composition should be revised. It should be merely an advisory body, its decisions being subject to ratification by the Executive Council. We believe that the conduct of examinations should be the concern of the Executive Council as well as the declaration of the results. It should also be the function of the Boards of Studies concerned to suggest the panel of persons both for internal and external examinerships, who may be considered suitable for appointment. The Standing Committee may recommend the award of stipends, scholarships, medals, prizes, etc. which should be approved by the Executive Council.

Finance Committee

As regards the Finance Committee, we have already made our recommendation.

Selection Of Teaching Personnel

In several of the memoranda that we have received and from the evidence tendered there seems to be considerable dissatisfaction at the manner in which teaching personnel have been selected for several years. There does not appear to have been a sound policy both in regard to the advertisement inserted and in regard to the constitution of the Selection Committee. It has been openly asserted that the advertisements are sometimes so drafted that they may keep out somebody or be extremely advantageous to some others. We realise that these criticisms may be made by persons who have been disappointed but, when such criticisms have been made and specific reference invited to certain of the advertisements, we feel that the manner in which advertisements are inserted requires looking into. At present, Principals are asked to send these advertisements and they do not consult heads of departments who are competent to advise on the qualifications to be prescribed for the persons to be recruited with a view to get proper persons for the Department. In this connection, our attention has been drawn to the advertisement for the Professor of Pharmaceutics in the University. The first advertisement required among essential qualifications "Good Master's Degree in Pharmaceutics". In the second advertisement, this essential qualification was changed into "Good Master's Degree in Pharmaceutics, or Pharmaceutical Chemistry or Chemistry". The first advertisement, it would appear, was based upon the draft given by the Principal and issued on March 28, 1957. The Head of the Department was not consulted and he had also a grievance in the matter. The revised advertisement containing modification in the qualification of the candidate required for the post was issued on August 2, 1957. It is stated that the original advertisement sent by the Principal was not strictly in accordance with the terms of the recommendations of the Visiting Committee of the All India Council for Technical Education. In any case, this has led to a great deal of controversy and unpleasantness.

We have had another unfortunate case placed before us. This has reference to an eminent Professor in the University, Dr. Joshi, who is a D. Sc. of the London University. This qualification was challenged by some of his colleagues in the University and an acrimonious correspondence was carried on with the authorities of the London University. In spite of their best efforts to explain that the qualification obtained by Dr. Joshi was a *bona fide* qualification and for technical reasons it had not been possible actually to confer the degree at a Convocation, the persistence with which efforts were made to belittle and belie the statements of Joshi finally resulted in a strong protest by the Principal of the London University. Both the Vice-Chancellor of the Banaras Hindu University and the Inter-University Board of India were apprised of these facts by the Principal of that University and it was only when a strong line was taken by the Vice-Chancellor that this unfortunate and unbecoming correspondence was stopped by the clique which was behind this move.

While we do not want to leave the matter relating to advertisements entirely to the heads of departments, we realise that the process should be far more thoroughly scrutinised and it should be possible in some cases at any rate to get expert advice from other Universities giving the scope of the work that is expected to be performed. A very large number of advertisements are no doubt published in various newspapers in India, but it has been stated that the composition of the Selection Committees leaves much to be desired. Some of the experts are persons who are more or less amenable to the wishes of some of those who have *ex officio* standing in the Selection Committees and, being drawn from the neighbouring Universities, a sense of mutual obligation is sometimes said to prevail with the result that the Selection Committees do not command the confidence that they ought to among the teaching staff concerned. Instances of this nature have been brought to our notice. We think therefore that the Selection Committee should be constituted under a statutory provision and it should consist, as in some other Universities, of the Vice-Chancellor as the head of the Selection Committee, the Dean of the Faculty concerned, and three experts nominated by the Executive Council as contemplated by us, two of these experts being outside the State of Uttar Pradesh. The experts should really be selected on an all-India basis. The Expert Committee should interview the candidates and, in some cases, they may even meet in other centres like Bombay, Delhi, Calcutta or Madras. If the post to be filled be of Reader or Lecturer, the head of the department may be associated with the Selection Committee, if he is not also the Dean. It should not be open for the Executive Council to overrule the advice offered by the Selection Committee by itself appointing such persons. We would prefer the Selection Committee giving suitable names in the order of priority and the Executive Council to select only the first of those recommended. If for any reason, the Executive Council finds that the candidates suggested by the Selection Committee are not obviously in the interests of the University, they may refer the question to another Selection Committee composed on an *ad hoc* basis and by experts as suggested. This practice has been working very well in some Universities and there is no reason why it should not work well in Banaras University. In no case should any member of the Selection Committee be eligible for the post.

Library

We are afraid that the Library in this University is not put to proper use nor is it functioning in any satisfactory manner. The librarian should be a person well-qualified and of experience, who will contact the Deans of Faculties and Professors and will be responsible for suggesting books to be acquired for the library. Grants given for the library should be distributed over the several Faculties in due proportion taking note of the requirements of the Faculties concerned. It is regretted that proper accession registers have not been maintained nor a card catalogue. It is very necessary that there should be a thorough check of the library and the books acquired over a period of years should all be accessioned and reported upon. A qualified librarian with sufficient staff should be available in the library. Books for the library should be ordered after getting the permission of the Vice-Chancellor and according to the requests made by the several Deans who should themselves consult the respective Faculties. The necessity for having small departmental libraries is obvious. In some of the institutions, it is very necessary that departmental libraries should be available. We suggest that in the Women's College, there should be ample provision for a library. We also suggest that certain of the text books necessary for students should not only be duplicated but multiplicated, perhaps half a dozen to a dozen copies being acquired for the use of students. So far as the teaching personnel is concerned, there should be a limitation in the number of books taken by a teacher and we suggest that a Professor should have 20 cards, a Reader 10 cards and a Lecturer 5 cards which he can utilise for taking books whenever necessary.

Office Reorganisation

We feel that there should be a thorough reorganisation of the office. It may be divided into different sections and the responsibility should be that of the Registrar and the Vice-Chancellor to see that these function properly. There is little or no necessity for the Professors to worry about the office and prompt registration and despatch of letters should be the rule. Sanction to all circulars sent out should be obtained. We feel that all circulars should be seen by the Vice-Chancellor so that no question of privilege should arise or criticism offered. We do not think it necessary to draft as Registrar or Assistant Registrar members of the teaching personnel. They are not best suited persons for administrative work and we would rather suggest open recruitment for such posts without any effort to manipulate some member of the teaching staff to any of these posts. We would also suggest that some of the persons may be qualified in Accountancy, Book-keeping, Commercial Correspondence and the way in which records should be kept. It is disheartening to note that certain of the official records disappear without anybody being held responsible for such disappearance.

Audit And Stock-Taking

The report of the honorary auditor and the recent reports of the Audit Department seive to show that the state of the accounts has not been very satisfactory for several years. While we greatly appreciate and are thankful to the honorary auditor for the good work that has been done, we feel that every year, according to the Act, a thorough audit of the accounts by a person appointed by the Central Government on the advice of the Comptroller-General or similar official of the Central Government should be made. We have also been distressed to note there was great disparity in the maintenance of the stock-registers by the different members. Regular stock-taking is not in vogue. There is loose financial control over the permanent imprest. It has been reported that there is enormous expense in the purchase of stamps and that service postage is used by Professors in private correspondence. Many of these irregularities should be checked by an annual stock-taking and maintenance of stock-registers for which the Professors concerned and heads of departments should be held responsible. Breakages and loss should be reported and verified by a small committee appointed by the Vice-Chancellor and, in cases where the loss cannot be accounted for, the persons concerned should be held responsible. In regard to expenditure, it has been brought to our notice that sometimes the expenditure far exceeds the budget allotment. The procedure to be adopted should be that all indents from Deans or other Professors should be sent to the Vice-Chancellor and that the Registrar should prepare, in each case, a statement which will show the provision in the budget before the indent is sanctioned. This should indicate: (i) the amount allotted in the budget, (ii) the amount already expended; (iii) the amount to be spent on orders already placed; (iv) the balance available, and (v) if the balance available is sufficient to meet the cost of the indent.

Construction Of Buildings

A large programme for the construction of buildings is now on hand. We are not in a position to say that these constructions can be effectively supervised by the machinery at the disposal of the University. When the grants come from the University Grants Commission for construction of hostels, construction of additional buildings and for laying of roads, underground drainage system, water supply and electrical connections and the various improvements that are to be made, we feel that it is very necessary that the Chairman of the University Grants Commission should appoint a person with the status of Executive Engineer for supervision with a small staff. It is entirely his responsibility to report on the progress from time to time, to check-measure all items of work, to scrutinise estimates, etc. and to call for tenders, and in every way to supervise all building operations in the same way as the Public Works Department is expected to do. After the building programme is over, there should be a permanent Engineer with a small staff who will be responsible for the supervision of the buildings, for the occupancy of such buildings by members of the staff, to see that no unauthorised occupants take possession of the buildings, to see to their repairs, and to ensure that the whole compound is kept tidy and that unauthorised sheds or *gumties* are not opened within the campus.

Ministerial Staff

We have been presented with a memorandum on behalf of the Ministerial Staff Association and representations have been made about their prospects, etc. We feel that this is a question that can be gone into by the new Executive Council in detail and wherever there is ground for improvement and wherever injustice is done, they could be rectified. We must express our surprise that the President of the Ministerial Staff Association is a Professor of a College and we think it very undesirable that any member of the teaching staff should have anything to do with the Association. We have noticed the correspondence that this Professor as President of the Association has had with the University. We take strong exception to such correspondence and we suggest that the Professor be required immediately to sever his connection with such associations.

Other Representations

We have also received representation from the Mazdoor Association i.e., Class IV employees. We feel that it is not possible for us to enter into consideration of all these grievances. They should really be left to the Executive Council of the future to look into. We are sure that due consideration will be given to their representation and steps taken on the recommendation of the Vice-Chancellor to improve their conditions.

Other Complaints And Grievances

We have received a number of other complaints and grievances but, within the terms of our reference and to the extent to which they are applicable we have taken note of them. We are not in a position to suggest remedies for such grievances. These personal grievances should be brought to the notice of the Executive Council of the future and we feel sure that the Vice-Chancellor will present the cases and the Council will decide on the issues.

Conclusion

We have, after careful consideration of all the issues involved and after studying the memoranda and examining several witnesses, come to the unanimous conclusion that radical changes are required if the University is to function as a University. We have given our detailed recommendations in the body of the report. We would like to mention that it is essential that the Visitor should take steps to see that the authorities of the University are suspended for the time being and that the affairs of the University are vested in a strong Committee such as the one we have suggested. We are also of opinion that the Act itself may need revision in the light of the suggestions submitted in the report. We have suggested that a Screening Committee should review the appointments made to the teaching staff and the work of the members of the teaching staff and, where necessary, suggest steps to be taken in the light of their findings. The indiscipline so frequently exhibited in this University is due to several factors which we have stated but it appears to us that the basic factor is the attitude of the teachers, some of whom play the role of teacher-politicians and are not disinclined to exploit the grievances of students. We have also stated that in regard to any of the University Unions and their activities, a sound convention should be established and there should be a limitation on the number of years within which students should aspire for these honorary places, as indeed there is in the field of sports. We fully realise that students have some handicaps and they should as soon as possible be remedied. We have given in detail some of the necessary amenities that the students should be given. We are of the opinion that the University should be a completely residential University and that, excepting for one college, the Kamachcha College, it should have no affiliations with other colleges; nor should it be in a position to hold examinations for private candidates and confer degrees and diplomas in such liberal measure as is being done at present. The whole object of a residential University is thus frustrated. We have made specific recommendations in regard to Selection Committees, Appointment of Examiners, Constitution of Boards, Councils, Court, Academic Council and other bodies. We have suggested that a high power committee should be appointed to study the Act in the light of this report and the information placed at our disposal and make suitable recommendations to the Government.

MINOR IRRIGATION COMMITTEE, 1957—REPORT

New Delhi, Ministry of Food and Agriculture, 1958. 147p.+vp.

Convener : Shri Mahavir Prasad.
Members : Shri S.R. Vasudev; Shri B.P. Saxena; Shri H.K. Nivas; Shri B.N. Banerji; Shri U.S. Mahida; Shri H. Anantachar; Shri J.C. Hardikar; Shri P.S. Rajagopalan; Shri P.V. Divatia; Shri C.M. Bennet; Shri Moti Ram; Shri H.M. Antani; Shri G.R. Nangea; Shri J.N. Mitra; Dr. J.C. Ramchandani; Shri S.D. Kalra; Shri U. Ananda Rao; Shri Narasimha Rao; Shri Fahim Beg; Shri F.P. Bulakani; Shri D.S. Sinha.
Joint Secretary : Shri M. Lal.

APPOINTMENT

The Minor Irrigation Committee was constituted under the Ministry of Food & Agriculture (Department of Agriculture) vide Resolution No.F.9-5/55-IRN, dated July 12, 1955, to study the work done in the field of Minor Irrigation and thereafter assess future possibilities and indicate steps that need be taken by the States to make the minor irrigation schemes more effective in the irrigation expansion of the country.

TERMS OF REFERENCE

(i) Collect available data with regard to minor irrigation works;

(ii) Examine the difficulties experienced by the States and the scope for further expansion; and

(iii) Render all possible assistance and guidance and to make suitable recommendations to enable the States to launch their schemes on a more sound footing.

CONTENTS

Introductory; Recommendations; Appendices I to V; Report of the Minor Irrigation Committee on: Hyderabad; Mysore; Erstwhile Rajasthan State; Madhya Bharat; Erstwhile Vindhya Pradesh State; Erstwhile PEPSU State; Saurashtra; Himachal Pradesh; Delhi; Orissa; Erstwhile Madhya Pradesh State; Uttar Pradesh; Bihar; West Bengal; Travancore-Cochin; Kutch; Bhopal State; Erstwhile Ajmer State.

RECOMMENDATIONS

Surface Water Diversion

For assured irrigation benefit, it is desirable that the minimum flow of the streams and its duration are invariably ascertained specially on streams that are flashy and whose discharge widely fluctuates. It is true that the age old practice of putting temporary embankments across the streams every year is now being replaced rapidly by pucca masonry constructions. The bunds should be satisfactorily completed to bring about lasting benefit from these works. With this end in view it would be desirable to study the use that the upstream water is already being put to. Such a study may bring out the advantages of combining two or more weirs at one place. State Governments should also examine the existing aiignments in the layout of the projected water distribution system as in the case of Sakhri and Kumri irrigation schemes in Bihar to explore the possibilities of an integrated layout.

Surface Water Storage

In the hilly and undulating regions, it is desirable to have small storage in order to avoid costly construction of water channels.

For an economic design of the storage schemes, basic hydrological data of flood discharge, minimum flow, co-efficients of yield and run-off need be determined.

For storage that are proposed in relatively drier parts of the country, the water yield from single catchments will have to be increasingly supplemented by diversion of flow from adjoining catchments.

Chain System Of Tank Irrigation

The State of Madhya Pradesh and Orissa should examine the possibilities of setting up chain systems of tank irrigation as in vogue in parts of Bombay and Mysore, as it is important that adequate surplusing arrangements are provided so that if any tank breaches, the tanks situated lower down are saved.

Surplusing Arrangement On Tanks

Every tank should be designed for passing the flood discharge from the catchment. The flood discharge should be carefully computed so that an economic design for surplusing can be decided.

Ample capacity for flood surplusing need be provided on tanks that are constructed in the areas frequented by cyclones.

Evaporation Losses On Tanks

In arid regions it would be desirable to decide construction of tanks in deep and lower area of water spread so that evaporation losses are minimised. It may be desirable to utilise the entire storage in rabi without attempting to carry over supplies to the following kharif.

Silting Of Tanks

In States where appreciable silting of tanks is observed, it would be desirable to provide initially for extra storage capacity.

It may be advisable to discourage cultivation in tank beds and also take special care of the foreshore area in order to reduce the silting of tanks.

The restoration of a silted tank will be relatively cheap if tank banks are raised instead of desilting the bed.

Restoration Of Old Tanks

It is important that proper standards are laid down for restoration of tanks with different irrigation capabilities.

Surface Water Lift Irrigation

At quite a few places, large pumping installations have been arranged at great cost without satisfactory arrangements for conveying rather large quantities of pumped water. It would be desirable to discourage large installations and thereby avoid over-capitalisation. As an alternative, it would be desirable to attempt a large number of small installations.

Kuhls In Hilly Areas

It is advisable to take care of the flow from all intervening drainage by providing suitable covers on the Khuls at suitable points.

Groundwater Utilisation

It would be desirable for the States to organise their own exploration with whatever drilling equipment they have with them.

Construction Of Open Masonry Wells

In the future construction of wells, care should be taken to see that the wells are not constructed too close and special steps taken to stop the retrogression in the nullahs.

Choice Of Pump Sets

It is important that the performance of the pump set is estimated on the de-rated horse power instead of the usual figure that is meant for a few hours' running.

Filter Points

Instead of driving the filter it is installed in a bore hole, the yield of water at the filter point would be improved.

Artesian Wells

Steps should be taken both by Madras and Andhra States to regulate the construction of artesian wells.

Tube Wells

For successful running of tubewells an assured source of power must be arranged. Steps should also be taken for introducing a pattern for intensive cultivation so that the tubewells are kept running all the year round.

Paddy cultivation in tube well command is not very congenial to successful tube well running.

Improvement Of Water Supplies On Wells

Cheapest manner of arranging new irrigation could be to tackle the existing wells for improved water supplies.

Power For Water Lifting

In the interest of lift irrigation, it is desirable that a definite allocation is made on all power schemes for use on agricultural pumping, at reasonable rates. Steps should also be taken to avoid wasteful installations so that electrical generation arrangement is put to maximum work. The Agricultural and Electrical Experts in the States should also scrutinise proposals before sanctioning finances for pumping set installations.

Water Distribution Channels

The water distribution system deserves as much attention as the main work. It would be desirable to leave the construction of small length channels to the beneficiaries as practised in Mysore and Madras.

Spray Irrigation

It may not be economically feasible for general use but it has its advantages when the water source is in limited quantity.

Bund Construction

Large scale construction by the local cultivators could be organised on the lines done in Sholapur and Poona districts of Bombay State.

Steps For Accelerated Construction

Sanction for the construction and the funds for payment should reach the field officers well in advance of the slack season. It is also desirable to sanction works in any area after taking into account the available labour strength and their maximum turn-out during the slack months.

Popular Contribution

Government should initially make available the entire required outlay and recover the local people's contribution in instalments.

Sanction Of Subsidy

It has been possible in Bihar to encourage the construction of a large number of works with the limited finances made available to them. The State does not ask for finances for the loan part and merely offers payments of the subsidy portion either in one lot on the completion of the work or in phased payments on partial completion. Other States can follow this example.

Record Of Completed Works

All completed works should be brought on record.

Legislative Enactments

The States of Madhya Pradesh, Madras, Andhra Pradesh, Mysore, Kerala and Bombay have already passed Acts and the remaining States should consider legislation on their lines.

Finances For Maintenance

In order to encourage maintenance, a levy on the entire irrigable area is imposed in the States of Mysore, Madhya Pradesh and Madras. The remaining States may also adopt a similar system.

Organisation For Maintenance

The States should recuit technical men with previous experience for looking after normal repairs and for special repairs the State PWD should take care. The maintenance responsibility of tanks with irrigation capability lower than 50 acres should be left to local organisations e.g., Panchayats, Gaon Sabhas, etc.

Shortage Of Technical Personnel

Shortages could be partially met by recruitment of Surveyors as Overseers. Local people with talent could also be utilised as Surveyors.

Assessment Of Irrigation Benefit

All States should arrange for random survey through an independent organisation like the statistical section at Bombay, Madras and Andhra Pradesh for assessing the benefit.

In Madras and Andhra Pradesh, the entire irrigable area is subject to a wet assessment. This is a good incentive for beneficiaries to take full advantage of the irrigation water. Other States, particularly Orissa, West Bengal and Bihar should examine the possibility of adopting this method.

Surface Water Diversion

A few completed diversion schemes have not fulfilled their irrigation targets because of insufficient water supplies being available at the end of the monsoon and towards the beginning of the cold weather. For assured irrigation benefit, it is desirable that the minimum flow of the streams and its duration should invariably be ascertained specially on streams that are flashy and whose discharge widely fluctuates.

At several places in Bihar and on bandharas in Bombay, there has been the age-old practice of putting temporary embankments across the streams every year. These embankments are washed away by the first floods in the following monsoon. Quite a large number of these embankments are being rapidly replaced by pucca masonry constructions. For a lasting benefit from these works, it will be desirable to attend to the marginal bunds along the flanks of the newly constructed weirs. Unless the bunds are satisfactorily completed and adequate length of water channels are dug, full benefit cannot be derived from the completed works.

Before deciding upon the masonry construction of a weir, it would be desirable to study the use that the upstream water is already being put to. Such study may bring out the advantages of combining two or more weirs at one place.

Similarly in the lay-out of the projected water distribution system, existing alignments be examined to explore the possibilities of an integrated lay-out. On Sakhri and Kumri Irrigation schemes in Bihar, this has been done for the benefit of larger area. Bihar and Bombay may have more instances where this could be profitably carried out. Other States may consider the suggestion while deciding upon the pucca construction of old weirs.

Surface Water Storage

Extensive investigations are being carried out with a view to locating all feasible sites for significant storage on major and medium schemes. Possibilities of small storage should, therefore, not be many. In several situations particularly those in the hilly and undulating regions covered by the Aravalli, the Satpura, Chhota Nagpur in the Vindhya and similar tracts in Western and Eastern Ghats, it may however be desirable to have small storage in order to avoid costly construction of long water channels over rolling country. This may be of particular utility in looking after the irrigation of small patches of cultivation in such tracts. All the head water regions of the streams need, therefore, be examined for locating minor irrigation tanks. This is for the consideration of States of Bombay, Madhya Pradesh, Bihar, Andhra Pradesh and Orissa.

For an economic design of the storage schemes, basic hydrological data of flood discharge, minimum flow, coefficients of yield and run-off need be determined. Such observations may have to be initiated in the areas of the former States of Saurashtra, Madhya Pradesh and Vindhya Pradesh where observation guages on streams may have to be set up at large number of places.

For storages that are proposed in relatively drier parts of the country, the water yield from single catchment will have to be increasingly supplemented by diversion of flow from adjoining catchments. This may be examined in the State of Rajasthan and for the area of the former Kutch State.

Chain System Of Tank Irrigation

In States of Mysore, former Hyderabad and in Satara District of Bombay, chain system of tank irrigation has been in vogue. In a valley, series of tanks are completed so that the surplus water from upstream tank is stored in the tank lower down. Maximum utilisation of water is thus aimed. The State of Madhya Pradesh and Orissa may examine possibilites of setting up similar chain systems of tank irrigation.

In a chain system of tank irrigation, it is important that adequate surplusing arrangements are provided particularly on the downstream tanks so that if any tank breaches, the tanks situated lower down are saved.

Surplusing Arrangement On Tanks

Every tank has to be designed for passing the flood discharge from the catchment. The flood discharge has to be carefully computed. Generally, it is determined from Dicken's formula, namely:

$$Q = CM^{\frac{3}{4}}$$

where 'Q' is the discharge in cusecs, 'M' is the sq. miles of catchment area and 'C' is the constant depending on the nature of the catchment. The value of 'C' is variable for different types of catchment and can be best determined by actual hydrological observations. If these are carefully taken and the value of 'C' accurately determined, an economic design for surplusing can be decided.

Good portions of States like Mysore, former Hyderabad and Saurashtra are frequented by strong cyclones resulting in heavy downpour either in the beginning or at the end of the monsoon period. Such cyclones require liberal provision for flood surplusing. Cyclones are, however, known to have different paths. It may be desirable to ask the Meteorological Department to mark out the particular path that the cyclonic storms usually take. Ample capacity for flood surplusing need be provided on tanks that are constructed in the areas frequented by cyclones.

Evaporation Losses On Tanks

On water spreads in arid regions of Rajasthan and of former Kutch, appreciable evaporation losses have been noticed. It would be desirable to decide construction of such tanks that are deep and have lower area of water spread, so that evaporation losses are minimised.

On tanks in such areas, it may be desirable to utilise the entire storage in rabi without attempting to carry over supplies to the following kharif.

Silting Of Tanks

Appreciable silting of tanks is reported in States of

Madras, Kerala, Rajasthan and former Kutch. Tanks in Madhya Pradesh, former Vindhya Pradesh and Hyderabad do not seem to have much of silting problem. In States where appreciable silting of tanks is observed, it would be desirable to provide initially for extra storage capacity. This will, however, have to be determined from studies that should be carried out of silt deposits on the tanks.

It may be advisable to discourage cultivation in tank beds. Also take special care of the fore-shore area as necessary in order to reduce the silting of tanks.

The restoration of a silted tank will be relatively cheap if tanks are raised instead of desilting the bed. Raising of banks will however submerge additional area. It could be adopted only where the damage, due to submergence, is not very appreciable.

Restoration Of Old Tanks

The work of restoration generally consists of :

(a) Strengthening or raising the banks ;

(b) Improving the surplusing capacity of the tank ; and

(c) Occasionally desilting the bed.

It is important that proper standards are laid down for restoration of tanks with different irrigation capabilities. Such standards would be of good guidance to the skeleton staff that has so far been possible to post to this important work. The States of Madras, Andhra and Mysore have already decided the standards for a large percentage of tanks in their States. Other States of Madhya Pradesh, Orissa and former Hyderabad need urgently lay down standards for the guidance of staff engaged on this work.

Surface Water Lift Irrigation

Attempts at lift irrigation have not so far been found economical. Main reason is commonly the non-availability of cheap power. At quite a few places, large pumping installations have been arranged at great cost without satisfactory arrangements for conveying rather large quantities of pumped water. It would be desirable to discourage large installations and thereby avoid over-capitalisation. This should be particularly important, as construction of large channels is not popular among cultivators with small holdings. As an alternative, it would be advisable to attempt a large number of small installations. Cultivators with small holdings will possibly find these more handy, as a lengthy construction of water channels would not be required and also heavy initial outlay would not be needed. The size of each installation would be decided on the extent of the area intended for irrigation. This would again depend upon the willingness of the cultivator to complete water channels.

Kuhls In Hilly Areas

A small minor irrigation arrangement has to be made for the small patches of cultivation in hilly districts of Punjab, former PEPSU, Himachal Pradesh, and Jammu & Kashmir. As most of the streams are snowfed, some water supplies are observed all the year round. Irrigation channels that are taken out by diverting the stream flow are commonly called 'Kuhls'. For the benefit of small areas, only diversion need be arranged. Not many storages have been felt necessary. It is however, important that minimum stream flow is observed, so that irrigation potentiality is accurately determined.

Usually, the water channels have to pass through porous soil. Hence, the seepage losses are appreciable. Lining of channels may have consequently to be done at good many places. The relative economics of a lined channel has to be compared with that of an unlined channel, on which frequent vertical falls may have to be provided. Each case can be decided on its merits, but it is important that this relative analysis is done in all cases before the construction of channel is undertaken. Of course, the low maintenance cost of a lined channel should also be taken into account.

For uninterrupted running of Kuhls, it is important to protect it from land-slides. Unless this is done, Kuhls will quite frequently get choked and inundated. It is, therefore, advisable to take care of the flow from all intervening drainages by providing suitable covers on the Kuhls at such points.

Ground Water Utilisation

Use of ground water has an important contribution towards irrigation development in the country. Nearly 30 per cent of the total irrigation in the country is from ground water. Among the minor irrigation schemes, ground water utilisation is responsible for over 50 per cent of the total irrigation. In the First Plan, construction of wells, tubewells and installation of water lifting appliances was encouraged. Search for new areas of ground water potentiality has been undertaken under the all-India Ground Water Exploration Project. This is primarily for locating tracts where State tube well irrigation could be introduced as a State enterprise. On the completion of this Project, it is proposed to continue exploratory drilling under a Second Ground Water Exploration Project. This project is aimed at locating areas with smaller ground water potentiality which though not sufficient for State tube well irrigation may be considered adequate for ground water utilisation by individuals or Cooperatives. As the unexplored areas are numerous and the Ground Water Project may not be able to expeditiously cover all areas, it would be desirable for the State to organise their own exploration with whatever drilling equipment they have with them.

Construction Of Open Masonry Wells

Construction of open wells is the most popular use of sub-surface water. Not many new areas with ground water potentiality have, however, been opened ; hence there is a tendency to overdraw on proven tracts. It was observed in Rajasthan and Bombay that fragmentation of family holdings has been responsible for the construction of increasing number of wells. New wells have even interfered and in some cases depleted the water supplies on existing wells. Wells are also getting into disuse in Bombay because of little care having so far been taken to protect the sources of water replenishment. Soil erosion in the nullah beds is one of the main reasons for a large number of wells getting into disuse in Bombay. In the future construction of wells, care should therefore be taken to see that the wells are not constructed too close and special steps should be taken to stop the retrogression in the nullahs.

Choice Of Pump Sets

In specifying pump sets, certain features have to be kept in mind. The pump set should not have a suction lift of more than 15 feet. This is important because with higher suction lift the efficiency sharply declines. In the choice of diesel engines for running pumps, the rating of the engine for continuous running should be ascertained. Normally, the specified horse power is for running the engines for a few hours. Only half of this horse power can be depended upon for continuous running. It is important that the performance of the pump set is estimated on the derated horse power instead of the usual figure that is meant for a few hours' running.

Filter Points

In the coastal areas of Madras, Andhra Pradesh and Kerala, ground water utilisation has been in vogue through the construction of filter points. These have been popular at places where the water table is not very deep and the ground water supply is plentiful, so that pumped water table is not deeper than the suction range of the pumping sets installed at ground level. Commonly, the filter point is completed by driving the filter. This is likely to compress the sands of sub-stratum and thereby reduce its water permeability. If instead of driving the filter it is installed in a borewhole, the yield of water at the filter point would be improved.

Artesian Wells

In the West Godavari District of Andhra Pradesh and South Arcot District in Madras, artesian wells have been located and tapped by drilling with four-inch and six-inch pipes. Their discharges have, however, declined mainly because:

(a) Unregulated tappings—too near each other, have been done with the result that the water supplies have been interfered with;

(b) The pipes have got choked; and

(c) Water under pressure of the artesian aquifer has taken to easy flow into the top strata.

Steps need be taken both by Madras and Andhra States to regulate the construction of artesian wells. Improved design would avoid (c) stated above.

Tube Wells

In tracts where gravity flow irrigation is not possible, it is advisable to take recourse to tube wells if the tract is ground water worthy. For successful running of tube wells, however, an assured source of power must be arranged. In addition, steps for introducing a pattern for intensive cultivation need be taken, so that the tube wells are kept running all-the-year-round.

Paddy cultivation in tube well command is not very congenial to successful tubewell running. It concentrates the water requirement to a short period with the result that the tube well command has to be curtailed to a smaller area. This does not offer a varied use for the tube well water.

Improvement Of Water Supplies In Wells

Cheapest manner of arranging new irrigation could be to tackle the existing wells for improved water supplies. Boring could be done in wells situated in alluvial tracts. Where the wells are resting on rocky tracts, their deepening by blasting the rock may increase the storage capacity and in addition tap new fissures for larger water supply. Several States have attempted this work but good progress has only been possible where sufficient work has been organised on sufficient number of wells in a compact block. Handling of scattered wells is very expensive and time consuming. States of Madhya Pradesh, Bombay and Rajasthan need organise these operations for improved turn-out.

Recharge Of Ground Water

Improvements in ground water recharge can be effected by the construction of percolation tanks and weirs. So far, these have not been encouraged because they are incapable of bringing about direct irrigation benefit. Their importance has, however, been recognised in a small way by the construction of Rapats in Ajmer. Importance of works that can suitably recharge the ground water should be of foremost concern to dry areas of Bombay including portions of Kutch and Saurashtra. It is suggested that observations may be carried out for assessing the area of ground water replenishment that water conservation measures, like the construction of percolation tanks and weirs, can actually bring about.

Power For Water Lifting

The ground water use is likely to get more in vogue if adequate arrangements are made for water lifting.

Electric power should be increasingly available with the completion of multi-purpose projects and rural electrification schemes. In the interest of lift irrigation, it would however be desirable that a definite allocation is made on all power schemes for use on agricultural pumping. All States need be asked for the steps they take in getting positive allocation of power at reasonable rates for agricultural pumping. In the past, States like Bihar, Hyderabad and Saurashtra did not have sufficient power to encourage agricultural pumping. Their rates were also high.

While availability of power is thus arranged, steps need also be taken to avoid wasteful installations, so that electrical generation arrangement is put to maximum work. In Mysore and Madhya Pradesh, several pumping installations have a higher horse power than necessary. At present, these pumping sets are running for fewer hours. With a lower horse power meter, the same irrigation benefit can be brought about by running the sets for longer hours. The owners prefer a higher horse power that need only run for fewer hours possibly because of labour difficulty. This is uneconomical for the electrical supply, as the non-agricultural consumers can make a fuller and more continuous use of electricity. For a more assured use of electric supply, the initial scrutiny of proposals need include consultations with the Agricultural and Electrical Experts in the State before sanctioning finances for pumping set installations.

Water Distribution Channels

While irrigation works were quickly completed for tapping available surface water, not all the desired attention has been paid to adequate conveyance of harnessed water supply. No irrigation benefit can accrue unless the harnessed water is distributed systematically to the fields. The water distribution system, therefore, deserves as much attention as the main work. Some of the States like old Hyderabad and even Bombay have entrusted the construction of water channels upto three cusecs carrying capacity, i.e., for as big areas as 200 acres, to local people. Because of lack of cooperation and non-availability of vacant land etc. channels have not been completed with the result that water is not reaching to all portions of the command that was originally projected. It would be desirable to leave the construction of only such small length of the channels to the beneficiaries as would be required for say 25 acres of irrigation. This practice has been successful in the States af Mysore and Madras, and is recommended for other States as well. It may be a good scheme to have the water courses constructed by the beneficiaries in advance of the actual execution of the works.

Spray Irrigation

Because of initial heavy outlay on equipment and recurring cost of pumping, spray irrigation may not be economically feasible for general use. It may, however, be economical to operate it in hilly parts at places where the hydrostatic head may even do away with pumping. Spray irrigation has its advantages when the water available is in limited quantity.

Bund Construction

In areas that have heavier texture of soil and where repeated application of irrigation water is likely to require special drainage arrangements it may be advisable to examine the extent to which construction of bunds could encourage cultivation. Bund construction may be popular if, in addition to heavier soil texture, the area is frequented by more rains during the later part of the monsoon. The construction of bunds would encourage conservation of moisture due to late rainfall in the heavier texture of the soil and thereby create favourable conditions for satisfactory growing of winter crop. Bund construction is not likely to be successful in tracts where the soil is light and the rainfall is heavy in the early part of the monsoon. Experiments are being conducted at Bellary in Andhra Pradesh for evolving satisfactory designs that could be adopted in the section of the bunds that are made with the heavy type of earth. Large-scale construction by the local cultivators could be organised on the lines done in Sholapur and Poona Districts of Bombay.

Steps For Accelerated Construction

Minor irrigation constructions aim at maximum utilisation of local resources and talent. As most of the constructions are planned in cultivated areas, the local labour and resource can best be available for the construction of minor irrigation schemes only during slack periods of agricultural activity. In certain parts of Rajasthan and North Bombay, construction works can perhaps be in full swing only after the first rain shower. Any construction that does not take full advantage of this slack period in agricultural activity will have to necessarily wait for the next season. It is for this reason that progress on minor irrigation works has been protracted for more than a year even though they are capable of being finished within a few months of concerted activity. In order that maximum use is made of the availability of labour in this period, it is very important that sanction for the construction and funds for payment reach the field officers well in advance of this slack season.

Some cases of protracted construction were noticed in Orissa and Hyderabad. Other States may have similar experience. There appears good scope for all States looking into and organising such procedure that would convey the sanction of works and funds to the field officers well in time for maximum construction progress during the slack period of agricultural activity.

In addition to improving the procedure for sanction of works and funds, it would also be advisable to take an account of the labour availability in the area. In fact, a prior census of labour would be extremely helpful in organising works. Labour does not find it convenient to leave their villages for construction works that are beyond five miles radius. It would therefore, be desirable to sanction works in any area after taking account of the available labour strength and their maximum turnout during the months of slack agricultural activity.

Popular Contribution

The most outstanding use of local resource and talent is evident on the commendable progress made in the construction of individually owned works like wells, installation of pumping appliances, etc. On group works, the contribution has been significant only in day areas where usefulness of irrigation is firmly established. Contribution in cash has been more popular than the offer of labour. This is generally true on works that are taken up in tracts that are already developed. In backward areas, people are too poor to pay in cash at the start of the work. On the construction of contour bunds in Sholapur and Poona Districts of Bombay, local labour has worked on payment of lower wages. Popular contribution has been relatively more for the construction of new works that are undertaken consequent to the initial suggestion of the local people. On restoration works, the popular contribution is generally feeble, as the people either expected the old landlords or the Government to restore the existing works. In Bombay, the State has been consistently insisting on a prior popular contribution before the Government part of the finances could be made available for starting the constructions. This has not been very popular and has frequently resulted in very poor progress of minor irrigation constructions. In the case of backward areas, it can be explained by the inability of the cultivators to muster up the necessary funds. It should, therefore, be desirable for the Government to initially make available the entire required outlay and recover the local people's contribution in instalments that would offer the beneficiaries a chance to improve their irrigated agriculture.

Sanction Of Subsidy

On individual works like wells, pumping sets, filter points, the GMF Rules permit subsidy being offered to the extent of 25 per cent which, in the case of backward areas, is permitted even upto 50 per cent. The total subsidy is equally shared between the State and the Centre. Balance amount required for completing the works is being offered as loan. The State of Bihar, however, does not ask finances for the loan part and has been merely offering payments of the subsidy portion either in one lot on the completion of the work or in phased payments on partial completion. In this manner it has been possible in Bihar to encourage the construction of a large number of works with the limited finances made available to the State. Other States may examine the possibilities of adopting similar practice as is prevalent in Bihar.

Record Of Completed Works

All completed works should be brought on record, so that their behaviour is regularly watched.

Estimates of works should be closed on completion, and further repairs should not be a charge on the initial finances.

Initial outlay on all individual works should be recorded, so that any later requirement of funds for repairs could be judged on the merits of earlier expenditure.

Legislative Enactments

Legislative enactments are necessary for authority to (a) enforce certain standards of maintenance and in case of lapses to take over the work and recover the expenditure incurred in its restoration; (b) provide penalties being imposed on those who interfere in systematic utilisation of water resources, and (c) declare a commanded area under irrigation work as compulsorily assessed and thereby making irrigation obligatory.

The States of Madhya Pradesh, Madras, Andhra Pradesh, Mysore, Kerala and Bombay have already passed Acts which provide for the above three clauses. Remaining States had better consider legislation on these lines. Clause (c) is worth serious consideration of States like Bihar, West Bengal and Orissa which have a higher annual rainfall. Because of high order of rainfall, water supplies on even minor irrigation schemes can be depended upon. It should, therefore, be possible to demarcate the irrigable area. Compulsory assessment on the other hand would stimulate irrigation and ensure satisfactory maintenance.

Having passed the Acts, all States do not seem to have enforced the provisions of clause (a) for ensuring adequate maintenance by the beneficiaries.

Care should, however, be taken to avoid what has happened in the case of a large number of breached tanks in Hyderabad. Irrigable area on all tanks was assessed at a uniform rate, but the beneficiaries were permitted a remission in their dues in case the water supplies from the tanks become uncertain. The beneficiaries have, in quite a large number of cases, taken advantage of this provision and have got the water supply from these tanks declared as "uncertain" even though it was within their capability to restore the breaches by doing some earthwork.

Finances For Maintenance

Individually owned works like those of wells, pumping sets, etc. will be looked after by the owners. Similarly, works that are constructed and maintained by a small group of cultivators would not require much finances for maintenance. This is particularly true of dry areas where the use of irrigation is fully recognised by the cultivators. There are, however, large number of works which have been restored by Government and whose maintenance thereafter has been entrusted to the beneficiaries. In order to encourage their maintenance, a levy on entire irrigable area is imposed. This practice is in vogue in the States of Mysore, Madhya Pradesh, Madras. The remaining States need impose similar levy.

Under a third category of works are those that have been restored by Government and are being maintained by them. Here again, the entire irrigable area should have a regular charge to defray the annual maintenance expenditure and for special repairs. Madras, Andhra Pradesh, Mysore, Hyderabad, and Bombay have arranged maintenance through Governmental agency on works that have sizable irrigation capability varying from 200 acres in Madras and Andhra Pradesh to 100 acres in Bombay.

Organisation For Maintenance

Minor irrigation works costing upto Rs. 10 lakhs are of different sizes. Starting from individual works like wells, pumping sets and filter points, there are small irrigation works of significant size. Some of the works are capable of looking after even 10,000 acres of irrigation. These require proper technical supervision in their maintenance. Such works are invariably in the charge of Engineering Department in the State. While Madras and Andhra Pradesh include in this category works that irrigate upto 200 acres, Bombay has kept it at 100 acres. For even smaller works in Mysore, the State P.W.D. is responsible, though Madras, Andhra Pradesh and Bombay entrust their Revenue or Community Development Department the responsibility for maintenance of such small works. These Departments are not, in all States, staffed with technical hands. It is desirable that these States recruit technical men with previous experience for looking after the normal repairs. For special repairs, the Public Works Department in the State need be consulted. It was also observed that special repairs have been felt necessary once in five years.

The maintenance responsibility of tanks with irrigation capability lower than 50 acres could be entrusted to local organisations like Panchayats, Gaon Sabhas etc. In States like Bihar, Bengal and Orissa where the irrigation works are only for supplemental use, the local people may not initially be alive to this responsibility. Consequently, Governmental set up will have to be more watchful till the irrigation benefits are finally established and grow into a recurring use.

Shortage Of Technical Personnel

Shortage of junior staff has been felt invariably by all the States. States like Himachal Pradesh, Tripura and Manipur which are isolated and have got difficult terrain have not been able to attract qualified hands from outside. Even those who join, very soon leave the assignment with the result that important levelling for initial survey and estimating has been sadly neglected. Work of levelling forms a major portion of the duties expected of subordinates. This shortage could perhaps partially be met with by recruitment of surveyors who are well up in levelling even though they have not got all the qualifications that make up an Overseer. The States may start training classes for a short-term course of, say, six months which would primarily be for training the hands in the work of levelling. Local people familiar with the area and with aptitude for cross-country work could be trained and thereafter employed as Surveyors. This may relieve the shortage of technical subordinates specially in the States like Himachal Pradesh, Manipur and Tripura.

Assessment Of Irrigation Benefit

Irrigation benefit on most of the schemes is at present being reported on the basis of the initial forecast. Actual figures of irrigation have so far been collected only for works that the Irrigation or Public Works Department in the State have under their control. On other works (particularly in States like Orissa, West Bengal and Bihar) no systematic measurement of benefit has been undertaken. In U.P., Bombay, Madras and Andhra Pradesh, the irrigation benefit comes under review in the normal routine of the Revenue staff during their assessment of agricultural cropping. While Orissa, West Bengal and Bihar need organise regular measurement of irrigation benefit in addition, it appears desirable for all States to arrange for random survey through an independent organisation like the Statistical Section of Bombay, Madras and Andhra.

In Madras and Andhra Pradesh, the entire irrigable area is subject to a wet assessment. This is a good incentive for beneficiaries to take full advantage of the irrigation water. It is suggested that other States particularly Orissa, West Bengal and Bihar may also examine the possibility of adopting this method.

STUDY GROUP ON SOCIAL SECURITY, 1957—REPORT

New Delhi, Ministry of Labour and Employment, 1958. 98p.

Chairman : Shri V.K.R. Menon.
Members : Colonel V.M. Albuquerque; Shri S.N. Mubayi; Shri B.N. Datar; Shri S. Krishnamurty.
Secretary : Shri K.K. Bhargava (died; replaced by Shri S.P. Jain).

APPOINTMENT

In pursuance of one of the recommendations on labour policy in the Second Five-Year Plan, the Government of India, Ministry of Labour and Employment, set up this Committee vide their Order No. L and E-3(5)/57, dated August 3, 1957.

TERMS OF REFERENCE

(a) Examine the experience gained by the working of existing social security schemes;

(b) Study how these schemes and any other privileges given to workers could be combined in a comprehensive social security scheme;

(c) Work out the administrative details of such an integrated scheme;

(d) Examine whether, without any appreciable increase in the total liability of employers and workers, additional advantages can be given to the working class; and

(e) Examine and make recommendations regarding conversion, wholly or partly of the present provident funds into suitable pension schemes as envisaged in the Second Five-Year Plan.

CONTENTS

Introduction; Conclusions and Recommendations; Achievements and Criticisms of Existing Schemes; Feasibility of an Integrated Scheme; The Scheme; Conclusion; Appendices I to IV.

RECOMMENDATIONS

Under existing conditions, any large extension of social security measures will not be possible either in terms of coverage or actual benefits. The aim should be to improve upon existing measures and to simplify administrative procedure, restricting additional financial levy for the time being, to what is required for this limited purpose.

(a) Existing enactments providing for some form of social security or social insurance in the accepted sense are:

Act	Contingencies Provided For
(i) Employees' State Insurance Act.	Medical care and treatment, sickness benefits, maternity benefits, employment injury including invalidity and dependants' pensions where death arises as a result of employment injury.
(ii) Employees' Provident Funds Act, Coal Mines Provident Fund and Bonus Schemes Act and Assam Tea Plantations Provident Fund Scheme Act. (The scheme of old age pensions introduced in the Uttar Pradesh is left out of account for present purposes.)	Old age or death while still in service.
(iii) Coal Mines Labour Welfare Fund Act, and Mica Mines Labour Welfare Fund Act.	Medical Care and Treatment.

Existing enactments providing for relief in certain contingencies but which are not measures of social security in the accepted sense as the liability in each case is placed directly on the individual employers:

Act	Contingencies Provided For
(i) Workmen's compensation Act.	Compensation in the form of single lump sum payments in case of permanent disability or death resulting therefrom and periodical payments in case of temporary disability.
(ii) Plantations Labour Act.	Medical care and treatment, sickness benefits, maternity benefits.
(iii) Maternity Benefit Acts of State Governments and Mines Maternity Benefit Act.	Maternity benefits.

Act	Contingencies Provided For
(iv) Industrial Disputes Act.	Payments in cases of retrenchment and lay-off—a form of limited unemployment relief.

One single agency should be set up—hereinafter referred to as the Organisation—which should as a first step assume administrative responsibility for the enactments mentioned on items (i) and (ii)(a) above. In case of workers covered by both the Employees' State Insurance Act and one of the Provident Fund Acts, employers will pay to this Organisation in one single payment, the contributions due under both. Inspectorate and supervisory staff will be unified. These and other consequential measures will aim at simplification and added convenience to both parties—employers and workers.

The coverage under items (i) and (ii) under (a) are not identical but the advantages of setting up the Organisation still exist. It should, however, be the aim to make the coverage under the two enactments identical as far as practicable and in stages by a prescribed target date. As one step towards facilitating this, action should be taken to delete the provision in the E.P.F. Act under which newly established factories are exempted from its provisions for the first three years. The deletion of this provision is necessary for another reason as well.

The present arrangements in respect of item (iii) under (a) by which the respective Welfare Funds are responsible for medical care and treatment of workers in coal and mica mines is working satisfactorily and should continue.

The quantum of cash benefits at present granted under the E.S.I. Act should be augmented as follows:

(i) Sickness benefit should be payable upto a maximum period of 13 weeks in any three benefit periods of 26 or 27 weeks each.

(ii) Extended sickness benefit, at full normal benefit rate may be granted in case of tuberculosis, or other prescribed long term diseases for a further period of 39 weeks but only to such persons as have completed at least two years of qualifying service.

(iii) The maternity benefit rate should be raised so as to be equal to the full average wage of the insured woman and subject to a minimum of Re. one per day.

There is considerable scope for improving the standard of medical care and treatment for workers covered by the E.S.I. Act. The provision of medical care and treatment (including hospitalisation) for families of workers is urgently needed as it is this omission that has brought in the largest and quite legitimate criticism from organisations of workers and individual workers themselves. All these improvements could be provided only if substantial additional funds are available. For this purpose, the levy on employers should be increased to the maximum that the law already provides for. The justification which existed for levying contributions at lesser rates has, with the considerable extension of the scheme, lost much of its force. The standard of medical care and treatment should be greatly improved and the scope extended to cover families. In fact, a beginning has already been made in this direction.

The enactments relating to Provident Funds have proved a real boon to workers covered thereby, in the form of provision for old age. But payment in lump sum has obvious disadvantages compared with a regular pension scheme. The time is ripe for converting the Provident Funds into a Statutory Pension Scheme to be administered by the organisation. A scheme of Old Age, Invalidity and Survivorship Pension-cum-Gratuity is recommended for adoption. This involves payment of a small gratuity sufficient to meet immediate needs and using the rest of the resources towards giving the maximum pensionary benefits. Though the Assam Tea Plantations Provident Fund Act is an Act of the State Legislature, it is hoped that it would be merged in the new Scheme. Otherwise, the workers in plantations in Assam would be deprived of a valuable benefit.

To provide pensions of reasonable amounts, the resources should be augmented by:

(a) Increasing the present rate of contributions of workers and employers to Provident Fund from 6-1/4 per cent to 8-1/3 per cent.

(b) While the statutory amendments and administrative arrangements required for the conversion into a Pension Scheme will take time, the increase of Provident Fund contributions (to 8-1/3 per cent) should be given immediate effect by amendment of the rules under the respective Acts. Delay in effecting the increase will adversely affect the insured workers as a year of contribution at the existing rate (6-1/4 per cent) will be taken as only nine months for reckoning length of service.

(i) Translated in terms of percentage contributions the recommendations regarding rates of contribution above imply that as a transitional arrangement rates for the three classes of factories may be laid down as follows:

(a) For factories, the employees of which would be eligible only to the benefits under the Employees' State Insurance Act, there will be no change. Their rates of contribution, when raised to the maximum that the law provides for, work out to about 4-2/3 per cent by employers and 2-1/3 per cent by employees.

(b) For factories, the employees of which would be eligible only to benefits under the proposed Scheme of Old-Age, Invalidity and Survivorship Pension-cum-Gratuity, their rates of contribution will be raised to 8-1/3 per cent by employers and 8-1/3 per cent by employees.

(c) For factories, the employees of which are covered

for the full range of benefits under the E.S.I. Act plus the proposed scheme of Old-Age, Invalidity, and Survivorship Pension-cum-Gratuity, their rates of contributions as under (a) and (b) above would work out to about 13 per cent by employers and 10-2/3 per cent by employees.

(ii) In addition, the employees will be liable to pay an administrative charge not exceeding 0.5 per cent of the total wage bill in cases under (b) and (c) above. No separate administrative charge will be leviable in cases under clause (a).

The Workmen's Compensation Act originally provided coverage for both workers in organised industry as also in several scattered employments. With the gradual extension of the E.S.I. Act more and more workers in organised industry will be governed by this Act. Several cases will still remain, particularly of scattered employments where the responsibility for payment of compensation will continue to rest with the individual employer concerned. A pension scheme can be adopted even in these residuary cases by requiring the employer to pay to the Organisation a lump sum amount and the Organisation then taking on the responsibility for making recurring pensionary payments to the injured worker or his dependants as the case may be. Steps should be taken to revise the relevant schedule to the Workmen's Compensation Act to increase the present scales of lump sum payments to meet the cost of the new pensionary liabilities.

While the provisions in the Industrial Disputes Act relating to compensation on retrenchment and lay-off have afforded some relief and acted as some deterrent to hasty retrenchment, certain unsatisfactory features have nevertheless been revealed. The permanent remedy may be in the form of a scheme of unemployment benefit but a scheme of this type will not be practicable for sometime to come. Till then, improvements should rather be in the direction of avoiding closures—and consequent retrenchment, as far as possible, as, e.g., by creation of a fund through which industrial units in temporary difficulties can be assisted and kept running where such a course is in the interests of the workers and the public interests at large. This subject will be studied and a supplementary report submitted if Government so wishes.

Comparative studies made of some countries in Europe by the I.L.O. show that the employer's liability towards cost of social security measures for the workers—expressed as a percentage of the wages—is, in many cases higher than what the Group has recommended—this, inspite of the fact that adequate standards of medical care, hospitalisation etc. are provided in these countries by the State for the population as a whole including industrial workers.

COMMISSION OF INQUIRY ON EMOLUMENTS AND CONDITIONS OF SERVICE OF CENTRAL GOVERNMENT EMPLOYEES, 1957-59—REPORT

New Delhi, Ministry of Finance, 1959. 640p.+xiip.

Chairman : Shri Justice Jagannadha Das.
Members : Shri V.B. Gandhi; Shri N.K. Sidhanta; Shri M.L. Dantwala; Smt. Maragatham Chandrasekhar.
Associate Secretary : Shri H.F.B. Pais.
Secretary : Shri L.P. Singh.

APPOINTMENT

The Commission was appointed by the Ministry of Finance, under Resolution No. 2474-Secy.(E)/57, on August 21, 1957.

TERMS OF REFERENCE

The terms of reference of the Commission will be as follows:

(i) Examine the principles which should govern the structure of emoluments and conditions of service of the Central Government employees;

(ii) Consider and recommend what changes in the structure of emoluments and conditions of service of different classes of Central Government employees are desirable and feasible keeping in mind the considerations mentioned below;

(iii) Recommend, in particular, the extent to which benefits to Central Government employees can be given in the shape of amenities and facilities; and

(iv) In making their recommendations the Commission will take into account the historical background, the economic conditions in the country and the implications and requirements of developmental planning, and also the disparities in the standard of remuneration and conditions of service of the Central Government employees on the one hand and of the employees of the State Governments, Local Bodies and aided institutions on the other, and all other relevant factors.

CONTENTS

Resolution; **Part I—Introductory:** Procedure of the Commission; Our Terms of Reference; General Description of Central Government Employees; **Part II—General Principles and Considerations:** Principles of Pay and Conditions of Service; Economic Conditions; Developmental Planning; Disparities Between Central Emoluments and those under State Governments, Local Bodies, etc.; Minimum Remuneration; Highest Salaries; Dearness Allowance; **Part III—Pay and Allowances:** Pay Scales; Headquarters Organisation of the Government of India; Office Staff outside the Secretariat; The Class I Central (Non-Technical) Services; Class II Services and Posts; Scientific Staffs; Engineering Staffs; Medical and Public Health Staffs; Economists and Statisticians; Class IV Staffs; Workshop Staffs; Some other Common Categories; Railways; Posts and Telegraphs Department; Civil Aviation Department; Central Board of Revenue; Audit and Accounts Departments; Ministry of Information and Broadcasting; Ministry of Defence; Government of India Presses; India Government Mints; Union Territories; Special Pay; Fixation of Pay in New Scales; Allowances; **Part IV—Conditions of Service, Amenities and Facilities, and Allied Matters:** Hours of Work; Weekly Off; Public Holidays; Overtime Allowance; Casual Leave and Special Casual Leave; Leave Entitlements; Age of Superannuation; Retirement Benefits; Medical Facilities; Housing Facilities; Educational Assistance; Uniforms; Protective Clothing etc.; Working Conditions; Canteen Facilities; Staff-Welfare; Leave Travel Concessions; Promotion and Character Rolls; Temporary Employees; Workcharged Staff, Casual Labour; Government Servants Conduct Rules; Political Rights; Right of Association; Machinery for Negotiation and Settlement of Dispute; Disciplinary Proceedings; Classification of Services; **Part V—Other Matters:** Efficiency in Public Service, Statistical Requirements; Cost of our Recommendations; Date of Effect of some of our Recommendations; Summary of Recommendations; Appendices I to V.

RECOMMENDATIONS

Principles Of Pay And Conditions Of Service

The structure of emoluments and conditions of service should be so designed as to ensure recruitment at different levels of persons with requisite qualifications and abilities and to keep them efficient.

The social position which a Government servant is traditionally expected to maintain should not in itself be a factor in the determination of his remuneration.

While the 'model employer' principle, as commonly understood, is not suitable for determination of remuneration, the social principles and standards which Government have laid down for, or commended, to employers generally should be taken into account. Further, in the matter of conditions of work and employment practices generally the Government may become the pace-setter—a model employer.

The minimum wage or salary should not be determined only on economic considerations, but should satisfy also social tests. Even above the minimum level Government should remunerate their employees fairly.

In the present circumstances, the principle of fair comparison with rates of remuneration in outside employment is not suitable for full and detailed application; but it is one of the important factors to be taken into account.

Once the demands of efficiency of the public service are satisfied, social considerations require limitation of disparities between the highest and the lowest salaries, and their reduction as far as possible.

With the minimum and maximum salaries having been determined on a combination of social and economic considerations, sound and equitable internal relativities constitute the most important single principle to be followed in the determination of the intermediate salaries.

Except in the broad sense of being an indicator of the level and the state of the economy, and thus of the resources which the Government can draw upon for their needs, the trend of national productivity cannot be accepted as a factor in itself relevant to the determination of salaries and wages of Government servants.

The level of consumer prices is among the factors relevant to the determination of rates of remuneration of Government servants.

Economic Conditions And Developmental Planning

Fluctuations in prices have occurred during the last twelve years, but the general trend, especially since 1955, has been upward. The growing tempo of investment in the economy and the relative shortage of foodgrains are the main factors responsible for the price increase.

Production and national income have increased over the last few years; the economic situation today is better and more promising than it was in 1947-48.

Indications are that there may not be a serious instability of prices in near future, but a slow rise of prices is likely; hence the need for caution.

There has been a growing shortage of internal resources needed for financing development plans. Rapid economic development requires restraint on consumption consistent, as far as possible, with the social objectives of planning.

Disparities Between Central Emoluments And Those Under State Governments, Local Bodies, Etc.

In the context of our constitutional structure the issue of disparities is a highly complex one, and tangled with other matters; it is not one that can be resolved in a simple way.

The suggestion that the Central Government employees posted in different States might be remunerated at the rates prescribed for the State employees, or, that, in the alternative, the dearness and other allowances alone might follow the State rates is not sound or feasible.

A scheme of recruitment to the non-gazetted posts under the Central Government by transfer of selected personnel from the appropriate services of the State Government may be considered.

The disparities should be regarded as a factor calling for restraint but not one that would justify the denial to the Central Government employees of the minimum improvement in remuneration which otherwise appears to be fair and desirable.

Minimum Remuneration

With the present magnitude of unemployment and under-employment in the country and the low levels of income, the present minimum of Rs. 75 is sufficient to attract recruits of the right type.

The present minimum remuneration of Rs. 75 in Central Government compares favourably with the average minimum rate in organised private industry.

A need-based minimum wage of the order of Rs. 125 per mensem proposed by the employees is not feasible economically and financially.

A diet capable of providing 2,600 calories and other nutrients of the requisite order would cost Rs. 52 per mensem for a family of three consumption units. Adding the requirements of clothing, housing, etc., a need-based minimum, permissible within the limits of the country's present output of foodstuffs would cost about Rs. 80.

With the Consumer Price Index at 116, a remuneration of Rs. 80 would restore the real income of employees on the lowest pay to the level at which it was fixed on the Varadachariar Commission's recommendations.

While it is necessary to keep inflationary pressures in check, a modest increase in minimum remuneration is called for on social considerations and in the interest of contentment of the staff. It is only as an element in an integrated economic and social policy that a sacrifice can reasonably be asked for from the lower grades of staff.

The minimum remuneration payable to a Central Government employee should be increased from Rs. 75 per mensem to Rs. 80 per mensem.

Highest Salaries

Keeping in view the necessity of maintaining a high standard of recruitment to the superior services, and the erosion of the real income which has taken place, reduction of the salaries at present prescribed for the highest grades is not recommended.

Dearness Allowance

While an upward tendency in prices is likely to persist, the possibility of a fall in the price level cannot be ruled out in view of likely fluctuations in agricultural production and other possible causes. Dearness allowance should, therefore, continue as a separate element in the remuneration of Central Government employees. It should, however, be limited for the present to employees whose salaries are below Rs. 300 per mensem.

Judging from the recent trends in prices, the consumer price index (1949=100) is not likely to drop below 100. The basic salaries of the lower paid employees should, therefore, be fixed in terms of the requirements at an index level of 100. No downward adjustment in basic salaries should, however, be made even if the index falls to 90.

The entire remuneration of the higher paid employees should be in the form of salary with no separate dearness allowance.

In future adjustments of the dearness allowance to meet rise in prices, employees in the pay-range of Rs. 300 and above but below Rs. 400 should, however, be grouped with those in the pay-range below Rs. 300.

Should the consumer price index continue to rise, the case of employees in the pay-range of Rs. 400 and above but below Rs. 1,000 for grant of dearness allowance may be considered in the light of all the relevant circumstances at the time.

There should not be automatic adjustment of dearness allowance with the price index. A substantial and persistent rise in prices, however, normally creates a *prima facie* case for compensation and it should be the Government's endeavour not to allow the standard of living of their employees in the lower range, of remuneration to fall.

For the present, employees drawing pay below Rs. 300 per mensem may be granted dearness allowance at the following rates:

(a) basic pay below Rs. 150 — Rs. 10 per mensem
(b) basic pay of Rs. 150 or above but below Rs. 300 — Rs. 20 per mensem

There should be marginal adjustments for employees drawing a basic pay of Rs. 300 or above but below Rs. 320.

These rates of dearness allowance should be taken as related to the consumer price index 115 (1949=100) and should continue unless the index falls below 100. If during a period of 12 months the index remains on an average, ten points above 115, the Government should review the position and consider whether an increase in the allowance should be allowed, and if so, at what rate. If thereafter the index falls by the same margin, and for the same period, the position may be similarly reviewed and appropriate adjustments made.

The benefit of dearness allowance should, in future upward adjustments, be extended to all employees drawing a basic pay below Rs. 400 per mensem in such a way that the total of basic pay and dearness allowance paid to any employee in the pay-range of Rs. 300 to Rs. 400 does not exceed Rs. 400.

Pay Scales

On promotion to a higher post, upto and inclusive of those from the present Class II level to Class I, the pay of an employee should first be increased by one increment in the lower scale and then fixed in the higher scale at the stage next above. No distinction should be made for this purpose on the ground that the lower post was held in a quasi-permanent or temporary and not permanent capacity.

Selection grades without functional differentiation are necessary in certain cases in order to provide incentives to employees who have no outlets, or very limited outlets, for promotion to higher posts.

The following typical scales of pay are recommended for Class I, II and III services and posts:

Class I

	Rs.
Supertime scales and fixed rates (Chapters XI, XIII, XV, XVI and XVII)	3000
	2750
	2500
	2250
	2000—125—2250
	1800—100—2000—125—2250
	2000
	1800—100—2000
	1600—100—1800
	1300—60—1600—100—1800
	1100—50—1300—60—1600—100—1800
	1300—60—1600
	1100—50—1400
Time scales:	
Indian Foreign Service	
Senior Scale	900—50—1300—1300—60—1600—100/2—1800
Junior Scale	400—400—500—40—700—30—1000
Class I (non-technical) Services	400—400—450—30—510—700—40—1100—50/2—1250
Scientific Services—	
Senior Scale	700—50—1250
Junior Scale	400—40—800—50—950
Engineering and some other Services—	
Senior Scale	700—40—1100—50/2—1250
Junior Scale	400—400—450—30—600—35—950
Medical Services—	
Senior Scale	850—45—1300—50—1400 (consolidated scale) or 675—35—850—40—1050—50—1150 plus non-practising allowance.
Junior Scale	575—25—600—30—750—40 1150 (consolidated scale) or 425—25—450—30—600—35—950 plus non-practising allowance.

Class II

Standard Scale . . .	350—25—500—30—830—35—900
Accounts Department .	590—30—830—35—900
Station Superintendents (Railways)	590—30—830—35—900
Medical Services . . .	475—25—650—30—950 (consolidated) or 325—25—500—30—800 plus non-practising allowance
Programme Executives in All India Radio, Grade III of the Central Information Service, Stores Officers, etc.	350—25—500—30—800
Research Assistants/ Technical Assistants etc.	325—15—475—20—575
Assistants in the Central Secretariat	210—10—290—15—530

Class III

Clerical Staffs :

Supervisory Grade I .	425—25—575
,, ,, II .	350—20—450—25—475
,, ,, III .	335—15—425
,, ,, IV .	210—10—290—15—380
Upper Division Clerk .	130—5—160—8—280—10—300
	130—5—160—8—280
Lower Division Clerk .	110—3—131—4—175—5—180

Stenographers . . .	320—15—530
	210—10—290—15—425
	150—5—160—8—280—10—300
	130—5—160—8—280—10—300

Scientific Staffs :

Research Assistants/ Scientific Assistant/ Laboratory Assistant etc.	325—15—475—20—575
	210—10—290—15—425
	150—5—160—8—280—10—300
	(If 4 grades are retained)
	or
	160—8—280—10—330
	(If 3 grades are retained)
	110—4—170—5—200

Engineering Staffs :

	450—25—575
	335—15—485
	335—15—425
	250—10—290—15—380
	205—7—240—8—280
	180—180—205—7—240—8—280
	180—6—240
	175—6—205—7—240
	150—5—175—EB—6—205—7—240
	110—4—170—5—200
	110—3—131—4—175—5—180
	with a special pay of Rs. 10 per mensem in some cases.

Accounts Staff :

S.A.S. Accountants . . .	270—15—435—20—575
Divisional Accountants	180—10—290—15—440

Revenue Staff :

Income Tax Department

Income Tax Inspectors (Selection Grade, only if there is direct recruitment to Class II)	325—15—475—20—575
Income Tax Inspectors (Ordinary Grade) .	210—10—290—EB—15—485
Notice Servers	75—1—85—2—95

Customs Department :

Preventive Officers Grade I/ Examiners (Selection Grade)	325—15—475—20—575
Preventive Officers Grade I/Examiners	210—10—290—EB—15—485
Preventive Officers Grade II	150—5—160—8—280—10 300

Central Excise Department :

Deputy Superintendents	350—20—450—25—575
Inspectors (Selection Grade)	320—15—485
Inspectors (Ordinary Grade)	210—10—290—15—380
Supervisors . . .	110—4—170—5—180
Women Searchers . . .	130—4—170—5—225

Posts and Telegraphs Department :

Operating Staffs—	
Supervisory Grades . .	335—15—425
	210—10—290—15—320
Basic Grades	150—5—175—6—205—7—240
	110—4—170—5—225
Assistant Superintendent of Post Offices and R.M.S. . . .	335—15—425
Inspectors of Post Offices and R.M.S. . . .	210—10—290—15—380
Wireless Operators / Repeater Station Assistants	270—10—290—15—350 (Selection Grade)
	150—5—160—8—240—EB—8—280—10—300
Telephone Inspectors	150—5—160—8—240—EB—8—280—10—300
Line Inspectors . . .	150—5—160—8—216
Mechanics, Cable Jointers	175—6—205—7—240 (Selection Grade)
	110—3—131—4—155—EB—4—175—5—180
Sub-Inspectors Telegraphs	105—3—135—EB—4—155
Head Postmen and allied categories . . .	135—4—155 (Selection Grade)
	105—3—135
Postmen, Linemen, Mail Guards	75—1—85—EB—2—95

Railways :

Scales of pay and main categoies under each scale :

Chief Controller Head Ticket Collector Head Travelling Ticket Examiner Inspector (Commercial) Inspector (Loco) Inspector (Transporation) Station Superintendent/ Deputy Station Supdt. Yard Foreman Yard Master	450—25—575

Deputy Chief Controller Head Ticket Collector Head Travelling Ticket Examiner Inspector (Commercial) Inspector (Transportation) Inspector (Loco) Power Controller Station Master Station Superintendent/ Deputy Station Supdt. Yard Foreman Yard Master	370—20—450—25—475
Loco Inspector Power Controller	335—15—485 (scale proposed if two existing grades Rs. 260—350 and Rs. 300—400 are grouped together)
Chief Wireless Inspector Driver Grade A Head Ticket Collector Head Travelling Ticket Examiner Inspector (Commercial) Inspector (Transportation) Inspector (Loco) Power Controller Section Controller Grade I Station Master Yard Foreman Yard Master	335—15—425
Section Controller . . .	270—10—290—15—425 (if Grades I and II are amalgamated)
Section Controller Grade II	270—10—290—15—380
Assistant Yard Foreman Assistant Yard Master Chief/Head Booking Clerk Chief/Head Goods Clerk Chief/Head Luggage Clerk Head Signaller Head Ticket Collector Head Travelling Ticket Examiner Head Trains Clerk Inspector (Commercial) Inspector (Transportation) Station Master Yard Foreman Yard Master	250—10—290—15—380
Driver Grade B	210—10—290—15—320—EB—15—380
Assistant Inspector (Commercial Assistant Inspector (Transportation) Assistant Station Master Assistant Yard Foreman Assistant Yard Master Chief/Head Booking Clerk Chief/Head Goods Clerk Chief/Head Luggage Clerk Conductor Driver (Licensed—Marine) Guard Grade A Head Signaller Head Trains Clerk Motorman Serang (Marine) Station Master Wireless Inspector Yard Foreman Yard Master	205—7—240—8—280
Serang (Marine)	175—6—205—7—240
Booking Clerk Driver Grade C Goods Clerk Luggage Clerk	150—5—160—8—240
Assistant Station Master Assistant Yard Foreman Assistant Yard Master Booking Clerk Conductor Driver (First Class Certificate—Marine) Goods Clerk Guard Grade B Head Signaller Head Ticket Collector Head Travelling Ticket Examiner Luggage Clerk Station Master Trains Clerk Yard Foreman Yard Master	150—5—175—6—205—EB—7—240
Wireless Operator . . .	130—5—160—8—200—EB—8—256—EB—8—280
Assistant Station Master Assistant Yard Foreman Assistant Yard Master Driver (Second Class Certificate—Marine). Guard Grade C Serang (Marine)	130—4—170—EB—5—200—EB—5—225

Yard Foreman	130—4—170—EB—5—200
Yard Master	—EB—5—225
Travelling Ticket Examiner	130—5—175—EB—6—205—7—212
Shunter Grade A . . .	130—4—170—EB—5—200
Shunter Grade B . . .	130—4—158
Fireman Grade A . . .	125—3—131—4—155
Shunting Jamadar	
Booking Clerk	
Goods Clerk	110—4—150—EB—4—170—5—180—EB—5—200
Luggage Clerk	
Signaller	
Ticket Collector	110—3—131—4—155—EB—4—175—5—180
Trains Clerk	
Cabinman	110—3—125
Shunting Jamadar	
Brakesman	100—3—130
Fireman Grade B	

Headquarters Organisation Of The Government Of India

The two grades of Section Officers should be amalgamated into a single grade carrying the standard Class II scale.

A slightly higher remuneration than that recommended would be justified for Lower Division Clerks if Government consider it necessary to have for the Secretariat a superior class of recruits even at that level.

Direct recruitment to the Upper Division grade should be stopped and promotion to a proportion of posts which are now being filled by direct recruitment should be made on the basis of a written examination conducted by the Public Service Commission.

Office Staffs Outside The Secretariat

Classification of offices into Attached and Subordinate offices should be made on a functional basis.

The Secretariat and Attached offices may be combined into a single headquarters organisation with a common 'office'.

Definite criteria should be laid down for determining as to what offices should be included in the Central Secretariat Service Scheme.

The question of direct recruitment above the level of Lower Division Clerk at the Armed Forces Headquarters should be examined.

The necessity for continuing the posts of Assistant-in-Charge should also be examined.

Posts of Upper Division Clerk now filled by direct recruitment should be filled by promotion on the basis of a limited competitive test, except where for any special reason a university degree is considered an essential qualification for the posts.

10 per cent of the posts of Lower Division Clerk should be in a selection grade in cadres in which the proportion of promotion posts is less than 50 per cent, of the Lower Division posts.

There should be a selection grade for Upper Division Clerks in the Indian Audit and Accounts Department and the Defence Accounts Department.

In the Railways, Typists should not be retained as a separate cadre but should be merged in the general clerical cadre.

In the Railways the system of employing Clerks as Telephone Operators may continue, but the necessity for, and the rates of, special pay granted to them should be reviewed.

The arrangement for employing Upper Division Clerks on supervisory duties on their grade pay plus a special pay is not satisfactory; if the duties are fully supervisory it should be considered whether posts of Head Clerk should not be created.

Lower Division Clerks in non-Secretariat offices may be permitted to compete for appointment to the grade of Lower Division Clerk in the Secretariat, and may be allowed suitable age relaxation for this purpose.

Stenographers and Stenotypists in non-Secretariat offices may be permitted to compete for posts in the lowest grade of Stenographer in the Secretariat and may be allowed relaxation of age limit for this purpose.

Class II Services And Posts

The existing arrangement of having both Class II services and a junior branch of the Class I service may continue.

Government may decide in which services promotion from Class II to Class I should be to the senior scale of the latter.

Scientific Staffs

All new recruits to Class I junior scale should be given up to two advance increments—one increment for every year of approved research before entering service.

In view of the pay structure and the nature of work in the scientific services it is recommended that the grade structure in research and development organizations should be such as to provide for a much larger proportion of posts in the senior and the higher grades together than in the junior grade.

A scheme of special merit promotion, providing for the creation *ad hoc*, of posts outside the normal strength of a grade, in the scale of Rs. 700—1250 or in a higher scale depending on the circumstances of each case, should be introduced for outstanding research workers.

A Scientific Civil Service on the lines of the all-India and some of the Class I Central Services is not feasible. But to ensure uniformity in the management of the different scientific services, and to facilitate occasional interchange from one such service to another, when this is in the interest of scientific work, a standing committee of representatives of various scientific Departments and organisations may be set up.

Medical And Public Health Staffs

Doctors who are in the whole-time employment of the Central Government for providing medical attendance and treatment to Government servants should not be permitted private practice.

Class IV Staffs

Excluding (a) categories peculiar to the Railways and the Posts and Telegraphs Department, and (b) a few other categories for whom new scales have been specifically recommended, all class IV staffs on the existing scales mentioned below should be brought on to the new scales noted against each. Class IV staffs on scales other than those mentioned below (their number is very small) may be fitted into one or the other of these new scales.

Existing Scales (Rs.)	Proposed Scales (Rs.)
20-½-25	55-1-60 (for under-age employees)
30-½-35	70-1-80-EB-1-85
35-1-40	75-1-85-EB-2-89
35-1-50 35-1-40-2-50	75-1-85-EB-2-95
40-1-50	80-1-85-2-95
35-1-50-2-60	75-1-85-EB-2-95-EB-3-110
35-1-40-2-60 40-1-50-2-60	80-1-85-2-95-EB-3-110
40-2-60	85-2-95-3-110
50-1-60	95-3-110

Including unskilled staffs in workshops, there are about seven lakhs employees in the scale Rs. 30—½—35. Their total remuneration including dearness pay and dearness allowance at present ranges from Rs. 75 to Rs. 80 per mensem. Their revised scale will be Rs. 70—1—85, which with a dearness allowance of Rs. 10 will raise ther minimum remuneration to Rs. 80 and the maximum to Rs. 95 per mensem.

Workshop Staffs

The following scales of pay are recommended for workshop staffs in general. The scales likely to be suitable, and generally adequate, in each important establishment have been indicated in paragraphs 21, 22 and 24 of the chapter.

	(Rs.)
Unskilled	70-1-80-EB-1-85
Semi-skilled and un-skilled supervisory	75-1-85-EB-2-95 75-1-85-EB-2-95-3-101-EB-3-110 85-2-95-3-110 95-3-110
Skilled	85-2-95-3-110 85-2-95-3-110-EB-3-128 100-3-130 100-3-130-EB-3-142 110-3-131 110-3-131-4-143 110-3-131-4-143-EB-4-155 110-3-131-4-143-EB-4-171 EB-4-175-5-180 125-3-131-4-155 125-3-131-4-163-EB-4-175-5-180 140-5-175 150 5-180
Highly Skilled	130-5-175-EB-6-205-7-212 150-5-175-6-205 150-5-175-6-205-EB-7-240 175-6-205-7-240 205-7-240

Unskilled staffs in the workshops whose work is exceptionally heavy, or whose normal duties involve special risks; should have, in addition to pay, a special pay of Rs. three per mensem.

There should be proper classification of "jobs", but no particular system of job-evaluation in preference to others is recommended.

The system of "basic tradesmen" in the Railways should be worked so as to provide a channel through which, in trades where there is no semi-skilled grade, unskilled workers may advance to the skilled grade; and posts of basic tradesmen created with this object should not be set off against posts in the skilled grade.

A suitable system of payment by results should be introduced wherever feasible; but the basic time-wage for the period worked should be guaranteed, and the piece rate determined after scientific studies and in consultation with the workers.

The task of fitting the workshop staffs in the new pay scales should be entrusted to specially constituted bodies consisting of two experts and a neutral chairman. The recommendations made by various bodies should be coordinated by a common chairman or a joint meeting of the chairmen of all the bodies.

Railways

A bonus scheme for running staffs as an additional incentive for punctual running of passenger trains and expeditious movement of goods trains has been suggested for consideration.

An *ad hoc* committee may be set up to review the pay structure of "Marine" staffs.

Posts And Telegraphs Department

The age limit of 45 years for promotion to the Postal Superintendents' Service Class II should be raised.

The basic pay for Task Work Messengers should be the same as for other Telegraph Messengers, and a new system of additional payments related to output above the prescribed standard may be evolved.

The strength of the cadre of Boy Messengers/Peons, and qualifications for their recruitment, should be so determined as to provide for their absorption in vacancies of Messengers/Peons as soon as possible after they have reached the normal age of recruitment to Government service.

Union Territories

Excepting Delhi and Andaman & Nicobar Islands, the rates of remuneration of the employees of a Union Territory should be fixed with reference to those of the employees in the neighbouring State. If, however, the Central Government find that the emoluments as in the neighbouring State fall below rates that would be fair on a consideration of the totality of the relevant circumstances, a suitable higher rate should be fixed.

The emoluments of the employees of the Union Territories should be so adjusted between basic pay and dearness allowance that they conform to the general pattern recommended for Central Government employees.

Special Pay

There should be a periodical review of special pays to ensure that a special pay is not granted except when the necessary conditions are satisfied and that special pays are not so large or granted so freely that they distort the pay structure.

Fixation Of Pay In New Scales

The initial pay may be fixed in the new scale on a point-to-point basis, subject to specified limiting conditions.

Allowances : I. Rent Free Quarters And House Rent Allowance

Rent free residence should be provided only if duties or conditions of work are such that a higher remuneration would be granted but for this concession.

Class IV staffs already enjoying the concession may continue to do so.

Railway employees who are provided with residences in future should pay rent as employees in other Departments.

Present classification of localities on basis of population should continue, but grant of house rent allowance in special cases may be considered on merits.

The revised rates of house rent allowance should be as follows:

	Class of Cities		
	A	B	C
	Rs.	Rs.	Rs.
Below Rs. 75	10	7.50	5
Rs. 75 and above but below Rs. 100	15	10.00	7.50
Rs. 100 and above but below Rs. 200	20	15.00	7.50 for those drawing below Rs. 150
Rs. 200 and above	10 per cent of pay.	7½ per cent of pay.	Nil

Where application of these rates results in reduction of house rent allowance being drawn at present, the reduction may be spread over three years or so.

The condition of residence within the limits of the qualifying city for the purpose of house rent allowance should be abrogated for both gazetted and non-gazetted staffs.

Employees whose place of duty, though outside, is in the proximity of a qualified city, and who, of necessity, reside within the city, may be given the house rent allowance admissible in that city.

II. Compensatory Allowance

The present basis, and general scheme of the city compensatory allowance do not call for revision; but the rates should be modified as follows:

	Class of Cities		
	A	B	C
	Rs.	Rs.	Rs.
Below Rs. 150	10 per cent of pay subject to a minimum of Rs. 7.50 and a maximum of Rs. 12.50.	Five per cent of pay subject to a minimum of Rs. five and a maximum of Rs. 10 for all persons drawing below Rs. 500 per mensem.	Nil
Rs. 150 and above but below Rs. 300	Eight per cent of pay subject to a minimum of Rs. 12.50 and a maximum of Rs. 17.50		
Rs. 300 and above	Six per cent of pay subject to a maximum of Rs. 75.		

Where the application of the proposed rates would result in reduction of the amount being drawn at present, the reduction may be spread over three years or so.

In Simla and Shillong compensatory allowance may be allowed at the following rates to employees drawing pay upto specified limits :

(i) house rent allowance	at the rate for 'B' cities;
(i) compensatory allowance	at the rate for 'A' cities; and
(iii) winter allowance	for five months, at half the compensatory allowance rates (paragraph 31).

In deciding whether a place should be declared a hill station for the purpose of allowances, classification made by the State Governments should generally be followed, but the rates may be different.

The existing scheme of hill allowances (except at Simla and Shillong) may continue, with adjustments in rates and slabs on the pattern of those in the compensatory and house rent allowances, etc., for cities.

In the case of remote locality allowance or bad climate allowance also no change is necessary except for adjustment in rates and slabs.

No allowance in the nature of a permanent addition to pay should be given for field service liability as such, as distinguished from actual field service (paragraph 38).

The discrimination against Clerks and Store Keepers under the Ministry of Defence, recruited before 1948, who are liable to lose their seniority if found physically unfit for field service, should end.

III. All India Transfer Liability

No special monetary concession or compensation is called for for all-India service liability.

IV. Travelling Allowance

The basis for sanctioning and the rates of fixed conveyance allowance should be revised.

The daily allowance rates, and the rates of allowance for incidental expenses in connection with tour, should be reviewed.

Certain categories of Posts & Telegraphs staff, who are now governed by special rules, should be granted travelling allowance under the ordinary rules, except for regular journeys on their fixed beats.

Postmen and Linemen should be entitled to an allowance when they have to spend the night away on duty.

Railway staff may not transport free of cost more personal effects than is permitted to other staffs, but they should be allowed incidental charges at the standard rates.

The present rates of allowance for incidentals for journeys on transfer should be halved, but in lieu of the other half an employee should be allowed half a month's pay subject to a limit of Rs. 150.

A retiring Government servant under certain conditions, or one invalidated from service, may be allowed travelling allowance for journey to his home town.

Workcharged staff in all establishments should be entitled to travelling allowance under the normal rules.

V. Transport Between Place Of Work And Residence

Loans for purchase of conveyance may be granted liberally.

No change is necessary in the present policy of not granting an allowance for travel between residence and place of work. But grant of transport concession in some form or other may be considered under certain exceptional circumstances.

Steps should be taken to ease the extreme transport difficulties of employees working in big cities.

Hours Of Work ; Weekly Off ; Public Holidays ; Overtime Allowance ; Casual Leave And Special Casual Leave

I. Hours Of Work

Weekly hours at present prescribed for various categories of staffs may continue. Working hours of office staff are on the low side and an increase would be justified, but an attempt should first be made to obtain better output within the present hours.

Uniformity in weekly working hours among various groups of employees is not necessary or feasible.

The Railway administration should examine whether the basis on which certain categories, such as Gatemen, have been classified for the purpose of working hours has changed on account of increased traffic, etc., necessitating reclassification.

In establishments in which industrial and non-industrial staff work together, the latter should observe the same hours as the former when the nature of their duties are such that their presence throughout is necessary for efficient working of the industrial staffs.

When night duty is such as to require continuous application it should be allowed weightage of 10 minutes for every hours worked, except when weightage for night duty is in effect provided in the shape of reduced weekly working hours.

Split duty should not ordinarily be required to be performed in more than three spells. Where the employee's residence is not close to the place of work, seven hours of split duty should be treated as equal to eight hours of normal duty.

II. Weekly Off

For office staffs who at present work a five-and-a half-day week alternate Saturdays should be full working days, and full holidays. Offices which have continuous dealing with the public should, however, continue to have a five-and-a-half, or a six-day week, as the case may be.

No change is recommended in the present arrangements for a weekly break for other employees, except that in the case of "operating" staffs the weekly off should be such as to allow a full night's rest, and it should not, as a rule, be less than 30 hours.

The staffs on call duty should have at least a fortnightly off and this should generally be possible by internal adjustment of duties. Where, however, there is a single employee on call duty and such an arrangement will not be possible, he should not ordinarily be kept at a one-man station or section for more than three to six months at a time.

A fortnightly, if not a weekly, break should be allowed to Cooks, Waiters, etc., by some suitable arrangement

For Chowkidars who have active duties requiring continuous alertness, a weekly off should be allowed. Chowkidars of different Departments stationed at the same place might be treated as a single group for the purpose of enabling them to have a weekly or a fortnightly off by rotation.

To office staffs and other employees for whom a compensatory holiday is not obligatory under the law, such holiday need not be allowed for occasional work on Sunday, which should not, however, become a regular feature.

To "operating" staffs generally, compensatory break should be allowed for work on an off day as soon thereafter as possible, and not later than two months.

An employee who is required to work on his off day, should normally have compensation in the form of another day's break. But where, in exceptional cases, monetary compensation has to be paid for such work it should be at one-and-a-half of the time rate. In no case should both, a compensatory break and a monetary compensation, be allowed for work on a weekly off day or on an authorised holiday.

III. Public Holidays

The number of public holidays should be reduced to 16 where they exceed that number.

Staffs who do not at present enjoy any public holidays should be considered entitled to the three National holidays, *viz.*, Mahatma Gandhi's Birthday, Independence Day and Republic Day ; and since, with some exception, they cannot be relieved of their duties on those days, they should be compensated by payment at one-and-a-half time the normal rate.

No change is recommended in the existing number of holidays for workshop staffs, except that it should not in any case exceed 16.

Non-industrial staffs employed in industrial establishments should have the same number of public holidays as the industrials.

For work on a public holiday to which an employee is entitled, overtime allowance should be paid at one-and-a-half of the time rate, except when he becomes entitled to a higher rate under the Factories Act, 1948, or under any other law.

IV. Overtime Allowance

Overtime allowance should be granted only to non-gazetted staffs drawing pay not exceeding Rs. 500 per mensem under specified conditions, and with the proviso in the case of office staffs (whose hours of work are relatively short) that claim to overtime allowance will arise only for duty in excess of 45 minutes beyond the prescribed hours on any working day.

In the case of workshop staffs who work for less than 48 hours the overtime allowance for work in excess of the prescribed working hours, but not in excess of 48 hours, should be determined by common criteria so that only such divergencies may be retained as have a rational basis.

Non-industrial staffs in workshops whose hours of work are the same as those of industrial workers should be governed by the same orders regarding overtime payment as are applicable to the latter.

Overtime allowances, should, in all cases, be calculated on the basis of pay and allowances, but excluding house rent allowance.

The rate of overtime allowance should be determined on certain specified general principles. An inter-departmental committee may review the present arrangements and work out a detailed scheme in the light of the general principles recommended.

Overtime allowances of Railway staffs should not be calculated on monthly basis; if there are practical difficulties in calculating it on weekly basis it may be calculated on half-monthly basis.

Cases in which overtime earnings are a regular supplement to pay, and where pay has been fixed taking this factor into account, a complete stoppage or substantial reduction of overtime earnings should be compensated by suitable adjustment of pay.

V. Casual Leave

Casual leave should be reduced to 12 days in a year for office staffs. Operating and other similar staffs who have either no public holidays or a restricted number of public holidays may have 15 days; and workshop and other industrial staffs seven days in a year.

Facilities for special casual leave for work connected with service associations etc., broadly modelled on those provided by the Department of Posts and Telegraphs or the Ministry of Defence to their civilian employees, may be extended to other employees representing recognised service associations.

Leave Entitlements

Earned leave should be admissible to non-industrial

staffs at the following rates:

During the first five years of service	1.75 days for each month of service
During the next 10 years of service	2.25 days for each month of service
After 15 years of service .	2.5 days for each month of service

Workshop employees in the Railways may continue to earn leave at the rates applicable to non-industrial staffs. But if casual leave is allowed to them there should be a proportionate reduction in the rate of earned leave.

Leave entitlements of industrial staffs in Departments other than Railways should be as follows:

(i) Earned Leave:

During the first five years of service	One day for each month of service
From the sixth to 15th year	1.25 days for each month of service
Above 15 years . . .	1.75 days for each month of service

(ii) Leave on half pay: 10 days for each completed calendar year of service, subject to a maximum of 30 days at a time, and 180 days during the entire service.

(iii) Extraordinary leave: Upto three months at a time, but extensible upto 18 months if suffering from a disease requiring prolonged treatment.

(iv) Sick leave on full pay: 10 days in a calendar year non-cumulative.

Heads of Departments, offices, etc. must plan their work in such a way as to permit employees to take a certain amount of leave annually, and a longer leave after some years, or according to any special necessity.

There should not be a monetary limit on leave salary when an employee has to take leave because of sickness, or when he is allowed longer leave for pursuing an approved course of study otherwise than on study leave terms.

While the normal limits of accumulation of earned leave should be reduced to 120 days, additional accumulation of upto 60 days should be permitted at the discretion of the sanctioning authority when leave applied for is refused in the public interest.

Hospital leave should be admissible to all low-paid employees, as also to those Class III employees whose duties involve the handling of dangerous machinery, explosive materials, poisonous drugs, etc., or the performance of hazardous task.

Industrial staffs should also be eligible for hospital leave upto three months on full pay, or six months on half pay, in a period of three years.

Maternity leave admissible to industrial staffs should be approximately the same as that admissible to non-industrial staffs. In the case of temporary and officiating service also, the period of maternity leave should count for purposes of increments.

Study leave may be granted for a study tour in which a Government servant may not attend a regular academic or semi-academic course; and for studies which may not be closely and directly linked with a civil servant's work but which will improve his capability etc. as a civil servant. Study leave should be liberally granted, particularly to scientific, technical, and administrative staff, and in suitable cases the staff should even be encouraged or advised to have such leave. Ordinarily it may not be necessary to extend the standard study leave terms to industrial staffs, but the question of providing them facilities for training and technical education may be considered.

The rates of leave salary during 'departmental leave' should be reviewed. Staff subject to 'departmental leave' should, while on duty, earn leave at the same rate as other staff, and not at a lower rate.

Leave salary may be calculated on the basis of the average of the rates of pay admissible during each of the 10 months in which an employee was on duty immediately prior to the month in which leave commences; but in the case of employees who proceed on leave from posts the maximum pay of which does not exceed Rs. 100 per mensem, leave salary may be based on the rate of pay drawn immediately before proceeding on leave.

An employee granted leave beyond the date of superannuation, or on the expiry of a period of extension of service, should not retain a lien on his permanent post during the leave, or count the leave as pensionable service.

The adequacy and basis of calculation of leave reserves should be reviewed.

Age Of Superannuation

The age of superannuation should be 58 years for all classes of public servants, including those for whom the retirement age at present is 60. But persons already in service may continue upto the age of 60, if they are at present entitled to do so.

Scientific and technical personnel may ordinarily be retained in service upto the age of 60 by grant of extension or re-employment for two years.

Retirement Benefits

Industrial staffs, on being made permanent, should be brought under the standard pension scheme, those already in service, however, being given the option to continue under their existing retirement benefit schemes.

The right to withdraw the whole or a part of a pension should be restricted to certain very exceptional, specified contingencies, and even then the power should be exercised, and where the original order is passed by a subordinate authority the appeal against it decided, only in consultation with the Union Public Service Commission.

The rate of gratuity should be changed so as to make the maximum amount available on completion of 30 years' qualifying service.

Temporary service when followed by permanency, whether in the same or any other post, should count in full for pension. Extraordinary service of certain employees in Defence establishments should count as half and not as one-quarter as at present.

Leave taken out of India should count for pension to the same extent as leave taken in India.

When the total period of qualifying service exceeds completed years by more than six months, an additional benefit of half a year's pension may be allowed for the purpose of determining the quantum of pension.

Officiating, special, and personal pay may continue to count in full in cases in which it so counts at present, but in other cases such pay drawn during the last three years of service should be taken into account in full or in half according to specified circumstances.

Non-practising allowance of doctors should count for pension.

Government may consider the question of granting some relief to persons whose pension does not exceed Rs. 200 per mensem, when there is increase in the cost of living.

The minimum gratuity admissible to the family of a permanent employee who dies before completing five years' qualifying service should be equal to six months' emoluments, except in cases in which death occurs in the first year of service, when the minimum may be two months' emoluments.

The family of an employee who is a subscriber to a contributory provident fund should be granted gratuity equal to the difference between the amount that would have been admissible had he been on pensionable establishment and the Government's contribution to his provident fund with accumulated interest. If such an employee dies before becoming eligible for admission to a contributory provident fund, the gratuity should be the same as for purely temporary employees.

A widow's and children's pension benefit scheme, on a contributory basis, should replace the existing family pension scheme.

Scientific employees of semi-Government institutions, financed from cess or Government grants, when appointed to permanent Government service, should be permitted to count in full their service in those institutions as qualifying service for pension, provided their previous employers are willing, in lieu of their contribution to the contributory provident fund, to pay to the Government pension contribution for the period of service with them.

To facilitate freer interchange of scientists and technologists between the Government and the universities, the pensionary contribution which the latter have to pay when they borrow the service of a Government servant should be restricted to the rate at which the university contributes towards the provident fund of its other employees.

Medical Facilities

Industrial staffs and their families should have the same facilities for medical care and treatment as non-industrial staffs.

The Central Government should have their own arrangements for the medical care of their employees in Calcutta.

Medical facilities for all Central Government employees should be placed on a contributory basis, and the pattern of medical care and treatment should, wherever there is a concentration of employees, be broadly similar to that available under the Contributory Health Service Scheme in Delhi.

Housing Facilities

Government should have a comprehensive programme for housing their employees.

There should be substantial expansion and acceleration of the present building programme, particularly in Bombay and Calcutta, and continuance of construction in Delhi on the present scale.

There should, in addition, be deconcentration of the Central Government offices from Bombay and Calcutta and any further concentration of offices in central parts of Delhi should be avoided.

Housing in small places where there is a large concentration of Central Government employees requires urgent attention.

Employees who are transferred from one station to another, should be given priority in housing.

Till the required number of permanent houses can be constructed, an emergent programme of construction of inexpensive, temporary accommodation may be taken up.

Government should encourage and assist employees to build their own houses specially on a co-operative basis.

The rent charged from the occupants of 'substandard' quarters, if any, should be appropriate to the accommodation provided.

The standard rent should be calculated at six per cent of the capital cost for all categories of employees in the Railway administration also.

The standard rent should be calculated after taking into account the cost of site.

The accommodation provided for Government servants in the highest pay ranges should not be of a type carrying a standard rent higher than 10 per cent of the occupants' pay.

The maximum rent recoverable from employees whose pay is below Rs. 150 per mensem, should be limited to seven-and-a-half per cent of pay.

Educational Assistance

In the interest of Centra Government employees as well as of other floating population in the country, the growth of schools with common syllabus and media of instruction and moderate fees, should be encouraged.

The Railway scheme of setting up hostels, with concessional lodging and boarding charges at a graduated rate, should be extended for the benefit of other employees drawing pay not exceeding Rs. 300 per mensem.

A scheme of educational assistance, similar to the one in operation in the Railways, may be introduced for other Central Government employees whose salary does not exceed Rs. 300 per mensem, to enable them to send their children to boarding schools of their choice when suitable schooling facilities do not exist at the station where they are posted.

Uniforms, Protective Clothing, Etc.

Uniforms, etc., are essential equipment for duty and not fringe benefits. Washing allowance need not be given to all employees who are supplied with uniforms, but may be granted to those drawing basic pay not exceeding Rs. 150 per mensem.

Working Conditions; Canteen Facilities; Staff Welfare

There should be a comprehensive examination of the rest house and retiring room facilities which operating staffs generally require. The difficulties of the R.M.S. staff call for particularly urgent attention.

There should be a planned programme (and fair as among the Departments) of construction of office buildings to ensure that within a few years all offices are satisfactorily housed.

There is wide scope for improvement of working conditions, and immediate improvement is possible in various matters such as cleanliness, lighting, heating and cooling arrangements, and office furniture and equipment.

At least a tiffin room should be provided wherever the number of employees is small, and a canteen where the strength of the staff exceeds 50. There should be a standard minimum provision of departmental assistance to canteens, tiffin rooms, etc. A Government-wide plan for providing suitable accommodation for canteens should be prepared, and put into effect within a reasonable period.

As a first step towards a co-ordinated welfare programme for the whole body of Central Government employees, there should be a central agency, or a committee drawn from different Ministries, to keep a general oversight on welfare activities and to maintain uniformity as far as possible.

In addition to social, cultural and recreational activities promotion of Co-operative Societies and schemes for relief to employees or their dependents in certain circumstances, deserve special attention.

Staff benevolent funds should be set up by the Departments on contributory basis.

The present expenditure on welfare activities should be substantially increased and the grant in different Departments should be more or less on the same scale.

A committee may be set up to make a review of the existing welfare arrangements and to make recommendations for their improvement.

Welfare measures should be administered with as full a participation of the staff as possible.

The working of the exisiting 'holiday homes' should be carefully examined before any new ones are started.

Leave Travel Concessions

The travel concession allowed to different Classes of Railway employees should be uniform, and in all cases reduced to one set of free passes and two sets of privilege ticket orders.

For other employees the present concession should be liberalised as follows: (a) It should be extended to such industrial and work-charged staffs as are entitled to regular leave; (b) employees who leave their families in their home towns may have the concession for themselves only, annually and (c) for employees unable to avail of the concession in a block of two years, the next block should count from the end of the first year; (d) an employee whose home place is not connected by rail should be allowed the concession also for journeys between his home and nearest railway station.

Promotion And Character Rolls

Revision of grade structures and complements may not be made merely for the purpose of increasing promotion opportunities.

With the exception of the upper division clerical cadre direct recruitment to the higher grades, where it is made at present, should continue.

Merit should continue to be the criterion in making promotions at higher levels. At lower levels the principle of seniority-cum-fitness is appropriate.

For promotions to grades in which specialised knowledge is necessary, qualifying examinations designed to test working (not academic) abilities may be useful; but with this exception, examination need not be adopted as a general method of selection for promotion.

There should be a system of promotion by a special limited competitive examination to provide young officers in Class II and Class III services an additional opportunity to enter any of the Class I or Class II services to which there is direct recruitment by a competitive examination.

The form in which confidential reports are drawn up should be related to the nature of the work of the particular class of employees, but should otherwise be as uniform as possible, and so designed as to provide for assessment under a number of specified headings, including potentialities of the employees for assuming higher responsibilities, as well as a general summing up.

A general grading of employees by the first reporting officer should not be obligatory; such grading should be done at a higher level, preferably at the level at which a whole cadre is dealt with for the purposes of promotion etc.

Confidential reports should be scrutinised at each higher level as soon as they are received to make sure that they had been prepared in accordance with the relevant instructions, and should be returned for rectification where necessary.

Unless it is proposed not to enter it in an employee's character roll, an irremediable as well as remediable defect should invariably be communicated to him.

The present arrangement of the immediate superior writing a confidential report may continue, but the next higher officer should be required to exercise a positive and independent judgment on the remarks of the reporting officer, and should clearly express his agreement or disagreement with the remarks particularly if they are adverse.

Temporary Employees; Workcharged Staff; Casual Labour

At present the number of temporary employees is disproportionately large for which there appears to be no justification.

The permanent requirements of all categories of staff should be speedily determined and thereafter the margin of temporary posts should be the same for all Classes.

One or two official committees may be set up to examine the permanent requirements of different Departments and to ensure that the revised orders of Government are given effect to within six months to a year.

Workcharged staffs whose services are likely to be required on a permanent or semi-permanent basis, should be made permanent, or given semipermanent status. They should be classified into industrial and non-industrial depending on the nature of their duties, and should have the same conditions of service as other industrial or non-industrial staffs.

Temporary workcharged staffs whose employment is not casual may have the benefits and concessions allowed to other temporary staffs, industrial or non-industrial, as may be appropriate.

Casual employment should be restricted to work of a truly casual nature; and in order to ensure that this is so there should be a review of the existing position.

The same rates of wages should be fixed for casual labour in "unscheduled employments" as are fixed for comparable "scheduled employments" under the Central Government (under the Minimum Wages Act). Or their wages may be fixed generally with reference to the minimum prescribed by the respective State Governments for comparable "scheduled employments".

All casual labour under the Central Government, including those to whom the minimum wages law is not applicable, should have the benefits and safeguards provided by Rules 23—25 of the Minimum Wages (Central) Rules, 1950, relating to weekly holidays, working hours, night shifts, and extra wages for overtime.

Long experience as casual labour should be taken into consideration while making selections for appointment to regular establishments.

Government Servants Conduct Rules

Instead of placing a general ban on public expression of views and then providing for some exceptions (as is the case at present), a general freedom of intellectual expression should be recognised and only such specific restrictions should be imposed as are necessary to meet the requirements of the public service.

Political Rights

Removal or relaxation of the existing restrictions on the exercise of political rights by employees would not be in the public interest, or in their own interest.

Right Of Association

The membership of an unrecognised association should not as such be a disciplinary offence. But if such an association takes recourse to or assists in activities which if resorted to by individual Government servants would constitute a breach of a provision of the Conduct Rules the Government servants concerned may be required to withdraw their membership on pain of disciplinary action.

The rules of recognition of associations should be conceived and recognition granted in a liberal spirit.

Public servants should not resort to strikes or threaten to do so ; but without amendment of the law a change should be brought about by the employees themselves abjuring the use of the strike weapon and demonstrations, and the Government accepting a convention that they would refer to arbitration any dispute concerning certain important matters which are not settled by negotiation.

Reasonable facilities should be provided for trade union activities.

Machinery For Negotiation And Settlement Of Disputes

A Whitley type machinery, with a central joint council representing the whole body of Central Government employees, both industrial and non-industrial, should be set up for negotiation and settlement of disputes. A committee of the central joint council may deal with matters peculiar to industrial staff.

There should be departmental joint councils also.

As a necessary complement to a joint machinery for negotiation, there should be provision for compulsory arbitration, open only to recognised associations and limited to pay and allowances, weekly hours of work, and leave, of employees not above the present Class II level.

The Ministry of Labour should be closely associated with important matters concerning staff relations. It should, in particular, be associated with the proposed central joint council, and should appoint the chairman of the board of arbitrators, should arbitration become necessary.

Disciplinary Proceedings

All memorials etc., as well as appeals, which come to the Central Government against imposition of major penalties, should be disposed of only in consultation with the Public Service Commission.

The power to withhold appeals, memorials or petitions under prescribed circumstances should be exercised by an authority higher than the one which had passed the orders against which the appeal, etc., is made.

A disciplinary enquiry should not be conducted by the immediate superior of the Government servant being proceeded against, or by an officer at whose instance the enquiry was initiated.

Classification Of Services

The present classification of services and posts into four Classes—I, II, III and IV—should be abolished.

Efficiency In The Public Service

The recommendations for improvement in the rates of pay and conditions of service have been made on the assumption that the employees will give, and the Government will take from them, a full day's work. It is suggested that an urgent and comprehensive review may be made of the whole problem of efficiency and productivity in Government offices, services (Railways, Posts & Telegraphs, etc.) and workshops.

Statistical Requirements

A systematic collection of data relating to wages, salaries and conditions of service in outside employment, and a continuous review of the data with reference to the rate of remuneration and service conditions etc., of Central Government employees, is recommended.

COMMITTEE OF PARLIAMENT ON OFFICAL LANGUAGE, 1957—REPORT

New Delhi, Ministry of Home Affairs, 1959 122, vip.

Chairman : Shri Govind Ballabh Pant.

Members

Rajya Sabha : Shri Purushottam Das Tandon; Shri K.P. Madhavan Nair; Shri Alluri Satyanarayana Raju; Prof. Dr. Raghu Vira; Sardar Budh Singh; Shri Bhagirathi Mahapatra; Dr. A. Ramaswami Mudaliar; Shri Perath Narayanan Nair; Shri Prafulla Chandra Bhanj Deo. **Lok Sabha**—Seth Govind Das; Shri P.T. Thanu Pillai; Swami Ramananda Tirtha; Shri B.S. Murthy; Pandit Thakur Das Bhargava; Shri Hifzur Rahman; Shri B. Bhagavati; Shri U. Srinivasa Malliah; Shri Frank Anthony; Shri Mathura Prasad Mishra; Shri Manikya Lal Varma; Shri Bhakt Darshan; Shri Shripad Amrit Dange; Shri Harish Chandra Sharma; Kumari Maniben Vallabhbhai Patel; Shri G.S. Musafir; Shri Atulya Ghosh; Shri Deorao Yeshwantrao Gohokar; Shri Hirendra Nath Mukerjee; Shri Pramathanath Banerjee.

Secretary : Shri R. Prasad.

APPOINTMENT

The Committee of Parliament on Official Language was constituted through the motion moved by the Minister for Home Affairs on September 3, 1957.

TERMS OF REFERENCE

To examine the recommendations of the Official Language Commission and to report to the President their opinion thereon.

CONTENTS

Introductory (Provisions of Article 344 relating to

Constitution and Duties of the Official Language Commission; Appointment of the Commission—Terms of Reference—Procedure; Submission of Commissioner's Report; Committee of Parliament on Official Language—Constitutional Provisions—Election of Members; Election of Chairman—Procedure and Rules of Business; Recommendations and Conclusions of the Commission—Scope of Committee's Duty; Meetings of the Committee—Method of Work Adopted—General Discussion—Detailed Examination of Recommendations; Materials Used—Acknowledgments; Plan of the Report); General Approach to the Problem (Constitutional Provisions relating to Official Language—Official Language of the Union—Official Language of the States—Language of Communication between the States and the Union and between One State and Another—Language of Legislation and High Courts—Special Directives; Salient Features of the Constitutional Settlement; Constitutional Settlement—An Integrated Scheme; Need for Replacing English by Hindi and Other Indian Languages; Practical Reasons why English cannot continue Indefinitely—Considerations of National Pride and Dignity; Hindi and other Indian National Languages capable of replacing English for Official Purposes; Development of Hindi as the Medium of Expression of India's Composite Culture; No Conflict between Hindi and other National Languages; Special Place of English in Certain Spheres; Manner in which Changeover should be brought about; Complete Changeover to Hindi by 1965 not Practicable; Need for a Plan of Work); Opinion of the Committee on the Recommendations of the Commission (scope of the Chapter); **Part I**—Section I : Progressive Use of Hindi for Official Purposes of the Union (Preparatory Measures to lay the Ground Work for the Changeover; Terminology; Translation into Hindi of Official Publications embodying Rules, Regulations, Manuals and Other Procedural Literature; Furnishing of Mechanical and Service Aids; Training of Administrative Personnel; Future Recruitment to the Union Services; Recruitment to Subordinate Posts in Local Offices of Central Government Departments; Selection of Candidates for Training Establishments; Recruitment to All-India and Higher Central Services; Propagation and Development of Hindi); Section II: Restrictions on the Use of English; Section III : Language of Legislation and of Higher Courts (Constitutional Provisions; Commission's Recommendations—Language of Legislation; Language of Parliamentary Bills, Acts, etc.—Committee's Opinion; Language of State Bills, Acts, etc.—Committee's Opinion; Language of the Supreme Court; Language of High Courts; Preparatory Measures for Changeover in the Field of Law); Section IV: Form of Numerals (Form of Numerals to be Used for Official Purposes of the Union); Section V: Preparation of a Time-Schedule; **Part II**—Statement giving the Recommendations of the Official Language Commission and the Committee's Opinions Thereon; Minutes of Dissent and Notes Recorded by Members; Annexures I to V.

RECOMMENDATIONS

The statement below gives the recommendations of the Official Language Commission in the order in which they are stated in their report and the opinions thereon of the Committee of Parliament on Official Language.

Serial No.	Recommendation of the Official Language Commission	Opinions of the Committee of Parliament on Official Language
1	2	3
	Chapter V	
	Terminology	
1.	In adopting terminology, clarity, precision and simplicity should be primarily aimed at. Doctrinaire insistence on 'language purism' is deprecated.	The recommendations one to five may be accepted.
2.	Promising sources for adopting new terminology should be available in the indigenous terms current in the past, and the terms currently used in actual life amongst various categories of craftsmen, artisans, etc. These should be explored. In suitable cases, international terminology may be adopted or adapted to the genius of the Indian languages.	
3.	The maximum possible identity in evolving new terminology for all Indian languages should be aimed at.	
4.	Suitable arrangements should be made for evolving terminology and for coordinating such work as between different authorities with reference to the Union language as well as the other regional languages.	
5.	On a review of the work done so far there would seem to be room for greater acceleration in the work and need for achieving more effective coordination as between different terminological efforts.	

1	2	3
	Chapter VII **Language in Public Administration—I** **Official Language Of The Union**	
	The pre-requisites of a change-over in the language for administration are: (1) Preparation and standardisation of the necessary special terminology used in the administrative field. (2) Translation into Hindi of official publications embodying rules, regulations, manuals, hand books and other procedural literature relating to the working of the administrative machinery. (3) Training of administrative personnel of different categories in appropriate standards of linguistic competence for the purpose of using the new linguistic medium with the requisite efficiency and facility of expression. (4) Development and furnishing in the new linguistic medium of the mechanical and service aids necessary for speeding up and facilitating office work, such as typewriters and typists, stenography and stenographers, printing and duplicating machines, teleprinters and other communication services adapted to the use of the new medium, etc. Regarding (1) above, it is a part of the general problem of terminology considered in Chapter V.	
6.	Regarding (2) above, it is necessary to ensure that a measure of uniformity is observed in the language used in the translations of all this procedural literature, and for that purpose it may be advisable to invest in a single agency of the Central Government the general responsibility for direction and superintendence over all such work.	This may be accepted.
7.	As regards (3) above, (training of personnel): the present arrangements made by the Government of India for training their employees on a voluntary basis in the Hindi language are reviewed. If experience shows that adequate results are not forthcoming under such optional arrangements, it would be legitimate and necessary for Government to impose, in pursuance of their language policy, obligatory requirements on Government servants to qualify themselves in Hindi within a reasonable period to the extent requisite for the discharge of their duties.	Government may prescribe obligatory requirements on Government servants to qualify themselves in Hindi.
8.	As regards (4) above, schemes should be adopted whereunder stenographers and typists are granted special leave and accorded special facilities to enable them to undertake training in stenography and typing in the new linguistic medium and to acquire knowledge of the Union language.	This may be accepted.
9.	The standard of linguistic ability in the English language normally associated with the academic education prescribed as a qualification for purposes of recruitment to various categories of posts and services would furnish a guide as to the standard of linguistic ability in Hindi to be aimed at for the different categories of Government personnel. During earlier stages perhaps a slightly lower standard might suffice.	This may be accepted in principle but during the transitional stages a slightly lower standard might suffice.
10.	Generally speaking, penalties would seem to be appropriate	This recommendation may be drop-

1	2	3
	with reference to failure to attain prescribed standard by the due date; incentives and rewards would seem to be appropriate with reference to performance above the minimum standard laid down.	ped.
11.	In certain segments of the administrative machinery of the Union Government, technical English terms might continue to be used for an indefinite time in the future at levels at which it is not considered necessary to evolve Indian terminology; similarly correspondence may be carried on in the English language where the work involves constant contact with foreign countries through that medium.	This may be accepted except that the Committee feels that it would suffice to provide for the continued use of technical English terms in the future for so long as it is not considered necessary to evolve Indian terminology, and not for an indefinite time as recommended by the Commission.
12.	Apart from the Ministries or Departments of the Government of India, the linguistic medium will have to change over in the administrative agencies and organisations, such as the Railways, the Posts and Telegraphs, the Excise, Customs, Income-tax Departments, and so on. Some of these organisations have units and branches located in different parts of the country and the language problem presents a special aspect in regard to them. It is necessary that these administrative organisations should evolve a measure of permanent bilingualism; that is to say, they will use the Hindi language for purposes of internal working and the respective regional languages in their public dealings in the respective regions.	This may be accepted.
13.	It is necessary that the staff structures of these administrative agencies and departments of the Government of India with a country-wide coverage should be reviewed and decentralised to conform to the requirements of such bilingualism. The recruitment methods and qualifications for recruitment may have also to be revised suitably.	The recommendations 13 to 15 may be accepted.
14.	As employers, these all-India departments and organisations have certainly the right to prescribe the standards of Hindi qualification (as of qualification, where necessary, in the respective regional languages) necessary for purposes of recruitment to the different categories of their establishment. It may be that for zonal and regional requirements, the standard of Hindi qualification could be somewhat lower than what would be necessary for the headquarters organisation of these offices as the work in the latter, as distinguished from the former, would be carried on wholly in Hindi.	
15.	In order that the employment opportunities in the different regions should not be curtailed during the transitional period, the requirements of Hindi knowledge may at the start be pitched somewhat lower having due regard to the progress of Hindi in the local educational system, any deficiency being made good by in-service training after recruitment. The standard may be progressively raised as facilities for instruction in the Hindi language improve in particular regions.	
16.	The language policy of these all-India administrative agencies of the Central Government, like the Railways, Posts and Telegraphs, in their dealings with the public should be framed principally with a view to the convenience of the	The recommendations 16 and 17 may be accepted.

1	2	3
	public whom they are designed to serve: the instrumentality of these departments should not be used as a 'lever' to force the pace of Hindi propagation at the cost of convenience to the public. Where Hindi terms and expressions are used on signboards, forms, etc. for the purpose of familiarising the public with them, the text should also be given in the regional language (or English where relevant) having regard to public convenience.	
17.	It is necessary to examine all new Hindi terms and expressions, especially those used by these all-India administrative agencies which come into intimate contact with the public, so as to ensure that the terms and expressions are not discordant with local forms of speech and associations; where certain Sanskrit words have come to acquire in different languages different specialised meanings the employment of inept or unsuitable expressions in disregard or ignorance of these is apt to bring the attempt at 'Indianisation' of the medium itself into disparagement and ridicule.	
18.	It would not be correct instead of training personnel in the new medium, to adopt the device of separate translation units or bureaux being maintained at additional cost to the public funds for translating the work done originally in the English language. While translation services would have their place in the administrative organisation both permanently and as an aid during the transitional stage, these cannot be a substitute for training the personnel to do its work originally in Hindi. In our view, the continuance of the original work in English and its translation at public expense at different stages into Hindi was not the sense in which the changeover of the linguistic medium for the business of the Union was enacted in the Constitution.	This may be accepted.
19.	The Union Government would be justified in prescribing a reasonable measure of knowledge of the Hindi language as a qualification for entry into their services by new entrants, provided a sufficiently long notice is given and the measure of linguistic ability prescribed is moderate, any deficit being made good by subsequent in-service training.	This may be accepted.
20.	In the case of officials of the age of 45 and above, the requirement to be prescribed should be for a 'comprehending knowledge' of Hindi rather than high levels of linguistic ability for purposes of expression corresponding to the levels of their ability in English. If necessary, separate tests may be devised for the purpose.	The Committee considers that there should be no obligation to learn Hindi in the case of officials of the age of 45 and above.
21.	We do not recommend that any restrictions should be imposed for the present on the use of the English language for any of the purposes of the Union.	This may be accepted.
22.	It has not been possible for us to furnish a regular time-table by dates and stages as to how Hindi should be introduced into the business of the Union so as to accomplish the general changeover within the period fixed by the Constitution. Since the Ministries of the Government of India are components of a single organic unity, the phasing of the progressive use of Hindi must, in general, be lateral and coherent in the different	The Committee desires the Union Government to prepare and implement a plan of action, for the progressive use of Hindi as the official language of the Union, in pursuance of the opinions of the Committee on the recommendations of the Official Langu-

1	2	3
	Ministries and Departments. We have not had the benefit of a provisional 'plan of action' by the Government of India covering all its Ministries and Departments and comprehending their special difficulties if any, estimates of workloads of basic preparatory work involved, the present linguistic capacity of all the Government staff and approximate dates by which they could be trained in the new linguistic medium etc. While we have therefore indicated the prerequisites, the general sequence of the phasing and the principles covering various related issues, the actual drawing up of a plan of action and the setting up of time schedule there-within must be left to the Government of India themselves to do after a study of the relevant factors.	age Commission.
23.	The special case of the Indian Audit and Accounts Department under the Comptroller and Auditor-General of India is examined. After a State has adopted its regional language as the official language, it will be necessary to arrange that the staff of the Indian Audit and Accounts department dealing with the affairs of the State is versed in that language sufficiently for the purpose of carrying out its duties of compiling accounts and the exercise of audit. This implies that the Accountant General's/Comptroller's office in a State should be capable of compiling accounts from returns submitted in the regional language and conducting audit with reference to noting and administrative decisions recorded in the regional language.	This may be accepted.
24.	'Provincialisation of audit was mentioned as a possible way of resolving this difficulty; it is however not necessary to consider such an alternative which would involve a major change in the constitutional arrangements currently in force. We feel that it ought to be possible to devise a solution within the framework of the existing constitutional arrangement whereby, on the one hand the establishment of the Accountant-General's / Comptroller's office in each State would be able to carry out their duties in respect of transactions recorded in the State language, and on the other, the present system, wherein the accounts and audit responsibility in respect of the Union as well as of the States is centred in the Comptroller and Auditor General working through a single Indian Audit and Accounts Department, is maintained. The organisation and methods of staffing of the Indian Audit and Accounts Department may have to be revised, somewhat similarly to the lines envisaged in respect of the Central Departments comprising activities spread over the whole country.	This may be accepted.

Chapter VIII

Language In Public Administration—II

Progress Made In The Use Of Hindi In State Administrations

1	2	3
25.	The States concerned will have to consider for themselves at what level administrative occasions would arise for their officers to enter into communication, oral or written, with officers of other States or of the Union. The State Governments must determine for themselves what staff would be affected and what precise steps should be taken for	This may be accepted.

1	2	3
	train their personnel at the appropriate levels for dealing with Hindi communications.	
26.	As in the case of the Union Government, the State Governments would be justified in imposing obligatory requirements for the acquisition of qualifications in the Hindi Language with reference to the staff embraced by the requirements of the new linguistic medium in the field of inter-State and State-Union communications. It would seem that acquisition of a knowledge of the Hindi language beyond these requirements should be on the basis of rewards and incentives rather than compulsion and penalties; however, this is an issue which must be decided by each State for itself.	Recommendations 26 and 27 may be accepted.
27.	Arrangements may be made for outgoing communications from the Union Government to a Hindi-speaking State being accompanied by a Hindi translation of the English text, whenever such a State makes a request to this effect. The employment of Hindi in actual work of administration before 1965 in this manner will help in establishing forms of address, expressions etc. in that language.	
	The Form Of Numerals	
28.	The international form of numerals is itself of Indian origin and as such is nothing but yet another mutation of the ancient Indian numerals, analogous to the several forms of numerals developed, together with their separate scripts, by the numerous Indian languages. It is to be noted that in the South the international form of numerals is in current use in the four great Dravidian languages, sometimes and to a varying extent, alongside of the numerals of their respective scripts.	This may be accepted.
29.	In certain States in the Hindi-speaking region the Devanagari form of numerals is used either exclusively or in addition to the international form of numerals for internal purposes of the State administration. It is for the respective State Governments to decide whether this should be so. So far as the Union Government is concerned, there should be a uniform basic policy depending on the public intended to be addressed as to the use of Devanagari numerals in addition to the international form of numerals in the publications of the different Ministries.	So far as the Union Government is concerned, the Committee considers that there should be a uniform basic policy as to the use of Devanagari numerals in addition to the international form of numerals in the publications of the different Ministries depending on the public intended to be addressed and the subject matter of the publication.
30.	We have no recommendation to make for the issue of directions by the President for the use of the Devanagari form of numerals in addition to the international form of Indian numerals for any purposes of the Union between now and the time when the issue will be re-examined by the next Commission to be appointed in 1960.	This appears to be unnecessary and need not be taken into consideration.

Chapter IX

Language Of Law And Law Courts—I

Language Of Legislation

1	2	3
31.	The practice as regards answering interpellations appears to vary. In some cases, provision is made, for furnishing, for the information of the other Members, written translations of the questions and answers in the prescribed language (s) of the legislative	Under the terms of reference, the Commission were expected to make recommendations as to the language to be used for all or any of the purposes mentioned

1	2	3
	body concerned when these have been rendered in another language. Such a practice might be generalised with advantage.	in article 348 of the Constitution. The question of language to be used in Parliament and State legislatures is not covered by article 348. These recommendations, therefore, go beyond the terms of reference and may be left out of consideration.
32.	It may happen that for a period of time after (i.e., after January 25, 1965, in the case of the Parliament) English has been replaced by Hindi in the Parliament and by the respective official languages of the States, in the State Legislatures, cases would arise in which a member may not be able to express himself adequately in Hindi/the State language concerned or in his own mother-tongue; and it would seem advisable that provision should be made to empower the presiding authorities in such cases to permit the members to address the House in English.	
33.	Apart from the authoritative enactment which, in our opinion, ought to be eventually in Hindi, both in respect of parliamentary legislation and State legislation, there may be need, for the sake of public convenience, to publish translations of the enactments in different regional languages. In respect of State legislation, this would be normally necessary in the regional language(s) prevalent in the State, whereas in respect of parliamentary legislation it may be necessary in all the important regional languages current in the country.	Until 1965 or until English is replaced by Hindi, parliamentary legislation should continue to be in the English language with an authorised translation in the Hindi language. Arrangements may be made for providing translations also in the official languages of the various States.
34.	We consider that it is essential, when the time comes for this changeover, that the entire statute book of the country should be in one language which cannot of course be other than Hindi. Therefore the language of legislation of the States as well as of Parliament and also of course consequently the language of all statutory orders, rules, etc., issued under any law, should be the Hindi language.	So far as the language of State legislation is concerned, the State legislature may adopt the official language of the State for this purpose but an authoritative text thereof has to be published in English under Article 348 (3). If the original text is in a language other than Hindi, a Hindi translation may also be published with it.

Chapter X

Languages Of Law And Law Courts—II

Language Of Law Courts

1	2	3
35.	So far as the language of the Supreme Court is concerned, eventually there can be only one language, i.e. Hindi, in respect of the entire court proceedings and records. including of course the judgments and orders. When the time comes for the changeover, the Supreme Court will have to function only in Hindi language. The authoritative texts of reported judgments of the Supreme Court will also be published in the same language.	Recommendations 35 to 37 may be accepted.
36.	Processes issued in Hindi by the Supreme Court, when addressed to a non-Hindi region or against a person whose mother-tongue is not Hindi, should be accompained by a translation for the convenience of the concerned party.	
37.	Provision should also be made for reliable translations of Supreme Court decisions being available in the State languages in separate regional language series.	
38.	The pros and cons of the regional and Hindi languages are carefully examined so far as the linguistic medium of the High Court is concerned. There are several strong and, in our opinion, conclusive	With the previous consent of the President. the official language of the State or Hindi may be used in proceedings in the

1	2	3
	reasons in favour of deciding that when the time for the changeover arrives, the language of the judgments, decrees and orders of the High Courts must be a common linguistic medium for the whole country and therefore, these should be in the Hindi language in all regions.	High Court under clause (2) of Article 348, but judgments, decrees and orders passed by High Courts have to be in the English language. The Committee is of the opinion that the President may be pleased to give his sanction to the introduction of a Bill in Parliament providing for the use optionally of Hindi and other official languages of States for purposes of judgments, decrees and orders also, with the previous consent of the President. Judgments, decrees and orders which are made in a language other than English, should be accompanied by a translation in the English language. Allreportablejudgments and orders should be translated also into the Hindi language.
39.	Since subordinate courts are guided by the determination of law given in the HighCourt judgments, there will have to be translations into the respective regional languages of all reportable High Court judgments. It would be necessary, in our opinion, to ensure that thesetranslations are sufficiently reliable and we could suggest, for consideration by the concerned authorities at the material time, that a "translation unit" may be established in each High Court for such translation of judgments.	
40.	So far as the processes, decrees and orders of High Courts are con cerned, we would suggest that, wherever necessary, it may be provided that they would issue in regional languages in their 'authorised translations', in addition, to their original issue in Hindi.	The Committee has already expressed its opinion as regards the language of decrees and orders under Serial 38. So far as processes are concerned, they may be in the regional language with a translation in the Union language.
41.	As in all other such cases, so in regard to the language of the law courts, we consider it important to concentrate on bringing about the general changeover in the linguistic medium for the system as a whole. Wherever it is necessary to make individual exceptions for a good reason, e.g., in order that we may continue to enjoy or to secure afresh the services of suitable personnel for the posts of judges in the Supreme Court and the several High Courts, dispensation as to the language should be readily granted. It may be that for a long time after such a general changeover in the language of the judiciary has taken place, there would still be individual judges, who would prefer to deliver their judgments in English. Such individuals must be accommodated.	This may be accepted.
42.	Having regard to the recommendations made by the States Reorganisation Commission regarding transfer of High Court Judges and the proposals about a single judicial service, it might be worth considering whether certain minimum language texts in appropriate regional languages and Hindi should not be adopted in the case of High Court Judges.	The Committee does not consider it appropriate to prescribe language tests for High Court Judges. It is, however, appreciated that a knowledge of Hindi and the official language of the State in which High Court is situated will be useful to Judges.
43.	Apart from the option of delivering judgments in English, there may be an option to High Court Judges to deliver judgments in their regional languages provided English or Hindi translations of such judgments are authenticated by them.	Vide opinion on Serial 38.
44.	Provision may be made for granting leave by presiding	This may be accepted.

1	2	3
	judges to counsel, in suitable cases, to argue in English in the Supreme Court and in English or the regional languages in the several High Courts even after the general changeover in the linguistic medium has taken place.	
45.	We would recommend, for consideration by the States concerned at the appropriate time, the making of a provision (at any rate) at the district levels, whereunder it would be open to parties or counsel to resort to the Hindi language at their option. We expect that this would be particularly necessary in larger towns; but if it is found necessary at lower levels as well, the principle ought to be extended.	The anguage of Courts subordinate to High Courts is not regulated by article 348. This recommendation is, therefore, not covered by the terms of reference.
46.	So far as the language of special tribunals is concerned, wherever their decisions or orders have a bearing not confined to a single region, it should be prescribed that their judgments and orders shall be delivered originally in Hindi. A translation into another language may be made available to the parties where necessary. As in the case of High Courts, we would envisage the English language being allowed to be used as the language of the judgment or order by individual judges of such special tribunals for a considerable transitional period.	This may be accepted.

Chapter XI

Language Of Law And Law Courts— *i*

The Dynamics Of The Changeover

1	2	3
47.	The following preliminaries appear to us to be prerequisite to the accomplishment of a changeover of the linguistic medium in the fields of legislation and administration of justice: (i) The preparation of a standard legal lexicon; (ii) Re-enactment of the statute book in Hindi in respect of both the Central and State legislation.	The Committee agrees with these recommendations, and considers that it would be necessary to constitute a Standing Commission or a similar high level body consisting of legal experts representing the different national languages of India for proper planning and implementation of the entire programme relating to translation of statutes and preparation of legal terminology and glossaries. It is felt that in so far as the question of translation of State Statutes into the official languages of the States are concerned, the State Governments might be advised to take necessary measures in consultation with the concerned Central authorities.
48.	So far as evolving of legal terminology is concerned, it seems to us necessary to adopt the following plan of action and to carry it out as rapidly as possible: (1) The present pace of evolving the necessary terminology for the Indian languages in the field of law must be greatly accelerated. (2) Steps must be taken for the publication, from time to time as they get ready, of glossaries of such terminology, as standard and recognised expressions under the 'imprimatur' of a suitable authority. (3) A rendering of the statute-book, both Central and State, into Hindi must be projected under the auspices of the Centre. It should be decided as to whether such Hindi versions of the law should not be enacted afresh by the appropriate legislative authority; precise arrangements in this behalf and a programme of action in respect of the Central as well as the State laws should be settled and pursued.	
49.	In order that original drafting may commence being attempted in Hindi by persons competent to do so and drafting practices gradually develop in	These recommendations may be accepted.

1	2	3
	that linguistic medium, it seems to us necessary to allow those States, who may want to do so, to undertake authoritative enactment originally in Hindi itself.	
50.	We envisage a transitional period of time during which the Statute Book as well as the case law would be partially in Hindi and in English, the Hindi language progressively assuming a larger proportion of the whole. During such a transitional period, resort may be had to the device of texts being made available in both Hindi and the English language, one of them being the original text for purposes of the law and the other an authorised translation.	

Chapter XII

The Union Language And Public Services Examinations

1	2	3
51.	For obvious reasons the linguistic media of the competitive examinations should be generally in keeping with the media of instruction in the educational system.	This recommendation may be dropped.
52.	It seems there has not been yet an overhaul of the linguistic media of instruction in some of the training establishments; and probably most of such training continues to be in English, although it may be susceptible of replacement, to more or less extent, by the Hindi medium. Such a review should be made, and steps taken for the language media for the appropriate entrance examinations, being related on the one hand to the medium of instruction in the different training institutions, and conforming on the other to the changes in the system of secondary education taking place in the country.	For some time, it will be necessary to continue English as the medium of instruction in the training establishments to which a reference has been made in the Commission's report. Suitable steps should, however, be taken to introduce Hindi as a medium for all or some of the purposes of instruction. So far as the medium of examination for entrance to these training establishments is concerned, English and Hindi should be adopted with choice for either with reference to any or all the papers, and an expert Committee should be appointed to examine the practicability of introduction of regional languages as media without bringing in a quota system.
53.	If in view of this, English has to be displaced partly or wholly as the medium for these examinations, it might be necessary to introduce regional language media in place of English, as secondary education in most parts of the country has now switched over from the English language medium to the medium of the regional language. This might entail a region-wise decentralisation of the entrance examination and, consequentially, a quota system. There are, however, very important distinctions between the adoption of the quota system for admission to training establishments and the adoption of such a system for purposes of actual recruitment to all-India services at the highest level of the administrative cadres, where the issue arises.	
54.	Having regard to the linguistic abilities that would be needed by members of the All-India and the Central Services in the future it would be legitimate in our view to introduce a compulsory paper in Hindi after due notice. In order that non-Hindi students may not be unduly handicapped in the transitional period, the paper may, to start with, be of a fairly low standard and treated as only a 'qualifying paper' and later on after due notice again it may be raised to the status of other compulsory papers as a 'marking' and fully competitive paper. Further, candidates having one of the South Indian languages as mother-tongue may be exempted from answering one or two stiffer questions in the Hindi paper which the candidates whose mother-tongues are closer to Hindi	As regards competitive examinations for the all-India and the higher Central Services the Committee considers: (i) English should continue to be the medium of examinations, and Hindi may be admitted as an alternative medium after sometime and both Hindi and English should be available as alternative media at the option of the candidates for as long as necessary. (ii) After due notice, there

1	2	3
	may be required to answer.	should be two compulsory language papers of equal standard, one in Hindi, and another in a modern Indian language other than Hindi to be selected by the candidate. (iii) There should be a compulsory paper in the English language even after the medium of examination is changed till English is completely replaced by Hindi for all official purposes. (iv) An expert committee should be appointed to examine the feasibility of introducing the regional languages as media without bringing in a quota system.
55.	To equate the Hindi candidates with the non-Hindi candidates, the former should be required to offer a paper, to be answered in their linguistic medium of the general examination, out of a variety of options including subjects of cultural interest bearing on South India and languages of the English Schedule other than Hindi.	
56.	We do not see sufficient justification for the suggestion that the 'compensatory provision' for Hindi candidates should be that they must offer a paper in a regional language (or a South Indian language) other than Hindi.	
57.	Provision may be made for testing candidates for the all-India services examinations in English through specific papers even after the medium of the examination is changed to a different language or languages.	
58.	As regards the language medium for the combined competitive examination through which candidates are recruited for the all-India and the higher Central Services, the principal difficulty arises out of the fact that for obvious reasons it will be prima facie extremely difficult to attain satisfactory standards of 'moderation' if the competition is held in linguistic medium anything as numerous as the thirteen regional languages. If the number of linguistic media for the examination exceeds the limits of manageability with reference to satisfactory standards of moderation, quota system may become inevitable unless the character of the examination itself is changed.	

1	2	3
	A quota system would break up the character of the existing all-India services and would lead to a fragmentation of the all-India competition and to deterioration in the quality of recruits to the all-India as well as the higher Central Services. Considering the present-day calls on the administrative personnel, we would strongly discountenance proposals leading to any such deterioration in the quality of the recruits to these services. In the case of the personnel of the all-India services, the chief consideration even from the point of view of each region exclusively regarding its own interest should be 'quality' and not proportionate share in the volume of employment. For like reasons quality is more important in the case of the higher Central Services as well than a proportionate region-wise distribution of the employment available. On the subject of the linguistic medium of the competitive examination for these services we, therefore, conclude as under: (a) So far as the all-India and Central Services are concerned (and this would apply, unless otherwise provided, also to other all-India services created hereafter), the alternative of the Hindi medium in addition to the existing English medium may be introduced after due notice. As and when other regional languages become a medium of instruction in the universities up to graduation stage as Hindi has done, the admission of other linguistic media will have to	

1	2	3
	be considered.	
	Suitable standards will have to be laid down as to what degree of progress as a medium should have been made in university education in respect of any language before its eligibility as a linguistic medium for the competitive examination for recruitment to these services may be considered.	
	The medium of the English language may be continued as an alternative for as long as may be necessary; if, eventually, a position should arise when this alternative could be dispensed with, such dispensation should of course be made after a sufficiently long notice.	
	(b) While 'moderation' might still be practicable so long as the number of linguistic media is manageable, having regard to the availability of examiners with suitable bilingual or multilingual qualifications, a stage might arrive when the admission of further linguistic media would be found impracticable.	
	Before such a stage is reached the Union and State Governments must take mutual counsel and decide whether, (1) they would accept a change in the scheme of recruitment to the all-India services or, in the alternative, (2) agree upon a limitation in the number of the linguistic media, or (3) make other appropriate changes in the system of the examination.	
	(c) We hope and trust that before the contingencies contemplated in (b) above eventuate, the progress of Hindi amongst non-Hindi speaking University graduates generally would have advanced sufficiently to admit of their competing on equal terms with Hindi-speaking candidates at these examinations through the medium of the Hindi language:	
	And until then, the availability of the English medium would give to such of the non-Hindi-speaking candidates as may need it an alternative sufficient to safeguard their legitimate interests:	
	Some of us entertain the hope that it would not, in the upshot, be necessary for the Union and State Governments to make the difficult choice presented by the alternatives in the last sub-paragraph of item (b) above.	
59.	As a measure of general encouragement to linguistic studies so badly needed in the special circumstances of this country, the concerned authorities should revise the list of optional subjects tenderable at the various Public Service Commission examinations and consider whether greater scope should not be allowed for the subjects of languages and literatures in the different Indian languages.	This may be accepted.

Chapter XIII

Propagation And Development Of Hindi And Regional Languages

1	2	3
60.	Since the adoption of the Constitution, this work has assumed a different aspect and it is now necessary that this responsibility is 'sponsored' officially.	This may be accepted.

1	2	3
61.	From what we have seen of the working of voluntary agencies in this field, it appears to us that steps ought to be taken in the following directions for the more systematic organisation and expansion of the work of propagation of Hindi: (1) Coordination of work among the various agencies, and where necessary demarcation of their activities. (2) Survey of their requirements for the purpose of adequate expansion of their allotted fields of activity. (3) The introduction of some measure of uniformity and comparability in standards of their examinations; and ensuring that proper methods are adopted and appropriate academic standards maintained in the conduct of the examinations. (4) Provision of aids for improvement of teaching methods and greater facilities for teachers' training. (5) Securing an appropriate and graded supply of suitable text books for the different regions of the country and for different categories of persons receiving Hindi instruction; supply of supporting reading matter and literature for the benefit of neo-literates and special classes of pupils, like children, women, etc. (6) Ancillary to the propagation of the Hindi language the provision of reading room and library facilities for those recently made literate in Hindi.	This may be accepted. It is felt that publication of some Hindi books in regional scripts would facilitate the learning of Hindi by adults in non-Hindi regions.
62.	We recommend that the Central Government should make liberal financial assistance available to the voluntary agencies for enlarging and improving their activities in the various ways referred to above.	This may be accepted.
63.	A greater and growing rapproachment amongst the various Indian languages and a wider understanding and comprehension of the varied cultural inheritance of India would be promoted by the encouragement of studies in the field of linguistic and philology; and such studies and research deserve every encouragement at the hands of the Union and State Governments.	This may be accepted. It is felt that encouragement should be given also to studies in the field of Indian literature.
	Reform Of The Devanagari Script	
64.	It is urgently necessary to finalise the type-writer keyboard and authoritatively adopt reforms to be made in the Devanagari script which can only be done on the leadership and under the auspices of the Centre.	The Committee agrees with this recommendation, and considers that early steps should be taken to resolve the differences that have arisen lately over the decisions taken at the Lucknow Conference, 1953, regarding reform of the Devanagari script.

WORKING GROUP ON INDUSTRIAL COOPERATIVES 1957—REPORT

New Delhi, Ministry of Commerce and Industry, 1958. 254p.

Chairman : Shri M.R. Bhide (resigned replaced by Shri J.C. Ryan).

Members : Shri M.P. Bhargava; Shri V. Subramanian; Shri H.D. Shourie; Shri L.C. Jain; Shri P.M. Mathai; Dr. D.K. Malhotra; Shri K. Subrahmaniyam Nayudu; Shri M.M. Vadi.

Secretary : Shri K.P. Parameshwaran.

APPOINTMENT

Village and small scale industries have been assigned an important place in the Second Five-Year Plan and Rs. 200 crores have been allocated for their development. Six All-India Boards viz., the Khadi and Village Industries Board, the All-India Handicrafts Board, the Handloom Board, the Small Scale Industries Board, the Central Silk Board and the Coir Board have been established to deal with their problems, as a result of which considerable increase in production and employment has already been achieved. In order to coordinate the activities of these Boards, in relation to functions, policy and finance, a "Coordination Committee of Small Industries" has been set up in the Ministry of Commerce and Industry. This Committee, presided over by the Minister for Commerce and Industry, at its first meeting held on June 8, 1957, decided to constitute a Working Group "to examine the question of development of industrial cooperatives during the period of the Second Plan". The Government of India, in its communication No. AC/-II/(2)/57-Coord., dated September 11, 1957 appointed the Working Group on Industrial Cooperatives.

TERMS OF REFERENCE

(i) To review the progress of industrial cooperatives for village and small-scale industries;

(ii) Examine the difficulties impeding the rapid progress of the formation of industrial cooperatives, including those connected with the registration and supervision of such societies;

(iii) Examine the financial, organisational, and marketing difficulties of industrial cooperatives; and

(iv) Recommend measures for ensuring accelerated development of industrial cooperatives with special reference to the objectives and programmes of the Second Five-Year Plan.

CONTENTS

Introductory; Cottage and Small Scale Industries; Industrial Cooperatives in India—Present Position and Organisational Problems; Raw Material and Equipment; Provision of Credit; Marketing; Training and Education; Administration; Other Related Matters; Summary of Recommendations; Appendices from A to N.

RECOMMENDATIONS

I. Organisational Problems

The members of a cooperative production society should be enrolled with reference to their skill in the manufacture of the products which the society intends to produce and should be drawn from a compact area such as a town or a group of villages.

Normally, there ought to be a separate society for each industry or craft. If, in any case, two or more industries or crafts are to be combined in one society, it should be carefully examined whether the members will have a community of interest and whether there is scope for the success of the society.

In the case of industrial cooperatives in which the worker members may not be able to provide leadership, capital, managerial ability or outside influence in the measure necessary for success, it is desirable that a few non-workers should be admitted into the society as members but their number should be restricted to 10 per cent of the total number of members and care should be taken to see that such "sympathisers" are genuinely interested in the workers' welfare.

There should be no objection to the conversion of a proprietory concern into an industrial cooperative society provided the entrepreneur and the workers join the proposed society as members and entrepreneur is not given any special privileges in the society and is entitled to only one vote and a reasonable remuneration and bonus for services rendered. Before the registration of such a society the Registrar should educate the member workers in their rights in the society so that their interests are not subordinated to those of the entrepreneur.

There should be no objection to the registration of an industrial cooperative society of small entrepreneurs provided (i) that the workers employed by each entrepreneur are also admitted as its members, and (ii) that no entrepreneur member employs more than 10 workers.

Additional workers required to complete the execution of an order by an industrial society as also apprentices, including minors, may be enrolled as associate members with a nominal share each but with no other rights in the society than that for wages and bonus on wages. Suitable provision may be made for this purpose in the cooperative law in force in each State.

When purchases of raw materials and sales of manufactured products increase in a production or service society, the suppliers and customers may be brought into the society as nominal members with nominal shares but without any rights in the society.

The procedure according to which loans are being provided for handloom weavers with a view to enabling them to take shares in a weavers cooperative society may be adopted by the Government in respect of all industrial cooperative societies.

Where, for the successful conduct of their business, industrial cooperative societies need more owned capital than what can be raised as share capital from members, the State Governments may contribute to the reserve fund of the society the required amount as foundation money.

The practice, according to which the Central Government, through the All India Handloom Board, provides State Governments with loans for contribution to the share capital of open weavers societies may be adopted in respect of the industries dealt with by the other Boards. An apex industrial society should also be entitled to receive a grant from the Government towards contribution to its reserve fund.

The Board of Directors of an industrial society should ordinarily be elected by its members from among themselves and the President should be elected by the Directors from among themselves. Separate representation may be given on the Board to sympathisers to the extent of not more than about 25 per cent of the total number of Directors.

It would not be proper to let the Registrar of Cooperative Societies nominate more than a-third of the Board of Directors, including the President of the Society, if necessary, for the first three years. In exceptional cases, the entire Board may be nominated for the first three years with the special sanction of Government.

The Board of Directors should be assisted by a competent manager and adequate staff. Where, with the help of a Government subsidy, the services of experienced men can be secured by the society from business organisations, Government should provide the subsidy for a limited period on a sliding scale.

The practice obtaining in some States of deputing experienced officers of the Cooperative Department to work as the managers of industrial cooperatives on foreign service terms under the direction and control of the Board of Directors of the societies, for a period of three years at a time, may be adopted, wherever necessary. Where a society cannot afford to pay for the services of such a manager, he may be deputed initially free of cost but within a period which should be specified, it should bear his entire cost on a graduated scale. During the period of deputation of such an officer, no contribution towards pension and leave salary should be collected from the society. Nor should the officer be transferred by the Department to other work during the period of his Deputation. Further, during this period, the society should train some one to take the place of the deputed officer in due course.

The manager and every member of the administrative staff of an industrial cooperative society should be eligible for its membership.

No industrial cooperative society should be registered without an on-the-spot study of its prospects of success. Such a study should find out particulars regarding (i) the market for the article to be produced, (ii) the availability of the raw materials needed, (iii) the availability of transport facilities, (iv) the need for and the availability of financial resources, (v) the cost of production per unit, (vi) the price at which the products can be sold and the margin of profit it will give, and (vii) the performance of other units of the same industry in the neighbourhood, etc. It should be examined whether the net profits of the society will be sufficient to set apart reserves, declare a dividend of at least three per cent on the share capital and a bonus of three per cent on wages after paying off instalments on loans, interest charges, rates and taxes, etc. and providing for depreciation. If the study reveals that the society will not pay its way for many years to come, say, even beyond four years, the society should not be registered.

In the case of industries which are being supported with subsidies in view of their importance from the point of view of providing employment, such subsidies should be taken into account in the on-the-spot study suggested. Even in their case, the society should not be registered if, in spite of the subsidies, the society will not pay its way year after year.

The Departments of Industries and Cooperation should study the technical and commercial aspects of the production of selected items of light engineering goods, electrical goods and goods needed by the building industry, and take steps to organise industrial cooperatives for the production of such items as offer prospects of business success. The Central and State Governments might secure large orders for these selected items from the railways and other State industrial enterprises and distribute them among the industrial cooperatives organised, for being executed according to specifications under competent supervision.

Industrial cooperative societies for other lines of business should also be supported where they exist and more such societies should be organised wherever there is a demand and the prospects of success are good. They should also be given all the aids recommended.

A relaxation of the maximum borrowing limit fixed at eight times the paid-up share capital and reserve fund of an industrial cooperative society is likely to lead to overtrading and losses. However, the various measures recommended for giving the society adequate owned funds are likely to provide it with a sufficient basis on which to borrow up to its needs. Further, loans given on the pledge of raw materials and finished products may be excluded from the maximum borrowing limit of eight times the owned funds.

The members of industrial cooperatives should be educated in the correct appreciation of their relationship with the society and their rights and duties. They should not seek outside interference but should govern their workshop by themselves.

The several types of assistance recommended for industrial cooperatives may be expected not only to stimulate the formation of a large number of cooperative societies in the sphere of cottage and small-scale industries but also to lead to the conversion of industrial units, which at present function otherwise than on a cooperative basis, into cooperative societies. Such conversions should be welcomed and encouraged, care being taken to see that the societies which are formed conform to cooperative principles. Further, the different types of assistance now being offered to cottage and small industries by Government should be channelled in an increasing measure through cooperative societies.

Every State should have a cooperative apex marketing society for industrial goods which will be both a business and promotional body. Every industrial cooperative society in the State should take shares in it. The Government should also take shares in it up to three times the capital subscribed by the societies and, in any case, not less than Rs. 10 lakhs for a State of the size and industrial prospects as Madras, Mysore, Punjab or West Bengal.

The functions of the apex society should be to (i) supply raw materials and equipment to member societies for cash; (ii) take over their finished products for sale on consignment basis or on an outright purchase and sale system, (iii) obtain orders from Government, Railways, large industrial firms, etc., and arrange for their production and delivery by the affiliated societies on a sub-contract system; (iv) recommend loans and advances to banks for industrial societies and, if necessary, to guarantee their repayment; and (v) run a research and publicity section.

The apex marketing society should open a branch with a godown-cum-sales depot at the headquarters of the State as well as at the headquarters of each district. The raw materials and equipment in demand from members should be stocked in the godown for sale on cash basis. The finished products of the members should be received at the sales depots, displayed suitably and sold to the public for cash. Each godown-cum-sales depot should be in-charge of a branch manager, assisted by an office and field staff.

Each branch should have an Advisory Committee, nominated for three years at a time by the Board of Management of the apex society and consisting of three representatives from the member societies in the district and one from the District Cooperative Bank, one from the Industrial Cooperative Bank, if any, and one each from the departments of Industries and cooperation in the State and the Small Industries Service Institute of the Central Government.

The management of the apex society should vest in a Board consisting of (i) one or two representatives from the member societies of each district; (ii) three directors nominated by the State Government, who should be Registrar of Cooperative Societies, Director of Industries and the Finance Secretary; (iii) the Director of the Small Industries Service Institute in the State; and (iv) a nominee of the National Small Industries Corporation. The president of the apex society should be elected by the members of the Board from among themselves.

While this Board may meet not more than once a quarter, an Executive Committee, consisting of the President, two directors representing industrial cooperatives and two other official directors, should carry on the business of the apex society, meeting once a month or more often if necessary.

The general body of the apex society consisting of one representative from every affiliated society and of the directors of the apex society will be the ultimate authority of the society.

Loan applications of affiliated industrial societies should be made to the branch manager who will place them before the Advisory Committee, which will take a decision as to the grant of the loan, and forward the application to the bank, whose representative on the Advisory Committee agrees to finance the society.

Where the lending bank asks for a guarantee, it should be given by the branch manager with the approval of the Advisory Committee up to a limit for which the Board of Management of the apex society have given him powers. Beyond that limit, the guarantee should be given by the Board of Management itself on the recommendation of the Advisory Committee.

Government should provide the apex society with a guarantee fund, by making a grant which might be about Rs. 10 lakhs initially and Rs. five lakhs during each of the next four years, depending upon the size of the State and opportunities for development of industrial cooperatives.

This guarantee fund should be invested by the apex society separately in trustee securities, and should not be drawn upon except with the consent of the Trustee appointed by the Government from among its nominees on the Board of Management of the apex society. The guarantee fund should be allowed to be drawn upon by the Trustee only to the extent of a percentage of the guarantee enforced against the apex society. This percentage should be as large as 75 per cent during the first five years, at the end of which period the Government may review the situation and reduce the percentage.

The running costs of the apex society should be borne by Government for the first five years in the case of the establishment at the headquarters. As regards the branches, its costs to Government may be reduced on a sliding scale over a period of eight years. In the interests of speedy development, a good part of the Government subsidy should come from the Central Government.

In the first five years of the working of the apex society, one half of the net profits and the entire dividend on Government share capital should be contributed to the reserve fund of the society.

Indirect aids from Government to industrial cooperatives recommended in this report—statutory, administrative and fiscal—should all be available to the apex societies also.

Existing apex weavers' societies should remain distinct and, where a common apex industrial society is now dealing with all varieties of industries including handloom weaving, the latter should be separated and a separate apex society established for weavers' cooperatives. Similarly, apex coir societies and federations of cooperative societies of village industries which are functioning well should be allowed to continue. There should be no regimenting of industrial cooperatives into the apex marketing society recommended by us though every society which wishes to join it should be free to do so.

A review of the working of the existing federations of industrial cooperatives may be undertaken in each State. Wherever the existing institutions are working on sound lines and may, therefore, be retained in their present form, such institutions may be allowed to continue and the aids recommended for the apex societies may, generally, be extended to them. A similar review may also be undertaken in the case of the existing district or regional organisations with a view to determining whether they could be suitably integrated with the proposed apex marketing society by affiliation.

II. Raw Material And Equipment

The supply of yarn to primary weavers' societies may be undertaken by apex weavers' societies in all the States and every endeavour may be made to ensure such supply at reasonable prices through wholesale purchase and economy in distribution costs.

Apex weavers' societies should follow the generally accepted cooperative principle of "sale at market price" and supply yarn to affiliated societies at the prevailing market price.

Apex weavers' societies may build up specific reserves to meet losses, if any, on yarn trade, carrying, if necessary, part of their profits on this business to such reserves.

The Central Government may actively assist State Governments with loans and grants, import licences etc., for establishing cooperative spinning mills at all important centres.

A review may be made of the current allocation of iron and steel and other commodities under control as between the several sectors or agencies and, with due regard to the increasing importance of small scale industries in our economy, their quota may be increased. Further, as an incentive towards organised effort, industrial cooperatives may be shown special consideration, including preference in special circumstances.

The import of raw silk may be liberalised so as to enable the level of employment to be maintained in the section of the silk-weaving industry in which imported raw silk is exclusively used.

When raw material is to be imported, special licences should be issued for the purchase of such material to industrial cooperatives on a preferential basis. In case an apex body is able and willing to import the material direct, Government should issue import licences to it direct.

Where raw material is in short supply and is controlled by Government, industrial cooperatives should be registered for quotas on a preferential basis and their demands met with due regard to the availability of the material in the country. The services of apex bodies should be utilised in the distribution of controlled commodities such as iron, steel, cement, etc.

Wherever Government has control over the release and distribution of raw material for public use, some preferential treatment in price etc., may be given to industrial cooperatives for a prescribed period.

Industrial cooperatives should be advanced loans on a liberal basis, for the seasonal purchase of raw materials and their stocking for distribution during the off-season.

Government may consider the question of providing loans and subsidies to large-sized industrial cooperatives for the construction of godowns for storage of raw material and finished goods in the same manner as the marketing cooperatives are assisted for the purpose.

The existing arrangements for the supply of equipment, machinery and tools to industrial cooperatives by the various All-India Boards, etc., should be continued and the following additional facilities should be provided : (i) Industrial cooperatives should be given preference in the matter of supply of machinery imported or in short supply within the country. (ii) In cases where the financial resources of a cooperative society do not permit immediate payment for machinery or equipment needed by it, the All-India Board or the State Government concerned should provide the necessary funds on a medium-term or long-term basis. (iii) In cases where machinery has to be imported, the apex industrial society or a primary society may be allowed to get it on a priority basis.

III. Provision Of Credit

The Reserve Bank of India may, in addition to these industries already selected for study, undertake the study of three more industries viz., those producing light engineering goods, electrical goods and goods needed by the housing industry with a view to financing them.

Every endeavour should be made, as early as possible, to place the financing of industrial cooperatives on an institutional footing. As the transition to institutional financing will be a slow and difficult process, Government should take the following steps so as to inspire confidence among the institutional financing agencies and improve their readiness to finance industrial cooperative societies.

(a) The many sided programme for the development of cottage and small scale industries should be pressed forward with a sense of urgency so as to make the prospects of their stability and survival demonstrably bright.

(b) Technical and supervisory staff should be provided at the cost of Government for the financing institutions for the first two or three years or the services of such staff employed by Government should be made available to them.

(c) Initially, to provide such experience to these banks as would help them understand and deal with small industrial units and their problems better, the funds intended to be provided by Government to industrial societies may, as a rule, be routed through the banks under suitable conditions.

(d) Government should provide such financial aids as loans for contribution to share capital, reserve fund grants, etc., to strengthen the owned funds of the industrial cooperatives and other financial aids necessary for making the structure of these societies stronger.

Ordinarily, it is to a Central Cooperative Bank that an industrial cooperative society should turn for its credit requirements. In order to ensure an increasingly active role on the part of cooperative banks in meeting the credit requirements of the industrial cooperatives, the following steps should be taken :

(i) There should be suitable representation for industrial cooperatives on the boards of management of cooperative central banks with due regard to their number and importance in the cooperative economy of the district or the region served by such banks.

(ii) An industrial sub-committee consisting of the President and three or four directors, including one or two representatives of industrial cooperatives and the nominees of the administrative department of the State Government which is concerned with industrial cooperatives, may be constituted to deal with all matters relating to industrial cooperatives, including the disposal of their loan applications. The sub-committee would act in an advisory and recommendatory capacity. Any special staff which a Central Cooperative Bank may employ for these societies, may work under the control and direction of this sub-committee. An annual report may be sent by this sub-committee to the Board of the central bank which may be incorporated in the bank's annual report together with such remarks as the Board may wish to make.

(iii) Central cooperative banks may, in consultation with the appropriate departments of Governments concerned, make an annual estimate of the probable financial requirements of industrial cooperatives in their jurisdiction and earmark part of their funds for these societies.

(iv) The Government should extend guarantees to financial agencies in particular circumstances or in the case of particular industries, as may be necessary, for a specified period of time.

(v) Wherever there is a fairly good concentration of industrial cooperatives in the jurisdiction of a central cooperative bank, the latter may employ a suitable person as deputy manager or deputy secretary to attend to matters connected with industrial cooperatives.

(vi) For the first three years, Government may help the bank with subsidies to meet the cost of this officer. Similar subsidies may be made available, on a sliding scale, towards the cost of the executive staff which the central bank may employ for the supervision of industrial cooperatives in its jurisdiction.

(vii) Whenever cooperative central banks require the services of the technical departments of Government, State or Central, which are interested in the promotion of cottage and small-scale industries, for scrutiny of loan applications, etc., the respective departments should place the services of such personnel at their disposal.

Wherever cooperative banks are not, for one reason or another, in a position to finance the industrial cooperatives, they may be financed by the State Bank of India.

The officers of the State Bank of India should be invited to attend and participate at the meetings of the organisations connected with the promotion of industrial cooperatives.

All the facilities, guarantees or nelp which have been proposed for cooperative banks, may, wherever necessary or justified, be extended to the State Bank of India in the initial stage.

With the resources of the State Financial Corporations, current and potential, they should reorient their policies and procedures, so that it may be possible for industrial cooperatives to obtain, in an expanding measure, their requirements of block capital from these Corporations.

In view of the servicing costs involved, the State Financial Corporations may not be interested in providing small loans or loans below a prescribed limit. In such cases, the Government may continue to provide medium or long-term loans.

An arrangement may, by agreement, be worked out by which the State Bank of India or the central cooperative bank which provides working capital to an industrial cooperative, also acts as an agent of the State Financial Corporation in so far as its medium-term or long-term loans are concerned.

Appropriate changes may be made in the constitution of the Boards of Directors of the Corporations so as to include a representative, where necessary, of industrial cooperatives, or a nominee of the department of the State Government dealing with industrial cooperatives or of the apex marketing society.

Steps may be taken so that the requirements of security demanded by the State Financial Corporations can be met, initially, by the provision of a guarantee by the State Government or by an apex marketing society of industrial cooperatives until the society get well established and the Corporations have gained sufficient experience in this line.

All the help, facilities and concessions recommended by us elsewhere for cooperative and other financing agencies, should be extended also to the existing industrial cooperative banks.

In areas where the credit needs of industrial cooperatives can be met adequately only by setting up industrial cooperative banks and where conditions favourable to their successful working exist, such banks may be established. In such cases, the decision to set up an industrial cooperative bank should be preceded by a careful examination of all the relevant factors, especially the following: (a) whether there is a large concentration of industrial units organised on cooperative basis in the locality to provide the bank with adequate share capital and adequate business; (b) whether there is a large potential for the growth of industrial cooperatives in the area; (c) whether the credit needs are not, or cannot be, met adequately by the existing financial agencies, and (d) whether the new bank will be in a position to attract deposits.

Some members of the Group were strongly of the view that industrial cooperative banks should, in deserving cases, be eligible for State partnership.

With funds becoming available to industrial societies from banks, apex weavers' societies, district industrial associations, etc., should give up the practice of combining trading with banking by supplying goods on credit.

In case of Government loans for working capital repayable in annual instalments over a period of years, no repayment should be demanded for the first two years and the loan may be made repayable in a period of 10 to 15 years, the first instalment being due at the end of the third or fourth year as the case may be. Besides, a further loan may be provided to a society in those circumstances where the payment of the instalment is likely to result in the shrinkage of its business.

The pattern of assistance for schemes connected with cooperative societies of cottage and small scale industries should not be made less liberal during the remaining period of the Second Five-Year Plan and a review may, if necessary, be undertaken at the end of this period.

Separate rules may be made in the States for advancing loans to industrial cooperatives under the State Aid to Industries Act.

The terms and conditions relating to the provision of loans to industrial cooperatives of scheduled castes and scheduled tribes should be liberalized to the maximum extent possible and this and other types of assistance recommended for industrial cooperatives should be extended generously to societies serving these sections of the population.

Where Government funds are provided the rate of interest on the loan should in no case exceed three per cent to industrial cooperatives.

Where Government funds are routed through cooperative or commercial banks or corporations, or these institutions provide such loans out of their own resources, Government may provide an appropriate subsidy to enable these banks to advance funds to the industrial cooperative societies at the rate of three per cent.

The concessional rate of interest recommended may initially be provided for a five-year period at the end of which the position may be reviewed.

As a rule, the State cooperative bank may be permitted a margin of one per cent and the Central cooperative bank, a margin of two per cent. While the margins should be sufficiently liberal in the immediate future so as to enable the banks to employ extra administrative and supervisory staff, create adequate reserves, etc., the position may be reviewed after five years.

The existing arrangements for the sharing of losses sustained by cooperative financing agencies in respect of their loans to cooperative societies for handloom weaving and small scale industries, may be adopted in respect of the financing of cooperatives of other industries as well.

In cases where guarantees against losses are given, they should be guarantees enforceable on losses ascertained at the end of every two or three years as may be agreed upon at the time the guarantee is given and there should be no avoidable delay in reimbursing the banks.

The following general considerations should govern the policy in respect of security for loans to small scale and cottage industries:

(i) Central cooperative banks may ordinarily provide clean accommodation to an industrial cooperative society to the extent of its owned funds. (ii) An industrial cooperative society should also be normally entitled to accommodation on the pledge of stocks of raw material, and finished goods held in a godown under the bank's lock and key. (iii) Where a society does not have adequate owned funds to merit a clean loan or sufficient stocks to obtain a pledge loan or does not find it convenient to pledge stocks to raise the funds it needs, certain special arrangements may be devised, e.g., the bank may make what is known as a "factory type" of advance. (iv) Where this type of arrangement is not possible accommodation might be provided against the security of fixed assets to be mortgaged, even though advances may be for working capital purposes. (v) Where even this cannot be done, banks may consider the possibility of financing the societies against a floating charge on all their assets. (vi) Advances against railway receipts in respect of goods despatched to such purchasers as Government, etc. may be allowed. (vii) Cooperative banks may, to the extent possible, undertake to provide industrial societies with those facilities which commercial banks ordinarily extend to their clients who are exporters.

The following precaution may generally be taken in financing industrial societies:

(a) It should generally be ensured that the borrowing society has a satisfactory past record, that it has an able and honest management, that it is technically competent to produce goods to specifications and, above all, that the goods are readily marketable. (b) The stocks of raw material purchased with the loan may be taken as pledge, to the extent possible. (c) Where feasible, advances made for the purchase of raw materials may be effected in the form of payments to the suppliers of raw materials. (d) For the liquidation of the dues to the bank, it may be arranged if practicable, that the purchasers of finished products should make their payments to the bank direct.

The purchasing departments of Government, both in the States and at the Centre, should make every endeavour to settle expeditiously, the bills for goods supplied to them by industrial cooperatives.

The Government should arrange for a speedy settlement of all the claims of weavers' societies and other cooperatives which are entitled to the reimbursement of rebate.

A concerted drive should be organised for promoting thrift and collecting savings from individual members of industrial cooperative societies.

IV. Marketing

Standardisation schemes should be drawn up and enforced by the departments of Government concerned, with the help of the Indian Standards Institution, at least in respect of the major products of cottage and small scale industries.

Arrangements should be made for the provision of financial accommodation on a specially liberal scale to industrial cooperative societies to enable them to hold stocks of finished products, when necessary, in sizeable quantities.

The following assistance may be given to cooperatives for cottage and small scale industries in purchases made by Government departments and institutions.

(a) Apart from a general preference provided for products of cottage and small scale industries, a further marginal preference may be shown to the products of industrial cooperatives as compared with private units at least in fields of intensive cooperative organisation.

(b) The decisions and directives of Government in this regard should be sufficiently clear and should not, in any manner, give room for evasion.

(c) It should be made clear to the various departments of Government that it is the accepted policy of the State to support industrial cooperatives through their purchasing programmes.

(d) Wherever possible, all purchases of Government stores should be centralised in one Department of the State Government.

(e) Wherever an order is placed by Government or on its behalf, e.g., by the National Small Industries Corporation, industrial societies may be given, without delay, detailed specifications and such technical guidance and assistance as may be necessary.

(f) A list of goods produced by cooperatives of small scale and cottage industries should be drawn up and circulated periodically among heads of departments.

(g) Appropriate provision should be made for liaison between industrial cooperatives and the authorities of the State Government who make purchases for various departments.

Suitable machinery in the appropriate administrative department may be constituted, for bringing to the notice of large-scale industrial units, the products which industrial societies can manufacture for them, and to the notice of industrial cooperatives the type of products which might be required by large scale units and which could be produced by them.

The National Small Industries Corporation and the

Regional Small Industries Service Institutes should take a more active interest in providing assistance for co-operative societies.

The schemes of the various All India Boards for publicity and propaganda should be extended to as many products of cottage and small scale industries as possible. Such publicity and propaganda should be undertaken on a larger scale than hitherto.

The Government of India should make liberal annual contributions to the apex marketing organisations of the industrial societies so that they may undertake suitable schemes for advertisement, publicity, exhibitions, etc.

With the help of our Embassies and High Commissioner Offices, foreign markets may be tapped for the promotion of sales of the products of cottage and small scale industries. Wherever there is sufficient scope for canvassing sizeable business, active steps may be taken to build up a suitable marketing organisation, taking care that there is no avoidable duplication in such arrangement.

Each State Government may draw up a list of industries for the products of which there is an assured demand for which specific orders can be collected from large-scale purchasers and efforts for the organisation of industrial cooperatives may be specially devoted towards these industries.

Fullest use should be made of the facilities for technical aid available from the Handicrafts Board and similar organisations, with a view to finding and cultivating a foreign market for handicrafts products.

The management of the emporia run by State Governments or certain specialised organisations for the marketing of products of cottage and small scale industries may, wherever possible, be progressively transferred to suitable cooperative institutions.

V. Training And Education

The official and non-official staff connected with industrial cooperatives may, with profit, join any of the training institutions established by the Central Committee for Cooperative Training, choosing industrial cooperatives as their optional subject.

The key officers of the proposed industrial apex marketing society will require training of a high standard which should be organised as a special branch of the Senior Officers' Training Course at Poona, with adequate emphasis on business management.

Every State should open one or two training schools on industrial cooperatives for the training of junior cooperative officers and employees of industrial societies. Each of these schools may train 80 candidates per year in two classes of 40 each. The teaching staff might consist of a Principal and three Lecturers, one for banking, business management and book-keeping, one having experience in working out the programmes of the various All-India Boards dealing with cottage and small scale industries and a third for industrial cooperatives, including cooperative marketing and supply. Concessions such as free tuition, monthly stipends, lump-sum allowance for tours conducted for practical training, etc. might be granted to candidates. In the initial stages, the entire expenditure on such schools should be met by the Government of India and the organisation and other matters connected with the establishment and running of these schools might be dealt with by the Central Committee for Cooperative Training.

The suitable agency to impart cooperative education to the members and office-bearers of industrial cooperatives will be the paid supervisory staff and the Block Level Extension Officers (Cooperation and Industries). These officials, who should visit the industrial cooperatives often, and attend the meetings of their general body as well as of their committee, should not only provide guidance on specific problems and instruction in principles of cooperation but should also cultivate a business sense among the members.

The basic principles outlined in the pamphlet on "Extension work in the cooperative movement" by Prof. A.F. Laidlaw in regard to the requirement and training of extension workers, methods of extension and the general approach to work of this nature should be adopted in connection with the programmes of Government for the development of industrial cooperatives.

The education programme for the members and office-bearers of industrial cooperatives should include instruction in regard to their special problems, organisational, administrative and financial, and the instructors should themselves be specially equipped for the purpose.

Periodical conferences might be held to popularise industrial cooperation as well as to educate different sections of the public in regard to its problems.

Elementary instruction in cooperation may be provided in the high schools and advanced courses of study in the subject may be introduced in the universities in the degree and honours courses in commerce and economics. Facilities for research in the various aspects of cooperation may also be provided in the universities.

The State Governments may, at an early date, undertake, with reference to the needs of their programmes for industrial cooperatives, a review of the arrangements for training and instruction of a technical nature, estimate the overall requirements in this field and take measures for their improvement to the necessary extent.

Full use should be made of the existing technical training organisations. Greater publicity and effective liaison between the various technical agencies associated with the All-India Boards and the authorities in charge of industrial cooperatives are necessary and should be ensured.

Increasing use should be made of industrial cooperatives for promoting the technical efficiency of cottage and small-scale industries by the introduction of improved methods and tools for production.

Artisans of proved competence may be selected from among members of industrial cooperative societies and deputed to large industrial concerns in the country and in foreign countries, for training in improved techniques. Where a well developed cooperative society is in a position to provide such facilities, to artisan members of other societies, the concerned society may be suitably remunerated.

Even in courses which are strictly intended for technical training, cooperation should be included as a subject and the trainees might be taken round a few industrial cooperatives in the neighbourhood.

A careful selection of trainees for the training courses is necessary with reference to their background, prospects of future employment, etc. Preference may be given to candidates sponsored or recommended by well established industrial units or employers, including cooperatives.

VI. Administration

For coordinated control and unified direction, it is desirable to keep the cooperative financing agencies and the societies financed by them under the administrative control of a single authority. As the pressure of work in regard to registration, financing, audit etc., increases, the Registrar of Cooperative Societies, whose responsibilities at present pertain mainly to agricultural cooperatives, may, in some States, have to be relieved of the responsibilities relating to industrial cooperatives, housing cooperatives, etc. and these latter duties may have to be passed on to others. Thus, within a State, there may be two or three Registrars dealing, say, with agricultural cooperatives, industrial cooperatives and other cooperatives. Duplication of office and field staff for these Registrars should, however, be avoided as far as possible. Where there are two or more Registrars of Cooperative Societies, the work of these Registrars should be properly coordinated by appointing a Registrar-General or by designating the Senior Registrar as Registrar-General or by constituting the proposed two or more Registrars into a single Board with the Senior Registrar as Chairman.

In this administrative pattern which is suggested tentatively there should be room for designating, where necessary, the Director of Industries himself as the Registrar in charge of industrial cooperatives, though the detailed inter-departmental adjustments that this would involve, should be worked out very carefully.

Those selected for appointment as Registrar or Registrar-General should be persons with aptitude for cooperative work and should invariably be given practical training in this field for a period of six months.

The Registrars of Cooperative Societies should not be disturbed from their posts before the completion of a minimum period of at least five years.

Liaison between the Departments of Industries and Cooperation should be established so that there is consultation between them in the formulation of their programmes and individual schemes and that, whichever department sponsors the organisation of a particular industrial cooperative, the guidance and help of the other will be readily available.

The Departments of Industries and Cooperation should ordinarily be placed under the same Secretary to Government and, if possible, under the same Minister.

The Officers of the Industries Department as well as the field staff might be given a brief training in cooperation as part of any technical training which is arranged for them. In cases where this cannot be done, they should be given at least a month's course of lectures and taken on visits to cooperative institutions.

At the district level, the Assistant Registrar of Cooperative Societies, who is in charge of all types of cooperative societies, should also be in charge of industrial cooperatives, but should be assisted, in this task, by a District Cooperative Officer for industries, or a Cooperative Sub-Registrar for industries.

An additional Assistant Registrar in the District to deal with industrial cooperatives alone might be appointed in those cases where their number and volume of activities are large enough to justify such an appointment. It such cases, coordination at the district level should be maintained by the seniormost Assistant Registrar in the district.

There should be adequate subordinate staff for the inspection and supervision of industrial societies.

The Block Level Extension Officers (Industries and Cooperation) should also be available for work relating to industrial cooperatives in the Community Development Blocks.

Gradually, as the apex industrial cooperative marketing society grows, it will be necessary, for ensuring coordinated development, that all such technical staff as are looking after industrial cooperatives should be transferred to this society from the Cooperative Department, the Industries Department and the other agencies employing such staff. It will be necessary that, for this purpose, the Government should continue to meet the cost of such staff till such time as the apex society is in a position to pay for their services.

There should be adequate audit staff, generally at the rate of one auditor for every 20 societies of average size, for doing at least one audit per year. In the case of large societies, provision should be made for concurrent or interim audit, at the rate of one auditor for every five societies.

As the audit of industrial societies is likely to be complicated and difficult, special training facilities may be provided for auditors of industrial societies.

Periodical inter-departmental conferences may be arranged by the Registrar at which the problems of the development of industrial cooperatives can be discussed with the participation of the concerned departments.

The officials of specialised departments e.g., the Public Works Department, the Forest Department, etc., may be invited to conferences of industrial cooperatives, so that they may have a better appreciation of the difficulties experienced by these societies and may also advise suitably.

To ensure suitable allocation of funds for schemes connected with industrial cooperatives from out of budget allotments for departments other than the Cooperative Department, liaison between the heads of departments concerned and the Registrar will be necessary and should be secured.

A senior officer with experience in cooperation may be appointed in the Ministry of Commerce and Industry, Government of India, with the necessary staff, exclusively to give active attention to the development of industrial cooperatives, and, among other functions, to pursue with the State Governments and others concerned, the implementation of the necessary measures recommended by us in this regard.

Every endeavour should be made, to keep the State Cooperative Advisory Council informed of the activities of industrial cooperatives and to seek its advice and cooperation on important issues of policy in this sphere.

VII. Other Related Matters

(a) Women's Organisations

Trained women organisers may be appointed for conducting regular propaganda among women-folk. The organisers should be carefully selected and trained in the principles and practice of cooperation, organisation, administration, accounts, etc., and also given technical instruction in a few important industries.

In particular, the possibilities of organising women's cooperatives in respect of the following industries may be fully explored:

(i) Spinning and weaving.
(ii) Mat-making.
(iii) Embroidery.
(iv) Tailoring.
(v) Toy-making.
(vi) Dolls manufacture.
(vii) Bamboo products.
(viii) Fish-net making.
(ix) Hand-pounding of paddy.
(x) Ornamental leather goods.
(xi) Cosmetics manufacture.
(xii) Making of thread ball, tape, ribbon, etc.
(xiii) Food preservation and canning.
(xiv) Pickles, etc.

The State Governments may undertake a review of the concessions now shown to women's cooperatives and extend to them the necessary incentives and concessions. Where necessary, assistance may be given by way of financial accommodation, supply of tools and equipment, free services of managerial staff in the initial stages, preferential purchases of the products of these societies, etc.

(b) Cooperative Housing

Such aids and facilities as are now available for providing houses and common facilities for weavers on a cooperative basis may be extended to other cottage and small industrial workers organised on cooperative lines, the particular type of cooperative industrial units eligible for help being determined in consultation with State Governments.

SCAVENGING CONDITIONS ENQUIRY COMMITTEE, 1957—REPORT

Delhi, Manager of Publications, 1961. 209p.+iip.

Chairman : Shri N.R. Malkani.

Members : Shri P.N. Rajabhoj; Shri K.L. Balmiki; Shri Rajkrishna Bose; Shri N.S. Kajrolkar.

Secretary : Shri O.K. Moorthy.

APPOINTMENT

At the instance of the Minister for Home Affairs, the Central Advisory Board for Harijan Welfare, at its meeting of October 12, 1957, set up this Committee.

TERMS OF REFERENCE

(i) Improvement of Scavenging condition;

(ii) Improvement of living conditions of scavengers.

CONTENTS

Introduction; Cleaning of Latrines; Transportation of Night-soil; Wheel Barrows; Implements; Night-soil Deposits; Dumping Grounds; Underground Drainage; Design of Latrines; Latrines on Railways; Customary Rights; Methods of Scavenging in Foreign Countries; Administrative Set-up; Some General Aspects; Summary; Appendices I to XV.

RECOMMENDATIONS

The Receptacle

The use of receptacles in private and public latrines should be made compulsory.

The receptacle should be made of iron sheets or M.S. Plates of suitable gauge to last at least a year or so and should be provided with a handle on one side and a slanting side on the other.

The non-use of receptacles of latrines should be made an offence and the defaulters dealt with properly.

The municipal bye-laws should be so framed as to penalise the use of a receptacle other than the prescribed size and make.

The house-owners left to themselves would not go in for the receptacles even though it is made obligatory and penalty imposed for failure to provide the receptacle. The receptacles should, therefore, be supplied, periodically, at least once a year or more if the first is broken or damaged, by the local body directly or through licensed shops on a no-profit-no-loss basis, and if necessary at subsidised rates.

It should be the duty of the scavenger and the area sanitary inspector to report to the local body about a receptacle which might have broken or been damaged.

The local body should recover the cost of receptacle along with the scavenging tax where such a tax is in force or with other taxes at the time of their realisation.

The floor of latrines is often 'kutcha'. It should be cemented and slanting outward.

The receptacle chamber should not be too wide to allow lateral or forward movement of the receptacle. It should be placed in a fixed spot so as to ensure that the aperture in the squatting plate is just over the centre of the receptacle. Fixed place can be ensured by making a slight depression of the size of the receptacle in the floor with smooth slanting sidings so that the receptacle may get fitted into the cavity and water if any accumulated can be wiped out conveniently. The depression should not be deeper than half an inch.

Providing of receptacles in public latrines should be the responsibility of the local bodies.

Bigger receptacles so as to cater to the needs of the place should be provided in public latrines, private latrines of big 'chawls', 'katras' or houses having large number of people.

The number of public latrines should conform to the demand for them in the area on the basis of their usage. It is desirable to prescribe a standard proportion to the population of the area and conform to it.

The structure of latrines where no receptacle can be placed at present should be got changed so as to make provision for a receptacle. This would not be costly and would not require much change.

As far as possible, all public buildings like offices, schools, hospitals etc., should have flush-out latrines failing which septic-tank latrines or aqua-privies be provided. But where this is not possible, it should be ensured that standardised receptacles are provided. Hotel owners and owners of places where large number of people stay should also follow this practice.

Wherever new buildings, colonies or townships are built by Government or with Government aid or by local bodies and in all industrial housing programmes, the latrines must be of sanitary types.

Night-soil, Urine And Ablution Water To Remain Separate

It would be better if the latrines are so modified as to ensure keeping night-soil and urine or ablution water separate. This can be done by having a slope in front of the seat so that urine is not mixed with night-soil. An additional step may be provided side by side so that the squatter shifts to the third step for purpose of washing.

The Scraper

It should be obligatory to use a standardised scraper which should be supplied by the local bodies to their employees and not left to the scavengers themselves.

In case of private scavengers, the local bodies should supply the standardised scraper directly or through licensed dealers at no-profit-no-loss basis and it should be made obligatory to use such a scraper.

The scraper should be of iron sheet or M.S. plates with a long handle at one end and a semi-curve at the other end. The sheet or plate should be of a suitable gauge so that it may not break while collecting the night-soil. The corners of the plate should be rounded.

It should be the duty of the scavenger and the area sanitary inspector to ensure that broken or damaged scrapers are replaced immediately.

The Rubber Gloves

Efforts should be made to encourage the use of rubber gloves, particularly at the pail-depots and dumping grounds.

The Head-load

Carrying of night-soil in basket, 'tasla' and drum etc., as head-load should be prohibited by law and made an offence.

For stopping carrying of night-soil as head-load, persuasive methods should also be adopted and they can be more effective than legislation.

The Bucket

In narrow lanes or lanes which are unpaved or have ups and downs, wheel barrows cannot ply conveniently and cannot be taken right up to the latrine seat. For such cases, there is no alternative but to introduce buckets. The bucket when full can be carried to the wheel barrow standing nearby.

In narrow lanes or roads of varying altitude, means like Kawar also known as Kawath, Kawad or Bengi may be used.

The local bodies should supply small buckets of not more than two to three gallons capacity, painted with coal-tar to its employees.

The lid of the bucket should be fixed with hinges as otherwise this is either thrown away or not used. The lid should be collapsible.

Private scavengers should also be compelled to use small covered buckets which can be supplied to them by the local bodies on no-profit-no-loss basis.

The broken or damaged buckets should be replaced immediately.

The Cess-Pools

Collection of night-soil in cess-pools is most insanitary and the inhuman ill use of scavengers engaged in cleaning them should be stopped.

The contents of cess-pools must not be carried as head-load.

Cess-pools maintained by local bodies particularly those attached to public latrines, should not be allowed to continue. All the pail-depots where night-soil is collected in big drums should be closed down.

Abolition of cess-pools in private houses is likely to take sometime. As long as these are in existence, the local bodies must introduce mechanical devices for cleaning them periodically. There should be a suction system.

In no case the contents of cess-pools should be removed by hand but only through mechanical devices.

Wherever feasible, lorries like Scampers should be introduced for sucking the contents of the cess-pools.

Lorries fitted with suction pump can be made use of.

Corporations or big municipalities or such local bodies as may afford, should think seriously in terms of introducing vacuum cars/lorries etc., as used in Japan for cleaning cess-pools.

Washing Of Latrines

It should be ensured that latrines are washed properly and regularly.

The scavengers should be given access to latrines.

Transportation Of Night-Soil

After collection night-soil is taken in basket, 'tasla', drum, etc., either as head-load or waist-load to the pail depot, carriage van or the place of disposal. This is most inhuman. The entire process of carrying night-soil as head-load or waist-load which is the root cause of all the troubles, has to be revolutionised.

For putting an end to the practice of carrying night-soil as head-load or waist-load, wheel barrows should be introduced.

The bullock or *bhensa* carts used for transporting night-soil are most insanitary and deserve to be abolished at once.

The man-drawn carts for carrying night-soil are an insult to human dignity and must be abolished.

There are various other types of carts drawn by bullocks which are all primitive. These need immediate replacement.

The open trucks are as bad as bullock carts. These should be discouraged.

The local bodies should introduce improved types of night-soil vans, tankers and trailers, etc.

Some local bodies collect night-soil in overhead tanks or big drums which have to be poured into night-soil vans for transportation. In some places, night-soil is churned and collected in pools before transportation. Such storage tanks and churning operations must not be allowed to continue.

In places of overhead tanks or pools used for collecting night-soil, the scientific system of providing trailors or night-soil tankers should be encouraged.

The night-soil barrels used for collection purposes should be placed at higher levels so that night-soil can be poured outright into the night-soil lorry tanker, or better still there should be a suction system.

Wheel Barrows

The crude type of wheel barrows already in use in some States should be discarded.

Some States are using drum wheel barrows of 15 to 40 gallons capacity. Such wheel barrows need replacement with better designs.

The design of wheel barrow as given in figure No. 49 is considered to be most useful, the introduction of which would facilitate the work of scavengers. This design could, however, be modified or improved in the light of local conditions.

The frame of wheel barrow should be all steel one with solid rubber type wheels with ball bearings. There should be two pails in the wheel barrow. The pails should not be of more than five gallons capacity each and the combined capacity of both the pails should not exceed the capacity of eight gallons when full. The lids of the pails should be collapsible and fixed with hinges to the body of the pails. The bottom of the pails should be such that night-soil does not stick.

Even women scavengers would not resist the use of such light wheel barrows. At some places, women have already taken up to wheel barrows.

The design of wheel barrow proposed would not normally cost more than Rs. 100 to Rs. 120 if made locally or Rs. 120 to Rs. 140 if imported from any other State.

The manufacture of the proposed type of wheel barrow on a large scale for requirements throughout a State could be centralised to some place for distribution to all local bodies in which case the cost of wheel barrow would definitely come further down and the design will conform to the required pattern uniformly.

A few of the municipalities are using wheel barrows with four pails. Such wheel barrow costs Rs. 175 to Rs. 200. These wheel barrows are quite heavy and the scavengers using them complained of their weight. Such wheel barrows can be used by men only and not women.

Wherever necessary, some administrative adjustments may be carried out. Men may do the pushing and women the cleaning. The wheel barrows may be kept moving from house to house along with the women workers.

For places where wheel barrows cannot ply conveniently, Kawath also known as Kawar, Kawad or Bengi may be used. Two pails each of four to five gallons capacity hanging at either end of a bamboo pole at a distance of about six feet or so and may be carried on shoulder like the milk cans which are found convenient in such cases. An iron hook at either end may also be fitted to the pole.

The main difficulty in popularising the introduction of wheel barrows is the passive attitude of scavengers. This requires tactful handling. The local authorities should make a beginning with a few intelligent scavengers and with the assistance of non-official organisations and social workers, persuade scavengers to use wheel barrows.

To begin with only a few wheel barrows may be put into use on an experimental basis and on their becoming popular, more wheel barrows may be pushed in.

The Public Health Officers can by persuasion and by amending the bye-laws etc., achieve substantial measure of success.

Even the local bodies which have plans for underground drainage system, must take up the scheme of wheel barrows without further delay.

The number of wheel barrows can be reduced with the extension of the underground drainage line.

For transporting night-soil, the bullock carts, *bhensa* carts, donkey gangs etc., which are used at present should be replaced with tractors and trailers or such other mechanical vehicles.

In places where the trailers may not be convenient to ply, the local authorities may make use of three-wheelers. The intake capacity of the three-wheelers is quite good and these can ply in narrow streets easily.

The trailers must be placed at places within easy approach of scavengers and where these are needed more.

The entire process of dealing with night-soil from latrine to places of disposal would thus involve:

(a) Collecting of night-soil from receptacle under the latrine-seat with a proper scraper into the pail of a wheel barrow or a bucket provided with a collapsible lid where wheel barrow cannot ply;

(b) Emptying of bucket into the pail of wheel barrow;

(c) Carrying of wheel barrow to the trailer or pail-depot wherever it is in use and emptying the pails into the trailer, etc.; and

(d) Drawing of trailer by the tractor to the dumping ground or the place of disposal.

Financial Aspects

For the administration of various schemes, the main burden will have to be borne by the local bodies concerned with or without the assistance from the State Governments. They will have to make necessary adjustments and provisions in their bye-laws, rules, etc.

The State Governments will have to ensure that their local bodies agree to adopt the measures uniformly throughout the State.

For purchase of wheel barrows, the local bodies find it difficult to find out adequate financial resources. The best course would be for Government of India to meet the entire cost towards the purchase of wheel barrows failing which :

(a) The poorest local bodies should be given 100 per cent assistance—75 per cent to be given by the Central Government and 25 per cent by the State Government—the entire amount to be treated as grant;

(b) For medium local bodies, the Government's grant can be 75 per cent—50 per cent to be given by the Central Government and 25 per cent by the State Governments and the local body to contribute only the remaining 25 per cent from its own resources;

(c) For the bigger municipalities and corporations etc., the Government of India's assistance should be 50 per cent, the rest to be borne by the local body alone or by the local body and the State Government concerned together.

The Union Territories being under the administrative control of the Central Government, the entire expenditure on schemes is borne by the Central Government. Being so, the Union Administrations are supposed to take a lead in the abolition of carrying night-soil as head-loads.

In all cases where the local bodies concerned need loans for meeting their share of expenditure, the State Governments should help the local bodies by advancing loans to them.

For purchase of other mechanical equipments like tractors and trailers or vans etc., the State Governments should find the fund which may be advanced to the local bodies as grants wherever possible or otherwise in the form of loans. If possible, necessary funds may also be found from the agricultural programmes for converting night-soil into manure. If the Ministry of Health provides any funds for such purpose that may be made use of.

The local bodies should earmark a fixed percentage out of their annual budgets for the improvement of scavenging conditions and the living conditions of scavengers.

Wherever wheel barrows are supplied to private scavengers, it should be the responsibility of the local body to watch the proper use and maintenance of the wheel barrows through the area sanitary inspectors.

Long-handled Brooms

Long-handled broom with a small 'Khurpi' (flat scraper) fixed at the other end for scrapping purposes would be found very convenient.

Implements

Implements' Allowance: Instead of giving implements allowance to scavengers, local bodies should supply all the necessary and proper implements to their employees to carry out their duties.

Besides the implements suggested by the Committee, the Public Health Officers should apply their minds to the problem and think about the continuous improvements of implements.

The local bodies by adopting necessary bye-laws should see that even private scavengers are equipped with necessary implements for use.

Night-Soil Depots

The number of pail-depots must be increased according to the needs. The pail-depots should be constructed at places where it is convenient and within easy reach of the scavengers.

In towns where due to over-crowding there is no place for constructing additional pail-depots, their trailers can be used more conveniently. These can be stationed at suitable places and taken away with the help of a tractor at periodical intervals.

The existing conditions of the night-soil pail-depots and the scavengers working there are extremely unsatisfactory and deserve the immediate attention of the local bodies.

The work at pail-depots must be carried out in hygienic conditions and efforts should be made to ensure that the scavengers avoid bodily touch with night-soil and rubbish.

Cess-pools for storing night-soil before transportation should not be allowed to continue.

The workers at night-soil-pail-depots must be provided with gum-boots, gloves, aprons, water-proof headgears, long spades and rakes etc., for pulling out cloth pieces etc., and avoid clogging.

The structure of such depots where perforce, the scavengers have to wade through night-soil must be altered. Provision of trailers can minimise the difficulty to a great extent.

The depots may be so constructed as to allow the trailers to clear the load in the mouth of the depot itself.

In case of dry pail-depots, platforms of proper height with a sloping siding at either ends just like railway platforms must be constructed so that the wheel barrows can be brought with ease over the platform and poured into the standing trailer.

At every pail-depot, there must be an attendant. It should be his duty to handle the load at the depot.

Amenities At Pail-Depots

At every pail-depot arrangements for the supply of sufficient water for washing the vehicles, wheel barrows, drums, the depot, etc., and for scavengers to bathe and wash their clothes must be provided.

There may be separate bath-rooms for men and women. A set for each can be sufficient in most of the cases. The number may be increased if necessary.

Wherever possible, arrangements for changing clothes before and after the work should be provided.

Disinfection Stations

Corporations, big municipalities and such other local bodies as can afford, should establish disinfection stations where clothes of the scavengers may be given steam treatment. The local bodies may extend the benefit to others such as labourers, hospitals, etc., also.

Wherever the scavengers do not find it convenient to keep the wheel barrows etc., at the places of their residences, arrangements for keeping the wheel barrows at the pail-depots may be made. Their cleanliness can also be ensured.

Persons Working In Gutters

For cleaning underground sewers, use should be

made of mechanical devices already in vogue in big towns. Safety of the life of persons working in gutters should be ensured and such implements, apparels, masks, etc., as may be considered necessary provided to them.

Dumping Grounds

Dumping grounds should be as far away from the towns as possible. Where towns have extended, dumping grounds should be shifted further beyond.

The size of the dumping ground should be sufficient so as to meet the requirements.

All the night-soil and refuse of the town should be brought to the dumping ground. This would increase the income from the sale of manure.

To collect all the night-soil and refuse from the town, proper vehicles for transport should be supplied and vigilance maintained to see that no night-soil is wasted by the scavengers or members of the public.

As at present, most of the dumping grounds are running at loss. With the exception of a few isolated cases, the position need not be so tight and there is no reason why the entire business should not be turned into a profit making one and at least the cost of maintenance be realised.

To suppress the stink and nuisance of flies at dumping grounds, use of the Swingfog or the Gammaxine Powder or any such other useful chemical must be made by the local bodies.

Workers At Dumping Grounds

Long gum-boots (up to the knee) are an absolute necessity for workers at the dumping grounds. They must be provided with gloves as well. An apron would also protect the clothes. Necessary implements for use should be given to the workers. They should be supplied with working uniforms and headgears.

The extra allowance of a rupee or so given by some of the local bodies to workers at dumping grounds does not meet the requirements.

At all dumping grounds, arrangements for the supply of sufficient water for washing vans, pails, etc., and for scavengers to take their bath and wash their clothes must be made.

Construction of a few bath rooms would be very useful.

For cleaning the vans etc., overhead water tanks and hoses can be more useful. The ground underneath should preferably be cemented.

At places where water supply is scarce, the local authorities must endeavour to supply as much water as possible. Digging of a well at the site may solve the problem to some extent.

In rocky areas, a well is not a practical solution. There the local bodies should make arrangements for bringing water in vans and storing in overhead tanks, etc.

Somehow or the other, water must be made available at the dumping grounds.

Supply of soap at dumping grounds and also at pail-depots is essential.

Arrangements for liquid soap or soap cakes may be made wherever possible.

Shelters may be provided at the dumping grounds under which the workers may rest during sun or rain.

Other amenities like place for changing clothes, medical aid, etc., can be considered wherever possible. Big local bodies at least should do this.

Agricultural Fields

In some parts of the country, people do not like to make use of night-soil for manuring purposes and there all the night-soil goes waste. To popularise the use of night-soil local bodies should attach agricultural fields to the dumping grounds. The manure prepared may be utilised in those fields which would serve as a model to others. It would also be a paying proposition to the local bodies.

Composting

The local bodies should ensure proper composting in the shortest possible time.

Gram Laxmi Gas Plant

The use of Gram Laxmi Gas Plant may be made in villages and towns where there are no agricultural fields or where no use of night-soil manure is possible.

Cooperative Societies

The local authorities may consider the possibilities of establishing cooperative societies for the purchase and sale of compost.

If cooperative societies of scavengers come forward they should be encouraged.

Private Dumping Grounds

No private dumping grounds should be allowed to continue.

Cleaning of night-soil and refuse from the town and its proper disposal is the primary responsibility of the local bodies and should be well looked after by them.

So long as customary rights are not abolished, the local bodies should ensure proper treatment of the night-soil at the private dumping grounds.

Efforts should be made to improve the conditions of work and workers at private dumping grounds.

If necessary, bye-laws and necessary legislation for the proper maintenance of private dumping grounds in the interest of sanitation should be passed and strictly enforced.

Some local bodies have already got some bye-laws

etc., which in many cases, are rarely implemented. There is great necessity for enforcing the municipal bye-laws and regulations strictly.

Underground Drainage

At least in all the towns already having some underground drainage system, the local bodies should make serious efforts to extend the lines so as to cover the entire towns.

In towns which are expanding rapidly, local bodies should make serious efforts to lay the underground sewers in all new colonies side by side with the provision of other amenities.

Sewage Disposal Plants

Local bodies should make use of Sewage Disposal Plants. They may follow the Madurai experiment for use and disposal of sewage of the town.

Local bodies can depute their officers to study the working of the farm at Madurai and adopt similar methods with improvements, if any, in their own towns.

After consulting experts, growth of vegetables, etc., on such farms may be encouraged.

Financial Aspects

A specific amount must be earmarked for the underground drainage schemes separately and at least one-third of the total allocations of the National Water Supply and Drainage Schemes should be earmarked for drainage schemes.

Grant Of Subsidy

Several towns have underground drainage schemes only on paper. Funds are not forthcoming. Such schemes are not workable without adequate subsidy from the Centre or the State Governments.

The Central Government must also give liberal subsidy to States.

The Ministry of Health may examine the possibility of giving subsidy under their Health and Sanitation Schemes.

State Governments which do not give any subsidy to their local bodies as yet must make necessary provisions for the purpose.

Connections With Underground Drainage System

In areas served with sewers, it should be made obligatory to connect house latrines with them. Defaulters should be dealt with properly.

Conversion Of Dry-Latrines Grant Of Loan/Subsidy

There are people who due to their poor financial position are not able to convert their dry latrines into water borne ones. For such people, local bodies should give loan/subsidy to house owners according to income slabs, or in the light of local conditions.

The Central Government should also give aid to State Governments by giving adequate assistance.

Wherever underground sewers have already been laid or are being laid, latrines must be converted into flush-out latrines and in places where flush-out latrines are not possible, latrines like septic-tanks, aqua-privies etc., may be adopted.

Rebate In Taxes

The local bodies may examine the possibility of allowing some rebate in house, latrine tax etc., to such of the parties who may like to convert their dry latrines into water-borne, etc.

The rebate given at present is insufficient but should be raised so as to induce sufficient number of people to convert their latrines.

Surface Drains

As long as surface drains exist, arrangements for keeping them clean should continue. At set of two persons—a cleaner and a bhishti—may be very useful.

The cleaners should have proper implements with them.

Wherever necessary, open surface drains should be covered.

There should be a short phased programme to make surface drains 'pucca' and at least by the end of the Third Five-Year Plan, all the surface drains must be made 'pucca'. These should be so constructed as to enable the water to flow easily and not stagnate.

Drains should be washed daily.

Sullage water from drains can be very well utilised in agricultural fields.

In towns where water supply is not sufficient, other arrangements for keeping the drains clean should be made.

Design Of Latrines

People must be educated and persuaded to construct latrines in their houses. The local bodies should pass bye-laws for having latrines compulsorily and the plans for construction of new houses should not be passed unless and until there is a provision of a sanitary latrine.

Bye-laws should also be passed for compelling owners of the existing houses which are without latrines to construct latrines.

Public Latrines

The number of public latrines should be increased keeping in view the demand for them.

In places of congestion where these are needed, the number of latrines should be increased.

Underground water-borne latrines at the cross roads would be found convenient.

As long as all the public latrines cannot be converted into water-borne ones, they should at least be made fly-proof. This would also prevent pig entry.

The local bodies should give serious thought to the models of public latrines. Primitive latrines must be remodelled and more sanitary latrines adopted.

As far as possible, public latrines should be water-borne with arrangements for the automatic flow of water after periodical intervals.

Public latrines should be constructed in the most crowded localities and places within easy reach. Latrines constructed at remote or far off places are not likely to be of much use and whenever these are used, these are misused.

Wherever possible, latrines should be built on a large scale underground.

Private Latrines

Roof-latrines as in Punjab must be brought down. Bye-laws should be framed that in new buildings roof-latrines are not allowed. Efforts should be made through legislation etc., or persuasion to bring down existing roof-latrines. Wherever space is available, sanitary latrines be constructed, otherwise standardised receptacles should be made use of.

Even roof-latrines may be converted into water-borne ones and connected with underground sewers where such sewers exist or to septic-tank which could be constructed on ground-floor. Where there is no space on the ground-floor or there are no sewers, septic-tanks may be constructed on cooperative basis at any available place in the street or where possible, just under the street itself and three or four houses may connect their latrines with them. Local bodies can help in keeping such septic tanks clean periodically.

All primitive latrines should be demolished. As long as these continue, no improvements in scavenging conditions can be expected. For remodelling primitive latrines, not only legislation, etc., but persuasion would also be required

Some of the improved type of latrines suitable for towns are :

(1) Flush-out Latrine.
(2) Automatic-flush-out Latrine.
(3) Septic-tank Latrine.
(4) Aqua-privy Latrine.
(5) Leach-type Latrine.

The local bodies should adopt the type of latrine they feel can be best suited to their towns. They may improve thereon making them more suitable to their towns according to the conditions prevailing locally.

Latrines On Market And Festival Days

Wherever markets or fairs are held regularly, permanent latrines should be provided which should possibly be water-borne failing which any other improved type may be adopted. Wherever receptacles are provided, their sizes and arrangements for keeping them clean must be specified. Extra scavengers should be provided on such days. Where markets etc., are held after long intervals or where permanent latrines are not possible, temporary latrines of improved types with arrangements for extra scavengers should be made.

Latrines In Rural And Semi-rural Areas

Latrines should be introduced in villages also progressively and people must stop present indecent and insanitary practice of easing everywhere. It is indecent to observe a large number of people squatting all along the railway lines, etc. Some of the better type of latrines suitable for rural and semi-rural areas are:

(1) 'Kucha' Trench Latrine.
(2) 'Pucca' Trench Latrine.
(3) Bore Hole Latrine.
(4) Gopuri Latrine.
(5) Dhanoli Type Latrine.

Latrines On Railways

The recommendations made in respect of the removal of night-soil, providing of receptacles, conversion of dry latrines etc., may under a phased programme be also adopted by the Indian Railways as well.

Where water-borne latrines are not possible, Indian Railways could construct fly-proof latrines.

Indian Railways have resources and technical talent to provide an abject lesson to the whole country in the matter of construction of various types of sanitary latrines. This would play a great psychological role on the minds of lakhs of people who see and use them daily throughout the country.

Customary Rights

Private scavengers have customary rights not only for cleaning latrines in certain localities but at some places over the possession and disposal of night-soil also. Such customary rights must not in any case be allowed to continue and be abrogated immediately.

The local bodies should pay reasonable compensation in cash to such of the scavengers who might be affected and do not get employment due to acquisition of customary rights.

The Governments at the Centre and State should come forward to finance such of the local bodies who are not in a position to pay reasonable compensation.

Wherever cash compensation is not possible, or the local bodies cannot offer employment under them, the affected scavengers must be taken in other services.

Most of the scavengers would be prepared to forego their customary rights if provided with municipal services.

Scavenging Cess

In places where there is no scavenging cess, such a cess should be levied and the scavenging services municipalised. The scavenging cess should be so adjusted that scavenging services may become almost self-supporting.

L.S.G. Departments

It should be the duty of the Local Self-Government Departments to initiate necessary legislation for the acquisition of customary rights. They should handle the problem at the State level through their legislature and ensure that a uniform policy is adopted by all the local bodies and fully implemented.

Small Committees To Be Appointed

The State Governments and Union Administrations should appoint small committees to go into the whole question of the abolition of customary rights. They should not merely study the legal aspects but go thoroughly into other problems as well connected with it. They should draw up a phased programme for the abolition of customary rights and see that the work is completed as soon as possible but not later than a fixed target date. They should determine the basis, mode of payment and the amount, etc.

Negotiations and mutual agreements between the local bodies and scavengers can bring in the desired effects. The local authorities would be well advised to tackle the problem in a friendly and persuasive manner. Cooperation of non-official organisations and social workers interested in welfare of scavengers may also be enlisted.

Administrative Set-Up

The problem of improving the scavenging conditions should be dealt with by the Local Self-Government Departments of the States/Union Administrations or such other Departments as may be concerned with it.

All the necessary legislation, policy, directive principles, etc., should be issued by the Local Self-Government Departments and they should evolve a machinery to ensure the implementation of their directives etc., fully and properly through the local bodies and such of their officers as they may like to appoint. Mere enacting of legislation or issuing directives would not be so much helpful as their proper implementation.

The State Governments/Union Administrations should appoint Special Officers exclusively to look after the problems of scavenging and scavengers.

Need For Central Officer

The Central Government must appoint an officer having the necessary background knowledge of the various problems of scavenging and scavengers in the country at the Centre to deal with these problems and watch their day-to-day development.

A small Vigilance Committee consisting of non-officials who are well acquainted with the magnitude of the problem and have shown serious interest in tackling it, should be appointed by the Ministry of Home Affairs to move about from State to State, meet and discuss with officials, social workers and members of the public about the urgency of the problem and mobilise their efforts for solving it.

The Ministry of Home Affairs who are concerned with the welfare of Scheduled Castes should initiate legislation for the abolition of customary rights, if necessary.

The ceiling for water supply and drainage schemes should be fixed separately. The ceiling for drainage scheme is too small in comparison to the cost and requirements of this scheme. The Ministry of Health should consider increasing this ceiling.

The Ministry of Health may consider giving some grants/loans to be recovered in convenient instalments to the local bodies through State Governments for the purchase of vehicles, etc., for transportation of night-soil and town refuse.

The Ministry of Food and Agriculture (Agriculture Department) may also consider what possible help they can give for converting night-soil into manure under agricultural programmes.

The State Governments/Union Administrations should help their local bodies technically, financially and otherwise.

The Cooperation Department of the Ministry of Community Development and Cooperation can also tender their advice and start some of the schemes if possible for the welfare of scavengers particularly those who may be affected due to abolition of customary rights, and also help in the collection, preparation and sale etc., of the manure on a cooperative basis.

Some General Aspects

Though the question of the improvement of the living conditions and environment of scavengers is beyond the scope of the terms of reference of the Committee, yet as this is an important aspect having direct bearing on the problem, some suggestions have been made which require urgent attention.

Housing

Quarters for conservancy staff should be as near their places of work as possible but never around the pail-depots, morgues, public latrines, dumping grounds, etc. Such location of scavengers' quarters at such places amounts to criminal neglect. A few quarters here and a few there may be built in colonies inhabited by others as well so as to avoid segregation and give an impression of a mixed colony.

It is of primary importance that the housing conditions of scavengers are radically improved. This would create a new sense of self-respect in them and particularly their children.

For the welfare of scavengers, maximum use of the Slum Clearance Schemes should be made. It is necessary to nave a special provision in the plan under the Works and Housing Ministry for providing houses to the conservancy staff of the local bodies.

The Low Income Housing Scheme

The local bodies should construct houses for scavengers under the Low Income Housing Scheme and as far as possible pass on the quarters to them on Hire-Purchase system.

Leaving aside the schemes under the Slum Clearance and Low Income Housing Schemes, it would be advisable for the local bodies to construct houses for scavengers and give them on Hire-Purchase system. This would enable the scavengers to own their houses after sometime and live in them permanently.

One-room tenements are not adequate. Scavengers have large families and even taking an average of five members per family, one-room tenements are too small. From the point of view of moral hygiene also every tenement must make provision for two living rooms. A kitchen, a bath room, a latrine—flush-out or any other sanitary type like septic-tank etc., built up cupboard, a slightly raised platform for fire place with a hood and chimney over it and possibly a hollow underneath for storing fuel and a verandah should be provided. Wherever possible, electricity must also be provided. Water supply is a necessity.

The quarters need not necessarily be completely 'pucca' and wherever the cost is on the high side, these may be 'semi-pucca' as well. The cost of each tenement for such quarters which are not to be owned by the scavengers on Hire-Purchase system, etc., may vary from Rs. 1,200 to Rs. 2,000 on the lines of the quarters built in Madras under Slum Clearance schemes.

It is very important that amenities like primary school, a welfare centre with a community hall which may be used as community centre, medical facilities etc., are provided in large colonies. A social worker should invariably be provided to be incharge of the welfare activities. There is a need for appointing a social worker for covering a population of 100 families.

Conditions Of Service

At present, conditions of service in different States are far below the minimum needs which is the principal reason for discontentment amongst scavengers. The better the service and working conditions, better would be the relations between the scavengers and the local bodies.

Wages

Wages should be paid to scavengers according to the Minimum Wages Act.

The State Governments/Union Administrations who have not done it so far, must appoint small committees to go into the whole question of wages and payment of other allowances to scavengers and suggest basic wages which should, however, not fall below the minimum wages. Question of payment of other allowances as may be admissible to scavengers must also be considered.

Unclean Work Allowance

Unclean Work Allowance should not be in cash but in the form of extra amenities such as gloves, water, etc., to make the occupation more clean. Extra allowance paid in cash is not utilised properly and the work remains unclean. Such a terminology should not be used. Unclean Work Allowance can very well be called like any other ordinary allowance.

Distribution Of Wages

Wages should be distributed in the presence of a responsible officer of the local body who should ensure that no creditors are allowed to throng the premises and harass the scavengers. Such an officer should also keep an eye on the supervisory staff of the local bodies directly in touch with the scavengers and who are often alleged to accept illegal gratifications.

Hours Of Work

For full time employees, the hours of work should not be more than seven hours per day of which only four to five hours may be reserved for scavenging work. Part-time worker should not be asked to work both in the morning and evening as this deprives them of any other work and causes them hardships.

Roll Call

The scavengers on duty should be called only twice for roll call—once in the morning and once in the afternoon.

Leave Rules

Local bodies should frame leave rules and the scavengers should be given the benefit of casual, privilege, earned leave, etc.

Women scavengers must be given pre-natal and post-natal leave. They should be given leave in case of miscarriage, etc., also.

Off-Day In A Week

State Governments/Union Administrations should see that at least in local bodies where the scavenging service is municipalised, scavengers are allowed a full day off in a week.

Uniform

All the local bodies should give sufficient and proper summer and winter uniforms both to male and female scavengers.

Proper kit for scavengers for cleaning underground drains should be supplied.

Permanency Of Service

Every effort should be made by the local bodies to give some security of employment to the temporary scavengers and avoid keeping them on a temporary basis for an indefinite period.

Full-Time And Part-Time Workers

Local bodies, as far as possible, should not appoint part-time scavengers. Full-time worker is bound to be more efficient.

Appointment Of Scavengers In Other Occupations

Scavengers who may like to leave their occupation should be appointed on other posts such as peons in other Departments, 'chowkidars', 'naka-walas', etc.

Vocational training may be imparted to such of the scavengers who may like to settle in a trade. After training some subsidy/loan may be given to them for settling in trades. They be given chances and opportunities for training as drivers, cleaners and mechanics etc., in municipal workshops and other gainful occupations.

Water Supply

Sufficient water for drinking and washing must be supplied to scavengers in or near 'basties' and at times when they return from work.

Soap

Arrangements for supply of soap at the place of work like pail-depots and dumping grounds etc., should be made.

Women Workers

Creches should be started in the colonies of scavengers where a paid worker preferably a trained lady worker may be appointed to look after the children. Children must be taught clean ways of living and habits so as to make them clean persons.

Community Centres

There should be established community centres where care of children is combined with training of women in some crafts and adult education. Such community centres should also be used for cultural purposes and amusements, etc.

Education

State Governments and local bodies should ensure that children of scavengers are provided easy admissions in schools and hostels irrespective of their caste. Efforts should be made to open primary schools near their 'basties' where children of scavengers and other communities may receive education.

Occupational Diseases

All State Governments etc., should conduct a medical survey and find out if the scavengers suffer from any disease due to their handling night-soil. If so, proper medical arrangements for them should be made. Scavengers must at least be examined periodically.

Name For Scavenger

In order to create a healthy atmosphere and psychological background, the scavenger should not be called by the age old name. He should be known by some more decent terminology according to local conditions and language.

The Pig

Rearing of pigs in any area of towns must not be allowed. If anybody wants to rear piggery, he should do so on the proper lines away from towns.

Urinals For Men And Women

Adequate number of urinals, preferably with automatic water arrangements, should be put at public places like bus stands, market places, parks, cinema halls, thoroughfares, etc. Urinals for women must also be provided in sufficient numbers. Urinals near latrines are bound to be misused and should be avoided. Efforts should be made to equip men's urinals with Western type basins which cannot be misused.

Dust Bins

Local bodies must provide dust bins at all suitable places which should be within easy reach and ensure their proper cleaning. The dust bin may be kept fixed on paved floors.

Legislation

State Governments/Union Administrations should explore possibilities of framing rules, bye-laws, etc., which they may consider necessary for the solution of various problems.

Propaganda

Various processes of scavenging problems such as use of defective and good latrines, methods of scavenging, working at pail-depots, dumping grounds and system of carriage etc., can be filmed by the Ministry of Information and Broadcasting in consultation with the Ministry of Home Affairs and the good and bad spots in the country presented before the masses who should be educated in the use of improved methods.

The documentaries, cinema slides, etc., prepared by the Films Division of the Ministry of Information and Broadcasting would be of great help in creating public opinion for improving conditions of scavenging and those of scavengers.

The Ministry of Home Affairs and the State Governments/Union Administrations should ensure that those non-official organisations who get financial assistance either from the Centre or the State Government must include schemes for the improvement of the conditions of scavenging and scavengers in their programmes. They should be asked to publish posters, leaflets, etc., propagating the need for improvement of the conditions. The organisations who have got cinema vans should be asked to make use of such vans for the purpose of schemes for putting an end to the practice of carrying night-soil as head-loads, conversion of dry latrines into sanitary ones, schemes for improvement of the scavenging conditions and those of scavengers.

This should be one of the compulsory schemes seeking assistance from the Centre and the States.

It is essential that State Governments and the Ministries of the Government at the Centre should draw up a phased programme for implementing the various recommendations and suggestions in a systematic manner by the end of the Third Five-Year Plan.

AD-HOC COMMITTEE ON COTTONSEED OIL INDUSTRY, 1957—REPORT

Delhi, Manager of Publications. 1960. 74p

Chairman : Shri N. Srinivasan.
Members : Shri K. Vyasulu; Shri F.G.T. Menzes; Shri E. Svendsen; Shri S.H. Turner; Dr. A. Chatrapati; Shri Tulsidas M. Vishram; Shri G.V. Sirur; Dr. R. Sankaran.
Member-Secretary : Shri V.A. Mehta.

APPOINTMENT

A conference was convened on August 17, 1957, in the Ministry of Commerce and Industry under the chairmanship of Shri Manubhai Shah, Minister of Industries, to discuss measures necessary for the development of cottonseed crushing on a priority basis. The meeting was attended by representatives of the Planning Commission, Ministries of Food and Agriculture and Finance; Council of Scientific and Industrial Research; East India Cotton Association; cottonseed crushers; vanaspati industry and acetate rayon manufacturers. In accordance with the decision taken at this meeting, Government of India, vide letter No. 11(29)/57-NF and MC, dated October 28, 1957, set up an ad hoc Committee for the industry.

TERMS OF REFERENCE

(a) To examine the immediate problems of the industry and suggest ways and means for its speedy development.

(b) To examine the present position of the industry, e.g. installed capacity, annual production etc., and suggest suitable locations for new units.

(c) To suggest fiscal measures which could give necessary incentive for the crushing of cottonseed and the consumption of cottonseed oil as cooking oil and in the manufacture of vanaspati.

(d) To suggest measures for developing the use of decorticated cottonseed cake.

CONTENTS

Introduction—Terms of Reference of Committee—Method of Work of Committee; Importance of Industry in India's economy—Progress made in other Countries—Growth of Industry in India; Present Position of Cottonseed Crushing in India and Availability of Cottonseed—Composition of Indigenous Seed—Location of Units—Production, Consumption, Exports and Price of Cottonseed Oil; Problems of the Industry; Plan for the Future Development of the Industry; Processing Operations; Cotton Linters; Cottonseed Hulls and Cake; Industrial Uses of Cottonseed Oil and its Soap Stock; Utilisation of Cottonseed Oil in the Manufacture of Vanaspati and Refined Oil; Recommendations of the Committee; Conclusion and Acknowledgements; Appendices from 1 to 13.

RECOMMENDATIONS

Crushing of Non-fuzzy Seeds: The crushing of non-fuzzy seeds which contain smaller percentage of linters could be advantageously undertaken in the unorganised sector by smaller units which are not equipped with delinting machinery. The Committee is of the opinion that this sector may be encouraged to crush non-fuzzy seeds.

Fuzzy Seeds: The objective of the industry in the organised sector should be to crush such seeds which are rich in linters (fuzzy) and at the same time have a higher oil content, it being immaterial whether they are of American or desi origin.

Installed Capacity: The Committee is of the opinion that the installed capacity of cottonseed oil mills in the organised sector ought to be rated not merely by the expeller capacity but by the capacity of the delinting machinery.

New Units Recently under Licensed Industries (Development and Regulation) Act: The Committee understands that a number of mills licensed under Industries (Development and Regulation) Act have not yet taken effective steps to set up their units. The Committee is of the opinion that Government should review their progress at an early date and take steps where necessary to revoke licences which block up the capacity. The revoked capacity may be allotted to other applicants from the same State.

Speculation in Cottonseeds: The Forward Markets Commission may keep a watchful eye on the speculative activities in the forward markets of cottonseeds so that such activities may not hinder the availability of cottonseeds for crushing purposes by pushing the prices beyond crushing parity.

The Forward Markets Commission may also consider whether the practice reported to be adopted at Bombay of excluding the fuzzy variety of cottonseeds from tendering against forward contracts can be extended to other exchanges dealing in cottonseeds.

Fiscal Policy: (i) The Government of India should persuade the State Governments to waive the sales tax, levy on cottonseeds on special considerations or at least not to discriminate and exempt cottonseed which is fed to cattle from payment of sales tax as this step would divert more and more whole seed instead of cake for cattle feeding. The State Governments should also be requested to advise local bodies to consider the abolition of octroi duty on cottonseeds.

(ii) Unlike other vegetable oils, there is at present no excise duty on cottonseed oil. Government of India have exempted cottonseed oil in order to give a stimulus to the crushing of cottonseeds. The Committee recommends that excise duty should not be levied on cottonseed oil for five years. The position may be reviewed thereafter. Such an announcement from the Government would help the rapid development of the industry.

Financial Assistance: (i) Government may advise State Finance Corporations to accord high priority to cottonseed oil industry in their scheme of assistance to private industrialists.

(ii) The Reserve Bank should be requested to advise all scheduled banks to consider the question of advancing loans on cottonseed and cottonseed products.

Transport Facilities and Railway Freight: (i) The Committee recommends that the Railway Board should consider reduction of freight on movement of cottonseeds on station to station basis within 400 miles, where a crushing mill is located at or near the railway station. Such a concession will no doubt apply to cottonseed meant both for crushing as well as for cattle feeding, as it will be difficult to prevent consignments being used by the farmers as well. It is suggested that this concessional freight may be half that of the normal rate charged for groundnut in view of the fact that the percentage of oil recovered from cottonseed is hardly 50 per cent of that recovered from groundnut.

(ii) The Railway Board should examine again the difficulties in connection with the loading of 300 maunds of cottonseed hulls in open wagons. The industry has pointed out that it is not possible to load more than 200 maunds in each wagon, although the railways have stipulated 300 maunds and also charge freight for this quantity. Similar difficulties are also faced on the metre gauge.

Import of Bleaching Earth and Activated Carbon: Import of bleaching earth and activated carbon should be allowed for refining cottonseed oil till indigenous products of satisfactory quality are available.

Import of Plant and Equipment: The proposal regarding the import of cottonseed preparatory machinery on a barter basis against cotton linters may be examined by the State Trading Corporation. The possibility of procuring preparatory machinery and continuous solvent extraction plants under the U.S. Export-Import Loan Fund and other Assistance programmes may also be explored by the Government.

Standards for Cottonseed Oil: Standards should be laid down for crude cottonseed oil by the Indian Standards Institution. Standards may also be prepared for cottonseed. The Indian Standards Institution may urgently re-examine the standards laid down for washed cottonseed oil in consultation with the manufacturers as well as the consumers of cottonseed oil e.g. vanaspati and soap manufacturers.

Research Problems: The Committee recommend that an investigational work on cottonseed and cottonseed products should be coordinated by the Council of Scientific and Industrial Research.

Association of the Industry: The Committee recommends that an Association of Cottonseed crushers be formed to consider common problems and assess the progress of the national plan for the industry.

Future Development of the Industry : (i) The Committee recommends a plan for the speedy development of the industry in two stages:

(a) Production on a minimum basis of 60,000 tons of cottonseed oil by the existing and licensed units and by establishing nine additional units each of capacity 12,000 tons per annum in terms of cottonseeds on the basis of 200 working days in a year. Out of these nine units, two should be set up in Madras, two in Madhya Pradesh, four in the Punjab and one in Rajasthan.

(b) The second stage would be to achieve a production of 70,000 tons of oil by the setting up of further five units of similar capacity, one in Madhya Pradesh and four in the Punjab.

(ii) The Committee is of the opinion, that in order to achieve the additional installed capacity, first preference should be given to existing regional vegetable oil mills and vanaspati factories. New units may, however be developed in case the existing oil mills and vanaspati factories do not take to crushing cottonseed expeditiously.

(iii) The Committee feels that special efforts may be necessary to develop cottonseed oil industry on modern lines in the Punjab.

(iv) The Committee considers that there is full justification for incurring the foreign exchange of Rs. 1.6 crores for the immediate development of the industry.

Organisation of the Industry on Cooperative Lines: While every encouragement may be given to the organisation of the industry on cooperative lines in accordance with the plan evolved by the Committee, existing oil mills, vanaspati factories and new entrepreneurs should not be prevented from setting up cottonseed oil mills on modern lines at approved locations.

Processing Operations: (i) The Committee is of the opinion that solvent extraction process for extracting oil from oilseeds and oil-cakes is particularly advantageous for cottonseed which has a lower oil content in comparison with other oil seeds.

(ii) The Committee recommends that continuous refining plants may be allowed to be imported as far as possible by those who wish to install such plants, as the continuous process is more economic than batch refining process.

Linters: (i) Increased cultivation of the improved variety of cottonseed—Active steps should be taken by the Government to extend the cultivation of the fuzzy variety of cottonseeds in different regions of the country.

(ii) The Committee recommends that the linter industry should be organised on the basis of production of first-cut and second-cut, as the latter is the most suitable raw material for high grade chemical cotton essential for the manufacture of plastics, rayon, films, explosives, lacquers, etc.

As there is no demand in the country for first-cut linters, in view of the availability of mill-waste, the first-cut may be allowed to be exported freely and to facilitate such exports, the export duty of 30 per cent ad-valorem which was abolished early in 1958 should not be reimposed for five years. The position may be reviewed thereafter.

(iii) The Committee recommends that linter pulp plants may be organised at suitable places to facilitate the conversion of linters into bleached pulp for industrial purposes.

(i) Cottonseed Cake: The Committee recommends that production of balanced ration for cattle composed of decorticated cottonseeds cake, hulls, rice bran, molasses, salt, etc., should be undertaken on a large scale.

(ii) **Propaganda:** Intensive propaganda may be undertaken for popularising cottonseed cake through Community Development blocks under Community Projects Administration and All India Radio.

(iii) The Central Oil-seeds Committee should give serious attention to propagation of use of cottonseed cake instead of the whole seed by the farmer.

(iv) The Committee recommends that Government dairies and farms should use cottonseed cake instead of whole seed. Ministry of Food and Agriculture may also advise the State Governments.

(v) **Standards:** The Committee recommends that uniform specifications should be laid down by the Indian Standards Institution for decorticated cottonseed cake based on analytical figures of cake produced by modern mills. The State Governments and Army Purchase Organisation should follow the I.S.I. standards while prescribing their requirements.

(vi) **Production of Undecorticated Cake:** The production of undecorticated cottonseed cake need not be discouraged. Delinting of seed should however be done in all cases; hulling may or may not be done. This would facilitate the disposal of cottonseed cake. As an animal feeding stuff, undecorticated cake can replace the whole seed more readily than decorticated cake in the initial stages.

Soap Stock and Soap Industry: (i) Soap Stock—Plants may be established in central locations for the production of fatty acids from refinery soap-stock and Government should provide facilities for the import of plant and machinery for this purpose.

(ii) The Committee recommends that five per cent of cottonseed oil may be used in the manufacture of soap.

Utilisation of Cottonseed Oil in the Manufacture of Vanaspati: (i) The Committee endorses the decision of the members of the Vanaspati Manufacturers Association to voluntarily use cottonseed oil in the production of Vanaspati—two-and-a-half per cent on an annual basis in 1958, five per cent in 1959, seven-and-a-half per cent in 1960 and 10 per cent in 1961. Cottonseed oil would be used in the manufacture of Vanaspati upto five per cent irrespective of the price difference between cottonseed oil and groundnut oil.

(ii) The Committee recommends the manufacture of special brands of vanaspati for the Army containing 25 per cent to 50 per cent cottonseed oil, in view of the possibility of larger consumption of cottonseed oil in such brands.

COMMITTEE FOR THE INTEGRATION OF POST-BASIC AND MULTIPURPOSE SCHOOLS, 1957—REPORT

New Delhi, Ministry of Education. 1960. 34p.

Chairman : Dr. P.D. Shukla.

Member : Shri Veda Prakasha.

Secretary : Shri D.I. Lall (Later Shri P. C. Sharma took over charge).

APPOINTMENT

In pursuance of the recommendation of the Standing Committee on Basic Education, the Union Ministry of Education appointed in November 1957, a Committee for the Integration of Post-Basic and Multipurpose Schools.

TERMS OF REFERENCE

The terms of reference were as follows :

(i) To undertake a comparative study of the syllabi of the Multilateral and the existing post-Basic schools ; and

(ii) To find out common points with a view to bringing the two types nearer to each other.

CONTENTS

Introduction ; Post-Basic and Multipurpose Schools; Recommendations; Summary of Recommendations; Appendix.

RECOMMENDATIONS

1. The study of crafts in post-Basic schools should be considered equivalent to the study of the electives in the Multipurpose schools and for doing this, proper standards should be laid down for both.

2. Necessary assistance should be provided to every post-Basic school to enable it to raise its standard of study in Humanities and Sciences to the same advanced level as is provided for them as electives in every Higher Secondary School.

3. While selecting schools for conversion to Multipurpose schools, the post-Basic schools should be given the same consideration for this conversion, wherever possible, as other Higher Secondary schools.

4. A common scheme of examination for both the post-Basic schools and the Multipurpose schools should be instituted by the State Boards of Secondary Education after giving due cognizance to the special features of the work done in post-Basic schools. This should automatically imply the issue of the same certificate for students of post-Basic schools as for those of other Higher Secondary schools.

5. During the interim period the Governments should recognise the school final examination of the post-Basic schools as equivalent to the certificates awarded to the students of other Higher Secondary schools for purposes of employment and urge upon the universities to accord the same recognition to that examination for purposes of admission to institutions of higher learning.

6. In order to enable post-Basic schools to improve the quality of their teachers and strengthen their laboratory, library, etc., the same financial assistance and guidance should be made available to the post-Basic schools as is being done to the Higher Secondary and Multipurpose schools.

7. As a matter of policy the products of post-Basic schools should, in the earlier stages, be given preference in the matter of employment on those special jobs for which their training has specially equipped them.

8. The recommendation of the All-India Commission for Secondary Education regarding the study of crafts as a compulsory subject should be implemented in all Higher Secondary and Multipurpose schools with due emphasis on the productive aspect of that work.

9. The technique of correlation should be specifically emphasised in all Higher Secondary and Multipurpose schools and utilised as an effective technique of teaching to the extent it is normally possible to do so at that stage of education.

10. Every post-Basic school should suitably add the words 'Higher Secondary' to its name.

EXPERT COMMITTEE ON COAL CONSUMPTION ON RAILWAYS, 1957—REPORT

New Delhi, Railway Board, 1958. 210p.+viip.+Plates.

Chairman : Shri Karnail Singh.
Members : Shri R. Krishnaswamy; Shri Ratan Lall; Dr. J. W. Whitaker; Shri P. M. Nayak; Dr. A. Lahari.
Secretary : Shri D. P. Mathur.

APPOINTMENT

The Export Committee on Coal Consumption on Railways was constituted under the Ministry of Railways vide their letter No. E 57 CO/ 133/ RBI, dated November 5, 1957, to study the Railway coal problem.

TERMS OF REFERENCE

I. To examine and to report on the factors responsible for increase in railway expenditure on coal, commenting particularly on:

(i) The extent to which the quality of coal is responsible for increase in consumption and expenditure and for poor performance;

(ii) The expenditure incurred on handling charges keeping in view the lead and lift involved;

(iii) The comparative merits and demerits of employing departmental or contract labour for coal handling;

(iv) The causes and quantum of wastage and losses of coal in transit, in sheds and otherwise;

(v) The extent to which the increase in expenditure on coal is due to increase in traffic, coal prices, freight charges of coal, etc.

II. To examine the Railways' future requirements of high grade coal for steam traction and the prospects of adequate supplies and to recommend measures for meeting any anticipated shortages.

CONTENTS

Preface; Introduction; **Part I—Coal Consumption and Expenditure**—Indian Coals: Grading and Pricing Structure; Trends in Expenditure on Railway Coal; Effect of Quality of Coal on Consumption and Costs; Other Factors affecting Coal Consumption; Losses and Wastages; Handling of Coal and Ashes—Merits and Demerits of Contract and Departmental Working; Handling of Sea-borne Coal at Calcutta Docks; Measures for reducing Coal Consumption and Expenditure.

Part II—Prospects of Future Supplies of Coal to Railways and Measures Necessary for Meeting Deficiencies—Coal Reserves, Production and Requirements of Various Grades of Coal for Railways under the Second and Third Five-Year Plans and anticipated Deficiencies; Measures necessary to Meet Deficiencies in Future Supplies; Scope for Reducing Coal Requirements by Electrification and Dieselisation; Resume of the Report, Summary of Recommendations; Appendices 1 to 23.

RECOMMENDATIONS

Quality Of Coal

The number of collieries from which coal for the Railways is drawn should be progressively reduced to facilitate inspection and control of quality. The target number to be achieved eventually may be taken as 250.

As loading of miscellaneous coal and dirt is now practised underground in the mines, it is essential that travelling picking belts should be provided on the surface to ensure efficient handling of shale and dirt and loading of coal to specified grades.

The Railways on their part should take immediate steps to set up an organisation for inspection of railway coal with a view to ensuring that the supplies are according to declared grades. The establishment of such an organisation is all the more urgent because the Railways will have to accept more and more non-coking coals in place of coking coals and the maintenance of quality is vital.

Railways should obtain their supplies by entering into contract with collieries and the contract should provide for penalties enforceable by Railways for failure to supply coal according to grade.

Coal quality surveys should be conducted twice a year by Railways preferably in collaboration with Central Fuel Research Institute.

The coals of Outlying Fields should be graded and suitably priced without any delay.

The present grading of Bengal and Bihar coals, which is now over 10 years old, should be revised.

Assessments Of Losses And Wastages

Reweighment checks of coal wagons at receiving sheds should be periodically carried out to keep a watch on transit losses.

The quantity of coal consumed in shed services should be assessed separately from that consumed in train working.

The calibration of locomotive tenders should be improved to enable accurate assessment of tender balances.

The Railways should be fully equipped to carry out

periodically coal trials for fixing correctly trip rations for various services so that coal consumption on line can be properly checked.

Handling Of Coal And Ashes

All coal handling operations should be departmentalised in sheds where losses of coal by pilferage are heavy.

Loading of coal on engine tenders should be departmentalised in sheds where this is done mechanically.

Mechanical loading should be introduced in all sheds where coal loading exceeds 70 tons per day.

Contracts relating to picking of cinders and handling of ashes should be terminated on Railways and departmental labour should be organised to handle the various operations as under:

(i) Cleaning of ashpits and loading of ashes into trucks for dumping at nominated sites should be undertaken by departmental labour controlled by loco sheds.

(ii) Picking of cinders, screening and grading of ashes and disposal of cinders and ashes including utilisation for Railway purposes should be handled by department al labour controlled by the Engineering Department on Railways.

At wayside stations, including traffic yards, all items of ash handling and cinder picking should be undertaken by the Engineering Department.

Experimental schemes should be organised by the Railway Testing and Research Centre to examine possibilities of large scale utilisation of ashes for construction purposes.

To save Southern Railway additional expenditure which they now incur on the supply of coal by sea, supplies of coal from Outlying Fields should be increased after steps have been taken to improve the quality of the coals produced in these fields.

The present contract arrangements for handling of Southern Railway coal at the Calcutta Docks should be terminated as early as possible and replaced by a departmental organisation under a Railway officer with sufficient commercial experience. He should be assisted by an experienced Senior Commercial Inspector and a Divisional Accountant in the management of the work now done by the shippers and in the settlement of monetary transactions relating to:

(i) Payment of colliery bills;

(ii) Verification and adjustment of Railway freight charges; and

(iii) Prompt payment of port dues and other charges in an authorised manner.

Control Measures

To control the quality of coal supplies, Railways should have the same freedom to select collieries (in collaboration with the Coal Controller) as non-Railway consumers have.

The setting up of the Railway Inspection Organisation in accordance with the pattern indicated by the Committee should be expedited.

Coal consumption on shed movement should be controlled by recording the time spent on shed services.

Trip rations for train services and a scale of allowances for extra consumption due to out-of-course stoppages and detentions should be fixed on the basis of properly conducted trials.

Facilities for training of shed and running staff should be increased to improve the standards of locomotive maintenance and firing technique. Further, a review of the maintenance organisation on Railways is necessary to meet the requirements of rapidly increasing traffic and rolling stock holdings.

Investigations regarding the specifications of lubricating cylinder oils should be finalised as early as possible.

Co-operation of the State Governments should be sought to regulate the sale of steam coal only through licensed dealers so that local authorities can question the sources of supply by examining their accounts and other means in the event of any malpractices being suspected.

The strength of Security Force with the Railways consider inadequate for keeping a watch over coal stacks in sheds and overloaded coal wagons standing in open yards, should be suitably augmented without delay; armed guards should be posted in sheds and yards as a drive against pilferage where necessary.

Although the expenditure on the provision of brick walls to prevent the entry of outsiders into loco sheds is heavy it is amply justified at sheds where pilferage is found to be heavy.

Severe disciplinary action should be enforced against drivers and other staff wherever reasonable evidence is forthcoming regarding their indulgence in the stopping of trains at vulnerable points and other malpractices leading to leakage of coal.

Fuel Organisations on Railways should be suitably strengthened to implement the control measures on the lines.

A centralised system of linking 'missing' and 'unconnected' wagons should be introduced as a safeguard against possible losses of complete wagon loads.

Initial compilation of coal and operating statistics should be decentralised to Divisions to facilitate exercise of better control by local authorities.

Before compilation of coal consumption statistics there should be a general reconciliation between the figures of coal consumption and issues of coal by sheds to locomotives.

The Railways should compile and publish statistical data relating to coal consumption separately for the following services:

(i) Passenger Services:

(a) Mail and Express;

(b) Passenger and Parcel;
(c) Local and Suburban;
(d) All Passenger;
(e) Proportion of mixed;
(f) Passenger and proportion of mixed.

(ii) Goods Services:
(a) Through goods;
(b) Pick-up and van goods;
(c) All goods;
(d) Proportion of mixed;
(e) Goods and proportion of mixed.

Coal Beneficiation And Other Measures

(i) In order to guarantee reliability and uniformity in quality of future supplies, the time is ripe for the establishment of washeries in certain fields to upgrade non-coking coal; and

(ii) In order to counteract any fall in the handling capacity of locomotives during the present difficult period, mechanical stockers should be fitted to heavy goods locomotives as far as practicable even though coal consumption may go up.

Detailed schemes should be worked out immediately for setting up washeries at Anuppur, Junardeo and Kothagudium so that the washeries may be in commission by 1961-62. For this pupose, the Central Fuel Research Institute should be requested to undertake investigations without delay.

Electrification And Dieselisation

Electrification should be undertaken as rapidly as foreign exchange, funds and availability of power permit, preference being given to sections on which high traffic density makes this step an operational necessity.

To meet the future requirements of both industries and Railways, the Cen'ral Water and Power Commission should coordinate the planning of power development, transmission lines, and service stations.

Government should speedily develop adequate capacity for the manufacture of heavy electrical machinery and traction equipment.

All shunting services should be progressively dieselised.

Dieselisation of main line services should be introduced where it is necessary to improve line capacity and electrification is not feasible.

High priority should be given to:

(a) Design and manufacture of diesel plant and equipment; and

(b) Increased production of diesel fuel and lubricants.

The existing refineries should step up production of diesel oil by conversion of furnace oil and the projected development of natural crude oil and refinery capacities in Assam should be utilised to the maximum extent for production of diesel oil.

Government should undertake pilot-scale investigations to study the technological and economic possibilities of the synthetic processes (b) and (c) referred to in para 100.

CENTRAL WATER AND POWER COMMISSION REORGANISATION COMMITTEE, 1957—REPORT

New Delhi, Ministry of Irrigation & Power, 1959.

Chairman : Shri B.K. Gokhale.

Members : Shri A.C. Mitra; Shri M.S. Thirumale Iyengar; Shri N.N. Iengar; Shri Indarjit Singh.

Secretary : Shri R.R. Bahl.

APPOINTMENT

The present Central Water and Power Commission was created by amalgamating the Central Water Power, Irrigation and Navigation Commission and the Central Electricity Commission. The functions of the Commission were described in Resolution No. EL.I.201(5), dated April 21, 1951, of the Government of India in the Ministry of Natural Resources and Scientific Research. The Government of India considered that in view of the changes that had since occurred, it would be appropriate to review the work of the CW and PC to assess whether the existing arrangements were adequate for the effective performance of the duties assigned to the Commission. It was, therefore, decided and this Committee was constituted vide Ministry of Irrigation and Power office Memo No. 40(10)56-Adm. I, dated November 29, 1957.

TERMS OF REFERENCE

(i) To review the organisational structure of the Commission and to indicate the directions in which it needs to be improved or strengthened;

(ii) To examine the methods of recruitment now adopted for staffing the organisations at various levels and to recommend modifications of those methods to ensure that the Commission possesses the 'expertise' expected of it as a consultative organisation, and functions in practice as a high level expert body;

In making their recommendations the Committee may take into consideration the desirability of imparting field training to the officers on the Commission who, after some years, tend of lose touch with reality.

(iii) To indicate what broadly should be the relationship between the Commission on the one hand, the Ministry of Irrigation and Power, the Planning Commission and the States on the other;

(iv) To make any other recommendations, which are calculated to improve efficiency and promote maximum utilisation of available water and power resources in India.

Later, the following Terms of Reference were added, [vide Irrigation and Power Ministry O.M. No. 40(10)/56-Adm.I, dated January 17, 1958]:

(v) To examine the directions in which the Power Wing of the Commission should be strengthened to make it an effective agency for rendering high level technical assistance and advice in regard to the generation, transmission and utilisation of power in the following sectors:

(a) heavy industries in the public sector;

(b) railway electrification schemes;

(c) production of power by nuclear energy; and

(d) manufacturing industries producing heavy and light electrical machinery and power consuming apparatus.

(vi) To examine whether in the context of accelerated development envisaged in the Power and Irrigation Sectors of the Second Five-Year Plan and the subsequent Plans and the proposals to entrust additional duties to the Power Wing, there is a case of bifurcation of the Commission and the setting up of two organisations, one dealing with Power and the other with Irrigation, Navigation and Flood Control.

In addition to the above, the following specific problems bearing on the organisation of the CW and PC were referred to the Committee:

(i) Setting up of a Statistical and Economic Unit in the Commission.

(ii) Setting up of a unit in the Commission for assessment of efficiency of operation, maintenance and management of the electric supply undertakings in the public sector.

(iii) Declaration of the post of Director in the Commission as 'non-tenure' post.

CONTENTS

Introductory; Historical Retrospect; Constitutional Position; Assessment of Existing Arrangements at the Centre and in the States: Principles of Re-organisation; Pattern of Organisation; Detailed Organisational Structure; Recruitment, Promotion, Training and other Personnel Matters; Other Administrative Matters; Conclusion; Appendices I to VI.

RECOMMENDATIONS

The functions of the C.E.A. other than arbitration, as laid down in Section 3 of the Electricity (Supply) Act, 1948, should, by an amendment of the Act, be taken out of its purview. The C.E.A. should be renamed as the Standing Arbitration Board.

The States which have not yet been able to equip themselves with technical organisations to reasonable standards, should be assisted to do so within as short a time as practicable. A time limit should be set for liquidating organisations created in the C.W.&P.C. for the purpose of rendering routine assistance to the States.

There should be a proper balance between the functions that should be organised at the Centre and in the States in the Power Sector.

An embargo should be placed on expansion of activities of the C.W.&P.C., if adequately trained staff is not available.

Each State Government/Electricity Board should have the following minimum organisations:

(i) an investigations and planning cell; and

(ii) a designs cell.

The States/Electricity Boards should make their own arrangements for load survey. Suitable measures, as suggested should be taken by the C.W.&P.C. to see that the States Boards do not inflate their figures.

A Plan of Assistance, on the lines of the Colombo Plan, should be organised to pool the experienced technical personnel of the Centre and the States in the I. & P. Sector, for use wherever they are needed most. The Planning Commission may appoint a Committee of two or three Engineer Consultants and a Senior Finance Officer with administration and management experience to make a quick assessment of the needs of the States in trained manpower in the I. & P. Sector.

The functions of the re-organised C.W.&P.C. should be generally to:

(a) Formulate an all-India Plan of action embracing the Centre and the States;

(b) Review the original work done in the States from an all-India angle; and

(c) Assist the States with the necessary technical staff in an emergency.

For an adequate technical appreciation of the Plan proposals, the C.W.&P.C. should consolidate relevant data basin-wise and develop plans from these data in order to check that the proposals made lead to the optimum use of the resources on an economic basis, and also that the schemes are technically sound, financially feasible, and have been fully investigated.

The responsibility of the C.W.&P.C. in the basin-wise studies should be (i) to lay down a time table for such studies, (ii) to apportion the work amongst the State Governments, and (iii) if necessary, to recommend measures for assistance to the State Governments for this purpose.

The major gaps in the basin-wise data should be filled within the next five years so that a greater degree of accuracy is imported into the planning of Irrigation and Power Projects than hitherto.

The C.W.&P.C. should not devote detailed attention to schemes costing below Rs. one crore. It may, if necessary, review such schemes broadly, when inter-State interests are involved.

The State Governments should plan in advance the priorities and types of projects costing below Rs. one crore and send to the C.W.&P.C. only a brief description of such projects in a proforma designed for this purpose, to enable the C.W.&P.C. to see (i) whether any inter-State ramifications arise, and (ii) whether an ordinary irrigation project is being included as a flood project. A detailed examination by the C.W.&P.C. will be necessary only if any projects answer the above description.

The C.W.&P.C. should plan the work of obtaining basic hydrological data necessary for basin-wise studies. The actual collection of such data should be entrusted to the States.

The Commission should lay down a definite time-schedule for basin-wise studies taking into account the part to be played by the States, and should place it before the Coordination Board of Ministers for adoption.

The Committee should periodically evaluate the basic studies and send regular reports thereon to the I. & P. Ministry and the States.

An additional post of Member should be created for a period of three to five years for implementing the programme of basic studies.

The C.W.&P.C. should continue to function as the Central Organisation for the preparation of designs of a complicated nature. Such work should be undertaken only on request and the technical officers of the State/Project concerned should be associated with the preparation of designs. A Scheme should also be drawn up for the utilisation of the experienced personnel for designs work from projects nearing completion.

Investigations should, in future, as far as possible, be taken up by the States only. The existing staff engaged on this work in the C.W.&P.C. should be dispersed to the States after the investigations in progress have been completed.

The C.W.&P.C. should prepare a programme for investigations and, in consultation with States, demarcate the staff required having regard to its total availability. Periodic conferences of the I. & P. Ministry and the States may be held in order to evaluate the progress made in respect of the investigations.

All projects costing below Rs. one crore should be dealt with by the State Chief Engineers except in cases where their inter-State implications are required to be examined by the C.W.&P.C.

A drill for authorisation of projects in future prescribed in this paragraph (5.32), has been suggested for adoption.

The C.W.&P.C. should not undertake construction work. The existing Erection Unit for small thermal plants may, however, continue until the States have equipped themselves for such work.

The Commission should concern itself with the progress of construction and phasing of projects by (i) receiving regular progress reports, (ii) personal visits, and (iii) by attending Central Board meetings. The evaluation of selected projects may continue to be organised by the Committee on Plan Projects.

The C.W.&P.C. should continue to function as an Attached Office. Neither its Chairman nor Members need be given any ex-officio status in the Ministry.

The following items of work should be transferred from the C.W.&P.C. to the Ministry:

(i) Allocation of foreign exchange;

(ii) Rationalisation and distribution of plant and machinery; and

(iii) Allocation of scarce materials.

Technical officers may be appointed in the Ministry to handle this work.

The C.W.&P.C. should, however, be kept informed about the material prepared in the Ministry on these subjects, and should also be associated with final discussions involving high level technical appreciation.

The work relating to Parliament questions should be handled in the Ministry as far as possible. The C.W.& P.C. should be consulted only where there is a likelihood of its making some contribution.

The Commission should examine the issues referred to it as a corporate body. Important matters including projects received for scrutiny should initially be placed before the Commission. Detailed examination in the Directorates should be undertaken only after the Commission has given its directions. The Commission should also review the work of each Directorate once a month.

It would add to the efficiency of the Commission if 25 per cent of the posts of Deputy Directors and below were reduced. The details of the lower staff should be worked out in consultation with the Ministries of I.&P. and Finance.

There is considerable scope for level-jumping in the flow of work, i.e., cases, other than complicated issues, can go from Deputy Director directly to the Member.

All fresh receipts should be seen by the Director, and he should submit the more important ones to the Member.

The work of the Commission would be adequately carried out by a Chairman, seven Members, and a Secretary.

Four out of the seven Members should deal with water resources; three with power development. The total number of Directorates should be 23.

The seven Members proposed will have the following broad distribution of work among themselves:

(1) Planning, Investigations and Water Utilisation;

(2) Designs;

(3) Projects;

(4) Basic Studies and Research;

(5) Thermal Power;

(6) Hydro Power and Power Systems; and

(7) Power Utilisation.

There should be no separate Flood Wing in the Commission. The various Members should deal with such aspects of floods as pertain to subjects included in their respective charges.

Member, Planning, Investigations and Water Utilisation, will be incharge of the following Directorates:

(i) Planning and Investigations;

(ii) Hydrology and Statistics;

(iii) Irrigation and Waterways; and

(iv) Union Territories (Temporary).

Member, Designs, will have the following Directorates under him:

(i) Canals including Flood Designs;

(ii) Dams.

He should be placed in exclusive charge of these Directorates to enable him to devote undivided attention to designs work.

Member, Projects, will deal with the following Directorates:

(1) Technical Examination;

(2) Cost Control; and

(3) Construction Plant and Machinery.

He will normally attend the meetings of the Control Boards except in cases where the presence of any other Member is necessary. He will also be incharge of miscellaneous work in the Commission, such as tendering advice to other Ministries and Projects. This work should be handled, under his guidance, by a Deputy Director.

Member, Basic Studies and Research, will have the following Directorates under him:

(1) Manuals and Standardisation;

(2) Basin-wise Studies; and

(3) Research Station, Poona.

Member, Thermal Power, will be solely in-charge of the work of planning and execution of installation of Thermal Stations. He will have the following three Directorates under him:

(1) Thermal Stations, layout and designs;

(2) Thermal Stations, specifications and contracts; and

(3) Planning Cell, Neyvelli (Temporary).

Active measures should be taken for training engineers in the techniques of large high pressure steam power stations.

Member, Hydro-Power and Power Systems, will deal with the following Directorates:

(1) Hydro Stations, layout and designs;

(2) Hydro Stations, specifications and contracts;

(3) Technical Examination; and

(4) Power Research, Standardisation and Manuals, Tele-Communication Coordination.

There is no justification for a separate Member for Transmission and Distribution of Power. A Senior Director should handle this work. He should also supervise hydro-electric power surveys.

The growth of low voltage distribution and rural supply lines should be reviewed in a separate Directorate in the Power Utilisation Section.

Technicians for erection and commissioning of large power generating plant should be rapidly trained and developed in the power systems of the States/Electricity Boards. The Irrigation and Power Ministry should collect from the States/Projects full details of expenditure on foreign technicians and consultants, separately for Water and Power Projects.

Two Erection Squads (one Hydro and one Thermal) may be built up in the Central Water and Power Commission on a temporary basis for helping areas that are relatively under-developed. These should in due course be transferred to the N.P.C.C.

Member, Power Utilisation, will have the following Directorates under him:

(1) Load Surveys and Rural Electrification;

(2) Statistics, Tariffs and Legislation; and

(3) Union Territories (Temporary).

The States Electricity Boards should themselves undertake load survey of the areas within their jurisdiction. The field staff of the Load Survey Directorate of the Canal Water and Power Commission together with the work in hand should be transferred to the States/ Boards.

It is not necessary for the Central Water and Power Commission to equip itself for rendering high level technical advice to heavy industries in the Public sector, railways, or manufacturing industries producing heavy and light electrical machinery, etc. The Commission should advise such industries only in regard to proper power supplies for their working, and standardisation of electrical equipment used by them to conform to practices employed in the field of general power supply.

To handle the ncreasing volume of work in this regard, two Deputy Directors may be appointed to head two Directorates in the Utilisation Section.

Administrative matters of the Commission should be handled in one place in a unified manner under the charge of the Chairman. The Chairman should be assisted by the Secretary to the Commission in managing common services.

The reorganised Commission will not have the following existing Directorates:

(1) Plant and Machinery;

(2) Silt and Construction Materials;

(3) Flood Control Designs; and

(4) Four Investigation Circles and two Flood Sections.

The work in respect of (1) will be largely transferred to the Irrigation and Power Ministry. The Directorate of Construction, Plant and Machinery, provided for under Member (Projects) would deal with construction plant layout aud other construction problems.

The Directorate at (2) should be abolished and the existing laboratory at Delhi amalgamated with the Research Station at Poona.

The work at present being done in the Directorate of Flood Control Design should in future be dealt with in the Canals Directorate under Member (Designs). Similarly, the work being done in the other two sections of the Flood Wing should be distributed among the appropriate Directorates according to the nature of work. Investigation work should be transferred to the States. Any residual work in respect of flood investigations and coordination may be done in the Directorate of Planning and Investigations.

The proposal to set up a unit in the Commission for assessment of efficiency of operation and management of electric supply undertakings in the public sector should be deferred till the electricity systems in the States have gone beyond the present developmental stage and get stabilised.

The posts of Members and the Chairman should continue to be tenure posts. The normal tenure of these posts should be five years. A Chairman or Member may continue to serve up to the age of 60 years provided his total term in the Commission as a Member, Chairman or both, does not exceed five years. The field of selection for Members/Chairman should be restricted to eminent Chief Engineers with construction experience of at least two years in the capacity of Chief Engineer. A Director of the Commission will become eligible for selection only if he has acquired experience for at least two years in the capacity of Chief Engineer in a State, Project or Electricity Board.

A Selection Committee should be appointed to advise the Ministry of Irrigation and Power in the choice of Chairman and Members.

One-half of the posts in the grades of Directors and Deputy Directors should be filled by Officers on deputation from the States, and the other half should be filled by promotion of officers of the Commission in the grades next below. One-half of the posts of Assistant Directors should be filled by officers on deputation from the States, and the other half by direct recruitment through the Union Public Service Commission.

The posts of E.A.D.'s should be abolished.

There should be no cadre of Design Assistants, Computors and Draftsmen should be employed instead, for technical jobs of routine nature.

The cadre strength of the various posts below the Director's level, should be reviewed and fresh recruitment suspended till the reorganisation is completed.

The States should be persuaded to enlarge their engineering cadres to provide for an adequate reserve for deputation to the Centre. If they do not accept the proposal, the programme of work should be curtailed.

A Committee should be appointed for selection of officers from the States. The States should be associated with the procedure of selection of officers for deputation to the Commission by giving them representation on this Committee.

The period of tenure should be strictly adhered to.

No officer should become eligible for promotion to the next higher rank unless he has adequate field experience in his grade. The Commission should depute its officers to the States, Projects and Electricity Boards for field training according to a carefully planned programme.

If the heavy backlog of untrained officers does not permit arrangements being made for their training, as recommended in the Report, some suitable interim arrangements may be made to provide them with the elements of essential experience required for manning the higher posts.

The training should at present be accommodated within the present strength of the C.W.&P.C. When the strength has been fixed on the basis of a detailed work-study, a suitable training reserve should also be provided.

Full use should be made of the N.P.C.C. for imparting field training to the officers of the C.W.&P.C., by drawing a certain proportion of the staff of the Corporation from the training reserve of the Commission.

When an officer with the requisite experience is not available for promotion to a particular vacancy the available officer, not ordinarily included in the field of selection, should not be promoted on a regular basis. He should be placed in charge of the higher post on his existing salary plus a small allowance.

The selection grades should be suitably revised. These should ordinarily be intended to prevent stagnation in a cadre when an officer in the ordinary grade has reached the maximum of the scale and avenues of further promotion are not available for the time being.

The grade of S.E. should be abolished.

The C.W.&P.C. should not be split up into two organisations.

The Commission should work as a corporate body. It should hold weekly meetings to consider important technical and administrative problems. A formal record of the proceedings should be sent to the Ministry who should scrutinise them to ensure that the Commission functions as a corporate body.

There is no justification for any considerable expansion of the responsibilities of the Power Wing for rendering assistance to heavy industries in the Public Sector, railway electrification schemes, production of power by nuclear energy or industries producing heavy and light electrical machinery.

A panel of consultants drawn from the ranks of outstanding retired engineers should be constituted for consultation concerning individual projects or problems and for checking up designs originally prepared by the C.W.&P.C.

The advice of the C.W.&P.C. in technical matters should be accepted by the Ministry of I.&P., the Planning Commission and the States.

The C.W.&P.C. should continue to handle the work relating to carrying out investigations and collecting and recording power data, and coordination of activities of the planning agencies in relation to the control and utilisation of power resources. The Electricity (Supply) Act, 1948, should be amended to relieve the C.E.A. of these functions.

The engineers employed in the Control Room should be replaced by statisticians as early as possible.

Officers of middling seniority from the Commission/States should find adequate representation in the composition of delegations sent abroad.

The C.W.&P.C. should be treated on the lines analogous to the various National Laboratories and provided with proper office and housing accommodation to facilitate high-level technical work.

COMMISSION OF INQUIRY TO ASCERTAIN THE CAUSES OF THE ACCIDENT TO I DOWN BOMBAY-CALCUTTA MAIL TRAIN BETWEEN PADALI AND ASVALI, CENTRAL RAILWAY ON THE NIGHT OF NOVEMBER, 23, 1957, 1957—REPORT

Delhi, Manager of Publications, 1958. 59p.

Chairman : Justice G.D. Khosla.
Members : Dr. P. Subbarayan; Shri J.N. Nanda.
Secretary : Shri P.B. Aibara.

APPOINTMENT

The Commission of Inquiry to Ascertain the Causes of the Accident to I Down Bombay-Calcutta Mail Train Between Padali and Asvali, Central Railway on the Night of November 23, 1957, was constituted under the Ministry of Railways vide their Notification dated November 29, 1957, to enquire into the causes of this accident.

TERMS OF REFERENCE

(i) Make an inquiry into the causes of the said accident and for that purpose take such evidence as may be necessary;

(ii) State its findings as to causes of the said accident and as to the person or persons if any, responsible therefor; and

(iii) Suggest safeguards against similar accidents in future.

CONTENTS

Introductory; The Cause of the Accident; Persons Responsible for the Accident; What Safeguards can be Suggested Against Similar Accidents in Future; Annexures A & B; Photographs; Explanatory Notes for Photographs.

CONCLUSIONS

The accident caused to the I Down Bombay-Calcutta Mail on November 23, 1957, was the result of a deliberate act of sabotage committed by some person or persons unknown.

It is impossible to suggest any measures which will

completely and effectively prevent sabotage or detect it in time to avoid an accident, but a substantial measure of security can be achieved by :

(a) The use of reversed jaw type sleepers in conjunction with the normal type on CST-9 plate-sleepered track at the rate of at least three per rail length. This measure does not involve any extra cost nor does it interfere with regular track maintenance.

(b) Welding of rail joints. This measure offers some resistance against sabotage attempts and apart from the saving in rail joints and maintenance expenditure, has the added advantage of affording smoother running and reduced wear and tear of rails and wheel tyres.

(c) A more powerful engine headlight with swivelling arrangement to light the track better and increase the possibility of detection of obstructions and track faults. The consideration of this matter should be entrusted to a high level Committee.

(d) Effective security patrolling over those sections which previous experience has proved to be vulnerable or where acts of sabotage may be expected. Complete coordination between the District Police, Railway Police and the Railway Protection Force at all levels is imperative. The system of patrolling should include an element of surprise by laying down varying programmes of which one may be chosen at random for any particular spell. A mobile vehicular patrol acting as a supervisory check over the system of foot-patrolling will have a salutory effect. The question of associating the residents of adjoining villages should also be examined.

(e) Special legislation to provide deterrent penalties on those found guilty of attempts at train wrecking.

(f) The offering of substantial awards to those who give information leading to the arrest of saboteurs.

CHAIRMAN INDEX

INDEX

COMMITTEES AND COMMISSIONS IN INDIA 1947-73

Details of Published Volumes

COMMITTEES AND COMMISSIONS IN INDIA 1947-80

(In 18 Vols.)

Vol. 1	1947-54	Rs. 1500
Vol. 2	1955-57	Rs. 1500
Vol. 3	1958-59	Rs. 1500
Vol. 4	1960-61	Rs. 1500
Vol. 5	1962-63	Rs. 1500
Vol. 6	1964-65	Rs. 1500
Vol. 7	1966	Rs. 1500
Vol. 8	1967	Rs. 1500
Vol. 9	1968-69	Rs. 1500
Vol. 10	1970	Rs. 1500
Vol. 11	1971-73	Rs. 1500
Vol. 12	1974	Rs. 450
Vol. 13	1975	Rs. 450
Vol. 14	1976	Rs. 450
Vol. 15A	1977	Rs. 450
Vol. 15B	1977	Rs. 450
Vol. 15C	1977	Rs. 450
Vol. 15D	1977	Rs. 450
Vol. 16A	1978	Rs. 450
Vol. 16B	1978	Rs. 450
Vol. 17A	1979	Rs. 450
Vol. 17B	1979	Rs. 450
Vol. 18A	1980	Rs. 450
Vol. 18B	1980	Rs. 450

COMMITTEES AND COMMISSIONS IN INDIA
1947-73

Volume IV
1960-61

Virendra Kumar

CONCEPT PUBLISHING COMPANY, NEW DELHI-110059

ISBN 81-7022-213-3 (Vol. IV)

First Published 1977
Reprinted 2005

Published and Printed by
Ashok Kumar Mittal
Concept Publishing Company
A/15-16, Commercial Block, Mohan Garden
NEW DELHI-110059 (India)

Phones : 25351460, 25351794
Fax : 091-11-25357103
Email : publishing@conceptpub.com

DEDICATED

TO

LATE DR. S.R. RANGANATHAN

INTRODUCTION

This Fourth volume attempts to understand and analyse the activities of the various 'Committees and Commissions' during the period of 1960-1961 which have been received as far as the previous volume is concerned scant attention from even bibliophiles and documentation experts. It is known that the governments all over the world largely rely on the Committees and Commissions for their decisions on particular subjects. Governments make an extensive use of the Instrument of the Public Enquiries which ultimately help in lessening managerial tensions as wellas quietening the allegations of misrule. According to John Stuart Mill, "A man seldom judges right, even in his own concerns, still less in those of the public, when he makes habitual use of knowledge his own or that of the public, or that of some single adviser". Thus the "Committee System"
greatly helps the proper functioning of a democratic set up.

A Commission is a "Governmental Agency created to perform a particular function such as special investigations or governmental regulations of business". It is appointed mainly when it is thought that a matter involves some financial questions. There are other reasons for which a Commission is appointed, e.g. in matters pertaining to the welfare of the state and its citizen and for improving the efficiency in an administration. The status of a Committee is also the same as that of a Commission, but it does not possess as wide powers as are enjoyed by a Commission and has to limit itself in relation to specific work assigned to it under its terms of reference. While arriving at decisions in the form of recommendations, a Committee or Commission ensures that such decisions are representative of interests of various types of people and also a safeguard against abuse of power.

The Committees and Commissions always advise a Government, offering valuable suggestions and recommendations for smooth operation and efficiency in administration for the welfare of the people.

A Committees or a Commission comprises a Chairman, the Members and Member-Secretary (sometimes there is also a Vice-Chairman and an Assistant Secretary). In some cases there are even one-man commissions and enquiries conducted by such Commissions are entrusted to an Official-on-Special-Duty or a Judge of the High Court.

The Chairman of a Commission is a person well versed in legal affairs and is often a retired Judge of a High Court or the Supreme Court of India. Occasionally, a member of Parliament is also appointed to the post of Chairman of a Commission. Regarding Committees, the Chairman is usually a specialist in the subject of the Committee. He can be a Leader or a Convenor also if he heads a Panel, Study Group, Working Group or a Delegation etc.

The members of a Commission, Committee, Panel, Study Group, Working Group etc., are specialists in their respective fields and provide valuable guidance to the Commission in making recommendations.

The Member-Secretary or Secretary is nominated from among the experienced officials who have the requisite competent knowledge of the subject on which the Commission or the Committee is appointed.

The Study of the "Committee and Commissions" is divided into two main parts :

(I) Pre-Independence :- From 1772 to August 1947 ; and

(II) Post-Independence :- From August 1947 to 1973.

The first volume in this series is devoted to the period August 1947 to 1954, and the second volume coversthe period 1955 to 1957. The third volume covers the years 1958 and 1959, and the present Volume covers the year 1960 and 1961.

The work provides information on subjects like Bibliographical Data of the Committees and Commissions ; Chairman, Leader, Convenor etc. of the Committees and Commissions ; Appointments ; Terms of Reference ; Contents and Recommendations.

Arrangements : The arrangement in the "Committees and Commissions" are Chronological and items have been arranged according to their dates of appointment and not according to their dates of publication. At the end of the book a separate Index of Chairmen and Subject Index has been appended to facilitate the utility of the book.

Suggestions made by reviewers and others have been taken into consideration in the preparation of this volume and improvements have been made as far as possible. I am indebted to my friends who have helped me a lot in the process of compilation of this volume. I am also grateful to my wife and children who have sacrificed their personnel comforts by providing me every facility to make this volume ready for publication within a reasonable short time.

NEW DELHI
Durga Ashthami
October 19, 1977

VIRENDRA KUMAR

CONTENTS

1961

1960

COMMITTEE ON EVALUATION OF THERAPEUTICAL CLAIMS OF YOGIC PRACTICES, 1960—REPORT

New Delhi, Ministry of Education, 1962. 72 p.+iip.

Convenor : Dr. B.K. Anand.
Members : Dr. S.S. Misra ; Dr. B. Narayana ; Dr. V. Narayanaswami,
Secretary : Shri R.L. Anand.

APPOINTMENT

In 1958, the Government of India had set up a Committee to make an on-the-spot study of the working of the Vishwayatan Yoga Ashram, Katra Vaishno Devi (Jammu and Kashmir State) and make recommendations to the Government of India in respect of the proposals put forward by the Yoga Ashram for the expansion and development of its activities. The Committee *inter alia* recommended as follows :

"Elaborate claims are being made regarding the therapeutical values of Yogic Practices. Government would do well to appoint a Committee of Medical Experts to study this so that benefits which may be observed can be given wider publicity and utilised in greater measures. If, on the other hand, the claims are proved not to be valid the public must be made known of the position,"

The above recommendation of the Committee was accepted by the Government of India in consultation with the Ministry of Health and appointed a Committee in 1960 to assess the therapeutic claims of Yoga and to make a report to the Government on the existing conditions and suggest measures for further development of this.

TERMS OF REFERENCE

(i) To study and evaluate the therapeutical values of Yogic Practices.

(ii) To visit the institutions and recommend suitable measures for developing them on scientific lines.

CONTENTS

Preface ; Appointment of the Committee ; Impressions about the institutions visited ; Evaluation of the Therapeutic claims of Yogic Practices ; Recommendations of the Committee ; Summary of Recommendations ; Appendices I to VI.

RECOMMENDATIONS

The Committee appointed by the Government of

India for evaluation of the therapeutical claims of Yogic practices sent out a questionnaire for eliciting relevant information to 71 Yoga Institutions. Based on these replies, the Committee visited 19 Institutions.

The Committee has come to the conclusion, based on the, visits to these Centres and by study of the records maintained by them, that as the records have not been maintained on proper scientific lines, it is not possible to evaluate the various therapeutical claims made for Yogic treatment of various diseases. Lack of proper records have mainly been due to want of resources and lack of knowledge of modern methods of scientific investigations, as well as lack of trained personnel. The Committee, therefore, feels that it is very essential, that conditions be created and facilities provided for, at some of the Centres for scientific evaluation and assessment of the effects of Yogic exercises, because in its view Yogic practices, if done on proper lines, may help those individual who suffer from diseases with predominant psycho-somatic disturbances.

In the light of above observations the Committee recommends to the Government of India that at 10 institutions proper facilities be provided for carrying out scientific investigations. These 10 institutions have been selected on the basis of the facilities already available with them and from the capacity and enthusiasm of the personnel of those institutions. It is very essential that the patients suffering from various diseases, who are treated by Yogic therapy, should be investigated and assessed by qualified medical personnel with the help of proper modern equipment. It, therefore, recommends to the Government of India that in all these centres investigative laboratories, having modern equipment, be set up and personnel for clinical examination provided. The Committee further recommends that at one of these Centres facilities for training disciples in Yogic techniques be also made available as mentioned in the report.

Although the Committee has mainly been concerned with the study of therapeutic uses of Yoga and has based its recommendations primarily towards that end, it is also of the opinion that Yogic exercises may play an important role in the prevention of disease and maintenance of positive health. It, therefore, recommends that the medical units created at the various Yogic centres for studying the therapeutic claims of Yoga, should also direct their attention to the study of prevention of disease by Yogic exercises. This will have to be studied on a long-range basis.

HIGH LEVEL TEAM ON TRAINING, 1960—REPORT

New Delhi, Ministry of Community Development and Cooperation (Department of Community Development), 1961. 51p.

FIRST COMMITEE

Leader : Shri S. Chakravarti.

Members : Prof. N.R. Malkani ; Development Commissioner of the State Concerned ; A Representative of the Ministry of Community Development and Cooperation ; Director of Extension Training, Ministry of Food and Agriculture.

Secretary : Principal, Institute for Instruction on Community Development, Rajpur

APPOINTMENT

In persuance of the recommendations made by the Advisory Board of the Central Institute, Mussoorie, the High Level Team on Training was Constituted by the Government of India to visit Training Centres and provide necessary technical guidance with a view to improving the quality of training of Community Development Personnel in 1960.

TERMS OF REFERENCE

To visit Training Centres and provide necessary technical guidance with a view to improving the quality of training of Community Development personnel.

CONTENTS

Machinery for Coordination and Supervision ; Inter-Institutional Relationship ; Use of Training Facilities ; Physical Environment, Manual Work, General Atmosphere ; Common Training and Composition of Courses ; Syllabus and Pattern of Courses ; Job Course, Syllabus ; Study Course Syllabus; Training Methods ; Problems of Trainees During and After Training ; Teaching Staff ; Touch with Field

Conditions and Development Trends ; Realism in Training.

SECOND COMMITTEE

Leader : Shri S Chakravarti.

Members : Shri Radhe Lal Vyas ; Shri Raghubir Sahai ; Development Commissioner of the State concerned ; Commissioner (Training), Ministry of Community Development and Cooperation ; Director (Social Education), Ministry of Community Development and Cooperation.

Secretary : Principal, Institute for Instructions on Community Development, Rajpur.

APPOINTMENT

In pursuance of the recommendation made at the first meeting of Committees I and II of the Advisory Board on Training the High Level Team on Training was reconstituted by the Ministry of Community Development) and cooperation (Deptt. of Community Development) to visit Training Centres and provide necessary technical guidance with a view to improving the quality of training of Community Development Personnel.

TERMS OF REFERENCE

To visit Training Centres and provide necessary technical guidance with a view to improving the quality of training of Community Development Personnel.

CONTENTS

Part A;—Machinery for Coordination and Supervision; Inter-institutional Relationship ; Use of Training Facilities : Quality of Trainees ; Physical environment : Manual Work, General Atmosphere ; Syllabus and Training Methods ; Teaching Staff ; Touch with Field Conditions and Development Trends : Realism in Training, Growth of Training Centre ; **Part B**—Machinery for Coordination and Supervision ; Inter-Institutional Relationship ; Use of Training Facilities Composition of Trainees ; Physical Environment : Manual Work, General Aptitude ; Syllabus and Pattern of Courses ; Training Methods ; Teaching Staff ; Touch with Field Conditions and Development Trends ; Realism in Training: Growth of Training Centre ; General ; Annexure (Decisions on Recommendations made in the First Report of the High Level Team on Training).

RECOMMENDATIONS OF :

First High Level Team

Recommendations of Machinery for Coordination and Supervision

Whilst machinery for the coordination and supervision of the training programme exists at the State level in the shape of a State Level Coordination Committee on Training and even at Regional level as at Ranchi where there is a Coordination Committee of all the Training Centres with the Commissioner, Chhota Nagpur Division as Chairman, the interest of the Development Commissioners in the sphere of training is neither sustained nor deep. This normal relationship has been to the serious detriment of the entire training programme ; basically it has chacked the line of communication from which should flow :

(a) effective interchange of personnel between training centres and the field and between training centers inter-se ;

(b) Constant and continuous picture of the latest trends in the development programmes ; and

(c) Realism in training stimulated by the cross check which Development Commissioners and their staff can provide in relation to their practical experience of the results and requirements of training as seen in the field.

It is, therefore, essential that the Development Commissioners should be more actively drawn into the work of the training centres. Three steps would appear to be necessary :

(a) The State Level Coordination Committee on Training has not met four months together in some States. One possible reason for this might be its weak composition and vague terms of reference. The Committee as constituated consists of the Departments Commissioner (Chairman), Head of Departments concerned as members and the Director of Training as the Secretary, and it is simply required to "review from time to time the working of the training Institutions on the basis of reports of inspection furnished by its members." It is suggested that the Committee be reorganised with the following revised composition and terms of reference :

Composition

Development Commissioner of State in which the Training Centre campus is located	...Chairman
Two or three Heads of Departments concerned Three or four non-officials All Principals/Directors	...Members
Director of Training	...Secretary

TERMS OF REFERENCE

(i) Plan in advance the programme for the courses in the different centres to ensure common talks, common discussions and common activities;

(ii) Ensure better inter- institutional coordination between training centres;

(iii) Arrange for inter-change of staff between training centres and the field and between training centres;

(iv) Ensure full utilisation of training centre capacity;

(v) Ensure adequate staffing;

(vi) Ensure efficient relationship between the training centres and the block attached thereto;

(vii) Bring about realism in training particularly through periodical discussion of the problems raised by the trainees at each of the courses. It is suggested that the Principal of each training centre should list out the problems raised by the trainees during each course and bring them up at a meeting of the committee at which staff members of training centres should also be associated, to the end that the staff can, as a result of the discussions, be posted with the latest thinking on the several problems and possible answers thereto. Indeed, such a discussion will be of advantage to the Development Commissioner and his staff as providing another line of communication to field problems.

(viii) Generally review the progress of courses at the several training centres and suggest measures for improving the quality of training.

It will be sufficint if the committee as reorganised above meets once three months; once in six months or once a year. It would be an advantage if the Development Commissioners of neighbouring States, whose trainees are sent for training to the particular training centre, also attend the meeting. There is precedent for this suggestion in the arrangements which already exist in respect of the Block Level Cooperative Officers Training Centre. The Local Committee in Himayatsagar, for instance, consists of the Development Commissioner, Andhra Pradesh (Chairman), Registrar of Cooperative Societies of Andhra Pradesh, Mysore and Kerela as members apart from a representative of the Reserve Bank, non-officials and the Principal of the training centre.

(b) The work of allotment of seats for the different courses in the O. & S.C.'s should be decentralised to the extent possible and the Principal made responsible for the allotment supported by a sub-committee of the above Committee to be designated as the local committee or advisory board under the Chairmanship of the Development Commissioner. (This proposal has since been accepted by the Ministry and orders also issued for forming on Advisory Board for each O. & S.C.). What is important to emphasise is that the Board should function for all practical purposes as the Local Committee referred to above. This will ensure that it is internally related to the State Coordination Committee on Training.

(c) Separate Sub-Committees may be formed to function as a local committee for each of the other Centres also.

In addition to Local Committees suggested above, it is necessary, where there is more than one training centre at a campus, that there should be a Committee of Principals, with one or two staff members drawn from each centre and, each Principal acting as a Convenor in rotation, mainly for the purpose of developing corporate life among the trainees in the compus; giving opportunities of learning and working together resulting in appreciation of the common objectives of the programme and the need for team work in the field; developing correct attitudes; coordinating training programmes in the campus and field programmes or villlage practicals and pooling common facilities and teaching skills in the total interest of all the training centres. A "Coordination meeting of the Principals of all the training centres within the campus" was recently convened at Himayatsagar, but it would appear that its attention was concentrated more on cultural activities. It is suggested that the *ad-hoc* arrangements for meetings should be institutionalised in the form of a committee and the scope and focus of its work enlarged as suggested above.

There is also need for a study circle of staff members of all training centres in a campus to provide a forum for the consideration of extra curricular professional activities of the staff and promotion of study among them. The study circle may meet once a month to discuss teaching and programme problems and arrange presentation of papers and case studies bearing on those problems with a view to improving the content and method of teaching and achieving unity of approach. The Chairmanship of the circle may rotate among the principals. In Bakshi-ka-Talab combined staff meetings have been held occasionally and in Nilokheri a Trainers' Study Circle was recently started. It is essential to systematise the position in all training centres.

It has been suggested to us that all training centres in a compus should be serviced by one common principal with a Vice-Principal for each centre both in the interests of effective coordination among training centres and development among trainees of correct attitudes in terms of team work required in the field. In the absence of an opportunity to work out the practical implications of this proposal, we do not propose to make specific recommendations in this regard. From the same angle and with a view to creating an academic atmosphere it is felt that any new centre to be opened should, as far as possible, be located in the campus of existing centres and where no such centre exists, in the campus of Universities.

Inter-Institutional Relationship: Himayatsagar And Ranchi.

Though there are many training centres in the campus, there is hardly any evidence of corporate and community life among the instructors and trainees. Different training centres are located in the same campus basically with a view to creating an academic atmosphere and providing the trainees even during trainining with opportunities of learning and working together and appreciating the common methods and objective of the programme. Apart from the necessary basis of factual information about the aims and methods of community development, the training courses are designed to instil proper attitudes on the part of the workers; the campus would be failing in one of its major objectives if a spirit of team work and sensitive appreciation of the villagers' problems through interchange between different levels of workers at different centres are not encouraged. It is, therefore, suggested that community life in the whole campus and composite training to the extent possible be developed in terms of canteen, library and playground facilities, *shramdan*, cultural activities, celebration of festivals, a common journal for all training centres, a common cooperative store, common lectures and discussions on certain core subjects, common seminars and symposia and even common village practical. The Committee of Principals suggested above, as providing a common forum, should help to improve the position in several of these directions.

All centres have a core of common subjects but as the institutions are independent, they employ separate staff instructors. It was found in some centres in Himayatsagar that instructors do not have sufficient work. It should be possible to combine the teaching staff in at least some of the centres.

Bakshi-Ka-Talab, Lucknow

The tradition of unified administration of three Centres—B.D.O.T.C., S.E.O.T.C. and E.T.C. under a common Principal during 1957-58 has had not a little to do with the continuance of coordinated working between these institutions even after the O, & S.C. created is November 1958 in place of the B.D.O.T.C. came under the administrative control of the Ministry Common prayer, common cultural programmes, common *Shramdan*, common programme of debate or symposia, informal consultations between Principals, combined staff meetings and talks to other centres by by Instructors of the O. & S.C. are features which training centres in other States may well emulate Some of these features require to be given institutional shape as recommended earlier. Pooling of vehicles and common village practicals have unfortunately been given up ; we feel that this requires to be reconsidered.

Use of Training Facilities

Better use of training facilities will undoubtedly be ensured by drawing in Development Commissioners more actively in the training programme as suggested earlier. Whether it will be necessary to go further and place the Orientation and Study Centres under the administrative control of the Development Commissioners as suggested by the Staff Conferences of Development Commissioners, needs detailed consideration. In the absence of the representative of the Ministry we did not have the opportunity of considering this issue in its several practical aspects. The under-use of training facilities is, however, a matter still causing concern, as the following figures for the O. & S.C. Bakshi-Ka-Talab for the six months period from August 16, 1959 to February 21, 1960 will show :

Allotted	254
Joined	186 (approx. 74 per cent)

A significant feature is that the under use is greatest in the home State *viz.*. U.P. for the same period the figures were :

Allotted	86
Joined	50 (approx. 59 per cent)

The position was no different in the O. & S.C. Ranchi, where in the words of the Principal they "have not had the full strength of trainees so far in any course" the number of trainees in the Job Course being particularly poor.

The large number of States from which trainees are drawn, alterations in the States getting allotments from time to time, and the absence of a decentralised authority to pursue with undivided attention the allotments once made might be contributory factors, apart from the lack of a Training Reserve, which it is hoped has since been made good. It is suggested that each training centre should be fed by a few States to be earmarked for the purpose. Such earmarking would enable the instructors to familiarise themselves with the rules, procedures and problems of the States concerned with added value to the entire training, that percentage allotments for a period of one year for each State so earmarked should be indicated by the Ministry to the Principal and the Advisory Board Local Committee made responsible for working out actual allotments and ensuring full utilisation. A procedure such as this will, we feel, improve the position and will certainly obviate the phenomenon of under-use in the home State itself. This procedure need not stand in the way of the Ministry making any special allotments to meet special demands.

Physical Environment, Mannual Work, General Atmosphere

The trainees come to the training centres with some

set habits of living and thinking and as attitude change is one of the set purpose of the training programme, there is need, apart from work in the class room, to demonstrate outside the desired attitudes in relation both to the daily conduct of the Instructors and the physical environment of the training centres. If it is desired to inculcate an attitude of sensitivity to rural requirements, trainees must line in that atmosphere even during the training period. There is great scope for improving the arrangements in training centres to provide models for the trainees for their work in villages. For instance, the food taken should be a model of balanced diet, *Chulhas,* both rooms and latrines could represent the types advocated for use in villages. None of the features was present at Himayatsagar, Bakshi-ka-Talab or Ranchi. At Sriniketan the sanitary arrangements were in the words of the 'Director not very satisfactory and rather primitive'. At Himayatsagar, Bakshi-ka-Talab and Ranchi there was a common Consumers' Co-operative Store which was dormant and which was in the process of being revitalised. Such stores require to be developed at all training compuses. Further as in Himayatsagar and Nilokheri an open air theatre can be constructed by the trainees themselves for providing facilities for recreation and cultural development both to the trainees and the staff. Similarly, latrines of the types advocated in the field can be constructed and used in all training centres.

Practicals should be so designed as to instil a sense of dignity in manual work, develop community life among the trainees and demonstrate during training practices to be advocated in the field. Such work was, however, confined in the O. & S. C. Himayatsagar to kitchen gardening only. In the Orientation and Study Centre, Bakshi-ka-Talab, the time was first utilised on *Shramdan* on such items as digging drains, pits, etc., and later, in the absence of projects of permanent utility, the time was spent by the trainees in learning the use of agricultural implements, digging compost and soakage pits, making smokeless *chulhas* constructing rural latrines, etc. *Shramdan*, whilst necessary for purposes of instilling a sense of dignity in manual work should, it is felt, be made purposive, if frustration freely expressed by the trainees in respect of this programme is to be avoided. This will be possible if manual labour is related to activities in the training programme and is made part of specific projects of continuing or permanent utility to the training centre ; this will also ensure better demonstrational impact. Three projects of this type immediately came to mind. Kitchen gordening can be a continuing operation covering day-to-day care in the growth of vegetables, digging of pits, collection of dried leaves and composting of manure, and can be extended to cover propagation of green manure plants and grafting etc. It was found that whereever farm facilities existed the trainees felt a sense of satisfaction in carrying out agricultural operations on the basis of improved implements, improved agricultural practices, etc. It is suggested that farm facilities should be provided in all training centres where they do not exist at present. Another possibility is paultry farming. In one of the E.T.C.'s, a Cooperative Society has been formed with the trainees as temporary share holders for the purpose of managing a paultry farm. The eggs are taken by the trainees at a concessional rate and the share capital is returned at the end of the training period, when new trainees become shareholders. A similar project in all training centres is recommended.

No less important than the physical environment is the atmosphere at the training centres. Basically, the training has to be self-training ; the educational process cannot be achieved unless time is available for study and reflection. Unfortunately, except at Sriniketan and Belurmath no training centre was free from the boarding school approach of filling the time of the trainees from early morning to late night and many Principals Directors proudly displayed the daily programme from 5 or 5-30 a.m. to 10.00 p.m. or 10.30 p.m. Three correctives are possible :

(a) The daily programme should be so organised that at least one or two afternoons in the week are left free for the purpose. The Principal, O. & S. C., Bakshi-ka-Talab is already endeavouring to this end. The experiment of one or two free afternoons was tried in the IXth course at the Central Institute with good results ; on the one hand trainees had more time for pursuing their own projects, e.g., intensified study of books or preparation of individual papers on their field problems and on the other, the criticism of regimentation so frequent in the earlier courses completely disappeared.

(b) The trainees should be encouraged, though their own committees to manage their own campus affairs—mess, lodging, manual work, recreation, seminars, symposium and debates. These activities have been well organised in the Orientation and study centres Himayatsagar and Bakshi-ka-Talab.

(c) At Bakshi-ka-Talab, Sriniketan and Belurmath the staff mix freely with trainees, participate in tournaments and invite the trainees in groups to their residences for informal talks. Such informal exchanges are extremely useful.

Where the courses are for periods longer than six months, mid-vacation breaks are desirable. Block

Level Cooperative Officers Training Centres impart **training** of 11 months duration with a mid-vacation of **one month** and there is no reason why the Mukhya **Sevikas** whose case is entirely similar, should not enjoy **a brief** break of at least a fortnight.

Common Training And Composition Of Courses

Different workers in Community Development are **trained** in different centres with their own curriculum **and** atmosphere and yet they are required to work as **a team** in the field. Inevitable though this heterogeneity of training is, to some extent, in terms of the **different** levels of workers to be trained and the different techniques and special requirements of various posts it is still necessary to seek out fields or **possibilities** where some common training to different **operators** can be given in the interests of instilling team **spirit**. At the Xth course of the Central Institute, **Mussoorie**, two Block Development Officers—one from **Rajasthan** and one from U.P.—were called in for the **first** time to participate in the course for a period of **four** days; their presence has been so valuable in **bringing** a sense of realism to the discussions about **the** problems connected with the role of Block Development Officers in the field that one was retained for a **period** of three weeks and it has also been decided to **call** Block Development Officers for the future courses **for** a period of a fortnight. Similarly, at the Orientation and Study Centres, we feel that it would be of **considerable** advantage if selected Village Level **Workers** could be associated with the training in the **orientation** and study courses. In all the training **centres** visited, this idea found ready acceptance **among** the trainees as well as the staff. Different **methods** of association may be tried out, viz., for a **week**, fortnight or entire course.

Apart from Block Development Officers and **Extension** Officers; it is necessary to give a short **Course** of orientation training to overseers and block **level** medical officers on the one hand and supervisory **officers** like Deputy Collectors, District Level Officers **on the** other. The Block Development Officer trainees **at** Himayatsagar were, for instance, unanimous in the **view** that unless the supervisors were trained in the **methods** and objects of Community Development, they **would** not get sympathetic understanding and support **from** them. It is understood that the Madras State has **already** arranged for short training courses at Gandhi**gram** for this purpose. In Andhra Pradesh, it was **indicated** during the discussions with the development Commissioner that they were considering the conduct **of** such courses for Deputy Collectors, District Heads **and** Secretaries of Zila Parishads. The Development Commissioners, U.P., stated that the training of District Level and Sub-Divisional Officers was proposed to be entrusted to Zonal Officers. We would like to emphasise the need for organising such short courses in all the States, for the categories referred to above. In addition, selected officers may be sent to the O. & S.C. for the orientation and study Courses also; in Orientation courses different methods of association may be tried out as the case of Village Level Workers.

In the job course at the Orientation and Study Centre, Himayatsagar, it was found that Block Development Officers who had previously received Orientation training as Extension Officers had been required to go through this course again on promotion as Block Development Officers. Such cases should go direct for job training.

In the Social Education Organisers' Training Centre Bakshi-ka-Talab, Lucknow, out of 110 Social Education Organisers trained so far, 10 were post-graduates, 83 graduates, 73 intermediates and 10 matriculates; whilst of the 79 Mukhya Sevikas trained three were post-graduates, 26 graduates, 10 intermediates, and 26 matriculates. Such a wide range of educational background may have adverse effects on the standard of training; the problem deserves some attention.

Syllabus And Pattern Of Courses Orientation And Study Centre

Syllabus for Orientation Courses:

The conference of Principals of Orientation and Study Centres held from December 23, 1959 to December 24, 1959, suggested the following reduction in the number of talks:

	At Present	Proposed	Remarks
Preamble	5	1 or 2	
Cultural trends in Indian History	2	Nil	
Historical Growth of National Movement	2	Nil	Cover under part C of syllabus-genesis of C.D.
Postwar problems	1	Nil	
Principles and philosophy of extension	20	14	Group allied Subjects.
Team-work and administration coordination	7	4	
Evaluation	6	2 or 3	

The time thus saved was recommended to be used for covering the following topics under Panchayati Raj in eight or 10 talks :

(i) Growth and concept of democratic decentralisation.

(ii) Functional democracy.

(iii) Comparative study of Acts and Programmes.

(iv) Role of officials and non-officials.

The following topics were also recommended to be added to the Orientation Course :

(i) Growth of Community Development in India.

(ii) Achievement and weaknesses of Community Development in India.

The following further additions are suggested :

(a) "Relationship between the three tiers." "Functions of the three tier bodies".

(b) "Farm planning" may be added as item (ix) after II-c. 7 (viii).

(c) Principles and methods of supervision.

(d) The object of Community Development is to change the traditional way of living of the people but this has been dismissed off in one talk and the syllabus spreads itself out in six talks on generalities like rural psychology and basic urges of man and cultural trends in Indian history. It is suggested that the social aspects of rural society should be more adequately covered in at least three talks and realism imported to the teaching by the use of the following case studies in teaching :

(i) Mckim Marriot—"Village India" published by the Chicago University Press.

(ii) "India's Villages" published by Government of West Bengal.

(iii) S.C. Dube : "An Indian Village" and "India's changing villages" published by Rontledge and Kegan Paul. London.

(iv) Programme Evalution Organisations :

(a) Group dynamics and Northern Indian Villages.

(b) Leader and groups in other Indian Villages, and

(c) Reports of Bench Mark Surveys of different blocks.

(v) Agro Economic Research Centre Visva-Bharati : study of Villages Shahjapur.

The stage would then be set for an exposition of the way in which the Community Development Programme seeks to change the traditional, social and economic structures.

The conference has suggested a reduction in the number of talks on extension from 20 to 14, by grouping allied subjects. We would like to go further, as a fundamental issue is involved. The syllabus contemplates 20 separate talks on extension and 22 separate talks on the programme. It is perhaps this dichotomy that partly accounts for the criticism that the Orientation Course is overladen with theory. For what could be easier for an instructor than to give a theoretical exposition on the several aspects of the programme unconnected with practical ways of extending the programme or to enumerate extension methods unrelated to their applicability to particular aspects of the programme ? We feel that once an understanding of the village situation (17 talks) has been covered, the practical aspects of the programme and the extension approaches relevant thereto should be combined to impart realism to the teaching. It is a necessary corollary that such an approach should, as far as possible, be on the basis of the experience of the working of the different programme in the various States. Case histories, *e.g.* of Result Demonstrations and other successful and unsuccessful attempts made in implementing the programme to try out the several extension methods, media and techniques should provide adequate teaching material for this purpose. The study being conducted by the Central Institute on the role of the Village Level Worker and Result Demonstration will, when completed, be extremely useful. What little material exists even now should be used molleffectively, *e.g.* Dr. Dube's book on "India's Changing Villages" which gives an account of the relevance of the several approaches in the village context. It should also be possible for the Instructors taking Refresher Courses to build up more material on the subject.

On the basis of this approach the number of talks can without difficulty be reduced from 42 to about 30; it can be reduced further as soon as the text literature suggested else where in this report. On the other hand, as stated earlier, the syllabus requires to be strengthened in terms of the requirements of Panchayati Raj.

At every centre the trainees were critical about the duplication in the Orientation and job courses. That there is some duplication cannot be gainsaid. For instance, 22 talks are scheduled on the "programme" in the Orientation Course and 57 on the same subject in the job course. This raises the fundamental overhaul of the syllabus, a question which requires very careful consideration particularly as the syllabus was brought into force only in October 1958. As a preparatory step a small study group on the syllabus may be constituted in the Institute for Instruction, Rajpur under the guidance of the Central Institute to collect the reactions of Principals and trainees from all training centres and the observations of the Development Commissioners, Rajasthan and Andhra Pradesh and consider the data in consultation with selected Principals and a few experienced Block Development Officers;

it will then be possible for the team to check in the field the provisional conclusions of the study group during its second round of visits in July-August, (when it is hoped the team will be fully represented) and reach fairly firm conclusions on the subject.

As an essential preliminary to the work of the group we have already requested the Principals of the Orientation and Study Centre, Himayatsagar, Bakshi-Ka-Talab and Ranchi to prepare a short paper on the subject.

One aspect of the matter is important. Wherever it is proposed to appoint a Syllabus Committee for the Orientation and Study Centres it is essential that if should be a joint committee for all the three courses—Orientation, Job and Study. Only such a body can take an integrated view of the syllabus : it can always coopt members where special problems relating to particular courses have to be considered.

A problem still causing concern is the need for coordinated working and team spirit among all operators in the field. Though all training centres stress this aspect, and the syllabus carries it prominently, we feel that it does not go beyond the stage of intellectual understanding of the problems on the part of the trainees. It can become part of their living experience only if the different operators in the field live and work together during the training period. A common core of Orientation training is indicated for all categories of officials and non-officials from the District down to the village, but the large numbers involved and other administrative difficulties might stand in the way of the Training Centres becoming a forum for this purpose.

Already the Orientation Courses intended for Block level functionaries such as Block Development Officers. Social Education Organisers and Extension Officers have been thrown open to M.L.A.'s, Presidents of Panchayat/Block Samitis and Cooperative Unions. This process can be extended further by associating a few selected Village Level Workers in the courses just as selected Block Development Officers are now being associated at the Orientation Courses at the Central Institute ; little adjustments like this are possible and necessary but the problem will still remain. To test out the alternatives for the conduct of this training it is suggested that the Central Institute should arrange a seminar for four days or so of selected representatives from different levels—about 30 in all—from Collector, District Level Head, Deputy Collector, Block Development Officer, Extension Officer to Village Level Worker and from Pramukh to Sarpanch—to consider the problems of working together in planning and implementation of the Block Programme.

JOB COURSE, SYLLABUS

Job training must necessarily be conducted in the context of the practical job to be done on the ground and not in terms of theory of "how soils are formed" or the "contribution of different species of livestock". Yet 57 talks out of a total of 84, overladen with theory, are scheduled to cover the various facts of the programme. The theoretical and general aspects can well be taken care of by text literature and on this basis a group of allied subjects now involving two or more talks can, as suggested later, be combined and introduced by the speaker with reference to practical problems of the village situation.

The use of the overall time saved thereby must first be considered in the context of the requirements of Panchayati Raj. The Conference of Principals of Orientation and Study Centres held in December 1959 recommended that six to eight talks should be given on the following additional subjects :

"(a) Role of Civil Servants in Democracy.

(b) Relationship of the B.D.O. in the new set up with reference to Pradhan, Panchayati Samiti Member, Pramukh, Zila Parishads, Extension Staff, Village Health Staff, District Staff.

(c) Responsibilities of the B.D.O.—

(i) Administrative,

(ii) Executive including programme extension; and

(iii) Financial."

These headings are some what generalised and in addition omit important facets of work like the work programme. The following specific items are accordingly suggested :

(a) Principles of Public Administration,

(b) Role of Civil Servants in a Democracy.

(c) Organisation and Methods.

(d) Personnel Management.

(e) System of Panchayati Raj.

(f) Relationship of—

(i) B.D.O. and the three basic village institutions, B.D.O. and V.L.W.'s.

(ii) B.D.O. and E. Officers, B.D.O. and Distt. Level Officers, E.O.'s and District Level Officers. Pradhan and B.D.O. Pradhan, and other Staff, Pradhan Standing Committees and Samiti Members.

(iii) Pramukh and Pradhan, Collector and Distt. Level Officers, Collector and Zila Parishad, Collector or Dy. Collector and Panchayat Samiti.

(g) Principles and methods of supervision as distinct from inspection.

(h) Financial Rules, Local Fund Audit.

(i) Works Programme—Talks to be increased from three to six (Estimating, Measurements, Standards and specifications for the different works programme).

15 talks and discussion periods will be required to cover the specific items suggested and pending a review of the time schedule for class room work in the light of the reduced load resulting from the use of text literature, etc., it may be possible to find the time by making the following reductions in the number of talks in the existing syllabus :

Topic			Existing No. of talks	Proposed
B 2	...	...	12	9
B 3	...	...	4	3
B 6	...	...	6	4
B 7	...	...	8	6
B 9	...	...	5	0 (covered by additional subjects suggested)
B 10	...	...	5	3
			40	25

The programme of study tours for a week has not subserved the purpose. The general impression we got at all centres was that these tours have generally tended to become sight-seeing tours and that the staff are unable to resist pressure from the trainees to visit selected places of interest. The main objective of the study tours to clarify details and sharpen receptivity is more often than not overlooked.

Many Block Development Officers come with short experience in new blocks and the result is that their sensitivity to village problems is not sufficiently stimulated when they take the job course. Many tend to become passive participants and come to regard what is taught as the last word. We, therefore, feel that Block Development Officers should be attached to Blocks for at least one week before they come to the job course. Such attachment as it would be in selected Blocks outside their home States will be of considerable educational value. The study tour may then be restricted for three days to a visit to Rajasthan or Andhra Pradesh, as the case may be, till other States implement and gain experience as a glimpse of the working of Panchayati Raj as an essential part of the job course. A gap of about a week between the Orientation and the Job course will also give a little time to the staff to examine the various group reports on and reports on village practicals, seminars, etc., and prepare summaries for use during discussions in the Job and subsequent courses. In the words of the Principal, O. & S.C. Ranchi "at present the staff hardly gets any time to look at these reports and no useful purpose is served by them".

The role of the B.D.O. covers many aspects of administration, service rules, budget, accounts, office management, personnel management, etc., It is, therefore, essential that the job training should be conducted in the context of the rules and regulations prevailing in the States from which the trainees come. If, as suggested, a few States are earmarked to particular training centres, it could then be made incumbent on Instructors to familiarise themselves with the administrative and accounting procedures and practices in those States.

Study Course Syllabus

We had an opportunity of participating in the Second Study Course at the Orientation and Study Centre, Ranchi. The attendance, at the course was poor with only 15 trainees comprising of seven B.D.O.'s, five District Level Staff and three non-officials. A discussion was proceeding on the new role of Cooperatives, but it was rather general and we were doubtful about the impact of such a discussion in problem solving at the village end. A disquieting feature was that even though the Regional Cooperative Centre was located at Ranchi, no attempt was made to associate the Cooperative trainees in the Syndicate Study or discussion on Cooperatives. Though the syllabus rightly attempts "to strike a balance between discussion of the theoretical principles involved and the practical problems which arise in the implementation of the programme and the solution of such problems", the latter aspect was not much in evidence. The trainees freely stated that the course was academic and was of little "executive value". Their further criticisms were :

(a) The talks, for instance, on agriculture covered theory rather than programme aspects ,

(b) Instructors rather than executive officers in the field gave many of the talks ;

(c) There was continuing disparity between the approach as taught in the Training Centre and the actual methods of work in the field.

These difficulties are real. A concerted effort is necessary to ensure that this training is not regarded as a mere continuation of the training already given and that the course centres round the actual problems, difficulties and experience of the field workers. The following suggestions are made :

(a) The programme for the II Study Course at Ranchi contained as many as 27 talks in a course of 21 days two hours being taken up by two talks on many days. There is clearly need for cutting down the number of talks : merely because the various facets of the programme from one head among the eight heads of the syllabus, the tendency has been to cover each one of the facets by a talk with resultant overloading on the theory side. It is suggested that the talks be cut down 10 to 12 at the most.

(b) The talks should be given by outside lecturers of

standing working in the field.

(c) Last minute concellations which are too frequent, imposing a burden on Instructors unfamiliar with the field to give a talk for talk's sake should be avoided.

(d) To enable the trainees to face up to the realities of the field situations and to discuss their problem in terms of actual village conditions, the problems raised by them should be grouped under appropriate headings and experienced and successful field workers of similar or slightly higher status invited, not to deliver a talk, but to listen and to discuss.

(e) The course should not start straightaway with talks by outside speakers but with an exposition by each of the trainees of his problems for two days. From these problems should flow subjects of common interest for syndicate study. In these studies field workers may also be associated.

(f) The talk of the Development Commissioner should not centre round a general subject, but round a resume of points drawn from the first two days session on problems and from the syndicate studies.

As the study programme at the Training Centres under the guidance of the Central Institute makes head way, it will become relatively easy for the elucidation of the problems and proposed solutions to be kept very close to real village situations.

Supplementary Specialised Course, S.E.O.T.C. Ranchi ; Syllabus And Other Special Problems.

The syllabus has been changed thrice and it would appear that even the final syllabus is so elaborate, that the principal very correctly had to prune it down to actual field requirements, after making some additions to cover the several aspects of Panchayati Raj.

Against the capacity of 40, there were only 21 trainees in the XIIth Course of whom four were tribals ; six were working in tribal areas and six were living with families in tribal areas. In spite of the attraction for the plains, it is essential that Social Education Organisers should be kept for sufficiently long period in tribal areas so that, among others, they can learn the tribal languages. We found one curious instance of a trainee from Orissa State after specialised tribal training in the Centre was proposed to be transferred to a non-tribal area. This is wasteful in every sense. We suggest that State Governments should be requested to post the Social Education Organisers after training at Ranchi invariably to tribal areas. The tribal posts should be made sufficiently attractive either by way of special allowances or special promotion for good work. The scale of allowances if any at present given in the different States requires consideration.

It was stated by trainees that progress criteria were in many cases the same for both tribal and non-tribal areas. At our instance the Social Education Organisers' Training Centre has undertaken to work out reasonable targets or norms for tribal areas which will be further considered at a syndicate study in the Central Institute.

The similarity in progress criteria is perhaps also due to the fact that the Block Development Officer is not trained in tribal work and his approach is based on non-tribal experience. It is suggested that State Governments should be requested to prepare panels of names of Block Development Officers likely to be posted to tribal areas over the next year or so and such Block Development Officers should receive a short course of training along with Social Education Organisers in the Ranchi Centre. In the meantime, it should be possible to hold common seminars between the Orientation and Study Centre and the Social Education Organisers Training Centre so that understanding of tribal problems can be ensured on the part of Block Development Officer trainees.

Except in Assam where village level workers are generally tribals, tribal areas in other States are serviced by village level workers drawn from the plains. It is important that the latter should also get a short spell of specialised training at Ranchi, if the programme is to succeed with the tribals.

Training Methods

Orientation And Study Centre, Himayatsagar

The main emphasis is on talks—there were as many as four to five each day—followed, as the Principal says "by discussion wherever possible." The trainees are also "divided into convenient groups and they are allotted a subject for group discussion and for writing their report". There is also a library hour every day for enabling the trainees to study for themselves with the guidance of an instructor whenever necessary." "During the course of training, symposia seminars and discussions are held for ascertaining the opinions of the trainees and the members of the staff and for eliciting their suggestions for the improvement of the training programme." There is also an associate Instructor, a senior and experienced Block Development Officer deputed by the State Government to assist the staff and the trainees with his field experience in group discussions and in talks as well as village practicals."

Orientation And Study Centre, Bakshi-Ka-Talab Lucknow

The lecture hours cover daily six periods of 45 minutes each and the talks are followed by "questions and answers or group discussions". The Principal was aware, in his own words, that the "method of giving lectures contend more towards group discussion" and pointed out that this method was followed successfully in the study courses. There is also a programme of syndicate and guided studies at this centre, beside seminars and symposia. In a recent symposium the trainees of all the three training centres participated. Evaluation of training during each course is a regular feature.

Orientation And Study Centre, Ranchi

"...besides class room work, which consists and discussions, the training programme includes village practical work, study tours, seminars and symposia, group discussions and library work". According to the Orientation course syllabus, four talks are expected to be delivered each day for 27 days, and only one period is available for discussion each day.

Orientation And Study Centre, Nilokheri

The training programme covers three or four talks per day mostly by the staff and partly by visiting lecturers syndicate studies, symposia and seminars in Orientation courses and assignment discussion in job courses and problem discussions.

Social Education Organisers' Training Centre, Bakshi-Ka-Talab, Lucknow

Talks are covered by guest lecturers and staff members and "there is hardly any deviation from the prescribed syllabus." The system of preparing lesson plans for teaching a given topic has been adopted and where this is not possible the staff maintain their own synoptic notes and bibliography. The Director stated that "discussions to involve the trainees for effective learning experience was being increasingly adopted." However, our observation of the discussion of the problem of organisation of an educational exhibition has not very encouraging: it was more a process of arguing back and forth rather than a group discussion. "Group studies are generally conducted during village camps....No other type of syndicate studies have been conducted so far." The trainees take part in seminars organised by other agencies and also participate in a weekly symposium. An evaluation of the training by the trainees is done at the close of each course.

Social Education Organisers' Training Centre, Ranchi

The programme consists of theory lectures by the staff on social Anthropology, Tribal Cultures of India, Applied Anthropology and Tribal Welfare Social Psychology; extension talks by outside experts; discussion classes and study circles twice a week at which trainees meet their Instructors in small groups and discuss various problems and difficulties arising from their study or class lectures; supervised study four times a week; MCD publication class once a week and field work. There is no course evaluation at the end of each course.

Social Education Organisers' Training Centre Sriniketan.

The training methods consist of "straight talks followed by questions and answers," "discussion on case studies," seminars, panel discussions, reference study, library work, etc. Synoptic notes are not given to the trainees, but instead monographs prepared by the staff on selected subjects have been placed in the library. The system of lesson plans has not been adopted, as it tends to make the instructions rigid. "Informal discussions between the trainees and staff are held towards the end of the course to collect their reactions on the training programme." "A winding up staff meeting is held after the trainees have left when the outgoing course is discussed threadbare."

Social Education Organisers' Training Centre, Belurmath.

Apart from talks and group discussions, there are tutorial classes, seminars, supply of selected bibliography, and reading from core books, followed by discussion. An evaluation of the course is done both during midterm and at the end.

By and large most of the centres are following the straight lecture method and we hardly noticed any lively interchange between the lecture and the class. At many centres trainees themselves complained of too many talks, lack of time for discussion, theory laden classes over comprehensive job syllabus somewhat unrelated to their field requirements and a great deal of regimentation allowing them little time for study or reflection.

There are several directions in which improvements are possible :

(a) The core of the syllabus does not vary in coverage from course to course. The problem of too many talks per day, sometimes four to five can be mitigated if on such core subjects, text literature is prepared by various specialists. The Institute for Instruction, Rajpur can prepare synopsis for various subjects and send them to the Central Institute for getting standard texts prepared by different authorities on the subject. The text literature can then be tested out at selected centres with reference to the receptivity of the trainees and thereafter the material can be arranged to be edited by the Central Institute. It is a matter of satisfaction that already both the Social Education Organisers' Training Centre, Sriniketan and Belurmath were using either monographs or core books with good results. Standard text literature prepared on these lines will ensure :

(i) Uniformity in all Training Centres, in the imparting of basic knowledge relating to Community Development.

(ii) Large reduction in the number of talks and increased time for real discussion. A group of allied subjects now involving two or more talks could then be introduced by the speaker in 15 to 20 minutes with particular reference to the problems posed by the subject in the village context, and the next half hour or so can be taken up for discussion. The experience of the Central Institute in respect of the new feature on individual papers introduced in the IXth course shows how lively the interchange between the class and the speaker can be on this basis.

(b) Nowhere was the Syndicate method of study properly developed and there was lack of understanding of its essential components—mode of selecting subjects, formulation of outlines, preparation of draft reports, consideration by groups, etc. It is suggested that the Central Institute should circulate to all Training Centres a paper on the subject.

(c) Assignment and problem discussion was an interesting innovation at Nilokheri, worthy of adoption elsewhere. The basic problem is of course how to keep the discussion close to the real village situations. Suggestions to this end have been made elsewhere in the report.

(d) One experienced B.D.O. from Andhra Pradesh and one from Rajasthan may be invited for short periods to participate in the different courses to give a realistic insight into the problems of Panchayati Raj. The Principal, Orientation and Study Centre, Ranchi has rightly pointed out that through "the change in the administrative set up as a result of the introduction of democratic decentralisation is now thrown open for discussion, the discussion remains confined only to the broad general aspects of the system" for lack of participants from Rajasthan or Andhra Pradesh.

(e) There is no evaluation of the course in some centres whilst in others, it is only held at the end of the course. It is suggested that there should be two evaluations—one during mid-term and one at the end of the course.

(f) A winding up staff meeting after the trainees have left such as is held at Sriniketan is worthy of adoption in all Training Centres.

(g) These suggestions together with the local committees and study circle of staff members recommended earlier will, it is hoped, help to tone up the present programme; the institutional arrangements suggested will provide continuing raw material for the State Level Coordination Committee for making further improvements to the quality of training.

Problems Of Trainees During And After Training

Though there is a great deal of contact between trainees and instructors in the daily routine of the training centre, the trainees at the several centres correctly desire to have more opportunities for informal contacts with the staff. Such contacts assist in the building up of right attitudes. The Principal of the Orientation and Study Centre, Bakshi-Ka-Talab has gone some way to meet this need by allowing maximum freedom to the trainees to manage their own affairs, holding tournaments and sports competitions in which members of the staff participate and occasionally inviting the trainees in groups to his residence for tea and informal conversation. At Sriniketan trainees are divided into groups and each group allotted to a staff member who meet the groups at regular intervals. It has been the experience that these contacts outside the class room encourage trainees to come out more frankly with their problems than they normally do even in group discussions. It is understood that in the Administrative Training School, Ranchi, an allowance has been granted to the Principal to meet the expenditure involved in such informal contacts. It is suggested that a sum of Rs. 50 p.m. or a lump sum Rs 600 per year be kept at the disposal of the Principal as sumptuary allowance to meet such expenditure.

The trainees of the Mukhya Sevikas' Training Centre, Sriniketan complained about the uneven pay and training allowance given to them during the period of training. The picture as presented by the trainees was as shown on page 14.

The standard of expenditure at the training centres being the same, uneven training allowances, in particular, create hardship and a sense of unequal treatment and thereby affect the receptivity of the trainees.

We also observed considerable delays in the payment of salaries and training allowances to the trainees during the period of their training. It is suggested that the Directors/Principals should be made responsible for disbursing the amount from a special fund, recoveries from the State Government being credited to it from time to time.

The morale of the trainees requires to be maintained at a high level during the training period and these disparities and delays deserve urgent consideration.

At the S.E.O.T.C., Sriniketan and Belurmath we noticed the absence of any proper relationship between the centre and the State Directorate of Education. As the S.E.O. is on the Education Cadre in West Bengal, the need for contact between the Directorate and the Training Centre is obvious.

Post training problems in S.E.O.T.C., Ranchi.

Teaching Staff

The absence of educational facilities in the Himayatnagar and Bakshi-Ka-Talab and other campuses is causing great concern to the staff members. It is understood that transport facilities have been provided free for school going children of staff members at the E.T.C., Himayatsagar. A similar concession should be extended to all training centres.

The academic qualifications of the staff at the S.E.O.T.C., Bakshi-Ka-Talab leave much to be desired. We observed that there was not a single member of the staff who had academic training in Sociology and social Welfare. The need for these qualifications in filling up existing vacancies requires to be kept in view.

Staff members should have sufficient time for extra curricular professional activities for the purpose of improving the content of teaching and teaching methods, and attending to the study programme. This has been dealt with more fully elsewhere in the report.

Systematic arrangements are necessary for interchange of staff between the training centre and the field.

In the study courses Principals of Orientation and Study Centres have been charged with the responsibility of training District Level Officers. The Centres have also been thrown open to M.L.A.'s. In this context, the junior status of many of the Principals is becoming a handicap. It is suggested that the status be raised and a line of promotion established between Principals and prospective Deputy Development Commissioners to be placed incharge of training. We came across an instance of this kind in Andhra Pradesh. The procedure requires to be systematised in all the States.

The staff of the Regional Cooperative Training Centres and Health Training Centres do not come for training to the Institute for Instruction, Rajpur. It is desirable that these categories are also drawn into

State	Deptt. from which the trainees were deputed	Qualifications	Basic Pay	Training allowance
Bihar	1. Development Deptt.	All qualifications covered	100	20 per cent of the basic pay
	2. C.S.W.B.			No pay 75 lump sum.
West Bengal	1. Development Deptt.	Matriculate	80	50
		Graduate	100	50
	2. C.S.W.B.			Only Rs. 75 lump sum as stipend.
Assam	1. Development Deptt.	Matriculate	80	50
		Graduate	125	50
	2. C.S.W.B.		115	Nil
	(If they were not in the job in advance only Rs. 75 paid as training allowance).			
Madhya Pradesh	1. Development Deptt.	Matriculate	75	Nil
		Graduate	110	50
	2. C.S.W.B.		75	—

It was also reported that some of those deputed by the CSWB had to forego their salaries during the training, if they were in position earlier and got only Rs. 75 as training allowance.

The position of S.E.O. trainees in the SEOTC, Belurmath was similar as the following table will show :

State	Qualifications	Basic Salary	Training allowance
		Rs.	
Orissa	Under-graduate	82 to 140	Nil
	Graduate	120 to 250	Nil
West Bengal	Under-graduate	82 to 180	50
	Graduate	100 to 225	50
Bombay	Irrespective of qualifications	70 to 200	50
Bihar	Do	100 to 190	20 per cent of basic pay.
Manipur	Do	100 to 150	No training allowance.

the training programme for Instructors.

It is desirable that Principals/Directors, Orientation and Study Centres and S.E.O.T.C.'s should attend the Orientation Courses at the Central Institute. A systematic programme for this purpose may be drawn up. It is particularly important that officers without field experience who have been appointed as Principals should participate in the course as a matter of urgency.

Follow-up tours important as they are, for contact with post trainees and for assessing the value of the training, are no less important for giving an opportunity to the staff to keep in touch with the field, draw materials for case illustrations and thereby improve the quality of training. Such tours are not planned properly but only sporadically undertaken as a roving mission in many centres : the arrangement for study tours would appear to be completely absent in the Regional Cooperative Training Centre and Extension Training Centres. It is hoped that the proposed Advisory Boards/Local Committees will coordinate and assist in the drawing up of an annual programme for the purpose. It is recommended, only a few States feed a Training Centre; there can be no objection to the staff undertaking follow-up tours in all these States.

It was particularly observed in Sriniketan that the Centre had undertaken additional courses of short duration during the last six months on behalf of the Ministry of Food and Agriculture, Ministry of Community Development and the State Government. Already the programme of training for S.E.O.'s and Mukhya Sevikas is run in quick succession and it must be ensured that by undertaking additional courses, the burden on the staff does not result in lowering the standard of training for the main categories. Uncoordinated framing out of courses by different authorities should therefore be avoided and one Central authority whether the Ministry or the State Government (State Level Training Committee) made responsible for this work.

Touch With Field Conditions and Development Trends Realism in Training

Except at Bakshi-ka-Talab and Sriniketan, there was no established relationship between the Training Centre and the adjoining block. At our instance the subject was included in the agenda of the conference of Principals of Orientation and Study Centres held from December 23 to 24, 1959, and the following conclusions were reached :

(i) "The Ministry of Community Development may address the State Governments to attach a block to each S.E.O.T.C. This Block will be selected by the Principals and the State Development Authorities in mutual consulation.

(ii) The Block Development Officer of the attached Block should work as a part-time staff-member in the O. & S.C. His responsibility will be to give talks off and on to the trainees and also to assist the O. & S.C. staff in the conduct of the field programme. Taking all factors into consideration, an honorarium of Rs. 75 per month is recommended for the B.D.O. for these additional duties.

(iii) Some funds should be placed at the disposal of the Principal to enable him to carry out certain projects in the Block area in consultation with the Block Authorities.

(iv) The Principal should be a member of the Block Development Samiti/Panchayati Samiti. This will enable him to have an intimate knowledge of the development programmes being chalked out for the Block."

It is suggested that these recommendations should be given high priority and implemented without undue delay. At Sriniketan the Director is already a member of the Advisory Committee of the local Block.

At Bakshi-ka-Talab the Officer-in-charge of the Extension Training Centre is in "superior charge" of the attached Block and, as institutional relationship between this centre and the other training centres is already on a fairly sound basis, all the training centres have had freedom to carry out ideas, experiments and studies in the villages with the help of the Extension staff. The women's programme constituted the main-field in this regard, but it is considered that in the villages around the training centres at least one model service cooperative should be organised. Some of these experimental activities require support to be followed through and some financial provision is required for the purpose, whether from the Block budget or otherwise.

The S.E.O.T.C. Sriniketan has gone a step further and is following a system of deputing its staff members to the Block for a period of three months by rotation to work as additional S.E.O. incharge of one V.L.W. circle. The staffs member in placed under the administrative control of the B.D.O. during this period and is given an additional allowance of Rs. 100 per month. The system is a commendable one and it is suggested that all staff members of training centres who have had no field experience whatever or those working continuously as Instructors for more than three years should be deputed to Blocks to work in their respective fields on lines similar to those now in force at Sriniketan.

A number of other staff managements are also possible for ensuring touch with field conditions :

(a) As far as possible departmental officers may be recruited as Instructors, direct recruitment being resorted to wherever necessary only for such specialised fields as rural sociology, research methodology, etc.

(b) Generally, no Instructor should remain in a Training Centre for more than five years, after this he should ordinarily go back to the field. In exceptional cases Block attachment for a period of three months, may be ensured before he returns to teaching.

(c) Even during his tenure as Instructor for three to five years, a Instructor should be attached to a Block every year for a fortnight subject to a three months attachment whenever necessary as suggested above.

Staff members particularly of the Orientation and Study Centres even though borne on the cadres of the State in which the Training Centre is located do not have any connection with their own departments. It is essential that they should be treated as and integral part of their parent department and supplied with copies of all circulars, etc., issued by them. In particular, they should be invited to attend important departmental meetings connected with the programme.

A live relationship with the office of the Development Commissioner is fundamental, but this was nowhere the case. The position will be remedied to some extent when the proposed Advisory Boards/Local Committees are set up. It is however, necessary to go further. Touch with development trends will not be possible through sporadic receipt of circulars from the Development Commissioner's Office : it can be achieved only if the Principals are regularly invited to attend the Coordination Meetings held by the Developments Commissioner with the Heads of Departments and Secretaries to Goveronment. Mere membership on the State Committee on Training will not also serve the purpose.

The study programme for Training Centres has already been generally approved. It will not, however be possible to make any headway with the programme unless the following consequential requirements are ensured :

(a) At our instance it has already been agreed that the number of courses at Orientation and Study Centres should be reduced and that an instructor should have at least two days in a week completely free for field work and two free months in the year for analysis and processing of data. It is hoped that the Ministry have issued orders on the adjustment and reduction of workload to give the study programme a fair start.

(b) The establishment of study wings at the Orientation and Study Centres and selected Social Education Organisers' Training Centres for which complete proposals have been sent by the Central Institute together with the early recruitment of staff is another *sine qua non*.

(c) The importance of the study programme is so obvious from the point of view to building up a body of knowledge for improving the training programme and creating research attitudes and experience among the staff and the trainees that the highest priority has to be given to all aspects of this work. Only thus can case studies be built up to provide "the kind of village material round which teaching and discussion should be planned to give it a realistic and not an idealistic lant".

RECOMMENDATIONS OF:

Second High Level Team

Decisions On Recommendations Made In The First Report Of The High Level Team on Trainings.

Reorganisation of State Local Coordination Committee On Training And Formation Of Level Committee Or Advisory Boad For Each O. and S.C.

Managing Boards have been chnstituted for each centre.

Allotment Of Seats.

Managings Board have been assigned this work.

Separate Committee For Other Training Centres

Accepted for S.E.O.T.C's.

Coordination Committee Of Principals/Directors For Centres In A Campus

Accepted and being implemented.

Study Circle of Staff Members

Accepted and being implemented.

One Principal For All Centres In A Campus

Not considered practicable.

Community Life In A Campus And Combining Teaching Staff For Common Core Of Subjects.

Campus coordination committees will be asked to examine how for these can be implemented.

Under Use Of Training Capacity

Managing Boards have been asked to look into this.

Specific States To Be Attached To Each Training Centre

Accepted and being implemented.

Allotment Of Seats To Participating States And Utilisation

Managing Boards have been made responsible for this.

Creating And Environment An Atmosphere In Keeping With The Training

Accepted and being implemented.

Purport Of Practicals

Accepted and being implemented.

Arrangement Of Daily Programme

Accepted.

Trainees Should Manage Their Own Affairs

Panchayats at Centre will take care of this.

Staff And Trainees To Mix Freely

Accepted and being implemented.

Mid-Vacation Breaks In Courses Longer Than Six Months

Accepted and being implemented.

Association Of Selected VLW's In Orientation And Study Centres

Accepted and being implemented.

Short Course Of Orientation Training To Overseas, Block Level Medical Officers, Deputy Collectors, District Level Officers

State Governments may arrange short courses for these personnel.

B.D.O.'s Who Have Received Orientation Training Not Required To Undergo Further Orientation Training On Promotion As B.D.O.'s

State Governments informed accordingly.

Wide range Of Educational Background Of Trainees

A Committee has been appointed to look into this.

Syllabus For Orientation Course

Study Group was appointed as recommended. A revised syllabus has been drawn up.

Syllabus Committees

This will be kept in view.

Coordinated Work And Team Spirit Among All Operators In The Field

This has been recommended to State Governments.

Syllabus For Job Training For B.D.O.'s

Revised syllabus has been drawn up.

Additional Talks On Panchayati Raj

Included in the revised syllabus.

Study Tours

Accepted. Instructions issues to centres.

Attachment Of B.D.O.'s To Blocks Prior To Job Course

10 days' Block attachment agreed.

Study Tour To Rajasthan And Andhra Pradesh

Not accepted.

Block Placement Prior To Job Training Course

Accepted and will be followed.

Job Training Should Be Conducted In The Context Of Rules And Regulations Prevailing In The States

Only a comparative picture of rules and regulations can be attempted and not detailed instructions.

Study Courses

Accepted and being implemented.

S.E.O.'s In Tribal Areas

The State Governments have been addressed.

B.D.O.'s should Receive Short Courses Training Along With S.E.O.'s In Ranchi

Accepted and details will be worked out.

Reduction In The Number of Talks One Third For Talks And Two Thirds For Discussions, Preparations Of Core Literature

Accepted. Institute for instruction on Community Development working on it.

Syndicate Method Of Study

Central Institute has circulated a note to Orientation and Study Centres.

Assignment of Problem Discussion

Being done.

Experienced B.D.O.'s From Rajasthan And Andhra Pradesh To Participate In Courses

Not necessary as problems differ from State to State.

Evaluation of Course

Accepted and being implemented.

Staff Meeting At The End Of The Course

Being implemented.

Sumptuary Allowance To Principal

Not accepted by Finance.

Delays In Payment Of Salaries And Allowances To Trainees

Being processed.

Need For Contacts With The State Directorate Of Education

Managing Boards will help achieve this.

Transport Facilities

Being examined.

Academic Qualifications Of Staff Of SEOTC, Bakshi-ka-Talab

Being examined.

Time For Extra Curricular Activity Of Staff Members

Accepted.

Interchange Of Staff Between The Training Centre And Field

Being implemented.

Raising The Status Of Principal

Not accepted.

Training of Staff of Regional Cooperative Training Centres And Health Training Centres At The Institute For Instruction On C.D., Rajpur

This has been taken up with concerned Ministries.

Participation Of Principals/Directors In Orientation Course at the Central Institute, Mussoorie

Accepted and being implemented.

Follows-up Tours

Managing Boards are looking into this.

Forming Of Courses

Managing Boards attend to this.

Relationship of Training Centre With Adjoining Block

Accepted and instructions issued.

Field Experienced For Staff; Attachment To Blocks For Three Months

Accepted and being implemented.

Staffing Of Training Centres

(a) As far as possible departmental officers should be recruited as instructors; (b) Generally no instructor should remain in a training centre for more than five years; (c) Even during his tenure as instructor for three to fieve years he should be attached to a Block elsewhere for a fortnight subject to three months attachment whenever necessary.

Accepted and being implemented.

Staff Members Should Be Invited To Attend Important Departmental Meetings Of the State

Development Commissioners have been requested accordingly.

Alive Relationship With The Office Of The Development Commissioner

Development Commissioner is the Chairman of Managing Board.

Study Programme

Accepted. Three months break provided in annual programme, weekly break is a local adjustment by Principal.

Recruitment Of Staff For Study Wings

Being recruited.

PANEL ON DELHI SCHOOL BUILDINGS, 1960—REPORT

New Delhi, Committee on Plan Projects, Planning Commission, 1969 19p., Maps & Charts.

Chairman : Shri V.R. Vaish.
Members : Shri J.P.J. Billimoria; Shri B.D. Bhatt; Shri B.L. Chadha; Shri T.S. Vedagiri.
Secretary : Shri Jagdish Singh.

APPOINTMENT

The Committee on Plan Projects, Panel on Delhi School Buildings was constituted under the Planning Commission in 1960.

TERMS OF REFERENCE

(i) Rationalising the area requirements per place so as to bring about economies without sacrificing functional efficiency.

(ii) Planning of requirements in such a way so as to get a high degree of design efficiency by restricting to the minimum the ancillary and circulation space.

(iii) Laying down norms for structural designs and specifications so as to bring about an effective balance between the structure and its functions.

CONTENTS

The Problem; Requirements of Space; Planning and Layout; Design and Specifications; Effect of Recommendations; Appendices I to IV.

RECOMMENDATIONS

Requirements of Space

The Changing Pattern Of Education

Rapid changes have taken place in designs and fashions in various sectors of ourlives and we have adopted ourselves to these. Few people, however, realise that there has been a revolution in the ideas and practice of education since after the First War and more so after the Second War. In India the post-Independence era is marked by two significant changes—acceptance of Basic education as a national pattern of primary education and the new structure of higher secondary education. Basic education is a departure from the traditional approach to class room teaching. Similarly, the emphasis in secondary education is on diversified courses and progressive methods of teaching. Those concerned with the designing of school buildings have, therefore, to take note of the changing needs of children for whom the schools are built. The Secondary Education Commission have stated, for example :

"Any design must, therefore, take note of this possibility of expansion as well as of the variety of courses that may be provided. It should be necessary to provide for workshops, for certain laboratories, certain special rooms for drawing, painting or music, etc., and it is desirable that any design for a school building should take these into consideration and so adjust the design that, in course of time, without much change of the original building, such additional accommodation may be provided."

The educational administrators usually ask for additional accommodation when new activities or subjects are added to the existing curriculum. A multipurpose use of the existing space is seldom thought of which, however, is closely linked with the type of school furniture being used. The traditional two-seated or multiple-seated desk has been discarded elsewhere since it is not conducive to the development of correct posture besides being cumbersome. There is an urgent need for evolving suitable designs of easily portable and stackable class room furniture. Investigations are already in progress in this field and will be dealt with in a subsequent report. The present report deals mainly with the building of a typical higher secondary school including furniture and other major fittings in science laboratories.

The Higher Secondary School

A Higher Secondary School in Delhi normally has six classes, three in the middle department (sixth, seventh and eighth) and three in the higher secondary department (9th, 10th and 11th). Each class has two or three sections. Usually, each section has a maximum strength of about 40 students. An average school has on roll approximately 650 students, in 16 sections, distributed as follows :

Three sections each in classes VI, VII, VIII and IX.	...	12
Two sections each in classes X and XI	...	4
		16

In a bigger school with an enrolment of 1000, the distribution of sections will be :

Five sections each in classes VI, VII and VIII	...	15
Four sections in class IX	...	4
Three Sections each in classes X and XI	...	6
		25

Class Rooms

A class room should, therefore, be adequate to accommodate 40 students seated on dual desks of size two ft. nine in.×three ft. six in. (being supplied by the Education Department at present). It was estimated that an area of 400 sq. ft. (37.2 sq. m.) would be sufficient for the purpose. However, the sanctioned strength of 40 is sometimes exceeded by a couple of students under pressure of heavy enrolment. Besides according to the standing regulations of the Board of Higher Secondary Education, Delhi, a minimum area of 480 sq. ft. (44.6 sq. in) is prescribed for a class room to accommodate 40 students. The Panel has, therefore, accepted this area for a class room for the present.

In addition to class rooms, a few other rooms are required for elective subjects. The size of these rooms will not be as big as the main class rooms since the number of students occupying these rooms at a time is not expected to be more than 20 or 25. The possibility of utilising the class rooms themselves for some of the elective subjects was also considered. On these considerations the Panel has come to certain conclusions regarding the number and size of class rooms to be provided in different types of schools, which are scheduled below.

(i) For 650-Pupil School

Total number of class rooms	...	22 (19 measuring 24′×20′ each, one measuring 2′0×20′ and two measuring 16′×20′ each).

These may be distributed as follows :

Class Rooms	...	16 (one for each section).
Art Room	...	1
Science Theory Room	...	1
History and Geography Room	...	1
Commerce Room	...	1
Craft Room	...	1
Activities Room	...	1

(ii) For 1000-Pupil School

Total number of class rooms	...	32 (29 measuring 24′×20′ each, one measuring 02′×20′ and two measuring 16′×20′ each).

The distribution may be :

Class Rooms	...	25 (one for each section)
Art Room	...	1
Science Theory Room	...	1
History & Geography Room	...	1
Commerce Room	...	1
Other Optional subjects	...	1
Craft Room	...	1
Activities Room	...	1

Laboratories

Normally not more than 24 students use the Physics and Chemistry laboratories for practicals. In Biology the enrolment is much less in a boys' school but in a girls' school the number of students taking this subject may exceed the number of those taking Physics and Chemistry. For Domestic Science, however, the position is different. All the girls in a section may have taken up this subject and may be expected to do practical work at one and the same time. These factors have, therefore, to be taken into account in determining the lay-out and specifications of each laboratory.

Studies conducted in a few representative schools revealed variations in the dimensions of laboratories as well as in the arrangement of furniture and fittings. It is thus clear that sufficient thought was not given to the planning of laboratories. In many cases provision was not made for the satisfactory conveyance of the service lines that are necessary in a laboratory. No provision was made for special facilities such as fuming cup-boards. On the whole a laboratory, even in the case of newly completed schools, had a number of improvisations which are not conducive to smooth and efficient working.

The planning of facilities within the laboratory naturally depends upon the type of work that is to be done in it. A satisfactory lay-out cannot, therefore be prepared unless a detailed study of the work within the laboratories is carried out. The Panel gave a lot of attention to this point and evolved a number of lay-out plans for the different laboratories in a school. These were discussed in detail in the Panel meetings as well as with school teachers and other educationalists.

The Panel considers that an area of 30 sq. ft. (2.8 sq. m.) per student would be adequate to meet the normal requirements of Physics and Chemistry laboratories. An area of 30 ft. × 24 ft. = 720 sq. ft. (66.9 sq. m.) should be more than adequate for these laboratories. The dimensions of these two laboratories in the proposed lay-out have been kept at 36 ft. × 20 ft. = 720 sq. ft. (66.9 sq. m.) to secure proper arrangement of laboratory tables and other fittings. In addition to this a store of 16 ft. × 10 ft. = 160 sq. ft. (14.9 sq. m.) has also been provided. The Biology laboratory measuring 32 ft. × 20 ft. = 640 sq. ft. (59.5 sq. m.) however, is slightly smaller as the number of students who take up Biology is less. The attached store of 16 ft. × 10 ft. = 160 sq. ft. (14.9 sq. m.) may be divided into two portions, one of which may be earmarked for installation of the gas plant with a niche provided for a fire extinguisher on the verandah side wall. In case a larger number of girl students take Biology, it is possible to interchange Biology with Physics Chemistry laboratories. Regarding Domestic Science the Panel considered that room measuring 32ft. × 22.5ft. = 720 sq. ft. (66.9 sq. m.) with an attached store of 160 sq. ft. (14.9 sq. m.), should be sufficient. If considered necessary, one of the rooms earmarked for elective subjects may be utilised as an additional room for Domestic Science.

Hall, Library And Staff Room

In most of the schools studied by the Panel, a hall having an area of 3,000 to 3,500 sq. ft. (279 to 325 sq. m. had been provided. It is mainly used for morning prayers and for some other occasional gatherings. The use co-efficient of this hall varies from 15 to 35 minutes per day. This does not warrant an expenditure of Rs. 30,000 to Rs, 35,000. The Panel, therefore, considered that it would be better to plan for a multi-purpose hall which can be put to other uses also.

Considering the other requirements of Higher Secondary Schools, such as library, staff room, etc. the Panel thought it would be ideal to utilise a portion of the hall as library and another portion as staff room with adjustable partitions in between. However, in a school with a capacity of 1,000 students an additional staff room measuring 16 ft. × 20 ft = 320 sq. ft. (29.7 sq. m.) may be provided on the second floor. Further, the educational authorities desired that provision should be made for audio-visual education. The stage portion of the hall can be profitably utilised for this purpose. The Panel decided that the hall should be so planned that there should be some class rooms adjacent to it which can be used as green rooms whenever necessary.

The dimensions of the hall for different types of schools are listed below :

Approximate Enrolment of Students	*Dimensions*	*Area (sq. ft.)*	*Remarks*
650	60′ × 30′ or 64′ × 30′	1800 or 1920 (167 or 178 sq. m.)	This includes the stage portion measuring 32′ × 20′ = 640 sq. ft. to be used for audio-visual purposes. The remaining portion of the hall will be divided into two sections are to be used as library measuring 32′ × 22-1/2′ = 720 sq. ft and the other as staff room measuring 32′ × 16-1/2′ 560 sq. ft. (52 sq. m.)
1000	64′ × 30′ + 32′ × 22-1/2′ Balcony	1920 + 720 = 2640 (245 sq. m.)	—Do—

Principal's And Clerk's Office

A Principal's office in a school is used by the Head of the institution for administrative purposes, for meeting the parents and for holding meetings. A room measuring over 300 sq. ft. (27.9 sq. m.) is usually provided as the Principal's Office with a separate Clerk's office of an area of about 500 sq ft. (46 4 sq. m.). The dimensions appear to be very much on the high side. It may be of interest to note that an area of 150 sq. ft. (13.9 sq. m.) is laid down in the V.K. for such an office. It has, therefore, been agreed that a single room measuring 20 ft. × 16 ft. = 320 sq. ft. (29.7 sq. m.), partitioned into two sections, may be provided, one portion of which may serve as the office of the Principal and the other as the Clerk's office and record room. Staff meetings may more conveniently be held in the staff room, which will further result in administrative convenience and saving on furniture.

Additional Accommodation

Keeping in view the expanding activities of a higher secondary school two additional rooms for various types of activities like Scouting (Girl Guiding), NCC, Red Cross, Crafts, etc., have been provided as per dimentions given below:

(i) Activities Room ... 20ft.×20ft.=400 sq. ft. (37.2 sq. m)

(ii) Craft Room ... 24ft.×20ft.=480 sq. ft. (44.6 sq. m)

Ancillary Accommodation

The following provisions have been suggested:

(i) **Genreal Stores**: Two (one on each floor in a =650 pupil school and three (one on each floor) in a 1,000 pupil school, each measuring 20 ft.×8 ft.=160 sq. ft. (14.9 sq. m.)

(ii) **Tuck Shop**: Wherever possible a tuck shop of size 16 ft.×12 ft may be provided near the main building and away from the compound wall so as to prevent its access to public.

(iii) **Water Rooms**: Located centrally on each flour, four water rooms in a school of two-storeyed building and six water rooms in a school of three storeyed building.

(iv) **Class IV Quarters**: The quarters, one for the sweeper and the other for chawkidar may be provided within the school compound at the back side. The areas of these quarters shall be according to the scale prescribed for class IV staff.

(v) **Sanitary Block**: WC's may be of squatting type. The floor of lavatory block on the first floor may be depressed by two ft. The roof of WC's. also may be similarly depressed so that storage tanks can be screened off from view. The urinals should be of the lipped type and, as an experimental measure, a stall type urinal with terrazo finish may be tried. It is preferable to have automatic flushing arrangements for urinals. The number of WC's and urinals may be as follows:

Enrolment	*No. of WC's*	*No. of Urinals*
(Boy's School)		
650	16	32
1000	24	48
(Girls' School)		
650	24	...
1000	40	...

A separate sanitory blocks may be provided for the staff.

Planning And Lay-Out

General Lay-Out

In the preceding chapter the Panel has considered the requirements of space and has laid down certain standards regarding the same. This would lead to sufficient reduction in expenditure, but for achieving efficiency in performance, it is necessary to consider in detail the planning and lay-out of various facilities. The efficiency of performance depends, to a large extent, on the proper juxtaposition of the various facilities and the correct sequence of their arrangements.

It is also a moot point to consider whether schools should be based on corridor or verandah pattern. The former would be economical from the point of view of space utilisation as circulation space in that case would be much less than in the latter. But from the point of view of lighting and ventilation, the verandah pattern would be more advantageous. The Panel would, therefore, recommend mainly this pattern for school building but with a view to achieving economy in space, short lengths of corridor can be interposed.

A number of lay-out diagrams based on the requirements as decided by the Panel were prepared and discussed. Two of the typical lay-outs are given in Appendix II. It is not the intention of the Panel to standardise the lay-out diagrams. The plans given in the Appendix represent only two of the solutions to the problem. Many more solutions are possible depending upon the individuality of the architect. The plans, therefore, should be taken as broadly indicative of the suggested arrangements of the various facilities in a school. The two plans have been conceived in such a way that they should be capable of adoption either for a girls' school or for a boys' school with a capacity of 650 or 1,000 students.

Both the plans envisage 2-storeyed construction for a strength of 650 and 3-storeyed construction for a strength of 1,000 students. This is inevitable due to pressure on land in a rapidly developing metropolis. In rural areas, however, where the pressure on land is not much, it is not necessary to go in for 2 or 3-storeyed construction. A single-storey lay-out in that case is desirable.

Design Efficiency

The total built up area of any school can be broken into following four categories:

(a) Area of teaching accommodation.

(b) Administration area which will include Principal's room, office, general store and staff room.

(c) Circulation and ancillary area which will include both horizontal and vertical area, toilet block, etc.

(d) Thickness of walls, columns, etc.

Leaving item (d) the rest constitute the floor area of the building which can be broadly divided into teaching and non-teaching accommodation. The break-up of teaching and non-teaching accommodation for the two lay-outs suggested by the Panel is given below :

Accommodation In Percentages

	Plate I		*Plate II (Alternative lay-out)*	
	Girls' School	*Boys' School*	*Girls' School*	*Boys' School*
Instructional	57.7%	56.1%	60.90%	59.5%
Administrative	6.2%	6.5%	6 0 %	6.2%
Circulation and Ancillary	36.1%	37.4%	33.1 %	34.3%

Area Per Student (In. Sq. Ft.)

	Plate I		*Plate II*	
	Girls' School	*Boys' School*	*Girls' School*	*Boys' School*
Instructional	22.6	22.3	23.6	22.3
Administrative	2.5	2.5	2.3	2.3
Ancillary and Circulation	14.2	14.2	12.8	12.8

It may be seen that teaching accommodation accounts for more than 55 per cent of the total floor space. This figure compares favourably with that achieved in the planning of school buildings in the U.K. and U.S.A. A range of 55-60 can, therefore, be legitimately fixed as a factor for design efficiency for school buildings. It must be the endeavour of architects and planners to achieve a design efficiency figure not less than this in the planning of schools.

Flexibility In Lay-Out

The lay-out suggested by the Panel has inherent flexibility for expanding the school in stages, if necessary. If the school is to be ultimately for a strength of 650 students, it need be only two-storeyed. Some portions shown as terrace in the first floor should be capable of being constructed later on to meet additional requirements. If, on the other hand, the ultimate strength of the school is to be one thousand, the foundation and the structure should be designed as for a three-storeyed construction though initially the construction may be restricted to two storeys. It can be further built up in stages as and when need arises.

The Chemistry and Biology laboratories have been located on the ground floor and Physics and Domestic Science laboratories on the first floor. In a school with a capacity of 1,000 boys, the Domestic Science Laboratory will be converted into a balcony over the hall and the attached store will be converted into a WC. In a girl's school for 1,000 students, the Domestic Science laboratory and the store will be located on the second floor over the portion of balcony and the attached store over the WC, on the first floor. In case there is difficulty in supplying water to the Domestic Science laboratory on the second floor in certain areas, a separate tank on the roof may be provided for this purpose in addition to those normally provided to feed the water closets.

Furniture And Fittings In Laboratories

The size and shape of various laboratories has been arrived at after carefully fixing up the numbers and size of furniture and fittings that are to go into each. The main item of furniture in laboratories is the laboratory table. These tables are normally designed for four to twelve students. The Panel feels that a table for six students or more would be unwieldy for small laboratories. In arriving at the size of tables, the Panel has taken care to see that the dimension of the table top, (6 ft. × 3-1/2 ft.) is kept the same for Physics, Chemistry, Biology and Domestic Science laboratories. The Chemistry table however, though of the same size, will have sinks and shelves mounted on it.

The height of the Chemistry table is two ft. nine in. and that of Biology and Physics laboratory table three feet. The Domestic Science table will be only 2 ft. six in. high. No drawers or cup boards have been provided for any of these tables as it is felt that, while adding to the cost and making the furniture bulky, they do not serve any useful purpose. As a matter of fact, they hamper free working It is better to provide for shelves and cup-boards along the walls for storage. Such cup-boards have been shown in all the laboratories. In the Biology laboratory, some extra ledges have been provided for keeping exhibits. In the Domestic Science laboratory, ledges and sinks have been provided for cooking, laundering, etc. A few shelves have been provided below the ledges for storage.

The provision for balances is another item that requires careful planning. In the Physics laboratory separate ledges have been provided for balances. The location of fume cup-boards, gas generation plant also have been shown in the lay-out of the Chemistry laboratory.

The plan at Appendix I (b) gives also the lay-out of services in the Chemistry laboratory which requires careful pre-planning.

In the Physics laboratory a small dark room is provided, the access to which is from the laboratory itself. Exhaust fams may be provided above the door of the dark room to secure adequate ventilation.

The stores attached to laboratories will have seven ft. (2·1 m.) high dwarf walls. The gas plant portion, however, would have wall right upto the ceiling.

Lay-Out of Class-Rooms

In the case of class rooms provision has been made for a built in cup-board in each room, partitioned horizontally into two portions with two separate shutters, one for the use of the teacher and the other for students. Wooden picture rails may also be provided on the carridor side between the louvered windows and also at available spaces in the front wall. Though these may add to the initial cost, this will ultimately result in savings on wooden cup-boards and other fittings and will add to utility and convenience.

With regard to black-boards in class rooms it is suggested that they may be in cement mortar with an admixture of black pigment. They should be three feet above the floor level and may be three ft. nine inches (1·1 m.) high.

A suggested lay out for a class room is given in Appendix IV. Only one door has been provided for each class room. A suggestion was made that every class room should be provided with two doors to ficilitate movement of students and for supervision. This however, would add substantially to the cost and also adversely affect the efficient utilisation of space within. Considering these the Panel thought that the disadvantages of providing an additional door would far out weigh the advantages that can be claimed for it.

Design And Specification

The cost of construction, to a large extent, depends upon the structural design and specifications adopted for a building. It seems worth while to lay down norms regarding structural designs and specifications to be adopted for school buildings with a view to achieving a certain measure of uniformity consistent with economy and functional efficiency. These are given below.

Structural Designs

As mentioned earlier, it is necessary for a developing city to go in for two or three-storeyed construction. The structure may be of the load-bearing type. The height of plinth should be two feet above the crest of the road. The floor to floor height need not be more than 12ft.

The walls on the ground and first floors may be 13-1/2 in. thick in portions other than the multipurpose hall. For the second floor outer walls may not be more than nine inches thick. Columns in verandah may be 9 in. × 13 1/2 in. in R.C.C. on the ground floor and of the same size in brick work on the first and second floors.

Specifications

Foundations : The design of foundations depend upon whether the school will ultimately be double-storeyed or three storeyed. In either case the foundation may be so designed as to facilitate building up of all portions except the hall shown as terrace in the plan.

Doors and Wind ows : The percentage of window area to floor area may be 20. The height of windowsill may be kept at three ft. Fan lights to windows may be eliminated. The doors may be of commercial flush type. On the corridor side no glass panes may be provided within the reach of students. However, for securing effective cross ventilation, glass louvers may be fixed at a suitable height. In places where electricity is not likly to be available in the foreseeable future, windows may also be provided on the verandah side to facilitate better ventilation. The doors and windows of Domestic Science laboratory should have fly proof shutters. The windows and ventilators in the stores attached to all laboratories should be provided with fixed wire gauze frames. The windows of laboratories on the ground floor and the Principal's Office may be provided with B.R.C. fabric or grill of suitable design.

Flooring : The flooring may be of 1-1/2 in. thick cement concrete over a base of lean cement concrete in all the rooms except for WC's, entrance hall and staircases where terrazo flooring is essential. In verandahs also this type of flooring is desirable in view of its durability and longer life. In W.C. blocks a dado of terrazo may be provided upto window sill level. In upper floors a screed 1-1/2 in. thick can be laid directly over the R.C.C. slabs.

Effect Of Recommendations

The original space requirements of Delhi Administration for administrative and teaching accommodation were 02, 020 sq. ft. (1952.82 sq. metres). To give this amount of floor space the built up area which will include circulation and ancillary area, thickness of walls pillars, etc. would be of the order of 37,000 sq. ft. (3437.41 sq. metres). According to the revised requirements laid down by the Panel, the area of teaching and administrative accommodation would be 16,320 sq. ft. (1516.38 sq. metres) which means a reduction of 22.3 per cent over the original requirements. By proper planning of space it should be possible to give this amount of accommodation together with necessary ancillaries and circulation space, within a built up area of 29,700 sq. ft. (2759.22 sq. metres). The difference in built up area would be of the order of 7,300 sq. ft. (678.20 sq. metres), which on the basis of the prevailing rates of construction, would mean a reduction of Rs. 73,000 in the capital outlay for each school. The effect of this reduction on the outlay on new Higher Secondary School buildings proposed to be taken up in the Third Plan will be of the order of Rs. 40 lakhs.

Apart from reduction in capital outlay, the norms given in the report would be of help in standardising the plans and estimates of school buildings. Such standardisation is absolutely essential to avoid frequent changes during execution which, in addition to causing delays add to the cost.

NATIONAL BUILDINGS ORGANISATIONS, PANEL ON HEALTH BUILDINGS, 1960—REPORT ON URBAN HEALTH CENTRE BUILDINGS.

New Delhi, National Buildings Organisation, 1963. 38p.

Chairman : Dr. T.P. Tiwari.

Members : Shri J.D. Shastri; Dr. Raghunath Sahai Chawla; Shri M.K. Jadav; Shri N.G. Joshi; Dr. B.V. Mulay; Shri C.B. Patel; Shri M.A. Hafeez.

Secretary Shri J.L. Sehgal

APPOINTMENT

To lay norms and standards to guide the designs of Dispensary and Health Centre Buildings an functional and economical lines, Government of India, Ministry of Works, Housing and Rehabilitation constituted a Panel on Health Buildings in 1960.

TERMS OF REFERENCE

To lay norms and standards to guide the designs of Dispensary and Health Centre Buildings on functional and economical lines.

CONTENTS

General; Functions; Location; Size; Land Requirements; Selection of Site; Building Requirements; out-Patient Unit; Personal Services; Routine Office Administr. tion and vital statistics; Indoor Patients Units; Ancillary Accommodation; Residential Accommodation; Traffic; Physical Environments; General Design considerations; Building Economy; List of Illustrations.

RECOMMENDATIONS

Location : Health Centre shall be located in areas having municipal status and population not less than 20,000 persons.

Size : The size of the reception area shall be so delimited that the population served is not more than 40,000 persons.

Maximum distance between the Health Centre and home is not more than three kilometres.

Average daily attendance rate does not exceed 600 patients.

Land Requirements : Four hectares.

The width of the plot at all places shall not be less than 31 metres.

Waiting Space : Aggragate waiting space for 100 persons should be provided as minimum.

A good spacing of benches from back to back is .9 m. and a bench length of .5 m. per person is adequate.

Allow .6 sq. m. per waiting seat provided exclusive of gangways.

Consultation Rooms : 15 sq. m. for general medical practitioners.

13 sq. m. for dental Surgeon.

15 sq. m. for Specialists.

Dark room of eight sq. m. should be attached to consultation room for specialist.

Clinical Laboratory : 15 sq. m.

Dispensary : 13 sq. m.

Dressing and Minor Operation : 19 sq. m.

Injection Room : Nine sq. m.

X-Ray (Future) : 19 sq. m. Radiographic room.

Six sq. m. Processing room.

11 sq. m. Radiologist Room.

Maternal and Child Health Waiting Space : 11 sq. m. inclusive of passages should be provided as minimum.

History Taking and Registration : 17 sq. m.

Consultation, Examination and Treatment : 15 sq. m.

Family Planning : 13 sq. m.

Immunisation and Prophylactics : 15 sq. m.

Routine Office Administration and Vital Statistics: 15 sq. m.

Wards : Eight Bedded maternity Ward.

Two Bedded Female Ward.

Two Bedded General Ward (three numbers).

One Isolation Ward.

5.6 sq. m. per bed.

Duty Room : 11 sq. m.

Linen and Equipment Store : .9 sq. m. per bed subject to a minimum of nine sq. m.

Labour Room : 13 sq. m.

Clean up and Waste Room : 5.6 sq. m.

Sterilization Room : 5.6 sq. m.

Ward Pantry : 11 sq. m. inclusive of provision store which may be four sq. m.

Storage : Nine sq. m. for medical store.

Eight sq. m. for Lumber room.

Eight sq. m. for disinfectants, chemicals, etc.

Public and Staff Convenience :

(i) Water closet with Ablution Tap :	One for every 100 males or part thereof and two for every 100 females or part thereof.
(ii) Wash Basin :	One for every 100 persons or part thereof.
(iii) Urinals :	One for every 50 males or part thereof.

Garages, Cycle Stands, etc. : Requirement and distribution of parking space would be guided by the mode of conveyance used in the locality.

One garage for ambulance of size 3 m. × 7 m.

Three garages or sheds for doctors' cars of size 2·8 m. × 5.5 m.

Residential Accommodation : Minimum requirement would normally be for two doctors, one pharmacist, two nurses, one health visitor, one mid-wife and four Class IV staff.

Traffic Interior : Corridors 2.1 metre wide.

Stairs 1.1 metre wide.

Ramp slope...less—than 5 (per cent).

PANEL ON UNIVERSITY BUILDINGS—HOSTELS, 1960—REPORT

New Delhi, University Grants Commission, 1960. 31p.+Charts

Chairman : Shri Bhailal Bhai Patel
Members : Shri H. Rahman; Shri T.S. Vedagiri.
Secretary : Shri R.K. Chhalra.

APPOINTMENT

During recent years, there has been rapid increase in the number of students entering our universities. The number of students in the universities and colleges at the beginning of the Second Five-Year Plan was 7,12,697 and it is estimated to be 9,00,000 at the end of the plan period. This naturally has had its effects on the standards of education. For improving the quality of college and university education, a number of measures have been taken by the University Grants Commission which include among others, improvement of buildings, libraries and laboratories, provision of more hostel facilities, etc. It was estimated that hostel facilities existed for about 15 per cent of the university and college students at the beginning of the Second Plan. It has been the endeavour of the University Grants Commission to raise this figure at least to 20 per cent during the plan period. This means that about 14.3 lakh sq. ft. of hostel accommodation has to be constructed during the course of the Second Five-Year Plan if the target mentioned above has to be attained. The financial implication of this can be placed at about Rs. 17.16 crores which covers only the buildings and internal services. It is expected that during the Third Plan period there will be an addition of four lakhs of students in the universities, and for providing hostel accommodation for 20 per cent of this student strength about 212 lakh sq. ft. of hostel accommodation has to be constructed during the Third Plan period involving an expenditure of about Rs. 27.5 crores.

The provision, however, for this in the Second Plan is about Rs. five crores which does not touch even the fringe of the problem. It may not be possible to allocate more funds for the construction of hostels without detriment to other essential items of development. This position makes it imperative for the authorities concerned to economise as much as possible on the actual cost of construction and see how far funds allotted for the purpose can be made to yield maximum results.

It is felt that there is a great scope for economy on buildings by improving space utilisation, rationalising design standards and specifications and by introducing, wherever possible, techniques of construction other than the conventional ones. This is more than amply illustrated by the work done in England and by the recent work of the Buildings Projects Team in India on different types of buildings. The study conducted by the Ministry of Education in the U. K. on training college hostels is quite revealing in the sense that an organised attempt has been made to reduce cost by improved space utilisation. The proportion of the living space to the total floor area which was as low as 50 per cent in some of the early post-war hostels has been increased to as much as 81 per cent by intelligent space planning. The Buildings Projects Team of the Committee on Plan Projects has similarly demonstrated how by improved planning of space, economy can be achieved in multi-storeyed buildings and in industrial estates. The Chairman of the University Grants Commission considered that it was quite worthwhile to initiate this sort of study with respect to buildings in universities, such as hostels, libraries, laboratories and college buildings and set up this Panel for this purpose in 1960.

TERMS OF REFERENCE

(i) To consider the question of hostel accommodation; and

(ii) To submit a report giving norms and standards for future adoption.

CONTENTS

Forword; Introduction; Observations; Planning of Hostel Buildings; Size of Hostels; Service Space; Drinking Water Facilities; Common Facilities (Lounge and Recreation); Provision for Hostel Staff; Provision for Utility Shops; Circulation Space; Efficiency of Planning; Design and Structural Considerations; Structural Arrangement; Design Considerations; Expansion Joints; Foundations; Specifications and Costs; Joinery; Flooring; Terracing; Finishing; Services; Furniture; Execution of Work; Ceiling on Cost; Financial Effects of the Recommendations; Summary of Important Recommendations; Appendices I and II.

RECOMMENDATIONS

Living rooms are to be arranged in such a way that they get the maximum benefit of the prevailing breeze and avoid as much as possible of western exposure.

An area of 85-90 sq. ft. (7.9 to 8.4 sq. m) for single seater room, 75-80 sq. ft. (7.0 to 7.4 sq. m.) per student for two seater and 70-75 sq. ft. (6.5 to 7.0 sq. m.) per student for a three seater room would be adequate for an undergraduate hostel. For post-graduate and research students the room area should not exceed 100 sq. ft. per student.

Dining area should be designed to accommodate not more than two-thirds strength of the hostel at the rate of 10-12 sq. ft. (1.0 to 1.1. sq. m.) per person and kitchen-pantry area at the rate of five to seven sq. ft. (0.5 to 0.7 sq. m.) per student.

The following provisions for toilet facilities are recommended:

(i) W.C.: One per 10 men students eight women students.

(ii) Urinals: One per eight students.

(iii) Wash basins: One per eight students.

(iv) Bath with a shower: One per eight men students/six women students.

Area for common room may be 500-650 sq. ft. (46.5 to 60.4 sq. m.)

It should be the endeavour of architects and planners to plan the hostel in such a way that the built up area per student is generally not more than 2.3 to 2.5 times the floor area per student within the room.

Increase in the working stress of concrete alone cannot lead to economy unless the working stress in steel is also correspondingly increased.

Economy in R.C.C. frame work depends to some extent on the judicious choice of the concrete mix for the various components. It is advantageous to use a mix of 1: 1-1/2: 3 or even 1:1:2 for members which are predominantly in compression. The normal 1:2:4 mix can be adopted for members subject to flexural stresses. It is, however, better to design the mix and use quality controlled concrete.

Where foundation exploration shows special features and where the structure is heavy, needing special foundation study, qualified foundation experts should be consulted. The data should be properly analysed and alternative foundation designs prepared in order to arrive at the most economical solution.

The area of windows may vary between 12 to 25 per cent of the room area.

The cost of normal internal water supply and sanitation should be about 7-1/2 per cent of building cost.

The cost of internal electrification should be about 7-1/2 to 10 per cent building cost. This will not include the cost of fan.

Ceiling cost of movable furniture may be Rs. 150 per student.

Ceiling cost for hostels may be worked out at any place on the basis of norms for space utilisation and specifications outlined in the report and the prevailing cost of construction.

REVIEW COMMITTEE ON EDUCATION, 1960—REPORT

New Delhi, University Grants Commission, 1966. 94.+pviiip.

Chairman : Prof. N.K. Sidhanta (Died) and Prof. K.G. Saiyidain took over as Chairman).

Members : Dr. E.A. Pires (Left Delhi); Prof. T.K.N. Menon; Dr. Salamatullah; Dr. A. Mujib; Shri K.L. Joshi.

Secretary : Dr. P.J. Philip.

APPOINTMENT

One of the statutory functions of the University Grants Commission is "to take, in consultation with the universities or other bodies concerned, all such steps as it may think fit for the promotion and coordination of university education and for the determination and maintenance of the standards of teaching, examination and research in the universities."

While considering the report of the visiting committee appointed by the University Grants Commission to examine the development of post-graduate studies in the University College of Education of the Osmania University, the Commission resolved that the whole question of the duration, contents, staff, admission qualifications, etc., of the post-graduate courses in Education be further examined.

This led to the appointment by the University Grants Commission of a Committee to examine the standards of teaching and research in the departments of Education in Indian universities and to make recommendations in regard to the manner in which adequate standards may be maintained in 1960.

TERMS OF REFERENCE

The Committee had wide terms of reference and was free to determine its programme and rules of procedure. The Committee was specially asked to go into all the details:

(1) Determine different types of courses which should be offered by the universities.

(2) Work out objectives of different types of courses, especially of studies at the Master's degree level.

(3) Recommend to the universities schemes of papers for each type of course with a view to providing specialisation.

(4) Recommend teaching methods suitable for teaching various parts of the syllabus and to lay down guiding principles for the conduct of examinations.

(5) Lay down the entrance qualifications of students for the various courses.

(6) Recommend duration of the course.

(7) Lay down minimum standards for passing the examinations and grouping of question papers for the purposes of examination.

(8) Indicate any other steps that may be necessary to achieve uniform and high standards, such as qualifications of teachers, etc.

CONTENTS

Foreword; Introduction; Post-Graduate Courses in Education in Indian and in Some Selected Foreign Universities; Post-Graduate Teaching in Education; Research in Education; Staff and Facilities; Summary of Observations and Recommendations; Appendices I to XIV.

RECOMMENDATIONS

Introduction

There has been a considerable expansion of facilities for teacher training in the country after Independence. The number of training colleges as well as their intake capacity has increased considerably. The number of training colleges stood at 36 in 1950-51, 75 in 1955-56 and 108 in 1958-59. Their total intake capacity increased from 3,490 in 1950-51 to 13,779 in 1958-59.

There is at present a certain lack of agreement in regard to the principles and practices, incorporated in the programme of study offered by various institutions in Education. The courses prescribed reveal considerable variations in regard to goals as well as the means for achieving them. Practices relating to admission, choice of the curriculum and type of research required of the students lack proper coordination. Such conditions make it difficult for various training institutions and departments of Education to make a real contribution to educational thinking and planning in the country.

Post Graduate Studies in Education

The M. Ed. course should have the following broad objectives:

(a) To produce competent teachers for the training colleges;

(b) To train personnel for undertaking higher studies and research in problems of education;

(c) To train educational administrators;

(d) To train persons for educational and vocational guidance of youth; and

(e) To produce competent educational workers with a thorough understanding of the role of planning and education is national development.

The content of the M.Ed. course should lead to at least one specialization and to a fair acquaintance with the methodology of educational research, besides promoting a desirable intellectual discipline. The curriculum suggested is given in the body of the report.

For admission to M.Ed. course, the candidate should generally have a good second class B.A./B.Sc. degree, preferably a good second class M.A./M.Sc. degree and a first or second class B.Ed. degree in both theory and practice. Direct admission to a two-year integrated course leading to the M.Ed. degree after at least a second class Bachelor's or Master's degree would be another way of attracting better and more promising candidates for the profession.

It would also be helpful if the M. Ed. degree is prescribed as a necessary qualification for certain posts like those of headmasters, district education officers and other supervisory personnel.

Incentives in the form of loans and scholarships should be available to meritorious students.

Under our present set-up, it is neither possible nor feasible to have an entirely independent staff for the B. Ed. and M. Ed. classes in the same college or university department. It is, therefore, desirable to ensure that teachers who teach M.Ed. classes are not normally over-burdened with supervision of the practice teaching of B.Ed. students.

Teaching at the M.Ed. level should be supplemented by tutorials seminars.

In most universities the M.Ed. course is at present a whole-time course of one year's duration. An extension of the course would not be immediately feasible in view of financial and other difficulties. One solution of great promise is the introduction of integrated B.Ed. and M.Ed. courses. The details and *modus operandi* of such a course will have to be worked out.

Dissertation as part of the M.Ed. programme serves a useful purpose but at present it usually does not come up to a desirable standard. It would be worthwhile to consider the possibility of undertaking group projects in which individuals contribute their part of study and research. Another possible alternative to dissertation could be the writing of good text-books. Preparation of measuring tools and tests in school subjects would also be a good substitute.

The practice of placing successful condidates in three classes may be abolished for the M.Ed. examination. Instead, the universities may give pass and distinction marks, pass marks at 45 per cent and distinction at 65 per cent. At least 20 per cent of the total marks for M.Ed. course should be earmarked for sessional work which should be assessed by committees consisting of faculty members. It should be possible to find ways and means of checking the objectivity, reliability and validity of internal marks. The *viva voce* should be a necessary part of the post graduate examinations. Besides gauging the depth of knowledge and mental alertness of the candidate, the *viva voce* examination could also serve as a useful check on the reliability of internal assessment.

Research In Education

No candidate should be admitted to a research course in Education unless he has shown sufficient evidence of his capacity for independent thinking and critical examination of theories and facts. A doctoral committee consisting of reputed scholars in the field of the candidate's research specialization should examine the candidate with regard to his general ability to pursue research on the topic selected by him. It would also be desirable to insist on one or two years' professional experience on the part of candidates before they are enrolled for research. The candidate should be allowed to supplicate for a research degree only in a department or place where adequate library facilities and qualified supervisors are available.

No person should be appointed as a supervisor unless he himself possesses a doctoral degree or has published recognised research work to his credit or is an eminent scholar in his field.

While fundamental research in Education should be encouraged far as possible, it would be advisable for a large majority of candidates to take up practical problems facing the country that need urgent solution.

Sufficient attention will have to be given to the preparation of suitable instruments of research.

Suitable incentives in the form of fellowships and scholarships should be available to departments of Education in order to attract talented students to careers of research and fellowship.

It will be necessary to build up sound traditions of research in Education and also to educate the consumers of research, viz., school teachers, principles, educational administrators, etc. They should be guided by the findings of research in their day-to-day work.

In general, there should be three examiners to evaluate a doctrol dissertation. The examiners should be scholars of repute. If qualified persons are not available in the country, specialists could be invited from abroad to act as examiners. Every candidate must be examined by means of a *viva voce* test. The candidate should be considered for the award of a doctoral degree only when the examiners recommend him unanimously.

It would be desirable to work out some criteria for the general guidance of examiners to achieve a high degree of objectivity in the evaluation of performance of candidates.

Staff and Facilities

Teachers of postgraduate departments of Education should have a sound academic background, some professional experience and adequate competence to guide and carry on research. The minimum qualifications for a postgraduate teacher in Education should be as under :

(a) **Lecturer** : (i) At least a second class Masters's degree in Education besides at least a second class Master's degree in any other subject.

(ii) Three year's experience of teaching and/or administration and/or research.

(b) **Reader** : (i) Same as for lecturer.

(ii) Five years' experience of teaching and/or administration and research (Research would connote a research degree in Education or published work of recognised merit).

(c) **Professor** : (i) Same as for lecturer plus a research degree.

(ii) Ten years' experience of teaching research and/or administration. The condition regarding experience may be relaxed in the case of a first class candidate who has published research work to his credit.

The teaching workload of a postgraduate lecturer in Education should not exceed 15 periods a week. The work of professors and readers should be distributed judiciously over teaching, research and guidance of research.

The number of senior posts in a department of Education should be about one-third of the total strength of the teaching staff.

The training colleges should endeavour to enrich the secondary schools by offering them help and guidance in their work and also, if possible, by associating their teachers in some of the college activities. Well qualified teachers of B.Ed. classes should also be encouraged to take up one or two papers in their fields of specialisation at the M.Ed. level.

That in all postgraduate institutions research colloquium should be arranged at suitable intervels in which the M.Ed. and Ph.D. students may be required to present their research problems with design and methods of study. It would be desirable to invite specialists from outside and from other departments to participate in discussions.

Regional seminars and workshops may be organised by teacher training colleges or departments of Education on current problems of education and other professional problems. It may be possible for the U.G.C. to provide the necessary financial assistance for the purpose.

An attempt may be made by the unitary universities to institute a system of inter-departmental teaching in some subjects.

Students should be exposed to the influence of books and guided to cultivate sound reading habits. A college/department which offers postgraduate course in Education should provide for its library at least Rs. 50,000 phased suitably over a period of 5 years, and Rs. 5,000 annually.

The standard of accommodation of 5,000 to 7,000 sq. ft. laid down by the U.G.C. for a postgraduate department should be adopted by postgraduate teachers colleges/departments of Education also.

Part-time evening courses leading to the M.Ed. degree may be arranged wherever possible, especially for in-service teachers, to enable them to improve their professional qualifications. It, is, however, necessary to ensure that this provision does not result in further deterioration of standards.

In order to attract better students to postgraduate studies in Education, the Ministry of Education and the Planning Commission may consider providing suitable loans and scholarships to deserving candidates for studies at the M.Ed. level.

STUDY TEAM ON RURAL-CUM-URBAN TOWNSHIP AT THE HEADQUARTERS OF C.D. BLOCKS, 1960—REPORT

New Delhi, Ministry of Community Development and Cooperation, Department of Community Development, 1961. 48p.

Chairman : Shri B. Mukerjee (replaced by Shri B.D. Pande).

Members : Dr. D.K. Malhotra; Shri M.S. Bhatia (replaced by Shri H.D. Nargolwala); Prof. V.L. D'Souza; Shri J.N. Tewari; Shri R.V. Ramiah.

Secretary : Shri Athar Husain (replaced by Shri C. Srinivasa Sastry).

APPOINTMENT

The Study Team on Rural-cum-Urban Townships at the Headquarters of C.D. Blocks was constituted under the Ministry of Community Development and Cooperation (Department of Community Development) vide their Resolution No. 8(VI)/BD/59, dated January 18, 1960.

TERMS OF REFERENCE

(i) To examine the trend of growth of population in a few selected Block Headquarters;

(ii) To examine the precise nature of the requirements in terms of the objective developments which have taken place and the different ways in which these might be approached;

(iii) To frame a type scheme to be taken up in the proposed urban-cum-rural units for generating additional employment opportunities on an agro-industrial base.

CONTENTS

Introduction; Terms of Reference; Method of Study Classification of Block Headquarters According to Population Changes; The Relation Between Initial Population and Rate of Increase in Population; Cases of Decrease in Population and the Influencing Factors; The Influence of the Location of the Block Headquarters on its Development; Factors that Govern the Growth of the Block Headquarters; Potentialities for Industrialisation; The role of Governmental Assistance; Categorisation of Block Headquarters Based on Potentialities of Population Growth; Funds for the Development of the Townships; Coordination at the State Level; Suggested Lines for Planning the Physical Growth of Townships; Block Headquarters in the Hilly and Tribal Areas and Under-Developed Areas; Summary of Conclusions; Appendices.

RECOMMENDATIONS

In a majority of the Block Headquarters, there is said to be scope for the promotion of industries based on agricultural produce and of village and cottage industries. In about half the Block Headquarters industries based on various local products like hides and skins, and miscellaneous manufacturing, processing and consumers good industries, could be established.

Governmental assistance has an important bearing on the growth of industries and consequently on the growth of population. A definite policy regarding the extension of electrification to the Block Headquarters and rural areas and the giving of connections to small scale industries in rural areas on a priority basis, would have to be adopted. The policy of Government in granting assistance for establishment of industries should be such that it would facilitate the geographical dispersal and structural decentralisation of industry. The exact types of industries that should be located in any particular Block Headquarters would have to be decided after a careful and detailed study. However, several of these industries could have an agro-industrial base, namely, that the industries could utilise or process local agricultural produce and other raw materials, and/or produce implements, improved tools, consumer goods, etc., which would be required by the agriculturists and the village artisans. In these ways a mutual relationship can be built up between the agricultural and the industrial sectors, between the surrounding rural areas and the township, each being supplementary and complementary to the other.

In the Block Headquarters which are situated in the orbit of influence of a big industrial centre or metropolis, medium and small scale industries should be established as ancillaries and feeders to the large scale and medium industries in the metropolitan centres. The new industrial units should be so located that the established industrial centres and the metropolices would actually aid them in their growth and not dwarf them. Such Block Headquarters, in turn, would prevent the unhealthy growth of metropolitan and industrial centres, and would also retard the drift of population from rural areas.

The exact types of industries to be established in a particular Block Headquarters, and the formulation of a comprehensive scheme for its development, need a careful study of the conditions prevailing in the local area.

Definite steps by Government need to taken in guiding the development, at present, of only those Block Headquarters where conditions conducive to rapid growth exist. In these cases Government have to play a vital role in (a) directing the physical growth of the township, (b) assisting the process of industrialisation and (c) providing essential amenities. Funds for the development of such rural-cum-urban townships can be drawn from various schemes which have been included in the Third Plan, like the Rural and Urban Water Supply and Sanitation Schemes, Housing Schemes, Rural Electrification Schemes, Village and Small Scale Industries, etc., are pooled together.

To ensure that there is a sufficient coordination, there should be a committee at the State level consisting, among others, of the Development Commissioner, Director of Industries, Chief Engineer for Roads and Buildings, Chairman of the State Electricity Board, Head of the Housing Department, Chief Town Planner, Registrar of Cooperative Societies. This Committee should select the Block Headquarters which are likely to grow and whose development has to be guided on proper lines, and the Committee should indicate the types of industries to be established and ensure that funds are channelised to the selected Block Headquarters according to their requirements. At the district and the Block levels, the Zila Parishad/District Development Committee and the Panchayat Samiti/Block Development Committee should be the coordinating authority for implementation.

For the proper growth of townships, and existing land use map, and a development plan should be prepared and the uses of land within the area of each township prescribed. This envisages the preparation of plans similar to "Master Plans" for which some provision is to be made in the Third Plan. The provision, for the present scheme, however, is meant for only the larger cities and industrial centres. The scope of this scheme should be enlarged to include the rapidly growing semi-urban and rural areas like many of the Block Headquarters. All the States may enact suitable legislation on the lines of the Model Town and Country Planning Act recently circulated by the Ministry of Health and the selected Block Headquarters may be declared as "Local Planning Areas", and the Block or Panchayat Samitis designated as the "Local Planning Authorities".

For the planned growth of townships, availability of land that could be put to non-agricultural use, is essential. Where Government land is already available, it may be reserved for this purpose. Definite steps for demarcating such land, if necessary, by acquisition, and its development into building sites and industrial sites have to be taken. For this purpose the scope of the scheme for the acquisition and the development of land already envisaged in the Third Plan should be enlarged so that the relatively smaller towns, like many of the Block Headquarters, could derive benefit from the scheme.

In the hilly, tribal and backward areas, left to themselves, the Block Headquarters may not have the necessary dynamism for development, but because of the importance of these areas in the scheme of national planning, definite steps would have to be taken for aiding and guiding their development. The industries that could be set up in these areas may be based on the produce of the area or the locally available raw materials, and the development of the Block Headquarters should be in keeping with the surroundings.

COMMITTEE FOR THE REVISION OF RULES REGARDING ALLOTMENT OF GOVERNMENT RESIDENCES IN DELHI/ NEW DELHI, CALCUTTA AND BOMBAY, 1960 --REPORT

New Delhi, Ministry of Works, Housing and Supply, 1962. 53p.

Chairman : Shri Anil K. Chanda.
Members : Shri M. Gopal Menon; Shri A.S. Naik; Shri S. Vohra; Shri R.S. Gae; Shri M.G. Kaul; Shri C. Balasubramaniam.
Secretary : Shri S.P. Saksena.

APPOINTMENT

The Committee for the Revision of Rules Regarding Allotment of Government Residences in Delhi/New Delhi,Calcutta and Bombay was constituted under the Ministry of Works, Housing and Supply vide letter No. 3/22/59-Acc, dated January 28, 1960.

TERMS OF REFERENCE

(a) Rules regarding allotment of regular residences in Delhi and New Delhi;

(b) Special Accommodation Rules, 1950;

(c) Rules regarding attotment of residences to Class IV officers;

(d) Rules regarding allotment of hostel accommodation;

(e) Principles for allotment of accommodation on out-of-turn basis and according to over-riding priority;

(f) The present classification of residences with a view to reducing their categories to a few broad ones;

(g) Procedure for granting allottees permission to share Government accommodation and procedure for conduct of enquiries and imposition of penalties in cases of unauthorised subletting of Government residences ;

(h) Procedure for retention of Government accommdation and counting of service rendered by officers in one pool on transfer to an office having a separate pool of accommodation ;

(i) Other allied questions.

CONTENTS

Constitution of the Committee and Terms of Reference ; Definition of 'family' Liberalisation of ; 'Date of priority' Liberalisation of ; Reduction in Number of Classes of Residences—Not Possible ; Compulsory Move of Officers to Residences of their Entitled Class due to Change on their Emoluments—not to be Enforced and Rate of Rent to be Charged ; (a) Concessional periods for which one can Retain Government Residences on the Occurrence of Certain Events ; (b) Concessions to be Granted to Officers going on Training to States or Abroad ; Period for which the Director of Estates may Grant Extension of Stay and Rate of Rent to be Charged ; Transfers in the Same Station from an Eligible Office to an Ineligible Office or to State Governments—Concessional Periods Admissible; Concessional period for Retention of Accommodation when Transfer is Proceeded by Leave; Period of Notice for Vacation of Residences—Reduction of ; Change of Residence in the Event of Death of the Allottee's Wife and/or Husband, Children, etc.—Change to be allowed even when Death does not take Place in the Residence Mutual Exchange of Flats in Buildings having more than one Floor—Permissible even if the Flats are in different Classes; Retention of Accommodation by Officers who after Retirement, Resignation or Termination of Services are employed without any Break or during the Concessional Period permissible for Retention of Residences; Allotment of Vacant Accommodation in Higher Classes—Conditions of; Period for which the Allottee may be Permitted to Sublet the Residences Allotted to him and the persons to whom the same can be Sublet; Bungalows having Garages, Stables and Servant Quarters attached to Flats—Prevention of Subletting; Servant Quarters attached to Orthodox and Unorthodox Chummeries—(a) Prevention of Subletting and (b) Conditions for Allotment; Submission of Annual Certificates by Allottees regarding Use of Stables, Garages, and Servant Quarters; Categories of Persons who can be Accommodated in the Servant Quarters; Penalties for Subletting—Enhancement of; Weightage to Officers, who are Debarred on account of Unauthorised Subletting after the Expiry of the period of Deparment—no Special Treatment to be Accorded; Persons Eligible to Share Accommodation with Allottee Officers; Permission to Share Accommodation—Procedure for and Action to be taken where the Allottee and Sharer fall out; Procedure for making Enquiries into cases of Subletting—Powers to enter upon Premises; Submission of Application for 'next below' Class by Officers Occupying Residences in Classes Lower than their 'Next Below' Class—not to be Compulsory except in case of Officers not Occupying any Government Residence; Upgrading of Residences—Compulsory Move of Officers not to be insisted—and Rate of Rent to be Charged; Special Accommodation Rules, 1950—discontinuance of and Special Provisions to be made in Regular Allotment Rules; Treatment of Delhi and New Delhi as one station for Allotment of Residences; Grounds on which Out-of-Turn Allotments may be Sanctioned; Procedure for Grant of Over-riding Priorities; Reconstitution of Special Accommodation Committees to include Representatives from other Ministries; Tenure Officers' Pool—Officers Eligible for; Senior Officers' Pool—Creation of; Procedure for retention of Government Accommodation and Counting of Service Renderd by Officers in One Pool on Transfer to an Office having a Separate Pool of Accommodation; Retention of Accommodation by Officers who are Transferred to Non-Family Stations—Procedure for; Allotment of Accommodation to Single Officers—Procedure for; Allotment of Accommodation to Officers—Owning Houses Change in the Procedure; Representations of the Ministry of External Affairs for Special Treatment; National Pay to be Taken into Account for Purposes of Priority Date in the Case of Certain Categories of Officers of the Ministry of External

Affairs; Representation of Certain Associations; Allotment to be Made to Officers having Large Family Members—Procedure for Determining Priority among Officers; Procedure for Allotment of Hostel Accommodation; Rules for Allotment of Class IV Residences and Procedure for Out-of-Turn Allotments; Note of Dissent; Appendices I to V.

RECOMMENDATIONS

The present definition of the family needs a change both from the point of view of the object to be served and in the context of joint family system prevalent in India. The Committee therefore recommends that the word 'wholly dependent' be replaced by the word 'dependent' only and the definition of 'family' be revised as below :

'Family' includes only the wife, or husband, as the case may be, children, step-children, legally adopted children, parents, brothers and sisters ordinarily residing with and dependent on an officer.

The Committee further recommends that where both husband and wife are in Government service and are entitled to allotment of accommodation under these rules, either of them should be allotted family accommodation and the condition regarding dependence on the officer should not apply.

The Committee recommends that the 'priority date of an officer in relation to a class of residence to which he is entitled under the Provisions of S. R. 317-B-3 (1), should mean the earliest date from which he has been continuously drawing emoluments of a particular class or a higher class irrespective of the place of his service under the Central Government anywhere in India or abroad.

The Committee further recommends as below :

That in the case of officers who are posted from an 'eligible' office to an 'ineligible' office and are retransferred to an 'eligible' office the service of the officers in the'ineligible' officers should be counted towards their priority date;

That in the case of Central Government officers who are sent on deputation to foreign service the periods spent on deputation should be taken into account towards their date of priority for allotrment of accommodation in Delhi/New Delhi;

That in the case of officers who are either permanent or hold administrative lien on posts under the Central Government and who are transferred to semi-Government autonomous bodies in Delhi/New Delhi/Simla, or outside these places, the entire period should count towards their priority date on their being re-transferred to an eligible post under the Central Government in these Stations;

That in the case of officers who are either permanent or temporary under the Central Government and who are transferred to semi-Government/autonomous bodies in Delhi/New Delhi/Simla who have their own pool of residences, should on their retransfer to posts under the Central Government be allowed to count the service rendered by them in those organisationss towards their 'date of priority';

That officers who are initially appointed in semi-Government/autonomous organisations and who are subsequently transferred to eligible offices in Delhi/New Delhi/Simla, should be allowed to count the Service rendered by them in these organisation towards their 'priority date' ; and

That in the case of the staff of the semi-Government bodies who have been declared eligible for residential accommodation, their priority date should be reckoned from the date they are declared eligible.

These liberalisations may also apply in determining the 'priority date' in the case of officers stationed at Bombay and Calcutta for allotment of accommodation under the administrative control of the Ministry of Works, Housing and Supply at these stations.

The Committee recommends that in cases where the transfer of the officer is ordered after the expiry of the leave granted to him, he may be allowed to retain the accommodation for the period of leave plus two months which are usually allowed in the case of transfer, provided that the total period including the concessional period of two months does not exceed the total period of 8 months on payment of normal rent. Accordingly, the Committee recommends that the period of notice may be reduced from 10 days to five days.

After taking into account the peculiar difficulties obtaining in the case of Bombay and Calcutta, the Committee recommends that in the case of flats in the same buildings—Government owned—which are in different classes having the same accommodation and carrying the same standard rents, mutual exchange of flats in different classes may be permitted subject to the condition that in such cases the allotments of the officers may not be changed and that if any of the officers who was a party to the mutual exchange vacates his residence for any reason ; the other officer would be required to move back to the flat actually allotted to him unless he can arrange fresh mutual exchange with the subsequent allottee.

The Committee has recommended the continuance of th concession whereby officers who resign their posts can retain the accommodation allotted to them on payment of normal rent for a period of one month from the date of resignation. There may be occasions on which such officers may be re-employed in eligible offices either without any break in service or during the concessional period of one month during which they can retain the residence allotted to them.

The Committee accordingly recommends that in both the types of cases referred to above, the officers concerned may be allowed to retain the residences allotted to them, as also their entitlement for allotment of accommodation under these rules.

The Committee further recommends that similar procedure may be followed in cases where officers occupying residences under these rules retire from Government service or whose services are terminated and who are subsequently appointed in eligible offices either without a break or during the concessional periods for which they can retain Government accommodation.

The Committee recommends that surplus accommodation in a higher class may be allotted in the following manner:

(i) To the applicant in that class who submitted his application late, and if there is no such applicant ;

(ii) To the applicant drawing the highest emoluments who is in occupation of accommodation in the class lower than the class to which the surplus residence belongs and if such an officer is not willing to accept the allotment/offer then ;

(iii) To the applicant, drawing the highest emoluments, who is not occupying any accommodation in the class next lower to the class to which the surplus residence belongs.

In one of the cases mentioned at items (ii) and (iii) should officers refusing the allotment of higher class accommodation be penalised.

The Committee further recommends that in order to avoid delay in the allotment of such vacant residences, if any, offers/allotments should be sent to at least 10 officers simultaneously in each category.

The Committee recommends that an officer may ordinarily be permitted to sublet the residence upto a period of six months during the allotment year, depending on the merits of each case.

On the question as to the persons to whom subletting may be permitted, the Committee recommends that subletting may be confined to Government officers entitled to accommodation under the rules, or to officers who are eligible to share accommodation with the allottee. Further, as far as possible, 'family' accommodation may be sublet to persons having families.

No garage may be allowed to an officer who does not possess his own car. An officer who initially secures an allotment of a garage may be required to surrender the same or his subsequently disposing of his car. If, however the interval between the selling of the car and the acquisition of the new car is within three months, the officer may be allowed to retain the garage but not otherwise.

The Committee further recommends that it would be desirable to obtain a certificate from the officers to the effect that they have not sublet the stables, garages and/or the servant quarters on rent for gain or profit. The Directorate of Estates may devise means by which yearly certificates are obtained from the allottees. The Committee also recommends that if subsequently any complaint is received and it is found that the officer had given a false certificate, the Directorate of Estates should take suitable action against such an officer for unauthorised subletting of the same.

The Committee recommends that the present orders regarding use of servant quarters contained in the Ministry of Works, Housing and Supply Office Memorandum No./26/4/58-Acc., dated September 28, 1959 (Appendix III) may continue.

The officers found guilty of subletting may be charged standard rent under F.R. 45-B, or twice the standard rent under F.R. 45-A, or twice the pool standard rent under F.R. 45-A, where the rents have been pooled or 15 per cent of the emoluments, whichever is the highest.

The Committee recommends that the present procedure for investigating cases of subletting may continue and in the allotment rules a specific provision may be made to enable the Director of Estates or a gazetted officer under him to enter the premises on his behalf to make enquiries with regard to the allegations of unauthorised sharing and/or subletting and recording the statements of the neighbours and if necessary to call such persons to his office for purposes of investigation.

The Committee recommends that the Special Accommodation Rules, 1950, may be discontinued and the following additional provisions may be made in the Regular Allotment Rules, Supplementary Rules :

(i) All the accommodation available in general pool may be divided into two parts, viz., Part I and Part II of the Schedule.

Part I may contain all the buildings now known as 'regular' and also the Government owned units of accommodation (excluding hutments) now classified as 'special'.

Part II may contain all the other units of accommodation, at present included in the special accommodation, viz., the leased and requisitioned houses and only other sub-standard accommodation which is not included in Part I.

(ii) The buildings in Part I may be allotted to officers according to their position on the waiting list; and the refusal of the same may attract the penal provisions contained in the Allotment Rules.

(iii) Future vacancies of residences in Part II may be allotted to officers who are sanctioned out-of-turn allotment.

(iv) Officers in occupation of residences which are

included in Part II may be shifted to residences in Schedule I in accordance with their position on the waiting list.

However, such officers as are in occupation of residences of their entitled class in Part II may have the option to retain the same, without any penalty, and be not compelled to move to residences in Part I.

(v) When an officer is required to vacate a leased/requisitioned house due to Government's decision to release the same, he may be provided with a residence, with over-riding priority either in Part I or II. The alternative accommodation may either be of the same class to which the residence to be released belonges, or in the 'next below' class of the officer or in the class to which the officer is entitled by virtue of his emoluments drawn on the first day of the relevant allotment year; and may as far as possible, be in the same locality.

The Committee further recommends that the Revised Regular Allotment Rules may also be extended to Bombay and Calcutta, and separate orders may be issued that officers drawing Rs. 2,250 or more per month will be entitled out-of-turn allotments at Bombay and Calcutta, as no special pools exist in the case of these two cities.

The Committee recommends that Delhi and New Delhi may be treated as one station with the following safeguards :

(i) That for purposes of allotment of residences, Old Delhi and New Delhi may be treated as one Station and officers be considered for allotment in any part of the capital —Delhi/New Delhi, the only option given to them being that they may be asked to express clearly in their application forms (1) Whether they would like to be considered for allotment in any of these Stations or only in one particular station and (2) whether they would be prepared to take an allotment beyond six miles from their places of duty. Allotment will be made in accordance with the options given and adhering as far as possible to the preferences given by the applicants to particular localities. This will not, however, apply to change of allotments which will be given from one zone to another zone and not in the same locality or the same zone.

(ii) That the residences in Old Delhi may be included in Parts I or II of the Schedule as the case may be.

In future applications for out-of-turn allotments may be considered only in the following three types of cases.

(i) For reasons of health of the officer himself or any other member of the family. (All such requests should be supported by a medical certificate and routed through the Ministry of Health in case of officers entitled to Contributory Health Service Scheme and in all other cases the application may be accompanied by certificate from the authorised medical attendants. In cases where the officers family is staying outside Delhi/New Delhi, medical certificate from a Civil Surgeon/Assistant Surgeon may be accepted.)

(ii) In the interest of 'public duty', if so certified by the Joint Secretary or the Head of Department, as the case may be, and

(iii) In any other case of grave hardship such as calamities caused by acts of God or the accommodation occupied by the officer becoming unsafe and uninhabitable.

The Committee recommends that a provision may be made in the allotment rules that where an officer is transferred to a non-family station, he may be permitted by the Director of Estates to retain the accommodation on payment of normal rent provided that the same is required for the bona fide use of the family.

Where the Special Accommodation Rules, 1950, should be discontinued the Committee recommends as below :

(i) That the accommodation intended for single officers drawing less than Rs. 500 p.m. may be included in Part III of the Schedule; and

(ii) That the same may be allotted to 'single officers' and to such 'family officers' as are not residing with their families and desired to be considered for the same.

It is not necessary to create a separate pool or set apart any separate residences for the I.F.S. officers or for other officers of the Ministry of External Affairs drawing less than Rs. 500 p.m.

The Regular Accommodation Rules may be extended to the allotment of Hostel accommodation in Delhi/New Delhi, Bombay and Calcutta with suitable modifications.

ENGLISH REVIEW COMMITTEE, 1960—REPORT

New Delhi, University Grants Commission, 1965. 56p.

Chairman : Prof. G. C. Bannerji
Members : Prof. K. R. Srinivasa Iyengar; Prof. V. K. Gokak; Prof. C. D. Narasimhaiah; Shri S. Mathai; Prof. A. G. Stock.
Member-Secretary : Dr. P. J. Philip

APPOINTMENT

The problem of strengthening the teaching of English in Indain universities and colleges has been engaging the attention of the University Grants Commission for some time. In 1955, the Commission appointed a Committee consisting of Pandit H. N. Kunzru, Prof. N. K. Sidhanta, Prof. V. K. Ayappan Pillai and Shri Samuel Mathai to examine the problems connected with the question of the medium of instruction and to recommend measures to ensure adequate proficiency in English at the university stage. The Kunzru Committee submitted its report in December 1957. The Committee stressed that in the interest of academic standards the change from English to an Indian language as the medium of instruction should not be hastened. Even when a change is effected, English should continue to be studied by all university students as a second language. It underlined the importance of a proper foundation in English being laid at the secondary school stage so that a student entering the university would be able to follow lectures in the English language and read books pertaining to his subject. Among the measures to be undertaken for strengthening the teaching of English in the Universities the Committee recommend that special attention should be given to English in the pre-university class and in the General Education Courses; also to the study of Linguistic both in the universities and in Teacher Training Colleges.

In 1958, the Commission convened a Conference of English teachers to consider the recommendations made by the Kunzru Committee. The Conference devoted itself to a consideration of the teaching of English at both the pre-university and the university level. It made recommendations in regards to the time to be set apart for the purpose, to teaching methods, the size of lectures and tutorial classes and to text books, examinations etc., in the compulsory English course. It also recommended that at each University there should be provision for the study of English language and literature as an optional subject both for the B.A. and M.A. degrees.

The Commission forwarded the reports of the Kunzru Committee and the English Teacher's conference to the Universities and to the State Governments for information and necessary action. These reports were also referred to the Central Institute of English, Hyderabad, for prepairng a plan of action for implementation of the recommendations. The programme drawn up by the Institute was circulated to the Universities for their consideration.

It is an undeniable fact that after Independence, insufficient attention was paid to the teaching of English in our universities and colleges. This was largely due to controversies of a non-academic kind about the future status of the English language in the country and also to a narrow view being taken regarding the role of English in relation to the development of the regional languages. A sharp decline in communication skills, as also in the working knowledge of English, among the students, was the result. The deterioration of standards in English adversely affected the standards in other subjects also. A situation threatened to develop in which students in our universities would be in danger of acquiring out dated knowledge isolated from current trends of thought in different areas of study.

The present position in all the States is that the regional language is the medium of instruction up to the secondary stage. At the undergraduate stage, the medium is either English or an Indian language, and an option is given to the students to write their answers at examinations in either English or the regional language. The medium of instruction at the post-graduate level in almost all universities is English though a few universities permit students to answer questions in Hindi or regional language.

These changes have created a number of complex problems for our universities and colleges. Firstly, we do not have competent teachers in sufficient numbers for teaching the different subjects through the medium of the regional language. We are also unable to provide a sufficient number of good text books, reference books in journals in these languages. Consequently the students have to rely mainly on cheap 'Notes', guide books, etc. Secondly, the abrupt change in the medium of instruction from the school to the university or from the under-graduate to the post-graduate stage overlooks the fact that with inadequate knowlege of English students will not be able to follow lectures delivered in English. Students also find it difficult to read books in English which reduces very considerably the usefulness of libraries in the university and colleges. It has further to be noted that the percentage of failures in English at all public examinations is much higher than that in other subjects. It would, therefore appear that it may not be possible to reduce the present student 'wastage' in the country without sufficiently strengthening the teaching of English weather it is used as the medium of instruction or studied as a second language.

In view of these developments, the university Grants Commission felt that a Committee of experts should examine the issues involved. The Commission accordingly appointed the Committee in February, 1960.

TERMS OF REFERENCE

(a) To define the objectives of teaching and learning English at the various levels of university education.

(b) To examine the standards of teaching in English language and literature both at the under-graduate and post-graduate levels.

(c) To examine the methods of teaching English used in our universities and colleges to equip students with the minimum competence required in this regard in the shortest possible time.

(d) To consider measures for re-organising the M.A. course in English to provide for an intensive study of the language as a tool of knowledge rather than as literature.

(e) To recommend the steps that may be taken to strengthen the teaching of English in the context of the medium of instruction in the Universities.

CONTENTS

Foreword; Appointment of the Committee; Introduction; The Present Position; English in the School; English in the University; Summary of Recommendations; Appendices; I. Summary of recommendations of the Kunzru Committee Report; II. Summary of Recommendations of the English Teacher's Conference held at Hyderabad; III. Plan of Action Based on the Two University Grants Commission Reports on Teaching of English; IV. Suggestions for Syllabuses and examination in English Language at the B.A. (Hons.) and M.A. Courses in Indian Universities.

RECOMMENDATION

1. Introduction

There are two aspects of the teaching of English which are quite distinct in their aims. One is to teach the language and the other is to teach the literature. Although there is no inherent conflict in the claims of one over the other, greater attention should be paid to the language aspect.

The regional languages have not yet developed to a point where they can replace English as a tool of knowledge and as a medium of communication. Even when the regional languages become sufficiently developed, English will remain our window to world knowledge. It has, therefore, to be ensured that the student is able to read books, journals reports, etc., in English in his subject of study.

Generally speaking, it is the responsibility of schools to train students in the effective use of language, so that they can follow instruction in the university without difficulty. For a variety of reasons, many schools in our country are not able to discharge this responsibility. Consequently, most students enter the university without even the basic skills of language. The universities have, therefore, to remedy the defects by making special efforts to teach the language in the pre-university course or in the first year of the Degree course.

In the universities where English is not the medium of instruction the aim should be to develop the reading comprehension, whereas the universities which have English as the medium of instruction the aim should be to develop also the skills of writing and speaking. In both types of universities, it would be necessary to teach English as a compulsory subject upto the final year of the degree course. Universities should start the teaching of English at the point at which it was left off by the schools. The effort should continue throughout the degree course.

2. English In The School

In order to raise standards at the university and college level, adequate attention has to be given to raising of standards obtaining in the high school. There is a widespread consciousness of the need for strengthening the teaching of English in schools but the number of years for which English has to be studied in schools varies from one State to another, English should be studied in schools for at least six years.

A possible line of action for training of English teachers could be the adoption of the Madras Governments 'snow ball' programme, under which groups of teachers were put through a training programme, who in turn trained others and so on. A more effective way would be to organise summer schools of a month's duration at which the syllabus and the reading materials for one year could be covered. In service training programme such as week-end classes, evening classes could be tired. It will also be necessary to set up a large number of institutions providing courses in the language and in the new method.

The aim of teaching English at the school should be that the student actually learns a select vocabulary of 2,500 to 3,000 words. The reading material in the school final year should consist of specially written passages intended to revise the more difficult structure and of simplified passages from good modern English literature. These should be accompained by suitable exercises. The schools should provide a minimum of eight periods per week for the teaching of English.

The question paper should keep in view the level of students' competence at the end of their school programme. The paper should contain questions on text as well as questions designed to test the skills in language vocabulary and grammar. It should also have questions on basic skills, which have been enumerated in the Report.

3. English In The University

As a positive step towards improving the knowledge of English of students who enter the university with inadequate knowledge of English, universities should organise special courses of three to four weeks' duration during the summer vacation or during the vacation between the first and second term or arrange special classes in English during the first term by cutting down laboratory work for science students and tutorials for arts students. Alternatively, English classes could be held outside the normal working hours of the university or college. These special courses should be planned as an intensive preparation of university work.

3.2 English In The First Year Of Pre-University Class

The teaching of English at the pre-university stage needs to be strengthened. The course should include two text-books, one of modern English prose and the other of short stories or plays or a short novel for rapid non-detailed reading. There should be a second course designed to improve language skills. The aim of this course should be to expand vocabulary, to establish control over structures and to improve the students' reading comprehension. One way of doing this is to encourage the student to speak in English on familiar themes and also in the course of conversation.

The pre-university course should provide eight periods per week for English, comprising three lecture periods and the rest tutorials. One lecture period can be used for teaching of prose text, another for the book of poems and the non-detailed text and the third period for reading comprehension, the fourth for vocabulary and spoken English and the fifth for work on the prose text and the poems. Lecturers should be used mainly for imparting fresh information and tutorials for discussion, questions and answers, and for practice in writing.

Tutorial work shou'd in no case be left to the care of junior teachers on'y. Substitution tables may be used to reduce the quantum of correction work, which a scheme of intensive tutorial work involves. Ideally speaking, each group should consist of not more than 10-12 students; in no case should the number exceed 25.

The examination in the course has to be related to the objectives of teaching and made more reliable and valid. It has also to be ensured that students attend the required number of tutorial classes and take periodical tests regularly. The question of giving credit for the essential work done by students may also be considered by universities.

It is desireable that all teachers of English should receive some training in the Central Institute of English, Hyderabad, and when this is not possible to attend special summer courses organised by the university. After they have been trained, they should have the freedom to select their teaching materials, organise their courses of study and use the new teaching techniques to the best possible advantage.

The language section of the library should be strengthened sufficiently. The library should also build up a good collection of interesting reading material. Physical facilities like tutorial rooms, facilities for cyclostyling material, recorded speeches on tapes or discs, recorded verse, dialogues, etc., should be provided to add interest to the study of English.

It is necessary to ensure that taxtbooks in other subjects are written in simple English so that students can read them without difficulty. Teachers of these subjects should also present their lectures in the simplest possible language, speak slowly and clearly, use the blackboard and distribute cyclostyled sheets of their lectures to facilitiate understanding.

In universities where a course in the regional language is a requirement, additional English or Hindi should be permitted as an alternative for those who have not studied the reginal language earlier. The texts for this course should be at a higher level.

3.3 Compulsory English In The Intermediate And Degree Course

There should be two courses in English which every student studying for a degree in arts or science or commerce should be required to offer. The first course should consist of two or three texts including short stories, essays, short plays, a certain amount of prose and verse and perhaps a novel. The second course should be concerned with the enlargement of the student's vocabulary and his command of structure.

There should be a provision of three periods a week for the first two years of the degree course in the first paper. The final examination in this paper should be held at the end of the second year. The second paper should be taught mainly through tutorials. The course should be spread over all the three years with the final examination at the end. Pass marks in the second paper should be much higher than in the first.

3.4. Optional And Honours English Courses For The B.A. And M.A. Degree

The optional and Honours courses at the B.A. level in the M.A. Course in English ought to form one integrated programme. Every student should have taken a paper on the English language at some stage before he obtains the M.A. degree in English.

Although the syllabus for the B.A. and M.A. courses in English would be decided by every university in the context of its resources, library facilities and specialisation of the teaching staff, it might be indicated that the optional papers for the B.A. (Pass) course shou'd have a broad cultural value and for this reason texts written in obsolete language, however good their literary value, should be avoided. History of literature should emphasise the study of representative works of a period rather than a broad survey of various literary movements. It should be taught in the context of the social and political background of English literature. The study of criticism and prosody is also important. The study of literary forms should be prescribed on'y when enough examples of the form are to be found in English as well as European literature.

The M.A. course in English should have the following objectives :

(a) A thorough acquaintance with the major classics and the main movements in literary history;

(b) The ability to think independently and form sound critical judgments on works of English literature;

(c) An emphasis on the study of language, its evalution, structure and behaviour.

In order to raise the standards of post graduate studies in English, admissions to the course have to be more selective. In universities where there is an honours course cnly such students as have done the honours course should be admitted to the M.A. course In other universities candidates must have offered English as an optional subject and must have obtained at least a second class in the B.A. examination. In exceptional cases students who have done B.A. in the first or high second class without the optional papers in English may be admitted for an interview. It would further improve matters if students are admitted upon the result of special entrance tests in composition and comprehension. External students should not b epermitted to take the M.A. examination without attending lectures.

M.A. teaching in English should be permitted, on a co-operative basis, only at centres where there are two or more degree colleges, after the university is satisfied about library facilities, requisite staff, etc. The university should encourage participation by teachers from affiliated colleges in its post-graduate teaching work.

The M.A. course should comprise a paper on the English language, there are four papers covering major classics in prose, poetry and drama, a paper on the principles and practice of criticism, one or two literary forms and two optional papers, e.g., Shakespeare, American Literature, Indian writing in English, etc.

It is not desirable to divide the M.A. examination into parts. The practice of offering 'dissertation' in lieu of one or two optional papers should be discouraged as it limits the study of English literature, particularly in universities where students come to the M.A. course without an honours degree in English. The testing of students by means of a *viva voce* is to be commended. The *viva voce* should be conducted by the entire board of paper setters and examiners, wherever practicable. In any case, an external examiner should always be associated with the *viva voce* examination.

3.5. Research

Research in English will mostly have to be confined to university teaching departments. If a college have the facilities for undertaking research and if there is an outstanding man on its staff, such a person should be recognised as a research guide. A research student has to be near his guide but in the case of bright young teachers an exception might be made and they could be allowed to supplicate for a research degree provided they meet the guides during summer vacations. The selection of topic for research can best be done by ascertaining the library facilities and the nature of available guidence. There could be no objection to the award of a Ph.D. degree on the translation of well-known Indian classics with suitable editing and biographical details. All research students should be given a course in the methodology of research. They should also be required to study the subject of research against its wider background.

3.6. Qualifications of Teachers

Lecturers and professors in colleges and lecturers in universities should have good degrees especially good M.A. degrees and some training at an Institute of English. Readers and Professors at the university should preferably have a good degree from a good

British or American university addition to a first or second class degree from an Indian University. They may also have a Ph.D. But the Ph.D. degree should not be insisted upon in all cases, for the essential qualification in the university professor is that he should be a 'scholar of repute'.

SCHOOL HEALTH COMMITTEE, 1960—REPORT

New Delhi, Ministry of Health, 1963 2 Vols.

Chairman : Smt. Renuka Ray.
Members : Smt. Tara Cherian; Dr. N. B. Kabbur; Shri K. R. Ramachandran Dr. M. Swaminathan; Dr. R. P. Devadas; Dr. C. Gopalan.
Co-opted Member : Smt. Pushpa Mehta.
Secretary : Dr. V. Ramakrishna.

APPOINTMENT

The School Health Committee was appointed by the Government of India vide Order No. F2/202/58PW (Pt), dated February 16, 1960, to assess the present standard of health and nutrition of school children and suggest ways and means of improving them.

TERMS OF REFERENCE

(i) To examine the present position of school health programme in the country in all its aspects (excluding physical education, games and sports), e.g., prevention of diseases, medical care and follow-up service, nutrition, health education, healthy environment, etc., of the students at all stages of education and to suggest:—

(a) Further survey of studies if required ; and

(b) How the work of various agencies such as medical, social and welfare associations can be co-ordinated to assist in the promotion of health of school children.

(ii) To examine studies and surveys so far made to assess the nutritional standard of school children and to indicate—

(a) Further survey or studies needed in any specific areas; and

(b) To give concerte suggestions to institute appropriate measures to improve standards of nutrition among school children recommending, inter alia, way and means for financing and organising such programme.

(iii) To examine and recommend the possibility of entrusting Primary Health Centres and other Organisations for conducting a comprehensive and realistic school health programme in association with the local education administration. The recommendations should include measures to develop an effective school medical service suitable to the country.

(iv) To examine the present facilities available for promoting nutritional standards of pre-school children and to suggest practical measures to improve the present position.

CONTENTS

Part: I—Introduction; School Health Services—Appraisal of Existing Situation; School Health Services—Functions of a School Health Service; School Meal Programme—Appraisal of Existing Situation—Purpose and Scope; School Meal Programme—Recommendations; Pre-School Child; School Health Education; Training, Studies and Research; School environment; School Health Administration; Summary of Important Recommendations; **Part II**—Appendices A to G.

RECOMMENDATIONS

School Health Services

School Health Services should form part and parcel of the general health services of the community.

All children should be provided with school health services for the proper development of their personalities and for their well-being. However, with the limited resources at our disposal, it is not possible to bring all children under the scheme at once. For the present, school health services may be made available to primary school children, i.e., children between six to eleven years.

It would be a mere waste of time and money to continue the present system of medical inspection of children. The unsatisfactory results of the present school health services are attributable to : (a) carrying out of the medical inspection in a perfunctory manner; (b) the non-availability of remedial facilities; and (c) lack of follow-up even in the cases of those declared as defective.

The functons of the school health services should be the provision of health measures both preventive and curative. These should include the detection and treatment of defects and the creation ana maintenance of a hygienic environment in and around the school. It should also provide measures for promoting positive health including the provision of supplementary food to improve the nutritional status of children, and health education. The school health services should also provide for the care of eyes, ear, nose and throat and of teeth.

All newly admitted childern should have medical examination first and then again after four years. The limited facilities available today do not permit medical examination at frequent intervals. Children who show serious conditions at entrance and those who show signs of defects and illness later, should have frequent examinations and follow-up.

The medical examination of each pupil should be thorough. Parents should be persuaded to be present during the medical examination of their children.

Adequate space should be made available for the medical inspection of school children.

Securing facilities for prompt treatment is one of the main functions of the school health service. Defects which can be treated at primary health units should be treated there and school health clinics should be held once a week.

Those which call for specialised treatment should be referred to nearest hospitals and transport provided for this purpose. Additional wards for children should be set up with the existing or new hospitals. The medical specialists should visit the primary health units periodically.

Prevention and control of communicable diseases in schools should be the responsibility of public health authorities. Care should be taken to promptly detect and isolate cases of communicable diseases. The class teacher, if properly trained, can spot out common communicable disease in his class.

Emphasis should be laid on compulsory primary and revaccination against smallpox immediately. Immunisation against diphtheria, whooping cough and tetanus should be made compulsory in the immediate future. Steps should be taken to manufacture the vaccine in India so that it may be supplied free. Steps should also be taken to immunise against polio in certain areas of the country where its incidence is reported. In areas where epidemics have known to occur with regular periodicity, it would be necessary to undertake such preventive measures as a routine.

In order to carry out the comprehensive school health service, it will be necessary to increase the staff of the primary health centre by at least one additional medical officer and four auxiliary nurse-midwives. But under the present circumstances, it will not be possible to achieve this ideal in the immediate future. Until such time as doctors become available in required numbers, one additional auxiliary nurse-midwife should be added to each centre to carry on the programme.

To attract the medical and health personnel to work in rural areas, certain incentives, such as better salary scales, facilities for housing, arrangement for schooling of their childern, attractive leave and travel facilities, periodical refresher courses in teaching institution and the grant of advance increments to those who work in rural areas should be given.

With adequate training in health education and school health services, it should be possible for the teacher to undertake certain functions connected with school health services such as : (a) observation of children with a view to spot out any deviations from normal health; (b) recording of height and weight and simple testing of vision and hearing; (c) maintaining of health records of children; and (d) giving First-aid.

The medical history and records of all students should be kept on cards filed in the schools. For the purpose of comparison, it will be necessary to develop uniform types of recording system containing relevant basic data.

Child counselling units in schools and child guidance clinics in the local health department should be established to start with in metropolitan cities where technical personnel and resources may be easily available for providing such services.

Till such time as the doctors and other trained personnel are available in adequate number for services in rural areas, school health services, as an interim measure, may be carried out in only a part of the area covered by the primary health unit. It should be possible for one medical officer to look after school health programme in a limited area covering about 2,000 children as against 6,000 children in the entire area.

In addition, four districts in each State may be selected during the Third Plan and school health services provided to all the children in the age group six to 11.

School health services may be provided in all the schools in corporations and municipalities. In any case, all the children studying in schools located in slum areas of cities and towns must be covered.

During the Fourth Plan period, school health services should be provided to : (a) all children in the age-group six to 11 in rural and urban areas; and (b) the children of middle and high schools in areas where facilities exist.

School Meal

The primary aim of the school meal programme should be to improve health and encourage sound dietary habits among children.

The school meal should provide approximately one-third of the dietary and nutritional requirements of children.

The school meal should be based on cheap nutrition and locally available foods. A sample menu may comprise a minimum of : cereals and millet—2.5 oz. ; pulses one oz. (or pulses 0.5 oz. and protein rich supplement 0.5 oz.); leafy vegetables—one oz.; non-leafy vegetables —one oz.; oil—1/4 oz.; and condiments and salt. This menu would cost roughly 10 nP. The cost of providing such a meal to each child would be roughly 12 nP per day including the cost of preparation of meals and other incidental charges of two nP.

As there is shortage of milk supply, at present, in our country, it should first be given to the infants, expectant and nursing mothers and pre-school children. There is, however, likelihood of some surplus milk which will be available to school children because for the next few years the majority of pre-school children cannot be reached as the number of institutions through which they can be reached is limited. It will thus be possible to provide milk to the lower age-group of six to seven years and possibly to others in the primary school age-group.

School meal for children should include the multi-purpose food or other locally available protein rich foods as a supplement. Plants for the manufacture of multi-purpose food produced at the Central Food Technological Research Institute, Mysore, should be set up in various parts of the country.

The catering colleges and catering centres planned to be set up by the Food and Agriculture Ministry to train personnel for catering establishments and prepare different types of delicious and nutritions foods should also undertake to prepare meals for being distributed in the schools located in the surrounding areas. They should also serve as modern central kitchens for the school meal programme and to popularise the use of inexpensive and nutritions food articles.

The potentialities in respect of production of fish and fish-meal which can constitute a part of school meal, should be explored. Facilities for improved haulage, quick refrigerated transport and cold storage of fish should be provided.

In every junior or senior basic school, wherever land is available, vegetables should be grown. Such fresh vegetables should constitute a part of school meal. Such facilities should also be provided at least in a few other schools in each of the community development blocks. Extension Division of the Agricultural Development should help the schools by giving seeds, implements, fencing material and technical guidance.

Expanded nutrition programmes similar to the one recently started in Orissa, should be taken up in other States. These projects should include the production and distribution of nutritionally valuable foods to vulnerable segments of population. They should also include nutrition education of people and training of personnel.

Every school should be provided with protected water supply and facilities for drainage; sanitary environment; facilities for storage; preparation and distribution of food; adequate space for feeding of children; and sanitary disposal of garbage.

It is necessary that the Government should support the school meal programme besides the contribution of the community at the rate of 50 per cent of the total cost.

For psychological and social reasons, there should be no discrimination between children from rich families and poor families in regard to serving of school meals. The parents from well-to-do families will naturally contribute more towards the community's share of the programme.

All children in the age-group six to 11 should be provided school meal during the Third Plan period. It is estimated that about 50 million children would be in Primary School by 1965-66. The number of children who may actually attend school, on most of the days, however, would be 40 million. It should not be difficult to provide meal to these 40 million children during Third Plan period if both internal resources and external assistance are utilised.

Any proposal about the external assistance towards this important programme, in the shape of food articles, should be favourably considered. The acceptance of external aid is suggested as an interim measure only. It should be possible to finance school meal programme through our own resources, as and when there is increased community participation, improvement in the internal resources, and in the food production in the country.

In case external assistance and community participation on a higher scale are not forthcoming in the early stages, school meal should be provided to roughly 11 million children during the Third Plan period. Apart from the community contribution in cash or kind, which is reckoned at 50 per cent of the total expenditure, the Government share on this programme would be roughly Rs. 42 crores. The remaining spillover will have to be carried over to the Fourth Plan period.

During the Fourth Plain period, the scheme of providing school meal should be extended to cover children of the middle schools also along with all the children of primary schools, who would have been covered by the end of the Third Plan period. Wherever possible, the students of high schools and colleges should also be covered.

Pre-School Child

A comprehensive health and welfare service for pre-school children should be introduced.

In order to provide such service, the existing institutions should be strengthened, and a machinery through which the activities of different social welfare organisations could be coordinated for undertaking programmes for improving nutritional status of pre-school children should be evolved.

The fist priority in regard to milk supply should be given to expectant and nursing mothers, infants and pre-school children.

In the past, large quantities of milk powder made available by UNICEF, have been left unused. The pre-school children in particular and even school children in many parts of the country did not receive milk due to unsatisfactory storage and distribution of milk powder. Immediate steps should be taken to remedy this situation.

Services of 'Balwadis', 'Mahila Samiti's', maternity and child welfare centres, health centres, clinics, and nursery schools, the pre-primary schools, pediatric centres of hospitals and social welfare and similar organisations should be utilised for the distribution of milk to pre-school children.

There is need to evolve suitable diets for pre-school children. This can be achieved by the judicious combination of the available food-stuffs which are rich in protein and others protective nutrients. It is necessary to produce such products on a regional basis.

It is estimated that, at present, it is possible to reach only 15 lakhs of pre-school children. They would require about 51 million lbs. of powder milk in a year if every child is given one-and-a-half oz. of milk powder per day. It is hoped that milk powder and vitamin supplements needed for distribution to these children would be made available by UNICEF and other agencies. The total cost of distributing 51 million lbs. of milk powder to 15 lakhs of children would be roughly Rs. 3.4 crores per year.

School Health Education

Health education should be included as a part of general education in the primary, middle and secondary schools. The Basic Education system, as expounded by Mahatma Gandhi, contains the essential ingredients of a school health education programme.

Steps should be taken to keep the school environment in a sanitary condition. The school administration should provide the right environment to promote health, prevent disease and furnish opportunities to children to practise food health habits.

School authorities should employ teachers who are in sound health and should take steps to see that conditions under which they are working are conductive to healthy living.

The health personnel should assist the teacher in carrying out his health education responsibilities. They should also help parents to provide facilities for the child to practise at home the health habits learnt at school.

The State Administration should play a vital role in the effective implementation of the school health education programme and in setting up standards in the State in accordance with the national policies.

The State Administration should take immediate steps to publish text-books on health education and to have health lessons included in other appropriate text-books. Books and teaching aids should be kept up-to-date with scientific health information and adopted to the developmental level of pupils for whom they are intended.

The Central Health Education Bureau, and the National Institute of Audio-visual Education in cooperation with appropriate advisers in various fields of education should develop "type" instructional material and teaching aids for use in school health education programme. These material should serve as guides for the States to develop their own aids and material.

In primary grades, the emphasis should be placed on practising healthful living. The teaching should be practical and related to the pupil's past experience, his home conditions and his present needs.

The learning experiences in middle classes should be 'life-centred' rather than 'book-centred'. In school where there are special subject teachers, the health content of the curriculum may be correlated with the specific subjects taught. Where the class teacher is responsible for all teaching in the class, he should be responsible for the health teaching as well.

The health curriculum for secondary schools should be carefully planned so as to avoid unnecessary duplications and serious omissions with appropriate health topics being incorporated with in the respective special subjects. Wherever facilities exist, health should be included in the list of optional subjects offered.

The draft syllabion health education for the children of the age-groups six to 11 11 to 14 and 14 to 17 prepared by the Committee on Health and Nutrition Education constituted by the Ministry of Education should be adopted for hea'th teaching in schools with slight modifications to suit lccal needs.

The School Health Education Section in the Central Health Education Bureau and the Student Health Education Units in State Health Education Bureau should be developed to provide leadership in different aspects of School Health Education.

Training Studies, and Research

The training programmes of the existing orientation and other training centres for doctors should be critical'y evaluated and re-organised to equip the trainees passing through them to play their role providing health care with understanding and faith in the preventive services.

The existing departments of hygiene run by part-time teachers in many medical colleges should be upgraded to the departments of social and preventive medicine Medical students should have sound background in the social and preventive medicine in their under-graduate curriculum.

The Indian Medical Council and Universities should examine the curriculum of social and preventive medicine with a view to provide sufficient emphasis on the health of the school child.

The field practising centres attached to the medical colleges should be provided with the required staff and equipment to facilitate provision of experience in the organisation and implementation of school health services.

Steps should be taken to arrange short-term cources and seminar with a view to provide adequate training to doctors in applied nutrition. Nutrition education should recieve special attention in the teaching of different subjects in medical colleges.

A short specialised course in school health service should be provided by the All-India Institute of Hygiene and Public Health for those who will be in-charge of administration of school health. Similar courses should be organised either at the field training centres attached to the medical colleges or at the proposed health demonstration districts.

The syllabus for the training of auxiliary nurse-midwives should be re-examined by the Indian Nursing Council with a view to include the subject of school health in the curriculum besides fundamentals of healthful school environment, principles of nutrition and treatment of minor ailments. The present curriculum of training of health visitors should also be reviewed with a view to see that sufficient emphasis is placed on the practical aspects of school health services.

For the training of sanitary inspectors, The curriculum formulated by the Director General of Health Services should be followed in all the sanitary inspectors' training courses.

In teacher training programmes, health education and school health should be a required part of training. The teacher should have the knowledge of the growth and development of children, personal hea'th, community health, school health practices and methods of health education.

One teacher in each teacher training college or institution should be made responsible for coordination of courses and activities in health education. All such teachers should receive special training in health education and in principles and practices in school and community health. Health education at the post-graduate level should be provided at the National Institute of Education and in the zonal institutes being set up by the Ministry of Education and at the post-graduate centre for health education to be developed by the Ministry of health.

For the teachers who are already in service, special short-term courses should be organised in the local school organisations with the technical assistance from the health personnel. The Central and State Health Education Bureaux should guide and assist in the training of teachers health education.

Short-term orientation courses should be organised by training colleges or by lccal administrations to provide in-service training on health education to administrators and education officers.

Future school health and school meal policies and programmes should be developed from the results obtained through scientific surveys and studies. Studies and research are quite essential for making school health programme efficient, effective and economical.

School Environment

School buildings should be simple, safe, attractive and sanitary. In selecting the location of a school, consideration should be given to sufficiency of space for buildings and playgrounds, availability of safe water supply, possibility of drainage and sanitation. The surroundings should be attractive and protected from traffic hazards. The construction and maintenance of school buildings should be in accordance with the rules formulated by the States.

Every school building in urban areas where public water supply is available should have water supply connection and adequate number of taps. In rural areas an independent water supply system is desirable for each school. If that is not possible, earthen pitchers properly covered and with taps fixed to them should be provided.

In urban areas whatever drainage facilities exist, these should be extended to all schools. In rural areas, drains should be constructed for the removal of waste water.

Wherever drainage facilities exist, there should be hand-flushing laterines connected to sewers, if feasible or to septic tank disposal systems. In other cases, hand-flushing latrines as per the type design approved by the Central Public Health Engineering Organisation of the Ministry of Health should be adopted. Where water is scarce, a bore-hole latrine should be used with a simp'e squat plate having an aperture which should be covered after use.

The garbage should be disposed of according to the methods approved by the health authority.

The scale of food by hawkers in and around the school shou'd be prohibited.

School Health Administration

The success and efficiency of school health and school meal programme depends largely on sound coordinated and effective administration. There should be greater understanding and cooperation between the health, education, agriculture and community development authorities at all levels. They should jointly assume responsibilities for policies and procedures for rendering these services.

As this should be one of the important projects for public participation under the Third Five-Year Plan, thle non-officials and the community should be closey associated in shouldering the responsibility for the programme.

The medical officer or the health officer of a particular area shou'd have responsibility in carrying out school health services of that area. The local health authority should supervise and assist the school administration in maintaining healthy environment of the school.

The school meal programme should be the responsibility of the local administration and the education authorities. The Headmaster or the Principal of a particular school will be responsib'e for the implementation of school meal service with the assistance of the local committee. The latter should be responsible for raising the community share of resources.

Any organisational set up at the national, State or other levels should recognise and mobilise voluntary efforts of the community and agencies concerned in the health and well-being of the children. It should also facilitate maximum utilisation of limited resources of every department.

At the Centre, there should be a National School Health Council. Such a Council will facilitate cooperation and coordination of many individuals and groops that are concerned with the health of the children. It should provide a simple and orderly way of bringing together representatives of the community, professional and voluntary organisations and official agencies both at the Centre and States so that they may share in planning and imp!ementing schoo! hea'th services.

The Nat'onal Council comprising 40 members including a non-official as Chairman should be the Chief Advisory Coordinating and Supporting Body appointed by the Government of India, Ministry of Education. Its tenure should be three years.

The Council should have a permanent full-time Secretary who will be assisted by three part-time technical Joint Secretaries drawn from the Ministries of Health, Education and Food and Agriculture.

There should be new divisions in the Ministry of Education, Hea'th and Food and Agriculture for giving effect to the School Health Programme, formulated on the recommendations of the National Council.

Each State should have a State Council of School Health comprising 25 members with a non-official as Chairman. The Director of Education and the Director of Health Services should alternative'y be Secretary and Joint Secretary of the Council.

There should be a 'school health bureau or section' in the Health Department and school meal and health education bureau or section, in the Education Department in each State to implement the programme.

At district level, School health and School Meal Committees should be set up as sub-committees of the District Development Councils. The District Health Officer and District Education Officer should alternatively be the Secretary and Joint Secretary of the Committee. The District Health Officer should be responsible for organising and conducting school health services and the District Education Officer for school meal and health education programmes. The District Food and Agriculture Officer should look after the storage and distribution of food.

The district health and education organisations should be strengthened appropriately to plan, implement and supervise this additional work.

There should be School Health Committees at the block level. These committees could be sub-committees of the Block Development Council. The medical officer of the primary health unit and the inspector of schools should be the Secretary and Joint Secretary of these Committees.

At village level, local school health committees should be constituted. These should include representatives of the village panchayat, representatives of welfare organisations, if any community leaders interested in school health and the local health staff, with the senior headmaster as the Secretary. These committees should mobilise the community to make programmes continous and self-supporting.

HINDU RELIGIOUS ENDOWMENTS COMMISSION, 1960—REPORT

Delhi, Manager of Publications, 1962. 524, III p.

Chairman : Dr. C.P. Ramaswami Aiyar.

Members : Shri Sankar Saran ; Shri Mahabir Prasad ; Swami Harinarayananand ; Shri P. Kameswara Rau ; Shri K. Vankataswami Naidu ; Shri K.C. Sen.

APPOINTMENT

By notification G.S.R. No. 233 dated the March 1, 1960, in the Ministry of Law (Legislative Department) the Government of India constituted on the March 1, 1960, under Section 3 of the Commissions of Inquriy Act, 1952 (60 of 1952), a Commision of Inquiry called the Hindu Religious Endowments for the purpose of making an inquiry into certain matters connected with Hindu public religious endowments.

TERMS OF REFERENCE

(a) To examine generally the institution of Hindu religious endowments and to recommend the classes of such endowments which should be treated as public religious endowments ;

(b) To inquire into the manner in which Hindu public religious endowments are being managed and the resources thereof are being utilised, and to recommend ways and means for the proper management of such endowments and the proper utilisation of their resources ;

(c) In particular, to inquire into the manner in which holders of offices in relation to Hindu public religious endowments are being chosen, whether by way of succession, nomination or otherwise ;

(d) To examine whether the existing arrangements in regard to the manner in which holders of such offices are being chosen are satisfactory and if not, to suggest ways and means for improving the same ; and

(e) To inquire into and report on any other matter relevant to any of the matters specified above, which, in the opinion of the Commission, requires to be inquired into.

CONTENTS

Introduction ; Historical Background of Temples, Mutts and other Religious Institutions ; Legislation ; Private and Public Religious Endownents ; Archakas, Pujaris, Pandas and Other persons connected with Temple Service ; Trustees ; Utilisation of Surplus Funds and Application of *cy-pres* doctrine ; Succession ; Jain and Buddhist Endowments ; Irregularities and Malpractices ; Management and Administration ; Religious Trusts Bill, 1960 ; Land Reform legislation in so far as it affects the Income of Endowments ; Amendment of the Constitution ; General ; Summary of Recomendations and a General Summing up Epilogue ; Appendices I to XX ; Bibliography.

RECOMMENDATIONS

This Commission is definitely of the opinion that those States where there are no enactments governing Hindu religious endowments (namely, Assam, Punjab, West Bengal and Uttar Pradesh) should speedily undertake suitable legislation in this behalf.

This Commission desired to suggest to the Central Government the desirability of bringing into operation a uniform pattern of lagislation dealing with the administration and management of religious endowments of all the communities in India whilst making such special provisions as may be necessary to deal with the special problems of the religious endowments of individual communities. Such legislation has, naturally, to be undertaken only after ascertaining the views of the communities, which have not been included in our survey.

Such uniform legislation may incorporate with advantage the provisions of clauses 5, 11, 12, 13, 14 and 15 of the Religious Trusts Bill, 1960.

The legislation recommended by us relates to topics which appertain to the concurrent list in the schedule to the constitution. Where State legislation has already been undertaken and implemented, the suggestions that we make will superseed the provisions of the local legislation to the extent to which they are inconsistent with our recommendations. Where States have not passed any legislation regarding religious endowments the provisions that we have recommended will be embodied in a statute which will apply *suo motu* to those States unless and until they pass legislation carrying out the objectives of our recommendations.

No claim of a proprietary nature on the part of archakas, pujaris or pandas in offerings made by devotees to temples should in our opinion be recognised.

Subject to what follows in (5) below, if offerings or gifts for his services are made to an archaka, panda or pujari personally on account of the veneration and respect due to that person, then they will inhere in the person in question and be treated as his own, but in such a case they should be received and kept separatly and distinctly and should not be mixed with the offerings made to the dity as a juristic entity. Where offerings are made to a temple without specially designating whether they are to the officiating priest, mahant, archaka, etc., or to the deity, then they should be treated as belonging to the deity as a juristic entity.

It is essential to lay down that where the public or a section of the public have traditional customary and unrestricted access to a temple, it should be treated as a public one and that even in cases where a temple is maintained within residential premises if offerings and gifts are received by the temple authorities from the public or a section thereof at the time of worship or other religious service, it should be treated as a public temple and should cease to be treated as private one.

In the case of temples, the trustee or shebait should not be allowed to claim any personal or proprietory interest in the management of the institution and the offerings and donations and gifts made by worshippers to the deity and should be strictly accountable to the public for them. The Constitution should, if necessary, be amended so as to make the position absolutely clear, thereby preventing the possibility of any trustee or shebait attempting to prefer any such claim to absolute or heritable ownership in future either in his office or in respect of gifts and offerings by devotees. Of course, if in any institution, a shebait, archaka or pujari engages in any religious service, he may be adequately remunerated for such service but the right to the office of shebair and emoluments thereof should not be regarded as private property.

Where offerings are made to the head of a mutt and are not earmarked or specially designated as personal gifts or donations to him they should be regarded as the property of the mutt and should be utilised for the purposes of the mutt.

All mutts should be treated as public religious endowments in the sense that the public or a substantial portion of the public is interested in their upkeep, conduct and management.

The original purpose of all mutt s should be recognised as comprising religious instruction and propagation of religious tenets of sampradayas and the teaching and training of monastic and lay disciples and followers.

Having regard to the long continued practice and traditions of many matts, the property rights of the head of the mutt in offerings known as padakanikas and pranamis may be recognised to the extent that while the head of a mutt has a right to disburse them at his discretion during his life time for furtherance of the objects and purposes of the mutts and religious and charitable objects consistent with those objects and purposes, any of those or their proceeds remaining undisbursed at the end of his life, should automatically vest in the mutt. It is of course to be understood that the head of a mutt being a religious preceptor and not a bare trustee is entitled to spend the income of the mutt whatever be the source for the maintenance, accommodation and legitimate travels of himself and his sishyas and disciples suitable to the status and dignity and traditions of the mutt and so as to carry out the essential objectives of mutts—namely the propagation of the tenets and sampradaya of the mutt in question and for the propagation of Hindu religion and culture generally.

There are provisions in the Civil Procedure Code exempting certain persons from personal appearance in courts. It is for consideration whether this privilege should not be extended to the accredited and recognised heads of mutts of accepted sanctity and authority.

Every State should set up in one or more important Hindu religious centres schools or institutions wherein archakas, pujaris and pandas are given instruction in agamas, archana, puja-paddhati, rituals, etc., according to a prescribed syllabus with provision for both elementary and advanced training. The elementary training should provide for (a) a working knowledge of Sanskrit, (b) a knowledge of the agamas, rituals and mode of worship of the respective sampradayas to which the archakas belong and the sthalpuranas of the institutions to which they may be, or are attached, and (c) a good working knowledge of the regional languages so as to enable them so explain to worshippers with facility the meaning and significance of the mantras and archanas.

Advanced training should in addition provide for the study of selected Shastras and the Darsanas or philosophies of Hinduism in general with particular emphasis on the tenets, etc. of the sampradaya to which the archakas belong. The institution should provide for refresher courses for the archakas already serving in the temples and part time courses for such Hindu students from secular educational institutions who may volunteer for such training in their leisure hours. There may be a system of awarding stipends to students who are willing to take up such training, preference being given as far as possible to the students from the families of the hereditary archakas and pujaris. The training should be organised in such a manner as would cater to the needs of the main sampradayas in the State. The institutions should be financed from the surplus funds of the religious institutions of the main sampradayas pooled together on a Central basis or in different centres or regions from the pooled funds of a group of temples pertaining to a particular sampradaya, whichever course may be found appropriate.

Provision should be made for prescribing minimum qualifications for the archakas to perform archanas or puja in the temples. We recommend that such qualiications may, subject to suitable modifications in view of the local conditions, be (a) working knowledge of Sanskrit, (b) a good knowledge of the mantras agamas, rituals and (c) a knowledge of the sthalapurana and traditions of the institution to which they are attached or may be attached.

They should in addition be proficient in the regional languages so as to enable them to explain with facility the meaning and significance of madtras and archanas to pilgrims, devotees and worshippers. Further they should possess a good moral character and basic learning so as to inspire reverence in the worshippers.

Hereditary rights of succession wherever archakas and pujaris enjoy such rights need not be abolished. However, every archaka, whether hereditary or non-hereditary, should be required to undergo some minimum tests of fitness and should qualify himself to perform his duties efficiently and properly. If the hereditary archakas are not so qualified, they may be required to appoint qualified deputies in their places until they or their descendants qualify themselves. In the matter of appointments first preference should be given to qualified persons who have a hereditary right.

As already indicated the archakas, pujoris, etc., should not be allowed to have a proprietary right to any part of the offerings made before the deity. They should also not enjoy any proprietary right of custody of the jewels and other valuable articles belonging to the temple. If necessary, the Constitution should be amended to make this point clear.

It is absolutely essential that archakas and pujaris should be ensured a minimum living wage and their emoluments fixed in suitable grades for various categories in order that they may not resort to beggary or extortion. They should al so be allowed the benefit of a provident fund and pension at least in the case of big temples which can afford the same. The facility of free residence, near the temple, should also be provided as far as practicable.

The minimum emoluments even in the case of archakas in small temples should be at least at Rs. 60 p.m. in addition to dearness allowance and other allowances admissible to persons in Government service in the corresponding grades in the State service.

In cases where temples are, out of their own resources, unable to afford such payments, the pooling system already adverted to in respect of the income of temples of the same sampradaya should be resorted to.

The conditions of service of archakas and pujaris should be prescribed by rules and should inter alia provide for fines and suspension or removal from their office for misconduct or negligence of duty, disobedience of the directions of the trustees or other authorities concerned with the affairs of the temples. Adequate provision should be made for a right of appeal to a superior authority against the decision of a subordinate authority awarding punishment particularly in the matter of suspension or removal from office or reduction in emoluments.

A code of conduct should be prescribed by rules for the archakas.

A tariff containing a regulated scale of fees payable by the worshippers at the temples concerned for services like utsavas, pujas abhishek, etc., should be prescribed and prominently exhibited in the temples. Persons should in all cases be issued receipts for the amounts paid by them.

The State laws wherever they exist or are under contemplation should make suitable provision to implement the foregoing recommendations.

As one of the primary objects of temples there should be a provision for reading and exposition of the scriptures. Puranas, etc., (especially of those relating to the institution and the presiding deity) and discourses thereon in a manner relevant to and in conformity with the sampradaya of the temple or mutt concerned and provision should be made for this purpose within the premises of the temple or the mutt or in some other suitable place. Provision should also be made for indicating religious and ethical ideals in the minds of worshippers and the visiting public by the exposition of scriptures and their episodes and extracts from the Puranas, Itihasas, etc.

Arrangements should be made daily and/or on the occasion of an utsava abhishekam or archana for the giving of a full account for the benefit of the pilgrims in the regional language, of the history of the temple and its traditions and significance. These discourses should be based on the relevant scriptures, Puranas and traditions and be designed to inform the lay public of the details regarding the temple and the import of the various ceremonies performed and the prayers actually offered. We recommend in this connection the system in vogue in the Badrinath temple and some other temples in the country.

Trained religious teachers may, wherever practicable, be employed on a whole-time basis to go round a manageable group of institutions belonging to a particular sampradaya placed under their charge in order:

(a) To guide and supervise the work of archakas and

ensure that worship in a temple is conducted properly in accordance with the tenets and usages of the sampradaya concerned; and

(b) To give discourses, lectures, etc., to the members of the Hindu public so as to bring about religious revival and enlightenment.

The State laws particularly in Northern India (wherever such exist or are under contemplation) should specifically provide for controlling and regulating the activities of the pandas. Their compulsory registry and a specified scale of fees and disciplinary jurisdiction over them in the case of misconduct or extortion should be invariably laid down.

Pandas in important Hindu religious centres should be encouraged to organise themselves to act as qualified pilgrim guides. Adequate arrangements should be made to help them by providing a short course of training.

A system of licensing of pandas should be brought into vogue and none other than those licensed should be allowed to officiate as priests or act as guides. A code of conduct should be prescribed by rules.

There should be provision in the State laws enabling Government to lay down the maximum and minimum charges for particular services randered by pandas and the scale of charges should be prominently displayed on notice boards in the temple; and pandas who take more than the prescribed maximum charges from pilgrims or harass them in any other manner should be dealt with by way of suspension or dismissal and cancellation of their licenses.

Some type of queue system should be introduced in all important temples where pilgrims in large numbers congregate. The system followed in Tirupati can with advantage be adopted.

Wherever pandas officiate as priests or perform other services in the temples, it should be insisted that they should be duly qualified for the duties which they are expected to perform. In the case of persons having hereditary rights, they should be required unless and until they are personally qualified to nominate qualified deputies for the jobs and to hold themselves responsible for all the acts done by their deputies.

Pandas also should have no proprietary right to any part of the offerings made by worshippers to the deity in the temples. Wholly voluntary gifts made to them personally stand on a separate footing and if specially meant for them personally and not for the institution they may be treated as their own.

In all States having at present no enactment with regard to religious endowments, it is necessary inter alia to set up by statute a well defined machinery to exercise effective control over trustees who are responsible for the day-to-day management and administration of the institutions, following the pattern set up by the States who possess such enactment, local variations may of course be found necessary.

There should be adequate provision in such legislation for the maintenance of proper accounts, audit of such accounts, framing of budgets, etc., by the trustees or other persons in charge.

The appointment of trustees, their selection or election, their administration in regard to religious matters and the power vested in them to use the funds of the trust with a view to furthering the objects of the trust may be regulated in accordance with general and local custom and usage in consultation, wherever practicable, with accredited and reputable representatives of the sampradaya concerned and others who may be specially qualified to advise on Hindu religion and religious practices. There should be however, adequate provisions so as to enable the authorities to interfere effectively, whenever it is found that the above objectives and purposes are not duly carried out or are frustrated.

In all cases, as regards the current revenues, if the budget is properly drawn up the true suprlus can be ascertained. Where the objectives of an endowment are clearly specified in a trust deed, court scheme or other document or are undisputed there will be no difficulty in finding out what sum would be left after those objects have been duly carried out such sum would be the surplus. Where no specific objects can be discerned from documents or the custom and usage of the institution the recommendation made below as regards obligatory objects and discretionary or optional objects should in our opinion apply, subject to such priorities as may be appropriate in each case and to the amounts considered adequate in respect of each of such objects. These two limitations would be matters for consideration when budgets are prepared.

If there are surpluses available in any religious institutions, we think that it ought to be their primary objective to arrange for intensive and liberal education in the ideals and doctrines that have found expression in these institutions. For this purpose the surpluses of institutions following the same sampradaya may usefully be pooled together to enable the starting of centres of instruction in selected places. The curriculum and course of studies may be framed on the analogy of the theological universities of the West and of Taxila, Nalanda and Kanchipuram in the past. With reference to Nalanda, especially, there are ample materials for such a purpose.

Contributions for the establishment of centres of instruction referred above may be made from endowments wherever possible voluntarily, but power may be taken by legislation to require the managements of endowments to make such contributions where there is a definite and ascertainable surplus.

A common good fund on the lines of that provided

for in Section 97 of the Madras Hindu Religious and Charitable Endowments, 1959 (22 of 1959), might be created in all States and funds thus available be utilised not merely for renovation and preservation of temple in need of help and for the promotion and propagations of the tenets common to all or any class of religious institutions but also as stated above, for the performance of the essential services in temples which have no resources even for such services.

It would be very advantageous if on a voluntary basis the same type of common good fund can be inaugurated in the case of the mutts either generally or mutts following the same sampradaya, for the purpose of carrying out either for the benefit of whole Hindu community or for the mutts of a particular sampradaya the original purposes of such institutions.

We consider that it would be desirable to divide the objects and purposes of religious institutions into two categories one obligatory and other desirable or optional for the purposes of utilisation of funds. We would suggest that the following may be considered to be the obligatory objects or purposes :

1. The due maintenance of the object of the institution and the proper performance of the services therein in conformity with or 'dittam' namely what is ordained or prescribed.

2. Payment of the salaries or allowances due to the archakas and pujaris and other servants of the institution and the adequate training of these functionaries such as archakas, adhyapakas, Vedaparayanikas and othuvars (reciters of holy texts).

3. The due discharge of liabilities of loans binding on the institution.

4. The repair, renovation or extention of the buildings connected with the institution. Due care should be taken that adequate provision is made for these purposes.

5. The contribution to the reserve fund of the institution which may be fixed at five per cent of the income.

6. Maintenance of a working balance.

The desirable or optional objects may be the following :

1. Arrangements for providing ameneties to the pilgrims, e.g., accommodation, food, water supply, lighting, sanitation and supply of wholesome food, where the custom of naivedyam or bhog obtains.

2. Grant of aid to other religious institutions which are poor or in needy circumstances, of the same sampradaya as far as possible.

3. Flower gardens and goshalas.

4. Propagation of the tenets of the temple and the fundamental of Hindu dharma common to all sampradayas.

5. Publication of agamas and history of the temple, provision of libraries with religious books and publication of religious literature and making them available to the public free of cost or at a nominal charge.

6. Provision for religious discourses and kalakshepams.

7. The grant of scholarships or stipends to Hindu students who study in educational institutions and also undertake to study the Hindu religion and be examined as to their progress.

8. Promotion of temple architecture, sculpture and fine arts.

9. Establishment and maintenance of institutions wherein both modern as well as Hindu religious education is imparted.

10. The establishment and maintenance of colleges or institutions for the study of Hindu religion, philosophy, vedas or the agama sastras or contributions thereto.

11. Establishment and maintenance of orphanages for Hindu children.

12. Establishment and maintenance of asylums for leper patients and/or persons suffering from other serious ailment.

13. Establishment and maintenance of poor homes for destitute and physically disabled Hindu widows, aged people and children.

14. Establishment and maintenance of hospitals and dispensaries for the benefit of pilgrims, worshippers and devotees.

In case of mutts, the funds should primarily be spent on the expounding and popularising of the tenets of Hinduism or of a particular sampradaya and for training and teaching disciples. Such teaching and training may be entrusted to persons belonging to the categories of qualified sadhus or qualified lay teachers. If any surplus is left after fulfilling the primary objects, it may be expended on desirable objects indicated above.

The doctrine of *cy-pres* should be applied to the surplus funds of religious institutions and where there is no statutory provision for such application definite provision should be made on the lines of those contained in Sections 35 and 56 of the Bombay Public Trusts Act, 1950, and Section 66 of the Madras Hindu Religious and Charitable Endowments Act, 1959.

Provisions on the lines of Sections 13 and 14 of the U.K. Charities Act, 1960, may also with advantage be adopted in our laws for the application of the doctrines of *cy-pres*. The doctrine of *cy-pres* in the opinion of the Commission is not in essence different from the basic Hindu definition of Ishta and Purtha as comprising both religious and charitable objects.

The system of hereditary succession to trusteeships or other offices in temples, wherever it exists, may be allowed to continue. It is, however, necessary for the administrative authorities to have control over the above functionaries in the same manner in which they are having control over the non-hereditary ones.

So far as succession to the headship of mutts and temples is concerned, each institution should be allowed to follows its own prevailing custom, usage or tradition, where it is clearly established.

The persons who succeed to the headship of mutts should possess the following essential qualifications :

(a) They should be men of unquestionable moral character and religious temperament.

(b) They should be fully conversant with the particular systems of philosophy of the institutions of which they are the heads and also be able to expound the tenets of the concerned sampradaya to the disciples and devotees.

Matters like claims to hereditary trusteeship and other similar offices in temples, succession to headship of mutts and determination of the suitability of persons who succeed to the headship of mutts with reference to their qualifications should in case of dispute be decided by a statutory Tribunal to be set up for the purpose.

The Hindu Succession Act, 1956, should not be made applicable to succession to headship of religious foundations.

The Hindu Succession Act, 1956, may be amended, if necessary, to make it clear that the property acquired by and belonging to a sanyasin would not pass to his blood relations in the poorvashrama family. Similarly, a sanyasin who has served connections with his natural family should have no claims to property of a non-sanyasin who was related to him by blood in his poorvaashrama days.

Hindu temples may with advantage pool their resources and undertake the work of repair and renovation on the lines on which this work is being done by the Jain Community.

Large accumulations of Jain trust funds particularly Devdravya and Gyandravya which are reported to be lying idle and unused should be diverted with suitable safeguards for utilisation on objects designated by those expressions elsewhere or on objects nearest to the original objects in the respective Kshetra. Surplus funds in the Gyan Kshetra or a substantial portion of such surplus on a percentage basis may be pooled together at least in States where Jain shrines and institutions are concentrated (for example, in Mysore, Maharashtra, Gujarat, Rajasthan and Bihar) and the money may be utilised towards organising some centres in the country on a zonal basis for the study and spread of Jain philosophy. Similarly, funds from the accumulated surpluses in Dev Dravya may also be pooled together for the purpose of repair and renovation of Jain temples.

The Tribunal contemplated by the Commission after consultation with the persons and interests concerned should be empowered to divert the surplus funds of a particular Kshetra to finance a deficit trust so as to be utilised for identical purposes. In the case of Digambar Jains this pooling or diversion of funds should be a comparatively simpler affair as they have a single fund known as 'Bhandar' which can be used for any good object.

The States concerned should scrutinise their laws so that a proper machinery for administering the aforesaid pooled funds may be brought into existence.

In all matters of importance, e.g., diversion of funds in the various Kshetras, utilisation of funds pooled from various sources, matters of religious practices, etc., the authorities including the Commissioners and the Tribunals should act in consultation with prominent Jains belonging to the Swetamber and Digambar groups, as the case may be, either in their individual capacity or as office holders of important and representative Jain organisations in a State.

Jain trusts, like all other trusts, should also be required to frame budgets, keep regular accounts and submit such accounts for audit.

As far as possible, no vested interest should be allowed to be created in the management and administration of Jain trusts.

We are of the view that the same type of supervision and control is appropriate in respect of Buddhist endowments as in the case of Jain endoments. In all cases of importance, the authorities before taking important decisions as to management and administration should consult accredited organisations and representatives of the Buddhist faith.

The authority in charge of Hindu religious endowments in each State should exercise the utmost vigilance in preventing alienations or misappropriations of their property, and where alienations have already taken place, he should take speedy action wherever practicable, to have such alienations set aside and the alienated properties restored to the endowments concerned. Alienated property and its proceeds should be followed in the hands of the alienees who should be made accountable for the proceeds.

We are definitely of the opinion that Articles 134B and 134C in the First Schedule to the Indian Limitation Act, 1908 (9 of 1908), should not apply to alienations by the incumbent of a mutt or the manager, trustee or dharmakarta of a temple, which are colourable or for inadequate consideration and that there should be no limitation in respect of proceedings to recover or to follow up and obtain an account of the proceeds of the institution in the hands of alienees.

Section 10 and Articles 134A, 134B and 134C of the

Indian Limitation Act, 1908 (9 of 1908) should, as indicated above, be amended so as to provide, whether against the trustee or his alienee, for suits in such cases to follow the trust property or its proceeds and to implement the accountability for the proceeds in the hands of those who are liable to such accounts. Such suits should be exempt from the bar of limitation.

If the implementation of the recommendation above attracts any of the provisions as to fundamental rights of property, the Constitution should be suitably amended so as to clarify and place beyond all doubts the status and obligation of the matadhipatis and dharamakartas, shebaits, managers and trustees of temples and other religious endowments.

Provisions on the lines of those contained in Section 109 of the Madras Hindu Religious and Charitable Endowments Act, 1959, should be embodied in other State enactments to prevent wrongful alienations. Provisin should also be made to declare that any alienation made in future without the requisite sanction of the authority concerned will be *ab initio* null and void.

We are strongly of the opinion that where the custom or usage is that the head of a religious institution should be a celibate, he should not be permitted to marry and that where he marries in violation of such custom or usage, steps should be taken to remove him immediately.

Six out of the seven members of the Commission are of the view that the executive administration of temples by a single officer will be more expeditious and efficient than administration by a body of persons or Board of Commissioners.

The appointment of Commissioners in the States should be made by the Governor of the State in his individual capacity after such consultation as he deems to be necessary with the religious and secular interests concerned.

We do not favour the continuance of advisory boards or committees whose utility has been shown to be very limited and which have in practice been very ineffectual. It has been found by experience that such bodies tend to the creation of factions and vested interests by reasons of which administration is impeded of nullified.

Whenever there is any disputed question relating to religious usage of a particular institution or sampradaya, the Commissioner should after consulting qualified persons belonging to sampradaya or sect concerned from out of a list of assessors to be maintained by him, be entitled in cases of emergency to pass orders subject to the ultimate jurisdiction of the Tribunal referred to hereinafter.

There may be a Central Committee composed of leading members (including both lay people and sadhus and sanyasis) who may be available for consultation so as to enable the Tribunal referred to hereinafter to obtain authoritative and practical solutions to the questions coming before it. The experiment of forming such a committee should be tried. It cannot be forgotten that the success of the experiment will be wholly dependent on the eminence and influence of the members of such a committee and their determination to take a detached view and arrive at harmonious conclusions.

The Commissioners in the States should have no powers of appointment and removal of trustees as under certain enactments now in force; such powers should be vested in the Tribunal referred to hereinafter. In cases, however, where a matadhipati dies or is removed or for other reasons is not able to function, and there is no one duly selected to succeed him, or where on account of any act of clear misconduct, misappropriation or other breach of trust, it becomes necessary to take urgent action the Commission may be empowered to suspend the person in default and where necessary, to make temporary appointments to the office concerned and to take all other requisite measures and make a report as soon as practicable to the Tribunal for final orders. His action should be operative and valid until such final orders are passed by the Tribunal. In the case of temple trustees, dharmakartas and other functionaries the powers vested in the Commissioner may be on the lines of those laid down in the Madras and Andhra legislation the subject.

Appeals against the decisions of the Commissioner may be preferred to a duly constituted Tribunal which may, besides appellate jurisdiction and revisional jurisdiction over State Commissioners have exclusive origional jucisdiction in the following matters:

(a) Succession and appointment to hereditary offices such as hereditary trustees, heads of mutts, etc.

(b) Determination of what are matters of religion or essential religious practices and what are ancillary accretions or unessential accretions.

(c) Such other matters of basic importance in relation to the conduct and management of temples and mutts as in their opinion demand adjudication or decision having regard at the same time to such proved custom, usage or tradition as the Tribunal may find to be established.

The tribunal may consist of five or more members who are Hindus by faith and conviction believing in Hindu scriptures and temple worship. It should include at least:

(a) A judicial member who has been or is eligible for being appointed as a High Court Judge and who is to be its President.

(b) A member who has held a senior administrative office under the Government and has had adequate administrative and or financial experience for not less than ten years under Government.

(c) A members who is specially conversant with Hindu scriptures and religion and religious practices and with the working of Hindu religious endowments.

The Tribunal should be empowered to consult as assessors such leaders of the denomination or sampradaya concerned and such others as are generally recognised to be fit to give advice in matters pertaining to the sampradaya, custom or usage coming up for decision before the Tribunal. Such other persons or organisations as may be specially competent in this behalf may also be consulted.

The Commissioner may be authorised to refer to the Tribunal for its opinion, advice or adjudication any matter or question as to which he feels the necessity for such guidance.

The members of the Tribunal will be appointed by the President of India on the advice of a committee of eminent and impartial advisers chosen by him. The members will enjoy a term of office of five years renewable for not more than an additional term at the discretion of the President. They will be governed by such conditions of service as may be prescribed by rules.

The Tribunal may function in as many benches as it considers expedient having regard to the quantum and nature of work. Every such bench will consist of at least three members with the qualifications as already indicated. Benches may be constituted as far as possible for each State or a group of contiguous States. Attention in this connection is invited to the constitution of the Income tax Appellate Tribunal. The Tribunal proposed by us may also be given the power to co-opt as full members not more than two persons on each occasion who are especially competent to offer opinion and advice on any particular matter or matters coming before them.

Appeals against the decisions of the commissiners at present lying to the State Government or courts concerned should hereafter lie exclusively or the Tribunal.

Litigation under Sections 92 and 93 of the Civil Procedure Code involves an often unrecompensed expenditure of money and energy on the part of the members of the public setting the law in motion. The person in possession is able to utilise the funds of temple or mutt in question and can prolong the litigation indefinitely. It should be provided that in all such legal proceedings the defendent should be made personally liable for costs when he has been in the wrong, and unless his contentions are found to be just and are upheld he will not be entit'ed to spend the funds of the institution.

Many trustees, archakas and pujaris have insisted that the quantity of grain, milk, ghee, oil, incense and many other articles required for worship in the temple must not be deviated from, not withstanding the changed circumstances and enhanced prices of the present day. The judgment of the Supreme Court in the Dargah Committee, Ajmer *versus* Syed Hussain Ali (A.I.R.1951 S.C. 1402) inter alia with regard to the question of what would constitute an essential or integral part of religion or as essential religious practices may be construed as indicating that the exact quantity of commodities required for worship should not be regarded as matter of fundamental religion but as a matter of religious practice or observance which can be modified to suit altered circumstances. It does not appear that the articles in the Constitution relating to non-interference with religion can and should be so applied as to stereotype quantities and values which may change from time to time. If, however, for any reason it is considered necessary to amend the Constitution to make the above position clear, this should be done.

It is absolutely essential that every religious institution should prepare and submit detailed budget estimates of income and expenditure and also maintain accounts in prescribed forms and that these accounts should be audited carefully, the author not necessarily confining himself to a mere formal scrutiny of vouchers placed legislation which is sought to be introduced or passed with reference to religious endowments.

It is desirable that provisions of the Religious Trusts Bill, 1960, should be made applicable to all communities like Muslims, Christians, Parsis, Jews, Sikhs, etc., and Clause 34 thereof omitted.

In sub-clause (1) of clause 11 of the above Bill, in the proviso, for the words 'five thousand' substitute the words 'one thousand'.

In regard to the proviso to sub-clause (3) of clause 12 of the Bill, the majority of the members are of the view that in the case of any trust having an annual income of less than 10 thousand rupees, the trustee may appoint a part-time or full-time accountant after consulting the commission.

With regard to clause 17 of the Bill we are of the opinion that the provisions of Sections 13 and 14 of the U.K. Charities Act, 1960, with suitable modifications, may be incorporated.

Clause 20 in the Bill is not necessary in view of our recommendations contained in the chapter relating to Management and Administration.

Lands held by religious institutions to the extent they

are under the direct management of such institutions may be kept out of the purview of the land ceiling provisions so that the institution may be able to utilise the income from the lands for their purpose.

So far as lands which are under the cultivation of tenants are concerned, it would be difficult and invidious to get them exempted for the normal provisions of the tenancy legislation applicable to lands owned by others. Where such lands are settled with tenants, institutions concerned should be given a perpetual annuity equal to the average annual income from these lands for, say, six years preceding the date of taking over of such lands. While fixing the annuity, due weight should also be given to the increase in the market prices of the lands.

In addition to our other recommendations for the amendment of the Constitution, the Constitution may also be amended to elucidate the following points:

(a) That temples, mutts and other institutions to which the public resort as of right and/or by tradition or custom for the purpose of worship or religious training or discharging vows and/or institutions that accept gifts, donations and offerings from the members of the public without the right to refuse such offerings should be treated as public trusts in the sense that the public or section thereof are interested in and have the right to enforce their proper administration and management. The special position of the matadhipati as different from a bare trustee has already been dealt with.

(b) The fact that the management of the temple or the mutt is in the hands of persons or groups historically connected with the foundation of the institution or in the hands of persons who claim to have acquired proprietary or other vested interests in the image or the temple associated with an image can make no differences with regard to the essential character of the institution.

(c) All mutts whether managed by celiberate or non-celibete persons, having been originally founded for the purpose of training and gathering together a band of persons commonly devoted to the study, under standing or propagation of particular doctrines, dogmas, rituals, practices or ideas and being primarily charged with the duty of instruction and propagation of particular aspects of religious belief can never be regarded as private institutions although the head of the institution or the matadhipati may on account of personal or traditional holiness or learning or possession of extraordinary gifts (e. g., of healing and so forth) attract a number of disciples and followers who are willing to recognize the personal status of the person by gifts or offerings. In these cases also these gifts and offerings are made to the personage concerned by virtue of his office in addition to his personal attributes. Such gifts and offerings can never be private property in the ordinary sense of the term as stated above although a portion of the income or accumulation of the mutt properties may be utilised for the maintenance and proper dignity and traditional status of the head of the mutt and the maintenance not only of the matadhipati but of his followers, sishyas, and his establishment and customary travels and the functions and ceremonies associated by custom and usage with the traditions of the mutt.

The Bharat Sadhu Samaj may become, if properly organised, regulated an disciplined, and instrument for carrying out the task of religious and ethical instruction of the masses and especially of the youth of the country and for the dispensing of relief to the poor, to the aged and to the diseased.

We feel that for the achievements of the objectives of the Samaj, that organisation required more thorough consolidation and carefully designed arrangements about preliminary screening and training of the Sadhus engaged in the tasks envisaged by the Samaj and also about the scrutiny of the activities of its units.

We have come to the conclusion that while there is a case for the training of Sadhu missionaries in the larger interests of the public in general and Hindus in particular, it is absolutely essential that the persons selected for such training should be thoroughly screened and the training confined only to undeniably qualified persons fit in all respect for the task. In our view such missionary activity, if at all it is to be effective and supplemental to the official and non-official efforts in welding together the centrifugal elements within the Hindu fold and achieving the wider perspective of emotional integeration of communities with varying creeds, beliefs and religions inhabiting our country, should eschew all activities and utterances tending to create or widen any schism between the various religions followed in India or between the various sects or sub-sects among Hindus or between religions which are in fraternity with the Hindu religion like Jainism, Buddhism and Sikhism.

Shri Badrinath Temple

Dr. Sampurnanand has suggested that some of the palatial buildings owned by the Badrinath Temples Committee at Dehradun, Lucknow, Calcutta, Bombay and at other places may be disposed of and the money utilised in constructing shelters for pilgrims where they are badly needed. We feel that this suggestion is valuable and should be carefully considered bv the authorities concerned.

The Temple Committee should build its own dharamshalas, rest houses, etc., at Badrinath and also at a few other convenient places en route Badrinath and have full control over them. Donations received in this behalf should of course be welcome and given due publicity and prominence in other suitable ways. The Committee should provide for a better equipped hospital with more beds.

The canteen run by the Committee at Joshi Mutt should be expanded and a few more canteens opened there to meet the needs of a large number of pilgrims. The Committee should also run a canteen at Badrinath and at least one on the route from Joshi Mutt to Badrinath.

The sanitary arrangements en route and at Badrinath are imperfect. Speedy steps should be taken to improve these amenities.

The work and programme of the Kali Kamliwala Trust may be scrutinised and if necessary supplemented so as to make for the more adequate convenience of the pilgrims.

Shri Kedarnath Temple

The Temple Committee should undertake the construction of rest houses equipped with flush latrines for the benefit of the pilgrims. There are many water-falls in the place and it should not be difficult to provide proper sanitary arrangements.

The Committee should run a canteen to provide wholesome food to pilgrims on moderate charges. They should also run a well-equipped hospital with at least 50 beds during the pilgrim season.

The Committee may have its own dandies and ponies to bring the pilgrims to Kedar. It may engage whole-time coolies for the purpose and pilgrims can be asked to pay coolie charges at the scheduled rates to the Committee itself.

In the matter of transport the example of Tirupati may be usefully followed.

The Committee should publish a proper and authentic guide book for the benefit of the public.

Glaciers are approaching the Kedar temple and the detritus is approaching very close to the temple. The State Government should have a geological survey undertaken and taken other timely preventive measures.

Temple of Shrinathji, Nathdwara

A careful assessment of the essential expenditure enjoined by the Pushtimarga doctrine should be made and ways and means found to effect economies in the expenditure now being incurred which, in our opinion, is certainly capable of reduction. The savings thus effected may be utilised for the propagation of the tenets of the Pushtimarga Sampradaya, the giving of scholarships to students and others studying those tenets and the provision of necessary amenities to the very large number of pilgrims visiting the holy shrine of Srinathji.

Triupati Temple

Scrupulous care should be exercised to ensure that the ever expanding activities of the temple which undoubtedly enhance the temple's popularity and income should not leave any right or wrong impression in the mind of the devotees that the temple is being run with a commercial slant or with a view to profit. A part of the jewellery accumulated with the temple valuing over a crore of rupees which is decided as not very essential to be preserved for decorating the diety according to usage and tradition may be disposed of and money invested in a productive form. Also some check should be exercised on new jewellery being made at huge cost only to replace the old kundalams, giritams, bracelets, mekhalas, etc., with a view to finding a scope for utilisation of the large surpluses which now result.

Care should be taken that in the educational institutions conducted and financed wholly or subsidised by the temple authorities, a religious and spiritual outlook and bias are maintained in curriculum and by means of adequate scholarships, fellowships, lectureships etc., tenable by students in those or outside institutions and devoted to the furtherance of Hindu idea's of life and religion.

Sri Jagannath Temple, Puri

It is absolutely essential that well designed amenities for pilgrims and shelters and dharamsalas for them should come into existence and that pilgrims should not be dependent upon the pandas whose quarters alone are now mainly available for them.

There should be a larger number of institutions in this holy place for the imparting of religious instructions to the vast numbers of people congregating here. There should also be provision for regular religious discourses and the recitation of the scriptures and Puranas in and outside the temple.

The archakas or pujaris in the temple should be men of learning and piety and there should be institutions in nd around Puri to train them for their work. They should be paid adequately so that their income does not accrue through a process of importunity or extortion.

Shri Viswanath Temple And Other Temples In Varanasi

Reforms on a comprehensive basis have to be carried out so that proper facilities may be given to the pilgrims by way of accommodation and religious enlightenment, the temple and its environment are conducive to peaceful worship and meditation and also proper atmosphere is preserved and maintained by learned and reverent officiating priests.

The services of the Benaras Hindu University and the Sanskrit University and their staff can be made easily available to produce an authentic atmosphere of piety, reverence and learning in the conduct of the temple's secular and religious affairs.

Hardwar

The temple of Gangeshwar and the Hari-ke-Charan (now called Hari-ki-Pauri) although resorted to by thousands of people annually have no proper arrangements in the matter of sanitation. Thousands of pilgrims resort to Hardwar. Greater attention should also be paid to their physical and religious needs.

Ganga

Though this is a place of great religious significance, the temples here are very imperfectly maintained. There are no shelters provided for pilgrims. The extortions of the pandas, most of whom are ignorant and rapacious, are proverbial and no fixed rates have been provided for the religious observances such as 'tarpans' and 'pindapradanas'. Ths state of another holy place here namely Vat Vriksha and Vishnupad is scandalous. There is an open drain on the way to Vat Vriksha and dirt all round. The priest allegedly incharge during our visit did not even know the name and significance of the images at the foot of the trees. The authorities, concerned should undertake immediate steps to remedy the above State of affairs.

Ujjain

Though the temple of Mahakali in Ujjain is kept in a fairly clear condition, no steps have been taken for maintaining the once celebrated literary and religious background of the place. Near Ujjain is also the reputed Asram of Sandipani under whom Sri Krishna and Balrama are reported to have studied. A great deal has to be done to keep alive the old memories clustering round the place and to impart to it the right atmosphere.

We cannot persuade ourselves to agree with the recommendation of the Sanskrit Commission that the diversion of surplus funds of religious institutions to secular charitable purposes should be absolutely prohibited by legislation. We have already expressed our views on this matter.

We agree with the recommendation of the Sanskrit Commission that so long as it is possible to utilise the funds earmarked for Sanskrit studies for the purpose of such studies, such funds should not be diverted to other charitable purposes.

The Archaeological Department should extend its activity in the field of excavation work in appropriate important religious centres.

The Archaeological Department may take charge of the archaeologically significant temples and at the same time allow worship to be conducted with such minimum precautions as they consider necessary to preserve the archaeological aspects of the temple.

Ancient and historic Hindu temples and shrines may be treated with the same amount of meticulous attention to their repairs and structural and other requirements as is now in a very praise worthy manner bestowed upon Juma Masjid, Taj, Sanchi, Bodh Gaya and other places.

A common good fund should be constituted with the aid of the compulsory contribution of a certain percentage of incomes of temples with a specified minimum income on the lines provided for in the Madras Hindu Religious and Charitable Endowments Act, 1959, and money utilised on a planned basis for repair and renovation work pertaining to poorer temples with small or no income or other resources and which are falling into ruin. This pooling of resources may be either for the whole State or region(s) in the State or for a group of temples within the fold of a particular sampradaya as may be found expedient.

The Commissioners of Endowments and other heads of Departments in charge of endowments in the States should at periodical intervals meet and exchange their ideas and experiences.

Some of the institutions like Tirupati and Srisailam in Andhra Pradesh and Madurai Palani and Tiruchendur in Madras are examples of fairly well managed institutions. Representatives of the endowment departments from other States may usefully visit such institution and study their working on the spot.

Government may consider the question of granting exemptions from income-tax in respect of funds donated to religious institutions as many such institutions are greatly in need of funds to carryout the schemes we have adumbrated.

Each State in the appropriate department should compile and publish a directory of temples and other Hindu religious institutions in the State. A guide book in English, Hindi and regional language concerned containing information helpful to pilgrims with details as to amenities for lodging and board available at the temples and religious places concerned, should also be prepared and made available for sale at a nominal price of all important places and religious centres in the country.

It should be the duty of the Commissioners of Endowments as well as the Tribunal envisaged in the Report to see that the benefit and advantage of spiritual and cultural instruction and enlightment should be at the disposal and be availed of by Harijans and all other backward communities and especially students belonging to those communities. All opportunities should be afforded to them to obtain a sound knowledge of Hindu ideals, doctrines, ethics and philosophy. It may be mentioned that though statutorily all temples are thrown open to all Hindu communities, yet in practice there are undefined but real impediments for their visiting and worshipping in the temple and taking advantage of the religious observances. Attempt should be made to remove such impediments.

A General Summing Up

Before concluding our Report to which we have appended a summary of our recommendations and certain explanatory Appendices, we deem it essential to make certain observations elucidatory of our approach to the problems that we have been called upon the privileged to examine.

The Members of the Commission are all Hindus belonging to many parts of the country and to several dinominations of the Hindu faith. Hinduism has been admirably defined by Dr. Radhakrishnan as "a way of life" and by its many-sidedness, its infinite adaptability during the ages and its marvellous tradition of tolerance. It has demonstrated the truth of this dictim. A reverent and religious attitude and a continuous quest for the realisation of the Supreme have been the feature of the long continuous history of Indian thought and experience. According to the extent of spiritual evolution and individual spiritial urge, Hinduism has recognised as equally valid every approach to the Supreme Being or Paramatman as an impersonal, formless and indescribable entity or as Iswara manifested in various forms and incarnations, supplication and prayer to whom and worship of whom, may satisfy the cravings of individual souls and enable them to concentrate on something beyond and above their normal range of consciousness. It is to satisfy these cravings and to cater to the manifold needs of individuals and groups that temples were established, worship and prayers in those temples organised, festivals contemplated and religious and cultural activities associated with temples dedicated to multiform manifestations and embodiments of the Supreme Being in one or other of its several aspects, whether those aspects comprise the idea of a Trinity of Vishnu and Lakshmi, Siva and Sakti, Ganesa, Karthikeya, or Subramania or even local, regional and other deities associated with particular localities or incidents. Various sects and groups have arisen in India dedicated to the worship of the one envisaged as a father, a mother, kinsman, a friend or lover. It may also be remarked that evolved souls like those of Sankaracharya, Ramanuja and Madhwa, not only advocated concentration on the abstract idea of the One Supreme Being but also preached and practised the worship of several incarnations and embodiments of the Supreme. This phenomenon is observable in all countries and in all epochs whether we turn to Egypt, Babylon, Greece, Rome, Arabia, Palestine or the Christian world, or to Jainism, Budhism, or Zoroastrianism. The glory of Hinduism is that it is not exclusive and gives to each person the liberty and privilege of approaching the divine through any of its historic or traditional incarnations or manifestations, thus disdaining no other religion and tolerant of all beliefs.

So viewed, a temple is regarded as a place where, by supplication and prayer to and adoration of one form of divinity, the soul gets satisfaction and solace. We have also indicated that temples serve not only as places of dedication and worship but as centres of all those cultural, artistic and beneficent activities that can elevate the human soul and bring it nearer to the divine ideal. We have also indicated that when the purity of the original faith in several denominations of Hinduism faded and abuses and materialistic and subversive ideas arose, mutts were founded beginning from early days and signalised by the activities of Buddha, Sankara, Ramanuja, Madhwa, Vallabha, Basava, Chaitanya and many others, to expound and propagate the ideals and doctrines of particular forms of the all-embraching Hindu creed.

The Members of the Commission, holding these views, have come to the conclusion that whatever may be the encrustations and later interpretations by vested interests or Courts and other authorities, it is essential for the revival and regeneration of the Hindu world and for the inauguration of an era of faith and tolerance, to resusciate and, by all practical and legislative-means, to re-establish the root idea underlying the institution of temples and of mutts. Thus, it follows that the divine entity symbolised by the image in a temple is the primary object of resort and worship and that the propagation of a particular form of faith and ideals and doctrines constitute the meaning and import of a mutt and that offerings laid at the feet of the presiding deity of a temple or of the head of a mutt or Guru of a particular mutt are to be regarded as meant prima facie for the purpose of forwarding the original ideas that led to the commencement and evolution of these institutions. It follows again from the above statement that unless specifically given to any particular person in or connected with a temple or mutt, all gifts and offerings are, and should be, the property at the disposal of the institution rather than of any individual. This does not preclude the gift to any particular person connected with a temple or a mutt to whom, out of personal devotion, reverence or love, gifts are made which, of course, will in here in him.

We are constrained to observe that the above idea has not always been kept in view either by Governments or by courts in dealing with the affairs of temples and mutts and we are, therefore, recommending that even if it be necessary to amend the Constitution for the purpose, steps should be taken to place the matter beyond controversy with reference to the ownership and rights over afferings and gifts to mutts and temples and with reference to claims of ownership in respect of the institutions themselves and their properties and offices connected therewith. When saying this, we should like to emphasise that we do not wish in any manner to detract from the status, dignity, perquisites and privileges of functionaries connected with temples and mutts both of which have illustrious histories and certain traditional honours and dignities appurtenant to them; nor do we wish to minimise the importance from the point of view of the worshipper, of festivals as a means of popular enlightenment and delectation, of poojas, archanas and special services as catering to individual needs or to those forms of gift and seva which may characterise the relations of and initiate, of a disciple and a Guru. But we wish, at the same time, to emphasise that, as observed by the Supreme Court in a recent case relating to the affairs of a Durgah at Ajmer, there is an essential difference between what is fundamentally a matter of religion and what may be regarded as encrustation or merely accidental or incidental practices which are not of the essence of religion.

Finally, we also wish to make it clear that the definition of the term 'property' and the provision in the Constitution in regard to the safeguarding of the property rights should not be extended in favour of heads of mutts, dharmakartas, shebaits, archakas or others so as to enable them to treat their propert'es as their individual perquisite to be spent on purposes even unconnect ed with the ideas underlying the foundation of mutts and temples. Any changes in the Constitution that may be necessary to carry out this idea are not only important but, in our opinion, essential for the purposes we have in view.

Lastly, we may point out that Hindu Scriptures. and Sastras, when defining the forms of charity and religious offerings, really made very little difference between Ishta and Purtha, namely, between the spiritual and charitable modes of application or wealth. This explains not only the building of temples and mutts and residences and dharmasalas and flower gardens attached to them but also the digging of wells, the construction of ponds and tanks, the relief and amelioration of human distress and disease which are the characteristics of the foundations of the past.

The doctrine of *cy-pres* is essentially an outgrowth of English ideas and should be understood in relation to English history involving the conflict between the church and the State and the differentiation made between religious and charitable uses. We have, there fore, adopted the wide definition of the recent English statute rather than those ideas as to *cy-pres* which seem to have dominated the minds of some of the judges deciding cases arising in India. We have endeavoured in our recommendations, therefore, to insist that surplus funds of temples and mutts, after carrying out to the full the obligations cast on those institution by the Deeds of foundations or by custom, usage and tradition and after providing for the implementation of the basic needs and ideals of those institutions, should be devoted to a variety of purposes which are called for at the present moment by the advance of ideas, by the necessities of our times, and, above all, the need to create an atmosphere and background in and around temples and mutts which will make them objects of reverential resort and also centres for spiritual enlightenment and the popularisation of tenets appertaining to particular institutions or groups of institutions and to Hindu thought in general. By such means alone will it be possible to effect that integration of Indian endeavour and that sublimation of ideals which are of special significance to resurgent India.

REVIEW COMMITTEE ON SOCIAL WORK EDUCATION, 1960—REPORT

New Delhi, University Grants Commission, 1965. 100p.+vp.

Chairman : Dr. Radhakamal Mukerjee.

Members : Dr. M.S. Gore; (left for U.S.A. and replaced by Shri S.N. Ranade); Dr. V. Jagannadham; Prof. A.R. Wadia; Mrs. V. Mulay (replaced by Shri P.C. Sharma),

Secretary : Dr. P.J. Philip.

APPOINTMENT

In recent years a number of schools of Social Work

have sprung up. While they are marked by enthusiasm, they do not have adequate financial resources and qualified personnel. The Advisory Board on Social Welfare had expressed their concern regarding this situation. This fear came to be shared by the Ministry of Education and the University Grants Commission. They, therefore, resolved to set up a Committee to Review the work of these schools and university departments. The Committee was appointed on March 2, 1960.

TERMS OF REFERENCE

The Committee had wide terms of reference and was free to determine its own programme and procedure of work. The Committee was particularly asked to consider the following:

(a) To review the present position of teaching, training and research in social work, particularly at the post graduate level;

(b) To exmine the existing inadequacies in this regard and suggest methods of improvement; and

(c) To suggest minimum standards of social work education in the country.

CONTENTS

Foreword; Introduction; Training Institutions—Historical Background; Some General Observations; Content of Courses; Teaching Staff; Field Work; Library Facilities; Coordination and Trainning Programmes; Organisation of Social Work Education; Undergraduate Programme in Social Work; Summary and Recommendations; Appendices I to VIII.

RECOMMENDATIONS

Importance of Social Work Training

Social work as a profession is of comparatively recent origin. As community life in the past was organised in small self-sufficient units such as joint families, caste orgnisations and village communities, the need for providing welfare programmes on a large scale was not felt. A limited section of the handicapped and destitute also received some help from charitable institutions and philanthropists. The situation has changed with the coming of independence and the establishment of a democratic Government in India. It is no longer possible to tackle welfare problems through voluntary effort alone. In the circumstances, the training of social workers has acquired a new importance and urgency.

Requirements Of Trained Welfare Personnel

It would be useful to have some idea of our requirements for trained personnel in the field of Social Welfare. The Study Team on Social Welfare and Welfare of the Backward Classes estimated the requirements to be of the following order:

Graduates	4150
Under graduates	3550
Matriculates	8C00

These appear to be underestimates. There is no doubt that our present output of graduates is inadequate to achieve the physical targets laid down in the Third Five-Year Plan for trained welfare personnel in fields like hospitals, family planning clinics, child welfare programmes, correctional administration and trible welfare. It would be desirable to expand the present facilities but such expansion should not lead to hasty establishment of schools without adequate resources. The short term *ad hoc* and in-service training programmes which are in operation in the country may continue in the transitional period but they should evolve their programmes in consultation with the school of social work. The schools may also start similar programmes provided they have the necessary facilities.

Recognition Of Training

The only area in which social work training has been given statutory recognition is that of labour. Similar recognition should be extended to other fields of training also by both the Central and State Governments by making training a necessary qualification for recruitment to all posts involving welfare functions. This would help in raising the quality of social work education.

Content Of Courses

(a) **Background Courses**: It is necessary for the social worker to have a basic knowledge of the social sciences as a background to social problems. The background courses thus form an important part of the social work curricula. These courses are at present not properly integrated. They should attempt to bring out clearly the inter-relationship between the different social and behavioural sciences. These can be grouped under two-broad heads (1) Man and Society and (2) Dynamics of Human Behaviour as suggested by the Mussoorie Seminar. Sufficient time should also be allotted for teaching the background courses. Teachers of these courses should have a good postgraduate degree in at least one of the social sciences.

(b) **Methods Courses**: The methods courses cannot be properly conducted without being closely related to field work. The courses have so far remained unrealistic as the schools mostly rely on foreign sources and have not been able to build up case records based on the experience of workers in India. Students hardly get an opportunity of testing theories in the field. In the absence of field experience on the part of teachers, instruction tends to become entirely theoretical. This factor should be borne in mind at the time of recruiting teachers to schools of social work. Alternatively, the teacher should be given opportunities to come in close contact with welfare agencies. The fields which need particular attention in the context of our present requirements are those of community organisation and social welfare administration.

(c) All the fields of social work cannot be covered adequately in a two-year training programme. It does not, however, seem feasible to extend the duration of the course as it will increase the cost of training and also affect the supply of trained graduates. The best solution under the present circumstances would, therefore, be to provide for a generic programme during the first year of training and specialised courses during the second year. The labour institutes which offer only a specialised course need to strengthen their generic base. Similarly the generic schools have to provide for some specialised courses. In each case the areas of specialisation should be selected keeping in view the resources of the school and the opportunities for field work and employment.

(d) The following distribution of time between the different courses may be found suitable :

Man and Society	120
Dynamics of Human Behaviour	120
Fields of Social Work	90
History and Philosophy of Social Work	60
Case Work	60
Group Work	60
Community Organisation	60
Welfare Administration	90
Social Research & Statistics	60
Specialisation	180
	900

Most schools rely on the lecturing method for covering the theoretical content of the courses. It is necessary to supplement lectures by tutorials and seminars. This will encourage students to have a good practice in writing and thinking. It will also be desirable to give them some training in research methods. This can be done by asking them to prepare a project report on a theme which may be of interest to the social welfare agencies or which may have some bearing on social problems in the region. For further encouraging research some fellowships should be made available to suitable graduates from the schools of social work.

Teaching Staff

One of the problems facing the schools of social work is that they are not able to attract and retain highly qualified teachers. There are many teachers who have neither sufficient experience nor adequate training. This difficulty, however, is not unique to social work education as a more or less similar situation prevails in other professional courses.

For raising the present level of training it is necessary that teachers employed by schools of social work possess high academic ability. Although a large majority of teachers should be persons with training in social work, persons from the related social sciences with some background of social work may also have to be employed during the transitional period. The following minimum qualifications are suggested for teachers in schools of social work :

(i) They must have least a good second class as a basic qualification.

(ii) Those having a postgraduate degree or diploma in social work should have at least a second class Master's Degree in one of the social sciences.

(iii) Those not having any training in social work should have had some experience of research on topics relevant to social work in addition to post-graduate qualifications in one or more of the social sciences.

(iv) Experience of work in a social welfare agency in a responsible capacity should be considered as a preferred qualification.

There should be at least one full time teacher for every 10 students. This provision does not include the post of the Director/Principal. Schools offering specialisation in rural or tribal welfare will require a sufficient number of field assistants in addition to normal staff. While schools may find it useful to have honorary social work practitioners helping them in their developmental programmes it is necessary that the teaching staff should be employed on a full-time basis. This applies to all schools whether functioning as a department of the University or as independent institution.

Provision should also be made for the training of teachers. The training programme may be of one year's duration. Admission to the course should be restricted to teachers of less than three year's standing. All candidates selected for training should have a postgraduate degree or diploma in social work. It will be necessary to provide financial assistance to schools conducting such training programmes and also to other schools for reimbursing the salaries of deputed teachers.

The salary scales in schools of social work should correspond with those of postgraduate teachers in the universities of that region.

It would be desirable for teachers of social work to engage in researches relevant to their field, particularly those which have a bearing on Indian social problems. There are a number of factors such as heavy workload of teachers, lack of adequate facilities, dependence on foreign text books and lack of adequate elementary data on social probtems which are responsible for the present lack of interest in research. Some of these difficulties can be met by organising research bureaux having a regular staff of research assistants and statisticians.

Field Work

Field work is an integral part of social work training and needs to be planned carefully. It requires selection of agencies, preparation of work outline, supervision arrangements and careful evaluation of performance. As most of the schools are not in a position to provide field work opportunities to their students, they will have to develop close contacts with social work agencies in the area.

It must be emphasised that field work as part of social work education implies not only collection of data but actual experience of working with people. In this sense it is different from field work done in other social sciences. In order to make field work more effective, it has to be properly supervised. The responsibility of guiding students will have to be borne by the teachers themselves as the agencies are generally not in a position to do so. The work should not be entrusted to junior teachers only. It should be supervised by the teachers concern with that particular field. It may be necessary to appoint field work supervisors to assist teachers in the conduct of field work especially in rural or tribal areas.

Students should be require to pass independently in field work. Field work performance should be evaluated on the basis of a detailed and systematic record of the work done by a student. The student should also have an idea of his day-to-day progress and should be given every possible opportunity to improve. It does not serve any educational purpose if the student is informed at the end of the training period that his field work has not been upto the mark.

Schools which have the necessary facilities may arrange study tours, observational visits, concurrent field work and work camps. The work camps may be particularly useful in a rural setting.

Library Facilities

Library facilities in schools of social work are generally inadequate. For proper development of library facilities, each school should have an independent library with an annual provision of at least Rs. 3000 for the purchase of books and periodicals. University departments of social work which depends on the central library for the bulk of their books may have a small departmental library. As schools of social work do not have well-qualified library staff, it has not been possible for them to provide documentation and reference services. It would be useful if a beginning is made in this direction in some of the more developed schools.

Coordination of Training Programmes

It would be desirable to set up a National Council of Social Work Education for the purpose of coordinating the training programmes in institutions of social work. The Council should have on it the representatives of the Association of the School of Social Work, Indian Conference of Social Work, the U.G.C.. the Ministries of Education, Health, Labour and Employment, Home Affairs and Community Development and Cooperation along with social work educators. It will be the function of the Council to coordinate and integrate programmes of training, assess personnel requirements, ensure absorption of trained workers and advise on maintenance of adequate standards of training.

Organisation of Social Work Education

It is not in the interest of development of social work education to organise it along with other courses in liberal arts and sciences. Social work has become a full-fledged profession and its needs cannot be adequately met if the schools do not function as independent units.

The financial position of the schools of social work needs to be considerably strengthened. They should be treated at par with other professional institutions for purposes of grant by the University Grant Commission and by the Ministry of Education. All grants should be channelled through the University Grants Commission.

Undergraduate Programme of Social Work

Welfare services in the country are expanding so rapidly that our needs in respect of trained personnel cannot be met by postgraduate institutions only. We have, therefore, to recognise the need for undergraduate programmes for training of workers at the lower levels. Many such training programmes are organised on an *ad hoc* basis. A few universities offer social work as an optional subject for the B.A. Degree. The Rural Institutes conduct a three-year training programme leading to the diploma in rural services. Such programmes are useful and may continue but they should not be regarded as substitutes for the training offered by the schools of social work.

Social work education at the undergraduate level should provide an adequate base for training programmes at the postgraduate level. It should include courses on Sociology, Economics and Psychology besides instruction in the following areas: (1) Historical background to Social Work, (2) Philosophy of Social Work, (3) Social Welfare policies and programmes, (4) Methods of working with people.

Field work must be properly emphasised. It should consist of observational visits to welfare agencies. Opportunities should also be provided to students of working with people specially in rural areas and in urban welfare centres. It may be necessary to give field orientation programmes to trained persons before they are employed in a particular field. The number of institutions providing undergraduate training will have to be related to our requirements of trained workers for lower position.

RAILWAY CONVENTION COMMITTEE, 1960—REPORT

New Delhi, Lok Sabha Secretariat, 1962. 26p.+iiip.

Chairman : Sardar Hukam Singh.

Members : Shri Chapalakanta Bhattacharyya; Shri Morarji Desai; Shri Bimal Comar Ghose; Shri Jagjivan Ram; Shri Jaipal Singh; Shri N.G. Ranga; Shri Jagannatha Rao; Shri M. Thiruwala Rao; Shri T.B. Viltal Rao; Shri Rameshwar Sahu; Shri Diwan Chand Sharma; Diwan Chaman Lall; Shri N.M. Lingam Shri M.P. Bhargava; Shri B. Parameswaran; Shri Rohit M. Dave; Prof. A.R Wadia.

Under Secretary : Shri Y.P. Passi.

Deputy Secretary : Shri V. Subramanian.

APPOINTMENT

The recommendations of the Convention Committee, 1954, which were approved by the Lok Sabha on December 16, 1954, and the Rajya Sabha on December 21, 1954, *inter alia*, laid down that a Parliamentary Committee should review the rate of dividend towards the end of the quinquennium 1955-1960 and suggest for the years following it, any adjustment considered necessary, in the light of the situation obtaining then. The 1954 Convention covered the period up to March 31, 1960. This period was, however, extended by one year, i.e., up to March 31, 1961, with the approval of the Parliament through a Resolution passed in the Lok Sabha on April 28, 1959, and in the Rajya Sabha on May 8, 1959, as it was considered by the Railway Ministry that it would facilitate a more accurate appraisal of the Railways' financial position, obligations and surplus resources in the context of the Plan if future Conventions synchronised with each Plan period. A Committee of both Houses of Parliament was, therefore, constituted this year in pursuance of the following Resolution adopted by the Lok Sabha on the April 22, 1960 and concurred in by the Rajya Sabha on April 28, 1960:

"That this House resolves that :

(i) A Parliamentary Committee consisting of 12 members of this House to be nominated by the speaker be appointed to review the rate of dividend which is at present payable by the Railway undertaking to the General Revenues as well as other ancillary matters in connection with the Railway Finance *vis-a-vis* the General Finance and make recommendations thereon by November 30, 1960; and

(ii) That this House recommends to the Rajya Sabha to agree to associate six Members from that Sabha with the Committee and to communicate the names of the Members so appointed to this House".

TERMS OF REFERENCE

At their first sitting held on September 14, 1960, the Committee drew up the undermentioned list of subjects for examination with reference to the above Resolution and asked the Railway Board to furnish detailed memoranda thereon.

(i) A review of the working of the Indian Railways during the six years 1955-56 to 1960-61, that is, the five year period covered by the Railway Convention Committee, 1954 (1955-56 to 1959-60) plus the one year of extension approved in Resolutions of the two houses of the Parliament in April-May, 1959.

(ii) The financial prospects of the Railway undertaking for the five-year period 1961-66, on the basis of the present rates and fares and the anticipated increase in traffic during the Third Five-Year Plan, and whether the anticipated net revenue would be sufficient :

(a) To meet the increased appropriation to Depreciation Fund annually which is becoming necessary;

(b) To pay the dividend to General Revenues at four per cent on the steadily increasing capital-at-charge; and

(c) To leave sufficient net surplus for credit to the Development Fund from which are financed certain works which are essential but not remunerative.

(iii) Assuming that the present method of contribution to General Revenues in the shape of a fixed dividend—expressed as a percentage inclusive of the element of interest—on the loan capital invested in the railway undertaking as computed annually, is to be preferred to any other method, whether this rate of four per cent on the Railways' capital-at-charge payable to General Revenues requires to be revised; if so, what should be the revised rate and how should it be met by the Railways ?

Having regard to the rate of growth of the Railways' capital-at-charge, what adjustments, if any, are called for in order to eliminate the element of over-capitalisation for the purpose of working out the dividend payable to the General Revenues, further to those which were recommended by the Railway Convention Committee, 1954.

(iv) The rate at which contribution to the Depreciation Reserve Fund should be made, in order to ensure that adequate funds are available for renewals and replacements of railway assets.

(v) Whether any alterations in the existing rules of allocation of railway expenditure between Capital, Revenue, Depreciation Reserve Fund and Development Fund, are considered necessary in the light of actual working ?

(vi) In particular, having regard to the fact that, during the period of the present Convention, the railway surplus has been inadequate to permit appropriations to the Development Fund sufficient to meet the charges to such Fund—with the result that existing balances have been wholly liquidated and a further sum has had to be borrowed from General Revenues—and the unlikelihood of the surplus materially improving in the Third Five-Year Plan period, what change is called for in regard to the incidence of works at present charged to the Development Fund and the method of financing them?

(vii) Whether the operating loss incurred by the Railways on strategic lines should be deducted from the contribution calculated for payment to General Revenues?

(viii) The desirability of creating an amortisation fund.

(ix) Whether the existing practice of expressing the rate of dividend in terms of a percentage on the capital-at-charge and the amount being paid annually through a fixed rate should continue?

The Committee also directed the Financial Commissioner (Railways) to furnish the following information :

(i) The capital invested on strategic lines.

(ii) The capital invested on the construction of quarters for the Railway staff and the return (house rent etc.) therefrom during the last five years.

(iii) Statement showing concessions given by the Railways to other Government Departments and Public undertakings e.g., Military Tariff Rates, Reduced Tariff on Industrial Raw Materials, etc.

(iv) The floating assets (stores) of Railways.

(v) The amount of loan received from the World Bank, the rate of interest payable thereon and terms and conditions of repayment.

(vi) The extent of over-capitalisation on the Railways.

(vii) The amount of passenger tax collected by the Railways during the years 1958-59 and 1959-60.

The Committee also desired to be furnished with a note on the financial working of Nationalised Railways in some of the Western Countries like U.K., Belgium, France, etc., with special reference to the mode of their contribution to the Exchequer.

CONTENTS

Composition of the Railway Convention Committee, 1960; Introduction; Report; Appendices I to III.

RECOMMENDATIONS

In the opinion of the Committee the present mode of contribution viz. a fixed rate of dividend by the Railways to General Revenues does not call for any change in the next five years.

The rate of dividend to be paid by the Railways to General Revenue should be fixed at 4.25 per cent during the five years 1961-66.

The annual loss in the working of strategic lines should be borne by General Revenues.

The Committee accept the suggestion of the Railway Board that the capital-at-charge of the North-East Frontier Railway, other than the clearly strategic portion thereof, should be regarded as unproductive and recommend that till such time as the line becomes productive or the next Convention Committee review the position, whichever is earlier, the rate of dividend payable on the capital-at-charge should be at the average borrowing rate of Government.

The total contribution to the Depreciation Revenue Fund should be Rs. 350 crores during the next quinquennium.

The Committee are inclined to accept the suggestion that the existing rules of allocation of the Railway expenditure between Capital, Revenue, Depreciations, Reserve Fund and Development Fund might be retained without any modification during the next five years.

The Committee are averse to the curtailment or limiting of expenditure on works met out of the Development Fund which in their opinion are as important as additions financed from capital. They, therefore, see no alternative but to continue the facility of providing temporary loans from General Revenues to finance the Railway Development Fund during the next five years, unless the net surplus is able to meet in full the requirements of the fund.

The Committee endorse the proposal of the Financial Commissioner (Railways) that the outstanding liability of the Development Fund to the General Finance as on March 31, 1961, should be liquidated in the *ad-hoc* manner indicated in the last sub-para of para 11 of this Report so that the Railways could start on the Third Plan period with a clean state in regard to this liability.

The Committee recommended that the Railway Development Fund, besides meeting the cost of Labour Welfare Works, etc., should include a minimum allocation of Rs. three crores per annum for users' amenities as hitherto.

The suggestion made by the Railway Board that the passenger tax at the existing rate might be merged with passenger fare from April 1, 1961 and that the State Governments might be paid a fixed amount based on the average collections in the period 1957-61 is reasonable. The Committee recommended that the fixed amount payable by the Railways may be Rs. 12.50 crores per year during the quinquennium 1961-66 representing the overage of the actual collections for the years 1958-59 and 1959-60.

While the Committee appreciate that the financial position of the Railways during the next quinquennium will not be favourable for the creation of an Amortisation Fund, they nevertheless feel that this question should not be lost sight of inasmuch as in the context of the repatriation of all the dollar loans, it will assume importance.

With reference to the recommendation of the Railway Convention Committee, 1954, contained in para 19 of their Report, the Committee are of the view that the deferred dividend on new lines should be paid from the sixth year onwards only if the net income of the new lines leaves a surplus after payment of the current dividend.

Paragraph 11 Mentioned in the Recommendations

The Financial Commissioner (Railways) also pointed out that, under the 1954 Convention Committee's Report only the cost of such new lines as were taken up for construction from April 1, 1955 is charged to capital; the cost of new lines under construction on that date is allocated under the earlier provisions of the 1949 Convention Committee's Report, in terms of which unremunerative new lines were financed from the Development Fund. The Financial Commissioner (Railways) suggested that, in order to liquidate the loans taken from General Finance for the Development Fund upto March 31, 1961, an *ad hoc*, adjustment may be made from Development Fund to capital of the cost of all new lines under construction on April 1, 1955 hitherto charged to Development Fund; and liability still remaining could be repaid from out of the balances in the Revenue Reserve Fund.

NATIONAL WATER SUPPLY AND SANITATION COMMITTEE, 1960 —REPORT

New Delhi, Ministry of Health, 1962. 167p.

Chairman : Shrimati Lourdhammal Simon.
Members : Dr. N.N. Kailas; Dr. Ram Subhag Singh; Shri H.C. Mathur; Shri N.V. Modak; Shri M.K. Kutty; Col. Barkat Narain; Shri K.S. Krishnaswamy.
Secretary : Shri S. Rajagopalan.

APPOINTMENT

The National Water Supply and Sanitation Committee was constituted under the Ministry of Health, Government of India, vide their order No. F. 12-1 (WS)/60, dated April 28, 1960, to make an assessment of the requirements of water supply, both urban and rural and to suggest ways and means for financing these programmes effectively.

TERMS OF REFERENCE

The National Water Supply and Sanitation Programme has now been operation for about five years. It was felt that it would be useful to make a critical review of the progress made so far and of the requirements of the future in the field of water supply and sanitation. The Committee will decide its own procedure but may visit the States to review progress and examine the problem on the spot.

A clarification of the terms of reference was given,

by Shri D.P. Karmarkar, Union Minister for Health while inaugurating the first meeting of the Committee. He referred to the fact that so far a correct and comprehensive assessment of the urban and rural water supply and sanitation requirements in the country has not been made and stressed the need for compiling a realistic forecast of the requirements now as well as in the future. He desired that the Committee should decide and recommend on the procedure to be adopted by the Central and State Governments to set about this task and come up with a realistic and authoritative assessment of the urban and rural water supply and sanitation needs and requirements in the country. He indicated that it was open to the Committee to widen and amplify the terms of reference to include subjects which, it considered, have a bearing on an overall assessment of the problem. He also suggested that the Committee should go fully into the problem of financing of the schemes, both water supply and severage, with special reference to the tax structure and revenue potential in the urban areas as also into the question of training and research as part of the problem of the organisation of the different States. He would also welcome the Committee's views in regard to the agencies in the States, technical and administrative, who should be entrusted with the implementation of the rural works, irrespective of the particular Ministry at the Centre or the State level which may be administering the plan, in order to ensure uniformity of procedure and efficiency and economy in construction and maintenance.

CONTENTS

Introductory; A Historical Retrospect; An Assessment of the Problem; Effective Measures for Stock-taking; The problem of Finance; Organisational Reforms; Special Aspects of the Rural Problem: Procedural Reforms; Production and Procurement of Materials; Water Resources Conservation and Water Pollution Control; Summary of Recommendations; Appendices I to V

RECOMMENDATIONS

Measures For Assessment Of The Problem

In order to make a complete and correct assessment of the urban and rural situation State-wise, and to facilitate a realistic planning in the future years, the State Governments may be advised to set up an Urban Assessment Committee and a Rural Assessment Committee for each State.

The Urban Committee may be headed by the Minister for Local-Self Government with the Chief Public Health Engineer of the State as the Secretary and include representatives from the State Legislature, Municipal Councils and the Directorate of Public Health. The Committee would carry out a preliminary survey and assessment of the urban water supply and sewerage position for the entire State to include a physical and demographic inventory, preliminary engineering forecasts, forecast of the magnitude of the total problem, a priority list for implementation within a specified period, and set out the details in regard to organisational and administrative reforms, production and procurement of materials and all allied matters.

The Rural Committee headed by the State Health Minister with members to represent the State Legislature, Development Department, Panchayati Raj institutions, Directorates of Public Health and Public Health Engineering, with the State Director of Public Health as the secretary, would likewise include in its assignment a physical inventory of existing facilities, village-wise for each Panchayat, nature, extent and cost of additional facilities required, and include recommendations on the financing pattern, maintenance problems, list of priorities to be followed; administrative and organisational set up for implementation of the programme and suggestions for evaluation of the programme at required stages.

Until a comprehensive and correct assessment of the problem is made available through such special committees, set up for the purpose, the approximate forecast of the funds required to complete water supply and sewerage schemes in all urban and rural areas based on the 1961 population figures could be roughly assumed as Rs. 950 crores for the urban and Rs. 200 crores for the rural programme.

Financing Problems

Considering the totality of the problem ahead, the Third Plan allocation may form but one-tenth of the total requirements for urban schemes. It is desirable to complete the entire urban phase of the programme within a period of 10 to 15 years, but from practical considerations the period may have to be spread over 25 years. Even such extended period may involve a capital outlay on urban schemes of the order of Rs. 40 crores per year. Such a heavy programme is not possible under the current methods of financing such schemes, where subsidies create an inhibiting tendency. The concept of water as a merchandise has to be popularised and local bodies encouraged to prosecute water and sewerage systems as a joint utility venture on a self-paying basis. Special help may, however, be necessary in the initial stages of the programme to encourage sewerage schemes being taken up side by side with water supply schemes.

Independent statutory bodies styled as "Water and Drainage Boards". either State-wise or on a region wise basis, may be set up, clothed with adequate statutory powers to promote and finance water supply and sewerage schemes for all urban local badies. The statutory bodies will exercise control on investigation, design, construction and operation of the projects on behalf of the local bodies in the same manner in which commercial enterprises are managed by buisness houses. Independent statutory bodies for the purpose are necessary to infuse confidence in the subscribings public that their investments on the urban schemes would be properly safeguarded.

The Union Health Ministry may set up a High Power Committee with members representing the fields of Public Health Engineering, buisness management, administration, financing and banking, for suggesting the measures to be taken by the State Government for creating such statutory boards, the legal enactments necessary for the purpose, organisational administrative and managerial reforms that will be needed and the Codes and Buy-laws applicable to the regional boards when set up.

The prospects of securing international and for the implementation of urban water supply and sanitation schemes should be explored. Similar assistance for establishing any industry or industries connected with the manufacture of proprietary materials required for the programme should also be explored.

Organisational Reforms

The question of organisation holds the key position, in the carrying out of the major programme ahead. The measure of efficiency of the organisation is the measure of achievement of success of the plan. The setting up of an independent Public Health Engineering Department in each State should no longer be delayed or be a subject matter for debate. The Department should have an independent cadre with service rules and prospects available to the officers as in other etablished departments of engineering. It is essential to integrate Municipal Engineers with the Department. Initial promotion of schemes, investigations, design, execution, operation and maintenance should all be unified under the Public Health Engineering Department with opportunities afforded to the officers to deal with all these aspects in their normal career.

The Local Self Government Ministry should have an effective voice in the implementation of all urban schemes and should have control over the Public Health Engineering Department. The officers manning the Department will then have their roots in the local bodies and will be in tune with their aspirations and needs and will be better able to do promotional work in the local bodies to sponser and pilot their schemes to better advantage. In any case, there is the need for greater liaison between the Health and Local-Self Government Ministries in the implementation of the schemes in future.

The Public Health Engineering Department of the State should gradually encompass within its activities all legitimate functions pertaining to environmental hygiene.

All Subordinate Municipal Engineering Services should be brought under a rationalised system establishing some uniformity in the qualifications and experience prescribed for such personnel and in the service rules and prospects applicable to them through their service in municipalities. Provision should also be made for their absorption in the State Public Health Engineering Department wherever their qualifications and experience befit them for the purpose.

The State Public Health Engineering Departments should carry out the technical services on behalf of the Regional boards, supplemented by private consultants, depending on the work load to be handled.

Concurrent steps should be taken for a continuing training programme for the Public Health Engineering personnel in all disciplines, including academic courses, refresher courses, seminars, conferences and the like.

Fundamental and applied research on all current problems arising in the Public Health Engineering field should receive constant attention so that engineering projects in the future may be based on rational factors applicable to local conditions rather than on conventional methods.

Special Rural Problems

Rural water supply and sanitation should receive very high priority as they have far reaching effects in rehabilitating rural health and economy. The programme needs vision and sustained drive for its success. The basic objectives should be to secure technical soundness and efficiency in the design, construction and maintenance of all types of rural schemes and at the same time adopt financial and administrative measures such as would draw the best out of the villagers and get them involved and interested in the programme.

The multiplicity of agencies employed on the rural programme at present operates as a handicap in the effective implementation of the programme. A unitary agency at the State level should have control over the entire field of activity irrespective of the number of Ministries administrating the different programmes.

Once the assessment of the problem is available, all planning should be carried out district-wise and block-wise. The Zila Parishad should be fully brought into the picture, with a Sub-Committee set up to include the concerned technical officers as members to deal with the entire subject of water supply and sanitation in the district.

The resources made available to the Zila Parishad should be allocated by it to the Panchayat Samities taking into consideration the latter's requirements and the funds available under all programmes for water supply and sanitation, and the extent to which voluntary contribution, etc., would also be available. The needs of backward and neglected areas should recieve high priority.

The State Public Health Engineering Department should be utilised as the single technical agency with a special rural wing at the Headquarters and technical units at the District level, to exercise overall control on the technical aspects of the programme with proper guidance, supervision and check over the field staff.

While preliminary investigations, drawing up of plans and estimates and supervision and guidance would be afforded by the technical personnel at the district level, actual construction of works, except in any special cases, may be entrusted to the Panchayat Samities, the technical supervision remaining with the district level organisation.

Maintenance of completed schemes should receive special importance. The technical responsibility for proper operation and maintenance should be ensured by the employment of minimum qualified technical staff either singly for any particular village system, or jointly for several contiguous villages, so that proper operation and supervision thereof is ensured all the time. The physical responsibility for operation and maintenance should be shouldered exclusively by the local Panchayat Samitis or Panchayat Unions without looking to the State Government for a subsidy even for this purpose.

Rural sanitation should form an integral part of the programme. A sanitory latrine for each village house should be promoted under a sustained programmes so that fifth-borne diseases may be banished from the rural areas as soon as possible. Sullage disposal in rural areas should also recieve special attention.

The existing procedure of subsidering rural water supply schemes under the National Water Supply and Sanitation Programme to population units of 5,000 and below may continue. Relaxation of the rule may be made in special cases upto a population of 10,000.

The semi-urban Communities with population between 5,000 to 20,000 may be brought under a slab system of subsidy for their water supply and sanitations schemes. The Central subsidy may be 35 per cent for units with population between 5,000 to 7,000 25 per cent for units between 7,000 to 10,000 and 15 per cent for units from 10,000 to 20,000.

Procedural Reforms

Procedural matters in processing urban or rural schemes from the stage of its initiation to the final stage of completion through the several agencies should all be streamlined in order to remove bottle necks wherever they exist.

The Union Health Ministry should lay down the guiding principles for design of schemes for the State Governments to follow under the programme, so that delays in preparation of schemes and their approval may be avoided.

The security of the schemes both at the State level and at the Centre should be expedited. There should be an interchange of officers between the Central Public Health Engineering Organisation and the State Public Health Engineering Department.

The State and Central Public Health Engineering Organisations should play their mutual role in establishing standards and techniques for dealing with all problems in design, construction and maintenance and arrange for bringing out technical journals, manuals, codes and brochures for keeping the members of the profession abreast of current trends and latest developments.

The Union Health Ministry should expedite approval to schemes from the State Governments without any reference to the Planning Commission, as it involves delay without any corresponding advantage.

At the State level, a Standing Coordinating Committee may be set up in the Secretariat composed of Ministries, Secretaries, Engineers, Legislators and Municipal Chairmen to meet periodically to study the movement of all schemes figuring in the programme to deal summarily with delaying factors against progress.

The progress of execution of schemes should be specially watched in order to avoid delays by timely action, wherever needed. It would also be necessary to build up a load on the water supply distribution system and on the sewerage system side by side with the execution of these schemes, so that when the local bodies take over completed schemes, the citizens would derive the expected benefits from these aminities without any long time-lag.

Procurement of Materials

It is common complaint that critical materials required for the programme are much in short supply at present, particularly C. I. Pipes in the smaller sizes, Cast Iron specials and valves and other water works fittings. The current rate of financial allocations and the procedure being followed for allotments hinders long-range planning not only in respect of preparation of projects by the States but also in regard to industries planning their production capacities. What is required is a comprehensive planning and decision to implement the total programme within a specified period which will give a proper indication of the future magnitude of the problem and the quantum of requirements needed for such a programme.

Nearly 60 to 70 per cent of the cost of urban water supply schemes comprises the value of C. I. Pipes and specials and the total quantity of such materials required for our schemes in the next 20 or 30 years would be of a significant measure. It will therefore be worthwhile for the State to participate in the manufacture of cost iron pipes and specials so that the quality and price of pipes would be controlled and regulated.

It is desirable that a judicious choice of materials is made in the pipes adopted in the several of the major and minor urban and rural schemes to that pipe materials used correspond to actual needs and scarce materials are conserved for meeting appropriate requirements.

The possibility of securing financial assistance for starting these important industries from International loan agencies may be explored. Reputable foreign firms are now getting interested in helping to increase production of scarce materials. What is required is to channelise the interest evinced by the several agencies into a fruitful line of action and to programme the future plan of production with vision.

The production of pumps and motors and similar water works appurtenances needs some stimulation for the starting of necessary industries so that under a planned programme of production, supply and demand could keep pace at all stages with a control over the quality and price range of all the materials produced.

The High Power Committee to be set up by the Union Health Ministry should also go into this major question, work out the details of future requirements and indicate the extent and scope of the industrial expansion needed in the field.

The District Centre would be the pivot of future activity for implementing the rural programme in future. It is desirable that the Centre is so developed that it has a manufacturing yard for the casting, curing and storage of different sizes of concrete pipes, special latrine pans, squatting slabs, traps, etc., required for rural water supply and sanitation works. A mechanical section under adequate supervision of the District Centre should be entrusted with the production, stocking, supply and distribution of all materials required for the programme. Each Centre could, in addition, train the required number of masons, carpenters, mechanics, mistries and other artisans in their respective works so, that they may handle the field work in rural areas to better advantage. The District Centres could, in addition arrange for the necessary orientation, refresher and training courses for the subordinate for technical personnel employed in the rural areas to better advantage. This District Centre could, in addition, arrange for the necessary orientation, refresher and training courses for the subordinate technical personnel employed in the rural programme.

Water Resources Conservation And Water Pollution Control

A Water Resources Conservation Programme is of supreme importance, in order to safeguard and regulate future development of all water supply systems, big and small. Advance action to conserve adequate supplies for the future needs of each city should receive special attention. The State Governments may detail an advance investigation division to conduct a preliminary survey and decide on the nature and extent of resources which will have to be harnessed for the present and future needs of all citizens and of special rural areas, and also to examine to what extent collaboration with other users of water from the same source is necessary and to initiate necessary measures to reserve adequate supplies for future needs.

A Water Pollution Control Programme is equally important to ensure adequate safeguards for preserving the quality of the supply from present and future sources. Almost all water courses in the country are getting increasing discharges of pollutional loads from waste waters and trade effluents which may impair the chemical and bacterial quality of such stream flows.

There are two aspects of the problem of water pollution control. The one is an initial assessment of its extent, nature and magnitude in the several States; and the other is the manner and method in which such pollution could be combated effectively and the administrative, technical and legal machinery to be set up for such a purpose. The engineering, economic and equity aspects involved in the problem and its solution deserve a discerning study of the local factors before regulations are to be enforced in each case on its merits. An overall assessment of the problem with statistical data on the present and future pattern of development is a prerequisite for working out the details of such a programme.

The Union Health Ministry may set up a compact High Power Committee to include Public Health Engineers and Public Health Officials from the Directorate General of Health Services and the Central Public Health Engineering Research Institute, Members from the Union Parliament and the State Legislatures, representatives from the industries and representative from the Union Ministries of Law and of Commerce and Industry to study and report on a comprehensive

Water Pollution Control Programme for the country. The Committee will make detailed studies of river velleys with special reference of water pollution, make a general survey and assessment of the water pollution State-wise make a comparative study of the existing laws and available technical and administrative machinery for controlling the problem in the States and advise on the legal, technical, administrative and general measures to be adopted by the States for bringing into effect a comprehensive water pollution control programme. It may also go into the allied question of setting up State-wise Water Pollution Control Boards, and indicate their constitution, set up and functions for administering the programme on a uniform basis throughout the country.

SCHEDULED AREAS AND SCHEDULED TRIBES COMMISSION, 1960—REPORT

New Delhi, Ministry of Home Affairs, 1961. 2 Vols.

Chairman : Shri U.N. Dhebar

Members : Shri D. Basumatari; Shri H.C. Heda; Shri Jaipal Singh; Shri T. Sanganna; Shri Manikyalal Verma; Shri Narayan Rao M. Wadiwa; Shri Subodh Hansda; Shri D.J. Naik; Shri Dharam Dev Shastri; Dr. Verrier Elwin.

Secretary : Shri S. Narayanswamy.

APPOINTMENT

Article 339 of the Constitution provides that:

"The President may at any time and shall at the expiration of 10 years from the commencement of this Constitution by order appoint a Commission to report on the administration of the Scheduled Areas and the Welfare of the Scheduled Tribes in the States.

The order may define the composition, powers and procedure of the Commission and may contain such incidental or ancillary provisions as the President may consider necessary or desirable."

In pursuance of the provisions of this Article, this Commission was appointed by the President under the designation, the Scheduled Areas and the Scheduled Tribes Commission, on April 28, 1960, by his order published in the Government of India, Ministry of Home Affairs Notification No. 11/6/59-SCT. IV, dated April 28, 1960.

TERMS OF REFERENCE

To report on:

(a) The administration of the Scheduled Areas under the Fifth Schedule to the Constitution, and, in particular, as to

(i) the functioning of the Tribes Advisory Councils

(ii) the laws applicable to the Scheduled Areas and the exercise by the Governors concerned of powers under paragraph 5 of the Fifth Schedule; and

(iii) the principles to be followed in declaring any, territory to be, or to form part of, a Scheduled Area or directing that any territory shall cease to be, or cease to form part of, a Schedule Area;

(b) The welfare of the Scheduled Tribes in the States and, in particular, whether the development plans in relation to matters connected with the welfare of Scheduled Tribes require any alteration in respect of objectives, priorities or details of working; and

(c) Any other matter connected with the administration of Scheduled Areas or the welfare of the Scheduled Tribes in the States which may hereafter be specially referred to the Commission for investigation and report.

CONTENTS

Introductory; **Part I**: Tribes and Constitutional Arrangements—The Problem; The Scheduled Tribes; The Condition of the Tribes Prior to Independence; The Constitution and the Scheduled Tribes; The Scheduled Areas; Governor's Powers under the Fifth Schedule; Tribes Advisory Council; Criteria for Scheduled Areas; Article 275 of the Constitution and Responsibility of the States; **Part II**: Review of the Progress and Recommendations—Assessment; Land and the Scheduled Tribes; Tribals and Forest Policy; Agriculture; Village and Cottage Industries; Community Development and Tribal Development Blocks; The Problem of Indebtedness; Cooperation; Eductional Development; Health; Housing; Communications; Impact of Industrialisation; **Part III**: Administration and Institutional Set up—Administration; Commiioner for Scheduled Castes and Scheduled Tribes;

Non-official Agencies; Training Programmes ; Representation in Services ; Role of the Traditional Tribal Councils ; Survey, Research and Evaluation : **Part IV** : State-wise Recommendations—Andhra Pradesh; Assam; Bihar ; Gujarat ; Kerala ; Madhya Pradesh ; Madras : Maharashtra ; Mysore ; Orissa ; Punjab ; Rajasthan ; West Bengal ; Andaman and Nicobar Islands ; Himachal Pradesh ; Laccadive, Minicoy and Amindivi Islands ; Manipur ; Nagaland ; NEFA ; Tripura ; Conclusion ; Summary of Recommendations ; Select Bibliography ; Notes on References ; Tables ; Appendices I to XIV (in Volume II).

RECOMMENDATIONS

The Scheduled Areas

Scheduled Areas have been constituted with two clear and straight-forward objectives—one is to assist the tribals in enjoying their existing rights unhindered by others and the second is to develop the areas and promote economic, educational and social progress among Scheduled Tribes. In this scheme protection of the interests of the Tribals in land, protection against exploitation by money-lenders and priority in the allotment of land come first. The Constitution has vested powers in the Governor to make regulations for the protection of the tribals but this power has been used very sparingly. This appears to be due to certain vagueness about the law making powers of the Governor and the absence of suitable directions. It is felt that without some directions from the Centre the State Governments may not realise the scope of the law making and rule making powers and their importance for the general development programme. The State Governments may be advised to utilise to the full provisions of paragraph 5 of the Fifth Schedule within a given period. The legislation that may thus be promoted should take into account the harm caused in the interim period and also to what extent it is possible to remedy it. The Union Government should state a time limit and pursue the matter with the State Governments so that the necessary legislation is completed within the given period.

There has been as much vagueness about the approach, priorities and methods of application in developmental activities, but inspite of the deficiencies considerable progress has been made in the field of education, health and community development and these have made an impact on the tribals.

Figures of developmental expenditure are maintained district-wise and unless the Scheduled Area is itself a district, it is impossible to get a picture of the physical and financial targets, achieved in the Scheduled Areas. The State Governments should be required to maintain figures of development expenditure separately for the Scheduled Areas, giving physical and financial targets achieved.

Governor's Powers Under The Fifth Schedule

The Governor's reports are intended to enable the Union Government to discharge their responsibilities to the tribes. It is only a medium on which further action is to be taken. No instructions have been issued by the Union Government about the formal contents of these reports with the result that State Governments have come to look upon them as departmental reports. The main purpose is thus not fulfilled. There is plenty of material available for the preparation of these reports. A proper use of this material can give a co-ordinated picture of the position in the tribal areas. The preparation of the annual report should not be left to the Tribal Welfare Directorate, but should be the responsibility of the Secretariat, who should collect the data from the Director and the staff in the field. The views expressed by the Members of Legislative Assemblies, Members of the Tribes Advisory Councils, non-official organisations and the Commissioner for Scheduled Castes and Scheduled Tribes should also be incorporated. The actual conditions in the tribal areas can provide a review of the reactions of a cross section of the people living or working on them. The State Governments as well as the President will thus have a carefully prepared document which can be of real use to the Union Government.

The preparation of this report can be better handled by the Chief Secretary who may have a small section to assist him for a couple of months in a year. After the report is prepared, it should invariably go to the Council of Ministers and only then be forwarded to the Governor and through him to the President.

The Tribes Advisory Council should also be invited to make suggestions for inclusion in the report on any matter of importance.

There is no special machinery in the States to consider the possible effect on the tribals of legislation proposed in Parliament or in the State Legislatures. The past 10 years have witnessed phenomenal, economic and social changes, many of which have been brought about through legislation. The application of these laws to the Scheduled Areas without any machinery to look into their possible consequences on the tribals is, in our opinion, a sad omission. It is recommended that—

(a) At the State level a section should be created in the Legal Department to undertake a study of the Central and State laws relating to (i) social matters, (ii) rights in land including tenancy laws, (iii) allotment of land and setting apart land for village purposes,

(iv) private money-lending and village management including establishment of village Panchayats, and to suggest modifications to protect the rights of the tribals in regard to these matters. This should be undertaken without any further loss of time.

(b) A survey should be undertaken in each State with a view to ascertain to what extent the interests of the tribals have suffered, which require restoration or retrospective legislative assistance.

(c) The Union Government should take up with the State Governments the necessity of having a definite and consistent policy of protection in relation to subjects mentioned in the Fifth Schedule.

(d) Early steps should be taken by the Union Government to evolve in consultation with the State Governments concerned a definite and consistent policy in relation to allotment of lands to the tribals.

Tribes Advisory Council

In the Punjab, Bihar and other States, the Chief Minister is the Chairman of the Tribes Advisory Council. This practice has been very helpful. The Chairman of a Tribes Advisory Council should accordingly be a person who has influence beyond the immediate department concerned, for he is expected to deal with problems that concern for he is expected is deal with problems that concern all the departments.

Since the maximum number of non-tribals that can be appointed to the Tribes Advisory Council is five, the representation of officials should be limited to one at the most so as to leave scope for the nomination of non-officials. It would be sufficient if the Chief Secretary is a member. He as the coordinating medium of the entire administration will be able to guide and control other Departmental Heads or Secretaries.

It is desirable to have on the Council persons who are non-tribals working in the field. This will provide a common forum for discussion and be a source of encouragement to them.

As regards the representation of tribal legislators, there is need for caution in the States where there is a large tribal population as in Bihar, Madhya Pradesh and Orissa. Government should try to ensure that all shades of opinion are given representation.

The rules regarding the composition of the Councils should be changed in the case of those States which include a number of officials and where there is only notional representation for non-official agencies.

The Rules of Business should be amended so as to define properly the functions of the Council and should include provisions enabling the members to initiate and bring up for discussion any matter concerning the welfare of the Scheduled Tribes or development of the Scheduled Areas.

In almost all the States, Tribes Advisory Councils have been given an opportunity to discuss the draft Third Five-Year Plan. Annual discussion on the progress of the Plan will be helpful in generating interest of the tribals in a planned approach, besides making them more and more development-conscious Simultaneously, it will enable them to understand their responsibility in making the plan success.

There is need for consultation with regard to legislation. There may be same laws which do not warrant any detailed discussion. At the same time there will certainly be others which under the Fifth Schedule, do warrant such a discussion.

There should be a periodical review of the work done in the Tribal Development Blocks and in other fields of development activity. Members of the Tribes Advisory Council should be given facilities to go round the state and visit important projects.

The Council should have a staff of its own with a Secretary who can do the follow-up work.

There should, in all the States and Union Territories, whether they have Scheduled Areas or not, be Tribes Advisory Councils to advise on the protection and development of the Scheduled Tribes.

Criteria For Scheduled Areas

The criteria for determining a Scheduled Area should be related to the objectives of the Fifth Schedule. These are (i) protection of the Scheduled Tribes; and (ii) raising the level of administration in the Scheduled Areas. In determining the criteria those factors which promote the objectives of the scheduled should invariably be present; others may or may not be.

The most important factor is the concentration of tribal population. The percentage of tribal concentration in any area proposed for declaration as a Scheduled Area should not be less than 50 per cent. This is particularly necessary when entensive efforts for protection and large-scale development are contemplated.

The compactness of the area is an important consideration since scheduling involves special administration. A sub-tehsil should be the unit. Wherever, there is a Tribal Development Block, the size of the sub-tehsil should correspond with it. Elsewhere sub-tehsils should be formed which could conveniently be converted into Tribal Development Blocks.

The area should be under-developed. It is possible to apply tests to assess the degree of under-development, e.g., the extent of cultivated and uncultivated land against the total land available, extent of irrigation, the mileage of roods in the area, the percentage of literacy and the number of dispensaries.

There should be marked disparity in the economic standards of the tribals living in the areas compared to the people in the surrounding areas. Areas where shifting cultivation is still in vogue or the size of holdings is less than 50 acres per capita (standard acre) and the per capita incomes are lower than half of the all-India incomes and the quantum of under-employment is severe that the people do not get work for more than 200 days in a year, should be reckoned as fulfilling this factor in the criteria.

All these four factors—

(1) preponderance of tribals in the population,

(2) compact and reasonable size,

(3) under-developed nature of the area, and

(4) marked disparity in economic standards of the people,

must invariably be present before any area can be considered eligible for declaration as a Scheduled Area. Other factors such as the primitive or distinctive way of life or the practice of shifting cultivation seem to relate to the condition of the people and not to the area and would be covered by the criteria stated above.

For the purpose of scheduling areas, no distinction should be drawn between the States and the Union Territories.

No existing area can be de-scheduled unless the government, after examination of all available data, is satisfied that it fulfils a certain standard and has developed economically and educationally and in point of health, communications and services to the limit when it can no longer remain scheduled. In the Commission's view no Scheduled Area has yet reached the State where descheduling can be considered.

In view of the changes that have taken place since the inception of the Constitution, we feel that it is no longer necessary to pursue the question whether a tribal area should be declared scheduled or a Scheduled Area should be de-scheduled. The Fifth Schedule was conceived as a temporary expedient and its objectives can be achieved by our alternative approach, which is simply that government should undertake a plan which would protect the Scheduled Tribes and ensure development of the tribal areas within a stated period. The State Governments should undertake general legislation applicable throughout the Scheduled and non-Scheduled Areas for protection of the rights of tribals, inland and forests, and protection from exploitation by money-lenders and this legislation should be implemented with a period of 10 years. Pending enactment of such general legislation, the regulatory powers of the Governor under paragraph 5(2) of the Fifth Schedule may be utilised for the promulgation of corresponding regulations for the Scheduled Areas. Simultaneously, all tribal areas should be grouped under Tribal Development Blocks so that the bulk of the tribal population is brought under intensive development schemes. The blocks should concentrate on the following four activities—economic development, education, health and communications and should have specific targets. With the fulfilment of the targets in all Tribal Development Blocks and the passing and implementation of protective legislation, the objectives of the Fifth Schedule would have been achieved and it could conveniently be abrogated.

If Government is unable to accept this programme, there is no alternative to declaring those areas, which after enquiry satisfy the criteria suggested by us, as Scheduled Areas despite the complications involved.

Articles 275 Of The Constitution And Responsibility Of States

The grants-in-aid under Article 275 are intended to supplement the general welfare programmes which are directed to the entire community including the Scheduled Tribes. The Andhra Pradesh Government has issued instructions to all heads of departments that three per cent of the total provision of each department should be earmarked for the welfare of the Scheduled Tribes during the Third Five Year Plan period. The other State Governments may consider the issue of similar instructions.

The distribution of grants-in-aid only on the basis of population will not be fair. There is no doubt that the criterian of population is a safe and easy one. But since the grant is intended also to develop the area, the relative under-development of an area and its present problems should be assessed. In the allocation of funds under Article 275, the following criteria may be followed:

(a) Population;

(b) Level of development reached by the State in welfare activity for Scheduled Tribes and level of administration in the Scheduled Areas;

(c) Financial position of the State.

In addition to these three factors the position of the border States in the north and north-eastern regions which have suffered a serious dislocation of their economy and trade due to change in the international atmosphere be taken into consideration in deciding the outlay for tribal welfare in all such areas.

Beyond allocating funds to the States, Union Government have no adequate machinery for ensuring that the funds given have been properly spent and for the purposes intended. It is suggested that the proposed Department of Tribal Welfare to be set up in the Ministry of Home Affairs should contain an Accounts Cell exclusively for the purpose of maintaining accounts of the funds disbursed to the State Governments, Union Territories and non-official organisations.

As the grants are specially intended to, raise the tribal

areas to the level of the surrounding areas, the large amounts that invariably lapse at the end of each financial year should be available for re-allotment for the same purpose. The machinery at the Centre to ensure such re-allocation is totally inadequate and to solve this problem, following alternatives are suggested :

(a) A procedure may be devised by which the grants sanctioned during a particular year are available for expenditure even in the succeeding year, thus giving the administration 12 months to implement the schemes in full.

(b) A non-lapsable Tribal Welfare Fund may be created on the lines of the Central Road Reserve Fund.

(c) The financial year may be changed from April-March to July-June.

A separate entry be made in the budget and accounts so that it becomes easier to obtain figures of provision, expenditure and balance left for purposes of re-allotment in subsequent years.

Delay appears to lie with the State Governments whose Finance Departments are reported to scrutinise the schemes further even after approval is given by the Union Government on the basis of their inclusion in the annual plans. The State Governments should devise a suitable procedure which would obviate reference to their Finance Departments of cases where the increase in the outlay does not exceed a particular percentage, say five per cent.

Six-monthly progress reports of the State Governments should be despatched promptly within three months after the lapse of the six-monthly report period; this should be made a condition of the grant.

As Article 275 does not envisage loans to the State Governments, the Union Governments, or the Reserve Bank should give loans to the State Governments for disbursement to the tribal people for economic development such as agriculture, industries, rehabilitation in a trade or even construction of houses.

It is recommended that all expenditure on the employment of additional staff in the field and at the headquarters and their training should be met out of funds given to the States

In view of the constitutional obligations in regard to the welfare of the Scheduled Tribes, the programme for the welfare of Scheduled Tribes should be kept separate from the general programme of social welfare and given a higher priority to these schemes at the time of annual plan discussions.

As the responsibility for the welfare of the Scheduled Tribes and raising the level of administration on the Scheduled Areas is primarily that of the State Governments, we feel that there is need for a change in their attitude. They should come foreward more enthusiastically and liberally to shoulder the responsibility.

Schemes with high priority such as economic development, health, drinking water supply, training of personnel, research and evaluation should be included under the Central sector whereas schemes for education, housing etc. should come under the State sector.

Assessment

The achievements in the positive field of development during the first and second plan periods are also limited. This has been due to diffusion of effort and lack of an integrated and planned approach which would give employment at least for 300 days a year on reasonable ages and food all the year round. The problem of economic development for the bulk of the tribals cannot be solved unless the resources of land, forests, cattle wealth, cottage and village industries are all mobilised in service. In other words improvement of techniques and an integrated approach in relating to all the four avenues of employment available in the tribal areas is the only answer.

Education has made an unmistakable impact upon the tribal mind and there is no place in India which is not demanding primary middle and high schools. There is outstanding contribution in regard to maleria control and eradication. The other diseases like yours, V.D. and T.B. have get to be tackled properly. The communications in the tribal areas have not been properly developed. The development plans have left a mixed impression on the minds of the people. Tnere have been serious shortfalls in financial and physical targets some of the State Governments, notably Madhya Pradesh, have explained to us the reasons for the shortfall. One of the reasons given by the State Governments is that since Tribal Welfare is dealt with as part of the bigger subject 'Social Services' they feel embarrassed in giving a higher priority to tribal welfare. It is recommended that Tribal Welfare should be separated from Social Welfare and given its own importance and priority.

In some of the tribal areas, the working season does not exceed three or four months. Even in the easier districts, it does not exceed eight or nine. Once snow begins to fall or the rainy season sets in, no work is possible. The rules (financial) should take into considerat on these special conditions.

One of the most important lessons that the shortfalls have to teach us is that there should be a constant watch upon expenditure and achievement in tribal areas. Dacisions have, therefore, to be taken well in advance. A periodical examination of such vital questions at the time of the annual appraisal of the Plan is necessary at the Union Government level. This appraisal would enable the Union Government to step in as and when the situation required.

Land And The Scheduled Tribes

Prevention Of Land Alienation

All existing Acts and Regulations affecting tribal's lands be examined by a Committee in each State and Union Territory with the ultimate object of completely preventing transfers of tribals' lands to non-tribals. It may be necessary in many cases to amend the present laws drastically. If this is likely to take time, the Governors may, in exercise of the powers conferred to them under the Fifth Schedule, issure the necessary Regulations without delay.

There should be a general prohibition of all transfers, whether by sale, mortgage, gift or lease under any kind of agreement to contract affecting the tribal's lands entered into by tribals in favour of non-tribals without the permission of the Deputy Commissioners or the Collectors. The Government should make rules in consultation with the Tribals Advisory Council governing the grant of permission by the Deputy Commissioner or the Collector after ascertaining the conditions prevailing in each area.

There should be a bar against sui... or applications against any such order made by a Deputy Commissioner or a Collector and the courts of law should be precluded from taking cognisance of all transfers of land, gift or lease or any other agreement or contract and from passing decree thereon unless arrangement has been entered into with the previous permission of the Deputy Commissioner or the Collector.

The Deputy Commissioners or Collectors should have powers *sup moto* or at the instance of the aggrieved tribal land holder within a period of 12 years to institute enquiries and restore possession of the land with or without payment of any compensation to the transferee. This provision should have retrospective effect from January 26, 1950. Adequate machinery should be created to implement these provisions.

All surrenders of lands should be only to the State, which should hold the surrendered land as a trustee for the tribals.

Non-official agencies should educate the tribals regarding the laws or regulations made for their benefit and render them necessary financial and legal assistance.

Impact Of Industrialisation

The scheme of rehabilitation of persons likely to be displaced as a result of any project should form a part of the project and adequate financial provision should be made for it as a part of the project expenditure.

In selecting alternative sites for their rehabilitation, the acquiring authorities should consult the tribals and their representatives.

So long as uncultivated land is available in the neighbourhood, land under cultivation should not be acquired for any project.

In following the principle of compensation of giving land for land and house for house, if the value of land allotted is less than the value of land acquired for any project, the difference should be made good by payment in cash.

Development of colonies for displaced persons should be completed before they are asked to vacate their lands and houses acquired for any project.

Persons likely to be affected as a result of a project should have preference in employment on the project work, subject to the consideration of technical qualifications where they are needed.

Land Allotment

In the Scheduled Areas and in the areas where there is a predominantly tribal population, first priority for land allotment should be given to the tribal people. In other areas they should rank for this purpose with the Scheduled Castes.

There should be a regular plan drawn up for every Scheduled Area and the areas where the Scheduled Tribes are in considerable numbers, for allotment of cultivable wasteland. A certain portion of the cultivable wasteland may be set apart for the future needs of the State, the general public or the villagers, other lands being distributed without any further delay. Only such number of families may be accommodated there as can maintain themselves upon the land.

The scheme for the allotment of land should also incorporate the following facilities for land allottees:

(a) Irrigation.

(b) Credit—not on some mechanical basis, but having regard to the tribals' need to clear the area, construct houses, dig wells and maintain themselves till the new harvesting season.

(c) Housing—the taste, tradition and needs of the tribals should be borne in mind. They should be permitted to build their houses from locally available material.

Surplus land that will be available in tribal areas as a result of legislations prescribing ceilings on holdings should be allotted to tribals on a preferential basis.

While allotting surplus or cultivable waste-land, the tribal cooperatives may have precedence but the land should not be tied up with any such condition.

Record Of Rights

The work of preparing the record of rights, as far as the tribals are concerned, should be completed as early as possible. Since most of the tribals are illiterate and ignorant of the implications of various exactments, the approach to this work should be human rather than legalistic, and should take full note of tribals' custom and tradition. Possession of a certain piece of land should be regarded as a *prima facie* proof to warrant recording of that land in favour of a tribal unless there are circumstances to show that it is illegally acquired.

Forest Policy

The forest policy as laid down in the Resolution of 1952 should be reviewed and the departures made by this policy in relation to release of forest lands for cultivation, supply of villagers' needs from the outlying areas in the reserved forests, village forests, grazing and shifting cultivation should be reconsidered. Government should accept in relation to the rights of the tribals in forests at any rate the position that obtained prior to Independence. The needs of the village communities should be kept in view and the present approach of government towards the tribal villages in forest areas be revised.

Government should take steps to eliminate the middlemen between the inhabitants of the forests and the Forest Development in relation to the exploitation of the forest. The system of monopoly should in any case be ended.

Settlers in the forest villages should be granted security of tenure. These settlers should not be required to work except on payment of wages at rates not lower than the wages payable under the Minimum Wages Act. These villages should be provided with all amenities including drinking water supply, education and health. The settlers should receive credit facilities both from the State as well as from the cooperative societies.

The right of individuals in the private forest be immediately abolished in those areas in the country, where it has not been abolished so far.

The Forest Department should be deemed to be charged as a branch of the government with the responsibility of participating in the betterment of tribals side by side with the development of forests.

In Relation To Execution

Steps should be taken to implement the policy decision of the government in regard to the village forests. There should be coordination between the Forest, Revenue and Development authorities for this work. The management of the village forests should be vested in village Panchayats and all revenue from these forests should go to them.

Suitable areas reserved for afforestation may be handed over to the local Panchayats, the Forest Department providing the necessary technical guidance. The Panchayats should not only have the responsibility of managing them but should also be given a right to appropriate the forest produce in a certain proportion subject to the rules and regulations of the Forest Department for the benefit of the village.

The Forest Department should promote growth of improved varieties of grass in forest areas especially in areas where afforestation is in progress and should also participate in the preparation of hay and silage-making. Grazing fees should be regulated.

The Minimum Wages Act should be scrupulously enforced in relation to the employees of the Forest Department and those of contractors and middlemen.

The Forest Department in consultation with Agriculture, Industries and Development Departments in each region should prepare a time schedule so as to provide work for the tribals all the year round. Such work should include services in the Forest Department as Forest Guards and for protection, conservation, regeneration and exploitation of forest and forest produce. It should include work on land utilisation schemes, collection of forest produce, processing of minor forest produce and exploitation of major forest produce.

The tribals residing in and around the forests should be organised into permanent labour corps for the purposes of obtaining labour of the right type for forest operations.

The Forest Department should assist in organising the Forest Labourers' Cooperative Societies. A time limit should be fixed to cover the entire forest area with such societies and all work pertaining to the exploitation of forest produce should be entrusted to them.

The State Governments should organise Cooperative Finance and Development Corporations on the model of the Andhra Scheduled Tribes Cooperative Finance and Development Corporation, with such modification as circumstances may require, with a view to consolidate and develop the economy of the tribals, particularly in relation to purchase of minor forest produce, supply of requirements of the members, processing and grading of forest produce for the benefit of the tribals, discharge prior debts and to act as an agent of the government for procurement, supply and distribution of agricultural and other produce. The programme should cover all the tribal areas by primary cooperatives which should function as agents of the Central institution.

Agriculture

In the tribal areas, agricultural production suffers from small holdings, fragmentation, poor quality of soil and elementary methods of cultivation. Improvement of agriculture for the tribes, therefore has to follow the same principles of intensive cultivation introduced in other parts of the country. This can only come with security of land tenure, irrigation, scientific jhuming, soil conservation and the promotion of animal husbandry.

One of the major problems in the tribal areas is that of shifting cultivation. Everyone agrees that shifting cultivation is not an ideal method. The total replacement of this system, if it comes at all, will be a long-term process.

Shifting cultivation is a mixed problem, partly connected with the physical conditions of the land and partly with social customs, traditions and beliefs. Any hurried departure may create complications.

An attractive solution of the problem is to convert shifting cultivation into terraced cultivation. Wherever the hill slopes permit and the soil is sufficiently deep, this holds out immense possibility of improvement, and in many places throughout the tribal areas, it has already been taken up with enthusiasm. It involves heavy initial expenditure of money.

The most reasonable policy is to regulate shifting cultivation on scientific lines so as to limit its disadvantages and promote the fertility of the soil. For this purpose we recommend the undertaking of research in every area where the jhuming cultivation exists on a wide scale. This is a very large and expensive programme.

The transfer of population from the shifting cultivation area to the lower regions down below does not appear to be a practical proposition that would yield results in the immediate future. It may well have to be phased over a period of 50 years.

In any land colonisation scheme, we suggest that special attention be paid to the following points even if this involves reduction in the number of families that can be accommodated :

(i) There should be adequate land. It should be properly demarcated and distributed, with title deeds.

(ii) Irrigation facilities should be available and provided.

(iii) The settlers should be provided necessary employment in clearing the land, constructing the houses, wells, approach roads and irrigation work immediately ofter their agreeing to be members of the colony.

(iv) The rates of labour should be fair. There should not be a contractor in between nor should there be any question of expecting the people to do the work on an *ad hoc* basis or on loan.

(v) They should be provided with bullocks, seeds and maintenance allowance for the period they work on the fields till they get the harvest.

(vi) Horticulture, depending on the soil, climate and irrigation facilities, should be encouraged.

(vii) The colony should be self-sufficient in every respect. There should be proper arrangements for drinking water, a school and a cooperative society.

The terrain which the tribals cultivate is mostly undulating. Continuous cultivation has considerably eroded the soil and reduced its fertility. The process is increased by winds, snow and turbulent water-courses in the hills. Soil conservation on a large and scientific scale is essential for these areas.

Regarding soil conservation, it is recommended that :

(i) A phased programme of conservation, including contour bunding, gully-pluggings, terracing and field bunding, should be prepared for every Tribal Development Block.

(ii) In preparing the schemes, those areas which have a tribal concentration should be given precedence.

(iii) Subsidies should be given for soil conservation measures an individual as well as community holdings. The tribals' contribution should be in the form of labour only.

(iv) Afforestation work should be taken up simultaneously. If necessary, research on local problems should be undertaken to find out—

(a) Suitable grass and legumes for the locality ;

(b) Suitable techniques for gully-plugging (reclamation) ; and

(c) fruit trees suitable for eroded soils.

Fruit trees, grass and legumes selected after research which would prove useful for erosion control should be multiplied in government nurseries and then distributed to the tribals free of cost.

(v) Construction of irrigation wells should be encouraged in these areas where there is scarcity of rain

(vi) Expenditure from tribal funds on schemes that predominantly benefit others should not be permitted.

Since for same time to come agriculture will be the mainstay of tribal economy and since their holdings are small, cultivation is the only way to build up their economy. Intensive cultivation is not possible without irrigation.

The approach to this problem of irrigation in a Tribal Development Block should be as follows :

(i) First a survey should be made of the tribals' land and the possible source of irrigation.

(ii) Those schemes of irrigation should get priority which would ensure irrigation of the lands of the tribals and other under-developed groups.

(iii) If there are schemes which can irrigate the lands, but not necessarily those of the tribals, they should be undertaken on condition that if they irrigate lands which have been acquired by individuals from the tribals, such lands should be redistributed and irrigation facilities provided to all.

(iv) In the areas where irrigation is not possible, if there are already irrigated lands which once belonged to the tribals, such lands should be redistributed.

The demand for irrigation is universal. The achievements so far bear no relation to the people's needs. It is recommended that :

(i) A special division with a Superintending Engineer at the top for survey and execution of minor and medium irrigation projects should be set up in each State.

(ii) State Government should fix targets for minor and medium irrigation works in tribal areas and earmark a substantial amount from its normal budget for these projects.

(iii) The rules in relation to returns be reviewed and revised. The question of return should be considered in the light of the condition of the people.

(iv) All existing irrigation sources--walls ond tanks should be repaired and improved.

(v) Irrigation wells should be constructed on full subsidy basis.

(vi) Improvement and extension of channels, installation of electric and diesel pumps and Persian wheels and boring of tube-wells should be taken up wherever possible.

There is considerable scope for development of horticulture and cash crops in the tribal areas. To encourage horticulture it is recommended that :

(a) Suitable lands including lands now classified under forest but without trees should, wherever they are available and there is a demand, be transferred to individuals and Panchayats for the development of horticulture ;

(b) The holder of land should have full rights over the trees and fruits ;

(c) Arrangements should be made to supply plants, seeds, manure and fertilisers ;

(d) Arrangements should also be made to supply insecticides and plant protection equipment ;

(e) Technical assistance and guidance should be given by the Agriculture and Forest Departments free of cost ;

(f) Fruit preservation units should be established where necessary ; and

(g) Transport and marketing facilities should be provided.

The major need of the tribal as soon as he gets irrigation water will be bullocks. The early establishment in each region of a suitable cattle-breeding farm is desirable. For this purpose it will be necessary that the type of the animal needed for each region should be fixed first. The Indian Council of Agriculture Research and the Ministry of Food and Agriculture may be asked to examine this question further.

For the development of animal husbandry the following measures are suggested :

(i) Establishment of proper unit for development of the animal husbandry to guide and direct Tribal Development Block agencies in the work of survey and development.

(ii) Establishment of a nucleus cattle farm in each region for developing a drought breed.

(iii) Survey of the milk and other dietic need of the tribals and the people of the area, assessment of the possibilities in the areas to meet these needs and the steps to be taken to do so.

(iv) Supply of veterinary services to the area for the protection and development of their stock.

(v) Arrangement for breeding, feeding and weeding of the cattie in tribal areas.

(vi) Training on a mass scale for spreading the knowledge about improvement of the stock and economic utilisation.

(vii) Training for Certificate, Diploma and Degree courses in animal husbandry of tribal students.

(viii) Developing facilities for credit and marketing the stock as well as its produce.

(ix) Rearing of goats, sheep, horses, mithons, yaks and chorus and development of poultry and piggery,

Village And Cottage Industries

The problem of distribution and the sub-normal standard of living in the tribal areas owing to the low potential of agriculture can be mitigated through development of village and cottage industries. Cottage industries can utilise and develop the creative faculties of the tribal people, provide gainful employment to them and offer an avenue for converting the raw materials into processed articles.

The problem of village and cottage industries is one of proper direction and of large-scale organisation. Owing to the lack of an organisation and absence of a clear-cut policy, the efforts at spreading village and cottage industries have been mostly superficial. There is very little of preliminary survey of the scope of such industries which are marketable,

The village industries in the tribal areas can be divided into three categories:

(i) Consumer goods industries;

(ii) processing industries, and

(iii) Handicraft and art pieces.

Talking consumer goods industries first there will not be much of a market for articles manufactured in tribal villages. Similarly, handicrafts and art pieces which depend on outside markets enquire survey or assessment of the potential markets. Where such an industry has a prospect a pilot project can be started with adequate financial investment and with training facilities. The prospects for processing industries, however, are bright and efforts have been made to organise such industries e.g., add leaves in Andhra Pradesh, brooms and baskets and many other major and minor forest produce.

Wherever there is raw material available and there is a market available locally or outside, the principle should be that the raw materials should not go in the form of raw material but should go as a processed article unless the cost is uneconomic or it involves technical or transport problems beyond the reach of administration in tribal areas.

The basic thing, however, is the need for an effective organisation for all the three types of village and cottage industries. It is only when there is an organisation solely devoted to the task of survey, study, piloting, and organisation that there will be any appreciable change in the situation.

It is clear that Khadi and Village Industries Commission and the All India Handicrafts Board are the proper agencies to undertake a large share of responsibility. What remains can be attended to by an organisation modelled according to their advice.

There shall by attached to each State institution representing them, a special section, to assist the field agencies with guidance, technical assistance, training facilities and financial heip. The Tribal Welfare Department with the assistance of the State Boards should set up a field organisation for the purpose.

A number of production-cum training centres for cottage industries have started. In some places the other youths out numbered the tribal and that too in centres opened by the Tribal Development Blocks. It was noticed that selection of tribals was not carefully done having regard to the neeos of the area and also the psychology of the people. Tannery should not be introduced in tribal areas so long as it carries the social stigma amongst the tribals. Satisfactory records have not been maintained of the follow-up efforts made to to rehabilitate the trainees on completion of their course.

There is scope for expansion of cottage industries in Assam, NEFA, Nagaland, Bihar etc. Orissa has a large scope for handloom, spinning, bamboo work and rope-making. Lahaul and Spiti and Himachal Pradesh can supply all types of woollen fabrics, if adequate quantities of wool are supplied to maintain industry.

Madhya Pradesh and Orissa are dominating the Indian scene in biri manufacture. There is no reason why processing of tobacco and preparation of bidi cannot be taken over by the tribals. Pilot schemes can be undertaken.

Community Development And Tribal Development Blocks

As far as the coverage of the tribal areas by the Tribal Development Blocks is concerned, the criterion of 66.6 per cent tribal population in the selected area as fixed by the Ministry of Home Affairs, is quite arbitrary and will lead to discrimination. The origional proposal made by the Committee on Special Multipurpose Tribal Blocks in this connection was a sound one. All the areas where there is a concentration of Scheduled Tribes should be grouped together for purpose of coverage under the Tribal Development Blocks and in intensive effort should be undertaken to raise the level in the spheres of economic development, education, health, housing and communications, to that of the neighbouring areas with a grap not exceeding five years. The question of coverage should, therefore, be revised and necessary regrouping be made. The Ministries of Community Development and Home Affairs will have to work out the details. The area of Tribal Development Block should in that case be between 150 to 200 sq. miles and the population approximately 25,000. Where these limits have been crossed, the Block should be reorganised.

There should be pre-extention stage even for a Tribal Development Block.

The term "schematic budget" should be substituted by some other term which is flexible. It may be called "model budget" or "illustrative budget". The budget for each Block should be prepared by the Block Development Committee in consultation with the local officers of the Tribal Development Block. The Collector may give them such guidance as he considers suitable.

The funds available under the Block Programme for education should be administered by the Education Department. The State should also allocate more funds from the general revenues for expenditure on education bearing in mind the relative backwardness in the Tribal Areas.

Before the commencement of the Block activities, it is necessary to have a preliminary socio-economic survey of the area.

On the basis of this survey, the State Government, in consultation with the District Development Committee, should indicate the general priorities in respect of important items such as economic development, communication, health, education and drinking water supply. The priorities suggested by the State Government would be for guidance of the project staff and the local people. They shall, however have the option to change the order of priority.

While doing this, care should be taken to avoid multiplicity of schemes, emphasis being laid on a few selected schemes in relation to matters for which there is a recognised felt need. In relation to schemes of economic development emphasis should be on the provision of productive employment. · Integrated developmental programme in the field of agriculture, animal husbandry, forest and industries should be undertaken,

Responsibility for the sucessful implementation of this programme by act vising the project staff and render ng necessary assistance and advice to the Block Development Committee should be that of the Collector. The Colleotor should be in a position to accord sanction or order modification on behalf of the State Government in respect of all schemes.

There should be a Forest Extension Officer attached to the Tribal Development Block.

The charge of a Gram Sevak should be reasonable. He should be in a position to pay a visit to every village at least once in a fort night in an agricultural season. Knowledge of the local language should be an essential qualification for a Gram Sevak.

With a view to introducing the staff gradually a Block should start with the minimum staff, viz., Project Executive Officer, Agricultural Extension Officer, Soil Conservation Officer, Medical Officer and Assistant Engineer. With the progress of the programme as drawn up, the other officers like Extension Officer for Animal Husbandry, veterinary Officer etc., may be introduced

The Problem Of Indebtedness

In the absence of reliable figures of the extent of indebtedness and the rates of interest charged, the magnitude of the problem cannot be fully assessed nor can the remedies proposed be determined as adequate. We would therefore, suggest that as a first step the State Governments should undertake forthwith sample surveys in the tribal areas to ascertain the quantum of indebtedness, the nature of violation of the provisions of the laws now in force and the extent of exploitative element in money lending transaction,

It is also necessary for the State Government to undertake an enquiry into the existence of bonded labour. In the case of indebtedness accompanied by oral customary or written agreements for bonded labour, legislation should be passed forth with treating the agreements as void, the debt as discharged and the labour as released. The tribal will not be in a position to stand up against the creditor of the burden of debt survives. An agreement of this nature should be declared not only illegal but an offence punishable severely.

Having regard to the handicaps under which the tribal operates, while the Commission does not wish to do away with his credit, it desires and recommends that effective control be exercised by licensing the money-lender, making it obligatory upon him to enter his transactions in certified books of account and by periodical examination of his books.

As regards the past debts, the Commission recommends the following steps:

(i) The creditor should be required by legislation to file all his claims against all his tribal debtors within a prescribed time after which the right of action should be earned and the debt should be deemed as discharged.

(ii) The creditor should be required to produce all his books or other proofs and deposit them in the court along with his claims.

(iii) No books of account or document or written proof not deposited in the court along with the claim should be admitted in evidence thereafter.

(iv) The onus of proving the loan and the amount, received should be on the creditor. Verbal evidence unsupported by books of account kept in regular course of business, should not be considered as sufficient. Promissory notes alone should not be deemed to be adequate proof of the loan in the case of tribals.

(v) The rate of interest should be fixed. All payments should be credited first against interest and the balance against the loans. The principles of 'Dam Dupat' shoul be applied. The account should be prepared on the basis of simple interest where there is no provision for compound interest. Where, however, there is such a provision, the compound interest should be calculated on the basis of yearly rates. If payments by the debtor as a result of preparation of such accounts exceed the loan and interest, a decree should be passed in favour of the debtor for the excess amount.

(vi) Any amount due to the creditor should be made payable by instalments at a nominal rate of interest. The government should not take over the responsibility of discharging these debts from its funds.

Non-official agencies should undertake the responsibility of educating the tribals about the harm borrowing does not only to themselves but to their future generations also and also the new legislation as and when introduced.

Cooperation

The cooperative movement, if it is to thrive in the tribal areas, has to concern itself with :

(i) The discharge of outstanding debts;

(ii) the day-to-day needs of the tribal including non-productive requirements ; and

(iii) the needs for development.

In regard to outstanding debts, a scheme for scaling down such debts and repayment by instalments has been suggested. In the question of current needs the Union Government must take a firm decision on the provision of adequate alternative credit with a view to eliminating all sources of exploitation existing in the Scheduled Areas. Till the tribals gather same experience in economic functioning in the modern world and attain maturity, arrangements will have to be made for giving loans for social purposes. There is no provision in the Cooperative Socities Act or rules which debars a society from lending money for social customs or other obligations. This may, however, be gradually discontinued as the economic status of the tribals improves. The ratio between the productive and unproductive loans may be fixed carefully in the light of conditions obtaining in the various States. There is no reason why this approach cannot succeed if a cooperative society has an effective charge on the produce.

The cooperative law will have to be amended to meet the needs of the tribals who own land in common as members of the tribals or in the name of their headman. In the case of those whose lands are hypothecated as security or who are cultivating as tenants, what were one time their own lands, the money can be advanced on the security of their produce, the cooperative society getting an effective charge thereon.

There has been a persistent demand for grain golas from the tribals. It is necessary to increase the number of grain golas and reduce the area of operation of each of them. At the same time, the stocks of grain should be sufficiently raised so as to meet the full requirements of the members who at present have to meet their requirements partly from the grain golas and partly from other sources, generally the money-lender. Proper check, control and supervision from time to time require to be exercised in order to make the scheme effective. It is desirable that the grain golas should develop a cash wing for advancing money on credit.

The Committee on Cooperative Credit has suggested various measures for revitalising the existing societies, the training of management, accounting and clerical personnel, the pattern of organisation and participation of government. These recommendations may be adopted for developing the cooperative movement in the tribal areas with suitable modifications.

There should be a separate department in the Reserve Bank of India dealing with the problem of tribal economy, on the lines of the Agricultural Credit Department set up in the Reserve Bank of India in 1935.

There should be, in each State, promoting or sponsoring agencies for spreading a network of cooperatives. The sponsoring body should begin by undertaking the work of purchasing the articles, the tribals produce, selling to them their needs and providing them credit with a view to replacing the middle man in that field.

The exact relationship between the sponsoring agency and the government can be worked out by the government, but the responsibility for organisation, trade and finance in the initial stages should be on the government.

Education in cooperation should be imparted to tribals in general and the Committee members of the societies in particular.

Every village should be served by a Cooperative Society with at least one member from each family as a member.

The society should embrace all the avenues of economic development such as agriculture, animal husbandry, forests and processing, consumers' goods as well as other village industries and handicrafts as a part of an integrated programme of economic development.

The Cooperative Societies Act should be amended for creating an effective change on the produce of its members.

Minimum credit of a member should be fixed on his capacity to raise crops in his land and not on the acreage of his holdings or multiple of rental assessment.

Steps should be taken to link credit with marketing.

The procedure for advance of loans should be simplified in keeping with the condition of tribal areas.

A thrift fund may be created for meeting demand for loans on account of social obligations, particularly of landless tribals.

The cooperative should pay special attention to the sale and marketing of the produce and supply of the tribals' requirements at reasonable prices. In areas where there is the problem of storage and marketing of perishable goods like fruits etc., marketing socities should set up processing and preservation units.

Care should be taken to see that the rich or the influential sections of the people do not dominate the cooperatives and monopolise their benefits.

Educational Development

The education of the tribal children is, and should be, the concern of the Education Ministry to the same extent as the education of non-tribals. The Ministry of Home Affairs should be associated at the thinking level. We recommend that a Board of Committee be established to study this question and formulate teprocedures that would ensure smooth and efficient functioning.

There should be one system, one policy making body and one operating channel in the tribal areas and since primary and secondary education is the responsibility of the State Governments they must take over the sole responsibility.

In granting recognition to schools and giving them grants-in-aid, the State-Government should satisfy itself that no institution which receives a grant from the government or is recognised by it, practises discrimination either in the recruitment of teachers or in the admission of students on the ground of caste, community or religion.

We realise that it is difficult to set up schools and hostels in small villages which are little more than hamlets and situated so far apart. Nevertheless, where 30 childern of school-going age are available in one locality, the school would not be located at a distance of more than one mile. In no case should a child be required to walk for more than two miles to go to school. In other cases there should be schools with hostels attached.

Vacations and holidays should coincide with agricultural and forest operations and social festivities in the locality. Reasonable hours and school timing should bear in mind the requirements of the people.

The emphasis in education should be on a craft or technical bias and as far as possible the idea of a residential school should be encouraged.

The teaching of drawing and art should be a port of the school curriculum and tribal children should be given full opportunity to satisfy their creative urge through school activities.

The teaching of folk songs, stories and riddles should not be ignored. The tribal games and archery as well as tribal music and dances should be organised as a part of the curriculum.

Even after primary education is over, facilities will have to be provided to the tribals in the form of night schools to undertake further studies.

It is necessary that discrimination between ordinary schools, basic schools and other types of schools should be kept down as low as possible. In no case should a Scheduled Tribe student be placed in a position where he cannot get admission at higher levels simply because he has gone to a school of a particular type.

Equipment in primary schools should continuously be improved. With a view to giving a touch of homeliness, the class-rooms should display pictures of vegetation, birds and animals common in the locality. The structure and decoration in the school building should be in tribal style. The class room should give a feeling of cheer and should not be shabby.

There should be a considerable expansion of technical education. The courses should include the certificate course, diploma course and degree course—including Agricultural Engineering. As far as possible there should be atleast one technical education centre in every district. The expansion of the certificate course is an urgent necessity.

Arrangements should also be made for sample workshop training to the boys as motor mechanics, motor drivers, fitters, for irrigation pumps and such other jobs. There is a great demand everywhere for these artisans and a workshop type of course, while cheap in running, will offer a solution of mass employment of trained personnel.

As regards the medium of instruction in the schools in the first two years, the lessons should be imparted verbally in the tribal dialect to make the tribal boys and girls follow the lessons. The teachers should invariably know the tribal language Lessons can be taught in the regional language from the third year

This solution should not result in forgetting the major tribal languages. Under Article 305-A of the Constitution, every State and every local authority within the State has to provide adequate facilities for instruction in the mother-tongue at the primary stage of education to children belonging to linguistic minority groups.

To say that it is impossible to prepare text books in the tribal language—there are so many of them—may not be a justifiable matter. There is no need to prepare books in the dialect of any small tribal group. Attention should be directed to the larger tribal languages which are spoken by a sufficient number of people.

The question of text books has to be viewed from two angles, viz., script and content. As regards the contents of the text books, the objective of integration should not be lost sight of. The tribal students are expected today to read the common text books for the State. The common text books should also include lessons depicting, the life of the tribals, their folklore, songs, history and the lives of important personalities in the social, religions and political fields. These subjects should be woven into the text-books.

A growing number of educated tribals are beginning to write books, pamphlets and articles in magazines. This new literature is always in the people's old mother-tongue. This is another argument in favour of emphasising the tribal languages at the school level. This movement may well provide us with many treasures and may prove an invaluable means of helping the tribals to attain self-expression. It should be encouraged in every possible way.

Adequate provision for midday meals, clothing, a small amount of pocket money say Rs. two a month, for the girls, the supply of free books, states and stationery would surely attract tribal boys and girls to schools in sufficient numbers.

It is suggested that where the progress in education is below the First Plan level in any region, approximately of the size of a Tribal Development Block, the number of scholarships be increased.

There have been compiaints regarding irregularity and delay in payment of scholarships To ensure that the scholarship amount reaches the student every month in time, it may be sent along with the salary of the teachers.

A teacher in the tribal areas must have a thorugh knowledge of tribal life and culture.

It is of the greatest importance that teachers should be provided with houses and should have a fixed tenure their schools. Over and above residential accommodation some additional inducement should be given.

There should be a separate cadre in the States for teachers in these areas for a period of 20 years. As the areas develop, and as communications develop and as the situation reaches the normal level, the cadre may ultimately be wound up.

Tribal boys and girls who pass out VII and VIII standards should be trained as teachers and posted to schools in tribal areas. To that extent, ordinary rules and conditions should be relaxed. There should be special provisions for a short-term training course for such students.

According to the scheme of the Teacher's Training Centre at Sudimalla in Andhra Pradesh, candidates are selected from village schools who have studied upto fourth standard and are taught in the Centre upto the sixth standard. The special teachers' training is given for one year and successful candidates are appointed as village teachers. During the training period, a candidate is paid Rs. 20 p.m. as stipend. This is a good experiment and should be carefully studied.

More effective inspection and supervising machinery should be provided and stern disciplinary action should be taken in case of recalcitrant teachers. Teachers may be placed under the administrative control of the Block or Project Officers who will have a far more direct contact with them than the other officers.

Before introducing compulsory primary education, the authorities should make sure about the availability of well qualified and experienced teachers who know the local language; and they should have the necessary text books ready, apart from other facilities referred to earlier.

Midday meals, supply of free books states and stationery will have to be provided, if compulsory education is to be introduced in the tribal areas An intensive propaganda campaign will have to be organised.

The tribal students experience some difficulty in securing admission in the secondary and collegiate courses. While there should be no lowering of standard it is felt that there should be a period of coaching before the tests are taken. The Tribal students should be admitted in the institution on their showing the minimum educational qualifications for admission. Necessary facilities can be provided to them for coaching, after which they may appear for the test.

Andio-visual education cannot be introduced in tribal areas. There is lack of transport and lack of adequate finance to cover all the principal tribal dialects. A beginning may be made with silent visual demonstration accompanied by explanation of the subjects in local dialect verbally.

There are groups of tribals who are comparatively speaking in the most undeveloped condition. They are not conscious of the benefits of education. In case of such groups special efforts should be made by the State Governments by undertaking special approaches. Nomadic tribes will also come in this category. The ordinary school will not be adequate to raise the level of education among these sects. The responsibility of supplying books, meals, clothing etc,, in such cases should be undertaken by government.

Health

There are four principal reasons for the shortfall in the adequate provision of medical and health facilities for the tribals: (a) the need for a correct approach; (b) the problem of personnel; (c) adequate of communications and (d) rules regarding supply of medicines.

One of the major difficulties is in persuading the tribals to take medical treatment in preference to their own doctors and herbal medicine. The essential thing is that the medical staff should take the right attitude to tribal medicine and the tribal priest. The most successful doctors have been those who have interested themselves in what we may call medical sociology, in such things as the tribal pharmacopoeia, the tribal theory of the influence of dreams on health, tribal methods of diagnosis to win the confidence of the people.

The doctors are working against heavy odds in the tribal areas and simple rules and procedures should be devised to make their task easy so that they may extend their work more widely. The present method of intending for medical supplies in the interior areas is very frustrating.

There is a great shortage of medical personnel and qualified nurses and for some time to come this position will continue. It has not been possible to attract men and women of the medical profession to work in tribal areas. There are difficulties of housing, education for the children, contact with the world outside; these cannot be calculated in terms of money. Leave rules and rules relating to service generally will have to be modified. The question has to be studied from two angles; sympathy towards the personnel posted in the tribal areas and consciousness of the urgency of the problem. The solution lives in having a special cadre for a period of 20 years for medical personnel required for the tribal areas. We do not think that it will be possible for the State Governments to secure the services of the requisite personnel on the terms offered in the plain areas. Except perhaps for 'dais' we think that this is only practical approach.

Effort must be made to train the local people. A time will come when they will be able to staff their own hospitals and this will be in 20 years. While there should be no difference in their emoluments, on the expiry of a period of 20 years, the tribal recruits will be absorbed in the general cadre on such terms and conditions as the government may then consider fit.

It would be advisable to have a large number of peripatetic dispensaries and mobile health units rather than the static dispensaries and hospitals for the tribal areas. It will be possible to cover in this way a large area and a larger number of people.

The mobile medical units should be adequately increased and must have an equally important preventive section which should work on such items as malaria control through spraying of D.D.T., tuberculosis control through B.C.G. vaccination, control of epidemics like cholera, etc., by proper inoculation and supply of milk and vitamins to children and expectant mothers.

The mobile units must also have a propaganda section fully equipped with projector, film and literature. The unit must carry all the necessary medicines, ayurvedic, allopathic and homeopathic. Thus, the multi-purpose mobile medical units will go very far in meeting the medical needs of the tribal people.

In view of the shortage of allopathic doctors, State Government may set up increased number of ayurvedic dispensaries to meet the need for treatment of diseases on scientific lines. The tribal are used to herbal remedies and tried and tested herbal medicines can be made available to them.

Medicine chests should be provided at all Panchayats, primary schools, middle schools, dormitories, etc. These chests should be kept under the charge of the Headmasters, or the Panch or the village level worker. Arrangement to refill them should be ensured. These chests should contain simple, harmless and patent medicines. A doctor should be put in charge of a certain number of these medicinal chests and tour from time to time to inspect and supervise their working.

Health education is very necessary in the tribal areas. A systematic programme with andio-visual equipment should be undertaken.

The recommendation of the Study. Team on Social Welfare regarding drinking water facilities is accepted.

(a) A phased programme should be undertaken for providing drinking water wells or clean water supply to all the villages. Priority should be given on the basis of population and distances and no person should be required to go for water more than four furlongs from his place of residence.

(b) Such wells should be sanitary and properly looked after.

(c) People's contribution should not be insisted upon in this programme.

(d) In the hills, the springs should be connected with pipes and clean drinking water provided.

A phased programme of maternity and child welfare centres should be taken up. An extensive programme for training 'dais' is also necessary, since the 'dais' are in contact with the tribals and will be in a better position to make maternity services more easily available. Best of all, tribal women themselves should be trained. These 'dais' should be given refresher courses continuously through a peripatetic arrangement and their standard raised to the level of midwife.

There should be a Maternity Home in each Panchayat Samiti with propaganda arrangements for sanitation, the care of children and the care of expectant mothers.

In the goitre affected areas, the medical section, with the assistance of the Revenue or the Community Developments Department, should make arrangements for the distribution of iodized salt at concessional rates.

Housing

Housing for the tribal people should be viewed from. the following four aspects.

(i) Shelter;
(ii) Sanitation;
(iii) Aesthetic tastes of the tribes; and
(iv) Comparative Cost.

Considering the great variety, extensive research should be conducted to ensure that the right people recieve help, the houses are adopted to the climate and that, wherever possible the style of building, evolved through centuries of experience, is followed.

There is very little reason why any normal tribal family who lives in a forest area should have a really good home. Provided the Forest Departments of the States are more liberal in allowing the extraction of building materials without permits, the tribals can go ahead with making roomy, well-ventilated and water-proof homes if they are given a little guidance and encouragement.

It most tribal areas, there is no need to change the architecture of the buildings. Small windows, double roofing or ventilators may be introduced to take away the smoke and let in more air. The need is to make the house more sanitary.

The housing schemes should benefit those who are in real need of houses. The aim should be to meet needs of the poorest and the needs of the dispossessed. Housing schemes for small and impoverished groups, as the Yerukulas, Yeuadis and Sugalis of Andhra Pradesh, the Khatkaris of Maharashtra, and Dublas and Naiks of Gujarat, the Gujjars of Himachal Pradesh, the Paniyans of Kerela and the Kurubas of Mysore, should have priority. The houses need not be costly nor built with imported materials.

The staff from the plains, ignorant of the local conditions, gives buildings to the tribals which are neither to their taste nor add to their comforts. It is essential that the P.W.D. specifications should be liberalised to permit the modification in the light of local conditions. The question of building cattle-sheds. pig-sties and poultry-runs is also important.

Housing colonies should not be undertaken unless it is possible to provide employment.

Instead of providing houses to all and sundry, which will involve considerable expenditure and divert funds from programme of greater priority, the limited funds available for housing should be used for the weaker groups who are really in need of better houses. In other cases funds should be utilised for improving the existing houses. Since the improvement of rural housing is more an educational them a construction programme, much could be done by persuasion and propaganda and the funds could be used for improvements, such as providing windows, drains, and sanitation facilities.

Full advantage should be taken of the tribal's own advise before and during the construction of a colony.

In Lahaul, Spiti and Himachal Pradesh, the Harijans and *Hanses* live under conditions of overcrowding. They should be helped to get more rooms.

The Spitians preserve the night soil for manure. A little technical assistance may go a long way in improving sanitation. In Assam tribal areas, the NEFA approach to housing sanitation should be adopted.

In areas where for four to five months in a year people have to live indoors and keep their fires burning continuously, smokeless "Chulha" or the system of "chemney" should be introduced.

A proper grain gola in every village should be organised to relieve the congestion and to enable the tribals preserve their food-stuff properly.

In the Santhal Parganas and many other places, we should not get away from the beautiful housing models that the tribals themselves follow. The existing pattern should be improved by giving them some technical advice. In all places, the basic architecture and village lay-out, which has evolved through centuries, should be followed with suitable improvements.

One great impediment to tribal housing in the attitude of the Forest Department in imposing great restrictions on the use of timber. The rules should be considerably liberalised to enable every tribal family to obtain easily and without delay their requirements of timber for house-building purposes.

Hurried programmes for housing with a view to fulfil the targets are not at all advisable and should be avoided.

Communications

Communications will spread in the tribal areas much more speedily than we imagine. In a mojority of cases the development of the tribal consciousness may not keep pace with the development of communications. A balance will have to be struck so that this unprecedented expansion does not place an inordinate strain on the tribals and wherever the new roads go, the State will have to protect them against exploitation.

The problem of communications may be considered from five aspects:

(i) roads and other communications indispensible for national needs and defence;

(ii) roads and other communications indispensible for industrial development;

(iii) roads and other communications necessary for administration;

(iv) roads and other communications needed from the point of view of trade and commercial interests; and

(v) roads and other communications needed in the interests of the tribals.

A correct approach will be to give the highest priority to (i) and (v) above; second priority to (ii) and (iii) and in relation to (iv) decide after close study on the basis of the trade and commercial data available and the relative advantage to the tribal population.

The present All-India average-length of roads per 100 square miles of area is 28 miles whereas the average length in many tribal areas is not even twelve miles. Thus, there is considerable leaway to be made up.

The government should undertake a programme of roads fulfilling the needs of the tribals. The tribal is more concerned in connecting his village with the forest or the weekly market or the school for his children. These roads should be planned in such a manner that they could be used all the year round and could be widened for purposes of cars and jeeps as occasion arises or funds permit. Similarly, if it is possible to link up a village with a hospital or dispensary, that also would be useful. A priority worked out on this basis will offset any feeling that the tribal interests are being given the lowest place in the matter of communications.

The majority of these roads should not be very expensive. Careful planning is, of course, necessary to spread their benefit to the largest possible number of people.

In fixing the relative priorities, consultation with the local people should be the rule.

Local material should be used unless the use of imported material is unavoidable.

A beginning should be made with foot-tracks or bridle paths. They should be so planned that the alignment, soiling, earth-work and culvert will be suitable for the use of the carts jeeps, and trucks when widened.

The work should be undertaken in the off-season

whenever possible when the tribals have comparatively little to do.

There are some special problems needing attention at the national level. One of these is the need for communications in the Assam Hills, especially in those areas which used to depend for their markets on places which are now a part of Pakistan. Partition destroyed the profitable trade in fruits, especially oranges and pineapples. The Hill people and the country at large will be greatly benefited if the necessary communications are established quickly.

Paddy and rice in Manipur have always been purchased from tribals at extremely low prices and the tribal farmers of this territory have suffered exploitation by merchants of the foothills, who have taken full advantage of the lack of adequate communications. Communications should be established quickly.

The forest and the Public Works Department roads should be planned as part of a single coordinated system of communications with proper regard to the protection and development of forests.

The possibilities of developing traffic on rivers and inland waters by boats may be explored. A small section in each State where there are perennial rivers should carefully study the question.

There have been complaints that tribal welfare funds have been utilised for arterial roads. The best thing is for the Union Government to specify what part of its grants for communications will be used in the States for arterial roads. The rest should be spent in village roads, bridle paths and inter-village communications. This will keep the position of the States and Centre clear before the public.

Regarding construction of roads, the P.W.D. should encourage cooperatives among the tribal labourers. Where this is not feasible, the department should see that the tribals get fair wages.

There are constant complaints about the shortage of field staff. Encouragement should be given to the local people to equip themselves through work and practice for the work of mistries, sub-overseers and so on. Educational qualifications need not be regarded as essential. The devotion and courage of the tribals, their vitality and stamina are famous and should be used to the full.

In some parts of the country roads have to be built under tremendous risks and difficulties. To this heroic effort, a human approach and some consideration for the tribals are necessary. In such risky operations the States should not only be considerate but prompt in meeting the claims of the living and helping the relations of the dead. Women and men should be paid according to the risk of the operations they are involved in, and not just as women and men as unskilled labourers. In these far off places there should be proper arrangement for shelter, water, medicine and education and arrangements for some training for higher jobs. Discrimination between local labour and imported labour in the matter of wages should be brought down as much as possible.

The telephone and wireless services of the Defence and Police Forces should be thrown open to the public on payment, subject of course to official work getting the necessary precedence. The linking of the tribal and forest areas of India, through the telephone or wireless service, as is done in NEFA and Nagaland, will bring about their earlier integration.

For the remote tribal regions the norms and rules of the Posts and telegraphs must be different.

Impact Of Industrialisation

There has been very scant research on the question of the impact of industrialisation on the socio-economy of the tribal people which would have given a greater insight into the steps to be taken. It is the responsibility of the Union Government, as a corollary to the central planning of industries, to undertake this research. Bihar, parts of Madhya Pradesh and Orissa will come under intensive industrialisation and though no data is available at the moment, there is room for confidence that as soon as research studies are conducted, adequate provision will be made to assist the tribal people to adapt themselves. By industrial impact is meant not only the impact of large-scale industries, but also that of mining, the immigration of labour and the entry of outside interests in the tribal areas. Surveys in specific areas of the various States will give a precise ideas of the rehabilitation programmes necessary.

It is necessary to set up a permanent machinery which will study every individual project and its impact upon tribal interests. This machinery should, besides following up the proper rehabilitation of tribal families through welfare schemes, be responsible for integrated planning right from the inception of the project. For instance, a multipurpose river valley project should, from the very beginning, take into consideration the proper rehabilitation without disturbance in the life of all the families affected. It should be accepted that such projects are intended to improve the existing condition of the families affected and not disturb them as to deprive them of their livelihood. We, therefore, consider it necessary that the scheme of rehabilitation should be part of the project itself; if this could be done the time lag between the actual displacement and rehabilitation could be avoided. By planning the project and phasing the programme of rehabilitation in advance, it would be possible to bring about simultaneously displacement with minimum inconvenience and rehabilitation.

Schemes for rehabilitation should include programmes for education, training and equipment of the displaced people.

To increase the employability of the tribal families affected by the projects, the establishment of industrial training institutes within the project areas is recommended. In the Interim Report, greater emphasis on technical education in such areas was recommended. It was proposed for Bihar, that one technical institution in the Scheduled Areas of Singhbhum District and 10 industrial workshops in the other Scheduled Areas to train as large a number of tribal boys as possible in industrial work should be established. On the lines of the Industrial Training Institute of Korba in Madhya Pradesh, the setting up of similar institutes in the tribal areas of Madhya Pradesh, Orissa and Bihar should be taken up to help the tribal youths to keep pace with the rapid advance of industrialisation.

In the case of families displaced by industrial or development projects, government should also consider establishing the tribals in the new economy set-up, not necessarily as landless labourers, but as producers of the primary needs of the township dwellers and factory workers. These needs include foodgrains, milk, eggs, meat and other requirements of the people.

The incentives offered by government or the project authorities in the colonies should be sufficiently attractive. It should be the responsibility of the project authorities to provide water supply, sanitation, provision for schools and medical relief. Facilities for open air life and the aminities offered should be such as to make the tribal people feel at home. They should not feel that they have been uprooted from their natural surrounding.

In the case of families receiving cash compensation, every effort should be made to rehabilitate them in some suitable employment within the project itself. We consider that the highest preference should be given in absorbing the tribal people in permanent employment. The Employment Exchanges should arrange to give preference to local tribals over outsiders, even though this may involve a relaxation in the prescribed qualifications. The heads of factories and employing departments should be advised accordingly.

Administration

It is felt that in the content of the specific targets fixed and the time limit of 10 years for their fulfilment, the existing arrangements in the Ministry of Home Affairs for dealings with tribal problems may not be adequate. A separate Ministry for this purpose is not suggested but a separate department devoted exclusively to tribal problems would be sufficient. This department may be placed under the exclusive charge of a Minister under the Home Minister. Its functions will include examination of the Governors' Reports, implementation of the provisions of the Fifth Schedule, functioning of the Tribes Advisory Council, Progress of Plan, General Administration of Welfare Schemes, training of personnel and coordination. Its actual set-up is a matter of administrative detail.

Evaluation in terms of physical and financial targets is the function of the Planning Commission and it may be improved and perfected. Again the Commissioner for Scheduled Castes and Scheduled Tribes should be changed with the responsibility of qualitative evaluation and the impact upon the tribals. The coordination of all further branches of tribal interests whether social, economic or cultural should be the function of the Mininistry of Home Affairs, which will also be the competent agency to evaluate the work of the research institutes. A vast programme of continuous evaluation can only be undertaken by the Ministry of Home Affairs.

The Ministry of Home Affairs should arrange for periodical research through a cell or cells specifically for the examination of various subjects in relation to tribals. Special cells in the Ministry to follow up actively the progress of work in the Tribal Development Blocks which constitute the largest single programme under the Tribal Welfare Programme and the Development of weaker sections of the tribes should be constituted.

Schemes received from States are referred to the Ministries concerned and the Commissioner for Scheduled Castes and Scheduled Tribes. This leads to duplication. The technical and financial examination by the State should be sufficient and the Ministry of Home Affairs should give its approval, without referring it to other Ministries and the Commissioner for Scheduled Castes and Scheduled Tribes unless on account of the nature of the scheme, the finances involved or other important reasons, it feels that it should have further advice.

In the States with a tribal population of one million and above, there should be a Minister exclusively in change of the portfolio of tribal welfare and responsible for the fulfilment of tribal policies and programme. He need not necessarily be a tribal.

There should be a separate Department for Tribal Welfare in the States where the tribal population is more than a million, viz., Bihar, Orissa, Andhra Pradesh, Madhya Pradesh, Maharashtra, Gujarat, Rajasthan and West Bengal. Assam is not mentioned here because the Sixth Schedule is in force and the constitutional arrangement is different.

States should have a section under the Chief Secretary to evaluate qualitatively and quantitatively the tribal welfare programme.

State Governments may bring about the required administrative flexibility by reorganising the procedures and methods of the Directorates dealing with tribal affairs. A small committee of officials from the Tribal Welfare, Agriculture, Veterinary, Forest, Irrigation and Roads and Medical and Public Health Departments should set up at the State level for coordination and effective implementation of tribal welfare programmes both in the Scheduled Areas and other tribal areas. The Committee may also be charged with the function of scrutinising the development programmes of these departments to ensure that their schemes also cover the Scheduled Tribes and the development of Scheduled Areas.

There would be an improvement in the administration as well as in the tempo of development if contiguous Scheduled Areas of different districts are formed into separate districts or if unwidely large districts are devided into two or more districts each under a separate Collector. The Collectors of these districts should be given greater powers.

To ensure more speedy and effective implementation of the developmental activities in the Scheduled Areas, the following scheme is suggested for the consideration of the State Governments:

(i) The Collector should be in overall charge of not only the revenue and judicial administration but also of development activities.

(ii) He should have the power to alter priorities of development schemes for the tribal areas and sanction schemes up to a limit prescribed by government.

(iii) All the heads of the departments in the districts and their subordinates to, whatever departments they belong, concerned with the work of the Scheduled Tribes will function under his supervision, guidance, and control.

(iv) He should have powers to punish erring class III and IV staff after proper investigation and write confidential records of Class I and II officers.

Above the Collectors in each of the States having Scheduled Areas, there should be an officer of the status of a Commissioner in overall charge of the tribal districts and all the powers of the State Governments should be delegated to him subject to the condition that he should consult the State Governments on all matters invovling a question of policy.

The field staff for work in tribal areas should be carefully selected and placed under the control of the Collector. As far as possible, trained staff with a background of tribal culture and way of life should be posted so that they may be able to handle the situation sympathetically and not try to overwhelm the tribals with too many schemes. The number of the officers should be kept to the minimum.

There should be greater provision of inspecting staff in Cooperation and Education Departments to go round, examine the wokings of the cooperative societies and schools and make suggestions for their improvement. The extension staff of the Agriculture, Animal Husbandry and Engineering Departments requires to be strengthened.

We suggest that a separate cadre of medical officers for service in these areas should be formed and that its terms and condition of service should be so framed as to induce the doctors to stay in the tribal areas for a period of time.

Commissioner for Scheduled Castes And Scheduled Tribes

The Commissioner's functions are to investigate and report on the working of the safeguards. This is done by an annual report to the President. This report is intended to assist the President, the Parliament and the Union Government to discharge their responsibilities under the Constitution. The report enters into a host of matters and the substance occasionally gets lost in a forest of details. The sense of urgency and priority, which should be the real concern at the Union Government and Parliament level, is lost.

The essential thing about the Commissioner's reports should be an assessment of the way the constitutional safeguards are being implemented in the States; justification or of lack of it, whenever there is remissness; the progress achieved in raising the level of administration of the Scheduled Areas; fields in which direction is required from the Centre; a qualitative evaluation of welfare work and the impact of all this on the tribal people.

The Commissioner should focus his attention on certain items of strategic importance and ensure that the States and the Centre work them out in accordance with a time schedule.

The office of the Commissioner should be given a status and rank that would attract a person of high status, calibre and wide influence.

The non-statutory functions of the Commissioner, namely, representation in the managing committee of non-official organisations, examination of the accounts of such organisations, advising the Union Government on schemes receieved from the State Government be withdrawn from him. These are not an essential part of his duty and in making this arrangement the Ministry has reduced the status of the Commissioner to that of a departmental head thereby prejudicing the discharge of his constitutional responsibility.

There should be a separate Commissioner for Scheduled Tribes.

The State Governments are not impressed with the

present arrangement of Assistant Commissioners. It will be necessary to consider whether the present arrangement should continue or how they should function with reference to the separate Commissioner for Scheduled Tribes suggested above. This is an administrative matter and should be examined in greater detail. It is doubtful if the present set up will be needed, if the Special Officer for Scheduled Tribes is relieved of his non-statutory functions.

If a senior officer with sufficient administrative background is selected for the post of Regional Assistant Commissioner, work should be considerably facilitated. He should preferably be an officer of the status of a Collector so that he may be able to pull his weight with the Collectors and the Commissioners.

The revision of the present set up of the Commissioner's Office both from the point of utility as well as compactness is recommended.

It is felt that Commissioner's report should have the status of the reports of the Estimates Committee and Public Accounts Committee of the Lok Sabha. Whenever his comments are adverse on the working of the State or Union Government, particularly in relation to the protective measures, the report should be accompanied by the explanations of the Government concerned which may be considered alongwith the reports in the Legislatures.

Non-Official Agencies

Non-official agencies are working mainly in the field of education and public health. They command the services of workers who have given their lives to the cause and have been able to create an impact on the tribals. They are slowly extending their work to cooperation, cottage and village industries, cultural activities, animal husbandry, legal assistance and prohibition.

Non-official organisations are necessary for the active participation of the people in the welfare activities both in planning and implementation. A certain measure of constructive activity should be done under non-official auspices. These agencies have the 'human touch' and can harness the latent energies of the masses into useful channels for their development. The scope of these organisations should, however, be clearly defined to avoid duplication of effort.

Accountant General's office in each State should maintain a list of qualified accountants who can be made available to non-official institutions in receipt of assistance on any substantial scale. The allowance or salary paid to the accountant should be given to the institution as an additional grant.

Some machinery to evaluate the true value of the work of non-official organisations will go a long way in infusing new vigour and new ideas in them. Such evaluation can be done at the instance of the non-official agency itself by any local research institute.

The Governor in his report to the President should invariably give an assessment of the work of every institution which is receiving a grant of more than Rs. 25,000 in a year.

Training Programme

The administrative officers working at and above the district levels should have an orientation course in tribal welfare at the Central Institute of Study and Research in Community Development at Mussoorie at the time they receive training in the Community Development programme.

The method of training will, as hitherto, be through seminars, study groups, syndicates. A detailed syllabus for this category of officers is not necessary but the subjects should include:

(a) Applied Anthropology;

(b) Psychology of Tribal People;

(c) Constitution and the Scheduled Tribes;

(d) Tribal economy with special reference to—

(i) land;

(ii) forest;

(iii) industries; and

(iv) finance;

(e) Study of problems pertaining to health, education, communications, etc.;

(f) Study of various schemes implemented by the Union Government and the State Governments for the welfare of Scheduled Tribes; and

(g) Socio-economic surveys.

The training proposed for Collectors/Commissioners, who are directly concerned with planning and implementation of tribal welfare programmes, should also be extended to other heads of Departments and Divisional Officers, e.g., the Chief Conservator of Forests, Director of Education, Registrar of Cooperative Societies, Chief Engineers, Roads and Buildings and Irrigation Director of Agriculture, Director of Land Records, Director of Public Health, Director of Veterinary Services, Director of Industries, Director of Cottage Industries.

Supervisory Officers at and below the district level should, as at present, be trained at the Tata Institute of Social-Sciences. The capacity of this Institute should be expanded or similar facilities should be provided at one or other similar institutes. The training should be improved to make it more "problem-centred", and practical training and visits to tribal areas should be arranged.

The Ministry of Community Development may be asked to earmark one of their Orientation and Study Centres exclusively for the training of the supervisory staff at the block level and district officers of other departments operating in the tribal areas.

Training should be confined to those officers who are likely to serve in the tribal areas for a period of at least three years. The training will embrace all the departments including Revenue, Forests, Public Works, Police, Agriculture, etc., and if it is possible, the training can also be arranged along with the supervisory staff working at or below the district level either at the Tata Institute of Social Sciences or other institute that may be selected for the purpose. The training should be curtailed to three months.

We suggest that the content of training and its duration be worked out for each category of personnel. These are technical matters and the representatives of the Ministries of Home Affairs, Education, and Community Development and Cooperation, the Tata Institute of Social Sciences and Research Institutes, should work out an appropriate syllabus for the purpose.

The training of field staff is as important as the training of the supervisory administrative personnel. This should be impressed on the State Governments and they should be asked to assess their requirements of field staff, arrange for their recruitment or selection well in time and complete the training before they are actually posted for working in the tribal areas. Those who are actually in the field now will have to be given either an in-service training or sent to the training centres for a short refresher course.

We should suggest that the existing training institutions run by government should, when they have capacity, undertake the training of the field workers of non-official voluntary agencies and similarly the centres established by the non-official agencies should undertake the training of government field staff, wherever possible. This will remove the existing barriers between official and non-official workers, and facilitate understanding of each other's point of view. There has been some difficulty in training women field workers such as Gram Sevikas. The State Governments have training facilities as well as non-official agencies like the Kasturba Gandhi National Memorial Trust. The facilities for training at the institutions conducted by the non-official agencies should be utilised to the maximum extent by the State Governments. The non-official voluntary agencies should be encouraged to establish additional training centres in selected areas through substantial subsidy from the Centre.

Institutes on the lines of Gram Sevak Training Centres may be opened at suitable areas for training of technical field staff in suitable areas. These training centres should be located in tribal areas so that facilities are readily available for practical training. As in the existing conditions, the number of non-tribals among the field staff will be quite considerable, arrangements should also be made at the training centres to teach them the tribal dialects.

Training of office-bearers of non-official voluntary agencies should be arranged along with the official at the Central Institute of Study and Research in Community Development.

For technical personnel of the non-official agencies, training may be arranged along with the supervisory government technical personnel either at the Tata Institute of Social Sciences or at the Research Institutes run by the Governments of Madhya Pradesh, Bihar and Orissa.

It will be necessary to give training to office-bearers and employees of the Panchayats and Cooperatives, so that they may adjust themselves to the tribal conditions and way of life. This training in the case of office-bearers who are tribals can be in-service training by holding camps in the villages as is being done by the various Community Development Blocks. Paid employees, however, will have to be trained at the institutions mentioned for the supervisory and field staff.

A programme of training of the tribal leaders will in the long run be advantageous to government and the tribals.

Tribals bias should be given to all training programmes and tribals should be recruited for some of the jobs at village and block levels. In case they do not possess the prescribed qualifications, a longer period of training may be arranged.

It is most important that adequate incentives should be provided to tribal candidates to join professional and technical training institutions so that eventually we will have a larger number of tribals working in the tribals areas.

We recommend that:

(i) As far as possible local tribals should be selected, the qualifications being relaxed, if necessary;

(ii) If outsiders are recruited, special arrangements should be made to teach them the local dialect before they are posted; and

(iii) While under training they should make themselves familiar with the tribal way of life and culture.

The training programme outlined will necessitate the expansion of facilities available at the existing institutions or the establishment of new institutes. These institutes will have to be staffed with teachers and instructors. Provision should be made for training these teachers. This aspect of the training programme be examined further by the Union Government in consultation with the State Governments and Research Institutes and suitable steps taken to ensure that the required number of additional teachers and instructors will be forthcoming.

Representation In Services

The All India and Central Services for which recruitment is made on an all India basis require higher educational qualifications and until education has progressed sufficiently amongst the tribals, it will not be possible for them to take full advantage of the reservation in their favour in these Services. There is gradual improvement and if the policy is pursued further with speed and vigour, representation of the Scheduled Tribes will improve appreciably in the next 10 years.

In the other branches of the Services both under the Union and State Governments, the position is not reassuring. The progress in the implementation of order is slow. There has been slackness on the part of the government to devise a proper procedure which would ensure adequate intake of tribal candidates.

In Andhra Pradesh, Rajasthan, Madras, Punjab, and to a certain extent Maharashtra, there is a combined percentage of reservation for Scheduled Castes and Scheduled Tribes, which is prejudicial to the tribal candidates State Governments should be requested to fix a separate percentage for Scheduled Tribes for all the State Services.

The quality of public service is important in recruitment to Class I and Class II services and posts. In regard to Class III and Class IV, where the work is mechanical and routine, it should be possible to recruit tribal candidates and arrange for their in-service training.

It is necessary to fix the percentage of reservation differently for different services and posts. In regard to Class I and technical posts, tribal candidates with the requisite qualifications may not be available and it will take a long time before they can fill up the percentage in Class I and Class II services and posts. If the quota is to be made up in the initial stages, the percentage of reservation in Class III and Class IV services and posts will have to be proportionately higher. The Orissa Government has fixed the quota for scheduled Tribes proportionately higher in Class III and Class IV services namely, 50 per cent. This experiment is commended for the other States.

It is suggested that while the overall percentage of reservation should continue at the figure already fixed, the State Governments may study the question with reference to local conditions, so that a higher percentage of reservation in certain categories of services and in certain departments may be fixed. This will go a long way in ensuring that the tribals get adequate representation in the services within the shortest possible time.

State Governments should instruct all the local authorities like the Municipalities, Panchayat Samities and Zila Parishads to follow the policy laid down by them in regard to representation of Scheduled Tribes in Services.

Suitable instructions be issued to Central and State undertakings in public sector to give adequate representation to Scheduled Tribes.

We would suggest that State Governments may take steps to issue instructions on the lines of instructions of the Union Government in regard to promotion and review of cases of supersession of officers belonging to Scheduled Tribes.

The following further suggestions in regard to the representation of Scheduled Tribes in the Services may be considered for implementation :

(i) At the moment, if a vacancy reserved for a Scheduled Tribes is not filled owing to the non-availability of a suitable candidate, the vacancy is kept open for a period of two years. It is suggested that, whatever the period for which the vacancy may be kept open, if the State Government can get a candidate who is near enough the prescribed qualification, he may be given coaching for a time, re-examined and recruited if he is found to have made satisfactory progress:

(ii) The existing orders of the Union Government which permit the appointment of Scheduled Caste candidates in the vacancies reserved for Scheduled Tribes, where suitable qualified candidates are not available, should be rescinded. The presence of such a permissive order brings about complacency. The recruiting authorities should make all possible efforts to find the Scheduled Tribe candidates.

(iii) The relaxation of the age-limit in regard to Gazetted and non-Gazetted posts is quite sufficient but there are States where this has not been done. This rule should be made applicable uniformly throughout the States.

(iv) In the case of local recruitment, there should be semebody on the Selection Committee, who can look after the interests of the tribals. The Tribal Welfare Officers in the district or the sub-division can be associated with the Selection Board.

(v) Adequate publicity should be given in the tribal areas about reserved vacancies. Social agencies could be used to spread this information. Publicity should not be confined merely to newspapers as many of the tribals live in inaccessible areas. Other means of publicity should be devised and checked periodically.

(vi) The rule that a name must be registered with the Employment Exchange before appointments are made should not be binding in the case of the tribal candidates because they cannot be expected to maintain contact with it.

(vii) Arrangements should be made to pay some allowance to a tribal candidate, who is expected to appear before the recruiting authority at his head-quarters, if this is at a distance from his normal place of residence. This has been done in Orissa and might be followed by other States.

(viii) It is necessary that a roaster of appointments on the Bihar model or on the lines of the instructions issued by the Union Government should be maintained and this should be made obligatory for all categories of services and in all the departments. Periodical checks should be made to find out, if, at every stage, proper care is being taken to ensure recruitment of Scheduled Tribe candidates against posts received for them.

Role of Traditional Tribal Councils

One of the functions of the Statutory Panchayats in the tribal areas or the Tribal Councils should be in relation to forests.

In areas where the population is mixed and where the tribal people do not preponderate and the trial councils have virtually fallen into disuse or have little authority, every effort should be made to revive them so that they can work alongside the Statutory Panchayats and settle their own religious and social affairs.

In all homogenous tribal areas such as Nagaland, NEFA, the autonomous hills districts of Assam, the hill areas of Manipur and suitable areas which are already Scheduled, where the Tribal Councils are strong and alive, advantage may be taken of the provisions in the Panchayat Acts whereby the Governor can exempt a specific area or areas from the operation of the Act. It will not be necessary to introduce new Statutory Panchayats in such places but a serious attempt should be made to develop the existing Councils and gradually transfer to them all the powers of the Statutory Panchayats, ultimately recognising them as such.

In other tribal areas, where there is a mixed population, wherever tribal councils are active and have some authority among the tribal people, they should be encouraged and developed to function side by side with the Statutory Panchayats. Here the traditional Councils will be conceived mainly with social and religious matters, and the Statutory Panchayats with administration and development.

The principle of election has to be explained to the tribals. They should be free to moderate the principle of election with a view to avoid internal frictions.

The Statutory Panchayats should take advantage of the influence of the traditional Councils in the matter of development activity. The village development programmes should always be prepared by the Statutory Panchayats in consultation with the tribal councils.

Wherever the statutory Panchayats and the Tribal Councils exist side by side, the Panchayat may entrust to the Council various aspects of development work, management of ordinary or forest cooperatives, and they should be encouraged to settle village and inter-village disputes without having resort to the ordinary courts.

Wherever a Statutory Panchayat is constituted in a tribal village, the rules should provide that fair proportion of members comes from the tribal groups.

It will not be possible for either the traditional Councils or the Statutory Panchayats to raise revenue or levy cesses and taxes for some time. No hurried effort should be made to earn revenues. By and by, as the economy and the consciousness develops, cesses and taxes may be gradually introduced.

Surveys Research And Evaluation

Special arrangements should be made for rapid sample surveys of selected representative tribal areas to be completed within a reasonable time. Such surveys should concentrate on certain items, collect data in relation to them and also find out the conveniences available locally which would enable the government to carry out the programme within the time limit fixed.

A similar survey should be conducted in a selected adjoining non-Scheduled Area so as to assess the disparity existing between the tribals and the non-tribals and the comparative backwardness of the tribal area.

In addition to the surveys mentioned above, the State Governments should conduct specific surveys in relation to specific problems faced in specific areas. These surveys should, as far as possible, be carried out through the Bureaus of Economics and Statistics. Universities, Tribal Research Institutes and Institutes like the Tata Institute of Social Sciences and similar other non-official agencies qualified to do this work. The State Governments should render them all possible help and financial assistance.

The functions of the Tribal Research Institutes should be redefined to include:

(i) Collection of basic socio-economic data for the use of Tribal Welfare Department in formulation and implementation of schemes for the economic development of the tribals;

(ii) Research on craft and industries which will be of immediate value for the economic development of the tribals by the utilisation of their skill and local materials and resources;

(iii) Examination of tribal welfare schemes with special reference to:

(a) the impact on their attitudes, skills, and knowledge;

(b) the socio and economic changes brought about by them;

(c) improvement of the programme,

(iv) Assistance to the State Governments, etc., in their training programme.

(v) Research in tribal philology with a view to preparing text books and primers in tribal languages, collection of folk songs, folk lore, stories of tribal heroes, etc.,

(vi) Teaching of tribal languages or dialects to the field staff of the Tribal Welfare Department.

A Central Institute of Tribal Welfare may be set up to coordinate research on an all-India level and take up studies of special problems which extend beyond the territorial limits of anyone State, as for example, shifting cultivation, impact of industrialisation on tribal society etc.

A beginning may be made with a coordinating body in the Ministry of Home Affairs to guide, supervise and coordinate the work of Research Institutes. For this purpose, a separate cell may be attached to the proposed Department of Tribal Welfare in the Ministry.

REVIEW COMMITTEE FOR CHEMISTRY IN INDIAN UNIVERSITIES, 1960—REPORT

New Delhi, University Grants Commission, 1963. 107p.+iii+iiip.

Chairman : Prof. T R. Seshadri.

Members : Prof. S. R. Palit; Prof. G. Gopala Rao; Prof. S. K. Bhattacharya; Prof. M.R.A. Rao; Prof. R. C. Mehrotra; Dr. (Mrs.) Asima Chatterjee.

Secretary : Dr. B. D. Laroia (since his retirement from U.G.C. in June 1962, Dr. D. Shanker Narayan, became the secretary of the Committee).

APPOINTMENT

During the past few years, the University Grants Commission has been giving liberal grants to various Universities in our country for purposes of rehabilitation and construction of buildings, purchase of new and modern equipment needed for research improvement of libraries and providing better wokrshop facilities. Since a systematic evaluation of the results achieved in raising the standards of teaching and in furthering research work as a result of these grants made by the University Grants Commission was not made for some time, the Commission, in early 1959, felt it desirable to undertake an assessment in the above line in various sciences subjects and the Chairman of the University Grants Commission appointed a few Review Committees of experts in specific fields.

The Chemistry Review Committee was appointed by the Chairman, University Grants Commission in May, 1960.

TERMS OF REFERENCE

The Chemistry Review Committee enjoyed wide terms of References and was free to make its own programme and procedure of work. In order to carry out its assignment satisfactorily, the Committee was, in particular requested to examine the following important aspects :

(i) The stage of development achieved so far in the specific field under reference, viz., chemistry;

(ii) Revision of the syllabi and suggestion for the modification in our present examination system;

(iii) Evaluation of research work done so far and examination of trends of research, their potentialities and relationship to the general needs of the development programmes in the country.

(iv) The action which may be taken for the development and expansion of training and research in certain special fields in Chemistry, keeping in view the avoidance of duplication of efforts;

(v) Measures for improving the teaching personnel;

(vi) Suggestion of ways and means of coordination between universities themselves and between universities and other Centres of Research like the National Laboratories.

CONTENTS

Foreword; Preface; Introduction ; Development of Chemistry in India—A Historical Sketch; Existing Facilities; Syllabi and Examination System; Future Lines of Development in Chemistry; Summary of Recommendations; Appendices I and II.

RECOMMENDATIONS

Model syllabi for undergraduate and post graduate courses are recommended in order to improve the standard of training in chemistry. The B. Sc. syllabus is given in three forms, viz., (i) B. Sc. (General) for students who offer chemistry as one of three science subjects of equal weightage; (ii) B.Sc. (Special) for those who have chemistry as the major; and (iii) B.Sc. (Subsidiary) for those who offer any other science subject as the major with chemistry as a minor subject.

M.Sc. course in chemistry will be two-year course after the B.Sc. degree. In the first year of the M.Sc., a student be expected to study organic, inorganic and physical chemistry and also carry out practical work in these three branches. The second year of the M.Sc. course will be devoted to the study of these three branches at the general level as far as theory is concerned. In addition, there will be a special paper in any one of the three branches. The practical work, however, will be confined only to the subject which will form the special subject.

Radiochemistry may be introduced at the second year of the M.Sc. course as one of the special subjects, i.e., as an elective subject. The syllabus for this course is also recommended.

In order to raise the standard of teaching, lectures should be coupled with demonstrations of all possible types. Holding conventions of college and university teachers to discuss teaching methods and examination systems may be highly useful. A journal devoted to this subject and capable of reaching all the teachers will be useful to pull up the level of teaching.

Due recognition should be given to sessional tests in assessing the capacities of students so as to reduce the dependence on one comprehensive annual examination at the end of the course. In order to do this, it is recommended that 40 per cent of the total marks may be allotted to sessional tests.

A maximum time limit of five years is recommended for completing the work for the Ph.D. degree. Candidates for this degree besides submitting a thesis should also appear for a written as well as an oral examination. They should give seminars from time to time and also attend a certain minimum number of seminars. They should put in a minimum period of one year in a teaching department of a University.

It is considered that post-graduate course should be confined to university departments while colleges may take care of undergraduate teaching.

Research centres which are specially active and which have already distinguished themselves in research should be raised to the status of premier centres of chemistry research and efforts should be made to bring them to an international level. The centres which are under-developed should be financially helped so as to come to a higher standard.

There should be arrangement for Visiting Professors.

Organisation of frequent Symposia and Summer Schools may help in the promotion of chemistry research in our country.

To raise the standard of publication of research papers and to avoid time lag between dates of communication and of publication of research papers, it is recommended that a single journal under the name 'Indian Journal of Chemistry' may be started in collaboration with the Council of Scientific and Industrial Research, New Delhi, which is already incharge of a number of publications.

Special requirements of chemistry laboratories particularly engaged in research work may be considered and grants may be made available for these.

The teacher-pupil ratio may require improvement. The teaching load of those who are engaged in post-graduate teaching and research should not be more than 14 hours per week. The ratio between senior and junior teachers should be brought to roughly 1:1. Large chemistry departments having the responsibility of post-graduate teaching should have a senior teacher (professor or reader) in each of the three branches, viz., organic, inorganic and physical chemistry and one in certain special fields for which facilities are available (e.g., nuclear chemistry).

To make the Head of the Chemistry Department free from routine administrative work, an Administrative Secretary may be appointed in the University Department.

COMMITTEE APPOINTED BY THE GOVERNMENT OF INDIA TO EXAMINE THE FEASIBILITY OF EVOLVING A SYSTEM OF PAYMENT BY RESULTS TO CERTAIN CATEGORIES OF EMPLOYEES UNDER THE BOMBAY AND MADRAS PORT TRUSTS AND THE BOMBAY DOCK LABOUR BOARD, 1960—REPORT

New Delhi, Ministry of Transport and Communications, 1962. 15p.

Chairman : Shri F. Jeejeebhoy.
Members : Shri V. Vaz; Shri T.K. Parmeswaran Nambiar (replaced by Shri V.A. Jaywant); Shri S.C.C. Anthoni Pillai; Shri M.G. Kotwal; Shri S.C. Sheth; Shri K.A. Khan.
Secretary : Shri Batuk H. Mehta.

APPOINTMENT

By its Resolution No. 23-PLA (103)/59, dated May 12, 1960, published in the Gazette of India Extraordinary, Part I—Section 1, No. 67, dated May 14, 1960, the Government of India in the Ministry of Transport and Communications (Department of Transport) constituted this Committee.

TERMS OF REFERENCE

(a) To examine the feasibility of extending the system of payment by results to the categories of tally clerks shed staff, stackers, mobile crane drivers, and wagon, loaders and unloaders employed by the Port Trusts of Bombay and Madras; and

(b) To devise suitable schemes for payment by results to the categories in respect of which such payment is considered feasible.

By its further Resolution of even number dated September 2, 1960, the Government directed that the tally and sorting clerks and registered stevedore khalasis employed by the Bombay Dock Labour Board should also be included within the scope of the Committee's enquiry.

CONTENTS

Report; On the Import Side; On the Export Side; Helping Gangs; Baroots and Stackers; Example; Tally Clerks; Mobile Crane Drivers; Example; Fork-Lift and Platform Truck Drivers; Sorters; Tally and Sorting Clerks; Cart and Wagon Unloaders; Appendices A to C.

RECOMMENDATIONS

The term 'feasibility' in the Government's Notification has no doubt an elastic connotation, but within the group of Port and Dock Workers under Reference; and we have examined all categories brought to our notice by labour as eligible for piece rates. The Committee has taken the view that not all of them are so engaged or placed as to attract piece rate schemes.

The Committee has arrived at the conclusion that in terms of the Reference, the following categories of dock workers of Bombay and Madras Ports, having regard to their functions as being in some way associated with the handling of cargo at the respective Ports, or as lying within the cycle of operations, or as working as tally clerks who have to be quick and accurate in checking out put and noting details of work on which payment to the workers is based, are eligible for induction into the general concept of the existing scheme of piece-rate by being geared to it in some appropriate manner:

(a) **On the Import Side:**

(1) "Helping Gang" of shore mazdoors employed by the Bombay Port Trust for long carry.
(2) Baroots at Bombay Port.
(3) Mobile crane drivers including operators of Tractors, Fork-Lifts, and Platform Trucks at Bombay and Madras when engaged on a ship unloading.
(4) Stackers of Madras, i.e., persons engaged to do stacking of cargo in course of discharge.
(5) Tally clerks engaged at the hook, both at Madras and Bombay, for tallying import cargo other than bulk cargoes while the ship is unloading.
(6) Sorters of Bombay and Madras.

(b) **On the Export Side:**

(1) Cart and wagon unloaders of Bombay Port Trust.
(2) Tally clerks engaged at the hook, both at Madras and Bombay, for tallying export cargo other than bulk cargoes while the ship is loading.
(3) "Helping Gang" of shore Mazdoors employed by the Bombay Port Trust for long carry.
(4) "Tally and sorting clerk" of Bombay Dock Labour Board.

The Committee is of the view, that taking into account all the factors relevant to the wage structure of these categories, as also their relative position *vis-a-vis* the categories covered by the major scheme of piece rates for handling cargo at the Ports as embodied in the decision of the Labour Appellate Tribunal, the following schemes of payment are adequately suited for the purposes of this Reference before this Committee.

Helping Gangs: Where "helping" men work with a shore hook gang at Bombay for long carry of export or import cargo, and the piece-rate wage of a gang worker exceeds his daily wage for the period occupied in doing piece-rated work, each helping man shall receive as premium an amount equal to the sum by which the piece-rate wage of the gang worker exceeds the daily wage for the said period.

Baroots and Stackers: The baroots of Bombay Port Trust and the stackers of Madras (i.e. persons engaged to do stacking of cargo in course of discharge) shall be given a premium whenever so employed as under.

Each baroot of Bombay or stacker of Madras shall receive a premium equivalent to the average of the piece-rate earnings over the daily wage of the workers of the hook gangs to which he is attached of that shift and vessel, subject to the condition that the premium to which the baroot or the stacker shall become entitled shall be in proportion to the average tonnage stacked by the baroots or stackers in relation to the average of the piece-rate tonnage handled by all the said hook workers in that shift of that vessel; provided that if the baroots or stackers have left cargo unstacked or done the stacking undifferently, the premium shall be deemed not to have accerued to the extent of such short stacking or indifferent stacking. In this connection it is assumed that the Port Trust concerned has employed a sufficiency of baroots or stackers.

Example: Supposing there are three hooks working on a vessel at Bombay in a shift to which the baroot is attached, and the piece-rate earnings over daily wage of each gang working of these three hooks is Rs. 10, nine and eight. The average piece-rate earnings over his daily wage of each gang worker will thus be Rs. nine. For earning this sum of Rs. nine, the total piece-rate tonnage of the cargo handled by all the three gangs was, say, 390 tons for that shift of that vessel. Then the average per hatch will be 130 tons, and the average per worker would be 10 tons. Supposing there are 20 baroots and they have stacked 240 tons, then the average effort of each baroot will be 12 tons.

Each baroot will receive $\frac{12 \times 9}{10}$ = Rs. 10.80

Tally Clerks: The tally clerk at Bombay, while engaged at the hook for talling import and export cargo, shall receive during the eight-hour shift a premium of three nP. for each hook for all cargoes excluding bulk cargoes.

The tally clerk at Madras, while engaged at the hook for talling import and export cargo, shall receive during the eight-hour shift a premium of 2-3/4 nP. for each hook for all cargoes but excluding bulk cargoes. But in the case of wheat discharged in bulk, 12 bags will be regarded as the equivalent of one hook.

The payment of premium as above, both at Bombay and Madras, shall be subject to the following proviso designed to secure the essential requirement of accuracy in tally.

"If tally is accurate between 99 and 100 per cent, the tally clerk shall receive the full premium; if the tally is accurate between 99 per cent and upto but not including 99 per cent, the tally clerk shall receive 90 per cent of the premium; if the tally is accurate between 97 per cent and upto but not including 98 per cent, then he shall receive 70 per cent of the premium; if the tally is accurate between 96 per cent and upto but not including 97 per cent, he shall receive 40 per cent of the premium; and if the tally is accurate between 95 per cent and upto but not including 96 per cent, he shall get 10 per cent, of the premium. Accuracy of tally below 95 per cent shall not attract any premium."

For the second and the third shifts at Bombay each, of six-hour duration, there shall be an adjustment by the addition of 33-1/3 per cent to the premium at the above rate. For the second and third shifts at Madras, each of six-and-a half hours duration, there shall be an adjustment by the addition of 23 per cent to the premium at the above rate.

The relievings tally clerk, both at Bombay and Madras, shall receive the average of the premium of the tally clerks whom then relieve.

Accuracy shall be accordings to number of packages and under the respective marks as shown in the manifest. The percentage of inaccuracies shall be ascertained shipwise; but whenever any particular tally clerk or relieving tally clerk is found responsible for an inaccuracy, his premium shall be reduced accordingly and his errors should be ignored in the case of the rest.

Mobile Crane Drivers: The mobile crane driver at Bombay (including thereby the tracter driver), shall receive a premium equivalent to the average of the piece-rate earnings over the daily wage of the shore crane drivers of that shift and vessel to which they are attached; subject to the condition that the premium to which they shall become entitled shall be in the proportion of the average tonnage stacked by them in relation to the average of the piece-rate tonnage handled by all the said shore cranes and derricks in that shift of that vessel to which they are attached; provided that if they have left cargo unstacked or done the stacking indifferently, the premium shall be deemed not to have occrued to the extent of such short stacking or indifferent stacking. For the purposes of accounting, where a derrick has been used, it will be assumed that a shore crane was employed and piece-rate earnings computed accordingly. Provided that the maximum premium earned by the above categories shall not exceed the maximum of the piece-rate earnings over the daily wage of the piece-rate crane drivers working at the relevant hooks for that shift and in that vessel or those vessels.

Example: Suppose in a shift, hatches Nos. I, IV and V are discharging with shore cranes Nos. 5, 7 and 8 and such cargo requires to be handled by six tractors and two mobile cranes. If the piece rate earnings over the daily wage of the crane drivers of shore cranes Nos. 5, 7 and 8 are Rs. 10, nine and eight respectively, the average piece rate earning over daily wage would be Rs. nine. If the total output of cranes Nos. 5, 7 and 8 is 120 tons, 100 tons and 80 tons respectively, the average output per shore crane will be 100 tons. Suppose out of 300 tons cargo discharged by the above three shore cranes, the six tractors and two mobile cranes together handled 150 tons of cargo, the average tonnage handled by each combined unit of three tractors and one mobile crane will be 75 tons. Then each of the six tractor drivers and each of the two mobile crane drivers shall be paid a piece rate premium of $\frac{75 \times 9}{100}$ = Rs. 6.75.

The mobile crane driver of Madras (and the tractor driver if engaged and the shore crane driver if and when employed in the place of a mobile crane) shall receive a premium equivalent to the average of the piece-rate earnings over the daily wage of the shore crane drivers or which drivers working on the vessel or vessels, whenever they are called upon to work in connection with the handling of any cargo discharged by the hooks of that vessel or those vessels; subject to the condition that the premium to which they shall become entitled shall be in the proportions of the average tonnage stacked by them in relation to the average of the piece-rate tonnage handled by the shore cranes and derricks at the hooks from which the cargo handled by the mobile crane driver, the tractor driver, and the said shore crane driver as the case may be, has been discharged. For the purposes of accounting, where a derrick has been used, it will be assumed that a shore crane was employed and piece-rate earnings computed accordingly. Provided that the maximum premium earned by the above categories shall not exceed the maximum of the piece rate earnings over the daily wage of the piece rate crane drivers working at the relevant hooks for that shift and in that vessel or those vessels.

Fork-lift and Platform in Truck Drivers: The fork-lift driver and the platform truck driver of Madras and the mobile crane driver of Bombay, while operating a fork-lift or a platform truck shall be paid a premium based on the tonnage calculations of the baroots of Bombay or the stackers of Madras, as the case may be; but the rate of his premium shall be calculated on the average of the piece-rate earnings over the daily wage of the shore crane drivers in that shift and working on the vessel. For the purposes of accounting, where a derrick has been used it will be assumed that a shore crane was employed and piece-rate earnings computed accordingly.

Sorters. A sorter when so employed by the Bombay Port Trust shall receive during the eight hour shift a premium of 1-1/5 nP. in the case of all cargoes, excluding bulk cargoes, for each hook coming down during the shift, provided that the cargo brought down by the hook has come under the sorter's work.

A sorter when so employed by the Madras Port Trust shall receive during the eight-hour shift a premium of 1-1/10 nP. in the case of all cargoes excluding bulk cargoes for each hook coming down during the shift, provided that the cargo brought down by the hook has come under the sorter's work.

This premium is payable to the sorter at Bombay and Madras subject to the condition that the sorter is always present at his post and actively pursues his work during the shift and that the sorting under his directions has been done properly.

For the second and the third shifts at Bombay, each of eight-hour duration, there shall be an adjustment by the addition of 33-1/3 per cent to the premium at the above rate for Bombay. For the second and third shifts at Madras, each of six and a half hour duration, there shall be an adjustment by the addition of 23 per cent to the premium at the above rate for Madras.

Tally-and-Sorting Clerks : The tally-and-sorting clerk registered with the Bombay Dock Labour Board when employed by a registered employer to act as a sorter for export cargo concurrently with the loading of the vessel shall receive a premium of 2-1/2 nP. per-hook of the cargo got ready by him for shipment according to the duties laid down by the Bombay Dock Labour Board; provided that if his duties are not properly performed. the premium shall be deemed not to have accrued to the extent of such shortcoming.

Cart and Wagon Unloaders : The cart and wagon unloader of the Bombay Port Trust shall receive, if his output exceeds seven tons in a shift, a premium at the following rates :

(a) Between seven tons and upto 13 tons, for every tons or part thereof, a premium of 65 nP. per ton.

(b) Beyond 13 tons, for every ton or part thereof his premium shall be at the rate of 75 nP. per ton.

Provided that he stacks all cargoes received at the shed properly as required by the authorities. He will also stack all cargoes other than bag cargo which may be unloaded by the shipper's labour. The premium shall be deemed not to have accrued to the extent of stacking not properly done. The Port Trust may re-group the cart and wagon unloaders for the more effective working of this scheme.

As regards the question of extension of piece-rates to shed staff, the Committee was of the opinion that while recognising the value of rewards in recognition of work done with more than ordinary zeal and fidelity by persons like shed superintendents, etc., this Committee recommends that this is a matter which calls for consideration by the Administration, but it is not a matter within the purview of this Committee's work.

COMMITTEE OF ENQUIRY INTO THE CONDITIONS OF SERVICE OF THE MARINE SERVICES OF THE PORT OF CALCUTTA, 1960—REPORT

New Delhi, Ministry of Transport and Communications (Department of Transport), 1960. 271+ivp.

Sole Member : Shri S.N. Guha Roy.
Secretary : Shri N.S. Ghosh.

APPOINTMENT

The One-Member Committee was appointed by the Government of India, Ministry of Transport and Communications, Department of Transport, (Transport Wing), in Resolution No. 9-PE(1)/60, dated June 17, 1960, published in Part I, Section (1) of the Gazette of India, dated June 25, 1960, for enquiring into the conditions of Service of the six Marine Services of the Port of Calcutta given below :

(1) Assistant Harbour Masters' Service.
(2) Dredger and Despatch Service;
(3) Hooghly Pilot Service;
(4) River Surveyors Service;
(5) Berthing Masters' Service; and
(6) Marine Engineers' Service.

TERMS OF REFERENCE

(i) To enquire into and report on the conditions of all categories of persons employed in the Port of Calcutta, which are detailed in the Schedule, and to make recommendations generally and with special reference to the following matters, keeping in mind the considerations mentioned in clause (iii) below :

(a) Scales of pay;
(b) Allowances and fees;
(c) System of turns, hours of work and periods of rest;
(d) Adequacy or otherwise of the strength of the existing cadres and the basis on which they should be fixed;
(e) Desirability of adoption of an interim scheme of remuneration for abnormal work as a result of shortages in existing cadres;

(ii) To examine whether the recommendations of the Ports Marine Services Enquiry Committee, 1955, should be amended or supplemented, regard being had to the representations submitted by the various Marine Services Associations of the Port of Calcutta.

(iii) In making their recommendations the Committee will take into account the prevailing pay scales, allowances and other conditions of service in similar services at other major Ports, the recommendations of the Central Pay Commission in regard to comparable Government Services and the historical background.

CONTENTS

The Committe, Its Terms of Reference and How it proceeded—The Port of Calcutta Proper, Its Approaches, The Jurisdiction of the Commissioners and the Field of Operations of the Six Marine Services of the Port; The Historical Background of the Six Marine Services of the Port; The Immediate Background of the Present Enquiry; General Principles to be Followed in Examining Demands for Enhancement of Emoluments—The Demands of Each of the Services and of the Lighting Officer under the Heading "Scales of Pay Allowances, Fees including Overtime", the Comments of the Commissioners thereon and the Findings of the Committee; System of Turns, Hours of Work and Periods of Rest—The Demands of the Services, the Commissioners, Case and the Findings of the Committee- Overtime

Allowances; The Strength of Cadres—Desirability of Adoption of an Interim Scheme of Remuneration for Abnormol Work Due to Shortages in Cadres; Administrative Matters of the Different Sections of the Marine Services—Sectional Independence—Creation of Additional Administrative Posts—Alteration of the Existing System of Holding Marine Enquiries—Changes in the Existing Mode of the Working of the Department—Retention of Superannuated Officers in Service and its Effect on the Other Members of the Service; Miscellaneous Demands; Administrative Officers—Sectional and General; Conclusions and Thanks—Summary of Findings and Recommendations; Appendices A to H.

RECOMMENDATIONS

Emoluments (Pay, Allowances, etc.)

Assistant Harbour Master : If the emoluments of the Assistant Harbour Masters are compared with the emoluments paid to other categories of civil servants or even other technical staff in the country, one would be justified in saying that the Assistant Harbour Masters are luckier than most. There is, therefore, no ground for recommending any further increase in their emoluments.

Since the night fee at 25 per cent of their basic pay, which they were in receipt of prior to 1938,—has already been merged in the structure of pay, there is no case for grant to them of night fee, as a separate item.

An Assistant Harbour Master when placed on special duty does not work overtime or moor/unmoor vessels. There is, therefore, no reason for their claiming compensation for loss of their earnings in mooring/unmooring fees and overtime allowance.

The mooring fee paid to the Assistant Harbour Masters at any rate or the present basis of calculation of such fee, is entirely wrong in principle and so is the principle on which overtime is calculated. The Port Commissioners may consider whether for future recruits, it will be expedient to do away with mooring/unmooring fees.

Hooghly Pilot Service : It will not be reasonable to recommend consolidation of the night fee at figures higher than the present figures, i.e., Rs. 350 for the Branch and Master Pilots and Rs. 200 for the Mate Pilots. If the present position is allowed to continue, by about 1965, provided the volume of shipping remains constant, the figures may reasonably be expected to come down to the figures at which the Commissioners have consolidated the night fees.

The demand that whenever a Pilot cannot work for the whole month on account of absence on leave, the number of ships for the purpose of overtime, should be reduced seems to be absurd on the face of it. He cannot in justice claim anything in the shape of an overtime allowance.

As they remain away from the town for about half a month and also because they do not have to do as much travelling on duty as the Assistant Harbour Masters do there is no reason for increasing their transport allowance to Rs. 175 per month.

To give retrospective effect from 1951 to the grant of mess allowance sanctioned from 1955 as a result of the recommendations of the Lokur Committee, would be wrong in principle.

The existing rate of the Sandheads mess allowance is adequate.

Dredger and Despatch Service : Since the grant of mooring/unmooring fee to the Assistant Harbour Masters is not considered reasonable, extension of the privilege to the officers of the Dredger and Despatch Service, would not be justified.

Since the Port Commissioners provide cooks, servants, crockery and cutlery, and other facilities, there is no ground for raising the existing rate of mess allowance of Rs. 5 per diem.

Grant of compensation to the Chief Officers taking command of the Tugs for the mere discomfort and hardship they have to undergo in these vessels would not be justified because the Tugs are used only in emergencies. The Commissioners should, however, see that normally these Tugs are commanded by Commanders.

The scale of pay of the Lighting Officer (Shri D.P. Choudhury) should be raised to Rs. 750-50-1,300.

Assistant River Surveyors : The claim that the pay and allowances of the Assistant River Surveyors should be at a par with those of other Marine Services, seems unreasonable.

There is no justification for a higher command pay for the Commanders of Survey Vessels.

The Assistant River Surveyors in-charge of Survey Parties in Dredgers may be granted a charge allowance of Rs. 100 per month.

It is not understood why it should be necessary for all the officers to undertake journeys to the stores, workshops, and the Head Office. These journeys should always be undertaken by the officers to whom a conveyance allowance is payable. If, on rare occasions any other officer has to be deputed, the cost of conveyance can not obviously be such as will justify grant of a general conveyance allowance for all the officers of the service, for on such occasions the individual officers may easily be compensated for the cost of the journeys on certificates of their respective Commanders.

The demand made by the Assistant River Surveyors for mooring/unmooring fee for mooring and unmooring servey vessels, does not seem to be at all justified because in the first place, the payment of mooring/

unmooring fee to the Assistant Harbour Masters, which has given rise to it, is unjustified and secondly, the Survey Vessels are much smaller than the vessels which the Assistant Harbour Masters are required to moor and unmoor.

The command pay should be treated as "Pay" for the purpose of calculating the "Away from Base" allowance for all the services eligible for grant of "Away from Base' allowance. The expression "Basic Pay" used in this' contex t, in the report of the Lokur Committee should be amended to include "Command Pay".

The existing rate of mess allowance is considered to be adequate.

Class I Marine Engineers : The decision of the Port Commissioners on the recommendations of the Special Committee as regards pay and allowances of the Class I Marine Engineers including Chief Engineers, are considered quite reasonable and should be sufficient to meet the legitimate grievances of the officers concerned. The decisions should be given effect from the date on which they were made by the Port Commissioners.

The conveyance allowance of Rs. 50 per month already sanctioned for the Second Engineers, Class I Vessels should be sufficient.

There is no substance in the demand that Second Engineers doing the duties of Chief Engineers in casual or short leave vacancies should be paid the pay of Chief Engineers. The existing practise based on the correspon-ding Government rules—on the subject should continue be followed.

There is no ground for extending messing facilities to the Engineers attached to the Port Dredging Unit. If Lascars—who bring food for the officers and are paid by the Port Commissioners for this, are not willing to do this work, the Port Commissioners should make alterna-tive arrangements for having the food of the officers concerned brought from their homes and ensuring that it reaches them on duty.

There is no justification for paying the Engineers of the Port Dredging Unit, any special fee for the supervis-ing the mooring and unmooring of the Bucket Dredgers.

From an analysis of the nature of their duties, it seems that the Port Dredging Chief Engineers have hardly any case for a conveyance allowance at all. They are, however, paid Rs. 100 per month as conveyance allowance. There is, therefore, no ground for increasing this allowance by another Rs. 75 per month.

Junior Marine Engineers The difference that exists at present between the scales of pay and total emoluments of the uncertificated Junior Engineers employed in the Port of Calcutta and of the uncertified Junior Engineers employed in the Merchant Marine, whether on Home Trade or Foreign-going Vessels, —does not seem to be unfair in any way to the uncertified Junior Engineers of the Port. As a matter of fact, the Inland Engineers particularly towards the end, are better off in the Port than in the Merchant Marine where they are treated as uncertified Engineers.

There is, however, some justification for the Junior Engineers—with Second Class Certificates,—getting in the initial stages, more than what they are in receipt of at present. Second Class Junior Engineers should be given 12 advance grade increments instead of three as at present. In other words, they should be given starting salary of Rs. 400 in the scale of Rs. 250-10-310, -15-400-20-500/E.B.-40-740, the Second Class Junior Engineers already in receipt of a pay above Rs. 400, but below the maximum of the scale, being granted one in-crement of every three years of service with Second Class Certificates subject only to this that the maximum pay of the scale is not exceeded. The above grade increment may be given effect from January 1, 1961, without any prejudice to their normal increments during the year.

As it is not necessary for all Junior Engineers to undertake journeys on official duty, there is really no case for a conveyance allowance to all Junior Marine Engineers,--the Engineers-in-Charge of Class II Vessels—already getting a conveyance allowance of Rs. 50 per month.

As the responsibilities of an Engineer-in-Charge, Class II Vessle, are those of a Chief Engineer of a Class I Vessel are not identical, there ought to be a difference in their rates of charge allowance. There is therefore, no justification for raising the charge allow-ance of Rs. 100 per month payable to an Engineer-in-Charge of a Class II Vessel to the level of Rs. 200 paid to the Chief Engineer, of a Class I Vessel.

There is no ground for departing from the Special Committee's recommendation on the questions of grant of mess allowance to the Relieving Junior Engineers attached to the vessels under repairs.

As the Junior Port Dredging Engineers have more or less fixed hours of duty and they do not have to go down the river for a number of days at a stretch, they cannot in justice claim in mess allowance. It is also not necessary to provide facilities for their messing on board the vessel.

The existing discrimination between the Navigating Officers and the Marine Engineers in the matter of eligibilty for mess allowance when on casual or special compensatory leave should be removed.

The demand that the officers should be paid overtime at double the rate of their basic pay, instead of at the single rate, does not seem reasonable.

Berthing Masters Considering their academic quali-fications, their age of entry into the Post service, and the period of training they have to undergo under the Port Commissioners and also having regard to the general conditions of employment and the scale of pay which candidates with similar general initial qualifications command in the country, the scale of pay of the Berthing Masters seems reasonable and there is no justification for raising it.

Since the decision of the Port Commissioners not to give effect to the Lokur Committee's recommendation for raising the initial salary of a Berthing Master from Rs. 300 to Rs. 420 is not unreasonable, the question of giving the recommendation of the Lokur Committee a retrospective operation hardly arises for the simple reason that the recommendation has not been made operative at all.

The demand that a Berthing Master acting as an Assistant Dock Master for seven days or more at a time should be given an acting allowance is not considered reasonable. The principal followed by the Port Commissioners in the matter of making acting arrangements and paying acting allowances are sound.

To nandle ships without power on the main engines, is a part of the normal duties of a Berthing Master. To pay special allowance for a piece of work which is a part of the normal duties of an officer because it happens to involve skill, care and alertness, would certainly be setting up an undesirable precedent. The demand for 'Non-Steam' allowance is, therefore, considered unjustified.

As they are already getting one day's basic pay for work on Sunday's or holidays, there is also no justification whatsoever for two days pay or additional casual leave being granted to the Berthing Masters for working on Sundays or public holidays.

Since there is no necessity for implementing the 'Lock to Lock' scheme at present, the question of raising the transport allowance in the event of such a scheme coming into operation, does not arise.

System Of Turns, Hours Of Work, And Periods Of Rest.

Assistant Harbour Masters: From the figures of hours of duty per day, made available to the Committee, it is clear that 18 turns fixed at the standard for an Assistant Harbour Master, is far from excessive.

As the officers who are 'first on turn' do not actually do any official work beyond holding themselves in readiness, for work. 'Being on first on turn', cannot justly be considered to be even duty, for less a turn.

On principle, the system of pooling of mooring/unmooring fees and overtime fees is wrong.

The Commissioners may find out of officers would like a change of the existing practice of pooling.

The recommendation of the Lokur Committee fixing 18 turns a month for an Assistant Harbour Master should be modified for the Assistant Harbour Master at Buadge Budge and the norm for him should be raised to 24 turns a month.

Hooghly Pilot Service: Reduction of the standard of work fixed by the Lokur Committee of the Branch Pilots will not be justified on the ground of their age or on any other ground.

There is no justification for putting the duty of attending the Head Office in connection with an examination or enquiry on a par with the duty of ship-handling either for an Assistant Harbour Master or a Pilot, though for both, it is a part of their periodical normal duties. Nor do such duties deserve from their nature, or duration, to be compensated by any extra payment.

The word 'turn' should be confined to the regular-ship handling work of an Assistant Harbour Master or a Pilot.

There is no ground for time being the pilotage of more than 18 hours as two jobs or in the alternative for treating an Ulubaria ship as two ships.

It will not be correct to treat the period of detention of a Pilot as an extra job which means an extra job of navigating a ship.

There is no reason why the 'Station Orders' should be regarded as 'turns' which for a Pilot should mean only the work of piloting ships. Although travelling as passengers on board ships for taking up duties either at the Sandheads or at Garden Reach constitutes duty, it is certainly a duty of a kind different from the normal duty of a Pilot which is to pilot a ship and because of this difference it should not be treated as a job for a Pilot.

The Commissioners may consider whether they should not have more Leadsmen with Second Mate's certificates and their initial emoluments should not be made more attractive.

Dredger And Dessatch Service: The monthly norm of dredgers to be down the river should be fixed at 20 days and the annual norm at 240 days. The monthly norm is something to be aimed at, though the exigencies of the service may not make it possible for the Port Commissioners to stick to this rigidly. So long as no one in service be asked to be down the river for more than 26 days in a month and more than 240 days in a year, it will not be really hard on the officers.

When the dredgers are in the Port, the officers will of course follow their usual routine of work.

When the annual norm is exceeded, the officer concerned will be eligible for overtime leave.

The norm for the 'Despatch Service' may be fixed at 18 days a month and 216 days in a year to be applied and worked exactly on the lines suggested for the dredgers. The maximum number of days for the Despatch Vessel should not exceed 24 days down the river in any month—the officers being eligible for overtime leave if the annual norm is exceeded. The officers will also have to do their normal duties, when their vessels are in Port.

The practice of treating the day of arrival and the day of sailing as one day for the purpose of grant of 'Away from Base' allowance is fair and should continue to be followed.

Assistant River Surveyors : For the three Surveys vessels and the Survey Parties attached to dredgers, the norm of work should be the same as for dredgers—i.e. 20 days in a month and 240 days in a year and the principle enunciated in connection with dredgers should be applicable to the officers attached to the Survey Vessels and the Survey Parties on dredgers. These officers should also do their usual round of duties when the vessels are in the Port.

The only standard of work for the Higher Reaches Survey Party should be 264 days work in a year on the monthly standard of 22 days, which cannot and need not be rigidly followed.

Officers of the Fairfields Station and the Hooghly Point Station should work for 26 days in a month of 30 days and 27 days in a month of 31 days, either in the office or in the river.

The Commissioners should be left to decide the question regarding increasing the number of survey units.

Class I Marine Engineers : The standard of work, i.e., the number of days down the river, for Class I Marine Engineers attached to vessels which have to go down the river should be the same as that fixed for the Navigating Officers of such ships.

If an officer is to be away from the Port for more than that period he will have to be compensated in the same way as the officers of the Dredger and Despatch Service.

Junior Marine Engineers : The Junior Marine Engineers normally work in eight hours shifts; some of them who are attached to the Port Dredging Unit, actually work for eight hours a day and if their work extends beyonds eight hours, they earn an overtime allowance. The Junior Engineers attached to the vessels which have to go down the river have sometimes to work for more than eight hours in an emergency. As they are ship's men and are in receipt of an 'Away From Base' allowance for the days they are away from the Port, payment of 'overtime' for any work beyond eight hours on a particular day would not be justified.

The standard of work of Junior Engineers in charge of Class II vessels which have to go down the river for a number of days at a stretch should be the same as fixed for the Navigating Officers of such vessels and then will be eligible for additional leave if the standard is exceeded exactly in the same manner as laid down for the Navigating Officers attached to the vessels.

Overtime Allowance

Assistant Harbour Masters : As the number of turns of the Assistant Harbour Masters fixed by the Lokur Committee is far from excessive and the same number of turns fixed for the Assistant Harbour Master at Buadge Budge is extremely low, there is no question of reducing the duration of a turn for an Assistant Harbour Master either in Calcutta or at Budge Buadge or for a reduction of the number of turns.

Hoogly Pilot Service : As there is no ground for reducing the number of turns for Branch Pilots to the number of turns for Master and Mate Pilots, the question of changing the basis of calculation of overtime allowance does not arise.

The demand that the Commanders of Pilot Vessels should be paid overtime whenever they are called upon to do special duty loses sight of the fact that these officers are ship's officers and their position is comparable to that of the Master of a ship or the Commander of a Dredger or a Despatch Vessel who are always on duty like the Commander of a Pilot Vessel. As these officers do not earn overtime, there is no reason why the Commanders of Pilot Vessels should be made eligible for it.

Dredger and Despatch Service : The officers of the Dredger and Despatch Service, should be compensated by extra leave to be calculated at the rate of one day for each day they spend down the river in excess of the yearly norm laid down for them. The special leave in lieu of excessive work should be calculated after the year is over so that the special leave will be due in the year following. If for any reason the Port Commissioners cannot allow the special leave to an officer who has earned it, in the year when it has became due even though the officer may then ask for it, he should be allowed to accumulate the leave to his credit for a number of years to be fixed by the Port Commissioners. In the event of dredging round the clock, some officers may have to work harder. The Commissioners may consider if some allowance for hard work is not likely both to provide an incentive for such work and to compensate the officers concerned.

Assistant River Surveyors : The officers attached to the dredgers and the survey parties and the Higher Reaches Survey Party should be compensated for work in excess of the norm fixed for them, by additional special leave on the same principle as enunciated for the dredger section of the Dredger and Despatch Service. As the officers at Fairfields and Hooghly Point will work for 26 days in a month of 30 days and 27 days in month of 31 days, their weekly off days are ensured. Their weekly off days may be given to them by turns; if necessary, and normally there should be no extra work for them.

Class I Marine Engineers : The Chief Engineers and Second Engineers, when they go down the river, are not restricted to any fixed number of hours of work as they are supposed to be on duty for 24 hours. It is fair that they should be compensated by a special leave if they have to go down the river for a period in the excess of the norm fixed for them, such leave being calculated as in the case of the Dredger and Despatch Service.

The demand for compensation for night work for the Engineers attached to Dredgers and Despatch Vessels, does not appear to be justified, first because there is little night work in Dredgers and secondly if in Despatch Vessels occasional night work may be involved, it does not appear to be sufficient to justify a special compensation.

The Strength Of Cadres

Assistant River Surveyors : If Government sanctions the five posts already sanctioned by the Port Commissioners, the strength of the service should be sufficient for the present.

The post of Officer-in-Charge, Port Dredging Survey should be restored to the service.

It is not understood how one ship-keeper can afford sufficient relief to all the men who have to go down the river in the Survey Vessels for fairly long spells. From the available materials, it is not possible to say whether any such post is really needed. The Port Commissioners may, however, examine the proposal and find out whether with the total strength standing at 43, officers cannot be relieved by turns so that each of them may have a number of evenings free.

As the survey work is carried out in units of two, three or four officers, it can only mean that there have been, throughout the existence of the shortage, one or two teams less or in other words, necessary work was left undone and not that there has been any increase in the work-load for any of the parties. Consequently, the question of compensating the officers for increased work-load, resulting from any such shortage, hardly arises.

Class I Marine Engineers : There is no necessity for creating five additional posts of Chief Engineers.

The question whether when an officer relieves another officer of the higher grade for a period less than a month, he should be paid an officiating allowance or not, is quite different from the question of how many officers are actually needed for the work. To introduce that in connection with the question of fixing the cadre strength, is to confuse the issue. The only consideration for fixing the strength of a service should be what strength is really needed for carrying out the work, and for relieving the officers when they go on leave. If a particular number is needed for the actual carrying out of the work, a leave reserve has certainly to be added to that number, but, then, there is really no need at all for appointing to the leave reserve, officers of a higher grade.

The Port Commissioners will no doubt consider the question of strengthening the cadre as and when they find it necessary.

The demand that a Senior Engineer from tho Port Dredging Unit instead of an Assistant Harbour Master should be appointed as the Officer-in-Charge, Port Dredging seems totally unjustified.

There is no reason why the designation of the Chief Engineer of the Bucket and Suction Dredgers of the port. Dredging Unit should be changed to Chief Engineer-cum-Dredging Master.

Junior Marine Engineers : There is no question of compensating an officer, when his casual leave is refused. Since with the existing strength, it is possible to allow officers to go on earned leave, the question of strengthening the cadre only for the purpose of enabling the officers to avail themselves of earned leave, hardly arises.

Berthing Masters : The Port Commissioners will no doubt, increase the cadre to the requisite strength if such an increase is justified by the requirements of the Port.

Desirability Of Adoption Of An Interim Scheme Of Remuneration Of Abnormal Work Due To Shortages In Cadres

Where shortages are of a purely temporary character lasting less than a month and cannot be foreseen, it is hardly possible to make any arrangements beforehand for such shortages. But where such shortages can be foreseen and occur for a substantially long period, it is only fair that the Post Commissioners should do something to compensate the officers concerned for the increase of their work-load as a result of such shortages, provided, of courses the shartage is in excess of a fixed percentage of the sanctioned strength, and provided further that the shortage really means a consequent increase in the work-load. Only those officers for whom there is no scheme for overtime allowance should be eligible to be benefited by the proposed interim scheme.

As a uniform scheme for all the services may not be practicable, the Commissionors should have a wide discretion the matter. Subject to this discretion the following general scheme may be adopted. Whenever of shortage occurs in a cadre by atleast 25 per cent of the total permanent cadre and this shortage lasts for more than a month, the officers whose work-load increased as a result of that shortage, should be compensated by a percentage varying between five and 10 of their basic salary according to the quantum of the increase and other relevant factors.

Administrative Matters

Sectional Independence : The demand for sectional independence is far from justified.

As far as routine matters are concerned, which can be disposed of by the Deputy Conservator himself, he can have a discussion with the Sectional Heads concerned and dispose of the matters dictating orders in the presence of the Sectional Head concerned and then directing copies thereof being sent to him. Where, however, the matter is of greater importance and requires to be put up before the Commissioners or the Chairman, the Deputy Conservator after examining it, may send up the original proposal together with a forwarding letter of his own in which he will give his own views and suggestions on the proposal as it originally emanated from the section.

The Deputy Conservator is not merely in charge of the conservancy services as Deputy Conservator but he is also in-charge of the operational part of the Marine Services. Whatever conflict there may be between these two wings, there is really no reason why the Deputy Conservator should not be able to rise above the conflicts and decide the matter justly and fairly to all concerned.

In order to ensure team work and coordination among the different sections, it is essential that there should be a responsible officer not to look into the day-to-day working of the different services but to know enough about all the sections to be able to see first that there is no conflict amongst them, secondly that each of the services renders to the Port the service that is expected of it and thirdly that whenever coordination between one service and another service is necessary, there is no lack of it.

It is difficult to understand why there should be any objection to the existing system of examination unless of course the position of the Port Pilotage Officer is made somewhat awkward not so much by the system itself, as by the manner in which the system is made to function. It is up to the Deputy Conservator as the Head of the Department to ensure that Port Pilotage Officer gives him the maximum possible help which can be expected from him.

There is hardly any reason why presiding over the enquiries by the Deputy Conservator or by the Senior Assistant Conservator should be objected to by the Sectional Heads one or the other of whom may have to be present at the enquiry.

The present system of a conference among officers before a draught forecast is made, is not only highly desirable in itself but absolutely essential and if a proper record is kept of the estimates of the different officers, it can easily be found out later on, if necessary, which of the officers was right and which wrong and which of the officers was nearest to the correct depth. For this purpose, a suitable printed form may be devised so as to enable each of the officers attending the Conference, to record his estimates in his own hand and the Deputy Conservator to record the final decision arrived at in the conference. If all the officers agree to the final decision, then all should sign it ; if some of them do not agree, then can say whether they disagree or whether they agree.

The grounds given by the Services would not justify the removal of the Deputy Conservators overall control of the Hooghly Pilot Service.

There is also no justification for the River Survey Service being taken out of the hands of the Deputy Conservator.

Creation of Additional Administrative Port

Assistant Harbour Masters : From the materials and evidences, it is not clear whether an additional post of Dock Master is really necessary in the interests of efficiency of the working of the Port. If an additional post is really necessary in the interests of the Port, it will be the Commissioners to decide what the nature of that additional post will be and whether an additional Deputy Dock Master will not be enough.

As the crew receive a preliminary training of some sort for three months in the school provided by the Government of West Bengal, the Commissioners can supplement that training as they have been doing at present by making them work with those who are already fully trained. That seems to be a better scheme than putting them under an additional Mooring Master (Personnel). The Commissioners may, however consider all the relevant materials at their disposal and decide whether such an administrative post is really necessary.

There is no ground for changing the designation of the Port Pilotage Officer to the Deputy Conservator, Pilotage.

Dredger and Despath Service : It is not a bad idea to place some one fully conversant with the work of the Dredger and Despatch Service in sole administrative charge of it. As the service itself suggests that as long as Shri B.L. Mital is the Senior Assistant Conservator, they would have no objection to his being placed in exclusive charge of it, that arrangement may be given effect to by redistribution of the work of the two Assistant Conservators. The Commissioners should find out what extra help they can provide to Shri Mital in the discharge of his duties without incurring any additional expenditure. It is just possible that one of the two Supernumerary Commanders might be used whenever they are available, for giving some relief to Shri Mital.

The demand for the second administrative post does not seem to be justified on its own merits.

Alternation Of The Existing System Of Holding Marine Enquiries

The rules as they stand, do not seem to contemplate a combination of a casualty enquiry and a disciplinary enquiry, but when this combination is found not merely desirable but also essential because witnesses attached to the ships which cannot be indefinitely detained, in the Port, have to be examined before their ships leave the Port, the officer conducting the enquiry can hardly help combining the casualty enquiry and the disciplinary enquiry in the same proceedings. When he does so, he must give the officers, he may eventually have to proceed against an opportunity of being present throughout the enquiry and also the right and opportunity of putting questions to the witnesses that are being examined and of generally making his submissions in his own defence. The executive instructions on the subject, therefore, call for a certain amount of modification in respect of proceedings, combining casualty enquiry and disciplinary enquiry. It is, however, always desirable, whenever it is possible, to separate a disciplinary enquiry from a casualty enquiry.

Change in The Existing Mode Of The Working Of The Department

The Commissioners are fully justified in not Implementing the 'Lock to Lock' schemes.

There does not seem to be any necessity for an Advisory Committee being formed to go into the matters affecting the Pilots. But if the Administration thinks that such a Committee will help the Pilot Service being administered smoothly, it may consider how this Committee should be formed and what its precies functions should be.

Dredger and Despatch Service : While it is certainly desirable that the Deputy Conservator should have at his disposal the best possible technical advice, he can have on the design and lay-out of a dredger, it is hardly desirable to tie down his hands in any way by the formation of a regular Committee.

It will be useful if the Commissioners have a small library of technical books and publications attached to the office of the Deputy Conservator for the use not merely of the Dredger and Despatch Service but of all other Marine Services.

The service rules may be printed and copies made available to the different services.

It is absurd to think in terms of seniority of ships because first, it is impossible to fix the seniority of ships according to any intelligible principle, and secondly, it may affect the question of appointment to a permanent vacancy by seniority among officers.

Assistant River Surveyors : The post of the 'model Officer', should continue to be a selection post and the post filled in accordingly.

In drawing up the order of seniority in respect of the four Probationary Assistant River Surveyors recruited in 1958, the order of precedence made by the selecting officer may be treated as entirely provisional. This provisional order of precedence may be changed according to the results of the first examination when an officer is confirmed his service on the distinct understanding that even this is provisional and the final determination of the order of seniority among the officers concerned is to be made on the combined results of the examinations at the end of the third, fourth and fifth years.

The above method is considered better than the existing method of determining seniority on the basis of the results of the first examination.

Junior Marine Engineers : The demand made on behalf of the Junior Marine Engineers that there should be a definite system of posting of Junior Marine Engineers to different vessels which should be graded for the purpose and postings made strictly according to seniority, seems totally impracticable.

It is open to the Commissioners to consider the rotational system of posting wherever that is possible.

In view of the fact that ships in the Hooghly require constant manoeuvring of the machinery and that the maintenance of the machinery has got to be of a very high order, the change in the existing system either in regard to the appointment of Chief Engineers and Second Engineers to Pilot and Despatch Vessels or to the posting of Inland Engineers as Engineers-in-Charge of Inland Vessels, would not be justified.

There is no necessity for engaging any more Ship keeping or Watcher Engineers.

There should be no objection in principle to the grant of a fixed day off to the Junior Engineers attached to vessels which are normally stationed in the Port. It is however, for the Commissioners to consider whether it will be practicable to do so.

As both the Engineers attached to each of the following vessels, Fire Float 'Alfa', Tug 'Stalwart', Crane Vessel 'Samson'—do not carry the same responsibility, there is no reason why both of them should be designated as "Engineers-in-Charge"

Clerical Establishment Under The Different Marine Services

It should be possible to make a fairer allotment of duties among the four clerks engaged to look after the River Survey establishments.

There is no reason why the clerk attached to a Dredger or Despatch Vessel should not be made to lend a hand to assist the Chief Engineer for certain kinds of work.

In the above suggestions are accepted it will not be necessary to post any more clerks either to the stations of the River Survey or to the vessels either of the River Survey Party or of the Dredger and Despatch Service.

Courtesy Title

There can be no reasonable objections to the use by the Commanders of Dredger and Despatch Vessels of the courtesy title of 'Captain'.

Miscellaneows Demands

There is no justification for a Pilot taking a servant with him on board the vessel and the Commissioners paying the cost.

The extension of the benefit of pension to the members of the Pilot Service, who are not entitled to it on the recommendation of the Lokur Committee, would not be justified for the present.

To expect the Commissioners to extend to all the officers the benefit of full pension five years before the superannuation is due, is on the face of it, an unsound proposition both an economic and general grounds and from that point of view the demand seems unreasonable.

The question of a Chief Engineers, Class I vessel, taking his family in the vessels, which provided no sufficient accommodation does not arise. On the 'Bhagirathi' and the two Pilot Vessels, the Commissioners, if they think proper, may allow the Chief Engineer to take his family at least occasionally with the permission of the Deputy Conservator.

As regards the scale of accommodation for Engineers, the accommodation provided on the existing vessels cannot be changed. In vessels to be constructed hereafter, what accommodation should be provided for the Engineers is a matter to be considered by the Commissioners. There is no doubt that they will try to do justice to all kinds of officers.

As long as the rules governing classification of officers remain, there is hardly any reason for making an exception in the case of the Berthing Masters, nor is there any sufficient reason for raising the maximum of their scale to Rs. 1000 just to place them in class I. The post of Dock Master should continue to be held by a Master Mariner.

Compensation For Accidents, Causing Injury And Loss Of Life To Officers On Duty

As the scale of compensation is regulated by rules applicable to all Government services, the question cannot be considered for the Port Officers only and if the matter has to be gone into, it should be gone into as a whole.

Compensatory Leave in Lieu Of Weekly Off Days

As the Commissioners have accepted the Lokur Committee's recommendation regarding grant of compensatory leave for loss of weekly off days, it is only fair that compensation should be provided in the shape of leave to those officers who could not be allowed these weekly off days.

If, officers are allowed 26 days' special leave in lieu of weekly off days, those of them who have been denied this weekly off day would have a sufficient measure of compensation both for the past failure of the Commissioners to implement the Lokur Committee's recommendation and for their failure in future.

In future, the Commissioners should see that each of these services—namely, the Pilots, the Dredger and Despatch Service, Assistant River Surveyors and the Engineers both Class I and Junior of outgoing vessels are completely relieved for a day a week, two days in two weeks, or three days in three weeks and so on by turns, so that each of the officers is allowed in this way at least 26 days off, for the other 26 days off they are entitled to, leave being credited to them in the manner already suggested.

If a particular officer has been granted some days off as weekly off days in a year, this leave should be proportionately curtailed.

An officer should be allowed to carry on his leave for a reasonably long period so as to enable the Port Commissioners to give during that period all these officers the leave already due to them. If, however, a particular officer does not avail himself of the leave during the period, the leave to his credit will stand cancelled.

These recommendations should have effect from the date when the Lokur Committee's recommendation on the point came into operation.

Extension Of Travel Facilities To All Officers

The rule, as it stands, governing grant of travel facilities, cannot obviously apply to officers living within 250 miles of the Port, because the whole of the cost of this part of the journey has in any case to be borne by the officers themselves under the rule. It seems that there is really no reason for an amendment of the rule so as to extend it to officers living within 250 miles of their headquarters.

The Commissioners may consider the feasibility of putting up extra garages to meet demand of the Class I Marine Engineers.

It will certainly be conducive to the maintenance of a high moral amongst the officers if occasionally the

Chairman could meet them.

If it is possible for the Commissioners to have quarters for all their officers as near the Port as possible, the members of the service will certainly find it more convenient to attend the different places where they have to work.

The Commissioners may consider the proposal regarding supply of refrigerators for the use of the officers of the Port Dredging Unit, on its own merits.

In the future allotment of quarters, Marines Engineers should be given priority.

The suggestion that the Commissioner should take lease of private houses for their employees does not seem to be a practical one.

The only practicable solution of the problem of the housing shortage in Calcutta, is to have more quarters built for the officers and to let them out to the officers.

There is no justification for grant of rent-free quarters to the officers attached to Despatch Vessels.

The ceiling of rent for Nimak Mahal flats cannot be lowered without at the same time lowering its scheduled rent which is already lower than that of the Portland Park and Dumayne Avenue flats. A reduction of the scheduled rent cannot be recommended.

A good deal of the doctors' time is wasted in transit. The Commissioners should devise ways and means for increasing the effective hours of duty of the doctors. They may also consider in this connection, the feasibility of opening one or more centres from which the External Service can be operated.

The grievance of the services an account of inadequacy of cabins is likely to be redressed in the near future, when the new Hospital is built.

The Commissioners should provide a waiting room for officers in each of the two Hospitals.

The demand of the officers for treatment by a doctor out of panel of doctors to be drawn up by the Commissioners or for treatment in nursing homes at the cost of the Commissioners cannot be justified.

Administrative Officers Sectional And General

There should be a difference of Rs. 50 between the pay of a supervisory post and that of the post immediately below.

Harbour Master's Section

There is no justification for grant of a car allowance of Rs. 150 to the Assistant Dock Master and the Deputy Dock Master.

There is no reason for raising the pay of the Administrative Officers of the Harbour Master's Service.

If because of the financial loss involved in the promotion of an Assistant Harbour Master to any administrative post, there is at any time any reluctance on the part of the officers, to accept these promotions, the officers concerned must be prepared to be passed over when their turn for promotion comes.

Pilot Service : There is no justification for raising the pay of the Commander of Pilot Vessel.

It is true that Branch Pilot on promotion to the post of Commander, Pilot Vessel loses financially. But these two administrative posts were created in pursuance of the demands of the service for more administrative posts. If they want the administrative posts, they should be prepared for serving in these posts even though it may amount in some cases, to a financial loss on their part. If the Branch Pilots as Commanders do not want to serve in these posts, the Commissioners may not consider them for such promotions in future.

The maximum fixed for the Assistant Harbour Masters exceeds that of the Dredger and Despatch Service by Rs. 100. Whether this maximum is reasonable or not is a matter, which the Commissioners may take into consideration when considering for future entrants what should be the scale of pay.

Grant of a special compensatory allowance at the rate of Rs. 350 per month that is at the rate of the consolidated night fees, to the Branch Pilots acting as Commanders for seven days or more would not be justified.

It is also unfair that the senior most Branch Pilot should be repeatedly called upon to incure this loss and no one else. To obviate all these difficulties, short leave vacancies or casual leave vacancies should be filled up from amongst the Branch Pilots on a strictly rotational basis.

Further liberalization of the passage rules would not be proper.

The basic salary of the Assistant Port Pilotage Officer and the Port Pilotage Officer on the 'C' scale should be fixed at Rs. 1,875 and Rs. 1,950 per month respectively.

River Survey Service : The basic pay of the Deputy River Surveyor should be raised to Rs. 1,850 and that of the River Surveyor to Rs. 1,950.

There is no ground for increasing the car allowance of the River Surveyor.

Marine Engineer's Section: It would not be proper to fix for the Assistant Engineer Superintendent, a scale higher than that of the Chief Engineer.

The scale of the Engineer Superintendent should be Rs. 1,200-50-1,500-75-1,950.

The Commissioners may consider reducing the scale of pay of the Harbour Master and the Deputy Harbour Master for future entrants.

The special Committee's recommendation that the senior-most Chief Engineer be designated as "Commodore Chief Engineer' and he be paid a special pay of Rs. 250 per month should be implemented.

The scale of pay of the post of Assistant Conservator held by Shri B. L. Mital, may be raised to Rs. 1,200-50-1,500-75-1,950.

To compensate Sri B. L. Mital, Senior Assistatnt Conservator, for loss as a result of his promotion to the Post of Assistant Conservator, he should, in all fairness, be given an advance grade increment with effect from January 1, 1961 without effecting his usual increments.

There is no justification for granting to the Assistant Conservator, the concession of rent-free quarters.

The new scale recommended for the Deputy cons.rvator is Rs. 2,000-100-2,200.

RAILWAY ACCIDENTS INQUIRY ON THE CASUALTIES AMONG ROOF TRAVELLERS ON NO. 12 UP KUMAON EXPRESS AT JAMUNA BRIDGE BETWEEN RAYA AND MATHURA CANTT. STATIONS, NORTH EASTERN RAILWAY ON 8TH JULY, 1960—REPORT

Delhi, Manager of Publications, 1962. 4p.

One Man Commission : Shri A. C. Khastgir.

APPOINTMENT

The Inquiry was constituted on July 8, 1960 under the Ministry of Transport and Communications (Railway Inspectorate) in accordance with Rule 9 of Railway Board's Notification No. 1926-T, dated March 19, 1930.

TERMS OF REFERENCE

To inquire into the casualties amongst persons unauthorisedly travelling on the roofs of coaches of 12 Up Kumaon Express on Jamuna Bridge at mile 215/17 to 216/0-1, between Raya and Mathura Cantt. Stations on the Kasganj-Agra Fort metre gauge section of North Eastern Railway at about 03.42 hours on July 8, 1960.

CONTENTS

Summary; Inquiry; Brief Description of the Accident; Casualties; Composition of the Train; Damage; Relief arrangements; Restoration of Communications; Number of passengers; Weather Conditions; Description of local Conditions; Summary of Evidence and Discussion; Conclusions.

CONCLUSIONS

On full consideration of all the facts and material evidence, I have reached the conclusion that the grave loss of life and grievous injuries sustained by persons unauthorisedly travelling on the roofs of coaches of No. 12 Up Kumaon Express, while the train was travelling over Jamuna Bridge between Raya and Mathura Cantt. On July 8, 1960, was the result of their own rash and heedless behaviour, in violation of the provisions in Section 118 (2) of the Indian Railways Act, 1890, and the instructions contained in para 11 (vi) of 'Important Hints to Passengers' of the North-Eastern Railway Time Tables, April, 1960.

I hold the persons who travelled on the roofs of the coaches of 12 Up Express themselves responsible for the accident.

I am satisfied that medical relief and other relief measures were provided promptly and in a satisfactory manner.

STAFF WELFARE REVIEW COMMITTEE, 1960—REPORT

New Delhi, Ministry of Home Affairs, 1962. 196p.+ivp.

Chairman : Shri Fateh Singh.
Members : Shri P. G. Zachariah Shri R. Anandakrishna; Shri K. P. Sircar; Dr. B. R. Seth; Shri B. S. Srikantiah; Shri B. N. Malhan.
Secretary : Shri O. T. J. Zacharias.

APPOINTMENT

The Commission of Enquiry on emoluments and conditions of service of Central Government employees, commonly known as the Second Pay Commission, recommended in para 28 of Chapter XLIII of their Report that a Committee may be set up to undertake a review of the existing welfare arrangements for Central Government employees and make recommendations for their improvement. In pursuance of this recommendation, the Staff Welfare Review Committee was set up in August 1960.

TERMS OF REFERENCE

(i) To undertake a review of the existing welfare arrangements for Central Government employees; and

(ii) To make recommendations for their improvement.

CONTENTS

Introduction; Working Conditions; Residential Accommodation; Educational Facilities; Medical Facilities; Transport; Canteens; Promotion of Cooperatives; Staff Benevolent Funds; Staff Clubs; Grants-in-Aid for Provision of Amenities; Holiday Homes; Griha Kalyan Kendras (Family Welfare Centres); Welfare Services and Duties of Welfare Officers; Welfare Organisation; Summary of Recommendations; Appendices I to XI.

RECOMMENDATIONS

Working Conditions

In view of the imperative need for providing adequate office accommodation in the general pool, the cut made in the construction programme during the Third Five-Year Plan should be restored and the full amount of Rs. 35 crores to complete the original programme sanctioned.

Departments not included in the general pool should also re-examine the position and step up their building programme.

Since new constructions would take time, more accommodation shoul be taken on lease as a temporary measure. For this purpose, the prescribed rent ceilings may be reviewed and the procedure simplified to enable the local Heads of Departments to hire suitable accommodation.

It may also be worth while in places like Calcutta, Bombay, Madras, etc., to enter into agreements with private parties who are willing to put up office accommodation on reasonable terms and in suitable localities and thus acquire as much accommodation as possible.

The position regarding maintenance and repairs to existing buildings taken on lease should be reviewed and steps taken to maintain and equip them at the cost of Government, if necessary.

In planning office buildings, proper provision should be made for records, canteens, tiffin and recreation rooms for the staff.

In order to afford some immediate relief, Ministries/Departments may consider inter-change of existing accommodation, removal of old records to record rooms and reclamation of accommodation in the basement, outhouses, annexes etc.

Existing out-moded furniture should be replaced by modern utility furniture. An Expert Study Group may be appointed to go into this question.

Cabinets, racks and cup-boards for keeping records in office rooms should be built into or fixed along-side the walls. Only current records should be kept in office rooms.

Storage of records in record rooms should be so arranged as to fully utilise the available space. Record rooms should be adequately lighted and should provide space for the staff engaged in the weeding of old files.

The Caretaker of each Ministry should be made responsible for the maintenance of cleanliness in office rooms including the fittings therein. He should also be responsible for the maintenance of water coolers and supervision of cleanliness in lavatories. He should be provided with adequate staff for these purposes.

Corridors should be well-lit and cleared of all furniture. All improvised structures in them should be removed.

Lighting arrangements in office rooms should be improved by providing flourescent tubes.

Heating and cooling arrangements should be improved. Replacement of the existing air-conditioning and heating plants in the North and South Blocks should be completed as early as possible. In hutments, desert coolers should be provided in every room. If for any reason, this is not possible the, Ministry/Department concerned should arrange for the provision of good quality *khas khas* well in time before the advert of summer. The multi-storey buildings in New Delhi as well as elsewhere which were designed for air-conditioning should be provided with such plants with least possible delay.

Sufficient number of water coolers should be provided and they should be maintained properly.

There should be covered cycle stands with proper lighting and garages near office buldings.

Toilet facilities in hutments and rented buildings should be improvéd. Adequate water supply for lavatories, etc., should also be assured.

Each Ministry/Department should have its own library providing books of general interest. If the Ministry Department is not able to make arrangement their indoor games clubs should be encouraged to do so by giving them financial and other assistance.

There should be a dispensary with adequate staff in or near office buildings where a sufficiently large number of employees work. Each office should also be provided with well equipped first-aid boxes.

Each Minister/Department should have a recreation room.

In or near each office buliding, there should be adequate postal and banking facilities.

Residential Accommodation

The cut imposed in the funds asked for construction of quarters in the general pool under the Third Five Year Plan should, as far as possible, be restored consistent with other imperative needs.

In order to cover the shortage of accommodation in the general pool, temporary constructions should be undertaken as recommended by the Pay Commission.

Departments not covered by the general pool should review the requirements and take steps to provide at least temporary accommodation to their staff, particular attention being paid to the requirements of staff-employed in outlying areas and of the lower pay-groups.

The question of providing Class IV staff in Delhi with two-room quarters and a ceiling fan should be reconsidered when conditions are more favourable.

The quarters in the DIZ area and Minto Road lack several amenities available in New Quarters of the corresponding classes. This anomaly should be set right.

The demand from the occupants of 'F' and 'G' type quarters for an additional ceiling fan should be considered when conditions are more favourable.

The proposed construction of two hostels in Delhi for single officers—separately for men and women—should be expedited.

Special attention should be paid to provide basic amenities in Central Government colonies in Delhi. These should be proper coordination between the local bodies and the *C.P.W.D.* Quarters, particularly those built in places far away from the Secretariat, should not be allotted until the colony is self-contained in every respect. Committees of residents of the colonies should be constituted to look after the arrangements and to take up matters with the authorities concerned. Constructional defects should also be looked into by the *C.P.W.D.* and rectified. All open grounds should be levelled and adequate drainage provided.

Suitable transit accommodation should be provided in all important places for officers who are transferred or are on tour. Arrangements should be made with the State Governments for the elimination of discriminatory Treatment in regard to provision of accommodation in Dak Bangalows, Inspection Bangalows, etc., to Central Government officers who proceed on tour.

Government employees should be encouraged to form cooperative house-buldings societies. For this purpose, they should be given necessary facilities by way of loans.

Some working arrangements should be arrived at whereby Central Governments employees in Bombay can be given advances to purchase flats.

Educational Facilities

The recommendations of the Pay Commission should be implemented without further delay by encouraging the growth of schools with common syllabus and media of instruction, etc.

Arrangements should be made for the reservation of seats in one or two schools in the region/circle for children of employees who are subject to transfer within a region/circle only.

The pattern of assistance given to employees of the railways whose salary does not exceed Rs. 300 p.m.; to send their children boarding schools away from the place at which they are posted should be extended to other Central Government employees in similar circumstances.

Schools started on the initiative of employees themselves should be recognised and aided by the Central Government.

The State Government should be persuaded to reserve seats in colleges and technical institutions for the children of Central Government employees subject to transfer.

In Delhi, new schools for boys and girls as well as nursery schools should be set up simultaneously as new colonies come into being.

Private bodies of standing should be encouraged to start schools which would conform to the standards prescribed by the Central Government by giving them facilities like land, etc., if Government or municipal authorities cannot do so.

New colleges should be opened in the neighbourhood of Government colonies.

Medical Facilities

In Delhi the Contributory Health Service Scheme should be improved by providing more dispensaries to cover areas where none exist at present. Each dispensary should have suitable accommodation. Where necessary, the staff in dispensaries should be increased. Regional laboratories for pathological tests should be set up. The existing orders regarding prescription and issue of special medicines should be reviewed and liberalised. More specialists should be appointed and they should be attached to dispensaries conveniently located. Facilities should be improved for hospitalisation either by providing more beds in the existing hospitals or by opening a new hospital.

Families of Government servants suffering for T.B. who are on long leave without pay should continue to be entitled to the benefits of the Contributory Health Service Scheme even though the Government servant has ceased to pay his contribution.

The pattern and medical care and treatment available to Central Government employees stationed in places other than Delhi should be similar to that available under the C.H.S. Scheme.

As an interim measure, the State Governments should be requested to increase the number of authorised medical attendants and to give the same facilities to Central Government employees and members of their families as are given to their employees in regard to admission to hospitals. The working of the present certificate which Central Government employees are required to produce in order to avail of treatment at residence in respect of members of their families should be modified so that domiciliary treatment is made available in all deserving cases. A system should be worked out whereby reimbursement of medical expenses is expedited. Specialists should be available for consultations at dispensaries one or two days in a week.

Dispensaries may be established near groups of Central Government offices and in colonies, wherever they exists, of Central Government employees.

Artificial limbs, hearing aids, etc., should be provided free of cost when such disability is sustained during the course of performance of duties.

Transport

Specific claims for transport allowances should be examined further in the light of the general principles enunciated by the Pay Commission and with reference to local conditions.

The Departments concerned should make transport arrangements for employees who have to work outside the city limits and have to be on duty at odd hours, until such time as they can be provided with residential accommodation near their place of duty.

New buildings for offices which are being planned should, as far as possible, be constructed near residential colonies.

In major cities, an acceptable scheme of staggering office hours should be considered to eliminate difficulties of peak-hour traffic.

Advances for purchase of conveyances should be granted to all employees applying for them and the budget provision in this regard enhanced, if necessary.

Canteens

In all buildings where a substantial number of persons work, canteen facilities should be adequate.

In buildings, where there are several canteens as in the North and South Blocks, etc., a separate block should be put up nearly to house a big central canteen.

Canteens should be run departmentally and should be given financial assistance by Government.

Government should provide free accommodation, equipment and furniture and also subsidise the wagee of the canteen employees. The entire charges on water and electricity should be borne by Government. The cost of fuel in whatever form of energy should be borne by canteen.

The management of canteens should vest in a managing committee consisting of the Ministry Depart ment and the employees. It should be presided over by an officer nominated by the Head of the Department. Steps may also be taken to give this Committee a legal status.

A proper machinery may be set up for periodical cost accounting and frequent inspection. Accounts of the canteens should also be subjected to regular audit.

Promotion of Cooperatives

In each important city where there is a large con centration of Central Government employees, a con sumer cooperative society with branches at convenient points should be set up.

Consumer cooperatives should be given financial aid and Government should subscribe as much as 50 per cent of the share capital.

Consumer cooperatives may be granted subsidy to meet their establishment charges at a graduate scale. They should also be exempted from the payment of sales tax for an initial period of five years or if this is not possible, each wholesale store should be granted a subsidy equal to the amount paid by way of sales tax.

The Head of the Department or a senior officer nominated by him should be on the Managing Committee of the cooperatives. A senior officer, who should be assisted by a number of Inspectors, drawn from the cooperative department should be appointed to assist the Chief Welfare Officer in organising and supervising the work. Proper arrangements should also be made for the audit of consumer cooperative societies by attaching necessary special staff to the Staff Welfare Organisation.

Consumer cooperatives should be provided with free accommodation and equipment. They would also be given facilities to import supplies cost indent supplies direct from manufacturers and wholesalers, permission to obtain supplies from Ordnance and other Government factories on a priority basis and at Government rates, and obtain supplies through the *D.G.S. & D* on the same basis as other Government departments. They should be given the same rail and other transport facilities as are afforded to other Government departments. They should also be given facilities for the recovery of dues from the pay bills.

Cooperative thrift and credit societies of employees should be encouraged by State participation in the share capital or advance of substantial loans at a nominal rate of interest, provision of adequate accommodation and furniture. Facilities should also be provided for the recoveries of dues through pay bills and classical assistance give wherever necessary for an initial period of upto three years. The Head of the Department or a senior officer nominated by him should be the President of the Managing Committee. The machinery proposed for the organisation, supervision, etc., of consumer cooperatives may also be made responsible for the promotion, supervision, etc., of thrift and credit societies.

Staff Benevolent Fund

Government should make a contribution to the Fund every year. In the first year, there should be an outright grant at the rate of at least Re. one per head for the entire staff. In the subsequent years, this amount should be at least equivalent to that raised by the employees by voluntary subscriptions, subject to a limit of Re. one per head per annum.

Organisation of a 'Benevolent Fund Day' or arrangement of special charity shows may be useful means for raising funds.

An insurance scheme under which members takes a life insurance policy through the agency of the Fund may also be considered.

Officers outside Delhi may have one Central Fund or separate funds in each of their units depending upon the number of staff in each organisation.

Staff Clubs

Each member of the staff should be made to interest himself on one sport or the other suited to his talents and genius. Welfare officers should be closely associated with the working of these clubs. All gazetted officers, more particularly senior officers, should also take greater interest in the affairs of the staff clubs and takes part in one activity or other.

In all places, one or more covered badminton courts should be provided.

The constitution of Sport Boards should be examined with a view to making them more efficient and buisness-like and also with a view to bringing about greater uniformity in the matter of maintenance of accounts, stock registers, audit, conduct of tournaments, etc.

In the interest of efficient working of the Boards, the President and Vice-President should be nominated by the Secretariat Staff Welfare and Amenities Committee and a specific provision made in the constitution of the Boards to the effect that no elected office-bearer should hold an office for more than two consecutive terms.

A high-power committee consisting of Secretaries of Home, Education, Finance and Works, Housing and Supply Ministries should be set up to direct and coordinate the activities of the various Sports Boards.

Teams of Government employees from outstations should occasionally be invited to Delhi.

A sufficient number of playgrounds and a stadium with a swimming pool exclusively for the use of Secretariat staff should be provided in Delhi and other places where there is a concentration of Central Government employees.

Grants-in-Aid For The Provision Of Amenities

The amount of grant permissible should be determined on the basis of total strength including gazetted officers.

For places other than Delhi, where there is concentration of Central Government employees, grants-in-aid should be given for organising inter-developmental tournaments and competitions on the same lines as is being done in Delhi.

Grants should also be given for the purpose of extending Grih Kalyan Kendra Scheme to all places outside Delhi where Government Colonies exist.

Holiday Homes

As the bulk of Central Government employees are stationed in Delhi, a holiday home for the convenience of Government employees should be set up in Simla. The Cart Road chummeries can be re-built and re-modelled to serve the need.

To enable officers to spent their holidays at a hill-station, a portion of the Grand Hotel in Simla should be made available at concessional rates.

Holiday homes should provide all reasonable facilities for which a nominal rent or a graduated scale based on the pay of an emyloyee can be charged.

Arrangements may be made with the Railways to allow the concession of double-journey on payment of single-fare.

Excursion trips to places of interest should be organised on a wider scale.

Grih Kalyan Kendras (Family Welfare Centres)

In addition to community halls, one or two rooms in a quarter which a resident is prepared to spare, or C.H.S.S. dispensaries during off hours, shops in markets in residential colonies and where these are not available a quarter in the locality may be considered for accommodating the Grih Kalyan Kendra Centres.

A suitable building should be provided by Government for accommodating the headquarters of the organisation.

Additional administrative staff in the Ministry of Home Affairs, which should form part of the staff welfare organisation should be provided.

The scheme should be extended in course of time to all places where there is a large concentration of Central Government employees and a substantial number of them is housed in Government colonies.

The question of giving a legal status to the Grih Kalyan Kendra organisation may be examined.

Welfare Services And Duties Of Welfare Officers

The Welfare Officer should be associated with the various committees for the management of canteens, consumer and credit cooperatives, staff benevolent funds, staff clubs etc., in the Ministries/Departments as well as with associations in Government colonies in or near the area in which he resides.

The Welfare Officer should be in constant touch with members of the staff and be able to gain the confidence of the employees and assist them in solving their personal problems.

Welfare Officers should be provided with facilities like the minimum necessary clerical and field staff, a separate room in office, telephones both in office and residence an allowance to enable them to maintain a suitable conveyance and an imprest to meet unavoidable expenditure in emergencies.

Welfare Organisation

Each large organisation should have an officer specifically charged with the responsibility for promoting the welfare of the staff.

In offices where the strength is between 100 and 300, a full time Assistant Welfare Officer (Grade II) should be appointed. In offices where the strength of the staff is between 300 and 750, an Assistant Welfare Officer (Grade I) should be appointed. In offices where the strength is between 750 and 1,500, Welfare Officer should be appointed. Where in a single establishment the number exceeds 1,500, the Welfare Officer should be given the assistance of an Assistant Welfare Officer (Grade II) for every 500 employees.

The Chief Welfare Officer should be assisted by a Deputy Chief Welfare Officer and adequate staff; since his duties and responsibilities would increase considerably, the question of raising his status may be considered.

Welfare Officers in Ministries should be of the rank of Under Secretaries. In other cases, the scale of pay should be in Welfare Officers—Rs. 900-1,250, Assistant Welfare Officer (Grade I) Rs. 350-900 and Assistant Welfare Officer (Grade II) Rs. 275-530.

There should be a separate Welfare Officer attached to the Ministry of Home Affairs with a few Assistant Welfare Officers (Grade II) to look after the interests of the Colonies of Central Government employees.

Officers selected from the Ministries/Departments should be put through a short course of training. Those selected from the Labour Pool should also be sent for refresher courses in suitable institutions.

Welfare Officers should not be changed frequently.

In all important places outside Delhi, a high-power committee consisting of the local heads of all Central Government Departments should be set up to arrange sports and coordinate welfare activities. A senior officer of the State Government concerned should also be represented on this Committee.

OIL PRICE ENQUIRY COMMITTEE, 1960—REPORT

Delhi, Manager of Publications, 1961. 121p.

Chairman: Shri K. R. Damle.
Members: Shri P. N. Sapru (resigned; replaced by Shri C. P. Sinha); Shri N. Krishnan.
Secretary: Shri N. R. Law.

APPOINTMENT

The Government of India, Minsitry of Steel Mines & Fuel, Department of Mines and Fuel, in their Memorandum No. 101 (II)/60-PPD, dated August 2, 1960, appointed a Committee to examine the principles and elements according to which the selling prices of various petroleum products in India should be determined after April 1, 1961.

TERMS OF REFERENCE

To examine and report on—

(a) The cost at which crude oil and the various efined petroleum products can be imported;

(b) Whether the "port charge element" in oil prices can be adjusted on a flat basis irrespective of the particular port to which any supply area is linked;

(c) in keeping with the relevant clauses of the existing agreement relating to the establishment of the two refineries at Bombay and the refinery at Visakhapatnam, how should be ceilings be determined for the ex-refinery prices of their products;

d) whether the time is opportune for evolving a railway freight pool system in respect of oil products;

e) whether along with such pooling, or irrespective of the same, for reduction of the imbalance in consumption particularly, principles can be evolved for having a common tariff of railway freight in respect of petroleum products irrespective of whether they are of the dangerous or non-dangerous category;

(f) to what extent more efficient and economic arrangements can be introduced for unloading, storage and distribution of petroleum product inland.

(g) the best manner in which the oil industry can enlist service cooperatives in the marketing and distribution of such petroleum products as are in daily use in almost every household like, particularly, Kerosene;

(h) in keeping with the needs of conservation of foreign exchange, stabilisation of prices, raising of internal resources, and the overall development of the planned economy, to what extent the pricing mechanisms in respect of petroleum products should be used for purposive influencing of production, transport, distribution and consumption patterns.

CONTENTS

Introduction; Establishment of Refineries; History and the Trading results of the Oil Companies; Pricing Procedure in the Past; Cost of imported crude oil; Cost of Refined Petroleum Products; Pricing Formula; Pricing of Indigenous Products ex-Digboi; Demand; Marketing and Disrtibution Charges; Packed-Bulk Differential; Pooling of Port charges; Pooling of Railway Freight; Common Railway Tariff for Dangerous and Non-Dangerous Products; Profit; Future Ceiling Selling Prices; Comparison of Proposed Basic Ceiling Selling-Prices with the Corresponding Existing Prices; General—Period of Pricing Formula and the Fluctuation in the Price Structure; Imbalance in Production and Consumption of Products; Unloading, Storage and Distribution of Petroleum Products; Service Cooperatives for Distribution of Petroleum Products; Summary of Conclusions; Acknowledgments; Statements 1 to 14; Annexure 1; Appendices I to III.

RECOMMENDATIONS

All the three coastal refineries obtain their requirements of crude oil from their overseas suppliers, who are themselves not original producers/suppliers of crude oil. The companies are unable to disclose the names of their original suppliers. We fail to see why the companies could not deal with the original producers/suppliers of crude oil or furnish information regarding the names of such original producers/suppliers. The oil companies with their world wide connections should normally be capable of dealing directly with the Consortium operating in Iran, in which their principals have interest, in respect of supplies through that source, and also with the original producers/suppliers at other places.

The prices of crude oil are based on the posted price thereof obtaining in the Persian Gulf, subject to discount on c. i. f. cost. With effect from 1st June, 1960 Burmah Shell obtained or discount of about eight per cent and from 1st July, 1960 S.V.O.C. obtained almost the same discount and Caltex too obtained almost the same discount with effect from August 1960. No discount was available on crude oil obtained from Indonesia.

Caltex should press its suppliers for equivalent discount on "Minas" crude oil obtained from Indonesia or consider the discontinuance of the use of this oil in favour of a discounted crude oil from the Persian Gulf; unless Government is satisfied that the continued use of "Minas" crude oil is advantageous to the overall economy and conducive to saving in foreign exchange in regard to furnished products.

The oil companies should recognise the advent of a new set of circumstances in a long term commitments of the nature of their Refinery Agreements and not insist on import of crude oil from sources of their choice only so long as the profitability of the refinery is not affected and at least, they should press on their suppliers for equivalent discount as available to India on a long term continuous basis on imports of the same quality of crude oil from sources other than traditional.

It is difficult to appreciate how the intermediary firms, through whom supplies are obtained, subsist without charging anything extra on transactions passing through their hands.

It should normally have been possible for the oil companies to successfully bargain for discounts on posted prices for their requirements of crude oil, long before discounts were conceded at the current rates. They should not only press on their suppliers for the continuance of discounts in future but also for increase in quantum thereof, consistent with the market trends prevailing from time to time.

The discounts on posted prices of crude oil should, in more or less equivalent measure, be reflected in the pricing of end-products. The recent discounts on crude oil are not reflected in the prices of end-products and the benefit thereof is absorbed by the refiners/consigners. To this extent, their margin has been enhanced above the expectation envisaged at the time of conclusion of the Refinery Agreements.

The availability of discounts on crude oil should be taken into account for allocation of foreign exchange.

For import of deficit refined products, the procedure followed by the three major oil companies is almost similar to that for crude oil and our observations regarding the latter are equally applicable in regard to Bulk Refined Products for Burmah Shell and Caltex.

The statement of the oil companies that the suppliers of Bulk Refined Products do not charge any fee or commission for the services rendered, apart from chargeing out-of pocket expenses, does not stand to reason, particularly when the services rendered include even arrangement for financing.

As discounts are admittedly available in crude oil, there is every reason to believe that the discounts should also be available on refined products.

Two oil companies admitted that they obtain their imports at discounted prices. The products imported by them are not identical and the rates of discount vary for the different products. This shows that the availability of discounts depends upon the bargaining capacity of the individual marketing company. The major oil companies, with their world-wide, connections and long experience in the oil business, should be able to exert sufficient pressure on the suppliers of Bulk Refined Products in obtaining discount on their supplies.

The stipulation in the Refinery Agreements for determination of prices products on "import parity" is not intended to preclude the availability of supplies in the Indian market of products from sources other than those of the major oil companies. Therefore, it would be quite appropriate to base the landed cost of products on imports at cheaper rates, if available, from sources other than those, which have been normally utilised by the major oil companies provided continuous supply of equivalent quality is guaranteed.

The inability of the oil companies to obtain discounts for the import of products from their supplies is no proof of the position sought to be established that discounts are not available in the Middle East.

The major oil companies have been quoting for supplies, particularly H. S. D., rates lower than the landed cost of imports from Russia. Such under-quoting would only be possible, if substantial discounts were available to them on f. o. b. postings.

Discounts at the following rates have been taken in the determination of parity prices and the same should also be adopted for the calculation of foreign exchange requirements for imports of deficit products :—

Kerosene (Superior & Inferior)	.... 10%	on f. o. b.
Aviation Turbine Fuel	.... 10%	"
High Speed Diesel Oil	.... 10%	"
Motor Spirit	.... 5%	"
Light Diesel Oil	.... 9.3%	"
Furnace Oil	.... 3%	"

S. V. O. C. should endeavour to reduce (and eventually eliminate altogether) the payment of charges to S. V. S. S., London and its New York Office.

A pricing formula is evolved only for Bulk Refined Products and Bitumen. 'Lubricants and Greases' and 'Specialities have been grouped for the purpose of control of distribution costs and profits. Hot Heavy Stock, Low Sulphur Fuel Oil, Liquified Petroleum Gas, Boiler Fuel and Chemicals have been excluded from the purview of the proposed pricing formula.

The f. o. b. cost of Bulk Refined Products shall be determined at the lowest posted prices of any company regularly posting in Abadan, as reported by Platt's Oilgram Daily Reporting Service.

In the prices evolved, f. o. b. quotations as applicable on 24th May 1961 (and reported in Platt's Oilgram Price Service No. 102, dated 25th May 1961) have been adopted, subject to discounts mentioned in paragraph 6.14.

Ocean freight has been calculated at the AFRA rate ex-Abadan as applicable in the second quarter of 1961.

Bombay has been taken on a single part discharge, Madras Visakhapatnam, Calcutta on a double port discharge at the Calcutta rate and Kandla/Okha/Cochin on a double port discharge at the Cochin rate.

Marine insurance, excluding War Risk Insurance has been included. War Risk Insurance will be added separately in case of emergency.

Ministry of Finance (Department of Economic Affairs) should take up with the Indian Insurance Companies Association, the question of undertaking marine insurance of petroleum products at the rates available to the oil companies from other sources. The risks covered should also be comparable to the risk covered under the arrangement at present followed by the oil companies.

Ocean loss has been included in the pricing formula as a percentage on c.i.f. cost on the basis of the past experience of the oil companies.

To convert the f.o.b. prices, ex-source of import into Rupees, at the landing port in India, we have adopted the following conversion factors :—

Product	A.G @ 60°F per long ton	I.G. @85°F per long ton	Factor of f o.b. A.G. to f.o.b/I.G.	Combined factor of cents per A.G. to Rs. per I.G. 4×0.0477	Combined factor of cents per A.G. to Rs. per kilo litre
1	2	3	4	5	6
Aviation Spirit 100/130 Octane	375.42	317.47	1.1825	0.0564	12.4066
Aviation Spirit 115/145 Octane	328.24	323.84	1.1803	0.0563	12.3846
Aviation Spirit 73 clear	378.65	320.21	1.1825	0.0564	12.4046
Aviation Turbine Fuel	341.90	288.44	1.1853	0.0565	12.4286
Motor Spirit	376.81	319.00	1.1812	0.0563	12.3846
High Speed Diesel Oil	323.10	271.74	1.1890	0.0567	12.4726
Kerosene Superior	340.26	287.06	1.1853	0.0565	12.4286
Kerosene Inferior	323.98	273.15	1.1861	0.0566	12.4506
Vapourising Oil	328.88	277.46	1.1853	0.0565	12.4286
Light Diesel Oil *	...	262.00	...	...	...
Furnace Oil	281.18	238.75	1.1802	0.0563	13.2292 per metric ton

* L.D.O. = 90% Kerosene Inferior (No. 2 Fuel) and 10% of Furnace Oil (Bunker C Fuel).

Rate of exchange has been adopted at U.S. Dollars 2.80 per Pound Sterling (within a range of Dollar/Sterling of $ 2.78 to $ 2.82). The current rate of exchange of Pound Sterling at Rs. 13.3565 has been adopted.

Basic Duties and Surcharges have been included in the prices as applicable for the imported counterpart adjusted to normal temperature of the landing port on an all-India basis taken at 29.4°c or 65°F at the standard conversion factors referred to earlier. In the event of variations in the level of Customs Duty and Surcharges resulting from discussions by the Oil Industry Metric Committee with the Ministry of Commerce and Industry, suitable adjustments should be made.

Rates of wharfage included in the prices are as applicable during January 1961.

Other compulsory landing charges are based on the past experience of the oil companies.

In the absence of posted price for Bitumen, f.o.b. cost is determined on the basis of the Suppliers invoices. For this, Bombay port landed cost is based on bulk parity, while for other ports, it is determined on packed parity.

Marine freight for bulk Bitumen is included at the rates for premium rated vessels as applicable in the second quarter of 1951. Marine freight for packed supplies has been included at the rates indicated by the London Freight Brokers Association on 12th January, 1961.

Insurance and Ocean loss have been provided on the same lines as for Bulk Refined Products.

Customs Duty has been calculated at the rate of 27 per cent on a provisional tariff value of Rs. 231 per metric ton for Straight Grades and Rs. 280 per metric ton for Cutbacks, both packed in drums. In case Bitumen Straight Grade is supplied in bulk, the relevant Customs Duty at 27 per cent on a provisional tariff value of Rs. 138 per metric ton will have to be substituted. In case of Bitumen ex A.O.C., the Customs Duty at 27 per cent on the respective tariff value will be substituted. In the event of the tariff valuation being different suitable adjustment should be made in Customs Duty.

To rationalise the distribution system for Motor Spirit and H.S.D., free delivery zone has been created for H.S.D., as for Motor Spirit. The oil companies should issue specific instructions, under advice to Government, that the dealers should not make a further charge on account of delivery of H.S.D., within the free delivery zone.

The expenses against which specific recoveries are made at present have been included in the prices. Delivery ex-Airfield pump will, therefore, no longer, involve payment of extra charges. The oil companies should bring this fact prominently to notice at the Airfields.

The charges for delivery beyond the companies' storage points of kerosene, Vaporising Oil, Furnace Oil, Light Diesel Oil and Bituman have been exclud de from the basic ceiling selling prices.

A differential between the selling prices at International Airfields and other International Airfields has been maintained.

The three major oil companies handle approximately 89 per cent of the entire trade in Lubricants and Greases and the balance is handled by smaller companies numbering about 175. The bulk of the sales of Lubricants and Greases is made from the main installations and only about 1/3rd of the sales are made at the up-country depots.

For 'Lubricants and Greases' and 'specialities', control should be imposed by fixing an overall ceiling limit for marketing charges and profit margin, on an average for all the products coming under these groups. The ceiling limit will be Rs. 123.02 per kilolitre for Lubricants and Greases and Rs. 31.28 per kilolitre for specialities.

The oil companies shall be permitted to recover the cost of materials, blending charges and the packaging and filling-in charges at actual rates. In case recovery towards marketing and distribution charges and profit margines per unit during a financial period exceeds the ceilings proposed. the oil companies should suitably revise the price structure of the various products within the respective group.

The prices for the A.O.C. products have been determined on parity with the prices ex f.o.r., Calcutta, subject to differential being maintained for lower diesel index of H.S.D.

There has been a progressive increase over the past years in the consumption of petroleum products and the demand will continue to increase considerably during the Third Plan Period.

The average increase in volume for each of the three years 1962-1964 is estimated at about 25 per cent for the three major oil companies.

The overall unit incidence in 1959 shaved a decrease specially in regard to Bulk Refined Products as a group in respect of all the companies. This is largely attributable to increase in the volume of sales in 1959 over 1958.

Burmah Shell and S.V.O.C. handle about 80 per cent of the total sales of petroleum products and would, therefore, represent the cross-section of the Industry. In each of the three years 1962-1964, the estimate of sales will be about 22 per cent over 1959 for Burmah Shell and about 25 per cent over 1959 for S V.O.C.

In estimating the future marketing and distribution charges, suitable provision has been made for (i) increase in expenditure or the higher anticipated volume of sales, (ii) for effecting free deliveries of Aviation Spirit/Gasoline and Aviation Turbine Fuel from the companies storage points to the Airfield outlets/Aircraft and Motor Spirit, Gasoline and H.S.D. at the Retail Pump Outlets within the free delivery zone in port and municipal towns and (iii) for unrecovered freight and bridging costs.

The weighted average of the marketing and distribution charges of Burmah Shell and S. V. O. C. has been adopted as the fair incidence for the Industry.

The packed-bulk differential for 18.18 litre tins (4 I. G.) is assessed at Rs. 1.88 per container, based on the price of Rs. 1407.4 per metric ton of tin plate.

Introduction of uniform port charges in the price structure is not considered advisable.

Introduction of a railway freight pooling system is also not considered advisable and the maintenance of **status quo** is recommended. B. O. C. (I. T.) Ltd., which has been operating a freight pool system in its area may, however, continue to do so.

The present classification of products into dangerous and non-dangerous categories in regard to railway freight should continue.

Based on the capital employed in 1959 of Burmah Shell and S. V. O. C., the requirements of capital employed for both the companies for their future sales have been estimated. A return of 12 per cent on capital employed has been allowed.

The basic ceiling selling prices for Bulk Refined Products as evolved should be applicable for delivery as under:—

Aviation Spirit/Aviation Gasoline and Aviation Turbine Fuel.	Ex-Oil Company's storage point and ex-Airfields/Air-craft.
Motor Spirit and H. S. D.	Ex-Oil Company's storage points and Retail pump Outlets within free delivery zone.
Kerosene, Vaporising Oil, Light Diesel Oil, Furnace Oil and Bitumen.	Ex-Oil Company's storage points.

Further charges will be payable, whenever applicable on account of railway freight, Local duties/taxes, specific delivery and supplies in returnable packages. Railway freight from companies' storage points to up-country points will apply at the bulk rate for bulk despatches and at the packed rate for supplies in packages.

The prices evolved should come into effect from 1st September 1961 and remain in force till 31st March 1965, subject to fluctuations as suggested. The control on Lubricants and Greases and Specialities should be valid for the same period.

The employment of price mechanism for the correction of imbalance is not favoured and the solution thereof should be sought in technological adjustments in production pattern and in findings alternative use for surplus products.

The oil companies do the loading/unloading through a system of contractors appointed as a result of tenders or by negotiations. The rates paid are not unreasonable.

If service cooperatives are capable of undertaking distribution of kerosene and other Petroleum Products, preference should be given to them.

Paragraph mentioned from the report 6.14

The products which have been discounted are mainly Kerosene, Aviation Turbine Fuel, High Speed Diesel Oil, Motor Spirit and Furnace Oil. The rates of discounts vary in the case of different sources. On the material available to us, we noticed that discounts generally fluctuate within the range 10 to 15 per cent in the case of Kerosene, High Speed Diesel Oil and Aviation Turbine Fuel. In the case of Motor Spirit and Furnace Oil, lower rates of discount have been disclosed to us and they vary between 3 to 5 per cent. We are informed that Light Diesel Oil is a combination of Inferior Kerosene and Furnace Oil in the proportion of 9:1. Since its components are subject to discounts, proportional discounts would also be available for the final products. We, therefore, consider that discounts at the following rates should be taken in the determination of parity prices and the calculation of foreign exchange requirements for import of deficit products:

	per cent
Kerosene (Superior & Inferior)	10
Aviation Turbine Fuel	10
High Speed Diesel Oil	10
Motor Spirit	5
Light Diesel Oil	9·3
Furnace Oil	3

THE COMMITTEE ON MANAGERIAL PERSONNEL, 1960—REPORT

New Delhi, Ministry of Education, 1964, 76p.

Chairman : Dr. A. Ramaswami Mudaliar.
Members : Dr. V.K.R.V. Rao ; Dr. M.V. Mathur ; Shri R. Prasad ; Shri Pitamber Pant ; Shri K. Khosla ; Shri Y.A. Fazalbhoy ; Prof. A. Das Gupta.
Secretary : Shri M.V.D. Nair.

APPOINTMENT

The Committee on Managerial Personnel was constituted under the All India Board of Technical Studies at its Meeting held on August 27, 1960, to assess the requirements of managerial personnel for the country's development programme in the private and public sectors.

TERMS OF REFERENCE

To assess the requirements of managerial personnel for the country's development programme in the private and public sectors.

CONTENTS

Terms of Reference and Definitions; Requirements of Managerial Personnel for Manufacturing Industries ; Managerial Personnel Requirement for Sectors other than Industry ; Management Cadres and Present Training Facilities ; Requirements of Managerial Personnel for the Third and Fourth Plans and Provision of Increased Facilities for Training in Management ; Appendices I to VII.

RECOMMENDATIONS

Definitions

In an industrial establishment "Management functions" are exercised in varying degrees from the lowest supervisor to the topmost executive. Supervisory personnel carrying out routine technical operations fell outside the scope of the work of the Committee. The term 'Manager' could better be defined in terms of his functions and position of responsibility. The major managerial functions are generally as under :

1. General Management.
2. Production.
3. Sales.
4. Research and Engineering.
5. Finance.
6. Law.
7. Personnel.
8. Public Relations.
9. Traffic.
10. Office Management.
11. Purchasing.
12. Plant Management.

A Manager is, therefore, a person who carries out one or more of the above functions.

The production functions may be stated to have the following contents in general :

1. Design and construction of plants.
2. Planning and justifying plant capital expenditure.

3. Supervision of production orders received.

4. Promise of delivery schedule of manpower equipment and material flaw, coordination with sales.

5. Planning of the production flow and assignment of orders.

6. Supervision of production.

7. Development of production controls, such as:

(a) Coordination with marketing and engineering.

(b) Quality control.

(c) Control of over-all production, machine and manpower performance, purchasing, design of plant and product, plant maintenance, inventory, industrial relations, research, traffic, safety, engineering and industrial engineering.

The content makes it clear that managerial training is essential for production personnel.

In pursuance of the decision taken at the first meeting, letters were sent to important industrialists, both in the public and private sectors, Managing Directors of Banks and commercial organisations, to obtain information necessary to assess the requirements of managerial personnel for the country's planned development. The letter conveyed that the purpose of the Enquiry was assess the requirements of managerial personal who may be trained in the theory and practice of management, with a view to determine the extent of facilities that should be organised in the country for the training of such personnel. To enable this to be done, information was sought on the existing managerial personal in the following fields of management.

(a) Technical Management comprising Production Management, Development Management and Transport Management.

(b) Commercial Management comprising Distribution Management, Sales Management, and Financial Management.

(c) General Management comprising Office Management, Personnel Management and General Management.

It was also pointed out that the Board of Technical Studies in Management had organised courses of study in Business Management and Industrial Management for persons working in industrial and commercial establishments who were graduates in Engineering, Science and Arts and who had a minimum of two years requisite supervisory experience. Suggestions were also sought as to additional centres which should be organised for providing facilities for training in management. Comments too were invited on the steps to be taken to promote management education.

The relative importance of requisite abilities of managerial personnel in industrial concerns generally varies with the size of the concern. The great French Industrialist, Henry Fayol, has drawn up a chart of the requisite abilities in the various types of concerns. These are as follows:

Requisite Abilities

	Managerial %	Technical %	Commercial %	Financial %	Security %	Accounting %	Total Evaluation %
One-man business	15	40	20	10	5	10	100
Small firm	25	30	15	10	10	10	100
Medium-sized firm	30	25	15	10	10	10	100
Large firm	40	15	15	10	10	10	100
Very large firm	50	10	10	10	10	10	100
State enterprise	60	8	8	8	8	8	100

From this table the following conclusions may be drawn:

(1) The most important ability of the head of the small industrial company is technical ability.

(2) In medium-size industries, managerial ability increases and that of technical ability declines.

(3) In large-scale industries, the managerial coefficient increases at the expense of the rest, which tend to even out, approximating upto one-tenth of the total evaluation.

Apart from the size, there are other factors which decide the number of managerial personnel in a concern. Two of these are: (1) competitive nature of the product; (2) end use of the commodity.

In the case of a competitive commodity, there are several establishments producing the same goods and large number of managerial personnel will have to be employed for the proper organisation of sales and services. Consumer industries employ a larger number of managerial personnel than industries manufacturing raw materials and chemicals required for industry itself.

An important factor that has to be taken note of in estimating the facilities required for the training of managerial personnel is that even if no facilities are provided, the industrial targets of production aimed at and the expansion of trade commerce, construction and transportation will not be physically affected though efficiency would be markedly less. The fundamental principles of organisation and administration which are common to different types of activities can be taught and should be taught. They can also be laboriously acquired by individuals by a process of trial and error. In Indian Industry at present, it is by this trial and error method that principles of management are imbibed by the large majority of persons in managerial positions. There are many countries in the world where even today there are no specially organised educational facilities for training in management and yet these countries have reached commendable industrial levels. The management movement in the country is in its infancy and better organisation of industrial production and business efficiency would ultimately depend on the success of the movement.

Requirements Of Managerial Personnel For Manufacturing Industries

The first step in the assessment of managerial personnel is the estimation of the managerial norm. The managerial norm is the over-all percentage of the number of managerial personnel to the total number of persons employed.

The managerial norms have to be fixed in relation to a particular point of time. The commencement of the Third Plan has been taken as the point of time for the purpose of calculation in this Report. Modern techniques of production, rationalisation, and increased efficiency would tend to lower manpower requirements. Consequently, there would be an automatic reduction in managerial personnel requirements also.

A change-over from a medium-sized industry to a large-sized industry, would increase the requirements of managerial personnel by 20 per cent. If an industry is nationalised, a still higher percentage of managerial personnel would be required. To the extent possible, these considerations have been taken note of in fixing norms for the industry The managerial norm for a particular industry or type of industry is decided on the basis of replies furnished to the questionnaire with such modifications as may be necessary taking into consideration the size of the concern and other relevant factors.

The requirements of management personnel industry-wise are indicated below.

Industrial Machinery Equipment Manufacturing Industries.

From the analysis of the figures of employment and production in the following industrial establishments, it has been deduced that for every crore of output the number of persons employed is 800 :

The managerial norms for the various industries are shown in column no. 2:

Name of the Industry	Norms for Technical management	Norms for General and Commercial Management
1	2	3
1. Industrial machinery	0.5%	0.5%
2. Equipment manufacturing industries	0.5%	0.5%
3. Iron and steel	0.38%	0.2 %
4. Aluminium	0.5%	0 5%
5. Copper, lead and zinc	0.5%	0.5%
6. Precision instruments (industrial and scientific)	1%	1.2%
7. Surgical instruments	1%	0.7%
8. Automobile and ancillary industries		
Passenger cars, commercial Vehicles, jeeps & station wagons	0.65%	0.45%
Sewing machines	0.4%	1.1%
Bicycles	0.4%	1.1%
Ship building expansion of Hindustan Shipyard and second shipyard dry docks	1.5%	0.5%
9. Fertilisers	0.5%	0.5%
10. Cotton textiles	0.3%	0.3%
11. Salt	0.4%	0.2%
12. Vanaspati	1%	1%
13. Paper and paper board	1%	1.5%
14. Cement	0.22%	0.33%
15. Glass and glassware	0.9%	1.00%
16. Soap	0.5%	1%
17. Synthetic rubber	1 26%	1.84%
18. Plastics	1%	0.5%
19. Refractors	1%	1%
20. Power and industrial alcohol	1%	1%
21. Industrial gases	0.9%	2.8%
22. Petroleum products crude oil	1%	2%

1. Hindustan Cables Limited.
2. Chittaranjan Locomotive Works Limited.
3. Ashok Leyland Limited.

In regard to three items, however, viz., Machine Tools, Gear Industry and Ceramic Refractories, this ratio does not apply as these industries employ more persons per crore of production. From the figures furnished by the Hindustan Machine Tools Limited the Indian Telephone Industries Limited, etc., it was observed that this type of industry requires 1,000 persons for every crore of production.

The managerial norm for the industry is 0.5 per cent for Technical Management and 0.5 per cent for General and Commercial Management. The following is the statement indicating the additional management personnel required for achieving the targets of production indicated in the Third Plan.

Sl. No.	Industry	Production 1960 (Rs. crores)	Tentative estimated Production (1965) (Rs. crores)	No. of Persons in Employment in 1960	Estimated Additional Employment	No. of Managerial Personnel Required	
						Tech. management	Genl. & commercial management
1	2	3	4	5	6	7	8
A.	Industrial machinery and equipment manufacturing industries :						
1.	Paper making machinery	Negl.	7.0	Negl.	560	3	3
2.	Sugar mill machinery	4.2	12.0	3,360	6,240	31	31
3.	Cement machinery	0.6	8.0	5,480	5,760	30	30
4.	Boiler machinery	0.5	30.0	400	23,600	120	120
5.	Textile machinery :						
	Cotton textile machinery	11.0	21.0	8,800	8,000	40	40
	Jute mill machinery	2.2	2.5	1,760	240	3	3
6.	Coal mining oil and other mining machinery and equipment						
	Coal mining, oil and other mining machinery etc.	Negl.	15 0	Negl.	12,000	60	60
	Coal washeries	Negl.					
7.	Structural (fabrication) and cranes :						
	(i) Structural	20.0	100.0	16,000	64,000	320	320
	(ii) Cranes	0.5	15.0	400	11,600	55	55
8.	Tractors and earth moving equipment :						
	(i) Agricultural tractors and implements	0.2	15.0	160	11,840	60	60
	(ii) Earth moving machinery and equipment	Nil	12.5	Nil	10,000	50	50
	(iii) Road rollers	1.5	3.0	1,200	1,200	6	6
9.	Chemical plants	1.4	20.0	1,120	14,880	75	75
10.	Power driven pumps	3.0	3.0	2,400	1,600	8	8
11.	Diesel engines	8.2	20.0	4,950	7,050	35	35
12.	Printing machinery	Negl.	1.6	Negl.	1,280	6	6
13.	Dairy machinery	0.2	2.3	160	1,680	8	8
14.	Gear industry	0.1	2.1	120	2,400	14	14
15.	Building and construction machinery	1.0	4.0	800	2,400	14	14
16.	Tea processing machinery	1.2	1.5	960	250	3	3
17.	Machine tools	10.0	45.0	10,000	35,000	175	175
18.	Compressors	1.5	5.0	1,200	2,800	15	15
19.	Industrial flour mill machinery	Nil	0.3	Nil	250	3	3
20.	Ceramics and refactory	0.1	0.6	160	800	4	4

1	2	3	4	5	6	7	8
21.	Locomotives, wagons and railway equipment :						
	(i) Locomotives	13.0	17.0	18,000	5,500	28	28
	(ii) Railway wagons	8.1	20.0	6,560	9,520	48	48
	(iii) Coaches	22.9	65.7	9,000	9,000	45	45
	(iv) Railway stores and equipment	21.6	61.5	21,600	40,000	200	200
22.	Conveyers and other material handling equipment	1.3	7.7	1,040	5,120	26	26
23.	Steel plant machinery	Nil	5.0	Nil	4,000	20	20
	Total	114.3	465.3	—	—	1,505	1,505
B.	Electrical machinery and equipment manufacturing industries :						
1.	Electric motors	8.3	25.0	6,640	13,360	67	67
2.	Transformers	6.6	20.0	5,180	10,720	54	54
3.	Switch gear and control gear	4.0	15.0	3,200	8,800	44	44
4.	Cable and wires	27.0	75.5	33,600	38,800	190	190
5.	Heavy electrical machinery and equipment	Nil	35.0	Nil	28,000	140	140
	Grand Total A & B	160.2	635.8	16,4250	408,170	2,000	2,000

Iron And Steel Industry

Tata Iron and Steel Company Ltd., has been taken as the representative firm in this category. In 1960-61, this firm produced about two million tons of Steel ingots and had a labour force of 38,000. On this basis, the then existing total labour force in the steel industry was 66,500. The total additional labour force for the production of additional 6.7 million tons of steel will, therefore, be 126,550. The managerial norm for iron and steel production is 0.38 per cent for technical management and 0.27 per cent for general management. This managerial norm applies to all types of production in this category. The additional 6.7 million tons will be distributed as follows :

	millions
Bhilai	2.0
Rourkela	1.8
Durgapur	1.6
Mysore Iron & Steel Works	0.1
Bokaro	1.0
Private Sector (Tata Iron & Indian Iron)	0.2
	6.7

The additional managerial personnel required for technical management is 483 and for commercial management is 335 for achieving this target.

Applied Tool And Special Steel

40,000 tons of applied tool and special steel were produced by the end of 1960-61. By 1965-66, it is expected that production would be of the order of 200.000 tons. The additional capacity will be in the following centres :

	Tons
Durgapur Plant	1,00,000
Ordinance Factory, Kanpur	25,000
Ordinance Factory, Ishapur	25,000
Private Industry	10,000
	1,60,000

For production of 25,000 tons of special steel, four managerial personnel under Technical Management and three for General Management is required. This would be the minimum irrespective of the tonnage produced. The total requirements of management personnel in this category is 28 for Technical Management and 18 for General and Commercial Management.

Grey Iron Castings, Steel Castings And Steel Forging

About 700,000 tons of grey iron castings, steel castings and steel forging were produced by the end of 1960-61. The Third Plan targets for these are 1.2 million tons of grey iron castings and 200,000 tons each for steel castings and steel forging. The following is the distibution of additional centres :

	Steel castings	Grey Iron castings	Steel Forgings
	Tons	Tons	Tons
Forge and Foundry, Ranchi	45,000	38,000	69,700
Durgapur Mining Machinery Plant	6,000	11,000	7,000
Hindustan Machine Tools, Bangalore	—	6,000	—
Durgapur, Bhilai, Rourkela	15,000	75,000	—
Chittaranjan Loco	10,000	3,000	—
Foundaries attached to Railway Workshops	—	6,000	—
	76,000	139,000	76,700

The followings will be the share of the private sector :

Steel Castings 74,000 tons

Steel Forgings 88,300 tons

On the basis of managerial norms as for special steel, the additional managerial personnel required is 100 for techninical mangement and 75 for commercial and general management. The total managerial personnel required for Iron and Steel Industry to achieve the planned target of production is 631 for technical management and 428 for general and commercial management.

Non-Ferrous Metals

In this category are aluminium, copper, lead and zinc. The following tables gives the actual production in 1960-61, estimated production in 1965-66, number of persons in employment in 1960-61, additional persons required for development and the additional managerial personnel for technical management and general commercial management.

Name of Industry	Production 1960-61	Production Estimated 1965-66	Number of Persons Employed 1960-61	Additional Number of Persons Required	Additional Number of Managerial Personnel Required	
					Technical Management	General and Commercial Management
	Tons	Tons				
1. Aluminium	18,500	87,500	14,000	69,300	350	350
2. Copper	8,900	22,000	7,000	10,000	50	50
3. Lead	3,500	8,500	3,500	8,500	43	43
4. Zinc	Nil	15,000	Nil	15,000	75	75
					518	518

The returns furnished by the Indian Aluminium Company have been taken as the basis for the calculation of managerial norms which are 0.5 per cent for technical management and 0.5 per cent for general commercial management. The additional number of managerial personnel required for the non-ferrous industries during the Third Plan is 518 for technical management and 518 for general commercial management. The development of the industry is in the following centres :

Aluminium

	Tons
Indian Aluminium Company's Plant Hirakund	10,000
Indian Aluminium Company's Plant, Alwaye	5,000
Smelter at Rihand	20,000
Smelter at Koyna	20,000
Smelter at Salem	10,000
Aluminium Corporation of India	5,000
Copper	
Khetri and Deribo Copper Mines	11,500
Zinc	
Zawar Mines, Rajasthan	15,000

Miscellaneous Industries

The following table gives the production in 1960-61, estimated production in 1965-66, persons employed in 1960-61, additional persons required for the development and managerial norms for technical management and general commercial management and additional managerial personnel required for technical and general management.

Sl. No.	Name of Industry	Produc- 1960-61	Estimated Production 1965-66	Persons in Employment 1960-61	Additional Persons Reqd. for Development	Managerial Norms: Technical Management	Managerial Norms: General and Commercial Management	Additional Managerial Personnel Reqd.
1	2	3	4	5	6	7	8	9
1.	Precision instruments (industrial and scientific)	3.6 crores	23 crores	3,000	23,000	1%	1.2%	230 276
2.	Surgical instruments	Nil	2.5 million pieces	Nil	2,700	1%	0.7%	27 19
3.	Automobile and ancillory industries							
	Passenger cars, commercial Vehicles, jeeps & station wagons	53,000	100,000	32,000	30,000	0.65%	0.45%	195 135
	Sewing machines	300,000	700,000	3,000	7,000	0.4%	1,1%	28 77
	Bicycles	1.05 million	2.2 million	5,000	5,000	0.4%	1.1%	20 55
	Ship buildings expansion of Hindustan Shipyard and Second Shipyard. Dry Docks	20,000	50,000	5,000	7,500	1.5%	05%	112 38

*These are two figures in column No. 9. The first represents number of persons required for technical management and the second for general and commercial management.

Chamical Industries

The largest and most important development under this head during the Third Plan will be in the field of fertilisers. The following is the capacity for nitrogenous fertilisers in the public sector :

	Tons
Existing capacity (Sindri, Nangal, FACT)	217,000
Rourkela	120,000
Neyveli	70,000
Trombay	90,000
Nahorkatiya	32.500
Further expansion of FACT	40,000
Gorakhpur	80,000
One more fertiliser undertaking in the public Sector	80,000
Total	729,500

The following development in the private sector has already been approved :

	Tons
Sahu Chemicals	20,000
Ennore, Madras	8,250
Madhya Pradesh	50,000
Visakhapatnam	80,000
Kothagudiam	80,000
Rajasthan	80,000
West Bengal	58,000

The production capacity in 1960-61 was 110,000 tons of nitrogenous fertilisers. This is expected to increase to 1,000,000 tons at the end of the Third Plan period. The number of persons in employment based on the analysis of the Sindri fertilisers was 16,000. The additional number of persons required for the development programme is 128,000. The managerial norms for this industry are one per cent technical management and 0.5 per cent general and commercial management. The additional number that will be required, therefore, is 128 for technical management and 64 for general and commercial management.

In the field of heavy chemicals, the most important for which development is planned are Sulphuric Acid, Caustic Soda, and Soda Ash.

In 1960-61, the sulphuric acid plants in the country produced 363,000 tons. By the end of the Third Plan, it is proposed to increase this capacity to 1,750,000 tons.

The following is the position regarding production in 1960-61 and targets for 1965-66 :

	1960-61	1965-66
Chemical Caustic	27,000	50,000
Electrolytic Caustic	97,435	450,000
Total	124,435	400,000
Soda Ash (Light)	2,20,000	370,000
Soda Ash (Heavy)	Nil	160,000

The investment for heavy chemicals comprising sulphuric acid, soda ash, caustic soda, calcium carbide, sodium hydro-sulphate and hydrogen peroxide is of the order of Rs. 420 millions. The managerial norms for this industry are estimated to be 1 per cent for technical management and 1 per cent for general and commercial management. The additional number of persons required are 120 for technical management and 120 for commercial and general management.

The following table gives the position regarding production of other chemical products and drugs and pharmaceuticals in 1960-61, estimated for 1965-66, capital investment proposed and additional number of managerial personnel required.

Name of Industry	Unit	1960-61 Production	Target (1965-66)	Capital Investment (Rs. crore)	Additional Managerial Personnel Required: Tech. Management	General and Commercial Management
1	2	3	4	5	6	7
Miscellaneous Chemicals						
(i) Carbon Black	000 tons	—	30	13.0	40	40
(ii) Industrial explosives						
(a) Blasting explosives	000 tons	6	20			
(b) Liquid oxygen explosives:	000 tons	2	9			
(c) Safety fuses	million coils	2	25.0			
(d) Detonators	million nos.	—	80			
(iii) Rubber chemicals	000 tons	n.a.	3			
Coke						
(a) Soft coke (low temperature carbonisation)	million tons	—	2.0	42.0	120	120
(b) Hard coke by-product	000 tons	500	1,160	29.2	80	80
(iv) Dyestuffs and organic intermediates						
(a) Dyestuffs	million lb.	11.5	22.4			
(b) Intermediaries	tons	—	25,000			
(v) Drugs and Pharmaceuticals						
(a) Sulpha drugs	tons	150	1,000			
(b) Penicillin	million mega units	40	205	28.0	80	80
(c) Streptomycin	tons	—	150			
(d) P.A.S.	,,	100	400			
(e) Anti-dysentery drugs	,,	30	75			
(f) I.N.H.	,,	30	100			
(g) Phytochemicals	,,	—	76.4			
(h) D.D.T.	,,	2,800	2,800			

Textile Industries

The requirement of cotton textiles at the end of the Third Plan has been calculated on the assumption that 8,450 million yards of cloth will be needed for domestic consumption and 850 million yards for exports. The actual availability of cloth in 1960-61 was of the order of 6,750 million yards. Out of the target of 9,300 million yards proposed, 3,500 million yards have been allocated as a share of handlooms, khadi, small pover looms, etc. The production target allocated to the mill sector is 5,800 million yards as against the effective capacity of about 5,000 million yards at present. The number of persons in employment in 1960-61 in the cotton textile industry is 150,000. The additional number for the development proposed is 24,000. In regard to the managerial norms, it may be pointed out that five textile mills have replied to the questionnaire and the figures of managerial personnel employed by them vary considerably. On this basis, the additional managerial personnel equired will be of the order of 72 for technical management and 72 for general and commercial management. The actual production of rayon filament and staple fibre is about 95 million pounds. This is proposed to be increased to 215 million pounds by the end of the Third Plan period. The additional number of persons that will be required is of the order of 36,000. On the basis of the managerial norms in the textile industry, the number of additional persons required is 108 for technical management and 108 for general and commercial management.

Food Industries

Salt: Production in 1960-61 for salt was of the order of 3.7 million tons. This is expected to be increased to 6.5 million tons by the end of the Plan period. The additional number of persons required is 1,000. The managerial norms for this industry are 0.4 per cent technical management and 0.2 per cent general and commercial management. The total number of managerial personnel required is four for technical management and two for general and commercial management.

Vanaspati: Estimated production of Vanaspati in 1960-61 was 330,000 tons. The development proposed is to increase this to 550,000 tons by the end of the current Plan period. The number of persons in employment in 1960-61 was 7,000. The additional number required for the development proposed is 5,000. Managerial norms are one per cent for technical management and one per cent for general and commercial management. Additional number of managerial personnel required for technical management is 50 and for general and commercial management 50.

Other Industries

The following table gives the production in 1960-61, target for 1965-66, number of persons employed in 1960-61, additional number required for development; managerial norms and additional number of managerial personnel required during the Third Plan.

Name of Industry	Production	Estimated Production	Persons in Employment	Additional Persons Reqd. for Development	Managerial norms: Tech. Management	Managerial norms: General & Commercial Management	Additional Managerial Personnel Required: Tech.	Additional Managerial Personnel Required: General & Commercial
1	2	3	4	5	6	7	8	9
Paper and Paper Board	375,000	970,000	18,750	29,750	1%	1.5%	300	450
Cement	8.5 million	15 million	28,000	23,400	0.22%	0.33%	52	78
Glass and Glass ware	84,000 tons	—	11,000	28,600	0.9%	1.00%	257	286
Soap	150,000 tons	500,000 tons	—	6,000	0.5%	1%	30	60
Synthetic Rubber	—	50,000 tons	—	12,000	1.26%	1.84%	151	220
Plastics	10,000 tons	85,000 tons	Not available	14,000	1%	0.5%	140	170
Refractories	0.52 million	2 million	"	13,000	1%	1%	130	260
Power and Industrial Alcohol	22 million gallons	72 million tons	1,100	5,000	1%	1%	50	50
Industrial Gases	790 million cu. ft.	2,550 million cu. ft.	6,400	14,000	0.9%	2.8%	126	392
Petroleum Products Crude Oil	5.67 million tons	10.77 million tons	Not available	16,000	1%	2%	160	320

The requirements of managerial personnel for production management and general commercial management for the Third Five-Year Plan period is given below. The basic assumption made in the calculation of personnel is that the targets of production as envisaged in the Third Plan would be achieved and that the allocation of industries in the private and public sectors would be in accordance with the Industrial Policy Resolution of the Government of India. To quote an example-private industries are not keen to take up the manufacture of fertilisers and this has resulted in the enlargement of the public sector and consequent reduction in the private sector. Such mid-Plan changes obviously could not be taken into consideration in the preparation of these estimates. Another assumption is that industrial efficiency would remain the same throughout the five-year period. At best, these estimates are an indication of the order of requirements for the development envisaged in the Third Plan.

Industary	Production management	General & Commercial Management
1. Industrial machinery and equipment manufacturing industries	2,000	2,000
2. Iron and steel	631	428
3. Non-ferrors metals,	518	518
4. Miscellaneous engineering industries : Precision instruments, automobiles; ship-building etc.	612	600
5. Chemical Industries :		
Fertilizers	128	64
Heavy chemicals	120	120
Miscellaneous chemical industries such as drugs, pharmaceuticals, dye stuffs liquid oxygen, etc.	280	280
6. Textiles :		
Cotton yarn and cloth	72	72
Rayon	108	108
7. Vanaspati	50	50
8. Miscellaneous industries such as paper, cement, soap, plastics, etc.	1,396	2,286
	5,915	6,506
or	5,900	6,500

Managerial Personnel Requirement For Sectors Other Than Industry

The Committee, at its meeting held on June 10, 1962, decided that it was necessary to have a separate questionnaire for commercial establishments. The questionnaire was drawn up in consultation with Dr. V.K.R.V. Rao and Shri R. Prasad. The questionnaire sought information regardings number of persons employed in managerial capacity in purchase and sales management, organisational and personnel management, and the total gross value of purchase and sales. Though this questionnaire was issued to about 100 business houses, only a few replied. The replies are analysed below:

Burmah Shell

Total gross value of annual business	Rs. 1,840 million
No. of personnel employed in managerial capacities	417
Approximate average per managerial personnel	Rs. 4.4 millions

Acharya Bros.

Total gross value of annual business	Rs. 15 million
No. of personnel employed in managerial capacities	7
Approximate average per managerial personnel	Rs. 2 million

Sen & Pandit (Pvt.) Ltd.

Total gross value of annual business	Rs. 41.4 millions
No. of personnel employed in managerial capacities	9
Approximate average per managerial personnel	Rs. 4.4 millions

State Tradings Corporation Of India

Total gross value of annual business	Rs. 650 millions
No. of personnel employed in managerial capacities	140
Approximate average per managerial personnel	Rs. 4.6 millions.

On an average, therefore, Rs. 4.5 millions is fixed as the norm for calculation of managerial personnel required by trade and commerce in the export and import business.

The total import at the commencement of the Third Plan was of the order of Rs. 10,720 millions and the total likely imports at the end of the Third Plan inclusive of P.L. 480 imports is estimated to be of the order of Rs. 12,700 millions. The increase in imports over the Plan period is, therefore of the order of Rs. 2,000 millions. The annual exports at the commencement of Third Plan is of the order of Rs. 6,140 millions. It is expected that by end of the Third Plan period, this would be doubled. The total increase in the value of import and export business is of the order of Rs. 8,140 millions and applying the norm of Rs. 4.5 millions to each managerial personnel, the number of additional personnel required is of the order of 1700.

Banking

Of the banks addressed, four replied to the questionnaire. They are :

1. Reserve Bank of India.
2. State Bank of India.
3. Punjab National Bank.
4. Bank of India.

The Reserve Bank of India have informed that they have their own arrangements for the training of their personnel and would not ordinarily depute persons for management studies. The Bank has a sandwich system of instruction under which training in the various departments of a bank is imparted together with theoretical instruction in such subjects as are necessary for banking personnel. The course of instruction covers certain management subjects. The reply of the State Bank is also in the same vein. The Bank of India has also informed that they utilise the training facilities organised for the Reserve Bank and hence do not propose to depute any persons for management training. The Punjab National Bank has 10,540 persons in employment out of which 1,800 persons come under the category of general management.

There are at present 83 scheduled banks in the country. The total number of offices of scheduled banks at the commencement of the Third Plan was 4,401. By the end of the Third Plan, it is expected that there would be a 20 per cent increase in the number of branches of the banks. The number of persons in employment at the commencement of the Plan was of the order of 60,000. At the end of the Plan, therefore, an additional number of 12,000 persons is likely to be employed. The figures furnished by the Punjab National Bank shows that about 17 per cent of the persons employed in the Bank have managerial responsibilities and supervisory functions. On this basis, the number of additional personnel required for banking in the Third Plan is 2,040. Since, however the Reserve Bank of India and the State Bank of India and others have their own arrangements for training which, inter alia, includes management subjects, the requirement of managerial personnel for banking establishment may be estimated at one-fourth of the number, i.e., say 500.

Insurance

The Chairman of the Life Insurance Corporation has informed that though he agrees in principle that training in management subjects would benefit the employees of the Life Insurance Corporation, yet as the present staff has to be trained in the Life Insurance itself, it becomes a question of priority and naturally priority has to be given to training of personnel in the techniques of Life Insurance business itself. In the circumstances, it has not been envisaged that the Life Insurance Corporation would be taking advantage of the training facilities for the management studies in the present juncture. In the overall calculation for managerial personnel, requirements of insurance industry need not be taken into consideration.

The Committee is, however, of the view that executives employed in Life Insurance business should have managerial training and it would be to their advantage if the junior and senior executives could be deputed to educational institutions imparting instruction in management.

Small-Scale Industries

In the estimates of personnel made in the report of the Third Plan the additional employment under small-scale industries is shown as nine lakhs. The National Productivity Council and the Small-Scale Industries Institutes have organised short-term courses of three-month duration for small-scale industries and such other persons desirous of equipping themselves with managerial known how and techniques are likely to prefer this course as it aims at imparting instructions in the modern industrial techniques in addition to management principles and practices. It is, therefore, doubtful whether many persons starting small-scale industries would take advantage of the training scheme for managerial personnel. In the circumstances, the requirements of the small-scale industries need not be taken into consideration in the overall estimates of the managerial personnel, though it is likely that a few persons desirous of having better knowledge in management theory and practice may join this course.

Construction And Transportation

The managerial norms for construction and transportation have been worked out on the basis of published statistics in the following reports.

Report on the Occupational Pattern of Employees in the Public Sector in India, and

Report on Occupational Pattern of Employees in the Private Sector in India (1961).

At the beginning of the Third Plan, the number of workers in construction industry in the private and public sectors was 118,500 and 531,193 respectively, totalling 649,693, or say 0.65 millions. Managerial personnel for construction industry fall into two categories, viz., (i) technical personnel, civil engineers and overseers, and (ii) business and commercial management personnel. The number of civil engineering personnel in construction industry was 3,115. The employment pattern in the industry is one civil engineering degree holder for every four overseers and hence 620 civil engineers with degree qualification may be presumed to be in position. This works out to 0.33 per cent and this may be taken as the managerial norm for technical personnel employed in construction industry. The number of non-technical managerial personnel is 5,400 for the total labour force of 0.65 millions. This works out to 0.38 per cent and this may be taken as the norm for general and commercial management.

In 1960-61, the national income under the head construction was Rs. 3,310 millions. At the end of the Third Plan, this is expected to increase to Rs. 5,400 million, i.e., an increase of 63 per cent. Providing for increased efficiency of construction due to mechanical devices and higher labour output and such other factors, a reduction of 2-1/2 per cent per annun, i.e., an overall adjustment of 12-1/2 per cent, may have to be provided to arrive at man-power requirements. Making this adjustment, the additional working force required to achieve the national targets of the Third Plan is 50 per cent, i.e., 0.325 millions. Applying the managerial norms, the number of managerial personnel required for technical management is 1,072 or 1070. For general and commercial management, it is 2,700.

Transportation

In this category are :

(i) Railways,
(ii) Shipping,
(iii) Airways, and
(iv) Road Transport.

The Railways

The Railways have been traditionally a store house of technical and managerial man-power which have been unstinctedly spared by the organisation for the development of public sector industry. The recent success of the Integral Coach Factory, Madras, and the Chittaranjan Locomotive Factory, West Bengal, are in no small measure due to their awareness of the latest techniques of production, the need for work study and other management practices leading to increased efficiency. In the circumstances, for the purposes of the estimates of managerial personnel, it may be presumed, the requirements of Railways would be in the main taken care of by the organisation itself.

Shipping

At the beginning of the Third Plan, the capacity of Indian shipping was 0.9 million G.R.T. It is expected to increase to 1.7 million G.R.T. by the end of the Third Plan. The share of the overseas shipping is expected to move up from 0.6 million G.R.T. in 1960-61 to 1.3 million G.R.T. in 1965-66. The managerial personnel required are for employment in the head office, representation in foreign countries and also in Indian ports. Additional managerial personnel has been estimated as two persons for every 10,000 tons and hence the total requirements of managerial personnel in the category of general and commercial management is 160.

Airways

The Third Plan provides for an expenditure of 255 millions on Civil Aviation which is distributed between the various categories as shown below :

(i)	Works at aerodromes	185 millions
(ii)	Aeronautical telecommunication equipment	50 "
(iii)	Air routes and aerodromes	10 "
(iv)	Training and education equipment	8.4 "
(v)	Research & Development equipment	1.6 "
	Total	255 millions

A sum of Rs. 295 millions for the expansion of the air corporations has also been included in the Third Plan. The Air India International had, at the commencement of the Third Plan, three Boeings and nine Super Constellations The programme for the Third Plan provides for the purchase of four additional jet aircrafts. The operating fleet of the Indian Airlines Corporation at the commencement of the Third Plan, consisted of 54 Dakotas, five Skymasters and 10 Viscounts. The programme in the Third Five Year Plan provides for the purchase of four Viscounts and 25 modern aircrafts to replace Dakotas. A provision of Rs. 150 millions' has been made in the Third Plan for the Corporation.

The managerial personnel required for the Airways fall into two categories :

(i) Maintenance Engineers required at the aerodromes ; and

(ii) General and commercial management personnel required at the head offices and branch offices in India and abroad.

Engineers and other personnel are eligible to work as ground engineers at the aerodromes and in workshop after obtaining a certificate issued by the Department of Civil Aviation. As these executives deal with the labour, it would be an advantage if some managerial training is given to them. Currently, this is not the practice. The functional courses organised by the National Institute for Training in Industrial Engineering, Bombay, National Productivity Council, would be able to cover the requirements in this respect. The Corporation requires general and commercial management personnel. On an average, one managerial personnel is required for Rs. four millions of capital investment and on this basis, the number of persons required would be about 60.

Road Transport

The number of personnel employed at the commencement of Third Plan is 90,000 and that of the managerial personnel is 2,900. The managerial norm is, therefore, 3.2 per cent. The position at the commencement of the Third Plan regarding commercial vehicles is as follows :

Goods Trucks	170,000
Passenger Buses	58,000
Total	228,000

This is expected to increase by 1,32,000 by the end of the Third Plan period : the increase in goods trucks is 110,000 and in passenger buses 22,000. The increase in vehicles, therefore, is of the order of 58 per cent. Providing for increased efficiency and optimisation of the facilities, the increase in personnel may be fixed at 50 per cent. Applying the managerial norm of 3.2 per cent, the additional General and Commercial Management Personnel required is 1,450.

Summary total for Transportation:

Road Transport	1,450
Shipping	180
Air Transport	60
Total	1,690

The following is the summary of the requirements of managerial personnel in the various non-manufacturing sectors.

The figures represent the requirements if the targets of export and import trade, shipping, road transport and construction as envisaged in the Third Plan, are reached. There have been mid-term variations. The shipping target is expected to be exceeded whereas the target for export is not likely to be achieved. The figures given indicate the order of requirement rather than the exact requirements.

	Technical Management	General and Commercial Management
Trade and Commerce	—	1,700
Banking	—	500
Construction	1,070	2,700
Transportation	—	1,690
Total	1,070	6,590

Management Cadres And Present Training Facilities

The estimates for technical personnel made in the previous two chapters are for managerial personnel with degrees in engineering or technology. The lower categories consisting of personnel with diploma qualifications and sometimes with no academic qualifications at all but having only experience are also in supervisory positions exercising managerial functions. It will be observed that cadres such as Foreman, Assistant Foreman, Senior Chargeman, Senior Draftsman, Overseer, Technical Assistant etc., exercise supervisory functions and in general a university degree in engineering is not considered essential for carrying out the duties assigned to these posts. Ordinarily, an Assistant Engineer or a person working in an equivalent rank is the lowest in the technical cadre for whom a degree qualification is almost obligatory. For every Assistant Engineer down the scale there are about three to four technical personnel exercising supervisory functions depending upon the nature of industry.

The Board of Technical Studies in Management have formulated four courses of study for the various cadres of management personnel. They are :

(1) Industrial Engineering ;
(2) Foreman Supervision ;
(3) Industrial Management ; and
(4) Business Management.

Industrial Engineering is a post graduate diploma course of one year's duration on full-time basis or three year on part-time basis, open to graduates in engineering. The course imparts instruction in managerial practice and principles and modern techniques of Production, Planning and Control. The following are the subjects taught in the post-graduate course :

Part I : 1. Structure and Economic Aspects of Industry and Commerce. 2. Personnel Management and Industrial Relations. 3. Management Principles and Practice. 4. Procurement and Inventory control.

Part II : 1. Work Study. 2. Materials Handling. 3. Statistical Methods and statistical Quality control. 4. Location of Industry and Plan Layout. 5. Product Design and Development.

Part III : 1. Production, Planning and Control. 2. Cost Control. 3.Quality Control and Metrology. 4. Operational Research. 5. Maintenance. 6. Job Evaluation and Merit Rating. 7. Project Work and Report (Instruction and Contact hours).

The syllabus of studies as approved by the Board of Technical Studies in Management course is offered on a full-time basis in the Indian Institute. of Technology, Kharagpur, and on part-time basis in the Victoria Jubilee Technical Institute, Bombay.

Foremanship and Supervision course is a certificate open to matriculates having three years experience in a supervisory position in industry. Instruction is imported in the following nine subjects :

Elements of supervision.

Industrial History and Industrial Relations.

Communications in Industry.

Elementary Principles of Management.

Elements of Personel Management.

Principles of Foremanship.

Principles of Production Planning.

Principles of Remuneration, Estimating and Costing.

Safety in Industry.

Syllabus approved for the course by the All India Board of Technical Studies in Management can be organised in an industrial establishment or in a technical institution. There are three courses at present in the country and all the three are on a part-time basis. One of them is at Jamshedpur and is organised by the Tata Iron and Steel Company Ltd., Jamshedpur. The Gujarat Textiles Association has organised a course in Baroda in collaboration with the Baroda University. The Victoria Jubilee Technical Institute, Bombay has organised a course in the Institution. There is a proposal for the consideration of the Board for setting up an institute which will impart instruction on a full-time basis in Foremanship and Supervision.

With the assistance from the United Nations Special Fund, Government have set up a National Institute for Training in Industrial Engineering. The Institute will conduct functional courses ranging from one week to 22 weeks in the following subjects :

Advanced work Measurement—Comprehensive Course.

Work Measurement—Comprehensive Course.

Production Planning and Control—Comprehensive Course.

Sales Organisation—Comprehensive Course.

Method Study—Comprehensive Course.

Operative Training Methods—Comprehensive Course.

Profit Planning and Financial Control.

Standardisation, Simplification and Variety Reductions.

Plant Maintenance.

Business Appraisal.

Estimatings and Pricing.

Design and Implementation of Incentive Schemes.

Job Evaluation and Merit Rating.

Clerical Organisation.

Stock Control, Tool Room Control and Storekeeping.

Purchasing Methods and Value Analysis.

Selection Methods and Procedures.

Product Engineering.

Plant Design and Layout.

Materials Handling.

Management Controls.

Profit Sharing Methods.

Industry Courses :

Cotton Textiles

State Transport

Building Industry

Jute Industry

Wood working Industry

Light Electrical Engineering

Foundry Industries

Sugar Industry

Radio Industry.

The course of study in Business and Industrial Management drawn up by the All India Board of Technical Studies in Management is open to those who are graduates and who have least two years experience in a responsible supervisory capacity. The course entends over a period of one year on a full-time basis and three years on a part-time basis. There is also provision in the scheme for the state system of instruction under which candidates are given three months full-time in struction in a year, the entire course being completed in three years. The subjects of study comprise : (a) Background subjects ; (b) Tools of Management ; (c) Management subjects ; and (d) Specialised operational Subjects.

The Background subjects are :

1. The Growth and Structure of Industry and Commerce.
2. The economic aspects of Industry and Commerce.
3. The Legal Aspects of Industry and Commerce.
4. Psychology.

The Tools subjects are :

1. Accounting
2. Statistical methcd
3. Work study and Organisation and Job Evaluation.
4. Budgetary and Higher Control.

The Management subjects are :

1. The History and Nature of Management.
2. Management Principles.
3. Management practice.
4. The Personnel Functions.

The Operational subjects are :

1. Manufacturing.
2. Development and Design.
3. Distribution.
4. Purchasing, Storekeeping and Transportation.

All the 12 subjects comprising the first three groups cover a body of knowledge essential to all those who aspire to higher levels of management whether in operational or functional division of an enterprise or in general management.

The post-graduate course in Business Management and Industrial Management are at present being offered in the following centres :

1. Delhi University.
2. Indian Institute of Social Welfare and Business Management, Calcutta.
3. Madras University.
4. Bombay University.
5. Osmania University (Business Management only).
6. Thiagarajar Educational Trust, Madurai (Business Management only).

The Board has also approved the starting of two courses at the P.S.G. Engineering College, Coimbatore, Allahabad University and Kerala University. The approved intake for each of the courses in 30.

With the assistance of the Ford Foundation, Government have set up two Institutions, one at Calcutta and the other at Ahmedabad named the Indian Institutes of Management, Calcutta and Ahmadabad which will inter-alia, conduct full-time courses of two years duration at the Master's degree level in Management. The course of study are at present designated as post-graduate diploma course in Business Administration. By the end of the Third Plan, it is expected that these two institutions will have an intake of 150 each in the post-graduate diploma course. Admission to this course is open to brilliant young graduates with proved aptitudes in management.

Administrative Staff College, Hyderabad

The College was established in 1957 on the model of the Administrative staff college, Hanley-on-Thames, England. Its object is to bring together under one roof Senior Executives of proved ability from different fields of activity to study the skills and techniques of higher management and leadership. By living and working together the participants are enabled.

1. To interchange and analyse ideas and experience.

2. To acquire a close acquaintance with the economic social and political environment in which they operate.

3. To get a deeper understanding of the inter-relationship between different sectors of the national economy and between Public Administration and Business management ; and to appreciate how their respective roles complement each other in the achievement of the common national objectives.

4. To enrich their personalities and increase their competence as administrators by developing greater insight into and a broader approach to executive problems.

The college admits 50-60 candidates to each session of 12 weeks.

The National Productivity Council of India and the All India Management Association have also a part to play in the promotion and development of management education. The former has annual programmes for short functional courses ranging from one week to 26 weeks dealing with different aspects of management techniques and practices relating to production. The latter has been arranging seminars on diverse management topics which attract top and middle management personel from all parts of India. In addition, every year there is an annual intensive programme of study of a selected topic in management which is attended by top management personnel in industry, educational institutions and Government.

Organised In-Service Training

The direct method of training management personnel is through planned and organised in-service training programmes. Such programmes may include theoretical instruction besides supervised on-the-job training. Several establishments in the private sector, notably Tatas, Hindustan Lever, Standard Vacuum, etc., have well-developed in-service training programmes. The Tatas have set up a staff training college at Jamshedpur for continuing attention to the in-service training and development of their supervisory and management staff at junior levels. They also maintain a college at Poona for the training of their middle and higher level management personnel. In the public sector, Hindustan Steel have set up a small management training centre at Ranchi. Generally speaking, however, adequate attention is not paid at present to the training and development of managerial personnel in many enterprises including public sector enterprises. There appears to be need for creating greater awareness among top management personnel of the importance of organised in-service training programmes for the development of managerial skills and talents.

Requirements Of Managerial Personnel For The Third And Fourth Plans And Provision Of Increased Facilities For Training In Management.

The Committee was entrusted initially with the assessment of managerial personnel for the Third Plan period. The Third Plan period is about to be over and planning for the Fourth Plan is under way. Hence, the Committee has made tentative estimates for the Fourth Plan. It would be possible to work out correct estimates only after the Plan targets for industry have been fixed and the financial ceilings decided. However, for purposes of preliminary estimates the figures used by the Planning Commission in their Rs. 220,000 million Plan for the Fourth Plan period can well be a guide. The following is a structure of manufacturing industries in India from 1960-61 to 1975-76 as anticipated by the planners :

Sl. No.	Items	Net Value of Production (Rs. million)			
		1960-61	1965-66	1970-71	1975-76
1.	Consumer goods Industries	4,236	5,468	8,146	11,920
2.	Intermediate goods Industries	3,491	8,518	18,926	32,097
3.	Machinery	1,513	4,227	9,899	15,422
4.	Others	68	128	254	403
	Large factories Sub-total	9,308	18,341	37,225	59,842
5.	Small factories	1,288	2,646	5,558	8,704
6.	House hold industries	8,190	9,990	15,210	22,340
	Total small enterprises (5)+(6)	9,478	12,636	20,768	31,044
7.	Adjustment for coverage	2,604	2,604	2,604	2,604
	Grand Total	21,390	33,580	60,600	93,490

It will be observed that the net value of production at the end of the year 1965-66 stands at Rs. 33,580 millions. It is estimated to increase to Rs. 60,000 millions at the end of the Fourth Plan period. This represents about 80 per cent increase in production on the prices obtaining in 1960-61. The number of management personnel required, therefore, is also 80 per cent more for industrial production than that estimated for the Third Plan period. The following (in col. 2) is the estimate of the number of managerial personnel required under technical management and general and commercial management for the Third and Fourth Plan Schemes :

Third Plan

	Technical Management	General & Commercial Management
Trade & Commerce	—	1,700
Banking	—	500
Construction	1,070	2,700
Transportation	5,915	6,506
	6,985	13,096

Fourth Plan

	Technical Management	General & Commercial Management
Manufacturing Industries	10,267	11,711
Banking	—	900
Trade & Commerce	—	3,060
Construction	1,926	4,860
Transport & Communications	—	3,042
	12,573	23,573

There are a number of factors which have to be taken into consideration in regard to the above estimates. As pointed earlier, the estimated requirements are based on the assumption that division of industry between private sector and public sector would be as in the Third Plan. If there is further rationalisation, the requirements of the managerial personnel would be higher. Further, these estimates are based on the norms as worked out for the Third Plan. There would be material variation in certain industries due to introduction of modern methods of production, increased efficiency and rationalisation. The assessment figures have therefore this limitation.

From the analysis of the replies received to the questionnaire, it is observed, of the 1,700 technical personnel employed in manufacturing industries, about 500 require training. This works out to about 30 per cent for technical managerial personnel and about the same percentage would be applicable to the other category of the general and commercial personnel.

The number of people to be trained in the category of Technical Management is, therefore, of the order of 4,000 and under General and Commercial Management about 7,200.

For the training of 4,000 industrial engineers during the five-year period, as the course is of 12-month duration, the number to be trained per annum is 800. The intake to this course on a full-time basis is 20 and hence the number that will be possible to train per annum would be considerably less. The target of training of industrial engineers for the Fourth Plan should be the training of 300 industrial engineers per annum. The following are likely places, among others, where such training could be organised :

(1) Indian Institute of Technology, Bombay.
(2) Indian Institute of Technology, Madras.
(3) Indian Institute of Technology, Kanpur.
(4) Indian Institute of Technology, New Delhi.
(5) Indian Institute of Science, Bangalore.
(6) Jadavpur University, Calcutta.
(7) Bengal Engineering College, Howrah.
(8) P.S.G. College of Engineering and Technology, Coimbatore.
(9) Victoria Jubilee Technical Institute, Bombay.
(10) Maulana Azad College of Engineering and

Technology, Bhopal.

(11) Regional Engineering College, Durgapur.

(12) Regional Engineering College, Rourkela.

(13) Regional Engineering College Jamshedpur.

(14) Faculty of Technology, Baroda University, Baroda.

(15) Bihar Institute of Technology, Sindri.

In regard to the lower caders of supervisory personnel, a concerted effort should be made to persuade as many industrial establishments as possible to undertake the organisation of this training. The All India Board of Technical Studies in Management has estimated the requirements of the course at Rs. 8,000 per course and this has been reported to be very inadequate and therefore an assessment of the requirements for the organisation of this training will have to be made afresh and future grants sanctioned on this basis. The principle to be observed is that an industrial establishment volunteering to start this course should not be handicapped with any financial liability on this account. The Tata Iron & Steel Co. has sponsored the proposal to start a full-time instruction in Foremanship and Supervision. This is a move in the right direction. The Committee is of the view that the Institute should be started as early as possible and that at least three institutions of this type should be established during the Fourth Plan period. The other two suitable centres are Bangalore and Bombay. The possibility of National Institute for Training in Industrial Engineering organising this course should be considered in the first instance. If for some reason, the National Institute for Training in Industrial Engineering is not able to organize this course, then only should another centre in Bombay be considered.

The questionnaire for managerial personnel had also sought information on the additional centres to be started for the organisation of part-time courses in Industrial and Business Management. The centres suggested are :

(1) Baroda

(2) Coimbatore

(3) Madurai

(4) Bangalore

(5) Durgapur

(6) Kanpur

(7) Ranchi

(8) Jamshedpur

(9) Ahmedabad

(10) Bhilai

(11) Hyderabad

Of these, the Board has already approved the starting of management courses in Madurai, Hyderabad and Coimbatore.

It will be observed that apart from Bombay, Calcutta, Jamshedpur, Madras, Coimbatore and Durgapur, at least as far as the Third Plan is concerned, there is no other suitable centre for the organisation of part-time courses in Industrial Management. The Committee would, therefore, suggest that requests for starting of part-time courses in Industrial Management should be limited to such centres where industrial development envisaged employment of large numbers of managerial personnel.

One of the bottlenecks in the organisation of part-time courses in Business Management and Industrial Management is the lack of properly qualified teachers to teach management subjects and industrial psychology. The Committee is of the view that this matter requires attention of the Board and would suggest for consideration that same collaborative arrangement may be worked out with the National Institute for Training in Industrial Engineering under which training in Management Principles and Practices and Industrial Psychology could be imparted by the personnel of these three institutions to those undergoing instruction in university institutions. There are two ways by which this could be achieved. The first and the most obvious is for the three institutes named above to depute the trained teachers for short periods for a month or so to university institutions. The other possibility is for the university institutions to send their students to the management institutions for short periods for receiving instruction in special management subjects. Further, the two Institutes of Management should organise regular courses for the training of teachers of management subjects in university institutions.

The Board has approved introduction of what is known as the slab system under which full-time instruction is imparted for three months in a year and the whole training is phased in three years. This system has not been introduced by the university institutions at present conducting part-time courses. Adoption of this method would extend the catchment area of the trainees for the university institutions and would benefit industrial and commercial establishments which are not in the immediate vicinity of the university institutions.

As already stated earlier, in the field of General and Commercial Management, facilities for full-time courses exist in the two Management Institutions set up at Ahmedabad and Calcutta. These two institutions have programmed for an admission capacity of 150 for their post-graduate Diploma Course in Business Administration. It is expected that this target will be reacted by the end of the current plan period. It was reported to the Committee that Government have under consideration, the question of increasing intake to these institutions to 300 during the Fourth Plan period. This is a move in the night direction and is supported by the Committee. The Committee recommends that two more institutions on the pattern of the existing institutions at Ahmedabad and Calcutta should be set up during the Fourth Plan period.

The Committee further recommends that intake to the institutions conducting part-time courses at present should be increased for Business Management and that new centres for business management be started wherever possible after ens ring that suitable teachers would be available. The Committee expresses its graceful thanks to the industrialists and organisations and people who extended their cooperation to the Committee and furnished necessary information.

THE COMMITTEE ON CHILD CARE, 1960—REPORT

New Delhi, Central Social Welfare Board, 1965. 447p.+xvp.

Chairman : Smt. B. Tarabai.

Members : Dr. B. H. Mehta; Smt. Pratibha Singh; Smt. Pushpa Mehta; Smt. S. Manjubhashini; Smt. M. S. H. Jhabvala: Smt. Tarabai Modak; Shri S.C. Pandit (replaced by Smt. P. K. Makhan Singh); Shri D. V. Kulkarni; Shri N. D. J. Rao; Shri Radha Raman; Smt. Sudha Majumdar.

Secretaries : Smt. B. Ghufran; Shri B. N. Dhar.

APPOINTMENT

When a nation becomes free freedom releases the impulses and initiative of the people to achieve a new national destiny. The people are inspired to build new foundations for the health and happiness of all citizens. The vision of the nation is guided by its awakened social consciousness to correct the errors of the past and fresh measures are taken to build foundations a new so that the future of the nation may be prosperous, bright and unable mished. Action is now being taken in India in all fields of national endeavour; yet in the execution of plans and programmes serious difficulties come across, many of which are due to neglect of correct social attitudes and endeavours to maintain the health and efficiency of the nation. The great importance of the human factor must be realised without delay, because man himself is the architect and instrument of his destiny. The shortcomings and imperfections of the human being are unnecessarily diminishing the harvests of our effort, and whatever be the complexity of the causes of our shortcomings, nobody could question the need of child care, or overlook the consequences and costs of neglected children.

Realising the need to study the problem of child care and child welfare, the Central Social Welfare. Board, at the instance of the Union Ministry of Education, decided at its 30th meeting held in October 19(0, to appoint a Committee to prepare a comprehensive plan for the care and training of children in the age-group 0-6.

TERMS OF REFERENCE

(I) To study in the light of changing socio-economic conditions in the country care and up-bringing of children in the family and the community with particular reference to the provisions of health, nutritional and recreational facilities in the home and in the neighbourhood;

(II) To examine the problems of children in need of special care and protection and to recommend measures for providing comprehensive child care services for them;

(III) To evaluate the nature, extent, and distribution (rural, urban, type of locality, etc.) of existing child welfare services with special reference to the management (government, proprietory, corporate non-official bodies, etc.) and pattern (Indian, Western, etc.) of pre-schools.

(IV) (1) To Study and evaluate the standards of pre-school education with reference to :

- (i) The pattern of staffing (trained and untrained, teacher-pupil ratio, etc.);
- (ii) The curricula and methods of teaching adopted;
- (iii) The type of equipment available and the manner and extent of its use; and
- (iv) Programme of recreation, rest nutrition, health, care and instruction.

(2) To work out a tentative plan for the development of pre-school education for the next five or 10 years with estimate of cost.

(V) To study the existing facilities for training of Child Welfare Workers in terms of the number of centres required and contents and standards of training and to suggest a long-term training programme for child welfare workers on a uniform basis.

(VI) To work out a plan for the manufacture of a standard recreational and educational equipment at moderate cost, suited to the requirements of Indian children. This could be linked up with the socio-economic programme of the Central Social Welfare Board.

(VII) To assess the financial position of child welfare institutions for this age group, to study their pattern of income and expenditure and to assess the problems of grant-in-aid, the nature ond volume of assistance required and the period for which it would be necessary.

(VIII) To recommend a pattern for the reorganisation and extension of the programme of community and institutional services for the proper physical, mental and emctional development of the child in the first six years, keeping in view the continuity of services for children that will follow from six to 11 and 12 years to adulthood,

(IX) To suggest methods of coordination among the large number of agencies working in the field of child welfare.

CONTENTS

Preface by Chairman, Central Social Welfare Board; Synopsis of Chapters; List of Tables; Introduction; Family and the Nation; Child Population and Family Planning; The Background and Concept of Child Care and Neglect; Infant Mortality and Diseases Amongst Children; Health and Infant Welfare; The Pre-School; Handicapped Children; Personnel and Training Programmes; Organisation and Management of Child Welfare Programmes and Institutions; Children's Recreation; Art, Literature and Play; Recommendations; Table 1 to 57; Appendices A to I.

RECOMMENDATIONS

Basic Recommendations

Campaign And Movement

The Committee recommends that there is a need to organise a campaign to promote a National Child Welfare Movement with defined objectives, using scientific methods, and promoting programmes of different kinds to suit the different regions and sections of the population in India.

Children's Act

That each State in the Indian Union must exact a Children's Act; and the existing national Children's Act, which serves as a model for all the States, should be thoroughly revised. Efforts should also be made to bring about some measures of uniformity in the State legislative enactments contemplated under the Acts.

Division

That a Division of Child Welfare be created in the Ministry of Education in order to provide specialised direction and guidance to all child welfare programmes in the country.

Coordination

That a National Council of Coordination be appointed by the Ministry of Education to achieve and maintain common standards, lay down basic policies, achieve maximum economy in the use of resources and personnel, and take advantage of available results of research and knowledge in all subjects which have a bearing on child welfare.

Advisory Board

That a National Advisory Committee of Child Welfare be appointed by the Ministry of Education to advise the Ministries concerned about the standard of care to be maintained in programmes and institutions child welfare legislation, registration of institutions, counselling, etc,

Section Of Child Welfare In The Central Social Welfare Board

That the Central Social Welfare Board, which has initiated a large number of welfare programmes in urban and rural areas, should develop a special wing for the exclusive promotion of programmes of child welfare and child study, and for improving the standard of child welfare services in the country.

Children's Bureau

That the division of Child Welfare in the Ministry of Education, or alternatively the Central Social Welfare Board, should create in course of time a National Bureau of Child Welfare which will serve as a clearing house for child welfare information and become the main source of guidance for child welfare activities in the field.

Central Institution

That a National Centre for the training of child welfare specialists and general personnel for leadership, administration and direction of field programmes be created in a suitable metropolitan area; and that such a centre should undertake pilot projects, programmes of child study and research, production of literature on child welfare, and other activities to direct and guide State and private agencies in their efforts to promote child care and welfare.

Resources

On the basis of the information received, it is found

that the resources actually provided for all the child welfare services in all the States are entirely inadequate to meet the demands of even a minimum child welfare service ; and therefore special measures be taken to strengthen the Prime Minister's Children's Fund and find other ways to develop financial and other resources by every means possible.

Financial Aid

That the existing National, State and local agencies for child welfare should be strengthened by enabling them to expand their services ; and to carry out programmes with the special financial assistance of the State, and additional resources provided by the communities.

Demonstration Project

That at least one Demonstration Child Welfare Project should be organised in every State. These projects will provide an intensive and integrated programme of child welfare including programmes for the welfare of children under six years. There should be at least five additional Demonstration Projects for the benefit of children in metropolitan areas. These programmes will function according to resources and plans to be provided by the Central Ministry of Education.

Guidance And Counselling Services

Competent guidance and counselling services should be created in each State consisting of Field Guides and Counsellors to assist State and private child welfare programmes organised in the State ; and a sum of Rs. 10 lakhs be set aside to give grants-in-aid to competent child welfare organisation Schools of Social Work and Universities, who are willing to provide such counselling services, be set up according to rules and procedures to be laid down by the Central Government

Minimum Standard Pre-Schools

That at least 1,000 pre-schools as minimum standard pre-schools, should be created in the third plan period ; and the annual recurring cost of such a pre-school will be Rs. 3,500 for one unit of 30 children between the ages of three-plans and five-plans years.

Pre-School Pilot Project

That at least one pre-school should be created in each District of India to function as a Pilot Project. The recurring expenditure of such pre-school will be about Rs. 10,000 per year, and the non-recurring grant in the first year may be Rs. 4,500.

Experiment Pre-School

Special types of Experimental pre-schools with a programme of child study should be attached to Universities, schools of social work, and child study institutions. They should be given grants-in-aid by the Central as well as State Governments.

Training Programme

One-year training programme for the training of Balsevikas must be organised in each State. The trainess should be given general information about the philosophy, objects, methods, and programmes of child welfare together with an intensive training to function as organisers and teachers of pre-schools.

That Central and State Governments should support all two-year programmes for the training of pre-school teachers by recognised voluntary agencies, universities and schools of social work.

National Toy Industry

That the Central Government should promoted a national industry for the manufacture of toys and educational requirements and materials ; and it should provide Rs. 15 lakhs to organise at least one such industry which will be able to supply cheap and standard equipment and materials for pre-schools, playgrounds, children's centres, and other child welfare organisations.

Research Programme

A sum of Rs. 10 lakhs be utilised for the promotion of a research programme in child welfare, in cooperation with the Research Programmes Committee of the Planning Commission.

That in order to meet the expenditures required for implementing programmes mentioned above, an additional allocation of Rs. 35 lakhs be sanctioned by the Planning Commission ; or in the alternative the Rs. 3 crores be redistributed to include the suggested programmes for the Guidance and Counselling Service, Research, and the promotion of an Industry for the manufacture of educational materials and toys.

Important And General Recommendations

An extensive programme of Social Welfare is being organised all over the country, it should be the national policy to consider child welfare as an integrated and comprehensive programme which must be implemented everywhere by properly constituted agencies of child welfare in all parts of the country ; and that the family and the community should play an increasingly important role in the execution of such programmes.

That, top priority should be given to the provision of adequate welfare services for children, giving proper consideration to the requirements if nutritions foods for infants and children, the dietary articles being supplied to urban slums and villages at every cheap rates.

That, as a matter of national policy, every effort should be made to promote the social health of the family and its integration. This has also to be attempted by counteracting those social forces which contribute towards family disorganisation and disintegration.

That, in the future policy of social welfare, the need for a proper reorientations in the welfare schemes for children should be taken into account ; and in social welfare, maternity and child welfare services should be given a very high priority.

That, the existing programmes of child care should be extended so as to benefit a large number of children ; and the existing efforts should be intensified so as to deal with all aspects of the life of the child. All the same time, the general quality of services should be improved in order to raise the standard of efficiency of child welfare programmes.

That, voluntary agencies should work as pioneers in the field of child welfare, dealing with educational and nutrition programmes not covered by normal social services, with experimental programmes for the improvement of existing services, and with programmes for the rehabilitation of children in need of special care. It should also be the function of voluntary agencies to act as mentors of the Government for speedy implementation and execution of child welfare, schemes and programmes promoting parental education.

That, utmost consideration be given to the provision of suitable environment to the child to protect him from climatic and environmental hazards so as to promote his chances for survival, growth and development. Suitable environment may be said to incorporate the following :

(a) Availability of adequate shelter in sanitary surroundings ;

(b) Protection from climate - especially protective clothings ;

(c) Provision of safety measures so as to afford protection against hazards of environment.

That, as the funds allotted for programmes of child welfare at present are entirely inadequate to meet the primary needs of survival and normal growth and development of the child, more funds should be raised, and allotments should be made after properly assessing the minimum needs of child welfare in each area.

That, existing programmes of grants-in-aid for the benefit of children under six years of age should be given a special priority so that as many children as as possible could be given help from the very beginning, and so that the cost of later welfare services may be reduced because of benefits derived from earlier assistance.

Social Policy

That a general social policy should now be laid down by the Central Government, and the following should be adopted as relevant articles dealing with problems and needs of children under six years of age :

(a) Having accepted the Declaration of Rights of Children as defined by UNICEF, all programmes relating to family and child welfare amongst all sections of the people must now be aimed at implementing, to the best of our capacity, the principles of the Charter.

(b) In view of the fundamental differences of approach by political ideologies and systems of Government, it is desirable that it should be the national policy to do everything to strengthen the family, and to promote its integration and comprehensive social health, so that the family may always remain the fittest institution to provide a proper environment to promote the health and welfare of the child.

(c) The true well-being of all families and children requires a careful and well organised programme of Family Planning ; and it should be the national policy to promote a coordinated and intensive programme of family planning along with child welfare.

(d) The nation must accept the equal importance of all the four stages of childhood-Intra-uterine stage, Infancy, Toddler's, and Pre-school stage-for the purposes of planning, organisation and development of child welfare. Local conditions and needs will determine priorities of child welfare activities within the general programme of social welfare.

(e) Immediate action must be taken to provide for the proper care of normal children, emphasis being laid on all programmes providing for the growth training and development of the normal child. The State should also take full responsibility for the care of abandoned children ; and it must recognise the special needs of handicapped, maladjusted and subnormal children.

(f) The State must recognise the need for assisting private social welfare agencies to promote experimental and special programmes of child welfare, especially those dealing with the study of children and the organisation and administration of pilot and experimental projects ; and when extensive programmes have to be developed for the welfare of all children in urban, rural and sylran areas, the State must bear the greater burden and responsibility for the promotion of such extensive and standard child welfare services.

Stages Of Childhood—Definitions

That, the following stages of childhood should be accepted with their implications in order to provide intensive care to children in the different stages of growth during the earliest period of life.

1. **Intra-Uterine : From Conception To Birth ;**

Programmes for maternity and antenatal care ; and parental education.

2. **Infancy** : From Birth To One Year; Programmes for preventing mortality and providing measures for promoting good health and growth of the child.

3. **Toddler Stage** : From One Year To Three Years: To emphasise the need of nutrition, healthy recreation and total environment care.

4. **Pre-School Stage** : From Three years to Six year. To emphasise the need of eduction and training. health, recreation and nutrition. (It must be noted that these are highly formative years when habits, character, and intelligence patterns are established.)

5. **Primary School Stage** : From Six years to 11 years: To emphasize the need of primary education, health and recreation.

Child Care And Neglect

That, the following should be accepted as the implied contents of a comprehensive concept of child care :

(a) Adequate nourishment for the child in terms of provision of the right type of food of good quality in adiquate quantity.

(b) Adequate shelter in sanitary surroundings.

(c) Protection from climate, especially protective clothing.

(d) Love and affection in the family environment.

(e) Protection against diseases, especially providing for comprehensive, frequent and timely immunisation against infectious diseases.

(f) Safety measures against hazards of environment.

(g) Opportunities for growth, development and activity in an atmosphere of freedom, and in association with other children.

(h) Opportunity for indoor and outdoor play.

(i) Opportunities for training and development of the child within his home, community, and/or institutional environment.

(j) Protection from unfit guardians, exploitation for material gain, and cruelty inflicted through physical punishment and injuries to his emotional and mental life.

(k) Adequate provision for early and immediate treatment of physical, mental, emotional and social handicaps and maladjustments.

That, 'Neglect' be defined as isolation of the child, leaving it without love, shelter and protection ; and the following be accepted as implied contents of the concept of neglect :

(a) Failure on the part of the family to provide shelter, nourishment and protection.

(b) Absence of attention to basic needs of children like affection, protection, security, play and companionship.

(c) Wilful exposure of children to unfavourable climatic conditions and insanitary surroundings.

(d) Failure to attend in time to minor ailments, physical handicaps and chronic sub-health.

(e) Exposure of the child to severe physical punishments, emotional shocks or mental injury.

(f) Absence of protection for the child from all kinds of exploitation.

(g) Association of the child with an unfit guardian.

(h) Permitting the child to live without a name or nationality.

Programmes

That, the following specific programmes be recognised as necessary activities for the purpose of promoting the welfare of children under six years of age :

(a) Family planning clinics and family counselling agencies.

(b) Clinics and community welfare programmes providing ante-natal and post-natal care ; and Health Visitors' service.

(c) Maternity hospitals, children's wards in hospitals, maternity homes, community dispensaries and hospitals for children.

(d) Creches and day nurseries.

(e) Pre-schools.

(f) Institutions and homes for children including institutions for the care of handicapped, maladjusted and sub-normal children.

(g) Schools of social work, social work department Universities, instutions promoting programmes for the training of child welfare personnel, and research and investigations dealing with living conditions, problems and needs of all children under six years of age.

Family Planning

That, a national network of family planning clincis should be initiated by powerful national and State organisations, and maximum use must be made of the press, cinema and radio to promote family planning in a national campaign.

That, efforts should be made to promote "spacing" as the chief objective of family planning, and parental education must promote a minimum spacing period of 30 months between the birth of the previous child and the conception of the next child. More extensive use of contraceptives must be recommended to parents who have three or more children to prevent a further increase in the size of the family.

That, the national association for the promotion of planned parenthood must receive maximun support from the State, and its plans and recommendations must be accepted, as far as possible, by all welfare organisations in the country.

Family And Mother's Welfare

That, the family should primarily undertake the responsibility of adequate child care and that it should receive all possible and necessary help from the regional community or the neighbourhood to which it belongs by implementing programmes contained in the other recommendations of the report.

That, in Community Development Programmes the social health of the family should receive as much attention as family economy. The Community Development Programmes should take special measures to promote and strengthen the family's spiritual and ethical backgrounds which had constituted in the past to sound social health and family and national integration.

That, a very careful study of women's participation in different aspects of national economy is required to ensure that the social health of the family is not affected when women undertake employment due to economic reasons.

The coordination and integration of programmes of health visitors, ante-natal, maternity and past-natal care, social education, housing management, community organisation and every type of domiciliary service is essential to spread the knowledge, and achieve the acceptance of family planning programmes in the shortest time possible.

Ante-Natal Care

That, the required services that an ante-natal programme should provide must be able to achieve the following objectives :

1. To create desirable psychological conditions to the expectant mother when she is primigravide, so that she is in a happy, hopeful and confident frame of mind, free of anxieties, sorrow and fears.
2. To diagnose and treat any early complications.
3. To increase the proportion of normal deliveries.
4. To lower the maternal mortality and morbidity rates.
5. To reduce the incidence of premature births, still-births and parental and neonatal deaths.
6. To improve the cleanliness, orderliness, and sanitary conditions of the house in which the expectant mother is living.
7. To give minimum parental education required by the mother, especially at the time of first delivery, in order to provide intelligent and affectionate care to the child from the very beginning, after birth.

Post-natal Care

The post-natal care must become an efficient instrument for ensuring the health and nutrition of both the mother and the infant during first 12 to 18 months after delivery. The mother should receive advice, assurance and instructions to protect the infant from neo-natal and other familiar infections.

That post-natal care must pay special attention to parental education with a view to increase "the mothers ability to cope with life" ; and due to inadequate personnel and facilites, this programme should become a primary element in all social education programmes in the country.

Health

That Health Services may be provided to children in the following ways :

(a) As part of basic services necessary for community health such as provision for adequate housing, safe water supply, improved sanitation, avoidance of over-crowding and slum conditions, etc.

(b) As specialised services for mothers and children, such as ante-natal maternity, post-natal and counselling services, creches, pre-schools, children's playgrounds, immunisation programme against infections diseases, etc.

(c) That, health and nutrition requirements should be integrated with every programme of child care.

Recognising that adequate efforts are being made to increase the number of women doctors in the country, and also recognising that even male doctors are inadequate in rural areas, it is still imperative to increase the number of women doctors in the country in such a way that at least one woman doctor is employed in rural areas either in the primary health centre or in charge of an important subsidiary centre.

That, a special allowance may be given in order to attract medical personnel to work in rural areas. In addition, housing and educational facilities for the children of such personnel should also be provided.

Vital Statistics

That, all vital statistics which are required for the purpose of social studies should be based upon organised, systematic and efficient registration in all parts of the country; and measures should be taken to perfect this machinery before the commencement of the next census in 1971.

Reducing Infant Mortality

That, every effort should be made in India as early as possible to see that it leaves the 'high' mortality bracket (with infant mortality above 100) by reducing infant mortality rate to the bracket where it is between 35 and 75; and this could be achieved by improved standards of housing and wages, maximum employment, improved standard of living, and by increasing and improving existing services for the family, mother and child welfare in terms of family planning and parental education programmes and ante natal, maternity, post-natal care, etc.

Immunisation

That, measures should be taken to protect the health of the child from contagious diseases, and the programme of timely and frequent immunisation should be extensively introduced to cover the entire population of children in the country.

That, whilst immunisation programmes are carried out through the various hospitals, clinics, primary health centres and dispensaries; this programmes should be accelerated with the cooperation of the urban and rural community welfare centres; and children should be given triple and single immunisations to ensure protection against T. B., small pox, dyphtheria tetanus and poliomyelitis. Moreover, innoculation against cholera and typhoid should be given to all the children before the age of 9 2/1 months.

Nutrition

That, attention must be given to the problem of infants who are not breast-fed. Humanised milk should be produced and distributed in cities where parents are able to afford their cost. Other mesures are needed to keep the supply of substitute powder milk and baby foods commercially produced to meet existing demands, especially in urban areas.

That, strong and effective measures should be taken to see that babies and children have the highest priority to obtain their needs from the local milk supply; and even rationing and control should be introduced whenever necessary, to prevent the use of whole milk in hotels and for commercial manufacture of sweets, pastries, ice-cream and such articles.

That, every effort should be made to discover and encourage the production of cheap foods. This work should be entrusted to State agencies, so that such foods can be supplied as subsidised foods and the cost of nourishment of children may be kept as low as possible.

Handicapped Children

That, for the welfare and treatment of all handicapped children, high priority should be given to preventive programmes and the detection of handicaps from as early an age as possible.

That, in each State the Ministry of Welfare should create "children's villages" for the care of abandoned children, and foundlings, and the village should be fed by sub-centres in urban and rural areas. These villages must consist of Homes which will function as rehabilitation centres which will include a reception service, a counselling service and case work service for parents and children, and it will also provide shelter, training, education, rehabilitation, etc., to the foundlings till he reaches the age of 18 years.

That, in order to reduce the pressure of orphanages and other institutions and also for assisting the child to avoid institutional care, foster home services should be organised by responsible organisations of child welfare in both urban and rural areas, and in cooperation with the authorities created for the enforcement of the Children Act.

That, adequate measures should be taken all over India to prevent blindness and for correction of defective vision, and for this purpose special measures should be taken for the detection of defective sights of children, in pre-schools, clinics, domiciliary programmes, community centres and all other agencies interested in the welfare of children. The investigation must specifically refer to blindness, and also V. D., small pox, trechoma caused by infection and as a result of vitamin 'A' deficiency.

Day Nurseries and Creches

That, for the benefit of working mothers and in environments which are evidently harmful for the health and growth of toddlers between one and three years of age, creches, day nurseries, or 'palnaghars' should be created to satisfy health and environmental needs and nutritive requirements of such children.

Pre-Schools

Since a large number of pre-schools are required in our country, it is desirable that the principles of simplicity of training and maximum economy in the management of pre-schools organisation should be adopted, especially in rural and tribal areas, to solve the problem of workers and funds. The pre-school should provide maximum variety of activities to occupy the time and interest of children.

That, leadership of pre-schools must come from special training institutions offering two or three years' graduate or post-graduate course in Universities, teachers' training colleges, and schools of social work, especially those offering specialisation in child welfare.

Considering the need for improved programmes for the training of all kinds of child welfare workers, it is recommended that a committee be set up to revise the existing programmes, curricula, methods of training, etc., in the various Ministries and departments of the State, as well as training programmes organised by the Universities, schools of social work, and private child welfare and educational agencies.

That, the following varieties of articles are needed for the use of children under six years of age; pre-school educational materials and apparatus; playground equipment; educational toys; general varities of toys to suit children at different ages and levels of growth and development; picture books story books and childrens literature; books printed on cloth.

Recommendations : Central Government

Vital Statistics

The recommendations of the W. H. O. regarding tabulation of live birth and foetal deaths be endorsed; and that tabulation of live births and foetal deaths be registered in the four groups according to the length of gestation measured from the beginning of the last menstruation.

That, a committee should be appointed to examine the existing methods of registration in the State and suggest possible improvements that can achieve the purposes of registration.

That, the classification of infant mortality rates in Census Report may be done on the basis of standard of living, rather than on the basis of religion and community as at present. The classification of infant mortality on the standard of living basis may be as follows :

(1) Agricultural and forest labourers, artisans and small cultivators;

(2) Shop-keepers, money lenders, village officials and small landlords;

(3) Big landlords and rural aristocracy;

(4) Industrial workers and other wage earners;

(5) Shop-keepers, clerks and lower middle class;

(6) Professional and other educated persons and middle class;

(7) Owners of property and wealth, industrialists, financiers, etc.

That, the disparity of prices at which importers of milk (either in powder form or manufacturing them as children's foods). Supply the market and the market price of the same products should be examined, together with the policy regarding the import of foreign milk in powder form, so that every effort is made to increase the supply of powdered milk and children's foods to meet the full demand of the market for baby foods. This should also be achieved through indigenous manufacture of baby foods.

That, the assistance given by the UNICEF to increase the milk supply for babies and children should be properly utilised ; and further assistance must be given by the Centre to State Governments so that such schemes may be able to serve other cities with a population of more than three lakhs in the first instance.

That, the import policy regarding babies' and children's food should be carefully examined so that political and economic considerations do not came in the way of the availability of maximum quantities of milk powder at the lowest price till such time as when the entire needs could be met by internal production and that when whole milk supply is inadequate in the country, the import of foreign in gredients for infants' food should be treated as of equal importance with the need of foodgrains for the use of the adult population.

That, special efforts should be made to establish one or more plants for the production of cheap and nutritive foods for infants and children.

Legislation

That, efforts should be made to enact legislation for enabling private trusts and Endowments to divert their funds from less fundamental purposes in order to provide for the care of children whenever finances are available for the purpose of charity. This should especially be done by taking into consideration the Cypre Act or Law.

That, a Committee should be appointed to prepare a Model National Midwifery Act to be followed by legislation on the subject in every State.

Teaching of Paediatrics.

That, paediatrics must became a compulsory subject and part of the curriculum in all programmes of medical education ; and paediatricts should be recognised as specialists of great importance, and they should be gradually made available to every primary health centre by the end of the Fourth Plan Period.

Pre-Schools

At the present stage of pre-school development, it is suggested that important experimental projects should be carried out in different types of regions and communities and progress should be made in child study and research dealing with problems of growth, heredity, environment and child development as a whole.

Special type of child study and experimental pre-schools should be attached to universities, schools of social work and child study institutions.

Children's Literature

That. the Ministry of Education should maintain a unit consisting of a permanent staff of artists, writers, photographers, cine-technicians, etc., for the writings of children's books, including story books, nursery rhymes and poetry, etc.; and their services should be available to assist the development of children's literature in the various States.

That, for the printing of children's books, including picture books. books printed on cloth, etc:, a national organisation is required with printing establishment equipped for photography, art work, and offset printing. A part of the produced materials without language inscription may be used by different States imprint the coloured printed materials with appropriate language description in the various regional languages.

Whilst appreciating the work done by the Children's Book Trust, the Committee recommends the extension of the work of the Trust in order to enable it to prove of benefit to all the linguistice regions of the country.

Recommendations : State Governments

United Nations Charter For Children

That, the Declaration of the Rights of the Child adopted by UNICEF on November 20th, 195), should be extensively circularised amongst Governments and Departments at all levels ; and every effort should be made by State Governments and private agencies to achieve the purposes of the declaration.

Administration For Child Welfare

That, since existing programmes of child welfare are being carried out by a large number of departments of the various State Governments, it is recommended that a Division of Child Welfare be created in an appropriate Ministry, in order to provide specialised direction and guidance to all child welfare programmes of the States.

That, a permanent and regularly functioning Co-ordination Committee should be set up in each State consisting of representatives of each of the Departments dealing with programmes of child welfare in order to serve common objectives, maintain common standards, avoid over-lapping and achieve cooperation between all departments to promote maximum economy and efficiency.

That, the Coordination Committee on Child Welfare in each State should create an appropriate machinery to promote intensive cooperation and close coordination of all State and private effort for child welfare.

That, in States where the post of a Lady District Welfare Officer has not been created to serve the rural areas, such a post be created with the view to appoint a qualified and trained child welfare officer to organise, guide and supervise all programmes of women and child welfare in the district.

Legislation

That, severe and corrective action is needed to deal with persons who are guilty of criminal neglect of any child under their protection, guardianship, or custody. It is necessary and desirable to promote legislation against cruelty and neglect of children, and the law should be effectively enforced and implemented to prevent the sufferings and hardships of any child. It is recommended that a Committee be appointed to review the existing legislation and suggest modifications where-ever necessary.

Housing

That, to strengthen the family socially, the problem of housing should be dealt with not only in terms of minimum housing standards, but also in terms of adequate, proper and systematic housing management where properties, good neighbourliness, health and human relation are looked after.

Vital Statistics

That, immediate measures must be taken to see that registration regarding births and deaths of children and causes of infant mortality are properly carried out so that the correct situation could be understood. As far as possible, all States should adopt a uniform method of registration of data pertaining to vital statistics and other information for demographic purposes.

That, there should be a permanent machinery in every State for the maintenance of all vital statistics, and annual reports should be available to cover all areas of the country without exception. If possible, there should be a Census Bureau in every State.

Family Planning

Whilst facilities for sterilisation and performance of vasectomy should be increased, including the use of mobile service, the training of the entire staff associated with the programme is necessary to increase its efficiency and efficacy. A follow-up service for a brief period is necessary to deal with such cases.

Health And Nutrition

Health services should be started for children of pre-school age so that periodical health check up of children of this age group may be carried out.

That, at least one children's hospital should be created in every State,

Efforts should be made to provide adequate milk to all the children, under-nourished children being given a priority.

That, programmes for the nourishment of children providing the right type of food of good quality and adequate quantity should be introduced in all pre-schools.

That, cooperative dairy farming should be developed in rural areas ; and milk distribution to methods and children should be done through the panchayats.

That, in order to prevent profiteering, welfare centres and cooperatives must become direct distributors of all commercial goods, including milk products produced and imported into the country.

That, every effort should be made to discover and encourage the production of cheap foods. This work should be entrusted to State Agencies, so that such foods can be supplied as subsidised foods and thus the cost of nourishment of children may be keept as low as possible.

Large scale production of protein rich foods which have already been perfected should be encouraged. That further research should be conducted to discover more articles containing high nutritive value in terms of protein to supplement and substitute the milk supply.

Health Visitors

That, a Health Visitors service is essential in all the States, and the domiciliary service along with properly organised ante-natal and post-natal clinics should function even when Public Health Nurses are available to assist the community under the control of the Ministry of Health.

Maternity Services

That, the existing training programmes for Dais need to be increased so that they may function as provisional Health Visitors and as parent educators and instructors in family planning wherever possible, and when special staff is not available for these programmes.

That, there should be done trained dai for every 20 villages ; and for every 10,000 of rural population by the end of the Third Plan period, to be increased to one trained dai for every five villages and 3,000 of rural population by the end of the Fourth Plan Period.

That, the prevailing system of attention to pregnant mothers in the community at the time of delivery should always be taken into consideration, and till such time as a national midwifery service is properly constituted and organised, the policy of compulsary registration of all the dais must be adopted, accompanied by a period of minimum training for such dais to be organised in every district of the country.

Post-Natal Care

The post-natal and well-baby clinics should be organised within primary health centres and M.C.H. Centres to supervise the cases up to the age of at least one year, and upto three years wherever possible.

Pre-Schools

Government should give substantial assistance to voluntary institutions running pre-primary schools.

That, different categories of aid should be given mainly to assist the pre-school with equipment, payment of salary of teachers, and to supplement the cost of pre-school feeding programmes, etc. A grant-in-aid should be paid by the Central Government to pilot and experimental projects ; and State Governments should promote pilot projects in each district ; and Municipalities should develop pre-schools mainly for the benefit of slum areas and to cater to children who do not have the advantage of being brought up in proper physical and human environments.

That, all under-privileged children should be given an opportunity for pre-school education ; but it is not desirable to create separate pre-schools for them.

That, wherever possible, States should enact a Pre-School Act and all pre-schools be registered under the Society Registration Act of 1860. All pre-schools should conform to minimum standards which the relevant Municipality or the State may lay down.

That, the age of admission to the pre-schools should be about three-and-a-half years in all general types of pre-schools ; and children who are two-and-a half years old may be admitted in pre-schools where there are sufficient number of assistant teachers, and the teacher is not called upon to lookafter more than 15 children under three-and-a-half years of age.

That, all pre-schools should be universally co-educational and all the children may wear a common type of dress.

That, ordinarily a child may spend a minimum of two years and a maximum of four years in a pre-school.

That, a normal unit of a pre-school should be of 25 children and one unit of pre-school should not have more than 40 children. In case there are more than 20 children in a unit, the unit should have are additional assistant teacher.

Recommended Scales

Graduate teachers with special two years training	Rs. 200 plus D.A. to Rs. 2:0.
Graduates with short-term training	Rs. 120 plus D.A. to Rs. 250.
Intermediate Arts with special two years training	Rs. 150 plus D.A. to Rs. 300
Matriculates with special training	Rs. 90 plus D.A. to Rs. 180.
Assistant Teachers—Matriculates with training	Rs. 90 plus D.A. to Rs. 150.
Assistant Teachers—Non-Matriculates (V.F.) with training	Rs. 70 plus D.A. to Rs. 150
Attendants, Sahayikas, Cooks and Servants	Rs. 40 plus D.A. or prevailing scales in the area.

Care Of The Handicapped Child

That, the following classes of handicapped children should be given special treatment in terms of institutional care and other programmes in order to provide opportunities for rehabilitation and normal growth and development.

1. Orphans ;
2. Foundlings ;

3. Blind and partially visioned, deaf and dumb ;

4. Children affected by chronic diseases like T.B., V.D., etc.

That, a few large hospitals and rehabilitation centres should be created in the various States to deal with the cases requiring long term care and intensive treatment for rehabilitation.

The Committee is of the opinion that the cost of maintenance of majority of children under six years of age in boarding institutions vary between Rs. 40 to Rs. 50 per month per head excluding the cost of treatment ; and adequate grants-in-aid be provided to enable such children to receive opportunities to grow up as normal children.

That, adequate services are not provided at present for children whose one parent is alive ; and therefore it is necessary to create Short Stay Homes where children could be looked after till their parents are able to undertake full responsibility for the care of children.

That, the traditional procedures connected with adoption of children are at present inadequate ; and effective measures are necessary to apply amended Adoption Act to all those who desire to adopt children ; and there should be a provision for screening, recommendation and acceptance for a short-term observation in order to protect the true interests of the adopted child.

That, in each State, the Ministry of Welfare should create "Children's Villages" for the care of foundlings and the village should be fed by sub centres in rural and urban areas. These villages must consist of Homes which will function as rehabilitation centres which will serve as a case work service for the parents and the child, and it will provide shelter, training, education, rehabilitation, etc. to the foundlings till they reach the age of 18 years.

That, a nation-wide census of handicapped children should be carried out and this work should be the responsibility of Gram Panchayats and District authorities in rural areas, whilst in urban areas the census must be carried out by Municipalities with the help of social welfare organisations and Universities.

That, in order to detect handi-capped conditions, the norms showing development of the child at various stages should be widely published and made available to hospitals, clinics, institutions and welfare agencies.

That, States should divert some funds from the finances earmarked for pre-school education to provide special pre-school for handicapped children.

That, for the detection of auditory defects, audiometric units should be created in hospitals, and in all institutions for deaf and mutes, etc.

Experimental day nurseries for the benefit of working and illiterate mothers should be organised in all rural areas where the integrated programme of child welfare will be introduced in the Third Plan period.

That, day nurseries should be organised in orphanages and foundling homes where infant and small children are admitted, and trained nurses should be employed in such institutions. Day nurseries are also needed in women's institutions, prisons where females are kept, in slum areas and in areas where ex-criminal groups reside.

That, training programmes should be organised, as far as possible, along with training programmes of balsevikas, health visitors and pre-school teachers for the benefit of special balsevikas to serve in creches and day nurseries. The day nurseries training curriculum should also become a part of the training of Public Health Nurses. Short-term training programmes should also be organised by aided programmes in schools of social work.

Training

That, training programmes may be developed in important cities, as well as in all the States, to give a comprehensive in-service training in problems, needs and programmes of child welfare to personnel who are employed to serve in different fields.

Recommendations : Municipalities And Zila Parishads

That municipalities and zila parishads should give high priority to welfare programmes for the mother and child by promoting funds for the organisation and efficient management of domiciliary services and M.C.H. centrer providing for ante natal and post natal care, family planning, pre-schools, and programmes for the feeding of under nourished children.

That, the development of services for the mother and the child should be based upon local needs of the particular place and the particular time.

That, as the funds allotted for programmes of child welfare at present are entirely inadequate to meet the primary needs of survival and normal growth and development of the child, more funds should be raised, and allotments should be made after properly assessing the minimum needs of child welfare in each area.

That, child welfare at the community level in urban and rural areas should now be carried out by a proper personnel selected and trained for specific functions ; and their numbers should be increased according to the increasing resources which are now to be provided for the execution of all integrated programmes, including family planning, health visiting, ante-natal and post-natal care, family contact and counselling and parental education, etc.

That, special measures should be taken in urban areas to reduce infant mortality especially in slum areas; and intensive programmes of child welfare and ante-natal and post-natal care should be extensively introduced in such areas as early as possible.

Children's food should be supplemented through milk centres for the poor in as many urban areas as possible.

That, the assistance given by the UNICEF to increase the milk supply for babies and children should be porperly utilised; and further assistance must be given by the Centre to State Governments so that such schemes may be able to serve other cities with a population of more than three lakhs in the first instance.

That, in order to provide improved care to new born children, pressure on maternity services in urban areas should be reduced; and this can be done by strengthening and increasing domiciliary services so that all the cases for normal delivery may be attended to outside the institutions.

That, the existing number of maternity beds in city hospitals should provided over and above their own requirements for accommodating five per cent to 10 per cent of the total births outside—properly equipped maternity homes and domiciliary service outside such hospitals.

That, wherever there is any kind of housing authority such as Housing Boards, Housing Cooperative Societies, Development Boards, etc., in existence, efforts should be made to create ante-natal and post-natal clinics in their area; and grant-in-aid should be given to them by municipalities and State Governments.

That, in localities where higher income groups are living, the private practitioner should open Family Planning and ante-natal clinics to serve the locality.

That, in slum areas and in the localities where lower income groups live, one health visitor or midwife (or public health nurse) should be provided at the rate of one to 400 families to provide medical assistance and guidance to them.

That, specialised services should be provided at materntiy and paediatric hospitals for mothers and children who are referred to them by maternity or child welfare centres, namely regional clinics for investigation and treatment of serious cases such as V.D., E.N.T., eye defects, etc.

That ante-natal clinics should carefully supervise the diet of pregnant women, and if required, should supplement them by free meal scheme.

That, ante-natal and post-natal programmes should be assisted by other welfare wokers like family planning counsellers, family connsellers, social education workers, community organisers, etc.

That, as deaf children are invariably mute also, and deafness is not normally detected till the child is 12 to 18 months old, post natal clinics should be mainly responsible for the detection all the sensory defects of the child.

Recommendations : Community Development

That, in a community development programme the social health of the family should receive as much attention as family economy especially through programmes of have economics, social education and family counselling wherever possible. The community development programmes should take special measures to promote and strengthen the family's spiritual and ethical backgrounds which had contributed in the past to sound social health and family and national integration.

That, all panchayats must be associated and made responsible for not only the registration of data, but the supervision of the registration machinery at the lowest level.

Child Health

That, coverage of primary health centres in rural areas, and municipal MCW centres in urban areas should be reduced to a number which could be effectively handled by the staff. The existing staff should not later to a population of more than 25,000 persons.

That, special nutrition rehabilitation centres should be started in community areas to provide simple and inexpensive meals to children to help them to recover from deficiency caused by diseases like rickets, beriberi,, etc.

That courses in nutrition may be included in school curricula; and besides, education about nutritional needs of children may be imported to mothers through various centres and domiciliary programmes. Demonstrations should be given dealing with methods of cooking articles and dishes so that the nutrition value of food may not be lost.

That, there should be one trained dai for every 20 villages; and for every 10,000 of rural population by the end of the Third Plan period, to be increased to one trained dai for every five villages and 3,000 of rural population by the end of the Fourth Plan period.

That, a nationwide census of handicapped children should be carried out and this work should be the responsibility of Gram Panchayats and District Authorities in rural areas, whilst in urban areas the census must be carried out by municipalities with the help of social welfare organisation and universities.

Recommendations : Pre-Schools

That, pre-school education must be single mindedly devoted to the true welfare, growth and development of the human child as a vital organism, and a unit of the human species,

That; the concepts of pre-school philosophy and principles are appropriate to Indian conditions and needs; that children must be healthy and active within their family and community environments, and grow up and develop during childhood to receive education and become worthy citizens of the nation.

That, the system of training must correspond to the fundamental needs of the child's comprehensive growth and development irrespective of any social, economic, political or philosophical considerations.

That, the pre-school programme should be based upon five factors which have been universally accepted and which are stated below:

(a) Heredity and environment of the child must receive very great attention because the growth and development of the child is largely dependent on these two factors.

(b) That, child at all times must live in an atmosphere which is full of joy, contributing to its total happiness.

(c) The child must grow up and develop in conditions of freedom.

(d) The child needs activity in order to spend its energy and to expand its total capacity and abilities, thus accumulating experience which contribute to its total growth and development.

(e) The child needs protection and assistance of parents and other competent persons who are aware of the special needs of children during the pre-school age.

In order to increase the number of pre-schools in the whole of India including urban, rural and sylvan areas, it is necessary to organisationally promote self-sufficient pre-schools which could be organised, if possible, without the assistance of the State to be managed by regional communities in urban neighbourhoods and large villages. A national pre-school association be created for this purpose.

Pre-schools shall be started in urban areas, where people can pay the cost of education of the children.

Responsibility for starting pre-schools should be left to voluntary organisations with adequate assistance from the Government.

That pre-schools should be of the following types:

(a) A half day organisation to be developed as "The Minimum Standard Pre-School". A pre-school of minimum standard should provide a playground, look after the health and cleanliness of children, inculcate in them good habits and correct behaviours, and provide such opportunities for training like Nature Study, and other subjects which can be easily dealt with by reasonably trained teachers and Balsevikas.

(b) Standard pre-schools following some kind of systems like the Montessori, the Pre-Basic, Azzisi and any other system suitable to rural areas; and any type of pre-school using programmes, methods and techniques suitable for different types of environments in urban areas.

(The true meaning of Pre-Basic should imply the acceptance of the "Principle of Activity" initiated and developed by a number of psychologists and educationist of Vienna. The types of activities must be suitable to the needs of the child and the community.)

(c) A pre-school project attached to the village primary school, to be located as far as possible in a separate structure so that classes of the pre-school and primary school are not held together.

(d) Infant classes in primary schools and high schools, with training and programme modified to conform to principles and programmes of the pre-school.

(e) Open air pre-schools with playgrounds may be created where facilities and resources are inadequate; or where there are inadequate numbers of children to promote a pre-school as a unit.

(f) (i) Pre-schools attached to institutions where unattached women with children are provided with boarding and lodging facilities.

(ii) Special pre-schools in urban areas for subnormal, feeble-minded and problem children with behaviour disorders.

(iii) Special types of pre-schools to help the care, training and rehabilitation of handicapped children.

(iv) Pre- schools attached to prisons for women with their children.

(v) Pre-schools with a high standard of service for areas where communities of ex-criminal groups live.

(vi) Pre-schools promoted as a special treatment for areas where juvenile delinquency is extensively present.

(g) Pre-schools organised in large housing schemes where a number of rooms and tenements are available for their use. Where there is no space for playgrounds, terraces may be suitably adjusted for the purpose in order to provide safety for the children.

That, all under-privileged children should be given an opportunity for pre-school education; but it is not desirable to create separate pre-schools for them.

That, a common nomenclature for all pre-schools is not desirable; but when names are given to pre-schools, they should not be, as far as possible, associated with names of systems and types of equipment used in each pre-school.

It is not desirable for pre-schools to have a very large number of children and as far as possible, a pre-school should not have more than four units.

That, during the whole period of stay of a child in

a pre school, it may go through three or four stages of training. Each stage of the child's training in a pre-school must conform to his physical conditions and nature of growth and development.

That, pre-school should, as far as possible, be located near places where a large number of families reside; and as far as possible, they may belong to regional communities, and may be entrusted to their care for management and supervision.

That, where children have to walk to the pre-school, they should not be expected to go more than one mile from their place of residence each day.

Transport facilities may be provided by institutions which are self-sufficient in their resources.

That, the presence of natural surroundings is necessary for the physical growth and emotional development of children; and when pre-schools are not open-air schools, gardens and playgrounds shall be attached to them.

Pre-schools in rural areas should be located in villages with minimum population of about 500 persons. Preference should be given to villages which agree to give a site for the structure and playground and bear part cost of structure, or at least provide labour for construction.

In tribal areas where people live in hamlets which are located at considerable distances with small population, the pre-schools should be located in villages where hamlets are close together, and where it will be possible for the children to walk small distances to attend the pre-school.

That heavy capital expenditure should not be incurred for the construction of pre-schools. Even open air schools, low cost structures or gardens or open spaces be considered adequate for the use of children.

That whenever possible simple structures may be constructed, and they could be 'kutcha' structures in rural areas, using local materials for their construction. The plan of the pre-school should allow sufficient space for kitchen and a washing place, dining and siesta.

That, a pre-school must have a playground, at least two rooms, a tap, bath room, lavatory and urinals.

That, municipalities, landlords, owners of public places like temples, churches and all citizens must do everything in their power to see that space and shelter are not denied to children for play and pre-schools.

That, playgrounds should be provided by all Housing Boards, or other types of housing authorities so that there is accommodation for an open-air pre-school with 80 to 100 children in a community of about 500 families.

That, for pre-schools with more available space about 100 sq. feet of ground and garden per child are needed for open air activities. For indoor activities there should be an assembly hall, which can also be used for siesta purposes, as well as space for group activities and indoor meetings. A store room and a kitchen, an office room, a staff room, and an isolation room could always be useful. There should be a locker room for children, if possible, adequate washing and bathing accommodation, and taps and toilet for all children, should be provided. At least one lavatory is needed for every 12 to 15 children.

That routine programme of activities of the pre-school must always be adopted to suit the place, the climate, the ability of teachers and the wish of children and pre-schools are invariably 'good weather' institutions, and children should not be called to participate in activities of pre-school during inclement weather, when there are heavy rains or cold. Pre-schools should function during seasons and months suitable for different types of pre-school activities.

That pre-schools should start there day in the morning assembly so that all children may gather, meet each other, and enjoy companionship. Daily programmes should be planned in advance by the pre-school teachers ; and varieties of subjects and activities should be introduced every day like play activities, learning activities, handwork activities, practicals, school service, etc. Children must enjoy open air and outdoor life as much as they can. The time allotted to different types of activities should vary according to the capacities of children to give attention and their interest in activities or subjects which are handled by the teacher.

That, children must participate in all important activities of the whole community, and this must be an important part of all pre-school activities.

That, at least a midday meal or snack should be served at pre-school ; and three meals should be given, if the family and the community are willing to contribute towards the expenses of a light morning breakfast with milk, lunch, and light evening snack with fruits.

That, a careful study must be made of the sleeping habits of children at home ; and there must be a daily siesta of 90 to 120 minutes after the midday meal. When the pre-school works only for half-a-day, and when parents insist that children should return home for their afternoon lunch, then parental education must make them realise that the child must have sleep and rest at home during the afternoon.

That, to meet all pre-school expenses, local contributions should be obtained from the community in cash, kind, labour or service towards programme of construction, nutrition, instruction, excursions and camps.

There should be team of the following scientists to assist pre-school workers' training programme and counsellors of pre-schools : Psychologists, Paediatricians,

Nutrition Experts, Educationists, Sociologist, Biologist, and other scientists dealing with the methodology of pre-school training. Their services may be requisitioned from regional Universities.

That, Balsevikas should be young women, preferably under 25 years of age at the time of employment, as small child normally responds affectionately to young persons or very old persons. The employment of young men (Balmitras) should not be ruled out for pre-school work, because they are useful as instructors for hand-work, playground activities and pre school social service.

That, pre-school with two or three units and not exceeding four units should have a Mukhya Shikshika, or Headmistress or Principal.

A large number of pre-schools and institutions with a high standard of child care and training programme will require a Director for the pre-school, while in rural areas persons will be required to direct, organise, and supervise a large number of pre-schools in each district. A woman District Welfare Officer should be entrusted with this work.

That, term like 'ayah' or 'servants' are in appropriate for pre-schools, but assistants and 'helpers' or 'Sahayika' are required for the maintenance of cleanliness, helping children to bathe and wash themselves, for the preparation of service of meals, cleaning of utensils, and helping to look after unmanageable children.

Pre-school attended by children with behaviour problems require a special person on the staff trained in psychology.

Recommended Scales

Graduate teachers with special two years' training	...Rs. 200 plus D A. to Rs. 350.
Graduates with short-term training	...Rs. 120 plus D.A. to Rs. 250
Intermediate Arts with special two years training	...Rs. 150 plus D.A. to Rs. 300
Matriculates with special training	...Rs. 90 plus D.A. to Rs. 180
Assistant Teachers—Matriculates with training	...Rs. 90 plus D.A. to Rs. 150
Assistant Teachers—Non-Matriculates (V.F.) with training	...Rs. 70 plus D.A, to Rs. 150
Attendants, Sahayika, cooks and servants	...Rs. 40 plus D.A. or prevailing scales in the area.

Recommendations : Miscellaneous

That, courses in nutrition may be included in school curricula; and besides, education about nutritional needs of children may be imparted to mothers through various centres and domiciliary programmes. Demonstrations should be given on methods of cooking articles and dishes so that the nutritive content and value of food may not lost.

That, specialised services should be provided at maternity and paediatric hospitals for mothers and children who are referred to them by maternity or child welfare centres namely regional clinics for investigation and treatment of serious cases, such as V.D., E.N.T., eye defects, etc.

That, anti-natal clinics should carefully supervise the diet of pregnant women, and if required, should supplement them by free meal scheme.

Family Planning

Family planning must become a regular habit amongst married adults in rural and urban communities, and extensive cooperative efforts of all social welfare organisations and medical and educational services must achieve this object through family contact programmes and parental education.

Anti-Natal Care

That, the required services that an ante-natal programme should provide must be able to achieve the following objectives :

(a) To create reasonably desirable psychological conditions to the expectant mother when she is primigravide, so that she is in a happy, hopeful and confident frame of mind, free of anxieties, sorrows and fears:

(b) To diagnose and treat any early complications.

(c) To increase the proportions of normal deliveries.

(d) To reduce the incidence of premature births, still-births and parental and neo-natal deaths.

(e) To improve the cleanliness, orderliness, and sanitary conditions of the house in which expectant mother is living.

(f) To give minimum parental education required by the mother, especially at the time of first delivery, in order to provide intelligent and affectionate care to the child from the very beginning, after birth.

That, wherever there is any kind of Housing Authority such as Housing Boards, Housing Cooperative Societies, Development Boards, etc., in existence, efforts should be made to create ante-natal and post-natal clinics in their area; and grant-in-aid should be given to them by Municipalities and State Governments.

That, the use of the Rhythm Method is useful to create the knowledge and consciousness of family planning, and to overcome the mental hesitation and antagonism to concepts of planned parent-hood.

In recommending and adopting the use of any kind of contraceptive, the psychological reactions of the users and the aesthetics of sexual relations must be kept in mind, together with a consideration for the general moral and social health of the family, youth and society as a whole.

That, parents, school teachers and Government Departments should be given sufficient guidance in adopting the right approach to the welfare of handicapped children.

That, for the purpose of early detection of handicaps and effective care and rehabilitation of cases, the following measures are suggested :

(a) A programme of parental education.

(b) Pre-school teachers, gramsevikas and balsevikas should have some elementary training to be able to detect early defects which can be referred to school, Health and Medical services.

(c) The staff of Primary Health Centres and even indigenous dais could be trained to detect defects at an early stage.

(d) Mobile Health Units in rural areas, and all child welfare agencies in urban areas can help the detection of handicapped.

That, parental education should be provided as an essential part of all day nursery programmes.

That, educational toys and materials should, as far as possible, be manufactured locally.

That, toys made of rubber, metal and plastics may be manufactured by the private sector; but they must be suitably guided by educational and child welfare agencies regarding design, construction, costs, etc.

PETRO-CHEMICAL COMMITTEE, 1960—REPORT

New Delhi, Ministry of Commerce and Industry, 1963. 120p.+iiip.

Chairman : Dr. G.P. Kane.
Members : Shri K.K. Sahni ; Dr. J. S. Ahluwalia ; Shri K. Vyasulu.
Secretary : Dr. A. Seetharamiah.

APPOINTMENT

A committee for the preparation of a plan for the development of petro-chemical industries during the Third and the Fourth Five-Year Plans was appointed in terms of Office Memorandum No. CH(1)—2(81)/60, dated October 10, 1960, issued by the Government of India in the Ministry of Commerce and Industry. The The Terms of Reference of the Committee as well as its composition were amended by a further Office memorandum No. CH (1)-2(81)/60, dated November 2, 1960, issued by the Ministry of Commerce and Industry. The background to the appointment of the Committee is stated as follows :

"During the last few years in many advanced countries of the world, products such as synthetic rubber, plastics, insecticides, detergents and organic solvents have been made increasingly as petro-chemicals. In view of the rapidly rising demands of such products in the country and the likely availability of suitable petroleum fractions for their production in the next few years, Government recognise the need to encourage the development of petro-chemical industries. It has, therefore, been decided to set a Committee to study the subjects in all its aspects so as to evolve a plan for organising such industries during the Third and the Fourth Five-Year Plans.

TERMS OF REFERENCE

(a) An assessment of the types and quantities of material whose production may have to be organised in petro-chemical industries ;

(b) A study of the integrated pattern of production of petro-chemicals in advanced countries and to evolve a suitable pattern for development in India ;

(c) To assess the extent to which aromatic as well as aliphatic raw materials may have to be produced as petro-chemicals during the period 1961 to 1971 ; and

(d) To recommend the pattern of development of petro-chemical industries in the country.

The above para (b) was substituted vide Memorandum No. CH (1)-2 (81)/60, dated November 2, 1960 as follows :

"To evolve a suitable pattern for development in India in the context of the integrated pattern of production of petro-chemicals in advanced countries"

CONTENTS

Introduction and Scope of the Committee's Work ; A Brief Review of the Development of Petro-Chemical Industry in Advanced Countries ; Availability of Raw Material Feed Stocks ; Organic Chemicals and Other Products to be Manufactured from Petroleum Products ; Facilities Needed for the Manufacture of Organic

Chemicals and Other Products and Related Matters; Estimated Current Availability of Organic Chemical and Related Products; The Extent to which the Demand for these Products would have to be Based on Petroleum and Non-Petroleum Feed-Stocks, Estimates Regarding Investment, Value of Production, etc.; Summary of Conclusions and Recommendations; Appendices I to VI.

RECOMMENDATIONS

The demand for organic chemicals; synthetic rubber plastics, pesticides, detergents, etc., is rising very rapidly in the country. The three chief raw materials for the Organic Chemicals Industry, viz., Petroleum and its products, coaltar products, vegetable matter and fermentation products thereof would become available shortly for the first time in the country in substantial quantities. The Organic Chemicals Industry, which can be said to have just started in the country, is therefore on the threshold of major developments and one may expect a spectacular growth and development of this industry during the next decade.

While the raw materials from carbonisation of coal are aromatic compounds, those from petroleum are largely aliphatic compounds. Since modern processes enable compounds of both types to be obtained from either, coal and petroleum may be regarded as complementary as well as supplementary sources of chemicals. Both are, therefore, necessary for the modern Organic Chemicals Industry.

In the industrially advanced countries the demand forecasts for different organic chemicals and other products are worked out on the basis of projecting the consumption rates in relation to current levels and the growth of income and their distribution in the country. The studies would also cover patterns and shifts in consumption expenditure. Such an approach is not feasible at the present stage in India, because the Organic Chemicals Industry is still in its infancy.

Further in a planned economy dependents on heavy imports for development, restraints on consumption are expected to operate. The Committee is not in a position to make assumptions about such restraints.

The restrictive factors acting as a brake on consumption would have been largely overcome by the end of the Third Plan and thereafter production could be expected to expand freely in response to demand.

Targets for more important products under the Third as well as the Fourth Five-Year Plan has been worked out taking into consideration estimated domestic demand, minimum economic size of manufacturing units export potentialities, etc.

Some of the more important products the production of which will have to be taken up first have been listed and targets of production for them under the Third and Fourth Plans have been suggested.

The Committee is of the view that if there are no restraints on consumption and investments nor abnormal price increases, the demand estimates worked out for the end of the Third and the Fourth Plans would definitely be reached. It is noted that the targets proposed for 1965-66 in the Report on the Third Plan for some of these products are lower than those suggested by the Development Council. The report, however, states that the revision of these targets open to consideration in the Third Plan period.

In order to ensure the production of adequate quantities of organic chemicals and other products, it would be necessary to ensure that the following primary raw materials which would be used as feed-stocks one made available to the extent indicated below for the Organic Chemicals Industry.

	1965-66	1970-71
	tons	tons
(1) Methanol	25,000	60,000
(2) Ethyl-Alcohol	200,000	290,000
(3) Ethylene	50,000	165,000
(4) Propylene	20,000	70,000
(5) N-Butane/N-Butylenes	60,000/45,000	160,000/120,000
(6) Isobutylenes	13,000	67,5000
(7) Acetylene	24,000	59,000
(8) Benzene	80,000	180,000
(9) Naphthalene	20,000	40,000

Production of methanol and ethylene could be organised either from coke-over gases or petroleum feed-stocks. Propylene, N-butane/N-butylenes, iso-butane iso-butylene would have to be based on petroleum feed-stocks.

The entire requirement of ethyl-alcohol would be obtained by the fermentation of molasses and it would not be necessary to produce ethyl-alcohol based on petroleum products.

Part of the requirements of benzene would be met from coal-tar source, the balance being met from petroleum source.

Almost the entire quantity of acetylene needed by the end of the Third Plan is assumed to be met from calcium carbide. During the Fourth Plan, there might be some production of acetylene from petroleum sources depending on its economics.

The demands for cis-4-polybutadiene poly-iso-prene and butyl rubbers are likely to be interchanged, and this fact would have to be taken into account while creating capacity for synthetic rubber. The position would be somewhat similar in the case of major plastrics, namely PVC, polyethylene and polystyrene,

In the past, the demand for benzene for the Organic

Chemicals Industry was small but during the next few years to demand is expected to increase very rapidly which would not be met by the benzene recovered from coal carbonisation units. This is so because coal carbonisation is linked mainly to steel production and the rate of increase in the production of organic chemicals would be much faster as compared to the rate of increase in steel production. Therefore, the gap between demand and supply of benzene would have to be bridged by the production of benzene from petroleum source.

Aromatic are generally made from petroleum source by catalytic reforming of naphthenic rich fractions. Several commercial catalytic-forming processes are available and the process best suited to meet the country's requirements will have to be chosen.

Toluene content in the reformate is higher than the benzene conten, but the demand for benzene is greater than for toluene. By selection of proper fractions it would be possible to rectify this imbalance.

The crudes refined at present in India are imported from Middle East and these certain comparatively small quantity of naphthenes since these are mixed base. These crudes, therefore, are not suitable for producton of aromatics.

We would have a very good source of crude for the manufacture of aromatics in the Nahorkatiya crudes which are very rich in aromatics as well as naphthenic hydro-carbons. Since there is likely to be a shortage of benzene in the country, it is necessary that the indigenous crudes are suitably processed for the recovery of aromatics.

While the light gasoline fraction of Combay crude is reported to contain 18.2 per cent naphtenes and 4.2 per cent aromatics, the light fraction of Ankleshwar crude is reported to contain 32.2 per cent naphthenes and 10 pre cent aromatics. These crudes, particularly the one from Ankleshwar, appear to be suitable for the production of aromatics.

Since the demand for benezene for the projects already sanctioned in the Western region of the country is about 20,000 tons/year and the naphtha-cracking units (stream-crackers) in that region would only meet about half of this requirement, there is need for additional benzene which can be met either by expanding the capacity of the naphtha crackers already sanctioned and/or by the catalytic reforming and isolation of aromatics. In this content the production of aromatics from Ankleshwar crude in the new refinery would deserve careful consideration.

Catalytic reformers and naphtha-crackers should, as far as possible, be set up in conjunction with refineries. There would be certain advantages in a refinery itself setting-up a catalytic reformer because the non-aromatic fractions of a reformate could be used with advantage by a refinery for gasoline blending and this would influence the economics of the aromatics plant as well as the refinery. Similar considerations would hold good in respect of steam-crackers also. Under exceptional circumstances, however, a stream-cracker may have to be set up independently.

Since the plants for the manufacture of aromatics are capital intensive, it is essential to ensure that the units are of economic size because it is important that the products are made available to the other industrial consumers at prices comparable with world prices for these commodities or in competition with supplies from steel plants in the country.

In addition to methane, propane, butanes and pentanes, considerable quantities of hydrogen would became available as a by-product in the catalytic reformers and these would have to be utilised to the best advantage.

Toluene obtained from coal carbonisation units and the catalytic reformers would be far in excess of internal requirements and its disposal would pose problem. A solution to this problem can be found either by adding it to motor gasolene as high octane component or by its conversion to phenol as well as to benzene by dealkylation with hydrogen. Exports, if feasible, will also provide another outlet.

While there would be a good demand for O-xylene for conversion to phthalican hydride—there might even be shortage of O-xylene—the disposal of m-xylene would be a serious problem. It may become necessary to adopt processes for the isomerisation of m-xylene to O-xylene and p-xylene mixture and thus reduce the magnitude of the problem.

The amount of naphthalene which would be recovered from coal carbonisation units would be inadequate to meet the demand for it in the country. The production of naphthalene from petroleum source is on its way for the first time even in U.S.A. Therefore the gap between demand and supply may have to be bridged by the use of an alternative starting material viz., O-xylene for the production of phthalic-anhydride.

Since the demand for ethlene and propylene would not be met by the two steam-crackers which have already been approved in the Bombay region, it is evident that further step-up of steam-cracking facilities would be needed even during the Third Plan vis-a-vis the demand forecasts for ethylene and propylene.

The production of indigenous raw rubber in the plantations in South India has not been able to keep pace with the rapidly increasing damands of the Rubber-Goods Manufacturing Industry. The demand for all varieties of rubber, which was of the order of 58,000 tons in 1960, is expected to rise to 141,000 tons in 1965 and to 282,000 tons in 1970. The production of natural rubber is expected to increase from the current level of about 25,000 tons to about 40,000 tons by 1965 and about 55,000 tons by 1970. It is, therefore, necessary to fill the gap between supply and demand by undertaking the production of synthetic rubber on a large scale. In view of the limited availabilty of natural rubber it will be necessary to undertake the manufacture of those varieties of synthetic rubbers which would need the least amount of natural rubber for compounding. On this score the choice would have to be in favour of manufacturing two stereo-specific rubbers, viz., cis 4-polybutadiene and cispoly-soprene. The manufacture of butyl rubber deserves further consideration. There would be no need for creating additional capacity for SBR type of synthetic rubber, since it cannot be used alone or in substantial quantities in admixture with natural rubber in the manufacture of giant tyres which would continue to constitute the bulk of automobile tyres produced in the country for a fairly long time to come.

The most profitable uses of surplus naphtha would be as a raw material for production of materials that would save maximum foreign exchange. Such materials are nitrogenous fertilisers, petro-chemicals and town gas for substitution of. Kerosene as a domestic fuel. The alternative suggestion is to use naphtha temporarily in admixture with gas oil. However, before marketing any such blend same administrative problems would have to be solved.

Use of naphtha for nitrogenous fertilisers production would save foreign exchange equivalent to about 10 times its value. Similarly, when naphtha is used for production of organic chemicals, plastics, etc., the value of the material produced per ton of naphtha would vary from three to seven times the cost of naphtha depending on the nature of the ultimate product.

In case adequate quantities of surplus naphtha from the indigenous sources are not available for the manufacture of nitrogenous fertilisers, organic chemials and other products, the shortfall would have to be made good by imports til the indigenors supply catches up with demand because it would cost less foreign exchange to imports naphtha than the import of finished products derived from it. In this connection, it would be advantageous to import suitable crudes and make available naphtha for the chemical industry after refining. The Committee is of the view that Government may proceed on the basis that naphtha will be available either from indigenous sources or, if necessary, for a very short period by imports to feed such schemes as may be considered important enough for licence under the Industries Act on import-saving or foreign exchange earning considerations. It is also recommended that projects which have already been approved may be processed on this basis.

With a view to ensure balanced development of different parts of the country and also to minimise the transport of chemicals and other finished products which would be necessary to set up naphtha-cracking units in the different regions. Since these crackers would have to draw naphtha from the refines, it stands to reason that while setting up new refineries, the natural supply area also would have to be taken into consideration. In this context, it would be necessary to set up a refinery in South India. This would obviate the need for transport of naphtha from Bombay to F.A.C.T., Alwaye and also would help in setting up petro-chemical industry in South India to meet the requirements of that region.

Plants for the manufacture of aromatics, olefins and organic chemicals, plastics, synthetic rubber, detergents, etc., are capital intensive and do not lend themselves to small scale operations. The setting up of such units can be justified only when large volume operations are feasible.

Decision regarding the location and size of unit should be based on economic considerations. While encouraging the setting up of crackers as well as other units during the Third and Fourth Five-Year Plans, an attempt must be made to ensure that the units set up are of economic size so that the cost of production is comparable with that in other countries. Under these circumstances, the Organic Chemicals Industry in the country would have a firm footing and its products would offer considerable scope for organising exports at least to neighbouring countries.

It is recommended that steps be taken for setting up four steam-cracking units in the western, eastern and southern zones of the country to meet the requirements of ethylene, propylene, butylenes, butadiene, benzene, etc. From economic considerations, it is essential to establish the steam-cracking units near refineries. The first steam-cracking unit should be established near the Bombay refineries; the second near the Barauni refinery; the third near the Gujarat refinery and the fourth near a refinery to be set up in South India.

By the end of the Third Plan, while there would be a surplus of motor gasoline, there would be deficits in all the other items, particularly the middle distillates. In order to reducing/removing these deficits, it is recommended that additional refining capacity should be set up in South India. This step, in addition to removing the deficits, would also yield additional naphtha for the Petro-Chemical Industry.

Utilising the starting materials obtained from the steam-crackers, petro-chemical complexes involving the manufacture of diverse products should be undertaken to fulfil the estimated demand indicated by the end of the Third and the Fourth Plan periods.

Depending upon the products to be included for production in these petro-chemical complexes, it would be necessary to decide whether steam-crackers would be of the low severity type or of the high-severity type.

The amount of C_4s available is rather limited and these should be utilised for the production of synthetic rubbers which are of strategic importance. C_4s should not be used as fuel in LPG. In order to augment the C_4s, it may be necessary to set up a special naphtha-cracking unit somewhere in North India.

The Committee is of the definite opinion that it is essential to build up the necessary technical knowledge not only with regard to production, separation, etc., of aromatics from petroleum feed-stocks but also with regard to diverse aspects of the Petro-Chemical Industry in the organisations such as the Development Wing, the Department of Oil (Ministry of Steel, Mines & Fuel) and the Planning Commission, which are closely associated with the development of the Petro-Chemical Industry in the country. The only satisfactory way of building up the necessary technical knowledge in the concerned organisation would be by the technical officers of these organisations visiting the petro-chemical units in the advanced countries. Unless this is done soon, it might be difficult to correctly assess the schemes submitted for the production of petro-chemicals and to exercise a check on the advice tendered by overseas consultants/experts, which are essential for ensuring the proper growth and development of this major industry in India.

It is necessary that naphtha used in the production of all chemicals and other products including nitrogenous fertilisers be exempted from payment of import and excise duty. In this context, it may be recalled that the removal of duty on imported hydro-carbon oil used for chemical synthesis, as recommended by the Ayne Committee (1944), was chiefly responsible for the development of a flourishing Petro-Chemical Industry in U. K. The gains by way of corporate tax, etc, accruing to Government by the establishment of new industries will more than compensate the loss of revenue from excise duty concession.

The demand and supply of naphtha for the Chemical Industry by the end of the South Plan appears to be very close to each other (about 2.15 million tons). If the rate of increase in motor gasoline consumption increases at a faster rate than 10 per cent per annum during the Fourth Plan and/or more than 50 per cent of the additional production of nitrogenous fertilisers during the Fourth Plan is based on naphtha, there would be a deficit which could be bridged by increasing the refining capacity in the country beyond 20 million tons.

The foreign exchange spent on direct and indirect imports of organic chemicals and related products in 1960 works out to approximately Rs. 30 crores. The estimated demand of organic chemicals and derived products excluding basics such as benzene, naphthalene, methyl-alcohol and ethyl-alcohol by the end of the Third Five Year Plan would be about 400,000 tons, valued at approximately Rs. 122 crores at current c.i.f. prices. Corresponding figures by the end of the Pourth Plan would be 960,000 tons, valued at Rs. 260 crores.

While by the end of the Third Plan, products equivalent to about 198,000 tons of carbon would be derived from non-petroleum sources, products equivalent to about 175,000 tons of carbon would be derived from petroleum sources including natural gas. A similar assessment indicates that by the end of the Fourth Plan, products equivalent to 293,000 tons of carbon may be derived from non-petroleum sources while products equivalent to 542,000 tons may be derived from petroleum sources.

While investment on plant and equipment alone for the production of basic feed-stock amounts to approximately Rs. 117 crores, the corresponding investment in respect of derived products amounts to about Rs. 200 crores making a total of Rs. 317 crores. The foreign exchange component in respect of plant and equipment for basis would be about Rs. 64 crores and about Rs. 101 crores for the derived products; thus the total foreign exchange component would be about of Rs. 165 crores It is likely that the total investment, starting from the basic feed-stocks to the ultimate distribution of commercially saleable products, would be of the order of Rs. 500 to Rs. 600 crores.

There is considerable enthusiasm on the part of overseas firms to invest in the field of Petro-chemical Industry in the country and it might be reasonably anticipated that a substantial portion of the foreign exchange required for the emport of plant and equipment could be obtained as overseas investment.

COMMITTEE ON DISTRIBUTION OF INCOME AND LEVELS OF LIVING, 1960—REPORT

Part I. Distribution of Income and Wealth and Concentration of Economic Power, New Delhi, Planning Commission, 1964. 107p.
Part. II. Changes in Levels of Living, New Delhi, Planning Commission, 1969. 114p.+9 Charts.

Chairman : Prof. P.C. Mahalanobis.
Members : Prof. V.K.R.V. Rao ; Dr. P.S. Lokanathan ; Dr. B.N. Ganguli ; Shri Vishnu Sahay ; Shri D.L. Mazumdar ; Dr. B.K. Madan ; Shri B.N. Datar.
Secretary : Shri P.C. Mathew.

APPOINTMENT

While moving in the Lok Sabha on August 22, 1960, that the draft outline of the Third Five-Year Plan be considered, the Prime Minister referred to the increase in the national income during the First and the Second Plan period, and stated that it would be desirable for an expert committee to enquire how this additional income has been spead in the country. The Prime Minister mentioned, 'Again it is said that the national income over the First and Second Plans has gone up by 42 per cent and the per capita income by 20 per cent. Now a legitimate query is made—where has this gone ? It is a very legitimate query ; to some extent of course, you can see where it has gone. I sometimes do address large gatherings in the villages and I can see that they are better-fed and better-clothed, they build brick houses and they are generally better. Nevertheless, that does not apply to everybody in India. Some people probably have hardly benefited. Some people may even be facing various difficulties. The fact remains, however, that this advance in our national income, in our per capita income has taken place and I think it is desirable that we should enquire more deeply as to where this has gone and appoint some expert committee to enquire into how exactly this additional income that has come to the country or per capita has spread.
This Committee was accordingly appointed on October 13, 1960, by the Planning Commission.

TERMS OF REFERENCE

(i) To review the changes in levels of living during the First and Second Five year Plans ;

(ii) To study recent trends in the distribution of income and wealth ; and in particular;

(iii) To ascertain the extent to which the operation of the economic system has resulted in concentration of wealth and means of production.

CONTENTS

Part I—Introduction ; Terms of Reference, Basic Issues and National Income ; Distribution of Income and Wealth ; Concentration of Economic Power; Statistical Tables ; Glossary of Abbreviations ; **Part II**—Introduction ; Changes in Levels of Living—Aggregate Indicators ; Changes in Levels of Total Consumption with Special Reference to Consumption of Cereals ; Chairman's Note on Consumption of Cereals with Comments by Dr. B.K. Madan ; Recommendations on Gaps in Statistics ; Annexures.

Part I—RECOMMENDATIONS

Terms Of Reference, Basic Issues And National Income

It may be recalled that the Preamble to the Constitution of India in 1950 solemnly resolved to secure to its citizens social, economic and political justice and equality of status and apportunity. Section 39 of the Constitution also mentions under Directive Principles of State Policy that :

"The State shall, in particular, direct its policy towards securing (a) that the citizens, men and momen equally, have the right to an adequate means of livelihood ; (b) that ownership and control of the material resources of the community are so distributed as best to subserve the common good ; and (c) that the operation of the economic system does not result in the concentration of wealth and means of production to the common detriment."

In the Third Five-Year Plan, the above objectives were reiterated, and it was stated :

"........development along socialist lines will secure rapid economic growth and expansion of employment, reduction of disparities in income and wealth, prevention of concentration of economic power, and creation of the values and attitudes of a free and equal society... The tendency towards concentration of economic power has to be countered in a variety of ways...firstly, through the extension of the public sector...secondly, through widening opportunities for new entrants and thirdly, through effective exercise of Government's powers of control and regulation and use of appropriate fiscal m asures." (Chapter I pp. 9, 13-14)

The broad social objectives are clear, namely, rapid economic growth, improvement in the level of living especially of the poorer people, equality of opportunities and access to facilities for education, care of health cultural amenities ; reduction of disparities in the level of living, income and wealth ; and countering the tendency towards concentration ot economic power.

National Income As A Measure Of Economic Growth

To attain the above objectives, it is essential to promote rapid economic growth. The rate of increase of national income is a convenient indicator of the growth of the economy. An estimate of national income is a convenient indicator of the growth of the economy. An estimate of national income is a measure of the total output of commodities and services during a given period, reckoned without duplication. The national income of India, in principle, can be thought of as having been obtained on the basis of the individual accounts of nearly 88 million private households, and a much smaller number of government and public agencies and corporate bodies of various kinds. However, it is not possible to use any direct method of aggregation for the preparation of national accounts, as very few or practically no households keep complete accounts. The national income and other entries in national accounts have to be estimated, therefore, in an indirect way, from the value of goods produced, the earnings of various occupational groups, or the expenditure incurred by different agencies or by private households. There are many conceptual and computational difficulties, especially in a country like India where most of the production takes place in the unorganised sector a good part of the production, especially of food, is consumed at home and never comes within the money economy of the market. In this situation, it is most important to have checks and cross-checks from independent sources to assess the validity of the estimates.

The national income can be utilised either for current consumption or for savings. Current consumption takes place either in the form of government or public current expenditure or in the form of private consumption of persons and households and non-profit organisations. Government current expenditure consists of two parts are of which, such as expenditure on education, health services, cultural amenities etc., contributes directly to the level of living of the people. The other part of government current expenditure for defence, provision of justice, general administration, etc., although not contributing directly to the level of living of the people, is essential for security, preservation of essential human rights and the stability of society as a whole.

Savings are utilised for investment. The accumulation of capital or means of production at a sufficiently fast rate to increase the future national income is the most important way of achieving rapid economic growth. Domestic savings, which form the chief means of increasing productive investments, thus play a most significant role in the development of the national economy.

The level of living of the people as a whole is determined mostly by that part of the national income which is used directly for private consumption ; to this should be added that part of government expenditure which is devoted to education, care of health etc. Per capita consumption is a convenient overall measure of the level of living.

The increase in the national income can be thus considered from three aspects. A part of national income goes to raise the level of private consumption and improve the level of living ; a part is used to increase government consumption expenditure (a part of which, again, is redistributed to improve the level of living) ; and the remaining part, which is saved, supplies a general measure of possibilities of future development of the economy. The trend of national income, analysed by the basic components of private consumption, government current expenditure and savings, would therefore supply a broad idea of changes in the general level of living over the decade under review and also give some idea of what has been done to promote future growth.

The Additional Income Of The Nation

It would be appropriate to start with the question : what has been the additioanl national income between 1950-51 and 1960-61, that is, during the period of the First and Second Five Year Plans and what has happened to this additional income ? The position in 1950-51, at the beginning of the decade and in 1960-61 the last year of the decade, is shown in the following statament.

(See statement (1) on Page No. 156 in this Report)

The national income increased from Rs. 88.5 abja (billion) in 1950-51 to Rs. 127.5 abja (billion) in 1960-61, with a rise of about 44 per cent over the decade. Governnment expenditure increased from Rs. 5.2 abja (bilion) to Rs. 10.3 abja (billion) showing an increase of about eight per cent. Domestic savings rose from Rs. 5.0 abja (billion), to Rs. 10.4 obja (billion) showing an increase of 108 per cent. Government expenditure and domestic savings taken together increased roughly by 103 per cent over the decade. This was brought about by curbing private consumption which had increased by only 36 per cent over the decade against arise of 44 per cent in income.

The description given above shows the changes in the composition of the national income and the rate of increase between the beginning and end of the decade.

Statement (1) : National Income And Its Composition In 1950-51 And 1960-61

Sl. No.	Items	Symbol	national aggregates		percentage composition		1960-61 as p. c. of
			1950-51	1960-61	1950-51	1960-61	1950 51
(0)	(1)	(2)	(3)	(4)	(5)	(6)	(7)
	In Rs. abja (=100 crores=1000 million=one billion) at factor cost at 1948-49 prices.						
1.	National Income	(a)=(d)+(c)	88.5	127.5	100.0	100.0	144
2.	Government Expenditure	(b)	5.2	10.3	5.9	8.1	198
3.	Domestic Savings	(c)	5.0	10.4	5.6	8.1	208
4.	Sub-total	(d)=(b)+(c)	10.2	20.7	11.5	16.2	203
5.	Private Consumption	(e)	78.3	106.8	88.5	83.8	136

National income, however, was not growing at a uniform rate every year. There were ups and downs in the growth of income and also of its components. To find what was the total additional national income, it is convenient to use a consolidated account for the 10 year period as a whole. A summary statement is given below:

Statement (2) : Consolidated Total Increase In National Income And Associated Items During The 10 Year Period 1951-52 to 1960-61

Base year 1950-51 : Population=357.6 million, national income= Rs. 88.5 abja (billion) at factor cost

Sl. No.	Item	Symbol	Rs. abja (billion) at 1948-49 prices	Percentage
(0)	(1)	(2)	(3)	(4)
1.	Total increase of national income in ten years	(a)	190.0	100.0
2.	Increase in Government expenditure	(b)	25.5	13.4
3.	Increase in Domestic Savings	(c)	25.2	13.3
4.	Sub-total	(d)=(b)+(c)	50.7	26.7
5.	Balance available for increase in private consumption	(e)	139.3	73.3
6.	Of which absorbed by increase in population	(f)	85.6	45.0
7.	Net available for increase in per capita consumption	(g)=(e)−(f)	53.7	28.3

The total additional income earned during the 10 year period was Rs. 190 abja (billion) of which a part, Rs. 25.5 abja (billion) was used in increasing government expenditure over the whole decade. Another part, Rs. 25.2 abja (billion), represented the additional domestic savings in 10 years. These two parts taken together, namely, Rs. 50.7 abja (billion) may be considered to have been used for purposes of development and expansion of investments to promote future economic growth.

The balance available for increase in private consumption was Rs. 139.3 abja (billion) for the whole of the 10 year period. If the population had remained the same throughout the decade then this amount would have been available to increase the per capita consumption of households. In actual fact, the population was also growing at the rate of about two per cent per year, or roughly by seven or eight million persons per year. A good part of the additional national income had to be used to provide these new additions to the population with same per capita consumption as in 1950-51, at the beginning of the 10 year period. Simple calculations show that Rs. 85.6 abja (billion) was absorbed to provide the new entrants into the population during the decade with a per capita consumer expenditure at the rate of 1950-51 for an appropriate number of years. Finally, the balance of Rs. 53.7 abja (billion) was the net amount available to increase the average per capita consumption of the whole population. Distributing this amount over the average number of persons over the decade, we get Rs. 2.5 as the share of each person per year in the increase in consumer expenditure. With Rs. 219 as the consumer expenditure per person in the base period (1950-51) the rate of increase was about 1.1 per cent person per year.

How The Additional Income was Used

Corresponding percentage figures using the total additional income of Rs. 190 abja (billion)=100, given in column (4) of statement (2), show the position very clearly. A little over 13 per cent of the additional income had been used to increase government expenditure and another 13 per cent represented the increase in domestic savings. The two taken together, about 27 per cent was used for development activities and for buiding up the foundations of future progress.

It would be noticed that about 73 per cent of the additional income was available for increase in private consumption out of which, 45 per cent, however, was required to provide that part of the population which was added during the decade with a per capita consumer expenditure at the rate of 1950-51. The largest part of the additional income during the decade thus had to be used to compensate for the growth of the population during the 10 year period. Any slowing down of the rate of growth of the population would help in improving the general level of living. The ballance of only a little over 28 per cent or a quarter of the additional available for the net increase in per capital consumption

The Plan Outlay During The Decade

Similar calculations, when made at current prices, would make it possible to compare our figures with the plan outlay during the 10=year period (1951-52 to 1960-61). Expressed at 1948-49 prices, the aggregate government consumption expenditure and domestic savings amount respectively to Rs. 77.5 abja (billion) and Rs. 75.2 abja (billion) during the decade under review; these figures correspond respectively to Rs. 80.9 abja (billion) and Rs. 78.8 abja (billion) at current prices. Taking out Rs. 56.0 abja (billion) which is 10 times the 1950-51 rate of government consumption expenditure, from Rs. 80.9 abja (billion), we get Rs. 24.9 abja (billion) as the increase in government current consumption over the decade. Out of this, Rs. 13.5 abja (billion) represents current outlays included in the first two Five Year Plans, and Rs. 11.4 abja (billion) as the increase in the current outlays outside the Plans. As India obtained Rs. 16.8 abja (billion) as external assistance over the two plan periods, the total resources available for investment amounted to Rs. 95.6 abja (billion) over the two plans periods, this figure is in broad agreement with estimates of investment given in the reports of the two Five Year Plans.

The expenditure on various social services and community development, included in the two Plans, amounted to Rs. 13.7 abja (billion). The breakdown was as follows : education Rs. 4.2 abja (Rs. 423 crores); health Rs. 3.3 abja (Rs. 326 crores); backward classes Rs. 1.1 abja (Rs. 115 crores); welfare activities Rs. 0.4 abja (Rs. 41 crores); rehabilitation Rs. 1.6 abja (Rs. 160 crores); and community development Rs. 3.1 abja (Rs. 305 crores). Most of these expenditures can be regarded as collective consumption contributing to same improvement in the level of living of the people. In a general way, the amount of Rs. 13.7 abja (Rs. 1370 crores) represents the additional affect made in this sphere.

The improvement in our capacity for future production on the other hand, is indicated by the estimate of investment. This was somewhat below Rs. 100 abja (billion) according to present calculations and agrees fairly well with the estimates given in reports on the two Five Year plans.

Expansion Of Strategic Sectors And Government Activities

The increase in investment during the decade led to significant developments in certain strategic sectors of the economy. The production of important industrial commodities had increased considerably during the period under review. The increase of output of machinery was 440 per cent, of aluminium 353 per cent, of electricity 206 per cent, of cement 191 per cent, of iron ore 194 per cent, of chemicals and chemical products 188 per cent, and of finished steel 131 per cent between 1950-51 and 1960-61.

Wages and salaries in government had increased by 100 per cent, that is, it had doubled showing a large expansion of government activities. Capital stock in public sector enterprises had also increased appreciably during the decades. The increase in the activities and investments of the public sector would help in building up rapidly the industrial foundations for the production of consumer goods in increasing quantities in future.

Indian economy is no longer stagnant. 10) years of economic planning have initiated some important structural changes, and have led to an appreciably increased production especially in the organised sector. Whether such a process of development has led to any increase in concentration of income and wealth and of economic power has become a matter of urgent study. Viewed in this way, the terms of reference (namely, changes in the level of living, trends in the distribution of income and wealth, and the concentration of economic power) represent different aspects of the historical process of transformation through which India is passing at the present time.

Distribution Of Income and Wealth

Introduction

The second term of reference of the Committee requires it to study recent trends in the distribution of income and wealth. The main purpose of such a study would be to examine how the increase in national income in recent years has been shared by different income and occupational groups and whether the inequality in incomes has increased or diminished over the first decade of planned economic development. Before entering into a substantive discussion on the issues involved, it would be useful to have an idea of the nature and adequacy of the statistical information which we have for examining, these issues at the present time.

Estimates of national income for India and its distribution by industrial origin have been published by the Control Statistical Organisation since 1948-49. These estimates of national income are available at current and constant prices. Despite their vary real limitations, they are the only source of information about national income and its variations. However, these data throw no light on the size-distribution of income. Thus the required data are not available, at present for a direct study of the question on income distribution referred to the Committee and no firm conclusions on the subject can be drawn.

The Committee, however, received a number of special papers prepared by the CSO, NCAER, ISI, RBI, Ministry of Finance and independent research workers bearing on the distribution of income. In some of these papers an attempt is made to trace the changes in income distribution while others endeavour to present the pattern of income distribution obtaining at a particular as point of time. The conclusion arried at in these paper are based on data obtained either from the income tax statistics available with the Central Board of Revenue or as a result of household sample surveys or from both the sources. These data are, however, object to rather serious limitations, the more important of which may be mentioned.

The Committee recognised that there are serious difficulties in using income-tax statistics. Even in 1960-61, the proportion of income recipients in the tax-paying group was less than one per cent (only about 0.74 per cent) of the total number of income recipients. Income in the tax statistics are derived only from non-agricultural sources ; though agricultural incomes are taxed in some States, detailed information relating to such assessments is not available. Because of tax evasion, the income-tax statistics do not accurately reflect the incomes of non-salary earners ; the margin of error here may be fairly wide. Substantial concealment of income assessable for tax would affect not only shares of income claimed by different groups by size of income but also the distribution among groups of the number of income recipients. One of the forms in which income is under-stated is through 'expense accounts' maintained by a number of business and other institutions. While the importance of 'expense accounts' is likely to have increased in recent years and, possibly, relatively more so in higher income groups, the extent of variation from one income-size-group, to another is not known.

In addition, there are conceptual difficulties. Tax statistics would depend on the legal definition of income for purposes of taxation and also on the definition of the recipient or assessee. Changes, for example, in legal exemptions, capital gains or permissible deductions, possibility of children or women having independent incomes and titles to wealth, etc., would affect the validity of comparison of the size distribution of income over time. There are also possibilities of legal manipulation in the manner in which income and wealth may be rearranged and spread overtime between members of the family or wider kinship groups by means of gifts, transfers, one-man companies, family settlements, discretionary trusts, etc., which tend to make it increasingly difficult to make a clear distinction between income and wealth. Changes in the demographic structure of the population in respect of age, sex, ratio of dependent to earning units, employment of children and women, age of retirement, etc., would also generally influence the size-distribution of income. Taking all these factors into consideration, the distribution of taxed income by namely conceived recipients (who are not even persons) cannot reflect the size-distribution of income on the basis of a rational economic concept.

The other data, which, in some studies, have been combined with the income-tax data are the NSS data a relating to consumer expenditure. However, they relate only to the distribution of total consumption expenditure into certain expenditure brackets and do not provide information on incomes as such. The NCAER has carried out sample surveys both in the urban and the rural sectors for obtaining information inter alia with regard to distribution of income. Such data, however, are available one for one year.

The validity of survey results depends on the extent the sample is representative of the population under study. There are special difficulties in a country like India where literacy is low and which has so many different languages, communities and classes. Further, survey results are subject to serious limitations due to sampling e rors besides reporting and non-response errors ; the magnitude of the sampling errors, again, depends on the size of the sample. Moreover, in India high income households may not be adequately included even in fairly large scale sample surveys. Also, some of the very poor people, who do not have any home, are usually excluded from the sample. Such deficiencies in coverage distort the picture of income distribution obtained from survey data.

With all their limitations mentioned above, the available data and estimates in the various studies on the subject relating to income distribution contained in the papers have been analysed to see if useful conclusions, even of abroad nature, could be drawn concerning changes in income distribution. The findings of these papers are briefly indicated in the following paragraphs.

Size-Distribution Of Personal Income

Utilising the income NSS data and the data relating to the income of the income-tax paying group, the distribution of income by monthly per capita income is estimated for the year 1955-56 by Lydall for the entire population covering both the urban and rural sectors and also separately for each other. According to these data, 86 per cent of the population had a per capita annual income of less than Rs. 360 and 69 per cent of the population had a per capita income per year of less than Rs. 240. On the assumption that persons with incomes falling between Rs. 240 and Rs. 360 are uniformally distributed over this range, it appears that approximately 72 per cent of the population in 1955-56 had an income lower than the average per capita national income (viz., Rs. 255) for that year, and their share in total personal income was of the order of 49 per cent. Thus, nearly 28 per cent of the population, having a per capita income higher than the average for the nation as a whole, claimed more than 50 per cent of aggregate personal income in 1955-56. The extent of inequality in income distribution is more clearly brought out by an analysis based an fractile groups; when classified by monthly per capita income, the top 10 per cent of population accounted for as much as 33 per cent of pre-tax income (i e., personal income), the top five per cent for 23 per cent and the top one per cent for as much as 11 per cent of income in 1955-56, while the bttom 25 per cent of population shared under 10 per cent of income. Consideration of post-tax income (i e..disposable income) does not significantly after this picture. This is only to be expected since the tax-paying group constitutes a negligibly small proportion of total population.

In a paper by Iyengar and Mukherjee, an effort is made to obtain the size-distribution of household income for the three years 1952-53, 1953-54 and 1956-57 utilising, again, the NSS data relating to the size-distribution of total consumer expenditure and adding to the estimated total expenditure of each expenditure size-group its share in aggreate saving; aggregate saving estimates worked out by the RBI are used for this purpose and the allocation of saving to different expenditure classes is done on certain assumptions. Estimates of income claimed by the top five and 10 per cent and the bottom 20 per cent of households when ranked by incomes are given for above-mentioned three years. These estimates seem to suggest an increase in the share in total income received by the top 10 and the bottom 20 per cent of the households implying thereby that the middle income groups became relatively worse off over the period 1952-57.

The RBI study on income distribution attempts to utilise all the available data for the purpose. The absolute magnitudes of the NSS data and the income-tax data are not used but the proportions revealed in these data are applied to the households independently estimated on the basis of population data and incomes on the basis of national incomes estimates. The estimates, therefore, manage to avoid some of the limitations of the income-tax data and the NSS data mentioned earlier. Since the NSS data on consumer expenditure are more reliable for a somewhat longer period than for a single year, the study uses two-year averages beginning from 1953-54. The period covered by this study is rather short—1953-54 to 1956-57; however, this is the period during which the tempo of development quickened. Thus, though it is not possible to derive the trend in income distribution over the whole decade from 1950-51 to 1960-61, the Reserve Bank of India study gives some idea of the direction of change. The main conclusions of this study are: (a) income distribution in the urban sector, is more unequal than that in the rural sector, and with the rural sector it is more unequal in the non-form sector than in the farm sector; (b) the degree of inequality in overall income disiribution does not seem to have changed significantly, though the degree of inequality in the urban sector appears to have increased and that in the rural sector to have declined.

The data on income distribution which are independently obtained utilising sample survey results are those available from the urban household saving survey and the rural household consumption survey carried out by the NCAER in 1960. The broad results of these surveys are indicated below.

The share of the top 10 per cent in both the rural and the urban sectors is higher than the share indicated in the Reserve Bank study, and the share of the bottom 20 per cent in both the sectors in the NCAER survey is about half of that estimated in the other stud es. The size-distribution of income before tax for the urban household sector covered by the NCAER survey indicates that 75 per cent of urban households received an income which was less than the average for all urban households while a major proportion of them (or nearly 42 per cent of all households) were actually subsisting at an income level of less than Rs. 1,000. Nearly 86 per cent of households received an income of less than Rs. 3,000 which is the current exemption limit for income tax; the share in aggregate income before tax of these households was 50 per cent. In other words, the top 14 per cent of urban households with a pre-tax income of Rs. 3,000 or more received as much as 50 per cent of aggregate income before tax in 1960,

The size-distribution of disposable income (i.e., after tax) in the NCAER survey was more or less similar to that of personal income, viz., income before tax. The only difference was that as a result of direct taxes, the share of the top five per cent of urban households declined from 31 per cent in pre-tax total income to 28.6 per cent in total disposable income.

The size-distribution of income based on the NCAER rural consumption survey data reveals that while the average income for all rural households covered by the study for 1960 was Rs. 1,126, roughly 61 per cent of rural households had an income of less than Rs. 1,000 in that year. Another 25 per cent of households received an income between Rs. 1,000—Rs. 1,999; while there were some seven to eight per cent of households in the next income bracket, i.e., Rs. 2,000—2,999. Thus, approximately 94 per cent of rural households had incomes under Rs. 3,000 in 1960 compared to 86 per cent of urban households in the same income bracket in the same year. A comparison of the share in total income of the households with incomes under Rs. 3,000 among the urban and rural sectors indicates that incomes are much less unequally distributed among the rural households than among the urban; bottom 86 per cent urban households with incomes under Rs. 3,000 shared 50 per cent of aggregate income before tax (or 52 per cent of income after tax) whereas the bottom 94 per cent rural households with incomss under Rs. 3,000 accounted for more than 77 per cent of aggregate rural income. The Reserve Bank study shows a similar result.

The fact that the distribution of income among the rural households is less concentrated than among the urban is further confirmed by studying the shares in incomes accruing to different fractile groups in each of these sectors. Each fractile group among the rural sector seems to account for a greater share in aggregate income than the corresponding fractile group among the urban sector with the exception of the top and the bottom 10 per cent of households. The top 10 per cent of households in the urban sector seems to account for a significantly higher proportion of aggregate income (42 per cent) than the corresponding group in the rural sector (34 per cent). However, it is also true that the share in income of the bottom 20 per cent of households in the urban sector is the same as the share in income of the corresponding group in the rural sector.

None of the estimates of distribution of personal income discussed here covers the entire period 1950-51 to 1960-61. Further, since there are methodological differences between the estimates, they are not comparable. As a result, it is not possible to draw any valid conclusions regarding the trends in income distribution over the whole period. However, between them these estimates provide a broad picture of the state of income distribution in India which is summarised in the following statement.

Statement (1) State of Personal Income Distribution : Different Periods

S. No.	Fractile group (p. c. of households)	1952-53	1953-54	1955-56	1956-57	1953-54 to 1956-57			1960	
						Total	Rural	Urban	Rural	Urban
(0)	(1)	(2)	(3)	(4)	(5)	(6)	(7)	(8)	(9)	(10)
1.	95-100	14.0	14.0	23 0	17.5	20.0	17.0	26.0	—	31.0
2.	90-100	24.0	23.0	34.0	25.0	28.0	25.0	37.0	33.6	42.4
3.	50-90	—	—	41.0	—	44 0	41.0	38.0	45.7	40.6
4.	0-20	7.5	8.0	9 5	8.5	8 0	9 0	7 0	4 0	4 0

To sum up, it appears from the estimates made by the Reserve Bank and Iyengar and Mukherjee that the top 10 per cent of the households account for 23 to 28 per cent of income, while the bottom 20 per cent for 7.5 to 8.5 per cent. According to the estimates of Lydall and the NCAER, the top 10 per cent of the households in terms of Lydall's estimates seems to be more or less the same as indicated in the estimates of the Reserve Bank and Iyengar and Mukherjee, while in terms of the NCAER estimates their share is about half that indicated by the other estimates.

Further, the estimates of the NCAER, as well as the Reserve Bank suggest that the distribution of income in the rural sector seems to be less unequal than that in the urban sector. From the Reserve Bank study, it appears that the income distribution in the non-farm rural sector is more unequal than that in the farm rural sector. The same study indicates that there has been probably no significant change in the degree of concentration in the overall income distribution though it may well be true that the degree of concentration in the urban sector may have increased somewhat. Again the rate of increase in the direct taxes does not seem to have kept pace with the rate of increase in the incomes of the non-salary earner group, indicating the extent of tax evasion.

Share In Aggregate Income Of Tax-Paying And Non-Tax-Paying Groups.

One method of approach to the problem of income distribution is to consider how the increase in income resulting from planned economic development has been shared by the population belonging to the upper and the lower strata representing the income-tax paying and non-tax-paying groups of income recipients. It is assumed that the number of income recipients for the country as a whole is equal to the number of persons in the working force as estimated by the CSO. Tax-paying income recipients include all individual assessees, Hindu undivided families and unregistered firms. It is assumed that on an average a Hindu undivided family or an unregistered firm contains three income recipients assessable for tax. A study of income shares in relation to the proportion of persons or households supported by each of these groups would have been more useful but this could not be attempted due to lack of data.

In 1950-51, the tax-paying income recipients constituted 0.6 per cent of all income recipients and had 4.7 per cent of total disposable income. In 1955-56, despite lowering the minimum taxable income limit to Rs. 3,000 from Rs. 4,200, the proportion of income recipients assessed to tax declined to 0.5 per cent reflecting the uncertain incidence of administrative factors ; the share in disposable income claimed by this group registered an increase from 4.7 per cent in 1950-51 to 5.2 per cent in 1955-56. Relative to the year 1955-56, there was a significant rise in the proportion of income recipients assessed to tax for the year 1960-61 to 0.7 per cent, but the share in total disposable income of this group registered only an increase to 6.4 per cent over this period.

The inconclusive nature of the change observed in in the distribution of income referring to particular years suggests the inadequacy of any attempt to derive any trends from a comparison of figures for individual years at intervals, as these are likely to be affected by peculiar factors. We have, therefore, made an effort to study the changes in income distribution referring to a longer accounting period than one year so as to smoothen out any abnormal effects pertaining to single years.

Judged by the share in income received in relation to the proportions of income recipients receiving that share, it appears that there was a small change in income distribution in favour of the tax-paying group in the middle period, viz., 1954-57, as compared to the first period, viz. 1951-54. However, in the last period, viz., 1957-60, the proportion of tax-paying income recipients increased considerably more than the proportion of income claimed by this group ; in other words, the tax-paying group taken as a whole appears to have became worse off over this period.

Such deterioration in the average income was, however, purely arithmetical, having arisen through the entry of a large number of persons of low income into the tax-paying group, and has no bearing on the size-distribution of income of the population.

Of course, these conclusions are subject to a number of limitations mentioned earlier, apart from the assumptions made to estimate the number of income recipients in the whole population as well as in the tax-paying group. Some of these limitations would have the effect of shifting income distribution in favour of the tax-paying group and some against it, it is not possible to work out the net effect of all these limitations on income distribution due to non-availability of the required data.

Distribution Of Income Within The Tax-Paying Group

Changes in the distribution of income within the tax-paying class have been studied in a number of papers submitted to the Committee by the CSO, the Ministry of Finance and the NCAER.

These studies indicate a slight fall in concentration of income among the individual income-tax assessees taken as a whole over the period 1953-54 to 1959-60. The same conclusion appears to emerge, on the basis of similar studies for various sub-groups among the tax-paying group except for pure salary earners. These conclusions are supported by other studies based on fractile group analysis as well as an analyis of changes in income distribution of a sample of common tax-payers. It may be noted in this connection that there are reasons to believe that the income-tax statistics relating to salary incomes would be more accurate than those for non-salary incomes.

For a proper appraisal of the changes which occurred in the distribution of income, it is necessary to study the changes in income distribution of specific population groups whose composition remains the same over the period under study, thereby permitting us to follow the trends over time in the incomes of the same population grouped by income at the beginning of the period.

The NCAER has carried out a special study of the changes in income distribution of a sample of common tax-payers over the period 1951-59 utilising the CBR income-tax data.

There was a decrease in the share in income received by the top 10 per cent of assessees, when ranked by income of each year (or period of time), while there was a slight increase in the share in income taken by the bottom 10 per cent but virtually no change for the bottom 30 per cent. The middle and upper middle class among the tax-payers seem to have slightly improved their comparative position over the period 1951—59. Owing to technical and conceptual difficulties inherent in the notion of "taxed income", which have been explained earlier, it is however not possible to infer whether there was any change in the inequality of distribution of income according to any rational economic concept.

As regards the income distribution among the tax-paying salary earners, these data indicate that either there was virtually no change in the distribution of income or a very small increase in the concentration of income among the top 10 per cent and the middle and lower middle income groups over the period 1951-59.

The share in income received by different fractile groups is shown for different years and period of time for all common assessees and separate for salary earners among them on the basis of the ranking of assessees by their average income during the initial period 1951-54 instead of by their changing income in each of the years and period to which the data on income relate. These data show a marked reduction in the degree of inequality in incomes among all tax-paying assessees and a slight reduction among the tax-paying salaried group—a result somewhat different from what was found in the fractile group analysis based on incomes relating to each year or period under study. In other words, when individuals or families are ranked by their initial income position so that the same persons can be followed over time, there is evidence of a clear tendency towards less concentration of income, while such tendency is not pronounced when persons are ranked by income in various years over this period and the relative shares of the high, medium and low incomes in each of these periods are compared. Thus, the richer persons in the earlier part of the period are relatively not so rich in the later part but, as a result of the rise of other persons in the income scale, there was little difference in the result over the period, in the relative share of the upper income groups.

The incomes of tax-payers can be analysed by their occupation to find out how the different occupation groups fared over the period 1951-59. That the contractors as a group greatly improved their position. Self employed people engaged in manufacturing, transport and financial business also fared well though not to the same extent as contractors. Tax-paying salaried employees also did well. The rise in income of professionals was much lower than the rise in per capita income for the country as a whole. Finally, persons who derive their income from property experienced a marked decline in their incomes over the period 1951-59. It is necessary to reiterate that the comparability of these trends is seriously vitiated by the highly varying extent of tax-evasion among different occupational groups, in particular as between salaried and non-salaried income-earners.

Trends In Wages And Salaries For Selected Occupation Group.

So far we have examined the available estimates relating to income distribution based on sample survey data or income-tax data and found that they could provide no definite conclusions concerning the changes in income distribution over the last decade. Another method of appraising the trends in income distribution is to study the relative in growth in incomes of different occupation groups. However, for drawing valid conclusions from a study of this type, it would be necessary to examine the growth in income of a large number of homogeneous occupation groups.

We do not have the necessary data for this type of study. All the information avaible at present relates to trends in incomes received by not more than a dozen occupation groups and very heterogeneous ones.

We shall first review the wage rates at current prices which prevailed in 1951. As should be expected, such rates varied widely. The annual earnings of agricultural labourers were as low as Rs. 300. The position of skilled rural workers was relatively better and on the average they earned between Rs. 600 and Rs. 750. Workers engaged in mining activity were more or less of the same income status as rural skilled workers. School teachers earned as much as rural skilled workers though they were at a lower income level than blue collar workers (factory employees). The blue collar workers were certainly better off compared to the other four wage earning occupation groups described above as well as school teachers.

Compared to the year 1950-51, mining workers in general and those working in coal mines in particular, seem to have made the greatest advance in their incomes, the index number of average earnings for this group having roughly doubled over the last decade. Next in order came factory workers drawing less than Rs. 200 per month who had an increase in tneir average income by 44 per cent over the period 1950-60. Central Government employees had an increase in their average income by 27 per cent over the last decade ; the railway employees group among them experienced a much higher increase (about 37 per cent). The income of rural skilled workers increased by 23 per cent during 1950-60. The growth in income of all four groups, thus, seems to have kept pace with or kept ahead of the growth in average income per employed person for the country as a whole over the last decade.

Wage statistics covering the full decade 1950-51 to 1960-61 are not available for other occupation groups. The available data, however, seem to indicate that the rate of growth in the salary incomes of school teachers and professors was ahead of the rate of growth in the average income per employed person at least up to the beginning of the Second Five-Year Plan. It also appears from available data that the plantation workers also experienced an increase in their relative income over the period 1953-60. The only group which does not seem to have made any advance in its income position is agricultural labourers.

Changes in the distritution of money income alone do not necessarily indicate the real changes in the economic position of different groups of population. We however, do not have price indices of commodities purchased by different income groups ; it is not possible therefore, to compare in a rigorous way the trends in the distribution of real income separately for different income groups of the population. However, as the distributions by size of income have been considered in this report mostly at current prices, a study of changes in wage and salary at current prices is relevant.

Social Services And Income Distribution

The entire increase in real income of various groups of population is not reflected in the data and estimates relating to the pattern of income distritution. Real incomes particularly of the low income groups are increasingly affected by the provision of various types of services by the State, which do not get reflected in the income data. Some of the services like low cost housing, health, free primary education and social welfare services improve the relative real income position of the low-income groups and thus tend to reduce concentration in the distribution of real income.

Distribution Of Wealth

It is generally difficult in any country to collect comprehensive information on asset holdings of different groups of the population as the households do not keep regular accounts and those that do would not normally reveal them. It is not surprising, therefore, that most countries do not have the required data for a systematic study of the annual or periodical changes in the distribution of asset holdings among the personal or household sector.

At persent we have one same rough estimates of aggregate wealth (value of reproducible tangible assets) by type of asset, owned individually (i.e. by households and single persons), jointly (i.e. by the limited and unlimited liability companies including partnerships) and publicly (i.e. by the Central and State Governments including local authorities) as at the end of March 1950 and March 1961. According to these estimates, the total value of reproducible wealth at the end of March 1950 and at the end of March 1961 was of the order of Rs. 17,086 crores and Rs. 32,164 crores, respectively.

The distribution of some items of reproducible tangible wealth among the three sectors—households, organised private business sector and government sector--is not accurately estimated but this does not seem to affect the broad picture significantly. A rough grouping of data in the aforesaid three categories indicates that the household sector accounted for 71 per cent of tangible wealth in 1950, while the shares of the organised private sector and government sector were 12 per cent and 17 per cent respectively. In 1961, the share of the household sector declined to 60 per cent, while the share of the other two sectors increased. The government sector's share increased substantially to 25 per cent, while the share of the orgainsed business private sector rose to 15 per cent.

The substantial increase in the share of the gorvernment sector is significant from the point of view of concentration in wealth distribution in the private sector. It provides an offset to the tendency towards concentration in the private sector. Further, it indicates the increasing proportion of goods and services generally in the nature of basic facilities provided to the economy by the government ; for example, the progressive development of transport and communication as well as power and irrigation enables the relatively, under developed regions to grow and thus acts as a catalytic factor for generating a higher rate of development.

From the available data, it is not possible to quantify either the degree of concentration in the private sector or the offsetting and dynamic effects on concentration in wealth distribution of the growing share of the government sector.

However, some indication with regard to wealth distribution in the private sector is provided by the data on land holdings, owner-occupied houses and the distribution of dividend income.

Distribution Of Land Holdings

In general, our finding is that both ownership and operational holdings are very highly concentrated. Also there was no appreciable reduction in inequality between 1953-54, and 1959-60, in spite of the fact that a good deel of land reform measures had been exacted during the period. In 1953-54, the top one per cent of the households owned 17 per cent, the top five percent owned 41 percent and the top 10 per cent of the honscholds owned 58 per cent of the ownership holdings of the households; in 1959-60, these proportions were 16 per cent, 40 per cent and 56 per cent respectively, The botton 20 per cent of the households did not own any land in either of these two years.

From the NSS data (eight round) referring to the year 1953-54 has been prepared for various population zones by omitting holdings of size less than 0.005 acre. It appears that the degree of concentration in land distribution is much greater in urban sector than in the rural. The top five per cent of urban households own 52 per cent of the total land belonging to households in the urban sector (and operate nearly 75 per cent of land) as against about 37 per cent share in terms of ownership as well as operational holdings of the top five per cent of households in the rural sector in the same year. The tob 20 per cent of households in the urban sector own 93 per cent of land and operate practically the entire land belonging to urban households. The bottom 20 per cent of households in the urban sector own or operate practically no land at all.

In the rural sector, the greatest concentration in land ownership (and operational holdings) is in South India while in urban sector the concentration is greatest in the Eastern part of the country in terms of ownership of land and North and North-West urban India in terms of operational holdings.

Distribution Of Wealth In The Form Of Owner – Occupied Houses

Statistics regarding home ownership and current market value of houses are available only for the urban household sector for the year 1960. These data were collected by the NCAER in the course of the study of urban income and saving referred to earlier. According to these data about 40 per cent of the households in urban India live in own houses, 51 per cent in rented accommodation and the rest in houses for which no rent is paid.

The data obtained in the above study are utilised for fractile group analysis of wealth held in the form of owner-occupied houses in the urban sector (non-home-owning households have been excluded from this study). This indicates that the top 10 per cent of home-owning house hold in the urban sector account for 57 per cent of the total wealth held in the form of owner-occupied houses, the tob 20 per cent for 73 per cent while the bottom 10 per cent account for less than one per cent. The average current market value of a house is about Rs.110 and Rs. 28,600 respectively for the bottom and the top fractile groups.

Distribution Of Other Assets

No data, not even scattered bits of information, are available for a direct study of the distribution of personal wealth held in other forms such as bank deposits, shares, securities and commercial property, even at a particular point of time. Nevertheless, in so far as wealth is related to the income it yields, some information regarding wealth distribution can be deduced for the tax-paying individuals from the available income-tax data. In view of the many severe limitations to which the income-tax data are subject, we shall confine our attention to studing the distribution of only one type of income from wealth, namely, dividend income and examine on this basis the implications of the holding of wealth in this form by the household sector as a whole.

The top 10 per cent of income-tax assessees, when they are ranked according to their dividend income, shared about 55 per cent of total dividend income received by all tax-paying households in 1955-56, while the bottom 10 per cent of assessees accounted for only about two per cent of dividend income. In 1959-60, the share in total dividend income of the top 10 per cent of assessees was 52 per cent while that of the bottom 10 per cent was 2.5 per cent.

If the share in dividend income can give a fairly good indication of wealth held in the form of company share holdings, the above statistic, derived on the basis of the CBR income-tax data, imply that more than 50 per cent of shares are held by the top 10 per cent of income-tax assessees, when ranked according to dividend income. Since the income-tax assessees, even if each of them is counted as a household, constitute no more than one per cent of all households, it is clear that the top one-tenth of one per cent of households when ranked by dividend income, own more than half of the total personal wealth in the form of shares. It would thus appear that ownership of shares is much more concentrated than the ownership of land holdings or residential house property.

The above conclusion rests on two assumptions : (a) neither the population receiving dividend income but not submitting income-tax returns for whatever reasons, nor the total dividend income received by such persons, is significant and (b) there are no benami shareholders. If the latter assumption is violated, it implies a greater concentration of share holdings than that observed here. It is difficult to assess precisely the effect on the distribution of dividend income if these assumptions did not hold good. However, it is not possible to say to what extent the observed slight decline of three percentage points in the share of dividend income received by the top 10 per cent of tax-payers can be taken to indicate some reduction in the degree of inequality in dividend income distribution, and consequently, in the ownership of share holdings.

Concluding Observations

The most important conclusion which emerges from

this study is that we do not have the required data for drawing valid conclusions concerning the changes in income distribution which might have taken place over the two plan periods.

The available estimates and data relating to size-distribution of income seem to suggest that the degree of inequality in income distribution is not higher in India than in some other developed or under-developed countries ; the distribution of income in the urban sector is more unequal, as in other countries, than that in the rural sector.

The analysis of the available income-tax data suggests some reduction in inequality of income among the tax-paying group as a whole and also for some of the sub-groups of this population over the period under study except for pure salary earners where the picture is mixed. However, in view of the deficiencies to which these data are subject, it is not possible to place much confidence in this conclusion or to make any generalisation on this basis. Also changes, if any, in the distribution of taxed income would not generally have any relation to the size-distribution of income in its economic sense.

Available estimates and data suggest no significant change in the overall distribution of incomes, though they do indicate a slight probable increase in inequality in the urban sector and some reduction in inequality in the rural sector. Again in view of the inadequacies of the data used for comparison purposes, it is not possible to be definite about this conclusion.

Trends in wages and salaries received by selected occupation groups over the decade 1950-51 to 1960-61 indicate that, with the notable exception of agricultural labourers, the growth in income of employees has generally kept pace with the growth in average income per employed person for the country as a whole. In particular there is evidence that the growth in incomes of the mining and the factory workers has kept ahead of the rate of growth in average income per employed person. Agricultural labourers as a group do not seem to have shared in the increase of incomes.

Analysis of the income-tax data, based on the occupation of common assessees reveals that over the period 1951-59 the average incomes received by contractors have registered the highest increase ; the rise in income of this group has been very much higher than the rise in the income per employed person for the country as a whole. Self-employed persons engaged in business (manufacturing, trade, transport and financial business) and the salaried class among the tax-payers also have increased their incomes, but in their case the rate of growth in income seems to have just kept pace with the rate at which average income per employed person has grown.

It should be noted that there is a general feeling, though the Committee could not collect the required data to support it, that an average person whether in urban or rural areas is better-fed, better-clothed and even better-housed in the 1960's than in the 1950's and that the working conditions have also improved generally over this period. On the other hand, since there is also some evidence that the rate of growth in income for certain high income groups has been as high as or higher than the rate of growth in income per employed person for the country as a whole, it has not been possible for the Committee to pronounce a definite judgment, even of a broad nature, on the changes in income distribution. However, it can be stated that there is no clear indication of a significant change in income distribution over the plan decade.

Much less information is available on the distribution of wealth, among different groups in the population than on the distribution of income.

Some scattered data obtained through household sample surveys indicate that there is a fair degree of concentration of personal wealth held in the form of land both among the rural and urban sectors. The distribution of personal wealth held in the form of owner-occupied houses is known only for the urban sector which indicates that there is less concentration of wealth in this form than in the form of land holdings.

The available income-tax data relating to dividend incomes indicate that there is a greater degree of concentration in personal wealth held in the form of company shares than in the form of land or owner-occupied houses.

Available fragmentary data relating to distribution of important items of wealth indicate that the degree of inequality in wealth distribution is higher than that in income dirtribution ; wealth distribution seems to be more unequal than income distribution as in some other countries.

If the question of income distribution is to be answered satisfactorily, there is a clear need for the Government to organise the collection of the required data ; the earlier we start on this job the better. The available data on the distribution of income and wealth are too meagre too draw any firm conclusions on the issues referred to the Committee.

Concentration Of Economic Power

Introduction

We were required, by our third term of reference, to ascertain the extent to which the operation of the economic system has resulted in the concentration of wealth and means of production. In a subsequent letter from the Planning Commission, it was also suggested that "the Committee might consider such data as are available for a factual study of the problems connected with financial control of industrial and economic activity". Concentration of wealth and means of production or of financial control, are only means to an end which is the concentration of economic power. We therefore, agreed that our study should be directed to this wider phenomenon.

We are aware that in studying the extent to which the operation of the economic system has led to concentration, it would have been useful to have had statistical data running over the entire period of the first two Five-Year Plans. Unfortunately, such data are not available, for the most part, in regard to concentration ; and even when available, as in the case of income-tax and allied data, it is difficult to use them without qualification. Moreover, it appears that no trends as such could be identified in terms of either bettering or worsening of the situation in respect of the broad pattern of distribution. Under the circumstances, we have confined ourselves in the main to an analysis of the situation as it prevailed at the end of the two plan periods, with of course, due attention to the extent to which the eperation of the economic system has resulted in facilitating the process and increasing the degree of concentration. Where possible however, we have also made use of data extending over the period.

Concentration : Basic Concepts And Issues

Concentration can be treated as a technical concept dealing merely with concentration ratios giving the share of the largest few firms in respect of some specific characteristics. In such a case, the measure of concentration may refer to "the share of the total gross output, net output or employment in a particular industry controlled by a given number (say three) of the largest units in that industry. 'Unit' would mean a single firm or aggregate of firms owned or controlled by a single parent company, control being defined as ownership of more than half of the capital (or voting power) of each firm. The term 'concentration' could also be based in a wider sense of a small number of individuals or groups having in their control significant volumes of economic power in terms of capital or income or employment or media of communication which, though not constituting a large percentage share of the national aggregate in each case, nevertheless sets them so much higher than any other individual or group in the relevant, content, that it gives them a disproportionately large influence and enables them to exercise economic power not measurable statistically by the mere ratios of concentration. Apparently, what the Planning Commission, and the public in general, have in mind is the latter rather than the former, though an analysis of concentration ratios is also relevant even from the point of view of a study of the wider aspects of concentration of economic power.

This concentration might exist is the form of either ownership, or management or even in mere indirect forms of operational control. Though majority ownership generally implies operational control, a minority ownership can and very often is sufficient to achieve such control. Similarly, the operation of the managing agency system as well as other forms of management, e.g., Secretaries, Treasurers etc., within the corporate sector might lead to considerable centralised control. So would interlocking of directors between different branches of activity or even between units within the some industry or activity when such interlocking does not follow from centralised ownership or management.

Economic power may be concentrated in a few hands within one particular sector such as 'industry' or 'agriculture' or within one particular group of production, e.g, 'engineering', 'Steel' or 'chemicals' or may be exercised over a number of economic activities simultaneously. Thus, for example, Tatas. one of the most prominent business groups in the country, have their main interest in steel, engineering and power, but also have interests in many other industries like cement, cotton, chemicals, vegetable oils, as well as in activities like insurance, investment and trade. Similarly, Birlas, another most important industrial group, are engaged in not only all varieties of industrial production other than steel and power but also control one of the largest banks in India and have a considerable interest in investment and trade. The study of concentration cannot, therefore, be confined to individual sectors of production or economic activity though this aspect of the study is also of importance.

Generalised Forms Of Concentration

We may begin our study with the more generalised forms of concentration of economic power. We have dealt in the previous chapter with the changes that have taken place in the distribution of income and property during the first 10 years of planning and drawn attention to the inadequacy of the relevant statistical data needed for drawing firm conclusions on this subject. We have also expressed the opinion that in the main there have not taken place such changes in the distribution of income and property as would indicate any significant trends in either direction. In this chapter, we may appropriately deal with the distribution position as it prevailed at the close of the first two plan periods with a view to determining whether it reveals the existence of any degree of concentration of economic power, and if so, to what extent

Income-tax statistics do not help in giving an idea of the overall national picture, not only because of their non-reliability due to avoidance and evasion of unknown magnitudes but also because they exclude from their purview agricultural income which accounts for half the national income as also the aggregate income of more than 70 per cent of the labour force. There are also the other statistical limitations to which we have made reference in the previous chapter. We have, therefore, to fall back upon two indicators of distribution, are based on NSS expenditure data of the 15th round covering the period July 1959 to June 1960, and the other based on the NCAER sample surveys of urban and rural households for 1960. Relevant figures are given in the following statements :

Statement (1) : Percentage Share Of Total Consumption Expenditure By Fractile Group NSS 15th Round, July 1959 To June 1960

(Percentage)

Sl. No.	Fractile Group	Share in consumption Urban	Rural
(1)	(2)	(3)	(4)
1.	0—10	3.33	3.40
2.	10—20	4.66	4.94
3.	20—30	5.67	5 82
4.	30—40	6 34	6.69
5.	40—50	7.44	7.68
6.	50—60	8.30	8.61
7.	60—70	10.21	9.93
8.	70—80	12.17	11.74
9.	80—90	15.83	14.42
10.	90—1000	26.00	26.77

Statement (2) : Percentage Share Of Household Incomes In the Aggregate Income Of Different Pre-Tax Income Tenths, 1960

(Percentage)

Sl. No.	Fractile Group	Share in the aggregate income before tax Urban	Rural
(1)	(2)	(3)	(4)
1.	0—10	1.3	0.7
2.	10—20	2.7	3.3
3.	20—30	3.6	4.5
4.	30—40	4.5	5.6
5.	40—50	5.4	6.6
6.	50—60	6.5	7.7
7.	60—70	8.1	9.5
8.	70—80	10.3	12 1
9.	80—90	15.2	16.4
10.	90—100	42.4	33.6

NSS data show that the top 10 per cent of the rural households accounted for 26.8 per cent of total expenditure, while the bottom 10 per cent accounted for only 3.4 per cent. NCAER figures show that the top 10 per cent of the rural households claimed 33.6 per cent of the total income, while the bottom 10 per cent accounted for only 0.7 per cent. Corresponding figures given by NSS for urban areas are 26.0C per cent and 3.33 per cent respectively, while those given by NCAER are 42.4 per cent and 1.3 per cent respectively. The NCAER figures present a grimmer picture partly because they pertain to income while the NSS data relate to expenditure. The wide range of variation that one finds between the top and the bottom tenths of the population clearly reveals the existence of concentration of economic power in the country in its most generalised form. That the imposition of taxation has not made much difference to the range of variation and therefore to the presence of concentration is clearly revealed by the following statement based on NCAER data of percentage shares in the post-tax or disposable income by income tenths.

Statement (3) : Share Of Household Incomes In Aggregate Income By Different Post Tax Income Tenths (Urban Only), 1960

percentage

Sl. No.	Fractile group	Share in the aggregate income after tax
(1)	(2)	(3)
1.	0—10	1.3
2.	10—20	2.8
3.	20—30	3.7
4.	30—40	4.7
5.	40—50	5.6
6,	50—60	6.7
7.	60—70	8.3
8.	70—80	10.7
9.	80—90	15.8
10.	90—100	40.4

The conclusion seems justified that even after 10 years of planning and despite fairly heavy schemes of taxation on the upper incomes, there is a considerable measure of concentration in urban incomes. This would also hold for rural incomes, as in their case, even the burden of taxation is not heavy on the higher ranges of incomes. It must be added that to a large extent the phenomenon of economic concentration in the Indian economy is the result, at one end, of unemployment and under-employment and consequent low productivity per unit of labour, that is to say, of inadequate economic development rather than merely structural inequalities of a distributional character, and at the other end, mainly of deficiencies in tax compliance or of tax evasion and avoidance rather than of an insufficiently progresive tax system. If this analysis is correct, it would seem to call for rethinking of the overall strategy of development adopted during this period in relation to the social goals. Since we are not required by our terms of reference to consider such issues, it is not necessary to pursue the matter further.

The data available on the distribution of wealth indicate that there is an even more marked degree of concentration than we have found in the case of income and expenditure. Thus, the distribution by size of holdings of agricultural land is extremely unequal. From the NSS data co lected in the eighth round (July 1954 to March 1955) and the 16th round (July 1960 to June 1961) on land holdings in the rural sector, it appears that though there was a mild trend towards redistribution of land holdings between 1953-54 and 1959-60, there was a high degree of concentration with regard to land distribution. In 1953-54, the top one per cent of the households owned 17 per cent, the five per cent owned 41 per cent and the top 10 per cent of households owned 58 per cent of all lands belonging to households ; in 1959-60, those proportions were 16 per cent, 40 per cent and 56 per cent, respectively. The botton 20 per cent of households did not own any land in either of these two years.

For owner-cccupied houses in urban areas, the NCAER survey for urban India in 1960 should that the bottom 20 per cent of households clained a shere of only 0.9 per cent in the aggregate market value of the owner-occupied houses, while the share of the top 20 per cent was 73.1 per cent, the top 10 per cent accounting for as much as 57.0 per cent.

As regards companies, which perhaps constitute economically the most significant form of property, no complete data are available regarding distribution by ownership of share capital. Income-tax statistics do not cover the entire sharholding population, as quite a number of share holders have incomes below the income-tax limit. A study made by the CBR for 1954-55 took into account not only assessees who received dividends but also refundees ; and it showed that of the estimated number of 101,033 share holders—itself an infinitesimal part of the total population, 1 4 per cent accounted for 31.5 per cent of the dividend income, while 50.3 per cent could claim only 10.8 per cent of that income. A more detailed study carried out by the Reserve Bank of India in March 1960 covered 70 compaines with paid up capital of Rs. 212 croses with a market value of Rs. 417 crores ; and it showed that 0.5 per cent of the total number of shareholders (without making allowance for duplication in the sense of some holders having shares in different compaines, but including company shareholders) had holdings of Rs. 50,000 and above, accounting for 56.5 per cent of the total value of the shares coverd by the enquiry. If allowance is made for multiple shareholding by individuals and also for the fact that some of the holdings are by companies, there can be no doubt, there is a high degree of concentration in the wealth represented by shares of joint-stock compaines. This is also shown by the income-tax statistics on dividend income by ranges according to which 1.5 per cent of dividend receivers accounted for 34.6 per cent of total dividend income assessed to tax in 1959-60.

The data given above do not indicate any trends in concentration. What they do reveal, however, is the existence at the end of 10 years of planning of a considerable degree of inequality in the distribution of economic assets and consequent concentration of economic power in the hands of a numerically small section of the population. It is true that a considerable measure of inequality in the distribution of income and wealth also exists in several other developed and developing countries. There also, it is cousing concern. But in the context of the Indian situation, it should be of even greater concern, as ours is a planned economy and we are pledged to follow policies that will further the twin objectives of lessening economic inequalities and promoting economic growth. To the extent, therefore, that there has been no appreciable reduction in the concentration in economic power during the last 10 years, this fact may be taken, as we have already stated earlier, as same evidence of the inadequacy of our current strategy of economic development in one of its important aspects.

Concentration In Private Corporate Sector

We may now pass on to consider the problem of distributive inequality and concentration of economic power in the significant part of the economy formed by the private corporate industrial sector which has a crucial place in planned development under Indian conditions. Industrial production in the private sector accounts for 16 per cent of the net national product and about a half of this production is orgainsed in corporate form. But the corporate sector is the most dynamic element of our developing economy and must claim special attention in any study of concentration of economic power. A study of joint-stock companies in India shows that while the number of companies is large a small number of companies accounts for a large portion of their paid-up capital. Thus, in 1960-61, the total number of compaines having a paid-up capital of less than Rs. five lakhs each constituted 86 per-cent of the total number of compaines at work during that year, but their share of the total paid-up capital was only 14.6 per cent ; as against this, the companies having a paid-up capital of Rs. 50 lakhs and above constituted only 1.6 per cent of the total number of compaines but claimed 53 per cent of the total paid-up capital. Though the increasing size of companies is by itself not necessarily an index of growing concentration in ownership of companies—and there is some evidence of an increasing dispersal of ownership as such—the phenomenon is conducive to greater concentration of control and economic power and as we shall presently see, it has facilitated the process.

It is also evident that the working of the planned economy has contributed to this growth of big companies in Indian industry. The growth of the private sector in industry and especially of the big companies has been facilitated by the financial assistance rendered by public institutions like the Industrial Finance Corporation (IFC), the National Industrial Development Corporation (NIDC), etc. Thus, as on June 30, 1963, loans had been approved by the IFC for a total sum of Rs. 127.7 crores. The number of conrcerns to which loans had been sanctioned was 244 ; 143 of these concerns were given loans of less than Rs. 50 lakhs each, the total amounting to Rs. 32.7 crores, while 101 concerns were given loans exceeding Rs. 50 lakhs, the total being Rs. 94.9 crores. Loans exceeding Rs.1 crore each were given to 22 concerns and accounted for Rs. 34.8 crores, while loans below 10 lakhs were given to 32 concerns, the total amounting to Rs. 1.8 crores. Lending by NIDC which totalled Rs. 3 crores upto March 1963, would also generally be to bigger companies.

Similar details are not available for the loans sanctioned by the State Financial Corporations, which totalled Rs. 49.8 crores upto March 31, 1962. However, loans given by the State Financial Corporations all fell in the category below Rs 10 lakhs and would have generally assisted medium and small industry. The amount of loans which could be classified as having been made to small industry in terms of a unit with fixed assets (including capitalised value of rental premises) of equal to or less than Rs. five lakhs was somewhat over a-quarter of the total loans, the rest being given presumably to medium-small and medium-sized enterprises.

One noteworthy feature of some of these loans has been pointed out by the Third Annual Report on the Working and Administration of the Companies Act of 1956, which we quote below in view of its relevance to the subject of concentration of economic power :

"Cases have came to notice where companies with large reserves have invested heavy amounts in shares of other companies in the same group while borrowing heavily from the Government and quasi-Government institutions. While these companies appeared to be financially sound and could have apparently met their needs for expansion or modernisation of their plant and machinery by converting their investments into cash, they have preferred to borrow from outside bodies. Presumably companies have, on balance, decided to keep their voting power intact in the companies in which shares were held by them or possibly, in same marginal cases, the realisation of the investments might have resulted in losses. In same cases, however, the investments industrial holdings have been found to be of the order of half a crore of rupees matched by an overdraft from State Bank of India for a like amount."

Government policy during the plan period has been responsible in other ways as well for the growth of the private sector and in the process specially of big companies. In addition to affording a protected market and the necessary overhead facilities and maintaining a budget policy with a mildly inflationary situation favourable to industry, the Government have been promoting the growth of private industry by extensive tax incentives. Under Section 150 of the Income-Tax Act, new ventures are given a tax holiday for five years and profits upto six per cent of the capital employed are exempted from both income-tax and super-tax. Under Section 10 (2) (vi) of the Act, new companies set up after March 31, 1954, are allowed to deduct 25 per cent of the actual investment towards depreciation of plant and machinery. Under section 56-A of the Income-tax Act, dividends received from companies engaged in certain specified industries are exempted from super-tax ; for inter-corporate investment in these industries, this concession together with the provision for income-tax credit which already existed, meant that such dividends were totally exempted from taxes There is no indication of the total tax rebate given to industries in this manner but the amount should be quite considerable. While these tax concessions and rebates promoted a climate favourable to investment by both small and big enterprises, it is evident that the latter were in a better position to take advantage of the same.

In commenting upon the growth of capital formation in the corporate sector, it is important to indicate the extent to which this has been financed by funds other than those obtained from shareholders either by way of new issues or bonus issues or by ploughed-back profits. The overall pattern of sources of finance of capital raised by non-government companies is indicated by the records of the Controller of Capital Issues where the distribution of consents and details of subscribed and paid-up capital by types of issues (viz. initial, further, bonus, debenture and loan) are available for each of the industries. Such data over the period 1955-60 have been collected and analysed by the CSO separately for government and non-government companies. Total long-term capital raised during 1955-60 by non-government companies amounted to Rs. 468 crores. The share of capital raised through debentures was Rs. 44.7 crores (9.5 per cent) while that through loans (from World Bank, Governments, LIC, IFC and SFC's) was Rs. 160.7 crores (34.4 per cent). Total increase in debt thus formed about 44 per cent of the total long-term capital raised, while capital raised through issue of shares formed 56 per cent. The following figures give the general pattern of financing of industrial expansion :

Statement (4) : Capital Raised By Non-Government Companies During 1955-60

	(Rs. Crores)	Percentage of total
Total Capital raised	467.5	100.0
1. of which increase in debt (a+b)	205.4	43.9
(a) debentures	44.7	9.5
(b) loans*	160.7	34.4
2. of wh ch share capital (a+b)	262.1	56.1
(a) bonus	33.5	7.2
(b) ordinary and preference shares	228.6	48.9

*Include (i) Loans from the World Bank ;
(ii) Loans from the Central and State Governments against the creation of company's fixed or liquid assets ;
(iii) Advances from the LIC on mortgaged property ; and
(iv) Loans granted by others (other than banks).

Bank credit has also played an impressive role in financing the growth of industry during the last seven or eight years. The Reserve Bank's studies of company balance sheets have shown that the proportion of bank borrowings to total sources of funds for all public limited companies was 14 per cent during 1959-60. For small companies, this was 20 per cent while for medium and large companies it was only 13 per cent. The absolute figures for the latter were, of course, very much larger.

The dependence of private industry on banks for financing its expansion is confirmed by a purpose-wise analysis of advances by scheduled banks. Thus, industry which accounted for 36 per cent of scheduled bank advances at the end of 1951, increased its share to 52 per cent by the end of 1961 and this from a total that was nearly double that in 1951. Of the total increase in bank loans of Rs. 722 crores between 1951 and 1961, Rs. 477 crores or 66 per cent was accounted for by industry, over half of the increase being shared by cotton textiles, sugar, engineering, iron and steel, and cement. The Reserve Bank of India has recently conducted a survey for ascertaining the extent of finance provided by banks in the form of term credit, to industries as at the end of April, 1962. The results of the survey revealed that the total 'term credit' outstanding amounted to Rs. 103.6 crores and formed 7.7 per cent of the total credit of these banks and 15.8 per cent of their industrial advances. Approximately, one half of the 'term credit' granted was in the form of medium-term loans with maturity of over one year ; the other half represented rolled-over credit consisting mainly of overdrafts and cash credits with a specific understanding that the credit would be renewed.

Analysis of the bank credit thus made increasingly available for the financing of industrial expansion during the last few years shows that the main beneficiaries have been the big and medium enterprises. Financial assistance provided by the commercial banks to small scale industries (with assets less than Rs. 5 lakhs was insignificant, amounting to only Rs. 28 crores or barely 5 per cent of their total advances to industries in 1960. The meagre absolute amount of credit extended to small industry is, however, to be considered against the very smallness of this sector ; the paid up capital of small public limited companies, below Rs. 5 lakhs each, formed barely 3 per cent of that all companies. At the same time, there is no doubt that part of the explanation for the practically insignificant share of small industries in bank advances is the lacuna in the structure in industrial financing in terms of which the credit requirements of small industry in the unorganised sector were left to be met by non-institutional sources. It is only in the last few years that some attention has been given to this problem and the share of small industry in bank advances has increased, fairly rapidly, from Rs. 20.7 crores in the first half of 1960 to Rs. 39.4 crores by the end of 1962. This has been partly stimulated by the guarantee scheme for small loans operated since July 1960 by the Reserve Bank as an agent of the Government ; the total amount of guarantees issued under the scheme amounted to Rs. 18 8 crores in respect of 5098 applications by 30th June, 1963. We have still to go a long way however, before reaching the stage when bank advances to small industry can be regarded as satisfactory either in terms of their absolute requirements (including their large non-corporate sector) or in comparison with the position of the big and medium enterprises.

In the light of the above general picture, it is interesting also to look at the sources of finance for the top 'complexes' analysed by R.K. Hazari, in terms both of changes over the period 1951-58 and the share of loans in the total liabilities for these Complexes. Thus, the increase during the period in loans was 34.8 per cent for the 10 complexes and 35.8 per cent for the four top-most complexes. In terms of absolute figures, the increase in loans amounted to as much as Rs. 154 crores for the four top-most complexes out of a total increase in gross liabilities of companies controlled by the Complexes of Rs. 430 75 crores. The share of loans as a proportion of total liabilities also increased substantially from 19 per cent in 1951 to 30 per cent in 1958 for the 10 complexes and within the complexes this share which for one group was already high at 31.8 per cent in 1951 increased to as much as 40.3 per cent in 1958.

The following statement brings out the considerable increase in the role of borrowing (loans) in the financing structure of companies and the relatively greater increase in reliance on borrowed funds by the twenty complexes covered in Dr. Hazari's stduy as compared to the 1001 companies in the Reserve Bank study:

Statement (5): Structure Of Combined Balance Sheet Of Public Companies

(Percentages)

	Liabilities	1951		1958	
		20 Complexes	R.B.I. Sample	20 Complexes*	R.B.I. Sample
(0)	(1)	(2)	(3)	(4)	(5)
1	Share Capital	35	35	28	29
2	Reserves	22	19	16	18
3	Loans	20	21	30	28
4	Other Liabilities	23	25	26	25

*Excluding banking and insurance but including finance companies.

Moreover, the commercial banks also increase their own holdings of shares in joint stock companies, as the size of the companies increases. The Life Insurance Corporation (LIC) which is a nationalised concern, also supports big business in private industry by its holdings of stock exchange securities, its total investments in this sector amounting to Rs. 92 crores as on December 31, 1960. The large companies and bigger enterprises have an easier access to the capital market, and banks, life insurance companies and trusts besides individuals have a preference for investing in shares of large companies. Thus, the operation of the economic system, with its criteria of credit-worthiness and security for lending and investment, tends to support the large and established enterprise against the small and struggling entrepreneur. There is, however, a compensatory element to the extent that the procedure followed in supporting the larger enterprises enables a more continious scrutiny on their operations by the lending interests. In any case, if the pattern of growth in a mixed economy has to be a simultaneous development of both large scale and small scale enterprises, the regulatory measures should not take the form of withholding finance to the larger units. It is necessary, however, to eliminate unhealthy competition between large and small enterprises, and ensure easy flow of finance to the latter.

It must be pointed out, however, that the growth of big business as such, though indicating the presence of economic concentration does not necessarily mean the deliberate adoption of an anti-social policy. There is such a thing as the economy of scale which works in favour of big business, on purely economic grounds; and economic considerations are certainly relevant especially in the context of our scarce resoures and the imperative need for our making the most economic utilisation of these resources. In many industries, the size of the domestic market is small in relation to the size of the plant at which maximum average costs begin to obtain; and any attempt to reduce the degree of concentration by breaking down economic-size units into a large number of uneconomic-size plants would only lead to economic waste. At the same time, there is no doubt that localised concentration of industry, even if unavoidable an economic grounds, must necessarily result in the accrual and possible exercise of monopolistic power. What is needed in such a case is not the break-up of large units as the adoption of a policy of regulation, continuous scrutiny and possibly, nationalisation which will help to prevent the emergence of anti-social consequences from the otherwise economically justifiable localised concentration in the form of big units in one industry or another.

As localised industrial concentration is an important aspect of concentration of economic power, it is necessary to examine the extent to which such concentration has emerged in Indian industry at the end of 10 years of planned economic development.

The following statement (on page no. 172, Statement 6) gives relevant date on producer concentration in selected industries:

It will be seen from the above statement that in the case of 12 out of the 21 industries listed above, the top units claimed a share of more than 50 per cent of production. In four of these cases, one unit claimed more than 50 per cent of production. It is true that in the case of steel and pig iron, there is now substantial production in the public sector, which reduces to a significant extent the share of the top units as also of the top unit in production. Also, the monopoly or semi-monopoly position enjoyed by a few concerns earlier has been considerably reduced as a result of a steady expansion of the industrial sector during the last decade or so. Thus, for example, the ACC in 1951 controlled 64 per cent of the total out put of cement; by 1960, its share had declined to 39 per cent, and is expected to decline further to 25 per cent by 1965-66. In match industry, WIMCO was more or less the sole producer of matches in 1951, as a result of differential excise and encouragement of A,B,C and D class of units, the share of WIMCO in total out put of match industry has been reduced to 60 per cent by 1960. The share of Titaghur Paper in the total out put of paper declined from 25 per cent in 1951 to 15 per cent in 1960. The Metal Box Company in 1951 enjoyed almost a monopoly in the matter of containers ; in 1960 its share has been reduced to 20 per cent. Hind Cycles accounted for 90 per cent of the out put of bicycles in 1951 ; its share in 1960 declined to about 15 per cent. Soap and vanaspati, electric cable manufacturing, aluminium industries, soda ash and other chemicals and several other areas of industry furnish instances of a declining trend in localised industrial concentration with new entrants in various fields of industry. An appreciable measure of such concentration in the private industrial sector, however, still remains. Even in the case of pig iron and finished steel, the fact of concentration remains as far as the private sector is concerned.

Statement (6) : Producer Concentration In Selected Industries

Sl. No.	Industay	Year	Percentage share of top-most units/group in total production/ capacity	Percentage share of stop.few units/groups in total production/ capacity	No. of units groups under column (4)
(0)	(1)	(2)	(3)	(4)	(5)
1.	Finished steel	1958	63.70	93.36	2 groups
2.	Pig iron	1958	54.63	90.08	2 groups
3.	Electric lamps	1960	40.00	88.70	14 units
4.	Sewing machines	1960	88.00	88.00	1 unit
5.	Soda ash	1958	52.25	84.68	2 groups
6.	Electric fans	1961	51.00	82.00	4 units
7.	Paper and paper board	1958	23.50	77.90	5 groups with 8 units
8.	Bicycles	1959	20.20	72.72	4 units
9.	Cement	1960	45.00	71.90	3 groups
10.	Soap	1957	30.75	69.11	4 groups with 8 units
11.	Superphosphate	1958	14.76	53.04	5 groups
12.	Hydrogenated oil	1958	14.01	47.09	6 units
13.	Paints and varnishes	1957	11.40	45.90	6 units
14.	Ceramics	1957	17.29	39.72	4 groups with 6 units
15.	Jute textiles*	1958	12.29	37.61	4 groups
16.	Matches	1960	60.00	60.00	1 group with 5 units
17.	Caustic soda	1958	14.76	28.51	2 groups
18.	Coal	1958	11.09	24.70	3 groups
19.	Sulphuric acid	1958	16.89	23.72	2 groups
20.	Cotton textiles*	1958	4.10	11.49	3 groups
21.	Sugar	1958-59	2.36	4.56	2 units

*Percentage of looms installed.

How far the position revealed by this study has justification in terms of economies of scale and what policy measures are required to safeguard the public interest are questions which need detailed study in the case of each industry ; what agency should undertake this task, whether departmental or otherwise, is a matter for consideration by Government.

More important than the existence of localised industrial concentration—for which perhaps there could be found some justification in terms of the economies of scale – is the more generalised concentration of economic power to which reference has been made earlier in this chapter. In the Indian context, it is the concentration of control in the industrial sector as a whole rather than in any one or other particular industry that presents the more menacing aspect of concentration of economic power. It has been pointed out already that shares in joint stock companies are held by an extremely small percentage of the population and that this represents a concentration of economic power that is significant enough to command attention. But more important than ownership is operational control. The normal behaviour of the large majority of share-holders whose individual holdings are quite small, does not indicate on their part any real interest in exercising the control that goes with ownership ; and the growing importance of impersonal holders like banks, trusts, companies and the like has increasingly tended to divorce individual ownership from control. As it is control which is significant from the point of view of economic power, a study has to be made of concentration of control by selected business groups within the corporate sector.

It is extremely difficult to obtain light on the concentration of control in the corporate sector without a full and detailed inquiry into operations of individual companies such as only a full-time agency with powers to call for books and examine accounts could undertake. In the absence of such an inquiry, are has to fall back upon such evidence as can be gathered by an analysis of the composition of Boards of Directors and their interlocking, the number and resources of companies operated by managing agencies, inter-corporate investments and subsidiary companies, and such identification as are make from indirect data of the presence of units of control sprawling over companies within the same industry and over many industries. We have been assisted in our work by a study undertaken by Dr. R.K. Hazari of the structure of the corporate private sector as also by working papers prepared by the Central Statistical Organisation and by the Reserve Bank of India. While the data either collected or used by us for determining the concentration of economic power in the private corporate sector through concentration of control is by no means as complete as we would have liked, it enables us to formulate same considered views on the subject.

Dr. Hazari's study is particularly notable for the light that it throws on the subject of concentration of control in the structure of the private corporate sector. He has attempted to identify groups in the corporate sector which exercise effective control over corporate decisions, even though they may have no separate legally-identifiable existence. A corporate group of this kind or a controlling interest is defined as consisting of units which are subject to the decision-making power of a common authority. It takes policy decision on prices ; profits, investments, production, purchases and sales on behalf of a number of companies and determines responses, to particular economic and political developments, It functions as a single organisation, though each of the companies it controls is a separate legal entity apparently independent of the others with which it is linked by this Controlling Interest. It is not necessary for the Controlling Interest, for the purpose of acquiring such control, to own the majority of shares in every company in the group. By a process of inter-corporate investment it is possible for it to acquire control over a number of companies with comparatively little investment ; in the simplest of cases, a Controlling Interest which owns the majority of shares in a comparatively small concern. A may gain control over the affairs of a larger concern B in which A holds the majority of shares, a second still larger concern C in which B holds the majority of shares, and so on ; even in the original concern A, the Controlling Interest's investment may be partly financed by borrowings from banks on the security of that investment itself. The picture could be made complicated by spreading the investment of each company among several companies of the group and by changing the pattern of investments over time. The control acquired by inter-corporate investment is supplemented by powers obtained under managing agency agreements and by the buying and selling of shares by Investment Companies belonging to the group.

The study divides the concerns subject to the decision making authority of a single Controlling Interest into Inner Circle concerns and Outer Circle concerns. The Inner Circles constitutes the group proper and consists of sole control and majority companies, while the Outer Circle consists of fifty-fifty, minority, and under-management companies in which the decision-making authority of the groups has a material influence but not controlling voice. The two Circles together are referred to as the Complex.

20 leading groups have been selected for study on the basis of various criteria to yield a cross-section of the corporate private sector. Among the criteria used are not only size of physical assets, but also age, occupation, corporate structure and pattern of financing, distribution of ownership, relative size of controlling blocks, and techniques of control. Caste and provincial origin have also been pressed into service in making the selection. Altogether they present a fair picture of the corporate sector in respect of concentration of economic power. Though the Complex is brought into give a comprehensive idea of the importance of the groups in the total corporate private sector, measurement of concentration is based primarily upon the size of the Inner Circle. Indeed, as Dr. Hazari observes : "The presence of control over the disposition of resources, in terms of which economic power has been defined, ends

at the boundaries of the group, i.e., the Inner Circle... To same extent, the interests even overlap between the groups studied. Consequently, the measurement of concentration has to be based primarily upon the size of each Inner Circle. The study covers the period 1951-58, and gives details for both the years 1951 and 1958.

The 20 groups studied have an interest of one kind or other in 983 companies with a share capital of Rs. 236 crores in 1951 and 1073 companies with a share capital of Rs. 352 crores in 1958 (excluding government companies), These companies accounted for 29.2 and 32.4 per cent of the share capital of non-government companies in 1951 and 1958 respectively. The statements below give details of share capital and physical assets for these 20 groups, as also for the 13 largest amongst them.

Statement (7) : Share Capital And Physical Assets Of 20 Groups (Public Companies Only)

(Rs. Crores)

Sl. No.	Circle	Share Capital		Net fixed assets		Net Capital stock		Gross Capital stock	
		1951	1958	1951	1958	1951	1958	1951	1958
(0)	(1)	(2)	(3)	(4)	(5)	(6)	(7)	(8)	(9)
1.	Inner	165.2	254.6	139.0	404.1	258.1	636.8	375.8	862.2
2.	Outer	65.0	112.4	58.5	153.9	98.0	244.4	141.3	337.2
3.	Complexes (gross)	230.2	367.0	197.5	558.0	356.0	881.2	517.1	1199.4
4.	Less overlap	27.5	56.7	22.0	79.2	38.6	121.8	54.5	165.6
5.	Complexes (net)	202.7	310.3	175.5	478.8	317.5	759.4	462.6	1033.8
6.	All non-govt. public Companies	591.0	756.0	464.0	1200.0	976.0	1956.0	1396.0	2675.0

Statement (8) : Share of the 20 Groups in the Share Capital And Physical Assets of All Non-Govt. Public Companies

(Percentages)

Sl. No.	Groups	Share Capital		Net Fixed Assets		Net Capital Stock		Gross Capital Stock	
		1951	1958	1951	1958	1951	1958	1951	1958
(0)	(1)	(2)	(3)	(4)	(5)	(6)	(7)	(8)	(9)
1.	20 groups :								
2.	Inner	27.95	33.28	29.95	33.67	26.44	32 56	26.92	32.23
3.	Complex (gross)	38.97	47.96	42.56	46.50	36.48	45.05	37.05	44.85
4.	Complex (net)	34.30	40.56	37.81	39.90	32.53	38.83	33.14	38.65
5.	13 Largest groups								
6.	Inner	26.78	31.67	28.64	32.40	25.25	30.89	25.78	30.52
7.	Complex (gross)	33.44	40.50	36.64	40.62	31.61	38.45	32.28	38.26
8.	Complex (net)	33.09	38.41	36.31	38.13	31.17	36.66	31.69	36.35
9.	All non-govt. public companies	100.00	100.00	100.00	100.00	100.00	100.00	100.00	100.00

Note : 'Complex (gross)' figures are simple aggregates in respect of all companies comprising the Inner and Outer Circles of each of the Complexes considered. In the process of aggregation of several Complexes, it often happens that some companies are counted more than once. 'Complex (net)' figures have been arrived at after making necessary adjustments for such double counting.

The 20 selected groups have increased their share of all corporate private capital, including both public and private companies, from 29.2 per cent to 32.4 per cent, during the eight years ending with 1958. The share capital of the companies controlled by the 20 groups in 1958 stood at Rs. 352 crores, net physical assets at Rs. 501 crores, net capital stock at Rs. 814 crores, and grass capital stock at Rs. 1102 crores. Their share of net physical assets was 37 per cent, of net capital stock 34.7 per cent and of gross capital stock 34.3 per cent. The figures reveal an impressive picture of concentration of economic power in the entire corporate private sector. The picture makes an even more massive impact if one considers the share of the longest 13 of these 20 groups.

Their share of the share capital of the entire corporate private sector increased from 27.9 per cent in 1951 to 30.6 per cent in 1958. Their share of net fixed assets stood at 35.2 per cent in 1958, of net capital stock at 32.2 per cent and of gross capital stock at 31.9 per cent.

Statement (9) : Share Of The 20 Groups In Corporate Private Capital (Public And Private Companies)

Sl. No.	Group	Share Capital 1951	Share Capital 1958	Net Fixed Assets 1958	Net Capital Stock 1958	Gross Capital Stock 1958
(0)	(1)	(2)	(3)	(4)	(5)	(6)
1.	All non-govt. companies (Rs. Crores)	810.00	1086.00	1353.00	2349.00	3204.00
2.	Percentage	100.00	100.00	100.00	100.00	100.00
3.	20 Groups : (Inner) (Rs. Crores)	192.01	283.54	416.17	664.90	895.62
4.	Percentage	23.70	26.11	30.76	28.31	27.95
5.	Complexes (gross) (Rs. Crores)	265.57	414.48	584.30	947.60	1279.74
6.	Percentage	32.79	38.17	43.19	40.34	39.94
7.	Complexes (net) (Rs. Crores)	236.19	352.27	501.04	813.86	1102.06
8.	Percentage	29.16	32.44	37.03	34.65	34.33
9.	13 largest groups Inner (Rs. Crores)	183.49	268.70	398.66	623.38	840.01
10.	Percentage	22.65	24.74	29.46	26.54	26.22
11.	Complexes (gross) Rs. Crores)	228.19	349.12	508.55	795.26	1078.16
12.	Percentage	28.17	32.15	37.59	33.86	33.65
13.	Complexes (net) (Rs. Crores)	225.89	331.95	476.53	757.24	1023.45
14.	Percentage	27.89	30.57	35.22	32.24	31.94

The picture of economic concentration that has been presented above gains added significance when one makes a further break-up of the 13 largest groups that have been dealt with. Thus 10 groups had an interest of one kind or other in 876 companies with a share capital of Rs. 205 crores in 1951 and 929 companies with a share capital of Rs. 297 crores in 1958. They accounted for more than 25 per cent and 27 per cent of the share capital of non-government companies in 1951 and 1958 respectively. Among these 10 groups; the top four showed a still higher degree of concentration, the companies controlled by these complexes accounting for a share capital of Rs. 147 crores in 1951 and Rs. 225 crores in 1958 or 18 2 per cent and 20.8 per cent respectively, of the share capital of entire corporate private sector. The top-most group controlled a share capital of Rs. 66.8 crores in 1951 and Rs. 108.2 crores in 1958 or 8.3 per cent and 10 per cent respectively of the share capital of the entire corporate private sector.

Measurement of changes in concentration has to take into account physical assets, but this is possible, as pointed out earlier, only for public joint-stock companies. The following statement gives the percentage share of the total for all non-government public companies in share capital, net capital stock, and gross physical stock for the 20 complexes taken to gether. 13 longest of these, 10 largest and four top complexes.

Statement (10) : Share Of 20 Groups In Share Capital Net Capital Stock And Gross Physical Stock Of All Non-Government Public Companies (Public Companies Only)

(Percentage)

Sl. No.	Groups	Share Capital 1951	Share Capital 1958	Net Capital Stock 1951	Net Capital Stock 1958	Gross Capital Stock 1951	Gross Capital Stock 1958	Difference in percentage Share between 1951 and 1958: Share Capital	Net Capital Stock	Gross Capital Stock
(0)	(1)	(2)	(3)	(4)	(5)	(6)	(7)	(8)	(9)	(10)
1.	Total non-government Companies.	100.00	100.00	100.00	100.00	100.00	100.00			
2.	20 Complexes (gross)	38.97	47.96	36.48	45.05	37.05	44.85	8.99	8.57	7.80
3.	13 " "	33.44	40.50	31.61	38.45	32.28	38.26	7.06	6.34	5 98
4.	10 " "	29.35	34.53	26.99	32.62	27.21	31.83	5.18	5.63	4.62
5.	4 " "	22.13	26.75	20.55	26.60	21.20	25.20	4.62	6.05	4.00
6.	1 " "	9.35	12.29	9.60	14.28	10.86	13.86	2.94	4.68	3.00

The data given above make it guite clear that concentration of economic power exists to a significant extent in the public non-government corporate sector and also that it has increased significantly between 1951 and 1958.

We have already seen that non-government public companies financed the greater part of their substantial expansion during the Plan periods from external resources. In the case of these 20 complexes, about 32 per cent of the gross total funds raised during the period came from loans and another 24 per cent from short-term liabilities, making a total of 56 per cent for borrowings. About nine per cent came from reserves and 19 per cent from depreciation. Only 16 per cent came from additional share capital. If one analyses the controlling blocks—and this is feasible only for Inner Circles and not for the entire Comlexes—one finds that the proportion of controlling block to Inner Circle equity share capital declined from 48 per cent in 1951 to 43 per cent in 1958, while the corresponding figures for preference shares were 23 per cent and 17 per cent respectively. Details for the 20 complexes are given below, as they show a great deal of variation from one another which have little to do with the size of each individual group.

Statement (11) : Controlling Blocks In Public Companies Of 20 Inner Circles

(Percentages of Share Capital)

Sl. No.	Group	Ordinary 1951	Ordinary 1958	Preference 1951	Preference 1958
(0)	(1)	(2)	(3)	(4)	(5)
1.	Tata	19.5	18.0	4.5	2.2
2.	Birla	61.0	61.1	55.5	28.0
3.	Martin Burn	25.9	23.7	7.4	3.1
4.	Dalmia-Sahu-Jain	65.2	54.8	36.3	24.2
5.	Bird Heilger	34.7	40.5	10.6	8.2
6.	Andrew Yule	43.3	45.7	43.0	43.1
7.	Bangur	79.8	68.8	46.5	25.4
8.	Thapar	57.6	61.1	11.8	23.7
9.	J.K.	72.8	74.7	46.0	36.4
10.	Shri Ram	46 3	43.9	58.2	26.9
11.	Shapoorji	72.3	35.5[1]	—	99.2
12.	Khatau	67 2	68.6	16.4	17.7
13.	Walchand	69.8	67.0	17.1	6.3
14.	Mafatlal	68.5	69.5	2.7	7.4
15.	Kasturbhai	23.4	20.1	36.2	31.3
16.	Seshasayee	8.7	6.1	4.9	2.7
17.	Ramakrishna	26.5	24.4	18.3	11.9
18.	Indra Singh	62.6	40.6	—	41.0
19.	Mahindra	8.0	37.8[2]	22.5	5.3
20.	Kirloskar	27.9	27.9	—	1.7
	Total	48.0	43.1	22.7	17.3

[1]Decline due to acquisition of Brady Group in 1958.

[2]Increase mainly due to the conversion of the principal company from private to public.

Inter-corporate investment is the main instrument, and an increasingly important are, for the control of companies. Roughly two-thirds of the controlling blocks were held by companies, with investment and industrial companies as the principal corporate holders. Of the additional share capital raised between 1951 and 1958 by Inner Circle companies, the controlling interest contributed only 37 per cent. About 83 per cent of this contribution came from companies mainly investment and industrial, 12 per cent from trusts, and only five per cent from individuals. The individuals who constitute the ultimate Controlling Interests provided only Rs. one crore out of the Rs. 38 crores contributed by individuals in general towards the expansion of the total share capital of the Inner Circle companies during this period. Dr. Hazari compares the technique of holding controlling investments to a chain breeding process.

He observes :

"The controlling families in most cases make same relatively small investments in a principal company or companies which initiate a breeding process—in some groups an inbreeding process—that takes care of nearly all subsequent controlling investments of significance, without calling forth further substantial investment, from the families. All complexes except Martin Burn, Shri Ram, Kasturbhai, Seshasayee and Kirloskar, have a large number of subsidiaries and joint subsidiaries. In 1958 the Tata Complex had 73 subsidiaries, on joint subsidiaries, Birla had 105, Dalmia-Sahu-Jain 30, Bird Heilger 44, Andrew yule 20, Bangur 47, Thapar 31, J.K. 27, Shapoorji 15,Khatau 14, Walchand 16, and Mafatlal 13. Even among the smaller groups Ramakrishna had three, Indra Singh four and Mahindra five subsidiaries and joint subsidiaries. In the aggregate, net of multiple counting, there were 163 subsidiaries and 266 joint subsidiaries out of the 1079 sample companies in 1958. In most of the remaining companies, also, inter-corporate investment played a key role but individuals and trusts too were important holders".

Company Law Administration does attempt to control inter-corporate investments but within somewhat restricted limits; whether the Administration could deal more effectively with such investments with suitable modifications in the existing laws is a question of policy which has to be left to the appropriate authorities.

We have not been able to assess whether and how far the undoubtedly larger area of concentration in industry was balanced to any extent by a dilution of the intensity of central associated with a decline in the ratio of share capital of the controlled sector owned by the Controlling Interest. Indeed, the procedures and processes of decision-making in the groups, and their significance for concentration of economic power would seem to be worth same further exploration for a fuller assessment of the problem. The groups in Indian industry differ in their structure and internal organisation, ranging from the rather loose to the closely knit organisation of the patriarchal type and with varying degrees of customary or formal devolution of powers. Some regard to these factors seems necessary when making use of Dr. Hazari's ratios of concentration. These qualifications would, however, apply more to the Outer Circles and the Complexes (gross) and do not substantially affect the conclusions regarding the extent of control based on Inner Circles.

There can be no denying the social significance of the concentration of economic power that exists and has grown over the Plan periods in the hands of a comparatively few individuals ; and it has become possible because ownership and investment of personal funds is not required for acquiring operational control over large segments of the non-governmental corporate sector. How far this concentration can claim economic justification in terms of optimum use of scarce entrepreneurial talent, to what extent the manner in which the concentration is obtained leads to anti-social consequences, what precisely its implications are in the operation of our democracy, the implementation of the constitutional directives on economic policy and an economic development, and what remedial measures are required, are all important problems that need answering. But this can be done only after a thorough and comprehensive inquiry by a full-time organisation created solely for the purpose of inquiring into the concentration of economic power in the non-governmental corporate private sector. We shall revert to this suggestion towards the end of this Chapter, but it is relevant to draw attention at this stage to the recently published report of the Commissioner of Inquiry on the administration of Dalmia-Jain companies, and the lessons that flow from it in regard to the possibilities of the anti-social consequences that can follow from both the attempts to build up concentration of economic power as also from an exercise of this power.

So far we have dealt with the concentration of ecomic power that rests in the hands of certain groups of Complexes who by ownership, inter-corporate investment and other means have acquired control over a significant volume of non-governmental corporate sector activity. But control need not be exercised only through the Controlling Interests relative share in the assets of the companies either through ownership or inter-corporate investment. It can also be exercised through managing agents, common directors and similar other forms which enable the controlling group or authority to participate actively in the day to day business of such undertakings

The growth of joint-stock companies managed by managing agents has been studied in a paper prepared by the Reserve Bank of India. A sample of 1001 public limited companies was selected for the purpose. The study showed a decline in the number of managing agents from 407 in 1955 to 355 in 1959, with the number of companies they managed falling from 715 to 597. Their control declined from 73.3 per cent to 65.7 per cent in terms of net worth and from 72.3 per cent to 66 per cent in terms of total assets. The number of managing agents managing smaller units with net worth or total assets of less than Rs. 50 lakhs declined substantially in 1959 as compared to 1955, whereas the number of managing agents managing bigger units, viz., with net worth or assets exceeding Rs. five crores increased somewhat during the period. The managing agents controlling units with net worth exceeding Rs. 20 crores controlled 23.0 per cent of net worth of 1001 companies in 1959 as compared to 15 per cent in 1955. In respect of total assets the managing agents in the corresponding class controlled 31.8 per cent of total assets of 1001 companies in 1959 and 28.2 per cent in 1955. Of the 10 most important managing agents studied in the paper, Tata Industries (P) Ltd., Martin Burn Ltd., and Birla Brothers (P) Ltd , were the first three leading managing agents measured both in terms of net worth and total assets. These three managing agents managed 25 companies in 1959 which accounted for 20 per cent in terms of total assets of 1001 companies while in 1955, these three units controlled 31 companies, which accounted for nearly 16 per cent of the total assets of 1001 companies. Although the number of companies managed by these three groups has decreased, the control both in terms of net worth and total assets has increased. Thus, while the reform of Company Law has reduced the role of the managing agent in corporate affairs, within the reduced number of managing agents, thg tendency is clearly visible of a strengthening of the influence of the bigger managing agents and consequently of concentration of economic power through the exercise of managing agency functions.

Besides managing agencies, common directors or inter-locking director-rates constitute another method fot bringing about concentration of economic power. Some light on the presence of this phenomenon in India is thrown by a special study of directorships in 331 companies with paid-up capital exceeding Rs. 50 lakhs each that has been made by the Company Law Administration. In terms of paid-up capital, these companies account for 60 per cent of the total paid-up capital of all companies at work in the country in 1956-57. The total number of directorships in the 331 companies selected for the study comes to 2,419 held by 1,502 persons acting as directors. However, these 1,502 persons have been found to be holding 7,366 other directorships besides the 2,419 directorships in 331 companies studied. The average number of directorships held by a person thus came to 6.5. Of the 1,502 persons, 26.6 per cent held single directorships, 53.2 per cent held two to ten directorships, 14.4 per cent 11 to 25 directorships and 5.8 per cent more than 20 directorships. In other words, 73.4 per cent of the persons acting as directors held multiple directorships and the total number of the directorships held by the directors holding single directorships accounted for about four per cent of the total of 9,785 directorships held by the 1,502 persons.

The Central Statistical Organisation has also undertaken a similar study of common directorships among 282 large sized public non-government industrial undertakings but for later year, namely 1959-60. The total number of directors of all these concerns put together was nearly 1800 indicating an average of six directors per unit. But several of these directors were found to be associated with more than one company. After making adjustments for repetition of names, the number was found to have come down to 1158. Distribution of these persons according to the number of directorships held showed that three directors held 11 or more directorships, 11 directors held eight to 10 directorships each and 37 directors five to seven directorships each. Of the rest, 215 held 2 to 4 directorships each and 892 directors held single directorships. Thus compared to 1956-57, the prevalence of multiple directorships showed a decline from the point of view of heavy concentration of directorships amongst a few directors, but inter-locking still continues to be an important feature.

As regards directors holdings in share capital this is only available for the earlier study and also only for 883 directors belonging to 121 companies, out of the 2,419 directors (inclusive of duplication) serving in the 331 companies covered in the study. The study reveals that these 833 directors of the 123 companies held among themselves directly in their own names, six per cent of the total paid-up capital of the companies of which they were directors. The percentage holdings of the directors in the companies managed by their managing agencies work out to around three per cent, whereas those of the directors of the companies which are managed directly by their boards of directors work out to around nine per cent. The financial stake of directors in the case of companies operated by managing agencies is low, because control in such companies is retained by the managing agency firm and not by the board of directors. As against this, the holdings of directors in the companies managed by boards of directors is higher as control and management of the companies are retained by the directors. From the point of view of control, the figure of nine per cent appears to be very low; however, it is likely that the directors, directly or indirectly, probably control a fairly, high proportion of the capital of the companies through their benamidar relatives, friends, financial institutions and companies. Further, due to disposal of share holdings over a large number of persons, a majority of whom do not take active interest in corporate, decisions, it is not necessary to have a majority of voting rights to get or retain control of a company, even a block of 10 to 20 per cent of the voting rights being enough sometimes to acquire control. In addition, substitutional holdings of share capital by disinterested financial institutions also encourage such control. Thus, without even a significant share of ownership, inter-locking of directors may lead to operational control of a big-sized industrial undertakings by one industrial house.

In this context, it is of interest to study the inter-locking between directorships of banks and non-government industrial undertakings within the economy. For the purpose, an analysis has been undertaken in the Central Statistical Organisation of the existing inter-locking between directors and managing directors of fourteen selected leading banks and the 296 large-sized non-government public companies with a paid-up capital of Rs. 50 lakhs or more in 1959-60. The total number of directors of the 14 banks was found to be 148. Out of these, 73 were not associated with any major industrial undertaking; 24 were directors of one industrial house each; 37 were directors of two to four undertakings each and the rest i.e. 14 were Directors of more than six industrial houses each. The distribution of directors by banks is as shown (at page 179) in Statement 12.

The dominance of industrial directors on the boards of commercial banks is seen to be much greater in the case of the first eight banks, in whose case they numbered 59 out of 77 or nearly 77 per cent of the total. It is evident from the above that there is a significant link in the form of common directors between the leading banks and the large-sized industrial undertakings.

Bank advances to concerns in which the directors of the banks concerned are interested, accounted for Rs. 184 crores in 1962. This constituted 12.4 per cent of the advance given by all scheduled banks. For the top 15 banks, the proportion was 14.1 per cent. It is significant that this proportion is the highest for the State Bank of India. Details are given in the following Statement No. 13 (on page 179).

Statement (12) : Frequency Distribution Of Directors Of 14 Major Banks According To Their Common Directorships In Industrial Houses, And The Percentage Of Industrial Directors To Total 1959-60

Sl. No.	Bank	Nil	Only One Industry	2-4 Industries	5 Industries and more	Total Number of Directors	p.c. of Industrial directors to total
(0)	(1)	(2)	(3)	(4)	(5)	(6)	(7)
1.	Bank of India	1	2	6	2	11	91
2.	Central Bank of India	2	—	7	1	10	80
3.	Punjab National Bank	3	1	4	1	9	66
4.	United Commercial Bank	3	5	5	—	13	77
5.	Bank of Baroda	2	2	4	4	12	83
6.	Allahabad Bank	2	1	1	1	5	60
7.	Indian Overseas Bank	1	4	1	—	6	83
8.	United Bank of India	4	2	4	1	11	64
9.	Sub-total	18	17	32	10	77	77
10	State Bank of India	11	5	1	4	21	48
11.	Indian Bank	10	1	1	—	12	17
12.	Canara Bank	8	+	—	—	8	—
13.	Union Bank of India	5	1	3	—	9	44
14.	Canara Industrial and Banking Syndicate	10	+	—	—	10	—
15.	Bank of Maharashtra	11	+	—	—	11	—
16.	Grand total	72	24	37	14	148	57

Statement (13) : Advances To Compaines Or Firms In Which The Directors Of The Bank are Interested As Directors Partners, Or Managing Agents Or In The Case Of Private Compaines As Members, 1962.

Sl. No.	Bank	Advances (Rs. crores)	Percentage to total advances
(0)	(1)	(2)	(3)
1.	State Bank of India	72.8	26.9
2.	Allahabad Bank	1.6	4.1
3.	Bank of Baroda	17.6	20.8
4.	Bank of India	31.2	24.5
5.	Canara Bank	0.8	3.0
6.	Central Bank of India	9.9	5.6
7.	Chartered Bank	5.5	10.8
8.	Devkaram Nanjee Banking Co.	0.5	1.7
9.	Indian Bank	2.1	6.8
10.	Indian Overseas Bank	1.6	6.6
11.	National & Grindlays Bank	7.9	6.6
12.	Punjab National Bank	2.9	2.9
13.	Union Bank of India	1.7	7.2
14.	United Bank of India	3.4	7.8
15.	United Commercial Bank	12.3	17.3
16.	Total for 15 banks	171.8	14.1
17.	All Scheduled Banks	183.5	12.4

(Contd.)

Note : Industrial banks' figures ore taken from the balance sheets for 1962. Figures relating to all scheduled bank have been taken from the "Statistical Tables Relating to Banks in India for 1915 and 1962", Reserve Bank of India.

The banking sector itself presents a picture of high degree of concentration. The aggregate share of the 15 top banks having deposits of Rs. 25 crores and over in total deposits of 363 Indian joint stock banks during the year 1959 was 78 per cent. If the Government owned State Bank is excluded—and looking to the composition of its Board of Dirctor, there is really no adequate reason for doing so—the percentage comes to 60. In stating this, we do not wish to suggest the continuance of unsound banking units merely because they are small in size. The present situation of a highly concentrated system, however, points to the need of effective steps to direct the resources of the system especially into the service of small and medium industries and business. We have already seen that the growth of the large Complexes, which represent concentration of economic power, is due largely to bank loans and that small industries get a very small share of bank finance. We have also seen the extent to which there is inter-locking between industrial houses and joint stock-banks through common directors. While it is not possible for the Committee to come to any categorical conclusions on this subject, the presumption seems strongly to be in favour of the thesis that there is an intimae relation between the growth of big banks and the growth of big business in the country during the Plan periods. How far this can claim justification on economic grounds and to what extent, if any, it represents a departure from the Constitutional directives and the Plan objectives for a reduction in the concentration of ceonomic power are questions that can be answered only as a result of a much more comprehensive inquiry and by a full time agency having much larger powers-to obtain data than has been the case with our Committee.

In this connection, the Committee thinks it worth while quoting the following observation which was made by the Governor of the Reserve Bank of India in August, 1960 :

"One of the structural features of Indian banking is this concentration of power which, in some cases, is enormous in relation to the capital actually employed. From time to time, we came across cases, in which a family or group has a controlling interest in a bank and it has become a major task of inspection to prevent the exercise of this interest in undesirable ways."

In view of the prevalence of mutual understanding among the big industrial complexes, banks might give assistance not only to industrial concerns is which their own directors have a major interest, but also to other industrial houses which might in turn reciprocate through the banks on which they have strong representation. By its very nature this is a very difficult field for investigation. The organisation referred to by us at the end of this chapter should be able to make same advance in the study of this phenomenon. It may be noted that the ratio of capitai and reserves to the aggregate deposits of the top banks in 1960 was only three per cent.

Case studies on the extent of inter-locking of company directorships in seven selected typical compaines belonging to seven leading Indian and foreign business groups have also been attempted to obtain some broad idea regarding inter-locking between competing compaines and inter-connection between manufacturing and financial compaines. The study of the seven compaines (Andhra Valley Power Company Ltd. in Tata Group ; Century Spinning and Weaving Company Ltd. in Birla Group ; Standard Mills Ltd. in Mafatlal Group ; Mclood and company Ltd. in Surajmull Nagarmull Group ; Kamarhatti Ltd. in Jardine Henderson Group ; and Bengal Coal Company Ltd. in Andrew Yula Group) reveals wide prevalence of inter-locking of directorships in compaines belonging to long-established and reputed houses. However, the effect on the policies of the two compaines with common director or directors would, to a certain extent, depend upon the personality of such common directors and the influence they wield on the strength of their associations with business houses etc. Subject to this limitation, it is seen that there is association of the seven companies studied, with financial compaines, particularly banks and investment, etc through common directors. Further, the inter-locking of directorships of these seven compaines with companies carrying on similar trade or manufacturing activity connotes horizontal integration which often results in common price and distribution and related policies which are of mutual benefit. The extact extent of such uniformity in business policy is, however, difficult to determine. The seven compaines studied are often linked with non-profit making associations and even Government compaines through their directors.

To explore further the inter-locking of directorship between distribution and industrial undertakings, the Department of Company Law Administration has undertaken a study which covers seventy-four marketing compaines with paid up capital of Rs. five lakhs and above. These compaines are connected with 1111 companies through 233 directors out of a total of 341 directors of 74 marketing compaines. Out of 1111 compaines inter-linked with marketing compaines, 414 are manufacturing compaines, 382 trading companies, 113 banking and financial companies, 19 electricity companies and 183 companies belonging to miscellaneous industrial groups.

41 out of 74 companies studied here are having a board of three or five directors. 18 companies have a board of six to eight directors. Four compaines are managed by boards consisting of nine to 10 directors. Only 11 companies have two-director boards. Thus, compared to the all-India average size of the boards of seven directors in the case of companies with paid-up capital of Rs. 50 lakhs and above, the average size of the board of directors of the marketing companies is comparatively small with only 4.6 directors.

The number of companies three-fourths or more of whose directors are interested as directors of other companies, come to 38. In case of 10 compaines, 50 per cent to 75 per cent of the directors hold directorships in other companies. In other 12 companies only 25 per cent to 50 per cent directors have directorship interest in other compaines. In the case of five companies, less than one fourth of the directors hold directorships in other companies. On the whole, it can be said that most of the directors of marketing companies are having multiple interests which are not confined to only marketing companies.

Out of 75 marketing companies, only nine companies do not have their directors common with any other companies. In respect of remaining 65, eight companies are connected with 40 campanies or more, 24 companies are connected to 11 to 39 companies through common directorships, and 33 companies have forged inter-locking of directorships with companies numbering 10 or less than 10. Thus, most of the marketing companies are inter-locked wite other companies through common directoships. It is, however, interesting to note that inter-locking of marketing companies does not depend much upon their size. Statement 14 gives the distribution of 74 marketing companies according to their size and their inter-locking with other companies and shows that on an average the marketing companies are connected with 10 other companies through their directors.

Statement (14) : Size And Inter-locking of Marketing Companies

Sl. No.	No. of Inter-locked companies	Number of Marketing Companies Number of Directors 2	3-5	6-8	9-10	Total
(0)	(1)	(2)	(3)	(4)	(5)	(6)
1.	0	3	6	—	—	9
2.	1—5	5	9	2	2	18
3.	6—10	2	6	6	1	15
4.	11—15	1	8	1	—	10
5.	15—20	—	3	1	—	4
6.	21—30	—	4	3	—	7
7.	31—39	—	2	—	1	3
8.	40 and above	—	3	5	—	8
	Total	11	41	18	4	74

One of the factors accounting for an increase in economic power of the large groups in recent years would appear to be the larger flow of foreign investment and technical know-how through joint ventures in Indian industry in collaboration with foreign interests. Established large industrial groups in India are in a much more advantageous position to obtain foreign capital and technical services. This itself may partly explain the increased concentration of control in the top business houses in recent years.

Last but not least in importance in the study of operational control is the inter-linking of directorship between private corporate undertakings and Government companies. This acquires special significance in view of rapid expansion of the public sector in the form of active participation in production and distribution activities. A study has been made by the Department of Company Law Administration of the inter-locking of directorship between Central Government companies and non-Government companies. State Government companies have been excluded from this study because of their relative smallness from the point of view of the investment therein. The number of Central Government companies covered by this study is 49 and includes companies jointly owned by Central Government and the State Governments, as they are administered by the Central Government. The paid up capital investment of the aforesaid 49 Central Government companies is Rs. 620 crores, forming 95 per cent of the total paid-up capital investment of all Central and State Government companies.

There were in all 428 directorships in these 49 Central Government companies and they were held by 311 persons of whom 86 were 'non-official.' Of the 49 companies, 13 have no 'non-official directors on their boards. In eight companies the 'non-official' directors held no directorships in non-Government companies. In the case of one company a representative of foreign collaborator is on its board. 42 of the 86 'non-official' directors did not hold directorships in any non-Government company. The remaining 44 'non-official' directors held 50 directorships in 27 Government companies and 334 directorships in 308 non-Government companies. The number of directorships in non-Government companies held by these 44 'non-official' directors has been studied further and result of the analysis are as follows :

Statement (15) : Directorships Held In Non-Government Companies By 'Non-Official' Directors In Government Companies

Sl. No.	Number of Non-Government Companies in which the 'Non-official Director of a Government Companies is a Director	Number of 'Non-official' Directors
(0)	(1)	(2)
1.	Below 5 companies	20
2.	5 to 10 companies	0
3.	10 to 15 companies	5
4.	15 to 20 companies	5
5.	20 companies and above	4
	Total	44

It is not possible to draw conclusions regarding the economic and social consequences of this inter-linking between government companies and directors of non-Government companies without a careful examination of the growth and working of the Government companies vis-a-vis the private undertakings where such common directorships exist. How far this helps the public sector by enabling it to obtain business expertise and how far it helps to increase the concentration of economic power in the hands of selected individuals in big business are questions that are partinent but that we are not in a position to answer. Perhaps these constitute a part of the puzzle that characterises a mixed economy such as the country is building through its planned development.

Economic power is exercised not only through control over production, investment, employment, purchases, sales and prices but also through control over mass media of communication. Of these, newspapers are the most important and constitute a powerful ancillary to sectoral and group interests. It is not, therefore, a matter for surprise that there is so much inter linking between newspapers and big business in this country, with newspapers controlled to a substantial extent by selected industrial houses directly through ownership as well as indirectly though membership of their boards of directors. In addition, of course, there is the indirect control exercised through expenditure on advertisement which has been growing apace during the Plan periods. In a study of concentration of economic power in India, are must take into account this link between industry and newspapers which exists in our country to a much larger extent than is found in any of the other democratic countries in the world.

An analysis of the ownership of newspapers in relation to their circulation shows that there was same increase during 1960 in the concentration of newspapers under common ownership as represented by Chains, Groups and Multiple Units and the circulation commanded by them. For the study of ownership of newspapers, with special reference to trends in the direction of common ownership, all papers (dailies as well as periodicals) coming under common ownership are divided into three categories, viz.)

(1) **Chains** : Publication of more than one newspaper under common ownership from more than one centre.

(2) **Groups** : Publication of more than one newspaper under common ownership from the same centre.

(3) **Multiple Units** : Publication of more than one newspaper of the same title, language and periodicity, under common ownership, from different centres.

According to figures available from the Annual Report of the Registrar of Newspapers for India, for the year 1960, as much as 67.5 per cent of the total circulation of dailies in India came under the ownership of Chains, Groups and Multiple Units. Out of a total circulation of 46.10 lakhs of dailies in different languages in the country, the share of those forming part of 17 Chains, 115 Groups and 27 Multiple Units was 31.10 lakhs. According to the same source, there were 10 owners representing five Chains (Express Newspapers, Times of India Publications, Hindustan Times and Allied Publications, Amrita Bazar Patrika and Jugantar, and Ananda Bazar Patrika), three Groups (Malayala Manorama, Free Press Journal and Hindu) and two Multiple Units (Thanthi and Statesman) which published 37 dailies with a circulation of 18.11 lakhs and this controlled 39.3 per cent of the total circulation of daily newspapers in the country. Taking the three categories separately, dailies forming part of Chains commanded 34.7 per cent of the total circulation dailies, of those belonging to Groups 23.8 per cent, and those coming under Multiple Units 9 per cent. In 1960, there was an increase in number of Chains from 14 to 17 and in Groups from 99 to 115 while the number of Multiple Units remained the same, viz., 23. In addition to 17 Chains mentioned above, the Communist Party of India is publishing a chain of 34 papers having a total circulation of 101,810.

The following statement shows the number of Chains Groups and Multiple Units in 1959 and 1960 and the number of papers controlled by them.

Statement (16) : Chains, Groups and Multiple Units In Newspapers

Sl. No.	Year	Chains		Groups		Multiple Units	
		No.	News-papers	No.	News-papers	No.	News-papers
(0)	(1)	(2)	(3)	(4)	(5)	(6)	(7)
1.	1959	14	101	36	99	23	63
2.	1960	17	103	42	115	23	60

While the data given above clearly establish the fact of concentration in our newspaper industry, it has not been possible for the Commitee to examine its interconnection with industry and with the Complexed and Inner Circles that control so much of economic power in Indian industry. Not only is this a time consuming task involving full-time work but also it requires larger powers of calling for data, scrutinising it and going into ramifications of accounts that only a full time agency can undertake. A study of concentration of economic powers cannot, however, be complete without such an inquiry ; and such inquiry could deal not only with the details of concentration within the newspaper industry but go further and examine the inter-connection that exists between newspapers and industrial Complexes and Inner Circles with a view to assessing its consequence on the concentration of economic power in the country. It would be specially necessary to examine the connection, if any, between the top units in industry prope and the top units in the newspaper industry,

The data we have given in the previous paragraphs do indicate the presence of concentration of economic power within the economy in terms of income, property and especially of control over the non-Governmental corporate sector. There can also be no doubt that, inpart at least, the working of our planned economy has encouraged this process of concentration by facilitating and aiding the growth of big business in India. How far this is an inevitable part of the process of economic development, how far it can be justified in terms of economy of scale and full utilisation of scarce managerial and entrepreneurial resources, how far it is consistent or is in conflict with the declared objectives of our Constitution and our planned economy, and how for the growth which has taken place is unhealthy and anti-social in its consequences all these are questions that we can only pose for further and detailed inquiry. It is true that except for the Complexes, statistics do not show any definite and significant trend in concentration ratios during the first 10 years of planning. It is also relevant to note that during this period, Government has sought to limit unhealthy growth through a series of counter-vailing measures such as Company Law reform, licensing of industrial units, control over capital issues, increasing scrutiny by the Reserve Bank and other allied measures. They have also sought to create countervailing power by public investment, deliberate expansion of the public sector in industry, encouragement of new-comers in the private sector in industry, special facilities and for small industry, and promotion of corporative organisation in industry and marketing.

Inasmuch as a major line of attack on the problem of concentration of economic power would lie in intensifying the countervailing action, it is useful to explain in somewhat greater detail the measures which have so far been taken in this direction.

Among the foremost of there is a relative expansion of the public sector in industry. As compared to 19:0-51, by the end of the Third Plan, the contribution of the public sector was expected to increase from less than two per cent to nearly a fourth in organised manufacturing industries and from less than a tenth to over a—third in mineral production. During the Third Plan period, public sector investment in industry and minerals is expected to be Rs. 1530 crores as against only Rs. 1050 crores in the private sector. These figures imply that the relative place of private sector industry in the total industrial Complex of the country will continue to shrink. In particular, the public sector is responsible for the development of the major key industries, which, if left to the private sector, would have increased concentration ; and once the growing investments in these industries fructify, concentration of economic power is likely to diminish.

Moreover, important industries which are in private hands are subject to State regulation in a number of ways e.g., through control of production, prices and distribution. Besides, industrial licensing seeks to regulate the expansion of new capacity and, to the extent possible, encourages entry of new medium-sized firms in competition with existing large enterprises. The licensing provisions seek to ensure, however imperfectly, a degree of regional and other diversification of industry and to prevent the emergence of industrial monopolies, though this objective has to be constantly balanced against the equally imperative need of promoting efficiency and productivity. Legislation governing the operation of companies attempts to eliminate abuses and malpractices and avoid excessive inter-company investment.

For encouraging the growth of new entrepreneurs and small industry, various institutions have been developed with a view to providing technical assistance, marketings facilities and credit. The setting-up of the National Small Industries Corporation, Small Industries Service Institutes, various Boards for different cottage and handicrafts industries, for Governmental, technical, financial and marketings assistance, establishment of State Financial Corporations, institution of the State Bank of India schemes of lending and the Credit Guarantee Scheme for encouragement of commercial banks' lendings to small industries are a few of the measures to broadbase the process of industrial development and combat the undoubted advantages enjoyed by large enterprises. In the same category falls the substantial assistance extended by Goverement to cottage and small industries through the setting-up of a large, number of industrial estates to provide an appropriate framework of basic facilities. These incentives and facilities granted to the new entrepreneurs are encouraging then emergence in increasing number. This is likely to have a salutary impact an economic concentration in Indian industry in the years and to come.

The fiscal instrument has, further more, been pressed into service to lessen inequalities in income a distribution through a sharply progressive tax system. The main task in this sector remains that of more effective enforcement of the tax levies, which is a function of improvement in tax administration.

Despite all the countervailing measures taken which have been recounted above, concentration of economic power in the private sector is more than what could be justified as necessary on functional grounds, and it exists both in generalised and in the specific forms. It is not within our terms of reference to suggest what should be done to remedy the situation and combine economic development with a steady diminution of the concentration of economic power. Undoubtedly, an extension of the scope and intensity of countervailing measures to alleviate the incidence and offset the effect of economic concentration indicates the general direction of attack on the problem. At the same time, for devising adequate corrective measures in consonance with the economic growth objectives, more comprehensive and detailed information regarding the many aspects and ramifications of economic power and controls in the private sector is required than has been available to us. Such information could be collected only by a full time agency as suggested earlier, if it is set up with both the necessary legal authority and competent full-time staff to enable it to carry out its task. The task is not easy. The country has a mixed economy; and the private sector has an important role to play in its planned economic development. Industrialisation has its own logic, and neither the economics of scale nor that of full utilisation of scarce talent can be ignored with impunity. Economic development within a democratic framework remains a paramount objective of national policy. At the same time, the country is pledged to the realisation of a socialist pattern of society; and diminution and eventual elimination of concentration of economic power in private hands is a part of that society. The task has to be attempted in terms of harmonious progress towards these goals; and the sooner the Government sets up the necessary machinery for collection, examination and analysis of all relevant data on the subject, the easier it would be for it eventually to formulate the necessary policy that will combine industrialisation with social justice and economic development with dispersal of economic power.

Part II : Recommendations

Gaps in Statistics

We were asked "to ascertain such statistical data as can be gathered at present, identify the gaps in the existing information and suggest step for removing these deficiencies in future".

By and large, the statistical information used by us can be classified under the following categories :

(i) Sample survey data on household consumption ;

(ii) Official national income statistics and output in different sectors ;

(iii) Official data on industrial production ;

(iv) Statistics of wages, earnings and prices of consumer goods ;

(v) Statistics of social and allied services like health education, transport, communications, housing, etc. ;

(vi) Income tax statistics ;

(vii) Statistics relating to companies ; and

(viii) Unofficial research papers.

It is difficult to lay down the criterion for assessing the quality of data culled out from unofficial research papers. However, the basic criterion we have adopted for examination and selection of valid data from other sources can be briefly considered at the outset. Any statistical information to be satisfactory must be a valid estimate of a character at a specified point of time. To measure a change, it is necessary to ensure that we have at least two such independent estimates as at two points of time. Once this is ensured, it is also necessary to see that the estimates are precise enough for the purpose in view. The gaps in statistics, thus can be considered under the following heads :

(a) When there are absolutely no data ;

(b) When the existing data are not considered as valid estimates ; and

(c) When the existing data are valid estimated but are not precise enough for our purpose.

Where no data exist, it is necessary to recommend ways and means for collection of fresh data ; in other cases, we have to suggest modifications in the procedure and increasing the number of units surveyed for ensuring validity of the measurement procedure and increasing the precision of the estimates respectively.

Bulk of the sample survey data on household consumption used by us comes from the National Sample Survey (NSS). We have presented data on average per capita told consumer expenditure, per capita physical consumption of some selected items, quantity and/or value, by fractile classes of per capita total consumer expenditure. The fractile distributions have been so adjusted that the estimated population in each fractile class is equal. Apart from this, we have also used NSS data on land holdings, village statistics, etc. We have also used data based on surveys conducted by the National Council of Applied Economic Research (NCAER). The NCAER data employed by us relate to incomes, savings and certain other characters of the respondents.

The sample survey data used by us constitute proper measurements of some population characteristics at specified points of time, and hence satisfy our basic criterion set down above. We would, however, stress that for measurement of change it is also necessary that uniform concepts and definitions are used at different points of time between which comparisons are made. On the other hand, for a continuing improvement of data collection, we are also of the view that concepts and definitions have to undergo continuous change so as to take into account the changing structure of the economy. We feel that a proper balance should be maintained between these differing requirements. This is possible only if the bulk of data obtained through sample surveys, is collected on a continuing basis so that there is automatic adjustment of the concepts and definitions and also that the comparability is not disturbed violently over successive periods.

The sample survey data used by us, in general were considered to be accurate enough for drawing broad inferences at the all India level. However, the surveys were not large enough for drawing inferences at regional level or on the consumption of such items as are used by households very infrequently or on changes in small and meaningful sub-classes of the population being studied.

Our recommendations on sample surveys are as follows :

(a) Sample surveys of household budgets are indispensible for the study of changes and disparities in the level of living. In respect of the sector of household consumption a large volume of data collected mainly by the NSS is already available ; so there is really no problem of absolute lack of data although the available material has its limitations as outlined above. We would therefore, recommend that the NSS household consumption survey should be undertaken on a continuing basis at suitable intervals. Periodically, the surveys should also be carried out on a fairly enhanced scale so that they could throw up valid information on the level of consumption not only for the general population at the all-India and the regional levels but also for various socio-economic groups.

(b) Successive Finance Commissions have felt the need for statistics of consumption of certain commodities although for a purpose other than study of changes in the level of living. The Second Finance Commission had suggested that arrangements for compilation of statistics of consumption of important item subject to excise duties may be made through agencies like the National Sample Survey. We would endorse this view and further suggest that in case ordinary rounds of the National Sample Survey are not adequate, special enquiries may be instituted for the purpose, preferably with a sample design based on multi-purpose stratification providing for regional variations in consumption as well as variations between rural and urban areas.

(c) We have amply stressed the need for adequate data on income in the absence of which we were not able to attempt an exhaustive study of changes in the distribution of income. The regular source of data on income in India is the All India Income Tax Revenue Statistics, which apart from their several other limitations, are not adequate for throwing light on the distribution of income as the data cover only the income-tax assessees who account for a very small fraction of the population of the Country. We have discussed these statistics in detail subsequently in this section. Here we are concerned with the collection of income. An attempt should be made to collect information on personal income of households on a continuing basis. We learn that the NSS has introduced with effect from the Nineteenth Round a special schedule known as the integrated house hold schedule which, inter alia, aims of at collecting comprehensive and continuing data on household receipt and disbursements. It may be hoped that the information so collected will go a long way in filling the gaps in the statistics of household income expenditure.

(d) No direct material on distribution of income and wealth is available and we have depended on statistical data from various sources. In India so far, no information on income has been available from the population census. Although questions on income are included in population censuses in several countries, the role of population census, as a source of information on income distribution has been rather insignificant. The large number of respondents, the broad scope of the questionnaire and difficulties encountered in interpreting the income consept, are some of the disadvantages associated with population censuses, which, in consequence, can generally throw up only rough estimate of income although the universal coverage of a census and the wealth of demographic information, it furnishes on the income recipient are some of its advantages, which may compensate for the low quality of estimates. In some countries, sampling procedures have been introduced in conjuction with census in an effort to improve the quality of response. In USA, a special sehedule for collection of information on income is distributed at the time of the decennial census to one-household in five. A similar procedure involving a 10 per cent sample of households, has been employed Ceylon and South Africa. A limited investigation on these lines as a part of the decennial censuses in India may be worthwhile to undertake.

(e) Periodic surveys like those on income and savings conducted by the NCAER should be encouraged, but the survey plans in such cases should also be drawn up as to ensure collection of data at least at two points of time separated by a number of years.

(f) What has been said in (e) about sample surveys on income, may be extended to the land holdings surveys of the NSS, as land holdings constitute a very important form of wealth especially in the rural sector.

Official national income statistics have been used by us in many of our tables in different chapters. The official estimates of national income are based on data of very uneven quality; likewise, while some of the official estimates of output appear to be reasonably good others do not appear to be so. In the absence of any alternative data, we have used the official national income data to assess the overall growth rate of per capita national income and consumption over the decade studied by us.

National income statistics are essentially derived and depend, by and large, on source material which cannot be regarded as the outcome of a process of measurement of a characteristic at a point of time. On account of the inadequacy of data as currently available, subjective judgement has to be used in deciding about the level of output in a number of important sectors. In some other sectors, the increase of output depends on regularly available official data which may also have limitations in some respect. Taken as a whole, the existing estimates of aggregate national income for any particular year cannot obviously be regarded as the outcome of a process of measurement. Such a position is quite unsatisfactory, and we would recommend that continuing attention be paid to the improvement of official national income statistics. We do not however, consider that it is necessary for us to go into details in this field because appropriate agencies exist for this task. It is considered necessary that the Advisory Committee on collection of data for National Income, which is already entrusted with this task, should reorient its programmes towards speedy collection of the minimum essential data required for improvement of national income statistics. In this connection it seems appropriate to have small groups within the Committee, each group assigned specific problems in respect of certain important aggregates. These arrengements are likely to result in more effective and expeditious working of the Committee.

National income estimates in respect of all the unorganised service sectors as well as non-factory manufacturing activities depend on annual estimates of labour force and the average per head earnings of the gainfully occupied persons in these sectors. It is suggested that appropriate methods should be devised for obtaining inter-censal estimates for these characters. Further, in view of the growing importance of regional planning, it is necessary to obtain all such statistics at a State level.

Regarding official production data in the field of agriculture, industry and allied fields,we feel again that it is the task of the Advisory Committee, on National Income to play an important role. We would suggest, however, that it would not be proper to be satisfied about this matter until a consensus of views is arrived at in respect of estimates of outputs of important commodities. This can be achieved only if scientific principles of measurement pre applied in all cases assiduously until doubts of various types vanish and the truth in the matter gradually emerges.

We would like to make a special observation in respect of the data currently available on industrial production. It would be worth while to collect and compile on a regular basis statistics of availability of more non-essential goods than are already covered by the regular official publication such as "Monthly Statistics of the production of Selected Industries of India". We have already collected and presented the data in respect of quite a few of such article, in the section on national aggregates but in an expanding economy such list can never be considered exhaustive or adequetely representative. The monthly statistics of the production of Sellected Industries of India already contains data on a number of items out of which a few may be considered to belong to the non-essential category. We would suggest inclusion of more items and are showing below a few of these by way of illustration :

1. Milk food.
2. Corn and wheat flakes.
3. Processed and rolled oats and oat flakes.
4. Cashewnut-Kernals (factory production).
5. Canned fruits.
6. Confectionery.
7. Foreign wines (Indian made).
8. Cheroots and cigars.
9. Face cream and snow.
10. Shaving cream and after-shave lotion.
11. Face powder.
12. Toilet powder.
13. Tooth paste.
14. Tooth powder.
15. Shampoo and other hair-dressing materials.
16. Terylene, synthetic fabrics.
17. Pressure cookers, gas cookers
18. Washing machines.
19. Box cameras.
20. Cigarette lighters.

In one of our tables, we have made use of data on wages and earnings of workers of various categories, deflated them with consumer price indices and compared them with real improvement in per capita national income and per capita consumer expenditure. These were about a dozen occupational groups, in all. While it is not possible to draw conclusive inferences from such data, we feel that material of this type has usefulness at a certain level. We would, therefore suggest that existing information on the subject be improved upon and more and more categories of wage and salary earners are gradually covered until we reach a stage when we have annual data in respect of the entire field of employee compensation. In more specific terms, we might recommend that data on earnings or wages of occupational groups such as teachers, employees in banks, shops, corporate bodies, etc., should be collected on a regular basis.

The deflator used in reducing wages or earnings to a constant price level should relate to the class which is under study. In the absence of consumer price indices applicable to various classes of wage and salary earners, the official working class consumer price indices which relate mainly to factory workers have been used to deflate the earnings in most cases. It will be useful to construct and publish separate consumer price indices in respect of different classes of employees, such as industrial workers, rural labour and non-manual employees. We note that steps are being taken to construct such indices. It is gratifying to learn that the Central Statistical Organisation has made a beginning by constructing consumer price index numbers with 1960=100 for urban non-manual employees for 45 centres including 16 capital cities.

Improvements in the availability of social-services have been discussed in our report on the basis of available statistics relating to educational facilities, medical facilities. Transport and communication facilities and housing conditions. We have depended mostly as regular official statistics for this purpose.

The data relating to educational, medical, transportation and communication facilities are derived from operational statistics, collected as a by-product of administration. The statistics attempt complete coverage but suffer considerably from non-response in several cases. For example, the statistics of educational focilities relate only to recognised institutions and do not cover unrecognised tutorial institutions and the like. The statistics of medical facilities include only the hospitals and dispensaries run by government and local bodies but do not cover private nursing homes, dispensaries, etc. Figures relating to the number of medical practitioners in government or private employment or in own account practice. The figures are obtained from the medical councils ; where no such councils exist, no data are available. Data on ancillary medical personnel also suffer from similar draw backs. We had, therefore, to take recourse to certain methods of estimation in arriving at the stock of doctors.

We feel that continuing action should be taken by appropriate agencies to obtain annual estimates of stock of doctors, teachers, and other key personnel both in the fields of health and education by employing both the methods of count, that is, through routine administrative methods supplemented by surveys and by the method of outern-less-attrition as used by us. In so far as private institutions or persons are concerned, this will require devising appropriate agencies and methods for compilation of required statistics, and the task is by no means easy, we would, however, emphasise that this is a field in which collection of required statistics would emply pay the cost. Secondly, we would recommend more prompt compilation and publication of the statistics of the existing type, and this in our view can be achieved by revitalising the existing agencies.

As statistics/relating to railways and communication services emanate from government agencies which are in sole charge of their operation, the short comings, if any, are very minor in nature and we would not recommend anything here. As regards road transport and inland water transport a considerable chunk of which is still under private management, little statistical information is available which could meet our requirements. The same applies to unorganised conventional forms of transport which are by no means insignificant in our rural economy. We would therefore recommend collection of data in these sectors on a systematic basis in the case of the former and at regular intervals in respect of the latter specially through sample surveys.

Housing is one of the major components of the level of living. The 1961 census did collect some data of housing conditions based an a sample of 20 per cent of census houses but as there was little information in the 1951 census, the variation over the inter censal decade could not be studied. The NSS has, on an exploratory basis, collected data on the distribution of households by type of wall, roof, etc., on the average number of persons per room, average floor area per person, etc., in a few rounds. We would recommend the continuance of collection of such data in greater detail through the census on the one hand and sample surveys on the other at regular intervals in the intercensal period.

Statistics pertaining to measures of social security of labour in factories, plantations and mines are available on a regular basis. These statistics may not always be striclty comparable over time an account of the varying nature of benefits extended to different classes of workers from time to time. Nevertheless, an increase in the magnitude of social security benefits does speak of the general improvement in the lot of workers. Social security for all groups of society is one of the ultimate objectives of government policies and as such collection of social security statistics, with wider coverage, covering all groups and with regional breakdown will be essential for a proper appraisal of welfare measures.

We have made some use of official income tax statistics published by the Central Board Revenue (CBR), mainly in Chapter 3 of the Report (Part I). These statistics are derived from the income tax returns submitted by the assessees and relate to the assessments of completed during the year. A large majority of cases of assessment of personal income are normally completed during the year, following the year to which the incomes relate.

In the cases of firms, however, the assessments take

longer time. It is not clearly known how far this type of lag affects the comparability of the series over time. Further, it is not unlikely that the assessments completed during the year in respect of an assessee relate is income of more than one year but in such cases the same assessee is counted more than once. In general, it is difficult to relate the concept of an assessee with that of a household or a person, concepts in which we are interested his economic analysis, we have discussed the major limitation of income tax data in the body of the report.

Studies based on income tax statistics in some countries reveal an apparent reduction in inequality over historical periods. Many discerning students of the subject could not regard this as a real change They. feel that there is a continuing social transformation by virtue of which the entities which enjoy income are to day willing to accept a lower nominal income compensated by a large increase in security title to assets of various sorts, economic power and overall stability and improvement in the level of living spread over the life span taken as a whole all acquired in lieu of sacrifice of shme current income. Thus more egalitarianism in terms of nominal incomes actually buy for entities enjoying it.

Taking an overall view, we do not hope to get very useful and reliable information out of income tax statistics, eventhough we have been forced to use these data. It is for this reason that we would refrain from making and detailed recommendations in this sphere, we would feel, however, that the following three lines of work would be very useful.

(i) A systematic effort may be made to establish a relation between economic concepts like persons and households and the tax concept of an assessee. This work can be taken up at a research level but in collaboration with the CBR.

(ii) A systematic study of under-reporting and evasion should be taken up, again at research level but in collaboration with the CBR and other government agencies.

(iii) Lastly "we feel that it is extremely important to make a sustained study of the problem we have considered in the last paragraph in the Indian context. In fact, it may be desirable to set up a working group for this study. In our study of concentration of economic power in Chapter 4 (Part I), we have made extensive use of data on manufacturing industries from the census and sample survey of manufacturing industries. Statistics of corporate sector published by the Company Law Administration, analysis of balance sheets of joint stock companies published by the Reserve Bank of India and various research studies based an industrial production and employment data as well as information given in company accounts. We do not propose to discuss the industrial production statistics again. We have briefly reviewed this earlier, when we pointed out that continuing efforts should be made for improvement in the data.

Statistics relating to joint stock companies refer to government as well as non-government companies (further classified into public and private) subject to the Companies Act and are based on returns submitted by the Registrars of Joint Stock Companies in the States. Figures relating to companies in existences, which depend on new registrations as well as closures are normally subject to revision as provisional figures are published as soon as available. Information relating to paid-up capital and changes therein is based on returns submitted by companies. Annual returns are required to be submitted within six weeks of the holdings of the annual general meeting of the Company. Firm figures of paid-up capital are therefore received normally with a time lag of more than one year. In the meantime provisional figures one published in respect of new companies on the basis of amounts paid on shares subscribed by the signatories to the memorandum and articles of association. Figures relating to paid up capital of newly registered companies are usually incomplete. Figures published is regard to liquidation and net changes in assets are also usually incomplete and Provisional. It would, therefore, appear that while figures for the earlier years may be regarded as relatively more reliable, those relating to the latest years are usually incomplete and subject to revision. It follows also that any comparison between the earlier and the latest year suffers from this difficulty. The analysis of the balance sheets and profit and loss accounts of joint stock companies made annually by the Reserve Bank of India at present relates to 1333 large and medium sized non-government public limited companies, which account for 69 per cent of the total paid up capital of all such companies. The coverage varies from 63 per cent in coal to 100 per cent in iron and steel. Although the number of companies covered in the study year after year remains the same, the companies are not identical in all the years; some companies whose balanee sheets could not be obtained are being replaced by others. The substitution does not, however, appear to have affected the comparability of the results materially. The results of the analysis, on the other hand, are not fully representative because of the deliberate choice of the sample from large and medium sized companies, figures relating to tax provision, profits after tax, dividends, etc., published are stated to be not comparable over different years because of changes in the system of company taxation. In some research studies used by us certain groups in the private corporate sector have been demarcated as each controlling a number of companies. Delimitations of these groups are partly based on subjective considerations and cannot possibly be very accurate, that is, we cannot be perfectly sure whether a particular company is under the control of a particular group. This is because the criterian adopted by the research worker, though plausible, cannot be regarded as perfect. further, one cannot reflect the underlying economic reality, even when the accounts might meet the legal requirements fully. It is possible to devise ways and means of inflating costs and showing profits as much less than what, they actually are. It is our feeling that even granting that company statistics supply useful information, a good deal of caution should be exercised in accepting those figures at their face value. We do not however, propose to make any recommendations apart from pointing out that there is room for patient research in trying to find out how far company statistics reflect the underlying reality.

Finally, in regard to some of the problems posed before us particularly in the sphere of economic power. for example, regarding interlocking of directorships, we do not propose to make any recommendations as the subject, forming as it does, a part of the wider problem of monopolies, has been considered in detail by the Monopolies Commission.

STUDY TEAM ON NYAYA PANCHAYATS, 1960—REPORT

Delhi, Manager of Publications, 1962. 227p.

Chairman : Shri G.R. Rajagopaul.

Members : Shri A. Prakash ; Shri K.R. Prabhu (resigned ; replaced by Shri L.M. Nadkarni)

APPOINTMENT

In Chapter 43 of its Fourteenth Report submitted to the Government in September, 1958, the Law Commission set out their conclusions with respect to panchayat courts in the following terms :

"(1) Panchayat courts are capable of doing a good deal of useful work by relieving the regular courts of petty civil litigation and criminal cases of the simpler type.

(2) The panchayats are in a position to dispose of simple cases more cheaply and expeditiously and with less inconvenience to all concerned than ordinary courts.

(3) An effort should be made to establish and popularise panchayat courts in States where they are not firmly established.

(4) Wherever possible, a panchayat court should be constituted for a group of villages situated in a nearly area.

(5) Nyaya panchas should be nominated by a suitable authority out of those elected panchas who possess certain prescribed qualifications like literacy.

(6) In order to provide continuity, the terms of office of nyaya panchas should be staggered.

(7) Nyaya panchas should be given training before they are allowed to exercise judicial functions.

(8) To get over the difficulty caused by the existence of factions, the panchas deciding a case might be required to belong to a neighbouring village, or each party to a dispute may be allowed to select his panch.

(9) The jurisdiction of panchayat courts should be exclusive.

(10) Nature of cases (civil) and the list of offences (criminal) triable by these courts are set out at length in the various State enactments and do not call for any enlargement.

(11) The upper limit of the civil jurisdiction of panchayats should be Rs. 200 or Rs. 250. In special cases with the approval of the High Court, their jurisdiction may be increased to Rs. 500.

(12) The criminal jurisdiction of panchayat courts should be limited to inflicting a fine of Rs. 50. They should not have the power to award sentences of imprisonment either substantively or in default of payment of fine or to find over parties to keep the peace cases in which such action is necessary should be made over to the regular courts.

(13) The court fee, if any, levied by the panchayat courts should be nominal.

(14) Panchayats courts should not be bound by procedural codes or by the law of evidence.

(15) Panchayat courts should wherever possible seek to effect an amicable settlement between the parties.

(16) Legal practitioners should not be permitted to

appear in these courts.

(17) A revision should lie from the decisions of the panchayat courts in civil and criminal matters to the munsif or sub-divisional magistrate, who should be empowered to transfer a case from one panchayat court to another or to the regular court for trial.

(18) The power of revision should not be given to the district judge nor should a right of appeal to a larger panchayat be allowed.

(19) The district judge should be empowered to direct the removal of panchas, if he is satisfied upon a report that the panch in question has been quilty of misconduct in the discharge of his judicial functions. There should be a provision for an appeal against such order of removal.

(20) Panchayat courts should be empowered to distrain or seize movable property in execution of their decrees and to send them if necessary to the collector for execution.

(21) A special officer or special officers should be appointed for the purpose of imparting training to panchas and to supervise the administration of panchayat courts.

(22) More detailed information should be collected and published regarding the working of the panchayat courts".

These conclusions were discussed among other matters, at a Conference of State Law Ministers presided over by the Central Law Minister held at Srinagar in June, 1960, and the Conference felt that the subject being an important one and that, having regard to the utility of these institutions as organs of cheap and speedy justice at the village level, a Committee representative of the States and the Centre may be nominated by the Law Minister to examine the question of the composition, jurisdiction and functions of panchayat courts.

It, was, however ultimately decided by the Central Cabinet that the subject of panchayats beings in the State List, it would not be necessary to appoint a committee as envisaged by the Law Minister's Confernce but that it would be sufficient of a Study Team, Consisting of the Special Secretary, Legislative Department, Ministry of Law and one representative each from the Ministries of Community Development and Home Affaris, after obtaining the needed reports from State Governments, undertook an on-the-spot study of panchayat courts functioning in the various States, associating the appropriate State official for the purpose in respect of each of the States visited.

In pursuance of the Cabinet decision, this Team was appointed by the Government of India in the latter half of October, 1960.

TERMS OF REFERENCE

After obtaining the needed reports from State Governments, undertook an on-the-spot study of panchayat courts functioning in the various States, associating the appropriate State official for the purpose in respect of each of the States visited.

CONTENTS

Introductory; Historical; Analogous Institutions in Other Countries; he case for Nyaya Panchayats; Constitution of Nyaya Panchayats; Special Provisions for Women and Scheduled Castes and Scheduled Tribes; Qualifications; Training; Jurisdiction; Conciliation; Procedure; Secretarial Assistance; Supervision and Control; Matters Incidental to the Proper Working of Nyaya Panchayats; Conclusion; Appendics I to V.

RECOMMENDATIONS

Nyaya panchayats are of respectable antiquity and their success in the past is a clear indication that by reviving and moulding them on the right lines, we will be taking a much needed step in the direction of making law and administration of justice reflect the spirit of the people and become rooted once again in the people.

A study of the participation of laymen In the administration of justice in some of the leading countries of the world clearly reveals that with appropriate safeguards, it would not be difficult to make any institution of lay-judges successful, if the need for it is there

The process of democratic decentralisation envisaged by article 40 of the Constitution and already ushered into to some extent has resulted in the general awakening of the people in the villages, and it is clear that given proper guidence panchayat institutions can be successfully worked.

Nyaya panchayats, wherever they are in existence, are serving a real felt need of the villages by disposing of cases more expeditiously and with minimum of inconvenience and expenses to parties. Although some of the criticisms directed against the nyaya panchayats may be justified, it is possible by suitable safeguards to remove the basis for any such criticisms.

The vesting of judicial functions in gram panchayts charged with executive functions is neither necessary nor desirable, and the principle of separation of the executive from the judiciary should hold good at the village level also.

To avoid the baneful effects of factions, unhealthy rivalries, etc., a nyaya panchayat may be set up for a group of villages, and the grouping may be made having regard to factors like area, population, contiguity, compactness, means of communication, etc. Where in view of the size and population of the village a separate nyaya panchayat has to be set up for a single village, the device of splitting up the village into a number of words can be adopted.

As to method of constitution of nyaya panchayats, the system of nomination in any form has to be ruled out. Villagers must be given a free hand and the choice lies between the system of direct elections and indirect elections. The method of indirect elections seems to afford for the time being the best solution and of the various possible methods of indirect elections, the best seems to be the type in which each of the gram panchayts in the nyaya panchayats circle elects a specified number of persons to serve on the nyaya panchayat.

It is not desirable to allow the same person to serve on both the gram panchayat and the nyaya panchayat.

All bona fide attempts to secure unanimity in the choise of personal to serve on panchayats deserve encouragement.

The chairman of a nyaya panchayat should be left to be elected by the members of that body for amongst themselves.

In order to provide for continuity, the terms of office of nyaya panchas should be staggered.

It would be extremely desirable to associate women in the trial of cases by nyaya panchayats and provision should be made for the cooption of at least two women of in the ordinary process of election they do not find a place therein.

It is necessary to make provision for cooption of members of scheduled castes to serve on nyaya panchayats so long as they require special protection under the constitution.

A minimum age of 30 years and ability read and write the regional language fairly fluently may be prescribed as qualifications for a person to be eligible to serve as a nyaya panch. No property qualification need be prescribed Relaxations of this minimum qualification may be necessary in backward areas.

To ensure the successful functioning of nyaya panchayats, it is essential that the panchas should be properly trained. A traning programme centring around a comprehensive but easily understandable manual and consisting of an initial training course followed up by refresher courses and supplemented by radio programmes and periodical literature will serve the purpose. For getting the best results all efforts in relation to training programmes may be made on an all-India basis.

The jurisdiction of nyaya panchayats should be enclusive.

The civil jurisdiction of nyaya panchayats may be confined to simple money and other suits of the type mentioned below:

The Civil Suits which may ordinarily be entertained by nyaya panchayats, as provided in almost all the Acts now in force, are:

(1) Suits for money due on contract, other than contracts in respect of immovable property ;
(2) Suits for the recovery of movable property or the value of such property ;
(3) Suits for compensation for wrong fully taking or injuring movable property.
(4) Suits for compensation for damage to property caused by cattle trespass.

The upper pecuniary limit of civil jurisdiction may be Rs. 250 which may go up to Rs. 500 if parties consent. Power may be taken to enhance these limits from Rs. 250 to Rs. 500 and from Rs. 500 to Rs. 1,000 respectively.

It would not be correct to rest unlimited jurisdiction in nyaya panchayats to decide suits merely because parties consent thereto.

The time for conferring jurisdiction in relation to matrimonial causes is yet to come, but nyaya panchayats may be utilised for making reports to magistrates making inquiries under Section 488 Cr. P.C. as to the amount of maintenance which may be made payable.

Nyaya panchayats may be given criminal jurisdiction in respect of petty matters where the punishment in the form of a fine would be an adequate corrective.

Nyaya panchayats may be empowered to inflict fines up to Rs. 50. The maximum limit of Rs. 50 may be increased to Rs. 100, if any State Government feels justified in doing so. Nyaya panchayats should, however, not be given power to award imprisonment, either substantively or in default of payment of fine.

It is neither necessary or desirable to confer on nyaya panchayats powers to issue prohibitory orders (for example, under Section 144 of the (Cr. P.C.) or powers to demand security for keeping the peace or for good behaviour, etc.

Grading of nyaya panchayats for the purpose of conferring enhanced powers on certain nyaya panchayats is not called for and may result in undesirable conseqences.

It would not be wise to rest any revenue jurisdiction in nyaya panchayats though the services of nyaya panchayats may be utilised by the concerned officials on an informal basis for getting reports as to questions of succession and transfers which have taken place in the village.

The importance of conciliation as a method of settling village disputes cannot be over emphasised and every endeavour should be made by a nyaya panchayat to bring about amicable settlement between the parties before taking up a case for adjudication.

There is no case for a separate body for effecting conciliation and the method and manner of bringing about conciliation may be left to the discretion of nyaya panchayats according to the circumstances of each case.

The categories of disputes which may be settled by conciliation should be co-extensive with those falling within the jurisdiction of the nyaya panchayats.

Nyaya panchayats should not be bound by the procedural codes or the Indian Evidence Act, Nyaya panchayat procedure should be of a simple character ; but care should be taken to see that principles of natural justice are complied with.

The Limitation Act may not be made applicable to nyaya panchayats and a period of three years in respect of civil matters and one year in respect of offences may be prescribed as the periods of limitation in respect of matters within the jurisdiction of nyaya panchayats.

In the disposal of any proceeding before it by a bench of nyaya panchayat, care should be taken to see that the bench includes at least one member from the village in which the plaintiff or complainant resides and one from the village in which the dependant or accused resides ; and where both parties reside in the same village, at least one member from that village.

A brief record of evidence of each of the witnesses appearing in a proceeding should be kept by the nyaya panchayat and judgments of nyaya panchayats should contain reasons.

No trial should be conducted in the absence of the accused, but suitable machinery may be provided for the production of an accused under arrest if need be with the help of the regular court.

Court fees and other fees leviable by nyaya panchayats should be nominal.

No legal practitioner should be allowed to appear before nyaya panchayats.

As to execution, a simple power to distrain and sell movable property as also a power to seize and deliver specific movable property may be vested in nyaya panchayats. Failing satisfaction by these methods, a decree or order may be transferred to the collector for execution in accordance with the procedure prescribed for recovery of arrears of land revenue.

Records of nyaya panchayats should be maintained properly and inspected periodically.

Nyaya panchayats may be provided with Secretarial assistance for the discharge of functions of a purely clerical and routine nature. Depending upon the workload, there may be one secretary for one, two or three nyaya panchayats. The secretary need not possess legal qualifications but he must ordinarily be a matriculate and he must be given proper training.

A separate cadre of panchayat secretaries may be organised in each State and they may be fitted into some Government department and given reasonable chances of promotion to higher posts. Disciplinary powers over secretaries may be exercised by the Government either suo moto or on reports of nyaya panchayats.

Special officers, or specified judicial officers may be appointed in consultation with the High Court whereever necessary, to supervise and guide the work of nyaya panchayats.

Power to remove any panch on the ground of any disqualification, particularly active association with any political party or with any religions, regional language, caste or communal group as also the power to dissolve any nyaya panchayat found to be not acting judicially may be vested in an appropriate authority. Provision may be made for appeals against such orders in suitable cases.

It is not necessary to make any provision for appeals from the decisions of nyaya panchayats.

Revision should lie from the decisions of nyaya panchayats to a senior judicial officer. The revisional authority may interfere only if he is not satisfied as to the correctness legality or propriety of the decision and should refrain from interfering if he is satisfied that substantial justice has been done.

It is necessary to make provision for the transfer of criminal cases from one nyaya panchayat to another or to a court and in hearing petitions for transfer, courts should not summon any nyaya panch as a witness though then may call for a report from the nyaya panchayat.

Power to quash civil proceedings before a nyaya panchayat may be allowed, if at all, only on serious grounds like apprehended miscarriage of justice and should be exercisable only by a senior judicial officer such as a district judge who should have the power to mulct an applicant in costs of the application for quashing a proceeding is found to be false, frivolous or vexatious.

Courts may not be empowered to withdraw cases from nyaya panchayats, but nyaya panchayats may be permitted to transfer a case to a civil or criminal court on the ground of its intricacy, etc.

Nyaya panchayats should be provided with the basic necessities such as a convenient place to hold sittings, requisite stationery, contingency funds, etc.

No salary or remuneration may be paid to nyaya panchas, but they should be reimbursed in respect of travelling and other out-of-pocket expenses.

Nyaya panchas should be accorded the status and protection due to them as members of a judicial body and should be treated as 'public servants'. All official agencies, particularly police, should extend the fallest co-operation to them.

There is great need for collecting and disseminating information relating to the work done by nyaya panchayats.

Devices such as awarding prizes to nyaya panchayats

or individual nyaya panchas may be adopted to enthuse the nyaya panchayats to work in a spirit of healthy competition.

There should be no difficulty in adopting a uniform pattern of nyaya panchayats in all the States.

CENTRAL EXCISE REORGANISATION COMMITTEE 1960—REPORT

New Delhi, Ministry of Finance, 1963. 369p.

Chairman : Shri A. K. Chandra
Members : Shri Babubhai M. Chinai, M. P.; Shri M. P. Nathwani, M. P.; Shri B. C. Ghose, M. P.; Sir J. D. K. Brown; Shri A. M. M. Murugappa Chettiar.
Secretary : Shri R. N. Misra.

APPOINTMENT

The Central Excise Reorganisation Committee (1963) was constituted vide Resolution No. 3 (21) 59-Ad. IV, dated Nov. 2, 1960, of the Ministry of Finance (Department of Revenue).

TERMS OF REFERENCE

(i) To examine generally the organisational and administrative set up of the Central Excise Department and advise Government on such reorganisation as may be necessary for achieving maximum efficiency at minimum cost.

(ii) To review the Central Excise Act and Rules and Procedures and recommend the steps required for their rationalisation, simplification and improvements wherever necessary so as to better adopt the machinery to the changing conditions.

(iii) To make any other recommendations germane to the objectives of the investigations.

CONTENTS

Introductory; **Part I** : A General Survey (Concept of Excise; Growth of Excise; Excise in the Constitution : Inter-relation of Central Excise and Sales Taxes; Use of Excise for Purposes of Economic Regulation; Pattern of Levy and Control; Manufactured Goods; Unmanufactured Products; Compounded Levy Schemes; Paripatetic Audit Control; Collection of Duty; Deferred Payment Schemes; The Central Excise Law); The Central Excise and Salt Act and Rules (The Act; Parliamentary Control; Inoperative Provisions; Anamolies in the Act; The Rules; Publication of the Central Excise Tariff and Manuals); Procedure for Levy and Collection of Duty (Basis of Assessment; Specific Rates of Duty; Ad Valorem Rate of Duty; Payment of Duty); Structure of Control (Licensing; Bonds; Accounts Vs. Physical Checks; Checks on Raw Materials; Checks on Manufacture; Assessment and Clearance; Compounded Levy Schemes); Multipoint Excise Review; Fiscal Reference; Refunds on Exports; Adjudication, Appeals and Revision Petitions; **Part II** : The Organisation of Central Excise (Headquarters Organisation; The Central Board of Revenue; Directorate of Inspection; Statistical and Intelligence Branch; Central Revenues Control Laboratory; Field Organisation; Collectorates; Ranges Circles; Divisions); The Central Board of Revenue and its Attached Offices; The Field Organisation (Executive; the Primary Unit; The Supervisory Hierarchy; Ministerial); Revenue Accounting and Audit; Structure of Staffing (Executive; Ministerial Intelligence and Preventive); Public Relations and Settlement of Operational Difficulties; Management Improvement and Staff Welfare : (Transport, Housing, Transfers and Overtime Allowance; Stationery, Office Equipment and Forms; Suggestions Schemes; Cadre Strength and Workload; Training Schemes; Uniforms); Costs of Collection; Textile Fabrics and Yarn (Cotton Fabrics and Yarn; Cotton Fabrics; Powerlooms; Rayon and Artificial Silk Fabrics; Woollen Fabrics and Yarn); Matches; Tea; Paper [(a) Paper; (b) Boards]; Soap; Footwear; Electric Batteries; Electric Wires and Cables; Patent or Proprietary Medicines; Coffee; Acids; Cinematograph Films; Exposed; Vegetable Non-essential Oils; Acknowledgements; Summary of Conclusions and Recommendations; Tables : Growth of Excise Revenue; Excise Revenue in Plan Resources; Revenue from Commodities Taxed since 1954-55; Un-manufactured Tobacco: Area, Production and Average Yield of Main Varieties; Powerloom Cotton Fabrics : Clearances and Revenue; Powerloom Cotton Fabrics : Average Incidence of Duty; Powerloom Cotton Fabrics; Comperative Incidence of Duty; Unmanufactured Tobacco : Production, Clearance and Revenue; Unmanufactured Tobacco: Offtake for Main Uses; Unmanufactured Tobacco: Arrears of Duty and Miscellanous Demands; Khandsari

Sugar: Production and Revenue; Matches: Comparative Duty Preference for Different Categories of Manufacturers; Matches : Categorywise Number of Match Factories and Production; Paper Production by Tarrif Categories; Paper : Newsprint : Production, Clearance, and Revenue; Soap : Production in Power and Non-power-operated Factories; Soap : Production and Revenue; Soap; Quantities Exempted and Revenue Foregone : Vegetable Non-essential Oils; Number of Millers, Production and Revenue; Vegetable Non-essential Oils : Estimated Utilisation; Appendices: Press Note; Main Questionnaire; Supplementary Questionnaire; List of Persons to whom Main Questionnaire was Issued; List of Persons who Replied to the Questionnaires; List of Industrial and Other Units Visited by the Committee; List of Witnesses Examined; Number of Licences in Force on May 1, 1962; Statistics of Breaches of Central Excise Law; Rewards Sanctioned for Detection of Central Excise Crime; Number of Appeals (Offences) Received, Dealt With and Pending; Central Excise Collectorates and the Major Indicators of Workload; General Organisation of a Collectoraters Headquarters Office; Central Excise Ministerial Establishments as on July 1, 1962; Central Excise Executive Establishments as on July 1, 1962.

RECOMMENDATIONS

PART I : General Survey

Use Of Excise For Purposes Of Economic Regulation

Incentives in different forms have been provided including preferential rate of, or exemptions from excise duties to give impetus to the growth of the village and small scale industries. Two conditions should be fulfilled if small scale industries are to make their full contribution to the national economy. Firstly, these industries should be largely complementary and, not competitive with organised industries and secondly, they must attempt at becoming self-reliant and self-supporting by adopting improved techniques and more efficient forms of organisation. In other words, reliance should not be on fiscal preferences.

2. Fiscal preference as an instrument of national planning and development is now new and has been used to protect developing indigeneous industries. Excise levies are also being used to subserve this purpose. Differential rates of duty and exemptions have, however, in certain cases, led to fragmentation to avoid payment of duty.

3. Excise duties have been used to conserve foreign exchange and to reduce domestic consumption for maximising exports. Other objectives have also influenced the evolution of the tariff.

4. The tariff has also been used as a measure of economic assistance to individual units and to whole industries in times of distress. The use of differential excise levies selectively as an economic regulator has not always fulfilled the purpose intended ; in some cases it has produced a contrary effect. It has also placed on the revenue administration responsibilities inappropriate to its main function.

5. Generally speaking low priced articles of high common consumption are best suited for excise levies. as also luxury articles. Capital goods in view of their place in the economic development of the country, should be lightly taxed. Commodities with relatively small revenue potential are best left alone. Administration of levy in these commodities is expensive and also difficult.

6. Increases in revenue attributable to new levies imposed in recent years have not been in proportion to the number of commodities added to the list.

7. It is not prudent to keep down the cost of collection by resorting to relaxation of standard checks.

8. The Schemes for allowing drawbacks or set off of duty on raw materials and Components used for making other excisable goods vary from commodity to commodity. They lead to a feeling of discrimination and do not always subserve the needs of internal economy or the export trade. A definite policy, even a philosophy should be evolved in taxing goods at different stages of manufacture.

9. Articles with low revenue potential should be taxed only when they can be and are used as substitutes for other taxed articles. Levies that entail disproportionate costs of collection and on articles which are produced largely by small dispersed units should be avoided.

10. The revenue from taxing fabrications of taxed basic materials could, sometimes, be raised more economically by increasing the rates of duty on the raw materials themselves.

11. It is not possible to apply any one principle rigidly in selecting commodities for taxation. The major consideration should, however, be that a levy does create such administrative problems as largely defeat its purpose and that it does not create psychological complexes which retard Production. It is best to explore the possibility of increasing yields by adjusting rates of established excises on goods already taxec before considering new levies.

Pattern of levy and Control

12. Each major industry has its distinctive features and its own pattern of production and distribution. It must necessarily have rules suited to its needs. It is

not possible to bring all commodities under a common code.

13. Abatement of duty on losses due to dryage and wastage of tobacco though reasonable in itself is a major source of friction between excise officers and assessees.

Central-Excise-Law

14. Apprehensions expressed when the consolidating Act was passed in 1944 that consolidation of statutes of dissimilar goods will create complications have materialised. These are sought to be met by frequent amendments and adoption of principles which are applicable to some but not to all. There is thus complaint of discrimination. Relaxtion of rules or checks is not the solution to the problem.

15. The normal scheme of excise control cannot be applied to many commodities. The scheme devised primarily for a few basic commodities is no longer suitable for the large range of goods now subjected to levy. A rationalisation of the law is necessary.

Central Excises And Salt Act and Rules

The Act

1. The act should be made comprehensive to include all substantive provisions of law; Procedural matters should be covered by subsidiary legislation.

Parliamentary Control

2. Rates approved by Parliament are largely treated as ceiling rates and effective rates are introduced by notifications. This is an encroachment of the prerogative of Parliament which often has no information of the changes made. Neither total revence for gone nor the revenue sacrificed in fostering growth of the small sector can be property estimated. Revenue forecasts prove also in correct and attract parliamentary and audit criticism. A scheme of subsidies should be considered as an alternative; if feasible it would remove many of the drawbacks of the present procedure.

3. As revenues estimates are framed on the basis of rates actually intended to be imposed by notification and there is time enough after in introduction of the Fiance Bill to make necessary enquiries which could not be made earlier on considerations of secrecy, Parliamentary approval should be sought to rates to be finally imposed and not to rates which are subsequently treated as ceilings.

4. With the power sought to vary the rates up-wards also, the Indian provisions are now comparable to the U.K. Scheme. The safe guards of the U.K. scheme should, therefore, be adopted to maintain parliamentary authority.

5. Full and complete research should precede farming of taxation measures. The unusual power to vary statutory rates by notification should be sparingly used; changes, if any, in rates proposed in the Finance Bill should be incorporated in the act itself. Other changes made by notification should by and large cover the whole range of taxed goods and should be brought before parliament for ex-post facto approval.

Inoperative Provisions

6. Provisions and references to salt in the Act and rules should be deleted.

Anomalies in the Act

7. Anomalies arising out of definitions, particularly of the term "Manufacturer" should be removed.

8. Tariff values should be determined with circumspection, the apparent conflict in the provisions relating to valuation and fixation of tariff values should be removed.

9. Provision should be made for determination of assessable value of taxable components of a manufactured article.

10. The law itself should provide for the status of a rule made when Parliament is not in session if it is later revoked when brought before parliament. The Question is important for regularising implementation during the intervening period.

11. (i) Courts of law should notify the excise officer of impending disposal of excisable goods under their control.

(ii) Infringement of licensing provisions should be brought within the ambit of departmental adjudication.

(iii) The ceiling for penalties should be realistic; it should be upto three times the value of goods involved.

(iv) Central excise officers empowered to summon persons for conducting enquiries should have the authority to impound the documents required and to impose penalties if the summons are disregarded.

(v) The law should provide that a. Central Excise Officer seizing excisable goods should, on demand, give the owner the reasons therefor.

(vi) Provisions should be made for review of original decisions.

12. The present arrangement of taxable items under different groups in the Schedule to the Act is unnecessary and should be discontinued.

The Rules

13. A common set of rules to regulate storage of excisable goods in the manufacturer's store-room and in bonded warehouses should be prescribed.

14. Common provisions of all compounded-levy schemes should be consolidated.

15. Rules regulating refund on export should similarly be revised and consolidated ; inoperative or out-moded provisions should be deleted.

16. Rules relating to exemptions and remissions of duty should be made more specific to conform more fully to the provisions of the Act. Delegation of powers to subordinate officers should be reviewed, rationalised and enlarged.

17. A period of limitation should be incorporated in Rules 10A.

18. A common set of rules should be drawn upto regulate returns of excisable goods for reprocessing.

19. Failure to comply with supplemental instructions should entail penalties.

Publication of Tariff and Manuals

20. There is no up-to-date compendium of the rules and the rates of duty inforce. A revised edition of the Central Excise Tariff should be published every half year as on 1st May and 1st December.

21. There is no uniformity in notifying procedural instructions to the sections affected. The demand for a periodical bulletin of rules, notifications, interpretations and instructions for public use is legetimate. Such a publication is also necessary for the excise officers. Supplemental instructions should be issued in printed sheets of a standard format.

Procedure For Levy And Collection of Duty

Basis of Assessment.

1. It is not possible to be dogmatic on the question of the basis of levy for every commodity. Though specific rates lead to difficulties, especially for the small sectors to industry, their definiteness out weights many of the disadvantages. Purely from the point of view of simplicity of administration, they are to be preferred to ad-valorem rates, the present system does not lead to equitable results even where ad valorem rates are prescribed.

2. The Administrative set up of the central exise Department is not suited for the proper administration of ad valorem duties. This is proved by the adoption in a number of cases of expedients to convert ad valorem to wholly or partially specific rates.

3 Constitutional, legal and economic objections to the present concept of assessable value for levy of duty ad valorem deserve consideration. The customs legislation which formed the Proto-type for administration of ad valorem exise duties has now itself been revised.

4. The tariff as now designed gives anomalous results for certain values of taxable tobacco products as it is arranged in slabs of values. This anomaly should be removed.

5. Specific rates are obviously feasible in those cases where the present tariff provides both for specific and ad valorem rates but as alternatives.

6. Specific duties should be prescribed where ad valorem levies are administered through specific rates fixed by exemption notifications.

7. Where specific, rates of duty cannot be evolved tariff values for goods chargeable ad valorem should be fixed after proper enquiry.

8. Determination of assessable value on cost of production plus a fixed margin is not practicable;

9. Determination of assessable value on list price less fixed deductions is of limited application.

10. Assessable value should correspond to ex-factory price less excise duty, without reference to any particular market. For this purpose, transactions in which there is no special relationship between the manufacturer and the purchaser should be distinguished from those in which there is such relationship.

11. In direct sales, assessment should be on in voice value less duty and other post-clearance changes.

12. For transactions involving special so arrangements between producer and buyer; rules should specific inclusions and exclusions to be made uniformly to arrive at the assessable value.

Payment Of Duty

13. There should be no reversion to the system of post-payment of duty ; its prepayment should continue.

14. Procedures for payment should be simplified by consolidating assessment forms into three basic documents.

15. One current account for all duties payable by a manufacturer for all products produced in the same factory should be authorised.

16. Departmental treasuries should be set up in major centres of concentration of excise work.

17. The scheme for payment by cheque should be made more attractive by liberalising procedural restructions and acceptance of a single cheque for all clearances made from a factory in the course of a day.

18. Payment of licence fee should continue through revenue stamps. Use of stamps for payment of other dues is not feasible.

19. Facilities for bonded storage of excisable goods in main marketing centres should be allowed in selected cases on recovary of extra costs incurred as supervision fees. The principle in selection should be to allow bonded storage for goods whose production is regionally concentrated and which are assessable at specific rates.

Structure Of Control Licensing

1. A single multipurpose license should be issued to

cover all manufacturing operations at the same factory. Similarly a single license should be sufficient for whole sale purchase and warehousing of unmanufactured tobacco.

2. Brokers and Commissions Agents not possessing or stocking unmanufactured tobacco need not be licensed.

3. Categories of licence fees should be fewer. The fee for a licence to manufacture more than one commodity might be made a multiple of a single manufacturing licence.

4. All manufacturing and major warehousing licences should be renewed triennially.

5. Renewal of licences should be staggered over the year instead of being concentrated in the months November and December each year.

6. The penal fee for failure to renew licences in time should be substantially enhanced.

7. Powers of Inspectors to issue and renew licences in certain cases are adequate but superintendents should be made the licensing authority for all other licences. Manufacturing licenses or those where a transfer of ownership or premises is involved should be approved and renewed by superintendents.

8. Licensing Provisions should be made more stringent as a deterrent to revenue mis demeanours.

9. The utility of bonds for securing safety of revenue is limited. The work involved in their execution, acceptance, custody, etc., is not commensurate with the revenue collected.

Accounts Vs. Physical Checks

10. Audit type of control should be extended to all Public Sector undertakings, and in the Private Sector to those whose products are normally assessable at uniform specific rates and/or whose book keeping is adequate for checking production and delivery. Licensee's own statutory auditors may also be appointed Government Auditors.

11. The standard procedure of control should be simplified ; deliveries may be permitted without excise officers' counter signature of gate passes, subject to surprise checks.

Checks On Raw Material

12. The procedures for routine verification and check of intake and utilisation of raw materials should be reviewed with a view to eliminating avoidable checks. Manufactürer's own accounts of raw materials supported by purchase vouchers should generally be accepted in lieu of officially prescribed accounts.

13. Revenue control should be ensured by periodical and systematic analysis of manufacturer's own accounts. Proper procedures should be formulated for this scrutiny. When results of such checks warrant, a deeper probe should be made.

Checks of Manufacture

14. Schemes of sampling of process materials and of physical attendance of exise officers should be reviewed to eliminate all those checks which do not contribute to the substance of revenue control.

15. Separate production and store-room entry books entail duplication and should be amalgamated where possible. Forms of account, where prescribed, should take account of different characteristics of excisable goods. Where a manufacturer's own accounts are adequate for proper exise control, they should be accepted in lieu of officially prescribed accounts.

16. Routine test checks of daily production and packing should be made at the filling or packing storage in surprise visits. Tolerances should be authorised to conform to those commonly current in the trade or permitted by legislation such as the Marchandise Marks Act,

17. Quantities of excisable goods taken for chemical analysis should be the minimum necessary. Re-tests should be conducted on duplicate or triplicate of the same sample. Test results should be speedly communicated to the assessee. Re-tests in better equipped institutions should generally be permitted.

Assessment and Clearance

18. While some notice of removal of excisable goods is necessary, loading for clearance need not await the arrival of the excise officer.

19. Routine opening and verification of contents of packages at the time of delivery is unnecessary. The power to make such checks should be retained but exercised only in cases of well founded doubt.

20. Assessment disputes should initially settled by the super intendent, whose order should be appealable. The limitation for rectifying short levies is adequate Resort to Provisional assessments is to be deprecated.

21. Excise officer's countersignature of gate pass should be dispensed with. 'Producers' own despatch invoice, etc. If it gives the information required should be accepted in lieu of gate pass.

22. Existing for formalities attendant on removal of samples are unduly detailed and rigid ; a more liberal attitude would not endanger revenue.

23. Sector officers should be authorised to permit overtime clearances subject to subsequent approval by the. Range Officer.

Compounded Levy Schemes

24. A common set of basic rules will obviate the need for frequent changes in Compounded Levy

Schemes.

25. Compounded Levy Schemes do not solve the problem of ensuring adequate revenue control where the small sector forms a large proportion of manufacturers. A better alternative would be to recast the tariff.

Multi Point Excise Levies

1. Although relief from multiple levies is afforded selectively, there is neither uniformity in the pattern nor is there any evident or expressly stated principle in these reliefs.

2. The scheme recently introduced for giving credit of study borne on specified components and raw materials used for manufacture of specified excisable goods entails additional documentation and leads to distortion of revenue accounts without meeting the general grievance as it is limited in scope,

3. The variegated pattern of selective ad hoc reliefs leads to contradictions and accentuates discrimination.

4. It is impracticable to achieve a single Point Levy Uniformly.

5. Collection of duty on raw materials and components on delivery from the producing factory blocks up working capital of manufactures using them for production of other excisable goods. Some relief is colled for. It should be provided by permitting transfer of duty liability with the goods, the duty being collected along with that leviable on the final product. Similar relief should be provided for goods to be refined or reprocessed. Costs of Administration of this relief should be recovered as supervision fee. This will facilitate also the determination of ad hoc rates of refund on export.

6. A detailed study should be made of the administration of Added value tax system (TVA) in France and certain other countries to explore the possibility of introducing it in India in future.

Fiscal Preference

1. The tariff of riddled with preferences, privilages and exemptions. Their Administration on creates practical difficulties. It is doubtful also if their benefits always reach the persons for whom they are intended.

2. Increase in rates of duty has accounted for the largest contribution to increased revenue and extension of excise coverage the smallest.

3. The small increase in revenue relatively to a much larger excise coverage has stretched the administrative machinery ; gaps between work-load and resources are bridged by ad hoc adjustments.

4. Schemes of fiscal preferences, beside reducing revenue potential, lead to fragmentation of larger units. Scope for malpractices and collusive frauds increases. The need then arises for greater administrative vigilance and more detailed schemes of surveillance over the free and preferred sectors. These ineffect becomes paper controls. Idle capacity also increases and the role which the plan assigns to small scale industry is defeated.

5. Fiscal concessions to units in the organised sector of industries are neither necessary nor beneficial.

6. Commodities of which the major part of the production is not concentrated in the organised sector units are administratively unsuitable for taxation.

7. Revenue for gone for schemes of fiscal preferences cannot readily be computed, without reckoning the effects of limiting production, in 1961-62 it may have been of the order of Rs. 80 crores with reference to tariff rates and Rs. 20 crores with reference to effective rates.

8. Fiscal preferences are largely ineffective in their promotional effect, firstely, because they come in driblets with each assessment and, secondly, because the distributive trade depressee the purchase price corresponding to the quantum of duty preference and eventually appropriates most of the benefit to itself. This has been particularly noticeable in vegetable non-essential oils and matches.

9. Rate concessions should be substituted by cash bounties paid periodically. Assessment in all sectors would then be simpler as uniform rates could be applied. Units in the preferred sector may claim and receive the bounty periodically with reference to their part production. This will not involve extra works. Revenue Security will improve and amounts incurred to assist the small scale sector will be known.

10. The principles and scales of subsidy for different classes of manufacturers should be determined after open enquiry by a body like the tariff Commission which should also review the working of the schemes periodically.

11. Periodical cash bounties will ensure that fiscal aid reaches those for whom it is intended and that it takes a more effective and tangible form. Possible initial hardship for small scale manufacturers should receive due consideration when coolving principles and scales of subsidy.

Refunds on Exports

1. Many provisions of the present multiplicity of procedures cannot be fully understood or applied. They also hamper exports as the full burden of excise duty is neither removed nor is it practicable to do so. Refunds, are not always admissible of duty borne by raw materials and components and, even where they are allowed, no abalements are given for wastages in manufacture.

2. There is no rationale in a bond not being allow-

ed to cover exports merely because the port of export is changed.

3. Different procedures govern payment of refunds which are made partly by the Central Excise and partly by the Customs Departments.

4. There is excessive docmentation and repeated verification of the same manufacturing formulate where ad hoc rates of customs and Excise drawbacks are authorised.

5. Whenever an excise officer supervises goods made ready for export, checks for customs purposes should also be entrusted to him. Goods may than be allowed to be shipped under his certificates of scales without routine opening in the docks at the time of shipment.

6. Producers should be devised so that full refund of the total amounts is paid promptly after shipment.

7. Common procedures applicable to all goods and all exporters should be devised and consolidated to ensure that goods exported are relieved to the total customs and excise duty burden. Formal notifications that refund will be payable as export of specified goods is avoidable. This should be restricted to instances where special conditions become necessary.

8. The actual exporter should be entitled to refund on goods exported and executive restrains against this should be revoked.

9. Ad hoc rates of rebate on account of customs and Central Excise duties should be fixed for as wide a range of goods as possible on broad estimates of the incidence of all such duties borne at every stage, including the duty borne by packaging materials. It is essential that the exporter should know the quantum of rebate which will accrue on the goods be exports. Subsequent procedures can thereafter be simplified.

10. The special procedure now restricted to specified ports should become the normal procedure.

11. Other refunds should also be speeded up. Verification of original payment may be made with excise records and refunds paid by cheques.

Adjudication. Appeals and Revision Petitions

1. Decline in incidence of detection of excise offences may be due to slackness resulting from inadequacy of manpower of enforcing the standard pattern of control. New techniques have therefore, to be evolved.

2. An efficient enforcement and investigating agency should be created. Selected officers should be trained in modern methods of investigation.

3. Rewards for detection are small; diligence and initiative should be better rewarded.

4. Graduates with legal qualifications should be employed in cadre posts at collectorate Headquarters for briefing counsel in law suits.

5. Powers of adjudication of officers should be substantially enhanced. The Deputy collector should have the same powers of original decisions as the collectors.

6. Appellate powers of officers require no change, but to expedite decisions, the collector and his Deputies should hear appeals also on their tours.

7. If a licence holds adequate excisable goods to cover penalty and duty, his appeal should be heard without pre-payment of the dues.

8. While the present appellate channels may continue, the final stage of the revision application should be abandoned; instead, an Appellate Tribunal which would go both into the facts of the case as well as points of law should be set up. The Tribunal shoula have one member of status and experience comparative to that of a serving or retired High Court Judge and one or two members with working experience of technical excise work. The Tribunal should not be subordinate to the Chief Excise Authority, but there is no objection to its being within the Ministry of Finance.

PART II: The Central Board of Revenue and its Attached Officers

1. Taxation policy is best formulated in the Economic Affairs Department of the Finance Ministry in Association with other economic ministries. The CENTRAL BOARD OF REVENUE should cease to be a department of Government. It should be the chief revenue authority concentrating an efficient management of the collecting agencies but its views on the feasibility or otherwise of each levy should continue to be obtained.

2. There has been no rationale in fixing the strength and status of Members of the Board from time to time. There should be an objective assessment of workload and responsibility to determine both the number of members and their and the chairman's status.

3. There should be two Boards, one for direct taxes and the other for indirect taxes, each with its own independent chairman.

4. The Board for indirect taxes, which may be called the Board of Central Excise and Customs, should set as a Board to consider all aspects of technical, administrative and establishment work. The strength of the Board and distribution of work among its Members should be determined by the volume of work. The chairman should be drawn from either wing of the Service. Besides co-ordinating the work of the Board, he should be the Finance Minister's adviser on indirect taxes. The Board should be responsible for implementing taxation measures and evolve requisite techniques. It should report to Government the difficulties of administration so that remedial measures could be taken.

5. The data now used to formulate new proposals is neither upto date nor complete. It is also insufficient

for consideration of excise levies. The Board of central Excise and customs should set up a tax research bureau to collect, collate, analyse and provide it with all relevant material and data. The Central Excise field force is best suited to collect the information required for the tax research bureau.

6. The Directorate of Inspection should be reorganised to concern itself with investigation and study of major revenue and tehnical problems and not with the routine inspections. Its regional offices will then be unnecessary.

7. The statistics and Intelligence Branch is hardly equipped to undertake any intelligence work. Little is gained by mechanical tabulation of the same statistical summaries which are also manually consolidated. It should be reorganised after a detailed study to be made by a committee of statistical experts. It should be equipped to build up fuller statistical information.

8. If articles to be taxed are properly defined, there should be little room for technical chemists in the day to day administration of excise levies. The principle function of Regional and the control Laboratories should be of carrying out analysis where duty liability depends upon the chemical composition of an article. Their needs in equipment and personnel should be reviewed in this light.

Field Organisation Executive

The Primary unit

1. The Multiple Officer Range Scheme has evoked to widespread criticism from official and non-official witness alike.

2. The main objectives of the scheme have not been achieved the grew a men of criticism :

(a) The Deputy Superintendent in charge of the municiple officer Range is unable to inspect his charge objectively.

(b) evidence is not conclusive that yields tobacco have increase following introduction of the scheme.

(c) delays are greater and there is lack of community of supervision;

(d) an extra rung in the hierarchy is introduced and the fixation of responsibility has become difficult.

(e) despite travelling longer distances licenses cannot readily find the proper officer and complaints of delays are frequent.

3. Concentration of staff farther from areas where work arises increases risks of smuggling and evasion. Frequent rotation has created a feeling that the administration lacks faith in its men and has affected too morale besides reducing scope for specialisation.

4. There is greater loss of time in travelling and more expenses. Rotation of officers dislocates family life besides causing other difficulties where accommodation is provided by factories. There is mutued bickering and rancour and the control of the Deputy superintendent is ineffective.

5. Multiple officer range scheme may be suitable for areas of concentration of industry but it is not so where production units are dispersed. Periods of rotation should be reduced to a minimum of one year to provide for continuity and specialisation.

6. The primary revenue unit should be a sector with workload manageable by an Inspector, and an adequate member of sectors should cover the whole country. The general pattern, except in areas of concentration, should be single officer sectors manned by Inspectors. The utility of Sub-Inspectors is extremely limited.

The Supervisory Hierarchy

7. Too many tiers of supervision and lack of adequate delegation delays resolution of difficulties. Both should be remedied.

8. Compact groups of sectors and Municiple officer Ranges should form a Range in charge of a class II superintendent whose office duties should be drastically curtailed. He should essentially be an inspecting and supervising officer. There is neigher room nor need for a non-gazatted supervisory officer between the sector officer and the superintendent, Range offices should not be offices of record but each Range should have one or more additional Inspectors for enforcement etc. work.

9. There is no justification for retaining two classes of superintendents.

10. Control over Ranges should vest in class I officers in charge of Divisions with adequate power to shoulder responsibility and take decisions.

11. The Divisional office should have three branches, each in charge of a class II superintendent for administration, technical including statistical and intelligence control, and adjudication work respectively.

12. Jurisdiction of collectorates should be based on our relevant considerations, the purpose being to make them as far as possible comparable. Collectorates comprising portions of two states should be avoided.

13. Collectors should be assisted at their headquarters by two Deputies so that they are not tied down to their desks.

14. Integration of customs and excise work outside major posts may continue but service conditions of officers engaged in customs work whether they are Customs or Central Excise Departments should be made comparable. There is not much scope for the merger of customs and central excise administration or for integration of their class II.

15. Collectors, Deputy Collectors and Assistant Collectors should be redesignated Commissioners, Deputy Commissioners and Assistant Commissioners respectively.

Ministerial

16. Ministerial and Executive cadres should continue to be separate.

17. A large proportion of Lower Division Clerks actually undertake upper Division Clerks work. Adjustments should be made in the strength of Lower Division Clerks who should be employed only on routine duties as emisaged by the Second Pay Commission.

18. There should be a common grade of Office Superintendent for all Collectorates. The numbers required should be determined on the strength of the establishment in each office.

19. Deputy Superintendents (Ministerial) and Head Clerks in Supervisory charges of sections in office should be replaced by a common grade of Deputy Office Superintendent. Their number should depend upon the number of sections in which an office is organised. Each of three branches in Divisional Offices should be in-charge of a Deputy Office Superintendent. In Ranges an Upper Division Clerk should be the clerk in-charge with a charge allowance.

20. Ministerial Cadres in the Directorates and the statistics and Intelligence Branch should be merged in those of the office of the Chief Central Excise Authority. Present anomalies in Career Prospects and emoluments should be removed.

21. The imbalance is the Steno-typists and Stenographers Cadres should be removed by creating more posts of ordinary grade Stenographers. Senior Officers should be provided with stenographers.

22. Deserving ministerial officers should be given the opportunity at a comparatively young age in the executive gazetted and not-gazetted grades as is already done in Customs and Income-Tax Departments. There should be a permissive provision but no reservation of Posts.

Revenue Accounting And Audit

1. The feasibility of departmentalising compilation of central excise revenue accounts should be further pursued.

2. The purpose of setting up Examinars audit parties in frustrated because accounts the work is entrusted to untrained personnel.

3. As audit procedure has not been revised with changes in taxing schemes and document realling the Chief Accounts Officer do not contain all particulars necessary, it is impossible to audit many types of demands and payments.

4. The audit procedure should be revised to make through checks possible.

5. The unimportant function of drawing and distribution bills and accounting and audit of expenditure has become the main function of Chief Accounts Officers to the detriment of their more important work of audit of revenue.

6. Personnel resources are totally inadequate for any worthwhile audit. Some Chief and Assistant Chief Accounts Officers have themselves had no training or experience of accounting and audit.

7. The Department has now no proper organisation or arrangements for audit of its transactions. This lacuna must be removed.

8. The Chief Central Excise Revenue Authority should include a Directorate of Audit. Chief Accounts Officers should be given status and pay appropriate to their functions and responsibilities which are comparable to those of a junior Accountant General. Half the number of Chief Accounts Officers required should be drawn from the Indian Audit and Accounts Officers and the other half found within the Department after an initial training of selected officers

Structure of Staffing Executive

1. Sub-Inspectors are either used for Inspector's or sepoy's work, mostly latter. Nothing is gained by retaining this cadre and it should be eliminated.

2. With increasing infusion of promoted men, the Inspector cadre is beginning to deteriorate, even though flow of promotions is slow. The deterioration will increase with time.

3. Inspectors should be recruited on the results of written examinations and viva voce on an all India basis- Entry of ministerial officers to the cadre should also be regulated by competitive tests to be taken within specified age units.

4. There should be some direct recruitment in the class II service of superintendents. One half of the promotion quota should be filled by selection on the basis of seniority-cum-merit and the other half by a competitive examination open to all Inspectors who have completed a minimum specified period of service.

5. Inter se seniority of officers in the combined class I service should be reviewed to remove existing general grievance.

6. Collectorates should as far as possiple be made comparable in work load and responsibility. Heavier or more complex charges should be headed by senior officers and a special pay should be attached to such posts.

7. The system of first promotion after 1956 of Deputy Superintendents according to a zonal seniority reckoned from date of confirmation has led to discontent

as other factors were not comparable. Promotion prospects have also become uneven in all lower ranks. The only practical way is to revert to the old basis of promotions upto class II rank on a collectorate basis.

8. The present cadre formation does not fall into a pyramidal pattern. It will become more rational and incidentally, prospects will become more equalised, under these proposals.

9. The future Range should consist of about six sectors. The Division of about six Ranges and the circle of four to six Divisions. Costs are not likely to be any greater.

10. The number of sepoys should be reduced by abandoning gate controls at factories and restricting them to customs and perhaps tobacco work as a peons in offices. The number of jemadar's posts should be increased.

Ministerial

11. There is no need for clerks in Sectors-Ranges should have an Upper Division Clerk in charge with a charge allowance, one other Upper Division Clerk and a Stenotypist.

12. Divisional Offices should generally be organised in three branches, one each for administration technical and judicial work. Lower Division Clerks shoutd be employed only for routine duties.

13. Collectorate Headquarters Offices should have three main branches for administration, technical and audit and accounting additional branches being formed if work loads justify. Administration and technical branches should be made up of sections in charge of Deputy Office Superintendents and each consisting of six to eight upper and two to three Lower Division Clerks. Branches should be controlled by office Superintendents.

14. Some direct recruitment at the Upper Division Clerk's level should be resumed. Promotions should be by selection after a qualifying examination open to Lower Division Clerks with three years service.

15. Advance increments pending actual promotion should be allowed to officers who qualify at selection examinations.

16. In audit and Accounts Branches original work should be done by 'Auditors', one half of whom should be recruited from amongst University graduates and the other half by selection of Lower Division Clerks after qualifying tests. 'Accountants' should be in supervisory charge of cells of auditors. They should be promoted from amongst auditors by selection after passing a qualifying examination. The whole branch should be under an office superintendents. This and class II posts of Assistant Accounts Officers, Deputy Head quarters Assistants and Examiners should be filled by promotion of Accountants.

Intelligence and Preventive

17. First consolidation of statistical returns should be in the Divisional Office from Sector Officers' returns. Comptometers and adding machines will speed up the work.

18. Inquiries into the feasibility of mechanising compilation and tabulation of statistical data in each collectorates or groups of collectorates should be entrusted to the proposed committee of statistical experts.

19. The intelligence organisation should be backed by an adequate and mobile force of trained officers for conducting investigations and collecting material also for the tax research Bureau.

Public Relations and Settlement of Operational Difficulties

1. Administrative arrangements should ensure quick decisions on problems.

2. Supervisory Officers should have larger powers to dispose of precedual and minor issues.

3. The scope for public relations officers is extremely limited.

4. Where policy impinges on Procedures, Advisory committees may be allowed to discuss it indirectly for a review on practical considerations.

5. Decisions on Regional Advisory Committees' recommendations should be taken expeditiously and also communicated to the Committees.

6. The size of Regional Advisory Committees should not be enlarged unduly but representatives of industries not already included amongst their members should be co-opted so that their problems can be discussed.

7. No major changes in Advisory Committees are necessary if assessees and responsible officers are brought in closer touch. Such Committees below the collector's level cannot be of much use.

Management Improvement And Staff Welfare

Transport, Housing, Transfers and overtime allowance

1. Living and working conditions in the Central Excise Department are somewhat peculiar and more exacting than in others.

2. Mere grants-in-aid for cultural and social activities are not enough unless working conditions can be alleviated.

3. Low paid employees like Lower Division Clerks should not be subject to routine transfers. Transfers of others upto and including class II officers should not involve inter-collectorate or inter-state moves.

4. There are few Government owned or hired buildings. This adds to the already difficult conditions

specially in rural areas and at land frontiers.

5. It is wrong in principle to place excise officers under obligation of manufacturers in regard to housing. Except in plantations and factories away from urban centres, manufacturers should not be required to provide residential accommodation.

6. Cost of travelling on duty within short distances is not fully reimbursed. Vehicles at each Divisional and cirlce head quarters and in heavy tobacco growing areas will improve mobility and revenue control. The principle to provide vehicles should be accepted but it may be implemented gradually.

7. There is no justification to distinguish between excise and customs officers as similar duties for purposes of overtime allowance. Common principle for cash overtime fees should be uniformly applied.

Stationery, office equipment and forms.

8. There is a chronic shortage of paper, articles of stationery and printed forms for reports and returns and many field officers rely for these requirements on their licensees. There are also inadequacies of furniture and fittings, telephones and office machines. As these have also been pointed out earlier, a beginning should be made now to remove these shortcomings.

9. Sample surveys should be made to estimate the time executive officers have to devote to office work which should then be systematically reduced. Forms of statistical reports, returns and registers should be printed and supplied to them.

Suggestions Seheme

10. More concrete forms of recognition may stimulate interest in the suggestions scheme.

Cadre strength and workload

11. Recruitment and promotion procedures should be imported so that no gaps remain between authorised staff and that in position.

12. All officers and men who have officiated in clear vacancies for two years should be confirmed and all temporary posts continued beyond three years made permanent.

Traning Scheme

13. There was never been a proper training scheme in the Department except for some refresher courses. Training "on the job" is not a satisfactory arrangement. To improve efficiency, a central residential training school for recruits to gazetted ranks and zonal residential schools for training recruits to non-gazetted ranks should be established. For the ministerial staff, training courses should be organised locally.

Uniforms

14. Central Excise officers should continue to wear uniforms. The existing scale of allowances is inadequate and should be revised. Additional allowance should be given for winter kit where necessary. No distinction should be made between uniform allowances of customs and Excise officers employed on comparable duties.

15. The new distinguishing badges of rank are confusing and should be rationalised.

Cost of Collection

1. Commodity-wise costs cannot be worked out under the present system of accounting. While employment of recognised techniques of cost accounting should enable determination both of commodity-wise costs as well as their comperative costs in different collectorates, the true position of real comparative costs may be obscured by a number of factors.

2. Steps should be taken to develop a fully integrated system of cost control.

3. Costing must be based on basic documents prepared at the time of assessment, overheads not relatable to any particular excise should be allocated empirically. Costs of Chief Central Excise Authority and its ancillary offices at New Delhi need not be allocated to collectorates for purposes of comparision.

4. Present cost of collection of Excise duties is not unreasonable and is comparable to that of the other two main sources of revenue, though compared to costs of collection of indirect taxes in some other countries, it is still high.

Part III : Textile Fabrics And Yarn

1. The separate levy of yarn consumed in manufacture of cotton fabrics in composite mills and powerloom units large than 49 Looms, should be converted into fabric duty.

2. There is no agreement on replacing physical-cum-accounts method of control by the audit type of control.

3. Duty may be charged on samples but the procedure should be simplified.

4. There should be closer and early consultation between representatives of industry and excise officers competent to settle procedural details and clear doubts whenever a new duty is levied.

5. Production has increased but the average incidence of duty on cotton fabrics of the compounded levy sector has been falling. Revenue sacrifice in compounding is estimated at Rs. 6 crores annually on the basis of 1961 rates of production.

6. Licensed powerloom units rose from 279 in 1955 to cover 26,000 in May, 1962.

7. Neither reduction of Looms per unit to constitute the free sector nor raising the compounded-levy rates is likely to improve revenue. The benefit of the revenue sacrified often goes to city financiers instead of powerloom owners. Anti-fragm ntation measures have not succeeded. Fragmentation has resulted in the costs of administration sometimes exceeding the revenue collection.

8. Schemes to relate the compounded levy to actual or potential production and grading it according to sizes of units will both entail excessive costs and perpetuate the tendency towards fragmentation.

9. Cotton powerloom fabrics should not again be exempted from the duty.

10. Duty from powerloom cotton fabrics should be derived by a levy on yarn delivered from spinning mills and excise control over powerlooms abandoned with economy is administrative costs. The exemption for coarser yarns delivered in banks should be revoked. All handloom fabrics will then again bear a modieum of tax. If protection than is to continue, this could either be done by refund of yarn duty to handloom fabrics will then again bear a modicum of tax. If protection for thom is to continue, this could either be done by refund of yarn duty to handloom co-operatives or by increasing the rate of handloomcess, preferably the former. Relief to different sections of powerloom industry may, if found necessary, be given as subsidy.

11. The monthly exemption slab for independent processing units should be replaced by a scheme of subsidy, the amount of subsidy rising as the quantities processed increase above a floor and upto a ceiling, after which there should be no subsidy.

12. The revenue from the second stage levy of processing duty on rayon and artificial silk fabrics, should be derived through revised rates of yarn duty. This will reduce admiuistrative costs and also remove the grivance that, unlike cotton fabric processors, artificial silk processors do not have an exemption slab. There should be no exemption slabs for them.

13. Conversion of the two stage levy on woolen fabrics into a duty on yarn is not feasible.

14. Avoidable documentation in completion of assessment memoranda and deduction for discounts, 'flag' allowances and the like should be eliminated.

15. Duty on yarn wasted in processing and milling should be taken into account when fixing rates of refund on export of fabrics.

16. Remnants of pieces used for cutting samples should be allowed to be delivered on recovery of duty.

Tobacco

1. The excise systems of other countries give no guidance for remodelling our scheme.

2. A scheme of assessing duty on cured produce, the liability being dischared by the first buyer but without subsequent control on the tobacco, is not feasible.

3. If the off take of cigarette production was higher and a tax on manufacture l biris adminis'ratively feasible, it would be possible to rise all revenue from these manufactured products and leave raw tobacco untaxed. But that is impract'cable.

4. There is no workable alternative to the present system of classification for assessment, but the large gap between lower and higher rates is an incentive to misuse of lower rated tobacco. Complaints of this are widespread though statistical study does not indicate any large scale increase in production of whole-leaf varieties.

5. The quality of Indian tobacco should be improved but not through compulsory grading of tariff preferences. There should be stricter restrictions, as in other countries, on collection of bottom, withered, etc., leaves and ratoon.

6. A flat rate of duty is desirable, but as a differential between tobacco for biri and for other uses has been maintained over a long period, a sudden change may upset the equilibrium the gap between the two rates should be gradually reduced so that a flat rate can ultimately be introduced.

7. Control over production of tobacco should be stricter.

8. The grower's entry book may be abolished and the curer's entry book restricted to professional curers only.

9. To help curers, some such agency as the Central ware housing corporation should set up public bonded ware houses for cured tobacco and make advances on stocks deposited.

10. A specified period adequate for the actual needs of the trade should be fixed for the storage of tobacoo in warehouses in bond. There should be no extensions and the period fixed should be uniformly enforced.

11. Revision of rates of duty to allow for losses due to dryage and withdrawl of the concession to condone such losses is to react adversely on the producer. But such condonation should be limited to losses on account of natural dryage, during a period to be fixed for each major variety, taking into account the time taken by freshly cured tobacco to lose its surplus moisture. Thereafter, no claims for losses should be entertained.

12. Condoning losses in curer's premises should be regularised by law.

13. In re-arranging jurisdictions care should be taken to see that primary revenue officers are able to realise the arrears and, in any case, to check any further rise in arrears. A mandatory penalty should apply to

amounts remaining unpaid. There is no need to demand interest, but curers may be allowed to pay arrears in instalments.

14. Amounts in arrears may be re-assessed on rate enhancement only where tobacco physically exists. Revising other demands where tobacco has already gone into consumption it for practical purposes of no value.

15. The law of enforce recovery of arrears is adequate. State administrations should realise that a part of the arrear is actually state revenue. There should be reliance on the normal organisation to realise arrears and not on employment of special squads.

16. Administration will become simpler and certain grievances of cigarette manufacturers will be met if the two stage levy, first on tobacco and then on cigarettes. Could be replaced by a single levy on cigarettes, but a specific tariff with reference to weight of tobacco in cigarettes does not appear practicable.

17. There is considerable evasion of cigar and cheroot duty and more and more cigars pass for non-taxable than could genuinely be marketed within the tax-free slab having regarded to prevailing price, wage, etc., levels. The collection being small, the duty should either be abolished or replaced by a flat specific levy related to weight of cigars and cheroots. Excise labels for cigars lose all meaning when a free slab exists and may be continued only if the free slab is abolished.

Sugar

1. Either the methods prescribed for testing sugar samples should be replaced by those which will not be open to objection on technical grounds or the earlier definition of excisable sugar should be restored.

2. Documentation and sampling for exise purposes and physical checks are excessive and should be reduced, Departmental chemists should only analyse samples in disputed cases and not become technical consultants or judges of operational efficiency. The scheme of technical control and scrutiny of process accounts should be modified accordingly.

3. Audit type of control should largely replace the present system of physical control.

4. The incidence of duty borne by khandsari sugar produced under compounded levy is much lower than under the notified rates which are themselves low.

5. The production of Khandsari sugar by sulphitation process is organised in small factories. The sugar they produced is also often indistinguishable from sugar made in vacuum pan factories. The rate of duty on sulphitation processed khandsari sugar should, therefore, be brought nearer the normal rate. This would be justified in itself and would also largely compensate for the loss of revenue by exemption ordinary khandsari sugar from the duty.

Matches

1. A simple levy has become extremely complex through successive changes in categorisation of factories and rates of preference applicable to individual producers.

2. Despite of duty preference for factories in the organised sector. Since 1961, their total production declined. Changes in gross benefits from rate concessions have led to lowering of output of "B" category factories, some of whom have closed down or fragmented into "C" category factories whose numbers and out put have shown a phenomenal increase.

3. Restriction on licensing of more than one factory belonging to members of the some undivided Hindu family is commonly circumvented and also complained of as discriminatory. Both this and the rule requiring approval of labels have in effect become dead letters and servce no useful purpose.

4. The exiting rate preferences are an incentive to fragment into smaller units or restrict output. The effective tariff should be recast to encourages consolidation and growth.

5. Revised duty differentials have not benefited those for whom they were intended, the labour engaged in small factories or the consumer. The objective of telescopic rates to encourage manufacturers to grow has not been achieved. The duty preference is largely passing into the distributive channels.

6. There is no justification to distinguish between the present 'B' and 'C' category factories for tariff purposes.

7. The criterion of the use of mechanical power may be an adequate one to distinguish factories in the organised from those in the small sector, ignoring such use of mechanical aids as, for instance, in grinding chemicals, cutting labels etc. There should be no preferential slab for manufacturers in the organised sector. There should be a common preferential rate for all manufacturers in the small sector. Aid to individual manufacturers in the letter sector should then be given through cash subsides, the amount of subsidy increasing as production rises. This will provide incentives to consolidation and growth.

8. Banderolling is preferred by all but as there is scope for substantial economy by eliminating banderolling, an alternative should be explored.

9. Rules relating to certificates specifying the price at which manufacturers may buy banderols need revision.

10. The Departmental Treasury at Sivakashi should be supplied banderols directly from the Security Press.

11. Marketing of retail prices on match boxes has not served any useful purpose. Uniform retail price

cannot be ensured without statutory price control and uniformity in other taxes levied on matches.

Tea

1. Warehousing of tea store in Calcutta and Cochin pending auction will relieve the financial burden on producing tea estates. Excise duty may be recovered on delivery from warehouses after auction. Where estates deliver tea directly to buyers, duty may continue to be recovered at the time of removal from the producing factory.

2. The suggestion to accept post-dated cheques on account of excise duty cannot be endorsed.

3. Tea cess levied on quantities of tea exported may be spread over the entire production and collected in the same way and along with excise duty to facilitate recovary and also lower the cost of tea exported.

4. Consumption of loose tea which does not bear the package tea duty is increasing. Levy of package duty puts a premium on unhygienic storage and chandling of loose tea. The savings of package tea duty is largely appropriated by the distributive Channels. The overall duty burden bears more heavily on the rural consumer than on hotels, restaurants, etc., who can order tea in large packs and avoid the package duty.

5. Revenue will improve considerably and the rural consumer also benefit it to the zonal rate was added, in substitution of the package duty, a common rate applicable to all tea going into internal consumption. Warehousing of tea in auction markets will facilitate this and reduce administrative costs.

6. Zonal rates should be fixed tacking into account, besides the average selling price, the cost of production also.

7. There is scope for reducing physical checks and excise accounts to eliminate those that are of little value or involve duplication.

8. Powers of officers to supervise distriction should be liberalised to meet day-to-day needs of production.

9. There is no need for a bond for tea waste which is ab initio exempted from the duty.

10. Central and state levies on tea can only be combined into a single stage recovery if constitutional difficulties and the objections of the states can be overcome.

Paper

1. The complaint that dissimilar varieties are grouped under the tariff at common rates of levy and that the same varieties are at times classified differently at different paper mills is not without substance. The present scheme leads to the grievance that officers usually assess at the highest of several rates applicable.

2. Grouping of varieties for tariff purposes should be on the basis of verifiable physical characteristics. The number of categories could be reduced from the present four to two. The higher rate may apply to varieties identifiable by physical characteristics, e.g. tissue other than cigarette tissue, blotting, toilet, cheque or art paper. The lower rate may include all other varities.

3. The rate preferences for newsprint is liable to abuse, the detection and prevention of which is difficult. A common rate of duty may apply to all newsprint however used, the mechanical woodpulp content being made the criterion to distinguish newsprint from other variaties of paper.

4. Enquiries which are made at the instance of the ministry of commerce and Industry to determine whether a variety of paper is provisionally recognised as handmade before it is exempted from duty may be entrusted to Excise officers.

Boards

5. As all boards are assessable at any one of two basic rates of duty, a more broad based tariff description will facilitate administration.

6. The existing procedure prescribes the same physical checks at successive stages in the packing room, store room and at the time of clearance. The scheme should be simplified and all test checks conducted mainly in the packing room, checking in subsequent stages being confined to such cases where there is reason to suspect substitution.

Soap

1. The out put of the power operated sectors has steadily increased after the levy of duty but there have been only minor improvements in the output of the taxable non-power operated sector.

2. The free slab in power operated sector accounts for four to five per cent of its total duty liability. The free and preferential slabs for the non-power operated sector lead to about 60% of the out put being free of duty. The revenue foregone in exemption slap in power operated sector is about Rs. 10 lakhs annually; the annual revenue from the non-power operated sector is Rs. 14 lakhs.

3. About 150 power operated factories yield nearly 94% of the total revenue from soap. 350 factories in the non-power operated sector contribute the balance of 6%. Another 1400 non-power operated factories are under excise control but as they pay little revenue the exise effort in surveillance over them is unproductive of revenue.

4. The non-power operated sector may be exempted from the duty ; the revenue loss should be offset by abolition of the exempted slab for the power operated sector and recasting the tariff. This will reduce costs without a major disturbance to the economy of the industry.

5 All household and laundry soap should be chargeable at as common rate.

6. As rates of duty for all other soaps are the same, the tariff can be rationalised into two rates, one for household and laundry soaps and another for all others.

7. Criteria such as the size of containers, alkalies used, design of labels, etc. for eligibility to exemption should be treated like other excisable components and raw materials ; all other deliveries should be subjected to the duty.

8. Correlation of raw material with production is incomplete if it is confined to consumption of vegetable non-essential oils only.

Footwear

1. Notified and executive exemptions have stultified the purpose of extension of the levy to footwear parts. Recovery of duty on excisable footwear parts is contingent as the fact whether they are made into footwear in the same or in any other footwear factory in the excluded sector.

2. Duty should be levied on all footwear and footwear parts produced with the aid of power.

Electric Batteries

1. Administration of ad valorem levy has presented more than the usual difficulties in assessment of batteries used by certain manufacturers. Changing the basis of levy to a specific rate with reference to the weight or other criteria of batteries should be explored.

2. Flat deduction from published list prices for assessment of batteries is not favoured by the industry.

3. On administrative considerations, battery plates produced by five worker factories whose out put of battery still exempt, should also be exempted.

Electric Wires and Cables

1. Preference in valuation for assessment is an incentive to production of non-standard cables. Sub-standard electric cables are hardly in the notional interest.

2. Simplification through tariff values for assessment is defeated by the fixation of values and preferences. Duty cannot be calculated in terms even of whole naye paise.

3. Revenue to be derived from cables can be realised more simply and cheaply by suitable revision of the rates of duty for electrolytic copper and conductor grade aluminium, or taxing rods drawn from such metals and insulating materials.

4. Such decisions as charging insulating types if the weight of cotton fabrics is them exceeds 40%, and an insulating enamels made from taxed imported resins, should be revoked. While not contributing any appreciable revenue, they create administrative difficulties and enlarge the area of conflict.

Patent and Proprietary Medicines

1. Instead of the intrinsic quality or the therapecutic value of a drug, the formal, design, colour or colours, borders, background effect of the lable under which it is marketed, determining its. liability to duty is irrational. There is also a large discretion to the assessing officer giving rise to uncertainty which is not healthy for the trade. If the intention is to siphon off a part of the extra profit, this cannot be achieved by charging the duty ad valorem.

2. From the practical point of view, the entire range of pharmaceutical products should be brought under excise levy with selective exemptions restricted to specified essential life saving drugs. The institution of the loan licensees should be reviewed specially as purity of drugs is so vital to the well being of the community. Excise administration will be simplified if loan licensees were abolished.

3. The limits for quantities permitted to be replaced free of duty or delivered as samples free of duty should be reviewed from time to time to conform to the normal practice in the trade.

4. Audit type of control is not feasible with a preponderance of small scale manufacturers, but it could be introduced for well organised laboratories with fully documented accounts only if the whole range of medicines is made excisable.

Coffee

1. Although the coffee board markets of bulk of the crop, it is neither advisable nor feasible to entrust excise administration to it.

2. All coffee could be subjected to a common rate of duty.

3. It is in advisable to convert the basis of levy to ad valorem to help inferior or low priced grades.

4. Facilities of bulking and garbling coffee should be allowed to all exporters.

5. In view of the importance of the Industry and its revenue potential a research foundation should be instituted to secure improved yields and quality of Indian Coffee.

Acids

1. Hydrochloric and nitric acids made with out the use of power by small manufacturer using duty paid sulphuric acid may be exempted out right as revenue is small and it is not possible to ensure compliance of all the conditions now prescribed.

Films

1. The suggested substitution of the excise duty on

exposed cinematograph films by an increased rate of duty on raw film is likely to bear harder on those producers who take fewer them 14 or 15 copies of each film but will lighten the burden on producers who take larger number of copies.

2. In view of the altered balance between import and excise duties under the finance Bill of 1963, the matter may be further examined.

Vegetable Non-Essential Oils

1. Although more oil was produced is successive years by a larger number of millers and the exempted and preferred sectors had been reduced in size, the revenue declined instead of improving, the share of the small scale sector in the total output rose in successive years and that of the organised sector declined. The incidence of duty borne by oil produced in the organised sector averaged Rs. 100 per tonne ; the incidence the small scale sector's oil fell from about Rs. 81.60 in 1959-60 to about Rs. 40-60 per tonne in 1961-62.

2. The Scheme of duty preferences induced larger units to fragment. Anti-fragmentation measures did not succeed.

3. Compounding led to swelling the profits of the exporters and the benefit of lower incidence in compounding did not accrue to the millers. A more marked distortion occured in the production pattern of castor oil.

4. Abolition of the exempted sector in March, 1959 was expected to yield about Rs. 4 crores additional revenue, but actual revenue collections fell by about Rs. 3.5 crores over the preceeding year, the revenue actually for gone may have even higher.

5. Fragmentation and growth of numbers of small millers affected also the solvent extraction plants and export trade in oil-cake.

6. As the number of factors which affects the production capacity of the same equipment is large, there is no method of arriving at a fair average production capacity for each equipment for crushing of oil seed.

7. For constitutional and other reasons compounding cannot be made compulsory.

8. Deriving the total revenue from vegetable non-essential oils by enhanced rates for other excisable goods made with oils as raw material might up set the balance and lead to other comlications.

9. A commodity is which half of the production is distributed in the Small Scale Sector is not a very suitable article for levy of duty. Government appear to have arrived broadly at the same conclusion as the duty has been exempted but a study of this levy gives an interesting in sight into practical and economic effects which an excise duty can have.

RAILWAY ACCIDENT INVESTIGATION ONTHE ACCIDENT OF 309 DOWN BOMBAY—POONA JANATA EXPRESS BETWEEN KHANDALA AND LONAVLA STATIONS (CENTRAL RAILWAY) ON NOVEMBER 14, 1960—REPORT

New Delhi, Ministry of Transport and Communications (Railway Inspectorate), 1963. 12p.

One Man Commission : Shri K.C. Pathak

APPOINTMENT

The Commission was constituted under the Ministry of Transport and Communications (Railway Inspectorate) in accordance with paragraph 9 of the Railway Board's Notification No. 1926-T, dated March 1 9,1930. The Investigation Team was appointed on November, 15, 1960.

TERMS OF REFERENCE

To inquire into the Accident to No. 309 Down Bombay-Poona Janata Express at Mileage 77/29 E-S, between Khandala and Lonavla stations on the Bombay Poona Broad Gauge Main Line Section of the Central Railway, on November 14, 1960.

CONTENTS

Summary ; Inquiry ; Description of Accident ; Casualties. Relief Measure ; Particulars of Train ; Damage ; No. of Passengers ; Local Conditions ; Weather ; Method of Working of the Electric Locomotive ; Summary of Evidence ; Discussion (Excessive Load on the Coupling ; Causes of Couplings being Strained Unduly ; Design of the Coupling ; Cause of the Accident ; Other Accidents of Coaching Trains Parting in Ghats ; What Caused the Tripping of Banking Engines ; Metallurgical Examination) ; Conclusions.

CONCLUSIONS

Cause Of Accident

After careful consideration of the evidence recorded by me and other evidence available and after an inspection of site, coaches and the engines, I have come to the conclusion that parting of No. 309 Down Janata Express of Nov. 14, 1960, at Mileage 77/29 E-S., between Khandala and Lonavla stations was the result of the snapping of the coupling of the 4th coach which connected it to the 5th coach. This failure of the coupling was the result of the conditions brought about by the tripping of the Engine No. 4500-EF/1, aggravated by a local change of grade on track from 1 in 36 to 1 in 55, and the faulty design of the couplings of I.C.F. type wherein a screw 20 inches long had been provided.

The tripping of locomotive No. 4500/EF/1 was brought about when the pantograph of the engine moved upward from a height of about 19 ft. above rail level to 19 ft. 6 in. above rail level between electric structure 77/17 and 77/18. In this range the tension changed from 30 lbs. 31 lbs. and there was probably certain time lag for the springs of the pantograph to adjustment themselves at a height of 19 ft. 6 in. above rail level. Thie caused a short break of contact between the pantograph and the contact wire.

Responsibility

I do not hold any particular person responsible for this accident.

Relief Measure

I consider that prompt action was taken to attend to the injured persons at the site of the accident and in the Khandala a Civil Hospital. The arrangements to convey the three injured persons to the Lonavla Railway Dispensary and the Sassoon Hospital, Poona, were satisfactory.

CENTRAL WAGE BOARD FOR TEA PLANTATION INDUSTRY, 1960—REPORT

New Delhi, Ministry of Labour, Employment and Rehabilitation, 1967. 122 p.

Chairman : Shri L. P. Dave.

Members : Shri T. Manaen ; Dr. R. Balakrishna (replaced by Shri V.L. D'Souza) ; Shri L.T. Carmichael (replaced by Shri B.C. Ghose) ; Shri J.B. Soutar ; Shri G. Ramanujam ; Shri B. Bhagwati (replaced by Shri M. N. Sarmah who died and Shri Jadu Nath Bhuryan was appointed in his place).

Secretary : Shri N. Ahmed.

APPOINTMENT

In pursuance of the recommendations contained in paragraph 25 of Chapter XXVII of the Second Five Year Plan, regarding the establishment of Tripartile Wage Boards for individual industries, the Government of India in the Ministry of Labour and Employment appointed the Central Wage Board for Tea Plantation Industry vide its Resolution No. W.B-3(12)/59, dated December 5, 1960.

TERMS OF REFERENCE

To work out a wage structure based on the principles of fair wages as set forth in the Report of the Committee on Fair Wages as far as practicable.

In evolving a wage structure, the Board should, in addition to the consideration relating to fair wages, also take into account :

(i) The needs of the industry in a developing economy ;

(ii) The system of payment by results ;

(iii) The special characteristics of the industry in various regions and areas ;

(iv) Categories of workers to be covered (this may be according to the definition of workmen in the Industrial Disputes Act) ; and

(v) Working hours in the industry;

Explanation

Whenever applying the system of payment by result the Board shall keep in view the need for fixing a minimum (fall-back) wage and also to safeguard-against overwork and undue speed.

CONTENTS

Introductory ; Interim Wage Increase ; Wage Structure ; Recommendations ; Staff Wages—North-East India ; North India (Punjab, Himachal Pradesh, U.P. and Bihar) ; Miscellaneous ; Appendices from I to VIII.

RECOMMENDATIONS

1. Extent Of Tea Industry Covered

Recommendations should apply to all tea plantations in which tea is being cultivated, produced and/or manufactured for commercial purposes.

2. Categories Of Employees Covered

All workers employed in tea plantations in fields, factories, workshops, offices, hospitals (including group hospitals), dispensaries, schools, welfare establishments, etc., in the tea plantations or connected with them and coming with in the definition of 'workman' in Clause(s) of Section 2 of the Disputes Act, 1947, should be covered by the Boards Industrial recommendations. All employees in tea plantations, whether they work on the plantation itself or at any place in the tea plantation district would also be covered. But employees working in any office situated at district or sub-divisional headquarter town would not be covered by the Board's recommendations.

3. Daily Rates Of Wages For Field Workers

The daily wages of workers should consist of basic wage and dearness allowance. The basic wage of field workers should be as mentioned in the statement given below:

4. Daily Rates Of Wages For Factory Workers

Existing differentials between rates of wages of field workers and factory workers in North-East India will continue. With effect from Jan. 1, 1967, factory workers (in Madras, Kerala and Mysore) are to be paid a differential over the new daily wage rates of the field workers at the rates on page no. 211 in col. 1 :)

Basic Rates of Wages

(in Rs.)

State / Region	Basic Wages effective from Jan. 1, 66			April 1, 66		
	Men	Women	Children	Men	Women	Children
A—NORTH EAST INDIA						
1. **Assam :**						
Dibrugarh sub-division of Lakhimpur district and Sibsagar district.						
(i) Assam Valley : (i) Tea plantations of 150 acres and above	2.23	2.05	1.08	2.25	2.07	1,09
(ii) Other tea plantations	2,20	2.02	1.07	2.22	2.04	1.08
Darrange district (except Mangaldai) and North Lakhimpur sub-division of Lakhimpur district.						
(i) Tea plantations of 150 acres and above.	2.16	1.99	1.05	2.08	2.01	1.06
(ii) Other tea plantations	2.13	1.96	1.04	2.15	1.98	1.05
Mangaldai in Darrange district	2.13	1.96	1.04	2.15	1.98	1.05
*United North Cachar and Mikhir Hills, Nowgong, Kamrup and Goalpara district	2.06	1.95	1.04	2.08	1.97	1,05
(ii) Chachar : Cachar and tea plantations within 10 miles area of Dimapur	1.70	1.60	0.91	1.72	1.62	0.92
2. **West Bengal:**						
Dooars						
For tea plantations of 500 acres and above	2.11	1.94	1.14	2.13	1.96	1.15
For tea plantations below 500 acres	2.08	1.91	1.14	2.10	1.93	1.15
Terai & Cooch Behar	2 05	1.88	1.12	2.07	1.90	1,13
Darjeeling*	1.73	1.62	0.94	1.75	1.64	0.95
3. **Tripura :**	1.51	1.32	0.74	1.53	1.34	0.75

*These rates are subject to the condition that no reduction from the present wages rates will be made.

(in Rs. P.)

State	Region	Basic wage effective from Jan. 1, 66 Men	Women	Children
	B—NORTH INDIA			
1. Punjab & Himachal Pradesh	Kangra and Mandi	1.20	0.94	0.55
2. Uttar Pradesh	Dehradun	1.60	1.60	—
	Bearing and Chokorie areas of Almorah district	1.20	1.20	—
	Other areas of Almorah and Garhwal district	0.86	0.86	—
3. Bihar	Ranchi	1.55	1.55	—

State	Categories of estates	Basic wages effective from Jan. 1, 66 Men	Women	Adolescent	Children
	C—SOUTH INDIA				
1. Madras	100 acres and above	2.25	1.80	1.35	1.13
	Less than 100 acres	2.11	1.66	1.29	1.13
2. Kerala	100 acres and above	2.25	1.80	1.35	1.13
	Less than 100 acres	2.18	1.76	1.33	1.11
3. Mysore	100 acres and above	2.25	1.80	1.35	1.13
	Less than 100 acres	2.11	1.64	1.25	1.13

Men : 20 paise over field men's wage.
Women : 15 paise over field women's wage.
Adolescents : 15 paise over field adolescents' wage.

5. Wages Of Pruners, Sprayers, Etc.

The present differentials, if any, between the wages of workers employed in pruning spraying, etc., and those employed in ordinary field work should continue.

6. Wages Of Supervisors/Mistries (In South India)

The supervisors/mistries should be paid wage increase from January 1, 1966, equal to the wage increase granted to an adult male worker in the field from the same date plus 20 per cent of the differentials existing between the total wages of supervisors/mistries as an December 31, 1965, and the wages of adult male workers in the field on the same date. In the case of Kote mistries in South India, the increase is to be six paisa per day plus the increase given to adult male worker.

7. Dearness Allowance

The dearness allowance is to vary in North-East India at 0.4 paisa and North India and South India at 0.75 paisa per day per point of increase (above 170 points) in the average All India Consumer Price Index number subject to a maximum increase of 16 points in North East India and South India (or six paise in North-East India) and 12 points in North India in any one calender year. Any excess over this limit, in any year, upto the level of 200 points, is to be carried over to the following year. No dearness allowance revision beyond 200 points before December 31, 1970, dearness allowance to be rounded off at the end of each month.

8. Price Rates

(i) In North-East India, the existing system of price rates, particularly plucking rates, should continue but may be revised by agreement between employers and labour so that the worker with normal diligence would earn at least the fair wages now agreed to for a day of eight hours work.

(ii) In South India, the existing system of piece rates in Kerala, Mysore and Madras should continue. The rates should, however, be revised so as to be in step with the increase agreed to for the daily rated worker.

9. Mixed Estates

Wages of workers in mixed estates in South India should be governed by existing practice.

Staff Wages

(a) North East India

10. Wage Increase From Jan. 1, 1966

From Jan. 1, 1966, the clerical and medical staff and technicians should be granted increase in their cash emoluments payable for the month of December, 1965, at 52 times the rate of increase granted to the daily rated workers, with effect from April 1, 1966, in the region. The other monthly rated workers should be similarly granted increase at 33 times the increase granted to the daily rated workers in the region.

11. Wages Structure From April 1, 1966

(i) The following should be the basic pay scales for the various grades of staff employed in the plantations in North-East India, with effect from April 1, 1966 :

Grade	For estates of 300 acres and above	Other estates
A—Clerical Staff		
I	Rs. 220-8-300-10-400	Rs. 150-6-210-7-280
II	Rs. 160-6-220- 8-300	Rs. 110-4-150-5-200
III	Rs. 125-4-165- 5-190-6-220	Rs. 90-3-120-4-160
B—Medical Staff		
I	Rs. 250-15-400-E.B.-20-600	Rs. 220-8-300-12-480
II	Rs. 160- 7-230-10-330	Rs. 120-4-160- 5-235
III	Rs. 130- 5-180- 7-250	Rs. 90-3-120- 4-180
C-As Artisans and Technicians		
A	Rs. 210-8-290-10-390	Rs. 180-8-260-10-360
B	Rs. 150-6-210- 7-280	Rs. 130-6-190- 7-260
C	Rs. 100-3-130- 9-170	Rs. 80-3-110- 4-150
D-Subordinate and monthly rated staff		
A	Rs. 80-3-140	Rs. 80-3-140
B	Rs. 70-2-100	Rs. 70-2-100
C	Rs. 60-2-100	Rs. 60-2-100

(ii) In the case of tea plantations of tess than 150 acres, grade 1 in the case of staff and grade A in the case of artisans and technicians will not apply.

(iii) All gardens between 151 and 450 acres in Darjeeling, Cachar, Tripura, North Cachar and Mikir Hills will pay the scales prescribed for gardens of less than 300 acres in these districts.

(iv) For gardens in Darjeeling, above 450 acres, the scales for gardens over 300 acres will apply but grade 1 in the case of clerical staff and grade A in the case of technicians will not apply.

12. Categorisation

Clerical and medical staff, and artisans and technicians, subordinate staff and other categories of employees in North-East India are to be categorised and fixed in the new grades according to the rules prescribed.

13. Fitment In The New Scale Of Pay

Fixation of employees in new scales of pay should be according to the conditions laid down.

14. Phased Implementation Of Wage Rise

In the case of employees who are much below the starting basic pay of the new scales, the maximum increase in basic pay would be Rs. 10 per year plus the equivalent of one increment in the new scales until the starting pay of the new scales is reached. The increments, where necessary should take effect from April, 1966. New recriuts are to start with basic pay one increment Lower than the lowest paid employee of the same category in an estate.

15. Conversion Of Daily Rated Into Monthly Rated

For conversion from daily rated into monthly rated, the daily rates should be multiplied by 26 for fixing the pay in the new scale.

16. Dearness Allowance

The fixed dearness allowance, with effect from April 1, 1966, should be 20 per cent of the new basic pay. The variable dearness allowance should be at 0.4 per cent of the new basic pay per point rise above 170 in the All India Consumer Price Index, for clerical, medical and technical staff and at 0.3 per cent per point rise for subordinate and monthly rated staff subject to a maximum of 16 points in any calendar year. Any excess over this limit in any year upto the level of 200 points is to be carried over to the following year. No dearness allowance revision beyond 200 points is to be allowed before December 31, 1970.

17. Servant Allowance

Subject to higher rate of servant allowance remaining unaffected and present grade C artisans (who are in receipt of this allowance at present) continuing to get it as personal pay, the servant allowance, wherever it is payable at present, should be at the following rates, with effect from April 1, 1966 :

Plantations of less than 300 Acres	Other Plantations
Rs. 35 per month from April 1, 1966	Rs. 35 p.m. from April 1, 1966
	Rs. 40 p.m. from April 1, 1967
	Rs. 45 p.m. from April 1, 1968
	Rs. 50 p.m. from April 1, 1969
	Rs. 55 p.m. from April 1, 1970

The servant allowance is to be regarded as part of basic pay for purpose of overtime payment, provident fund contribution and bonus.

(b) North Indi

18. (i) Pay Scales

The new pay scales in North India tea plantations, with effect from April 1, 1966, should be :

1. Minimum grade for staff Rs. 90-3-120-4-160
2. Minimum grade for sub-staff Rs. 60-2-100

(ii) Dearness Allowance

The fixed and the variable dearness allowance are to be at the same rates as in North-East India.

19. Categorisation And Fitment

Categorisation and fitment of staff in North India are

to be according to the principles laid down.

In South India pay scales, dearness allowance, servant allowance, categorisation and fitment (given below) are the same as modified by staff settlement dated May 4, 1965 :

20. Scales Of Pay With Effect From Jan, 1, 1966

Large Estates in all the three states :

General Grade	Rs. 40/50-3-56-4-80/ EB-5-120-EB-6-180
Senior Grade 'A'	Rs. 90-6-120-EB-7-148 EB-8-196-200
Senior Grade 'B'	Rs. 150-10-280

Medium Estates in Madras and Kerala :

General Grade	Rs. 40-50-3-56-4-80- EB-5-130
Senior Grade (for heads of Depts. only)	Rs. 90-6-120-EB-8-180- 10-220

Medium 'B' Estates in Mysore :

General Grade	Rs. 40/50-3-60-4-80-EB-5- 135
Senior Grade	Rs. 90-6-120-EB-7-148-EB 8-196

Medium 'A' Estates in Mysore :

General Grade	Rs. 4o-3-55-4-75-EB-5-105
Senior Grade	Rs. 90-5-120-EB-6-156

Note : The definition of large, medium, medium 'A' and medium 'B' estates are the same as in the staff settlements of 1957 and 1958.

21. Categorisation, Fitment And Promotions

According to the provisons in the State Settlement dated May. 4, 1965.

22. Dearness Allowance

The dearness allowance, with effect from Jan. 1, 1966 is to be according to the UPASI revised scales of Dearness Allowance, a schedule of which is attached to Staff settlement dated May 4, 1965.

23. Servent allowance

Servant allowance @ Rs. 35 except in the case of general grade in small A estates in Mysore, where it is Rs. 17.50 per month.

24. Promotion Procedure In Certain Cases

Promation in certain cases such as those of nurses without nursing certificate, medical staff of grade III, subordinate staff reaching top of their grade and grade C artisans, are to be according to the procedure laid down.

25. Relife In Certain Cases

Cases of members of the staff reaching maximum of the new scales, as a result of Board's proposals, are to be considered by the industry sympathetically for giving relief.

Miscellaneous

26. Period Of Enforcement

Recommendations to remain in force from January 1, 1966 to December 31, 1970 in respect of labour in the entire country and from April 1, 1966 to March 31, 1970 in respect of staff in North-East India. The revised wages for staff in South India, are to remain in force from January 1, 1965 to December 31, 1969.

27. Splitting Of Tea Estates

Splitting of tea estate is not to affect wage rates.

28. Employment Of Family Members

Whenever extra hands are to be engaged, members of workers' family are to be given preference.

29. Supply Of Foodgrains

All tea plantations in India should be supplied with foodgrains regularly by Government and the employers should supply the same in North-East India at the existing concessional prices or at such rates as may be revised by agreement between the parties and in South India on 'no profit no loss' basis, in addition to providing rent free storage and free clerical and other services for distribution.

30. Revision Of Prices Of Cereals

The question of revision (upgrading) of concessional prices of cereals in North-East India may be discussed on regional basis between employers and labour. The quantities and prices should be switched on to metric system.

31. Cold Weather Tasks In North East India

Parties may make such adjustments in cold weather tasks as can be performed by a worker of normal diligence in seven to eight hours, by mutual agreement.

32. Existing Amenities, Benefits, Etc., To Remain Unaffected

Board's recommendations are without prejudice to the existing amenities and benefits and the concessional supply of foodgrains in North-East India.

33. Payment Of Arrears

If back wages accumulate for a period exceeding six months, the industry is to be allowed to pay the accumulated wages in two equal instalments, one within one month of the date of publication of the Government notification and the other within another month

34. Constitution Of Committee

Committees are to be constituted with equal representatives of workers and employers organisations with Labcur Commissioner of the respective State as Chairman to go into the difficulties of over-staffed or otherwise handicapped gardens in North-East India due to partition of India and other allied reasons and to devise remedial measures.

35. Machinary Of Interpretation

Disputes arising out of the interpretation of the Boardi recommendations are to be decided by arbitration of a sitting or retired High Court Judge, whose decision would be final and binding upon the parties.

STUDY GROUP ON THE WELFARE OF THE WEAKER SECTIONS OF THE VILLAGE COMMUNITY, 1960—REPORT

New Delhi, Ministry of Community Development and Cooperation, 1961. 70p.+vp.

Chairman: Shri Jayaprakash Narayan.
Members: Shri Anna Saheb Sahasrabudhe; Mrs. Sucheta Kripalani; Shri M. R. Krishna; Shri Braj Raj Singh; Shri B. Sivaraman; Shri L. M. Shrikant.
Secretary: Shri R. Jagannathan.

APPOINTMENT

The Study Group on the Welfare of the Weaker Sections of the Village Community was constituted under the Ministry of Community Development and Cooperation vide their Notification No. 10 (3)/60-Panch, dated December 8, 1960.

TERMS OF REFERENCE

(a) To study how far and in what manner the Community Development Organisation and/or Panchayati Raj institutions at Village, Block and Zila levels can promote the economic development and welfare of the weaker sections of the community.

(b) To suggest steps by which the development schemes of the Central and State Governments and Local Authorities and the financial assistance available can be effectively utilised for the benefit of the weaker sections of the community.

CONTENTS

Introduction; Objectives and Approach; Definition and Size of the Problem; Minimal Requirements for the Welfare of the Weaker Sections; Block Programmes and Funds; Role of Cooperatives; Role of Panchayati Raj Institutions; Organisational setup at the Centre and States; Supplementary Note by Shri Braj Raj Singh; Main Conclusions and Recommendations.

RECOMMENDATIONS

Objectives And Approach

The uplift, welfare, and emancipation of the weaker sections cannot be accomplished without a comprehensive non-violent Social Devolution, encompassing all facts of Indian Society. A distinguishing feature of the Indian revolution must be the destruction, root and branch, of the caste system, without which the bulk of the weaker sections can never come into their own.

Size Of The Problem

About 80 per cent of the rural households have an income of less than Rs. 1,000 per annum, and 50 per cent, who form the lower rung of the ladder, have an income of less than Rs. 500 per annum. This lower rung comprises agricultural labourers, and cultivators with very small landholdings, artisans and small craftsmen and, at the lowest level destitutes with no means of livelihood at all.

A Means Test is suggested. Families whose income is less than say Rs. 1,000 a year would cover cases of chronic economic backwardness. Following Gandhiji's concept of "Antyodaya", within this low income classification, priority of assistance should be given to those families whose income is less than Rs. 500 a year. A beginning should be made from the lowest rung of the ladder. Lastly, families whose income is less than Rs. 250 per annum should be regarded as destitutes.

The entire scheduled castes and scheduled tribes may be regarded as forming part of the weaker sections and means test if necessary in their case.

Minimum Requirements

The following requirements must be fulfilled in order

that the weaker sections are assured a minimum level of well-being and their rightful place in society.

1. Full employment;
2. Housing and drinking water;
3. Education.
4. Health;
5. Protection from economic exploitation;
6. Freedom from social and cultural disabilities;
7. Reform and prevention of wasteful and ruinous habits and customs.

Agriculture

Petty holdings, which are far greater in number, are responsible for keeping both agriculture and the majority of the cultivators in a chronically depressed condition. Here is an obstinate socio-economic [disease that calls for a radical remedy. Village ownership and management of land is the only complete answer to the problems of our agriculture at once from the point of view of social justice and of development of agriculture and preparing favourable conditions for rural industrialisation. The following two recommendations are made in that connection:

(a) One of the objectives of Community Development is "to develop a spirit of community life among the people by promoting cooperation and mutual sharing leading ultimately to voluntary community ownership of the basic means of production, such as land ..."

This objective has not received the attention from the C. D. Organisation and its non-official collaborators and supporters as it deserved. We, therefore, recommend that encouragement and promotion of common ownership of land be taken up as a prominent part of the educative and reorientation work of the Organisation and all its ancillary bodies.

(b) The C. D. Ministry should institute a scientific study of a suitable programme of villagisation of land by legislation as a means both of social justice and agricultural and industrial development.

Employment In A Public Works Programme

Government should undertake and make a declaration to that effect-to guarantee employment to every citizen who is prepared, and fit, to do manual labour. Such guarantee and declaration would work a psychological transformation and lift up the pall of despair and discouragement that over shadows millions of Indian homes. It might, indeed prove to be the spark to kindle the energies of a somnolent giant.

Rural Industries

Rural industrialisation is the supreme requirement both for lifting the rural economy from the morass it has fallen into as also for raising the standard of living of the economically and socially week. It should be rated higher than agriculture because, though agriculturel development is necessary for industrial growth, there is a limit to its growth and to the pace of it. Industrialisation on the other hand, whether rural or urban, is capable of rapid and large expansion. Rural industrialisation is not to be conceived of as being limited to what are termed at present as "rural industries" or to merely agricultural processing industries. There can be and should be an unlimited variety and an even spread of industries throughout the countryside. At present there is no single authority at any level whose particular responsibility it is to think, study, plan and act in this behalf. Rural industrialisation must be viewed as a single integrated program and not be dealt with piecemeal by different agencies, even though they may coordinate their activities. Government of India should, therefore, create (out of the existing bodies, or by establishing a new one) a single comprehensive authority, with the necessary powers and resources and charged with the responsibility of rapidly industrialising the rural areas.

Education

The following facilities should be provided:

(1) Subject to a "means test", free education upto Higher Secondary stage;

(2) Subject to a "means test", free board and lodging in mixed hostels for students upto the Higher Secondary stage;

(3) Scholarships for higher education subject to competence qualification;

(4) Mid-day meals for all children in the primary classes;

(5) Free dress, states, pencils and books for pupils of the primary classes from the weaker sections.

The village school has to integrate itself with the community. Its teachers and students must participate in the community activities—in transplanting, harvesting and freeplanting, composting, dramatics, sports, festivals, adult education, etc. The Primary schools should be the responsibility of the Panchayats and the Middle Schools of the Samities.

Health

One way of overcoming the shortage of doctors in rural areas would be to obtain a bond from all students who are admitted to Government Medical Institutions that they would, if required, serve in rural areas for a period of at least two years after their graduation. (A si ilar step may be followed in regard to over coming shortages in regard to other technical personnel.) We would also recommend grant of rural allowance to all doctors incharge of primary health centres.

The village community should be educated to feel its

responsibility towards the medical care of those who might he indigent, disabled to work, orphans, etc. For this purpose, every village panchayat, through voluntary contributions, should create a fund with which to assist helpless persons in times of illness.

In view of the fact that State Health Services are likely to remain inadequate for a considerable period as also with a view to further the basic aim of people's self Government and self-reliance, voluntary as well as State agencies should encourage and help the people to form their own Health Insurance Societies. The State Government should assist these societies on a half-and-half basis. The existence and operation of these societies should exercise a healthy influence upon the State services and private practitioners.

Drinking Water

In some States, assistance for well-construction is conditional on the beneficiaries providing a suitable plot of land. More often than not, Harijan families do not have any such land. Where drinking water is concerned, no conditions should stand in the way of its supply, and it should be the duty of the State (again counting the Panchayati Raj Institutions) to see that a source of pure drinking water supply is within the easy reach of every one in the rural area.

Protection From Economic Exploitation

The weaker sections suffer from a virulent form of economic exploitation at the hands of money-lenders and traders. The only effective manner in which this evil can be fought is by organising and extending as fast as possible, cooperative credit, production and marketing. The cooperative movement has here a great challange to answer.

Freedom From Social Disabilities

School teachers at the orientation courses, should be impressed with the necessity of inculcating in their students the values of human equality. In all the three bodies of Panchayati Raj, there should be committees to deal with questions relating to the scheduled castes (and tribes where they exist). These committees should exercise vigilance in respect of social disabilities also.

The caste of scavengers must immediately be emancipated.

(a) Head carrying of might soil should be prohibted by law;

(b) Old latrines should be converted as soon as possible into septic flush latrines and no new house should be permitted to be built unless it provides for a septic latrine.

The necessary financial assistance to individuals and municipalities should be provided as a measure of urgent national development.

The largest single wasteful habit of the weaker sections is that of drink. State policy in regard to prohibition, therefore, should be carried out with greater vigour and efficiency in the entire rural area of the country. Official and non-official agencies should both join their talents and resources to wage this compaign effectively.

C.D. Programme

Community Development should be regarded not only as a means but also as the end. The C.D. programme, as well as the funds allotted to it in the schematic budget should, therefore, have a single focus, viz., developing the village community.

The improvement of the economic condition of the weaker sections cannot be brought about by the efforts of the weaker sections alone. The community as a whole should cooperate in this endeavour and its equally necessary to reorient the outlook of the more well-to-do sections who have a district role to play in view of their better social, cultural and economic condition.

Having regard to the national priorities laid down in the Third Five-Year Plan, funds under grants and loans should, as a rule, be devoted only to schemes involving community participation specially benefiting the weaker sections, besides extension work including demonstration. Schemes to give financial benefit to individual well-to-do farmers should be discouraged. Where the nature of the scheme is such that only individual assistance could be given, it should be given to members of the weaker sections, starting with families having an annual income of less than Rs. 500, with priority to those belonging to scheduled castes and scheduled tribes.

Funds for staff quarters which are no doubt necessary, should not form part of the funds provided for community development. They should be provided for from other sources, for instance as loan from the Life Insurance Corporation.

In order to achieve uniform development in all the blocks, it would be desirable to give a further measure of assistance to specially backward areas and in areas or blocks where there is a larger concentration of economically weaker sections. A specified amount say Rs. 10,000 (loan Rs. 5,000 and grants-in-aid Rs. 5,000) should be pooled from each block and kept as a reserve or equalisation fund at the district. The zila parished could then examine the position of each such backward area and allot supplementary funds from this reserve.

Consequential on decentralisation of authority there is need for removing the uncertainty in the Panchayat Samiti's mind as to the quantum of funds which it is likely to get year to year from the Community Development budget. As the Community Development budget is a five-year budget, it would help if the Panchayat

Samiti is given power to spend upto a ceiling of one-fifth of its five year allocation of Block loans and grants every year and to adjust the expenditure towards the termination of stage I or II as the case may be, without such certainty, the block Samiti's initiative for planning effort is dimmed for a certain period every year until annual budget allotments are received from the State headquarters months after the commencement of the financial year, even though some ad hoc arrangements operate in the States for incurring expenditure pending such allotment.

Other Departmental Programs

In regard to loan-funds given for productive schemes in Agriculture, Irrigation. Animal Husbandry, Fisheries and Small Scale Industries the rules for the grant of loans and subsidies should be liberalised in favour of the weaker sections and they should be given priority in the allotment of funds. Also the quantum of aid should be equal to the requirements of the productive purposes for which they need the aid. In most cases, it is insufficient and the poor farmers are driven to the money-lender for the balance. The requirement of two sureties may be dispensed with where the scheme for which the loan is sought is part of the accepted village production plan.

In regard to the social services schemes, the bulk of them should be applied to the benefit of the weaker sections. In the Third Five-Year Plan, certain minimum amenities have been indicated as essential for every village viz., drinking water supply, school, and road communication from the village to the nearst main road or rail head. These minimum amenities should be made available as first priority especially in the areas occupied by the Scheduled Castes and other weaker sections in the village.

Provision for rural housing should be utilised exclusively for the weaker sections.

As regards Local Development Works, the bulk of these should be applied to areas occupied by the weaker sections allowing such special reduction in the scale of people's contribution as may be decided by the Panchayat Samitis concerned.

Special Schemes

Irrigation and Land Development: Attemps may be made to living together lands of the weaker sections of the community in one block by exchange with other owners through consolidation processes. Thereafter, a higher rate of subsidy may be paid to the weaker sections for digging irrigation wells. Each well will irrigate land of more than one person, as ordinarily the weaker sections have very small holdings. In the alternative, Panchayats may assume the obligation of providing irrigation wells and recover the cost in easy instalments from the cultivators. The same procedure may be followed in regard to reclaiming and developing the marginal holdings of the weaker sections.

In the preparation of village production plans, the the problems of the cultivators of marginal holdings should be studied and specific programs prepared for helping them. Where landless labourer is resettled on land, a subsistence allowance should be given to him until the first crop is harvested and he is able to stand on his own.

Demonstration of improved agricultural practices should, as far as possible, be taken up in lands belonging to the small cultivators. Loss, if any, should be reimbursed to the cultivators.

Milk Supply Schemes: A deliberate effort should be made to link agricultural labour with the program of milk production and supply. This is feasible particularly in the rural areas which are proposed to be linked with urban markets through Government sponsored milk production and distribution programs. At least 25 per cent of the plan outlay provided for developing milk and poultry production in rural areas should be utilised for the benefit of the landless agricultural labour.

Poultry Development Schemes: A short period of training should be arranged in modern methods of poultry-keeping on a wide scale, so that a large number of persons can be trained; supply of improved variety of cocks for upgrading local birds, poultry feed at subsidised rates, and help from the block organisation for marketing eggs.

Development of piggery: Many families among the weaker sections of the community would take to this occupation if sufficient help is given. Supply of improved types of animals and also supply of pig feed at subsidised rates in the initial period should be arranged. If necessary, help will have to be given through block organisation in marketing the produce.

Literacy: A literacy campaign aimed especially at the weaker sections of the community should be undertaken. In such a campaign sufficient incentive should be offered to illiterate persons who become literate, such as paying a few naye paise more per day to labourers in government work if they sign their muster role instead of putting their thumbprint.

Education and Training: Special attention should be given to education and training the members of the weaker sections of the community for occupying key-posts in the block development programs, particularly in supervisory and higher grades. This will ensure satisfactory implementations of schemes approved by government for the improvement of the weaker sections.

Welfare Schemes

The following welfare measures are suggested for

consideration :

(i) The Government of U. P. has a scheme of old age pension introduced sometimes ago, Madras and Andhra Pradesh Governments propose to introduce are shortly. A similar scheme may be considered by other State Governments.

(ii) A Life Insurance Scheme for the benefit of families of agricultural labourers may be taken up by labour cooperatives. A "mass insurance scheme" may also be considered.

(iii) Social welfare schemes being implemented by State Governments and other authorities seem to have an urban bias. Orientation of effort towards rural destitute households is necessary.

Role Of Cooperatives

The risks of cultivation of marginal lands are much more than that of lands in general. Even with the risk fund placed before the agricultural cooperative system, the risk of loss in marginal lands being quite heavy, no primary credit society will undertake the risk of including this class of cultivators on the principle of credit worthly purpose. The risk fund should be suitably augmented and societies which are prepared to undertake this risk should be helped suitably.

The chronic indebtedness makes it impossible for the cooperative credit system to help the petty cultivator to improve his lands or improve his agricultural practices or get out of a below subsistence level of economy. The State has to stop it and give him the base from which there can by a jumping off to a better economy. The rural works program can be suitably oriented to meet the expenditure for improvement of the land of the petty cultivator. If the works program takes up land reclamation of these petty cultivators on a complete relief basis and also provides for small irrigation sources and contour-bunding, ridging and such works which will be of benefit to the lands of the petty cultivator, the problem will be substantively solved.. Waste lands on which the landless are reseltied can also be improved similarly by schemes of land reclamation on a complete relief basis and provision of irrigation etc., made.

Processing of agricultural produce for local consumption and marketing of surplus to other consuming centres can be tackled by the regional marketing societies already established. The marketing societies now undertake supplies of production requirements to the agriculturists. They can take back the produce from the agriculturists in payment for supplies or for better marketing. It is only are step forward for these marketing societies to put up their own processing industries to process the produce, supply local demand and market the surplus in the best possible way. As the scheme is one to help out the agriculturisr it should be possible to extend Reserve Bank credit for agriculturists to meet the situation.

Semi-processing of agricultural produce can similarly be undertaken by the regional marketing societies though factories of their own. Oil-seeds of various kinds including the non-edible oilseeds, can be pressed and the oil exported instead of oil-seeds. This saves transport and also gives oil-cakes for local utilisation as manure and cattle feed. Here again, extension of Reserve Bank credit for such ventures would go a long way towards solving the problem.

The program suggested for the improvement of the handloom industry can be applied without much deviation to the production of any other group of artisans in the rural areas. These production groups suffer from the same disabilities as the Handloom Weavers used to suffer. Forming cooperatives of the artisans who are located within a reasonable distance of suitable centre and linking them up with a power unit at the centre would definitely improve the economics of such a group. The industries plan contemplates provision of such service centre and also provision for training in better methods. But if the Reserve Bank credit now given for the agricultural field can be extended to these artisans also through the cooperative banking structure there will be no need to confuse schemes and confuse sources of credit. The industries program has its limitations in the matter of the quantum of credit available for running expenditure. The Cooperative banking system can extend credit according to the requirements of the problem without too much of red-tape. It is, therefore, suggested that for rural industrialisation similar credit, to that given by the Reserve Bank for agricultural production should be extended through a heirarchy of industrial banks in the cooperative field.

The wider sections of the community comprising artisans and those who live by occupations such as, those of fishermen, are very much in the position of the handloom weavers. The cooperative structure by itself will not help them unless certain other facilities are also given to them as has been given to the handloom weavers, e. g. :

(a) Membership payments of a cooperative supply agency initially to be made by the State and subsequently repaid from profits;

(b) Better equipment on a subsidy basis to be provided by the State or through State help by the cooperative system;

(c) Teaching of better technique at State expense;

(d) Marketing of facilities, if necessary, with State aid till the jumping off position is reached;

(e) Protection from large industries or ventures in

the same field by reservation of items of production or fields of production;

(f) Limiting handicrafts to items of production where the artisan can show his individuality; and

(g) Organisation of artisans as group to take advantage of small machinery for bulk production of articles.

If the Rural Works Program is prepared in advance for a Panchayat Samiti area after taking into consideration the amount of under-employed labour that can be gathered for the local works in the off-season, it will be possible to work in advance a program of employment of the under-employed labour. The labour in such cases will be attached to their present location of employment and will get remunerative work in the off-season from the works program. Panchayat Samities should be brought into this program actively and asked to plan out the minimum employment for every landless labourer who wants seasonal employment when his normal employer is unable to give him work.

Details relating to the working of the labour cooperatives in the Punjab have recently been circulated by the Ministry of Community Development and Cooperation to all the State Governments. This movement has great potential for benefiting the landless labour, who are one of the weakest sections of the community.

Cooperative Farming

The following conditions and facilities should be given to cooperative forming societies :

(i) The pooling of land should be for a minimum period of 10 years;

(ii) Loans should be provided to enable farm labourers to take shares in cooperative farming societies ; and

(iii) As a general principle, 40 per cent of the produce (after meetings interest, revenue, labour, and other charges) should be distributed to those who have contributed land to the cooperative 40 per cent to labour; and the remaining 20 per cent should go to reserve.

The land originally pooled should be valued on a certain unitage based on production, and it should again be valued on a similar unitage basis after the improvements have been effected. If the improvements have been planned and executed properly, there is bound to be a substantial increase in the unitage of the farm. It should be divided between the landowners and the landless in the preparation of one-third to the landholders and two-thirds to labour. As the unitage also has relation to land, the landless labour will become owners over these units of land in the farm at the end of the improvement period.

Large agriculturists should be made to invest a part of their earnings from the land in land improvement. This can be hastened by the imposition of an improvement surcharge which can be waived if a certain volume of investment is made per acre of the land surcharged.

Small landholders should be helped to join together and form a cooperative society of their own. Improvement of their lands, mostly marginal, is impossible, unless all the land can be taken in one common lot where development can be done easily. To face this difficulty of fragmented and scattered holdings, it is suggested that wherever the small landholders are willing to join together, there should be consolidation of holdings, and their holdings should all be consolidated in one compact part of the village. This will enable the full benefit of the development schemes reaching these small landholders. A pilot scheme can be started in those villages where small landholders own a large extent of land. This will at least give the experiment a surer foundation till other forces reacting enable us to link up the big and the small.

The landless should be given waste lands available and be persuaded to form themselves into a small land owners' cooperatives and be further helped by direct state aid for improving their land production.

Role Of Panchayati Raj

The whole bias of panchayati raj institutions has to be towards the weaker sections of the village community. Responsibility should be vested in the Village Panchayats in regard to :

(i) Providing full employment either in the works programs of the panchayats themselves, or by the utilisation of idle manpower in public works under the proposed government's guaranteed employment scheme. A register of unemployed should be kept, and where employment has to be found outside, the sarpanch should take it up with the Panchayat Samiti.

(ii) Providing the minimum essential social services needed by village community

There should be an evaluation of the progress made every year. This evaluation should be made by the Panchayat Samitis. In addition, the evaluation, of the effects of economic development on the weaker sections of the rural population should be one of the main functions of the Program Evaluation Organisation of the Planning Commission.

Panchayats should help the economically weaker sections of the community to became members of cooperative societies by 'making available financial resources to enable them to purchase shares in cooperative societies, e.g. :

(a) Panchayats can provide grant or loan for this purpose. If the panchayats are given grants, the necessary matching contribution may be made either by the

Panchayat Samitis or by the State governments to the panchayats.

(b) Funds should be provided under the scheduled castes and scheduled tribes schemes to panchayats to enable them to help a certain number from these sections of the community every year to become members of cooperative societies.

Panchayat Samitis should be empowered to waive the condition regarding the people's contribution or suitably to reduce it having regard to special circumstances and hardships. The principle should be that a working labourer should be paid his wages.

Organisational Set-up

The existing organisation at the Centre in the Ministry of Community Development and the Development Commissioners' set up in the States should be responsible for promoting the welfare of the weaker sections of the village community. Their annual reports should specifically cover this subject and should be reviewed initially by a sub-committee of the Cabinet and later by the Informal Consultative Committee of the Legislature at the Centre and the States.

There should be the closest consultation and coordination between all the Central Ministries concerned with rural development and welfare. A committee may be constituted consisting of representatives of the Ministry of Community Development and Cooperation, Ministry of Food and Agriculture, Ministry of Commerce and Industry, Ministry of Education, Program Evaluation Organisation, Ministry of Home Affairs and the Commissioner for Scheduled Castes and Scheduled Tribes. This committee should be responsible for ensuring effective implementation of program, removing defects and deficiencies pointed out in the evaluation reports and otherwise, and charging the development program with the necessary dynamism and vision.

1961

COMMITTEE ON CHILD-CARE, 1961-62—REPORT

New Delhi, Central Social Welfare Board, 1965. 447p.

Chairman : Smt. B. Tarabai

Members : Dr. B.H. Mehta; Smt. Pratibha Singh; Smt. Pushpa Mehta; Smt. S. Manjubhashini, Smt. M.S.H. Jhabvala; Smt. Tarabai Modak ; Sri S.C. Pandit was replaced by Sri. D.V. Kulkarni ; Smt. P.K. Makhan Singh; Sri. N.D.J. Rao; Sri Radha Raman; Smt. Sudha Majumdar.

Secretary : Smt. B. Ghufran and Shri B.N. Dhar

APPOINTMENT

Realising the need to study the problem of child care and child welfare, the Central Social Welfare Board, at the instance of the Union Ministry of Education, decided at its 30th Meeting held in October 1960, to appoint a Committee to prepare a comprehensive plan for the care and training of children in the age-group 0-6. This particular age-group was specified because various other Committees have been appointed from time to time to study problems of children after reaching the primary school age. The Committee was inaugurated at New Delhi on March, 25, 1961, by Smt. Durgabai Deshmukh, Chairman of the Central Social Welfare Board. She provided the initial leadership in setting at right tone to the Committee's work when she said that" recent thinking on social welfare had recognished that child welfare was a special field and, in future planning, the welfare of children should be accorded the highest priority". She particularly drew attention to the fact that while many studies have been made on the welfare needs of school-going children, no comparable study has so far been attempted on a country-wide basis to report on the welfare needs of children up to the age of six. It was, therefore, necessary that the Committee should make a detailed survey of the nead and requirements of children in this age-group and make suitable recommendations for their welfare.

TERMS OF REEERENCE

(I) To study in the light of changing socio-economic

conditions in the country, care and the community, with particular reference to the provision of health, nutritional and recreational facilities in the home and in the neighbourhood.

(II) To examine the problems of children in need of special care and protection and to recommend measures for providing comprehensive child care services for them.

(III) To evaluate the nature, extent, and distribution (rural, urban, type of locality, etc.) of existing child welfare services with special reference to the management (government, proprietory, corporate non-official bodies, etc.) and pattern (Indian, Western, etc.) of pre-schools.

(IV) (1) To study and evaluate the standards of pre-school education with reference to:

(i) The pattern of staffing (trained and untrained, teacher-pupil ratio etc.,)

(ii) The curricula and methods of teaching adopted.

(iii) The type of equipment available and the manner and extent of its use.

(iv) Programme of recreation, rest, nutrition, health, care and instruction.

2 To work out a tentative plan for the development of pre-school education for the next five or 10 years with estimates of cost:

(v) To study the existing facilities for training of child welfare workers in terms of the number of centres required and contents and standards of training and to suggest a long-term training programme for child welfare workers on a uniform basis.

(vi) To work out a plan for the manufacture of a standard recreational and educational equipment at moderate cost, suited to the requirements of Indian children. This could be linked up with the socio-economic programme of the Central Social Welfare Board.

(vii) To assess the financial position of child welfare institutions for this age group, to study their pattern of income and expenditure and to assess the problems of grant-in-aid, the nature and volume of assistance required and the period for which it would be necessary.

(viii) To recommend a pattern for the reorganisation and extension of the programme of community and institutional services for the proper physical, mental and emotional development of the child in the first six years, keeping in view the continuity of services for children that will follow from six to 11 and 12 years to adulthood.

(ix) To suggest methods of coordination among the large number of agencies working in the field of child welfare.

CONTENTS

Family and the Nation; Child Population and Family Planning; The Background and Concept of Child Care and Neglect; Infant Mortality and Diseases amongst Children; Health and Infant Welfare; The Pre-School; Handicapped Children; Personnel and Training Programmes; Administration, Organisation and Management of Child Welfare Programmes and Institutions; Children's Recreation; Art, Literature and Play; List of Tables from 1 to 57; List of Appendices from A to I.

RECOMMENDATIONS

Section 1 : Basic Recomendations

Compaign And Movement

The Committee recommends that there is a need to organise a campaign to promote a National Child Welfare Movement with defined objectives, using scientific methods, and promoting programmes of different kinds to suit the different regions and sections of the population in India.

Childern's Act

That each State in the Indian Union must enact a Childern's Act, which serves as a model for all the States, should be thoroughly revised. Efforts should also be made to bring about some measures of uniformity in the State Legislative enactments contemplated under the Acts.

Division

That a Division of Child Welfare be created in the Ministry of Education in order to provide specialised direction and guidance to all child welfare programmes in the country.

Co-ordination

That a National Council of Co-ordination be appointed by the Ministry of Education to achieve and maintain common standards, lay down basic policies, achieve maximum economy in the use of resources and personnal, and take advantage of available results of research and knowledge in all subjects which have a bearing on child welfare.

Advisory Board

That a National Advisory Committee on Child Walfare be appointed by the Ministry of Education to advise the Ministeries concerned about the standard of care to be maintained in programmes and institutions, child walfare legislation, registration of institutions, counselling, etc.

Section Of Child Walfare In The Central Social Welfare Board

That the Central Social Walfare Board, which has initiated a large number of welfare programmes in Urban and Rural areas should develop a special wing for the exclusive promotion of programmes of child welfare and child study, and for improving the standard of child walfare services in the country.

Children's Bureau

That the Division of Child Welfare in the Ministry of Education, or alternatively the Central Social Walfare Board, should create in course of time a National Bureau of Child Walfare which will serve as a clearing house for child welfare information and become the main source of guidance for child walfare activities in the field.

Central Institution

That a National Centre for the Training of Child Welfare Specialists and general personnel for leadership, administration and direction of field programmes be created in a suitable metropolitan area; and that such a centre should undertake pilot projects programmes of child study and research, production of literature on child welfare, and other activities to direct and guide State and private agencies in thier efforts to promote child care and welfare.

Resources

On the basis of the information received, it is found that the resources actually provided for all the child welfare services in all the States are entirely inadequate to meet the demands of even a minimum child welfare service; and therefore special measures be taken to strengthen the Prime Minister's Children's Fund and find other ways to develop financial and other resources by every means possible.

Financial Aid

That the existing national, State and local agencies for child welfare should be strengthened by enabling them to expand their services; and to carry out programmes with the special financial assistance of the State, and additional resources provided by the communites.

Demonstration Project

That at least one Demonstration Child Welfare Project should be organised in every State. These projects will provide an intensive and integrated programme of child welfare including programmes for the welfare of children under six years. There should be at least five additional Demonstration Projects for the benefit of children in metropolitan areas. These programmes will function according to resources and plans to be provided by the Central Ministry of Education.

Guidance And Counselling Services

Competent guidance and counselling services should be created each State consisting of Field Guides and Counsellors to assist States and private child welfare programmes organised in the State; and a sum of Rs. 10 lakhs be set aside to give grants-in-aid to competent child welfare organisations, schools of social work and universities who are willing to provide such counselling services according to rules and procedures to be laid down by the Central Government.

Minimum Standard Pre-Schools

That at least 1,000 pre-schools, described in the report as Minimum Standard Pre-Schools, should be created in the Third Plan Period; and the annual recurring cost of such a pre-school will be Rs. 3,500 for one unit of 30 children between the ages of three-plus and five-plus years.

Pre-School Pilot Project

That at least one pre-school should be created in each District of India to function as a pilot project. The recurring expenditure of such a pre-school will about Rs. 10,000 per year, and the non-recurring grant in the first year may be Rs. 4,500.

Experimental Pre-Schools

Special types of Experimental Pre-Schools a programme of child study should be attached to universities, Schools of social work, and child study institutions. They should be given grants-in-aid by the Central as well as State governments

Training Programme

One year training programme for the training of Balsevikas must be organised in each State. The trainees should be given general information about the philosophy, objects, methods, and programmes of child welfare together with an intensive training to function as organisers and teachers of pre-schools.

That Central and State governments should support all two year programmes for the training of pre-school teachers by recognised voluntary agencies, universities and schools of social work.

National Toy Industry

That the Central Government should promote a national industry for the manufacture of toys and educational requirements and materials, and it should provide Rs. 15 lakhs to organise at least one such industry which will be able to supply cheap and standard equipment and materials for pre-schools, playgrounds, children's centres and other child welfare organisations.

Research Programme

A sum of Rs. 10 lakhs be utilised for the promotion of a research programme in child welfare, in co-operation with the Research Programmes Committee of the Planning Commission.

That in order to meet the expenditure required, for implementing programmes mentioned above, an additional allocation of Rs. 35 lakhs be sanctioned by the Planning Commission, or in the alternative, Rs. 3 crores be redistributed to include the suggested programmes for the Guidance and Counselling Service, Research, and the promotion of an industry for the manufacture of educational materials and toys.

Section 2 : Important And General Recommendations

As extensive programmes of social welfare are being organised all over the country, it should be the national policy to consider child welfare as an integrated and comprehensive programme which must be implemented everywhere by properly constituted agencies of child welfare in all parts or the country; and that the family and the community should play an increasingly important role in the execution of such programmes.

That top priority should be given to the provision of adequate welfare services for children, giving proper consideration to the requirements of nutritious foods for infants and children, the dietary articles being supplied to urban slums and villages at very cheap rates.

That as a matter of national policy, every efforts should be made to promote the social health of family and its integration. This has also to be attempted by counteracting those social forces which contribute towards family disorganisation and disintegration.

That in the future policy of social welfare, the need for a proper reorientation in the welfare schemes for children should be taken into account; and in social welfare, maternity and child welfare services should be given a very high priority.

That the existing programmes of child care should be extended so at to benefit a large number of children ; and the existing efforts should be intensified so as to deal with all aspects of the life of the child. At the same time, the general quality of services should be improved in order to raise the standard of efficiency of the child welfare programmes.

That voluntary agencies should work as pioneers in the field of child welfare dealing with educational and nutrition programmes not covered by normal social services, with experimental programmes for the improvement of existing services, and with programmes for the rehabilitation of children in need of special care. It should also be the function of voluntary agencies to act as mentors of the Government for speedy implementation and execution of the child welfare schemes and programmes promoting parental education.

That utmost consideration be given to the provision of suitable environment to the child to protect him from climatic and environmental hazards so as to promote his chances for survival, growth and development. Suitable environment may be said to incorporate the following :

(a) Availability of adequate shelter in sanitary surroundings.

(b) Protection from climate-especially protective clothings.

(c) Provision of safety measures so as to afford protection against hazards of environment.

That as the funds allotted for programmes of child welfare at present are entirely inadequate to meet the primary needs of survival and normal growth and development of the child, more funds should be raised, and allotments should be made after properly assessing the minimum needs of child welfare in each area.

That existing programmes of grants-in-aid for the benefit of children under six years of age should be given a special priority so that as many children as possible could be given help from the very beginning, and so that the cost of later welfare services may be reduced because of benefits derived from earlier assistance.

Social Policy

That a general social policy should now be laid down by the Central Government, and the following should be adopted as relevant articles dealing with problems and needs of children under six years of age :

(a) Having acecpted the Declaration of Rights of Children as defined by UNICEF, all programmes relating to family and child welfare amongst all sections of people must now be aimed at implementing, to the best of our capacity, the principles of charter.

(b) In view of the fundamental differences of approach by political ideologies and systems of Government, it is desirable that it should be the national policy to do everything to strenghten the family, and to promote its integration and comprehensive social health, so that the family may always remain the fittest institution to provide a proper environment to promote the health and of the welfare of the child.

(c) The true well-being of all families and children requires a careful and well organised programmes of family planning; and it should be the national policy to promote a coordinated and intensive programme of family planning alongwith child welfare.

(d) The nation must accept the equal importance of all the four stages of childhood-intra-uterine stage, infancy, toddler's, and pre-school stage—for the purposes of planning, organisation and development of child welfare. Local conditions and needs will determine priorities of child welfare activities within the general programme of social welfare.

(e) Immediate action must be taken to provide for the proper care of normal children, emphasis being laid on all programmes providing for the growth, training and development of the normal child. The State should also take full responsibility for the care of abandoned children; and it must recognise the special needs of handicapped, maladjusted and sub-normal children.

(f) The State must recognise the need for assisting private social welfare agencies to promote experimental and special programmes of child welfare, especially those dealing with the study of children and the organisation and administration of pilot and experimental projects; and when extensive programmes have to be developed for the welfare of all children in urban, rural and sylvan areas, the State must bear the greater burden and responsibility for the promotion of such extensive and standard child welfare services.

Stages Of Childhood—Definitions

That the following stages of childhood should be accepted with their implications in order to provide intensive care to children in the different stages of growth during the earliest period of life :

1. **Intra-uterine : From Conception to Birth** : Programmes for maternity and antenatal care; and parental education.

2. **Infancy : From Birth to One Year** : Programmes for preventing mortality and providing measures for promoting good health and growth of the child.

3. **Toddler Stage : From One year to Three Years** : To emphasise the need of nutrition, healthy recreation and total environmental care.

4. **Pre-School Stages : From Three Years to Six Years.** To empasise the need of education and training health, recreation and nutrition. (It must be noted that these are highly formative years when habits, character, and intelligence patterns are established.)

5. **Primary School Stage : From Six to Eleven Years** : To emphasise the need of primary education, health and recreation.

Child Care And Neglect

That the following should be accepted as the implied contents of a comprehensive concept of child care :

(a) Adequate nourishment for the child in terms of provision of the right type of food of good quality in adequate quality.

(b) Adequate shelter in sanitary surroundings.

(c) Protection from climate, especially protective clothing

(d) Love and effection in the family environment.

(e) Protection against diseases, especially providing for comprehensive, frequent and timely immunisation against infectious diseases.

(f) Safety measures against hazard of environment.

(g) Opportunities for growth, development and activity in an atmosphere of freedom, and in association with other children.

(h) Opportunities for indoor and outdoor play.

(i) Opportunities for training and development of the child within his home, community, and/or institutional environment.

(j) Protection from unfit guardians, exploitation for material gain, and cruelty inflicted through physical punishment and injuries to his emotional and mental life.

(k) Adequate provision for early and immediate treatment of physical, mental, emotional, and social handicaps and mal adjustments.

That NEGLECT be defined as isolation of the child, leaving it without love, shelter and protection ; and the following be accepted as implied contents of the concept of neglect :

(a) Failure on the part of the family to provide shelter, nourishment and protection.

(b) Absence of attention to basic needs of children like affection, protection, security, play and companionship.

(c) Wilful exposure of children to unfavourable climatic conditions and insanitary surroundings.

(d) Failure to attend in time to minor ailmentss, physical handicaps and chronic sub-health.

(e) Exposure of the child to serve physical punishments, emotional shocks or mental injury.

(f) Absence of protection for the child from all kinds of exploitation.

(g) Association of the child with an unfit guardian.

(h) Permitting the child to live without a name or nationality.

Programmes

That the following specific programmes be recognised as necessary activities for the purpose of promoting the welfare of children under six years of age :

(a) Family planning clinics and family counselling agencies.

(b) Clinics and community welfare programmes providing ante-natal and post-natal care ; and health visitors' service.

(c) Maternity hospitals, children's wards in hospitals maternity homes, community dispensaries and hospitals for children.

(d) Creches and day nurseries.

(e) Pre-schools.

(f) Institutions and homes for children including institutions for the care of handicapped, maladjusted and sub-normal children,

(g) Schools of social work, social work department in universities, institutions promoting programmes for the training of child welfare personnel, and research and investigations dealing with living conditions, problems and needs of all children under six years of age.

Family Planning

That a national network of family planning clinics should be initiated by powerful national and State organisations, and maximum use must be made of the press, cinema and radio to promote family planning in a national campaign.

That efforts should be made to promote "Spacing" as the chief objective of family planning, and parental education must promote a minimum spacing period of 30 months between the birth of the previous child and the conception of the next child. More extensive use of the contraceptives must be recommended to parents who have three or more children to prevent a further increase in the size of the family.

That the national association for the promotion of planned parenthood must receive maximum support from the State, and its plans and recommendations must be accepted, as far as possible, by all welfare organisation in the country.

Family And Mother's Welfare

That the family should primarily undertake the responsibility of adequate child care and that it should receive all possible and necessary help from the regional community or the neighbourhood to which it belongs by implementing programmes contained in the other recommendations of the report.

That in community development programmes, the social health of the family should receive as much attention as family economy. The community development programmes should take special measures to promote and strengthen the family's spiritual and ethical backgrounds which has constituted in the past to sound social health and family and national integration.

That a very careful study of women's participation in different aspects of national economy is required to ensure that the social health of the family is not affected when women undertake employment due to economic reasons.

The coordination and integration of programmes of health visitors, ante-natal, maternity and post-natal care, social education, housing management, community organisation and every type of domiciliary service is essential to spread the knowledge, and achieve the acceptance of family planning programmes in the shortest time possible.

Ante-Natal Care

That the required services that an ante-natal programme should provide must be able to achieve the following objectives.

1. To create desirable psychological conditions to the expectant mother, when she is primigravide, so that she is in a happy, hopeful and confident frame of mind, free of anxieties, sorrow and fears ;
2. To diagnose and treat any early complications ;
3. To increase the proportion of normal deliveries ;
4. To lower the maternal mortality and morbidity rates ;
5. To reduce the incidence of premature births, still-births and parental and neo-natal deaths ;
6. To improve the cleanliness, orderliness, and sanitary conditions of the house in which the expectant mother is living ; and
7. To give minimum parental education required by the mother, especially at the time of first delivery, in order to provide intelligent and affectionate care to the Child from the very beginning, after birth.

Post-Natal Care

That post-natal care must become an efficient instrument for ensuring the health and nutrition of both the mother and the infant during first 12 to 18 months after delivery. The mother should receive advice, assurance and instructions to protect the infant from neo-natal and other familiar infections.

That post-natal care must pay special attention to parental education with a view to increase "the mother's ability to cope with life", and due to inadequate personnel and facilities, this programme should become a primary element in all social education programmes in the country.

Health

That health services may be provided to children in the following ways :

(a) As a part of basic services necessary for community health, such as provision for adequate housing, safe water supply, improved sanitation, avoidance of over crowding and slum conditions, etc.

(a) As specialised services for mothers and childern, such as ante-natal maternity, post-natal and counselling services, creches, pre-schools, children's playgrounds, immunisation programmes against infectious diseases, etc.

(c) That health and nutrition requirements should be integrated with every programme of child care.

Recognising that adequate efforts are being made to increase the number of women doctors in the country, and also recognising that even male doctors are inadequate in rural areas, it is still imperative to increase the number of women doctors in the country in such a way that at least one woman doctors is employed in a rural area either in the primary health centre or in-charge of an important subsidiary centre.

That a special allowance may be given in order to attract medical personnel to work in rural areas. In addition, housing and educational facilities for the children of such personnel should also be provided.

Vital Statistics

That all vital statistics which are required for the purpose of social studies should be based upon organised, systematic and efficient registration in all parts of the country ; and measures should be taken to perfect this machinery before the commencement of the next census in 1971.

Reducing Infant Mortality

That every effort should be made in India, as early as possible, to see that it leaves the 'high' mortality bracket (with infant mortality above 100) by reducing infant mortality rate to the bracket where it is between 35 and 75 ; and this could be achieved by improved standards of housing and wages, maximum employment, improved standards of living ; and by increasing and improving existing services for the family, mother and child welfare in terms of family planning and parental education programmes, and ante-natal, maternity, post-natal care, etc.

Immunisation

That measures should be taken to protect the health of the child from contagious diseases, and the programme of timely and frequent immunisation should be extensively introduced to cover the entire population of children in the country.

That whilst immunisation programmes are carried out through the various hospitals, clinics, primary health centres and dispensaries ; this programme should be accelerated with the cooperation of the urban and rural community welfare centres ; and children should be given triple and single immunisation to ensure protection against T.B., Small Pox, Dyphtheria, Tetanus and Poliomyelitis. Moreover, inoculation against cholera and typhoid should be given to all the children before the age of nine-and-a-half months.

Nutrition

That attention must be given to the problem of infants who are not breast-fed. Humanised milk should be produced and distributed in cities where parents are able to afford their cost, Other measures are needed keep the supply of substitute powder milk and baby foods commercially produced to meet existing demands, especially in urban areas.

That strong and effective measures should be taken to see that babies and children have the highest priority to obtain their needs from the local milk supply ; and even rationing and control should be introduced whereever necessary, to prevent the use of whole milk in hotels and for commercial manufacture of sweets, pastries, icecream and such articles.

That every effort should be made to discover and encourage the production of cheap foods. This work should be entrusted to State agencies, so that such food can be supplied as subsidised foods and the cost of nourishment of children may be kept as low as possible.

Handicapped Children

That for the welfare and treatment of all handicapped children, high priority should be given to preventive programmes and the detection of handicaps from as early an age as possible.

That in each State, the Ministry of Welfare should create Children's Villages, for the care of abandoned children, and fondlings, and the village should be fed by sub-centres in urban and rural areas. These villages must consist of homes which will function as rehabilitation centres, which will include a reception services, a councelling service and a case work sarvice for parents and children, and it will also provide shelter, training, education, rehabilitation, etc., to the fondlings till he reaches the age of 18.

That in order to reduce the pressuse of orphanages and other institutions and also for assisting the child to avoid institutional care, foster home services should be organised by responsible organisations of child welfare in both urban and rural areas, and in cooperation with the authorities created for the enforcement of the Children's Act.

That adaquate measures should be taken all over India to prevent blindness and for correction of defective vision ; and for this purpose special measures should be taken for the detection of defective sights of children, in pre-schools, clinics, domiciliary programmes, community centres and all other agencies interested in the welfare of children. The investigation must specifically refer to blindness, and also V.D., Small Pox, Trachoma caused by infection and as a result of Vitamin 'A' deficiency.

Day Nurseries And Creches

That for the benefit of working mothers and in environments which are evidently harmful for the health and growth of toddlers between one and three years of age, creches, day nurseries or 'palnaghars' should be created to satisfy health and environmental needs and nutritive requirements of such children.

Pre-Schools

Since a large number of pre-schools are required in our country, it is desirable that the pinciples of simplicity of training and maximum economy in the management of pre-school organisation should be adopted, especially in rural and tribal areas, to solve the problem of workers and funds. The pre-school should provide maximum variety of activities to occupy the time and the interest of children.

That leadership of pre-schools must come from special training institutions offering two or three year's graduate or post-graduate course in universities, teachers training colleges, and schools of social work, especially those offering specialisation in child welfare.

Considering the need for improved programmes for the training of all kinds of child welfare workers, it is recommended that a committee be set up to revise the existing programmes, curricula, methods of training, etc., in the various Ministries and Departments of the State, as well as training programmes organised by the universities, schools of social work, and private child welfare and educational agencies.

That the following varieties of articles are needed for the use of children under six years of age; pre-school educational materials and apparatus; playground equipment; educational toys; general varieties of toys to suit children at different ages and levels of growth and development; picture books, story books and children's literature; books printed on cloth.

Section 3 : Recommendations : Central Government

Vital Statistics

The recommendations of the W.H.O. regarding tabulation of live births and foetal deaths be endorsed; and that tabulation of live births and foetal deaths be registered in the four groups according to the length of gestation measured from the beginning of the last menstruations.

That a Committee should be appointed to examine the existing methods of registration in the States and suggest possible improvements that can achieve the purposes of registration.

That the classification of infant mortality rates in the Census Report may be done on the basis of standard of living, rather than on the basis of religion and community as at present. The classification of infant mortality on the standard of living basis may be as follows:

(1) Agricultural and forest labourers, artisans and small cultivators;

(2) Shopkeepers, money lenders, village officials and small landlords;

(3) Big landlords and rural aristocracy;

(4) Industrial workers and other wage earners;

(5) Shopkeepers, clerks and lower middle class;

(6) Professionals and other educated persons and middle class ;

(7) Owners of property and wealth, industrialists, financiers, etc.

That the disparity of prices at which importers of milk (either in powder form or manufacturing them as children's foods) supply the market and the market price of the same products should be examined, together with the policy regarding the import of foreign milk in powder form, so that every effort is made to increase the supply of powdered milk and children's food to meet the full demand of the market for baby foods. This should also be achieved through indigenous manufacture of babyfoods.

That the assistance given by UNICEF to increase the milk supply for babies and children should be properly utilised; and further assistance must be given by the Centre to State Governments so that such schemes may be able to serve other cities with a population of more than three lakhs in the first instance.

That the import policy regarding babies and children's food should be carefully examined so that political and economic considerations do not come in the way of the availability of maximum quantities of milk powder at the lowest price till such time as when the entire needs could be met by internal production and that when whole milk supply is inadequate in the country, the import of foreign ingredients for infant's food should be treated as of equal importance with the need of food-grains for the use of the adult population.

That special efforts should be made to establish one or more plants for the production of cheap and nutritive foods for infants and children.

Legislation

That efforts should be made to enact legislation for enabling private trusts and endowments to divert their funds from less fundamental purposes in order to provide for the care of children whenever finances are available for the purpose of charity. This should especially be done by taking into consideration the Cypre Act or Law.

That a committee should be appointed to prepare a Model National Midwifery Act to be followed by legislation on the subject in every State.

Teaching of Paediatrics

That paediatrics must become a compulsory subject and part of the curriculam in all programmes of medical education; and paediatricts should be recognised as specialists of great importance, and they should be gradually made available to every primary health centre by the end of the fourth plan period.

Pre-Schools

At the present stage of pre-school development, it is suggested that important experimental projects should be carried out in different types of regions and communities and progress should be made in child study and research dealing with problems of growth, heredity, environment and child development as a whole

Special type of child study and experimental pre-schools should be attached to universities, schools of social work and child study institutions.

Children's Literature

That the Ministry of Education should maintain a unit consisting of a permanent staff of artists, writers, photographers cinetechnicians, etc., for the writing of children's books, including story books, nursery rhymes and poetry, etc., and their services should be available to assist the development of children's literature in the various States.

That for the printing of children's books, including picture books, books printed on cloths, etc., a national organisation is required with printing establishment equipped for photography, art work, and offset printing. A part of the produced materials without language inscription may be used by different States to imprint the coloured printed materials with appropriate language description in the various regional languages.

Whilst appreciating the work done by the Children's Book Trust, the committee recommends the extension of the work of the Trust in order to enable it to prove of benefit to all the linguistic regions of the country.

Section 4 : Recommendations : State Governments

United Nations Charter For Children

That the Declaration of the Rights of the Child adopted by UNICEF on November 20, 1959, should be extensively circularised amongst Governments and Departments at all levels; and every effort should be made by State Governments and private agencies to achieve the purposes of the Declaration.

Administration For Child Welfare

That existing programmes of child welfare are being carried out by a large number of departments of the various State Governments, it is recommended that a Division of Child Welfare be created in an appropriate Ministry, in order to provide specialised direction and guidance to all child welfare programmes of the States.

That a permanent and regularly functioning Co-ordination Committee should be set up in each State consisting of representatives of each of the departments dealing with the programmes of child welfare in order to serve common objectives, maintain common standards, avoid over lapping and achieve cooperation between all departments to promote maximum economy and efficiency.

That the Co-ordination Committee on Child Welfare in each State should created an appropriate machinary to promote intensive Co-operation and close coordination of all State and private effort for child welfare,

That the States where the post of a Lady District Welfare Officer has not been created to serve the rural areas, such a post be created with a view to appoint a qualified and trained child welfare officer to organise, guide and supervise all programmes of woman and child welfare in the district.

Legislation

That severe and corrective action is needed to deal with persons who are quality of criminal neglect of any child under their protection, quardianship, or custody. It is necessary and desirable to promote legislation against cruelty and neglect of children; and the law should be effectively enforced and implemented to prevent the sufferings and hardships of any child. It is recommended that a committee be appointed to review the existing legislation and suggest modifications whenever necessary.

Housing

That to strengthen the family socially, the problem of housing should be dealt with not only in terms of minimum housing standards, but also in terms of adequate, proper and systematic housing management where properties, good neighbourliness, health and human relation are looked after.

Vital Statistics

The immediate measures must be taken to see that registration regarding births and deaths of children and cause of infant mortality are properly carried out so that the correct situation could be understood. As far as possible, all States should adopt a uniform method of registration of data pertaining to vital statistics and other information for demographic purposes.

That there should be a permanent machinery in every State for the maintenance of all vital statistics, and annual reports should be available to cover all areas of the country without exception. If possible there should be a Census Bureau in every State.

Family Planning

Whilst facilities for sterilisation and performance of vasectomy should be increased, including the use of mobile service, the training of the entire staff associated with the programme is necessary to increase its efficiency and efficacy. A follow-up service for a brief period is necessary to deal with such cases.

Health And Nutrition

Health services should be started for children of pre-school age so that periodical health check up of children of this age group may be carried out.

That at least one children's hospital should be created in every State.

Efforts should be made to provide adequate milk to all the children, under nourished children being given a priority.

That programmes for the nourishment of children providing the right type of food of good quality and adequate quantity should be introduced in all pre-schools.

That cooperative dairy farming should be developed in rural areas; and milk distribution to mothers and children should be done through the panchayats.

That in order to prevent profiteering, welfare centres and cooperatives must become direct distributions of all commercial goods, including milk products produced and imported into the country.

That every effort should be made to discover and encourage the production of cheep foods. This work should be entrusted to State agencies, so that such foods can be supplied as subsidised foods and thus the cost of nourishment of children may be kept as low as possible.

Large scale production of protein such foods which have already been perfected should be encouraged. That further research should be conducted to discover more articles containing high nutritive value in terms of protein to supplement and subsitute the milk supply.

Health Visitors

That a health visitors service is essential in all the States, and the domiciliary service along with properly organised ante-natal and post-natal clinics should function even when public health nurses are available to assist the community under control of the Ministry of Health.

Maternity Services

That the existing training programmes for dais need to be increased so that they may function as provisional health visitors and as parent educators and instructors in family planning wherever possible, and when special staff is not available for these programmes.

That there should be one trained dai for every 20 villages, and for every 10,000 of rural population by the end of the Third Plan period to be increased to one trained dai for every five villages and 3,000 of rural population by the end of the fourth plan period.

That the prevailing system of attention to pregnant mothers in the community at the time of delivery should always be taken into consideration, and till such time as a national midwifery service is properly constituted and organised, the policy of compulsory registration of all the dais must be adopted, accompanied by a period of minimum training for such dais to be organised in every district of the country.

Post-Natal Care

The post-natal and well-baby clinics should be organised within primary health centre and M. C. H. centres to supervise the cases upto the age of atleast one year, and upto three years wherever possible.

Pre-Schools

Government should give substantial assistance to voluntary institutions running pre-primary schools.

That different categories of aid should be given mainly to assist the pre-school with equipment, payment of salary of teachers, and to supplement, the cost of pre-school feeding programmes, etc. A grant-in-aid should be paid by the Central Government to pilot and experimental projects; and State Governments should promote pilot projects in each district; and municipalities should develop pre-schools mainly for the benefit of slum areas and to cater to children who do not have the advantage of being brought up in proper physical and human environments.

That all under privileged children should be given an opportunity for pre-school education; but it is not desirable to create separate pre-schools for them

That wherever possible, States should enact a Pre-School Act and all pre-schools should be registered under the Society Registration Act of 1860. All pre-schools should conform to minimum standards which the relevant municipality or the State may lay down.

That the age of admission to the pre-schools should be about three-and-a-half years in all general types of pre-schools; and children who are two-and-a-half years old may be admitted in pre-schools where there are sufficient number of assistant teachers, and the teacher is not called upon to look after more than 15 children under three-and-a- half years of age.

That all pre-schools should be universally co-educational and all the children may were a common type of dress.

That ordinarily a child may spend a minimum of two years and a maximum of four years in a pre-school.

That a normal unit of a pre-school should not have more than 40 children. In case there are more than 20 children in a unit, the unit should have one additional assistant teacher.

Recommended Scales

Graduate teachers with special ...Rs. 200+D.A. to

two year's training	Rs. 350
Graduate with short-term training	...Rs. 120+D.A. to Rs. 250
Intermediate Arts with special two year's training	...Rs. 150+D.A. to Rs. 300
Matriculates with special training	...Rs. 90+D A. to Rs. 180
Assistant teachers—Matriculates with training	...Rs. 90+D.A. to Rs. 150
Assistant teachers—Non matriculates (V.F.) with training	...Rs. 70+D.A. to Rs 150
Attendants, sahayikas, cooks and servants	...Rs. 40+D.A. or prevailing scales in the area.

Care Of The Handicapped Child

That the following classes of handicapped children should be given special treatment in terms of institutional care and other programmes in order to provide opportunities for rehabilitation and normal growth and development.

1. Orphans ;
2. Fondlings ;
3. Blind and partially visioned, deaf and dumb ;
4. Children affected by chronic diseases like T.B. and V.D., etc.

That a few large hospitals and rehabilitation centres should be created in the various States to deal with the cases requiring longterm care and intensive treatment for rehabilitation.

The Committee is of the opinion that the cost of maintenance of majority of children under six years of age in boarding institutions vary between Rs. 40 to Rs. 50 per month per head excluding the cost of treatment ; and adequate grants-in-aid be provided to enable such children to receive opportunites to grow up as normal children.

That adequate services are not provided at present for children whose one parent is alive ; and, therefore, it is necessary to create Short Stay Home where children could be looked after till their parents are able to undertake full responsibility for the care of children.

That the traditional procedures connected with adoption of children are at present inadequate ; and effective measures are necessary to apply amended Adoption Act to all those who desire to adopt children ; and these should be a provision for screening, recommendation and acceptance for a short-term observation in order to protect the true interests of the adopted child.

That in each State, the Ministry of Welfare should create "Children's Villages" for the care of fondlings and the village should be fed by sub-centres in rural and urban areas. These villages must consist of homes which will function as rehabilitation centres, which will serve as a case work service for the parents and the child, and it will provide shelter, training, education, rehabilitation, etc., to the fondlings till they reach the age of 18 years.

That a nation-wide census of handicapped children should be carried out and this work should be the responsibility of gram panchayats and district authorities in rural areas, whilst in urban areas the census must be carried out by municipalities with the help of social welfare organisations and universities.

That in order to detect handicapped conditions, the norms showing development of the child at various stages should be widely published and made available to hospitals, clinics, institutions and welfare agencies.

That States should divert some funds from the finances earmarked for pre school education to provide special pre-schools for handicapped children.

That for the detection of auditory defects, audiometric units should be created in hospitals, and in all institutions deaf and mutes etc.

Experimental day nurseries for the benefit of working and illiterate mothers should be organised in all rural areas where the integrated programme of child welfare will be introduced in the Third Plan period.

That day nurseries should be organised in orphanages and fondling Homes where infant and small children are admitted, and trained nurses should be employed in such institutions, prisons, where females are kept, in slum areas and in areas where ex-criminal groups reside.

That training programmes should be organised, as far as possible, along with training programmes of balsevikas, health visitors and pre-school teachers for the benefit of special balsevikas to serve in creches and day nurseries. The day nurseries training curriculum should also become a part of the training of public health nurses. Short-term training programmes should also be organised by aided programmes in schools of social work.

Training

That training programmes may be developed in important cities, as well as in all the States, to give a comprehensive in-service training in problems, needs and programmes of child welfare to presonnel who are employed to serve in different fields.

Section 5 : Municipalities And Zila Parishads

That municipalities and zila parishads should give high priority to welfare programmes for the mother and child by promoting funds for the organisation and efficient management of domiciliary services and M.C.H. centres providing for ante-natal and post-natal care, family planning, pre-schools, and programmes for the feeding of under nourished children.

That the development of services for the mother and the child should be based upon local needs of the particular place and the particular time.

That as the funds allotted for programmes of child welfare at present are entirely inadequate to meet the primary needs of survival and normal growth and development of the child, more funds should be raised, and allotments should be made after properly assessing the minimum needs of child welfare in each area.

That child welfare at the community level in urban and rural areas should now be carried out by a proper personnel selected and trained for specific functions; and their numbers should be increased according to the increasing resources which are now to be provided for the execution of all integrated progrommes, including family planning, health visiting, ante-natal and post-natal care, family contact and counselling and parental education, etc.

That special measures should be taken in urban areas to reduce infant mortality especially in slum areas, and intensive programmes of child welfare and ante-natal and post-natal care should be extensively introduced in such areas as early as possible.

Children's food should be supplemented through milk centres for the poor in as many urban areas as possible.

That the assistance given by the UNICEF to increase the milk supply for babies and children should be propeny utilised; and further assistance must be given by the Centre to State Governments so that such schemes may be able to serve other cities with a population of more than three lakhs in the first instance.

That in order to provide improved care to new born children, pressure on maternity services in urban areas should be reduced; and this can be done by strengthening and increasing domiciliary services so that all the cases for normal delivery may be attended to outside the institutions.

That the existing number of maternity beds in city hospitals should provide over and above their own requirements for accommodating five per cent to 10 per cent of the total births outside properly equipped maternity homes and domiciliary service outside such hospitals.

That, however, there is any kind of housing authority such as housing boards, housing co-operative societies, development boards, etc., in existance, efforts should be made to create ante-natal and post-natal clinics in their area; and grant-in-aid should be given to them by municipalities and State Governments.

That in localities where higher income groups are living, the private practitioners should open family planning and ante-natal clinics to serve the locality.

That in slum areas and in the localities where lower income groups live, one health visitor or midwife (or public health nurse) should be provided at the rate of one to 400 families to provided medical assistance and guidance to them.

That specialised services should be provided at maternity and paediatric hospitals for mothers and children who are referred to them by maternity or child welfare centres, namely regional clinics for investigation and treatment of serious cases such as V.D., E.N.T., eye defects, etc.

That ante-natal clinics should carefully supervise the diet of pregnant women, and if required, should supplement them by free meal scheme.

That ante-natal and post-natal programmes should be assisted by other welfare workers like family planning counsellors, family counsellors, social education workers, community organisers, etc.

That as deaf children are invariably mute also, and deafness is not normally detected till the child is 12 to 18 months old, post-natal clinics should be mainly responsible for the detection of all the sensory defects of the child.

Section 6 : Community Development

That in a community development programme the social health of the family should receive as much attention as family economy especially through programmes of homes economics, social education and family counselling, wherever possible. The community development programmes should take special measures to promote and strengthen the family's spiritual and ethical backgrounds which had contributed in the Past to sound social health and family and national integration.

That all panchayats must be associated and made responsible for not only the registration of data, but the supervision of the registration machinery at the lowest level.

Child Health

That coverage of primary health centres in rural areas, and Municipal MCW Centres in urban areas should be reduced to a number which could be effectively handled by the staff. The existing staff should not cater to a population of more than 25,000 persons.

That special nutrition rehabilitation centres should be started in community areas to provide simple and in expensive meals to children to help them to recover from deficiency caused by diseases like rickets, beri-beri, etc.

That courses in nutrition may be included in school curricula; and besides, education about nutritional needs of children may be imparted to mothers through various centres and domiciliary programmes. Demonstrations should be given dealing with methods of cooking articles and dtshes so that the nutrition value of food may not be lost.

That there should be one trained dai for every 20 villages; and for every 10,000 of rural population by the end of the Third Plan period, to be increased to one trained dai for every five villages and 1,000 of rural population by the end of the Fourth Plan period.

That a nationwide census of handicapped children should be the responsibility of gram panchayats and district authorities in rural areas, whilst in urban areas the census must be carried out by municipalities with the help of social welfare organisations and universities.

Section 7 : Pre-Schools

The pre-school education must be single-mindedly devoted to the true welfare, growth and development of the human child as a vital organism, and a unit of the human species.

That the concepts of pre-school philosophy and principles are appropriate to Indian conditions and need that children must be healthy and active within their family and community environments, and grow up and develop during childhood to receive education and become worthy citizens of the nation.

That the system of training must correspond to the fundamental needs of the child's comprehensive growth and development irrespective of any social, economic, political or philosophical considerations.

That the pre-school programme should be based upon five factors which have been universally accepted and which are stated below :

(a) Heredity and environment of the child must receive very great attention because the growth and development of the child is largely dependent on these two factors.

(b) That child at all times must live in an atmosphere which is full of joy, contributing to its total happiness.

(c) The child must grow up and develop in conditions of freedom.

(d) The child needs activity in order to spend its energy and to expand its total capacity and abilities, thus accumulating experience which contribute to its total growth and development.

(e) The child needs protection and assistance or parents and other competent persons who are aware of the special need of children during the pre-school age.

In order to increase the number of pre-schools in the whole of India including urban, rural and sylvan areas, it is necessary to organisationally promote self-sufficient pre-schools which could by organised, if possible, without assistance of the State to be managed by regional communities in urban neighbourhoods and large villages. A national pre-school association be created for this purpose.

Pre-schools shall be started in urban areas, where people can pay the cost of education of the children.

Responsibility for starting pre-schools should be left to voluntary organisations with adequate assistance from the Government.

That pre-schools should be of the following types :

(a) A half-day organisation to be developed as "The Minimum Standard pre-school." A pre-school of minimum standard should provide a playground, look after the health and cleanliness of children, inculcate in them good habits and correct behaviours, and provide such opportunities for training like nature study, and other subjects which can be easily dealt with by reasonably trained teachers and balsevikas.

(b) Standard pre-schools following some kind of systems like the montessori, the pre-basic, azzisi and any other system suitable to rural areas; and any type of pre-school using programmes, methods and techniques suitable for different types of environments in urban areas,

(The true meaning of pre-basic should imply the acceptance of the principle of Activity" initiated and developed by a number of psychologists and educationists of Vienna. The types of activities must be suitable to the needs of the child and the community.)

(c) A pre-school project attached to the village primary school, to be located as far as possible in a separate structure so that classes of the pre-school and primary school are not held together.

(d) Infant classes in primary schools and high schools, with training and programme modified to conform to principles and programmes of the pre-school.

(e) Open-air pre-schools with playgrounds may be created where facilities and resources are inadequate, or, where there are inadequate numbers of children to promote a pre-school as a unit.

(f) (i) Pre-schools attached to institutions where unattached women with children are provided with boarding and lodging facilities.

(ii) Special pre-schools in urban areas for sub-normal, feeble-minded and problem children with behaviour disorders.

(iii) Special types of pre-schools to help the care, training and rehabilitation of handicapped children.

(iv) Pre-schools attached to prisons for women with their children.

(v) Pre-schools with a high standard of service for areas where communities of ex-criminal group live.

(vi) Pre-schools promoted as a special treatment for areas where juvenile delinquency is extensively present.

(g) Pre-schools organised in large housing schemes where a number of rooms and tenements are available for their use, where there is no space for playgrounds, terraces may be suitably adjusted for the purpose in order to provide safety for the children.

That all under privileged children should be given an opportunity for pre-school education; but it is not desirable to create separate pre-schools for them.

That a common nomenclature for all pre-schools, they should not be, as far as possible, associated with names of systems and types of equipment used in each pre-school.

It is not desirable for pre-schools to have a very large, number of children and as far as possible, a pre-school not have more than four units.

That during the whole period of stay of a child in a pre-school, it may go through three or four stages of training. Each stage of the child's training in a pre-school must conform to his physical conditions and nature of growth and development.

That pre-school should, as far as possible, be located near place where a large number of families reside; and as far as possible, they may belong to regional communities, and may be entrusted to their care for management and supervision.

That where children have to walk to the pre-school, they should not be expected to go more than one mile from their place of residence each day.

Transport facilities may be provided by institutions which are self-sufficient in their resources.

That the prence of natural surroundings is necessary for the physical growth and emotional development of Children; and when pre-schools are not open-air schools, gardens and playgrounds should be attached to them.

Pre-schools in rural areas should be located in villaages with minimum population of about 500 persons. Preference should be given to villages which agree to give a site for the structure and playgrounds and bear part cost of structure, or at least provide labour for construction.

In tribal areas, where people live in hamlets which are located at considerable distances with small populaton, the pre-schools should be located in villages where hiamlets are close together, and where it will be possible for the children to walk small distances to attend the pre-school.

That heavy capital expenditure should not be incurred for the construction of pre-schools. Even open air schools, low cost structures or gardens or open spac's be considered adequate for the use of children.

That whenever possible, simple structures may be constructed, and they could be 'kutcha' structures in rural areas, using local materials for their construction. The plan of the pre-school should allow sufficient space for kitchen and a washing place, dining and siesta.

That a pre-school must have a playground, at least two rooms, a top, bath room, lavatory and urinals.

That minicipalities, landlords, owners of public places like temples, churches and all citizen must do everything in their power to see that space and shelter are not denied to children for play and pre-schools.

That playgrounds should be provided by all housing Boards, or other types of housing authorities so that there is accommodation for an open-air pre-school with 80 to 100 children in a community of about 500 families,

That for pre-schools with more available space, about 100 sq. feet of ground and garden per child are needed for open air activities. For indoor activities there should be an assembly hall, which can also be used for siesta purposes, as well as space for group activities and indoor meetings. A store room and a kitchen, an office room, a staff room, and an isolation room could always be useful. There should be a locker room for children, if possible adequate washing and bathing accommodation, and taps and toilet for all children, should be provided. At least one lavatory is needed for every 12 to 15 children.

That routine programmes of activities of the pre-school must always be adopted to suit the place, the climate, the ability of techers and the wish of childern, and pre-schools are invariably good weather" institutions, and children should not be called to participate in activities of pre-school during inclement weather when there are heavy rains or cold. Pre-schools should function during seasons and months suitable for different types of pre-school activities.

That pre-school start their day in morning assembly so that all children may gather, meet each other, and enjoy companionship. Daily programmes should be planned in advance by the pre-school teachers; and varieties of subjects and activities should be introduced every day like play activities, learning activities, hand work activities, practicals school service, etc. Children must enjoy open air and outdoor life as much as they can. The time allotted to different types of activities should vary according to the capacities of children to give attention and their interest in activites or subjects which are handled by the teacher.

That children must participate in all important activities of the whole community, and this must be an important part of all pre-school activities.

That at least a midday meal or snack should be served at pre-school, and three meals should be given, if the family and the community are willing to contribute towards the expenses of a light morning breakfast with milk, lunch, and light evening snack with fruits.

That a careful study must be made of the sleeping habits of children at home; and there must be a daily siesta of 90 to 120 minutes after the midday meal, when the pre-school works only for half-a-day, and when parents insist that children should return home for their afternoon lunch than parental education must make them realise that the child must have sleep and rest at home during the afternoon.

That to meet all pre-school expenses, local contributions should be obtained from the community in cash, kind, labour or service towards programme of construction, nutrition, instruction, excursions and camps.

There should be a team of the following scientists to assist pre-school workers, training programme and consellors of pre-schools. Psychologists, paediatricians, nutrition experts, educationists, sociologists, biologist, and other scientists dealing with the methodology of pre-school training. Their services may be requisitioned from regional universities.

That balsevikas should be young women, preferably under 25 years of age at the time of employment, as small child normally responds affectionately to young persons or very old persons. The employment of young men (balmitras) should not be ruled out for pre-school work, because they are useful as instructors for hand work, playground activities and pre-school social service.

That pre-school with two or three units and not exceeding four units should have a Mukhya Shikshika, or Headmisterss or Principal.

A large number cf pre-schools and institutions with a high standard of child care and training programmes will require a Director for the pre-school, while in rural areas persons will be required to direct, organise, and supervise a large numbers of pre-schools in each district. A Woman District Officer should be entrusted with this work.

The term like "Ayah" or "Servants" are in appropriate for pre-schools, but assistants and 'helpers' or 'Sahayika' are required for the maintenance of cleanliness, helping children to bathe and wash themselves, for the preparation of service of meals, cleaning of utensils, and helping to look after unmanageable children.

Pre-school attended by children with behaviour problems require a special person on the staff trained in psychology.

Recommended Scales

Graduate teacher with special two years training	...Rs. 200 plus D.A. to Rs. 350
Graduates with short term training	...Rs. 120 plus D.A. to Rs. 250
Intermediate Arts with special two years training	...Rs. 150 plus D.A. to Rs. 300
Matriculates with special training	...Rs. 90 plus D.A. to Rs. 180
Assistant teachers Matriculates with training	...Rs 90 plus D.A. to Rs. 150
Assistant teachers-non matriculates (V.F.) with training	...Rs. 70 plus D.A. to Rs. 150
Attendants, sahayika, cooks and servants.	...Rs. 40 plus D.A. or prevailing scales in the area.

Section 8 : Recommendations : Miscellaneous

That courses in nutrition may be included in school curricula, and besides, education about nutritional needs of children may be imparted to mothers through various centres and domiciliary programmes Demonstrations should be given on methods of cooking artic'es and dishes so that the nutritive content and value of food may not be lost.

That specialised services should be provided at maternity and paediatric hospitals for mothers and children who are referred to them by maternity or child welfare centres, namely regional clinics for investigation and treatment of serious cases, such as V.D., E.N.T., eye defects, etc.

The ante-natal clinics should carefully superwise the diet of pregnant women, and if required, should supplement them by free meal scheme.

Family Planning

Family Planning must become a regular habit amongst married adults in rural and urban communities, and extensive co-operative efforts of all social welfare organisation and medical and educational services must achieve this object through family contact programmes and parental education.

Ante-Natal Care

That the required services that an ante-natal programme should provide must be able to achieve the following objectives :

(a) To create reasonably desirable psychological conditions to the expectant mother when she is primigravide, so that she is in a happy, hopeful and confidant frame of mind, free of anxieties, sorrows and fears.

(b) To diagnose and treat any early complications.

(c) To increase the proportion of normal deliveries.

(d) To reduce the incidence of premature births, still births and parental and neo-natal deaths.

(e) To improve the cleanliness, orderliness, and sanitary conditions of the house in which expectant mother is living,

(f) To give minimum parental education required by the mother, especially at the time of first delivery, in order to provide intelligent and affectionate care to the child from the very beginning, after birth.

That whatever there is any kind of housing authority such as housing boards, housing co-operative societies, development boards, etc., in existence, efforts should be made to create ante-natal and post-natal clinics in their area ; and grant-in-aid should be given to them by municipalities and State Governments.

That the use of the Rhythm Method is useful to create the knowlege and consciousness of family planning, and to overcome the mental hesitation and antagonism to concepts of planned parent hood.

In recommending and adopting the use of any kind of contraceptive, the psychological reactions of the users and the aesthetics of sexual relations must be kept in mind, together with a consideration for the general moral and social health of the family, youth and society as a whole.

That parents, school teachers and Government Departments should be given sufficient guidance in adopting the right approach to the welfare of handicapped children.

That for the purpose of early detection of handicaps and effective cure and rehabilitation of cases, the following measures are suggested.

(a) A programme of parental education.

(b) Pre-school teachers, gramsevikas and balsevikas should have some elementary training to be able to detect early defects which can be referred to school, health and medical services.

(c) The staff of primary health centres and even indigenous dais could be trained to detect defects at an early stage.

(d) Mobile health units in rural areas, and all child welfare agencies in urban areas can help the detection of handicapped.

That parental education should be provided as an essential part of all day nursery programmes.

That educational toys and materials should; as far as possible, be manufactured locally.

That toys made of rubber, metal and plastics may be suitably guided by educational and child welfare agencies regarding design, construction, costs, etc.

KRISHNA-GODAVARI COMMISSION, 1961—REPORT

Delhi, Ministry of Irrigation & Power, 1963. 18 Vols.

Chairman : Shri N. D. Gulhati
Member : Shri D. D. Jaini
Secretary : Shri R. C. Hoon

APPOINTMENT

The Krishna-Godavari Commission was constituted under the Ministry of Irrigation & Power in 1961.

TERMS OF REFERENCE

(1) To report on the availability of supplies in the Krishna on the basis of annual flow at Vijayawada and other points taking into account upstream utilisation and allowing for regeneration :

(i) for 86 per cent dependability as assumed in 1951;
(ii) for 75 per cent dependability; and
(iii) for such other criterion of dependability as may be considered appropriate.

(2) To report on the requirements of the projects on the Krishna :

(i) in operations in 1951;
(ii) as approved by the Government of India for executions;
(iii) included in the Plans but not yet approved by the Government of India;
(iv) further proposed by the States; and
(v) such minor schemes as may have been sanctioned up to March, 1961.

(3) To report on the availability of supplies in the Godavari on the basis of annual flows at Dowlaishwaram and other points taking into account upstream utilisation and allowing for regeneration :

(i) for 86 per cent dependability as assumed in 1951;
(ii) for 75 per cent dependability; and
(iii) for such other criterion of dependability as may be considered appropriate.

(4) To report on the requirements of the projects on the Godavari :

(i) in operation in 1951;
(ii) as approved by the Government of India for execution;
(iii) included in the Plans but not yet approved by the Government of India;
(iv) further proposed by the States; and
(v) Such minor schemes as may have been sanctioned upto March 1961.

(5) To report on the feasibility of diverting any surplus supplies in the Godavari to the Krishna indicating the grantity to be diverted and the order of the cost involved.

RECOMMENDATIONS

General

The Commission suggests that the possibilities be

examined of collecting general statistics, particularly data of land utilisation, by river basins and sub-basins.

Land And Water Utilisation

It is necessary to review the number and distribution of rain-gauge stations in the two basins and to establish new stations to fill in such gaps as exist. It is also important that the daily rainfall data for all these stations should be published on a monthly basis by sub-basins. Machinery should be established for a regular study and analysis of these data.

Evaporation

It is necessary to establish an extensive network of evaporation measuring stations, throughout the two basins, particularly at the sites of existing and proposed reservoirs.

Systematic observation of evapo-transpiration under various crops needs to be carried out in selected stations throughout the two basins.

River Flow

The Commission strongly recommends, as a matter of first urgency, the establishment on a permanent basis and on scientific lines, of daily discharge observations at 38 sites of the Krishna River System and 38 sites on the Godavari River System. The river flow data to be obtained at these sites are essential for the preparation of individual projects, for the preparation of an integrated basin-wide plan, for the subsequent operation of such a plan and the regulation, to best advantage, of the available river waters in any year.

As a number of dames are being constructed in these river basins, it is necessary that, besides taking discharge observations, systematic data should also be collected with regard to the sediment carried by river waters. These data would be of considerable use in the design of the dams and in estimating the probable life of reservoirs.

The Commission regards the collection of river discharge and sediment data as a fundamental work of national stock taking and recommends that, like meteorological data and general surveys, the Central Government should assume the responsibility for this important work and set up a special organisation of this purpose under the Ministry of Irrigation and Power.

It is necessary to formulate detailed rules for each project laying down the manner in which river flow will be withdrawn, or abstracted for storage, during any part of the years under varying conditions of river supply. The operation of all projects in different States will have to be carried on in a coordinated manner.

Arrangements should be made by each State Government:

(a) To make accurate measurements of the daily withdrawals by all major irrigation canals and power channels and an estimate, from gauze discharge curves of the withdrawals by other canals and power channels; such gauze discharge curves to be regularly checked and kept up-to-date;

(b) To measure river flow and prepare water accounts at the sites of all storage projects and diversion weirs in operation; and

(c) As soon as a new project is conceived, to set up as a first priority, regular discharge and sediment observations at that site.

Ground Waters

It is important that regular observations should be made by all State Governments of the position of the ground waters and their fluctuations during the year. The methods to be adopted would vary in different parts according to local conditions. This information is necessary to maintain a close watch on the behaviour of ground waters, particularly in view of the large scale new developments undertaken and contemplated, and for the due exploitation of ground waters separately or in conjunction with canals.

The Commission recommends that important data for individual tanks should be collected and an up-to-date record maintained. The area irrigated annually by each tank should be measured and recorded, together with an estimate of the quantity of water applied to irrigation.

A survey of each tank should be carried out periodically, say, every five years, to watch the loss in capacity, if any.

The Commission recommends that discharges of drains should be observed regularly and the data compiled.

Working Statistics of Canals And Distributaries

The Commission is of the view that complete working statistics of canals and distributaries should be compiled annually and printed in a suitable form so as to be available as a permanent record for future reference.

The Commission recommends strongly that an immediate review be made of the developments undertaken since 1951, in each State, in order to as certain how the construction of the engineering works can be expedited to attain the optimum rate of development on each work. Such additional funds (including foreign exchange) and such personnel, as may be required should be allocated to these projects in preference to any new project. New projects should be sanctioned only if men, material and money are available surplus to the requirements of the projects already undertaken.

It is necessary that the crop pattern on these projects should be reviewed and the irrigation facilities provided spread over a larger area and to a larger number of cultivators.

The Commission recommends that the effect of each project undertaken since 1951 on the supplies available for projects downstream of it should be examined, the relative priorities on river flow for each project determined and, where necessary and to the extent now possible, the design of each project should be revised to comply with the requirements of integrated operation.

New Projects And Adequacy Of River Supplies Therefor

Immediate steps be taken to prepare an integrated plan incorporating the power and irrigation developments proposed by different States in the lower Godavari area and the Polavaram-Vijayawada Link and the Godavari-Pulichintala Link. It should be possible on the basis of the information contained in this report, field reconnaissance and some preliminary surveys to be carried out to prepare a preliminary project report in about six months and establish the feasibility, or otherwise, and scope of the proposed diversions from the Godavari to the Krishna.

As soon as this preliminary project report has been prepared, final decision can be taken in regard to :

(i) The scope of the Nagarjunasagar Project in the light of the diversions from the Godavari;

(ii) Sanction to or abandonment of the Nagarjunasagar Hydroelectric Project; and

(iii) The scope of the Srisailam Project.

It is clear that the Srisailam Project would fit in any scheme and from this point of view, there should be no objection to starting work on the Srisailam Projects, the only hydroelectric development left in the lower Krishna area. The scope of the project would, however, have to be reviewed as soon as the preliminary plan mentioned above has been prepared.

In view of the regulated supplies that would be available to the projects, existing and proposed, on the Krishna [below Nagarjunasagar, from the Godavari diversions, and to the canals at Nagarjunasagar, from Srisailam, the crop pattern now proposed on the basis of four to six months' supply should be revised to take advantage of the regulated flow.

A preliminary survey be made of the proposed Penganga-Pochampad Link and this survey be taken into account before according sanction to the Penganga Hydroelectric Project.

Administration And Management

An important provision, which does not appear adequately in any existing legislation, is with regard to the obligation of the irrigation to prepare his land for receiving irrigation waters. Such a provision is important for the Krishna and Godavari basins.

Need For A New Policy

The Commission recommends that the State Governments concerned should all agree to tune their policy regarding irrigation and the administration and management of irrigation works to the requirements of optimum development of a scare and expensive natural resource.

Some of the steps which should be undertaken immediately in furtherance of this objective are as follows :

(a) Limit the irrigation of paddy to the rainy season, in order to reduce the use of irrigation supplies to the minimum and (i) to areas of high rainfall such as sub-basins G. 8, G. 9, G. 10, G. 11 and G. 12 and the narrow strip along the Western Ghats where the data for paddy should not be more than about two feet; (ii) valley-bottoms and low lying areas where, because of the seepage from upland irrigation no other crop can be grown and paddy can be grown with advantage; or (iii) to the delta lands.

(b) Adopt a crop pattern which would (i) take full advantage of seasonal rainfall; and (ii) not require any stored water after February, so that the reservoirs are emptied by that date. This will save the high evaporation loss from March to May.

(c) Develop the use of ground waters to the maximum; investigate the likely sites and develop the use of underground reservoirs, artificially charged the rainy season.

(d) Limit perennial crops to (i) only those areas where the irrigation supplies required between, say, January to May, can be obtained from ground waters or from artificially charged underground reservoirs; or (ii) to those areas where irrigation waters are obtained from the regulated flow below a power project. In such cases, the perennial areas should be in convenient blocks, so that it is not necessary to run any irrigation channel with a capacity factor of less than 0.5 in any month.

(e) In case of multipurpose projects, the crop pattern should be such as would require irrigation supplies more or less uniformly all the year round.

(f) Reorganise the Public Works Department, where necessary, to enable it to manage all irrigation projects, major, medium, minor or small tanks, and all stages of planning, construction, operation and development including the assessment of water charges. It is necessary that all aspects of the development of water resources for irrigation and of their ultimate use should be under unified control.

(g) While no control need be exercised, at this stage, with regard to development or irrigation from wells, except where such development is an integral part of a canal system, it is necessary to have in the irrigation Department officers to advise cultivators with regard to developments from wells and who should maintain a record of well operations. These officers should also maintain records of the operation of private irrigation works and watch the effect, on the hydrology of the basin, of contour bunding and land treatment in non-irrigated areas.

(h) Introduce necessary legislation along uniform set of principles facilitate optimum development of the water resources of the two river basins, laying down appropriate powers for government and the rights and obligations of the cultivators. A more or less uniform basis for charges for irrigation water supplies and betterment levy etc., should be established.

(i) The present system of administrative account of irrigation projects should be reviewed and revised to take note of the changed conditions such as the new direct receipts from agricultural commodities or the processing of agriculture produce. An appropriate basis should be established for taking note of indirect benifits in the administrative accounts.

There should be in every Irrigation Department, a soil survey wing, whose duty should be not only to carry out a scientific soil survey of all areas proposed to be supplied with irrigation nature but also, periodically, to carry out soil survey of the areas already under irrigation in order to study the effect of irrigation supplies on the soil characteristics so that the necessary ameliorative measures can be taken and irrigation ensured as a permanent feature of agriculture.

Need For Co-operative Approach

The Commission recommends that an inter-State body, a Reiver Board or by whatever name called should be established without any delay, for bringing about a cooperative approach and establishing the necessary coordination in the planning and operation of various developments in the two river basins. The integrated operation of all projects, which is indispensable, would not be possible without such a coordinating body.

Irrigation Extension Service

The Commission recommends for serious consideration that, in each State, an Irrigation Extension Service should be introduced as a part of the Irrigation Department.

REVIEW COMMITTEE FOR LIBRARY SCIENCE IN INDIAN UNIVERSITIES, 1961—REPORT

New Delhi, University Grants Commission, 1965. 86p.

Chairman : Dr. S.R. Ranganathan.

Members : Dr. C.P. Shukla; Dr. K.A. Isaac; Shri S. Bashiruddin; Shri P.N. Kaula; Dr. Jagadish Sharma; Shri S. Das Gupta; Shri B.S. Kesavan.

Member-Secretary : Dr. P.J. Philip.

APPOINTMENT

The Committee was appointed by the University Grants Commission in 1961 to consider the question of improving the standards of teaching and research in the departments of Library Science in the Universities.

TERMS OF REFERENCE

The Committee had the following terms of reference :

(a) To determine the different types of courses which should be offered by the universities ;

(b) To work out the objectives of the different types of courses ;

(c) To recommend to the universities schemes of paper for each type of course with a view to providing specialisation in a particular field ;

(d) To work out agreed syllabus in each of the subjects for the different courses, including the relative place of theory and practice in each subjects in the curriculum ;

(e) To recommend methods suitable for teaching the various parts of the syllabus and to lay down guiding principles for the conduct of examinations ;

(f) To lay down the entrance qualifications of the students for the various courses ;

(g) To lay down minimum standards for passing examination and grouping of question papers for the purposes of the examinations ;

(h) To recommend any other steps to achieve uniform and highly developed standards.

CONTENTS

Foreword; Introduction; Existing facilities of teaching and Research; Syllabus; Sectors for Research in Library Science; Recommendations; Appendices I and III;

General Statement Nos. 1 to 20.

RECOMMENDATIONS

Minimum Qualification For Admission

It was not possible so far to attract students of a high calibre to courses in library sceince as the conditions of working librarians were far from satisfactory. Now that the emoluments and general conditions of service of the library staff have been sufficiently improved, only those students should be admitted to the courses who are intellectually mature and who can really benefit from the course. The course of library science is a professional course. One peculiar feature of the liabrary profession is that it has to cater to the intellectual needs and requirements of different types of readers. It is a profession which requires a high standard of performance. In order to raise the present standard of library service in the country, it would be necessary to restrict admissions to students who have a good educational background. We would suggest the following minimum qualifications for admission to the various courses.

1. **Certificate Course** : High School certificate or an equivalent qualification.

2. **B. Lib. Sc. Course** : A second class Bachelor's degree of a recognised university.

M. Lib. Sc. Course : Second class B. Lib. Sc degree.

4. **Ph. D. Course** : (1) Either a second class M. Lib. Sc. degree, or a second class B. Lib. Sc. degree plus a second class Master's degree in any subject of a recognised university.

(2) The candidate must have shown sufficient evidence of capacity for research.

Pre-admission Course

In the earlier years, practically all the students admitted to the various courses in library science were those who had some experience of working in a library. They were familiar with the routine work as well as with the various kinds of reading material usually found in a library. With the change of circumstances, even raw graduates are now admitted to the library science course. Very often they are ignorant of reference books, bibliographies, and periodi als. They have no idea whatever of the ordinary routine involved in the day-to-day library work. The result is that much time has to be spent during the course of the year in giving the student the necessary training in repetitive routine and also in acquainting him with different kinds of publications. This should be avoided as it cuts into the time available for the substance of the post-graduate professional course. It is, therefore, necessary to admit the students provisionally some months in advance and insist on their taking an apprenticeship course for a period of about six months in an approved library. For this purpose the department of library science should keep itself in touch with the approved libraries and ensure that the apprentices are given the right type of training. It would be desirable if the syllabus for the apprentice course is worked out by the head of the department of library science in consultation with the heads of the approved libraries. The practice of asking the students to take apprentice course after the completion of the course in library science does not serve educational purpose to an equal extent. This is now being realised even in other professional courses and pre-course apprenticeship is being introduced in place of post-course apprenticeship.

University Courses Of Library Science

We attach great importance to the question of determining the courses in library science, which should be conduted by other bodies. For historical reasons, some of the earlier universities started with courses leading to a certificate in library science. This was necessitated by the fact that at that time there was no other agency in the country for preparing semi-professionals. The circumstances have changed now. In a number of States, the Library Associations, the State Governments, and other bodies are conducting certificate courses to train non-graduates for managing small libraries and for working in junior positions in larger libraries, such as college, university, public and research libraries. There appears to be no need, therefore, for the universities to continue the responsibility of teaching to the certificate standard in the present conditions. Moreover, if teachers of library science have to engage themselves in teaching at the lower level, they will not have sufficient time for doing research to gain and maintain competence to teach at a higher level and to guide students in research work. It would be as much an anomaly to make the university department of library science to train semi-professionals as it would be to ask the university depar ments to train laboratory assistants or to teach in school classes. The main emphasis today is not on teaching or research alone, but on a fruitful combination of teaching and research. Both the Adviso y Committee of library science appointed by the Government of India and the Library Committee of the University Grants Commission have, therefore, recommended that training for certificate in library science should not be the responsibility of the universities. After considering various issues such as the demand and supply of certificate holders in library science in the country, we feel that the certificate course should be left out of the purview of the university departments of library science. The universities should be concerned only with the Ph. D., M. Lib. Sc., and

B. Lib. Sc. courses. The statement of this policy does not preclude this committee making suggestions for the content, duration, etc., of the certificate courses to be conducted by other agencies. On the other hand, the suggestions may be of use to the nation. It is for this reason that section VI (A) has been included in this report.

Equivalence Of Diploma And Bachelor's Degree Course In Library Science

At the beginning, some of the universities called the postgraduate course in library science as diploma course. In due course the content and the standard of work in the diploma course in library science have been gradually improved and today it has attained the same standard as the B. Lib. Sc. Course. We are, therefore, of the view that the diploma course in library science in these universities should be redesignated as the post-graduate B. Lib. Sc. Course and should enjoy the same status. For the purpose of appointment and promotion in libraries and in the departments of library science, and for admission to the M. Lib. Sc. course the holders of the postgraduate university diploma of the past should be treated at par with the holders of the B. Lib. Sc. degree of the present. It is neither educationally sound nor necessary (in view of the course content) to make such diploma holders either take an additional course or the examination over again in order to gain the status of the B. Lib. Sc. degree holders.

Method Of Teaching And Relative Place Of Theory And Practice

While it is true that the library profession is an intellectual professon, it does not mean that no routine has to be performed by librarians. Most of the techniques like book selection, cataloguing, maintenance of accounts, management and circulation work require an understanding of basic principles and they also involve actual work. For this reason, it is desirable that the total number of hours devoted to the various courses in library science is equally divided between formal lesson and tutorial work on the one hand and actual practice any observation work on the other. Formal lessons should not all be in the form of lectures, putting the students in the passive mood of listening or taking notes. Most of the lessons should involve a two-way flow of thought between the teacher and the taught.

The aim should be to rouse the curiosity of students to make them seek information to satisfy the curiosity, to induce in them a good capacity to analyse a problem for all angles, to make them arrive at valid conclusions from the observed data and the assumptions of laws and principles made to regulate thought, and to develop in them the capacity for collective thinking and team work.

Non-Professional Subjects

We find that some universities include in the library science course one or two non-professional subjects in addition to the professional subjects. Thus, for example Bombay, Calcutta, Karnataka and SNDT Women's universities have a paper on general knowledge; the Calcutta University has a paper on language and the Bombay University has a paper on cultural history in the diploma course. Historically, non-professional subjects were included in the library science curriculum at a time when non-graduates were admitted to the courses. In India at present the admission to the B. Lib. Sc. course is restricted to graduates, who already have maturity and some understanding of subjects like cultural history, general knowledge, language, etc. The necessity for including non-professional subjects does not, therefore, arise hereafter. Moreover, the curricular load of the B. Lib. Sc. course is heavy by itself. If we add non-professional subjects, it would increase the load beyond the proper limit and also lower the standard of the professional content.

Examinations

We are not in favour of the present practice of examining the candidates by means of viva-voce test with the help of external examiners. A test of this type is conducted usually on the basis of sessional or project work done by the candidates under the guidance of teachers. Such work should be more appropriately assessed from time to time by the teachers of the department. Moreover, external examiners, on account of the number of candidates involved, do not often get the necessary time to go through each candidate's sessional or project work before the viva-voce test. The character of the test becomes too general and tends to suffer from superficiality. We would further recommend that all the papers for the B. Lib. Sc. and M. Lib. Sc. degree should be written ones.

Working Hours

The time-table of the B. Lib. Sc. course should provide for at least 400 working hours during a session comprising lectures, tutorials, and class practicals (under a teacher's guidance). About one-half of the :e time table hours should be assigned to lectures ard one-half to class practicals and tutorials. The time-ta bloe the M. Lib. Sc. course should provide for 300-325 hours for lectures, tutorials and seminars. The time needed for guiding the M. Lib. Sc. students in their project work or for practicals should be in addition to the provision s ggested above.

Minimum Qualifications For Teachers

In order to raise the standard of teaching and

research in the subject, we suggest the following minimum qualifications for teaching posts, which should be insisted upon in the case of all fresh appointments ;

Professor

Second Class M. Lib. Sc. degree plus doctorate in library science plus experience of guiding research plus 10 years teaching experience or five years experience of having worked as a Reader in library science.

Reader

Second class M. Lib. Sc. or second class Master's degree in some subject with first class B. Lib. Sc. plus teaching experience of at least five years.

Lecturer

M. Lib. Sc. degree or second class Master's degree in some subject plus B. Lib. Sc. in the second class.

Staff Requirement

In the present circumstances, we consider a staff-student ration of 1 : 10 at the B. Lib. Sc. level and 1 : 5 at the M. Lib. Sc. level as reasonable. Here staff means full-time staff. In our view, a department of library science conducting the B. Lib. Sc. course should have a minimum staff of one reader and two lecturers and a department conducting M. Lib. Sc. course should have a minimum staff consisting of one professor, two readers and four lecturers. The old practice of employing the university library staff as part-time teachers should be discontinued as early as possible.

Physical Facilities

A department of library science should generally provide for accommodation to meet the following requirements :

(a) Two lecture rooms.
(b) One practical or laboratory room.
(c) One reading room.
(d) Staff room for individual teachers.
(e) One seminar room.
(f) One room for demonstration and use of Library equipment.
(g) One office room.

Books

We consider a lump sum initial provision of Rs. 50,000 for basic books and a recurring provision of Rs. 8,000 per annum as the minimum requirements for a department of library science.

Training Of Teachers

The quality of work of a teacher in library science should be judged on the following grounds :

(a) He must have a good grasp of the subject to be taught.

(b) He should also have a proper training in the methods of teaching.

With the expansion of courses in library science in the country, there has been a decline in the quality of teaching offered by the departments. We, therefore, recommend a regular training in teaching methods which should include the methods of teaching, psychology and special techniques of teaching the different branches of library science. Facilities should be provided for training at least 10 teachers in library science every year.

Research

Research in library science has a special importance. First, library techniques require constant improvement based on research. Secondly, with the extension of library service, organisational work in the libraries will have to be adopted to the changing social needs of the country. While considerable research work is in progress in the country, this will have to be augmented further. The new sectors of research in library science are indicated in chapter four of the report. We further suggest the institution of research fellowships (about three each year). We also recommend the provision of scholarships to deserving persons and holding of seminars, conferences and refresher courses for the research of library science in order to raise the standards of teaching and research in the subject.

Survey Of Trained Personnel-Needs And Quality

The University Grants Commission should arrange a survey of the need for professional librarians of different categories in the country and also carry out an assessment of the quality of the trained personnel turned out by the universities from the viewpoint of both the employers and the employees.

Cooperation Between The Departments Of Library Science And The Library

There should be a close cooperation between the library and the department of library science in a university. It would be useful for the teachers of library science to work in the library for short periods and similarly it would be useful for the librarians to maintain an academic interest in the subject by delivering a few lectures in the department. While we would welcome a close association between the departments of library science and the library in a manner to be determined by the universities, we are not in favour of the present practice of employing part-time teachers in the department of library science drawn from the university libraries. This, in our view is not conducive to efficiency. Part time use of the members of the university libray staff for teaching library science was possible in the past when the annual library fund was at a low level and there was not much research work in many of the departments of study. These conditions have now changed. Library departments are all active with research work, not only by the teachers themselves but also by a number of research students. Service to them requires the full attention of the university library staff. Further, the annual university finance has now increased considerably due to the grants from the University Grants Commission and from other sources. Therefore, the administrative work of the library also has reached a level calling for the full-time attention of the members of the university staff. Therefore, it is not proper to continue any longer the practice of asking the university library staff to be part-time teachers in the departments of library science. The department of library science should enjoy the same status in regard to leave, vacations, academic matters, representation on university bodies, etc., as the other departments of the university.

REVIEW COMMITTEE FOR PHILOSOPHY IN INDIAN UNIVERSITIES, 1961—REPORT

New Delhi, University Grants Commission, 1966. 108p.

Chairman : Prof. N.A. Nikam.

Members : Prof. N.V. Banerjee ; Prof. T.M.P. Mahadevan ; Prof. T.R.V. Murti ; Prof. P.J. Chaudhry (following the sad demise of Prof. P.J. Chaudhry in 1964, Dr. (Mrs.) P. Chatterjee was appointed members of the Committee) ; Prof. Kalidas Bhattabcharya

Member-Secretary : Dr. P.J. Philip

APPOINTMENT

With a view to examining the standards of teaching and research in philosophy and considering the problems that concerns the future of philosophical studies and research in our universities, the University Grants Commission appointed a Committee of experts in 1961.

TERMS OF REFERENCE

The terms of reference of the Committee are as follows :

(a) To define the objectives of teaching and learning philosophy at the various levels of university education ;

(b) To examine the standards of teaching and research in philosophy in Indian Universities ;

(c) To suggest measures for promoting the study of philosophy in Indian Universities, and to attract bright young scholars to philosophical studies ; and

(d) To consider the problems of the future growth of philosophy as an intellectual discipline.

CONTENTS

Foreword ; Introduction ; Historical Background ; The Present Position ; Objectives of Teaching Philosophy (Including Syllabi) ; Improvement of Instruction ; Research in Philosophy ; The Role of Philosophy in Eduction ; Summary of Observations and Recommendations ; Appendices from I to X.

RECOMMENDATIONS

The Role Of Philosophy In India

Among the liberal arts subjects, philosophy has an important place. The analytical and synoptic ways of thinking that philosophy fosters are of great benefit to university life. The study of philosophy not only enriches the humanities but also includes in its critical purview the social sciences.

India has a long and respected philosophical tradition of her own. If, however, interest in the study of philosophy as an academic discipline has somewhat dwindled in recent years and departments philosophy do not attract bright students. The reason is to be sought in the fact philosophy in India has not yet become resourceful enough to meet the pressing demands and complex situations of modern life.

Philosophy can make a positive contribution to the clarification of our goals and offer valuable guidance when different ideals and courses of action are in conflict, if a modern approach is brought to bear upon it. This would mean that in the universities appropriate changes have to be brought about in the content of courses of study and research.

Objectives Of Teaching Philosophy

At present courses of study in philosophy in Indian

universities are largely related to the study of traditional systems of Indian philosophy and the history of western philosophy. They do not take account of the various changes that have taken place in recent times in philosophical thinking. Many university syllabi prescribe out of date text books and courses at the B.A. (Hons.) and M.A. levels are often duplicated, There is also an undesirable compartmentalisation of papers. It is, there fore, necessary to define clearly the objectives of teaching philosophy at the different levels.

The B.A. pass course in philosophy should have the following objectives :

(i) to introduce the students to the world philosophy it its several aspects ;

(ii) To promote liberal education ;

(iii) To train the mind of the students ; and

(iv) To stimulate interest in the further study of philosophy.

The following schedule of papers is recommended for the B.A. pass course :

(i) **Logic and Scientific Method** : An attempt should be made to introduce a certain amount of modern logic in the content of this paper.

(ii) **Ethcis and Social Philosophy** : Basic ethical concepts should be critically studied with reference to actual texts. Some topics which usually come under political philosophy should be included in this paper.

(iii) **Basic Philosophical Concepts and Theories (Epistemological and Metaphysical)** : This paper should be taugh with reference to both Indian and eastern philosophy and centre round selected readings.

The main objective of the honours course in philosophy should be to prepare students for postgraduate studies in the subject. This would require a concentration of papers in the main honours subject with two or three papers in subsidiary areas like history and Sanskrit.

The following papers are suggested for the B. A. (Hons.) course in philosophy :

1. **Selected Western Philosophers** : Intensive study of such philosophers as Plato, Aristotle and Kant.

2. **Indian Philosophy** : A study of the traditional schools of philosophy with special attention to one or two schools and to a few selected problems.

3. **Modern Logic** : Stress should also be placed on an intensive study of the scientific method and its application to the social sciences in particular.

4. **Ethics** : It should centre round selected texts with special reference to their contemporary relevance.

5. **Contemporary Western Philosophy** : A critical study of current trends of special interest in western philosophy with reference to selected texts.

6. **Social and Political Philosophy** : A critical study of the main trends of political thought and their relevance to social change.

7. and 8. Any two of the following :

(a) **Philosophy of Religion** : This should be studied with special reference to Hinduism, Christianity and Islam.

(b) **Special Indian Philosophy** : Texts either in the original or in translation.

(c) **Special Western Philosophy** : Texts.

(d) **Philosophy of Sciences.**

(e) **Modern Metaphysics.**

(f) **Linguistic Analysis.**

It may be desirable to institute a combined honours course in philosophy in which philosophy could be studied along with one or two other subjects like economics, politics or sociology, which are of great interest and practical utility. Graduates who have taken the course would be well qualified to participate in various forms of public service.

The combined honours course should have the following objectives :

1. To make an intensive study of the relevant aspects of the subjects offered under the course. Such a study would not be difficult as the combined honours course would be open only to the intellectually abler students. It would, however, be necessary to develop an inter-disciplinary approach to the study of these subjects.

2. To develop in the student a thyrough understanding of modern philosophy.

3. To provide for specialisation in any of the various subjects offered.

The course might consist of nine papers including three papers in philosophy viz.:

(i) Seleted Western Philosophers;

(ii) Ethics; and

(iii) Contemporary Western Philosophers.

The main aim of the postgraduate course should be to produce teachers and research scholars. The course should develop in the student a high degree of competence so that he could take to careers of teaching, research and other kinds of academic work. He should have the capacity to make contributions to his subject and to communicate his knowledge to others.

The following schedule of papers is recommended for the M. A. course.

Paper 1 : Ancient and Medieval European Philosophy;

Paper 2: Modern European Philosophy upto Hegel and Schopenhauer.

Paper 3 : Indian Philosophy : An effort should be made to relate the basic concepts of Indian philosophy to the contemporary philosophical situation.

Paper 4 : Logic : Critical review of the historical background of the subject and intensive study of the basic problems of modern logic should be undertaken.

Paper 5 : Ethics : Study of selected texts including contemporary works.

Paper 6 : Philosophical Analysis with reference to Texts.

Papers 7 and 8 : Any two of the following :

(a) Philosophy of Science.
(b) Social and Political Philosophy.
(c) Modern Schools of Metaphysics.
(d) Linguistic Analysis.
(e) Philosophy of Religion.
(f) Aesthetics.
(g) Special Indian Philosophy (Advanced Texts).

Improvement Of Instruction

Since expansion of numbers is not easily compatible with the maintenance of high standards, increase in the number of students in philosophy should be brought about with great care and deliberation. If a choice has to be made quality should be the goal and not quantity.

Pressure is often exercised on college authorities to introduce Hindi or a regional language as the medium of instruction, but there is often a dearth of good books in these languages and lack of competent teachers to teach through their medium. We have, therefore, to ensure that pass course teaching does not suffer on account of lack of suitable preparation to introduce Hindi or a regional language as the medium of instruction

An essential condition for starting an honours course, whether pure or combined, should be the provision of adequate facilities in the college or university concerned for conducting tutorials and seminars to inculcate independent habits of study, consultation of texts and provide opportunities for discussion. Every effort should be made to attract bright student to the honours course in philosophy. The participation of postgraduate teachers in the honours teaching programme is essential for its success. Teaching courses have also to be pooled in order that more teachers can be released for tutorial work.

In the interest of high standards, universities must satisfy themselves about the fulfilment of requisite conditions before postgraduate colleges or departments of philosophy are started. The proper method of developing postgraduate work would be to keep the postgraduate courses confined to institutions which offer an honours courses so that the students for M. A in philosophy can be drawn mainly from the honours stream. Such an arrangement would also have the advantage of enabling them to hold combined seminars for honours and postgraduate students, which would be of benefit to both.

As many postgraduate colleges do not have facilities for conducting tutorial closses inspecialised fields, there should either be centralisation of tutorial work under the supervsion of university departments or the specialised fields should be developed in selected centres only.

At the postgraduate level tutorials should be supplemented by seminars, which would not only stimulate discussion but alo encourage students to study original works. The students should be able to follow important articles printed in academic journals.

There is also a need for the translation of important texts in Indian philosophy so that students do not have to depend on second hand accounts. It may be helpful to have some outstanding pundits in the languages concerned in the departments of philosophy.

The study of languages like Sanskrit, Greek and Latin would be of great benefit to the study of philosophy. Facilities for the teaching of these languages have, therefore, to be augmented.

In order to attract meritorious students to the study of philosophy, scholarships should be made available on a generous scale. Scholarships should be specially earmarked for various subjects, including philosophy, intead or making them available for humanities, social sciences, sciences, etc., in a general way.

While objective tests are not suited for evaluation in philosophy, it is necessary to break away from the stereotyped examination system by assigning more marks to discussion-type questions. Due credit should be given for independent thinking. More questions should be asked on recent developments in the subject, particularly during the last 30 years or so.

Refresher courses, summer schools and workshops should be arranged regularly to provide an opportunity for teachers to exchange ideas and to become acquainted with the latest developments in their subject. Teachers should also attend regular seminars in their own universities so that their interest in philosophy is kept alive. Suitable incentives could be offered to those who undertake research work. The philosophy teachers should be a person of wide general culture, aware of contemporary problems and alive to the latest developments in his subject.

Research In Philosophy

It is necessary to admit only such students to the research courses in philosophy as have the necessary aptitude, ability and motivation for research. The linguistic equipment of the students should be of a high order. Those ignorant of Sanskrit should not be allowed to offer subjects in Indian philosophy.

The registration of a research scholor should be subject to the approval of a small department committee comprising the head of the department, dean of the faculty and the supervisor and such registration should be provisional. A test should be given to the condidate at the end of six months or one year in order to ascertain whether he has the capacity to continue his work. The test should concern the background material relevant to the topic selected. During the preliminary period the candidate should prepare a thorough bibliography relating to his subject. Attendance at Seminars arranged for doctoral students should be compulsory.

The duration of the research course should ordinarily be three years, i.e., two years after one year of apprenticeship. Teachers of three years' standing may be allowed to submit their theses in two years' time without undergoing the preliminary test or examination. No student should be enrolled for the Ph. D. for more than five years.

Departmental teachers only should undertake supervision in the case of subjects of which they have specialised knowledge. No supervisor should enrol more than six students.

The examiners for the Ph. D. theses should be well-known scholars in the subject. At least three examiners should be appointed to evaluate Ph. D. theses. It would be desirable to have one examiner from a forign university. The supervisor should not ordinarily be a referee, but may be associated with the viva-voce examination of the candidate. The viva-voce test should not be regarded as merely a routine matter. It should enable the examiner to check whether the work is the candidate's own, as also his general standard of philosophical competence.

Departments of philosophy should be given suitable grants to enable them to publish papers presented at seminars and books and research papers produced by teachers and research scholars.

Some of the research projects undertaken by university departments could, with advantage, be concerned with philosophy teaching itself, for example, with new ways of presenting Indian philosophy or modern logic. Centres of advanced study in philosophy have a special contribution to make in this regard.

There is a great need for evolving modern schools of Indian Philosophy. In fact, one of the tasks of research in philosophy should be a reinterpretation of the traditional systems of thought in India and recreation of philosophical schools.

Funds should be provided to enable universities to hold seminars, invite outstanding philosophers and make provision for endowment lectures. Encouragement should be given to undertake the translation of leading texts. Even doctorate degrees could be awarded on such works.

Formal supervision is not necessary for research work leading to the award of the D. Litt. degree. The degree should be dependent on published work of outstanding merit. The minimum qualification for permission to supplicate for the D. Litt. should be a Ph. D., but exemption may be granted in very exceptional cases to teachers and postgraduates of five to 10 years standing. All the examiners for the D. Litt. degree should be external.

Teachers may be granted sabbatical leave for studies and research and also relieved of some of their teaching load to enable them to undertake investigations. They should be given incentives by way of increments and/or promotion to do research.

The Role Of Philosophy In Education

Though philosophy is a theoretical discipline concerned with concepts and doctrines, it has also an intimate relationship with the actual situations of life. Philosophy can respond to the complex problems and challenges of modern life only if it is made contemporary.

Firstly, emphasis needs to be placed on modern logic, which provides a useful training for the mind. Our students should be able to think cogently and to draw correct inferences and detect fallacies.

Secondly, there is a great need for a critical evalution of our own heritage. Traditional values and schools of philosophy should be studied in the light of present-day condition and forms of thought and restated.

Thirdly philosophy should have an important place in any system of "general education" and all first year students, whether of arts or science subjects, should be encourged to study some philosophy. Along with pure philosophy courses, there can be courses of philosophy which are oriented towards particular subjects. Such adaptability presupposes a great deal of flexibility on the part of the philosophy teachers.

Fourthly, close contact needs to be maintained between philosophy and other subjects like the social sciences, history and the classical languages. A multi-religious country like India should also strengthen courses of study in comparative region in selected universities.

Fifthly, some universities should be encouraged to take up research projects in the philosophy of education-a subject which has remained somewhat neglected as falling neither under the umbrella of philosophy nor within the purview of conventional courses in education.

Philosophy has much to offer to subjects like politics, sociology, economics, history, etc. By entering intimate relationships with them philosophy is also able to enhace its relevance for contemporary situations and problems.

The philosopher should regard as part of his business to reinterpret old doctrines like 'karma', 'dharma', etc., define new concepts like 'standards' and 'secularism' and to analyse political, economic and social affairs, if this task is not undertaken by the philosopher, the danger is that others less qualified than him would do it.

CONTRIBUTORY HEALTH SERVICE SCHEME ASSESSMENT COMMITTEE, 1961—REPORT

New Delhi, Ministry of Health, 1962. 58p.+iip.

Chairman : Shri Radha Raman. Shri M.P. Bhhargava ;
Members : Dr. R. Viswanathan ; Shrimati K. Mankekar ; Shri P.G. Zachariah ; Dr. R.S. Chawla;
Secretary : Dr. W. Mathur.

APPOINTMENT

The Committee was constituted under the Government of India, Ministry of Health, vide their letter No. 4 (I)-34/60-H (II), dated March 4, 1961.

TERMS OF REFERENCE

(i) To review the working of the Contributory Health Service Scheme and to report how far it has succeeded in improving the medical care facilities to Central Government Servants in New Delhi and Delhi ;

(ii) To make a comparison between the medical care facilities available to the Central Service (Medical Attendance) Rules and those provided under the Contributory Health Service Scheme ;

(iii) To determine whether the results achieved are commensurate with the expenditure incurred on the Scheme ; and

(iv) To make an assessment of the quality of the service received by the beneficiaries and their reaction to the Scheme.

CONTENTS

Introduction ; Organisation and Scope ; How the Contributory Health Service Scheme Functions ; Assessment of work ; Recommendations ; Appendices I to V.

RECOMMENDATIONS

Dispensary Services

The Committee considers that the Dispensary service is the backbone of the Contributory Health Service Scheme organisation. It is, therefore, essential that everything possible should be done to make this service as efficient and comprehencive as possible.

Accommodation

Because of the fact that many of the difficulties experienced in providing an efficient dispensary service are due to obvious lack of physical facilities, the Committee is of the opinion that the highest priority be given to the question of providing separate permanent buildings for all the dispensaries. At present practically all of them are located in residential premises which are quite unsuited for providing adequate dispensary service, inspite of the best efforts made by the authorities in making suitable alterations.

The new dispensary building should be planned in such a manner as to provide one consulting room separately for each doctor two or three dressing rooms as the case may be, one sterilising room, an Injection room, a dispensary with separate counters for men and women with a small attached store room, one clinical side-room-for simple laboratory examinations, office for the doctor incharge, a registration room, one main waiting room, in addition to waiting spaces in front of doctors' consulting rooms, dressing room, injection room and dispensary, two store rooms one for drugs and another for sundries, and adequate number of lavatories. Ordinarily, a dispensary should be planned only for five doctors. If additional load is to be catered for in any particular region, it will be advisable to have another small dispensary at a distance.

Since family planning constitutes an integral part of medical care, such of those dispensaries in which family planning units are located should provide for additional accommadation and other facilities for the purpose.

The Committee is of the view that all the dispensary staff should reside within the dispensary premises. For this purpose, residential quarters should be constructed either within the dispensary premises or in close proximity to it.

Staff

Overcrowding in all the Contributory Health Service Scheme dispensaries no doubt speaks for the popularity which these dispensaries have gained. At the same time it should be pointed out that the crowding of patients at any particular moment in any of the dispensaries is primarily due to the inability of the existing staff to cope with the situation. The only way by which overcrowding can be obviated is by increasing the number of doctors. One doctor at present sees about 120 cases a day on the average during six hours of duty. During the peak period, the attendance per doctor per day rises even to 150. The Committee is of the view that a doctor should be made to see not more than 12 patients in an hour. This means he will be able to see only about 70 to 80 patients a day. As the average sickness incidence on the basis of dispensary attendance, old and new, works out to about four per cent, the Committee recommends that there should be at least one doctor for every 2,000 beneficiaries. As it is advisable to have one dispensary for every 10,000 beneficiaries, there should be five doctors working in such a dispensary. The staffing pattern for a dispensary catering to 10,000 beneficiaries will be as follows :

Medical Officers (male)	3
Medical Officers (female)	2
Clerks	3
Nurses	2
Pharmacists	4
Medical Store Keeper	1
Laboratory Technician	1
Dresser (male)	2
Dressers (female)	1
Nursing Orderlies	2
Female Attendants	2
Peons	2
Sweepers	2
Chowkidar	1

Equipment

Each dispensary should be adequately equipped for the minimum laboratory facilities contemplated including a microscope. Instead of providing one diagnostic set to each doctor as at present, it will be sufficient if a set for each dispensary is provided. In addition, an electric torch, an ordinary nasal and aural speculam and a torgue depresser should be supplied to each doctor. It is recommended that sterilised dressings should be provided at each dispensary through a central supply service. Since electrical equipments go often out of order, it will be advisable to provide an ordinary instrument sterilizer which can be heated either on a hot plate or a burshane gas burner.

The Committee very carefully considered the question of the working hours of the dispensary. It recommends that the present system of the functioning in the morning and evening with a break in the middle may continue. Considering the climatic conditions of Delhi, the Committee does not recommend that the dispansary should be kept open continuously for 12 hours as was suggested by some of the beneficiaries.

Domiciliary Visits And Night Duty

At present the doctors are called for domiciliary service during dispensary hours. The doctor on night duty has to do full day duty the next day. The Committee feels that the present system is unsatisfactory and recommends that the dispansary medical officer should be free from domiciliary visits and night duty and these functions should be entrusted to a separate group of medical officers located at the Regional Poly Clinics, recommendations about which have been made elsewhere in this report. Pending the change over and the adoption of the newly contemplated emergency service, the Committee recommends that no medical officer after he performs night duty should be made to work the next morning at the dispensary.

Mobile Dispensaries

The Committee is of the opinion that Mobile Dispensaries may continue to cater to the needs of beneficiaries residing in outlying areas. It, however, recommends that proper arrangements for the waiting of the patients be provided at the halting places of the mobile dispensaries.

Specialist And Laboratory Services—Poly Clinics

The Committee is of the view that the present arrangement to centralise the specialist and laboratory services in the two hospitals, namely, Willingdon and Safdarjang, is unsatisfactory. The Committee feels that decentralisation of these services will ensure better efficiency and promptness. At present, the Committee has been informed that there is considerable delay in providing both specialist as well as laboratory services. It is, therefore recommended that at least five poly clinics in different areas should be established. Each of these poly clinics should provide the following facilities :

(i) Specialised laboratory examination.
(ii) Radiological examination and electro-therapy :
(iii) Specialist services.
(iv) Domiciliary and emergency service.
(v) Initial supply of specialist medicines.
(vi) Ambulance service.

Specialised Laboratory Examination

While routine examinations of urine, blood, stool, etc., will be undertaken at the dispensary itself, all other types of specialised laboratory investigations should be undertaken in the poly clinic. For this purpose, the laboratory at each poly clinic should have three sections namely, clinical pathology, bacteriology and biochemistry. Each of these sections should be in-charge of a trained medical officer with adequate number of trained laboratory technicians and laboratory attendants to assist.

Radiological Investigations

The X-ray department in the poly clinic should be fully equipped for all types of radiological investigations. It should be in-charge of a competant radiologist of staff surgeon status. There should also be facilities for electro therapy, like infra ed, ultraviolet and diathermy.

Specialist Services

The Committee observed that the quantum of work being undertaken is much more than can be handled by the specialist staff. Further, emergency references and direct calls (at the consultation room or visits at home) on the specialists by a class of beneficiaries of higher income group also dislocate the work. The Committee recommends that the concession of direct consultation with the specialist without a reference through the dispensary doctor should be withdrawn forthwith. Further the specialist should normally give a home visit only on the request of the dispensary or emergency doctor. This will obviously remove the existing invidions distinction between different class of employees.

In regard to the work load, the Committee recommends that a consultation should not be required to see more than 12 and the specialist more than 15 classes per day. It further recommends that arrangements for specialist consultations in all specialities should be made at the poly clinics.

Because of the fact that all the specialists are concentrated in the two hospitals, considerable delay has been experienced by the beneficiaries in obtaining specialist consultation. If the specialists are located at the poly clinics, there will be division of work and consequent minimising of delay. Facilities should be provided for specialities like medicine, surgery, dentistry, ear, nose and throat, ophthalmology, gynaecology and paediatrics Each of the specialist departments should be in charge of one staff surgeon trained in that particular speciality. In so far as medicine is concerned, because of the heavier volume of work, there should be a junior staff surgeon to assist the medical specialist. The surgical specialist should be in a position to do minor operative work for which purpose there should be a small operation theatre at the poly clinic. The ophthalmologist may be assisted by a non-medical refractionist for refraction work.

Domiciliary And Emergency Services

After very careful consideration, the Committee has decided to recommends the adoption of a new procedure for providing domiciliary and emergency services. The new arrangement has been suggested not only for the purpose of ensuring efficiency and promptness of these services but also to allow the dispensary doctors to devote their entire time to the patients attending the dispensaries. The Committee recommends that domiciliary services should be centralised at the poly clinics. For this purpose, each poly clinic should have six medical officers so as to provide round the clock service by two doctors at a time. There will be one nursing orderly attached to each of the doctors. In order to facilitate domiciliary services two vehicles should be attached to each of the poly clinics. Direct telephone should be provided exclusively for the use of the domiciliary service department. Once the new system comes into operation, the dispensary doctors will not have the responsibility of answering any of the domiciliary calls. Hence no conveyance allowance need be paid to them. The savings thus effected can be utilised for meeting the expenditure in connection with employing extra doctors and other staff for manning the domiciliary and emergency services.

The specialist should not be called directly by any beneficiary for domiciliary visits. They can only be called in consultation with any one of the doctors employed under the scheme.

The Committee recommends the following staff for each poly clinics—

Consulting And Diagnostic Service

Staff Surgeon (Physician)	1
Staff Surgeon Junior (Physician)	1
Staff Surgeon (Surgeon) (Ear, Nose and Throat)	1
Staff Surgeon (Eye)	1
Staff Surgeon (Gynaecology)	1
Staff Surgeon (Radiology)	1
Staff Surgeon (Dental)	1
Clinical Pathologist	1
Biochemist	1
Bacteriologist	1
Refractionist (non-medical)	1
Sister	1
Staff Nurses	5
Staff Nurse (X-Ray)	1
Clerks (specialists) Clerks (X-ray) Clerks (Laboratory)	6
Pharmacists	2
Laboratory Technicians	3
Laboratory Assistants	3
Radiographers	2
Dental Hygienist	1
Dark Room Assistant	1
Physiotherapist	1
Nursing orderlies	2
Peons	10
Sweepers	3
Chowkidar	1
Staff for Central Sterilisation and Supply	
Nursing orderlies	4

Domiciliary And Emergency Service

Medical Officers	6
Nursing Orderlies	6
Drivers	6
Cleaners	2

The central suppy service will supply sterilised dressings, etc., to the zonal dispensaries and to the specialists at the poly clinics.

Specialist's Medicines

Since specialists services are to be centralised at the poly clinics level, arrangement should be made for the patients to get special medicines prescribed by the specialist at the poly clinic. It should, however, be ensured that only two days' medicine will be made available to the patients. It medicines are prescribed for more days, they should be obtained from the respective dispensaries for the remaining periods.

The poly clinic should be specially designed and constructed in such a way that all the services enumerated above are provided adequately. Broadly speaking, there should be a consulting room for each specialist, a laboratory with three sections for clinical pathology, bacteriology and biochemistry, an X-ray department with rooms for Radiography, fluoroscopy, developing and for electro-therapy, a minor operation theatre with its own wash-up and sterilising room, accommodation for central sterilization supply services, dispensing room with store room, office for the officer-in-charge and administrative staff, duty rooms for the two emergency duty doctors, adequate number of lavatories, garages for the vehicles and ambulances. Pending the construction of permanent buildings for the poly clinics, the committee recommends that rental accommodation may immediately be obtained so that the poly clinics should start functioning without delay.

It is suggested that one of the poly clinics might be located at each of the two main hospitals, Safdarjang and Willingdon. This will mean that the specialist wings of the two hospitals will not only continue but will also be expanded to provide all the services enumerated above. The Poly Clinics located in the hospitals should have in addition to the staff already mentioned, a senior staff surgeon (consultant) for each of the specialities. The surgical and medical divisions should be further strengthened each by the addition of two Junior Staff Surgeons. The hospital poly clinics will no doubt have their own laboratories and X-ray facilities intended exclusively for the Contributory Health Service Scheme. The Committee is strongly of the view that while the consultants will continue to be located in the hospital poly-clinics permanently, the staff surgeons will be rotated between the regional poly clinics and the hospital poly clinics. This will enable the specialits to do hospital work periodically.

Ambulance Service

When separate hospitals under the scheme are established, the Ambulance Service may be located at the hospitals. In the interm period, the Committee suggests that one ambulance may be stationed at each of the five poly clinics.

Hospitalisation

The Contributory Health Service Scheme at present does not provide for separate hospital facilities. The beneficiaries have to take their turn in getting admissions to hospitals with other patients. No doubt once they are hospitalised their treatment is free. The present arrangement, however, is unsatisfactory because it involves considerable amount of delay particularly for those suffering from chronic ailments and for those who require cold surgery. The Committee recommends that Contributory Health Service Scheme should take up the responsibility for hospitalisation as well. For this purpose, it is essential to establish two hospitals with 250 to 300 beds each. Out of the 600 beds which might be made available in both the hospitals put together, 150 to 200 should be reserved for obstetrics and gynaecology. Since, however, all the needs for maternity service may not be met in the two hospitals, present arrangement that has been made with maternity and child welfare centres and the women's hospitals in the city may continue and extended if necessary to other hospitals. The Committee is of the view that when certain highly specialised services like cardiac surgery, neuro-surgery, special treatment for respiratory diseases are needed, facilities available in other institutions, like the All India Institute of Medical Sciences and the Vallabhbhai Patel Chest Institute, etc., may be utilised.

Medicaments

For the Contributory Health Service Scheme the establishment of a separate medical stores is a must. The accommodation provided for it at present is inadequate. The Committee recommends that a separate building for the medical stores may be constructed for the purpose. On the establishment of the two proposed hospitals under the Scheme, the Committee recommends that the medical store-depot may be located at each of the Hospitals.

The medical stores depot is inadequately staffed to handle the work of indenting and supply of medicines to 40 and odd dispensaries. The Committee recommends that staffing pattern should be the same as that of the Government medical stores depots under the Directorate General of Health Services.

In regard to the procurement of medicines the

Committee recommends that the Vocabulary Medical Stores items may continue to be indented from the medical stores depots under the Directorate General of Health Services. Other special preparations of proprietary nature account for about two-thirds of the total expenditure on medicaments and are at present being procured through the Director General of Supplies and Disposals, which constitutes the main bottleneck in the procurement of medicines It is recommended that the Director, contributory Health Service Scheme, be authorised to procure all these preparations direct from manufacturers or sole distributors after inviting tenders.

One of the complaints of the beneficiaries was about the quality of preparations at the dispensaries. The Committee recommends that the Disectorate General of Health services may draw up a list of manufacturers of standing and repute and quotations may be called from them.

The Committee further recommends that all the dispensaries should be adequately stocked with the preparations on the general and specialist. The local purchases should be the minimum. The general list should be progressively enlarged by transfering more preparations from the specialist. These lists should be periodically reviewed.

It is also recommended that no patent medicines, vitamins or hormons should be given to any persons as tonics.

Positive Health And Prevention

The Committee notes with satisfaction that the authorites have made some important beginnings in regard to the promotion of positive health and prevention of diseases.

Physical Check-up : At present, there is one physical check-up unit which, in the opinion of the Committee, is inadequate. To begin with, it is suggested that one physical check-up unit should be located at each of the poly clinics. The physical check-up should include routiue radiological examination ; hence the need to locate the check-up unit at a place where facilities for this purpose exist.

Yoga Classes : The Committee welcomes the yogasanas scheme recently organised under the contributory Health Service Scheme, but is not in a position to offer any observations on the benefits accruing of it. As a matter of fact it is too early to evaluate the results.

Family Planning : Judicians spacing of additions to the family is desirable not only from the point of view of the health of the mother but also from the point of view of the control of population. The Committee recommends that more emphasis may be given to family planning programme. For this purpose additional family planning centres may be established to have one centre for 20,000 beneficiaries.

Prophylaxis : Immunisation programme against diphtheria tetanus and pertussis is still in early stages and is yet to get into full swing. The Committee hopes that adequate steps would be taken to ensure systematic immunisation of the susceptible population among the beneficiaries. For this purpose, it would be worthwhile to maintain special records of all children under 10 years of age. Such records may be maintained at the dispensaries showing the dates of immunisation with triple vaccine. It may be necessary to engage special clerical and inocculation staff for a period of a year or so.

It would also be relevant to emphasise the importance of T.A.B. vaccination. The heavy incidence of enteric group of fevers all the year round and the consequent high cost of curative treatment makes such a measure imperative both from prophylactic and financial points of view. The Committee was informed that in the first six months of 1961, the cost of one drug (chloramphenical) alone amounted to about Rs. 21,000. The Committee suggests that intensive publicity should be undertaken to popularise the value of prophylactic measures against diphtheria, whooping cough and enteric group of fevers through posters exhibited at all dispensaries. The services of the Family Planning Field staff may also be utilised for this.

Morbidity Survey And Vital Statistics

The Committee notes with great satisfaction the progress made by the Statistical Section of the Contributory Health Service Scheme in making morbidity survey of the population covered by the Scheme. This is being done in collaboration with the Indian Council of Medical Research. Such a survey will have to be a continuing process in order that reliable data can be obtained periodically. The Committee, however, feels that it is essential to strengthen, the statistical organisation of the Scheme in order that comprehensive vital data can be collected and collated. Such data will be not only useful for the Contributory Health Service Scheme but also for the country as a whole particularly in view of the fact that very little reliable morbidity data are available.

Central Workshop

To ensure maintenance of vehicles in working condition as also to put them back on road without avoidable delay, it is suggested that a central workshop under the charge of a trained engineer may be set up for the servicing and repairs of the ambulances, and other vehicles attached to the medical stores depot and poly clinics. This workshop could preferably be located along with the Medical Stores Depot.

Extension Of The Scheme

While recommending the continuation of the contributory Health Service Scheme in Delhi and New Delhi, the Committee feels that the present working may be consolidated and the Scheme extended to such other Central Government servants at Delhi as are not at present covered by it.

Other Systems Of Medicine

During the course of evidence, a number of beneficiaries pointed out that they should, under the Scheme, be able to have access to other systems of medicine. The Committee feels that the Government may consider the desirability of providing consultation in other systems of medicine.

Other Relations Of The Employee

A certain section of beneficiaries suggested that the definition of 'family' may be enlarged to include brothers and sisters who reside with the employee. The Committee does not recommend the inclusion of any other category of relative over and above those now entitled to medical care.

Name Of The Scheme

The medical officers said that the prefix "contributory" in the name of the Scheme gave an impression of its being financed out of the contributions of beneficiaries ; the patient has thus a false idea of his essentially being a giver. They suggested that the Scheme may be called. "The Central Government Health Service Scheme". The Committee feels that the acceptance of this suggestion will not in any way affect the genuine partnership between the individual and the State for the proper working of the Scheme. It, therefore, recommends the dropping of the word "contributory" and renaming of the Scheme as suggested.

Compendium Of Rules And Instructions

A Scheme of the nature of Health Insurance creates an array of rights and obligations. To give effect to them adminstrative routine must be laid down. The Committee observed that the criticism of the scheme was partly due to the beneficiaries, not having its proper appreciation. It was informed that the beneficiaries, even in the higher wage groups, were not aware how to get medical care in a real emergency. The Committee recommends that the Government should undertake to put out precise instructions for the guidance of beneficiaries detailing the different services and the method of availing these.

Training Programme

The Committee is of the view that it is essential for the doctors employed in the Contributory Health Service Scheme to be up-to-data in their knowledge of different branches of medical science particularly because of the fact that enormous advances are being made every year in this field. For this purpose, it will be necessary to provide proper facilities for conducting Refresher Courses periodically. Such courses can be arranged in conjunction with the different teaching institutions in Delhi.

As promotions in the service will necessarily depend upon postgraduate training and qualifications, the junior doctors in particular should be provided with opportunities for undergoing the different postgraduate courses in which they are interested. For this purpose, they should be given study leave periodically. Some of them, particularly the specialists, might be given fellowships to go abroad solely for the purpose of gaining more practical experience in their respective fields. It will also be desirable to send senior specialists periodically on short observation tours in order to enable them to get acquainted with rent developments made in medical sciences in other countries.

The Committee is of the view that the Contributory Health Service administration should periodically meet different categories of staff and arrange for talks on personnel management, doctor patient relationship, community health, corporate life, etc. It will be desirable to inculcate the spirit of service in the minds of all categories of staff. Since the mind has considerable influence over the body, people practising the act of healing will accelerate the process of recovery in a patient by adopting a sympathetic attitude and by kind words of comfort and solace.

Incentives

In any field of human-endeavour, healthy competition contributes to rapid progress and development. There should be annual competition among dispensaries and a shield should be awarded for the best dispensary service. Similarly, awards should be introduced for those among the different categories of staff who have been found most efficient during the year. The Committee feels that provision of such incentives will greatly assist in the successful working of the Scheme.

Regional Councils

Mention has been made previously of the working of the Contributory Health Service Scheme Advisory Committee, its constitution and functions. The Committee, considers that it may be a good idea to extend the area of such collaboration with the representatives of the beneficiaries at the periphery also. It is, therefore, suggested that Regional Councils be constituted for the purpose. These councils will have on them the welfare officers, all medical officers incharge of all dispensaries of the group, representatives of different services and of resident associations and such other nominated element which might be considered helpful. They shall function as advisory bodies within the rules to be framed for the purpose and will enable all sectors concerned to occasionally set together and discuss such matters, as might crop up from time to time and have local significance, and find solution for them without their having to go to higher levels.

Administrative Organisation

With the increasing number of benificiaries to be catered to and the consequent expansion of the Contributory Health Service Organisation as a whole, it is considered necessary to augment and strengthen the administrative set-up. The Committee is strongly of the view that the Director of the Scheme should be a wholetime officer without any collateral duties to perform. Though in the beginning stages of the Scheme, the administration could be administered by the officers of the Directorate. General of Health Services, it is not possible to do so at present as the Scheme has expanded enormously.

The expenditure itself shows nearly 135 per cent increase during the last few years. Medicines worth nearly Rs. 38 lakhs are bought and disbursed annually. Several hundreds of officers and other categories of staff are employed under the Scheme. It is also very likely that the scheme will be expanded in the very near future in order to make it more efficient and comprehensive. In the circumtances, the Committee feels that there should be a provision of an Assistant Director General and an Assistant Director Statistics in addition to the existing administrative staff at the headquarters.

Besides the above, it will be desirable to strengthen the other categories of staff as well.

Financial Implications

It is estimated that the additional expenditue involved on the basis of the recommendations made in this Report would come to the tune of about Rs. 6.6 lakhs as non-recurring and Rs. 20.6 lakhs annually on recurring items. A break-up of th s may be summarised as under :

(a) Non-recurring :

	Rs.
(i) Five X-Ray Plants for Screening as well as Radiography	2.50,000
(ii) Laboratory Equipment—Five sets	1,25,000
(iii) Five Ambulances	1,25,000
(iv) Ten Domiciliary Duty Vehicles	1,60,000
Total Non-recurring	6,60,000

(b) Recurring :

(i) Expenditure on Additional Dispensary Staff	7,85,000
(ii) Expenditure on Poly Clinics	9,85,000
(iii) Emergency Staff	2,90,000
Total Recurring	20,60,000

Total recurring annual cost of the Scheme as a result of incorporation of these recommendations is expected to rise from Rs. 66.65 lakhs to the tune about Rs. 87.25 lakhs. This raises the average annual cost per employee per annum to Rs. 82.31 as compared with Rs. 62.8 at present. The net expenditure payable by the Government would, however, came to the tune of Rs. 54.00 lakhs as against Rs. 33.40 lakhs actually incurred by the Government during the year 1960. This works out to Rs. 50.94 per employee per year as against Rs. 31.51 at present. The Committee is of opinion that the extended nature of the medical facilities proposed would bring greater satisfaction both to the Government and the beneficiaries.

As the setting up of poly clinics is likely to take some time in order to afford immediate relief to the medical officers; action should be taken for the appointment of night duty medical officers on the basis of one doctor for each group of dispensaries joining togther for this purpose. The cost of this will only come to about rupees one lakhs per year.

IMPORT AND EXPORT POLICY COMMITTEE, 1961—REPORT

Delhi, Manager of Publications, 1962, iiip.+iiip.

Chairman : Shri A. Ramaswami Mudaliar.

Members : Shri G. L. Bansal ; Shri E.P.W. Da Costa ; Shri P.A. Narielwala ; Shri J.M. Lall (died, His place was taken by Shri N.M. Wagle) ; Shri S.M. Shah ; Shri H.L. Khanna ; Shri

B.K. Kochar.

Secretary Shri M.P. Mathur (replaced by Dr. S.P. Chablani).

APPOINTMENT

The Import and Export Policy Committee was constituted under the Government of India, Ministry of Commerce and Industry vide their Resolution No. 7/2/61-Imp. Pol., dated March 30, 1961.

TERMS OF REFERENCE

(i) To enquire into the working of Import Trade Control with particular reference to :

(a) The procedures followed in the formulation of import policy and methods followed in dealing with applications for import licences to the different categories of applications ;

(b) The organisation of the existing machinery for Import Control ;

(c) Any other matter incidental to the working of Import Control Organization.

(ii) To examine questions relating to allocations for import of raw materials and capital goods with special references to the requirements of the Third Five-Year Plan.

(iii) To review the efficiency of the existing export promotion measures and to make recommendations with regard to measures necessary to step up exports in the Third Five-Year Plan period.

CONTENTS

Preamble ; The Problem ; Import Policy and Procedure ; Export Promotion ; Rupee Payment Arrangements State Trading, etc. ; Miscellaneous Matters ; Summary of Conclusions and Recommendations ; List of Appendices A to J.

RECOMMENDATIONS

The Problem

The Third Five-Year Plan

The Third Plan starts with a legacy of valuable past experience of large-scale planning, as well as with depleted exchange reserves, a sizeable foreign debt; with virtually no net 'invisible' over-sea income, and a yawning gap in balance of payments. The country has taken in hand the formidable task of creating, within the course of a decade, a self-propelling economy, capable of supporting a high level of investment and employment.

Foreign Exchange Requirements

The balance of payments position will continue to remain under severe strain for many years. If the bill for 'Maintenance' imports goes up, the country would have to redouble its efforts to augment its exports to honour its financial commitments and maintain its credit in the international market. The annual import requirements of the succeeding plans will be even larger; so will be the repayment obligations on account of debt services and interest charges. Already, the country is functioning under a system of stringent import and exchange restrictions. There is little scope for further curtailment of foreign exchange expenditure.

Defence Requirements

We have not dealt with the import requirements of our Defence industries and the export possibilities of some of them. A great deal could perhaps be done to conserve—and earn—foreign exchange through an integral policy for the whole economy. A Commission of Enquiry may be appointed to go into the matter, necessarily working "in camera".

The Task

Overall, it will be necessary to see to what extent the available resources in foreign exchange can be used more economically ; how best the country's stock of resources can be distributed to yield an optimum return; to what extent existing capacity can be more fully utilised to enlarge production and augment exports; how far indigenous sources can be more fully tapped for the supply of equipment and raw materials ; what measures of import-saving and export promotion can be installed.

Export Targets

The task of elevating India's exports to twice their present level by the end of the Fourth Plan, will require effective measures which will demand the whole hearted cooperation of all sectors of the economy.

Import Policy And Procedure

Objectives Of Import Control

The objectives of Import Control as enunciated by official spokesmen are unexceptionable ; but the question is one of translating these principles into practical terms, and of evolving the right kind of import priorities.

Maintenance Vs. Development Imports

The present controversy is due to a misconception about "industrial capacity". For an objective assessment of the problem, only the "effective capacity" can be taken into consideration. 'Maintenance' and 'Development' of the economy are two facts of the same phenomenon, and there can be no hard and fast dividing line between them. There are certain 'developments' which are necessary for keeping even the existing industrial units in full production, such as, for instance : (a) power, (b) transport and (c) industries producing raw materials and components for the existing units which are presently being imported and vice versa.

It is also sometimes forgotten that considerable new 'development', apart from being necessary in itself, is financed out of the 'tied aid', which is not available for financing 'maintenance' imports. There is, therefore, little choice in these cases. Also in order to keep the wolf of inflation at bay, the country has per force to 'maintain'/'develop' industries catering for the primary needs of the population. Precedence has also to be given to the 'development' of 'export-oriented' industries. Thus, there can be no rough and ready solution to the theory of 'maintenance' first and 'development' afterwards and vice versa. The country can neither freeze pattern of the economy, nor allow its stagnation. A balance has to be struck pragmatic and selective, designed to stimulate the dynamic spread of the cumulative process of economic growth and to disperse and diversify the economy in consonance with the objectives of the Plan.

All considered, the policy, in brief, should be to give facilities for the import of raw materials and components, etc., to all existing industries, subject to overriding priority being given to certain types of new industries described in para 11.

The criteria followed at present in respect of the licensing of industrial establishments or the import of capital goods are still somewhat general. What is necessary is a systematic and scientific review, industry by industry, to determine how best production can be augmented, costs reduced, imports saved and exports developed. The relative merits of 'maintenance'/'development industries would have to be objectively assessed. The progress of some of the typical existing 'maintenance' and 'development' industries should be evaluated.

Unutilised Capacity

A part of the industrial capacity in the country is unutilised. But in the absence of precise information, it is difficult to make an assessment of the extent to which the country is industry is under-utilised or otherwise; and to guage the extent to which production could be augmented by providing balancing equipment and other feeders of industry.

The development wing may, therefore, be charged with the special responsibility of constantly reviewing the problem of under-utilisation of industrial capacity and of recommending remedial measures. The results of such reviews should be published annually.

Study Of Problems Of Import Substitution

It is also necessary to study more closely the question of substitution of imported materials in its widest connotation and to see to what extent and in what manner indigenous products can effectively replace the imported stores ; how they can be commercially developed and used. Whichever may be the agency responsible for this task, the assistance of institutes like the National Laboratories could well be enlisted in solving some of the technical problems.

Scope For Further Import Restriction Limited

The solution to the problem of bringing the balance of payments in equlibrium lies not in further import restrictions—the scope of which is severely limited, but within limits, in augmenting specific imports to remove the bottle neck exports. The present stringent import restrictions and rigid exchange allocations may continue in respect of production destined for the domestic market. But where exports can be really assured, Government should have no hesitation in making available such raw materials and balancing equipment as are essentially required.

The volume of incentive to be given to emerging industries will need to be substantially larger than in the case of our traditional items of exports. The differential which exists between Indian costs and those of our competitors will have to be considerably abridged if our products are to enter significantly into international trade.

Need For Good Understanding

There would have to be a basic understanding between Government and the mercantile community, and mutual respect and sympathy for the difficulties, needs and obligations of either side. A selective approach may be made, to start with, with the more well run units of industry. They may be invited—on the basis of a proper assurance of all round assistance—to come forward with an integrated programme of industrial and export expansion.

Primarily, this assistance should be given to stimulate additional exports ; and there should be no objection to giving assistance on a 'loan basis', subject to necessary safeguards, where government is satisfied on the merits and bona fides of the case.

Every proposal of this kind would require detailed examination. After completion of the technical scrutiny the case should invariably come up before an inter-ministerial sub-committee.

Complementary Advance Of Agriculture

The cardinal importance of the complementary advance of commercial crops and their impact on industrial development and export promotion has not been sufficiently appreciated. A serious attempt should be made to review the role which agriculture, horticulture, fisciculture and forestry can play in our economic progress.

Licensing Procedure

Imort procedure plays a vital part in the execution of import policy. The procedure should be capable of efficient execution of policy.

Import control is a service organisation. The public pays for its services and, naturally, expects from it a high degree of proficiency, quick disposal and integrity. Despite improvement of efficiency in the C.C.I's office (the pendencies being only 0.6 per cent), there has been general complaint of delays, which can have far-reaching consequences, and cost the country dearly in foreign exchange. This aspect should be impressed on all concerned.

Solution Of Delays

The solution of delays lies in simplification of procedure, decentralisation of work, etc. Our suggestions in this regard are detailed below.

Simplification Of Procedure

Annual Licensing

All important licensing should, in future, be done on an annual basis. Development of indigenous production is by no means so revolutionary as to justify halfy-yearly revisions of import policy. The basic content of an import licence, over the year, should remain intact. If possible, exchange, budgetting, too, should be done on an annual basis. If, on grounds of foreign exchange, it becomes necessary to follow a more stringent policy for the second part of the licensing year, a general percentage reduction could be applied by one single public notice to all import licences. Annual licences should be issued on the basis of a single application, duly accompanied by twice the normal fee (in taken of two licences issued in one operation).

Period Of Validity Of Import Licences

In view of the genuine difficulties of importers, it is proposed that: (i) the initial validity should be one year in the case of Actual Users' and Established Importers' licences and two years for CG/HEP licences except CG/HEP licences issued against 'tied' credits such as the 'Ex-im Bank' Loans, in which case the validity period should be one year, as at present; (ii) Actual Users' licences should be revalidated upto six months, and CG/HEP licences upto one year, upon request, without requiring the licences holder to produce evidence as to the unavailability of supplies; (iii) except in the cases of licences issued against 'tied' credits, the power of revalidation should be delegated to the regional licensing authorities; (iv) normally, the validity of Established Importers' licences would not be extended; but in special circumstances, such licences may be extended by three months.

I.V.C. Number

On balance, it is proposed that the present system of I.V.C. numbers may remain; but henceforth they should be valid for three (annual) licensing periods.

S.S.I. Committee

The regional offices have to refer certain cases to Headquarters for instructions regarding disposal. These cases are considered by the S.S.I. Committee, whose recommendations are transmitted to the licensing authorities along with the applications/files for disposal. Time would be saved if instead of remitting the cases back to the licensing authorities, the execution of the S.S.I. Committee's recommendations is done at Headquarters. The clarifications/appeals, too, could be attended to at Headquarters.

C.C.I.'s Ad Hoc Committee

C.C.I.'s Ad hoc Committee should be more fully representative of the concerned technical officers of the development wing; and it should be possible to take decisions on the applications in the committee itself, in the same way as does the S.S.I. Committee. Cases, involving special difficulty, could be seen on the file by the technical officers concerned, wherever necessary.

Scheduled Industries

There is a general complaint about the long delays in the disposal of applications for the import requirements of scheduled industries. It is proposed that where an application has to be scrutinised by more than technical Directorate, the sponsoring Directorate should try to clear it at an inter-Directorate meeting. The institution of such meetings, to be held every week or fortnight, should be encouraged.

Non-Scheduled Industries

While issuing the 'Essentiality Certificates' the Directors of Industries do not always follow a uniform policy C.C.I. should evolve, on the eve of the licensing period, the general criteria for assessing 'essentiality, in consultation with the Directors of Industries.

Register Of Raw Material, Components, Plant And Machinery

The Development Wing should bring out annually a comprehensive register indicating the availability of raw materials and components, plant and machinery produced in the country, the names of the producers and full information in regard to their installed capacity, actual production, specification, etc.

Monetary Ceilings

Information regarding monetary ceilings for each licensing head should reach all the licensing authorities on the eve of the licensing period.

Simplification Of Application Forms

The application forms for the various categories of import licences admit of some simplification. C.C.I.& E. should carefully go into this matter.

Decentralisation

Decentralisation Of Licensing work

There is still scope for further decentralisation. It is suggested that : (a) licensing of fresh fruits from Pakistan could well be decentralised, under a general policy laid down by the Chief Controller; (b) licensing of newsprint could be decentralised, as it is not necessary to consult the Registrar of Newspapers on each case ; (c) other requirements of printing industry (e.g., printing machinery, etc.) could be dealt with by the C.C.I.'s Ad Hoc Committee. Whenever necessary, the Registrar of Newspapers could be invited to be present ; (d) as C.C.I. has a full-fledged investigation division under him, all cases of investigation now dealt with by the 'news print cell', may in furture, be handled by the investigation division, in consultation with the Registrar of Newspapers, whenever necessary ; (e) quota licensing of greases and lubricants should be done at the regional offices.

Transfer Of Quotas

The entire T.Q.R. work can now be decentralized. Each regional office could have a small T.Q.R. Cell for the purpose. Cases of special difficulty could be referred to Headquarters for advice.

Public Relations

It has been complained that interviews cannot easily be had with the officers of the C.C.I. nor is it always possible to get a precise answer to the applicant's problems. The importance of good relations with the public should be underscored to all officers.

Attached to the personal staff of the C.C.I. should be a public Relations Officer of the rank of a Deputy Chief Controller *au fait* with the problems of Import Control, who should be able to sort out the importers' difficulties. The regional offices, too, should be assisted by P.R.O.'s of the rank of Controller/Assistant Controller.

Organisational Changes

It is suggested that : (a) the regional office in Rajkot should be abolished ; and, instead, a regional office may be established in Ahmedabad, under a Deputy Chief Controller ; (b) there should be a similar office in Kanpur, with jurisdiction over U.P. ; (c) in view of transit difficulties, specially in winter, a sub-office, under and Assistant Controller, may be opened at Srinagar, with jurisdiction over the State of Jammu & Kashmir ; (d) there should be a similar office in Bangalore, with jurisdiction over the State of Mysore.

Miscellaneous Problems

Established Importers Vs. Actual Users

Status quo may remain. However, in the case of industries, with a large number of units, it will be an advantage if the imports of components, etc., are canalised through established importers to prevent undue locking up of foreign exchange.

Small value licences

Small value licences are wasteful of foreign exchange. But the abolition of the present system might lead to displacement of a large number of established importers. Recommend status quo. However, established importers may be permitted to effect their imports through agents on the basis of 'Letters of Authority,' which may be given freely to allow of 'clubbing' of 'small value' licences to prevent wasteful expenditure of exchange.

Ad Hoc Licensing

An exhaustive policy should be framed in respect of items licensed on ad hoc basis, by reviewing all cases over the past two years, and case laws evolved. There should be, basically, no ad hoc licensing, except in cases of emergency, or where the necessity of the import of any particular item could not be fore shadowed or a formal policy could not, for any reason, be evolved.

I.T.C. and I.C.T. Classifications

The institutional arrangements for resolving classification difficulties seem to be in order. But the existing arrangements need to be published. The I.T.C. authorities are planning to adopt the S.I.T.C., which is a detailed instrument of trade classification in international usage. If the customs authorities, too adopt the same, it might solve many of the classification difficulties. Also, the description of goods in the import licences should be as detailed as possible. If even so, there is a difference of opinion, the interpretation of the I.T.C. authorities should prevail for purposes of clearance ; the customs authorities being free to levy such import duty as they deem appropriate. A formal understanding to this effect should be reached between the two authorities.

Appeals

There should be a separate 'Appeals section' at each of the regional offices, so that the 'first-appeals' could be considered more formally and dispassionately.

Investigation

It should be impressed on the special police establishment that, normally, their investigations in respect of import control cases should be completed within 12 months. Where, however, an investigation cannot be completed so soon, the van on the issue of import licences should be removed after the expiry of two (half-yearly) licensing periods. This would mean that import licences in such cases would remain suspended for two licensing periods, and a final decision on the type and quantum of punishment would be taken in the light of the results of investigation. The proposal would perhaps necessitate an amendment of the Import Control Order, etc.

Legal Cell

There are over one hundred writ petitions against the C.C.I. It is highly necessary that the C.C.I's office should scan the 'Law Reporters' for the past several years and prepare a compendium of all judgements so far delivered, duly indexed and annotated in consultation with the Ministry of Law. A separate small 'Legal Cell' should be constituted at Headquarters to undertake the early compilation of the 'compendium of judgements' and to attend to the defence of the numerous writ petitions.

Export Promotion

Intricacies Of The Task

The task of doubling the country's exports and raising them to Rs. 1,300-1,400 crores per annum by the end of the Fourth Plan, would be a formidable one for any country. The export demand for our traditional items is by no means buoyant. It is also difficult to foreshadow what repercussion the 'economic communities' will have on the future course of Indian trade; but undoubtedly, India will have to make much more than ordinary efforts to boost her export business. The whole nation will have to crusade for the export markets-not only in traditional lines but along the entire front of exportable products.

The domestic market, ready at hand, offers more attractive, quick and easy returns. The incentives to efficiency become relatively weak; costs tend to go up, the quality goes down. The country has also not developed any great export tradition; much less the necessary export apparatus. A considerable part of India's overseas trade, specially her exports, goes via the entrepot countries; and only a fraction of trade is manned by Indian merchants.

Lacunae In Promotional Effort

The country has touched only a fringe of the export problem. Whereas targets of a high order have been theoretically drawn up, adequate steps have not yet been taken to dovetail the import-export targets with the plans and projects of development in the private and in the public sector and to lay the foundation of a big trade. This deficiency is beginning to be repaired, though slowly. The current arrangements are no more than mere 'promises' to export. Where the country's future is mortgaged, any casual acceptance of illusory export prospects at their face value is likely to lead to difficulties. Special attention should be paid to this problem and the 'promises' should be properly appraised in each case; appropriate bank guarantees obtained; failure to export would need to be suitable penalized; genuine difficulties will have to be gone into. A special, section, to be created in the Directorate of Export Promotion, should watch the performance of the assisted industries and ensure that the export obligations are duly respected.

A detailed and organised study should be made, industry-wise and commoditywise of the items that could be or should be released for export. These studies should be undertaken urgently, and actually, reflected in the export plans which should be an annual feature of the economy.

Export Climate

The high task of export promotion as envisaged in the plans will demand the willing and enthusiastic co-operation of every sector of the economy. The State Governments do not always seem to be alive to the primacy of export promotion; and source of their policies, particularly, in the fiscal field, have hindered the even flow of exports. The nation cannot afford to think and function compartmentally.

Export Business Must Become Worth Doing

The Government will have to carry the business community with it in its effort to make a break-through in the world market. The promotion of our trade depends upon the efficiency of our merchants and manufacturers. It is the business community that would have to shoulder the mainburden of responsibility of augmenting the country's export trade.

The mercantile community cannot be expected to be guided by altruistic or patriotic motives and will expect to receive, for its efforts in the export market, a return which stands in a reasonable relation with the profits on domestic sales. It would be government's responsibility to compensate the trade for its export effort through selective concessions, fiscal reliefs and other incentives to make the export business worthwhile over the long haul.

Revitalisation Of The Administrative Machinery

It will be necessary to have a coordinating machinery, sufficiently powerful to be able to cut through the tangles of conflicting inter-departmental interests, re-orient the thinking of the State Governments and reconcile their stand-points with the national objectives of export promotion. It should be capable of taking quick decisions on the day to day issues and of translating them into practical terms. The problem of securing surpluses for exports, cannot be left to the unaided efforts of private enterprise. It is a matter of supreme national concern—one in which the State must take a direct hand.

It is understood that government is proposing to strengthen the organisation for Export Promotion. This is a step in the right direction. We trust it will be adequately staffed and headed by an officer of sufficiently high status, so that the organisation may be able to pull its weight with other departments of government; secure recognition in the mind of the nation of the vital need for an all round, substantial, expansion in India's exports and make export promotion a profitable, and yet respectable and patriotic avocation.

The Directorate of Export Promotion should have a 'Policy Cell' like the 'Import Policy Cell' under the C C.I. It should be responsible for framing the export policy for specific items, and constantly review the aids and incentives given in other countries with the object of examining how far they can be adopted with advantage in India.

Aids And Incentivies

The incentives so far given have been only moderate and, indeed, often ineffective. India will have to emback on a much more adventurous policy of 'aids and incentives' to augment her export trade.

Increased Allocation Of Raw Materials

One of the most effective aids would be to permit of an increased allocation of raw materials to industry. A substantial part of the unutilised capacity is by far and large a reflex of shortage of imported raw materials, components and replacements. If additional raw materials could be imported say for Rs. 100 crores per annum, as suggested by Sir Donald Macdongall, they may well serve as the first basis for a substantially new attempt to break the bottleneck of raw materials. The fringe benefits flowing from increased production/additional exports may far outweigh the increased expenditure on the marginal imports required for a fuller utilisation of the industrial capacity or intensification of agriculture.

It is highly important that the existing export-oriented industries should be assured prompt and adequate supplies of essential raw materials at international prices so that they do not suffer from a price disadvantage in relation to their competitors abroad. On balance, India would stand to gain by under-writing in full the foreign exchange required for manufacturing goods for export. The production costs would thus be reduced; and it may well be that much of the differential that exists in some industries can be overcome merely by this provision.

A search will have to be made to find a foreign exchange allocation for these additional imports. If internal allocation of foreign exchange does not allow of any significant importation of marginally needed raw materials, stores and replacement equipment, the case studies could be put to the friendly countries; and perheps, on this plane, it may be possible to secure further assistance to put the Indian economy in an even keel.

Import-Export Stabilisation Fund

It may also be possible to finance the import of these additional raw materials through the media of a revolving fund which may be specially created for the purpose. There is reason to believe that groups of international banks may be agreeable to provide credits for import of raw materials to be used by approved exporters, who can be relied upon to fulfil undertakings on exports. It would be imperative to ensure that the foreign exchange so lent would be translated into export earnings to form the basis of what may be termed as the 'Import-Export Stabilisation Fund' which could be used to enhance the import of raw materials for the export industry. The arrangement would imply the matching of additional 'import credits' with export performance so as to augment both sides of the equation and to improve India's balance of payments in the process.

It will be necessary to have an Agency which will have all the authority of the Government to ensure high priority to these activities, but will also carry the conviction abroad that the funds made available for this purpose would not be diverted to domestic production. An autonomous body may be set up as soon as possible under the caption of 'Export Stabilisation Board'. The example of I.C.I.C.I. should serve as a useful guide. It wold have control over the export earnings and also possess statutory authority to negotiate credits for the import of raw materials to be translated into export earnings. When the revolving fund has attained the desired level, any surplus foreign exchange that may accrue would revert to Government.

For a provisional figure designed to increase India's exports by say Rs. 100 crores per annum, it might be necessary to place at the disposal of the 'importer-exporters' an additional sum of possibly Rs. 25 to Rs. 30 crores as a revolving fund to finance the requisite imports and to supplement them by indigenous stores, whenever possible, at prices corresponding to the competitive world standards.

Certain American firms have also shown interest in financing the import of raw materials and components required for our export-oriented industries, against rupee payments. The rupees so earned will be used by them for buying Indian commodities for their home market. Such arrangements—affording a line of 'untied' credit for the import of raw materials—need to be encouraged if, on merits, the terms offered by them are mutually beneficial.

Income-Tax Relief

One of the most powerful incentives for export promotion would be remission of income-tax on export earnings. Such a relief has been given by way of 'exporters' 'compensation' in some of the most advanced countries like Germany, France, Japan with considerable success. India might do something similar. Our initial idea was to confine the grant of income-tax remissions only to earnings from additional exports. But on further reflection it seemed to us that this may not be a step in the right direction, for—unless effective measures are taken to buttress our exports—their present level cannot be taken for granted. It is also felt that unless the remission of income-tax on additional export earnings is linked with the rebates on the basic exports, the system would fail, with serious loss of revenue to Government.

Having regard to all aspects of the case, a three-fold system of income-tax remission is proposed viz. :

(a) A tax remission of seven-and-a-half per cent on profits on 'Basic' exports ;

(b) A tax rebate of five per cent on all export earnings to enable the exporter to build an 'Export Development Reserve' ;

(c) A special tax remission of 10 per cent on earnings on 'additional' exports i.e. exports over the basic norm.

It is important to the success of this significant measure that the method of calculating the tax rebate should be simple. The Income Tax rebates proposed in this report would be based on the exporters' internal and exports turn over ; and it would not be necessary to make a meticulous calculation of their actual earnings by reference to their books of account. A tax remission based on a meticulous calculation might lead to acrimony between the exporters and the income tax Department.

The system proposed is so devised as to prevent the possibility of exporters' abusing the concession.

The details of the arrangement proposed have been explained at length in paras 37—46 at pp. 29—33

Enlargement Of The Scope Of Export Promotion

The incentive of 'currency retention has been tried with varying degrees of success in many countries. It is, however, not necessary to let the Indian exporters have a free hold on any percentage of their export earnings. Instead, the scope of the present 'Export Promotion Schemes' should be widened. The exporter's choice to import should not be limited to one or two items as is the case at present ; and exporters/manufacturers, under this arrangement, should be able to use their licences for any raw materials, components or equipment which they may care to import for the manufacture of the 'export product', subject to certain restrictions (vide para 50). Furthermore, the export Promotion Schemes need not, necessarily, be limited to certain specified items as is now the case, but should cover the whole range of items entering the export market. Further, if the imported Commodities are not required for a particular industry, they may be allowed to be sold to a sister industry. The aforesaid concession may be open to manufacturers as well as to exporters, though the entitlement of the mere exporter (or the manufacturer who does not intend to use the stores himself) may be only two-thirds of the manufacturer/exporter.

Freight Concessions

As Indian Commodities are facing intense competition, and as our oversea salesmanship is still weak, it will help the export effort is the Railways give a general rebate of, say, 25 per cent on all goods put on board. Where a Commodity requires a freight rebate beyond 25 per cent, a case would have to be made out. As export freight traffic is only a fraction of the total traffic of the Railways, the proposed concession is not likely to weigh heavily on the Railways.

Specific Assistance To Selected Commodities

The specific difficulties confronting our export industries will have to be tackled. For instance, tea, which is our foremost exchange earner, was not receiving its full requirements of fertilizer ; nor was it getting the supplies of fertiliser at the rare at which it is available to the agriculturists'. Curiously, the export of tea is still controlled, when supplies are plantiful. Export of tea should be decontrolled. Similarly, the exports of coffee suffer from fluctuating supplies. The possibility of stabilising the export quotas through the creation of a 'buffer stock' should be examined, and a larger proportion of 'plantation coffee', which yields a better price abroad, should be earmarked for exports. Exporters of marine products, too, are said to be charged exhorbitant prices for tin containers. Their refrigeration and quality control arrangements also need to be improved. As the industry offers promising prospects, its difficulties should be looked into more minutely.

Removal Of Disincentives

Drawback Of Import And Excise Duties

The incidence of import and excise duties on typical representatives of Commodities eligible for drawback should be worked out in consultation with the representatives of the industries concerned. On the basis of such a study a tariff of drawbacks should be drawn up for all, or at least the more important, items of export. An exporter claiming a drawback would have merely to produce evidence of having exported the particular cammodity in requisite quantum and value and having received the right amount in foreign exchange. No reference to his books of account would be necessary; and there would be no need to argue over the exact value of the imported raw material content in the exported commodity. Something in this direction is already being done; but the scope of the scheme needs to be enlarged to cover all, or at least the more important, items of export.

Remission Of Sales Tax

Most countries in the world give remission of Sales Tax an exported goods. In India Sales Tax is a State subject; and State Governments are highly averse to parting with their revenues. To cut through the tangles of this vexed question, the Central Government should assume the responsibility for the remission of sales tax entering into export costs; and they may make such financial readjustments with the State Government as they deem appropriate. The method of tax remission should be a simple one. A uniform rebate of say two per cent would be a help to the export effort.

Reimbursing Authority

For the sake of convenience of exporters, the drawback of import duties, the Excise and the Sales Tax should all be given at one central point most convenient to the exporter e.g. Collector ot Customs.

Other Measures

Participation In International Fairs

Indian pavilions in International Fairs are in the nature of 'grand exhibitions'. The participation is at Government level; and Indian merchants conversant with the intricacies of their business are conspicuous by their absence. Little business has flowed from our participation, except perhaps in East European countries where buying is canalized through State agencies. International fairs are forums of being business; then attract the world's foremost suppliers and biggest buyers. In such a setting the kind of 'Exhibition' which India generally offers does not fit in. India's policy in this regard, therefore needs to be re-oriented; and if an adequate number of the right type of Indian exporters/merchants/producers do not come forward, India need hardly participate in international fairs at all. But Indian exporters may find the task too venturesome. Government, therefore, could assist them by bearing (i) the rent of pavilion, incidental expenses, and the cost of management, publicity, freight of exhibits to and from the destination (This is already being met); and (ii) a part of the travelling costs of Indian participants. Subsidization of participants in international fairs is done even by an advanced country like Germany.

The best way perhaps would be entrust the entire work of participation in International Fairs to an independent 'body'—located in a city like Bombay or Calcutta. It might consist of nominees of Government, but should largely represent the chief exporting interests and be presided over by a distinguished member of the mercantile community. The composition of the proposed agency is described in Para 76. The Directorate should be redesignated as the 'Directorate of Fairs' and duly reorganised to deal only with questions of policy.

Liaison With Indian Merchants Abroad

There are hundreds of Indian Merchants playing a prosperous business abroad for generations. Their energies should be harvessed in the service of the nation. They should be called in conference, and the Directorate of Export Promotion should be in regular consultation with the Associations of our oversea merchants. Our Embassies and Consulates should be enjoined to make a vigorous effort to establish a close liaison with the Indian Merchants residing with in their beat.

Role Of Chambers Of Commerce

The Chambers of Commerce can play an important part in export promotion. They can liaise between trade and Government; they could keep government abreast of the happenings abroad; then can disseminate market information vital to the trading community. Chambers of Commerce in the advanced countries have their representatives abroad; and then supplement the work of the Trade Mission in servicing the country's foreign trade.

Tourism

India is a tourists' paradise. But tourism is not well developed in the country. It has been estimated that the country has lost over Rs. 2-1/2 crores last year, because of shortage of acceptable accommodation and lack of air passage. The economic possibilities of tourism should be objectively assessed; and measures should be devised to obviate the difficulties which discourage potential tourists.

It is suggested that (a) steps should be taken to augment proper hotel accommodation throughout the country and to improve travel facilities for the convenience of tourists; (b) facilities for cashing of traveller's cheques should be liberalised; (c) possibility of giving tourists' discounts, as in France and U. K. may be explored; (d) Customs officials should be more helpful; (e) in order to avoid inconvenience to the tourists, the Emigration and the Customs officials should invariably board the ship along with the pilot in mid-stream as was done in the past; and all formalities should be completed before the boat touches the pier, and the tourists allowed to disembark straightaway. Liquor permits, too, should be given to them on Board; and (f) there should be also a sizeable shopping centre at each air port to attract the custom of tourists.

Rupee Payment Arrangements, State Trading, Etc.

Rupee Payment Arrangements

Much has been said for and against the 'Rupee Payment Arrangements'. There may have been an element of diversion of some of our exports, but, on the whole the 'rupee payment' countries have offered in the net a worthwhile outlet as well as a new source of supply for essential goods at a time when foreign exchange has been particularly scarce. However, fullest care should be taken to ensure that imports from these countries are limited to such goods as are essentially required for the economy; and there should be no easing of the import restrictions just because the goods are comming under a rupee arrangement.

To safeguard against undue price mark up on goods coming from rupee-payment countries, it is necessary to have adequate price data. It is proposed that a study unit be instituted in the Ministry of Commerce and Industry. It should constantly enquire, review and compare the prices of products imported from the rupee sources as well as other centres of supply. We attach great importance to the collection of this data, and feel that it could be veritable source of exchange-saving.

A review of the pattern of export trade with these countries, when made with reference to the provisions of our trade agreements with them would suggest that some of these countries are not lifting the quantities prescribed in the Agreements. We feel that the situation would be remedied if all the contracts with the rupee payment countries were registered, so that the follow of our trade could be adequately studied and, if necessary, rearranged. It is strongly recommended that all export contracts should be registerd.

Role Of S.T.C.

Since its inception in 1956, the S.T.C. has come to play a significant role in the country's foreign trade. But there is a great deal of criticism of its activities.

The S.T.C. performs some important functions and has been created as an additional organ of trade to give effect to some of the economic policies of Government.

Consistently with its objectives, the S.T.C. has also to be a self-financing organisation. We do not think that the corporation's role was intended to be confined to trade merely with the certain countries, as has often been suggested, although trading with State Organisations and 'monopolies' would have to remain its principal activity. There is, on the whole, a field in which the S.T.C. can co-exist with private enterprise.

There is perhaps some justification in the criticism that the corporation has not quite succeeded in arranging timely imports; in ensuring satisfactory procurement arrangemenis from the point of view of price and quality; in holding the price line. The S.T.C., however, works under the directives of Government. If Governments were to issue its directives to the S.T.C. utilized the services of trade more fully, with proper safeguards against profiteering and malpractices, many of the complaints against the S.T.C. would disappear. The S.T.C. should also make greater use of the Chambers and Associations in the distributive trade and notify its ceiling prices for the information of the public. Clearly, the S.T.C. need to improve its public relations which seem to have been some what neglected.

It is also necessary that all export contracts with the 'Rupee payment' countries should be registered with the S.T.C, so that the implementation of the 'trade Plans' could be watched and it could be ensured that they remain in better balance. To keep the interested public abreast of the Import-Export arrangements with the 'Rupee payment' countries, the 'trade plans' should be published.

Barter Tarde

Trade is opposed to Barter trading. But in the conditions of today, barter arrangements often become necessary. Therefore, there need be no wholesale condemnation of the system, if additionality of trade, and a fair price return, could be assured.

Miscellaneous Matters

Compulsory Exports

It will not be in the best interests to make exports compulsory by statute. Instead the better course perhaps would be to undertake a campaign of public education to restrain consumption and to awaken the mercantile community to their responsibility to shoulder the burden of export promotion. Perhpas the leaders of Industry and Trade could be induced to levy a small voluntary cesson the product for domest'c consumption as has been done by the B:cyc'e industry. A Similar course is capable of wider application.

Quality Control

In view of the fact that Agmark and I.S.I. seals are unacceptable to various buyers abroad, having their own specifications, we feel that compulsory quality control or pre-shipment inspection is not feasible. There would be no point in imposing Indian Standards on the foreign importer. What is necessary to ensure is that the goods exported are in accordance with the specifications prescribed in the export contract. It is suggested that the Associations of trade must organise their own 'Inspectorate' to effect quality control and pre-shipment inspection. They must impose upon themselves a code of self discipline. Offenders could be put on the black list, which should mean their debarment from receiving any incentives or consideration proposed in this report.

Directory Of Exporters

The Indian Directory of Exporters leaves much to be desired. The preparation of the 'Directory' is a specialised job; and it would be well worth seeking the assistance of an expert under the T.C.M. or the German Technical Assistance Programme.

Export Risk Guarantees

In keeping with the Berne Convention, ERIC should guarantee expot risks upto a period of five years.

India will progressively become an exporter of Capital Goods and Equipment, and her 'construction Industries' are likely to play an increasingly important part in the future as earners of foreign exchange, the more so if we were to encourage the setting of 'consultation Bureaux' in collaboration with foreign enterpri es, so that India may be able to supply consultative service over a large technical field. ERIC would have to guarantee, in the future, export risks of much larger dimensions. Its scope should, therefore, be enlarged. Alternatively, the export risks beyond ERIC's prescribed powers could be either guaranteed by Government or re-insured with an organisation like the L.I.C. ERIC's management, too, should be enlarged to command greater confidence in the public mind.

Staff Of C.C.I. & E.

As the fortunes of trade depend so much on prompt action, it is apt to become impatient of any delays on the part of the Import Cartrol authorities; and complaints in this behalf have been voiced everywhere. It is felt that one of the causes of delay is the shortage of Staff which seems to be fully stretched. A realistic view of the staff requirements of the C.C.I. & E. should be taken, so that the organization may be able to function more effectively and proficiently.

Some of the measures which have been proposed on the procedural side are likely to ease somewhat the burden of the C.C.I. & E.'s office. But, on the other hand, it will have to prepare and issue 'certificates of basic export performance' to exporters, preferring claims for remission of income-tax which have been proposed. Their number would be considerable. Due regard need to be paid to this aspect of C.C.I.'s work, when sanctioning his staff. The C.C.I. & E. also does not seem to be adequately equipped to meet any sudden on rush of work such as may emanate, for instance, from the signing of a new trade agreement which may tend to trigger off a series of new problems in the initial stages. The best way to cushion his difficulties would be to place at his disposal a small 'squad', under a controller, which may be used to bulldoze any pendencies or arrears in whichever section then may be.

Application Fees

If necessary, the application fees for import licences could be revised to meet the extra expenditure on the additional staff. The trade should not mind a small increase in the scale of fees, provided it could be assured of prompt disposal of their cases. The revised fee structure is given in Appendix G.

Breath Of Fresh Air

One more fact which militates against efficiency is the present lack of mobility of the C.C.I. E's staff. They are not transferable, and gain no experience even of the departments dealing with other aspects of foreign trade. The system leads to inbreeding and stagnation and creates problems of vigilance. We are afraid that a similar situation is likely to arise in the Directorate of Export Promotion which is now being strengthened if, from the very inception, a system of 'inter-change' or 'delegation' is not conceived. It will be an advantage for the C.C.I. & E. and the Directorate of Export Promotion to have a common cadre so that the members of the staff would acquire more varied experience and introduce a breath of fresh air in the organisation. An interchange of officers between the Import and Export Control the Directorate of Export Promotion and the C.B.R. would also be mutually beneficial. It could be a simple system of delegation for a tenure, on a reciprocal basis, so that the inter se seniority of officers in the various organisations would not be affected, and, at the same time, they would acquire a more integrated experience.

Indian Trade Representatives Abroad

In the coming years the task of trade and economic promotion is going to be vitally important to the course of our economic development; and India's trade representatives will have to play an important part in the promotion of trade. The various tasks which they will be called upon to perform have been described in para 24, at p. 49 of the Report. In a word, India's Trade Representatives will have to be at once the eyes and the ears of the business community. This is by no means an amateur's job. It requires specialized knowledge and practical training in commercial and economic work, which many of the Indian trade representatives abroad do not possess. Often they do not have even the aptitude for this type of work; and, on the whole, the Indian business community, is none too enamoured of the performance of our accredited trade representatives abroad.

On Trade Representations abroad need to be vastly strengthened both in numbers and in the quality of personnel. It is our considered view that a greater measure of flexibility should be introduced in the staffing arrangements. The Ministry of Commerce and Industry have the primary responsibility for the maintenance and promotion of trade; and, naturally, they should have a major voice in the selection of officers for the commercial and even consular posts. It is also felt that all Consulates and Consulates-General should function primarily as trade promotion centres; and in selecting personnel for these posts due consideration should be given to qualifications, experience and aptitude in commerical economic matters.

India would do well to follow the British model under which the trade post's are manned partly by the Foreign Sercice personnel and partly by representatives of the Board of Trade. A pool of officers could be drawn from the Ministries of External Affairs and Commerce and Industry, including its attached offices of the Office of the Chief Controller of Imports and Exports and the Directorate of Export Promotion and to same degree from the open market. It would be a system of secondment of hand-picked officers of the two Ministries to the pool who would devote the better part of their life and energy to the promotion of economic matters overseas. The officers of the Ministry of Commerce and Industry would not, normally, be posted or promoted to the chancery; whereas the foreign service personnal of the pool would have occasional turns of 'political' assignments, and be entitled to rise as heads of 'posts' or 'missions' in course of time. But, overall, the emphasis in the career of such officers would be on the commercial and economic aspects; and they would be a class of 'commercially-oriented' officers of the Forign Service.

The officers of the pool should have a common cadre of inter se seniority so that then could aspire to legitimate promotion in their own turn as counsellors, Ministers, Consul-Generals or as Senior Trade Commissioners. The advantage of the proposed pool would lie in its flexibility, and in its capacity to offer a relatively large base of staff from which to draw 'oversea' officers for commercial posts. It would facilitate cross-fertilization of ideas between the home and oversea elements, and field more fruitful results.

Normally, the tenure of a commercial officer' abroad should be five years.

Our overseas officers on the commercial and economic side, need a great deal more grounding in their specialised fields; before then leave for their posts, it should be ensured that then go well equipped to their task.

REVIEW COMMITTEE FOR SOCIOLOGY IN INDIAN UNIVERSITIES, 1961—REPORT

New Delhi, University Grants Commission, 1966, 72p.

Chairman : Prof. M. N. Srinivas,

Members : Prof. S.C. Dube; Prof. Narmadeshwar Prasad; Prof. I.P. Desai.

Member-

Secretary : Dr. P. J. Philip.

APPOINTMENT

The Review Committee in Sociology, was appointed by the University Grants Commission in April 1961.

TERMS OF REFERENCE

The terms of reference of the Committee are as follows :

(i) To examine the standards of teaching and research in Sociology in Indian Universities ; and

(ii) To make recommendations with regard to the modernization and improvement of the course of study provided in this subject in our universities.

CONTENTS

Foreword ; Development of Sociology in India ; Existing Facilities ; Sociology as an Intellectual discipline ; Place of Sociology in Indian Universities ; The Objectives of Teaching Sociology ; Research in Sociology ; Summary of Observations and Recommendations ; Appendices from I to VI.

RECOMMENDATIONS

Sociology As An Intellectual Discipline

All societies in space and time constitute the subject matter of sociology, and the sociologist has to bring to bear a comparative approach to the study of the institutions in any one society. He has also to relate every feature of social life—economic, political, religious and legal—to the total social framework.

In recent years new and important specialisms are developing in sociology : the sociology of economic institutions, political sociology, sociology of knowledge, sociology of religion, sociology of education, sociology of law, sociology of kinship, etc. We need to train not only general sociologists but also sociologists in each of the above specialisms.

The relationship between sociology and other social sciences is one of mutual interdependence. In the analysis of various aspects of society sociologists need to take note of other disciplines such as history, economics and politics. At the same time sociological analysis of problems will provide new perspectives and insights for other scholars.

There is also a need for establishing a closer relationship between anthropology and sociology. While physical anthropology has only limited relevance to the study of sociology, the study of social anthropology is vital to the proper understanding of sociology. In universities which have strong departments of sociology, social anthropology should be developed within their fold. Similarly, in universities with sociologically-oriented departments of social anthropology, studies in sociology could be initiated with great advantage.

It is necessary to distinguish between sociology and social work. Social work is action-oriented and social work departments have to establish contracts with a variety of organisation for giving proper training to their student. In addition, involvement in social work produces an attitude of mind which may not be conductive to the development of sociology as an intellectual discipline which has as its aim the scientific understanding of the nature of human societies. A knowledge of sociology is, however, indispensable to social work both at the preparatory and research levels.

It would be desirable to have a combined honours course in the social sciences on the model of the Oxford PPE course. This would give the future social scientists, administrators and teachers a proper understanding of the close relationship between the different facets of social life.

Place Of Sociology In Indian Universities

There is at present a certain lack of uniformity in the content of courses, the number of prescribed papers and the core-compulsory and non-corepapers in sociology offered in the universities. It is necessary to give thought to the problem of bringing about some uniformity in the content and pattern of the courses while at the same time respecting the individuality of each department.

While it would not doubt be useful for the student to be familiar with the programmes followed in other countries at the undergraduate and postgraduate levels, the courses of study in our universities have to be organized to suit our own conditions and requirements. Sociological studies in the country have to be related to the social environment around the student.

Objectives Of Teaching Sociology

The intimate relation between sociological theory and empirical work must be brought home to the student at every stage. This will involve giving the student a certain amount of familiarity with social and political theory. These facts have to be borne in mind when framing syllabuses.

An empirical bias to the teaching of sociology can be imparted in several ways. Firstly, the papers at different levels may include the study of actual institutions such as marriage, family, class, caste and religion, particularly in papers relating to Indian Social Institutions and Social Change. Secondly, the student should be made to realise the importance of field work for the study of social institutions. It may not be possible to have field work at the B. A. (Pass) or (Honours) level. It is nevertheless necessary to ensure that there are some practical exercises at the B. A. (Honours) and the students are asked to collect censuses, describe elections, weddings, etc. It is necessary to have a paper on Field Work Methods and Techniques at the M. A. level, and it is desirable that students base their doctoral dissertations on field-research.

At the B. A. Pass or general level students may offer

only two or three papers in sociology as part of a 'liberal' education. The following papers are recommended :

(a) Elementary Sociology.

(b) Indian Social Institutions.

(c) Social Change.

The B. A. Honours course should also include these papers but they should be taught at a more advanced level. In addition, there ought to be a paper on Social Structure and Social Stratification, and a paper on Techniques and Methods of Research. Regarding 'non-core' papers, each department should have the freedom to choose them according to the specialisation of staff members. Some of the subjects which may be considered in this connection are : Social Psychology, Sociology of Kinship, Sociology of Religion, Sociology of Political Institutions, Sociology of Economic Institutions, Educational Sociology, Sociology of law, and the Sociological Study of a period in Indian History.

At the M. A. level there is usually a provisions for offering a dissertation in lieu of one of the optional papers. If dissertation are to be introduced at the M. A. level, they ought to be confined to those students who have passed B. A. honours with sociology obtaining at least high second class marks. The dissertations should not involve field-work as field work cannot be satisfactorily carried out while studying seven papers for the M. A. course. Facilities for field-work by M. A. students are also lacking in most sociology departments.

Research in Sociology

It may be desirable to introduce an intermediary degree, M. Litt., between M. A. and Ph. D. which will serve both as a terminal point and also as a preparation for the Ph. D. The M. Litt. course should consist of a dissertation and it may also include two or three papers. Where papers are part of the M. Litt. course, they will be used to deepen the student's grasp of theory enlarge his acquaintance with the problems of area etc. The dissertation should be between 100 to 150 pages. Candidates successful in the M. Litt. course should have no difficulty in obtaining the Ph. D. after two or three years of work. M. Litt. will prevent wastage at the Ph. D.

Only candidates with suitable qualifications, temperament and motivation should be registered for the Ph. D. degree. All registrations should be provisional in the first instance, and registrations should be confirmed or cancelled after a year depending on the progress shown by the student.

As research is a whole-time activity, it needs the full-time attention and devotion of the research scholar. Students should stay at the university while they are studying for the Ph. D. and meet their supervisors as frequently as they are required to do so. They should be allowed to remain absent from the university only if the nature of their research work necessitates this. Similarly, the tendency of Ph. D. students to take up jobs while they are working at their theses should be firmly discouraged. However, regular attendance and presence at the place of research may not be insisted upon in the case of teachers in the affiliated colleges and university departments but even they should be required to meet their supervisors at regular intervals.

Every university should impose a ceiling on the number of Ph. D. students that a teacher may guide. A teacher may take about three-four candidates and in no case should the ceiling exceed 10 students.

The recognition of a teacher for research guidance should not be automatic. The teacher's academic qualifications should be such as to enable him to be a supervisor. It would be good if each faculty has a committee of senior scholars to decide whether a teacher is qualified to guide Ph. D. students.

The Ph. D. degree should be awarded only when all the examiners appointed to evaluate the thesis unanimously agree that the candidate merits the award of the degree. The candidate should also be examined by means of a viva voce test.

Funds should be made available for the publication of approved theses, and also for encouraging research in the fundamental aspects of the subject which are at present being somewhat neglected.

Pursuit Of Excellence

Teachers should be enabled to take a term or two off from teaching in order to carry out research and to write up its results. The teacher-student ratios in departments of sociology will have to be favourable enough to enable teachers to do field-work. Block grants will perhaps be necessary for every department of sociology for carrying out field-work. The work of a department should be so arranged that the head's time is not taken up in administration and committee work. Administrative duties should be shared by all the teachers in the department and university rules should permit delegation and decentralization.

A few good departments in the country should be developed as centres of advanced study and be assisted liberally. To begin with, the programme should include the setting up of six centres, each with a different focus. These should be for sociological theory rural studies, urban studies, social change (including planning and development) methodology and communications.

PANEL FOR SCIENCE LABORATORIES AND EQUIPMENT HIGH/ HIGHER SECONDARY SCHOOLS, 1961—REPORT

New Delhi, Committee on Plan Projects, 1962. 42p., 1 Chart

Chairman : Dr. K.N. Mathur.
Members : Shri S.K. Sen; Smt. S. Doraiswami; Shri M.H. Pandya; Shri G. Baderia; Shri G.S. Barotia (replaced by Shri Rajendra; Prasad); Shri T.P. Singh; Shri B.K. Ishrish.
Member-Secretary : Shri Jagadish Singh.

APPOINTMENT

At the instance of Delhi Administration a panel for Delhi Higher Secondary School Buildings was set up by the committee on Plan Projects in June, 1960. The panel studied in detail the building requirements of higher secondary schools as suggested by the Education Department, Delhi, keeping in view particularly the specific needs of the comprehensive syllabus prescribed by the Board of Higher Secondary Education. The Government School Buildings constructed, heretofore, were meant for high school classes where the syllabus was not as extensive and the existing buildings could not, therefore, meet the need of the higher secondary syllabus. Besides, working out the details of the instructional, administrative and ancilliary accommodation required in a higher secondary school, the Panel made a study of the needs of laboratories and their furniture and fittings, keeping in view the special needs of the higher secondary syllabus.

The report on Delhi School Buildings embodying these recommendations was circulated to the State Governments who evinced great interest in the norms laid down in the report. The Government of Mysore held a Seminar on School Buildings. At their request the Committee on Plan Projects deputed two of their representatives to participate in the deliberations. The norms laid down by this Panel were accepted at this Seminar. Bihar Government also set up a "Committee for Secondary School Buildings" to examine the question of construction of buildings and laboratories for high/higher secondary schools/multipurpose school especially with a view to reducing construction cost while ensuring adequate accommodation.

Since the scope of study of this Panel was restricted to the special requirements of higher secondary schools in Delhi, it was felt desirable to make a more comprehensive and extensive study to lay down norms and standards for science laboratories and equipment for high/higher secondary schools at an all India level. This was considered all the more necessary since the number of higher secondary schools by the end of the Third Plan is expected to rise to 6,390 from 3,121 at the end of the Second Plan. The Third Plan also gives special importance to science education. In addition to providing general science in all the secondary schools as a compulsory subject more than 9,500 out of 21,800 secondary schools are to have science as an elective subject.

Accordingly, a broad based and composite Panel for Science Laboratories and Equipment was set up. The Panel was constituted in May, 1961.

TERMS OF REFERENCE

The terms of reference of the Panel were as follows :

(i) To fix norms and to suggest lay-outs for science laboratories for Physics, Chemistry, Biology and Home Science in High/Higher Secondary Schools;

(ii) To suggest standard sets of equipment and apparatus both for practical work and demonstration for all the various laboratories;

(iii) To lay down specifications and standards for equipment and apparatus and suggest procedure for quality control.

(iv) To suggest simplification of procedure for allotment of funds and procurement of equipment, etc.;

(v) To examine the possibilities of having a centralised agency for the manufacture and procurement of science equipment.

(vi) To consider the possibilities for simplification of method of work in the laboratories.

CONTENTS

Introductory; Planning of Laboratories; Equipment and Apparatus; Other Recommendations; Appendix I List of Equipment and Apparatus; Appendix II-Layout Plans.

RECOMMENDATIONS

Planning Of Laboratories

Basic Requirements

Since the main function of a laboratory is to impart scientific education in an efficient way, its design should, therefore, be based on functional requirements. In determining the total area for a laboratory, the following factors were taken into consideration :

(a) The number of pupils working at a time.

(b) The minimum space necessary for each pupil for comfortable work, taking into account the subject of study and the prescribed syllabus.

(c) The necessity for providing some flexibility in the accommodation to give an opportunity to the teachers to regroup the classes so that demonstration experiments could be carried out conveniently with the participation of the pupils. This will also allow for changes in syllabus that may be necessary to keep pace with scientific progress.

(d) Ancillary accommodation such as :

(i) Room far storage of equipment and apparatus;

(ii) Dark-room, for certain experiments,

(iii) Balance room for chemistry laboratory, and

(iv) Room for a gas plant.

(e) Special provision necessary for certain laboratories such as fume cupboards for Chemistry, museums for Biology, kitchen and wash rooms for Home Science, etc.

Function Planning

Location Of Laboratorie

The Panel considers that in the interest of economical distribution of layout and services, it would be advisable to locate the laboratories for Chemistry and Home Science on the ground floor and those for Physics and Biology on the first floor over these laboratories if the school buildings have a double-storeyed structure. For a single-storeyed structure, the grouping of Home Science with Chemistry and of Biology with Physics may still be kept intact. Both Chemistry and Home Science laboratories require special layouts for water and drainage which will be best arranged if they are both on the ground floor and adjacent to each other.

Laboratory Space

Keeping in view the requirements described above the Panel reconsidered the sizes of laboratories and of the various items of furniture as also the total space recommended in various reports* published on the subject. The Panel is of the view that all the four laboratories, viz., Physics, Chemistry, Biology and Home Science could be of the same size i.e., 10.0 m × 6.0m. =60 sq. m (32 ft ×20 ft =640 sq. ft) with a space of 6.0 m×3.7m=22.2 sq. m. (20 ft. × 12 ft.=240 sq. ft) provided for ancillaries for each laboratory. The Panel feels that the space requirement of 60 sq. m. for a batch of 24 students is the minimum that could be recommended for each laboratory. In making this recommendation the Panel has given considerable thought to the operational requirements in each laboratory and paid visits to several institutions with a view to find how best the economy of construction could be combined with efficiency, texibility, practical layout of workables, movement of supervising staff, layout of water and gas lines, etc. The Panel has even considered factors like proper placement of doors and windows and standardisation of layouts of electricity and gas fittings in the most economical way possible in addition to preserving interchangeability and structural economy as mentioned before.

Laboratory Lighting

The factor of light, apart from affecting visual and physical comfort of students, involves the question of economy also in respect of the size and type of windows and of the disposition of light fittings. The chief purpose of lighting is to provide comfortable visual observation for laboratory work and the conservation of the vision of the young workers. It is desirable to make maximum use of day-light by proper location of doors, windows and sky-lights. Windows are best placed at a standard still height of 1.2 m (4 ft) from the finished floor level, as this would give a good distribution of light over the work tables whose hight may very between 85 cm. and 90 cm. (2 ft 9 in. and 3 ft). The save on capital as well as recurring expenses artificial lighting needs to be provided only for occasional work, for instance during certain hours in winter in monsoon months. Windows and doors should be so disposed as to provide as evenly distributed illumination as possible. A window are of 20 per cent of the floor area is considered to be adequate for general laboratory work. In terms of lumens, the amount of day light illumination of the order of 15 to 20 lumens per sq. ft. is considered to be adequate. The following reflectance standards are recommended for obtaining a desirable brightness level inside the laboratories :

Ceilings : 85 per cent of the total amount of light received by the surface.

Walls : 60 per cent of the total amount of light received by the surface.

Floors : 15 to 30 per cent of the total amount of light received by the surface.

Light and colour are closely inter-related so that in determining a suitable colour scheme inside the laboratory, the reflectance value should always be taken into

---

* Report on Delhi School Buildings, Committee on Plan Projects, Planning Commission, 1960. Planning Higher Secondary School Buildings, National Buildings Organisation, Ministry of Works, Housing & Supply 1961. Planning Schools for India, Ministry of Education, 1959.

account. White is not considered suitable for laboratory walls as it causes glare and shows dirt very prominently. Light cream or silver gray may be preferable.

Laboratory Services

We recommend the provision of services in the various laboratories as follows :

1. Physics Laboratory

(a) Power points (230 volts, single phase, 10 amps) :

(i) Two each on the two side walls.

(ii) One in dark room for exhaust fan.

(iii) One on demonstration table.

(iv) One for charging batteries.

(b) Plug points from light circuit (230 volts, single phase, 5 amps) :

(i) Two points distributed in the laboratory.

(ii) Four points in dark room.

(c) Gas supply :

(i) One gas tap on the demonstration table.

(ii) Three two way gas taps on the three tables on one side (to be fixed underneath the tables with connecting tubes for using the tap on the tables).

(d) Water supply :

(i) One tap with a sink on demonstration table.

(ii) Two taps with sink for general use, one in the laboratory and one in store-cum-preparation room.

2. Chemistry Laboratory : (a) Power Points (230 volts, single phase, 10 amps.).

(i) Two points for two exhaust fans.

(ii) Four points evenly spaced in the laboratory.

(iii) One Point on demonstration table.

(iv) One point in the preparation room.

(b) Gas Supply** :

(i) Two 2-way gas taps for each work table.

(ii) One 2-way tap on demonstration table.

(iii) One tap in the preparation room.

(c) Water Supply :

(i) Two taps to each work table with a common sink.

(ii) One tap for demonstration table with sink.

(iii) One tap for preparation room with sink.

3. Biology Laboratoy : (a) Power Point (230 volts, single phase, 5 amps) : One power point on demonstration table.

(b) Plug point from light circuit (230 volts, single phase, 5 amps.). One on demonstration table.

(c) Light point : One to each table (for microscopic work), if necessary.

(d) Water Supply :

(i) Two taps with sinks at work tables as indicated in the plan.

(ii) One tap on the demonstration table with sink.

(iii) One tap in preparation room with sink.

4. Home Science Laboratory : (a) Power points (230 volts, single phase, 10 amps.) :

(i) Two for electric irons.

(ii) Two for electric hot plates.

(iii) One extra point.

(b) Gas Supply***

Four gas taps suitably placed in the laboratory and the kitchen.

Laboratory Furniture

Work table is the most important item of furniture and needs careful consideration. The size and design of this not only affects the size of the laboratory but has a bearing on cost. The Panel, therefore, considered this in detail in arriving at optimum standards.

Studies and serveys carried out by the Panel revealed considerable variation in the size and design of laboratory tables, for example, it is usual in the U.K. and U.S.A. to provide table surface area ranging from five to 15 sq. ft. per students while in the laboratories visited by the Panel the average varies between four-and-a-half and eight sq. ft. The Panel, after careful consideration of the functional requirements, now makes the following recommendations :

1. Size of the work table need not be the same for all the four laboratories since the work carried out differes in each case.

2. Work tables in the Physics, Chemistry and Home Science laboratories and need not have drawers or closed cupboards. Biology tables, however, may preferably be provided with drawers. In Physics laboratory the work tables may be provided with 2 feet. wide intermediate shelves about one foot above the floor level.

3. Provision for tables should be made for 24 students in each laboratory.

4. Sizes of work tables should preferably be as follows :

Physics (for a group of four students) :

1.8 m × 1.1 m × 90 cm (6 ft—0 inch × 3 ft—6 inch × 3ft.—0 inch) with a plain top and an intermediate shelf placed about 1 foot from the floor level.

Chemistry (for a group of four students) :

1.8 m × 1.1.m × 85cm (6 ft—0 inch × 3 ft—6 inch × 2 ft—9 inch) with acid resistant top, with one sink in the middle having two taps and two reagent bottle racks on either side of the sink. These racks should be 60 cm × 20 cm × 45 cm (2 ft—0 inch × 8 inch × 1 ft—6 inch) with intermediate tiers and should be constructed as separate pieces from the main table while capable of

** Care should be taken in selecting good quality gas taps as some of the cheaper makes start leaking very soon.

*** Where gas supply is not available, non-pressure type safety stores may be substituted. Use of petrol gas plant is, however, recommended.

being screwed on the tops.

Biology : General work tables 1.8 m × 1.1 m × 85 cm (6 ft × 3 inch - 6 inch × 2 ft—9 inch) with two sinks, one at each end, for dissection. Side tables of size 2.0m × 50cm × 85cm (6 ft—6 inch × 1 ft—8 inch × 2 ft—9 inch) to be placed against walls and close to windows for microscopic work. These tables will have drawers and small cupboards below allowing sufficient space between cupboards as leg room.

Home Science : Suitable number of tables for :

(a) **Cooking**—50 cm wide × 80 cm high × length to suit the wall length (1 ft—8 inch × 2 ft—6 inch) ;

(b) **Sewing Machines**—dimensions according to requirements ; and

(c) **General Purposes**—1.8 m × 90cm × 80 cm. (6ft—0 inch × 3 ft—0 inch × 2 ft—6 inch).

In addition to the above furniture, all the laboratories, except Home Science; should have a demonstration table 2.5 m × 80 cm × 90 cm (8 ft—0 inch × 2 ft—6 inch × 3 ft—0 inch) with a sink at one end. A chalk board should be provided on the wall.

The laboratories should also have, in addition, soft pinning boards and wall show cases as indicated in typical lay-outs appended.

As for the material for furniture, the Panel feels that looking to the present conditions, timber is the most economical and easily available material in various parts of the country although steel facilities lighter and neat-looking construction.

Note : For sketch designs of Physics & Chemistry tables, the Report on Delhi School Buildings may be referred to.

Ancillary Accommodation

The Pannel has noticed that in most laboratories ancillary accommodation such as storage and balance room is often not provided or is grossly inadequate. It is, therefore, strongly recommended that such accommodation must form an essential part of the laboratory itself and should be well planned in the same manner as the laboratory.

The Panel recommends the following standards for each laboratory :

1. **Physics** : (a) Dark room : 3.7m × 2.7m = 9.99 sq.m. (12 ft—0 inch × 9 ft - 0 inch = 108 sq. ft)

(b) Store-cum-Preparation room : 3.7m × 3.3m = 12.21 sq.m (12 ft—0 inch × 11 ft - 0 inch = 132 sq. ft).

2. **Chemistry** : (a) Balance room : 3.7m × 2.7m = 9.99 sq.m (12 ft—0 inch × 9 ft—0 inch = 108 sq.ft).

(b) Store-cum-preparation room : 3.7 m × 3.3m = 12.21 sq.m (12 ft × 11 ft = 132 sq.ft).

3. **Biology** : (a) Museum-cum-preparation room : 3,7m × 3.3m = 12.21 sq.m (12 ft × 11 ft = 132 sq.ft).

(b) Store room 3.7 m + 2.7 m = 9.99 sq.m. (12 ft × 9 ft. = 108 sq. ft).

4. **Home Science** : (a) Kitchenette-cum-preparation room : 3 7m × 3.3m = 12.21 sq.m. (12 ft × 11 ft = 132 sq. ft).

(b) Store room : 3.7m × 2.7m = 9.99 sq.m. (12 ft × 9 ft = 108 sq. ft).

The Panel considers that there is no necessity of providing spacious store rooms for keeping stores and equipment. A comparative smaller room, with well-designed shelving carried up to the celling, can provide enough storing space for the purpose. For reasons of economy and durability shelves and ledges of precast concrete type are recommended. Where, however, a store is used as a preparation room, a portion of the bottom shelf may have shutters forming lockable cupboards.

Height of Laboratories

This aspect, though not vital from the point of view educational requirements, is very important from the point of view of economy in construction. A height of the order of 12.14 and even 16 feet is quite common in our country especially for public buildings in hot and dry regions. This can be conveniently reduced. The Panel, therefore, considers that a height of 3 3m (11 ft) may be adequate. This will permit required depth of structural beams as well as sufficient room for fan and light fixtures.

Equipment and Apparatus

Equipment and Apparatus in Science Laboratories : The Board of Higher Secondary Education, Delhi, (now designated as the Central Board of Secondary Education) had drawn up a detailed list of equipment for Physics, Chemistry, Biology and Home Science Laboratories. The schools have, therefore, been guided by this list for placing orders for the quipment required by them for each laboratory. This list was recently revised by the Board. A list of apparatus and equipment was also drawn at a "Workshop" organised by the Directorate of Education, Delhi in May 1962. The Panel made a detailed study of these lists. Besides, the list of equipment, actually available for each of the four science subjects in a few representative schools of Delhi, were also prepared. Discussions were held with the science teachers and principals of several schools. As a result of the data collected from all those sources and the subsequent discussions in several meetings, the Pannel prepared its own list of apparaturs and equipment for various laboratories.

The Panel made a detailed study of the cost involved in equipping the various laboratories. It was, however, not possible to arrive at correct figures in view of the varying prices given by the schools as also by the firms. Another factor which proved a handicap in making correct estimates of the co t was the availability of different makes of the same apparatus at highly divergent prices. For purpose of our study, we took into account the prices given by the "workshop" mentioned above. As explained in subsequent paragraphs, the Panel decided to recommend that the procurement of equipment and apparatus for a school which was to introduce science subjects afresh may be spread over a period of three to four years. In the case of a school which is already imparting instruction in these subjects, the requirements will vary with reference to the available equipment and need for future development within the limits of the Panel's list.

An effort has been made to reconcile the apparently conflicting aims of economy and efficiency in equipping science laboratories. In order to obviate the necessity of incurring heavy expenditure in the initial stages for which there may not be adequate financial provision, the items have been grouped separately as "essential", "desirable" and "supplementary" indicated in the note to the list.

Other Recommendations

The Panel's datailed recommendations about the first two items of the Terms of Reference have been given in earlier chapters. The panel gave considerable thought to the remaining four items and makes the following recommendations ad seriatum :

Laying Down Specification and Standards for Equipment and Apparatus and Procedure for Quality Control. The Panel feels that the laying down of specifications and standards for equipment and apparatus will greatly improve the quality of instruments at present being supplied to schools and recommends that the necessity for Standards Institution and the Central Scientific Instruments Organisation with the request that they may expedite the laying down of standards of atleast those items of science apparatus which are already being manufactured in the country.

Procedure for Allotment of Funds and Procurement of Equipment: The Panel very strongly recommends that the allotment of funds, both capital and recurring, should be made as early as possible so that the funds could be utilised before the end of the financial year. It has been brought the notice of the Panel by several manufacturers that orders are usually placed with them so late in the year that they find considerable difficulty in supplying the articles in time. The Panel was made aware that many suppliers take advantage of the delay by dumping the worst quality materials at the very fag end of the financial year, and the school authorities could only reject the supplies at the resk of losing the grants. The Panel strongly recommends that the schools should be given the allotted grants before they close for the summer vacation and they should be instructed to place the orders for equipment before the schools reopen. Staps should then be taken for obtaining the equipment soon after the reopening of the schools.

Possibility of having a Centralised Agency for the Manufacture and Procurement of Scientific Equipment: The Panel feels that, since a large number of firms are already engaged in the manufacture of scientific instruments, there is no necessity for a centralised agency for their manufacture. The procurement of science equipment, however, can be improved considerably if, for the new schools, package units, conforming to the prescribed equipment, were available to the schools by bulk purchases made through a quitable agency. It has come to the notice of the Panel that most of the Government purchasing agencies have to accept the lowest tenders according to the established procedure. This has led to deterioration in the quality by manufactures. The procedure of bying on the lowest tender needs to be replaced by a more rational system whereby producers of quality goods may get an equitable proce for their product. Where standards are available, purchases should be made strictly in accordance with the Indian Standards Institution standards or any other available standards.

Simplification of Methods of Work in the Laboratories: The Panel feels that, at present, there is considerable over-simplification of practical work. In most science laboratories only one teacher is available. With 20 to 24 students working at a time and trying to complete an experiment within a period of about 80 to 90 minutes the teacher is hardly able to do justice to the personal requirements of the pupils The possibility of providing two demonstrators in each class deserves to be fully explore. It is also recommended that, wherever possible, full use should made of the laboratory during the working hours and the possibility of two or more schools collaborating in practical work may be kept in view. If this is possible the number of science teaching laboratories will not have to be increased in the same proportion as the number of schools.

STUDY TEAM FOR SELECTED EDUCATIONAL SCHEMES, 1961—REPORT

New Delhi, Committee on Plan Projects, 1964. 206p.

Leader : Shri B. N. Jha.
Members : Shri K. L. Joshi; Prof. T. K. N. Menon ; Shri I. N. Menon.
Member-Secretary : Shri Jagdish Singh.

APPOINTMENT

The expansion of education in compliance with the constitutional directive for free and compulsory education has brought in its wake several broblems. One of these is the provisions of adequate number of properly trained teachers at various levels of education. The Committee on Plan Projects in the Planning Commission, which has been organising studies in various fields, therefore, with the concurrence of the Planning Commission and the Ministry of Education, set up a Study Team for Selected Educational Schemes in May, 1961, and entrusted to it the detailed examination inter-alia, of the programmes relating to teacher training at various levels.

TERMS OF REFERENCE

The terms of Reference of the Study Team were as follows :

(a) To enquire into and report on the present position of various types of programmes undertaken at the Centre and in the States in the following Sectors of Education :

(i) Teacher Trainings.
(ii) Social Education; and
(iii) Rural Institute.

(b) Make suggestions on any aspects of the programme with a view to :

(i) Effecting economy and efficiency in the utilisation of resources; and
(ii) Expediting the working of the programmes.

(c) The teacher training programmes may be studied particularly from the point of view of the requirements for :

(i) Enforcement of compulsory education for the age-group six to 11;
(ii) Expansion of Middle/Junior, High/Senior basic education for the age-group 11-16; and
(iii) Expansion of secondary education.

(d) In addition, to make such recommendation for improvement as may be relevant to the success of the programmes referred to above.

For assisting the Team in detailed studies, a Panel of experts, with the undermentioned composition was constituted :

Chairman : Shri B. N. Jha.
Members : Shri K. L. Joshi; Prof. T. K. N. Menon; Shri J. P. Naik; Dr. R. K. Singh; Dr. S. N. Jha; Miss G. R. Samuel; Shri P. L. Shrimali; Shri S. R. Chaturvedi; and Shri B. D. Srivastava.
Member-Secretary : Shri Jagdish Singh.

Shri B. N. Jha, Leader of the Education Team died on April 13, 1964. So the entire responsibility for revising the Report in the light of the comments of the State Governments and Union Ministry of Education, fell on Shri K. L. Joshi.

CONTENTS

Introduction; Objectives of Teacher Education and Trends of Development; Procedure and Preparation; Present Position; Some Aspects of Teacher Education; Problems of Teacher Education; Teacher Education—Suggestions for Administration and Organisation Summary of Conclusions and Recommendations; Appendices from I to XXVI.

RECOMMENDATIONS

Objectives of Teacher Education and Trends of Development

Modern education aims at the education of the whole person. So every teacher should have a deep knowledge and understanding of children and skill in applying that knowledge and understanding.

Overwhelming majority of men and women can only become good teachers if the training programme is built on a sound foundation of theoretical knowledge and supervised practice.

The problem is to examine whether the required number of teachers during the Plans is being properly trained in institutions established for the purpose, keeping in view both economy in training programmes and efficiency among men and women trained.

The following points need to be included in a programme of teacher training ;

(i) To enable the trainees to require the skills and techniques needed to teach young children with the help of modern knowledge of child psychology and methods of teaching ;

(ii) To inculcate in the educants the ideals of accepted behaviour patterns of the society in which they live and whose purposes they serve ; and

(iii) To develop in the teacher trainee certain attitudes, values and interests in conformity with the ideals of democracy and our developing economy.

The following are the recent trends in Teacher Training Programme :

(i) Entrance qualification for primary teacher is being raised to a pass in matriculation or equivalent ;

(ii) Training schools have increased to 1,358 and training colleges to 216 in 1960-61 ;

(iii) More women students are seeking admission to training institutions ;

(iv) Financial allocation for teacher education is not being proportionately increased through plans ;

(v) The question of teachers' salaries cannot be dissociated from the question of training programmes ; and

(vi) Separation between elementary and secondary teacher education has led to a lack of participation of professional persons in the same objectives of teacher education.

Procedure and Preparation

There were in 1960 61, 1,358 training schools and 216 training colleges whose working and effectiveness have been assessed in this study.

Programmes of training in each State have been summarised in the heading under Present Position.

It is not intended to cover the ground already cleared in certain studies examined by the Committee.

It seems to us that while making financial allocations through the Plan, sufficient attention to adequate staff, building, equipment, etc., has not been paid.

State Departments of Education have not been able to supervise and control this programme with efficiency needed in relation to the immensity of the task.

Appendix IX indicates that in primary schools, non-matriculate teachers have been decreasing from 78 to 71 per cent and matriculate teachers rising from 22 to 29 per cent. In middle schools, the non-matriculate teachers are about 45 per cent and matriculates and graduate 55 per cent.

In 1957-58, in secondary schools, 48 per cent were graduate teachers 52 per cent non-graduate teachers.

During the last 10 years, recommendations of the Secondary Education Commission in regard to the Teacher Training Programmes have not been implemented fully probably because of financial limitations.

Report of a study by an International Team made certain recommendations which have been partially implemented but even now a dynamic approach to improve the existing institutions has yet to be made.

The supply of trained teachers for elementary schools is not related to the actual requirements

Location of training institutions is more fortuitous than planned.

There is no uniformity of courses for training of primary teachers in different States and the old traditions of admitting students after the middle school education continue in a number of States.

Physical facilities in majority of training schools are lacking.

Present Position

There is confusion of nomenclature in respect of training institutions. One suggestion is that the training schools for primary teachers be described as Junior Training Colleges. In this document the current terms 'training schools' and 'training colleges' have been employed.

In estimating teacher requirements, if qualitative improvement is taken into consideration, more trained teachers will be required at all stages.

Appendix XX, giving financial provision over the Plans for training programmes, indicates that provision in different States is not necessarily related to the requirement of teacher training programme in the States concerned.

Appendices XIII (a), (b) and (c) indicate various types of training and while training courses in the colleges indicate certain uniform practices, the variety of training courses at the training schools level cannot be reduced to uniform pattern.

The objectives of T.D. courses as obtained in States of Gujarat and Maharashtra conducted by colleges affiliated to universities are commended to other universities from the point of view of supply of middle school teachers.

A study of special courses in teacher's training for specialised teachers should be undertaken by a committee of experts to examine in details the objectives of such courses and syllabus or curriculum as well as the duration. They would be in a position to examine how some of these courses are outmoded and could be eliminated and other could be properly combined in useful and effective courses.

We generally observed that women's training institutions showed a high morale compared with the institutions for men.

We recommend coeducational pattern for training colleges from the point of view of administrative economy and tone of efficiency.

Current practice of separate training schools for men and women may continue along with coeducational institutions.

In the Second and Third Plans, financial provisions for teacher training programme in terms of percentage of the total amount provided for general education indicates lack of progress.

Some Aspects of Teacher Training

We recommend that universities should take interest in the appointment of staff to the training colleges.

To staff training schools, teachers drawn from secondary schools are not suitable and, therefore, they should go through an orientation course of at least two three months to make themselves familiar with the problems of the primary schools.

Scales of pay of teachers in the training colleges should be same as recommended by the University Grants Commission for teacher in Colleges of Arts and Science.

We recommend that State Governments may consider giving teachers of secondary schools appointed to training schools either a special allowance for working as Lecturers in the training schools or some other incentive.

The whole question of staff, salaries, conditions of service will need to be examined by different State Governments in relation to other salaries for similar type of work.

In majority of teacher training institutions the problem of selection does not appear to be a serious one.

We found that in some training institutions there was shortage of candidates and the intake capacity was not fully utilised. While in others there was a much larger number of applicants than the capacity.

Certain selection methods are commonly used in institutions where selection from among the applicants is necessary.

Departmental candidates are selected by the Directors of Education in Government institutions and the number of deputed teachers form a considerable majority as compared to freshers, for whom the choice of selection has to be exercised.

Appendix VII indicates data about variations in the methods employed in selection procedures, quality of trainees and the number of trainees.

There is an urgent need for evolving a suitable and objective set of measures of assessment for selection of trainees. Minimum standards have to be established for admission to training institutions whether the number of applicants is more than the capacity or less.

For teachers with set habits, above the age of 35 or with an experience of more than seven years of teaching, other methods of training included in in-service training programmes should be employed.

In selecting candidates, the following criteria, with suitable modifications, may be found helpful :

(i) Past achievements and academic records of the candidates ;

(ii) Results obtained by the candidates in aptitude test ; and

(iii) Interview by a selection committee.

There is a wide gap between what the training institutions produce and what is required in a school.

In the course of studies prescribed, quite a lot of dead wood appears to have been collected and needs to be cleared through a new approach.

Statements of aims and objectives in relation to prescribed syllabi will be found helpful.

There was a general complaint of heavy burden on the students in the prescribed courses of theory and practice.

Appendix XVI gives various courses in methodology. However, the choice of students is not related very often to the requirement of the subject teachers in the schools.

We would recommend about 30 lessons, i.e., 15 each in two school subjects as the optimum for the purpose of practice teaching.

The practical training should also include attendance at demonstration lessons given by masters of methods and other outstanding teachers, observation of lessons, delivering criticism lessons, working on educational projects, preparation of teaching aids, etc.

All practice teaching lessons should be planned under guidance, given under supervision and discussed later by the supervisor.

Appendix XVII indicates allocation of marks for theory and practice.

A moderate and balanced contribution can be struck (in examination of the trainees) by placing proper weightage on internal assessment and checking up by external examiners in a greater proportion. An informal interview of a few minutes for the trainees by the internal and external examiners can also be very useful, in having a proper and balanced estimate of the trainees capabilities.

The details of any proper evaluation and weightage in marks and also in the system of examination in practice teaching, in our opinion should require a review by academic bodies.

In the case of primary teacher training institutions, a suty included in the report (Education of Primary Teachers in India, 1961) bring out wide differences in quality and load of the syllabi from State to State.

We feel that different types of experiments in training programmes have to be encouraged and we commend the Kurukshetra experiment and the experiment of the four Regional Colleges being established by the

Ministry of Education under the National Council of Eductional Research and Training.

We notice that institutions with higher enrolment reduce the cost per capita without endangering the examination results or efficiency of training.

Large-sized institutions are found in some of the advanced countries and we have examined the advantages of such institutions which showed that an academic atmosphere could be established in the campus of such an institution without difficulty. A small training school or college may be educationally ineffective and costly. McNair Report says, "We doubt whether a college of much less than 200 is capable of being staffed, equipped and organised, both efficiently and economically."

Standardised cost pattern for recurring and non-recurring expenditure in the case of training schools or training colleges has to be evolved.

Appendices XXII (a) and (b) summarising cost patterns of institutions in different States indicate interesting variations.

Appendices XXIV (a) and (b) indicate the wide range of pattern of expenditure and lack of uniform models for training institutions.

It is recommended that an estimate of financial provision for different types of training programmes, including those of correspondence courses, evening and vacation courses should be done by an Experts Committee which should take into account suggestions made by the Association of Training Colleges in India.

We had complaints from all concerned regarding non-avilability of text-books for teachers and trainees.

Lack of hand-books leads students to a state of despair and they depend on teachers who employ the method of dictation of notes which they themselves will discard as a method of teaching.

The publication of suitable text-books in Indian languages has to be undertaken on a national scale.

In training schools the use of modern teaching aids has to be very much encouraged.

Facilities of workshops and those for craft training have to be provided in a much greater measure in the training institutions.

Recommendations made by the Working Group of the All India Association of Training Colleges in regard to provision of library facilities should be considered.

Certain training schools and training colleges are attached to high schools of Arts and Science Colleges. We suggest that this arrangement might continue provided the staff requirements are properly met and other physical facilities are made available.

In the case of postgraduate studies and research in education, we have noted disturbing variation and constant deterioration in the practices relating to admission, choice of courses of study and also in the quality of research work required of students.

Teacher education at postgraduate and research level did not always attract the type of students who had either facilities or the capacity to attack research problems in education.

The best minds should be induced to take up research in education and this could be achieved by taking not only those who have done the B. Ed. degree at the graduate level but also others who have done either a good degree in humanities or science. For the latter, a course of slightly longer duration may be desirable.

Extention centres and units in training programmes have given a new lead in teacher education and they will soon cover a very large number of secondary schools in the country.

Extension programme is proposed to be introduced through training schools in elementary schools. The experiment will be watched with interest.

Problems Of Teacher Education

Dimension of the problem of teacher training in terms of numbers is formidable as it includes the training of additional teachers required for expansion of school educational facilities, the backlog of untrained teachers and replacement.

Advancement in training of teachers has proceeded in India, as in other countries, on many fronts without coordination and without any overall or commonly accepted plan. Progress had to be made wherever and whatever it could be made with whatever adjustments in programme or practice were made necessary by the demands of specific local or institutional situtations.

A uniform standardisation of programme would appear to be necessary.

A balance between liberal and pedagogical elements has to be established and specific needs in training have to be identified.

We recommend that if any untrained teaher is appointed to a teaching post, he should be given the scale of pay of the post prescribed for a trained teacher. After he gets training qualifications, he should be granted two increments in the scale. This would also mean that a trained teacher, if freshly appointed, has to be started with two advance increments in the scale.

Our attention was drawn to a certain lack of morale, particularly in training schools-a subject which is related to selection of proper teachers and trainees in the training schools and provision of physical facilities such as buildings, library and equipment, as well as the scope for initiative of the trainee.

If the universities took more interest in the training schools, the latter will not only get academic status but there will also be greater freedom in giving proper initiative to the trainees and the members of the staff.

Some of the existing deficiencies in the training institutions like uneconomic and inefficient training units, absence of well-designed programme for location of training schools and inadequate number of seats in some of the institutions could be avoided after the introduction of the A.T.O. and Correspondence Courses.

Teacher Education-Suggestions For Administration And Organisation

Another line of research has to be undertaken for establishing relationship between the supply of subject teachers in secondary schools who are scarce and the undergraduates in those subjects in the universities.

We are of the view that in the present circumstances in the country, the minimum qualification for elementary teacher should be at least of matriculation or equivalent standard followed by a two-year training course well linked with the content of courses in primary schools with necessary courses in pedagogy.

At the secondary stage, teachers have to know their subjects and the more advanced the grade the more important it is for the teacher to have good training specifically in his particular field.

For secondary teachers, knowledge of subjects to be taught is very essential along with the knowledge of methods of teaching.

A teacher should have wholeness of personality and mind and wholeness of experience and he must be given time and opportunity in his training course to think about education.

Many teachers are taught unscientific psychology for which they are hardly ready, by unimaginative teachers.

The universities can play a decisive part in the training of all teachers.

We recommend that a suitable machinery should be employed to involve universities and university colleges of education to take leadership in the programmes of training schools.

The machinery for this purpose has been a matter of debate.

Considerable thinking done in the McNair Report, in a Study by an International Team and by the Council of Elmentary Education, Ministry of Education, indicates the lines of administrative reforms.

Since the matriculation or equivalent qualification is recognised as a suitable admission qualification for training of primary teachers, the universities should be interested in their training. We recommend that the univerities be made responsible for the academic control of the total training programmes so that the primary and secondary levels and Government and private institutions may continue to have the administrative control.

Some universities have been conducting a T.D. course for those who have passed matriculation or equivalent examination and are supplying the needs of middle school teachers.

We recommend for the consideration of the universities and State Governments, the possibility of setting up Area Training Organisation (A.T.O.) which will integrate and supervise training of teachers at all levels in respective areas, with the assistance of an advisory council.

We recommend that as many of the existing 216 training colleges as possible may be encouraged to develop into the new type of comprehensive or multipurpose teacher training institutions. This should be possible within the recommendations made about A.T.O.

We feel that correspondence should be introduced immediately of the same duration as the institutional courses, for teachers who are untrained, to deal with the problem of backlog of untrained teachers.

The correspondence courses have been recommended in the study of the All India Council of Elementary Education and an account of their success has been given in the Ministry of Education publication "Education in the Soviet Union".

Correspondence courses could also be considered for training of teachers for middle schools and secondary schools under the proposed A.T.O.

We recommend organisation of in-service training programmes through evening and vacation courses.

We suggest that trained graduate teachers in the same scale of pay they would have drawn in the high schools, should be gradually appointed as Headmasters of Middle Schools, and also of some of the large-sized primary schools.

COMMITTEE ON EMOTIONAL INTEGRATION, 1961—REPORT

Delhi, Manager of Publications, 1962. 277p.+xvip.+2 Vols.

Chairman : Dr. Sampurnanand.

Members : Shrimati Indira Gandhi ; Prof. T M. Advani ; Prof. Hiren Mukerjee ; Shri M. Henry Samuel ; Prof. M. N. Srinivas ; Shri Bhai Jodh Singh ; Shri A. E. T. Barrow ; Shri Asoka Mehta ; Shri. A. A. A. Fyzee ; Shri. K. Kuruvila Jacob ; Dr. B. S. Haikerwal.

Secretary : Kumari K. Nair.

APPOINTMENT

At the Conference of Education Ministers held in November, 1960, one of the subjects discussed was the distressing frequency with which disruptive tendencies were making themselves felt in the country. While expressing its concern at such tendencies which, if unchecked, it said, might threaten the unity of the country, the Conference stressed the importance of the role of education in counteracting such divisive trends and in fostering unity. It recommended that a Committee should be set up by the Union Ministry of Education to study the problem and suggest positive educational measures for promoting integration. This was followed by the appointment of the Committee in may, 1961, under the Resolution of the Government of India in the Ministry of Education, No. F. 29-7/60-SE-1, dated May 15, 1961.

TERMS OF REFERENCE

(i) To study the role of education in considering and promoting the processes of emotional integration in national life and to examine the operation of tendencies which come in the way of their development.

(ii) In the light of such study, to advise on the positive educational programmes for youth in general and students in schools and colleges in particular, to strengthen in them the processes of emotional integration.

CONTENTS

Synopses of Chapters ; Introduction ; Historical Background ; Trends Undermining, and Factors Fostering, Unity ; The Philosophy of Education ; General and Major Policy Suggestions ; Language and Script ; School Education ; University Education ; Youth Programmes ; Adult Education ; Teachers ; Curriculum ; Textbooks And Other Reading Materials ; Summary of Recommendations ; Conclusion ; Note by Prof. H. N. Mukerjee ; Appendices 1 to 35.

RECOMMENDATIONS

General And Major Policy Suggestions

It is necessary to evolve an effective national policy in education, the implementation of which will bring the States and Union Territories closer together. For this, in any matter of educational policy of an all-India character, the Centre, on its own motion or at the instance of the States or statutory bodies like the University Grants Commission, should confer with the State Government and other interested parties and arrive at a decision in consultation with them. Such a policy arrived at by majority decision shall then become an all-India policy and all States shall necessarily follow it.

The Union Education Ministry should set up suitable machinery at the Centre to watch the progress in the implementation of such policies, and should suggest, in consultation with the State Governments concerned, any other measures needed to implement such policies.

All necessary Constitutional changes should be made in order to implement the recommendations made above.

There should be a common pattern of education in the country which will minimise confusion and coordinate and maintain standards. Similar opportunities for education should be made available in all parts of the country.

Education must be planned to suit the aptitudes and abilities of the pupils as well as to meet the economic and social needs of the country.

There should be more terminal stages in the pattern of education where pupils can branch off to vocations or semi-vocational training.

A high school stage at the end of 10 years is a necessity ; 12 years of education before the degree course is equally a necessity. The two-year classes following the high school stage will either be attached to the schools and called the higher secondary classes, or attached to degree colleges as pre-university classes. These two classes may also be an independent unit called the junior college which can be controlled and recognized by the State education department or the university, or both. Students successfully completing the higher secondary, pre-university and junior college courses may be awarded a diploma to establish their qualification for entry into the different avenues of employment available to them.

Higher secondary and junior college classes should

be planned as multipurpose or comprehensive institutions providing (a) preparatory courses for students proceeding to college ; (b) all-round terminal education with a semi-vocational or semi-professional preparation ; and (c) terminal education for a vocation. Students from higher secondary courses and junior colleges should be competent to enter many of the public services now open only to those with university degrees.

The technical courses provided in higher secondary classes and junior colleges should be planned in coordination with those in polytechnics.

Junior colleges should serve the local community by providing evening continuation courses of different kinds and different durations for cultural enrichment and professional improvement.

The objectives in the field of education have to be clearly stated and perspective planning is necessary in relating the pattern of education to the employment potential of the country. The Union Ministry of Education should immediately initiate action in this respect.

The number of post-matriculation scholarships given to poor and talented students needs to be enhanced considerably to cover as many students as possible for all types of education.

As a long-term measure, steps should be taken to correct deficiencies noticed in pupils while they are in primary schools so that they get proper opportunities for the growth and development of their talents.

The Government of India should take necessary steps in consultation with the State Governments and other authorities to create a pool of competent and experienced educationists and educational administrators, which the State and the Centre can draw upon for their additional requirements.

The recommendations made in the interest of emotional integration should be classified under national priorities and it is of the utmost importance that speedy and effective action is taken to implement them. Suitable machinery should be set up by the Central Government to watch the progress of implementation. The schemes proposed in this respect will be Centrally sponsored schemes but the responsibility for implementation will rest with the States.

Language And Script

The use of the Roman script may be permitted in certain areas for an interim period to enable persons to improve their acquaintance with Hindi.

Throughout India the international numerals must be used.

To reduce the burden of three scripts, Hindi may be learnt in the non-Hindi areas in the regional script.

To popularise the study of Hindi in non-Hindi-speaking areas a beginning may be made with the publication of Hindi books in the Roman script and the compilation of simple dictionaries in Hindi-Other Languages, also in the Roman script.

Hindi books may be published in the regional script and the Compilation of Regional Language-Hindi dictionaries should be encouraged.

A complete language formula recommended for Hindi and non-Hindi areas is given in para 5.29.

At the high school stage, Hindi must be taught in the Devanagari script, keeping in view the Constitutional provision.

The two link languages--Hindi and English—should be effectively taught at university level so that conditions of emotional and intellectual isolation are not created.

It is necessary to ensure that in implementing any language policy the rights of minorities are adequately protected.

Periodic consultations should be held at Central and State levels for eliciting non-official opinion from minority communities on educational policies which concern them.

School Education

Towards expanding pre-school education steps should be taken for the establishment of play centres for the pre-school age-group three to five years. Such centres should be provided in all mills and factories.

The principles of Basic education emphasised by Gandhiji and the objectives outlined at the 11th session of the UNESCO General Conference in 1960 should be kept in mind in planning courses and teaching methods for primary schools.

Steps should be taken by the Centre and the States to strengthen facilities available at present for school architecture.

Provision should be made for research in the design and construction of school equipment.

Minimum standards must be observed in schools concomitant with the quantitative expansion of primary education, in the absence of which, recognition should be withdrawn.

Schemes for the expansion of girls' education and the training of women teachers which have been discontinued should be revived in order to accelerate the tempo of primary school enrolment.

Effective steps should be taken for the implementation of a national policy to employ women teachers in increasing numbers through special incentives and facilities to attract them to the teaching profession.

The Ministry of Education, in collaboration with other agencies, should immediately finance a well-coordinated scheme to provide midday meals to cover all primary school children by pooling funds including public donations, and by encouraging voluntary contributions.

The qualifications of teachers in the higher secondary classes and junior colleges should be similar to that of teachers for pre-university classes. Also accommodation and equipment for these three parallel stages should be similar.

The low minimum mark accepted now a days for a pass in examinations needs looking into, as the recognition of low standards of attainments for a pass is likely to have unfortunate effects on the character of individuals.

Schemes to provide continuation education should be taken up to cater for those children, who for reasons of economic necessity, leave school between the ages of 11 and 14.

Any training course envisaged in such continuation classes should contain instruction in the regional language and in the rudiments of Indian history and geography as social studies.

The establishment of more trade and industrial schools and more polytechnics is essential. Schools for agriculture, horticulture and forestry may be run by the Union and State Ministries of Education in cooperation with the Union and State Ministries of Food and Agriculture, as such practical diversification will go a long way in stopping the present wastage and consequent frustration.

Greater emphasis should be placed on intensifying educational and vocational guidance services at the secondary stage, and an estimate of employment opportunities to be created in connection with our Plans made available to vocational guidance bureaux.

It is desirable to have a uniform for school children; one common uniform for the whole of India is not necessary; schools may have their own preference in regard to colour and pattern but the uniform should be neat and practical and worn by all the children. Where-ever possible, parents are expected to supply the uniform. The village cooperatives or school cooperatives should be encouraged to stitch them for sale so that the cost can be kept to the minimum. The State would have to povide uniforms for those children whose parents cannot afford to buy the necessary material.

Children should be taught to sing the National Anthem in unison and behave in a disciplined way when it is sung. They should also be taught the meaning of the verses. One of the first duties of citizenship is to be taught the meaning of the versus. One of the first duties of citizenship to be taught at the very earliest stage is reverence for the Flag and the Anthem.

National Days-January 26, August 15 and October 2—should be celebrated by schools with the full participation of the teachers and the community.

The handbook of suggestions for teachers should be give practical suggestions on ways of celebrating these National Days.

Recorded music by the All India Radio should invariably be used in schools as a guide both to instrumental and vocal rendering of the Anthem.

Special meetings of the school assembly should be held at the beginning of each term when the headmasters speak to the children on any topic dealing with the unity and oneness of the country.

At these special meetings children take a pledge of loyalty to India. The taking of the pladge which should be an all-India pledge must be preceded by the a flag hoisting ceremony and followed by the singing of the Anthem.

The Government should encourage children to go on excursions outside their State by offering them partial assistance and maximum travel concessions. Educational authorities or institutions in the area visited, should provide free accommodation in their school buildings or hostels for such students, on a reciprocal basis.

A scheme to allow a number of school parties in one State to travel to wortwhhile places to every other State every year should be drawn up. Children should be chosen only from the senior classes of the primary schools and above.

Such tours should be planned well in advance, the number of participants being limited; the programme should be well organised and suitable follow-up, ensured. The various Ministries concerned with travel and tourism and education should pool their resources for an effective scheme of assistance to schools for such excursions.

Educational and travel documentaries with particular emphasis on various aspects of Indian Scenery, flora and fauna, on various developmental and reconstruction programmes should be produced for use in schools.

Films for high school children should include documentaries on some of our important educational institutions and on what is done by children in other parts of the world.

Every trained teacher in secondary schools should have some knowledge of audio-visual techniques.

A scheme to produce childrens films and cartoons dealing with brief historical tales or legends should be launched by the Ministry of Information and Broadcasting.

The cooperation of the film industry may be sought for suggestions and for tapping histrionic talent.

There are various schemes for the production of films/films strips/documentaries in different ministries of the Government of India. A competent committee including representatives of the departments concerned and of the film industry should be entrusted with the responsibility of Planning, producing and arranging distribution of such films for the use of schools.

A regular programme to show films/posters/documentaries to children and their parents, should also be drawn up by this committee.

With properly conceived and coordinated projects the maximum number of students and their parents can be covered under this programme by an effective use of the mobile vans and projectors now available under the field publicity programmes of the Governments.

Posters should be increasingly used in schools to give children a clear and vivid picture of various aspects of Indian life. Pictures of eminent leaders of all-India fame in all spheres of life should also be displayed in schools.

A comprehensive scheme for the design and distribution of posters to all schools on subjects which help to promote the process of integration should be drawn up by the Union Ministry of Educations. This scheme should be implemented in consultation with the Ministry of Information and Broadcasting through their Department of Visual Publicity.

Schools may conduct several projects which improve their general knowledge of the country. For instance, a 'Known Your Country' project can be undertaken during which children may share in the collection of information about a State in the Indian Union other than their own.

Open-air dramas as recommended in our Preliminary Report should be encouraged.

Every school should have a pupils' committee on which students staff are both represented to see that a regular programme of activities on the suggested lines is implemented.

These projects should be dealt with in detail in a handbook of suggestions for teachers.

The programmes suggested for school children for emotional integration in Chapter VI should have broad similarly in all the States and Union Territories so that the Centre would then be able to evaluate on a comparative basis the impact which these programmes have made. The co-curricular activities taken up should also be similar wherever possible.

University Education

If universities are to play an effective part in providing leadership and fostering the necessary climate for emotional integration, they must maintain uniformly high standards through a judicious basis of admission, and the recruitment of staff on the basis of academic qualifications, character and personality.

Able students drawn from the poorer sections of the people should be helped to evercome their social and economic disab lities not only through financial support but through proper guidance and advice from student-counsellors.

The students who have no room available for quite study at home, need to be provided with facilities for day hostels.

Provision of proper leisure-time activities for collage students is essential and should be expanded to cover the entire university population.

University students should increasingly participate in social service programmes and work camps so that they can acquire some training in service to the community.

A scheme should be worked out with the employment bureaux in the States to ensure that every university should have employment bureaux to assist graduates in securing suitable employment. These bureaux should maintain close liaison with the local employment exchanges.

Collage buildings, wherever possible, should be put to constructive use after normal working hours to avoid 'wastage' in this respects. Their premises could be used for further education classes.

An extended programme of financial assistance should be given to poor but able college standard on the basis of means and merit. If it is difficult to end at once the reservation of seats in educational institutions for backward classes, a phased programme covering five or, at the most, 10 years should be worked out.

The selection of teachers on the basis of caste and community should, on no account, be encouraged and universities must make a determined effort to fight casteism and communalism in all their manifestation.

Caste or communal hostels should not be permitted, where separate hostels have been built for Harijans out of funds set apart for non-Harijans.

It is necessary to foster mutual appreciation of the various religions in the country and universities can assist in this matter by encouraging research on various topics which help towards a greater understanding of and sympathy with different religious faiths.

The University Grants Commission should institute research fellowships for the purpose.

Monographs published as a result of such research should be carefullyselected and published conducted by the Universities Grants Commission.

Courses of an extamural nature should be conducted by universities on subjects of social and political significance in addition to educational programmes.

There should be no migratory res rictions imposed on students. No preference should be shown to students from any particular area in the matter of admission to a university and immediate steps should be taken to remedy such a State of affairs, wherever it exists.

It is desirable in the interest of students that recommendations made by the Inter-University Board in respect of the recognition of degrees are accepted by all our universities. This is a matter which needs further examination.

Centres for advanced study and research in different subjects in the various universities of India are a necessary step in integration.

Distinguished professors should also be deputed periodically to different universities so that a larger range of students can benefit from their experience.

College lecturers should be given periodic in-service training through seminars and summer institutes and funds for such seminars and institutes should be provided by the University Grants Commission.

To attract to the teaching profession young men and women of talent who now opt for more lucrative posts, the scales of pay suggested by the University Grants Commission should be adopted as widely as possible in colleges.

Steps should be taken by the Union Ministry of Education and the University Grants Commission to make the scheme for research scholarships in the humanities more popular through wide and effective publicity and the liberalisation of rules.

Every student who takes up science should have some background in the humanities and a compulsory paper on India's cultural heritage, just as students in the humanities should have some knowledge of general science.

The use of Indian languages as the medium of instruction from the lowest to the highest stage of education is a matter of profound importance for national integration, as only the adoption of regional, languages as media of instruction right up to university level will bridge the gap between the intellectual elite and the mass of the people. Safeguards have to be devised, however, to prevent the lowering of standards.

The change-over to the regional language must be preceded by preparation of textbooks and arrangements for translation from English and, wherever possible, from other modern languages.

In order to maintain inter-university and inter-State communication special attention must be paid to the teaching of the link language, Hindi and English, when the change-over to regional languages is accomplished.

Special efforts must be made to forge links between universities in different parts of the country when the regional languages become media of instruction, or else, wide gaps will be created not only between universities but also between different States.

For purely intellectual purposes students in universities should have a good knowledge of the English language so that they can express themselves with facility. It is necessary, therefore, that they can express themselves with facility. It is necessary, therefore, that they should frequently listen to lecrures and write tutorials in English.

To ensure that the universities are not cut off from one another, that common standards are maintained and gifted Indians are enabled to reach the highest degree of excellence in their chosen fields of knowledge, there should be provision for English as an associate medium of instruction in the universities. This is a necessary corollary to the recognition of English as an associate official language. The use of this associate medium of instruction can be made in some selected colleges, in a university or in some divisions in a large college. Details in this connection will have to be worked out by the universities to suit varying conditions and requirements.

Indian students who go abroad on scholarships or at their own expense, have a duty to the country and to themselves to see that they are fully conversant with India's diverse cultural heritage, her plans for economic progress and security and the background of her struggle for freedom. A special subject dealing with national integration should be made compulsory for all college students throughout the country at the degree level. Failure in the paper would not amount to failure in the whole examination but students should be encouraged to take up a course of this kind through the institution of prizes or awards for outstanding performance in the subject. Special mention should be made in the degree certificate of all those students who have taken this additional paper successfully.

The University Grants Commission may set up a small committee to draw up the details of such a paper and to prepare text books with a national approach, on these subjects.

Pending the introduction of such courses, and as a temporary measure, students who go abroad on scholarships should be given an orientation course on India before they leave and presented with two or three books which give some basic information about the country.

Youth Programmes

The Union Ministry of Education should initiate action to plan a minimum programme of recreational and social activities for young people in the age-group 14-25, to cater for those in schools and colleges and also for those who have left school.

Some of the funds for labour and social service camps could be increasingly diverted to campus work projects through which children help in building stadia, pavilions and other similar amenities for schools and colleges.

An annual inter-State work camp should be held where students in considerable numbers should participate during the vacation in the construction of projects of national importance.

An All-India Youth Council should be set up to coordinate all the youth programmes taken up by the Central and State Governments and also to help these various agencies to extend their efforts.

Training for youth leadership should be one of the courses offered in universities teacher-training institutions and schools of social work.

The Junior Red Cross should be given every encouragement to flourish and its activities spread amoung as many schools as possible.

Scouts and Guides, in addition to their camping and outdoor activities, should be induced to take up small tasks in keeping their town on the village clean.

A National Playing Fields Association should be founded to organise a nation wide drive to enlist non-official cooperation for donations of land, equipment and funds for providing playing fields.

Every town should at least have one playing field which children from local schools can use.

The scheme of rendering compulsory national service for a period of about one year, before entering life or continuing higher education, should be tried out in certain selected areas as a pilot project.

Holiday camps for young people deserve special attention and voluntary organisations should be given every encouragement to open holiday camps at hill and sea resorts.

Increased facilities for road travel through the provision of special buses or tourist coaches should be provided to enable young people to visit places of historical and industrial interest.

A net work of youth hostels should be established all over India and there should be a better distribution of such hostels in the country.

Accurate information should be obtained from the States as to the use made from all these hostels. Examination and follow-up is necessary.

Non-student youth should be enabled not only to have continuation education but also recreational facilities. There is need for long-range planning in this respect.

A committee should be set up with representatives genuinely interested in the problem, to conduct a socio-economic survey to identify youth interest, their recreational pursuits, the degree of casual employment or unemployment, their occupational interests and educational attainments.

On the basis of the study, the question of creating new employment opportunities for youth should first be taken up by the Ministries of Labour and Education in mutual consultation.

Suitable training schemes to cover non-student employed youth, taking into account training programmes already in existence run by various Ministries and voluntary organisations, should then be formulated.

The youth welfare boards in the various States should undertake full responsibility for the implementation of these programmes although the Centre will be responsible for coordination.

Continuation classes for the age group 14-17, to ensure suitable further education for them, should be planned. The system of one-day-in-the-weak instruction in special colleges for this category of young people deserves detailed examination and a pilot scheme should be worked out for the establishment of one or two such colleges in every State and for the special training of teachers who will be required to staff them.

Schools for young workers to improve their general education and vocational efficiency should be set up.

Adult Education

Education organised for the adult population should also be further education which mainly stems from individual interests-economic, cultural and social.

It is necessary to have adequate motivation for adult education programmes which should, therefore, be linked with the occupational interests of the people.

Suitable programmes should be organised to give them the necessary education in the acquisition of certain simple skills to help them to utilise their spare time.

People working at the lower levels of industry, service or even agriculture should be encouraged to improve their educational qualifications and/or acquire better skills to improve their vocational efficiency.

Employees, government or non-government, should give these workers necessary encouragement; a comprehensive scheme for further education of various types for skilled and unskilled people should be drawn up by the Union Education Ministry in consultation with other Ministries or organisations concerned.

Training must progressively be concentrated on providing more opportunities for those who have left formal studies to take up work. A gradual network of day colleges as suggested in the chapter on Youth Programmes should be established in the country to cater for the needs of non-students. Long range planning in this respect is necessary.

The social education organiser and the block development officer should ensure that the school and community work in close cooperation for the spread of literacy.

Worker's education should cover the entire country enabling workers to take an intelligent and constructive part in citizenship. The programmes launched by the Central Board of Workers' Education need evaluation so that steps may be taken, wherever necessary, to introduce changes to keep abreast of the changing needs in working conditions.

Although the worker's education scheme is now completely financed by the Central Government, regional boards for workers' education for implementation at State level should also be established.

The present syllabus of the workers' training course may be modified to include general lectures on the cultural heritage of India, the deversity of her trade and handicrafts and her natural wealth.

Special orientation courses should be conducted by teacher-training institutions in the field of workers' education.

Background pamphlets on the institutions and way of life of people in different parts of India should be specially prepared for workers.

It should be the responsibility of adult education organisers to use mass media with discrimination and judgment in adult education programmes.

A combined adult education programme may be drawn up by the Ministries concerned for utilizing museums, libraries, the film and the radio in the education of adults.

In the adult schools and industrial training schools, certain immediate programmes should be included which will help adults to have a basic knowledge of their contry and to realise the need for whole-hearted cooperation in its developmental activities.

Teachers

The Union Ministry of Education should implement a scheme providing for a national minimum scale of salaries for teachers in the primary, middle and secondary schools.

Every attempt should be made to ensure that the scales recommended by the University Grants Commission are adopted in colleges and universities.

A Pay Revision Committee, Consisting of representatives from the Planning Commission, the Ministries of Education and Finance and representatives from the teaching profession, should be immediately, set up to work out the full financial implications and operative details of implementing the scheme for a national minimum scale of salaries for teachers with the help of subcommittees at State levels, if necessary. This work should be completed as expeditiously as possible.

Steps should be taken to ensure security of tenure for all trained teachers.

Other ancillary measures to improve the economic and social status of teachers will also have to be taken up on a country wide basis.

A scheme should be evolved by the Union Ministries of Education and Health and the State Governments to provide free medical aid for teachers and their families.

Adequate provision should be made in States Plans for free education upto the secondary stages, at least for the children of teachers.

Teachers should be given free quarters and this facility should be extended in the first instance to women teachers.

The construction of quarters should be taken up as an integral part of the construction of school buildings.

Prospects of higher promotion for teachers and the triple benefit scheme of insurance, provident fund and pension for them should be provided by all the States.

Teachers should not be asked to apply for the annual national awards, but the selection should be made by the authorities concerned based on record of work.

The status accorded to teachers by the public should be related essentially to the role played by them in the service of the community. Provision to enable teachers to serve on committees set up in regard to various expansion programmes for education, should be made.

A Central Council of Teachers with corresponding counterparts at State and district level to coordinate the inter-State programmes recommended for achieving emotional integration, may be formed.

A scheme of further education in the teaching line should be formulated.

There should be selection grades for all types of teachers on the basis of qualifications, efficiency and length of service. The financial implications of such a measure may be referred to the Pay Revision Committee already recommended.

A clear-cut programme for teacher training which will promote a national outlook, sense of citizenship and unity should be drawn up after evaluating present practice.

Teacher-training programmes should be enriched by introducing compulsory courses in group dynamics and cultural. Anthropology and by making specialisation any one subject of the higher secondary school also compulsory.

Excursions, inter-school visits, community work and cultural activities should form part of the carefully planned training given to pupil-teachers.

Geography should receive more attention in teacher-training programmes.

Every geography student in training colleges should have basic training in the use of audio-visual material and a thorough training in the use of geographical maps.

Research scholarships in economic and human geography should be made available for study at selected institutions of higher education.

The State Governments should depute their curriculum experts to work in mutual consultation and draw up a suitable curriculum for all training institutions keeping the national objectives in view.

The duration of the teacher-training courses should not be less than two years at any level.

For staffing training colleges, teachers of proved competence should be selected and given higher professional education in institute of education or universities. Universities and institutes of education should provide special professional education for this purpose.

The minimum age for admission to training schools should be 16.

The minimum qualification for men recruits should be a pass in class X. For the time being, this condition may be relaxed for women teachers.

Teachers should be given in-service training at least once in five years to enable them to keep in touch with new trends of development in the field of education and teaching techniques.

A handbook of suggestions should be produced by the Union Government for use in training institutions.

Similar handbooks of suggestions should be prepared for the use of teachers in primary and secondary schools with special reference to the social studies and languages.

These handbooks should give a brief outline of current problems and suggest a number of practical programmes for teachers to work out as part of curricular and co-curricular activities which help to foster the feeling of Indianness.

A panel of names from the teaching profession should be drawn up from which the most competent should be commissioned to write these handbooks.

Curriculum

Although it is not possible to provide religions education as a part of the curriculum for schools in a secular State, education will be incomplete if students are not helped to appreciate the spiritual values which the various religions present to the people. Talks, open to all, on the teachings of various religions by able and competent persons may be arranged in schools.

The overloading of the curriculum in number and content of subjects should be examined at all stages of school study.

Detailed curricula for all syllabuses and detailed syllabuses for different subjects in the curricula should Worked out.

Criteria and methods of evaluating whether the objectives set down for the curriculum are actually attained through the educational programmes, should be evolved and improvements suggested.

Basic research should be conducted in the problem of the conditions under which changes in human behaviour occur.

An efficient and well-staffed curriculum research unit should be set up in each State and also at the Centre under the National Council of Educational Research and Training. These units should work in close cooperation with textbook bureaux in teacher-training colleges and the result of their research should form the basis of curriculum construction and criteria for textbooks.

Fellowships for curriculum research should be instituted in selected teacher-training institutions.

The idea of national unity and the unity of man kind should be introduced from the very outset in the curriculum with due regard to children's age and understanding. The teaching of geography should be made compulsory.

Textbooks And Other Reading Materials

A well-thought-out and comprehensive scheme of publication in Indian languages should be launched without delay.

A large programme of translations must be launched. It is also necessary to produce original work in different branches of study written by Indians in Indian languages.

The University Grants Commission should be create a special fund for an imaginative programme of publishing worthwhile books in the Indian languages.

Immediate steps need to be taken to lift our textbooks from the neglect and low levels to which then have fallen.

Judicious selection of writers and proper coordination between the State Governments and publisher is necessary to get good textbooks written for our schools and colleges.

Potential talent in teachers should be developed by training them in the technique of writing textbooks.

A sufficient number of scholarships should be instituted annually for training abroad in textbook writing and publication.

History and geography textbooks, as the subjects demand all-India treatment, should be Centrally produced.

Supplementary books which deal with local history and geography may be produced by the State Governments in the respective regional languages and English so that they can also serve as useful material for inter-State understanding.

Textbooks especially in languages and the social studies imported from abroad for use in India should be screened and care teken to see that no books are suggested for schools which lead to bias or the creation of stereotypes.

The Central Government should be responsible for effective coordination of the activities of the State Governments in the field of textbook publication and selection.

The Central Bureau of Textbook Research, now under the National Council of Educational Research and Training should be strengthened to enable it to function as the secretariat of a national body dealing with all matters pertaining to textbooks.

The Bureau will prepare model textbooks for all the States and will have the sole authority of producing history and geography textbooks for distribution to all the States.

State textbooks committees will have Central representation and the States will be represented on the Central textbooks Committee.

The Central Bureau of Textbook Research may publish a journal to disseminate information in regard to the latest techniques in textbook writing and production.

The Bureau should have a library of textbooks from all over the world and from the States of Indian Union in the charge of a full-time librarian.

In view of the security of good illustrations a wing of the library should contain blocks for illustration, available on loan to all the States.

The Bureau will maintain liaison with the universities to ensure that textbooks written for them are also free from religious and communal bias.

Unfair suppression of detail should be avoided and facts of history should not be distorted in the attempt to promote integration.

The approach to history teaching and consequently in the writing of history textbooks, should stress cultural and social relationships of our people down the ages.

Geography textbooks should show children that we live today in an inter-dependent world.

The present shortage of up-to-date atlases and maps should be looked into and immediate action taken to meet this inadequacy.

The institution of prizes for children's books written with imagination and originality should be given a wider field.

Every facility should be provided to voluntary organisations to encourage talent in the writing of children's books.

The production of more children's magazines of a high standards, with translations in Hindi and English, would meet a long-felt need.

The help of newspapers which have the advantage of a wide coverage to attract talent should be utilised as fully as possible in getting suitable stories for children.

The best 20 or 30 stories in such a collection can then be compiled for publication in book form.

Newspaper offices which non publish annuals for the adult public may also bring out similar annuals for children with stories and articles about various parts of the country and the world attractively got-up and presented.

The establishment of a syndicate for children's literature might help in meeting the present dearth of good writing in this field through adequate scouting of of talent and maintenance of high standards in illustration and get-up.

The Government of India in collaboration with the National Book Trust, the Sahitya Akademi and the Children's Book Trust, should formulate a scheme for the immediate production of a series of reference books for adults and children on the different States and Union Territories of India.

Brief, attractively illustrated booklets for children on various subjects of Indian economy and planning should be published.

Books should be produced on traditional folklore and folk-songs from various parts of India together with the transliterated texts and the translation. Other books on various aspects of India should also be brought out.

Good reading habits should be cultivated not only in children but also in adults. One of the primary objectives of library development should be the promotion of school libraries and the training of teacher-librarians to run them. These libraries should be supplemented by public libraries running a children's wing, with a separate reading room for children.

The 'book mobile' or mobile library which now serves the adult population should also increasingly cater for children in the villages.

School libraries and children's libraries should have facilities to link books with pictures, maps, films, filmstrips and recordings. A scheme may be worked out to establish such a library in every secondary school in the country to begin with.

The holding of annual book fairs should be encouraged and every incentive given to promote quality in independent publishing.

The free flow of books to this country should not in any way be impeded by trade and import restrictions. Any policy imposing such restrictions should be reviewed. There should be effective liaison between the educational authorities and the customs so that essential books are not held up by red tape. Reduction in postal and freight charges would help the reading habit.

Textbook seminars should be held to highlight methods of production in India and in other countries.

Travelling book exhibitions should be held featuring books in the various Indian languages to help to stimulate public interest in our major languages and their literature.

The scheme for the production of literature for neo-literates operated by the Union Ministry of Education should be strengthened so that the work it has attempted so far can be expanded and improved.

The Central Bureau of Textbook Research should undertake research in regard to this most important field, to ensure that the books produced for the newely literate cater for all type of adults.

To promote the reading habit among neo-literates, picturestrips with suitably graded reading matter should be produced, as this is bound to be popular. The need for objective and effectively graded illustrations is important.

The highest priority should be given, in programmes for emotional integration, to the proper writing, illustration and production of textbooks at all levels of education and the building up of a storehouse of attractive and imaginative supplementary reading material.

CENTRAL WAGE BOARD FOR COFFEE PLANTATION INDUSTRY, 1961—REPORT

New Delhi, Ministry of Labour and Employment, 1965. 223p.

Chairman : Shri L. P. Dave

Members : Shri T. Manean ; Dr. R. Balakrishna (Replaced by Shri V. L. D'Souza) ; Shri U. K. Lakshman Gowda ; Shri M. B. Cariappa ; Shri M. C. Narasimhan ; Shri P. Variddhagiri.

Secretary : Shri N. Ahmed.

APPOINTMENT

In pursuance of the recommendation in paragraph 25 of chapter XXVII of the Second Five-Year Plan regarding the establishment of tripartite Wage Boards for individual industries, the Government of India, in the Ministry of Labour and Employment, by its resolution No. WB-3 (5)/61/1,dated July 7, 1961, set up a Centrol Wege Board for the Coffee Plantation Industry.

TERMS OF REFERENCE

To work out a wage structure based on the principles of fair wages as set forth in the report of the Committee on Fair Wages as far as practicable.

In evolving a wage structure, the Board should, in addition to the considerations relating to fair wages, also take into account :

(1) The need of the industry in a developing economy ;

(ii) The system of payment by results ;

(iii) The special characteristics of the industry in various regions and areas ;

(iv) Categories of workers to be covered (this may be according to the definition of Workman in the Industrial Disputes Act) ; and

(v) Working hours in the Industry.

Explanation : Whenever applying the system of payment by results, the Board shall keep in view the need for fixing minimum (fall-back) wage and also to safeguard against overwork and under speed.

CONTENTS

Introductory ; Interim Relief ; Wage Development in coffee Plantation Industry ; Staff Wages ; Paying Capacity of the Coffee Plantation Industry ; Board's Terms of Reference and Recommendations ; Reviseed Wage Structure ; Miscellaneous ; Appendices from I to XIII ; Annexures from A to M.

RECOMMENDATIONS

Terms Of Reference And Parties' Views

The Board has to work out a wage structure based on the principles enunciated in the Fair Wages Committee Report, keeping their practical aspects in view. And while evolving such a wage structure, the Board has to take into account the categories of workers which should be covered by the Board's recommendations ; working hours in the coffee plantation industry ; special characteristics of the industry in the various regions and areas ; needs of the industry in a developing economy, etc. The Board has also to make a study of the system of payment by results and in applying any such system it has to keep in view the need for fixing minimum (fall-back) wage and also the safeguards which should be provided against overwork and undue speed.

As mentioned above, the Board has to evolve a wage structure based on the principles of fair wages set forth in the Report of the Committee on Fair Wages. It would require consideration of several matters which have been dealt with in the Report of the Committee on Fair

Wages. In connection with the consideration of fair wage, the Board has to keep in view, among other things, the productivity of labour, the prevailing rates of wages in similar occupation in the same or neighbouring locality ; the level of national income and its distribution and the place of the industry in the economy of the country. In connection with the fixation of wages for the categories of workers, other than the lowest paid, the Board has to give due consideration to the several factors which determine the wage differentials such as skill, training, experience, etc. which have been enumerated in the Fair Wages Committee's Report. This is one aspect of the Board's work. But these considerations are also dependent upon the considerations of paying capacity of an industry. The capacity of the industry has been the central and pivotal point in all the deliberations of the Board. It opens out a very wide field requiring an objective study of the principles of measuring paying capacity, etc., laid down by the Fair Wages Committee with the help of a purposeful and detailed analysis of the financial data. Not merely this, the board, by its very terms or reference, has been required to investigate into the needs of the industry in a developing economy. This condition has added considerably to its responsibilities. Opinions widely differ in connection with the needs of the industry as these have to be viewed and determined in the context of the industry's future needs, at least for a period of five years.

Significance Of The Words "As far as Practicable"

The employers have laid great emphasis on the addition of the words "as far as practicable" to the Board's terms of reference. They consider the absence of these words in the terms of reference of any of the previous wage boards, other than Plantation (Tea, Coffee and Rubber) Wage Boards, as of considerable significance. It is their argument that while the terms of reference place outside limits on the scope of the Board's work, its direction, within the four corners of the terms of reference, is unfettered and the Board is free to vary, modify, combine or reject the norms laid down by Fair Wages Committee to make the Board's recommendations about wages national and practicable.

Omission Of The Factor Of 'Social Justice'

There is yet another point which the employees have raised on the Board's terms of reference. They hold the view that the omission of the factor of social justice from the Board's terms of reference is not without significance particularly when it found a place in the terms of reference of other wage boards. The employers wish the Board to draw an inference that by this omission Government intended that social justice is not to be taken as imperative and the Board should be guided by the practical considerations of he economic needs and the special circumstances of the industry.

Norms Of 15th Session Of Indian Labour Conference

The question whether the norms of need based minimum Wage recommended by the 15th Session of the Indian Labour Conference have a bearing on the Board's investigations and its deliberations in connection with the working out of a wage structure on Fair Wages Committee's principles was also a subject of considerable discussion. The Wage boards have been giving due consideration to these norms. The 15th Indian Labour Conference has resolved that the minimum wage is 'need based' and should ensure the minimum human needs of the industrial worker irrespective of any other considerations and that the norms laid down by the conference for calculating the need based wage should guide all wage fixing authorities including minimum wage committees, wage boards, adjudicators, etc. These norms have assumed importance as the Conference, recognising the existence of instances where implementation of its recommended norms would be difficult, has itself directed that wherever the minimum wage fixed was below the recommendations of the Conference, the wage fixing authorities should justify it by giving circumstances which prevented them from adherence to the norms laid down by the Conference. These norms of the need based minimum wage are discussed later on in this chapter. But, while on the question of Board's terms of reference, it may be pointed out that the workers' side attached great importance to the resolution of the 15th Indian Conference prescribing the need based wage formula and was not willing to accept any alterations therein. On the other hand, the employers expressed the view that the Board was strictly bound by its terms of reference and the criteria laid down by the 15th Session of the Indian Labour Conference did not form part of the terms of reference. They also tried to establish that the need based wage formula is not applicable when wage revision in the coffee plantation industry is being contemplated. They referred to the proceedings of the 10th Session of the Industrial Committee on Plantations to show that the question of applicability of otherwise of the need based wage formula to the plantation industry was left to be looked into by the concerned wage board.

Briefly stated, the employers' point of view has been that the Board should not consider the norms of the 15th Indian Labour Conference and the resolution is to be regarded as extraneous as far as the Board's enquiry is concerned. In regard to the recommendation of Fair Wages Committee also, they are opposed to the Board following them as they are and have urged, in respect of every recommendation of the Committee, that the practical aspect of it should not be ignored. As has been pointed out (in Chapter IV) in connection with the Board's discussions on paying capacity of the industry, the industry would not like the Board to go by the representative cross section of the industry in a region. According to the industry, the practical way of fixing wages was by determining the capacity of the marginal and uneconomic units of the industry.

The Board does not propose to express any opinion on the arguments of the employers which they have advanced in support of their contention that the Board should not follow Fair Wages Committee's principles of wage fixation and should consider itself free to amend them to sit the requirements of the industry. It may, however, be pointed out that wage fixation is not a simple matter of arithmetical calculations. Other wage boards have fixed the wages to suit the peculiar conditions obtaining in the industry concerned including the extent to which the industry could bear the burden. Even in highly industrialised centres, wages differ from industry to industry and from unit to unit despite efforts having been made to bring about uniformity in wages by the wage fixing authorities. It shows that wage fixing authorities are usually guided, to a large extent, by the practical aspects of wage fixation. The 15th Indian Labour Conference's resolution was before all the wage boards, They gave due consideration to the need-based formula enshrined in this resolution, but no wage board appears to have recommended a need based wage, according to the money value of these norms, irrespective of any other considerations. The employers in the coffee industry are also aware of this position. In support of their contention that the need based wage formula should not be followed in its present form, they have pointed out that the Central Pay Commission the Sugar Wage Board, the Cement Wage Board and the Bank Tribunal have rejected the need based wage norms of the 15th Indian Labour Conference as impracticable in the present stage of the country's economy and have regarded them as distant goal to be reached. The labour, however, did not agree with these views. The approach of this Board also would not and could not have been different in this respect from that of the previous wage boards even in the absence of any specific mention about the application of the Fair Wage Committee's principles of wage fixation to the coffee industry in a practical manner. Even so, the Board might make it clear that at no stage of its deliberations, the practical aspects of wage fixation and the needs and requirements of coffee industry were lost sight of while recommending a wage structure for this industry.

Wage Structure Suited To The Industry

As stated earlier, by the very terms of reference, the Board has to consider :

(i) The special characteristics of the industry in the various regions and areas ;

(ii) The place of the industry in the economy of the country ; and

(iii) The needs of the industry in a developing economy.

The idea of a wage board is that there should be a practical approach to the problems under its consideration. With equal representatives of workers and employers, it has the advantage of expert knowledge of the special problems of the industry. Any wage structure that may be evolved by such a board would bepractical and 'suited to the conditions obtaining in the trade'. The wage structure that is being recommended by this Board is a wage structure which has been devised after having taken into consideration all points discussed in the Report of the Committee on Fair Wages including the paying capacity of the industry. The Board has also taken into account the pecular conditions in the coffee plantation industry as a whole. Any appreciation of the new wage structure in the industry, therefore, is not possible without at least a brief study of the various aspects of the industry including the three mentioned above. Some important features of the coffee plantation industry are, therefore, dealt with below.

Historical Background

Coffee Plantation began as small proprietory farms. More successful among the early pioneers later combined into partnerships and company ownerships. The industry began to expand and by 1872, India was able to export a little over 25,000 tons of coffee and the area under cultivation was 3,00,000 acres. But a series of reverses followed. Keen competition in the world market from foreign coffees, general depression in the thirties and slump in the coffee production resulted in the decline of Indian coffee industry which was depending, very largely, on its export market. The area under coffee shrank to 1,81,000 ares in 1940-41. To meet the situation, Indian Coffee Market Expansion Board was constituted on December 21, 1940, under the Coffee Expansion Ordinance* with the object of controlling and marketing coffee in India and abroad. This Board was the predecessor of the present Coffee Board and since its formation the industry entered into a period of recovery and stability.

Caltivation Of Coffee

The Coffee trees begin to yield from the fourth year though they attain maturity only from the seventh year. There is only one crop in a year in India. Coffee trees blossom in March/April with the first showers received after the preceding dry period. The berries mature and

*No. XIII of 1940.

ripen in the course of the next six to eight months. In some areas the crop is ready as early as in September, while in others it is as late as in January. The harvesting of crop is done in three rounds to ensure that only fully ripe berries are picked in each round and, therefore, in some areas the harvest season lasts till May.

Coffee Growing Areas

Coffee cultivation is confined mostly to the three States of Southern India, viz., Mysore, Madras and Kerala. Besides these, there is a small area under coffee in the States of Andhra Pradesh, West Bengal, Orissa, Assam, Madhya Pradesh and Andamans. The area planted with coffee in different States during 1963-64 season is given below :

State	Planted area under Coffee (in acreas)
Mysore	180,179
Madras	67,554
Kerala	71,336
Other States	737
Total	3,19,806

The important coffee growing regions, Statewise, are :

(a) Mysore State	Area Under Coffee (1963-64) (in acres)
1. Chikmagalur	76,895
2. Hassan	26,720
3. Mysore (Billigiria)	1,327
4. North Coorg	32,393
5. South Coorg	42,515
6. Others	329
Total	180,179
(b) Madras State	**Area Under Coffee (1963-64)**
1. Nilgiris	15,490
2. Nilgiris-Wynaad	6,970
3. Madurai (Palnis)	30,255
4. Coimbatore (Anamallais)	3,420
5. Salem (Shevaroys)	9,924
6. Others	1,495
Total	67,554
(c) Kerala State	**Area Under Coffee (1963-64)**
1. Palghat (Nelliampathies)	4,695
2. Cannanore (North Wynaad)	14,008
3. Kozhikodi (South Synaad)	43,633
(Contd.)	
4. Kottayam (Kanan Devan)	7,270
5. Eranakulam	1,312
6. Others	418
Total	71,336
(d) Other States	737
Grand Total	319,806

Two Important Varieties Of Coffee

The main varieties of coffee grown are Arabica and Robusta. Out of the total crop of 69,000 tonnes in 1963-64 season, Arabica coffee accounted for 39,125 tonnes and Robusta 29,875 tonnes, i.e., in terms of percentage Arabica coffee account for 57 per cent and Robusta 43 per cent of the total production.

Arabica coffee is grown at the attitudes of 2500 feet and above. It requires shade to protect it from the heat of the sun and the standard of care, attention and cultural practices are of higher order. Arabica coffee is more susceptible to insects and fungus attacks. Robusta coffee cultivation is not much different from Arabica except that it flourishes at lower elevations and can withstand extremes of climate. It is more disease resistant and its cultivation is less difficult. Since Robusta plant is bigger in size, it can be easily distinguished from the Arabica tree. Arabica coffee fetches far higher prices than Robusta in the market.

The State-wise production of Arabica and Robusta varieties of coffee in India during the year 1963-64 was as follows :

State	Estimated Production In 1963-64 (in tonnes)		
	Arabica	Robusta	Total
Mysore	32,880	19,635	52,515
Madras	5,515	1,365	6,880
Kerala	670	8,875	9,545
Other States	60	—	60
Total	39,125	29,875	69,000

Important among Arabica growing regions are Mysore district (including Bababuddin), North Coorg, Nilgiris, Nilgiri-Wynaad, Palnis and Nelliampathies. The Robusta growing areas are Mysore district, South Coorg, Malabar-Wynaad, Travancore and Palnis. The table given below shows the distribution of area under Arabica and Robusta in the various district of growth during the year 1950-51, 1954-55 and 1959-60 :

District of Growth	1950/51 (Area in Acres) Arabics	Robusta	Total	1954/55 (Area in Acres) Arabics	Robusta	Total	1959/60 (Area in Acres) Arabics	Robusta	Total
				Mysore State					
Mysore (including Bababudin)	72756	14059	86815	72510	20161	92671	74375	23965	98340
Biligiris	1060	—	1060	1297	—	1297	1313	—	1313
North Coorg	21168	1553	22721	21455	2895	24360	27343	4797	32140
South Coorg	8144	13543	21687	6873	20304	27177	6739	29545	36284
Total	103128	29155	132283	102145	43360	145505	109770	58307	168077
				Madras State					
Nilgiris	14758	180	14938	15000	221	15221	14747	694	15341
Nilgiri-Wynaad	6310	1014	7324	5194	1432	6626	3980	2396	6376
Shevaroys	10385	—	10385	10538	1	10539	10039	—	10039
Palnis	25485	625	26110	27344	1214	28558	28571	2722	31293
Anamallais	2287	484	2771	2186	844	3030	2340	925	3265
Total	59225	2303	61528	60262	3712	63974	59577	6737	66314
				Kerala State					
Malabar-Wynaad	2627	29009	31636	1595	36669	36264	1371	46223	47594
Nelliampathies	1499	946	2445	2299	1309	3608	1904	2031	3935
Kanan Devans	NA	NA	NA	702	—	702	703	—	703
Travancore	NA	NA	NA	28	2300	2328	292	7453	7745
Total	4126	29955	34081	4624	38278	42902	4270	55707	59977
Grand Total	166479	61413	227892	167031	85350	252381	173617	120751	294368

Regional Peculiarities

In view of the cooperative pooled system of marketing followed in coffee, it is unnecessary to go into the quality characteristics of coffee grown in different regions such as their cup quality, flavour, etc. The entire coffee is pooled under a few specified grades and marketed. Since marketing is not on the basis of individual estate crops or the production of a particular coffee region, individual characteristics have no relevance to the price realised by a producer. The type of coffee produced namely, Arabica or Robusta, and the grades into which they are processed, namely, peaberry, plantations, cherry, flats, etc. determine the sales realisations. The regional differences have therefore, to be traced out to the type of coffee produced, i.e., whether it is Arabica or Robusta and the yields or production trends in each region.

All the coffee districts in Madras, except the Anamallais, come within the North East Monsoon belt and all the districts in Mysore and Kerala and the Anamallais come within the South West Monsoon belt. There was a drop of nearly 500 acres in Arabica in S.W. Monsoon area between 1941-42 and 1949-50 but in the following decade ending 1959-60, the increase was by over 9000 acres. On the other hand, Arabica area in the N. E. Monsoon region increased by more than 13,000 acres in the first decade as against only 500 acres in the second. If Palnis were excluded, this area actually shows a decline of about 4000 acres during the second decade. Many estates in these districts were at one time well known for high quality coffees. The decline is attributed to attacks of pests and diseases as well as to the wide fluctuations in coffee yields caused seasonal vagaries in the region.

Trends In Production

Yield and production, above all other factors, mark the regional differences in the coffee industry. At any rate these are the reliable factors to be gone into the considering the question of wages for the different regions. The distribution of coffee crop among the States of Mysore, Madras and Kerala for the period after the States of Reorganisation is analysed below. As coffee is liable to wide crop fluctuation, any year's production or yield is not safe to take and therefore average over a period of years is invariably taken for such comparisons.

Yearly Average Production For the Years 1955-56 to 1959-60 (In Tonnes)

State	Arabica	Percentage	Robusta	Percentage	Total	Percentage
Mysore	20,652	75.4	9,978	65.2	30,630	72.2
Madras	6,360	23.2	752	4.9	7,112	16.7
Kerala	360	1.4	4,560	29.9	4,920	11.1
Total	27,372	100 00	15,290	100.00	42,662	100.00

It will be seen that both Arabica and Robusta production is concentrated in Mysore State. Madras and Kerala take second and third places but much lower than Mysore. Arabica production in Kerala is only 1.4 per cent of the total Arabica crop, but is next to Mysore in the matter Robusta.

The five years average annual production of Arabica and Robusta by districts from 1941 to 1960 and their respective increase of output are given below :

Arabica and Robusta Production by Districts of Growth Averaged for 1941-42/1944-45 and Five Years ending 1949-50, 1954-55 and 1959-60 (In Tonnes)

Districts of Growth	1941-42/ 1944-45		1945-46/ 1949-50		1950-51/ 1954-55		1955-56/ 1959-60		% increase of 1955-56/ 1959-60 over 1941-42/ 1944/45	
	Ara.	Rob.	Ara.	Rob.	Ara.	Rob.	Ara.	Rob.	Ara.	Rob.
Mysore (including Bababudin)	5522	1008	5553	1503	6516	1740	12205	4017	121	299
Billigiris	108	—	201	—	323	—	495	—	358	—
N. Coorg	2644	51	2671	105	4092	163	6079	458	130	798
S. Coorg	1092	1114	1050	1900	1293	2468	1873	5501	72	394
Nilgiris	—	—	1310	11	990	20	1652	43	26*	291*
Nilgiri-Wynaad	—	—	604	67	625	88	708	186	17*	178*
Anamallais	443	136	399	176	401	178	571	242	29	378
Shevaroys	929	—	1071	—	933	—	1764	—	90	—
Palnis	595	90	845	111	756	156	1665	281	180	212
Malabar-Wynaad	70	1151	64	1743	2	2117	9	4105	—87	257
Nelliampathies	63	27	95	82	133	129	249	212	295	615
Kanan Devans	47	—	76	—	43	—	54	—	15	—
Travancore	—	280	13	201	10	228	18	243	38	13

*The percentage increase is over 1965-46/1949-50 ; since separate figures for Nilgiris and Nilgiri-Wynaad are not available for 1941-42/1944-45.

According to the trend of production the chief Arabica growing districts are Mysore (including Bababydan). North Coorg, Nilgiries, Shevaroya and Palnis. Mysore (121 per cent), North Coorg (130 per cent) and Palnis (180 per cent) have more than doubled their crop by the late fifties. Notwithstanding its greater percentage rise in output, Palnis' yield per acre has not kept pace with other districts. Shevaroya recorded 90 per cent and South Coorg 72 per cent increases in their Arabica output. Although Billigiris and Nelliampathies recorded an increase of 358 per cent and 295 per cent respectively, these are not strictly comparable with the districts mentioned earlier because of their considerable smaller area under coffee.

In Robusta, South Coorg registered the highest increase (394 per cent) with Mysore district coming second (299 per cent) and Malabar-Wynaad third (257 per cent). North Coorg, Nilgiris, Nilgiri-Wynaad, Palnis and Nelliampathies also recorded marked increases in Robusta output Billigiris and Shevaroys have not produced any Robuts crop worth noting.

Yield Per Acre

The average yield per acre periods of five years is given in the table below which will show that district accounting for a larger share of production need not necessarily have a higher productivity per acre :

Average Yield per Acre according to District of Growth for Periods of Five Years ending 1949-50, 1954-55 and 1959-60 (in Cwt/acre)

District of Growth	1945-46/49-50		1950-51/54-55		1955-56/59-60		Percentage Increase of Col. 4 over Col. 2	
1	2		3		4		5	
	Ar.	Rob.	Ar.	Rob.	Ar.	Rob.	Ar.	Rob.
Mysore	1.52	2.36	1.79	2.00	3.48	3.51	129 p.c.	49 p.c.
Billigiris	NA	—	5.47	—	8.42	—	—	—
North Coorg	2.52	2.19	3.84	1.42	5.10	1.83	102 p.c.	16 p.c.
South Coorg	2.45	3.43	3.38	2.96	6.12	4.28	150 p.c.	25 p.c.
Anamallais	NA	NA	3.54	6.58	4.95	6.25	—	—
Nilgiri/Nilgiri-Synaad	1.77	1.67	1.54	1.47	2.39	1.89	35 p.c.	13 p.c.
Shevaroys	2.08	—	1.78	—	3.37	—	62 p.c.	—
Palnis	0.69	3.00	1.16	4.32	1.28	3.41	85 p.c.	14 p.c.
Malabar-Wynaad	—	1.42	—	1.32	—	2.13	—	50 p.c.
Nelliampathis	1.29	1.96	1.04	1.92	2.01	2.40	56 p.c.	22 p.c.
All India	1.67	2.17	1.93	1.94	3.33	2.93	99 p.c.	35 p.c.

Billigiris' is the highest yield per acre of Arabica but it is not strictly comparable with the yield of other districts because of its small acreage. From among the other districts, South Coorg had the best record of average Arabica yield as well as rise in productivity. North Coorg was behind South Coorg during 1955-56/1959-60 which was the result of new area planted with Arabica since 1955.

The average yield of Mysore (including Bababudin was below the all-India average during the periods 1945-46/1949-50 as well as 1950-51/1954-55. It showed a sudden and appreciable increase after the mid-fifties and there was a rise of per acre yield from 1.52 cwts. and 1.79 cwts. per acre to 3.48 cwts. per acre.

Malabar-Wynaad has the lowest yield of Robusta coffee. Apart from the topography and climate, one of the important contributing factors is the larger per centage of small holdings in this area. The number of holdings below five acres in Malabar-Wynaad in 1959-60 was 9.168 (83 per cent) out of a total of 11,089 compared to 4,250 (76 per cent) out of 5, 986 in South Coorg and 5,095 (66 per cent) out of 7,686 in Mysore.

The N.B. Monsoon districts are generally low yielding regions compared with the S.W. Monsoon districts. It is for this reason Shevaroys and Nilgiris have lower yield per acre. Palnis has the lowest Arabica yield per acre inspite of its impressive increase in output.

Small Growers

Small grower is defined in the Coffee Rules, 1955, as a registered owner who is not a larger grower. A large grower is defined in the same Rules as a registered owner owning land planted either with Arabica or Robusta or both aggregating not less than 50 acres ; whether the land is in one estate or in more than one estate.

There is a predominance of small growers in the coffee plantation industry and this is its important feature. The table below shows the distribution of the acreage and production according to sizes in Mysore, Madras and Kerala :

Size of Holdings In Acres	Mysore	Madras (Acreage)	Kerala	Total	Total Production (1959-60* in Tons.)
Below 50	72,113	36,056	44,788	152,957	18,375
50-100	17,686	4,353	2,756	24,795	4,256
100-200	26,428	8,172	4,574	39,174	8,302
200 and above	51,872	17,985	7,859	77,716	18,857

*1959-60 figures as available in the Coffee Statistics.

Estates of below 50 acres from 50 per cent of the total acreage. The holdings between 50-100 acres account for 8.67 per cent of the total coffee area. The holdings between 100-200 acres are 13.68 per cent and those of 200 and above 27.15 per cent. Company owned properties in coffee is about 20 per cent of the total coffee area. The distribution of holdings shows that out of a total area under coffee (of 272,298 acres in 1960), company owned properties account for 53,959 acres, i.e., just about 20 per cent. Out of this, however, companies holding 300 acres and more account for 18.25 per cent.

The small growers may not be able to produce as efficiently as large growers can. The small scale operations deprive the small growers of the benefits of advance management and large scale economy. But the small growers have also some advantages. They do not have the over-head charges like those of large estates and their tax liabilities are very much limited. Most of them also are free from the provisions of labour laws. Much of the coffee on small holdings is grown along with other crops like pepper, cardamum, oranges, paddy, etc. The small growers who have diversified crops do not suffer as much as the large growers due to crop cycles and low prices of coffee.

Mixed Estates

Coffee estates, in some cases form part of estates of tea, rubber, cardamum, etc., and are managed as one unit; such units are called 'mixed estates'. The table given below furnishes information* about the mixed estates having majority coffee acreage in the three Southern States, Mysore, Madras and Kerala:

State	No. of Units	Area under Coffee (in Acres)	Percentage of Coffee	Percentage of other Crop	Total Acreage on planting: In the State	Total Acreage on planting: Under mixed Estates
Mysore	122	29,722	91.65	8.35	154,007	31,528
Madras	51	10,072	72.97	27.03	67,324	17,922
Kerala	22	4,769	67.32	32.68	49,581	8,619
Total	195	44,563	—	—	270,912	58,069

Source: UPASI—Planning Directory of Southern India—1958.

The mixed product estates pose a problem in Madras due to difference in the conditions between the plantations of various products. In Mysore, however, acreage under tea and rubber plantations being negligible, the problems of mixed product estates are not serious.

Coffee Board

Contribution of the Coffee Board towards the development of coffee has been remarkable. Its constitution is broad based and representation has been given to all the interests directly or indirectly connected with the coffee, industry. Including the Chairman, it consists of 33 members; three representing Parliament; three representing the Governments of Mysore, Madras and Kerala; 12 coffee growers; three coffee traders, one coffee owner, three consumers; four labour; and three others. The Coffee Board is responsible for the quality of coffee, its collection, processing, marketing, propaganda, research and development. It functions through sub-committees. The Chairman is the Chief Executive of the Board and also presides over the meetings of the Board and committees. The Coffee Board conducts investigations and researches to attain healthy and prosperous growth of coffee plantations by taking the fruits of researches to the door steps of the planters. Through its development wing, the Coffee Board gives long term loans for intensive and extensive cultivation to registered estates in the 5.50 acreage group. supplies approved coffee seeds to the estates and makes equipment and machinery available on hire purchase terms to estates upto 50 acres. It also renders technical and advisory services through demonstration plots, trial plots, etc.

Marketing Of Coffee

The most important function of the Coffee Board is to organise colletion of coffee from the growers and after rendering it marketable,.arrange for its sale to the best advantage of producers and consumers. Coffee produced in the country is marketed through a common pool in which all registered owners participate. These registered owners deliver all the coffee produced by them except such quantities of coffee as may be permitted by the Board to be retained for seed purposes and domestic consumption. The Board makes an estimate of the current season's coffee crop and after making an estimate for the internal market, the balance is allocated for release in the export market. The Board has opened a number of pool depots at convenient centres in the coffee growing areas to enable the small growers to deliver their produce without having to transport it over long distances. Large growers deliver their produce to the pool agents appointed by the Board at the main coffee curing centres. The small growers are paid Rs. two per point immediately towards the price for coffee delievered. The balance is paid in instalments. The large growers are, however, paid in instalments as and when sale prices are realised.

The Coffee Board's estimate of cost of production and actual return to the growers per point value in the last few years are given below:

*Latest figures is not available.

Years	Board's Estimates of Cost of Production. (Value per Point on 50 kg.)	Actual Return to the Grower per Point Value per 50 kg.
	Rs. P	Rs. P.
1956-57	2.18	2.78
1957-58	2.29	2.47
1958-59	2.23	2.46
1959-60	2.11	2.29
1960-61	2.18	2.02
1961-62	2.07	2.26
1962-63	2.02	2.30
1963-64	2.00	2.50 (payment so far made)

There are no serious complaints about the sales realisations in the internal market. The industry, however, seems to be dissatisfied with the sales realisations in the export market. It has been represented to this board that in the last few years because of the lower export prices, return to the grower had been steadily falling. The industry is not, however, in favour of raising internal prices unduly so as to cover export losses as it considers it against the long term interests of the growers.

Progress Of Coffee Industry

The progress of coffee plantation industry in the last, one decade has been phenomenal, as may be seen from the table* given below. Along with the steady growth in output, internal consumption and exports have also gone up during this period.

Year	Area in Acres	Production in Tonnes	Consumption in Internal Market (In Tonnes)	Exports** (In Tonnes)
1955	252686	25427	22646	10334
1956	554449	35028	24189	3115
1957	260401	42572	26622	19508
1958	268472	44490	27570	12109
1959	272298	46915	30105	16513
1960	294929	49790	30004	14985
1961	297320	68020	33873	19582
1962	308126	46050	34651	29690
1963	319806	56200	33634	20376
1964	319806	69000	35200	33000

The significant factor of the industry is that coffee production has more than doubled in the last 10 years with only 20 per cent increase in the acreage. The increase in production has, therefore, been on account of intensive cultivation and higher yield per acre. During the Second Plan, the yield per acre was 168 kg. ; it has already gone upto 216.59 kg. per acre and is expected to rise to 250 kg. per acre by the end of the current plan. The above table also reveals that there has been substantial rise in the internal consumption and exports have also been rising. India's exports of coffee rose from 19582 tonnes in 1960-61 to 33,000 tonnes in 1963-64. No targets of production were fixed for the First and the Second Plans. The target for the Third Plan was fixed at 80,000 tonnes to be achieved by 1965-66, out of which 35,300 tonnes were to be consumed internally and 44,700 tonnes were to be exported. The actual achievement for the year 1963-64 is 68,922 tonnes of production out of which 35,200 tonnes have been consumed internally and 33,005 tonnes have been exported. The target of production for the Fourth Plan by 1970-71 is 85,000 tonnes out of which 40,000 tonnes are meant for internal consumption and 45,000 tonnes are proposed to be exported.

The coffee industry's prospects primarily depend upon the cost of production of coffee. To reduce the cost of production all steps are being taken by the industry with the assistance and cooperation of the Coffee Board, which is providing facilities for increasing the yield per acre. The employers have become extremely productivity conscious and have been adopting every possible measure within their means to curtail and cost of production. Not only the operations considered necessary in the past for maintaining a coffee plantation are being restricted, but some operations which were previously , carried on by manual labour are now being conducted more economically and efficiently with the help of machines. The employers have fully realised, nad have given expression to their views that labour cannot be wastefully employed when wage costs were rising and mechanisation and technological improvements in the method of production could bring down the cost of production. The land-labour ratio seems to be going down and expectations are that in future less labour might be required to produce large crops.

There is a growing tendency amongst the planters to adopt improved methods of cultivation and processing of coffee. There has been an increase in the demand for fertilizers, machinery and accessories. The growers' fortunes depend, to a large extent, on the timely blossom showers in March-April and the backing showers, thereafter, at appropriate intervals. But due to the vagaries of nature, blossom showers do not always oblige the growers. Absence of blossom showers and occurrence of inadequate showers spell disaster but the growers have now become conscious of the benefits of sprinkler

*Source—Coffee Board.

**Exports figures are for financial years.

irrigation equipment which could come to their aid in ensuring a good crop inspite of uncertain weather conditions. They are, therefore, going in for such equipment. As has been pointed out in the Board's discussions on paying capacity, the increased production of coffee has been to a very large extent due to the scientific methods of cultivation adopted by the planters and the assistance rendered to them by the Research Department of the Coffee Board. This has led to high hopes about the future of the coffee industry in the country and in the Fourth Plan yield per acre is expected to be further increased as against 250 kg. at the end of Third Plan and as against 216.59 kg. at present. Some coffee estates hold reserve lands which are available for immediate coffee plantation and expansion. Coffee growing areas in Andhra Pradesh and other States also are expected to develop. There is a great scope of coffee growing in these area and large areas are expected to be brought under coffee cultivation. But the increase in coffee production is aimed at mainly by a higher yield per acre. The old and obsolescent coffee plants are being replaced by higher yielding ones and the replacement programme spread-over a period of 12 years at the rate of 10,000 acres per annum is under consideration. The Coffee Board's programme for rehabilitation of coffee provides for long term loans and the depreciation provision made for replanting in the assessment of coffee prices is expected to enable the planters to fulfil the programme of replanting. The employers have some apprehensions of glut of considered by some to be misplaced. There is a growing demand of coffee in the world and this commodity has a potential market at home. It is expected that 80 thousand tonnes of coffee that might be produced in the last year of the Third Plan would be consumed; a large portion of it in the internal market. The pirces of coffee in the internal market have been considered to be satisfactory. There is a competitive export market in which only quality and lower prices would help India to sell its coffee. The planters and the curers are becoming increasingly conscious of this fact and are studying modern teachniques for improving the quality of coffee. The Coffee Board is, there to render them every possible assistance in this respect.

Place Of The Industry In The Economy Of The Country

The contribution of coffee plantation industry to the general economy of the country is not insignificant. Its part in the economy of Southern India, particularly of Mysore State, is very great. Besides giving livelihood to the planting community consisting of some 48,000 growers, the coffee plantation industry gives direct and indirect employment to be large number of persons. The average daily number of persons directly employed in the coffee estates is 2,85,444*. Besides, the industry gives employment to a large number of persons in coffee curing works, coffee trade and other ancillary institutions and firms. The industry supports many other subsidiary industries depending on it as suppliers of goods and services. By its distribution in Mysore State and by its location in the sparesely inhabited Malnad areas, the coffee industry plays a significant role in the economy of this region.

The industry pays excise duty and customs duty to the national exchequer and sales tax and agricultural income-tax to the various States of its location. The contributions of the industry by way of central excise duty and customs duty are on the increase. The central excise duty has increased from Rs. 50 lakhs in 1949-50 to Rs. 165 lakhs in 1960-61 and the customs duty has increased during the same period from Rs. 67,344 to Rs. 7,74,868. The figures of agricultural income-tax collected from coffee estates in the States of Mysore, Madras and Kerala are not available for all the years but from the figures available for certain years it appears that this industry makes a substantial contribution the State revenues by way of agricultural income-tax.

Moreover, from the point of view of national economy coffee is now assuming an important position as foreign exchange earner. In the fiscal year 1963-64, it had contributed Rs. 8.30 crores to the country's foreign exchange earning and elsewhere it has been pointed out that the industry has already earned Rs. 11.31 crores of foreign exchange upto the end of October 1964. It ranks sixteenth amongst the foreign exchange earning commodities of the country.

World Coffee

The total area under coffee cultivation in India accounts for about one per cent of the total world area under this crop. The principal coffee growing areas are situated in four continents namely North and South Americas, Africa and Asia. The largest contribution to world coffee comes from the South American countries of which Brazil is the premier coffee producing country. Brazil's production of coffee has fallen during the last three years and consequently the total production of South American countries has come down from 38.89 million sacks (132 lbs, or 60 kg. each) in 1960-61 to 21.52 million sacks in 1964-65. During the same period, the North American countries production of coffee has, however, slightly increased from 9.5 million sacks to 10.27 million sacks. Among the Asian countries, India and Indonesia are the principal producers of coffee. Production of both the countries is increasing. From

*Figures for the year 1960-61.

3.71 million sacks in 1961-62, it has increased to 4.31 million sacks in 1964-65. The important coffee growing countries in Africa are Angola, Guinea, Ethiopia, Congo and Uganda. Production of coffee has gone up in almost all the African countries. As against 13.8 million sacks in 1960-61, the production has rise to 16.6 million sacks in 1964-65. The world total production has, however, gone down from 65.5 million sacks in 1960-61 to 52.6 million sacks in 1964-65. It may be pointed, out that world production had recorded a substantial increase in 1961-62, but it fell in 1962-63 to the level of the base year 1960-61. It showed a slight increase in 1963-64 and from a production of 67.8 million sacks, it came down to 52.6 million sacks in 1964-65.

The average yield per acre in India is low when compared to the yield in other coffee growing countries. A comparison with the yields in some of the other important coffee growing countries such as Brazil, Mexico, Tanganiyka and Indonesia indicated that the yield per acre in India is just about 70 per cent of the yield in these countries.

International Coffee Agreement

The world annual production of coffee is now around 52 million sacks, 15 million sacks fewer than a year before. The world consumption of coffee has now reached an average of 44 million sacks. The consumption is increasing and yet a large surplus is left over after current consumption and coffee stocks have been after accumulation in the past few years. The latest estimate of carry over stock of coffee has been put at equivalent of the word requirement for three years. Since 1957, leading world producers of coffee have been trying to organise themselves with a view to arresting the steady decline in coffee prices by regulation the production and export of coffee. The International Coffee Agreement was reached in 1958 and it was followed by the formation of the Federation of Central American Coffee Growers and the Federation of African Coffee Producers. Despite a quota system introduced since 1958, the world stocks of coffee have been accumulating in most of the coffee producing centres and consequently the coffee prices in the world markets are showing a downward trend. The prosperity of Indian coffee is closely associated with the world prosperity. India is, therefore, a signatory to the International Coffee Agreement as one of the 47 countries. The export quota of coffee is governed by the International Coffee Agreement which came into force in September 1962. The Agreement has fixed a basic quota of 21,600 tonnes in 1962-63 exclusive of India's exports to the non-quota countries. India exports to as many as 31 quota countries and 30 non-quota countries. Important amongst the quota countries are West Germany, U.S.A., Italy, Yugoslavia, France, Netherlands, Norway, Sweden, Belgium, Bulgaria and Pakistan. Important non-quota countries are U.S.S.R., Poland, Iraq, Saudi Arabia and Bahrain Islands. In so far as quote countries are concerned. India's share in the international coffee trade is thus restricted and at present there is not much scope of increasing the exports of the quota countries as to the non-quota countries.

The International Coffee Agreement aims, inter alia, at achieving reasonable balance between supply and demand on a basis which will ensure adequate supply of coffee to consumers and market to the coffee producers at equitable prices. It also aims at contribution to the development of productive resources and/or to the promotion and maintenance of employment and income in the member countries, thereby helping to bring about fair wages, higher living standards and better working conditions.

Needs Of The Industry

The Board has to consider the needs of the industry in a developing economy and in order to ascertain these needs views were solicited through specific questions in the questionnaires. The replies reveal that the parties hold somewhat different views. The workers' organisations have expressed the view that the essential need in a developing-economy are to step up production to meet the growing demand for coffee by increasing yield per acre and by giving a 'square deal to the workers'. It is their contention that not only the industry has got its needs in a developing economy, the workers also have their needs in a developing economy. According to them developing economy is resulting in developing inflation bringing in its wake a progressive diminition in the purchasing power of the wage earners. In the context of the developing economy, therefore, the workers' organisations have advanced the view that safeguarding the rights of the workers and their purchasing power are also the essential needs of the coffee industry. The employers have, however, enumerated the various measures that should be taken to reduce the cost of production, which, according to them, can be achieved only by increasing the yield and by avoiding imposition of new or higher imposts upon the industry. The replanting and replacement of average yield stands with high yielding materials even if such stands are not averaged, have been considered as essential needs of the industry. The Board realises that the rehabilitation, development and expansion of the industry will require capital resources. Its future depends upon the price at which coffee could be placed in the internal as well as in the foreign markets. The industry has, therefore, a strong case for cost control. While workers' output and their contribution to the production should increase, the growers should concentrate upon producing quality coffee and the planters and curers should study modern techniques adopted in other coffee growing countries to raise the quality of Indian coffee. The prices of Robusta are satisfactory.* But it is a fact that in the export market there had been significant fall in coffee price. The Coffee Board is aware of the price trends in the external markets and it is adopting all possible measures to safeguard the industry's interests. It has introduced open auctions from April 1964 as against the previous system of closed tenders. This method of sale was expected to attract more enterprising bidders from the country and abroad. But the prices received in the open auction have also revealed a downward tendency. The Coffee Board is of the view that the performance of open auction system may have to be observed for a further period before coming to a difinite conclusion whether the desired objective could be achieved or not. The conditions of supply and demand in the world market influence the level of prices in the export sales. There is a considerable demand for quality coffee. There were some complaints that the quality of Indian coffee was going down. It may be one of the causes for lower prices as compared to those in Kenya or Columbia. India is also faced with difficulties in the shipment of coffee without allowing its quality to deteriorate. While African coffees are being shifted in fast moving steamers within a few days of placing an order, it has come to the notice of this Board that the Indian coffee is being shifted months after the sales are concluded. This results in quality deterioration. Adequate shipping facilities are, therefore, required to be made at Mangalore and Calicut in order to ensure the supply of quality coffee.

A few important needs of the industry have been discussed above in view of the Board's specific terms of reference and the Government's directive to the Board that such needs of the industry should be considered while devising a wage structure for coffee plantation industry. It may, however, be pointed out that coffee is, in a way, controlled industry and the Coffee Board is fully aware of the industry's needs and requirements. The Coffee Board has taken effective measures in the past for the industry's benefit and for its development and it is largely on account of the interest taken by the Coffee Board that the industry has achieved such spectacular results. It can be safely presumed that the Coffee Board will not allow the genuine needs of the industry to suffer for lack of attention.

*Coffee Board Chairman's speech at the annual meeting of the Board.

Revised Wage Structure

Workers' Estimates Of Minimum Requirements

The parties were requested by the Board to state the fair wage which was justified in their opinion for the lowest category of unskilled manual worker and for other categories of worker connected with coffee plantations keeping in view the recommendations of the Fair Wages Committee and norms of the 15th Section of the Indian Labour Conference on need based wage. The estimates of fair wage submitted by the workers' organisations for the lowest paid worker are between Rs. 160 and Rs. 200 per month. These are the minimum estimates expenditure for a standard family consisting of three adult consumption units. For a middle class family, a minimum expenditure of Rs.316 per month has been considered essential. It appears that the estimate of Rs. 160 per month is on the basis of the norms laid down by the 15th Indian Labour Conference, although some departures have been made here and there. But it is not clear on what basis an estimate of Rs. 220 per month has been arrived at as the minimum requirements of a working class family. The estimate of Rs. 316 per month for middle class family seems to have been arrived at by providing for better type of food, highest standard of clothing and a number of miscellaneous requirements which are no usually considered essential in estimating minimum requirements of a working class family. In the miscellaneous requirements for middle class family, boarding expenses of two children, tooth paste, brush, face powder, travelling expenses and a number of other items have been included.

Parties Views Of Need Based Wage

Much was discussed about the need based wage both in the written statements and while making submissions to the Board. The parties have tried to deal with this subject very exhaustively. The workers' representatives would like the Board to accede to their demand of need based wage on the basis of the 15th Indian Labour Conference formula, irrespective of the capacity of the industry, the needs of the industry and the return which the industry should get on its capital. The workers' case is that the need based minimum wage should be calculated on the basis of the norms recommended by the 15th Indian Labour Conference providing for balanced diet and that the need based wage recommended by the Board should be sufficient to maintain a family of three consumption units including the wage earner. The employers have opposed this demand. They have taken a stand that the existing wage is a fair wage not only for the unskilled manual workers but also for other categories of employees and hence the entire wage structure in the coffee plantation industry is a fair wage structure. They not only consider a wage in terms of the Fair Wages Committee's recommendations as impractical but also hold the view that the Board is not bound by the 15th Indian Labour Conference recommendations and should not accept it as a basis for wage fixation.

In the light of the terms of reference, the Board has to base its recommendations on the principles of fair wages as enunciated by the Committee on Fair Wages. The first question that arises is : 'What is a fair wage according the Fair Wage Committee ?' The fair wage as such has not been defined by the Committee. It has, on the other hand, defined the minimum wage and the living wage and has left the fair wage concept dependent upon various facters. It has, therefore, to be determined by the wage boards after taking those factors into consideration. The Fair Wages Committee's principles of wage fixation have never been regarded as inflexible. The commitee has laid down some broad principles of wage fixation and, whether the terms of reference require it or not, these principles have to be applied in each case taking the practical and common sense point of view of all the relevant matters before the Board.

Minimum Fair Wage is Need Based Wage

For the purpose of Board's deliberations, it would be enough if for the time being the Committee's concept of minimum wage is considered. According to the Fair Wages Committee, the minimum wage must provide merely for the bare sustenance of life but for the preservation of the efficiency of the worker. For this purpose the minimum wage must also provide for some measure of education, medical requirements and amenities. The minimum wage obviously is not the same as the bare subsistance wage. It is something more. It has been regarded as the need based wage and the minimum level of the fair wage. It is in this context that the norms of the 15th Indian Labour Conference assume considerable importance. The Fair Wages Committee has only prescribed the broad suggestive principles of need based wage in its definition of minimum wage and has not defined them in quantitative terms. The first attempt in this direction was made by the resolution of the 15th Indian Labour Conference. The norms laid down by this resolution have attracted attention of almost all wage fixing bodies including all the wage boards and these norms have been discussed threadbare from all points of view. It is not, therefore, necessary for this wage Board to repeat them here. But it does not mean that the Board attaches less importance to them. Its non-inclusion in the Board's terms of reference does not make any difference. It is a tripartite agreement and has been so worded that it is not necessary for all wage fixing bodies to adopt the norms laid down therein toto. It has been recognised by the framers of resolution that in some cases it may not be possible to adhere to the norms mentioned in that resolution. What is expected is only a justification of the circumstances which prevent any wage fixing body from adhering to them. In the resolution itself, therefore, the practicability of its application is both implied and expressed. In the circumstances nothing should deter this Board from giving the consideration that the resolution deserves in the light of the peculiar circumstances of the coffee plantation industry.

Board's Office Estimates Of Need-based Wage

The Board's office has, therefore, worked out estimates of minimum requirements for one consumption unit both on the basis of the balanced diet and improved diet for the coffee growing areas and for which price data and other information were available. These estimates have been worked out in the manner they were prepared by the previous wage boards by taking help of the diet formula mentioned in the agenda papers of the 15th Indian Labour Conference on the basis of which the food norms of the need based wage were devised. The weights, (proportional to the expenditure) forming basis of the consumer price index number at a place and the level of prices for September 1963 for those places have been taken to work out the estimates. Expenditure in respect of other items, clothing, housing and miscellaneous requirements—has been calculated in the manner indicated by the need based formula. In the case of the clothing items the yearly expenditure based upon weight and prices (mentioned above) has been calculated for 21.85 metres (24 yards) per unit and in this calculation no allowance has been made for woollen and silk clothing, bedding and footwear. Nothing has also been provided for stitching charges. The standard rent of a small two roomed tenement of Rs. 14 a month has been taken on the basis of the rent fixed by the Ministry of Works, Housing and Supply, under the Subsidised Housing Scheme. As the estimates are for one consumption unit, proportionate house rent cost per month has been taken to be Rs. 4.67 The expenditure on fuel, lighting and miscellaneous requirements has been taken as 20 per cent of the total minimum wage or 25 per cent of the expenditure on the other three items. On the basis of these calculations, the cost of monthly minimum requirements for coffee plantation workers for one consumption units works out on page No. 299

Centre	Total (In Rs.) with Balanced Diet	Improved Diet
Chickmagalur	50.65	39.23
Ammathi (Coorg)	56.55	39.95
Gudalur	55.14	46.58
Madurai	41.45	35.65
Coimbatore	46.56	36.74
Kozhikode	51.64	47.20
Valparai	42.03	38.31

Employers' Estimates Of Minimum Requirements

The employers have also worked out estimates of cost of living of coffee plantation workers. While doing so their main criticism is directed towards food norm of the 15th Indian Labour Conference formula. The food expenditure has been worked out on the basis of their own formula providing for (i) 2,200 calories; (ii) 2,600 calories; and (iii) Second pay Commission's formula providing for 2,600 calories. In the matter of clothing, the employers budget markes a provision for 15.5 yards per capita per year, i. e. 66 yards per family instead of 72 yards prescribed by the need based wage formula. This has been justified on plea of per capita availability of cloth in the country. No provision has been made for woollen clothings as the two cumblies, which plantation workers of estates of 25 acres and more are intitled to get, have been considered to be adequate to cover the needs for woollen clothings in cold climate. The employees consider that the actual need of a plantation worker for clothing is very much lower than 18 yards per annum and therfore, 15.5 yards provided by them is a generous provision. The cost of clothing has been estimated at the rate of Re. one per yard, as was done by the Sugar Wage Board, the report of which was published in 1960 No provision has been made for housing since, according to the employers, it is provided free under statute. In the miscellaneous group also, the employers have taken only such items on which the plantation workers actually incur expenditure and which have been revealed by the family budget enquiries made in the plantation households and not the 25 per cent of the cost of food, clothing and housing. They have argued that no expenditure is incurred by the plantation workers on fuel, as according to them, firewood is collected free by the workers from the estates. The only expenditure which deserves to be included in the miscellaneous group for fuel is on lighting and match box and kerosene oil. The employers have actually taken 20 per cent of the cost of food and clothing as adequate expenditure on miscellaneous requirements. The total cost of the three budgets for coffee plantation workers' family has thus been worked out on the basis of prices available for Hassan in Mysore State. The details of prices have not been given. The summary of the employers' budgets is given below :

	Budget I (2600 calories)	Budget II (2600 calories)	Budget III (2600 calories, taken by Second Pay Commission)
	Rs.	Rs.	Rs.
Food	43.44	51.87	52.44
Clothing	5.17	5.17	5.17
Miscellaneous	9.72	11.41	11.52
Total	58.33	68.45	69.13

The cost of the coffee plantation workers' budgets providing for three different types of vegetarian diets amount to Rs. 58.33, Rs. 68.45 and Rs. 69.13. Taking the highest priced budget, which is regarded by the employers as a need based wage for a coffee plantation worker's family, it has been argued that the daily wage rate will work out on the basis of 2.25 wage earners and three consumption units at Rs. 1.44 for men, Rs. 1.08 for women and Re. 0.72 for children. It has been further argued that even if it is assumed that only the male worker and his wife are employed, the daily wage rates will be Rs. 1.52 for men and Rs. 1.14 for women. They have compared these rates with the wage rates in Mysore region. Inclusive of the interim wage increase in Mysore, which is the highest wage region in coffee plantation industry, daily wages are Rs. 1.65, Rs. 1.25 and Re. 0.82 for men, women and children, respectively. Thus the employers tried to establish before the Board that the current rates of wages in the coffee plantation industry were such that they could be regarded as higher than the estimated need based wage and, therefore, a fair wage was already in force. In their subsequent arguments the employers have also claimed that inclusive of the non-cash benefits such as provident fund, gratuity, free housing, free medical facilities, lay off compensation, annual leave with wages, etc., the coffee workers' wages have all the attributes of a living wage as conceived by the Fair Wages Committee. This view of the employers would be discussed later, but for the time being a few observation about the budget estimates submitted by the employers may be made here.

The employees have adopted their own standards in respect of almost every item of the workers' budget. The Board is aware of the fact that a food norm of the need based wage formula is not free from controversy, ever since the norms of the need based wage have been discussed by the Second Pay Commission. The Second Pay Commission has adopted a vegetarian diet of the calorific value of 2,600 and worked out its cost at prices prevailing in Delhi and a uniform wage was fixed for the entire country. There could be a difference of opinion about the type of diet as the need based formula of the Indian Labour Conference did not specifically provide for it. But the norms adopted in respect of the expenditure on clothing, housing and other requirements need some consideration. The Second Pay Commission has taken expenditure on these items in accordance with the norms recommended by the Indian Labour Conference. What the need based formula has provided is a norm of clothing and within the yardage fixed by it different types of clothing depending upon the climatic conditions have to be provided. If the principle is accepted that the workers' requirements in respect of clothing should be in keeping with the per capita avilability of cloth in the country. It will amount to a progressive increase and continuous revision of this norm depending upon the availability of cloth. The cloth production is rising. As the employers have themselves pointed out, the availability of cloth is expected to rise to 17.2 yards per capita by 1965-66. Now that the Third Five-Year Plan period is ending, 17.2 yards, instead of the provision made for 15.5 yards in the employers budget estimates, may have to be adopted. The norm of clothing will thus be subject to revision from time to time.

The workers' contention is that the Kamblis are an occupational necessity and are not an alternative to woollen clothing requirements in cold climate. The employers, however, contend that Kamblis will take care of the needs of woollen clothing for the workers. The price of cloth at Re. one per yard in the context of the prevailing prices of cloth also requires consideration.

Nothing has been provided for housing on the argument that when a Statute provides for an amenity, it must be presumed that it has been actually provided. It has also een contended that if housing is not provided, an employer may be prosecuted for non-implementation of the Plantations Labour Act ; but it would not mean that provision for housing should be made in working out the wages of a worker. The Plantations Labour Act requires an employer to provide and maintain necessary housing accommodation for every worker and his family residing in the plantation. It would thus appear that the employers are required to provide houses only to such of the workers as are residing in the coffee plantations. An idea can be had about the number of houses available for the plantation workers from the report of the Working Group on Plantations Labour Housing, published in 1964. In Mysore State, 65,461 workers are in employment ; 19,206 houses are required out of which 14,910 are available and there is a shortfall of 4,296 houses. In Madras State, 83,244 workers are employed in plantation (Tea, Coffee and Rubber) ; 34,507 houses are required and only 23,048 houses are available showing a shortfall of 11,450 houses. This gives some idea about the availability of houses for plantation workers. But even if it is accepted that housing is provided free to almost every worker, the notional house rent should have been taken for calculating the amount of the miscellaneous requirements.

In justification for taking 20 per cent of the expenditure on food and clothing only for miscellaneous group the employers arguments are as follows :

"In view of the fact that the weight of the miscellaneous group can be ascertained from the actual family budget survey by the Labour Bureau, we have adopted that weight (i.e. 16.3 per cent) for our calculation of the expenditure. This corresponds to 19.5 per cent of the expenditure on other items. Rounding off, we arrive at 20 per cent which we have adopted in our calculations."

Wage Earners In A Family

Apart from discussions about the norms of food, clothing, housing and miscellaneous requirements, there have been very lengthy arguments before the Board about the wage earners in a plantation workers' household. Both the Fair Wages Committee and the resolution of the 15th Indian Labour Conference envisags a working class family consisting of three consumption units and one wage earner. The Committee's decision is that if the standard family is reckoned as one requiring three consumption units and providing one earner, it would be in accord with the results of the family budget inquiries. The resolution is more specific in this respect and in view there the earnings of women, children and adolescents have to be disregarded. As has been stated earlier, the employers and workers hold very strong but divergent views on this subject. Workers are not prepared to compromise for anything less than three consumption units for a wage earner. The employers, on the other hand, have argued strongly in favour of adopting the principle of 2.25 wage earners maintaining three consumption units on the basis of family system of employment in plantations. The employers contend that, if in determining a worker's wage, needs of his family have to be ascertained, the actual income of a household to maintain a standard of life intended to be allowed should also be ascertained. In so far as the Fair Wage Committee's principle of three consumption units and one wage earner is concerned, the employers desire that the Board should ignore it by considering that this principle was recommended by the Committee with reference to a living wage standard. Even otherwise they suggest that this principle could be modified by applying the caution of practicability in the Board's terms of reference in this respect also. The resolution of the Indian Labour Conference is considered by them as one dealing with employments in general and not with any particular industry. It was also contended that an assurance was given to the plantation industry in the 10th Session of the Industrial Committee on Plantations to the effect that the norms of wage fixation would be decided by the Wage Board.

The industry is not, therefore, in favour of determining wages in coffee plantations on the basis of each adult male worker being presumed to have to satisfy the needs of three adult consumption units. It has been argued that for agricultural community working on plantations almost in a family group, the earnings of a household consist of the total earnings of all the earners in that household. It has further been argued that all the minimum wage committee have recommended need based minimum wage in plantations and while doing so they have accepted the fact of family employment and fixed wages accordingly.

Position Of Family System Of Employment

The Board has given most careful consideration to the question of family system of employment in coffee plantation. Family system of employment in the plantation industry has a historical background. When the plantations started for the first time, most in uninhabited areas, labour had to be imported from far off places; recruitment of labour had to be resorted to on family basis through the recruiting agents. This system of recruitment was also necessary as some operations in coffee plantations, particularly the picking of coffee berries is better carried on by the women labour. In the absence of any organised machinery for wage fixation for the plantation workers, the wages were low and every member of the family had to work to balance the budget. Family system of employment is still in vogue in the coffee plantations although it does not appear to be the same as it was before. It is not a statutory condition that the employers should engage labour on family basis. There is also no condition that only families are to be employed in the industry. It is not possible for the Board to specify the extent to which family system of employment are, however, available in the family Budget Enquiries conducted in 1944 which have been referred to by the Fair Wages Committee in Appendix III of its Report. In Madras and Coorg Coffee plantations, there were 2.05 earners, 0.75 dependents and the earner dependent ratio was 1.37. However, the Deshpande enquiry into the cost and standards of living of plantation workers in South India in 1947 reveals 2.41 wage earners, 1.89 dependents in a family of 3.80 units in Madras and in 1952 the Minimum Wage Committee in Travancore-Cochin State found 2.39 wage earners and 1.85 dependents in a family of 4.25 units. These figures show the factual position as it was in existence in 1947 in Madras and in 1952 in Travancore-Cochin. While replying to the questionnaire of the Board, the Madras Government has favoured the adoption of three consumption units for one wage earner. The Kerala Government is also of similar view. The Mysore Government has expressed no specific opinion in this respect. An ILO survey in 1949 found that women labour constitute 40 per cent in coffee plantations. But since 1949 changes have taken place which may have reduced the family system of employment. The regulation of working of living conditions in plantations, fixing of statutory minimum wages, provision for maternity benefit may have contributed to the gradual diminution of family system of employment. Another ILO Report on plantations published in 1961 shows that the population in the plantation areas has increased to such an extent that the problems of immigrant labour have now given place to the problems of acute unemployment.

The family system of employment is conspicuous in plantations but it is not a unique feature of this industry as this system of employment is also prevalent in industries like textiles, chemicals, matches, bidi making, tobacco curing, iron ore, manganese, limestone, mines, etc. On a careful balancing of the materials available before the Board and the submissions made by the parties and the data supplied by the State Governments to the Board, it appears that while the family system of employment still persists in the coffee plantations, the number of dependents in the plantation areas is more now than what it was in the past. Expression of a more definite view by the Board on the question of wage earners is not considered necessary as in the fixation of a revised wage the Board has not been guided merely by one factor.

Employers' Contention Of Present Wage Being Fair

The employers consider the present wage in the coffee plantation industy as one which is on the higher side of the fair wage and has given the ingredients of a living wage. The employers' arguments are on the following lines.

According to the Fair Wages Committee any wage between the minimum wage and the living wage is a fair wage because it says that while the lower limit of the fair wage is the minimum wage the upper limit is equally set by what may be called the capacity of the industry to pay. The lower limit of the minimum wage is on which would provide not merely for the bare sustenance of life but for the preservation of the efficiency of the workers by making provision for some measure of education, medical requirements and amenities. The wages paid in the coffee plantation industry are fair wages because the minimum wage committee, when they recommend minimum wages for the first time in 1952 in the coffee plantations, did so with the object of providing sustenance to the worker and his family and for the preservation of his efficiency as a worker. This was subsequently raised by two voluntary agreements, in Mysore, one in 1956 and the other in 1960, raising the minimum wage by 42 per cent and 62 per cent respectively. The incentive rates in coffee picking provide considerable higher earning to the workers in the harvesting season. The annual bonuses further add to the earnings.

Employers' Contention Of Present Wage Being Living Wage

The employers' contention is that in addition to the cash earnings, the coffee plantation workers' real earnings are augmented by the addition of non-cash benefits such as provident fund, gratuity, annual leave with wages, etc., and they claim that the coffee plantation workers' wages have all the attributes of a living wage even if the standards are lower because according to the employers these wage components fulfil the conditions laid down by the Fair Wages Committee in regard to the living wage. According to the Committee a living wage should enable a male earner to provide for himself and his family not merely the bare essentials of food, clothing and shelter but a measure of frugal comfort including education of children, protection against ill health, requirements of essential social needs and a measure of insurance against the more important misfortunes including old age. The employers have asserted that by their wage, besides providing the bare essentials, frugal comforts have also been provided. The claim of the employers that their wage is a living wage is thus based upon their other claims, namely (1) that the workers have been provided with free housing facilities according to the standards prescribed by the plantations Labour Act; (2) medical facilities, water-supply, sanitation and protective clothings, have been arranged for the workers which protect them against ill health; (3) free primary education is available for the children between ages of six and 14; (4) 12 weeks' maternity leave with maternity benefit, rest period, weekly holidays, seven festival holidays with wages, annual leave with wages at the rate of one day for every 20 days' work, creches and recreational facilities, ensure the requirements of essential social needs and constitute frugal comforts; and (5) the provision of provident fund, retirement gratuity, workman's compensation constitute the element providing against the more important misfortunes including old age.

The employers are, therefore, of the view that wages in coffee industry, considered along with the fringe benefits, have all the attributes of a living wage, as conceived by the Fair Wages Committee, and the only omission, according to them, is the requirement that one male wage earner should earn enough to provide for the whole family.

This is the point of view of the employers. There can be a difference of opinion about a wage being minimum fair, adequate, etc , depending upon the background in which it is judged. It is not, therefore, intended to express any opinion for or against the view expressed by the employers about the nature of the existing wage. It may, however, be pointed out that the benefits enumerated above are not such that everyone in coffee industry enjoys. The per capita additional burden in the wage will has been calculated by the employers on the basis of the returns received from company owned plantations. These amenities are not universally provided to all the workers by all the estates and the benefits are also not uniform. As has been pointed out earlier, most of these benefits are statutory and several plantations do not come within the purview of the Plantations Labour Act or the Provident Fund Act. Several plantations are not also covered by agreement by which bonuses have been paid and other facilities and benefits have been extended to the workers. Furthermore, while discussing the question of paying capacity, the employers have urged that in view of the peculiar character of the industry, viz , perdominance of small holdings and small growers, their capacity to pay a given wage rate should have primary consideration. But when the question of adequacy of wages and fringe benefits was being considered they have taken for comparison purposes wages, benefits and facilities available to the employees in large company managed coffee plantations in support of their assertion that the present wage is not only fair but to a certain extent it is living wage.

Board's Approach

The Board has to see whether the minimum wage, as defined by the Fair Wages Committee, is being paid in the industry at present or not. The wage should be such as would provide for not only bare sustenance of life but also for education, medical requirements and certain amenities. The need based wage formula of the Indian Labour Conference is only a quantitative measure to judge whether present wage in the coffee plantation industry is a minimum fair wage which is another way of expressing the need based wage. The existing wage of men workers per day, inclusive of interim wage increases, are between Rs. 1.47 and Rs. 1 65. Some rough estimates of the need based wage were made by the Board. Allowing even for an economic vegetarian diet and other requirements according to the Indian Labour Conference formula, it was found that the present wages required to be enhanced In coming to this conclusion, besides the considerations of increase in the cost of living, the Board's decision was also influenced by other factors such as the progress which the industry has achieved in the past one decade, the desire of labour to attain better standards of living, etc. A contented labour is also a need of the industry.

In connection with the quantum of which the present wages can be enhanced, the Board gave due consideration to the matters like the place of the industry in the economy of the country and its regional characteristics, capacity of the industry to pay higher wages, productivity of labour, prevailing rates of wages in the same or similar occupations and the level of national income and its distribution, and also desirability of gradually bringing up wages in areas where they are very low at present to the same level as in other areas and inadvisability of giving very steep rises. The Board has already discussed the place of the industry in the economy of the country and its other features in the earlier part of this chapter. The capacity of the industry has also been considered in Chapter IV. It is now intended to deal with the other three factors influencing wage fixation.

Productivity Of Labour

The employers' contention is that they are not against higher wages if the increase in wages does not result in higher cost of production. They therefore, emphasise that any wage increase should come from a higher productivity and should be as a result of it. They have repeatedly brought to the attention of the Board the Fair Wages Committee's observation that the wage fixing machinery should relate to fair wage to a fair work load. The employers have, therefore, been pleading for a proper appraisal of the work-load in coffee plantation industry and desired that, if 'necessary, by means of a work study the relationship between the wages and the work norms should be determined.

The employers accept that there is improvement in production and yield per acre on account of :

(a) Greater and more scientific application of fertilizers.

(b) Preventive measures taken against pests and diseases.

(c) More scientific methods of cultivation.

(d) Improvement in the care of soil and better field management.

(e) Replanting and new planting with higher yielding and disease resisting material, and

(f) Introduction of improved machinery and equipment on estates.

The workers also claim to be given due credit for a part of increase in production and productivity on the plea that even though the area under coffee cultivation has gone up, the number of workers employed per acre has remained the same and in the output there have been increases of substantial nature. It is argued that the labour works harder and is now better organised and, therefore, loss of production on account of strikes and other labour disputes is not frequent now; labour gives full cooperation to management in their efforts to increase productivity even if such measures cause some hardship to labour. The employers, in their replies to the questionnaire, had favoured a time and motion study for the purpose of fixing reasonable workloads. But at the time of submissions to the Board, they expressed the view that the 'work study' was a possible way of assessing the work loads in the plantations and desired that proper workloads should be fixed after 'work study'. They have not explained the significance and meaning of 'work study' in clear terms. No scheme of 'work study' has been submitted by them either. From the "Introduction to Work Study" by I.L.O. they have, however, quoted the following definition of 'work study': "Work study is a term used to embrace the techniques of method study and work measurement which are employed to ensure the best possible use of human and material resources in carrying out a specific activity." The employers had expected that the Board would conduct a work study. This was too much of an expectation from the Board which had no means to take up such a vast and complex study. At the later stages of Board's deliberations the employers have suggested a system of piece rates for Mysore State devised by the Mysore State Planters' Association and desired that it might be adopted by the Board. This scheme has nothing to do with work study. It will be discussed in connection with the piece rates in coffee industry.

The United Planters' Association of Southern India is best suited to carry on a work study, if it is practical. But the Board understands that nothing had been done so far in their direction. The Board had no means to undertake a work study. A time and motion study was considered to be thoroughly impracticable. Such studies may be useful in industries which are mechanised and wherein workers are employed only to operate machines, and as such there is scope for standardisation of workloads. In the coffee plantations, conditions differ from estate to estate and even in the same estate conditions differ from one season to the other. There was a suggestion that the employers and workers should conduct experiments and fix workloads by mutual agreements. This suggestion has the full support of the Board. Productivity should improve. Any improvement in productivity is in the best interests of the industry, the wage earners, the country and every one concerned. The figures of absenteeism available for plantations in Mysore State reveal the bitter reality that absenteeism is rising from 1955 onwards. As against 16.9 per cent in 1955, it was 21.5 per cent in 1962. The reasons for absenteeism can be many and it would be desirable to make an objective study to ascertain reasons for this higher rate of absenteeism and efforts should be made by the industry and the labour to eliminate it. Less absenteeism will improve productivity and workers' earnings. It may, however, be pointed out here, as has already been accepted by the Fair Wages Committee also, productivity is the net result of several factors which include the conditions of work and the level of managerial efficiency. It is, therefore, necessary that a thorough and an impartial study should be made at the level of each unit to climate waste and to improve productivity.

Prevailing Rates Of Wages

According to the Fair Wages Committee, the prevailing rates of wages in the same or similar occupations in the same or neighbouring localities should be taken into account before granting a wage increase. In connection with such comparison of wages in relation to coffee plantations different views have been expressed by the parties. The workers have expressed the view that prevailing rates of wages only in organised industries should be taken as a guide while fixing fair wages for coffee plantation workers. The employers, on the other hand, have come out with the argument at the time of the Board's public sittings that all the operations in coffee plantations are comparable only with those in agriculture and coffee plantation labour is therefore comparable by the nature of its work with agricultural labour alone. They have, therefore, emphasised that the nature of work performed by the coffee plantation workers should first be fully understood and no comparison should be made with the manufacturing industries and with wages and conditions of service obtaining in such industries. They have, therefore, tried to establish the agricultural character of the plantation industry before the Board. The workers' representatives, in their counter arguments, have been very keen to prove that the coffee plantations had all the attributes of an industry and should be regarded as such. The determination of the nature of work in the coffee plantations, agricultural or industrial, will not affect the wage proposed to be recommended by the Board, and the arguments in this respect are more of an academic nature. There have, however, been some interesting discussions before the Board on this point. While emphasising the importance of the industry in the economy of the country, the employers have urged upon the Board to consider the coffee plantation industry as one of the more important industries in the agricultural sector. Coffee plantations are not, therefore, purely agricultural organisations nor can they be treated on par with manufacturing industries. For a similar reason wages and working conditions in purely agricultural operations cannot justifiably be compared with those in plantations. Agriculture is not an organised industry and the wages in Agriculture have never been regarded as satisfactory in view of the fact that the agricultural labour is unorganised and, for the time being, has few opportunities of bargaining a proper wage. Moreover, a distinctive feature of agriculture is absent in plantations. Agriculture is a seasonable activity and wages depend upon the availability of labour at the time when it is mostly needed. The system of payment of wages in kind in agricultural operations is another attraction which is not available in the coffee plantation work. There are also other reasons on account of which it is difficult to treat coffee plantation workers like those in agriculture. Coffee plantations are situated in areas remote from the centres of other economic activity. It is, therefore, not possible to determine wage rates for coffee' plantation workers in comparison with the wages of other workers also. Some iron ore mines have been opened out recently in Chickmaglure region and the wages in these mines and in road construction and building activities can provide some rough idea about the prevailing rates of wages although the condition of the same or similar industry is not fulfilled in this comparison.

National Income

The Fair Wages Committee requires consideration of the level of national income and its distribution. The national income, in a way, reflects the general economic condition of the country and can, therefore, have a relevance in connection with the wage fixation. The Fair Wages Committee has itself realised that the level of the country's national income was so low that linking of national income with living wage was difficult. The employers in organised industries have always been insisting that the wages of the workers should not be very much out of line with what is justified by the country's national income. The workers, on the contrary, have been opposing this view of the employers and did not want the considerations of national income to be brought in when the wage fixation is being contemplated. The oft-quoted objection of the workers is that the national income of the country include seventy per cent of the rural earnings and since the rural population is only partially employed, the figures of national income can only be used to the detriment of the industrial workers. But the approach of the workers' organisations in the coffee plantation industry had been a little different on the question of giving importance to the national income in connection with the new wage structure for the workers represented by them. They consider that the per capita income of a coffee plantation worker is lower than the national per capita income and therefore they urge that the per capita income of the plantation workers should in no case be lower than the national per capita income. The employers in the coffee plantations have stated that national income could only provide a broad indication of the possible wage levels and should be taken into consideration in fixing wages. The per capita national income at 1948-49 prices was Rs. 294.70 in the year 1962-63. The corresponding figure at currant prices was Rs. 399.40. The discussions on national income in connection with wage fixation have been of an academic nature and, as far as it is known, there are no guide-lines available to indicate the extent to which national income can be utilised in any wage fixation. This factor can, however, be kept in view in the determination of a suitable wage structure and it need not be said here that the Board has given due consideration to the general economic condition of the, country and the national income and the coffee plantation workers position therein, while revising the wages of the coffee plantation workers.

Place Of Amenities And Fringe Benefits In Wages Fixation

The question of amenities and fringe benefits has been the subject of earlier discussions. It requires some further consideration as the employers attach considerable importance to the amenities and benefits which they are providing to the coffee plantation workers. It has been submitted to the Board that the following benefits and amenities, under statutes or agreement, are available to the workers :

Bonus
Provident fund
Gratuity
Free housing
Free education
Free medical aid
Sickness benefit
Maternity benefit
Protective clothing
Annual leave with wages
Seven festival holidays with wages
Lay off, compensation
Workmen's compensation
Creches
Recreational facilities
Fire-wood collection facilities

Employers' contention is that amenities and benefits provided by them have workers from expenditure as, in their absence, any expenditure in respect of them would have had to be meted out of the wages received by the workers. Since the standard of living of a working class family is the result of cash income and the non-cash benefits available to workers, they desire that the workers' emoluments in cash should be judged in the background of the various fringe benefits and amenities provided to them.

The Fair Wages Committee is of the view that before a wage fixing machinery decides to make an allowance for benefits, statutory or otherwise, it should examine the nature and the extent of these benefits and where benefits are such that they reduce the expenses of a worker on items of expenditure which are taken into account for the calculation of fair wage, they should be taken into account in fixing the actual fair wage payable. The benefits which have no connection with the items of expenditure on which the fair wage is calculated are to be ignored.

As has been pointed out earlier, these are difficulties in the way of assessing the money value of the amenities and benefits accruing to the coffee plantation workers in general on account of the reason that these amenities and benefits differ considerably in standard from unit to unit. They are not also available to all the workers, particularly to the workers employed on plantations to which the Plantations Labour Act is not applicable. The Fair Wages Committee was also conscious of this position. In respect of housing facility, for instance, it has remarked that an important item of welfare work which involves considerable expenditure is the provision of housing; but some employers have provided first rate housing, while others have either done nothing in this matter or only made a show a providing housing. The employers have tried to give to the Board an idea about the cost per worker on account of the statutory and other benefits; but only in respect of some organised big coffee companies. Cost per worker per day in such companies has been worked out at Rs. 174.76 for 280 working days or 62.04 paise per day in the manner shown below :

	Cost of Per Worker
	Rs.
Labour Bonus	27 04
Gratuity	12.24
Provident Fund	28.80
Leave with wages	22.84
Sickness benefit	6.34
Maternity benefit	6.22
Medical aid	24.52
Other Labour benefits	46.76
	174.76

Applying the criterion laid down by the Committee on Fair Wages referred to above, the Board carefully examined the amenities and benefits listed above to see how far they reduced the expenses of a worker so that to that extent account may be taken in the calculation of wages. The facilities of free housing, free medical and education are no doubt such that, if they are free or subsidised, the savings thereby could reduce the expenses of a worker. Expenditure on such items is taken for the calculation of a fair wage. In case of housing facilities, for example, where houses have been provided or there is a system of paying house rent allowance in lieu thereof, the norm of expenditure on housing need not be taken into account while calculating workers expenses of minimum requirements. Employers' views on the benefits to workers on account of provident fund have been contested by the other side. The workers argue that not only no deduction should be made from their wages on this account, their take-home-pay-packet should be exclusive of the contribution they made towards provident fund.

To be fair to the employers who incur expenditure on providing amenities to their workers, such expenditure should be considered carefully by the wage fixing authorities. But there is a difference when such expenses are considered for an Industry as a whole and for a particular unit whose wage structure is being reviewed. In the case of the industry an assessment of the expenditure on amenities and benefits in exact terms is difficult. A fair idea of the expenditure incurred by an employer on amenities and benfits and the extent to which the workers were saving expenditure on them could be had only when wages of workers in specified units are under examination. The amenities and benefits provided by large coffee companies, though beneficial to the workers employed on them and desirable too from every point of view, could not be taken by the Board as representative of the entire industry. The facilities available to some workers employed by large companies is the result of their association with establishments of better paying capacity. Similarly, workers in profit earning concerns get profit sharing bonus more than the others. In the circumstances of an industry like coffee in which conditions differ so widely in its various units and wherein quite a large number of units are beyond the purview of any statute or agreement, providing for amenities and benefits, it is difficult to draw any specific conclusions with regard to the monetary value of the benefits available to the workers in general. In the case of staff, on the other hand, there is a general system of allowing a servant or a servant allowance. This is a concrete and specific facility which the staff is enjoying and cannot, therefore, be ignored while considering the adequacy or otherwise of their emoluments.

The guidelines suggested by the Fair Wages Committee are not, therefore, capable of practical application when a wage is under consideration for an industry as a whole consisting of units with widely differing conditions. Even so, the Board feels that by custon s and usage the plantation workers are getting some amenities of varying nature and this Board has given due consideration to the overall effect of amenities and benefits on the wages of the coffee plantation workers.

Other Points For Consideration

The other important points which remain for consideration are whether the wages should be uniform for the industry or regional characteristics and size of the plantations should be given d u consideration, whether wages should be the same for men and women or different wages should be fixed in view of the nature of work performed by them in coffee plantations. The Board has also to consider whether a consolidated wage should be fixed or basic wage and dearness allowance should be separately prescribed. The system of payment by results also require discussion.

Wage Differences Based Upon Region And Acreage

At the time of Board's deliberations the coffee growing areas were found to be distributed into broad regions of Mysore State, Coimbatore (Anamallais), Nilgiris, Salem and Madurai Districts (Shevaroys and Palnis) in Madras State and Malabar (Wynaad) and Nelliampathis in Kerala State. In the submissions made before the Board, the workers appeared to be against given weightage to the regional differences. They have urged that uniform wages should be fixed for the whole of South India, regarding it as one region. The employers reacted to this suggestion by expressing the view that any wage fixation without giving due considerations to regional differences would be arbitrary and impractical.

While discussing the various aspects of the industry, the special characteristics of the coffee plantation industry in the different regions of South India have been explained. The Board has noted that the average yield per acre differ considerably from region to region. The yield per acre is closely linked up with the paying capacity and hence the regional wage difference appears to be inevitable.

When minimum wages were fixed for the first time in Mysore by notification and in Madras on the advice of the Minimum Wages Committee, no differentiation was made on account of the size of the coffee plantations. The workers, who appeared before the Board, were not in favour of any discrimination between coffee plantations on the basis of acreage and their arguments in this respect were more or less the same as in the case of fixation of different wages for different regions. The employers, however, hold the view that the same wage cannot be fixed irrespective of the size of holdings as, according to them, the paying capacity of a large grower cannot be the same as the paying capacity of a small grower. In connection with uniform wages fixed under the Minimum Wages Act. the employers have pointed out that the minimum wages committees, when they recommended minimum wages, were not so much concerned, at that stage, with the paying capacity. They argued that when fair wage is proposed to be fixed, the size of the holding should be taken into account as that would reflect the paying capacity of the employers.

Although at the stage of minimum wage fixation uniform wage was fixed for the entire industry in a State, by the time this Board was constituted, the practice of fixing different wages on the basis of the size of the coffee plantations had already come into existence. Divison of estates according to acreage had come into effect as a result of agreements between the parties. At the stage of granting interim relief, it was found that the plantations were divided in Mysore into two categories—(i) below 50 acres and (ii) 50 acres and above. In Kerala State the divisions of coffee plantations were (i) below 300 acres and (ii) 300 acres and above. There was no division on acreage basis in Madras. By the Board's interim wage re-commendations, new divisions were created for Madras as (i) below 100 acres and (ii) 100 acres and above.

At the time of the Board's deliberations on the question of final wage structure, the employers had suggested that the acreage division in Mysore should be below 50 acres and 50 acres and above, i.e., the same as the existing ones. For other areas, however, it was suggested that the acreage divisions should be below 100 acres and 100 acres and above. No acreage division was considered necessary by the employers in Shevaroy's and Madurai and a uniform wage was preferred for these areas irrespective of the size of holdings.

In connection with the regional differences it may be pointed out that the Fair Wages Committee favour fixation of wages on industry-cum-region basis and under the various agreements reached between the parties in Mysore, Madras and Kerala States, before this Wage Board was set up, different wages had been fixed for different coffee growing regions. The practice of dividing estates according to area was initiated by agreements, as prior to such agreements the wages were uniform in a region. But the differentiation of plantations in the region on the basis of acreage goes against the practice of wage fixation on an industry-cum-region basis. The predominance of small growers in the coffee plantation industry and the existence of the agreements relating to industry indicating the Will of the parties for making such differentiation has, however, impelled the Board to retain the existing wage differentials on the acreage basis.

In the result, the Board's conclusion is that the present regional differences and the acreage differences should be allowed to continue both in respect of the wages of the labour and the scales of pay, etc., of the staff except for minor adjustments wherever necessary. The regional differences as well as the acreage differences are not the same for labour and staff. This is because not only the paying capacity had to be considered but also the nature of duties performed.

Different Wages For Men And Women

The Board is aware that it is a Directive Principle of the State Policy under the Constitution of India that there should be equal pay for equal work for both men and women. The Fair Wages Committee's view is where employment is on piece-rates or where the work done by men and women is demonstrably identical, no differentiation should be made between men and women workers regarding the wage payable. But the Committee justifies a lesser wage for women who are employed on work exclusively done by them or where they are admittedly less efficient than men.

There is a general practice of fixing different wages in coffee plantations for men and woman workers. In fact, for men and women different wages have been fixed and are being paid in the States of Mysore and Kerala. But in the old Madras State minimum wages were fixed not for men and women workers but for Grade I and Grade II workers. This is still the current practice in Madras and in Malabar part of Kerala State. The Board considered the desirability or otherwise of adopting this practice. It has come to the Board's notice that there has been a misuse of the terms Grade I and Grade II workers to the detriment of the workers' interest in certain coffee growing areas. While fixing different wages for Grade I and Grade II, the Madras Government had indicated that this differentiation was based upon physical capacity, skill, efficiency and out-turn of work. Taking advantage of this explanatory note, certain employers have employed men and Grade II workers. The Board, therefore, considered it inadvisable to fix wages according to Grade I and Grade II.

Unusually, women workers in coffee plantations are required to do less strenuous work than men workers. Further, the tasks assigned to women workers are lower than those assigned to men wokers. Because of this, there has been a practice of fixing different time rates of wages for men and women. On a careful consideration of all facts, the Board has decided to continue the present practice.

There can, however, be a dispute about the extent of disparity between the wages of men and women workers that should be allowed. The present practice is that as between the wages of men and women there is a ratio of 8 : 6. On considerations of differences in the wages of men and women in other plantation areas, the Board decided to alter the present differentiation between men and women in order that the difference between their wages may be less.

Wage Composition

The question before the Board was whether consolidated wages should be fixed for separate basic wage and dearness allowance should be prescribed. It was natural for the workers' organisations to argue that separate basic wage and D.A. should be fixed and the amount of D.A. should be such as would fully neutralise the rise in the cost of living of the lowest paid employee and the future variations in the cost of living should be compensated by linking the D A. with the rise and fall in the consumer price index numbers of the region. The employers favour continuation of the existing system for labour and staff which means that labour wages should be consolidated and staff wages should consist of basic wage and D.A., the latter being the same as the UPASI scales of D.A.

It was brought to the notice of the Board that in the past a separate D.A. system for the plantation workers had been prescribed but later on it was discontinued. The Madras Minimum Wages Cammittee had recommended separate basic wage and D.A. and a scheme of variation in D.A., linked with Madras city consumer price index. But the Government of Madras fixed a consolidated wage. The Travancore-Cochin Minimum Wages Committee had recommended separate basic wage and D.A. and a scheme of variation in the dearness allowance on the basis of the changes in the Ernakulam consumer price index number. The Travancore-Cochin Government accepted this recommendation with minor changes in the quantum only. But later on, the parties mutually agreed to abolish the sliding scales of dearness allowance notified by the Government (Notification No. LI-9632/51/DD, dated June 30, 1952). In Coorg also the Minimum Wages Committee recommended a scheme of variations in the dearness allowance linked up with the consumer price index numbers. But it was not accepted by the Coorg Administration even though the Committee's recommendation for a separate dearness allowance was given effect.

The matter was discussed before the Board. The member representating employer and those representing labour had private discussions and negociations on the point. Ultimately, they found a way out. Instead of fixing a separate D.A., they agreed to contiune the present system of consolidated wages for the workers (labour), but they also agreed to a regular rise in the wages from year to year (twice in the first year). They expected that the rise in the cost of living would be compensated by the regular increments.

For the staff, there has been a system of separate dearness allowance; but it is not linked with the cost of living indices. The parties, after discussion and negotiations, have thought it desirable to continue the present dearness allowance.

The Board, and especially the Chairman and independent members, realise that this is by no means an ideal arrangement. They have, however, accepted it as parties have agreed to it, being the best under the circumstances. To some extent, it solves the difficulties of both sides.

Payment By Results

Yet another matter which is required to be considered by the Board in connection with the fixation of wages for the workers in coffee plantation industry is the system of payment by results. The terms of reference require that while applying the system of payment by results, the Board should keep in view the need for fixing minimum (fall-back wage and also to safeguard against over work and undue speed. The employers' contention is that normally there are no piece rates in coffee plantations; there are time rates plus incentive jobs; purely time rated jobs and task rated jobs. For example, picking and gleaning are time rated plus incentive jobs; spraying, manuring, pruning are time rated; and shade lopping, weeding, pitting, trenching are task rated. There is, however, no uniform practice followed as regards tasks and time rated jobs. Items which are given on task on some estates are performed purely as time rated jobs and vice versa on some other estates. In fact all jobs on coffee plantations are, in a way, piece rated. There is a task fixed for almost every job and this makes the job not much different from piece rated ones. The employers favour conversion of the incentive rates into piece rates as it is applicable to tea and rubber plantations in Kerala. They also desire that some of the present field operations conducted on time rate basis should be converted into piece rates after making a proper 'work-study'. The employers suggest that the fall-back wage should be fixed lower than the prevailing time rate. They are also of the view that opportunities should be provided to enable a deligent worker to earn more than the time rate for a normal day's work. They do not, however, favour an incentive rate which increases with increased output as they fear that it may cause damage and result in bad work in certain operations. The workers do not consider that the occupations, other than the picking work, can be brought under pieces rate system.

The tasks differ from one region to another and even from estate to estate depending upon the field conditions and, therefore, tasks cannot be prescribed or standardised by the Board. The tasks may be determined by mutual agreements between the parties at the level of the estates or the regional level. The picking rates also cannot be prescribed for the entire industry. The picking rates are fixed each season depending upon the size of the crop. Different rates are laid down for Robusta and Arabica coffees and for the main picking and the secondary picking, i.e , gleaning. The Board, therefore, did not find it feasible to standardise the picking rates throughout the industry. The Mysore State Planters' Association has, however, submited a system of piece rates of wages to be adopted for the Mysore State. These proposals have been given in Appendix VIII. The Mysore State Planters' Association's Scheme provides piece rates for not only the picking operations but also for weeding, thinning, pitting, trenching,, manuring, pruning, shade lopping and for a number of other operations. It has been submitted to the Board that this scheme of the Mysore State Planters' Association has been devised after a careful study of the past and present performances in connection with the extension of the system of payment by results to as many operations as possible where some measuring of the output of work was found to be feasible. The board could not study the practical implications of this scheme and, therefore, it is not in a position to adopt it and make any recommendation in respect of it. The Board, however, appreciates the effect made by Mysore State Planters' Association and would command the scheme to the parties for giving it an impartial and careful consideration.

Board's Recommendations

Having considered in detail the various aspects of the industry and the principles of wage fixation and the parties' views thereon, it now remains for the Board to deal with the various points referred to it by Government in the terms of reference. The points for Board's decision are the determination of the coverage, i.e., the extent of the industry to which the Board's recommendations should apply, the employees who should be covered by its recommendations and working hours. Besides, the Board has to recommend wages for the time-rated workers, piece-rated workers, clerical, medical and other staff.

Extent Of Industry Covered

Coffee plantation industry is mainly concerned with the cultivation or production of coffee for commercial purposes. The Board's enquiry was confined to such departments of the coffee plantations as are directly or indirectly connected with the cultivation and production of coffee and, therefore, its recommendations should apply to all coffee plantations wherein coffee is being produced for commercial purposes.

Coffee Curing Works Excluded

The question of including the coffee curing works had been the subject of detailed consideration by the Board. On a representation from the workers organisations in the coffee curing works. the Government of India had referred the matter to the Board for its decision. According to the Coffee Act, coffee curing means the application to raw coffee of mechanical process other than pulping for the purpose of preparing it for marketing and a coffee curer is a person who undertakes the curing of coffee. There are a number of curers, large and small, firms and individuals and cooperative societies in South India employing large number of workers during the season in their curing yards or curing establishments. Detailed information was collected about the coffee curing works and the employers' and workers' associations connected with coffee curing were addressed for their views about bringing in the curing works within the Board's purview. The Board considered the replies received from the parties and also visited some of the coffee curing works to acquaint itself with the nature of work and employment in the coffee curing establishments. Representatives of the parties in coffee curing works and Chief Marketing Officer of the Coffee Board were heard on the specific question of inclusion of the coffee curing works under the purview of the Board's enquiry. After considering the written and oral submissions made by the parties, the Board came to the conclusion that even though workers in coffee curing works may be said to be workers in coffee plantation industry, they should not be brought within the purivew of the Board's recommendations for reasons and practical difficulties mentioned below :

(i) Cofiee curing works are mostly situated away from coffee plantations ;

(ii) Workers in coffee curing works are not under the control of the coffee planters, nor are they paid by them ;

(iii) Coffee planters have no direct control over their product as soon as it is haned over to the coffee curers ;

(iv) Coffee curers function mainly as agents of the Coffee Board ; and

(v) Workers in the coffee curing works are mostly governed by the Factories Act.

In view of the exclusion of coffee curing works from the purview of the Board's recommendations, its recommendations should apply to all the departments connected with the coffee plantations such as coffee fields, offices, hospitals, workshops, schools, centres of welfare activities like canteens, creches, etc.

Workmen To Be Covered

According to clause (iv) of paragraph 4 of the Board's terms of reference, the Board has to consider the categories of workers which should be covered by its recommendations. In a coffee estate there is no elaborate system of staffing and the usual practice is to employ the same members of the staff, within the prescribed working hours, to carry out a number of duties. Any single duty may not be such that it may occupy the whole day. There is, therefore, no specific categorisation of staff according to the jobs performed by the workers. The workers are broadly classified according to the departments in which they work. The coffee plantations consist of coffee fields, offices, workshops, hospitals, schools, etc. The workers are, therefore, generally known as field workers, office staff, workshops employees, medical staff, school staff, etc. Most of the field operations, being of an agricultural nature, are carried out by men, women and children and persons working there are referred to as field workers. If, however, the field operations, which are usually performed by the field workers, are to be enumerated in order that an idea may be had about the nature of work in coffee plantations, it may be pointed out that they are : (i) weeding in the fields ; (ii) digging trenches ; (iii) manuring ; (iv) pruning i.e., cutting branches other than the main ; (v) hoeing, i.e., loosening of the earth ; (vi) lopping the shade trees ; (vii) uprooting diseased plants ; (viii) spraying the plants to prevent leaf diseases; (ix) picking coffee crop ; and (x) gleaning, which is secondary picking of berries. These are the jobs done by the workers in the field. Everyone who is performing these jobs need not have a designation. The persons doing weeding, pruning, spraying and picking are generally known as weeders, pruners, sprayers and pickers. The persons in charge of manure mixing, shade lopping and hoeing, are sometimes called manure mixing mazdoors, lopping mazdoors and hoeing mazdoors.

The other employees engaged in coffee plantations are building supervisors, lorry or car drivers, tractor drivers, mechanics and artisans. The staff consists of field staff (such as field conductors and writers) and office staff (consisting of clerks and their assistants, stenographers, typists and store-keepers). The hospital staff including medical officers, nurses, pharmacists/ compounders and malaria surveyors, headmasters, teachers and their assistants come within the category of school staff.

The workers, organisations desired that all categories of workmen employed in the field, workshops, offices, hospitals and schools should be covered by the Board's recommendations. There was also a demand to apply the Board's recommendations to the staff working in the head offices of the coffee plantations. A demand was also made for the simplification of the nomenclature which according to the workers' organisations, varied at present widely from estate to estate. They urged that in the interest of uniformity and in order that same wage might be ensured for the same and similar operations within the industry, a standardisation of nomenclature was necessary. They were also against the existing classification of workmen into permanent, temporary, casual, etc., and desired that a simpler classification of workmen should be introduced.

The employers categories the employees in coffee plantations into : (i) estate managers, assistant managers and other employees on individual contract ; (ii) clerical, field and medical staff and field staff on monthly pay scales ; (iii) non staff categories, namely, artisans, craftsmen, drivers, mechanics, watchmen, messengers, etc. ; (iv) labour supervisors on daily rated wages ; and (v) daily rated labourers working on the estate. The employers desire that the above categories, except those mentioned in (i) i.e., estate managers, assistant managers and other employees on individual contracts should be covered by the Board's recommendations.

In view of the present practice of classifying workmen according to the departments and not according to the nature of work in coffee plantation industry, the Board did not feel it necessary to take up the categorisation of the employees according to specific jobs. It has come to the notice of the Board that same operations are performed by workmen known by different designations depending upon the situation of the coffee growing areas. The Board understands that these nomenclature have their origin in the language spoken in the region and have been in use from the inception of the coffee plantation industry. It was, therefore, felt that a standardisation of nomenclature though extremely desirable from every point of view, may not prove to be very helpful in so far as the wage fixation in the coffee plantation industry is concerned.

In regard to the application of the Board's recommendations to the workmen in coffee plantations, it may be pointed out that in the terms of reference itself the Government have indicated that the categories of workmen to be covered by the Board may be the same which come within the definition of 'workman' in the Industrial Disputes Act. The Industrial Disputes Act's definition of 'workman' is sufficiently wide. According to this definition, a workman means any person (including an apprentice) employed in any industry to do any skilled or unskilled manual, supervisory, technical or clerical work for hire or reward. It does not, however, include army and police personnel and managerial and administrative staff and supervisory staff drawing wages exceeding Rs. 500 per month. This definition is capable of covering all types of workmen except those specifically excluded. It also includes apprentices, contract labour and does not make any differentiation between permanent, temporary or casual workmen. The word 'Industry' used in the definition itself had been very liberally interpreted. The Board, therefore, recommends that all workers employed in coffee plantations in the fields, workshops, offices, hospitals, schools, welfare establishments, etc., who are governed by the definition of workman given in Section 2 of the Industrial Disputes Act, 1947, should be covered by the recommendations of this Board. It may, however, be pointed out that the workmen employed in curing of coffee should be considered as excluded from the purview of the recommendations of this Board.

Contract Labour

There is a practice in some coffee estates of giving on contract some of the normal plantation operations such as, weeding, pitting, trenching, etc. Moreover, the estates have, on occasions, jobs of building construction road construction and repairs to buildings, roads and machinery. These are casual jobs. Such works are usually contracted out by the estates. The Board recommends that no contract labour should be employed in connection with the normal work of coffee plantations. Contract labour may, however be employed when an estate is required to get some work done urgently owing to extraordinary circumstances. All workmen employed in connection with any contract work should also be considered as covered by the recommendations of the wage Board and no differentiation should be made in the matter of wages between contract workers and regular workmen of the estate. Whenever contract labour is employed, the principal employer should be liable for payment of wages to the contract workers and it should be the responsibility of the principal employer to see that all laws relating to labour are implemented.

Working Hours

It is the directive of the Government that in evolving a wage structure in the coffee plantation industry the Board should also take into account Plantations Labour Act, 1951, which applies to coffee plantations which admeasure 25 acres or more and whereon 30 or more persons are employed. This Act has prescribed the maximum working hours for adults, adolescents and child workers. They are 54 hours a week for adults and 40 hours a week for adolescents or children. A child is a person whose age is below 15 years and an adolescent is one whose age is between 15 and 18 years. The rest are adults. The Minimum Wages Act, 1948, applies to all employments in any coffee plantation and since this Act applies to all plantations irrespective of the acreage and the employment it may be presumed that the maximum Rules are applicable to the coffee plantations. According to the State rules the working hours are eight per day or 48 per week for adults and four-and-a-half per day for children. The working hours for the adolescents are the same as for the adults or children depending upon the certificate granted to them to work as adult or child. The wage rates recommended by the Board are related to the daily working hours, i.e., a full eight hours work for adults and four-and-a-half hours work for children. Since many items of field work are performed on task basis and the task is fixed keeping several factors in view including the working hours, there could be no specific hours of work in respect of the workers employed on the basis of a task.

New Wage Structure

The Board has already discussed various principles by which it has been guided in evolving a new wage structure for the coffee plantation industry. The revised wages that are being recommended by the Board reflect the cumulative effect of a large number of factors which were considered relevant to the circumstances of the industry with which the Board was concerned. This wage structure is peculiar to the industry. The Board was keen to evolve for the coffee plantation industry a rational and practical wage structure from all points of view. It is the result of a compromise between the points of view of the employers and labour. Here is a wage structure which, in the opinion of the Board, should be acceptable to all. In devising the new wage structure, the difficulties of small growers have also been taken into account. The capacity of the industry has been given very careful consideration. In fixing wages not only the regional considerations have weighed with the Board but also the size of the coffee plantation and the inadvisability of giving steep rises in wages, especially in low wage areas. The Board has fixed difference in wages for men, women, adolescents and children in keeping with the existing practice, but the ratios between their wages have been altered from 8 : 5 : 4 to 10 : 8 : 6 : 5.

The wage structure for the staff in the past has emerged as a result of a series of agreements between the staffs' union and the employers. The wage structure, which is now being recommended by the Board, has the consent of the parties directly concerned and that is why it has been accepted by the Board.

Period Of Enforcement

The wage structure recommended by the Board is for a period of five years. In case of certain categories, the new wage structure is to come into force from July 1, 1964, and in case of others, from January 1, 1965.

Time Rates Of Wages For Field Workers

The following should be the minimum rates of wages per day of the daily rated field workers in coffee plantations, other than mistries:

(1) All Estates of 50 Planted Acres and Above in Mysore State and Madras State (except Maduri and Salem Districts) and Estates of 300 Planted Acres and more in Wynaad in Kerala State

From		Men	Women	Adolescents	Children
July 1,	1964	1.80	1 40	1.10	0.90
January 1,	1965	1.85	1.45	1.12	0.92
July 1,	1965	1.90	1.50	1.15	0.95
,,	1966	2.00	1.60	1.20	1.00
,,	1967	2.10	1.68	1.26	1.05
,,	1968	2.20	1.76	1.32	1.10

(2) All Estates below 50 Planted Acres in Mysore

From		Men	Women	Adolescents	Children
July 1,	1964	1.71	1.37	1.03	0.85
January 1,	1965	1.76	1.42	1.06	0.88
July 1,	1965	1.82	1.45	1.10	0.90
,,	1966	1.90	1.52	1.15	0.95
,,	1967	2.00	1.60	1.20	1.00
,,	1968	2.12	1.70	1.28	1.05

(3) All Estates below 50 Planted Acres in Madras

From		Men	Women	Adolescents	Children
July 1,	1964	1.78	1.42	1.08	0.88
January 1,	1965	1.78	1.42	1.08	0.88
July 1,	1965	1.82	1.45	1.10	0.90
,,	1966	1.90	1.52	1.15	0.95
,,	1967	2.00	1.60	1.20	1.00
,,	1968	2.12	1.70	1.28	1.05

(4) All Estates in Madurai and Salem Districts of Madras State

From		Men	Women	Adolescents	Children
July 1,	1964	1.65	1.32	1.02	0.82
January 1,	1965	1.70	1.36	1.05	0.85
July 1,	1965	1.78	1.42	1.08	0.90
,,	1966	1.88	1.50	1.12	0.95
,,	1967	2.00	1.60	1.20	1.00
,,	1968	2.12	1.70	1.28	1.05

(5) All Estates below 300 Planted Acres in Wynaad

From		Men	Women	Adolescents	Children
July 1,	1964	1.68	1.32	1.02	0.82
January 1,	1965	1.72	1.36	1.05	0.85
July 1,	1965	1.78	1.42	1.08	0.90
,,	1966	1.88	1.50	1 12	0.95
,,	1967	2.00	1.60	1.20	1.00
,,	1968	2.12	1.70	1.28	1.05

(6) All Estates, other than in Wynaad, in Kerala State

From		Men	Women	Adolescents	Children
July 1,	1964	1.83	1.45	1.10	0 90
January 1,	1965	1.88	1.50	1.12	0.92
July 1,	1965	1.90	1.55	1.15	0.95
,,	1966	2.00	1.60	1.20	1.00
,,	1967	2.10	1.68	1.26	1.05
,,	1968	2 20	1.76	1.32	1.10

A statement giving wages in coffee plantation industry existing on June 30, 1964, and the recommended wages is in Appendix IV.

Maistries Wages

(a) Mysore State

The daily rates of wages of maistries should be as follows :

From		In Mysore State except Coorg.	In Coorg area of Mysore State
		Rs.	Rs.
July 1,	1964	2.10	2.30
January 1,	1965	2.15	2.35
July 1,	1965	2.20	2.40
,,	1966	2.30	2 50
,,	1967	2.40	2.60
,,	1968	2.50	2.70

(b) Madras And Kerala States

Existing wages of maistries in Madras and Kerala States differ not only from estate to estate but also from person to person even in the same estate. The Board's recommendations with regard to maistries/supervisors in these States are as follows :

(i) The wages of maistries as on June 30, 1964, on all estates employed on daily wages, inclusive of commission or headmoney merged under the memorandum of settlement dated November 4, 1958, in Madras State and the memorandum of settlement dated September 20, 1962, in Kerala State*, should be increased by 24 paise from July 1, 1964. The subsequent increase in their wages should be as follows :

From				
From	January 1,	1965	—	5 paise
,,	July 1,	1965	—	5 paise
,	,,	1966	—	10 paise
,,	,,	1967	—	10 paise
,,	,,	1968	—	10 paise

(ii) Kole-maistries, who were in service on June 30, 1964, should also be paid the above increases in wages.

(iii) With effect from July 1, 1964, the wages of maistries absorbed as supervisors without commission or headmoney under the memoranda of settlement referred to in (i) above and of those appointed since then by promotion from the ranks of labour, should be the minimum time rate of the adult male worker, for the

*Memoranda of settlements reproduced in Appendix XIII.

time being in force, plus a differential of 60 paise per day.

(iv) With effect from July 1, 1964, the supervisors directly recruited by the estate by 50 planted acres and above, after the memoranda of settlements referred to in (i) above should be placed in the scale of Rs. 2.50-0-20-90 and their wages should be fixed in that scale in accordance with the provisions for fitment in paragraph 5.122.

(v) The daily wage of supervisors directly recruited by estates of below 50 planted acres should be as follows :

From			Rs.
July 1,	1964	—	2.30
January 1,	1965	—	2.35
July	1965	—	2.40
,,	1966	—	2.50
,,	1967	—	2.60
,,	1968	—	2.70

Fitment of the supervisors placed in the scale of Rs. 2.50-0-20-3.90 should be effected by adding 10 per cent of their wages as on June 30, 1964, subject to a minimum of 30 paise per day. If the amount so arrived at is less than Rs. 2.50 per day, the supervisor concerned should be fixed on Rs. 2.50 per day with effect from July 1, 1964. If the amount so arrived at is not a stage in the new scale, the pay of the supervisor should be fixed at the next higher stage in the scale. If by reason of fitment, the pay of the supervisor exceeds the maximum of the new scale, the excess amount should be treated as personal pay. Any increases granted to these supervisors as a result of the Board's recommendation dated December 9, 1964 (Appendix XII) should be adjusted against these fitment increases.

Piece Rates

The Board did not find it feasible to fix picking rates, which are piece rates in the coffee plantations because conditions differ from region to region and estate to estate in the same region and in some cases even in the different parts of the same estate depending upon several factors. For this reason there can be no standardised piece rates for picking. The picking rates are, however, fixed by the employers every year taking in view condition of the crop and a number of other circumstances. The wages of time rated workmen have been increased as detailed above and the picking rates would also require to be correspondingly increased. The Board recommends that picking rates should be revised every year bearing in mind the increased wages which the time rated workers would be getting at the time of such revision and the relevant factors which are now being taken into account while fixing the picking rates.

Staff's Pay Scale In Madras And Kerala States

The revised pay scales, with effect from January 1, 1965, for the staff in coffee plantations in the States of Madras and Kerala should be as follows :

(A) For staff in Small estates, as defined hereunder :

(1) General Grade—Rs. 40-3-70-4-90.

(2) Senior Grade (for Heads of Departments) —Rs. 90-5-120-EB-6-

(B) For staff in Medium Estates, as defined hereunder :

(1) General Grade—Rs. 40/50-3-56-4-80 EB-5-130.

(2) Senior Grade (for Heads of Departments only) —Rs. 90-6-120-EB-7-148-EB-8-180-10-220

Note : A probationer in the general grade mentioned in (1) should start at Rs. 40 per month and the probationery period should not exceed one year.

(C) For staff in Large Estates, as defined hereunder :

(1) General Grade—Rs. 40/50-3-56-4-80-EB-5-120-EB-6-180.

(2) Senior Grade A—Rs. 90-6-120-EB-7-148-EB-8-196-200.

(3) Senior Grade B—Rs. 150-10-280.

(4) Selection Grade I—Rs. 250-12 -350.

(5) Selection Grade II—Rs. 300-15-420.

Note : A probationer in the general grade mentioned in (1) should start on Rs. 40 per month and the probationary period should not exceed one year.

Estate Grading

The following are the definitions of the Large, Medium and Small Estates :

(a) **Large Estates** : Large Estate owned by companies or proprietors whose total area in Madras State or Kerala State, taking each State as a separate unit, comprises more than 600 acres of coffee or more than 400 units of mixed products, reckoning as one unit, one acre of tea, one-and-a-half acres of coffee or two acres of rubber and other plantation products.

(b) **Medium Estates** : Estates which do not come under the category of Large Estates or Small Estates.

(c) **Small Estates** : Estates owned by companies or proprietors whose total area in Madras State or Kerala State, taking each State as a separate unit, comprises 300 acres or less of coffee, or 200 units or less of mixed products reckoned as mentioned in connection with the definition of Large Estates.

Staff's Pay Scale In Mysore State

The revised pay scales, with effect from January 1, 1965, for the staff in coffee plantations in Mysore State should be as follows :

(A) **Small Estates 'A'** : 51 acres to 80 acres. General Grade—Rs. 30-3-45-4-65-5-75

Small Estates 'B' : 81 acres to 150 acres. General Grade—Rs. 35-3-50-4-70-5-80-EB-5-90

Provided that if a senior member of the staff employed in small estates of 120 acres of above is required to exercise considerable degree of independent managerial responsibility, he should be fixed in the grade of Rs. 80-5-90-6-120.

(B) **Medium Estates 'A'** : 151 acres to 300 acres. General Grade—Rs. 40-3-55-4-75-ES-5-105

Senior Grade – Rs. 90-5-120-EB-6-156.

Medium Estate 'B' : 301 acres to 450 acres. General Grade—Rs. 40/45-3-60-4-80-EB-5-135

Senior Grade—Rs. 90-6-120-EB-7-148-EB-8-196.

Note : A probationer in the general grade should start on Rs. 40 per month and the probationary period should not exceed one year.

(C) **Large Estate** : 451 acres and above. (1) General Grade—Rs. 40/50-3-56-4-80-EB-5-120-EB-6-180.

(2) Senior Grade 'A'—Rs. 90-6-120-EB-7-148-EB-8-120-196-200.

(3) Senior Grade 'B'—Rs. 150-10-200.

(4) Selection Grade 'I'—Rs. 250-12-1/2-350.

(5) Selection Grade II—Rs. 300-15-420.

Note :—A probationer in the general grade mentioned in (1) should start on Rs. 40 per month and the probationary period should not exceed one year.

Explanation

The acreage planted with coffee as registered with the Statutory Board, irrespective of the total acreage of ownership, should be the basis for classification of estates into Large, Medium and Small Estates, subject to the following provisions :

(i) Where there exists a practice of interestate transfer within the same ownership, the acreage of the total ownership and not the individual estate should determine the size of the estate for the purpose of grading.

(ii) Where a member of the staff, though employed by a single registered estate, works permanently and regularly for differently registered estates, the aggregate of the planted acreage of all such estates will form the total which should be taken for estate grading.

(iii) In the case of mixed estates, one acre of tea should be reckoned as one acre of coffee and one acre of rubber should be reckoned as half acre of coffee.

Employees In The "Excluded Categories"* (In Madras And Kerala States)

The scales of pay of the qualified mid-wives, lorry, tractor and ambulance drivers and non-SSLC teachers and non-SSLC K.PS (Kanaka pillais), who at the time Madras and Kerala Settlements of October 1975 and November 1957, respectively were on the scale of Rs. 35-3-53-4-65-5-100 should be revised and with effect from January 1, 1965, the new scale of pay should be Rs. 35-3-53-4-65-5-110.

Fitment For Staff And 'Excluded Categories'

Members of the staff and employees in the "excluded categories" mentioned in paragraph 5.127 should be given one additional increment in their existing scale of pay as on January 1, 1965. Those who have already reached the maximum of any scale should be given one increment as a personal allowance at the rate equal to the increment last drawn. This personal allowance should not attract any benefits or allowance, except dearness allowance, overtime allowance and provident fund, and should be continued in the case of those to whom it is granted until their retirement or promotion, as the case may be ; provided that in the case of promotion to a higher scale of pay, such employees should be fitted at that point in the higher scale which is immediately above the sum of the basic pay and the personal allowance, referred to earlier, and on such fitment the personal allowance should be considered as merged in the basic salary.

Dearness Allowance (Revised)

With effect from January 1, 1965, the United Planters Association of Southern India scale of dearness allowance mentioned in Appendix IV, for staff (in Mysore, Madras and Kerala States) and excluded categories (in Madras and Kerala States) should be revised in the manner shown below :

(1) A sum of Rs. 26 should be added to the existing dearness allowance for the members of the staff drawing a basic pay of Rs. 104 and below, per month :

(2) A sum of Rs. 32 should be added to the existing dearness allowance for the members of the staff drawing a basic pay of Rs. 105 and above, per month ;

(3) In addition,

(a) An amount equal to 10 per cent of the sum arrived at as above should be added in respect of the members of the staff drawing a basic pay of upto Rs. 75/ per month ; and

(b) An amount equal to 17-1/2 of the sum arrived at as above should be added in respect of the members of the staff drawing a basic pay of Rs. 76 and above, per month.

Note : The interim increases granted according to the recommendations of the Wage Board should be absorbed in the above increases in the dearness allowance and all interim increases so granted should not be payable from January 1, 1965.

*Proviso 3 of the Madras and Kerala Staff Settlements, dated October 28, 1957, and November 7, 1957, respectively mentioned in Appendices V and VI.

The interium increases paid since January 1, 1965 should be adjusted towards the amounts due under this revision. A table showing the revised rates of Dearness Allowance is given in Appendix X.

Servant Allowance

The Servant Allowance should continue to be paid in cash at the rate of Rs. 350 per month on all estates except Small 'A' Estates in Mysore State, where it should be paid at the rate of Rs. 17.50 per month.

Pay Scales Of 'Non-Staff' Categories Of Employees (Other Than "Excluded Categories" In Madras And Kerala States)

(a) The following should be the pay scales (consolidated, i.e., all inclusive) of car drivers and tractor drivers employed on coffee estates coming into effect from January 1, 1965.

For Estates of :

(i) More than 50 planted acres :

Daily rated—Rs. 2.75-0.15
Rs. 3.80-0.20
Rs. 4.80

Monthly rated—Rs. 72-4-100-5-125.

(ii) 50 planted acres & less :

Daily rated—Rs. 2.75-0.75-3.80-0.20-4.00.

Monthly rated—Rs.72-4-100.

(b) The following should be the pay scales (consolidated i.e., all inclusive) of vehicle drivers and heavy vehicle drivers, coming into effect from January 1, 1965 :

Daily rated—Rs. 3.20-0.15-3.80-0.20-6.00.

Monthly rated—Rs. 84-4-100-5-155.

(c) **Mechanics** : The following should be the pay scales (consolidated, i.e., all inclusive) of mechanics, coming into effect from January 1, 1965 :

Daily rated—Rs. 3.20-0.15-3.80-0.20-6.00

Monthly rated—Rs. 84-4-100-5-155.

(d) **Mode of Employment of Tractor and/or Vehicle Drivers** : The estates may continue their practice of employing mechanics, tractor drivers and/or vehicle drivers on daily basis or on monthly basis.

(e) **Fitment** : The pay of mechanics, tractor drivers, car drivers, vehicle drivers and heavy vehicle drivers, who were in serviee of the estates on January 1, 1965, should be fitted in the new scales of pay by granting increase of 10 per cent subject to a minimum of Rs. 7.80 in case of monthly rated workers and 30 paise in case of daily rated workers over and above their total emoluments as on December 31, 1964. If the amount so arrived at is not a stage in the new scale, the pay of the worker conserned should be fixed at the next higher stage in the scale. If by reason of fitment, the pay of a worker exceeds the maximum of the new scale, the excess amount should be treated as personal pay.

(f) The following should be the pay scales (consolidated, i.e., all inclusive) of peons, office attenders, ward-boys and watchmen, coming into effect from January 1, 1965 :

Daily rated—Rs. 2.50-0. 10-3.00-0.15-3.90.

Monthly rated—Rs. 65-2-75-3-96.

(g) **Fitment** : The pay of the peons, office attenders, ward-boys and watchmen, who were in service on January 1,1965, should be fitted in the new scales by granting an increase of 10 per cent of their total emoluments as on December 31, 1964, subject to a minimum of Rs. 3.90 in case of monthly rated workers and 15 paise in case of daily rated workers over their total emolument as on December 31, 1964. If the amount so arrived at is not a stage in the new scale, the pay of the workman should be fixed at the next higher stage in the scale. If by reason of fitment, the pay of the workman exceeds the maximum of the new scale, the excess amount should be treated as personal pay.

Explanation : 'Total emoluments' mentioned in the fitment clause (e) and (g) above mean the sum of basic pay, dearness allowance, if any, and the first interim wage increase.

Wages Of Artisans Like Carpenters, Blacksmiths, Etc.

Artisans like, carpenters, blacksmiths, etc., are not usually borne on the regular pay rolls of the coffee estates and hence no pay scales for these categories of employees are being prescribed. In case, however, such categories of workmen are borne on regular pay roll of any estate, such workmen should be paid increases in wages in the manner shown below :

From July 1, 1964, 25 paise per day (less second interim wage increase of 20 paise per day) over their wages as they stood on June 30, 1964.

From January 1, 1965, a further increase of 10 paise per day.

From July 1, 1965, a further increase of 15 paise per day.

From July 1, 1966, a further increase of 15 paise per day.

From July 1, 1967, a further increase of 15 paise per day.

From July 1, 1968, a further increase of 15 paise per day.

Gratuity

Gratuity schemes have been evolved both for labour and staff by agreements between the parties. By Staff Agreement dated May 4, 1965, the gratuity scheme for the staff has been revised. Gratuity schemes for labour and staff, as they are applicable at present, are given in

Appendix XI. The Board is satisfied that a very large section of workers engaged by coffee plantation industry is covered by these schemes and they are being benefited by them. It is the desire of the Board that all the workers employed in coffee plantation industry should be covered by these gratuity scheme-

Miscellaneous

Splitting Of An Estate Not To Affect Wages

Any split of coffee estate, as it existed on June 30, 1964, hereafter into smaller units for any reasons whatsoever, should have no effect upon the wages of the workers and they should be paid at the same rate at which they would have been paid if there had been no such split.

Supply Of Foodgrains

After considering the demand of the labour representatives for supply of foodgrains at concessional rates to the workers by their employers and the difficulties expressed by the employers' representatives in supplying foodgrains regularly due to the lack of supply by the Government concerned, the Board recommends to government that the coffee estates should be supplied with foodgrains regularly and to the employers it recommends that, on foodgrains being so supplied to them by the Government, they should supply the same to their workman on no profit and no loss basis, bearing, in addition, all expenses incurred in connection with storage and distribution of foodgrains.

Permanent Workers

Every estate should make permanent not less than 75 per cent of the average number of workers, who actually worked on it in the year from April 1, 1964 to March 31, 1965, excluding the picking season. The Board makes it clear that by making this recommendation, it does not fix land-labour ratio.

Employment level

Complaints have been made before the Board that the level of employment in coffee plantations are going down, which is due to employers reducing the number of workers and employing casual and contract labour. The Board learns that a similar complaint was also made at the 11th Session of the Industrial Committee on Plantations and, as decided at the said Session, the Government of India has appointed One Man Fact Finding Committee to go into all aspects of the question of employment in plantations. Its terms of reference are as follows :

(i) To find out how and to what extent the vacancies that have arisen since 1959 due to natural wastage or otherwise have been filled.

(ii) To find out whether there has been any increase the ratio of employment of contract/temporary/'bigha' labour in plantations to permanent labour since 1959.

(iii) To find out whether there has been a material change in the land-labour ratio since 1959 and if so, to what extent ?

(iv) To find out by means of a sample survey or otherwise whether there has been any significant increase in the workload by plantation workers since 1950, and to assess broadly the extent of such increase.

(v) To find out whether there has been sizeable reduction of employment in the plantation industry as a whole since 1959, and, if so, the reasons therefor.

(vi) Any other related matters that the Committee may deem fit to consider.

The findings and the report of the Fact Finding Committee will bring out facts on the subject and as such the Board concluded that unless definite findings of the said Committee on the points mentioned above are available, the Board cannot express any opinion. The Board has, therefore, abstained from making any recommendation on the subject.

Part Implementation

It may be mentioned that the Board's recommendations about wages of field workers in coffee plantations were to come into force from July 1, 1964 and January 1, 1965, have already been notified by Government through resolution No. WB-3 (26)/64, dated January 14, 1965 (Appendix III).

CENTRAL WAGE BOARD FOR RUBBER PLANTATIONS, 1961—REPORT

New Delhi, Ministry of Labour and Employmen, 1966. 179, 22,4,4,23,7,4,11p.

Chairman : Shri L.P. Dave.
Members : Shri T. Manaen ; Dr. R. Balakrishna, (resigned and replaced by Shri V. L. D'Souza), Shri M.M. Varghese ; Mr. C.H.S. London ; B.K. Nair ; Shri P. Ramalingam.
Secretary : Shri N. Ahmed.

APPOINTMENT

In pursuance of the recommendations contained in paragraph 25 of Chapter XXVII of the Second Five Year Plan, regarding the establishment of Tripartite Wage Boards for individual industries, the Government of India in the Ministry of Labour and Employment appointed a Central Wage Board for Rubber Plantation Industry by its Resolution No. WB-3(5)/61/II dated July 7, 1961.

TERMS OF REFERENCE

"To work out a wage structure based on the principles of fair wages as set forth in the report of the Committee on Fair Wages as far as practicable".

In evolving a wage structure, the Board, in addition to the considerations relating to fair wage, has also to take into account.

(i) The needs of the industry in a developing economy ;

(ii) The system of payment by results ;

(iii) The special characteristics of the industry in various regions and areas ;

(iv) Categories of workers to be covered (this may be according to the definition in the Industrial Disputes (Act) ; and

(v) Working hours in the industry.

Explanation : Whenever applying the system of payment by results, the Board shall keep in view the need for fixing a minimum (fall-back) wage and also to safeguard against overwork and undue speed

CONTENTS

Introductory ; interim wage increase ; wage Structure in Retrospect ; Staff Wages-Fair Wage Structures ; Wage and Working Conditions ; New Wage Structure ; Miscellaneous ; Appendices from I to XII.

RECOMMENDATIONS

(1) Daily Rates Of Wages

The following are the daily rates of wages :

	FROM				
	1.5.64 Rs.	1.4.65 Rs.	1.4.66 Rs.	1.4.67 Rs.	1.4.68 Rs.
I. For Estates of 100 Acres or More					
	(a) Kerala and Madras States Field Workers				
Men	2.10	2.20	2.25	2.30	2.35
Women	1.80	1.90	1.95	2.00	2.05
Adolescents	1.31	1.38	1.41	1.44	1.47
Children	1.05	1.10	1.13	1.15	1.18
Factory Workers					
Men	2,30	2.40	2.45	2.50	2.55
Women	1.95	2.05	2.10	2.15	2.20
Adolescents	1.44	1.51	1.54	1.57	1,60
	(b) Mysore States				
Field Workers					
Men	1.80	1.90	2.00	2.10	2.20
Women	1.40	1.50	1.60	1.68	1.76
Adolescents	1.10	1.15	1.20	1.26	1.32
Children	0.90	0.95	1.00	1.05	1.10

1	2	3	4	5	6
Factory Workers					
Men	1.90	2.00	2.20	2.20	2.30
Women	1.50	1.60	1.68	1.76	1.84
Adolescents	1.15	1.20	1.26	1.32	1.38
II. For Estates Of Less Than 100 Acres					
(a) Kerala and Madras States					
Field Workers					
Men	2.03	2.13	2.18	2.23	2.28
Women	1.76	1.86	1.91	1.96	2.01
Adolescents	1.29	1.36	1.39	1.42	1.45
Chiidren	1.03	1.08	1.11	1.13	1.16
Factory Workers					
Men	2.23	2.33	2.38	2 43	2.48
Women	1.91	2.01	2.05	2.11	2.16
Adolescents	1.39	1.46	1.49	1.52	1.55
(b) Mysore State					
Field Workers					
Men	1.71	1.81	1.91	2.01	2.11
Women	1.29	1.39	1.49	1.57	1.65
Adolescents	1.05	1.10	1.15	1.21	1.27
Children	0.90	0.95	1.00	1.05	1.10
Factory Workers					
Men	1.81	1.91	2.01	2.11	2.21
Women	1.39	1.49	1.57	1.65	1.73
Adolescents	0.95	1.00	1.06	1.11	1.16

(2) Field Classification

Rubber fields are to be classified into seven classes in the manner shown below :

Class	Yield Per Acre	Standard Output Per Tapping Block
I	Upto 110 kg.	1 kg.
II	More than 110 kg. upto 180 kg.	3 kg.
III	More than 180 kg. upto 270 kg.	5 kg.
IV	More than 270 kg. upto 360 kg.	7 kg.
V	More than 360 kg. upto 450 kg.	10 kg.
VI	More than 450 kg. upto 540 kg.	12½ kg.
VII	More than 540 kg.	15 kg.

(3) Tapping Blocks

Tapping blocks for (a) ordinary tapping ; (b) ladder tapping ; (c) assisted collection tapping are to be as follows :

(a) In ordering tapping, 250 trees, where stand per acre is 100 or below and upto 300 trees in other cases as at present.

(b) In ladder tapping—135 trees.

(c) In assisted collection tapping (under prescribed conditions) : (i) 375 trees in the first year in which the system of assisted collection tapping is introduced ; (ii) 400 trees in the second and subsequent years ; (iii) Higher tasks by mutual agreement.

(4) Safeguards Against Retrenchment

Recommendations in respect of tasks and assisted collection tapping are subject to the condition that there should be no retrenchment of any tapper as a result thereof.

(5) Price Rates

In addition to the fall-back wage mentioned below (paragraph 6), the price rates for tappers to be as follows :

Class of the Rubber Field	Rate in Paise per 1/2 kg. upto Standard Output	Rate in Paise per 1/2 kg. for output above the Standard Output
I	39	7
II	20	7
III	13	8
IV	9.5	8
V	8.30	10
VI	6.64	10
VII	5.50	10

(6) Fall-Back Wage

Tappers are to be paid a fall-back wage at the rates mentioned below :

From	Kerala & Madras	Mysore
1.5.64	Re. 1.04	Re. 0.74
1.4.65	,, 1.11	,, 0.81
1.4.66	,, 1.15	,, 0.90
1.4.67	,, 1.18	,, 0.98
1.4.68	,, 1.22	,, 1.07

(7) Safeguards For The Existing Level Of Earnings Of Tappers In Malabar

Recommendations for uniform piece rates through out Kerala are subject to the condition that the higher earnings of the existing tappers under the old system should remain uneffected by granting them the difference between the earnings under the old system and those under the revised piece rates as personal pay.

(8) Rubber Industry Covered

Recommendations are to apply to all rubber holdings and estates as defined under the Rubber Act, 1947 in the States of Kerala, Madras and Mysore.

(9) Categories Of Employment Covered

Recommendations are to apply to all workers on Rubber Plantations, whether they work on the plantation itself or at any place in the rubber plantation itself or at any place in the rubber plantation district, coming within the purview of the definition of workman in clause (s) of Sec. 2 of the Industrial Disputes Act, 1947. Employees working in any office situated at a district headquarter town are to be excluded.

(10) Working Hours

The time rated workers, for whom a task is not fixed, should work for eight hours a day.

(11) Time Rated Tappers

Time rated tappers, who are employed exclusively for tapping, should be paid not less than 40 paise more than the respective wage rates for the ordinary daily rated workers.

(12) Supervisors/Maistries

The supervisors/maistries in rubber plantations are to be fitted in all inclusive scale of Rs. 85-4-125-5-150 in the manner prescribed.

(13) Staff Wages

The pay scales, dearness allowance and servant allowance, and provisions for fitment (mentioned below) are the same as modified by the staff settlement dated May 4, 1965.

(i) **Scales Of Pay With Effect From January 1, 1965**
Large Estates in all the three States :

General Grade : Rs. 40/50-3-56-4-80-EB-5-120-EB-6-180.

Senior Grade 'A' : Rs. 90-6-120-EB-7-148-EB-8-196-200.

Senior Grade 'B' : Rs. 150-10-280.

Medium Estates in Madras and Kerala :

General Grade : Rs. 40/50-3-56-4-80-EB-5-130.

Senior Grade (for Rs. 90-6-120-EB-7-148-EB-8-180-10-220 heads of Depts. only).

Medium 'B' Estates in Mysore :

General Grade : Rs. 40/50-3-60-4-80-EB-5-135.

Senior Grade : Rs. 90-6-120-EB-7-148-EB-8-196.

Medium 'A' Estates in Mysore :

General Grade : Rs. 40-3-55-4-75-EB-5-105.

Senior Grade : Rs. 90-5-120-EB-6-156.

Note : The definitions of large, medium, 'A' and medium 'B' estates are the same as in the staff settlement of 1957 and 1958.

(ii) Fitment is to be according to the provisions made in the staff settlement dated May 4, 1965.

(iii) Dearness allowance, with effect from Jan. 1, 1965, is to be according to the United Planters Association of Southern India's revised scales of dearness allowance; a scheduled of which is attached to staff settlement dated May 4, 1965.

(iv) Servant allowance at the rate of Rs. 35 p.m., except in the case of small A estates in Mysore where it is Rs. 17.50 p.m.

(14) Mixed Estates

Recommendations are to apply to all workers in rubber areas of the mixed estates.

Miscellaneous

(15) Period Of Enforcement

Recommendations in respect of daily rated workers and supervisors/maistries are to take effect from May 1, 1964, and to remain in force till March 31, 1969, and the recommendations for the staff should take effect from January 1, 1965, and remain in till December 31, 1969.

(16) Spliting Of Rubber Estates

Spliting of rubber estates is not effect wage rates.

(17) Contract Labour

No contract labour is to be employed on normal work on plantations. All workmen employed on contract are to be considered as covered by the Board's recommendations and no discrimination is to be made in the matter of wages between the contract workers and regular workers. The principal employer should be responsible for payment of wages and implementation of Labour Laws.

(18) Board's Recommendations Without Prejudice To Existing Earnings And Benefits

Recommendations are without prejudice to the existing earnings, amenities and benefits, etc.

Machinery For Interpretation

Any dispute about recommendations to be referred to the Labour Commissioner of the State concerned for interpretation, with the cooption of a representative each of the employers and labour in the rubber plantations in the State.

COMMITTEE ON TAKAVI LOANS AND COOPERATIVE CREDIT, 1961—REPORT

New Delhi, Ministry of Community Development & Cooperation, 1963. 113p.

Chairman : Shri B. P. Patel.

Members : Shri B. D. Pande; Shri G. D. Goswami; Shri Y. N. Verma; Shri Satish Chandra; Shri L. N. Bongirwar; Shri T. P. Singh; Shri R. Tirumalai; Shri V. Kodandarama Reddy; Shri K. P. Pande; Shri T. Satyanarayana Rao.

Secretary : Shri B. S. Dhavle.

APPOINTMENT

In its meeting dated the November 8 and 9, 1958, the National Development Council adopted a resolution on cooperative policy in which it was considered essential that by making takavi loans and other facilities available through cooperatives, conditions should be created in which every peasant and rural worker will find it to his advantage to join the village cooperative. The new policy was communicated by the Government of India to all State Governments in May, 1959. While communicating the new policy, the Government of India had suggested that, exopts in the case of distress takavi all assistance to farmers should be channelled through cooperatives organisations. While a few State Governments took steps to channel takavi loans through cooperatives in specific areas and/or for specific purposes, the progress by and large was not appreciable. It was felt that the various organisational, procedural and administrativs difficulties that came in the way of successful implementation of the policy called for careful consideration. Accordingly, under Notification No. F. 6-9/61-UT, dated July 26, 1961 issued by the Department of Cooperation, the Government of India in the Ministry of Community Development and Cooperation, appointed a Commitee to examine the whole question and suggest suitable procedures for the implementation of the policy.

CONTENTS

Introductory; Background; Takavi Loans and Cooperative Credit Present, Position; Need and Scope for Channelling Takavi Loans through Cooperatives; Specified Issues and Recommendations; Conclusions; Appendices from I to VII.

RECOMMENDATIONS

Statistical data relating to takavi operations are not readily available with State Governments. They should, therefore, arrange for the maintenance of department-wise and consolidated uptodate information relating to takavi operations.

Cooperatives should be accepted as institutional agency to provide credit to agriculturists for normal production and land improvement purposes subject to certain expections and government should discontinue the issues of such loans to them directly..

There are certain purposes for which because of the echnical nature of the operations or the financial risks involved or delayed returns on investments, it will not be possible for the cooperatives to finance agriculturists. Government will have to continue to provide finance directly to the agriculturists for these purposes.

The responsibility to provide the entire finance required by agriculturists for normal production and land improvement purposes, excluding those purposes which it will not be possible for them to finance for special reasons, should be transferred to the cooperatives according to a phased programme.

When cooperatives become the sole agency to provide credit to agriculturists for normal production and land improvement purposes, the funds available with government for making advances to agriculturists should be utilised to supplement the resources of the cooperatives.

After transfering to the cooperatives the responsibility to finance agriculturists, government should continue to make budgetary provisions in an increasing measure for financing agriculturists and utilised such provisions for strengthening the structure and resources of the cooperatives.

All development departments of government should continue to provide the technical guidance and other assistance that will be required in preparing and processing applications for loans evenafter cooperatives take over the work.

Some States have not yet taken effective steps to rationalise the central banking structure so as to have one central cooperatives bank for each district. The concerned State Government should take steps to complete this programme as quickly as possible.

Cooperative banks have to make more determined efforts to attract deposits not only by offering competitive rates of interests but also by providing certain essential banking facilities and services. Among the minimum of such facilities would be issue of cheque books and demand drafts coupled with making effective arrangements for clearing such documents at the various clearing houses in the country.

One of the services which the depositing clients expect from their banks is occasional overdraft accommodation-which is different in character from the grant of loans and other credits-to help them tide over emergent temporary difficulties. Cooperative banks should, therefore, have the freedom to offer occasional and small overdrafts to their depositing clients-both individuals and public institutions. There should be specific limits both in regard to individual accommodation (which should bear a proportion to monthly income) and total limits so granted which should not exceed a specified proportion of the overall deposits of the institution concerned.

The implementation of the scheme of opening branches by central cooperative banks should be accelerated and States should provide adequate assistance to central cooperative banks to cover that might be incurred by their branches till they become self supporting.

The short and medium term credit structure in the nine States of Andhra Pradesh, Gujarat, Maharashtra, Kerala, Madhya Pradesh, Madras, Mysore, Punjab and Uttar Pradesh is sufficiently developed both organisationally and financially except for certain specific pockets to be identified as areas of inadequate cooperative development. Government in these nine States should, therefore, discontinue issuing of short and medium term takavi loans for purposes of normal production and land improvement and entrust the work exclusively to the cooperatives, leaving out certain pockets and certain purposes which it will not be possible for them to finance for varous reasons.

The development of the cooperative structure has lagged behind, for various reasons, in certain parts of Jammu and Kashmir, Orissa, Rajasthan and West Bengal. In Bihar, huge takavi overdues, in some districts, have handicapped cooperative development. Governments of these five States of Jammu and Kashmir Orissa, Rajasthan, West Bengal and Bihar should in the first instance discontinue issuing of short and medium term takavi loans for normal production and land improvement in selected cooperatively developed districts areas only. The scheme should be extended to other district areas as and when the cooperative structure these gathers adequate strength so that ultimately no district/area is left outside the purview of the scheme.

Government of Assam should continue issuing of takavi loans and simultaneously take steps to revitalise and strengthen the cooperative institutions. The question of channelling takavi loans through cooperatives in Assam should be considered by the State Government only after the process of rehabilitation is completed.

The principles that have applied to the States in deciding the question of channelling takavi loans through cooperatives should apply to Union Territories also.

The land mortgage banking structure in any State should ultimately be a federal one with a Central Land Mortgage Banks at the State level and primary land mortgage banks at a lower level. In State where Central land Mortgage Banks are financing agriculturists directly through branches, it would be advantageous to organise primary land mortgage banks at the district level.

In States, where primary land mortgage banks are functioning at the district level, there should be some agency at a level below the district which is easily accessible to the agriculturists. The primary land mortgage banks in such States should take steps to open branches at the tehsil or taluka/block headquarters if they have not already done so.

With a view to reduce delays in the sanctioning of loans power to sanction loans upto certain limits should be delegated to primary land mortgage banks and their branches and the branches of central land mortgage banks.

As in the cases of Maharashtra and Gujarat States, the other States also may consider the amendment of the Cooperative Societies Act to include provisions extending to land mortgage banks the special privileges that are available to Government in the matter of security and recovery of loans under the Land Improvement Loans Act which would induce land mortgage banks to advance loans in an increasing measure and help to reduce delays in the sanctioning of loans.

The land mortgage banking system has gained considerable strength in Madras, Andhra Pradesh, Mysore, Maharashtra and Gujarat. Government in these five States may, therefore, discontinue issuing of long term takavi loans, except for those purposes which the land mortgage banks are not in a position to finance at the present juncture and entrust the work exclusively to the land mortgage banks. In other States, a purposewise and regionwise phasing will have to be adopted.

The recommendations of the Committee on Cooperative Credit to raise the Reserve Banks annual contribution to the Long Term Operation Fund to Rs. 15 crores should be implemented as early as possible for augmenting the medium term resources of Cooperatives.

Cooperatives should be helped to raise substantial amounts by way of time-deposits by introducing some measure comparable to the deposit insurance scheme introduced in the case of commercial banks. Attention is also drawn in this connection to the guarantee scheme introduced by the Government of Madras in respect of fixed deposits with cooperative banks for more than three years.

The quantum of medium-term funds that would be made available to central cooperative banks through reimbursement should not be less than that available under the credit limits applicable to them in accordance with the recommendations of the Mehta Committee.

The funds earmarked by Government for making short-term and medium-term advances to agriculturists for normal production and land improvement purposes, excepting those for implementing schemes which the cooperatives are not in a position to finance at the present juncture, should be utilised mainly to supplement the medium term resources of the cooperative structure.

Government funds which can be utilised for supplementing the resources of co-operatives should be made available to the Cooperative structure, preferably in the form of medium-term loans.

In exceptional cases where the owned funds of cooperative institutions need strengthening a part of government funds can be routed through cooperatives and may be utilised for share capital participation in cooperative institutions, if it is found difficult to obtain funds for this purpose from the Reserve Bank of India.

Government loans to supplement the resources of the cooperative structure should be routed through the State cooperative banks.

The rate of interest on Government loans for supplementing the resources of the cooperative structure may be the same as that charged by the Reserve Bank of India on the medium-term advances made by it to the State cooperative banks. If for any reason, a State Government is unable to advance loans at this rate, the rate of interest may be equal to the pooled rate of interest incurred by the State cooperative bank concerned on its deposits or the rate at which the State Government obtains loans from the Central Government, whichever is less.

To overcome the difficulty experienced by Central Land Mortgage Banks in obtaining and utilising interim accommodations being provided by the State Bank of India, State Governments should sanction continuing guaruntees in respect of such accommodation and State Bank of India should renew the accommodation from time to time on the basis of such continuing guarantees. This procedure should apply to interim accommodation from State cooperative banks as well.

State participation in the share capital of Central Land Mortgage Banks should be related to their requirement of interim finance and matching contribution should not be insisted upon in such cases.

The rate of interest on interim finance provided to Central Land Mortgage Banks by State Governments should be the same as that at which they raise funds from the Central Government or open market.

Interest rate on the interim finance being provided by the State Bank of India to Central Land Mortgage Banks should not exceed by one-and-half per cent to basic rate at which the State Bank of India is eligible for accommodation from the Reserve Bank of India on the security of government paper.

The recommendations made by the Committee on

Cooperative Credit for securing assured support from the various agencies in the public and cooperative sector for the debentures floated by land mortgage banks should be implemented.

The Government of India should expedite the setting up of the proposed Refinance Corporation for Agriculture so that it may help the Central Land Mortgage Banks in finding long term resources.

Well established Central Land Mortgage Banks should be permitted to issue debentures in excess of the amount covered by mortgages to enable them to muster enough funds to maintain continuity in their loaning operations.

State Govrnments should make over to the cooperative land mortgage banks at least fifty per cent of the dividend due to them in excess of the interest payble to the Reserve Bank on the amounts borrowed for investment in the shares of cooperation land mortgage banks for strengthening their Agriculture Credit (Stabilisation) Funds for enabling them to give short postponements of instalments in years of scarcity and to meet unforeseen contingencies.

State Governments should continue to make budgetary provisions for advancing long term loans to agriculturists for such purposes as have been transferred to the land mortgage banks and such provision should, after meeting the requirement for managerial grants and other subsidies, be utilised primarily for supplementing the medium term resources of the cooperative structure. Such funds may also be utilised for meeting the shortage of interim finance experienced by cooperative land mortgage banks and for purchasing debentures floated by them where necessary.

While assessing the credit needs of an agriculturist, all his needs should be taken into account. Societies should be assisted to organised ad-hoc chit funds for meeting the social needs of members. They should also be encouraged to build up special funds for meeting special needs of members. Societies which show tangible results on these lines should further be permitted to utilise a portion of their owned funds for these purposes if this can be done without affecting adversely their borrowing capacity for purposes of production.

Land mortgage banks should, while concentrating on financing development works, be free to issue loans for liquidating all categories of secured prior debts.

Effective measures should be taken wherever necessary to adjust the burden of prior debts, especially government debts, incurred under conditions of distress and to arrange for their repayment in easy instalments over a period consistent with the repaying capacity of the debtors, so as to enable cooperatives to make advances to their members in a normal business like manner without fear of the first charge of Government on their properties standing in the way of effecting recoveries.

Cooperatives in backward areas should be treated on a special footing and given adequate managerial grant which may be on a more liberal scale and for a longer period than that to societies in developed areas.

Cooperatives may continue to charge their economical lending rate on short and medium term loans even after becoming the sole institutional agency to provide all such loans required by agriculturists for normal production and land improvement purposes.

The economic lending rate of cooperatives on short term and medium term loans should not be more than seven-and-a-half per cent to eight per cent, depending upon the development of the cooperative movement in each area.

Central cooperative banks in Kerala should work out a pooled rate, taking into account the interest paid on all borrowings and deposits and make advances to cooperatives at a uniform rate of interest irrespective of the source of funds.

Socities which are charging higher rates of interest may be given some special assistance to enable them to bring down their lending rates to the level prevailing in the cooperatively developed States or areas. This special assistance may take the form of additional managerial grant over and above the normal grant of Rs. 900 spread over a period of five years and the Central Government should offer encouragement to the States in this regard by recognising the additional expenditure for Central assistance in the proportion already prescribed for sharing managerial assistance.

Cooperatives should review their economic lending rate from time to time with a view to bringing them down to the extent possible.

The rate of interest on long term loans advanced to agriculturists for undertaking works of agricultural development should be kept reasonably low. It is for the State Government to decide as to what should be this reasonable rate, but it should not be above six-and-a-half per cent.

State Governments should assist the land mortgage banks in advancing loans for developmental purposes at reasonably low rates of interest by liberalising grants for meeting overhead costs on the technical and managerial staff employed by them and their branches and by providing subsidy at a rate equal to the difference between their economic lending rate and the prescribed reasonable rate of interest.

Adequate number of land valuation officers—as far as possible one for each branch or principal office of a primary land mortgage bank—should be placed at the disposal of the land mortgage banks. The financial assistance from government for the land valuation officers and for the managerial and supervisory staff attached to primary land mortgage banks and branches of primary and Central Land Mortgage Banks should be available for four years instead of three years on the same pattern as in the eastern States, viz., full cost in the first two years and two-thirds and one-third cost in the subsequent two years.

Long term loans for redemption of prior debts and purchase of lands have to be treated on a different footing and they may not call for concessional rates of interest.

The preparation of production plans may be the responsibility of Panchayati Raj institutions while the responsibility to such plans should be that of the cooperatives.

Cooperatives should be closely associated with the preparation of production plans at all stages. They should, however, be free to make advances to agriculturists after paying due regard to the objectives of the production plans.

Cooperative institutions will be in a position to give an indication of their resources position and quantum of funds that may be available with them for making advances during a particular season. These should be taken into account while preparing production plans and cooperatives should be expected to provide funds only up to such limits.

The loans policy of the cooperatives and other matters in which the panchayats are legitimately interested may be discussed in joint meeting of the panchayats and the managing committees of the cooperatives. The panchayats may formulate suggestions on the activities of the cooperatives on the basis of such discussions and communicate them to the zila parishads which may take them up with district level cooperative institutions or with departmental officers, if necessary.

An agriculturist desiring to avail of institutional credit should join as member of the local cooperative society recognised by the government for this purpose and confirm to the usual terms and conditions applicable to borrowing members.

Cooperatives should implement as early as possible the recommendation of the Committee on Cooperative Credit relating to financing upto Rs. 200 of persons who do not have enough money to purchase the requisite number of shares in one instalment.

Agriculturists who do not desire to continue as members of cooperatives after repaying the amounts borrowed by them should be given facility to withdraw from membership and to obtain refund of the share capital invested by incorporating necessary provisions in the bye-laws of cooperatives.

Land mortgage banks should also finance cultivators not eligible for loans under normal rules irrespective of whether they are small holders or persons having for all practical purposes permanent right though not transferable rights on the lands cultivated by them or persons whose ownership of land cannot be confirmed in law provided (a) the loans are required for implementing production schemes which on examination are found to be technically sound; (b) the cultivators are adjudged to have sufficient repaying capacity; and (c) government guarantees to make good the losses arising out of such financing to the extent of the short fall in the security.

Special committee should be constituted at the level of primary land mortgage banks consisting of representatives of primary land mortgage banks, community development organizations and government for examining the loan applications of cultivators who are not eligible for loans under normal rules. The applications recommended by such committee only need be sanctioned by land mortgage banks. Government should by a general order extend guarantee to all loans sanctioned by the land mortgage banks on the recommendations of these committees.

To enable cooperatives to play the role that is expected of them, the recommendations of the Committee on Cooperative Credit relating to (i) pattern of organisation at the village level; (ii) State partnership in primary credit societies; (iii) increasing resources of cooperatives; (iv) relaxing the standards for fixing the credit limits of cooperative banks; and (v) avoiding competition between national small savings and savings through cooperatives should be implemented by all concerned as quickly as possible.

Takavi loans for relief of distress should be indicated as such in govenment records.

Recovery of cooperative dues should be given priority as against the outstanding of distress takavi loans.

Effective measures should be taken for the timely recovery of takavi loans issued for genuine production and land improvement purposes so that those who have taken takavi loans for these purposes will not remains defaulter on account of takavi dues and will not be debarred from obtaining loans from cooperatives.

Cooperatives should change over to the system of making available production credit to agriculturists on the basis of their repaying capacity and on their producing adequate sureties irrespective of whether they are owners, tenants or lessees without further delay so that even defaulters on account of takavi dues may be able to obtain necessary credit for seasonal agriculture operations.

Grant of loans for relief of distress shall as a rule

be the responsibility of government.

Cocperative of a particular area effected by natural calamities may be permitted to disburse distress takavi loans if they are financially strong enough and consider that they can undertake the work without detriment to their normal business, provided they function purely on an agency basis with being required to bear the risks involved and obtain the specific sanction of the Registrar of Cooperative Societies in each case.

THE COMMITTEE ON CONTEMPT OF COURTS, 1961—REPORT

New Delhi, Manager of Publications, 1963. 68p.

Chairman : Shri H. N. Sanyal.
Members : Dr. W. S. Barlingay; Shri G. R. Rajagopaul; Shri L. M. Nadkarni.
Secretary : Shri H. C. Daga.

APPOINTMENT

The Committee on Contempt of Courts was consituted under the Ministry of Law, vide their Order No. F. 49/61-Adm. dated July 29, 1961.

TERMS OF REFERENCE

(i) To examine the law relating to contempt of courts generally, and in particular, the relating to the procedure for the punishment thereof.

(ii) To suggest amendments therein with a view to clarifying and reforming the law wherever necessary; and

(iii) To make recommendations for codification of the law in the light of the examination made.

CONTENTS

Introductory; Historical; Constitutional Provisions relating to Contempt; Definition and Classification; Contempt in Relation to Pending Proceedings; Contempt in relation to imminent proceedings; Contempt in relation to Innocent Dissemination; Contempt in relation to Proceedings in Chambers or in Camera; Defences; Practice and Procedure; Right of Appeal; Conclusion; Appendix.

RECOMMENDATIONS

Confidence in the administration of justice is essential for the preservation of our liberty and nothing should be done which may tend to undermine that confidence.

At the same time, as the jurisdiction to punish for contempt trenches upon two important fundamental rights, namely, the right to personal liberty and freedom of speech and expression, rights which are of vital importance in any democratic system, the law of contempt of court should be viewed mainly from the stand point of these rights rather than on the basis of its origin or its present position in other countries.

The Contempt of Courts Act, 1952, though sound so far as it good, touches only the fringes of the subject. While the existing provisions should be continued, there is need for widening considerably the scope of the Act.

Want of knowledge of a pending proceeding, whether civil or criminal, should afford a complete defence to a person accused of contempt.

The rule of contempt in relation to imminent proceedings may be abolished so far as civil cases are concerned. As regards criminal cases, want of knowledge should be a complete defence as in the case of pending proceedings. Further, where in respect of an offence, no arrest has taken place, a presumption should be drawn in favour of the alleged contemner that proceedings are not imminent.

A case which has reached the stage of execution shall not be deemed to be a pending case for the purpose of the law of contempt.

An innocent distributor of a newspaper or other publication, that is to say, a person who had no reasonable grounds for believing that a publication distributed by him contained any offending matter, small not be guilty of contempt of court.

The burden of establishing any of the defences aforesaid shall be on the alleged contemner.

No contempt proceeding in respect of the publication of the text or a fair and accurate summary of the whole or any part of an order made by a court sitting in chambers or in camera small be competent unless the court has expressly power conferred by any enactment for the time being in force.

Contempt proceedings in relation to cases of secrecy should be initiated only when no other punishment is prescribed.

Some of the existing defences open to an alleged

contemner may be given express statutory recognition. These are :

(i) That a person shall not be guilty of contempt for publishing a fair and accurate report of a judicial proceeding or any stage thereof;

(ii) That a person shall not be guilty of contempt for publishing any fair comments on the merits of any case which has been heard and finally decided or on the conduct of any judge of it be for the public good, the question of public good being in each case a question of fact; and

(iii) That a person shall not be guilty of contempt in respect of any statement made by him in good faith concerning the presiding officer of any court subordinate to a High Court, say, to the Chief Justice of that High Court.

In the case of contempts committed in the face of the court, the present summary powers of courts have to be continued and a simple procedure consisting of oral appraisal of the charge to the contemner, the giving of an opportunity to him to make his defence and provisions as to bail and custody, on the lines suggested in paragraph 4 of the Chapter X, may be adopted.

Applications for transfer of proceedings for contempt committed in the face of the court may be entertained by the judge in whose presence the contempt is committed and if he feels that in the interests of proper administration of justice the application should be allowed, and that it is practicable to do so, he should cause the matter to be placed before the Chief Justice for his directions.

A criminal contempt (other than a contempt committed in the face of the court) should be heard only by a Bench of not less than two judges except in cases where the court consists of one judge, e. g., court of the Judicial Commissioner. That contempt may be taken cognisance of only of a motion or on a reference made by some other agency. That is say, in the case of the Supreme Court, the motion may be made by the Attorney-General or a person authorised by him, and, in the case of a High Court, by the Advocate-General or a person authorised by him. Such motion may be made either on the initiative of lhe Attorney-General or the Advocate-General, as the case may be, or at the instance of the court concerned. Where the contempt is that of a subordinate court, action may be taken on a reference made by that court.

A provision may be made that no court shall punish any one for contempt unless the contempt is of such a nature as substantially to interfere with due course of justice.

The provisions of the Contempt of Courts Act, 1952, as to punishment and apology may be continued but it may be made clear that in cases of civil contempt, where fine is not an adequate punishment, the punishment of simple imprisonment to be awarded should consist of detention in a civil prison for a term not exceeding the prescribed statutory period.

It may also be provided that in cases where the person found guilty of contempt in respect of any undertaking given to a court is a corporation, the punishment may be enforced, with the leave of court, by the detention in a civil prison of the directors or principal officers of the Corporation.

Every order of punishment for contempt shall state the facts constituting the contempt, the defence of the person charged, the substance of the evidence taken, if any, as well as the finding and the punishment awarded.

Provision may be made for an appeal as of right from any order or decision of a High Court in the exercise of its jurisdiction to punish for contempt. The appeal should be to a Bench of Judges of the High Court and where the order of decision is of a Bench, the appeal should lie to the Supreme Court.

The rule of practice as to 'purge' of contempt may work hardship in many cases and, therefore, both the appellate court and the court from whose judgment or order an appeal is being preferred should have the power to stay execution of the sentence, to release the alleged contemner on bail and to here the appeal or allow it to be heard, notwithstanding the fact that the appellant has not purged himself of the contempt.

The Supreme Court may, in the interests of university, be conferred power to make rules to supplement where necessary the rules of procedure recommended by us. It may also be provided that the Supreme Court may make rules in relation to High Courts only after consulting the High Courts.

COMMITTEE ON STANDARDS OF UNIVERSITY EDUCATION, 1961—REPORT

New Delhi, University Grants Commission, 1965. 282p. Charts.

Chairman : Prof. N.K. Sidhanta.
Members : Shri S. Govindarajulu ; Dr. A.C. Joshi ; Shri G.D. Parikh ; Shri G.C. Bannerjee ; Shri R.M. Roy ; Dr. R C. Majumdar ; Dr. George Kurian ; Prof. A.B. Lal ; Shri T.K N. Menon ; Dr. G.J. Datta.
Member-Secretary : Dr. P.J. Philip.

APPOINTMENT

One of the important functions of the University Grants Commission is to take, in consultation with the Universities or other bodies concerned, all such steps, as it may think fit, for the promotion and coordination of University education and for the determination and maintenance of standards of teaching, examination and research in Universities. The University Grants Commission appointed a Committee in August 1961.

TERMS OF REFERENCE

The terms of reference of the Committee are as follows:

To undertake a systematic and objective investigation of problems relating to the standards of higher education in Indian Universities.

CONTENTS

Preface ; Aims of University Education in India ; Evaluation of Standards ; Admission Policy ; Courses of Study ; Undergraduate Education ; Postgraduate Education ; Science Education ; Improvement of Teaching ; Medium of Instruction ; Examination Reform ; Colleges ; Organizations of Universities ; Maintenance and Coordination of Standards ; Summary and Main Recommendations ; Appendices from 1 to 36.

RECOMMENDATIONS

The Standards Committee was appointed by the University Grants Commission to make a systematic and objective assessment of standards of university education and to suggest various measures of improvement. In addition to using the questionnaire method, the Committee visited a number of university centres in India and held discussions with Vice-Chancellors, educationists, teachers and students. The main conclusions and resulting recommendations of the Committee are summarised below.

Aims Of University Education In India

Recent developments in the economic, social and political spheres in the country call for a reappraisal of the functions of the Indian university. In the context of the far reaching economic and social changes taking place in India, universities should lay much greater stress on development-oriented education.

The pursuit of liberal values should, however, be a perennial activity of every university, irrespecive of its courses of study. Even in institutions which are primarily concerned with training in professional skills, the inculcation of these values has to be promoted.

The preservation and communication of existing knowledge is an important function of the university. It is, however, essential to transform teaching from routine instruction to acquisition of knowledge by bringing about a living contact between students and teachers.

The university has also to advance the frontiers of knowledge. This has, however, to be done in combination with teaching. Experience has shown that these two activities communicate strength to each other and flourish in combination.

While many Indian universities encourage the study of subjects like Indian languages, Indian history, Indian philosophy, etc., they have, on the whole, failed to create a modern intellectual tradition of their own. Apart from imparting to their students and understanding of India's cultural heritage, universities in India should try to develop in them a modern Indian outlook. This requires a reinterpretation and adaptation of our traditional values in the context of the contemporary situation.

Universities in developing countries like India have firstly to ensure that they reflect and respond to the life of the people living around them. It is mainly through the intellectual and moral leadership of our universities that a tradition-bound and stagnant society is to be transformed into a modern and progressive community. It should be considered obligatory on the part of the university to make an intensive study of problems faced by its neighbourhood as well as by the nations. Universities are expected to influence the thinking and planning activities of the government and other bodies.

A national outlook and purpose has also to be cultivated in our universities by a deliberate pursuit of national ends in preference to local interests. Universities as national institutions should devote themselves to a study of this problem in all its aspects.

Evaluation Of Standards

For a variety of reasons, a categorical answer cannot be given to the question whether standards have deteriorated during the last 10 or 15 years. Standards are said to have declined from the point of view of examination results as also with reference to the expectations entertained by employing agencies and the general public.

It is a fact that courses of study in many universities are not related to well-defined educational objectives The conditions under which teaching and learning are carried on are also far from congenial.

The general opinion, however, seems to be that while the quality of the best students is as good as ever, the average product of an Indian university does not compare favourably with his counterpart in some of the well known universities in the world.

On the other hand, it has to be recognised that many of our scholars and scientists have done outstanding work and that the various schemes of national development have been implemented by personnel trained in our universities.

Further, the various steps taken by the University Grants Commission have made a definite contribution to improvement of facilities in the universities and colleges. It has, however, necessary to point out that the resources placed at the disposal of the Commission have been far from adequate to deal effectively with this problem.

Admission Policy

In the interest of standards, it is of the utmost importance to adopt a bold and imaginative policy in respect of admission of students to university courses. Current practices lead to a great many students, who are neither emotionally nor intellectually prepared for higher education, entering the universities.

There are several ways in which a more careful selection of students could be made such as approving only such students as have secured a fairly high percentage of marks at the school examinations or special weightage being given to marks in important subjects like languages and mathematics. A consideration of their cumulative record at school or a viva voce or written test is also desirable. Each university will have to identify by investigation over a number of years the particular method or combination of methods which is likely to yield the best results.

We should provide for alternative training programmes for those who are not admitted to the universities but possess the necessary aptitude for vocational training. Existing facilities in this regard need further expansion and improvement.

The school system should contain a number of terminal points from which students could be diverted to technical and vocational courses and removed from the passage to the university.

Another solution consists in a large scale expansion of facilities for correspondence courses, part-time courses, etc. It will also be desirable to institute two streams of undergraduate education—a pass as well as an honours. Admission to the honours course will have to be limited to the intellectually abler students, with provision for shifting students from the pass to the honours courses and vice versa according to their aptitutde and ability.

Some have commended the setting up of central institutions of higher education in different parts of the country, where admissions could be strictly controlled and based exclusively on merit.

Universities should agree on the minimum age for entrance to the degree course. It would be desirable to have 17 plus as the minimum age but as a first step, a minimum of 16 plus may be prescribed.

Universities should also agree on the core subjects required for admission to degree courses. All students who aspire to enter the university should have an adequate grounding in science, mathematics, history and geography, apart from languages. Universities should further demand a fairly high standard of English for entrants.

Courses Of Study

The problem of formulating suitable courses of study in Indian universities has to be judged in the light of the rapid advances being made in the field of knowledge, particularly in science and technology. The general impression one gets is that, except in a few universities, no serious attempt is made to evaluate syllabuses in the light of modern developments. Universities should devote themselves more assiduously to a definition of what is expected of students at particular points of their education.

There are several reasons why courses of study have not been rationalised and modernised in our universities. One reason is that the procedure of revision is at present complicated and cumbersome. There is also a lack of competent teachers for imparting instruction in the new areas. Sometimes the universities do not have the required equipment and physical amenities for carrying out reforms.

It is necessary to make the Boards of Study solely responsible for formulation and modification of syllabi. The Boards should include a number of young teachers who are acquainted with the latest developments in the concerned areas.

The reports of the Review Committees appointed by the University Grants Commission to examine courses of study in different disciplines give valuable guidance in this direction and full advantage should be taken of the recommendations made by them. Such reviews should also be undertaken periodically.

The University Grants Commission should explore the possibility of instituting standing review committees for continual study of university courses in the light of modern developments in the respective fields.

The universities may also appoint review committee periodically to carry out a critical evalutaion of their courses.

There should be a regular programme of seminars and conferences of teachers in different subjects for considering issues relating to objectives of teaching, content of courses, organisation of research, teaching methods, etc.

It may be desirable to make permanent arrangements for year-round refresher courses and seminars to which teachers may be exposed for short periods in groups.

The centres of advanced study, set up by the University Grants Commission, should have an extension section for offering facilities of refresher courses and research to selected teachers from universities and colleges.

It is necessary to have a built-in device in every university to look after the maintenance and improvement of courses of study.

Undergraduate Education

All universities in India with the exception of the University of Bombay and the four State Universities in U.P., have accepted the three-year degree course pattern but many of the conditions essential for its implementation have not been fulfilled.

In recent years, there is a general agreement on the total duration of school and university education being 15 years. Most of the members of the committee support this proposal. It is, however, necessary to ensure that the new pattern is harnessed to conditions which are conductive to a refinement of both school and collegiate education.

The period of 15 years may be split up in a convenient way. It does not seem possible to have a 12-year school education except in exceptionally good schools. The pattern of having 10 years of school education followed by two years in an intermediate or a junior college and three years in a degree college deserves serious consideration. The junior college could provide an opportunity to a large number of students to acquire a university degree without having to proceed further, besides being a point for dispersal to vocational and technical courses.

The pre-university course needs to be reorganised, keeping in view the capacity of students as also the need for giving them an adequate grounding for higher studies Special attention should be directed to the teaching of English in the pre-university course.

There is a considerable lack of uniformity in regard to the honours courses in the universities. While we should make provision for a variety of courses and combination of subjects to suit different kinds and degrees of ability, it is essential to have a clear idea of their specific objectives. The honours course should aim at greater specialisation on the basis of which the student could proceed to postgraduate studies.

The idea of "general education", interpreted, imaginatively and in a flexible way, could serve as a rational principle of reorganisation of undergraduate education to make it more balanced and appropriate to the intellectual and spiritual needs of students in the modern world.

Postgraduate Studies And Research

In recent year there has been a rapid expansion of postgraduate studies in the Indian universities. It is a matter of satisfaction that, by and large, results at the postgraduate level the qualitatively as well as quantitatively superior to those at the undergraduate level. But a great need exists for strengthening and consolidating these gains to make them comparable to the best international standards.

The chief aim of postgraduate education should be the acquisition of specialised knowledge. The courses should produce competent scholars and scientists for employment mainly in the learned professions.

Universities do not seem to be careful in permitting colleges to start postgraduate studies. Postgraduate colleges should be allowed to come into existence only if they fulfil requisite stringent conditions, particularly in respect of research.

The proper method for developing postgraduate education in the colleges is to orgonise it in places where at least three to four good colleges may pool their resources in equipment and teaching personnel. Universities should also appoint some professors and readers, who could visit these colleges and deliver lectures.

It would be desirable to lay down that universities should consult a body like the University Grants Commission before postgraduate colleges are started. This will also enable them to resist local pressures and have at their disposal the advice of an expert body in the matter.

Though the research activites of the universities have gained considerable momentum in recent years, such more remains to be done in this regard. While it is true that a good deal of research is being done by institutions and organisations outside the universities, it is in the universities that research can grow in a natural way.

A greater coordination between the departments of different universities in the matter of research programmes seems desirable.

Universities should also make use of the research facilities available in institutions outside the university, e.g., in national laboratories, as in a country like our's research resources are scarce and should be made the best use of.

There seems to be a tendency in some universities to register candidates without due attention being paid to their research aptitudes. It is also doubtful whether the research degree committee in the university has sufficient time to consider the large number of applications placed before it. The chief responsibility for acceptance or refusal of research candidates should belong to the professor/supervisor.

Research students should be admitted only provisionally, to begin with, their confirmation being related to good work. They should be introduced to the methodology of research and asked to prepare a bibliography and read widely.

Universities should ensure careful supervision of research work. The practice prevailing in some departments of permitting eight to 10 candidates to register under one professor should be discontinued.

These should be referred only to competent scholars in the field. The candidate should also be given a viva voce test with a view to finding out more about his suitability for award of the doctorate degree.

It would be desirable to introduce an intermediary degree, viz., M.A./M.Sc. by research, especially in the languages, in order that standards of the Ph. D. may be maintained at a high level.

Teachers should be given necessary facilities for quiet reading, writing and research. It may be desirable for universities to give due consideration to the research work done by teachers before they are confirmed or promoted.

Science Education

Science education in India has grown fairly rapidly during the past four or five decades. The proportion of science students to the total enrolement in the Indian universities compares favourably with a large number of countries but the same cannot be said about the number of students enrolled in the professional faculties.

The resources available to the universities for the development of science departments have not been commensurate with their requirements, considering the great need for improving standards of science education in the country.

There are several factors which have adversely affected the standards of science education. Although the quality of science teaching has not declined at the higher levels and it has probably improved, it cannot be claimed that instruction is satisfactory in the case of a large majority of students.

Standards of science teaching should be improved at the school level in order to provide adequate foundation for upgrading standards at the university level. Science text books for schools should be written by top scientists in the universities. It is also necessary to ensure that science is taught at the school level by first-rate teachers.

The programme undertaken by the University Grants Commission of organising summer institutes for improving the teaching of science in schools needs considerable expansion.

Students with scientific potentialities should be identified sufficiently early and given special attention and care.

Students for science courses in the universities should be selected very carefully, with particular emphasis on their mathematical ability and capacity to do practical laboratory work.

In view of the rapid advance of scientific knowledge in recent years, it is of the utmost importance that courses of study in different science subjects should be reviewed from time to time and made uptodate. Requisite facilities by way of laboratories, equipment, etc., should be provided to enable universities to introduce modern teachniques in teaching science.

It is desirable to provide more diversity in the selection of subjects both at the undergraduate and postgraduate levels. There should be far greater communication between science subjects which are closely related.

Universities should also encourage students to build up their own apparatus and to improvise methods of their own to develop far greater skill and insight into practical work.

It is understood that in some departments very little work is being done with the equipment available to them. In such cases, equipment should be transferred to other departments, where it can be used more effectively.

Although the government has taken several steps for encouraging scientific research in the country, provision for research and development appears to be highly inadequate. Apart from difficulties such as foreign exchange, laboratory facilities, books, etc., there is also a shortage of well-qualified personnel.

Indian scientists working abroad should be offered congenial conditions of work and encouraged to return to the country.

It is important to recognise the international aspects of science and to explore the possibilities of fruitful collaboration between Indian universities and universities abroad. Full advantage should be taken of the assistance available under various foreign aid programmes, particularly at the level of research.

Information about scientific careers and opportunities should be disseminated widely to impress upon promising young people in the universities the attractive rewards which science offers in the developing situation of our country.

Improvement Of Teaching

Conditions in which teaching and learning are carried on in the Indian universities and colleges are unsatisfactory. This is largely due to the enormuous expansion of numbers which has diluted the available resourses such as staff, libraries, etc.

Very little attempt is made in Indian universities to involve the students in the learning process through direct contact with the aid of the teacher. The emphasis is mainly on lecturing, which is not supplemented by other recognised methods of instruction.

The dictation of notes in university classes should be discouraged as it develops a tendency among students to rely on guide books, bazar notes, etc., and encourages memorisation. It will, however, be useful if the teacher prepares a synopsis of his lectures containing carefully selected bibliography and makes it available to the students for their guidance.

Students should be persuaded to take part in academic discussions. Some time should be left at the end of each lecture period for questions.

Encouragement should be given to students to go to the library, select books and read for themselves. One method of doing this would be to insist upon more written assignments and tutorials during the course of the year.

Tutorials should have an important place for writing. The size of the tutorials should be kept reasonably small. It may not be possible to provide separate tutorials for each subject, but with the limited staff available, every student could be given at least one tutorial per week.

At the post-graduate level, tutorials should be supplemented by seminars. Postgraduate students should be encouraged to do independent thinking and to take part in group discussions of an inter-disciplinary nature.

The generally prevailing idea that lectures should "cover" the syllabus must be given up. Syllabuses could also be broken up into suitable parts, each part being dealt with by different teachers.

An attempt should be made to select more promising students and give them better facilities in the laboratories and libraries, instead of dealing with all students alike.

Universities are facing an acute shortage of good teachers. Conditions have, therefore, to be created for attracting and retaining in the teaching profession the services of well-qualified people.

Salaries paid in the universities should be comparable to those in the National Laboratories, Institutes of Technology, etc, which, at present, are higher. No further revision of salaries in the allied secots should take place without due consultation with the University Grants Commission.

Salaries of college teachers are very low and it has not been possible for a number of colleges to introduce even the Second Plan scales of pay recommended by the Commission. The existing gap in the salaries of teachers in the affiliated colleges and those obtaining in the university departments should be narrowed.

There is an urgent need to make the rules for provident fund or pension benefits, health services, etc., as attractive as those prevailing in the administrative and other sectors.

Apart from increasing residential accommodation in the university and college campuses, the possibility of making loans available to teachers on easy terms for building houses in the vicinity of the campuses should be considered.

University rules should provide for 'sabbatical leave' for study and research by teachers. The leave should be provided for professional work and confined to deserving cases only.

The right of universities to appoint their own teachers should be preserved and protected. Universities on the other hand should act with a high sense of responsibility as cases are not uncommon of considerations other than academic; merit being brought to bear upon the appointment of teachers.

It would be desirable to lay down fairly well-defined qualifications for teachers of different categories for the guidance of selection committee.

It would be of great advantage to appoint one or two experts from universities on the selection committees of colleges.

University teachers should have some orientation in the techniques of teaching. They should also be frequently brought together at refresher courses, summer schools; seminars, etc, for exchange of ideas and modernisation.

Teaching aids like radio, television, teaching machines, films, tape recorders and so on can be used with great advantage by Indian universities and colleges. It would be necessary for a central agency like the University Grants Commission to collect and communicate to the universities and colleges information about such equipment and also periodically to organise exhibitions at suitable centres in regard to their uses.

Medium Of Instruction

By and large, English continues to be the chief medium of instruction of university education. Some universities have, however, changed over to Hindi or a regional language at particular stages or permit their use in examinations. It is doubtful whether these changes have been brought about after necessary deliberation and assessment of facilities.

Changeover to the regional language as the medium of instruction at the university stage requires careful preparation as the area of pertinent knowledge to be covered is large and the technology of acquiring knowledge in the universities differs widely from the one used in schools. Unless an Indian language has grown upto its full academic stature, it would be unwise to introduce it as the medium of instruction at the university stage.

Before any changeover is brought about, universities must satisfy themselves about the competence of teachers to teach in the language concerned and about the availability of sufficient number of good books.

Where the medium of instruction changes from the school to the university stage or from the undergraduate to the postgraduate level, it has to be ensured that students do not suffer from it.

It would be desirable to undertake some experimental studies concerning the relative performance of students who study through the English medium and others. It is claimed that at present the best students elect English as their medium and that their standards are also higher.

Even when the medium of instruction is changed to a regional language, it would be necessary to provide for imparting adequate knowledge of English, for English is a great integrating factor, both for unity in India and for access to world literature especially in science, technology, etc. English will also be helpful as a common link for inter-university communications not only within India but also between India and other countries.

The teaching of English should begin sufficiently early at the school stage. Special methods which have been evolved recently for teaching English as a foreign language should be widely introduced in our institutions. Teachers of English should also be given special training at such places as the Central Institute of English at Hyderabad.

Summer schools and refresher courses should be organised on a large scale for teachers of English and use should be made of equipment specially designed for language teaching.

Examination Reform

Examinations have many important functions to perform, such as measurement of the student's competence and his suitability for employment or continuation of studies, etc.

The present examination system in Indian Universities lacks sufficient reliability and validity and has come in for much adverse criticism in recent years.

The aim should be to remove the sources of error in the present method rather than to replace it by some other method which may prove to be equally unsatisfactory. There should, in fact, be a combination of different methods of evaluation as well as the objective and written types of examination.

The main difficulty in regard to internal evaluation has been that in some of the affiliated colleges attempts are sometimes made to raise the value of the sessional work with a view to improving the position of their candidates in the final examination. Internal marks should, therefore, be scaled to the same mean and standard deviation for each college. Another way of making internal assessment more reliable will be to award to each student along with his university diploma, a separate record of the internal tests and other relevant information without adding these marks to the score in the final examination. Yet another alternative would be to confine internal assessment to objective tests, which are easy to administer and quick to score.

Universities should also arrange convenient spacing of examinations. The system of holding a final comprehensive examination has become outdated in view of the rapidly growing content of knowledge which has considerably heightened the burden of the student.

The question papers set at university examinations have a number of defects such as poor sampling of content, ambiguity and lack of standard answers. Paper setters do not devote sufficient time to the framing of questions. Every paper should be related to such educational objectives as recall of knowledge, comprehension, application, analysis, synthesis and evaluation. It should also define the direction and scope of the answers desired. The paper setters should prepare a tentative outline of answers to ensure uniformity in evaluation.

Marks in different subjects should be scaled to a common mean and standard deviation before they are combined. Results should also be moderated with reference to approved statistical procedures of the kind outlined in the University Grants Commission publication, "Three Studies in Examination Technique".

Earnest attempts should be made by universities to reduce the time consumed by examinations. Use may be made of mechanical aids for purposes of tabulation and analysis of marks. Universities should also lay down clearly the maximum number of answer books that a teacher may examine during a year, either from his own university or from outside.

Colleges

Colleges occupy a pivotal position in the present day pattern of higher education in India. The fact that nearly 85 per cent of students are enrolled in the colleges and that they have 83 per cent of the total number of teachers in the universities, is significant. It shows that standards cannot be improved without raising the quality of collegiate education.

The assistance so far made available by the University Grants Commission for providing facilities for affiliated colleges has not been adequate.

Even government colleges and missionary colleges which were noted for their high standards in the past are finding it difficult to maintain them under the present conditions. In a community of colleges weaker colleges have a tendency to pull down standards in the better institutions.

Colleges are allowed to be set up these days under the influence of political pressure, regional rivalry, parochial sentiments, etc. This situation calls for regulative control. A number of colleges in India do not have adequate enrolment, with the result that they cannot be considered viable economic or intellectual units. Before new colleges are started, due consideration should be given to the existence of such institutions and attempt should be made to explore the possibility of utilising them to the fullest extent.

There should be a reasonably uniform system of granting affiliation to colleges all over the country. The norms and conditions formulated by the college Committee of the University Grants Commission in regard to staff requirements and physical and other facilities should be strictly adhered to. The power of granting affiliation should vest in the university and there should not be any interference or pressure from government or any other agency in this matter.

Efforts should be made to bring universities and colleges closer together and the universites should concern themselves more actively with collegiate education.

A certain number of good colleges should be given an "autonomous" status to experiment with new techniques of teaching, courses of study, internal examinations, etc. Special assistance should also be made available to selected colleges for the pursuit of excellence.

A number of outstanding colleges all over the country should be chosen for treatment in the same way as 'centres of advanced study' are in respect of post-graduate teaching and research.

The possibility of every university setting up a college or 'centre' under its own auspices to serve as a 'pace-setter' for other colleges should be explored. Such colleges can in turn grow into full-fledged universities in due course.

The system of government meeting 90 per cent of the deficit of the constituent colleges of Delhi University should be extended to other colleges also. Instead of determining grants on an ad-hoc basis, there should be a grant-in-aid code to regulate financial assistance to colleges.

Colleges should organise extension lectures by distinguished scholars and scientists from the university and outside to explose their students and teachers to the influence of experts in their respective fields.

Organisation Of The University

Universities should have a high degree of autonomy. They should have the freedom to choose their students, to appoint their staff, to organise their courses of study, etc.

Universities in India enjoy freedom in many of these matters, but there are occasions when its exercise is threatened. Some of the methods now employed in the election or selection of Vice-Chancellors, for example, impinge on the autonomy of universities.

The Vice-Chancellor should be an able and academically minded person, preferably with a record of teaching and research. He should be given full authority and facilities to discharge his duties in an efficient way.

There is no inherent conflict between the principle of accountability and the idea of autonomy. State governments should follow the example and procedures initiated by the University Grants Commission in dealing with the universities.

While universities should enjoy autonomy in academic matters to the fullest extent, they should on their part be fully alive to and aware of their social obligation in respect of training leaders and administrators in various walks of life.

Participation of aly-men in the legislative and administrative organs of the university may be desirable, but in no case, should they be allowed to become a hampering factor in the performance of academic activities. The Senate and the Syndicate should be concerned mainly with administration and academic programmes should be left, by and large, to academic men.

The constitutions of our universities which were modelled to suit different circumstances are not suitable for the present conditions which require quick action and efficiency. An attempt should be made to get rid of large and cumbersome bodies and also to do away with unnecessary administration.

There should be a Board of Undergraduate Education and parallel to it, a Board of Postgraduate Education. The boards might jointly constitute the Academic Council, or operate under it, but should have sufficient authority to organise the work of the university in their respective spheres.

There is an urgent need for streamlining the present methods of administration involving such procedures as filling up of unnecessary forms, maintenance of useless records, etc.

Many heads of departments, specially in science subjects, have so much routine work to do that they have practically no time left to devote themselves to study and research. The possibility of dividing administrative work over as many members of the department as possible should be explored.

Maintenance And Coordination Of Standards

In pursuance of the functions entrusted to the University Grants Commission under the University Grants Commission Act of 1956, the aim of the Commission is to raise the levels of university education ; firstly, to the highest standards obtaining in our own country, and secondly, to raise the best attainable in our country to international standards.

Although, education is a State subject in India, the function of the University Grants Commission to coordinate university education signifies that issues have to be judged in a wider context and a proper coordination of university education brought about with resources as well as requirements.

The Commission would also be able to organise development and strengthening of academic facilities among universities on a regional basis to ensure optimum utilization of material and personnel resources particularly in respect of highly specialised subjects.

The University Grants Commission has dealt with the problem of university autonomy with great tact and wisdom. The Commission has to continue to provide effective leadership to the universities in the sphere of standards. The legal powers of the Commission in this behalf cannot however, be exercised to the fullest extent and with beneficial results unless resources are made available to the Commission on a scale much higher than has been the case hitherto

The academic activities of the University Grants Commission such as the holding of seminars and conferences, appointment of review committees, setting up of centres of advanced study, etc., need to be strengthened further.

While expenditure of an order undertaken by advanced countries may not either be applicable or possible in India, unless the present outlay on higher education, as also the cost per student is sufficiently increased, many of our institutions will not be able to rise above sub-standards.

In India, education in general arts and science subjects is being given to far too many students. It would be necessary to pay particular attention to and expand those sectors of education, which are of more direct value to the developmental programme of the country.

A strict control should be exercised by the Central Government on the establishment of new universities by State Governments.

Concerted efforts have to be made for promoting among teacher and students a sense of pride in the university as also for raising their morale and bringing into being a truly academic community.

DERAILMENT OF 2TF DOWN PASSENGER TRAIN BETWEEN MAINPURI AND BHONGAON STATIONS (NORTHERN RAILWAY) ON OCTOBER 29, 1961—REPORT

New Delhi, Ministry of Transport and Communications (Railway Inspectorate), 1964. 12p.

One Man Commission : Shri A. C. Khastgir.

APPOINTMENT

The Commission was constituted under the Ministry of Transport and Communications (Railway Inspectorate) in accordance with Rule 9 of Railway Board's Notification No. 1926-T, dated March 19, 1930.

TERMS OF REFERENCE

To inquire into the accident No. 2 TF Down passenger train at Km. 1268.69 between Manipur and Bhongaon stations on the Shikohabad—Farukhabad section of the Northern Railway at 10.35 hrs. on October 29, 1961.

CONTENTS

Summary; Inquiry; Brief Description of the Accident; Casualties; Composition of the Train; Damage; Relief Measures; Restoration of Communications; Number of Passengers; Weather Conditions; Description of the

Locality; Description of Permanent Way; Distances; Booked and Permissible Speeds; Summary of Evidence; Observations and Tests; Discussion (Possible Causes of the Accident; Tampering of Track; Defect in Track or Obstruction on Track; Defect in Mechanical Equipment; Excessive Speed; Riding Qualities of AWD/CWD Engines; Probable Sequence of Events); Conclusion.

CONCLUSIONS

After full consideration of all the facts, and material and circumstantial evidence, I have reached the conclusion that the derailment of No. 2 TF Down Passenger train at Km. 1268-69 between Mainpuri and Bhongaon stations on October 29, 1961, was caused by the train attaining the high speed of 45 miles per hour, which is far in excess of the maximum permissible speed of 30 miles per hour on the section for AWD engines. The high speed caused excessive flange forces and violent oscillation of the engine followed by distortion of track and derailment. The sudden application of the brakes caused a rapid loss of speed and almost instantaneous capsizement of the engine and the consequent telescoping of the following four coaches. I hold Driver Bhagita, who unfortunately lost his life in the accident, responsible for driving his engine at such a high speed, in contravention of GRs 89 (a) and (b).

I am satisfied that the medical relief afforded was prompt and satisfactory, inspite of the comparatively large number of casualties. This was possible, because the accident occurred at a place where the main road between Shikohabad and Farukhabad crosses the railway track and buses and trucks plying on the road were requisitioned to remove the injured to the hospitals.

DERAILMENT OF NO. 16 UP SAURASHTRA EXPRESS BETWEEN BROACH & ANKLESHWAR STATIONS OF THE WESTERN RAILWAY ON OCTOBER 4, 1961—REPORT

New Delhi, Manager of Publications, 1967. 13p.

One-Man Commission : Shri K. C. Pathak.

APPOINTMENT

The Commission was constituted under the Ministry of Transport & Communications (Railway Inspectorate) in accordance with paragraph 9 of the Railway Board's Notification No. 1926-T, dated March 19, 1930.

TERMS OF REFERENCE

To inquire into the Derailment of No. 16 Up Express at Km. 322/1-2 T. P., between Broach and Ankleshwar stations on the Bombay—Baroda Broad Gauge Main Line (Double Line) Section of the Western Railway on October 4, 1961.

CONTENTS

Summary; Inquiry; Description of the Accident; Casualties; Information of the Accident and Relief Measures; Restoration; Particulars of Train; Damage; Local Conditions; Summary of Evidence; Discussion (Speed of the Train; Examination of the Coach; Inspection of Site; Weather Conditions; Occurrence of Creep and Buckling; Cause of Derailment; Responsibility of Mate Isale Umar; Responsibility of Permanent Way Inspector; Responsibility of the Assistant Engineer); Conclusions.

CONCLUSIONS

Having inspected the site of accident and having considered the recorded as well as material evidence. I have arived at the following conclusions :

(a) **Cause :** The derailment of No. 16 Up Saurashtra Express at km. 322/1-2 T. P., at 12.14 hours on October 4, 1961, was the result of the track having buckled under the train, while it was passing over the spot. The buckling, which occurred during the hottest part of the day, was due to excessive creep which already existed at the site, the expansion gaps having disappeared and the rail joints having jammed hard, and the end of the creeping rails being followed immediately by track consisting of 210 feet long welded panels of rails laid on new steel through sleepers with loose jews which held the rails firmly keyed to the sleepers and prevented any creep.

(b) **Responsibility :** (i) I consider the Permanent Way Inspector, Shri Stanley D'Lima, primarily responsible for the accident because he did not take steps be times to pull back the rails for adjustment of creep in spite of having received a request from the Gang Mate of the length to do so:

(ii) I also consider Shri J. N. Marfatia, Assistant Engineer, Broach, responsible for the accident in that being himself ignorant of the dangerous condition of the track that existed at the site of the accident he did not give necessary directive to the Permanent Way Inspector when the latter failed to take the initiative himself.

The action taken by Shri M. H. Ahmed, Station Master, Broach, in rushing to the site of the accident and conveying the injured passengers to the hospital by commandeered motor vehicles, is indicative of commendable presence of mind and initiative on his part.

(c) **Relief Measures :** The injured persons were taken proper care of in the Sarvodaya Hospital at Broach after their admission there by 13.15 hours,

STUDY GROUP ON THE TRAINING OF ELEMENTARY TEACHERS IN INDIA, 1961—REPORT,

New Delhi, Ministry of Education, 1963, 72p.

Chairman : Shri Raja Roy Singh.

Members : Dr. Salamatullah; Shri L. R. Desai; Shri K. S. Radhakrishna; Shri A. C. Devegowda; Shri S. P. Verma; Shri D. P. Nayar; Shri T. K. N. Tandon: Shri J. K. Shukla.

Secretary : Shri J. P. Naik.

APPOINTMENT

This Study Group on Training of Elementary Teachers in India was appointed by the All India Council for Elementary Education in its first meeting held at New Delhi on October 30 and 31, 1961.

TERMS OF REFERENCE

The following were the terms of reference of this Study Group :

(i) To prepare a programme for the improvement of teacher training at the primary stage.

(ii) To study and report on the following topics referred to by the All India Council in its meeting held on and October 30 and 31, 1961, viz.

(a) The need of specific training in the theory and practice of primary education for those who are requir d to work as te chers in primary training institutions and inspectors of primary schools.

(b) Measures to effect qualitative improvements in the preparation of elementary teachers.

(c) A time limit should be laid down with regard to the realisation of minimum educational qualifications for recruitment and training of candidates of scheduled castes, scheduled Tribes and women candidates as teachers.

(d) The maximum upper age limit for admission in the training schools should be prescribed.

(e) Making provision for deputing teachers in service for training, specially in States where there are a large number of untrained teachers in service.

(f) Education of primary teachers in India.

(g) Report of the first national seminar on the training of primary teachers in India.

CONTENTS

Introduction; The Education of Elementary Teachers in India; A Historical Survey (1800-1961); The Present Situation; An Appraisal; Pre-Service Education of the Teacher In-Service Teacher Education; Towards a Comprehensive Organisation for Teacher Education; Summary of Recommendations; Annexures; Statistical Tables.

RECOMMENDATIONS

In the three preceding chapters, we have made a number of recommendations relating to a programme of action for the improvement of teacher education at the elementary level. For convenience of reference, these have been briefly summarised in this concluding chapter.

Significance Of The Programme

No other single factor can make such a vital difference, for the better, as a proper system of teacher education and a "break-through" here is urgently necessary. It does not really involve any 'additional' expenditure; all that it implies is the incurring of an expenditure, which will ultimately have to be incurred under any circumstances, but which would lead to great improvement in quality, if incurred in the near future. This programme should, therefore, receive high priority in the remaining period of the third plan as well as in the fourth plan. (Paras 64-66)

Clearing The Backlog Of Untrained Teachers

By the end of the Third Plan, there would be a backlog of about 4,00,000 untrained teachers in primary and middle schools. Special measures should be devised for training these teachers. We recommend the following:

(i) A substantial number of these untraind teachers would be above 35 years of age and would have put in a service of 10-15 years. Little useful purpose is likely to be served by sending them for a regular course of pre-service training. Their training should be undertaken through short-term in-service course.

(ii) For teachers below the age of 35, who have put in five to 10 years of service, the pre-service training course should be of one year.

(iii) Full-term training courses would be required for those untrained teachers who have put in less than five years of service and are below 35 years of age. The number of additional training places would have to take account of these untrained teachers. (Paras 72-74)

Correspondence courses are particularly suited for clearing this backlog of untrained teachers. They would not take away the teachers from their schools for any length of time; and teachers in categories (i) and (ii) above may be trained effectively through correspondence, supplemented by some short-term courses, mainly for practical work. A committee of experts should be appointed to work out the details of the correspondence courses in collaboration with the National Institute of Education and a pilot project should be started in each State to try out this method. It may be expanded suitably in the light of practical experience.

Expansion Of Training Facilities

A large expansion of training facilities is necessary and steps to secure this should be taken immediately. In estimating the requirements of additional places in training institutions for elementary teachers, a pupil-teacher ratio of 45 may be adopted. This would mean of pupil-teacher ratio of about 50 in classes I-V and of about 40 in classes VI-VIII. The target of enrolment to be reached by 1975-76 should be 100 per cent enrolment in the age-group six to 14 in all areas where an enrolment of 60 per cent or above has been reached by the end of the Third Five-year Plan. In the remaining areas, the target of enrolment should be 100 per cent enrolment in the age-group six to 11 and 75 per cent in the age-group 11-14.

The minimum size of a training institution should be 160, preferably 200. This would secure efficiency as well as economy.

The facilities for teacher training should be so expanded that the annual output of training institutions would match the annual requirement of additional teachers. To achieve this equilibrium between the supply and demand for trained teachers is the most significant programme in the "breakthrough" we have urged for teacher education. The programme for each State and Union Territory should be so drawn up that this goal would be reached by 1967-68, the first year of the Fourth Plan, and steps towards it should be taken from now. (Paras 75-78)

Appointment Of Study Groups

Each State and Union Territory Administration should immediately set up a Study Group to :

(a) Work out detailed estimates, on the lines indicated in Annexure I, of the additional enrolment in the elementary schools upto 1975 and the additional teachers required annually ;

(b) Assess the size of the existing backlog of untrained teachers and prepare a detailed scheme for clearing the backlog;

(c) Examine the possibilities of expanding the capacity of existing institutions;

(d) Determine the additional training places which need to be created so that, by 1967-68, the output on the basis of a two-year course should match the annua requirements (estimates to be worked out separately for primary and middle schools);

(e) Assess the requirements of teachers for the special categories, e.g., women teachers, teachers for remote areas, teachers for tribal areas, etc., and

(f) Work out the estimate of the cost and the phasing of the whole programme.

The Study Groups should starts functioning immediately and complete their work by March, 1963. The plans prepared by the Study Groups should be combined for the over all plan of teacher education for the country. (Para 79)

Location And Planning Of Training Institutions

The location and planning of training institutions should be done with great care. The following general principles are suggested in this regard :

(a) A district should be taken as the unit of planning and each district should be provided with as many training institutions as are required to meet demand of elementary teachers within its area;

(b) Since 80 per cent of the population is rural, about four-fifths of the training institutions should be located in rural areas;

(c) As the training institutions need practising schools of a fair size, an ideal location for a training institution would be a township with a population between 5,000 and 15,000. This will provide the necessary facilities of a practising school on the desired scale without detracting from the rural character of the location; and

(d) The institutions should be so located that they would be easily accessible from all parts of the district. There is a proposal that each training institution should provide extension services to primary and middle schools within its neighbourhood. The location of training institutions should, therefore, be so planned, that when these services are started, it should be possible to cover most of the primary and middle schools in the district. (Para 80)

Cost Of The Programme

Each State and Union Territory should prepare a blueprint of an elementary training institution of the optimum size and work out the details of its total cost-both capital and recurring. It should also prepare a detailed estimate of the capital and recurring costs involved in raising the existing training institutions to the desired level in size and efficiency as well as in the establishment of the new institutions required. (Para 81)

General Education Of Elementary School Teachers

The following policies should be adopted in respect of the general education of elementary school teachers :

(a) As soon as practicable, and in any case not later than 1965-66, the recruitment of teachers for primary and middle schools should be only from those who have passed the matriculation or equivalent examination.

(b) Beyond the deadline fixed for the recruitment of matriculates only, the selection of a non-matriculate teacher should be permitted in the following exceptional cases :

(1) For tribal or remote areas, if suitable matriculate teachers are not available; and

(2) Women teachers in rural areas, if no matriculate women teachers are available.

(c) Even in the exceptional cases mentioned in (b) above, suitable measures should be adopted to see that the need to recruit non-matriculate teachers disappears as quickly as possible and at a date which does not extend beyond 1971.

(d) The employment of graduate teachers in elementary schools should be encouraged. It is desirable that the headmaster of every primary school with more than 250 children should be a graduate. (Paras 82-88)

Duration of the Training Course

The duration of the elementary course should be two years for all teachers who have completed secondary school, or the higher secondary or even the intermediate course. For those who have not completed the secondary school, the duration of the training course should-be three years which should be divided into two period a continuous pre-service training programme of two years followed by an in-service training programme of one year. (Paras 89-92)

Revision of Syllabi

The existing syllabi of training institutions for elementary teachers need considerable revision. The programme can be helped if a model syllabus can be evolved to serve as the general framework within which such adaptation as may be required to suit the conditions of different States may be made. This work should be undertaken by the National Institute of Education in collaboration with the representatives of the State Governments and selected Principals of training institutions. (Para 93)

Training of Teacher Educators

Special in-service training courses should be organised for teacher educators. It is desirable that universities provide specialised courses at the M. Ed. level to prepare teacher educators for training institutions. It would also be a distinct advantage if persons taking such specialised courses become familiar with methods of infant teaching. (Para 94)

Improving The Physical Conditions In Training Institutions

A blueprint of the minimum essential needs of a training institution for elementary teachers should be prepared and immediate steps should be taken, during the Third Five-Year Plan itself, to improve the physical conditions in training institutions such as buildings for classrooms, hostels, staff quarters, laboratories, land for the farm and teaching equipment. The Study Groups proposed to be set up in States and Union Territories should examine the existing position in this respect and prepare development programmes with estimates of cost. (Para 95)

In-Service Teacher Education

In-service teacher education is of the highest importance and a beginning should be made in the Third Five-Year Plan itself for developing a nation-wide network of in-service training programmes. The ultimate objective should be to give, to every elementary teacher, in-service training of not less than two months' duration in every five years of service.

The in-service training programmes have to be institutionalised; and an adequate provision for this purpose should be made, either in existing institutions, or in special institutions created for the purpose.

In-service training programmes should also be organised for headmasters and members of inspecting staff. (Paras 96-99)

Extension Services

The scheme of the National Council of Educational Research and Training for establishment of extension service centres in training institutions for elementary teachers is welcome. The number of such centres should be increased to 240 at least by the end of the Third Plan and 50 per cent of training institutions should be covered by the end of the Fourth Plan. (Para 100)

State Institutes Of Elementary Education

State Institutions of Elementary Education established as early as possible and should be charged with the following functions :

(i) To provide in-service training to teachers Self educators and the inspecting staff connected with elemen tary education;

(ii) To undertake studies, investigation in all problems of education and research in methods of teaching and the curriculum in elementary schools;

(iii) To prepare instructional material and teaching aids for the use and guidance of the teachers; and

(iv) To carry out periodic evaluative studies of the programmes of training institutions, extension activities and the progress of elementary education in general and of basic education in particular. (Para 102)

Incentives And Facilities For Further Self-Education

Adequate incentives and facilities for further education should be provided to elementary school teachers. For this purpose :

(i) The conditions governing the grant of study leave should be liberalised;

(ii) Advance increments or higher scales of pay should be given to teachers who acquire higher academic or professional qualifications;

(iii) The possibilitiesi nherent in the correspondence courses should be examined with a view to providing to elementary teachers opportunities for acquiring higher professional qualifications. A beginning in this direction can be made through the State Institutes of Elementary Education; and

(iv) The teachers who acquire higher qualifications should be eligible for promotion to the inspecting cadre and to the training institutions. (Para 103)

Productional Of Education Literature In Indian Languages

The non-availability of adequate educational literature in Indian languages is one of the main handicaps of the elementary teacher in India. Steps will, therefore, have to be taken to produce this literature in all the Indian languages. The primary responsibility for this programme should be on the National Council of Educational Research and Training and the State Institutes of Elementary Education. The organisations of teachers have a particularly important role to play in this sector and should be encouraged in all possible ways to assume a share of this responsibility. (Paras 104 & 105)

Comprehensive Organisation For Teacher Education

The programme for the reform of teacher education cannot be implemented effectively through adhoc measures; it must be supported by an adequate organisation. We are firmly of the conviction that a time has come to create a permanent organisation at all levels which would be charged with the responsibility for improving teacher education and which should be giving continuous thought to its problems. (Paras 106-108)

State Councils Of Teacher Education

In every State, there should be a State Council of Teacher Education, consisting of the Director of Education, representatives of the University Departments of Education, representatives of training colleges for secondary teachers, representative of the Principles and teachers of training institutions for pre-primary and elementry teachers, and non-official educationists. The Council will deal with teacher education at all levels, pre-primary to secondary, and have the following functions :

(i) To prepare programmes for the development of teacher education and supervise their implementation;

(ii) To set standards for teacher education;

(iii) To confer recognition on institutions which fulfil the requirements prescribed by the Council;

(iv) To prepare the curriculum and syllabuses according to which the training programmes, both pre-service and in-service should be carried out;

(v) To conduct examinations and award Certificates and Diplomas;

(vi) To arrange for the inspection and supervision of the training institutions recognised by it;

(vii) To coordinate the training programmes and collaborate with other agencies in the State and outside in the furtherance of its objectives. (Paras 109 & 110)

Special Officer For Training Institutions

Every State should have a Special Officer (or any other suitable administrative machinery) whose wholetime responsibility would be for the programmes of training institutions and that the annual inspection of the training institutions should be carried out by panels of experts.

Department Of Teacher Education In the NIE

The decision to establish a Department of Teacher Education in the National Institute of Education is welcome. The Department should have the following functions :

(i) To act as a clearing house of ideas and information;

(ii) To provide advanced level training courses in teacher education;

(iii) To conduct research in various aspects of teacher education;

(iv) To prepare instructional literature in Hindi and other regional languages for the use of training institutions; and

(v) To provide consultative services to the States.

(Paras 113 and 114)

Financial Implications

The total cost of a programme of teacher education, both pre-service and in-service, would be of the order of Rs. 112 crores spread over a period of 10 years. This would be about five per cent of the total direct expenditure on elementary education.

A beginning should be made for implementing this programme by providing a sum of Rs. 20 crores in the Third Five-Year Plan. A sum of about Rs. 60 crores would be needed in the Fourth Five-Year Plan for this programme. (Paras 115-117)

PUNJAB COMMISSION, 1961—REPORT

New Delhi, Manager of Publications, 1962. 16p.

Chairman : Shri S.R. Das.

Members : Dr. C.P.Ramaswami Aiyar ; Shri M.C. Chagla

APPOINTMENT

The Punjab Commission was constituted under the Government of India vide their Resolution No. 40/12/61-Poll. (I), dated October 31, 1961, to inquire into the general question of discrimination and examine any charges of alleged differential treatment or grievances of the sikhs in the Punjab.

TERMS OF REFERENCE

To inquire into the general question of discrimination and examine any charges of alleged differential treatment or grievances of the Sikhs in the Punjab.

CONTENTS

Resolution ; Order ; Report ; Resolution.

RECOMMENDATIONS

As regards charges of alleged discrimination against non-Sikhs we are clearly of opinion that the same cannot be entertained by as substantive cases and independently of charges of alleged discrimination against the Sikhs in the Punjab. If any case were put forward alleging discrimination against the Sikhs in the Punjab, those parties contesting that case might conceivably be permitted to allege discrimination against non-Sikhs only by way of rebuttal of the charges of discrimination against the Sikhs in the Punjab. In other words, they might have been permitted to plead discrimination against non-Sikhs only to disprove the case of discrimination against the Sikhs in the Punjab. They cannot, we hold, be allowed to allege discrimination against non-Sikhs independently of the question of discrimination against the Sikhs in the Punjab. In view of the terms of reference construed as aforesaid we are unable to entertain the cases of discrimination against non-Sikhs as no case of discrimination against Sikhs has been made or pressed before us.

The individual grievances put forward before us refer to denial of employment, official promotions, fair allotment of lands and matters of dismissal from service or the like. Some of these cases refer to a period before or immediately after the partition of the country in 1947. It is true that discrimination against individual Sikhs may go to make up a general case of discrimination aganist the Sikhs as a community. But the memoranda submitted before us are very few and there are also memoranda filed by non-Sikhs making similar complaints. Stray cases of injustice against individuals cannot ipso facto be accepted as discrimination against the community to which he belongs. Apart from the question of construction of our terms of reference outlined above, the investigation of such individual grievances would properly be a matter either for the Public Service Commission or for the courts, involving examination of materials and witnesses. This Commission cannot sit in judgment upon the decision of the appropriate authorities, executive or judicial. A writ procedure may be approoriate where it is alleged that individual rights and privileges have been infringed by reason of discrimination contravening the provisions of the Costitution. We are, therefore, of opinon that it is not possible for us to deduce from such instances any general conclusion of discrimination against the Sikhs as a community in in the Punjab.

The question of refusal to grant transport licences by the West Bengal Government to the Sikhs and the eviction of Sikhs from land in the Terai region of Uttar Pradesh obviously are outside the scope of our reference for, these do not constitute discrimination against the Sikhs in the Punjab. But that strict construction apart, in those two States, there is no problem of Sikhs versus non-Sikhs. What happened is that the respective Governments concerned have tried to do something for the benefit of citizens other than Sikhs who they considered, had not a fair chance in the matter of obtaining transport permits or allotment of land for cultivation. Giving a fair chance to every section of citizens and particularly to bring about nationalisation of an essential trade or a public utility service cannot ipso facto, be called a discrimination against any particular community. If there is discrimination at all, it is against the non-Bengalis is one case and against the non-Terai peasants in the other.

The question which has been seriously urged and equally earnestly contested before us relates to the case made by the Nationalist Sikhs of non-implementation, of the Regional Formula and introduction of the Punjabi language in Gurumukhi script upto the Secretariat level. It is to be noted that no memorandum has been filed on behalf of the Akali Dal or any other community alleging discrimination against the Sikhs as such. Indeed the statements made by Master Tara Singh as early as June 19, 1947, and January 21, 1955, and referred to by Shri Virendra of the Hindi Raksha Samiti in the course of his arguments were that the real grievance of Master Tara Singh and the Akali Dal was the non-formation of the Punjabi Suba. As a matter of fact, in his statement made on January 21, 1955, Master Tara Singh stated categorically that he did not believe in a linguistic Punjabi State but wanted a Sikh State. To the same effect is the statement of Master Tara Singh reported in the Indian Express in its issue of December 12, 1961 that the only discrimination against the Sikhs was about the non-formation againt the Punjabi Suba. The demand by Master Tara Singh, therefore, was not based on any emphasis on the Punjabi language but his argument, in substance, was that the Hindus had got a State, the Muslims had got a State and, therefore, the Sikhs must have a State for themselves. This is, however, a question which has not been referred to this Commission.

In the statement filed on behalf of the Nationalist Sikhs, the Nationalist Sikhs stated categorically and emphatically that the Sikhs as a community have no grievances rising out of discrimination under any of four heads referred to in their memorandum, namely,

(1) Constitutional and legal,

(2) Political and social,

(3) Public services, and

(4) Government patronage to business and industry.

The Nationalist Sikhs concede that there is nothing whatsoever in the Constitution of India or in any law passed by any legislature which has denied equal treatment to the Sikhs or an honoured place to the Sikhs as citizens of India. Every adult Sikh, man or woman, has the right to vote and to practise and propagate his or her religion. The Nationalist sikhs maintain that in the Punjab Legislature as well as in the Parliamant, the Sikhs have political representation commensurate with their historical and social importance. Though they are only 34 per cent in the Punjab population, their representation in the Punjab Cabinet ever since independence has been 40 to 50 per cent and they had always had a sikh in the Central Cabinet ever since 1947. The present Chief Minister of the Punjab is a sikh. There is a Sikh Governor of an Indian State and several Sikh Ambassadors and holders of important political positions. The Sikhs in and outside the Punjab are an heonoured part of the Indian Society. As regards representation in public services, the Sikhs cannot have any grievance as the figures show, if anything, that they are over-represented. Except for a few sporadic cases of injustice immediately after the partition, the Nationalist Sikhs have not been able to find any case for grievance under this head. In other important services like engineering, medical, veterinary, revenue, cooperation, judiciary and administrative services their number is no way less than what their population warrants. They believe that they are maintaining their historic position in the Indian Army both in the officers rank and in the men's rank. As regards the grievance that there are no industrial undertakings in the Punjab, the Nationalist Sikhs recognise that it is not a grievance of the Sikhs above. If there had been any grievance, it is of all the the Punjabis. Factually, it is not correct as pointed out by some of the other parties, because, there is a big fertiliser factory in Nangal, next in importance to Sindri. Further, a number of industries are being started round about Delhi within a belt of 18 miles of the capital city. The figures given by the Haryana Lok Samiti and the Punjab Hindi Raksha Samiti and also by the Punjab Government in their respective memoranda fully support the view that the Sikhs as such cannot complain of discrimination under any of the four heads mentioned above. This clearly disposes of the case sought to be made out by Sardar Bhagat Singh Chawla. The only grievance that the Nationalist Sikhs have stressed before us is based on (a) a non-use of the Punjabi language as the official language of the Punjab State at the Secretariat level to which the Government stands committed and (b) the non-implementation of the Regional Formula which the Government claims they have done. According to the Nationalist Sikhs the whole trouble in the Punjab would be set at rest if the Regional Farmula had been scrupulously and promptly applied. Reference is made by the Nationalist Sikhs to the observation by the Prime Minister that Punjabi is the dominant language of the Punjab and the observation made by Malik Hardit Singh reported in the Times of India in its issue of October 5, 1961, and the joint statement of Sardar Teja Singh, former Chief Justice, PFPSU, and Sardar Ujjal Singh, former Finance Minister of Punjab reported in the Times of India on Septmber 10, 1961, and finally to the editorial in "Jathedar" in its issue of October 28, 1961, to the effects that if the Regional Formula had been implemented in the spirit in which it had been conceived by the Central leadership under the guidance of Pandit Jawaharlalji, then no further trouble would have arisen in the Punjab. The question of division of the Punjab into two regions, Hindi and Punjabi, the Sachar Formula and the Regional Formula and the setting up of the Regional Committees have been very severely criticised and opposed by the All-India Bharatiya Jan Sangh, the Haryana Lok Samiti and the Punjab Hindi Raksha Samiti. They maintained that although Punjabi is understood by the vast majority of people in the Punjab, it is nothing more than a spoken language, or a mere dialect. They maintain that the demand for a Punjabi Suba has been given a new twist and is now presented in the garb of a demand for the Punjabi language in Gurumukhi script. Gurumukhi, is a religions script of the Sikhs and cannot be foisted on non-Sikhs. Formerly, Punjabi used to be written in Persian, Devanagari and Gurumukhi scripts and there is no reason why a scriptural should be made compulsory. It has been further pointed out to us that in the interest of the Punjabi language itself, it would be a mistake to insist on Gurumukhi as the only script. For the purpose of our Report, it is not necessary for us to express any opinion one way or the other, for we hold that the case put forward by the Nationalist Sikhs regarding the non-implementation of the Regional Formula cannot be said to amount to a complaint of discrimination against the Sikhs. All that it implies is that certain decisions taken by the Government which they approve of as being in their favour are not being implemented fast enough and their only grievance is that they are not getting all the fruits of their victory. This we feel, is not a case of discrimination at all so as to come within the purview of our Commission. There are strong arguments advanced before us on both sides but we express no opinion their respective merits, for we do not conceive ourselves to be a Language Commission. Accordingly we simply draw the attention of the Government to the memoranda filed by the respective parties for such consideration as they may think fit to bestow on them and to take such action on them as they think fit to do.

It is clear from what has been stated above that the Commission, which was constituted mainly, if not exclusively, by reason of the agitation carried on by Master Tara Singh and his Akali Dal and the demands made by them, can only record the fact that no formal complaint of discrimination against the Sikhs in the Punjab has been placed before it. The Commission records the fact that none of the individuals or organisations that appeared before it has alleged any discrimination against the Sikhs in the Punjab as such and these have, in fact, expressly repudiated that there has been any such discrimination. In the result, the Commission holds that, on the materials before it, no case, of discrimination against Sikhs in the Punjab has been made out.

ACCIDENT TO NO. 14 DOWN MADRAS-BOMBAY JANATA EXPRESS AT KOSGI (SOUTHERN RAILWAY) ON NOVEMBER 9, 1961—REPORT

New Delhi, Manager of Publications, 1964. 15p.

One-Man Commission : Shri H. S. Hart.

APPOINTMENT

The Commission was constituted under the Ministry of Transport and Communications (Railway Inspetorate) in accordance with Rule 9 of the Railway Board's Notification No. 1926-T, dated March 19, 1930.

TERMS OF REFERENCE

To inquire into the accident to No. 14 Down "Madras-Bombay Janata Express" at Kosgi station of the Guntakal-Raichur Broad Gange main line section of the Southern Railway at about 02-30 hours on November 9, 1961.

CONTENTS

Summary; Inquiry; Restoration of Communications; Number of Passengers; Weather Conditions; Description of Local Conditions (Description of the Locally; Description of the Station and Method of Working; Description of the Permanent Way; Permissible Speeds;) Summary of Evidence; Observations and Tests; Discussions (Time of the Accident; Permanent Way; Signals and Interlocking; Speed of the Train; Brakes; Condition of the Engine; Driver's fitness to Perform his Duties; Conclusions.

CONCLUSIONS

Cause Of The Accident

From the evidence available, I have come to the conclusion that the accident to No. 14 Down "Madras-Bombay Janta Express" at Kosgi station on the Guntakal-Raichur Broad Gauge main line section of the Southern Railway at about 02-30 hours on November 9, 1961, was the result of the train passing the Down Main Starter Signal in the 'ON' position and entering the Sand Hump taking off the main line just beyond the Down Main Sterter signal.

Responsibility Of The Accident

The Driver, Shri A. J. D.'souza, was responsible for the accident, in that he failed to control his train and passed the Down Main Starter signal in the 'ON' position without authority. He thereby violated General Rules 76 (a) and (b), and 79.

The driver was 34 years of age and had over 13 years' service, having been first promoted as a 'C' Grade Driver in May, 1955, and confirmed in that grade in May, 1957. He had a fairly good record of service, and, since November, 1954, had only had the following punishments meted out to him :

(a) Increment with held for three months with effect from Ianuary 3, 1955, for having misjudged traffic signals white performing shunting and derailing an engine.

(b) Increment withheld for three months with effect from November 29, 1960, for having failed to examine his engine thoroughly before leaving the shed which resulted in an engine failure.

(c) Increment again with held for three months for negligent working of a goods train resulting in an engine failuer.

(d) Censured for not being alert and failing to examine his engine in August, 1960, which resulted in the derailment of the engine during shunting operations in a siding.

Relief Arrangements

(i) The two fireman were apparently killed instantaneously. The driver was not killed outright, but the Asstt. Surgeon, Southern Railway, Gooty, stated that his life could not have been saved without modern hospital facilities being available within half an-hour of the accident, and this statement has been endorsed by the Asst. Medical Officer, Southern Railway Guntakal. It is obvious that making available such facilities in so short a time was quite impossible.

(ii) The Civil Asst. Surgeon at Kosgi stated that he arrived at the station at 02-55 hours and immediately went to see the driver who had by this time expired. On the other hand, the Guard stated that this doctor examined the driver at 03-55 hours and this statement was corroborated by the Station Master. It would appear, therefore, that this Civil Assistant Surgeon only arrived at about 03-55 hours, i. e., one hour and 10 minutes after being informed. This delay may be pointed out to the Andhra Pradesh Government.

(iii) The Station Master Adoni, tried to procure the services of a doctor and an ambulance to go out to Rosgi from Adoni. His evidence reveals that two private doctors (Drs. Narayana Rao Phone—No. 78, and Krishnaswamy Iyengar Phone No. 112) would not come out, one giving as an excuse at an urgent case and the other that he was unwell. Again when he contacted Dr. Raghavan of the Government Hospital, the latter stated that he had urgent work and could not go out. As a result, there was considerable delay before the ambulance set out from Adoni for Kosgi. The attention of the Andhra Pradesh Government may also be drawn to this.

(iv) The Medical Relief Van was called out from Gooty at 02-45 hours, but only left at 03-40 hours as against the 15 minutes' time limit allowed. The Southern Railway should take up this delay and ensure that such delays do not recur.

(v) The Officers' Special left Guntakal only at 03-55 hours and arrived Kosgi at 06-05 hours, having been delayed at Adoni for 12 minutes for detaching a vehicle with a hot axle. This delay should also be looked into by the Southern Railway.

(vi) Kumari Pratibha Shenoy, aged 11 years, who was rendered first-aid and sent to Raichur Government Hospital for further investigation, was not X-rayed at Raichur, but treated there by the doctor for a minor injury. On return to Madras, an X-ray revealed that she had sustained injuries at the base of the neck and middle of the spirel which would necessitate her being in a clinic for atleast a month. It is not understood why the Civil Docter at Raichur did not X-ray this patient, but classified the injury as 'simple'. The attention of the Mysore Government may be drawn to this lapse.

(vii) More than one person testified to the help rendered by one of the passengers (Shri Abdul Munaf) in trying to extricate the driver when the latter was struggling to get out of the engine. This passenger also went to the nearly mill and helped in getting an electric connection to the spot. His efforts were indeed praiseworthy and deserve special mention.

(viii) The help rendered by Shri K. Ramachandra Setty, merchant at Kosgi, who arranged for temporary electric lighting from his oil mill, to light up the scene of the accident, also deserves special mention.

THE REAR END COLLISION BETWEEN RMR (MG) GOODS PILOT AND NO. 4 ATF (BG) PASSENGER TRAIN BETWEEN RAJA-KI-MANDI AND AGRA CITY STATIONS, CENTRAL RAILWAY) ON NOVEMBER 25, 1961—RFPORT

New Delhi, Manager of Publications, 1964. 9p.

One-Man Commission Shri K. C. Pathak.

APPOINTMENT

The Commission was constituted under the Ministry of Transport and Communications (Railway Inspectorate) in accordance with Rule 9 of Railway Board's Notification No. 1926-T, dated March 19, 1930.

TERMS OF REFERENCE

To inquire on the Rear end Collision of the R. M. R. Goods Pilot and No. 4 ATF Passenger train in the tunnel between Roja-Ki-Mandi and Agra City stations on the Jhansi Division of Central Railway at about midnight of November 25, 1961.

CONTENTS

Summary; Description of Accident; Casualties; Relief Measures; Particulars of the trains; Damage; No. 4 ATF Passenger; Local conditions; System of Train Working Weather Conditions; Summary of Evidence; Discussion; Conclusions.

CONCLUSIONS

Cause of the Accident : Having gone through the proceedings of the Committee and the Remarks and Reasons given by them, I agree with their Conclusions generally, and find that the collision between R. M. R. Down Goods Pilot and No. 4 ATF Down Passenger between Raja-Ki-Mandi and Agra City stations on November 25, 1961, was Caused by allowing No. 4 ATF Down Passenger to enter the Block Section between Raja-Ki-Mandi and Agra City, while it was still occupied by R. M. R. Down Metre Gauge Pilot.

Responsibility : (a) Assistant Station Master B. D. Arora of Agra City station exhibited extreme carelessness after having granted Line Clear for the R. M. P. Down Goods Pilot in having cleared the section before that pilot had been admitted and had cleared that Block

Section. He was further guilty of having granted Line clear for No. 4 ATF Down Passenger while the Down R. M. R. Goods Pilot was still waiting at the outer signal. He breached General Rule 248 (a) and is primarily responsible.

(b) Driver Bhimchand of Down R. M. R. Metre Gauge Pilot was responsible for inaction in not sending anybody to the station even when he was detained at the outer signal for over an hour. He breached General Rule 125 and was accessary to the occurrence of this accident. He made his case worse by freely prevaricating in which his fireman loyally initiated him.

(c) Guard Rawtani of Down R. M. R. Metre Gauge Pilot did not protect his train in the rear and did not fix the tail lamp in the rear end of the brake van; thereby he breached General Rule 144. Had he done so, this accident would not have occurred. By his inaction he proved himself to be accessory to the occurrence of this accident.

I am satisfied that the injured persons, whose number was small and injuries simple, were given adequate attention at the site by the Railway Staff.

FINANCE COMMISSION, 1961—REPORT

New Delhi, Manager of Publications, 1962. 118p.

Chairman : Shri Ashok Kumar Chanda.
Members : Shri P. Govinda Menon ; Shri Divigendra Nath Roy ; Prof. M. V. Mathur.
Member-Secretary : Shri G. R. Kamat.

APPOINTMENT

In pursuance of the provision of article 280 of the Constitution of India and of the Finance Commission (Miscellaneous Provisions) Act, 1951 (XXXIII of 1951), the President is pleased to constitute a Financial Commission under his Order Notification No. FC.5.(1)-A/60, dated December 2, 1960.

TERMS OF REFERENCE

The terms of reference are as follows :

In addition to the matters on which the provisions of sub-clauses (a) and (b) of Clause (3) of Article 280 of the Constitution, the Commission is required to make recommendations ; the Commission should also make recommendations in regard to :

(a) The States which are in need of assistance by way of grants-in-aid of their revenues under article 275, and the sums to be paid to those States other than the sums specified in the proviso to Clause (1) of that article, having regard, among other considerations, to :

(i) The requirements of the Third Five-Year Plan, and

(ii) The efforts to be made by those States to raise additional revenue from the sources available to them ;

(b) The changes, if any, to be made in the principles governing the distribution amongst the States under article 269 of the net proceeds in any financial year of estate duty in respect of property other than agricultural land ;

(c) The changes, if any, to be made in the principles governing the distribution among the States under article 296 of the net proceeds in any financial year of the additional excise duties levied on each of the following commodities, namely : (i) cotton fabrics ; (ii) rayon or artificial silk fabrics (iii) woollen fabrics ; (iv) sugar and (v) tobacco including manufactured tobacco, in replacement of the States sales taxes formerly levied by the State Governments.

Provided that the share accruing to each State shall not be less than the revenue realised from the levy of sales tax in the financial year 1956-57 in that State.

. The recommendations of the Commission shall, in each of the above cases, cover the period of four years commencing from April 1, 1962.

CONTENTS

Constitution of the Commission and its Terms of Reference ; Procedure Addopted ; Distribution of Assigned Taxes ; Devolution of Union Taxes/Duties ; Distribution of Aditional Duties of Excise ; Grants-in Aid ; General Observations ; Summary of Recommendations ; Acknowledgements ; Minute of Dissent by Shri G. R. Kamat ; Observations on the Minute of Dissent ; Appendices from I to VII.

RECOMMENDATIONS

Our recommendations to the President are set out below :

I. Estate Duty

For a period of four years with effect from April 1, 1962 :

(a) Out of the net proceeds in each financial year of estate duty in respect of property other than agricultural land, a sum equal to one per cent be retained by the Union as proceeds attributable to Union Territories ;

(b) The balance of the net proceeds be apportioned between immovable property and other property in the ratio of the gross value of all such properties brought into assessment in that year ;

(c) The sum thus apportioned to immovable property be distributed among the States in proportion to the gross value of the immovable property located in each State ; and

(d) The sum apportioned to property other than immovable property be distributed among the States as follows :

State	Percentage
Andhra Pradesh	8.34
Assam	2.75
Bihar	10.78
Gujarat	4.78
Jammu and Kashmir	0.83
Kerala	3.92
Madhya Pradesh	7.51
Madras	7.80
Maharashtra	9.16
Mysore	5.46
Orissa	4.08
Punjab	4.71
Rajasthan	4.67
Uttar Pradesh	17.10
West Bengal	8.11

II. Grant Of Rs. 15.5 Crores In Lieu Of The Tax On Railway Passenger Fares

With effect from April 1, 1961, a sum of Rs. 12.5 crores be distributed each year during the quinquennium 1961-66 among the States as follows :

State	Rupees in Crores
Andhra Pradesh	1.11
Assam	0.34
Bihar	1.17
Gujarat	0.68
Kerala	0.23
Madhya Pradesh	1.04
Madras	0.81
Maharashtra	1.35
Mysore	0.56
Orissa	0.22
Punjab	1.01
Rajasthan	0.85
Uttar Pradesh	2.24
West Bengal	0.79

III. Income Tax

For a period of four years with effect from April 1, 1962 :

(a) The percentage of the net proceeds in any financial year of taxes on income other than agricultural income, except in so far as those proceeds represent proceeds attributable to Union Territories or to taxes payable in respect of Union emoluments, to be assigned to the States by 66-2/3 (sixty-six and two-thirds) ;

(b) The percentage of the net proceeds of taxes on income which shall be deemed to represent proceeds attributable to Union Territories be 2-1/2 (two-and-a-half) ;

(c) The percentage of the net proceeds assigned to the States be distributed as follows :

State	Percentage
Andhra Pradesh	7.71
Assam	2.44
Bihar	9.33
Gujarat	4.78
Jammu and Kashmir	0.70
Kerala	3.55
Madhya Pradesh	6.41
Madras	8.13
Maharashtra	13.43
Mysore	5.13
Orissa	3.44
Punjab	4.49
Rajasthan	3.97
Uttar Pradesh	14.42
West Bengal	12.09

IV. Union Excise Duties

For a period of four years with effect from April 1, 1962, a sum equal to 20 (twenty) per cent of the net proceeds of the Union duties of excise on the articles scheduled below be paid out of the Consolidated Fund of India to the States and distributed among them as follows :

Schedule of Articles

1. Suger
2. Coffee
3. Tea
4. Tobacco
5. Kerosene
6. Refined diesel oils and vaporizing oils
7. Diesel oil, not otherwise specified
8. Furnace oil
9. Asphalt and bitumen
10. Vegetable non-essential oils
11. Vegetable products
12. Pigments, colours, paints, enamels, varnishes, blacks and cellulose lacquers

13. Soap
14. Tyres and tubes
15. Paper
16. Rayon and synthetic fibres and yarn
17. Cotton fabrics
18. Silk fabrics
19. Woollen fabrics
20. Rayon or artificial silk fabrics
21. Cement
22. Pig iron
23. Steel ingots
24. Aluminium
25. Tin plate and tin sheets including tin taggers and cuttings of such plate, sheets or taggers
26. Internal combustion engines
27. Electric motors and parts thereof
28. Electric batteries and parts thereof
29. Electric lighting bulbs and fluorescent lighting bulbs
30. Electric fans
31. Motor vehicles
32. Cycles, parts of cycles other than motor-cycles
33. Footwear
34. Cinematograph films exposed
35. Matches.

Schedule of Distribution

State	Per centage
Andhra Pradesh	8.23
Assam	4.73
Bihar	11.56
Gujarat	6.45
Jammu and Kashmir	2.02
Kerala	5.46
Madhya Pradesh	8.46
Madras	6.08
Maharashtra	5.73
Mysore	5.82
Orissa	7.07
Punjab	6.71
Raiasthan	5.93
Uttar Pradesh	10.68
West Bengal	5.07

Additional Duties Of Excise

For a period of four years with effect from April 1, 1962, out of the total net proceeds of the additional duties of excise levied in replacement of sales tax on cotton fabrics, rayon or artificial silk fabrics, silk fabrics, woollen fabrics, sugar and tobacco (including manufactured tobacco):

(a) A sum equal to one per cent of the net proceeds be retained by the Union as attributable to Union Territories;

(b) A sum equal to one-and-a-half per cent of the net proceeds be paid to the State of Jammu and Kashmir; and

(c) A sum equal to the balance of the net proceeds of the duties, i.e., after the deduction of the amounts mentioned in sub-paragraphs (a) and (b) above, be distributed as follows:

(i) The sums mentioned below, representing the income of the States in 1956-57 on account of sales taxes by whatever name called, on the six commodities, be first paid to them:

State	Rupees in lakhs
Andhra Pradesh	235.24
Assam	85.08
Bihar	130.16
Gujarat	323.45
Kerala	95.08
Madhya Pradesh	155.17
Madras	285.34
Maharashtra	637.77
Mysore	100.10
Orissa	85.10
Punjab	175.19
Rajasthan	90.10
Uttar Pradesh	575.81
West Bengal	280.41
	3254.00

(ii) The remaining sum, if any, be distributed as follows:

State	Percentage
Andhra Pradesh	7.75
Assam	2.50
Bihar	10.00
Gujarat	5.40
Kerala	4.25
Madhya Pradesh	7.00
Madras	9.00
Maharashtra	10.60
Mysore	5.25
Orissa	4.50
Punjab	5.25
Rajasthan	4.00
Uttar Pradesh	15.50
West Bengal	9.00

Grants-in-aid

(i) Under the substantive portion of article 275 (1) of the Constitution, in each of the four financial years beginning on April 1, 1962, the sums shown in the table below be charged on the Consolidated Fund of India as grants-in-aid of the revenues of the States mentioned against them:

State	Rupees in Lakhs
Andhra Pradesh	1200
Assam	900
Bihar	800
Gujarat	950
Jammu and Kashmir	325
Kerala	850
Madhya Pradesh	625
Madras	800
Mysore	775
Orissa	1600
Punjab	275
Rajasthan	875
Uttar Pradesh	200
West Bengal	850

(ii) Under the substantive portion of article 275 (1) of the Constitution in each of the four financial years beginning on April 1, 1962, the following further sums be charged on the Consolidated Fund of India as grants-in-aid of the revenues of the States mentioned against them for improvement of communications;

State	Rupees in lakhs
Andhra Pradesh	50
Assam	75
Bihar	75
Gujarat	100
Jammu and Kashmir	50
Kerala	75
Madhya Pradesh	175
Mysore	50
Orissa	175
Rajasthan	75

BONUS COMMISSION, 1961—REPORT

New Delhi, Manager of Publications, 1964. 154p.

Chairman : Shri M.R. Meher.

Members : Shri M. Govinda Reddy; Dr. B. N. Ganguli; Shri S.R. Vasavada; Shri S.A. Dange; Shri N. Dandekar; Shri D. Sandilya (resigned and replaced by Shri K. B. Mathur).

Secretary : Shri K.R. Wazkar.

Assistant-Secretary : Shri M.B. Prabhoo.

APPOINTMENT

The Government of India (Ministry of Labour and Employment) have decided to set up a commission to study the question of Bonus to workers in the industrial employment and to make suitable recommendations vide their Resolution No. WB-20 (9) 161, dated December, 6, 1961.

TERMS OF REFERENCE

(1) To define the concept of bonus and to consider in relation to industrial employments, the question of payment of bonus based on profits and recommend principles for computation of such bonus, and methods of payment.

Note : The term "Industrial employments" will include employment in the private sector and in establishments in the public sector nor departmentally run and which compete with establishments in the private sector.

(2) To determine the extent to which the quantum of bonus should be influenced by the prevailing level of remuneration.

(3) (a) To determine what the prior charges should be in different circumstances and how they should be calculated.

(b) To determine conditions under which bonus payments should be made unit-wise, industry-wise, and industry-cum-regionwise.

(4) To consider whether the bonus due to workers, beyond a specified amount, should be paid in the form of National Savings Certificates or in any other form.

(5) To consider whether there should be lower limits irrespective of losses in particular establishments, and upper limits for distribution in one year and if so, the manner of carrying forward profits and losses over a prescribed period.

(6) To suggest an appropriate machinery and method for the settlement of bonus disputes.

(7) To make such other recommendations regarding matters concerning Bonus that might be placed before the Commission on an agreed basis by the employers' (including the public sector) and the workers' representatives.

CONTENTS

Appointment of the Bonus Commission and the

Terms of Reference, Historical Background-Evoluation of the Full Bench Formula of the Labour Appellate Tribunal; Proposals of some Employers' Association to abolish Bonus as a Long-Term Objective-Experience of Profit Sharing Systems in other Countries-The Concept of Bonus in India-Divergent Views of Employers' Association and Unions-Views of the Commission; Proposal of Some Employers'. Associations to link Bonus based on Profits with Productivity/Production Considered; Some Formula proposed by Unions considered; Principles of Bonus-Whether Bonus should be Unitwise, Industrywise or Industry-cum-region-wise; Principles of Bonus (Continued)-whether Bonus should be subject to a Minimum or Maximum-Whether Profit of the Particular Year should be taken as the Basis, or the Average of Two or Three Years; Recommendations on the Formula for Bonus-Computation of Profit for the Year; Our Recommendations on the Formula of Bonus (Continued); Recommendations on the Bonus Formula (Continued)-Proportion of the Available Surplus to be Allocated as Bonus-Minimum and Maximum Bonus and Set-off and Set-on Proposed; Application of the Formula to Particular Industries-The Jute Industry and the Plantation Industries; Application of the Formula to the particular Industries (Continued)-The Coal Industry; Application of the Formula to Particular Industries (Continued)-Bank and Insurance Companies; Application of the Formula to Particular Industries (Continued)-The Sugar Industry; Application of the Formula to Particular Industries (Continued)-Miscellaneous Industries; Application of the Formula-The Public Sector; Miscellaneous; Note by Dr. B.N. Ganguli; Minute of Dissent by Shri N Dandekar; Summary of Conclusions and Recommendations; Appendices from A to B.

RECOMMENDATIONS

Concept Of Bonus

It is difficult to define in rigid terms the concept of bonus but it is possible to urge that, once profits exceed a certain base, labour should legitimately have a share in them. In other words, we think it proper to construe the concept of bonus as sharing by the workers in the prosperity of the concern in which they are employed. This has also the advantage that in the case of low paid workers such sharing in prosperity augments their earnings and so helps to bridge the gap between the actual wage and the need based wage. If it is not feasible to better the standard of living of all the industrial and agricultural workers as aimed at in Article 43 of the Constitution, there is nothing wrong in endeavouring to do so in respect of at least those workers whose efforts have contributed to the profits of the concern in which they have worked. The validity of such a conception of bonus is not affected by the difficulty of determining or quantifying precisely the 'living wage' or even the 'need-based wage' at any given time and place.

It appears to us that a properly conceived bonus system that is linked to profit also imparts a measure of desirable felexibility to the wage structure. The workers are enabled to share in the prosperity of the concern, without disturbing the underlying basic wage structure.

It would neither be feasible nor desirable to require industries to incorporate existing schemes of varying bonus payments into the wage structure permanently with a view to eliminate bonus, for while profits are variable, wage rates are fixed on the industry-cum-region basis and not on the basis of the particular unit's ability to pay. This is not peculiar to this country.

The profit bonus system has little direct incentive effect. Bonus is usually paid to all workmen at the same rate in terms of monthly basic wages in some cases, or in some cases in terms of consolidated wages. The efficient as also the inefficient worker gets bonus at the same rate. An annual but uncertain bonus varying from year to year and paid long after the close of the financial year can hardly act as an incentive to greater effort. Incentives, to be effective, have to be given soon after the effort which it is sought to reward. Besides, the best incentives are those applied to results achieved by individuals or small groups of workmen; the incentive becomes weaker when applied to large groups and when the factory is treated as a unit, the incentive is too weak to have any influence on the quantity or quality of work turned out by the individual worker. Profit bonus is in reality a very different thing from incentive bonus, for incentives to efficiency operate only under properly conceived production bonus schemes which establish a direct relationship between better production, efficiency and higher earnings.

No case for evolution for Bonus

Having taken into consideration the role that profit bonus has played in the past and is playing at present in the industrial system in India, we are unable in the present circumstances to support the proposal of some Employers' Associations and individual employers that we should recommend the abolition of bonus altogether. If bonus disputes have led to strife and litigation, it should not be overlooked that industrial disputes on other subjects have also led, unfortunately, to industrial strife and it cannot, therefore, be an argument of denouncing the bonus system which has served and is serving a useful purpose. The remedy is to evolve a satisfactory bonus scheme. The worker is habituated to this system in which he receives a lump sum payment every year. It suits the workers' pattern of consumption for spending, at least once in a year, on some articles of additional and diversified consumption and on needs which cannot be conveniently met from the monthly wage packet. In any event, we do not think it feasible or advisable to abolish this long standing system by attempting to the merge bonus in wages.

In our openion the formula for computing bonus need not, however, be perfectly logical or aim at giv.ng mathematical justice; it would be futile to attempt to do so. It should be a formula which is not complicated, which is easy to understand and broadly just and fair to all concerned. In making our recommendations we have kept aims in view.

Linking of Bonus with production

In view of the objection to the proposal by a large sections of employers, as well as by almost all the Unions, and the practical difficulties inherent in any such proposal, we are unable to recommend that the concept of bonus based on profits should be replaced by an annual bonus linked with production or productivity. It is doubtless true that properly devised incentive systems in manufacturing concerns form a useful part of the substitute to replace the annual profit sharing bonus. Where in particular companies, as in the case of Indian Aluminium Co. Ltd., the employer and the Union have adopted or, in future, opt for such a scheme in substitution of bonus based on profits, it would be a different matter; and our recommendations would then have no application to such cases.

Bonus as a certain percentage of Gross Profit

We are unable to recommend that bonus should we determined at a certain percentage of the gross profit after deducting only depreciation, for the following reasons:

(1) It is not possible to work out a percentage satisfactorily for each industry. The proportion between bonus and paid in the past and the gross profits (after depreciation) in the relevant years may reveal wide disparity between various units even in the same industry.

(2) The formula would also necessitate a separate examination of each unit, as a single rate for the whole industry would be impracticable; a percentage acceptable to labour would be quite unacceptable to the companies in the industry and vice versa.

(3) The calculation of the percentage is complicated by too many variable factors such as the type of industry, whether the industry is capital-intensive or labour-intensive, the proportion of bonus paid by different units to the profits made by them in the past, etc. The capital employed for units of identical capacity may be different; and to apply a uniform percentage for determining bonus would not take account of disparities in the quantum of employed capital and the composition of the capital, i.e., the proportion of owned capital and borrowings.

(4) It gives the highest priority to bonus without regard to the claims of capital for even a minimum return or to the needs of the indusry.

We appreciate that it may be feasible for particular concerns to enter into long-term agreements with the unions concerned on the basis of percentage of bonus to the profits after deducting depreciation and after taking into consideration the proportion of bonus paid in the past year the prospects of the concern and other relevant factors; but the Commission cannot recommend any such formula for general application as it is impracticable to determine bonus as a certain percentage of the profits applicable to all units in the different industries.

Bonus Pool

There is a system of pooling bonus to a limited extent in the tea industry in North East India, but it is by industrywise agreement in which bonus is payable on the basis of a certain percentage of the profits. There is also a minimum bonus in those cases where there is a loss or only a small profit. Most employers are strongly opposed to any such pooling arrangement. We think there is force also in the objection that a bonus pooling system puts a premium on inefficiency by requiring the profits an employer who has made profits to be distributed to workmen of loss making units. This may be not also be welcome to the workmen of the profit making units. If one of the aims of a profit bonus system is to create in the workers a sense of belonging to concern, to the have a stake in the industry and its continued prosperity," this cannot be achieved if bonus is unconnected with and dissociated from the profit made by the concern, and is payable, in case of loss, from the profits of other concerns.

It seems to us doubtful whether the bonus scheme prevalent in the tea estates in West Bengal, Assam and Tripura, which is acceptable to the employers and the workmen in the tea industry could be worked out for other industries.

In the plantations in South India, bonus is paid at a certain percentage of the annual earnings and this arrangement appears to have worked satisfactority.

Whether Bonus should be Unitwise, Industrywise or Industry-Cume-regionwise

We are of the opinion that ordinarily the computation and payment of bonus should be unitwise in accordance with the formula recommended by us in the succeeding Chapter. We are of the unable to recommend a formula for a uniform rate of bonus for all industries generally or for the cotton textile industry in Southern India or for the plantations. Where industrywise arrangements already exist, the parties are at liberty to renew agreements with such modifications, if any, as may be agreed to by them. If the Employers and Employees' Associations can agree to make or continue industrywise agreements on a basis acceptable to them, the formula proposed by us in our recommendations in the succeeding Chapters would not apply. The formula proposed by us would also not apply during the currency of any industrywise or unitwise agreements, except where such agreements stipulate that the formula recommended by the Bonus Commission should apply in modification or substitution of existing arrangements.

Minimum and Maximum Bonus

There can be no doubt that bonus should be subject to a reasonable maximum.

It there is a maximum so that however high the profits in a year, the workers cannot be given more bonus than at a certain rate expressed in terms of wages, it stands to reason that there should be a minimum also. Labour cannot be expected to accept as reasonable a formula which provides for a ceiling on bonus without also providing for a floor. An arrangement of minimum and maximum would have the added advantage of evening out bonus payments over the years and thus avoid the obvious disadvantages of widely fluctuating bonus, with years in which there may be no bonus at all and others in which the bonus would be very large. In some industries there have been agreements providing a formula for bonus with a minimum and maximum and a set-off and set-on arrangements. If a reasonable minimum and maximum are fixed, linked with system of set-off of deficiencies and set-on of excess in the succeeding years, it would be a satisfactory arrangement both from the point of view of employers and labour. An exception would, however, have to be made in the case of new concerns upto a certain period.

Bonus Based On single year's Profits

The opinion of the representatives of Employers' Associations who appeared before us was generally in favour of continuing the present practice of taking the profits of the particular year as the basis. The Unions were also not in favour of taking the average of two or three years as the basis. In the circumstances, we think it would be best that bonus for any particular year should be related only to the profits of that year.

Computation Of Profits

The first step in the formula must necessarily be the ascertainment of the gross profit of the accounting year for the purposes of the bonus formula.

Extraneous Profits

We have considered the question whether extraneous profits, i.e., profits unrelated to the efforts of workmen should be excluded from the computation of profits for the purposes of bonus. In actual practice, the question of extraneous profits has led to much controversy and litigation as to what should be considered as extraneous profits. To attempt to scan too closely profits unrelated to the efforts of workmen serves little useful purpose. We are of the opinion that only the following items should be excluded from the profit computed for the purpose of the bonus formula ; (a) profit or loss from the sale of immovable property or fixed assets of a capital nature (other than those on which depreciation has been allowed) comprised in the undertaking unless the business of the company consists, wholly or partly, of buying and selling such property or assets ; (b) income, profits and losses from businesses outside India ; (c) income of a non-Indian concern from investments outside India ; and (d) refund of income-tax paid for previous years and any excess provision for income-tax for previous years written back to the profit and loss account.

Donations

It is usual for companies and firms to make donations to charities, both to maintain the goodwill of the public and also to make a contribution through the exercise of reasonable charity towards the public welfare, which to some extent is to be expected of every prosperous concern or individual in the country. We have not heard that shareholders have objected to such reasonable donations to charities, and we do not believe that workman are as a rule averse to it. The Income-Tax Act allows donations to charities as expenditure within certain limits. Such donations have sometimes to be made to help flood relief and for other landable objects, and a large number of companies have contributed according to their mite to the Defence Fund. It would be unreasonable to add back such amounts to the profits and consider them notionally available for bonus. But donations in excess of the amount admissible under the Income-Tax Act stand on a different footing and cannot be allowed as expenditure for the purposes of the bonus formula.

The manner in which the gross profits of the accounting year should be computed for the purpose of bonus formula in the case of companies is indicated in the proformla reproduced below. The same mode of computation would apply, mutatis mutandis in the case of proprietory and partnership conceres.

Computation Of Gross Profits (Before Depreciation And Taxation) For Purposes Of Bonus

Accounting year ending ....

Item No.	Particulars	Amount of Sub-Item	Amount of Main Items'	Remarks
1	2	3	4	5
		Rs.	Rs.	
1.	Net profit as per Audited profits and Loss account.			
2.	Add back provision for :			
(a)	Bonus			
(b)	Depreciation			
(c)	Direct Taxes, including the provision (if any) for previous years			See foot note (1)
(d)	Development Rebate Reserve			See foot note (2)
(e)	Any other Reserves			See foot note (2)
	Total of Item (2)	Rs.		
3.	Add back also :			
(a)	Payment of bonus, if any, relating to previous years.			See foot note (2)
(b)	Donations in excess of the amount admissible for Income-tax.			
(c)	Capital Expenditure and Capital Losses (other than losses on sale of capital assets on which depreciation has been allowed for Income-tax).			See foot note (2)
(d)	Losses of, or Expenditure, relating to, any business situated outside India. Total of Items (3)	Rs.		
4.	Add also : Income, profits or Gains (if any) credited indrectly to Reserves, other than :			
(i)	Capital Receipts and Capital Profits (including Profits on the sale of Capital assets on which depreciation has not been allowed for Income-tax).			
(ii)	Profits of, Receipts relating to, any business situated outside India,			
(iii)	Income of non-Indian Companies from Investment outside India.			
	Net Total of Item (4)	Rs.		
5.	Total of Item 1, plus 2, plus 3, plus 4.		Rs.	
6.	Deduct :			
(a)	Capital Receipts and Capital profits (other than profits on the sale of assets on which depreciation has been allowed for Income-tax.			See foot note (3)
(b)	Profits of, Receipts relating to, any business situated outside India.			See foot note (3)
(c)	Income of non-Indian companies from Investment outside India.			See foot note (3)

1.	2	3.	4.	5.
		Rs.	Rs.	
(d)	Expenditure of losses (if any) debited directly to Reserves, other than :			
(i)	Capital Expenditure and Capital Losses (other than loss on sale of capital assets on which depreciation has not been allowed for income-tax).			
(ii)	Losses of any business situated outside India.			
(e)	In the case of non-Indian concerns proportionate Administrative (overhead) expenses of Head office allocable to Indian business.			See foot note (4)
(f)	Excess provision, if any, of previous years relating to Bonus, Depreciation, Taxation or Development Rebate if written back.			See foot note (3)
	Total of Item (6)	Rs.		
7.	Gross Profit for purposes of Bonus. [Item (5) minus (6)]		Rs.	

(1) This includs Income-tax, Super-tax Corporation Tax Super Profits Tax and other Taxes on Income.

(2) If, and to the extent, charged to Profit and Loss Account.

(3) If, and to the extent, credited to Profits and Loss Account.

(4) In the proportion of Indian Gross Profit (Item 7) to Total World Profits [as per consolidated Profit and Loss Account, adjusted as in Item (2) above only].

Note : The computation of Gross Profit for purposes of Bonus as above should bear a certificate as to its correctness by the Company's Auditors.

Depreciation

In our opinion depreciation should be the first prior charge on the gross profits. In fact, it can be said that the real profit of the accounting year is ascertained only after deducting depreciation. Depreciation is an estimated sum representing the loss incurred by wear and tear of an asset and must be written off to keep the capital intact.

Depreciation under the Income-Tax Act is allowed on the "written down value" system, i.e., at the prescribed rates of depreciation applied to the full costs of the assets in the first year and to their reducing values in subsequent years (that is to say, the value as reduced by the amount of depreciation). If this is understood as the "normal" depreciation, then under the Labour Appellate Tribunal formula it is the "notional normal" depreciation that is to be allowed as a deduction, for purposes of Bonus.

Since that decision, the "initial" depreciation and "additional" depreciation allowances which were admissible under the Income-Tax Act on assets installed after March 31, 1948, which necessitated the concept of "notional normal" depreciation have been abolished. The initial depreciation has been replaced by the development rebate. Meanwhile, the concept of "notional normal" depreciation in bonus computation has, in practice, led to much litigation, though fortunately, in the case of machinery installed after the abolition of the additional depreciation allowances referred to above, the notional normal depreciation and the income-tax normal depreciation would be the same.

We have given much thought to the question of the computing depreciation and, in particular, to the alternatives suggested, viz., straight line depreciation and a formula of "wear and tear depreciation" suggested by some Unions. We are not in favour of imposing a new type of depreciation and requiring employer to maintain separate books and accounts for calculating such depreciation. Even if the straight line method were now adopted for the purposes of the bonus formula, it could only be adopted in respect of new companies ; and in the case of old companies, it could readily be adopted only in respect of plant installed after the coming into effect of our recommendations for otherwise a portion of the depreciation which has been already written off would have to be written back after laborious calculations. The formula would also work out unevenly as between new companies and old companies, and as between old companies, some of whom may instal considerable new machinery and others who get on with the bulk of the old machinery. The straight line basis required keeping a separate record of each asset and each addition to an asset, while the reducing balance method is simple of calculation and has been increasingly followed in this country.

Having given careful consideration to the matter, we are in favour of allowing as prior charge only the normal depreciation admissible under the Income-Tax Act (including multiple shift allowance). Though in the initial years of the life of assets, such depreciation is higher than on a straight line basis, in later years the expenditure on repairs and maintenance increasing as the plant becomes older, and so the increasing charge on repairs offsets, to some extent, the diminishing charge for depreciation. Besides, in the case of existing companies, while the income-tax depreciation in the case of new plant will be higher in the initial period, it will be much lower on the older plant, so that the sum total of the normal depreciation admissible under the Income-Tax Act (including multiple shift depreciation) is, on the whole, likely to be a more appropriate prior charge for the purposes of the bonus formula than depreciation calculated in other alternative way. We recommend, therefore, that the normal depreciation including multiple shift allowance admissible for income-tax should be a prior charge both for existing and new companies.

There are, however, cases in which bonus has been determined and paid in the past after deducting from the profits the "notional normal" depreciation. In such cases, if a switchover is now made to the normal depreciation admissible under the Income-Tax Act, the company may not get the benefit of the entire depreciation of certain assets for the purposes of the bonus formula and a portion of the depreciation would lapse. We, therefore, recommend that in any case where bonus has been paid in the past under an Award or agreement after allowing "notional normal" depreciation from the profits, the depreciation to be deducted from the profits for the purpose of the bonus formula should at the option of such company, continue to be the "notional normal" depreciation.

Taxation

The next prior charge to be deducted should be the income tax and super tax. In the case of companies these should be deducted at the current standard rate applicable for the year for which bonus is to be calculated. In the case of plantation companies, agricultural income-tax would also have to be deducted on the portion of income taxable as agricultural income.

We have recommended in the previous Chapter that the present practice of determining bonus on the basis of the profits of the particular accounting year for which bonus has to be determined should be continued. Since this involves that losses or arrears of depreciation of previous years are not taken into account, it stands to reason that the concession given in income-tax on account of previous years' losses or arrears of depreciation should not also be taken into account in deducting the income-tax and super tax at the standard rate from the profits. This is equitable and also secures indirectly to the company some degree replenishment of previous losses and arrears of depreciation.

The tax should be deducted at the standard rate; but when the rate is less on account of double taxation, e. g., investment income from shares in companies, income from subsidiary companies, the tax leviable on that portion of the income would be at the lower rate applicable. In deducting tax, we would, however, leave out account rebate in tax given by the Finance Act in respect of income from articles exported, as the saving in tax is specifically intended as an inducement to export. So also the concession given in section 84 of the Income-Tax Act in respect of certain new undertakings should not be taken into account.

Development Rebate

Under the Income-tax Act development rebate is not part of the depreciation allowance and is granted over and above the depreciation allowance. It is a special allowance to encourage Companies to install new machinery. In a year in which installations of machinery are very large, the inclusion of the whole of the development rebate together with the statutory depreciation, as prior charge, might wipe off or substantially reduce the available surplus, even though the working of the concern may have resulted in very good profit. Development rebate has not been treated as a prior charge under the Labour Appellate Tribunal formula and we are also of the view that it should not be deducted as a prior charge.

It seems to us that if development rebate is not allowed as a prior charge, it is fair that the concession in tax on account of development rebate should not be taken into consideration in deduction income-tax and super tax in the bonus formula.

Super Profit Tax

We are of the opinion that in the calculations for the purposes of the bonus formula no deduction need be made on account of super profits tax for the following reasons :

(1) Bonus paid upto a reasonable amount is allow-

able as expenditure under the Income-Tax Act.

(2) The super profits tax has been notified by the government as a tax on excess or abnormal profits, under Section 349 (4) (d) of the Companies Act.

(3) Super profits tax is leviable an the ' chargeable profits" as defined in Section 2 (5) of the Super Profits Tax Act, read with the First Schedu'e to the Act.

(4) Super Profits Tax is chargeable at certain rates on so much of the chargeable profits as exceeds the standard deduction, i. e., 6 per cent of the capital, computed in a certain manner. The calculation of super profits tax itself is beset with complications. It is desirable not to make the bonus formula unnecessarily complicated.

(5) Another reason for not deducting the super profits tax as a prior charge is that the tax should be payable only if the surplus left to the company is sufficiently large, for only the portion of income over the standard deduction is liable to tax.

Different Rates Of Tax

In the case of companies in which the public are not substantially interested, according to the definition given in Section 2 (18) of the Income-Tax Act, the deduction of tax should be only at the standard rate applicable to companies in which the public are substantially interested.

In the case of non-resident companies, tax should be deducted at the chargeable (higher) rate. As in such cases the available surplus would be greatly reduced by the higher rate of tax, while the saving in tax on bonus paid would be larger, we are of the opinion that in the case of such Companies the percentage of the available surplus allocated as bonus should be increased by seven per cent, so that it should be 67 per cent instead of 60 per cent in the case of other companies as recommended by us in Paragraph 12.1.

In the case of co-operative societies, income-tax should be deducted from the tax 'profit, at the rate if any, at which the society is liable to pay tax according to the provisions of Section 81 of the Income-tax Act, but the amount required by statute to be transferred to the reserves should be allowed as a prior charge.

In the case of partnership concerns, the tax to be deducted as a prior charge should be the aggregate of the tax payable by the partners on their shares of the profit from the concern as if it was their sole income, plus the income-tax and super-tax payable by the firm.

In the case of proprietory concerns, the tax should be deducted on the same basis, viz., the tax payable by the proprietor on the profit from the concern in which he workmen are employed, as if it is his only income.

Rehabilitation

Having considered the complications created, the resulting litigation in respect of calculations of rehabilitation requirements which the employers themselves have conceded as matters of guess work, and having regard to the fact that the formula proposed by us leaves a fair surplus for the company, we are of the view that no specific provison need be made for rehabilitation in addition to the normal depreciation in the formula. If rehabilitation were allowed at a certain arbitrary percentage of the available surplus, it would have to be different in respect of companies engaged in manufacturing and companies engaged both in trading in general and also in manufacturing. In respect of non-manufacturing companies, rehabilitation would be required only for buildings owned by them, on the assumption that depreciation allowances are insufficient. Thus no satisfactory method of calculating rehabilitation requirements can be devised.

We are of the opinion that computation of rehabilitation at a certain percentage of the available surplus or a certain percentage of depreciation or of the block would be arbitrary and without reference to the real requirements of the company, the state of the machinery and buildings and the funds available with the company for rehabilitation from out of its reserves and surplus profits. The same objection would apply to computing rehabilitation as a certain percentage of the gross profits after deducting depreciation. We have, therefore, come to the conclusion that no special provision for rehabilitation need be made as a prior charge in the bonus formula. The formula proposed by us provides for the normal (including multiple shift) depreciation allowed under the Income-Tax Act, and indirectly for half of the development rebate, but not taking into account the saving in tax on account of development rebate. Further, we are proposing a substantial portion out of the available surplus, after meeting the prior charges to be left to the company or concern. This amount together with the tax relief on the amount payable as bonus would be available, among other things, for rehabilitation.

Return On Paid-Up Capital

Having given careful consideration to the representations made before us, we are of the view that the return on paid-up capital to be allowed as a prior charge in the bonus formula should be at seven per cent. We are of the opinion that on preference share capital the return should be at the actual rate at which divident is payable, and in the case of participating preference share capital the return should be at that rate of dividend payable on them when the dividend on ordinary shares is declared at seven per cent.

Computation of Capital of Foreign Companies

In the case of foreign companies whose business in India is confined to trading and/or who have no paid-up capital in India, capital for the purposes of return in the bonus formula should be computed as the sum of amount of the net fixed assets, plus the amount of current assents minus the current liabilities. When capital is thus computed, the amount of current assets minus the current liabilities. When capital is thus computed, the amount, if any, appearing as due to or advanced by the Head Office is not to be included in the current liabilities, and the interest, if any, paid to the Head Office is not to be included as expenditure for the purposes of the formula.

Return On Reserve

We are of the opinion that in the bonus formula the prior charge of return on reserves should be at a lower rate than on paid up capital and that it should continue to be at the rate at which the return is usually allowed on reserves used as working capital under the existing formula, viz., at four per cent. This return should be allowed on all reserves and surplus shown in the balance sheet at the beginning of the year including profit carried forward from the previous year. Provision for taxation should not be considered as reserve, but a specific reserve for taxation (in addition to the full provision) should be included. Return is to be allowed on the reserves and surpluses proper, not on items such as the amount appropriated towards dividends but remaining with the company for some months until the dividend is paid. It is to be noted that depreciation cannot be included in the reserves entitled to a return. But depreciation reserve specifically created out of additional depreciation provided over and above the amount of normal depreciation under the Income-Tax Act and figuring as such on the liabilities side of the balance sheet should be treated like any other reserve and allowed a return.

Remuneration For Working Partners

We think it desirable, in order to avoid unnecessary controversy and litigation, that for the purposes of the bonus formula the remuneration of the working partners should be determined on the analogy of managing Agency Commission. We recommend as a general rule that the total remuneration of the working partners may be fixed at 25 per cent of the gross profits after deducting normal depreciation admissible under the Income-tax Act. If the terms of the partnership deed provide for remuneration which is lower than this figure, then that remuneration would be allowable, subject to a maximum of Rs. 48,000 for each working partner or the working proprietor, as the case may be If the terms of the partnership provide for a higher remuneration, it would be subject to a maximum of 25 per cent or a sum calculated at Rs. 48,000 per annum for each working partner or the working proprietor, as the case may be, whichever is less.

Allocation Of The Available Surplus As Bonus

It is not necessary in each case to take into consideration the prevailing level of remuneration in the concern in allocating a proportion of the available surplus as bonus. The fixing of a certain proportion of the available surplus (after meeting the prior charges recommended by us) to be distributed as bonus, subject to a minimum (coupled with an arrangement for set-off and set-on) in the formula which we recommend, would lead to an equitable result. We recommend that this proportion should be 60 per cent. The balance left with the concern would be 40 per cent and this would be increased by the saving in tax on bonus payable. The aggregate balance thus left with the industry is intended to provide for gratuity and other necessary reserves, the requirements of rehabilitation in addition to the provision made by way of depreciation in the prior charges, the annual provision required, if any, for redemption of debentures and return of borrowings, payment of super profits tax, if any, and additional return on capital.

Bonus To Be In Terms Of Basic Wages And D.A.

We are of the opinion that the distinction between basic wages and dearness allowance for the purposes of expressing the bonus quantum should be done away with and that bonus should be related to wages and dearness allowance taken together. But all other allowances such as overtime wages and incentive, production and attendance bonus including attendance bonus under statutory bonus schemes, should be excluded. The inclusion of such allowance would introduce anomalies in regard to bonus as between workmen not getting such allowance and workmen getting such allowance. On the other hand, Puja bonus and other customary bonus, if paid, should be considered as bonus paid "on account" and deducted from the amount finally payable as bonus under the formula recommended by us.

Quantum Of Minimum And Maximum Bonus

The minimum bonus we recommend is equivalent to four per cent of the total basic wage and dearness allowance paid during the year (excluding all other allowances and other bonuses such as production bonus, attendence bonus, statutory attendence bonus, etc.), or Rs. 40 to each workes, whichever is higher. This amount of Rs. 40 would be payable to workmen who have worked for all the working days of the year (including periods of privilege leave and maternity leave with pay, casual or sick leave with pay). In the case of children the minimum should be equivalent to four per cent of their basic wage and dearness allowance, or Rs. 25, whichever is higer. For employess who have worked for a lesser beriod, the amount payble would be pro rata. The maximum bonus should be equivalent to 20 per cent of the total basic wage and dearness allowance paid during the year.

We are of the opinion that bonus payable in accordance with our recommendations should ordinarily be paid not later than eight months after the close of the accounting year.

We recommend that in the bonus formula proposed by us, the portion of the available surplus allocated for bonus should be deemed to include bonus to employees drawing a total basic pay and dearness allowance (taken together) upto Rs. 1,600 p.m., regardless of whether they are "workmen" or "non-workmen" as defined in the Industrial Disputes Act or any other relevant Act, with the proviso that the quantum of bonus payable to emyloyees drawing total basic pay and dearness allowance over Rs. 750 p.m. shall be limited to what it would be, if their pay and dearness allowance were only Rs. 750 per month. As regards officers and supervisory staff drawing over Rs. 1,600 p.m. it would be open to the Company or concern, if it considered necessary, to pay them bonus out of the balance (40 per cent) of the available surplus left to it under this formula.

New Units

we recommend that the general bonus formula proposed by us should not apply to new concerns until they have recouped all early losses including all arrears of normal depreciation admissible under the Income-Tax Act, subject to a time limit of six years. In other words, in such cases we recommend that the liability to pay bonus (including minimum bonus) in accordance with our formula should commence only.

(a) from the year in which there is for the first time an overall net profit, i.e., sufficient profit, after providing for that year's normal depreciation, to wipe off all accumulation; or

(b) from the sixth year following the year in which the undertaking begins to sell its products and/or services; whichever may be earlier.

This recommendation applies also to existing concerns in respect of new industrial units or undertakings established by them, whether in the same industry (e.g., a new cement factors established by an existing cement manufacturing concern) or in a different industry (e.g., a new cement factory established by a jute manufacturing concern). Where, however, it has been the practice of such concerns to pay bonus to its workmen at a unifrom rate on the basis of a consolidated profits computation in respect of all their units (whether limited to the consolidation of all units engaged in the same industry, or extending also to the consolidation of all units regardless of the industry to which they belong), that practice should continue in respect also of new units started by that concern. What we have stated in this paragraph applies equally to new concerns and new units of existing concerns in the public sector.

The Bonus Formula

The general bouns formula recommended by us, subject to the explanations and particular provisions set out in the various Chapters, is as under:

Gross Profit for the year computed as as per Chapter VIII Paragraph 8,10	Rs.
Less-Depreciation as per Chapter IX paragraph 9.2.	Rs.
Less-Income-tax and Super-tax as per Chapter IX paragraph 9.6	Rs.
Less-Return at the actual rate payable on Preference Share Capital and at seven per cent on Ordinary Capital, plus at four per cent on reserves as per Chapter XI paragraph 11.13.	Rs.
Balance	Rs.

The balance would be the "available surplus". Of this balance, 60 per cent shall be allocated as bonus subject to a minimum equivalent to four per cent of the annual basic wages and dearness allowance (excluding all other allowances and bonuses such as production bonus, attendance bonus, etc.) or a minimum amount of Rs. 40 whichever is higher (Rs. 25 in the case of children). The amount of Rs. 40 (or, Rs. 25 as the case may be) would be the sum payable to a worker who has worked for all the working days in the year (including periods of privilege leave with pay, casual leave with pay, sick leave and maternity leave with pay). For a worker who has worked for a lesser period the amount payable would be pro rata.

Set Off And Set On

Where the amount allocable as bonus exceeds the maximum, i.e., exceeds the equivalent of 20 per cent of the earninigs as defined above, then the excess upto a limit of a further 20 per cent is to be carried forward to be "set on" in the succeeding years upto a maximum period of the next four years. Where there is no available surplus, or the amount of the available surplus allocable as bonus is a sum less than four per cent of the annual earnings as defined above, then the whole of the quantum of four per cent, or the amount necessary to make up four per cent as the case may be, should carried forward and set off in the succeeding years, the amount of set on or set off brought forward from the earliest year should first be taken into account.

Any amount left undistributed out of what has been specifically allocated for distribution as bonus should be carried forward to the bonus account or the following year and dealt with on the lines already discussed.

Jute Industry

Having carefully considered the representations of the employers and the unions and the views expressed unanimously by the Tripartite Wage Board for the jute industry, we are of the opinion that the plea of employers in the jute industry that the bonus system should not be introduced in the jute industry cannot be accepted. We are of the view that the general bonus formula recommend by us should apply to the jute industry also, unless the Employers' Associations and the Unions concerned agree to any other arrangement.

Plantation Industries

In reference to plantations in South India, we would urge on the Employers' Associations and Unions concerned to continue industrywise agreements with such modifications, if any, as may be agreed to by them. What we have said applies also to plantations in Bengal, Assam and Tripura. If the parties are unable to renew industrywise agreements, our general bonus formula should apply. We are of the opinion, after taking into consideration the history, progress and present position of the plantation industries, that they would be in a position to pay the minimum bonus recommended by us. Bonus higher than the minimum would be payable only if adequate profits are made. We see no good reasons for recommending exemption from the general bonus formula recommended by us in the case of the plantation industries, nor do we recommend any modification of the formula in its application to these industries, if they are unable to renew industrywise agreements for bonus.

Coal Industry

It has to be borne in mind that profit bonus is also paid in industries which have incentive bonus schemes; and merely because in the coal industry there is a statutory bonus scheme linked to attendance as part of the wage structure, it is not a valid reason why the workmen should not, as in the case of other industries, be allowed to participate in the prosperity of the industry. We may, however, mention that coal is a very labour-intensive industry and the price of coal is controlled. Some rough calculations made by us give ground for the belief that if the general bonus formula were applied to the coal mining industry, the workers would probably get only minimum bonus in a large majority of cases It might also transpire that in the case of this industry which has never paid profit bonus, the payment of a minimum bonus may necessitate some though not an appreciable increase in the price of coal. If the payment of a minimum bonus necessitates a rise, we think that it would be preferable to the discontent that might be caused by singling out this industry for excluding the workers in it from the benefits of a profit bonus scheme. It has to be borne in mind that coal mining is one of the most strenuous of occupations. We have, therefore, come to the conclusion that our general bonus formula should apply also to the coal industry.

Mining Industry

What we have said about the application of our bonus formula to the coal mining industry applies also to the mining industry generally.

Banks

Having considered the representations made to us, we are of the opinion that the entire formula of the Desai Award (including the computation of gross profits) should continue to be applicable in future with the following modifications :

(1) Where for any earlier year bonus has been paid after making deduction of notional normal depreciation, should continue. In all other cases the depreciation admissible under the Income-tax Act should be deducted from the profits.

(2) Our recommendations in regard to super profits tax, donations, extraneous profits and losses will also apply to banks.

(3) There should be no specific provision for rehabilitation.

(4) The distinction between reserves used as working capital and reserves not so used should be abolished (vide Chapter XI Paragraphs 11.14 to 11.17). And as regards return on reserves, depreciation should not count as reserve except in the circumstances indicated in Chapter XI Paragraph 11.17.

(5) The percentage of the available surplus allocable as bonus after meeting the prior charges should be 60 per cent.

(6) The distribution of the quantum of bonus to employees, should be on the same basis as in the case of other industries, as proposed in Chapter XII, with a minimum equal to four per cent of the wages (inclusive of basic wages and dearness allowance) and a maximum equal to 20 per cent, with provision for set off and set on up to four years.

State Bank Of India

It might be mentioned that the Award of Justice Shri Desai in regard to banks does not apply to the State Bank of India which was not a party to the reference. Having considered the different views on the question of bonus to employees of the State Bank of India, we are of the opinion that the formula proposed by us in regard to Banks generally should also apply to the State Bank of India.

Insurance Companies

The bonus formula of the Labour Appellate Tribunal has not in the past been applied to the insurance companies on account of the provisions of Section 31 A (1) (c) of the Insurance Act. And in view of these provisions, we feel that our recommendations should not, in terms, apply to employees of general insurance companies. It would, of course, be open to the parties concerned to come to mutual agreements concerning the matter, and also for the Department of the Government of India concerned to consider whether in giving its sanction to any proposal for bonus under the proviso (vii) to Section 31 A (1) (c), such agreements and/or the principles recommended by us in respect of bonus should be applied, with such modifications, if any, as may be necessary.

Sugar Industry

We are of the opinion that the general formula proposed by us should be applicable to the sugar industry unless the Employers' Associations and the Unions concerned agree to any other arrangement or formula in their respective regions.

Tile, Cashes And Coir Manufacturing Industries In Kerala

We are of the opinion that if the representatives of industries and unions concerned can come to an agreement on the subject matter of bonus on an industry wise basis, it would be a good thing, and such agreement should of course be acted upon. Failing such agreements, however, the general bonus formula recommended by us should also apply to industries in Kerala referred to above.

Electricity Undertakings

At present disputes regarding bonus in Electricity Undertakings when referred to Industrial Tribunals are decided in accordance with the Full Bench formula of the Labour Appellate Tribunal. We are of the view that there is no good ground for exempting electricity undertaking from the general approach of bonus. Our general formula would, therefore, apply, subject to this that, as in the case of banks and co-operative societies, the amount required to be transferred by statute from the profit of the year to the reserves should be allowed as a prior charge. The formula would, of course, not apply to electrical undertakings run by municipalities, for the terms of reference to us exclude industries in the public sector run departmentally.

Seamen On High Seas

Section 150 (9) of the Merchant Shipping Act lays down that the Industrial Disputes Act shall not apply to any disputes between seamen and the owners of ships and such disputes have to be referred to special tribunals. It is, therefore, doubtful whether seamen come within the purview of the reference to us.

In the view we have taken, our recommendations would not apply to seamen. Even otherwise, the quistion of bonus to them raises certain difficulties which must be borne in mind. If Indian shipping companies engaged in foreign trade were required to pay bonus to seamen, it would put them at a disadvantage to competition with foreign shipping companies and it would be difficult to attempt to apply the bonus formula to foreign shipping companies. Any attempt to force the bonus formula on them would discourage the employment of Indian seamen, and foreign companies may well prefer to employ seamen from other countries. It may, therefore, be unwise to apply the bonus formula in respect of these employees.

We were informed at one of our meetings that one Indian company, viz., the Bombay Steam Navigation Co. (1953) Ltd., which is a subsidiary of the Scindia Steam Navigation Co. Ltd., and engaged wholly in coastal trade, pays bonus to seamen engaged in costal ships. The bonus is one the same scale as that paid to the shore staff of the Scindia Steam Navigation Co. We hope this practice willbe continued by the company.

Stevedore Labour

We are of the opinion tnat stevedore labour should not *per se* be ineligible for bonus. It has not been suggested that stevedoring is less profitable in Calcutta than in Bombay. The circumstance that employment is from a pool, rotation and intermittent, is not a good argument against giving bonus and there should be no practical difficulties since a record is regularly maintained of the persons who have been employed under each stevedore.

Since stevedoring is done by some firms in addition to other business and it may be difficult to go into the accounts and separate the profit in stevedoring from other lines of business and in view of the past practice, it, is desirable that the present practice in Bombay which has worked well should be continued. So far the Stevedore's Association has been able to come to an agreement with the Transport and Dock Worker's Union about the rate of contribution by the employers to the bonus pool. We hope that this will continue to be the case. If in future, the parties cannot for any year agree as to the rate of contribution to the bonus pool and/or as to the manner of its distribution among the entitled workmen, we recommend that the same should be determined by arbitration. If in any year the parties do not agree to arbitration, the machinery of the Industrial Disputes Act would be available for settlement of the dispute. In view of the particular circumstances in which stevedore labour is employed under the decasualisation scheme, we are clear that our general formula would be inapplicable; so also any system of minimum and maximum bonus. We recommend further that the bonus pool system for stevedors labour in Bombay should also be applied at other ports, including Calcutta, subject to such modifications as local conditions may require. In the event of disagreement the matter should be referred to arbitration or adjudication.

Small Shops And Trading Establishments

Having given consideration to the matter, we recommend that the general bonus formula proposed by us should not apply to all small units employing less than 20 persons except those which are factories as defined in the Factories Act.

Institutions

We recommend that the bonus formula should not apply to institutions such as Chamber of Comerce, Red Cross Associations, universities, schools, colleges and hospitals and social welfare institutions. Such institutions are not established with a view to make profits, though they may have a surplus of income over expenditure.

Industries Run By Charitable Institutions

We are of the opinion that employees of industrial establishments engaging 20 or more persons and factories within the meaning of the Factories Act, owned by charitable institutions for profit should be eligible for bonus according to the bonus formula; but we agree that in such cases income-tax and corporation tax should be deducted as a prior charge at the full rate applicable to companies notwithstanding that no tax may, in fact, be chargeable. Organisations operatting concerns of this type should not be deprived of the benefit of tax concession which is given for promoting the charitable purpose.

Building Workers

These workers get minimum wages fixed under the Minimum Wages Act. Most of them are unskilled. Workers engaged directly by construction companies would be getting bonus according to our formula if they have worked for the company for not less than 30 days in the year. But the question of bonus to workers engaged through contractors raises difficulties. Such workers are engaged for a particular contract job. To attempt to pay them bonus according to the profits of the particular job would create serious practical difficulties. We think that the problem relating to workers on building construction engaged through contractors is one of evolving and enforcing a proper wage structure. It is not feasible to apply the bonus formula to such workers engaged through contractors on building construction work, and we recommend accordingly.

The Public Sector

We recommend that if not less than 20 per cent of the gross aggregate sales turnover of a public sector undertaking consists of sales of service and/or products which compete with the product and or services produced or sold by units in the private sector, then such undertakings should be deemed to be competitive and our formula should apply to such units. We recommend further that in the event of any disputes in particular cases as to whether any anomalous and marginal cases fall within or outside the dividing line of being "20 per cent competitive" the machinery for deciding them should be that recommended by us in paragraph 10.23 Chapter XIX for the settlement of bonus disputes generally.

We may mention here that we are aware that some non-competitive public sector enterprises have in the past been paying bonus in some form to their workers by mutual accommodation. They are, of course, outside our purview. But we trust they will not, merely for that reason, discontinue the payment of bonus in future.

Proof Of Items in Balance Sheet And Profit And Loss Account

If a prima facie case is made out showing that the balance sheet or profit and loss account is incorrect, the Tribunal or other authority may go into the question of the correctness or incorrectness of the items. The Tribunal deciding a bonus dispute may, in its discretion, permit unions to obtain clarification of items in the balance sheet or profit and loss account or major break up figures of large items. But we consider that tribunals and Arbitrators should not embark on investigations into questions such as whether stocks have been correctly valued, whether a portion of the revenue expenditure which has been the adequacy of remuneration to Directors and Managing Agents of companies, whether expenditure on travelling allowance is excessive, etc. The Companies Act and other Acts provide ample safeguards against malpr ac tices. There are also provisions under the Companies Act for directing investigations into the affairs of companies in certain circumstances.

Accounts Of Partnership And Proprietory Concerns

In a bonus dispute, the Tribunal may, if it thinks it necessary, require the accounts in such cases to be audited. When they are audited and certified to be correct the same principles should apply as in the case of audited accounts of companies.

Audited Accounts of Banks

We are of the opinion that in a bonus proceeding audited accounts of banks should not be permitted to be challenged or gone behind. Unions may, however, be permitted to obtain from the bank such information as is necessary for working out calculations according to the bonus formula, e.g., figures of basic wages and dearness allowance, bonus for previous years included in the account of the year, whether provision for bonus is included in expenditure for the year etc.

Minimum Attendance To Quality For Bonus

In a number of agreements between companies and unions a minimum period of work in a year is specified to qualify for bonus. We are of the view that there should be a minimum period of 30 days' work in the year for qualifying for bonus. In the profit sharing system in other industrialised countries there is usually a minimum qualifying period. A minimum qualifying period, is, on principle, desirable. It would also avoid administrative difficulties caused to companies by having to keep records of attendance of casual and temporary workers who may have worked at any time during the year and to verify that bonus payments claimed are made to the right persons.

Non-Payment Of Bonus Due To Misconduct

Bonus certainly carries with it the obligation of good behaviour which helps sustaining the industry.

According to the existing practice, bonus is withheld only in the case of misconduct, causing financial loss to the company to the extent of the loss.

We recommend that, for the present, the existing practice may continue, but with the addition that bonus may be withheld for dismissal only in cases of riotous or violent behaviour on the works premises, theft, fraud, misappropriation or sabotage of property of the concern.

Payment Of Bonus in Cash

We are of the openion that the amount of bonus payable to the workers should be paid in cash and not in the form of National Saving Certificates or any other form.

Machinery for Settelement of Bonus Disputes

Since we have simplified the bonus formula and reduced the factors of uncertainty in its operation, there should be less scope for disputes and for litigation. The formula could be worked out, in the large majority of cases, without difficulty. There may, however, be a residue of cases where the parties do not agree on the calculations of bonus or some other minor issues may be involved. In such cases, we would recommend that the matter be referred to arbitration, each party appointing one arbitrator. The arbitrators before entering on the reference should choose an umpire to whom the matter would be referred in case of disagreement between the two arbitrators. If the parties are not willing to refer the dispute to arbitration, the machinery of the Industrial Disputes Act would be available for the settlement of the dispute.

Retrospective Effect To Our Recommendations

We suggest that our recommendations should apply to all bonus matters relating to accounting year ending any day in calendar year 1962 other than those cases in which settlements have been reached or decisions have been given.

COMMITTEE ON NATURAL RESOURCES, 1961—REPORT

New Delhi, Planning Commission, 1962. 57p.

Chairman : Deputy Chairman, Planning Commission.

Vice - Chairman : Member (Education), Planning Commission.

Members : Director-General, Council of Scientific and Industrial Research; Chairman, University Grants Commission; Chairman, Central Water & Power Commission; Chairman, Atomic Energy Commission; Member (Production), Oil and Natural Gas Commission; Vice-President, Indian Council of Agricultural Research; Inspector General of Forests; Scientific Adviser, Ministry of Defence; Director-General, Geological Survey of India; Director, Indian Bureau of Mines; Surveyor-General, Survey of India; Director-General, Survey of India; Director-General, Meteorological Department; Director, Indian Standards Institution; Director, Central Statistics Organisation; Director, Indian Statistical Institute; Mineral Adviser to the Government of India; Director-General, National Council of Applied Economic Research.

Secretary : Adviser, Natural Resources, Planning Commission.

APPOINTMENT

The First and the Second Five-year Plans were formulated on the basis of available information concerning the land, water, mineral and the energy resources of the country. In recent years various organisations concerned with the survey and utilisation of natural resources have been expanded and have undertaken a series of new investigations. These investigations have led to a greater knowledge of the nation's natural resources and have also brought to light gaps in information and deficiencies in relation to future requirements. As envisaged in the Third Five-Year Plan and with a view to drawing up long-term plans of development, it is necessary to take a comprehensive view of the information available in respect of the Country's main natural resources. The principal gaps which exist, the surveys required and the further measures needed in relation to specific long-range objectives in the development of irrigation, power, steel, coal, oil and minerals, and land and forest resources have to be identified. For achieving long-term goals, it is also necessary to assess the resources and requirements in relation to different regions. The Third Five-Year Plan has stressed the need for a coordinated and continuing efforts on the part of the Planning Commission, the various organisations of the Central and the State Governments, leading institutions engaged in scientific and economic research, and the universities to ascertain the nature and extent of the country's natural resources and the requirements of development and to suggest appropriate measures. In pursuance of these recommendations, it has been decided to constitute a Committee on Natural Resources. The Committee was Constituted under the Planning Commission, vide their resolution No. F. 6/40/61-S. R. dated December 23, 1961.

TERMS OF REFERENCE

(i) To assess from time to time the available information regarding the natural resources of the country and to identify gaps in it in relation to programmes of planned development;

(ii) To arrange for the formulation, in collaboration with the various organisations concerned, of coordinated programmes for surveys of natural resources in different parts of the country in relation to plans for long term economic development;

(iii) To initiate studies on problems relating to natural resources;

(iv) To make recommendations bearing on the conservation, utilisation and development of natural resources; and

(v) To disseminate information concerning the country's natural resources through publications.

CONTENTS

Organisation; Staff; Problems Proposed for Study; (a) Long-Term Studies; (1) Land, (2) Water. (3) Minerals (4) Energy; (b) Short-Term Studies; Studies and Surveys approved by Committee on Natural Resources: (1) Land, (2) Water, (3) Minerals, (4) Energy; Appendix.

RECOMMENDATIONS

Long-Term Studies

Land

Resource maps at State level, e. g., climatic maps, maps showing areas liable to regular flooding, land use potential of waste lands, areas which have been water-logged or subject to salinity, and permanent fallows, etc., will be prepared. The methods and scale of mapping will be standardised.

Agricultural Crops

The major need of India is the production of food crops and commercial crops. If a concentrated attack is made on this problem and resources are conserved, better results could be expected. A good deal of money which is now being spent on animal husbandry and dairying in States where there is no prospect of their development could be better utilised by its use on more productive schemes.

A State like Kerala is most suitable for the production of tropical crops like spices, coconut, arecanut, rubber, coffee, etc., which the rest of India cannot produce. In such areas emphasis should be on these crops.

The role of prices and their stability from year to year requires consideration.

Forests

A total survey of forest resources is urgently required.

There is need of a more dynamic forest policy and we must make effective use of existing knowledge regarding fast growing trees of economic value.

Fisheries

An urgent need is a complete survey of waters which do not dry up during summer and which can be stocked with fish.

India's marine fisheries resources have not been properly assessed and there is need of a comprehensive survey.

Water

It will be necessary to clearly demarcate the assured rainfall areas in the country.

A close analysis of the minor irrigation surveys is required so that the States which have not undertaken such surveys may be asked to do so.

Minerals

The most pressing needs in the context of programmes of planned industrial development were (i) systematic and detailed surveys and investigations by the Geological Survey of India, and the Indian Bureau of Mines, and the National Laboratories with a view to quantitative and qualitative assessment of the reserves of the more important minerals and their proper utilisation ; and (ii) a broad National Policy with particular attention to systematic exploitation of minerals with due regard to conservation.

There is an urgent need to investigate and prove fresh reserves of quality limestone required for the steel industry. In the context of the rapidly increasing demand for petroleum products, it would be necessary to intensify search for petroleum and prove indigenous resources to conserve foreign exachange.

Energy

Fuel resources can be conserved by improving efficiencies.

Short Terms Studies

Surveys of forests in which close coordination is required between the Survey of India and the authorities concerned with forests in the Government of India and the States could be more effectively organised. It will also enable the Planning Commission to develop coordinated programmes for surveys of natural resources in relation to plans for long-term economic development.

For preparing a sound inventory of our agricultural resources, it is very necessary that full use should be made of the Patwari agency and revenual records system of the different States are studied on a coordinated basis and improved keeping in view the requirements of national planning. New the aim should be to make these records a tool for fostering agricultural production.

A coordinated study of the fibre resources as well as of connected problems as a whole can be very paying.

It would be examined whether the use of cement sleepers would not be in national interest as compared with wooden sleepers.

Present fertiliser use and allocations used to be reviewed critically and future fertiliser use and allocation planned in light of best experimantal evidence and best export knowledge.

A modest number (perhaps 24 to 40) districts or areas where available irrigation water is not being used effectively should be identified. A programme for most efficient, immediate productive use of available water in these districts should be formulated and the requirements and programmes necessary to achieve the programme of water use requires to be set forth specifically in quantitative terms.

A systematic study of the ground water table should be made.

Exact methods of assessing flood damages should be evolved and the subject requires further studies. It will be necessary to develop and standardise the techniques of assessing flood damages.

Forestry plans to ensure an adequate supply of raw materials also require to be formulated.

Present forest legislation in the various States should be analysed and the extent to which the forest legislation is actually effective should be ascertained by means of field studies; gravity of forest denudation and the degree to which inadequate legislation or inadequate enforement is responsible should be determined and in specific terms, a programme of forest protection and afforestation should be formulated.

No data is available on the quantity of water being used by Indian industries. A comprehensive survey is, therefore, called for.

At present, only a few hundred tons of potassium chloride are recovered from bitterns against a possible total of about 80-90 thousand tons, though our requirement of potash (K_2O) for agriculture are considerable. Similarly, bromine is recovered to the extent of 25-30 tons per year against a possible total of several thousand tons.

A study should be made to be extent these minerals should be extracted, and the economics of extraction as well as use in ancillary industries.

The utilisation of blast furnace slag in India for cement making and for various other purposes, e. g., road making, stag wool manufacture, stowing of mines, etc., requires to be studied.

CHAIRMAN INDEX

INDEX

COMMITTEES AND COMMISSIONS IN INDIA 1947-73

Details of Published Volumes

COMMITTEES AND COMMISSIONS IN INDIA 1947-80

(In 18 Vols.)

Vol. 1	1947-54	Rs. 1500
Vol. 2	1955-57	Rs. 1500
Vol. 3	1958-59	Rs. 1500
Vol. 4	1960-61	Rs. 1500
Vol. 5	1962-63	Rs. 1500
Vol. 6	1964-65	Rs. 1500
Vol. 7	1966	Rs. 1500
Vol. 8	1967	Rs. 1500
Vol. 9	1968-69	Rs. 1500
Vol. 10	1970	Rs. 1500
Vol. 11	1971-73	Rs. 1500
Vol. 12	1974	Rs. 450
Vol. 13	1975	Rs. 450
Vol. 14	1976	Rs. 450
Vol. 15A	1977	Rs. 450
Vol. 15B	1977	Rs. 450
Vol. 15C	1977	Rs. 450
Vol. 15D	1977	Rs. 450
Vol. 16A	1978	Rs. 450
Vol. 16B	1978	Rs. 450
Vol. 17A	1979	Rs. 450
Vol. 17B	1979	Rs. 450
Vol. 18A	1980	Rs. 450
Vol. 18B	1980	Rs. 450

COMMITTEES AND COMMISSIONS IN INDIA 1947-73

Volume V
1962-63

Virendra Kumar

CONCEPT PUBLISHING COMPANY, NEW DELHI-110059

ISBN 81-7022-214-1 (Vol. V)

First Published 1977
Reprinted 2005

Published and Printed by
Ashok Kumar Mittal
Concept Publishing Company
A/15-16, Commercial Block, Mohan Garden
NEW DELHI-110059 (India)

Phones : 25351460, 25351794
Fax : 091-11-25357103
Email : publishing@conceptpub.com

DEDICATED
TO
MY UNCLE
LATE DR. JAI DEO KULSRESHTHA

INTRODUCTION

The Fifth Volume attempts to understand and analyse the activities of the various "Committees and Commissions" during the period 1962-1963 which have received as far as the previous volumes are concerned scant attention from even bibliophiles and documentation experts. It is known that the government all over the world largely rely on the Committees and Commissions for their decisions on particular subjects. Governments make an extensive use of the Instrument of the Public Inquiries which ultimately help in lessening managerial tensions as well as quietening the allegations of misrule. According to John Stuart Mill, "A man seldom judges right, even in his own concerns, still less in those of the public, when he makes habitual use of knowledge but his own or that of some single adviser." Thus the "Committee System" greatly helps the proper functioning of a democratic set-up

A Commission is a "Governmental agency created to perform a particular function such as special investigations or on governmental regulations of business". It is appointed mainly when it is thought that a matter involves some financial questions. There are other reasons for which a Commission is appointed, e.g., in matters pertaining to the Welfare of the State and its Citizens and for improving the efficiency in an administration. The status of a Committee is also the same as that of a Commission, but it does not possess as wide powers as are enjoyed by a Commission and has to limit itself in relation to specific work assigned to it under its terms of reference. While arriving at decisions in the form of recommendations, a Committee or Commission ensures that such decisions are representative of interests of various types of people and also a safeguard against abuse of power.

The Committees and Commissions always advise a Government, offering valuable suggestions and recommendations for smooth operation and efficiency in administration for the Welfare of the people.

A Committee or a Commission Comprises a Chairman, the Members and the Member-Secretary (sometimes there is also a Vice-Chairman and an Assistant Secretary). In some cases there are even One-Man Commissions and enquiries conducted by such Commissions are intrusted to an Official-on-Special Duty or a Judge of the High Court.

The Chairman of a Commission is a person well versed in legal affairs and is often a retired Judge of a High Court or Supreme Court of India. Occasionally, a Member of Parliament is also appointed to the post of Chairman of a Commission. Regarding Committees, the Chairman is usually a specialist in the subject of the Committee. He can be a Leader or a Convener also if he heads a Panel, Study Group, Working Group or a Delegation etc.

The Members of a Commission, Committee, Panel, Study Group, Working Group, etc., are specialists in their respective fields and provide valuable guidance to the Commission in making recommendations.

The Member-Secretary or Secretary is nominated from among the experienced officials who have the requisite Competent knowledge of the subject on which the Commission or the Committee is appointed.

The Study of the "Committees and Commissions" is divided into two main parts :

(I) **Pre-Independence** : From 1772 to August 1947 ;

(II) **Post-Independence** : From Augest 1947 to 1973.

The first Volume covers the period from August 1947 to 1954. The Second Volume covers the period from 1955 to 1957. The Third Volume covers the period from 1958 to 1959. The Fourth Volume covers the period from 1960 to 1961. This present book, Volume V, in the series covers the period from 1962 to 1963.

The Work provides information on subjects like Bibliographical Data of the Committees and Commissions, Chairman, Leader, Convener, etc. of the Committees and Commissions ; Appointments ; Terms of Reference ; Contents and Recommendations.

Arrangements : The arrangements in the "Committees and Commissions" are Chronological and items have been arranged according to their dates of appointment and not according to their dates of publication.

I am sure that this reference work will continue into a number of Volumes for it is unique in nature. I have spared no efforts to make it a comprehensive reference work and it will be of great use to the research scholars, sociologists, historians, economists, students of political science, as well as to all those connected with the study of administration and legal affairs. I have tried my level best to rectify all errors and omissions that I noticed in the previous Volumes. It will be my effort to go on improving these Volumes. The introductory part in Volume I deals with the *why*, *what* and *how* of the "Committees and Commissions".

In the end I must express my gratitude to the Press that reviewed and appreciated the work. I am also indebted to my wife and children who have sacrificed their personal comforts by providing me every facility to make this Volume ready for publication with in a reasonable short time.

New Delhi
Deepavali
November 10, 1977

VIRENDRA KUMAR

CONTENTS

1963

1962

COMMITTEE ON PREVENTION OF CORRUPTION, 1962—REPORT

New Delhi, Ministry of Home Affairs, 304p.

Chairman : Shri K. Santhanam.

Members : Shri Santosh Kumar Basu ; Shri Tika Ram Paliwal ; Shri R.K. Khandilkar ; Shri Nath Pai ; Shri Shambu Nath Chaturvedi ; Shri L.P. Singh ; Shri D.P. Kohli :

Secretary : Shri T.C.A. Ramanujachari

APPOINTMENT

The Committee on Prevention of Corruption was constituted under the Ministry of Home Affairs in 1962.

TERMS OF REFERENCE

(i) To examine the organisation, set up, functions and responsibilities of the Vigilance Units in the Ministries and Departments of the Government of India and to suggest measures to make them more effective.

(ii) To examine the organisation, strength, procedures and methods of work of the Special Police Establishment and the difficulties experienced by it, and to suggest measures to further improve its working.

(iii) To consider and suggest steps to be taken to emphasize the responsibilities of each Department for checking corruption.

(iv) To suggest changes in law which would ensure speedy trial of cases of bribery, corruption and criminal misconduct, and make the law otherwise more-ffective.

(v) To examine rules relating to disciplinary proceedings and to consider what changes are necessary in order to expedite these proceedings and to make them more effective.

(vi) To suggest measures calculated to produce a social climate both amongst public servents and in the general public in which bribery and corruption may not flourish.

(vii) To examine the Government Servant's Conduct Rules and to recommend changes necessary to ensuring maintenance of absolute integrity in the public services.

(viii) To suggest steps for securing public support for anti-corruption measures.

(ix) To consider special measures that may be necessary in corporate public undertaking to secure honesty and integrity amongst their employees.

CONTENTS

Introduction ; Nature of the problem ; Extent of Corruption ; Conduct Rules ; Disciplinary Rules; Preventive Measurs ; Law and Procedure relating to Corruption ; General Recommendations ; Vigilance Organisation ; Special Police Establishment ; Social Climate ; Miscellaneous ; Conclusion ; Summary of Conclusions and Recommendation Annexures I to XVI; Appendices I to VII.

RECOMMENDATIONS

Section 4

The existing rules governing the conduct of Government servants did not make any radical changes in the rules that were in force prior to the commencement of the Constitution with the results that in respect of many matters the rules were either silent or inadequate.

The rules pertaining to integrity should be uniform.

The more important changes recommended are :

1. A duty has been cast on Governments servant holding supervisory post to keep a watchful eye on the integrity of the staff working under them.

2. Every Government servent should take full responsibility for his actions and orders, except where he acts under the directions of his official superior.

3. The conduct expected of every Government servant in case of conflict between public duty and private interest has been clearly stated in Rule 3 (4) which bring out some of the points that were hitherto implied but left unsaid.

4. Rule 10 deals with the question of receipt of gifts and states the position more precisely and also liberalises the existing rules so as too prevent to much interference in private life. The financial limits have been suitably modified.

5. Government servants should submit periodically a complete statement of their assets and liabilities instead of the annual immovable property statements which have been found to serve no useful purpose. In these periodical statements the value of movable property except articles of daily use, like cloths, utensils, crockery and books should be stated including the value of jewellery.

The need for continuance of the exemptions granted in 1959 to industrial employees drawing a pay of Rs. 500 or less and holding non-gazetted posts may be re-examined and in the meant'me the exemptions may continue to be in force

The rules may apply to Government servants appointed to any civil service or post in connection with the affairs of the Union.

While the manner of promulgation of the rules is a matter of detail any modification or liberalisation of the rules should be made only in consultation with the Central Vigilance Commission and with the concurrence of the Ministry of Home Affairs.

Section 5

The constitutional protection given to Government servents by Article 311 which limits the doctrine of pleasure was first given by the Government of India Act, 1935.

Judicial interpretation of Article 311 of the Constitution has resulted in making disciplinary proceedings highly involved.

The latest amendment of Article 311 has not improved the position. It would not be an unreasonable classification to treat disciplinary proceedings involving charges of bribery, corruption and lack of integrity as separate category and to provide for a simplified for a procedure. Article 314 should not come in the way of dealing effectively with members of the former Secretary of States Services. In such cases the jurisdiction of courts shou'd be limited. Another clause some-what on the following lines may be added as Clause (4) to Article 311 :

"Notwithstanding anything contained in Parts III, IV, VI, and XIV of the Constitution, Parliament may, by law, regulate all matters relating to maintenance of integrity and honesty in the services and posts under the Union and States, including the jurisdiction of Courts in respect of such matters.

The power to legislate in this behalf should be added as an item in list of Schedule VII of the Constitution.

In view of the Constitutional requirements and judical pronouncement sit is not possible to radically simplify the producer unlsss the constitution is suitably amended.

The more important of the recommendations contained in the interim report dated August 23, 1963 (Annexure IV) are :

(i) There should be only one set of Discipline and Appeal Rules in respect of Government servants serving in connection with the affiars of the Union or appointed by the Union Government. The definition of the term "Government servant" has therefore been enlarged to include members of the All India Services ;

(ii) The President may impose any of the prescribed

penalties and institute disciplinary proceedings against any Government servant including a member of the All-India Service (Rule 8) or direct a disciplinary authority to institute such proceedings (Rule 9) (i) ;

(iii) The Central Government may institute proceedings against a member of an All-India Service if the circumstances of the case are such that the Central Government is satisfied that it would be in public interest to institute such proceedings provided that before doing so the Central Government shall consult the State Government ;

(iv) The power to institute departmental proceedings has been given to the President, specified disciplinary authorities and such other authorities as may be empowered by the President by general or special order. (This last recommendation was made in view of the recommendation of the Committee that the Directorate of Vigilance of the Central Vigilance Commission should have the power to determine the nature of disciplinary proceedings to be initiated and to initiate, conduct and complete such proceedings. Though in the scheme of the Central Vigilance Commission, as accepted by the Government, the power to initiate, conduct and complete such proceedings has not been given to the Central Vigilance Commission, the provisions made in the rules may be allowed to stand.

(v) The penalties of withholding or withdrawing in full or in part the pension which can now be imposed under Civil Services (Regulation 351) (A) and Rule 8 of the All India services (Death-cum-Retirement Benefits) Rule 1958 have been included in the categories of penalties prescribed under Discipline and Appeal Rules and the procedure for imposing such penalties has been made part of the Discipline and Appeal Rules.

(vi) The requirement of the accused officer submitting a written statement of defence after the framing of charges has been dispensed with.

(vii) The rules relating to suspension, regulation of the period of absence from duty after reinstatement of an officer who had been dismissed, removed or suspended provide for removed of certain difficulties that have arisen out of some recent pronouncements of the courts.

(viii) The requirement of submitting an appeal or a memorial through the authority which passed the order which is subject matter of the appeal or memberial has been despensed with to minimise delay.

The Government should have the power to compulsorily retire a Government sarvant who has completed 25 years of qualifying service or has attained 50 years of age without giving any reason and without any liability for special compensation.

There should be a committee with the Central Vigilance Commissioner as the Chairman and two Secretaries to Government as members to review the cases of all gazetted officers who are due to complete 25 years of qualifying service or to attain 50 years of age during the ensuring year and recommend the name of the officers who are to be compulsorily retired.

There should be one or more committees, State wise on Departmentwise, as may be convenient, with ; nominee of the Central Vigilance Commissioner as the Chairman of each Committee to review such cases in regard to non-gazetted employees and make appropriate recommendations.

The Central Government should have the power to take action under Rule 17 (as amended in May 1963) and Rule 20 of the All India Services (Death-cum-Retirement Benefits) Rules 1958, after consultation with the State Government Concerned.

Section 6

Preventive measures, administrative, legal, social, economic and educative, should be carefully planned and effectively implemented.

A systematic and thorough review of the laws, rules procedures and practices should be undertaken for the purposes of listing (a) discretionary powers (b) levels at which such powers are exercised (c) the manner of exercise of such powers (d) the control exercised within the hierarchy over the exercise of such powers (e) the points at which citizens come into contact with the Minisitry/Department and the purposes for which they do so.

A thorough study should be made in respect of each Ministry/Department/undertaking of the extent, the possible scope and modes of corruption, preventive and the remedial measures prescribed, if any, and their effectiveness. Such studies should be started on a priority basis in respect of each Ministry/Department/undertaking and the Central Vigilance Commisson should also pay attention to this important piece of work for which purpose Government may provide the necessary staff and other facilities.

Serious thought should be given as to how trade associations or their representatives could be associated in the matter of granting licences and allocation of scarce goods. Membership of a recognised trade organisation should be a necessary condition of eligibility for obtaining a licence or a permit. The organisation should screen the capacity of the applicants, their past performance and conduct and make recommendations to the licensing authority. These organisations may also be usefully associated in investigating modes of misuse and mis-utilisation of goods obtained under served advantage.

Administrative delay must be reduced to the utmost extent possible and firm action should be taken to eliminate all such caused of delays as provide scope for corrupt practices.

(a) Each Ministry/Department/undertaking should immediately undertake a review of all existing procedures and practices to find out the cause of delay, the points at which delay occurs and to devise suitable steps to minimise the possibility of delay.

(b) Time-limits should be prescribed, if not already done, for delaing with receipts, files etc., and these should be strictly enforced. Superior officers should consider it their responsibility to find out whether in any particular matter there has been any avoidable delay and call the persons responsible for the delay to account.

(c) All notings at the level lower than that of Under Secretaries should be avoided. The responsibility of the Section should be only that of putting up previous papers and precedents. This procedure should be strictly observed in Ministries/Departments which have to deal with the grant of licences or permits of various kinds.

(d) The levels at which substantive decision could be taken should be prescribed and any attempt to involve as many as possible should be discouraged and dealt with severely, if found to be persisted in.

In all those fields where Government interferes to regulate and control there is scope for abuse. It would be desirable for each Ministry/Department to undertake a review of the regulatory functions which are its responsibility and also examine whether all of them are necessary and whether the manner of discharge of those functions and of the exercise of powers of control are capable of improvement.

Discretionary powers are exercised by different categories of Government servants all of whom are not endowed with a high sense of dedication and integrity in equal measures. While it would not be possible to completely eliminate discretion it should be possible to devise a system of administration which would reduce to the minimum, even is there is a seeming loss of perfection, the need for exercise of personal discretion consistently with efficiency and speedy disposal of public business. Various methods of control devised in the more advanced countries should be studied and a suitable system of control should be devised keeping in view the difficulties that may arise on account of the vastness of our country and the basic principles which are enshrined in our Constitution and jurisprudence.

As many of the citizens of our country who have to seek the help of the administration in many matters are not equipped or trained, they find it necessary to seek the assistance of touts and intermediaries. A serious attempt should be made to educate the citizens in regard to such matters and also make suitable arrangements which would provide an easy access to administration without the intervention of touts and intermediaries.

It may be worthwhile in the country's interest to examine whether the categories of officials who have to exercise considerable discretion in matters relating to taxation, issue of valuable permits and licences, or otherwise deal with matters which requir high degree of integrity, should not be given special attention regarding status and emoluments. Undue economy in the number of officers is not desirable. It would be worthwhile to review the proportion of direct recruits and promotees in the various services as there is a general belief (we do no fully endorse any sweeping generalisation on this point) that the standard of integrity of direct recruits is comparatively higher.

Housing and medical facilities for the Government servant and his family and facilities for the education of his children should be provided.

Till such time as Government is able to construct the required accommodation houses should be requisitioned or taken on lease and let to the Government servants. Accommodation should, to the extent possible, be in colonies.

Informal codes of conduct for different categories of Government servants working in Ministries/Departments dealing with the economic affairs of the country and which spend large sums of monies on construction and purchases should be complied regarding participation in entertainment and availing themselves of other facilities from those who may have or are likely to have official dealings with them. The example must be set superior officers.

Every officer of superior status under whom a number of Gazetted officers are working directly should take steps to as certain personally whether there is any reason to sought or suspect the integrity of any of these officers.

Some of the other preventive measures are :

(i) Great care should be exercised in selecting officers for appointment to high administrative posts. Only those whose integrity is above board should be appointed to these posts.

(ii) At the time of making selections from Non-Gazetted to Gazetted ranks for the first time all those whose integrity is doubtful should be eliminated.

(iii) Every officer whose duty is to sponsor a name for promotion should be required to record a certificate that he had seen the record of service of the Government servant and he is satisfied that the Government servant is a man of integrity.

(iv) Exigencies of public service require grant of extension or re-employment of Government servants who have attained the age of superannuation and are about to retire or retired. Such servants are also employed in the public sector undertakings. We recommend that an essential condition for the grant of extension or re-employment should be that the person concerned has had a good reputation for integrity and honesty. If this condition is not fulfilled the person concerned should not be considered eligible for grant of extension or re-employment.

(v) A good deal of harm is done by vague talk about corruption. This can be reduced only if there are agencies which a person with a genuine complaint can approach for redress, with the assurance that he will be fully protected and that promt and adequate action will be taken where found justified. The Central Vigilance Commission and the Vigilance organisation should be able to meet this need in matters relating to complaints of corruption, harassment, etc. It is essential that bona fide complainants should be protected from harassment or victimisation. The Ministry of Home Affairs should consider itself as having a special responsibility in this regard.

(vi) Enquiry-cum-Reception Offices should be established in all Ministries/Departments which deal with licences/permits and to which members of the public frequently go. All visitors should enter their names and the purpose of their visit in a register to be kept at the Reception Office.

(vii) Steps should be taken to prevent sale of information. One of the causes of this type of corruption is the undue secrecy maintained in regard to all types of matters in respect of which it is not necessary to do so. A clear distinction should be made as to what information should be treated as "secret" and what should be made freely available to the public. Any member of the public who wants to have information of the later category should be able to approach some specified officer in each Ministry/Department/undertaking for that purpose and get what he wants. Difficulties are experienced in obtaining the necessary forms required to be submitted for obtaining licences/permits etc. Arrengement should be made for easy supply of forms whether free or on payment.

There is a column in the annual confidential report regarding every public servant where the superior officer has to comment on his integrity. In cases where the reporting officer is not in a position to make a positive report about integrity he should leave the column blank and submit a secret report if he has reasons to doubt the integrity of the officer on whom he is reporting stating the reasons for his suspicions. The Government or the heads of Department who receive such secret reports should take suitable steps to find out the correctness or otherwise of the report.

There should be a complete ban against Government servants accepting private commercial and industrial employment for two years after retirement. Reasons have been given in the interim report dated 20th December, 1963 (Annexure V)

The existence of large amounts of unaccounted black money is a major source of corruption.

There is no justification to treat income-tax returns and assessments as secret. Publication of such returns and assessments would have a salutary effect on those persons in business and professions who are inclined to take advantage of secrecy provisions to evade income-tax.

To buy and sell properties at prices much greater than those recorded in the conveyance deeds has be come a common method of cheating the central Government of inoome-tax and other taxes and the State government of the stamp duty etc. If the special corporations set up for the purchase can be empowered to step in and acquire such properties that have been deliberately under valued it will strike a blow against black money.

The habit of charging "pugri" or "premium" for renting houses and flats is a similar source of corruption for which some drastic steps have be taken.

(i) No official should have any dealing with a person claiming to act on behalf of a business or industrial house or an individual unless, he is properly accrediated, and is approved by the Department, etc., concerned. Such a procedure will keeping out persons with unsavoury antecedents or reputation. There should, of cource, be no restriction on the proprietor or manager, etc, of the firm or the applicant himself approaching the authorities.

(ii) Even the accredited representatives should not be allowed to see officers below a specified level the level being specified in each organisation after taking into consideration the functions of the organisation, the taking into consideration the functions of the organisation, the volume and nature of the work to be attended to, and the structure of the organisation. However, care should be taken to limit permissaible contacts to levels at which the chances of corruption are considered to be small. This would often mean that no contact would be permitted at the level of subordinate officers.

(iii) There should be a system of keeping some sort of a record of all interviews granted to accredited representatives.

(iv) There should be a fairly senior officers designated in each Department to which an applicant etc., may go if his case is being unreasonably delayed.

It is necessary that a proper procedure should be devised in consultation with the Central Vigilance Commission for accrediting and approval by the Department. Before granting approval the antecedents of the person proposed to be accredited should, if possible, be verified. In any case no person who is not definitely employed by an established undertaking, who will be responsible for his contact and actions should be approved.

Officers belonging to prescribed categories who have to deal with these representatives should maintain a regular diary of all interviews and discussions with the registered representatives whether it takes place in the office or at home. The general practice should be that such interviews should be recorded. Any business or discussion which is not so recorded should be recorded. Any business or discussion which is not so recorded should be deemed to be irregular conduct. Of which serious notice should be taken by the superiors.

Companies and businessmen should be obliged to keep detailed accounts of the expenditure in their expense account. Whenever an income-tax officer feels that amounts have been spent for entertaining high officials, or other purposes for which satisfactory explanation is not forthcoming, it should be his duty to refer the matter to the Chief Vigilance Officers in the department concerned. If there is any legal difficulty for passing on such information, under the present law, it should be removed.

It will be desirable to create a special cell in the Home Ministry consisting of representatives from All India Radio, Press information Bureau and the Films Division to evolve effective propaganda and publicity measures. Representatives of the press may also be associated. The general principles to be followed are :

There should be no publicity at the time of investigation or during departmental inquiry, but effective and widespread publicity to cases resulting in dismissal, removal or compulsory retirement should be given. In cases of prosecutions before courts, important cases will in the ordinary course be given publicity by the press. What is required is to ensure that true facts an d arguments are available to those who edit the cases. The cell proposed should offer to provide the necessary assistane. A perodical summar, say once in three months, of important cases dealt with either by departmental inquiries or prosecutions in courts should be supplied to the press. It may also be hoped that the report of the Vigilance Commission which will be placed before Parliament will attract wide publicity.

Section 7

The Indian Penal Code does not deal in any satisfactory manner with acts which acts which may be described as social offences having regard to the special cirucumstances under which they are committed. And which have now become a dominant feature of certain powerful sections of modern society. Such offences may broadly be classified into :

1. Offences calculated to prevent or obstruct the economic development of the country and endanger its economic health.

2. Evasion and avoidance of taxes lawfully imposed.

3. Misuse of their position by public servants in making of contracts and disposal of public property issue of licences and permits and similar other matters.

4. Delivery by individuals and industrial and commercial undertakings of goods not in accordance with agreed specifications in fulfilment of contracts entered into with public authorities;

5. Profiteering, black-marketing and hoarding;

6. Adulteration of foodstuffs and drugs;

7. Theft and misappropriation of pub'ic property and funds ; and

8. Trafficking in licences, permits etc.

Some of these offences have been made punishable by special enactments. It is desirable to add a new chapter to the Indian Penal Code bring together all the offences in such special enactments and supplementing them with new provisions so that all social offences will find a prominent place in the general criminal law of the country. Government may consider whether this work should be undertaken by a special legal committee or referred to the Law Commission.

Section 21 of the Indian Penal Code should amended as stated below :

(i) The words 'public servant' should be defined to mean 'every person in the service or pay of the Government, a local authority or a Corporation established by a Central or State Act, or a Government Company as defined in Section 617 of the Companies Act, 1956 and/or who is remunerated by fees or commission for the performance of any 'public duty'.

(ii) Every Minister including Ministers of State, Deputy Ministers and Parliamentary Secretaries holding such office in the Union or State Governments.

(iii) The words 'engaged in any trade or industry' may be deleted from the twelfth clause of Section 21 of the Indian Penal Code.

(iv) Any person entrusted with adjudicatory functions in the course of enforcement of any law for the time being in force. (A revised draft incorporating the above amendments is given).

Offering of bribe or attempt to offer bribe should be made a substantive offence and not merely an abtment as at present by adding a new Section in the terms suggested as Section 161 A.

Offerences under Chapter IX of the Indian Penal Code should be made non-bailable.

The presumptions enunciated in Section 4 (1) and

4 (2) of the Prevention of Corruption Act should be made available in respect of Sections 5 (1) and 5 (2).

(The Committee is suggesting extensive amendment to Section 5).

(i) The words in the discharge of his duty should be deleted frcm Section 5 of the Prevention of Corruption Act.

(ii) Possession of assets by a public servant disproportionate to his known sources of income for which he cannot satisfactorily account should be brought within the definition of criminal misconduct and treated as a substantive offence.

(iii) Habitual corrupting of public servants or abetment of such conduct should be made a substantive offence by the addition of a new sub-section. A draft of Section 5 incorporating the above suggestion is given.

Section 5 A of the Prevention of Corruption Act may be amended so as to authorise all Inspectors of the Special Police Establishment and such Officers of similar rank of the Anti-Corruption agencies of the State Government to be specified by the respective State Governments by general or special orders to make investigations without obtaining the permission of a Magistrate.

Section 4 (p) of the Criminal Procedure Code or Section 5 of the Delhi Police Establishment Act may be amended to include Officers of the special Police Establishment of the rank of a sub-Inspector, an Inspecor and a Deputy Superintendent of Police within the definition of 'an officer in charge of a Police Station' so that they may be able to exercise, in the discharge of their functions in any area in a State any of the powers which an officer in charge of a Police Station can exercise under the Code of Criminal Procedure.

Section 94 of the Criminal Procedure Code and Section 5 of the Bankers' Book (Evidence) Act should be suitably amended to enable the Officers of the special Police Establishment and/or of the State anti-corruption agencies and/or any other officer notified in this behalf by general or special order by the Central or State Government, as the case may be, to obtain certified copies of the accounts and of all other documents relevant to the entries in the books of accounts relating to any person in respect of whom an inquiry or an investigation is being made whether under the provisions of the Code of Criminal Procedure or any other law or rule for the time being in force or in any other manner whatever.

Section 222 (2) of the Code of Criminal Procedure may suitably be amended so as to cover offences under Section 5 (1) (c) of the Prevention of Corruption Act and dishonest misappropriation of movable property other than money.

Sub-section (6) of Section 251 A may be amended to make it obligatory for the accused to file a list of witnesses and documents he proposed to rely upon in his defence immediately after the charge is framed. There is however no objection if such a list is furnished at subsequent stage but on the closing of the evidence for the prosecution.

A proviso may be added to sub-section (IA) of Section 344 of the Code of Criminal Procedure to provide that adjournment or postponment of trial or inquiry need not be granted or made only on the ground that a party to the proceedings intends to take up in revision before a higher Court the legality, properiety or correctness of an order passed by the Court.

A proviso may be added to sections 435 to 439 to provide that higher courts may not grant stay of proceedings without giving a reasonable opportunity to the opposite party to show cause against grant of stay and to require that reasons should be recorded to show that it is not necessary in justice to stay the proceedings.

Section 435 of the Criminal Procedure Code may be amended to provide that the records of the lower court should not be requisitioned without hearing the opposite party or in cases whare the purpose could be served by the filing of certified copies.

Section 492 of the Criminal Procedure Code should be amended to empower the Central Government to appoint Public Prosecutors, in any case, or in any specified class of cases.

Section 540 A (2) may be amended to enable the court, in its discretion, to proceed with the trial or inquiry and to record evidence even in the absence of the accused subject to the right of the accused to recall the witnesses for cross-examination.

Section 198B of the Criminal Procedure Code may be amended by-

(i) Deleting sub-section (13)

(ii) Deleting the words other then the offence of defarmation by spoken words' in clause (1);

(iii) Casting the burden of proving the month of imputation on the accused; and

(iv) Requiring the accused to prove that he acted in good faith and in public interest,

Section 5 of the Imports and Exports (Control) Act, 1947, may be amended so as to raise the punishment provided for there under two years rigorous imprisonment and also to make it obligatory to pass the minimum sentence of six months imprisonment except where the court, for reasons to be recorded in writing, considers that a sentence lesser than the minimum should bs imposed.

A provision may also be made to the effect that the principal office bearers would also be liable for punishment for offences committed by a company or partnership concern or any incorporated body or an association of individual and that the burden of proving their innocence should lie on them.

Sections 7 and 8 of the Essential Commodities Act may be so amended by the Act by adding the words or any direction given under any order made thereunder, may order made under Section 3.

Article 311 of the Constitution may be amended by adding the following clause as clause (4).

"Notwithsta ding any thing contained in Parts III, IV, VI, and XIV of the Constitution, Parliament may by law regulate all matter relating to maintenance of integrity and honesty in the Services and posts under the Union and States including the jurisdiction of courts in respect of such matters."

The power to make such legislation should be added as an item in List I of Schedule VII of the Constitution.

Powers to summon and compel attendance of witnesses and production of documents should be conferred on the inquiring authorities in departmental proceedings by suitable legislation.

The need for continuing the provisions prescribing a period of limitation for initiation of any proceeding for any thing done or ordered to be done under the powers given by special enactments such as the Central Excise and Salt Act, 1944, should be examined and if possible be totally done away with ; if it is not possible to do so the period of limitation should be enlarged and it should start running from the date of knowledge of the act or order and not from the date of accrual of the cause of action.

Section 8

The instructions issued by the Ministry of Home Affairs on 27th July 1962 regarding the procedure for dealing with anonymous complaints strike a balance between the view that such complaints should be ignored and the view that they should be ignored.

Some of the circumstances under which it would be appropriate to place a Government servant under suspension are:—

1. Cases where an investigation whether by the Police or departmental authorities, has commenced regarding.

(a) any offence or conduct involving moral turpitude;

(b) Corruption; embezzlement or misappropriation of Government money; possession of disproportionate assets; misuse of official powers for personal gain ;

c. Serious negligence and derliction of duty resulting in considerable loss to Government;

(d) Allegations which, if proved, may result in dismissal, removal or compulsory retirement;

2. Wherever continuance in office will prejudice the investigation trial or any inquiry (e.g., apprehended tampering with witnesses or documents).

3. Whenever it is decided to prosecute the Government servant for offences which, if proved, are likely to end in his conviction and consequent dismissal removal or compulsory retirement from public service ;

4. Desertion of duty;

5. Refusal or deliberate failure to carry out written orders of superior officers.

6. Where continuance in office is likely to subvert discipline in the office in which the public servant is working.

Some of the principles to be observed in dealing with requests or petitions for withdrawal of a prosecution are ;

1. when once a case is put in a court it should be allow d to take its normal course.

2. If in any case if becomes necessary to consider a petition for withdrawal such a petition should be disposed of on the advice of the Central Vigilance Commission, provided that.

(a) The court has not commenced recording evidence.

(b) It is clear from the records that the competent authority had not examined the merits of the case before according sanction; and

(c) Facts have come to light which would show that no offence had been committed by the accused.

In the event of a Government servant being vonvicted by a court, his tenure should forthwith be put an end to even if he has filed an appeal, if the legal advice is that there is no reasonable chance of the conviction being set aside; in other cases, the Government servant should be under suspension.

Consultation with the Union Public Service Commission may be dispensed with in cases where a penalty is proposed to be imposed on the ground of conduct that led to the conviction of a Government servant by a court.

In Ministries/Departments which have to deal with grant of contracts and licenses and which deal with assessment, collection and refund of taxes, depost facto scrutiny of disposed of files should be made to find out the nature of mistakes and irregularites as has been done in the Directorate General of Supplies and Disposals.

There should be a machinery for verification of proper fulfilment of conditions of different kinds of licenses granted by Government.

In the Ministries/Departments which have to deal with grant of contracts for construction and supplies, an attempt should be made to classify those matters which are best left to be decided by a Committee and those which are better left to be decided be individual officers.

To the extent possible transaction of Government business should be open and in accordance with declared principles and there should not be any undue secracy.

Care should be taken to see that non-official institutions which receive grants from Government function properly. These institutions should submit annual reports and audited accounts and it should be the responsibility of some specified officer to certify proper utilisation of Government grants.

Section 9

The Administrative Vigilance Division functions substantially in an advisory capacity. The Time has come to put the entire Vigilance Organisation on a proper and adequate basis without in any way undermining the general principle that the Secretaries and heads of departments are primarily responsible for the purity, integrity and effeciency of their departments

Sub-offices of the Central Vigilance Commission may be established at Bombay, Calcutta, Delhi and Madras in charge of serving Government servants of a sufficiently high rank and to discharge such functions and duties as may be allotted to them by the Central Vigilance commission.

The Vigilance organisation in the Railways requires to be considerably improved. The Organisation should be reorganised as follows :—

Member (Vigilance)

- Joint Director (Vigilance)
  - Deputy Director (Engineering)
  - Deputy Director (Store Purchases)
- Joint Director (Investigation)
  - Deputy Director (Traffic)
  - Deputy Director (Investigation)

The Joint Director (Vigilance should ordinarily be an officer belonging to a service other than the Railway Service, preferab'y an I.A.S. Officer. The Joint Director (Investigation) should be a Police Officer of the rank and status of the Deputy Inspector-General of Police. Adequate investigating staff should be provided at Headquarters.

In the Zonal railways, the Vigilance Officer should have the status of a departmental head and be given full freedom to investigate into complaints received by him.

There should be one Chief Vigilance Officer in each Ministry/Department/Corporate undertaking. The Chief Vigilance Officer and the Vigilance Officers should be of a sufficiently high rank so that they may be able to function effectively. There should be Vigilance Officers in all subordinate and attached offices, and in important departments of the public sector undertakings.

The Central Board of Revenue has now been split into two Boards. There shall be two Chief Vigilance Officers in the Ministry of Finance one for the matters dealt with by the Direct Taxes Board and the other for the matters dealt with by the Indirect Taxes Board.

The Chief Vigilance Officers should be appointed in consultation with the Central Vigilance Commission and the Vigilance Officers in subordinate and attached offices should be appointed in consultation with the Chief Vigilance Officer of the Ministry/Department. No person whose appointment as Chief Vigilance Officer is objected to by the Vigilance Commissioner should be so appointed. The Chief Vigilance Officer and other Vigilance Officers, besides being the link between the Central Vigilance Commission and the Ministry/Department, should, as at present, continue to be the special assistants to the Secretary or the Head of Department/undertaking in compating corruption, misconduct and malpractices in the Ministry/Department/undertaking. The Chief Vigilance Officer will be responsible for coordinating and guiding the activities of other Vigilance Officers in the attached and subordinate offices and other organisations for which his Ministry/Department is responsible.

(ii) Whole-time or part-time assistance of a Deputy Superintendent of police from the Central Bureau of Investigation may be made available to the Chief Vigilance Officer (s) of each of the Ministries/Departments/ Undertakings.

The Chief Vigilance Officers and the Vigilance Officers should have complete independence to investigate complaints of corruption and malpractices.

Those working in the Vigilance Organisation should have an assurance that good and efficient work in the Vigilance Organisation will enhance their opportunities for promotion and not become a sort of disqualification.

Those posted to the Vigilance Organisation should not have the far of returning to their parent cadre after a short period with the possibilities of facing the anger and displeasure of those against whom they made inquiries.

It should be the invariable practice to obtain integrity clearance from the Vigi'ance Organisation in matters relating to confirmation and promotion.

The Chief Vigilance Officers and Vigilance Officers in Departments and establishments having field organisations should have an adequate investigating staff so that such of those complaints or cases which are not handed over to the Central Bureau of Investigation may be investigated by them. The strength of the investigating staff should be determined by each Ministry in consultation with the Central Vigilance Commissioner.

All departmental proceedings against Class I and Class II officers and other important cases should be entrusted to Commissions for Departmental Inquiries attached to the Central Vigilance Commiss'on. For this purpose, the number of the Commissioners for Departmental Inquiries should be suitably increased and Officers from different departments like Railways, Central Public Works Department Income-Tax Central Excise and Customs, Posts and Telegraphs should also be appointed as Commissioners for Departmental Inquiries.

The Chief Vigilance Officers in other Ministries/ Deparments, the Member, Vigilance, in the Railways and the Chief Vigilance Officers in the public sector undertakings should have the power to scrutinise the correctness of the findings and conclusions arrived at in a Departmental inquiry and the adequacy of punishment and initiate action for review if he considers that the punishment awarded inadequate. Similarly, the Delhi Special Police Establishment should also be authorised to move for review of findings and punishment in cases started on their report. In all these matters the advice of the Central Vigilance Commission should be freely obtained.

Training Courses should be organised for the Vigilance Officers and the programme for training should include instructions in the various laws and rules departmental procedures, methods of investigation, inculding collection of information and processing the same procedure for Departmental proceedings, etc. The syllabus should be devised by the Central Vigilance Commissioner in consultation with the Director of Central Bureau of Investigation. It should be open to the State Governments also to send their officers for training.

It is desirable that the Special Police Establishment should be able to spare some officers for Vigilance work and its strength should be reviewed for this purpose.

Section 10

The wing in the Special Police Establishment which deals in the malpractices and offences occurring in connection with the management of joint stock companies and infringement of Import/Export regulations should be expanded and strengthened to take up cases of breaches of foreign exchange regulations and important cases of smuggling, evasion of customs duty, under-invoicing and over-invoicing.

In order to secure cooperation between the special Police Establishment and the Ministries/Departments of the Central Government, separate directives had been issued by the Ministry of Home Affairs, Railway Board and the Army, Naval and Air Headquarters and Defence Production organisation. These separate directive issued from the Ministry of Home Affairs for which purpose the Central Vigilance Commission should undertake a review of these directives.

It should be the duty of every Vigilance Officer and head of department and undertaking to report to the Special Police Establishment for investigation of all cases in which allegations of bribery and corruption are made against public servants.

The present practice of obtaining prior concurrence for investigating cases against Railway Gazetted Officers should be discontinued.

All records and documents required by the Special Police Establishment should be made available to them for inspection and scrutiny ordinarily with a fortnight and positively within a month from the date of the receipt of the request.

Superintendents of Police in charge of Special Police Establishment Branches should also be authorised to write to Accountant General Concerned direct and to requisition the documents in the possession of audit which are relevent to any inquiry or investigation made by the Special Police Establishment.

In cases where the Special Police Establishment are investigating serious charges, request for transfer of such Government servants should be complied with quickly.

Government servants required for examination by the Special Police Establishment should become available for that purpose quickly.

Requests for statements regarding pay, allowances, etc. of Government servants against whom investigations of the allegation of possession of disproportions assets are being made should be made available Special Police Establishment within a month of receipt of such request by the audit and for this purpose it would be desirable to designate a specified officer whom the Special Police Establishment could approach.

Officers of the Special Police Establishment should be allowed to go foreign countries whenever inquiries of a complicated nature on important points are necessary, if this is certified by the Central Vigilance Commission.

There should be a Central Organisation to conduct examinations and inspections and to give technical opinion on all cases relating to constructions, works diggings etc. irrespective of the Ministry or Department to which he may relate. This Central organisation should include other specialist and should be placed under the Central Vigilance Commission.

Proposals for strengthening the Government Examiner of Questioned Documents Establishment which are reported to be under consideration should be finalised quickly.

Research Centres and Laboratories which are under the control of State Governments should also deal with the request from the Special Police Establishment on a priority basis.

The Central Figure Print Bureau, Calcutta, should undertake comparison and opinion work in Special Police Establishment cases.

Request for granting sanction to prosecute should be dealt with expeditiously.

As a general rule, public servants found guilty of bribery, corruption or other criminal misconduct should be prosecuted in the first instance if the evidence is sufficient for that purpose. In other cases, departmental action should be taken in the first instance and the question of the prosecution would not generally arise. Difference of opinion as to whether prosecution in a court or departmental action should be taken in the first instance should be referred to the Central Vigilance Commission for advice.

In all States except one, Special Judges and Magistrates for trying Special Police Establishment cases are notified by a general order but in one State, the State Government have to pass orders allotting each case to a Special Judge or a Magistrate. The Practice in this regard should be the same as is followed in all the other States.

If the Special Judge or Magistrate appointed to try Special Police Establishment cases is also allotted other work such a Judge or Magistrate should accord priority to Special Police Establishment cases.

All the State Governments should be persuaded to issue instructions that the Special Police Establishment cases should be conducted by the Government Advocate or the Senior Assistant Government Advocate in the High Courts. If this is not possible, the Special Police Establishment should be authorised to engage its own counsel.

Departmental inquiries against all Gazetted officers should be conducted by Commissioners for Departmental Inquiries. Such inquiries against non-gazetted employees should also be conducted and completed expeditiously.

In cases investigated by the Special Police Establishment the inquiry record should be made available to the Special Police Establishment quickly so that they may be in a position to review that the adequacy of the punishment if the Special Police Establishment recommend a review and, if there is a difference of opinion, the matter should be referred to the Central Vigilance Commission.

Informants and witnesses should be afforded sufficient protection and should be saved from harassment.

The Special Police Establishment should be strengthened and the proposed additional strength is given in Annexures XIV to XVI.

(i) There should be two more posts of Deputy Inspectors General of Police.

(ii) Branches should be established for the States of Kerala and Jammu and Kashmir.

(iii) There should be a Branch at Ranchi.

(iv) There should be 5 wings of the Central investigating Agency.

(v) The Special Police Establishment Branches at Delhi, Ambala, Bombay and Madras, should be strengthened to deal with anti-corruption work in the Union Territories.

(vi) There should be a small Special Police Establishment Unit at Manipur with jurisdiction over Manipur and Tripura. This unit should be work under the overall control of the Superintendent of Police, Special Police Establishment, Shillong.

(vii) Another post of Deputy Legal Adviser should be created.

(viii) The grade of Assistant Public Prosecutor should be abolished and there should be only two grades, namely, Senior Public Prosecutor and Public Prosecutor.

Overseers Sectional Officers of the Central Public Works Department, Railway Engineering Service and the Military Engineering Service may be taken on deputation in the Special Police Establishment in all the branches except the Central Investigating Agency Branch. An officer of the grade of Executive Engineer should be taken on deputation at the Special Police Establishment.

Inspectors from the Income-tax, Central Excise and Customs Department should also be taken on deputation. One post of Junior Technical Officer (Accounts) should be created in the Branches at Bombay, Calcutta and Madras.

A percentage of posts in the ministerial cadres of the headquarters of the Central Bureau of Investigation shall be excluded from the Central Secretariat Service.

The scale of special pay/allowances should be improved so that the total emoluments are commensurate with the important and difficult duties with the Special Police Establishment Officers have to perform, particularly, in respect of those officers who are taken on deputation.

Adequate housing facilities should be provided for the Special Police Establishment Officers and other staff. If Government houses are not available buildings should be taken on rent by Government and given to its officers.

Section 11

There is a large consensus of opinion that a new tradition of integrity can be established only if the example is set by those who have the ultimate responsibility for the governance of India. Namely the Ministers of the Central and State Governments. In the interest of the future of public life, the following steps should be taken :

(i) A code of conduct for Ministers including the provisions suggested for public servants relating to acquisition of property, acceptance of gifts and disclosure of assets and liabilities should be drawn up. This code of conduct should be placed before Parliament and States Legislatures. The Prime Minister and Chief Ministers should consider themselves responsible for enforcing the code of conduct.

(ii) Specific allegation of corruption on the part of a Minister at the Centre or a State should be promptly investigated by an agency whose findings will command respect. If a fromal allegation is made by any 10 members of Parliament or a Legislature in writing addressed to the Prime Minister or Chief Minister through the Speakers and Chairman, the Prime Minister or Chief Minister should consider himself obliged, by convention, to refer the allegations for immediate investigation by a Committee as has been suggested hereinafter.

This would be in addition to the reponsibilities of the Prime Minister and Chief Ministers of States to take note of allegations made in the Press or which otherwise come to their notice. In respect of such allegations also the Prime Minister and the Chief Ministers should be free to refer the matter to the Committee referred to above. In all other cases the Ministers against whom the allegations are made should, as a rule, institute legal proceedings by filing a complaint for criminal defamation and the Ministers concerned should be given legitimate assistance by the Government of which they are Ministers.

In cases where the Ministers are unwilling, the Prime Minister or the Chief Ministers of States, as the case may be, should consider themselves, obliged by convention, unless there is irrefutable proof of integrity of the Minister concerned, to advise the President or the Governor, as the case may be to withdraw his pleasure, which would mean the Minister will have to go out of office, unless he himself resigns.

The Central Vigilance Commission should not deal with complaints against the Ministers nor would it be desirable to establish any permanent tribunal. The proper course would be for the President to constitute, on the advice of the Prime Minister, a "National Penal". Whenever allegations against a Minister require to be inquired into an ad hoc committee should be selected out of this penal by the President. The Committee may consist of three persons one of whom at least should have held or should be holding a high judicial office. It should be the duty of the Committee to ascertain whether there is a prima facie case. The Committee should have the power to direct the Central Bureau of Investigation, in suitable cases, to investigate and report. If the Committee wishes to make any inquiries otherwise than through the Central Bureau of Investigation, it would be given all the necessary facilities and assistance including free access to all documents, files etc., without being hampered by any claim of privilege. On the completion of the inquiries either through Central Bureau of Investigation it should be given all the necessary facilities and assistance including free access to all documents, files, etc., without being hampered by any claim of privilege. On the completion of the inquiries either through the Central Bureau of Investigation or otherwise the Committee should consider the available material and advise as to further action, if any, that may be necessary. It may advise that a regular case be registered for investigation with a view to prosecute the Minister concerned or a commission of inquiry under the Commissions of Inquiry Act, 1952 be appointed. If the Committee makes such a recommendation the Minister should resign as a matter of convention and should remain out of office till the completion of the proceedings. If the Minister is found guilty of the allegation or is found to have been corrupt, he should be dismissed and should also become ineligible for becoming a Minister or for holding any elective office. The necessary legal instruments for giving effect to this provision should be brought into existence. Until such time as the necessary legislation is made, there should be a convention which would give effect to this provision. As publicity would be an effective instrument there should be a convention that the findings of the Committee would be placed before Parliament or State Legislatures. Suitable legal provisions should be made to afford protection from proceedings for defamation in regard to the proceedings and the findings of the Committee.

The integrity of Members of Parliament and of the Legislatures in the States will be a great factor in creating a favourable social climate against corruption. It has been talked about that some Members use their good offices to obtain permits, licences and easier access to Ministers and Officials for industrialists and businessmen. In the case of Legislators who are in the employment of private undertakings for legitimate work, it is desirable that such legislators should declare the fact of such employment so that it may be open and known. Such legislators should not approach Ministers or Officials in connection with the work of the employers and also should not participate in the discussion or voting on demands or proposals in which the undertakings or firms are interested. Other legislators, who are not such bona fide employees, should on no account undertake, for any valuable consideration or other personal advantage, to promote the interests of or obtain favours for any private party either in the legislature or with Government. It is desirable that a code of conduct for legislators embodying these and the other principles should be framed by a Special Committee of the Parliament and Legislatures nominated by the Speakers and Chairmen. The Code shou'd be formally approved by resolutions of Parliament and the respective Legislatures and any infringement of the code should be treated as a breach of privilege to be inquired into by the Committee of privileges. If a breach is etablished, action including termination of membership, may be taken. Necessary sanctions for enforcing the code of conduct should also be brought into existence.

The conduct of political parties should be regulated by strict principles in relation to collection of funds of electioneering. A total ban on all donations by incorporated bodies to political parties and for political purposes will clear the atmosphere. All political parties should keep a proper account of their receipts and expenditure and should publish annual audited statement of such accounts giving details of all individual receipts. Failure to do this should debar a political party from recognition by the Election Commission, the Postal authorities and Banks. Those who receive donations for political purposes should have to account for them in their own audit account and include them in their total income for purposes of income-tax.

Central and State Governments should make it a point to scrutinise carefully all complaints and allegations appearing in responsible newspapers and investigate them thoroughly. Editors and reporters should be encouraged under a pledge of secrecy to communicate to the Chief Vigilance Officers or the Central Vigilance Commissions about suspected corrupt practices and all such reports should be promptly inquired into. The Press should be informed of the result.

Drastic action should be taken against irresponsible newspapers which make reckless allegations It should be the invariable practice to prosecute such newspapers unless they can establish the truth of their allegations. It should not be left to individual Officers or Ministers to take such action and for this purpose the existing law and procedure must be reviewed.

Voluntary public organisations willing to Assist Government in combating corruption should be invited to cooperate with the Government in the fight against corruption. The reports from organisations should be protected and treated as confidential unless the organisations concerned agree to there publications.

The responsible heads of the Panchayat Raj Institutions, namely, the Sarpanches, the Chairman and Presidents of the Panchayat Samities and the Zila Parishads should consider it as part of their duties to report to Government all cases in which corrupt practices are suspected. The enthusiasm of these persons can be maintained only if their reports are given prompt and serious consideration, and they are informed of the results of investigations based on such reports.

It is desirable to create a situation in which those officials who have been found guilty of corruption feel not only that they lost their jobs but also feel socially degraded.

A similar mobilisation of public opinion against persons who corrupt the officials or evade taxes, or indulge in other anti-social practices is necessary. Ministers and high officials should take particular care to avoid any situation which is likely to created the impression that such persons enjoy their confidence, support or patronage.

It should be one of the important functions of the Central Vigilance Commission to explore all possible methods of mobilising public opinion against corruption in public life and services. It should become the fearless champion of integrity and fair-dealing.

Section 12

Our general recommendations relating to conduct rules, disciplinary rules, preventive measures and procedural matters relating to contracts, purchases, etc., will apply to the Ministry of Defence and its establishments except in so far as other provisions have been made in the Army, Navy and Air Force Acts.

The Chief Justice of India in consultation with the Chief Justices of the High Courts should arrange for a thorough inquiry into the incidence of corruption among the judiciary, and evolve, in consultation with the Central and State Governments, proper measures to prevent and eliminate it. Perhaps the setting up of vigilance organisations under the direct control of the Chief Justice of every High Court coordinated by a Central Vigilance Officer under the Chief Justice of India may prove to be an appropriate method.

The University Grants Commission and the Inter-University Board should take immediate steps to institute an inquiry into the malpractices that may be prevailing in the universities and evolve measures to fight them.

An important condition of assistance given to non-official organisations should be that these bodies are free from any corrupt practices and measures. Including audit, should be devised to enforce this condition.

COMMITTEE ON RESIDENTIAL ACCOMMODATION FOR STUDENTS AND TEACHERS, 1962—REPORT

New Delhi, University Grants Commission, 1965. 25p.

Chairman : Dr. M.S. Mehta.

Members : Dr. B. Prasad ; Dr. G.D. Parikh; Shri P.T. Chandi ; Shri Chandran ; D.S. Devanesan ; Shri P. G. Mavalankar ; Shri K.N. Sen ; Dr. R.K. Singh.

Secretary : Shri R.K. Chhabra;

APPOINTMENT

The University Grants Commission appointed the Committee on Residential Accommodation for Students and Teachers in 1962.

TERMS OF REFERENCE

The terms of reference of the Committee were as follows :

(i) To enlarging and improving facilities for residential accommodation in the universities ;

(ii) To study the problems in all aspects and prepare a broad outline plan for consideration of the Commission.

CONTENTS

Introduction ; Students Hostels ; Staff Quarters ; Future Policy And Programme ; Summary of Recommendations ; Appendix.

RECOMMENDATIONS

Student Hostels

Efforts should be made to maintain the present proportion of students provided with hostel accommodation. If possible this proportion should be increased in the years to come.

Since the physical environments of the residence exert a powerful influence on the character and attitude of the individual, the planning of a hostel should be efficient, logical and pleasant. The building should be so planned that it provides for quiet individual work and for the growth of community feeling.

To realise the full benefit of hostel life, different wards of the hostel may be organized on the basis of 'houses' and 'fraternities'.

The local authorities or the State Governments may be persuaded to grant exemption of ground rents and reduction of rates and taxes on the hostels which will ultimately reduce the hostle fees charged from the students.

The expenditure on hostels should be treated as an admissible item of grant for the universities and colleges.

The schedule of hostel fees should be adjusted in a way as can provide for rent free accommodation to about 5 to 10 per cent of the students living in hostels who could be selected on the basis of merit.

Effort should be made to provide hostel accommodation to about 75 per cent of the students in institutions of All-India character. The possibility of granting financial aid to students in these hostels to cover all their expenses may also be explored.

Certain types of work in the hostel may be distributed among the students on payment of small remuneration and a 'mutul assistance fund' started in the hostels for the benefit of needy students.

Every hostel should have essential provisions like sick room, indoor games, reading room and a place for congregation for purposes other than intellectual and academic.

The hostels should have common kitchens and common messes. The messes should be organised on co-operative basis.

The University Grants Commission should provide grants for the renovation of existing hostel buildings.

Some senior students may assist the Warden in supervision the hostel in return for some remuneration.

The hostels for postgraduate students should be planned differently from those of undergraduate so as to provide proper facilities for a congenial environment and for a quiet place for study.

On account of the growth of collegiate education in the rural areas the accommodation problem for both students and teachers requires greater attention and suitable grants should be provided by both State Government and the University Grants Commission on liberal scale for this purpose.

With the spread of education among middle-class women a large provision for hostels for them has become essential and should be planned in a systematic way, The universities should be encouraged to undertake a programme of promoting these facilities.

It is not desirable at this stage to encourage common hostels for men and women. Women hostels may be organised as distinct units and wherever possible located on the campus.

The warden may not necessarily be a senior teacher. If a junior teacher possesses requisite qualities, there should be no bar in his functioning as warden of the hostel.

A big hostels do not provide sufficient opportunites for enough contact, small hostels of say 50-60 seats may be encouraged. However, where it is not possible provision should be made for sub-warden. The warden's and subwarden's house should be located either in the hostel itself or close to the hostel. The University Grants Commission should assist the universities for the construction of houses which may accommodate senior teacher and about 10-12 students living together as a single family.

The University Grants Commission should liberalise the rules for the grant of assistance for the construction of hostels so as to obviate the necessity of procuring matching funds.

The approach of comparatively more emphasis on university hostels hitherto adopted should be revised and improvements in the living conditions of college hostels given an equally high priority.

It is not possible to lay down a uniform pattern of hostels for all cases. The norms and standard of accommodation of dining and sanitary arrangements suggested by the University Grants Commission panel on hostels should be kept in view as guiding principles.

In the rural areas and provincial cities hostels accommodating 8-12 students who live together, cook their food themselves may be set up on experimental basis.

Students Homes

In order to provide facilities to students for quiet study the universities and colleges should be encouraged to establish 'Students Homes' or 'Day Hostels' which should provide reading accommodation and have small library and cafetaria.

Staff Quarters

Steps should be taken to provide residential accommodation for 50 per cent of the teachers in universities and colleges by the end of the Fourth Plan.

The houses for teachers may be of two types and the accommodation provided need not be related to the position of the teacher.

It would be preferable to provide outright grants to universities and colleges for the construction of staff quarters. If grants to the extent necessary are not feasible, interest free loans may be given by the University Grants Commission or the local Governments. Such loans may be given to teachers for building houses on convenient terms.

For the residential accommodation provided by the institution to the teachers a subsidised rent @ 5 per cent of the salary may be charged as in the case of armed forces.

The University Grants Commission may involve the Central Ministry of Works and Housing in the programmes of residential accommodation for students and teachers.

The University Grants Commission may consider setting up of a research cell for examining the methods through which the cost of building could be reduced.

CENTRAL WAGE BOARD FOR IRON AND STEEL INDUSTRY, 1962—REPORT

New Delhi, Department of Labour and Employment, 1965, 232, VIII,III,II,IVp.

Chairman : Shri G. K. Shinde
Members : Shri Akbar Ali Khan ; Prof. M. L. Dantwala ; Shri M. S. Rao ; Shri Sardindu Gupta ; Shri Michael John ; Shri Gopeshwar
Secretary : Shri V. R. Kulkarni.

APPOINTMENT

In pursuance of the recommendation contained in para 25 of Chapter XXVII of the Second Five Year Plan regarding the establishment of tripartite Wage Boards for individual industries, the Government of India have set up a Central Wage Board for the Iron and Steel Industry Vide its Resolution No. WB-II (I) 61 dated January 5, 1962.

TERMS OF REFERENCE

(a) To determine the categories of employees (manual clerical, supervisory, etc.), who should be brought within the scope of the proposed wage fixation ;

(b) To work out a wage structure based on the principles of fair wages set forth in the report of the

Committee on Fair Wages.

CONTENTS

RECOMMENDATIONS

Scope : The scope of the Wage Board extends to six Steel plants located at Jamshedpur, Burhanpur, Bhilai, Rourkela, Durgapur and Bhadravati.

Vertical Scope : Workmen getting a basis wage upto Rs. 500 p.m. (marginal cases to be included) be included within the scope of enquiry, Apprentices and trainees should be excluded. The special Staff of the Indian Iron and Steel Co. Ltd. should included.

Horizontal Scope : Employees employed outside the plants in service like, town, medical, educational, municipal, Water Works Departments, etc. should be included within the scope of enquiry.

Head Office Staff : Employees of the Head Office and Sales Offices situated outside the plant town be excluded from the scope of enquiry.

Other Categories Of Employees : All employees who work in the existing plants for production, repairs, alterations, should be treated on par with the employees employed inside the plant.

Administrative Office Employees : All such employees employed at the plant location and working in administrative offices like those of General Manager's Office, Account's Office, Works Engineering Office etc. though located outside the plant will be included within the scope of enquiry.

Minimum Wage For Men Production And Maintenance : The Board is of the view that it would be appropriate to fix Rs. 125 per month as the need based wage for unskilled men engaged in Works Department of the Steel Plants on Production or maintenance jobs. Only in the case of the Mysore Iron and Steel Ltd. slightly lower minimum wage i.e. Rs. 115 per month has been recommended.

Minimum Wage For Men (Service And Outside Works) : The minimum wage for men in Service Departments and those engaged outside the works would be Rs. 120 per month. Only in the case of the Mysore Iron and Steel Limited it would be Rs. 110 per month.

Minimum Wage For Women : The minimum wage for the lowest paid unskilled women will be Rs. 115 per month. Only in the case of the Mysore Iron and Steel Ltd. it would be Rs. 105 per month (Production and Maintenance) and Rs. 104 per month (service and outside).

Grades : The following graded scales have been recommended for the lowerst paid workers.

For Iisco Lisco And H.S.L

Men (Production, Maintenance)	—Rs. 125—135
Men (Service & Outside works)	—Rs. 120—130
Women (Production, Maintenance) (For H.S.L. 115—130)	—Rs. 115—135
Women (Service & Outside works)	—Rs. 115—130

For Mysore Iron And Steel Ltd.

Men (Production, Maintenance)	—Rs. 115—125
Men (Service & Outside works)	—Rs 110—120
Women (Production, Maintncance)	—Rs. 105—125
Women (Production & Outside works)	—Rs. 104—120

Equal Pay For Equal Works : In fixing the above scales for men and women it is understood that differentiation will be justified only if there is difference in their job content.

Dearness Allowance For the Lowest Paid Unskilled Worker : The revised deaness allowance for the lowest paid unskilled worker will be :

Tata Iron and Steel Co. Ltd.	Rs. 64
Indian Iron and Steel Co. Ltd.	Rs. 64
Hindustan Steel Limited	Rs. 45
Mysore Iron & Steel Limited	Rs. 50

Split Of Wages In Dearness Allowance And Basic Wage : The split of the total wages of the lowest paid unskilled worker into basic wage and dearness allowance shall be as under.

Production and Maintenance

Organisation	Basic Pay		D.A.	Total	
	Women	Men	All	Women	Men
TISCO	Rs.	Rs.	Rs.	Rs.	Rs.
LISCO	51-2-71	61-2-71	64	115-135	125-135
H.S.L.	70-1-71-2-85.	80-2-90	45	115-130	125-135
MISL	55-2-75	65-2-75	50	105-125	115-125
Service And Outside Works					
TISCO	51-1,85-	56 2-66	64	115-130	1"0-130
IISCO	62.10-1.95-66				
H.S.L	70-71-2-85	75-2-85	45	115-130	120-130
MISL	54-2-70	60-2-70	50	104-120	110-120

Note : The cash coke subsidy granted by the Tata Iron and Steel Co. Ltd. and cash value of subsidised sale of coke by the Indian Iron and Steel Co. Ltd. which is said to be Rs. 9 shall be part of dearness allowance. The coke shall be continued to be supplied o the employees by these companies as at present but at the controlled rates. House Rent of Rs. 4 in the case of the employees of the Indian Iron and Steel Co. Ltd. who are not provided with quarters should be merged in dearness allowance. If, however, the management and the recognised union of the Indian Iron come to an agreement that the present system of supply of coke and payment of house rent allowance should continue, the Board would have no objection of such an arrangement; but in that case the dearness allowance payable would be reduced correspondingly.

Cost of Living Index: The wages be linked with the All India Consumer Price Index (1949=100). The wages already recommended by the Board are related to the average of the All India Consumer Price Index for the year 1964 which is 152.

Adjustment In Dearness Allowance: The dearness allowance should be variable. The rate of increase or decrease should be of Rs. 1.50 for every two points rise or fall in the all India Consumer Price Index 1949=100, provided that:

(i) There will be no change in the dearness allowance, either upward or downward, for the first six months from the time of the introduction of the revised wage structure; and

(ii) There will be no downward revision unless the index falls below 144.

The dearness allowance should be revised every three months in the months of March, June, September and December, on the basis of the average all India consumer price index number of the previous quarters, October to December, January to March, April to June and July to September. It is recommended in paragraph 12.6 that the revised wage structure should be introduced from 1st April, 1965. This would mean that there will be no charge in the dearness allowance for the months, April 1965 to September 1965, upward or downward, and the first change would be made as soon as the figures of the all India Consumer Price index for October 1965 to December 1965 are available.

Neutralisation: The adjustment in dearness allowance recommended above gives 100% neutralisation in the rise or fall of the cost of living for lowest paid worker tapering off gradually as the wages rise.

Production/Incentive Bonus: For producation/incentive bonus schemes bonus earnings will continue to be determind on the same basic wage in each case as applicable prior to these recommendations. The Board recognises that with the change of circumstances the production/incentive bonus can be modified at the appropriate time.

Retiring gratuity: The Present scheme of paying retiring gratuity in the Tata Iron and Steel Co. Ltd. and the Indian Iron & Steel Co. Ltd. is to continue. The Hindustan Steel Limited has no scheme of retiring gratuity at present. The basic wage and dearness allowance for the circulation of gratuity, shall be those recommended by the Board.

Conversion Of Daily-Rated Scales Into Monthly Rated Scales: All the daily rated scales be converted into monthly rated scales. The monthly rated scales are for a calender month with the usual weekly off which must be available to all the workers.

Acting Allowance: After conversation of daily rated scales into monthly rated scales the privilege of the daily rated employees getting acting allowance when they act in higher rated jobs even for a day or part of a day shall continue.

Leave: After conversation of daily-rated scales into monthly rated scales the employees of the Tata Iron and Steel Co. Ltd., the Indian Iron and Steel Co. Ltd. and the Mysore Iron and Steel Ltd. should be allowed five days casual leave. The Hindustan Steel Limited will continue give casual leave as now. No other additional leave benefits for the daily rated employees on being converted into monthly scales shall be available. All the future entrants to these converted scales will continue to get privilege leave at the rate of one day for 20 days work performed as at present and they will not be entitled to any furlough leave in the Total, Iron and Steel Co. Ltd. and the Mysore Iron and Steel Ltd. wherever these recommendations are at variance with the certified standing orders of the company, the management and the recognised union will approach the certifying officer for an amendment of the certified standing orders in accordance with these recommendations and the implementation of the recommendations will be subject to such certification. Meanwhile the employees should be paid the total emoluments as now recommended by the Board through calculated on daily rated basis.

Practice Of Taking Work In Breach Of Section 51 And 52 Of The Factories Act In The Indian Iron And Steel Co. Ltd: The practice to take work from the employees of the Indian Iron and Steel Co. Ltd. for all the seven days in a week without a weekly off should be stopped in doing so it must be ensured that no existing worker suffers any reduction in total emoluments including the amount earned due to his having to work even on the weekly off days in the month) provided the workers are prepared to take on themselves without (increase in manning as far as practicable the additional worked arising from the change over to shift cycle and weekly off as required under Factories Act.

National Holidays: All the Steel Plants should give the following paid national holidays:

Republic Day	26th January
Independence Day	15th August
Mahatma Gandhi's Birth Day	2nd October.

The Tata Iron and Steel Co. Ltd. would continue to

give Founder's Day on the 3rd March as a paid holiday.

Scales Of Dearness Allowance: The proposed scales of dearness allowance shall be as per paragraph 8.24, 8.26, 8.27 and 8.28 for the Hindustan Steel Limited, the Tata Iron and Steel Co. Ltd, the Indian Iron and Steel Co. Ltd. and the Mysore Iron and Steel Ltd, respectively.

Wage Structure: The revised wage structure is given in Schedule I, II, III and IV attached to the report.

Explanations And Safe Guards: In the case of the Indian Iron and Steel Co. Ltd, the scales for the security Guards, special staff and Medical Department could not be finalised.

They should be settled between the management and the recognised union. The scales for the daily rated personnel in town, watch and ward and sanitary services will be the same as corresponding revised scales for works.

In the case of Mysore Iron and Steel Ltd., Bhadravati, the scales, for the Hospital, canteen, school town, watch, and ward etc, departments could not be finalised. They should be settled between the management and the recognised union by mutual negotiations.

It is possible that some of the existing wage scales may have been omitted in the schedules. It is expected that the Managements and the recognised unions concerned will negotiate a suitable wage scale; in all such cases, -keeping in view the differentials indicated in the other similar revised wage scales.

It is recommended that so far as the production/incentive bonus schemes, which are at present in operation in the various plants, are concerned, the bonus earnings of the employees will continue to be determined on the same basic wages in each case as applicable prior to the coming into force of these recommendations. The Board, however, recognises that, with the change of circumstances, the production/incentive bonus schemes can be modified at the approppriate time.

Revised Scales Of The Ministerial Staff: The revised lowest scales of the Ministerial staff shall be as under:

(1) TISCO...Rs 90-5-100-10-220-15-265
(This will give Rs. 158 at the minimum and Rs. 364 at the maximum).

(2) H.S.L Rs. 117-8-149-10-189-Test-12-285-15-300
(This will give Rs. 162 at the minimum and Rs. 355 at the maximum)

(3) IISCO Rs. 95-5-125-7-160-EB-8-200.
This will give Rs. 165 at the minimum and Rs. 275 at the maximum and in addition Prodction Bonus).

(4) MISL Rs. 85-4-97-5-112-EB-7-140.
(This will give Rs. 140 at the minimum and Rs. 200 at the maximum).

Explanations

In the case of the Hindustan Steel Limited the present lowest two grades of Rs. 110 to Rs. 180 and Rs. 130 to Rs. 280 have been merged into one Rs. 117-300.

In the case of the Indian Iron and Steel Co. existing grades A, A'& B and B have been merged into a single grade of Rs. 95-200.

In the case of the Mysore Iron and Steel Ltd. the existing lowest three grades, viz. III Division and II Division Clerks and typists have been merged.

In the case of the Hindustan Steel Ltd. the present incumbents on the post of Lower Division Clerk shall be subjected to a test after reaching the stage of Rs. 189, only successful condidates will be eligible for the subsequent increments. This present incumbents of the post of Upper Division Clerk in the Hindustan Steel Ltd. and Senior Clerks in the Indian Iron and Steel Co. Ltd, will not be subjected to this test, similarly, in the case of the Indian Iron, there will be an Efficiency Bar at Rs. 160.

For future recruits the managements of the Steel Plants may revise the minimum qualifications for recruitment of ministerial staff.

Scales Of Lalaries: Scales of salaries and revise of dearness allowance for Ministerial staff in each of the Steel Plant shall be as in Schedule V.

Eitment: The following procedure should be followed in fitting the existing employees in revised scales;

Employees would be fitted at a step in the revised scale nearest to their own rate of pay in the existing scale so that the benefit received is not less than one scale increment of the revised scale.

Pro-Rata Payment: The existing daily rated employees who have been converted into monthly rated in departments or units in the Plant which work less than 18 shifts in a week will be paid pro-rata as at present.

Weekly Off: We have already recommended that all the employees should be given one full day's weekly off. Such of the existing daily rated employees in the town & medical departments of the Tata Iron and Steel Co. Ltd. who at present work for half-day on Sundays (but get full day's wages at present) will be given a full day weekly off, on their being converted into monthly rated, and an allowance equivalent to two day's basic wages will be paid as personal to them.

Safe Guards: Merely as a consequence of implementation of the recommendations of the Board, any facility, privilege, amenity, benefit monetary or otherwise, or concession to which an employee might be entitled, by way of practice, or usage shall not be withdrawn, reduced or curtailed without an agreement with the reconised union, unless there is a specific direction to that effect in these recommendations:

Disputes Regarding Fitments : If there be any dispute in respect of implementation of the recommendation of the Board regarding the fitment of employees in the proposed scales the same may be resolved by bipartite negotiations between the management of the Steel Plant and it's recognised union.

Date From Which The Recommendations Should Be Given Effect To : The recommendations of the Board shall come into effect from the 1st April, 1965.

DERAILMENT OF NO. 110 UP TRIVANDRUM-MADRAS PASSENGER AT SUNDARAPERUMAL KOIL STATION (SOUTHERN RAILWAY) ON 2ND MARCH, 1962—REPORT

Delhi, Manager of Publications, 1964 12p.

One-Man Commission : Shri H. S. Hart.

APPOINTMENT

The commission was constituted under the Ministry of Transport of Communications (Railway Inspectorate) in accordance with Rule 9 of the Railway Board's Notification No. 1926-T dated 19th March, 1930.

TERMS OF REFERENCE

To inquire into the derailment of No. 110 Up Trivandrum-Madras Passenger at Sundaraperumalkoil Station on the Mayuram-Thanjavur Metre Gauge Main Line Section of the Southern Railway at about 19-46 hours on the 2nd March, 1962.

CONTENTS

Inquiry ; Description of the accidents ; Disposition of the engine and first two Coaches ; Casualties ; Composition of the train ; Damage ; Relief Arrangements ; Restoration of Communications ; Number of Passengers; Weather Conditions ; Description of Local Conditions (Description of the locality ; Description of the station and method of working ; Description of the Parmanent Way ; Permissible speeds) ; Summary of Evidence Observations and Tests (Track ; Engine and Rolling Stock ; Braking Test) ; Discussion (Time of the Accident ; Condition of the Points and Signals ; Possibility of Sabstage ; Condition of the Brakes ; Condition of the Engine ; Condition of the Coaches ; Speed of the train ; Responsibility of the Driver ; Condition of the Track ; Responsibility for the sharp curvature of the turn-in portion to road No. 3 ; Conclusions.

CONCLUSIONS

Cause Of The Accident

From the evidence available I have come to the conclusion that the derailment of No. 110 Up "Trivandrum-Madras Passenger" at Sundaraperumalkoil station on the Mayuram-Thanjavur Metre Gauge Main Line section of the Southern Railway at 19-46 hours on the 2nd March 1962 was due to the spread of gauge on the 50 lbs. B.H. cast iron pot sleeper road on the turn-in portion of the second loop at the Thanjavur end. I have also come to the conclusion that the spread of gauge was caused by the track being subjected to excessive flange forces exerted by the engine No. YP 2052 which in turn was due to :

(a) The curvature of the turn-in portion of road No. 3 at the spot being sharper than what is laid down in the Metre Gauge Schedule of Dimensions and the Indian Railways Way and Works Manual, and

(b) The spead of entry of No. 110 Up into the second loop being appreciably in excess of the prescribed maximum of 10 m.p.h.

Responsibility For The Accident

(i) The Permanent Way Inspector, Shri L. Amalraj, was responsible for the accident, in as much as he failed to check the curvature of this turn-in curve to the second loop and ensure that the curvature was within the prescribed limits. He thereby violated G.R. 198 (a).

This Permanent Way Inspector, who was meaning 55 years at the time, was originally appointed as a substitute clerk in November 1925, but later transferred as a temporary Permanent Way Sub-Inspector in September 1928. In October 1947, he was first promoted as a Permanent Way Inspector and had been in charge of this section since August 1961. During his 36 years' service, he had only the following adverse entries made against him in his service record :

(a) Warned in April 1942 for failure to maintain the Permanent Way in a yard during the hot weather.

(b) Warned for failing to report a contractor in connection with the manufacture of windows in November 1943.

(c) Censured in April 1953 for not having brought to the notice of his Assistant Engineer or Divisional Engineer the loss of sand ballast.

(ii) Driver Shri T.V. Dharmalingam was also responsible for the accident, inasmuch as he failed to reduce the speed of his train to 10 m.p.h. While entering the second loop, thus violating G.R. 90 (a).

This Driver, who was 53-1/2 years at the time, was originally recruited as a Cleaner in November, 1929. He was first promoted as a Driver in July 1946 and later promoted to officiate as Driver 'B' Grade with effect from June 1957, though reverted back as Driver 'C' Grade in April 1959. He was again promoted to officiate as a 'B' Grade Driver in July 1960. He had been last medically examined in September 1961 who he had been considered fit for service in Class A (i) with glasses. With regard to his general record, there had been a very large number of adverse entries in his service Record during the previous ten years, but mainly to the effect that his monthly fuel consumption had been heavy.

Relief Arrangements

I am satisfied that the first aid and medical relief rendered to the injured were both prompt and adequate. In this connection, special mention may be made of the services rendered by Dr. Swaminathan (a passenger in the train) and Dr. Paramahamsan of the Local Government Dispensary. Credit is also due to the prompt action taken by Dr. M.R. Kesavan (Resident Medical Officer, Government Hospital, Kumbakonam) and Drs. Ganapathy and Veerabhadran (Civil Surgeon and Assistant Surgeon, Thanjavur, respectively) who rushed to the site with ambulances and removed the more seriosuly injured passengers to the hospitals at Kumbakonam and Thanjavur. I have also to commend the sense of duty displayed by Shri S. Murugesan, Brakesman of No. 110 Up Passenger, who, despite having sustained a grievans injury himself, rendered help in rescuing the injured and attending to them after the accident.

JUTE COMMITTE, 1962—REPORT

New Delhi, Ministry of International Trade, 1963. 54p.

Chairman : Shri N.C. Srivastava.
Members : Shri K. V. Venkatachalam; Shri A. Bakshi; Shri S.C. Chaudhri.
Member - Secretary : Shri A. Mozoomdar.

APPOINTMENT

A target of 9,00,000 tons has been fixed for export of Jute manufactures in the Third Five Year Plan. Jute Manufactures occupy a very important position in the economy of the country inasmuch as they contribute the major share in the foreign exchange earnings of the country. It is important, therefore, to ensure that the industry fulfills the role assigned to it. With a view to examine the various factors affecting a steady increase in the exports of Jute manufacture, both in terms of quantity and value, and to suggest ways and means by which the industry can be enabled to achieve the target fixed in the Third Plan.

The Jute Committee was set up by the Government of India, Ministry of Commerce and Industry by its Memorandum No. 5 (1)-Tex (D)/62 dated March, 6/7, 1962.

TERMS OF REFERENCE

(1) The steps necessary to increase production of Jute goods in order to achieve the Third Plan target;

(2) The need for further modernization and expansion of the Jute industry;

(3) The steps required to maintain stability in the prices of Jute goods;

(4) Trend in the Indian Jute goods exports and the steps required to keep their prices competitive;

(5) Diversification of production for the manufactures of special fabrics/goods required by foreign countries;

(6) Availability of adequate supplies of raw materials (including jute cuttings) at economic prices;

(7) Measures required to improve the quality of Jute goods and;

(8) Machinery to deal with complaints against quality/specifications from foreign importers.

CONTENTS

Introduction; Consumption and Export Trends of Jute Manufacturers; Production Targets for Jute Goods; Raw Material Supply; Price Stabilisation;

Marketing of Jute Goods and Export Promotion ; Competition in Export Markets ; Summary of Conclusions and Recommendations ; Annexures From I to X.

RECOMMENDATIONS

India's Production And Export Of Jute Goods

The Indian Jute industry has passed through a series of upheavals in the years since Independence. Due to the war time diversion of jute manufactures to military purposes jute had lost a significant part of the packaging market in the U.S.A. and Europe to substitutes. With the partition of India in 1947, the Indian jute industry's source of raw material became insecure. Self-sufficiency in this material was attained only in 1959. The industry has modernised itself and has rationalised its production and increased the output of specialities. These are not able achievements. However, India's output of jute goods has not increased in proportion to the rise in the world consumption of goods in last decade. India's exports in the period 1950 to 1960 fluctuated between 8.5 lakh tons per annum. Whatever may have been the circumstances which in the past prevented a larger share of the increased world market from coming to the Indian jute industry it appears necessary to take energetic measures now to increase exports and take the fullest possible advantage of the increased world demand.

Growth Of World Consumption Of Jute Goods

The Committee considers that on the basis of the current trend in the world consumption of jute goods, there is likely to be additinal consumption of jute goods to the extent of 10,41,000 tons by 1970.

India's Share Of Export Markets

Indian exports of major types of jute goods are given in Annexure III. It is considered that there will be increased opportunities of exports of Indian jute goods to both Eastern and Western Europe and to those parts of Africa, Asia and Latin American which do not have facilities for developing jute industries of their won.

Internal Consumption Of Jute Goods

Internal consumption of jute goods has been steadily increasing. The average annual rate of increased in consumption during the First and Second Plan periods were 15,200 tons and 17,600 tons respectively. It is expected that the internal consumption will increase by about 30,000 tons a year in the remainder of the Third Plan reaching the level of 4 lakh tons per annum in 1965-66. Further it is considered that in the period 1966-71 an average annual increase in internal consumption should be planned at 40,000 tons raising the consumption level to 6 lakh tons in 1970-71.

Targets In The Third And Fourth Plans

The production and export targets included in the Third Plan and proposed tentatively for the Fourth Plan a-e as follows : –

	Unit	Third Plan by 1965-66	Fourth Plan by 1970-71
Export of jute goods	Lakh tons	9.00	11.00
Internal consumption of jute goods	,,	4.00	6.00
Total Production of jute goods	,,	13.00	17.00
Requirement of fibre	Lakh bales	75.00	98.00

The industry needs expension and the necessary planning should be taken in hand without delay.

The Working Time Agreement Of The I.J.M.A.

The installation of the additional capacity and the level of production in jute industry are at present strictly controlled by I.J M.A. under its working Time Agreement, which controls 96% of the jute looms installed in India and has been virtually unchanged since 1938.

As it appears that there are certain grave disadvantages inherent in the Working Time Agreement, the Committee has come to the conclusion that in view of the achievement of self-sufficiency in raw material and the rising demand for jute goods both internally and externally, there is no need for the continuance of the Agreement.

Priorities For Expension

While recognising the need for expansion, the committe suggests the priorities thus : (a) first priority should be for existing uneconomic units (b) the next priority may be for those units which, though economic, can achieve additional economies by expansion and (c) the establishment of new units may be taken up on the basis of regional needs provided raw materials and other facilities are available.

The Problem Of Power Supply

The Power available to the jute mills-about 88 MW is barelly sufficient to run the equivalent of single shift capacity of all the registered looms of the member mills of the I.J.M.A. The power requirements of 1,000 additional broad looms to be installed by the end of 1963 are estimated at 10 MW. Further, for increasing production by operating the full installed capacity for yarn continuously throughout the week, the power requirements have been estimated at 10 MW. It is necessary to ensure by some means that in the short term, the working of this vital export industry is not hammpered by the dearth of power. If by the end of the Fourth Plan period, the production of jute goods is to rise by 4,00,000 tons over the Third Plan target, additional power requirement will be about 40 MW. This should be kept in view while planning for power requirement of the Calcutta area in the Fourth Plan.

Trends Of Raw Jute Production

The area under jute in Indian the last 15 years and the area under mesta in the last 10 years are shown in Annexure VI.

The Committee considers that the area under jute and mesta in the Third and subsequent plans should be stabilised at around 20 lakh acres and 8 lakh acres respectively. The targets of fibre output should be achieved by raidly raising they yield per acre of both jute and mesta and not by encroachment in the area under food grains.

Shortfall In Second Plan Targets

There were serious shortfalls in the targets set in respect of use of improved seeds, fertilisers and improved methods of cultivation.

Measures To Increase Yield Per Acre

The yield per acre in certain areas has not shown any appreciable improvement in the last few years. It should be possible by the end of Third Plan period to increase the average yield to 3.3 bales per acre could be achieved. The Committee considers that a fresh programme of saturation of all the jute growing areas with the best available seed within a period of say 3 years should receive priority and should be executed by the end of the Third Plan. It is estimated that about 1.8 lakh maunds of improved seed would be required to cover 20 lakh acres under jute. The requirement of improved seed would thus be about 60,000 maunds per year against the output at present of only 6,000 maunds a year. The Committe has also recommended grant of increased subsidy, seed multiplication by registered grower outside main jute growing areas, payment of fair price to them etc.

The allotment of fertilisers for jute cultivation should receive priority and the allocation for mesta should be on the same basis as for jute. The distribution machinery should be reviewed by the respective States and the Ministry to ascertain whether additional distribution points ; batter storage and more fertiliser loans could accelerate the consumption of fertiliser for jute and mesta cultivation. The need for concession on the fertiliser price for remote and inaccelerate the concession on the fertilizer jute growing areas in Assam, North Bengal & North Bihar should be examined in view of the high transport cost.

Retting facilities should be improved at a more rapid pace. The model scheme drawn up by the I.C.J.C. should be implemented.

Schemes should be undertaken for the development of mesta also by the production of improved better yielding strains, seed multiplication, fertiliser distribution assistance for improved practices, plant protection measures etc.

Jute Development Board

With a view to facilitating the effective implementation of the development programmes, and to achieve a break through in this vitally important matter of increasing jute yield, the Committee suggests that the Union Government should set up a high powered jute Development Board under the control of the Ministry of Food & Agriculture. The major jute growing State may be represented on the Board through their Secretaries of Agriculture. The functions of the Board should also cover jute marketing, stabilization of jute prices and jute transport. The Board should be associated with the Burffer Stock Agency. It should also come in the picture of promoting measures for stabilising prices of jute manufactured goods.

The staff under State Governments dealing with jute development should be strengthened.

Import Of Long Jute And Cuttings

With the expansion in the manufacture of specialities, the requirements of high grade long jute will grow, and if the output of the best qualities, of Indian jute is not adequate more long jute may have to be improved. The import of limited quantities of cuttings is also recommended by the Committee provided by adequate price support machinary, foreign exchange is available and the price of imported cuttings are reasonable.

Measures To Ensure Stability In Price Of Jute Goods

Instability of prices has been single most important adverse factor affecting competitive position of jute manufactures in world markets. A policy of supporting the price of jute above pre-determined "floor" by means of buffer stock operations was adopted for the first time in the 1961-62 season.

The committee considers that the Government should have full operational control over any Agency which may be entrusted with buffer stock operations and price support arrangements.

The availability of adequate storage capacity in Calcutta for buffer stock should be checked and warehousing facilities in the main terminal markets expanded. Additional storage facilities in the mofussil areas should also be developed.

It is necessary to ensure that in the peak marketing

period each season the purchase of jute by the mills matches the quantity of jute on offer. The Committee also recommends that derivative prices corresponding to the "floor" price at Calcutta should be fixed at all secondary markets and supported by buffer stock operations.

High priority should be given by the State Governments to the establishment of a series of "regulated markets" in the jute growing areas so that no jute grower has to take his jute more than five miles to reach such a market. States which do not have law in regard to the establishment of regulated markets should enact necessary legislation and take other steps to set up these markets. Sales in these markets would be by open bids, weights would be checked and unfair practices would be largely eliminated.

Further, Cooperative Jute Marketing and ware housing organizations should be developed on a much larger scales than has hither to been possible. As much as possible of the buffer stock purchases should be made through the cooperatives.

To minimise fluctuations in the prices of jute goods due to seasonal or short-term changes, the Committee recommends the establishment of Jute Goods Buffer Stock. The same Buffer Stock agency could handle both the raw jute and jute goods buffer stock. The buffer stock of goods should aim at restricting the fluctuations in jute and jute goods prices to (say) 5 % either way. The jute Development Board recommended in paragraph 16 should come in the picture in regard to the Jute Goods Buffer Stock also.

The Committee also recommends a further strengthening of the checks which the Forward Markets commission has in recent years imposed on speculative dealings in the jute and jute goods markets several steps have been specifically recommended.

D.G.S. & D. should make purchases in a way which would assist in stabilishing prices of jute goods.

Market Intelligence And Demand Forecasting

Further efforts to study and develop markets abroad in a systematic manner on long-term basis should be made. The export potential to the U.S.S.R. and Eastern Europe has not been sufficiently assessed. The consumption trends in East and West Africa, the Middle East and South East Asia should also be studied.

The Committee suggests that the office of the Jute Commissioner should create an effective system of market intelligence for all the consuming countries. To enable the Jute Commissioner's office to under take market reasearch and short and long term domand forecasting, the organisation should be suitably strengthened.

Trade With Eastern Europe

Large increase in the planned economies of Eastern Europe. The Committee suggests that these should be consultations between the Government of India and these countries to determine the extent to which India's production of jute goods can be coordinated with the five or Seven Year Plans of each of these countries. It should be possible to develop longer-term agreements for the export of jute goods to these countries in lieu of the current annual trade agreements.

Trade With Western Europe

The total trade of India with Western European countries constituted 8.9 % of India's total exports of jute goods Trade with these countries could not develop. Substantially mainly due to quota restrictions except in U.K. for coventional goods.

The Committee suggests that the effect of Indian jute goods exports due to quota restrictions in these countries should be studied in detail so that effective steps could be taken to negotiate with these countries to increase India's share of the market for jute goods.

Diversification And Product Development

Jute can hold its ground against substitutes like synthetic fibres only if it shows the same degree of adaptability to technological change and awareness of consumers' requirements and taste. Indian Jute industry has so far played little or no part in this process of adaptation and new product development, and is unwilling to take up orders for small lots of "non-standard" items with consequent loss of orders.

The Committee recommends the creation of a Product Development. Cell in the Jute Commissioner's Organisation under the supervision of a experienced jute technologist. The cell which should maintain close liaison with I.J.M.A. Research Institute & Techonological Research Laboratories of I.C.J C. should keep a breast of the latest technological developments abread, suggest new lines of applies research to the laboratories, examine the need for pilot plant trials etc.

Broadlooms

One of the most important developments in the jute industry in recent years has been the growth in the production of wide hessian of high quality used in the manufacture of tufted carpets.

The Committee understands that there is considerable scope for expanding the export of carpet-backing to Australia and West Europe. For the Planned development of carpet-backing production, the Jute Commissioner's Office should make a detailed study on a priority basis of the trends in the production and consumption tufted carpets so as to be able to make a reasonable forecast of the future demand for wide hessian.

The Committee further suggests that the possibility

of manufacture of tufted carpets in India for export should also be considered.

Quality Control

The Committee endorses the recommendations made by the ad hoc Committee on quality Control and Preshipment Survey that (i) the ISI standards for jute manufactures for inspection within the mills at the stage of production should be finalised without delay ; (i) there should be a procedure for inspection within the mills at the stage of production in accordance with I.S.I. Certification Marks Scheme.

Complaints

The arbitration provisions in the standard export contract from need not be altered ; but representatives of foreign buyers' associations may be included in the arbitration panel at Calcutta if they so desire. Indian exporters should be registered by the Jute Commissioner's office and the registering authroity should intervence to settle disputes here necessary. There should be provision for deregistration in the event of unfair trade practices.

Competition

The Committee is of opinion at the extent of competition other than from Pakistan is not immedately significant but the growth of production in all the competing countries should be closely watched by the proposed market intelligence organisation so that effective steps may be taken at the right time to present loss of export markets to India.

Tariff And Quota Restrictions

The Committee views with concern India's inability to obtain reductions in protective duties especially in U.S.A. Japan, Argentina and Canada.

With the proposed entry of U.K. into European Common market, not only will the U.K. Jute control disappear but the tariff and quota restrictions policy of the E.C.M. will assume greater importance to the future of Indian jute goods export. It appears that the E.C.M. will insist on a 18 to 20% common external tariff on all types of jute goods.

The Committee considers that in the negotiations leading to a trade treaty between India and the enlarged. E.C.M. the following objectives must be sought to be achieved :

(a) There should be a nil tariff or a very low tariff on export of sacking to Western Europe ;

(b) The common external tariff on hessian should be gradually reduced ;

(c) The continuance of the existing quota restrictions and any attempt to introduce new quotas whether country wise or for the common market as a whole must be resisted ; and

(d) The planners of the European Common Market have to be urged in these negotiations to keep in mind that the Common market should lead to a larger volume of trading with countries outside the market. Protection to the relatively high cost European industry against exports of manufactured goods by the developing countries would be inconsistent with this objective.

Measurers To Reduce Costs

Considerable economies have been achieved in recent years by modernisation, improved processing and formation of larger units by amalgamation of mills. The Committee feels what when additional jute goods production becomes necessary, it should be achieved by working more looms on double shift.

The remaining old prepartory and spining machinery should be replaced at the earliest. It is necessary that every assistance including foreign exchange for imports where necessary, should be given by Government to enable the industry to replace worn out and obsolete carding equipment and to instal high-speed winding equipment and pre-beamers, which improve both quality and output. Arrangements for giving loans for modernisation should be made.

A phased programme for loom modernisation should be drawn up by the jute Commissioner. Early decision should be taken as to the alternative types of automatic looms offered by U.K. manufacturers.

Supply Of Jute Mill Machinery & Foreign Exchange Requirements

The committee recommends that out of the foreign exchange allocation for Jute industry, the highest priority should be given to the machinery manufacturers' needs of imported capital goods and components. At the same time the manufacturers of Jute mill machinery should prograssively increase the indigenous components up to 80% in 3 years. As the Jute industry is an important foreign exchange earner, its needs of foreign exchange should be given priority. The Committee has also recommended prorities within the Jute industry itself.

Export Incentive In The Form Of Machinery

The Committee has recommended that as an incentive to export, a scheme may be worked out for import entitlemen's in respect of essential Jute machinery. Further, as a special case, in view of the high export potential of this industry, the import of machinery may be extend even to machinery for priority industries other than Jute.

Increased Productivity

It appears to the Committee that there is considerable scope for cost reduction by way of checking stores consumption and developing suitable methods of inventory control, undertaking work-study, introduction of statistical quality control system, etc. The committee welcomes the study by the National Productivity Council.

The committee recommends the adoption of "unform costing" by the Jute industry leading to a system of regular inter-firm comparisons of operating data, costs of production and marketing and utilisation of resources.

COMMITTEE TO EXAMINE THE EXISTING SYSTEM OF GRANT OF SUBSIDY AND SUBVENTION TO THE FLYING AND GLIDING CLUBS, 1962—REPORT

New Delhi, Ministry of Transport and Communications, 1963. 153p.

Chairman : Shri G. Narayanaswami.
Member : Lt. Col. G. V. Raja.
Member-Secretary : Shri Babar Mirza.

APPOINTMENT

On the recommendations made by the Master Committee in 1953, the Government of India had evolved a scheme for payment of subsidy and subvention to the Flying Clubs in India. The scheme was brought in force with effect from the Ist April, 1954 vide the late Ministry of Communications letter No. 14-A/6-(53)/2 dated July 31, 1954/August 2, 1954. A scheme for the payment of subsidy and subvention to the Gliding Clubs/Gliding Wings of the Flying clubs has also been sanctioned vide Ministry of Transport and Communication (Departments of Communications & Civil Aviation) letter No. 15-VE (27)/59, dated September 22, 1959. Certain difficulties have been brought to the notice of the Government of India in connection with the working of these schemes. The Government of India, Ministry of Transport and Communications (Departments of Communications and Civil Aviation) Constituted a Committee to examine the existing system of the grant of subsidy and subvention to the Flying and Gliding Clubs and to recommend the procedure to be followed in maintenance of the accounts by the Clubs, by their Order No. 15-VE (35)/61 dated March, 20, 1962.

TERMS OF REFERENCE

(i) To work out the standard cost of operation of the Gliding Clubs, and of Class I, II, III and IV Flying Clubs and their branches based on different types of aircraft operated by the Flying Clubs, having regard to the changes that have taken place in the Flying pattern of the clubs and the increased cost of spare parts, fuel and other materials and the pay structure of their employees;

(ii) To review the working of the existing subsidy scheme and to determine whether the results achieved by the grants-in-aid sanctioned to the Flying Clubs and Gliding Clubs under the existing orders are commensurate with the expenditure incurred, and to make recommendations for the modification of the existing schemes, having particular regard to:

(a) the cost of operation of the clubs as determined by the Committee;
(b) the various sources of revenues of the Clubs, including the grants-in-aid sanctioned by the Central Government and the State Governments;
(c) the amounts of insurance for which the Pilot-Instructors of the Clubs should be compulsorily insured.

(iii) To study the existing instruction for accounting of the grants-in-aid sanctioned by the Central Government and the assistance received from other sources including State Governments and to recommend :

(a) rate of contribution to the Accident Reserve Fund;
(b) rate of contribution to the Replacement Fund;
(c) instructions to be followed in preparing the annual balance sheet and the income and expenditure account with a view to ensuring that the grants are spent for the purpose for which they are intended and the monies are accounted for properly.

CONTENTS

Introductory; Development of Flying Clubs; Terms of Reference of the Committee and scope of Enquiry; Review of Revenue and Expenditure of Flying Clubs;

Standard Cost of operation of Flying Clubs; Factors Affecting the cost of operation of the Flying Clubs under Standard Condition; Scheme of Subsidy and Subvention to Flying Clubs; Reserve Funds; Accounting Instructions; Miscellaneous Matters Relating to Flying Clubs; Gliding Clubs; Summary of Recommendations; Acknowledgements; Appendix I to XV.

RECOMMENDATIONS

Control Over Expenditure

Action should be taken for preparation of detailed estimates of all expenditure including expenditure on spares and stores required for the following year. Purchase should be made according to need.

Trainer Aircraft For Ab-Initio Training

Government should keep a reserve of suitable aircraft for supply to Clubs. If training Aircraft and equipment in the Clubs is standardised and made uniform there would be considerable saving in the annual recurring expenditure.

Aircraft For Advanced Flying

Government should take appropriate steps in order that the Clubs could be equipped with one or two aircraft with R/T equipment suitable for ad night flying and long distance cross-country.

Disposal Of Aircraft In Excess Of Requirement

The Clubs which are unable to make justifiable use of the full fleet should store their surplus aircraft without incurring any expenditure on their maintenance and annual overhaul. They should be brought into use only if any when flying potential is increased. Such Clubs may also consider selling surplus aircraft to other Clubs in need.

Utilisation Of Aircraft

Minimum utilisation should be fixed at 500 hours per year per airworthy aircraft. It should be possible for a Club to have 75 per cent of its working fleet in a serviceable condition and to achieve 500 hours per annum on each of such aircraft.

Strength Of Staff

The Committee has fixed the standard strength of various categories of staff in the different classes of Clubs. Clubs should try to confirm gradually to the standard strength and economise their expenditure.

Pay Scales Of Technical And Other Staff

Standard rates of pay and allowances should be fixed for all staff. No further additions to pay such as conveyance allowance or bonus are necessary once proper scales of pay and allowances have been fixed. Scales of pay and allowance of subordinate Engineering staff and staff connected with the administration of the Clubs should as far as possible not exceed the scales of pay and allowances laid down by the State Government under similar conditions. The standard scales of pay as recommended by the Committee take into account the past recommendations made by the Aero Club of India. The Clubs should in the coming years be in a position to fix the pay of their staff on the standard scales recommended by the Committee.

Cadre Of Chief Pilot Instructors And Cheif Engineers

For the enforcement of standard scales of pay and for effecting a better administrative control and the systematic training of pilots, the Committee recommends that the Chief Pilot Instructors and Chief Engineers working with the clubs should be borne on two separate cadres under the administrative control of the Director General of Civil Aviation. They will be treated as Government servants on loan to Clubs. The cadres may contain their own leave reserve and promotions to them regulated by the Director General of Civil Aviation from the Junior Instructors and Engineers working in the Clubs. A scheme of Contributory Provident Fund and grant of retirement gratuities may also be instituted.

Service Conditions Of The Staff

Rules and regulations regarding conditions of appointment, promotion, leave scales of pay, grant of increment conduct, discipline, right of appeal against punishment, etc., should be laid down by the management of the Clubs preferablly on a uniform basis.

Contributory Provident Fund should be instituted in all the Clubs. Rate of interest which the amounts in the Provident Fund should carry should be laid down and annual accounts given to each member of the staff. The Fund should be administered either by the Provident Fund Commissioner or by an independent Trust consisting of representatives of employees and the employer. The Amount should be invested in Securities on the advice of the Provident Fund Commissioner.

Uniform rules should be made by the Clubs for grant of advances to the employees.

Pay and allowances of the staff should be disbursed promptly. Managing Committee of each Club should review its financial position frequently to avoid delays in payment.

Insurance Of Pilot Instructors

The Pilot Instructors should be covered by Personal Accident (Adviation Risks) insurance only. The amount of insurance for the various categories of Instructors as recommended by the Committee are :

	Rs.
Confirmed Chief Pilot Instructor	35,000
Officiating Chief Pilot Instructor	30,000
Pilot Instructor holding independent charge	25,000
Pilot Instructor working under Chief Pilot Instructor	20,000
Assistant Pilot Instructor	15,000

Concessional rates of premia may be obtained from Aviation Insurance in case the insurance policies of all the Club Instructors are taken with them. There is no objection to a Flying Club paying an amount towards extra premium on the Life Policy of an Instructor in lieu of Accident Insurance provided the Instructor indemnifies the Club against all accident risks and the amount paid by the Club does not exceed the premium payable in respect of the Accident Insurance for the Instructor.

It is not necessary for a Club to pay for insurance against loss of licence in addition to Accident Insurance.

Honorary Instructors at the Clubs may be insured for accident risks if they enter into agreement to serve the Club for the period for which the insurance is effected.

Performance Of Pilot Instructors

A Chief Pilot Instructor should be able to do a minimum of 400 hours of annual instructional flying and other Pilot Instructors and Assistant Pilot Instructors should do a minimum of 500 hours in a year in addition to imparting ground instructions to the trainees.

Scheme Of Subsidy And Subvention To Flying Clubs

The most rational way of determining the method which should govern the grant of subsidies and subvention should be based on the estimated expenditure of the Clubs under the standard conditions. On this basis the scheme of subsidy recommended by the Committee for 4 classes of Clubs is :

	Rs.
Class IV Below 1600 hours of instructional flying	50,000
Class III Below 2400 hours of instructional flying	75,000
Class II Below 3200 hours of instructional flying	1,00,000
Class I Below 4000 hours of instructional flying	1,20,000

Clubs doing more than 4000 hours will get a subsidy of Rs. 1,30,000. All the clubs will get subvention at a uniform rate of Rs. 50 per hour of the instructional flying. For flying hours done by the HT-2 aircraft an extra subvention of Rs. 20 per hour may be given. The subsidy includes a bonus of Rs. 400 for each Private Pilot's Licence trained at a Club. The Club would also get in addition Rs. 150 for each trainee who obtains a Private Pilot's Licence in the year. This amount is to be disbursed to the trainee.

The bonus of Rs. 400 may be distributed to the Instructional and Engineering staff. The Committee discourages any further payments by the Clubs to their Instructors and other staff, in the shape of bonus over and above the grant of Rs. 400 for each Private Pilot's Licence trained.

Subsidy Scheme For Satellite Centres

A Statellite Centre should be expected to do a minimum of 500 hours of instructional flying per year and paid a fixed subsidy of Rs. 25,000 per annum and a subvention @ Rs. 50 per hour flown. A Satellite Centre achieving a minimum of 1200 hours may be treated as a full fledged Club and subsidised under the main scheme.

Accident Reserve Fund

The present minimum in the Accident Reserve Fund of Rs. 6,000 per aircraft of Rs. 30,000 whichever is greates for dispensing with insurance of aircraft should be raised to Rs. 10,000 per aircraft or Rs. 50,000 whichever is greater. The contribution to the Accident Reserve Fund should be at the same rates as at present. Clubs should cover their fleet with the Accident Reserve Fund when the amount in the Fund reaches the above limits. The maximum amount in the Accident Reserve Fund should be the total value of the aircraft in the Club, Excess amount over this maximum may be permitted by the Director General of Civil Aviation to the transferred to Replacement Reserve Fund, if required. Withdrawals from the Accident Reserve Fund may also be permitted to be made for replacing major components when the expenditure is large. Insurance against ground risk is not necessary when the fleet is covered by the Accident Reserve Fund but a Club can, at its discretion, take such a cover provided it is Dispensed with when the amount in the Accident Reserve Fund has reached the maximum limit.

Replacement Reserve Fund

Contributions to this Fund should be made regularly at the prescribed rates both for Club owned aircraft and Government loaned aircraft.

Accounting Instruction

Separate Income & Expenditure accounts should be prepared in respect of the Flying and Social activities of the Clubs. A separate account, in addition to the annual published accounts, should also be prepared to show the direct and indirect expenditure incurred on the maintenance of State Government aircraft and for services rendered.

Clubs should prepare annually estimates of their Income & Expenditure in the form prescribed. They should also prepare monthly statement of expenditure for the last 5 months of the year and send them to the Director General of Civil Aviation. No Capital expenditure beyond a reasonable limit say Rs. 2,000 should be incurred without the approval of the Director General of Civil Aviation.

Social Activities

Social activities are recognised as necessary at each Club. Common items of receipts and expenditure of the Club should be allocated between the Flying side and the Social side on an equitable basis as recommended by the Committee in order that the Flying side accounts may present a true picture.

Clubs which do not have any Social activities at present may be permitted to fund the portion of the receipts into a Fund (Social Amenity Fund) to be utilised later.

Procedure For The Accounting Of Stores

The Procedure recommended in Appendix X may be followed in all the Clubs as a defective procedure was noticed in certain Clubs.

The management of the Clubs should be tightened up so far as flying activities are concerned. Managing Committee should ensure that the programme of training for the pupils is adhered to.

No trainee should be allowed to continue as a member without voting right for more than 3 months if he has obtained a Private Pilot's Licence.

The provision that the Managing Committee or the Board of Directors shall consist of 1/3rd active flying members should be made mandatory. Government may, grant exemption in specific cases.

The Honorary Secretary of a Club should be assisted by a full time assistant to supervise the day to day working of the Club and to bring to the notice of the Managing Committee all matters connected with management, discipline, training, etc. The Chief Pilot Instructor or any other member of the staff should not be on the Managing Committee.

A senior officer of the Civil Aviation Department assisted by an accounts staff should be periodically deputed to inspect the records of the Clubs to ensure that the training is properly imparted and the initial accounts are properly kept.

This unit will also look into the difficulties which the Clubs may have in their day to day working.

Concession To Office Bearers

The expenditure on the grant of concession to the office bearer and staff should be economised and regulated on a uniform basis.

Extravagant Expenditure : The clubs should economised expenditure on all items particularly on motor transport telephones and nonrevenue flying.

Purchase Of Spare Parts : The Clubs should take steps to regulate their expenditure on stores to prevent large accumulations.

Workshop Facilities : Facilities for overhaul of engines should be concentrated at selected Clubs in such a manner that other Clubs can avail of the facilities at reasonable cost.

The economise expenditure on Certificate of Airworthiness of aircraft, it is suggested that it may be carried out on completion of prescribed number of hours of flying instead of annually. The Committee presumes that the Director General of Civil Aviation will issue instructions in the matter.

Scheme Of Scholarship : Aptitude of trainees selected for the grant of scholarships should be tested and those who are well grounded in science or other subjects should be preferred. Scholarships are to be awarded only to deserving, pupils irrespective of the consideration of their parental income subject to usual reservation for Scheduled Castes and Scheduled Tribes candidates.

Policy of the grant of scholarships by certain State Governments for advanced training should be reviewed.

Scholars whose parent's or guardian's income is less than Rs. 300 per month may be given a sum of Rs. 200 in suitable instalments to meet their out of pocket expenses.

Scholars and/or their guardian should sign an undertaking to refund the cost scholarship in case the trainee discontinues his training before its completion.

Written examination for the issue of a Private Pilot's Licence may be on the American Quiz system to test the knowledge of the trainees and they may be held as frequently as possible, if not once in a month.

The number of subsidised hours of scholarships should be raised from 40 to at least 75 hours with reference to the new Licensing Rules. State Governments should also be informed.

Training Of Instructors : Immediate steps should be taken to train sufficient number of Instructors and to evolve a machinery to subject the existing Instructors to appropriate check. Training should be on voluntary basis and trained personnel expected to find jobs on their own.

Charges For Flying Training : All persons upto 37 years of age may be allowed subsidised flying @ Rs. 10 per hour upto the number of hours fixed per annum. Those above the age of 37, should be required to pay Rs. 25 per hour. Lt. Col. G. V. Raja, a member of the Committee, however, considers that the rate should uniformly be Rs. 10 per hour irrespective of age.

The non-subsidised rate may be fixed at Rs. 60 per hour and the full rate at the standard cost of operation of the Club according to its classification. Actual extra expenditure incurred on night and cross-country flying by a member of the Club (other than an ab-initio trainee) may be recovered from him by the club.

Flying charges for foreign nationals should be the same as for Indian nationa's.

Joy Rides And Charter Flights : Joy rides help in spreading airmindedness. Rates recommended are Rs. 5 and Rs. 10 per flights of 5 and 10 minutes duration respectively. Rates for charter flights may be fixed by the Director General of Civil Aviation with reference to the standard cost of operation of each Club.

Insurance Of Engineering And Other Technical Staff : The Chief Engineer or the Aircraft Maintenance Engineer who may be required to fly on test flights may be insured at Club expense for Rs. 15,000 or Rs. 10,000 respectively for a maximum of say 25 hours. Insurance of any other staff is not necessary.

Expenditure on insurance of trainee pilots should not be a burden on the Clubs The trainees could, however, do so at their own expense.

Clubs At Uncontrolled Landing Grounds : Suitable Civil Aviation Department representative should be posted at such places primarily to check the flying records on the basis of which financial assistance to a Club is determined.

Commercial Pilot's Training : Some Flying Clubs may be selected and permitted to impart training for obtaining a Commercial Pilot's Licence and the selected trainees may be given training at a reasonably subsidised rate without guaranteeing any employment.

Remunerative Activities At Clubs And Incentive For Pilots : The Clubs may be encouraged initially to engage in such remunerative activities which may not need acquisition of any additional equipment of any specialised training of pilots. To give an incentive to pilots, acquisition of a Private Pilot's Licence may be recognised as a preferement for employment.

Aero Club Of India : Its functions should enlarge and it should play a better role for the benefit of the Flying and Gliding Clubs to justify grants from the Government of India.

Air Rallies : Rallies may be held at periodical intervals. The Committee presumes that Government would continue the same concessions and also render financial assistance as have been given in the past.

Aeromodelling : It may be encouraged and introduced as an item of sport in Schools and Colleges.

Training Of Instructors And Winch Operators : Adequate facilities should be provided for training such personnel.

Gliding And Other Equipment : If gliders and winches are to be loaned to the Clubs by Government, adequate steps should be taken to give the minimum number of gliders any winches in order that the activities may not be hampered. Government may sanction an outright grant for the purchase of a jeep to Clubs which are not in a position to acquire it from their own funds.

Cables should be procured by Government on an estimate of annual requirement and their conditions of service should be standardised as in the case of Flying Clubs so that no Gliding Club could exceed the standard cost as worked out.

Fees For Training And For Joy Rides : The existing rate of Re. 1 per launch may continue.

Revised Rates Of Subsidy And Subvention For Gliding Clubs

Fixed subsidy:

	Rs.
For Clubs performing 15000 to 3000 launches	20,000
For Clubs performing 3000 to 4500 launches	25,000
For Clubs performing 4500 to 6000 launches	30,000

Subvention

Flat rate of Rs. 6 per launch (including joy rides) Gliding Clubs may be given an additional subvention @ Rs. 3 per launch to build up a reserve for eventual owning of gliders if it is proposed that ultimately the clubs would be expected to own gliders.

New Gliding Clubs

The minimum number of members for starting a new Club may be fixed at 50. The minimum number of launches required under the Subsidy Scheme viz. 1500 may be relaxed in special circumstances.

Accounting Instructions And Other Recommendations For the Economic Running Of The Gliding Clubs : The recommendations made in the case of Flying Clubs should be deemed to be equally applicable in the case of Gliding Clubs as far as may be relevant.

Gliding By NCC Cadets : National Cadet Corps gliding scheme may be coordinated with the activities of the Civil Gliding Clubs.

General

The Gliding Clubs should, as far as possible, be organised at places separate from the Flying Clubs and preferably near centres of education. Possibility of Starting new Clubs at airstrips and landing grounds where there is not much of air traffic may be explored.

WORKING GROUP SET UP BY COMMITTEE ON ADMINISTRATION FOR SIMPLIFICATION OF THE PUBLIC WORKS ACCOUNT CODE, 1962—REPORT

New Delhi, Cabinet Secretariat, 1963. 60p 11p.

Chairman : Shri A. K. Mukherji
Members : Shri R.N. Vasudeva ; Shri U.J. Bhat (not joined with the Committee) ; Shri B. K. Guha ; Shri D. P. Karnik.
Representative of the M.E.S. : Col. G. Benjamin.
Secretaries : Shri T. S. Vedagiri ; Shri P.K. Biswas.

APPOINTMENT

The Working Group for simplification of the Public Works Account Code was constituted under the Cabinet Secretariat, Department of Cabinet Affairs, Organisation & Methods Division vide their Memorandum 40/2/62-O&M dated May 2, 1962.

TERMS OF REFERENCE

For the simplification of the Public Works Account Code.

CONTENTS

Introductory; Works Accounts; Stores; Accounts; Suspense Accounts; Transactions with other Divisions; Departments and Governments; Submission of Accounts to Audit; Miscellaneous; Summary of Recommendations; Annexures.

RECOMMENDATIONS

It is not necessary for Audit to be supplied with Administrative Approvals.

Technical sanctions need be communicated to the A.G. only in respect of works relating to projects costing more than Rs. 2.5 lakhs and non-project works costing more than Rs. 10 lakhs.

Copies of the abstract of Estimates need not be supplied to Audit unless specifically asked for.

The existing restriction in the second proviso of para 77 of the C. P. W. A. Code regarding the processing of excess expenditure over an estimate viz., that the amount upto which an officer is empowered to sanction an original estimate should not be exceeded, should be removed.

A revised expenditure sanction should be necessary only if the actual expenditure exceeds the amount of original sanctions by more than 10%, instead of 5%, as at present.

The minimum monetary limit for classifying a work as "Major" work should be raised from Rs. 20,000 to Rs. 1 lakh.

In case of works executed through contractors the maintenance of accounts by sub heads may be dispensed with.

In the case of works done departmentally, or through contractors where the contract is for labour rates only, sub-head accounting may be confined to works costing more than Rs. 1 lakh.

The existing limit of sub-heads prescribed in para 258 of the C.P.W.A. Code may be raised from Rs, 2,000 to Rs. 20,000/.

Material-at-Site Accounts need not be maintained in respect of works executed through contractors.

In the case of works done departmentally, or through contractors, where the contract is for labour rates only, a M.A.S. Account may be maintained only if the estimated cost of the work is more than Rs. 1 lakh. This amount may be only a numerical account.

It is not necessary to maintain M.A.S. Account for "Minor" and repair Works.

Forms 25 and 27 in C P.W.A. series may be abolished and Forms C.P.W.A 26 (as revised, vide Annexure 3) may be used for all running and final payments.

Advance payments for works done but not measured, may be made at pre-determined levels, which may be indicated in the sanctioned Estimates.

Form C.P.W.A. 32, as revised (vide annexure 4) may be used in all cases in which its use is authorised.

The preparation and submission of Labour Reports may be dispensed with, except in the case of Muster Rolls containing names of more than 15 persons.

Part II of the Muster Rolls may be abolished.

A register of Unpaid Wages may be maintained in the Form given in annexure 5.

It is not necessary for the Divisional Accountant to recheck the entries made in the Measurement Books during the course of their "Annual Review".

The existing percentages for the scrutiny of Contractors' Bills and Muster Rolls with reference to Measurement Books in the Divisional and Sub-Divisional Offices should be reduced.

An uptodate Priced Vocabulary of Stores, showing the correct description and identifying code numbers of the various items (completed in respect of Issue Rates by the Divisions concerned) should be prepared and adopted throughout the Central P.W.D.

The, Register of Stock Receipts/Issues (form C.P.W.A.8) may be replaced by B in Cards.

The Abstract of Stock Receipts (Form C.P.W.A. 9) may be replaced by Goods Received Sheets.

The exi ting Form of Indent for Stores may be revised so as to provide separate columns for Stores indented and stores actually issued.

The Abstract of Stock Issues (Form C.P.W.A. 10) may be abolished and a monthly summary of Indents introduced instead.

The Half-yearly Balance Return of Stock (form C.P.W.A. 11) and the Half-yearly Register of Stock (Form C.P.W.A. 12) may be replaced by a Priced Stores Ledger).

A Division-wise Ledger of issues of Stores may be introduced.

The issue rate of an article of Stock may be fixed at the beginning of the year and it is not necessary to review/revise the same every half-year, and the issue rate need be revised only when material variations in the purchase rates are noticed.

Adjustment of profit or loss on stock and the allocation of the balance under the sub-head of stock among the works at the end of the year is not necessary and that the "profit" or "loss" should be taken into account while reviewing and fixing the issue rates for the next year.

A suitable percentage based on carriage and other incidental charges of the previous year should be worked out for haulage and added to the issue rate.

The storage charges may be fixed at the beginning of a year and added on a percentage basis so as to form part of the issue rate.

The receipt and issue of Tools and Plant may be entitled in the "Tools and Plant Received Sheets" and "Tools and Plant Indents" and a quantity ledger of Tools and Plant may be maintained in each sub-division.

The head "London Stores" may be abolished and the value of stores purchased through the India Stores Deptt., London, passed through "Purchases".

The cheque forms to be used for settlement of inter-divisional transactions should bear a distinct marking viz., "Payment by Book Adjustment only".

For supplies received through the D.G.S. & D., the Pay and Accounts Officers should obtain reimbursement of the payments (initially made by them to the suppliers) directly from the indenting Divisions, instead of claiming the amounts from the Accounts Officers, as at present.

The Land Acquisition Officers may be financed by the P.W. Divisional Officers direct and the advances made by the latter debited direct to the Works Accounts under a suspense head "Land Acquisition".

The submission of Rent Returns to Audit may be dispensed with altogether.

The form of the Extracts of Revenue Realised/ of Revenue may be simplified.

The submission to Audit of vouchers relating to payments made to Class IV Work-charged staff may be discontinued.

The possibility of converting as much of the W.C. Estt. as possible to regular Estt. should be explored.

The limit of vouchers not required to be submitted to audit should be raised to Rs. 250.

The levy of percentages on account of Estt. & Tools and Plant charges may be confined to Capital Works or Works where actual recovery is involved, i.e., those executed on behalf of other Govts., Railways, Defence Deptts., Commercial undertakings on non-Govt. bodies.

The percentage charges determined on the basis of the estimated costs of a work, may be levied annually on the expenditure incurred during the year.

The percentage for Estt. and Tools of Plant Charges may be revised once in every 5 years.

The Divisional Officers may send their first reply to an Audit Inspection Report direct to the A.G.

ANNEXURE 3

RUNNING ACCOUNT BILL

(C.P.W.A. Code, paragraphs 212, 215 and 217)

Final payments must invariably be made on forms printed on yellow paper which should not be used for intermediate payments.)

For Contractors—This form provides for (1) Advance Payments, and (2) Payments for measured works. The form of Account of Secured Advances, which has been printed separately, should be attached, where necessary.

Division...Sub-division.

Cash Book Voucher No...Dated

Name of Contractor..

Name of work...

Serial No. of this bill...

No. and date of his previous bill for this work...

Reference to Agreement No..

Date of written order to commence work..

Date of actual completion of work..

1 – Account of work executed

Item of work (grouped under "sub-head" and "sub-works" of estimate)	Unit	Rate	Quantity executed upto-date as per measurement book	Payments on the basis actual measurements. Up-to date	Since previous bill.	Remarks
1	2	3	4	5	6/7	
		Rs. np.		Rs. np.	Rs. np.	

Total value of work done to date (A)
Deduct value of work shown on previous bill.
Not value of work since previous bill (F)
Figure (F) in words-Rupees

When there are two or more entries in column 6 relating to each sub-head of estimate they should, in the case of works the accounts of which are kept by sub-heads, be totalled and the total recorded in column 7 for posting the works Abstract.

II Certificates and Signatures

The measurements on which are based the entries in columns 1 to 6 of Account I were made by.................... ....and are recorded at page.............................of measurement Book Nos.....................

Certified that in addition to and quite apart from the quantities of work actually executed as shown in column 4 of Account 1, some work has actually been done in connection with several items, and the value of such work (after deducting therefrom the proportionate amount of secured advances, if any, ultimately recoverable on account of the quantities of materials used therein) is in no case, less than the advance payments as per item of the Memorandum of Payments made or proposed to be made, for the convenience of the contractor, in anticipation of, and subject to the results of, detailed measurements, which will be made as soon as possible.

Dated signature of Officer preparing the bill ....
(Rank)......................................

....

Dated signature of contractor.

Dated signature of Officer authorising payment ....
(Rank)......................................

This signature is necessary only when the Officer who prepares the bill is not the Officer who authorises the payment. In such a case the two signatures are essential.

III—Memorandum of Payments

Total value of work actually measured, as per Acct. I, Col. 5, Entry (A) Rs. np. Total "up-to-date" advance payments for work not yet measured, as per details given below :

Rs. np. (B)

(a) Total as per previous bill...

(b) Since previous bill......................................as per page..............................of M.B. No................

Total "up-to-date" Secured Advances on security of materials, as per Annexure (Form 26 A). Col. 8. Entry (C).

Total (Items 1+2+3)..

Deduct amount withheld :

Figures for works Abstract

Rs. np.

(a) From previous bill as per last Running Account Bill

(b) From this Bill...............................

Balance, i.e. "up-to-date" payment...(Items 4-5). (K)*

Total amount of payments already made as per Entry (K) of last Running Account Bill No......................... of..................................forward with accounts for...........................19...........Payments now to be made, and detailed below :

*This figure should be tested to see that it agrees with the total of items 7 and 8.

	Rs.	np.	Rs.	np.
(a) By recovery of amounts creditable to this work :			(a)	
Total 5 (b)+(a) (G)				
(b) By recovery of amounts creditable to other works or heads of accounts :			(b)	
(c) By cheque				
Total 8 (b)+(c).......................(H)				

Pay Rs. (..................................)..................................**by cheque

Dated initials of Disbursing Officer.

Received Rs. (..................)..............as per above memorandum, on account of this work.

Dated the (Amount in vernacular)

Stamp,

†Witness........................ Full signature of Contractor

Paid by me, vide cheque No...dated...19

Dated initials of person actually making the payment.

**If the net amount to be paid is less than Rs. 10 and it cannot be included in a Cheque the payment should be made in cash, this entry being altered suitably and the alteration attested by dated initials.

Here specify the net amount payable vide items 8 (c).

The payee's acknowledgement should be for the gross amount paid as per items 8 (i.e. a+b+c.)

†Payment should be attested by some known person when the payee's acknowledgement is given by a mark, seal or thumb impression.

IV--REMARKS

(This space is reserved for any remarks which the Disbursing Officer of the Divisional Officer may wish to record in respect of the execution of the work, check of measurements or the state of contractor's account).

FORM 26 A

(To be annexed to Form 26 where necessary)

Division...Sub-division..

Name of Contractor..Name of Work..

S. No. of the Bill to which the.........Account pertains..............Cash Book Voucher No................dated...........

Account of "Secured" advance allowed on the security of materials brought to site.

Quantity outstanding from previous bill	Deduct quantity utilised in work measured since previous bill	*Quantity outstanding (including quantity brought to site since previous bill)	Full rate as assessed by the Divisional Officer	Description of Materials	Unit	Reduced rate at which advance is made	**Up-to-date amount of advance	Reference to Divisional Officer's written orders authorising the advance.	Reasons for non-clearance of advance when outstanding for more than three months.
1	2	3	4	5	6	7	8	9	10
			Rs. np.			Rs. np.	Rs. np.	No. Date	

Total amount outstanding as per this account..(C)

Deduct amount outstanding as per entry (C) Annexure to the previous bill.................

Net amount since previous bill (in words)...........Rupees.......................................(D)

*Entries relating to each description of materials should be posted thus column 3. First enter difference between quantities in columns 1 & 2.

Then show below this entry, the quantities, if any, brought to site against which a further advance has been authorised, this entry being prefixed by the plus sign. Finally, strike the total of the two entries, which will represent the total quantity outstanding.

**Entries in column 8 show the money values of the total quantities outstanding as per column 3.

*Certified, (1) that the plus quantities of materials shown in column 3 of the Account above actually been brought by the contract or to the site of the work and the contractor has not previously received any advance on their security (2) that these materials are of an imperishable nature and are all required by the contractor for use on the work in connection with items for which rates for finished work have been agreed upon, and (3) that a formal agreement in Form 31 signed and executed by the contractor in accordance with paragraph 288(a) of the Central Public Works Account Code is recorded in the Divisional Office.

Dated signature of officer preparing the Bill..............

(Rank)..............

**Dated signature of officer authorising payment.................

(Rank)..............

*These certificates must be signed by the Sub-Divisional Officer.

**This signature is necessary only when the officer who prepares the bill is not the officer who authorises the payment. In such a case the two signatures are essential.

ANNEXURE 4

PETTY WORKS REQUISITION AND ACCOUNT FORM C.P.W.A. 32

PART III—Summary of Charges

Breif Particulars	Cash book voucher or transfer entry book item No.	Final charges	Suspense Account (To be operated when necessary)	Total cost	Total of the month	up-to date total	Initials of S.D.O.	Initials of Divisional Accountant
Grand Total								

The work was completed on.................... Checked and found correct Remarks of Divisional Officer for Passing excess.

Signature of Sub-Divisional Officer Divisional Accountant Divisional Officer

ANNEXURE 5

REGISTER OF UNPAID WAGES

Name of Work.......................

Sl. No.	Muster Roll	Name of labourer	Father's name	Period to which the amount relates	Amount due	Amount paid	Initial of the SDO	Cash voucher No. and date	Remarks
1	2	3	4	5	6	7	8	9	10

Note :—The name of work should be mentioned at the top before recording the entries relating to that work.

COLLISION BETWEEN V. 414 DOWN MILITARY VEHICLES SPECIAL AND 1590 UP GOODS AT SIVARAMAPURAM STATION, SOUTHERN RAILWAY ON 24TH MAY, 1962—REPORT

Delhi, Manager of Publications, 1970. 20p.+ip.

One-Man Commission : Shri H. S. Hart.

APPOINTMENT

The Commission was constituted under the Ministry of Tourism and Civil Aviation (Commission of Railway Safety) in accordance with Rule 9 of the Railway Board's Notification No. 1926-T, dated the 19th March 1930.

TERMS OF REFERENCE

To inquire into the head-on collision that occurred between V. 414 Down Military Vehicles Special and 1590 Up Goods at Sivaramapuram Station on the Arkonam-Guntakal Broad Gauge Single Main line section of the Southern Railway at about 02-25 hours on the 24th May 1962.

CONTENTS

Corrigendum; Summary; Inspection and Inquiry; Preamble (Description of the accident; Casualties; Composition of the trains; Damage and disposition of the vehicles; Escorts; Weather conditions); Relief Measures (First-aid and medical assistance; Restoration of communications;) Local Conditions (Description of the Site; Description of the Station and system of working; Permissible Speeds); Summary of Evidence; Observations and Tests (Local of V. 414 Down; Braking Distance Tests); Discussion (Time of the accident; Cause of the accident; Safeguards provided in connection with the working of Sivaramapuram Station; Speed of V. 414 Down at the time of the collision; Condition of the brakes of the leading and the banking engines attached to V. 414 Down ; Brake Power of V. 414 Down; Responsibility of the Train Examining Staff; Responsibility of the Driver of the leading engine handling V. 414 Down; Probable causes of V. 414 Down getting out of control); Conclusions; Recommendations made by the Commission of Railway Safety in Connection with Collision between V. 414 Down Military Vehicles Special and 1590 Up Goods at Sivaramapuram Station Southern Railway, on 24th May, 1962; Annexures I and II.

CONCLUSIONS

Cause Of The Accident

From the evidence available, I have come to the conclusion that the collision between V. 414 Down Military Vehicles Special and 1590 Up Goods at Sivaramapuram station on the Arkonam-Guntakal Broad Gauge Single Main line section of the Southern Railway at about 02-25 hours on the 24th May 1962 was due to the train crew of V. 414 Down losing control of the train and passing the Down approach signals of Sivaramapuram station in the 'ON' position without authority, and colliding with 1590 up goods which was at the time being received into the station on signals.

Responsibility For The Accident

(a) The Driver of the leading engine of V. 414 Down Shri K. C. Venkataraman, was primarily responsible for the collision in terms of General Rule 77, in that he failed to exercise sufficient care, lost control of his train, and passed the Down approach signal's of Sivaramapuram station in the 'ON' position without authority.

This Driver whose evidence was tendered in a very straight forward manner, is 30 years of age and has been in service for the last 11 years, having been engaged as a Fireman Apprentice in March 1951. He was promoted as a Driver 'C' Grade with effect from May 1958 and has had the following punishments :

(i) Censured for overstayal of leave without prior sanction in April 1954.

(ii) Increment due in 1956 withheld for one month for being absent without leave or medical certificate.

(iii) Increment due in 1959 withheld for 3 months in connection with detention to a Goods train.

(iv) Increment due in 1960 withheld for 2 months for being held responsible for the parting of a Goods train.

He was last medically examined in December 1959 and passed in Class A !

(b) The Driver of the banking engine of V. 414 Down, Shri C. Obalesu, was also responsible for applying the vaccum brake, thereby vitiating to some extent the attempts of the Driver of the leading engine to restore the vaccum by blowing up with the large ejector. He thereby violated the provisions of Subsidiary Rule 77 (iii) (b) and paras 6 (h) (ii) and (iii) of the Southern Railway's "Pamphlet Containing the Rules and special Instructions for the use of the Automatic Vacucum Brake on Trains". It cannot, however, be said with any certainty that his applying of the vacuum brake made any significant contribution to the accident.

This Driver is 52 years of age and was appointed as a Fuel Cooly in January 1929. He was initially promoted as a 'C' grade Driver in November 1954 and was confirmed as such in January 1957. Since 1950 he has had the following punishments :

(i) Censured in July 1952 for being responsible for a late start to a goods train.

(ii) Censured in August 1955 for not creating sufficient vaccum while banking No. 9 Mail.

(iii) Suspended from duty from December 1956 to April 1957---this being later regularised as suspension period only.

(iv) Increment due in April 1958 withheld for 21 months for poor engine manship.

(v) Censure for excessive fuel consumption in December 1958.

(vi) Censured in September 1959 for obstructive working.

(vii) Censured in February 1960 for mismanagement of his engine while banking a goods train.

(viii) Increment due in April 1961 withheld for 21 months.

(ix) Censured for being heavy in fuel consumption in September 1960.

The Driver's record is not good. His replies were also inclined to be evasive and were not given in a straight-forward manner.

Relief Measures

The Assistant Station Master Cuddapah stated that an engine and brake van were ready on the platform by 03-00 hours, but that the Assistant Surgeon only brought the necessary medical equipment to the station by 03-50 hours. The Station Master Cuddapah also stated that the Assistant Surgeon only came to the station with his equipment at about 03-45 hours, and this has been corroborated by the Traffic Inspector. The Assistant Surgeon, however, in his evidence stated that he came to the station with his equipment by 03-30 hours and that the engine and brakevan were not ready at the time. The train only left Cuddapah at 03-55 hours and this avoidable delay should be investigated by the Railway Administration.

Information was given by Control to Nandalur to start the Medical Van Special at 02-45 hours, but it only left at 03-15 hours. The delay in starting this Medical Relief Van Special from Nandalur should be looked into by the Railway Administration.

MOTOR VEHICLES INSURANCE COMMITTEE, 1962—REPORT

Delhi, Manager of Publication 1963. 146p.

Convenor : The Deputy Secretary Incharge of Road Transport Division in the Ministry of Transport & Communications, Department of Transport, New Delhi.

Members : The Controller of Insurance, Simla or his representative; Secretary to the Government of West Bengal, Home, (Transport) Department, Calcutta; Member, Motor Accident Claims Tribunal, Bombay; Shri D. S. Dikshit ; Shri A. A. Jasdenvala ; Shri G. A. Desai ; Shri A. Niyogi ; Shri S. Krishnamurty Shri K. Srinivasan.

APPOINTMENT

The Government of India have received several suggestions for amendment of Chapter VIII of the Motor Vehicles Act, 1939, relating to compulsory insurance of motor vehicle against third party risks. Since the proposals involve substantial changes in the existing provisions of the Act and require thorough examination from the point of view of the insurer, the insured and the public, the Government of India, decided to appoint a part-time Committee to Study the various proposals and make recommendations in respect thereof. So The Motor Vehicle Insurance Committee was Constituted by the Ministry of Transport and Communications, Department of Transport (Transport Wing) Vide Resolution No. 2-TL (26)/59 dated May 24, 1962.

TERMS OF REFERENCE

1. To survey and report how far the existing provisions relating to compensation, third party insurance and claims Tribunals serve the purpose for which they were meant.

2. To examine and report on the following specific suggestions :

(a) Extension of time limit for filing applications

before the Claims Tribunals;

(b) Increase of amounts for which third party insurance policies should be taken;

(c) Making it incumbent upon the insurer to pay a third party claimant a certain minimum sum of money, depending upon the nature of the loss sustained and indicating such minimum;

(d) Prescribing the minimum compensation payable for various injuries;

(e) Making the insurer a party in compensation proceedings before Claims Tribunals;

(f) Authorising Claims Brokers to contest claims on behalf of aggrieved parties before claims Tribunals.

(g) Suo moto action by claims Tribunals.

3. To make any other recommendations germane to the above subject.

CONTENTS

Introductory; Recent Developments in other Countries; Road Accidents Statistics; Third Party Victims; Compulsory Insurance of Transport Vehicles; Damage to third party property; Claims tribunals; Miscellaneous Summary of Main Conclusions, Recommendations and Acknowledgements; Note of Dissent; Appendices.

RECOMMENDATIONS

Road Accident Statistics

The National Road Safety Council, the establishment of which is under the Government of India's consideration, should, study the reasons why the number of cases in which compensation is actually paid is much less than the number of cases in which, according to accident reports, the driver is in the wrong.

The recording and reporting of full particulars of all accidents resulting in third party property damage should be made obligatory under the Motor Vehicles Act, which, at present, contains provisions covering only third party injuries.

A provision should be made in the Motor Vehicles Act requiring the maintenance of an accident register for every transport vehicle operating on an inter-State route.

The Road Accident Report Form evolved in the First Study Week in Traffic Engineering and Highway Safety organised by the Government of India in 1959 at Bombay under the auspices of the ECAFE, may be adopted in this country. In addition to the information covered by this, further essential details about the insurance of the Vehicle involved in an accident should be obtained. All India statistics of uninsured vehicles, hit-and-run accidents, etc, should also by systematically collected. The insurers should also be asked to furnish particulars of their annual premium receipts, compensation payments etc., to the National Road Safety Council as well as the Controller of Insurance.

The National Road Safety Country should be vested with the statutory responsibility for not merely processing accident data through an Accident Record Division and coordinating any researches and are necessary, but also publishing the results of its studies. The Police authorities should be required to send copies of their First Information Reports to the Council within 48 hours of each accident.

Third Party Victims

The Motor Vehicle Taxation Acts in the different States should be suitably amended to make it impossible for a vehicle owner to pay the tax for a period extending beyond the period covered by the insurance of the vehicle.

Claims Tribunals should be empowered to recover adjudicated damages like arrears of land revenue from the owner or driver of a vehicle which is not insured or liability in regard to which is repudiated by the insurer on valid grounds. The power should also be available in the case of a transport vehicle when the damages awarded exceed the amount of insurance.

The Motor Vehicles Act should amended to provide also for penalty up to Rs. 1,000 for deliberate misrepresentation by an owner of a vehicle for securing a certificate or policy of insurance and for any vexatious attempt by the insurer to wriggle out of his liability by any false statement of facts.

Insurers should be required to make a separate deposit for Act liability cases by an amendment of the M. V. Act. The exact amount of deposit should be prescribed by the Comptroller of Insurance, taking the insurer's volume of Act liability business into account in accordance with a formula which he can evolve in consultation with the insurers. The deposit should be earmarked for payment of any claims that are unreasonably delayed or that may be settled after the insurer goes into liquidations, such course of action in every case being subjected to the prior scrutiny and sanction of the Controller of insurance.

The agency commission for Act liability insurance should reduced to 10 per cent from the present rate of 15 per cent.

A Central Third Party Insurance Fund should be set up for compensating innocent victims of accidents involving (i) uninsured vehicles. (ii) vehicles with effective certificates or policies of insurance, (iii) unidentified vehicles, (iv) stolen vehicles and (v) insolvent insurers, and also victims of accidents in which there is no contributory negligence on the part of either the owner or driver or victim himself. This fund should be administered by a Special Committee of the National

Road Safety Council which should include the Controller of Insurance and representatives of the insurers. Contributions should be collected for this fund in the form of a surcharge equal to 5 per cent of the third party compulsory insurance premium payable by vehicle owners and also from the following sources :

(i) The premium that should have been paid in the normal course by the owner of an uninsured vehicle for the period he has not taken a valid insurance policy for it, together with penality for the default, which should be equal to the amount of arrear premium.

(ii) Contribution from State Transport Undertaking based on the premium that will be payable by them but for their exemption from insurance.

Payments from the fund should be restricted to claims settled by a Claims Tribunal or a Civil Court, subject to a maximum of Rs. 10,000 per individual and Rs. 20,000 per accident exclusive of interest and cost. The national Road Safety Council should be entitled to sue the owner or operator or driver of a vehicle for reimbursement of any amount paid by it in pursuance of the Tribunal's/court's order. It should be allowed to be impleaded as a defendant in all cases where it is called upon to make the compensation payment.

Insurance Of Transport Vehicles

The owner of every stage carriage and contract carriage should be required to take a policy of insurance that will compensate the passengers in the event of an accident for which neither the owner nor the driver of the vehicle was responsible, unless there is contributory negligence on the part of a victim.

The existing limits of the amount of insurance policy for employee and third party liability for a transport vehicle should be increased from Rs. 20,000 to Rs. 50,000 for a vehicle under Section 95 (2) (a) and (b). There should also be a further increase in the amount of policy for passenger risk insurance from Rs. 2,000 to Rs. 5,000 per individual passenger if it is a bus and from Rs. 4,000 to Rs. 10,000 per passenger if it is a taxi under Section 95 (2) (b). A vehicle capable of carrying upto 30 passengers may be compelled to insure for Rs. 50,000 a vehicle with a carrying capacity ranging from 30 to 60 for Rs. 75,000 and a vehicle with a large capacity for Rs. 1 lakh.

Third Party Property Insurance

Insurance against damage to third party property for a sum of Rs. 2,000 on accident should be made compulsory ; claims should be required to be lodged before Claims Tribunals in all cases where they do not exceed this amount. Even if the claim for damage to property exceeds Rs. 2,000, the victim of an accident, who has suffered personal injury before a Claims Tribunal should be entitled to prefer the property damage claim also before the Tribunal Fees may be levied in respect of property claims on the same ad-valorem basis as in the civil courts.

Claims Tribunals

The Kerala, Utter Pradesh, Mysore, Andhra Pradesh, and Rajasthan Governments should constitute Tribunals without further delay, thus obviating the need for an amendment of the Motor Vehicles Act for setting up Tribunals compulsorily.

Full particulars of the insurer, driver and the owner of a vehicle involved in an accident and of the witnesses to the accident, including occupants of the vehicle, should be obtained and recorded by the police in the first information. Report or as soon thereafter as possible and these should be forwarded to the National Safety Council promptly.

The Motor Vehicles Act should be amended to empower a Claims Tribunal to summon the driver or owner of a vehicle as a witness, and also impose a fine on the delinquent driver who remains absent or fails to produce the evidence in his possession, up to a maximum of Rs. 2,500 and/or suspend, cancel the driving licence/permit/registration certificate.

A Claims Tribunal should also be enabled to permit an insurer to defend an action directly where it is satisfied that—

(i) There is lack of cooperation on the part of the insured or his agent who was in possession of the vehicle or of other persons connected with him, or

(ii) There is collusion between the insured and the person who preferred the claim.

In every case of accident in which the Police commence prosecution of the owner or driver of a vehicle, and also every case of hit-and-run accident, the Police should be instructed to let the victim of the accident or his legal representative simultaneously have a circular in the regional language explaining the remedy that is available, the procedure for application for compensation and the time for filing it. The Union Ministry of Transport should draft a model circular for this purpose.

The criminal courts should be requested by a general circular or draw the attention of the victim of an accident to his right to move the Tribunal for compensation at the time of pronouncing a judgment of conviction and to state at the foot of the calendar which accompanies the judgment that they have made the above direction.

Copies of police records should not be withheld from the parties of a claims case during the pendency of the criminal proceedings on the mere ground that the case is subjudice.

The period within which an application for claims should be filed before the Claims Tribunal should be increased to six months from the date of the accident.

A court fee of Re. 1 should be charged if the claim in a case of accident is confined to special damages. If any further general damages are claimed, an advalorem fee should be charged on the aggregate of the special and general claims on the following scale :

Amount of claim	Amount of court fee
Upto Rs. 5,000..................	Rs. 10
Rs. 5,00—50,000.............	1/4% of the amount of claim
Rs. 50,001—100,000...........	1/2% of the amount of claim
Above Rs. 100,000............	1% of the amount of claim

Penal interest at the rate of four and half per cent should be payable on the amount of compensation in arrear, unless the Tribunal has itself allowed extension of time for payment of any part of the amount for any reason. This penal interest should be charged even in cases in which the compensation has already been paid from the Central Third party Insurance Fund and the National Road Safety Council files a suit against the owner or driver of the vehicle either jointly or severally.

Miscellaneous

The insurance should be required to notify not merely cancellation or suspension of policies but particulars of all vehicles the policies in respect of which have not been renewed by them, the Transport Commissioner/Controller/Director of Transport of the State where the vehicles were last registered.

The insurers should be required to keep separate proforma accounts for Act liability insurance and submit them to the Controller of Insurance as a separate revenue account in terms of the Insurance Act and statistics regarding the different kinds of motor insurance policies, premium receipts, claims, etc. should also be furnished along with the revenue accounts.

Suitable rules should be made under Section III of the M. V. Act requiring insurance furnish (i) periodical returns of the number of Act liability policies issued for the vehicles in each State and (ii) such specific information as may be needed by the State Governments and the National Road Safety Council, in regard to particular policies.

The National Road Safety Council should be in active touch with the legal aid societies where they exit, and have panels of lawyers where there are no such societies for free aid in cases where applications are made in forma pauperies and also in cases where the claimants are women and males who have not attained majority or whose annual income does not exceed Rs. 1,500. The system of claims brokers is undesirable.

The State Transport undertakings should conform strictly to the relevant rules prescribed by the Central Government regarding motor vehicles third party insurance funds.

The Transport Department of each State Government should maintain a record of the Government vehicles which are exempt from insurance and also details of accidents in which the vehicles are involved including the compensation paid to claimants in these accidents and basis on which the compensation is paid.

An accident should be deemed to have occurred in a public place notwithstanding that the person injured or the property demaged is actually not there if the cause of accident or the error of amission or commission which had led to it had occurred there.

The owner of a vehicle who wants to sell it and also transfer the unexpired policy of compulsory insurance covering it to the vendee should, by an amendment of the motor Vehicles Act, be required to give minimum notice, say of a week, commencing from the date of receipt of his letter by the insurer, for this purpose and the insurer's failure to respond to it within this week should be taken to amount to concurrence.

The National Road Safety Council should underwrite the third party risk in cases where the insurers-decline to renew a policy, on such terms and at such premium rates as it considers fit.

The National Road Safety Council should try to bring about settlement out of court; but the judicial procedure should not be dispensed with, where a compromise does not materialize.

The minimum amount of compensation should be prescribed for certain injuries and the amount of additional compansation payable with reference to the impairment of the earning capacity of the enjured should be left to the discretion of the Claim Tribunals.

The minimum should be fixed on the basis of the amount prescribed in the Workmens Compensation Act for a person in the lowest income group.

The claiment and the defendant in every claims case should be required to furnish information about their relationship, if any, and about prior accidents in which either of them was involved.

Copies of all orders awarding compensation should be required to be sent by the Claims Tribunal to the Licensing or Regional Transport Authorities concerned for appropriate action against the drivers and owners of the vehicles in case either criminal proceedings have not already been initiated against them or they have prove unsuccessful for lack of evidence.

The National Road Safety Council should examine, in the light of the conditions obtaining in the different States the steps necessary for giving adequate publicly to the provisions of Chapter VIII.

Acknowledgements : We have received a full measure

of cooperation from State Governments, State Transport Undertakings, Insurance Companies and the Insurance Association of India, Road Safety Associations, Automobile Associations, the Indian, Road and Transports Development Association, Chambers of Commerce, Automobile Manufacturers & Dealers, the All India Motor Unions' Congress and other Associations of transport operators and drivers, and various other organisations and individuals interested in road transport and road safety.

Our thanks are due to Dr. M. K. Ganguli, for interpreting some of the statistical information for us and for suggesting the form in which sum of the essential date can be collected in future. He was ably assisted in this work by Shri K. C. Saksena and Shri G. Ramachandran.

We did not trouble the Government for separate staff for our enquiry but availed of the services of the staff of the Road Transport Division in the Transport Ministry. We place on record our appreciation of the rare efficiency and diligence with which Shri R. C. Gupta, who is at present an Officer on Special Duty with the Ministry, has assisted the Committee in its task and the very competent and willing Secretariat work turned out by Sarvashri R. S. Ohri, Dharampal Singh and Santokh Singh Meen.

COMMITTEE ON TRAFFIC IN DELHI, 1962—REPORT

Delhi, Ministry of Home Affairs, 1963, 86p.+various pages+Maps

Chairman : Shri Bhagwan Sahay.

Members : Chaudhuri Brahm Prakash ; Shri Daroga Mal ; Bawa Bachittar Singh ; Mir Mushtaq Ahmad ; Shri S.L. Puri ; Shri R.R. Bahl ; Shri B. B. Banerji ; Shri P.K.J. Menon (replaced by Shri K. A. Khan) Shri G. Mukharji ; Shri T.S. Khanna.

Co-opted Members : Shri L. O. Joshi (replaced by Shri K. Kishore) ; Shri S. G. Bose Mullick ; Shri Gajraj Singh ; Shri C. S. Gupte ; Shri B. G. Fernandes ; Shri M. P. Singh ; Shri K.L. Rathee.

Member-Secretary : Shri P.K. Dave.

APPOINTMENT

The Committee on Traffic in Delhi was constituted under the Ministry of Home Affairs vide their Resolution dated 21.6.1962.

TERMS OF REFERENCE

To conduct investigation into all aspects of the problem of traffic in Delhi and make the recommendations to Government on the subject.

CONTENTS

Preamble :—The Nature of the Problem ; Improvement of the Circulation System ; Public Transport ; Regulation and Enforcement ; Organisation, Coordination and Direction ; Summary of Conclusions and Recommendations ; Appendices from A to I ; 6 Graphs ; 3 Maps.

RECOMMENDATIONS

We consider that the techniques of both "place" and "time" segregation should be applied to the traffic problem of Delhi in a scientific manner.

An efficient machinery for timely repairs of roads should be maintained by the authorities concerned on a decentralised basis.

The Nature of The Problem

The rapid urbanisation of Delhi from the time it became the capital of British India, through the Second World War and in the ost-independence years has been traced. Since 1931, the rate of urbanization has been extremely high ; it was accentuated during the war years and a phenomenal increase was registered with the refugee influx immediately following Independence. The population projections for the Delhi urban area for 1971 and 1981 have been mentioned to indicate roughly the magnitude of the problem likely to be faced.

The importance of Delhi as a centre of trade and commerce and its emergence after Independence as the national capital and an international centre have all contributed to its traffic and its break down into trips in public transport vehicles, hired vehicles and private transport have been indicated.

The characteristics of the existing circulation system have been noted. By and large, the growth in vehicular traffic has not been attended with equivalent growth in road capacities and mileage. Insufficient road-width and the mixed nature of traffic contribute to the traffic problem of Delhi. Connected approaches to the highways and to the various localities are not readily available ; intersection designs are faulty and not only cause accidents but also act as bottlenecks ; footpaths and cycle tracks are inadequate and are of faulty design ; driver visibility and road lighting are poor ; road condition is unsatisfactory. Access between Delhi and New Delhi present very great difficulties.

Vehicular accidents have increased almost four fold between 1957 and 1962. The increase being contributed largely by the fast moving vehicles. Fatal and major injuries have more than doubled in the same period and minor injuries have increased nearly three-fold and collisions more than five fold. Pedestrians are the greatest sufferers both in killed and injured.

The various factors which influence driver performance and the accident rate have been noticed.

Traffic in Delhi is mixed in character, consisting of slow moving bullock-carts, tongas, rehras and bicycles along with high speed scooter and motor-cycle rickshaws, private cars taxis, buses and goods carriers. Provision, of separate tracks for pedestrians and bicycles is inadequate and inefficient. There is great pressure of competing users of different speeds and this not only causes confusion and congestion but reduces the capacity of the roads. Frequent obstruction of footpaths and kerbs by hawkers and vendors is a special feature of Delhi roads, which forces pedestrians on to the main carriage way thus creating a road hazard and obstructing flow of traffic.

Delhi is fast developing into an inter-city and inter-state road terminus ; but the buses and goods vehicles have tended to congregate at certain key points resulting in problems of congestion.

The bicycle is the main vehicle of personal transportation and in 1957 survey, 7 out of 10 vehicles on Delhi roads were found to be bicycles. The passengers on these bicycles are largely people going to and from the principal work centres ; this creates unprecedented problems of congestion.

The Delhi Transport Undertaking has increased its services from a mileage of 19,000 in 1951-52 to 75,000 in 1962 63 ; passengers carried per day have increased from 79,000 in 1951-52 to 6,00,000 in 1962-63. This developments encouraging but the increase in the number of buses itself creates great problems of traffic ; bus terminals are in adequate, bays for parking of buses are virtually non-existent and guard rails and queuing rails are only now being introduced,

Congestion points caused by road-rail crossings have been noted.

The special problems of parking and frequent openings on to main road caused by multistoreyed constructions in areas served by relatively narrow roads have been noticed.

One of the principal contributory factors of congestion is the concentration of the work centres in three or four well-defined complexes. Mass transport media have proved inadequate for clearing the traffic to and from these work centres. The D.T.U. is making good efforts to cope with the problem but there are no other mass transport media available. The limited suburban train service makes an insignificant impact and even the projected ring railway will prove of little value. The very welcome decision of Government to stagger working hours for offices has reduced the problem some what but the full impact of this measure has yet to be achieved.

The problem of congestion during special occasions has been dealt with by another Committee appointed in 1959 and its recommendations have resulted in considerable improvement. But the problem itself cannot be permanently solved by mere regulatory measures.

Enforcement of traffic laws by the Traffic Branch of the Delhi Police suffers for want of adequate personnel and modern aids like mobile patrols with wireless communication, automatic devices for speed testing, enforcement research etc. This inadequacy adds to the traffic situation.

A few specific studies and some research on the traffic proplems of Delhi have been done, but a comprehensive view was taken for the first time in the Master plan for Delhi which provides a considerable amount of basic material for our report.

Improvement of the circulation system

The essentials of an ideal circulation system have been discussed with treatment in some detail of the four major factors—roads, land use, vehicles and the users.

The development of a good circulation system will require coordination of various policy making, planning and administrative, executive and regulatory agencies. The importance of traffic engineering to the development of a sound circulation system has been emphasized. Traffic engineering has been defined and its application discussed. We have expressed the hope that its importance will be maintained and that it will come to stay as one of the principal means of solving the traffic problems of the capital.

Measures for the improvement of the circulation system have to be considered in two parts short-term and long term. The short-term measures deserve to be implemented immediately with such addition and alterations in the Third Five Year Plan outlay as may be required ; the long term measures are essentially projects for implementation over a longer period but a beginning should be made on several of them from now.

We have discussed the peak hour problems of road congestion and transportation which are becoming more acute as time passes. We consider that it is clearly beyond the capacity of a road transport organization which has to be run on economic lines to take on the whole burden. The staggering of working hours is an obvious immediate solution and we are glad to note that while our committee was in session, the Government of India have introduced this in their offices. We consider, however, that it is necessary that this principle should be given wider acceptance. It will be necessary for Delhi Administration to persuade the business establishments to fall in line with this measure.

We consider that the techniques of both "place" and "time" segregation should be applied to the traffic problem of Delhi in a scientific manner. Detailed Recommendations have been made in the chapter on "Regulation and Enforcement". The policy in this regard will have to be constantly under review and research to cope with the development problem.

The condition of roads and of the road surface in Delhi have been discussed. We consider it essential that an efficient machinery for timely repairs of roads should be maintained by the authorities concerned on a decentralised basis. We have examined the expedient of providing a small repair agency under the Traffic Police but do not recommend it. The work should rest squarely on the agency for the maintenance of a particular read way but steps should be taken to streamline the machinery. Each such agency should have a traffic cell to detect surface deterioration and to execute urgent minor works expeditiously. The traffic Police should also report the development of broken surfaces to the agency responsible.

We suggest that the practice obtaining in other busy cities of conducting repair work at night or at least during the off-peak hours should be introduced in Delhi.

Whenever roads are to be cut for various kinds of repairs etc., advance information should be given to the traffic authorities so that they can make certain that proper diversions are provided and adequate signs and danger signals placed. We would strongly recommend that once a warning has been issued to the authorities concerned, the police should prosecute all persons not observing the safety and traffic requirements.

In planning new road works, the departments concerned should take coordinated action to plan and to provide for electric, sewer and water pipelines so that occasions for cutting of the road to not arise in future. Pipes should be buried at suitable points to enable cross connections for electricity, telephone, sewers and water supply lines. This would require a high degree of coordination which we trust, the Depatrment of Traffic recommended in Chapter V will be able to achieve.

The problem of storm water flooding of the road surface has assumed inconvenient proportions and we recommend that the storm water drainage system should be designed for effective run-off 1/2" per hour in main drain, and 3/4" in branch drains as recommended by the Flood Control Committee. Road-side drainage should also be improved effectively. In our view, the problem deserves concentrated attention.

Lighting of Delhi roads, footpaths and cycle tracks at night time is inadequate and defective. This not only reduces road capacity but creates accident hazards. Orders prohibiting the use of head lights cannot be enforced on badly lit roads. We recommend that the lighting of Delhi roads, inter-sections, cycle tracks and footpaths should be done on top priority basis. The position should be kept under constant review to cope with the growing intensity of traffic.

As major roadways and streets of the city become well lit, the use of head-lights on them should be prohibited, and the prohibition rigorously enforced.

At least on the important roads, all the road signs and direction boards should be lit. This will be all the more important when use of headlights is prohibited.

The principal factor militating against the free flow of traffic in Delhi is the inadequacy and faulty lay-out of road intersections. Some work has been done to improve matters and reasearch is also going on under the Central Road Research Institute. We consider that the pace of this work should be expedited. We have given in Appendix 'A' a list of the road intersections which require urgent improvement. The improvement and redesigning of intersections will remain a continuing function of the Department of Traffic recommended by us in chapter V.

We recommend that all obstructions which impede the free flow of traffic should be removed. Removal of these obstructions would go a long way in speeding up the flow of traffic.

It inherant vendors need to be severely restricted and their parking rigorously controlled. Over-hanging branches of trees which reduce visibility need constant attention. Permission to strack building materials on roads and permits for holding marriages and other functions on the streets should be strongly discouraged.

Vehicle break downs and traffic accidents should not be allowed to remain in streets obstructing traffic for long periods. We consider it necessary to have a mobile recovery service with central telephone points so that such obstructions can be removed without loss of time. The accident investigation squad should be geared up to be able to complete the investigation on the spot in less than half an hour of the occurrence of an accident.

Pavement should be improved and freed from obstructions in order to draw in pedestrians from the carriage way. Municipal authorities should take active steps with the help of the police for the clearing of all existing obstructions.

Fresh permits to hawkers, rehriwalas and tongas should be issued by the Corporation and the transfer of ownership of permits should also be curbed so as to eliminate such obstructions in due course. There should be a joint drive by the police and the Corporation to check existing licences and rehbazari chits so that forged documents may be dealt with according to law.

For pedestrian safety, we recommend the provision of guard rails at busy interesections, introduction of pedestrian crossing lights, prominent marking of pedestrian crossings and their inforcement, increase in the number of such crossing preventing jay-walking on the roadways and where feasible, construction of subways and over-bridges. On wide roads, pedestrain refuges may be provided in the middle of the road. Pedestrian crossings should, as far as may be possible, be a few yards behind a bus stop. In certain parts of the old city, the creation of "pedestrian precinets" may be considered.

Cycle tracks should be improved and made attractive to the cyclists. The number of openings of roads leading to the bungalows which obstruct cycle tracks should be reduced. Arrangements should be made for clearing bicycle traffic at important intersections. A beginning must be made with the provision of new cycle tracks and the proper maintenance of the old ones. We have given a list in Appendix 'B' of cycle tracks which we consider essential.

There are already several schemes for the widening of roads and bridges which act as serious bottlenecks. In Appendix 'C' we have given a list of works in order of priority which we consider necessary. The works given top priority in our list must receive the most urgent attention of Government.

There is urgent need for increasing the number of crossings over the river Yamuna. In addition to two bridges at Wazirabad and Humayn's Tomb provided in the Master Plan, two more bridges should be built, one north of Rajghat and the second between the Wazirabad barrage and the existing Yamuna Bridge. To speed up traffic on the existing rail-come-road bridge, the track should be concreted immediately. To prevent vehicle breakdowns blocking traffic, we recommend the maintenance of a break-down recovery service at or near the bridge all the 24 hours of the day.

We recommend grade separation of road from railway lines at certain congested points.

The problems of parking in Delhi are growing apace. We endorse the recommendations of the Master Plan, some of which are already under implementation. We have also made general recommendations to solve this problem. Certain studies on parking have been given in Appendices 'D' and 'E'.

Bus stops on congested street stend to become "Black spots" for accidents. We recommend reduction of bus stops on busy streets and their staggering, and the provision of bays away from the carriage way for the buses to stop and for the passengers to assemble ; such bays should not interfere with footpaths and bicycle tracks.

We endorse the recommendation of the Master Plan for the construction of godowns and warehouses on the outskirts of the city to remove congestion from busy areas. The development and allotment of land for this purpose should be given high priority. Until this is done, loading and unloading may be permitted in the existing premises with such safeguards and restrictions as can be imposed. The Delhi Corporation and NDMC might consider the licensing of such premises as a further measure of control.

Long-term Measures

We have emphasized the inter-relationship between scientific land use and transportation. We endorse the Master Plan recommendations for a traffic circulation plan with such changes as may be necessary at the detailed planning stage. We have also recommended the redevelopment of the Connaught place area according to the Master Plan and the provision of multi-storeyed parking facilities on Esplanade Road and at Gandhi Grounds near Fountain on a priority basis.

We recommend that the Old Delhi Main and New Delhi Railway Station Yards should be redesigned to cope with growing traffic, and provided with openings and passenger access terminalson two sides. Additional parking space should be provided opposite New Delhi Railway Station as recommended in the Master Plan.

For the vast expanding needs of South Delhi, the Nizamuddin Railway Station should be expanded.

We endorse the proposal in the Master Plan for the development of mineral sidings at Tughlakabad, Sahibabad, Azadpur and Kirt nagar.

Unless a satisfactory mass transit system is developed all measures of improvement of the circulation pattern are likely to remain mere palliatives. This has been discussed in detail in Chapter III."

We have stressed the importance of continuing research and studies in traffic problems, without which the arrangements will always lag behind the growing requirements.

In Map I, the major recommendations for the improvement of the circulation system have been shown.

Public Transport

We have stressed the decisive role of mass transit facilities in the development and growth of big cities and the need for ensuring that such facilities keep pace with the development of a city and its suburbs. The D.T.U., which is the sole facility for mass transit in Delhi, is unlikely to provide the answer and there is need to take stock of the requirements, analyse the problems and work out solutions both on short and long-term basis. We recommend that in the interests of the future integrated development of Greater Delhi, a comprehensive survey of the transportation and traffic situation should be carried out by a team of experts.

The mere addition of surface transport vehicles will not solve the problem of additional transport capacity and may, in fact cause, complication while we urge the rapid development of the ring railway with many as radial connections as may be possible, this scheme may not provide the ultimate solution. We have, therefore, emphasized the need for perspective planning of other kinds of rapid transit systems ; this should be taken in hand immediately so that a decision can be reached and the land required for the chosen scheme reserved in advance to prevent future complications.

Measures for improving the coverage and turnover of the D.T.U. have been recomended by us in Chapter II. Additional measures, such as the creation of focal points for bus services to minimise route lengths and improve utilisation of crew and vehicles have been suggested. The Master Plan recommendation for the establishment of inter-state bus terminals has been endorsed.

We suggest that the D.T.U. should provide basic amenities to its passengers and crew. A beginning should be made with the focal points recommended by us.

To maximise the use of the existing fleet, we have recommended that D.T.U. should be authorised to carry more standing passengers during peak hours.

Although provision of separate lanes for public transport vehicles may be somewhat difficult in view of the heterogeneous traffic, we recommend that all efforts should be made in this direction.

We have recommended a number other measures to reduce the unnecessary movement of heavy traffic in congested areas.

For facility of transport operators and the general public, we recommend that all Government offices dealing with transport licensing and control should be one building easily accessiable both from old and New Delhi.

We do not recommend subsidising of public transport services to eliminate the bicycle from the Delhi roads. But we suggest that the resources of the D.T.U. should be augmented and the organisation enabled to raise funds in the open market and its securities made negotiable. This will enable the D.T.U. to prepare plans on a long range basis.

The duties of the Police in traffic management and formulation and enforcement of traffic policies have been broadly described.

We consider that modern traffic conditions require a well-equipped agency for inforcement and regulation. We have emphasized that modern aids for improving the flow of traffic and scientific regulatory measures do not reduce in any way the need for effective policing ; the presence of uniformed Police Officers on the road is the most effective way of encouraging the good behaviour of road users, and the best deterrent against traffic offences. We consider mobile Police patrols, we trained and directed, a very important adjunct of a modern traffic Police branch.

We have recommended a careful review of the Traffic Police strength but have been unable to make specific proposals for enhancement of the strength. For facility, we have given in Appendices 'F' and 'G' certain statistics and the recommendations of our Sub-Committe which went into this matter in detail.

It is not possible to offer to the Traffic Police full transferability to the regular Police branches and therefore, we have recommended that suitable incentives in the form of special pays and allowances and promotion prospects should be built into the terms of service of the Traffic Police.

The conditions at various points of duty should be improved so as to protect Constables from the inclemencies of the Delhi weather.

The principal functions of moble partrols have been broadly defined.

We consider the use of Traffic Wardens a useful expedient not only for relieving the Traffic Police of certain relatively minor duties but also of bringing forth the cooperation of the public in enforcement measures. We recommend that this system may be introduced on an experimental basis in selected parking areas and at congested points near schools and other educational institutions. For the present, we do not recommend giving power to the Wardens to prosecute offenders or to collect fines.

We have recommended that arrangements be made for the systematic training of the Traffic Police including their refresher and advanced training.

Regulatory measures to improve flow of traffic have already been dealt with in Chapter II. The formulation and implementation of all such measures will depend upon a continuing study of the traffic problem on a scientific basis. In Appendix 'H' we have given an illustrative list of measures for 'time' and (Place) segregation. We have advocated, a considerable increase in the installation of automatic traffic lights at intersections.

On busy roads we have recommended the implementation of right-turn and 'U' turn restrictions after careful surveys.

We feel that there is room for frequent review of speed restrictions and for prescribing more rigorous lim'ts in some areas and relaxations in others.

We consider that enforcement of the law and regulatory measures is an aspect of Public education and should be handled as such by the Police. In our view, motoring offences are largely the outcome of ignorance of the principles of road conduct, and if prompt on-the-spot advice is given to the road users in a courteous and considerate manner the lesson of enforcement will have a more lastin effect than by spasmodic checking and prosecution. Subject to this general observation, enforcement of the traffic law and regulatory measures should be vigorous and comprehensive, and deliberate repetitive or vicious voilations should not go unpunished.

We have specially noted the congestion and accident hazard resulting from the large bicycle traffic in Delhi. We consider that apart from construction and improvement of cycle tracks, it is necessary to enforce the traffic rules firmly and, after giving due publicity, the police would be justified in carrying out drives for prosecuting offenders.

There is obvious need for streamlining the investigation of road accidents. We recommend the posting of Accident Investigation Squads should be equipped with all necessary scientific aids and should be able to complete the preliminary investigation so as to enable the removal of the vehicles and other impediments within a maximum period of half an hour. It will be necessary to station at least two recovery vehicles in the city for removing obstructions caused by serious collisions.

The time-lag at present in the disposal of cases in courts is quite considerable. Apart from provision of adequate Police staff for the prosecution of cases, we have also suggested a review of the Magistrates' strength in Delhi. In this connection, we have emphasised the importance of the institution of Honorary Magistrates for traffic offences to associate the public in a obstructive way with enforcement. We have suggested that the magistracy should realise the importance of deterrent sentences in cases of deliberate, repetitive or vicious violations. We are of the view that good results can be expected if most of the enforcement work is dealt with on-the-spot by mobile Magistrates operating with enforcement staff.

We see that the existing procedures for payment of compensation to victims of traffic accidents should be examined so as to speed up the award of compensation. At least for the transport services, including the D.T.U., a system of ad hoc and ex-gratia payment even before the finalisation of wards should be introduced.

We have emphasized that the pedestrians being the most under-privileged of the road users, deserves the fullest sympathy of the Traffic Police who should assist him at all times. At the same time, it is the function of the Police to ensure that pedestrians use the footpaths and the prescribed crossings and, after due notification, encroachments on the carriage way by pedestrians should be firmly discouraged.

Drivers of hired vehicles appear to show scant regard for traffic regulations. In the interest of the passengers, and of road users generally, we recommend strict control over hired vehicles.

Delhi is very poorly served by traffic signs and slogan boards. We recommend that a drive should be organised to resite and repair the old signs and slogan boards and to place new ones at suitable points. The use of non-standard road signs should be discontinued. We consider it advisable to give the authority for the placement and shifting of signs and slogan boards to the Police who may be given a small budget by the Delhi Corporation and the N.D.M.C. for this purpose. We have recommended in Chapter II that an important streets, the signs and slogan boards should be lifc up at night.

We suggest that the recommendations of the Committee on Traffic for Special Occasions appointed by the Home Ministry in 1959, should be implemented where this has not already been done.

We consider that an inspection of vehicles and licensing of drivers have a bearing on road accidents, this work should be transferred from the State Motor Transport Controller to the Traffic police the staff being suitably augmented, wherever necessary.

We consider that there should be provision for calling in for a test any vehicle, which, from the registration documents, seems to have outlived it life, or which has been involved in a major accident.

The tests prescribed for the initial issue of driving licences should be mad; fairly comprehensive and strict, knowledge of the "highway code" should be thoroughly tested and traffic situations simulated to observe reactions. This policy should be followed even more rigorously in the case of commercial licences. There should also be provision for calling up for a re-test and instruction, drivers should be intensively tested, given proper instruction and, if necessary, placed on a period of probation. We would not hesitate to recommend very strong measures against drivers who are known to be accident prone, or are consistently inconsiderate to road users and violate traffic regulations. Consumption of alcohol, by drivers, whenever detected, must be dealt with sternly and the licences impounded, or even cancelled. For a proper implementation of this policy, complete Police records about delinquent drivers should be built up and prosecutors should urge courts to endorse driving licences of persons convicted of serious violations.

It seems to us necessary to require the production of a medical certificate at the time of initial issue of a driving licence. If a licence has been endorsed for accidents, or for traffic violations where disregard of signals is alleged, a repeat medical examination should be insisted upon. These provisions are of particular importance for drivers of commercial vehicles, or vehicles plying for hire.

We consider that Government owes it as a duty to prospective drivers to ensure that driving schools which have come up in large numbers, are fully qualified to impart training. The Traffic police should supervise the training schools, or at least, introduce a test for the instructors. Such schools as employ qualified instructors may be permitted to designate themselves as "Approved by the Government."

The consideration of the need for amendment or extension of traffic laws is a continuing duty of the Traffic Police, the Municipal authorities and the proposed Department of Traffic. Certain suggestions for amendments have been given in Appendix 'I'. We recommend that these may be examined in detail by Government and appropriate action initiated.

The question of delegating power to suspend driving licences of persistent or serious defaulters to the Superintendent of Police (Traffic) may be examined by Government after ascertaining the practice in other cities.

We consider that the most important programme of traffic regulation and enforcement is the education of the road users. We recommend an intensive programme for this purpose with the full cooperation of the public, automobile associations, traffic safety associations, transport organisations and drivers' unions. In the schools, the subject should be introduced through selected teachers adequately briefed by the Police and also by selected Police officers themselves. Audiovisual aids like film strips, traffic safety films etc. and the television network of Delhi should be used in an organised manner. Traffic safety weeks should be observed. It would also be advisable to buy up advertisement space in newspapers and periodicals to educate the public through persuasion and correction with a tactful hint of the strong arm of the law. We believe that the results of a vigorous programme in this direction will achieve quick and lasting results. Incentives for accident-fee driving have already been introduced by the D.T.U. and we recommend that similar incentives should be introduced by other transport operators.

It would be a good idea to introduce children to traffic control by allowing them to control traffic and parking near school crossings, and, gradually at other more important points.

Organisation, Coordination and Direction

There are several agencies dealing with various aspects of the traffic and transportation problems of Delhi which are extremely complicated and involve the use of a number of specialist services. It is not possible to bring all such specialist services under one single authority but we consider that the problem of effective coordination between them will govern the totality of traffic regulation and improvements. We are of the view that a Department of Traffic with experienced technical staff with the techniques of planning, effective road circulation, pedestrian control, accident prevention and traffic education and enforcement must be established for Delhi immediately. This agency should make detailed recommendations for policy formulation based on scientific studies of the various aspects of traffic and transportation. The research and studies of the proposed Department of Traffic should be confined to the subjects in which more than one agencies have interests and should work in collaboration with each other, the specialist agency should at the same time continue research and studies in their own spheres. But such research etc. should be coordinated by the Department of Traffic.

The Department of Traffic should be placed in charge of a qualified traffic engineer who is also fully familiar with sociological economics, and the legal and enforcement aspects of traffic. He should be given the assistance of specialists in various fields.

This Department must be directly under the control of Delhi Administration and should be closely linked with the traffic Branch of Delhi Police and the Department of transport. There should be a high level Committee to guide and advise the Department.

We trust that the approach of the Municipal authorities of Delhi to this Department will be one of wholehearted cooperation.

STUDY TEAM ON THE POSITION OF GRAM SABHA IN PANCHAYATI RAJ MOVEMENT, 1962—REPORT

Delhi, Ministry of Community Development & Cooperation, 1963. 80p. various pages

Chairman : Shri R. R. Diwakar
Members : Shri R. K. Patil; Shri S N. Dwivedy; Smt. Sarojini Mahishi; Shri J.N. Pahadia; Shri S. M. Joshi; Shri Raghubir Sahai; Shri G.P. Jain; Shri B.S. Mehta; Shri G. Venkatachalapathi; Shri Bhagwant Singh;
Secretary : Shri S. Das gupta.

APPOINTMENT

The fifth meeting of the Central Council of Local Self Government held in 1959 recommended that the Gram Sabha should be given statutory recognition and legislation should provide for its participation in the formulation of programmes and the review of progress. This was reiterated by the sixth meeting of the Council held in 1960 and by the Conference of State Ministers of Panchayati Raj held in 1961. Though a number of States have recognised the Gram Sabha statutorily and assigned them certain specific functions, it is yet to develop into an institution capable of exerting its effective influence on the village Panchayat.

The extention of the process of democracy to the people in the real sense should mean that the Panchayat functions as the executive body to give concrete shape to the wishes and aspirations of the village community as represented by the Gram Sabha. The objective of Panchayati Raj is to established a participating democracy so that at the village level the Gram Sabha, consisting of all adult residents of the village, should not only deliberate, but also participate with its executive, namely, the Gram Panchayat in planning and implementing the various programmes. The mode of achieving this objective requires to be examined.

If decentralisation and the sharing of powers and responsibilities by people's representatives at the various levels are to be real, these powers and responsibilities must be exercised institutionally. In this connection the powers conferred on the Chairman of the panchayat Samiti and the Sarpanch need to be analysed with a view to providing effective safeguards to ensure that they function institutionally.

These problems precipitated by the working of Panchayati Raj in different States have been exercised the mind of the Government for some time. The Government of India have accordingly decided to set up a Study Team On the Position of Gram Sabha in Panchayati Raj Movement was constituted under the Ministry of Community Development and Cooperation vide their Resolution No. 4/78/61-Panch dated June 26, 1962.

TERMS OF REFERENCE

(i) To study the working of the Gram Sabha, Gram Panchayat and the Panchayat Samiti with special reference to:

(a) the extent to which the Gram Panchayat is influenced in its policies and decisions by the views and mandate of the Gram Sabha and the extent to which Gram Sabha is involved in the implementation of Programmes.

(b) the extent to which the existing powers and functions of Sarpanches of village Panchayats and Pradhans of Panchayat Samiti are consistent with the institutional functioning of the panchayats and Panchayat Samitis.

(ii) To suggest measures necessary to ensure that:

(a) The Gram Sabha is built up as the basis of Panchayati Raj, and

(b) Sarpanches (Panchayat Presidents) and Pradhans (Presidents of Panchayat Samities) function institutionally.

CONTENTS

Letter of Transmittal; Introduction; Objectives and Approach; Gram Sabha—its Role; Functions of the Gram Sabha; Gram Sabha, Panchayat Samiti and Zila Parishad; Summary of Main Conclusions and Recommendations; Notes of Dissent and Annexures.

RECOMMENDATIONS

Objective And Approach

To secure development of participating democracy as compared to representative democracy which functions at the level of the higher tiers, should be one of the fundamental objectives of the Panchayati Raj movement. A true participating democracy could however, be effectively promoted only at the level of the lower tiers of Panchayati Raj, that is, at the level of Panchayat and Gram Sabha. The question of bringing Gram Sabha into picture and endowing it with a definite role and responsibility, therefore, needs serious consideration. Although there are many, who feel that strengthening of Gram Sabha may weaken the Panchayat and the time of endowing it with powers of control over the Panchayat is not yet due. Gram Sabha will have to be gradually brought into picture by assigning to it a definite status, role and set of functions.

The development of the institution of Gram Sabha, however, depends upon the growth and regeneration of the village community ; the concept of an integrated willage community has not yet taken shape in our country and will be realised, only over a period of time. It will, therefore, taken some time before, the institution of Gram Sabha becomes vocal and effective. The existing role of the Gram Sabha as it is found in some of the States, where it is used as a primary village assembly and offers benefits of consultation and advice and acts as a check and balance over the Panchayat needs to be recognised on a country-wide basis. The Gram Sabha must have, thus, a legal entity, some specific formal functions and a definite relationship with the Panchayat. The full development of the institution of Gram Sabha, as a body to whom the Panchayat will be ultimately responsible, cannot, however, be achieved merely by conferral of statutory powers on it. It is only through constant practice of its immediate role of consultation assigned to it that the Gram Sabha will be able togather necessary momentum and grow into an effective organisation of the village people.

It is generally agreed that in days to come and in the final pattern of relationship, the Gram Panchayat should be responsible to the Gram Sabha but the question with which we concerned at the moment is whether this relationship should be allowed to develop gradually through a process of convention, or should it be laid down by law as a pattern to be followed immediately by all the States. The issue appears to us to be largely academic, in view of the present development of the institution of Gram Sabha whose meetings are hardly attended by its members and in whose affairs the members show practically no concern. Once the Gram Sabha starts functioning, it is bound to influence the thinking and decisions of the village Panchayat. To make its previous consent necessary for all decisions and actions of the Panchayat, therefore, appears unnecessary and may act as a fetter on some Panchayats.

Status and Role of the Gram Sabha

The Gram Sabha should be statutorily recognised in each State and its meetings should be held more frequently, that is at least once in each quarter as against the existing practice of twice a year. The Gram Sabha should consider the following at its meeting :

(i) Plan and budget of the Panchayat,

(ii) A note on the Progress of village production plan and its implementation,

(iii) Six-monthly report on the working of different functional committees,

(vi) Annual report and accounts of the Panchayat,

(v) Summary of the annual report of the Panchayat.

(vi) Summary of the annual report of the Panchayat Samiti.

(vii) A six-monthly report on the community works under constructions.

(viii) A quarterly report on utilisation of medium and long-term-loans.

(ix) A review of the working of village Volunteer Force Defence Labour Bank.

In order to strengthen the Gram Sabha, it is, however, necessary to strengthen the Panchayat itself and to enable the two to work out a proper relationship between them. Since Panchayat is the executive of Gram Sabha, strengthening of the executive and defining the role and relationship of the Panchayat and Gram Sabha, will strengthen the Sabha itself. The Panchayat may have, accordingly, the following functions :

(i) Panchayats should be authorised to deal with matters relating to mutations, allotment of agricultural land, grazing grounds, forest rights of the village, distribution of water for irrigation and such other functions.

(ii) Lower grade officers at the village level should be guided by the Panchayat.

(iii) Development departments should not deal with individual villagers except through the Panchayat.

(iv) Nation-building departments should function in collaboration with the Panchayat, especially at times of village emergency.

We visualise that in the future pattern of growth of the Panchayat, it will develop into a stronger body and even take up functions of control on police and maintenance of law and order.

The Gram Sabha should review the working of the Panchayat in all the above matters, which will now fall within the Jurisdiction of functions of the Panchayat. There shall be a question hour in Gram Sabha meetings when any member would be free to raise questions and seek redress regarding any of the matters mentioned above. Apart from the question hour, our view is that the Panchayat should seek the consensus of Gram Sabha and look forward for the benefit of consulting it in all matters which fall within the scope of functioning of the former. The Panchayat Samiti and the officers of the Block, district and higher levels should, similarly, take the views of the Panchayat into consideration when they organise any activities of take any decision regarding the village concerned. The last two steps would ensure that the Gram Sabha will have opportunities to have its say in all matters concerning the village.

Strengthening the Gram Sabha

In order to activise the Gram Sabha, we suggest the following measures :

(i) Gram Sabha meetings should be held in rotation in each of the constituent villagers. The venue in each village shoùld however to common.

(ii) Gram Sabha meetings should be held at a time and in a day when the villagers are not busy in their agricultural operations.

(iii) A recreational programme or film show be organised immediately after the meeting of the Gram Sabha.

Size And Meetings Of Gram Sabha

Having regard to the considerations of viability and community characteristics, a population of about 400 to 500 should have a Gram Sabha.

In order to enable Gram Sabha to be wiedly and a functioning body, it is desired that the Gram Sabha in a big village, with a population exceeding 1,500, should consist of word-wise Up-Gram Sabhas, which may hold meetings and convey their decisions for consideration of the whole Gram Sabha. In such a village where there will be Up-Gram Sabhas, the meetings of the Gram Sabha in addition to those of Up-Gram Sabhas may be held twice a year, whereas the meetings of the Up-Gram Sabhas be held once in a quarter.

There should be a quorum both for original and adjourned meetings of the Gram Sabha and such quorum in both the cases should be formed by attendance of 10% of adult voters in the Panchayat area. Ten per cent of adult voters should similarly have the power to requisition a meeting of the Gram Sabha.

Decision Making In Gram Sabha

Decision-Making in Gram Sabha meetings should, as far as possible, be achieved through arriving at consensus. If, however, a decision has to be acquired through voting, two-third majority of the members present should be insisted upon.

Functional Committees

To realise the objectives of participating democracy in full, the Panchayat should set up a number of functional committees including members of the Gram Sabha on such committees and with a member each of the Panchayat as the convener of each of such committees. Each of these functional committees should be entrusted with the management of one or other of the developmental subjects of the village. The functions of these committees should be mainly advisory, their suggestions and advice being be warded to the Panchayat for necessary action and for being discussed in the Gram Sabha as well.

Village Production Plans

Where as village production plans should be of main interest to that section of the village population, who own land and participate in cultivation in some way or the other, the Gram Sabha as a whole would be interested in schemes relating to utilisation of surplus labour force and in such matters which ensure more effective corrodination between the supply line and their productional prerequisites. The Gram Sabha should and thus could, be fully associated with the implementation of village production plans.

In order to make the village production plans simpler and more comrehensible to the villagers, the present practice of having elaborate plans running into serveral columns of complicated data, may be re-examined and in view of the fact that the village production plans contain today many unnecessary items, it may be revised and that the total requirements of essential supplies of credit, seed and fertilizer required to cultivators may only find place in it. This would make the plan more comprehensible and suitable for discussion in Gram Sabha.

To stimulate production, a few good farmers, who perform essential labour by themselves on their holdings may be selected by the V.L.W. and the production plans of the former vigorously and conscientiously supervised by him; and if this could induce them to follow all the cultural practices, which are today inserted in the village production plans. This would go a long way in securing their adoption by the rest of the cultivators.

The Panchayat should levy a betterment tax for improvements effected through shramdan by members of the whole community, on the assets of particular individuals/sections of the community and which benefit these particular individuals/sections of people. The funds thus realised could be credited to the Defence Labour Bank. This would stimulate those sections of the village community who have no assets to improve, but contribute their labour through shramdan or the Village Volunteer Force.

Village Volunteer Force

The Village Volunteer Force may form a permanent feature of our rural development activities. The Force should consist of persons between the age of 18 and 45.

The functions of the V.V.F. should be the following :

(i) maintenance of law and order in the Panchayat area.

(ii) Checking spread of rumours.

(iii) Fighting fire and epidemics.

(iv) Offering first-aid and removal of casualties to

hospital.

(v) Discharge of other civic responsibilities e.g., management of fairs.

(vi) Night patrolling and protection of property and life in the Panchayat area.

To secure popular support for the scheme, it would be desirable if the Dalpati is coopted on the Panchayat as a non-boting member.

Organisation of V.V.F. at the village level should be integrated with corresponding organisations at the Block, Tehsil, district, divisional and state levels.

Panchayat And Cooperative

In addition to one service cooperative in each village, the Panchayat Samiti should organise, in the shape of agro-industrial projects, larger cooperatives catering to the needs of a number of Panchayats, in order to secure fuller employment for the un and under-employed members of the village community as well as for the weaker sections.

All cooperative assistance, other than loans to the individual villagers, should be offered through the Panchayats should take special steps to ensure that the credit and other needs of the weaker sections are adequately attended to.

In order to secure better coordination between the Panchayat and the Cooperative, and especially for securing effective emplementation of the village production plans, a member of the Panchayat should be a member of the managing committee of the Local Cooperative Society, without right to vote. Similarly, a member from the Cooperative Managing Committee should be coopted on the Panchayat sub-committee for village prduction plans.

The Panchayats, wherever they are in a position should subscribe, out of their funds, to the share capital of the cooperatives, so that the former could help to strengthen the cooperative movement of the villages.

Welfare Of Women And Weaker Sections

In order to secure participation of the women members of the Gram Sabha, it is suggested that (a) two women members should be coopted on the village Panchayat (in case no women members were duly elected) and (b) the issues concerning the women-fold of the village may be discussed in a Mahila Mandal meeting preceding the Gram Sabha meeting, so that the women members could put forward their views in a more effective manner.

While drawing up the Budget, the Panchayat should give special attention to the needs of the scheduled castes/tribes and the Zila Parishad may call for an annual report from all Pradhans in its jurisdiction in order to ensure that the problems of the weaker sections have been effectively dealt with in their respective areas. The Panchayat should also form a sub-committee to look after the welfare of the scheduled castes/tribes.

It is recommended that at least a member of the scheduled cates/tribes be coopted on the Panchayat Samiti, provided that they form to per cent of the total population of the area and unless a representative of this group has been elected to these bodies through the normal process of election notwithstanding the fact that local M.Ps. and M.L.As. may already be on these bodies as ex-afficio members. Subject to the above stipulations, one of the posts of Sarpanch/Up-Sarpanch of the Panchayat, or Pradhan/Up-Pradhan of the Panchayat Samiti should also go to a member of the scheduled castes/tribes.

Executive Assistance For Panchayat And Gram Sabha

The Panchayat should have the services of a Panchayat Secretary to look after its working. A specific functionary, working at the village level and trained in extension methods for development of Panchayat and Gram Sabha, should also be appointed. There are now a number of functionaries such as the V.L.W Panchayat Secretary and so on, who function at the level of the Panchayat but sometimes have more than one Panchayat to attend to. We feel that the whole question of having a specific village functionary for each Panchayat, who could attend to the working of the Panchayat administration as well as extension activities, should be thoroughtly enquired into.

Panchayati Raj Tiers

The Panchayat should be composed of elected members and all adult members of the area should elect the Sarpanch. The Sarpanch should be the ex-officio member of the pachayat Samiti. The Panchayat Samiti should thus be composed of all the Sarpanches of the area and a few others elected by an electoral college composed of the Panch as of the area. The total numbership of the Panchayat Samiti. No member, other than those belonging to the scheduled castes/tribes, should, however, be coopted on the Panchayat Samiti, if he had lost any primary elections.

Tenure

With a view to reduce political favour, which is usually associated with elections, we feel that the Panchayat should be a self-continuing, body, one-third of its members (then exact number depending on size of Panchayat) retiring every year. Every Panch, under the scheme, should be hold office for not more than three years as a result of each election, after which he should retire. He may, however, be eligible for re-election but not for more than two consecutive terms, that is, he will not be in office for more than six years at a stretch.

Panchayati Raj Courts

State Governments may explore the possibility of appointing apprciatic Panchayati Raj court-one for each district, with an officer of the rank of sub-Divisional Officer having adequate knowledge of and sympathetic approach to village problems, to settle disputes arising between the Panchayats and individual villagers.

Evaluation

It would be a welcome idea of the State Governments could effectively evaluate the working of the Panchayats and Panchayat Samitis and allot more funds to the deserving Panchayats thereby offering impets for Panchayats to work effectively. An evaluation organisation should, therefore, be appointed in each State preferably under non-official auspices and functioning outside the organisation of the Development Commissioner and/or Director Panchayats, for evaluating the performances of the various Panchayat and Panchayat Samiti on the basis of a well-draw in up criteria which would include, inter alia, the interest taken by these institutions in the development of Gram Sabha.

Training And Education

The question for consideration before the Team in this regard were :

(a) relationship between the people's representatives and the officials working at each tier ;

(b) relationship between the officials of the same department working in the different tiers ;

(c) the relationship between the people's representatives in the different tiers ; and our recommendations are that services in our country, as is the pattern in some States, could be divided into all-India, Central, State and Pachayati Raj services. It is important to secure that ascertain proportion of services in a higher cadre is reserved for promotion from the lower cadre and there should be possibilities of promotion from Panchayati Raj services to State services.

With regard to officials like clerks, peons, etc., whom the Panchayats employ for their work, the Panchayat should be in full control and authority over them.

The second category of personnel working in the Panchayat area, but having more than one Panchayat areas in their charge, e.g., Patwari, irrigation 'Patrol', tube well operator, officials belonging to forest and public health departments, etc., their confidential reports should be recorded in the first instance by the Sarpanches of the Panchayat areas in which they operate. In cases of complaint about their work, a convention should be established that complaints from the Sarpanches should be promptly dealt with.

With regard to the third category of officials, which would include police constables, forest guards and officials of other non-development departments, the procedure of making complaints to their superior officers and securing replies to these in the meeting of Panchayat Samiti should be followed.

At the level of the Panchayat Samiti, the B.D.O. should be responsible to the Pradhan and the latter's supervision over the Panchayat Samiti staff be exercised through the B.D.O. The Pradhan should also write the confidiential reports of all the extension officers including the revenue officer, posted at Block headquarters. In so far as the B.D.O. is responsible for coordiantion, the pradhan should be able to avoid direct dealings with the extension staff. This is a matter of proper orientation and should be dealt with by the training programme provided for Pradhans and similar classes of non-officials.

The Block Development Officer should have the status of a Provencial Civil Service Officer so that he could command confidence and ensure smooth functioning of the administration of the Panchayat Samiti. This would help him to work out a proper relationship with the non-official members.

In determining the relationship between various officials working in the same department in the various tiers we consider that the administrative and technical responsibility of the departments should remain undesturbed. This would include not only offering of technical advice and directives, but also grant of leave, provision of substitutes, etc., which should be the responsibility of the departments. We do not think that this would come in the way of drawing up programmes of work at the village level.

The general import of working out proper relationship between people's representatives in the different tiers, is to secure coordination between the work of various bodies within the jurisdiction of the higher tier, while leaving them sufficient freedom to plan development programmes suitable to their local conditions. The village Sarpanch should be unfettered in selecting programmes of work which they have to finance exclusively from their own resources. In addition to the general supervision and direction laid down in the Acts there would be at the higher level officials whose duty it would be to inspect and guide the working of these institutions so that the duties laid down in the Acts could be adequately discharged by the body concerned. The responsibility for any decisions on reports regarding of lower tiers should be taken by the appropriate representatives of the people and not left to the reporting Officer.

A revenue official may be associated with the Block organisation. With headquarters at the Block, so that prompt action may be taken on villagers' grievances regarding allotment of land, removal of encroachments mutations, etc.

Institutional Functioning

The Panchayat should keep its electorates informed of the developments that take place in Panchayat meetings.

One of the ways of securing that the office-bearers of the Panchayat act institutionally is to ensure that their work is regularly supervised. The Zila Parishad and Panchayat Samiti should, therefore, consititute small sub-committees to supervise the working of the Panchayat Semiti/Panchayat, as the case may be, with the special objective of the securing that they function institutionally.

Training programme for the officials should include a particular course each in the manner and method of implementing programmes of guidance and pointing out lapses without causing unnecessary offence. Directions given to tiers on the basis of spervision and guidance should invariably, be by the Head of the higher tiers, in consultation with the sub-committees set up for the purpose.

The Panchayat Samiti may appoint specific functional sub-committees for supervising the work of lower tiers and thereby ensure association of the members of the Panchayat Samiti with the working of the institution. There should be provision for holding a meeting, at least once in a year, of all the Panchas of the area with a view to secure more effective association of the Panches with the working of the Samiti.

To safeguard against misuse of financial powers of the Sarpanch, it should be made obligatory on his part to inform the members of Panchayat about the condition of the Panchayat funds at each meeting of the Panchayat and what is the balance deposited.

Panchayat elections and Political parties

Elections to the Panchayat should be non-political inasmuch as political parties should be refrain (a) from announcing/nominating candidates (b) allotting party symbols and insignia for different contestants in Panchayati Raj elections.

Those panchayats where elections have been unanimous may be offered inducements in the shape of additional grants either in lump or as recruing measure.

In order to prevail upon the political parties to take a non-political view of the Panchayat elections, we feel that a meeting of all political parties should be convened be some organisation of standing (e.g.., All-India Panchayati Raj Parishad) in order to help them to come to an agreed decision that the political parties should not contest Panchayat elections on party basis, so that they may agree so set up candidates who would be elected unanimously.

STUDY TEAM ON PANCHAYATI RAJ FINANCES, 1962—REPORT

Delhi, Ministry of Community Development and Cooperation, 1963. 2 parts.

Chairman : Shri K. Santhanam

Members : Shri Shree Narayan Dass ; Shri M.Y. Ghorpade ; Prof. M. V. Mathur ; Shri C. Narasimhan.

Secretary : Shri R. Saran.

APPOINTMENT

The Study Team on Panchayati Raj Finances was constituted under the Ministry of Community Development & Cooperation vide their Resolution No. 4/78/61-Panch, dated July 29, 1962.

TERMS OF REFERENCE

The Study Team will examine, within the broad frame work and provisions of the Third Plan, the resources and finances of Panchayati Raj institution in different States and make recommendations on the following subjects :

(a) With due regard to functions transferred, sources of revenue (including land revenue) which should be handed over in full or in part to Panchayati Raj instituions and arrangements for earmarking of certain resources for maintenance of services and institution under Panchayati Raj bodies;

(b) Grants by State Governments and the conditions to be attached to such grants,

(c) Mutual financial relations between the Panchayati Raj institutions,

(d) Steps to develop the existing resources and to build up revenue yielding assets or Panchayati Raj institutions; and

(e) Steps to attract gifts and donations and mobilise voluntary contributions by the people.

CONTENTS

Part I : Introductory; General Approach ; Structure and Functions; Resources of Panchayats; Expenditure of

Panchayats; Resources Panchayat Samitis; Zila Parishads; Loans to Panchayati Raj Bodies; Budget, Accounts and Audit; general Conclusions; Summary of Recommendations and Suggestions; Annexures I to VIII.

Part II: State and Union territory reports.

RECOMMENDATIONS

Section 4 - Resources of Panchayats

House Tax, profession tax and vehicle tax should be compulsory taxes of Panchayats Minimum and maximum rates of compulsory taxes should be prescribed. House tax may be levied on the basis of capital value of the house. There should be no exemption from the levy of house tax. An independent agency for valuation of houses may be set up. The maximum and minimum rates of house tax based on capital value of houses may be as follows :

(a) On a house of capital value not exceeding Rs. 250.	Minimum 25 nP. and Maximum Re. 1
(b) On a house of capital value ranging from Rs. 251 to Rs. 500.	Minimum 50 nP. and Maximum Rs. 2.
(c) On a house of capital value ranging from Rs. 501 to Rs. 1000.	Minimum Re. 1 and Maximum Rs. 5.
(d) On a house of capital value of over Rs. 1000.	For every increase of Rs.500 or part thereof the increase in the minimum and maximum rate to be 50 nP. and Rs. 2.50 respectively.

For town Panchayats, the rates may be higher. Profession tax should be levied at rates similar to those proposed in the Andhra Pradesh Panchayats Bill 1963. The rate of cycle tax should be fixed by Panchayat Samiti and made uniformly applicable throughout its area 7/8 Steps should be taken to see that municipalities within the area of Samiti levy the tax at the same rate.

Vehicle tax should be levied on all vehicles including bicyles. Motor vehicles should continue to be exempted. The minimum rate of vehicle tax should be Rs. 2 per annum, for all vehicle and the maximum Rs. 4 per cycle and Rs. 10 per bullock-cart. The circumstances and property tax imposed by the States of Bihar, Orissa and West Bengal should be split up into its component parts, viz. house tax and land tax, for greater precision, certainty of imposition and case of collection. Kollagarum, a tax on produce sold in village by weight, measurement or number, may be an optional tax of Panchayats.

The State Governments should consider the possibility of replacing octroi where levied, by other progressive taxes.

Pilgrim tax should preferably be levied by Panchayat Samiti or Zila Parished, a part of the proceeds being given to Panchayats in the area of which pilgrim centres are located and the rest utilised for the common benefit of the area of Samiti or of the district. The expenditure incurred in this connection should be shared suitably by concerned Panchayat, Samiti and Zila Parishad.

The State Governments should consider the possibility of providing for levy by Panchayats of a tax on animals.

The levy of fees for water supply, drainage, street lighting and conservancy should be optional. Where water supply, drainage or electric lighting is provided through loans, Panchayat should have the right to charge a fee from beneficiaries. The basis for fixing the rate of such fees may be the amount needed for servicing the loan or for covering the liability incurred in providing the service.

In regard to the levy of licences and fees, the position in each State should be reviewed in the light of levies in different States so as to make the powers of Panchayats as comprehensive as possible.

The expenditure on Naya Panchayats should be met by the Government on the net cost basis, preferably at the Samiti level.

Unless specailly exempted, all public land, trees, ponds and tanks with fishery rights therein, unreserved forests, choultries, rest houses and other buildings situated in a Panchayat area and not belonging to a private party should be transferred to that Panchayat.

The proceeds of sale of abadi land should be used only for expenditure which will create permanent assets for Panchayat.

Alienation of immovable property by a Panchayat should be subject to permission or approval of a prescribed authority.

In Panchayats where there are large unassigned areas of cultivable land, a minimum of one cent of land per capita should be given to Panchayat as non-alienable Community property, while the rest may be retained with the Government for future assignment of landless labourers and others.

When there is not enough land available, the State Governments should acquire and hand over to each Panchayat not less than 5 acres to be used as community property for house sites, compost making, tree planting nursery and such other purposes.

Management of fishery ponds, even where fishery rights belong customarily to local communities of fishermen, should vest in Panchayats.

Cattle pounds should be the property of Panchayats, who should be given the right to fix rates for them.

In the case of markets classified as Samiti and Zila Parishad markets, a reasonable share of net income, may one-third, subject to a maximum of one rupee per capita should be given to Panchayats in the area of which fair is held or market is organised.

The question of sharing the income from markets, organised by Market Committees or Societies, with Panchayati Raj institutions should be carefully examined by the State Governments. Panchayats and Samitis should be allowed to participate actively in the organisation of these markets.

Surcharge on stamp duty not exceeding 5 per cent of the value of property should be levied and collected by State Government. The proceeds within the area of a Samiti should be distributed in an equitable manner among that Samiti and its Panchayats.

The whole or a part of entertainment tax collected by State in rural areas should be shared with Panchayats and Samitis. Panchayats and Samitis may levy a show tax in addition.

The State assistance, if any, for the whole or part of the salary of Secretary of Panchayat should be in the form of purposive grant. Secretary should be paid directly Panchayat.

The Governments, who derive income from the sale of Kendu leaf, may consider the desirability of sharing this income with Panchayts or Samitis.

The entire tax demand of a Panchayat, excluding arrears, may be taken as the basis for matching grant and, if collection of 75 per cent is made in a year an amount equal to 15 per cent of such collection should be given as matching grant which should increase atleast by one per cent for every additional five per cent collection.

The matching grant for panchayats in backward areas should be on more liberal basis.

A basic minimum maintenance grant of Re. 1 per capita should be given to every Panchayat and this should be shared equally by State and Central Governments.

For executing specific development projects, panchayats should have powers to levy special tax on land revenue house tax, or on some other basis.

In case voluntary contribution in cash or labour is insufficient to execute a development project, recourse may be had to labour tax, Defence Labour Bank or special levy, payable in cash or labour. Voluntary contribution may be adjusted against these levies.

Expenditure Of Panchayats

The expenditure on administration should not ordinarily exceed 25 per cent of the total income of a Panchayat.

Wherever revenue authorities feel confident and Panchayats agree, the work of revenue collection may be transferred to Panchayats.

Every Panchayat should have a Secretary who may perform also the duties of collection of land revenue and Panchayat taxes or that the Village Level WorKer but a VLW should not be given the task of revenue and tax collection.

An over-head tank, a pipe line and taps for water supply at convenient centres should be an objective of all Panchayats.

Every Panchayat, which can afford, should engage one or more sweepers. Street sweepings, should, as far as possible, be converted into compost. Special attention should be paid to the maintenance of village road. Special assistance, a part of which may be in the form of loan, should be given to Panchayats in areas which are badly in need of drainage facilities.

Electrification of villages should be speeded up.

Community broadcasting in the villages may be universalised and a proper maintenance organisation established for servicing community listening sets.

Where Panchayat has funds, a portion may be earmarked for construction of Panchayat building.

Where a development project common to several Panchyats and accepted by a majority of them is held up for want of voluntary contributions from a few Panchayats, Panchayat Samiti concerned should be able to endorce a special levy on recalcitrant Panchayats.

The procedure followed in Madras of pooling all grants under the community development schematic budget and those from State Departments and of evolving a development schematic budget for Samiti may be examined by all other State Governments. The Government of India should encourage the States to adopt the procedure.

An annual average per capita grant of Re. 1 should be made to each Samiti to be shared equally by the State and Central Government and to be earmarked for maintenance of staff on an agreed pattern. The Centre's share of the grant may be met by suitable adjustments within grants now being made by it.

To enable Samitis to participate in the evolution of the Forth Plan, the Central and State Government may intimate to them in advance the minimum and maximum financial limits that can be made available to them by way of grants and loans.

In the implementation of the plan, limitations imposed on Samitis should be in terms of broad categories like education, health, roads, etc. and so long as they conform to national pattern, the Samitis should have freedom to read just the plan in the light of actual experience and the changing needs of the people.

An amount of Rs. 400 crores @ Rs. 10 per capita of rural population should be alloted in the Fourth Plan for unspecified local development works to be given on a matching basis.

Elementary education, a natural and essential function of the Panchayat Raj, should be transferred to

Samiti or Zila Parishad. Its actual day to day management may vest in a Board set up by Samiti or Zila Parishad in which not only members of that body but also others with special knowledge and experience in the proper development of education should find a place.

The entire expenditure on elementary education should be met out of grants and resources transferred specially for the purpose by the State Government.

Every Samiti should have some additional funds at its disposal for initiative in effecting educational improvements.

Not more than half the proceeds of resources transferred to Samitis, like share of land revenue of cess, stamp duty, entertainment tax, etc. should be earmarked for committee expenditure on schemes and institutions transferred to them and the balance of such expenditure should be finaned by the State partly by general and partly by specific grants.

Grants for maintenance of roads may be on the basis of mileage and those for repair and maintenance of irrigation sources, on the basis of acreage irrigated.

There should be no confusion and overlapping in the taxation powers of Panchayat Samiti and Zila Parishad.

Contributions from Panchayats should be shown on the receipt side of the budget of every Samiti and the total expenditure on works belonging to the Samiti shown on the opposite side.

The salaries and allowances of all staff working under Samiti should be paid from its funds and shown in its accounts.

A Samiti should be free to add to the strength of its staff so long as it is able to meet the expenditure from the one rupee per capital grant and its own resources.

Where it is too big to be managed by Panchayats, Samitis should be entrusted with the management of fairs, markets, ghats and ferries, tanks and plantations and share the proceeds with Panchayats where these are located or organised.

Every Service or institution serving exclusively the area of a Samiti and being its legitimate function should be transferred to it.

Section 7-Zila Parishads

It is necessary to transfer some more elastic sources to Zila Parishad in Maharashtra so that is can be an effective organ of local Government at the district level. Even a purely Advisory District Council can render useful service if the matters on which it should be consulted are listed with imagination and precession and a convention established for modification or rejection of its recommendation only by the State Cabinet.

There should be definite principles and criteria for distribution of funds to Samitis through Zila Parishads. Where the distribution is more or less automatic, the funds may be sent directly to Samitis or Panchayats concerned without being channeled through Zila Parishads.

The rights and duties of Zila Parishads, Samitis and Panchayats in any particular sphere of activity should be precise and beyond dispute. Zila Parishad or Samiti should not be empowered to levy contributions from body belonging to a lower tier, except for executing development projects in the area of that body. The salaries of all staff working under a Zila Parishad should be paid from the Zila Parishad's funds.

Section 8-Loans To Panchayati Raj Bodies

Every State Government should establish a Panchayti Raj Finance Corporation. State Governments should fix the authorised capital subject to a minimum of one crore of rupees and maximum of 5 crores of rupees.

Its authorised capital should be divided into fully paid up shares of Rs. 100 each to be issued among Panchayati Raj institutions, State Government, Central Reserve Bank of India, Life Insurance Corporation, Cooperative Banks, Sheduled Banks, Insurance Companies and other financial institutions.

The corporation may give loan to Panchayat, Samiti or Zila Parishad for public utility undertakings; construction of shops, markets. hotels, etc. purchase of tractors, pumping sets and bore well units; plantation and afforestation; scientific agriculture and small-scale and medium industries.

The corporation may give loan to Panchayati Raj institutions seeking loans on the financial, technical and other aspects of the projected undertakings.

Section 9-Budget, Accounts And Audit

For inclusion in the budget of a Panchayati Raj institution the items of assistance which depend on actual receipts of a tax, fee, etc., should be calculated by the State Government on the basis of the actual collections of the first half and the estimated collection of the second half of the year preceding the budget year. These amounts should be intimated to the Panchayati Raj institutions well in advance of the time fixed for preparation of their bedgets.

The State Governments should make special efforts to arrive at decisions on the schemes to be executed by Panchayati Raj institutions and the amounts to be given to them for the purpose by way of grant and loans and to intimate the same to the institutions concerned well in advance of the preparation of the budgets.

The Panchayats and Samitis should make provision in their budgets only for such taxes as are to be actually levied in the budget year, and the proceeds from which can be resonable estimated.

Samiti should adopt the practice of deciding upon schemes to be executed through Panchayats at least six months in advance of the budget year. A suitable penalty, say of 10 per cent, may be levied on all arrears of taxes and this penalty utilised by the revenue authorities or Samities for appointing special staff for collection of arrears.

Generous prizes may be offered to Panchayats which collect hundred per cent of their assessment.

Wherever Samiti is required to approve the budgets of its Panchayats, the power should be delegated to its Finance Committee.

The form of Panchayat accounts should be simple and should indicate independently the normal recurring receipion one side and the committed expenditure on the other. Special grants, contribution its own contibution and loans, for development projects should be special grants, contributions, its own matching contribution and loans, for development projects should be separately shown on the receipt side and expenditure on development works either is own or of Samiti, should be shown on the expenditure side.

The budget of Samiti should reflect all receipts and expenditure, whether of the community development programme, its own resources, grants from development departments, contributions from Panchayats, or loans raised by it. The expenditure should include the salaries of all staff even if they are paid directly by Government. The payment by Government for this purpose should be shown as receipt. Grants to panchayats by Samiti for their works, like drinking water supply or Panchayat roads, should be shown separately.

Samiti should show in some manner or the other the cumulative value of all permanent assets created either through grants, contributions, loans, or its own resources.

Wherever a public utility or remunerative undertaking has been financed by loans, proper commercial accounts should be maintained.

Every Panchayat should be inspected at least once in three months by Panchayat Extension Officer to ensure that there is no misappropriate on or falsification of accounts.

A weekly statement of receipts and expenditure should be sent by each Panchayat to its Samiti office where it should be scheduled or Cooperative Bank or Post Office Savings Bank and money for expenses drawn strictly according to rules and procedures.

Panchayats should not be encouraged to make longter n investments merely for earning interest, but, should be persuaded to use their balances for constructive purposes including development of remunerative undertakings.

A special branch in the office of the Examiner of Local Fund Audit should be organised in each State to carry-out regularly the audit of the accounts of Panchayati Raj institutions.

It should be impressed upon Panchayats, and Samitis that defects pointed out by auditors should be promptly remedical and satisfactory explanation offered_to meet the audit objection.

A special meeting of Panchayat/Samiti should be held for consideration of the audit report within 30 days of its receipt, and the result of discussion should be sent to supervising authority.

Section 10-General

As frequent changes in their structure, functions, and resources will prevent Panchayati Raj bodies from taking root and will create around them an atmosphere of uncertainty, revision of laws and rules should be undertaken only after sufficient experience of their working has been gained.

The salaries, allowances and other conditions of service of the employees of Panchayati Raj bodies should as far as possible be the same as those of State Government employees of similar categories.

Training in budgetary and accounting procedure should be particularly emphasized in the case of Panchayat Extension Officers and Secretaries.

In order to facilitate the work of Panchayati Raj Finances Corporation, there should be an institute in each state to study the scope of remunerative undertakings in particular areas and to undertake pilot project. It is desirable that it should have wings for evaluation and studies relating to Panchayati Raj.

All high schools should provide for teaching about Panchayati Raj and this should be supplemented by periodic voluntary service camps of boy scouts, National Cadet Corps, etc. In colleges and Universities, the study of problems relating to Panchayati Raj should be encouraged by making it a special subject or an integral part of social science.

All grants and subventions, including specific and purposive departmental grants, may be pooled at the State level and disbursed in a consolidated form to various Panchayati Raj institutions.

A High level officer should, at least in bigger States be exclusively in charge of financial matters concerning Panchayati Raj bodies. Ministers in charge of Panchayati Raj should devote special attention to the development of cordial relations between the departmental officers and Panchayati Raj bodies.

Samitis, Zila Parishads and State Governments should prepare annually consolidated statements of income and expenditure of the institutions under them. The consolidated statements for all the tiers at the State level should be published and presented to State Legislature every year.

The Ministry of Community Development and co-operation should prepare consolidated statements for the country as a whole and publish them with Statewise tables of income and expenditure.

Panchayats and Samitis may be classified into three or four groups according to their capacity to raise resources to ensure that proportionately greater assistance is given to poorer categorties.

As the three tier system may not be quite suitable in peculiar circumtances of backward area, particularly hilly tracts inhabited by scheduled tribes, special institutions and procedures may be devised for them.

The State Governments may consider the possibility of sharing the income from forests, quarrying and mineral royalties with Panchayats which have every little agricultural land and consequently insignificant land revenue. All donations for purposes such as those of National Defence Fund and expenditure on receptions and cerremonial occasions, in excess of a small minimum, should be prohibited.

Special attempts should be made to assist Panchayats in overcoming difficulties to obtain title or possession of land and property transferred to them by Acts or rules and orders made under them. When they get involved in litigation, legal advice and financial assistance should also be extended to them. The authorites concerned should give preference to Panchayat in its corporate capacity, for agencies in respect of National Savings Scheme and Life Insurance Corporation.

Help to the disabled and destitutes should be given by Government through Panchayati Raj institutions which should also share the burden to some extent, wherever possible.

Panchayats should endeavour to attract gifts and donations.

It may be worth while considering whether some degree of uniformity should be attempted in the nomenclature of Panchayati Raj institutions and their presiding officers to avoid confusion in inter-state comparisions and all India reports.

When Panchayati Raj institutions have come to be firmly established in all states, the problems of mutual cooperation between Panchayati Raj bodies and cooperative may be re-examined by representatives of both sides.

Section 11-Conclusion

After Panchayati Raj bodies have functioned for some years, there should be enquiries at State level on a uniform basis, by agreement among State Government, to review their resources and finances. This should be followed by an enquiry for the whole country instituted by the Government of India.

WORKING GROUP ON PLANTATIONS LABOUR HOUSING, 1962—REPORT

Delhi, Manager of Publications, 1964. 113p.

Chairman : Shri N. N. Chatterjee.

Members : Shri K. N. Valenkar ; Shri A. S. Bam or Alternately Shri W. Simpson ; (left and replaced by Shri K.M. Kidwai) ; Shri S.S.B. Raghavan ; Shri Gurudev Saran ; (left and replaced by Shri G.S. Bhasin ; Shri B. Krishnamurti ; (replaced by Shri M.K. Kochar).

APPOINTMENT

The Ministry of Labour and Employment according by issued orders setting up the Working Group on Plantation Labour Housing Vide their Letter No. PL-15 (8)/60 dated August 5, 1962.

TERMS OF REFERENCE

(a) To assess the total cost of provision of houses of approved standards for plantation workers and thei families not yet provided with such houses and the resources available to employers for this purpose including loan facilities under the Plantation Labour Housing Scheme and those provided by banks.

(b) To suggest how the existing loan facilities may be improved, whether further facilities for loans should be provided, and whether loans can be had from the life Insurance Corporation for construction of workers houses under the Plantation Labour Act.

(c) To recommend whether, in addition to loans, assistance by way of subsidies should be provided by Government and if so, how and to what extent such assistance should be given.

(d) To consider whether the entire cost of construction of worker's houses could be charged to the revenue account so that 100 per cent development rebate would be allowable to employers for purposes of income tax without affecting the profits for disbursement of bonus to plantation workers.

(e) To examine whether the annual rate of construction of worker's houses prescribed in the Plantation Labour Rules should be modified ; and

(f) To make any other suggestion for completion of the housing programme for plantation workers within a reasonable time.

CONTENTS

Introductory ; Assessment of the total Cost of Provision of Labour Housing Resources available to the Employers ; Financial Assistance for Labour Housing ; Request of Plantation Industry for grant of 100 per cent Rebate for Income tax in respect of Expenditure Incurred on Construction of Houses for Labour ; Whether the Anunal rate of Construction of Houses for Plantation Labour as Prescribed under the Plantation Labour Rules should be Modified ; Housing Cooperatives of Workers ; Construction of Housing Colonies by Government ; Standards and Specifications for Worker's Houses in Plantations ; Summary of Conclusions and Recommendations ; Appendices from I to XV.

RECOMMENDATIONS

The financial burden on the plantation industry has increase considerably since the target for construction of houses for 8 per cent of the resident workers per annum was laid down in 1950 on account of additional taxation, increase in wages & fringe benefits and increased cost of construction of labour Housing.

Against a total number of 4,51,670 houses required to be constructed only 2,40,329 houses of the approved standard were in existence on the 31st Dec, 1962. According to the present cost of construction per unit in the various States, a capital of about 87.66 crores would be required to complete the housing programme.

The position regarding finances avaible to the plantation industry from within their own resources, cannot be generalised. The financial condition of the industry differs not only from State to State but also from one area of another in the same State and from one plantation to another plantation in the same area.

No appreciable impact can be made in the speeding up of the housing programme by diversion of reserve funds to the construction of houses.

In certain cases, there is room from curtailing expenditure on over head charges by decreasing the remuneration paid to the Managing Agents and Secretaries by abolishing or restricting the commission paid to managers etc. and by rationalising the salary structure of the managerial cadre.

There is a prima facie case for rationalising the existing high rates of divided paid by certain companies so as to provide more funds for labour housing while ensuring a fair return to share holders.

A reasonable balance should be maintained between expending of money on developmental charges and on labour housing and neither of the two should take precedence over the other.

The State Governments should on the analogy of the practice followed by the government of the West Bengal, accept bank guarantees from planters, as security for repayment of loans under the plantation Labour Housing Scheme.

On the analogy of action taken by the Government of West Bengal, the State Governments should draw on the loan facilities available from the funds of the Life Insurance Corporation for providing financial assistance to needy planters.

Some units of the plantation industry are definitely in need of financial assistance if they are to fulfil the housing programme according to the target of construction of houses at the rate of 8 per cent of resident workers per annum.

Efforts should be made to ensure that the 8 per cent target is adhered to as far as possible.

Early action is called for on the part of the State Government concerned in regard to the creation of the Pool Guarantee Fund.

Where there is a recognised building progromme & where the plot numbers upon which houses are to built can be identified it should not be difficult for the bank to agree in writing that the particular plots not with standing the hypothecation on the estates as a whole, would be excluded, so that the plots may be mortgaged together with the houses built thereon as security for repayment of loans under the Plantation labour Housing Scheme.

Administrative delays in sanctioning loans should be avoided and the amounts sanctioned made available as expeditiously as possible.

It is necessary to provide assistance in the form of subsidy to the plantation industry as in the case of other Industeries. The plantation labour Housing scheme, may be modified to provide for grant of subsidy to the extent of 25 per cent of the cost and the grant of loans to the extent of 50 per cent of the cost, on the lines of the subsidised Industrial housing scheme.

The panchayats should not levy house tax on houses constructed under plantations Labour Act 1951 as these houses are rent free and the panchayats do not provide the civic amenities normally expected of them in plantation areas.

The State Governments should not revise the standards and specifications for construction of worker's Houses in way that will increase the cost of construction considerably. The Group commends for the consideration of State Governments that houses once built according to specifications should continue to be treated as "standard" houses for the rest of their life.

There is a very strong case for providing some relief to the plantation Indu try by allowing them higher rates of depreciation allowance than are admissible at present, in respect of expenditure incurred on provision of houses constructed according to approved standards for labour. The rate of depreciation allowance should be corelated to the type of houses constructed so that the amorlization period coincides with the life of house. The following rates of depreciation allowance should be adopted.

(a) **Pucca type** :—No change in the existing rate; viz. Normal depreciation allowance of 7.5 per cent per annum plus a special depreciation allowance of 20 per cent during the first year.

(b) **Semi-pucca type** :—Normal rate of depreciation allowance of 7.5 per cent per annum should continue, but special depreciation allowance during the Ist year should be raised from 20 per cent to 40 per cent.

(c) **Kutcha type** :—Normal annual depreciation allowance should be 25 per cent per annum and special depreciation allowance during the 1st year should be 40 per cent.

The concession to charge the expenditure to revenue should be allowed in cases of renewal of all kutcha type houses conforming to the approved standards.

The grant of income tax rebate at higher rates as suggested above should not affect in any manner the quantum of bonus payable to plantation labour.

All State Governments should allow rebate for assessments of agriculture on income-tax on the same rates as have been recommended in Item 18 above of for purposes of assessing central Income tax.

There is no justification for a general whole sale reduction in the existing target for construction of worker's houses at the rate of 8 per cent per annum. Specific cases should be considered by State Governments on merits & exemption from the fulfillment of the housing target for particular years sanctioned by them.

Cases of exemptions should be dealt with expeditiously and State Govts. should provide adequate staff to deal with these cases.

If in a particular year, the housing programme can't be proceeded with according to the fixed target due to the shortage of building materials or similar other reasons, the estates should set aside an appropriate amount out of theire net profits for the year for heing expended position of availability of building materials improves.

Construction of houses by housing co-operatives outside plantations; worker's cooperatives may be tried out only where suitable location is available. Govt. may either acquire suitable land for this purpose and give it to workers' cooperatives or help them in getting suitable land. Assistance as is available under the subsidised Industrial Housing Scheme to workers' co-operatives may be provided.

Construction of houses by workers' cooperatives inside plantations. It may be possible to acquire suitable land at the outer periphery of some plantations where an approach road may be available. In such cases, the planters will not be put to any trouble. They may also have no objection to the occupation of the house by a family even after the retirement of a worker provided at least one member of the family continues to work in the plantation. The pattern of assistance to be provided to the co-operatives may be as follows :

(i) The land on which houses are to be constructed should be made available by the planters on a long term lease basis with a provision for renewal of these.

(ii) The planters should subsidise 50 per cent of the cost of houses and services. Once the houses are constructed, the entire expenditure on their maintenance and repairs will be the responsibility of co-operatives of workers.

(iii) The remaining 50 per cent of the cost should be met by grant of loans & subsidies and share capital raised by the society.

The main test for setting up a new agency to provide the various welfare facilities including housing facilities to plantation workers will be whether this will result in speedier implementation of the welfare provisions of this Act. As this can't be ensured, acceptance of the proposals for construction of workers' houses and provision of other facilities by a Govt. agency which will also be more costly is not recommended.

Govt. should have power to construct houses & realise costs where employers fail to provide housing accommodation as prescribed under the Rules, unless such failure is for reasons beyond their control.

Small estates which are contigous may be allowed to set up housing colonies on a joint basis, wherever feasible, so as to have a layout plan for the colony & to provide common services like drinking water etc. at less cost.

As the 8% formula has to be applied, Assam Govt. should hold in obeyance the new standards prescribed untill the finance position of the tea Industry demonstratively improves. If Assam Govt. can't keep the revised standards in obeyance, the following steps are suggested.

(i) They should not declare houses constructed under the standards prescribed before Feb., 1963 as sub-standard, calling for remodelling of existing houses.

(ii) The tea gardens should have a discretion to construct kutcha or semi-pucca houses only on revised standards (which no doubt, would be constlier in the long run, but would not entail heavy investment initially).

(iii) Assam Govt. should be prepared to offer the tea gardens a subsidy over & above the form of assistance recommended by the working group to make up for the difference in outlay caused by their revision of standards.

The working group recommends the design produced by the Indian Tea Association for the consideration of State Govt. in the Eastern Region. The Group would not like to indicate any minimum all-India standard as there are enormous local variation in climate, environments housing requirements etc.

As local housing conditions vary from State to State, the working group considers that the State Govt. are in a better position to decide about the standards & specifications for workers' houses.

If sufficient supply of building materials like cement etc. is not available, the State Govt. may consider relaxation of the standards & specifications in suitable cases, to enable the employers to make a more liberal use of locally available material for construction of semi-pucca or kutcha houses of improved design.

Suitable arrangements should also be made for the supply of requisite quantities of building materials to planters. For this purpose the planters should draw up a forward programme of their requirements where it is not being done at present.

SECOND WORKING GROUP ON INDUSTRIAL COOPERATIVES 1962—REPORT,

Delhi, Manager of Publications, 1964. 236p.

Chairman : Shri B.P. Patel ;

Members : Shri K.V. Venkatachalam ; Shri M.P. Bhargava ; Shri Brahm Prakash ; Shri D.A. Shah; Shri V. Sivaraman; (replaced by Shri P.D. Kasbekar) ; Shri M.L. Batra ; Shri M. Gandharva Sain; Shri F.N. Rana; Shri S.R. Varma ; (resigned replaced by Shri B.K. Chatterjee) ; Shri P. Sabanayagam ; Shri Tarapado Chaudhary (expired and replaced by Shri Nagendra Kumar Bhattacharyya).

Member-Secretary : Shri L.N. Renu

APPOINTMENT

The Second Working Group on Industrial Cooperatives was constituted under the Ministry of Commerce and Industry in Consultation with the Planning Commission and the Ministry of Community Development vide Memorandum No. 9 (25) 62-I CC dated September, 1962, to review the present position of Industral cooperatives reommend special programmes and physical torgets during the third plan and indicate the lines of development Industrial cooperatives in the Fourth Plan.

TERMS OF REFERENCE

(i) To review the present position of industrial cooperatives.

(ii) To recommend specific programmes and physical targets for the organisation of cooperatives during the Third Five Year Plan period and to make recommendations for allocating to cooperatives a certain position of the funds provided for the entire sector;

(iii) To suggest patterns of financial assistance from the Government;

(iv) To assess financial requirements of cooperatives at various levels and suggest ways and means of meeting them ; and

(v) To indicate the lines of development of industrial cooperatives in the Fourth Plan.

CONTENTS

Introduction; Present Position of Industrial Cooperatives; Third Five Year Plan; Pattern of Government Assistance; Institutional Finance; Fourth Plan ; Conclusions; Summary of Recommendations; Appendics: Statements ; Explanatory Notes on Societies of Small Industrialists.

RECOMMENDATIONS

1. (i) Amongst the industrial societies there are those that undertake production and others that only provide to their members. They are organised in most cases on a single industry basis and in special cases on a multi-industry basis. Among the production type there are workshops set up by workers in special trades. In

order to distinguish them from industrial cooperatives of other types these societies may be called "workshop cooperatives."

(ii) There is another type of production society where members continue to work in their cottages or original workships but the society takes the risk of production

(iii) There are societies which offer services to their members by supplying raw materials, tools and equipment, selling their products or providing credit or other facilities. These may be called "industrial service societies."

2. (i) The aim should be to bring about 30% of the working in household industries under cooperative organisation by the end of the Third Plan. This would mean an upward revision of the existing programme to about 15,000 new industrial cooperatives and in addition of 15 lakh members. The target for working capital will be Rs. 300 per individual member i.e. Rs. 120 crores (an addition of Rs. 67 crores during the Plan) and for paid up capital of an additional amount of Rs. 20 crores. The borrowing of these societies from the government would be Rs. 25.92 crores including the amount passed through the Khadi & Village Industries Commission, from cooperative banks Rs. 26.65 crores and from coop the state financial corporations, the Industrial Finance Corporation, the Life Insurance corporation and other sources Rs. 23.43 crores. Of the plan provision under the head "village and small industries" Rs. 84 crores may be utilised towards development of cooperative societies, of which Rs. 46 crores would be by way of government loans to societies, their members and banks and by way of share participation. Share capital loans and share participation by Government may account for Rs. 16.01 crores, government loan of or working capital, equipment and other purposes to the societies Rs. 19.49 crores and government loan to the banks for being advanced to industrial cooperative societies Rs. 10 crores.

(ii) We hope that sales machinery of weavers' societies will be geared up to attain a turn-over of three times their working capital by 1966.

(iii) Separate provisions for handicraft cooperatives should be made by those states which have not already done so and the provisions suitably stepped up by all states to reach a target of 50% of the Third Plan provisions for handicrafts.

(iv) We recommend that 25% i.e. Rs. 11.1 crores of the small scale industries provision in the State Plans should be utilised for the development of industrial cooperative societies. Some states have laid down targets for the development of societies in this group. Others may also do so.

3. Coir co-operatives should be encouraged to purchase raw husk, undertake its retting and sell retted husk to members in addition to their usual activities of sale of yarn and their finished products of their members. The cooperative banks should be agreeable to advance loans to those societies against the security of husks in the process of retting, subject to such safeguards as may be necessary in practicie to protect their interests.

4. Along with the necessity of paying due attention to the formation of workers cooperatives, the need for the organisation of societies of crafts man and small manufacturers cannot be ignored. It is expected that a substantial number of such societies would be organised during the Third Plan in the field of handicrafts, coir and small scale industries on an industry-wise basis. This would include societies of (i) aritisans (ii) master craftsmen and (iii) small industrialists. A distinction will be necessary in regard to the nature and quantum of assistance that would be provided to the 3 categories of societies, care being taken to see that special assistance meant for the societies consisting of workers and artisans is not utilized by the societies formed by the well-to-do master craftsmen and industrialists.

5. The scheme for utilizing the services of urban cooperative banks be reconsidered and a rivised scheme worked out for utilising the agency of new or existing urban cooperative banks for industrial loans on a pilot scale. Upto six such banks may be selected/organised in each state in towns which have not got facilities of industrial cooperative banks of the mixed type. A bank selected under the scheme should have a minimum paid up captail of Rs. 50,000. Government should assist those banks whose capital is below this figure by meeting the difference by share participation. The guarantee referred to in paragraph 126 should be extended to these banks. They should be given managerial grants by the Government to enable them to appoint a special deputy manager, an accountant and an inspector for industrial work. Where it is intended to assist them with government funds, these should be made available through central financing agencies and not directly. The latter should make the required funds available to them at a rate not higher then the Reserve Bank of India rate viz four and a half per cent. Loans should be made available by these banks to their members at a rate of interest not much above that charged by the State Bank of India i.e. at about six and half per cent. A subsidy of 3 to three and a half per cent be paid by government on funds advanced by the central financing agencies to urban banks for industrial purposes. Where the margin of 2% or so available to urban banks is found to be inadequate, the central financing agencies may consider the granting of a more favourable rate than four and a half per cent or the urban cooperative banks may be permitted to charge a somewhat higher rate of interest to the borrowing units. In areas where selection cannot be made out of the

existing urban cooperative banks, new banks may be organised for the purpose. The results of the pilot experiment may be reviewed at the end of 3 years.

6. The agricultural primary credit societies should be made aware of their responsibility to finance village craftsmen and should be encouraged to pay due attention to their needs.

7. The supply and sales societies would be well advised to appoint experienced salesmen for canvassing and booking orders. It would be easier to deal with wholesalers and exporters if the societies set up an agency for collecting information on the products in demand and on the market trends so that they could forewarn their members. They should develop ancillary production by booking orders with larger industrial concerns for manufacture of components and parts and undertake job orders on behalf of their members. These societies should continue to adjust their prices according to the market trend even when market prices decline to a rate lower than that at which the society purchased its stock.

8. Cooperative societies can maintain an accounts unit to keep the accounts of members and fill in the numberous forms required under different Acts and prepare the tax raturns for them on payment of a regular fee.

9. The possibility and utility of organising cooperative credit guarantee organisations need to be explored.

10. (i) It is advisable to encourage the members of production and sales societies to contribute to the working funds and to share as much risk as possible for wastage etc. in manufacture of goods ;

(ii) A voluntary quantity control should be introduced by common facility workshops as well as other societies that undertake production either in their own or the members workshops.

(iii) These societies should create a provident fund for the workers in their workshops and a depreciation fund for the replacement of worn out machinery.

(iv) They should observe the conditions laid down under the Factories Act and other labour legislation.

(v) Wages in the production societies should be paid on a piece rate basis as far as possible. These should not be higher then those prevailing in similar factories.

(vi) Special emphasis should be laid on periodical cost accounting to keep an eye on sale price and profits.

(vii) These and other societies should ensure that the credit facilities allowed to them by suppliers do not increase their liabilities beyond reasonable limits and timely payments are made.

(viii) As far as credit sales are concerned, the societies should include in their supply vouchers, the terms of credit and the rate of interest chargeable in case of delayed payment.

11. For the orderly growth of industrial cooperatives, it is essential that the authorities concerned with the organisation and registration of new societies discuss with the promotors the prospects of the proposed cooperative becoming a viable unit in terms of the government policy for the industry concerned within a reasonable period of time. The scale of operations of a society has to be at least as much as will provide it with a net income sufficient to meet overhead costs. From this point of view it becomes necessary to ensure before hand that the society will have adequate as well as dependable membership. Model schemes which would indicate in broad terms some of the minimum pre-conditions of viability should be worked out for the more important among the traditional house hold type of industries in which the industrial co-operatives are expected to play a significant role.

12. (i) Federations of industrial cooperatives may be set up at importınt marketing centre on a single of muti-Industry basis, according to loal circumstances provided a need is felt by the primary cooperative for arranging supply, sales, common wrok shop facilities or other services.

(ii) At the state level there should be at least one industrial cooperative federation. While separate state level federations may be organsed for these industries in which it is possible to run the economically, multi-industry federations are required to serve other industries and such federations may be organised in those states which this has not been done.

(iii) Possibilities of handloom federation selleing the products of handicraft cooperatives deserve serious Consideration.

(iv) There is a need for a separate all India federation of Coir cooperatives that can undertake export of products of coir cooperatives and develop domostic market.

(v) As the number of KVI cooperatives increases, it may be possible to form state Khadi and village cooperative federations in some States.

(vi) There is a need to organise a National Federation of industrial cooperatives whose memberhsip may extend to the all India federations organised on a single industry basis as well as the apex industrial cooperative bodies.

13. (i) An experiment be tried of organising special training of member and directors of industrial cooperatives by the committee for Corporation Training of the National Cooperative Union of India.

(ii) We would suggest the organisation of special orientation courses of 2 to 3 weeks 'duration for those Industries officers who are in charge of providing technical, financial and other facilities, supplies of controlled materials, issue of essentiality certificate for import licences, recommending units for government stores purchases and for hire purchase of machiery.

14. Data on all cooperatives in each state should be available with a single agency. We recommend preparation of a standard classification of industries, introduction of standard forms for collection of data and fixation of responsibility of compilation and supply of data on a statistical cell in the Cooperative Department, even in those states where industrial cooperatives are under the directorate of industries or any other department. Statistics should be published on cooperatives in imporant industries and the Reserve Bank of India may examine the inclusion in the statistical statement of items mentioned in this Report.

15. (i) Standing Advisory Committees for Cooperatives should appointed by the Central silk Board, the Coir Board and the Small Scale Industries Board.

(ii) Selected officers of the Small Industries Service Institute, the National Small Industries Corporation and different boards should be trained in industrial cooperation so that pointed attention could be paid by them to the promotion of this sector.

(iii) It would be necessary to have in the Ministry of Commerce & Industry a stronger organisation which could study the different problems of the industrial co-operative and pursue with the State governments more vigorously the introduction and implementation of the programmes for industrial cooperatives. The various recommendations in the report require sustained action on the part of an officer higher in status than a Director at the centre. The Ministry of Commerce and Industry's original proposal to have a commissioner for Industrial Cooperatives supported by adequate staff should be revived and given effect to.

16. (i) The question whether the administration of industrial cooperatives should remain with the Cooperative Department or the industries Department continues to be raised from time to time. All things considered, the balance of advantage lies in keeping industrial cooperatives under the control of the Registrar of Cooperative Societies except, it seems, in the case of mechanised type of industries which may be placed under the Director of Industries.

(ii) While the decision whether the work relating to the industrial cooperatives should remain with the cooperative department or be transferred to the Industries Department has to be left to the discretion of the State Government to suit the local needs of cooperatives and the set up of different administrative departments, we suggest that if the Registrar is in charge, he should be assisted by a technical officer of the status of a Joint Director of Industries preferably on deputation from the Industries Department. He should obtain the help of the technical staff of the Industries Department with regard to the economic and technical feasibility of the schemes. The State Government should place at his disposal necessary funds from out of developing the societies and the Director of Industries should offer them technical guidance, quotas of controlled and imported raw materials and certificates required from him by different authorities in the same way as he would if they were under his control.

(iii) If the Director is in charge he should be assisted by a Joint Registrar belonging to the cooperative cadre and with previous training and experience in cooperation and his field staff should get the help of inspectors in the Cooperative department in framing the bye-laws of the society, and ensuring that the cooperative banks, cooperative unions and other cooperative institutions offer their unstinted services to develop the society.

(iv) The authorities registering the societies should also have statutory power of inspection which should be done through entirely separate field staff. In other words, if the Director of Industries is in charge, he should have separate field staff available at all levels for inspection and the industrial inspectors should, in such cases, obtain special training in cooperation. Similarly, if the Registrar of Cooperative Societies is in charge, he should earmark some inspectors for industrial work and they should receive special training on the technical side of industries.

(v) Promotion, organisation, registration, inspection and liquadation should be the tradition and compilation of statistics should remain with the cooperative department in either case. In respect of societies registered by officers of the Industries department, the Registrar may reprepare a panel of arbitrators in consultation with the Director of Industries and appoint nominees in consultation with him.

(vi) For ensuring coordination between the two departments, a two-man committee may be constituted, at the Secretariate level consisting of the Secretaries of Industries and Cooperation with the senior of the two as Chairman. If there is a separate Secretary in-charge of village and small industries, he should also be a member of this committee. The Director of Industries and the Registrar of Cooperative Societies should be invited to the meeting of this Committee which should be held once a month.

(vii) State Government should pay special attention to the supervision of societies and appoint adequate number of supervisors for industrial cooperatives, who should not ordinarily be entrusted with any other work. The supervisors may be appointed at the average rate of 1 for every 20 industrial co-operatives in all states for the next few years.

(viii) The supervisors and other officers in charge of industrial co-operatives should not be transferred as far as possible for a period of three years.

(ix) While the power of audit should remain with the Registrar of Cooperative Societies in all States, a separate group of auditors be trained for industrial cooperative work and maintained in every state in adequate numbers as a distinct group and a panel of certified auditors should also be drawn up whose services can be utilised to supplement the work of the departmental staff. In States where the Director of Industries is made responsible for all other regulatory functions, he should be associated with the preparation of the programmes for the audit of industrial cooperatives. Where there is a backlog of audit, it may be cleared as quickly as possible by the appointment of ad hoc staff.

(x) The Registerar should be authorised to exempt cooperative societies working at loss from the whole or part of the levy of audit fees in deserving cases.

(xi) Norms may be fixed for the work output of supervisors and auditors for different types of socieites and work load determined on the basis of number and type of than on a territorial basis.

(xii) Forms of audit report be studied, suitable forms evolved and uniform standards for audit classification of different types of socities introduced.

17. It would be desirable to orient officers in revitalisation work so that they would have the correct mental attitude towards languishing and dormant socities and can deal with their problems efficiently. Seminars of three or four days' duration for the field staff of Government departments, cooperative institutions and also non-official workers from one or more districts in which discussions are stimulated and guided by one or two experienced persons would be the most suitable means of achieving the desired results fairly quickly. The subject of revitalisation of languishing and dormant socieities. should also form an important part of the syllabus of cooperative training colleges, schools, and special classes where training in industrial cooperation is imparted. A regular revitalisation programme will require careful examination of the working and position of each individual society at the hands of a competent person. Specific officers at the district and higher levels should be made responsible for seeing that approved revitalisation schemes of industrial cooperative are implemented and whatever action is necessary for that purpose is taken expeditiously and in time. The services of central financing agencies such as industrial cooperative banks, federations and prominent non-official leaders of well-managed socities should be fully utilised for the revitalisation work. The latter should be paid out-of-pocket expenses if they have to tour outside or traval long distances in the same city. Relaxation of rules may become necessary in certain cases. Six thousand socities should be retalised by the end of the Third Plan. The fulfilment of the target will involve some additional expenditure on staff, management, grants to societies, fresh finance, etc. but such expenditure will be fruitful and fully justified.

18. The Central and State Governments and the National and State cooperative unions fully explore the ways and means of bringing, for business and production purposes, socieities in the same and different sectors together by creating organisational and other contracts between them at various levels, work out details and take steps to disseminate the knowledge of the schemes that may be prepared.

19. The State Governments should get their respective Cooperative Societies Acts examined in respect of the needs of industrial cooperatives.

20. (i) We are of the opinion that Government assistance to augment the share capital of primary industrial cooperative societies should ordinarily by way of share capital loans to their members, at the same time the present practice of Government participation in the share capital of those primary industrial cooperative societies in whose case special circumstances require this type of assistance on an ad hoc basis should be continued.

(ii) Government assistance in the form of participation in share capital is particularly suited to the federal type of cooperatives whose share capital has to be raised from other cooperative socities who are themselves usually weak.

(iii) In the case of federal cooperatives that undertake initial, intermediary or final processing and that of industrial cooperative banks participation by Government may normally be on a matching basis.

(iv) We recommend share participation by government in the case of service type of federations upto three times the amount subscribed by the members.

(v) The responsibility for redemption of government shares will have to be undertaken by the members who, in the case of primary society, should make it a convention to invest about 5 per cent of their earnings in its shares The societies on the other hand should as a convention invest atleast 10 per cent of their additional paid-up capital in the shares of the federation.

(vi) It needs to be ensured that the society retains at least 50 per cent of its owned funds for its own operations.

21. (i) The system advocated in the case of other industries is for the Director of Industries to give a loan to the member through the agency of the society which undertakes to collect the applications, bonds, receipts, etc. from him and make the required recoveries from his wages or sales proceeds. But the liability to repay the loans remains with the member, who issues a certificate entitling the government to forfeit his share and transfer

them to any other member in case of default or desertion. The system is recommended to be preferred since the member assumes full responsibility for repayment of the loan and is made aware that he is investing the money in the society.

(ii) Concerted efforts should be made by the government to use a larger portion of its provision for advancing share capital loans both to existing and prospective members of the societies.

22. (i) The period of repayment of loans advanced for land and buildings for workshops, etc. for SSI and other cooperatives be raised to 15 years and the first instalment be made repayable on the 4th Anniversary of the disbursement of the loan.

Industrial cooperatives that receive unconditional grants for equipment and other fixed assets under different programmes should, as a convention, transfer such grants to a depreciation fund.

(iii) The amounts of contribution by the members to purchase additional shares, the cumulative total of which should not be less than the amount required to meet the in statement, should be determined before the society approaches the government or a financing agency for a term loan.

23. (a) Managerial grant from government to SSI and other cooperatives should cover the cost of (i) a manager or a secretary (ii) an accountant, (iii) an enginear, designer or similar other technician and (iv) a qualified or experienced salesman, appointed by the society.

(b) While we agree that the cooperative industrial estates should not get any assistance higher than what their members would have received, had they occupies government owned estates, it would be desirable to assist the cooperative industrial estates by meeting a portion of their overhead costs on salaries of adequately qualified and experienced persons. Government may therefore, extened to them a grant on a sliding scale of 100% for the first year, 75% for second year, 50% for the third year and 25% for the fourth year towards the salary of a manager, an engineer and an accountant. The total incidence of this grant in our view will be lower than the concessions that are available to small industrialists in government woned industrial estates.

(c) The pattern for service federations should include, in addition to the salaries of the manager, accountant, technical staff, one inspector and a salesman, rent of office accommodation on the basis of 100% for the first year, 75% for the second year, 50% for the third year and 25% for the fourth year.

24. Specific allocations should be made in each state budget for the development of industrial cooperatives under each group and also separately for such schemes as apply to more than one industrial group. (e.g. loans and grants of banks, associations training institutions. etc.)

25. (i) The possibilities of organising cooperative societies of small industrialist occupying the worksheds in the departmentally managed industrial estates to take over the ownership and management of these estates should examined and a programme of gradual handing over of such estates to cooperatives should be prepared in each state.

(ii) The possibilities of formation of cooperative societies of those small industrial units, which have been regularly making use of the services of departmentally run common facility workshops, should be considered and a programme prepared of gradually handing them over to such cooperative societies.

26. In circumstances where it is not feasible to meet the full requirements of industrial cooperatives on account of shortage of materials, the authorities concerned should allot at least sufficient quotas to keep them in continued and effective operations without incurring losses. We, therefore, recommend the allocation of separate quotas on these lines for controlled commodities to industrial cooperatives. These quotas should be channelled through the apex industrial cooperative institutions.

27. It is observed that those State governments that have come to grips with the problems of the industrial cooperative societies have considered it fit to allow industrial cooperative societies a 10% price preference over that allowed to small scale industrial units. In our view it would be necessary for other State governments as well as the Central Government to take similar steps in order to make their assistance to industrial cooperative effective. We recommend that the industrial cooperative societies should be allowed a price preference of not less than 6% as between the quotations of the small scale industrial units, and in the case of the Central government and those State Governments which have not already introduced a more liberal pattern, a 15% preference over the quotations of the large industrial units.

28. The facilities available to industrial cooperatives should be made available by the Ministry of Commerce & Industry to all types of cooperative processing units.

29. Industrial cooperatives whether federations or primaries can take the net profits accruing to them due to fluctuations of prices to separate price fluctuation reserve. If however, a cooperative incurs a substantial loss on account of price fluctuations in its early years before sufficient reserves are built up, it faces a crisis. By way of a tentative solution of this problem it is suggested that State Governments or preferably the Khadi & Village Industries Commission should create a guarantee fund for the benefit of such cooperatives according to the particular needs of each State.

30. (i) Rethinking about the specific content and corresponding amendment of Section 17(2) (bb) of the Reserve Bank of India Act would be necessary to ensure the assistance of the Reserve Bank of India to enable the co-operative central financing agencies to extend adequate credit to industrial cooperatives.

(ii) Direct incentive in the form of specific limits for financing industrial cooperatives as such would be more efficacious at the present juncture, and the Reserve Bank may in any case be requested, in implementing its declared policy, to evolve a suitable procedure so as to ensure that the accommodation it makes available to central financing agencies does in point of fact induce them to use their own resources for financing industrial cooperatives.

(iii) The accommodation provided by the Reserve Bank of India is in the nature of a credit limit sanctioned to a State Cooperative Bank on behalf of a Central Cooperative Bank or an apex/regional weavers society. The State Governments may issue to the Reserve Bank of India a blanket guarantee within which may be accommodated the requirements of individual borrowing institutions recommended by the Registrar of Cooperative Societies.

(iv) The central financing agencies which do not have experience of industrial financing have a fear that their overdues may be relatively high on account of this business. It will be necessary therefore, for the Reserve Bank of India to deal with this aspect of Industrial finance in a way that would promote the integration of industrial finance with their other business,

31. Systematic efforts need to be made by the apex banks to pay due attention to the financingof industrial cooperatives. It is necessary that a special wing is created in each apex cooperative bank for this purpose with a separate deputy manager and a cost accountant supported by adequate staff. This wing should work under a special committee for industrial finance, composed of the chairman and some directors of the bank, connected with industrial cooperatives, the Registrar of Cooperative Societies and the Director of Industries.

32. (i) The Central financial agencies in all districts except those which are served by an industrial cooperative bank should similarly have separate wings for industrial finance with a deputy manager or a deputy secretary or any other special officer of the same rank, who should preferably have cost accounting knowledge and who should be supported by an adequate number of the inspectorial and other staff. Separate committees should be set up and representation allowed to industrial cooperatives on their boards by these agencies on the lines suggested by the First Working Group on Industrial Cooperatives.

(ii) Government should pay to the Central financing agencies a grant equivalent to 1% of the average outstanding amounts of loans and credits drawn by production type of industrial cooperative in the course of any given year. This contribution should be kept in a special bad debt fund to be maintained by the central financing agencies but not to be drawn upon except with the approval of the Registrar. Government should continue to make such payment every year until the special bad debt reserve amounts to 5% of the loans and credits sanctioned by central financing agencies and drawn by societies, Industrial cooperative banks also should be eligible for this assistance.

(iii) A definite number say 20% of the central financing agencies should be persuaded to adopt all the measures suggested by the First Working Group on Industrial Cooperatives every year. Sustained efforts will have to be made by the State governments and the Reserve Bank of India in this direction and a specific programme with targets indicating the central financing agencies and the amounts they would be expected to invest in industrial finance will have to be prepared and implemented. The central financing agencies should be able to provide additional credit to industrial cooperatives to the extent of Rs. 15 crores in the last year of the Third Plan.

33. (i) It would be desirable not to disturb the present position of the Mysore State Cooperative Bank as the apex bank for the Central Cooperative Rural Industries Financing Bank may be oriented in banking practices and the methods of work of a regional industrial cooperative bank. It should have a trained and competent staff at the head quarters and in the field, convert itself into a regional bank and confine its activities to a compact area in which it can work intensively for promotion and development of cottage and small scale industries. It may, at the same time, continue to deal with the affiliated 'taluk' societies and urban banks in the State until they can be afficiated to appropriate central financing agencies including district industrial cooperative banks wherever they exist.

(ii) It will be avilable for the U.P. Industrial Cooperative Bank to confine its activities to two or three districts. As weavers' and other industrial cooperatives from the whole State are members of the bank, some of the shares of such societies in the industrial bank could be transferred to central financing agencies. The bank has recently employed a retired officer of the State Bank of India as its manager and at our instance sent him and the Deputy Registrar of Industrial Cooperatives to visit the regional bank at Surat and the district bank at Sholapur. Whatever they saw and learnt at Surat and Sholapur it should be utilised early for reorienting the working of the bank.

(iii) New district industrial cooperative banks may be organised where there is considerable concentration of small industrial units organised cooperatively or otherwise, there are fair prospects of their ability to raise deposits and the credit needs of the industrial cooperatives cannot be met adequately by the existing central financing agencies.

(iv) A district industrial cooperative bank should be registered after a minimum of Rs. 1.5 lakhs has been collected as initial share capital and an assurance to collect Rs. 1.0 lakh more in the course of the next two years is forthcoming. Government should contribute equity share capital on a matching basis equal to the paid-up capital otherwise collected by the bank. There should be no objection if government nominates the first board of directors for a period of two years but the official members of the board of directors for a period of two years but the official members of the board should not be more than three and the rest of the directors should be drawn from representatives of industrial co-operatives, small scale industrialists and sympathisers of good standing who are conversant with banking and business practices. Exclusive of the officials, the representatives of industrial cooperatives on the board should be in a majority. It would be desirable for the banks to use the bye-laws of the Southern Gujarat Industrial Cooperative Bank as a model with such modifications as may be required to suit local circumstances. Subsidies should be given to the banks under the staff subsidy scheme. They should be used as agency for routing Government funds to industrial cooperatives and to small industrialists. Care will have to be taken to initiate the necessary measures for appointment of trained staff etc. It would be a great advantage if important members of the administrative and inspectorial staff are allowed an apportunity at Government cost to visit the industrial bank at Surat and Sholapur and spend at least ten days at each place studying the working of the banks at headquarters and at branches and accompanying inspectors on their inspection tours.

(v) The position in regard to deposits has changed somewhat radically of late on account of the deposit insurance scheme introduced for joint stock banks. Unless a similar scheme is also devised for industrial cooperative banks. It would not be fair to except the new banks to attract substantial deposits. The subject is understood to be engaging the attention of all concerned for all cooperative banks. We assume that the insurance scheme that will this emerge will be applicable to the industrial cooperative banks as well.

(vi) The formula of the Reserve Bank of India for weavers' finance, which was evolved keeping in view of other limits allowd to the normal central financing agencies, becomes distinctly restrictive in its application to industrial cooperative banks who have no other limits. We have, therefore, to suggest that the Reserve Bank may consider allowing accommodation upto a higher multiple of owned funds in regard to these banks.

(vii) The industrial cooperative banks should be allowed to attract the surplus funds of those urban co-operative banks which do not enjoy credit facilities from the other central financing agencies and which are engaged largely in industrial finance.

34. Government and Khadi & Village Industries loans should be routed through central financing agencies and not through central financing agencies and not through 'panchayat samitis'.

35. For the benefit of societies in industries other than cotton handlooms, loans should be made available to the apex banks by government in place of Reserve Bank of India loans.

Government loans may be made repayable by the banks in ten years, in 5 equal annual instalments, the first instalment falling due on the sixth anniversary of the drawal of the loan. As far as the industrial cooperatives are concerned. This should be advanced on a short term or medium term basis and conditions. The quantum of the funds to be advanced to an apex bank may be determined on the basis of the estimated requirements during the disposal of the central cooperative banks by apex banks and the former may continue to receive the same ninty per cent guarantee and may thus bear no more than the same ten per cent risk. This system will enable the central financing agencies to advance larger funds from out of their own resources to societies in industries other than handloom. As these instalments are repaid, it is expected that the cooperative banks would replace them by further advances from their own funds. Funds may be advanced to the apex banks at a rate of interest equivalent to the Reserve Bank of India rate, namely, four and half per cent and the banks may be paid a subsidy by government to meet their overhead expenditure at the rates suggested by us in para 260.

36. Ordinarily at the point of production, the rate of interest to be charged to a small industrialist or an industrial cooperative society should be somewhat favourable but not higher than what the medium and large scale industrialist the rates shall be fixed in such a way that they are uniform for the same purpose irrespective of the source of funds, that is, whether the funds come from government or are raised by cooperative banks from the public. Ordinarily the rate of interest to be charged to an industrial cooperative should not be less than the Reserve Bank rate i.e. four and half per cent. It may be necessary to charge lower rate to groups of societies that are organised with socioeconomic considerations and require a longer period of promotional assistance.

This may be also necessary in case of conversion of rebates into a consolidated concession in the form of reduced rates of interest. The rate to be charged to an individual small industrialist may reasonably be placed at two per cent higher than that charged to an industrial cooperative in the same category of industries. The rate of interest on government loans to them would accordingly be six and half per cent which will be on par with the rate charged by the State Bank of India under its liberalised scheme for financing small industries. The state should, however, give adequate grants to the financial institutions to cover their overhead costs and also an element of risk of losses so as to enable them to advance loans at the prescribed reasonable rate of interest. This grant would be at the rate of 3 to theree and half per cent on the average of daily balance of advances of the central financing agencies to industrial cooperative societies and urban cooperative banks for industrial purposes. For the sake of convenience and easy calculation, however, an a'ternative arrangement would be to give them a grant at the prescribed rate on the advances outstanding on a date to be agreed upon between the apex bank and the State government. The rate of grant for the overheads may be correspondingly reduced if a higher rate of interest is prescribed by government in favour of particular losses of industrial cooperatives. Conversely, the grant may be increased in case a lower rate is prescribed. On loans advancedby the industrial cooperative banks and district cooperative banks to individual small industrialists and craftsmen directly, the grant would be 1 to one and half per cent. Except in states where the central financing agencies are well developed and have a large turnover, the grant for overhead expenditure may be fixed so as to allow the apex and the district central banks to have a total margin of three and half per cent between the borrowing rate of the apex bank and the ultimate lending rate to industrial cooperatives.

37. (i) Both the credit guarantee scheme and the 90% guarantee schemes have their advantages and it would be for the financing agency to choose which of the two schemes will offer to it greater security in the light of the age and strength of the industrial cooperatives to be financed.

(ii) In the case of some industrial cooperatives like those in KVI and those of the economically backward members a 100% guarantee would be necessary to presuade the banks to finance them. The standing of each rush society can be reviewed every two or three years to decide when the 100% guarantee could be stopped and it could be brought under the 90% guarantee scheme.

38. (i) A list of the areas where the State Bank of India and its subsidiaries and expected to operate should be conveyed to them early by the state governments and the benefits of the 90% guarantee schemes and the concessional rate of interest scheme should be extended to loans advanced by them.

(ii) Details of participation arrangements between industrial cooperative banks and the State Bank of India should be worked out and tried out on an experimental basis in the first instance.

39. Accommodation from the state financial corporations and the Industrial Finance corporation could be facilitated if the margin of security could be relaxed in certain cases against State government guarantees.

40 (i) The cooperative Acts may be suitably amended to allow the registration of hypothecation charges with the Registrars of cooperative societies so that the banks can get security from these charges as they do in the case of joint stock companies.

(ii) The forms of agreements in case of government loans should be suitably modified so as to restrict the charge of government to the assets created out of the loans or to include a clause to the effect that so far as short and medium term loans advanced by banks against the pledge or hypothecation of goods are concerned, they would have the first charge and the Government's charge would be subordinated to it.

41. (a) In the Fourth Plan attention needs to be directed to strengthening the industrial cooperatives and putting them on a sounder footing whereby they could provide better service and fuller employment to their members. Greater emphasis will therefore, have to be placed on augmenting the owned funds of the industrial cooperatives and, with this end in view, a larger portion of government funds may have to be used for share capital loans. The main programme for the weavers' cooperatives should aim at (i) increasing their self-sufficiency in the supply of yarn by setting up a larger number of cooperative spinning mills and (ii) improving production through different types of common processing units. The main increase in the number of cooperatives and their membership should be in other industries where an attempt should be made to organise 50% of the small factories and industrial households, in the urban and rural areas into cooperatives. While it will be necessary to continue the existing grant pattern, steps will have to be taken to see that the proportion of grants to the total Fourth Plan provision is reduced as a result of larger expenditure on technical improvements and share capital loans. In the field of machanised industries, we expect a faster growth in the cooperatives of small industrialists, most which will be service cooperatives.

(b) Our estimates are 68,000 industrial cooperatives at the end of the Fourth Plan with a membership of 65 lakhs and working capital of Rs. 2.50 crores.

(c) Government expenditure on grants, rebates, development measures and other revenue items may be

Rs. 65 crores and on share capital loans, share participation, loans for equipment, work sheds, etc., to societies and loans to banks Rs. 100 crores. Our estimate thus is a Fourth Plan provision of Rs. 165 crores by Government for cooperation development of industries.

COMMITTEE ON PLAN PROJECTS, AGRICULTURE TEAM ON IMPROVED AGRICULTURAL IMPLEMENTS IN INDIA, 1962—REPORT

Delhi, Planning Commission, 1967. 117p.+various pages

Leader Shri A.P. Jain
Members Dr. Arjan Singh; Shri B.M. Lakshmipathy; Dr. G.V. Chalam

APPOINTMENT

The Committee on Plan Projects was set up by the National Development Council in September 1956, with a view to securing economy and efficiency in the implementation of projects included in the plans. In pursuance of these objectives, the Committee on Plan Projects set-up the Agriculture Team Vide its Memorandum No. COPP/7/3/62 dated September 7, 1962.

TERMS OF REFERENCE

The Team will make an appraisal of the various schemes, both of the Central and State Governments, relating to Agricultural implements and make such suggestions as it may consider necessary with a view to achieving economy, efficiency and expedition in the working of the schemes.

For the purpose of the study by the Team, Agricultural Implements will be divided into the following categories ;

(a) Bullock drawn implements;
(b) Small power implements ;
(c) Hand tools and garden implements ;
(d) Irrigation appliances and machinery
(e) Plan protection equipment ; and
(f) Supplementary implements and equipment.

The team will study, and report thereon, all aspects of the progress of various schemes, both of the Central and State Governments, and their efficiency and effectiveness in relation to the manufacture, population and distribution of agricultural implements, particularly the following :

(i) **Research**—
(a) Progress made in research at the levels at the Central and State Research Stations ;
(b) Testing and trials, including the work done at Regional Testing-cum-Training Centres ;

(ii) **Manufacture**—
(a) Availability of raw materials with special reference to the quality of iron and Steel required for the manufacture of the implement ;
(b) Arrangements for quality control of implements ;
(c) Adequacy of organisation, both public and private, indifferent States and the country as a whole, for the manufacture of improved implements ;

(iii) **Training**—
(a) Study of training facilities in agricultural engineerings, training standards, number of trainees, scope for their employment, etc. ;
(b) Arrangements for training of village artisans and farmers ;
(c) Follow-up in the field of the training programmes for artisans and farmers ;

(iv) **Sale and distribution**—
(a) Review of the methods and organisations employed for the sale and distributions implements and their effectiveness ;
(b) Role of the cooperatives and departmental seed stores and the distribution of agricultural implements ;
(c) Linking of credit facilities with the distribution of agricultural implements grant of loans in kinds ;

(v) **Population**—
(a) Review of the arrangement for demonstration at the village and block levels, the methods and techniques adopted and need and scope for strengthening of the village and block level set up ;
(b) Arrangements for repairs and maintenance at the various levels and the role and working of rural workshops ;
(c) Purchase and hiring of implements by Cooperatives and Panchayats ;

(vi) **Administrative arrangements**—

(a) Need and scope for strengthening the Agricultural Engineering staff at the District, Regional and State levels ;

(b) Coordination among different agencies concerned with research, manufacture, popularisation and distribution of implements.

The Team will carry out case studies of the different prototypes of important Agricultural Implements and hand tools with a view to judging their efficiency, economy and contribution towards increased production. With a view to facilitating studies and making them realistic, the Team will consult and hold discussions with Progressive farmers, manufacturers of agricultural implements and officers and staff of the State Agriculture and other concerned Departments, etc. The Team may coopt representatives of various interests in the field of manufacture, supply and use of agricultural implements in different States.

CONTENTS

Physical and Agro-economic Features ; Research Manufacture and Marketing ; Education, Training and Extension ; Financial Aspect in the Fourth Plan ; Summary of Recommendations ; Terms of Reference ; Annexures from I to XV.

RECOMMENDATIONS

In order to strengthen and stabilize the rural economy speedy execution of land reforms is necessary.

In order to assess the progress in the introduction of improved agriculture implements and machinery, steps should be taken by the Directorate of Economics and Statics (Ministry of Food, Agriculture, Community Development and Co-operation) to enumerate all important agricultural implements at the time of quinquennial livestock censuses.

In the context of modern trends in the farming methods in India and abroad, mechanisation in agriculture is assuming considerable importance. It is, therefore, essential to examine in detail its scope and formulate a definite policy.

Each State has taken up research on a number of implements. It, however, seems necessary to clearly indentify the problems of the various categories of farmers and pay special attention to those, which are of most urgent nature for the maximum goods of the different sections of the agricultural community.

Since agro-climatic conditions vary from region to region in a State, it is necessary to set up adequate number of research sub-stations for conducting trials of implements designed at the State Research Stations. So as to modify them, if necessary, according to the draft capacity of the local animals and soil and climatic conditions.

Since experimental data on the role played by the improved agricultural implements in increasing production is very meagre and lacking, it is necessary to draw up a well-planned programme of cost-benefit research.

The All-India surveys of indigenous implements, have provided valuable basic material in respect of their design, construction, weight, cost, output, quality of work and estimated life etc. In order to find out their real worth, it is necessary to test them under field conditions and work out their efficiency, economy, cost of operation and power requirements in relation to the draft capacity of the bullocks.

There is considerable overlapping in the research programmes of various Research-Testing-cum-Training centres and the State Engineering Sections. Though some overlapping is inevitable, yet maximum benefit could only be derived if specific problems of a region or crop are tackled on a co-ordinated basis.

The Research-Testing-cum Training Centres must carry out more intensive research and field tests on the various types of hand tools, which form an essential part of farm equipment. It is also necessary to start technical studies on their improvement so as to obtain maximum efficiency and output and determine most suitable postures for work, size of blades, handle attachment etc.,

While the problems of All-India importance and fundamental nature may be tackled at the Agricultural Engineering Division of the I.A.R.I., the simpler and routine type of work connected with testing of farm implements and their modifications to suit local conditions, may be attended to by the State Research Centres.

The crop-oriented research on agricultural implements should mainly be conducted and co-ordinated by the Central Crop Research Institutes.

Most of the implements, which have been awarded prizes by the Indian Council of Agricultural Research have not yet found their way to the cultivators ; adequate arrangements must, therefore, be made to promote their use.

Regular exchange of ideas amongst the Research Workers, particularly by circulating monthly progress reports and organising meetings at different centres, should be encouraged.

Instead of schematic approach, to research it will be desirable to build up a strong Agricultural Engineering Section in each State by pooling all the available resources.

In order to utilise effectively the available animal power in the country, there is an urgent need for making detailed and systematic study of harnesses, hitching devices and methods of hitching.

Concerted efforts should be made to design animal-drawn multipurpose implements, which could cover a wide range of operations, reduce the capital cost and recurring expenditure to the farmers.

It is necessary to carry out a proper survey of different types of handtools, commonly used in the country, with due regard to their uses, shapes, sizes, economies, efficiency, production cost etc.

Detailed studies and intensive field trials of tractors and power tillers, in different horse power ranges, require to be conducted at important stations, on a co-ordinated basis, for drawing up realistic programme of promoting their use and manufacture.

In view of vast scope in increasing agricultural production in irrigated areas, special attention requires to be paid to the implement for land levelling, channel making, bund forming, etc.

In order to ensure more effective use of fertilizers, the development of proper seed-cum-fertilizer drill needs special attention of the research workers.

Transplanting of rice seedlings, which is done during the peak period of labour requirements, has, so far, defied machanisation. Intensive efforts required to be made to develop a suitable device for this purpose.

There is a great need for research on sprayers and dusters, with a view to ensuring the application of pesticides evenly and thoroughly for effective control of pests and diseases.

Special attention requires to be paid for the development of suitable power and bullock-drawn threshers for the grain crops.

At the harvest time, Kuravi paddy crop in South India is damaged by rains, resulting in deterioration of quality and discoloration of grains. Development of a simple dryer is, thus, a matter of great importance.

Existing procedure of indenting for controlled items of iron and steel is very lengthy and cumbersome. Since the control is now exercised only on a few items, it should be feasible to authorise the State Iron and Steel Controller to indent for a specific quantity of iron, equivalent to the quantity supplied in a specific year, taken as a base, directly from the producers.

A representative of the Ministry of Food, Agriculture, Community Development and Co-operation may be taken as a Member on the Steel Priority Committee.

Requirements of steel for the manufacture of tractors, power tillers and improved agricultural implements should be given high priority, second only to the Defence needs.

Arrangements should be made to meet the requirements of the iron and steel of the village artisans, through the Co-operatives, from the Steel Stock Yards, proposed to be set up in the States.

The arising of industrial scrap should be made available to the fabricators of implements on priority basis.

Due to over-all shortage of high carbon steel, it will be helpful if the high carbon scrap available from the Railways and Defence Departments is made available to the manufacturers through the State Governments.

In order to keep down the prices and improve the quality, the State Governments may encourage specialisation in the manufacture of implements, by helping suitable production units for the production of only those implements so as to provide them with necessary facilities and draw up realistic manufacturing programme.

The Co-operative Societies should be encouraged to enter into the field of manufacture and distribution of agricultural implements, with the assistance of the Agro-Industrial Corporation.

It will be desirable if the public and private sectors work in co-operation with, and as complementary to one another in the manufacture of agricultural implements while the vital parts of the agricultural implements like shares, points, discs, blades, etc., which require high carbon steel and high technical skill, may be manufactured in the public sector at the State or Regional level and supplied to the approved fabricators, the private sector may manufacture the remaining parts of the agricultural implements.

The manufacture of light-weight small engines (0.5 to 3.00 H.P.) required for plant protection enquipment and other similar farm machinery require to be specially encouraged by affording necessary facilities to the manufacturers.

There is no quality control on agricultural implements either in regard to correctness of the design in relation to prototypes or the material used in their manufacture, which has given rise not only to unhealthy practices but also to the under-mining of the confidence of the cultivators in improved agricultural implements. It is, therefore, necessary to set up an organisation in each State for inspection and quality marking of implements and their components.

The States, which so far, have no arrangements for the preparation of the prototypes of improved implements and supplying them to the fabricators should set up State workshops for this purpose.

There seems to be a great necessity of setting up Agricultural Implements and Machinery Corporation in the public sector, in each State, and in the case of small States for a group of States with homogeneuous conditions, so as to ensure the manufacture and distribution of improved agricultural implements on a planned basis.

A critical review of the schemes running on subsidised basis required to be made so as to restrict the use of subsidy only to essential items in the initial states.

In view of anticipated increase in the requirements of the Agricultural Engineers in relation to their availability, it is necessary to augment the admission capacity of the existing Agricultural Engineering Colleges, and to introduce this subject in other Agricultural Universities.

The courses of study in agricultural engineering at the Agricultural Colleges should aim at more practical and field work by ensuring closer coordination between the Agricultural Engineers and Agronomists.

The Implements Museum at the Agricultural Colleges should keep up-to-date set of improved agricultural implements, recommended by the State Departments of agriculture, as also those developed in other States, particularly in the neighbouring areas, so as to broaden the student's outlook.

There should be periodical assessment of the courses of study taught at the Agricultural Engineering Colleges so as to include up-to-date developments in agricultural technology.

The present arrangements of imparting training to the village artisans in workshops attached to the Gram Sewak Training Centres are not considered satisfactory. It is necessary to examine the working of these workshops and take necessary steps to improve them.

In view of acute shortage of trained tractor operators and livelihood of increased demand for them in the Fourth Five Year Plan, it is essential to set up more tractor training centres in the country.

A training programme may be drawn up at the central or regional level for the periodical training of skilled employees, preferably of the cadre of foremen in the modern technique of implements manufacture.

Short courses may be organised to train farmers, village volunteers and rural youths in the use of improved agricultural implements.

Refresher courses should be organised, on a regular basis, for the village level workers, agricultural engineers, District Agricultural Officers, Block Development Officers, Agricultural Extension Officers and overseers, with a view to refreshing their knowledge and acquainting them with the latest developments in the field of agricultural implements.

The Chief Instructor and other Instructors and the workshop wings of the Gram Sewak Training Centres should be kept in touch with the recent developments in modern fabrication and techniques, by arranging refresher courses at selected institutes from time to time.

The quantum of financial assitance made available to the trained artisans requires to be substantially raised.

Periodical surveys of trained village artisans should be carried out in order to keep a regular contract with them and exchange ideas for the solution of the problems encountered by them in the field.

Apart from the handtools and bullock-drawn implements a few tractors, power implements oil engines, power sprayers, dusters, irrigation appliances, should also be kept at the workshop wings for imparting adequate knowledge in respect of their maintenance and minor repairs etc., to the village artisans.

The trainees at the workshop wings should be given on the-job training by attaching them for a short time with experienced trained artisans in the surrounding areas of the Extension Training Centres.

Adequate facilities by way of land, raw material and power should be provided to the trainees to set up their workshops in the Industrial Estates and rural areas.

Besides workshop wings at the Extension Training Centres, private, co-operative and State Industrial Units, engaged in the manufacture of agricultural implements, may also be utilised for the training of village artisons.

Since improved agricultural implements contribute in several ways towards increased production, it is necessary that exclusive demonstrations on the use of agricultural implements to prove their economics and utility to the cultivators, should laid out, on a well-planned basis.

Where ever Farm Mechanics are appointed for the demonstration of improved agricultural implements, they should be required to work in close collaboration with the village level workers.

At present, every State is maintaining a long list of improved agricultural implements, some of which are now out-of date. The list, therefore, requires to be critically examined and curtailed so as to retain only those implements which are of proven utility and economic significance

The implements kept at the village level worker centres and panchayats require similar review with an idea of keeping the number of implments in a set to the barest minimum. Proper procedure also requires to be laid down for their use and maintenance.

Since mechanisation is now assuming great importance a set of power tillers and other machinery should be kept at the block level for demonstration purposes.

The scheme for landing implements to the cultivators suffers from a number of draw-backs. In order to obtain larger participation of cultivators in the scheme, it seems necessary that a nominal rent may be charged for the use of implements and a proper procedure may be laid down which should be rigidly followed.

At a number of Government agricultural farms, indiginous implements are still being commonly used. It should be incumbent on them to use the recommended implements so as to improve their working efficiency as also serve as demonstration units.

In orter to ensure closer co-ordination between the activities of various sections and implementation of programmes. As senior technical officer, higher in status than that of the heads of Sections, requires to be appointed in the Ministry of Food, Agricutre, Community Development and Co-operation.

Suitable status, at par with other equivalent technicians in the State services, requires to be given to the heads of State Agricultural Engineering Sections.

The State Agricultural Engineering Sections are, by and large, inadequately staffed, especially at the lower level. They need to be thoroughly re-organised keeping in veiw the requirments of the State.

The Full Finance scheme, as experimented on a pilot basis by the Co-operative Departments, Madras, so as to meet the entire credit requirements of the farmers in an area, required to be tried in the rest of the country.

The procedure for advancing loans to the cultivators requires to be simplified and recovery made in easy instalments. To safe guard against the misuse, it is necessary that loans should be advanced, as far as possible, in kind.

As to other small units, the small Scale Inustrial Sector should also advance loans to the manufacturers of improved agricultural implements.

The entire question of giving subsidy on improved agricultural implements requires to be throughly scrutinised by the Central and State Goverenments.

The maintenance of a fleet of tractors, power tillers and other power machinery at one centre in a State for hiring out to the cultivators at 'no profit no loss basis' is not likely to prove of much use. It is doubtful if it can be run on self financing basis.

The supply of spare parts by the Government organisation can be useful only to a limited extent. This service should generally be left to the private and co-operative sectors, subject to the rigorous control of the State Departments of Agriculture on the procurement sale price and distribution of spare parts.

STUDY GROUP ON TRANSPORT COOPERATIVES, 1962-64—REPORT

Delhi, Manager of Publications, 1965. 124p.

Chairman : Shri S.N. Bilgrami

Members : Shrimati Subhadra Joshi; Shri S.S. Panda (retired and noother person was appointed on the Group); Shri V.P. Johar; (Membership was withdrawn by the Govt. of Punjab and his vaccancy was also not filled); Shri M.L. Batra; Shri D.P. Singh; Shri K. L. Luthra; Shri A. Sarkar; Shri K.T. N. Nambiar

Member-Secretary : Shri K. Srinivasan

APPOINTMENT

The policy laid down in the third-five year plan was that cooperation should increasingly become the principal basis of organisation in many branches of the economic life. It was felt that the implementation to this policy would be facilitated if the activities in the different sectors of the country's economy were separately studied and specific programmes drawn up for shaping them in conformity with the desired pattern of development. The Planning Commission suggested accordingly that working groups should be constituted for each of the major sectors for not merely reviewing the progress so far made but indicating the lines of development for the balance of the Third Plan period and the Fourth Plan period.

In persuance of this recommendation the Ministry of Transport appointed a Study Group on the 11th September, 1962.

TERMS OF REFERENCE

(i) To examine the scope for the cooperative form of organisation in the field of transport.

(ii) To draw up a pattern of organisation for transport cooperatives ;

(iii) To assess the financial requirements of transport cooperatives and suggest ways and means of meeting them ;

(iv) To suggest patterns of financial assistance from the Central and State Governments to transport cooperatives;

(v) To recommend specific programmes and physical targets for the organisation of transport cooperatives during the Third Plan period;

(vi) To make recommendations for allocating to transport cooperatives, a certain portion of the funds provided for the entire cooperative sector ; and

(vii) To indicate the lines of development of transport cooperatives in the Fourth Plan.

CONTENTS

Introductory ; Earlier Studies of Transport Cooperatives in India ; Trends in other Countries ; Review of Transport Cooperatives in India; Pattern of Organisation of Bus and Truck Cooperatives ; Financing of bus and Truck Cooperatives ; Taxi-Cab Cooperatives ; Inland Water Transport ; Jin and Cycle-Rickshaws and Auto-Rickshaws ; Miscellaneous ; Summary of Recommendations; Acknowledgements; Annexures from I to XIII.

RECOMMENDATIONS

A society in which almost all the members are its employees and "sympathiser members" are negligible in number, represents the most desirable form of transport corporation. A formula on the following lines may help in distinguishing a workers' cooperative from others :

(a) The society should be mainly engaged in the business of, or its Memorandum of Association should provide that its main business would be transport of goods or passengers or both from one place to another in motor vehicles ;

(b) The motor vehicles of the society should be used exclusively for its business ;

(c) At least 75% of the members of the society should be its employees; and in the case of a society the number of whose shareholders exceeds the number of its employees, at least 90% (rounded off to the nearest whole number) of its employees should be its members ;

(d) At least 50% of the members of the society should not be related to each other ; a member being deemed to be related to any other member if that member is the husband, wife, brother or sister or a lineal ascendant or descendant of that other member.

Users' cooperatives are not very common in this country at present but this form of cooperation has a widening horizon with improvement in rural roads and production of one-ton vehicles. It can be organised either village cooperative societies or Panchayati Raj institutions to carry crops from the centres of production to the markets, and the goods the farmers require on their journey to the villages. The membership of the society can be broad-based including farmers, other users and the drivers and cleaners of the vehicles.

The changing pattern of rural life also for regular passenger transport services to knit the small scattered communities closely, and bring them nearer the urban areas. The aim of any cooperative that is set up to meet such a traffic demand should be to achive a membership covering not less than twenty five per cent of the adult population of the satellite towns/villages. It will not be worth registering any society if it has a membership of less than 500 persons.

An ideal service cooperative will be one which has a membership of at least 10 different bus owners or 15 truck owners with 25 vehicles in all, and undertakes the following services for them :—

Essential

(a) Booking and forwarding agency ;

(b) A garage for repairing and serving their vehicles ;

(c) Procurement and supply of spare parts, tyres, tubes, and, if possible, oil petrol, etc.

(d) Settlement of their motor vehicles tax and goods tax, passenger tax libility ; and

(e) Arrangements for vehicle fitness inspection.

Desirable

(a) Recruitment and training of drivers and maintenance of a complete record of their antecedents and their service ;

(b) Cooperative insurance under Section 108 of Motor Vehicle Act ; and

(c) Settling claims and attending to other litigation involving the vehicles of the society.

Ex-servicemen's socities should be formed as far as possible, with ex-servicemen who become employees of the society in some capacity or other-conductor or drivers or clerks, managers.

Societies of route permit holders should convert themselves into workers 'societies or users' societies as early as possible and should not be given any new routes by the Transport authorities till such conversion is effected.

Societies of scheduled castes and scheduled tribes should also, especially where there are organised under government initiative or with government loan assistance, conform to the pattern of workers cooperatives.

Other societies, including societies of vehicle owners, should imbibe the spirit of cooperation and admit workers into their fold in adequate numbers or should reorganise themselves as users/service cooperatives.

Since cooperation is a State Policy and can serve as a satisfactory alternative or adjunct to nationalisation, the State Government may, where it is not proposed to extent the public sector to any new route or to a feeder route, consider the feasibility of encouraging passenger transport cooperatives to supplement the services provided by the public sector undertaking. If they want to hold their own against the tide of nationalisation, the existing operotors should voluntrily organise themelves into cooperatives.

Since it is unlikely that there will be any programme for large scale nationalisation of the goods transport services for several years, the State Governments should give all possible inducements for the formation of goods transport cooperatives, particularly those which constitute viable units.

The financing agencies would normally be the State

and District Cooperative Bank and the State Financial Corporations which should, in their turn, be able to secure the necessary funds from the State Governments or the State Bank of India on State Government guarantee.

Instead of promoting too many societies, which only result in the dissipation of the limited resources available, it is advisable to organise a small number of societies in each State for stage carriages and goods vehicles, preferably the latter. A reasonable target will be, 1000 societies for the entire Fourth Plan period of about 10 societies per State per year. It will be the responsibility of the Registrar of Cooperative Societies and the Transport Department of the State concerned to organise these societies, watch their working and ensure that they do not founder.

An economic unit will be five vehicles in the case of stage carriages and 10 vehicles in the case of trucks. However, there should be no objection, in the initial stages, to extending assistance to societies which have a smaller number of vehicles.

Each member of the society should contribute Rs. 1,000 to the society as his share money, out of which a sum of Rs. 500 should be paid immediately and the balance recovered later by deduction from his monthly salary.

Government should also participate in the share capital with 50% holding, from the outset, which will work out to Rs. 50,000 in a society consisting of 50 members. Requirements of funds in excess of the share capital and the contributions of the members and the Government, which may be of the order of Rs. 3,50,000 in the case of a society with 10 trucks, should be obtained either from the State Financial Corporations or other institutions.

Government capital should be retired as soon as the members are able to run the society with their own resources. The loan capital should be repayable within a period of five years, in monthly instalments, the first of which should be due six months after commencement of business by the society.

Preference should be given to (a) workers' cooperatives, (b) users cooperatives and (c) service coopertives in that order of priority in dealing with loan applications.

A provision of Rs. 20 crores should be made in the Fourth Plan of the Central Government and an equal amount in the plans of all the State Governments together, for permanent investment in road transport cooperatives either directly or through the State Financial Corporations. The sum of Rs. 40 crores represent Government investment in the form of share capital as well as loans in 1,000 societies during the Fourth Plan period. It will also cover subsidies for managerial assistance for a period of two years at the rate of about Rs. 4,000 per society.

The number of societies be organised in the different States/Union Territories will obviously depend on the extent to which they have developed road transport. The Central loan assistance of Rs. 20 crores can be distributed among the various States either in proportion to the number of goods vehicles they have or the capital Corporations. Which may undertake to finance the cooperatives on behalf of the Government. In the latter case, the funds can remain with the State Financial Corporations as some kind of an "imprest" fund, which will continuously be in circulation as loans to the road transport cooperatives; money repaid by one society will be advanced to another and so on.

The interest payable by the coopreatives should not normally exceed the rate charged by the Reserve Bank by more than 4%

Light vehicles, which are likely to be manufactured in sufficient numbers during the Fourth Plan period and which may not involve a large capital outlay for the operaters, will have a valuable role in improving the rural economy. The Zila Parishads and other authorities should advise any rural transport cooperative they may organise to go in for one-ten vehicle. It will be less difficult co secure adequate cargo and keep these vehicles working to full capacity than medium or heavy vehicles.

Loan assistance to service cooperatives should be restricted to specific purposes e.g., constructing a workshop organising a training school, etc.

The Bihar State Financial Corporation seems to have decided that no assistance should be made available by it to those owners/undertakings who have more than 3 vehicles. Such a restriction will be a disincentive to the formation of viable cooperative units and should be withdrawn.

Proper arrangements should be made by Government for providing guidance and supervision to a society, particularly in its early stages. The departmental staff, where loaned, can later be partly replaced by Society's supervisory staff.

Every vehicle that is acquired with Government loan should be comprehensively insured with the Life Insurance Cooporation or the Oriental Fire and General Insurance Company or a recognished cooperative General Insurance Society and the policy should be assigned to the concerned financing institution.

The society must also undertake to purchase its oil from petrol pumps of the Indian Oil Company, unless it is explained to the satisfaction of the Government nominees in the Governing Body that this is inconvenient or impracticable in the circumstances of any particular case.

It has been represented that one of the reasons for

the reluctance cf hire-purchase financiers and Banks to advance loans for the purchase of vehicles is the absence of any substantive provision in the Motor Vehicles Act enabling any endorsement on the certificate of Registration of a vehicle to indicate that the vehicle is covered by a hire-purchase deal or is hypothecated against a loan. The Motor Vehicles Act should be amended to permit such an endorsement.

Banking organisations, oil companies, insurers and manufacturers or dealers in motor vehicles should be encouraged to combine to accommodated the operators either by direct loans or by deferment of their dues. Transport cooperatives can take advantage of such syndicates when they come into existence.

The best form of taxi cooperative is one which involves not merely the concept of self-help but the pooling of resources and joint working of the members to mutual advantage, though societies which secure cheap credit for taxi drivers and improve their resources, also have a useful purpose.

Since the chances of adequate return in the smaller towns are not bright and since embarking on a cooperative scheme simultaneously in all towns is a formidable task, State Governments should concentrate attention on a few important cities during the Fourth Plan period. At least one society for every city with a quarter million population appears to us to be a practical target.

As for central financial aid, it will be necessary to make a total provision of Rs. one crore in the Fourth Plan.

According to the 1961 Census, there were 38 cities/towns in India whose population exceeded 2.5 lakhs. The proposed provision of Rs. one crore will help the formation of 70 societies with 10 taxis each, costing Rs. 1, 50,000 during the Fourth Plan period.

The funds can be made available to tax cooperative societies through the State Financial Corporation or directly through the State Governments subject to the States Governments concerned taking the responsibility for organising the cooperatives. Providing them managerial assistance and supervising their working till they repay their loans. The pattern of managerial and financial assistance followed in West Bengal is commendable and may be adopted in other States.

If an economic, dependable and efficient inland water transport service is to be built up with the least dislocatcr. to the existing boatimen in Kerala, and other States with navigable waterways, a two-pronged drive for mechanisations of country craft and their formation into co-operatives should be carried through will vigour. It is obvious that cooperation cannot be achieved by compulsion but the supply of powered craft by Government may effectively secure the twin objectives, viz., replacement of obsolete and slow-moving craft by fast-moving tugs and barges of flats and of unhealthy competition by collective ownership.

The optimum size of an inland water transport cooperative will be about 100 members. Preference should be given in the selection of members to boat-men operating in areas where societies are proposed to be set up. The order of preference should be as under :

(a) Boat-men who own their boats and will sell them to the cooperatives if the boats conform to prescribed specifications ;

(b) Boat-men who have been working in the area but do not own any boats ; and

(c) Boat-men from other areas.

Every one of the members should be called upon to serve as an employee of the society. The initial subscription could be a nominal amount, say Rs. 100 per member, to be increased by deductions from monthly salary to Rs. 1,000/ per member over a period of two years.

The primary security for the Government loan is the members' character, the tug being only the additional security. Care should therefore be exercised in the selection of members.

The members should have three tugs which can push suitably designed flats or barges or pull as many boats as possible. For operation over small stretches of sheltered waters, boats with out-board engines may be used.

Government should give the societies long term credit facilities and should be entitled to re-possession of all the assets acquired with their loan if there is reason to believe at any stage that the assets have not been properly maintained or if there is any default in the repayment of the loan.

Obsolete craft should be systematically replaced and adequate reserves built up for return of Government loan and for other purposes.

The craft and other assets acquired with Government loan should be full insured.

Each society should have a booking, forwarding and distributing agency at important loading centres.

Arrangements should be made to ensure (a) booking of bulk cargo, as far as possible, (b) speedy movement of goods, (c) regularity of services, (d) safety of the cargo, and (e) warehousing facilities at important centres.

What is needed is intensive and not extensive development. Instead of dissipating resources in scattered areas in the State where the water-borne traffic is not heavy or where cooperation has not taken root, concentrated action should be taken in areas where there is comparatively greater scope for achieving cooperative economy in this sector.

An apex society should be established in Kerala, if possible, to serve as the forum for bringing the problems of the primary societies to the Government's notice and also to provide common repair and workshop facilities.

The aim should be to organise a net work of cooperatives in water ways where Government are not themselves providing the services. The State, which is potentially the best suited for such a project, is Kerala. The State can pioneer with a target of 50 societies in the Fourth Plan period.

Provision should be made for loans to State Governments in the Central Fourth plan to the extent or Rs. 1 crore altogether. Out of this amount, Rs. 50 lakhs should be earmarked for Kerala for facilitating the establishment of at least 50 societies. Other States, which set up pilot cooperative units on the above lines, with any modifications that local conditions may require, may be given a loan of Rs. 10 lakhs each. If prompt measures to execute the project are not taken by any of them within the first two years of the Fourth Plan, the funds set apart for the defaulting State may also be diverted to Kerala.

Central Government can supply out board engines, tugs, barges or flats and the equipment necessary for putting up small dockyards or shipways for repairs and maintenance of craft. It should be the duty of the apex society proposed in above to construct dockyards etc. as near the centres of operation of the cooperatives as possible. It may not be difficult to accommodate the financial needs of an apex society within the Plan provision proposed by us above.

In addition to the loans, the Central Government may also make a grant not exceeding Rs. 5 lakhs for starting a training institution in Kerala with provision for training about 100 men each year in the operation and maintenance of power craft as well as cooperative principles and procedures. The State Government, who were asked to establish a training school two years ago, expressed a desire to defer the proposal for the duration of the current emergency. It is advisable for them to reconsider it, inspite of the continuance of the emergency.

The earlier Jin and cycle-rickshaw as are off our roads, the better. A sweated trade, which treats men like best of burden, is incompatible with the pattern of society to which the country is wedded, and the process of its elimination requires, therefore, to be speeded up.

The first step in the conversion of cycle-rickshaws into auto-rickshaws is to license and bring the existing rickshaw pullers together within the fold of a cooperative society. This will serve to improve their present plight, while the acquisition of auto-rickshaws will support and strengthen the society and will be the means of their attaining better standards of life. The State Governments have a duty to promote such societies not merely on this major humanitarian consideration, but also in the interest of cheap transport for people in the middle and low, income groups. Who cannot affort to hire taxis in urban areas.

A Standing Committee, consisting of the Transport commissioner, Registrar of Cooperative Societies, Labour Commissioner and the Managing Director of the State Financial Corporation should be constituted in every state to review the position periodically, but not less than twice a years from the following points o view.:

Surveying and licensing of all the existing rickshaws and rickshaw-pullers ; (No new rickshaw licence should be given except to cooperative societies).

Necessity for granting new permits for operation of auto-rickshaws in the different towns/cities in the State, taking the rising traffic demand into consideration ;

Scope for replacement of cycle-rickshaws (coopting representatives of the local bodies concerned when this is examined;) and Practical measures required for giving effect to on a firm footing.

Where a cycle rickshaw is not plied by its owner but by an employee, tha licence for the rickshaw should be cancelled, if necessary, by suitable legislation and if the owner is prepared to sell the rickshaw to a cooperative society in which the erstwhile rickshaw pullers are members, the licence may be transferred to the society for the duration of the life of the rickshaw. This may be effected as a gradual process.

The U.P., M.P., A.P. and other State Governments should take positive active to organise at least one society in each city with a population exceed in, 1,00,000 where auto-rickshaws are not banned on grounds of traffic regulation and control. It will make a great and salutary difference not merely from the transport angle but also from the point of view of the cooperative movement.

An effective programme for auto-rickshaw cooperative may entail a total provision of Rs. 50 lakhs for all the States together for the entire Fourth plan period and the assistance, which should take the form of loans at a nominal rate of interest, can be channelised through State Governments. In addition to loans on liberal terms the State Governments should also see that permits are not withheld from these cooperative societies, unless, the tronsport Authorities are satisfied that either the traffic in the area in question cannot bear an additional permit or that the members of any particular society are bad characters and the society must be screened off in the public interest. As a condition for the issue of permits, the State Government may also insist on a society building a shed or garage and setting up a workshop, (preferably a mobile one) either individually or jointly with other societies ; and any financial help that this may involve also be extended by the Government.

Preferential treatment should be given to a cooperative in the grant of route permits as long as there is no reason for any misgiving about its ability to cope with the traffic requirements.

Within the framework of the existing provisions of the Motor Vehicles Act and without prejudice to the policy of State Governments in regard to nationalisation of road transport, fillip can be given to the development of transport cooperatives. What is required is that the existing provisions of the Act should be implemented in their spirit and cooperatives given their legitimate share on all routes, including long distance route.

It is possible and also desirable for the Registrar of cooperative Societies to be a member of the State Transport Authority which is the body which coordinates and regulates the activities and policies of the Regional Transport Authorities of the entire State, in order to ensure that the interests of cooperatives are not neglected. Where, however, there are Regional Transport-Authorities with more than one member, representation may be given to the Cooperation Department on them.

Only ownership of vehicles, and not their mere ocntrol by a cooperative society, shold make it eligible for the grant of permits.

The Delhi Motor Vehicles Taxation Act, 1962 has provided 50 per cent tax relief for workers cooperatives. A similar concession should be extended by all State Governments to vehicles owned by transport cooperatives, under their respective Motor Vehicles Taxation Acts.

A differential tax levy i.e, an increased exemption limit is justifiable in the cases of transport cooperatives. Since the optimum size of a viable transport cooperative will be 10 trucks with a membership of about 50 people, the exemption limit of Rs. 15,000 may be increased in these cases to Rs. 50,000 and a worker's cooperative may be defined on the lines of Section 14 of the Delhi Motor Vehicles Taxation Act, 1962 for this purpose.

Audit fee should not be regarded as a measure of taxation but correlated to the actual cost of the service rendered by the auditors. Audit should be either departmental or through an approved penel of auditors. Steps should, however, be taken to see that a society does not suffer undue expenditure by prolonged audit.

The Registrar of Cooperative Societies should, in consultation with the transport authorities concerned, simplify the system of accounts that transport cooperative should follow and, if possible, arrange for the supply of forms and books to the societies. Since these societies cannot afford to employ qualified accountants and do not understand the principles and practices of commercial book keeping it is essential to evolve a procedure by with the required information can be recorded even by men with little or no accounting experience.

Managerial subsidies may be provided to transport cooperatives for four or five years. It will very useful to obtain the service of qualified Government officials. Preferably from State Transport Undertakings or the cooperation department, wherever possible, for a period of two or there years on deputation basis, free of charge, to put the working of the societies on sound footing. The persons as selected may be trained in all aspects of transport operation and cooperation before they are given this assignment.

A desirable objective is the development of a professional managerial class familiar not merely with transport operation but also with the methods and ideals of cooperation. This will be practicable if the Registrars of Cooperative Societies draw up a programme for the recruitment of qualified men with business aptitude, who can be sponsored for training for two or three years in the State Transport Undertakings the Central Road Transport Research and Training Institute which is shortly proposed to be established by the Ministry of Transport and also any central institution that may be organised for providing training in cooperation on an all-India basis. The transport societies can be made to engage them either jointly or individually, depending on the extent to which their services are needed, and to contribute to their salary accordingly.

There will be need for apex societies of Federation at State and all India levels only if transport cooperatives come up in large numbers in the different States.

Appointment of a few service cooperatives as agents of the manufacturers or importers may obviate all causes of complaint from transport cooperatives about difficulties in the procurement of spare parts, etc.

While it is not possible to compel a manufacturer in the private sector to extend any special concessions or patronage to transport cooperatives. There should be no difficulty in Government's instructing all public sector undertakings, including State Trading Corporation, Indian Oil Company, etc., to encourage cooperatives to the maximum possible extent, e.g. in allotment of petrol station by Indian Oil Company, distribution of tyres by the State Trading Corporation etc. The Postal Department should likewise give preferential treatment to applications from Stage carriages operated by transport cooperatives in the award of contracts for carriage of mails. Similar preference should also be extended by other Government departments/public sector undertakings.

A cell should be created under a senior officer in the Ministry of Transport to plan and watch the development of transport cooperatives and to maintain liaison with the co-operation and other departments and the various public sector undertakings.

Though it is desirable to promote cooperative insurance societies, there is no justification for any amendment of the Motor Vehicles Act for this purpose. A society which wants to undertake comprehensive motor vehicle insurance should so after complying with the provisions of the Insurance Act 1938.

The Kerala Government have asked for loan assistance for promoting a second unit under the Union Transport Ministry's pilot Scheme for organising tran port cooperatives for educated unemployed. It need not be a "Pilot" society, since the pilot society that was registered in 1959 appears to have gained in strength and come of age. Financial assistance can be given for the second unit as a part of the general effort to promote cooperation. It is, however, prematures to consider extension of the current pilot scheme, as such elsewhere.

COMMITTEE ON MODDLE PLANNING LEGISLATION, 1962—REPORT

New Delhi, Ministry of Health ; 1965. 48p.

Chairman : Shri Gian Prakash.

Members : Lt. General D. N. Chakravarthy; Shri B. T. Talim; Shri K. N. Misra; Shri D. G. Karanjgaokar ; Director of Town & Country Planing; Shri C. Govindan Nair;

Secretary : Shri C. S. Chandrasekhar;

APPOINTMENT

The Model Town and Country Planning Law was prepared by Central Ragional and Urbrn Planning Organisation in 1960 on the basis an earlier draft by the Institute of Town Planners, India. The Model law was considered by the 1st Conference of State ministers for Town and Country Planning held at Bangalore in 1961, which set up a Committee Ministers to examine the model and to make suitable recommendations thereon. This committee cosisting of the Ministers from Madras, Mysore and West Bengal examined the Model Law in great detail and after giving careful consideration to a large number of comments received from the State Governments particularly from the Government of West Bengal revised it suitably and commended it for consideration of the 2nd Conference of State Ministers for Town and Country Planning held in Trivandrum in 1962. The Conference after considering the report of the Committee and the revised Model Law agreed with the committee's views that no Model Law could meet the requirements of each state individually and that it would have to be adopted to meet the requirements of individual states. At best the Model could provide the basic guidance in regard to essential requirements of a Law relating to Comprehensive planning and leave it to the State Government to adopt it to meet their requirements. The conference also recognised that in a dynamic society like ours ; Where constant changes were taking place, the requirements which a law on town and country planning would have to meet will also undergo change and it would be necessary to take note of these changing requirements periodically. Accordingly the conference commended the version of the Model Law as finalised by the committee to the State Governments for their consideration and adaptation.

Acting on this recommendation of the conference most State Governments have been taking steps to revise their existing planning laws. Some of the State Govenments have enacted laws on the basis of the model; while others are revising their existing law to meet the present day requirements. With a view to examine the matter in detail the Government of West Bengal, set up a separate commission for Lagislation on Town and Country Planning in October, 1962.

TERMS OF REFERENCE

The committee after examining the general views and detailed recommendations on the several clauses of the West Bengal Legislation Commission on the Model Planning Law as also the experience gained so far in adapting it to the requirements of the various States.

CONTENTS

Report of the Committee on Model Planning legislation; Summar of Recommendations; Report of the Committee on Model Planning Legislation; Annexures I to III.

RECOMMENDATIONS

The Committee after examining the general views and detailed recommendations on the several clauses of the West Bengal Legislation Commission on the Model

Planning Law as also the experience gained so far in adapting it to the requirements of the various States came to the following conclusions :

1. The Committee reiterates the views of the conference expressed earlier that no Model Law could meen the requirements of each State individually and that it would have to be adapted to meet the requirements of individual States. In a dynamic society like ours, where constant changes are taking place, the requirements which a Law on Town & Country Planning will have to meet, will also have to change and it would be necessary to take note of these changing requirements periodically.

2. A study of the suggestions made in regard to the State Town & Country Planning Authority, indictates that a State Town & Country Planning Boards of the type recommended in the Model Law is necessary so that there is available an overall plan advisory body consisting of various heads of departments of State Governments to advise the State Government and to give realistic appraised to any plan prepared for a local area or a region within the State. There was, however, no objection to the setting up of a State Planning Authority as proposed by the Commission as a small body of experts to prepare the plans in cases where the local authorities are not able to do, and also to make studies, publish literature, to control the enforcement of the plan and also to hear appeals. The composition of such an authority would have to be left to each State Government to decide upon.

3. The composition of a local planning authority to be given in a Model Law should leave enough flexibility for the State Government to appoint an authority which can truly represent the various interests at the local level and also to function effectively. Any detailed definition of this authority beyond that proposed in the Model Law may defeat the purpose of such representation.

4. Referring to Comments of the Commission suggesting longer time intervals between different stages of the Development Plan the Committee draws attention to the existing provisions in the Model Law providing for extension of time at each stage by the State Government if there was sufficient justification.

5. The Committee agrees with the Commission's view that the time for calling objections on existing land use map may be extended to one month and that this should prove sufficient for the purpose of verifying whether the use of any property in the planning areas is correctly shown or not.

6. In regard to the sale of maps and reports the committee felt that as the documents were to be published as public notification they should be available for sale and further the local planning authority may have to put out simplified literature to mobilise public support.

7. The requirements of publicity included in the Model Law provide the minimum required according to Law and the Committee emphasizes the need for having a much larger publicity to enlist public's Co-operation and to mobilize its support in plan implementation. Such publicity programme, the committee felt, can be undertaking better by direction from the State Government than by Law.

8. The Committee recommends that the terminology used in the Model Law, which takes note of the current usages of terms and concepts both in India and abroad and which also expresses fully the intent in each case be used in preference to terms like Master Plans or General Plans which have been found by experience to have certain rigidities and ambiguities in their meanings.

9. The Committee recommends that, where a local authority is appointed as local Planning authority the local authority* should be required to set up a separate committee of the status of a Standing Committee of the Local Authority to undertake the preparation of the Plan, process it and enforce it.

10. The Committee recommends that, for making minor changes which do not affect either change in land use or prescribed densities the planning authority should be able to take a final decision provided its decisions were given appropriate publicity. For all other changes the procedure prescribed in the law should be followed.

11. In regard to effect of other laws, the Committee felt that Sub-Section 2 (a) of Section 71 will need a proviso indicating that the grant of planning permission does not absolve the owner of obtaining such permissions as may be necessary from other authorities and such payments as may be necessary to be made for undertaking the development by a Planning authority.

12. The Committee felt that certain norms and standards assumed in preparing the Plan may not be considered obligatory but may be included in the development plan to give general indication of the basis on which the plan is prepared.

13. The Committee after considering the procedure for appeal included in the Model Law felt that the procedure for filing of appeals should be as far as possible decentralised in order to avoid harassment and expenses to those who file appeal against the refusal of grant of planning permission or against the levy of development charge. The Committee recommends that appellate authorities should be made available at the district or divisional level and such appellate authorities may consist of a Town Planner, a Superintending Engineer and a non-official, whose decision may be taken as final except in some cases such as levy of development charge, where a second appeal may be provided to the State Planning Authority, who may appoint a Sub-Committee to hear such matters, if needed.

14. The detailed changes suggested by the Commis-

sion are in the nature of verbal changes, elaborations to clarify the meaning and intent of a certain section or a sub-section and errors in printing. These have examined thoroughly and the extent to which these could be usefully incorporated in the revision of the Model Law is indicated in Annexure I to the report.

15. The Committee recommends that the Model Law may be suitably revised in the light of the recommendations given in its report and circulated to all the State Government.

STUDY GROUP ON COOPERATIVES UNDER RAILWAYS AND POSTS & TELEGRAPHS DEPARTMENT, 1962—REPORT

New Delhi, Ministry of Community Development and Cooperation (Department of Cooperation), 1963. 124p.

Cairmans : Shri G.D. Goswami ;
Members : Shri S.C. Sen Gupta ; Shri D.G. Jadhav ; Shri L.C. Jain ; Shri Ram Krishna Prasad.
Member-Secretary : Shri J,K. Verma.

APPOINTMENT

The question of speedy development of Cooperatives under the Railways, Posts and Telegraphs Department, etc. have been under the consideration of Government. The Planning Cammission have recommended that a Study Group may be appointed for the purpose. It has accordingly been decided to constitute a Study Group to Examine the present condition and problems of cooperatives under Railways, Posts and Telegraphs Department, etc. and suggest specific programmes for their promotion and development on sound lines.

The Study Group on Cooperatives under Railways and Posts and Telegraphs Department was Constituted under the Ministry of Community Development, Panchayati Raj and Cooperation (Department of Cooperation) vide their Resolution No. 13-34/64-Coord, dated October 9, 1962.

TERMS OF REFERENCE

(i) To examine the present set-up of the organisation of cooperatives under the Railways, Posts Telegraphs Department ; etc.

(ii) To examine the present pattern of organisation and financial assistance and suggest changes if any ;

(iii) To recommend specific programmes and physical targets for the organisation of the above cooperatives during the third Plan ;

(iv) To indicate the lines of development of these cooperatives in the fourth plan.

CONTENTS

Introductory ; General Background and Approach ; Cooperative Credit Societies on the Railways Consumer Cooperative for Railway Staff ; Other types of Cooperaivte on the Railways; Cooperative Cradit Societies under the P & T Department ; Consumers' Cooperatives for P & T Staff ; Other Forms of Cooperatives under P & T Department ; Administrative Arrangements for organisation and Supervision ; Summary of conclusions and Recommendations ; Appendices I to VII.

RECOMMENDATIONS

Cooperative Credit Societies on the Railways

The objects of some societies include the "introduction of housing schemes". A credit society should not get involved in acquiring houses sites or starting colonisation schemes which should be appropriately taken up by saparate housing cooperatives.

The employees credit societies can help consumers' cooperatives by sanctioning loans to members for making 3 trade deposits in consumers' cooperatives. The may also honour the credit chits of approved consumeres cooperatives and debit the amount as loan against the member.

Some societies are having arrangements with certain recognised dealers whose credit chits are honoured by the society and the amounts debited as loans against the members. This system is objectionable as it breeds favouritism in the matter of selection of traders.

Taking up welfare activitis for their members and their children is none of the specific objective mentioned in the by-laws of the credit societies. A part of the profits of the credit societies should, therefore, be set apart for specified welfare activities.

The societies on Railways being very big, do not have direct participation of members in the annual general meetings. However in the case of Jackson Cooperative Bank having over one lakh members, general elections are conducted on basis of voting by each shareholder. This is unrealistic. When the membership and jurisdiction are big, the annual general meeting should be held on a delegate system.

The general problem of throwing up new and younger leadership is common to the entire cooperative moment. A great deal would naturally depend on the efforts made to educate the members about their rights and responsibilities. A suggestion was made that the by-laws might contain a clause preventing a person for standing for election for more than two consecutive terms. This is a broad question and will have to be examined in detail by the farmers of cooperative policy.

The General Managers and the F.A. & C.A.O. are in many cases functioning as ex-officio chairmen and vice-chairmen of credit societies. The interest taken by them is partly responsible for the impressive growth of the cooperative credit structure on the Indian Railways. The societies have now gained sufficient strength and in the present contest of de-officialisation, holding of ex-officio positions by railway officials should be dispensed with. Many of these societies employ a large number of staff to conduct their day-to-day business and it is very necessary that suitable accommodation should be arranged for them. Wherever cooperative societies are in a position to construct their own buildings, the railway administration should help them as they have done in the case of Jackson Cooperative Bank, Bombay.

Thrift is anessential part of cooperative credit. There are some societies which have not yet introduced any scheme of 'thrift deposits. Steps should be taken to introduce the system. Wherever it does not exist. The scales of thrift deposits suggested by the Railway Board should be adopted.

All the credit societies on the railways should get themselves affiliated to the respective state cooperative banks who should provide credit and other facilities to these societies to the extent necessary. These societies should use the cooperative bank as their bankers. The Registrar of Cooperative Societies should not permit the credit societies to open accounts with the joint stock banks. This would enable the state cooperative banks to play the balancing role for which they were intended. Long-term investments of the credit societies should preferably be made in the debentures floated by the central land mortgage banks.

For a cooperative credit society which accepts deposits, maintenance of fluid resources in accordance with the prescribed standard necessary. It was noticed that some of the societies were not regularly maintaining such cover. The Registrars of cooperative societiess should review the position obtaining in their states and ensure that fluid cover is maintained as follows :

40 per cent of deposits at call, cash credit, overdraft sanctioned but not drawn ; 25% of saving deposits ; 25% fixed deposits maturnig within next three months ; 100% of thrift deposits falling due within next 30 days.

The procedure for disbursement of loans is not uniform. As the members of bigger societies are spread over a large area, the practice of disbursment of loans through cheques to be cased from the station earnings is satisfactory. This system may be adopted wherever it does not exist. provided the socities keep adequate deposit for this purpose with Chief Cashier and the Pay Master of the Railway.

There is diversity in the rate of interest charged on loans by the societies. This depends upon many factors such as the rate at which obtains loans and deposits. The rate of interest charged from members should, therefore, be reviewed from time to time and efforts made to maintain them at a reasonable level.

Recovery of loans is done through pay sheets of members for which the railway administration charges a fee of 4 annas per cent which is credited to the welfare fund of the society if such a fund is constituted by the Society. As the deduction of the due of cooperative societies from the salaries of the members is a statutory obligation of the employers, the levy of this charge may be discontinued.

One of the problems facing the cooperative credit Societies on the railways is the recovery of loans amounting to Rs. 59.53 lakhs from members who have gone to Pakistan. Steps may be taken to have the matter settled early.

In the case of Jackson Cooperative Bank, the Engineering Department on the railways has given active assistance in the construction of the society's buildings. Such assistance might be extended to other societies also.

The railway administration has not given direct financial assistance by way of loan except in one case. It is difficult for a new society to have sufficient working capital. Initial loan assistance might be given to such infant societies and may be recovered in 10 years time. Only 54% of the railway staff are members of the credit societies. Efforts should be made to cover at least 75% of the employees by the end of third five year plan.

At present the staff of N.E.F. Railway is being served by two credit societies located at Calcutta. A separate society for N.E.F. Railways with its headquarters at

Pandu may be set up.

Consumers' Cooperative for Railway Staff

The Railway Board decided that a primary consumers' store should normally cover a radious of 20 miles with about 600 railway men. With this it should be possible to have a minimum of 250 members and a turnover of about Rs. 1 lakh to make the store a vialble unit. The unitary type of store is more suitable for residential areas while in big cities the branch-type of store may merit with the setting up of consumers' cooperative stores under the centrally sponsored scheme in towns and cities having population of over 50,000 the railway men's stores should seek affiliation to the nearest whole sale society under this scheme.

The consumers' cooperative stores have not made any efforts to take up simple processing and manufacturing activities. The consummers' stores may set up small processing and manufacturing units wherever possible in order to provide better services to their members.

The managing committee of most of the consumers' stores is elected entirely by the members. There is no need for any officials holding positions in their ex-officio capacity. Wherever the railway administration participates in the share capital, they may nominate their representative up to one third of the strength of the management or three directors whichever is less.

In order to attract membership from class IV staff, at least one or two members should be taken from this category.

A cooperative store has to take note of the habits of the clientele it serves. It will not, therefore; be practicable to prohibit credit sales altogether. In some stares, credit sales are allowed to the extent of of paid-up share capital. There is also an overall limit of one/third of the total salary of the member. Credit sales should be subject to both these restrictions.

Correct pricing of goods plays an important part in the success of cooperative stores. Practices very in this respect. The best method would be charge the market prices and distribute the surplus as rebate. In the initial stages, the rebate need not be disbursed in cash but converted into share capital.

Women all over the world have played a very important role in this field. The membership of consumers' cooperative stores should therefor be open to the wives of the railway employees and they should be given adequate representation on the managing committee.

Inadequate and unsuitable accommodation has contributed to a large extent to the slow growth of consumers' cooperative stores. Suitable premises should be constructed by the administration providing adequate space to run different sections of the stores. The existing shop premises allotted to consumers stores should be suitably remodelled. The present pattern of assistance does not provide for share capital contribution or working capital loan. Lack of sufficient capital has stood in the way of expanding the business of many stores. The stores in N.E.F. Railway deserve particular attention. The Ministry of Labour has recommended a sca'e of financial assitance to be provided employers in the private sectors. This envisages share capital contribution of Rs. 2,500 on matching basis, and working capital loan upto to Rs. 10,000 per store. The Railway Board should provide assistance on the same scale to all new societies to be organised and to the existing societies which are in need of such assistance.

Consumers' Cooperative stores should be in a position to meet competition from provate trade. However, initially certain protection in needed. The railway administration may discourage shopkeepers from opening shops in railway colonies. Wherever consumers' cooperative stores are functioning. Licences of existing shopkeepers might not be renewed as soon as a consumer cooperative store is organised. The staff posted in outstations and railway tracks find difficulty obtaining in their supplies. Selected consumers' stores can run a mobile van and the cost may be recovered by a suitable surcharge on the prices.

The success of the stores movement depends to a great extent on the training given to employees of the stores. A phased programme for the training of the employees of the stores can be drawn up by the railway administration in consultation with the Committee for Cooperative Training.

It is essential that the welfare inspectors who are charged with the responsibilty of supervision of consumers' cooperative stores should be conversant, with cooperative principles and procedures. Those who have not been trained earlier should undergo a course of training in this behalf in the regional training centres.

The present number of consumers' cooperative stores in about 200 and another 100 societies will be needed to serve the entire staff. The aim should be to enrol 7.5 lakh members by the end of the fourth plan.

Other Types of Cooperatives on the Railways

A separate study group appointed by the Ministry of Works, Housing and Rehabilitation is examining the question regarding housing cooperatives. However, a suggestion was made that out of the funds available under middle and low income group housing schemes, separate allotment should be placed at the disposal of the Railway Ministry so that railwaymen's cooperatives may not have to take a chance with others in the matter of securing loans from the State Government. This suggestion should be examined by the Ministry of Works, Housing and Rehabilitation.

Big contractors sometime obtain a number of vending points and sublet them. A cooperative will enable self regulation among the venders and render the task of the railway administration easier. The only long-term answer to tho persistent complaints about the quality of catering on the railways is to evolve an organisation under which the actual workers engaged in catering have a full sense of involvement in the success of the enterprise. The best way of securing such involvement is organising them cooperatively and to provide them with managerial talent and financial assistance. The organisational pattern and financial assistance should be as follows:

(a) The vendors cooperatives will have to operate in a compact area to secure effective member participation and it should have at least 50 members in order to be viable. If a coopertive obtains contract for running a restaurant or a refreshment room, the society might also be given the vending contract on that station.

(b) Membership of these societies should be open only to cooks, bearers and the actual vendors including those who run stalls on railway stations. There is no need for sympathiser members. The responsibility for organising these cooperatives will have to be assumed by the railway administration.

(c) The members themselves will not intitally be able to take shares of substantial value. A system of compulsory monthly share deposit at the rate of 5% of the earnings of each vendor should be introduced. The administration should subscribe Rs. 25,000 towards share capital on a matching basis which may be retired over a period of 15 years, the retirement commencing from the fifth year.

(d) The railway administration should provide a manager subsidising his cost on a tapering scale for 4 years as 100% in first year, 75% in the 2nd year, 50% in the 3rd year and 25% in the 4th year and from 5th year onwards the cost will be borne in full by the society.

(e) (i) Wherever vendors' cooperative societies have been organised, no contractors should be appointed to carry on vending and as and when vending cooperatives come up, the existing departmental catering and vending should also be transferred to the cooperatives.

(ii) In the initial stages for a period of 5 years, the vendors cooperatives should be charged nominal rent for office premises as well as fixtures and fittings and kitchen equipment. After the society has been full established, reasonable rent should be charged. The railway administration should ensure that unhygenic accommodation is not given and the equipments supplied are of standard quality.

(iii) Licence fee should be calculated on an average for the past three years.

(iv) In case of termination of contract which should be with the approval of the Railway Board in each case, departmental catering may be taken up and in no case should the contract be given back to a private contractor.

(v) As the entire scheme will be implemented through the agency of the railway administration, there is no need to accept any security deposit from the cooperatives.

There may be about 8,000 to 10,000 vanding points on all the railways, besides 400 to 450 refreshment rooms and restaurants. There will be enough scope for the formation of about 300 cooperatives of vendors and caterers. The railway administration will have to work out a detailed programme for organisation of these societies and to strengthen the cooperative wing in the Railway Board for promotion and supervision of these societies. It may also be necessary to work out training arrangements for a cadre of managers of vandors cooperatives in consultation with the committee for Cooperative Training.

When sufficient number of cooperatives of vendors are formed one each railway, it should be possible to set up a federation for such regional federations, each railway should have an advisory committee with the Chief Commercial Superintendent as Chairman.

Contractors are given by the railway for loading and unloading of goods, parcles., coal, for picking up cinders etc. Inspite of the positive policy adopted by the Railway Board, the share of the cooperatives in handling the work is not significant. These labourers consitute the under-privileged section of the community and the only method of increasing their earnings is to eleminate contractors and form them into cooperatives. The organisational pattern and financial assistance should be as follows:

(a) A composite type of society should be organised at a station or a group of stations for taking up all types of work. Different items of work can be done by different groups of labburers and the wages should be paid according to the customary rates. A society with 100 members which can handle contracts of the value of about Rs. 10,000 a month should be a viable unit.

(b) The respensibility for organisation of such societies will have to be taken up by the railway administration itself. The assistance of the-social service organisations like Bharat Sewak Samaj and Rama-Krishana Mission may be obtained wherever possible.

(c) The society should have a good and efficient manager-cum-accountant. It may be possible to depute some railway staff for this purpose. The pay of the manager may be subsidised by the railway administration for the first 4 years on a tapering scale as 100% in first year; 75% in 2nd year, 50 % in 3rd year and 25% in the 4th year.

(d) Share capital is required by the society for employment of casual workers and for payment of security deposits. The railway administration might contribute Rs. 2,500 on a matching basis, retirement of which may commence after 5 years.

(e) (i) As the railway administration is associated with the working of the societies, security deposit at the rate of 5% may be obtained from the cooperative instead of at 10% as at present.

(ii) The railwag admin:stration should allot some office space to the society at nominal rent. The administration should also provide a proper shed so that the workers may rest, relax and take their mid-day meal.

(iii) The scale of demurrage should be reduced suitably.

(iv) The railway administration should permit station masters and locoforemen to be associated with the management of the societies.

(v) 75% of the bill may be paid as ad hoc advance on presentation, the balance being paid latter after scrutiny.

(vi) There is no need to call tenders wherever there is a cooperative society for handling contracts. The value of contract may be fixed in consultation with the society.

(vii) Railway passes should be given to the representatives of the societies to collect labour from other stations.

When sufficient number of cooperatives are organise, a federation of such societies may be formed on each railway. Pending organisation of such federations, advisory boards with the Chief Commercial Superintendent as the Chairman should be set up. A national Federation of all handing contract cooperative societies is also visualised.

The aim should be to organise 200 cooperatives during the remainting years of third plan and in the first two years of the fourth plan. Decasualisation of licensed porters at railway stations was introduced except at Allahabad and Kanpur. If cooperative societies of porters were to be formed, the Railway Administration would be relived of this responsibility.

In spite of sympathetic attitude of Railway Board, there has been no marked progress in the organisation of labour construction cooperatives for execution of railway works. The pattern of organisation, financial assistance and other facilities to be given to these societies may be as follows :

(i) A labour contract and construction society should have a minimum membership of 50 with prospects of increasing it to 200. The area of operations may be flexible to cover a number of sympathiser members should not exceed one/tenth of the total membership. The casual workers may be admitted as nominal or associate members.

(ii) There may be share capital contribution of Rs. 2,000 on a cadre to be maintained by them. The average pay of the manager will be about Rs. 200 p.m. and the railway administration may bear the cost on a tapering scale for the first four years. The railway administration should also make an initial advance up to 25% of the value of contract. Further working capital can be obtained from Central Cooperative Banks.

(iii) Unskilled works without any limit and skilled works up to Rs. 50,000 exclusive of the cost of materials should be reserved for labour cooperatives wherever they exist. Some weightage may be given to cooperatives for tenders submitted by them beyond this limit. When skilled works include large components of unskilled work awarded to labour cooperative societies. The schedule of rates should be revised regularly on a rational basis in respect of works entrusted to cooperative societies without calling for tenders. Payment of bills may be ensured fortnightly on completion of each stage of work. Independent tribunals should be set up for deciding disputes that may arise in connection with execution of works and settlement of bills.

(iv) Labour cooperatives should be exempted from payment of earnest money and security deposit.

(v) A Labour Welfare Inspector should be attached to the Civil Engineering Department for ensuring prompt settlement of the bills.

The Welfare Organisation on the railways has to be suitably strengthened and the railway administration should take initiative for the formation of these cooperatives. The assistance of social welfare organisation like the Bharat Sewak Samaj, Ramakrishna Mission might also be obtained in promoting such cooperatives.

400 societies may be formed during the remaining years of the third plan and during the fourth five year plan period at the rate of 50 societies per year. By the end of fourth/five plan, the aim should be to have 500 societies on the railways.

There is no need to form district level federation of such societies. A federation of all labour construction cooperatives working on a particular railway may, however, be necessary. Till such federation comes up, Advisory Committees may be constituted.

A cooperative canteen should aim at providing cheap and whole some meals to its members rather than earn large profits. It must, however, run strictly as a business organisation. The Railway Board are reviewing the question of providing canteen facilities for the staff as a result of the recommendations of the Second Pay Commission and as the Staff Welfare Review Committee report does not cover these employees. Hence no specific recommendations are made in this behalf. However, pending this, the railway administration should examine the cases of cooperative canteens which have not got adequate and proper accommodation and should provide them if necessary by undertaking the construction of additional accommodation. The existing canteens run by staff committees should be converted into cooperative societies, as registered societies will have a definite advantage in respect of audit etc. by the cooperative department. Canteens run by contractors and the departmentally managed canteens may be converted into cooperative socities. A phased programme of cooperativising the canteens may be drawn up and completed in the next three years.

There is some surplus land all along the railway line to meet the demands of future expansion. With the increased emphasis on Grow More Food, these lands are leased out for growing food crops subject to certain conditions by the State Governments. Out of a total 76,588 acres available for cultivation, only 32,046 acres have so far been leased out leaving a balance of 44,542 acres. The State Governments should utilise the available surplus and for increased agricultural production and lease out these lands on a long-term basis to cooperative joint farming societies consisting mainly of landless agricultural labourers organised for this purpose.

There are about 250 out agencies on Indian railways for carrying goods and parcels to places not connected by rail. It is possible to work these contracts through existing transport cooperatives. Preference should be given to genuine transport cooperatives over the contractors in the operation of the out-agencies.

The railway administration is running handicraft centres for providing part-time employment to wives of railwaymen, the expenditure on this being met from the staff benefit fund. These centres are run departmentally. The railway administration can relieve themselves of a part of their responsibility by cooperativising these centres wherever possible. The administration may provide working shed at nominal rent to cooperative working shed besides managerial personnel.

Cooperative Credit Societies under the P.&.T. Department.

An administrative unit in the P.&T. department comprises of a division and there are 266 such divisions. It should be the aim to organise one society per division. On this basis, there is need for organising 150 new societies besides reorganising the existing societies so as to avoid overlapping of jurisdiction.

The recommendations 1 to 4 will apply to the credit societies of P.&T. employees also.

The credit societies can take up the work of providing fidelity guarantee bonds for their members. They can also undertake life insurance business as an agent of the Life Insurance Corporation.

In the initial stages, not exceeding three years of the divisions or one of the senior officers may function as Chairman of the society so as to help its growth. The recommendations No. 6 and 10 apply to cooperative societies of P.&T. also.

Thrift deposits should be introduced in all the societies on the scale as recommended for societies of railway employees and they should maintain fluid cover as per recommendation No. 11.

On the railways, the societies keep a part of their funds with the Chief Cashier and Pay Master against which cheques are encashed from the station earnings. The P.&T. administration may examine whether similar arrangements can be evolved for P.&T. credit societies so that the members are spare the burden of paying money order commission both at the time of securing and repaying the laons.

The preparation of recovery statement every month involves considerable labour. This should be dispense with and the recovery may be incorporated in the acquittance roll itself as is done in the case of societies on railways.

Consequent on reorganization of sates and the postal circle, there are some difficulties in recovering dues of members transferred outside the state. Till the legal position is cleared, the P.&T. department should extend fullest cooperation in this behalf.

Cooperative credit societies formed in the backward areas may require financial assistance from the Government. In suitable cases, a working capital loan up to Rs. 15,000 free of interest may be advanced recoverable in a period of ten years. The P.&T. administration should continue to spare the services of their staff on deputation to such societies.

The Welfare organisation of the P.&T. department should be suitably strengthened by taking a few inspectors from the state cooperative departments for exercising proper and adequate supervision on them. Alternatively, the existing welfare inspectors may be trained in Cooperative principles.

Consumers' Cooperatives for P. & T. Staff

Unlike on railways, there are no established colonies for P.&T. staff hence consumers' cooperative stores in residential areas cannot be organised for them. The stores have to be located in the places of work until the P.&T. colonies come up.

A centrally sponsored scheme been launched for organisation of consumer stores in different cities and towns with a population 50,000 or more. Under another scheme, the primary marketing cooperative societies are assisted for supplying consumer articles to village societies are assisted for supplying consumer articles to village societies. The Ministry of Home Affairs have approved a scheme of setting up one central cooperative stores of Central Government employees at Delhi and the scheme is likely to be extended to other major cities. The staff of the P.&T. department may take advantage of all these schemes.

There may be group of postal employees living in outlying areas which may not be served by any consumers' stores. They should be encouraged to join the nearest consumer stores by arranging a system of home delivery, the cost being met by a surcharge on prices.

In areas covered by public sector undertakings, consumers' cooperative stores will be set up as per the decision communicated by the Ministry of Commerce and Industry.

The P.& T staff working in these areas should be encouraged to join these stores.

When the P.&.T colonies come up, it should be possible to set up consumers' cooperative stores in every colony having at least 200 houses.

A special survey might be taken up in 1963-64 to collect data about the strength of different offices in each place so as to draw up programme of organisation of independent consumers, cooperative stores of P.&T. employees. On the basis of this survey, action might be taken to setup consumers' cooperative stores during the remaining years of third plan.

Adequate accommodation is to be provided to the stores and where accommodation is not available new buildings may be constructed so as to provide a minimum of 1,000 sq. ft. floor area.

The pattern of financial assistance should be same as indicated in recommendation No. 30, besides managerial subsidy on a tapering scale for 4 years.

It is not practicable to set up a separate whole sale store for P.&T. employees. The retail stores should be affiliated to the wholesale societies set up for the general public.

The recommendation No. 23 to 28, 31, 33 and 34 would apply to consumers cooperative stores of P.&T. employees also.

Other Forms of Cooperatives under P. & T. Department

The P.&T. department assisted three housing societies at Bombay, Madras and Patna. The scheme in operation at Patna considered suitable for adoption in other areas. The administration may also permit the recovery of monthly instalments from pay sheets.

The recommendation No. 36 applies to housing cooperative societies of the P.& T. employees also.

(i) As the business of canteens involves trading risks cooperative credit societies should not undertake this activity.

(ii) There is no need to run separate canteens for different categories of staff and they should amalgamated into one wherever necessary.

(iii) Contract system should be abolished and the canteens should be cooperativesed.

(iv) The P.&T. administration should not provide less financial assistance than the scale recommended for other Central Govt. employees by the Ministry of Home Affairs.

Administrative Arrangements for Organisation and Supervision

The programme of organising different types of cooperative societies during the third and the fourth five year plan period is fairly large and beyond the capacity of the existing machinery to handle. The Labour and Welfare Adviser who is of the status of Director is attending to labour welfare and cooperative department who should at least be of the rank of the Joint Registrar. Assistance from a few technical assistants will also be necessary to handle all technical matters relating to cooperation. On the bigger railways, a post of class I officer of the rank of senior personnel officer should be created and should be manned by an offiicer of the status of Joint Registrar or Deputy Registrar taken from the state cooperative department. On the North-eastern and North-east Forontier Railways, a post of class II officer should be created and manned by officers taken from the state cooperative department. At the divisional level, a cooperative inspector should be provided in the welfare organisation.

Similarly, a senior officer of the rank of Joint Registrar from the cooperative department might be taken by the Director General, P.&T. at headquarters. It will be necessary to provide one cooperative inspector in each Post Master General's circle and other circles, the pay scale being Rs. 300-20-400. No changes in the existing cooperative Societies Acts are necessary. The present arrangement for audit and inspection by the Regisitrar of Cooperative Societies should continue.

CENTRAL WAGE BOARD FOR THE COAL MINING INDUSTRY, 1962—REPORT

New Delhi, Ministry of Labour, Employment and Rehabilitation, Department of Labour and Employment, 1967. 2 Vols.

Chairman : Shri Salim M. Merchant.
Members : Shri P. R. Chakravarti; Shri S.S. Marathe; Shri Rasiklal Worah; Shri R. Lall; Shri Kanti Mehta; Shri Devan Sen; Shri J. G. Kumaramangalam; Dr. Mrs. Maitreyee Bose.
Assistant Secretary : Shri K. S. Rama Iyer.

APPOINTMENT

In pursuance of the recommendations made in para 25 of the Chapter XXVII of the Second Five year Plan, and in para 30 of Chapter XV in the Third Five Year Plan, the Government of India in the Ministry of Labour and Employment has by two Resolutions, Nos. WB-16 (1) 62 of the 10th August and 17th October 1962, respectively Constituted a Central Wage Board for the Coal Mining Industry of India.

TERMS OF REFERENCE

(a) To determine the categories of employees (Manual, clerical, supervisory, etc.) who should be brought within the scope of the proposed wage fixation.

(b) To workout a wage structure based on the principle of fair wages as set forth in the report of the Committee on Fair Wages.

Explanation

In evolving a wage structure, the Board should, in addition to the considerations relating to fair wages, also take into account :

(i) The special features of the coal mining industry;

(ii) The needs of the industry in a developing economy;

(iii) The impact of the wages structure so evolved, on the cost of production of coal and ultimately the effect of this on various industries consuming coal;

(iv) The need for adjusting wage differentials in such a manner as to provide incentives to workmen for advancing their skill; and

(v) The desirability of extending the system of payment by results.

In applying the system of payment by results, the Board shall keep in view the need for fixing a minimum (fall-back) wage and also to safeguard against over work and undue speed.

(c) To consider demands of labour for an immediate interim wage increase pending submission of the final report.

(d) To consider the demand for the introduction of a gratuity scheme on an industry wise basis.

CONTENTS VOL. I

Introductory; Interim Wage Increases; Coal Industry and Plan Targets, Scope of Inquiry; History of Wage Fixation; Principles of Wage Fixation; The Minimum Wage; Our Wage Structure; Outlying Coalfields and ancillary Undertakings; The Coal Mines Bonus Scheme 1948; Gratuity; Allowances including Shri Kumaramangalam's supplemental Note; Leave and Railway Fares; Contract Labour and C. R. O.; Other Matters; Impact on Costs and on other industries including Kumaramangalam's note; Explanation; Conclusions and Acknowledgements; Summary of Recommendations; **Vol. II** :— Appendices from I to XIX.

RECOMMENDATIONS

Interim Wage Increases

The Board unanimously recommended two interim wage increases, the first of Rs. 0.37 paise per day or Rs. 9.75 per month with effect from 1st March 1963 and the second of Rs. 0.19 paise per day or Rs. 4.87 per month with effect from 1-10-1965. Both these recommendations were accepted by Government, and as a consequence Government raised the selling price of coal by Rs. 0.81/82 paise per tonne in the first instance and by Rs. 0.41/41 paise in the second.

Scope of Enquiry

The Neyveli Lignite Corporation was excluded from the scope of the reference to the Board by Government's decision dated 18-12-1962 (para 6).

The reference would cover all employees in the coal mining industry who fall within the definition of the term "Workmen" in Section 2(s) of the Industrial Disputes Act 1947 (Act XIV of 1947) including miners and other sirdars (Para 2).

The ancillary undertakings, departments, offices and establishment whose workmen would came within the scope of the Board's enquiry are listed in paras 3 and 5.

Minimum Wage

The Board is of the opinion that the minimum wage of category I surface worker of Rs. 5 per day at All India Average Working Class Consumer Price Index Number 166 (Base 1949=100) would be fair and reasonbale. Inclusive of bonus payment at the rate of 10 per cent of basic pay pro-rata on attendance, the lowest paid category I surface worker will be entitled to Rs. 5.50 per day or Rs. 143 per month (Paras 24 and 25). Shri Worah, however, had his reservations on payment of bonus pro-rato on attendance.

Scheme of Dearness Allowance "For every point's rise over the Index No. 166, to which the Board's wage structure is linked, the dearness allowance shall be 3 paise per day. The method of calculation of the Index shall be on the basis of the average of six months; i.e. from January to June and July to December, in each year and the adjustments will be made on 1st October and 1st April each year respectively as at present. If there are fractions in the average the next higher integer will be taken."

The Board has made it clear that if there is a fall in the average cost of living Index No. for any period of six months from the average Index No. for the previous period of six months, the dearness allowance will be reduced to the extent of such fall at the rate of 3 paise per point per day, but not if the Index No. falls below 166 (Para 28).

Our Wage Structure

A. Time Rated Categories

The existing are the scales of pay for the six daily rated categories (Para 15), as shown in Appendix V.

The following are the scales of pay for the six daily rated categories at All India Average Working Class Consumer Price Index No. 166 (Base 1949=100) (Para 19).

Categories	Daily wage Minimum	Increment	Daily wage Minimum	period	Attendance Bonus
I	5.00	0.10	6.00	10 years	+10%
II	5.35	0.12	6.55	10 years	+10%
III	5.90	0.15	7.40	10 years	+10%
IV	6.90	0.20	8.90	10 years	+10%
V	7.95	0.28	10.75	10 years	+10%
VI	10.90	0.40	14.90	10 years	+10%

B. Collieries of National Coal Development Corporation, Including Categorisation of the Excavation Section, Deep Shaft and Mechanised Mines

Monthly paid staff of the National Coal Development Corporation who are at present governed by the Central Pay Commission scales of pay, Railway Rules, Corporation Rules or by other rules should be allowed to opt for the scales of pay and other service conditions recommended by the Board for similar monthly rated staff in the private sector collieries. Such option shall be exercised within 12 months from the date the recommendations of the Board come into effect and the option once exercised shall be final and binding.

The Board recommends the following scales of pay for workmen of the excavation section.

Category E	Rs. 6.75—0 .20—8.75
Category D	Rs. 10.75—0.40—14.75
Category C	Rs. 12.00—0.60—18.90
Category B	Rs. 13.50—0.70—20.50
Category A	Rs. 16.00—0.90—25.00

New appointees in category "F" should be given the scales of the clerical grade III, with option to the existing employees to continue in category V daily scale or to opt for the monthly scale. Job descriptions for these categories given in the Award in Reference No. 57 of 1959, should stand. Operators of shovel/draglines of 10 cubic yard capacity and above or dumpers of 45 tonne capacity and above should be given 25 per cent higher wages than what they draw in their present categories.

Daily rated categories of NCDC governed by existing awards will get the scales which are applicable to like categories in the market collieries.

Shaft Sinking : The existing scheme (special cadre scheme) should continue with a modification that on adoption of new categories recommended by the Board, the provision should be that initial recruitment should be in new category I and thereafter the workmen should be promoted to new categories III, IV and ultimately to VI. The initial probationary period of 3 months may be extended to another term or terms at the discretion of the management.

Drifting Mazdoors : The existing scheme of recruitment should be suitably modified as under :

Initial recruitment will be in category I with provision for promotion after 6 months to category III on the terms indicated the scheme and after a further period of 4 months to category IV in terms of the scheme. Where, however, mechanical loading is employed such workers will be promoted to category V after a further period of 4 months provided they acquire the skill to operate such loaders.

Winding Engine Khalasis : On recruitment, Winding Engine Khalasis should be placed in new categary IV. They would be promoted to new category V as soon as they are found fit for independent operation of these winders. After further 6 months, they would be promoted to new category VI.

N. B.—If the Mines Department introduces a regulation stipulating that winding engine operators must possess Second Class of First Class Certificates before they are authorised to operate winding engines, winding engine operators with Second Class and First Class Certificates should be placed, in new categories V and VI respectively.

The above applies to conventional drum type winders. If such operators are asked to operate Koepe winders, they should be placed in technical and supervisory Grade "B" at the minimum of the scale; in the case of smaller Koepe winders up to 5,000 B.O.B. Operators employed on Koepe winders of higher capacity should be given three advance increments in this scale.

Signal Men : New category V is recommended for signalmen connected with the operation of these new type winders.

The operators of continuous miners should be given the same scale as has been recommended for Grade "A" in the mechanised excavation mines. For loaders and shuttle car operators, the Board recommends Grade "C" of the mechanised excavation mines. Helpers to all these operators should be placed in new category IV and redesignated as Assistants to the Operators.

Barkarkhana and Kobra Workshops : The employees in these workshops should be given the same scales of pay as recommended by the Board for equivalent categories in Excavation Section. For other categories, revision of wages may be done by negotiation at unit level.

C. Piece-Rated Workers

The Board has classified the piece-rated workers into 5 groups as indicated in para 35.

For these 5 groups, the Board recommends the following wages structure with its fall-back wage (minimum guaranteed wage) for each group, as shown below at the All India Average Working Class Consumer Price Index Number 166 (Base 1949=100) :—

	Basic Wage Rs.	Fall-Back Wage Rs.
Group I	5.25	5.00
Group II	5.40	5.00
Group III	5.90	5.25
Group IV	6.00	6.00
Group V	6 75	6.00

The Board recommends the following work-loads for earning their group-wage :

Pick Miner—1 tub of 36 cft. or 36 cft.
Machine Loader—2 tubs of 36 cft. or 72 cft.
Quarry Pick Miner—1.1/6 tubs or 36 cft, or 42 cft.
} Fixed by Majumdar Tribunal and modified by L. A. T.

Quarry Miner—1.2/3 tubs of 36 cft. or 60 cft.
Drill Coal Miner—1.1/2 tubs or 36 cft. or 54 cft.
Quarry Loader—2.1/3 tubs of 36 cft. or 84 cft.
C. P. Miner—1.1/3 tubs of 36 cft. or 48 cft. (as fixed by L. A. T.)

Wagon Loader—Workload same as fixed by L. A. T. i.e. 22 tons per gang of 5 wagon loaders in an eight hour shift.

The Board recommends the following progressive reduction in the workloads of the outlying areas for earning their group wages :

At present	Revised workloads recommended
(a) Where workload is 90 cft. or less	72 cft.
(b) Where workload is more than 90 cft.	90 cft. immediately 81 cft. after 1 year and 72 cft. after 2nd year

Sarvashri Lall and Worah, however disagreed and were of the opinion that the existing workloads in the outlying areas should continue.

D. Clerical Staff And Their Scales

The following are the scales of pay for clearical staff at the All India Average Working Class Consumer Price Index No. 166 (Base 1949-100)

Grade III-Rs. 180-5-2?0-7-265 plus 10% attendedce bonus.

Grade II-Rs. 205-7-275-10-325 Plus 10% attendence bonus.

Grade I-Rs. 245-10-325-15-385 Plus 10% attendance bonus.

Special Grade-Rs. 305-15-425-20-505 Plus 10% attendance bonus.

Shri Rasiklal Worah, however, disagreed on bonus being earned pro-rata on attendance (Para 15).

E. Technical And Supervisory Staff

The Board has decided that the Technical and Supervisory staff should be divided into eight grade (A to H) and recommend the following pay scales at the All India Average Working Class Consumer Price Index No. 166 (Base 1949-100).

Grade A-Rs. 405-20-605-25-730
Grade B-Rs. 305-15-395-20-575
Grade C-Rs. 245-10-305-15-440
Grade D-Rs. 205-7-247-10-337

Grade E-Rs. 180-5-210-7-273
Grade G-Rs. 146-3 176-4-184
Grade H-Rs. 140-3-170-4-178 (Para I)

The Board recommends the following pay scales for the Grades mentioned above in respect of the different categories in the various departments as given below :

Mining Department

Existing designation with Basic Scales of Pay	New Designation	Grade	New Consolidated Basic Scale of Pay
Head Overman Senior Overman Overman-in-Charge Rs. 85-5-150-200	Head Overman	B	Rs. 305-15-395-20-575
Overman Rs. 75-5-105-6-111	Overman	C	Rs. 245-10-305-15-440
Mining Sirdar Class I Rs. 55-3-85 Mining Sirdar Class II Rs. 52-3-73	Mining Sirdar Class I	D	Rs. 205-7-247-10-337
Mining Sirdar Class II Rs. 46-3-61. Mining Sirdar Class IV Rs. 43-3-52	Mining Sirdar Class II	E	Rs. 180-5-210-7-273
Shotfirer Rs. 43-3-52	Shotfirer	E	Rs. 180-5-210-7-273

The existing incumbents in the categories of Deputy Overman, Junior Overman or Assistant Overman in the existing scale of Rs. 65-5-95 will be placed in grade D and will start at Rs. 226 in that scale, in other words their pay scale will be Rs. 226-7-247-10-337.

Survey Department

Existing designation with Basic Scales of Pay	New Designation	Grade	Revised consolidated Basic Scales of Pay
Surveyor Rs. 95-10-205 ...	Surveyor	A	Rs. 405-20-605-25-730
Asst. Surveyor (qualified) ... Rs. 50-4-90-5-100.	Asst. Surveyor (qualified)	C	Rs. 245-10-305-15-440
Asst. Surveyor (unqualified) ... Rs. 40-3-52-4-76	Ass. Sureveyor (unqualified)	E	Rs. 180-5-210-7-273
Tracer Rs. 40-3-52-4-76 ...	Tracer	E	Rs. 180-5-210-7-273
Head Chairman ...	Head Chairman	E	Rs. 180-5-210-7-273
Ferro-Printer Rs. 30-1-40-2-46 ...	Ferro Printer	F	Rs. 165-4-205-5-230
Chairman Rs. 30-1-34 ...	Chairman	F	Rs. 165-4-205-5-230

Engineering Department

Existing Designation	New Designation	Grade	New Consolidated Basic Scales of Pay
1	2	3	4
1. Electrical Supervisor Electrical Chief-Foreman Electric Sr. Foreman Electrical Foreman-in-Charge.	Foreman-in-Charge Technical	A	Rs. 405-20-605-25-730
2. Mechnical Chief Foreman Senior Mechanical Foreman Foreman-in-Charge (Mechanical)	Foreman-in-Charge Mechanical	A	Rs. 405-20-605-25-730
3. Head Electrical Foreman Electrical Foreman Electrical Chargeman	Electrical Foreman	B	Rs. 305-15-395-20-575
4. Head Fitter	Head Fitter	B	Rs. 305-15-395-20-575

(Contd.)

1	2	3	4
5. Foreman Mechanical Chargeman Machanical	Mechanical Foreman	B	Rs. 305-15-395-20-575
6. Asst. Foreman Elec/Mech ; or Junior Asst. Chargeman Shift-in-Charge Elec/Mech. Asst. Electrician.	Asst. Foreman Electrical/ Mechanical.	C	Rs. 245-10-305-15-440
7. Asst. Head Fitter.	Asst. Head Fitter	C	Rs. 245-10-305-1 5-440

Medical Department

Existing Designation	New Designation	Grade	New Consolidated Basic Scales of Pay
Doctor (M.B.) Rs. 200-20-300-25-400	Doctor (M.B.)	A	Rs. 405-20-605-25-730
Doctor (L.M.F.) Rs. 100-10- 150-15-210	Doctor (L.M.F.)	B	Rs. 305-15-395-20-575
Nursing Graduate of Senior Trained Nurse (with or without Midwifery Certificate) Rs. 75-5-110-6-134.	Senior Trained Nurse or qualified Midwife.	C	Rs. 245-10-305-15-440
Compounder qualified Rs. 60-5-90	Compounder qualified	D	Rs. 205-7-247-10-337
	Creche Nurse Registered		Rs. 205-7-247-10-337
	Pharmacist.		Rs. 205-7-247-10-337
	Junior Trained Nurse	D	Rs. 205-7-247-10-337
Compounder (unqualified) Rs. 45-3-75	Compounder (unqualified) Nursing Orderlies	E	Rs. 180-5-210-7-273
	(untrained or apprentices nurse) Operation Theatre	E	Rs. 180-5-210-7-273
	Assistant.	E	Rs. 180-5-210-7-273
	Dai-unqualified Midwife.	H	Rs. 140-3-170-4-178
Dressers, Ward boys, Vaccinators Rs. 28-1-45	Dressers, Ward boys Vaccinators.	H	Rs. 140-3-170-4-178
Creche Ayahas Rs. 28-1-30	Creche Ayahas	H	Rs. 140-3-170-4-178

Doctors (L.M.F.) with six or more years service in a colliery or group of collieries under the same management should be placed in Grade A in the pay scale of Rs. 405-20-605-25-730.

Existing Designation	New Designation	Grade	New Consolidated Basic Scales of Pay
	Watch and Ward Staff		
	Head Chowkidar, Havildar, Jamadar, Head Peon, Head Watchman, Head Guard	F	Rs. 165-4-205-5-230
Night Watchman Rs. 30-1-42	Night Watchman	G	Rs. 146-3-176-4-184
Watchman, Peon, Chawkidar, Chaprasis Rs. 28-1/2-30-1-40	Watchman, Peon, Chowkidar, Chaprasis	H	Rs. 140-3-170-4-178

Canteen Staff

Existing Designation	New Designation	Grade	New Consolidated Basic Scales of Pay
Canteen Supervisor or Manager Rs. 48-3-57-4-93	Canteen Supervisor or Manager	Cl	Rs. 205-7 275-10-325
Asst. Supervisor or Asst. Manager Rs. 43-3-82	Asst. Supervisor or Asst. Manager	Cl. III	Rs. 180-5-230-7-265
Canteen Cooks Rs. 30-87-2.08-43-35	Canteen Cook	F	Rs. 165-4-205-5 230
Canteen Boy Rs. 27.62-0.78-32.30	Canteen Boy	Cl. II	Rs. 140-3-170-4-178

Teacher

Existing Designation	New Designation	Grade	New consolidated Basic Scales of Pay
	Graduate Teachers	Cl. I	Rs. 245-10-325-15-385
Matriculate Trained Teachers	Matriculate Trained teachers	Cl. II	Rs. 205-7-275-10-325
Matriculate untrained or non-matriculate trained teachers Rs. 43-3-82.	Matriculate untrained teachers, teachers or non-matriculate trained teachers.	Cl. III	Rs. 180-5-230-7-265
Non Matriculate untrained teachers Rs. 40-2-52	Non-Matriculate untrained teachers.	F	Rs. 165-4-205-5-230
Welfare Officer	The Board recommends	A	Rs. 405-20-605-25-730

The above scales are the lowest below which no colliery should be allowed to go. In collieries where higher scales of pay then what the Board has recommended are prevailing they shall be continued and the Board trusts they will be further improved upon. Shri Worah had his reservations on the recommendation.

The above scales are basic pay scales and in addition the staff be entitled to dearness allowance, attendance bonus at 10 per cent of basic pay and other allowances to which they are entitled.

Section-F

The Board has devised the undernoted method of adjustment.

Method of Adjustments

(a) When the total emoluments of the workers as on 1.10.1966 made up of basic wage plus dearness allowance plus variable dearness allowance plus interim wage increases recommended by the Board, is below the minimum of the prescribed wage scale for their category, they shall be brought upto the minimum prescribed by the Board ; if they are in between two stages of their wage scale, they shall be placee at the stage next above in their prescribed wage scale ;

(b) After adjustment as aforesaid the, workmen shall be given one increment for every three completed years of serviee, those with less than three years service not being entitled to any increment.

(c) Those with service of three years and more but less than six years shall be entitled to one increment in the prescribed scale ;

(d) Those with service of six years and more but less than nine years shall be entitled to two increment in the prescribed scale ; and

(e) Those with service of mine years and more shall be entitled to three increments in the prescribed scale.

If by the above method of adjustment the total emoluments of a workman as aforesaid plus the amount of attendance bonus at 10% as proposed by the Board, does not give him an increase of 10% over his total emoluments as computed above plus attendance bonus at the existing rate as if it had been earned, then the following method of adjustment shall be adopted.

To his total emoluments as on 1-10-1966 computed as in para 1 above will be added the full attendance bonus to which he would have been entitled under the existing Coal Mines Bonus Scheme as if it had been earned. The amount so arrived at will be adjusted in the new scale applicable to his category at the nearest point in the scale. On the amount so adjusted in his new scale, he would be entitled to the new attendance bonus at the rate of 10% of his consolidated basic wage/salary.

Outlying Coalfields And Ancillary Undertakings

Ancillary undertakings : In the absence of specific agreement between the parties the Board recommends that its proposed categorisation and wage scales should be made applicable to all employees in the Ancillary Undertakings (mentioned in para 3 of Chapter IV). The fitment of employees into the new scales recommended should be affected at unit level in consultation with the workmen or their representatives, the difference (if any) being settled at unit level.

Andhra Pradesh : Coal cutters in this field should be placed in new category IV.

Subject to the board agreements (reached between the representatives of the management of Singareni Collieries and the representatives of the Unions) the wage structure and the proposed categorisation for Bengal and Bihar should be made applicable to the Singareni Collieries Co. Ltd. with necessary modifications and changes, occasioned by their special condition.

Madhya Pradesh, Orissa And Maharashtra : Categorisation proposed by the Board for Bengal and Bihar should be adopted in the outlying coalfields of Madhya Pradesh, Maharashtra and Orissa. In the case of specific categories not mentioned in the categorisation proposed by the Board the managements and the unions concerned should at local level, by agreement, fit in such workers in the appropriate categories on the basis of their present emoluments, skill involved and other relevant factors.

Workers employed in private power stations and railways should also be fitted in the proposed categorisation recommended by the Board.

Assam : The existing separate categorisation of surface and underground workers will be replaced by one categorisation for both surface and underground workers and the differential between surface and underground workmen, will be maintained by a separate underground allowance as in the rest of the country. All time rated daily paid workers shall be placed in six categories as shown in appendix VA with the following basis consolidated scales of pay at All India Working Class Consumer Price Index No. 166.

Categories	Daily wage minimum	Increment	Daily wage Maximum	Period of Scale	Attendance and bonus deferred
	Rs.	Rs.	Rs.		
I	5.75	0.11	6.85	10 years	plus 10%
II	6.15	0.14	7.55	10 years	plus 10%
III	6.80	0.18	8.60	10 years	plus 10%
IV	7.95	0.23	10.25	10 years	plus 10%
V	9.15	0.32	12.35	10 years	plus 10%
VI	12.55	0.46	17.15	10 years	plus 10%

Clerical Staff : Basic consolidated scales of pay at All India Working Class Consumer Price Index No. 166.

Clerical Grade III	Rs. 205-6-265-8-305 (15 years)	Plus 10% attendance bonus and deferred bonus.
Clerical Grade II	Rs. 235-8-315-12-375 (15 year)	-do-
Clearical Grade I	Rs. 280-12-376-16-440 (12 year)	-do-
Special Grade	Rs. 350-16-430-20-570 (12 years)	-do-

Technical And Supervisory Staff: Scales of pay at cost of living at All India Working Class Consumer Price Index No. 166.

Grade A...	Rs. 475-20-575-25-825	(15 years)	plus 10% attendance and deferred bonus.
Grade B...	Rs. 350-16-430-20-630	(15 years)	-do-
Grade C...	Rs. 280-12-340-16-500	(15 years)	-do-
Grade D...	Rs. 235-8-275-12-395	(15 years)	-do-
Grade E...	Rs. 205-6-235-8-315	(15 years)	-do-
Grade F...	Rs. 190-5-215-6-275	(15 years)	-do-
Grade G...	Rs. 106-4-206-5-216	(15 years)	-do-
Grade H...	Rs. 160-4-200-5-210	(12 years)	-do

The categorisation and grades will be the same as the ones recommended for the rest of the country. In the case of categories not covered or any other difficulty in categorisation the matter should be settled by mutual negotiation failing which by arbitration or adjudication.

Workers will continue to be supplied with food-grains and other articles at concessional rates as at present.

Scheme of Dearness Allowance: For every point's rise beyond the index number 166, the dearness allowance will be 2.25 paise per point per day or 58.6 paise per month. Other terms and conditions of payment of dearness allowance will be the same as for the rest of the country.

Categories like doctors, surveyors, senior overmen whose existing scales of pay are better and higher than that recommended by the Board should be put in the next higher scale. In cases where even the highest scale may not give some of these employees any benefit the Board recommeneds that the management should evolve a scale which is higher than the one, they are enjoying, at present, taking into account the general wage increase and the adjustment formula recommended by the Boards.

Price Rated-Workers : The present consolidated ratio should be increased by 23% in the same manner as the Board has recommended for the price-rated workers the rest of the country. The fall back wage of local cutters (whom the Board has been given to understand are the only piece-rated workers in the ARTC) shall be 15% higher than the group fall back wage that has been recommended for similar categories in the rest of the country on a pro-rata weekly basis. In other words the fall back wage will be Rs. 0.90.

Underground Allowance : The rate of underground allowance shall be 10% of the basic consolidated rate with a maximum of Rs. 50 per month. This allowance shall be increased by 1% with a corresponding increase of Rs. 5 per month in the maximum after every 12 months from the date the recommendations of the Board come into effect until it reaches a rate of 15% of the basic consolidated pay with a maximum limit of Rs. 75 per month. Sarvashri Worah and Lall do not agree with that part of the recommendation which provides for a phased increase of 1% each year.

The allowances for difficult mining conditions which the Board has recommended in Chapter XII of the report should not be extended to workers in Assam. This however does not apply to underground and tub pushing allowance, lead and lift payments and to allowances other than for difficult mining conditions, e.g., officiating allowance, over-time allowance, etc.

The Coal Mines Bonus Scheme 1948

The provisions in Para 8 of the Scheme relating to forfeiture of bonus because of participation in an illegal strike, should be removed.

Bonus should become a definite part of the wage of the worker and it should no longer be conditional on a minimum attendance qualification.

The Board recommends that the Bonus should be paid quarterly as hitherto, but prorata on attendance, (Para 27). Shri Worah, however disagreed with the recommendation for payment on pro-rata attendance.

Bonus should be calculated at 10% of the new consolidated basic wage and the same should be paid quarterly pro-rata on attendance to all employees who are covered by the Board's recommendations and whose new basic pay does not exceed Rs. 730 per month.

Gratuity

The Board recommends an industry-wise scheme of gratuity. Such a scheme should be met out of a fund to be created by the levy of a cesson despatches of coal. The scheme should be administered by the Board of Trustees of the Coal Mines Provident Fund or a similar tripartite autonomous body.

Workmen shall be entitled to the payment of gratuity from the cess with effect from 1-1-1967 irrespective of the date from which the gratuity scheme is put into force. All past services shall count for payment of gratuity. Sarvashri Lall and Worah do not agree that the scheme should be introduced with effect from 1-1-1967.

Workmen entitled to the payment of gratuity under an existing scheme shall have the right either to opt for the existing scheme or the scheme of gratuity recommended by the Board.

The Board recommends 60 years as the age of superannuation.

The Board except Shri Worah, who submitted an alternative scheme, recommmends the following scheme of Graduity

GRATUITY SCHEME

Events entitling gratuity	Quantum of gratuity payable
1. On death or on physical/mental incapacity whilst in service, which renders the workmen unfit for further service...	15 days' wages, for each completed years of service, subject to a maximum of 15 months' wages.
2. On superannuation at the age of 60 years...	
3. On voluntary retirement or resignation of—	
(i) surface workmen (ii) underground workmen—	
(i) Surface Workmen—	
(a) Upto 10 years of service ...	Nil
(b) Over 10 years but below 15 years of service ...	10 days' wages, for each completed years of service.
(c) Over 15 years of service ...	15 days' wages for each completed years of service subject to a maximum of 15 months' wages.
(ii) Underground Workmen—	
(a) Upto 5 years of service ...	Nil
(b) Over 5 years but below 10 years of service ...	7 days' wages for each completed years of service.
(c) Over 10 years and below 15 years of service ...	**10 days' wages of each completed years of service.**
(d) Over 15 years of service ...	**15 days' wages for each completed year of service subject to a maximum of 15 months wages.**

(Contd.)

N.B.—In the event of a workan (whether surface or underground worker) voluntarily retiring on attaining the age of 50 years or above provided he has put in 5 years' service, he shall be entitled to payment of gratuity at the rate of 10 days' wages for each completed year of service.

4. On termination of service by the employer :

(a) Upto 5 years of service	...	Nil
(b) Over 5 years of service	...	15 days' wages for each completed year of service, subject to maximum of 15 months' wages.

Allowances

Underground Allowances: Underground allowance shall be paid to all those who are entitled to receive it at present at the rate of 5% of the new consolidated pay with a maximum of Rs. 25 per month. This allowance shall be increased by 1% with a corresponding increase of Rs. 5 per month in the maximum after every twelve months from the date the recommendations of the Board come into effect until it reached the rate of 10% of the basic pay, with a maximum limit of Rs. 50. Sarvashri Lall and Rasiklal Worah do not agree with that part of the recommendation which provides for a phased increase at the rate of 1% each year.

Lead and Lift

Distance		Rate
Lead (For tubs of 36 cft to be converted into cubic-metres)		
		Rs.
0 to 50 ft.	...	Nil
50 to 100 ft.	...	0.225
100 to 150 ft.	...	0.675
150 to 200 ft.	...	1.125
200 to 250 ft.	...	1.800
for every additional 50 ft. beyond 250 ft.		0.700
Lift (36 cft. tubs to be converted into cubic meters)		
0 to 10 ft.	...	Nil
10 to 15 ft.	...	0.225
15 to 20 ft.	...	0.425
20 to 25 ft.	...	0.675
for every additional 5 ft. above 25 ft.		0.450

Managements and Unions at unit level may negotiate of lead payable from 0' to 150' into the tub rate of pick miners and loaders and other price-rated workers to whom lead is payable.

Shri Rasiklal Worah does not agree with the quantum of lead and lift rates or with the distances for which they are recommended.

Overburden Removal Workers Lead: For every 50' or part of 50' over the first 100' Rs. 7.30 per 1000 cft of overburden. Lift-For every 5' lift or part of 5' over the first 10', Rs. 3.65 per 1000 cft. of overburden.

Tub Pushing Allowance for Miners : A consolidated rate of 0.075 per tub of 30 cft. should be paid for every 100 ft or part thereof in excess of the first 100'.

Stacking and Reloading Allowance : The general practice of paying the full rate for cutting and stacking coal should be made uniform For reloading the same rate as for loading machine cut coal should be paid. Two of the employee's representatives are of the opinion that for cutting and stacking 36 cft of coal the rate should be Rs. 4.50 as against Rs. 6 for cutting and loading 36 cft of coal.

Overtime for Persons Holding Position of Supervision and Management and Doing Confidential Work : Notification No. GSR 975 should be suitably amended and all such workers whose wages are less than Rs. 500 should be paid at overtime rates when called upon to work overtime. The drivers of cars, trucks and other vehicles shall have the option of overtime as recommended above or to the benefit of existing rates of khoraki payable to them, but shall not be entitled to both. Where the existing practice is to grant both the overtime payment and khoraki, the practice should continue.

Lead And Lift For Wagon Loaders : Lead—For every 50' or part of 50' over the first 100' paise per tonne of coal.

Lift—For every 5' lift or part of 5' over the first 10', 15 paise per tonne of coal.

Sarvashri Lall and Worah have disagreed with the recommendation.

Officiating/Acting Allowance : Where an employee in a lower category works in the place of a workman of a higher category he should be entitled to payment of officiating allowance which shall be the difference between his wages and the minimum of the higher category, if such minimum is higher than his existing pay. In case by this method of adjustment, he gets less than one increment in the officiating scale, he should be given one increment in that scale. In the event of the existing pay of the officiating workman being higher than the minimum of the higher category in which he works, then his existing pay should be adjusted into the next higher step in the higher category's scale and he should be given one increment in that scale. Where, however, existing terms regarding payment of officiating allowance are more favourable the same shall be continued.

Water Seepage/Bailing Allowonce : Miners and/or loaders who are called upon to do the work of bailing mazdoors should be compensated by payment equivalent to the wages of time-rated bailing mazdoor or mazdoors who would have been otherwise required to do the work. The full rates payable to each bailing mazdoor should be equally divided and paid to the gang of miners and/or loaders.

Dressing Allowance (For Miners and Loaders): These Miners and Loaders should either be designated as drill coal miners (whom the Board has placed in group IV and for whom it has fixed a workload of 54 Cft) or in the alternative they should be compensated by payment equivalent to wages of time-rated dresser or dressers who would otherwise have been required to do this work. Two of the employers representatives have their reservations on this recommendations;

Thin Seam Allowance : The piece-rated workmen should be paid the following minimum allowances :

(a) For seams of 1 to 1.5 metres thickness : 5% of the consolidated basic rate wage.

(b) For seams of 1 metre and below 10% of the consolidated basic rate wage.

First Aid Allowance for Workers who Quality for St. John Ambulance Association Certificate First Aid : Workmen who are required to obtain such a certificate under a statute or at the behest of the employers should be paid a suitable al'owance. Those management which at present paying such allowance should continue to pay it.

Thick Seam Depillaring Hard Coal/Stone Band Allowance and Steep Gradient Allowance : Should be negotiated at unit level.

Surplus Allowance : Wherever the management cuts wages for shortage, the workmen will be entitled to be compensated for the surplus.

Bad Ventilation Allowance : Question of compensation for bad ventilation must be settled at unit level.

Allowances Claimed by Singareni Collieries Workers' Union, Cycle, Motor Cycle, Typing, Stenographer, Comptometer, Parade, Project and Payment Allowances : The question of increasing the rate of the allowances should be negotiated between the workers and management.

Conveyance Allowance : This demand should be negotiated and settled at unit level.

Long Distances Walking Allowance : The Board recommends that this demand should be negotiated at unit level.

Night Shift Allowance : When there is rotation of shifts there is no justification for payment of any extra allowance for night shift working. The representatives of the workmen however contended that coal mining is not a continuous process industry and hence the workers are entitled to Night Shift Allowance.

Sarvashri Lall and Worah had their reservations on some of these recommendations as recorded by them in their separate minute of dessent.

Leave and Railway Fares—Chapter XIII

The Board makes the following recommendations—

Leave

Priviledge leave or annual leave with wages (Majority recommendation) :

(a) A workmen employed underground in a coal mine shall be entitled to annual leave with wages at the rate of one day for every twelve days of work performed by him.

(b) A workman who is employed otherwise than as stated in (a) above shall be entitled to annual leave with wages at the rate of one day for every sixteen days of work performed by him.

Casual Leave : Five days paid casual leave in the year with liberty to prefix or suffix casual leave to Sundays, weekly rest days of paid festival holidays should be granted to workmen. (This is a majority recommendation Shri Worah dissenting).

Sick Leave : All workmen shall be entitled to 15 days sick leave in the year on full pay or 30 days in the year on half pay with a right to the workmen to accumulate sick leave for a period of 60 days and 120 days respectively, in the entire period of service. (Majority recommendation one member dissenting).

Paid Festival Holidays : The existing provision for seven paid festival holidays in the year is adequate and should continue. If, however, any unit is granting more than seven paid festival holidays, it shall be continued.

Leave Without Pay : One month's leave without pay in the year should be granted.

Quarantine Leave : The provision of the Model Standing Orders, shall stand.

Paid leave for T.B. Cancer, Leprosy, Mental Diseases, Paralysis and Occupational Diseases like Pneumoconeosis, Silicosis etc : Special leave with pay on medical certificate for at least six months in the first instance should be granted and paid by the Coal Mines Welfare Fund. If within a period of six months it is found that the disease is curable, longer leave should be granted depending on the circumstances of each case.

Injury Leave : The question of extending the applicability of Rules 83 and 83A of the Fundamental Rules to the Coal Industry should be gone into by the Industrial Committee on Coal Mining.

Railway Fare : The condition of three month's uninterrupted service on return from leave should be rescinded and all workmen should be paid return railway fare within a week of their being allowed to resume duty on return from leave.

Railway Fare concessions should be allowed to be accumulated for a period of two years. The members representing the industry do not agree with this recommendation.

Railway Fares should include boat fares wherever payable.

The class by which the workmen shall be entitled to travel will be as follows :

If the workman's basic wage is Rs. 165 or less per month — III Class

If the workman's basic wage is above Rs. 165 and upto Rs, 265 per month — II Class

If the workman's basic wage is above Rs. 265 per month — I Class

Contract Labour and C.R.O.

In the interest of securing social justice and industrial peace the Government should take effective steps for the expenditious implementation of the recommendations of the Dave Court of Enquiry, on the employment of contract labour.

C.R.O., or Gorakhpuri labour : The C.R.O. system should be abolished at the earliest in the interest of healthy employer employee relationship. Sarvashri R. Lall and Rasikal Worah, did not agree with this recommendation of the Board.

Other Matters

Incentive Production Bonus : It would not be within the Board's powers to frame an incentive or production bonus scheme for the whole industry when none exists at present. The Board, however, fully supports the introduction of incentive/production bonus scheme at individual collieries, which should be worked out in consultation with the workmen's representatives. Where incentive or production bonus schemes are existing at present in individual collieries, whether of the public or private sector undertakings, the same shall be continued.

Apprentices and Learners

The Government should co-ordinate the existing training programmes and schemes and explore the possibilities of further improving and extending them so as to provide trained and skilled personnel to the coal industry.

Apprentices and trainees, who are not governed by separate contracts, should receive the minimum wage of the category in which they are asked to work and that in no case should such apprentices and trainees receive less than the minimum wage that the Board has recommended for an unskilled category I workmen.

Conversion of Weekly Paid, Time-Rated and the Piece-Rated Workers into Monthly System of Payment

Wherever conversion into monthly system of payment is desired it should be negotiated at unit level.

House Rent Allowance

House rent allowance of Rs. 8 per month should be paid from 1st January 1967 to all workmen who are not provided with free housing. Those who are offered accommodation and do not avail themselves of the offer, will not be entitled to payment of the house rent allowance. The three employer's representatives on the Board do not agree with this recommendation.

No house rent should be charged to workers who are provided with housing accommodation.

Alternative Light Employment for Disables Workmen

Government should look into the matter and formulate a proper scheme to ensure that every disabled workman who is capable of performing lighter work is provided with such alternative employment.

Free Fuel

Free fuel should be supplied to all workmen in the coal industry. Where such practice does not exist it should be introduced and where free fuel is being supplied, the existing practice, quantity and manner of supply should be continued.

Interchangeability

Extension of the practice of interchangeability and team-work is desirable provided (1) it is done in agreement with the workers and their representatives (2) does not result in retrenchment and (3) the workers receive an equitable share of increased productivity. Dr. Mrs. Maitreyee Bose and Shri Deven Sen disagreed with the recommendation.

Impact on Costs and Other Industries

The Board has not been able to arrive at an agreed quantitative assessment of likely increase in the costs of production resulting from the wage structure which it has recommended. It is, however, the consensus of the Board that a change in the wage structure of the order recommended in this Report will have some impact on production costs ; and it will necessitate a review of coal prices. Such a review is already being undertaken by the Tariff Commission and the extent of price of adjustment or any other policy changes which might be deemed necessary in the context of the new wage structure will have to be considered and decided upon by Government.

The employer's representatives disagree with this view and have expressed their views in separate notes.

Conclusions and Acknowledgements

The recommendations on each issues are the minimum below which no colliery management shall be permitted to go. All existing higher and better rates of wages, allowances and amenities which are more favourable than those recommended shall be protected.

All recommendations, unless otherwise specifically stated, shall come into force from 1st January 1967. The employer's representatives do not agree with this recommendation.

If the recommendations come into effect from 1st January 1967 or on any subsequent date before 1st April 1967, the workmen should get dearness allowance on cost of living index No. 177, which is the average of the first 6 months of 1966. This would work out to 33 paise per day or Rs. 8.58 per month. The dearness allowance will again be revised on 1st April 1967 and further every 6 months thereafter as earlier recommended by the Board. If, however, the recommendations come into effect on or after 1st April 1967 the workmen should get dearness allowance on the basis of the average cost of living index No. of the second half of 1966.

COLLISION OF NO. E. 160 UP AND THE REAR OF E. 158 UP AT SAIDAPET STATION (SOUTHERN RAILWAY) ON 9TH NOVEMBER, 1962—REPORT

Delhi, Manager of Publications, 1967. 18p.

One Man Commission : Shri H. S. Hart,

APPOINTMENT

The Commission was constituted under the Ministry of Transport and Aviation (Commission of Railway Safety) in accordance with Rule 9 of the Railway Board's Notification No. 1926-T, dated the 19th March, 1930.

TERMS OF REFERENCE

To inquire into the collision of E. 160 up with the rear of E. 158 Up at Saidapet Station the Madras Beach-Tambaram Electrified Suburban Metre Gause section of Southern Railway at about 18-25 hours on the 9th November 1962.

CONTENTS

Summary; Inspection and Inquiry; Preamble (Description of the accident; Casualties; Composition of the trains; Damage; Number of Passengers ; Weather Conditions); Relief Measures (Medical Assistance; Restoration of Communications); Local Conditions; (Description of the locality; Method of Working; Description of the Up line from Guindy to Saidapet; Appendix G; Permissible Speeds); Summary of Evidence; Observations and Tests; Discussion (Time of the Accidents ; Condition of the Signals; Conditions governing the passing of an Automatic Signal in the 'Or' position; Speed of E. 160 Up at the time of collision; Condition of the breaks of E. 160 Up; Effect of the 'dead' section on observance of General Rule 277; 'Responsibility of the Motorman of E. 160 Up: Responsibility of the Guard of E. 160 Up; Protection of a train Stopped in an automatic signalling section; Responsibility of the Guard of E. 158 Up; Responsibility of the Assistant Station Master, Saidapet; Responsibility of the Gateman at level Crossing No. 12); Conclusions; Recommendations made by the Commission of Railway Safety in connection with collision of E. 160 Up with the rear of No. E. 158 Up at Saidapet Station on the Madras-Beach-Tambaram Electrified Suburban (M. G.) Section of the Southern Railway on 9th November, 1962; Annesure I.

CONCLUSIONS

Cause of the accident

From the evidence available, I have come to the conclusion that the collision of E. 160 Up with the rear of E. 158 Up at Saidapet station on the Madras Beach-Tambaram Electrified Suburban Metre Gauge section of the Southern Railway at about 18-25 hours on the 9th November, 1952, was due to the failure on the part of the Motorman of E. 160 Up to control his train.

The failure on the part of the Guard of E. 158 Up to protect the rear of his train in accordance with prescribed rules also contributed to the accident.

Responsibility for the accicent

(i) The Motorman, Shri C. G. Sampson, of E. 160 Up was directly responsible for the accident, in that he failed to control his train and did not comply with the rules prescribed for passing an automatic stop signal in the 'ON' position, breaching General Rule 277 and subsidiary Rule 277.

His reponsibility should be viewed in the context of the following unfavourable circumstances obtaining at the time.

(a) E. 158 Up having stopped not at Saidapet station platform; as might have been expected, but off the platform and to the rear of it.

(b) The rear of E. 158 Up not having been protected.

(c) Visibility ahead of Level Crossing No. 12 immediately in the rear of E. 158 Up being restricted.

(d) The necessity for his train having to gain sufficient momentum before approaching level Crossing No. 12 in order to clear the 'dead' section—he had failed in this 'dead' section on two previous occasions which had made him over anxions to ensure that he did not fail a third time, particularly as the "peak-hour" rush was on.

This Motorman, aged 43 years, was originally recruited as a Temporary Laboures in May 1947, and worked his way up, having been promoted as a Temporary Motorman in May 1959. He has a fair record of service, having been only punished thrice as detailed below :

January 1957—Promotion with held for 3 months for derailing a train while shunting.

June 1957 —Annual increment withheld for 1 year for derailing a train while shunting.

August 1962 —Annual increment withheld for 3 months for failing to cut out a defective pair of motors while working a train.

He was last certified medically fit in Class A, in January 1960, and had more than 24 hours rest before coming on duty.

His evidence was given in a straight forward manner.

(ii) The Guard of E. 158 Up, Shri M. S. Ramanjulu was also in part responsible for the accident in that he failed to protect the rear of his train even though it had been standing at Saidapet Station for more than 5 minutes before the accident occurred. He thereby breached General Rule 280.

His responsibility should be viewed in the context of the fact that the "peak hour" rush was on, and he was expecting the power to come on at any minute after which his train would normally have left the Station after E. 156 Up.

This Guard, aged 46 years, was originally appointed as a Temporary Porter in September 1937, first promoted as a IV Class Guard in January 1945, and had been working as a 'B' Grade Guard Since July 1959.

His record of service is hardly fair and he has had the following adverse entries made in his service record since 1957.

August 1957—Censured for unauthorised absence.

July 1953—Censured for failing to padlock a Brake-van with parcels.

September 1959—Failed in Guard's refresher course.

March 1961—Annual increment with held for 6 months for threatening Station Master, Tambaram.

September 1961—Annual increment further withheld another 3 months for not being readily available to work trains.

He was rast certified medically fit in Class A-2 (with glasses for reading only) on 20-6-1962, and had more than 24 hours rest before coming on duty.

His evidence was given in a straight forward manner.

Relief arrangements

I am satisfied that these were prompt and adequate.

THE EXPORT SECTOR COMMITTEE ON AGRICULTURAL COMMODITIES AND AGRICULTURE BASED INDUSTRIES, 1962—REPORT

New Delhi, Ministry of Commerce, 1965. 287p.

Chairman : Shri V. Shankar

Members : Shri A.D. Pandit; Shri P.L. Tandon; Shri P.A. Narielwala; Shri M.N. Pittie; Shri C.V. Mariwala; Shri S.R. Nanawati; Shri P.B. Kurup; Shri D.P. Goenka; Shri Ram Das Kila Chand; Shri Madan

Mohan Ruia; Shri Charat Ram; Dr. J.S. Patel; Dr. S.M. Sikka; Shri L. Sahai (retired replaced by Dr. P. Bhattacharya; Shri G.P. Kane; Shri N.P. Chatterjee (replaced by Shri R T. Mirchandani);

Member Secretary : Shri F.C. Gera.

APPOINTMENT

The Export Sector Committee of the Board of Trade decided at its meeting on the December 5, 1962 to set up a number of Study Groups to carry out an intensive study of the Commodities that figure in India's export trade. So the Study Group (Export Sector) on Agricultural Commodities and Agriculture based industries was Constituted Under Ministry of Commerce on December 5, 1962.

TERMS OF REFERENCE

(i) To review the export targets of different commodities an envisaged in the Third Five Year Plan and the Fourth Five Year Plan.

(ii) To identify different commodities which have a reasonable export potential and increasing future possibilities of exports. For the production of such quantities of these products, the Committee would examine the existing structure of different agricultural products and industries and may recommend, inter alia.

(a) Diversification wherever necessary of the existing units;

(b) Establishment of new capacities either in the existing industrial units or as entirely new units. Economics of scale will be specially considered and prescribed by the Committee;

(c) Special advantages of suitable locations for different items of exports;

(d) Advantages and rationalisation of tansport facilities with respect to specified export commodities, and

(e) Measure to increase productivity in agricultural commodities which have a prominent export angle and also measures for improving the production, quality, grading and marketing of such agricultural commodities which are alikely to play a prominent role in exports.

(iii) To review the different incentives granted under the Export Promotion Schemes and to make suitable recommendations as to the manner and quantum of such incentives that may be granted as a packet, if found more desirable to the Export Sector Commodities and Industries.

(iv) To study and recommend, in order to maximise export earnings of different commodities, the formulation of suitable export houses, export agencies, export complexes, firms and organisations, involving different treatment for different commodities viz, canerlisation through one or few selected organisations or agencies, prescribing floor and/or celling prices.

(v) To undertake specific studies of the overseas demand and the potentialities of growing markets as well as threat of substitutes for our traditional goods developing in foreign markets.

(vi) To study the possibilities of further processing and manufacturing out of such articles as are today made in foreign countries from exported raw materials and semi-processed goods from India.

CONTENTS

Preface; Fundamental problems and policies; Oilseeds, Vagetable oils and Oilcakes; Sugar and its bye-products; Cashew Kernels; Tobacco, Spices other than Cardamoms; Raw Cotton, Raw Wool; Fish and products; Lac; Natural gums and Resins; Onions; Raw Jute; Essential oils; Meat and its bye- products; Fruits and fruit Vagetable products; Walnuts; Pulses; Animal (including sheep) Cansings; Potatoes; Cocoa products; Garlie; Dairy products; Sisal fibre Repacking of dates and dry fruits; Concluding remarks.

RECOMMENDATIONS

Role Of Foreign Trade

Foreign trade, besides earning valuable and indispensable foreign exchange, strengthens the news of economic development in several ways. It gives a fillip to transport, shipping, insurance, banking and other economic activities. A target of Rs. 5,100 crores has been adopted for exports in the Fourth Plan period. To achieve this, exports will have to be stepped up by about 40 per cent during the Fourth Plan period.

Import substitution and export expansion have to be among the most important planks of our growth policy. Even afterwards a careful check will have to be kept on foreign trade trends to ensure that there is no unhealthy drain of our foregin exchange resources.

The rise in our exports has been much slower than that in our national income and in imports. It also compares unfavourably with that of other countries and the world average. The year 1958-59 makes a turning point in the matter of our export performance. Since than not only have our exports risen by about 37 per cent but our imports have also been kept in check.

Agricultural Exports

Importance : Agriculture being by far the most important industry in India agricultural products account for over fourty per cent of our average annual exports. If we add the agricultural content of the manufactures, the share of the agricultural sector will become much larger. In the next 10 to 15 years, till the manufactures and semi-manufactures are able to establish external markets, agricultural commodities will have to occupy apivotal role in the export trade of India. But the capacity to discharge this role is likely to be considerably circumscribed by the growing demands of consumption within the country, let alone the trend of increasing costs.

Commodity Composition : Our export trade is built round a few commodities tea, oilcakes, fruits and vegetables including cashew, sugar, tobacco vegetable oils (non-essential), spices, cotton (raw and waste). Any other developing countries, e.g., Ceylon, Pakistan, Burma, Malaysia, Thailand and Mauritius have a similar pattern of exports. Diversification of export trade become difficult partly because of the difficulties in transferring resources from the traditional export sector and partly because of handicaps in adjusting domestic consumption to the needs of exports. We have also to allow for the growing tendency in many countries to restrict imports and for the growing competition from substitutes and synthetics.

Annual Fluctuations : The export earnings have shown a consistently rising trend in the case of oilcaks, fruits and vegetables and tobacco. On the other hand, they have been on the decline in the case of spices, vegetable oils, cotton and lac. In 1963-64, the vegetable oil exports showed a marked recovery. The magnitudes and the frequency of fluctuations in the volume of exports were very pronounced in some cases ; pulses, sugar, potatoes, linsed oil, some oilseeds and oilcakes.

Unit Values : The unit values realised from our export crops very widely and ranged between Rs. 15,931 in 1963-64. Onions and oilcakes are in the lowest group and lemongrass oil, raw wool, tobacco and pepper in the highest. Still more noteworthy are the annual fluctuations. These were pronounced for ginger, groundnut, defatted groundnut meal and lemongrass oil.

Destinations : India's export trade continues to be concentrated in a few countries U.K. and U.S.A. are still our most important customers. But their share (as per cent of the value of our total exports) has declined from about 44 per cent in 1950-51 and 1955-56 to 36 per cent in 1963-64. On the other hand, there has been a rise in the relative importance of U.S.S.R. and Japan each of which now accounts for 7 per cent of our total exports (by value). Most of our agricultural exports go to U.K., U.S.A. and U.S.S.R. An even distribution of exports provides a better distribution of the risk of demand fluctuation over a number of markets. Some notable changes are taking place in the destinational pattern. During the past few years we have developed our exports of tobacco with U.S.S.R. and of sugar with U.S.A. and Canada. The bilateral trade agreements which we have entered into have been instrumental in developing our exports with some countries.

Export Expansion

(a) **The determinants :** Export expansion calls efforts in three interdependent direction (a) creation of supplies for export, (b) developing exportability and (c) maximisation of net export earnings. Export supplies—Extension of cultivation—Efforts should be made to reclaim waste, including marshy and water-logged, land available for the purpose in different States, such reclamation, being costly, calls for a State or organised, corporate, including co-operations to be set up. The corporations can plan for the development of a scientifically-organised and systematically oriented export sector in agriculture.

(b) **Yields :** India is trailing far behind in regard to yields of agricultural crops. It is essential that the reasons for our chronically low productivity are understood and the requisite remedial measures taken. Amongst the most important of them is the needs to orient the community development programme to its true purpose, viz., development of enthusiasm, care and skill in the cultivator. What matters with the cultivator is really the economic superiority and feasibility. The effectiveness of extension is marred greatly because the importance of this realistic approach is not sufficiently realised or allowed for, consequently, the block personnel are not able to put through their programmes and recommendations on economic grounds and demonstrate to the cultivator the economic value and practicability of measures and methods being sponsored.

(c) **Size of holding :** The important foreign exchange earning crops like oilseeds, tobacco, cashew-nuts should be exempted from the ceiling laws.

(d) **Conservation of supplies:** Efforts are also called for, for conserving what we produce, substantial quantities can be saved out of production, if adequate and economic storage facilities are provided. Another avenue of saving is from economics in seeds rates.

(e) **Utilisation of available resources and techniques :** If sustained efforts are made in areas having irrigation facilities to make the best of the available resource, e.g., fertilisers manures, improved seeds, agricultural implements, pesticides and water, a marked headway in improving yields can be made particularly in respect of commercial crops which are directly or indirectly of export importance.

(f) **The pull of domestic demand :** Our exports did not keep pace with production in many cases. Apart from caster, groundnut and linseed oil and groundnut and linseed cakes, exports can be said to constitute insignificant proportions of the production of oilseeds and their products. Among other commodities only black pepper and sugar have shown a predilection towards exports. The spurts in sugar exports during the last two years were quite exciting and promising, but the lustre has somewhat worn off in 1963-64 and may not revive in 1964-65.

In a number of cases the export percentage fell in one or more years since 1955-56 with a rise in the production, e.g., tobacco, linseed, cashew kernels, pluses, chillies, fish and fish products.

(g) **Per capita availability trends :** If we analyse the factor, pull of domestic demand further, we find that it is not due only to a rise of incomes. Statistics of per capita domestic availability show that it has been generally, upward in several cases, viz., tobacco (except in 1960-61).

There is, thus, need to take measures, obligatory or economic, to ensure the flow of available supplies in the desired directions. Exports should receive priority in respect of commodities whose levels of consumption are not short of the requirements of a balanced diet, e.g , sugar and those which are not essential and have a good foreign demand, e.g., tobacco. cashew kernels, chillies, black pepper. Consumption can be pegged at certain appropriate levels in such cases. It is only a planned level of consumption on these scientific lines that can release commodities for exports according to our export needs and foreign demands. It must be bore in mind that these markets can be held not by fluctuating but only by assured exports. Scientific planning postulates a determined long term policy and decisions which may be inconvenient or unpalatable but nevertheless in the interests of the country, as a whole.

Exportability (a) Factors of exportability : Exportability depends on the existence of actual or potential external demand and the relative competitiveness. The factors which influence exportability are multifarious, world- wide an changing.

(b) **Demand :** There has been an all-round expansion in the world demand of many agricultural products during recent years. Our exports of many commodities e.g., pepper, tobacco, wool oilceeds, oils, oilcakes and groundnut meal have no kept pace withthe world demand with the result that their shares in world exports have been declining.

In order to develop exportability, a thorugh knowledge of the overseas demand is needed. A continuous study of the trends and projections of demand in the traditional and new markets is the sine qua non of an effective programme of export expansion. We should send delegation to overseas countries to investigate into the potentialities for the sale of our export products. These delegations should consist of not only commodity specialists but also of others who can supplement their talents in an essential chain of enterprise.

(c) **Adaptation of the Productive System :** (i) Production pattern Crop pianning should be done in order to achieve a proper balance between production for domestic and export needs and secure the best returns from the agricultural resources. Planning need not always be physically enforced; preferences and incentives often succeed in breaking down the bariers of resistance more efficiently than legal regulation.

(d) **Dehydration and Processing :** Dehydration and processing should be estended to commodities like potatoes, banana, garlic, oinion. As between raw products and processed goods, the aim should be to export processed goods, as they fetch a high rate of return and foster other economic activities in the country. A composite view of export perfomance. Potentialities and policies should be taken of the raw materials and their products. The aim should be to earn the largest foreign exchange from a group of commodities and not necessarily from each of them separately and to restrict the export of primary products to the unavoidables. Ways and measures may be devised for improving the competitive strength of the processing industry.

(e) **Marketing Improvements :** Several marketing improvements, such as fumigation, cold storage, refrigerated shipping should be under taken. Compulsory quality control and pre-shipment inspection should be introduced as early as possible for the remaining agricultural export commodities. A geneuine consciousness and conscientiousness about the importance of quality and honesty in trade .and also about the need for raising the standard of quality right from the stage of production has to be developed. Cooperative marketing should be encouraged. When cooperatives are unable to deliver the goods, there should be no hesitation in supplementing or supplanting them. There is need for setting up trade of fices in countries where they do not exist in order to improve the publicity of our exports.

(f) **Price factor :** Prices of many goods, which India exports are over of line with world prices, Crop planning and regional and purposive specialisation should make for lower costs of production.

Agricultural cess has become an anachronism and should be abolished.

Research in export crops should be intensified in

order to evolve methods of lowering costs of production and improving quality and to discover new uses of by products, such as meat, rice, cotton seed and tobacco seeds. This could yield considerable economic returns' lower the costs of production and augment the supply of goods for internal use as well as export. The economic utilisation of the commodity and as such, may prove to be valuable agent of export promotion.

(g) Co-ordination with imports: While emphasizing export expansion the need for import substitution should not be overlooked. The foodgrain crops and some commercial crops, like jute and cotton, officer good opportunities for emport substitution.

(h) Maximisation of export earnings: The relative profitability of commodities from the point of view of unit value and per acre yield of foreign exchange should be taken into account in formulating export policies. An analysis on these lines may induce a better sense of proportion and priorities in devising export promotion measures and may be of inesteemable value in achieving the objective of export expansion.

Role of the Government

Vigorous efforts have been made during recent years to invigorate the export sector and the results have been gratifying. During the Fourth Plan, exports have to be stepped up by 40 per cent which is twice rate of rise in the Third Plan. The task is a gigiantic one, particularly, in the light of difficulties and efforts involved. If concerted efforts are made keeping in view the present trend of international trade on bilateral lines, significant improvments can be made with a large number of countries, in Europe and East Asia. Concerted efforts are needed in several directions.

Indian yields are extremely low. Teachnological progress has the effect of contracting the demand for raw materials, quality has to be improved. Market knowledge and experience are inadequate. Then there are trade barriers. The most difficult problems is the maintenance of a balance between the domestic and export sectors, sacrifices in consumption and in revenue will have to be faced. These are all matters which only a firm, determined and planned policy can solve.

Foreign demand as well as methods of production and sale in countries which are our competitors have to studied. Gaps in the availability of statistical data on production and exports have to be removed. Policies have to be constantly reviewed and stops taken to ensure their implementation. Government intervention in the market may be needed to ensure the flow of supplies in the export channels to the required extent. A wide range of other measures-production incentives, acreage payments, price differentials, export quotas, subsidy payments may have to be taken.

We have to realise that exports are the symbols of development and that every one has apart to play in making a success of export programmes and policies. The State Governments should associate themselves more actively with the national export effort. Educative and publicity programmes have to be intensified in order that this export consciousness may permit throughout the whole process.

Oilseeds, Vegetable Oils and Oilcakes

We have lost ground in a number of countries in respect of the exports of mustard seed. We gave also lost ground in respect of groundnut oil in Burma and Netherlands. Imports of linseeed oil by Australia have practically stopped and have declined in Rumania and U.K. efforts should be made to recover our position in as many countries as possible.

For tackling the problems arising out of the vagaries of the monsoon, as suitable system of crop insurance in selected areas of production should be introduced.

Efforts should be made to increase the yields of through the introduction of better farming practices by strengthening the extension system.

The manufacturers should also been encouraged to aropagate improved methods of oilseeds cultivation in the areas supplying them the raw materials.

The question of permitting imports of American expellers should be examined. There is need to conduct a thorough study of the economics of oil milling.

Efforts should be made to set up cattle feed industry in the country on a substantial scale so that we could improve the quality of cattle feed in the country and earn more foreign exchange by exporting cattle feed than by exporting oilcakes. Some of the indigenous grasses and molasses could be used along with the oilcakles of or this industry.

Out of over 3 lakh metric tons of rice bran, estimated to be available for oild extraction, only 17,000 tonnes are actully used for this purpose, efforts should be made to increase the production of rice bran oil. Steps should also be taken to increase the collection of non-edible oilseeds from trees like muhua, neem Karanj, Undi which grow in the forest and non-forest areas. Efforts should be made to increase the production of mahua oil by persuading the State Goverments, to abstain from cutting down the mahua trees in pursuance of their prohibition policy.

The Indian Central Coconut Committee should consider what steps are necessary for increasing the production of coconut oil and for growing red palm in the country on a plantation basis.

The present pace of development of the cotton seed oil industry should be intensified. The increasing supply of cotton seed oil may keep prices of other edible oils at reasonable levels and thus promote exports of other oils and cotton seed cakes.

Persistent complaints are received from shippers that the conference lines hold a substantial amount of money with them and also dicate terms to the shippers on pain of forefeiting the rebate. It is suggested that net rate should be charged so that the amounts are not locked up.

There is need for the Port Trusts to provide storage tanks, pumping units, tank barges etc. at the ports. They could charge out-of-pocket expenses from the users of these facilities.

Export Targets—The following export storage may be fixed for the end of the Third/Fourth plan period.

Commodity	III Plan	IV Plan	Para No.
Groundnut kernel	50,000	70,000	31
Castor oil	45,000	50,000	31
Groundnut oil	75,000	1,50,000	31
Oilcakes	10,00,000	20,00,000	32
Kardi oil	1,000	3,000	33

The important countries importing Indian cane Jaggery are Ceylon and Malaysia. Exports have fallen appreciably during 1962-63 and 1963-64. Afghanistan and Singapore, which imported from India cane Jaggery worth Rs. 3.11 lakhs and Rs. 3.99 lakhs respectively during 1961-62, have practically not imported and cane jaggery from us during 1962-63 and 1963-64.

Palmyra Jaggery some limited quantities of palmyra Jaggery are also being exported from India, as will be evident from the following figures of exports :

Table 9

Exports of Palmyra Jaggery

years	quantity (Metric tons)	value (Rs. in lakhs)
1961-62	192	1.25
1962-63	74	0.76
1963-64	39	0.55

The important contures importing Indian Palmyra Jaggery are Ceylon, Afghanistan, Malaysia and Singapore. The exports of Palmyra jaggery have fallen appreciably during 1962-63 and 1963-64. Malaysia, Afghanistan and Singapore, which imported Indian palmyra jaggery worth a few thousand rupees during 1961-62, have practically not imported any palmyra jaggery during 1962-64 and 1963-64

Sugar and its Bye-Products

Efforts should be made to raise the yield Per acre of sugarcane in Indian through better agronomic practices, better irrigation facilities and effective pest control measures. There is also need to effect improvement in the quality of sugarcane so that it may yield more sugar.

As the Indian sugar is unable to compete in the international markets, quays and means should be found for reducing the cost of production and the cost of transport.

Experiments of far conducted indicated that, if suitable equipment were available, there would be no difficulty in producing sugar from beet in India. Efforts should be made to grow beet on a commercial scale.

Raw sugar has considerable potentialities for export to many contures. It will be necessary to plan in advance the manufacture of raw sugar to meet the export requirements.

Japan provides a very good market for our sugar. For acquiring a strong hold in this lucrative market, it is imperative for us to draw up a positive and sustained programme for export of sugar to Japan on the lines recommeded by the sugar Delegation which visited Japan under the leadership of Shri V. Shankar, I.C.S. in May, 1964.

A special cell may be set up at the National sugar Institute, Kanpur, for undertaking researeh on problems relating to the manufacture of raw sugar under the Indian conditions.

Greater attention should be paid to quailty factors, viz., polarisation, colour value and grain size.

There is need to phase the shipment programme and give sufficient margin for delays. It might be worth considering whether the responsibility for chartering vessels may be placed squarely on the buyers with usual sateguards for utilising Indian ships.

Factories in India might be given permission to pack in different sizes instead of in one standard size of one quintal.

The possibility of manfacturing food yeast and sugar easter might be explored.

The Japanese refineries have a definite preference for bulk transport of sugar. The world market is progressing towards bulk transport and mechanised handing. We have to pay serious attention to this development.

Mutual exchange of visits of manufacturers, delegations and technical experts between India and Japan is very desirable for some years to come. The possibility of entering into a long-term agreement with Japan might be explored.

It would be desirable to produce high polarisation and low polarisation raws in different regions to avoid inter-maxing.

A faw factories may be selected for production of raw sugar.

The target of export could be fixed at 5 lakh metric tons at the end of the Third Plan and 7.5 lakhs metric tons at the end of the Fourth plan.

Efforts should be made to build up a sizeable cattle feed industry in India using molasses, de-oiled cake and wild grasses. We should attempt to export cattle feed.

It would be desirable to study the possibilities of manufacturing rum and gin in India from molasses for export purposes.

Reasonable facilities should be provided to the factorise recently licensed for the manufacture of fodder yeast so that they start manufacturing yeast quickly. We can then consider the possibility exporting this product.

Efforts should be made to start manufacture of lactic acid in the country from molasses. This would mean saving of foreign exchange at present spent on imports of lactic acid.

By proper rehabilitation and modernisation of some of the sugar factories in north India, considerable quantities of bagasse could be saved for the manufacture of paper and pulp. This would also mean saving in foreign exchange at present spent on imports of paper and pulp. The possibility of concessional railway freight on the transport of bagasses may be examined.

The manufacture/export of sugarcane wax should be encouraged by (a) allowing liberal imports of machinery and equipment and (b) undertaking a survey to gauge the probable demand for this product in the overseas markets.

Efforts should be made to augment exports of confectionery by affording certain facilities to maunfacturers such as provision of imports of special colours, essences and packing materials which are not produced in the country.

Cashew Kernels

Cashew processing factories should be set up in the vicinity of plantation areas. There is also need for introducing modern methods of processing.

Pilot processing units have started functioning in the cashew-nut producing centres of Africa. Consequently, our share in the imports of cashew kernels by U.S.A. has declined during the sixties by about 7 per cent, There is need for us to have a long-term programme for the import of cashew nuts and also to generate a sufficiently strong consumer preference for our cashew in several countries of America, Asia and Europe.

In U.S.A. propaganda for popularising the uses of cashew kernels in the confectionery and backing industry, specially for lower grades of cashew kernels, would give a fillip to the demand for cashews. If our cashew-nuts are found to retain their flavour after dehydration, their use in choclates could increase substantially,.

Considering the relative economic prosperity and per capita consumption of cashew, the countries of Latin America, Africa and Western Europe offer an excellent opportunity to increase our cashew exports. Market surveys should be undertaken in these countries to guage the extent of demand and the nature of consumer preference.

The best method of entering the sophisticated West European markets seems to be through collaboration with firms in those countries to ensure attractive packaging and-effective distribution arrangements.

There is an urgent need for a vigorous publicity compaign in these countries, e. g., U.K., other European countries, Canada, Australia, New Zealand and Japan, which offer the greatest potentialities for our cashew exports. Several measures are needed to make our publicity effective in these countries.

The Government should assist cashew exporters with quotas/import licences for important articles needed by them.

The data on area and production of cashew nuts and on the scope for extending cashew cultivation are not reliable enough. A scientific survey is called for.

In view of the large-scale programme for cashew cultivation, adequate provision for research and development should be made.

Suitable incentives, e.g., exemption from ceiling laws, provision for loans and subsidised supply of fertilisers should be offered to cultivators to evoke the requisite responsible for the amitious programme of cashew cultivation. The producers should get a legitimate share of the price fetched by cashew-nuts.

Marketing co-operatives capable of collecting cashew-nuts from the producer's farms should be set up.

The desirability of setting up a Cashew-nut Board as has been formed in Tanganyika, should be examined.

Compulsory pre-shipment inspection and quality control on export of cashew introduced recently has had a salutary effect on exports. Quality control schemes should be run for the benefit of the producers.

Irrecoverable subsidies like those given for rubber should be given for cashew also.

There is little justification for the imposition of agricultural cess on cashew kernels exported from India in the context of our attempt to boost exports.

The State Governments may be requested to consider the question of having a uniform rate of sales tax on cashew-nuts, if they cannot be persuaded to abolish it altogether.

Railway freights should be reduced on raw-nuts, cashew kernels and cashew shell oil.

Use of modern machinery like oil bath unit, for the extraction of cashew oil is the need of the day.

There is need to undertake research on new uses of cashew shell oil.

The Indian Central Spices and Cashew-nut Committee or the Council of Scientific and Industrial Research may examine the possibility of setting up a plant for the manufacture of beverages, syrups, chutneys and drinks etc. from cashew apples.

The target for the export of cashew kernels should be 58,000 tonnes per year by the ends of the Third Plan and about 70,000 tonnes per year by the end of the Fourth Plan.

Tobacco

Agricultural Marketing Adviser should be requested to introduce a composite grade of tobacco as desired by some countries so that there may be no need to mix the tobaccos again at the time of manufacture.

The Indian Central Tobacco Committee should interest tobacco growers in the production of Bureley Tobacco.

Efforts should be made to publish periodically up-to-date statistics about Indian tobacco crop and prices as soon as they become available.

The project being carried out to grow varieties of tobacco suited to the West German markets should be completed quickly as, due to the cancer scare, demand for tobacco with low nicotine content is also likely to come from other countries.

The Tobacco Delegation has reported that there was demand in Belgium, Poland, East Germany and West Germany for our eigar filler tobacco. This should be further investigated.

The Ad-hoc Committee recently constituted by the Commerce Ministry has recommended a number of measures, e.g., invitations to foreign delegations, greater publicity, reduction or elemination of tariffs. These should be examined and necessary action taken expeditiously.

The Tobacco Export Promotion Council have addressed the London Chamber of Commerce requesting them to adjust the timing and period of their marketing operations so that the cultivators can wait for cring till the leaves becomes fully ripe. The matter should be pursued.

It is essential to adopt scientific methods for the redrying of tobacco as this would improve the quality. It is understood that licences have been issued for the import of ten more redrying plants. Efforts should be made to see that these are installed early. If there is demand for more redrying plants, it would be a false economic not to meet it.

Efforts should be made to effect a general improvement in the yield by adoption of better agronomic practices.

Efforts should be continued to increase the production of Virginia tobacco. Care should be taken to see that the cultivators are supplied fertilizers in adequate quantities, specific allocation of fertilizers exclusively for tobacco would be helpful.

The Ad-hoc Committee has recommended a number of measures for increasing yield and production of Virginia tobacco. These should be examined and given effect to as far as possible.

There is a good demand for Indian cigar tobacco. Till the production of improved cigar wrapper tobacco is developed on a commercial scale, it may be allowed to be imported Efforts should be made to grow cigar tobacco which suits American needs. In other countries too, due to the cancer scare, there is a shift in demand from cigarettes to cigars. Advantage should be taken of this by us.

The grading and marketing of tobacco should be improved by (a) extension of regulation to tobacco in Andhra Pradesh, (b) establishing a large number of rural grading centres, (c) organising co-operative societies, which may pool and grade members' tobacco under Agmark before sale, and (d) evolving simple grade specifications and providing trained technical personnel.

Efforts should be made to get the present system of deferred payment of freight replaced by a net foreign rate.

State or/and Central warehouses m y be set up for providing scientific storage and facilitating grant of bank credit against warehouse receipts.

To develop facilities of institutional credit to tobacco growers, the pilot scheme initiated in Ongole taluq by Andhra Pradesh Government should be extended to the entire Guntur District and to other tobacco growing areas.

The quality control and pre-shipment inspection procedure needs to be tightened up.

Effort should be made to provide adequate supplies of coal for flue-curing and redrying of tobacco.

In the context of the need to boost exports, the present levy (1/2 per cent advalorem) on exports of tobacco under the Agricultural produce Cess Act., 1940 should be abolished.

The feasibility of forming a Tobacco Board on the lines of the Coffee/Tea Board may be considered.

At least 60 per cent of India's production of Virginia tobacco and about 20 per cent of cigar and cheroot tobacco should be exported. The target of total tobacco exports can be fixed at about 75,000 metric tons in view of the production target of 4,68,000 metric tons of tobacco by the end of the Fourth Plan.

Spices Other Than Cardamoms

There is room of augmenting foregin exchange returns from the exports of black peper and curry paste and powder by developing trade with countries from where we realise higher returns per metric ton of our exports.

Efforts should be made to develop the cultivation of minor spices with a view to making available increased quantities for export.

Figures of production of several important export spices are not being collected regularly. Efforts should be made to collect them.

Efforts should be made to raise the yields of different spices through better agrounomic practices.

Adequate pesticidal facilities should be provided for celery seed.

Compulsory quality control and pre-shipment inspection in respect of chillies have been in force since 1st January 1963. Some complaints about the quality of chillies have been received even after this control was imposed. Most of these were in respect of non-specified grades. Requisite changes in the Chillies Grading and marking Rules are being made. The control measure should also be tightened up.

Compulsory quality control and pre-shipment inspection should be enforced on celery, coriander and cumin seeds, curry paste and powder, fennel and fenugreek seeds.

There is need to encourage the production of fibreless ginger in India. If necessary, we should import ginger seed from Jamaica for suppling to growers in selected areas. There is also need to undertake scientific peeling and drying of ginger.

There is need for developing proceeding facilities for most of the spices in order to convert them into power and to make other preparations. New products like oleoresin from pepper should be developed. Particulars of oleores in likely to be in demand in overseas countries may be procurred. Efforts should be made to procure proper machines for the manufacture of essential oils of peper, ginger, chillies etc. The Central Food Technological Research Institute. Mysore should undertake research with a view to evolving new products from spices and for processing chillies in forms like capsic in acceptable to foreign buyers. Efforts should be made to export cumin, coriander, fennel and fenugreek seeds in power form in polythene bags and to manufacture oil from these seeds, and from tejpat for export to industrially advanced countries.

The leading exporters of back pepper are reported to be generally agreeable to constituting a "Pepper Exporters' Corporation" to avoid unhealthy competition among themselves and to put forth a collective effort against competition from the rival producing countries. This point needs to be given serious consideration.

The Indian Central Spices and Cashew-nut Committee may be asked to set up a pilot plant for the manufacture of white pepper and to popularise the manufacture of white pepper to meet the needs of the countries who prefer white pepper. A suggestion has been made that one of the methods of preparing white pepper is by polishing black pepper. Efforts should be made to get the polishing machines from abroad.

Efforts should be made to give adequate publicity to the method of packing chillies in a compressed form evolved by the Central Food Technological Research Institute, Mysore, and to the method of re-drying and compressed packaging of chillies evolved by the Directorate of Market and Inspection.

Exporters of spice and curry powders should be helped with requisite foreign exchange to import the right type of machinery and plants for grinding etc.

Exports should be given facilities to import packing materials. For this purpose, they may be granted 10 per cent import entitlement on the F.O.B. value of their exports.

Intensive propaganda and publicity should be undertaken to popularise curry powder and paste in countries which import these from us.

India's traditional exports of ginger are in the dried, bleached and unbleached forms. Efforts should be made to expolore the possibilities of exporting ginger in other forms, e.g., powdered, pickeled, fresh.

Efforts should be made to develop the manufacture of ginger powder, oil and resin of ginger, ginger pickles, ginger syrup, preserved ginger etc., with a view to introducing these items in the overseas markets. Possibility of exporting fresh ginger should be explored.

Suitable measures should be taken to check sudden fluctuations in the internal prices of turmeric so that the importer could be assured of its supplies at a steady price.

The possibility of manufacturing suitable units fitted with magnetic separators for grinding turmeric should be investigated. If necessary, liberal imports of such machines should be allowed.

A new and simple method for removing dirt and fibrous roots from turmeric replacing the conventional use of cow-dung and chemichrome (lead chromate) has been developed by the C.E.T.R.I. ? Mysore. Efforts should be made to popularise this method.

The targets for the export of various spices suggested are shown in the given on page 109.

Raw Cotton

Stress is at present laid on increasing the production of medium and long stape varieties of cotton with a view to meeting the requirements of the Indian Cotton Textile industry and progressively reducing our dependence on imports. As increased production of medium and long stape varieties facilitates the capacity of the mill industry to export cloth, the present policy is already indirectly export-oriented.

In order to be able to cater to the increased demand for cotton textiles for export and internal consumption and to meet the reqirements of cotton for the manufacture of surgical cotton, khadi etc. and for export, we

Table 2

Export Targets Of Spices

(Metric tons)

Spices	Third Plan	Fourth Plan	Para No.
1. Black Pepper	23,000	28,000	28
2. Chillies	11,000	16,000	29
3. Celery seed	1,800	2,200	30
4. Coriander seed	5,500	8,000	31
5. Cumin seed	500	750	32
6. Curry paste & powder	2,250	3,500	33
7. Fennel seed	2,000	2,500	34
8. Fenugreek seed	—	—	35
9. Ginger	8,000	10,500	36
10, Tejpat	500	6C0	37
11. Turmeric	3,500	5,000	38

should stop up our effort so as to increase the production of raw cotton by about 30 per cent. We should concentrated on increasing the yield per acre through improved techiniques of production.

The Government of India should examine the possibilities of untilizing in the country itself, as far as possible, the cotton at present being exported for the manufacture of finished goods for export. The possibilities of securing collaboration with Japan or some other country in the manufacture of matresses etc. should also be examined and explored. However, until any export oriented schemes of utilisation of deshi cotton in the country itself come into force it would be desirable to maintain the export of deshi cotton at least at the existing levels.

During recent years there has been a fall in the exports of cotton to our traditional markets, viz. U K. and U.S.A. It would be worth-while investigating the reasons for this. The Indian Embassies in these countries may be requested to ascertan the scope for increasing the import of short stape cotton from India and to indicate measures needed to achieve this end.

Our Missions in Japan and Hongkong (who are our major buyers or short stape cotton) may also be asked to investigate whether there was scope for increasing the exports of deshi cotton to these countries. If these investigations indicate the possibility of these countries being able to absorb large qualities of Indian deshi cotton, the Ministry of Food and Agriculture should take measures to increase the production of deshi cotton. Form the export angle, we should mainly concentrate on four varieties, viz., Bengal Deshi, Oomras, Dholleras Comilleas. Any imports of American under PL 480 Agreement should not act as a disincentive for the production of cotton in the country.

The staple fibre industry in India should be suitably developed so that more of these fibres could be used for the cloth industry and our dependence on imported cotton could be reduced.

Until any export-oriented schemes for utilisation of deshi cotton in the country itself come into force, it would be desirable to maintain the exports of deshi cotton at lest at the existing levels. The target of exports by the end of the Fourth Five Year Plan should be four lakh baies.

Raw Wool

The relative importance of U.K. and U.S.A. as buyers of Indian wool declined and that of U.S.S.R. went up considerably during 1961-62 and 1962-63. During 1963-64, this tendency was reversed. Exports to Russia should cause no regret but we should also try to retain our traditional markets. There is, therefore, need to increase production of wool so that we can feed both the traditional and new markets apart from meeting increasing indigenous demand.

It is for consideration whether we could not encourage setting up of a few sheep farms in compact blocks in suitable areas in Rajasthan. The sheep farms could be set up either by Government or private parties. In the latter case, it might be desirable to exempt the sheep farms from the operation of the ceiling laws.

It is necessary to plan for the production of Pashmina woold in the country, Breeding of Pashmina yielding goats is possibe by crossing Ladakh type with breeds from U.S.S.R. ? U.S.A. and Afghanistan. Efforts should be made to obtain the necessary number of goats from Afghanistan, U.S.S.R. and U.S.A. The scheme to breed pashmina goats should be vigorously pursued.

The possibility of manufacturing carpets, with the help of carpet weaving plants deserves to be investigated. The switch-over should be gradual so that the cottage carpet industry is not affected.

At present almost the entire production of tannery wool of South India is exported abroad for making felt. If the felt making industry could be set up in India and, instead of the wool, the felts were exported, our foreign exchange earnings could be higher.

The Acts under which warehouses have been set up both at Central and State levels do not include 'wool' in the schedule of commodities to be accepted by warehouses. Steps may, therefore, be taken to amend the relevant Acts so as to enable the Central and State Warehousing corporations to set up warehouses in the wool producing areas and in the terminal markets of Bombay.

An auction market for wool should be set up at

Bombay.

With a view to eliminating malpractices, rationalising market charges and ensuring a fair deal to the producers, the important markets in the wool producing States should be brought under the purview of Agricultural Produce Markets Acts.

For increasing the return of the producers, cooperative, processing and marketing need to be organised. Concerted and sustained efforts have, therefore to be made in the wool producing areas, chiefly in Rajasthan and Saurashtra, for promoting cooperative processing and marketing of wool, including grading.

In view of the growing indigenous needs, any steep increase in exports would not be possible but we should aim at increasing our exports by one thousand metric tons every year over the previous year.

Fish And Fish Products

Considering the volume of shark landings the export of shark fins could be easily doubled with concerted to cut the fins and process them for export.

Indigenous manufacture of diesel engines should be encouraged till such time as the indigenous production becomes sufficient. Adequate foreign exchange should be made available for the import of engines from abroad.

Adequate foreign exchange should be made available for the import of nylon to ensure increased production of marine fish.

Efforts should be made to export Laminated Bombay duck packed properly in attrative packing. We curing Shinghala may also be tried for export to Singapur and Ceylon.

We should set up ice factories near storage centres and provide a fleet of fishing boats for the various reservior projects.

With a view to securing the collaboration of Japan for the development of our fisheries, a delegation led by Shri V. Shankar, I.C.S. paid a visit to Japan in May, 1964. Collaboration has been secured in several directions. The Department of Food should follow up the recommendations speedily.

The Fisheries Corporation should aim at development of marine fishery resources as well as marketing fish abroad. It should explore the shrimp resources of deep waters beyond the reach of the Indian fishermen.

A resources survey should be undertaken in potential areas to assess the availability of raw materials for setting up large scale processing plants. Apart from surveys being done by the Indo-Norwegian project, the Indian Oceanographic Surveys should prove very valuable.

Research on production and conservation of frogs is called for.

We should form a panel of technical experts to guide the extension services.

It is necessary to have an agency to report the market trends for fish and fish products in the countries where they are exported. It is also necessary to collect samples of fishery products popular in foreign countries, so that the Indian laboratories could be asked to produce similar products in India for export purposes.

Efforts should be made to achieve the Third Plan target for ice and cold storages.

Efforts should be made to induce the exporters of India shrimp to give suitable brand names to their products. Besides, packaging should be attractive.

It is essential for the Indian producers to realise that, unless they produce and store dried fish under hygienic conditions and pack it in dust-proof containers our exports of dried fish are likely to suffer.

Effort should be made to standardise the method of packing live lobster with a view to increasing its exports.

At least 10 more canning factories can be set up between Cochin and Ratnagiri to utilise the Mackerel and Sardine catches. The canned fish can be exported.

The possibilities of producing fish oil should be explored.

Quality control should be introduced for the main varieties of export fish. Efforts should be made to improve the quality of dried and frozen fish by mechanization and popularization of hygienic methods of handling. It is essential to improve the quality of fish meal.

The tin-plate subsidy should be revived and continued at least till the end of the present Plan.

Incentives should be provided to expand the export of processed fish from new areas by giving sudsidies on marketing of fish in the internal market or in the manuacturer of fish meal, as hardly 5 to 10 per cent of fish landings consist of exportable varieties. Unless the rest of the fish is marketed properly in the interior of the country, there would be no incentive to increase fiish landings.

For the Fourth Five Year Plan, a target of Rs. 25 crores worth of fish and fish products for exports would appear to be reasonable.

Lac

(a) There is need to improve our production techniques so that we are able to meet the demand for bleached lac.

(b) It may be desirable to discuss with the foreign synthetic resin industry the possibility of adding lac to some of the synthetic products in foreign countries. Every effort should be made to encourage the use of shellac with synthetics in India as well.

The most important problem in the export expansion of lac and lac products is to meet the situation arising out of competition from Thailand. To counter act tihs, the price of Indian lac should be kept at a reasonable level.

The following recommendations made by the Indian Delegations sent to Thailand deserve to the pursued.

(a) a formal shape may be given to the existing arrangement made by the Thai Lac Association to control the production and prices of lac.

(b) The resources for research in order to discover new used of lac and for undertaking marketing surveys, advertisement and publicity. should be pooled together by the Indian and That Government.

(c) Increased production over normal output should be attempted by both these countries only after new uses of lac have been discovered so that there is no imbalance between demand and supply.

There is need for promoting research in collaboration with foreign exports and organisations on wider industrial uses of lac.

For ensuring reasonable prices to the growers of lac as well as for keeping the export prices competitive in the world markets, it is necessary to provide an organised marketing system, steps should, therefore, be taken for encouraging and fostering cooperative marketing.

At present quality control on exports is exercised on behalf of buyers. This is not always fair to the sellers. For effective and fair system of quality control this control should be exercised by Government.

There is need to draw up an agreed international standard specification for this important commodity of international trade.

More cold storage units should be set up at the assembling and terminal markets so that deterioration in quality could be prevented.

There is need for providing more refrigerated wagons for movement of lac from up country centres to Calcutta. Development of refrigerated storage godowns at Calcutta is also needed.

It is for consideration whether it would not be desirable to set up a lac development and export cooperation which should replace both the Lac Cess Committee and the Shellac Export Promotion Council and though which all exports should be channelised.

We may try to maintain the present level of exports, i.e., about 21,000 metric ton per year till the end of the Fourth Five Year Plan.

Natural Gums and Resins

Investigations are being taken up at the Forest Research Institute. Dehradun, to evolve a suitable method of tapping the trees yielding Gum Karaya. The objective is to secure yields with the last damage to the trees. The institute may be asked to accord priority to this project.

Efforts should be made to collect for export more gum karaya from trees known as cochlospôrmum gossypium D.C. and Sterculia Villasa Roxb.

Investigations are being taken up the Forest Research Institute. Dehradun, to evolve a suitable method of taping and economic utilisation of the trees yielding salai gum. The Institute may be asked to accord priority to this project.

There is need to introduce compulsory quality control on Gum Karya for purposes of export.

Researches conducted at the Forest Research Institute, Dehradun, have revealed that a good substitute for Canada balsam can be prepare from salai gum for mounting microscopic slides. There is an export market for this. This fact needs to be given adequate publicity with a view to drawing the attention of foreign buyers to this new use of this gum.

Efforts should be made to make an assessment of the scope for commercial exploitation of (i) Pins Griffithi M' Clell, (ii) Pins Khasya Royle and (iii) Pinus Genadiana Wall the trees yielding resins.

Adequate data do not exist about the extent to which production of gums and resins could be stepped up. Nor are there data about the extent to which foreign markets could absorb additional supplies of gums and resins if these were available. It is, therefore, necessary to conduct intensive studies to collect data regarding to the production, internal consumption and prospects for export of various gums and resins.

Onion

A survey of the traditional markets for Indian onions should be undertaken to assess the scope for the expansion of our exports to those.

We should try to raise production by at least 50,000 tonnes per year and increase exports by about 25,000 tonnes per year. The export target should be 2,00,000 tonnes by the end of the Third and 3,00,000 tonnes by the end of the Fourth Plan.

Efforts should be made to increase the per acre yield of onions by adoption of improved agricultural practices. Some of the measures required to step up yields area.

(i) Production of onion seeds of improved varieties for distribution in the Pilot Project areas.

(ii) Package programme for the production of onions in the onion growing districts of Maharashtra, Andra Pradesh, Madras, Gujarat and Mysore.

There is need for the addition of refrigerated ships to the Indian merchant fleet in order to capture the U.K. and other European markets.

There is need to introduce compulsory quality control and preshipment inspection standards for onion.

Facilities for cold storage and refrigerated warehousing are also needed. Researches have indicated that with the spraying of Maleic Hydrazine on onion crip 8-10 days before harvest, onions can be safely stored for 3-4 months in cold storage with 30-35°F as temperature and a relative humidity of 85-90 per cent. The spraying cost is Rs. 10-12 per acre or about Re. 1 per 1000 lbs. of onions at an average yield of 15,000 lbs, per acre. This needs to be given publicity through extension organisation.

Setting up of onion dehydration and powdering plants in areas of good onion production should be encouraged. A survey conducted by the Ministry of International Trade has revealed that there is ready demand for dehydrated onions in Kuwait, Bahrain and West Germany, and that, in some countries e.g., Czechoslovakia, Switzerland, Malasia and Singapore, a market for dehydrated onions can be created if sufficient efforts are made to popularise their use.

Raw Jute

Availability of raw jute and mesta is as essential prerequisite for the production and export of jute goods. For India to be able to cater to the increased demand for jute goods for export as well as for internal consumption, it is essential to increase the production of raw jute and mesta. We should concentrate our efforts on raising the yield per acre through improved growing techniques, because on account of competing demand of the crops, it would be difficult to bring more area under jute.

We should decide every year what quantities of raw jute, if any, should be allowed to be exported depending upon our supply position and the need to fulfil the trade agreements with the East European and other countries.

Considering the potentialities of world demand for ute goods the target for the production of raw jute may be put at 80 lakh bales at the end of the Third and at 100 lakh bales at the end of the Fourth Plan.

Essential Oils

The Indian Missions in West-Indies should be requested to make a comparative study of the variety of lemongrass grown and of the method of extraction of oil in India and in those countries with a view to enabling us to know what measures need to be taken by us to compete effectively with these countries.

Efforts for the manufacture of onions and synthetic Vitamin A from lemograss oil should be stepped up as there is danger of shrinkage in the exports of oil itself due to competition from Gautemala and synthetics.

The cultivation of palmarosa grass in the forest areas should be taken up on a planned basis. Such cultivation would present by bridation of the plant and would ensure that a pure strain of grass is used for distillation. Steps should also be taken to introduce better methods of distillation so that the perfumery value of the oil is not impaired.

Concerted efforts should be made to increase our wealth of sandal trees by planting more trees on a systematic basis and also by fighting the menace of the spike disease.

The target of production of vetiver oil may be fixed at 12 tonnes by the end of the Third Five Year Plan and 18 tonnes by the end of the Fourth Five Year Plan.

The target of production of cedarwood oil may be fixed at 18 tonnes per annum during the Fourth Five Year Plan period.

Large-scale cultivation of Mentha arvensis, the source of peppermint oil should be taken up. The Central Indian Medicinal Plants Organisations should be asked to give a very high priority to this work.

The cultivation of citronellain the vicinity of lemon grass. Palmarosa or ginger grass plantations should be discouraged because this may give rise to the mixture of these aromatic grassess. It would be desirable to demarcate suitable areas in the Madras State, preferably on the Nilgiris, under citronella where lemongrass and palmarosa have been tried and found to grow well.

The cultivation of patchouli, the source of patchouli oil, as an undercrop should be encouraged.

There is need to introduce scientific cultivation of geranium so that we get a better yield of oil.

The cultivation of Cinnamonum Zeylanicum, the source of cinnamon leaf oil, should be developed. The Central Indian Medicinal Plants Organisation and the concerned State Governments should be asked to look into this.

The Central India Medicinal Plants Organisation has drawn up a programme for the development of certain oil-yielding plants like dill seed, eucalystus. They should be asked to give a very high priority to these schemes. It should also conduct research on the agricultural aspects of the production of lemongrass, sandalwood, rosha grass and several other types of grass, plants and berries and on the technological aspects of extraction and recovery of oils of economic value.

About 33 per cent of the total production of sandalwood oil is consumed within the country in the manufacture of soaps, cosmetics and attars. Attars are being exported in considerable quantities from the country. One of the difficulties that the attar industry in the country is facing is regarding the availability of good quality sandalwood oil. There have been requests for quality control on the internal trade of this oil so that not only the quality of attars is improved but foreign exchange is earned by exporting them. This point needs to be considered.

Himalayan wood oil has good export prospects. It is, however, desirable to take steps for maintaining the quality of this oil. Its grading under Agmark should be made compulsory before export. In fact, quality control measures would be conducive to the export promotion of all the essential oils.

Efforts should be made to explore markets for lemongrass oil in the East European countries.

According to the current scheme, the State Trading corporation purchases lemongrass oil at the minimum support prices, viz., Rs. 11.00 per kilo ex-factory for oil of 78 per cent citral content with a premium of rupee one per kilo for oil of 82 per cent citral content. The premium should be given at a progressive rate with the increase in the percentage of citral content instead of giving it at a flat rate.

Efforts should be made to maintain the price of sandal-wood oil within a reasonable limit so that buyers may continue to buy the natural product and are not led away to go in for imitations like Sandela GD etc.

Imports of sandalwood oil into U.S.A. are subjected to an import duty of 10 per cent advalorem. The U.S.A. Government should be requested to abolish the duty on this oil so as to make it at par with sandalwood oil

There is scope for improving the quality of vetiver oil produced in Malabar. At present the roots are distilled in crude stills-sometimes emprovised from oil G.I. drums—and the method of distillation is not standardised. This imparts a very dark colour to the oil which is a serious drawback for its use in perfumery. Effects should, therefore, be made to improve the methods of distillation.

A comparative study of the quality of palmarosa oil manufactured in Java and Madagascar should be made with a view to making improvements in our methods of cultivation and distillation.

The following export target per annum are suggested to different essential oils :—

Essential oils	End of III plan	End if UV Plan (metric tons)	Para No.
Lemongrass	1,000	1,000	12
Sandalwood	100	115	27
Palmarosa	40	55	19
Vetiver	5	10	34
Cedarwood	—	10	37

Meat And Its Bye-Products

There is an export market for frozen meat in countries like the Middle East and Far East in view of less stringent requirements of veterinary certification and method of slaughtering and our competitive prices. But in view of the present and potential demand for mutton in the country, there is hardly scope for exporting it in the near future.

In the Fourth Plan one hundred carcass utilisation centres are proposed to be set up at a cost of Rs. 3 lakhs each. This should give an impetus to the exports of bye products of meat.

In order to obtain precise data on the waste an utilisation of bye-products in slaughter houses, it is desirable to conduct a special survey of licensed slaughter houses in the country.

To increase the production of animal casings, blood meal, bones etc. 200 producers co-operative societies for the manufacture of animal casings and 200 Co-operative bone collecting centres should be set up.

The modernisation of 100 slaughter houses in selected towns with a population of 50,000 and over should be taken up immedi·.tely.

The schem' or the setting up of an Animal Quarantine and Health Centification Service should be sanctioned and implemented at the earliest.

Considering the export potentialities of bye-products of meat, it is recommended that a separate organisation should be set up in the Ministry of Food and Agriculture for handling the problems connected with the production of various bye-products for export purposes. The work of conducting the survey may also be entrusted to this organisation.

If the measures proposed above are taken, exports of meat and its products stepped up by about 100 per cent in 5 years.

Fruits And Vegetable Products

Imports of certain citrus fruits at present allowed from Pakistan under the Indo-Pakistan Trade Agreement should be stopped.

Effort should be made to encourage exports of limes.

It is necessary to improve the condition of marketing of citrus fruits and mangoes by improving the standard of marketing services and promoting cooperative marketing.

Efforts should be made to create export markets in the European countries for some of the renowned varaieties of mandarin oranges, particularly Nagpur Santra and Coorg. Darjeeling and Khasi mada in oranges which are being produced in the country in large quantities. Adequate publicity should be given to the advantages of treating citrus fruits and mangoes with wax.

Trial consignments on the lines of those sent recently by the Directorate of Marketing and inspection should be sent to European countries so that the economics of the transactions may be worked out.

Provision of adequate refrigerated space in the ships should be made for the transport of citrus fruits and mangoes.

Compulsory quality control on the export of citrus fruits and mangoes should be enforced.

The export Credit and Guarantee Corporation should be persuaded to cover the export risks of citrus fruits and mangoes.

Publicity and market research in order to determine cost structure and consumer preferences for citrus fruits should be conducted in foreign countries.

A mango delegation should be sent to U.K. France and West Germany to explore export possibilities and to establish contacts.

A modest target of 6,000 tonnes per annum of citrus fruits for export may be fixed for the end of the Fourth Plan against 1,729 tonnes of export in 1963-64.

It would be reasonable to fix a target of 3,000 tonnes of mangoes for export per annum by the end of the Fourth Plan against the exports in 1963-64 of 1,595 tonnes.

Apples And Grapes

We may request our trade representatives in neighbouring countries like Ceylon, Pakistan, Malaysia, Burma to gauge the scope for exporting India apples and grapes to these countries. The possibilities of exporting apples to U.K. and other European countries should also be investigated.

Bananas

We should tap fresh markets by sending sample consignments of bananas to European countries like Yugoslavia, West Germany, France.

There is need to set up a Banana Export Corporation to organise larges-scale export of bananas. The shares of the Corporation should be held by the Central Government and the important banana producing States.

The manufacture of banana products should be organised keeping in view the potential demand in foreign countries.

The measures suggested by the Banana Delegation to develop the marketing aspects viz. quality control, modern carners, elevator conveyors, suitable warehousing. Creating and transport should be considered as early as possible.

Exports should be made through foreign companies like United Fruit Co., and Cogis who are well versed in the transport and packing of banana. Some of the companies should be persuaded to enter into contracts with the cooperative Societies in India.

Efforts should be made to expand exports to the East European countries. U.S.S.R, Japan, Italy, Middle East and Iran, as recommended by the Banana Delegation. There is prospect of our developing exports to the West Asian countries to the tune of about 15,000 tonnes and to Iran to the tune of 10,000 tonnes per year.

Fruits And Vegetable Products

Indian fruit and vegetable products have so far been exported to cater to demand from Indian nationals settled abroad. The foreigners have yet to develop a taste for these. Efforts should be made to give adequate publicity to various fruit and vegetable products exported from India.

By far the most important raw material used in the fruit canning industry is sugar. A special quota of sugar may be allotted by the Government of India directly to the manufacturers for this purpose every year.

At present a cash incentive at the rate of 10 per cent is allowed on foreign exchange earned through exports of fruit and vegetable products. This is rather inadequate and should be raised.

A subsidy at the rate of Rs. 500 per ton of tin plate consumed in the manufacture of canned products was being given till 31-3-63. The trade has represented for the restoration of this facility. This may be considered.

Efforts should be made to provide foreign exchange for the import of up-to-date automatic or semi-automatic processing machines required by the industry.

Railway transport needs to be improved. Wooden ventilated wagons should be provided for the transport of fruits and vegetables from the centres of production to the factories.

Exporters desirous of popularising their products in foreign countries may be allowed to spend abroad a certain percentage, say 5 per cent of their export earnings on publicity of their products.

Fruit and vegetable products factories and dehydration plants should be set up in areas of large-scale production of the fruits and vegetables concerned.

Proper ware-housing facilities for fruits and vegetables, the basic raw materials of the industry, should be provided.

Fruit products shall have to be improved in respect of quality as well as hygienc. The idea that fruit surpluses and culls should go into the can is out-moded concept of the fruit products industry demands, the utilisation of the raw produce specifically grown for the purpose.

Efforts should be made to produce more dehydrated vegetables like Hima peas for export.

Efforts should be made to get the ocean freight for fruit, and vegetable products reduced. While the rate from Australia to U.K. is 169 sh. per 40 c.f., that from India to U.K. is 995 sh. This descrimination should be removed.

Efforts should be made to introduce new item of fruits and vegetable products for export. These are tomato paste, pineapple products, fruit juice powders, dehydrated onions, mango cereal flakes, papain and pectin, neera, mango juice, preserved litchi bulbs, guava, raspeberry etc.

An export target of 5,000 tonnes per annum of fruit and vegetable products may be fixed for achivement by the end of the Fourth Plan as against the existing exports of 3249 tonnes.

Walnuts

The factors which made it possible to earn higher rate of exchange, when the volume of exports rose by 87 per cent in 1960-61, should be examined with a view to finding out whether advantage can be taken of them for fomulating export policies.

The exporters of walnuts should be persuaded to clean and grade their produce before export with a view to getting better prices.

There is need to pay increased attention towards unconventional markets like Switzerland, Sweden, Holland, West Germany and Australia who import substantial quantities of walnuts. East European countries, U.S.S.R. and Middle Eastern countries also offer potentialities of export.

Adequate publicity measures need be taken to promote exports of walnuts. The industry should introduce and popularise ready to use attractive consumers, packes of in-shell walnuts and roasted and salted kernels to capture new markets.

Efforts should be made to develop exports of brown-coloured walnut kernals.

We should try to create an overseas demand for our kagzie-in-shell walnuts.

The production of walnuts should be stepped up through the adoption of better agronomic practies, introduction of prolific varieties and expending the cultivation to new areas.

The cultivators should be persuaded to develop the cultivation of walnut plants on village waste-lands, foothills, croded lands. etc.

An effective organisation need be set up for the collection and remuncrative disposal of walnuts in the near and prospective areas like Kulu Valley. Himachal Pradesh and hilly districts of Uttar Pradesh, where scattered walnut trees exist.

There is need to raise good nut-hearing varieties of walnuts as has been successfully done in the case of cashewnuts in Madras State.

The walnut producing Stares should, to start with, conduct a survey of acreage (if possible, variety-wise) and production of walnuts. Thereafter, these estimates may be collected after every ten years as, without these statistics, any scientific plan augmenting production is hardly possible.

The research and extension organisations of the State Government concerned need be geared up to extend technical help and supply grafted and budded plants of quality walnuts at subsidised prices of cultivators.

The schemes sanctioned by I.C.A.R. designed to effect improvements in the technique of cultivation of walnuts etc. in Punjab, Uttar Pradesh and Himachal Pradesh should be implemented expeditously.

The Government should set up a Research Station for walnuts at some suitable place in Jammu and Kashmir which may undertake studies and initiate research on various aspects of walnut cultivation and suggest suitable measures for effecting improvement in this sphere. This station may also deal with research pertaining to other allied crops like almonds pistachio etc.

Attempts should be made to build up and expand our exports of shelled walnuts.

Efforts should be made to promote a better utilization of by-products of walnuts like shell waste, walnut oil, walnut cake etc. The C.S.I.R. may be requested to undertake an intensified programme of research on the export-oriented uses of walnut by products.

The difficulties suffered by the trade, e.g. inadequate accommodation facilities, levy of town duty, fortnightly sailaing, want of cold storages, absence of proper dehydrators, non-availability of bleaching powder, need be tackled.

There is need to endorce rigid quality control on exports of walnuts. The staff engaged in the grading and quality control of walnuts should undertake extension education programme with a view to imparting theoretical and practical training to producers for the preparation of better quality in-shell and shelled walnuts.

Apricot kernels, almonds, etc. are some of the tree nuts which need be developed. In order to plan devise ways and means to push up exports of these commodities, a Board composed of leading businessmen. Directors of Agriculture in States like Jammu and Kashmir, Uttar Pradesh, etc. representatives of the Forest Departments of these States, may be set up in the Ministry of Food and Agriculture.

A target of 6,500 metric tons of walnuts for export every year till the end of the IV Five years plan is suggested.

Pulses

At the present juncture, when production is downward, the scope for the exports of pluses which constitutes an important item of the common man's diet, is limited. The first requisite, therefore, is to increases the production of pulses.

There is also need to orient the production plants and efforts to export seeds. Lentil is the most important export pulse of India. U. P. Bihar and West Bengal are the most important States producing lentil. Efforts should be made to increase the production of lentil in the selected districts of these States.

The principal measures called for increasing production are use of improved seeds and superphosphates. To encourage their use, the subsidy on superphosphates should be increased from 25 per cent to 75 per cent.

Besides, cultivation should be encouraged on lands which remain fallow for long periods, e.g., rice fallows in Orissa, West Bengal and Eastern U. P.

Measures need to be devised for overcoming the competition in Ceylon from low quality pulses exported by Syria and Lebanon.

The need for a concession in the railway freight may be examined. Quality standard should be laid down.

Exports should be evenly spread out during the year so that prices do not rise unduly.

The target of exports should be 50 thousand tonnes for the end of the Third Five Year Plan and 1 lakh tonnes for the end of the Fourth Five Year Plan.

Export Targets

There are also possibilities of enhancing our foreign exchange earnings by developing exports of animal casings to more remunerative markets.

There is ample scope for increasing the exports of animal and sheep casings.

The manufacture and export of casings products under the method evolved by the Leather Research Institute should be encouraged.

The programme of modernisation of slaughter houses should be speedly executed.

There are immense possibilities of further processing of guts. Small amounts of foreign exchange, needed for important machinery for the processing of goods be made available to the processors.

Potatoes Production

Saudi Arabia used to import considerable quantities of Indian potatoes but has practically stopped importing them now. This needs in-vestigation.

There is scope for expanding our export trade in potatoes to Afro-Asian Countries.

Efforts should be made to raise the yield of potatoes through intensive cultivation methods. Our sim should be to increase production by 5 per cent per year.

At present export of potatoes is allowed within specified quotas which are not announced to the trade. These should be published so that prospective exporters may know the quantities released for export from time to time.

Rigid compulsory quality control should be enforced on exports of potatoes.

The Indian Merchant Fleet should acquire a few refrigerated ships for the export of fruits, vegetables and other perishables including potatoes.

There is considerable spoilage of potato crop for want of transport facilities in the potato-growing areas. Transport facilities should be therefore, developed in those areas.

A Potato Development Board may be set up in the Ministry of Food and Agriculture to develop the production, marketing and export of potatoes.

Efforts should be made to export potatoes to the extent of 2 per cent of production. Our aim should be to achieve a target of 25,000 metric tons by the end of Third Five Year Plan and 50,000 metric tons by the end of Fourth Five Year Plan.

Cocoa Products

The indigenous cocoa-based industries depend on imports, as stated earlier, for their requirements of cocoa beans. Therefore, our plans for the development of these industries and, consequently, for exports of cocoa products have to be linked with the imports of cocoa beans to the extent it is unavoidable. This could be as paying proposition from the foreign exchange angle, as raw material would always be cheaper than the manufactured product. But the possibilities of earning net foreign exchange would be greater if other costs, i.e., manufacture, transport etc. are kept to the minimum. Assuming that adequate quantities of cocoa beans would be forthecoming to meet the demands of the industry, the following targets of exports are suggested :

(a) **Cocoa Powder** : At present we are exporting only about 31 per cent of our production. Export of 140 metric tons per year by the end of the Third Plan period would be a reasonable target for this item. For the Fourth Plan the annual traget may be 250 metric tons per year.

(b) **Cocoa Butter and Paste** : The exports of cocoa butter and paste during 1960-61, 1961-62 and 1962-63 were 10 metric tons, 16 metric tons and 20 metric tons respectively. An export target of 40 metric tons per year by the end of the Third Plan period and of 80 metric tons by the end of the Fourth Plan period is suggested for this items.

(c) **Chocolate Preparations Including Chocolate**

Confectionery : The exports of chocolate prepèrations including chocolate confectionery during 1960-61, 1961-62 and 1962-63 were 2 metric tons, 1 metric ton and 62 metric tons respectively. A target of 100 metric tons per year by the end of the Third Plan period seems to be reasonable for this item. The annual target by the end of Fourth Plan period should be 200 metric tons.

Garlic

A survey of the existing and potentional demand in existing overseas markets, as well as exploration of new markets, is required for assessing the total demand for garlic in foreign markets. A Study Team should be sent abroad to survey not only the markets for garlic but also those for other related commodities. An integrated study of this type would be very useful for a proper planning of an export promotion drive. This could be brought up-to-date from time to time with the assistance of our Commercial Attaches abroad.

Efforts may be made to raise the productivity of garlic by better agronomic practices.

Compulsory quality control on garlic before export should be introduced.

Facilities for cold storage and refrigerated warehousing in producing centres and at the export ports should be developed.

Facilities for cold storage and referigcrated warehousing in producing centres and at the exports should be developed.

There is need to develop refrigerated rail transport and refrigerated shipping for the export of garlic and other perishables.

There is need to set up plants for making garlic powder for export as well as home consumption.

Dairy Products

Every effort should be made to set up quickly the plant licensed for the manufacture of milk powder and to run them to their full capacity so that we may meet our entire requirements internally and do away with imports.

Butter is a bye-product of the organised dairy industry and a part of the production of butter could be set apart for export purposes with due regard to our domestic requirements.

The Kaira-Mil Union could, perhaps, be encouraged and, if necessary, subsidised to export butter and ghee to West Asian countries.

Efforts should be made to export Indian melted butter ghee to Malayasia for the needs, of people of Indian origin.

The question of effecting a reduction in the fat content of the milk supplied to the consumers by Indian dairies with a view to making a larger quantity of ghee and butter available for export needs to be examined.

The following annual targets of export till the end of the Third Five Year Plan period are suggested.

	(Matric tons)
Butter	25
Ghee	125
(Paras 17 and 19)	

Sisal Fibre

In any attempt that might be made in future for making India self-sufficient in regard to its requirements of sisal fibre of for-export purposes, emphasis will have to be laid on the cultivation of Agave sislana species of sisal.

If private enterprise is not willing to take up production of sisal, a corporation should be set up by the Government for the purpose. The manufacturing units should be set up along with the production units. This corporation could also take up the growing of ramie and sann hemp.

If the method of collecting fibre from sisal is improved so that is bye-products by cogenene and sisal wax could be collected and utilised, we could not only effect savings in foreign exchange by reducing imports but also earn foreign exchange from the exports of hycongenene.

Repacking of Dates and Dry Fruits

There is scope for developing export/re-exports of figs (dried) and raisins. The technique for drying and processing figs/grapes has to be improved so that we get good quality dried figs/raisins both for internal consumption and for export. The Central Food Thechnological Research Institute, Mysore, may be requested to investigate into this problem and examine the possibilities of developing an efficient unit for the drying and processing of figs/raisns on scientific lines.

1963

TECHNICAL COMMITTEE ON CROP ESTIMATES, 1963—REPORT

Delhi, Ministry of Publications 1958. 127p.

Chairman : Shri S.R. Sen ;
Members : Shri K.R. Nair ; Shri D.B. Lahiri ; Shri S.P. Pande ; Shri G.R. Seth ; Shri J.S. Sarma; Shri M.N. Murthy Shri; V.R. Rao.

APPOINTMENT

The Technical Committee on Crop Estimates was constituted under Planning Commission in January, 1963.

TERMS OF REFERENCE

(i) Examine the results of type-1 studies undertaken in Rajasthan and Bihar ;

(ii) Formulate the detailed proposals for type-2 studies (to be undertaken along with the eighteenth round (1963-64 of the NSS) ;

(iii) Consider the schedules and instructions of the NSS Crop Survey for the eighteenth round for ensuring appropriate comparison between the two Series; and

(iv) Study the data collected by the NSS in the past and the results of any other enquiries and Surveys with a view to suggesting-improvement in the existing agricultural statistics.

CONTENTS

Introduction; Type-1 and 2 Studies: Comparison of NSS and official series of crop estimates ; Conclusions and recommendations; Statistical tables; Charts; Appendices.

RECOMMENDATIONS

A striking feature of the NSS and official estimates of production was that they were consistently different throughout the period of study the former being higher than the latter. The magnitude of this difference was much larger during the earlier period (1957-58 to 196162), ranging between 15 and 24 million tons ; the difference narrowed down to 5 to 8 million tons in the subsequent years (1963-64 to 1965-66). Even during the later years, while estimates of production of rice revealed fairly close agreement, the estimates for wheat, Jowar and Maize continued to differ to a marked extent. At the State level, NSS estimates (for 7 Cloreals) were substantially higher than the official estimates in the case of Assam, Bihar, Gujarat and Maharashtra, and lower in the case of Kerala and West Bengal.

The divergence between the two series can arise because of differences in the estimates of (a) area and (b) yield rates, which in turn may be due to differences in the technical procedures of selection, compilation, estimation, etc. as also operational differences in the field and processing work. In regard to estimates of area, the different concepts used in the two series, 'gross' in the NSS and 'net' in the official series, were a handicap in ascertaining the reasons for divergence between the two series. The Committee's attempt at securing comparability by having the NSS obtaining crop area according to procedures followed in the official series, could not materialize. The wide divergences between the trends of the two series of area estimates, sometimes in contradictory directions, would however tend to the conclusion that are contributed materially to the overall divergence in production.

Several factors could have accounted for the divergence between the two series of area estimates. In the official series, the practices followed for recording net areas happen to be different from State to State and sometimes even in a State. It is not certain that the procedures laid down in the Land Record Manuals for this purpose are carefully followed by the primary agency and adequate precautions taken in arriving at appropriate net area in all cases. This is a matter for further investigation and improvement both by laying down well considered concepts and procedures for recording area under crop mixtures and adequate training of the primary staff and supervision over their work. The Committee understands that considerable progress has been made in this direction through the efforts of Ministry of Food and Agriculture, which need to be pursued actively in future.

Another factor influencing the official estimates of area could be the cumulative effect of errors in recording aggregating and transfer of area statistics from village level upto the State level. The number of persons engaged in the compilation of area statistics at various levels is far too large to completely avoid such errors. It should, however, be possible to ensure that the cumulative effect of such errors does not vitiate the accuracy of the final estimates of area at the State level. The Committee intended to have a study undertaken in 3 or 4 States to assess the overall effect of errors inaggregation and transfer. This was ultimately carried out only in one district of Andhra Pradesh (Nalgonda) for want of time and facilities. The results of this limited study, though not quite representative of conditions obtaining even in Andhra Pradesh, not to speak of other States, did reveal the existence of errors at almost all levels, namely, village, tehsils and districts, which could not be completely ignored. The Andhra Pradesh study would thus underline the need for a more detailed investigation on a large scale in this regard.

One factor affecting the NSS series could be the change in the procedure of building up area estimates from 1961-62. The earlier procedure is known to result in consistent over-estimates as compared to the subsequent procedure. This apparently arose out of inaccuracies in the compilation of geographical area at various levels. A detailed study on the extent of, and the reasons for, these inaccuracies should be undertaken.

Among the factors contributing to the divergence in yield rates could be the size of the ultimate sample cut used for crop-cutting experiments. From the type-1 and type-2 studies organised at the instance of the Committee on different crop, it was seen that the large divergence observed in the NSS and official estimates of production was not ascribable to the different types of sample cut used in the two series.

There could be a number of other factors affecting the estimates of yield rates which could not be examined by the Committee. They require laborious and time-consuring studies and the committee can at best suggest the course of action in this regard for future consideration. One of the possible sources of divergence in the estimates of yield rate is the cumulative effect of various type of non-sampling errors to which both series were subject, such as response rates (proportion of the number of crop-cutting experiments analysed to the number of experiments planned), biases in the selection of sampling units due to departure from strict probability sampling procedures at various stages, biases due to deviations from appropriate procedures of estimation, and the choice of appropriate expansion factors particularly which regard to yield rates of crops shown in mixtures, errors in driage ratios (of dried grain to harvested produce), and finally, the short-comings of the primary field agencies in carrying out the programme of crop cutting work according to prescribed procedures. There has, no doubt, been considerable improvement in the recent years in the quality of field work, response rates an attention to technical details, due to the growing awareness of the importance of crop surveys. Nevertheless greater attention need to be paid to study the over all effect of varying practices followed for obtaining the yield estimates. In this connection, it will be worth while to subject the data of the two series to a critical examination, on the lines indicated in Appendix 10.

In the view of the committee, it is important that all possible measures should be taken to improve the quality and time lines of official series of crop statistics, as no other series can ever completely replace the official series. Apart from careful scrutiny of the procedures of compilation and estimation, and securing as far as possible uniformity in concepts and definitions for inter-state comparability it is necessary to provide for a fairly intensive supervisory check over the primary field work in regard to both area and yield estimates. The normal departmental supervision should be strengthened for this purpose. In order to ensure objectivity, it should be supplemented by supervision based on a probability sampling, both of field enumeration and compilation procedures, with the help of higher levels of departmental staff (at least at two levels higher than the level of the primary agency). Such supervision will provide the necessary authority for taking corrective measure as well as provide a quality check. There should be a concurrent sample check by a Central Agency on a sufficiently large scale to provide estimates of crop area and production at the State and All-India levels for administrative and policy requirements of Government of India.

Appendix 10

List Of Items For Special Research Studies

NSS Series

(i) Frequency distribution of yield observation by crop and years (for important States).

(ii) Distribution of unweighted yield rates for pure crop and mixed crop.

(iii) Percentage recovery of dried grain from harvested produce for individual State-crops and years from 1957-58 onwards (sub sample wise figures).

(iv) Investigations into the biases (if any) in production estimates due to the use of inaccurate (or out-of date) driage factors and/or due to the application of the driage ratios at in appropriate stages.

(v) Relative merits (bias and variance) of estimates of acreage and production of crops according to different selection and estimation procedures including those actually used.

(vi) (Investigations into the reasons for divergence or inconsistency among different official series of geographical areas, and their relative role in respect of the resulting) inaccuracies in estimates of area and production due to the use of in accurate expansion factors for other similar reasons.

(vii) Study of biases (if any) in the estimates of yield rate of given crops due to the rule or procedure of allocation of sample cuts to pure and mixed crops in any of the rounds.

(viii) Study of bias in production estimates in case (if any) the methods of apportionment of area survey and (b) for sample crops cuts different in any of the rounds.

(ix) Characteristics of the 'non-responding' units ; assessment of related bias, Nature of 'substitutions' and assessment of bias.

(x) Investigations into the possibility of double count or omission in crop acreage enumeration in repeated visits in different seasons.

(xi) Comparison of repeat samples (villages/survey numbers) between successive rounds (years) to assess the reliability of data.

(xii) Study of trends in gross area in selected States (and comparison of NSS trends with 'official trends').

(xiii) Comparison of State matching sample estimates with central sample estimates ; study of reasons for divergence (if any)

Official Series

(i) Frequency distribution yield observations by crops and years (for important States).

(ii) Distribution of unweighted yields rates for pure crop and mixed crop.

(iii) Percentage recovery of dried grain from harvested produce for individual States-crops and years from 1957-58 onwards.

(iv) Investigations into the biases (if) in production estimates due to the use of inaccurate (or out-of-date) driage factors, and/or due to the application of driage ratios at inappropriate stages.

(v) Relative merits (biases and/or variance) of different modes of complication, derivation or estimation of acreage under crops. and of different modes of selection and estimation for crop production, including those actually used.

(vi) (Investigation into the reasons for divergence or inconsistency among different official series of geographical areas, and their relative role in respect of the resulting) in accuracies in the figures or estimates of area and production due to the use of inaccurate expansion factors or for other similar reasons.

(vii) Study of biases (if any) in the estimates of yield-rate of given crops due to the official rule or procedure of allocation of sample cuts to pure and mixed crops.

(viii) Study of bias in production estimates in case (if any) the methods of apportionment of areas under each component of mixed crop (a) for area survey and (b) for sample crop cuts differ.

(ix) Characteristics of the non-responding or 'non-reporting' units : assessment of related bias, Nature of substitutions and assessment of bias.

(x) Investigations into the possibility of double count or omission in crop acreage enumberations in repeated visits in different seasons.

(xi) Comparison of repeat tehsils/villages/survey numbers (samples) between the successive seasons and the successive years to assess the reliability of the data.

(xii) Study of trends in gross area in States where the required data are available (and comparison of the 'official trends' with the 'NSS trends.')

(xiii) Comparison of official acreage estimates with data collected according to official procedure by the NSS (central). Cases of divergence (if any).

(xiv) Assessment of errors of recording, aggregation, and transfer of official area statistics at different levels-village, tehsil, district and State. Study of comulative effect of such errors.

(xv) Investigations into the effect of non-compliance of intructions in the Land Records Manual Formation of well-considered concepts and procedures for recording area under crop mixtures so as to arrive at appropriate net area in all cases.

General

(i) Reasons for divergence between different series of official geographic area figures.

(ii) Relationship between weather conditions and the area and production of crops.

COMMITTEE ON RATIONALISATION OF STEEL SECTIONS, 1963—REPORT

Delhi, Manager of Publications, 1968. 101p.

Chairman : Shri Suku Sen

Members : Shri T.R. Subramanian ; Shri Ranbir Sen ; Shri B.S. Krishnamachar ; Shri K.N.P. Rao : Shri A.K. Gupta ; Shri M.M. Panje; Shri R.K. Chatterjee ; Shri V. Subramaniam; Mr. C E. Cargin ; Shri R.C Sen,

Convenor : Shri S.C. Mukherjee

APPOINTMENT

Structural shapes in which steel products are commonly rolled comprise of beams, channels, sheet piles, equal angles, unequal angles, bulb angles, tees, squares, round bars and flat bars. The number of such sections included in the relevant Indian Standards alone is about 516. There are many other sections like crossing sleepers, 'Z' sections, etc. which have not yet been standardised by the Indian Standards Institution. The number of sections at present being rolled by Indian Producers is also considerable about 300. Existence of such a large number of sections from which Engineers are permitted to select for designing structures has given rise to two difficult problems :

(a) **The Problem of Matching Steel** : Often the Engineers call for, along with large quantities of certain sections comparatively small quantities of certain other sections, which are, according to them more economical. It often so happens that the supply of popular sections are received fairly quickly but even if such supplies com.r prise of about 90 per cent of total steel required fo fabrication of the structures, the work cannot be taken on hand until the remaining 10 per cent of 'matching steel' is available. If the Engineers were aware of the difficulty of getting this 10 per cent of the materials, they could have certainly designed their structures in such a way as to avoid to use of these sections which are uncommon and frequently rolled.

(b) **The Problem of Economic rolling Tonnage for the Producers** : The present output of structural steel sections in India (including bars and rods) is about 2.5 million tons. Out of these sections, the annual demand of some popular ones ranges between 50,000 tons to 1,000,000 tons. As a result, total annual demand of several sections is very small. Both of operational efficiency and economics of production, there is a minimum tonnage which could and should be produced in any particular mill. This economic rolling tonnage of course, varies from mill to mill, for the fast modern mills which are now installed in all the Steel Plants, the minimum economic tonnage is quite high, ranging from 1,000 tons to 3,000 tons per section per rolling. As a result, they find it difficult to produce sections for which the demand is less than the minimum economic tonnage. Even if the demand is up to this minimum tonnage, such sections with relatively smaller demand can be produced only once or twice a year depending on the total demand. Consumers needing such sections as matching stee', therefore, have to wait for a long time to complete their jobs.

With a view to finding a solution to the problems mentioned above the Iron and Steel controller has been considering the question of 'rationalising' the number of sections thereby reducing the number of sections to be produced in the country. This matter is obviously a complicated one as it involves not only steel plant operational problems but also problems of engineering construction. The sections to be rationalised should be such as could be more economically produced by the existing steel plants. At the same time a suitable range of sections should be provided for the Engineers to design structures with, without seriously affecting the Govt's declared policy of steel economy. The Iron and Steel controller obtained the services of Shri Ranbir Sen of Tata Iron and Steel Co. Ltd., to study this matter and to make suggestions. Shri Ranbir Sen visited all the Steel Plants, discussed the problems with the Technical Officers of the various Steel Plants. Thereafter he also discussed this question with the Indian Standards Institution in Delhi with Central Water and Power Commission and the Railway Board, the two important consumers of Structural Steel. He also had discussions with leading structural fabricators of the country. As a result of these discussions with the Steel Plants Shri Ranbir Sen came to the conclusion that some of the structural sections standardised by the Indian Standards Institution needed some. modifications to enable the existing mills to produce them without difficulty. This matter was brought to the notice of the Indian Standards Institution by Shri Ranbir Sen and the Institution in its turn prepared a paper giving their views as to why the producers should try to roll the standardised sections.

Simultaneously, the Indian Engineering Association also undertook an independent study of this difficult problem. The Association produced a comprehensive report which was of great assistance to the committee. It provided useful technical data and also recommended a complete list of sections which to be rationalised.

The Iron and Steel Controller circulated the following documents to the Main Steel Plants, Indian Engineering Association and the Indian Standards Institution and convened a meeting to discuss the matter further :

(a) Notes by Shri Ranbir Sen on his discussions with various interests concerned.

(b) Notes prepared by the Indian Standards Institution on the proposal of Shri Ranbir Sen for modification of certain ISI standards sections.

(c) Report of, the Indian Engineering Association giving their views about the sections which should be rationalised.

The papers mentioned above were discussed at a meeting held on 22nd August, 1963. The meeting generally approved the line of approach recommended by Shri Ranbir Sen and the Indian Engineering Association. It was, however, felt that a number of details about the exact nature of modification required in the existing ISI sections, the exact number of sections that should be rationalised and the producers to whom such rationalised sections should be allotted will have to be gone into and that this could be more conveniently done by a small committee. The Committee on Rationalisation of Steel Sections was therefore set up by the Government of India, Ministry of Steel and Mines, Department of Iron and Steel, Iron and Steel controller vide their letter No. SC (e)—4 (1)/63 dated July, 24, 1964.

TERMS OF REFERENCE

(i) Recommending modifications, if necessary, of certain ISI sections for acceptance by the Indian Standards Institution,

(ii) Selection of sections to be rationalised, and

(iii) Allocation of the proposed rationalised sections among different producers.

CONTENTS

Report and Recommendations; Appendices from 1 to 5.

RECOMMENDATIONS

On the first two points, the committee has come to unanimous decision. Their recommendations are the following :

(a) **Modification of Sections :**

Beams

Section	Flange Width	Flange Thickness	Wed Thickness	Slop	tf./tw	Wt. Kg./m
1. ISMB 100		tf.	tw.			
Standard	75	7.2	4	98°	1.8	11.5
Proposed	70	7.5	4.5	98°	1.67	*
2. ISMB 125						
Standard	75	7.6	4.4	98°	1.73	13
Proposed	70	8.0	4.8	98°	1.67	*
3. ISMB 150						
Standard	80	7.6	4.8	98°	1.58	14.9
Proposed	75	8.0	5.0	98°	1.60	*
4. ISMB 175						
Standard	90	8.6	5.5	98°	1.56	19.3
Proposed	85	9·0	5.80	98°	1.55	*

ISMB 200 to 600: As a temporary measure, relaxation be given in the Web thickness by increasing it by 2 per cent and the sectional weight of the new section with increased web thickness has to be calculated.

Channels

Section	Flange Width	Flange Thickness tf.	Wed Thickness tw.	Slop	tf./tw.	Wt. Kg/m
1. ISMC 75						
Standard	40	7.3	4.4	96°	1.66	6.8
Proposed	40	7.5	4.8	96°	1.56	*
2. ISMC 100						
Standard	50	7.5	4.7	96°	1.60	9.2
Proposed	50	7.7	5.0	96°	1.48	*
3. ISMC 125						
Standard	65	8.1	5.0	96°	1.62	12.7
Proposed	65	8.2	5,3	96°	1.55	*
4. ISMC 150						
Standard	75	9.0	5.4	96°	1.67	16.4
Proposed	75	9.0	5.7	96°	1.58	*
5. ISMC 175						
Standard	75	10.2	5.7	96°	1.70	19.1
Proposed	75	10.2	6	96°	1.70	*

(* to be calculated by the ISI)

ISMC 200 to 400: The same relaxations as in the case of Beams ISMB 200 to 600 recommended for these sections.

With regard to tolerances, the Committee recommend as follows:

Beams

(A) Tolerances on Flange Width:

(i) Flange width upto and including 100 mm ±2 mm

(ii) Flange width above mm and upto 200 mm +3 mm −4 mm

(iii) Flange width above 200 mm ±2 per cent

(B) Tolerance on Depth:

Depth in mm	Tolerances in mm Plus	Minus
75—125	3	1.5
150—200	3	2
225—400	3.5	2.5
450—600	4	3

Channels

(A) Tolerance on Flange Width:
Same as in the case of Beams

(B) Tolerance on Depth:

Depth in mm	Tolerance in mm Plus	Minus
75—200	3	2
225—400	3.5	2.5

At the request of the Committee, the above recommendations regarding modification of ISI sections were communicated by the Iron and Steel Controller to the Department of Iron and Steel and the Indian Standards Institution. The matter has also been considered by the Indian Standards Institution and they have agreed to accept these modifications for a period of 2 years. The Indian Standard Institution excepts that the producers would be able to switch over to the standard sections within this period.

(b) With regard to the second problem, viz. selection of sections to be rationalised.

In addition to these rationalised sections the following special sections will also have to be rolled to meet certain specific important demands:

1. Crossing Sleepers—BG and MG
2. Bearing Plate Bars.
3. Telegraph Channels
4. Bulb Angles
5. Z Section
6. Sheet Piling Sections
7. Crane and Bridge Rails
8. Electric Transmission Pole Section (116 mm× 110 mm).

It will be seen that the Committee has suggested rationalisation of only 153 sections. With regard to the Tee Sections, the Committee would suggest that the possibility of producing them by slitting the Beam Sections should be explored by the producers. As and when slitting arrangement is made, it should be possible for the producers to offer a larger range of Tee sections to meet the country's requirements. This will incidentally save rolls now required to produce Tees. In selecting the rationalised sections, the Committee has taken into account both the engineering properties of these sections and also the present trend of demand of these sections in the country. To enable the producers to achieve maximum productive capacity, the Committee recommend rationalisation of only medium section which are not only comparatively easier to produce but also give a reasonable quantum of out-put per section. According to the calculations made by the Indian Engineering Association, the additional consumption of steel involved in replacement of certain traditional sections by the rationalised sections for several important jobs now under execution would range between 0·01 per cent to 8.56 per cent but mostly within two and half per cent, which may be considered negligible.

In putting forward this scheme, the committee recommend that any reduction in the number of available sections and sizes should be regarded as a temporary expedient. The long term aim should be to provide steel to consumers in India with a wider range of sections and sizes to enable them to approach closer to the Engineering ideal of maximum strength or efficiency for minimum steel (and hence minimum cost). In the export sphere it is particularly important that Engineering firms should not be handicapped by having access to a relatively limited range of steel sections and sizes as compared with the much larger range available to exporters in other countries. To this extent a more flexible import policy is essential to ensure that exporters of fabricated steel are not unduly restricted in their choice of matching sections.

The committee recommend that the Government of India should immediately take all possible steps to ensure that all the rationalised sections are available to consumers as early as possible. All consumers should also be requested to indent for sections on the basis of the Rationalised list only. If any producer desires to develop any non-rationalised sections for which they anticipate sufficient demand, approval of the Joint Plan Committee should be obtained before any preliminary action is taken in the matter.

With regard to the third problem viz. allocation of sections to different producers the committee could not come to any unanimous decision. It is felt that with the statutory decontrol of structural sections and establishment of the Joint Plan Committee, this problem should more appropriately be referred to that committee to tackle.

This report is confined to the sections to be rolled by the Main Producers. The Re-rolling industry should be left free to roll any other section if sufficient demand are received.

COMMITTEE ON URBAN LAND POLICY, 1963—REPORT

Delhi, Manager of Publications, 1965. 98p.

Chairman : Shri S.M. Fazlur Rahman
Members : Shri S.M.A. Majid ; Dr. Rafiq Zakaria ; Shri Prabodh Chandra ; Shri Dharma-Vira ; Shri H.C. Daga ; Shri S. Dutt ;
Member-Secretary : Shri Gian Prakash

APPOINTMENT

The Committee on Urban Land Policy was constituted under the Ministry of Health at the Joint Session of the Central Council of Local Self-Government and the Ministers for Town & Country planning vide its Resolution No. 11 in 1963.

TERMS OF REFERENCE

To examine the problems of urban land policy in the light of the note prepared by the Town and Country Planning Organisation and the draft Model Land Acquisition Act and the note submitted by the West Bengal Government and considered by the Conference in 1961.

CONTENTS

Introduction ; Background of the Problem ; Need for a Long Term Urban Land Policy ; Classification of Urban Land ; Measures for Developed Urban Lands ; Measures for Undeveloped Urban Land ; Measures for Urbanisable Limits ; Measures for Mopping up Unearned Increases ; Other Anti-speculation Measures ; Land Acquisition Procedure and Compensation Policy ; Land Development and Disposal Policy ; Organisational and Administrative Machinery ; Summary of Conclusions ; Appendix ; Annexure.

RECOMMENDATIONS

Need For A Long Term Urdan Land Policy

The facts about the declining man-land ratio, the pitiable urban conditions and the urbanisation perspective make it absolutely clear that a comprehensive long range urban and policy is imperative for India today. But without an effective urban land policy, planned development of the urban and the rural areas is quite inconceivable so also the achievement of many a social objective which the country has set before it.

Background Of The Problem

1. The average per capita availability of land in India is not only comparatively very low but, because of population pressure, it has been declining continuously over successive census decades. In three of the five Census Zones the per capita availability of land is less than the national average of 1.84 acres.

2. Our country has at present about 1.1. acres of cultivable land per capita as against 1.2 acres in 1950-51. As population grows, this figure will go on declining as food requirements go on increasing. The trend cannot be viewed complacently.

3. Analysis demographic data reveals the relatively fast growth of urban population and urban areas especially of Class I cities. This clearly denotes the lopsided distribution of population as between the urban areas of varying status and the degree of concentration and congestion in the well established major urban areas. Such a situation is undesirable and not conductive to balanced urban development in the country.

4. Most of the urban areas, particularly the matropolitan cities, present a pathetic picture of congestion, over-crowding, slums and blight while within many of them utilisation of land is extremely inequitable. A large majority of them lack even basic services like water supply. Housing conditions are extremely depressing. There are huge backlogs in community facilities etc. All these deficiencies have to be removed and better urban living conditions provided at the earliest. Any attempt to do so is bound to have repercussions on the problem of land, its acquisition, development, distribution and use.

5. The process of urbanisation and urban development does change the characterof land from agricultural to non-agricultural and of the population affected in the process from rural to urban. At the same time urbanisation being a direct consequence of economic and industrial development has an element of inevitability and may even be considered a progressive and desirable development provided it is not allowed to take place in the present chaotic manner.

6. For urbanisation to be really conducive to economic development and human welfare, it must be well planned and well directed. This pre-supposes that urbanisation policy will be intimately and rationally linked with the industrial and other investment decisions and the location of industries etc. The Planning and direciion of urbanisation process will have to be in accordance with the pattern of urban development outlined in the Five-Year-Plans.

7. With accelerated economic development the problem of towns is becoming more and more acute and unless it is now tackled boldly it will become increasingly difficult and more expensive with the laps of time. We, therefore, urge the Planning Commission and the State Governments to lay down in the Fourth Five Year Plan in clear terms the policies towards the process of urbanisation and urban development and provide adequate funds for urban development schemes.

8. If a measure of urbanisation is inevitable or desirable the conversion of some land from agricultural to non-agricultural use cannot be helped. Utmost care, would, therefore, have to be taken to see that the urbanised land is put to optimum use.

Need For A Long Term Urban Land Policy

9. The facts about the declining man-land ratio, the pitiable urban conditions and the urbanisation perspective make it absolutely clear that a comprehensive long range urban policy is imperative for India today. But without an effective urban land policy, planned development of the urban and the rural areas is quite in conceivable so also the achievement of many a social objective which the country has set before it.

10. While a long range land policy is essential and desirable the emphasis on the various objectives or purposes to be served by it will vary from place to place and time to time so also the methods and techniques depending upon the special circumstances and situations to be tackled. These measures, methods and techniques will have to be woven into the texture of the overall progammes and policies for these places.

11. We, however, feel sorry that our country does not yet have a clear urban land policy. The existing legislation concerning the control, regulation and compulsory acquisition of land is far too in adequate in the context of India's changed social setting. It is mainly preoccupied with compulsory acquisition of land.

12. Any blue-print of urban land policy must necessarily cover the multi-farious aspects of the problems of urban land in their entirely and find lasting satisfactory solutions for them. This would naturally imply a series of co-ordinated measures-legislative, administrative, financial and planning to take care of the various aspects of the problem.

Social Objectives Of Urban Land Policy

13. The principal social objectives of urban land policy laid down in TCPO's paper are to :

(a) Achieve an optimum social use of urban land ;

(b) Make availability of land in adequate quantity, at the right time and for reasonable prices to both the public authorities and the individuals ;

(c) Encourages co-operative community effort and bonafide individual builders in the field of land development, housing and construction;

(d) Prevent concentration of land ownership in few private lands and safeguard specially the interests of the poor and under privileged sections of urban society.

14. The only known method of organising the land use in the socially desirable optimum manner is that of regional and urban land use planning. Land use planning even when it is focussed on a particular urban area must be regional because from development point of view each community is inter-related in regard to economic, physical and social factors. The administrative limits of the urban areas may not always be coterminus with "planning areas" or areas of socio economic and cultural interaction.

15. Regional planning offers an approach that may prevent undesirable social effects of urbanisation and permit industrialisation without the growth of unmanageable urban centres and slums.

16. The regional and urban plans should be formulated within the overall frame work of the National and State Five-Year Plan Policies, objectives and targets.

17. The Third Five-Year-Plan has recommended the broad objective of "balanced development between large, medium-sized and small industries, and between the rural and urban areas" and stated the four main ingredients of development policy. These policy directions of the Third Five-Year-Plan can be concretised only through the preparation, enforcement and implementation of comprehensive regional plans.

18. The broad dynamic definition of "urban land" adopted by us also necessitates that in urban planning the concept adopted is regional.

19. The regional planning concept is especially significant for big metropolises and major urban or industrial centres where the solutions of the urban problems may lie in creating foci of growth in regions where migration originates or in planning and establishing self-contained communities or "ring towns" or "satellites".

20. The fulfilment of the second, third and fourth objective would imply firstly, a policy of effective public control over land particularly through large scale public acquisition ; secondly a rational and equitable compensation policy ; thirdly, breaking the stranglehold of speculation in land ; fourthly, positive encouragement of bona fide builders and co-operative and lastly, sympathetic treatment to poor and vulnerable sections of society.

21. We find ourselves in full agreement with these social objectives as they are quite consistent with planning principles, national planning goals and the national objectives of a socialist pattern of society. While these social objectives are unexceptionable and must be pursued vigorously, utmost effort should be made to finance as far as possible, the urban development and improvement programmes out of the urban land resources themselves. In some cases substantial financial assistance may have to be provided by the Central and the State Government also.

Classification Of Urban Land

22. Urban land is not a homogeneous mass but 'a heterogeneous structure comprising lands of various descriptions'. A proper classification of urban land is necessary as the nature of problems and their solutions in each distinct category of urban land are bound to be different.

23. The classification of urban land into the following four broad categories has much to commend itself :

(a) Developed Urban Land i.e. land within the city limits which is developed and largely built upon. There may be some vacant plots within it which would also fall in this category.

(b) Undeveloped Urban Land i.e. land within the city limits at any point of time which is not yet developed in and built upon.

(c) Land within the Urbanisable limits, i.e. land presently agricultural or un-urbanised but likely to get urbanised within the next 10 or 15 years.

(d) Land beyond the Urbanised Limits. This would naturally be purely rural land and the greater its distance from the city limits the lesser would it be subject to the forces of rural-urban interaction.

24. To this classification we wish to suggest the addition of the following category which we treat as separate and distinct because the problems it raises are somewhat different than in the other categories and call for special attention.

Land, the use of which is frozen as green belt or for agricultural purposes and also land which is reserved for community use.

Measures For Developed Urban Land

25. In developed urban land the major problems are: congestion and over-crowding blight and slums, non-conforming uses, lack of civic services and community facilities, rising land prices, growing unearned increments and underutilization of land. The measures required to tackle these problems are master plans, zoning regulations, effective enforcement of municipal

bye-laws and urban renewal schemes.

26. It is a pity that in a country which has advanced in the field of national economic planning, regional and urban land use planning should still be in a nascent stage. We need hardly emphasize that the preparation of comprehensive regional and urban plans and programmes deserves very high priority if urban development has to be guided, as it must be, along right lines.

27. Regional and/or urban master plans prepared with comprehension in approach and thoroughness in details and implemented with undaunted determination are the best guarantee to ensure optimum use of the scarce land resources of the nation. These are also the best means to make the urban areas more healthy, comfortable and functionally efficient entities.

28. We strongly recommend that the State Governments strengthen their Town Planning Departments and have Master Plans prepared at the earliest for all their growing urban areas. Where the preparation of Master Plans is likely to take time, interim or outline development plans should be prepared urgently. The State Government will be will advised to seek the technical assistance of TCPO in this matter.

29. We recommend that the Union Government extend liberal financial help to the State Government and Local Authorities not only for the preparation but also for the implementation of Master Plans.

30. It is very necessary that the State Governments have a town planning law based on modern scientific concepts of planning. It should, inter alia, enable the preparation and enforcement of regional plans. Those States which do not yet have an upto date Town Planning Act should expeditiousty enact such a law.

31. In order to enable the State Governments and local authorities to plan their cities and regions it is necessary to provide sufficiently large number of town planners. This calls for increase in the facilities for their training. We recommend that the Central Government should establish a number of regional training institutions. Wherever, the Central Government are unable to establish such institutions themselves, they should offer generous financial assistance to the States for the purpose.

32. There is need also to improve the quality of training imparted to the students of town planning courses. The implementation aspects should be given adequate emphasis in the training.

33. More important than the preparation of plans is their implementation. One of the best methods to ensure that the master plans are implemented is to prepare simultaneously with the land use plan a capital improvement programme and a fiscal plan. The same can be evolved into or integrated with the city development plan (Programme) envisaged by the Planning Commission. The City development Plans should, as Planning Commission also desires, be integrated in an organic way with the State Five Year Plans.

34. We very strongly recommend that the State Governments issue necessary directives to their town planning, local self-governments and planning departments to prepare city development plans (Programmes) for every urban area and particularly that for which a master plan has been prepared. The State Government may very well benefit from the experience of the Town & Country Planning Organization, Ministry of Health, on this subject.

35. Zoning and sub-division Regulations are not in vogue in this country. We would like to recommend that the State Governments and their town planning organizations give serious thought to evolving zoning and sub-division regulations and making them applicable within the jurisdiction of all urban local bodies. The draft zoning regulations evolved by the TCPO and the zoning provisions forming a part of the Master Plan for Delhi could well form the basis for the State Governments to start with. The TCPO's assistance in this task would be available to the State Governments and we hope they will make good use of the same.

36. Where municipal bye-laws and zoning regulations are not compatible, the municipal bye-laws should be revised suitably. The Town Planning Acts should also include a provision that the municipal bye-laws conform with zoning and sub-division regulations. The State Planning Departments should assist the local bodies in having the municipal bye-laws revised suitably.

37. We suggest that the State Government appoint expert committees to modernise the municipal building bye-laws so that they lend support to Master Plans and zoning regulations.

38. There is a good deal of merit in the suggestion that municipal licensing system should be made comrehensive so as to cover, as far as possible, every viable unit of trade, business and industry located within the municipal jurisdiction. A good comprehensive municipal licensing system would, through the exercise of licensing powers help, prevent blight and slums, aid the enforcement of land use plans and give greater regulatory powers particularly test over-industrial units not covered either by the Industries Development & Regulation Act or the Factories Act. Implementation of this suggestion may need amendment of the municipal acts.

39. In evolving and enforcing such a licensing system the urban local bodies should establish close co-ordination with the authorities administering the Shops and Commercial Establishments Act, the Factories Act and the Sales and Excise Taxes.

40. To tackle the problem of the congested and

overcrowded areas three alternatives may be considered, namely (1) wholesale demolition and thorough redevelopment, (2) a programme of selective urban renewal, and (3) a pogram me of gradual improvement.

41. Wholesale demolition and redevelopment of large built up areas, particularly those which are historically old, will mean sudden displacement of thousands of families and their rehabilitation and any other place would confront the public authorities with administrative, economic and human problems of stupendous magnitude. Such a programme is, therefore, practically out of the equestion.

42. Urban renewal is a good coomprehensive concept Under this programme the present thoroughly decayed or deteriorated urban areas, particularly in the old but central parts of the cities and towns could be redeveloped to their optimum capacity without extra expenditure on services. Urban renewal programme in the context of the overcrowded areas of big cities should be instrumental in reducing the densities and making available the much needed open spaces.

43. We are inclined to suggest that it may be a good idea to try the programme of urban renewal on a pilot basis in some selected urban areas. Preference in urban renewal projects should, in the first instance, be given to the presently underutilised but potentially valuable pockets of land in cities and towns. Wherever urban renewal is tried it should be done as an integral part of the land use plan and city development plan (programme) mentioned earlier. The Union Government should give reasonable financial assistance to the State Governments for approved urban renewal projects.

44. The third alternative has significant for most of our urban areas, specially the metropolitan cities. This alternative envisages undertaking measures like provision of water taps and drains, minimum necessary street pattern and community facilities etc, or the toning up of the environment with the least possible dislocation.

45. The municipal and/or development authorities should have for the congested areas (1) a systemetic policy of gradual decongestion and (2) detailed long-term redevelopment schemes ready, so that new developments fall into the pattern envisaged for the future.

46. In the context of our economic and financial limitation such a gradual but steady improvement programme seems to us the most economical and practicable way of making a dent on the physical living conditions of the vast majority of people living in overcrowded localities.

47. A majority of the houses in the congested areas are substandard. Most of them being rent controlled and the rents from then being very low, the owners have hardly any incentive to improve these houses. The programme should not therefore be confined to toning up of the environment only. In those cases where the improvement depends upon the co-operation of the land owner, as for example, in covering dry latrines into water-borne flush latrines, a combination of incentives, coercion and financial assistant may be tried. Financial assistance may be particularly necessary in the case of property owners in the every low income brackets.

48. As rent control laws are responsible for hampering urban development and optimum utilisation of land, there is a strong case revising and rationalising the system of rent control. If the rent laws could be suitably amended permitting eviction of the tenants by the landlords in the event of the latter undertaking to redevelop the properties to the optimum capacity in accordance with the Plans and programmes of development, at least in the big cities most of the landlords would be willing to redevelop their land and construct modern buildings thereon. This will lend to fuller and proper utilisation of land and will be in the interest of the community. We, therefore, recommend that suitable provisions in the Rent Control Acts for the eviction of tenants from old and dilapidated buildings should be made.

49. Such eviction will, however, cause hardship to a number of old tenants paying nominal rents and, therefore, some reasonable compensation not exceeding five years' rent may be paid to them in order to facilitate their rehabilitation at other places. In the alternative the evicted tenants could be given an option to occupy portions of the newly constructed buildings on controlled rents. The local authorities may also, if possible, provide some transit accommodation for such tenants to mitigate their hardship.

50. In regard to sub-letting of the premises also the Rent Control Legislation should be amended to discourage, to the maximum extent possible, such a practice.

51. In so far as the "non-conforming uses" are concerned. the obnoxious or hazardous uses should be immediately removed. For others there should be a phased programme of removal depending upon the period of grace granted to them. To expedite their shifting to proper locations, they could be subjected to reasonable administrative and financial measures and denial of facilities for further expansion. Some positive inducements, like tax relief for a few years or a more lenient treatment in the grant of power supply and loan assistance, will also have to be given.

52. In cases where non-conforming uses do not shift even after the period of grace, prosecutions should be launched and recurring fines for each day be prescribed by the law.

53. Vacant sites amount to wasteful non-utilisatson of land and services. We unreservedly endorse the idea of subjecting them to normal municipal property taxes.

As regards the imposition of a penal tax on vacant sites, a large number of the owners of vacant sites, keen on constructing houses, find themselves quitehelpless because they do not get the building materials. In quite a few cases the vacancy may be for other bonafide reasons like poverty and lack of finances. Under these circumstances we would suggest ; firstly that there should be a limit to the size up to which a vacant plot may not be subjected to a penal tax. For plots and sites beyon d the exempted size a penal tax should be levied after five years from the time all essential services have been made available.

54. We should also recommend that out-right public acquisition of vacant sites, where these are absolutely necessary for making good the deficiencies in regard to community facilities should be undertaken.

Measures for Undeveloped Urban Land

55. Within many municipal limits there is undeveloped land on which pre-mature spotty development takes place. This development is wasteful of land and of a substandard nature. It necessitates the stretching of roads and utility services. Such a State of affairs is neither in the interest of the public authorities nor the individuals. Premature spotty development, should, therefore, be discouraged and compact development promoted.

56. In most of the urban areas, particularly the bigger ones, spotty development generally takes place because of narrowly conceived and uncoordinated activities of the various public authorities themselves. To the extent the scattered spotted development is due to this factor, better coordination among the developments and authorities and the State Town Planning Department could considerably ease the problem.

57. Where individual developer is responsible for scattered spot development, imposition of stringent conditions subject to which alone development or construction may be permitted outside of the compact area seems the only way to improve the situation.

58. The programmes of public utilities and community facilities should be so evolved as to be consistent with the idea of encouraging compact development. Future development in the presently undeveloped areas should be on the basis of planned neighbourhoods forming an integral part of the master plan of the city, if one exists.

59. Speculative transfers take place on a substantial scale in undeveloped land lying within the municipal limits. But as the obligation to obtain prior permission for each transfer with a view to prevent speculation is considered untenable on constitutional grounds the imposition of a levy on such transfer is the only alternative. Such a levy should be imposed in the form of a conversion tax. Where the transfer involves non-agricultural land the development tax should be levied.

Measures for Urbanisable Limits

60. Urbanisable land beyond the city limits is vulnerable to haphazard growth particularly alone the highways. Over this land industrial units also come to be established in a chaotic manner. The suggested measures for this category of land are: (1) extension of the municipal limits to cover the urbanisable area and (2) declaring the area as a "controlled" one as has been done under the Chandigarh Periphery Control Act.

61. We see no objection in generally agreeing with the above suggestions. We are, however, afraid that in actual practice extension of municipal limits may not always be workable. We would, therefore, suggest a cautious approach in the matter. Each case of extension of municipal limits should be decided on its merits.

62. Where extension of municipal limits is not feasible or immediately desirable municipal jurisdiction in the of essential planning controls could be extended up to five miles beyond the municipal limits. The other alternative of declaring the area as controlled also appeals to us but we would leave the discretion of either using the Municipal Act or having a separate legislation for the purpose to the State Governments.

63. To check speculatory increase in land prices within urbanisable limits and for other reasons of development it is necessary that public authorities gain ownership of land either through mutual negotiations or through compulsory acquisition. Weighing the pros and cons of these two alternatives we are of the view that the purchase of land through negotiations may bristle with too many formidable difficulties.

Measures for Land Beyond Urbanisable Limits

64. The use of land beyond the urbanisable limits should be governed by a regional land use plan. Even where a regional plan does not exist some simple special interim measures are necessary to exercise control over major developments.

65. While the setting up of small agro-industrial units in this category of land may be permitted, large industrial units which are likely to change the character of the area should not be allowed in a haphazard manner but strictly in accordance with regional land use plan.

66. In the matter of establishing industrial units there is certainly a great need for co-ordination between concerned rural local body, the urban local body, Director of Industries and the Town Planner of the State Government. Wherever, such industrial units come up in accordance with the regional land use or subject to other safegurds, the rural local body concerned should subject them to adequate taxation, licensing and other

controls.

67. Where some regions show signs of extraordinarily rapid development, it is desirable that early steps are taken to regulate growth of buildings etc. by creating an overall authority controlling development activities therein.

68. It is suggested that necessary legislation for controlling ribbon development along highways should be passed by all State Governments as soon as possible and more important than that enforced efficiently. The Executive Engineer of the appropriate authority should be made responsible for watching developments along the highways and given summary powers of demolition.

Measures for Mopping up Unearned Increases

69. Unearned increments in urban land and property values being in the nature of social surpluses must be mopped up for the benefit of the society as a whole. The Third-Five-Year Plan recommends the mopping up of these unearned increases to combat speculation and as a measure to achieve social and economic equity. We also unreservedly endorse this idea.

70. While there is every justification in siphoninh off unearned uncreases the real difficulty comes up in deciding a suitable measure or measures thereof. The measures discussed in the following paragraphs have, however, been considered.

71. Theoretically enhancement of stamp duty or the levy of an additional surcharge on it should be helpful in mopping up unearned increments. This duty is already being levied almost everywhere in India but its yield is hardly significant partly because of the rate of surcharge being low but mainly because of the widespread deplorable tendency to understate the consideration values. Unfortunately there does not seem any effective check against this evil practice. Enhancing the Stamp Duty or the rate of surcharge thereon may, we are afraid, accentuate the tendency to under-quote the valuations in registration. Assessing the measure as a whole, surcharge on Stamp Duty may not be an effective instrument for mopping up unearned increases.

72. Development charge is payable when a land use is instituted or changed or when any 'development' is carried out. Not being based on quid pro quo, the West Bengal Government had doubted its legality unless it was imposed by way of a tax. Even by making it a tax the problem is not solved and a number of handicaps, like its overlap with other property taxes, inability to operate unless development is applied for and discouraging effects on the process of development, limit its usefulness. We therefore, feel that while a modest development charge may attend the grant of planning permission, subject to its co-ordination with other local and State taxes on property much realiance on it cannot be placed in so far as the larger question of mopping up unearned increase is concerned.

73. The general experience of betterment levy, already being collected under some State Town Planning Acts, is reported to have been not very happy. Due to difficulties in its administration and applicability to limited areas betterment levy as a general measure for mopping up unearned increases does not appear to satisfactory.

74. A tax conversion of land from agricultural to non-agricultural use could be useful device in so far as the lands around urban areas are concerned where the extent of speculation is more than anywhere else. We recommend the adoption of this tax and further suggest that it should have a differential rate schedule for conversions residential, commercial and industrial uses. Being a measure of limited application we would like the Conversion Tax to be accompanied by some board-based measure having universal application.

75. An annual tax on unearned increments suggested in the TCPO's Note on Urban land Policy, has, no doubt, many more merits than in other measures. Such a tax would be quite broad-based and effective. The practical difficulties amending such a levy are bound to be quite serious. The question of its levy may, nevertheless, be examined by the Central Government. We are of the view that having a new tax the existing taxes should be so framed as to mop up unearned increases to the maximum extent possible.

76. As regards changing the basis of municipal property taxation from annual to capital value, it is very difficult for us to hazard any definite views on this subject. All that we may observe is that there is definitely an urgent need to rationalise the system of municipal properly taxation.

77. Another related issue is separate rating of site and development and the application of lower rates on development and graduated higher rates on site value. As this measure will introduce drastic changes in the system of municipal property taxation, necessitate complex valuation machinery and give rise to many administrative difficulties, we are not inclined to endorse it.

Other Anti-Speculation Measures

78. One of the major issues in urban land policy concerns speculation in land. We fully share the view that no proper solution of the urban land problem would be possible so long as wide-spread speculation in land continue.

79. Besides other measures discussed earlier, TCPO's note suggested that the public authorities assume the right of pre-emption at the price indicated by the owner. Even though we appreciate its effectiveness as an anti-speculation measure, we are unable to

recommend pre-emption because legal experts consider it too serious an infringement of Article 19 of the Constitution.

80. Though the enforcement of a ceiling on urban land holdings bristles with numerous complications, yet we feel very strongly that the idea should be in principle be accepted and implemented in all new allotments of land made by the public authorities hereafter for residential purposes.

81. The public authorities must make it a policy (i) of not allotting a plot of residential land area already owns a residential plot in the urban area and (ii) of not alloting to any one individual land beyond a reasonable maximum size. Exemption from this rule may, however, be given to (i) registered organization like the co-operatives and public and private limited concerns engated in the business of land development and disposal; (ii) persons constructing dwellings, groups houses or flats for rental purposes and (iii) people living in congested localities or in houses built on very small plots or those owning a small share in joint family houses.

82. Though theoretically there is nothing wrong in prescribing a time limit for completing constructions, yet in view of the prevailing shortage of building materials we feel that such a limit should not exceed five years after the services have been provided. Only thereafter should a heavy tax, increasing with the passage of time, be made applicable.

Land Acquisition-Procedure and Compensation Policy

83. The most complex but crucial of the problems of urban land policy relates to compulsory public acquisition of land. It has been suggested that large scale public acquisition of land should be undertaken in the undeveloped areas and in areas within the urbanisable limits. We, too are of the view that there is no escape from it. We would even observe that it would really be in the best interest of the society as a whole. It is by far the best and perhaps the only way to put an end to speculation in land, capture subsequent increases in land values, enable proper planned development and use of land and to enable the public sector to extend its control over vital land resources.

84. Advance acquisition of land could be possible by the Government notifying under Section 4 of the Land Acquisition Act the entire area of land it wishes ultimately to acquire. While there is no legal impediment to freezing large areas, we do not feel quite happy that large area should be notified for acquisition and the actual possession of the same should be taken after the lapse of a number of years. At the same time we cannot resile from the stand that large scale advance ecquisition is necessary and desirable. We, have, therefore, to strike a proper balance in reconcilling this conflict between the social and the private interest.

85. Our suggestion is that Government may notify in advance large areas for acquisition. But where the Government fails to take possession of the land within a period of five years, it should assume the liability of paying, in addition to the compensation, interest on the amount of compensation at the bank rate for the period in excess of the first five years from the date of notification. As this is not permissible under the Land Acquistion Act of 1894, necessary amendment to the Act should be made. Considering the fact that the land after notification remains (till taken possession of by Govt.) in the possession of the owner who can continue using it, payment of interest should be a more than adequate recompense for losses, if any, sustained by him due to uncertainty. On the other hand, liability to pay interest would deter the Government from erring on the side of excess in notifying land for acquisition.

86. Even though large scale advance acquisition of land is within the realm of feasibility, we would like the public authorities to undertake this systematically. They should assess the land requirements for a few years and evolve phased annual programmes for acquiring, developing and disposing off land.

87. We consider it desirable that instead of different local bodies and development agencies handling the work of land acquisition etc. each in a limited isolated way, these functions could be better performed by a high powered Board or Authority. Tho problem of finances may also be easier in the case of the Board/Authority.

88. By and large, compulsory public acquisition of land is governed by the land Acquisition Act of 1894. There are a few special acts also under which land can be acquired. It is, however, found that the acquisition provisions of the special Acts have not generally been utilised.

89. The non-utilisation of the special provisions governing acquisition indicates the inherent practical difficulties in making any departures from the general practice of paying compensation as provided in the land Acquisition, Act. We are convinced that there should not be separate enactments governing the acquisition of land as the use of separate enactments embodying different compensation formule may be accused of being highly discriminatory, legally untenable and socially undesirable. The only exception to this should be Acts governing Slum clearance.

90. Experience all over the country shows that the entire procedure of acquiring land is highly dilatory with the result that work on projects of public interest suffers. The Law Commission have also made a pointed reference to these procedural delays.

91. The Law Commission have suggested a few amendments to the existing land acquisition Act to make

the acquisition proceedings more expeditious. The Commission have, in fact tried to stipulate a definite time limit for each step in the acquisition proceedings and an overall time limit for the completion of the proceedings by the Land Acquisition Officer.

92. The suggestions made by the Law Commission are, no doubt, good but even after incorpo ating them delays in acquisition proceedings are likely to be considerable. The commission have themselves suggested the appointment of special courts where public authorities undertake large scale acquisition of land. We feel that in addition to special courts for disposing of references arising out of cases of land acquisition, special land acquisition officers dealing exclusively with this job should be appointed.

93. A point for our consideration was whether references against compensation awards should be made to the ordinary law courts or to Tribunals presided over by a person of the rank of not less than a District judge and cosisting of an assessor, estimator and other experts like engineers etc. We are greatly impressed with the idea of such Tribunals as these are so constituted as to have special expertise on valuation problems and would help in reducing delays in deciding references by simplifying the procedures of hearings, evidence etc. Some members of our Committee do not, however, approve of the Tribunals and desire the ordinary law courts to continue deciding such cases. They suggest that wherever large scale acquisition of land is involved special judges' courts in requisite number should be appointed to deal exclusively with land acquisition references.

94. The Land Acquisition Act of 1894 enjoins that compensation should be based on 'market value' of land as on the date of preliminary notification under Section 4. In addition, Section 23 (2) of the Act requires a solatium of 15 per cent to be given. The Law commission have recommended the continuance of both market value and solatium.

95. As against the Law Commission's recommendations, TCPO's Note on Urban Land Policy contends that by paying compensation based on market value the public exchequer makes payment not only for the actual worth of land but also for unearned increases and speculative values and that only way in which accumulated unearned increments and potential developments values could be removed from the compensation-calculus was to peg land values to some 'earlier date' subjected to further necessary modifications.

96. We would not deny that the above arguments against market value are quite well founded and that one of the ways to rid the compensation liability of illegitimate speculative elements is to ante-date compensation. We were skeptical and ante-dating mey not be held constitutional and legal. The position would appear to be that if ante-dating is such as to render compensation illusory or to be no principle of compensation at all it would be unconstitutional; but if it is rational and bears some proximate relationship with relevance to the date of preliminary notification under and Section 4 it would not be bad.

97. Even though ante-dating may be legally feasible in actual practice it will be extremely difficult to fix any particular date or dates to which compensation should be pegged down. This practical difficulty apart, the need for ante-dating does not arise once large scale advance acquisition of land is undertaken. The effect of large scale advance acquisition is practically the same as that of ante-dating compensation. Of the two alternative we prefer advance ecquisition of ante-dating. There, however, may be instances where subsequent to the publication by the Government its intention to undertake a scheme or to prepare a master plan speculative activity may precede Govt's notification for acquisition. In such cases which, in our opinion, should be an exception rather than the rule, the compensation may well be ante-dated to rid the compensation liability of speculative increases in land values.

98. Another related issue is the question of compensation for areas shown as open spaces, parks and gardens or reserved for similar community uses in the Master Plans. Once land is earmarked for such a use the owner is deprived of his right to develop the property. Under the existing law no compensation for it is payable and the provisions are that such lands should be acquired by the public authorities. Where public authorities are under a legal obligation to acquire such plots of land a time limit within which they should do so must, however, be stipulated. A time limit of 10 years is considered reasonable by us.

99. The provision of solatium does not exist in the special acts and a majority of the public authorities do not consider it necessary to give any solatium. The Law Commission have, on the other hand, recommended the payment of solatium.

100. We are of the view that the payment of solatium should not be necessary or justified in each and every case of public acquisition. We are more inclined to treat this issue as a part of the larger problem of rehabilitation of the dispossessed persons. In any acquisition proceedings each and every individual will not need public assistance in getting rehabilitated. It is, therefore, desirable that simultaneously with the launching of acquisition proceedings a proper survey is made to identify and classify people who would need to be rehabilitated. Suitable measures (mentioned in the report) for their rehabilitation should be undertaken.

Land Development And Disposal Policy

101. It is imperative that public authorities engaged in land acquisition should have a proper land development and disposal policy.

102. In land development and disposal the general practice seems to be to allot land after its proper development by the public authorities themselves. It has been stated that development of land should not be left in private hands because development cannot be ensured according to prescribed standards. We too share these apprehensions. We, however, realise that quite often the public authorities may be able neither to muster sufficient resources nor to maintain the required speed with which land should be developed and disposed off.

103. In the above context it is not only useful but essential to make the best use of the agency of private colonisers, co-operative societies or other persons holding sizeable areas of land.

104. In order to check the activities of those permitted to develop colonies it is necessary to acquire land and then lease it out to them for development and disposal also charging alongwith premium the cost of external development.

105. Only a certain percentage of the area approved for development through the private agency should be available to it for disposal on predetermined terms and conditions. After the developer's selling the land to the actual user, the latter should enter into a lease-deed with the improvement Trust or the Development Authority.

106. Where public authorities undertake to develop land themselves, it is highly necessary that they create the required organisation and procedure the needed finances so that land development is completed expeditiously.

107. To minimise the administrative, financial and organisational burden involved in the development of land and to expedite the process of making it available to the public, development agencies may dispose of raw land to other public authorities, registered co-operative societies and registered bonafide colonisers subject to proper safeguards.

108. On considering the relative merits of lease-hold and free-hold, we fully favour the former because it retains the ownership of land with Government, allows greater control and manoeuvreability and enables the Public authorities to capture part of unearned increments in land values at the time of transfer.

109. The terms and conditions in the lease deed should, among other things. (1) make it incumbent on the lease-holder to obtain prior permission for transfer of land; (2) provide for re-capture of unearned increment and (3) stipulate the right of pre-emption exercisable by the public authority in cases where consideration values are prima-facie understated. As regards the period of lease generally speaking, a period of 30 years is considered normal with optional renewal upto 90 years. At the time of each renewal the lease money could be enhanced upto one a half times of the original.

110. In executing the programme of land disposal, adequate land should be earmarked for industrial, commercial and other uses and the land property subdivided subject to a minimum and maximum plot size. Great care should be exercised in fixing the minimum and maximum plot sizes for industrial and commercial uses.

111. Another significant aspect of land disposal policy relate to price policy. We are glad that some short of a descriminating price policy is already being practised. There, however, is need to refine the policy further. Its overall objective should be to help the poorer sections and to encourage uses which are in the larger interests of the community. The financial soundness of the Scheme as a whole should not however be jeopardised.

Organisational And Administrative Machinery

112. Unless the various measures suggested by us are evolved in a co-ordinated manner and enforced simultaneously it will not be possible to make any impact on the problem of urban land. Partial acceptance and enforcement of these measures may be discriminatory and cause more harm than good.

113. The implementation of the various measures suggested by us calls for an effective organisation and a high degree of administrative and organisational co-ordination, collaboration and concerted action. Under the existing administrative and organisational framework there does not seem any particular public authority which may be considered suitable for the purpose of bringing about the required co-ordination and integration in policies and programmes bearing on urban land problems.

114. We are of the view that the task is much more difficult than what can be tackled by isolated agencies and recommend that there should be in every state a statutory high powered Board or Authority which should be the planning and co-ordinating agency for resource and metropolitan regions and major urban areas where the problems may transcend the local jurisdictions.

115. In a number of areas it is found that there is multiplicity of agencies doing same work with considerable overlap and clash of jurisdictions. We recommend that wherever, possible this multiplicity of authorities should be done away with, and an attempt made to rationalize and consolidate them. This authorily besides generally guiding and advising State Governments, urban local bodies and development agencies on matters

pertaining to urbanisation, urban development and planning would work as the co-ordinating agency for planning and development. It will also endorce the plans prepared by it and may also undertake the implementation of various development schemes itself.

116. For the Board/Authority to perform such a wide range of functions it will become necessary for it to set up its units in the areas where it has to operate effectively. The Board/Authority should have a whole-time Chairman, two or three whole-time members. Besides it should have as its members very senior officers of the concerned State departments and one or two members of the Parliament, State Legislature or local authorities. Its principal executive head should be vested with sufficient financial and executive powers.

117. In view of its large responsibility this Board/Authority should have a well equipped team of technical and administrative personnel. Where the Board set up an agency at the local or regional level it would be useful to have a Local Advisory Committee.

118. Where the State Board/Authority is not in a position to establish its units it may entrust the urban development functions to a suitable local agency subject to its general direction and control. In such instances the State Government should ensure that the local agency is adequately empowered and properly financed. Even here a local Advisory Committee would be highly useful to seek inter-agency co-operation and co-ordination.

119. Our recommendations may need certain modifications. We would still urge the State Governments to so modify our recommendations as not to impair their basic character.

120. The idea of a Valuation Organisation has some merit and we wish to commend it to the State Governments for their very sympathetic consideration. Such an organisation can certainly be utilised for many related assignments. If Valuations organisations are established, appeal against their assessments may be referred to the Tribunal recommended earlier.

121. We recommend to the Planning Commission and the Central State Governments to give adequate attention to the problems of urbanisation, and high priority to town development and improvement and hope that sufficient funds would be provided in the Fourth Five-Year-Plan for the purpose. No less important and urgent is the question of creasion of adequate machinery for the implementation of schemes and carrying out suggestions made in our report.

ENERGY SURVEY OF INDIA COMMITTEE, 1963—REPORT

New Delhi; The Ministry of Irrigation and Power, 1965. 441p.

Chairman : Shri M.R. Sachdev

Joint Chairman : Mr. Walker Cisler; Prof. Austin Robinson:

Members : Mr. Louis de Heem; Mr. Jacques Desrousseaux ; Shri K.R. Damle ; Shri K.P.S. Nair ; Shri P.R. Nayak ; Shri A.B. Guha ; Shri S.S. Kumar ; Shri S. Bose ; Shri M.N. Chakravarti ; Shri B.S. Nag ; Shri P.S. Lokanathan ; Dr. V.K.R.V. Rao ; Dr. M. S. Randhawa ; Shri Pitambar Pant ; Shri V. Nanjappa ; Shri C.S. Krishnamoorthi.

Advisor : Prof. M.S. Thacker ; Shri C.M. Trivedi ; Dr. H.J. Bhabha

APPOINTMENT

The Energy Survey of India Committee was constituted under the Ministry of Irrigation & Power vide their Memorandum dated 3-1-1963.

TERMS OF REFERENCE

The Energy Study would cover present and prospective demands and supplies of energy, both total and in respect of all constituents of energy on a national, regional and sectoral basis. It would be expected to provide the Government of India basic material for development planning in the field of energy upto 1981. In making this study, the Committee will give consideration, among other things, to u e of energy in rural areas.

The Committee will also study development of power resources-hydro-electric, thermal (including coal, lignite, oil and gas) and atomic energy, and make recommendations as to phasing in which these should be brought into use progressively. The Committee will also study the question of fuel for thermal power stations, availability of fuel, best location and sizes of plants. The fuels to be considered would be coal, oil, gas and atomic energy."

CONTENTS

RECOMMENDATIONS

General

In this final chapter we bring together the principal conclusions and recommendations of our Survey. We begin with general considerations and then go on to present our principal conclusions regarding each of the main sectors of demand and sources of energy.

The total energy resources of India are adequate but not abundant for the present stage of Indian economic development. Much of the coal is made difficult to use by its high ask content. The indigeneous oil supplies are not sufficient to meet more than a relatively small fraction of India's prespective requirements and unless new discoveries are wholly different in scale from those yet known ; a large part of the demand for oil will have to be met by import.

Much of the coal, and all of the coking coal, is moreover situated in the Bihar/West Bengal coal field in North East India. While other coal exists and is likely to be increasingly developed as time goes on, there are large parts of Southern, Western and North Western India that are distant from any coal supplies.

The limitations imposed by the geographical distribution of the coal fields are in considerable degree mitigated by the fact that the hydro resources of India are largely in those parts of Southern, Western and North Western India which are distant from coal resources.

In planning the economic development of India it will be important to have clearly in mind these geographical limitations of the fuel supplies. In all advanced countries energy supplies have been very powerful factors in determining the location and development of industries. The costs, efficiency and competitive position of the heavy metallurgical industries are particularly sensitive to the delivered prices of their materials and fuels, including transport costs. The iron and steel industries have tended to grow up either where coal has been available on the sport (as in the Ruhu and in most of the traditional locations in the United Kingdom), or where coal could be very cheaply transported, usually by ship or barge, to the source of the iron ore. In India the location of all coking coal in the Bihar/West Bengal area will impose limitations on the choice of sites where costs in the iron and steel industry are generally competitive. If other more distant sites are to be adopted, it will be necessary to consider very carefully in advance the possible method of economic transport of coal or coke to the site concerned. Our investigation suggest that for some of these sites imported coke or coking coal may possibility be more economic than Indian supplies.

But in a broader sense the most economic use of India's natural resources and energy resources may require recognition of the advantages of locating in fairly close proximity to the coking coalfields those industries which are energy intensive and must depend on actual direct use of coking coal and on the other hand locating in those parts of India which are more remote from such coal resources a larger share of the industries which are not energy intensive. The availability of cheap energy in the Bihar/West Bengal area in the form of by product coals from the wash-heries may give opportunities to locate in that region energy-intensive industries producing cheaply for export markets.

The pattern of the Indian energy economy will be dictated by the relative advantages and relative costs of different fuels. The trend of almost all of the economically advanced countries is at present towards an oil-based energy economy. There are evident signs in India of a similar trend ; but some caution is needed before assuming that this trend should be accepted and encouraged in Indian conditions. Oil is an indigencous and very plentiful fuel both in the U.S.A. and in the U.S.S.R. The trend towards oil is moving much more slowly in most of the European countries which are more similar to India in having little or no indigenous oil and in being necessarily concerned with the possible effects on the balance of payments of large imports of oil.

In the case of India our first estimates suggested a very high future dependence on oil, more particularly if one had assumed that some of the difficulties of supplies of domestic energy that we foreses would be solved by very substantial increase of the use of kerosene. But even on the basis of the revised estimates that we have presented in this Report, the share of energy imports (including both crude oil and products and all the capital equipment used in the energy sector) in the total of imports increase from about 19% in 1970/1, to 24% in 1975/6 and to 38% in 1980/1. These represent a very formidable charge on India's prospective imports and we feel serious doubts whether the Goverment of India would be in any position to provide for larger oil imports than we have assumed.

We have estimated the demands for energy both in total and in all forms. The amount of energy that will be required for Indian development will clearly depend on the rate of that development. At the time of our Survey the Planning Commission had not completed its work on the next Plan Period nor had it officially formulated assumptions about more distant periods. We have therefore though it best to present alternative calculations. Based on alternative assumed rates of growth. These are presented in detail. In view of the high cost of investment in energy it will be important to secure that. While keeping abreast and actually developing needs, it does not run far a head of the realities and actual development in practice.

Coal

While supplies of non-coking coal are (as was said above) abundant in quantity, supplies of cooking coal are not abundant, though probably sufficent to meat needs until the end of this century. Economy of coking coal is most important. At present, only about 40% of the coking coal that is in the ground in the seems that are being worked is recovered and brought to the surface only about 60% at most of what is recoverd from the mine is delivered as 17% ask content washed coal from the washeries to the coke-ovens. Thus in total less than 25% of the potential coking coal is actually available to be used for the purposes for which it is essential. It is important that improvement of this performance should be sought in every may ; through economy of coke in the blast furnances ; through acceptance of as large a fraction of the total assis practicable by the coke-ovens from the washeries ; but above all through recovery from the mine of a substantially larger proportion of all coal that is available in the seams. We know that all these problems are being actively examined by the Department of Mines and Metals and that there is hope of a significant increases in the recovery rate and of lower ratios of coke to pig-iron. But the matter is so important that we hope even greater efforts will be made to achieve economies. We recommend that any necessary resources be made available to put into practice both the improved mining methods and even greater economy of use of coke that is proposed.

Whatever may be done to conserve coking coal, it is clear that with the progressive expansion of the iron and steel industry there will be increasing demands for washed coking coal and increasing supplies of coking coal by products. We have examined with care the relative economies of using two-product and three-product washery processes. We are convinced that the two-product process will produce by product coals which can find an economic market, principally for thermal electricity and that this process is to be preferred.

We have examined with care the economic problems of transporting these by-product coals and using them economically. We are satisfied that, if suitably priced, a market can be round for all the by-product coals that we likely to be produced.

These coking coal by-products are likely, however, to find markets principally in uses which are normally met by non-coking coals. Having regard to the substantial amounts likely to be available, there may be no more than a small additional requirement for non-coking coals in the next Plan period. By-product coking coals, if suitable priced and transported in closed-circuit train loads can meet the requirements for coal for thermal electricity stations and other purposes at points as far as and beyond most of the outlying coalfields that it has been proposed to develop. We suggest that the wisdom of developing in the near feature some of these outlying coalfields be re-examined.

In addition to the problems created by the by-product coking coals there are further problems created by the large amounts of slack coal that are produced as part of the process of mining the non-coking coals.

More incentive is desirable to encourage mining methods which will reduce the proportion of slack to a minimum. But a considerable output of slack is inevitable. We recommend that there be price at levels that will encouage its consumption in all uses for which it is suitable. We recommend also the urgent examination by the Central Fuel Research Institute of the possibilities of producing from this slack a domestic fuel that will relieve the present excessive pressure of the demand for firewood.

The long-term success and prosperity of the coal industry must depend on increasing the efficiency of coal-mining. The output per head is at present very low in many of the older private-sector mines. All that is possible should be done to increase their productivity.

The demands for coal estimated in this Survey are appreciably below other estimated that have been made. One important source of difference has been the use of existing inputs of energy to calculate requirements in later years. While this is a normal and proper procedure, some allowance needs to be made for the progressive economies of the use of fuel which have greatly affected the trends of demand in more advanced countries. Some of the errors has been due to use of "ready reckoners" of demand for coal in thermal generation of electricity which seriously exaggerate the probable requirement.

There is a strong trend towards greater dependence on oil as a source of energy. It will be desirable explore all possible ways in which Indias oil supplies can be increased. Much is already being done to explore the possibilities of further indigenous supplies. But unless discoveries are made on a scale wholly different from any hitherto, a very large proportion of Indian oil supplies will have to be imported (were estimate the proportions in 1975/76 as about 75%). It is of great importance to explore all possible ways, by trade agreements and otherwise of increasing and making more certain India power to purchase these necessary supplies.

At present relative costs of coal and oil, the use of oil is more economic on the highly industrial regions of western and southern India. There is a likelihood that demands may increase in those and other regions even beyond Indias capacity to finance imports, and it may at some stage necessary to take measures which will make the use of indigenous fuels more attractive.

The principal increases of demand for energy in the form of oil seem likely to arise in transport (where both the growth of road transport and the proposed dieselisation policy of the railways will substantially increase demand) and in the domestic sector (if the shortage of firewood that we foresee leads to increased dependence on kerosene). The longer-term repercussions of a dieselisation policy on the balance of payments will need to be considered in advance.

The pattern of Indian consumption of oil products does not accord easily with the potential out-turn of Indian refineries from the most easily available crude oils. In the past India has been short of Kerosene. In future India seems likely to be short of middle distillates generally as the result of the prospecctive growth of demands for diesel oils. On the other hand India is likely on the present and prospective pattern of demand in the absence of policy changes to have surplus supplies of gasoline and naphtha at one end and possible of fuel oil at the other end, even when the out-turn of refineries have been adjusted so far as possible to meet the changing pattern of demand. It may not be easy to export the surplus gasoline at reasonable prices to neighbouring markets or to acquire consideration needs to be given to the wisdom of present taxation policies which tend to discourage consumption of gasoline and encourage consumption of diesel oils.

The net effect of a continuation of the present taxation is likely to be an increase rather than a decrease of the total required net cost of imports of oil and oil products, even when allowance is made for the lower consumption per kilometer of road transport using diesel oils. It is probably in the national interest to encourage gasoline consumption in all forms of transport that can reasonably use it to take advantage of the cheaper initial cost of internal-combustion engines designed to use gasoline.

There is also likely, in the absence of changes of policy, to be a surplus of naphtha. This can probably be absorbed without great difficulty by suitable planning of fertiliser and petro-chemicals production and possibly by use to economies coke in the iron and steel industry.

If there is not to be a surplus of fuel oil, it is desirable to encourage its consumption in those areas near to refineries and distant from coal fields where it is likely to be an economic source of energy in industry or the generation of thermal electricity.

Electricity

Policy in the planning of electricity needs to be coordinate completely into a national and regional energy policy. The location of thermal power station should be made with full consideration not only of the trends in the development and location of demand but also of the availability and location of the cheapest sources of primary energy. The large volumes of coking coal by products in the regions of the iron and steel industry washeries will excercise a very important effect on the desirable locations, which are likely to be increasingly supply-oriented rather than demand-oriented.

Examination has been made of the relatives costs of using newly development coal mines nearer to the demand-centre or by-product coal carried by rail in a closed circuit operation. This has shown that at distance up to and above 1000 Kilometres, it is likely to be more economical to use the by-product coals. Examination has also been made of the relative costs of carrying coal by rail to a demand oriented power station transmission lines from a supply-oriented power station near to the coal washery. This has shown that for large blocks of energy there is an economy in constructing such transmission lines and adopting the wishery location.

Examination has been made of the relative economies of generating plant of different sizes. The economies are such that there is advantage in a progressive move towards larger size, but not necessarily towards greater complexity, so far as this is achievable with the present experience and resources of the heavy electrical industry.

The relative costs of generating electricity in thermal, hydro and nuclear stations have been analysed in detail and in terms of the prospective costs of constructing and providing fuels for each in Indian conditions. This analysis shows that in certain locations at a distance from cheap coal supplised and where hydro is not available, nuclear energy is already competitive. For the next ten to fifteen years while experience is being gained with nuclear energy there are adequate other sources of energy available of required. Thus, the decision to build nuclear stations should be reached on purely economic ground. During the 1970's when the problems of using thorium have been statisfactoily resolved, nuclear energy is likely to become increasingly competitive.

The same analysis makes it clear that the best ultimate strategy of electricity generation is to use hydel increasingly to meet peak loads and to carry the base loads on steam plant using wherever available by products coals and in some regions on nuclear plant. There are likely to be some regions, particularly in Northern India where the development should probably be based wholly on hydel.

The full and effective use of large thermal and nuclear station and their integration with hydel stations is impossible unless transmission lines are available to the necessary extent. Indian investment in transmission and distribution has been inadequate and a large investment is necessary in the next Plan Period if full use is to be made of nuclear and other generating plant already planned and beginning construction. A beginning with the construction of extra high voltage transmission lines is recommended before 1970-71.

Careful consideration has been given to the organisation electricity supply that is most appropriate to the changing technical conditions and to the need for greater integration than has existed in the past. We welcome the creation of Electricity Supply Regions. We hope that this very necessary integration of the planning and operation of the generation of electricity may be acheived without any formal re-organisation and by the voluntary co-operation of the State Boards within the various Regions and of the Regions themselves. It will, however be necessary to watch carefully the progress of co-operation on this basis and it may at some stage be necessary to consider whether a greater degree of central ownership and control of generating is a necessary condition of an effective generating policy. If that should sometime become necessary, it will remain desirable that state Boards should be responsibile for all distribution. And in any new organisation that may be worked out, effective decentralisation of day-by-day operations will be absolutely essential. We make certain subsidiary proposals for the strengthening of the state Boards.

We have considered the problems of the pricing of electricity. We recommend that every effort should be made to reduce costs and to make prices as low as is compatiable with an efficient and healthy industry. But we recommend that the state Boards should be encouraged to earn a reasonable economical return (which we estimate at 10%) on their invested capital and to provide from their retained earnings and depreciation funds a substantial part of the capital funds needed for expansion.

In the interest of improved efficiency we suggest that careful attention be given well in advance to the training of the technical staff that will be necessary. We believe that overseas suppliers of equipment would be prepared to collaborate in such training both in India and, where appropriate, in similar large stations abroad.

Rural electrification should be expanded as rapidly as possible to all places of suitable size in rural electrification on a strictly commercial basis. Having regard to the very large rural population of India and the importance of the electricity supply industry retaining adequate funds for the expansi n of its general activities it is not likely to be possible for rural electrification on a large scale to be subsidised to the extent that it is in most advanced countries by Urban electrification. We recommended that rural electrification be regard more as a social service than as a strictly economic enterprise and possibly financed in part from general revenues.

The Domestic Demand

There are grounds for very serious concern regarding the supplies of energy to the domestic sector. Principally for cooking but partly also for lighting, fans and air-conditioning and other purposes. The domestic demand have largely been met from traditional non-commercial sources, including firewood, cattle dung and waste products, but partly also in recent years from kerosene and electricity. The statistics are inevitably somewhat uncertain but recent inquiries have made it possible to present more accurate estimates. In 1960-61. In non-commercial forms of energy probably provided about three-fourth of the total energy used in India and about nine-tenths of the energy used in the domestic sector.

This large supply of non-commercial energy has only been made possible by the cutting annually of about 100 million tonnes of firewood. This almost certainly exceeds the growth of available timber and involves the progressive deforestation of India. The growth of demand in the domestic sector that we forecast will, if nothing is done, rapidly denede increasing areas of India.

We fear that if there are no immediate steps taken, shortage of firewood will cause grave hardship and lead to much larger demands for kerosene than Indian potential imports are likely to be able to provide. We recommended that immediate and active measures are taken jointly by the Government of India and the State Governments to formulate and implement a policy for expanding the growth of quick-growing timber suitable for use as firewood this will require the assignment to this use of considerable areas of land.

In addition we recommend that measures be taken to produce and popularise the use for domestic purposes of commercial fuel is based on indigenous coal supply.

The Pricing of Energy

A satisfactory national policy for energy requires that all consumers of energy shall use those forms of energy which, having regard to the circumstances of India, can be most economically provided to meet their needs. It is of the essence of a satisfactory energy policy that consumers shall have the fight incentives to use the right fuels. We have set out what we believe to be the essentials of an energy pricing policy. We recommend that the various bodies concerned in the making of prices for energy products take full account of the importance of establishing the right incentives for consumers to use the most economic fuels.

If the present pricing policies are not revised, we foreseen serious surpluses of unsaleable coking coal by products and non-coking coal slacks. The disposal of these would cost considerable sums and be a grave waste of national resources. From a national planning point of view these surpluses are available at zero cost. They should be clear the market. At present the incentives to use them are inadequate.

There are likely to be similar problems in the pricing of oil products which in this case are affected by taxation policies. We recommend that taxation policies should take account of the probable deficits and surpluses of different types of oil products.

Investment in Energy

We have estimated the probable investment required in energy at different dates down to 1980-81. The ratio of investment in energy to total investment is about that which might be expected on the basis of similar inquiries in European Countries.

We have estimated also the proportion of the gross investment which is likely to take the form of imports in the basis of present trends. We think that it will be important that India shall as rapidly as possible reduce the dependence on imported equipment to a minimum so as to reduce also the necessary foreign expenditures below those that we have estimated. Part of the large dependence on imports a ears to result from the desire to progress in respect of installation of types of equipment rather more rapidly than Indian capacity is likely to be able to progress in respect of their manufacture. It will be necessary to hold a balance and to put heavy embasis on the manufacture in India of type of equipment which at each stage can be produced with a low import content.

Plans for investment in energy need to be based on the best possible estimate of the future requirements for energy. In the case of electricity such estimate are provided both by the recently established Annual Electric Power Survey of India and by such studies as have been made on behalf of our Energy Survey. We have found discrepancies in respect of 1970-71 between our own estimates based on the probable requirements of KWH in different industries in India as a whole and the estimates of the Power Survey. We believe that both the methods of estimation of future requirements are valuable. But we take the view that better short term estimate extending over two or three year ahead can be provided (as does the Electric Power Survey) by building up detailed local estimates of future connected loads. We take the view that estimates for more distant dates can better be made and better escape errors different industries and the corresponding energy requirements. Each method provides for intermediate dates a valuable check on the other.

The Making of Energy Policy

We are convinced that it will be desirable to keep constantly under review the trends of energy consumption and to reformulate policies as circumstance change. We greatly welcome the establishment within the Planning Commission of a unit that will be concerned under one Member of the Commission with energy problems. We recommend that this unit be charged with the responsibility for the collection and organisation of the statistics that are essential to any such work.

We would expect that it will be desirable to repeat at intervals of about five years same such survey as we have undertaken in order that it may be seen whether circumstances have so changed that a change of policies is required. We estimate at this stage to recommended that it should be conducted on the same basis as this survey has been. But we would emphasis the advantages that this survey has enjoyed through the close cooperation of representative of the several ministries under which energy problems are divided at present and of experts drawn from a number of fields in India and abroad and possessing a wide variety of relevant experience.

In the intervals between such reviews, we suggest that great advantage could be secured by provision of inter-departmental arrangements for regular consultation between the Secretaries of the various Ministers concerned with energy problems. We understand that such provision has already been made.

ENERGY SURVEY OF INDIA COMMITTEE, 1963—REPORT

New Delhi, Planning Commission, 1965. 441p.

Chairman : Shri M.R. Sachdev.

Joint-Chairman : Shri Walker Cisler ; Prof. Austin Robinson.

Members Mr. Louis de Heem ; Mr. Jacques Desrousseaux ; Shri K.R. Damle ; Shri K.P.S. Nair ; Shri P.R. Nayak ; Shri A.B. Guha ; Shri S.S. Kumar ; Shri S. Bose ; Shri M.N. Chakravarti ; Shri B.S. Nag ; Shri P.S. Lokanathan ; Dr. V.K.R.V. Rao ; Dr. M.S. Randhawa ; Shri Pitambar Pant ; Shri V. Nanjappa ; Shri C.S. Krishnamoorthi.

Members-Appointed To Advise The Committee : Professor M.S. Thacker ; Shri C.M. Trivedi ; Dr. H.J. Bhabha ;

APPOINTMENT

The Energy Survey of India Committee was appointed by the Government of India, Ministry of Irrigation and Power Vide their Memorandum of January 3, 1963.

TERMS OF REFERENCE

The Energy study would cover present and prospective demands and supplies of energy, both total and in respect of all constituents o f energy on a national, regional and sectorial basis. It would be expected to provide the Government of India basic material for development planning in the field of energy upto 1981. In making this study the committee will give consideration, among other things, to use of energy in rural areas.

The Committee will also study development of power resources-hydro-electric, thermal (including coal, lignite, oil and gas) and atomic energy, and make recommendations as to phasing in which these should be brought into use progressively. The Committee will also study the question of fuel for thermal power stations,' availability of fuel, best location and sizes of plants. The fuels to be considered would be coal, oil, gas and atomic energy.

CONTENTS

Foreword ; Preface ; Abbreviations and Equivalents ; Terms of Reference ; The Energy problems of India ; Recent trends of Energy Consumption ; Estimates of Future Demands ; Forecasts based on sectoral projections, Transport ; Forecasts based on sectoral Projections, Industry ; Energy use in Agriculture ; The Domestic Sector ; Final Estimates of Demands ; The Regional Distribution of Demands ; Problems of Coal Supplies ; Problems of Oil Supplies ; Problems of Electricity Supplies ; Capital Investment in Energy ; Summary and Conclusions ; Annexures from 1 to 6.

RECOMMENDATIONS

The total energy resources of India are adequate but not abundant for the present state of Indian economic development. Much of the coal is made difficult to use by its high ask contect. The indigenous oil supplies are not sufficient to meet more than a relatively small fraction of India's prospective requirements and, unless new discoveries are wholly different in scale from those yet known, a large part of the demand for oil will have to be met by import.

Much of the coal, and all of the coking coal, is moreover situated in the Bihar/West Bengal Coal field in North-East India. While other coal exists and is likely to be increasingly developed as time goes on, there are large parts of Southern, Western and North Western India that are distant from any coal supplies.

The limitations imposed by the geographical distribution of the coal fields are in considerable degree mitigated by the fact that the hydro resources of India are largely in those parts of Southern, Western and North Western India which are distant from Coal resources.

In planning the economic development of India it will be important to have clearly in mind these geographical limitations of the fuel supplies. In all advanced countries energy supplies have been very powerful factors in determining the location and development of industries. The costs, efficiency and competitive position of the heavy metallurgical industries are particularly sensitive to the delivered prices of their materials and fuels, including transport costs. The iron and steel industries have tended to grow up either where coal has been available on the spot (as in the Ruhr and in most of the traditional locations in the United Kingdom), or where coal could be very cheaply transported, usually by ship or barge, to the source of the iron ore. In India the location of all coking coal in the Bihar/West Bengal area will impose limitations on the choice of sites where eosts in the iron and steel industry are generally competitive. If other more distant sites are to be adopted, it will be necessary to consider very carefully in advance the possible methods of economic transport of coal or coke to the site concerned. Our investigations suggest that for some of these sites imported coke or coking coal may possibly by more economic than Indian supplies.

But in a broader sense the most economic use of India's natural resources and an energy resources may require recognition of the advantages of locating in fairly close proximity to the coking coalfields those industries which are energy intensive and must depend on actual direct use of coking coal and on the other hand locating in those Parts of India which are more remote from such coal resources a larger share of the industries which are not energy intensive. The availability of cheep energy in the Bihar/West Bengal area in the form of by-product coals from the washeries may give opportunities to locate in that region energy-intensive industries prodocing cheaply for export markets.

The pattern of the Indian energy economy will be dictated by the relative advantages and relative costs of different fuels. The trend of almost all of the economically advanced countries is at present towards an oil-based energy economy. There are evident signs in India of a similar trend; but some caution is needed before assuming that this trend should be accepted and encouraged in Indian conditions. Oil is an idigenous and very plentiful fuel both in the U.S.A. and in the U.S.S.R. The trend towards oil is moving much more slowly in most of the European countries which are more similar to India in having littel or no indigenous oil and in being necessarily concerned with the possible effects on the balance of payments of large imports of oil.

In the case of India our first estimates suggested a very high future dependence on oil, more particularly if one had assumed that some of the difficulties of supplies of domestic energy that we foresee would be solved by very substantial increase of the use of kerosene. But even on the basis of the revised estimates that we have presented in this Report, the share of energy imports (including both crude oil and products and all the capital equipment used in the energy sector) in the total of imports increase from about 19% in 1970-71, to 24% in 1975-76 and to 38% in 1980-81. These represent a very formidable charge on India's prospective imports and we feel serious doubts whether the Government of India would be in any position to provide for larger oil imports than we have assumed.

We have estimated the demands for energy both in total and in all forms. The amount of energy that will be required for India development will clearly depend on the rate of that development. At the time of our Survey the Planning Commission had not completed its work on the next Plan Period nor had it officially formulated assumptions about more distant periods. We have therefore, thought it best to present alternative calculations, based on alternative assumed rates of growth. These are presented in detail. In view of the high cost of investment in energy it will be important to secure that, while keeping abreast and actually developing needs, it does not run far ahead of the realities and actual development in practice.

Coal

While supplies of non-coking coal are (as was said above) abundant in quantity, supplies, of coking coal are not abundant, though probably sufficient to meet needs until the end of this century. Economy of coking coal is most import-out. At present, only about 40% of the coking coal that is in the ground in the seams that are being worked is recovered and brought to the surface; only about 60% at most of what is recovered from the mine is delivered as 17% ash content washed coal from the washeries to the coke-ovens. Thus in total less than 25% of the potential coking coal is actually available to be use for the purposes for which it is essential. It is important that improvement of this performance should be sought in every way: through economy of cake in the blast furnaces: through acceptance of as large a fraction of the total as is practicable by the coke-ovens from the washeries, but above all through recovery from the mine of a substaintially larger proportion of all coal that is available in the seams. We know that all these problems are being actively examined by the Department of Mines and Metals and that there is hope of a significant increase in the recovery rate and of lower ratios of coke to pig-iron. But the matter is so important that we hope even greater efforts will be made to achieve economices. We recommend that any necessary resources be made available to put into practice both the improved mining methods and even greater economy of use of coke that is proposed.

Whatever may be done to conserve coking coal, it is clear that with the progressive expansion of the iron and steel industry there will be increasing demands for washed coking coal and increasing supplies of coking coal by-products. We have examined with care the relative economies of using two-product and three-product washery processes. We are convinced that the two-product process will product by-product coals which can find an economic market, principally for thermal electricity and that this process is to be preferred.

We have examined with care the economic problems of transporting these by-product coals and using them economically. We are satisfied that, if suitably priced, a market can be found for all the by-product coals that are likely to be produced.

These coking coal by-products are likely, however, to find markets principally in uses which are normally met by non-coking coals. Having regard to the substantial amounts likely to be available, there may be no more than a small additional requirement for non-coking coals in the next Plan Period. By-product coking coals, if suitably priced and transported in closed-circuit train loads, can meet the requirements for coal for thermal electricity stations and other purposes at points as far as and beyond most of the outlying coolfields that it had been proposed to develop. We suggest that the wisdom of developing in the near future some of these outlying coalfields be re-examined.

In addition to the problems created by the by-product coking coals there are further problems created by the large amounts of slack coal that are produced as part of the process of mining the non-coking coals. More incentive is desirable to encourage mining methods which will reduce the proportion of slack to a minimum. But a considerable output of slack is inevitable. We recommend that this be priced at levels that will encourage its consumption in all uses for which it is suitable. We recommend also the urgent examination by the Central Fuel Research Institute of the possibilities of producing from this slack a domestic fuel that will relieve the present excessive pressure of the demand for firewood.

The long-term success and prorperity of the coal industry must depend on increasing the efficiency of coal-mining, The out-put per head is at present very low in many of the older private-sector mines. All that is possible should be done to increase their productivity.

The demands for coal estimated in this Survey are appreciably below other estimates that have been made. One important source of difference has been the use of existing inputs of energy to calculate requirements in later years. While this is a normal and proper procedure, some allowance needs to be made for the progressive economics of the use of fuel which have greatly affected the trends of demand in more advanced countries. Some of the error has been due of "ready reckoners" of demand for coal in thermal generation of electricity which seriously exaggerate the probable requirement.

Oil

There is a strong trend towards greater dependence on oil as a source of energy. It will be desirable to explore all possible ways in which India's oil supplies can be increased. Much is already being done to explore the possibilities of further indigenous supplies. But unless discoveries are made on a scale wholly different from any hitherto, a very large proportion of Indian oil supplies will have to be imported (we estimate the proportion in 1976-77 as about 75%). It is of great importance to explore all possible ways, by trade agreements and otherwise of increasing and making more certain India's power to purchase these necessary supplies.

At present relative costs of coal and oil, the use of oil is more economic in the highly industrialised regions of western and southern India. There is a likelihood that demands may increase in those and other regions, even beyond India's capacity to finance imports, and it may at some stage prove necessary to take measures which will make the use of indigenous fuels more attrective.

The principal increases of demand for energy in the form of oil seem likely to arise in transport (where both the growth of road transport and the proposed dieselisation policy of the railways will substantially increase demand) and in the domestic sector (if the shortage of firewood that we foresee leads to increased dependence on kerosene). The longer-term repercussions of a dieselisation policy in the balance of payments will need to be considered in advance.

The pattern of Indian consumption of oil products does not accord easily with the potential out-turn of Indian refineries from the most easily available crude oils. In the past India has been short of kerosene. In future India seems likely to be short of middle distillates generally as the result of the prospective growth of demands for diesel oils. On the other hand India is likely, on the present and prospective pattern of demand in the absence of policy changes, to have surplus supplies of gasoline and naphtha at one end and possibly of fuel oil at the other end, even when the out-turn of refineries have been adjusted so far as possible to meet the changing pattern of demand. It may not be easy to export the surplus gasoline at reasonable prices to neighbouring markets or to acquire considerable additional supplies of middle distillates. Thus more consideration needs to be given to the wisdom of present taxation policies, which tend to discourage consumption of gasoline and encourage consumption of diesel oils.

The net effect of a continuation of the present taxation is likely to be an increase rather than a decrease of the total required net cost of imports of oil and oil products, even when allowance is made for the lower consumption per kilometer of road transport using diesel oils. It is probably in the national interest to encourage gasoline consumption in all forms of transport that can reasonably use it to take advantage of the cheaper initial cost of internal-combustion engines designed to use gasoline.

There is also likely, in the absence of changes of policy, to be a surplus of naphtha. This can probably be absorbed without great difficulty by suitable Planning of fertiliser and petro-chemicals production and possibly by use to economise coke in the iron and steel industry.

If there is not to be a surplus of fuel oil, it is desirable to encourage its consumption in those areas near to refineries and distant from coal fields where it is likely to be an economic source of energy in industry or the generation of thermal electricity.

Electricity

Policy in the planning of electricity needs to be co-ordinated completely into a national and regional energy policy. The location of thermal power stations should be made with full consideration not only of the trends in the development and location of demand but also of the availability and location of the cheapest sources of primary energy. The large volumes of coking coal by-products in the regions of the iron and steel industry washeries will exercise a very important effect on the desirable locations, which are likely to be increasingly supply-oriented rather than demand-oriented.

Examination has been made of the relative costs of using newly developed coal mines neares to the demand-centre or by-product coals carried by rail in a closed-circuit operation. This has shown that at distances up to and above 1000 kilometres it is likely to be more economical to use the by-product coals. Examination has also been made of the relative costs of carrying coal by rail to a demand-oriented power station and of carrying electricity by extra-high-voltage transmission lines from a supply-oriented power station near to the coal washery. This has shown that for large blocks of energy there is an economy in constructing such transmission lines and adopting the washery location.

Examination has been made of the relative economies of generating plant of different sizes. The economics are such that there is advantage in a progressive move towards larger size, but not necessarily towards) greater complexity, so far as this is achievable with the present experience and resources of the heavy electricals industry.

The relative costs of generating electricity in thermals, hydro and nuclear stations have been analysed in detail and in terms of the prospective costs of constructing and providing fuels for each in Indian conditions This analysis shows that, in certain locations at a distance from cheap coal supplies and where hydro is not available, nuclear energy is already competitive. For the next ten to fifteen years while experience is being gained with nuclear energy, there are adequate other sources of energy, available if required. Thus, the decision to build nuclear stations should be reached on purely economic grounds. During the 1970's, when the problems of using thorium have been satisfactorily resolved, nuclear energy is likely to become increasingly competitive.

The same analysis makes it clear that the best ultimate strategy of electricity generation is to use hydel increasingly to meet peak loads and to carry the base loads on steam plant, using wherever available by-product coals, and in some regions, particularly in Northern India, where the development should probably be based wholly on hydel.

The full and effective use of large thermal and nuclear stations and their integration with hydel stations is impossible unless transmission lines are available to the necessary extent. Indian investment in transmission and distribution has been inadequate and a large investment is necessary in the next Plan Period if full use is to be made of nuclear and other generating Plant already planned and beginning construction. A beginning with the construction of extra high-voltage transmission lines is recommended before.

Careful consideration has been given to the organisation of electricity supply that is most appropriate to the changing technical conditions and to the need for greater integration than has existed in the past. We welcome the creation of Electricity Supply Regions. We hope that this very necessary integration of the planning and operation of the generation of electricity may be achieved without any formal reorganisation and by the voluntary co-operation of the State Boards within the various Regions and of the Regions themselves. It will, however, be necessary to watch carefully the progress of co-operation on this basis, and it may at some stage be necessary to consider whether a greater degree of central ownership and control of generating is a necessary condition of an effective generating policy. If that should sometime become necessary, it will remain desirable that State Boards should be responsible for all distribution. And in any new organisation that may be worked out, effective decentralisation of day-by-day operations will be absolutely essential. We make certain subsidiary proposals for the strengthening of the State Boards.

We have considered the problems of the pricing of electricity. We recommend that every effort should be made to reduce costs and to make prices as low as is compatible with an efficient and healthy industry. But we recommend that the State Boards should be encouraged to earn a reasonable economical return (which we estimate at 10%) on their invested capital and to provide from their retained earnings and depreciation funds a substantial part of the capital funds needed for expansion.

In the interest of improved efficiency we suggest that careful attention be given well in advance to the training of the technical staff that will be necessary. We believe that overseas supplies of equipment would be prepared to collaborate in such training both in India and, where appropriate, in similar large stations abroad.

Rural electrification should be expanded as rapidly as possible to all places of suitable size in rural areas. It is not likely to be possible to carry out rural electrification on a strictly commercial basis. Having regard to the very large rural population of India and the importance of the electricity supply industry retaining adequate funds for the expansion of its general activities, it is not likely to be possible for rural electrification on a large scale to be subsidised to the extent that it is in most advanced countries by urban electrification. We recommend that rural electrification be regarded more nearly as a social service than as a strictly economic enterprises and possibly financed in part from general revenues.

There are grounds for very serious concern regarding the supplies of energy to the domestic sector, principally for cooking but partly also for lighting fans and air-conditioning and other pusposes. The domestic demands have largely been met from traditional non-commercial sources, including firewood, cattle dung and waste products, but partly also in recent years from kerosene and electricity. The statistics are inevitably somewhat uncertain but recent inquiries have made it possible to present more accurate estimates. In 1960-61, non-commercial forms of energy probably provided about three-fifths of the total energy used in India and about nine-tenths of the energy used in the domestic sector.

This large supply of non-commercial energy has only been made possible by the cutting annually of about 100 million tonnes of firewood. This almost certainly exceeds the growth of available timber and involves the progressive deforestation of India. The growth of demand in the domestic sector that we forecast will, if nothing is done, rapidly denude increasing areas of India.

We fear that, if there are no immediate steps taken, shortage of firewood will cause grave hardship and lead to much larger demands for kerosene than Indian potential imports are likely to be able to provide. We recommend that immediate and active measures be taken jointly by the Government of India and the State Government to formulate and implement a policy for expanding the growth of quick-growing timber suitable for use as firewood, this will require the assignment to this use of considerable areas of land.

In addition we recommend that measures be taken to produce and popularise the use for domestic purposes of commercial fuels based on indigenous coal supplies.

The Pricing of Energy

A satisfactory national policy for energy requires that all consumers of energy shall use those forms of energy which, having regard to the circumstances of India, can be most economically provided to meet their needs. It is of the essence of a satisfactory energy policy that consumers shall have the right incentives to use the right fuels. We have set out what we believe to be the essentials of an energy pricing policy. We recommend that the various bodies concerned in the making of prices for energy products take full account of the importance of establishing the right incentives for consumers to use the most economic fuels.

If the present pricing policies are not revised, we foresee serious surpluses of unsaleable coking coal by-products and non-coking coal slacks. The disposal of these would cost considerable sums and be a grave waste of valuable national resources. From a national planning point of view these surpluses are available at zero cost. They should be priced at levels which will ensure their use and clear the market. At present the incentives to use them are inadequate.

There are likely to be similar problems in the pricing of oil products, which in this case are affected by taxation policies. We recommend that taxation policies should take account of the possible deficits and surpluses of different types of oil products.

Investment in Energy

We have estimated the probable investment required in energy at different dates down to 1980-81. The ratio of investment in energy to total investment is about that which might be expected on the basis of similar inquiries in European countries.

We have estimated also the proportion of the gross investment which is likely to take the form of imports on the basis of present trends. We think that it will be important that India shall as rapidly as possible reduce the dependence on imported equipment to a minimum, so as to reduce also the necessary foreign expenditures below those that we have estimated. Part of the large dependence on imports appears to result from the desire to progress in respect of installation of types of equipment rather more rapidly than Indian capacity is likely to be able to progress in respect of their manufacture. It will be necessary to hold a balance and to put heavy emphasis on the manufacture in India the types of equipment which at each stage can be produced with a low import content.

Plans for investment in energy need to be based on the best possible estimates of the future requirements for energy. In the case of electricity such estimates are provided both by the recently established Annual Electric Power Survey of India and by such studies as have been made on behalf of our Energy Survey. We have fouud discrepancies in respect of 1970-71 between our own estimates based on the probable requirements of Kwh in different industries in India as a whole and the estimates of the Power Survey. We believe that both the methods of estimation of future requirements are valuable. But we take the view that better short-term estimates extending over two or three years ahead can be provided (as does the Electric Power Survey) by building up detailed local estimates of future connected loads. We take the view that estimates for more distant dates can better be made, and better escape errors of duplication, by making estimates of total output of different industries and the corresponding energy requirements. Each method provides for intermediate dates a valuable check on the other.

The Making Of Energy Policy

We are convinced that it will be desirable to keep constantly under review the trends of energy consumption and to re-formulate policies as circumstances change. We greatly welcome the establishment within the Planning Commission of a unit that will be concerned under one Member of the Commission with energy problems. We recommend that this unit be charged with the responsibility for the collection and organisation of the statistics that are essential to any such work.

We would expect that it will be desirable to repeat at intervals of about five years some such survey as we have undertaken, in order that it may be seen whether circumstances have so changed that a change of policies is required. We hesitate at this stage to recommend that it should be conducted on the same basis as this survey has been. But we would emphasize the advantages that this survey has enjoyed through the close co-operation of representatives of the several Ministries under which energy problems are divided at present and of experts drawn from a number of fields in India and abroad and possessing a wide variety of relevant experience.

In the intervals between such reviews, we suggest that great advantage could be secured by provision of inter-departmental arrangements for regular consultation between the secretaries of the various Ministries concerned with energy problems. We understand that such provision has already been made.

WORKING GROUP FOR THE STUDY ON WASTELANDS INCLUDING SALINE, ALKALI AND WATERLOGGED LANDS AND THEIR RECLAMATION MEASURES, 1963—REPORT

New Delhi, Planning Commission, 1963. VI, 237p., 15 Charts.

Convener : Dr. S.P. Raychaudhuri.
Members : Dr. B.N. Uppal ; Shri R.D. Dhir ; Dr. R.V. Tamhane ; Shri K.P. Sagreiya ; Shri U.S. Madan ;

APPOINTMENT

The Committee on Natural Resources at their meeting held on December 1961, approved a study on Water Logged, Saline and Alkali Lands and Wastelands of India. The Technical Committee on Land set up a Working group on January 3, 1962.

TERMS OF REFERENCE

(i) To collect all the existing information on the occurrence of Saline, Alkali and water logged Lands,

(ii) To examine all the reclamation measures for such lands ; and

(iii) To analyses the data available with a view to suggesting policy measures. The economics of reclamation of such areas by the application of different methods was also to be studied.

CONTENTS

Foreword ; Introduction ; Wasteland in India ; Kans infested Waste-land ; Saline and Alkali Soils, extent, Location, Reclamation Measures Suggested for Prevention of extension of such areas ; Problems of Coastal Saline soils ; Review of the work done in the survey of ground water demarcation of areas and sweet and saline ground water ; Suitable trees, grasses and crops for Saline and Alkali Soils ; The extent of water logged laads, their classifications and rate of change ; Problems of surface drainage ; A review of work done in some States to tackle the problem of water-logging with suggestions for future work ; Suitable trees and grass spices for water-logged areas fish crops suitables for water-logged area and culture in paddy fields ; Review of work on Soil Conservation and reclamation done during First and Second Plan Periods and Schemes of Third Plan; Use of aerial photography in soil mapping and land use classification with particular reference to waste lands including saline and alkali and Waterlogged lands; The economics of reclamation of wastelands; Recommendations; Bibliography; References; Appendices I and II.

RECOMMENDATIONS

General

(1) (a) There are large gaps in our knowledge of land resources. To obtain quick result it is necessary that land surveys using photogrammetric techniques (aerial photographs) should be undertaken, and data on land use, lond improvement, reclamation of water-logged, saline and alkali lands and their productivity should be collected in systematic manner with a view to drawing up future plans.

(b) It is recommended that the Ministry of Food and Agriculture may set up a small working group of 2 or 3 persons for drawing up a practical scheme for resettlement in bigger plots, indicating priorities and phasing the programme taking into consideration the limited available funds. The basis of financing may be Rs. 1000/ par family including supply of water, provision of road, residence, etc. apart from the cost of reclamation of land which may be put at Rs. 150 per acre amounting to Rs. 1050 for reclaming 7 acres of land, the total cost per family being abut Rs. 2000. For smaller plots Rs. 500 per family may be taken as the initial expenditure.

(ii) It is recommended that a Land development sub-Committee may be set up under the Agricultural Production Committee in the States for looking after the land development work.

(iii) In view of rapidily expanding areas under irrigation, it is necessary to establish a suitable central organisation to conduct intensive investigation in the field of irrigation, drainage and anti-waterlogging.

(iv) Co-ordinated studies on land records in different states should be conducted so that they provided a sound basis for agricultural planning. Even today agricultural statistics are not available for about 86 million acres of land, and among those which are in the reporting category, statistics for over 90 million acres are rough estimates.

(v) There is primary need for establishing agency to implement the programme and land development for irrigation to carry out works such as provision of field channels, grading and levelling of land and extension of sound irrigation practices. This should be made the primary responsibility of state Land Development sub-Committee under the Agricultural Production Committee.

2. **Waster lands**: (i) The Ministry of Food andagriculture should take effective steps for early implementation of the recommendations of the wastelands Survey and reclamation Committee and also of the centrally sponsored schemes for the survey of wastelands in block of less than 250 acres, by establishing a cell in the Ministry.

(ii) In respect of reclamation of kans-infested waste lands, enquiry may be made from the state to find out what help they want for such reclamation work and how far the work may be carried out without foreign exchange and subsidy.

(iii) Large tracts of waste'and are found in the riverain belts along the beds of rivers. The reclamation of such areas should be assigned high priority. It is recommended that comprehensive schemes should be prepared fore reclaming these tracts which should include the construction of roads provision of electricity for pumping water for irrigation and grant of loans to cultivators for purchasing tractors for cultivation and pumping sets.

It was agreed that the programme of work may be co-ordinated with the scheme of reclamation in big plots which will be drawn up by the working group of the Ministry of Food and Agriculture proposed under Recommendation.

(iv) There should be balanced use of wastelands. Definite areas of waste land should be reserved for the production of fire-wood and fodder according to land capability classes.

(v) Agricultural wastelands in the country are mostly held by small owners who are not in a position to meet the cost of their reclamation. Such wastelands total to a considerable area. The reclamation of such was te'ands may be subsidised by Government who should bear a larger proportion of the reclamation cost then at present.

(vi) Before allotting wastelands for cultivation, these lands should be reclaimed by the State Government and apporpriate soil and water conservation measures carried out consistent with their land capabilities. The Government should take adequate steps to ensure that appropriate follow on practices are adopted by the allottees.

3. **Saline and alkali lands**: For fundamental work on salnie and alkali soils, three regional salinity laboratories are to be set up under the Third Plan and it is recommended that these laboratories should be established without any delay. One of these laboratories should be established in the existing agricultural institutes.

For the successful reclamation of saline and alkali lands, cooperation between various professional groups including agricultural chemists, irrigation engineers and drainage specialists is essential and should be ensured.

Sufficient information is available on the methods of reclaming saline, saline alkali and alkali lands. What is now needed is to demarcate these areas in each state based on their soil characteristics. For this purpose it is necessary to print large sized maps of the districts showing the location of saline and saline alkali lands of different categories. Detailed information regarding such lands in blocks of 5 acres or more, should also be obtained for the different tehsils in the district, and for this purpose survey may be conducted.

The reclamation of saline alkali soils on a national basis has already been recommended by the Crops and Soils Wing of the Board of Agriculture and Animal Husbandary in India during its meeting in similar held in 1956. This recommendation should be given high priority under the Fourth Five-Year Plan programme. The expenditure on this account can be met partly from the povision made for the reclamation of saline and alkali and anti-soil erosion by the Ministry of Food and Agriculture and partly from the amount carmarked by the Ministry of Irrigation and Power for flood control drainage and anti-water logging where salinity is accompanied by water-logging.

Detailed soil survey of the saline and alkali lands should be carried out before undertaking reclamation measures.

For the reclamation of saline-alkali soils, the eultivation of dhaincha (sesbania aculeata) and the addition of fertilisers and manners and gypsum to the soil are very useful. Dhaincha seed should be supplied free of cost, and gypsum and fertilisers at concessional rates for reclamation.

The growing of salt-tolerant bushes and trees, such as kikar (Acacia arabica), and (prosopia, juliflora) and frash (Tamarix articulata) etc. is very helpful in the amelioration of Kallar-affected soils. It is recommended that these plants should be extensively grown on lands which are lying waste.

Intensive studies are needed on the improvement of black soils in Andhra Pradesh which have been rendered unfit for cultivation of virginia tobacco due to the development of salinity.

There is evidence that saline water containing small amounts of plant unitients like nitrate and potash can be used for raising successful crops. This suggests that with the more intensive use of fertilisers and mannures it may be possible to use saline water for irrigation in marginal lands.

Since irrigation is the cause as well as the cure of salinity and alkalinity in soils has been carried out in countries where the average yield per acre is much higher than that in India. Accordingly it is recommended that similar studies should be conducted in India for the purpose of establishing, suitable limits for Indian conditions.

It is generally recognised that agroclimatic conditions drainage and physical and chemical characteristics of the soil determine the suitablity of a method of soil reclamation. Detailed investigations should be conducted to ascertain as to which of the methods in vogue are economically feasible.

(4) (i) Despite the extension of canal irrigation, ground water is an important source of irrigation supply.

It is recommended that a reconnaissance survey of ground water resource should be carried out, particularly in the Punjab, Delhi, Uttar Pardesh, Rajasthan, Madhya Pradesh, Gujarat and Maharashtra,-pherever good quality of ground water is found in sufficient quantities as supplement to irrigation from canals. This will not only ensure better utilisation of natural resources, but will also help in mitigating the menance of water-logging.

(ii) It is desirable that the ground water Division of the Geological Survey of India, should work in close collaboration with the Agriculture and Irrigation Departments of the different states and plan its activities in consultation with these Departments.

(iii) The system of analysis of irrigation water and the interpretation of results as recommended by the technical Committee on quality of water set up by the Central Water and Power Commission, should be followed all over the country, so that the results are comparable.

The use of tube-well water for irrigation should be made economical by (i) charging the water on volumetric basis, and (ii) making irrigation water charges for both canal and tube-wells uniform. It is understood that the Maharashtra State is doing some work in this direction. A small group representing the Ministry of irrigation and power and the Ministry of Food and Agriculture may visit the Maharashtra State to see what has been done in that State and what could be done for other State in the light of the experience gained in Maharashtra State.

(iv) The ground water quality should be considered an integral part of soil survey and the suitability of water for irrigation should be determined with respect to the soil and crops.

(v) In some States the changes in the ground water table of the soil are being investigated by the Irrigation Departments. Similar studies should be made in other states.

Water-logging

The drainage of water-logged lands should be planned on the watershed basis.

Perennial canal irrigation should be avoided in areas where the waver a table is already high or tending to rise and in such areas recourse may be had to a system of canal cloures.

Encouragement and subside should be given to cultivators for using water from tubwells or open wells within the ayacut of an irrigation system. This would help to control the rise of the subsoil water table in the area. A certain percentage of the irrigated tract depending on the type of soil, sub-soil water level etc. should be reserved exclusively for lift irrigation.

Use of shallow tubewells for depressing the subsoil water table as an anti-waterlogging measure should be given extensive field trials.

The scope of vertical drainage to recharge drier strata of the underground for reclamation of water-logged areas should be investigated.

In the state in which there are sizeable water-logged areas the Indian Council of agricultural research in collaboration with State Government concerned may take up research on crops suitable for such areas.

Feasibility of planting deep rooted trees having high water consumption in areas where the water table shows a raising tendency requires to be studied as it might be helpful in averting the rise of the water table.

Reclamation of swamps and water-logged areas by drainage should be possible in many tracts. But a careful survey should be made as some of these areas should be better developed for fish culture or for recreation and preservation of wild life.

Drainage : Drainage problems have received inadequate attention in the past. The subject requires serious consideration from the investigation and also from development point of view. Studies should be undertaken for assessing drainage requirements, optimum depth and spacing of drainage and economic of drainage system.

Intensive surveys should be initiated throughout the country jointly by experts in flood control, transport engineers, agriculturists and soil scientists, to locate areas which are subject to drainage congestion. These investigation should preferably be carried out in a self-contained "doab" and a Master Plan clearly demarcating the different regions should be prepared. These programmes should contain clear cut programme of construction priorities, and indicated the economic benefits of draining to different tracts. Such a scientifically designed plan will indicate the best use for which each tract is naturally suited-whether it can advantageously-be utilised for agriculture pasture, forestry. colonisation, etc.

While surveys and investigations are in progress and before actual implementation of the Master Plan of the "doab" is taken up, information should be widely diseminated regarding the cultivation of crops by way of field experiments on an extensive scale. All the available knowledge in respect of canal lining, including the experience of the Nagal Power Channel, the Rajasthan Canal, etc. should be collected and made available for use in future works.

The efficacy of providing sub-surface drainage should be investigated and field trials conducted to assess the economic feasibility of the measure. Also experiments to standardise the material, size and shape of the sub-surface drain should be undertaken.

Field demarcation (Through the Community Development Organisation) should be laid down throughout the country to educate the public in general and the farmers in particular, on the importance of drainage and dangers of the extravagant use of irrigation water.

The possibility of making it obligatory for village panchayats to keep water courses in proper shape and also, if possible, to have them lined, needs to be carefully investigated.

There should be common land for providing natural drainage along roads, railway and canals, including chos. Where consolidation of holdings has not taken place, common lands must be set apart for natural waters; where consolidation of holdings has already been done, the land along the sides of the natural drains should be acquired and afforested.

Work on the execution of drainage projects which are technically sound and economically feasible should be taken up forth with.

The borrow pits along highways, railways and canals should be connected and properly shaped so as to facilitate the movement of storm water.

The Ministry of Food and Agriculture may set up a technical group representing the Ministry of food and Agriculture, Ministry of Irrigation and power and the Planning Commission which will scrutinise these recommendations and classifiy them into two categories viz. (i) which recommendations can be implemented in the Third Plan without nay foreign exchange and extra allotment of funds, and (ii) which recommendations may be taken up during the Fourth Plan. After this scrutiny has been made the report with modifications made at this meeting along with suitable convering letter will be issued to the States by the secretary, Ministry of Food and Agriculture (Department of Agriculture).

POWERLOOM ENQUIRY COMMITTEE, 1963—REPORT

Delhi, Manager of Publication 1964. 208p.

Chairman : Shri Asoka Mehta

Members : Shri A.R. Bhat ; Shri G.K. Devarajula Naidu ; Nawab Aizaz Rasool ; Dr. D K. Malhotra ; Shri M. Somappa.

Member Secretary : Shri K.R. Aravamuthan

APPOINTMENT

The Powerloom Enquiry Committee was Constituted under the Ministry of Commerce and Industry vide their Resolution No. 10 (2) TEX (C)/62 dated 8-1-1963.

TERMS OF REFERENCE

(i) To examine the structure and growth of the powerloom industry with special reference to the types, holdings, ownership, appliances, supply of raw material, sorts of fabrics produced, processing of fabrics marketing, financing and other factors relating thereto ;

(ii) To examine the remunerativeness of the powerloom industry taking into account the costs of production and efficiency of working and the conditions of workers,

(iii) To consider the relative role to be played by the powerloom industry *vis-a-vis* that of the handloom and mill industry and to recommend targets of production,

(iv) To account for the phenomenal growth of unauthorised powerlooms in the post and devise means to prevent future unauthorised expansion ;

(v) To examine the desirability and scope for the conversion of handloom cooperatives into powerloom cooperatives, and

(vi) To make suggestions for the establishment of the powerloom industry on a stable footing within the field of operation which should be allotted to it.

CONTENTS

Introduction ; General Review of the Textile Industry ; Government Policy on Powerlooms ; Raw Material for Cotton Powerlooms ; Processing, Finance and Marketing ; Conversion Scheme of Handlooms to Powerlooms ; Economics of Working of Cotton Powerlooms ; Excise Duty on Cotton Textile Industry ; Art Silk and Silk Powerlooms ; Woolen Industry ; Supply of Looms and Accessories ; Targets of Production ; Powerlooms in a Socio-economic Perspective ; Future Role of Powerlooms (Note of Dissent and Explanation by Shri A.R. Bhat) ; Summary of Conclusions and Recommendations ; Annexure I to VII.

RECOMMENDATIONS

The pattern of yarn consumption may be revised in round figures to 68% by handlooms, 22% by powerloms and 10% by hosiery, rope making, etc,

We consider that both these sectors (handlooms and powerlooms) should draw their yarn supplies from a common pool. A compartmentalisation would unduly restrict flexibility in supplies and manufacture. In the future set-up, as envisaged by us, the replacement of handlooms by powerlooms will assume considerable importance and it would not be proper, therefore, to earmark spinning mills exclusively for either the handlooms or the powerlooms.

Conclusion and Recommendations

The handloom industry is the oldest industry in the country. From the point of view of its sizes and the number of persons depending on it, the industry ranks only next to agriculture.

The organisation of the weavers on co-operative basis formed the fulcrum in the implementation of the different developmental schemes for the handloom industry.

The organisation of weavers in the co-operative fold construction of housing colonies to facilitate working of handlooms in the weaver's own cottages and other various measures of assistance were devised so as to reserve this household and cottage character and develop the industry to give the weavers better earnings.

The various measures implemented by the government of India for developing the handloom industry had no doubt the effect of stabilising the industry and instilling in the minds of weavers a sense of confidence.

The bringing in of a large number of weavers in the cooperative fold with its attendent element of loyalty to the institution was the main factor which contributed to the organisational stability to such an extent that quite apart from other aspects, the tendency has been for the handloom weavers to expect establishment of co-operative spinning mills exclusively for their benefit for the supply of yarn of the desired counts.

The total capital employed in the handloom sector

ôn cotton yarn may be assessed at Rs. 100 crores.

The inducements for the establishment and development of poerlooms till 1955 were of the normal kind which operated in many small industries. There is no doubt that the powerloom had, by then come to occupy a place though not very significant one in the textile industry consisting of the textile mill sector on the one. hand and the large multitude of handlooms on the other.

It will be correct to state that the order of growth has been chronologically the handlooms, textile mills and powerlooms, the increase in and the geographical spread of supply of electric power together with the availability of looms discarded from the mills provided a strong base for the growth of powerloom in certain centres. The facility to improve one's earnings by switching over from handlooms to power-operated looms involving only a relatively small capital investment naturally induced a number of better placed handloom weavers to set up powerlooms.

The part played by the private entrepreneurs the mill workers thrown out of job having the necessary technical know-how the availability of second hand-powerlooms on account of mill closures and replacements of looms by mills the availability of electric power covering wider areas, a sense of ownership of a better. Cheaper quicker and easier method of weaving by employing power the local initiative and encouragement for setting up of powerlooms instilling a sense of gradual but increasing participation in the industrial development in the areas and above all the urge of the handloom weavers to employ power to better their standard of living and for lessening the strain of work-together with the scope provided by the increasing demand for cloth in the country on the pegging of loomage in the mills, all these contributed to the steady growth of powerlooms in the different parts of the country till it reached a total strength of about 27,000 by 1956.

The policy of the Government to peg the weaving capacity of the textile mills and the deliberate policy of not allowing expansion in the powerloom side also except to the extent provided for in the second five year Plan for replacement of handlooms by powerlooms in the co-operative fold automatically put a seal on both expansion and addition to the large powerloom factories. This did not however quell the increasing urge on the part of the weavers in the country to switch over to power-operation to earn more.

The growth of powerlooms in the recent years has been very rapid and phenomenal Induced by certain extraneous factors of which excise levy formed the most attractive even outsiders stepped into the field solely to get the benefits of excise exemption.

A large number of powerloom were thus set up in an unauthorised manner. A number of intermediaries and even textile mills induced the handloom weavers as also others not in the weaving profession to set up powerlooms in large numbers. They provided all the required financial and other measures of assistance as a purely business proposition. Records to scrapped looms from mills by itself could not meet this upsurge in demand and this in turn, encouraged local technical talent and skill to set up small workshops for fabrication on assembling of looms adopting ingenous methods and improvisations. Almost the entire growth of powerlooms in the recent years being in contravention of law, the ancillary activity of fabrication, repairs, assembling of looms etc. in small workshops with local talent and skill also necessarily assumed the form of unauthorished growth. There is no doubt however that the owners of the looms who acquired and installed them by straight or surreptitious means were prompted to do so in the hope of using them for a living. The social, economic employment and other factors are very relevant in the consideration of the problem of unauthorised growth of powerlooms.

Broadly, the structure of the powerloom sector as it exists now should be considered as consisting predominantly of small units of four looms and less with a bare 5 per cent accounted for by large units coming under the Industries (development and Regulation) Act, 1951 and another 5 per cent in the mid segment of five looms and above not coming under this act.

In regard to the small units of four looms and below master weavers, intermediaries and in some cases, even textile mills are reported to have set up powerlooms on benami basis. The extent of such fictitious ownership is difficult to measure but from what the Committee could gather from knowledgeable sources, it may be put at not more than 25 per cent.

The picture that emerges from a study of the various; phases of the textile industry is one of virtual stagnation of the mill weaving capacity and activities accompanied by a marked expansion and intensification in the activities of the decentralised sector of the textile industry omprising powerlooms and hand looms. In this intensification of activities of the decentralised sector, the spinning section of the textile mill industry has no doubt played significant part.

It was represented to us that while government had been solicitous in regarding regularising the unauthorised powerlooms persons who had previously applied to the textile commissioner for setting up powerlooms and as law abiding citizen did not instal powerlooms without permission were not given the opportunity to instal looms in preference to those who had installed the looms in contravention of law.

The executive instructions for scrapping of looms and rendering them unsuitable did not have the desired effect either because the dismantlement of scrapping was not in all cases done with a scrupulous adherence, to the instructions or because of the fact that the indigenous technical skill and practical workmanship of the artisan were so excellent that it was not beyond their capacity to make good the deficiencies in the looms dismantled.

Whenever powerlooms have come up almost the entire community in those areas, turned the powerlooms for livelihood and therefore, there have been no large scale complaints.

We are convinced that as a practical proposition it would be difficult if not impossible to depend purely on power connections either to assess the number of powerlooms or restrict their growth.

The all India policy relating to control or regulation of powerlooms did not have that much effective and practical follow-up and support which it should have had from the State Governments concerned.

Of the present supply of yarn to the internal market of about 316 million kgs. per year almost fortyfive per cent is supplied by composite mills and fifty-five per cent by spinning mills in the country.

The assumption that 90 per cent of the total yarn availability as representing the consumption by the handloom and powerlooms taken together would in our opinion still hold good.

On the existing conditions, the pattern of yarn consumption may be revised in round figures to 68 % by handlooms, 22% by poerlooms and 10% by hosiery rope making etc. The average count of yarn spun by spinning mills was 27.5 in 1959 and this is reported to have gone up to 29.4 in 1962 while in the case of composite mills, the corresponding increase during the same period is reported to be from 24.3 to 25.1.

We consider that both these sectors (handlooms and powerlooms), should draw their yarn supplies from a common pool. A compartmentalisation would unduly restrict flexibility in supplies and manufacture. In the future set-up as envisaged by us. The replacement of handlooms by powerlooms will assume considerable importance and it would not be proper, therefore, to earmark spinning mills exclusively for either the handlooms or the powerlooms.

We recommend that irrespective of any other regulations there should be a strict control exercised on the quality of yarn made available by the textile mill indusry for handlooms and powerlooms and suitable quality standards fixed forward and weft yarn with appropriate price for each.

It is apparent that under the existing level of availability of yarn the unauthorised powerlooms which have come up in the recent years, cannot work to their full capacity.

As Indian cotton would still be largely of short and medium staples only there is no doubt that almost together additional production of cloth which could be envisaged for the next two or three plan periods, should be of coarse and medium cotegories only. Therefore, a need both from the short and long term point of view to impress in the textile mill industry as also the powerlooms and handlooms to adjust their pattern of production with greater emphasis on the manufacture of medium varieties of cloth.

It is desirable that powerloom owners should be enabled to market their cloth direct so as to derive the full benefit arising from the sale of processed cloth. Processing factories should therefore, be established in the different centres in the country. These processing establishments may preferably be on co-operative lines but we do not rule out such facilities being provided by private entrepreneurs.

It is clear that the existing set up of processing establishment in the country is not aligned with the geographical distribution of powerlooms. It was also explained that there was an overall shortage in the facilities available for appropriate processing of powerloom cloth.

We recommend that the processing capacity in the textile mills should in future be allowed to be expanded purely on the basis of the textile mill sector's own requirements. In addition in a period of three years on a phased programme the present permission to mills to process outside cloth may be discontinued.

We consider that the spread of electricity to wider areas would inevitably lead to the substitution of manual processes by mechanised processes and this evolution has got to be recognised. We have therefore provided for mechanised pre-weaving facilities being organised and integrated with the set up of the powerlooms in different centres.

We recommend that the common service facilities should be capable of being utilised by handlooms and powerlooms both within and outside the co-operative fold. Wherever possible, such facilities should also be utilised by the art silk weaving sector.

The total investment required for one powerloom with the proportionate investment on the preparatory processes etc. and for working capital would be about Rs. 8,700 powerlooms spread over the next 10 to 12 years at current prices would involve an investment of Rs. 21 crores for looms only and a similar amount would be needed for ancillary preparatory and processing facilities. The aggregate estimate for rehabilitation of the cotton powerloom industry spread over the next 10 to 12 years may therefore be place at about Rs. 40 to 42 crores.

Our enquiries have revealed that almost the entire capital for the purchase of looms has been found by the loom owners themselves and in many cases by selling jewellery or morgaging property, etc. In a number of cases the more prosperous handloom weavers have been able to find finance from their own resources. In the case of benami ownership, intermediaries and even textile mills are reported to have financed the setting up of looms. For obtaining finance for working capital generally the powerloom weavers are found to be virtually in the grip of cloth merchants and moneylenders.

We would lay considerable emphasis on the importance of adequate working finance for the proper functioning of the powerloom industry in the country. In the light of the important role which the decentralised sector will have to assume in supplying the clothing needs of the country in future all efforts should be made to ensure that the powerlooms obtain necessary finance at fair rates of interest. The State Finance Corporations, Government loans under the State Aid to Industries Act and Commercial Banks particularly the State Bank of India may have to step in a big way to fill the gap. The resources of these financing institutions may have to be adequately augmented in order to make them take up these responsibilities.

The growth of the powerlooms in the recent past having been haphazared and almost wholly in contravention of law, there has not been any regulated development in so far as marketing activity is concerned.

The vicissitudes in the textile mill cloth market have their immediate reactions on the powerloom cloth as the textile mill cloth rules market. The trade representative explained to us that other factors remaining the same, there is a vis-a-vis the mill cloth of the same variety and answering the same quantity and description. It was stated that as compared with the mill cloth of identical quality and description powerloom cloth would fetch a price 10 to 12 per cent less in the market.

We recommend the formation of co-operative marketing institutions for the powerlooms in the different centres.

The scheme sanctioned during the Second plan period for the installation of powerlooms in the handloom co-operative fold did not meet with full success not because the weavers did not take to the scheme with enthusiasm but mainly because of insufficient financial assistance provided for working capital imposition of condition for allowing the powerlooms in the handloom co-operatives in rural areas with population less than 30,000 absence of simultaneous arrangement for providing pre-weaving facilities and post-weaving finishing arrangements and absence of arrangement to ensure that in the allocation of looms in the co-operatives the benefits arising the reform did really get distributed among all the members of the co-operatives. It is clear that the efficient working of the powerlooms does not depend merely on the powerlooms as such but on the ready availability of facilities for preparatory and finishing process etc. which cannot be made available in all cases in rural areas. The gravitation of the looms to places near about the cities obviously followed the natural course in the prevailing circumstances.

As the apprehensions of weavers and State Governments were being overcome and the initial process of implementation of the scheme was gathering momentum in some of the States, the scheme was discontinued. Thus even in those States where the potentiality for the conversion of handlooms into powerlooms was strong the conversion scheme was abruptly terminated and as a result a very useful measure of helping the lot of the handloom weavers was denied to them, We recommend the revival of the scheme to benefit the handloom weavers in those societies which are located in the vicinity of main cities and towns where the required facilities are available.

Powerlooms as such play at present only a complementery role to the textile mills in the matter of supply of cloth, although powerloom products have to compete with the mill products in the cloth market.

The handicap suffered by powerlooms in the matter of yarn prices as compared with the mills is between 21 and 28 per cent. This was the extent of handicap at the time of the costing of the units in the middle of 1963.

The committee has been informed that in some centres weavers attempt to increase the yardage production by reducing picks despite deterioration in quality as larger yardage per loom shift in the case of looms subject to the compounded system of excise levy means less incidence of excise levy per yard. This has been admitted as an unhealthy practice.

Taking an over picture in the country as a whole the average shift working of the powerlooms could be assumed at 1-5 per day of 8 hours per shift.

Powerloom establishments in their working fall under four broad classifications :—

(1) Owner operated units mostly single looms.

(2) Units operated both by owners and hired labour.

(5) Operated exclusively by hired labour.

(4) Units rented out on monthly payment basis.

The first two categories are generally owned by traditional weavers who have switched over from handloom to powerlooms as also weavers coming out from textile mills who had started their own weaving establishments. Hired labour is employed in these establishments wherever family members are not available to work additional shifts. The working of the first two categories is largely household and domestic in character employing up to four looms where the return on capital is not distinguishable from the return on effort put in. The third and fourth categories have sprung up as purely commercial enterprises and function as such although in a number of cases they are shown as small units with independent existence and and ownership. The excise disparities have contributed to their growth inducing both middlemen and financiers to enter the field purely in expectation of higher return on investment available in their working. This category also includes the big sized weaving factories mostly owned as partnership or private or public limited companies formed as a medium or large scale industrial enterprise a number of years ago when the powerlooms were not within the excise fold.

The earning of a powerloom weaver owner or a paid weaver is Rs. 100 per month in several of the principal centres accounting for about two-thirds of the total number of powerlooms. In other centres accounting for one-third of the total number of powerlooms it varies from Rs. 50 to 90 per month. The weighted average earning for the total number of powerlooms for which data have been collected comes to Rs. 86.50 per month. The gross return to the owner may be around Rs. 75 per month.

In certain centres representations were made to us that even the powerloom sector would like to instal automatic looms. We do not, however, visualise that in the present context with the powerloom establishments working with old type and discarded looms the transformation to the adoption of automatic looms could take place in any foreseable period.

Overall the "wage" element in the cost of production in the powerloom may be assumed at round about 50 per cent of the cost in the mills even allowing for the lower productivity on the powerlooms. The element of power and fuel in the total cost of production in the powerlooms is more or less the same as in the mills. The repair cost in powerlooms in much less than in the textile mills. There is not much of a difference between the mills and the powerlooms in regard to depreciation. The expenditure on sundry expenses and overheads in powerloom establishments is almost 400 to 500 per cent of that in mills. It has been explained to us that the interest charges incured by the powerloom establishments are heavy which is one of the factors for the high incidence of overheads in the powerloom sector.

Unlike the textile mill industry powerlooms being largely decentralised quite a number of factors come into play pushing or reducing the cost from unit. This makes it difficult to determine a centralised pattern which could be applied uniformly to the powerloom establishments according to the different size groups. The cost study, however, has shown certain indicators which will hold good only for an overall assessment and will not be suitable for individual application. Taking together the elements of cost excluding "wages" in the manufacturing charges according to the above cost data the net handicap suffered by the powerlooms vis-a-vis the mills are about 25 per cent in the manufacturing charges excluding "wages" and an advantage of 50 per cent in "wages". The net handicap suffered by the powerlooms at the production end will be 8 per cent vis-a-vis the mills.

It has been brought to our notice that several mills having modernised processing equipment take over powerloom cloth and after processing and stamping their own brand names are able to market the same fabrics at prices at which their own products are sold. This points to the need for the powerloom establishments to organise the modernised processing facilities and also modernised methods of publicity and sales so that the advantages which are now being derived by the mills could also be obtained by the powerlooms.

From what we could gather, the marketing disability for powerloom cloth including the consumer's bias may be assumed at about 10 to 12 per cent vis-a-vis the mills.

As a rough guide we may take the overall handicap suffered by the powerlooms at about 18 per cen vis-a-vis the mills.

We are inclined to agree with the technical opinion placed before us that the economic size in the medium range of powerloom establishments should be between 24 and 36 looms.

On balance of consideration, it would be in the interest of the bigger powerlooms units to get themselves either fragmented or converted into regular composite textile mills.

The remunerativeness of the working of small powerloom establishments depends on factors like location and varieties of cloth produced.

The big sized units are finding it difficult to continue working in view of the high rates of excise levy.

The committee does not consider it proper that the excise authorities after deliberately allowing the excise concession, should have taken indirect steps to penalise fragmentation by prescribing certain higher rates of excise duty in such cases.

We consider that prima facie the measure of protection given to the small powerloom units by way of exemption from excise levy should be such as to enable them to market their goods at competitive rates and obtain a reasonable margin as means of livelihood. The entire objective would get defeated if outsiders entered the field and appropriated the benefits of such concessions.

It appears that to certain extent instead of powerlooms establishing themselves on their own and then going in for financial and other assistance, textile mills, intermediareis and other financiers had, for their own advantage set up small powerloom units in an unauthorised manner merely with a view to take advantage of the fiscal concessions involved. The growth of the powerloom sector in this manner cannot be considered as in any way normal or healthy. While we appreciate the normal role which the trade should play in the marketing of the powerloom cloth in the country we do not consider that a fortuitous benefit should accrue to a class of intermediaries by whatever name they are called, particularly where it is a question of Government sacrificing revenues, nor would it is be in the long term interests of the powerloom owners to reduce themselves to the position of wage earners. From the evidence available to the committee it is clear that the small powerloom owner weavers are very much in the grip of these financiers and intermediaries and are being exploited and put to hardship.

The present definition of "independent processor" adversely affects those powerloom units which have their own processing equipment as excise duty is charged at full rates as for composite mills for fabrics processed by them. This has led to the closure of some powerloom working in these units. We recommend that this should be remedied and these factories treated as independent processors. On the same analogy we also recommend that independent sizing factories which have been given the concession of paying 80 per cent of the surcharge on sizing of yarn as applicable to mills may be allowed the concession even if they work powerlooms and/or have other yarn processing operations.

We have come to the conclusion that the system of charging excise duty at different rates or different sizes of powerloom units and concessions allowed for small units had been a major factor in causing an unhealthy and undesirable distortion in the structure of the powerloom sector in the country.

We recommanded that :

(1) The existing exemption for powerloom establishments of 4 looms and below as also the levy on the larger powerloom establishments whether at compounded rates or otherwise may be discontinued and the incidence shifted as a high duty at the two key points-yarn and processing where excise surveillance will be more effective.

(2) Yarn in hank form upto and including 40s count should bear no duty. This exemption is intended to assist the handlooms weavers. Handlooms are already enjoying this concession Yarn of and above 40s supplied in hank form should continue to enjoy concessional rates as at present. Cone yarn and yarn in all forms other than hanks of all counts should be subjected to excise levy.

A higher rate of duty on yarn delivered on sized beams, whether sized by the composite mills or independent sizing factories may be levied. This may be in the form of a surcharge over the duty on cone yarn. It should be easy and necessary to bring mechanised sizing factories under excise control.

The existing system of charging processing duty on powerloom and handloom cloth may be continued. The rates may be increased suitably taking into account—

(a) The complete abolition of excise duty either on compounded rates or on other basis for the powerloom establishments, and.

(b) The need for rationalising the excise rates so that different types of processing might bear different rates of duty, the rates themselves being higher for more sophisticated processing.

With the above changes the excise pattern on grey mill made cloth may be revised to provide for the following :

(1) An increase in the excise levy on yarn to equate with the increased levy on yarn, which goes to the decentralised sector.

(2) A suitable reduction in the basic duty on grey cloth the additional excise duty in lieu of sales tax being continued.

(3) Increase in the excise duty on different types of processing to provide for progressively increased rates for more reined processes after taking into account the reduction in the basic duty for grey cloth.

The excise duty on processing by the independent processors may also be correspondingly increased for the different types of processing with due provision for exempting in initial quantity and for charging reduced rates of excise for powerlooms and handlooms.

It is necessary that in relation to the future development of the industry the role of excise levy should be clearly thought out. In the lesson of the past there is a sufficiently good basis for deciding the approach in regard to excise levy for the future. One of the lessons is that the rate and pattern of growth of the industry should not be left to be determined by the vagaries of excise levy but that on the other hand, the excise policy itself should be so shaped as to subserve the objectives laid down in regard to the growth of the industry. There are two decisions implied in this, Firstly in so far as levy as instrument for raising revenue for government it should be employed like any other taxation measure with due reference to paying capacity and the differentials as between different sections of the industry should be so framed that the relative positions and internal structures of the sections are not disturbed. Secondly, in so far as the excise levy has to be employed as a means for realising certain developmental objectives it should be so adjusted that it helps in achieving them. The Committee cannot at this stage go beyond stating the approach in these broad terms but it would recommend that this matter should be gone into by Government in relation to the recommendations we have made elsewhere in this Report in regard to the production targets and pattern of growth of the powerloom industry.

We do not consider that in the near future, raw material supply for art-silk looms could be made fully sufficient as scarity conditions have themselves generated the growth of the powerlooms.

The existing policy of feeding the art-silk industry by the import of yarn under the Export Promotion Scheme has given a spur to the growth of the powerlooms. Our estimate of the current total of art-silk cloth production on the powerlooms is 630 to 650 million yards and the handloom production about 70 million yards.

We would place the estimate for rehabilitation and modernisation of the art-silk industry in its present size at about Rs. 40 crores. The pace of rehabilitation could be spread over to two plan periods covering ten years.

The export incentive scheme has served to give increasing stimulus to the production of art-silk fabrics and to their exports.

The ribbon manufacturing powerloom industry in the country is a compact organised and generally prosperous industry and the Committee considers that there is good scope for expansion subject to adequate supply of raw material.

The Committee considers that it would be a good step to segregate the ribbon, tapes, braiding, labels and other similar powerlooms and allow free expansion of the industry as this sector is entirely distinct from cloth powerlooms.

The Committee does not consider that any conversion of these ribbon looms to cloth looms should be allowed.

The committee suggests that purely with a view to watching the development of the tape, ribbon, lace newar and similar powerlooms and assisting the industry whenever necessary it would be advisable to have free registration of these looms and ensure at the same time that they are nursed properly and given all the required help. The industry should be allowed to develop and seek its own level, government authorities only coming in for registration without compulsion or restriction.

In the art-silk weaving sector the analysis made by our study teams discloses that on an average a weaver gets Rs. 110 to Rs. 120 per mensem for working on powerlooms while the earning of an owner is about Rs. 50 per loom for two loom establishments increasing to 70 per loom for four looms and even Rs. 125 per loom in larger units.

The committee argees with the suggestion that co-operative marketing facilities might be set up for marketing the production of art-silk weavers.

We do not consider that there is any advantage in developing the art-silk industry on a vertical basis by allowing the rayon spinners to set up their own looms.

A unit of four powerlooms may be considered as a fairly average sized unit to be worked by a weaver's family.

The picture of the art-silk weaving industry in future would be a cluster of art-silk powerlooms with technical and other services, finance marketing preparatory and postweaving processes, preferably established on co-operative lines.

The working capital requirement for art-silk powerlooms may be placed at Rs. 4,000 to Rs. 5,000 per loom. We recommend that facilities for providing finance should be extended by the State Finance Corporations. Loans should also be made available under the State Aid to Industries Act. Alternative sources of financing should be commercial banks.

The investment in the art-silk powerlooms sector is about Rs. 8 crores on looms. Including preparatory and processing facilities the total capital investment may be estimated at about Rs. 16 to 17 crores.

We consider that it should be possible to bring as many varieties as possible of art-silk cloth under the scheme of standardisation so that both in the matter of export and in internal consumptions these standards could serve to create confidence in the consumers about quality and durability. This would also emphasise the need for a machinery to ascertain the changes in the fashions and tastes of consumers so as to tune production to the changing tastes.

We do not agree with the view that the cotton textile mills should be debarred from using staple fibre and other man-made fibre yarn.

The woollen powerloom industry cannot be considered as an owner-operated industry. Almost the entire weaving labour is hired and the owner of the establishment attends generally to the managerial and sales activities. This is a peculiar feature of this sector which distinguishes it from the cotton and art-silk powerloom sectors.

It was suggested that in the future expansion of the worsted spinning industry due consideration should be given to the needs of the small woollen powerloom establishments by allowing them to set up their own spinning mills, preferably on co-operative lines. We agree with the suggestion.

The practice of composite or spinning woollen mills taking over the capacity in the small powerloom sector should both be permitted.

It would be to the advantage of the woollen powerloom industry if efforts were made to set up co-operative processing factories.

The studies of our team have shown that the profit per loom per shift per month varied from Rs. 107 to

Rs. 357 depending on the types of fabrics produced and the continuity of working. The monthly earning of a weaver was assessed at Rs. 100 to Rs. 150.

Our estimate of the total requirement of looms every year till the end of the Fourth Plan would work out to an average of about 32,000. A phased programme for increasing the indigenous production of looms has to be drawn up linking it with the phased programme indicated for the installation of powerlooms in the handloom sector.

We do not see the need for placing restrictions on new entrants to the field of manufacture of powerlooms.

We consider that in order to provide technical guidance to the small scale factories in the matter of designing and fabrication of looms, suitable technical service guidance or assistance unit will be necessary. In this respect the Textile Research Association as also the Small Scale Service Institute in the different parts of the country could play a very useful part. We have proposed that the entire responsibility for the development of the decentralised sector of handloom and powerlooms should be vested in the All India Handloom Board as reconstituted into a statutory, in the matter of ensuring that the necessary facilities are brought into existence in the different parts of the country for the supply of looms and loom parts to the decentralised sector.

Research in the matter of improving weaving techniques should be such as to fit in with the small scale nature of operation of the powerlooms and should not be focussed only on the application of modern automatic techniques which are conducive to centralised and mass production.

The estimate of powerloom cloth production currently lies between 1,000 and 1,100 million yards. This would mean that the balance of 2,050 to 2,150 million yards is accounted for as the production by handloom sector.

Overall we may not visualise the planned target production of yarn being halted by shortage of spinning capacity in the country, as with the abundant licensing of additional spindleage even a part materialisation would go to fulfil the requirement.

Cloth production at the end of the current Plan may turn out to be only about 8,500 to 8,600 million yards, which would mean that during the remaining period of the plan the production should be stepped up by about 500 to 600 million yards. The mill cloth production might go up to 5,000 to 5,100 million yards from the current level of 4, 850 million yards. There will still be gap of 250 to 350 million yards which should be made up by stepping up the production of the decentralised sector.

While we do not discount the possibility of stepping up production to some extent by the handloom industry as it exists today, any large scale agumentation of production could be achieved only by a regulated transition of handlooms to powerlooms.

We recommend as an immediate measures that a policy announcement should be made that while every assistance would be given to set up additional looms that have agreed to both in the composite mills and in the spinning mills no further expansion in loomage in the mill sector is contemplated till the end of the Fourth Plan period.

We consider that the handlooms sector should be enabled to step up its production by the process of installation of powerlooms and accordingly recommend the installation of 10,000 powerlooms in the handloom sector being started immediately and the looms brought into production as far as possible during the remaining period of the current Plan on a priority basis.

We consider that the cotton production in the country may reach a level of a little over 70 lakh bales only by the end of the Fourth Plan under normal conditions. The total cloth production at the end of the Fourth Plan period would be 10,100 million yards worked out on the basis of availability of cotton. This figure might go up if larger imports are allowed. We recommend that the entire additional cloth production in the Fourth Plan period should be earmarked for production by the decentralised sector to give full benefit to the handloom weavers by a phased programme of replacement of handlooms by powerlooms.

For obtaining the extra production the number of additional cotton powerlooms required will be about, 60,000.

We visualise that the per capita availability of man-made fibre fabrics has to be raised to 4 yards from the Third Plan target of 1.8 yards. In terms of yardage the increased production of man-made fibre fabrics in the Fourth Plan would be of the order of 1,500 million yards. Allowing for a 20 per cent production by the handlooms for some of the fabrics being knitted we consider that the loomage on the art-silk side will have to be expanded by at least about 40,000 powerlooms during the Fourth Plan period.

The total number of additional powerlooms both on art-silk and cotton which may be introduced in the handloom sector during the Fourth Plan period may be estimated at one lakh. We recommend that there should be a phased programme for getting these one lakhs powerlooms installed half in the handloom co-operative and the other half in the sector outside the co-operative fold. The phased programme should also keep pace with the increase in the supply of cotton yarn and man-made fibre yarn.

We reөommend that the State-wise allocation of additional powerlooms to be introduced in the hand-loom in the co-operative sector and outside may be on the basis of the number of handlooms registered in the different States. The spinning capacity to feeding these cotton powerlooms should, as far as possible be located round the clusters of powerlooms in the different parts of the country.

The total outlay per cotton powerloom including working capital, preparatory machinery and processing facilities is assessed at Rs. 10,000 and for art-silk powerloom Rs. 11,000 to Rs. 12,000. The total outlay therefore, for the powerloom to be installed as recommended by us would be of the order of Rs. 104 to 108 crores, half of which will require financing by Government.

The entry of the decentralised sector in a big way in the supply of cloth during the Fourth plan should serve to exert a healthy influence to the advantage of the consumers. This is in addition to the many gains social and economic like diffusion of enterpreneurship and mobilisation of capital in the dispersed areas flowing from decentralisation of industrial activity.

We recommended that the production of dhoties and sarees by the textile mills may be pegged at 1963 level.

We also recommended that the production of coloured sarees should be reserved exclusively for handlooms. Small powerloom establishments with four looms and below at present are free to manufacture these sarees. It will be necessary to take positive measures for increasing the protection offered to those who would still continue to ply the handlooms by preventing the production of coloursed sarees by the small powerloom also whether they are in the co-operative fold or outside. We recommend that Government may take all the steps necessary to ensure that adequate facilities to obtain sized beams are provided within a period of three years for the weavers in Burhanpur, Malegaon and Jabalpur so that the powerlooms in these centre, whether in the Co-operative sector or outside simultaneiously could change over the weaving of fabrics other than coloured areas.

The data in regard to employment on powerlooms are also significant, The employment provided in certain cases may be as much as 2.5 per loom and in other may as low as 2 per loom on an average working of 1.5 shifts in the country. Thus for 82,000 cotton powerlooms in the different parts of the country on the basis of 1.5 shifts working the employment provided will range between 1.64 lakhs to 2.1 lakhs which includes the owners and men employed. On preparatory equipment etc. but excludes the employment afforded in the processing of powerloom cloth distribution and marketing. The employment provided by an art-silk powerloom may be assumed at abont 2.3 on an average working of 1.75 shifts working the employments provided would range between 1.40 lakhs to 1.80 lakhs.

Our considered view is that the scope for setting up powerlooms in the rural areas with a view to providing rural employment and improving the economic condition of the rural population is at present rather limited.

We consider that construction of industrial estates of the type now being established in the country is likely to be an expensive proposition and the rent payable for the sheds may be found burdensome by the powerloom weavers. We suggest the alternative course of establishing common weaving sheds, preferably co-operatively owned.

The merchant middleman is in a peculiarly strong position in this industry because he provides essential services of yarn supply finance and marketing and it will not be easy to dispense with or displace him untill efficient cooperatives or other agencies take over these functions. For the long term growth of the industry on a selfreliant basis and on healthy lines, it will be necessary to re-fashion the structure of many of the existing economic relationships. The steps to be taken to achieve this object have been indicated in our recommendations in the appropriate chapters of this report.

A pattern of growth for the powerlooms industry which seems to be feasible would be based on clusters of about 300 powerlooms each-not under one rocf but in small units within convenient distance of one another-established in and around small towns fed by yarn from a mill, preferably a cooperative spinning mill; sizing facilities being provided by a cooperatively owned sizing unit; finance being provided by either existing banking institutions or special powerloom corporations; processing establishments again preferably cooperatively owned and marketing arrangements (not necessarily co-operative) which do not operate to the detriment of the powerloom weaver.

For another important reason also viz. the availability of yarn, watch will have to be kept over the rate of growth of powerloom industry. We recommend that installation of looms on cotton or art-silk without any registration by the textile commissioner should be entirely at the risk of the parties who install the looms and Government should publicise that in the event of looms being installed no Governmental assistance by way of ensuring supply of yarn should be expected. Further till such time as the man made fibre yarn supply in the coubtrt catches up and becomes available in sufficient quantities application for registration powerlooms to be employed on art silk yarn should be scrutinised by the Textile Commissioner and registration allowed only at his discretion after satisfying himself about the availability of raw material.

However, looking ahead over a period of the next ten or twelve years, powerlooms are likely to continue to be a part of the country's industrial economy and their growth should be planned as a part of the overall strategy of development.

The emphasis in the developmental schemes for the handloom indus'ry has so far been largely governed by the overall limitation that handloom should continue to be handloom. We have, however, now come to a stage where unless as a matter of policy, Government would embark on a large scale scheme of giving the handloom weavers a more efficient instrument of production to improve their lot the efforts and moneys spent from the exchequer for the different measures of amelioration of the condition of the weavers would largely be set at nought.

We recommend removal of control in regard to acquisition, installation etc. of powerlooms in the decentralised sector as these have proved ineffective and resulted in several malpractices.

We recommend a registration scheme under which powerloom may formally be registered on payment of fee.

While in the case of cottonlooms application for registration when made will be admitted and registered as a formal measure on payment of the fee as prescribed the Textile Commissioner may be given the discretion to refuse registration in the cases of art silk looms depending on the supply position of art silk yarn is also convertion of cotton looms into art silk looms may be allowed to be registered only at the discretion of the Textile Commissioner. Installation of looms on cotton or art silk without any registration by the Textile Commissioner should be entirely at the risk of the parties installing them. Government should publicise that, in the event of looms being installed no Governmental assistance by way of supply of yarn etc. should be expected.

The existing controls and other regulations for the installation and working of woollen powerlooms may be continued and their administration made more effective.

We consider that the scope of the studies on the handloom industry at present undertaken should be expanded to cover powerlooms also,

As registration of powerlooms will be freely allowed and will not also be compulsory, it will be necessary to introduce a biennial census of powerlooms and handlooms to enable collection of relevant data.

While we generally agree with the pattern of assistance adopted for the conversation of handlooms into powerlooms under the old scheme, we suggest that the conditions for installation of the looms should also be modified in terms of our recommendation and the working capital provided should also be suitably increased. We also recommend that in regard to the looms already installed under the conversion scheme, the amount of working capital should be raised as recommended in this report.

We consider that in order to make this transformation of handlooms to powerlooms take place effectively and in meaningful and satisfying manner, the All India Handlooms Board should be made responsible for the implementation of the scheme of replacing the handlooms as recommended by us as also for the task of ensuring that the handlooms and the existing powerlooms maintain and improve their production.

We recommend that the All India Handloom Board should be made into a statutory body and charged with all the functions indicated in our report and provided with the required funds so as to be able to work with a budget of its own. . In consultation with this Body, the State, Government should work out the organisational set up at the States level for the propose of successful implementation of the schemes relating to each state.

AGRICULTURE TEAM ON IMPROVED IMPLEMENTS FOR THE MADRAS STATE, 1963—REPORT

New Delhi, Committee on Plan Projects, 1963. 106p.

Leader : Shri A. P. Jain.
Members : Dr. Arjan Singh; Shri B. M. Lakshmipathy; Dr. G. V. Chalam.

APPOINTMENT

The Agriculture Team appointed by the Committee on Plan Projects, Planning Commission, undertook the studies of Improve Agricultural Implements in the Madras State, in accordance with the terms of reference Circulated to the State Government Vide Committee on Plan Projects letter No. COPP/7/10/62 dated Febuary 12, 1963.

TERMS OF REFERENCE

The Team will make an appraisal of the various schemes, both of the Central and State Governments, relating to Agricultural Implements and make such suggestions as it may consider necessary with a view to achieving economy, efficiency and expedition in the working of the schemes.

For the purpose of the study by the Team, Agricultural Implements will be divided into the following categories :—

(a) Bullock drawn implements ;

(b) Small power implements ;

(c) Hand tools and garden implements ;

(d) Irrigation appliances and machinery ;

(e) Plant protection equipment, and

(f) Supplementary implements and equipment.

The Team will study, and report thereon, all aspects of the progress of various schemes, both of the Central and State Governments, and their efficiency and effectiveness in relation to the manufacture, popularisation and distribution of agricultural implements, particularly the following :—

(i) Research : (a) Progress made in research at all levels at the Central and State Research Stations ;

(b) Testing and trials, including the work done at Regional Testing-cum-Training Centres ;

(ii) Manufacture : (a) Availability of raw materials with special reference to the quality of iron and Steel required for the manufacture of implements ;

(b) Arrangement for quality control of implements ;

(c) Adequacy of organisation, both public and private, in different States and the Country as a whole, for the manufacture of improved implements ;

(iii) Training : (a) Study of training facilities in agricultural engineering, training standards, number of trainees, scope for their employment, etc.,

(b) Arrangement for training of village artisans and farmers ;

(c) Follow-up in the field of the training programmes for artisans and farmers ;

(iv) Sale and Distribution : (a) Review of the methods and organisation employed for the sale and distribution of implements and their effectiveness ;

(b) Role of the cooperatives and departmental seed stores in the distribution of agricultural implements ;

(c) Linking of credit facilities with the distribution of agricultural implements and grant of loans in kind ;

(v) Popularisation : (a) Review of the arrangement for demonstrations at the village and block levels, the methods and technique adopted and need and scope for strengthening of the village and block level set up ;

(b) Arrangements for repairs and maintenance at the various levels and the role and working of rural workshops ;

(c) Purchase and hiring of implements by Cooperatives and Panchayats ;

(vi) Administrative Arrangement : (a) Need and scope for strengthening the Agricultural Engineering staff at the District, Regional and State levels ;

(b) Co-ordination among different agencies concerned with research, manufacture, popularisation and distribution of implements.

CONTENTS

General Background ; Organisation ; Research ; Raw-material ; Manufacture ; Distribution ; Training ; Extension ; Credit facilities ; Economic and Improved Implements and scope of power Machinery ; Summary of Recommendations ; Terms of Reference ; Annexures from 1 to X.

RECOMMENDATIONS

In order to watch the progress of introduction of improved implements and machinery, steps should be taken to enumerate them separately at the time of quinquennial livestock census.

The facilities available at the Annamalai University for the post graduate studies in Agricultural Engineering are inadequate and need to be augmented to a considerable extent.

Closer coordination between the Departments of Industries and Agriculture in the matter of supply of raw material and manufacturing programme of agricultural implements is recommended. It will also be desirable to associate the Joint Director of Agriculture (Engineering), in the formulation of annual programme of implements manufactured by the industrial units.

In order to avoid duplication of efforts and waste of time and expenditure on research in agricultural implements, it is necessary to bring about close integration and coordination of activities of the Agricultural Research Institute, Coimbatore and Agricultural implements workshop at Thanjavur. While the Research Testing and Training Centre may be converted into the main research station by amalgamating the research section of the college, regional sub-stations may be set up in important agricultural zones of the State.

The inter changeability and coordination amongst the agricultural engineering staff of various schemes should be established so as to enrich and improve the working efficiency of the department.

Since only a few of the large number of implements recommended by the department are popular with the ryots, it is suggested that the list may be carefully examined and only those implements may be retained in it which are of real economic use and within the reach of the cultivators.

It will be desirable to enlarge the objectives and

functions of the Research Testing and Training Centre and include small tractors, power implements and machinery such as power threshers, power sprayers, etc., in the programme of work.

Special attention requires to be paid to the designing of a dryer for paddy seeds.

As hand-tools are still extensively used, particularly in hilly areas, it is necessary to initiate technical studies on them with a view to obtaining maximum efficiency and output by determining the most suitable posture for workers and shape and size of blades, handles and angle of attachment, etc.

Detailed study of various parts of implements, quality of material required for their manufacture and the measures that could be taken to reduce the cost of implements, without reducing their usefulness or working life, should be taken and the results of study published for the information of manufacturing units and extension agencies.

As the ordinary cultivator does not have the means to go in for a large variety of single-purpose implements, concerted efforts are required to be made to evolve suitable multipurpose implements.

At present, the estimates of requirements of iron and steel for agricultural implements are made, more or less, on an ad hoc basis, taking into consideration previovs year's figures. It will be desirable to draw up a clear-cut programme regarding the number of implements to be manufactured and estimates for iron requirements should be framed on the basis of schedule recommended by the Team.

The present arrangement of excercising check on the utilisation of iron and steel by the fabricators, needs revision. It will be desirable to ensure this work to the Assistant Engineers instead of the District Agricultural Officers.

Since the present procurement procedure is lengthy and cumbersome, it is suggested to curtail it by long-term planning and doing away with the practice now followed of routing indents through the Ministry of Food and Agriculture.

The policy of equi-distribution of iron and steel out of the agricultural quota to fabricators requires to be stopped. The team recommends that the raw material should be supplied to the fabricators on their previous year's production, installed capacity and future manufacturing programme.

Like iron and steel and coke and coal, separate quota of pig iron requires to be fixed for Agricultural purposes.

There appears to be an urgent need of carrying out survey of agencies engaged in the manufacture of implements and categorise them with reference to their capacity and suitability.

In order to keep down overhead cost of production, it is suggested that the State government may encourage suitable production units for the manufactures of special implements in which they possess the requisite technical know-how and experience.

Utilisation of cooperatives in the manufacture of implements deserves special attention and in order to achieve it, it will be desirable to draw up a definite programme jointly by the Director of Agriculture and Registrar of Cooperative Societies.

In order to ensure standardization of implements and their spare parts, some experienced and well-to-do manufacturers may be encouraged to equip their workers with modern machinery and take up the manufacture of standard implements on a mass scale.

One of the State workshops may be suitably equipped for taking up the manufacture, on a mass scale, of some vital parts of implements such as the discs, blades, etc., which require high carbon steel. All these parts must bear the hall mark of the department and made available in sufficient numbers to fabricators who should be required to make use of them and allotted iron only for the other parts of the implements.

A special committee consisting of joint Director of Agricultural Engineering, Research Engineer (Research Testing and Training Centre), Agricultural Engineer (Inspection), Agronomist, Deputy Directors of Agricultural and few progressive farmers may be set up for the standardization of designs, testing of implements and bringing them on the approved list of the Department.

Arrangement should be made for the quality-marking of implements manufactured by various agencies, including industrial units, by appointing a small subordinate staff and utilising the services of Assistant Engineers in the Districts.

The blue prints and specifications prepared by the Team in cosultation with the Research Engineer may be published in the form of leaflets for Distribution amongst fabricators and other interested persons.

The industrial units engaged in the manufacture of agricultural implements should draw up their own regular programme of manufacture in consultation with the extension organisations and make arrangements for direct sales to the cultivators either through cooperative societies or retail sellers.

At times, Industrial Units despatch the implements in unassembled condition and send various component parts in several lots which creates great problem for extension agency in assembling them into a finished product.

The scope and function of the workshop wings of Extension Centres may be restricted only to the training of village level workers.

The training of village artisans may be done at the

Industrial Units.

While the inservice training for District Agricultural Officers and Assistant Engineers may be arranged at the Research Testing and Training Centre, Coimbatore, training course for A.E.O.S., village level workers and farmers may be organised at Agricultural Farms and Extension Training Centres.

For the demonstration of improved agricultural implements and machinery, a well-organised programme requires to be taken up, particularly to show the increased or additional production or saving in labour through the use of improved agricultural implements.

While composite type of demonstration is, no doubt, good, the single-purpose demonstration in the case of implements is also necessary for convincing the farmers of the economy and efficiency of a specific process or item.

The programme of planning, laying out and recording of demonstration of implements requires to be reviewed so as to bring it on a sound footing.

As the demonstration of new implements can best be done by the extension workers fully familiar with local agro-economic conditions, there seems to be no need to appoint an agricultural supervisor in each district for this purpose.

The scheme for the provision of demonstration sets of implements with V.L.W's,. B.D.Os. and panchayat unions, requires to be examined so as to improve its working efficiency and retain or add only those Implements which are absolutely essential.

For Implements lent out to cultivators for practical use and demonstration, no charge should be levied.

On some seed and demonstration farms, it will be desirable to have power tillers and small tractors with necessary implements for demonstration to the cultivators of surrounding areas.

On all agricultural exhibitions and shows, improved implements, suited to local conditions, should be exhibited and simple leaflets in local language, giving briefly use, economics, method of handling, availability of implements, their spare parts and prices, should be distributed amongst the visitors.

A conspicuous space should, be reserved for the exhibition of improved implements in the important markets of agricultural commodities and leaflets should also be freely distributed at these places.

It should be possible for important fabricators to combine their production programme with the training of village artisans and theireby use the latter for introducing and promoting the sale of implements.

All short-term and medium-term loans for agricultural implements and machinery should be advanced through the Cooperative Societies and Revenue Department and Banks should stop issuing those loans.

Since the available experimental data in regard to the increased production as a result of the use of improved implements are very meagre, it is suggested that a well planned programme of research may be immediately undertaken covering all aspects of tillage operations and implements necessary to produce tilth for optimum crop production and economics of various implements in relation to their capacity.

The usefulness of Melur and M.B. Plough, which are at present being distributed throughout the state on subsidised basis, should be carefully examined in the light of results of experiments obtained at different Agricultural farms and their use should be popularised only in areas where their utility is fully established.

Because of equitable tropical climate and extensive irrigation system. Madras offers considerable scope for multiple cropping and introduction of labour intensive crops. In the light of these conditions, the scope of mechanisation in Madras agriculture requires to be studied, in detail, so as to formulate a definite policy and initiate steps to implement it.

COMMITTEE ON PLAN PROJECTS, AGRICULTURAL TEAM ON IMPROVED AGRICULTURAL IMPLEMENTS IN HIMACHAL PRADESH, 1963—REPORT

New Delhi, Planning Commission, 1967. 55p.

Leader : Shri A. P. Jain.
Members : Dr. Arjan Singh; Shri B. M. Lakshmipathy; Dr. G. V. Chalam.

APPOINTMENT

The Agricultural Team on Improved Agricultural Implements in Himachal Pradesh was constituted under the Committee on Plan Projects, Planning Commission vide their Memorandum No. COPP/7/10/62 dated 12-2-1963.

TERMS OF REFERENCE

The team will make an appraisal of the various schemes, both of the Central and State Governments, relating to Agricultural Implements and make such suggestions as it may consider necessary with a view to achieving economy, efficiency and expedition in the working of the schemes.

For the purpose of the study by the Team, Agricultural implements will be divided into the following categories:—

(a) Bullock-drawn implements;
(b) Small power implements;
(c) Hand tools and garden implements;
(d) Irrigation appliances and machinery;
(e) Plant protection equipment; and
(f) Supplementary implements and equipment.

This Team will study, and report thereon, all aspects of the progress of various schemes, both of the Central and State Governments, and their efficiency and effectiveness in relation to the manufacture, popularisation and distribution of agricultural implements particularly the following:—

(i) **Research** : (a) Progress made in research at all levels at Central and State Research Stations;

(b) Testing and trials, including the work done at Ragional Testing-cum-Training centres ;

(ii) **Manufacture** : (a) Availability of raw materials with special reference to the quality of iron and steel required for the manufacture of implements;

(b) Arrangements for quality control of implements;

(c) Adequacy of organisations, both public and private, in different States and the country as a whole, for the manufacture of improved implements;

(iii) **Training** : (a) Study of training facilities in agricultural engineering, training standards, number of trainees, seope for their employments, etc.

(b) Arrangement for training of viliage artisans and farmers ;

(c) Follow-up in the field of the training programmes for artisans and farmers ;

(iv) **Sale and Distribution** : (a) Review of the methods and organisations employed for the sale and distribution of implements and their effectiveness;

(b) Role of the cooperatives and departmental seed stores in the distribution of agricultural implements ;

(c) Linking of credit facilities with the distribution of agricultural implements and grant of loans in kind ;

(v) **Popularisation** : (a) Review of the arrangement for demonstrations at the village and block levels, the methods and techniques adopted and need and scope for strengthening of the village and block level set-up ;

(b) Arrangements for repairs and maintenance at the various levels and the role and working of rural workshops ;

(c) Purchase and hiring of implements by cooperatives and Panchayats ;

(vi) **Administrative Arrangement** : (a) Need and scope for strengthening the Agricultural Engineering staff at the District, Ragional and State levels;

(b) Coordination among different agencies concerned with research manufacture, popularisation and distribution of implements.

The team will carry out case studies of the different prototypes of important Agricultural implements and Hand Tools with a view to judging their efficiency, economy and contribution towards increased production. With a view to facilitating stndies and making them realistic the Team will consult and hold discussions with progressive farmers, manufacturers of Agricultural implements and officers and staff of the State Agriculture and other concerned Departments, etc. The Team may coopt representatives of various interests in the field of manufacture supply and use of agricultural implements in different states.

CONTENTS

Geographical and Agro-economic Features; Programmes and Problems ; Perspective Planning ; Summary of Recommendations ; Terms of Reference ; Annexures.

RECOMMENDATIONS

In order to watch the progress of the introduction of improved implements and machinery, it is necessary that steps are taken to enumerate systematically all categories of improved implements at the time of quinquennial livestock censuses.

The programme of general development of hand tools at the Research Testing and Training Centre, Mandi may also include systematic all categories of improved implements at the time of quinquennial livestock censuses.

The programme of general development of hand tools at the Research Testing and Training Centre, Mandi may also include systematic studies on their shape, size and angle of adjustment in relation to the physical capacity of the field worker.

The working of the Research Testing and Training Centre, Mandi needs to be closely examine and streamlined with regard to the appointment of technical staff, equipment of workshop building and supply of raw materials.

In the absence of any scientific data on the field performance of Agro Uni versal power tiller, any proposal for its large scale distribution amongst the cultivators is fraught with risk. It is, therefore, desirable to conduct exhaustive field trials with regard to its suitability, economics, efficiency etc. before recommending it to the cultivators.

Steps may be taken to expedite the appointment of a Lecturer in Agricultural Engineering at the Himachal Agricultural College, Solan so that the syllabus in Agricultural Engineering is fully and comprehensively covered.

The horticultural kit developed by the Workshop Wing at Mashobra may be taken up for further trials at the Research. Testing and Training Centre, Mandi and if found suitable, should be encouraged for mass production.

Immediate steps should be taken to restart the training of village artisans at the Workshop Wing, Mashobra. Urgent action is also needed to fill up the post of Chief Instructor in implements.

The Workshop Wing should have its own full-fledged workshop building with ample working space and training facilities for the village artisans.

The revolving fund provided by the Ford Foundation and lying idle up-till now, may be utilised for advancing loans to the trained village artisans by simplifying the financial procedure.

The training course in blacksmithy and carpentry at the Government Cluster Centres may be organised on sound basis so as to impart comprehensive practical training in the manufacture and handling of common agricultural implements to the trainees. Adequate funds may also be made available to these centres for the purchase of complete sets of implements commonly in use in that area for the benefit of the trainees.

It would be desirable to include elementary knowledge of agricultural implemenls and hand tools in the carpentry course tanght at the Industrial Training Institute, Solan.

The lengthy and cumbersome procedure with regard to the supply of iron and steel to the cultivators needs to be reviewed critically and cut short by long term planning. The Government may also consider the possibility of making bulk purchase of decontrolled items at the State level for distribution to the cultivators and village artisans at no profit no loss basis.

The Government Foundry, Nahan may take up mass production of improved implements and fast-moving parts of standard design and specifications in consultation with the State Department of Agriculture.

The Rural Common Facility Workshops should be encouraged to take up mass production of hand tools under the technical guidance of the Research Engineer, Mandi.

The system for the sale of improved implements through cooperative societies introduced in Mandi District should be extended to all well-established cooperative societies in the rest of Himachal Pradesh. A proper survey and assessment of specific types of implements, particularly in Chamba and Kinnaur District, needs to be conducted and only such implements as are really found suitable under the local conditions should be recommended to the cultivators.

The possibility of including the Village Panchayats or big landlords to purchase land thrashers for hiring them out to the cultivators at nominal rate may be explored.

There is a need to develop light but durable bullock-drawn implements like iron plough, trimular bar harrow, etc., specially suitable for the hilly terrain Small-sized fields and poor animal power.

In view of vast scope of garden tools in Himachal, concerted efforts may be made to arrange their production locally rather than continue importing them indefinitely from outside the State.

It would be useful to bring out simple leaflets on all important implements and hand tools giving their photographs use economics, and extension workers.

Audio-visual aids should be employed on a large scale to make the cultivators implement-minded.

The programme of demonstrations on improved agricultural implements lacks sustained efforts and needs to be adequately strengthened. The demonstration sets should be kept in perfect working order and proper record of demonstrations maintained at all levels.

The causes for the non-issue of loans to the cultivators for the purchase of improved implements need to be looked into and removed in order to avoid hardship to the cultivators.

Adequate funds,may be placed at the disposal of the cooperative societies for issuing loans to the cultivators at a uniform nominal rate for the purchase of agricultural implements.

The State Government may examine the question of setting up a separate Agricultural Engineering Section for the demonstration and popularisation of improved agricultural implement more effectively and efficiently.

The Research Testing and Training Centre, Mandi should pay prior attention to designing a suitable clod crusheer.

Intensive research and exhaustive field trials are necessary on the economics and efficiency of various German machines and implements before they are recommended to the cultivators for large scale adoption.

The blue prints and specifications of implements and hand tools evolved at the Research Testing and Training Centre and their sectionwise iron and steel requirements may be prepared for the use of the fabricators.

There is need to set up a well-equipped Agricultural Engineering Workshop at the Himachal Agricultural College. Solan for providing adequate teaching facilities and practical training in agricultural engineering to the students. The workshop may also include a set of implements and hand tools designed and development at the Research Testing and Training Centre, Mandi.

The workshop Wing, Mashobra may include a complete set of improved bullock-drawn implements in the training course of village artisans to acquiant them with the use, maintenance and repairs of all types of improved implements in use in the Territory.

Agreement entered into with the village artisans at the time of their training at the Workshop Wing may be modified making it compulsory for them to take up the repair and manufacturing of agricultural implements in their home village for a certain minimum period after the successful completion of the training.

Long-term loans at low interest may be offered to the trained village artisans enabling them to equip their workshops with necessary tools and instruments.

The State Government may consider the possibility of setting up small workshops at the Block level and rent them out to the experienced village artisans at nominal charges.

The Director of Agriculture should be associated with the Board of Management of Nahan Foundry to render technical advice on the manufacturing programme of implements.

Efforts may be made to set up small fabrication units for agricultural implements on cooperative basis at suitable places, preferably, near the Rural Common Facility Workshops.

Short-term refresher course in the case and maintenance of improved agricultural implements may be started for the District Agricultural Officers, Block Development Officers and Agricultural Inspectors at the Research Testing and Training Centre, Mandi.

A conscise programme indicating a definite number of demonstrations on improved implements may be determined for the whole Territory. Splitting them further at district, block and village level season-wise and fixing the responsibility of each extension worker to achieve the target.

It is desirable to institute a system of awarding cash prize or certificates of merit to the extension workers, as an incentive who achieve the annual target of demonstrations, in full.

The Department of Agriculture may make a careful selection of improved implements to be included in the demonstration sets according to the local needs and agro-climatic conditions.

All the Government farms may be equipped with only improved implements and machinery for increasing the efficiency of operations as well as to serve as model to the cultivators.

Arrangements may be made to supply adequate number of spare parts of improved Agricultural implements to the trained village artisans so that implements are repaired without causing any dislocation in the normal schedule of farm operations.

THE AD-HOC COMMITTEE ON TOURISM, 1963—REPORT
New Delhi, Department of Tourism, 1963. 93p.

Chairman : Shri L.K. Jha.
Members : Shri Y.T. Shah ; Shri S. Mullick ; Shri Fateh Singh ; Shri M.G. Abrol.
Secretary : Shri S.N. Chib.

APPOINTMENT

The Ad-hoc Committee on Tourism was constituted under the Department of Tourism (Ministry of Transport) on 1st March, 1963.

TERMS OF REFERENCE

(i) Examine, generally, the conditions prevailing in the country from the point of view of promoting tourist traffic and to suggest ways and means of improving these conditions with a view to achieving an expansion in that traffic by at teast 20 per cent a year in the next three years, and thereafter at a progressive rate of increase.

(ii) In particular—(a) assess the requirements of tourism in respect of hotel accommodation and transport arrangements and suggest necessary measures for the speedy provision and improve of these facilities; (b) examine the present rules and procedures regarding Visas, customs, and other formalities with a view to facilitating entry and exist of tourists ; and (c) recommend necessary reorganisation of publicity programmes and other steps required to bring about the desired expansion of traffic.

(iii) Suggest measures necessary to ensure that the foreign exchange earned from tourism and resulting from its expansion is protected against leakage.

CONTENTS

Introduction ; The Value of Tourism; The Potential and the Performance; Formalities; Facilities at Airports; Transport Facilities ; Hotels ; Publicity and Promotion ; Development of Tourist Centres ; Shopping and Entertainment ; Training of personnel for Tourism ; Leakage of Foreign Exchange ; Building up an Organisation ; Appendices.

RECOMMENDATIONS

Introduction

After a fairly rapid increase until 1959, tourist traffic began slowing down in 1960 and 1961. In 1962 there was a decline of 3.9 per cent, part of which had taken place before the Emergency.

The Committee was appointed to enquire into the causes of the decline in tourism and to suggest ways and means of expanding tourist traffic.

The Value Of Tourism

Earnings from tourism amounted to about 3 per cent of our total exports in 1961, a performance which was bettered by only five other items on our export list.

To assess the potentialities of tourism in augmenting our foreign exchange resources, it is worth noting that international travel expenditure in a single year is far more than the foreign exchange gap for our Third Five Year Plan as a whole. Countries like Spain, Italy and Austria have been able to wipe out their trade deficits and build up large reserves of foreign exchange mainly through measures to attract tourists.

Foreign exchange apart, the tourist industry benefits the domestic economy on account of its high employment potential, because of the personal service provided by hotels, restaurants and transport operators as well as the sale of handicraft products. Possibly 15 per cent of what the tourist spends in the country goes to augment the revenues of the Central and State Government as well as of Municipal authorities.

On all these considerations, it is essential that State Governments and Municipal authorities should offer their fullest cooperation in encouraging foreign tourists to come to India.

To cater for the tourist, it is not necessary to provide luxury standards which may be beyond our resources. The kind of standards of clearnliness and decor, of sanitation and hygiene which the tourist needs should and could be beneficial to a developing country rather than a strain on its resources.

The value of tourism in promoting greater international understanding should not be forgotten.

The Potential And The Performance

Few countries in the world can surpass India in the range of attractions offered to the tourist-places of scenic beauty, ancient monuments, shikar and other sports, as well as things of cultural, economic and potential interest.

Despite these advantages, India was visited by only 139,804 tourists in 1961, whereas Italy earned about Rs. 359 crores in foreign exchange from 18.9 million tourists in the same year. While tourist traffic all over the world has been increasing at an annual rate of about 13% and many countries in Asia and Africa have had a steady increase in their tourist traffic, the traffic to India has been declining since the beginning of 1962.

A steady growth in tourism can be achieved by us—provided there is a nation-wide recognition of its value and a concerted effort on the part of the Central, State and local authorities.

Formalities

The formalities that a tourist has to comply with have to be made as simple as possible if he is to feel that he is welcome visitor.

A more liberal policy in the granting of visas is necessary. Applications for visas who hold a return/onward ticket need not be asked to give any bank guarantee.

If any tourists arrive without visas, landing permits valid for at least 72 hours should be issued liberally. Such landing permits should also enable the holders to do local sightseeing and in case they desire to visit nearby places, they should be able to get the necessary permission speedily on application. Special arrangements should be made for the issue of collective visas to passengers arriving for a stay of 72 hours or less by chartered aircraft.

Certain countries have been able to abolish visa regulations on a reciprocal basis and this has greatly facilitated the flow of tourist traffic between those countries. To what extent such an approach would be possible for us, may be considered by Government.

The measures adopted to ensure that high-value article like cameras and radios brought by the tourist are taken out by him when he leaves the country, could be further simplified. The re-export form need contain only four columns, viz., (i) make or brand, (ii) marticles (iii) prices paid; and (iv) number of years and certain article which tourists are not likely to part with, such as a reasonable amount of tourists are not likely to part with, such as a reasonable amount of personal jewellery and photographic equipment, may be allowed in without being entered in the re-export form. Tourists sometime carry large stocks of unexposed film on account of doubts regarding their availability in the countries visited. They need not be called upon to obtain an import licence for them. Similarly, no monetary ceilings or other limits should be imposed on what the tourist can bring in, excepting that articles of high value may be entered on the re-export form.

There should be no limit on the quantity of Indian goods which a tourist may take out with him. If the value is particularly large, customs should check with the foreign exchange booklet carried by the tourist to see whether the goods have been purchased with the foreign exchange which he has cashed in the country.

Much of the irritation voiced by tourists against customs would be eliminated if the opening of their baggage by customs is reduced to the minimum. The discretion to reduce the percentage of test-check is rarely exercised. It is suggested that the baggage of tourists coming by air should ordinarily not be checked, unless there are grounds for doing so.

India's policy regarding prohibition does not include its enforcement on foreigners, particularly those who are temporary visitors. In practice, however considerable inconvenience is caused to tourists, because the regulations vary from state to State—Arrangements to issue all-India liquor permits for tourists should be introduced quickly and Tourists Offices should issue these permits even after office hours and on holidays. Similarly, arrangements should be made for the sale of liquor to tourists on dry days at approved establishments. In areas such as Delhi, where consumption of alcohol in a public place is not permitted a room should be set apart in each hotel where both food and alcoholic drinks can be served, admission to such rooms being restricted to foreigners and/or residents.

Facilities At Airports

The first and last, and perhaps the most lasting, impression on a tourists mind is that of the treatment he receives at the time of his arrival and departure, usually at one of the four principal airports of India. Much of the criticism against various formalities and regulations stems from the fact that our facilities at airports are poor.

The terminal building need improvement and in this task, the advice of competent firms abroad who have experience in this field may be sought. The possibility of new air terminal buildings exclusively for the use of international airlines should be explored,

Special attention should be paid to the air-conditioning of those areas of the air terminals where tourists have to spend considerable time. The airport building should provide adequate rest room facilities for the Customs, Police and Health staff who have to be on duty at odd hours. The senior most officials in charge of customs and of immigration formalities should be given residential quarters at the airports.

Postal, banking and exchange facilities should be available at every airport round the clock. Arrangements to make hotel and transport reservations should exist in the terminal building. A few retiring rooms should also be provided.

Catering and shopping facilities at airports should be considerably improved. Duty-free shops should also be provided to enable tourists to purchase articles of day-to-day use such as photographic material, alcoholic beverages, tobacco products, toilet requisites etc.

The most important factor is the human element ;

special training should be given to personnel at airports who shuold have a reasonably long tenure of service and should possess a reasonably fluency in English so as to avoid misunderstandings in dealing with tourists.

The immigration staff at airports should be under the control and direction of the central government.

The aerodrome officer should be fully responsible for the management, upkeep and maintenance of the terminal building and should hold periodic meeting with the heads of the customs, police and health staff to ensure coordination of effort.

The aerodrome officer should be given financial powers to incure reasonable expenditure on maintenance, petty repairs, etc. a readily available source of finance for this could be found by levying a cess of Rs. 3 per international passenger at the time of departure.

Transport Facilities

In 1962, 67 per cent of the tourists came to India by-air. Earlier surveys indicated that 75 per cent of American tourists and 60 per cent, of European tourists chose air transport for most of their journeys within the country.

The Indian Airlines Corporation have a distinguished and enviable record of safety in their services. However certain difficulties and drawback from the tourists point of view need to be removed.

The Indian Airlines corporation should get itself better known abroad, both through travel agents and through Government of India Tourist Offices. It should not only advertise its flight schedules long in advance, but should ensure that the change in timings are duly notified in foreign countries.

Speedy confirmation of bookings is essential for the tourist traffic. As a rule, tourist should be able to get confirmed bookings at 15 days notice. About 10 per cent of the seats on all routes normally used by tourists should be kept in reserve for them until one week before each flight and 2 to 3 seats upto three days before departure to enable tourists to make changes in itineraries.

Until all stations of the IAC have been linked up by teleprinter the IAC should put through extra telephone calls (without necessarily recovering the cost from the tourist) to facilitate bookings from immediate stations.

Some of the Dakotas likely to be rendered surplus should be retained by the IAC for introducing additional flights during the peak season and for charter flights.

The IAC should pay special attention to tourist traffic to earn foreign exchange which it needs for the maintenance and expansion of its service. At present it is estimated to be earning about Rs. 2.75 crores in foreign exchanges per annum. This figure could steadily grow. The IAC might well run some services which purely in rupee terms may not seem so attractive. If thereby it is able to carry a large volume of tourist traffic as for instance a Dakota flight between Agra and Jaipur.

Next to air transport, tourists prefer travelling by road on short sectors. Motor vehicles are, therefore, necessary both for group travel and for those desiring to travel in privacy.

Special motor coaches equipped with large glass-panes trained guides, public address system and other amenities are essential for sightseeing in large cities like Bombay, Delhi, Calcutta and Madras. Attention should be given to the improvement of existing tourist bus service, and it might be an advantage to give the operational charge of these buses to the Department of Tourism at least for a limited period.

In order to maintain an efficient car transport service for tourists who want to do sight seeing in privacy it would be necessary to import cars which should preferably run by a governmental agency so as to ensure that the cars are used only by tourists on payment in foreign exchange. Cars allotted to private operators should be under stricter control to ensure that they give preference to tourists, charge approved rates and account for earnings of foreign exchange.

Railway are now used by tourist mainly to visit places not linked by air. For the benefit of those who travel by rail, western-style dishes of good quality should be supplied on demand by charging higher prices, if necessary bed rolls should be available at short notice even at smaller station of tourist interest. Facilities should also be made available to tourists to make speedy return or onward reservations from intermediate railway stations.

Hotels

India has at present only about 11,000 hotel beds suitable for tourists. There is a marked absence of moderately-priced hotels of a suitable standard in large cities. The growth of the hotel industry, in general has not kept peace with the increase in the number of tourists.

The incentives given by government to the hotel industry include release of foreign exchange for import of essential equipment loans from the Industrial Finance Corporation and State Finance Corporations and income-tax exemption for new hotels. Despite these incentives, only five new hotels of a good standard with a total of about 341 beds, have come up in recent years.

The main difficulties are insufficiency of capital and non-availability of suitable sites. Not many hoteliers have asked for loans from the IFC or SFCs. Suitable sites for good hotels are difficult to get in larger cities except at prices which would make it difficult for a medium-priced hotel to be built.

The Tourist Department estimates that to provide the additional hotel accommodation to cope with the antcipated growth in tourist traffic, about Rs. 20 crores wou'd have to be invested in the next five years. It is doubtful if private enterprise can find so much capital. Private enterprise is also more likely to concentrate on luxury hotels, rather than on modestly-priced hotels. The public sector will, therefore, have to play a major role in providing additional hotel accommodation.

State Governments may be able to participate in financing the construction of hotels by making available suitable sites owned by them. Their value being the State government share in the equity capital private investment in public sector hotel should be ruled out.

It would be preferable to entrust the day-to day operation and management of state-owned hotels to hotel-operators India or foreign. The latter would have the advantage of helping to attract tourists through their international contracts.

While there is no objection, in principle to the creation of a separate agency for providing loans to the hotel industry it would be more practicable to rely on the existing financial institutions. For this a somewhat more flexible approach in the part of the existing institutions, taking into account the special features and requirements of the hotel industry, can be needed. The Life Insurance Corporation could constructing hotel buildings in places where there is accute scarcity of hotel accommodation.

It would be advantageous if institutions and countries offering credits for economic development could be persuaded to make their loans useable for the hotel industry. In addition, private foreign investment should also be encouraged.

It is necessary to ensure that hotel prices are kept within reasonable limits and are not increased without adequate justification.

The construction of low-period accommodation should be encouraged by subsidising organisations which are essentially non-profit-making. Suitable sites in important cities of Bombay, Calcutta, etc. should be specifically earmarked for hotel construction. The rates of permit for allowing hotel construction in important areas of Delhi, particularly in residential areas where only partial utilisation of land is allowed, should be re-examined.

For better utilisation of land which is highly expensive, new hotels should be allowed to design a majority of rooms as double rooms and the prescribed minimum of single rooms for income-tax exemption may be reduced from tofifty 25 per cent of the total accommodation. Income-tax exemption should be allowed even if the party owning the building and the party operating it are different.

Publicity and Promotion

Tourist publicity overseas is concentrated in a few countries and mainly takes the shape of distribution of tourist literature, contacts with the travel trade and press publicity.

For tourism no less than for other reasons, the image of India and the Indian people has to be projected abroad in a way that it reaches not merely the elite and the erudite, but also the average man. Publicity through editorials, newspaper and magazine articles, radio and television is of great value for this. It can be arranged through public relations, agencies as well as by inviting foreign journalists, travel writers, photograpers, television film producers etc., or familiarisation tours of India. The shooting foreign cinematographic films in Indian settings should be encouraged on a more liberal basis.

While from the available statistical data, it is not possible to say conclusively that the increase in the inflow of tourist from particular regions where Tourist Offices have been opened, was in fact, and if so, to what extent, attributable to the opening of these offices, India will, in order to compete with other countries trying to attract tourists, have to open additional tourist offices from time to time. The opening of an office in Japan and an increase in the number of offices in the United States would seem most worthwhile at the juncture. In addition, small teams may be sent to particular areas from time to time to make an impact by delivering lectures. arranging television programmes, briefing travel agents and other similar means.

Indian Missions abroad can and should be used to provide tourist information and encourage tourism. Similarly, the possibility of using the services of Indian Banks overseas and indeed, of the resident Indian community in certain areas for this purpose, should be explored.

Tourist publicity material should be of the very best quality and the best artists, designers, writers, printers, photographers, film producers etc., available in the country should be engaged for its production, so that the publicity material does not suffer in comparison with what is put out by other countries.

Development of Tourist Centres

Approximinately 150 places in India have the potential of being developed into good tourist centres. As our resources are limited, instead of spreading them thinly over too wide a field, we should concentrate on a few selected centres and provide all the necessary facilities there in the first instance.

Preference for immediate development should be given to place which have features most likely to attract foreign tourists and which are easily accessible, preferably by air. The list should include at aleast one or two centres in each State.

For purposes of development it would be practical to divide the selected tourist areas into two groups-those where basic facilities of transport, accommodation and other amenities already exist, and those which have to be developed from scratch. In the first category may be included Bombay, Calcutt a, Delhi and Madras as well as Agra, Jaipur, Banaras, Srinagar, Madurai, Hyderabad, Mysore, Chandigarh, Ahmedabad, Darjeeling, Cochin and Bhubaneshwar. In these places, further development should not only include hotel and transport facilities but also exploitation of local festivals and folklore. In the second category the inclusion of Kaziranga, Jim Corbett Park, Fatehpur Sikri, Bodh Gaya, Nalanda, Rajgir, Puri Konarak, Pahalgam, Gulmarg, Bhakra, Manoli, Udaipur, Sanchi, Mandu, Khajuraho, Ellora, Ajanta, Goa, Halebid, Mahabalipuram, Kovalam beach and Lake Periyar is suggested.

The master plans prepared by the working Groups appointed by the Department of Tourism should be implemented expeditiously. At other potential centres of tourism not mentioned above, the State Government should continue to develop basic amenties to attract mainly domestic visitors for holiday and tourism for the present.

Shoping and Entertainment: Tourists generally spend some time-and money-on shopping entertainment. According to an economic survey by the Institute of public opinion, tourists from America and Europe spend a total of nearly Rs. 2.00 crores annually on shopping alone. Tourists also took for various forms of entertainment. Tourist expenditure on these things can considerably help the promotion and development of handicrafts and also of cultural activities, besides yielding foreign exchange.

To help the tourist, a brochure giving a list of recommended shops in Delhi, Bombay, Calcutta and Madras has recently been brought out of the Department of tourism. More tourist be similarly covered.

Shops dealing with merchandise in which tourists are interested should be encouraged to form local associations so as to impose internal discipline on their members. Those showing a high earning of foreign exchange form tourists and a good record of No complaint service to tourist should be granted certificates by the Department of Tourism.

Special attention on the part of the authorities concerned with handicrafts and handloom products should be paid to the kind of "Souvenirs" which the tourist wants to buy. Souvenirs should be light, easily packed and not too fragile so that transportation by air presents no problem.

There is a paucity of good cultural entertainment, particularly in the light idiom. Instead of night clubs and foreign cabaret artistes, Indian style entertainment of a lighter variety, for performence in existing theatre halls and auditoriums as well as in hotels and restaurants, should be developed.

Private cultural organisations should be persuaded to plan their shows and festivals with an eye on the tourist traffic and in close collaboration with the Department of Tourism to ensure advance and adequate publicity-such as the Republic Day Parade in Delhi or the Dussehra festivities in Mysore already receive.

The possibilities of developing special programmes involving light and sound spectacles centred on some of the historic sites, particularly in Delhi should be explored.

Arrangements should be made for temporary membership of clubs for tourists to enable them to participate in sports such as golf, polo, tennis, etc. The development of winter sports in the himalayas and other forms of sports should be exploited for touristic purposes also.

Sampling local gastronomic delicacies is another form of evening entertainment for tourists, and hotels and restaurants should make efforts to popularise not only tandoori dishes but other specialities selected judiciously, prepared without too much of spices and served in a manner suitably adopted to western needs. Special attention should be paid to the taste and flavour of the tea and coffee served in Indian hotels, necessary technical assistance from the Indian Tea Board and Coffee Board.

Training of Personnel For Tourism

Apart from the need for specialised training for airport staff already mentioned it is necessary that hotels, travel agencies and tourist offices should be manned by personnel specially trained for their work.

In particular, attention should be paid to training facilities in hotel management. With a view to improving standards of the existing institutions set up for this purpose foreign instuctors, preferably under some aid programmes, should be employed, and some of the staff in training institutions may be sent overseas on short specialised courses.

Facilities for training in institutional catering should be provided in different parts of the country by setting up a number of craft training centres so that trained personnel are available for working in restaurants, railway dining cars, canteens etc.

There should be further discussion between the Department of Tourism and the State Governments as well as travel agencies to pursue the project of having short-term training courses in the off-season when the staff does not have its hands full.

A comparative study of tourists arrivals in India and

the foreign exchange earned from tourism during the last seven years, would show the earnings have not been increasing in proportion to the increase in the number of tourist arrivals. There was a 20 per cent increase in tourist arrivals in 1960 as compare to 1959, whereas the increase in earnings was about 7 per cent only.

This imbalance cannot be attributed to a change in the pattern of tourist expenditure. No doubt there has been a small increase in tourists belonging to middle income groups and also a slight decrease in the average duration of stay, but on the other hand the prices of hotels food transportation, entertainment etc. have been increasing. The imbalance could, therefore, only be the results of foreign exchange.

In any country suffering from acute shortage of foreign exchange, there are always anti-social elements attempting to secure foreign exchange by illegitimate methods. In considering precautionary measures, care has to be exercised to ensure that the measures adopted do not have the effect of defeating their own purpose by discouraging tourists from coming to India.

The steps to be taken to stop a leakage of foreign exchange would fall broadly in the following categories;

(a) There should be some simple measures which would make the tourist conscious of the fact that it is an offence to make sales of foreign exchange to unauthorised people at more than the official rates of exchange.

The tourist should in addition be made to feel that by cashing his traveller cheques at the right place and dealing with reputable organisations and agencies, he gets better value for his money.

The people who encash travellers' cheques should for their part, have the feeling that by surrendering the foreign exchange, they stand to benefit in respect of such of their normal legitimate activities as are dependent on their earning of foreign exchange.

The enforcement machinery should be active against all those who try to acquire foreign exchange from the tourist for illegitimate purposes.

The effectiveness of the recently introduced booklet recording foreign exchange transactions of tourists in stopping the leakage should be reviewed after six months experience.

People who get import licences in order to cater for the tourist trade should submit an account of their foreign exchange earnings and in the grant of licence due weight should be given to the amount of foreign exchange earned and surrended by them.

Building Up An Organisation

The success of the effort to promote tourism requires continuous attention to the ever-changing problems and prospects in this field. In the memorandum submitted to the Committee and in the oral evidence before it, it was emphasized, time and again, that the effort to promote tourism suffered, because its importance was not receiving the recognition that it deserved at the hands of Central Government Department, the State Governments and the public at large.

It is disappointing to note that very little of the Third Plan allocation of Rs. 8 crores-Rs. 3.5 crores for the centre and Rs. 4.5 crores for the states-has been utilised so far.

Apart from the recommendations embodied in this report to deal with new problems as they arise and for the various tasks which lie ahead, a proper organisational framework has to be built up.

In view of the value of tourism to the economy the public sector should assume a more active and positive role in matters related to tourism.

Apart from activities like hotel building referred to earlier, it would be an advantage for a public sector agency to organise for sale through travel agent etc. "package tours" in which the tourist will be able to pay at all-inclusive rates for internal travel, accommodation and sight-seeing. Such tours would be more attractive to visitors who can spend only a limited amount of time and money, would be easier to organise and eliminate the risk of leakage of foreign exchange. Then again, items like road transport facilities for tourists, supply of imported goods at reasonable prices to tourists and other similar activities would for various reasons be more suitably handled by a public-sector agency.

For such activities as would be essentially a commercial in character, a Corporation should be set up under the Companies Act, rather than as a Statutory body. Most of the activities of the Corporation would be self-supporting in nature, though a certain amount of promotional work may have to be undertaken. The resource required to set up the Corporation could be found out of the Third Plan provision for the Promotion of tourism the utilisation of which is proceding at a very slow pace.

The corporation could take over some of the functions of the Department of Tourism, such as publicity abroad. The department of Tourism could concentrate on activities which are, directly connected with the working of Government Departments and the exercise of regulatory control, where necessary.

Regulatory control over hotels, transport operators etc, should, as far as practicable, be exercised through executive rather than legal, authority. It would however, be advisable to take powers by law to license travel agents and regulate their activities.

A positive and nation wide feeling in favour of tourism has to be generated by inspiration from the top. Tourism should not be somthing extraneous but woven into the pattern of Indian life and Indian economy.

COMMITTEE OF MEMBERS OF PARLIAMENT ON HIGHER EDUCATION, 1963—REPORT

New Delhi, Ministry of Education, 1964. 65p.+ivp.

Chairman : Shri P.N. Sapru.

Members : Shri C. K. Bhattacharyya ; Shri M. P. Bhargava ; Shri Amar Nath Vidyalankar ; Shri Sidheshwar Prasad ; Shri P. Muthiar; Shri Satya Charan (expired) ; Shri P.K. Vasudevan Nair ; Shri R.M. Mehta.

Secretary : Shri Triyogi Narain (for some time he took leave and Shri C.L. Dhingra acted as secretary).

APPOINTMENT

At a meeting of the Informal Consultative Committee of Members of Parliament on Education held on the 6th of March, 1963, a resolution was moved by Shri Sidheshwar Prasad recommending that university education should be made a Union subject. In the discussion on the resolution, opinions were expressed in favour of the view that the Union Government should assume a greater responsibility than it has done hitherto in the field of higher education. Suggestions were made that the country should have a more or less uniform pattern of higher education. As the debate had raised some basic issues, Dr. K.L. Shrimali, the then Education Minister, suggested that members should agree to the appointment of a small committee from among members of the consultative committee to consider the constitutional provisions in all its aspects relating the coordination and determination of standards for institutions for higher education including research, scientific and technical education. The proposal appeared to be acceptable to the Members of the Consultative Committee and ultimately it was decided by the Government of India, in pursuance of the observations made by Dr. Shrimali, to appoint this committee.

TERMS OF REFERENCE

(i) To examine the provisions of the Constitution regarding the responsibility of the Central Government in the field of higher education with a view to finding out the extent to which the centre could assume greater responsibility in this field ; and

(ii) To suggest appropriate steps to be taken for the purpose.

CONTENTS

Introduction ; Historical Background ; Higher Education—Before and After Independence ; Guiding Principles ; Constitutional and Legal Position ; Maintenance or Standards ; Some other Aspects of Higher Education ; Role of the Union Government ; University Grants Commission A Review of Its Work ; The Gujarat University Case and Its Implications ; Recommendations ; Appendices I to IV.

RECOMMENDATIONS

1. We think that while Entry 66 of List I gives exclusive authority to the Union Government to coordinate and maintain standards it needs to be supplemented by an arrangement which would enable the Union Government to review the work and purposes achieved by university enactments and bring them, where necessary, into conformity with national requirements. We, therefore, recommend that university and higher education should be transferred from the State List to the Concurrent List, retaining intact Entry 66 in the Union List. Under this arrangement the State Governments will continue, as at present, to be responsible for the maintenance of universities. We have explained in the chapter on the Gujarat University case the exact impact of Entry 66 according to the view taken by the Supreme Court.

2. We have pointed out that the University Grants Commission is the main agency through which the Central Government has exercised the obligations imposed upon it by Entry 66. We are satisfied that under existing conditions, the University Grants Commission should have 15 members, of whom at least five should be full time members. It goes without saying that they should be men of the highest standing in the educational world and we, therefore, recommend that they should be persons of the status of Vice-Chancellors,

We have also been forced to come to the conclusion that it is undesirable that a person who is for the time being holding full time appointment as a Viee-Chancellor should be appointed Member of the Commission. We, therefore, recommend that serving Vice-Chancellors should not be appointed as Members of the Commission. Our reason for making this suggestion is that it is undesirable to place a person in a position where he may have divided loyalties. The prestige of the University Grants Commission depends upon its being an independent and impartial body. The composition of the Commission should be such as to give no impression to the public that it is not completely independent.

3. We have emphasized the importance of university education and research. They are vital for our national development. No country can afford to neglect them. Our considered opinion is that the grant for allotment for university education and research placed at the disposal of the University Grants Commission is very meagre. as was emphasized by Dr. Kothari, Chairman of the University Grants Commission in his statement before us. Without committing ourselves to any figure, we are strongly of the opinion that in the Fourth Five Year Plan, a very much larger amount should be placed at the disposal of the Commission.

4. Our enquiry has disclosed that the system of matching grants has not worked satisfactorily. Both State Governments and universities find it difficult to provide matching funds. We, therefore, do not favour the system of matching grants and feel that depending on the merits of the case, the condition of grant should be liberalized.

5. We are strongly of the view that the University Grants Commission should recognize, in consultation with the universities concerned, more and more institutions, as provided in clause (f) of Section 2 of the University Grants Commission Act, 1956, for purposes of financial aid. This will enable institutions which do not at present come within the purview of University Grants Commission Act to come under it.

6. We are distressed to find that the pay scales in aided colleges are grossly inadequate. We, therefore, recommend that steps should be taken to see that more and more colleges adopt the pay scales prescribed by the Commission for affiliated colleges.

7. We have emphasized in our report how education must be regarded as one integrated whole. Professional education cannot be completely divorced from general education. We, therefore, recommend that professional education including Medical (Basic), Agricultural, Engineering and Law should also come within the purview of the University Grants Commission.

8. A real improvement in university education is not possible without a corresponding increase in the efficiency of our secondary education. We, therefore, recommend that vigorous steps should be taken to improve the quality of secondary education. We refrain from going into further details in this matter as it is not within our purview.

9. Poverty should be no bar to the acquisition of the highest knowledge. It should be possible for common people to start life without avoidable handicaps. Provided a candidate has merit he should be enabled to join our higher educational institutions. We, therefore, recommend that the number of scholarships and sizarships for university education and research should be considerably increased in institutions of higher education. We attach importance to the question of amount as it should be one which would cover all reasonable expenses of a student.

10. The importance of the education of women cannot be over-emphasized. Women hold the key to the future progress of the country. The number of scholarships and sizarships for higher education for women students should be considerably increased.

11. We are not in favour of single-faculty universities, for neither the literatures, nor philosophies or the sciences can be separated one from the other. Nevertheless, we recognise that there is a place in our educational system for institutions of national status specializing in various disciplines in our country. We, of course, assume that there will be no complete divorce in these institutions between the humanities and the sciences.

12. We have examined in our Chapter on the University Grants Commission the working of that body. We have been disturbed by the fact that there have been occasions when a State Government has not consulted the Commission before setting up a university. We, therefore, recommend that the University Grants Commission Act should be so amended as to make it obligatory on the part of a State Government to consult the Commission before setting up a new university. We may point out that this change cannot be effected if education is not made a concurrent subject. Indeed, this is one of our main reasons for recommending that education should be brought on the Concurrent List. We feel that University Grants Commission Act should have specific provision which would enable the Commission to consistently refuse to give any financial aid to universities established without its prior consultation.

13. There are agencies at present for consultation between the universities and State Governments. The time has come now when a convention should be formally established for frequent consultations with State Governments and universities on all important policy issues. We are in favour of making the Inter-

University Board a more effective body and it should more and more be regarded as the spokesman of university opinion.

14. We think that the universities should give attention to the question of minimum age of entry. We think that there should be a minimum age. What that age should be is a matter for the universities to consider and decide. We are also of the opinion that the universities should pursue a common policy in regard to admissions and that admission particularly to professional institutions be based upon merit consistently with due regard to the interests of Scheduled castes, Scheduled tribes and other socially and educationally backward classes of society. It would, of course, be the concern of the universities to lay down the tests for merit.

15. One way in which the centre can play a greater part in promoting higher education is to establish at least one central institution of the highest standard in every state to serve as an example to other educational institutions in the State.

16. Our universities have a duty to perform towards those who are not able to complete their education and who desire to have the benefit of higher education. We recommend establishment of morning, evening colleges and correspondence courses for the benefit of those who are unable to pursue regular courses.

HEAD-ON COLLISION BETWEEN 35 UP PASSENGER AND 2 DOWN AVADH-TIRHUT MAIL AT UMESHNAGAR STATION (NORTH EASTERN RAILWAY) ON 4TH JANUARY, 1963—REPORT

Delhi, Manager of Publications, 1969. 15p.

One-Man Commission : Shri D.C. Desai ;

APPOINTMENT

The Commission was constituted under the Ministry of Tourism and Civil Aviation (Commission of Railway Safety) in accordance with Rule 9 of Railway Board's Notification No. 1926-T, dated the March 19, 1930.

TERMS OF REFERENCE

To inquire into the collision between No. 2 Down Avadh-Tirhut Mail and No. 35 Up Passenger, which took place at about 4.00 hours on the morning of 4th January, 1963 at Umeshnagar Station on the Katihar-Barauni Section (M.G.) of the North Eastern Railway.

CONTENTS

Summary ; Inspection and Inquiry ; Preamble (Description of accident ; Casualties ; Composition of the Trains ; Damage ; Passengers ; First aid and Medical Assistance ; Refreshment ; Restoration of Communications) ; Local Conditions (Description of locality ; System of Working) ; Oral Evidence ; Material Evidence; Discussion (Possible causes of Accident ; Driver of 35 Up passing signals at danger ; Down Signals taken off after replacing Up signals ; Up signals taken off after replacing Down signals ; Taking off through signals for 2 Down ; Driver of 2 Down passing signals at danger ; Priority of reception ; Reasons for Driver's failure ; Setting of Training points for a different line; Provision of outer signals ; speed of trains) ; Conclusion ; Recommendations made by the Commission of Railway Safety in connection with 'Head on collision between 35 Up Passenger and 2 Down Avadh Tirhut Mail at Umeshnager Station, N.E. Railway, on 4th January, 1963.

CONCLUSIONS

Cause Of Accident

Having considered all the oral, material and circumstantial evidence available during my enquiry and inspections, I have come to the conclusion that the collision between 2 Down Mail and 35 Up Passenger at Umeshnagar was caused by the Driver of No. 2 Down Mail having passed the Down flome signal at danger while entering the station.

Responsibility

I hold the Driver, R.D. Roy, of No. 2 Down Mail responsible for momentary inattention to the duty of observing the aspects of signals while approaching a station, thus violating G.R.'s 76 and 122. He is 48 years old and has put in 31 years' service. He had passed the eye sight examination on 27th January, 1962 with a pair of glasses which were in his possession. He had been punished on a few occasions for losing time on the run or turning up late on duty but not for causing any accident.

Relief Measures

(a) There was a delay of 1 hour in starting the Medical Van from Samastipur. The Railway Administration have investigated into the reasons for this delay and taken up with the staff responsible. Apart from this, the relief measures organised by the railway were prompt and satisfactory.

(b) The magistrate, police officers and the S.D.O., Shri Sahai, of Khagaria gave all possible assistance in the rescue operations promptly and in adequate measure. The Secretary, Thana Congress Committee, Khagaria, took charge of the dead bodies and performed the cremation rights according to custom. The Nagrik Sewa Samiti paid for the cost of food, clothes and blankets. A number of other social organisations from Ballia and Monghyr also helped in the relief arrangements.

(c) Special mention should be made of the yeoman's service rendered by Shri Kedar Narain Singh Azad, M.L.A. of Khagaria who contacted civil, police and medical authorities in addition to the local social and volunteer organisations immediately on hearing of the accident. He personally went to the Government Hospital, met the Deputy Superintendent and brought medical staff and equipment for relief work to the station. He informed the local volunteer corps and called upon the Nagrik Swayamsevak Samiti to collect clothes, food, blankets, tea and other refreshments. All these were sent in the medical relief van from Mansi under his personal supervision to Umeshnagar. He also despatched another train from Khagaria with a relief party, blankets, medicines and other materials to the site of accident. Finally, he went by motor trolley to Umeshnagar with the District Engineer and two civil doctors of Khagaria Hospital and assisted in the rescue operations.

(d) I am satisfied that all civil, railway and police officials as well as local volunteer organisations rose to the occasion and organised relief and rescue work in a praiseworthy manner. I suggest that the Railway Board may send letters of appreciation and commendation to the persons and organisations concerned.

ACCIDENT TO NO. 26 UP BANGALORE CITY COCHIN HARBOUR TERMINUS EXPRESS AT KUPPAM STATION OF SOUTHERN RAILWAY ON 21ST MAY, 1967—REPORT

Delhi, Manager of Publications, 1970. 16p.

One-Man Commission : Shri V. Venkataramayya.

APPOINTMENT

The Commission was constituted under the Ministry of Tourism and Civil Aviation (Commission of Railway Safety) in accordance with Rule 10 of the Railway Board's Notification No. 59-TTV/42/1 dated 11th April, 1966.

TERMS OF REFERENCE

To inquire into the accident to train No. 26 Up Bangalore City-Cochin Harbour Terminus Island Express at Kuppam Station, on Bangalore City-Jalarpet Broad Gauge Main line section of the Southern Railway at about 21-50 hours on 21st May 1967.

CONTENTS

Corrigendum ; Summary ; The Accident ; Casualties ; Inspection and Inquiry ; The Train ; Number of Passengers ; Damage ; The Relief ; Restoration of Traffic ; Local Conditions (The locality ; System of working ; The Permanent Way ; Permissible Speed ; Weather and Visibility) ; Summary of Evidence ; Inspection, Observation and Tests ; Discussion (Time of the accident ; Speed of the train ; Permanent way ; Signals and Interlocking ; The condition of the Engine ; Brakes) ; Conclusions ; Annexures I and II.

CONCLUSIONS

Cause Of The Accident

From the evidence available and from my detailed observations, I have come to the conclusion that the accident to No. 26 Up "Bangalore City-Cochin Harbour Terminus" Island Express at Kuppam station on the Bangalore City-Jalarpet Broad Gauge Main line section of the Southern Railway at about 21-50 hours on 21st

May, 1967 was caused by the inability of the Driver to control the train, which ran past the Starter Signal of the platform loop line in the 'ON' position and crashed into the Sand Hump.

Responsibility for the Accident

The Driver Shri G. Jeremiah was mainly responsible for the accident. He started his train from Tyakal station with insufficient vacuum in contravention of Rules 3 (b), 5 (c) and 6 (g) of the Rules and special Instructions for the use of the Automatic Vacuum Brake on trains. When he found that the train vacuum pipe had cracked and that he could not create sufficient vacuum, he should have stopped his train at Tyakal and arranged for changing his engine. He had mis-judged his ability to stop the train on a descending gradient with partial vacuum in the train and with steam brake on the engine.

Shri G. Jeremiah, aged 45 years, was originally appointed on 7-3-1940 as Fireman Apprentice and was later promoted as Fireman on 16-4-1942. He was promoted as Driver 'C' on 27-8-1949 in which capacity he worked till 19-7-1962 when he was promoted to officiate as Assistant Foreman/Running, Jalarpet. He was reverted as Driver 'B' at his own request with effect from 17-8-1964 and subsequently promoted to officiate as Driver 'A' on 28-10-1964. He had no punishments during the last 10 years as a Driver in connection with working of his train.

Guard Shri C.R. Ekambaram was also responsible for the accident. He should have detained the train at Tyakal station, as there was not sufficient vacuum. He contravened the subsidiary Rules 113 (ii) (a) and (b) of the General Rules and also Rules 3 (b), 5 (c) and 6 (d) of the Rules and special Instructions for the use of the Automatic Vacuum Brake on Trains. He had not been vigilant and had not cared to consult the Driver when there was not sufficient Vaccum in the rear brake van.

Shri C.R. Ekambaram, aged 57 years, was originally appointed as Training Pupil on probation on 26-7-1929 and was confirmed as Train Clerk on 7-4-1930. He was promoted as III class Guard on 4-2-1940 and as II class Guard from 20-3-1947. He was promoted as temporary 'A' Grade Guard with effect from 27-12-1954 and was later confirmed in that capacity on 1-12-1957. In connection with the train operation he was once censured for failure to ensure that train No. 604 on 19-9-1957 was stopped clear of failing mark to enable train No. 611 to be started in time which resulted in 35 minutes late start to the train.

The senior Train Examiner of Bangalore City Station (Shri P.S. Sripathy) failed in his duty to rectify the defective brake cyclinders or to give a correct Brake Power certificate. He cannot, however, be considered responsible for the accident, which was caused by the driver attempting to work the train with insufficient vacuum after the vacuum pipe had cracked. His (Shri Sripathy's) contribution to the cause of the accident can, if any, be considered as indirect and marginal only.

Relief Arrangements

The local doctors and the public had been very prompt in reaching the site. They spared no efforts in extricating the injuried and in giving medical attention. Their help and assistance were very commendable. The Road crane of Bharat Earth Movers Limited had rendered invaluable assistance in shifting and lifting the parts of the buckled coach and in extricating the injured passengers. The Railway Administration might like to convey their appreciation to all of them.

The Relief Medical Van from Jalarpet reached the accident site promptly but the Break-Down Special from Bangarapet was detained at Gudupulli for nearly half an hour. This detention could have been avoided.

Considering the tragic circumstances and resulting confusion at the time, I am satisfied that medical attention had been prompt and adequate.

STUDY TEAM ON FIVE YEAR PLAN PUBLICITY, 1963—REPORT

New Delhi, Ministry of Information and Broadcasting, 1965. 194p.

Chairman : Amar Nath Vidyalankar ;
Members : Radha Nath Rath ; P. Range Reddi ; Roshan Lal Chaturvedi ; S.M. Joshi ;
Secretary : A.R. Baji ;

APPOINTMENT

The Study Team was appointed Under the Resolution No. 9 (70)/59-PP dated 3rd April 1963. The Government of India have been considering for some time the question of undertaking an Assessment of the impact of various programmes of Publicity for the five year plans which is carried on through different media of Mass Communication under the Ministry of Information and Broadcasting. The department which are dealing with such publicity are the Directorate of Field Publicity, the All India Radio, the Press Information Bureau, the Directorate of Advertising and Visual Publicity, the Films Division, the Publication Division, the Photo Division and the Song and Drama Division. Public Co-operation and public opinion constitute the principal force behind planning in any country. THE GOVERNMENT HAVE ACCORDINGLY decided to set up a Study Team to make a detailed study of the impact of the measures taken to publicise the Plan and to report to Government about steps which should be taken for better utllization of the existing staff and resources. The team will also examine the question of the more effective utilization of the Publicity and Audio-Visual material produced by the Ministry of Community Development and Cooperation and distributed for the purpose of propagating the philosophy and objectives of Panchayati Raj, Sahakari Samaj & Community Development movements.

TERMS OF REFERENCE

The terms of reference of the Study Team will be to Study and report on :

(1) The Plan publicity being carried on by different media units of the Ministry of Information & Broadcasting and its impact on the Public with a view to improving its efficiency and broadening its impact, with particular reference to the following aspect :

(i) Arrangements for publicity

(ii) Co-ordination and activities between

(a) The different Media Heads of the Ministry

(b) The Centre and the States ; and

(2) The Utilization of the Publicity and audio-Visual material produced by the Government of India for the Purpose of propagating the philosophy and objectives of Panchayati Raj, Sahakari Samaj & Community Development movements. And to recommend to the Government ways and means for the better utilisation of the Publicity programmes undertaken by the Ministry of Information and Broadcasting and the Ministry of Community Development & Cooperation.

This Study team was required to submit its report within a period of six months. The period has been extended up to August 31, 1964.

CONTENTS

The report is in 3 parts :

Part I : Introduction, Scope and method of study ; Concept and approach of plan publicity ; the problem and the performance ; Coordination.

Part II : Broadcasting ; Film ; Field Publicity ; Songs and Dramas. Advertising and Visual Publicity ; Press ; Publications ; Publicity for Community Development ; Panchayati Raj Sahakari Samaj.

Part III : Summary of Conclusions and recommendations ; Appendices (A) Resolution of the Government of India ; (B) Questionnaires on Plan Publicity through Films, Broadcasts, Songs & Drama, Adversiting and Visual Publicity, Publications and Mobile Units, Mailed to Non-Officials ; (C) Total, Category-wise and Media-wise, Despatch and receipt of mail questionnaires ; (D) Questionnaires issued to Heads of media units and Regional Officers under them ; (E) States/Union Territories, District and Places visited ; (F) Questionnaires issued to Development Commissioners and Registrars of Cooperative Societies in the States.

RECOMMENDATION

This is a study of "What the Publicity arrangements are at present" and a report on "What they should be". Mass Media have not been oriented in method and approach to suit the needs of a developing society. The Appointment of the Team is an indication of Governments desire to take stock before embarking on expansion and recognition.

Mere adjustments and practical improvements within existing resources offer no solution. Available resources—Manpower and Material—have to be pooled effectively through planned publicity efforts and through fully bringing the State Publicity Organisations into the picture.

The Core of the Study is to assess the Impact of Plan Publicity with the objective of widening its scope through more efficient planning and excution of the publicity programmes.

The Methods of study employed including inviting written memoranda from Public, sample survey through mail, questionnaires sent to officials and the public, information from different publicity media units concerned, discussoin within Central and State Ministers and official concerned with information and publicity, legislators, Presidents and Members of the Zila Parishads, Panchayat Samitis and Panchayats and villagers, representatives of public organisations, members of public and on the spot field investigations in rural areas in mine States and three Union Territories. 89 out of 186 districts were covered by field investigations.

The findings may be challenged as being contrary to statistical information ; but these are a faithful reflection of what a cross-section of people at the receiving end think.

A radical departure from existing coordination arrangements with States is needed to bring into existence an effective mass communication mechinery.

The entire publicity effort—whether general or plan—must be pervaded and informed by the Socials ideals that the nation is striving for.

Concept and Approach of Plan Publicity : Plan publicity should generate among the masses a clear understanding of the "Vission of the future" projected in our plans and prepare the minds of people to meet the challenge of social problems that would arise due to industrialization, urbanization and modernization of the economy.

Government alone cannot shoulder the responsibility. A total mobilization of all opinion-moulding cadres of leadership is needed.

The concept of socialist pattern of society the urgency of the task of development and the role of the individuals and groups in this task should be communicated to the masses in a dynamic way and with missionary zeal. The essential basis of publicity programmes should be to bring the masses into action and to make the principal beneficiaries of development the Chief instruments and architects of the new society.

Publicity personnel in the field should establish the closest liasion with extension staff and ensure that general plan bulicity is linked with informational services emphasising improved techniques of farming and better rural living.

The research aspect of Plan publicity, which has received scant attention so far, needs to be strengthened in the most immediate future.

The objective of publicity, generally speaking should be to inform, persuade and inspire to make peoples minds receptius, to familiarise them with social and economic changes and to develop local executive for deision-making.

Problems and the Performance : Permanent cures and not palliatives are needed to free publicity policy, approach and method from the restrictive and inhibiting influences of today, some basic facts of publicity have been glassed over for too long.

The fundamental aim of the Plan publicity should be the motivation of group and individual action for realisation of the 'good life'. We are seeking for the masses. Information service should generate a wide spread understanding of basic aspects of democratic planning.

Developmental communication is a two-way traffic of 'information services' and 'intelligence services.'

The size and character of the masses to be reached and the tools and equipment available for this purpose have to be reckoned with in judging the performance.

The impact on the people of the existing programmes has been the srtenuous, vague and diffused and no section of the population has been touched in a forceful manner. Publicity has lacked purpose and has been weak in approach.

Publicity effort in urban areas needs point, direction and purpose and should be based on research and survey. In rural areas, it should be more broad-based and exclusively and imaginatively presented.

Radio, Film, Song & Drama and Exhibitions are the most productive media for publicity among rural masses ; 'printed word' publicity under present circumstances is a comparatively wasteful effort.

Semi-urban population, essentially rural in its background and an effective Channel of Communication with rural areas is a target of the highest importance to Plan Publicity but ill-served at present. The effective media for this section are Radio, Film, Exhibitions and language newspapers.

In urban areas, printed word is the most effective means of addressing the educated sections, should be reached through organised radio listening and documentary exhibition.

Students need to be converted to the new faith of democratic socialism.

A major public criticism has been that actual achievements fall short of what publicity projects. The content of publicity should confirm of realities.

There is no clear conception of the role of publicity functionaries ; they lack an intelligent understanding of the requirements of the new society being established on democratic socialism.

Publicity of the radical socio-economic changes aimed at in the Plan should be planned and organised on a nation wide war footing. Some of the basic principles of publicity campaigns should be that themes are planned and fixed periodically, ruling the different sections of the community and bearing relation to current problems, the basic social and economic conecpts, the change in emphasis as public opinion demands and the need of peoples participation. Departmental approach and publicity should be abandoned and achievements should be projected as national attainments.

Communication with the masses has been approached with apathy and indifference. Allocations for publicity have been very meagre and are regarded as a drain on the economy rather than investment in human resources. While Govt. has come to regard, publicity functionarie's as 'status symbols', the general public has come to view them as Propaganda boys of Government.

Expansion of media of mass communication in post-independence era, though striking in itself, has been inadequate compared to the requirements of reaching the vast numbers dispersed over wide areas.

The media units accord a low priority to plan publicity, conforming to budgetary allocations which are infinitesimally small. The dyarchic system of Central and State publicity has also encouraged disipation of the scarce resources.

Scientific planning and methodical execution, which have been conspicuously ladening so far, are essential to success of publicity. Publicity Planning Groups should be established at the Centre and in the States. A Director-General of Plan Publicity should organise, supervise and guide the total national effort.

It is mismanner to call the existing Research and Reference Division, providing as it does mainly reference services. Its research activity should be reoriented for scientific communication research under qualified directorial and research staff.

The cumulative impression of governmental publicity is that it is still a desk-bound service purveying facts and figures of no meaning to the common man. Publicity effort should be correlated with problems and issues agitating the public mind.

There is at present probably nothing like satisfactory field intelligence available to publicity programme planners.

The existing Directorate of Field Publicity should be converted into the Directorate of Plan Publicity Evaluation and intelligence.

No official participation is publicity, already being evaluated by a separate committee, needs to be broad-based and its integration with official publicity secured.

Present publicity is largely directed to urban based educated classes, with disproportionate emphasis on English educated sections, rural population in major clients, have not yet received a square deal.

Generally, publicity through the metropolitan press is sought with a heavy emphasis on coverage of ministerial pronouncements, conference proceedings and factual accounts of achievements in isolated sectors of the economy. This imbalance should be rectified, among other methods, by extending the work of Information Officers to cover advising an publicity through all media.

Imbalance in publicity resulting from an over-emphasis on publicity though personalities needs rectification.

There has been a disconcerting insensitivity to public criticism which has damaged governmental public relations and for which policy-makers rather than the functionaries should take the blame. The fault lies in the failure to depart from the pre-independence approach of only selling Government to people without reflecting peoples needs in governmental policies.

Publicity organisations have become "ineffective agents of action on behalf of the planners". The position can be profitably revered by recognising publicity as an integral part of the machinery of adult education.

Coordination : Communicating with masses requires the closest coordination between various State agencies from Panchayat but no machinery at present exists to secure effective co-ordination.

The greater the number of agencies, the greater is the need of their co-ordination action. Like a military campaign, publicity should aim at striking results.

The high-powered committee for Direction & Co-ordination has done commendable work, but a handicap has been its infrequent meetings, the limited scope of its composition, the inadequate follow-up machinery and the absence of assistance of a professional group of publicity planners.

The conferences of State Ministers and State Directors of Information have concerned themselves mostly with administrative details rather than policy and methodology. They have not reviewed action taken on their recommendations, which lack constitutional or conventional sanction, and have not succeeded in bringing about co-ordination.

The durational and functional vicimiludes of the post of Adviser on plan publicity have resulted in his ineffective functioning.

The Inter-Media Standing Committee can serve only a limited purpose and cannot provide the close coordination necessary.

The State Publicity Co-ordination Committee rarely meet, and do not cover much ground. Centre-State Co-ordination in the field is operating on personal basis which has genearally not yielded profitable results.

The general assessment is that existing co-ordination arrangements are not conductive to efficiency or economy, resulting in fragmentical, diffused and directionless publicity effort.

The Centre has a clear responsibility to import a rational purpose of the entire plan publicity programme. This is the theory behind the recommendations made in the Report.

Publicity should be a joint venture with Centre providing planning, direction, guidance and leadership and States implementing the directives. The main outlines of the scheme recommended are : uniformity in publicity policy and guidance secured through States' association in policy making at the highest level; a basic pattern of methodology and techniques for publicity campaigns to be evolved Centrally; provision for assessment and public reaction analysis under central auspicies; implementation of field programmes under supervision of State authorities and provisions of training facilities by the Centre for all publicity personnel.

All Central media should continue to render services as here to fore, but field execution should be carried out by States on behalf of the Centre which has the advantage of joint responsibility, unified policy and planning.

Policy directives should issue from the existing Committee for Co-ordination and Direction, where jurisdiction should extend to State programmes. The Committee's membership should include three to four State Ministers of Information, and it should normally meet once every three months to review progress and issue directives.

The Committee should brief all State Information Ministers at annual conferences and seek their advice. The Conferences should have powers to commit financially and administratively the State Governments to schemes approved by it.

Central Ministers concerned with development departments should exchange views with the Committee at alternate meetings. Secretaries of the departments should clear inter-Ministerial financial and administrative details in meetings held every four months.

There should be a Committee for Direction and Co-ordination at the State level, meeting once in three months, and functioning in the same manner as the Central Committee.

To plan publicity campaign strategy, a Central Publicity Planning Group should be set up in the Ministry of Information and Broadcasting with a Director-General of Plan Publicity as the chief technical executive to plan and direct the publicity programme. He should not be saddled with administrative duties.

A Planning Group should be formed to be associated with the Director-General in discharging his functions.

The Director-General should have under his control the Directorates of Communication Research and Plan Publicity Evaluation and Intelligence; the existing Research and Reference Division and the Directorate of Field Publicity should form the nuclear of these Directorates manned by experienced, trained personnel. Half of the existing units of the Field Publicity Directorate should be utilised as the field organisation for the Directorate of Plan Publicity Evaluation and Intelligence. The Director of Song and Drama of Plan Publicity Evaluation and Intelligence. The Director of Song and Drama and the officer advising on the mechanics of communication in Indian languages should have a small organisation to assist them in day-to-day work, which should be provided out of the existing Song and Drama Division.

Similar Planning Groups should also be set up in State Capitals, to work as agents of the Central Planning Group in giving effect to the Central directives.

The State Director of Information should be the chief executive agent on behalf of the Central and State Governments for all publicity activities and he should have appropriate ex-officio status in the Development Commissioners'.officer.

The machinery at the District Block and Panchayat levels should compromise the District Publicity Officer, the publicity supervisor, the Social Education Officer and the Panchayat Secretary or School Teacher, with their respective duties defined.

A regional Director of Plan Publicity should be appointed in each state on behalf of the Central Government to control and administer all Central media activities.

The CIS officer needs to be given in service training and orientation including the importing of knowledge of the goals and objectives of democratic planning and socialist pattern of society.

It is desirable and advantageous to bring the State Publicity personnel within the scope of the CIS. A general upgrading of salary scales of Central and State personnel is needed.

Close coordination is urgently needed not only between Centre and States but also between the different Central Ministers and Departments doing Plan publicity. CIS officers should supervise and control publicity units in all Ministeries concerned as is now in operation in such Ministeries as Railways, Community Development and Food and Agriculture.

All publicity functions of the State Govts. should be unified in the State Departments of Information.

Broadcasting. In India, Radio is the most powerful medium of information, education and entertainment. In the context of economic and social reconstruction it has a sensitive and significant role to pay.

Radio programmes have shown an undue concern with publicity to personalities and departments of Govt. instead of projecting achievements as national efforts in which people have a large share. AIR has a moral obligation to serve as the voice of the people as much as the mouthpiece of Government. Plan publicity programmes comprise only a very small proportion of total broadcast programmes ; the transmission and listening facilities need augmentation. Yet the impact of radio programmes for rural listeners has been quite improcosive, direct and decisive, as compared to other media. This is a clear case for a more intensified and efficient use of the radio in rural India.

The impact of Plan publicity programmes for urban listeners has been less impressive and less direct and decisive. They have to be effectively tackled by more organised and determined efforts.

The daily rural programme are very popular and received with enthusiasm and eagerness by the audience.

The new content of rural programmes is suffering from imbalance of urban-biased news, which needs to be corrected. Language, duration and timing of programmes are unsatisfactory in certain areas. For deep psychological impact broadcast of unedited recordings of reactions of villagers is desirable. The presentation of rural characters as ignorant backwoods men should be discouraged. The programmes do not contain much of interest to backward and non-farming sections. (a) A news gathering network should be organised and rural news coverage in the existing bulletins should be stepped up and ultimately a special rural news bulletin should be introduced (b) Rural preference should be taken into account in programme planning, the planners should keep in constant touch with rural life by periodical tours, and also provide guidance, advise and information on problems as they arise, (c) The duration of the programmes should be extended and adequate provision should be made in the Fourth Plan for the purpose. (d) The timings of the broadcasts should be fixed according to the requirements of regional and seasons, based on broader-based consultations. (e) The number and scope of mobile field units of AIR shoud be increased and their working, including visits to less accessible areas, toned up. (f) Solutions should be found to the difficulties in more extensive broadcasts to Adivasi areas and transmission and listening facilities in border areas should be given priority consideration.

The community listening scheme, though implemented at a slow pace, has made the rural listeners the most widespread, organised and receptive patrons of AIR programmes. The Radio Rural Forums have the potential to help the decision-making process at the village level to gain momentum. Above all, a state-owned radio system should cater to the informational educational and entertainment needs of the rural masses.

The proposal to increase community listening sets by 1.75 lakhs in the current plan should be implemented early In the Fourth Plan a 100 percent coverage in respect of both transmission and community listening facilities should be aimed at.

A systematic survey of replacement requirements of community sets should be instituted immediately with quick follow-up action. The Centre should bear 50 per cent of the cost of replacement of condemned sets. The local communities have necessarily to bear a part of the cost and should build up replaeement funds over ten years

Manufacturing defects have been detected in community sets even at initial delivery. Steps should be taken to ensure that no such lapses occur in future

All demands for the sets should be met, the centre should either ensure expeditious delivery or permit states to arrange supplies on their own.

Govt. subsidised schemes providing domestic sets to rural communities should be abandoned. But in the Fourth Plan a 100 percent coverage in respect of both values on community sets, which would involve extra cost which should be borne by the communities.

From 1964-65 only transisterised sets should be supplied under the community listening scheme, which offer many advantages.

The feasibility of setting up a radio manufacturing plant in the public sector should be examined.

The capacity of the single supply firm on contract to Govt. for dry battery packs for community listening sets should be augmented, or contracts should be given to other firms also to improve the supply position.

Short-term training courses on handling and maintenance of the sets should be organised and a sense of responsibility included in those who handle them.

State Govt. should lay down and enforce satisfactory procedures for inspection and report on the working of the community sets.

All India Radio should arrange, with State Government Corporation, for a model scheme of in-service training for mechanics.

In view of the meagre resources of State Information Departments, the Central Govt. should accept in principle the proposal to share a part of the maintenance expenditure, the actual quantum to be agreed upon between the Central and State Governments.

The Audio Rural Forums programme deserves a first priority in plan publicity.

The memberships of the Forums should be more broadbased that at present; mostly the advanced sections of the rural community alone are the members to day.

The informational and instructional broadcasts in the programme should be followed up by distribution to relevant literature and demonstration by Block Staff.

Special cells should be set up in State Information Departments to collect and classify all relevant data for ready reference and quick access to information needed for Forum programmes.

The District Publicity Officer should supervise the work of Block Officers in respect of organising and activating the Forums.

The Chief Organiser, the official responsible for organising and energing the forums, should be a fairly senior officer working on a full-time basis, and assisted by deputies and officers of the Central Directorate of Plan Publicity, Evaluation and Intelligence.

The Third Plan target of 25,000 Forums should be

achieved, in the Fourth Plan a Forum should be established in each of the two lack panchayats in the country. Chairman and Conveners of the Forums should be imparted short-term training in discussion procedures and follow-up action.

Block officers should show keener interest in the Forums, responsible development department officers should work as liason officer and Zila Parishads and Panchayat members should be responsible for creating awareness of the implications of the Forum schemes.

Government of India should take up with State Governments and management associations the question of compulsory provision of wireless sets in industrial establishments and speedy implementation of the Industrial Listening Forums Scheme, recommended at a 1962 seminar in Ahmedabad, for the benefit of the industrial working class. All India Radio should also extend the wire broadcasting service to workers colonies in major industrial centres. Labour representatives comments and views should also be broadcast in the programmes.

Courses on development planning should form an integral part of school curriculum. Special broadcasts on planning for schools should be organised and listening facilities provided in high schools on the Farm Forums model.

Serious-minded student youth should be brought into the Radio clubs, their interest in the clubs sustained and a general knowledge paper on plans, based on the broadcasts, prescribed.

AIR should establish organised listening groups in all towns and semi-urban areas where the listeners are the most receptive audience for Plan publicity.

Television, a powerful medium, but still in experimental stage in Delhi only, should be extended to the country in the forseeable future.

Film : Film-going in urban areas has become almost a national habit.

A medium of communication, film has an important and substantial part in developmental programmes.

Film has an emotional appeal, added to it is the glamour attached to film stars. No film, including the ones carrying social purpose, has proved as much a box office success as those featuring popular stars.

The demand for more extensive exhibition of documentaries, newsreels, and other films in widespread both in rural and urban areas.

Commercial exhibition of documentaries, newsreel, etc., in Bombay, Madras and Delhi has been very popular and should be extended to other urban centres. University Film Council should also be pressed into service and film clubs formed all over the country; documentary festivals should also be organised. The law of compulsory screening of approved films should be enforced strictly wherever it may now be violated.

while the best among the Film Divisions documentaries can stand international comparison and compilition, the rest are works of less than imaginative art.

Eminent producers should be, engaged in producing more Film Divisions documentaries than has been done so far.

Subjects of documentaries are determined by the sponsoring Ministeries and thereby lend to project personalities and achievements. There is considerable scope for improvement of scripts and the quality of their translation into regional languages. A portion of the documentaries should have a regional complexion.

Spoken language of the people should be employed more liberally in commentary writing, and the reading should be less rapid.

Colour films on development subjects are in great demand. Cartoon films create great impact and should be produced in larger numbers.

The proposed colour processing laboratory for the Films Division should be set up in the near future.

Half of the Films Divisions annual documentary production should be shot in the different States, which need not be dubled in all languages; each such documentary should be produced in the majority language of a State for exhibition in that State only. The other half may be produced as in the past but with emphasis on diverse regional coverage.

The production wing of the Films Division should be decentralised to secure wider coverage of different regions.

Newsreels should contain news of local interest for exhibition in the local areas. A monthly or two-monthly newsreel should also be produced for exhibition in rural areas.

At least two feature-type documentaries should be produced annually.

Private producers should be commissioned to produce feature films of educative and entertainment value under some guarantee scheme. Film industry may also contribute its share to the national effort by stars offering honorary services or on token payment for starring in films of this category.

Film strip production should be taken on hand soon.

The number of documentaries on tribal life should be increased as also the requirements of border areas met.

Field Publicity : The objective of field publicity is laudable. The aim of Central organisation is to provide a national ideological base to the common mans understanding of planned development.

Public reaction consenous is that the performance of field units has been neither adequately impressive nor fully purposive. The smallness of the Central organisation, the paucity of its resources, the indifferent skil of personnel and lack of adequate control and supervision of the field programmes have conditioned its performance.

At least half the film shows organised by the field units are held in urban areas or within easy reach of such centres. Distribution over districts is erratic, uneven, irrational the less accessible areas being neglected. Introductory remarks are not informative on the themes of the films and their linking with the national objectives. Selection is indifferent.

In the selection and organisation of song and drama functions, the performance of the officers has not been satisfactory.

Oral communication which should have been the main means of publicity aided by film, song and drama performances has generally been relegated to the background.

The quality and content of oral communication leave scope for anxiety and concern. The main handicaps appear to be inadequate knowledge and appreciation of local conditions and problems and inability to assimilate and utilise the guidance material received.

Little preparation and thought is bestowed on themes and content of symposia and seminars. Regional Officers, better equipped for organising the activities, have little time as they are preoccupied with headquarters duties and routine inspection.

Some definite achievements have been made in respect of programmes directed to women and children.

Selection of personnel has generally not been according to the standards of competence, zeal and enthusiasm necessary.

The status and the hard life of field officers resulting from the nature of their duties has also contributed to their poor performance.

Regional officers should control all the Central media units in a State and actively associate with the planning of Plan publicity.

In the organised set-up proposed, the Director will be one of the principal advisers to the Director-General of Plan publicity, in his new role as the Director of Plan Publicity Evaluation and Intelligence.

State-Central Coordination is based largely on personal equation than on an institutional basis.

The main cause of the improductive effort of field publicity has been the dyrachical approach to conceptual and organisation aspects.

From the view point of physical means of publicity, in valuation to the millions to be reached, there is no duplication of effort between the Central and State organisations. There is diffusion rather than duplication of effort.

Central personnel have more freedom to perform their primary task of publicity than the State personnel who have multiple demands to satisfy.

State Governments have meagre facilities while capacity of centre to operate in the field is limited, joint responsibility and participation is the answer.

The custody and display of publicity aids should be entrusted to the school teacher or panchayat secretary.

At the Block level, publicity should be the principal charge of the social Education Officer who should be responsible of the District Publicity Officer in this regard.

Field units, are in every five Blocks, should be set up with mobile cinema vans to organise more cinema shows in the rural areas. The Publicity Supervisors, in charge of the units, should organise song and drama activities and secure services of local leaders for oral communication of publicity. For this, all existing Central and State vans. which will be sufficient for the purpose, should be placed under the State Directorates of Information which should be the channels of all field publicity Central or State.

The District Field Publicity Officer should be entrusted chiefly with a supervision, inspection, guidance and direction of Publicity Supervisors and Social Education Officers, among other related activities.

Half the number of central units should be retained for special assignments in strategic areas or for other special accassiars. They should be under the charge of the Regional Director of Plan Publicity. The remaining half should be taken over by the Directorate of Plan Publicity Evaluation and Intelligence as its field units.

Publicity functionaries at all levels working in the field should have common designations.

Song and Drama: Song and Drama, touching the deepest emotions of the illiterate millions, is a matchless medium of propagating planned development.

It is difficult to reach the masses without utilising this medium which has the advantage of personal, intimate and traditional appeal.

The Medium's limitation is that it can be only supplemented to other media, as its appeal is emotional rather than personal and its purpose is to inspire rather than inform.

Incompetently written and produced dramas can produced no desired effect. A great majority of the dramas produced by registered troupes fall in this category.

Good script have not been available. To rectify this, more attractive terms to playwrights, who have shown a lack of involvement in national reconstruction, and less insistence on carrying direct messages in the scripts are some of the steps required to be taken.

The procedure for approving scripts should be further simplified, composition of the Scripts Committees should be reviewed and public spirited citizens with interest in theatre should be brought to serve on the Committees.

The quality of registered troupes is below standard. Good performers are generally attracted to perform in the cities. Also, there is an interdepartmental competition in commissioning the troupes. A standardised fee should be determined and the Song & Drama Division should raise the maximum of its payment. Amateur and College dramatic Clubs should be subsidised for a limited number of performances State Government troupes should also be commissioned on subsidy basis.

A local theatrical group should be formed for every 15 Blocks with a nominal Central financial grant, first on a pilot basis and later extended to the whole country if the results so warrant.

Song and drama activities, currently being organised through the Regional Offices of the Directorate of Field Publicity, should be organized through qualified officers of the State Information Directorates.

Drama festivals should be organised on a regional basis throughout the country under Central auspices with Cooperation of State Governments concerned.

The Central Drama Troup, while efficient in itself has not been able to satisfy the requirement of experimenting with new plays and evolving standards of private troupes to follow. It should be transfered to one of the neighbouring Hindi-speaking States under the Sponsored Drama Troupes Scheme.

The Departmental Troupe for U.P. and Bihar should also be transferred to either U.P. or Bihar. Also, the Centrally sponsored troupes scheme, a sound publicity Venture, should be implemented soon.

At least one ballet should be produced every year and staged in different parts under Central auspices.

The Song and Drama should be attached to the Central Publicity Planning Group as adviser to the Director-General of Plan Publicity to assist him in planning and directing the Song & Drama Programme in the country.

Advertising & Visual Publicity : Publicity, through display advertisements, posters, folders, etc. has not yielded results commensurate with the investment made. A principal drawback of the Directorate has been the absence of survey and research which would be rectified by the proposed Communication Research and Plan Publicity Evaluation and Intelligence Division.

Exhibitions and outdoor publicity have been effective and should be exploited more extensively.

Persuasiveness has been found wanting in Plan and Development advertisements.

Improvements in advertisements need to be made in regard to size, frequency, layout and typography. More judicious selection should be made for advertising in the periodical press.

The services of private advertising agencies should be utilized in an advisory capacity for major publicity campaigns. The DAVP should also be empowered to commission outside talent for major campaigns.

A wide section of the people can be reached through the Indian language, rather than the English, papers.

Govt. should review its advertising policy so as to encourage a positive role in development publicity in newspapers.

The lakhs of posters printed and supplied have been insufficiently and poorly displayed.

The posters should be produced imaginatively to make them attractive and inelligible to the people.

Regional language posters should be produced by State Directorates of Information. Posters in English should be displayed only in cities and large towns. The existing type of posters should not be distributed in rural areas and only hoarding-size posters should be displayed there.

Printed literature for rural areas should be confined to illustrated folders, which should be directly despatched to the Panchayats. For urban areas, different folders should be produced for different sections of the population.

Big-sized cement hoardings should be put up in all Panchayat Samiti head-quarters; large hoardings should also be set up at most frequented public places and select prints on railway trunk routes.

Metallic tableus should be displayed in all passanger trains and on State-owned and private buses.

One mobile exhibition van should be provided on all passanger trains and on State-owned and private buses

One mobile exhibition van should be provided for every six districts, during the Fourth Plan. These should be Central units but should operate under control of the State Directors of Information.

Two-coach exhibition units should be provided on each Railway Zone.

Two exhibition trains should be commissioned on the broad gauge and metre gauge systems dedicated to Jawaharlal Nehru the Prime Planner and projecting the cause of planning through his inspiring words.

Press

The Press Information Bureau's most favoured clients are the metropolitan newspapers central round Bombay, Calcutta, Madras and Delhi, but their coverage of Governmental publicity material is the smallest.

The press in State capitals and other cities has given better coverage to development news, but even so it is not adequate to the needs. A more liberal allotment of newsprint and an extensive development news service should be provided to this sub-metropolitan Press.

The future of newspapers as a medium of mass communication lies in a systematic development of the mofussil Press. But it is faced with a number of limiting factors and weaknesses.

The periodical Press, an important avenue, has not been properly utilised.

Generally, the language Press inadequately served by the Bureau. However, the material, seemingly prepared for the English Press, is not translated properly to be intelligible to the readers of this section of the Press. The language services should be freed from the bandage to the service in English and strengthened.

The feature service should be reoriented to serve as an imaginative service.

(i) In regard to the metropolitan and sub-metropolitan papers, the PIB should arrange unconducted tours for individual correspondents. The Bureau in co-operation with the Community Development Organisation should issue a fortnightly digest of rural and small town development news for use by newspapers. A background and reference service should be provided. A feature service of high quality should be organised by the Bureau for use by a select number of papers on exclusive basis. The Principal Information Officer should establish close liasion with leaders of the profession to ensure that a sense of pride in achievement is cultivated among readers.

(ii) For the non-metropolitan Press, the Bureau should arrange a special regional photo-cum-feature service, mailing of literature to correspondents in cities and districts, a fortnightly round-upon Plan and its progress, and a photo panel service for Sunday Magazine sections.

The organisational side of the Bureau should be improved.

The Photo Division should be enabled to plan and project photo publicity for the Plans. Government, through the Zila Parishads, should start small weekly newspapers of educative value dedicated to local needs, first on a pilot basis and later extended to the country, if found useful.

Publications

Disciplinary requirements of Govt. service have conditioned the literary effort of Govt. publicists, resulting in an apologetic approach to publicity.

The bewildering variety of reading requirements and tastes of different sections of the community and the failure to plan the publicity literature in accordance with the requirements of the target audiences have resulted in the relative ineffectiveness of the publications to create the necessary impact.

Printed publicity can have a deep and lasting impact.

Publications take time to issue, lack intimacy and personnel touch and, therefore, the impact gets diluted.

The language and content of the publications division's popular pamphlets directed to audiences of various levels are little different from one another and are of poor production value. The Division should evolve a more scientific assessment of the reaching lastes through the proposed Planning Group of the Divison.

Printed publicity for rural areas is a waste of effort and resources. Extensive survey and research into the vocabulary of village literates is needed for satisfactory results. The bulk distribution of the discontinued in rural areas. The resources should be diverted to printed publicity among people with higher literacy. Literature for neo-literates should, however, be produced.

The impact on the fairly educated class in urban areas has been encouraging, distribution arrangements among these sections should be improved.

Govt. should take immediate steps to ensure that the publications are displayed permanently and utilised properly in schools and colleges. Plan literature should also be made compulsory reading in schools and colleges.

Regional language publications can brought out in irrational order of preference, much later than their English versions, and with much lower production standards.

There is little original writing in the Publication Divisions regional language publications, which should except for Hindi, be entrusted to State Govts.

While the priced publications are of good production values the impriced Plan publications are not so, and need to be improved in this respect also.

Hoarding-size posters should be installed at Block Head-quarters. Panchayat Samitis should be set up cement structures and Central and State Govts. should supply posters to suit the size of hoardings.

It is desirable and feasible to have one mobile cinema for every five Blocks. The target for the Fourth Plan should be a mobile cinema van for every three Blocks and for the Fifth Plan and van for each Block. Film strips should be produced and, as their production gains momentum, each Block should have a film strip projector.

Radio is the most powerful medium in rural areas. The importance of working the community Listening and Radio Rural Forum Schemes should be forcefully brought home to the official workers of Community Development and elected representatives of Panchayati Raj Movements.

Publicity material reaches the Block headquarters, but is not fully distributed to the ultimate targets. The display of posters is disappointing. The material should be directly mailed to responsible officials like Panchayat Secretary or School teacher. The Social Education Officer should make inspection of actual utilisation and report to appropriate authorities.

Social Education and publicity go together. The Social Education Officers or the Education Extension

Officers should be redesignated as Extension Officers (Publicity) and suitable training should be imparted to them particularly in organising Radio Rural Forums.

The Study Team on Information and Community Centres has made recommendations regarding Information Centres and we endorse them.

The blue print of an integrated publicity machinery has been provided in the section on "Co-ordination"

COMMITTEE ON COOPERATIVE ADMINISTRATION, 1963—REPORT

New Delhi, Ministry of Community Development & Cooperation, Department of Cooperation, 1963. 266p. (Memograph)

Chairman : Shri Vaikunth L. Mehta.

Members : Shri R. Dasaratharama 'Reddy' Shri G.D. Goswami, Shri P. D. Kasbekar; Shri M. L. Batra.

Member Secretary : Shri G. V. Ramamurthy.

APPOINTMENT

The Committee on Cooperative Administration was constituted under the Ministry of Community Development & Cooperation vide their Notification No. F11 19/63-Coord. dated Aprils 15, 1963.

TERMS OF REFERENCE

(a) To review the existing departmental set up in the various State and to suggest the broad lines for determining the strength departmental staff at various levels, namely, at headquarters, divisional, district and lower levels;

(b) To make recommendations regarding the special staff required to be provided at various levels to deal with special items of work, like cooperative farming, cooperative marketing, processing, industrial societies and other types of societies;

(c) To make recommendations regarding the criteria for determining the strength of the audit staff at various levels;

(d) To suggest criteria for fixing the strength of supervisors whether employed by Government, Cooperative unions or by financing banks as the case may be;

(e) To suggest measures necessary for ensuring adequate training to the staff at various levels, and

(f) To suggest broadly procedures for recruitment at various levels with a view to securing continuity of policies and programmes.

CONTENTS

Introductory; Cooperation Under the Third Five Year Plan; Administrative set-up of Cooperative Department; The Registrar; Structure of Cooperative Department; Division of Departmental Machinery; Audit; Supervision; Loaning of Departmental Staff; Recruitment and Training; Federal Agencies—Transfer of Duties, Functions and Powers; Democratic Decentralization and Cooperative Administration; Conclusion; Summary of Recommendations; Appendix I to VIII.

RECOMMENDATION

The Registrar

It is the duty of the co-operative department to satisfy itself before a cooperative society is registered that it has reasonable prospects of success in co-operative functioning and in its business aspirations. The Department has also to help in designing a framework in which the institution can function satisfactorily without detriment to its co-operative character and the structural requirement of its business. Once the preparatory arrangements are made and the co-operative enterprise is launched, the Department has watch not only that the society and its members discharge the co-operative responsibilities enjoined on them by the by-laws accepted by then at the time of starting the enterprise. but also that the society receives all the assistance it is entitled to under he lan in matters like financing credit, raw materials, technical know-how marketing, etc.

In the context of the responsibilities develoving on the co-operative Department specially under the five year plans, the balance of advantage would seem to lie in keeping the service of a registrar from the I.A.S. cadre.

Before an I.A.S. officer is selected for the Registrar's post it is necessary to see whether he is temperamentally in tune with the aims and objects of the movement. The aptitude for understanding the features of different types of business activity and for being effective in the building up relations with non-officials is also an essential qualification that should be possessed by him.

There is no better way of testing the suitability of I.A.S. officers than by having a number of them taken though the mill of the co-operative Department in the same way as they are taken through postings in districts and in the secretariat.

Equipping a number of I.A.S. officers with co-operative experience will take time even if the State Government begin implementing the above recommendation without any delay. Meanwhile, some ad hoc arrangments will be necessary. Well before the resent incumbent of the post of Registrar is due to be transferred to some other post arrangments should be made to appoint another I.A.S. officer of the requisite seniority as Additional Registrar or Joint Registrar. Such an officer should get training for a period of at least one and half to 2 years before the steps into the post of the registrar.

In some states, I.A.S. officers who are posted of the co-operative department as additional or Joint registrars do not get special pay which they would have got if they joined some other departments or one of the secretariate departments. Such disincentives wherever they exist should be removed.

If in any State the present incumbent to the post of the registarar is due to complete his tenure shortly and it is found that there is no I A.S. officer available who has had prior training in the co-operative Department the State Government should make a selection from among senior officers of the co-operative Department. If an officer with the requisite experience and competence is not available the alternative course will be to extend the term of the present incumbent until a suitable I.A.S. officer is available.

While deparmental officers should be eligible for being posted as Registrars it may be an advantage if they are recommended for being appointed to the I.A S. Their inclusion in the I.A.S. will not only confer on them the status required to carry out effectively such functions as involve contact with other departments of government but also enable them after their promotion to the I.A.S. to get experience outside the Co-operative Department and thus widen their outlook before they get appointed as Registrars.

The co-operative department's share in the promotion quote in the I.A.S. cadre should be at least proportionate to its relative strength in class I officers and above (permanent as well as temporary) as compared to the total of such posts in all the state services which are at present considered at the time of filling the promotion quota in the I.A.S.

For the discharge of the very exacting and onerous duties to be performed by the registrar, the officer appointed to the position should be one who has at least twelve year's standing in the I.A.S., including about two years in the Cooperative department. (This would not easily to co-operative departmental officers who are absorbed in T.L.S.).

If the post of the registrar is to attract the right type of officers and if the registrar to be effective in his dealing with other development department, his status should in no case, be lower than that of any of the heads of other development departments. In most states, the heads of major development departments are likely to rank equal or nearly or equal to secretaries to Government. Where such is the case, it is recommended (i) that in the states where the posts of secretaries to government are not super time scale posts, the status of the Registrar should be equated to that of a secretary to Government and (ii) that he should not rank lower than any other head of a development department.

In states where the co-operative movement has attained wide ramifications covering many aspects of economic activity, it would be an advantage if the post of the Registrar is elevated to the status of a commissioner.

In order to ensure continuity in the functioning of the cooperative department the status of the post of Registrar should be so fixed that the likelihood of frequent upward transfers is obviated to a large extent. Even where such tranfers would be otherwise unavoidable, these could be avoided by resorting to the expedient of the temporary upgrading of the Registrar's post.

An officer once appointed as Registrar and found suitable should remain in the post for not less than 3 years and, preferably, for a period of 4 to 5 years. This period will be exclusive of the qualifying period of training or understudy.

Structure of Co-operative Department

The functional advisers of the registrar at headquarters should be officers of the status of Joint Registrars.

Irrespective of the size of a state, there should be Joint Registrar each for (i) audit, (ii) banking and credit, (iii) co-operative marketing and processing of agricultural produce, and (iv) industrial co-operatives. For the somewhat difficult programmes like (v) co-operative stores there may have to be one joint registrar each as recommended by the Ministry of community development and co-operation. In states where the sector of cooperative processing has developed of is likely to develop to a significant extent, it may be necessary to have a separate cost of joint registrar to deal with that subject.

So far as technical expertise is concerned it would be impractical to provide for it wholly within the Co-operative Department. The services of persons required, therefore, should be obtained on lowan from the departments concerned. They should function purely as technical consultants within their limited fields, assisting the functional advisers concerned and the field staff wherever necessary.

In states where divisioned offices of revenue department have been established, divisional offices of the cooperative Department should also be created with identical jurisdiction. In other states such officers may be considered only if : (i) other development department have found it necessary to have a divisional office in the cooperative department would to a significant extent (a) facilitate the work of administrative supervision over district offices and (b) provide to the public in the districts a more accessible recourse for dealing with cooperative matters than the headquarters of the Registrar. In such States, the Jurisdiction of the divisional offices may be so demarcated that each divisional office as a charge of about 5,000 societies.

The fallowing functions can conveniently be delegated to divisional offices :

Administrative

(i) Supervision and control over district offices; inspection of the offiices at least once a year;

(ii) Approval of tour programmes and scrutiny of tour diaries of discrict officers;

(iii) Inspection of a few primary, district and regional societies at frequent intervals to gain first hand knowledge of societies and generally to guide the work of district and lower officers;

(iv) Annual inspection of societies in the division having juristiction exceeding one district.

(v) Appointment and transfer of prescribed categories of non-gazetted staff.

(vi) Grant of casual leave to district officers.

Financial

(i) Exercise of financial control over the expenditure in the district offices in the division.

(ii) Sanction upto prescribed limits of orginary non-recurring contingent expenditure.

Statutory

(i) Exercise of all powers of the Registrar under the co-operative Societies Act except those reserved for being exercised by only the Registrar.

(ii) Hearing of appeals against the decisions of district or lower officers.

In certain circumstances and within certain limits it may be possible to delegate to the divisional officers some of the powers of the Registrar pertaining to sanctioning of financial assistance to co-operatives under various plan schemes.

The status of the officer posted in the divisional office will have to be higher than that of the highest officers of the Co-operative Department in the Districts. Whether this should be equal to that of the functional specialist at the head-quarters or should constitute a somewhat lower level in the administrative hierarchy in between the highest level of district officers and the level of the Joint Registrar, is a matter which may be examined by each State with reference to its conditions.

For the discharge of the functions which have been suggested, the divisional officer should be given the assistance of a gazetted officer with the necessary ministerial staff.

It would be an advantage to have an officer who could represent the co-operative Department so far as the district as a whole is concerned in its dealings with other departments of Government at the district level as also with federal and district level co-operative institutions. This officer should be also incharge of one of the circles in the district in addition to keeping himself in tough with the work of the other circle officer or officers. It may be desirable to make the post of this co-ordinating officer a Class I post as against the Class II status of the circle officer.

In districts comprising more than one circle and where there is a sufficiently large number of particular type of co-operative societies e.g. industrial co-operatives it may be possible to entrust the latter on a functional basis to one of the circle officers under the co-ordinating officer.

The officer in charge of a circle should given the assistance of at least two Inspectors of the senior category.

The recommendations relating to the structure of the Co-operative Department will entrail the creation of a Co-operative service in the gazetted rank with four levels viz. Assistant Registrar Class II ; District Registrar Class I ; Deputy Registrar Class I, Higher Grade and Joint Registrar Class I, Selection Grade or super time scale.

Below the circle officer, there should be two tiers of field staff designated as Inspectors Grade I and Inspectors Grade II. Where supervision over primary societies is with the Department, the 'Supervisor' would constitute the third level in the non-gazetted service, being slightly lower in status and emoluments than the Inspector Grade II.

In assessing the requirements for sale officers, the needs of each area with reference to the quantum of work involved will have to be worked out and necessary staff provided. It would be an advantage to borrow for this purpose staff from the Revenue Department.

For speedy disposal of liquidations work, the Department should maintain separate staff for the purpose at the rate of one Inspector Grade 1 for 20 societies under liquidation or for every Rs. 5 lakhs of liabilities to be discharged by societies under liquidation.

The delegation of statutory powers to officers 22 at different levels should be on a rational basis, the importance and extent of powers delegated to officers at lower levels being in conformity with the responsibilities which they carry in the departmental administration. The following power should necessarily be retained by the Registrar himself: (a) the power to direct amendments to by-laws by general or special order; (b) to superseede committees of societies; (c) to sanction the institution of any prosecutions under the Act; (d) to levy surcharge; and (e) to order liquidation of district level and higher institutions.

In States where there is no provision in the Co-operative Societies Act for the Registrar to undertake inspection of a co-operative society on his own motion, action may be initiated to get the Act suitably amended.

Division of Departmental Machinery

At the stage of formulation of a scheme of Co-operative endeavour in whatever may be the field of activity, proposals can better be dealt with in the headquarters of the Co-operative Department in active collaboration with the top level consultants of the technical department concerned. These would include the optimum scale of operations, and the working out of the pattern of financial assistance from Government and the financing institutions.

After co-operatives have been established in any line, the continual attention they need has to be provided both by the Co-operative Department and the technical department concerned. Theoretically, it matters little which department is held to be in charge provided both render their allotted services. The Co-operative Department provides certain essential services which are common to all types of societies. The services are to be rendered by the technical departments are not in their regular line and have to be organized for the sake of the Co-operatives through staff appointed specially for the purpose. On balance, therefore, it would ordinarily be an advantage to keep the administrative charge of Co-operative enterprises of all kinds with the Co-operative Department, with responsibility enjoyed on the special wings of the technical departments to provide the Co-operatives with such of the services as they are best fitted to render.

Division of administrative machinery of control over the working of special groups of societies should be exceptional. It is only in the following circumstances that such division may be considered : (i) the special group of societies constitues an important sector of the movement in a State and Co-operative Department would find it difficult to supervise and develop it effectively; (ii) the working of these societies involves techniques and skills, guidance and direction in respect of which cannot be provided satisfactorily by the Co-operative Department without building up a staff some special kind of assistance which the Co-operative Department may not find it easy to render; and (iv) there are satisfactory arrangements for the provision of credit for these societies under the Plan schemes or from other sources.

When any Department other than the Co-operative Department is placed incharge of any specific group of societies, it should arrange to borrow officers from the Co-operative Department to supervise the socities in the field and to advise the technical officers at the headquarters about the co-operative aspects of their working.

Where it is decided to take out of the purview 113 of the Co-operative Department, for purposes of administrative control, a specific group of societies, there should be no bifurcation of the audit machinery and audit should continue to remain unified for all types of societies under the overall control of the Registrar.

When a certain group of societies has been transferred from the co-operative Department to another department and the latter decides to give training in co-operation to its officials, it need not organise separate arrangements for that purpose but should make use of the existing co-operative training institutions.

Societies which are under the administrative control of functional departments should not be treated as having been out off from assistances from co-operative banks. It should become the duty of the Co-operative Department to act in co-ordination with the functional departments and to make sure that no discrimination is shown by co-operative banks.

Where co-operative societies in a State are in charge of more than one department, the Registrar should be consulted in matters of overall co-operative policy. When proposals for exentension of the scope of work or for new developments or for changes in structure are to be considered, there should be, invariably, preliminary consultation with the Registrar. He should also be consultation about proposals connected with prosecutions under the co-operative law, with the registration of societies that have adopted by-laws different from model by-laws, with important amendments of by-laws, with interpretation of by-laws and similar matters. It may also be provided that in case of difference of opinion between the Registrar and the head of the functional department on any point, the matter may be referred to representatives of Government for final decision.

For better co-ordination, the system obtaining in some States of having committee at different levels of development departments is favoured. In this connexision, the recommendation of the Second Working Group for the constitution of a committee at the secretarial level is endorsed.

Audit

The objectivity of, co-operative audit can be ensured by having within the Co-operative Department a separate wing exclusively for the purpose of audit, under a Chief Auditor who would be of the rank of Joint Registrar. The feeling of Independence is ensured by avoiding a mixing up of functions and by providing a separate line of command for audit below the Registrar. The advantage of this arrangement is that while it can ensure independence of audit, it also makes it possible for the audit staff to consist of persons with the right background.

In order to ensure that the staff entrusted with audit have a Co-operative background, the audit wing of the Co-operative Department should be manned by personnel who have had opportunities of working on the general side of the department and thus of developing within themselves the appropriate outlook in relation to the working of co-operatives.

The retention of audit with the Registrar has the advantage that on the basis of audit carried out by persons who have not only the professional competence but also the requisite orientation, he can keep himself in close touch with the movement. This aspect would assume more and more importance as supervision over societies gradually gets transferred to federal organisations.

In Uttar Pradesh, the only State where the contred of audit is not with the Registrar, the position may be re-examined early.

Within the Co-operative Department there should be a separate audit wing whose duties partain exclusively to audit wing whose personnel do not have take orders from the general side. This can be acheved by keeping the audit organization under a Chief Auditor of the rank and status of a Joint Registrar, who will be subordinate only to the Registrar. The officer should be assisted by adequate staff at the district and lower levels.

So far as the non-gazetted staff of the Department is concerned, there should be interchangeability of staff between the general and the audit sides. As regards the gazetted staff, it would perhaps be an advantage to maintain two distinct cadres, with the proviso, however, that every officer in the audit cadre should be made to work in the gazetted posts of the general side for a period of at least three years.

The minimum sacle that should be adopted for appointment of staff for audit of primary societies should be as under :

Type of societies	No. of Societies per auditor	Category of staff to be entrusted with audit
Credit Societies		
(a) Agricultural		
(i) Primary credit societies (small-sized)	40	Junior Auditor
(ii) Large-sized credit societies and credit unions	15	Senior Auditor
(iii) Primary land mortgage banks	25	Senior Auditor
(b) Non-Agriculture		
(i) Employees credit societies and Urban banks	25	Senior Auditor
(ii) Other types e.g. artisans, fishermen, etc.	40	Junior Auditor
Non-Credit Societies		
(i) Primary consumer's stores	15	Senior Auditor
(ii) Primary marketing societies (iii) Primary weavers' societies	15	Senior Auditor/ Junior Auditor*
(iv) Milk supply societies (v) Fishermen's societies (vi) Farming societies (vii) Housing societies (viii) Industrial societies other than weavers	20	Senior Auditor
(ix) Miscellaneous societies		
Societies under liquidation	40	Junior Auditor

*The work should be allotted depending upon the nature of transactions of the society. Where the transactions are not considerable a Junior Auditor may be entrusted with the work.

The catogories of Junior and Senior Auditors mentioned above should correspond to the Grade I and II Inspectors.

In allotting societies to each auditor, care will have to be taken to see that he has to traverse as compact an area as possible. As this would involve the audit of more than one type of society, the actual number of societies that will have to be entrusted to an auditor will have to be worked out by giving appropriate weightage to the different types of societies to be audited in accordance with their relative workloads as emerging from the norms indicated earlier. There is no objection to the developing of auditors in a district in such a way that certain auditors are entrusted with one type of societies, provided this is feasible without unduly transgressing the principle that the geographical area to be covered by an auditor is kept to the minimum possible.

The Co-operative Department may undertake from time to test audit of some of the institutions that are audited by chartered accountants where such a practice has been introduced, so as to satisfy itself that the audit has been properly done.

The audit of a society should be entrusted to only those auditors who have had at least two years intitial experience on the general side i.e. in the matter of reorganization supervision and inspection of societies.

In respect of societies having departmental officers as their cheif executive officers, care should be taken to see that audit of such societies is not entrusted to auditors of a rank lower than that of the deputed departmental officer. Alternatively, audit of such societies should be entrusted to qualified chartered accountants.

Ordinarily, no society should be made to pay a fee for departmental audit during the first few years of its existence. This period should be fixed according to types of societies having regard to the circumstances in each State. In regard to societies which cater to classes which are economically backward, fees should not be charged if the societies are in loss. Subject to the above, the scale of fees should be so fixed that generally a society does not have to pay as audit fee an amount exceeding the actual cost incurred by the Department or what a professional auditor would have charged, whichever amount is lower.

The Chief Auditor of the Department should preferably be drawn from within the Department. If for special reasons, an officer has to be appointed either from other departments or from outside, he should give the necessary orientation in co-operation before placing him in charge of the work.

At the district level, there should be for each district a District Co-operative Audit Officer of the same rank and status as an officer incharge of a circle on the general side. Where a district is small, it may be joined to the charge of the District Co-operative Audit Officer of a neighbouring district.

The District Audit Officer need not be under the control of the divisional officer on the general side. Where the number of District Audit Officers is large, the State Government may consider whether it is necessary to place under the Chief Auditor at head quarters or at divisional level gazetted officers of the rank and status of Class I Officers to supervise the work of District Audit Officers and also to conduct the audit of federal and other large institutions.

The District Audit Officer should undertake the test audit of a few societies that are audited by Senior Auditors. Similarly, Senior Auditors attached to the district offices should take up the test audit of a few societies whose accounts have been audited by Junior Auditors. The system of test audit may be introduced wherever it is not in vogue.

Supervision

It is necessary that in all States, not only should the functions of a supervisor be difined clearly, but measure should also be taken to see that the supervisor effectively discharges all the functions entrusted to him.

The central banks are the appropriate agencies to assume responsibility for supervision of Primary credit societies. Where the responsibility of supervision is not with the central financing agencies, there should be a phased programme for transferring the responsibility to them.

Ulitmately the supervision of societies other than primary credit societies should get transferred to appropriate federal agencies. Until, however, systematic arrangements for supervision are made within the co-operative sector, supervision has to remain the direct responsibility of the Co-operative Department.

Officials of the status of Inspectors Grade I may be allotted for work relating to marketing societies, consumers' stores, weavers and other types of industrial societies with have undertaken production activities, farming societies and housing societies. The remaining types of societies may be supervised by Inspectors Grade II.

In the development of Supervisors/Inspectors care will have to be taken to see that each supervisor has to cover as compact an area as possible. As this would natural involve the supervision of more than one type of society, the actual number of societies to be allotted to a supervisor will have to be determined by giving appropriate weightage to the different types of societies to be supervised in accordance with their relative work-loads as emerging from the norms indicated above.

Tanking all relevant factors into account, the following norms are recommended for appointment of supervisory staff :

Type of societies	Name of socities per Supervisor/ Inspector
Credit societies	
(a) **Agricultural**	
(i) Primary credit societies (small-sized)	25
(ii) Large-sized credit societies and credit unions.	12
(b) **Non-agricultural**	
(i) Employees-credit societies and Urban banks.	'15
(ii) Other types e.g. artisans, Fishermen etc.	25
Non-Credit societies	
(i) Primary consumers' stores	12
(ii) Primary marketing societies	12
(iii) Primary weavers' societies	10
(iv) Milk supply societies	15
(v) Fishermen's societies	15
(vi) Farming societies	10
(vii) Housing societies	20
(viii) Industrial societies other than weavers	10
(ix) Miscellaneous societies	20

For district federations, big processing units, wholesale stores, insurance societies, etc., additional staff would have to be provided to ensure effective supervision. It would be desirable for the circle or district officer concerned or a higher officer to conduct the inspection of such societies at least once a year. For purposes of supervision the State federation, sugar factories, spinning mills, etc. should be under the direct charge of a Joint Registrar.

Where central financing agencies are already responsible for supervision over agricultural credit societies, the present pattern of assistance on a tapering scale should continue to be extended for appointment of additional supervisory staff. Where supervision which has remained so far with the Co-operative Department is proposed to be transferred to central banks. The State Government should subsidise the cost of supervisory staff to the full extent in the first year, to the extent of 75 per cent in the second year and 50 per cent in the third year. Assistance to the extent of 50 per cent of the total cost should continue for a period of five years thereafter. Whether or not assistance should be continued and if so, to what extent, may be reviewed at the end of the Fourth Plan.

Loaning Of Departmental Staff

For co-operative institutions to borrow the services of departmental staff as a regular arrangement is not healthy and detracts from their autonomous character. To secure services of Government officials on deputation should be an exception rather than the rule. Extensive use of an expendient like that under F.R. 127 in Andhra Pradesh and Madras should be discouraged and where necessary, the services of Government officials should be lent to co-operative institutions only on the normal deputation terms.

If the board of directors of any society decides to ask for the services of a Government official on deputation, then the proper course would be for it request the Registrar to send it a panel of names of suitable Government officials along with their character rolls ; the selection should be made by the board of directors of the society itself. During the period of such deputation, the president of the board of directors of the society should be entitled to enter in the confidential file of the Government official remarks regarding his conduct and work. The board of directors should also be entitled to recommend disciplinary action against the Government official concerned, if after following the prescribed formalities it comes to the conclusion that he has b een remiss in the performance of his duties.

In many States, in the present stage of development of the movement, the number of institutions that will be served by a particular cadre, the uneven size and business of the institutions and the uncertainty of the broads of such institutions being attracted to the idea of a cadre, it may be premature to think in terms of 'cadres' of personnel to cater to different types of institutions such as central financing agencies, primary marketing societies, primary land mortagage banks, etc.

In a few States, the Co-operative Department has prescribed minimum qualifications that should be stisfied by the staff of co-operative institutions and these and other service conditions have been incorporated in the by-laws of the societies. This should ensure that the cooperative institutions are manned by qualified persons, besides providing some security and permanence of service to the employees. In States where this has not been done, the Cooperative Department may, in consultation with the appropriate federal organizations, lay down the qualifications, etc. that should govern the appointment of staff in different types of co-operative institutions.

The federal organizations should assume responsibilities to ensure that their affiliated organizations are manned by adequately qualified and trained staff.

If cadres for co-operative institutions cannot be created for the reasons mentioned earlier, the services of departmental officers may have to be lent to co-operative institutions in certain circumstances, until federal organizations are able to provide the necessary personnel or extend support as suggested above. While deputing staff care should be taken to see that the normal work of the Department is no affected in any manner.

Recruitment And Training

Even though technical qualifications are not a prerequisite of recruitment into the Co-operative Department, a fairly high degree of intellectual equipment is essential in the staff to be recruited for the Co-operative Department. In order that such persons are attracted to the Department, the Co-operative Service should not only comprise levels indicated in Chapter IV but also provide for status, pay scales, special pays and other benefits at the various levels, which are not lower than those enjoyed by their counter parts in other development departments in the State.

The State Governments may re-examine the existing pay scales of staff at different levels of the Co-operative Department in the light of the responsibilities attaching to them advise them in such a way as would attract to the department the type of personel that it needs.

As the .posts of Joint Registrars carry considerable responsibility and officers holding them are expected to advise the Registrar and control and guide the work of divisional and district officers, only those officers should be considered for promotion as Joint Registrar who have put in at least five years in the higher grade of Class I (divisional officers) or ten years in Class I (officers incharge of districts), or an equivalent combination of both.

Where the post of the divisional officer should be held by an officer who has had at least four years' experience in Class I (i.e. the level of officers in charge of whole districts) or ten year's experience in Class II or an equivelent combination of both. Direct recruitment of officers to fill the posts of divisional officers is not recommended.

The post of the officer incharge of a district should be held by an officer who has served at least for three years as circle officer (i.e Class II) and has acquired experience in the administration of societies.

In regard to the appointment to the posts of circle officers (Assistant Registrars), it would be desirable to reserve fifty per cent of the posts for direct recruitment should be on the basis of a competitive examination which may be held in common with other services as well. For appointments to the co-operative service, some weightage may be given during the Viva Voce test to candidates who hold degrees in co-operation, economics, commerce, agriculture or statistics. A diploma in co-operation in addition to a degree in some other subject should also entitle a candidate to a similar weightage.

For promotion to the posts of circle officers (Assistant Registrars) a minimum period of five years of field experience at the level equivelent to Grade I Inspector or Senior Auditor should be prescribed so as to ensure the requisite experience.

Recruitment to the posts in higher level of non-gazetted staff file. Inspectors Grade I, need not be direct. These posts should be filled by promotion of suitable persons from the rank of Inspectors Grade II or Junior Auditors with a prescribed minimum period of experience. At the lower level (i.e. inspector Grade II) seventy five per cent of the posts may be filled by direct recruitment on the basis of a competitive examination. The minimum qualification at this level should be a university degrees. The scale of pay should be such as would attract graduates at this level. The remaining twenty-five per cent of the posts may be filled by selecting suitable employees of Co-operative institutions (supervisors of central Banks, secretaries of large-sized societies etc.) and supervisors and ministerial staff of the Co-operative Department.

As the various plan programmes are drawn up sufficiently in advance, it should be possible for the Co-operative Departments to assess the requirements of staff one year in advance and to take steps to have the necessary staff sanctioned ; recruited and trained.

The question of creating an All-India Co-operatives Service should be kept open, and a final decision taken only after detailed examination in the light of the situation that will emerge after the proposal to constitute an All-India agricultural Service is finally disposed of.

Any expansion of the Department without adequate arrangements for the training of the staff at different levels is not conducive to sound co-operative administration audit and supervision. As the programme of recruitment and training should go hand in hand, the State Governments should provide for a 'training reserve' while making recruitment so that the staff appointed get trained soon after appointment and in any case before they are put on the field. Five per cent at each of the lowest levels gazetted and non-gazetted ranks is suggested this purpose.

In the context of the rapid growth of the movement in different directions, it is necessary that officers of the Department at different levels should go through a refresher or re-orientation course once in 5-7 years. Such refresher courses should also include visits to well-developed institutions in the traditional and new fields of activity and to other states, if feasible. Apart from these refresher courses it may be useful for the Co-operative Department to convene seminars at which officers of the Department could meet and discuss the common problems that they face in their day-to-day work.

In the light of the programmes drawn up for organising institutions in the special fields of co-operative activity, the co-operative Department will have to estimate its requirements of staff to be put in charge of these activities and make suitable arrangements with the National and State Co-operative Unions to provide the necessary training facilities.

As the staff of the co-operative Department have to be conversant with the problems and difficulties faced by co-operative institutions and of how they can best be met under a certain set of circumstances, it would be conducive to the efficiency of the staff if they are given practical training before they are called upon to take charge of responsible duties. The directly recruited Assistant Registrars may be given one year's field training besides going through the Intermediate Officers' Training Course. At the level of intermediate officers, the period may be six months, besides the above theoretical training course. For Junior officers, the period may be fixed at three months besides the basic training course. For junior officers, the period may be fixed at three months besides the basic training course at a Junior School. During the period they undergo of different functions so that they acquire a general idea of the various functions of the Co-operative Department.

The possibilities of providing experience in other department of Government to co-operative departmental officers may be explored.

Deputation of co-operative departmental officers on a tenure basis to the Ministry of Community Development and Co-operation and other national institutions viz. the National co-operative Development Corporation and the Reserve Bank of India, will help to widen their experience. A regular programme of inter-state study can also be usefully arranged for the benefit of the officers.

It would be advantageous to depute one Class officer at a time to the Secretariat Department for a short period to get trained in the methods, procedures etc., followed by the Secretariat Department dealing with Co-operation.

Federal Agencies—Transfer Of Duties Functions And Powers

The State Governments should promote the formation of federal bodies where they are not in existence, review the working of existing federal institutions charged with certain functions (e.g. supervision, training) and consider early the questions of transferring to them some of the statutory powers of the Registrar. For enabling State Governments to do so in areas where the conditions are favourable, the Co-operative Societies Act should be amended suitably to provide for the transfer of powers to federal organizations.

Democratic Decentralization And Co-Operative Administration

It is necessary to ensure that extraneous forces, political or otherwise, not allowed to influence the working of co-operatives, which are essentially business organizations. Care should be taken to see that their efficiency and soundness are not impaired and that their autonomy is safeguard. Moreover, any transfer of powers to panchayati raj institutions will dilute the responsibility of the Co-operative Department and will impede progress towards the transfer of authority to federal agencies which will make the movement self-disciplined and self regulatory.

Panchayati Raj organizations should interest themselves in such items as promotion, development and planning i.e drawing up proposals for the registration of new societies, the expansion of membership in existing societies the revitalization of weak institutions, the preparation of production plans, the planning of the general programmes for the supply of credit seeds, fertilizers and other requisites. The Co-operative extention staff should be utilized to attend to these items. Where supervision over primary societies is the responsibility of the Co-operative Department, the Co-operative extension officer should be available for the purpose.

As regards control over the staff deputed to Zila Parishads and/or Panchayat Samitis, there should be a clear understanding between the district officer of the co-operative Department and the Chief Executive Officer of the Panchayat Samiti. While the latter may continue to have administrative control over the extension staff in keeping with the general pattern of administration under the decentralized set-up, it should be made obligatory on him to carry out with the help of the extension staff the instructions of the officer of the Co-operative Department at the district level.

The Co-operative Department should have full powers of transferring the staff allotted to the Panchayti Raj organizations in order to ensure that every member of the staff has at least two years' experience on the general side before being entrusted with audit work.

Conclusion

It must be ensured that the statutory duties like audit, inspection, arbitration and liquidation, rectification of defects and prompt action to remove irregularities do not get neglected.

The recommendations made in the Report in regard to the staff to be maintained at different levels represent the minimum strength that the Department should have if it has to fulfil the role assigned to it in the planned development of the country. The actual strength of the staff in a State will, however, be determined by the numerical size, the volume of operations, the types of activities covered and other local conditions such as means of communication, etc.

Any increase in the size of the Co-operative Department should not lead to any interference in the day-to-day working of co-operative institutions such as would adversely affect their freedom and autonomy.

The administration of the Co-operative Department becomes less difficult and can be carried on successfully even with a limited staff where there is a large body of non-official workers, who take interest in and give their attention to the building up of the movement.

STEADY TEAM ON PROHIBITION, 1963—REPORT

Delhi, Manager of Publications, 1964 II, 548p.

Chairman : Justice Tek Chand.
Members : Shri R. S. Krishnaswami (replaced by Shri L. M. Shrikant); Dr. A. M. Khusro.
Secretary : Shri S. Narayanaswamy.

APPOINTMENT

The Government of India recently reviewed the position in consultation with the State Governments and decided that the working of the Prohibition programme should be studied for the country as a whole. Such a study will cover problems connected with the enforcement of Prohibition and Excise Laws, measures intended to reduce illicit traffic in liquor, improving administrative efficiency and securing to the maximum extent public support for the programme through the Co-operation of both official and non-official agencies. So the Planning Commission constituted the Study Team on Prohibition vide their Resolution No. 16(5)/63-PUB., dated April 29, 1963.

TERMS OF REFERENCE

(i) To make an assessment of the magnitude of illicit distillation and illicit sale and other abuses prevalent in both wet and dry areas.

(ii) To suggest practical measures for reducing illicit traffic in liquor and combating other abuses and malpractices.

(iii) To advise as to how better implementation of the Prohibition Programme could be ensured through official and non-official agencies.

(iv) To examine the existing legislations on Prohibition and make suggestions for removing defects and for Securing effective enforcement.

(v) To examine the existing administrative set-up in the States with particular regard to the personnel, their recruitment, their training, the powers entrusted to them in their methods of work.

(vi) To make suggestions for securing to the maximum extent the cooperation of voluntary organisations in the implementation of the programme and mobilization of people in support of Prohibition.

(vii) To study the financial aspects of the Prohibition Programme, both inregard to the actual loss in excise revenue and the cost of enforcement.

CONTENTS

Part one : Section One: Introductory:

Introduction; Terms and Phrases; Dry and Wet Regions and Prevailing Proof Strengths;

Section Two: Drinking In Ancient Societies & Modern International Experience :

Drinking in Ancient Societies with Particular Reference to India; History of Temperance and Prohibition in America; Experiment in Liqour Control in Scandiavian and other countries.

Section Three : Basic Considerations About Alcohol And Its Detection :

Alcohol Raises Several Problems ; Alcoholism ; Alcohol and the Armed Forces; The Drinking Driver and the Mechinist; Alcohol and Medical Science; Action of Alcohol and Detection of Inebriety; The Appliances for Determining Alcoholic Content ;

Section Four: Illicit Activity In Relation To Liquor :

The Problem of Illicit Distillation and Illicit Tapping;

The Problem of Smuggling; Bootlegging and Gangsterim; Racketeering, Craft and Corruption; Impact of Drinking by the World of Fashion and Officials; Divertion and Misuse of Duty-free Imported Liquor Intended for Embassies and Missions in India; The Problem of Toddy and Neera; Misuse of Spirituous, Medicinal, Toilet and Other Preparations; Prevention of Misuse of Molasses; The Control of other Raw materials; The Relative Success of Prohibition in Gujarat and Madras; The Attitude of West States towards Liquor Revenue; Liquor Strength reduced to Increase consumption;

Section Five : Economic and Financial Analysis

The nature and Pattern of Drinking in India ; The Magnitude of Illict Distillation and the Drinking Bill ; Financial Losses and Gains;

Section Six : Implementation of Prohibition Policy

The Nature of Remedies ; Problems of Law Enforcement ; Law and Liquor ; Public Opinion and Human Nature—Some Misconceptions ; Role of the Press ; Prohibition through Mass Education and Publicity ; The Role of Voluntary Organisations ; Administrative set up ; The Economics of Intoxicating Liquor in Wet Areas ; Policy for Wet Areas ; Foreign Visitors and Prohibition ; The Basis of Permit System for Hard Liquors ; The Economic Containment of Illicit Distillation—Case for Mild Liquors ; Case for Liberalization of Toddy ; A Critique of the Recent Liquor Policy Announced in Maharashtra ; Conclusions ; Summary ; Summary of Recommendations.

RECOMMENDATIONS

Alcohol Raises Several Problems

False value attached to liquor as worry-dissolvent is to be counteracted by widespread knowledge of is deleterious effects on the individual and the society.

Social censure of inerbriety by the community is desirable.

Alcoholism

A modern treatment of alcoholism is to be developed by means of sensitisation therapy by using drugs, like disulfirma, Orinase and Diabinese under medical superision.

Adjunctive therapies should be tried to build up euphoria by suing Adrenal steroids and Adrenocorticotrophic hormone along with vitamins under medical advice.

A programme of treating alcoholics in institutions may be drawn up.

Alcoholics should be encouraged to receive guidance from Alcoholics Anonymous.

Public education on alcoholism will forewarn its likely victims as to what is in store for them if they cannot curb their desire for liquor.

Alcohol and the Armed Forces

A special study may be made on the alcoholic ravages vis-a-vis armed forces, particularly on its harmful effects on sight, hearing, sense of smell, accurate thinking, quick decisions, prolonged endurance, steady nerves and on ability to fix attention.

In no case should army personnel be permitted to consume alcoholic beverages from contraband sources.

The Drinking Driver and the Machinist

A complete ban should be imposed on drinking by the driver while in charge of an automobile and on the machinist who is required to operate dangerous or delicate machines.

(ii) Law should raise an irrebutable presumption that a person in whose system the blood alcohol content is 0.05% or above, is under the influence of liquor.

There should be no liquor shops along frequented roads. There should be a dry belt of 5 to 10 miles 'width on each side of the highways.

All pilots incharge of aircraft, before flying, should be subject to compulsory Alcometer test.

A driver whose blood alcohol is 0.05% or more should be deprived of driving privilege for a year even it there has been no accident, besides a suitable deterrent sentence on conviction.

Intensive educational capaign against the hazards of drinking while driving should be carried on through different media of communication.

Alcohol and Medical Science

The widespread misconception as to the stimulating effects or curative properties of alcohol should be removed by disseminating the views of eminent medical authorities and its toll on health and longevity as discovered by medical science should be publicised, as also, that when taken internally it has no the rapeutic use.

The leading members of the medical profession should take it upon themselves to inform medical men of the dangers involved in prescribing alcoholic beverages as remedies for ailments.

The demonstrable scientific truths regarding alcoholic harm may be publicised by the physicians as that would help in creating a public opinion in favour of prohibition.

Action of Alcohol and Detection of Inebriety

Till applicances for detecting inebriety, like Alcometer,

Drunkometer, etc., are introduced, the test for determining inebriety should be on the basis of a scheme requiring the noting down of history, general behaviour, memory and mental alertness, pulse, temperature, mouth, smell of the breath, eyes, visual acuity, muscle co-ordination, gait, stance, etc.

The standard for determining sobriety should be rigid and receive statutory acceptance. We have suggested 0.05% of alcohol in the blood. It should be mandatory upon the courts to accept this standard.

Over blood tests, urine and breath tests have certain advantages and these should be tried.

The Appliances for Determining Alcoholic Content

In preference to analysis of blood, the tests by Drunkometer, Alcometer, Intoximeter, Breathalyser, etc. are recommended, as they have the advantages of simplicity and accuracy.

These tests eliminate delays and also help in exonerating the innocent.

In order that the breath testing applicances should win acceptance by the courts and the community, their working should be generally demonstrated and explained to law enforcement officers, to the members of the bench and bar, to the gatherings of automobile operators, to the members of automobile associations, to the student community and to the press.

The Problem of Illicit Distillation and Illicit Tapping

The Problem of Smuggling

Bootlegging and Gangsterism

As illicit distillation and illicit tapping are widespread and present several problems, their close study by the agents of the enforcement and the public is recommended. We have a similar suggestion in regard to the problem of smuggling.

As smuggling of liquors is intra-state, inter-state and also international, the powers and jurisdiction of the police both in the sending and in the receiving areas should be concurrent to enable pursuit and arrest of smugglers and seizure of their goods across the boundaries of a State.

For chasing illicit distillers and smugglers and for seizing cotraband goods and searching premises and for getting to grips with bootleggers and gangsters, the police should have better equipment in the nature of fast moving transport vehicles and launches, telephone and wireless equipment. Better manoeuevrability and more personnel besides the inebriety selecting appliances mentioned in chapter XIII.

Racketeering, Graft and Corruption

Greater vigilance is recommended to the government regarding racketeers and the corrupt government personnel. Closer watch and effective action is needed to counter the influence of the bootlegger in the departments of the Government, in polities and in the society, as they are not only responsible for contravention of the laws but are encouraging general disrespect for law.

As the members of enforcement who are themselves given to drinking cannot enforce dry laws with vigour and determination, in the selection of the enforcement agents, a close screening is necessary for enecking their integrity and personal habits.

The activities of the anti-social elements in America during prohibition need being studied as they give a warning of what might happen in this country where the price for corrupting an official is less and hunger for wealth is more, and the menance of wealth-producing crime is likely to impose a heavy strain on administration. No expense should be spared for containing the anti-social elements and for curbing their character-under-mining activities.

Impact of drinking by the world of Fashion and officials

The convivial drinking by the upper state should be curbed by creating a public opinion whereby it may be considered unfashionable to drink. The drinking youth will desist the moment drink is deposed from the high pedestal of prestige.

Youth is to be prevented from drinking by means of psychotherapy and by driving home to them its harmful effects.

The drinking parents have to abandon double standards and have to be themselves sober in order to stops their children from becoming inebriate.

Half the battle for prohibition will be won if the government servants will stand fast by the dry cause and shed luke-warm attitude. In order that prohibition should succeed. The enforcement should be manned by officials who are teetotallers by conviction.

The present incumbents of Government post who drink may be allowed to do so on permits.

For the new entrants, abstinence from drinking should be a condition of servive.

The drinking government servants may not drink or serve drinks in public.

The public men and social works can serve the cause of prohibition better by their example as better sermons have been preached with one's life than with one' slips.

Those who are interested in prohibition have to break the delusive spell of glorification which has been cast by votaries of Bacchus. The alcoholic beverages before they can be banished must be deglamorised.

A strong public opinion along with governmental disapprobation of drinking can contain and curb the leanings of the society people and the officials.

Diversion and misuse of duty free imported liquor intended for Embassies and Missions in India

In order to prevent diversion and misuse on duty free imported liquor intended for embassies and missions in India, the following recommendations are made :

The government may appeal to all the foreign missions explaining that while it is not the intention to impose any restriction on the use of liquor by the mission or their staff, they should assist in restricting import to the absolute minimum necessary.

A suitable procedure for siging/counter-signing the exemption certificate by the head of the mission or any official specially authorised by him be introduced.

The goods may be cleared or delivery taken by some embassy official against the authority issued by the head of the diplomatic mission of the diplomatic officer authorised in this behalf.

Intimation of the receipt of the goods in the embassy premises or by diplomatic officer for his personal consumption may be sent immediately on the receipt to the local excise authority.

The stock of liquor of the mission may be kept under the charge of some responsible officer.

The head of diplomatic missions may request the individual diplomats not to order supply of duty free liquor more than the genuine requirements.

The liquors supplied to missions and other previleged organisations should be contained in distinctive containers or bottles with specially embossed or marked labels possession of such liquor or such containers by a person who is not authorised to import this liquor to be an offence. The burden of proof should be on the accused to show how he acquired such liquor.

Payment of all such liquor may be by official cheques signed either by the head of the mission or by one of its senior officials duly authorised.

The Problem of Toddy and Neera

The neera parlours, especially among the industrial workers given to today should be popularised, by opening in industrial areas, attractively designed neera bars.

Special efforts need being taken to make sure that Neera, which is suceptible to fermentation, stays unfermented or is consumed before fermentation sets in.

The palm industry needs developing on a large scale as it would materially ameliorate the economic conditions of the people.

The Tad Gud and Shilpa centres like the one in Dahanu (Maharashtra State) should be increased with a view to develop large scale potentialities of the industry.

Misuse of Spiritutous, Medicinal, Toilet and other Preparations

Quotas of alcohol should be given to the manufacturing firms with reference to individual preparations after ascertaining their legitimate needs and not a general quota as at present.

In or 'er to check misuse of spirit based medicinal and toilet preparations, the quantity manufactured should be reduced and the manufacture of certain tinctures which serve no medicinal purpose should be stopped.

There are a number of defects in the Drugs Act and it has to be suitably amended.

The excise staff in the bonded laboratories should consist of qualified chemists and pharmacists.

Only those drugs which are the rapeutically active and are safe for use should be permitted to be manufactured.

A list of tinctures and other spirituous pharmacopoeial preparations which are essential may be drawn up and these alone should bear duty at concessional rate and the rest at a higher rate.

The recommendation of the Central Health Council that tinctures should be manufactured by government only and their total quantity should be fixed, is endorsed.

The Government should consider the production of all classes of spirituous preparations in the public sector as that would guarantee standardisation and purity and prevent misuse.

On the distribution side, the government should control the supply and restrict it to genuine needs.

There should be a quality control over alcohol based on Aurvedic preparations.

As these preparations contain only self-generated alcohol, their manufacture by the addition of alcohol or by process of distillation should be prohibited. Ayurvedic preparations should be brought under the purview of Drugs etc.

Ayurvedic pharmacopoeia should be prepared. But as this would take time it would be desirable to lay down standards for some of the more common preparations like Asavas, Arishtas, Suras and Sudhas, without avoidable delay.

The manufacture of homoeopathic tinctures should be restricted to bare requirements for bonafide purposes. These preparations should be packed in small containers, preferably. —OZ. phials.

It would be worthwhile investigating whether dilutions can be made by substances other than alcohol. It should be investigated whether all or most of the dilutions can be made by means of lactose instead.

To prevent misuse of denatured spirit, better denaturants than caoutchancine and pyridine should be employed. There are more than 60 effective denatured to avoid its misuse aspotable liquor.

The manufacturing houses and chemists and druggists

dealing in spirituous preparations should maintain proper records so that persons to whom sales are being made may be traced.

Chloral hydrate should not be allowed to be sold except to bona fide partities guaranteeing utilisation for bonafide use.

We endorse the eleven recommendations which were suggested by the Central prohibition Commiittee in 1961.

Prevention of misuse of molasses

In order to prevent premature setting in of fermentation in the molasses by addition of water, covered storage should be provided. The government should insist on the sugar factories providing covered storage and also assist sugar manufacturing co-operative societies.

Proper inspection of factories and constitution of a co-ordinating committee for more efficient utilisation of molasses is recommended.

Molasses produced by khandsari units should be collected at a few centres for use by the distillers and their sale in the open market prevented.

Ways and means should be devised to ensure that the entire quantity of molasses produced is utilised for manufacture of industrial alcohol and the essential industries are not in short supply in consequence of illicit distillers purchasing molasses on payment of high prices.

Any surplus molasses should be exported rather than made available to the illicit distiller.

Rigid control over the distribution of molasses will prevent the prevailing misuse.

Control of Other Raw Materials

The control of other raw materials which are being used as base material for making liquor is difficult, but a general watch should be kept over sources of misuse.

The Relative Success of Prohibition in Gujarat and Madras

Prohibition has achieved relative success in Gujrat and Madras, but there are at least five ways resorted to for making liquor available. Which need prevention.

The Attitude of Wet States Towards Liquor Revenue

The wet states should be induced to give up vicebred liquor revenue. Lowering of the rate of liquor tax will to some extent reduce the profit of the illicit destiller.

Sales Tax is A More Equitable Substitute For Excise Tax

Liquor Strength Reduced to Increase Consumption

The wet states while reducing liqour strength ought not to attempt to increase the sale of liqour in order to raise the revenue by making more people drink.

The Nature and Pattern of Drinking in India

Very little is being spent on recreation. More money should given to drinking and the potential drinkers.

The Magnitude of Illicit Distillation and the Drinking Bill

The dynamics of illicit distillation are compelling and deserve close examination. This is an essential step before effective means are devised to curb it.

Apart from ascertainable cost of drink there has to be taken into consideration the enormous though incalculable cost in terms of broken homes, neglected children, wasted lives, traffic accident, damage to property, etc.

Financial Losses and Gains

Such decline in excise revenues as will result on the introduction of prohibition in the wet states can be more than offset by the gain to the community by savings made on the drinking bill and also through other taxes.

There is need for an integrated policy to reduce the popular preferences for liquor on the one hand and to conduct an onslaught on illicit distillation on the other.

The Nature of Remedies

The onslaught of the illicit distillers and smugglers can be more successfully resisted by an all out effort on an integrated basis throgh several measure ; legal, administrative, education and economic.

Problems of Law Enforcement

The success of social legislation will depend upon the extent of determination with which the law supporting forces can stand against the law defeating forces. The balance can be imposed in favour of the former by propaganda and education.

When honest and sincere attempt is made to enforce a social reform legislations, it does not become futlie simply because considerable resistance might be offered at the outset, provided the law has the backing of strong moreal consensus.

The law should not be over-strained by making it do the work of the home, the church and the school, as it cannot supply the deficiencies of other agencies of social control.

In order to secure ready enforcement, the principle underlying the law has to be rooted in the habits and customs of men.

Laws contribution is felt only through human agencies which must be honest, earnest and efficient.

Both coercive and educative methods have to be employed, in order to create a favourable social climate. We cannot recommend relinquishment of effort because of occasional or even recurring set backs :

Law and Liquor

Witnesses

The law should make it incumbent upon certain specified persons to assist the police or other enforcement agency not only by giving information of the commission of the liquor offence but also to assist at the time of raids and rearch and seizures of exciseable articles as contemplated in Sections 44 and 45 of the Code of Criminal Procedure.

Just as there is maintained a list of Jurors-vide Sections 321-322 of the Cr. P.C. there should be a similar list of men from the public who may be associated for assisting the enforcement at the time of the raids, searches and seizures. A list of such persons should be maintained for every city, taluka of village.

The accompaniment of witnesses to search and seizure (panch or mahazar witnesses) may be dispensed with where presence is not easily procurable. In such cases, the testimony of the police-men should be considered sufficient for the purpose of conviction if it is other-wise creditable. But such police personnel should be of the rank of Assistant sub-Inspector or above.

Summary Trials

Offences against Prohibition under the liquor laws should be triable summarily and Section 360 of the Code of Criminal Procedure should be suitably amended.

Non-bailable Offences

The liquor offences, on the whole, should be made non-bailable with the exception of comparatively minor or technical offences.

Mobile Courts

Mobile Courts should be provided to try offences under Excise Law.

Judicial Panchayats & Hony. Magistrates

Judicial Panchayats, wherever they are functioning should be entrusted with disposal of prohibition cases where the offences is comparatively minor. Similarly, the institution of Honorary Magistrates wherever it functions will be useful in disposing of similar prohibition cases.

Providing Minimum Sentences

In all cases of repetition of offences, there should be provided a minimum sentence of imprisonment and in more serious cases even the first sentence should be a term of imprisonment besides a fine.

Register of Previous Convicts

There should be a central office in every State with branches in the district headquarters where lists of persons convicted under various penal Acts including liquor offences are maintained, containing entries giving necessary particulars of their convictions.

Onus on Accused

Where consumption of an intoxicant is an offence and where it is found that the accused person had consumed liquor and the concentration of alcohol in his blood was not less than 0.05% by volume, then the burden of proof that the consumption of liquor was in circumstances which do not make it an offence, should be on the accused.

Onus as to Jurisdiction

An amendment in Section 66 (b) of the Bombay Prohibition Act, 1949 is called for and it is suggested that the point in above decision will be met if a sub-section were to be added reading as under :—

> "In a prosecution under Section 66 (b), for consumption of an intoxicant, it shall be presumed, unit the contrary is proved by the accused that he consumed alcohol within the jurisdiction of the court where he was found."

Destruction of Stills, etc.

The law should confer a power upon officers of the enforcement of certain rank and above to destroy stills and other paraphernalia without obtaining the permission of the magistrates.

Imposition of Collective Penalties

Where illicit distillation goes on persistently, the law should provide that after giving warning, such areas may be notified and collective penalties imposed.

Special Taxes

Where illicit distillation is rampant recourse may be had to provisions of levying special taxes which may be enacted in the State laws.

Removal And Exclusion From Certain Areas

On the analogy of Section 57 (C) of the Bombay Police Act 1951, power should vest in the District Magistrate or some other authority in the district, of directing a person who has been convicted of violating prohibition laws to remove himself outside the area for a specified period within the local limits of his jurisdiction and not to enter or to return to the area, if there is reason to believe that such a person is likely again to engage himself in the commission of an offence, similar to that for which he was convicted.

Execution Of Bonds For Good Behaviour

Where a magistrate receives information that any person habitually commits, or attempts to commit or abets the commission of an offence of import, export, transport, manufacture, etc. of intoxicants or possesses them illegally, he may require such a person to show cause as to why he should not be ordered to execute a bond with sureties for his good behaviour for a period not exceeding three years.

Forfeiture Of Real Property

In the case of breach of liquor laws, even immoveable property which is being used for that purpose can be forfeited.

In view of extreme severity we hesitate to recommend adoption of such a drastic measure except perhaps in cases of incorrigible offenders who cannot otherwise be deterred.

Electoral Disqualification

In case a person has been convicted under liquor offences, he should be disqualified either to contest election or to be nominated for membership of panchayat, samiti, parishad, Legislative Assembly, Legislative Council, Lok Sabha, Rajya Sabha or hold any other electoral office.

If a person has been convicted during the period when he is the member of above said bodies, he should cease to hold such an office. The disqualification in such cases should exist for a period of five years, from the date of conviction.

Government Servants

Government servants, village officers, lambardars, Zaildar, Sufaidposh, Patels, Karnams, Talaiyaris or by whatever name they are called in any part of the country may be made liable to removal on being found guilty of such offences.

Chemical Analysts In Each District

The provisions should be made for having chemical analysis done in every district.

In order to expedite the trials of such cases, a pprovision should also be made that the statements of the witnesses should be recorded by courts without waiting for the report of the chemical analyst.

Joint Possession

The person in respect of whom there is reason to believe that he was aware of the existence of such intoxicating liquor or drug in the premises, vehicle or other place, should be liable to punishment unless he proves to the contrary. Section 35 of the Arms Act furnishes a model for adoption.

Contraband Sources

It should be a very grave offence for a person entitled to the use of liquor on account of his being in military service, who misuses the quota intended for him for unprivileged persons.

Club Licences

The laws with regard to clubs, if they are at all allowed to hold liquor licences, should be modified on the pattern of Sections 91 and 97 of the Licensing (Consolidation) Act, 1910 of the United Kingdom.

There should be restriction for sales on credit. No person shall either by himself or by any servant or agent sell or supply in any licenced premises or club any intoxicating liquor to be consumed on the premises ; or consume any intoxicating liquor in such permises or club unless it is paid for before or at the time when it is sold or supplied.

New Provisions In Liquor Laws

The laws relating to intoxicating liquors in the United Kingdom and the United States of America are far more stringent and comprehensive than the laws in our country and we will recommend that some of them should find place in our states. The provisions should relate to ;

(a) The duties of the keepers of liquor shops ;

(b) Burdening the accused with costs of prosecutions ;

(c) Punishment for witnesses refusing to give evidence;

(d) Drunken riotous person ;

(e) Drunken person incharge of any vehicle ;

(f) Drunken person incharge of minor under 7 ;

(g) Protection given to the husband and wife against inebriate partner ;

(h) Attempting to procure liquor for drunken person ;

(i) Person sending minor under 14 in a liquor shop etc ;

(j) Supplying liquor to constable on duty ;

(k) Restrictions on pawn brokers ;

(l) Spending some part of fines for development purposes ;

(m) Limitations on use of intoxicants in field of medicines etc ;

(n) Ban on advertisements ;

(o) Definition of intoxicating liquor ;

(p) Plea of ignorance of contents of liquor ;

(q) Vicarious responsibility in case of manufacture

of intoxicants, sales etc. by the wife, children, etc ;

(r) The place of manufacture of liquor to be common nuisance ;

(s) The vehicles rooms etc. where offences relating to liquor laws are committed being subject to lien for fines etc.

Changes In Laws Other Than Liquor Laws

"Under Influence Of Drinkes"

The expression "drunkenness" or "intoxication" in various enactments should be substituted by "under influence of drink or drugs".

Air Force Act, Army Act, And Navy Act

For the words "guilty of drunkenness" as used in Section 52 of the Navy Act and "found in a state of intoxication" as used in the Air Force Act, 1950 and the Army Act (Section 48), the words "under the influence of drink or a drug" should be substituted.

Inland Vessels Act Railway Act

Section 63 of the Inland Vessels Act, 1917 refers to "drunkenness" and Section 100 of Indian Railways Act to "state of intoxication" on the part of respective personnel. Wherever "drunkenness" or "intoxication" is punished, the standard should rather be of being "under the influence of drink or drug".

Government Servants

Absolute sobriety should be insisted upon by law, from Government servants and others, who are called upon to discharge duties requiring high standards of discipline, responsibility, efficiency or accuracy, e.g. members of medical services, nurses, teachers, prison officers, persons engaged in factories, mines, etc.

Section 510 Of The Indian Penal Code

Punishment under Section 510 of I.P.C. (1860) under Section 34 of Police Act (1861), be enhanced and in the case of a subsequent offence, the offender should receive a compulsory sentence of imprisonment.

Indian Telegraph Act

Section 28 of the Indian Telegraph Act ought to be amended, so as to make all servants of the Telegraph Department liable to punishment if they discharge their duties while "under the influence of liquor or intoxicating drug".

The Merchant Shipping Act

Driving or attempting to drive a motor vehicle on a road or other public.

In Sections 243 and 377 of the Merchant Shipping Act, 1958 "drunkenness" should be substituted by the words "under the influence of drink or drug".

Motor Vehicles Act

Driving or attempting to drive a motor vehicle on a road or other public place when a person is unfit to drive through drink or drug should carry besides the conviction under Section 117 of the Motor Vehicle Act (1939) also an obligatory disqualification for a period of at least 12 months from the date of the conviction, unless the court for special reasons thinks fit to reduce the period of disqualification to six months.

Section 17 and 117 and allied Sections should be modelled on Section 6, 11, 104, 109 and 111 and Schedule 11 of the English Road Traffic Act, 1960.

Operating of the car may also be made punishable though it may not be an attempt to drive.

The fact of conviction should be endorsed on the licence and the licensing authority should also be informed so that on the relevant register an entry of conviction and disqualification for holding a licence to drive may also be entered. Bicycle Riding etc.

On the pattern of Section 11 of the English Road Traffic Act, 1960 law in our country should provide punishment for a person riding a bicycle on a road or other public place while he is unfit to ride through drink or drugs.

Penalties should also be imposed upon persons driving vehicles other than motor vehicles whether animal driven carriages or other machanically propelled vehicles.

Changes Proposed In Laws Of Evidence

We suggest the following amendments in the Laws of Evidence relating to liquor offences :

In the case of intoxicants courts should take judicial notice of the intoxicating properties of well-known alcoholic beverages ;

A court may take judicial notice of the facts,

(a) That the essential elements in all spirituous liquor is alcohol ;

(b) That certain articles are commonly used in the manufacture of prohibited liquors ;

(c) That well-known alcoholic beverage have distinctive odour,

(d) That the intoxication increase the probability of being involved in an automobile accident ;

(e) That intoxicated person is capable of particular intent.

The Legislature should make provision as to what may be prima facie evidence. Such presumptions may be.

(a) That the essential elements in all spirituous liquors is alcohol, violation of law;

(b) That a certificate of public analyst is a prima facie evidence of the alcoholic contents of liquor ;

(c) That the defendant had no legal permit or authority to possess, sell transport, export, import intoxicating liquor ;

(d) That the liquor was not intended to be used for chemical, mechanical, medicinal, pharmaceutical, sacramental scientific or industrial perposes ;

(e) Presence of drunken persons, materials used in distillation etc. are prima facie proof of nuisance ;

(f) Possession of intoxicants above a certain quantity should be prima facie proof that they were intended for sale ;

In the case of drinking drivers the following presumptions may be made :

(a) Where there is less than 0.05% alcohol in the blood or equivalent amount in other body fluids or breath the subject shall be presumed not to be under the influence of alcohol ;

(b) Where there is 0.05% or more alcohol in the blood or other body fluids or breath the subject shall be presumed to be under the influence of drink.

The following amendments may be incorporated in the Laws of Evidence :

(a) An inference of guilt may be drawn from attempts to suppress evidence or destory intoxicating liquor, its containers, apparatus, still etc.

(b) On a prosecution for sale of liquor to a habitual drunkard his general equation be considered.

(c) Opinion evidence based on sight tests and smell of intoxicants may be admissble.

(d) The opinion evidence of non-expert should be made admissible as to whether a person is intoxicated.

(e) Evidence of an expert based on tests conducte by him shou'd be made admissible.

(f) Evidence based on smell alone should be made admissible ; without being able to describe the odour.

(g) Evidence of witness who recognises liquor by its odour should be admissible.

(i) Ana ; utoca ; resi ; ts made in blood samples taken from an unconscious person should be admissible.

(j) The testimony furnished by the drunkometer tests may carry persuation of correctness.

(k) Tests of intoxicants from breach, urine of blood should be made admissible, whether done with or without the consent of the accused.

The test for determining alcohol one shown to have been conducted by a competent person should be treated as conclusive.

Our law should recognise that every person who operates a motorvehicle on the public highway of the state shall be deemed to have given his consent to submit to a chemical test of his breath, blood urine or saliva for the purposes of determining the alcohical contents of his blood. If the accused refuses to give a sample for testing his licence to drive ought to be revoked.

The following presumptions may be raised :

(a) A label on the bottle may be presumed as indicative of its alcoholic contents ;

(b) The appearance of the vendee may be admissible on order to determine his age ;

(c) The reputation of the consigner as trafficker may be admissible ;

(d) The knowledge of the less or about his premises may be inferred from the repution of the place.

New Civil Damages Law Recommended

Vicarious Liability

The law should hold the furnisher of intoxicating beverages vicariously liable for the injury caused by a person to whom drink was furnished for his consuption.

Injury Or Loss To Property

The plaintiff should be entitled to obtain damages in case of injury or loss to his property occasioned by the defendents sale or furnishing of intoxicating liqour from him.

Damages For Injury To Means Of Support

The law should provide right of action for injury to means of support.

Care Of The Person Intoxicated

The seller of liquor should be made liable for the care of the person being intoxicated in consequences of the sale of liquor to him.

Service Of Notice On Seller

The wife or the others specified relatives of a person who is a habitual drinker should be given a right to give notice to liquor seller not to supply him with liquor. If despite notices liquor is supplied an action for damages may be allowed.

Right Of Parent Or Guardian Of Minor

A right should be given to a parent or a guardian of a minor to institute a suit for damages where intoxicants have been furnished to a minor.

Suit by Depandants

An action may be allowed where a person's drunken condition has deprived him of the normal use of his faculties so as to in capacitate him from protecting himself against danger to which by reason of intoxication he has been exposed.

Minimum Danger

The law should indicate a minimum sum which may

be allowed as damages in the events in the plaintiffs suit being decreed.

Right To Sue Be Given To Specified Persons

The persons on whom the status may confer the right to sue the supplier of drink may be specified.

Seller To Be Liable For Agent's Acts

The liability of the seller of drinks should be made vicarious and he should be liable in damages for injuries caused by his agents or servants acting within ordinary scope of their employment.

Insurance Policy

In order to ensure the realisation of decretal amount on execution being sued out, law should made it obligatory upon the liquor seller to take out a policy of insurance similar to the one contemplated by Section 94 of the Motor vehicles Act, 1939 against third party risks.

Special Law For Habitual Drinkers Retreats And Reformatories

Law For Habitual Drinkers

Law should provide for the special treatment of habitual drunkards.

Retreats And Reformatories

To types of retreats and inebriate reformatories can be provided where admission can be ordered by courts and where admission can be sought by the inebriate at his own desire.

Propery To Be In Custodialegis

The property of the habitual drunkard should be put under the custody of the court and should not be disposed of except under court's order.

Suit By Or Against Inebriate

The drunkard may be enabled to sue or be sued through a committee or the guardian appointed.

Reformatories

Two classes of reformatories may be provided :

(i) To which are sent such habitual drunkard where there is expectation of reformation ;

(ii) To which are sent worse type of offenders. These may be like prisons.

Inebriates In The United Kingdom

Our laws should be odelled on the pattern of the inebriates Act 1898 of the United kingdom authorising detentions of inebriates, repeatedly convicted for specified offences.

Trial To Be Given To Retreats and Reformatories

Detention in retreats, and reformatories and in suitable cases, probation should be given a trial.

Hints For Investigating Officers

The statement of the witnesses should be recorded under Section 161 of the Criminal Procedure Code:

Photographers should be associated at the time of raids.

The prosecution should provide full proof the incriminating links from the time of seizure till the time of reaching the office of the analyst should be supplied,

Sufficient proof of conscious possession of the incriminating article should be given.

Public opinion and human nature : Some misconceptions.

The opinion an individual expressed in public is not the opinion of the public though claimed as such. Every tendentions writing in a newspaper is not public opinion.

The prohibitionists should realise the cause of prohibition suffers less from the onslaught of those who believe in freedom to drink than at the hands of those whose themselves do not drink but dare no voice their opposition.

Role of the Press

The press can promote prohibition by bringing to the notice of the readers, the risks and danger of addition to alcohol by publicising alcohol caused evils in the sphere of home health economics accidents crime etc. The press can term light on incontrovertible scientific fact as to the harmful properties of alcholic baverages.

The newspapers should tell how drinking drivers cause accidents.

The press can censure lax enforcement and bring to light weaknesses in the enforcement including corruption. The press should pull its weight on the side of sobriety. The approach should be objective avoiding as much suggestion false as supperessiovery.

Prohibition Through Mass Education and Publicity

In order to propagate the cause of prohibition, information based on factual data is likely to carry a deeper appeal than suasion on an emotional plane.

Prohibition campaigns shonld be organised on the pattern of the Anti-saloon League of America which published books leafiets and weekly and monthly magazines by the billion.

The campaign by the National Committee of Poland in 1961 which arranged 14,000 lecures, 200 exhibitions,

250 cultural events provided material for 10 movies and and distributed 2 million leaflets and posters, is worthy of enulation as also the campaign by an organisation of 1200 medical students.

Efforts should be directed to dispel the pessimistic mood of apathy, listlessness and inertia which impedes the reformers work.

A warm, vibrant living public opinion should be created against drinking and in support of prohibition.

Strong laws, vigorous enforcement and stiff penalties will deter the violators to some extent ; but more so, a vigilant and determined public made alive to the dangers of inebriety.

A nation-wide effort on the basis of a systematic nation-wide programme will be productive of batter results. The sinister resistance to prohibition from liquor lobbyists and venal enforcement should be arrested.

The approach of social workers should be scientific rather than sanctimonious and the work must be entrusted to persons imbued with a living faith in prohibition.

The medical profession should undergo a refresher course in order to re-equip itself with medical truths regarding alcoholic caused harm which should be brought to the notice for the masses.

The mass media of communication inculding press pulpit and the screen, should be utilised in publicising alcohol caused depradation in the form of pauperism, domestic infelicity, neglected children, delinquency, disease, promiscuity and crime as also alcohols death dealing role on the road.

There is a great scope for religions the apy as the founders of all religions, the saints, the sarvants and distinguished men, have reprocated the use of alcoholic drinks. Their injunctions and savings can be collected and these will furnish a good basis for influencing the minds of the youth and of the religious minded men and women and for illistration vide paras 18, 19 and 20.

The views of great sportsman who acquired fame by eschewing liquor need being better known among the teenagers and the adolescent.

The Bharat Sadhu Samaj should take up the work as they have got a great held in certain section of Indian society.

The educators should study the basic facts and philosophy and bring home to the people the unfortunate results on account of the impact of alcohol.

The numerous alcohol caused problems should be the highlighted.

The tempo of educational campaign has to be kept up at a steady pressure.

Those who are interested in the prohibition work should be able to refute half-truths and false arguments usually advanced to mislead the gullible and the impressionable.

The growing awareness of the alcoholic danger should be brought home by devising special programmes including audio-visual aids, seminars, special periods in schools and colleges, cultural programmes dramatic performances, poetical symposia' shivirs, etc.

Womens organisations on the pattern of women's crusade in America will go a long way in bringing home the good results of prohibition.

The text-book crusade is equally important as it will have abiding effect upon the minds of the school-going children.

A relentless and ruthless exposure of the liquor evil should be pursued with vigour and determination.

Role of Voluntary Organisations

We endorse the recommendations made in the Third Plan.

The state government should associate voluntary agencies with the work of prohibition.

It would be desirable to open a net work of Nasha Bandi Lok Karya Kshetras throught the country. There should be one such Kshetra in every district and in important industrial projects and urban areas.

Government may consider the possibility of opening at least five Kshetras in each State, directly from the Centre, to give initial push to the programme.

There should be effective non-official coordinating agencies at the Central State and District levels.

Steps may be taken to open prohibition councils in all the States and their units at a district level.

These councils may be strengthened and given necessary financial assistance. They should be under All India Prohibition Council which has been started.

The Government should consider be possibility of associating All India and State Prohibition Council with Lok Karya Commitees.

The workers should be trained for carrying their task effectively. The training cover all aspects-economic, social, psychological and also the matters and techniques of approaching the people.

The training should be such as would help the workers to acquire proper skill and sympathy to handle the addicts and new victims.

The Planning Commission is setting up a Central Training and Research Institute on Public Co-operation. This Institution should be developed as a National Institution.

The Institution should impart theoretical, field and practical training.

It will be descrable if the elective system is eliminated in the matter of selection of non-officials, persons may be taken representing different interests, groups and social strata.

There should be separate wing of women prohibition workers and university students.

The Central and State councils should on the advice of the publicity experts chalk out a programme and produce literature in the form of tracts, pamphlets, charts, stastistics bills posters, cartoons, pictures, etc. etc.

The members of the non-official organization should develop direct contacts with the people including those who are addicts and also their dependents.

Every panchayat should be made to realise and shoulder the responsibility of readicating the drink evil from the village.

A scheme for awarding prizes to the villagers may be formulated for making the prohibition a success.

The Government should not open liquor or toddy shops at religious fairs and festivals.

Advantage should be taken of kathas and such other functions in order to propagate prohibition.

The mobile parties of good singers of folk songs should go round the village propagating about prohibition. Similarly 'shivirs' and dramas should be arranged.

Welfare and recreation activities in healthy atmosphere can play an important part.

People should have restaurants-cum-clubs where they could gather and refresh themselves with non-alcoholic beverages.

Special films on prohibition should be exhibited at prohibition 'shivirs' and 'sammelans'. The radio should also be used for the work of prohibition.

Attractive magazines in all regional languages will go a long way in instructing, entertainining and educating the readers.

Research studies and surveys are necessary for effective handling of the problems of enforcement by the State Governments.

The matter of prohibition should be taken in the Central Committee on prohibition. The Central Government may consider sympathetically for making a finencial provision which should not be less than Rs. 1 crore.

Administrative Set Up In The States

Enforcement of prohibition should be the responsibility of the police.

The staff at the station house level and the circle level be increased by 10%.

A careful analysis should be made either by the D.I.G. or by the I.G. of police to assesss the quality of work,

A mobile force should be at the disposal of the circle inspector and the deputy supdt, of police for stamping out illicit distillation in their area.

A separate transport, a jeep, motor cycle, etc. should be supplied at each police station.

A mobile squad should be constituted for each of the districts where illicit distillation and sale of liquor is found to exist on considerable scale.

The corruption in the force can be guarded against to some extent by :—

(a) Surprise visits by higher officials (incognito) ;

(b) Creation of mobile squads ; and

(c) Prompt attention to the posts from the public against corrupt officials.

There is no arrangement for a foundational course of training for the inforcement staff except on a very limited scale in some of the states. Adequate arrangements should be made for such training courses. Periodicals refresher courses may be also be organised.

The personnel deployed for prohibition should have belief in the prohibition programme and should be able to resist temptation and do their job effeciently. A system of special reward for meritorius work and also severe punishments for lapses on their part should be instituted.

Wider opportunities for discussions and exchange of intelligence among the officers related to the difficulties encountered during enforcement of prohibition laws should be provided.

A journal should be brought out by the Prohibition Intelligence Bureau giving the techniques adopted by the illicit distillers and bootleggers, practical difficulties encountered in detecting cases.,

The Minister incharge of the enforcement agency should also hold the portfolio of prohibition.

At the state level State Prohibition Boards should be created with the Home Minister for Prohibition as its president and consisting of non-officials to advise the government. Such non-official bodies should also be constituted at the district and taluka levels.

The Economics of Intoxicating Liquor in Wet Areas.

The system of granting licences during good behaviour with a nominal licence fee has great advantages over the alternate system of bidding and a heavy licence fee.

Policy for Wet areas.

The recommendations made in Third Five Year Plan detailed in para, 1 are endorsed. They call for early implementation.

For wet areas we recommend a four phased programme as detailed in Paras 4 to 13.

Though 12 years is outside limit, it would be better if the wet states could condense the four phases within a shorter period preferably by 30th of January, 1970 when the birth centenary celebrations of Mahatma Gandhi are going to conclude

Minimum guarantee system would not suit the phased programme.

The proof strength of liquor be reduced and the liquor be bottled in distillery or the warehouse instead of at the retail shop.

In the second phase public consumption of alcohol may be stopped by concelling all on-licences and the iicences for clubs, hotels and other public places should be gradually curtailed.

Finally the liquor trade must not be run for private profit and there should be full control over bonded warehouses breweries and distilleries, and if need be they should be shifted to the public sector.

Foreign Visitors and prohition

In places outside the three dry states, where rules forbid drinking in public, a room may be set apart in high class hotels for the exclusive use of foreign tourists residing in the hotel and their guests, where they may have the facility for meals and alcoholic drinks.

In the case of other foreign residents in India such as diplomats, technicians businessmen, etc. the same facilities should be allowed. The production of the passport should be sufficient evidence of a person being a foreigner.

The rules equiring the obsetvation of dry days may be relaxed in the case of a foreigner.

The place from where the foreigner purchases his drink, whether a hotel or a shop, should maintain record indicating the purchaser's name, address and the passport number.

For the purposes of obtaining drinks persons of Indian origin but domiciled abroad may have the same facility as any other foreigner.

The basis of permit system for hard liquors.

At initial stage alcoholic drinks of very mild variety, in particular those which are not harmful and do not cause drunkenness in the generality of cases, may be allowed on permits, under controlled conditions and the permit system for hard liquors may be strictly rationalised.

For addicts and habitual drinkers the use of alcohol should be allowed in order to relieve acute distress. The permits on ground of addiction or habitulation must not be granted to persons below the age of 40. Persons below 40 years may seek permits for milder varieties.

It is necessary that the date by which applications for hard liquors should be made be specified. No application after the late date should be entertained for hard liquors.

The grant of permits should be confined on medical grounds alone to addicts who may suffer from sudden stoppage of liquor. No permits should be granted on grounds of health.

Before issuing permits the level of the income of the applicant, the number of dependents and other circumstances should be taken into consideration.

A board consisting of a nominee of the executive authority, a reputable social worker and a representative of the medical department should examine the applications for permit.

Persons engaged in certain hazardous occupations must under no circumstances be given hard liquor permits.

The economic containment of illicit distillation ; The case for mild liquors.

If mild alcoholic beverages are allowed on permits and under controlled conditions the phenominal profits made in illicit liquor may be reduced.

In the case of light liquors no permit be issued to persons below 30 years.

The authority to issue permits for light liquors of foreign variety need not be board but a nominee of the executive authority.

Case for liberalisation of toddy.

The toddy may be allowed to be served subject to the following safeguards :—

(i) A ceiling of 5 per cent alcohol in bulk should be fixed ;

(ii) The production and the sale of toddy should be under government control ;

(iii) Wherever possible, bottling to guarantee standard, and refrigeration to stabilise alcoholic strength should be provided ;

(iv) The drink may be consumed only at the place of sale and not be allowed to be taken home ;

(v) The quantity of toddy that can be served to an individual should be suitably limited and the vendor or barman should be under statutory obligation not to violate this condition ;

(vi) The price of toddy and the tax element if unavoidable should be kept as low as possible with a view to dissuade people from drinking the hard product of illicit distillation ;

(vii) Drinking should be allowed only within regulated hours ;

(viii) Steps should be taken to remove the possibility of stale drink being served or of injurious substance being mixed.

(ix) The production and sale of toddy within a radius of five to 10 miles of palm gur centres should be stopped ;

(x) There should be an age limit of 21 years below which no consumer may be served the drink.

The suggestions with regard to toddy as given above are not intended to be adopted by the States of Gujarat and Madras.

In order to give effect to the proposals certain safeguards will have to be built into the system.

In case of scheduled tribes and adivasis a change has to be brought about in their mental approach and social outlook through the more enlightened members of their community, than through pressure of law.

The following measures are suggested in the case of adivasis and scheduled tribes :

(i) The adivasis or scheduled tribes with whom drinking is traditional may be allowed to brew such beverages to which they are accustomed for their consumption only ;

(ii) They should not be allowed to raise the alcoholic strength by adding strong catalytic agents;

(iii) For serious crimes committed under the influence of liquor, no lenity need be shown by reason of the fact that the accused had primed himself with liquor in order to mentally prepare himself for commission of the crime.

The states which are satisfied that no relaxation of prohibition in the case of scheduled tribes or adivasis living there is called for, need not liberalise drinking facilities.

A critique of the recent liquor policy announced in Maharashtra. The permit system according to the recent policy of Government of Maharashtra will be perpetuated and this must be avoided.

The free availability without permits of mild alcoholic drinks will add to the number of addicts.

No permit should be allowed on health grounds, but only on grounds of addiction and serious habituation.

No liquor permits for hard drinks should be allowed to persons below 40 years. The rule for granting permits on the certificate of a registered medical practitioner is no check for the bonafides of the applicant.

There is no justification for liberalisation of the grant of permits for mild drinks to persons from the age of 21 years.

The proposed stepping back will not enable the government to spring forward.

Conclusions

If the recommendations are adopted by the Governments concerned, it will be desirable that the Union Government sets up a Committee after a suitable time to assess the implementation and progress of the integrated programme.

COMMITTEE ON UTILISATION OF EXTERNAL ASSISTANCE, 1963—REPORT

New Delhi, Ministry of Finance, 1964. 59p.

Chairman : Prof. V. K. R. V. Rao.
Members : Shri B. N. Adarkar; Shri P. Govindan Nair; Dr. I. G. Patel.
Secretary : Shri V. K. Ramaswami.

APPOINTMENT

The Committe on utilisation of External Assistance was constituted under the Ministry of Finance, Department of Economic Affairs vide their Resolution No. F 12/35/63 EF Co-ord. dated Jnne 6, 1963.

TERMS OF REFERENCE

(i) to consider problems associated with the utilisation of external assistance from all sources and in all forms;

(ii) to hold discussions for this purpose with representatives of Government Departments as well as of the public sector enterprises and private trade and industry ;

(iii) to examine the problems encountered by private sector in its search for foreign technical collaboration or foreign capital investment.

CONTENTS

Introduction; Analysis of Assistance Received, Present Procedures for Negotiation of Assistance; Causes of slow utilisation; steps to Improve Aid Utilisation in the Public Sector; Procedures for Disbursement of Project Aid, Problems of the Private Sector; Policies and Procedures of Aid-giving Countries; Foreign Exchange Budgeting and the Use of Assistance; Summary of Main Conclusions and Recommendations; Appendices I to IV.

RECOMMENDATIONS

The Government should publish periodically statistics of ordering against available assistance, in addition to data regarding disbursements.

The middle ground between the overall mapping of resources and the detailed study of particular projects is not adequately covered. Considerably greater attention must be paid to geological, metrological, soil, water and forest resources studies. Assistance may be sought from the U.N. Special Fund and the World Bank for these surveys.

With regard to individual projects, the real initial stage is the preparation of a feasibility report. No project should be proposed for aid unless a feasibility report has been completed. Large numbers of feasibility studies must be prepared in order that schemes for which it would be worth while to prepare detailed project reports may be identified. The feasibility studies must be cover both economic and technological aspects and must of a high standard so that they are acceptable to the institutions and countries providing assistance.

It would be useful to draw up lists of Indian and foreign firms qualified to prepare project reports in different fields. The institutions and countries providing assistance could be requested to agree to finance the foreign exchange cost of the preparation of projects reports, without being committed to financing the projects themselves.

A major cause of delay has been the change in the scope of projects at a late stage. Such changes should be avoided.

Another cause of delay has been with regard to acquisition of land, the erection of township, etc. Government should review the legal position and take whatever steps are necessary to speed up land acquisition subject to certain safeguards.

In the case of certain industries the practice is followed of setting monetary limits for the import of standard plants, and there is no detailed scrutiny of the list of goods. The practice of relying on monetary ceilings rather than on detailed scrutiny of items should be extended to a number of other industries also.

The existing procedures of detailed check of lists of items to be imported by units with fixed assets of less than Rs. 25 lakhs should be relaxed; such units should be allotted a certain overall amount of foreign exchange and within this overall ceiling, subject, of course, to banned items not being imported and the capacity to as proposed being established, the unit should allowed to import equipment as it chooses. For the larger projects prior screening of lists of imported equipment seems justified but delays here could be minimised of project authorities consult the D.G.T.D. at as early a stage as possib e.

Much greater effort should be devoted by the D.G.T.D. to the collection of really detailed and up-to-date informat'on regarding the equipment manufactured in the country and the order look position of individual manufacturers. This information should be kept on cards, should be accessible to public and private sector industry, and should be cross-checked on the basis of reports from customers.

While items for which indigenous capacity is sufficient to meet all requirements should be banned in the import trade control policy, a liberal view should be taken with regard to the import of actual users of other items of the capital equipment.

Attention should be paid to the price aspect when screening import applications. Collection of price data is essential, both for determining whether import should be allowed or not and to choose between alternative foreign sources of supply. The D.G.S. & D. and the D.G T.D. could cooperate in the collection of such information. Government agencies abroad could assist in the work.

The private sector should be asked to actively assist in collection of information regarding the indigenous availability of various items particularly of capital equipment. If the units requiring equipment and the manufacturers can agree on what items can reasonably be allowed for import, many of the present delays can be eliminated. There could be separate committees with regard to each major type of equipment, and the Federation of the Indian Chambers of Commerce and Industry and their Associated Chambers should be requested to organise such committees.

Prior clearance by the D.G.T.D. should not be necessary with regard to the import o f components and raw materials by public sector projects. Reporting of orders placed may however be insisted on.

This procedure may also be extended to the private sector, at least for priority industries.

Once foreign exchange from specified sources has been allocated for the import of equipment, there should be no further need for the project authority to make a reference to the administrative Ministry or the Finance Ministry. Similarly, the project authority should be given full freedom to order components and raw materials against half-yearly allocations of exchange made from different sources, without having to make a reference to the administrative Ministry/Ministry of Finance.

The new entrepreneurs should be assisted to develop projects in a manner acceptable to financing institutions and collaborators and capable of being implemented speedily. The Indian Investment Centre should expand its activities in this field, and provide detailed advice regarding the feasibility of proposed projects.

Government should publish periodically information regarding availability of credits from different sources for financing the import of the equipment. This will help businessmen to choose sources of supply for which funds are available.

Industrial units should be offered as wide a range of choice as possible with regard to the sources of supply.

The non availability of adequate rupee finance has operated to delay the implementation of a number of priority projects for which foreign exchange has been earmarked. The I.F.C. and the I.C.I.C.I. have been of assistance, but the institutional arrangements in this regard require further review by Government.

The possibility of laying down standard foreign collaboration terms for different industries should be examined by Government.

Non-project assistance should form a larger part of the total. Project assistance should be defined to include components needed for the manufacture of capital equipment and the initial stock of components of machinery manufacturing industries whose equipment is financed by aid.

The delay between pledges at the Consortium meeting and actual commitments can be reduced if selection of programmes and projects is made as part of the Consortium exercise.

It will be of considerable help if at least 10 per cent of the aid given for a project is made available for purchase in third countries.

The World Bank the I.D.A. should agree to relax the requirement that the lowest tender should be accepted in order to permit placing or orders on indigenous suppliers who may charge higher prices but who would require less foreign exchange.

The U.S. authorities may be requested to relax the requirement that their should be tendering confined only to the United States if American assistance is to be forthcoming. The results of global tenders should be accepted.

The minimum value restriction on use of external assistance should be done away with to the extent feasible.

The use of assistance of different types and of free foreign exchange should be carefully coordinated. It should be possible to forecast minimal availabilities of foreign exchange for a few half years a head. On the basis of these estimates medium term plans for the utilisation of both external assistance and free foreign exchange could be prepared.

ESIS REVIEW COMMITTEE, 1963—REPORT

New Delhi, Ministry of Labour, Employment and Rehabilitation (Department of Labour and Employment), 1966. 310.+vip.

Chairman : Shri C. R. Pattabhi Raman.
Members : Shri R. Jaganath Rao; Shri M. Bhaktavatsalam; Shri Bijoy Singh Nahar; Shri Shantilal H. Shah; Shri D. C. Kothari; Shri R. K. Parikh; Shri G. V. Puranik; Shri G. Ramanujam; Shri Bagaram Tulpule; Shri G. V. Chitnis.
Secretary : Shri S. K. Wadhawan.

APPOINTMENT

The committee was constituted by the Government of India, under the Ministry of Labour and Employment vide their Resolution No. 1(45)/62-HI, dated the 26th June, 1963.

TERMS OF REFERENCE

To review the working of the Employees' State Insurance Scheme and to recommend what modification or change in the structure and organisation of the Employees' State Insurance Corporation would be necessary to ensure more satisfactory functioning of the Scheme.

CONTENTS

Introduction; Historical Development of Social Security Legislation in India; Growth and Development of the Corporation; Coverage under the Employees' State Insurance Act; Contributions; Cash Benefits; Disbursement of Cash Benefits; Medical Benefits—Administration; Medical Benefits—Outdoor Case; Medical Benefits—Indoor Medical Care and Treatment in Special Diseases; Medical Benefits—General; Adjudication Machinery; Financial Control and State Contribution; Administrative Structure; Organisational Set-up; Comprehensive Scheme of Social Security; Acknowledgements; Summary of Conclusions and Recommendations; Note of Dissent; Appendices I to XIV.

RECOMMENDATIONS

Growth And Development Of The Corporation

Slow Progress of Implementation

The delay in the progress of the implementation of the ESI Scheme was largely due to lack of sufficient enthusiasm on the part of some of the State Governments. Difficulties regarding the acquisition of suitable premises for the dispensaries, the arrangement for medical and para-medical personnel, procuring of equipment, making arrangement with the hospitals for indoor treatment, and settling of terms with the panel doctors, could have been anticipated and steps taken to overcome them. The duality of functions in the State Governments largely added to this delay.

There is a constant log between the resources of the State Governments in the matter of medical personnel and necessary finances and their responsibilities in regard to the provision of medical benefit to the general public. They could not do any better for the insured persons under the scheme which forms only a fraction of the total population of the state. The serious bottleneck in the arrangements for the medical care facilities in the states was the inadequacy of hospitals and specialists' services.

Complaints And suggestions

In a nation wide scheme of the magnitude and the size of the Employees' State Insurance Scheme, complaints and criticism from various sources had to be expected. It must be said to the credit of the organisation that the Corporation has been taking notice of all complaints, criticism and suggestions and they have tried to solve and smoothen out as many of these as possible by means of administrative instructions and amendments to the Regulations.

The Corporation had to build up an organisation for which there was not much previous experience. By and large it has performed this difficult task well.

Scope Of Coverage Under the E.S.I. Act.

Extension Coverage

Priority must be given to extending the scheme to those groups of workers who have no protection at all at present rather than trying to cover those sectors which have some measure of protection even if it is not quite adequate.

The limitations of resources and personnel particularly in the medical field as well as administrative difficulties in enforcing the provisions will not permit immediate extension of the scheme to very small establishments. However, the Scheme should immediately cover all factories as defined in the Factories Act, 1948.

Extension To Mines

The extension of the E.S.I. Scheme to cover mines would in effect mean shifting of the part of the responsibility for providing medical benefits from the employers to the colliery workers. The dispersal of the collieries in outlying areas and absence of concentration of workers in large numbers in any one area call for a specialised organisation to deal with their special problems. The mines should not for the present be included in the purview of the E.S.I. Act. The possibility of schemes for joint hospitals and dispensaries in sparse areas so that both those insured under the Employees' State Insurance Scheme and those entitled to benefit under the Mines Welfare Fund may be able to get adequate standard of medical relief, is however not discounted.

Extension To Plantations

Plantations by their very nature have to be in sparse areas away from the cities. The medical facilities have largely to be on the wheels and the provision for medical personnel and ancilliary staff has to be much more liberal. A large bulk of plantation labour will be exempted from payment of employees' contribution because of low rates of wages. Extension of the Act to plantation labour at this stage is, therefore, bound to make serious in roads into the funds of the Corporation. The Corporation should not enter this new field of activity immediately. The position might be reviewed after a period of about five years in the light of the development and resources of the Corporation at that time.

Priorities

The extension of the Scheme may follow progressively the following order in the next ten years or so :

(a) **Immediately**

(i) Factories using power and employing ten or more persons; factories not using power employing twenty or more persons ;

(ii) Running staff of road transport undertakings not at present covered.

(b) **During The Fourth Five Year Plan Period**

(i) All factories whether or not using power employing ten more persons;

(ii) Shops and Commercial establishments employing ten or more persons;

(iii) Trade and Commerce employing ten or more persons.

(c) **Thereafter**

(i) All undertakings under (b) above employing five or more persons;

(ii) Mines and plantations employing ten or more persons whether or not power is used.

Power of extension of the scheme under Section I(5) of the Act should rest with the Central Government which should, of course, consult the State Governments concerned before issue of the notification.

Exemptions

The provisions in the Act for grant ot exemption should be tightened and exemption may be given only in exceptional circumstances when the prevailing benefits are superior on an overall assessment to those that could be provided under the Scheme, and the employees themselves desire exemption. No distinction should be made between private sector and public sector in the grant of exemptions.

Enlargement Of The Scope Of The Term 'Employee'

The definition of the term 'employee' must be such as to bring in all classes of emplopees in a factory, except those about a certain wage ceiling.

Relief For Clerical Employees

It would be undesirable to prescribe a relief or diminution in contribution in case of class of employees not so much exposed to the risk of employment injury as that would amount to matching of the components of the contribution to each risk.

Wage Ceiling

The wage limit for coverage of an employee should, in the first instance, be raised to Rs. 1,000 per month. A provision should also be made for giving the Central Government powers to raise the wage ceiling from time to time.

Coverage Of Casual, Temporary And Badli Workers

It would be a retrogade step to exclude from the Scheme the large number of persons working as casual, temporary and badli workers.

It would not be desirable to specify any minimum period of continuous employment for coverage of an employee.

Contributions

Transitional Provisions

The transitional provisions which were introduced as a short term arrangement connot be continued for an indefinite period. These should be dropped and the contribution should be collected as per Schedule I to the Act.

Freezing Of Contribution And Benefit Rates

There should be a freezing of contribution and benefit rates at the persent maximum rates and no further wage group need be added with the raising of the wage ceiling to Rs. 1,000.

Exemption Limit for Payment Of Employees' Coutribution

In order to give relief to low paid employees, raising of the wage limit to Rs. 2 per day is recommended for exemption from payment of employees' contribution immediately with a provision for review of the position at the time of the next valuation.

Contribution Stamp System

The present system of collection of contribution through contribution stamps should not be given up. Nevertheless, the search for simpler system should continue and the O & M Division of the Corporation should concentrate on it.

Return Of Contribution Cards

The Return of Contribution Cards should be sent by the employer in triplicate.

System of calculation of contributions

Amendments in the Contribution and Benefit schedule as proposed are a considerable improvement over the present position and also over the percentage method of calculating the rate of contributions. No change is, therefore, suggested in the system of calculation of contributions.

Chalan Form For Purchase Of Contribution Stamps

One copy of Chalan Form should be returned to the employer for his record in case of purchase of contribution stamps.

Abolition Of Sets

The system of dividing the insured persons in three sets 'A', 'B' and 'C' may by abolished.

Fixation Of Unit For Payment Of Contribution

Another contribution table may be added in the Act to provide for payment of contributions on monthly basis in cases where the wage period is a month. Corresponding changes may be made in the contributory conditions for title to benefit.

Limitations For Recovery Of Contributions From employers

There should be a reasonable period of limitation for recovery of contributions payable by the employer. The provision of three years period for this purpose as proposed in the Amendment Bill would be adequate.

Transfer of Liability for Payment of contributions on Transfer ownership

It should be possible to provide in the E.S.I. Act that the liability to pay arrears of contributions, if any, passes on to the transferee along with the transfer of ownership of the factory.

Cash Benefits

Lumpsum Payment of Permanent Disablement Benefit

It should be provided in the Act itself that payment of permanent disablement benefit shall be made in the form of a lumpsum of the rate of benefit is less than 50 paise a day.

Appropriate provision may be made in the Regulations to the effect that Medical Board may also certify the correctness of the age declared by the insured person at the time of assessment of the extent of loss of earning capacity, which will operate in the absence of adequate proof of age.

Rate Of Sickness Benefit

No change in the present quantum of sickness benefit rate is recommended.

Reduction In The Sickness Benefit Rate During Hospitalisation

It would not be a proper step to reduce the rate of sickness benefit of an insured person while he is undergoing treatment as an indoor patient in a hospital.

Maximum Duration Of Sickness Benefit

Duration of sickness benefit should be increased from 56 days to 13 weeks (91 days) as a first step with an ultimate objective to increase the maximum duration to 26 weeks.

Qualifying Conditions For Extended Sickness Benefit

The qualifying period for extended sickness benefit should be reduced from two years to one and a half years. An insured person who has qualified in any of the three contribution periods during the previous four consecutive contribution periods, should be eligible for extended sickness benefit. The extended benefit may be allowed for the second and subsequent spells if there is an interval of not less than twelve months after the termination of the previous spell and the insured person has qualified for sickness benefit in the intervening contribution periods.

Increase In Rate Of Employment Injury Benefit

The rate of employment injury benefit should be 30% over and above the sickness benefit rate.

Expert Committee to Review The Schedule Pertaining To Assessment of Loss Of Earning Capacity

An expert committee should be appointed to review the schedule on which the assessment of the percentage of loss of earning capacity for purposes of permanent disablement is based and to make suitable recommendations taking into account the practice in other countries. A certain degree of discretion must be given to the Medical Boards in assessing cases involving combination of injuries and non-schedule injuries.

Grant-In-Aid To Safety Associations

The E.S.I. Corporation should actively associate with the National Safety Council for the setting up of which the President's Conference on Industrial safety held in New Delhi recently has made certain proposals.

Review Of Rates Of Certain Benefits

There should be quinquennial review of the rates of permanent disablement benefit and dependents' benefit at the time of the valuation. The increase should neutralise the rise in the working class cost of living.

Provision Of Waiting Period

The provision of waiting period in case of sickness benefit is based on sound principles and no alternation in this provision is suggested.

There is no particular objection to making the waiting period conditional on an insured person being certified sick for a continued period of three weeks, and paying the benefit from the very first day once he crosses the limit laid down except that this may increase administrative work and perhaps, also the cost. The Corporation may in due course examine by reference to the actual number of cases where the spells of sickness for last there weaks and more and the financial implications of the proposal.

Provision Of Death Grant

Death Grant is another useful suggestion for consideration as an additional benefit under the scheme in course of time.

Invalidity And Survivorship Pensions

There is need for provision of invalidity and survivorship pensions. The better course would be to tag them on to the old age pension scheme when it comes.

Increase In Absenteeism

There is no evidence to show that absenteeism in industry has shown a significant increase after the introduction of the ESI Scheme or that there has been malingering on a large scale.

No Claim Bonus

No claim bonus is not likely to solve the problem of absenteeism. In principle, there may be no objection to a provision for the extension of the maximum duration of benefit in the succeeding year for insured persons who do not claim sickness benefit during a year but this would not be of much benefit. This question may be further examined by the Corporation at a future date.

Disbursement Of Cash Benefits

Simplification of Procedures

The present system of claims taking and payment of cash benefits at the Local Offices is complicated and there is great need for making the procedure simple and straight-forward.

The process of decentralisation should be continued till it is ensured that all matters concerning determination of claims for short term benefits are finally settled at the local office level without reference to the Regional Office except in cases of doubt. The contribution cards should also be received in the local offices and work with regard to exit and re-entry of insured persons should also be done there. There is need for constant vigilance and Organisations and Method study for gradual improvement.

Review Of "No Contribution Card" Cases

To ensure prompt payment of benefit there should be a procedure for picking out 'no contribution card' cases immediatly after the end of the contribution period. In cases where there is reasonable evidence that the insured person was in employment he should be deemed to have paid contributions even if his contribution card is not received.

Benefit Files And Ledger System

The benefit file system has not worked well. The loose-leaf ledger system may be more suitable to the conditions in which the local offices have to work and may eliminate most of the difficulties of the present system.

"Teller" System

To speed up the payments, "Teller" system may be adopted with a machinery to check up claims and post the benefit files ledger subsequently. The counter clerks may be authorized to make the payment after quick determination of titles etc. upto Rs. 25 on the basis of the claim presented by the insured person. Subsequent payments in the same spell, even if exceeding Rs. 25 may also be made by the counter clerk,

Delays In Payment Of Long Term Benefits

Efforts should be made to reduce the time required for award of permanent disablement benefit after the termination of temporary disablement benefit to the minimum by treating such cases as Emergency Cases. Medical Officer Incharge of the case should send his report and recommendations well before the issue of final certificate on receipt of which local office should initiate action immediately. Thereafter the case should proceed from stage to stage on a "High Priority" basis. The arrangements for medical boarding should be made adequate wherever there are deficiencies and no one case should be allowed to wait for more than a few days for placing before the Medical Board.

Papers For Medical Board

Papers for the Medical Board should invariably be scrutinised by the Medical Officer of the Corporation, and should reach the Chairman of the Board at least three prior to the date of the meeting. The recommendations should also be routed through the Medical Officer in the Regional Office who can advise if an appeal or a review is necessary.

One Man Medical Board

In large industrial areas where the number of insured persons exceed one lakh, there may be two types of Boards, one on which three members sit, to deal with the cases of non-schedule injuries and the other with only one member to deal with the cases of schedule injuries.

Provisional Payment Of Permanent Disablement Benefit

In cases where the estimated disablement is more than 25% provisional payment upto 75% of the benefit may be made and adjusted later when the award of the Medical Board is available.

Time Limit For Payment Of Benefits

The time limits for payment of benefits particularly for maternity benefit, permanent disablement benefit and dependant's benefit are excessive and should be reduced to fourteen days, one month and three months, respectively. Satisfactory machinery should also be devised to inform the claimant, in the first instance, all that he is required to do.

Remittance By Money Order

The option for payment by money order should be freely publicised. The local offices should have specific machinery for disposal of applications for remittance by money orders and normally all requests for money orders received on a particular day should be disposed of the same day.

Refund Of Benefit Paid In Excess

If there are any impediments in the E.S.I. Act against refund or adjustment of over-drawn payments from future receipts, then should be removed. It should be ensured that intimation regarding excess amount paid is issued within twenty-four hours of payment.

Alternative Evidence Of Incapacity

While it is difficult to suggest that there should be no provision to deal with the exceptional cases where the insured person has necessarily to produce a certificate from the private doctor, there should be an effective machinery for proper check-up of such certificates.

Working Of Sub-Local Offices And Pay Offices

While a sub-local office may be economical it is unsatisfactory from the point of view of prompt and efficient service. The sub-local offices should be converted into small size local offices and a junior officer with powers to pass claims for short term benefits should be posted here.

The pay offices, should be replaced by the system of remittance by money orders.

In heavily congested areas payment of cash benefits to employees of large undertakings may be made at the employers premises by sending the cashier there once or twice a week as may be necessary.

Medical Benefits—Administration

Provision Of Ayurvedic System Of Medicine

Ayurveda being in great demand in certain areas, it is recommended that sufficient and satisfactory facilities should be made available for Ayurvedic treatment.

Responsibility For Administration Of Medical Benefits

While taking note of the arguments pro and con with regard to the Employees. State Insurance Corporation taking over the administration of medical benefits, it is felt that it would not be expedient to make any radical change in this regard at present. On the other hand, every effort should be made to gear up the machinery set up by State Governments to the needs of the scheme and to ensure that proper and effective liaison is maintained between the corporation and the State Governments. For the day-to-day functioning of the medical side of the scheme, the State Governments should have a free hand but then should be answerable to the corporation for any lapses. The administration of medical benefit may be entrusted to the corporation wherever the State Government feel that this step would be in the larger interest of the State and the efficient administration of the scheme.

Administration Of Medical Benefit In Delhi

The administration of medical benefits in Delhi where these are administered directly by the corporation is not very satisfactory. The dispensaries were found in a bad state of repairs. The buildings had not been white washed for several years. This was said to be the responsibility of the C.P.W.D. The corporation is an autonomous body and should make its own arrangements.

Consumption of drugs in Delhi had increased considerably and the dispensaries were running out of stock again and again. Strengthening of inspection machinery is indicated.

Medical Benefits—Out-Door Care

Doctor-Patient Relations

There is need for an extensive programme of information and education aimed at promoting a better understanding by each side of the difficulties and obligations and rights of the other. Some systematic orientation programmes should be regularly conducted by the corporation for the IMO/IMPs and other medical personnel.

Inspection

The Administrative Medical Officers should function more effectively than at present and then must have adequate inspecting staff to make routine checks and to speedily follow up specific complaints.

List Of Medicines

There should be only one list of drugs from which the doctors, including specialists, should be required to prescribe. Such a list must be comprehensive enough and must be kept up-to-date by fairly frequent revision.

Need For Training In Industrial Health

Steps should be taken to ensure that doctors working in the employees' State Insurance Scheme have proper training in the field of industrial health and medicine.

Domiciliary Visits

Steps should be taken to educate the insured persons of their rights and it should be deemed a major default if an IMP/IMO fails to pay a domiciliary visit when called upon to do so unless he can show that the call was a frivolous or vexations one.

Service System Versus Panel System

Service system offers better possibilities of giving satisfactory medical service to the insured persons and their families. However, conditions in some centres are such that adoption of the service system may not be possib'e. In such places the State Governments should give high prority to the setting up of atleast a few conveniently located service dispensaries and the insured persons may be given a choice whether to enrol with an IMP or at the service dispensary. This, in course of time, will show whether the insured persons under similar conditions show any clear preference for one or the other.

Steps To Make Improvements In Panel System

It is necessary that early steps are taken to remove the deficiencies that have been noticed in the Panel System.

Rate Of Capitation Fee

The present capitation fee of Rs. 17.50 per family unit per year is not low and does not need any upward revision at this stage. In areas where capitation fee prescribed at present is only Rs. 13.50 it needs to be revised to make it comparable with the fee paid in other areas.

Inadequacy Of Number Of IPs On The IMP's List

Any IMP who fails to have at least 100 insured persons on his list at the end of six months, after his enrolment in the Panel, should be removed from the Panel and similarly in any area which already has more than an adequate number of IMPs for the total number of IPs in the area, no new doctors should be admitted to the Panel.

Supply Of Drugs and Medicines

To meet the extremely unsatisfactory situation in the matter of supply of medicines in the Panel areas the following steps are suggested :

(i) State Governments should establish several drug depots, conveniently located in each panel area. These depots could be located at Government or Municipal hospitals and dispensaries as also at other premises already at the disposal of the State Government ;

(ii) The payment of the bills of approved chemists should be speeded up and time limit for payment fixed ;

(iii) Cooperative consumer stores should be encouraged to enter the field of E.S I. drug distribution ;

(iv) Approved chemists failing to hold adequate stocks should be removed from the list ;

(v) IMPs should not be permitted to be associated with the sale or distributions of drugs, whether in the scheme or outside ;

(vi) No approved chemists shop should be permitted to have any kind of association with any medical practitioner connected with the E.S.I. Scheme ;

(vii) Representatives of the Employees' State Insurance Corporation should be associated with committees dealing with supply, manufacture, distribution and pricing of drugs.

Inadequacy Of Diagnostic Centres

The number of diagnostic centres must be increased and then must be brought closer to the insured persons. Rigid time limits should be imposed for various kinds of investigations. Hours of attendance by specialists should also be extended, if necessary, by acquisition of the services of more specialists.

To improve the situation, a panel of specialist should be created. Group practice by specialists should also be permitted. The diagnostic centres may concentrate on pathological work which may be separated from specialist consultation.

The E.S.I. hospitals should also provide diagnostic and specialist consultation facilities for outdoor insured patients.

Inadequacy Of Ambulance Service

There is a glaring inadequacy of ambulance service. E.S.I. authorities should explore the possibilities of getting some firms interested in the manufacture of ambulance bodies on indigenously manufactured chassis. It is recommended that the E.S.I. Corporation should attend to this since State Governments may not be able to do it expeditiously. The importance of proper upkeep and manning of the ambulances available at present is further stressed so that then may be used to the maximum possible extent.

Medical Benefit : Indoor Medical Care And Treatment In Special Diseases

Inadequacy Of Hospital Beds

While there has been some progress in hospital construction during the past four years, the position is still far from satisfactory. The number of beds available is inadequate. The deficit is more shocking in the case of T.B. beds. The deficit is actually increasing as the rate of construction is behind the rate of extension of the scheme. Lack of adequate interest on the part of some State Governments has been one of the principle causes of this poor performance and it is clear that only a radical change in the present approach to the task can offer any hope of significant improvement.

Steps For Expediting Construction Of Hospitals

To speed up the construction of hospitals following steps should be taken :

(a) The responsibility and initiative should be entirely transferred to the corporation, which should have a civil engineering division to plan and look after the engineering aspect of the work ;

(b) The Regional Directorates of the Corporation should estimate the bed requirements in their regions, make plans, look for suitable sites and get estimates made etc. As sites are located, after getting approval of the Regional Boards, then should approach the State Governments for their acquisition ;

(c) Corporation should be authorised to call for tenders for actual construction, and to give contracts ;

(d) The Government should give high priority to the Corporation in the allotment of steel and cement for the construction of hospitals ;

(e) The present emphasis on very large hospitals should go. Instead, the Corporation should build a large number of medium and small hospitals even in big industrial centres. Where land is no problem, barrack type construction may further speed up the work. Such medium and small hospitals need not be equipped for all possible Specialities. The few cases that might need more specialised attention can be transferred to the large, well equipped hospitals which have been built in most of the larger centres. The State Governments should set aside space for such medium and small hospitals whenever they undertake any industrial housing projects.

(f) For the industrial workers who live away from the families in industrial housing colonies, one house in the block of workers' houses may be converted into a "sick-bay" and placed under the general supervision of a Medical Officer.

The delay in hospital construction is really a breach of a solemn promise given to the insured persons and a major failure of the Corporation and the State Governments in the discharge of their responsibility.

Standards Of Construction Of The E.S.I. Hospitals ;

Their Staffing And Services

There should be no difficulty in prescribing reasonable uniform and satisfactory standards in the construction of hospitals, in their staffing and in the standards of services given by them. The Medical Benefit Council should give careful thought to this matter and should evolve suitable and definite norms to be observed in all the States.

The superintendents of all the major E.S.I. hospitals should be enabled to pool their experiences.

Complaints And Suggestions Regarding Working Of The E.S.I. Hospitals

The Regional and Local Medical Benefit Councils with an adequate representation on behalf of the IPs, should be given facilities to keep in touch with the working of the E.S.I. hospitals and to deal with complaints and suggestions regarding them.

Treatment For Tuberculosis

Hospitalisation facilities for T.B. patients under the E.S.I. Scheme are regrettably meagre. Adequate number of T.B. hospitals should be constructed.

Till adequate number of hospitals are constructed, there should be greater emphasis on domiciliary treatment which should be supplemented by better facilities for X-ray and sputum smear examination.

Treatment Of Cancer And Mental Diseases

The Scheme should make standing arrangement with the institutions which specialise in the treatment of cancer and mental diseases on payment of normal fees and the insured persons should get the same standard of treatment and facilities as the other paying patients at these institutions.

Provision Of Special Wards In The E.S.I. Hospitals

Provision of special facilities under the Scheme for the use of insured persons in the higher income bracket is not recommended. Facilities available under the E.S.I. Scheme should be uniform for all insured persons regardless of their income.

The suggestion that the E.S.I. hospitals should have special wards which may insured person could avail of on a prescribed fee is not acceptable.

Reservation Of Beds In The E.S.I. Hospitals For Treatment Of General Public

Surplus beds in E.S.I. hospitals may be made available for the use of the general public on payment by the State Governments. If there is any impediment in the Act against this, that may be removed by suitable modification. It should, however, be ensured that no E.S.I. beneficiary is deprived of the hospitalisation facility simply because the beds have been made available for the general public.

Medical Benefits-General

Preventive And Restorative Care

The E.S.I. Scheme should address itself to preventive as well as restorative work and should make adequate plans therefore without delay.

The preventive and restorative care may consist of :

(i) Extensive health education programme for the insured persons and their familier ;

(ii) Immunisation of infants and children.

(iii) Preventive compaign against tuberculosis starting with centres and areas where the incidence of T.B. is known to be high among the insured populations ;

(iv) Coordination of T.B. preventive service with the public health programme.

Analysis Of Morbidity Data

The Corporation should have a suitable machinery to analyse the data on abnormal incidence for particular ailments in particular areas and States for necessary follow up.

Medical Check-Up Of Insured Persons Who Suffer Frequent Spells Of Sickness

All insured persons who suffer from frequent spells of sickness, should be referred to specialists for complete check-up. Any pathological investigations that may be recommended should be carried out and the insured persons should be put on a regimen prescribed by the specialist.

Family Planning

The E.S.I. Scheme should pay all possible attention to family planning among the insured persons. The details of the programme should be worked out in collaboration with the family planning units of the respective State Governments.

The State Governments should not deny the cash allowance to the insured persons which is being paid to other citizens of the State who undergo sterilisation operation. The payment of cash allowance by the Corporation as an incentive to insured persons for undergoing sterilisation operation is not favoured.

Rehabilitation Measures

The Corporation should undertake an effective programme of rehabilitation, retaining and re-employment of permanently disabled insured persons and institutional rehabilitation care should be provided. Every E.S.I. hospital in centres with an insured population of 50,000 family units or more, should have a properly equipped and staffed rehabilitation unit. Besides, there should be established in bigger industrial centres like Bombay and Calcutta, full-fledged medical rehabilitation centres with arrangement for whole day institutional care.

The medical training institutes in the country should be encouraged and assisted by the Corporation to provide and extend the facilities for specialised training in rehabilitation work on an adequate scale.

Health Homes And Convalescent Homes

The E.S.I. Scheme need not go in for health homes and convalescent homes for the present.

Certification By Panel Doctors

For proper certification, the panel doctors should lay down collectively the standards and enforce them through collective action.

Acceptance Of Alternative Evidence Of Incapacity

An outside certificate submitted by an insured person who has in the past also done so regularly, should be checked upon for genuineness. Similarly, if a particular medical practitioner from a particular place is found to be issuing an unusually large number of certificates, all certificates coming from him should be checked. On the other hand, certificates issued by public hospitals or dispensaries and reputed medical institutions should normally be accepted without question.

Supervision Of Medical Care Facilities

An adequate medical inspecting staff should be provided for detailed and day-to-day supervision of medical facilities. Local Medical Officers should be appointed at all the centres which have an insured population of 25,000 or more.

Incapacity References

Administrative machinery for incapacity references and for general supervision should also belong to the State Governments. The work of incapacity references should form part of the duties of the local medical officers. They should not only assist the Administrative Medical Officer in the supervision and inspection of arrangements, but should also attend to incapacity references received from the local offices of the Corporation.

Programme Of Information And Education

The Corporation should give immediate and adequate attention to developing such programmes of information and education calculated to promote healthy attitude among those who are concerned with the working of the scheme—particularly the insured persons, the doctors and the administering staff.

Writing Of Certificates

The certificates should continue to be written by the medical officers and this work should not be entrusted to clerks. If, however, any simplification of the certification procedure in other respects is possible, it should certainly be tried.

Intimation To Employers

The doctors will find it difficult to send intimation to the employers directly as their patients come from many different establishments and the doctors do not have their addresses. The present practice may be permitted to continue.

Text Of Final Certificate

The text of final certificate may be modified as follows :

"The Insured Person would not require medical treatment and attendance and abstention from work on medical grounds from."

Grant Of Certificate Of Permanent Incapacity

The insurance doctors may be empowerd to grant certificates of permanent incapacity for work, to the insured persons for the purposes of grant of gratuity. Disputed cases may be referred to competent medical specialists under the scheme.

Lapse Of Title To Medical Care

The Regulations should provide that an insured patient, whether the insured person or a member of his family, will continue to get treatment once started till the spell of sickness ends or in the case of long term ailments, so long as the patient requires active treatment, even if during the treatment the insured person becomes disentitled to medical care.

Supply Of Dentures And Spectacles

It would neither be practicable nor feasible financially to supply dentures and spectacles free of charge at this stage. There is, however, need to ensure that the facility regarding supply of spectacles on "no profit no loss" basis is actually made available. Similar arrangements for supply of dentures should also be made under the scheme.

Pre-employment Medical Examination

Pre-employment medical examination is not favoured. Facility for physical check-up should, however, be provided at the time of admission to the scheme. This could suitably be made an occasion for preventive inculations and prophylactic measures to be followed up with periodical inoculations as may be required.

Employment Of Partially Disabled Persons

There should be a statutory obligation on employers to continue in employment and to assign suitable work to persons who become partially disabled as a result of industrial accidents in the employers' establishment.

Medical Institutes

Full-fledged medical colleges should be started at places where there are large and well equipped E.S.I. hospitals, either directly by the E.S.I. Corporation or by the state with the help from the Corporation. In cases where the Corporation contributes financially to medical training, the students or trainees concerned should be under an obligation to serve the E.S.I. Scheme for a specified period which should not be less than 5 years, after achieving full qualifications. The E.S.I. hospitals should also be utilised for the training of nurses and other para-medical staff.

Minimum Professional Experience For E.S.I. Doctors

Complaints of the insured persons against being entrusted to the care of raw and in experienced doctors is legitimate. Doctors posted in E.S.I. dispensaries or hospitals should have not less than 3 years' professional experience.

Adjudication Machinery

Constitution Of Medical Boards And Medical Appeal Tribunals

It is not necessary to provide for a further right of appeal to the E.I. Court after the decisions of the Medical Appeal Tribunal. The proposal in the Amending Bill to allow an appeal against the decision of the Medical Board to the E.I. Court also seems unnecessary. Modification of the proposed legislation is suggested accordingly. Disablement questions should be completely taken out of the purview of the E.I. Courts.

Employees' Insurance Courts

The working of the Employees' Insurance Courts shows that the proceedings are generally prolonged, cumbersome and formal. The common pattern of ordinary Civil Courts is followed which is not suited to a scheme of social insurance where there is more need for promptness rather than precision.

The Employees' Insurance Courts should follow the summary procedure.

The Employees' Insurance Court Rules should provide a time limit of three months for adjudication of claim.

Informal Tribunals

There are very few disputes regarding payment of benefits which can be entrusted to informal tribunals. Therefore, no change is suggested in the present system.

Decision On Questions Of Coverage And Insurability

The questions of coverage and insurability should be reserved for the judgment of the Director General. His decision should be final subject only to appeal on questions of Law to the High Court. Where legal enquiry is likely to assist in reaching decision, the Director General may appoint a legal officer to conduct a legal enquiry and report to him.

Book Of Precedents

Books of precedents which should include brief proceedings and decisions of the E.I. Courts in the various States should be compiled.

Whole-Time E.I. Courts

The part-time arrangement for the Employees' Insurance court has not been found satisfactory. Whole-time E.I. Courts should be set-up. There should be one or two whole-time E.I. Courts in each State with jurisdiction extending to the whole of the state. If necessary, these may be supplemented by a part-time court.

Setting Up Of Appeal Tribunals

The delay in setting up of Appeal tribunals is difficult to understand. Immediate steps should be taken to establish Appeal Tribunals in States where these have not so far been set up.

Composition Of Medical Appeal Tribunals

The Medical Appeal Tribunals should continue to consist of a legal chairman assisted by one or more medical experts and one or more officials of the Trade Unions as assessors.

Recovery Of Contribution From Employers On Conviction

The Act should provide that on conviction the employer should also be required to pay the contribution not paid in addition to five imprisonment that may be imposed.

Penalty For Continuous Offence

The employers should be required to submit contribution cards even when the contribution due is recovered through a court decree. Failure to do so should attract a fine which may extend to Rs. 50 per day during which the default continues.

Employees' Contribution Trust Money

Non-payment of employees' contributions, which has already been deducted by the employer from the wages of the employees, should be treated as a breach of trust and a provision to that effect may be made in the Act itself.

Application Of Fines

A provision should be made in the E.S.I. Act to the effect that the court imposing any fine may direct that the whole or any part of the fine shall be applied in or towards the payment of costs of the proceedings.

E.S.I. Contribution-Preferential Payment

The contribution due under the E.S.I. Act for the previous three years should be treated as preferential payment for the distribution of the property of the in solent or in the distribution of a company being wound up.

Financial Control And State Contribution

Autonomy Of The Corporation

To ensure adequate autonomy for the Corporation and expeditions conduct of its business, the E.S.I. Corporation should be able, on its own initiative and decision, to raise funds, to invest money, to allocate expenditure for purposes of the scheme, to plan its objectives, to choose among the available operating alternatives and to formulate its own reserve and appropriation policies, subject to over-all accountability to the Parliament.

Control By Central Government

The list of items on which the Central Government alone has power to sanction expenditure or where prior approval of the Central Government is required, should be reviewed. While it is essential to keep an overall control with the Central Government, it is desirable to leave the management of the affairs of the corporation in the hands of the representatives of the interests concerned.

Matters To Be Dealt With By The Central Government

The Central Government need concern itself directly only with the following matters :

(i) Constitution of the Corporation, the Standing Committee and the Medical Benefit Council, their functions and conduct of their business ;

(ii) Appointment of the Director General ;

(iii) Prescribing the form for maintenance of accounts and appointment of auditors ;

(iv) Publication of accounts and audit reports ;

(v) Approval of budget estimates.

Steps may be taken to amend the Act and the Central Rules accordingly.

Investment Of Funds

While safety of the funds is of paramount importance and it has to be ensured that no investment is made in equity shares, the avenues for earning higher rate of interest on funds not immediately required, should not be closed.

Investment Committee

To evolve a broad-based investment policy, which may give freedom for investing a specific proportion of the available funds in other channels, it is necessary to have a small investment committee of the Corporation to advise the Director General. The powers of approval to deviate from the Rules presently retained by the Central Government, may be transferred to the Corporation.

Central Government Contribution

The Central Government should bear a fair proportion of the cost of the scheme. The Central Government's share should be on a per capita basis calculated with reference to the total number of employees covered under the scheme from year to year, the amount payable, however, being not less than the aggregate contribution of all the State Governments for medical care.

State Government's Contribution

The States' share on medical benefit for the insured persons should, in no case, be less than the per capita expenditure on other citizens of the state.

Provision Of State Share In The Act

The State's share should be specified in the Act itself and not left to any agreement to be arrived at between the Employees' State Insurance Corporation and the State Government. The share of the State Government should be worked out as follows :

(a) 1/3rd of the cost of the medical care for insured persons ;

(b) 2/3rd of the cost of medical care for members of the family of the insured persons ;

(c) The excess cost of sickness benefit to insured persons in the State over the average rate for the country as a whole.

Administrative Structure

Administrative Machinery

The present arranagement of administering the scheme through a statutory autonomous body like the Corporation is the correct one, since it permits the special problems of social insurance being given specialised attention and also ensures a degree of freedom from governmental routine and procedures.

Representation Of Interests Concerned

It is necessary to remove the feeling which representatives of the beneficiaries have that the Government representation on the Corporation is disproportionately high while the representation of the workers and employers is not adequate. The employers, employees and the Government, including other interests, should be represented in the ratio of 1:1:2 respectively. The strength of the Corporation should be raised to forty, out of which the employers and the employees should have ten representatives each. The rest may be distributed between the Central and the State Governments, medical profession and members of Parliament.

Routing of correspondence and participating in the deliberations of the Corporation through the Department of Labour is an avoidable duplication which can be eliminated by nominating a representative of the Department of Health on the Corporation and by handling all matters dealing with the working of the Employees' State Insurance Scheme in that Department. The Department of Health should, however, take the advice of the Labour Department in all administrative matters and delegate to that Department the work in connection with the grant of exemption and Employees' Insurance Courts.

If an eminent person connected with or having knowledge and experience of the field of activities of the Corporation is included among the nominees of the Central Government, it will strengthen the Corporation.

Representation Of Workers And Employers On The Standing Committee

With an increase in the representatives of workers and employers on the Corporation and following the same principle, the number of seats for these interests on the Standing Committee may also be increased to five each. This will raise its strength to 20 members. The remaining ten members will represent the Central and the State Governments and other interests concerned.

Nomination of Medical Experts By The Central Government On The Medical Benefit Council

Considering the specific functions of the Medical Benefit Council, it would be desirable to give more representation to medical experts on this body. The Central Government should, in addition, have powers to nominate on the Council five medical experts who may be specialists in medicine, chest, surgery, orthopaedics and indigenous system of medicine.

Participation By The State Government in the Medical Benefit Council

The participation of the State Governments in the deliberations of the Medical Benefit Council should be at the highest level and all State Governments should be represented through their Directors Health Services or the Surgeon-General.

Meetings Of The Corporation, Standing Committee And Medical Benefit Council

The Corporation, the Standing Committee and the Medical Benefit Council should meet regularly on due dates and there should be a suitable machinery at the Headquarters office of the Corporation for proper liaison between the functions of these bodies.

Constitution Of Regional Boards

In order to ensure adequate representation of the employers and the employees on the Regional Boards and consistant with the principle enunciated earlier, the Regulations should provide that where the number of employers and employees representatives on the Regional Board is less than three each, including the ex-officio members, the Chairman shall nominate additional representatives of employers and employees to bring their number upto three.

Functions And Powers Of The Regional Boards

The Regional Boards should not be encumbered with the day-to-day administration and it is not necessary to delegate to them powers relating to routine administrative matters which could safely be entrusted to the local executives. The Regional Boards should be entrusted with the following specific functions which would be in addition to those already mentionnd in the Regulations at present:

(i) Deciding, within the broad framework of the general decisions of the Corporation, questions like geographical extension of the Scheme, any special measure to meet peculiar conditions in the area or Region; improvement in benefits; extention of medical care to families; provision of indoor medical treatment; rehabilitation arrangements for partially disabled insured persons; ensuring compliance by employers and so on;

(ii) Exercising general supervision, without interfering with day-to-day administration, over the operation of the Scheme including working of local offices, processing of permanent disablement benefit cases etc;

(iii) Looking into general grievances and difficulties of insured persons, employers, medical personnel, Corporation staff etc., and promoting healthy relations among them.

The Regional Boards may set up suitable sub-committees for carrying out the different functions and they may also take assistance of the local committees.

Action On The Recommendations Of The Regional Boards And Local Committees—Setting Up Of A Screening Committee Of The Standing Committee

There should be a systematic consideration of the recommendations of the Regional Boards in the Corporation. The suggestions received from the Regional Boards should be placed before the Standing Committee for consideration and decisions thereon should be communicated to them without delay. Depending on the frequency and volume of such recommendations, the Standing Committee may have a screening committee which could meet more frequently to consider suggestions from the Regional Boards and Local Committees before they are placed before the Standing Committee. Suggestions which are clearly unacceptable should be referred back to the Regional Boards explaining why they are not being placed before the Standing Committee.

Regional And Local Medical Benefit Councils

It is necessary to have at least at the regional level expert machinery to advise the regional organisation on medical matters. Suitable Regulations be framed for the constitution of Regional Medical Benefit Councils and for delegation to them of necessary powers and functions to assist in the administration of medical care benefit under the Scheme.

Delegation Of Powers And The Role Of Accounts Officers

It would be mere expeditions if responsibility was placed on the Regional Directors and the administrative expenditure incurred by them is subjected to audit in the normal way. The Regional Assistant Accounts Officer in the Region should essentially be an audit officer but he should be available to the Regional Director for financial advice where such advice is sought by him.

Organisational Set-Up

Control Of Administrative Division By A Senior Officer

The control of the Administrative Division of a senior officer of the status of Principal Officer is a deside ratum which needs to be made up without delay.

Professional Experience For Appointment Of Principal Officers

Reorientation of the administration with bias towards expertise is strongly recommended. Social security administration is a highly technical subject and calls for high degree of professional skill and experience. It is of utmost importance that the Insurance Division is also manned by officers with suitable qualifications, experience and training in social security administration.

Appointment Of Deputy Director General

It is advisable to provide a deputy to assist the Director General and to coordinate the work of other Technical Divisions.

Appointment Of Principal Officers By The Central Government

It is unnecessary to burden the Central Government with the responsibility for appointment of Principal Officers. The appointment of Director General alone need to be made by the Central Government. The other Principal Officers should be appointed by the Corporation itself through normal channels.

Financial Adviser

Absence of Financial Adviser is a deficiency in the

organisational set up of the Corporation. The Chief Accounts Officer is at present performing the functions of the Financial Adviser, though his duties according to the rules laid down by the Central Government are confined to maintenance of accounts and carrying out of internal audit. He should either be designated as Financial Adviser or a separate post created for this purpose.

Statutory Provision Regarding Number Of Officers etc.

The Corporation should be free to modify its top organisational structure to suit its current requirements A statutory provision fixing the number and functions of a certain grade of officers irrespective of the size or growth of the organisation is an unusual and unrealistic feature.

Organisation And Method Division

There is need for strengthening of the machinery for Organisation and Method which would keep procedures under constant review and revision. The O. & M. Division should concentrate on a realistic appraisal of present work standards, potential improvements and simplifications with a conscious effort at economy in costs and operations, exploration of methods suited to the special needs and requirements of the organisation and effecting alternations and adjustments after proper experimentation so as to choose ultimately what best fits the needs of the organisation. In addition, the O & M. Division should engage itself in studying methods of eliminating the time wastage due to several factors and for prescribing certain minimum standards of efficiency and performance.

Staff Training

There should be a machinery for staff training. The staff training branch should engage itself in the programme of training of employees not only at the time of initial recruitment but also as a continuing process for intermediate levels and those at the top management level. There should be re-orientation courses, refresher courses and appreciation courses including re-orientation of mental attitude of the staff. There should be inter-regional meetings, seminars, publication of house magazines, participation in international seminars and conferences, availing of the facility for training available under the United Nations Programme of Technical Assistance and under the Colombo Plan and encouragement by means of monetary incentives for professionals training.

Public Relations Machinery

There is need for creation of a regular public relations organisation at the Headquarters and at the Regional offices, to disseminate information and experience.

Reorganisation Of Regional Offices

There is no advantage in retaining Assam as the solitary Grade IV Region. It should be possible to merge it with the West Bengal Region without any difficulty.

The two Grade I Regions viz., Maharashtra and West Bengal, have now become rather unwieldy. Bifurcation of Maharashtra region with two Regional Directors separately incharge of defined areas would be more purposeful. West Bengal Region should also be subdivided into two Regions—one comprising of Calcutta and Howrah and other of 24-Parganas and Hooghly.

It may be useful to amalgamate Bihar with Orissa and Delhi with Rajasthan Region.

After bifurcation and consolidation of the Region, all the Regions would be of practically the same grade and can have a uniform staffing pattern.

Status Of Regional Directors

There is great need for an effective and continuous liaison between the Corporation and the State authorities. It is possible only if the Regional Directors are of sufficient status who can effectively represent and commit the Corporation in negotiations with the State Governments.

Zonal Set-Up

It will be necessary to decentralise the functions of the Central Headquarters Office. For an effective decentralised machinery the country should be divided into four zones, the zonal offices being in Delhi, Bombay, Calcutta and Madras. The Regional Offices may then be renamed as Divisional Offices under the control of the Zonal Offices. The chief executive officer of the Zonal Office may be designated as Zonal Commissioner who may be of the same status as the Principal Officers at the Headquarters.

Set-Up At The Headquarters

The set-up at the Headquarters is essentially clerk-oriented. The set-up and the staffing and working methods must be systematised and carefully replanned. There is no merit in imitating the customary government procedures and practices which are completely unsuited to the Corporation's working. The staffing pattern at the Headquarters should be more officer-oriented. Excessive noting should be done away with. If a decision has to be taken at the level of a Principal Officer, the initial examination of the reference may be by the Section Officer. Officers should be required to do more original work and clerical assistance need be provided mainly for connecting relevant files, precedents and references. Officers who have an aptitude for independent and quick decision and for work connected with policy and planning should be considered particularly fit for the Headquarters.

The provision of a Section Officer and another Junior Officer (Assistant Insurance Commissioner, Assistant Medical Commissioner, Deputy Administrative Officer or Assistant Accounts Officer) to supervise the work of each Section is a peculiar feature which is both unusual and unnecessary. Papers from Section Officer should pass directly to the deputy Principal Officer. If necessary, there may be two or more deputies to assist the Principal Officer. The Corporation should give this matter serious consideration and the posts of Assistant Insurance Commissioner etc., in the Headquarters should be abolished.

Double File System

The double file system could be reduced to the minimum. The system may, however, continue as far as policy files and others of a long-term value are concerned. The system of de-novo examination of inter-Division references at clerical levels should be avoided and a file referred to the other Divisions for advice should be dealt with at the level equal to or higher than the level at which the reference has come.

There should be a Central Registry at the Headquarters which would make it unnecessary for papers to be diarised once again in the branches.

The remarks regarding double file system, the system of *de-novo* examination of inter-division references to clerical level and the desirability of maintaining are Central Registry equally apply to the Regional Offices.

Set-Up Of Regional Office

The set-up at the top should consist of a Regional Director assisted by a Deputy of an appropriate status and such number of Branch Officers (DRD/ARDs) as may be considered necessary.

Survey Branch

Each Regional Office should have a survey branch under the control of an officer of the rank of a Deputy or an Assistant Regional Director. This branch should arrange a periodical survey of each local office in the region by a team of officers, the chief of which should be of a status equal to or higher than that of local office manager whose work is to be inspected.

Staff complements for the local offices

It is necessary to evolve a proper scientific system of staff requirement. The local offices should send a periodical return of the items of work attended to. These returns should be consolidated at the Headquarters and based on the estimated time involved in each operation total requirement of staff complement for the Region may be worked out once at the end of each year. The Regional Director may then be left free to distribute the staff to the local offices on the basis of the work load in each local office.

Provision Of Office Accommodation And Equipment

Most local offices are housed in premises which have been improvised for the purpose. The space available is neither adequate nor entirely suitable for the business to be conducted. The execution of the plan for construction of regional offices and local offices is extremely slow and needs expedition. In most of the offices the equipment particularly the steel cabinets for storage of benefit files and contribution cards etc., is not sufficient, The Regional Directors should carefully work-out the requirement of the filing equipment and ensure their provision to the local offices. The records which are not required should be weeded out.

Staff Quarters

The construction of staff quarters and pending the construction, the arrangement for hiring buildings for letting out to the staff should be given due attention. This is a matter which merits urgent and careful attention of the Corporation.

Pay And Allowances

There is some discontentment among the employees of the Corporation in the matter of their service conditions. It is imperative that for the success of the scheme, the Corporation has full and whole-hearted cooperation of the staff. The employees naturally look forward to improvement in their emoluments commensurate with their responsibilities. The officers, seem to be particularly sore on lack of sufficient avenues of promotion and lack of immediate monetary benefit even on promotion due to overlapping of scales of pay. The Corporation should settle these matters in consultation with the organisations of their employees. The Corporation should give due consideration to all these matters.

Recruitment

The Corporation should fill up 75% of the posts at the lowest Class I level (A.I.C., D.R.D. etc.) from outside and 25% by departmental promotion. Higher posts should be filled 100% by departmental promotion.

The present provision regarding appointment to the posts carrying a maximum pay of Rs. 500 and above being made in consultation with the Union Public Service Commission should be amended. The Corporation should be free to recruit its staff through its own Service Selection Board.

Administrative Expenditure

There is scope for economy in administration. Efforts should be made to obtain maximum results. The officers of the Corporation particularly at the middle and lower levels and those deployed in the field must be oriented towards need for economy in administrative expenditure. There is a tendency in the Corporation to duplicate nearly every step in the process of work by providing for 100% checking. While certain processes do require checking of the original operation, most others need not be duplicated.

Institution of internal audit is another item which may be carefully reviewed with a view to rationalising the work and reducing the quantum of staff deployed thereon.

Comprehensive Scheme Of Social Security

Planning For Comprehensive Social Security Scheme

Plans are already under consideration for the introduction of limited schemes of unemployment insurance and old-age pensions. A caution is necessary against any haphazard and unplanned growth as was the case in many other countries. We should take advantage of a late start, learn from the experience of other countries and plan on the basis of a unified scheme. It would be wasteful to follow the process of evolution undergone by other countries. The seed of the idea to evolve a comprehensive social security scheme, covering, in a single enactment, various risks of cessation of income or wage less to which a wage-earner is exposed, have already been sown and planning can and should now proceed on this basis.

Economy In Administrative Cost

Economy in administrative costs is bound to flow from an administrative merger of the Employees' State Insurance Corporation and the Employees' Provident Fund Organisation.

Administrative Convenience

Both employers and workers would find it more convenient to deal with a single administrative agency and inspectorate and supervisory staff if the schemes were unified.

Maintenance Of Separate Funds And Accounts

As a safeguard against the use of funds means for long term benefits for the health insurance scheme, there may be a provision in the legislation itself that the funds for the two types of schemes should be kept separate. There should be no mixing up of funds. The contributions may be received in a single combined payment but the respective shares should be credited to the two accounts.

Administrative Merger Of The E.S.I. Scheme And The E.P.F. Scheme

Action should be initiated forth with to bring about an administrative merger of the two Schemes. Steps should be taken to examine the problem in all its details and to accomplish this with the least delay.

Merger Of Coal Mines Provident Fund etc. In The Unified Schemes

Merger of the Coal Mines Provident Fund and the Assam Tea Plantations' Provident Fund with the Employees' State Insurance Scheme may be postponed for the time being.

Review And Simplification Of The Comprehensive Scheme And Standardisation Of Rates Of Benefits And Contributions

It will be necessary to revise the Scheme to make it simple for both those who have to administer it and for those who have to benefit by it. The cost of the Scheme will have to be worked out afresh on the basis of the latest available mortality tables and the expected yield on investments in the future.

Expert Machinery

The Government should, in consultation with the Indian Labour Conference, set up an expert machinery to evolve a "blue print" for a comprehensive scheme of social security, which should also form a strong financial and administrative base for inclusion of benefits which are at present not available,

COMMITTEE ON MANGANESE ORE, 1963—REPORT

Delhi, Manager of Publications, 1966. 152p.

Chairman : Shri M. Butt (replaced by Shri R.N. Vasudeva).

Members : Shri T.V. Rama Rao; Shri S. Rajagopalan (replaced by Shri H.P. Sathaye); Shri R.S. Stead (resigned); Shri S. Lal; Shri J.C. Gandhi; Shri K. Sadagopan;

Secretary : Shri A.M. Hussain.

APPOINTMENT

The export trade in Indian manganese ore has been passing through a period of recession from 1958 onwards. Exports which were valued at about Rs. 32 crores in 1957 dropped to a figure of Rs. 14 crores in 1960 and later in 1963 declined to an all-time low level of Rs. 8.00 crores. The situation, as it developed became a matter of great concern to Government. It also came up for a general review at the periodical deliberations of the Board of Trade of the Ministry of Commerce. It was increasingly felt that besides taking short term measures, it would be desirable to make a comprehensive study of the problems of manganese mining industry with particular reference to the need for reducing costs in the face of growing competition from other manganese producing countries. It is against this background that the late Ministry of Commerce and Industry in consultation with the then Ministry of Mines and Fuel (now Department of Mines and Metals) constituted a special committee i e. "Committee on Manganese Ore" under the Government of India Resolution No. 20 (3)/63-BOT dated June 29, 1963.

TERMS OF REFERENCE

(i) To review and report on the present state of affairs of the manganese mining industry in all sectors such as mining, labour, transportation, port facilities etc. in so far as any of those aspects has a bearing on export of manganese ore;

(ii) To examine the projected developmental measures that are contemplated by the industry in the next five year period;

(iii) To study the nature and extent of the competition being faced by the industry in export trade in some of our principal export trade markets such as U.S.A., Japan and U.K.;

(iv) To examine, if possible, the conditions obtaining in the countries which are our principal competitors and assess the impact of the developments in those countries in our own exports; and

(v) To recommend on the basis of (i), (ii), (iii) and (iv) above, appropriate measures for the rationalisation and modernisation of the manganese mining industry in its various sectors (such as labour, management of mines, blending and beneficiation, transportation including facilities at ports) with a view to securing a firm position for the industry in the foreign markets.

CONTENTS

Introduction; World Resources of Manganese Ore—A Survey of Reserves in India and other countries; Physical and Chemical characteristics of Manganese Ore; Uses and Specifications; Beneficiation and Blending; Transportation and Port Handling; Mining, Mines Management and Mine Financing; Mining Legislation and Fiscal Levies; Marketing; Conclusions and Recommendations; Maps; Corrigendum.

RECOMMENDATIONS

World Resources Of Manganese Ore-A Survey Of Reseves in Indian and Other Countries

Conclusions

Almost seventy per cent of the world resources of manganese ore is accounted for by the USSR and the remaining thirty per cent is distributed among various other countries chiefly India, Brazil, Ghana, Union of South Africa, Union of Galon and Morocco.

During recent years, large scale prospecting operations have been carried out in some of these countries which have resulted in considerable additions to the known resources of manganese ore. According to the Mining Journal Annual Review—1963, the manganese ore resources of the USSR, were estimated at 2,000 million tons in 1961. This represents a great advance over the 1956 estimate of 550 million tons of 28-50% Mn.

The resources at Amapa, Brazil are estimated at 14 million tons of ore with 45 to 47% Mn. Besiedes, additional reserves are reported to have been discovered recently underlying the known deposits at Amapa mines which is the largest producer of manganese in the Western hemisphere. The Bethlehem Steel (U.S.A.) are associated with development and mining of these deposits.

Very promising manganese ore deposits have recently been discovered at Maonda, Gabon. These deposits are among the largest and richest in the world. Reserves of the order of 200 million tons of ore of 50% Mn. have been estimated. These deposits are being explored and exploited by the Compagnie Minerie de logone (Comilog) in which U.S. Steel has a major interest.

All major steel producing countries of the world excepting U.S.S.R. and China continue to have either very poor or no resources of manganese ore.

The United States of America has several large deposits of low grade refractory material containing sizeable quantities of manganese which could be recovered only under favourable conditions of improved technology, higher prices or both.

RECOMMENDATION

Intensive e ploration of manganese bearing areas in India is necessary for proving additional reserves. Government should accord high priority to exploration of manganese ore through the agencies of the Geological Survey of India, Indian Bureau of Mines and State Government's departments of geology in this respect.

Large scale mapping followed by exploratory drilling is the well established procedure. Geo-chemical and Geo-physical survey techniques should be pressed into service where possible. Magnetic and gravity surveys conducted by the Geological Survey of India have yeided good results in Madhya Pradesh and Andhra Pradesh. It will be useful if the results of these surveys could be made available to interested prospectors and mining interests through the medium of published monographs.

From the point of view of economics of exports, it will be necessary to accord priority to exploration of these deposits which are located near the sea coast, as for example in Mysore (North Kanara) and Goa. To meet the indigenous requirements of ferro-manganese producers and the steel plants, similarly, particular attention would have to be given to deposits in close proximity to these plants. Some of these 'near-plant' deposits could serve, with advantage to industry, as a captive source for the ferro-manganese producers and steel mills.

Physical and Chemical Characteristics of Manganese Ores :

Conclusions

Indian manganese ores are fairly hard, lumpy and easily reducible ; these characteristics are favourable for smelting ferro-manganese.

Indian ores have, however, low Mn ; Fe ratio of generally 6 : 1 as compared to Caucasian ore ratio of 50 : 1, Ghana 10 : 1 and Brazil 10 : 1. This is below specifications for the manufacture of ferro-manganese, which requires a high Mn-Fe ratio.

High phosphorus ores especially of Andhra Pradesh and Panch Mahals are also not very suitable for ferro manganese industry.

In view of these characteristics of ores, blending of ores of various grades is a necessity.

RECOMMENDATIONS

There is ample scope for blending ores of different types to produce standard mixtures with acceptable percentages of various constituents, particularly manganese, iron and phosphorous. Blending operations if they are to be productive of optimum results, would require careful control of the grade of ingredients, i.e., different types of ores which go into the final mixture. This will be greatly facilitated if the entire operation is carried out by or under the direction of an expert agency which has control of or access to the different grades of ores.

Blending of ores should be done at a few selected points having regard to the extent and quality of production from particular manganese producing areas. Variation in composition of the ores is no bar to blending. In fact such variations within a certain range provide scope for ingenuity of the "blender". It is possible to mix ores for production of a few standard grades acceptable to the foreign buyers. Some of the well known grades are 'Oriental' and 'standard' mixture of MOIL and CPMO, 'Sandur A' and 'Sandur B' of Messers. Sandur Manganese and Iron Ore (P) Ltd.

There is great scope for beneficiation of ores which deserves more attention than hither tofore. Full details of the problems of beneficiation have been discussed under Chapter V.

There is need for intensive research to achieve reduction of phosphorous content of ores. The Indian Bureau of Mines should be asked to pay special attention to this matter and undertake further research. The National Metallurgical Laboratory has recently commissioned an integrated pilot plant on the beneficiation of low grade manganese ores at a capital cost of Rs. 35.00 lakhs. The N.M.L. could be requested to conduct studies into the methods of reducing phosphorous.

Beneficiation and Blending

Conclusions

Almost all important manganese ore producing countries of the world such as Brazil, Galon, Ghana etc. undertake beneficiation processes which do not result in the production of concentrate fines. Coarse concentrates do not require agglomeration.

In Brazil, the preparation of ore consists of crushing,

screening, washing and dewatering. Almost a similar process is followed in Gabon. Ores are washed to remove clay impurities in Ghana.

Russian ores require crushing, washing and agglomeration of fine concentrates, At times flotation, jigging and tabling is also employed.

In India the main operations are breaking and hand sorting. Jigging and washing are employed on a limited scale. There is only one heavy media separation plant in the country.

From the point of view of beneficiation, the Indian Ores have broadly been divided into four groups i.e., simple, ferruginous, garnetiferous and complex. From the work carried out by the National Metallurgical Laboratory and the Indian Bureau of Mines, it is seen that only a small proportion of the manganese ores in India can be classified under simple ore requiring comparatively simple treatment like gravity concentration etc. There is a preponderance of ferruginons and garnetiferous ores and these require more elaborate and costly beneficiation plants. From the data of research work, however, it can be seen that most of the ores are amenable to beneficiation and the concentrates obtained are generally suitable for ferro-manganese production. The concentrates of the complex ores would need blending with other suitable concentrates to meet the specifications.

RECOMMENDATIONS

The problem of beneficiation in India has to be viewed in two ways (a) production of beneficiated coarse concentrates (b) production of concentrate fines and their agglomeration.

The former should receive immediate attention. The lump ores could be up graded to a considerable extent by crushing, screening, washing and jigging. Such ores could be carefully blended with ores from other regions to produce clean standard grade ore required by the foreign buyers. This may not be feasible in the present state of affairs of the industry where the bulk of production is accounted for by a very large number of producers and exports are similarly handled by numerous exporters. In the circumstances, beneficiation of ores and expert blending of different ores could be successfully undertaken only by a cooperative organisation of producers and exporters of manganese or any other centralised agency which would have resources, organisation and expertise to handle ores from a large number of mines and adopt beneficiation techniques at reasonable cost without affecting the economics of export. It should be possible to set up in North Kanara, Orissa, Madhya Pradesh and Maharashtra a few relatively simple beneficiation units employing crushing, screening, jigging and washing techniques.

Heavy media separation holds considerable promise. It can serve as a pre-concentration unit to reject waste rock from the run of mine ore and deliver an enriched sink for further concentration. It thus allows for indiscriminate mining without any laborious selection. By discarding the waste rock at an early stage, the mill gets an enriched feed and, for the same throughout, a larger production is obtained. This process brings about a greater reduction in the amount of material passing through the various crushing, grinding and concentration plants. It is applicable only to those areas in which a fair amount of mineral is liberated at coarse size. The minerals should also be separable at specific gravity less than 3.3. Manganese minerals of India generally possess a specific gravity of about 4 and therefore can be concentrated by heavy media separation from quartzitic or schistose rocks. The Committee recommends installation of a few more heavy media separation plants in Madhya Pradesh and Maharashtra region.

It may be possible to blend North Kanara ores with Panchmahal ores, and Orissa ores with Srikakulam ores. Due to wide variations in the composition of ores from one mine to the other, it may also be possible to blend ore locally in accordance with a carefully drawn up detailed scheme.

As has already been stated above different categories of manganese ores of India are amenable to beneficiation. The beneficiated ore, i.e. concentrate, is in the form of powder which would have to be agglomerated before use. Concentrates of complex ores would need careful blending. The Committee recommends the beneficiation of such ores and its use in the ferromanganese plants after suitable agglomeration in the country. This would release lumpsy ores for exports. The prospects of exporting agglomerated or nodulised concentrates could also be explored.

This Committee notes that a committee constituted in 1957 under the earstwhile Ministry of Natural Resources and Scientific Research, had gone into the problem of the beneficiation of low grade manganese ore particularly ores from Karwar, Madhya Pradesh and Rajasthan. The Committee had recommended, inter alia, the installation of pilot plants at Nagpur and Jamshedpur for pilot plant studies on low grade manganese ore by the Indian Bureau of Mines and National Metallurgical Laboratory. Based on these studies, the setting up of beneficiation plants was also advocated. This Committee observes that, although a couple of years have lapsed, no progress seems to have been made on the above recommendations.

It is recommended that pilot plant studies on low grade manganese ores for various regions in India should be completed by the Indian Bureau of Mines and the National Metallurgical Laboratory on top priority basis and the designs of beneficiation plants should be worked out by them. The new agency should take care of the matters connected with installation and working of these plants.

The Committee recommends that concessional royalty rate should be charged for beneficiated ore in order to provide an incentive for adopting beneficiation techniques to upgrade low quality ore. This could be fixed at 50% of the rate of royalty applicable to the grade of unbeneficiated ore.

The other incentive in the form of special railway freight rate for ore meant for beneficiation is also to be recommended. This is necessary because for one ton of beneficiated ore about 3 tons of low grade ore have to be transported. This may be fixed at 50 per cent of the prevailing freight rate for exports.

In order to ensure a regular supply of the feed of low grade ore for the beneficiation plants, it will be desirable to attach suitable captive sources of supply to such plants. In case of large efficient units, preference in the matter of grant of leases of additional areas should also be accorded.

Transportation and Port Handling

Conclusions

The cost of transportation has always been regarded as one of the major factors in the F.O.B. cost which determines the competitive position of Indian minerals in foreign markets. In other manganese ore producing countries of the world such as Russia, Brazil, Galon, Union of South Africa and Ghana, great advance has been made in the development of transport facility.

For transporting ore from the mines to the rail-head, use is made of the aerial ropeways on an extensive scale. For example, the mining areas of Chiature (Georgia, Russia) are serviced by an aerial tramway to a 21 mile spur of the main line of the Trans Cancasus railways. In Galon, a 45 mile cable-way with a capacity of 850,000 tons a year has been built to carry the ore from the mines near Franceville to rail-head at 'M' Binde. In India rope-ways have been used to a very limited extent. M/S Manganese Ore India Ltd., are operating two rope-ways from their Ukwa mine to Bharweli siding, a distance of 18 miles and from Ramdungri mine to Gumgaon mine, a distance of about a mile. M/s Sandur Manganese and Iron Ores (P) Ltd., have two rope-ways 8,000 ft. and 10,000 ft. each at their Sandur mines, Mysore. The rest of the producers have to transport ore by road to the rail-head excepting one or two large firms who have railway sidings near the mines. The average ton-mile cost of road transportation is Re. 0.75.

In almost all manganese producing countries, ore is transported by rail to the ports for export. In Brazil a railway line of more than 200 km has been constructed from the Amapa mines to the Ports Macapa. In Galon, 180 mile rail road has been built from 'M' Binda to a junction point near Dolisie on the Congo Ocean rail road which runs into Atlantic Port of Point Noire. In Russia Trans-Cancasus Railways carry ores from Chiature area to Betum (125 miles) or Poti (90 miles) on the Black Sea. The ores in Ghana are transported on Sekondi-Kumasi railway line to Tekoradi port, a distance of 39 miles. There have been innovations in the use of rail equipments for the handling and carriage of ores. At Amapa, Brazil the washed ore is drawn from the bottom of 550 tons ore bins into railroad cars on a single loading track under the bins which is designed with a slight grade permitting an entire ore train to be loaded and assembled by gravity with no locomotive required. A 70 tons car can be loaded in one minute. The ore reaches the port in 70 tons bottom dump cars.

The expenditure on transportation of ore from mine to the port is an insignificant factor of cost in other countries. The rail-haul is comparatively short. In India, excepting in Andhra Pradesh and Goa, ore has to cover an average distance of more than 400 kms. before it is shipped from the port. Similarly the freight cost per ton of ore is in the neighbourhood of Rs. 18.00.

Steady increase in the size of vessels is bringing about a marked reduction in the ocean freight and shipment of ore. Improved facilities for handling cargo is another factor which has a beneficial effect on the competitive position of minerals in the world market.

In India the port charges generally approximate to Rs. 10.00 per ton as compred to $ 1.00 a ton at most of the ports of other countries. The loading rate at the Indian ports is in the neighbourhood of 600 tons per day as against the loading rate of 2,000 tons per day at Portos Macapa, Brazil and 4,000 tons per day at Port Elizabeth, South Africa. Production from Galon is shipped through the Atlantic Ocean Port of Point Noire where automatic loading facilities have been installed. Ghana ores are exported through the Port of Tekoradi which has excellent mechanical facilities for handling limited traffic. The slow loading rate at the Indian ports results in abnormally slow turn around of vessels which makes for less favourable freight terms.

RECOMMENDATIONS

Road Transport : (a) In India, mining areas have the poorest roads and this is responsible for high maintenance charges and fuel consumption for transport vehicles. The Committee recommends that intensive road construction or improvement programmes for mining areas should be undertaken. As far as possible new roads should be built to support heavy traffic. Increasingly, the present light trucks would have to give place to heavy diesels. During the study tour of Orissa mining areas the Committee inspected Joda-Dubna Road under construction by the State Government and it was found that this road was not very suitable for heavy ore traffic. The matter has already been brought to the notice of the State Government. It may be desirable for the Central Government to ask the State Governments to particularly bear in mind the needs of heavy load traffic when they implement their road programmes.

Apart from the construction of new roads, it would be essential to modernise existing roads in mining areas. Attention of the State Governments may be immediately drawn to this aspect. During its tour of Mysore State, the Committee had an opportunity to recommend to the State Government the importance of the repairs of Joida Diggi road and construction of an additional 8 miles road-link to the road on Goa side. The Committee hopes that the State Government would find it possible to accept and implement the suggestions. Similarly there is a strong case for modernising the existing tract between Sarkunda area and newly opened railway station at Barsua in Orissa State for manganese ore traffic in Orissa.

The Committee is of the view that the Planning Commission should utilise funds at their disposal in consultation with the State Governments and Ministry of Steel and Mines for construction of new roads, as also repairs to and modernisation of the old roads for movement of manganese in various areas.

The Minerals and Metals Trading Corporation should be provided with certain funds by Government for giving grants to mine owners or for the construction of new roads and modernisation of the existing roads in the mining areas in consultation with the Ministry of Steel and Mines.

Apart from the construction of the main roads in the mining areas as outlined above, attention may also be given to the construction of access roads to an individual mine or group of mines. But the development of such feeder roads upto a distance of 5 miles from the mines should be the responsibility of the individual mine owner or group of mine owners who will be the principal beneficiaries.

Rail Transport : (b) The incidence of railway freight has been a subject of great controversy between the representatives of the industries and the railway authorities. The former are of the view that the railway freight has steadily registered a disproportionate increase, but the latter have contended that this is the result of a general rise in basic costs and that the present rates barely meet the operational expenditure.

The Committee is of the view that frequent changes in freight rates have subjected manganese industry to unforeseen additional strains. As manganese is a sensitive commodity in the world market, these frequent changes must be avoided in future as far as possible. Although, the present concessional rates are considered somewhat excessive and do not satisfy certain sections of the industry, the Committee recommends, as a compromise, that there should be no increase beyond the level of the current rate (as effective from 1-4-63) for another five years from now.

The Committee is of the view that the railways have to keep abreast of the problems of industry while allotting wagons and insisting on the movement of ore in a rake of box wagons, for the reasons already explained in this chapter.

It would be essential that the wagons are supplied at each separate loading point as per the indent of the producer or prorata thereof to enable him to take his ore at the port in a definite proportion for blending etc.

The insistence of the railways on the use of rake of box wagons has created another problem. At the port, the stacking space frontage for a paricular party being limited, it is not possible to take rakes for unloading. This results in serious delays in the supply of right type of ore. The Committee recommends that depending on the merit of the case four wheelers may be allowed for manganese ore movements.

It is further recommended that separate sidings should be provided for manganese ore at all the important loading point and weighment facilities given wherever possible.

Rope-ways : (c) As Rope-ways are relatively economical modes of transport, suitable surveys should be carried out in selected mining areas for installation of rope-ways systems.

Ocean Transport : (d) It is the cosidered view of the Committee that facilities at the ports should be improved so that a ship can be loaded in two days. The Committee feels that the port authorities are in a better position to plan necessary improvements. Plans for modernisation of loading facilities and berthing of large carriers are already under discussion in relation to particular commodities such as iron ore. The Committee recommends that the needs of managanese ore should also be kept in view when such plans are drawn up and implemented.

All present manganese ore is generally exported in liners of about 10,000 tons capacity as against charters of 30,000 tons capacity in other countries. The rates of liners are generally much higher as compared to charters. There would be appreciable reduction in c.i.f. cost if manganese ore is exported in charters of 20,000 tons capacity. Interest of manganese trade has suffered partly due to a multiplicity of exporters selling small packages in different markets. Now that Government have taken a decision to canalise all trade of manganese through two public sector agencies i.e. Minerals and Metals Trading Corporation and Manganese Ore (India) Limited, it should be possible to secure better prices for Indian manganese ore through a co-ordinated operation in the traditional and new markets. It should also be possible to achieve economies of large charters.

There is no room for any increase in port charges.

Port-wise Recommendations

Visakhapatnam : An important point which came to the notice of the Committee during its tour was the difficulties experienced by the exporters due to the insistence of the railway to transport ore in rake of box wagons. The Committee recommends that, on account of the peculiarities of this trade arising out of the numerous grades and a need for their blending, the railways should not insist on rakes and they should allow the movement of ores on four wheelers.

There is uniform skip rate of Rs. 2.00 per skip both for high grade and low grade ores at the port. The Committee recommends that there should be another slab for low grade ores.

Madras Port: The Committee recommends that berth South Quay may be used for manganese ore shipment. Stocking space of 10,000 tonnes is available at the key of the basin but the vessels may be mainly fed from the present managanese depot which is about a mile away. In the event of contingencies stocks at the key should be used. Thus the loading time will be minimised as also the loading rate will increase. The Commitee further recommends that ore may be brought from Manganese depot on trollies with flat tubs.

The port officials informed the Committee that as soon as iron ore programme is completed, Scoda cranes would be available. Shift derricks would also be available and work can be started as soon as basin is ready. The Committee recommends the implementation of there programmes.

The Committee is confident that a loading rate of 3,000 tonnes per day can be achieved at Madras Port if the above suggestions are implemented. Although the present traffic of manganese ore at the port is limited, more of it will be attracted once higher loading rate and better facilities are achieved.

The port charges at Madras are high because of high labour cost. The Committee feels that this can be cut down if idle labour hours are avoided.

Calcutta Port: The Committee recommends that there should be complete coordination between the port officials and the shippers in order to attain efficiency at the port. The sailing dates, the quantity to be loaded and the type of ships requisitioned should be made available to the port officials well in advance.

The railway should provide four wheelers instead of box wagons.

The stocking depot for manganese ore is in close proximity to other minerals such as iron ore and the chances of contamination are serious. Manganese ore should be so stocked as to avoid any contamination.

Bombay Port: The movement of vessels from one berth to the other for loading results in abnormal delays at the port. It is suggested that dredging may be done in some cases. The movement of vessels consumes considerable time and the shippers have to undergo lot of difficulties. Quick loading and unloading is an important element which has to be considered. The Committee recommends that the port authorities may take into consideration the above points while planning modernisation programmes.

The Committee recommends that the exisiting wagons of the trust railway, most of which are in an advanced stage of dilapidations, may be immediately replaced by 100 K. L. type wagons to be procured from railways.

The weigh-bridge provided by the Trust is inaccurate giving shortages amounting to 5 per cent. The Committee recommends that either two weigh-bridges should be maintained or alternatively, an automatic recorder should be provided at the existing weigh-bridge, or a weigh-bridge with punch card system may be installed.

It may be possible to use grab fitted mobile cranes for loading and unloading wagons.

Marmugao Port: The Committee is of the view that Marmugao Port can handle larger quantities of manganese by wagons and barges combined. Low grade ores of North Kanara, Mysore and also Sandur ores may be exported through this port. Necessary facilities may be provided for this.

Minnig, Mine Management and Mine Financing Conclusions

Manganese Mining Operations in various parts of the world cover a wide range of modes of production, from manual quarrying dating back to about a century to modern sophisticated methods and techniques. The major portion of world's manganese ore production is, however, derived from open pit or shallow underground workings.

Open pit mining is the pattern which obtains in case of the majority of mines in India, South Africa, Brazil and Congo. Underground mining is generally the rule in USSR, USA, Chile, Morrocco, Cuba and is also a prominent feature of a few important deposits in

India.

The Russian mines have been developed to an annual production capacity of ten million tons. Brazilian and Gabonese mines are at persent geared for a million ton each per annum.

In India, small mines are a pre-dominent feature of the manganese industry. In the year 1962, 475 mines accounted for a total production of 1.2 million tons out of which small-scale units producing less than 10,000 tons per year were responsible for 48% of the production. There were only two mines with annual production range of 60,000 tons.

In a highly competitive market as manganese, only sizeable units which can adopt modern techniques of mining and realise economies of scale can afford to remain in production in the long run.

With the exception of a few companies, majority of mine-owners have slender financial resources, which at times are supplemented by financial assistance from promoters. The total capital investment in manganese industry would be of the order of Rs. 5 crores only. As against this investment in the development of Brazilian deposits amounted to $ 50 million in 1958 for a production of about 600,000 tons of manganese ore and in Galon in 1961 a capital outlay of $ 12 million was in relation to a production of 500,000 tons (expandable to one million ton) per annum.

RECOMMENDATIONS

In order that Indian manganese industry may face the present competitive conditions of world market, it is necessary for mining units to adopt scientific techniques of mining and operate on an economic scale of production.

As all mine-owners are not in a position to acquire, service and maintain costly mining machinery such as buldozers, compressors, transport vehicles, preumatic rock drills etc., it should be possible to constitute a pool of such essential equipments at a central point from where it could be handled by either a cooperative of manganese miners or a Government department like the Indian Bureau of Mines or a public undertaking like the M.M.T.C., who are at present, the largest single organisation for buying and marketing of manganese ore.

The present concession of intitlement for import of mining machinery against 10 per cent of foreign exchange earnings, should be extended upto 25 per cent of thevalue of exports.

Cooperative departments of the State Governments or Central Agencies responsible for production or procurement or marketing should provide necessary leadership for organising wherever possible, small mining units into cooperative societies for one or several purposes e.g., provision of. capital finance, purchase of equipment, operational know-how marketing and sales.

To encourage mechanisation and adoption of modern scientific techniques, Government might consider a suitable scheme of fiscal and tax incentives.

For major ore deposits containing reserves of two to 2.5 million tonnes or higher the economic scale of production of a mechnised mine would be of the order of 50,000 tonnes per annum. In case of smaller deposits containing reserves of the order of one to 2 million tons an annual production of 30,000 tonnes could be planned on partially mechanised or unmechanised basis.

To meet the requirements of capital investment on equipment and machinery, the existing agencies like Industrial Credit and Investment Corporation, National Investment Development Corporation and Industrial Finance Corporation should be specially oriented to look after the needs of manganese industry. Taking into consideration the conditions of the mining industry in the country in general, the Committee feels that there might be a case for the creation of a Mining Finance Corporation in the Fourth Plan which would particularly cater to the needs of mining industry in all important basic minerals.

Mining Legislation and Fiscal Levies

Conclusions

Considering the risks and hazards inherent in mining ventures, it is important that suitable incentives should be built in mining and fiscal laws to attract interprising prospectors and to induce enterpreneurs to deploy their managerial skills and capital resources in the field.

Besides direct governmental levies such as royalty, income-tax, sales tax etc., stringent legislation on mineral disposition, safety and labour amenities are adversely affecting the exports of manganese.

Income Tax : In most of the advanced countries a new mine is given the opportunity to recover, before the imposition of taxes, a large part of the capital expenditure. A three year tax-exempt period for new mines, income tax allowances for pre-production costs generous depletion and depreciation allowances are some of the concessions given to the mining industry in Canada. Similar reliefs are also available in Australia, U.S.A., U.K. etc.

In India the Income Tax Act, 1961 and the Income Tax Rules, 1962, provide only for depreciation allowance and development relate which are much low as compared to other countries. A few other concenssions prevalent in the above countries are non-existent in India.

The freight earning of a shipper is taxable under the Indian laws which inflates the actual ocean freight charges from Indian ports to the consuming markets.

Sales Tax: There are two types of sales tax viz. Central Sales Tax levied under the Central Sales Tax Act on sales in the course of inter-State sales and the other local sales tax levied under the Sales Tax Acts of various State Governments on intra State sales. When a mine-owner exports a commodity directly, the sale is not liable to tax, but where he sells it to another dealer who in turn exports it, the first sale attracts the provision of the sales tax, but the second does not. Method of taxation is complex and it varies from state to state.

Canal Toll Dues: Vessels carrying mineral ores have to pay to the Suez Canal Authorities canal toll dues which has the effect of inflating the actual ocean freight.

Local Taxes: Some of the mining areas have been brought under the purview of municipal taxation and gram-panchayat taxes which are contributing to the high cost of production of manganese ore.

Royalty: International prices for manganese ore are still low. As the out-look for future is uncertain, the present rates of royalty do not appear to be justified and have brought about additional burden on the industry.

Disposition of Mineral Rights: Large areas of manganese ore have been reserved in various states for exploitation in the public sector. Even though the State Governments have no plans to work the areas, the same are not being released to the private parties.

Some of the State Governments are granting renewal of leases for a period of 10 years only although under the Mines and Minerals (Regulation and Development) Act, 1957, maximum period of 20 years is provided. This will in-hibit investment, planning and production.

Safety in Mines and Labour welfare: The need to provide for safety and welfare of workers in mines can hardly be ignored. At the same time it has to be ensured that such measures do not put undue strain on the mine-owners and obstruct their normal working. Some of the provisions in the Mines Act and Mines Rule could be oriented to suit the needs and working conditions at the manganese mines.

RECOMMENDATIONS

Income Tax: The following reliefs are recommended with regard to the levy of income tax on manganese mines :—

(a) Expenses incurred on prospecting and exploration of manganese mines to be treated as revenue expenditure.

(b) Tax holiday for 3 years for new mines ;

(c) Increase of the permissible depreciation allowance to 30% for mining machinery and equipment ;

(d) Expenses incurred on research and pilot plants in beneficiation or up grading of ore to be treated as revenue expenditure.

Sales Tax: The Committee recommends that the State Governments should be requested to exempt sales tax, central as well as local on manganese ore intended for export. Alternatively, they should be requestd to adopt the West Bengal system of taxation in the case of manganese ore.

Canal Toll Dues: Efforts should be made to secure some relief from the above dues for manganese ore.

Local Taxes: The Committee recommends that the mining townships were suitable amenities, such as, facilities for hospitals, creches and canteens, conservancy sanitation and other services are already provided by the mine-owners, should be exempted from gram-panchayat or municipal taxation. However the areas where adquate facilities are not provided by the mine-owners and the said services are provided by the local bodies, the levies may be imposed at the minimum rates provided under the Rules.

Royalty and Dead-rent: The Committee recommends the following rates of royalty on manganese ore :

Dioxide Ore (Mn O/2 78% and above Fe 4% Maximum)	Rs. 10.00 per tonne
45% Mn. and above	Rs. 4.00 per tonne
35-45% Mn.	Rs. 2.00 per tonne
Below 35% Mn.	Re. 1.00 per tonne

It is further recommended that the dead-rent on manganese ore for the last 3 years should be waived in view of depressed market conditions

Further, the Committee considers that the State Governments should be advised to collect arrears of dead-rent in instalments equal to the amount of royalty chargeable per tonne of ore on resumption of production. This will act as an inducement to the mine-owners to start mining operations.

With regard to the question of levy of royalty at the pit-head value of minerals, the Committee recommends that wherever departmental rules or instructions are not accordance with the principle enunciated by Mysore High Court, immediate steps should be taken by concerned State Governments to modify or amend such rules and instructions wherever these are due.

The Manganese Mines Labour Welfare Fund: The

legislation may not be enforced till manganese ore industry is fully rehabilitated and attains prosperity.

Disposition of Mineral Rights : The Committee recommends that manganese bearing areas reserved for state exploitation should be released for exploitation in private sector of the State Governments do not have any definite plan of the development and working of the areas within a reasonable period from the date of reservation. Special consideration should also be given to granting leases of suitable areas to the ferro-manganese industry so that wherever possible it can depend upon its own captive mines for a uniform and regular supply of ore.

The Committee is of the view that the renewal of mining lease should not be granted for less than the maximum period provided under the Mines and Minerals (Regulation and Development) Act, 1957, unless a lessee himself applies for a shorter period. The renewal of the lease for a shorter period will inhibit investment, planning and production.

The Committee further recommends that applications for mining leases in the reserved area should also be considered for minerals other than the ore for which it has been reserved provided that the working of the additional minerals in the areas applied for will not affect the development of the remaining part of the reserved area.

Power of Rivision of Central Government : The Committee recommends that the power of the Central Government in the matter of regulation and control of mining rights having been clearly defined in the Constitution, the State Governments should take steps to give immediate effect to the orders passed by the Central Government on applications made to them under the provisions of Mineral Concession Rules, 1960.

A reasonable time limit for the disposal of revision applications should be provided in the Mineral Concession Rules, 1960, so that redress to aggrieved parties is not unduly delayed or denied when it is most needed.

Labour and Safety : The requirements laid down under rule 33 of the Mines Rules regarding laterines and urinals in mines should not apply to manganese mines. Similarly rules 64 to 71 regarding provision of canteens in mines may be relaxed.

Marketing

Conclusions :

The annual world market of manganese or is likely to increase to 10 million tons by 1975 against the present level of 5 million tons. Captive sources of supply developed by the principal consumers of manganese ore can be expected to meet 50% of this demand leaving a "free demand" of 5 million tons per annum available to mine-owners and suppliers of manganese not committed to particular users.

The figure of 5 million tons of "free demand" is considered substantial especially when compared to the present volume of trade viz. 2 million tons per annum. As India is one of the largest producers of manganese ore among "non-captive" sources, it can reasonably hope for a larger share in total world exports provided the present production is expanded to produce the requisite quantities with due regard to the prime need for reducing costs. The increased world demand, however, need not necessarily imply any significant rise in international prices as the major portion of production will be derived from those sources where costs of production are low and better port facilities are available.

Under the existing pattern of trade, the demands of ore are pooled and met by a few intermediate ore purchasing agencies collectively for all consumers. This places the buyer of ore in relatively advantageous position with reference to sellers, because while interise competition among the former is practically eliminated the suppliers continue to operate on an individual basis. In India, apart from the disparity between the uneconomic costs of production and the international prices, the multiplicity of small exporters and other similar factors continue to operate against the prospects of Indian exports.

RECOMMENDATIONS

The Committee feels that with a view to maximising exports, it is desirable to canalise the exports of manganese through one or two central agencies which by means of carefully coordinated operations can obtain the best prices and terms for Indian manganese ore. The Committee notes that the Government of India have taken a decision to canalise exports of manganese ore through (i) Minerals & Metals Trading Corporation of India Ltd., (ii) Manganese Ore (India) Ltd. which are both public sector undertakings. The working of the new arrangements should be carefully reviewed from time to time from the point of view of significant gains in India's export trade and foreign exchange earnings. The Committee also recommends that M.M.T.C. being the only agency for purchasing ore raised by small mine-owners, it should take an itself an active role in providing technical and wherever possible managerial and financial assistance in developing and modernising their mines, with a view to maintaining quality or grade and reducing costs of production.

COMMITTEE OF DIRECTION ON COOPERATIVE FARMING 1963—REPORT

Delhi, Ministry of Community Development and Cooperation, 1966. 236p.

Chairman : Prof. D.R. Gadgil.
Members : Sardar Gurbaksh Singh ; Prof. A. M. Khusro ; Shri Ameer Raza ; Dr. J. P. Bhattacharjee ; Shri S. C. Chaudhri.
Secretary : Shri M. P. Bhargava.

APPOINTMENT

The National Cooperative Farming Advisory Board set up by the Government of India formulated a scheme of assessment and evaluation of Progress of Cooperative farming societies and evaluation of pilot projects. The Board has also recommended that at the central level, in initial stage i.e., for the first three years, the responsibility for processing data, progress, observation and analysis should be with Board. The Board should discharge this responsibility through a Committee which should be so constituted and allowed to function that its findings inspire general confidence. More recently, the Conference of State Ministers, incharge of cooperation, 1963, has also recommended that arrangement should be made for a systematic and careful evaluation of the progress achieved in pilot project from time to time.

In pursuance of the recommendations, the Government of India, Ministry of Community Development and Cooperation, in the Memorandum No. 10-9/63-CF dated July 9, 1963, appointed the Committee of Direction on Cooperative Farming for the assessment of Progress and evaluation of the pilot projects.

TERMS OF REFERENCE

(a) To examine the question of (i) base line survey regarding economic condition of members, (ii) progress of a society vis-a-vis other societies and individual farms, (iii) attitude survey and to devise methods, techniques and organisational set up for the same ;

(b) To analyse the data collected in the field and formulate conclusions ;

(c) To report the achievements and difficulties of the programme and suggest measures for solving the problems ;

(d) To make or help in the detailed study of the specific operational aspect e.g., preparation of production programmes, employment schemes, cooperative farm management, etc., and

(e) To undertake such other cognate measures as are germane and relevant to the scheme of assessment of progress and evaluation of pilot projects.

CONTENTS

Part I—The Background :-Introductory ; Review of Progress ; Part II—Summary of the Results of Investigation-Summary of the results of Investigation made by Agro-Economic Research Centre, Poona, for the States of Maharashtra and Mysore ; Summary of the results of investigation made by Agro-Economic Research Centre, Madras, for the States of Madras, Andhra Pradesh and Kerala ; Summary of the results of investigation made by agro-Economic Research Centre, Delhi, for the States of U.P., Punjab and Delhi ; Summary of the results of investigation made by Agro-Economic Research Centre, Visva-Bharati, Santiniketan, for the States of West Bengal, Bihar and Orissa ; Summary of the results of investigation made by Agro-Economic Research Centre Jorhat, for the State of Assam ; Summary of the results of investigation made by Agro-Economic Research Centre, Vallabh Vidyanagar, for the States of Rajasthan and Gujarat ; Summary of the results of investigation made by Agro-Economic Research Centre, Gwalior, for the State of Madhya Pradesh ; Note on the present position of some societies studied by the Working Group on Cooperative Farming ; Part III—Assessment and Recommendations Overall Assessment ; Recommendations ; Part IV—Summary of Recommendations ; Appendices.

RECOMMENDATIONS

The pooling of lands affords an opportunity to the cooperative, the pooling of labour may be said to present it with a challange. though initially a joint cooperative farming society is directed mainly towards farming and agriculture, it must as.

Report of the Committee of Direction on Cooperative Farming

SUMMARY OF RECOMMENDATIONS

The programme of cooperative farming is directed, in the main, towards the solution of problems presented by the class of small or "uneconcmic" cultivators in the Indian economy. The number of families in the countryside in this class is very large and the area of cultivated land controlled by it is estimated at not less than 15 per cent of the total Programmes as that of technical assistance and of cooperative credit and marketing find the greatest difficulty in serving this class effectively. The land surface controlled by them is, therefore, even less well-used than the average and the class suffers from a very high degree of under-employment, Cooperative joint farming by bringing together, under one management, lands held by a large number of uneconomic holders creates a land base on which technically efficient and economic operations become possible.

Efficient management of pooled lands implies that the total input of labour on the cooperative joint farms, for the same types of productive enterprise, is less than that on scattered individual holdings of which they are composed. The development of pooled land resources will absorb some labour in the initial stages and if such development results in intesifying agricultural activity, there would be some permanent increase in the level of demand for labour on the cooperative joint farm. Sooner or later, cooperative joint farms even when they succeed in considerably improving the use of pooled lands, find agricultural activity insufficient to employ the pool of labour in the families composing the membership of the cooperative farming society.

The pooling of lands affords an opportunity to the cooperative, the pooling of labour may be said to present it with a challenge. Though initially a joint cooperative farming society is directed mainly towards farming and agriculture, it must as a continuing organisation, be looked upon as a business which is set up with certain pooled resources and which is under compulsion to undertake diversified economic activities for the fuller utilisation of its pooled resources of labour.

All the steps relating to cooperative farms have to be considered in the context of the human problems. Such a society differs strikingly from most other types of cooperative activity. In a joint cooperative farming society, the household as a consumption unit alone remains separate ; usually as a production unit it loses identity both as to activity and as to command over resources. Against the background of normal operations in a rural society of family farmers, this loss of initiative and independence is bound to be keenly felt and must create many complex problems, human and administrative. It would be possible to deal with these adequately only if the total performance of the joint cooperative farming society is outstandingly different from that of independent small holders and the standard of living and opportunities afforded by it to member families are demonstrably better than those enjoyed by independent small holders.

The potentialities of this form of organisation to solve the problems of small farmers must be widely recognised and a sufficiently large number of groups of such farmers must be encouraged to form societies and must be carefully guided and assisted in the period of development. Non-official leadership and official, technical and financial assistance must work together in this cause.

Categories of farmers, other than small holders, may also form joint cooperative farming societies and these may achieve a much better utilisation of pooled resources through joint effort. However, the national programme of cooperative farming is not directed essential towards these. This is because even as independent units they can achieve a minimum level of efficiency in the use of resources and take advantage of and participate in national programme of development; and because specially strong efforts and strong motivation are needed to make a success of their joint farming. Moreover, experience shows that in many instances the formation of societies by members of other categories is wrongly motivated. Therefore, it is imperative to frame the programme in such a way as to give the least scope for such opportunities. The scheme of concessions and aid should, therefore, be framed specifically in relation to the needs only of societies of uneconomic holders.

It is imperative that non-official leadership should take an increasingly active interest in the programme. In particular, the support of non-official leaders of the cooperative movement itself, leaders of political parties believing in the efficacy of the programme, members of panchayati raj institutions and cons ructive social organisations, is essential to create a widespread understanding of the raisen d'etre of the programme and to dispel the doubts arising from hostile propaganda which has not hitherto been countered effectively.

In this, the cooperative leadership has a primary responsibility. It should encourage and sustain the programme, so that, by the results achieved and by its own example, it can educate and influence other leaders of opinion towards a fuller understanding of the National Cooperative Union of India should crystalise non-official cooperative opinion for this purpose and formulate a programme of action in consultation with the State Cooperative Unions. The National and State Cooperative Unions should constitute standing commitees for this purpose.

Other cooperative institutions like apex and central cooperative banks, marketing societies, etc. should lend full support and impart strength to the programme. The example of the Maharashtra Apex Cooperative Bank, which has constituted a separate cell for looking after the problems of the weaker sections, is commended to the Apex Banks of other states.

Panchayati Raj institutions which play an important role in the preparation and implementation of schemes of rural development should pay particular attention to this programme. Every effort should be made to associate the members of these institutions with the programme.

The programme should also draw assistance from constructive social organisations. Leadership of such agencies is particularly valuable when societies are formed by landless labourers. In such cases, the association of such agencies should not only be promotional and educative, but active guidance and assistance should also be provided in the day to day working of the societies.

In certain areas, the programme of cooperative farming has begun to create its own leadership. For the growth of such leadership, formation of federations of cooperative farming societies at the district and state levels is important. These federations would not only mobilise public opinion, but would also serve to disseminate knowledge of techniques of management and operation. As the programme gathers momentum and the number of district and state level federations increases, a national federation of farming societies may be formed. Such a federation should be necessary by the last year of the 4th plan.

Attention should be focussed mainly, on farming societies among small and medium cultivators, as they require the benefits of cooperative activity most. However, the programme need not be confined to any single type of society.

Where societies are formed with a heterogenous membership, it is of utmost importance to limit the interest and returns of bigger farmers, through a system of distributing income which fully safeguards the interest of members participating in farm operations.

A cooperative farming society should not subserve the interest of a restricted group of families to the detriment of that of other members. However, there appears obvious advantages in drawing members from a similar background, who face similar problems. The danger in such societies is two-fold. They may either be formed to avoid tenancy and ceilings legislation, or, in certain cases, the members of the dominant family, or families, may deliberately exclude others from membership.

Where the members have lived in independent households and maintained separate cultivating units, they may constitute the unit of membership even though they belong to one family, subject to two important safeguards. Firstly under no circumstances, shou'd minors and non-working persons be enrolled merely to fulfil the minimum numerical requirements of registration. Secondly, the number of independent landowning households, cultivating their units separately, should, at least, be the minimum prescribed for the registration of a society. In addition, it is absolutely essential to ensure that attached and landless labourers, who regularly work on the farm, are enrolled to full membership of the society.

No change is necessary in the present rule that the number of absentes and non-working members, taken as a group, should not exceed 25 per cent of the total membership. In this connection, a working member should be considered as one who obtains the major part of his employment on the farm or other activities of the society. Those who engage in farm operations only for a few days, by way of a ritual, should not be considered as working members. Members engaged in supervisory functions should be considered as working members, subject to the condition that they supervise the work for the major part of the year and that the number of members engaged in supervision is not larger than that strictly required for the organisation and conduct of the activities.

In case of societies organised by small land owners, the land base on which the societies operate is frequently very narrow. It is, therefore, necessary that cooperative farming societies operate on a wider and more diversified economic base. This will imply not only a more intensive use of the existing land resource, through suitable changes in cropping pattern, techniques of cultivation and land improvement measures, but, in addition, the increasing creation of employment opportunities for members through agro-industries and other allied activities.

Before the registration of a society, members should fully understand the implications of joining together and, in every case, the effort should be to pool fully the lands of members or to have a definite programme of total pooling by stages within a reasonable time. As an exception, however, in a State like Kerala, where the holdings of members are spread over a wide area and the local terrain makes their complete pooling difficult, the society may decide which plots should be pooled.

If, for any reason, the society after registration feels that it is not economic or worthwhile for it to operate or manage a particular plot of land belonging to a member within the general pool, it may make other arrangements for its management. All the pooled lands with a society need not be managed in the same way or administered by one set of persons. The society is the "firm" which controls many pieces of land and other assets. All major decisions regarding those connected with risk bearing, investment and production will be taken by the society ; but it may for greater convenience of management split its total business into a number of "plants". Such special arrangement is not to be confused with partial pooling, as in this case, the ultimate directing authority and the bearing of risks is that of the society.

In societies where partial pooling has taken place, corrective measures should be applied without delay to pool the remaining land of the members. Societies formed for the development of a particular tract of land, which forms merely a portion of the land owned by members in the area of operation of the society, should not be encouraged unless members take a firm decision to pool their remaining land. The actual process of pooling, may, however, be phased in a manner which the society, as the firm, considers most appropriate.

Where the holdings of members are scattered, efforts should be made to ensure that members are drawn, as far as possible, from amongst those whose lands can be pooled into a reasonable number of conveniently located and viable plots.

It is desirable that consolidation of holdings should precede or accompany the organisation of societies. However, the organisation of societies even under existing conditions leads to a measure of consolidation and represents an improvement on prevailing conditions.

In areas where consolidation of land holdings proceedings are being conducted, the cooperative farming society should be recognised as a 'single unit' for purposes of consolidation. Where the existing consolidation laws do not provide for this, they should be suitably amended.

The desirable size of a cooperative farm depends upon a number of factors; by and large the standards prescribed by the State Gevernments have been along right lines. In certain areas the societies below the prescribed minimum size were organised. Formation of such societies should be discouraged.

The capacity of the societies to step up employment increases with the undertaking of land improvement measures and capital works, greater intensity of cultivation and by undertaking allied activities like dairying and sheep rearing, and the development of non-farm occupations. The importance of these activities should be fully recognised. In respect of each society that is formed, a long-term plan of development should be formulated. This plan should specifically provide not only for land development but also for a programme of increasing employment to members and their families.

For societies to work on a wider economic base, programmes of agro-industries should be considered as an integral part of their activities. The schemes for such activities should be economically and technically viable. Whenever possible, activities undertaken by the societies should be dovetailed with the general schemes of the area. Technical and financial assistance should also be available to the societies from the general schemes.

As the limits on rent prescribed under the tenancy laws of the States vary, no uniform or rigid pattern for the payment of a return for ownership of land can be suggested for the country as a whole. However, in no case should he return for ownership of land exceed the limits prescribed under the tenancy legislation of that State. Further, the income obtained for land should not be larger than the total rent obtained on the eve of formation of the society, i.e. the return for ownership should be frozen at the initial level in the same manner as rents have been frozen under tenancy laws.

In the distribution of the surplus, full regard should be paid to basic cooperative principles. A larger part of the surplus should accrue to members in relation to the extent to which they actively participate in the operations of the society. Relatively lower priority should be given in this matter to the contribution of capital assets. The bulk of the surplus should be paid to members as bonus for work.

The administrative machinery and federations of farming societies should pay special attention to this aspect of the programme.

Little experience is available in matters of budgeting, accounting, work procedures, types of investment etc. As......these are complex issues, a deeper study of these aspects is needed. The National Cooperative College and Research Institute, Poona, should set up a well-equipped unit for this purpose. It should also impart training to key personnel engaged in this programme.

There is need to rationalise and simplify the records to be maintained.and, at the same time, to relate them more directly to the purpose of accounting, namely, more efficient farm management. It is suggested that a small technical group should go into the details of the records to be kept and formulate simple, but scientific, methods of so doing.

The proper training of secretaries of societies as also their office-bearers and members is of vital importance for the training of secretaries greater emphasis should be given in the existing six-month's course, to job-training in accounts and farm management. Special efforts should also be made to develop a knowledge of improved agricultural practices and skills in allied activities. Where the secretaries of societies have adequate agricultural experience, a short training course of four to six weeks, with special emphasis on accounts and farm management, may be organised.

The main responsibility for member education should devolve on the National and State Cooperative Unions and federations of cooperative farming societies, Government should, however, make available necessary financial assistance to them for carrying out this work.

Short orientation course should be organised regularly, for block and other staff responsible for technical guidance.

The National Cooperative College and Research Institute, Poona, should be equipped to organise short orientation courses for key personnel.

The Government and the National and State Cooperative Unions should formulate suitable measures to educate public opinion about cooperative farming.

A rigid pattern of assistance, unrelated to the size of the farm, the resources of members and specific projects of development has proved unsuitable. To be meaningful, financial assistance should be related to the long-term plan of development formulated by the society and the resources of members. It should take into consideration the requirements of the society in their totality.

A society, particularly of small holders would require assistance in the initial stages, for promoting and for establishing operations, which will have to be obtained from outside, i.e., in the form of assistance, both grants and loans, from Government. On the other hand, an established society will require finances for development and current production and other business needs. All such requirements should be met in the normal manner from appropriate cooperative financing institutions. In addition, there are also a number of specialised agencies, which look after financing of particular activities appropriate to farming societies. It must be ensured that assistance from all such agencies flows to cooperative farming societies speedily and appropriately.

(i) Assistance Under Cooperation Plan

Joint Farming Societies

The flate rate of Rs. 4,000 per society prescribed under the existing pattern of assistance, which works out to an average of Rs. 40 per acre, has proved inadequate. This was so in spite of the fact that a further diversion of the loan component of Rs. 3,750 made for construction of godown-cum-cattleshed was also allowed to be diverted for land development. Assistance for land development should therefore be related to the size of the farm and provided at an average rate of Rs. 100 per acre, subject to a ceiling of Rs. 20,000 per society.

No changes are necessary in regard to the quantum of share capital participation by Government (Rs. 2,000) and the extent of managerial subsidy (Rs. 1,200).

Whilst the provision of Rs. 5,000 for the construction of the godown-cum-cattleshed is adequate, such assistance should be given only after examination of the needs of each society. For purposes of an overall allocation of funds, provision might be made for about 25 per cent of the joint farming societies formed.

Collective Farming Societies

As the needs of the collective farming societies are greater both in respect of overall requirements, and investment per acre, assistance for land development may be provided by Government at the rate of Rs. 150 per acre, subject to a ceiling of Rs. 30,000 per society.

As these societies are generally in greater need of technical and managerial guidance, which is difficult to be found from within, the societies have generally to draw managers from outside. In view of this, the quantum of managerial subsidy may be raised from Rs. 1,200 to Rs. 2,100 per society, spread over a period of three to five years.

As in these societies difficulties are experienced in raising share capital from members on a matching basis, Government contribution to share capital may be related, to the capital subscribed by the members. Subscribed capital may be collected from members in instalments and the Government contribution made as soon as the members have collected and paid 1/10th of the subscribed capital.

As most of the collective farming societies would need the facility of a cattleshed-cum-godown, overall provision might be made, at the current rate, for assisting about 80 per cent of the collective farming societies that are formed.

Whilst the outlay for the programme may be calculated on the above lines, the State Governments, should assess the requirements of individual societies and provide resources to them.

(ii) Assistance From Other Department

Cooperative farming societies should be treated as single units for purposes of assistance. Existing rules and procedures, should be modified without any delay, where necessary. Intensive efforts should also be made to ensure that the resources of the developmental departments are made available increasingly to cooperative farming societies.

Steps such as those taken by Maharashtra Government, to provide cooperative farming societies with departmental resources for soil conservation, construction of community wells etc., should be adopted by other States.

For the Fourth Plan, instructions have already issued that 75 per cent of the overall resources for programmes relating to poultry, piggery and dairying should be earmarked for the cooperative sector. A further reservation should take place, in each State, to see that the requirements of cooperative farming societies are fully met and an integrated approach adopted for the formulation of schemes, providing of technical guidance etc.

The Khadi and Village Industries Commission should review its existing procedures and take measures to ensure that the benefits derived by societies in some areas are more widely spread. In certain areas, where a large number of societies have been formed, the Khadi and Village Industries Commission should intensify its activities.

Central Cooperative Banks should direct their attention immediately to providing short-term credit to cooperative farming societies according to their production plans. As short-term credit alone would not be enough, medium term loans should also be provided.

The Land Mortgage Banks provide long-term loans to cooperative farming societies. This will mean, in many cases, amending the byelaws of primary land mortgage banks. In other cases, it might mean clarifying the liability of members in respect of the repayment of such loans even in the event of the society ceasing to exist after the period of pooling is over. The procedure suggested by the Maharashtra Apex Land Mortgage Bank to its primary banks, it commended for adoption.

Members of the cooperative farming societies may need short-term consumption loans, as also loans over a longer period in order to meet expenses connected with ceremonial and contingent purposes, old debts, etc. As far as short-term consumption loans are concerned, the practice suggested to service cooperative in IADP districts should be followed : i.e., loans upto a limit of Rs. 50 per member should be advanced for consumption purposes. This amount should form part of the production programme against which loans are advanced and come within the overall credit limit of the borrower. Central cooperative banks should take a similar view in respect of the requirements of a cooperative farming society.

As the members pool their entire land, a method should be evolved to assist them in the repayment of old debts and to meet ceremonial and contingent expenditure. In regard to old debts, it is suggested that, at the time of admission of a member, the society should obtain a declaration of his debts. Where it is possible for the society to secure the scaling down of these debts, this should be done. After this, the society should assist the member in discharging the debt by advancing a loan to him against his return for ownership of land and remuneration for work. The loan may be recovered in suitable instalments. Where the debts declared are heavy and not easily repayable, the person concerned should not be admitted to membership. A similar procedure may be adopted by the society for providing loans to members for meeting ceremonial and contingent expenses.

As the financing of cooperative farming societies is the legitimate function of the cooperative banking structure, it is necessary for it to work out the exact manner in which this programme can be assisted. For this purpose, it is essential to study further the various practices and procedures currently followed for issue of short, medium and long-term loans. The All India State Cooperative Banks' Federation should set up a small committee in construction with the All India Union of Land Mortgage Banks to go into the details of this question as a matter of priority.

The technical staff viz., extension workers of the block, special staff appointed for cooperative farming staff of various other departments, have a vital role in this programme. The technical and administrative guidance provided to the societies should be adequate and of a high order.

At the State level, there should be one whole-time Joint Registrar or Deputy Registrar, who should be assisted by an officer of the Agriculture Department.

In States where 250 or more societies have been formed, state-level federations should be formed. These institutions should provide the technical know-how to the societies. For enabling the federation to provide such services, a grant of Rs. 40,000 may be given in the first year as suggested in the scheme formulated by the Ministry of Community Development and Cooperation. In the succeeding years, the assistance may be provided on a tapering scale.

In districts where a large number of societies are organised, it would be desirable to provide technical guidance through the district federations of farming societies. Such a federation may be provided with the whole-time services of an agricultural graduate. Action should be taken at the earliest to set up district federations on the lines of the scheme formulated by the Ministry.

As envisaged in the scheme, it is suggested that a grant of Rs. 10,000 may be given to each such federation for the first year. The assistance may, however, be tapered in the subsequent years. Where the federations set up a workshop or undertake other business activities, they may also be provided with a loan of Rs. 10,000.

If, any single district an adequate number of societies does not exist to warrant the formation of a federation, a federation may be formed for two or three contiguous districts of for a division.

At the project level, the special staff for the programme should include one worker of the extension officer rank. In addition, one village level worker should be appointed for each group of 10 societies.

At present, no special arrangements exist for non-pilot societies. It is suggested that one village level worker should be posted for every 10 such societies. His headquarters should be located in the light of local conditions.

It must also be ensured that the block staff and the various technical officers of the district, take special interest in this programme. The job charts of extension staff should provide for making available technical guidance on a continuing basis. The Block Development Officer should be responsible for seeing that the societies formed are adequately guided and assisted.

Panchayati Raj bodies, like the Zila Parishads and Panchayat Samities should be associated closely with the Programme. They should review their problems periodically and resolve their difficulties.

The programme of cooperative farming has immense scope on government waste lands, surplus lands and lands reclaimed as a result of large irrigation projects. It is essential that Government itself sets an example by encouraging cooperative farming on lands under its control.

Whilst the policy of the Government of India to utiise Government waste lands for cooperative farming has been clearly laid down, the implementation of the policy leaves much to be desired. This gap should be bridged.

Wherever government waste lands are available in compact blocks, forming viable units, these be allotted to cooperative farming societies. In making such allotment the priorities fixed by the State Government in this regard to the various categories of persons entitled to such lands, should be followed.

The allotment should be made promptly and the land should be given on a permanent or long-term basis. It should be ensured that the lands allotted can be cultivated in an economic manner. Failing this, the societies will face the problems of high cost and low returns.

Where large tracts of Government lands have re-claimed as by the Rajasthan Canal and Chambal projects, a sizeable area should be earmarked for cooperative farming. It should be possible to plan and develop such areas as models of agro-industrial enterprise. Similarly, special programmes should be formulated for areas covered by Tungabhadra project. Early steps should be taken to implement the schemes already prepared for these areas. In areas where resettlement of displaced persons is being undertaken, as in Dandakaranya, cooperative farming should be introduced

In Maharashtra, a beginning should be made to introduce cooperative farming on the lands acquired by the State Government as a result of imposition of ceilings on the holdings of private sugar factories.

The working of stagnant and disintegration societies should be carefully examined and steps taken to put them on the right lines. As such societies create an adverse reaction all round, this aspect of the programme should receive the closest attention.

For stabilising thss programme, cooperative farming societies would need careful nursing and guidanee : measures should also be taken to ensure that the benefits of joint management continue to flow over the years in an equitable and planned manner.

The areas of success have been those in which there was a conjuction of favourable circumstances. Having discovered these areas, special attention must be paid to conservation of results achieved and utilisation of the favourable climate for further progress. It should also be possible to find out other areas in which all these factors are present to some extent. A programme of such purposeful selection of areas is recommended for initiating and establishing intensive programme in the Fourth Plan.

At the same time the wider effort needed for promoting the programme need not be stopped. Such effort, if conducted continuously, with discrimination, is likely to yield at least some results in un-expected quarters. Moreover, the work of dissemination of ideology which is of vital importance would be greatly assisted by such widespread effort.

The programme is in its infancy and would take another 10-15 years before a significant impact is made on the country as a whole. It is therefore, emphasized that results should not be expected hastily and that there are no short cuts to solving the problems of marginal and submarginal cultivators.

Most of the successful societies are in the initial stages of their developments and special efforts should be made to see that they make continuous progress. The programme in relation to both the established successful areas and potentially successful areas must be intensive. In these areas, plans for development of each individual society must be drawn up separately, indetail, and financial assistance, technical guidance etc. must be ensured. In such of the areas, the formation of a further 50 to 60 societies is envisaged.

Besides the programme of intensive development consolidation and reorganisation of the movement along right lines should receive the utmost attention. At present, the programme is under way in about 300 pilot projects. In addition to the reorganisation of those amongst the existing societies which are defective, it should be possible to organise 10 to 15 new societies in the pilot projects already selected. With purposeful selection, the programme may be extended to continuous blocks and other suitable areas in each of which another 10 to 15 societies should be formed over a period of 5 years.

The programme of cooperative farming on government wate lands surplus lands, reclaimed lands etc.

will depend largely on the initiative of the Government.

In the Fourth Plan, about 10,000 new societies should come into existence, if support and guidance are made available to the programme in the manner outlined in the report.

COMMITTEE ON DEVELOPMENT OF SMALL TOWNS IN HILL AND BORDER AREAS, 1963—REPORT

Delhi, Manager of Publications, 1965. 107p.

Chairman : Shri C. B. Sharma.

Members : Shri Prabodh Chandra; Shri Karam Singh; Shri M. Koireng Singh; Shri S. M. Sen Gupta ; Shri S. K. Sahu; Dr. S. R. Sen.

Member-Secretary : Shri Gian Prakash.

APPOINTMENT

In the Joint Session of the 9th meeting of the Central Council of Local Self Government and the Fourth Conference of State Ministers for Town Planning held at New Delhi in September 1963, the Government of Himachal Pradesh had rightly drawn attention towards the relative backwardness of the Hill and border areas. It was contended that in Hill and border areas the size of towns is relatively small and neither the Planning Commission's programme of preparing Municipal Development Plans for cities with a population of over one lakh nor the Community Development and National Extension Service was of any avail to the hill towns.

Appreciating the force of the above contention, the Conference Vide its Resolution No. 10 appointed this Committee to study the problems and requirements of small towns in hill and border areas in 1963.

TERMS OF REFERENCE

(i) The overall occupational pattern ; (ii) agricultural and industrial sectors ; (iii) economic infra-structure consisting of transport ; (iv) communication and power ; and (v) social overheads like education and health.

CONTENTS

Foreword ; Introduction ; Scope of the Committee work ; General setting of hill towns ; Problems of Smell hill towns; Conclusion and Recommendations; Summary of Conclusion and Recommendations ; Appendix A, Statistical Tables ; Appendix B Questionnaire.

RECOMMENDATIONS

General

1. The small towns in hill and border areas suffer from a triple handicap. They are not only backward in themselves but happen to be located in relatively backward regions. Most of the States in which the hill areas form a large proportion of land and population are also relatively less better off. Backwardness is writ large in almost every aspect of their socio-economic conditions.

2. The problem of hill and border towns can not be treated in isolation. Any attempt to raise the hill towns without a similar corresponding effort in their hinterlands and wider regions will be put artificial and they will not be able to sustain the momentum given to them initially. Their development has, therefore, to be an integral part of a larger programme for the over-all development of the hill regions themselves and the problem has to be tackled with utmost inter-departmental collaboration, co-ordination and understanding.

Regional Plans For Hill Areas

3. There is need to formulate economic development plans and programmes for the hill and border areas as distinct regional plans which are bold in conception, of higher urgency in terms of priority and more liberal in the matter of financial and technical assistance from the Central and State Governments. A programme like the one which the Planning Commission's Team actually drew up for the backward eastern ragion of U.P. should be formulated for the hill areas after a thorough study of their problems, resources and potentialities. In the regional plans there should be a proper integration of economic and physical (land-use) planning.

4. In the context of the Chinese aggression and our strained relations with Pakistan the question of overall development of the hill and border areas and their small towns assumes the full character and urgency of a

national problem. This consideration makes the development of hill regions and their small towns as much of a defence problem as it is a socio economic one. The defence effort should, therefore, be co-ordinated with economic development.

Agriculture

5. Once the above basic premises are conceded attention has to be given to major aspects of economic development of hill areas and their small towns.

6. Since 80 per cent of hill population subsists on the primary sector, agricultural economy should be strengthened. The net sown area per capita in the hill areas is very small and there is not much scope for expanding the area under cultivation. In the face of this paradox, the development strategy has to be to concentrate on the development of horticulture and mixed farming or on raising the productivity of land in terms of money returns rather than on traditional foodgrains cultivation.

Horticulture

7. The scope for development of horticulture on the hill areas is immense. Climatic conditions also favour the growth and maintenance of orchards within certain attitudes.

8. In view of the additional cost involved in terracing and fencing, the proposal by the amount of loan for the new orchards under the scheme drawn up by the Indian Council of Agricultural Research should be raised from Rs. 500 to Rs. 1,000 per acre and made interest free for the first five years deserve sympathetic consideration. The State Governments may also distribute "taccavi" loans so that the farmers who have converted their farms into orchards can meet their foodgrain and other consumption requirements till the orchards begin to yield.

9. Regional Horticultural Research Stations should be set up in the following five regions namely Jammu & Kashmir, Punjab and Himachal Pradesh, U.P., West Bengal and Assam. These Regional Station should be established and financed entirely by the Government of India.

10. A comprehensive survey should be undertaken to demarcate the areas which can be brought under different types of fruits. Demonstration farms and seed production and distribution centres and centres of research, experimentation and training should also be established by the State Government.

11. The provision of cold storage and grading facilities at centres of collection and marketing of fruits and vegetables should be provided as development of horticulture grows apace. The State Governments in consultation with the Marketing Adviser, Ministry of Food and Agriculture, Government of India may have these aspects examined in detail.

12 Co-operativisation in the sphere of fruit and vegetable marketing transportation and rural credit and banking should also be encouraged as a part of agro-horticulture development programme. The procedures and rules for granting co-operative and bank credit in the hill areas may be simplified and suitable relaxed to make credit reach the really needy farmet and horticulturist. The State Registrars of Co-operatives may examine these aspects.

Potato Development

13. There is good potential for the development of potato cultivation in many hill areas (names listed). Potato being a high income yielding crop of the hill areas there is need to extend the areas of its cultivation and boost its production to meet the local and outside requirements.

14. Potato foundation seed farms should be located in different areas in the high hills to meet the local requirements. These farms should be run by the State Governments under trained technical staff. The disease-free nucleus seed stock should be supplied by the Central Potato Research Institute, Simla.

15. The State Departments of Agriculture should organise potato development sections-similar to the one in Himachal Pradesh-for watching the multiplication of foundation seeds.

16. A sound certification programme with sufficient inspection staff to help in spraying, growing grading and packing should be drawn by the State Governments. Apart from distribution of better seeds and the need for co-operative marketing societies of potato growers there is need to set up more potato research centres the results of whose experiments could be extended to the growers.

17. In view of the heavy application of fertilizers needed for potato cultivation adequate supply of the same should be ensured in the potato growing areas.

18. Transportation c st may make the use of fertilizers prohibitive. The State Governments should, therefore, consider subsidizing the difference in the cost of transports.

19. Due to high incidence of pests and diseases of which potatoes are vulnerable, the Plant Protection Wing of the Ministry of Food and Agriculture should study them and make special arrangements for the distribution of insecticides.

20. A large number of fruit preservation and canning factories should be established at important centres of collection and marketing of fruits and vegetables. Potatoes and vegetable dehydration plants, plants to manufacture concentrates of fruit juices

and factories for manufacturing jams, jellies, and pickles may also be set up. Industry for the manufacture of strong-light-weight packing materials should be encouraged. Industrial units engaged in fruit preservation and canning should be given loans on liberalised terms by State Governments.

21. A Central Hill Research Institute on the lines of the Central Arid Zone Research Institute should be set up. The institute should have various sections (names listed) and work in close collaboration with the Regional and State Research Stations. The benefit of its research should be extended to the farmers and horticulturists.

Animal Husbandry

22. Efforts should be made to improve the breeds of the cattle, reduce the number of useless cattle and to provide adequate feed for the cattle population. In the hill areas at altitudes above 8,000 feet rearing of sheep and yake should be promoted.

23. Efforts should be made to improve the existing pastures through improved practices. Particular attention should be paid to the development of these areas where the improvement of indigenous and foreign breeds of animals have been introduced. To overcome the present deficiency of milk supply and also to diversify the agricultural economy, dairy, poultry and piggery farming need also to be developed. Provision of adequate veterinary facilities is a necessary part of any development programme for animal husbandry.

24. The existing schemes for wool and sheep development like the establishment of sheep farms for production of stud rams, establishment of sheep and wool extension centres, rearing of imported sheep and regional research centres for sheep and wool improvement, shold be extended to those hill areas where these have not yet been introduced.

Irrigation

25. The possibilities of adopting the portable sprinkler irrigation system in the steep hill areas and more specially for high value horticulture and plantation crops may be experimented.

26. A survey of the rivers, streams and nallas to determine the technical feasibility of providing more stable irrigation facilities in the most economical manner should be carried out. The State Governments may in this respect solicit the technical assistances of the Central Water and Power Commission which in its own turn should extend its fullest co-operation to the concerned State Governments. On the basis of the surveys irrigation schemes should be formulated and liberal provision for the same made in the State Five Years Plans.

Soil Erosion

27. To tackle the problem of soil erosion, a many sided approach is required. In the sphere of agriculture there is need to enforce scientific farming practices and more intensive utilisation of land. The community project officials and village panchayats should do their best to encourage soil conservation measures.

28. On the side of forestry, measures should be taken to regulate the management or privately owned forests; control of fellings and forest fires and afforestation programmes. Farm forestry, i.e. growing trees within and around villages should be practised. The village panchayats should undertake this programme and the State Forest Departments should render to them necessary technical assistance.

29. For the urban areas the soil control measures are the provision of proper drainage facilities, planting of trees and construction of walls to prevent landslide.

30. Indiscriminate cattle grazing should be prevented and entry should be prohibited in some places of those animals whose grazing habits are known to be severely damaging.

31. To sustain efficient use of soil the scope should be enlarged from soil erosion control to complete treatment, management and land use adjustment and the new programme framed accordingly.

Forests

32. As the area under forests in most of the hill areas in much below the national forest policy standard of 60 per cent an ambitious afforestation programme in the hill areas should be undertaken.

33. The possibilities of growing costlier timber and such varieties of trees which yield valuable industrial raw materials may be explored by the Forest Department.

34. The development of forest-based industries (discussed in the Section dealing with Industries) will go a long way in raising the level of income of the people in the hill areas.

35. For proper utilisation of the forest resources a network of forest roads and the improvement of existing methods of extracting timber are necessary.

36. Development of sericulture on the lines of the Punjab Government Scheme merits examination and adoption by other States in their hill areas.

37. Collection, cultivation and production of herbs and medicinal plants, at altitudes of 8,000 feet and above should be promoted on a large scale through well organised agencies which the State Governments should establish. This agency could be departmental or co-operative. For the processing of and research on herbs and medicines, the State Governments should establish

laboratories and processing plants.

Minerals

38. Geological survey of hill areas should be done on a priority basis by the Geological Survey of India and the Indian Bureaus of Mines in collaboration with the State Bureau of Mines.

Transport and Communication

39. Development of transport and communications should be undertaken in a big way on a priority basis and in an integrated manner. There is need, not only to improve the existing roads and to widen one-way roads into two-ways roads but also to establish new road links wherever, required. The development of good roads assumes added urgency because of the constant vigilance that India's borders call for. The possibilities of building airports in the hill and border towns may be explored, taking into account strategic requirements and traffic loads.

40. In the Planning of border roads the concerned authorities should as far as, possible try to link up the intervening small towns. Thus the border roads would not only serve the defence requirements but will also be instrumental in promoting economic growth of such towns. . Where the border roads cannot connect the inlying hill towns, the State Governments should establish proper road links between the towns and border roads.

Power

41. The Central Water and Power Commission may undertake the required studies and investigate into the power problems of the Union Territories and also render technical assistance to the State Governments in the matter. These surveys should be linked up with the surveys suggested earlier for irrigational purposes. The relative merits of small diesel and hydel stations in the peculiar conditions of hill areas and their small towns should also be examined.

Industries

42. The major plan of industrial policy for the hill towns should be to develop local industries to meet local demand and also to establish those industries whose products can bear the burden of high transportation cost in the out-lying markets.

43. Small scale and cottage industries hold good promise in the small hill and border towns. Among these the important ones are fruit preservation wood-based stationery items, wood working units, box and tin making, wool and cotton spinning and weaving, leather tanning, handicrafts, sericulture, herbal medicine and bee-keeping.

Urbanisation

44. Not only should there be co-ordination in the planning and development of cantonments with the civil townships, but public utility services and community facilities should also be jointly conceived, executed and operated. The cost of jont services may be shared, in accordance with mutually agreed formulas. In such co-ordinated efforts the defence considerations should naturally have an over-riding priority.

45. To tackle the problem of urbanisation it is vital that the urban areas are prepared well in advance. The urban areas should be suitably selected for the location of appropriate industrial, commercial and other economic activities to lend them a measure of occupational balance.

Master Plans

46. Advance preparation for the anticipated urbanisation must begin with the preparation of master plans. For preparation of master plans, the centrally sponsored scheme of giving 100 per cent grand should be extended to the small hill towns.

47. The concerned State Government may give special allowance to attract overseers for preparation of base maps.

48. Besides preparing Master Plans for the hill towns, it is necessary to prepare town development programmes on the line of those envisaged by the Planning Commission for the bigger cities. These should be made an integral part of the regional plans suggested earlier and the State Five Year Plans. The State Governments may seek the assistance of the Central Town & Country Planning Organisation in preparing town development programme.

Water Supply, Sewerage and Drainage

49. Separate Engineering Survey and Investigation Units should be created to survey problems of water supply, sewerage and drainage of the small towns. Where such units exist, these should be augmented and strengthened to cover these small towns on a priority basis. State Governments should appoint Regional Water and Sewerage Boards to look after the establishment and maintenance of these services in small towns. The financial and material requirements of such programmes should be worked out in advance.

50. The National Water Supply and Sanitation "Scheme should cover, besides the pilgrim centres, "tourist centres and small towns in the hill and border areas". In case of these small towns, the pattern of assistance may be the same as the one approved by Planning Commission for rural areas from time to time. The Scheme applicable to small towns in hill and border areas should be a Centrally sponsored one. So far as

tribal areas are concerned the existing pattern of Central assistance should continue.

Health

51. For improving the health facilities in the hill towns, existing standards of hospital and dispensary facilities should be raised. Specialised services should be made available for treatment of disease prevalent in the hill areas.

52. With a view to evolve necessary measures for the prevention and cure of the disease prevailing in the hill areas, it is necessary to collect data in respect of these diseases. The Ministry of Health may arrange to carry out special surveys to determine the prevalence of various diseases.

53. Health education and social education should be provided through the community development blocks in rural areas and the civic authorities in urban areas.

Social Reforms and Social Welfare

54. The Central and the State Government Organisations departments concerned with the welfare of the scheduled castes and scheduled tribes should organise special intensive reform and welfare programmes in the hill and tribal areas on a priority basis.

Internal Roads

55. In the case of town area and notified area committees matching contribution against grants given for roads should not be insisted upon. Even in regard to the small municipalities the grants may be given on the basis of 25 per cent as against 100 per cent matching which is the practice at present.

Housing

56. With a view to improve the housing conditions, the terms and conditions of the Slum Improvement Scheme of Government of India should be liberalised to cover small hill towns also. The hill towns should be given priority in the matter of grant of loans under the various Housing Schemes.

57. Research work to find out cheaper building materials and methods of construction should be undertaken by the National Building Organisation on a priority basis. The building materials should be exempted from taxes by the local bodies. The State Government should also earmark special quotas of these commodities for the hill areas and hill towns.

Sanitation

58. One of the urgent requirements is to convert dry latrines into flush latrines wherever, water-borne sewerage system exist. Construction of inexpensive hand flushed latrines designed by the Government of U.P. should be encouraged. House-owners in the low-income group should be given loans recoverable in easy instalments to undertake such constructions.

59. Where water-born sewerage system does not exist, frequency of scavenging services should be increased and the staff therefore augmented suitably. Hand flushed pit type latrines should also be encouraged wherever, possible. To enable the local bodies to meet the additional expenditure on these, the State Government should provide liberal grants.

Tourism

60. Hill towns offer immense potentialities for tourist trade. A tourist traffic promotion programme on a big scale may be launched for the benefit of the hill towns.

61. Adequate residential accommodation to suit persons in different income groups should be created. Games and sports, cultural and literary programmes, conducted tours and shikar parties etc. should also be organised as a part of a co-ordinated overall programme for the development of tourism. The public and private organisations concerned should form committees to chalk out concrete programmes. The tourist bureaus of the State Governments in the hill towns should be strengthened. Well organised publicity compaigns are also necessary.

62. Tourist facilities should not only be concentrated in the larger hill towns but also extended in an increased measure to smaller ones so that they may have a chance to grow quickly. Special efforts should also be made in popularise them.

63. Concessions should be given in the bus fares for journeys to the smaller tourist towns. Special concession to students and sports' parties should also be given. Similar concessions in air transport may also be desirable.

64. Instead of tackling the problem in bits, a well-coordinated, phased and integrated programme after a detailed survey of present and potential tourist centres should be drawn up and priorities in regard to the development of small centres assigned. In this venture the collaboration of the State Governments with the Department of Tourism, Ministry of Transport may yield valuable results.

Educational and Research Institutions

65. As the scope for the development of industry and commerce in the hill towns is limited, possibility of establishing in them, institutions of higher learning and research laboratories connected with problems of the hill areas should be explored and encouraged wherever possible. Such institutions will help in raising the intellectual and cultural plane of the small

communities.

66. It is desirable that in the existing universities and technical institutions, special courses having a close bearing on the problems of hill areas should be devised and introduced.

67. Educational and training camps should be held in these small towns during the slack season.

Administration

68. Out-moded revenue systems like Zamidari still persist in many hill areas. The need to introduce land reforms in hill areas is urgent for raising the productivity of land. Those states where land reform laws have not yet been passed or passed but not effectively enforced should take necessary steps in this direction at an early date.

69. Cadastral Surveys of the hill areas should be carried out quickly and steps taken to convert 'non-reporting areas' into 'reporting areas'.

70. In many hill areas the revenue officials are performing police functions also. A separate police department should be created as distinct from the revenue department, as it will be conducive in promoting better security so essential for prosperity and even to help tourism.

71. The size of a 'patti' should be reduced to enable the 'Patwari' to function efficiently.

72. A special central pool of officers should be constituted for the hill areas particularly for the staff employed in agriculture, horticulture, engineering, soil conservation, forestry and animal husbandry and given a special allowance if posted in the hill areas of the States and territories concerned.

73. The State Government could as well make it compulsory for officers in administrative and technical cadres to serve in the hill and border areas for at least a term of three years, before they could be considered eligible for promotion.

74. The long term solution of the personnel problem lies in building up local talent. The concerned State Governments should follow a policy of selecting promising youngmen belonging to hill and tribal areas for award of scholarship for higher studies. They should also explore possibilities of reserving some quota in the technical institutions and outside their own States for students hailing from the hill and border areas.

75. A seperate senior officer under the Development Commissioner should be appointed by State Governments to look after the implementation of the Five Year Plan and Programmes in the hill areas.

76. A special officer should be appointed by the State Governments in the L.S.G. Departments for guiding, advising and directing the local bodies of the hill and border areas. This officer should ensure that areas classified as urban by the Census authorities have urban local bodies establishing for them. These urban local bodies should be given adequate financial assistance during the first few years. Efforts should also be made to strengthen the revenue structure of these urban local bodies.

Conclusion

77. Detailed Surveys about physical, economic, social and other aspects of the hill areas including the areas at high altitudes should be conducted. The Research Programmes Committee of the Planning Commission and/or the State Governments could take the initiative in having such surveys made. The State Governments may refer some important technical problems to appropriate national or other laboratories for proper research.

78. The Planning Commission and the Central and the concerned State Governments are urged to give these recommendations very sympathetic consideration.

COMMITTEE OF MINISTERS ON AUGMENTATION OF FINANCIAL RESOURCES OF URBAN LOCAL BODIES, 1963—REPORT

Delhi, Manager of Publications. 1965. 566p.

Chairman : Shri Rafiq Zakaria ;
Members : Shri S.M. Fazular Rahman ; Shri Allapati Venkataramiah ; Shri S.M. Abdul Majid ; Shri Prabodh Chandra ;
Secretary : Shri K.A. Ramasubramaniam ;

APPOINTMENT

The Eight Meeting of the Central Council of Local Self-Government held at Calcutta in 1962, passed the following Resolution :

The council having considered the question augmentation of the financial resources of Urban local bodies and having regard to the recommendations of the Taxation Enquiry Commission and the Local Finance Enquiry Committee recommended that information should be collected from the State Governments regarding :

(i) The types of taxes that can be levied by the urban local bodies under existing laws ; (ii) the taxes actually levied by the local bodies ; and (iii) the percentage of collection in local bodies of different sizes. The Council notes that the existing sources of revenue for local bodies are not adequate for their requirements.

The Council further resolves that a Committee consisting of Ministers for Local Self-Government from (i) Maharashtra, (ii) West Bengal, (iii) Punjab, (iv) Madras and (v) Andhra Pradesh may study the problem of augmentation of the financial resources of the urban local bodies in all its aspects and on the basis of their study the matter may be taken up with the Finance Ministry. The Committee was appointed at the 9th Meeting of the Central Council of Local Self-Government held in New Delhi in September 1963.

TERMS OF REFERENCE

To examine the proposals that have been made in the note of the Govt. of Kerala for introducing amendments in the Reserve Bank of India Act. to enable the bank to give long-term loans to urban local bodies for implementing development plans ;

To meet the Union Minister for Finance and discuss with him its proposals with a view to obtain increased financial resources for development plans of local bodies ;

To examine in details the note of West Bengal Government to the Central Council of Local Self-Government on basis of property tax by Local Bodies, in which a suggestion was made that the basis of property taxation should be changed from the present system which is based on annual rental Value to Capital Value.

CONTENTS

Pt.I. : Introduction ; The magnitude of Problem ; Financing Urban Development Schemes ; The Gap between needs and resources ; Better utilisation of existing resources ; Sharing of State revenues ; Grants-in-aid ; Borrowing of Urban Local bodies in India, New sources of revenue ; Summary of main recommendations ; Bibliography ; Annexure from A to F ; Charts ;
Pt. II : Analysis of date ; Charts ;
Pt. III. : Appendices from I to XLIX.

RECOMMENDATIONS

All schemes pertaining to urban development should be brought together and executed in a co-ordinated manner within the frame work of a master plan of comprehensive development. Every master plan should be translated into a master programme consisting of a number of specific schemes and each local bodies should prepare five-year City Developments Programmes in accordance with which the various schemes in order of priority would be executed. The programmes should also indicate how much the local body would be able to contribute out of its own resources towards their implementation and what should be the extent of subsidy from the State or from the Centre. Once such City Development Programmes are worked out and they are integrated with the State Plan and ultimately in the National Plan, the problem of finding resources for implementation of the Master Plan would become very much simpler.

A statutory Urban Development Board should be set up in each State which should be empowered to acquire lands and properties wherever necessary and undertake most aspects of town development. The Board may also statutorily undertake water supply and sewerage schemes in respect of specified regions. It can also junction as Central Loans Institution which would supply long-term as well as short-term credit to the local bodies. The initial capital for the Urban Development Boards should come out of the total provisions made in the plan for urban development. The boards should also be empowered to raise resources of their own and should also explore the possibilities of financial assistance from various international AID Agencies.

The Property tax should be administered under conditions which would give best results. To utilise this tax properly, the following measures are recommended :

(a) A Central Valuation Department, should be set up in each State to get the work of assessment of properties in different municipalities, done and also take up systematically at regular intervals, re-assessment of urban properties ;

(b) The Property Tax should be freed from the restrictive influence of the Rent Control Act either by imposing a 25% surcharge on the existing property tax and allowing the property owner to shift the entire burden of this surcharge on the tenants or by a suitable legal provision which would enable recovery of the difference between the property tax based on the reasonable annual rental value and the property tax based on standard rent from the property owner and allowing him to treat this difference as arrears of rent for the purpose of recovery ;

(c) The definition of "Lands and buildings" should be suitably modified on the lines of practice prevailing in England. A Comprehensive Code for Assistant of rental value should be drawn up with the assistance of one or two Assessors and Legal Expert ;

(d) In every State there should be a separate cadre of municipal employees and the Chief Executive Officers of all urban local bodies should be deputed from this cadre except for certain specified posts ;

(e) A standard percentage of collections should be prescribed and any municipality which fails to achieve this percentage without adequate reasons should be disqualified from receiving any Government grant or loans ;

(f) If the collection percentage in a particular local body falls below the prescribed percentage, the State Government should direct severe disciplinary action being taken against the Chief Executive Officer and the Collection Staff. Action may also be taken against the President of municipality and even inspite of this, if there is continued neglect, this should be considered as sufficient ground for supersession of the municipality;

(g) A Statutory minimum and maximum should be fixed for property tax. A provision should also be made in the Municipal Act to enable the State Government to impose property tax at any rate considered resonable by the State Government if the municipality fails to impose tax at that rate ;

(h) The State Government properties and Central Government properties should be subjected to property tax and service tax in the same manner as any private property ;

(i) The practice prevailing in England in respect of assessment of Machinery and plant, should be adopted by our urban local bodies so that industries are made to contribute adequately to the cost of services provided by urban local bodies.

Octroi in its present form should be gradually replaced either by a turnover tax or by a surcharge on sales-tax or by some other method which may cover the same sphere of taxation but would be free from the evils of the octroi system.

The maximum limit of profession tax in the case of an individual should be raised from Rs. 250 to Rs. 500 and in the case of companies to Rs. 2,000 by suitably amending the Article 276 of the Constitution. The levy of profession tax should be made obligatory.

Licensing system should be made more efficient and more comprehensive.

Urban local bodies encouraged to take up remunerative activities which would create permanent assets yeilding perennial non-tax income. As far as possible these remunerative activities should be financed out of a revenue fund.

As recommended by the Taxation Enquiry Commission, the following taxes should be reserved for exclusive utilisation by or for the local bodies :

(i) Tax on lands and buildings popularly known as property tax.

(ii) Tax on entry of goods into the area of local authority for consumption, use or sale therein.

(iii) Tax on professions, trades and callings.

(iv) Tax on vehicles other than mechanically propelled.

(v) Tax on animals and goats.

(vi) Tax on advertisements other than newspaper advertisements.

To begin with at least 25 per cent of the proceeds of the entertainment tax should be earmarked for urban local bodies and this percentage should be gradually raised so that ultimately the entire proceed of this tax are assigned to the urban local bodies. The entire proceeds of any surcharge that is being levied on the entertainment tax should be straightway handed over to the local bodies. The theatre tax and the show tax could be administered by the local bodies themselves but in cases where taxes are levied by the States, their proceeds should be earmarked for the local bodies. The proceeds of the entertainment and other allied taxes need not necessarily be distributed on the basis of population or the source from which the tax originated. The State Government should have the discretion to distribute it on the basis of needs of different categories of local bodies.

At least 25 per cent of the proceeds of the motor vehicle tax should be earmarked for local bodies and a formula should be evolved to distribute the proceeds to the different local bodies on the basis of population, mileage of roads maintained by them, volume of traffic, etc.

As recommended by the Taxation Enquiry Commission each State should have a Grants-in-aid code embodying certain well-defined principles, and that there should be a basic general purposes grant for each local body in addition to specific grants for particular item and services. For the purpose of evolving the principles in accordance with which such grants should be made, the urban local bodies should be classified into six groups :

(a) Class A—Corporations—metropolitan cities and big industrial centres ;

(b) Class B—Corporations municipalities covering cities with more than five lakhs population ;

(c) Corporations and municipalities with more than one lakh but less than five lakhs population ;

(d) Municipalities with more than 50,000 but less than one lakh population ;

(e) Municipalities with more than 20,000 but less than 50,000 population ;

(f) Municipalities, town area Committees and notified area committees with less than 20,000 population.

The Committee recommends that the Urban local bodies should get a recurring annual per capita basic general purposes grant at the following rates :—

(1) Class A Corporations—metropolitan cities and big industrial centres ;	—25 paise
(2) Class B Corporation Municipalities covering cities with more than five lakhs population ;	—25 paise
(3) Corparations and municipalities with more than one lakh but less than five lakhs population ;	—50 paise
(4) Municipalities with more than 50,000 but less than one lakh population ;	—75 paise
(5) Municipalities with more than 20,000 but less than 50,000 population ;	—Re. 1.00
(6) Municipalities, town area Committees and notified area Committees with less than 20,000 population ;	—Rs. 1.50 paise

With regard to specific grants, the Committee is of opinion that for Water Supply and drainage schemes, grants should be made on the following lines :

(1) Class A-Corporations—Metropolitan cities and big Industrial Centres.	No grant should be givin but State and Central Governments should give all assistance in securing loans on liberal terms.
(2) Class B-Corporation Municipalities covering cities more than five lakhs population.	Some grant may be necessary but this may be decided by the State Government after taking into consideration all the relevant factors with a view to make the project a practical proposition.
(3) Corporations/Municipalities with more than one lakh but less than five lakhs population.	10 per cent of the total cost of the Scheme should be contributed by the municipality. 66-2/3 per cent to be raised as loans by the Municipalities and the State Government would give the necessary guarantee. 23-1/3 per cent would be given as grant.
(4) Municipalities with more than 50 000 but less than one lakh population.	10 per cent contribution by the Municipalities. 50 per cent loan to be raised by the Municipalities with Government guarantee. 40 per cent grant.
(5) Municipalities with more than 20,000 but less than 50,000 population.	10 per cent contribution by the Municipalities. 40 per cent loan to be raised by the Municipalities with Government guarantee. 50 per cent grant.
(6) Municipalities town, area committees and notified area committees with less than 20,000 population.	10 per cent contribution by the local bodies. 30 per cent to be raised as loans with Government guarantee. 60 per cent grant.

A more liberal pattern of financial assistance should be adopted for large pilgrim centres, places of tourists' interests, hill towns and towns where due to technical difficulties the cost on water supply schemes is unusually high. In the cases of these local bodies, a minimum contribution by the local body need not be insisted upon and the percentage of grant assistance can be increased according to the circumstances of each case.

For developmental activities such as public health measures, parks and gardens, sports stedia, theatres, libraries, swimming pools, etc., grants may be given to the extent of 25 per cent.

To cover the increased administrative costs over payment of increased salaries, cost of living allowance etc. at least 50 per cent grant should be given.

Certain services like water supply, severage, drainage, public health measures, primary education, maternity and child welfare etc., though local in character, are National in importance. The Central Government as well as the State Government should, therefore, share the responsibility for providing these services to the urban population.

The debt of remunerative enterprises should be a charge on the revenue derived from these enterprises. There, should, however, be staggering of dates for paying instalments for the repayment of loans at least for such period till the enterprise really becomes remunerative. Local bodies should not be allowed to borrow indiscriminately from the open market but should borrow their entire loan requirements either from the State Government or from a Central Loans Institution like the Urban Development Board.

The proposed Bill for levy of terminal tax on passengers and goods carried by rail should now be enacted by the Government of India. For such time, till the bill is enacted, the railways should make recurring annual grants to the State Governments for the development of the urban areas from where the rail earnings mainly arise and this grant should be based on the approximate estimated yield from the terminal tax if it is actually levied in terms of the proposed bill.

To tax "Floating" population who come to metropolitan cities and important centres of trade and industry from a distance of within 150 miles, a tax which should be in the nature of a small surcharge on railway fares and bus-fares should be levied. The entire proceeds of this tax should also be made over to the urban local bodies concerned.

For mopping up unearned increments in land values an urban land tax should be levied on the market value of urban land irrespective of the value of the building standing on it. When the property is proposed to be put to more profitable use, a development charge may be levied before permission is given to change the land use. The proceeds of these taxes should be made over to the urban local bodies wherever they are responsible for implementation of the master plan or to improvement trusts or development boards as the case may be.

Where the States are already levying tax on the consumption of electricity, a surcharge should be made available to the urban local bodies. Where no such duty is in force, the urban local bodies by suitable amendment of the municipal enactments, should be authorised to impose tax on the consumption of electricity at a rate not exceeding 10 per cent of the existing electricity rates.

INFORMAL GROUP ON GOLD CONTROL, 1963—REPORT

New Delhi, Ministry of Finance, 1963. 12p.

Chairman : Shri S.S. Khera.
Members : Shri P.C. Bhattacharya ; Shri S. Bhoothalingam ; Shri L. K. Jha ; Shri V. T. Dehejia.
Secretary : Dr. I. G. Patel.

APPOINTMENT

At the request of the Finance Minister, an Informal Group of Officials was constituted on September 5, 1963 to review the working of the Gold Control Order in all its aspects and to suggest ways of improving, simplifying and rationalising the control.

TERMS OF REFERENCE

(i) To review the working of the Gold Control Order in all its aspects ; and

(ii) To suggest ways of improving, simplifying and rationalising the control.

CONTENTS

Introductory ; General Assessment ; The Problem of Goldsmiths ; Administration of the Gold Control ; Procedural Matters ; Ancilliary Questions.

RECOMMENDATIONS

General Assessment

In its general assessment of the working of the Gold Control, the report is convinced that the provisions of the Gold Control which seek to reduce smuggling, by control over individual holdings of non-ornament gold and by control over refineries and big dealers, have succeeded in their central objective and that at least for the time being, there has been a significant reduction in the extent of smuggling. The fact that the internal price of gold today is no higher than what it was when the control was introduced (and in fact lower than what it was a year ago) is a clear indication of the fact that, for the time being at any rate, there has been a significant decline in the demand for gold in the country. The task for the future is essentially one of preserving, consolidating and extending the gains of the past few months.

The Report points out, however, that though the policy underlying the Gold Control is essentially well-conceived, certain factors have led to disaffection, in regard to its working, on a scale which requires immediate attention if the prospects of successful implementation of a rational gold policy are not to be vitiated by lack of popular support. These, in its opinion, are:

(a) The lack of concertcd political support for the Gold policy;

(b) The somewhat tardy response to the legitimate complaints of thousands of small goldsmith; and

(c) The lack of adequate machinery for effective and equitable enforcement of the control.

The Problem Of Goldsmiths

In regard to the problem of goldsmiths, the recommendations of the report are:

The Problem of Unlicensed Goldsmiths (Section VII and Postscript)

(1) A quick, generous and publicity-informed approach to the problem of unemployed goldsmiths is at the very heart of the matter of making the gold policy succeed by making its implementation equitable and, therefore, generally acceptable. At the same time it must be realised that if the demand for gold in the country and the extent of smuggling are to be held in check, the scope for employing goldsmiths on the basis of the use of gold as such is bound to diminish considerably.

(2) The suggestion that Government should import a certain amount of gold, or use a part of the gold it already has, in order to release it in the form of 14 carat bars to goldsmiths in the country would be self-defeating in the long run. The release of a certain amount of gold by Government will not put an end to smuggling, there would be no rational way of distributing small quantities of go'd among thousands of goldsmiths and sooner or later, Government will be driven to open the flood-gates officially conceding to demands for more and more import of legal gold.

(3) The report of the Group did not favour the suggestion that goldsmiths may be permitted to make ornaments of purity higher than 14 carat atleast in so far as conversion from existing ornaments is concerned, because it felt that the 14 carat rule was an important part of the long-term gold policy and any attempt to go back on it would give a further impetus for the demand for gold and might also marginally increase the scope for smuggling.

After a study of the Report, the Finance Minister drew attention to the fact that the continuance of a virtual ban on any activity by thousands of goldsmiths would aggravate their economic distress as the rehabilitation measured proposed would necessarily take time to implement. The Finance Minister desired that this aspect of the matter should be further studied. The chairman and othor members of the Group available in Delhi met again to consider the problem from this aspect. They recognised that if self-employed goldsmiths were permitted to work only on 14 carat ornaments, it was not likely to result in any significant volume of employment for the simple reason that even a minimum supply of 14 carat gold could not be ensured without import of primary gold involving expenditure of foreign exchange. They also recognised that the measures of rehabilitation proposed in the report would necessarily take some time to produce results, even if implemented with great vigour. There was, therefore, a real transitional problem which had to be met by some concession. On the other hand there was the inherent disadvantage of postponing the time when no ornaments other than 14 carat would be manufactured. After careful consideration of these two aspects, and in view of the scale of the human problem these members of the Group come to the conclusion that same limited concession could be permitted, for such minimum period as may be found really necessary, without serious violence to the basic objectives of the Gold Control. In this light, they agreed in a postscript to the report that conversion of existing ornaments of higher than 14 carat purity to ornaments of a purity not exceeding the original could be permitted subject to the following safeguards:

(i) The concession should be confined to self-employed goldsmiths.

(ii) To prevent abuse, the maintenance of accounts in

a simple form should be prescribed.

(iii) No new gold should be issued.

These members of the Committee also recommended that as a further safeguard, steps should be taken to call for declaration of holdings of gold ornaments beyond a certain limit.

(4) The report is unable to accept the argument that the best way of reducing the demand for ornaments would be to put a low ceiling on individual holdings of ornaments without bothering about the purity of such ornaments. The country is not yet ready for accepting or administering such a suggestion, especially if the ceiling is kept low enough to have a real meaning in our circumstances.

Extension Of licensing facilities (Section VIII) : (1)

The Gold Board had approved a scheme whereby out-workers will be issued primary gold of 14 carat (or less) purity by the licensed dealers in order to enable the out-workers to execute orders placed on them by the licensed dealers. This scheme may be adopted without delay so that this part of the problem of unemployment among goldsmiths at any rate is met, to the extent possible.

(2) As regards the small goldsmiths who are self-employed, provision should be made for a special licence on nominal fee which might be issued in the first instance for one year. The holders of the special licences might be permitted to hold at any given time a limited amount of primary gold in the form of 14 carat or less. The submission of regular return by the special licences is not suggested in view of the administrative burden it would involve; the check on them would essentially be a physical one.

(3) No one who does not hold either a regular licence or a special licence should be allowed to deal in gold. Special licences should be disqualified for rehabilitation licence but will be free to surrender the licence and opt for rehabilitation, if they so choose. The right either to rehabilitation or the licence should be limited to those families who can substantiate, before competent authority, that they had a significant buisness in gold in the past. The right should be related to each family rather than to each individual member of it.

Rehabilitation Of Goldsmiths (Section IX) : (1) Efforts to rehabilitate goldsmiths have not been so far as determined, widespread or generous as they needed to be. Whatever the machinery at the Centre, the detailed task of rehabilitation must necessarily be entrusted to the States. The first thing is for the Centre to prepare an overall scheme of rehabilitation in consultation with the States. The major emphasis in such a scheme should be on loans for productive purposes. As far as possible attempt should be to rehabilitate goldsmiths at or near their present place of residence.

(2) It is difficult to determine the financial implications of such a programme. On a rough estimate, the cost may be of the order of Rs. 20 crores. An expenditure of even this order would be justified in view of what is at stake.

Desiderata For a Successful Policy Towards Goldsmiths :

Two things, in the opinion of the report, are vitally important for the successful operation of the measures outlined above. One is a clear reiteration of policy on the part of Government to the effect that the Gold Control has come to stay, that its basic provisions are sound and would if any thing be implemented more strictly in future, and that the scope for employing the goldsmiths as goldsmiths in the years to come would inevitably be much less than it has been in the past. It is only on such a clear statement of policy that the goldsmiths as a class can be expected to turn away from the futile course of agitation seeking to restore the status qua to a more responsive frame of mind towards attempts to rehabilitate them in other occcpations.

The second imperative for the successful implementation of the scheme is that the Government should be earnest, generous and quick in so far as the task of rehabilitating the goldsmiths in other occupations is concerned. This task is central to the whole problem of resolving the dissatisfaction against the Gold Control.

Administration Of the Gold Control

The other major area of the Gold Control, in which the Report makes several important recommendations, is the administration of the Gold Control. These are as follows—

The Administration of the Gold Control (Section XII):

(1) The actual work arising out of the Gold Control can broadly be sub-divided into four groups:

(a) Administration (including inter alia formulation of policies and procedures, licensing, obtaining, collution and scrutiny of returns etc.);

(b) Detection and enforcement (including watch on and random inspections of licences, raids, seizures, prosecutions) ;

(c) Rehabilitation of former goldsmiths ; and

(d) Persuasion (use of publicity and propaganda to mean people away from gold).

The first three are principally administrative functions where an official is more likely to deliver the goods than any non-official. It is in the last item viz., organising the means of persuasion that a suitable non-official may be in a better position than an official.

Considering all the circumstances, the Board form as the administrative agency should be given up.

(2) Instead, the administration of the Gold Control machinery should be entrusted to a senior official who may be designated the Gold Control Administrator. To assist him and to act as a two way bridge between him and the public, there should be in addition an Advisory Board (or Committee). The Advisory Board (or Committee) should have on it a number of non-officials and, if so considered necessary, official representatives as well from some State Governments where the rehabilitation problem may be more acute. Its Chairman should be a non-official.

(3) Immediately as he is appointed, the Administrator should be asked to formulate detailed proposals for the implementation of Control in all its aspects for the approval of Government.

(4) The Administrator may start with his head office in Delhi with a self-contained staff for work relating to administration and policy and licensing.

(5) The central responsibility for enforcement and the field work relating to gold must continue to rest with the Central Excise Department acting in close collaboration with the Central Customs Department. The efforts of the Central Excise Department must be supplemented by the enforcement agencies of the State Governments that have wide coverage in the field and somewhat similar training and responsibilities. A practical arrangement would be for the Central Excise Department to earmark, in the jurisdiction of each collector of Excise, another officer of that Department of suitable rank to have whole-time responsibility in respect of the Gold Control in that jurisdiction. This officer, while being subject to the local control of the Collector of Central Excise, would in other respects be directly responsible to the Gold Control Administrator.

(6) The Administrator should be contained within the Department of Revenue in the Ministry of Finance and also be designated as an Additional Member of the Central Board of Revenue.

(7) There should be an official co-ordinating Committee in each State and a small Standing Committee or Group of Secretary level at the Centre to provide internal assistance and guidance to the Administrator in regard to any major difficulties that he may have to face.

(8) The programme of rehabilitation of goldsmiths should be implemented through the State Governments within the broad framework of the policy laid down by the Centre. A separate Central Agency for the purpose is not necessary.

(9) The task of persuasion and propaganda, at official levels should be the responsibility of the Ministry of Information and Broadcasting. In the discharge of this responsibility they should be associated closely with the Administrator and the Advisory Board (Committee). In this particular field efforts of the official machinery alone will not suffice, considerable amount of work will have to be done by and through non-official agencies.

Procedural Matters

The report makes a series of recommendations for improving, simplifying and rationalising Gold Control procedures in its sections on 'Declarations by individuals,' 'Control over Refineries', 'Control over licensed dealers' and 'Provisions concerning industrial users'. In summary, these are ;

Declarations by Individuals (Sections IV):

(1) In all major cases where violations of the provision to declare non-ornament Gold have already been detected, immediate steps should be taken to launch prosecutions and to secure the exemplary punishments permitted under the law; the enforcement machinery must be strengthened and special efforts made to unearth further cases of non-declaration.

(2) It is not necessary to call for declarations of ornaments possessed in excess of a certain limit, at this stage. But powers to call for declaration of ornaments in specific cases may be assumed and general powers in this regard incorporated when the Gold Control is put on a permanant legislative footing at an appropriate stage.

(3) Government should provide a ready and free facility, such as at the offices of the State Bank, for tendering of declared non-ornamental gold, and of gold ornaments, in exchange for standard 14 carat gold bars.

Control Of Refineries (Section V) :

(1) The licensing of refineries, whether power operated or not, should be completed without delay. All those who have applied for licence, and who were in the legitimate business of gold refining before the Control, should be given a licence on specified conditions. As soon as practicable, refining of gold except under bond should be eliminated. Provision should be made for the primary gold produced by refineries to have a standard identifying mark.

(2) A cautions attitude should be followed towards extension of licensed refining facilities. The long-term objective should be to centralise gold refining activity as far as possible, and ultimately, in the hands of the Government.

Control Over Licensed Dealers (Section VI) :

(1) There should be an intensive drive to obtain regular returns, as required under law, from licensed dealers and to punish non-compliance by revocation of

licenses.

(2) The returns should be systematically scrutinised and possible cases of violations detected and punished.

Provisions Concerning Industrial Users (Section X):

(1) While it is recognised that the needs of industrial users must be met, search for substitutes must be encouraged and their use facilitated by suitable fiscal devices.

(2) With a view to avoid the danger of malpractices, bonding of major producers of liquid gold, and if possible, of zari makers could be considered.

Ancilliary Questions

Two ancilliary matters dealt with in the report are 'Impact of the Gold Control on Rural Credit' and 'Measures to supplement Gold Control'. Its recommendations on these matters are:

Import of Gold Control on Rural Credit (Section XI)

(1) As regards bank credit, it is not desirable that the long-term policy of discouraging bank advances against gold should be modified. At the same time, as far as the valuation of gold or ornaments for the purposes of determining credit limits is concerned, commercial banks should be free to be guided by their own best judgement of the market.

(2) Wherever rural credit has declined as a result of the Gold Control, special steps might be taken to step up credit operations by other agencies such as land mortgage banks cooperative societies and the like.

(3) The special problem regarding pawn brokers in States where jewellery not redeemed can under the law be sold only through recognised auctioners could be resolved in consultation with the State Governments concerned by providing that such auctioning could be undertaken by suitable officers such as District Magistrates.

Measures To Supplement Gold Control (Section XIII:

(1) Suitable forms of investment should be devised which should be endowed by law with the same quality of "Streedhan" that gold ornaments have at present.

(2) Facilities for obtaining credit against investments in forms other than gold should be liberalised and the habit of insurance spread further in the rural areas.

(3) Sooner or later, the Gold Control, which is at present operating as a part of the Defence of India Rules, should be given a separate and permanent legislative footing. This should be done at an appropriate time and in an atmosphere of reason when the immediate problem of rehabilitating the gold smiths has been tackled in right earnest.

INDUSTRIES DEVELOPMENT PROCEDURES COMMITTEE, 1963—REPORT

Delhi, Manager of Publications, 1964. 26p.

Chairman : Shri T. Swaminathan.
Members : Shri Bharat Ram ; Shri A.R. Foster ; Shri Lakshmipat Singhania ; Shri A.M. Murugappa Chettiar ; Shri P. Chentsal Rao ; Shri N.C. Srivastava ; Shri P. Govindan Nair ; Shri V.K. Ramaswami.
Secretary : Shri K.J. George.

APPOINTMENT

The Committee was constituted under the Ministry of Industry vide their Resolution No. 4 (22) Lic. Pol./63 dated 24th September, 1963.

TERMS OF REFERENCE

To examine the operation of the controls applicable to the establishment of additional industrial capacity under the Industries (Development and Regulation) Act, 1951, the import of capital goods, the issue of capital and foreign investment and collaboration.

CONTENTS

Resolution; Main Recommendations in the Final Report; Other General Recommendations of the Committee; Government's decision on the Committee's recommendations; Order; Final Report of Industries Development Procedures Committee; Import Licence for spare parts either received short or in damaged condition and replacement of which is made free of cost either by the supplier or on payment by Insurance Company; Procedure followed by the Industrial Credit and Investment Corporation of India and Industrial Finance Corporation for the grant of loans-special procedure for 'Key' industries; Reconstitution of the Committee after a year; Acknowledgements; Annexures I to V.

RECOMMENDATIONS

Procedure for Industries Other Than 'Key' Industries : In respect of Industries other than 'Key' industries, the Committee has expressed, the view that for various practical reasons, including the foreign exchange shortages which make difficult the prompt clearance in all cases of import of capital goods, it would not be practicable to follow the special procedures recommended for 'key industries'. It has, therefore, suggested that, wherever the availability of foreign exchange 'is not the main limiting factor, after the issue of a letter of intent, all subsequent clearances, such as the import of Capital Goods, approval of foreign collaboration terms, and issue of Capital should be given with in three months from the date of receipt of the respective applications. A procedure for keeping a close, watch on timely clearances has also been prescribed.

Special Procedure for Certain Industries Other Than 'Key' Industries Which are Import-Saving Or Substantially Export-Oriented : The Committee has listed a few industries in which substantial imports are at present taking place. It has recommended that the special procedure for 'key' industries should be made applicable to these industries and also in the case of any other industries which Government consider to be of special importance from the point of view of earning substantial amounts of foreign exchange through exports.

Procedure Relating To Licensing Of Raw Materials/Components : As delays in the issue of licences for raw materials affect industrial production, the Committee has suggested that ways and means should be found of issuing licences within three months from the commencement of each licensing period. If, for any reason, this procedure is not found practicable in the interests of ensuring continuous production, the Committee has recommended that ad hoc licences equal to 50 per cent of the value of the licence for the first half of the previous licensing year should be issued. For the second half, the Committee has recommended that all licences should be authorised by a General Notification to utilise at least 50 per cent of the value of the licence for the second half, pending the final announcement of policy for this period. The Committee has also suggested that while issuing licences for raw materials, the limitations should normally be value-wise and not quantitative, so that the licensee has the descretion to import any of the permissible items listed in the licence in such proportions as may be necessary.

Forms Of Application For Industrial Licences For The Import Of Capital Goods: The Committee has suggested some modifications to these forms, mainly with a view to ensure simplification in some ways. Another consideration that has been taken into account is the extent of detailed information likely to be available to the applicant at the time of his application.

The Committee has recommended the submission of two applications for industrial licence, one, a preliminary application (along with the Treasury Challan) to enable the issue of a 'letter of intent' speedily, and the other a final application at a later stage at the time of the issue of a formal industrial licence. The consideration which has guided the Committee in suggesting two applications instead of one application as hitherto is that at the time of initial application, the entrepreneur does not have a detailed, clear picture of all the items prescribed in the application form. It is not unlikely that in respect of many of the items on which information has been furnished by the applicant in the preliminary application the position may change substantially after consultations and negotiations with foreign collaborators and machinery suppliers, both indigenous and foreign. As the licensing Sub-Committee's final decision on the conversion of a 'letter of intent' into an industrial licence would depend on a correct final appraisal of all material factors, a final application is also proposed. In the case of 'key' industries this final application is to be considered along with the simultaneous consideration of the subsequent clearances relating to capital goods, foreign collaboration terms, issue of capital etc. In the case of the remaining industries, the final application is to be submitted either along with the capital goods application or at some other suitable point of time when all the relevant final details are available to the applicant. This final application is to be considered by the administrative Ministry concerned before conversion of the 'letter of intent' into an industrial licence.

Recommendation of the Committee After a Year: The Committee has stated that it is important that the actual working of the revised procedures, should be studied over a period of time. Accordingly, the Committee has recommended that it may be reconstituted after a year, with the same composition as far as may be, to study the results of the working of the revised procedures and to make suitable recommendations to Government.

Other General Recommendations

The Committee has also made recommendations regarding:

(i) residual action in cases where letters of intent, licences have already been issued for 'key' industries ;

(ii) form of 'letter of intent';

(iii) issue of import licence for spare parts either received short or in damaged condition and replacement of which is made free of cost either by the supplier or on payment by Insurance Company; and

(iv) procedure, in the case of 'key' industries, for consideration of application for grant of loans by the Industrial Credit and Investment Corporation of India and the Industrial Finance Corporation.

WORKING GROUP ON SMALL SCALE INDUSTRIES, HANDICRAFTS AND SERICULTURE—SUB-GROUP ON SMALL SCALE INDUSTRIES, 1963—REPORT

Delhi, Manager of Publications, 1966. 347p.+vp.

Chairman : Shri K. V. Venkatachalam.

Members : Dr. D. K. Malhotra; Shri A. R. Bhat; Shri N. K. Mukarji (replaced by Dr. S. T. Merani); Shri T. R. V. Chari; Shri L. N. Renu (replaced by Shri P. M. Mathai); Shri K. L. Nanjappa; Shri C.V.R. Panikar (replaced by Shri R. Mahadevan); Dr. S. L. Sharma; Shri P. M. Mathai (replaced by Shri J. C. Verma); Shri B. C. Mathur; Shri H. Nanjundiah; Shri Baldev Kapoor (replaced by Shri G. R. Bhai); Shri Anil De; Shri M. Samiyuddin (replaced by Shri A. B. Malik); Shri B. K. Chatterji; A representative of the Director-General of Employment and Training.

Convenor : Shri S. V. S. Sharma.

APPOINTMENT

A Working Group on Small Scale Industries, Handicrafts and Sericulture was set up by the Ministry of Industry, Government of India (vide Office Memorandum No 22 (3)/63-1cc(i) dated the 20th August, 1963, issued by the Ministry of Industry), for assisting the progress of the Third Plan and for carrying out the ground work for the formulation of projects for the Fourth Plan. At its first meeting held on 11th September, 1963, the Working Group decided to appoint three Sub-groups, one each on Small Scale Industries, Handicrafts and Sericulture to carry out the terms of reference.

TERMS OF REFERENCE

(i) To make a critical review of the progress of the programme and schemes of the Small Scale Industries, Handicrafts and Sericulture in the Third Plan period.

(ii) To assess, in the light of the current trends and other available data, the position likely to be reached at the end of the Third Plan period.

(iii) To formulate proposals for the Fourth Plan in the perspective, wherever possible, of 15 year period, 1966-81.

CONTENTS

Introduction; The Present Position; Approach to Fourth Plan; Development Policy; Spatial Decentralisation Growth Centres; Raw Materials; Industrial Areas; Credit Facilities; Technical Assistance; Training; Marketing; Export Promotion; Government Stores Purchase Programme; Hire Purchase of Machinery; Ancillaries; Industrial Cooperatives; Small Industry Associations; Organisational Arrangements; Financial Outlays and Targets; Summary of Conclusions and Recommendations.

RECOMMENDATIONS

1. The growth of small scale Industries during the last decade is one of the most significant features of planned economic development in the country. Considerable progress has been achieved in expanding the sector, volume of production, employment opportunities created, entrepreneural skills developed, increase in productivity, achievement in industrial dispersal, capital mobilised for industrial purposes, contribution to total industrial production etc.

2. The various types of assistance provided by the CSIO during the First and Second Plan periods resulted in the growth of the small scale industries into something more sophisticated and at the beginning of the III Plan, it was poised to play a much greater and significant role. Articles requiring high degree of technical skill, many of them being previously imported, began to be produced in the small scale sector, and notable progress was made amongst the newly developing industries like plastic and chemicals. With

this, the demand for foreign collaboration also increased.

3. During the Third Plan, in addition to increase and diversification of production, the aim was set for securing closer integration between small scale and large scale units over a wide range of industries and development of small industries as ancillaries.

4. The International Perspective Planning Team recorded in 1963 that (a) with equal access to raw materials there are many lines of industry in which the skill, flexibility, low costs, location advantages, other competitive factors favouring small units assured them of continuing and healthy growth; (b) this growth can and should be achieved without special financial subsidies or concessional benefits; (c) small factories are not confined to consumer goods but already contributed significantly to the manufacture of producers' or investment goods; (d) small manufacturers had shared very closely in the total expansion of factory output in the last decade which had approximated an average rate of 8%; (e) the principal criterion by which the small scale industry is to be judged should be its positive contribution to development.

5. (a) By 1963 nearly 59,000 units were registered by the State Directorates of Industries under the system of voluntary registration of small scale units. As on 31st March, 1965 the figure was 85,000.

(b) The capital invested and production in the small scale sector have been steadily increasing and the rate of growth, particularly in electrical and mechanical engineering lines had been note-worthy.

6. The IPP Team came to the conclusion that small factories, even excluding units not registered under the factories Act, contributed a surprisingly large share of the manufacturing out-put. It has also been recorded that (a) small registered factories have their greatest out-put, employment and investment in the basic necessities of life; food products, grain milling, ginning and pressing of fibres and textile weaving and finishing; (b) metal working and machinery industries are the next most important sector for small registered plants, confirming the well known evidence in their recent growth; (c) the third set of industrial group based mainly on direct conversion of primary resources and centring on construction goods related to tanneries, wood and cork, products of stone, clay, cement and glass etc. (d) the last group consisted of chemical groups, and rubber products, printing, motor vehicles repair etc.

7. (a) The central object of the CSIO's technical, management and development services related to about 16,500 small registered factories (in 1960) employing 6.15 lakh persons with a gross output valued at about Rs. 530 crores.

(b) The number of non-registered non-household small factories potentially under CSIO coverage is between 2 to 2.5 lakhs the number involved being so large, only the most highly promising of these can be given CSIO technical assistance.

8. (a) The total expenditure during the Third Plan is estimated to be Rs. 95.25 crores against Rs. 114.2 crores originally proposed. The State Governments had to reduce allocations for the small scale sector soon after the declaration of the emergency. On an average 40% of the total outlay on small industries was used for block loans in the States. Service schemes and commercial schemes can next in order of amount utilized.

(b) Apart from the fact that the pattern of outlay varies quite substantially between different States, even amongst the States in which small industries schemes have made an appreciable progress, there is no discernible uniform pattern of utilisation of funds on different schemes. A more detailed examination is called for.

(c) The subsidy on supply of power having been restricted to units using less than 20 H.P. has not worked as an effective instrument for developing small industries.

(d) There is need for an evaluation of the physical achievements made by the small scale industries sector in the different states during the Third Plan.

9. (a) During the Third Plan it is estimated that for a total fixed investment of Rs. 240 crores, the employment opportunities created would have been 10 lakhs. (8 lakhs direct and 2 lakhs indirect).

(b) The contribution of small scale factories alone to the total out-put of all factories in the country amounted to 31% (gross) and to 25% (net). This excludes the contribution of the non-factory, non-household sector which is bound to be substantial.

10. A review of the overall position of the small scale sector discloses the following important deficiencies and limitations in the programme:

(a) the change in priorities consequent on the declaration of the emergency has adversely effected small scale sector;

(b) allocations for small industries have been revised downwards and in some cases deferred;

(c) the CSIO programme of assistance does not include the entire range of small sector manufacturing activity. It should be done and the scope for decentralisation of conventional industries on a cooperative basis using improved technology should be explored;

(d) the common production programme has not been pursued in the Third Plan;

(e) no real progress has been made in making arrangements for collection of comprehensive data on the small scale sector;

(f) production capacities and employment potentialities remain significantly unutilised due to shortage of scarce raw materials;

(g) the technical assistance of programme the CSIO should be reviewed so that applied research gets adequate attention;

(h) particular attention should be given to special programmes like export promotion, dispersal of industries, development of ancillaries etc.

11. Greater emphasis should be given to developmental measures whereas proposals which are restrictive in nature are to be worked lightly and reviewed from time to time.

12. Main objectives of the Fourth Plan should be to: (a) promote the coordinated development of large scale and small scale industries (b) decentralise the industrial sector (c) foster development of technical and managerial aspects of small industry and (d) encourage the organisation of cooperatives by small scale entrepreneurs.

13. The CSIO should conduct initial studies in respect of industries proposed for common Production programmes or complete reservation for the small scale sector.

14. (a) By the end of the Fourth Plan the gross output of the small scale registered factories should increase to about Rs. 4,500 crores. The same is estimated at Rs. 2,244 crores by the end of the Third Plan. (Please see Recommendation No. 145.) ;

(b) The additional fixed investment that will be required to achieve the gross output target mentioned at (a) above will be Rs. 425 to 480 crores; Rs. 120 to 130 crores from Government sources, Rs. 225 to 280 crores from private sector and the balance from institutional sources.

15. The fixed investment mentioned in recommendation 14(a) will create employment opportunities for 15 lakhs persons during the Fourth Plan Period—12 lakhs direct and 3 lakhs indirect.

16. It is expected that during the Fourth Plan the number of registered small scale units would nearly double, thus providing opportunities to about 50,000 new entrepreneurs to enter the industrial field.

17. Apart from creating clusters of industrial activity in all towns with a population exceeding 50,000 "growth centres" should be developed in nearly half of the towns and villages with a population exceeding 15,000.

18. The strategy to be adopted in order to obtain the targets set for the Fourth Plan would be (a) consolidation of existing position and fuller utilisation of present capacities, (b) greater emphasis on quick maturing investments with high out-put prospects, (c) provision of adequate quantities of scarce raw materials to small scale industries, obtaining them through special foreign aid, if necessary, (d) enabling small industries to sustain growth in the agricultural sector, (e) modernisation and cooperative sat up of agricultural processing, beverage and food industries, service industries etc. and utilisation of opportunities afforded by newer industries like electronics, petro-chemicals etc., (f) increased demand of consumer goods to be met wherever possible by the small scale sector, (g) coordination of small industries development with other development programmes like technical training, housing, construction, town planning, export promotion, defence etc., (h) foster the growth of particular industries in selected places by discriminating use of subsidies and other forms assistance, (i) special studies to be undertaken to assess the requirements of different categories of machinery and equipment with a view to producing them in the small scale sector, (j) a research programme to enable small scale industries to adopt appropriate technologies (k) vigorous exploitation of the potentialities for the development of ancillaries and utilisation of the Government stores purchase programme as a more effective means of small industry development and (l) intensified provision of the assistance now being provided for industrial designs, prototype production, and improvement of traditional technologies etc. (Please see Recommendation No. 70).

19. Examination of the problem with a view to ensuring adequate and continuing supply of raw material to small scale units which have crossed the limit of Rs. 5 lakhs capital. (Please see Recommendation No. 140).

20. Provision of fixed capital requirements to the increasing number of small industries organised by engineers, technologists etc.

21. The following measures will have to be adopted to reorient the licensing policy for quick growth of the small scale sector:—

(i) the CSIO should be more closely associated with licensing and pre-study of applications;

(ii) licensing for the Fourth Plan should be done only after a realistic estimate of production capacities available in the small scale sector is taken into account;

(iii) over-licensing in the large scale sector should be avoided while fixing targets of production for different industries and the capacity and end-products should be co-related;

(iv) the assembly or fabrication of end-products, wherever possible, should be left to the small scale sector;

(v) licences to large scale units both in the public and the private sector should contain definite requirements regarding the development of anciliaries;

(vi) small scale units should be encouraged to expand and enter the medium scale and large scale sector and wherever possible, while creating additional capacities, preferences should be given to established small units over new units in the large scale sector;

(vii) the CSIO should be associated with DGTD in scrutinising applications for registration under the liberalised procedure whereby units having a fixed capital of less than Rs. 25 lakhs are exempted from the present licensing procedure. An evaluation study of the results of this relaxation should also be undertaken. (Please see Recommendation No. 117).

22. In implementing the common production programme during the Fourth Plan the following should be ensured :—

(a) since the programme has not attained the desired degree of success it should be revised suitably and extended to many more industries;

(b) the targets proposed in the Report for some items may be considered as tentative and should be finalised only after detailed studies are completed ;

(c) though generally speaking, industries in which the economies of mass production and distribution are offset by increased production and marketing costs are suitable for implementing the common production programme, particular industries should be selected only after careful studies are made with reference to the existing capacities in the large scale and small scale sectors;

(d) there should be a careful election of small scale units for participation in the programme with reference to the size, record of production, equipment etc.;

(e) raw materials and components, both imported and indigeneous, should be made available on equal terms to participating units both in the large scale and small scale sectors;

(f) the entire expansion should be reserved for the small scale sector in the case of industries in which the small scale units have demonstrated their capacity by accounting for a major portion of production;

(g) studies should be initiated immediately to determine the industries in which common production programme or exclusive reservation is to be resorted to, (Please see Recommendation No. 114).

23. For the rapid development of ancillary industries.

(a) Licences of large scale units should be endorsed with suitable provisions regarding development of ancillaries;

(b) raw material and other resources should be directly provided to ancillary units;

(c) components and parts should be purchased from small scale units by suppliers to the DGS & D in the large scale sector; (Please see Recommendation No. 116).

(d) close scrutiny of applications for licences in the large scale sector at the State level with a view to determining the parts and components which should be made in the small scale sector;

(e) provision of technical and managerial assistance; and

(f) closer liaison between the DGS & D and CSIO.

24. (a) Agricultural processing industries and service industries including repairing workshops should be brought under the ambit of the programme for development of small industries;

(b) The conventional or processing industries should be developed on a cooperative and decentralised basis ;

(c) In relation to the supply of electric power to a large number of additional villages during the Fourth Plan period, the scope for production of domestic electrical appliances and electrical accessories should be assessed and exploited;

(d) Efforts should be made to utilise opportunities available in the field of packaging industries to develop small industries;

(e) Continuous study of various types of industrial and agricultural wastes and other newer raw material should be undertaken with a view to utilising them for the development of the small scale sector.

(f) A separate cell should be created in the CSIO for undertaking the planning and development work of agro-industries. (Please see Recommendation No. 72).

25. (a) It should be the Government's policy to encourage the development of small scale units in suitable clusters in industrial estates or suitably developed industrial areas;

(b) Apart from providing the infrastructure in industrial estates/industrial areas, the Government should also provide common facilities, quality marking, testing etc., facilities, raw material depots etc ;

(c) Intensive studies should be undertaken to decide cluster of industries suitable to "growth centres"

26. The Government's stores purchase programme should be shaped as a more effective means for the development of small scale industries especially of engineering, chemical and other newer type of industries, for which there should be a policy agreement between the Departments of Industry and Supply.

27. (a) The CSIO should be made responsible for the coordination work in respect of export drive and the NSIC should undertake the actual implementation of the programme;

(b) Cooperative export houses should be started in the States. (Please see Recommendation No. 131).

(c) For units participating in the export work, scarce raw materials should be provided, preferably by opening revolving fund. (Please see Recommendation No. 91) ;

28. Compaigns for contacting local entrepreneurs in the rural and semi-urban areas should be intensified to make the programme of "growth centres" a success. (Please see Recommendation No. 36).

(29) In regard to the supply of raw materials, the following measures should be adopted during the Fourth Plan periods :—

(1) The system of sector-wise allocation raw materials should be discarded ; it should be allotted on the basis of production capacity without reference to the size of the unit.

(2) Special allocation of scarce raw materials should be made to small industries producing essential consumer goods and services, where they do not have their counterparts in the large scale sector.

(3) Detailed studies should be initiated on the impact of the introduction of the price tax system recommended by the Ford Foundation Team in place of the existing allocation system.

(4) The representatives of the small industries should be associated in scrutinising the eligibilities of the individul units for supply of scarce raw materials.

(5) While new entrants requiring scarce raw materials should be subject to a system of "guidance" by the State Directors of Industries, those based or indigeneous and freely available raw materials should continue to be "free" as at present.

(6) Capacities of existing small scale units requiring scarce raw materials should be scientifically and uniformly assessed.

(7) Existing units should be assisted to switch over from low priority to high priority products.

(8) Special imports would be justified if greater employment and higher output is achieved through fuller utilisation of existing capacities.

(9) All the recommendations made by the Lokanathan Committee on Raw Materials are supported.

(30) The question of special legislation to promote the growth of the small scale sector may be deferred for the time being. (Please see Recommendation No. 139)

(31) (a) The present ceiling of Rs. 5 lakhs for defining a small scale unit may continue with the modification that the figure of Rs. 5 lakhs sbould be taken to refer only to plant and machinery (Please see Recommendation No. 140).

(b) Subsidies and other assistances should be programmed in such a way as to encourage the smaller units and those coming up in smaller towns and "growth centres".

(32) A vast programme of decentralised industrial development should be energetically implemented to provide social and economic linkages between rural and urban areas which will minimise the imbalance in the living standards between the two.

(33) Spatial decentralisation should aim at creating clusters of efficient modern small industries at selected "growth centres".

(34) Various types of developmental activities should be assessed, coordinated and concentrated at the "growth centres".

(35) All towns with a population between 15,000 to 50,000 should be selected as "growth centres" and developed as such during the Fourth Plan period.

(36) The programme of development of about 700 "growth centres" during the Fourth Plan will involve (a) identification, techno-economic survey, preparation of blue prints for phased programmes etc., for about 120 centres every year, (b) provision of infra-structure including residential quarters through suitable cooperatives or other organisations to absorb bulk of the population moving into urban areas in the next decade, (c) establishment of training institutes, industriale states, common facilities centres, tool rooms, testing laboratories, raw materials depots etc., (d) intensive compaigns to locate prospective entrepreneurs (e) provision at concessional rate of interest for finance, supply of power at subsidised rates, special price preference, assured raw materials etc., and (f) adequate staff at both the Centre and State level. (Please see Recommendation No. 28).

(37) Surveys with the end products as the basis should be initiated immediately to determine priority and scope for further growth of small industries.

(38) The CSIO should play a more positive role for ensuring liaison between the representatives of small scale sector and allocating Ministries to obtain scarce raw materials in time.

(39) The work relating to the distribution of allocated raw materials should be taken over by State Small Industries Corporation which would be able to bulk the requirements and arrange for import procurement for further distribution. Subsidy may be given to meet the administrative costs of the Corporations for a short period

(40) The inspection procedures of utilisation of allocated raw materials should be stream-lined and made uniform. The number and level of inspectors should be increased and annual inspection of all small scale units requiring scarce raw materials should be conducted.

(41) The scope for substitution of scarce raw materials should be carefully explored in collaboration with concerned National Laboratories and Small Industries Associations.

(42) According to the present estimates the due share of the small scale sector for steel would be 40 % of all categories of steel supplied for industrial purposes or 25% of finished steel (total 3 million tonnes p. a. by 1970-71) produced in the country.

(43) The small scale sector would require foreign exchange allocation to the time of Rs. 20 crores p. a. for import of steel in the last year of the Fourth Plan.

(44) Non-ferrous metals to the value of Rs. 20

crores p.a. would be required (by the small scale sector) in the last year of the Fourth Plan (40 to 50 thousand tonnes of copper and 32 to 35 thousand tonnes of zinc).

(45) The availability of aluminium to the small scale sector should immediately be increased to at least 40 thousand tonnes p.a.

(46) The value of imported components/spare parts for the small scale sector in the last year of the Fourth Plan would be about Rs. 35 crores.

(47) Foreign exchange to the extent of Rs. 5 crores will be required for import of other scarce raw materials (specially chemical items) by the last year of the Fourth Plan. The total foreign exchange requirements in the last year of the Fourth Plan for imported raw materials would accordingly be Rs. 80 crores.

(48) (1) Even in the case of urban industrial estates where chances of success are greater, a more intensive planning and promotional effort is required.

(2) In the case of estimates in semi-urban and rural areas, a coordinated approach through integrated planning is necessary to provide other facilities like residential areas, educational facilities etc. besides the infra-structure to overcome locational disadvantages.

(49) Unless more intensive planning and promotional activities are undertaken by State authorities in consultation with local small Industries Service Institutes, the programme of industrial estates in semi urban and rural areas is not likely to succeed.

(50) During the Fourth Plan efforts should be made to set up an industrial estate (if it is not already there) in each of the towns with a population over 50,000 and in half of the towns with a population between 15,000 to 50,000. This would mean setting up of 700 industrial estates of varying sizes of which 112 will be urban estates and the rest at "growth centres."

(51) All urban estates should be established on the cooperative pattern unless special circumstances exist at a particular place for a Government industrial estate of the conventional type.

(52) Industrial estates organised in the "growth centres" should also be on the cooperatives lines if conditions are favourable.

(53) In future, industrial estates-areas should be let out on lease-hold terms to entrepreneurs and the rental part of terms reviewed every 5 year, the upward revision being subject to a ceiling of about 50% after every review. A concession in the ground rent may be allowed during the first 5 years of the existence of industrial estates in semi urban and rural areas.

(54) As a matter of policy the State/Central Government should establish common facilities centres, quality marking centres, raw material depots, technical information centres etc., in all cooperative industrial estates, which may also be financially assisted in the construction of service buildings.

(55) Conventional industrial estates may be constructed at "Growth centres", providing all facilities, in consultation with prospective occupiers.

(56) Adequate concessions and incentives should be provided to those willing to develop the smaller towns and "growth centres".

(57) While the general policy should be to encourage establishment of cooperative company type of estates, those in the urban areas (except cooperative estates) should be taken over by State Small Industries Corporation. Estates in the "growth centres" may continue to be administered by the State Directorates of the Industries.

(58) In all public sector projects there should be provision for establishment of ancillary estates. Private sector undertakings may also be encouraged to set up ancillary estates by providing loans to the extent of 50% of the cost of such estates.

(59) The following measures may be adopted for providing long term finance :

(a) In order to achieve institutionalisation of finance all loans under the State Aid to Industries Act/Rules exceeding Rs. 5,000 should be routed through State Financial Corporations. The responsibility of providing the entire finance to all the units in the urban areas should be that of the State Financial Corporations and other institutions.

(b) State Financial Corporations should be encouraged to lend out of their own resources at least twice as much as they lend under the agency arrangement ; guaranteeing of such loans should continue.

(c) Possibilities of the LIC and Industrial Development Bank of India contributing to the resources of State Financial Corporations should be explored.

(d) State Financial Corporations should reorientate their attitude and cultivate a "development outlook" towards the small scale sector.

(e) State Financial Corporations may constitute wherever possible their own "technical wings" ; in the alternative, they should make firm arrangements with SISIs to provide technical assistance, if necessary, on payment.

(f) The Reserve Bank of India in consultation with State Financial Corporations should undertake a study of the financial requirements of small scale units organised by technicians-managers and if found necessary take active steps to set up financing institutions for the purpose.

(g) While the rate of interest charged to the industrial cooperatives may continue to be 2-1/2%, a concessional rate of 3% should be given to small scale units situated at "growth centres". Commercial rate of interest may be charged for all other loans granted either by the State Directors of Industries or by SFC's.

(h) As a matter of policy larger amounts should be earmarked for block loans.

(i) It is preferable to give loans at concessional rate of interest even to technicians and others ; however in case of state participation in equity capital it should be done through the SFCs or other institutions and the participation should not exceed 50% of the total equity capital.

(60) In respect of short term finance the following measures should be adopted :

(a) The entire working capital requirements (over and above 20% approximately brought in by entrepreneurs themselves) should be met as for as possible by financing institutions.

(b) State Bank should invariably establish a branch at each "growth centre".

(c) Nominal fee may be charged by the CSIO for providing technical assistance to the State Bank and other Commercial Banks. Wherever feasible the State Bank may establish its own "technical wing".

(d) The State Bank should treat all branches as intensive centres and review the effectiveness of the working groups.

(e) The working groups should ensure that all units which have a bank account get finance to the full extent from the banks.

(f) Intensive efforts should be made to provide the smaller of the small scale units with working capital loans.

(g) As a special inducement to participate more fully in the credit guarantee scheme, the rate of fees may be reduced by 50% to all those banks which get all their loans to small scale units covered under the scheme.

61. During the Fourth Plan the quantum of both long term and short term institutional finance would be (a) Rs. 30 crores for loans under State Aid to Industries Act/Rules, (b) Rs. 50 crores as loans from State Financial Corporations/other institutions and (c) Rs. 600 to 700 crores in the last year of the Fourth Plan as working capital limits, half of which may have to be provided by the State Bank of India.

62. In the metropolitan and urban areas, all services and technical assistance to various types of industries should be pooled together at centres which will take the shape of branch institutes. During the Fourth Plan 50 to 60 such integrated training centres should function as branch institutes all over the country. Existing centres might be recognised/shifted handed over to respective State Governments to achieve the above objective.

63. Full fledged branch institutes should be established in Union Territories and smaller States (Himachal Pradesh, Manipur, Tripura, Nagaland, Pandicherry) and at suitable places in some of the bigger and underdeveloped States like Madhya Pradesh, Rajasthan, Bihar etc.

64. A well equipped central cell should be established to conduct systematic study and research of the numerous technical problems to rectify the lacuna of the absence of the applied research in the existing pattern of Industrial Extension Service.

65. The establishment of a technological information and documentation centre may be taken up as part of advance action fort the Fourth Five Year Plan.

66. Recruitment and training of additional technical managerial and economic staff (approximately 50% of the existing strength) should be taken up in a phased manner in order to meet the emerging situation during the Fourth Plan.

67. Suitable arrangements should be made to awail the services of consultants whose honorarium might be shared by the Government and beneficiaries.

68. The reorganised extension centres should be in a position to provide management consultancy services for which a nominal fee might be charged.

69. The practice of SISI Extension Centres providing technical assistance to State Bank of India may be extended to cover all other banks which offer to assist small industries on similar terms.

70. As a measure of evolving "appropriate teahnologies" the SISIs should encourage development of proto types of new machines which can be used in semi-urban and rural areas by resourceful entrepreneurs. (Please see Recommendation No. 18).

71. The proposal for the establishment of an institute for "appropriate technologies" in the CSIO together with a coordinating committee to guide its activities should be undertaken as part of advance action for the Fourth Five Year Plan.

72. Planning and Statistical cells should be established in the CSIO and in the different State Directorates of Industries which among other duties will hasten the process of import substitution, develop ancillaries, conduct surveys and select suitable location fof growth points and industrial estates, analyse production data, publish directory of small scale industries etc., (Please see Recomendation No. 24 (f)].

73. The compaigns to stimulate local entrepreneurship and bring aut local capital should be revived and conducted in large numbers so that by the end of the Fouth Plan almost all the districts of the country would be covered.

74. The Planning and Statistical cell (proposed vide Recommendation No. 62) at the CSIO should have a machine tabulation unit to process the data, collection of which should be improved by implementing suggestions such as (a) the ASI census sector should be gradually extended to cover all registered factories

(b) the non-household, non-factory sector should be covered by an annual sample survey, and (c) operational data collected by State Directorates should be systematically tabulated and analysed at the State level and coordinated by the CSIO for under taking all India analysis.

75. The publication work undertaken by the CSIO should be improved and augmented; the Bulletin of Small Industries should be made a priced monthly publication both in English and in Hindi. Model schemes, techincal bulletins etc. are also to be improved.

76. Services rendered by the Industrial Extension Service may be changed a nominal fee; to start with it may be done in metropolitan and urban areas, later on to be extended to other areas.

77. (a) While the present technical training programme should be continued more intensively to up grade the skills of small industry workers who had no opportunity to acquire formal industrial training, courses of an advanced nature should also be conducted.

(b) The CSIO should concentrate more on advanced traninig at its institutes.

(c) Suitable training programmes for supervisors/ Foremen/Chargemen etc., working in small scale units should be drawn up.

(d) The CSIO should take the responsibility as a coordinating agency in respect of training programmes being implemented in the common facility service schemes by the State Governments and at the rural workshops of the Ministry of Community Development.

(e) Officers who are functioning as trainers in the various technical trades should themselves be adequately trained and suitably equipped.

(f) Suitable arrangements should be made to provide training while the artisans continue to work.

(g) Management training should be made practice-oriented.

(h) The cooperation of small industrial association should be enlisted to put in practice what is taught at the appreciation courses and specialised courses in management.

(i) "Open House" method of discussion should be fully exploited.

(j) Trainers (technial and management) should be deputed to large scale units to study the methods and practices obtaining there.

(k) Personnel of Industrial Extension Service should be encouraged to participale in seminars and training courses in their respective trades within the country and abroad.

78. The SIETI should be enable to undertake research programmes and expanded in such a way as to provide training for 3 to 4 hundred persons at a time.

79. (a) The training given at the Prototype Production and Training Centres should cater to the needs of small industrialists rather than work as post-ITI training centres.

(b) More intensive work will have to be done on the production of prototypes of machines which are now largely imported and the work relating to adaptation of modern machines to suit the conditions within the country should continue.

(c) Each Prototype centre should have a joint committee consisting of representatives of CSIO, State Directors of Industries and NSIC to guide prototype development and research programme and maintain closer liaison between the field units.

(d) PTCs may undertake mass production of developed prototypes, only when private entrepreneurs are not forthcoming to do it.

(e) During the Fourth Plan six more Prototype Production Centres should be established—both general and for specialised industries.

80. Marketing assistance through indirect channels should be continued and intensified. State Governments should also subsidise the participation of small industrialists, through their associations, in industrial exhibitions in the country. The NSIC should similarly participate in International exhibitions.

81. Directories of small industries being published by the State Governments and FASII at the national level should be improved and the periodicity increased.

82. (a) The quality marking system should be extended to cover all products intended for export, all producer goods and sophisticated consumer goods.

(b) The CSIO should coordinate and ensure uniformity in standards of the quality marking sceme implemented by different states; close working relations should also be established between the Indian Standards Institution and the quality making centres.

(c) The CSIO should arrange for the drawing up of suitable standards, where ISI-standards are not available; reasonable substandards may also be provided, if necessary.

(d) Sampling percentage for quality marking testing should be laid doun by the CSIO for the guidance of the States.

(e) The State Governments may be allowed to charge a nominal fee for the quality marking service rendered.

(f) Small scale units should be enconraged to become members of the ISI and get the ISI mark. The ISI in turn should constitute a separate small industry wing to study the problems of standardisation in small scale industries.

83. Bulletins on marketing information should be published by the Small Industries Corporations.

84. The hire-purchase scheme of the NSIC should be utilised to encourage the manufacture and supply of

machinery by small scale units.

85. "Trade Centres" on the lines organised by prefactures in Japan should be organised by State Governments through State Small Industries Corporations and in cooperation with State Small Scale Industries Associations.

86. A separate Export Promotion Division should be created in the CSIO with a full time Director-in-charge of it. Full-time Export Promotion Officers, should also be appointed in each State Directorate of Industries and SISI.

87. Export Associations of small industrialists should be established in each State with in the next 2 years. Where possible, the associations might be started on a products basis also. Suitable financial assistance should be provided by the Government.

88. Export Promotion Division (as proposed in Recommendation No. 86) should function as the central clearing house for export marketing information apart from conducting studies, rendering service after sales etc.

89. Delegations of small industrialists should be encouraged to visit foreign countries which offer potential for export.

90. Annual target should be set for important items of exports.

91. An immediate beginning should be made to provide raw materials to the State Depots to be kept on 'imprest' basis for issue to exporters. [Please see Recommendation No. 27 (c)].

92. Functional industrial estates should be specially organised for items which have export patential.

93. The Industrial Design Cell should be further strengthened to pay special attention to designs of products.

94. Establishment of cooperative societies of small industrialists should be encouraged to provide export services.

95. Small industrialists should be given representation in the Export Promotion Councils though their Associations, and as an incentive may be allowed to pay reduced fees.

96. The special scheme with liberalised term for providing export credit to small industrialists drawn by the State Bank of India may be finalised soon and circulated to all other commercial banks for adoption.

97. The CSIO should work in close coordination with State Trading Corporation for increasing exports of small scale sector products.

98. (a) A technical review of the list of items purchased by the DGS & D should be undertaken so that capable small scale engineering and chemical units might be encouraged to quote for those items. The review should also lead to additions to the list of Group (4) items. By the end of the Fourth Plan this list should contain at least 150 items. (Please see recommendation No. 16 also).

(b) The aim should be to ensure that by the end of the Fourth Five Year Plan small scale units supply at least 50 per cent of the DGS & D purchases in Group (3) items.

(c) The DGS & D should evolve a procedure whereby tenderers for Group (2) items who agree to sub-contract to small scale units enlisted with the NSIC, get some special preference.

(d) State Directorates should nominate an officer to specially look after the stores purchase programme of the DGS & D.

(e) By the end of the Fourth Plan the aim should be to enroll 50,000 units for participation in the above programme.

(f) State Directorates of Industries and SISIs should maintain and suitably index details of the enlisted units.

(g) The DGS & D should recognise more test houses and laboratories.

(h) Test houses proposed to be set up by the Ministry of Commerce should be recognised by the DGS & D as their testing agency. Similar recognition may also be given to SISIs and Extension Centres where facilities exist.

(i) DGS & D should clearly indicate to those small scale industries who are registered with them directly that such registration will not carry any special treatment.

(j) Libraries of specifications and museums of items regularly bought by the DGS & D should be established at all important centres (50 to 60 during the Fourth Plan).

(k) Apart from giving a special price preference of 50 per cent to units located in growth points, the DGS & D should also undertake final inspection of then products at the factory itself and arrange for its transport at Government's expense.

99. The CSIO should arrange to ensure that in course of time small scale units become regular suppliers of defence needs.

100. A separate Directorate should be created in the CSIO with a full time Director-incharge to look after the entire work regarding participation of small scale industries in Govenment stores purchase programme.

101. State Governments should formulate schemes (on the lines of the scheme operated by the NSIC) and issue instructions to all purchasing Departments, regarding Government stores purchase.

102. The NSIC guarantee scheme in respect of Government contracts currently implemented by the

State Bank of India should be operated by other commercial banks also.

103. DGS & D should make special arrangements to release raw materials to small scale units as soon as Government contracts are awarded to them.

104. The NSIC should concentrate on semi-urban and rural areas in implementing the scheme of hire purchase of machinery for which the following priorities may be adopted :

(a) Applications from units established or proposed to be established at growth centres or other smaller areas—first priority.

(b) Applications from units established or proposed to be established in towns with a population below 1 lakh—second priority.

(c) Applications from all other towns excepting the 11 big cities—third priority.

(d) Applications from units in those 11 cities—last priority.

105. Concessional rates of intrest and service charges should also be allowed on the same priorities as given in Recommendation 104.

For this purpose a suitable schedule of rates will have to be worked out by the NSIC.

106. For units in urban and metropolitan areas it should be possible for the State Bank and other commercial banks to advance loans on instalment credit system for the purchase of machinery.

107. (a) Popular machine tools should be indigenously manufactured by the NSIC through its Prototype Production Centres.

(b) Arrangements should also be made for the regular supply of machine tools on a priority basis with parties like HMT.

108. There is enough room for both the NSIC and State Small Industries Corporations to operate in the field of hire purchase of indigenous machinery. The former might establish a branch in each State for this purpose.

109. The loans advanced to NSIC should be treated as long term loans so that it might be constituted as a 'revolving' fund.

110. The NSIC should continue to encourage applications for balancing equipment, modernisation, replacement of machinery and applications for smaller values.

111. (a) Services of State Directors of Industries, Small Industries Service Institutes, Small Industries Associations etc. should be pressed for collecting dues.

(b) Possibilities of obtaining PL 480 funds should be explored for operating the hire purchase scheme.

112. Keeping in view the instalment credit system operated by Banks and the proposed revolving fund at the disposal of the NSIC a provision of Rs. 35 crores would be necessary to operate the programme of hire purchase of machinery during the Fourth Plan period (Rs. 25 crores as Rupee provision of which 10 crores should be in the form of free foreign exchange ; and Rs. 10 crores of foreign exchange from AID sources).

113. A sum of Rs. 5 crores of free foreign exchange should also be provided for direct import of machines by small scale industrialists.

114. Special surveys should be undertaken to study the extent of the activities and the problems faced by small units supplying parts/components to large units and public sector undertakings [Please see Recommendation No. 22 (g)].

115. In view of the fact that it would be their own interest for large scale units to resort to procurement of parts/components from small scale units, the Federation of Indian Chambers of Commerce and Industry and similar other associations should take special steps to foster this ancillary relationship between their member firms and small scale units.

116. Raw materials should be supplied directly to small scale ancillary units on a priority basis and suitable deductions made in the entitlements of corresponding large scale units. [Please see Recommendation No. 23 (c)].

117. (a) The representatives of the CSIO should be associated with the licensing of large scale units so as to ensure the secrutiny of applications from the ancillary point of view. Such components/parts which could be made in the small scale sector should not be licensed and it should be the responsibility of the large scale units to locate ancillaries. (Please see Recommendation No. 21).

(b) List of standard parts/components that could be made in ancillary units prepared by the CSIO should be widely publicised and copies provided to all Government Departments, DGTD, members of the Licensing Committee, etc.

118. (a) The agreed list of items to be farmed out to ancillaries made by the CSIO in consultation with DGTD should be considered by the Licensing Committee for suitable endorsement in the licence.

(b) A copy of the application for licence should also be endorsed to the Director, SISI of the concerned State to enable him to examine it from the point of view of ancillaries which will be placed before the Licensing Committee.

119. (a) The DGTD should publish a quarterly bulletin with a view to stimulating the ancillary relationship between large scale and small scale units.

(b) Preference should be given for tenderers of Group II Items who will sub-contract to small scale units and develop ancillaries ; periodical evaluation of the use made of ancillaries should also be undertaken.

120. Ancillary units housed in industrial estates established by private sector undertakings should be free to supply to the replacement market and also other large scale buyers. They should also have an option to produce parts other than those required by the concerned large scale units.

121. (a) The C.S.I.O. should be associated in the preparation of project reports for public sector undertakings for indicating the possibilities of establishing ancillary industrial estates.

(b) At least 50 per centof the cost of the ancillary estate may be given to the project company as a long term loan. Alternatively traditional or cooperative industrial estates may be established in the vicinity of the project.

122. (a) Regional Committees of the Standing Committee on Ancillary should be established in all States.

(b) The Standing Committee on Ancillary should be further strengthened with the addition of representatives of small scale industries and the regional committees should co-op. representatives.

123 Industrial cooperatives in the small scale sector is largely confined to industries of simple nature ; the progress in the more sophisticated types, like engineering industries, chemical industries, metal working and machine tool industries etc. has been slow.

124. A distinction should be made in assistance provided to the worker's or artisans' societies on the one side and the entrepreneurs societies on the other.

125. The recommendations made by the Second Working Group on Industrial Cooperative are endorsed and the idea that the small scale entrepreneurs could be brought togetner into industrial cooperatives even if the workers in those units are not made members of the society should be given a fair trial.

126. (a) Promotional and developmental measures in the field of industrial cooperatives should be intensified for which (a) The Director of Industries should be made responsible for this work who should be assisted by a Joint Director who has experience in cooperative work. Where the Registrar is himself responsible for promotional activities he should be assisted by a Joint Registrar who has industrial experience. In either case, the officer should be exclusively earmarked for this work.

(b) Standing Committee on Industrial Cooperatives should be constituted in each State.

(c) An officer of the rank of a Deputy Director should be earmarked to coordinate work for development of industrial cooperatives in all the SISIs ; technical, managerial and other assistance should also be provided.

(d) Case studies of successful industrial cooperatives snould be undertaken and results widely published.

127. Efforts should be made to organise cooperative societies in sophisticated industries ; development of ancillaries on a cooperative basis should be encouraged and industrial estates in all urban areas should be started on a cooperative basis.

1.8. The element of subsidy in the pattern of assistance should as far as possible be eliminated except in the case of societies formed by artisans/workers.

129. Cooperative assembling units should be organised on the lines of functional industrial estates. Members should be free to work then individual enterprise in certain spheres while coming together to cooperate with each other in certain other spheres ; such cooperation would be mutually beneficial.

130. The recommendation of the Japanese Delegation on small scale industries that common service facilities should be organised on a cooperative basis should be accepted and implemented. Existing common facilities centres should be handed over to industrial cooperatives.

131. Export houses should be started in each state on cooperative basis and packing units and forwarding services etc. can also be provided by entrepreneurs themselves on similar lines. [Plase see Recommendation No. 27 (b).]

132. (a) Officers of the State Directorates of Industries, Smrll Industries Service Institutes etc. should be trained specifically in industrial cooperation.

(b) Intensive training should be given to managers and supervisors of industrial cooperatives in industrial management.

133. Industrial cooperatives should be made self-supporting institutions by gradually reducing grants and subsidies.

134. (a) The Federation of Associations of Small Industries of India and the local Associations should devote more attention to improving the working efficiency of their member units.

(b) Marketing research and statistical sections should be set up in the Federation and local Associations to study and advise on problems of growth of small scale industries.

135. Federation of Associations of Small Industries of India should take up among others, functions mentioned below :

(i) Popularise modern management practices amongst small industrialists.

(ii) Cooperative with CSIO in conducting productivity studies—for this purpose a separate productivity section may be added within the Federation.

(iii) Induce its members to adopt modern methods of book-keeping, cost accounting, etc.

(iv) Train permanent staff in the working of such Associations abroad.

(v) Strengthen the public relations section and enhance its role as an interpreter of the Policy of the Government on one side and of the problems of small industrialists on the other.

(vi) Bring out annually the hand-book and directory on small industries.

136. The Government should assist the Federation financially for continaing its present activities and for taking up additional activities mentioned in Recommendation No. 125.

137. Establishment of Management Associations should be encouraged by the Federation to focus the attention of members on the scope for improving efficiency and reducing cost by adopting better management practices.

138. Selected small industries associations in the metropolitan areas should be encouraged to run extension centres, common facility centres etc. on a cooperative basis.

139. In the matter of legislation to govern the development of small industries, the greatest advantage would seem to lie in leaving matters as they are, at least for the time being. (Please see Recommendation No. 30).

140. The definition of the small scale unit should be revised that the Rs. 5 lakhs limit of capital should be deemed to include only plant and machinery (at original price as now reckoned). [Please see Recommendation No. 19 and 31 (a)].

141. Special concessions in the matter of technical assistance, hire purchase of machinery etc. should be given to small scale units with an investment of less than Rs. 50,000 in plant and machinery and to those located in areas with a population of 50,000.

142. The efforts of the CSIO and the State Directorates should be more and more combined and coordinated especially in programmes like financial assistance, participation in Government stores purchase programme, industrial estates etc.

143. (a) In the long run, it may be advantageous to make the NSIC a purely commercial undertaking.

(b) The NSIC, as an experimental measure, might finance small scale units by participating in their share capital.

144. (a) The management of conventional industrial estates in urban areas and departmentally run production units should be transferred gradually to the SSI Corporations.

(b) The raw material depots established by the SSI Corporations should be recognised as registered/controlled stockists for distribution of steel and as agents of the State Directorates for distribution of steel and of other scarce raw materials, imported parts/components, basic raw materials/intermediates etc.

(c) A provision of Rs. 3 crores should be made to strengthen the capital base of SSI Corporations.

(d) State Governments may guarantee loans advanced by the State Bank of India to the SSI Corporations.

(e) The flow of raw materials to small scale units should be systematised and rationlised so as to minimise leakages into the open market and stabilise prices.

(f) State Governments should provide the SSI Corporations with sufficient finance to undertake hire purchase of machinery, particularly indigenous machinery.

145. In the last year of the Fourth Five Year Plan the small scale sector in expected to achieve a gross output of about Rs. 4,500 crores. (Please see Recommendation No. 14).

146. The doubling to the present gross output will therefore mean an additional net output of about Rs. 500 to 600 crores in this sector during the last year of the plan.

147. A fixed investment of the order of Rs. 425 to 480 crores will be required to attain the targets mentioned in recommendation No. 145 and 146.

148. The estimated total Government outlay will be about Rs. 195 to 210 crores for the Fourth Five Year Plan for the development of small scale industries State Government 90 crores, Central Schemes 60 crores, Industrial Estates 45 to 60 crores.

149. A sum of Rs. 75 crores (approximately is expected to be provided to small scale industries for obtaining fixed assets by :

(a) State Financial Corporations and similar other institutions : Rs. 50 crores ;

(b) State Bank of India under its medium term loan instalment credit system : Rs. 10 to 15 crores ; and

(c) LIC for industrial estates : Rs. 19 crores.

150. Foreign exchange to the tune of Rs. 107 crores (approximately) will be required during the Fourth Plan —Rs. 27 crores for capital goods and Rs. 80 crores for raw materials.

THIRD REVIEWING COMMITTEE OF THE COUNCIL OF SCIENTIFIC AND INDUSTRIAL RESEARCH, 1963—REPORT

New Delhi, Council of Scientific And Industrial Research, 1964. 96p.

Chairman : Sir A. Ramaswami Mudaliar.
Members ; Shri K. T, Chandy; Sir Patrick Linstead; Dr. S. Dhawan; Sir Charles F. Goodeve Prof. P. C. Mahalanobis; Dr. S. N. Sen Gupta; Dr. D. S. Kothari (discontinued after attending the first meeting on November 4, 1963).
Secretary : Shri Baldev Singh.

APPOINTMENT

The Third Reviewing Commitee was appointed in November, 1963 by the Prime Minister in his capacity as President of the Council of Scientific and Industrial Research.

TERMS OF REFERANCE

To review the work and progress of the Council of Scientific & Industrial Research and to recommend the lines on which the activities should be directed in the national perspective

CONTENTS

Part I Introduction; History and Brief Description of CSIR; Technology and the Problem of India: Evidence and Comments; Part II—General Principles; Laboratories of the Council—Central Institutes; Regional Research Laboratories and Field Stations; User 'Participation—Research Associations; The Headquarters and Technical Services; Governing Body, Executive Councils and Scientific Committees ; Part III—Staff; Links with universities; Bridging the Gap; Operational Research (O.R.); Future Development of CSIR Activities; Part IV-Summary and Principal Recommendations ;

RECOMMENDATIONS

The Flexibility in Functions of the CSIR

It is recommended that the CSIR maintains its present flexibility in function to enable it to discharge its wide responsibilities for initiating or supporting research in fields where gap exist. At the same time it should invite other government departments to take over partial or complete responsibility for fields with which they are concerned.

Relations with other Departments

It is recommended that machinery be set up and strengthened by the CSIR for its collaboration with the Planning Commission, Ministry of Industry, the Director General of Technical Development and other agencies responsible for the collection of essential information and action in respect of the nation's economy, with the object of ensuring that national plans and problems become the basis for the programmes of its research establishments.

Relations with other Research Organisations

Machinery should also be set up for inter-communication and exchange with other research organisations and technical agencies of the Government, in particular, those associated with the Agriculture, Medicine, Defence, Railways, Posts and Telegraphs, and the Atomic Energy.

Expenditure on Research

If India is to make headway as a developing country its research effort in terms of quantity, quality and effectiveness will have to be increased manifold and limited only by the availability of trained personnel and resources.

It is recommended that CSIR's part in the Fourth Plan should be implemented to the full and extended where fresh needs arise.

Governing Body of CSIR

The Governing Body is the supreme body of the Council responsible for its broad policy and external relations.

It is recommended that this body should be a compact one, to strength of which could be reduced from its present number without sacrificing the representation on it of the principal organisations. Consideration to introducing some fresh members should be given at the time of its reconstitution.

Board Of Scientific And Industrial Research

The Board should continue to assist the Governing Body and to concern itself with the programme of the CSIR and those of its institutes.

It is recommended that its strength should be limited to 20-25 and consideration should be given to introducing some fresh members at the time of its recommendation. It is also recommended that the Board should set up a limited number of specialist committees to advise on those aspects which would require more detailed consideration than the Board will haue time to give.

Councils Of The National Laboratories And Institutes Of The CSIR

It is recommended that each of these Councils should be limited to a membership of 12-15. Each Council should be assisted by 'panels of experts' in the formulation of research programmes. It is also recommended that the present policy of decentralising administration and giving of more powers to the Councils and the Directors should be further extended, with the headquarters maintaining an effective contact and ensuring that the policies of CSIR are carried out.

Research Programmes

The programmes of the laboratories of the CSIR should be mainly concerned with applied research and its related basic research. They should be framed in the context of the country's plans for industrial and economic development. The programme should be made up of well defined projects with clear objectives and the applied research projects should be time-targeted and normally not extended beyond a period of three to five years.

Posts Of Directors

Posts of Directors should be filled as expeditiously as possible to ensure the proper functioning of the research organisations and temporary appointments should be avoided as far as possible. Where, however, the Selection Committee feels unable to make a permanent appointment of a Director with complete confidence, it could be the appointment on contract or for a probationary period. It is recommended that in or either case this period should not exceed one at the most two years before confirmation or termination.

Posts Of Other Scientific Personnal

It is recommended that the administrative routine for recruitment to posts upto that of Scientists Grade 'E' (Rs. 1300-1600) should be handled by the Laboratories in accordance with standards laid down by Headquarters and appointments made by compentant authority according to rules therefore.

Location Of Research Institutes

It is also recommended that the following principles should operate in the siting of Institutes: Industry oriented laboratories should be located in an area containing a concentration of the industry but should avoid crowded parts of cities. An important consideration should be the availability of sufficient area for its future growth and accommodation of field stations of other laboratories and auxiliary institutes. On the other hand, out of the way places without social amenities and supporting engineering services should also be avided. Proximity to a university should play a part in the siting of a discipline-oriented or a regional laboratory. Where more than one institute or field station is to be located in the same city they should as far as possible be in the same campus and share common services as far as possible.

Regional Research Laboratories

It is recommended that a careful analysis of various aspects including finances and availability of personnel should precede the setting up of Regional Research Laboratories. Such should be multi-purpose in character, but at the same time should specialise in one or two fields depending on the nature of the problems in the area of their location.

Field Stations

It is recommended that the CSIR encourage its laboratories to set up a certain number of field stations preferably where these are supported by the concerned local industry and that common services are used as in recommendation.

Research Associations

Research carried out as a partnership between industry and government has proved to be a highly efficient mechanism for the selection of problems and for the application of results. This machanism permits a ready and effective means of decentralising responsibility, while at the same time permitting coordination. It is recommended that this should be extended. It is also recommended that existing research associations should look upon the inclusion of routine testing and quality control as a temporary function which should be handed over as early as possible to individual companies.

National Chemical Laboratory, Poona

The balance between fundamental and applied work which at present is about 50/50 should be altered nearer to 20/80 and the fundamental work should become mainly related to the applied projects or for the development of expertise in general chemical knowledge and techniques. The Laboratory should concentrate its research effort on selected protects in fields, such as organic intermediates, high polymers, fermentation chemicals, in organic chemicals, dye-stuffs and textile auxiliaries, catalysts and chemical engineering and pilot plant techniques. The number Ph.D. students and fellowships should be progressively reduced until it is not more than one-tenth of the permanent scientific staff.

National Physical Laboratory, New Delhi

The Primary emphasis should be on applied work, including standards and testing. On particular importance are the fields of radio components, radio propagation, electronics, ceramics, acoustics, optics, time measurement and applied mechanics, and in each of these fields objective basic work should form a substantial part. It is important that the Laboratory should build up an esprit de corps only possible in a well led single unit and it should not be divided into two wings with a separation of fundamental work from the applied.

National Metallurgical Laboratory, Jamshedpur

Research in the field on non-ferrous metallurgy should be increased in collaboration with the industry. The design facilities to enable the laboratory to act as consultants help to partly fill a gap in the application of research results and the these should be extended.

Central Fuel Research Institute, Jealgora

It is recommended that the objective basic research at this establishment should be increased in order to sustain its important applied research. The whole of such fundamental work should continue at Jealgora and not be separated. The coal survey stations should be organisationally separated from the Institute while retaining communication links.

Central Glass And Ceramic Research Institute, Calcutta

The four industries related to the four divisions of this Institute should be brought into even more active participation in the work and share in the finances, Advisory panels from industry should be set up for these four divisions.

Indian Institute Of Biochemistry And Experimental Medicine, Calcutta

The shifting of the Institute from its present congested locational Yadavpur may be carried out in due course.

Central Electrochemical Research Institute, Karaikudi

This institute should be transferred from its present isolated location to Madras as soon as possible.

Headquarters

The role of headquarters is broadly the formulation of policy, the coordination of research, and the provision of central technical services with the objects of supporting the country's planned development.

It is recommended that the Headquarters should divest itself of responsibility for routine administration of its establishment and retain only such functions as may be consistent with the above role.

Technical Service Units At Headquarters

In view of the importance of these services, it is recommended that they should be strengthened and expanded with special reference to the following points.

Coordination Units should be organised for contact and exchange of information with ministries and research organisations in Agriculture, Health, Railways, Posts and Telegraphs, etc. The Defence Coordination Unit should add to its responsibilities the encouragement of civil utilisation of results arising out of defence research. The Central Design and Engineering Unit should grow into a full-scale organisation for the design, engineering, erection and commissioning of pilot plants and industrial plants in order to assist the industry to bridge the gap between research and application. It should include technical and economic evaluation among its functions. Existing scientific and learned societies should be encouraged and financially supported to enable them to raise the standard of their publications. The servicing activities of the Indian National Scientific Documentation Centre should be extended and their costs should be reduced, Publications activity of this centre should be examined in the light of abstracts and documentation services available from agencies abroad.

Links With Universities

Support to the Universities by the CSIR is an act of enlightened self-interest and it is recommended that the CSIR continues to increase this support as fast as possible and in collaboration with the university Grants Commission. In particular it should support schemes for 'Institutes for Advanced Studies' through providing funds for equipment, the creation of professorships, etc. The Maintenance Grants and Fellowships Scheme have already achieved excellent results, but the number of such grants should be increased to keep pace with the demand for skilled manpower.

Industrial Participation In Research And Development

The greatest weakness in the present organisation is the lack of association of industry in taking a share of the responsibility for Government supported research and it is recommended that every possible step be taken to effect an improvement here. The research association mechanism is an excellent one for achieving this, but positive help is required to overcome the initial problems in starting such additional associations. Alternative or intermediate forms of cooperation with industry should be explored.

User Government Departments

Much of the work of some of the Institutes, such as food, building, road and public health engineering, is essential to the progress of the fields which are the responsibility of other government departments. Such departments should take a greater part in the supervision of such research and to underline this responsibility should provide part of the finances. Each such government department should have a special unit of its own staff charged with responsibility of the application of results of research.

National Research Development Corporation Of India

It appears to be the general opinion that this organisation has not been able to match the country's need and should be reorganised and substantially strengthened. Although it may remain a separate entity, it is recommended that for operational purposes, it should function under the control and direction of the Director-General of CSIR.

Operational Research

It is recommended that the development of Operational Research be given a high priority in the plans of the Council and the CSIR focus its first efforts on certain establishments.

Population Control

It is recommended that the CSIR should in cooperation with the ICMR, give vigorous support to research on population control and to the communication and application of the results in the widest and most efficient manner as this problem requires urgent solution.

Periodic Reviews

Periodic review of the work of the CSIR in relation to the research effort of India serves a useful purpose, and it is recommended that these should take place every five years, timed to precede the beginning of each five-year plan by about one year. A review of each individual laboratory or institute should take place before the overall review.

COMMISSION OF ENQUIRY ON CERTAIN ALLEGATIONS AGAINST S. PRATAP SINGH KAIRON, CHIEF MINSTER OF PUNJAB, 1963—REPORT

Delhi, Ministry Of Punjab, 1964. 298+vp.

One Man Commission
Chairman : Shri Sudhir Ranjan Dass

APPOINTMENT

By Notification No. S.O. 3109 dated November 1, 1963 issued by the Ministry of Home Affairs and published on the same date in Part II-Section 3-Sub-Section (ii) of the Gazette of India Extraordinary, the Central Government in exercise of the powers conferred on it by Section 3 of the Commissions of Inquiry Act, 1952 (Act No. 60 of 1952) constituted the present commission to enquire into and report on the allegations made in the said memorandum.

TERMS OF REFERENCE

(a) Issue a notice to every person, who in its opinion should be given an opportunity of being heard in the inquiry, to furnish to the Commission a statement relating to such matters as may be specified in the notice ;

(b) Issue a notification to be published in such manner as it may deem fit, inviting all persons acquainted with the subject matter of the inquiry to furnish to the Commission a statement relating to such matters as may be specified in the notification. Sub-rule (2) requires an affidavit to be filed in support of the facts set out in the statement and sub-rule (3) refers to documents which have to be furnished to the Commission along with the statement. Rule 3 lays down the procedure to be followed by the Commission after the statements are furnished to it under Rule 2 Sub-rule (1) of Rule 3 prescribe as follows:—

The Commission shall examine all the statements

furnished to it under rule 2 and if, after such examination, the Commission considers it necessary to record evidence, it shall first record the evidence, if any, produced by the Central Government and may there after need in such order as it may deem fit :

(a) The evidence of any person who has furnished a statement under rule 2 and whose evidence the Commission, having regard to the statement, considers relevant for the purpose of the inquiry ;

(b) The evidence of any other person whose evidence in the opinion of the Commission, is relevant to the inquiry.

CONTENTS

Conclusion

As a result of our investigation, we have come to the conclusion that there is non basis at all for any corruption; that in some of the chatges relating to his family members or others associated with him, certain improprieties were committed while Sardar Partap Singh, might not have been personally aware of these, a person in his position must be deemed to be constructively responsible; and that there were certain procedural irregularities in Administrative matters.

The Commission is free to concede that a father cannot legally or morally prevent his sons from carrying on business but exploitation of the infiuence of the father who happens to be the Chief Minister of the State cannot be permitted to be made a business of. Such exploitation cannot possibly be a legitimate business and the father's influence and powers cannot be permitted to be traded in. In the delicate situation in which S. Partap Singh Kairon holding such exalted high office, was placed as a result of the activities of his sons and relatives and Government officials, even assuming he personally had not lent a helping hand in relation to them, the least he could do was to give a stern warning, in private and if necessary publicly, to his sons, relatives, colleagues and subordinate officers against their alleged conduct even if such conduct had not been proved to be time. There is no getting away from the fact that S. Pratap Singh Kairon knew or had more than ample reason to think or suspect that his sons and relatives were allegedly exploiting his influence and powers. But, as his own affidavit shows, he made no inquiry, gave no warning to anybody and took no step whatever to prevent its recurrence but let things drift in the way they had been going, assuming he had no hand in it. In the premises he cannot now be heard to say that he had no knowledge of any wrongful conduct on the part of his sons, or relatives, or the officers under him. The allegations stared him in the face; he paid no heed to them. He cannot now plead ignorance of facts. In view of his inaction in the face of the circumstances here in before alluded to he must be help to have connived at the doings of his sons and relatives, his colleagues and the Government officers.

WORKING GROUP ON CLASSIFICATION OF BLOCKS FOR INTENSIFIED APPROACH TO SELECTED PROGRAMMES, 1963 –REPORT

New Delhi, Ministry of Community Development and Cooperation, 1965. 33p.

Chairman : Shri B. Mukerji.
Members : Dr. Douglas Ensminger; Dr. J. S. Patel; Shri D. P. Singh.
Secretary : Shri M. M. K. Wali.

APPOINTMENT

The question of intensive development in the field of agriculture production on a selected basis was discussed at the Annual Conference on Community Development and Panchayati Raj held at New Delhi in 1963, which recommended that with a view to concentrating efforts the Blocks should be classified according to their potential for quick agricultural development. The Ministry of Community Development and Cooperation consequently set up this working Group vide their O.M. No. 1 (1) (3)/63-Agr., dated November 2, 1963.

TERMS OF REFERENCE

(i) To suggest the criteria to be adopted for classification of Blocks for purposes of implementing selected programmes in the field of agricultural production;

(ii) To recommend in broad terms the programmes for each category of Blocks on which resources should be concentrated in that field;

(iii) To consider the need for other intensive programmes to diversify the rural economy and the basis on which a scheme for this purpose should be formulated; and

(iv) To recommend the administrative arrangements therefor.

CONTENTS

Introduction; Intensive Approach; Classification of Blocks; Basis for Selection; Assured Water Supply; Category II; Category III; Planning and Implementation; Staffing; Training; Supplies and Services; Incentives; Other Programmes; The Final Word; Summary of Recommendations; Annexures I to IV.

RECOMMENDATIONS

The idea of making an intensified approach to agricultural production in terms of local potential is not a new one. The programme of Community Development itself was intended to be oriented to this approach, though it has not been systematically and consistently applied in practice. Then came the Intensive Agricultural District Programme, the intensive Crop Cultivation Programmes and Intensive Fishery, Poultry and vegetable programmes, based on the concept of concentration of effort in favourable areas.

In the light of this the Working Groups considered that the main value of their report would lie in reiterating this approach in a practical form and suggesting such basis of selection as are practical and simple in application but crucial from the operational point of view.

The Blocks should be categorised into the following three broad categories:

(a) **Category I** : Those Blocks where impact programmes of agricultural development can be immediatele taken up.

(b) **Category II** : Blocks where agriculture is precarious and in significant but there is considerable potential for undertaking intensive programmes of Animal Husbandry, Dairying, Fishery, sheep and wool development etc.

(c) **Category III** : Blocks where programmes of water and land development in the nature of irrigation, soil conservation, drainage, flood control, levelling, etc., will have to be first undertaken before intensive production programmes become possible.

Immediate attention should be concentrated on Category I, as it offers the advantage of quick response to a programme of increased agricultural production.

Basis of Selection

A. Category I

(i) "Assured water" (assured irrigation or rainfall) should be the only criterion. Though factors responsible for increased agricultural production are diverse, yet this factor holds the key to the whole situation of farming at present. The crucial importance of assured water increasing agricultural production is borne out by a study of Dr. V. G. Panse, Statistical Adviser, Institute of Agricultural Research Statistics, ICAR, on "Yield Trend of Wheat and Rice in the First Two Five-Year Plans in India". Besides, this factor would be easier of practical application, than a complicated and sophisticated formula based on several factors. It is also of the highest importance from the farmer's point of view.

(ii) The actual Selection of Blocks in terms of this criterion should be done by local experts and planners who would know best whether an area fulfils this condition with reference to the agronomical situation cropping pattern and the predominant crops in the area.

(iii) The guiding principles in interpreting area of "assured water" should be as follows :

(a) **Assured Irrigation Areas** : The "command" of an irrigation project, major, medium or minor, to be taken into account should be realistically defined. It has been often noticed that the "command" is fixed at a much higher figure than the source can actually cope with.

(b) **Assured Rainfall Areas** : Here the Working Group has chosen an indirect and circumstantial index because of the practical difficulty in envolving a direct indicator. Blocks selected under "assured rainfall" should be those which have high spread and high yield or medium spread and high yield or high spread and medium yield of the various crops in the State. The high, medium or low yield/spread would be determined by taking the mean yield per acre/mean spread of a given crop for the State as base. This formula will automatically take into account of requirements of moisture for different crops, capabilities of land, etc.

(iv) As Block-level estimates of production are not yet available the determination of areas of assured rainfall on the above basis should be done in terms of districts and the relevant Blocks falling in those districts selected for implementation of intensive programmes.

(v) No arbitrary figure of minimum percentage-coverage of an area by irrigation for determining the eligibility of a Block for selection. All Blocks which come under this category should be so classified. In actual implementation, priorities should be determined by the availability of resources, Blocks having largest areas under assured irrigation being taken up first. But some consideration may also be given to selection of Blocks in compact region for facility of administration.

(vi) If due to inadequacy of resources intensive programmes cannot be taken up in all Category I Blocks, priority in selection should be given to areas with assured irrigation over those with assured rainfall.

(vii) Along with intensive programmes of agriculture programmes of dairying poultry and fishery (if applicable) should also be promoted.

(viii) Areas subject to frequent floods should be excluded from the application of this intensified approach.

B. Category II

(i) These are the Blocks which receive a rainfall of 15 inches and blow or the area where extensive areas are under forests or where lands are saline, alkaline or eraded. In such Blocks, depending on the potential in each Block the programmes of Animal Husbandry. milk production, poultry (common to all categories), and sheep and wool development, etc , could be taken up. Instead of agricultural crops the lands could best be utilised for growing grasses or trees.

(ii) Dairying should be promoted on an extensive scale in areas having good cattle breeds through a number of milk collection schemes of optimum size, without being necessarily linked up with large urban consuming centres. The milk could be sold in liquid form to smaller towns which live within the milk shed of each such scheme and the surplus processed.

(ii) For sheep and wool development also an integrated programme of improvement of stock, shearing facilities, and of grading, carding and marketing should be drawn up.

C. Category III

(i) This category is arrived at by eliminating the Blocks under Category I and II. Areas requiring land and water development would be classified under this ;

(ii) The first requirement in these Blocks is to have surveys carried out for various measures of Resource-development, e.g., irrigation, drainage, soil conservation, etc., reclamationand Master Plans of development of the area prepared.

(iii) Priority for development should be given to those Blocks where sizeable areas could be brought under major, medium or minor irrigation schemes.

The preliminary selection of Blocks in terms of these categories should be done by the Regional-level Officers of Agriculture, Animal Husbandry, Fishery, Horticulture, etc., in collaboration with the District-level Officers and then finalised by the Zila Parishads and Panchayat Samitis concerned. The ultimate phasing of the programme would be course be done by the State Governments in the light of the resources available, or likely to be available.

Soil conservation, minor irrigation and plant protection wings would need to be strengthened in most States.

There is need for evolving strains of seeds which

would absorb heavy doses of fertilisers.

Staffing

(a) **Category IA**: "type" pattern of staffing for all Blocks should be avoided. Strength of the staff should be determined on the basis of the requirements of each area. Indeed, in some Blocks where the standards of cultivation are high, there may be need to increase the number of Extension Officers rather than VLWs or to provide VLWs (and also Extension Officers) with higher qualifications.

(b) **Category II.**: The staff required would be in the nature of specialist VLWs and Extension Officers depending on the nature of the programme taken up, e.g., Animal Husbandry, poultry, sheep and wool development, etc.

(c) **Category III**: The additional staff required would be in the nature of higher level technical experts to survey, prepare and execute plans of Area Development.

Improvement in the quality of staff is of far greater importance than more increase in number.

It is of utmost importance that the necessary supplies and services are made available in terms of the requirements of each Block. The size of the programme should be strictly determined by the available resources, and any discriminate expansion avoided.

If cooperative structure in any area is not strong enough to handle the distribution of supplies efficiently there should be no hesitation in making alternative departmental arrangements, much as the Group would like to keep technical functionaries out of it. This however should be purely a temporary phase.

A study should be made as to what positive incentives, by way of better service conditions, could be provided to the Village Level Worker. The incentives so far given do not go far enough.

A study should also be made as to what incentives could be given to Panchayati Raj institutions, such as would provide them with added motivation to organise programmes of increased agricultural production.

As regards other intensive programmes to diversify the rural economy (are of the Terms of Reference of the Working Group), the Working Group felt that this would largely pertain to the programmes of Rural Industrialisation. Rural Industrialisation is a complicated subject and to make any worthwhile recommendation thereon, studies would have to be undertaken industry and technology-wise. The Working Group has no means to make such studies and therefore recommends that this should be studied separately.

Finally, the Working Group is of the opinion that "intensive approach" in favourable area is useful only as a short term measure. Miracles should not be expected of this approach in the overall agricultural situation, for such favourable areas occupy only a small part of the Indian agricultural landscape. A deep impact can be made on agricultural production if millions of farmers all over the country and adequately motivated to produce more. The pre-requisites for this are a proper price structure, easy availability of the needed supplies and services and provision of essential overheads like communications and rural electrification.

COMMITTEES FOR CATEGORISATION OF THE GOVERNMENT OF INDIA PRESS WORKERS, 1963—REPORT

New Delhi, Ministry of Works Housing and Rehabilitation (Department of Works & Housing) 1964. 75p.

Chairman : Shri V. Balasubramanyam (replaced by Shri P. K. Sen)

Membres : Shri P. K. Sen; Shri G. S. Bhasin; Shri B. C. Sen Gupta.

Secretary : Shri N. C. Sanyal.

APPOINTMENT

The Committee for Categorization of the Government of India Press Workers was constituted under the Ministry of Works, Housing and Rehabilitation (Department of Works and Housing) vide their Resolution No. 4(8)/63-PI dated November 26, 1963.

TERMS OF REFERENCE

(i) To review the classification of the posts of industrial workers, in the Printing Presses under the control of the Chief Controller of Printing & Stationery into the categories of unskilled, semiskilled, skilled, highly-skilled and supervisory;

(ii) Where necessary for the purpose of such review to examine the qua'ifications, and the field of recrui:-ment/promotion laid down for each part'cular post and to suggest modifications therein.

CONTENTS

Introductory; The organisation of the Printing Presses in the Government of India; Views of the workers and their Unions; Principles of Categorisation; the anno-malies in pay scales and classification; Pay structure in Government of India Press; The existing categories and Classification; Promotional Channels and methods of recruitment to various categories in the Presses; Method of implementing the recommendations; Some general aspect of Government of India Press establish-ment; Conclusion; Summary of Recommendations; Appendix A to G.

Report Of The Committee For Categorization Of The Government Of India Press Workers 1964

RECOMMENDATIONS

Packer should be semi-skilled. Whether it is at all necessary to retain this category should be looked into by the Department.

Cylinder Proof Pressman and Forme Proof Pressman should be elassfied as skilled with a pay scale of Rs. 110-131. The Galley Proof Pressman and (Hand) Proof Pressman should continue as semi-skilled and be given a Pay scale of Rs. 85-110 instead of Rs. 75-95.

A suitable percentage of Compositors should be upgraded to the highly skilled categories with a pay scale of Rs. 175-205. This group should comprise of persons selected from existing compositors. Type Store Keepers and Standing Forme Keepers.

There should be a Selection Grade for Binders.

The Category of Metal Melter should be upgraded as skilled with a pay scale of Rs. 110-131.

The Category of Gold Finisher be upgraded to the highly-skilled group with a pay scale of Rs. 175-205.

The Category of Assistant Mechanic (Mechanical) should be classified as semi-skilled with a pay scale of Rs. 85-110.

A category of Assistant Mechanic (Lino/Mono) should be created in the skilled category with a pay scale of Rs. 110-131.

The existing supervisory categories of Government of India Presses are Foreman Class I(General); Fore-man (Machine); Foreman (Bindery); Foreman (Stereo); Foreman Class I (Case); Foreman, Class III; Assistant Foreman Class I and Assistant Foreman, Class II. As against these categories, the Committee recommended two categories of Foreman viz, (1) Foreman in the scale of Rs. 240-380 and (2) Section Holder into the scale of Rs. 200-280.

Paste Supplier in the unskilled group should be up-graded to a semi-skilled status with a pay scale of Rs. 75-95.

Mono Caster Operator should have a pay scale of Rs. 110-131 and a selection Grade should be created for them with a pay scale of Rs. 125-155.

Category	Existing pay scale	Recommended Pay scale	Remarks
1	2	3	4
	Rs.	Rs.	
1. Mounter and Finisher	140-175	85-110	Recommended as Mounter (Page 18, Chapter V).
2. Blacksmith	110-180	110-155	p.18-19 Chapter V
3. Carpenter	100-130	110-155	p. 19, Chapter V
4. Binder	100-130	110-155	p. 19, Chapter V p. 31, and Chapter VII
5. Feeder	110-180	110-155	p. 20, Chapter V
6. Foreman	200-380	240-380	p. 21, Chapter V
7. Welder	125-155	110-155	p. 20, Chapter V
8. Etcher Class 1	168-280	175-280	p. 21, Chapter V
9. Dark Room Assistant	125-155	125-180	p. 21. Chapter V
10. Gold Finister	110-143	175-205	p. 21, Chapter V
11. Stereo Typer	100-130	110-155	p. 21, Chapter V
12. Prover	168-320	175-320	p. 21, Chapter V

1	2	3	4
13. Head Mechanic (Mechenical)	200-320	205-340	p. 22, Chapter V
14. Asstt. Mech, (Mechanical)	100-130	85-110	p. 22, Chapter V
15. Trimmer	95-110	85-110	p. 30, Chapter VII
16. Asst. Carpenter	75-95	85-110	p. 30, Chapter VII
17. Machineman (Falcon)	100-130	110-155	p. 32, Chapter VII
18. Machineman (Platen)	100-130	110-155	p. 32, Chapter VII
19. Machineman (Cylinder)	100 142	110-155	p. 32, Chapter VII

III. Abolition and Creation of new Categories

Clause 'A'

The following categories have been recommended to be abolished

1. Tilter
2. Bindery Despatcher
3. Mounter and Finisher
4. Bindery Finisher
5. Impositors
6. Distributor
7. Blacksmith and Mechanic
8. Checker (Machine)
9. Roller Boy
10. Embosser
11. Outturn Checker
12. Rotary Printers
13. Workshop Mechanic (Photo Litho Wing)
14. Correction Checker
15. Binder-cum-Guillotine Operator
16. Asst. Foreman Class I & II (all grades of Foreman excepting one)
17. Half-tone Etcher
18. Developer (Photo)
19. Boiler Attendant-cum Roller Moulder
20. Motor Attendant
21. Camera Assistant
22. Assistant Standing Formkeeper
23. Assistant Type Store Keeper
24. Elictrical Mistry
25. Counter
26. Bindery Examiner
27. Machineman (Platen)
28. Machineman (Cylinder)
29. Machineman (Falcon)
30. Blacksmith & Mechanic

Clause 'B'

The following new categories have been recommended to be created or merged :—

1. For Bindery work of a higher order a selection grade upto not more than 33-1/3 per cent of skilled binders in the scale of Rs. 155-180 be created.

2. The category of Automatic Machineman be redesignated as Machineman Selection Grade (or some other suitable separate designation), and classified as highly skilled with a pay scale of Rs. 175-205.

3. A selection grade of Rs. 125-155 for the Mono Caster Operators for the operation of super-caster machines is recommended.

(b) Merger and New Creations.

4. Two or three unskilled categories viz., Fly-boy, Mazdoor or Labourer are recommended to perform all normal manual work as against several unskilled posts.

5. Cleaner Driver be redesignated as Cleaner with their existing pay scales.

6. The Roller Moulder and Roller Caster should be merged with a single pay scale of Rs. 75-110.

7. The category of Embosser should be abolished and the job performed by them should be entrusted to the Warehouseman.

8. Rotary Printers recommended to be abolished should be merged with Automatic Machineman.

9. The category of Correction Checker should be abolished and on abolition of this category the work should be entrusted to the highly-skilled compositors recommended by the Committee.

10. There should be two categories of Etchers. The category of Half-tone Etcher should be abolished. The category of Etcher Class II should be in the pay scale of Rs. 140-175 and the Category of Etcher Class I should be in the scale of Rs. 175-280 with a suitable Efficiency Bar.

11. (a) The category of Developer (Photo) should be abolished and on abolition of this Category incumbents may be merged with the Dark Room Assistant category.

(b) The pay scale of Dark Room Assistant should be revised from Rs. 125-155 to Rs. 125-180.

12. There should be a category of Boilerman in the scale of Rs. 110-131 instead of Boiler Attendant-cum-Roller Moulder.

13. The category of Motor Attendant is recommended to be abolished and the work entrusted to the existing Electrician and Wireman.

14. The category of Camera Assistant is recommended to be abolished and merged with the category of Dark Room Assistant.

15. The designation of Machine Operators in all grades should be changed Office Mechinemen Grade I and Grade II with a pay scale of Rs. 210-425 and Rs. 175-320 respectively.

16. The category of Assistant Mechanic (Lino/Mono) is recommended a pay scale of Rs. 110-131 with skilled status.

17. The designation of Electrician-cum-Armature Winder may be replaced by that of Electrician.

18. The post of Tilter should be abolished and a semi skilled category with a pay scale of Rs. 85-110 be created with a separate designation.

19. The category of Mounter should be equated with the Assistant Carpenter.

20. The categories of Machineman (Platen), Machineman (Cylinder), Machineman (Falcon) should be merged with the newly created category of Machineman in the skilled grade in the scale of Rs. 110-155.

21. Machineman in the highly-skilled group as are required to handle multi-colour work should be given an extended pay scale of Rs. 175-205 to Rs. 175-240.

22. If all the recommendations of the Committee are accepted the number of categories will come down to 70 excluding the categories of posts in the Reading Branch and those carrying a starting pay of more than Rs. 240.

23. Pay Scales :-

The First Pay Commission recommended 6 basic pay scales for the industrial workers of the Presses. The Second Pay Commission had recommended 13 pay scales for Government Presses, following more or less the pattern as existed in 1959. The Committee have adopted 8 basic pay scales with minor variations by merging two scales or splitting up the basic scale into two parts as the guiding scales for the Press workers. As far as practicable, they stuck to the recommendations of the First Pay Commission translated in accordance with the recommendations of the Second Pay Commission.

General

1. The Committee has not dealt with the undermentioned categories of workers in the presses :

(a) Workers employed in the Reading Branch as a writ petition is pending in Punjab High Court.

(b) The categories of posts having a starting pay above Rs. 240 (on the analogy of the Second Pay Commission which has recommended prescribed scales upto Rs. 240 generally for the workshop staff all over India).

2. Industrial workers should be governed only by Industrial Rules and Regulations applicable to other industrial workers. A definition for the te m Industrial Workers, in the Industrial Sector under the Government, is essential. Pending such a definition, the Committee had gone solely by the criteria of those engaged in the production work and manual workers together with their supervisor and not by the lists suggested either by the workers or the Administration.

3. There is urgent necessity of yardsticks and norms in the Presses.

4. The Incentive Bonus Scheme should be introduced in its entirely i.e. with penalties for future recruits.

5. It is not desirable to have permanent and piece workers working side-by side.

6. Promotion chances as far as practicable should be the same in all the Government of India presses.

7. Firm Recruitment Rules and channel for promotion should be prescribed immediately.

8. Basic tradesmen as well as aspirants for skilieds jobs may be classified from unskilled to semi-skilled.

9. Highly-skilled workers may be classified along with skilled superviory.

10. The categories beyond highly-skilled group and supervisory categories over highly-skilled artisan may be classified as merely supervisory workers.

11. Pay scales of Operative Workers are too short. This is true of all industrial workers of Government of India. Supervisory pay scales in the Government of India Presses are rather in ordinately long.

12. There should be atleast one promotional step for each worker.

13. A ratio of direct recruitment and promotion from unskilled categories should generally be only 50:50.

14. Direct Recruitment to Selection Grades and supervisory categories should be abolished.

15. Except in exceptional cases the direct recruitment should not be resorted to in the highly-skilled category.

16. Promotion of Binders category upto 50 per cent may be made from Warehousemen. It has also been suggested that the ratio between the Warehouseman and the Binders should be 50:50.

17. The promotion quota of the Assistant Mechanic to the grade of Mechanic should be increased from 50 per cent to 75 per cent or 66-1/3 per cent.

18. There should be no direct recruitment to category of Head Mechanic (Mechanical), Head Mechanic (Lino) and Head Mechanic (Mono).

19. The apprentices should be treated as outside nominees for the purpose of direct recruitment.

20. The post of Lino/Mono Operators should be filled 100 per cent by direct recruitment and not from Compositors learners.

21. No direct recruitment should be made in the categories of Barman and they should be tested for the post of Assistant Mechanic (Lino).

22. Except as indicated in clause 31 below, the recommendation should not be given retrospective effect.

23. All recommendations wherever favourable, will be applicable to the existing categories. Where it is not favourable the existing incumbents will be protected and the recommendations will be applicable only to new

recruits.

24. The screening of persons where category has been recommended to be abolished for absorption in the equivalent grades is necessary. All existing incumbents of the categories where upgradition has been recommended should not automatically be upgraded but allowed the higher status only after passing a trade test. This will not apply to cases where the pay scale has only been revised upwards.

25. After merger the previous service of the incumbents should count in full for seniority in the merged category.

26. Workers not found suitable for merger with the existing categories should be allowed to continue on and at the time of their retirement they may be confirmed against supernumerary posts even in the categories which have been recommended for abolition.

27. The existing piece rates need revision.

28. With the creation of Senior and Junior Foreman for effective supervision, the Sections should be reorganised comprising of 15 to 20 skilled workers in each Section.

29. It is not possible to create posts in operative and ancillary categories according to fixed formulae.

30. Promotional quota for industrial workers to the grade of Overseer may be reviewed.

Miscellaneous

The prescribed pay scale of Rs. 90-120 of the category of Moulder and Finisher has apparently not been revised in accordance with the recommendations of the Second Pay Commission. This revision should be done now with retrospective effect from July 1, 1959.

COMMITTEE ON EDUCATION AS AN ELECTIVE SUBJECT AT THE UNDERGRADUATE STAGE, 1963—REPORT

New Delhi, University Grants Commission, 1966. 30p.

Chairman : Prof. A.R. Wadia.
Members : Dr. (Miss) S. Panandikar; Prof. A Mujib; Dr. S.N Saraf ; Shri K.L. Joshi ;
Member-Secretary : Dr. P.J. Philip later replaced by Dr. J. N. Kaul.

APPOINTMENT

The Suggestion to introduce "Education" as an elective for the B.A./B.Sc. degrees has been put forward on several occasions in recent years. The University Grants Commission has also discussed from time to time the relative advantages of introducing "Education" as an optional subject at the first degree stage. The University Grants Commission appointed a Committee in December, 1963.

TERMS OF REFERENCE

The terms of Reference of the Committee are as follows :

(i) To examine the question in various aspects, and

(ii) To make suitable recommendations in this regard.

CONTENTS

Foreword ; Appointment of the Committee ; Information received from the Universities ; Report ; Summary of recommendations ; Appendices from I to VI.

RECOMMENDATIONS

The Committee make the following specific recommendations:

The study of 'Education' as an elective subject at the undergraduate level may not be treated as adequate preparation for teaching in high/higher secondary schools. It will be neither possible nor desirable to include a teacher training programme in the undergraduate studies.

The study of 'Education' as an elective subject may however, serve the following four purposes:

(i) It may be a good independent and academic discipline which could promote cultural and liberal educational values;

(ii) It might get some students interested in teaching as a career. The course in 'Education' ought to promote the imaginative consideration of various general principles underlying a teacher's carrier;

(iii) It would be a useful subject for women condidates who intend to take up social work and home Economics or who terminate their studies at the undergraduate state;

(iv) 'Education' as an elective subject at the undergraduate level could also be introduced for those candidates who intend to take up a two year masters' degree course in 'Education', wherever it is available.

Objects of teaching 'Education' as an optional subject at the undergraduate level should be clearly identified.

Reading and reference material, produced on a co-operative basis by the experts in various disciplines, should be provided to the students. If necessary, U.G.C. may provide assistance in this regard to one or two universities selected for this purpose.

COMMITTEE ON SETTING UP A UNIVERSITY FOR THE NORTH EASTERN REIGON OF INDIA, 1963—REPORT

New Delhi, University Grants Commission, 1965. 50p.

Chairman : Prof. A. R. Wadia.
Members : Dr. S.K. Bhuyan; Dr. H.J. Taylor; Prof G.G. Swell, Shri R.P. Nayak; Shri Mayangnokch Ao; Shri P.B. Singh.
Secretary : Dr. P.J. Philip.

APPOINTMENT

The tribal people inhabiting the North-Eastern region of India comprising Nagaland, N.E.F.A., Manipur and the Hill areas of Assam have for some time been feeling the need for educational advancement. Until recently, facilities for higher education in the region were extremely meagre. Further, people in these areas have also been anxious to bring about a fuller integration with the rest of India.

On August 9, 1963 a meeting of representatives of tribal communities in shillong resolved 'to move the Government of India to establish a central federal University in the Hill Areas. Four members of Parliament, representing these areas, also wrote to the Prime Minister in September 1963 regarding the need for setting up a new university at a suitable centre to serve their educational and cultural requirements. They emphasized that the special needs of the tribal people were not being adequately met by the Gauhati University and also drew attention to the difficulties created for them by the declaration of Assamese as the official language of Assam. The Prime Minister forwarded the letter to the Chairman of University Grants Commission. The Commission appreciating the need for developing educational facilities in this region, considered it desirable to constitute a small Committee of educationists and representatives of the area to examine the question in all its aspects.

The Committee on setting up a University for the North Eastern Region was constituted by jointly by the University Grants Commission and the Ministry of Education, Government of India in December, 1963.

TERMS OF REFERENCE

(a) to assess the present facilities for higher education in the north-eastern areas of India (Nagaland, NEFA, Manipur and Hill Areas of Assam);

(b) to consider the pattern and development of higher education best suited to the needs of these areas; and

(c) to examine whether it would be desirable to set up a University in the region or an autonomous institution 'deemed to be a University' under the UGC Act of 1956.

CONTENTS

Appointment of the Committee; The Background of the Problem ; The Case for a University in the Hill Areas; Recommendations; Appendices; Acknowledgements.

RECOMMENDATIONS

For a variety of reasons, there is strong case for the provision of special facilities of higher education in the North Eastern Region comprising Nagaland, NEFA, Manipur and the Hill areas of Assam.

It is necessary to think out a fresh ways of organising teaching, research and examinations in order that the education offered by the university may be a high quality.

A university of the unitary type conducting both undergraduate and postgraduate teaching in a single campus cannot satisfy the needs and aspirations of vastly scattered areas and their people. On the other hand, an affiliating university will not be able to develop the feeling of oneness among the colleges for them to feel that they are part of an academic community. The situation can best be met by establishing a federal type of university with a constituent college in each important centre.

The university colleges should be developed, in the first instance, as centres of undergraduate teaching, with honours in the main subjects. They should be sufficiently large, well staffed and properly equipped. The staff, or part of the staff, would be appointed by and responsible to the university.

The University Colleges should become, in course of time, full-fledged centres of postgraduate teaching and research. Some colleges may conduct postgraduate teaching and research from the very beginning.

The university should have the function of conducting vocational and technical education at an appropriate level. In the first instance a polytechnic for boys and a nursing college for girls may be set up.

The structure of undergraduate education will need re-organisation and strengthening to provide a sound base for postgraduate teaching and research. The university should concern itself directly with undergraduate teaching instead of regarding it as a matter of secondary importance.

It would be necessary to bring teachers together through conferences, seminars, refresher courses etc. in order that they may keep themselves abreast of the latest developments in their respective fields.

Much attention and thought will have to be given to evolving a suitable pattern of courses. The pre-university course should be used mainly for preparing the student for university studies by giving him a through grounding in English.

The Court (or Senate) of the university, which represents varied interests, should largely function as an advisory body. The real authority of the university should be vested in a small body of high professional competence.

There should be a board of undergraduate education and paralled to it a board of postgraduate education. The boards might jointly constitute the Academic Council, or operate under it, but they should have the necessary freedom to organise their courses of study.

It may be desirable to set up a special board of part-time education to deal with the problem of night colleges and night shifts in the day colleges.

The proposed university should be established at Shillong. The actual site of the university may however be somewhere in the vicinity of Shillong.

The D.M. College, Imphal should become a university college and an important centre of the university to begin with.

The colleges at Tura, Aijal, Haflong and Kohima should be provided with necessary facilities to develop into university colleges for their respective areas.

Other Colleges in the Hill areas may be affiliated to the university with a closer bond with the university than is usually found in the case of affiliating universities.

The norms of the university should be such as will reflect the scope and purpose of the university and its relation to the Government of India.

Steps will have to be taken by the Union Government for establishing in the Hill areas a full-fledged university or an institution deemed to be university under Section 3 of the U.G.C. Act.

CHAIRMAN INDEX

INDEX